Maloney's

ANTIQUES & COLLECTIBLES

RESOURCE DIRECTORY

Seventh Edition

David J. Maloney, Jr., ISA CAPP, AOA CM

©2003 Sales Online Direct
Published by

 **kp** **krause publications**
An F&W Publications Company

Our toll-free number to place an order or obtain a free catalog is 800-258-0929.

Library of Congress Catalog Number: 2001090488

ISBN: 0-87349-732-5

Printed in the United States of America

To the memory of my father

Lt. Col. David J. Maloney, Sr. USAF (Ret.)
1916 - 2001

A veteran of three wars and seven kids.

Some have referred to his as "The Greatest Generation"

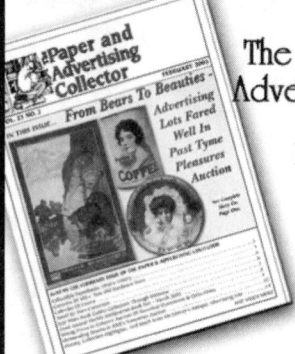

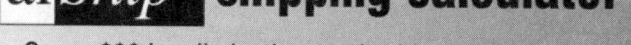

TABLE OF CONTENTS

ABOUT THE AUTHOR

David Maloney, ISA CAPP, AOA CM, is a Certified Appraiser of Personal Property and a nationally known appraiser, author, radio talk-show guest, public speaker, and appraisal course writer and instructor. His reputation is based on more than 32 years of practical experience, extensive academic and personal study, writing, teaching, and lecturing.

Maloney received his bachelor's degree from the US Coast Guard Academy and his master's from the Naval Postgraduate School. After a career in the Coast Guard, he operated an antiques business for several years prior to founding Frederick Appraisal, Claims & Estate Services in 1982.

For over twenty years, Maloney has been a full-time professional personal property appraiser specializing in the valuation of antiques, collectibles, residential contents, vehicles, and business equipment for insurance, probate, business valuation, divorce, and charitable contribution purposes. He has also provided appraisal consulting services to bank trust departments, personal representatives, accountants, lawyers, estate planners, insurance agents, and the moving industry. In addition, he's advised clients on the best options available for disposing of antiques and collectibles.

In addition to appraisals, Maloney provides damage claims and inspection services for major van lines operating in the Maryland, Washington, D.C., Virginia, and the West Virginia area. He has served as a member of the board of directors of the moving industry's Claims Prevention and Procedure Council, and he has written and spoken extensively on the role of an appraiser in the claims process. He is also a contributing author of the *California Household Goods Carriers Claims Training & Reference Manual.*

Maloney served in a leadership capacity with the International Society of Appraisers (ISA) for nearly twenty years, both at the chapter and the national levels. He was the ISA's vice president and was twice elected to the ISA's board of directors. As ISA's Education Committee chairman, Maloney was instrumental in writing ISA's Core Courses in appraisal theory and practices — courses he maintained and taught across the country and in Canada for more than six years. Maloney also served as the ISA's representative to The Appraisal Foundation Advisory Council (TAFAC) in Washington, D.C., where he served as chairman of the TAFAC Emerging Issues Committee, and where he was recognized for his contributions to the development of the Personal Property Appraiser Qualification Criteria.

For his efforts, Maloney has earned numerous ISA awards including, the Lamp of Knowledge Award, Distinguished Service Award, Member-of-the-Year Award, and the President's Award. Recently the ISA presented Maloney with the coveted Lifetime Achievement Award in recognition of his years of dedicated service to the ISA and the appraisal profession.

For more than twelve years, Maloney has authored *Maloney's Antiques & Collectibles Resource Directory,* now in its seventh edition. Called "the bible" of the industry by *U.S. News & World Reports*, *Maloney's* is considered a "must-have" on every collector's bookshelf.

Maloney also served as co-host of the Public Television series *Collecting Across America* and as chief appraiser on the PAX TV collectibles show, *Treasures in Your Home: The World of Collecting.*

Maloney currently serves as Secretary/Treasurer and webmaster for the Association of Online Appraisers (AOA). The AOA offers its members Maloney's unique 550-page *Complete Online Course in Personal Property Appraising* at **AOAonline.org**. Maloney also serves as Chief Appraisal Officer for CollectingChannel.com and its parent company, Sales Online Direct. In addition, he is the architect and Appraisal Manager of CollectingChannel.com's popular online appraisal service at **AsktheAppraiser.com**.

Maloney resides with his family in Frederick, Maryland.

FOREWORD

I first "met" David Maloney via email, when he contacted me because he was putting together the very first *Maloney's Antiques & Collectibles Resource Directory.* He invited me to be listed in the book, and I jumped at the chance to participate in what would prove to be the most comprehensive resource in the field of antiques and collectibles. When the book was published, I acquired a copy, and it changed my professional life.

David and I met face-to-face a few years later, on the set of the television show *Treasures In Your Home,* and we have remained fast friends and professional associates ever since, having collaborated on many different projects. Through the years my reliance on *Maloney's Antiques & Collectibles Resource Directory* has been constant and so complete that I could never get through the business day without it at my side.

As any professional appraiser will tell you, good research is the basis of the science of valuation — good research is what produces an accurate, reliable appraisal. And *Maloney's* is the best research tool there is, a resource so all-encompassing that there is virtually no person, group, store, place or service not present within its covers. If you need to know who, what, when, where or how about an antique or collectible, common or obscure, *Maloney's* is the place to find it.

Of course, it is not only appraisers who need *Maloney's Antiques & Collectibles Resource Directory.* It's an important reference for collectors, dealers, libraries, insurance adjusters, lawyers and those who work in the transit claims industry as well. Its also great if you've just dropped Aunt Hattie's wedding gift on the floor, watched it be smashed it to smithereens, and now need to find a matching service. Best of all, the material handed up by its pages is far superior to what one finds through Internet searches, where such an enormous amount of irrelevant information is turned up with every query. And who wants to wade through all *that?*

In short, I don't think there exists a better, more complete, tried and tested, comprehensive, all-in-one resource for those with an interest in the antiques and collectibles field than *Maloney's Antiques & Collectibles Resource Directory.* Now, if I haven't convinced you that you really, really need this book, then I've failed to do my job. I urge you to buy the book anyway, as you will realize its importance and value the very first time you use it. Trust me on that!

Judith Katz-Schwartz
Author, "Protecting Your Collectible Treasures: Secrets of a Collecting Diva"
January 2004

INTRODUCTION

Welcome to the seventh edition of *Maloney's Antiques & Collectibles Resource Directory*. This massive compilation contains thousands of resources to assist you in the location, study and authentication, replacement, repair, valuation, or buying and selling of nearly 3,200 categories of art, antiques, collectibles, and other types of personal property, including gems and jewelry, race cars and boats — even airplanes and meteorites!

Maloney's is a pioneer in gathering and disseminating information about antiques-related resources to the public. Since its debut twelve years ago, this book has been hailed as the "best one-volume research tool in print" by the Gannett News Service and has been listed as a *"Best Reference Book"* by the *Library Journal. Kipplinger's Personal Finance Magazine* refers to *Maloney's* as "the industry bible" This book is a unique and comprehensive, all-in-one resource for hard-to-find information about the personal property you own. And now with 20,000 listings (most of which have e-mail and Web addresses) in many new categories, the seventh edition of *Maloney's* is better than ever!

Specialized resources contained within *Maloney's* include buyers, collectors, dealers, experts, appraisers, periodicals, suppliers of parts, reproduction sources, reference book sellers, manufacturers/distributors/producers, clubs, societies and associations, museums and libraries, centers for specialized research, matching services, repair/restoration/conservation specialists, vendors to the trade, unique Internet resources, and mail-bid, Internet and gallery auctions. Many other miscellaneous services ranging from freelance writers and antique buying trips to computer software for the collector and bottle cleaning kits are also included. Please note that a listing should not be considered an endorsement, and no guarantee of satisfactory service is made. Comments I receive regarding service will be weighed in considering those to be included in future editions.

In addition to thousands of new and updated listings and scores of new categories, the seventh edition of *Maloney's* includes the following important features:

> — A greatly expanded **cross-referencing system**. Readers are directed to other relevant categories that might contain information of interest. No other publication has ever cross-referenced the world of antiques and collectibles to this degree.

> — A redesigned and highly-detailed **index**.

> — Over 11,000 listings with Internet **Web sites** and over 14,000 with **e-mail** addresses.

The goal of this book is to place as much information as possible at the user's fingertips to allow him or her to make decisions based on knowledge and fact. Veteran dealers and collectors are well aware that knowledge and information are the keys to success in the world of antiques and collectibles. Unfortunately, such informational resources are minimal in scope, widely scattered, and often short-lived or frequently changing.

Prior to *Maloney's* there was no organized method to capture, preserve, collate, and distribute collector resource information to efficiently keep the public accurately informed on a continuing basis. *Maloney's* is designed to overcome this shortfall through frequent updating and regular publication.

My personal experience as an appraiser demonstrates quite dramatically that most noncollectors are unaware of the value and historical/cultural significance of many of their own possessions. Even when people do realize that their collectible items are valuable and/or of interest to others, they are often at a loss as to how to determine value, find a buyer (should they choose to sell), or locate information to learn more about what they have.

This directory is an ideal source for locating potential buyers. Individual buyers are listed as are associated clubs (*Maloney's* lists nearly 2,000) and periodicals (more than 2,100) which are themselves excellent sources of information about and advertisers to potential buyers. In addition, the listed auction services (often specializing in a narrow area of collector interest) provide alternatives to selling to individuals.

Staying current in the fast-paced world of antiques and collectibles and with ever-changing values is difficult at best. New research, repair techniques, theft and fraud alerts, reproductions, and a fluctuating value structure makes trade periodicals, specialized serial publications, and collectors' clubs and their associated Web sites more important than ever as primary sources of current and topical news in all fields of antiques and collectibles. The past few years have witnessed countless dedicated collectors and dealers designing Web sites to share their hard-earned information with beginning and advanced collector alike. *Maloney's* includes it all.

For professionals, such as appraisers, dealers, estate liquidators, restorers, attorneys, and claims adjusters, *Maloney's Antiques & Collectibles Resource Directory* is the unrivaled source of information to find those who can aid in the authentication and valuation of antiques and collectibles, help settle a legal dispute, or help with the successful resolution of a loss or damage claim. Experts found among dealers, appraisers, collectors, clubs, and specialized periodicals offer an unparalleled source of specialized knowledge to help in confirming bona fide claims or in disproving fraudulent ones.

Of special interest to the moving, claims, and repair industries, *Maloney's* lists suppliers of such items as replacement crystals for chandeliers, furniture hardware, curved glass, tools, lamp parts, upholstery and caning supplies, clock parts, refinishing supplies, and other obscure and hard-to-find items, such as icebox and kitchen cabinet hardware. The directory also lists matching services for silver, crystal, dinnerware ("china"), conservation and repair supply sources, specialized repair services, and, through the dealer listings, replacement sources for just about anything antique or collectible. Also listed are computer programs for collectors and sources of supplies for the collector and dealer, such as bubble wrap, Mylar sleeves, acid-free storage containers, and display cases.

Maloney's further provides public awareness resources that disseminate information about recognizing fakes and reproductions, and reporting and recovering stolen art. In addition, there are listings for federal and state offices that provide information regarding the laws that govern the gathering, owning, transporting, or selling of items made from endangered species or of items classified as heritage resources such as certain Native American Indian relics or buried historical artifacts.

We are always interested in correcting, updating, and adding sources of information and in improving category nomenclature and structure. Please e-mail, write, or call with your suggestions for changes. At the end of this directory you will find a "Listing Registration & Change Form," that you can submit at any time to either change your present listing or to add a new one. (By the way, listings in *Maloney's Antiques & Collectibles Resource Directory* are free.)

A special thanks to all those who are listed, and to our users for their feedback, suggestions, and overwhelming encouragement. I continue to strive for excellence in providing a thorough, accurate and all-encompassing antiques and collectibles resource directory. To that end, I encourage and welcome your comments and suggestions.

David J. Maloney, Jr., ISA CAPP. AOA CM
P.O. Box 2049
Frederick, MD 21702-1049
phone: (301) 228-2279
fax: (301) 695-6491
dave@maloney.com

USER'S GUIDE

Description of the Listings

Maloney's Antiques & Collectibles Resource Directory contains over 20,000 specific entries in more than 3,200 subject categories arranged alphabetically by primary classification. Primary classifications are in CAPITAL LETTERS. Subclassifications appear (in upper- and lowercase letters) where there are recognized subcategories.

Of particular importance is the extensive and comprehensive cross-referencing system (which is found within both the Listings as well as in the Index), which directs the user to related subject matter and is unique to this publication.

The following is a sample of headings and subheadings found in the Listings:

> **ADVERTISING COLLECTIBLES**
>> (see also BREWERIANA; BUTTONS, Pin-Back; COFFEE; GAS STATION COLLECTIBLES; GLASSES; LABELS; MAGAZINES, Covers & Tear Sheets; PAPER COLLECTIBLES; POCKET MIRRORS; TIN COLLECTIBLES)
>> **Alka Seltzer**
>> **Beer & Soda**
>
> **AIR LABELS**
> **AIRLINE MEMORABILIA**
>> (see also AIRPLANES; AVIATION; AVIATION MEMORABILIA; LUGGAGE LABELS; STAMP COLLECTING, Air Mail Related; TOYS, Airplane Related; TRANSPORTATION COLLECTIBLES)
>> **Baggage I.D. Labels**
>> **Models, desk**
>> **Pan-American Airways**
>> **Pilot Wings**

Each entry contains as much of the following information as is applicable and available:

> 1) **PRIMARY CLASSIFICATION**
> 2) **Subclassification**
> 3) Entry type (i.e., dealer, collector, club, etc.; entries are in ZIP code order)
> 4) Contact person's name
> 5) Business, organization, club, or museum name
> 6) Periodical type and name
> 7) Postal address
> 8) Phone and fax numbers
> 9) E-mail address
> 10) Internet Web site
> 11) Descriptive comment

Primary Classifications and Subclassifications

Of critical importance was the establishment of a classification system that employs a well-defined system that is sensitive to nomenclature currently in vogue within the collecting community. A bi-level system of nomenclature that includes primary classifications and, where necessary, subclassifications, was adopted. Additional flexibility is afforded within either level by employing parenthetical divisions such as **CERAMICS (AMERICAN)**, **Stoneware**, or **GLASS, Carnival (Post-1960)**.

Entry Types

The entry type heading identifies the listing as an appraiser, auction service, bookseller, collector, collector club, dealer, expert, manufacturer/distributor/producer, matching service, miscellaneous service of special interest, museum or library, online service, periodical, repair/restoration/conservation service, reproduction source, or supplier. Entries are listed *alphabetically by entry type* and then in *ZIP code order* for ease in locating services or specialists in your area. Entry types are self explanatory, but the following warrant additional comment:

- ■ "Collectors" buy or trade primarily for their own enjoyment, and with any profit motive being secondary.

- ■ "Dealers" buy, sell, or trade. They may also be "collectors," but dealers anticipate making a profit.

- ■ "Experts" (while they may also be a "collector" and/or "dealer") are considered to be expert because they have lectured or written extensively on the subject, have authored books or articles, have curated exhibits or managed collections, have dealt extensively in the subject, appraise within a specialized field, have conducted lengthy studies on the subject, or otherwise have such a degree of experience that they are recognized within the trade as having an uncommonly high degree of knowledge about the subject.

- ■ "Man./Dist./Prod." are businesses that either manufacturer, distribute or produce items such as modem collectibles or reproductions.

- ■ "Suppliers" are sources of replacement parts or supplies. Included in this category are vendors who cater to the needs of collectors, dealers, repairers and restorers, conservators, etc.

- ■ As a general rule, only "periodicals" (newsletters, magazines, newspapers, journals, etc.) issued more than once a year are included in this directory. Books about antiques and collectibles are not listed as they are simply too numerous and often out-of-print; however, they are available through your local library or from the booksellers listed in *Maloney's* under **BOOKS, Reference**. General interest periodicals are listed under the category **PERIODICALS**. Specialty periodicals are listed within their respective specialty category. Periodicals, such as newsletters or magazines, issued by a club or society are listed with that club listing within its specialty area and are not also listed separately as a "periodical." (Many fine club periodicals are available to members only, so you may wish to join in order to receive them.)

NOTE: Always check the comment lines in each listing for additional information. For instance, often *collectors* or *experts* might also buy and sell, supply parts, do repairs, or provide other services relevant to the classification.

Names, Addresses and Phone Numbers
As appropriate, listings include a contact person's name, a business and periodical name, address, phone and fax numbers. Requests not to list a street address but rather only phone numbers or e-mail addresses have been honored. A requirement for being listed in *Maloney's* is that there be either a bona fide mailing address or e-mail address listed (preferably both).

E-Mail Addresses
More than 14,000 of the listings in this edition of *Maloney's* are also accessible via e-mail. With the growing popularity of online communications and the abundance of resources now on the Internet, savvy antiques and collectibles enthusiasts are speeding down the information super-highway to take advantage of information often found nowhere else.

Internet Web Sites
Over 11,000 listings in *Maloney's* also feature an Internet Web site. With millions of users, the Internet offers an unparalleled opportunity for you to learn more about what you own and who shares your particular areas of interest worldwide! The Internet can also increase the world's awareness of you and improve your efforts to gain publicity for your group, business, or area of interest.

Comment Lines
Most entries include a comment line containing amplifying information that users will find extremely valuable. Comment space was limited, so at times, editorial license was taken to shorten or otherwise modify comments submitted by those listed.

Tips for Searching *Maloney's*

■ Sellers of new books focusing on antiques and collectibles are listed under **BOOKS, Reference.**

■ Repair, restoration, and conservation services will be found:
  1) under the heading **REPAIR/RESTORATION/CONSERVATION**, or
  2) within their specialty classification under the entry type *Repair Services*.

■ Objects made of fired clay (pottery, earthenware, stoneware, and porcelain) will be found under the primary classification of **CERAMICS**, which is further subdivided according to place of origin and type, e.g., **CERAMICS (AMERICAN ART POTTERY), Roseville Pottery Co.** By cross-reference, users are directed to such related areas as **COOKIE JARS, FAIRINGS,** and **DINNERWARE** (a generic classification that contains most "china").

■ Matching services locate replacement pieces for dinnerware, glassware, and flatware tableware services. Matching services will be found primarily under the categories **DINNERWARE; FLATWARE; GLASS, Elegant,** and **GLASS, Crystal.**

■ Sports-related collectibles are listed alphabetically by sport subclassification under the primary classification of **SPORTS COLLECTIBLES.** (By the way, **SPORTS COLLECTIBLES** should not be confused with **SPORTING COLLECTIBLES.** The latter includes items relating to the hunting sports, such as decoys, hunting prints and paintings, sporting art, target shooting, fishing lures, duck game calls, etc.)

■ Contemporary collectibles, including limited editions, can be found under **COLLECTIBLES (MODERN).**

■ Many supplies for the dealer and collector can be found under **ANTIQUES DEALERS & COLLECTORS, Supplies for.** Certain specific categories such as **STAMP COLLECTING, Supplies for,** and **COINS & CURRENCY, Supplies for** also list sources of supplies for those specialties.

■ Listings with the **subcategory** *Computer Programs For* contain vendors of computer programs for cataloging and maintaining collections. As an example, see **STAMP COLLECTING, Computer Programs For.**

■ Although many listings now include an Internet Web site, those listees who operate solely or primarily on the Internet can be found listed within their specialty area under the entry type *Internet Resources*.

■ The category **REPRODUCTION SOURCES** (sometimes catering only to the wholesale trade) lists businesses offering copies of antiques and collectibles — everything from R.S. Prussia porcelain, and oak furniture to Diamond Dye lithographed tin advertising signs, and jukeboxes.

■ See the categories **HERITAGE RESOURCES** and **ENDANGERED SPECIES** for federal and state resources that disseminate information regarding the regulations governing the gathering, owning, and selling of certain types of artifacts and items made from parts of endangered species.

The Index

Maloney's offers a detailed index to help you quickly find both major and minor subject categories of interest. The index features an exhaustive cross-referencing system that will efficiently guide you to other categories of related interest.

Skim through the index. You'll be amazed at the diversity of items people collect. The index will also help you think of things you might own that may be valuable.

Can't locate information about an item? Try looking under related subjects. Our extensive cross-reference will usually guide you, but use your imagination. Many collectibles are crossovers, i.e., they have collector appeal in more than one field. For instance, an early 20th century calendar depicting bicyclists has appeal not only to paper collectors but also to bicycle enthusiasts.

Useful and Important Suggestions

■ When writing and requesting a reply from those listed, always send a long self-addressed and stamped envelope (LSASE) to help ensure and expedite a reply. Many collector clubs operate on a shoestring budget and require that a request for information be accompanied with an LSASE. Everyone will appreciate your courtesy. Include your phone number as well so the party can call you if he/she needs additional information concerning your query. If you are selling, many would-be buyers are anxious to speak to you personally as soon as possible. They will often have specific questions to ask that can be best answered over the phone.

■ When calling, DON'T CALL COLLECT, unless otherwise directed (and very few people do!); respect time zone differences and don't leave telephone or answering service messages unless you want the call returned collect. Suggest a time that the party should call back collect to ensure that you will be there. When calling about an item you own, be prepared. Have the item in hand (or good photographs of the item), along with notes on its dimensions, maker's mark, condition, signature, and any other identifying marks such as a patent number or date, model/serial number, etc.

■ Don't send items without first notifying the receiving party and getting his/her permission. Items sent without permission can be considered "gifts" and do not need to be returned. When sending photographs or digital images, be sure that they are clear, close-up and in focus. Polaroids are seldom useful. Often, relatively flat objects, such as small textiles, medals, ribbons, or paper items, can be photocopied.

■ If selling, always state the price you would be willing to sell the item for. Most authorities agree that it's up to the seller to set the asking price, although some dealers or buyers will help you. Unable to determine a fair price to ask? Your options are 1) to seek comparable items that have sold online or that are valued in one of many price guides available today (booksellers are listed under **BOOKS, Reference**), 2) use an online appraisal service such as AsktheAppraiser.com, or 3) retain the services of an expert, dealer, or traditional appraiser to assist you. Locate a traditional appraiser by contacting a professional appraisal society such as the ISA, AAA, or ASA (listed under **APPRAISERS**) for a free referral. (By the way, the person you retain to do the appraisal should have no interest in purchasing the items you are selling. That would constitute a conflict of interest.)

■ When you receive a reply from someone to whom you've offered to sell an item, make sure you respond promptly. If the party wants to buy the items you are offering, make sure you let the person know of your final intentions to sell to the him/her or otherwise. Don't keep them wondering whether you even received their reply. Often, listees spend their valuable time and money in researching and/or corresponding with you. Make sure you are courteous and thoughtful in return.

■ When asking for help in identifying or authenticating an item, in addition to photos, send complete descriptions, including dimensions, maker's marks, materials, how long you've had it, how you acquired it, and its provenance (who owned it before you and for how long).

■ When contacting someone for assistance, do not assume that services are offered without charge. Be sensitive to the possible need for paying for services rendered, such as an appraisal or authentication. While some will share willingly without cost, others make their livelihood in the antiques and collectibles business. They should — and do — charge for their knowledge and time. Make sure to ask if there are charges.

■ If an expert is not listed for your particular area of interest, try contacting a related collector's club or periodical. Often the club's contact person or the periodical's editor or publisher are themselves experts. In any case, they are almost always excellent sources of information.

■ Finally, when looking for an expert, advice, or service, don't forget to contact your own neighborhood resources. Museums, libraries, historical societies, and moving company claims departments (a great source for locating talented repairers) are just a few of the local sources to turn to when seeking advice. Don't forget to consult your local telephone *Yellow Pages*, too. Look under "Antique - Dealers," "Antiques - Repairing & Restoring," "Appraisers," "Furniture Repairing & Refinishing," "Jewelers," "Lamps," and "Moving & Storage" for local businesses that may also be able to help. If you locate an unusual source, let us know about it, too. We'd love to include it in the next edition of this book.

If you specialize and wish to be listed in a future edition of the *Maloney's Antiques & Collectibles Resource Directory*, complete and return the form located at the end of this book. Remember, there is no charge for being listed in *Maloney's*.

007

(see CHARACTER COLLECTIBLES, Spy Memorabilia [James Bond]; TELEVISION SHOWS & MEMORABILIA, Private Eye)

1930s TO 1960s

(see MODERNISM; POPULAR CULTURE; SOCIAL CAUSES)

20TH CENTURY

(see ART, Outsider; ART DECO; ELECTRICITY RELATED ITEMS, Appliances; MODERNISM; POPULAR CULTURE; SOCIAL CAUSES)

3-D PHOTOGRAPHICA

(see also CAMERAS & CAMERA EQUIPMENT; OPTICAL ITEMS; STEREO VIEWERS & STEREOVIEWS)

Clubs/Associations

John W. Bordner
National Collectors Association of Die Doubling
Newsletter: Hub, The
P.O. Box 15
Lykens, PA 17048-0015
ph: 717-453-9530
jwb209@epix.net
http://www.geocities.com/ ResearchTriangle/Facility/4968/ NCADD.html
Club is devoted to the study of die varieties; bi-monthly newsletter with information covering die varieties; attributions, micro and macro photography available.

Collectors

Harry Poster
P.O. Box 1883
South Hackensack, NJ 07606-0483
ph: 201-794-9606
fax: 201-794-9553
hposter@att.net
http://www.harryposter.com
Buying Tru-Vue rolls and viewers, View Master singles and three packs; wants Military, Cactus, Wildflowers, gold centers, Movie Pre-views ($50 ea.!); VM and Tru-Vue dealer displays, advertising, Novel View, and similar stereo slides.

Sheldon Aronowitz
487 Palmer Ave.
Teaneck, NJ 07666-3251
ph: 201-837-9508 or 800-982-7401
fax: 201-861-8648
Specializes in View-Master, Tru-Vue, Stori-Vue, Anaglyph, Lenticular, holograms, stereo cards, 3-D literature, 3-D cameras, 3-D views.

Kyle Spain
423 Knight Way
La Canada, CA 91011
ph: 818-952-2154
kyle.spain@warnerbros.com
Collector wants to buy 3-D/stereo slides (4" x 1 5/6") made by amateur photographers from 1950s stereo cameras; also wants viewers.

Christopher Perry
Photoplay Orchestra
7470 Church St., Ste. A
Yucca Valley, CA 92284-3248
ph: 760-365-0475
fax: 760-365-0495
evildoctor3d@yahoo.com
http://www.photoplayorchestra.com
Buys anything that is 3-D: 3-D cameras, projectors, viewers, Viewmaster, Tru-Vue, Realist slides, lenticular 3-D pictures, holograms, novelviews, 3-D filmstrips; 3-D magazines that you view with 3-D glasses or viewer; and any other 3-D items.

Dealers

Dalia Miller
3Dstereo.com, Inc.
1930 Village Center Circle, PMB 3-333
Las Vegas, NV 89134
ph: 702-838-7015 or 702-838-7021
fax: 702-838-7016
ddd@3dstereo.com
http://www.3dstereo.com
Buys and sells 3-D supplies, equipment, stereo cameras, projectors, viewers, lenticulars, books, stereorama, View-Master reels and packets, Tru-Vue strips; great catalog.

David Starkman
Reel 3-D Enterprises, Inc.
P.O. Box 2368
Culver City, CA 90231-2368
ph: 310-837-2368
fax: 310-558-1653
reel3d@aol.com
http://stereoscopy.com/reel3d
A catalog about 3-D photography and 3-D equipment collecting.

John Saddy
Jefferson Stereoptics
50 Foxborough Grove
London, Ontario N6K 4A8 Canada
ph: 519-641-4431
fax: 519-641-2899
john.saddy.3d@sympatico.ca
http://www3.sympatico.ca/ john.saddy.3d/home.htm
Specializes in stereoviews; buys, sells, and operates a specialized stereoview phone and mail auction; wants boxed

sets, reels, quality accumulations, View-Master and Tru-Vue; specializes in consignments; also buys antique photography.

Experts

Roger T. Nazeley
4921 Castor Ave.
Philadelphia, PA 19124-2411
ph: 215-535-9021 or 215-743-8999
fax: 215-288-8030
Buy, sell, trade View-Master reels and packets, Tru-Vue cards & film strips, look-a-like View-Masters, etc.; author of book on subject.

John Waldsmith
Collector's Auctioneer, The
P.O. Box 83
Sharon Center, OH 44274
ph: 330-239-1944 or 330-239-2212
vansywalsy@aol.com
http://www.YourAuctionPage.com/ Waldsmith
Wants stereoscopic views, View-Master reels, photographica; conducts mail/phone auctions on regular basis; also direct sales; author of "Stereo Views: An Illustrated History and Price Guide."

Mike Aversa, ISA
Aversa Estate & Appraisal Service
P.O. Box 863
Yorba Linda, CA 92885
ph: 717-777-3848 or 714-749-3887
AversaAntiques@mindspring.com
http://www.aversaantiques.com
Buys and sells stereo cards, stereo viewers, View Master viewers and reels, Tru-Vue, and all 3-D stereographica.

Internet Resources

MaryAnn & Wolfgang Sell
View-Master Homepage, The
3752 Broadview Dr.
Cincinnati, OH 45208
ph: 513-871-1026 or 513-871-1657
fax: 513-321-5398
vmmasell@cinti.net
http://www.cinti.net/~vmmasell
View-Master expert and general interest 3-D information source; curators of Holmes Stereo Research Library in Cincinnati.

Periodicals

Dalia Miller
3Dstereo.com, Inc.
Magazine: Inside 3-D
1930 Village Center Circle, PMB 3-333
Las Vegas, NV 89134
ph: 702-838-7015 or 702-838-7021
fax: 702-838-7016
ddd@3dstereo.com
http://www.3dstereo.com
Quarterly publication for 3-D enthusiasts; information on stereo cameras, projectors, viewers, View-Master, Tru-Vue and other 20th century 3-D.

Tru-View

Experts

Tom Martin
8305 Westbend Rd.
Minneapolis, MN 55427
ph: 763-591-9453
tlmartin@bitstream.net
http://www2.bitstream.net/~tlmartin/vtca
Has been collecting Tru-Vue, Novelview, View-Master and other 3-D transparencies for several years; has written articles on the subject; currently writing a book on Tru-Vue; writes online Tru-Vue and View-Master newsletter.

View-Masters

Appraisers

Mike Aversa, ISA
Aversa Estate & Appraisal Service
P.O. Box 863
Yorba Linda, CA 92885
ph: 717-777-3848 or 714-749-3887
AversaAntiques@mindspring.com
http://www.aversaantiques.com
Appraises, buys and sells stereo cards, stereo viewers, View Master viewers and reels, Tru-Vue, and all 3-D stereographica.

Clubs/Associations

Tom Martin
View-Master & Tru-Vue Collectors Association
Newsletter: ReView
8305 Westbend Rd.
Minneapolis, MN 55427
ph: 763-591-9453
tlmartin@bitstream.net
http://www2.bitstream.net/~tlmartin/vtca

Mary Ann Sell, Pres.
National Stereoscopic Association
Magazine: Stereo World
P.O. Box 86708
Portland, OR 97286
ph: 503-771-4440
vmmasell@cinti.net
http://www.stereoview.org
Members collect stereo views, stereoscopes, stereo cameras; View-Master reels, viewers, packets; all other 3-D collectibles; the glossy colorful magazine is published six timer per year.

Collectors

Jim Rohacs
9721 Lomond Dr.
Manassas, VA 22110-3104
ph: 703-369-5578
Wants to buy View-Masters and similar 3-D items.

Howard & Jane Hazelcorn
6731 Ashley Ct.
Sarasota, FL 34241-9696
ph: 941-921-1815
mrpropane@aol.com
Wants to buy early viewers and rare reels.

Bob Zeuschel
1638 Highland Valley Ctr.
Chesterfield, MO 63005-4919
ph: 636-537-3145
Wants to buy View-Masters, Tru-Vue 3-D slide formats.

Kyle Spain
423 Knight Way
La Canada, CA 91011
ph: 818-952-2154
kyle.spain@warnerbros.com
Collector wants to buy View-Master reels and packets; all types especially scenic, "Made in Belgium" reels (scenic).

Dealers

Steve Schuler
ph: 419-738-7551
sschuler@bright.net
http://www.bright.net/~sschuler/vmfs.html
Site has lots of reels for sale.

Diane Davison
A Different View of the World
1517 Reisterstown Rd., Ste. 101
Baltimore, MD 21208
ph: 410-486-0900
fax: 410-486-0901
diane@lawgal.net
Collects, buys and sells View-Master, 3-D, stereoscopy.

John & Dana Achziger
PMB #154
9116 E. Sprague
Spokane, WA 99206
ph: 509-924-9199
johna@unix.ieway.com
Have a large variety of View-Master reels for sale.

Experts

Walter Sigg
3-D Entertainment
10 Stonewall Dr.
Hamburg, NJ 07419
ph: 973-823-0968
ws3Dent@nac.net
Buys and sells View-Master, Tru-Vue, 3-D cameras, projectors, reels, and most 3-D items; also early single View-Master reels and the three reel packets, and reels and 3-D cameras by Sawyers and G.A.F.

Sheldon Aronowitz
487 Palmer Ave.
Teaneck, NJ 07666-3251
ph: 201-837-9508 or 800-982-7401
fax: 201-861-8648
Specializes in View-Master, Tru-Vue, Stori-Vue, Anaglyph, Lenticular, holograms, stereo cards, 3-D literature, 3-D cameras, 3-D views.

John Waldsmith
Collector's Auctioneer, The
P.O. Box 83
Sharon Center, OH 44274
ph: 330-239-1944 or 330-239-2212
vansywalsy@aol.com
http://www.YourAuctionPage.com/Waldsmith
Wants stereoscopic views, View-Master reels, photographica; conducts mail/phone auctions on regular basis; also direct sales; author of "Stereo Views: An Illustrated History and Price Guide."

MaryAnn & Wolfgang Sell
View-Master Homepage, The
3752 Broadview Dr.
Cincinnati, OH 45208
ph: 513-871-1026 or 513-871-1657
fax: 513-321-5398
vmmasell@cinti.net
http://www.cinti.net/~vmmasell
View-Master expert and general interest 3-D information source; curators of Holmes Stereo Research Library in Cincinnati; author of a 300-page history of View-Master.

Internet Resources

Keith Baird
View-Master Ultimate Reel List
701 Winflo
Austin, TX 78703
ph: 512-474-6759
http://ccwf.cc.utexas.edu/~number6/vm
Lists of reels, history of View-Master, numbering system.

A.C. GILBERT

(see TOYS, Construction Sets [Erector]; TRAINS, Toy [American Flyer])

ABRAHAM LINCOLN

(see CIVIL WAR ARTIFACTS; PERSONALITIES [HISTORICAL], Abraham Lincoln)

ACCOUNT BOOKS

(see also PAPER COLLECTIBLES)

Collectors

Roy C. Kulp
P.O. Box 264
Hatfield, PA 19440-0264
ph: 215-362-0732
Wants to buy account books and day books by farmers, carpenters, blacksmiths, coffin & carriage makers, and weavers; also wants pre-1890 handwritten travel diaries.

ACTING

(see PERFORMING ARTS)

ADDING MACHINES

(see also CALCULATORS; OFFICE EQUIPMENT; TYPEWRITERS)

Collectors

Peter Frei
P.O. Box 500
Brimfield, MA 01010-0500
ph: 413-245-4660
peterfrei@prodigy.net
Wants to buy handpowered vacuum cleaners, pre-1875 sewing machines, typewriters, calculators, and adding machines.

Anthony Casillo
Antique Typewriter Collecting
325 Nassau Blvd.
Garden City, NY 11530-5313
ph: 516-489-8300 or 516-742-4919
fax: 516-489-6501
typebar@aol.com
http://www.typewritercollector.com
Wants to buy old and unusual pre-1920 adding machines.

Arthur Cheslock
514 St. Paul St.
Baltimore, MD 21202
ph: 410-962-8580
fax: 410-752-8112
Wants pre-1945 calculators, adding machines and scientific instruments; also wants related literature.

Darryl Rehr
P.O. Box 641824
Los Angeles, CA 90064-6824
ph: 310-477-5229
fax: 310-268-8420
dcrehr@earthlink.net
Wants adding machines (machines that only add) of unusual and early designs; send SASE for free information packet.

ADIRONDACK

(see FURNITURE [ANTIQUE], Rustic)

ADS

Magazine

(see ADVERTISING COLLECTIBLES; MAGAZINES, Covers & Tear Sheets; PAPER COLLECTIBLES)

ADVERTISING COLLECTIBLES

(see also BREWERIANA; BUTTONS, Pin-Back; COFFEE; DINNERWARE, Advertising; GAS STATION COLLECTIBLES; GLASSES; LABELS; MAGAZINES, Covers & Tear Sheets; PAPER COLLECTIBLES; POCKET MIRRORS; POPULAR CULTURE; THERMOMETERS; WATCH FOBS)

Auction Services

Randy Inman
Randy Inman Auctions, Inc.
P.O. Box 726
West Buxton, ME 04093
ph: 207-872-6900
fax: 207-872-6966
inman@inmanauctions.com
http://www.inmanauctions.com
Conducts specialty auctions for advertising, coin-op, gambling devices, automata, soda pop, Coca Cola, breweriana, robots and space toys, cast iron and tin toys, Disneyana, mechanical music, and mechanical and still banks.

James D. Julia Auctioneers Inc.
Rt. 201, Skowhegan Rd.
P.O. Box 830
Fairfield, ME 04937
ph: 207-453-7125
fax: 207-453-2502
jjulia@juliaauctions.com
http://www.juliaauctions.com
Conducts specialized auctions of advertising and country store items; one of the leaders in the field; trade signs coin-operated items, gambling devices, syrup dispensers; uses nationally recognized experts to catalog specialty sales.

Howard Parzow
Howard B. Parzow, Auctioneers
P.O. Box 3464
Gaithersburg, MD 20885-3464
ph: 301-977-6741
fax: 301-208-8947
hparzow@aol.com
http://www.hbparzowauctioneer.com
Conducts specialized auctions of country store, advertising, drug store, apothecary and medical related items, and Americana; advertises nationally; auction house located at 10 South Main St., Mt. Airy, MD.

Richard W. Opfer, Jr.
Richard Opfer Auctioneering, Inc.
1919 Greenspring Dr.
Lutherville Timonium, MD 21093-4113
ph: 410-252-5035
fax: 410-252-5863
info@opferauction.com
http://www.opferauction.com
Specializes in auctioning paintings, furniture, antiques, toys, dolls, games, black memorabilia, and advertising items; monthly eclectic collector sales feature a wide variety of collectibles; weekly auctions include general estate merch.

Dave Beck
Beck Auctions
P.O. Box 435
Mediapolis, IA 52637-0435
ph: 319-394-3943
fax: 319-394-3943
adman@mepotelco.net
Conducts mail auctions of advertising watch fobs, mirrors, pin-back buttons, etc.; send stamp for illustrated auction catalog.

Larry & Sheri Manos
Buffalo Bay Auction Co.
5244 Quam Circle
Saint Michael, MN 55376
ph: 763-428-8480
buffalobayauction@hotmail.com
http://www.buffalobayauction.com
Conducts bi-monthly online antiques and country store consignment auctions.

Steve Howard
Past Tyme Collectibles
PMB #204
2401 San Ramon Valley Blvd.
San Ramon, CA 94583
ph: 925-484-6442
fax: 925-484-2551
pasttyme1@attbi.com
http://www.pasttyme.com
Specializes in the auction sale of advertising collectibles: signs, trays, tins relating to hunting and fishing, tobacco, breweriana, soda, coffee, general store, sporting goods, saloon Americana.

Clubs/Associations

Ephemera Society of America Inc., The
Magazine: Ephemera News
P.O. Box 95
Cazenovia, NY 13035-0095
ph: 315-655-9139
fax: 315-655-9139
info@ephemerasociety.org
http://www.ephemerasociety.org
The major organization for collectors and dealers of paper collectibles; focuses on the preservation and study of ephemera (short-lived printed matter); "Ephemera News" published quarterly; also publishes "The Ephemera Journal."

David Schnakenberg
Farm Machinery Advertising Collectors
10108 Tamarack Dr.
Vienna, VA 22182-1843
schnakenbergdd@erols.com

Antique Advertising Association of America
Newsletter: Past Times
P.O. Box 5851
Elgin, IL 60123
aaaa@bblocksonline.com
http://www.pastimes.org
Dedicated to collecting ALL forms of quality advertising: tobacco, coffee, whiskey, beer, candy, gum, clocks, country store, cabinets, etc.

Collectors

Barry Hunsberger
2300 Meadowlane Dr.
Easton, PA 18042
ph: 610-253-2477
Beer, soda, whiskey, other advertising lithos: calendars, signs, trays, match holders.

Jerry A. Phelps
1500 Van Buren Rd.
Mount Eden, KY 40046-9552
ph: 502-859-4063
phelps-vbv@dcr.net
Wants pre-1900 country store and advertising items: signs, broadsides, clocks, tins, bins, display cases, etc.

Mark S. McNee
1009 Vassar Dr.
Kalamazoo, MI 49001-4483
ph: 269-343-8393
nostrums@chartermi.net
Wants to buy all forms of early advertising including signs, posters, tin containers, and store displays.

Tom Rutledge
3015 Bever Ave., SE
Cedar Rapids, IA 52403-3028
ph: 319-399-1427
Wants country store advertising items, calendars, signs, broadsides, tins, posters for all types of products, especially ammunition, beer, whiskey, tobacco, and soft drink companies; also old mail order catalogs and flyers.

Mike Kranz
463 Stage Line Rd.
Hudson, WI 54016-7849
ph: 715-386-7333 or 715-386-9212
Wants to buy old store stock and store advertisements.

Steve Ketcham
P.O. Box 24114
Minneapolis, MN 55424-0114
ph: 952-920-4205
s.ketcham@unique-software.com
Seeking pre-1940 advertising signs, trays, mirrors, calendars, posters, etc. for all types of products, especially beer, whiskey, patent medicine, tobacco; send SASE with all inquiries.

Roger V. Baker
P.O. Box 620417
Redwood City, CA 94062-0417
ph: 650-851-7188
fax: 650-851-7188
Wants signs, calendars, trays, etc. advertising firearms, ammunition, beer, whiskey, tobacco, and general store companies.

Neal Austinson
P.O. Box 1691
Windsor, CA 95492-1691
ph: 707-838-9015
Wants to buy old advertising collectibles including signs, trays, etc.

Dealers

Leila Dunbar
Dunbar's Gallery
76 Haven St.
Milford, MA 01757-3821
ph: 508-634-8697
fax: 508-634-8698
dunbars@dunbarsgallery.com
http://www.dunbarsgallery.com
Mail order Americana - no reproductions; buys, sells and specializes in vintage character and comic toys, banks, advertising, automobilia, and Halloween related items.

Rudy Franchi
Nostalgia Factory, The
50 Terminal St., Bldg 2
Charlestown, MA 02129
ph: 617-241-8300 or 800-479-8754
fax: 617-241-0710
posters@nostalgia.com
http://www.nostalgia.com
Buys and sells all forms of old advertising, from Victorian trade cards to contemporary billboards; 25 years in business.

Phelps Fullerton
Great Bay Trading Co.
281 Atlantic Ave.
North Hampton, NH 03862-2103
ph: 603-964-7093 or 603-964-9928
pfullerton@aol.com
Buys and sells paper, tin, porcelain, and wood advertising signs, trays, tins, calendars, die-cuts, mirrors, display cases, country store items, etc. for all types of products.

Mary Ann Hahn
Second Hand Mary Ann's
103 Ocean Point Rd.
Boothbay Harbor, ME 04538
ph: 207-633-2426
fax: 207-633-2586
maryann@gwi.net
Wants to buy old advertising die-cuts (cardboard signs with easels on back).

Marc Zydiak
Star Archives
P.O. Box 285
Westfield, NJ 07091-0285
ph: 908-654-6505
mzunderstood@hotmail.com

Alice Kasten
Alice's Advertising Antiques
131 Allenwood Rd.
Great Neck, NY 11023
ph: 516-466-8954
alicek13@aol.com
http://members.aol.com/AliceK13
Buys and sells advertising collectibles; thousands of trade cards, advertising blotters, pamphlets, etc. on database; can send list tailored to your wants.

Harvey Leventhal
Harvey's Antique Advertising
412 Circle Dr.
Ellwood City, PA 16117
ph: 724-752-1068
harvey@antiqueadvertising.com
http://www.antiqueadvertising.com
Web site filled with photos, facts, fun and links to other antique advertising sites; lots of old tins, antique advertising and country store items.

John Cuddy
2768 Willits Rd.
Philadelphia, PA 19136-1026
ph: 215-552-9855
cuddymailpouch@aol.com
Buys and sells illustrated advertising mailing envelopes dating from 1870s to 1940s from US manufacturers; please no stamps or 1st day covers.

Mark & Sharon Weaver
Tin Man Antiques
P.O. Box 1663
Hockessin, DE 19707
ph: 302-998-7191
Specializes in advertising collectibles.

J. Glen & Violet Moore
Main St. Antiques
47 W. Main St.
P.O. Box 627
New Market, MD 21774-0627
ph: 301-865-3710
Buys and sells antique advertising items; signs (including neon), catalogs, trade cards and more; large selection specializing in earlier items; appointments preferred.

Gary Metz
Muddy River Trading Co.
263 Key Lakewood Dr.
Moneta, VA 24121
ph: 540-721-2091
fax: 540-721-1782
Buys and sells advertising collectibles: collections, signs in quantity, Coca-Cola, die-cuts, stand ups; tin, paper, cardboard, porcelain, country store items.

Willisia Holbrook
Armbrook Antiques
531 Doub Rd.
Lewisville, NC 27023
ph: 888-393-8025 or 336-945-9477
fax: 336-945-9914
Buys and sells early country store advertising items; Web site has full

online catalog including descriptions and photos.

George Goehring
Dennis & George Collectibles
323 Sandpiper Lane
Delray Beach, FL 33483
ph: 561-243-3072
dandgtins@aol.com
With Dennis O'Brien runs collectibles mail order firm; collectors and dealers of upright pocket tobacco tins, advertising, etc.

Vic Kroll
Kroll's Kollectibles
3451 Nighthawk Ct.
Punta Gorda, FL 33950-6675
ph: 941-575-0303
beer104@comcast.net
Buys, sells, trades beer, whiskey, soda and tobacco advertising items.

Ron Davison
TV Toy Memories
618 South Northwest Hwy. #179
Barrington, IL 60010
ph: 847-542-7473
cerealboxman@yahoo.com
http://www.tvtoymemories.com
Buys and sells 1950s through 1990s TV related memorabilia: toys, coloring books, advertising memorabilia, paper dolls, cereal dolls; most items are unused and many are autographed by the TV celebrity.

Mike Schwimmer
Collectors Center
325 East Blodgett
Lake Bluff, IL 60044-2112
ph: 847-295-1901
Collector of cigar memorabilia; dealer in all forms of vintage advertising; buys and sells.

Robert M. Levine
#2 Troll Court
Ballwin, MO 63011-4036
ph: 636-394-4370 or 314-518-4872
fax: 636-394-8557
boblevine@hotmail.com
Buys, sells, trades and collects advertising items with company logo; must be at least 25 years old.

Jim & Rita Hinton
Collector's Choice
P.O. Box 104284
Jefferson City, MO 65110-4284
ph: 573-636-7567

Don Creekmore
Nations Attic, The
ph: 316-371-1828
dcreekmore@cox.net
http://www.nationsattic.com
Wants to buy vintage pre-1970 advertising display material: signs (metal, cardboard, paper, neon, etc), clocks, in-store displays, etc.

Dale B. Peterson
Past Times Treasures
22762 Woodridge Dr.
Claremore, OK 74017
ph: 918-341-5475
cpeters2@mail.com
http://www.geocities.com/cdpet1
Actively seeking drug store and country store show globes, pedestal candy jars, old shelf stock, advertising, and especially counter top containers used for serving or displaying candy, gum, nuts, etc.; appraisals given.

Stephen Hansrote
Griffin Trading Company
159 Howell St.
Dallas, TX 75207
ph: 214-747-9234
fax: 214-747-0660
griffintc2@aol.com
http://www.griffintradingantiques.com
Buying and selling all types of American and European advertising such as displays, props, figures, paper goods, wood and metal signs.

John D. McKenna
McKenna Bros. Wholesale
801 W. Cucharras St., #803
Colorado Springs, CO 80905-1619
ph: 719-630-8732 or 719-488-0818
Always buying, selling, trading antique signs, tins, trays, posters, and country store items; best prices paid for mint condition items.

Ruth A. Miller Knott
Paperpreneur, The
1248 Ash St.
Lynden, WA 98264
ph: 360-318-8193
ruthie@nas.com
http://www.thepaperpreneur.com
Offers a unique selection of quality paper ephemera and historical documents: advertising, Americana, agriculture, Colonial, maritime, transportation, maritime, reward or merit, fraternal; does research, will answer questions.

Alma
MPA Collections
20, rue des Poissonniers
Neuilly sur Sein
Paris, 92200 France
ph: 01 40 8 01 52
info@mpacollections.com
http://www.mpacollections.com
Specializes in antique advertising, tins, toys, vintage Disney.

Experts

B. J. Summers
233 Darnell Rd.
Benton, KY 42025
Author of "Value Guide to Advertising Memorabilia."

Bob & Sharon Huxford
Huxford Enterprises
1202 7th St.
Covington, IN 47932
Authors of "Huxford's Collectible Advertising."

Craig Stifter
218 South Adams St.
Hinsdale, IL 60521
ph: 630-789-5780
mcstifte@gsb.uchicago.edu
Wants to buy older Coca-Cola, Pepsi-Cola, Dr. Pepper, Orange-Crush, Hires Root Beer and other brand soda memorabilia; writes columns for several antiques periodicals; also interested in items pertaining to country (general) stores.

Internet Resources

Ad*Access, John W. Hartman Center for Sales, Advertising & Marketing History
Duke University
Durham, NC 27708-0185
ph: 919-660-5827
fax: 919-660-5934
hartman-center@duke.edu
http://scriptorium.lib.duke.edu/adaccess
*The Ad*Access Project presents images and database information for over 7,000 advertisements printed in US and Canadian newspapers and magazines between 1911 and 1955: radio, television, transportation, beauty & hygiene, and WWII.*

Museums/Libraries

National Museum of American History, Archives Center, Smithsonian Institution
14th & Constitution Ave. NW
Room C340, MRC 601
Washington, DC 20560
ph: 202-357-3270 or 202-357-1789
fax: 202-786-2453
webmaster@si.edu
http://www.si.edu/organiza/museums/nmah/nmah.htm
Dedicated to advertising and American business ephemera from the late 1700s to 1980; also ethnic ephemera from 1890s to present.

American Advertising Museum
211 NW Fifth Ave. & Davis St.
Portland, OR 97209
ph: 503-226-0000
fax: 503-238-6674
info@admuseum.org
http://www.admuseum.org
A major exhibition, research and education center; the industry's most comprehensive collection of advertising and business artifacts.

Periodicals

Denise M. Sater, Ed.
Newspaper: Paper & Advertising Collector (P.A.C.)
P.O. Box 500
Mount Joy, PA 17552-0500
ph: 717-492-2540 or 800-800-1833
fax: 717-653-6165
dsater7650@aol.com
http://www.paperandadvertisingcollector.com
Specialty publication for collectors of paper, advertising, ephemera, country store, etc.

Alan R. Blakeman
B.B.R. Publishing
Magazine: British Bottle Review & Collectors Mart
Elsecar Heritage Centre
Nr Barnsley, South Yorks S74 8HJ U.K.
ph: 01226 745156
fax: 01226 361561
sales@onlinebbr.com
http://www.onlinebbr.com
Published for over 22 years; full color magazine; the world's longest continuous running publication covering the multitudinous areas of antique bottles; including world news; published quarterly.

Repair Services

Chuck Kovacic
9337 Sophia Ave.
North Hills, CA 91343-2820
ph: 818-891-4069
fax: 818-891-4069
cfkovacic@aol.com
Repairs antique advertising including porcelain tins and trays, paper, cardboard, and metal.

A & P Items

Dealers

Syd E. Pitzer
Cherished Antiques & Collectibles
425 Old Bethel Church Rd.
Winchester, VA 22603-4050
ph: 540-667-4255

Absinthe

Dealers

Mike Lavarone
Absinthe Collectibles
611 Marengo Ave.
Forest Park, IL 60130-1916
ph: 312-407-5639
Offering the finest in French bistro, absinthe and pastis items: spoons, glassware, books, posters.

Absolut Vodka

Clubs/Associations

Pam Brown, Sr. Ed.
Absolut Collectors Society
membership@absolutsociety.com
http://www.absolutsociety.com
Collectors interested in Absolut Vodka advertisements and associated paraphernalia.

Collectors

David Bell
318 Maxim Dr., 1st Fl.
Hopatcong, NJ 07843
ph: 973-601-0575
justgoodstuff@aol.com
Wants to buy any Absolut Vodka advertising items: postcards, ties, scarves, watches, store displays, clothing, art work, etc.

Alka Seltzer

Collectors

Darlene Shidler-Petrat
58999 Lower Dr.
Goshen, IN 46528
ph: 574-534-3903
precmom48@aol.com
Wants Alka Seltzer and Miles Laboratories, Inc. (Elkhart, IN) items: bottles, boxes, toys, "Speedy" figures, advertising, etc.

Ammunition

Collectors

Bill Bramlett
P.O. Box 12600
Florence, SC 29504-1965
ph: 843-629-1965 or 843-662-0702 x102
BillBramlett@webtv.net
Wants to buy 1890-1931 calendars, posters and signs advertising shotgun shells and cartridges from companies such as Peters, Austin, Remington, US Cartridge Co., The Black Shells, Western.

Aunt Jemima

Collectors

Lynn Burkett
P.O. Box 671
Hillsdale, MI 49242-0671
ph: 517-437-2149
slburkett@dmci.net
Wants Aunt Jemima pancake advertising: recipe booklets, flyers, maps, paper masks, signs, posters, product containers, premium items, china, etc.

Beech-Nut

Collectors

Bruce A. Van Evera
94 Montgomery St.
Canajoharie, NY 13317-1213
ph: 518-673-3522
vanevera@adelphia.net
Wants to buy Beech-Nut Brand glass, tin or cardboard containers with paper label intact: catsup, mustard, chili sauce, slice beef, ginger ale, sarsaparilla, peanut butter, jams, K-rations, gum, biscuit tins, cookie & candy containers.

Biblical

Collectors

Burke O. Long
14 Baxter Lane
Brunswick, ME 04011
ph: 207-725-8920
fax: 207-725-3495
blong@bowdoin.edu
Does not buy bibles; wants old advertising using Bible scenes, quotes, or themes: paper, postcards, trade cards, signs, celluloids, tin, etc.

Billboard Signs

Dealers

Randy Littlefield
Billboards of the Past
5654 S.E. King Rd.
Portland, OR 97222
ph: 503-659-0266
billboardsofthepast@attbi.com
http://www.billboardsofthepast.com
Offers original full size billboard signs dating from 1945 to 1967; subjects include auto, beer, Coca-Cola, gas, oil, Levis, food, politics, tires, tractors, household, and many others.

Black & White Scotch

Collectors

Paul Stookey
Olde Towne Collectables
24724 Brightwater Ct.
Leesburg, FL 34748
ph: 352-435-6169
stock22@aol.com
Wants to buy any "Black and White" Scotch advertising: signs, trays, bottles, back bar pieces, all black and white dogs, etc.

Buster Brown

Collectors

Jim Mitchell
70-D Pascal Lane
Manchester, CT 06040
Wants anything related to Buster Brown and the Brown Show Co.

Marty Goldman
5 East Genesee St.
Auburn, NY 13021
ph: 315-253-0236
yellowkid@tds.net
Advanced collector of all pre-1920 Buster Brown memorabilia; always looking for paper to pin-backs; also Yellow Kid.

Counter Jars

(see also BOTTLES; CANDY CONTAINERS, Jars; FRUIT JARS; JELLY CONTAINERS; TOBACCO COLLECTIBLES, Jars)

Collectors

Steve Boggs
644 Dayton Rd.
Waynesville, OH 45068
ph: 513-519-5786
SteveBoggs@juno.com
Avid collector of antique store jars with fired-on logos; specializes in 1 and 2 gallon cylinder jars and their matching side-loaders, with special focus on metal replacement lids.

Experts

Craig Ehlenberger
Abalone Cove Antiques
7 Fruit Tree Rd.
Rancho Palos Verdes, CA 90275
ph: 310-377-4609
fax: 310-544-6792
CEhlenberger@cox.net
Collector, dealer, expert; collects, trades, deals in pre-1950 counter display jars, glass trays, etc.; primarily those with names embossed in the glass, but also all others.

Figures

(see also DOLLS, Advertising; PHONOGRAPHS, Nipper)

Collectors

Roland Coover
1537 E. Strasburg Rd.
West Chester, PA 19380-6380
ph: 610-692-3112
rlcoover@aol.com
Wants to buy figures of trademark characters such as Speedy Alka-Seltzer, Mr. Clean, Reddy Kilowatt, Quisp, Otto the Orkin Man, Raid Bug, etc.

Dealers

Marty Blank
P.O. Box 405
Flushing, NY 11365-0405
ph: 516-485-8071
Wants to buy Elsie, Campbell Kids, Reddy Kilowatt, Coke, figural vinyl advertising and Country Store items.

Museums/Libraries

Creatability Toys Museum of Advertising Icons
1550 Maruga Ave., Ste. 504
Miami, FL 33146
ph: 305-663-7374
fax: 305-669-0092
http://www.toymuseum.com
Museum has over 650 nostalgic advertising icons; Web site allows you to search and obtain detailed descriptions and identification of all items in the collection.

Figures (Charlie Tuna)

Clubs/Associations

Cathy C. Runyan, Pres.
Charlie Tuna Collectors Club
7812 N.W. Hampton Rd.
Kansas City, MO 64152-4940
ph: 816-587-8687 or 816-587-1203
fax: 816-587-8687
marbleldy@aol.com

Experts

Cathy C. Runyan
Right Brain Publishing
7812 N.W. Hampton Rd.
Kansas City, MO 64152-4940
ph: 816-587-8687 or 816-587-1203
fax: 816-587-8687
marbleldy@aol.com
Collector, appraiser and specialist in Charlie Tuna memorabilia and promotional items.

Figures (Reddy Kilowatt)

Collectors

C. T. Little
183 Rainbow Dr., #8348
Livingston, TX 77399-1083
ladylight2000@yahoo.com
Collects and specializes in light bulbs; wants light bulbs with tips or unusual light bulbs, Glow Lamps (neon) with figurals inside, meters, sockets, bulbs with figural or decorative filaments, Edison, Westinghouse, Reddy Kilowatt, etc.

Experts

Warren Dotz
2999 Regent St., Ste. 300
Berkeley, CA 94705-2118
ph: 510-652-1159
fax: 510-540-0325
wellipsis@aol.com
Buys & specializes in advertising character figural store displays, banks, statuettes, and dolls; cartoonish trademark characters (Speedy Alka Seltzer, Reddy Kilowatt, Elsie the Cow, etc.); author of "Advertising Character Collectibles."

Firearms Related

Collectors

Bill Bramlett
P.O. Box 12600
Florence, SC 29504-1965
ph: 843-629-1965 or 843-662-0702 x102
BillBramlett@webtv.net
Wants 1890-1931 firearms-related advertising items such as calendars, signs and posters that advertise firearms, shotgun shells, gunpowders from Remington, Marlin, Peters, U.M.C., DuPont, Winchester, US Cartridge Co., Savage, etc.

Gerber Baby

Experts

Joan Stryker Grubaugh
2342 Hoaglin Rd.
Van Wert, OH 45891
ph: 419-622-4411
fax: 419-622-3026
Author of "Gerber Baby Dolls & Advertising Collectibles."

Hershey's

Clubs/Associations

Collectors Club of Hershey's Memorabilia
Box 153, 150 Moseywood Rd.
Lake Harmony, PA 18624
ph: 570-722-1020
dewolfe@ptd.net
http://www.candycollectorsclub.com
For the collector of Hershey's memorabilia.

Hormel

Museums/Libraries

SPAM Museum
P.O. Box 800
Austin, MN 55912
ph: 507-437-5345
Museum of the Hormel Company; history, artifacts, advertisements, SPAM history and exhibit.

Loose-Wiles

Collectors

Liz & Dick Wilmes
38W567 Brindlewood Ave.
Elgin, IL 60123-7976
ph: 847-697-9679
fax: 847-742-1054
Bblocks@bblocksonline.com
Wants to buy items produced by or for the Sunshine Biscuit Co. (or formally Loose-Wiles Company): display racks, containers, photos, trade cards, artwork, signs, toys, stationery, brochures, invoices, pins, calendars, etc.; SASE for reply.

Lucky Strike

Collectors

Harvey Leventhal
Harvey's Antique Advertising
412 Circle Dr.
Ellwood City, PA 16117
ph: 724-752-1068
harvey@antiqueadvertising.com
http://www.antiqueadvertising.com
Collects Lucky Strike tobacco items and displays them on his Web site.

Monarch Food Products

Collectors

Bruce & Nada Ferris
Ev'ry Nook & Cranny
3094 Oakes Dr.
Hayward, CA 94542-1234
ph: 510-581-5285
fax: 510-581-4469
Nada.Ferris@ncal.kaiperm.org
Wants Monarch food products items from the 1920s: glass items with paper labels, tins, Monarch cookbook, teenie weenie popcorn, etc.; also Toledo, OH advertising, Atlas, Woolson Spice & Coffee, Toledo Biscuit, Buckey Beer.

Nabisco Food Group

Clubs/Associations

Charlie & Prissy Brown
Inner Seal Club
Newsletter: Colophon, The
6609 Billtown Rd.
Louisville, KY 40299
ph: 502-231-9379
A club dedicated to the collection and discussion of antique and nostalgic items carrying or relating to the INNER SEAL trademark of the Nabisco Foods Group; National Biscuit Company (NABISCO), Americana, country store.

Old Spice

Internet Resources

Ray Dupont
OldSpicers.com
admin@oldspicers.com
http://www.oldspicers.com
An Internet based forum for those who collect, buy, sell, trade Old Spice/ Shulton collectibles and memorabilia.

Phillip Morris

Collectors

Stuart Morrell
8925 Laureate Lane
Richmond, VA 23236-4406
IBuyComics@aol.com
Wants old Phillip Morris items.

Piano Related

Collectors

Philip Jamison
17 Sharon Alley
West Chester, PA 19382
ph: 610-696-8449
fax: 610-696-8449
mortier@netreach.net
http://www.streetorgan.com
Wants piano related material such as advertising signs and posters, catalogs, photographs of factory interiors, piano trade publications, etc.

Janice E. Kelsh
633 Pennsylvania Ave.
Hagerstown, MD 21740-3769
ph: 301-797-7675
fax: 301-827-7039
mpec2000@hotmail.com
http://www.angelfire.com/music2/ miniaturepianoclub
Wants to buy piano advertising items; also piano related trade cards and postcards.

Pillsbury

Collectors

Doughfan
doughfan@doughfan.com
http://www.doughfan.com
Lots of great information about Pillsbury Doughboy: pictures, message board, links, and more.

David Wendel
F.E.I. Collectibles
P.O. Box 1187
Poplar Bluff, MO 63902-1187
ph: 573-686-1926 or 573-785-2075
fax: 573-686-8450
dwendel@ldd.net
Wants advertising and other memorabilia related to Pillsbury Doughboy, Green Giant, Sprout.

Dealers

R. Wiltfong
23709 W. 95th
Lenexa, KS 66227
ph: 913-782-0607
doughboy@planetkc.com
http://www.planetkc.com/frogs/ doughboy1.htm
Wants to buy older Pillsbury Doughboy collectibles.

Potteries Related

Collectors

Harvey Duke
577 Ave. Y
Brooklyn, NY 11235
Wants catalogs, brochures, flyers and other paper material from US potteries; also wants advertising signs, dealer signs, ceramic Christmas cards and calling cards, sample plates, plant visit souvenirs, etc. from US potteries only.

Signs

Clubs/Associations

Robert C. English
Porcelain Advertising Collectors Club
P.O. Box 381
Marshfield Hills, MA 02051-0381
ph: 781-837-0111
Informal membership that acts as a clearinghouse for collectors & dealers interested in porcelain signs in all categories. e.g., country store & automobile products as well as directional and street signs; 1900-1950; call for more info.

Collectors

Paul G. Engelke
23399 Rio Del Mar Dr.
Boca Raton, FL 33486-8504
ph: 561-338-3332
keytelco@bellsouth.net
Wants to buy porcelain signs that advertise any type of merchandise: food, gas, oil, services, etc.

Michael Bruner
2615 Echo Lane
Ortonville, MI 48462
ph: 248-627-6351
Wants pre-1950 American or Canadian porcelain signs with good colors or graphics.

Richard Trautwein
Toys N Such
437 Dawson St.
Sault Sainte Marie, MI 49783-2119
ph: 906-635-0356
Especially interested in porcelain advertising signs, neon clocks, and Coca Cola items.

Dealers

Robert C. English
P.O. Box 381
Marshfield Hills, MA 02051-0381
ph: 781-837-0111
Buys and sells porcelain signs including country store and automobile products as well as directional and street signs; 1900-1950.

Chick Darrow
Darrow's Fun Antiques
1101 1st Ave.
New York, NY 10021-8737
ph: 212-838-0730 or 888-DARROWS
fax: 212-838-3617
george@fun-antiques.com
http://www.fun-antiques.com
Buys & sells antique games, toys, ad signs, animated art, jukeboxes, slot machines, comic watches, bicycles & memorabilia of all types; also prop rentals.

Walt Feiger
Walt's Antiques
2513 Nelson Rd.
Traverse City, MI 49686-8557
ph: 231-223-7386 or 231-223-4123
feiger@pentel.net
http://www.pentel.net/antiques
Wants to buy old porcelain or tin advertising signs.

Dave Beck
P.O. Box 435
Mediapolis, IA 52637-0435
ph: 319-394-3943
fax: 319-394-3943
adman@mepotelco.net
Buys all kinds of signs in any quantity; may be fairly new (but not reproductions) or 100 years old; tin, porcelain, cardboard, or paper; advertising soda, beer, tobacco, farm related items, or anything else.

Doug Clemence
Treasure Chest
436 North Chicago
Salina, KS 67401-2020
ph: 785-827-9371 or 785-825-4111
Buys, sells, trades old advertising signs.

Nick Ciovica
550 B Ave. J East
Grand Prairie, TX 75050
ph: 972-641-0977
Buys, sells, restores porcelain signs.

Robert Newman
17220 Silver Lane
Encino, CA 91316
ph: 310-559-0539
Buying "picture" or graphic signs in better (8+) condition for any known brand names; also soft drink, oil, gas, auto, tires, jeans, food, ice, tobacco, and bus signs along with big outdoor neon signs; no reproductions or foreign.

Museums/Libraries

Larz Anderson Auto Museum
15 Newton St.
Brookline, MA 02146
ph: 617-522-6547
fax: 617-524-0170
director@mot.org
http://www.mot.org
The museum collection includes many unique and remarkable vehicles as well as many other significant historic artifacts.

Tod Swormstedt
American Sign Museum
407 Gilbert Ave.
Cincinnati, OH 45202
ph: 800-925-1110 or 513-421-2050 x336
fax: 513-421-5144
tod@signmuseum.org
http://www.signmuseum.org
Preserves, archives, displays a historical collection of signs in their many types and forms; documents and surveys the products and equipment used in the design and manufacturing of signs; a 501(c)3 tax-exempt organization.

Repro. Sources

Steve Jelf
SignPast
3203 East Birch Ave.
Arkansas City, KS 67005
ph: 620-442-1626
skj@hit.net
http://www.signpast.com
Makes over 100 reproduction auto, gas and oil, and other baked enamel signs.

Seay Marketing
1325 Tarman Circle
Norman, OK 73071
ph: 405-321-8797 or 800-729-7086
seaymktg@hotmail.com
http://www.seaymarketing.com
Offers high quality reproduction advertising signs for the shop of gameroom: automotive dealership, beverage, petroliana.

Sunshine Biscuit

Collectors

Liz & Dick Wilmes
38W567 Brindlewood Ave.
Elgin, IL 60123-7976
ph: 847-697-9679
fax: 847-742-1054
Bblocks@bblocksonline.com
Wants to buy items produced by or for the Sunshine Biscuit Co. (or formally Loose-Wiles Company): display racks, containers, photos, trade cards, artwork, signs, toys, stationery, brochures, invoices, pins, calendars, etc.; SASE for reply.

Telephone & Telegraph

Experts

Michael Bruner
2615 Echo Lane
Ortonville, MI 48462
ph: 248-627-6351
Co-author with Bob Alexander of "A Collectors Guide to Telephone, Telegraph and Express Co. Advertising."

Tin Vienna Art Plates

Dealers

Tom Lavely
Neat Olde Stuff
16935 N. Main St.
P.O. Box 9
Galesville, WI 54630-0009
ph: 608-582-2082
fax: 608-582-2180
tglavely@aol.com
Collector, expert and dealer in tin Vienna Art Plates; collecting since 1965.

Experts

Howard & Jane Hazelcorn
6731 Ashley Ct.
Sarasota, FL 34241-9696
ph: 941-921-1815
mrpropane@aol.com
Authors of "Hazelcorn's Price Guide to Tin Vienna Art Plates;" tin advertising plates made from the 1890s to the 1950s. (Vienna Art is a trademark used by the H.D. Beach Co., OH.)

Tins

Collectors

Michael R. Reilly
W259 N9116 City Rd. J
Hartland, WI 53029-9010
ph: 414-246-3017
Collector of antique and collectibles tins.

Julia Ball
10650 Steppington #116
Dallas, TX 75230
ph: 214-750-5113
RobjBall@juno.com
Collects small pre-1980 tin containers in which spices were sold.

Ken Kennedy, Sr.
7824 South 113th St.
Seattle, WA 98178-3238
ph: 206-772-4358
spiceking@isomedia.com
Wants to buy colorful old spice tins with interesting graphics.

Dealers

Ed Natale, Jr.
Retro Petro
P.O. Box 222
Wyckoff, NJ 07481-0222
ph: 201-493-7172
jednat@att.net
Wants to buy automotive related tin container: oil, grease, bulb, fuse, spark plug, tube patch, etc.; motorcycle, household oil, handy oil, gun oil; also related signage: tin, porcelain, paper; photos helpful.

Charles & Joan Rhoden
Rhoden Books & Publishing, Inc.
8693 N. 1950 East Rd.
Georgetown, IL 61846-6264
ph: 217-662-8046
rhoden@soltec.net
Wants to buy pre-1960 lard tins and spice tins; send brand name and describe, include photo if possible.

Tin Shop, The
Market Vaults
Scarborough, North Yorkshire YO11 1EU U.K.
ph: (44) 1 723 341905 or (44) 1 723 351089
tin.shop@virgin.net
http://www.tinshop.net
An online store offering advertising material: tins, packaging and memorabilia.

Trade Cards

(see also TRADING CARDS, Non-Sport)

Auction Services

Russell Mascieri
Victorian Images
P.O. Box 284
Marlton, NJ 08053
ph: 609-985-7711
fax: 609-985-8513
RMascieri@aol.com
http://www.tradecards.com/vi
Conducts specialized trade card mail and telephone auctions.

Murray Cards (International) Ltd.
51 Watford Way
Hendon Central, London NW4 3JH U.K.
ph: 0181-2025688
fax: 0181-2037878
murraycards@ukbusiness.com
http://www.murraycards.com
Stocks and auctions trade cards; also publishes "Cigarette Card Values" - a catalog of cigarette and other trade cards.

Trevor Vennett-Smith
T. Vennett-Smith Auctioneers & Valuers
11 Nottingham Rd.
Gotham, Nottingham NG11 OHE U.K.
ph: +44 (0)115 983 0541
fax: +44 (0)115 983 0114
info@vennett-smith.com
http://www.vennett-smith.com
Great Britain's leading professional autograph auction house, specializing in bi-monthly auctions of fine and varied autographs; also postcards, trade cards, ephemera, sporting memorabilia.

Clubs/Associations

Dave Cheadle
Trade Card Collector's Association
Journal: Advertising Trade Card Quarterly
3706 S. Acoma St.
Englewood, CO 80110
ph: 303-761-7906
TrdCardGuy@aol.com
http://www.tradecardcollectors.com
Helps unify advertising trade card collectors through informative publications and an annual national convention.

John W. Townsend
Cartophilic Society of Great Britain
15a Brooks Road
Chiswick
London W4 3BL U.K.
companysec@csgb.co.uk
http://www.csgb.co.uk/
Non-profit club founded in 1935 devoted to the research and collecting of all trade advertisement cards, especially tobacco/cigarette/gum.

Collectors

Paul Davis
308 Landsende Rd.
Devon, PA 19333
ph: 610-644-1216
pwbsdavis@msn.com
Wants insert and trade cards of tobacco companies from 1890 to 1920, Bubble Gum cards from 1930 to 1950, Liebig cards, Au Bon Marche cards and European trade cards.

Dealers

Dave & Nancy Dawson
P.O. Box 750
Marstons Mills, MA 02648-0750
ph: 508-420-3872
dawson95@aol.com
Has an inventory of thousands of trade cards in addition to a variety of other 19th century ephemera such as rewards of merit, valentines, business cards, broadsides, billheads.

Kit Barry
Kit Barry Ephemera
136 High St., Box 3
Brattleboro, VT 05301
ph: 802-254-3634
kbarry@surfglobal.net
http://www.tradecards.com/kb
Specializes in fine ephemera, scarce

and rare, including trade cards, billheads, labels, and posters; also sells a complete line of ephemera supplies: plastic pages, matchbook pages, rigid print holders, soft plastic sleeves, et.

Jean & Howard Berg
P.O. Box 343
Granby, CT 06035
ph: 860-653-7982
JandHBERG@aol.com
Buys and sells quality trade cards, seed and garden trade catalogs, and related ephemera.

Alice Kasten
Alice's Advertising Antiques
131 Allenwood Rd.
Great Neck, NY 11023
ph: 516-466-8954
alicek13@aol.com
http://members.aol.com/AliceK13
Buys and sells advertising collectibles; thousands of trade cards, advertising blotters, pamphlets, etc. on database; can send list tailored to your wants.

Stephen C. Jones
P.O. Box 267
Homer, NY 13077-0267
ph: 607-753-8822
Wants pre-1910 advertising trade cards illustrating products or services, mechanical bank trade cards, Currier & Ives trade cards, Victorian scrapbooks, illustrated business cards, cigar box sample labels and sample books of labels.

Marguerite Cantine
Cantine Kilpatrick
223 Southeast 37th Ave.
Ocala, FL 34471-3045
ph: 352-694-4514
fax: 352-694-4514
designbycantine@aol.com
Wants advertising trade cards and postcards from 1800s to 1915; none later than 1915; prefers children, chromolithographs, and product ads; no photographs; no city or state cards; send photocopy and price by mail, fax, email.

Ron Schieber
Mad Money
P.O. Box 72057
Akron, OH 44372
ph: 330-836-9442
dschiebe@neo.rr.com
Author of a series of 30 checklists of Trade Cards and other ephemera.

Jimmy & Amanda Greene
A & J Trade Cards
9453 Carlton Hills Blvd.
Santee, CA 92071-2504
ph: 619-562-0320
http://www.inetworld.net/jgreene
Buys and sells trade cards; wants Victorian trade card categories such as food-related items and odds and ends as long as they're attractive and/ or bizarre.

Bob Coalbran
Card Mine, The
P.O. Box 56
Telford, Shropshire TF1 3WQ U.K.
http://www.cardmine.co.uk
Specializes in European thematic and Victorian advertising collectible trade cards (sport and non-sport); regular auctions on Web site.

Leon
Creamofcards
9 Sir John Moore Ave.
Hythe, CT21 5DE U.K.
ph: 01303 264401
http://www.creamofcards.com
Specializes in quality cigarette cards and trade cards on a wide range of subjects: birds, dog breeds, glamour, movie stars, soccer players, sports, transporting, and much more.

Experts

Ben Crane
Trade Card Place, The
P.O. Box 4885
Wheaton, IL 60189
ph: 630-665-5662
fax: 630-665-2826
bcrane@tradecards.com
http://www.tradecards.com
Author of "The Before and After Trade Card;" Web site is about Victorian trade cards that advertise American goods and services during the late 1800s; Web site has biweekly online auctions, articles, collectors and dealers, organizations,

Internet Resources

Bob Coalbran
Card Mine, The
P.O. Box 56
Telford, Shropshire TF1 3WQ U.K.
http://www.cardmine.co.uk
Specializes in European thematic and Victorian advertising collectible trade cards (sport and non-sport); regular auctions on Web site.

Trade Cards (Tobacco)

(see also CIGARETTE COLLECTIBLES; SMOKING COLLECTIBLES)

Auction Services

Murray Cards (International) Ltd.
Newsletter: Cigarette Cards
51 Watford Way
Hendon Central, London NW4 3JH U.K.
ph: 0181-2025688
fax: 0181-2037878
murraycards@ukbusiness.com
http://www.murraycards.com
Stocks in excess of 20M cigarette & trade cards; monthly specialist auctions; publisher of card values & books on card collecting.

Bob Coalbran
Card Mine, The
P.O. Box 56
Telford, Shropshire TF1 3WQ U.K.
http://www.cardmine.co.uk
Specializes in European thematic and Victorian advertising collectible trade cards (sport and non-sport); regular auctions on Web site.

Collectors

William Nielsen
1379 Main St.
Brewster, MA 02631-1723
ph: 508-385-9247
Wants US tobacco related trade cards.

Paul Davis
308 Landsende Rd.
Devon, PA 19333
ph: 610-644-1216
pwbsdavis@msn.com
Wants insert and trade cards of tobacco companies from 1890 to 1920, Bubble Gum cards from 1930 to 1950, Liebig cards, Au Bon Marche cards and European trade cards.

Ron Stevenson
4920 Armoury St.
Niagara Falls, Ontario L2E 1T1 Canada
ph: 905-358-5497
Interested in American cigarette cards and albums; Brooke-Bond/Red Rose Tea cards and related ephemera; Liebig trade cards, English language; also other Lieberg ephemera.

Dealers

David Grimes
P.O. Box 354
Hopewell, NJ 08525
ph: 609-466-0303
fax: 609-466-8790
noblegb@aol.com
http://members.aol.com/noblegb/Page/ Text.html
Buys and sells 19th and 20th century American cigarette and tobacco cards, silks, leathers, etc.

Franklyn Roberts
Franklyn Cards
26 The Parade
Walton on the Naze
Essex, CO14 8EA U.K.
FranklynCards@bigfoot.com
http://www.franklyncards.com
One of the best resources on the Internet for 1880 to 1940 cigarette cards.

Internet Resources

Colin Smith
Cigarette Cards Central
29 Birchwood St.
King's Lynn, Norfolk PE30 2AG U.K.
cardking@cigcards.com
http://www.cigcards.com
A major Internet resource for collectors of cigarette cards, tobacco cards, and all cartophily related items.

Periodicals

David Stuckey
Magpie Publications
Magazine: Card Times
70 Winifred Lane
Aughton
Ormskirk, Lancashire L39 5DL U.K.
ph: 01695 423 470
fax: 01695 420 185
david@cardtimes.co.uk
http://www.cardtimes.co.uk
A monthly magazine focusing on trade cards, cigarette silks and cards, also trade cards of celebrities, politicians, athletes, etc.; club activities, sales/ show calendars, ads.

Typewriter Related

Collectors

Darryl Rehr
P.O. Box 641824
Los Angeles, CA 90064-6824
ph: 310-477-5229
fax: 310-268-8420
dcrehr@earthlink.net
http://home.earthlink.net/~dcrehr/ collecting.html
Wants pre-1920 ads for typewriters and office equipment; also trade catalogs and business magazines, e.g., "Business Man's Monthly."

Woolson Spice Co.

Collectors

Bruce & Nada Ferris
Ev'ry Nook & Cranny
3094 Oakes Dr.
Hayward, CA 94542-1234
ph: 510-581-5285
fax: 510-581-4469
Nada.Ferris@ncal.kaiperm.org
Wants Monarch food products items from the 1920s: glass items with paper labels, tins, Monarch cookbook, teenie weenie popcorn, etc.; also Toledo, OH advertising, Atlas, Woolson Spice & Coffee, Toledo Biscuit, Buckey Beer.

Experts

Randy Webb
42217 Cochran Mill Rd.
Leesburg, VA 20175
ph: 703-777-3600 or 540-668-6071
fax: 703-478-1160
thewebbs3@aol.com
Wants Wooson Spice Co. (Lion Coffee) items: bags, cans, cards, diecuts, premiums, store posters, games, etc.; these materials needed for entry into database and book on everything Woolson Spice Co.

AFRICAN & TRIBAL ART

(see also ART; ART, African-American; BLACK MEMORABILIA)

Appraisers

Norman Hurst, ISA CAPP
Hurst Gallery
53 Mount Auburn St.
Cambridge, MA 02138-5030
ph: 617-491-6888 or 212-744-6488
  (NYC)
fax: 617-661-0439
NHurst@compuserve.com
http://www.hurstgallery.com
  Buys, sells, appraises African,
  Oceanic, Native American,
  PreColumbian and Asian art; dealing
  in, authenticating and appraising
  African art and artifacts for over 25
  years; sculptures, masks.

Glenn A. Long
Long & Manzi Fine Art Services, Inc.
ph: 518-854-3388
fax: 518-854-3999
topappraisers@hotmail.com
  Private dealers and appraisers
  serving collectors and museums for
  over 25 years; specializes in art,
  drawings, paintings, photography &
  photographs, 19th and 20th century
  sculpture, African, Native American,
  Precolumbian.

Mona Gavigan
Gallery Affrica
2010 1/2 R St. N.W.
Washington, DC 20009
ph: 202-745-7272
http://www.affrica.com
  Specializes in the appraisal of African
  masks, figures, pottery, furniture,
  textiles, implements, currency and
  adornment.

Tara Ana Finley
Anubis Appraisers & Estate Services,
  Inc.
1042 Sorolla Ave.
Miami, FL 33134-3560
ph: 305-446-1820 or 786-486-8042
fax: 305-648-1939
tara.finley@worldnet.att.net
  Thirty years experience appraising
  African and Oceanic art for
  insurance, donation or probate
  purposes.

Auction Services

Norman Hurst, ISA CAPP
Hurst Gallery
53 Mount Auburn St.
Cambridge, MA 02138-5030
ph: 617-491-6888 or 212-744-6488
  (NYC)
fax: 617-661-0439
NHurst@compuserve.com
http://www.hurstgallery.com
  Buys, sells, appraises African,
  Oceanic, Native American,
  PreColumbian and Asian art; dealing
  in, authenticating and appraising
  African art and artifacts for over 25
  years; sculptures, masks.

Hesse Galleries
53 Main St.
Otego, NY 13825
ph: 607-988-6322
info@hessegalleries.com
http://www.hessegalleries.com
  Specializes in the auction sales of
  African and tribal arts.

Clubs/Associations

Alice Kaufman, Ex. Dir.
Antique Tribal Art Dealers Association,
  The
Newsletter: ATADA Newsletter
215 Sierra SE
Albuquerque, NM 87108
ph: 415-863-3173
fax: 415-431-1939
acek33@aol.com
http://www.atada.org
  Offers buyers a guarantee that objects
  members sell are as represented
  regarding age, authenticity and extent
  of restoration (if any); members also
  guarantee refunds if objects prove to
  be other than represented.

Collectors

Jon Lewin
622 Raleigh Ave., Apt. 3
Norfolk, VA 23507-2034
ph: 757-625-6732
  Wants any relics from the ancient
  world or tribal cultures: tools,
  weapons, coins, fetishes, masks,
  sculptures; African, Aboriginal,
  Native American, PreColumbian,
  Egyptian, Roman, Mideast.

Dealers

Tim Hamill
Hamill Gallery of African Art
2164 Washington St.
Roxbury, MA 02119
ph: 617-442-8204
fax: 617-442-8204
thamill@tiac.net
http://www.hamillgallery.com
  Buys and sells African and tribal art.

Norman Hurst, ISA CAPP
Hurst Gallery
53 Mount Auburn St.
Cambridge, MA 02138-5030
ph: 617-491-6888 or 212-744-6488
  (NYC)
fax: 617-661-0439
NHurst@compuserve.com
http://www.hurstgallery.com
  Buys, sells, appraises African,
  Oceanic, Native American,
  PreColumbian and Asian art.

Dominick Cardella
Artifactory
641 Indiana Ave. NW
Washington, DC 20004
ph: 202-393-2727
  Sells new and old African, Asian and
  other foreign souvenir, arts and craft
  items including carvings and textiles.

Charles Jones
Charles Jones African Art
6716 Barren Inlet Rd.
Wilmington, NC 28411-9602
ph: 910-686-0717
fax: 910-794-3366
cjart@bellsouth.net
http://www.cjafricanart.com

John Buxton
Shango Galleries
6717 Spring Valley
Dallas, TX 75254
ph: 972-239-4620 or 972-239-9943
fax: 972-239-9766
jbuxton@arttrak.com
http://www.arttrak.com
  Buys, sells, and appraises African,
  Precolumbian, Oceanic, and American
  Indian art.

Pierre G. Bovis
Bovis Primitive Arts
P.O. Box 5529
Santa Fe, NM 87502
ph: 505-474-6598 or 505-577-4723
fax: 505-474-6598
louberlugan@earthlink.net
http://www.bovisprimitivearts.com
  Specializes in Oceanic, African, and
  North American artifacts.

Pierre G. Bovis
Bovis Primitive Arts
P.O. Box 5529
Santa Fe, NM 87502
ph: 505-989-1339 or 505-577-7992
fax: 505-989-1339
louberlugan@earthlink.net
http://www.bovisprimitivearts.com
  Buy, sells, appraises cowboy
  memorabilia, primitive arts, American
  Indian arts, Napoleonic artifacts; also
  Polynesian, Hawaiian, New Guinea,
  Pacific Islands and African art
  including Shaman items, weapons,
  fine carvings.

Joel & Michael Malter
Malter Galleries, Inc.
17003 Ventura Blvd., Ste. 205
Encino, CA 91316
ph: 818-784-7772 or 888-784-2131
fax: 818-784-4726
mike@maltergalleries.com
http://www.maltergalleries.com

Marsha L. Vargas, ASA
Xanadu/Folk Art International
871 Santa Cruz Ave.
Menlo Park, CA 94022
ph: 650-329-9999
fax: 650-328-3918
info@folkartintl.com
http://www.folkartintl.com
  Interested in Asian, African and
  Oceanic antiques and works of art;
  has one of the largest collections on
  the West Coast of fine antique
  Tibetan//Nepalese bronzes and works
  of art as well as exceptional Khmer
  sculpture.

B.C. Galleries Ancient & Tribal Art
1069 High St.
Armadale, Victoria 3143 Australia
ph: +61 3 9804 3353
fax: +61 3 9804 3353
b.c.galleries@bigpond.com.au
http://www.bcgalleries.com.au
  Buys and sells ancient and tribal art:
  Oceanic, Melanesia, New Guinea,
  Pacific Islands, Australian Aboriginal,
  African tribal, tribal arts of Asia and
  of the Americas.

Experts

Scott Nelson
1636 Nicholson St. NW
Washington, DC 20011
ph: 202-726-6003
  Wants authentic African, Oceanic, and
  American Indian art and artifacts;
  consultant to "Schroeder's Antiques
  Price Guide."

Internet Resources

Tribal Art Directory
Flitcroft St.
London, WC2H 8DH U.K.
ph: +22 (0)20 7836 6747
fax: +44 (0)20 7379 0789
curator@elms-lesters.demon.co.uk
http://www.tribalartdirectory.com
  An online directory devoted to
  dealers, galleries, museums and
  services specializing in tribal and
  non-Western arts.

Museums/Libraries

SMA African Art Museum
23 Bliss Ave.
Tenafly, NJ 07042
ph: 201-894-8611
fax: 201-541-1280
http://www.smafathers.org/society/
  tenafly.htm

National Museum of African Art
Smithsonian Institution
950 Independence Ave.
Washington, DC 20560-0001
ph: 202-357-4600 or 202-357-2700
fax: 202-357-4879
webmaster@si.edu
http://www.si.edu/organiza/museums/
  africart/nmafa.htm
  Museum's primary focus is collecting
  & exhibiting the traditional arts of
  Africa south of the Sahara; also
  collects & exhibits the arts of other
  African areas, including the arts of
  northern Africa; also ancient and
  contemporary arts.

Periodicals

Jonathan Fogel, Ed.
Tribarts, Inc.
Magazine: Tribal Arts
2261 Market St., #644
San Francisco, CA 94114
ph: 415-552-6884
fax: 415-431-8321
jmfogel@pacbell.net
http://www.tribalarts.com
  The only magazine about the art,

ethnography, and culture of tribal and ancient cultures around the world.

AFRICAN-AMERICAN

(see AFRICAN & TRIBAL ART; ART, African-American; Art, Outsider; BLACK MEMORABILIA)

AGRICULTURE RELATED ITEMS

(see FARM COLLECTIBLES; FARM MACHINERY; TOYS, Farm; TRACTORS)

AIR LABELS

(see AIRLINE MEMORABILIA; LABELS, Luggage)

AIRGUNS

(see also TOY GUNS, BB Guns)

Clubs/Associations

Mike Ahuna
Carolina Airgun Club
Newsletter: Carolina Airgun Club Newsletter
689 Highland Ridge Rd.
Mooresville, NC 28115
ph: 704-660-3400
fax: 704-660-3401
The Club holds Target Matches, Field Target Matches, and Silhouette Matches the year round; Matches are open to the public and Club members.

American Airgun Field Target Association
Newsletter: AAFTA Newsletter
P.O. Box 218
Hernando, MS 38632
ph: 601-429-4663
questions@airguns.net
http://www.airguns.net/aafta/aafta.html

Dealers

Mike Ahuna
Mike's Crosman Service
689 Highland Ridge Rd.
Mooresville, NC 28115
ph: 704-660-3400
fax: 704-660-3401
Buys and sells old and new airguns; authorized Crosman airgun service station, and is an authorized Beeman 5 Star Dealer.

Experts

Dean Fletcher
6720 N.E. Rodney Ave.
Portland, OR 97211
ph: 503-289-5837
FletcherOR@aol.com
http://members.aol.com/vintairgun
Author of several books focusing on vintage airguns.

Internet Resources

Dean Fletcher
Vintage American Airguns
6720 N.E. Rodney Ave.
Portland, OR 97211
ph: 503-289-5837
FletcherOR@aol.com
http://members.aol.com/vintairgun
Site covers the collecting, history and shooting of vintage American airguns.

Periodicals

Barry Abel, Ed.
Newsletter: Airgun Ads
P.O. Box 33
Hamilton, MT 59840-0033
ph: 406-363-3805
fax: 406-363-4117
airgunads@bitterroot.net
Published monthly to enable subscribers to buy and sell airguns of all types, from Olympic match grade to smooth bore, including parts, accessories and literature.

AIRLINE MEMORABILIA

(see also AIRPLANES; AIR SICKNESS BAGS; AVIATION; AVIATION MEMORABILIA; LABELS, Luggage; MODELS, Aircraft; STAMP COLLECTING, Air Mail Related; TOYS, Airplane Related; TRANSPORTATION COLLECTIBLES)

Clubs/Associations

Bill Demarest
World Airline Historical Society
Magazine: Captain's Log
P.O. Box 660583
Miami Springs, FL 33266
fax: 786-331-7024
worldairsociety@aol.com
http://www.wahsonline.com
Members are interested in the collecting of airline memorabilia and in the study of airlines, airliners, kits, models and related items.

Collectors

Jay T. Schulz
Advanced Air Cargo Logistics
134 Rossevelt Blvd.
Hauppauge, NY 11788
ph: 516-234-0103
anjcrane@aol.com
Wants airline memorabilia from the 1970s: public relations materials, photos, wings, safety cards, aircraft models, etc.

Steve & Larry Charter
8249 Cavalry Run
Mechanicsville, VA 23111
ph: 804-779-3142
lcha370941@aol.com
Wants to buy airline memorabilia: playing cards, wings, matchbooks, metal travel agency display model airplanes, etc.

Charles C. Quarles
204 Reservation Dr.
Spindale, NC 28160-1534
ph: 828-286-2962 or 828-245-7803
fax: 828-286-3224
airliner@rfci.net
http://www.rfci.net/airliner
Wants pilot and steward/stewardess wings, hat badges, metal travel agency display model airliners, etc. from 1930s to 1960s US airlines.

Randy Ridgely
447 Oglethorpe Ave.
Athens, GA 30606-2236
ph: 706-549-6264
erie@negia.net
Wants railroad, steamship and airline items.

Bill Rosenbloom
1893 Worcester
Saint Paul, MN 55116-2614
ph: 651-699-2784
junk@fishnet.com
http://www.airlinecollectibles.com
Wants all older logoed airline items: playing cards, schedules, posters, kiddie wings, and all other logo-marked items.

Dick Wallin
P.O. Box 1784
Springfield, IL 62705-1784
ph: 217-498-9279
rrwallin@aol.com
Wants airline logo items: dishes, glassware, playing cards, crew wings and badges, silverplate pitchers, creamers; also large travel agency size plane models, chrome ashtrays with plane models.

Dealers

Bizarre Bazarre
130 1/4 East 65th St.
New York, NY 10021-7007
ph: 212-517-2100
fax: 212-517-2283
Wants museum quality aviation models, metal models of propellered aircraft, airline and travel agent display airplane models, factory and industrial design models.

William Gawchik
88 Clarendon Ave.
Yonkers, NY 10701
ph: 914-965-3010
fax: 914-966-1055
mrpanam@yahoo.com
http://mrpanam.freeyellow.com/ewr.html
Expert, dealer, collector, appraiser wants to buy pilot and steward(ess) wings, hat badges, and other logo-marked items from the 1930 to 1970s for Pan Am and other domestic airlines; pre-1990 kiddie wings (and cards) also wanted.

Jeffrey D. Boutin
JB Airline Collectibles
705 White Bluff Ave.
Savannah, GA 31419-3140
ph: 912-920-9907 or 912-657-0171
fax: 912-920-9906
Sells memorabilia from US airlines, past or present: postcards, flight schedules/timetables, table settings, baggage tags, etc.; wants to buy memorabilia from Northeast Airlines which merged into Delta Airlines in 1972.

Vernon Ford
18119 Sandy Pines Cir.
Fort Myers, FL 33917
ph: 239-567-0819
v8ford1@juno.com
Buys and sells airline memorabilia, especially pre-1970.

Dan Wells
Dan Wells Antique Toys
P.O. Box 7
Goshen, KY 40026
ph: 502-386-3453
jagdan@aol.com
Wants to buy all miniature/toy aircraft, especially travel agency and factory models.

Mike Fleming
Mike Fleming Antiques & Aviation Collectibles
432 S. Main St.
Princeton, IL 61356
ph: 773-267-8595
fax: 773-267-8596
FAAsale@aol.com
http://www.FAAsale.com
Wants aviation items that display airline and manufacturing logos: playing cards, travel agency models, manufacturer's models, ashtrays, lighters, timetables, company annual reports, flight manuals, crew items, hat badges, service pins.

Ered Matthew
Cabin Class Collectibles
P.O. Box 740474
Dallas, TX 75374-0474
ph: 972-235-8639
fax: 972-235-8614
mailroom@cabinclass.com
http://www.cabinclass.com
Buys and sells fine ocean liner, airline, and other transportation memorabilia on the Internet.

Craig Morris
Craig's Aviation Collectibles
105 Silver Willow Ct.
Galt, CA 95632-2442
ph: 209-745-4539
cmorris@softcom.net
http://www.thepostcard.com/craig
Wants to buy airline memorabilia: 1920-1960 airline postcards, time tables, posters, paper ephemera, etc.; will pay postage.

Experts

Larry McLaughlin
17 Seventh Ave.
Smithtown, NY 11787-4508
ph: 631-265-9224
larrymak@erols.com
Buys, collects and specializes in airline items: travel agency models, ashtrays, lighters, timetables, crew hat badges, pins, wings, commercial or military models, helmets, manuals; also wants tin airplane toys.

John R. Joiner
130 Peninsula Circle
Newnan, GA 30265
ph: 770-502-9565
propjj@numail.org
Wants pilot and flight attendant wings, hat badges; also wants display models, early signs, anniversary pins, postcards, time tables, playing cards from commercial airlines, pre-1970s; no military items, please.

Dick Wallin
P.O. Box 1784
Springfield, IL 62705-1784
ph: 217-498-9279
rrwallin@aol.com
Author of "Airline Collectibles General Information;" he will try to answer questions and provide information on buying and selling of specific items, or he will direct you to someone who can.

Internet Resources

Bill Rosenbloom
AirlineCollectibles.com
1893 Worcester
Saint Paul, MN 55116-2614
ph: 651-699-2784
junk@fishnet.com
http://www.airlinecollectibles.com
Purpose of this Web site is to promote the collecting of airline-oriented memorabilia.

Museums/Libraries

Arthur Thomas
Don Thomas Foundation
5134 Sugar Camp Rd.
Milford, OH 45150-9674
ph: 513-248-0485
rtmiloh1@juno.com
Sells and specializes in airline memorabilia; Don Thomas is author of "Nostalgia Panamerican," and "Poster Art of the Airlines."

Periodicals

Airways International, Inc.
Magazine: Airways
P.O. Box 1109
Sandpoint, ID 83864-0872
ph: 208-263-2098 or 800-440-5166
fax: 208-263-5906
airways@nidlink.com
http://www.airwaysmag.com
International bi-monthly magazine devoted to airlines and commercial aircraft; a global review of commercial flight; periodically
contains articles of interest to the collector of airline memorabilia.

Air Sickness Bags

Collectors

Larry Nadon
Barf O Rama
barf@sfmac.com
http://www.sfmac.com/barf
Bag images, links to other collections, commercial bags, non-commercial bags.

Steve Silberberg
Air Sickness Bag Virtual Museum
159 Nantasket Rd.
Hull, MA 02045-2629
ph: 781-773-1115
curator@airsicknessbags.com
http://www.airsicknessbags.com
Curator of the On-Line Air Sickness Bag Museum; collects all kinds of air sickness bags but specializes in one-of-a-kind bags usually not found on commercial flights; seeking a Space Shuttle bag.

Bruce Kelly
1087 Potlatch Circle
Anchorage, AK 99503
ph: 907-274-7122
fax: 907-275-2050
abkelly@alaska.net
Alaska collector wants air sickness bags and airline safety cards, either singles or collections; will purchase or trade; accepts donations.

Dr. Walter Brinker
Niedernfeld 2
Radevormwald, 42477 Germany
ph: 49-219540928
fax: 49-21956517
walter.brinker@t-online.de
A collector with about 1,600 air sickness bags from 720 air lines.

Rune Tapper
Sweden
ph: +46 70 5750232
rune@tapper.com
http://home1.swipnet.se/~w-14429/puke.htm
Collector of barf bags from airlines all over the world; bags to swap listed on Web site.

Graham Curran
Vomitorium, The
Greenacres, Old Hall
Hanmer, SY13 3BX U.K.
ph: +44 (0) 1948 830461
http://www.vomitorium.co.uk
Bags of fun from the colorful world of international air sickness; see what nauseous air travelers have in their laps.

Internet Resources

Ernest Cox
Barf Bag Central
xocpe2@aol.com
http://www.geocities.com/CollegePark/Theater/7314/BBHOME.htm
A central repository for information
related to collecting airline sickness bags (barf bags); featured bags, barf bag news, barf bag carousel, other collectors.

Baggage I.D. Labels

(see also LABELS, Luggage)

Experts

H. Van Dyk
7 Birchwood Ave.
Peabody, MA 01960
ph: 978-535-0353
Author of "Catalog of Baggage I.D. Labels, Vols. 1 & 2 , U.S.A. & Canada," and "Europe & Middle East;" buys airline baggage I.D. labels (for travelers' name/address); 1st Class, cabin baggage, crew, fragile, etc.; no destination labels.

Models

Collectors

Michael Walters
P.O. Box 31
Scottsdale, AZ 85252-0031
ph: 602-946-7454
fax: 602-946-8729
michwalt@aol.com
Collector wants good condition chrome desk display pieces and ashtrays that have plane models attached.

Models (Desk)

(see also TOYS, Airplane)

Collectors

Ira S. Kuperstein
22 Brush Hill Terrace
Butler, NJ 07405-2439
ph: 973-283-2420 or 800-526-5177
fax: 973-283-2426
kuperstein@nac.net
Wants to buy airplane display models.

David Ostrowski
5411 Masser Lane
Fairfax, VA 22032-3817
ph: 703-323-6674
Wants to buy military and civilian aircraft models, ID/recognition aircraft models, photos/negatives/slides of military and civilian aircraft.

Experts

Larry McLaughlin
17 Seventh Ave.
Smithtown, NY 11787-4508
ph: 631-265-9224
larrymak@erols.com
Wants to buy airplane, rocket, missile desk models: manufacturers' display models, travel agency models, commercial or military, etc.; has written articles for aviation toy magazines; staff editor for "Miniature Aircraft Quarterly."

Pilots Wings

(see also AVIATION MEMORABILIA, Military Insignia)

Collectors

Philip Martin
Pilot Wings of the World
3640 E. 10th St.
Long Beach, CA 90804
ph: 562-434-6701
wingman@earthlink.net
http://home.earthlink.net/~wingman
Buy, sell, trade pilot wings of the world.

Michael Dusek
1058 Lupin Dr. #5
Salinas, CA 93906
ph: 831-757-2526
Wants to buy military wings, civilian wings, sterling silver wings; also wants China, Burma, or India bracelets related to aviation.

Playing Cards

Collectors

Fred Chan
Top Flite Information
P.O. Box 2744
Sequim, WA 98382-2744
ph: 360-681-4671
fax: 360-681-4671
topflite@olympus.net
Author of the new 3rd edition of "Airline Playing Cards - An Illustrated Color Reference Guide" and annual supplements (3,328 cards, with prices); buys, sells, trades airline playing cards; appraises airline playing card collections.

Timetables

Collectors

Jerry Hughes
Jerry's Airline Timetable Collection
843 W. 146th St.
Gardena, CA 90247-2711
ph: 310-769-6208
fromfay@aol.com
http://members.aol.com/fromfay
A private collector of airline timetables from very old to present from all around the world.

AIRPLANES

(see also AIRLINE MEMORABILIA; AVIATION; AVIATION MEMORABILIA; MODELS, Aircraft; TOYS, Airplane Related)

Appraisers

Michael Bonventre
MJB Aviation
P.O. Box 1136
Seaford, NY 11783
ph: 516-328-0847
fax: 516-783-2536
airdrv@aol.com
Airplane appraisal and consulting service: valuations, estates, bankruptcy, tax appeals, repossessions, matrimonial, insurance, corporate, condemnations, condition surveys.

Michael Bonventre
Mountain Bay Airport
100 Ponderosa Ct.
Greentown, PA 18426
ph: 570-857-2611
fax: 570-857-9366
airdrv@aol.com
Airplane appraisal and consulting service: valuations, estates, bankruptcy, tax appeals, repossessions, matrimonial, insurance, corporate, condemnations, condition surveys.

George H. Campbell, ASA, NBAA
Campbell & Associates, Ltd.
6901 W. Okeechobee Blvd.
D5-332 PMS
West Palm Beach, FL 33411
ph: 352-684-9091 or 877-977-9444
fax: 352-684-9092
info@aircraftappraisers.com
http://www.aircraftappraiser.com
Domestic and international aircraft appraisals, consulting and leasing valuation services, mergers & acquisitions, commercial & corporate aircraft, industrial materials and handling.

National Aircraft Appraisers Association
12620 Lamplighter Sq.
Saint Louis, MO 63128
ph: 636-285-4768
naaa@plane-values.com
http://www.plane-values.com
The trade association for professional aircraft appraisers; since 1980 the Certification entity for professional aircraft appraisers in the U.S and abroad.

Donald R. Bell, ISA
Bell Associates Aircraft Services
2312 Minor Ave. E., #A
Seattle, WA 98102-6523
ph: 206-325-5929
fax: 206-325-0848
bellUpAway@aol.com
http://hometown.aol.com/bellupaway
Specializes in the appraisal of light aircraft, experimental aircraft, antique aircraft, aircraft equipment and components.

Auction Services

Jon Baddeley
Sotheby's
34-35 New Bond St.
London, W1A 2AA U.K.
ph: 44 171 293 5000
fax: 44 171 293 5989
http://www.sothebys.com
Conducts regular specialized auctions of vintage aircraft.

Clubs/Associations

L.E. Opdycke
World War I Aeroplanes, Inc.
15 Crescent Rd.
Poughkeepsie, NY 12601-4405
ph: 845-473-3679
http://www.aviation-history.com/
ww1aero.htm
A service organization devoted to

those magnificent flying machines of 1900-1919 and 1920-1940; for builders, museums, restorers, historians, modelers and collectors; publishes the journals "WWI Aero" and "Skyways."

Richard Bennett, Ed.
Great War Aeroplanes Association, The
Newsletter: Great Times, The
15815 Thompson Rd.
Thompson, OH 44086
ph: 440-298-3797
komodo@alltel.net
http://www.gwaero.org
This organization is for anyone that has an interest in WWI, especially aviation.

Robert Taylor, Pres.
Antique Airplane Association, Inc.
Magazine: Antique Airplane News & Digest
22001 Bluegrass Rd.
Ottumwa, IA 52501-8569
ph: 515-938-2773
fax: 515-938-2773
aaaapmhq@pcsia.com
http://www.aaa-apm.org/aaa
The organization for antique and classic airplane owners, pilots and enthusiasts.

Mike Barton
Antique Aeroplane Association of Australia, Inc.
Magazine: Rag & Tube
P.O. Box 1036
South Melbourne, Victoria 3205
Australia
thebartons@bigpond.com
http://www.antique-aeroplane.com.au
Australia's only dedicated old aeroplane magazine; published four times per year.

Graham Newby, CEO
Popular Flying Association
Magazine: Popular Flying
Term. Bldg., Shoreham Airport
Shoreham-by-Sea, Sussex BN43 5FF
U.K.
ph: (+44) 0 1273 461616
fax: (+44) 0 1273 463390
office@pfa.org.uk
http://www.pfa.org.uk
The United Kingdom's association of amateur-built and vintage aircraft restoration.

Dealers

Bob Von Willer
Exotic Aircraft Company
1719 North Marshall Ave.
El Cajon, CA 92020
ph: 619-562-7467
fax: 619-448-2110
baroness@barnstormers.com
http://www.barnstormers.com
Specializes in the restoration and marketing of antique aircraft, including warbirds; appraiser, dealer, expert, collector, and repair services offered.

Experts

Bob Von Willer
Exotic Aircraft Company
1719 North Marshall Ave.
El Cajon, CA 92020
ph: 619-562-7467
fax: 619-448-2110
baroness@barnstormers.com
http://www.barnstormers.com
Specializes in the restoration and marketing of antique aircraft, including warbirds; appraiser, dealer, expert, collector, and repair services offered.

Periodicals

L.E. Opdycke
World War I Aeroplanes, Inc.
Journal: WWI Aero
15 Crescent Rd.
Poughkeepsie, NY 12601-4405
ph: 845-473-3679
http://www.aviation-history.com/
ww1aero.htm
A quarterly magazine for collectors, restorers, replica builders, historians, and modelers focusing on 1900-1919 aircraft.

L.E. Opdycke
World War I Aeroplanes, Inc.
Journal: Skyways
15 Crescent Rd.
Poughkeepsie, NY 12601-4405
ph: 845-473-3679
http://www.aviation-history.com/
ww1aero.htm
A quarterly magazine for collectors, restorers, replica builders, historians, and modelers focusing on 1920-1940 aircraft.

Trader Publishing Company
Magazine: Aero Trader & Chopper Shopper
P.O. Box 9059
Clearwater, FL 34618-9059
ph: 727-712-0035 or 800-548-8889
fax: 727-712-0034
idowu@traderonline.com
http://www.traderonline.com

TAP Publishing Co.
Newspaper: Trade-A-Plane
174 Fourth St.
P.O. Box 509
Crossville, TN 38557
ph: 800-337-5263 or 931-484-5137
fax: 931-484-2532
webmaster@trade-a-plane.com
http://www.trade-a-plane.com
Published three times each month; huge advertising newspaper containing everything to keep you flying: from antique airplanes to parts, electronics and related services.

Christina Gargano
Heartland Communications Group, Inc.
Magazine: Aviators Hot Line
1003 Central Ave.
P.O. Box 1052
Fort Dodge, IA 50501
ph: 800-247-2000 or 515-955-1600
fax: 515-574-2233
libbie@hlipublishing.com
http://www.hlipublishing.com
The national and international marketplace for active buyers and sellers of corporate and general aircraft, parts and service.

H.G. Frautschy
Vintage Aircraft Association
Magazine: Vintage Airplane
P.O. Box 3086
Oshkosh, WI 54903-3086
ph: 800-843-3612 or 920-426-4800
fax: 920-426-4828
vintage@eaa.org
http://www.vintageaircraft.org
Nearly 10,000 members strong, the Vintage Aircraft Association brings together people from around the world who share an interest in the pre-1966 aircraft of yesterday.

H.G. Frautschy
Experimental Aircraft Association
Magazine: Sport Aviation
P.O. Box 3086
Oshkosh, WI 54903-3086
ph: 800-843-3612 or 920-426-4800
fax: 920-426-4828
vintage@eaa.org
http://www.vintageaircraft.org

H.G. Frautschy
Experimental Aircraft Association
Magazine: Sport Aerobatics
P.O. Box 3086
Oshkosh, WI 54903-3086
ph: 800-843-3612 or 920-426-4800
fax: 920-426-4828
vintage@eaa.org
http://www.vintageaircraft.org

Paul Wyatt
Primedia Price Digests
Price Guide: Aircraft Bluebook - Price Digest
9800 Metcalf Ave.
Overland Park, KS 66212
ph: 800-654-6776 or 913-341-1300
fax: 800-633-6219
http://www.aircraftbluebook.com
Comprehensive quarterly index of the value of used fixed wing aircraft and helicopters; controlled availability; no vintage, antique, military, kit or experimental planes; available only to aircraft dealers, service centers, lenders, etc.

Steven D. Werner
Werner Publishing Corp.
Magazine: Plane & Pilot
12121 Wilshire Blvd., Ste. 1220
Los Angeles, CA 90025-1175
ph: 310-820-1500
fax: 310-826-5008
editors@planeandpilotmag.com
http://www.planeandpilotmag.com
Articles on general aviation from light single-engine planes to medium-weight twins and related products.

Fancy Publications, Inc.
Magazine: Private Pilot
3 Burroughs
Irvine, CA 92718
ph: 714-855-8822
fax: 714-855-3045

Sclair Ben
Newspaper: Flyer
P.O. Box 39099
Tacoma, WA 98439
ph: 800-426-8538
fax: 253-471-9911
comments@flyer-online.com
http://www.flyer-online.com
Bi-weekly newspaper serving the aviation industry nationwide; containing thousands of ads for aircraft, avionics, equipment, instruction, aviation businesses, etc.

Ford Tri-Motors

Dealers

Tim O'Callaghan
305 St. Lawrence Blvd.
P.O. Box 512
Northville, MI 48167
ph: 248-449-2652
timothyo@ameritech.net
http://www.hfha.org/fordtrimotor.htm
Author of "The Aviation Legacy of Henry and Edsel Ford;" producer of the video "Henry Ford's Aviation Ventures 1924-1936;" buys and sells Ford Tri-motor memorabilia; always willing to answer questions.

Model

(see also KITS; MODELS)

Clubs/Associations

Larry Clark
Society of Antique Modelers
Newsletter: Sam Speaks
P.O. Box 528
Lucerne Valley, CA 92356
ph: 714-542-8294
CWReich@aol.com
http://www.antiquemodeler.org
Focuses on the collecting, restoring and operating of free flight and R/C model model airplanes of vintage design; chapters worldwide.

Periodicals

Erika Daileda
Wise Owl Worldwide Publications
Magazine: Scale Aircraft Modeling
5150 Candlewood St., Ste. 1
Lakewood, CA 90712-1900
ph: 562-461-7574
fax: 562-461-7212
info@wiseowlmagazines.com
http://www.wiseowlmagazines.com
A monthly English publication; gives details, historical facts, and photos on specific aircraft each month.

Racing

Collectors

John Garrett
2215 Harbor Blvd.
Costa Mesa, CA 92627
ph: 949-646-0275 or 949-631-8806
fax: 949-646-0287
Collects air racing and air meet items: programs, photos, negatives, posters, tickets, artwork, buttons, patches, postcards, first day covers, calendars, other related memorabilia.

Sailplanes

Clubs/Associations

Vintage Sailplane Association
Magazine: Bungee Cord
1709 Baron Ct.
Daytona Beach, FL 32124
raulb@earthlink.net
http://www.vintagesailplane.org
Soaring enthusiasts who are keeping our gliding history and heritage alive by building, restoring, flying gliders from the past; interested in vintage sailplanes (pre-1958) and classic sailplanes (25 years or older but post-1958).

Geoff Moore, Mem. Sec.
Vintage Gliding Club
Magazine: VGC News
Arewa
Shootersway Lane
Berkhamsted, Herts HP4 3NP U.K.
ph: 01442 873258
geoffmoore@cwcom.net
http://www.vintagegliderclub.org.uk
Members focus mainly on gliders designed during the 1930s, but includes some earlier and later; vintage gliders throughout the world, rallies, history.

AIRSHIPS

(see also KITES; STAMP COLLECTING, Covers [Balloon Related])

Balloons

Clubs/Associations

Dr. A.D. Topping
Lighter-Than-Air Society
1436 Triplett Blvd.
Akron, OH 44306
aa208@freenet.akron.oh.us
http://spot.colorado.edu/~dziadeck/lta.html

Collectors

Mark Walberg
P.O. Box 130
Sunbury, PA 17801
ph: 570-286-1617
fax: 570-286-9686
Wants anything with balloon subjects: letters, medals, drawings, fans, books, posters, prints, coins, etc.; 18th century to 19th century.

Alan Zimkus
1290 Creek Point Dr.
Rochester, MI 48307-1727
ph: 800-886-3766
fax: 704-992-0750
azimkus@aol.com
Wants to buy items relating to early gas balloons: postcards, posters, memorabilia, books, medals, etc.

Dirigibles, Zeppelins, Blimps

Collectors

Hank Loescher
90 Scofield Rd.
Bridgeport, CT 06605-2953
ph: 203-368-4983
hlenterprises@snet.net
Wants zeppelin or dirigible related items: books, charts, photos, relics, souvenirs, fabric, personal items, info., etc.

Art Bink
609 Hamilton Dr.
Cinnaminson, NJ 08077-4250
ph: 856-829-3959
Advanced collector of airship memorabilia.

Frederick Lingenfelser
814 Byram St.
Reading, PA 19606-1446
lingy@afo.net
Wants to buy pre-1945 Zeppelin items, must be passenger lines: postcards, letters, deck plans, books, tickets, brochures, dinnerware, souvenirs, models, menus, etc.

Alan Zimkus
1290 Creek Point Dr.
Rochester, MI 48307-1727
ph: 800-886-3766
fax: 704-992-0750
azimkus@aol.com
Wants to buy items relating to dirigibles, zeppelins, and blimps: postcards, posters, memorabilia, books, medals, etc.

Experts

Art Bink
609 Hamilton Dr.
Cinnaminson, NJ 08077-4250
ph: 856-829-3959
Historian not dealer wants airship items: zeppelin, blimp, dirigible memorabilia; pieces, toys, photos, books, medals, china, etc.; no balloons; collecting since 1942.

Charles Ira Sachs
TransAtlantic Research
P.O. Box 8797
Universal City, CA 91618-8797
ph: 818-985-1345
fax: 818-985-1345
onrs@earthlink.net
Buys/sells/specializes/lectures on ocean liner and zeppelin history & memorabilia from the high seas (i.e., none from coastal or river steamers) dating from 1840 to 1960s; posters, postcards and related material for collectors/museums.

Museums/Libraries

Navy Lakehurst Historical Society
P.O. Box 328
Lakehurst, NJ 08733
ph: 732-244-8861
fax: 732-244-8897
info@nlhs.com
http://www.nlhs.com
Non-profit organization dedicated to preserving the distinguished history of Naval Air Station Lakehurst, located in Lakehurst, NJ.; remembered for rigid airships Shenandoah, Los Angeles, Akron, Hindenberg disaster.

ALARM BOXES

Collectors

Tom Mills
P.O. Box 424
Spencer, MA 01562
ph: 508-885-9550
Wants fire alarm and police boxes especially ones with dates cast into them; seeks cast iron signs and street letter pickup boxes marked "U.S. MAIL;" best to write and send photos.

ALBUMS

Autograph

(see also AUTOGRAPHS; CELLULOID ITEMS; PAPER COLLECTIBLES; RECORDS)

Dealers

Barbara & Richard DePalma
Deer Park Books
609 Kent Rd., Route 7
Gaylordsville, CT 06755
ph: 860-350-4140
deerparkbooks@earthlink.net
http://www.deerparkbooks.com
Fine books bought and sold; antiquarian books, modern first editions, children's and illustrated;

also maps, autographs, etc.; all subjects; also wants handwritten diaries, travel journals, scrapbooks, albums.

Melco Antiques
125 Elizabeth St.
Buchanan, MI 49107
flynn@triton.net
http://www.yoursandmineantiques.com
Buys and sells autograph albums.

ALCOHOLICS ANONYMOUS ITEMS

Dealers

Clark Phelps
Amusement Sales Co.
7610 Main St.
Midvale, UT 84047-7106
ph: 801-255-4731
clarkp@aros.net
Historian and book seller wants AA books, pamphlets, etc. before 1974.

Experts

Charles Bishop, Jr.
Bishop of Books, The
46 Eureka Ave.
Wheeling, WV 26003-1424
ph: 304-242-2937
bishopbk@stratuswave.net
Buy, sell, appraise books, magazines, posters, postcards, etc. relating to alcoholism or Alcoholics Anonymous.

ALMANACS

(see BOOKS)

ALUMINUM

Hammered

Clubs/Associations

Dannie Woodard
Hammered Aluminum Collectors Association
Newsletter: Aluminist, The
P.O. Box 1346
Weatherford, TX 76086
ph: 817-594-4680
al1310@aol.com
Newsletter provides updated information on prices, patterns, ads and companies; group organized in 1990; 200 members.

Collectors

Mike Landis
P.O. Box 814
Adamstown, PA 19501
ph: 888-248-2291
landis2@ptd.net
Wants to buy hammered aluminum with the following marks: Arthur Armour, Palmer Smith, Cellini; also wants old Wendell August; call toll free or send picture and information.

James Londe
10374 Chimnet Rock Dr., #5
Saint Louis, MO 63146-5751
fax: 314-692-7071
jamlon@charter.net
Wants to buy most hammered aluminum with special interest in works of Palmer Smith and Clayton Sheasley.

Bonita Campbell, Ph.D.
P.O. Box 3151
Granada Hills, CA 91394
hcspc003@csun.edu
Collector and researcher actively engaged in academic research of artisans, companies, marks, times of production, and other information pertinent to hammered aluminum; also preparing research monographs as appropriate.

Dealers

John M. Rowley
Eye-Openers
HC 63, Box 356
South Acworth, NH 03607
ph: 603-835-2281 or 8888-OPENER
Buys and sells kitchen collectibles, gadgets, openers, and especially hammered aluminum.

Experts

Ed Gangawere
American Dream Collectibles
5128 Schultz Bridge Rd.
Zionsville, PA 18092-2542
ph: 215-679-2254
Buys, sells, collects hammered aluminum; National Hammered Aluminum Show held the last full weekend in October; call for location and time.

Dannie Woodard
P.O. Box 1346
Weatherford, TX 76086
ph: 817-594-4680
al1310@aol.com
Author of "Hammered Aluminum - Hand Wrought Collectibles Book II."

Man./Prod./Dist.

Wendell August
P.O. Box 109
Grove City, PA 16127
ph: 800-923-4438
fax: 724-458-1614
info@wendell.com
http://wendellaugust.com
Manufacturer of hammered aluminum ware since 1923.

AMERICAN BANDSTAND

(see also MUSIC, Rock 'N' Roll)

Clubs/Associations

Dave Frees
American Bandstand 1950's Fan Club
Magazine: Bandstand Boogie
P.O. Box 131
Adamstown, PA 19501-0131
ph: 717-738-2513
popfrosty@webtv.net
http://www.fiftiesweb.com/davey-frees.htm
Focuses on "American Bandstand" from the 1950s and 1980s; magazine published twice a year; sells "Dave's Collectables Catalog" ('50s through '80s photos, magazines, etc.) for $1 - free to members.

AMERICAN INDIAN

(see NATIVE AMERICAN)

AMMUNITION & EXPLOSIVE ORDNANCE

(see also ADVERTISING COLLECTIBLES, Ammunition; ARMS & ARMOR; CANNONS; CIVIL WAR ARTIFACTS; FIREARMS; MILITARIA; TOYS, Cannons; TRENCH ART)

Auction Services

Dr. J.R. Crittenden Schmitt
Crittenden Schmitt Archives
Court House Station
P.O. Box 4253
Rockville, MD 20849-4253
ph: 301-439-4346
csaschmitt@juno.com
Only video auctions in the world of ordnance material: collector ammunition, bombs, grenades, mines; inert only, from all countries; includes reference material in all formats and languages.

Clubs/Associations

International Cartridge Collectors Association
Journal: International Ammunition Journal
5032 Grave Run Rd.
Manchester, MD 21102

Shotshell Historical & Collectors Society
222 Redfield St.
Lodi, OH 44254
Focuses exclusively on shotshells.

Bob Cameron
Sioux Empire Cartridge Collectors Association
14597 Glendale Ave. SE
Prior Lake, MN 55372

Don MacChesney
Greater St. Louis Cartridge Collectors Association
634 Scotsdale
Kirkwood, MO 63122

Gary Muckel
Nebraska Cartridge Collectors Club
Newsletter: NCCC Newsletter
P.O. Box 84442
Lincoln, NE 68501
ph: 402-483-2484
Appraisals and buyers located; items identified; assistance offered to locate antique wants in small arms ammunition; bimonthly newsletter.

International Ammunition Association, Inc.
Journal: International Ammunition Journal
6531 Carlsbad Dr.
Lincoln, NE 68510
lcurtis@msn.com
http://www.cartridgecollectors.org
Association has over 1,000 members; membership open to all; Journal published bimonthly for members only.

Rocky Mountain Cartridge Collectors Association
Newsletter: Rocky Mountain Bullet, The
P.O. Box 757
Conifer, CO 804330757
ph: 303-697-0838
For those interested in collectible types of ammunition.

Rick Montgomery
California Cartridge Collectors Association
1728 Christina
Stockton, CA 95204

Graham Irving
European Cartridge Research Association
Newsletter: Cartridge Researcher, The
P.O. Box 55
Spa, 4900 Belgium
ph: +32 (0)87-77-43-40
fax: +32 (0)87-77-27-51
girving@skynet.be
Publishes its monthly bulletin in English, French, German and Dutch; holds cartridge meetings in Belgium, Holland, Germany, Switzerland, and France; has members world wide.

Collectors

Ron Willoughby
2281 Lime Kiln Rd.
North Haverhill, NH 03774
ph: 603-787-2060
fax: 603-787-2060
swillo@together.net
Wants to buy shotshell boxes, gun company posters and calendars, glass target balls and traps, gunpowder cans, pin-back buttons, and related items; a very serious buyer; free appraisals; estate purchases.

Guy Hildebrand
Cartridge Collector's Exchange
6748 Johnstown Loop
Tallahassee, FL 32308
ph: 850-893-9503
mg64guy@aol.com
http://members.aol.com/~mg64guy/
index.htm
*Interested in collecting old cartridges
and related boxes.*

Francois-Louis Dragon
4184 Kensington
Montreal, Quebec H4B 2W1 Canada
ph: (514) 485-8131
*Collects deactivated grenades from all
countries and periods but specializes
in British Commonwealth grenades;
also has interest in all grenade related
material such as books, and in other
inert ordnance such as bombs, shells,
mines.*

Dealers

Ray T. Giles
RTG Sporting Collectibles, LLC
P.O. Box 670894
Dallas, TX 75367
ph: 214-361-6577
ray@rtgammo.com
http://rtgammo.com
*Buys and sells antique and obsolete
ammunition in original boxes;
specializing in US sporting calibers;
no military or reloaded ammo; very
few shotshells, mostly metallics
wanted; no lists; see Web site or call.*

John Spangler
John Spangler Professional Services, LC
P.O. Box 711282
Salt Lake City, UT 84171
ph: 801-947-9442
hq@oldguns.net
http://www.oldguns.net
*Buys and sells ammunition for the
collector.*

Experts

Dr. J.R. Crittenden Schmitt
Crittenden Schmitt Archives
Court House Station
P.O. Box 4253
Rockville, MD 20849-4253
ph: 301-439-4346
csaschmitt@juno.com
*Family in business since 1849; full
line of consulting expertise in all
areas of munitions: grenades, land
mines, bombs, etc.; ordnance
consulting support for government,
industry, entertainment and private
collectors.*

Periodicals

Magazine: Artilleryman, The
234 Monarch Hill Rd.
Tunbridge, VT 05077
ph: 802-889-3500 or 800-777-1862
fax: 802-889-5627
mail@civilwarnews.com
*Published quarterly, the only
magazine exclusively for the 1750-
1898 artillery enthusiast: artillery*

*history, safety, places to visit, unit
profiles, etc.*

Badges

Collectors

Dr. J.R. Crittenden Schmitt
Crittenden Schmitt Archives
Court House Station
P.O. Box 4253
Rockville, MD 20849-4253
ph: 301-439-4346
csaschmitt@juno.com
*Wants only metal badges & pins
relating to bomb squads, explosive
ordnance disposal units, ammunition
& weapons companies of the world.*

Shell Casings

Collectors

Charles E. Eberhart
Lead Cannon, The
3616 Seward
Topeka, KS 66616-1652
ph: 785-235-1016
*Wants to buy large brass military
casings - the larger the better; also
wants to buy decorated "Trench Art"
shells.*

AMUSEMENT PARK ITEMS

(see also CAROUSELS &
CAROUSEL FIGURES; CARNIVAL
ITEMS; COIN-OPERATED
MACHINES, Arcade Games; ROLLER
COASTERS; TARGETS, Shooting
Gallery)

Auction Services

David A. Norton
Norton Auctioneers of Michigan, Inc.
50 W. Pearl St.
Coldwater, MI 49036-1967
ph: 517-279-9063
fax: 517-279-9191
nortonsold@cbpu.com
http://www.nortonauctioneers.com
*Specializing in the auctioning of
amusement rides, carousels,
amusement parks, arcades, museums,
etc.*

Clubs/Associations

Brett Johnson
Historic Amusement Foundation
Newsletter: HAF Times
4410 North Keystone Ave.
Indianapolis, IN 46205
ph: 317-841-7677

National Amusement Park Historical
Association
Magazine: NAPHA News
P.O. Box 83
Mount Prospect, IL 60056
ph: 412-831-6315
fax: 412-831-2658
info@napha.org
http://www.napha.org
*The world's only educational and
enthusiast's organization dedicated to
all aspects of the amusement park;
publishes "NAPHA News" magazine*

*six time each year; also publishes the
monthly newsletter "NAPHA
NewsFLASH!!!."*

Collectors

Ty Fluharty
P.O. Box 83
Mount Prospect, IL 60056
*Collector of amusement park
memorabilia.*

Jim Abbate
7936 Park Ave.
Skokie, IL 60077-2725
ph: 847-675-4511
amuspark@aol.com
*Wants roller coaster, carousel,
amusement park ephemera; photos,
brochures, stationery, ride manufacturers catalogs, tickets, sheet music,
letterheads, matchbooks, signs,
advertisements, pamphlets, trade
cards, postcards, etc.*

Tom Keefe
P.O. Box 464
Tinley Park, IL 60477-0464
mr.rollercoaster@attbi.com
*Wants signs, tickets, carousel horses,
tokens, photos, movies, letterheads,
ride manufacturer's catalogs, posters,
advertising items.*

Peter Dusza
305 Mathew St.
Santa Clara, CA 95050
ph: 408-988-8161 or 408-723-0722
fax: 408-988-2206
pdusza@ix.netcom.com
*Wants to buy roller coaster souvenirs
and memorabilia: coffee cups,
drinking and shot glasses, pins,
patches, postcards, posters, and
buttons.*

Experts

Thomas G. Morris
Prize Publishers
P.O. Box 8307
Medford, OR 97504-0307
chalkman@cdsnet.net
http://chalkman.homestead.com
*Specializing in carnival chalkware
figures; author of "The Carnival
Chalk Prize Vol. I and II;" will assist
with information or appraisals on the
subject.*

Museums/Libraries

Knoebels Amusement Park & Carousel
Museum
P.O. Box 317, Rte. 487
Elysburg, PA 17824-0317
ph: 570-672-2572 or 800-ITS-4FUN
magicusa@microserve.net
http://www.microserve.net/~magicusa/
knoebels.html

ANCIENT COINS

(see COINS & CURRENCY, Coins
[Ancient])

ANGELS

Clubs/Associations

Kay Ham, VP
Angels Collectors' Club of America
Newsletter: Halo Everybody!
107 Meadowlark Dr.
Altamonte Springs, FL 32701
ph: 407-331-0477
angelksh@juno.com
*Over 1,000 members who collect
angels in any form.*

Jeanne Kehe
Angel Collectors Club
Newsletter: Angels of the World
14 Parkview Ct.
Crystal Lake, IL 60012-3540
ph: 815-459-9259
*Members are collectors of any type of
angels; membership is limited to 225;
newsletter published 6 timer per year.*

Collectors

Barbara Lopatin
P.O. Box 1847
Annapolis, MD 21404
ph: 410-349-1158
fax: 410-349-1158
Blopatin@aol.com

ANIMAL COLLECTIBLES

(see also ANIMAL CONTROL
COLLECTIBLES; ANIMAL
TROPHIES; AQUARIUMS; BOOKS,
Poultry; DINOSAURS;
ENDANGERED SPECIES; FARM
COLLECTIBLES; FIGURINES,
Mortens; HORSES; INSECTS;
LICENSES, Animal; VETERINARY
MEDICINE ITEMS)

Collectors

John N. Case, Jr., BS, DVM
Veterinary Corps Museum & Archives
5462 North University Dr.
Lauderhill, FL 33351-5006
ph: 954-749-0551 or 954-629-6688
fax: 954-749-5462
JCase74683@aol.com
http://hometown.aol.com/jcase74683/
myhomepage/index.html
*Wants military artifacts of the
Veterinary Corps of each nation, any
era; also military farriers,
doghandlers, and Carrier pigeoneers:
insignia, badges, medals, uniforms,
hats/caps, documents, photos, IDs,
books, etc., museum information.*

Gary Bagnall
3090 McMillan Rd.
San Luis Obispo, CA 93401-6730
ph: 805-542-9988
fax: 805-542-9295
zoomed@zoomed.com
*Collects old pet items including old
dog dishes, collars, products, pet store
items, old pet magazines, etc.*

Dealers

Barbara Framke
"Just Animals"
15525 Fitzgerald
Livonia, MI 48154-1805
ph: 734-464-8493
fax: 734-464-8454
justanimals@justanimals.net
http://www.justanimals.net
*Buys and sells animal collectibles,
especially rabbit, horse, and dog
figurines.*

Bears

(see SMOKEY BEAR ITEMS; TEDDY
BEARS)

Cats

(see also CERAMICS [AMERICAN],
Black Cats; HALLOWEEN
COLLECTIBLES)

Clubs/Associations

Florette Schilkraut
Northeast Regional Cat Collector's Club
8 Tracey Court
New Hempstead, NY 10977
ph: 914-362-6369
jeffrey9@aol.com
http://www.hairballs.com

Karen Shanks
Cat Collectors
Newsletter: Cat Talk
P.O. Box 150784
Nashville, TN 37215-0784
ph: 615-297-7403
fax: 615-383-1359
musiccitykitty@yahoo.com
http://www.catcollectors.com
*Established in 1982 for those enjoying
collecting cat figurines, books,
artwork, advertising, calendars,
postcards, stamps, paper ephemera,
needlework, jewelry, antiques, bottles,
teapots and any object bearing the
image of a cat.*

Collectors

Marilyn Dipboye
33161 Wendy Dr.
Sterling Heights, MI 48310-6473
ph: 810-264-0285

Renae Giles
P.O. Box 6
Carver, MN 55315-0006
ph: 952-448-7046
zelda0555@aol.com
*Advanced collector seeks good quality
cat collectibles, especially Hagen-
Renaker, Freeman-McFarlin, Josef
Originals, Lowell Davis, Border Fine
Arts, Goebel, Rosenthal, and
Hutschenreuther.*

Mercedes DiRenzo
Jazz'e Junque
4107 N. Pulaski Rd.
Chicago, IL 60641
ph: 773-463-3687
fax: 773-463-3687
cookejarlayde@aol.com

Peggy Way
11334 Mesa Verde Lane
Parker, CO 80138
ph: 303-805-5884
purrrr@att.net
http://home.att.net/~purrrr/
homepage.html
*Cat collector specializing in Shafford
and Wales Black Cats, antique toy
cats, games featuring cats, cookie jars
and teapots in a cat motif, jewelry, etc.*

Dealers

Billie J. Parsons
431 Thomas Dr.
Webster, NY 14580
ph: 716-671-9388
*Specializes in canine, equine, and
feline collectibles: large dog figurines,
Western Hartlands, Kay Finch,
Hagen-Renaker, Breyer Horses.*

Experts

Marbena "Jean" Fyke
132 North Montgomery, Ste. D-12
Walden, NY 12586-1163
ph: 845-778-7327
fax: 845-564-1421
marbenaj1@aol.com
*Author of "Collectible Cats," Books I
and II (Collector's Books).*

Joyce McCandless
Krazy Cat Collectibles
P.O. Box 1192
Emmitsburg, MD 21727
ph: 301-271-9851
KrazyCatCo@aol.com
http://www.krazycatcollectibles.com
*Specializing in unique and interesting
old cat items: toys, postcards,
advertising, jewelry, pictures, cookie
jars, sale & peppers, plates, vintage
clothing, figurines, etc.; will buy one
piece or entire collection.*

Marilyn Dipboye
33161 Wendy Dr.
Sterling Heights, MI 48310-6473
ph: 810-264-0285
*Wants antique cat memorabilia in all
collecting categories.*

Cats (Goebel Figurines)

Experts

Linda Nothnagel
6721 Shelby, CRN 453
Shelbina, MO 63468
ph: 573-588-4958 or 816-781-5291
katzen630@hotmail.com
*Wants out-of-production Goebel cat
figurines and Goebel cat related
items.*

Cats (Kliban)

Collectors

Sue Lucente
115 Marbeth Ave.
Carlisle, PA 17013-1626
ph: 717-249-9343
Sooloo@webtv.net
*Wants ONLY black-and-white B.
Kliban cat items, no others: teapots,*

candy dishes, pillows and sheets,
*Christmas items, figurines, banks, salt
& pepper shakers, mugs, cookie jars,
cat feeders, book ends, stuffed
animals, kitchen towels, etc.*

Deer

Dealers

Elyce Litts
DeerLiteFul Antiques & Crafts
P.O. Box 394
Morris Plains, NJ 07950-0394
ph: 973-361-4087
happy-memories@worldnet.att.net
http://home.att.net/~deerliteful
*Buys and sells themed antiques,
collectibles and crafts including, but
not limited to, deer, doe, fawn, buck,
elk and gazelle figurines, glassware,
planters, lamps, jewelry, unique
handicrafts.*

Dogs

(see also LICENSES, Dog;
TELEVISION SHOWS &
MEMORABILIA, Lassie)

Collectors

Jeffrey Jacobson
860 Graegin Place
Dyer, IN 46311-2215

Jane Swanson
10290 Hill Rd.
Erie, IL 61250
ph: 309-659-2166
jane.swanson@ararental.org

Dealers

Annie Alpert
Dog Collector, The
400 Springfield Ave.
Cranford, NJ 07016-1809
ph: 908-276-2847
fax: 908-276-2954
annie@dogcollector.com
http://www.dogcollector.com
*Carries interesting dog art for the
collector including the full line of Ron
Hevener dog figurines.*

Billie J. Parsons
431 Thomas Dr.
Webster, NY 14580
ph: 716-671-9388
*Specializes in canine, equine, and
feline collectibles: large dog figurines,
Western Hartlands, Kay Finch,
Hagen-Renaker, Breyer Horses.*

Denise Hamilton
899 Latta Brook Rd.
Elmira, NY 14901-9226
ph: 607-732-2550
*Buys dog collectibles: figurines, old
dog postcards, jewelry with dogs in it,
etc.; Borzoi (Russian Wolfhound),
greyhound, all Morten Studio and
Erphila dogs and animals.*

Meg Weitz
Tigger's Dog Stuff
601 Rockwood Rd.
Wilmington, DE 19802-1120
ph: 302-762-8939
fax: 302-762-1050
dog4hire@aol.com
http://www.tiggersdogstuff.com
*Buys and sells fine dog collectibles
and prints.*

Jo Ellen Arnold
Dog Lady, The
P.O. Box 2641
Springfield, VA 22152-0641
ph: 703-644-5201
fax: 703-644-5401
Specializes in fine canine collectibles.

Jane & John Carroll
2894 John Tyler Highway
Williamsburg, VA 23185-1335
ph: 757-258-9322
fax: 757-258-9552
carroll@visi.net
*Buys and sells canine collectibles; a
poodle authority.*

Jennifer Mellin
Unique Dog Art
3061 NE 41 St.
Fort Lauderdale, FL 33308
ph: 954-695-2323
uniquedogart@yahoo.com
http://www.uniquedogart.com
*Sells dog art for the dog lover: dog
paintings, prints, ceramics,
photography, sculpture, jewelry,
woodcraft and more.*

Barbara Framke
"Just Animals"
15525 Fitzgerald
Livonia, MI 48154-1805
ph: 734-464-8493
fax: 734-464-8454
justanimals@justanimals.net
http://www.justanimals.net
*Buys and sells all dog related items,
especially figurines and collector
plates, both current and secondary
market; current sale lists available for
SASE; if selling, please price and
describe items.*

Museums/Libraries

Barbara Kolk, Lib.
American Kennel Club, Inc. Library
260 Madison Ave., 4th Floor
New York, NY 10016
ph: 212-696-8245 or 212-696-8348
fax: 212-696-8281
library@akc.org
http://www.akc.org/insideAKC/depts/
library.cfm
*Research library open to the public;
17,000 volumes on dogs and related
areas.*

American Kennel Club Museum of the
Dog
1721 S. Mason Rd.
Saint Louis, MO 63131
ph: 314-821-3647
fax: 314-821-7381
dogarts@aol.com
http://www.akc.org/love/museum/
index.cfm
*Commemorates every aspect of a
dog's life; collection includes dog art
and artifacts.*

Antiquibles Mall Dog Museum
P.O. Box 155244
Waco, TX 76715
ph: 254-829-0120 or 254-829-1921
fax: 254-829-0101
antiquible@aol.com
http://www.antiquibles.com
*Over 6,000 antique and collectible
dog related items; over 100 cross-
collectible categories.*

Dogs (Collies)

Collectors

Joan L. Neidhardt
P.O. Box 1000
Abingdon, MD 21009
JLNCollies@aol.com
http://www.lassie.net
*Wants to buy anything relating to
Collies or to Lassie; old, new, unique;
toys, figurines, character collectibles.*

Experts

Karen Pfeiffer
8417 West 400 South
Hanover, IN 47243-9111
ph: 812-866-4405
rpfeiffe@seidata.com
*Buys, sells, collects collie and Lassie
items: ephemera, toys, jewelry, etc.;
also collects collie items pertaining
specifically to Sunnybank and Albert
Payson Terhune.*

Dogs (German Shepherds)

Collectors

Henry Heiman, III
P.O. Box 316
South Salem, NY 10590-0316
*Wants to buy German Shepherd dog
items.*

Dogs (Poodles)

Collectors

Melody M. Teller
3465 Pelican Circle
Titusville, FL 32796
ph: 321-268-9653
fax: 321-385-1355
MommieDearest321@cfl.rr.com
*Has a collection of over 2,500 poodle
related items.*

Mickey Kern
NewMont Toy Poodles
124 North Crawford Ave.
Hardin, MT 59034
ph: 406-665-1097 or 406-679-1170
fax: 406-665-6127
*Collects, dealer, expert in poodle
items; prefers high quality items,
spaghetti, slaw, and similar varieties;
please no stuffed, mechanical, or
plastic poodles; also does not want
poodle hats, musical instruments, or
glasses.*

Dealers

Betty Hannigan
Way Back When Antiques
12509 Biscayne Dr.
Philadelphia, PA 19154
ph: 215-632-7247
waybackantiques@aol.com
*Carries a selection of spaghetti
poodles.*

Jane & John Carroll
2894 John Tyler Highway
Williamsburg, VA 23185-1335
ph: 757-258-9322
fax: 757-258-9552
carroll@visi.net
*Buys and sells canine collectibles; a
poodle authority.*

Dogs (Scotties)

Periodicals

David Bohnlein
Magazine: Scottie Sampler
P.O. Box 450
Danielson, CT 06239-0450
ph: 860-564-6660
dbohnlein@snet.net
http://www.scote.com/sampler
*A quarterly publication with historical
data, current market prices, photos,
ads, etc. for Scottie collectors and
dealers.*

Elephants

Clubs/Associations

Richard W. Massiglia
National Elephant Collectors Society,
The
380 Medford St.
Somerville, MA 02145-3810
ph: 617-625-4067
For information send LSASE plus $1.

Collectors

Rosita Williams
14357 Georgia Ave., Apt. T-2
Silver Spring, MD 20906
ph: 301-871-3135

Michael Knapik
15804 East Greystone Dr.
conscioussystems@mindspring.com
*Avid collector of elephant figurines,
advertisements, coins, inkwells,
incense burners, bookends, etc.;
collection includes over 3,000 items.*

Experts

Richard W. Massiglia
380 Medford St.
Somerville, MA 02145-3810
ph: 617-625-4067

Periodicals

Joan L. Huegel
Newsletter: Jumbo Jargon
1002 West 25th St.
Erie, PA 16502-2427
*Quarterly publication; free ad for
subscribers; articles, meet other
collectors, "from the expert" column,
classified ads, etc.; available only by
subscription.*

Flamingos

Collectors

Suzy Holleron
624 Morningside Dr.
San Antonio, TX 78209-2808
ph: 210-826-6663
*Known as the "Flamingo Lady;"
collects everything with a flamingo
motif.*

Lynn Rogers
P.O. Box 5495
Coos Bay, OR 97420
ph: 541-888-4177
Wants flamingo items.

Frogs

(see also FLOWER "FROGS")

Clubs/Associations

Ms. Merelaine Haskett, Ed.
Frog Pond, The
Newsletter: Ribbit Ribbit
P.O. Box 193
Beech Grove, IN 46107-0193
*Newsletter has articles and buy/sell/
trade ads; open to all who are
interested in collecting frog related
items.*

Dealers

Louise Mesa
"Frog Fantasies" Museum & Frogs Only
Gift Shop
151 Spring St.
Eureka Springs, AR 72632
ph: 479-253-7227
info@frogfantasies.com
http://www.frogfantasies.com

Museums/Libraries

Louise Mesa
Frog Fantasies Museum, The
151 Spring St.
Eureka Springs, AR 72632
ph: 479-253-7227
info@frogfantasies.com
http://www.frogfantasies.com
*Has over 6,000 frogs of every
description and made of every
conceivable material: porcelain,
majolica, wood, jade, cork, coconut
shell frogs, frogs carved from cedar
roots; frogs of woven plant fibers and
even of metal.*

Horse Related

(see also FARM COLLECTIBLES;
HORSE-DRAWN VEHICLES;
HORSES; LEATHER; RIDING TOYS,
Rocking Horses; SADDLES; SPORTS
COLLECTIBLES, Polo; SPORTS
COLLECTIBLES, Thoroughbred
Racing; WESTERN AMERICANA)

Collectors

James Cole
October Farm Horse Books
2609 Branch Rd.
Raleigh, NC 27610
ph: 919-772-0482
fax: 919-779-2325
octoberfarm@bellsouth.net
http://www.octoberfarm.com
*Wants carriage and wagon trade
catalogs, photos of old stagecoaches,
pre-1960 polo ephemera, old horse
books of all kinds.*

Bill Mackin
1137 Washington St.
Craig, CO 81625-1613
ph: 970-824-6717 or 970-824-6360
fax: 970-824-7175
*Author of "Cowboy and Gunfighter
Collectibles" price guide; sells books
for Old West collectors by mail and at
shows; over 45 years collecting; wants
nice gun leather and cowboy gear;
appraises, consults, lectures.*

Linda Paich
Bookends
P.O. Box 445
Los Olivos, CA 93441
ph: 805-688-3484
fax: 805-688-0307
*Wants items relating to horses:
postcards, books, statues, antique
Western tack, etc.; antique and out-of-
print on all types of horses and horse
sport; buys and sells.*

Dealers

Equine Antiques & Collectibles
256 Meaderboro Rd.
Farmington, NH 03835
ph: 603-330-0944
oldhorsestuf@metrocast.net
http://www.equineantiques.com
*Sells horse related antiques and
collectibles.*

Pam Pramuka
Horsies.net - Model Horses Great &
Small
122 Sunrise Hill Rd.
Norwalk, CT 06851
ph: 203-846-8246
pzp@horsies.net
http://www.horsies.net
*Expert, dealer buys and sells Breyer
model horses; also Hartland and
Peter Stone horse and animal models;
vintage, special-run, new-in-box,
hard-to-find; search service available.*

Billie J. Parsons
431 Thomas Dr.
Webster, NY 14580
ph: 716-671-9388
  Specializes in canine, equine, and feline collectibles: large dog figurines, Western Hartlands, Kay Finch, Hagen-Renaker, Breyer Horses.

Jim Cole
October Farm Books
2609 Branch Rd.
Raleigh, NC 27610-9213
ph: 919-772-0482
fax: 919-779-6265
octoberfarm@bellsouth.net
http://www.octoberfarm.com
  Buys and sells horse books and paper ephemera, especially relating to polo, carriages & driving, Morgan horses, American Saddlebred horses, and veterinary medicine; also old farm horse equipment and catalogs; mail order only.

Barbara Framke
"Just Animals"
15525 Fitzgerald
Livonia, MI 48154-1805
ph: 734-464-8493
fax: 734-464-8454
justanimals@justanimals.net
http://www.justanimals.net
  Buys porcelain and ceramic horse figurines, especially by Hagen-Renaker, Beswick and Goebel; also wants horse related books; all items considered.

Deborah Rashkin
Horsetiques
1822 E. Bruce Ave.
Gilbert, AZ 85234
ph: 480-730-0947
horsetiques@aol.com
http://www.horsetiques.com
  Collects, buys and sells items relating to horses: pottery, paintings, iron, jewelry; also anything relating to the equestrian lifestyle.

Experts

Felicia Browell
Other Stuff
123 Hooks Lane
Canonsburg, PA 15317-1835
ph: 724-746-2529
fbrowell@nauticom.net
http://www.nauticom.net/www/fbrowell
  Author of "Breyer Animal Collectors Guide" with concise descriptions and realistic values; also author of "Breyer Animal Quick Reference" with line-drawings, mint market values, good for taking inventories.

Deborah Rashkin
Horsetiques
1822 E. Bruce Ave.
Gilbert, AZ 85234
ph: 480-730-0947
horsetiques@aol.com
http://www.horsetiques.com
  Author of "Horse Antiques & Collectibles" (Schiffer).

Museums/Libraries

Tolley Graves, Dir.
American Saddlebred Museum
4093 Iron Works Parkway
Lexington, KY 40511
ph: 859-259-2746 or 800-829-4438
fax: 859-255-4909
ashm@mis.net
http://www.american-saddlebred.com/museum
  Represents the traditions and heritage of the American Saddlebred horse through the collection, preservation, and display of artifacts, fine art, and photography.

Bill Cooke, Dir.
International Museum of the Horse,
  Kentucky Horse Park
4089 Iron Works Pike
Lexington, KY 40511
ph: 859-233-4304
fax: 859-259-4212
khp26@mis.net
http://www.kyhorsepark.com
  Largest museum in the world dedicated to the horse; special gallery exhibitions April through October.

Horse Related (Draft)

Collectors

Jim Richendollar
46141 Harris Rd.
Belleville, MI 48111
ph: 734-699-3805
  Wants draft (work horse like Clydesdales) horse memorabilia: books, magazines, photos, prints, paintings, sale catalogs, statues, figurines, etc.

Horse Related (Horse Brasses)

Clubs/Associations

National Horse Brass Society
2 Blue Barn Cottage
Blue Barn Lane
Weybridge, Surrey KT13 0NH U.K.
ph: 01932 354 193
  For collectors of brass horse harness decorations.

Internet Resources

Jimmy Iddon
UK Brass
P.O. Box 1123
Campletown, NSW 2560 Australia
ph: 61 2 9820 1188
fax: 61 2 9820 3053
steptoe88@hotmail.com
http://www.ukbrass.com
  Medallions, martingale straps and horse bridle and harness ornaments.

Horse Related (Models)

Clubs/Associations

Daralyn Wallace
Equine Miniaturists & Collectors
  Association of Texas
Newsletter: EMCAT News
1311 Garden Lane
Bryan, TX 77802
RaunFalcon@aol.com
http://hometown.aol.com/emcattx/index.htm
  Formed for the purpose of promoting interest and involvement in model horse collecting and showing; all are welcome.

Chris Wallbruch, Rec. Sec.
North American Model Horse Shows
  Association
3518 West Kiltie Loop
Flagstaff, AZ 86001
wombats@earthlink.net
http://www.namhsa.org
  Organization of model horse shows; entrants at these shows exhibit accurate scale models of horses both in "halter" and "performance" and compete for prizes; model horses are composed of plastic, resin, or ceramic; new and antique.

Collectors

Chelle Fulk
1793 Ivy Oak Sq.
Reston, VA 20190-4723
ph: 703-471-1968
anthem2@juno.com
http://www.musicbyanthem.com/chelle/collection.htm
  Wants plastic horses, dogs, etc.: Breyer, Hartland, others; any size, condition, color.

Jessica Prior-Jennings
116 Isbell St.
Howell, MI 48843
ph: 517-545-5526
revjennings@yahoo.com
http://www.wasmi.net
  Collector of English-made Julip model horses, riders, stables, and tack; the horses are made of latex rubber with hair manes and tails; will also consider other types of model horses such as Breyer, Hartland, chinas.

Dealers

Alison L. Beniush
World of Model Horse Collecting, The
30200 Stoneybrooke Dr.
Salisbury, MD 21804-2487
ph: 410-543-8972
twmhc@intercom.net
http://www.geocities.com/twmhc
  Specializes in online orders of animal figurines including Hagen-Renaker, Cheval Ceramics, and Loza Electricas.

Susan Schutz
Horse Collector, The
1249 Edward Rd.
Naperville, IL 60540
ph: 888-294-5740
fax: 630-717-1459
breyerhrs@aol.com
http://www.horsecollector.com
  Offers fine porcelain horse sculptures, also Breyers.

Black Horse Ranch
1024 Nobles Court
Minden, NV 89423
ph: 800-360-5BHR
modelhorse@aol.com
http://www.bhranch.com/models.htm

Internet Resources

Model Horse Web
kira@metronet.com
http://www.lightsphere.com/model-horse
  Web site packed with resources for model horse hobbyists; dealers, classified ads, clubs, publications, artists, art supplies, shows, etc.

Model Horse Enthusiasts' Site
emilynchris@geocities.com
http://www.geocities.com/Heartland/Plains/6871
  For collectors of plastic, porcelain, pottery, or resin model horses.

Gail J. Berg
Model Horse Gallery
P.O. Box 390010
Mountain View, CA 94039-0010
curator@modelhorsegallery.info
http://www.modelhorsegallery.com
  The largest and only model horse gallery in the world; over 14,000 photos, 200 galleries and over 1,700 pages.

Periodicals

Tina Ferro, Ed.
Magazine: Hobby Horse News, The
14 Garraux St.
Greenville, SC 29609
thhn2000@aol.com
http://www.hobbyhorsenews.com
  Bi-monthly magazine with hobby horse articles, shows, ads, etc.

Sheryl Leisure
Horse Power Graphics, Inc.
Newsletter: Model Horse Trader, The
34428 Yucaipa Blvd., #E119
Yucaipa, CA 92399
ph: 909-446-0233
fax: 909-795-2474
  Ads-only newsletter consisting of dealers' lists from across the country; not a reference or price guides; models identified only be model number; send $15, photos and LSASE for appraisals; checks payable to Sheryl Leisure.

Repair Services

Sue Thiessen
25115 Cemetery Rd.
Middleton, ID 83644-5103
ph: 208-585-3243
Specializing in restoring model horses, Roseville, and other pottery; also collector of Hagen Renaker horse and animal figurines.

Horse Related (Models/Breyer)

Clubs/Associations

Breyer Collectors Club
Magazine: Just About Horses
14 Industrial Rd.
Pequannock, NJ 07440
ph: 973-694-5006
fax: 973-633-5090
comments@reevesintl.com
http://www.breyerhorses.com
A company-sponsored club; offers information on model horse collecting and hobbying including customization, vintage models & horse model showing; no paid ads.

Collectors

DeLayne Milby
16642 MLC Lane
Rockville, VA 23146
ph: 804-746-4564
fax: 804-749-4902
Collector of Breyer horses.

Kimberly Falat
525 N. Quenton Rd., #111
Palatine, IL 60067
Publishes a value guide of ALL Breyer models ever created; buys collections.

Dealers

Sue Coffee
Laysville Hardware
10 Saunders Hollow Rd.
Old Lyme, CT 06371-1126
ph: 860-434-5641
fax: 860-434-3640
SueCoffee@aol.com
http://www.suecoffee.com
Over 500 retired Breyer in stock; send SASE with .76 postage for list or visit Web site; also wants Breyer from the 1950s and 1960s, especially woodgrains and decorators (gold, blue and dapple.)

Pam Pramuka
Horsies.net - Model Horses Great & Small
122 Sunrise Hill Rd.
Norwalk, CT 06851
ph: 203-846-8246
pzp@horsies.net
http://www.horsies.net
Expert, dealer buys and sells Breyer model horses; also Hartland and Peter Stone horse and animal models; vintage, special-run, new-in-box, hard-to-find; search service available.

MyBreyer.com
P.O. Box 7526
Pittsburgh, PA 15213-0526
ph: 412-488-8800
fax: 412-621-8939
davesmusicmine@aol.com
http://www.mybreyer.com
Buys and sells Breyer horse and animal models.

Pat Morgan
KTM Breyer Horses
3884 Mill Rd.
Collegeville, PA 19426
ph: 610-489-9615
breyerktm@hotmail.com
http://www.breyerktm.com
Sells full line of Breyer model horses and animals.

Karen Hoagland
P.O. Box 204
Shartlesville, PA 19554
ph: 610-488-7742
horsiekat@aol.com
Buys and sells Breyer horse models.

Arlene Bentley
Bentley Sales Company
642 Sandy Lane
Des Plaines, IL 60016
ph: 847-439-2049
fax: 847-439-2071
bentley@modelhorses.com
http://www.modelhorses.com/bentley
Carries entire Breyer Model Horse line plus limited editions, discontinued and special run models.

Experts

Felicia Browell
Other Stuff
123 Hooks Lane
Canonsburg, PA 15317-1835
ph: 724-746-2529
fbrowell@nauticom.net
http://www.nauticom.net/www/fbrowell
Author of "Breyer Animal Collectors Guide" and "Breyer Animal Quick Reference."

Kimberly Falat
525 N. Quenton Rd., #111
Palatine, IL 60067
Author of "Breyer Model Collector's Value Guide;" detailed descriptions and production years of regular models, special runs, lamps, night lights, music boxes; contains current market values, photos, etc.

Nancy Atkinson Young
Nancy Young's Books
268 Ross Court
Claremont, CA 91711-3139
fax: 909-621-7872
Nancy_Young@earthlink.net
http://home.earthlink.net/~nancy_young
Author of "Breyer Molds and Models," (available from author) the most comprehensive book available on Breyer model horses and other animals; does not do appraisals; please include SASE when writing.

Internet Resources

Pam Pramuka
Horsies.net - Model Horses Great & Small
122 Sunrise Hill Rd.
Norwalk, CT 06851
ph: 203-846-8246
pzp@horsies.net
http://www.horsies.net
Great Web site by expert, dealer who buys and sells Breyer model horses; also Hartland and Peter Stone horse and animal models; vintage, special-run, new-in-box, hard-to-find; search service available.

Man./Prod./Dist.

Reeves International, Inc.
Magazine: Just About Horses
14 Industrial Rd.
Pequannock, NJ 07440
ph: 973-694-5006
fax: 973-633-5090
comments@reevesintl.com
http://www.breyerhorses.com
Manufacturer of Breyer fine porcelain and resin horse sculptures.

Mice

Experts

Dr. Albert H. Eschen
2200 S. Ocean Lane
Fort Lauderdale, FL 33316
albieboy@webtv.net
Author of book on "Collectible Mice: Art, History & Legend," an identification and value guide; specializes in mouse collectibles made from glass, ivory, bronze, pewter, gold, silver, platinum, porcelain, etc.

Monkeys

Collectors

Chad Kahrs
P.O. Box 45223
Kansas City, MO 64171
Has hundreds of monkey collectibles: figurines, organ grinders, salt-and-pepper sets, monkey fabrics, masks, mechanical monkey toys, etc.

Mules

Collectors

Gene Hammerlun
1350 Cal Ct.
Gardnerville, NV 89410-6123
ph: 775-782-5945
hammerlun@gbis.com
Wants to buy anything related to mules: pictures, advertising, stories, etc.

Periodicals

Magazine: Western Mule Magazine
P.O. Box 46
Marshfield, MO 65706
ph: 417-859-6853
fax: 417-859-2814
ben@westernmulemagazine.com
http://www.westernmulemagazine.com
Pleasure, cutting, show and pack mules' training, health, trail riding, mule rodeos and more.

Penguins

Collectors

Keith Cimino
ktcpengwin@aol.com
Has been collecting penguins (including "Chilly Willy") for over 20 years; over 1,500 items.

Pigs

Clubs/Associations

Carol E. Blackman
Happy Pig Collectors Club, The
Newsletter: Happy Pig, The
4542 N. Western Ave.
Chicago, IL 60625-2117
ph: 773-878-8328
happypigclub@ameritech.net
http://www.happypigcollectors.org
For collectors of pigs items, so that they may gain more enjoyment from their hobby and mingle with others cursed with the same strange affliction; it's respectful to say "When I see a Pig, I think of you."

Collectors

Arlene McNaught
136 Edwards St.
Kewanee, IL 61443-3538
ph: 309-853-4960
happypig@theramp.net

Gene Holt
P.O. Box 17
Oneida, IL 61467-0017
ph: 309-483-6192

Experts

Mary Hamburg
Tootsie's Antiques
20 Cedar Ave.
Danville, IL 61832-1525
ph: 217-446-2323 or 217-442-2725
tootsies@allarounddanville.com
Buys, sells, collects, and specializes in German china pig figurines; advisor to "Warman's Americana & Collectibles Price Guide."

Plastic Models

Collectors

Chelle Fulk
1793 Ivy Oak Sq.
Reston, VA 20190-4723
ph: 703-471-1968
anthem2@juno.com
http://www.musicbyanthem.com/chelle/collection.htm
Wants plastic horses, dogs, cattle, wildlife, etc.; especially Breyer; any size, condition or color.

Rabbits

Dealers

Barbara Framke
"Just Animals"
15525 Fitzgerald
Livonia, MI 48154-1805
ph: 734-464-8493
fax: 734-464-8454
justanimals@justanimals.net
http://www.justanimals.net
*Buys and sells rabbit collectibles
including figurines, collector plates,
prints, and Royal Doulton Bunnykins.*

Reptiles

Experts

Mark F. Miller
Herpetology.com
P.O. Box 52261
Philadelphia, PA 19115-7261
ph: 215-464-3561
fax: 215-464-3561
reptiles@earthling.net
http://www.herpetology.com
*Author of numerous articles regarding
reptile care, reptile books, and
collecting reptile literature,
sculptures, prints, and postcards; past
Editor or the "Bulletin of the
Philadelphia Herpetology Society;"
DO NOT send items on approval.*

ANIMAL CONTROL COLLECTIBLES

Collectors

Wayne M. Besenty
9060 Hegel St.
Bellflower, CA 90706-4216
ph: 562-925-8574 or 562-570-3057
CaSrACO@webtv.net
*Collector of historical animal control
and Humane Society items: patches,
badges, pins, banners, animal humane
magazines, posters, photographs of
dog catchers, animal control or
humane officers, ASPCA, trucks;
anything animal control.*

ANIMAL TROPHIES

(see also ENDANGERED SPECIES;
SKELETONS; SPORTING
COLLECTIBLES)

Auction Services

Gerard Giguere
Giguere Auction Co.
P.O. Box 1272
Windham, ME 04062-1272
ph: 207-892-3800 or 207-675-3207
fax: 207-675-3441
info@giguereauction.com
http://www.giguereauction.com
*Conducts sporting auctions: fishing,
hunting, decoys, sporting art,
taxidermy.*

Dealers

Bob Hoffman
Moose River Lake & Lodge Store
69 Railroad St.
Barnet, VT 05821
ph: 802-748-2423 or 802-633-4031
webmaster@allroutes.to
http://www.allroutes.to/mrl
*Old taxidermy; deer, moose, elk,
caribou antlers; skulls, folk art, prints,
paintings and photos; snowshoes,
pack baskets, creels, rustic & camp
furnishings; open daily.*

Gene Harris
Art By God
50 Upper Alabama, Store No. 248
Underground Atlanta
Atlanta, GA 30303
ph: 404-577-7311 or 800-940-4449
fax: 305-573-9343
artbygod@netside.net
*Mineral specimens, fossils, gems, sea
shells, animal mounts, animal pelts,
insects/butterflies, snail shells, skulls.*

Gene Harris
Art By God
3705 Biscayne
Miami, FL 33137
ph: 305-573-3011 or 305-573-3691
fax: 305-573-9343
artbygod@netside.net
*Mineral specimens, fossils, gems, sea
shells, animal mounts, animal pelts,
insects/butterflies, snail shells, skulls.*

Edward Leep
American Natural Resources
128 N. Broad St.
Griffith, IN 46319-2219
ph: 219-922-6444
http://www.leepstaxidermy.com
*Sells mounts from around the world:
full mounts, shoulder mounts, bear
rugs, birds, etc.*

David Boone
Boone's Trading Company
P.O. Box 669
Brinnon, WA 98320
ph: 360-796-4330 or 800-423-1945
fax: 360-796-4551
sales@boonetrading.com
http://www.boonetrading.com
*Buys and sells legal ivory, scrimshaw,
furs and skulls: scrimshaw, netsuke,
Eskimo artifacts, carvings, walrus,
hippo, warthog, mammoth, jewelry,
pistol grips, ivory beads, old trade
beads, scrimshaw supplies and
reproductions.*

Experts

Gerard Giguere
Giguere Auction Co.
P.O. Box 1272
Windham, ME 04062-1272
ph: 207-892-3800 or 207-675-3207
fax: 207-675-3441
info@giguereauction.com
http://www.giguereauction.com
*Conducts sporting auctions: fishing,
hunting, decoys, sporting art,
taxidermy; very knowledgeable about
the regulations related to the sale of
animal parts.*

Museums/Libraries

David George, GM
Buckhorn Saloon & Museum, The
318 E. Houston St.
San Antonio, TX 78205
ph: 210-247-4000
fax: 210-247-4020
destenter@aol.com
http://www.buckhornmuseum.com
*The undisputed largest collection of
animal trophies: the museum includes
the Hall of Horns, Hall of Fins, Hall
of Feathers; since 1881.*

Suppliers

Van Dykes Restorer's
39771 S.D. Hwy. 34
P.O. Box 278
Woonsocket, SD 57385-0278
ph: 800-787-3355 or 605-796-4425
fax: 605-796-4085
http://www.vandykes.com
*Issues large catalog of taxidermy
supplies.*

ANIMATION FILM ART

(see also AUDIO-VISUAL; CARTOON
ART; CHARACTER COLLECTIBLES;
SCIENCE FICTION)

Appraisers

Debbi Grossfeld
Gremlin Animation
Newsletter: Celmail
646 Richville Rd.
P.O. Box 1787
Manchester Center, VT 05255
ph: 877-GREMLIN or 802-362-4766
fax: 802-362-4745
gallery@thegremlin.com
http://www.thegremlin.com
*Animation film art dealer, expert and
appraiser; one of the largest
resources in the world for animation
art from all studios; currently
maintains an inventory of over 25,000
original cels, drawings and limited
editions.*

Pamela D. Scoville, AAA
1554 Greenwood Lake Turnpike
Hewitt, NJ 07421-3300
ph: 973-657-0560
fax: 973-657-0561
TheAAGLtd@aol.com
*Offers appraisal services for
animation film art; certified member,
Appraiser Association of America.*

Pam Martin
CEL-EBRATION!
P.O. Box 123
Little Silver, NJ 07739
ph: 732-842-8489 or 842-842-0494
fax: 732-842-8489
cel-ebration@monmouth.com
http://www.cel-ebration.com
*Appraises, buys and sells vintage and
contemporary animation art from all
studios; storefront in Red Bank, NJ;
also mail order; offers hard-to-find
rare cels.*

Melanie Smith, ISA
Seaside Art Gallery
2716 Virginia Dare Trail South
P.O. Box 1
Nags Head, NC 27959-0001
ph: 252-441-5418 or 800-828-2444
fax: 252-441-8563
info@seasideart.com
http://www.seasideart.com
*Accredited member of the Interna-
tional Society of Appraisers;
specializes in fine art (paintings,
graphics, sculpture) and animation
art.*

Norbert Hernandez
Classic Animation
4524 Sterling Lane
Plano, TX 75093
ph: 214-641-4464 or 972-519-0066
nhernan770@aol.com
*Accredited member of the Interna-
tional Society of Appraisers;
specializes in the appraisal of
animation art, toys, film mementoes.*

Michael Austin
Great American Ink
11633 San Vicente Blvd.
Los Angeles, CA 90049
ph: 310-552-2847 or 800-552-2847
fax: 310-447-1831
Grins@CartoonGallery.com
http://www.cartoongallery.com
*Appraiser, collector, dealer and
expert in animation artworks from the
early 1900s through the 1960s; strong
collector of Disney, Lantz, Warner
Brothers Studios original production
artworks including cels, story
paintings, backgrounds.*

Clubs/Associations

Pamela D. Scoville
Animation Art Guild, Ltd.
Newsletter: Update, The
1554 Greenwood Lake Turnpike
Hewitt, NJ 07421-3300
ph: 973-657-0560
fax: 973-657-0561
TheAAGLtd@aol.com
*Established in 1990; offers reliable,
unbiased information; member
services include book finders, auction
hotline, appraisal services, flash
advisories, art theft advisories,
world's most comprehensive database
on animation art values.*

Nancy McClellan
Animation Art Collectors Club of
Washington
2972 Yarling Ct.
Falls Church, VA 22042-4475
ph: 703-876-0891 or 202-364-0842
fax: 202-364-0002
antiques@erols.com
http://www.antiquesdc.com
*Regional club interested in promotion
and education of animation as an art
form.*

Steven Worth
Association Internationale Du Film
  D'Animation (ASIFA)
725 South Victory Blvd.
Burbank, CA 91502
ph: 818-842-8330
fax: 818-842-5645
sworth@vintageip.com
http://home.earthlink.net/~asifa
  A worldwide organization dedicated
  to the art of animation.

Dealers

Steve Grossfeld
Newsletter: Celmail
P.O. Box 1787
Manchester Center, VT 05255
ph: 802-362-4766
fax: 802-362-4745
CELMAIL@thegremlin.com
http://www.thegremlin.com/
  CELMAILhome.html
  An online animation film newsletter;
  join to be connected to thousands of
  other enthusiasts who share the
  hobby; member participation and
  monitored by industry professionals,
  industry publications and galleries
  alike.

Herb Barker
Barker Animation Art Galleries
1188 Highland Ave.
Cheshire, CT 06410-1624
ph: 800-227-5372 or 800-995-2357
fax: 203-699-1188
fun@barkeranimation.com
http://www.BarkerAnimation.com

Gallery Lainzberg
20-26 Industrial Ave.
Fairview, NJ 07022
ph: 877-422-4642
allanimationllc@yahoo.com
http://www.allanimation.com
  Oldest and most well established
  animation gallery in the country.

Pam Martin
CEL-EBRATION!
P.O. Box 123
Little Silver, NJ 07739
ph: 732-842-8489 or 842-842-0494
fax: 732-842-8489
cel-ebration@monmouth.com
http://www.cel-ebration.com
  Appraises, buys and sells vintage and
  contemporary animation art from all
  studios; storefront in Red Bank, NJ;
  also mail order; offers hard-to-find
  rare cels.

Animazing Gallery
474 Broome St.
New York, NY 10013
ph: 800-303-4848 or 212-226-7374
fax: 212-226-7428
heidi@animazing.com
http://www.animazing.com
  Featuring vintage and contemporary
  animation art, fine art that is fun, and
  fine craft; cells and drawings from all
  studios; a Disney exclusive gallery;
  hosts industry events; publishers of
  Underdog artwork.

Debbie Weiss
Wonderful World of Animation Art
51 E. 74th St., Ste. 1R
New York, NY 10022
ph: 212-472-1720
debbiew@animationartgallery.com
http://www.animationartgallery.com
  Buys, sells, appraises animation art;
  specializes in original art from
  Disney, Simpsons, Warner, Hanna,
  and others; over 2,000 original
  production pieces in stock.

Agnes O'Keefe
American Royal Arts Corp.
123 Frost St., Ste. 201
Westbury, NY 11590
ph: 516-997-2220 or 800-888-9449
fax: 516-997-2460
sales@AmericanRoyalArts.com
http://www.AmericanRoyalArts.com
  One of the nation's largest supplier of
  animation art: original production
  cels, limited edition cels, drawings
  and model sheets from a wide range of
  animated films; appeared on PAX
  TV's "Treasures in Your Home."

Stu & Miriam Reisbord
Cartoon Carnival Gallery, The
2 Rabbit Run
Wallingford, PA 19086-6218
ph: 610-566-4343 or 610-566-1292
fax: 610-566-2727
stureis@erols.com
  Specializing in Disney vintage
  drawings, cels and backgrounds for
  over 20 years; also original pen & ink
  classic syndicated art.

Bryan Guarnieri
Animation & Fine Art Galleries
University Mall
201 S. Estes Dr.
Chapel Hill, NC 27514
ph: 919-968-8008
fax: 919-968-8064
bryan@animationandfineart.com
http://www.animationandfineart.com
  Specializes in original production
  animation art cels and drawings as
  well as original paintings, drawings
  and sculpture by world-renowned
  museum-exhibited 20th century artists.

Melanie Smith, ISA
Seaside Art Gallery
2716 Virginia Dare Trail South
P.O. Box 1
Nags Head, NC 27959-0001
ph: 252-441-5418 or 800-828-2444
fax: 252-441-8563
info@seasideart.com
http://www.seasideart.com
  Wants original oils, graphics,
  sculpture, and animation film art; also
  buys and sells old and new animation
  art; Accredited Member of the
  International Society of Appraisers.

Dan & Mary Anne Ergezi
Art-Toons
P.O. Box 670600
Northfield, OH 44067-0600
ph: 330-468-2655 or 888-468-2655
fax: 330-468-2644
ArtToonsart@aol.com
http://www.art-toons.funurl.com
  A business dedicated to giving the
  public the enjoyment of owning
  animation art at affordable prices:
  Japanese/anime, Warner Bros., Walt
  Disney, commercials, MGM, super
  heroes, cult classics such as Heavy
  Metal, Wizards, Hanna Barbera.

Cartoon Factory Animation Art Gallery
1400 South Foothill Dr.
Salt Lake City, UT 84108-2300
ph: 801-583-3700
fax: 801-583-3713
gallery@cartoon-factory.com
http://www.cartoon-factory.com
  Large selection of animation art on
  the Web; original and limited edition
  art cels from Disney, Warner Bros.,
  Hanna-Barbera, The Simpsons,
  Peanuts, and many other studios.

Michael Austin
Great American Ink
11633 San Vicente Blvd.
Los Angeles, CA 90049
ph: 310-552-2847 or 800-552-2847
fax: 310-447-1831
Grins@CartoonGallery.com
http://www.cartoongallery.com
  Appraiser, collector, dealer and
  expert in animation artworks from the
  early 1900s through the 1960s; strong
  collector of Disney, Lantz, Warner
  Brothers Studios original production
  artworks including cels, story
  paintings, backgrounds.

Acme Vintage Toys & Animation Art
  Gallery
9976 Westwanda Dr.
Beverly Hills, CA 90210
ph: 310-276-5509
brad3845@aol.com
http://www.acmetoys.com
  Specializes in mint and boxed tin toys,
  Japanese robots, cartoon cells, and
  classic animation art from Disney,
  Warner Brothers, 20th Century Fox,
  Dreamworks, Hanna Barbera and
  other legendary Hollywood studios.

Ron Silverstein
Silver Stone Gallery
2005 Palo Verde Ave., Ste. 205
Long Beach, CA 90815-3399
ph: 562-598-7600
fax: 562-598-7700
silverston@aol.com
  A private gallery for the discerning
  collector, specializing in buying &
  selling Disney Studio vintage
  animation art.

Joseph Cesaro
Sunday Funnies LLC
10010 Canoga Ave., Ste. B1
Chatsworth, CA 91311
ph: 818-341-9040 or 800-693-2369
fax: 818-341-4850
joecesaro@sundayfunniesllc.com
http://www.sundayfunniesllc.com
  Sells animated art: production cells,
  limited edition cels, and seri-cels;
  includes Archie, Fat Albert, Heckle &
  Jeckle, Blondie, Beetle Bailey, Star
  Trek, Star Wars, Lone Ranger, Lassie,
  etc.; represents Filmation, Lucas
  Films, etc.

Stephen Worth
Vintage Ink & Paint
5701 Klump Ave. #7
North Hollywood, CA 91601
ph: 818-980-7637
sworth@vintageip.com
http://www.vintageip.com
  Buys, sells, repairs, appraises; the
  leading authority on animation art
  authentication & restoration; all
  paints manufactured in-house using
  same formulas and techniques used at
  Disney Studios; has worked with
  several major studios.

Steve Oakley
Acme Animation Art Cel Galleries
10938 Magnolia Blvd.
North Hollywood, CA 91601
ph: 909-899-5400 or 888-988-6667
fax: 909-899-0492
art@acmeanimation.com
http://www.acmeanimation.com
  A premier animation art gallery
  specializing in fine animation cels and
  cartoon character art as well as
  figurines and other collectibles.

Richard L. Trethewey
Rainbo Animation Art
8 Duran Court
Pacifica, CA 94044-4231
ph: 800-647-5085 or 950-359-0221
fax: 413-643-0711
webmaster@rainbo.net
http://www.rainbo.net
  Carries a wide range of animation art
  from production cells to posters; also
  carries animation collectibles
  featuring Toy Story toys and
  collectibles.

Vincent Sean Monico
Animation Artshop, The
P.O. Box 10014
Anchorage, AK 99510-0114
ph: 907-274-1894 or 800-646-5967
animate@alaska.net
http://www.alaska.net/~animate
  Collects, buys and sells all types of
  original Disney production artwork.

Jack Skorochod
Animation Connection
365 Eglinton Ave. W.
Toronto, Ontario M5N 1A3 Canada
ph: 416-482-5111 or 800-700-1173
contact@animationconnection.com
http://www.animationconnection.com
  Buys, sells and trades fine animation

art, cels and drawings from Chuck
Jones, Warner Bros., The Simpsons
and more; original and limited edition
animation cels and cartoon art; studio
authorized animation art gallery.

Experts

Debbi Grossfeld
Gremlin Animation
Newsletter: Celmail
646 Richville Rd.
P.O. Box 1787
Manchester Center, VT 05255
ph: 877-GREMLIN or 802-362-4766
fax: 802-362-4745
gallery@thegremlin.com
http://www.thegremlin.com
Animation film art dealer, expert and
appraiser; one of the largest
resources in the world for animation
art from all studios; currently
maintains an inventory of over 25,000
original cels, drawings and limited
editions.

Bryan Guarnieri
Animation & Fine Art Galleries
University Mall
201 S. Estes Dr.
Chapel Hill, NC 27514
ph: 919-968-8008
fax: 919-968-8064
bryan@animationandfineart.com
http://www.animationandfineart.com
Specializes in original production
animation art cels and drawings as
well as original paintings, drawings
and sculpture by world-renowned
museum-exhibited 20th century artists.

Ron Stark, ISA
S/R Laboratories, Animation Art
Conservation Center
Newsletter: Today
31200 Via Colinas, Ste. 210
Westlake Village, CA 91362-3939
ph: 818-991-9955
fax: 818-991-5418
srlabs@earthlink.net
http://www.srlabs.com
Appraiser, dealer, restorer, expert in
animation art; also Disneyana.

Stephen Worth
Vintage Ink & Paint
5701 Klump Ave. #7
North Hollywood, CA 91601
ph: 818-980-7637
sworth@vintageip.com
http://www.vintageip.com
Buys, sells, repairs, appraises; the
leading authority on animation art
authentication & restoration; all
paints manufactured in-house using
same formulas and techniques used at
Disney Studios; has worked with
several major studios.

Internet Resources

Jenia Ciomek
Cel Block, The
P.O. Box 175
Geneva, OH 44041
ph: 440-466-9406
jenia@cel-block.com
http://www.cel-block.com
Offers an online fee-based animation
art auction price guide; lists pieces
sold at auction as well as prices
realized; each item includes an image,
detailed description, date sold, price
realized; sorted by studio, character;
cross ref.

Animation World Network
5700 Wilshire Blvd., Ste. 600
Los Angeles, CA 90036
ph: 323-634-3400
fax: 323-634-3350
info@awn.com
http://www.awn.com
Animation art headline news, hot
spots, newstands, special publication,
search, companies, schools,
animators, festivals, associations, fan
sites, gallery exhibitions, vault
databases, discussion forum.

Museums/Libraries

Herb Barker
Barker Character, Comic & Cartoon
Museum
1188 Highland Ave.
Cheshire, CT 06410-1624
ph: 800-227-5372 or 800-995-2357
fax: 203-699-1188
fun@barkeranimation.com
http://www.BarkerAnimation.com
Features comic character collectibles,
television collectibles, cartoon
character collectibles, toys, and comic
memorabilia.

Museum of Modern Art, The
11 W. 53rd. St.
New York, NY 10019
ph: 212-708-9400 or 800-447-6662
comments@moma.org
http://www.moma.org

Periodicals

Magazine: Animation World
5700 Wilshire Blvd., Ste. 600
Los Angeles, CA 90036
ph: 323-634-3400 or 323-634-3350
editor@awn.com
http://www.awn.com/mag

Magazine: Animation Magazine
30101 Agoura Court, Ste. 110
Agoura Hills, CA 91301
ph: 818-991-2884 or 800-996-TOON
fax: 818-991-3773
animag@aol.com
http://www.animag.com
A monthly magazine about the
animation industry: animators, special
effects, commercials, festivals,
contests, fans, international
animation, collecting animation art,
ads for dealers selling animation art
and related services.

Directory: Animation Industry Directory
30101 Agoura Court, Ste. 110
Agoura Hills, CA 91301
ph: 818-991-2884 or 800-996-TOON
fax: 818-991-3773
animag@aol.com
http://www.animag.com
The most comprehensive reference
guide to the people and companies
active in the animation industry today.

Repair Services

Ron Stark, ISA
S/R Laboratories, Animation Art
Conservation Center
Newsletter: Today
31200 Via Colinas, Ste. 210
Westlake Village, CA 91362-3939
ph: 818-991-9955
fax: 818-991-5418
srlabs@earthlink.net
http://www.srlabs.com
First and only animation art
conservation center in the world
featuring restoration, ink & paint lab,
frame shop, accredited appraisals,
expert witness and trial consultation,
and much more.

Stephen Worth
Vintage Ink & Paint
5701 Klump Ave. #7
North Hollywood, CA 91601
ph: 818-980-7637
sworth@vintageip.com
http://www.vintageip.com
Buys, sells, repairs, appraises; the
leading authority on animation art
authentication & restoration; all
paints manufactured in-house using
same formulas and techniques used at
Disney Studios; has worked with
several major studios.

ANTIQUE & PERIOD JEWELRY

(see GEMS & JEWELRY; GEMS &
JEWELRY, Costume; GEMS &
JEWELRY, Vintage & Estate)

ANTIQUES & COLLECTIBLES

(see also ANTIQUES DEALERS &
COLLECTORS, Supplies For;
ANTIQUES SHOP DIRECTORIES;
ART; ART THEFT & FRAUD;
BOOKS, Reference [Antiques]; FLEA
MARKET GUIDES; INTERNET
CLASSIFIED FOR COLLECTORS;
POPULAR CULTURE;
PAWNBROKERS; PERIODICALS;
TOURS/BUYING TRIP)

Appraisers

(see also Appraisers listed within
specific categories throughout this
Directory.)

AsktheAppraiser.com
4 Brussels St.
Worcester, MA 01610
ph: 781-821-0199
ata@collectingchannel.com
http://www.AsktheAppraiser.com
The premiere online appraisal service
offered by CollectingChannel.com; all
appraisals comply with the "Uniform
Standards of Professional Appraisal
Practice" and with the standards of
the Association of Online Appraisers.

Association of Online Appraisers, Inc.
P.O. Box 2049
Frederick, MD 21702-1049
ph: 301-228-2279
fax: 301-695-6491
info@AOAonline.org
http://www.AOAonline.org
Not-for-profit association for online
as well as traditional appraisers;
establishes standards of appraisal
ethics & professional practice; offers
550+ page "Complete Online Course
in Personal Property Appraising" free
to members.

International Society of Appraisers
Newsletter: Professional Appraisers
Information Exchange
1131 SW 7th St., Ste. 105
Renton, WA 98055
ph: 206-241-0359 or 888-472-4732
fax: 206-241-0436
ISA@isa-appraisers.org
http://www.isa-appraisers.org
Largest assoc. of professional
appraisers devoted solely to personal
property; over 1,300 members
specializing in all areas of antiques &
residential contents, gems & jewelry,
fine art, machinery & equipment;
member directory on Web site.

Clubs/Associations

Dora Lerch
World of Collectibles - Collector Club
International
P.O. Box 245
Garnerville, NY 10923-0245
ph: 914-362-4657
fax: 914-362-3258
WorldofCollectibles@juno.com
Over 200 members.

Questers, The
210 South Quince St.
Philadelphia, PA 19107
Offers members a unique opportunity
to study and appreciate antiques; new
chapters are organized whenever
eight or more interested people apply
for a charter from the International
Organization.

Association of Online Appraisers, Inc.
P.O. Box 2049
Frederick, MD 21702-1049
ph: 301-228-2279
fax: 301-695-6491
info@AOAonline.org
http://www.AOAonline.org
Not-for-profit association for online
as well as traditional appraisers;

establishes standards of appraisal ethics & professional practice; offers 550+ page "Complete Online Course in Personal Property Appraising" free to members.

Betty McKenna, Pres.
American Antique Arts Association
Newsletter: A.A.A.A. Journal
1240 Colonial Rd.
Mc Lean, VA 22101-2965
ph: 703-827-0867
The AAAA is devoted to the appreciation, study and preservation of American antiques, architecture, art, crafts and local history; the 14 chapters with 1,000 members in MD, N. VA, and DC invite membership of any interested individual.

Victorian Homeowner's Association
Newsletter: Victorian Homeowner's Association Newsletter
P.O. Box 846
Sutter Creek, CA 95685-0846
ph: 209-267-0774
For owners of Victorian homes; home renovation, antiques and collecting info.

Robbie Miller
Southern Oregon Antiques & Collectibles Club
P.O. Box 508
Talent, OR 97540
ph: 541-535-1231
contact@soacc.com
http://www.soacc.com
Southern Oregon association of those interested in learning about antiques and collectibles; annual antiques show to benefit kids and local library.

John Cherepanik, Pres.
Wild Rose Antique Collectors
Newsletter: Dig & Pick
P.O. Box 1471
Main Post Office
Edmonton, Alberta T5J 2N5 Canada
ph: 780-437-9722
jcherepanik@netscape.net
Large club of antiques and collectibles enthusiasts; meets monthly with speaker program; organizes a Spring and a Fall antiques show.

Gail Al-Omar
Bath & Bradford on Avon Antique Dealers Association
280 High St.
Bathesaston
Bath, BA1 7RA U.K.
ph: +44 1225 851494
fax: +44 1225 851120
info@babaada.com
http://www.babadda.com
More than 70 antique dealers in Bath and surrounding towns of Somerset & Wilshire offering a full range of antiques.

Experts

George E. Michael
P.O. Box 2087
Merrimack, NH 03054-2087
ph: 603-424-7400
fax: 603-424-7400
gitius@aol.com
Specialist in fine arts and antiques: appraiser, expert witness, auctioneer, writer, editor, consultant, lecturer and instructor.

Judith Katz-Schwartz
Twin Brooks Antiques & Collectibles
E-zine: Antiques & Collectibles Newsletter
P.O. Box 6572
New York, NY 10128-0006
ph: 212-876-3512
fax: 212-876-3512
twinb@msjudith.net
http://www.msjudith.net
Appraiser, collector, dealer in a broad range of antiques and collectibles; specializes in antique kitchen implements, antique paper ephemera, antique and vintage toys and games, World's Fair, vintage clothing & jewelry, dolls, Disneyana.

Harry L. Rinker
Rinker Enterprises, Inc.
5093 Vera Cruz Rd.
Emmaus, PA 18049-9554
ph: 610-965-1122
fax: 610-965-1124
rinkeron@fast.net
http://www.harryrinker.com
Maintains research files, library (books, periodicals, etc.), photos and slides covering over 1,500 antiques & collectibles categories.

Internet Resources

CollectingChannel.com
4 Brussels St.
Worcester, MA 01610-2904
ph: 508-791-6710
fax: 508-797-5398
info@collectingchannel.com
http://www.collectingchannel.com
Internet Web portal for covering all aspects of collecting from eight micro-channels (devoted to Antiques, Entertainment, Jewelry/Gems, Stamps/Coins, Collectibles, Glass/Pottery, Toys/Dolls, and Sports).

ArtFact, Inc.
Price Guide: ArtFact
1130 Ten Rod Rd., Ste. D202
North Kingstown, RI 02852-4158
ph: 401-295-2656 or 800-278-3228
fax: 401-295-2629
sales@artfact.com
http://www.artfact.com
A computerized online price guide having almost 6 million auction sales results of fine art, antiques and collectibles; complete lot descriptions, prices realized with on-screen images.

Karen Lee
Collectics Reference & Education
P.O. Box 397
Riverside, CT 06878-0397
ph: 203-358-9433
karenlee@collectics.com
http://www.collectics.com/education.html
An online reference and education program presenting a variety of articles, essays, analysis, and photographs about major artists, manufacturers and design periods for the decorative arts.

About.com Hobbies
220 East 42nd St.
New York, NY 10017
pr@about-inc.com
http://home.about.com/hobbies
Online source for information about action figures, antiques, book collecting, coin collecting, collectibles, comic books, costume jewelry, dolls, mineral collecting, pin collecting, sports and trading cards, stamps, toy collecting.

Lee Bernstein
Lee Bernstein Antiques & Collectibles
Newsletter: Attic Muse, The
1631 Novo Dr.
Schererville, IN 46375
ph: 219-322-4272
info@elee.com
http://www.eLee.com
Lee Bernstein is a monthly columnist for the "New England Antiques Journal;" offers Attic Muse, a free quarterly online newsletter that helps collectors buy, sell, and avoid making mistakes; author of eBay's Collectibles "Inside Scoop."

Stephanie Benes
MuseumSpot.com
1840 Oak Ave.
Evanston, IL 60201
feedback@museumspot.com
http://www.museumspot.com
A site that can link you to the home pages of every major museum and nearly every other museum, no matter how small and obscure; quickly & easily locate museums by city, state, country, name and topic; explore museums, search for exhibits.

Don Thompson
Vintage Toy Encyclopedia, The
P.O. Box 8701
Kansas City, MO 64114
http://www.toynfo.com
Great Web site with informative articles about scores and scores of action figures, dolls, toys and other collectibles.

Ron McCoy
CollectingBuzz.com
E-zine: Antiques & Collecting Newsletter
131 E. 57 St.
Tulsa, OK 74105-7714
ph: 918-747-1344
ronmccoy@cox.net
http://www.collectingbuzz.com
Free antiques & collectibles online monthly newsletter available to anyone with an email address; keeps subscribers informed and up-to-date on general news/tidbits regarding the antiques and collecting hobby.

John Blatt
Planet Earth Antiques & Collectables E-Mail
876 Curtis St., Ste. 2709
Honolulu, HI 96813
ph: 808-596-8708
fax: 808-596-8708
support@peacelist.com
http://www.peacelist.com
A FREE listserve which allows subscribers to reach a targeted audience of subscribers worldwide to buy, sell, or publicize.

Antiques World
U.K.
antiquesworld@spence.globalnet.co.uk
http://www.antiquesworld.co.uk
A leading UK Internet gateway to information about antiques and collectibles: feature articles, book reviews, bookshop, research & education, calendar of events including antiques shows, exhibitions, tours, study courses.

Freeserve Collectables
Freeserve.com
Marylands Ave.
Hemel Hempstead, Hertfordshire HP2 7TG U.K.
ph: 0870 909 0666
fax: 01442 355 790
editor.fscollectables@freeserve.com
http://www.freeserve.com/collectables
The latest news, features, books, clubs, fairs, auctions, etc. in the field of antiques & collectibles; also great free price guide for many types of antiques.

Misc. Services

Leon Castner, ISA CAPP
National Appraisal Consultants
P.O. Box 482
Hope, NJ 07844
ph: 800-323-5996 or 908-459-5996
fax: 908-459-4899
castner@garden.net
http://www.nacvalue.com
Popular and knowledgeable speaker, teacher, seminar leader in most areas of antiques & collectibles; offers both lighthearted and serious presentations to civic groups or national organizations.

Jerri Dodd
AskAboutAntiques.com
P.O. Box 450
Warwick, NY 10990
info@askaboutantiques.com
http://www.askaboutantiques.com
A fee-for-service Web site offering thousands of articles and references on all fields of art and antiques.

Jeff Savage
Savages Guide
ph: 707-824-1711
jsavage@savagesguide.com
http://www.savagesguide.com
Online database of antiques & collectibles related resources and information.

Museums/Libraries

John Sonata
National Register Publishing
Directory: Official Museum Directory
121 Chanlon Rd.
New Providence, NJ 07974-1541
ph: 800-473-7020
fred.marks@renp.com
http://www.officialmuseumdir.com
Profiles more than 7,600 American institutions in 85 categories; aquariums, historic homes, museums, zoos; handy for those looking for information about specific types of antiques, fine art & collectibles; annual.

Museums of the World
Koenigsalle 106
Duesseldorf, 40215 Germany
ph: +49 211 30122260
fax: +49 211 30122261
http://www.museum.com
The international online magazine with news and stories about museum activities: exhibits, events; hundreds of museums categorized and listed.

Periodicals

National Register Publishing
Directory: Official Museum Directory
121 Chanlon Rd.
New Providence, NJ 07974-1541
ph: 800-473-7020
fred.marks@renp.com
http://www.officialmuseumdir.com
Profiles more than 7,600 American institutions in 85 categories; aquariums, historic homes, museums, zoos; handy for those looking for information about specific types of antiques, fine art & collectibles; annual.

David J. Maloney, ISA CAPP
Sales Online Direct, Inc.
Directory: Maloney's Antiques & Collectibles Resource Directory
P.O. Box 2049
Frederick, MD 21702-1049
ph: 301-228-2279
fax: 301-695-6491
dave@maloney.com
http://www.davidmaloney.com/aboutbook.htm
Publishes major resource information

source for collectors, sellers, claims adjusters, etc.: includes experts, buyers, clubs, periodicals, repairers, museums/libraries, appraisers, auctioneers, matching services, dealers, etc.

Appraisers

(see APPRAISERS category as well as specialized Appraisers listed under specific categories throughout this Directory.)

Auction Services

(see AUCTION SERVICES category as well as specialized Auction Services listed under specific categories throughout this Directory.)

Canadian

Appraisers

Kathryn Minard, ISA
Contemporary Fine Art Services Inc.
184 Pearl St., Ste. 201A
Toronto, Ontario M5A 1L5 Canada
ph: 416-366-9770
fax: 416-366-8541
art.advisory.biz@on.aibn.com
Art expert and appraiser specializing in Canadian contemporary and historical art; also Canadian Indian and Inuit.

Charles T. Cripps, ISA CAPP
Townsend Antiques & Appraisals, Inc.
15227 81 Ave.
Edmonton, Alberta T5R 3P2 Canada
ph: 780-486-5012 or 780-487-7180
fax: 780-484-2836
townsen@shaw.ca
Specializes in the appraisal of 18th and 19th century British and Canadian furniture, paintings, and silver; extensive experience in division of property, estate and matrimonial settlements.

Auction Services

Maynards Auctioneers
415 West 2nd Ave.
Vancouver, British Columbia V5Y 1E3 Canada
ph: 604-876-6787 or 604-531-0166
fax: 604-876-2678
antiques@Maynards.com
http://www.maynards.com
Quarterly auctions of Canadian, American & Western European fine art, antiques, silver, jewellery, china, glass, carpets and specialty collectables; Accredited Member of International Society of Appraisers.

Collectors

Colin R. Voorneveld, MD
27 Roncesvalles Ave., #408
Toronto, Ontario M6R 3B2 Canada
ph: 416-516-4751
fax: 416-516-4751
Avid collector specializing in pre-1900 medical and pharmaceutical antiques; actively seeks medical

instruments, spectacles, historic medicine, etc.

Dealers

Angey Sabourin
Do You Remember When
311 Elm St.
Sudbury, Ontario P3C 1V6 Canada
ph: 705-673-4430

Periodicals

Paul Fiocca
Trajan Publishing Corp.
Magazine: Antique Showcase
103 Lakeshore Rd., Ste. 202
St. Catharines, Ontario L2N 2T6 Canada
ph: 905-646-7744
fax: 905-646-0995
fiocca@trajan.com
http://www.antiquesshowcase.net
National magazine with diverse articles, show and auction reports, museum exhibits, book reviews, upcoming trends, etc.; also contains lots of display and classified ads for buyers of Canadian, US and European antiques; 9 times per year.

German

Auction Services

Auction Team Breker
Bonner Str. 528-530
Koln, D-50968 Germany
ph: 49 221 387049 or 941-925-0385 (US Rep)
fax: 49 221 374878
auction@breker.com
http://www.breker.com
German auction company specializes in the sale of old office equipment, scientific instruments and devices, photographica, and old technology including toasters, typewriters, sewing machines, tools, telecommunications, etc.

Irish

Dealers

James O'Brien
Collectors' Shop, The
19a Main St.
Blackrock
Dublin, Co Dublin Ireland
ph: ++44 771 239 7118
JJJOBrien@aol.com
http://members.aol.com/jjjobrien/stamps
Carries an extensive stock of Irish collectibles including beer mats, coins, phonecards, postcards, prints and stamps.

Mexican

Collectors

Joe Liberkowski
P.O. Box 2161
Medford, NJ 08055-7161
Wants American Indian items; also pre-1940 Mexican and South American Santos, Retablos, Ex Votos, crucifixes, religious, historical autographs/documents.

Dealers

El Paso Saddle Blanket Co.
601 N. Oregon
El Paso, TX 79901
ph: 800-351-7847 or 915-544-1000
fax: 915-533-7209
info@elpasosaddleblanket.com
http://www.elpasosaddleblanket.com
Wants to buy old Mexican rugs, blankets, Sarahs; also old Navajo rugs and weavings, Tarahumara Indian art, Mexican ranch collectibles.

Michael D. Higgins
Michael D. Higgins & Son Antique Indian Art
4429 N. Campbell Ave.
Tucson, AZ 85718
ph: 520-577-8330
mdhiggins@earthlink.net
http://www.mhiggins.com
Appraises, buys and sells antique American Indian, PreColumbian, Mexican and Spanish Colonial antiques; since 1972; also wants paintings of the American West; museum references available.

Saints & Martyrs
404-A San Felipe NW
Albuquerque, NM 87104
ph: 505-224-9323
info@saints-martyrs.com
http://www.saints-martyrs.com
Specializes in devotional antiques of Mexico: statues, reliquaries, folk art, Spanish Colonial Santos, retablos, furniture.

Periodicals

(see PERIODICALS category as well as specific Periodicals listed under specific categories throughout this Directory.)

Repair Services

(see Repair Services listed under REPAIR/RESTORATION/CONSERVATION and within other specific categories throughout this Directory)

Reproductions

Experts

Norman S. Young
Fake Publications
P.O. Box 766
Nassau, NY 12123-0766
ph: 518-766-3445
fax: 518-766-9826
nsyoung@aol.com
http://www.antiekllc.com
Author of "Fabulous But Fake" (H/C book), the professional's guide to fake antiques; available from the author for $44.95.

Periodicals

Mark Chervenka
Newsletter: Antique & Collectors
  Reproduction News
P.O. Box 12130
Des Moines, IA 50312-9403
ph: 515-274-5886 or 800-227-5531
  (orders)
fax: 515-255-4530
acrn@repronews.com
http://www.repronews.com
  *Monthly newsletter showing
  differences between old originals &
  new reproductions and fakes; 30-60
  close-up photos of new and old side-
  by-side in each issue; all subjects;
  printed on glossy paper; annual
  index.; orders 800-227-5531.*

Repro. Sources

Upper Deck, Ltd.
P.O. Box 1705
New Bedford, MA 02741
ph: 508-992-5424 or 508-992-3827
fax: 508-997-2123
  *Sells reproduction tin toys,
  weathervanes, decoys, glassware, etc.
  to the trade only.*

G.R.'s Trading Post
108 Chester Rd.
Derry, NH 03038
ph: 603-434-0220
fax: 603-425-2199
grtrde@aol.com
http://www.tradingpostantiques.com
  *Sells repro. roll top desks, ice boxes,
  lamps, dolls, baskets, wicker, iron
  banks & toys, clocks, prints, pie safes,
  iron & brass beds, china cabinets, etc.*

Renovator's Supply
P.O. Box 2515
Conway, NH 03818
ph: 800-659-2211 or 603-447-8500
fax: 603-447-1717
  *Offers catalog of Victorian reproduc-
  tion accessories, lighting, hardware,
  bath fixtures, and door, window and
  cabinet hardware.*

Sturbridge Yankee Workshop
90 Blueberry Rd.
Portland, ME 04102-1989
ph: 800-343-1144
fax: 207-774-2561
info@sturbridgeyankee.com
http://www.sturbridgeyankee.com
  *Furniture, floor coverings, lamps &
  lighting, framed prints, household
  textiles, garden & hearth, mirrors &
  wall art; Shaker, Country, Mission
  styles.*

Artique Inc.
259 Godwin Ave.
Midland Park, NJ 07432-1807
ph: 201-444-8989
  *Repro. clay pipes, fraktur, advertising
  memorabilia, Christmas tree
  ornaments, pottery, flags, 19th century
  engravings, old maps, bells, sleigh
  bells, etc.*

A.A. Importing Company, Inc.
30 Northfield Ave.
Raritan Center
Edison, NJ 08837
ph: 732-225-0770
info@aaimporting.com
http://www.aaimporting.com
  *Repro. Orientalia, porcelains,
  stoneware, cast iron banks and toys,
  simulated ivory, weathervanes, oak
  furniture; to the trade only.*

Museum of Modern Art, The
11 W. 53rd. St.
New York, NY 10019
ph: 212-708-9400 or 800-447-6662
comments@moma.org
http://www.moma.org

Castle Antiques & Reproductions
515 Welwood Ave. & Rte. #6
Hawley, PA 18428
ph: 800-345-1667 or 570-226-8550
fax: 800-374-4440
http://www.castleantiques.com
  *They publish a full catalog of a large
  line of antique reproductions.*

Fred & Dottie's Antiques Inc.
6711 Perkiomen Ave.
Birdsboro, PA 19508
ph: 610-582-1506
  *Reproduction ceramics, glass, cast
  iron; wholesale only.*

Merritt's Antiques, Inc.
1860 Weavertown Rd.
P.O. Box 277
Douglassville, PA 19518-0277
ph: 610-689-9541
fax: 610-689-4538
info@merritts.com
http://www.merritts.com
  *Carries a large line or reproduction
  clocks, ceramics, brass, dolls,
  furniture, glass, etc.*

Winterthur Museum
Direct Mail Marketing Office
Winterthur, DE 19735-0001
ph: 800-448-3883
webmaster@winterthur.org
http://www.winterthur.org
  Sells museum reproductions.

John White
Avalon Forge
409 Gun Rd.
Baltimore, MD 21227
ph: 410-242-8431
avlonfrg@bcpl.net
http://www.avalonforge.com
  *Offers documented 18th century
  replicas for living history such as
  military goods, farm and home items.*

A.A. Importing Company, Inc.
7700 Hall St.
Saint Louis, MO 63147
ph: 314-383-8800
fax: 314-383-2608
info@aaimporting.com
http://www.aaimporting.com
  *Repro. Orientalia, porcelains,
  stoneware, cast iron banks and toys,
  simulated ivory, weathervanes, oak
  furniture; to the trade only.*

ReproCrafters, Inc.
11578 Industrial Park
Forney, TX 75126
ph: 972-564-4441
fax: 214-552-9867
reprocr1@airmail.net
http://www.reprocrafters.com
  *An import-direct warehouse carrying
  reproduction carousel horses, wicker
  doll carriages, bird cages, ship
  paintings, tricycles, sleds, etc.*

A.A. Importing Company, Inc.
352 Shaw Rd.
South San Francisco, CA 94080
ph: 650-589-4422
info@aaimporting.com
http://www.aaimporting.com
  *Repro. Orientalia, porcelains,
  stoneware, cast iron banks and toys,
  simulated ivory, weathervanes, oak
  furniture; to the trade only.*

Switzerland

Collectors

Donald G. Tritt
81 Donald Ross Dr.
Granville, OH 43023
ph: 740-587-0213
tritt@denison.edu
  *Wants pre-1930 Swiss ephemera:
  books, travel brochures, postcards,
  stereoviews, trade cards, luggage
  labels, maps, playing cards, prints,
  posters, poster emblems, tobacco silks,
  cigar felts, enameled souvenir spoons,
  etc.*

ANTIQUES DEALERS & COLLECTORS

Clubs/Associations

National Antique & Art Dealers
  Association of America
220 East 57th St.
New York, NY 10022
ph: 212-826-9707
fax: 212-832-9493
naadaa@dir-dd.com
http://www.dir-dd.com/naadaa.html
  *Trade group represents art and
  antique dealers; sponsors antique and
  art exhibitions; promotes ethical trade
  practices among its members; free
  membership directory available.*

Diane Grimes
Antiques Dealers Association of
  Maryland
P.O. Box 303
Olney, MD 20832
ph: 301-774-3596
g113@mindspring.com
http://www.antiquesinmd.com
  *Established in 1974 for dealers in
  Maryland to work together to promote
  the highest standards in the antiques
  trade and to preserve Maryland's rich
  heritage.*

Larry L. Krug
National Association of Collectors
Newsletter: NAC News
18222 Flower Hill Way, #299
Gaithersburg, MD 20879-5300
ph: 301-926-8663
fax: 301-926-7648
info@collectors.org
http://www.collectors.org
  *Identifies and addresses those needs &
  concerns that are common to all
  collectors including information on
  security and insurance, collection
  management, displaying techniques,
  dispersal and estate planning; offers
  NAC insurance program.*

Jim Tucker
Antiques & Collectibles Dealer
  Association
Newsletter: ACDA News
P.O. Box 4389
Davidson, NC 28036
ph: 800-287-7127 or 704-895-9088
fax: 704-895-0230
info@antiqueandcollectible.com
http://www.antiqueandcollectible.com/
  acda.shtml
  *Provides a variety of services to
  dealers, such as insurance, merchant
  services, newsletter, seminars, travel
  and product discounts and more.*

Jim Tucker
National Association of Antique Malls
P.O. Box 4389
Davidson, NC 28036
ph: 800-287-7127 or 704-895-9088
fax: 704-895-0230
info@antiqueandcollectible.com
http://www.antiqueandcollectible.com/
  naam.shtml
  *Association for owners and managers
  of antiques malls; membership
  benefits include a newsletter directed
  at specific problems and needs of the
  antique mall, insurance benefits,
  merchant services, supply discounts,
  annual meetings.*

Internet Resources

Universal Currency Converter, The
http://www.xe.net/ucc
  *Convert one national currency to
  another; rates updated every minute.*

Martin Marcus
Antique Advertiser, The
P.O. Box 608
Marblehead, MA 01945
webmaster@antiqueadvertiser.com
http://antiqueadvertiser.com
  *An online only advertisement source
  and antique shop directory for
  Eastern Massachusetts antiques
  buyers and sellers: articles, free
  advertising, complete directory of
  dealers.*

Kovels Online Price Guide
P.O. Box 22200
Beachwood, OH 44122-0200
ph: 800-829-9158 or 800-829-9158
fax: 216-752-3115
kovels@palmcoastd.com
http://www.kovels.com

Stacie Berger
Antique Trader OnLine Price Guide
P.O. Box 1050
Dubuque, IA 52004-1050
ph: 800-482-3158 or 800-480-6169
fax: 800-531-0880
stacie.berger@fwpubs.com
http://www.collect.com/priceguide
Antique Trader's annual price guide database with a huge number of items priced in thousands of categories.

Ron Heath
Antiques Web
U.K.
antiques-web@gifford.co.uk
http://www.antiques-web.co.uk
This Web site lists antiques centers, dealers and shows in the U.K.; impartial advice for anyone planning a U.K. antiques tour.

Misc. Services

Clifford Barbara
Elegantantiques.com
2 Hannah Lane
Wanaque, NJ 07465
ph: 973-835-2367
info@elegantantiques.com
http://www.elegantantiques.com
Offers Web site design services for the antique and collectible community.

Periodicals

Antoinette Knopp Powers, Pub.
AMQ Group Ltd.
Magazine: Professional Antique Mall
 Owner/Manager
P.O. Box 219
Western Springs, IL 60558-0219
ph: 708-246-4990
fax: 708-246-1559
A quarterly periodical with antique mall related ads, articles, computer software.

Computer Programs For

Man./Prod./Dist.

Tom Bilotta
Carlisle Development Corp.
Software: Collector's Assistant
P.O. Box 291
Carlisle, MA 01741-0291
ph: 800-219-0257
carlisleDC@aol.com
http://www.carlisledevelopment.com
Software for collectors and dealers; standard versions are available for over 40 collectibles categories: coins, currency, figurines, toys, autographs, sports cards, knives, military, etc.; custom versions available.

ArtFact, Inc.
Price Guide: ArtFact
1130 Ten Rod Rd., Ste. D202
North Kingstown, RI 02852-4158
ph: 401-295-2656 or 800-278-3228
fax: 401-295-2629
sales@artfact.com
http://www.artfact.com
A computerized online price guide having almost 6 million auction sales results of fine art, antiques and collectibles; complete lot descriptions, prices realized with on-screen images.

Software: AntiquesOnTheMac,
 Collector's Edition
Yellow House
RR #1, Box 155
Reading, VT 05062
ph: 802-484-7799
antmac@sover.net
http://www.antmac.com/AntMac.html3
Software solution for managing a collection; no copy or paste; no calculator needed; scrollable fields, inventory descriptions up to 30,000 characters.

Software: AntiquesOnTheMac, Dealer's
 Edition
Yellow House
RR #1, Box 155
Reading, VT 05062
ph: 802-484-7799
antmac@sover.net
http://www.antmac.com/AntMac.html3
An integrated hyper-relational business program for managing antiques & art dealer's businesses; manages clients, correspondence, mailing lists, inventory, consigned inventory, consignment to group shops, shows, partners, layaways.

Rebecca Silverstone
Collectify MyStuff
Software: Collectify
60 E. 42nd St., Ste. 3112
New York, NY 10165-3197
ph: 800-932-5811 or 514-932-1500
fax: 514-932-8990
info@collectify.com
http://www.collectify.com
A personalized collection cataloging software program; record, track or consign your items; create your own piece of personal history and maintain control over your collection expenses, valuations, insurance needs.

Antique & Art Information Network, Inc.
43-08 209th St.
Flushing, NY 11361
ph: 718-225-9877
aain@aain.com
http://www.aain.com
Inventory and business management software for antique, art and collectibles dealers and collectors.

Ken Smith
KLS Training Corp.
Software: Collector's ShowCase
P.O. Box 491
Lewiston, NY 14092
ph: 888-751-9230
fax: 905-468-0774
ksmith@klstraining.com
http://www.lazydayssoftware.com/
 CS.html
This program will handle all your collections; can store up to 60 different collections and control them all from one screen.

Russ Wood
Collector's Marketplace
Software: Intelligent Collector Software
RD 1 Box 213B
Montrose, PA 18801-9779
ph: 570-278-2099
cmonline@epix.net

Andy Kaufman
Real Time Antiques Market
4460 Hodges Blvd., Ste. 818
Jacksonville, FL 32224-5209
ph: 904-992-0958
rtam@rtam.com
http://www.rtam.com
Internet auction software and e-commerce designed for auctioneers and dealers of antiques; online store fronts, online bidding, Web site design and technical support.

John Silling
Niche Software, Inc.
Software: KollectAll!
7118 NW Terrace
Parkland, FL 33076
ph: 954-344-6561
marketing@collectiblessoftware.com
http://www.collectiblessoftware.com
Different programs designed for collectors of: Beanie Babies; bottles and glass; books, magazines and paper; Civil War relics; coins; dolls & figurines; comic books; toys & diecast cars; guns; knives; sports; stamps; sports, Elvis, etc.

GEW
Software: Collector Series, The
1224 S. Federal Highway
Lake Worth, FL 33460
gardian@gardian.com
http://gardian.com/collectr.htm
Sells several different software programs for collectors of coins, stamps, baseball cards, autographs, silverware; also orchids and videos.

Linda Hiatt
Dimark Group
Software: Collectorpro 97
2205 Osburn Rd.
Arrington, MO 37104
ph: 615-395-4670
fax: 815-377-0653
info@collectorpro.com
http://www.collectorpro.com
Software to catalog collections; keep track of item information, financial information, customer information and expense tracking; record sales

and track sales tax; many reports and labels; stores and prints photos; WIN only.

J. Phillip, Inc.
Software: Collectibles Database for
 Collectors
5870 Zarley St., Ste. C
New Albany, OH 43054
ph: 800-407-4147 or 614-933-0887
fax: 614-855-7893
info@collectiblesdatabase.com
http://www.msdatabase.com
Organize and appraise your collectibles with this software: Longaberger baskets, Precious Moments, Hallmark, Harbour Lights, Boyds Bears, Christopher Radko, Dept. 56, Disney Classics, Forma Vitrum, Cherished Teddies and more.

Charles E. Crume
Charles Crume Software
Software: Charles Crume Software
P.O. Box 5054
Cincinnati, OH 45205
ph: 513-885-0479
fax: 513-885-0479
cc@charlescrumesoftware.com
http://www.charlescrumesoftware.com
Software program for antique and craft malls, consignment shops, cooperatives, and auction houses; optional modules for archive reporting, bar coding, credit card verification, extended inventory info, phone bid auctions, and more.

Randy Seba
Sebacom, Inc.
14444 W. 126th St.
Olathe, KS 66062-5844
ph: 913-238-7384
rseba@kcsolutions.com
http://www.tinkerware.com
Software for antique dealers and collectors to track inventory, sales and expenses for one or multiple locations.

Collector Oasis Software
1605 N. Fleming St.
Garden City, KS 67846
ph: 316-275-7740
fax: 316-275-7784
Offers computer software for a variety of collectibles.

James S. Nixon
Whirlwind Technologies
Software: Collect!
P.O. Box 450907
Garland, TX 75045-0907
jnixon@wwtech.com
http://www.wwtech.com/coll.htm
A system that allows you to work with collections of any type; program your own collection information in minutes; pre-defined templates for 15 types of collections including coins, stamps, comics, antiques, books, videos and more.

Innovative Logic Corp.
Software: Collector Pro
330 Jasper Highway
Smith Falls, Ontario K7A 4S5 Canada
ph: 613-284-0647 or 800-242-4775
http://www.innovativelogic.com/
collector
*Computerized collections database
program.*

Jose Nunez
Anteq Software Corporation
Software: Anteq Collection Manager
6600 Trans-Canada Highway, Ste. 615
Pointe-Claire, Quebec H9R 4S2 Canada
ph: 877-525-3336 or 514-426-2557
fax: 514-426-1642
admin@anteq.com
http://www.anteq.com
*Software for antique dealers, shops,
malls and collectors.*

PrimaSoft PC, Inc.
Software: Collectibles Organizer
P.O. Box 456
Surrey, British Columbia V3T 5B7
Canada
ph: 800-371-7520 or 604-951-1085
fax: 604-951-7797
support@primasoft.com
http://www.primasoft.com
*For beginners and advanced users;
designed to help to store information
about different types of collectibles
such as bears, dolls, miniatures, house
plants, jewelry, Precious Moments
figurines, Coca-Cola memorabilia,
etc.*

Insurance

Misc. Services

Anthony Bucci
International Collectors Insurance
Agency
P.O. Box 6991
Warwick, RI 02886-6991
ph: 800-691-1114
fax: 401-823-0240
*Insurer of collections; specializing in
china, porcelain, glass, crystal,
ceramics, figurines, pottery;
comprehensive coverage including
accidental breakage, flood and
earthquake.*

American Collectors Insurance, Inc.
P.O. Box 8343
Cherry Hill, NJ 08002-0343
ph: 800-360-2277 or 856-779-7212
fax: 856-779-7289
aci1@americancollectors.net
http://www.americancollectorsins.com/
collectibles
*Provides all-risk, low-cost, "agreed
value" insurance protection for a
wide range of collectibles (e.g., dolls,
model trains, vintage toys, limited
edition figurines, plates/steins,
ornaments, etc.).*

W. Danforth Walker
Collectibles Insurance Agency, Inc.
P.O. Box 1200
Westminster, MD 21158-0299
ph: 410-876-8833 or 888-837-9537
fax: 410-876-9233
info@insurecollectibles.com
http://www.collectsure.com
*Insurance for collectibles, collectors,
dealers and collector/dealers; all risk
coverage; no listing required unless
an item is over $5,000 in value; no
appraisal required; specialized
collectibles coverage for over 30
years.*

Unirisc, Inc.
2000 N. 14 St., Ste. 500
Arlington, VA 22201
ph: 800-424-9500 or 703-797-3300
fax: 703-524-7559
unicover@unirisc.com
http://www.unirisc.com
*Provides fine arts insurance coverage
for shops, galleries and collections;
also coverage for shipping and
storing.*

Jim Tucker
Association Insurance Administrators
P.O. Box 4389
Davidson, NC 28036
ph: 800-618-1787 or 704-895-9209
fax: 704-895-0230
acda@ix.netcom.com
http://www.antiqueandcollectible.com
*Provides property and liability
insurance to all dealers, mall owners,
collectors, show promoters; programs
sponsored by the Antiques &
Collectibles Dealer Association.*

Mercy A. Komar, CIC
Insurance Center, The
P.O. Box 271
Warren, OH 44482-0271
ph: 330-394-6444 or 800-546-6444
fax: 330-393-8118
insurancecenter@neonet.net
http://www.inscntrs.com
*Specializing in insurance for dealers
and collectors; member of Antiques &
Collectibles Dealers Association and
of the Society of Certified Insurance
Counselors.*

Collectors Insurance Online (UK), Blake
Marston Priest Insurance Consultants
52 Station Rd.
Egham
Surrey, TW20 9LF U.K.
ph: 44 (0) 1784 431213
mail@blakemp.freeserve.co.uk
http://www.collectorsinsurance.co.uk
*Offers collectors' insurance in U.K.
for hobbyists and collectors of
diecasts, dolls, Victoriana, cigarette
cards, postcards, etc.*

Services For

Misc. Services

David & Becky Beane
Beane's Antiques & Photography
92 River Rd.
Benton, ME 04901
ph: 207-453-6790
fax: 207-453-6790
*A photography business specializing
in illustrations of antiques for
antiques publications, auctions, dealer
advertisements and all relating
photography; travels and covers the
northern New England area.*

Andrew Katz
Windham Antiques Research Service
P.O. Box 1212
Norwich, VT 05055-1212
ph: 802-649-5712
windham@bmark.com
http://bmark.com/windham.antiques
*Specialty is research providing
identification, documentation,
historical and biographical
background information pertaining to
antiques, silver, ceramics and fine art
for dealers, appraisers, and
collectors.*

Edward J. Pfeiffer
361 Lovely St.
Avon, CT 06001-4071
ph: 860-673-4120
fax: 860-673-4120
*Publicity & public relations services
for auctions, shows, dealers,
museums; writing speeches, scripts,
presentations.*

Stanley & Bob Block
Block's Box
P.O. Box 233
Trumbull, CT 06611-0051
ph: 203-926-8448
fax: 203-261-7033
blockschip@aol.com
http://www.marblecollecting.com
*Produce video tapes & catalogs for
auctioneers and appraisers; full state-
of-the-art video tape production
facility.*

Richard Michael Gramly, PhD
Great Lakes Artifact Repository
79 Perry St.
Buffalo, NY 14203-3037
ph: 716-849-0149
fax: 716-852-0093
*Stores, sells, and conserves artifacts
from all parts of the world in a secure,
fireproof, climate-controlled working
room and vault; examining room with
drafting and photographic facilities;
cataloguing of incoming collections,
etc.*

Harry L. Rinker
Institute for the Study of Antiques &
Collectibles
5093 Vera Cruz Rd.
Emmaus, PA 18049-9554
ph: 610-965-1122
fax: 610-965-1124
rinkeron@fast.net
http://www.harryrinker.com
*Educational organization that offers
seminars and workshops designed to
improve business and object skills in
the field of antiques and collectibles.*

Donald L. Raleigh
Period Antiques Delivery Service, Inc.
P.O. Box 205
Millington, MD 21651
ph: 410-778-4357 or 800-962-1424
pads@dmv.com
http://www.padsinc.com/index.html
*Specializes in the professional
transportation of antiques and works
of art.*

Joan C. Browning
Papilion Lane Press
P.O. Box 436
Ronceverte, WV 24970-0436
ph: 304-645-6799
fax: 304-645-6799
oma00013@mail.wvnet.edu
http://myweb.mvnet.edu/~oma00013
*Syndicate distributing antiques/history
features to subscribing newspapers
and periodicals; publicist for history/
antiques entities on contract basis;
research in material culture; lectures
to historical organizations & college
classes.*

Asheford Institute of Antiques
775 Gulf Shore Dr., #33
Destin, FL 32541
ph: 850-654-1585
fax: 850-654-5524
antqcourse@aol.com
http://www.asheford.com
*Offers a home study course for those
wishing to start an antiques business
for profit or pleasure; Diploma
program.*

Joe Cohen
North East Adult Community School
Antique Classes
3090 North Couse Dr., Apt. #107
Pompano Beach, FL 33069
ph: 954-917-4676
jccohen3@attbi.com
*Fifteen antiques classes: introduction
to antiques, clocks & watches,
porcelain, silver and silverplate,
advertising antiques, music boxes and
automata, furniture, jewelry, and
more.*

Robert Reed, Ed.
Antique & Collectible News Service
P.O. Box 204
Knightstown, IN 46148-0204
ph: 765-345-7479
fax: 765-345-7479
ACNS@aol.com
*Provides articles and book reviews to
publications around the US and*

worldwide; more than 500 topics; lists available.

Judy L. Campbell
Attic Antiques
5500 Summerset Dr.
Midland, MI 48640-2931
ph: 989-631-9263 or 989-631-4874
fax: 989-631-4874
go4nteks@aol.com
http://www.judycampbell.com
Antiques columnist specializing in answering readers' questions regarding the history and status of their antiques and collectibles in today's market; also refers readers to specialists, clubs and other related resources.

Mary Antoine deJulio
Antoine & Associates
317 S. Wacouta Ave.
Prairie Du Chien, WI 53821
ph: 608-326-8225 or 608-326-6626
fax: 608-326-8225
Assistance in the care, management, protection, conservation, research, and documentation of American 18th and 19th century antiques.

Jim Crawford
Crawford Direct Marketing
7944 Curtis Ave.
Omaha, NE 68134-2162
ph: 402-571-0736
jim@crawforddirect.com
http://www.CrawfordDirect.com
An Internet marketing consultant specializing in the Antiques and Collecting industry; offers creative ideas on how to design and promote successful Web sites.

David Lisot
Advision, Inc.
3100 Arrowwood Lane
Boulder, CO 80303
ph: 303-444-2320 or 800-876-2320
sales@advisionvideo.com
http://www.advisionvideo.com
Advision specializes in producing and distributing videotapes about coins and collectibles; currently over 400 video titles available.

John Woracker
Thesaurus Group Ltd.
Mill Court
Furrlongs, Newport
Isle of Wight, Hampshire PO3O 2AA
U.K.
ph: (44) 1983 826000 or (44) 1714 868252
fax: (44) 1983 826201
john@thesaurus.co.uk
http://www.invaluable.com
A pre-sale auction search service checking traditional auctions worldwide, searching 7500+ catalogs per year; a fee based service for subscribers to get advanced notice of upcoming items for sale at auctions around the world.

Supplies For

(see also ANTIQUES & COLLECTIBLES; ANTIQUES DEALERS & COLLECTORS, Computer Programs For; AUCTION CATALOGS; BLACKLIGHTS [UV LAMPS]; GEMS & JEWELRY Suppliers; REPAIR/RESTORATION/ CONSERVATION, Archival Supplies For; REPAIR/RESTORATION/ CONSERVATION, Woodworking)

Suppliers

Bill Cole Enterprises, Inc.
P.O. Box 60
Randolph, MA 02368-0060
ph: 781-986-2653
fax: 781-986-2656
bcemylar@cwbusiness.com
http://www.bcemylar.com
Preservation supplies for comics, movie posters/stills, paperback books, sports cards, magazines, maps, currency, newspapers, legal documents, animation cels, phonograph records; archival repair and cleaning supplies.

Arlington Industries
2617 Vermont Route 7A
Arlington, VT 05250-8882
ph: 802-375-6139 or 888-308-4333
fax: 802-375-9549
info@plateholders.com
http://www.plateholders.com
Sells sturdy, safe and crystal clear plateholders for museums, galleries and collectors.

Kit Barry
Kit Barry Ephemera Supplies
136 High St., Box 3
Brattleboro, VT 05301
ph: 802-254-3634
kbarry@surfglobal.net
http://www.tradecards.com/kb
Sells ephemera supplies: plastic pages, matchbook pages, rigid print holders, soft plastic sleeves, et.

Russell Norton
Photographic Antiques
P.O. Box 1070
New Haven, CT 06504-1070
ph: 203-281-0066
http://www.stereoview.com
Carries 14 sizes of clear 2.5 mil polypropylene archival sleeves for photos and postcards up to 16" x 20".

Collector's House
710 New Brunswick Ave.
Rahway, NJ 07065
ph: 732-388-2649
fax: 732-388-8705
info@collectorshouse.net
http://www.collectorshouse.net
Showcases, tabletop display cases, jewelry displays, display mounts/ butterfly boxes, fitted table covers, wrapping pads, hobby supplies, plastic bags, plate stands.

George Glove Company, Inc.
301 Greenwood Ave.
Midland Park, NJ 07432
ph: 201-251-1200 or 800-631-4292
fax: 201-251-8431
roy@georgeglove.com
http://www.georgeglove.com
Carries a variety of art handling gloves that allow worry-free handling of prints, antiquities, books, coins, and similar items.

Sigrid Hostetter
Dealers Supply, Inc.
P.O. Box 717
Matawan, NJ 07747
ph: 732-591-2883 or 800-524-0576
fax: 732-591-8571
dlrsply@worldnet.att.net
http://www.dlrsupply.com
Carries fire retardant table covers and drapes, aluminum show cases, display risers, gridwall displays, canopies, lights, alarms, etc.

Chris Midkiff
Art Display Essentials
2 West Crisman Rd.
Columbia, NJ 07832
ph: 800-862-9869 or 908-496-4951
fax: 908-496-4956
info@artdisplay.com
http://www.artdisplay.com
Sells display items: general holders and easels, plate & bowl stands, picture hanging, display accessories, jewelry stands, risers, blocks, bases, humidity control, display cases and shelves, mineral and fossil stands, specific holders.

Dennis Blaine
Cutlery Specialties
22 Morris Lane
Great Neck, NY 11024-1707
ph: 516-829-5899 or 800-229-5530 (orders)
fax: 516-773-8076
Dennis13@aol.com
http://www.restorationproduct.com
Preservation products for flatware: waxes, polishes, cleaners, glues, epoxies, adhesives, chamois, buffs, putty: Renaissance Wax/Polish to restore, refresh, protect antiques, cutlery, furniture, precious metals, armory and more.

Robbins Container Corp.
222 Conover St.
Brooklyn, NY 11231-1033
ph: 718-875-3204
fax: 718-797-3529
Carries corrugated mailers, cartons, boxes, stretch film, stackable cardboard bins, tote boxes, storage chests, strapping and sealing tape, foam, polystyrene chips, mailing envelopes, twine, bubble wrap, etc.

Mega-National Industries Inc.
P.O. Box 538
Round Lake, NY 12151-0538
ph: 518-899-6190 or 518-827-4443
Supplier of canopy tent units, and dealer display equipment; also

archival quality protection polysleeves, archival rigids, semi-rigid sleeves for postcards, currency, stereoviews; archival pocket pages, backing boards, etc.

Bags Unlimited
7 Canal St.
Rochester, NY 14608-1910
ph: 800-767-2247 or 716-436-9006
fax: 716-328-8526
info@bagsunlimited.com
http://www.bagsunlimited.com
Sells collector supplies: poly and paper sleeves, mailers, filler pads, album jackets, storage boxes, divider cards, etc.

Brodart Company
P.O. Box 3037
Williamsport, PA 17705
ph: 800-820-4377 or 570-769-3265
fax: 800-283-6087
SusanWinterle@brodart.com
http://www.brodart.com
Carries clear protective covers for books; protect book dust jackets - they may represent half or more of the value of a book.

SAFE Publications, Inc.
P.O. Box 263
Southampton, PA 18966-0263
ph: 215-357-9049
fax: 215-357-5202
sales@safepub.com
http://www.safepub.com
Sells collecting systems for postcards, covers, documents, pins, medals, badges, stamps, coins, banknotes, telephone cards, etc.; crystal clear sleeves are PVC free.

W.C. Golden, Sr.
Golden's Antique Supply
311 Independence Way
Woodstock, GA 30188
ph: 888-202-1029 or 770-924-8528
fax: 770-924-5991
wcgolden@antiquesupply.com
http://www.antiquesupply.com
An extensive online site for antique related supplies and equipment for the beginner to the professional.

Terri Harlan
Mylan Enterprises
P.O. Box 971002
Boca Raton, FL 33497-1002
ph: 800-852-8119 or 561-852-0861
fax: 561-852-0862
sales@mylanusa.com
http://www.mylanusa.com
Carries a wide assortment of Wrapping Pads, Bubble Packs and Bubble Bags.

Joan Wurmbrand
Good Buy Girls
2691 East Main St., Ste. 102
Bexley, OH 43209
ph: 614-231-0437 or 866-886-0467
fax: 614-231-3140
goodbuygirls@tias.com
http://www.goodbuygirls.com
Carries glass domes, doll cases, plate

stands, easels, plate frames, plate hangers, thimble domes, lighted stands, turntables, display cabinets, Lucite stands and risers, sports cases, ornament stands; egg, marble and paperweight stands.

Capital Collectors Plastics
P.O. Box 543
Massillon, OH 44648-0543
ph: 330-832-4287
fax: 330-832-4416
collector@capitalplastics.com
http://www.capitalplastics.com
Manufactures hard plastic holders and displays for coins, currency, baseball cards, stamps, postcards, first day covers, medals, medallions, money, tokens, gaming chips, discs, pictures and documents.

Allan Koskela
Allan Koskela Restorations
1417 Third St.
Webster City, IA 50595
ph: 515-832-2437
repair@wmtel.net
http://
restorationmaterials.safeshopper.com
Sells extremely durable high impact polyethylene containers; never wear out; light weight; airtight lockable; safer and more cost effective than cardboard boxes or wooden crates.

Demco, Inc.
P.O. Box 7488
Madison, WI 53707-7488
ph: 800-962-4463 or 608-241-1201
fax: 608-241-1799
custserv@demco.com
http://www.demco.com
Carries clear protective covers for books; protect book dust jackets - they may represent half or more of the value of a book.

Kurt Keifer
Kiefer Supply
417 Stanton Ave.
Fergus Falls, MN 56537
ph: 218-736-7000 or 888-543-3377
fax: 218-736-7474
kurtkiefer@aol.com
http://www.kiefers.com
Acrylic stands, wrapping pads, banners, blacklights, bubble wrap, cartons, cash boxes, dollies, easels, fasteners, forms holders, inventory items, jewelry tags, knobs & finials, labels, laminated signs, magnifiers, pennants, etc.

James Moran
Telequest
1566 W. Algonquin, #165
Hoffman Estates, IL 60195-1575
ph: 847-991-1228
telequest@usa.net
http://www.telequest.biz
Sells storage and care supplies for the collector of coins, phone cards, sports cards, stamps, casino chips, pins, and ephemera.

Ronald Nootbaar
Roberts Colonial House, Inc.
570 W. 167th St.
South Holland, IL 60473
ph: 708-331-6233
fax: 708-331-0538
Sells plate hangers, plate stands, Plexiglass display cubes, quilted vinyl china cases, and over 1,600 other items; send for catalog.

Boss Mfg. Co.
221 West First St.
Kewanne, IL 61443
ph: 800-447-4581 or 309-852-2131
fax: 309-852-0848
Carries a line of nylon tricot inspectors gloves for the safe handling of silver, glass, jewelry, etc.

Steve Eyer
P.O. Box 123 -MAC
Mount Zion, IL 62549-0123
ph: 217-864-4321
fax: 217-864-3021
steve@eyersworld.com
http://www.eyersworld.com
Specializes in Microscopes and Photo Assist products for collectors and jewelers.

Sports Collectibles Supplies
1933 E. Pomona St.
Santa Ana, CA 92705
ph: 714-259-0550 or 800-366-1425
fax: 714-259-0550
sales@cardboardgold.com
http://www.cardboardgoldstore.com
A leading supplier of trading card supplies and sports memorabilia displays: semi rigid holders, pocket pages, cube displays for balls, and more.

American Plas-Tech Distribution
P.O. Box 1230
Concord, CA 94522-1230
ph: 925-609-9947 or 800-695-0332
fax: 925-609-9953
postmaster@americanplastech.com
http://www.americanplastech.com
Carries plastic display cases for collectibles and toys, Beanie Baby cases, tag protectors, comic book supplies, bags, backing boards, boxes, dividers, top loaders, trading card supplies, postcard and record supplies.

Jones West Packaging Co.
P.O. Box 1084
Rohnert Park, CA 94927-1084
ph: 707-795-8552
Supplier of all sizes of ZIP CLOSE plastic bags and flat bags in small or large quantities; since 1981; credit cards accepted; catalog available.

Collector Items
P.O. Box 55511
Seattle, WA 98155
ph: 206-365-1188
fax: 206-367-1188
collector-items@msn.com
Sells nylon bubble bags.

Supplies For (Safes)

Suppliers

Sportsman Steel Safes
6311 Paramount Blvd.
Long Beach, CA 90805
ph: 800-266-7150 or 562-984-5445
fax: 562-984-8277
http://www.sportsmansteelsafes.com
Carries large selection of safes for gun and other collectors.

Supplies For (Showcases)

Man./Prod./Dist.

J.W. Winchester Co.
307 B. Bryant St.
Ojai, CA 93023
ph: 805-646-5411
fax: 805-646—9635
jwwinchester@aol.com
Manufactures reproduction custom-built antique showcases in over 80 styles.

TECNO Display, Inc.
201 South Hill Dr.
Brisbane, CA 94005
ph: 415-468-6766 or 800-255-3536
fax: 415-468-6368
tecno@tecnodisplay.com
http://www.tecnodisplay.com
Manufacturer of pre-assembled glass display cases with halogen lights; counter to cases, wall units, free standing cases.

Suppliers

Daniel Neufield
Showcases by Lin Terry
185 6th Ave.
Paterson, NJ 07524
ph: 973-345-6677
fax: 973-345-5551
linterry@aol.com
http://www.linterry.com
Sells handcrafted acrylic collectible display cases for trains, dolls, ships, sports memorabilia, comic books, magazines, wax boxes, figurines, etc.; many sizes; call or write for free catalog.

Hank Coen
Coen Displays
30 Gertrude Ave.
Rochelle Park, NJ 07662
ph: 201-712-9637
fax: 201-712-1293
HankCoen@worldnet.att.net
http://www.CoenDisplays.com
Home, office, business custom made display cases.

Dave Cohen
Dave Cohen & Associates
1107 Highway 35
Ocean, NJ 07712
ph: 888-742-4242
fax: 732-663-9700
info@showcaseshowplace.com
http://www.showcaseshowplace.com
Supplier of glass display show cases for antiques shops, malls, co-ops, and private collectors.

Monique G. Caron-Krug, CEO
Showcase Sales Gallery, Inc.
360 Main St.
P.O. Box 312
Otego, NY 13825
ph: 607-988-2883 or 800-246-2940
fax: 607-988-9173
showcase@telenet.net
http://www.showcasesales.com
Showcases, display cases, cabinets, point of sale counters, jewelry showcases, wall and upright showcases; framed, frameless/knock down displays; various styles and sizes.

K & S Industries, Inc.
1801 Union Center Highway
Binghamton, NY 13905
ph: 877-742-5567 or 607-798-7156
fax: 607-798-7440
pleximan@888pickkns.com
http://www.888pickkns.com
Manufacturers of acrylic display cases for die-cast automotive collectors; made of clear acrylic with mirrored backs.

Dennis Bard, Pres.
Custom Display Cases, Inc.
3058 S. Queen St.
Dallastown, PA 17313
ph: 717-246-0137
fax: 717-246-8887
Customdisplay@cyberia.com
http://www.customdisplaycases.com
Sells quality acrylic display cases for collectibles.

Jay's Sports Connection
49 W. Aylesbury Rd.
Timonium, MD 21093
ph: 410-252-7700 or 800-628-2352
jaysport@erols.com
http://www.jaysports.com
Distributes Allstate aluminum showcases.

Chris R. Jensen
Streamwood, Inc.
Newsletter: Scout Stuff
121 Gulf St.
P.O. Box 1841
Easley, SC 29641-1841
ph: 864-859-2915
fax: 800-453-0398
cjensen@streamwood.net
http://www.streamwood.net
Sells BoxWare display cases made from tough injection molded plastic, not cardboard; latched lids so no more straight pins; replaceable glass or acrylic lenses; stocks 29 sizes of polyethylene zip lock bags.

Roger Kleinschmidt
Golf Ball Art & Custom Displays
5303 Park Place Circle
Boca Raton, FL 33486
ph: 888-296-4133 or 561-417-5010
fax: 561-417-5010
golfart@gate.net
http://golfballart.com
Builds golf ball display cases for collectors or to be given as awards of gifts; unique because of a new concept

of attaching balls to a surface; made of oak or acrylic and of any size; takes up less wall or desk space.

Bluegrass Case Company
272 Airport Rd.
P.O. Box 386
Stanton, KY 40380
ph: 606-663-9871 or 800-668-9871
fax: 606-663-6369
bluegrasscase@bluegrasscase.com
http://www.bluegrasscase.com
Sells black collector frames; also walnut, cherry or oak frames with locks.

Janie Jinks-Weidner
13706 Robins Rd.
Westerville, OH 43082
ph: 614-965-2868 or 800-444-1280
fax: 614-965-5913
janiew48@aol.com
http://members.aol.com/JanieW48
Sells hand-held display frames good for displaying scouting, arrowheads, knives, jewelry, fossils, minerals, militaria, Indian artifacts, spoons, Civil War relics, poker chips; 186 different sizes.

Sales Dept.
Jamar Company
P.O. Box 5330
Akron, OH 44334-0330
ph: 330-239-2889
fax: 330-239-2889
Manufactures and sells a wide selection of acrylic display cases and cabinets.

GEMO Display Cases
6952 Ponteberry St.
Canton, OH 44718
ph: 330-499-2023
fax: 330-499-3382
info@gemodisplays.com
http://www.gemodisplays.com
Glass and mirror contemporary design display cases; anti-static, dust proof, scratch proof, non tarnishing; large sizes available.

Robert Brickner
Cases for Collectibles
1600 Irma Ave.
Hamilton, OH 45011
ph: 513-856-9475
fax: 513-856-9133
caseman45011@yahoo.com
http://www.casesforcollectibles.com
Sells crystal clear acrylic display cases for dolls, antiques, toys, and other fine collectibles.

Charles Wood
Company C Wood-Shop
P.O. Box 27
Bethel, OH 45106
ph: 513-734-7374 or 888-684-7227
fax: 513-734-7047
woodc@goodnews.net
http://www.cwoodshop.com
Makes antique type chests, gun and knife cases; Civil War period camp chests, antique style gun and knife

cases, logo golf ball display cases, custom jewelry boxes.

Douglas Hammetter
Creative Store Design, Inc.
3728 N. Fratney St.
Milwaukee, WI 53212-1749
ph: 800-865-9595 or 414-963-1900
fax: 414-963-4445
Sells upright display cases or trophy cases; full vision, glass cube displays, countertop showcases; delivery and setup available.

Showcase Designs
315 Atwater St.
Saint Paul, MN 55117
ph: 651-489-5328 or 800-833-2226
fax: 651-489-7795
info@showcasedesigns.biz
http://www.showcasedesigns.biz
Makes specialized showcases.

Michael Cosentino
Marble Show-Case
6936 N. Overhill Ave.
Chicago, IL 60631
fax: 773-594-9479
mikecoz@mc.net
http://www.marbleshowcase.com
Sells display cases for marbles and other small collectibles; also sells and appraises marbles.

Militaire Promotions
P.O. Box 34679
Chicago, IL 60634
ph: 773-777-0499 or 800-383-0330
fax: 773-777-4017
mail@milprom.com
http://www.milprom.com
Sell J-mount display boxes; glass-top display boxes for small collectibles: jewelry, watches, buttons, badges, etc.; all sizes.

Garrett's Antiques
1264 East 2073 Rd.
Eudora, KS 66025
ph: 785-542-2339 or 800-447-7508
Sells black collector frames and aluminum or cherry sales/display/ show cases.

Mike Pratt
UsaDisplay Case Co.
512 North Spruce St.
Valley, NE 68064-9670
ph: 402-359-5539
fax: 402-359-5539
sales@usadisplay.net
http://www.usadisplay.net
Manufactures unique inexpensive cases to display, organize, and protect small collectibles of all types including marbles; send SASE for more information.

Action Figure Display Case Co.
512 North Spruce St.
Valley, NE 68064-9670
ph: 402-359-5539
fax: 773-395-3495
sales@usadisplay.net
http://www.usaidsplay.net
Manufactures high quality display

cases for all 12" action figures; full color combat backgrounds or cityscapes for Barbie; perfect for gifts, home or office.

Custom Craft Plastics
13660 Bora Dr.
Santa Fe Springs, CA 90670
ph: 562-407-1515
fax: 562-407-1518
ken@customcraftplastics.com
http://www.customcraftplastics.com
Manufacturer of acrylic display cases and accessories; literature holders, collectibles showcases, retail displays, custom designs and silk-screening.

ANTIQUES SHOP DIRECTORIES

(see also FLEA MARKETS, Directories)

Internet Resources

Joanne Bennett
Cape Cod Antiques & Collectibles
273 Tubman Rd.
Brewster, MA 02631
ph: 508-896-5026
fax: 508-896-1514
ask@capecodantiquesandcollectibles.com
http://
  www.capecodantiquesandcollectibles.com
The first and only site devoted entirely to listing antiques and collectibles shops in all of New England: shops, local flea markets, auctions, and more.

Herb Breese
Multidealer Antiques Shops, Malls, Co-Ops
3 Aurora St.
P.O. Box 428
Moravia, NY 13118-0428
ph: 315-497-0033
herbbreese@compuserve.com
http://ourworld.compuserve.com/
  homepages/herbbreese
Searchable online database listing most of the group shops in the US and Canada.

Periodicals

David & Kim Leggett
Three Rivers Press
Directory: Leggitts' Antique Atlas, The
201 East 50th St.
New York, NY 10022
ph: 212-572-2537
fax: 212-940-7868
crownpublicity@randomhouse.com
http://www.randomhouse.com
A comprehensive guide to antiquing in America: over 15,000 shops and malls.

Southern Antiques
Directory: Southern Antiques Shop
  Guide
P.O. Drawer 1107
Decatur, GA 30031-1107
ph: 404-289-0054 or 888-800-4997
fax: 404-286-9727
southernantiques@msn.com
Lists the South's best antiques shops, hundreds of antiques shows, top auction houses, and special products and services.

Bruce Causey
Magazine: Antiques & Art Around
  Florida
P.O. Box 980
Keystone Heights, FL 32656
ph: 352-475-1336 or 800-248-9430
fax: 352-475-5326
antartfl@aol.com
http://www.aarf.com
Full color guide to Florida's antique shops; maps, shows, museums; feature articles on antiques and FL heritage.

Judy Lloyd
FDS, Inc.
Directory: No-Nonsense Antique Mall
  Directory
P.O. Box 188
Higginsport, OH 45131
ph: 937-375-4395
fax: 937-375-4394
info@antiqueguide.net
http://www.AntiqueGuide.net
Nationwide antique mall directory with over 5,000 multi-dealer listings; all states, easy to use; alphabetical format by state and city; name, size, address, phone, hours, directions.

Connie Swaim
DMG World Media
Directory: AntiqueWeek Antique Shop
  Directory
P.O. Box 90
Knightstown, IN 46148
ph: 765-345-5133 or 800-876-5133
fax: 800-695-8153
connie@antiqueweek.com
http://www.antiqueweek.com
AntiqueWeek Shop Guide is an annual directory that lists antique shops and malls; two editions are published: Eastern and Central.

Janice Reittinger, Pub.
DJ's Publishing
Directory: Iowa's Complete Guide to
  Antique Shops & Malls
424 1st Ave. East
Dyersville, IA 52040-1301
ph: 319-875-8640 or 877-226-5351
http://www.hairwork.com/
  guides.iowa.htm
The most extensive and only Guide covering all of Iowa; over 800 shops with name, address, phone numbers, specialty items, repair, shows, maps, and wanted-to-buy section.

Connie Gewecke, Ed.
CarPac Publishing Co.
Directory: Antiques Shops Directory
1800 W. D St.
P.O. Box 601
Vinton, IA 52349-0601
ph: 319-472-4763 or 319-472-4764
fax: 319-472-3117
connie@collectorsjournal.com
http://www.collectorsjournal.com
*Lists antiques shops in Illinois,
Nebraska, Wisconsin, Kansas,
Minnesota, Missouri, South Dakota,
Texas and Iowa.*

Shepard C. Swift
Moonlight Press
Directory: Taylor's Guide to Antique
Shops in IL & So. WI
P.O. Box 5095
Buffalo Grove, IL 60089
ph: 847-465-3311
fax: 847-465-3307
stiver@ix.netcom.com
http://www.collectoronline.com/guides/
taylors.html
*Address and phone numbers of all
known antique shops in northern
Illinois and southern Wisconsin;
includes antiques show dates; repair
people; maps; published every April.*

Antoinette Knopp Powers, Pub.
AMQ Group Ltd.
Directory: Antique-ing Trip Planner
P.O. Box 219
Western Springs, IL 60558-0219
ph: 708-246-4990
fax: 708-246-1559
*Compiled quarterly by the editors of
"Professional Antique Mall Owner/
Manager;" lists every multi-dealer
antiques shop, antiques shop and flea
market in the Midwest.*

Jan Lindenberger
Directory: Antique Buyer's Guide
P.O. Box 7224
Colorado Springs, CO 80933
ph: 719-591-9558
fax: 719-591-9558
*Covering the states of KS, OK, NM,
CO, MO, NE and TX; addresses, ads,
maps.*

Bliss Cochran
Cochran Publishing
Directory: Cochran's Collector's Guide
to California
P.O. Box 1582
Gualala, CA 95445
ph: 800-648-0526 or 707-884-9239
fax: 707-884-3198
collectorsguide@cochrans.com
http://www.cochrans.com
*A travel-size annual map directory
including sections on antique show
schedules and shops throughout
California; free at participating shows
and store; $5 by mail.*

ANTIQUES SHOW PROMOTERS
Clubs/Associations

Antiques Council, The
P.O. Box 1508
Warren, MA 01083
ph: 413-436-7064
fax: 413-436-7066
info@antiquescouncil.com
http://www.antiquescouncil.com/
home.htm
*An association of approximately 80
members across the nation who
manage antiques shows for charity
sponsors; members abide by code of
ethics; show schedule now includes
seven annual shows; founded in 1990.*

C. Mitchell Sorensen, Ex. Dir.
Professional Show Manager's
Association
P.O. Box 30
One Regency Dr.
Bloomfield, CT 06002
ph: 860-243-3977
fax: 860-286-0787
msorensen@ssmgt.com
http://www.psmashows.org
*Promotes a Code of Ethics for the
benefit of the consumer show industry
and to facilitate the exchange of
information among show managers of
consumer shows.*

Jim Tucker
Antiques & Collectibles Show Promoters
Association
P.O. Box 4389
Davidson, NC 28036
ph: 800-287-7127 or 704-895-9088
fax: 704-895-0230
info@antiqueandcollectible.com
http://www.antiqueandcollectible.com/
acspa.shtml
*Provides benefits directed solely to the
show promoter and manager; 5
regions nationwide with annual
meetings in each region and
nationally; benefits include a
newsletter with contributions from
show managers, networking,
insurance.*

Misc. Services

David Lamberto
Jeanne Hertan Antique Shows
P.O. Box 628
Somers, CT 06071
ph: 860-763-3760 or 413-245-9872
fax: 860-749-9485
hertansbrimfield@att.net
http://www.hertansbrimfield.com
*Quality antiques shows held in May,
July and September in Brimfield, MA.*

Vivien Cord
Cord Shows, Ltd.
4 Whippoorwill Lane
Armonk, NY 10504
ph: 914-273-4667
fax: 914-273-4656
shows@cordshows.com
http://www.cordshows.com
Has been running antiques shows and

*fine art and crafts fairs for over thirty
years.*

Bob Smith
Dolphin Promotions, Inc.
P.O. Box 7320
Fort Lauderdale, FL 33338
ph: 954-563-6747
fax: 954-566-1982
DolphinPromotions@worldnet.att.net
http://www.dolphinfairs.com
Antiques show organizers.

Madison Rink
Caskey-Lees
P.O. Box 1409
Topanga, CA 90290
ph: 310-455-2886
caskeylees@earthlink.net
*Show producers of high end art and
antique shows.*

ANTIQUITIES

(see also ARCHAEOLOGY; COINS &
CURRENCY, Coins [Ancient];
PRECOLUMBIAN; PREHISTORIC
ARTIFACTS)

Appraisers

Dr. Jerome M. Eisenberg
Royal-Athena Galleries
153 East 57th St.
New York, NY 10022
ph: 212-355-2034
fax: 212-688-0412
ancientart@aol.com
http://www.royalathena.com
*Specialist in the appraisal of Greek,
Etruscan, Roman, Egyptian and Near
Eastern art.*

Tara Ana Finley
Anubis Appraisers & Estate Services,
Inc.
1042 Sorolla Ave.
Miami, FL 33134-3560
ph: 305-446-1820 or 786-486-8042
fax: 305-648-1939
tara.finley@worldnet.att.net
*Thirty years experience appraising
antiquities including Egyptian, Greek,
Roman and Islamic works of art;
appraisals done for insurance,
donation or probate purposes.*

Frederick P. Dose, Jr.
Frederick Dose Appraisals Ltd.
778 Pleasant Ave.
Highland Park, IL 60035-4613
ph: 847-433-7870 or 847-433-1090
fdoseappraisals@comcast.net
*Appraises Egyptian, Greek, Roman,
etc. art for insurance, corporate,
private, and attorneys; references on
request; 6 year full-time as University
art historian.*

Auction Services

Greg Manning
Greg Manning Auctions, Inc.
775 Passaic Ave.
West Caldwell, NJ 07006
ph: 973-882-0004 or 800-221-0243
fax: 973-882-3499
gmauction@aol.com
http://www.gregmanning.com
*Since 1905, a leading auctioneer of
Americana, glass, stoneware, and
antiquities.*

Christie's
20 Rockefeller Plaza
New York, NY 10020
ph: 212-636-2000
info@christies.com
http://www.christies.com

Howard Rose
Arte Primitivo Gallery
3 East 65th St., Ste. 2
New York, NY 10021
ph: 212-570-6999 or 212-570-0393
fax: 212-570-1899
info@arteprimitivo.com
http://www.arteprimitivo.com
*Specializes in Classical and Egyptian
antiquities, Precolumbian art,
ethnographic art, Asian antiquities,
and books; conducts absentee/
callback auctions biennially and
publishes lavish color catalog with
each auction.*

Alex G. Malloy
Alex G. Malloy, Inc.
P.O. Box 38
South Salem, NY 10590-0038
ph: 203-438-0396 or 203-438-9652
fax: 203-438-6744
alexmalloy@aol.com
http://members.aol.com/AlexMalloy/
agmalloy.htm
*Issues fixed price lists and mail bid
sales of ancient and medieval coinage,
and of ancient art and antiquities for
sale; author of "Official Price Guide
to Artifacts of Ancient Civilizations."*

Clubs/Associations

Antiquities Dealers' Association
c/o Faustus Ancient Art & Jewellery
41 Dover St.
London, W1X 4NS U.K.
ph: +44 (0) 20 7930 1864
fax: +44 (0) 20 7495 2882
http://www.the-ada.org
For antiquities dealers and collectors.

Collectors

Jon Lewin
622 Raleigh Ave., Apt. 3
Norfolk, VA 23507-2034
ph: 757-625-6732
*Wants any relics from the ancient
world or tribal cultures: tools,
weapons, coins, fetishes, masks,
sculptures; African, Aboriginal,
Native American, PreColumbian,
Egyptian, Roman, Mideast.*

Dealers

John Ambrose
Fragments of Time
P.O. Box 376
Medfield, MA 02051
ph: 508-359-0090
fax: 508-390-0090
fragments@aol.com
http://www.antiquities.net
Collector, dealer, expert, and appraiser of ancient Greek, Roman, Egyptian, Etruscan and Near Eastern art; known worldwide for museum-quality art at competitive prices; authenticity guaranteed.

Norman Hurst, ISA CAPP
Hurst Gallery
53 Mount Auburn St.
Cambridge, MA 02138-5030
ph: 617-491-6888 or 212-744-6488
(NYC)
fax: 617-661-0439
NHurst@compuserve.com
http://www.hurstgallery.com
Has been consulting, appraising and dealing in Ancient art for over 25 years: Greek, Roman, Middle Eastern; Egyptian, ancient glass, pottery, stone, sculpture, bronze, faience; AAA appraiser certified in Ethnographic art.

Allen G. Berman
Allen G. Berman Professional
Numismatist
P.O. Box 605
Fairfield, CT 06824-0605
ph: 845-434-6090 or 845-434-6079
fax: 845-434-6079
agberman@aol.com
http://www.bermania.com
Medieval, Byzantine and European seals including sealed documents, lead seals to modern times, medieval pilgrim badges; consultant to auction houses on attribution of seals, oil lamps and pottery; no New World or Far Eastern handled.

Edgar L. Owen
Edgar L. Owen, Ltd.
P.O. Box 714
Lake Hopatcong, NJ 07849
ph: 973-398-9557
fax: 973-398-8082
EdgarOwen@worldnet.att.net
http://www.edgarlowen.com
One of the largest inventories of antiquities in the world; from prehistory through the great ancient civilizations.

Sadigh Gallery
303 Fifth Ave., Ste. 1603
New York, NY 10016
ph: 800-426-2007 or 212-725-7537
fax: 212-545-7612
sales@ipgroup.com
http://www.ipgroup.com/sadigh
Framed antiquities, arrowheads and stone tools, ancient coins and jewelry, fossils, biblical artifacts, Persian ceramics.

Alex G. Malloy
Alex G. Malloy, Inc.
P.O. Box 38
South Salem, NY 10590-0038
ph: 203-438-0396 or 203-438-9652
fax: 203-438-6744
alexmalloy@aol.com
http://members.aol.com/AlexMalloy/
agmalloy.htm
Issues fixed price lists and mail bid sales of ancient and medieval coinage, and of ancient art and antiquities for sale; author of "Official Price Guide to Artifacts of Ancient Civilizations."

Ancient Art International
P.O. Box 4350
Vero Beach, FL 32964-4350
ph: 772-231-0744
fax: 772-231-3919
rbrockway@mindspring.com
http://www.ancientartinc.com
Fine art from the ancient worlds: Greek, Roman, Egyptian, Near Eastern, Islamic, Chinese.

David Markarian
Markarian Ancient Artifacts
P.O. Box 2476
Rancho Mirage, CA 92270-1087
ph: 760-202-5000
orion@inland.net
http://www.ancientart.org
Buys, sells ancient art; specializing in Egyptian, Precolumbian, and all others.

Dr. Geoffrey A. Smith
Antiquities in Design - CoinSold
P.O. Box 1004
Redlands, CA 92373
ph: 858-442-7835
fax: 858-759-7835
coinsold@aol.com
http://hometown.aol.com/coinsold
Buys, sells, appraises and specializes in ancient coins, jewelry and artifacts; GIA trained and certified in gemology - ancient and modern gems, metals, and jewelry; has up-to-date CEU and forensics certification.

Allan Anawati
Medusa Ancient Art
8380 Darnley Rd.
Montreal, Quebec H4T 1M4 Canada
ph: 514-735-8080 or 877-363-3872
fax: 514-733-2082
support@medusa-art.com
http://www.medusa-art.com
Dealing in Egyptian, Greek, Roman, and Near Eastern antiquities for over 30 years.

Internet Resources

Julia Hayden
Ancient World Web, The
feedback@julen.net
http://www.julen.net/ancient
An Internet index site containing major links relating to the ancient world: theories, archaeology, art, buildings, monuments, cities, daily life, general resources, history, institutions and organizations, mythology, religion, more.

Museums/Libraries

Abbe Museum
P.O. Box 286
Bar Harbor, ME 04609
ph: 207-288-3519
abbe@midmaine.com
http://www.abbemuseum.org
Discover 10,000 years of Maine Native American culture through changing exhibits, hands-on programs and workshops taught by Native artists; the museum store offers a fine selection of Maine Native basketry and other crafts.

British Museum, The
Great Russell St.
London, WC1B 3DG U.K.
ph: 020 7323 8605
fax: 020 7323 8614
info@afbm.org
http://www.thebritishmuseum.ac.uk
World famous collections housed in beautiful neoclassical building; covering humankind's artistic achievements from Ancient Egypt, Greece and Rome to Anglo-Saxon England and Renaissance Europe.

Periodicals

Kerry K. Wetterstrom, Ed./Pub.
Magazine: Celator, The
P.O. Box 839
Lancaster, PA 17608-0839
ph: 717-656-8557
fax: 717-656-8557
kerry@celator.com
http://www.celator.com
A monthly magazine focusing on ancient Greek, Roman and Byzantine coins: ads, articles, auction reports, etc.

Jerome M. Eisenberg, Ed.
Aurora Publications Ltd.
Magazine: Minerva
14 Old Bond St.
London, W1X 3BD U.K.
ph: 44 171 495 2590
fax: 44 171 491 1595
minerva@minervamagazine.com
http://www.minervamagazine.com
The international review of ancient art and archaeology; a bi-monthly illustrated magazine focusing on ancient art, antiquities, archaeology and numismatic discoveries worldwide.

Egyptian

Dealers

Norman Hurst, ISA CAPP
Hurst Gallery
53 Mount Auburn St.
Cambridge, MA 02138-5030
ph: 617-491-6888 or 212-744-6488
(NYC)
fax: 617-661-0439
NHurst@compuserve.com
http://www.hurstgallery.com
Has been consulting, appraising and dealing in Ancient art for over 25 years: Greek, Roman, Middle Eastern; Egyptian, ancient glass, pottery, stone, sculpture, bronze, faience; AAA appraiser certified in Ethnographic art.

David Markarian
Markarian Ancient Artifacts
P.O. Box 2476
Rancho Mirage, CA 92270-1087
ph: 760-202-5000
orion@inland.net
http://www.ancientart.org
Buys and sells Egyptian artifacts.

Allan Anawati
Medusa Ancient Art
8380 Darnley Rd.
Montreal, Quebec H4T 1M4 Canada
ph: 514-735-8080 or 877-363-3872
fax: 514-733-2082
support@medusa-art.com
http://www.medusa-art.com
Dealing in Egyptian, Greek, Roman, and Near Eastern antiquities for over 30 years.

Henk F. Dijkstra
Anubis Ancient Art
P.O. Box 24352
Rotterdam, 3007 DJ Netherlands
ph: +31 (10) 4332236
fax: +31 (10) 4332236
sales@artcollecting.com
http://www.artcollecting.com
Buys and sells high quality ancient Egyptian, Roman and Greek art; specializes in Egyptian art.

Greek & Roman

Dealers

Allan Anawati
Medusa Ancient Art
8380 Darnley Rd.
Montreal, Quebec H4T 1M4 Canada
ph: 514-735-8080 or 877-363-3872
fax: 514-733-2082
support@medusa-art.com
http://www.medusa-art.com
Dealing in Egyptian, Greek, Roman, and Near Eastern antiquities for over 30 years.

Museums/Libraries

Ellen Reeder
Walters Art Museum
600 N. Charles St.
Baltimore, MD 21201
ph: 410-547-9000
klavin@thewalters.org
http://www.thewalters.org
One of only a few museums worldwide to present a comprehensive history of art from the third millennium B.C. to the early 20th century.

Toledo Museum of Art, The
2445 Monroe St.
P.O. Box 1013
Toledo, OH 43697-1013
ph: 419-255-8000 or 800-644-6862
marketing@toledomuseum.org
http://www.toledomuseum.org
Internationally recognized collection

of Greek vases, as well as glass, paintings, and decorative arts.

Medieval

Museums/Libraries

Dr. Gary Vikan
Walters Art Museum
600 N. Charles St.
Baltimore, MD 21201
ph: 410-547-9000
klavin@thewalters.org
http://www.thewalters.org
One of only a few museums worldwide to present a comprehensive history of art from the third millennium B.C. to the early 20th century.

Repro. Sources

MacKenzie-Smith Medieval Arms & Armor
12116 Highland
P.O. Box 3315
Truckee, CA 96160
ph: 530-587-5974 or 800-829-1974
(orders)
info@mackenziesmith.com
http://www.mackenziesmith.com
Excellent quality replica weapons and armor for collectors, history buffs, reenactors.

ANTLERS

(see ANIMAL TROPHIES; FURNITURE [ANTIQUE], Antler & Horn)

APOTHECARY ANTIQUES

(see MEDICAL, DENTAL & PHARMACEUTICAL)

APPLE PARERS

(see also KITCHEN COLLECTIBLES)

Clubs/Associations

Gerald W. Laverty
International Society of Apple Parer Enthusiasts
Newsletter: ISAPE Newsletter
735 Cedarwood Terrace, Apt. 735B
Rochester, NY 14609
ph: 716-654-6998
http://www.collectoronline.com/clubs/ISAPE
Holds conventions; 12-page newsletter contains articles, old ads, patents and a buy/sell section; to date over 100 photos of different models have been presented.

Collectors

Johnny Appleseed
8060 Sierra St.
Fair Oaks, CA 95628-7549
ph: 916-961-7174
Apple peelers wanted; give patent dates, model and description.

APPLIANCES

(see ELECTRICITY RELATED ITEMS, Appliances; FANS, Mechanical; KITCHEN COLLECTIBLES; STOVES; RANGES; TOASTERS, Electric)

APPRAISERS

(see also Additional Appraisers who are also listed under specific categories throughout this Directory.)

Clubs/Associations

Victor Wiener, Ex. Dir.
Appraisers Association of America
Newsletter: Appraiser, The
386 Park Ave. S. #2000
New York, NY 10016-8804
ph: 212-889-5404
fax: 212-889-5503
aaa1@rcn.com
http://www.appraisersassoc.org
Nonprofit association of personal property appraisers with approximately 1,000 members in more than 600 subspecialties in all areas of fine art, antiques, and collectibles; membership directory available.

Appraisal Foundation, The
Newsletter: Foundation News
1029 Vermont Ave. NW, Ste. 900
Washington, DC 20005-3517
ph: 202-347-7722
fax: 202-347-7727
staff@appraisalfoundation.org
http://www.appraisalfoundation.org
Authorized by Congress as the source of appraisal standards and appraiser qualifications.

Edwin W. Baker, Ex. VP
American Society of Appraisers
P.O. Box 17265
Washington, DC 20071
ph: 703-478-2228 or 800-272-8258
fax: 703-742-8471
asainfo@appraisers.org
http://www.appraisers.org
The only appraisal organization in the US representing all the disciplines of appraisal specialists; call 800-ASA-VALU for free referral or membership directory, or visit Web site.

James Jolliff
National Association of Jewelry Appraisers, The
Newsletter: Jewelry Appraiser, The
P.O. Box 6558
Annapolis, MD 21401-0558
ph: 410-897-0889
Members perform gem and jewelry, silver flatware and hollowware, and watch valuations exclusively.

Association of Online Appraisers, Inc.
P.O. Box 2049
Frederick, MD 21702-1049
ph: 301-228-2279
fax: 301-695-6491
info@AOAonline.org
http://www.AOAonline.org
Not-for-profit association for online as well as traditional appraisers; establishes standards of appraisal ethics & professional practice; offers 550+ page "Complete Online Course in Personal Property Appraising" free to members.

Robert Bridel, Ex. Dir.
American Gem Society
8881 West Saraha Ave.
Las Vegas, NV 89117
ph: 702-255-6500
fax: 702-255-7420
http://www.ags.org
Founded in 1934 to protect consumers in their purchases of fine jewelry.

Appraisers National Association
25602 Alicia Parkway
PMB 245
Laguna Hills, CA 92653
ph: 949-349-9179
info@ana-appraisers.org
http://www.ana-appraisers.org
Nonprofit professional association dedicated to personal property appraising; provides referrals to appraisers of antiques, collectibles, art, furniture, other household items.

International Society of Appraisers
Newsletter: Professional Appraisers Information Exchange
1131 SW 7th St., Ste. 105
Renton, WA 98055
ph: 206-241-0359 or 888-472-4732
fax: 206-241-0436
ISA@isa-appraisers.org
http://www.isa-appraisers.org
Largest assoc. of professional appraisers devoted solely to personal property; over 1,300 members specializing in all areas of antiques & residential contents, gems & jewelry, fine art, machinery & equipment; member directory on Web site.

Misc. Services

ArtFact, Inc.
Price Guide: ArtFact
1130 Ten Rod Rd., Ste. D202
North Kingstown, RI 02852-4158
ph: 401-295-2656 or 800-278-3228
fax: 401-295-2629
sales@artfact.com
http://www.artfact.com
A computerized online price guide having almost 6 million auction sales results of fine art, antiques and collectibles; complete lot descriptions, prices realized with on-screen images.

William D. Hoefer, FGA, GG
Hoefers' Gemological Services
5016 Alan Ave., Ste. B4
San Jose, CA 95124-5741
ph: 408-264-0670
fax: 408-264-0725
editor@appraiserunderoath.com
http://www.appraiserunderoath.com
Offers expert consultation and expert testimony to attorneys on personal property appraisal methodology, legal research, etc.

Periodicals

David J. Maloney, ISA CAPP
Sales Online Direct, Inc.
Directory: Maloney's Antiques & Collectibles Resource Directory
P.O. Box 2049
Frederick, MD 21702-1049
ph: 301-228-2279
fax: 301-695-6491
dave@maloney.com
http://www.davidmaloney.com/aboutbook.htm
Publishes major resource information source for collectors, sellers, claims adjusters, etc.: includes experts, buyers, clubs, periodicals, repairers, museums/libraries, appraisers, auctioneers, matching services, dealers, etc.

Online

Appraisers

AsktheAppraiser.com
4 Brussels St.
Worcester, MA 01610
ph: 781-821-0199
ata@collectingchannel.com
http://www.AsktheAppraiser.com
The premiere online appraisal service offered by CollectingChannel.com; all appraisals comply with the "Uniform Standards of Professional Appraisal Practice" and with the standards of the Association of Online Appraisers.

Erik Kafrissen
WhatsItWorthToYou.com
48 Wilson St., Ste. 4
Perth, Ontario K7H 2N4 Canada
ph: 613-264-9032
fax: 613-264-0199
info@whatsitworthtoyou.com
http://www.whatsitworthtoyou.com
Has network of experts from around the world; able to provide appraisals based on information you submit on their Web site.

Clubs/Associations

Association of Online Appraisers, Inc.
P.O. Box 2049
Frederick, MD 21702-1049
ph: 301-228-2279
fax: 301-695-6491
info@AOAonline.org
http://www.AOAonline.org
Not-for-profit association for online as well as traditional appraisers; establishes standards of appraisal ethics & professional practice; offers 550+ page "Complete Online Course

in Personal Property Appraising" free to members.

AQUARIUMS

Collectors

Tim LaGanke
14054 Sweetbriar Lane
Novelty, OH 44072
ph: 440-338-8745
Wants to buy antique and old aquariums; also wants old toy and model divers.

Gary Bagnall
3090 McMillan Rd.
San Luis Obispo, CA 93401-6730
ph: 805-542-9988
fax: 805-542-9295
zoomed@zoomed.com
Buys and sells antique aquariums and related pet products.

Ornaments

Collectors

Darryl Rehr
P.O. Box 641824
Los Angeles, CA 90064-6824
ph: 310-477-5229
fax: 310-268-8420
dcrehr@earthlink.net
Wants attractive aquarium ornaments used in home aquariums: castles, sea creatures, divers, etc.

ARCHAEOLOGY

(see also NATIVE AMERICAN;
ANTIQUITIES; HERITAGE
RESOURCES; NATURAL HISTORY;
FOSSILS; MINERAL SPECIMENS;
PREHISTORIC ARTIFACTS;
TREASURE HUNTING)

Clubs/Associations

Archaeological Institute of America
Magazine: Archaeology
656 Beacon St.
Boston, MA 02215-2006
ph: 617-353-9361
fax: 617-353-6550
aia@aia.bu.edu
http://www.archaeological.org
Has phone numbers and addresses for all state archaeological departments; "Archaeology" is published bi-monthly; also publishes the "American Journal of Archaeology" quarterly; write for details.

Society for American Archaeology
900 2nd St. NE, #12
Washington, DC 20002
ph: 202-789-8200
fax: 202-789-0284
headquarters@saa.org
http://www.saa.org
Promotes interest in American archaeology; stimulates research, fosters professional associations, advocates the conservation of artifacts; works to eliminate the commercialization of antiquities.

Society for American Archaeology
Magazine: American Antiquity
900 Second St. NE, #12
Washington, DC 20002-3557
ph: 202-789-8200
fax: 202-789-0284
headquarters@saa.org
http://www.saa.org
An international organization dedicated to the research, interpretation, and protection of the archaeological heritage of the Americas; over 6,600 members.

Carol Ebright, Pres.
Archeological Society of Maryland, Inc.
305 Wembley Rd.
Reisterstown, MD 21136-3513
ph: 301-293-2708
cebright@sha.state.mu.us
http://www.smcm.edu/Academics/soan/asm/home.htm
Does not buy or sell artifacts; all artifacts recovered from excavations of prehistoric or historic sites in Maryland are preserved at the Maryland Archaeological Conservation Lab for study by anyone interested.

Piedmont Archaeological Society of
North & South Carolina
159 Marshdale Ave. SW
Concord, NC 28025
ph: 704-782-9253
packrat1@etinternet.net
http://www.pasnsc.org

Steve Beasley, Sec.
Peach State Archaeological Society of
Georgia
3327 Woodview Dr.
Smyrna, GA 30082-2422
ph: 770-436-2976
http://www.geocities.com/Heartland/Acres/6910

Dennis Bushey, Pres.
Rebel State Archaeological Society of
Alabama
113 Pine Forest
Selma, AL 36701
ph: 334-875-5299
cb2@zebra.net
A non-profit organization to promote ethical artifact collecting; hosts six Indian Artifact shows a year throughout Alabama.

Jim Butler, Sec./Treas.
Volunteer State Archaeological Society
of Tennessee
510 N. Russell St.
Portland, TN 37148-2009

Barbara Tully
Green River Archaeological Society of
Kentucky
P.O. Box 923
Benton, KY 42025-0903

Pete Schwinn, Sec.
Indiana Archaeological Society
14378 N. 400 W. Elwood
Elwood, IN 46036-9230

Darrell Largen, Pres.
Wolverine State Archaeological Society
of Michigan
Newsletter: Wolverine Barb
10086 W.M. Ave.
Kalamazoo, MI 49009-9492
dl10086@msn.com

Belinda Filbrandt, Sec./Treas.
Hawkeye State Archaeological Society of
Iowa
3967 Highway 22
Blue Grass, IA 52726-9400

Cathy Norton
Badger State Archaeological Society of
Wisconsin
Journal: Central States Archaeological
Journal
W7103 Cty C.
Monticello, WI 53570-9790
cnorton@utelco.tds.net

Illinois State Archaeological Society
Newsletter: Field Notes
7941 St. James
Moro, IL 62067-1229
jarco@prodigy.net
http://www.tocynbro.com/ARCHAEOL-OGY/illarch.htm
Collectors of prehistoric Native American and Pre Columbian artifacts: arrowheads, axes, pottery, inc.

John Crowley, Editor
Central States Archaeological Societies,
Inc.
Journal: Central States Archaeological
Journal
11552 Patty Ann
Saint Louis, MO 63146-5471
C21stlouis@aol.com
http://www.csasi.org
Endeavors to develop a better understanding among students and collectors of archaeological material, professional and nonprofessional, as well as museums and institutions of learning.

Janet Miller, Sec.
Greater St. Louis Archaeological Society
662 Tufwood Dr.
Ballwin, MO 63301-6275

Jeff Holder, Pres.
Arkansas Archaeological Society
Newsletter: Fieldnotes
2475 N. Hatch Ave.
Fayetteville, AR 72704
ph: 501-575-6545 or 501-575-3556
fax: 501-575-5453
jeff@arkansasheritage.org
http://www.uark.edu/depts/4society/index.html

Lone Star State Archaeological Society
of Texas
1610 West Main
Eastland, TX 76448
ph: 254-629-2549
sam@arrowheads.com
http://www.arrowheads.com/lonestar

Michael J. Rodeffer
Society for Historical Archaeology
Newsletter: Historical Archaeology
P.O. Box 30446
Tucson, AZ 85751
ph: 520-886-8006
sha_web@mindspring.com
http://www.sha.org
The largest scholarly group concerned with the archaeology of the modern world (A.D. 1400 to present); promotes scholarly research and the dissemination of knowledge concerning historical archaeology.

Collectors

Tommy W. Bryden
7941 St. James
Moro, IL 62067-1229
jarco@prodigy.net
http://www.tocynbro.com/ARCHAEOL-OGY/illarch.htm
Collector of prehistoric Native American artifacts such as arrowheads, axes, pottery.

Internet Resources

Hugh Jarvis
Lithics Site, The
hjarvis@acsu.buffalo.edu
http://wings.buffalo.edu/anthropology/lithics.html
Great page with lots of links to all kinds of archaeological resources: lithics research projects, literary resources, related institutional sites, archaeological courses on lithics, artifact information, commercial concerns.

Julia Hayden
Ancient World Web, The
feedback@julen.net
http://www.julen.net/ancient
An Internet index site containing major links relating to the ancient world: theories, archaeology, art, buildings, monuments, cities, daily life, general resources, history, institutions and organizations, mythology, religion, more.

Periodicals

Boston University Scholarly Publications
Journal: Journal of Field Archaeology
985 Commonwealth Ave.
Boston, MA 02215
ph: 617-353-4106
abw@crsa.bu.edu
http://jfa-www.bu.edu
This quarterly journal publishes articles that deal with reports of field excavations and surveys the world over; provides coverage of studies of methodological and technical matters

as well as scientific advances in archaeology.

Athena Publications
Journal: Athena Review
P.O. Box 10904
Naples, FL 34101
fax: 941-594-2163
athenarev1@aol.com
http://www.athenapub.com
Quarterly journal of archaeology, history and exploration.

Sean Kingsley
Aurora Publications Ltd.
Magazine: Minerva
14 Old Bond St.
London, W1X 3BD U.K.
ph: 44 171 495 2590
fax: 44 171 491 1595
minerva@minervamagazine.com
http://www.minervamagazine.com
The international review of ancient art and archaeology; a bi-monthly illustrated magazine focusing on ancient art, antiquities, archaeology and numismatic discoveries worldwide.

ARCHITECTURAL ELEMENTS

(see also DOORKNOBS; FIREPLACE ITEMS, Mantels; GARDEN FURNITURE, Furniture & Ornaments; PLUMBING; STAINED GLASS)

Auction Services

Julie Lewis
Great Gatsby's, The
5070 Peachtree Industrial Blvd
Atlanta, GA 30341
ph: 770-457-1903 or 800-GATSBYS
fax: 770-457-7250
internet@greatgatsbys.com
http://www.greatgatsbys.com
Specializes in the sale of architectural antiques.

Dealers

Aardvark Antiques
475 Thames St.
Newport, RI 02840
ph: 800-446-1052 or 401-849-7233
fax: 401-849-1591
ardvarkan@aol.com
http://www.aardvarkantiques.com
Lighting, stained glass, statuary, planters, sconces, pedestals, fountains, fireplaces, gates, fences, marble, iron, cast iron.

H. Weber & Jill Wilson
WebWilson.com
P.O. Box 506
Portsmouth, RI 02871
ph: 800-508-0022
fax: 401-683-1644
jill@LooLooDesign.com
http://www.LooLooDesign.com
Sells architectural antiques; garden ornaments, vintage plumbing, quality furniture, antique door hardware.

Chris McMahon
Architectural Salvage, Inc.
3 Mill St.
Exeter, NH 03833
ph: 603-773-5635
fax: 603-642-4348
arch@ttlc.net
http://www.oldhousesalvage.com
Deals in all types of old house parts from the smallest hardware to grand entrance ways and everything in between.

Allan Soll
Soll's Antiques
P.O. Box 307
Route 2
Canaan, ME 04924-0307
ph: 207-474-5396
solantiq@somtel.com
http://www.antiquestainedglass.net
Carries over 150 architectural c. 1900 stained and beveled glass windows; also antique doors, mantles, lighting fixtures, and other architectural items; also wholesales antique furniture.

United House Wrecking
535 Hope St.
Stamford, CT 06906-1316
ph: 203-348-5371
fax: 203-961-9472
unitedhouse.wrecking@snet.net
http://www.unitedhousewrecking.com
Sells architectural elements; stained and beveled glass, fireplace mantels and accessories, antique furniture, chandeliers and other lighting fixtures, etc.

Matthew White
Recycling the Past
381 N. Main
Barnegat, NJ 08005
ph: 609-660-9790
whitey99@cybercomm.net
http://www.recyclingthepast.com
Specializing in iron gates and fencing, garden urns, doors, windows, mantels, statuary, terracotta building parts, fireplace mantels, building parts of wood and metal, lighting, hardware.

Jeffery Venturella
Architectural Emporium
207 Adams Ave.
Canonsburg, PA 15317
ph: 724-746-4301
salesml@architectural-emporium.com
http://architectural-emporium.com
Carries a full line of architectural antiques; specializes in restoring antique lighting, chandeliers, and sconces.

Architectural Antiques
715 North Second St.
Philadelphia, PA 19123
ph: 215-922-3669
aaexchange@aol.com
http://www.architecturalantiques.com
Specializes in bars, mantels, stained glass, doors, ironworks and other architectural antiques.

Stephen G. DelSordo
Heritage Resource Group
305 Oakley St.
Cambridge, MD 21613
ph: 410-228-8934
fax: 410-221-8061
sdelsordo@comcast.net
http://www.heritageresource.com
A cultural resource management/ historic preservation firm that has contracts to locate, provide, authenticate artifacts for museums and collectors; areas of expertise include architecture, industry, domestic, agriculture, and maritime.

Salvage One
1524 South Sangamon St.
Chicago, IL 60608
ph: 312-733-0098
fax: 312-733-6829
staff@salvageone.com
http://www.salvageone.com
Maintains large inventory of American and European architectural elements from the 18th through 20th centuries.

Architectural Antiques
403 Dawson St.
San Antonio, TX 78202
ph: 210-226-6863
http://www.urweb.net/ architectualantiques1.htm
Buys and sells architectural elements including antique hardware, old pine doors, mantles, porch spindles and posts and brackets, old iron fencing, etc.

Don Hooper
Vintage Plumbing Bathroom Antiques
9645 Sylvia Ave.
Northridge, CA 91324-1756
ph: 818-772-1721
fax: 818-772-4647
vintageplumbing@juno.com
http://www.vintageplumbing.com
Buys, sells unusual c. 1900 American bathroom fixtures: bathtubs, toilets, sinks, showers, footbaths, sitz baths, nickel plated brass accessories.

Perry Prince
Perry S. Prince, Asian Antiques
P.O. Box 1364
Ashland, OR 97520
ph: 541-488-1989
fax: 541-488-1989
perry@asianarts.com
http://www.asianarts.com
Carries architectural antiques, Southeast Asian, Asian art, Asian antiques, interior decorating, interior design, Asian folk art, salvage, Chinese antiques, Chinese architecture.

Scott Lappa
Traders of the Lost Art
5915 1A St. SW
Calgary, Alberta T2H 0G4 Canada
ph: 403-229-0234
tradersofthelostart@shaw.ca
http://www.traderstoo.com
Specializing in architectural salvage:

decorative iron, chandeliers, garden statuary, primitive pieces, country doors, fireplace mantels, fixtures and fittings, etc.

John Rawlinson
Original Reclamation Trading Co., Ltd.
22 Elliott Rd.
Love Lane Estate
Cirencester, Gloucestershire GL7 1YS U.K.
ph: +44 1 285 653 532
fax: +44 1 285 644 383
Offers period stone, wood and cast iron fireplaces, oak flooring and doors, quality stone items for the garden, statuary, panelling, period garden seats.

Alexander Puddy
Architectural Heritage, Ltd.
Taddington Manor, Taddington
Nr. Cutsdean
Cheltenham, Gloucestershire GL54 5RY U.K.
ph: 01386-584414
fax: 01386-584236
puddy@architectural-heritage.co.uk
http://www.architectural-heritage.co.uk
In business since 1976; carries one of the largest stocks of fine quality architectural antiques and garden ornaments.

Internet Resources

Thornton Kay
Salvo
P.O. Box 33
Cornhill on Tweed
Northumberland, TD12 4YJ U.K.
ph: +44 1890 820333
fax: +44 1890 820499
tk@salvo.co.uk
http://www.salvo.co.uk
Has been providing information on antique and reclaimed materials for buildings and gardens since 1992; great source for information about antique and reclaimed materials for buildings and gardens worldwide.

Museums/Libraries

Octagon, The; The Museum of the American Architectural Foundation
1735 New York Ave., NW
Washington, DC 20006
ph: 202-638-3105
fax: 202-626-7420
aaf@aia.org
http://www.archfoundation.com/ TheOctagon.htm
Oldest museum in the US devoted to architecture and design.

Periodicals

Hanley-Wood, Inc.
Magazine: Old-House Journal, The
Two Main St.
Gloucester, MA 01930
ph: 800-234-3797
jbutterf@hanley-wood.com
http://www.oldhousejournal.com
Monthly magazine focusing on the repair of old houses; publishes "The Old-House Journal Catalog"-

hundreds of sources for products & services.

Hanley-Wood, Inc.
Directory: Old-House Journal Restoration Directory
Two Main St.
Gloucester, MA 01930
ph: 800-234-3797
jbutterf@hanley-wood.com
http://www.oldhousejournal.com
Sourcebook listing companies large and small which manufacture and sell traditional hard-to-find items for the old house owner: sinks, siding, lumber, plumbing, stoves, etc.; also call 800-931-2931.

Ray Shepherd
Magazine: Traditional Building
69A 7th Ave.
Brooklyn, NY 11217-3618
ph: 718-636-0788
fax: 718-636-0750
htcstaff@traditional-building.com
http://www.traditional-building.com
Great source for products for historical buildings.

Victorian Gingerbread

Suppliers

Vintage Woodworks
Highway 34 South
P.O. 39, MSC 2534
Quinlan, TX 75474
ph: 903-356-2158
fax: 903-356-3023
mail@vintagewoodworks.com
http://www.vintagewoodworks.com
Sells solid wood gingerbread suitable for Victorian homes: brackets, fretwork, gables, moldings, spandrels, screen doors, window cornices, porch posts, newel posts, balusters, etc.; send $3 for a copy of their 192-page catalog.

ARCHITECTURAL TOYS

(see TOYS, Construction Sets)

ARCHITECTURE & RELATED ITEMS

(see ARCHITECTURAL ELEMENTS; CATALOGS, Trade [Homebuilding]; FRANK LLOYD WRIGHT; HARDWARE; PLANNING ITEMS)

ARCTIC EXPLORERS

Museums/Libraries

Bowdoin College, Peary-MacMillan Arctic Museum
Hubbard Hall
9500 College Station
Brunswick, ME 04011-8495
ph: 207-725-3416
nwagner@bowdoin.edu
http://academic.bowdoin.edu/ arcticmuseum
Named for Arctic explorers &

Bowdoin graduates Robert E. Peary and Donald B. MacMillan, the museum is a center for the study of human cultures and natural environments found in Arctic regions; exploration gear, artifacts, specimens, Inuit.

ARMS & ARMOR

(see also NATIVE AMERICAN, Tomahawks; BAYONETS; EDGED WEAPONS; FIREARMS; HERALDRY; KNIVES; MILITARIA; ORIENTALIA; POWDER HORNS; SWORDS)

Appraisers

Erik Farrow
Erik's Edge
erik@eriksedge.com
http://www.eriksedge.com
Specializes in the appraisal of arms & armour.

Frank Pereny
Saisho International
P.O. Box 176
Spring Grove, PA 17362-0176
ph: 717-225-0176
fax: 717-225-9221
Collector for over 30 years; full-time dealer since 1980; Accredited Member of the International Society of Appraisers.

Auction Services

Christie's
20 Rockefeller Plaza
New York, NY 10020
ph: 212-636-2000
info@christies.com
http://www.christies.com

Sotheby's
1334 York Ave.
New York, NY 10021
ph: 212-606-7000
fax: 212-606-7107
http://www.sothebys.com
Over 70 collecting areas are featured at Sotheby's auctions including toys, dolls, porcelain, furniture, silver, art, books; exhibitions are free and everyone is welcome; for a free copy of "Sotheby's Newsletter," call 212-606-7245.

Bonhams & Butterfields
220 San Bruno Ave.
San Francisco, CA 94103
ph: 415-861-7500 or 800-223-2854
fax: 415-861-8951
info.US@butterfields.com
http://www.butterfields.com
Auctioneers and appraisers of antiques, fine art and collectibles in all categories; specialty sales include posters, toys, decorative arts, furniture, photography, etc.; the largest full service auction in the West.

Roy Butler
Wallis & Wallis
West St. Auction Galleries
Lewes, East Sussex BN7 2NJ U.K.
ph: 01273-480208
fax: 01273-476562
wallisandwallis@mcmail.com
http://www.wallisandwallis.co.uk
Britain's specialist auctioneers of arms, armor, militaria and military orders.

Clubs/Associations

Minnesota Weapons Collectors Association
P.O. Box 662
Hopkins, MN 55343
ph: 612-721-8976
fax: 612-721-8976
info@mwca.org
http://www.mwca.org
For arms collectors: antique arms, edged weapons, modern day arms, ammunition, accessories, accouterments.

Arms & Armour Society, The
P.O. Box 10232
London, SW19 2ZD U.K.
ph: 01323 844278
fax: 01232 449430
edmund@jbgreenwood.force9.co.uk
http://www.armourer.co.uk/arms.htm
To further the study of arms & armour; two journals and four newsletters per year.

Collectors

Jon Lewin
622 Raleigh Ave., Apt. 3
Norfolk, VA 23507-2034
ph: 757-625-6732
Wants worldwide arms and armor: breast & back plates, helmets, swords, shields, spears, halberds, battle axes, clubs, etc. from any culture; also wants cannon, mortars, flintlocks, wheellocks, matchlocks, plug bayonets, cross bows.

Jim Manteris
1613 Barnard Way
Bowling Green, KY 42103
ph: 270-846-4931
manteris@insightbb.com
Specializes in ethnographic weapons from Indonesia, Philippines, India, Africa, any type of club; wants police clubs, saps, billy clubs, blackjacks, brass knuckles, and old knives; also wants African and Asian weapons.

Dealers

Terry Porter
Fine Antique Arms
P.O. Box 870337
Mesquite, TX 75150
ph: 214-679-7418
fax: 972-681-8992
Terry.Porter@FineAntiqueArms.com
http://www.fineantiquearms.com
Dealing in fine antique arms, rapiers, swords, pistols, guns, muskets.

Hal Siegel
TherionArms
P.O. Box 187
Del Valle, TX 78617
ph: 512-247-3578
fax: 512-247-3578 *51
therion@therionarms.com
http://www.therionarms.com
Carries antique and reproduction arms and armor from around the world, with an emphasis on history and education.

Robert B. Miller
LionGate Arms & Armour, Inc.
P.O. Box 14952
Scottsdale, AZ 85267
ph: 480-948-6348
hussar@antiqueswords.com
http://www.antiqueswords.com
Buys and sells fine antique edged weapons and armour; specializes in European swords.

Brian R. Price
Arms & Armour
4226 Cambridge Way
Union City, CA 94587
ph: 650-961-2187
brian@chronique.com
http://www.chronique.com
Arms & armor dealer, expert, repair and reproduction source; Web site focuses on medieval times and has a complete online glossary for arms and armor.

Experts

Charles H. Clements, III
Gryphon Studio
1741 Dallas St.
Aurora, CO 80010-2018
ph: 303-364-0403
fax: 303-739-9824
chas@pcisys.net
http://www.combase.com/~carregal/ kuntao/chas.htm
Appraises and specializes in arms & armor, hunting, gaming, military and leisure material for men, frontier, fur trade and Indian artifacts, etc.

Internet Resources

Brian R. Price
Arms & Armour Glossary of Terms
4226 Cambridge Way
Union City, CA 94587
ph: 650-961-2187
brian@chronique.com
http://www.chronique.com
Web site with extensive glossary of arms & armor terminology.

Museums/Libraries

Higgins Armory Museum
100 Barber Ave.
Worcester, MA 01606-2444
ph: 508-853-6015
fax: 508-852-7697
higgins@higgins.org
http://www.higgins.org
Step in the Higgins Armory Museum and step back in time to medieval and Renaissance Europe, feudal Japan,

and even to the Mediterranean cradles of civilization; has 70 suits of armor - the heroic legacies of another world and time.

Periodicals

Brian R. Price
Journal: Journal of Chivalry, The
4226 Cambridge Way
Union City, CA 94587
ph: 650-961-2187
brian@chronique.com
http://www.chronique.com
A quarterly print journal.

Repair Services

Hal Siegel
TherionArms
P.O. Box 187
Del Valle, TX 78617
ph: 512-247-3578
fax: 512-247-3578 *51
therion@therionarms.com
http://www.therionarms.com
Carries antique and reproduction arms and armor from around the world, with an emphasis on history and education.

Repro. Sources

Pamela Lemieux
Swords n Stuff
123 Wolf Neck Rd.
Freeport, ME 04032
ph: 800-286-4143 or 207-865-3542
fax: 207-865-0385
webmaster@swords-n-stuff.com
http://www.swords-n-stuff.com
Offers a large selection of replica swords, daggers, shields and armor from medieval, Renaissance, Celtic and Roman times.

Iron Guard
155 North May St.
Southern Pines, NC 28387
72774.2240@compuserve.com
http://www.skirmisher.com/
SWORDS.htm
Sells high quality swords from all periods of history.

Museum Replicas Limited
P.O. Box 840
Gees Mill Rd.
Conyers, GA 30012
ph: 800-883-8838
fax: 770-388-0246
mrlcustserve@atlantacutlery.com
http://www.museumreplicas.com
Sells authentic replica edged weapons, battle gear, period clothing; swords, daggers, axes, shields, helmets, tunics, etc.

Kruno Kovacic
Historical Weapons & Stuff
C/Cuenca 15o - 1a
Valencia, AL 46007 Spain
ph: 34-96-3849435
fax: 34-96-3825029
historicalweapons@europe.com
http://www.historicalweapons.com
Carries a large selection of replica handmade arms and armour including

swords, military sabers, dagger, knives, shields, miniature cannon, helmets, Japanese and Oriental swords, ship models, etc.

Japanese

Collectors

Raymond Macy
P.O. Box 11
West Alexandria, OH 45381-0011
ph: 937-839-5721 or 937-839-5203
yarycam@voyager.net
Wants Japanese swords, daggers, sword parts, matchlock guns, anything samurai.

Don Beck
P.O. Box 15305
Fort Wayne, IN 46885-5305
ph: 2609-486-3010
Wants Japanese swords and sword items, guns, medals, daggers, head gear, from any war 1860 to 1945.

Japanese (Swords)

Appraisers

Frank Pereny
Saisho International
P.O. Box 176
Spring Grove, PA 17362-0176
ph: 717-225-0176
fax: 717-225-9221
Collector for over 30 years; full-time dealer since 1980; Accredited Member of the International Society of Appraisers.

Clubs/Associations

John Prough, Sec.
Metropolitan New York Japanese Sword Club/NY Tokenkai
P.O. Box 1119
Rockefeller Center Station
New York, NY 10185
ph: 201-656-0117
jpro@bellatlantic.net
Non-profit corporation dedicated to the study and education of its members and the general public as to the history, culture, and art of the Japanese sword (nihonto) and related items such as tsuba and koshirae; does not do appraisals.

Timothy P. Pepin
Society for the Preservation of Japanese Art Swords, The
Journal: SPJAS Journal
P.O. Box 718
Grant Park, IL 60940
ph: 800-435-5119
samuraisword@attglobal.net
http://www.samuraisword.com
About Japanese swords, tsuba/fittings, rubbing inscription of the tang,, evaluation sheet, items for sale, related links; members receive a Japanese language journal four times per year.

Japanese Sword Society of the United States, Inc.
Newsletter: Japanese Sword Society of U. S. Newsletter
P.O. Box 513
Albuquerque, NM 87103-0513
barry@hennick.ca
http://www.jssus.org
Focuses on the study and preservation of Japanese swords.

Roger W. Davis
Japanese Sword Society of Southern California
1039 Katella
Laguna Beach, CA 92651-3519
rog-di@worldnet.att.net
Formed in the late 1950s to study and appreciate the Arts of the Japanese Sword; meets once a month and publishes a monthly newsletter on various aspects of the Japanese Sword.

San Francisco Japanese Sword Society
P.O. Box 12235
San Francisco, CA 94112
ph: 415-334-7260
fax: 415-334-7260
Sfkatana@aol.com
http://members.aol.com/SFkatana
For the true Japanese sword enthusiast and collector; teaches an understanding of Japanese history, language, philosophy to those with strong commitment, desire and seriousness; free appraisals, inscription readings - send rubbing.

Peter Richards
To-Ken Society of Great Britain, The
23 Suffolk Close
Holland-on-Sea
Essex, CO15 5SQ U.K.
ph: +44 (0) 1255 814388
Peter@to-ken.com
http://www.to-ken.com

Collectors

Hank McGonagle
26 Broad St.
Newburyport, MA 01950-2103
ph: 978-462-2354
saber12@mediaone.net
Seeking edged weapons and Japanese swords.

S.J. Moore
S. J. Moore Jewelers
5 E. Genesee St.
Skaneateles, NY 13152-1317
ph: 315-685-8758
moore90w@adelphia.net
Buys and sells Japanese samurai swords and fittings: tsuba, menuki, fushi, kashira, kogai, kazuka, scabbards.

Robert Navrotski
1024 4th St.
Canonsburg, PA 15317-1910
ph: 724-745-4840
Wants to buy Samurai swords; free information and appraisal.

Greg Souchik
P.O. Box 161
Custer City, PA 16725-0161
ph: 814-362-2642
fax: 814-362-7356
Mg34@mg34.com
http://www.mg34.com
Wants to buy all WWII German and Japanese swords and daggers.

Mark Walberg
P.O. Box 130
Sunbury, PA 17801
ph: 570-286-1617
fax: 570-286-9686
Wants to buy Japanese swords, sword fittings, matchlock rifles, Samurai armor.

Ed Hicks
P.O. Box 42324
Fayetteville, NC 28309
ph: 910-425-7000
edhicks82@aol.com
http://www.warpathmilitaria.com
Wants Japanese swords and armor: daggers, bronzes, iron teapots, helmets, masks, lacquer, matchlock guns, Samurai relics, sword guards, sword fittings, metal work, tea ceremony artifacts and ceramics; free research on Samurai.

R. W. Lightner
P.O. Box 320042
Cocoa Beach, FL 32932-0042
ph: 407-783-0314 or 800-752-6135
Japanese swords and sword items; also guns, medals, daggers, head gear; member NBTHK, Tokyo.

Bill Simmons
181 NW 78th Ave.
Margate, FL 33063
ph: 954-984-9647
wsim1206@aol.com
Wants any and all Japanese and Chinese swords and daggers: military, ivory, Katanas, short, long.

K. Wiley
719 Baldwin SE
Grand Rapids, MI 49503-4470
ph: 616-451-8410
Wants Japanese swords, daggers, sword parts. Also German 3rd Reich daggers, swords, bayonets. References available.

Ron Hartmann
5907 Deerwood Dr.
Saint Louis, MO 63123-2707
ph: 314-832-3477
swords@usroute66.net
Wants to buy Japanese swords, daggers, sword guards, and other parts; over 20 years experience; life member of Japanese Sword Society; always willing to help others realize fair price for their items; send photos and SASE with inquiries.

Dealers

Erik Padison
15127 Frederick Rd.
Rockville, MD 20850-1109
ph: 301-424-0053
elnor57@comcast.net
*Buys, sells, collects, appraises,
specializes in Japanese swords and
militaria.*

Fred Coluzzi
Frederick's Swords
6919 Westview Dr.
Oak Forest, IL 60452-1566
ph: 708-687-3647
fax: 708-687-3695
coluzzi113@aol.com
http://www.frederickantiqueswords.com
*Buys and sells antique swords and
daggers from all countries and all
periods; issues 3 to 4 major catalogs
per year: Japanese, US, German,
Turkish, Moro, Indonesian,
Philippine, Chinese.*

David Pepin
SamuraiSword.com
P.O. Box 718
Grant Park, IL 60940-0718
ph: 800-435-5119 or 815-465-6619
samuraisword@attglobal.net
http://www.samuraisword.com
*Buys, sells, appraises Samurai
swords; Web site contains many good
sword related links; free appraisals -
visit Web site for a sword evaluation
form for your sword.*

Experts

Dale Garbutt
7 St. Paul St., Ste. 1400
Baltimore, MD 21202-1626
ph: 410-347-8710 or 410-358-1228
fax: 410-347-9475
dgarbutt@wtplaw.com
*Collects Japanese swords, sword
fittings, matchlocks, and armor;
member of the Japanese Sword
Society of the US and of The Society of
Japanese Art Swords, Tokyo, Japan;
will provide no-obligation evaluation
by mail or in person.*

Richard Fleming
P.O. Box 8394
Virginia Beach, VA 23450-8394
ph: 757-622-1343 or 757-463-2800 x205
fax: 757-463-3052
rfleming@milcom-systems.com
*Specializes in Japanese swords
brought back by our veterans and
servicemen; also interested in WWII
Army Air Force, Troop Carrier
Command, and Airborne items; free
translation of signed swords; book
about 1868-1945 swords available.*

David McDonald
P.O. Box 265
Sidney, MT 59270
ph: 406-482-3243
jswords@mcn.net
http://www.mcn.net/~jswords
*Collector, dealer, expert in Japanese
swords; swords and fittings bought,*
sold appraised and repaired;
specializes in Japanese sword Tsuka-
maki (hilt wrapping) services.*

Jim Kurrasch
1039 Katella
Laguna Beach, CA 92651-3519
rog-di@worldnet.att.net
*Specializes in Japanese swords and
some Japanese armor and fittings;
does not sell or charge for services.*

Fred Lohman
Fred Lohman Co.
3405 N.E. Broadway
Portland, OR 97232
ph: 503-282-4567
fax: 503-287-2678
lohman@katana4u.com
http://www.Japanese-Swords.com
*The ultimate source for parts and
supplies relating to the restoration
and maintenance of the Japanese
sword; restoration service backed up
with 30 years of Nihon-to experience
(references available.)*

Internet Resources

Richard Stein
Japanese Sword, The
P.O. Box 339
Locust Grove, VA 22508
http://home.earthlink.net/~steinrl
*Japanese sword history, care,
illustrated glossary, articles, clubs,
sword sites, Japanese military swords,
sword care, martial arts, etc.; links to
related sites that contain great
research information about swords.*

David McDonald
Nihonto Classified Ad Web Page, The
P.O. Box 265
Sidney, MT 59720
ph: 406-482-3243
jswords@mcn.net
http://www.montanairon.com
*A free service for posting for sale ads
and wanted ads for all Japanese
swords and related items.*

David Pepin
SamuraiSword.com
P.O. Box 718
Grant Park, IL 60940-0718
ph: 800-435-5119 or 815-465-6619
samuraisword@attglobal.net
http://www.samuraisword.com
*Buys, sells, appraises Samurai
swords; Web site contains many good
sword related links.*

Alan Quinn
Nihonto - Japanese Sword
U.K.
alan@meiboku.demon.co.uk
http://www.meiboku.demon.co.uk
*Provides a wealth of information
about Japanese swords.*

Man./Prod./Dist.

Fred Lohman
Fred Lohman Co.
3405 N.E. Broadway
Portland, OR 97232
ph: 503-282-4567
fax: 503-287-2678
lohman@katana4u.com
http://www.Japanese-Swords.com
*Thirty years as a "hands on"
manufacturer of all Japanese sword
parts.*

Museums/Libraries

Museum of Fine Arts, Boston
465 Huntington Ave.
Boston, MA 02115-5523
ph: 617-267-9300
webmaster@mfa.org
http://www.mfa.org
*Home to more than 500 swords and
thousands of sword fittings.*

Repair Services

David McDonald
P.O. Box 265
Sidney, MT 59270
ph: 406-482-3243
jswords@mcn.net
http://www.mcn.net/~jswords
*Collector, dealer, expert in Japanese
swords; swords and fittings bought,
sold appraised and repaired;
specializes in Japanese sword Tsuka-
maki (hilt wrapping) services.*

Bushido Japanese Sword Polishing &
Restoration
P.O. Box 61783
Honolulu, HI 96839
ph: 808-988-9908
fax: 808-988-9908
bushidoswd@aol.com
http://togishi.com
*Specializes in Japanese sword
polishing and restoration.*

Fred Lohman
Fred Lohman Co.
3405 N.E. Broadway
Portland, OR 97232
ph: 503-282-4567
fax: 503-287-2678
lohman@katana4u.com
http://www.Japanese-Swords.com
*The ultimate source for parts and
supplies relating to the restoration
and maintenance of the Japanese
sword; restoration service backed up
with 30 years of Nihon-to experience
(references available.)*

Suppliers

Fred Lohman
Fred Lohman Co.
3405 N.E. Broadway
Portland, OR 97232
ph: 503-282-4567
fax: 503-287-2678
lohman@katana4u.com
http://www.Japanese-Swords.com
*America's major supplier of all
domestic and imported sword*
supplies, materials and maintenance
items.*

Miniature

Clubs/Associations

Carmen A. Gianforte, Pres.
Miniature Arms Collectors/Makers
  Society
Magazine: Miniature Arms Journal
6156 Bonaventure Ct.
Sarasota, FL 34243-4805
ph: 041-351-9421
gin40@msn.com
http://www.miniaturearms.com
*Dedicated to the making, collecting,
and sharing of information on all
types of miniature arms.*

Dealers

Joel Morrow
Imperial Miniature Armory
10547 S. Post Oak
Houston, TX 77035
ph: 713-729-8424 or 800-MINIATURE
fax: 713-729-2274
miniguns@direcway.com
http://www.1800miniature.com
*Worlds largest maker and distributor
of high quality miniature arms and
armor.*

Experts

Joel Morrow
Imperial Miniature Armory
10547 S. Post Oak
Houston, TX 77035
ph: 713-729-8424 or 800-MINIATURE
fax: 713-729-2274
miniguns@direcway.com
http://www.1800miniature.com
*Author of "The Art of Miniature
Firearms."*

ARROWHEADS & POINTS

(see NATIVE AMERICAN;
ARCHAEOLOGY; PREHISTORIC
ARTIFACTS, Arrowheads & Points)

ART

(see also AFRICAN & TRIBAL ART;
ANIMATION FILM ART; BRONZES;
CARTOON ART; FOLK ART;
FRAMES; ILLUSTRATORS;
ORIENTALIA; PAINTINGS &
DRAWINGS; PERSONALITIES
[ARTISTS]; PIN UP ART; PRINTS;
PRINTS [MODERN]; REPAIR/
RESTORATION/CONSERVATION,
Art; SCULPTURE)

Appraisers

AsktheAppraiser.com
4 Brussels St.
Worcester, MA 01610
ph: 781-821-0199
ata@collectingchannel.com
http://www.AsktheAppraiser.com
*The premiere online appraisal service
offered by CollectingChannel.com; all
appraisals comply with the "Uniform
Standards of Professional Appraisal*

Practice" and with the standards of the Association of Online Appraisers.

Peter C. Sorlien, ASA
Accredited Appraisers
17 1/2 State St.
Marblehead, MA 01945-3536
ph: 781-631-5956
fax: 781-631-6550
appraisr@shore.net
Professional art and marine appraisals; experience with divorce, donation, estate, insurance, litigation, and tax matters; does not buy or sell.

S. Lamont McEvitt
Farmington Fine Arts, LLC
P.O. Box 1413
Farmington, CT 06033-1413
ph: 860-676-9996
fax: 860-678-7327
lmcevitt@farmingtonfinearts.com
http://www.farmingtonfinearts.com
Fine art appraiser specializing in American art and works by black American artists; considered an expert on Charles Ethan Porter; president of a fine arts auction house.

Patricia Sheeleigh
Patricia Sheeleigh Fine Arts
39 Old Eagle Rock Ave.
Roseland, NJ 07068-1433
ph: 973-228-4362
fax: 973-228-6509
SheeleighAndCleaver@compuserve.com
Appraises 18th through 20th century American and European paintings, prints, watercolors; Impressionists are a specialty.

Zia Ghahary, ISA CAPP, AAA
AAA Appraisals
240 Heather Lane
Franklin Lakes, NJ 07414-1111
ph: 201-337-5577 or 888-299-5577
fax: 201-337-0404
Zghahary@aol.com
Specializes in the appraisal of paintings, sculptures, manuscripts, miniature paintings, furniture, Orientalia, European and American rugs and tapestry, antiquities; Middle Eastern Egyptian, Islamic and Judaica Art.

Carolyn Remmey, Pres.
Remmey Antiques & Fine Art
P.O. Box 197
New Vernon, NJ 07960
ph: 212-427-2500 or 305-296-6546 (FL)
remmey@rcn.com
Specializes in the sale and appraisal of fine art.

M. Barden Prisant, FRICS
Telepraisal
32 Union Sq., #1016
New York, NY 10003
ph: 212-614-9090 or 800-645-6002
fax: 212-780-9539
info@telepraisal.com
http://www.telepraisal.com
For over 21 years, Telepraisal has been gathering pricing data on approximately 200,000 artists and

sales of their works; printouts of the data can be purchased for $35 per search, or more formal appraisals can be generated.

Debra J. Force
Debra Force Fine Art, Inc.
14 E. 73rd St., #4B
New York, NY 10021
ph: 212-734-3636
fax: 212-734-1042
debra@debraforce.com
http://www.debraforce.com
Specializes in the appraisal of American paintings, drawings, prints and sculpture of the 19th through 20th centuries.

Denise J. Levy
Art Find Associates, Inc.
135 Central Park West, Ste. 2 South
New York, NY 10023
ph: 212-595-5267
fax: 212-595-7666
djjl@nyc.rr.com
Fine art appraiser specializing in Modern and Contemporary art of all media: site-specific, prints, paintings, sculpture, unique works on paper; appraisals for insurance, charitable gift, estate planning, division of property.

Ellen J. Epstein
AARC Group
33 Park Dr..
Mount Kisco, NY 10549
ph: 914-666-7690
fax: 914-242-0232
ee27@erols.com
http://www.theartappraiser.com
Specializes in the appraisal of contemporary Russian art, sporting art, American paintings, drawings, sculpture, multiples, and in fine art in general.

James Martin
Marmargar
32 Maple St.
Broadalbin, NY 12025
ph: 518-883-3354 or 518-866-9181
mmartin5@nycap.rr.com
Appraises, repairs, restores, conserves all fine art: canvas, paper and mixed medium; all work is museum quality and fully insured; member of the ISA and the American Institute for Conservation of Historic & Artistic Works (AIC).

Dr. Charles J. Semowich
Charles Semowich Fine Arts
242 Broadway
Rensselaer, NY 12144-2705
ph: 518-449-4756
semowich@att.net
Appraiser of art, antiques and decorative arts.

Glenn A. Long
Long & Manzi Fine Art Services, Inc.
ph: 518-854-3388
fax: 518-854-3999
topappraisers@hotmail.com
Private dealers and appraisers

serving collectors and museums for over 25 years; specializes in art, drawings, paintings, photography & photographs, 19th and 20th century sculpture, African, Native American, Precolumbian.

Pamela E. Mayo, ISA
710 Washington St.
Sewickley, PA 15143-1845
ph: 412-749-0760 or 412-390-3707
fax: 412-390-3708
pandjr@usaor.net
Fine art appraiser (paintings, drawings, prints, sculpture), specializing in 19th and early 20th century American art with a general background in 18th-20th century American and European art; specializes in sporting art and Southern art.

Cecilia Gillespie, ISA CAPP
Perry Arts, The
212 Pine Court
Pittsburgh, PA 15237
ph: 412-364-8500 or 412-364-3063
fax: 412-364-3063
perryart@aol.com
Certified Member of the International Society of Appraisers; Certified, Professional Picture Framers Association; specializing in appraising fine art; restoration services, conservation services.

Rochelle Eisenberg, ASA
Art Directives, Inc.
455 Pennsylvania Ave., Ste 130
Fort Washington, PA 19034
ph: 215-646-0233
fax: 215-646-1894
info@artdirectives.com
http://www.artdirectives.com
Appraiser, consultant, writer, lecturer, author, advisor for Montgomery County newspapers, appeared on "Chubb Antiques Roadshow," instructor at Temple University.

Randall C. Hunt
Fine Arts Appraisals
3503 Fulton St., NW
Washington, DC 20007-1438
ph: 202-333-4035
randallhunt@starpower.net
Specializes in the appraisal of fine art including American and European 18th through 20th century paintings, prints and sculpture; Certified Appraiser, Appraisers Association of America.

Edwin W. Baker, Ex. VP
American Society of Appraisers
P.O. Box 17265
Washington, DC 20071
ph: 703-478-2228 or 800-272-8258
fax: 703-742-8471
asainfo@appraisers.org
http://www.appraisers.org
The only appraisal organization in the US representing all the disciplines of appraisal specialists; call 800-ASA-VALU for free referral or membership directory, or visit Web site.

P. Raab Christhilff
Alex Cooper Auctioneers, Inc.
908 York Rd.
Baltimore, MD 21204
ph: 410-828-4838
fax: 410-828-0875
info@alexcooper.com
http://www.alexcooper.com
Specializes in the appraisal and auction sale of fine art.

Association of Online Appraisers, Inc.
P.O. Box 2049
Frederick, MD 21702-1049
ph: 301-228-2279
fax: 301-695-6491
info@AOAonline.org
http://www.AOAonline.org
Not-for-profit association for online as well as traditional appraisers; establishes standards of appraisal ethics & professional practice; offers 550+ page "Complete Online Course in Personal Property Appraising" free to members.

Melanie Smith, ISA
Seaside Art Gallery
2716 Virginia Dare Trail South
P.O. Box 1
Nags Head, NC 27959-0001
ph: 252-441-5418 or 800-828-2444
fax: 252-441-8563
info@seasideart.com
http://www.seasideart.com
Accredited member of the International Society of Appraisers; specializes in fine art (paintings, graphics, sculpture) and animation art.

Luke Biggs
L. L. Biggs Conservator
P.O. Box 3091
Summerville, SC 29484-3091
ph: 843-851-9293
fax: 843-873-0165
biggsconservator@msn.com
Appraises and restores fine art and frames.

William Gordon
Gordon's Fine Art
5665 Highway 9, Ste. 103
Alpharetta, GA 30004
ph: 678-777-9034
fax: 770-569-1255
bill@gordonsfineart.com
http://www.gordonsfineart.com
Specializes in the sale and appraisal of fine art paintings and prints by listed 20th century artists; Associate Member of the International Society of Appraisers specializing in the appraisal of fine art, paintings, and prints.

Mark Moore
Regency Fine Art
6458 Dawson Blvd.
Norcross, GA 30093
ph: 770-840-7701
fax: 770-840-7721
mark@regencyfineart.com
http://www.regencyfineart.com
Specializes in the appraisal of 20th

century works on paper (serigraphs, lithographs, watercolors), original oils and bronze sculpture.

Mark Alexander, ISA
Art Services 2000 Ltd., Co.
P.O. Box 1205
New Smyrna Beach, FL 32170
ph: 386-428-2980 or 386-748-3531
fax: 386-428-2981
artserv2000@yahoo.com
http://www.artservices2000.com
Fine art consulting, documentation, research, appraisals, curatorial services; also offers fine art packing and transportation services; appraisals for insurance, charitable donation, liquidation, equitable distribution, estate planning.

Richard Carta, Administrator
International Association of Fine Art Appraisers
6401 East Rogers Circle, Ste. 9
Boca Raton, FL 33487
ph: 561-997-8007 x203
fax: 561-997-6653
artpikr@artpickers.com

Joan Kropf
16111 Redington Dr.
Saint Petersburg, FL 33708
ph: 727-399-1915
rljk@ij.net
Specializes in the appraisal of Salvador Dali art and in 19th and 20th century.

William C. Tregoning, III
Tregoning Fine Art & Services
100 North Main St.
Chagrin Falls, OH 44022
ph: 440-247-1690
fax: 440-247-6180
tfas@multiverse.com
http://www.tregoningfas.com
Specializes in works of art from 1700 to 1950, with special emphasis on art created in Northern Ohio from 1880 to 1950; appraisals prepared in conformance with USPAP and the American Society of Appraisers standards.

James Corcoran, ISA
Corcoran Fine Arts Limited, Inc.
2915 Fairfax Rd.
Cleveland, OH 44118-4015
ph: 216-431-0025 or 216-397-0777
fax: 216-397-0222
corcoranfa@aol.com
http://www.corcoranfinearts.com
Appraises European, American, Canadian and Latin American art: paintings, drawings, prints, sculpture; Renaissance to Contemporary; also contemporary glass appraisals.

Caroline Ashleigh
Caroline Ashleigh Associates, Inc.
800 E. Lincoln
Birmingham, MI 48009
ph: 248-613-4056
fax: 248-792-2545
carolineashleigh@appraiseyourart.com
http://www.appraiseyourart.com
Specializes in professional appraisals of fine art, antiques, textiles, residential contents; participating appraiser in the "Antiques Roadshow;" Certified Senior Member and Regional Representative of the Appraisers Association of America.

Patricia M. Knight
Finetooth Comb Antiques Research & Appraisal Service
P.O. Box 1177
Ames, IA 50014-1177
ph: 515-292-9028
ftcres@aol.com
Consultant and qualified appraiser of 19th century and early 20th century oil paintings; also Oriental images on paper; please send SASE for reply; does not purchase; send SASE if requesting return of photos.

Dennis Tesdell
Fine Art Investments
150 S. Prairie View Dr., Unit 401
West Des Moines, IA 50266
ph: 515-226-0606
fax: 515-226-1121
dennis@fineartinvestments.org
http://www.fineartinvestments.org
Appraisers of fine art and antiques for insurance, divorce, estate purposes; since 1973; brokerage services for collectors, heirs and others for most types of high quality fine art and antiques.

Daniel Erickson, ISA
Dan Erickson & Associates
1023 Grand Ave., #2
Saint Paul, MN 55105
ph: 651-276-7930
danielerickson@msn.com
http://www.fabulousfindsestatesales.com
Specializes in the appraisal of art, silver, arts & crafts.

Jacqueline McMillan
McMillan Appraisal Group, Inc.
3340 Brownlow Ave.
Minneapolis, MN 55426
ph: 952-926-1000 or 612-423-1323
fax: 612-339-8691
jmcmillan@mcmillanappraisals.com
Over 12 years experience in the appraisal of fine art.

Frederick P. Dose, Jr.
Frederick Dose Appraisals Ltd.
778 Pleasant Ave.
Highland Park, IL 60035-4613
ph: 847-433-7870 or 847-433-1090
fdoseappraisals@comcast.net
Appraises US, British, Continental paintings and furniture, prints, porcelain, silver, decorative arts, coins, antiquities; for corporate, private, and attorneys; references on

request; 6 year full-time as University art historian.

Victoria L. Scogland
Victoria L. Scogland Fine Art, Inc.
414 West Deerpath Rd.
Lake Forest, IL 60045
ph: 847-6151-1098
fax: 847-615-1132
vscogland@aol.com
Fine art appraiser, consultant, dealer.

Sybil Tillman, ISA
Artco Inc.
3013 Harrow Gate Dr.
Woodstock, IL 60098-7410
ph: 815-338-3600
SybilTillman@msn.com
http://www.e-Artco.com
Specializing in fine art appraisals and research; also buying and selling 19th and 20th century, Old Masters, important and contemporary American artists and American Indian Art; Accredited member of the ISA, Member of AAA.

Robert H. McHarg
Fine Arts Gallery of New Orleans, The
636 Burdette St.
New Orleans, LA 70118
ph: 504-866-4287
fax: 504-866-4287
fineartsgallery@yahoo.com
http://www.fineartsgallery.com
Specializes in the appraisal of paintings, graphics, watercolors, drawings, sculpture; American & European; 17th through 20th centuries.

Jody Kerr
Jody Kerr Antiques & Fine Art
7908 North Western
Oklahoma City, OK 73114
ph: 405-842-5951
okcjokerr@earthlink.net
Specializes in the appraisal of fine art, porcelains and furniture.

Brenda Mohle, ISA CAPP
Signet Art
2211 High Point Dr.
Carrollton, TX 75007-1705
ph: 972-306-1963 or 972-849-3053
fax: 972-306-1963
signetart@attbi.com
http://www.signetart.com
Appraiser of prints, paintings, drawings, sculptures and other fine art.

Beth Szescila, ISA CAPP
Szescila Appraisal Services
224 Birdsall
Houston, TX 77007
ph: 713-869-4088
fax: 713-869-3728
BethSzescila@ev1.net
http://www.houstonappraiser.net
Specializes in the appraisal of antiques and fine art.

Rachel Pabst, ISA CAPP
Rachel Pabst Estate Sales & Appraisal Associates
ph: 713-626-0179
fax: 713-877-8087
r_pabst@yahoo.com
Certified appraiser specializing in fine art and Americana; over 16 years experience; Attingham, Winterthur Institute, Bayou Bend docent, Sotheby's and Christie's courses.

Genae Fields, ISA
Image One International
16126 Rainbow Lake Rd.
Houston, TX 77095-4053
ph: 281-856-8866
fax: 281-550-8618
gfields@imageoneinternational.com
http://www.imageoneinternational.com
Specializes in 19th and 20th century art: Impressionist, Modern, Contemporary; also 20th century sculpture.

Cecily Horton
MKG Art Management
2825 Colquitt
Houston, TX 77098
ph: 713-526-4146
ceh@mkgart.com
http://www.mkgart.com
Specializes in the appraisal of European and American fine art including paintings, sculpture, and works on paper; also provides inventory management and acquisition advice on an hourly fee basis.

Suzanne Staley, ISA CAPP
Fine Art & Antiques Appraiser
P.O. Box 1288
Houston, TX 77251-1288
ph: 713-222-6309 or 888-758-1118
fax: 713-223-3116
suzanne@suzannestaley.com
http://www.suzannestaley.com
Specializes in the appraisal of fine art including paintings, prints, drawings, sculpture; American as well as European; also religious art, folk art, outsider art.

Richard Casagrande, ISA CAPP
Casagrande Appraisals
8546 Broadway, Ste. 203
San Antonio, TX 78217
ph: 210-820-3097
fax: 210-820-3097
rlcasagrande@sbcglobal.net
Appraiser specializing in 19th century American art; also the art of Texas and the San Antonio region.

Carol O'Brien English, PhD, ASA
I.C., Inc.
9920 West 34th Dr.
Wheat Ridge, CO 80033-5764
ph: 303-238-2882
fax: 303-238-1617
drenglish@attbi.com
http://www.appraisers.org/pages/
   memberpage.cfm?id=10178
Specializes in appraising Spanish, European, and American art; also

Spanish colonial fine and decorative arts; Accredited Senior Appraiser.

Jan Wilson
Jan Wilson Gallery
P.O. Box 6649
Ketchum, ID 83340
ph: 208-622-7799
fax: 208-726-5975
Specializes in appraising fine art, prints & sculpture.

Corinne Cain, ISA, ASA
Corinne Cain Ltd.
326 West Harmont Dr.
Phoenix, AZ 85021
ph: 602-906-1633
fax: 602-906-0677
corinne@savvycollector.com
http://www.savvycollector.com
A veteran art appraiser for over 25 years selling fine art and Native American arts online; guaranteed condition, authenticity verified, value is assured; Accredited Senior Appraiser, Certified Appraiser of Personal Property.

Elizabeth Dore, ISA
ABD Antique Appraisers
5809 West Glendale Ave.
Glendale, AZ 85301
ph: 623-931-0235
fax: 623-931-0235
medore@mindspring.com
Specializes in the appraisal of paintings and prints, Western art from the 20th century; appraisals for personal, IRS and legal purposes; entire estate appraisals making use of a team of specialists.

Jnanideva Shanmuga
Appraisal & Connoisseur Associates
620 Sierra Dr. SE
Albuquerque, NM 87108-3377
ph: 505-265-2842
jshan@nmia.com
Appraisers, artists and brokers serving the Southwest in painting, prints and sculpture; also appraise residential contents nationwide.

Joanna S. Stearns, ISA CAPP, GG
J. Stearns & Associates
7412 Silver Palm Ave.
Las Vegas, NV 89117-1442
ph: 702-360-8991
fax: 702-360-8938
joannastearns@earthlink.net
Specializes in the appraisal of fine art, residential contents, and gems & jewelry.

Kathleen DeBolt, ISA
Debolt Fine Art
18353 Sycamore Creek Rd.
Escondido, CA 92025-2302
ph: 858-676-5913 or 619-857-5913
fineart@adnc.com
http://www.onlineartline.com
Specializes in the appraisal of 19th and 20th century American Art, California Impressionism, American scene, New Mexico modernists, Western art.

Fran Preisman
Fran Preisman Fine Art
1626 Buckingham Dr.
La Jolla, CA 92037
ph: 858-459-2684
fax: 858-459-0480
Appraises paintings, drawings, prints, sculpture.

Patricia Saultman, ISA CAPP
Patricia Saultman & Associates
309 Willow Ave.
Corte Madera, CA 94925
ph: 415-788-3344
fax: 415-788-3344
Specializes in the appraisal of European and American paintings, prints and sculpture; also English, European, French and American furniture.

Nancy Burke Bosch, ISA
Bosch Appraisal Service
1610 Northstar Dr.
Petaluma, CA 94954-6607
ph: 707-773-3970
fax: 707-773-3974
nbbosch@pacbell.net
http://www.appraiseyourantiques.com
Specializes in appraising European & American furniture, fine art, decorative art & accessories, china, crystal, silver, American wicker, quilts, linen, other textiles, other appreciable residential contents; consultations, estate sales.

Linda Dunn
Dunn & Associates
8724 McCarty Ranch Dr.
San Jose, CA 95135
ph: 408-223-1095
fax: 408-223-1095
tpart@aol.com
http://www.art-appraiser.com
Specializes in 19th and 20th century European and American paintings, contemporary limited edition prints, and frescos and murals.

Mandy Sabbadini, ISA
Sabbadini Appraisal Services
P.O. Box 2476
Carmichael, CA 95609
ph: 916-944-1401
fax: 916-944-1236
mandysab@hotmail.com
Specializes in the appraisal of fine art; also residential contents and collectibles.

Richard C. Frey, ISA CAPP
R.T.L.H. Enterprises
1275 East Ave.
Chico, CA 95926-1020
ph: 530-343-4528 or 800-567-7854
fax: 530-343-9380
RFREYRTLH@aol.com
http://www.richardcfreyfineart.com
Certified appraiser of American and European art, paintings, watercolors, drawings, prints, sculpture, bronzes, etc.; appraises for estates, arbitration, and has testified as expert witness.

Susanne L. Gavigan, ISA, CPF
Artiques Appraisal Service
16425 Trail Dr.
Redding, CA 96001
ph: 530-244-2100 or 530-244-6147
fax: 530-244-0166
gartiques@aol.com
http://www.appraisalsbyrequest.com
Art dealer, expert, collector, conservator and appraiser since 1970: paintings, water colors, drawings, etchings, original prints, sculpture, etc.; Accredited Member of the International Society of Appraisers;

Scott Zema, ISA CAPP
Ark Limited Appraisals, Inc.
ph: 425-486-6310
scottzema@msn.com
http://www.arklimited.com
Appraises private and institutional art and art collections; also offers art investment advisory and consultation.

International Society of Appraisers
Newsletter: Professional Appraisers Information Exchange
1131 SW 7th St., Ste. 105
Renton, WA 98055
ph: 206-241-0359 or 888-472-4732
fax: 206-241-0436
ISA@isa-appraisers.org
http://www.isa-appraisers.org
Largest assoc. of professional appraisers devoted solely to personal property; over 1,300 members specializing in all areas of antiques & residential contents, gems & jewelry, fine art, machinery & equipment; member directory on Web site.

Lorraine Pierce-Hull, ISA
Pierce-Hull Art Appraisers & Advisors
23 Seaforth Rd.
Kingston, Ontario K7M 1E1 Canada
ph: 613-542-2228 or 877-205-5866
fax: 613-542-1474
piercehull@sympatico.ca
Appraiser of Canadian and European paintings, textiles, sculpture, photographs and prints.

Edith Yeomans, ASA
Appraisal Associates
80 Richmond St. West, Ste. 1101
Toronto, Ontario M5H 2A4 Canada
ph: 416-368-4334
fax: 416-368-6679
emy@appraisalassociates.ca
http://www.appraise.org
Specialist in the valuation of fine art, antiques, decorative art, including Canadian, American and European art.

Stephen P. Sweeting, ASA
Appraisal Associates Consulting Inc.
80 Richmond St. West, Ste. 1101
Toronto, Ontario M5H 2A4 Canada
ph: 416-368-4334
fax: 416-368-6679
sps@appraisalassociates.ca
http://www.appraise.org
Specialist in the valuation of fine art, antiques, decorative art, including

Canadian, American and European art.

Graham Ospreay
G. P. Ospreay & Associates
76 Eves Court
Newmarket, Ontario L3Y 7P4 Canada
ph: 905-895-2699 or 416-819-6218
fax: 905-895-1582
gospreay@rogers.com
Specializes in the appraisal of fine art including works on paper, prints and paintings; authentication services, forensic document examination, forgery & counterfeit identification, art & document security analysis.

Sharon London Liss
Sharon London Liss, Inc.
Canada
ph: 416-444-0075
fax: 416-444-1176
s.londonliss@rogers.com
Specializes in the appraisal of 20th century fine art and in large corporate collections being reintroduced to the secondary market.

Kathleen Laverty, ISA
Laverty Fine Art
P.O. Box 47055
Denman Place
Vancouver, British Columbia V5G 1J3 U.K.
ph: 604-602-0440
klaverty@shaw.ca
http://www.lavertyfineart.ca
Specializes in the appraisal of contemporary and historical Canadian art in all mediums: paintings, sculpture, prints, drawings.

David Peckman
U.K.
dpeckman@btinternet.com
Specializes in the appraisal of European and American art, primarily works on paper including prints, photography, drawings, and watercolors from the 20th and 21st centuries.

Auction Services

Michael B. Grogan
Grogan & Company Auctioneers
22 Harris St.
Dedham, MA 02026
ph: 781-461-9500
fax: 781-461-9625
grogans@groganco.com
http://www.groganco.com
Auctioneer and appraiser specializing in 18th through 20th century American & European paintings, sculpture, oriental rugs, and fine silver; accepts consignments year round for two semi-annual sales.

Willis Henry
Willis Henry Auctions, Inc.
22 Main St.
Marshfield, MA 02050
ph: 781-834-7774 or 800-244-8466
fax: 781-826-3520
wha@willishenry.com
http://www.willishenry.com
*Specializes in the sale of American
antiques of all kinds, particularly
Shaker, American Indian and Early
American.*

Colleene Fesko
Skinner, Inc.
63 Park Plaza
The Heritage on the Garden
Boston, MA 02116
ph: 617-350-5400
fax: 617-350-5429
info@skinnerinc.com
http://www.skinnerinc.com
*Established in 1971, Skinner Inc. is
the fourth largest auction house in the
US; has offices in Boston and Bolton,
MA.*

Philip C. Shute
Shute Auction Gallery
850 W. Chestnut St.
Brockton, MA 02401
ph: 508-588-0022 or 508-588-7833
fax: 508-559-6687
*Antique and custom furniture, art,
silver, glass and china, collectibles,
etc.*

George M. Young
Young Fine Arts Auctions, Inc.
P.O. Box 313
North Berwick, ME 03906
ph: 207-676-3104
fax: 207-676-3105
*Complete no-frills online art auction
catalogs; every lot illustrated with
jpeg image; prices listed after each
auction; four to five auctions per year;
specializes in pre-1950 American &
European paintings.*

S. Lamont McEvitt
Farmington Fine Arts, LLC
P.O. Box 1413
Farmington, CT 06033-1413
ph: 860-676-9996
fax: 860-678-7327
lmcevitt@farmingtonfinearts.com
http://www.farmingtonfinearts.com
*Conducts auction sales of 19th and
20th century fine art.*

Gene Shannon
Shannon's Fine Art Auctioneers
354 Woodmont Rd.
Milford, CT 06460
ph: 203-877-1711
fax: 203-877-1719
info@shannons.com
http://www.shannons.com
*Specializes in the auction sale of
American and European paintings,
bronzes and prints of the late 19th
century to early 20th century.*

Caroline Birenbaum
Swann Galleries, Inc.
104 E. 25th St.
New York, NY 10010-2977
ph: 212-254-4710
fax: 212-979-1017
swann@swanngalleries.com
http://www.swanngalleries.com
*Oldest/largest US auctioneer
specializing in rare books, autographs
& manuscripts, maps, atlases,
photographs, and works of art on
paper including vintage posters.*

Phillips de Pury & Luxembourg
450 West 15th St.
New York, NY 10011
ph: 212-940-1200
fax: 212-688-1647
inquiry.desk@phillips-dpl.com
http://www.phillips-dpl.com
*Specializes in the auction sale of
American art, Contemporary art,
Impressionist and Modern art,
jewelry, photographs, and 20th and
21st century Modern design.*

Christie's
20 Rockefeller Plaza
New York, NY 10020
ph: 212-636-2000
info@christies.com
http://www.christies.com

Sotheby's
1334 York Ave.
New York, NY 10021
ph: 212-606-7000
fax: 212-606-7107
http://www.sothebys.com

Amory Spizzirri, Client Svc.
William Doyle Galleries
175 E. 87th St.
New York, NY 10128-2205
ph: 212-427-2730
fax: 212-369-0892
info@doylegalleries.com
http://www.doylegalleries.com
*Holds over 50 auctions annually of
furniture and decorations, paintings
and sculpture, jewelry, books and
prints, couture and textiles, 20th
century art & design, majolica,
Lalique, Asian works of art and other
specialty categories.*

Nicole Arnn
Weschler's
909 E St. NW
Washington, DC 20004-2006
ph: 202-628-1281 or 800-331-1430
fax: 202-628-2366
fineart@weschlers.com
http://www.weschlers.com
*Conducts specialized auction sales of
art, paintings, prints and graphics.*

Frank Boos
Frank H. Boos Gallery, Inc.
420 Enterprise Court
Bloomfield Hills, MI 48302
ph: 248-332-1500
fax: 248-332-6370
artandauction@boosgallery.com
http://www.boosgallery.com
*Specializes in the auction and
appraisal of fine art, antiques and
decorative arts.*

Coeur d'Alene Art Auction
P.O. Box 310
Hayden, ID 83835
ph: 208-772-9009
fax: 208-772-8294
drumgallery@nidlink.com
http://www.cdaartauction.com
*Specializes in quality Western and
wildlife paintings 1840-1940.*

Julia Walker
Spink & Son, Ltd.
69 Southampton Row
Bloomsbury
London, WC1B 4ET U.K.
ph: +44 (0) 20 7563 4000
fax: +44 (0) 20 7563 4066
info@spinkandson.com
http://www.spink-online.com
*Auctioneers and dealers of coins
(ancient to present), banknotes,
medals, orders, tokens, decorations
and other numismatic items; also
stamps and postal history as well as
fine European, Indian and Islamic art.*

Clubs/Associations

Archaeological Institute of America
Magazine: Archaeology
656 Beacon St.
Boston, MA 02215-2006
ph: 617-353-9361
fax: 617-353-6550
aia@aia.bu.edu
http://www.archaeological.org
*Has phone numbers and addresses for
all state archaeological departments;
"Archaeology" is published bi-
monthly; also publishes the
"American Journal of Archaeology"
quarterly; write for details.*

National Antique & Art Dealers
Association of America
220 East 57th St.
New York, NY 10022
ph: 212-826-9707
fax: 212-832-9493
naadaa@dir-dd.com
http://www.dir-dd.com/naadaa.html
*Trade group represents art and
antique dealers; sponsors antique and
art exhibitions; promotes ethical trade
practices among its members; free
membership directory available.*

Donna Carlson, Dir.
Art Dealers Association of America
575 Madison Ave.
New York, NY 10022-2511
ph: 212-940-8590
fax: 212-940-6484
adaa@artdealers.org
http://www.artdealers.org
*Non-profit organization of nation's
leading dealers in fine art.*

Sharon Flescher, Ex. Dir.
International Foundation for Art
Research (IFAR)
Magazine: IFAR Journal
500 Fifth Ave., Ste 935
New York, NY 10110
ph: 212-391-6234
fax: 212-391-8794
kferg@ifar.org
http://www.ifar.org
*Clearinghouse for information on art
theft, fraud, forgery; promotes
recovery of stolen art & prevention of
circulation of forged works; publishes
Stolen Art Alert notices of art thefts
and recoveries; organizes lectures.*

International Association for Professional Art Advisors
433 Third St., Ste.
Brooklyn, NY 11212
ph: 888-682-2722 or 718-788-1425
fax: 804-391-3730
*Professional organization committed
to developing and maintaining high
ethical standards among its members
as well as the art advisory profession
at large; members are qualified to
provide guidance in art acquisition,
deacquisition, etc.*

American Association of Museums
1575 Eye St., Ste. 400
Washington, DC 20005
ph: 202-289-1818
fax: 202-289-6578
aaminfo@aam-us.org
http://www.aam-us.org
*A professional society of museums
which has established an accrediting
system for museums.*

Association of Online Appraisers, Inc.
P.O. Box 2049
Frederick, MD 21702-1049
ph: 301-228-2279
fax: 301-695-6491
info@AOAonline.org
http://www.AOAonline.org
*Not-for-profit association for online
as well as traditional appraisers;
establishes standards of appraisal
ethics & professional practice; offers
550+ page "Complete Online Course
in Personal Property Appraising" free
to members.*

N. J. Fregin
American Society of Artists, Inc.
Newsletter: Art Lovers & Craft Fair
    Bulletin
P.O. Box 1326
Palatine, IL 60078
ph: 312-751-2500 or 847-991-4748
asoa@webtv.net
http://www.americansocietyofartists.com
*National professional membership
organization; membership is juried,
with a crafts division - American
Artisans; presents shows, has lecture
and demonstration service; "ASA
Artisan" published quarterly for
members.*

Ruth Redmond-Cooper, Dir.
Institute of Art & Law
Journal: Art Antiquity & Law
1-5 Cank St.
Leicester, LE1 5GX U.K.
ph: +44 (0)116 253 8888
fax: +44 (0)116 251 1666
info@ial.uk.com
http://www.ial.uk.com
*A small independent institution,
founded in 1995, that aims to bridge
the divide between the worlds of art
and law by organizing seminars and
publishing books and periodicals;
membership is open to the public;
many related links.*

Collectors

Steven N. Jackson
1774 Highway 421 N.
Boone, NC 28607
ph: 828-264-8034
stevejackson@email.com
*Seeks oil paintings featuring scenes of
New York, Paris, Florida, Hawaii and
Tahiti by listed American artists;
please include SASE for extensive
want list.*

Dealers

Kennedy Galleries
730 Fifth Ave.
New York, NY 10019
ph: 212-541-9600
fax: 212-977-3833
inquiry@kgny.com
http://www.kgny.com
*Specializes in buying and selling
American art from the 19th and 20th
centuries.*

Hirschl & Adler Galleries, Inc.
21 East 70th St.
New York, NY 10021
ph: 212-535-8810
fax: 212-772-7237
gallery@hirschlandadler.com
http://www.hirschlandadler.com
*American and European paintings,
watercolors, drawings, and
sculptures; 18th century to present;
also American prints and decorative
arts 1810 to 1910.*

Bryan Guarnieri
Animation & Fine Art Galleries
University Mall
201 S. Estes Dr.
Chapel Hill, NC 27514
ph: 919-968-8008
fax: 919-968-8064
bryan@animationandfineart.com
http://www.animationandfineart.com
*Fine art, paintings, drawings,
sculptures, and prints experts, dealers
and appraisers; also offers repair
services.*

Melanie Smith, ISA
Seaside Art Gallery
2716 Virginia Dare Trail South
P.O. Box 1
Nags Head, NC 27959-0001
ph: 252-441-5418 or 800-828-2444
fax: 252-441-8563
info@seasideart.com
http://www.seasideart.com
*Wants original oils, graphics,
sculpture, and animation film art; also
buys and sells old and new animation
art; Accredited Member of the
International Society of Appraisers; in
business for over 40 years.*

Robert Thames
Robert Thames Art & Antiques
P.O. Box 4175
Ormond Beach, FL 32175
ph: 904-677-8835
rthamesa@bellsouth.net
*Specializes in fine art: paintings,
drawings and prints.*

Jerry Bengis, ISA
Bengis Fine Art
1440 Coral Ridge Dr., #166
Pompano Beach, FL 33071
ph: 954-757-2444
fax: 954-757-6222
yascha7@netrox.net
http://www.bengisfineart.com
*Fine art appraiser specializing in
prints (especially Salvador Dali),
graphics (Miro, Chagall, Picasso,
Warhol), etchings, engravings, prints,
bronzes.*

William C. Tregoning, III
Tregoning Fine Art & Services
100 North Main St.
Chagrin Falls, OH 44022
ph: 440-247-1690
fax: 440-247-6180
tfas@multiverse.com
http://www.tregoningfas.com
*Specializes in works of art from 1700
to 1950, with special emphasis on art
created in Northern Ohio from 1880
to 1950; appraisals prepared in
conformance with USPAP and the
American Society of Appraisers
standards.*

Gerald E. Czulewicz
Antiques Americana
25699 Highway 65 NE
Isanti, MN 55040
ph: 763-444-9216
fax: 763-444-9218
charliezebra@msn.com
*Buys and sells American paintings,
watercolors, drawings, prints,
sculpture.*

David Cook
David Cook Fine American Art
1637 Wazee St.
Denver, CO 80202
ph: 303-623-8181
fax: 303-623-4817
info@davidcookgalleries.com
http://
www.davidcookfineamericanart.com
*Buys, sells, collects and appraises
antique Native American art; also
interested in American paintings
(specializing in Colorado and New
Mexico artists), sculpture, and arts &
crafts.*

Corinne Cain, ISA, ASA
Corinne Cain Ltd.
326 West Harmont Dr.
Phoenix, AZ 85021
ph: 602-906-1633
fax: 602-906-0677
corinne@savvycollector.com
http://www.savvycollector.com
*A veteran art appraiser for over 25
years selling fine art and Native
American arts online; guaranteed
condition, authenticity verified, value
is assured; Accredited Senior
Appraiser, Certified Appraiser of
Personal Property.*

Keith Bartelheim
Fallen Leaf Gallery
3675 Baker Lane
Reno, NV 89509
ph: 775-826-7477
fax: 775-826-7477
fallenleafgallery@yahoo.com
*Specializes in buying, selling,
appraising fine art including 19th and
20th century prints and graphics.*

Richard C. Frey, ISA CAPP
R.T.L.H. Enterprises
1275 East Ave.
Chico, CA 95926-1020
ph: 530-343-4528 or 800-567-7854
fax: 530-343-9380
RFREYRTLH@aol.com
http://www.richardcfreyfineart.com
*Buys, sells and appraises fine art:
paintings, watercolors, prints,
drawings, sculpture, bronzes, etc.;
American or European; Accredited
Member of the International Society of
Appraisers.*

Elizabeth Wenner-Madison
ARTLister
12162 SW Scholls Ferry Rd., Ste 117
Portland, OR 97223
ph: 503-579-9295
fax: 503-590-3546
*Assisting dealers and private
collectors in pricing, marketing, and
shipping of limited edition prints,
sculpture, and original fine art.*

Lewis & Bond Fine Art
209 W. Houghton St.
Medford, OR 97501
ph: 541-988-5484 or 800-667-0562
sales@lewisbond.com
http://www.lewisbond.com
*Brokers, buys and sells most well-
known artist works; originals, limited
edition prints and posters; Red
Skelton, Bob Byerley, Norman
Rockwell.*

Experts

Myreen Moore
West Ghent Arts
1404 Gates Ave.
Norfolk, VA 23507-1131
ph: 757-623-4448 or 757-623-7827
fax: 757-855-4312
irine7@aol.com
*Art appraiser; also repairs, restores
art, paintings, prints; twenty-five
years experience as researcher/artist/
writer; staff writer for "Mid-Atlantic
Antiques Magazine;" listed in "Who's
Who in American Art."*

Alan Bamberger
ArtBusiness.com
2510 Bush St.
San Francisco, CA 94115-3002
ph: 415-931-7875
fax: 415-922-3580
alanb@artbusiness.com
http://www.artbusiness.com
*Author of "Buy Art Smart," "Art For
All," and "The Art of Buying Art;"
syndicated columnist who answers
questions about art, and offers online
art appraisals and consulting through
his Web site.*

Internet Resources

ArtFact, Inc.
Price Guide: ArtFact
1130 Ten Rod Rd., Ste. D202
North Kingstown, RI 02852-4158
ph: 401-295-2656 or 800-278-3228
fax: 401-295-2629
sales@artfact.com
http://www.artfact.com
*A computerized online price guide
having almost 6 million auction sales
results of fine art, antiques and
collectibles; complete lot descriptions,
prices realized with on-screen images.*

Artnet.com
61 Broadway, 23rd Floor
New York, NY 10006-2701
ph: 800-427-8638 or 212-497-9700
fax: 212-497-9707
support@artnet.com
http://www.artnet.com
The portal to the world of art for dealers, collectors, artists and enthusiasts; online auctions of blue-chip art; inventory from over 700 galleries; database of auction results and previews, fine art auction database; online magazine.

U.S. National Library of Medicine (NLM)
8600 Rockville Pike
Bethesda, MD 20894
ph: 888-346-3656 or 301-594-5983
publicinfo@nlm.nih.gov
http://www.nlm.nih.gov
Image library of nearly 60,000 images in prints and photograph collection; search by keyword or browse.

Christopher Witcombe
Art Resources on the Web
Sweet Briar College
Sweet Briar, VA 24595
ph: 804-381-6100
witcombe@sbc.edu
http://witcombe.sbc.edu/
ARTHLinks.html
One of the most comprehensive art-related sites on the Web; resources for all period of art organized by period, geographical area, genre.

Art.com
1321-101 Kirkland Rd.
Raleigh, NC 27603
ph: 919-838-1171 or 800-952-5592
fax: 919-831-0017
questions@art.com
http://www.art.com
Contemporary artist biographies, great hyper-linked online dictionary of art and antiques terms; also sells prints covering a wide variety of categories.

Scott Kublin
Art Directory
P.O. Box 1616
Rincon, GA 31326
ph: 912-826-6840
admin@artframing.com
http://www.artframing.com
Centralized resource for businesses in the art and framing industry.

World Wide Arts Resource
761 Franklin Ave.
Columbus, OH 43205
ph: 614-221-7661
fax: 614-221-1933
contact@wwar.com
http://www.wwar.com
The biggest gateway for the arts on the Internet: events, exhibitions, museums, cyber galleries, art schools, galleries, museums, art for sale, arts publications, arts agencies, literary

and theatre resources, crafts, antiques.

Art Brokerage, Inc.
P.O. Box 3730
544 East Fork Rd.
Ketchum, ID 83340
ph: 208-788-1484 or 208-788-1491
fax: 208-788-1492
drose@earthlink.net
http://www.artbrokerage.com
Online service for buying and selling art; specializes in selling limited edition prints and sculpture; accepts consignments; list your artwork for sale in classifieds.

AskArt.com
P.O. Box 8009
Scottsdale, AZ 85252-8009
ph: 480-423-8131
info@askart.com
http://www.askart.com
The world's most comprehensive database about North American artists: auction records, biography, image gallery, book and periodical references, dealers, museums, exhibitions; Impressionist, Hudson River School, Sculptors, Modernists, etc.

Art Buys
369 Montezuma Ave., Ste 422
Santa Fe, NM 87501
ph: 505-988-5484 or 800-667-0562
sales@artbuys.com
http://www.artbuys.com
Online classified ads for art; Red Skelton, Chagall, Peter Max, Steve Kaufman, Thomas Kinkade, Joan Miro, Leroy Neiman, Norman Rockwell, Salvador Dali, and many others.

John Malyon
Artcyclopedia, Inc.
51 Tuscany Hills Terrace N.W.
Calgary, Alberta T3L 2G7 Canada
ph: 403-547-9692
fax: 403-547-1506
jmalyon@artcyclopedia.com
http://www.artcyclopedia.com
A definitive and comprehensive Web site guide to museum-quality fine art on the Internet; currently lists 5,500 artists along with locations of their works either on exhibit or for sale; also lists of museums with online art presence.

John Laroche
artelino - The Magic of Art
Joh.-Seb.-Bach-Str. 11
Pullach, Bavaria 82049 Germany
webmaster@artelino.com
http://www.artelino.com
Art auctions, galleries and forum for art prints, old maps, Japanese art, Ukiyo-E, Orthodox icons; also contemporary artists, art resource listings and classifieds; extensive articles on art, prints, icons, etc.

Davie Cirese
Net-ArT Virtual Space for Art & Photography
via Palermn 6/a
Rome, 00184 Italy
ph: +39 06 4883253
fax: +39 06 48916583
cirese@net-art.it
http://www.netart.it
Internet art resource from Italy; presenting international art and artists; offers useful free search services for art-workers; go to the Web site to subscribe to Net-ArT Newsletter, a free online newsletter.

icollector.com Art Price Guide
Price Guide: Art Price Guide
United House
9 Penbridge Rd.
London, W11 3JY U.K.
ph: +44 (0)20 7313 2300 or +
fax: +44 (0)20 7221 7463
customer.services@icollector.com
http://www.icollector.com
Online price guide containing more than 1,100,000 auction records of sales from auction houses in 40 countries from 1987 to 1998.

Misc. Services

OmniGuard Corporation
730 Fifth Ave.
New York, NY 10019-4105
ph: 800-808-2882 or 212-577-9000
fax: 212-577-9220
info@omniguard.com
http://www.omniguard.com
Guarantees the authenticity of fine art; also registers art.

Sharon Flescher, Ex. Dir.
International Foundation for Art Research (IFAR)
Magazine: IFAR Journal
500 Fifth Ave., Ste 935
New York, NY 10110
ph: 212-391-6234
fax: 212-391-8794
kferg@ifar.org
http://www.ifar.org
Nonprofit educational and research organization; offers a unique authentication service which examines works of art to assist in the resolution of questions of authenticity and attribution; for individuals, art dealers, museums, etc.

Jerri Dodd
AskAboutAntiques.com
P.O. Box 450
Warwick, NY 10990
info@askaboutantiques.com
http://www.askaboutantiques.com
A fee-for-service Web site offering thousands of articles and references on all fields of art and antiques.

Wendy Reaves, Cur.
National Portrait Gallery
Prints & Drawings
750 Ninth St., Ste. 8300
Washington, DC 20560-0973
ph: 202-275-1738
fax: 202-275-1887
npgweb@npg.si.edu
http://www.npg.si.edu
Will authenticate prints & drawings brought in for inspection; make an appointment first; may be able to work from good photographs.

National Gallery of Art
Dept. of Education Resources
6th & Constitution Ave. NW
Washington, DC 20565-0001
ph: 202-842-6273
der-info@nga.gov
http://www.nga.gov/education/ep-main.htm
FREE loan program of VHS, laser discs, CDROMs, and slide/tape programs covering many facets of art and antiques; American, Ancient, Asian, Baroque & Rococo, Medieval & Renaissance, Neoclassic, Impression-ism, sculpture; send for catalog.

Gordon's Art Reference, Inc.
Price Guide: Davenport's Art Reference & Price Guide
306 West Coronado Rd.
Phoenix, AZ 85003-1147
ph: 602-253-6948 or 800-892-4622 (orders)
fax: 602-253-2104
office@gordonsart.com
http://www.gordonsart.com
Comprehensive bi-annual directory of over 240,000 artists, including biographical information, type of work, auction dates, and price.

Elizabeth Wenner-Madison
ARTLister
12162 SW Scholls Ferry Rd., Ste 117
Portland, OR 97223
ph: 503-579-9295
fax: 503-590-3546
Assisting dealers and private collectors in pricing, marketing, and shipping of limited edition prints, sculpture, and original fine art.

Veronique Paluch
Artprice.com
B.P. 69
St. Romain au Mont d'Or, 69270 France
ph: 33 478 220 000
fax: 33 478 220 606
info@artprice.com
http://www.artprice.com
A data bank of over 2 million auction results for cataloged works of art; more than 180,000 artists listed, updated daily; for paintings, prints, drawings, posters, sculpture, photography, ceramics & more; online & in CD-ROM and book form.

Duncan Hislop
Art Sales Index, Ltd.
194 Thorpe Lea Rd.
Egham, Surrey TW20 8HA U.K.
ph: 44 (0) 1784 451145
fax: 44 (0) 1784 451144
asi@art-sales-index.com
http://www.art-sales-index.com
Art auction results online computer art database (also on CD-ROM) of art auction prices since 1970 (over 2.3 million records); also publishes the Annual Art Sales Index.

John Woracker
Invaluable
Mill Court
Furrlongs, Newport
Isle of Wight, Hampshire PO3O 2AA U.K.
ph: (44) 1983 826000 or (44) 1714 868252
fax: (44) 1983 826201
john@thesaurus.co.uk
http://www.invaluable.com
A pre-sale auction search service checking traditional auctions worldwide, searching 7,500+ catalogs per year; a fee based service for subscribers to get advanced notice of upcoming items for sale at auctions around the world.

Museums/Libraries

Rhode Island School of Design Museum
224 Benefit St.
Providence, RI 02903-2723
ph: 401-454-6500
fax: 401-454-6556
mshaw@risd.edu
http://www.risd.edu/museum.cfm
Apparel, architecture, furniture, graphic design, industrial design, interior architecture, landscape architecture.

Newark Museum, The
49 Washington St.
Newark, NJ 07101
ph: 973-596-6550 or 800-7-MUSEUM
fax: 973-642-0459
webmaster@newarkmuseum.org
http://www.newarkmuseum.org
The museum's long-standing dedication to American Art has produced a collection of work from Colonial to Contemporary that ranks among the finest of any museum its size in the US.

Archives of American Art, New York Research Center
1285 Avenue of the Americas
New York, NY 10019
ph: 212-399-5015
fax: 212-307-4501
yeckleyk@aaany.si.edu
http://artarchives.si.edu
Important source of biographical material on American artists; maintains records of paintings by subject & artist; Washington, DC, New York City, and San Marino, CA.

Whitney Museum of American Art
945 Madison Ave. at 75th St.
New York, NY 10021
ph: 212-570-3676 or 877-WHITNEY
feedback@whitney.org
http://www.whitney.org

Heidi Rosenau
Frick Collection and the Frick Art Reference Library, The
1 East 70th St.
New York, NY 10021-4967
ph: 212-288-0700
fax: 212-628-4417
info@frick.org
http://www.frick.org
Housed in the Gilded Age mansion of Henry Clay Frick (1849-1919), the museum is one of the most important private collections of Western fine art and decorative arts in the world: Bellini, El Greco, Rembrandt, Titian, Whistler.

Metropolitan Museum of Art
1000 Fifth Ave.
New York, NY 10028-0198
ph: 212-535-7710
fax: 212-794-9316
http://www.metmuseum.org
One of the largest and finest art museums on the world; over 2 million works of art spanning more than 5,000 years of world culture.

Philadelphia Museum of Art
P.O. Box 7646
Philadelphia, PA 19101-7646
ph: 215-684-7860 or 215-763-8100
fax: 215-235-0050
pr@philamuseum.org
http://www.philamuseum.org
More than 400,000 works in the permanent collection; 3rd largest museum in the country; more than 200 galleries containing a myriad of artistic treasures from many continents and cultures.

Pennsylvania Academy of Fine Arts
118 N. Broad St.
Philadelphia, PA 19102
ph: 215-972-7600
pafa@pafa.org
http://www.pafa.org/museum/exhibitions
Founded in 1805, the Academy is America's oldest art museum and school of fine arts; collects and exhibits the work of distinguished American artist; renowned for its reputation in training artists from the US and across the world.

Corcoran Museum of Art
1701 E St.
Washington, DC 20002
ph: 202-639-1700 or 202-639-1725
webmaster@corcoran.org
http://www.corcoran.org

National Museum of Women in the Arts
Magazine: Women in the Arts
1250 New York Ave. NW
Washington, DC 20005-3920
ph: 202-783-5000
fax: 202-393-3235
http://www.nmwa.org
Brings recognition to the achievements of women artists of all periods and nationalities by exhibiting, preserving, acquiring, and researching art by women and by educating the public concerning their accomplishments.

National Museum of American Art
Catalog: Smithsonian Art Index
8th & G Sts. N.W.
Washington, DC 20560
ph: 202-357-2504
nmaainfo@nmaa.si.edu
http://www.nmaa.si.edu
Identifies drawings, prints, paintings and sculpture in Smithsonian divisions but not part of the museum collection.

National Museum of American Art
Catalog: Peter A. Juley & Son Collection
8th & G Sts. N.W.
Washington, DC 20560
ph: 202-357-2504
nmaainfo@nmaa.si.edu
http://www.nmaa.si.edu
Over 127,000 photographic negatives of art now lost, destroyed or altered.

National Museum of American Art
Catalog: Slide & Photograph Archives
8th & G Sts. N.W.
Washington, DC 20560
ph: 202-357-2504
nmaainfo@nmaa.si.edu
http://www.nmaa.si.edu
Over 60,000 35mm color slides and over 200,000 photographs and negatives for visual documentation of American art.

National Museum of American Art
Catalog: Pre-1877 Art Exhibition Catalogue Index
8th & G Sts. N.W.
Washington, DC 20560
ph: 202-357-2504
nmaainfo@nmaa.si.edu
http://www.nmaa.si.edu
A computerized index from over 700 rare catalogs of exhibitions held between 1790 and 1876; art unions, fairs, museums, etc.

National Museum of American Art
Catalog: Permanent Collection Data Base
8th & G Sts. N.W.
Washington, DC 20560
ph: 202-357-2504
nmaainfo@nmaa.si.edu
http://www.nmaa.si.edu
A computerized listing providing information on the over 300,000 objects in the museum's permanent collection.

Susan Cary, Registrar
Archives of American Art, Washington D.C. Center
Journal: Archives of American Art Journal
901 D St. SW
Washington, DC 20560-0937
ph: 202-314-3900
carys@aaa.si.edu
http://artarchives.si.edu
Important source of biographical material on American artists; maintains records of paintings by subject & artist; Washington, DC, New York City, and San Marino, CA.

Joaneath Spicer
Walters Art Museum
600 N. Charles St.
Baltimore, MD 21201
ph: 410-547-9000
klavin@thewalters.org
http://www.thewalters.org
One of only a few museums worldwide to present a comprehensive history of art from the third millennium B.C. to the early 20th century.

Chrysler Museum of Art, Art Reference Library, The
245 West Olney Rd.
Norfolk, VA 23510-1587
ph: 757-664-6200
fax: 757-664-6201
museum@chrysler.org
http://www.chrysler.org

High Museum of Art, The
1280 Peachtree St.
Atlanta, GA 30309
ph: 404-733-4400
fax: 404-733-4502
http://www.high.org
A leading art museum in the Southeastern US; collections include African art, decorative arts, European art, folk art, modern and contemporary art, and photography.

Toledo Museum of Art, The
2445 Monroe St.
P.O. Box 1013
Toledo, OH 43697-1013
ph: 419-255-8000 or 800-644-6862
marketing@toledomuseum.org
http://www.toledomuseum.org
One of America's finest art collections American and European paintings in a building of exceptional beauty

Cleveland Museum of Art
11150 East Blvd.
Cleveland, OH 44106-1797
ph: 216-421-7340
info@cma-oh.org
http://www.cma-oh.org
One of the world's great art museums with a collection of more than 30,000 works of art ranging over 5,000 years, from ancient Egypt to present; masterpieces from Europe, Asia, Africa and the Americas.

Detroit Institute of Arts
5300 Woodward Ave.
Detroit, MI 48202
ph: 313-833-7900
Erickson@dia.ci.detroit.mi.us
http://www.dia.org
*The fifth largest fine arts museum in
the US with holdings of over 60,000
works: paintings, sculpture, and
graphic and decorative arts.*

Art Institute of Chicago
111 S. Michigan Ave.
Chicago, IL 60603
ph: 312-443-0849
webmaster@artic.edu
http://www.artic.edu

Sam Duncan, Act. Librarian
Amon Carter Museum Library
3501 Camp Bowie Blvd.
Fort Worth, TX 76107-2695
ph: 817-738-1933
fax: 817-377-8523
webmaster@cartermuseum.org
http://www.cartermuseum.org
*Has large and distinguished collection
of paintings and sculpture by Frederic
Remington and Charles M. Russell
along with other masterpieces of 19th
and early 20-th century American art
and photography.*

Los Angeles County Museum of Art
5905 Wilshire Blvd.
Los Angeles, CA 90036
ph: 323-857-6000
publicinfo@lacma.org
http://www.lacma.org

Getty Center, The
1200 Getty Center Dr.
Los Angeles, CA 90049
ph: 310-440-7300
info@getty.edu
http://www.getty.edu
*J.Paul Getty Museum of European and
American art and sculpture; The Getty
Research Institute for the History of
Art and the Humanities; The Getty
Conservation Institute; The Getty
Information Institute.*

Archives of American Art, West Coast
Research Center
Huntington Library
1151 Oxford Rd.
San Marino, CA 91108
ph: 626-583-7847
fax: 626-583-7207
aaawcrc@aaa.si.edu
http://artarchives.si.edu
*Important source of biographical
material on American artists;
maintains records of paintings by
subject & artist; Washington, DC,
New York City, and San Marino, CA.*

Musee du Louvre
75058 Cedex 01
Paris, France
ph: (33) 01 40 20 51 51
fax: (33) 01 40 20 54 42
info@louvre.fr
http://www.louvre.fr

Periodicals

Sabro, Inc.
Magazine: Fine Arts Trader, The
P.O. Box 1273
Randolph, MA 02368
ph: 800-332-5055 or 781-961-9045
fax: 781-961-9044
info@fineartstrader.com
http://www.fineartstrader.com
*Published monthly to bring buyers
and sellers of fine art together; ads,
articles, happenings, upcoming
antique shows.*

Sandra Sandler, Pub.
Magazine: Fine Arts Trader, The
P.O. Box 1273
Randolph, MA 02368
ph: 800-332-5055 or 781-961-9045
fax: 781-961-9044
info@fineartstrader.com
http://www.fineartstrader.com
*Black and white publication that
focuses on buying and selling both
American and European fine art.*

John Sonta
National Register Publishing
Directory: Official Museum Directory
121 Chanlon Rd.
New Providence, NJ 07974-1541
ph: 800-473-7020
fred.marks@renp.com
http://www.officialmuseumdir.com
*Profiles more than 7,600 American
institutions in 85 categories;
aquariums, historic homes, museums,
zoos; handy for those looking for
information about specific types of
antiques, fine art & collectibles;
annual.*

Newspaper: Art Newspaper, The
80 East 11th St.
Rooms 224 & 226
New York, NY 10003
ph: 212-475-4574
fax: 212-475-4615
c.ruiz@theartnewspaper.com
http://www.theartnewspaper.com
*US editorial office for "the interna-
tional journal of art;" prints,
paintings, antiques, sculpture; news,
politics, articles, reviews, previews,
schedule of events, museum & gallery
exhibits, fairs; published 11 times per
year in England.*

Magazine: Art & Auction
11 East 36th St., 9th Floor
New York, NY 10016
ph: 800-777-8718 or 212-447-9555
fax: 212-447-5221
edit@artandauction.com
http://www.artandauction.com
*Covers the international art markets,
from antiquities to contemporary art;
articles include pieces on artists or
schools of art/furniture, analyses of
trends in the market, auction reviews
and previews, calendar of events, etc.*

Art & Auction Magazine
Directory: International Directory for
Collectors
11 East 36th St., 9th Floor
New York, NY 10016
ph: 800-777-8718 or 212-447-9555
fax: 212-447-5221
edit@artandauction.com
http://www.artandauction.com
*One issue per year of "Art & Auction
Magazine" includes the Annual
Directory of Galleries and Auction
Houses International (including
shows, art associations, fairs, art
services, appraisers, conservators,
etc.).*

Newsletter: ARTnewsletter
48 West 38th St.
New York, NY 10018-6211
ph: 212-398-1690
fax: 212-819-0394
info@artnewsonline.com
http://www.artnewsonline.com
*A biweekly international business
report of the art market; has the latest
news on auctions and trends in the art
market.*

Kennedy Galleries
Journal: America Art Journal, The
730 Fifth Ave.
New York, NY 10019
ph: 212-541-9600
fax: 212-977-3833
inquiry@kgny.com
http://www.kgny.com
*Outstanding articles on American
painting, sculpture, decorative arts,
photography, architecture, and
cultural history.*

Journal: Art On Paper
39 E. 78th St., #501
New York, NY 10021-0213
ph: 212-988-5959
fax: 212-988-6107
info@artonpaper.com
http://www.artonpaper.com
*Published bi-monthly, this journal
reports on the entire print and
photograph market and is considered
a must by print collectors and dealers;
also contains scholarly articles and
reviews, and auction results.*

Walter de Gruyter, Inc.
Magazine: International Journal of
Cultural Property
200 Saw Mill River Rd.
Hawthorne, NY 10532-1525
ph: 914-747-0110
fax: 914-747-1326
wdg-info@deGruyter.de
http://www.degruyter.de
*Addresses such issues as contested
attributions, ethics of art historians
and museum personnel, looting,
national retention and protection,
legal issues and evolving law
regarding art.*

Haworth Press
Journal: Art Reference Services
Quarterly
10 Alice St.
Binghamton, NY 13904-1580
ph: 800-429-6784 or 607-722-5857
fax: 607-722-6362
getinfo@haworthpressinc.com
http://www.HaworthPress.com
*Publication geared to art librarians
focusing on reference services for art
history, architecture, and the studio
arts; legal resources for art, index to
reviews of art reference titles, book
reviews, etc.*

David J. Maloney, ISA CAPP
Sales Online Direct, Inc.
Directory: Maloney's Antiques &
Collectibles Resource Directory
P.O. Box 2049
Frederick, MD 21702-1049
ph: 301-228-2279
fax: 301-695-6491
dave@maloney.com
http://www.davidmaloney.com/
aboutbook.htm
*Publishes major resource information
source for collectors, sellers, claims
adjusters, etc.: includes experts,
buyers, clubs, periodicals, repairers,
museums/libraries, appraisers,
auctioneers, matching services,
dealers, etc.*

Carolyn Proeber
Magazine: Art Calendar
P.O. Box 2675
Salisbury, MD 21802
ph: 410-749-9625
fax: 410-749-9626
Carolyn@ArtCalendar.com
http://www.artcalendar.com
*A monthly magazine with artist and
dealer interviews plus articles on art
fraud, art scams, artist block,
internships, shows, artist opportunities.*

Carolyn Proeber
Directory: Annual Artists' Resource
Directory
P.O. Box 2675
Salisbury, MD 21802
ph: 410-749-9625
fax: 410-749-9626
Carolyn@ArtCalendar.com
http://www.artcalendar.com
*Annual containing art consultants,
arts agencies and councils, college
galleries, resources for art materials
and framing supplies, artwork
insurers, etc.*

Billian Publishing Inc.
Magazine: Art & Antiques
2100 Powers Ferry Rd.
Atlanta, GA 30339
ph: 770-955-5656
fax: 770-952-0669
editor@artantiquesmag.com
http://www.ArtandAntiques.net
*Glossy magazine focusing on the fine
and decorative arts and in antiques:*

colorful ads, articles, auction reports, detailed listings, etc.

Tom Kellaway, Pub.
Magazine: American Art Review
12230 State Line Rd.
Shawnee Mission, KS 66209
ph: 913-451-8801
amartrev@aol.com
Bi-monthly magazine devoted to America's artistic heritage; high quality fine art publication; art reviews, gallery source.

Anthony R. Westbridge
Westbridge Publications Ltd.
Newsletter: Westbridge Art Market Report
1737 Fir St.
Vancouver, British Columbia V6J 5J9 Canada
ph: 604-736-1014
fax: 604-734-4944
info@westbridge-fineart.com
http://www.westbridge-fineart.com
A bi-monthly newsletter for fine art collectors and investors; extensive auction coverage, including results and analysis, as well as market movements and trends, interviews, advice and opinion pertinent to art as an investment.

Magazine: Apollo Magazine
1 Castle Lane
London, SW1E 6DR U.K.
ph: 020 7233 6640
fax: 020 7233 7159
editorial@apollomag.com
http://www.apollomagazine.com
The international magazine of art and antiques; an English monthly publication with detailed articles and glossy color photos; for US postal subscriptions write P.O. Box 47, North Hollywood, CA 91603-0047.

Magazine: ArtReview
Hereford House
23-24 Smithfield St.
London, ECIA 9LB U.K.
ph: +44 (020) 72364880
info@art-review.co.uk
http://www.art-review.co.uk
The UK's leading independent visual arts magazine designed to serve the art buyer and gallery visitor; useful information for both the experienced collector and for those looking to buy on a limited budget.

Repro. Sources

Van Key
Art Brokers International
3830 South A1A, Ste. C-3
Melbourne Beach, FL 32951
ph: 800-844-8046
fax: 800-844-8046
VanMonet@aol.com
http://www.oil-paintings.com
Artists hand paint museum quality recreations of fine art, family or pet.

Isabel Art Gallery
66 Av. des Champs Elysees
Paris, F-75008 France
http://www.isabel.com
Hand painted high quality reproductions of fine works of art.

David Gibbons
ArtUnframed
Regency Towers
3 East Ave.
London, E17 9NG U.K.
ph: 01524 859332
info@artunframed.com
http://www.artunframed.com
Offers museum quality reproductions of fine art; each painting is hand painted in the original medium on Belgian linen canvas.

Philip J. Chapman
Filman Fine Art
York House
Chichester Rd.
Dorking, Surrey RH4 1LR U.K.
ph: +44 (0) 1306 880779
customerservice@filmanfineart.co.uk
http://www.filmanfineart.co.uk
Hand painted Old Masters recreations; offers a no-risk guarantee and free shipping worldwide.

African-American

Appraisers

Camille Brewer, ISA
4ArtWorth
P.O. Box 21391
Detroit, MI 48221
ph: 313-282-4694
fax: 313-863-1426
cabrewer@4artworth.com
http://www.4artworth.com
Specializes in the appraisal of museum quality fine art by African-American artists.

Alabama

Dealers

Marcia Weber
Marcia Weber - Art Objects
1050 Woodley Rd.
Montgomery, AL 36106
ph: 334-262-5349
fax: 334-567-0060
weberart@mindspring.com
http://www.marciaweberartobjects.com
Specializes in locating and selling antique art by important Alabama artists: Anne Goldthwaite, J. Kelly Fitzpatrick, Zelda Fitzgerald, Bill Taylor and the artists of the New South group; gallery opened by appointment.

Andy Warhol

Museums/Libraries

Andy Warhol Museum
117 Sandusky St.
Pittsburgh, PA 15212-5890
ph: 724-237-8300
fax: 724-237-8340
information@warhol.org
http://www.warhol.org
Focuses on the American artist, Andy Warhol; also is a primary resource for anyone who wishes to gain insights into contemporary art and popular culture.

Asian

(see also ART, Oriental; INDONESIA; ORIENTALIA)

Appraisers

Norman Hurst, ISA CAPP
Hurst Gallery
53 Mount Auburn St.
Cambridge, MA 02138-5030
ph: 617-491-6888 or 212-744-6488 (NYC)
fax: 617-661-0439
NHurst@compuserve.com
http://www.hurstgallery.com
Buys, sells, appraises African, Oceanic, Native American, PreColumbian and Asian art.

Dr. Daphne L. Rosenzweig, ISA CAPP
Rosenzweig Associates
P.O. Box 3976
Sarasota, FL 34230-3976
ph: 941-371-4643
fax: 941-342-6893
rosetwig@aol.com
Asian/Islamic art, Japanese prints, jades, Asian ceramics, sculpture, metalworks, cloisonne, scholar's studio objects, ivories, netsuke, paintings, screens, Himalayan, Indian, Southeast Asian Buddhist art, Indian & Persian miniatures.

Elisabeth Douglas, ASA, ISA
China Coast, The
P.O. Box 610
Austin, TX 78767
ph: 512-330-9524 or 512-789-7507
fax: 512-330-9348
wien@texas.net
http://www.asianartappraisals.com
Active in the field of Asian art and antiques for over twenty years; specializing in damage, insurance and IRS appraisals; also offers brokerage of Chinese, Japanese, and Southeast Asian Art.

Fuji Murakami, ASA
Asian Art Appraisal Service
P.O. Box 24999
Denver, CO 80224-0999
ph: 303-758-8379
fax: 303-758-0816
fmarkm@qwest.net
Bronze, Asian ivory, netsuke, ceramics, costumes/robes/embroideries, jade and other mineral carvings, snuff bottles, paintings, calligraphy,

prints, screens and scrolls, textiles of China, Korea, Japan, Southeast Asia, some India/Tibet.

Christine Zachary
P.O. Box 82906
Portland, OR 97282-0906
ph: 503-234-8143 or 503-777-5813
christineZC@aol.com
Specializes in collecting, selling, appraising SE Asian art and antiques of the Himalayan regions as well as China; main expertise is in painted Buddhist thangkas and bronzes; also Chinese ceramics, textiles, statuary.

Book Sellers

Paragon Book Gallery, Inc.
1507 S. Michigan Ave.
Chicago, IL 60605-2812
ph: 312-663-5155
fax: 312-663-5177
paragon@paragonbook.com
http://www.paragonbook.com
Carries rare, out-of-print, and scholarly books on Asia; specializes in books on Asian arts and Asian studies; new and out-of-print.

Clubs/Associations

John van Breeman
Asia Society of Central Florida
Newsletter: ASCF Bulletin
2599 Via Tuscany
Winter Park, FL 32789
ph: 407-644-5190
A non-profit cultural organization; members interested in Asian art and culture; monthly meetings held Sept. to May with lectures and demonstrations on art of all Asian countries.

Collectors

John Rudak
32 Princess Lane
North Stonington, CT 06359-1117
ph: 860-599-8489
Wants Asian Buddhist & Hindu art; all representations desired; interested in all Asian artistic mediums including metalwork, wood carvings, porcelain, pottery, works on paper, etc.; special interest in Buddhist art & artifacts.

Dealers

Norman Hurst, ISA CAPP
Hurst Gallery
53 Mount Auburn St.
Cambridge, MA 02138-5030
ph: 617-491-6888 or 212-744-6488 (NYC)
fax: 617-661-0439
NHurst@compuserve.com
http://www.hurstgallery.com
Buys, sells, appraises African, Oceanic, Native American, PreColumbian and Asian art.

Subaash Kapoor
Art of the Past
1242 Madison Ave.
New York, NY 10128-0515
ph: 212-860-7070
fax: 212-876-5373
ArtofPast@aol.com
http://www.artofpast.com
Specializing in paintings, sculptures, textiles, Islamic and other works of art from India, Tibet, Nepal, and Southeast Asia.

Peaceful Wind
129 West San Francisco St.
Santa Fe, NM 87501
asianart@nets.com
http://www.asianart.com/pw
Expert and dealer specializes in high quality Asian art and antiquities, with a special emphasis on Himalayan art from Tibet and Nepal, and the art of Southeast Asia.

Perry Prince
Perry S. Prince, Asian Antiques
P.O. Box 1364
Ashland, OR 97520
ph: 541-488-1989
fax: 541-488-1989
perry@asianarts.com
http://www.asianarts.com
Carries architectural antiques, Southeast Asian, Asian art, Asian antiques, interior decorating, interior design, Asian folk art, salvage, Chinese antiques, Chinese architecture.

Christopher Krokos
ThailandTradeNet.com
79/41 Moo 2 Highway
Chiang Mai, Doi Saket 50220 Thailand
ph: +66-53-867-497
fax: +66-53-867-497
webmaster@thailandtradenet.com
http://www.thailandtgradenet.com
Specializes in Asian art: jade sculptures, Thai benjarong, sterling silver, fine porcelain, woodcarvings, tapestry, lacquerware, furniture, marble and bronze sculptures, etc.

Experts

Pratapaditya Pal, Cur.
Los Angeles County Museum of Art
5905 Wilshire Blvd.
Los Angeles, CA 90036
ph: 323-857-6000
publicinfo@lacma.org
http://www.lacma.org
Senior curator of Indian and Southeast Asian Art; author of "Tibetan Paintings;" specializes in Indian and Himalayan arts; Tibetan thankas, Hinduism and Buddhism.

Internet Resources

Ian Alsop
Asian Arts
129 "B" West San Francisco
Santa Fe, NM 87501
ph: 505-983-7658
fax: 928-223-0086
ian.alsop@asianart.com
http://www.asianart.com
The online journal for the study and exhibition of the arts of Asia; offers buy and sell service.

Museums/Libraries

Hiram Woodward
Walters Art Museum
600 N. Charles St.
Baltimore, MD 21201
ph: 410-547-9000
klavin@thewalters.org
http://www.thewalters.org
One of only a few museums worldwide to present a comprehensive history of art from the third millennium B.C. to the early 20th century.

Los Angeles County Museum of Art
5905 Wilshire Blvd.
Los Angeles, CA 90036
ph: 323-857-6000
publicinfo@lacma.org
http://www.lacma.org

Pacific Asia Museum
Newsletter: Pacific Asia Museum
  Member Newsletter
46 N. Los Robles Ave.
Pasadena, CA 91101
ph: 818-449-2742
fax: 818-449-2754
PacAsiaMus@aol.com
http://www.pacasiamuseum.org
Preserves, presents, and interprets to the public the arts and culture of the Pacific Islands and Asia.

Periodicals

Wendy Holden, Co-Ed.
Journal: Newsletter, East Asian Art & Archaeology
Dept. of the History of Art, 40 Tappan Hall
Univ. of Michigan
Ann Arbor, MI 48109-1357
ph: 734-763-2874
fax: 734-647-4121
nhilgen@umich.edu
http://www.umich.edu/~hartspc/NEAAA.html
Published three times per year, NEAAA focuses on current exhibitions, symposia, newly published books, scholarly news, etc.

Elizabeth Knight, Pub.
Orientations Magazine Limited
Magazine: Orientations
200 Lockhart Rd., 17th Floor
Hong Kong
ph: 2511 1368
fax: 2507 4620
omag@netvigator.com
http://www.orientations.com.hk
Brings readers informed articles on all aspects of the arts of East Asia, the

Indian Subcontinent and Southeast Asia; beautifully illustrated articles on the ancient arts of painting, calligraphy, bronzes, ceramics.

HALI Publications, Ltd.
Magazine: HALI
St. Giles House
50 Poland St.
London, W1F 4AX U.K.
ph: 020 7970 4600
fax: 020 7578 7222
hali@centaur.co.uk
http://www.hali.com
"HALI" is the leading bi-monthly international publication in the field of carpet and textile art; an invaluable encyclopedic source of information with original research articles, reviews of museum collections, etc.; high color.

Australia

Dealers

Ian Johnson
Harden, Johnson & Assoc.
1616 Whisper Way
Goose Creek, SC 29445-4655
ph: 843-572-7968
fax: 843-572-7968
24 years experience in Australian, New Zealand, South African paintings, drawings, and watercolors from 1797 to present; also specializing in British, Scottish, and Irish paintings from 1880-1950; daily contact with these countries.

Martin Wardrop
Aboriginal Art Online
5 Ganges St.
Brisband, QLD 4101 Australia
ph: (61) 7-3846 7766 or (61) 7-3846 2746
fax: (61) 7-3846 4111
contact@aboriginalartonline.com
http://www.aboriginalartonline.com
Offers quality paintings, limited edition prints and didjeridus by Australian Aboriginal artists; plus information to help understand these artworks.

B.C. Galleries Ancient & Tribal Art
1069 High St.
Armadale, Victoria 3143 Australia
ph: +61 3 9804 3353
fax: +61 3 9804 3353
b.c.galleries@bigpond.com.au
http://www.bcgalleries.com.au
Buys and sells ancient and tribal art: Oceanic, Melanesia, New Guinea, Pacific Islands, Australian Aboriginal, African tribal, tribal arts of Asia and of the Americas.

Automotive

Appraisers

Howell Lee Davis
P.O. Box 1420
Brighton, MI 48116-7920
ph: 810-227-5644
fax: 810-227-4809
howell_davis@yahoo.com
Specializes in the appraisal of special interest cars, petroliana (glass pump globes, gas pumps, advertising signage, promotional items) and automotive art (original paintings, signed, numbered or remarqued prints, bronzes, etc.).

Bad

Internet Resources

Vito Salvatore
Vito Salvatore Virtual Collection
vito@badart.com
http://www.badart.com
Scours the US for the most appallingly bad art; much is on this online virtual gallery.

Museums/Libraries

Museum of Bad Art
E-zine: MOBA news
73 Parker Rd.
Needham, MA 02494
ph: 781-444-6757
fax: 781-433-9991
moba@world.std.com
http://glyphs.com/moba
Museum is located at 580 High St., Dedham MA 02026; a community-based, private institution dedicated to the collection, preservation, exhibition and celebration of bad art in all its glory.

Botanical

Museums/Libraries

Hunt Institute for Botanical Documentation
Journal: Huntia
Carnegie Mellon University
Pittsburgh, PA 15213-3890
ph: 412-268-2434 or 412-268-2440
fax: 412-268-5677
HIBD-Huntbot+@andrew.cmu.edu
http://huntbot.andrew.cmu.edu/HIBD/HuntInstitute.html
Collection documents botanical imagery from Renaissance onward; center for research/documentation into botanical science, history, art, biography, bibliography; conducts exhibitions of botanical art and illustration; no appraisals.

British

Auction Services

Ian Johnson
Harden, Johnson & Assoc.
1616 Whisper Way
Goose Creek, SC 29445-4655
ph: 843-572-7968
fax: 843-572-7968
24 years experience in Australian, New Zealand, South African paintings,

drawings, and watercolors from 1797 to present; also specializing in British, Scottish, and Irish paintings from 1880-1950; daily contact with these countries.

Dealers

Ian Johnson
Harden, Johnson & Assoc.
1616 Whisper Way
Goose Creek, SC 29445-4655
ph: 843-572-7968
fax: 843-572-7968
24 years experience in Australian, New Zealand, South African paintings, drawings, and watercolors from 1797 to present; also specializing in British, Scottish, and Irish paintings from 1880-1950; daily contact with these countries.

Jeffery Measamer
Art Connections
8315 E. Copper Village Dr.
Houston, TX 77095
ph: 281-861-0244
fax: 281-861-0266
artconnections@sbcglobal.net
http://www.houstonarts.com
Specialists in fine prints and drawings from 1750-1950; deals primarily in British prints and drawings; always has a wide selection of American and European works in stock.

Museums/Libraries

Duncan Robinson, Dir.
Yale Center for British Art
P.O. Box 208280
New Haven, CT 06520-8280
ph: 203-432-2800 or 203-432-2850
fax: 203-432-9695
bacinfo@yale.edu
http://www.yale.edu/ycba
Largest museum and research center for British paintings, sculpture, prints, drawings, and rare books outside England; no decorative arts.

Byzantine

Museums/Libraries

Dumbarton Oaks Research Library & Collection
1703 32nd St. NW
Washington, DC 20007
ph: 202-339-6400
DumbartonOaks@doaks.org
http://www.doaks.org

Canadian

Appraisers

Kathryn Minard, ISA
Contemporary Fine Art Services Inc.
184 Pearl St., Ste. 201A
Toronto, Ontario M5A 1L5 Canada
ph: 416-366-9770
fax: 416-366-8541
art.advisory.biz@on.aibn.com
Expert and appraiser specializing in Canadian contemporary and historical art; also Canadian Indian and Inuit.

Elizabeth L. Reynolds, ISA
Reynolds Associates Limited
12 Kent Place
St. John's, Newfoundland A1B 1V5 Canada
ph: 709-722-4546
fax: 709-722-2040
ereynold@lightpost.ca
http://www.fineartservices.ca
Specializes in Canadian paintings and prints.

Shelli L. Cassidy, ISA
Cassidy Fine Art Services
174 Broadway Ave., Unit 1
Toronto, Ontario M4P 1Vp Canada
ph: 416-545-0560
fax: 416-967-6320
shellicassidy@hotmail.com
Specializes in art research and appraisal of Canadian fine art (historical and contemporary): paintings, sculptures, works on paper; consultant for corporate and private art collections.

Peter Blundell
P.O. Box 6
Vernon, British Columbia V1T 6M1 Canada
ph: 250-542-4540
petersblundell@shaw.ca
Former gallery owner, also available for general art & old print appraisals.

Donald Ellis
Donald Ellis Gallery
RR#3
Dundas, Ontario L9H 5E3 Canada
ph: 905-648-1837
ellisgal@interlynx.net
Dealer and appraiser specializing in North American Indian art in Canada: 18th and 19th century Northwest Coast and Eskimo art indigenous to Canada.

Auction Services

Waddington's
111 Bathurst St.
Toronto, Ontario M5V 2R1 Canada
ph: 416-504-9100 or 877-504-5700
fax: 416-504-0033
info@waddingtonsauctions.com
http://www.waddingtonsauctions.com
Canada's oldest and largest auction house specializing in decorative arts, jewelry, antique furniture, Inuit and native Canadian arts, European and Canadian arts, books, militaria, Orientalia, toys, ceramics, etc.

Periodicals

Wendy Ingram, Pub.
Canadian Art Foundation
Magazine: Canadian Art
56 The Esplanade, Ste. 310
Toronto, Ontario M5E 1A7 Canada
ph: 416-368-8854
fax: 416-368-6135
info@canadianart.ca
http://www.canadianart.ca
A charitable organization established to foster and support the visual arts in Canada; "Canadian Art" is Canada's

most widely circulated art magazine and chronicles the Canadian art scene.

Magazine: C International Contemporary Art
P.O. Box 5, Station B
Toronto, Ontario M5T 2T2 Canada
ph: 416-539-9495
fax: 416-539-9903
general@cmagazine.com
http://www.cmagazine.com
Published by C The Visual Arts Foundation, a non-profit educational organization and focusing on international contemporary art.

Magazine: Arts Atlantic
P.O. Box 36007
RPO Spring Garden
Halifax, Nova Scotia B3J 3S9 Canada
ph: 902-420-5045
fax: 902-491-8624
gillian.collyer@stmarys.ca
http://www.artsatlantic.ca
Atlantic Canada's only arts periodical; features and reviews work of practicing painters, print makers, sculptors, photographers and craftspeople; also performances staged by theatre and dance companies.

Magazine: Border Crossings
500-70 Arthur St.
Winnipeg, Manitoba R3B 1G7 Canada
ph: 204-942-5778
fax: 204-949-0793
bordercr@escape.ca

Magazine: Innuit Art Quarterly
2081 Merivale Rd.
Ottawa, Ontario K2G 1G9 Canada
ph: 613-224-8189
fax: 613-224-2907
iaf@inuitart.org
http://www.inuitart.org
The only magazine dedicated to the art of the Inuit; IAG gives a voice to the artists and provides in-depth coverage of their art and the issues that concern them.

Canvas Marks

Collectors

Alexander Katlan
Alexander Katlan Conservation Inc.
56 - 38 Main St.
Flushing, NY 11355-5046
ph: 718-445-7458
fax: 718-445-7458
Interested in collecting American canvas marks or maker's labels found on the backs of paintings; please send photos or fax.

Commercial Advertising

Man./Prod./Dist.

Craig Wolfe
Name That Toon Icons of Happiness
28 Mountain View Ave.
San Rafael, CA 94901
ph: 415-456-3452
fax: 415-456-9045
response@namethattoon.com
http://www.namethattoon.com
World's largest publisher of commercial advertising/animation art; framed and matted prints: Coca-Cola, Anheuser-Busch, M&M/Mars, Pillsbury, Hershey's, Campbell Soup, Nabisco, Planter's, Life Savers, Oreo, Ritz, etc.

Contemporary

Appraisers

Helen S. Shlien, ISA
P.O. Box 204
Cambridge, MA 02138
ph: 617-661-0121
hshlien@excite.com
Specializes in the appraisal of contemporary and 20th century art.

Trudy Rosato
Connors-Rosato Fine Art & Antiques
39 Great Jones St.
New York, NY 10012
ph: 212-473-0377
fax: 212-477-0096
trudy.rosato@verizon.net
Specializes in the appraisal of contemporary art.

Chris Ingalls
Ingalls & Associates
771 NE 125 St.
Miami, FL 33161
ph: 305-981-7900
fax: 305-981-3105
ingallsgallery@aol.com
http://www.ingallsassociates.com
Specializes in contemporary and modern art and design: sculpture, painting, works on paper, photography, installations, curatorial projects, decorative objects, furniture, rare and out-of-print books.

Perri Guthrie, ISA
3432 Hanover Ave.
Dallas, TX 75225
ph: 214-987-2988
fax: 214-987-9747
perriguthrie@aol.com
Specializes in the appraisal of 20th century painting, drawing, prints, and photography.

Maria-Josefa Velazquez, ISA
Art Appraisal Services International
1422 C. Stonehollow Dr.
Humble, TX 77339
ph: 281-358-9967 or 281-610-7067
fax: 281-360-3309
MJVelazquez@ArtAppraisalServices.com
http://www.artappraisalservices.com
Fine arts appraiser and consultant specializes in the appraisal of Latin American art, Spanish colonial art,

Western, American and European art, and contemporary art; published author, art history degree, lecturers, ISA Accredited Member.

Pamela Leeds
Pamela Leeds Fine Art
P.O. Box 1339
Topanga, CA 90290
ph: 310-455-4227
fax: 310-455-4227
ArtProPL@earthlink.net
27 years experience in art advising/ consulting, forming and curating collections for private and corporate collectors, and planning and executing customized art tours for groups and individuals.

Andrea Moody
Andrea Moody Fine Art Appraisals
1944 Pacific Ave., #605
Tacoma, WA 98402
ph: 253-274-8378
amoody@harbornet.com
Specializes in the appraisal of modern and contemporary American art; by appointment only.

Auction Services

Christie's
20 Rockefeller Plaza
New York, NY 10020
ph: 212-636-2000
info@christies.com
http://www.christies.com

Dealers

Knoedler & Company
19 East 70th St.
New York, NY 10021
ph: 212-794-0550
fax: 212-772-6932
info@knoedlergallery.com
http://www.knoedlergallery.com
Specializes in post-WWII and contemporary art with a focus on the New York School; since 1846.

John Dupree
Creighton-Davis Gallery
3222 M St. NW
Washington, DC 20007
ph: 202-333-3050
fax: 202-338-4470
info@rareart.com.
http://www.rareart.com
Specializes in contemporary, old and modern print artists with national and international reputations; also sells sculptures and paintings by newly emerging as well as established artists.

Sybil Tillman, ISA
Artco Inc.
3013 Harrow Gate Dr.
Woodstock, IL 60098-7410
ph: 815-338-3600
SybilTillman@msn.com
http://www.e-Artco.com
Specializing in fine art appraisals and research; also buying and selling 19th and 20th century, Old Masters, important and contemporary

American artists and American Indian Art; Accredited member of the ISA, Member of AAA.

Museums/Libraries

Museum of Modern Art, The
11 W. 53rd. St.
New York, NY 10019
ph: 212-708-9400 or 800-447-6662
comments@moma.org
http://www.moma.org

William Johnston
Walters Art Museum
600 N. Charles St.
Baltimore, MD 21201
ph: 410-547-9000
klavin@thewalters.org
http://www.thewalters.org
One of only a few museums worldwide to present a comprehensive history of art from the third millennium B.C. to the early 20th century.

Contemporary Arts Center
115 E. Fifth St.
Cincinnati, OH 45202
ph: 513-345-8400
fax: 513-721-7418
admin@spiral.org
http://www.spiral.org

Cranbrook Art Museum
39221 Wodoward Ave.
Bloomfield Hills, MI 48303
ph: 248-645-3323
fax: 248-645-3324
artmuseum@cranbrook.edu
http://www.cranbrookart.edu
A contemporary art museum located at the heart of Cranbrook Educational Community.

Museum of Contemporary Art
220 East Chicago Ave.
Chicago, IL 60611-2604
ph: 312-280-2660
fax: 312-397-4095
webmaster@mcachicago.org
http://www.mcachicago.org

Periodicals

Magazine: Artforum International
350 7th Ave., 19th Floor
New York, NY 10001
ph: 212-475-4000
fax: 212-529-1257
generalinfo@artforum.com
http://www.artforum.com

Brant Art Publications
Magazine: Art in America
575 Broadway
New York, NY 10012
ph: 212-941-2800 or 800-925-8059
fax: 212-941-2897
brantpubs@aol.com
A full-color monthly magazine focusing on contemporary art.

Art in America Magazine
Directory: Annual Art Directory
575 Broadway
New York, NY 10012
ph: 212-941-2800 or 800-925-8059
fax: 212-941-2897
brantpubs@aol.com
The August issue of "Art in America" includes an annual directory of art galleries, museums art associations, fairs, art services, appraisers, conservators, etc.

Magazine: ARTnews
48 West 38th St.
New York, NY 10018-6211
ph: 212-398-1690
fax: 212-819-0394
info@artnewsonline.com
http://www.artnewsonline.com
A monthly magazine that reports on the contemporary art forms, personalities, issues, exhibitions, trends, and events that shape the international art world; subscriptions call 800-284-4625

Newspaper: West Art
P.O. Box 6868
Auburn, CA 95604-6868
ph: 530-885-0969
West Coast biweekly art publication; information and photographs of current West Coast fine art and craft exhibitions.

Magazine: Modern Painters
52 Bermondsey St., 3rd Floor
London, SE1 3UD U.K.
ph: +44 (0)20 7407 9246
fax: +55 (0)20 7407 9242
info@modernpainters.co.uk
http://www.modernpainters.co.uk
An English quarterly journal of the fine arts.

Georgia O'Keeffe

Museums/Libraries

Georgia O'Keeffe Museum
217 Johnson St.
Santa Fe, NM 87501
ph: 505-946-1000
contact@okeeffemuseum.org
http://www.okeeffemuseum.org
Presents exhibitions featuring works by O'Keeffe and her American Modernist contemporaries; has permanent collection of more than 140 works by O'Keeffe, the largest in the world.

German

Collectors

Tony Vehr
5101 E. Monterey Way
Phoenix, AZ 85018-6623
ph: 602-957-0653
fax: 602-957-1631
tony@vehrwebbstudio.com
Wants to buy pen and ink sketches and prints by German artist Heinrich Kley.

Museums/Libraries

Busch-Reisinger Museum, Harvard University Art Museums
32 Quincy St.
Cambridge, MA 02138-3845
ph: 617-495-2317 or 617-495-9400
fax: 617-496-2359
huam@fas.harvard.edu
http://www.artmuseums.harvard.edu/ busch
Harvard University Art Museum's collection of Germanic art: masterpieces of Vienna Secession art, German Expressionism, 1920s abstraction, decorative arts and architectural drawings; late Medieval, Renaissance, Baroque sculpture.

Grandma Moses

Museums/Libraries

Bennington Museum, The
West Main St.
Bennington, VT 05201
ph: 802-447-1571
fax: 802-442-8305
bennmuse@sover.net
http://www.benningtonmuseum.com
One of the finest regional art history museums in the country; works by Grandma Moses, American glass, VT furniture, Bennington pottery, the oldest Stars & Stripes in existence, the 1925 luxury touring car "The Wasp," and much more.

Haitian

Dealers

Warren Kahn
MedaliaArt - The Art of Haiti
6 Fox Rd.
East Setauket, NY 11733
ph: 631-246-5527 or 800-984-2065
webmaster@medalia.net
http://www.medalia.net
Buys and sells Haitian art.

Bill Bollendorf
Galerie Macondo
5536 Bryant St.
Pittsburgh, PA 15206
ph: 412-661-1498
macondo@telerama.com
http://www.artshaitian.com
Devoted to informing collectors on trends in Haitian art, price trends, news of the Haitian art community and interviews with established and emerging artists.

Irish

Dealers

Ian Johnson
Harden, Johnson & Assoc.
1616 Whisper Way
Goose Creek, SC 29445-4655
ph: 843-572-7968
fax: 843-572-7968
24 years experience in Australian, New Zealand, South African paintings, drawings, and watercolors from 1797 to present; also specializing in British, Scottish, and Irish paintings from

1880-1950; daily contact with these countries.

Islamic

Auction Services

Julia Walker
Spink & Son, Ltd.
69 Southampton Row
Bloomsbury
London, WC1B 4ET U.K.
ph: +44 (0) 20 7563 4000
fax: +44 (0) 20 7563 4066
info@spinkandson.com
http://www.spink-online.com
Auctioneers and dealers of coins (ancient to present), banknotes, medals, orders, tokens, decorations and other numismatic items; also stamps and postal history as well as fine European, Indian and Islamic art.

Dealers

Mehmet Nabi Israfil
Fil Caravan Inc.
240 East 56th St., Ste. 2E
New York, NY 10022
ph: 212-421-5972
fax: 212-421-5976
filcaravan@att.net
http://www.filcaravan.com
Established in 1976, Serves an international clientele in all aspects of Islamic Art including antiques, jewelry, textiles and fine Oriental rugs; has large selection of authentic Russian samovars.

Italian Renaissance

Museums/Libraries

Marketing Director
Isabella Stewart Gardner Museum
280 The Fenway
Boston, MA 02115-5809
ph: 617-566-1401 or 617-566-5643
fax: 617-232-8039
information@isgm.org
http://www.gardnermuseum.org
Museum is the remarkable achievement of Isabella Stewart Gardner, who formed the collection, designed the building; opened in 1903; built in the style of the 15th century Venetian palazzo; houses 2,500 works of art spanning 30 centuries.

Jasper F. Cropsey

Museums/Libraries

Newington-Cropsey Foundation
25 Cropsey Lane
Hastings On Hudson, NY 10706
ph: 914-478-7990
ams@newingtoncropsey.com
http://www.newingtoncropsey.com
Concentrates on figurative and classical works, with good color illustrations, and comments on art, architecture, and culture in general.

Jewish

(see also JUDAICA)

Museums/Libraries

Vladimir Levin, Pub. Coord.
Center for Jewish Art, Hebrew
   University of Jerusalem
Journal: Jewish Art
Mount Scopus
Humanities Building
Boulevard, Jerusalem 91905 Israel
ph: 972-2-5882281 or 972-2-5882288
fax: 972-2-5400105
cja@vms.huji.ac.il
http://www.hum.huji.ac.il/cja
Dedicated to research, documentation, publication and education in the field of Jewish art.

Jo Mora

Collectors

Terry Ahlberg
1000 Irvine Blvd.
Tustin, CA 92780-3527
ph: 714-730-1000 or 949-856-9395
fax: 714-730-1752
emailit@earthlink.net
Collecting all art of Jo Mora (a.k.a. J.J. Mora, Joseph J. Mora, J.M.M.) (1876-1947) including posters, pictorial maps, sculpture, illustrated and/or authored books, photos of Mora or his art.

Latin American

Appraisers

Jose Alonso
Alonso Arts, Inc.
200 SW 30 Rd.
Miami, FL 33129
ph: 305-854-1010
fax: 305-854-1590
alonsofa@bellsouth.net
Specializes in Latin American and Cuban art, from Masters to contemporary artists; member of the International Society of Appraisers.

Frederic "Ric" Emmett
Modernism Gallery
1622 Ponce de Leon Blvd.
Miami, FL 33134-4012
ph: 305-442-8743 or 888-217-2760
fax: 305-443-3074
artdeco@modernism.com
http://www.modernism.com
Appraiser of Latin American art for over 20 years; has done shows of some of the finest artists such as Amelia Pelaez and Wifredo Lam.

Maria-Josefa Velazquez, ISA
Art Appraisal Services International
1422 C. Stonehollow Dr.
Humble, TX 77339
ph: 281-358-9967 or 281-610-7067
fax: 281-360-3309
MJVelazquez@ArtAppraisalServices.com
http://www.artappraisalservices.com
Fine arts appraiser and consultant specializes in the appraisal of Latin American art, Spanish colonial art, Western, American and European art, and contemporary art; published author, art history degree, lecturers, ISA Accredited Member.

Internet Resources

Paul Elwood
LatinArt.com
ph: 310-247-8885
pelwood@latinart.com
http://www.latinart.com
The definitive source of Latin American art; interviews of prominent Latin American artists, articles pertaining to art issues and collector issues; comprehensive digital displays of Latin American art; detailed art glossary.

Marine

(see also NAUTICAL ANTIQUES)

Appraisers

Peter C. Sorlien, ASA
Accredited Appraisers
17 1/2 State St.
Marblehead, MA 01945-3536
ph: 781-631-5956
fax: 781-631-6550
appraisr@shore.net
Professional art and marine appraisals; experience with divorce, donation, estate, insurance, litigation, and tax matters; does not buy or sell.

Sara Conklin, ISA
Nautical Appraisals
P.O. Box 30203
Blairsden, CA 96103
ph: 415-467-6249 or 800-464-4208
fax: 415-467-6249
sconklin2@pngusa.net
http://home.earthlink.net/~sconklin2
Managed the collections of the National Maritime Museum in San Francisco for ten years and is an expert in appraising marine fine art.

Dealers

James P. Marenakos
Quester Gallery
77 Main St.
P.O. Box 32
Stonington, CT 06378
ph: 860-535-3860
fax: 860-535-3533
info@questergallery.com
http://www.questergallery.com
Internationally recognized as a leading source for exceptional 18th, 19th and 20th century marine and sporting paintings; features works by artists such as James Butterworth, Montague Dawson, Jack Gray, Antonio Jacobsen, and John Stobart.

Rod & Becky Cardoza
West Sea Company
2495 Congress St.
San Diego, CA 92110-2820
ph: 619-296-5356
fax: 619-216-1097
wsco@cox.net
http://www.westsea.com
Buys, sells all types of marine paintings, scrimshaw, ships' carvings, ship models, navigational and scientific instruments, sailor handcrafts, campaign furniture, hard hat diving, antique marine photography, nautical books, naval ceramics.

Experts

Sara Conklin, ISA
Nautical Appraisals
P.O. Box 30203
Blairsden, CA 96103
ph: 415-467-6249 or 800-464-4208
fax: 415-467-6249
sconklin2@pngusa.net
http://home.earthlink.net/~sconklin2
Managed the collections of the National Maritime Museum in San Francisco for ten years and is an expert in appraising marine fine art.

Internet Resources

Marine Art Information Center
ph: 212-772-2737
fax: 212-861-4754
info@marineart.com
http://www.marineart.com
An online resource center for all manner of topics relating to marine art, including a link to The American Society of Marine Artists.

Periodicals

Robert R. McKenna, Ed.
Magazine: Nautical Collector
One Whale Oil Row
New London, CT 06320
ph: 860-444-0127
fax: 860-444-0129
nautworld@aol.com
An authoritative bi-monthly magazine on the antiques, collectibles, art, artifacts, literature and memorabilia associated with the seas, lakes and waterways.

New Mexico

Dealers

Peter Eller, ISA
Peter Eller Gallery & Appraisers
206 Dartmouth
Albuquerque, NM 87106
ph: 505-268-7437
fax: 505-268-6442
pelgal@nmia.com
http://www.peterellergallery.com
Specializes in works by Albuquerque artists and minor New Mexico artists, traditional and modernist, 1925-1965, for beginning and intermediate collectors; appraising art, antiques, Spanish Colonial, religious and SW Indian artifacts.

New Zealand

Dealers

Ian Johnson
Harden, Johnson & Assoc.
1616 Whisper Way
Goose Creek, SC 29445-4655
ph: 843-572-7968
fax: 843-572-7968
24 years experience in Australian, New Zealand, South African paintings, drawings, and watercolors from 1797 to present; also specializing in British, Scottish, and Irish paintings from

1880-1950; daily contact with these countries.

Oceanic

Appraisers

Norman Hurst, ISA CAPP
Hurst Gallery
53 Mount Auburn St.
Cambridge, MA 02138-5030
ph: 617-491-6888 or 212-744-6488 (NYC)
fax: 617-661-0439
NHurst@compuserve.com
http://www.hurstgallery.com
Buys, sells, appraises African, Oceanic, Native American, PreColumbian and Asian art; one of the leading appraisers of the Pacific including Melanesian, Polynesian, Micronesian, and Southeast Asian art.

Tara Ana Finley
Anubis Appraisers & Estate Services, Inc.
1042 Sorolla Ave.
Miami, FL 33134-3560
ph: 305-446-1820 or 786-486-8042
fax: 305-648-1939
tara.finley@worldnet.att.net
Thirty years experience appraising African and Oceanic art for insurance, donation or probate purposes.

Dealers

Norman Hurst, ISA CAPP
Hurst Gallery
53 Mount Auburn St.
Cambridge, MA 02138-5030
ph: 617-491-6888 or 212-744-6488 (NYC)
fax: 617-661-0439
NHurst@compuserve.com
http://www.hurstgallery.com
Buys, sells, appraises African, Oceanic, Native American, PreColumbian and Asian art; one of the leading appraisers of the Pacific including Melanesian, Polynesian, Micronesian, and Southeast Asian art.

John Buxton
Shango Galleries
6717 Spring Valley
Dallas, TX 75254
ph: 972-239-4620 or 972-239-9943
fax: 972-239-9766
jbuxton@arttrak.com
http://www.arttrak.com
Buys, sells, and appraises African, Precolumbian, Oceanic, and American Indian art.

B.C. Galleries Ancient & Tribal Art
1069 High St.
Armadale, Victoria 3143 Australia
ph: +61 3 9804 3353
fax: +61 3 9804 3353
b.c.galleries@bigpond.com.au
http://www.bcgalleries.com.au
Buys and sells ancient and tribal art: Oceanic, Melanesia, New Guinea, Pacific Islands, Australian Aboriginal,

African tribal, tribal arts of Asia and of the Americas.

Oriental

(see also ART, Asian; BRONZES, Oriental; CERAMICS [ORIENTAL]; COLLECTIBLES [MODERN], Sculptures [Japanese Themes]; ORIENTALIA; PRINTS, Woodblock [Japanese])

Appraisers

Marley Rabstenek
347 East 85th St., #4W
New York, NY 10028
ph: 212-879-4596
marleyrab@aol.com
Specializes in the appraisal of Chinese and Japanese works of art.

Dr. Daphne L. Rosenzweig, ISA CAPP
Rosenzweig Associates
P.O. Box 3976
Sarasota, FL 34230-3976
ph: 941-371-4643
fax: 941-342-6893
rosetwig@aol.com
Asian/Islamic art, Japanese prints, jades, Asian ceramics, sculpture, metalworks, cloisonne, scholar's studio objects, ivories, netsuke, paintings, screens, Himalayan, Indian, Southeast Asian Buddhist art, Indian & Persian miniatures.

Frank Castle
Castle Fine Arts, Inc.
P.O. Box 557
San Ramon, CA 94583
ph: 925-735-3149
info@castlefinearts.com
http://www.castlefinearts.com
Specializes in 18th through 20th century Japanese prints and other Oriental art.

Auction Services

William P. Weschler, Jr.
Weschler's
909 E St. NW
Washington, DC 20004-2006
ph: 202-628-1281 or 800-331-1430
fax: 202-628-2366
fineart@weschlers.com
http://www.weschlers.com
Conducts specialized auction sales of antique Oriental Art.

Dealers

Floating World Gallery
P.O. Box 148200
Chicago, IL 60614
ph: 312-587-7800
fax: 312-587-7888
artwork@floatingworld.com
http://www.floatingworld.com
Seeking paintings and prints from the Far East; antique to the present; Japan, Philippines, Indonesia, Singapore, Bali, China.

Experts

Dr. Daphne L. Rosenzweig, ISA CAPP
Rosenzweig Associates
P.O. Box 3976
Sarasota, FL 34230-3976
ph: 941-371-4643
fax: 941-342-6893
rosetwig@aol.com
Consultant and appraiser dealing with Oriental Art; author of the books "Selected Works from the Fine Arts Group of Later Chinese Painting," "The Appraisal of Oriental Art," and of Chinese jade and other Orientalia catalogues.

Misc. Services

Arthur M. Sackler Gallery
Smithsonian Institution
1050 Independence Ave. SW
Washington, DC 20560
ph: 202-357-3200
edsonmi@asia.si.edu
http://www.asia.si.edu
Will authenticate your Japanese, Chinese, Near East and South & Southeast works of art; call for an appt.; limit 5 items/visit, 10 items/year; may be able to work from good photographs.

Museums/Libraries

Arthur M. Sackler Museum, Harvard University of Art Museums
485 Broadway
Cambridge, MA 02138
ph: 617-495-9400
huam@fas.harvard.edu
http://www.artmuseums.harvard.edu/sackler
Houses collections of Ancient, Asian, Islamic, and Later Indian art: the world's finest collection of Chinese jades, Korean ceramics, and Chinese cave temple paintings and sculpture, Japanese woodblock prints, Chinese bronzes, etc.

Milo Beach, Dir.
Freer Gallery of Art
Smithsonian Institution
12th & Jefferson Dr. SW
Washington, DC 20560
ph: 202-357-4880 or 202-357-2700
edsonmi@asia.si.edu
http://www.asia.si.edu
The Freer Gallery of Art and the Arthur M. Sackler Gallery are the two national museums of Asian art at the Smithsonian Institution.

Arthur M. Sackler Gallery
Smithsonian Institution
1050 Independence Ave. SW
Washington, DC 20560
ph: 202-357-3200
edsonmi@asia.si.edu
http://www.asia.si.edu
The Freer Gallery of Art and the Arthur M. Sackler Gallery are the two national museums of Asian art at the Smithsonian Institution.

Periodicals

Nathan Hilgendorf, Ed.
Newsletter: Newsletter, East Asian Art & Archaeology
Dept. of the History of Art, 40 Tappan Hall
Univ. of Michigan
Ann Arbor, MI 48109-1357
ph: 734-763-2874
fax: 734-647-4121
nhilgen@umich.edu
http://www.umich.edu/~hartspc/NEAAA.html
Published three times per year, NEAAA focuses on current exhibitions, symposia, newly published books, scholarly news, etc.

Tuyet Nguyet, Pub.
Magazine: Arts of Asia
1309 Kowloon Centre
29-39 Ashley Rd.
Kowloon
Hong Kong
ph: (852) 23762228
fax: (852) 23763713
info@artsofasianet.com
http://www.artsofasianet.com
A bi-monthly fully illustrated, scholarly magazine about the Oriental arts.

Repair Services

Dennis Dobson
Dobson Studios
810 N. Daniel St.
Arlington, VA 22201-1944
ph: 703-243-7363
fax: 703-243-2382
ddobson@erols.com
Conservator of Oriental screens, scrolls and wood block prints; repairs and conservation to other paper items as well.

Outsider

(see also ART, African-American; FOLK ART)

Appraisers

Suzanne Staley, ISA CAPP
P.O. Box 1288
Houston, TX 77251-1288
ph: 713-222-6309 or 888-758-1118
fax: 713-223-3116
suzanne@suzannestaley.com
http://www.suzannestaley.com
Specializes in the appraisal of fine art including paintings, prints, drawings, sculpture; American as well as European; also religious art, folk art, outsider art.

Auction Services

Steve Slotin
Slotin Folk Art Auction House
5967 Blackberry Lane
Buford, GA 30518
ph: 770-932-1000
fax: 770-932-0506
folkfest@bellsouth.net
http://www.slotinfolkart.com
Leading venue for self-taught,

Outsider, Folk Art and Southern folk pottery.

Kimball M. Sterling
Kimball M. Sterling Inc.
125 W. Market St.
Johnson City, TN 37601
ph: 423-928-1471 or 423-975-0600
fax: 423-928-8697
kimsold@tricon.net
http://www.outsiderartauctions.com
Conducts live specialty outsider art and folk art auctions monthly.

Clubs/Associations

Jeff Cory
Intuit: The Center for Intuitive & Outsider Art
Newsletter: Outsider, The
756 N. Milwaukee Ave.
Chicago, IL 60622
ph: 312-243-9088
fax: 312-243-9089
intuit@art.org
http://outsider.art.org
Committed to fostering and expanding the awareness of outsider, intuitive, and visionary art.

Dealers

Frank Maresca
Ricco/Maresca Gallery
529 W. 20th St., 3rd Floor
New York, NY 10011
ph: 212-627-4819
fax: 212-627-5117
rmgal@aol.com
http://www.riccomaresca.com
Deals in American self-taught, folk and outsider art.

William K. Jones
Folk Art Net
4026 Melrose Ave.
Roanoke, VA 24017
ph: 800-476-5781 or 540-362-3751
fax: 540-362-1822
info@folkartnet.com
http://www.folkartnet.com
Collects, buys and sells self-taught, folk, outsider art.

America - Oh, Yes
17 Pope Ave. Executive Park, Bldg. 4
P.O. Box 3075
Hilton Head Island, SC 29928
ph: 843-785-2649
folkart@hargray.com
http://www.americaohyes.com

Matt Lippa
Artisans
P.O. Box 256
Mentone, AL 35984-0256
ph: 256-634-4037
fax: 256-634-4037
artisans@folkartisans.com
http://www.folkartisans.com
Buy and sell folk art, outsider art, fine art; Internet WWW site offers links to additional dealers; also offers non-profit clubs and museums with an outlet to post notices, press releases, calendar items, etc. at no charge.

Marcia Weber
Marcia Weber - Art Objects
1050 Woodley Rd.
Montgomery, AL 36106
ph: 334-262-5349
fax: 334-567-0060
weberart@mindspring.com
http://www.marciaweberartobjects.com
Has specialized in collecting art created by self-taught artists for many years; has an inventory of over 400 works available through photographs sent to prospective purchasers; gallery opened by appointment only.

Anton Haardt Gallery
2714 Coliseum St.
New Orleans, LA 70130
ph: 504-897-1172
anton@antonart.com
http://www.antonart.com
Specializes in contemporary folk art from the Deep South.

Lois Zetter
Zetter Collection, The
3261 Celinda Dr.
Carlsbad, CA 92008-2070
ph: 760-730-4630
fax: 760-730-4632
lzetter@pacbell.net
http://www.zetteroutsider.com
Specializing in outsider, folk, art brut, self-taught artists.

Bonnie Grossman
Ames Gallery, The
Newsletter: Ames News
2661 Cedar St.
Berkeley, CA 94708-1933
ph: 510-845-4949
fax: 510-845-6219
info@amesgallery.com
http://www.amesgallery.com
Specializes in self-taught, visionary, and outsider art; carved canes, quilts, hooked rugs, tramp art, whirligigs, and whimseys; emphasis is on homemades and handmades; call for appointment.

Internet Resources

William Swislow
Outsider Pages, The
billsw@interestingideas.com
http://www.interestingideas.com

Periodicals

Journal: Raw Vision
163 Amsterdam Ave., #203
New York, NY 10023-5001
ph: 212-714-8381
rawvision@btinternet.com
http://www.rawvision.com
A quarterly journal devoted to outsider art (works ignored by the conventional art press).

Paint-By-Numbers

Internet Resources

Larry Rubin
Le Salon de PAINT-BY-NUMBERS
eddertoo@paintbynumberz.com
http://www.paintbynumberz.com/directory.html
History of paint-by-numbers, articles, conservation tips, photos, related links.

Paint By Numbers, National Museum of American History
http://americanhistory.si.edu/paint/introduction.html
On this Web site the National Museum of American History presents the paint-by-number phenomenon as "...a window on the history of creativity, leisure, and domesticity in postwar America."

Periodicals

Larry Rubin
Newsletter: By The Numbers
2100 N.E. 52nd Ct.
Fort Lauderdale, FL 33308
rubin@pstcomputers.com
http://www.paintbynumberz.com/larry.html
A quarterly paint-by-numbers publication containing history, auction reports, preservation, pricing tips.

Polynesia

Collectors

Mark Blackburn
Mauna Kea Galleries
65-1298 Kawaihae Rd.
Waimea, HI 96743
ph: 808-887-2244
fax: 808-887-2226
mkg@interpac.net
http://www.maunakeagalleries.com
Wants to buy over 50-year-old-art and artifacts from Polynesia; coral pounders, wood bowls, god figures, jewelry, personal adornment items, wood headrests, tapa cloth; from Tahiti, Cook Islands, New Zealand, Samoa, Fiji, Hawaii, etc.

Prison Related

Dealers

Matt Lippa
Artisans
P.O. Box 256
Mentone, AL 35984-0256
ph: 256-634-4037
fax: 256-634-4037
artisans@folkartisans.com
http://www.folkartisans.com
Buy and sell folk art, outsider art, fine art; Internet WWW site offers links to additional dealers; also offers non-profit clubs and museums with an outlet to post notices, press releases, calendar items, etc. at no charge.

Pulp

Collectors

Timothy F. Isaacson
1002 Clinton
Oak Park, IL 60304
ph: 708-383-5646
moeknows1007@msn.com
Wants to buy original (cover) paintings; paintings that were used for the cover art for pulps, magazines, paperback and digest books, and movie posters: lurid, sleazy dames, hard boiled detective action, sexy gals, monsters, sci-fi, etc.

Remington

Internet Resources

D. Green
FredericRemington.net
FredericRemington@MyOldWest.com
http://www.fredericremington.net
This Frederick Remington portal is all about the famous Western artist: paintings, bronze sculptures.

Museums/Libraries

Frederic Remington Art Museum
303 Washington St.
Ogdensburg, NY 13669
ph: 315-393-2425
fax: 315-393-4464
info@fredericremington.org
http://www.fredericremington.org
The only museum dedicated to the life and works of the renown artist of the Old West, Frederic Remington.

Sid Richardson Collection of Western Art
309 Main St.
Fort Worth, TX 76102
ph: 817-332-6554
fax: 817-332-8671
info@sidrmuseum.org
http://www.sidrmuseum.org
Permanent exhibit of 56 paintings by the premier Western artists Frederic Remington and Charles M. Russell.

Rodin

Museums/Libraries

Maryhill Museum of Art
35 Maryhill Museum Dr.
Goldendale, WA 98620-4601
ph: 509-773-3733
fax: 509-773-6138
MaryHill@gorge.net
http://www.maryhillmuseum.org
The museum contains an internationally recognized collection of sculpture and drawings by the great French master Auguste Rodin.

Musee Rodin
77 Rue de Varenne
Paris, 75007 France
ph: 00 33 (0) 1 44 18 61 10
fax: 00 33 (0) 1 45 51 17 52
penseur@musee-rodin.fr
http://www.musee-rodin.fr

Scottish

Dealers

Ian Johnson
Harden, Johnson & Assoc.
1616 Whisper Way
Goose Creek, SC 29445-4655
ph: 843-572-7968
fax: 843-572-7968
24 years experience in Australian, New Zealand, South African paintings, drawings, and watercolors from 1797 to present; also specializing in British, Scottish, and Irish paintings from 1880-1950; daily contact with these countries.

South Africa

Dealers

Ian Johnson
Harden, Johnson & Assoc.
1616 Whisper Way
Goose Creek, SC 29445-4655
ph: 843-572-7968
fax: 843-572-7968
24 years experience in Australian, New Zealand, South African paintings, drawings, and watercolors from 1797 to present; also specializing in British, Scottish, and Irish paintings from 1880-1950; daily contact with these countries.

Southern

Collectors

A. Everette James, Jr.
St. James Place
205 New Castle Place
Chapel Hill, NC 27514
ph: 919-933-6853
fax: 919-942-0437
everette@nc.rr.com
Specializes in Southern Art from the period 1840 to 1950.

Dealers

Robert B. Mayo
Gallery Mayo, Inc.
11758 River Crest Dr.
Gloucester, VA 23061-2516
ph: 804-693-2516
hightide@visi.net
Buys and sells 19th through early 20th century American art, with a specialty in Southern and sporting art.

Henry Barnet
Your Town, Inc.
516 Maverick Circle
Spartanburg, SC 29307-3707
ph: 864-579-2112
hbbarnet@cs.com
Buys, sells and appraises 18th through 20th C. American art, specializing in Southern art, genre, rare and collectible books, sporting art; originals and prints.

Spanish

Appraisers

Carol O'Brien English, PhD, ASA
I.C., Inc.
9920 West 34th Dr.
Wheat Ridge, CO 80033-5764
ph: 303-238-2882
fax: 303-238-1617
drenglish@attbi.com
http://www.appraisers.org/pages/memberpage.cfm?id=10178
Specializes in appraising Spanish, European, and American art; also Spanish colonial fine and decorative arts; Accredited Senior Appraiser.

Museums/Libraries

Mitchell Codding, Dir.
Hispanic Society of America, The
613 W. 155th St.
New York, NY 10032
ph: 212-926-2234
fax: 212-690-0743
info@hispanicsociety.org
http://www.hispanicsociety.org

Sporting

(see also ART, Wildlife; SPORTING COLLECTIBLES)

Appraisers

Pamela E. Mayo, ISA
710 Washington St.
Sewickley, PA 15143-1845
ph: 412-749-0760 or 412-390-3707
fax: 412-390-3708
pandjr@usaor.net
Fine art appraiser (paintings, drawings, prints, sculpture), specializing in 19th and early 20th century American art with a general background in 18th-20th century American and European art; specializes in sporting art and Southern art.

Collectors

Robert B. Mayo
Gallery Mayo, Inc.
11758 River Crest Dr.
Gloucester, VA 23061-2516
ph: 804-693-2516
hightide@visi.net
Wants American sporting art through the mid-20th century; author of "America, The Sporting View."

Dealers

Sportsman's Eye, The
11-B Whiting St.
Hingham, MA 02043
ph: 781-740-0250
olruff@netzero.net
http://www.sportsmanseye.com
Specializes in American sporting art by Frank Benson, Pleissner, Frost, Ettinger, Ripley, others; also high-quality decoys specializing in New England decoys.

Stephen B. O'Brien, Jr.
268 Newbury St.
Boston, MA 02116
ph: 617-536-0536
fax: 617-536-2238
info@americansportingart.com
http://www.americansportingart.com
Buys and sells quality antique decoys; also folk art, and American paintings; offers appraisals, auction representation, brokerage, and collections management services.

James P. Marenakos
Quester Gallery
77 Main St.
P.O. Box 32
Stonington, CT 06378
ph: 860-535-3860
fax: 860-535-3533
info@questergallery.com
http://www.questergallery.com
Internationally recognized as a leading source for exceptional 18th, 19th and 20th century marine and sporting paintings; features works by artists such as Frank Benson, Jack Gray, Donald Curley, David Hagerbaumer, and Arthur Tait.

J.N. Bartfield
J.N. Bartfield Galleries, Inc.
30 West 57th St.
Third Floor
New York, NY 10019
ph: 212-245-8890
fax: 212-541-4860
bartfield@aol.com
Buys and sells sporting, Western, and 19th century American art.

Tony Laws
Woods & Water, Inc.
1019 McFarland Blvd.
Northport, AL 35476
ph: 205-333-1214 or 800-383-9020
fax: 205-339-9573
info@woods-n-water.com
http://www.woods-n-water.com
Buys and sells sporting art: paintings, prints, drawings, classic firearms, rods & reels, sporting bronzes, wood carvings, advertising art, catalogs, brochures, books.

Robert Krause
Ravenwood Gallery
38745 Butternut Ridge Rd.
Elyria, OH 44035-8372
ph: 440-458-4929
Wants to buy paintings, prints, etchings, calendars, and posters relating to hunting and fishing, birds, dogs, guns, ammunition and power companies; also duck and crow calls, decoys, sporting books, bamboo fly rods, rods, reels, etc.

Frank J. Mikesh
1356 Walden Rd.
Walnut Creek, CA 94596-3158
ph: 925-934-9243
fax: 925-947-6113
natscibooks@netvista.net
http://www.netvista.net/~natscibooks
Interested in out-of-print natural history, hunting, fishing, sporting, and wildlife books, and related art.

Sports

(see also SPORTS COLLECTIBLES)

Museums/Libraries

National Art Museum of Sport, Inc.
Newsletter: Museum of Sport Newsletter
850 W. Michigan St.
Indianapolis, IN 46202-5198
ph: 317-274-3627
fax: 317-274-3878
arein@iupui.edu
http://namos.iupui.edu
Promotes sports art, e.g., paintings, sculptures, prints depicting fishing, track, boxing, racquet games, auto racing, baseball, etc.

Supplies For

Suppliers

Chris Midkiff
Art Display Essentials
2 West Crisman Rd.
Columbia, NJ 07832
ph: 800-862-9869 or 908-496-4951
fax: 908-496-4956
info@artdisplay.com
http://www.artdisplay.com
Sells display items: general holders and easels, plate & bowl stands, picture hanging, display accessories, jewelry stands, risers, blocks, bases, humidity control, display cases and shelves, mineral and fossil stands, specific holders.

Western

(see also NATIVE AMERICAN; WESTERN AMERICANA)

Appraisers

Cynthia Hale
7930 S. Hudson
Tulsa, OK 74136
ph: 918-524-9338
cj-hale@swbell.net
Specializes in the appraisal of Native American art; also other fine art, paintings, sculpture.

Sarah Ann Bowler-Hill
Peter Eller Gallery & Appraisers
12432 Prospect Ave. NE
Albuquerque, NM 87112
ph: 505-249-3925 or 505-268-7437
fax: 505-268-6442
bowlerhill@yahoo.com
http://www.peterellergallery.com
Appraising Southwestern and contemporary Native American arts, antiques and general residential contents; video and photographic inventory services available.

Dealers

J.N. Bartfield
J.N. Bartfield Galleries, Inc.
30 West 57th St.
Third Floor
New York, NY 10019
ph: 212-245-8890
fax: 212-541-4860
bartfield@aol.com
*Wants anything of American
Historical interest, especially having
to do with the West: paintings,
bronzes, drawings, water colors;
Cowboy and Indian, Western
landscapes, Remington, Farny,
Hansen, Krieghoff, Bierstadt, Homer,
etc.*

William L. King
Bozeman Trail Gallery
190 N. Main
Sheridan, WY 82801
ph: 307-672-3928
btg@bozemantrailgallery.com
http://www.bozemantrailgallery.com
*Wants 19th and early 20th c. Western
art, especially by Joe DeYong, E.W.
Gollings, Hans Kleiber; also wants
No. Plains Indian beadwork and
related items, cowboy equipment, Colt
Bisley's, mod. 1885 Remington pistols.*

Michael D. Higgins
Michael D. Higgins & Son Antique
Indian Art
4429 N. Campbell Ave.
Tucson, AZ 85718
ph: 520-577-8330
mdhiggins@earthlink.net
http://www.mhiggins.com
*Appraises, buys and sells antique
American Indian, PreColumbian,
Mexican and Spanish Colonial
antiques; since 1972; also wants
paintings of the American West;
museum references available.*

Peter Eller, ISA
Peter Eller Gallery & Appraisers
206 Dartmouth
Albuquerque, NM 87106
ph: 505-268-7437
fax: 505-268-6442
pelgal@nmia.com
http://www.peterellergallery.com
*Specializes in and appraises
American, Southwest, and "Western"
art; also Pueblo pottery, Navajo rugs
and other weavings, Spanish colonial
artifacts of the Southwest.*

Don Bennett
Don Bennett & Associates
P.O. Box 283
Agoura Hills, CA 91376-0283
ph: 818-991-5596
fax: 818-991-6866
artofwest@aol.com
*Collects, buys, sells and appraises
high quality antique Native American
items: Navajo, baskets, etc.; also
paintings by deceased Western artists;
since 1968.*

Experts

Bruce M. Shackelford
Western Services
P.O. Box 15707
San Antonio, TX 78212
ph: 210-698-3217
fax: 210-698-0073
bruce@bshack.com
http://www.bshack.com
*Specializes in art from the Southwest
by Native Americans.*

Museums/Libraries

Rockwell Museum, The
111 Cedar St.
Corning, NY 14830
ph: 607-937-5386
fax: 607-974-4536
info@rockwellmuseum.org
http://stny.lrun.com/rockwellmuseum
*Collections include the finest in
traditional and contemporary America
Western and Native American art:
paintings, sculpture, and more;
considered by many to be "The Best of
the West in the East."*

M.J. VanDeventer
National Cowboy & Western Heritage
Museum
Magazine: Persimmon Hill
1700 N.E. 63rd St.
Oklahoma City, OK 73111-7906
ph: 405-478-2250
fax: 405-478-4714
info@nationalcowboymuseum.org
http://www.nationalcowboymuseum.org
*Preserves the rich heritage of the Old
West and honors both deceased and
living people who have made positive
contributions to the heritage of the
West; collections include barbed wire,
Western art, fashion, guns & gun
leather, more.*

Periodicals

Tom Tierney
Duerr & Tierney, Inc.
Magazine: Art of the West
15612 Hwy. 7, Ste. 235
Hopkins, MN 55345-3559
ph: 612-935-5850
fax: 612-935-6546
aotw@aotw.com
http://www.aotw.com
*Magazine featuring art of the West:
cowboys, American landscapes,
western wildlife, etc.*

Wildlife

Dealers

Bob Dumaine
Sam Houston Duck Co.
Newsletter: Duck Report, The
P.O. Box 820087
Houston, TX 77282-0087
ph: 281-493-6386 or 800-231-5926
fax: 281-496-1445
bdhouduck@aol.com
http://www.shduck.com
*Specializing in Wildlife Art, including
originals, prints, sculptures, and gifts.*

Museums/Libraries

National Museum of Wildlife Art
2820 Rungius Rd.
Jackson, WY 83001
ph: 800-313-9553 or 307-733-5771
fax: 307-733-5787
info@wildlifeart.org
http://www.wildlifeart.org
*The nation's premier public collection
of fine art devoted to wildlife; nearly
2,300 works of art in the collection.*

Periodicals

Pothole Publishing, Inc.
Magazine: Wildlife Art Magazine
1428 E. Cliff Rd.
Burnsville, MN 55337
ph: 952-736-1020 or 800-626-0934
fax: 952-736-1030
publisher@mail.winternet.com
http://www.wildlifeartmag.com
*Largest magazine focusing on art
relating to animals, birds, and art of
the natural world; international in
scope; full-color award-winning
magazine; artists from around the
world; painters, sculptors, wood
carvers, etc.; bi-monthly.*

William Aiken Walker

Experts

John Fowler
P.O. Box 15529
New Orleans, LA 70175
ph: 504-888-2380
fax: 504-899-0843
*Currently researching the works of
William Aiken Walker (1838-1921) in
the preparation of a catalogue
raisonne.*

ART DECO

(see also ARCHITECTURAL
ELEMENTS; CERAMICS; CLOCKS;
ELECTRICITY RELATED ITEMS,
Appliances; FRANKART;
FURNITURE [ANTIQUE]; GEMS &
JEWELRY; GLASS; MODERNISM;
RADIOS; SALOON & BAR
COLLECTIBLES, Cocktail Shakers)

Appraisers

Vivian Riegelman, ISA CAPP
AAA Appraisal Co., Inc.
10612-D Providence Rd., #225
Charlotte, NC 28277
ph: 704-843-4033
fax: 704-843-7562
vivri@carolina.rr.com
*Certified Member of the International
Society of Appraisers and the
American Society of Appraisers.*

Frederic "Ric" Emmett
Modernism Gallery
1622 Ponce de Leon Blvd.
Miami, FL 33134-4012
ph: 305-442-8743 or 888-217-2760
fax: 305-443-3074
artdeco@modernism.com
http://www.modernism.com
Dealer and appraiser of Art Deco

*furniture, lighting, art and period
objects for over 20 years.*

Sylvia Fitzgerald, ISA
A.A.E.S.
P.O. Box 2509
Sacramento, CA 95812
ph: 800-471-9841 or 916-448-2428
sylfitz@compuserve.com
*Accredited ISA appraiser specializing
in Art Nouveau, Art Deco, Arts &
Crafts, art glass, art pottery, and fine
porcelains.*

Auction Services

Amory Spizzirri, Client Svc.
William Doyle Galleries
175 E. 87th St.
New York, NY 10128-2205
ph: 212-427-2730
fax: 212-369-0892
info@doylegalleries.com
http://www.doylegalleries.com
*Holds over 50 auctions annually of
furniture and decorations, paintings
and sculpture, jewelry, books and
prints, couture and textiles, 20th
century art & design, majolica,
Lalique, Asian works of art and other
specialty categories.*

Savoia's Auction Inc.
Rte. 23
South Cairo, NY 12482
ph: 518-622-8000
fax: 518-622-9453

Ronald Piekarz
Art Deco Auction House
1600 Whitman, Ste. 100
Wheaton, IL 60187
ph: 630-665-5279
fax: 630-665-5279
service@virtualauctions.com
http://www.virtualauctions.com/
ArtDecoAuctionHouse
*If you are the type of person who fully
appreciates all types of distinctive Art
Deco, this is the place for you; from
sparkling chrome cocktail shakers to
elegant telephones, you will find them
at this live, interactive auction.*

Bonhams & Butterfields
7601 Sunset Blvd.
Los Angeles, CA 90046-2714
ph: 323-850-7500
fax: 323-850-5843
info@butterfields.com
http://www.butterfields.com
Two specialty auction each year.

Clubs/Associations

Tony Fusco, Pres.
Art Deco Society of Boston
One Murdock Terrace
Brighton, MA 02135-2817
ph: 617-787-2637
fax: 617-782-4430
fuscofour@aol.com
*Purpose is to educate, and to preserve
items and architecture relating to the
Art Deco period.*

Maury Panton, Mem.
Art Deco Society of New York
Newsletter: Modernist
P.O. Box 160
Planetarium Station
New York, NY 10024
samnoid@msn.com
http://www.artdeco.org
Dedicated to the study, preservation and celebration of all forms of Art Deco, from Cassandre posters to Donald Deskey furniture, from Bakelite radios to the Chrysler Building.

Art Deco Society of Washington
Newsletter: Translux
P.O. Box 42722
Washington, DC 20015-2722
ph: 202-298-1100
info@adsw.org
http://www.adsw.org
Non-profit organization to foster public awareness and appreciation of the Art Deco period (1925-1950) through volunteer actions to preserve the decorative, industrial, architectural, and cultural arts of that era.

George Neary
Miami Design Preservation League
Newsletter: Impressions
1001 Ocean Dr.
P.O. Box 190180
Miami Beach, FL 33119
ph: 305-672-2014 or 305-672-1836
fax: 305-672-4319
info@mdpl.org
http://www.mdlp.org
Non-profit Art Deco preservation society devoted to preserving, protecting and promoting the cultural, social, economic, environmental, and architectural integrity of the Miami Beach architectural district.

Sharon Koskoff, Pres.
Art Deco Society of the Palm Beaches
Newsletter: Streamline
325 SW 29th Ave.
Delray Beach, FL 33445
ph: 561-276-9925
fax: 561-276-9925
artdeco@adelphia.net
http://community.gopbi.com/artdeco
A non-profit organization dedicated to the preservation, education and awareness of Art Deco Architecture and design; custom Art Deco design services also available; newsletter published quarterly.

Art Deco Society of Cleveland
Newsletter: Newsreel
P.O. Box 210134
Cleveland, OH 44121
ph: 216-382-3283 or 216-721-2274

Detroit Area Art Deco Society
Newsletter: Modern, The
P.O. Box 1393
Royal Oak, MI 48068-1393
ph: 248-582-3326
membership@daads.org
http://www.daads.org

Chicago Art Deco Society
Magazine: Chicago Art Deco Society Magazine
950 Stonegate Dr.
Highland Park, IL 60035-5147
ph: 847-291-4440
fax: 847-291-6677
Promotes the appreciation of the Art Deco era through publications and meetings.

Art Deco Society of Louisiana
P.O. Box 1326
Baton Rouge, LA 70821-6367
ph: 225-275-6367

Art Deco Society of Los Angeles
Newsletter: Exposition, The
P.O. Box 972
Los Angeles, CA 90078-0972
ph: 310-659-3326
fax: 310-659-3326
adsla@ix.netcom.com
http://www.adsla.org
Since 1983, has welcomed individuals with a fondness for Art Deco and an interest in exploring its inexhaustible causes and effects; dedicated to the appreciation of Art Deco in all of its historic significance; tours, studies, workshops.

Art Deco Society of California
Magazine: Sophisticate, The
100 Bush St., Ste. 511
San Francisco, CA 94104-3908
ph: 415-982-DECO
halglatzer@sprintmail.com
http://www.art-deco.org
Society honors the aesthetic achievements of the first half of the 20th century, especially 1920s through 1940s (the Art Deco period); a not-for-profit membership organization that endeavors to increase public awareness of the era.

Richard Unger
Sacramento Art Deco Society
Newsletter: Moderne Times Newsletter, The
P.O. Box 162836
Sacramento, CA 95816-2836
ph: 916-736-1929
Non-profit organization dedicated to preserving all aspects of the Art Deco period (1925-1945); monthly lectures on architecture, design, jewelry, music, art, etc.; offers walking tours; educational and fun events.

Donald Luxton
Canadian Art Deco Society
470 Granville St., #470
Vancouver, British Columbia V6C 1V5 Canada
ph: 604-688-1216
donaldluxton@telus.net
Formed in 1984 to assist in the preservation and awareness of the Art Deco styles; holds annual lecture series, and occasional special events; member of the International Coalition of Art Deco Societies.

Collectors

John M. England, Jr.
103 Old River Rd.
Lincoln, RI 02865
Buys, sells, collects Art Deco items, industrial design, Moderne furnishings, radios, streamline.

Richard Trautwein
Toys N Such
437 Dawson St.
Sault Sainte Marie, MI 49783-2119
ph: 906-635-0356
Collector, dealer wants to buy quality Art Deco items in glass, ceramics, sculpture, metalwork, silver, jewelry, and rugs.

Clint Miller
1604 N. Harrison St.
Little Rock, AR 72207-5322
ph: 501-664-8424 or 501-340-6123
Wants to buy Art Deco bookends, radios, paperweights, book jackets, posters, etc.

Wilma Schiebel
No Place Like Home Collectibles
2200 S. Hwy 62-65
Harrison, AR 72601
ph: 870-741-9494
nplhc@alltel.net
Wants anything Art Deco.

Dealers

William Sakas
20th Century Antiques
P.O. Box 1725
Montclair, NJ 07042
ph: 973-783-7174
decobill@aol.com
http://members.aol.com/decobill
Buys and sells 20th century antiques, furniture, and collectibles; specializes in radios, cameras and paper items.

Sandi Berman
Deco Deluxe
993 Lexington Ave.
New York, NY 10021
ph: 212-472-7222
fax: 212-588-0645

Carl Ratner
94 Mechanic St.
Reinholds, PA 17569-9701
ph: 717-484-1021
artdeco@epix.net
Buy, collects, sell, trade a wide range of Art Deco items: Chase, Manning Bowman and Revere chrome; clocks, cameras, lighters, radios, telephones; Frankart; lamps and lighting fixtures; kitchen appliances; Roseville Futura pottery, etc.

Bob Aibel
Moderne Gallery
111 N. 3rd St.
Philadelphia, PA 19106-1903
ph: 215-923-8536
fax: 215-619-0068
raibel@aol.com
http://www.modernegallery.com
Wants to buy Art Deco items - glass, ceramics, furniture, sculpture, paintings, catalogs, etc.; specialty areas include Ruba Rombic art glass and Nakashima furniture.

Bruce Marine
Cherub Antiques Gallery
2918 M. St. NW
Washington, DC 20007-3713
ph: 202-337-2224
fax: 202-337-2224
Buys and sells Art Deco glass, artwork, and metal wares.

Ken Forster
5501 Seminary Rd., Ste. 1311 South
Falls Church, VA 22041-3907
ph: 703-379-1142
kencforster@aol.com
Dealer in American art pottery and tiles, specializing in American tiles from 1860 to 1940; also Art Nouveau, Art Deco, Georg Jensen silver, and American Modernism.

Frederic "Ric" Emmett
Modernism Gallery
1622 Ponce de Leon Blvd.
Miami, FL 33134-4012
ph: 305-442-8743 or 888-217-2760
fax: 305-443-3074
artdeco@modernism.com
http://www.modernism.com
Wants to buy Deco and 1950s furniture by Deskey, Rhode, Nelson, Frankl, Nakashima, Mont, and other designers; also wants lamps, pottery, glass, bronzes, chrome and Mexican silver.

Connie Zeigler
Durwyn Smedley Antiques
431 Massachusetts Ave.
Indianapolis, IN 46204
ph: 317-822-0102
Buys and sells 20th century design: Arts & Crafts era, Art Deco, Mid-Century Modern, upscale '50s; art pottery from all eras and designer dinnerware; the first Indiana antique shop in the World Wide Web.

Steve Savitt
Josie's
545 Ridge Rd.
Wilmette, IL 60091-2439
ph: 847-256-7646
fax: 847-256-7604
josies545@attbi.com
Specializes in Art Deco, 20th century Modern, art pottery, art glass and jewelry; no reproductions.

Ronald Baker
Art Deco Auction House
1600 Whitman, Ste. 100
Wheaton, IL 60187
ph: 630-665-5279
fax: 630-665-5279
service@virtualauctions.com
http://www.virtualauctions.com/ArtDecoAuctionHouse
Buys, sells, collects and has an online auction of Art Deco items.

Anita Cochran
Anita's Antiques
2730 Virginia Place
Homewood, IL 60430-1135
ph: 708-957-2241
anita.cochran@usdoj.gov
Buys and sells Art Deco; also Depression glass and china; collects Art Deco figurines.

Norman Karp
Time & Again Antiques
4796 Willow Glen Dr.
Las Vegas, NV 89147
ph: 702 889 1917
deco4u@aol.com
Buys and sells Art Deco & Art Nouveau ivory & bronzes and lamps; also Tiffany glass, Steuben glass and high-end small items.

Frank Piccolo
Piccolo Pete's
13814 Ventura Blvd.
Sherman Oaks, CA 91423
ph: 818-990-5421
fax: 818-990-5421
First Art Deco establishment in Los Angeles' San Fernando Valley; Art Deco furniture, glassware, pottery, jewelry, period lighting, etc.

J. Peter Linden
Decodence, Inc.
1684 Market St.
San Francisco, CA 94102
ph: 415-553-4525
fax: 415-553-4521
peter@decodence.com
http://www.decodence.com
Carries high-end European Art Deco pieces ranging from French 1930s furniture to 1920s and 1930s art glass by designers LeVerre Francais, Daum Nancy, and Lalique.

Art & Decoration 1920-1930
Wilhelminastratt 11
4818 SB Breda
The Netherlands
ph: +31-76-5221763
info@art-deco1920-1930.nl
http://www.art-deco1920-1930.nl
Buys and sells original 1930s Art Deco: furniture, figures, lighting, Bakelite, chrome, glass, mirrors, clocks, etc.

Experts

Tony Fusco
Fusco & Four, Associates
One Murdock Terrace
Brighton, MA 02135-2817
ph: 617-787-2637
fax: 617-782-4430
fuscofour@aol.com
Author of "The Confident Collector Identification and Price Guide to Art Deco;" offers appraisal and brokerage services for 1909-1939 Art Deco collectors; appraise and broker fine Art Deco European and American decorative arts.

Ira & Miriam Raskin
Try To Remember
5120 Wilson Ln.
Bethesda, MD 20814-2436
ph: 301-652-1695
fax: 301-986-4528
ieraskin@aol.com
Buys and sells functional nostalgia from the 1920s to 1950s: radios, clocks, watches, jewelry, books, etc.; sells at Beaver Creek Antique Mall, Hagerstown, MD (Exit 32A off I-70).

Greg Stevenson
University of Wales, Dept. of Archaeology
Lampeter
Ceredigion, Wales SA47 8ED U.K.
g.stevenson@lamp.ac.uk
Material culture historian specializing in British ceramics 1927-1937; lectures in design history and the work of designers Clarice Cliff, Keith Murray and Susie Cooper; author of "Art Deco Ceramics," and "The 1930s Home."

Internet Resources

Adam Schoolsky
ArtDeco.com
P.O. Box 95
Nashua, NH 03061
ph: 603-883-7931
fax: 603-882-3781
adam@ArtDeco.com
If it's from the 1920s-1940s, you'll find it here: music, fashion, designers, lifestyles, and much more; secure online multi-dealer Art Deco store.

Museums/Libraries

Cooper-Hewitt National Design
 Museum, Smithsonian Institution
2 East 91st St.
New York, NY 10128
ph: 212-860-6868 or 212-849-8300
publicinfo@ch.si.edu
http://www.si.edu/ndm

Frederick R. Brandt
Virginia Museum of Fine Arts
2800 Grove Ave.
Richmond, VA 23221-2466
ph: 804-340-1400
fax: 804-340-1548
webmaster@vmfa.state.va.us
http://www.vmfa.state.va.us
Fine arts museum covering the entire range of history of art.

Repro. Sources

Kenneth F. Kalbleish, Sr.
Sun Foundry
299 S. Lake St.
Burbank, CA 91502
ph: 818-841-7979 or 800-367-3479
fax: 818-955-9690
sunbronze@pacificnet.net
http://www.sunbronze.com
Carries 360 time-proven masterpieces: museum-quality bronzes: Art Deco, Western Art, Equestrian, Animalier, and more.

Chase Brass & Copper Co.

Book Sellers

Jo-D Books
81 Willard Terrace
Stamford, CT 06903-4927
ph: 203-322-0568
Books on Art Deco chrome, especially by Chase.

Clubs/Associations

Barry L. Van Hook
Chase Collectors Society
2149 West Jibsail Loop
Mesa, AZ 85202-5524
ph: 480-838-6971 or 480-965-1217
fax: 480-965-8314
vanhook@asu.edu
http://www.public.asu.edu/~icblv/chase.htm

Collectors

Barry L. Van Hook
2149 West Jibsail Loop
Mesa, AZ 85202-5524
ph: 480-838-6971 or 480-965-1217
fax: 480-965-8314
vanhook@asu.edu
http://www.public.asu.edu/~icblv/chase.htm
Avid collector of items made by the Chase Brass & Copper Company of Waterbury, CT.

Lamps & Lighting

Dealers

Jack Beeler
Decorum
1400 Vallejo St.
San Francisco, CA 94109-2608
Specializes in buying and selling French and American Art Deco lighting.

Neon

Dealers

Dennis Clark
Off the Wall Antiques, Inc.
7325 Melrose Ave.
Los Angeles, CA 90046
ph: 323-930-1185
fax: 323-930-1595
weirdstuff@earthlink.net
http://www.offthewallantiques.com

ART MODERNE

(see MODERNISM)

ART NOUVEAU

(see also CERAMICS; FURNITURE [ANTIQUE]; GEMS & JEWELRY; GLASS)

Appraisers

Vivian Riegelman, ISA CAPP
AAA Appraisal Co., Inc.
10612-D Providence Rd., #225
Charlotte, NC 28277
ph: 704-843-4033
fax: 704-843-7562
vivri@carolina.rr.com
Certified Member of the International Society of Appraisers and the American Society of Appraisers.

Sylvia Fitzgerald, ISA
A.A.E.S.
P.O. Box 2509
Sacramento, CA 95812
ph: 800-471-9841 or 916-448-2428
sylfitz@compuserve.com
Accredited ISA appraiser specializing in Art Nouveau, Art Deco, Arts & Crafts, art glass, art pottery, and fine porcelains.

Paul G. Bailey, ISA
Antique Appraisal & Estate Services
12819 SE 38th St., PMB 320
Bellevue, WA 98006-1395
ph: 425-746-2777
fax: 425-746-3793
antiquabailey@aol.com
30 years experience buying, selling, brokering, appraising Art Nouveau items: ceramics, clocks, furniture, glass by Daum, Galle, Lalique, Loetz, Tiffany; jewelry, lighting, metalware, etc.

Auction Services

Bonhams & Butterfields
7601 Sunset Blvd.
Los Angeles, CA 90046-2714
ph: 323-850-7500
fax: 323-850-5843
info@butterfields.com
http://www.butterfields.com
Two specialty auctions each year.

Dealers

Bruce Marine
Cherub Antiques Gallery
2918 M. St. NW
Washington, DC 20007-3713
ph: 202-337-2224
fax: 202-337-2224
Buys and sells Art Nouveau glass, artwork, and metal wares.

Paul G. Bailey, ISA
Antique Appraisal & Estate Services
12819 SE 38th St., PMB 320
Bellevue, WA 98006-1395
ph: 425-746-2777
fax: 425-746-3793
antiquabailey@aol.com
30 years experience buying, selling, brokering, appraising Art Nouveau items: ceramics, clocks, furniture, glass by Daum, Galle, Lalique, Loetz, Tiffany; jewelry, lighting, metalware, etc.

Museums/Libraries

Frederick R. Brandt
Virginia Museum of Fine Arts
2800 Grove Ave.
Richmond, VA 23221-2466
ph: 804-340-1400
fax: 804-340-1548
webmaster@vmfa.state.va.us
http://www.vmfa.state.va.us
Fine arts museum covering the entire range of history of art.

ART POTTERY

(see CERAMICS [AMERICAN ART POTTERY]; CERAMICS [ENGLISH], Art Pottery; CERAMICS [CONTINENTAL], Art Pottery)

ART THEFT & FRAUD

Appraisers

James Corcoran, ISA
Corcoran Fine Arts Limited, Inc.
2915 Fairfax Rd.
Cleveland, OH 44118-4015
ph: 216-431-0025 or 216-397-0777
fax: 216-397-0222
corcoranfa@aol.com
http://www.corcoranfinearts.com
Certified Fraud Examiner; active bar admissions in Ohio, New York, Massachusetts and California; insurance, loss and damage claims, expert witness services.

Clubs/Associations

Sharon Flescher, Ex. Dir.
International Foundation for Art
   Research (IFAR)
Magazine: IFAR Journal
500 Fifth Ave., Ste 935
New York, NY 10110
ph: 212-391-6234
fax: 212-391-8794
kferg@ifar.org
http://www.ifar.org
Clearinghouse for information on art theft, fraud, forgery; promotes recovery of stolen art & prevention of circulation of forged works; publishes Stolen Art Alert notices of art thefts and recoveries; organizes lectures.

Ruth Redmond-Cooper, Dir.
Institute of Art & Law
Journal: Art Antiquity & Law
1-5 Cank St.
Leicester, LE1 5GX U.K.
ph: +44 (0)116 253 8888
fax: +44 (0)116 251 1666
info@ial.uk.com
http://www.ial.uk.com
A small independent institution, founded in 1995, that aims to bridge the divide between the worlds of art and law by organizing seminars and publishing books and periodicals; membership is open to the public; many related links.

Internet Resources

Art Theft/Most Wanted Art/Recovery
   Project
saz@saztv.com
http://www.saztv.com
Major cases, stolen art, art recovery, art theft links, art intelligence.

FBI, National Stolen Art File
MT/TCU, Room 5096
935 Pennsylvania Ave., NW
Washington, DC 20535
ph: 202-324-4192
fax: 202-324-1504
http://www.fbi.gov/hq/cid/arttheft/
   arttheft.htm

Larry L. Krug
Theft Reports
18222 Flower Hill Way, #299
Gaithersburg, MD 20879-5300
ph: 301-926-8663
fax: 301-926-7648
info@amres.com
http://www.theftreports.com
Theft resources, education, news, resources.

Lost Art Internet Database
Koordinierungsstelle fuer
   Kulturgutverlustre
Kantstrase 5 / City Carr=E9
Magdeburg, Saxonia-Anhalt 39104
   Germany
ph: (0049) 391 / 5 448 709
fax: (0049) 391 / 53 539 633
mfranz@lostart.de
http://www.lostart.de
A German database for registering and locating cultural assets that were relocated, transported, and also with regard to Jewish citizens, confiscated as a result of their persecution during WWII and the NAZI period.

Alert All - The Stolen Property Guide
Box 24109
Stockholm, 104 51 Sweden
ph: +46 8 663 86 60 or +46 70 471 35 81
fax: +46 70 511 07 08
http://www.alert-all.se
Enables insurance companies, police authorities, auction houses, antique dealers, collectors, burglarized individuals to give and receive information about stolen valuables: clocks, paintings, vehicles, jewelry, yachts, prints, etc.

Ton Cremers
Museum Security Network
Rechter Rottekade 171
Amsterdam, 3032 XD The Netherlands
ph: +31 10 4653837 or +31 62 4224620
fax: +31 10 4653837
TonCremers@museum-security.org
http://www.museum-security.org
Web site collects and disseminates information about incidents and the trade involving stolen cultural property; offers related information such as publications, security products, safety and salvage plans, and related links.

Misc. Services

OmniGuard Corporation
730 Fifth Ave.
New York, NY 10019-4105
ph: 800-808-2882 or 212-577-9000
fax: 212-577-9220
info@omniguard.com
http://www.omniguard.com
Guarantees the authenticity of fine art; also registers art.

Art Loss Register, New York Office
666 Fifth Ave.
New York, NY 10103
ph: 212-262-4831
fax: 212-262-4838
artloss@artloss.com
http://www.artloss.com
A service to register lost art to assist in recovery; a permanent computerized database of stolen and missing works of art, antiques and valuables, operating on an international basis to assist law enforcement agencies.

Sharon Flescher, Ex. Dir.
International Foundation for Art
   Research (IFAR) Authentication Serv.
500 Fifth Ave., Ste 935
New York, NY 10110
ph: 212-391-6234
fax: 212-391-8794
kferg@ifar.org
http://www.ifar.org
Nonprofit educational and research organization; offers a unique authentication service which examines works of art to assist in the resolution of questions of authenticity and attribution; for individuals, art dealers, museums, etc.

Robert E. Spiel
Robert E. Spiel Associates
Newsletter: Art Intelligence Newsletter
855 Skokie Hwy., Ste. N
Lake Bluff, IL 60044
ph: 847-234-1786
fax: 847-234-1784
spiel@arttheft.com
http://www.arttheft.com
Offers global stolen art investigations & security services for appraisers, conservators, private & corporate collectors, dealers, insurance professionals, interior designers, museums, private & public investigators, moving companies.

Art Loss Register, London Office
12 Grosvenor Place
London, London SW1 X7HH U.K.
ph: 0171 235 3393
artloss@artloss.com
http://www.artloss.com
A service to register lost art to assist in recovery; a permanent computerized database of stolen and missing works of art, antiques and valuables, operating on an international basis to assist law enforcement agencies.

Periodicals

Robert E. Spiel
Robert E. Spiel Associates
Newsletter: Art Intelligence Newsletter
855 Skokie Hwy., Ste. N
Lake Bluff, IL 60044
ph: 847-234-1786
fax: 847-234-1784
spiel@arttheft.com
http://www.arttheft.com
Articles and commentary on art crimes; typical art fraud and their discovery; criminal techniques; former FBI Special Agent, Mr. Spiel dedicated most of his 20-year career to the recovery of stolen fine art and rare collectibles.

John Woracker
Trace Ltd.
Magazine: Trace Magazine
Mill Court
Furrlongs, Newport
Isle of Wight, Hampshire PO30 2AA
   U.K.
ph: 44 1983 826000
fax: 44 1983 826201
Trace@thesaurus.co.uk
http://www.trace.co.uk
A monthly, glossy published monthly; focuses on locating and retrieving stolen art, antiques and collectibles; the database interactively searches auction catalogs for fine art and antiques that have been misplaced, stolen, or lost.

ARTIFACTS

(see NATIVE AMERICAN; ANTIQUITIES; HERITAGE RESOURCES; NATURAL HISTORY; FOSSILS; MINERAL SPECIMENS; PREHISTORIC ARTIFACTS; TREASURE HUNTING)

ARTILLERY

(see CANNONS; CIVIL WAR ARTIFACTS; MILITARIA; AMMUNITION & EXPLOSIVE ORDNANCE)

ARTS & CRAFTS

(see also ARCHITECTURAL ELEMENTS, Arts & Crafts; CERAMICS [AMERICAN]; FRANK LLOYD WRIGHT; FURNITURE [ANTIQUE], Stickley; COPPER ITEMS, Stickley)

Appraisers

Paul Royka
AppraisalDay.com
210 Park Avenue, #295
Worcester, MA 01609
ph: 978-582-8207
fax: 978-582-8207
appraisalday@aol.com
http://www.appraisalday.com
Author of "Mission Furniture" (Schiffer).

Shawn Voils
430 Redding #1911
Breckinridge Court
Lexington, KY 40517
ph: 859-245-1089
shvoils@aol.com
Specializes in Arts & Crafts: metal work, pottery, lighting; Dirk van Erp, Gustav Stickley, Roycroft, Jarvie, Rookwood, Newcomb College, Grueby, Marblehead, and Old Mission Kopperkraft.

Alan Winston
Winston Studio & Imports
4448 West Lovers Lane
Dallas, TX 75209
ph: 214-357-0081 or 214-824-2842
fax: 214-821-8583
wsimports@aol.com
http://www.alanwinstonsmith.com
Specializes in the appraisal of arts and crafts, particularly in fiber arts, wood sculpture, silver smithing, casting of jewelry design in lost wax in both gold and silver; GIA graduate gemologist.

Sylvia Fitzgerald, ISA
A.A.E.S.
P.O. Box 2509
Sacramento, CA 95812
ph: 800-471-9841 or 916-448-2428
sylfitz@compuserve.com
Accredited ISA appraiser specializing in Art Nouveau, Art Deco, Arts & Crafts, art glass, art pottery, and fine porcelains.

Auction Services

John Fontaine
Fontaine's Auction Gallery
1485 West Housatonic
Pittsfield, MA 01201
ph: 800-448-7828 or 413-448-8922
fax: 413-442-1550
info@fontaineauction.com
http://www.fontaineauction.com
Conducts periodic Arts & Crafts auction sales of period furniture, metalwork, lighting, and pottery; full-color catalogs, national delivery, absentee bids welcome.

Jane Prentiss
Skinner, Inc.
63 Park Plaza
The Heritage on the Garden
Boston, MA 02116
ph: 617-350-5400
fax: 617-350-5429
info@skinnerinc.com
http://www.skinnerinc.com
Established in 1971, Skinner Inc. is the fourth largest auction house in the US; has offices in Boston and Bolton, MA.

Don Treadway
Treadway Auctions
2029 Madison Rd.
Cincinnati, OH 45208
ph: 513-321-6742
fax: 513-871-7722
treadway2029@earthlink.net
http://www.treadwaygallery.com
Specializes in the sale of Arts and Crafts pottery.

Bonhams & Butterfields
7601 Sunset Blvd.
Los Angeles, CA 90046-2714
ph: 323-850-7500
fax: 323-850-5843
info@butterfields.com
http://www.butterfields.com
Two specialty auction each year.

Clubs/Associations

Kitty Turgeon, Ex. Dir.
Foundation for the Study of the Arts & Crafts Movement
Roycroft Campus
31 South Grove St.
East Aurora, NY 14052
ph: 716-652-3333
fax: 716-655-0562
rycrft@aol.com
http://www.roycroftshops.com
The foundation's mission is to study, teach & preserve the philosophical and artistic legacy of the International Arts & Crafts Movement; meetings, seminars, appraisals, consultations.

Roycrofters-At-Large Association
Newsletter: RALA Newsletter
P.O. Box 417
East Aurora, NY 14052
ph: 716-652-0213
tomboj@buffnet.net
http://www.roycrofter.com/rala/rala.html
Studies the Arts & Crafts Movement and fosters new crafts people at the Roycroft Campus in East Aurora, NY; lecture series, tours, sponsors a winter and a summer crafts show.

Collectors

Terry Seger
880 Foxcreek Ln.
Cincinnati, OH 45233-1462
ph: 513-941-9689
Wants to buy Arts & Crafts furniture.

Richard L. Sasicki
P.O. Box 3113
Glen Ellyn, IL 60138-3113
ph: 630-682-8706
artware@sprynet.com
http://home.sprynet.com/~artware
Wants to buy books, catalogs, pamphlets, or any ephemera related to American Art Pottery and Ceramics or to the Arts & Crafts period.

Bruce Richards
508 N. Belmont Ave.
Los Angeles, CA 90026-4124
ph: 213-413-4517
Wants Roycroft, Karl Kipp, and The Too Kay Shop handwrought copper items in good condition with original

patina: letter openers, bookends, candlesticks, desk sets, vasettes, vases, trays, bowls.

Dealers

Jim Messineo
JMW Gallery
144 Lincoln St.
Boston, MA 02111-2523
ph: 617-338-9097
fax: 617-338-7636
mail@jmwgallery.com
http://www.jmwgallery.com
Buys, sells and specializes along with co-owner Mike Witt in the Arts & Crafts movement. Mission furniture: Lifetime, Limbert, Stickley; American Art Pottery 1875 to 1950s: Grueby, Newcomb, Marblehead, etc.; metalwork, Roycroft.

John S. Zuk
106 Orchard St.
Belmont, MA 02478-2940
ph: 617-484-4800 or 617-588-5709
fax: 810-283-5371
Buys and sells metal work (Roycroft), furniture (Stickley, Limbert), pottery (Newcomb, Marblehead, SEG, Grueby, Rookwood) in the Mission period.

Rosalie & Aram Berberian
ARK Antiques
P.O. Box 3133
New Haven, CT 06515
ph: 203-498-8572
fax: 203-776-4397
ark_antiques@yahoo.com
Wants American craftsman silver, jewelry and metal of the first half of the 20th century.

David Rago
Perrault David Rago Gallery
117 South Main St.
Lambertville, NJ 08530
ph: 609-397-1802
fax: 609-397-5543
perraggal@ragoarts.com
http://www.ragoarts.com
Wants American art pottery, and Arts and Crafts items such as furniture and metal items by Stickley, Rohlfs, Wright, Roycroft, etc.

Dave & Debbie Rudd
Daltons American Decorative Arts
1931 James St.
Syracuse, NY 13206
ph: 315-463-1568
fax: 315-463-1615
rudd@daltons.com
http://www.daltons.com
Specializes in c. 1900-1920 Arts and Crafts period furniture and accessories including Gustav Stickley, J&JG Stickley, Roycroft, mission oak.

Bruce A. Austin
c/o RIT/College Liberal Arts
92 Lomb Memorial Dr.
Rochester, NY 14623-5604
ph: 585-475-2879 or 585-387-9820
fax: 585-475-7732
baagll@rit.edu
Wants to buy L & JG Stickley, Stickley Bros., Gustav Stickley, Limbert, Roycroft, Rohlfs, Mission Oak furniture, clocks, art pottery; also hammered copper and lighting by Roycroft, Dirk Van Erp, Jarvie, Tiffany, Heintz, Albert Berry.

Steve Traband
P.O. Box 7064
Saint Petersburg, FL 33734-7064
ph: 813-896-2308
Buys and sells Mission style furniture: Stickley, Roycroft, Limbert, Lifetime, Rohlfs, F.L. Wright, etc.

Tony McCormack
McCormack & Company
P.O. Box 49093
Sarasota, FL 34320
ph: 941-952-1244 or 941-350-2785
birdkey@aol.com
http://www.birdkey.net
Dealer, expert appraiser specializing in American art pottery and the Arts & Crafts Movement; always buying Rookwood, Grueby, Newcomb College, Teco, Marblehead, Overbeck; dated Van Briggle, George Ohr, Weller & Roseville pottery; member ISA.

Don Treadway
Treadway Gallery, Inc.
2029 Madison Rd.
Cincinnati, OH 45208
ph: 513-321-6742
fax: 513-871-7722
treadway2029@earthlink.net
http://www.treadwaygallery.com

Connie Zeigler
Durwyn Smedley 20th Century
431 Massachusetts Ave.
Indianapolis, IN 46204
ph: 317-822-0102
Buys and sells 20th century design: Arts & Crafts era, Art Deco, Mid-Century Modern, upscale '50s; art pottery from all eras and designer dinnerware; the first Indiana antique shop in the World Wide Web.

John Toomey
Treadway Gallery, Inc.
2029 Madison Rd.
Cincinnati, OH 45208
ph: 708-383-5234
info@treadwaygallery.com
http://www.treadwaygallery.com
Conducts Arts and Crafts auctions in association with Don Treadway.

Michael FitzSimmons
Michael FitzSimmons Decorative Arts
311 West Superior St.
Chicago, IL 60610
ph: 312-787-0496
fax: 312-787-6343
contact@fitzdecarts.com
http://www.fitzdecarts.com
Specializing in 20th century architecture and decorative arts especially Frank Lloyd Wright and the Prairie School of design; also Gustav Stickley and others.

Experts

Rosalie & Aram Berberian
ARK Antiques
P.O. Box 3133
New Haven, CT 06515
ph: 203-498-8572
fax: 203-776-4397
ark_antiques@yahoo.com
Specializing in American Arts & Crafts Movement silver, jewelry and metal items.

Carole Hibel
Carole Hibel Art & Antiques
181 Broadview Rd.
Woodstock, NY 12498
ph: 845-679-2966 or 800-426-3357
fax: 845-679-9101
efshnc6@nyc.rr.com
Author of "The Fulper Book," wants to buy Fulper, Grueby, Marblehead, Teco, etc. pottery, Gustav Stickley, L & JG Stickley, Limberts, Roycroft, Van Erp furniture and lamps, etc.

Fritz Gram
357 North Shore Rd.
Cuba, NY 14727-9227

Bruce Johnson
25 Upper Brush Creek Rd.
Fletcher, NC 28732
ph: 828-628-1915
fax: 828-628-4070
bj1912@aol.com
http://www.arts-craftsconference.com
Writes furniture repair/refinishing column. Wrote "Price Guide to Arts and Crafts Movement" items.

Internet Resources

Carol Kamm, Dir. of Oper.
Arts & Crafts Society
1194 Bandera
Ann Arbor, MI 48103
ph: 734-665-4729
fax: 734-213-0045
info@arts-crafts.com
http://www.arts-crafts.com
Interactive electronic community dedicated to the philosophy and spirit of the original Arts & Crafts Movement of the late 19th and early 20th centuries.

On-Line Arts & Crafts Movement Resource Directory
2612 Clermont St.
Denver, CO 80207
ph: 303-388-2560
stermitz@ragtime.org
http://www.ragtime.org/ Ragtime_Resources.html
Online Arts & Crafts movement resource directory dedicated to the Craftsman period (1890-1920).

Periodicals

David Rago
Journal: Style: 1900
333 North Main St.
Lambertville, NJ 08530
ph: 609-397-9374
fax: 609-397-9377
info@ragoarts.com
http://www.ragoarts.com
The only periodical devoted entirely to the Arts & Crafts movement.

John Brinkmann
Magazine: American Bungalow
P.O. Box 756
Sierra Madre, CA 91205-0756
ph: 626-355-3363 or 800-350-3363
fax: 626-355-1220
john@ambungalow.com
http://www.ambungalow.com
Focusing on Bungalow and Arts & Crafts architecture, design, how-tos, sources, interior and exterior decor, furniture, craftsmen, etc.

Furniture

Dealers

Douglass White
Classic Interiors & Antiques
2042 N. Rio Grande Ave., Ste. E
Orlando, FL 32804-5644
ph: 407-839-0004
Wants to buy American Arts & Crafts period furniture.

Experts

Bruce Johnson
25 Upper Brush Creek Rd.
Fletcher, NC 28732
ph: 828-628-1915
fax: 828-628-4070
bj1912@aol.com
http://www.arts-craftsconference.com
Writes furniture repair/refinishing column; wrote price guide to arts and crafts movement items; host of annual Grove Park Inn Arts & Crafts Conference & Antiques Show, third weekend in February, Asheville, NC.

Roycroft

(see also BOOKS, Roycroft)

Collectors

Richard Blacher
209 Plymouth Colony Rd.
Branford, CT 06405-4753
ph: 203-481-3321
dblacher@javanet.com
Wants all types of Roycroft items, especially books; also wants other

American Private Presses of the period, especially limited editions, illuminations, illustrations, and fine bindings; please describe and price; all quotes answered.

Gary Wood
733 Myrtle Rd.
North Brunswick, NJ 08902-2549
ph: 732-821-7633
woodrasp@aol.com
Collector seeks single issues or bound volumes of all Roycroft magazines including "The Philistine," "Roycrofter," "The Fra," as well as books published by The Roycroft Press and craft items bearing the Roycroft cross-and-orb mark.

Francesca Gern
P.O. Box 2161
Hudson, OH 44236-0161
ph: 330-655-9325
fax: 330-655-9347
rumrill2@aol.com
Wants to buy Roycroft desk sets, vases, sconces, candleholders, lamps, etc.

Experts

Fritz Gram
357 North Shore Rd.
Cuba, NY 14727-9227
Appraises and specializes in Roycroft items.

Internet Resources

Roycroft Copper Online Price Guide
bigfatty@roycroftcopper.com
http://www.roycroftcopper.com
Focuses exclusively on Roycroft art metal; photographs, descriptions, estimated current values on selected pieces of Roycroft copper; also history, tips of identifying, and more.

Museums/Libraries

Elbert Hubbard Roycroft Museum
363 Oakwood Ave.
East Aurora, NY 14052-2319
ph: 716-652-4735 or 716-634-1231
ebert@earthlink.net
http://www.roycrofter.com/museum.htm

Van Erp-Style Lamps

Repro. Sources

Jerry Cohen
Aurora Studios
109 Main St.
Putnam, CT 06260
ph: 860-928-1965 or 800-448-7828
fax: 860-928-1966
jerry@mypinelake.com
http://www.artsncrafts.com
Since 1986 has made handcrafted, hammered copper lighting fixtures, from exact reproductions of Dick Van Erp and Gustav Stickley to custom work designed by Michael Adams or his clients; architectural lighting, table and floor lamps, & more.

William Morris

Clubs/Associations

William Morris Society (US)
Journal: Journal, The
P.O. Box 53263
Washington, DC 20009
us@morrissociety.org
http://www.morrissociety.org
Founded in 1955, the Society aims to make the life and work of Morris and his associates better known: lectures, conferences, tours, museum visits, social gatherings; publishes books and pamphlets dealing with Morris.

William Morris Society of Canada
Journal: Journal, The
52 Berkeley Court
Unionville, Ontario L3R 6LP Canada
ph: 905-475-9370
fax: 905-940-8698
canada@morrissociety.org
http://www.hedgerowhouse.net/ wmsc.html
Exists to foster knowledge about the life, works and philosophy of the gifted and multi-faceted 19th century artist, author and craftsman William Morris (1834-1896.)

William Morris Society (U.K.)
Kelmscot House, 26 Upper Mall
Hammersmith
London, W6 9TA U.K.
ph: 020 8741-3735
fax: 020 8748-5207
uk@morrissociety.org

ASHTRAYS

Collectors

Roger Rose
127 E. 61st St.
New York, NY 10021
ph: 212-838-8758
fax: 212-838-1494
Wants to buy chromo-litho and potmetal souvenir ashtrays made from the 1940s to 1960s; mint condition only; state shaped, US cities, US tourist spots.

Patrick Batzler
8118 Virginia Circle North
St. Louis Park, MN 55426
ph: 952-525-9590
fax: 952-545-7662
patrickbatzler@aol.com
Ashtray collector seeking "big-mouth," "smoker," and other unusual ashtrays.

Casino

Experts

Art Anderson
P.O. Box 4103
Flint, MI 48504-0103
ph: 810-234-3400 or 810-659-4446
fax: 810-234-8656
cashtrays@aol.com
http://members.aol.com/cashtrays
Author of "Casinos and Their Ashtrays."

Tire

Collectors

Jim Olean
115 MacBeth Dr.
Lower Burrell, PA 15068-2628
candy46man@aol.com
Avid collector of tire ashtrays, toy candy containers and American glass target balls.

ASPHALT

Museums/Libraries

Scott Gordon, Cur.
World Famous Asphalt Museum
6000 J St.
Sacramento, CA 95819
ph: 916-278-7946
gordonvs@ecs.csus.edu
http://ecs.csus.edu/~gordonvs/asphalt/asphalt.html
A breathtaking exhibit of famous asphalt from such notable byways as Route 66 and Hwy 1 (Pacific Coast Highway).

ASTRONAUT MEMORABILIA

(see SPACE COLLECTIBLES)

ASTRONOMICAL ITEMS

(see also INSTRUMENTS & DEVICES, Scientific; MINERAL SPECIMENS, Meteorites; SPACE COLLECTIBLES)

Comets

Experts

Stuart Schneider
Halley's Comet
P.O. Box 64
Teaneck, NJ 07666-0064
ph: 201-599-4250
fax: 201-599-4251
Stuart@wordcraft.net
http://www.wordcraft.net
Collector, writer wants items relating to Halley's comet; author of "Halley's Comet - Memories of 1910."

Telescopes

Clubs/Associations

Antique Telescope Society
Journal: Journal of the Antique
   Telescope Society
1878 Robinson Rd.
Dahlonega, GA 30533
njastro@erols.com
http://www.webari.com/oldscope
Members collect, study, restore, preserve and use antique telescopes & other early astronomical instruments, books, atlases, & related items; glossy stock journal published quarterly: technical, historical, restoration articles.

Experts

Bart Fried
P.O. Box 444
Conshohocken, PA 19428
ph: 610-825-6600
Specializes in the history of telescopes, astronomical instruments, atlases, astronomical books; special area of interest is in 19th & 20th century telescope makers; will assist with appraisals, restorations problems, authentication.

John W. Briggs
Yerkes Observatory
373 W. Geneva St.
Williams Bay, WI 53191-0258
ph: 505-434-7098 or 505-682-2000
fax: 505-434-5555
jwb@hale.yerkes.uchicago.edu
Specializes in early American telescopes; familiar with details relating to value, original construction, and restoration; historian of the various makers.

Repair Services

Bart Fried
P.O. Box 444
Conshohocken, PA 19428
ph: 610-825-6600
Specializes in the history of telescopes, astronomical instruments, atlases, astronomical books; special area of interest is in 19th & 20th century telescope makers; will assist with appraisals, restorations problems, authentication.

ATLASES

(see also BOOKS; GAS STATION COLLECTIBLES, Road Maps; GLOBES; MAPS & CHARTS)

Dealers

Murray Hudson
Murray Hudson Antiquarian Books,
   Maps, Prints & Globes
109 S. Church St.
P.O. Box 163
Halls, TN 38040-0163
ph: 731-836-9057 or 800-748-9946
fax: 731-836-9017
mapman@ecsis.net
http://www.murrayhudson.com
Buys/sells pre-1900 antique maps (especially pocket, wall, Civil War and railroad maps) & books with maps (e.g. atlases, travel guides, geographies, land surveys, etc.); esp. of S.E. & S.W. US; also wants pre-1950 world globes.

Paul Mahoney
Old Map Gallery, The
1746 Blake St.
Denver, CO 80202
ph: 303-296-7725
fax: 303-296-7725
oldmapgallery@denver.net
http://www.oldmapgallery.com
Wants atlases and folding pocket maps.

Lahaina Printsellers, Ltd.
636 Luakini St.
Lahaina, HI 96761
ph: 808-667-7843 or 800-669-7843
info@printsellers.com
http://www.printsellers.com
Wants to buy pre-1900 atlases.

AUCTION CATALOGS

Book Sellers

Andrew Rose
Catalog Kid
P.O. Box 2194
Ocean, NJ 07712
ph: 800-258-2056 or 732-502-9153
fax: 732-502-9156
catalogs@catalogkid.com
http://www.catalogkid.com
Distributes post sale auction catalogs from Christie's, Sotheby's, Phillips, Lelands, Treadway, Craftsman, Butterfield, Bourne, Icon20.com, Antiquorum at remaindered prices; domestic and foreign sales.

Kathe Quinn
Auction Catalog Company, The
1000 Plaza Ave.
Miami, AZ 85539-1007
ph: 520-617-0440 or 800-487-0428
fax: 520-617-0491
Kathe@AuctionCatalogCompany.com
http://www.AuctionCatalogCompany.com
Sells most definitive, up-to-date references in art, antiques & collectible market: Sotheby, Christie, Butterfields, Skinner post-auction catalogs; also offers photocopies from library of 30,000 catalogs 1970 to present for nominal charge.

Dealers

Wendy Kenney
EphemerArts
229 E. 31st St., #1
New York, NY 10016
ph: 212-481-0138 or 888-518-6610
fax: 212-689-3860
wendy@ephemerarts.com
http://ephemerarts.com
Carries auction catalogs, exhibition catalogs, reference books and out-of-print books on antiques & collectibles; online catalog includes Asian arts, Americana, decorative arts, dolls, pottery, porcelain, glass jewelry, toys, etc.

Misc. Services

Stanley & Bob Block
Block's Box
P.O. Box 233
Trumbull, CT 06611-0051
ph: 203-926-8448
fax: 203-261-7033
blockschip@aol.com
http://www.marblecollecting.com
Produce video tapes & catalogs for auctioneers and appraisers; full state-of-the-art video tape production facility.

AUCTION SERVICES

(see also Specialized Auction Services listed under specific categories throughout this Directory.)

Auction Services

Anthony Caropreso
Mac-Caro Antiques
P.O. Box 643
Lee, MA 01238-0643
ph: 413-243-4647
fax: 413-243-4687
Antique dealer, auction and appraisal service; estate liquidations.

Douglas P. Bilodeau
Douglas Auctioneers
Rte. 5
South Deerfield, MA 01373
ph: 413-665-3530
fax: 413-665-2877
info@DouglasAuctioneers.com
http://www.douglasauctioneers.com
Auction sales year-round, specializing in antiques, fine art, estates, and appraising; also conducts Auctioneering School.

Michael B. Grogan
Grogan & Company Auctioneers
22 Harris St.
Dedham, MA 02026
ph: 781-461-9500
fax: 781-461-9625
grogans@groganco.com
http://www.groganco.com
Auctioneer and appraiser specializing in 18th through 20th century American & European paintings, sculpture, oriental rugs, and fine silver; accepts consignments year round for two semi-annual sales.

Willis Henry
Willis Henry Auctions, Inc.
22 Main St.
Marshfield, MA 02050
ph: 781-834-7774 or 800-244-8466
fax: 781-826-3520
wha@willishenry.com
http://www.willishenry.com
Specializes in the sale of American antiques of all kinds, particularly Shaker, American Indian and Early American.

Skinner, Inc.
63 Park Plaza
The Heritage on the Garden
Boston, MA 02116
ph: 617-350-5400
fax: 617-350-5429
info@skinnerinc.com
http://www.skinnerinc.com
*Established in 1971, Skinner Inc. is
the fourth largest auction house in the
US; has offices in Boston and Bolton,
MA.*

F.B. Hubley
364 Broadway
Cambridge, MA 02139
ph: 617-876-2030
hubleyauct@aol.com
http://www.hubleys.com

Philip C. Shute
Shute Auction Gallery
850 W. Chestnut St.
Brockton, MA 02401
ph: 508-588-0022 or 508-588-7833
fax: 508-559-6687
*Antique and custom furniture, art,
silver, glass and china, collectibles,
etc.*

John H. Schofield
Eldred's
P.O. Box 796
East Dennis, MA 02641-0796
ph: 508-385-3116
fax: 508-385-7201
eldreds@capecod.net
http://www.eldreds.com
*Auctioneers and appraisers for over
45 years.*

David Rietter
New Hampshire Auctions
345 Currier Rd.
Hill, NH 03243
ph: 603-770-2647 or 603-934-6998
nha@worldpath.net
*A complete auction service; from
online to live estate and merchandise
auctions and appraisals; licensed and
bonded in NH.*

Richard W. Withington, Inc.
590 Center Rd.
Hillsboro, NH 03244
ph: 603-464-3232
fax: 603-464-4901
withington@conknet.com
http://www.withingtonauction.com

Ronald Bourgeault
Northeast Auctions
93 Pleasant St.
Portsmouth, NH 03801-4504
ph: 603-433-8400
fax: 603-433-0415
NEAinfo@ttlc.net
http://www.northeastauctions.com
*Holds five major cataloged auctions a
year in March, May, August and
November; the August sale includes
an Americana auction which is the
kickoff event for the NH Antiques
Week in Manchester, NH.*

Paul McInnis
Paul McInnis, Inc.
155 Lafayette Rd., Ste. 8
North Hampton, NH 03862
ph: 603-964-1301 or 800-242-8354
fax: 603-964-1302
Paul@PaulMcInnis.com
http://www.paulmcinnis.com
*Providing auction and appraisal
services for estates and collectors for
nearly 30 years.*

Cyr Auction Company
P.O. Box 1238
Gray, ME 04039
ph: 207-657-5253
fax: 207-657-5256
info@cyrauction.com
http://www.cyrauction.com
*Auction sales of Americana,
Victoriana, estate and Continental
antiques.*

Randy Inman
Randy Inman Auctions, Inc.
P.O. Box 726
West Buxton, ME 04093
ph: 207-872-6900
fax: 207-872-6966
inman@inmanauctions.com
http://www.inmanauctions.com
*Conducts specialty auctions for
advertising, coin-op, gambling
devices, automata, soda pop, Coca
Cola, breweriana, robots and space
toys, cast iron and tin toys,
Disneyana, mechanical music, and
mechanical and still banks.*

Thomaston Place Auction Galleries
P.O. Box 300
15 Atlantic Highway
Thomaston, ME 04861
ph: 207-354-8141
fax: 207-354-9523
johnh@kajav.com
http://www.kajav.com

James D. Julia
James D. Julia Auctioneers Inc.
Rt. 201, Skowhegan Rd.
P.O. Box 830
Fairfield, ME 04937
ph: 207-453-7125
fax: 207-453-2502
jjulia@juliaauctions.com
http://www.juliaauctions.com

Eaton Auction Service
RR 1, Box 333
Fairlee, VT 05045
ph: 802-333-9717

Linda Stamm
Winter Associates, Inc. Auctioneers &
   Appraisers
21 Cooke St.
P.O. Box 823
Plainville, CT 06062
ph: 860-793-0288
fax: 860-793-8288
info@winterassociatesinc.com
http://www.winterassociatesinc.com
*Appraises and conducts estate
liquidations of antiques, fine furniture,*

*paintings, jewelry, porcelain, glass,
etc.*

Christina's Auction Gallery LLC
24 Maple St.
Danielson, CT 06239
ph: 860-779-7732
fax: 860-774-2823
christinas@snet.net
http://www.christinas.biz
*Full service auction service
specializing in fine antiques, estates.*

Joseph Arman
Collector's Sales & Services
P.O. Box 6
Pomfret Center, CT 06259
ph: 860-974-7008 or 860-974-7009
*Specialize in mail-bid auctions for
historical Staffordshire, Quimper,
American glass, French and American
paperweights, bottles, etc.*

Norman C. Heckler
Norman C. Heckler & Company
79 Bradford Corner Rd.
Woodstock Valley, CT 06282-2002
ph: 860-974-1634
fax: 860-974-2003
info@hecklerauction.com
http://www.hecklerauction.com
*A full-service auction company for
antique glass and bottles, period
decorative arts, single art objects and
estates.*

Greg Manning
Greg Manning Auctions, Inc.
775 Passaic Ave.
West Caldwell, NJ 07006
ph: 973-882-0004 or 800-221-0243
fax: 973-882-3499
gmauction@aol.com
http://www.gregmanning.com
*Since 1905, a leading auctioneer of
Americana, glass, stoneware, and
antiquities.*

Bob & Clara Koty, ISA CAPP
Koty & Associates, LLC
P.O. Box 475
Farmingdale, NJ 07727
ph: 732-751-0504
fax: 732-751-9190
Bidtaker@compuserve.com
http://www.kotyauctions.com
*Specializes in the auction sale of
antiques, collectibles, household
contents, estates, etc.; certified
appraisers of appreciable and
depreciable residential contents.*

Robert F. McCook, Jr.
B & M Auctioneers & Appraisers
P.O. Box 482
Keyport, NJ 07735
ph: 800-300-4870 or 888-237-7580
topbidder@aol.com
http://www.bfsauctioneers.com
*Residential sales, machinery &
equipment, inventories, vehicles,
antiques & collectibles.*

Leon Castner, Pres.
Castner's
P.O. Box 920
Branchville, NJ 07826-0920
ph: 973-948-3868
fax: 973-948-3919
castner@garden.net
http://www.castnerauctions.com
*Specializing in the sale of local estate
contents including antiques and
residential contents; gallery auctions;
on site auctions; estate liquidations in
NJ, NY, and PA.*

Ken Dawson
Dawson's
128 American Rd.
Morris Plains, NJ 07950
ph: 973-984-6900
fax: 973-984-6956
info@dawsons.org
http://www.dawsons.org
*Specializes in the auction sales of
antiques, art, silver, jewelry, toys and
collectibles.*

Carolyn Remmey, Pres.
Remmey Antiques & Fine Art
P.O. Box 197
New Vernon, NJ 07960
ph: 212-427-2500 or 305-296-6546 (FL)
remmey@rcn.com
*Conducts on-site auction sales of
residential contents and antiques
including fine art, fine and costume
jewelry, American & European silver,
toys, collectibles, American and
English furniture, etc.*

333 Auctions
333 North Main St.
Lambertville, NJ 08530
ph: 609-397-9374
fax: 609-397-9377
info@333auctions.com
http://www.333auctions.com

Robert S. Bottone
BFS Auctioneers
P.O. Box 610
Brick, NJ 08723-0610
ph: 732-785-9411 or 888-237-7580
fax: 732-785-9413
Bob@bfsauctioneers.com
http://www.bfsauctioneers.com
*Conducts auction sales of residential
property, real estate, machinery,
equipment, inventories, bankruptcies,
vehicles, antiques, collectibles and
memorabilia.*

Frank French
French's Auction Service
820 Bluestone Lane
Bridgewater, NJ 08807
ph: 908-526-3072
fax: 908-253-0021
flfauction@aol.com
http://www.frenchauction.com

Ronald Norris
Ronald Norris Auctioneer & Appraiser
183 Chestnut St.
Bridgewater, NJ 08807-2700
ph: 908-685-1252
fax: 908-685-1252

Caroline Birenbaum
Swann Galleries, Inc.
104 E. 25th St.
New York, NY 10010-2977
ph: 212-254-4710
fax: 212-979-1017
swann@swanngalleries.com
http://www.swanngalleries.com
Oldest/largest US auctioneer specializing in rare books, autographs & manuscripts, maps, atlases, photographs, and works of art on paper including vintage posters.

Phillips de Pury & Luxembourg
450 West 15th St.
New York, NY 10011
ph: 212-940-1200
fax: 212-688-1647
inquiry.desk@phillips-dpl.com
http://www.phillips-dpl.com
Specializes in the auction sale of American art, Contemporary art, Impressionist and Modern art, jewelry, photographs, and 20th and 21st century Modern design.

Christie's
20 Rockefeller Plaza
New York, NY 10020
ph: 212-636-2000
info@christies.com
http://www.christies.com
Call 212-546-1199 on a touch tone phone to access a data base to obtain post-sale prices; have sale number and lot number handy.

Sotheby's
1334 York Ave.
New York, NY 10021
ph: 212-606-7000
fax: 212-606-7107
http://www.sothebys.com
Call 212-606-7000 on a touch tone phone to access a data base to obtain post-sale prices; have sale number and lot number handy.

Arlan Ettinger
Guernsey's Auction
108 East 73rd St.
New York, NY 10021
ph: 212-794-2280
fax: 212-744-3638
auctions@guernseys.com
http://www.guernseys.com
Auctions unique commodities and collections, e.g., vintage automobiles, sports artifacts, political memorabilia, vintage cigars, Soviet art, posters and more.

Amory Spizzirri, Client Svc.
William Doyle Galleries
175 E. 87th St.
New York, NY 10128-2205
ph: 212-427-2730
fax: 212-369-0892
info@doylegalleries.com
http://www.doylegalleries.com
Holds over 50 auctions annually of furniture and decorations, paintings and sculpture, jewelry, books and prints, couture and textiles, 20th century art & design, majolica, Lalique, Asian works of art and other specialty categories.

Robert H. Snyder
Cohasco, Inc.
P.O. Drawer 821
Yonkers, NY 10702-0821
ph: 914-476-8500
fax: 914-476-8573
info@cohascodpc.com
http://www.cohascodpc.com
In business over 55 years, specializing in paper collectibles, autographs, documents, Americana, ephemera, etc.; mail auction catalogs issued.

Jean-Paul Napoli
South Bay Auctions, Inc.
485 Montauk Highway
P.O. Box 303
East Moriches, NY 11940
ph: 631-878-2909
fax: 631-878-1863
info@southbayauctions.com
http://www.southbayauctions.com
Family-owned auction house with a big reputation for handling quality consignments; single items to entire estates.

Patrick T. Guariglia, Jr.
Patrick Thomas & Partners
858 Blue Mountain Rd.
Saugerties, NY 12477
ph: 914-247-8888
fax: 914-246-0589
Full service auction gallery specializing in American & European fine art, antique furniture, decorative arts, and collectibles; consignments from a single item to entire estates accepted.

Savoia's Auction Inc.
Rte. 23
South Cairo, NY 12482
ph: 518-622-8000
fax: 518-622-9453

Michael Fallon
Copake Auction, Inc.
P.O. Box H, 266 Rt. 7A
Copake, NY 12516
ph: 518-329-1142
fax: 518-329-3369
info@copakeauction.com
http://www.copakeauction.com
Conducts auctions specializing in the sale of Americana, period furniture, folk art, collectibles and classic bicycles.

Robert A. Doyle, ISA, CAI
Absolute Auction & Realty, Inc.
P.O. Box 1739
#45 South Ave.
Pleasant Valley, NY 12569
ph: 845-635-3169 or 800-551-5161
fax: 845-635-5140
hikertwo@aol.com
http://www.absoluteauctionrealty.com
Antiques and estate auctions approximately every two weeks; offers free newsletter.

Iroquois Auction Gallery
P.O. Box 736
Brewerton, NY 13029
ph: 315-668-2346
Semi-annual upscale art and antique auctions; also regular estate art & antique auctions; over 20 years of service; graduate of Sotheby's Style in Art course; always interested in buying quality art & antiques, paintings, art work, etc.

Hesse Galleries
53 Main St.
Otego, NY 13825
ph: 607-988-6322
info@hessegalleries.com
http://www.hessegalleries.com
Specializes in the auction sales of African and tribal arts.

David W. Mapes
Mapes Auctioneers & Appraisers
1729 Vestal Pkwy. West
Vestal, NY 13850-1156
ph: 607-754-9193
fax: 607-786-3549
info@mapesauction.com
http://www.mapesauction.com
Auctions and appraisals since 1966: estates, collections, fine and decorative art, toys, jewelry, oriental rugs, American furniture, European furniture and decorations, Arts & Crafts; no modern collectibles.

Richard Bronstein, CRA, CREA
R.W. Bronstein Corp.
3666 Main St.
Amherst, NY 14226
ph: 716-835-7400
fax: 716-835-7419
value@bronstein.net
http://www.bronstein.net
Valuation and marketing of all types of chattels and realty since 1950.

Samuel J. Cottone
Cottone Auctions
15 Genesee St.
Mount Morris, NY 14510
ph: 716-658-3119
fax: 716-658-3152
scottone@rochester.rr.com
http://www.cottoneauctions.com
Specializes in the auction sale of fine art and antiques.

Ann Marszalek, ISA
ANN & CO. Auctions
150 Orchard St.
Webster, NY 14580
ph: 585-872-9150 or 585-729-1215
Auctionfever@aol.com
http://www.anncompany.com
Appraiser/auctioneer conducts auctions of entire estates or quality consignments.

Dargate Auction Galleries
5607 Baum Blvd.
Pittsburgh, PA 15206
ph: 412-362-3558
fax: 412-362-3574
dargate@dargate.com
http://www.dargate.com

Steven D. Reinoehl
Total Auction Services
RD #2 Box 173B
Cherry Tree, PA 15724
ph: 724-254-4514
fax: 724-254-5141
totalauction@yourinter.net
http://www.yourinter.net/totalauction
Complete auction service for estates, antiques, collectibles, firearms, businesses; on site or off.

John McClain
York Town Auction Inc.
1625 Haviland Rd.
York, PA 17404
ph: 717-751-0211
fax: 717-767-7729
info@yorktownauction.com
http://www.yorktownauction.com
Antique & specialty auctions, lecture & appraisal services; antiques also purchased; American & English furniture, related specialties & accessories, Americana, folk art, jewelry, art, clocks & watches, militaria, steins, Oriental rugs.

Ted Hake
Hake's Americana & Collectibles Auction
P.O. Box 1444
York, PA 17405-1444
ph: 717-848-1333
Ted@hakes.com
http://www.hakes.com
Always purchasing, consigning items for 5 mail-bid & online auctions per year; hundreds of categories including toys, character collectibles, Disney, cowboy heroes, premiums, television, politicals, pin-back buttons, advertising and more.

Conestoga Auction Company
768 Graystone Rd.
P.O. Box 1
Manheim, PA 17545
ph: 717-898-7284
fax: 717-898-6628
ca@conestogaauction.com
http://www.conestogaauction.com

Rick Roan
Roan Inc. Auction Gallery
RR 4 Box 118
Cogan Station, PA 17728
ph: 570-494-0170 or 800-955-ROAN
fax: 570-494-1911
info@roaninc.com
http://www.roaninc.com/roan

T. Skinner
Skinner's Auction Company
P.O. Box 3070
Bethlehem, PA 18017
ph: 610-868-9985
skinnauct@aol.com
http://www.skinnersauction.com
 *Auctioneers specializing in antique
 auctions; estate liquidators;
 appraisers of antiques and collectibles; licensed and bonded; over
 15 years experience.*

Jim Ridolfi
Aston Trade Company, Inc.
1012 Westminster
Wilkes Barre, PA 18702
ph: 570-654-3090
fax: 570-655-2145
aston@epix.net

Tony Nard
Nard Auctions
U.S. Rte. 220
Milan, PA 18831
ph: 570-888-9404
fax: 570-888-7723

Cindy Stephenson
Stephenson's Auction
1005 Industrial Blvd.
Southampton, PA 18966-4006
ph: 215-322-2260
fax: 215-364-4395
info@stephensonsauction.com
http://www.stephensonsauction.com
 *Weekly general auctions of residential
 contents; quarterly auctions of
 antiques and decorative arts;
 additional specialty auctions.*

Michael Wilson
Wilson's Auctioneers & Appraisers
342-344 Valleybrook Rd.
P.O. Box 478
Chester Heights, PA 19017
ph: 610-565-1616
fax: 610-565-5840
sold@wbauction.com
http://www.wbauction.com
 *Fourth generation auction service;
 since 1911; three certified appraisers
 on staff.*

Freeman's Auction Gallery
1808 Chestnut St.
Philadelphia, PA 19103
ph: 215-563-9275
fax: 215-563-8236
proberts@freemansauction.com
http://www.freemansauction.com
 *America's oldest auction house:
 Continental, English and American
 furniture, paintings, silver and
 decorative arts; Oriental rugs, rare
 books, fine jewelry, Orientalia.*

William Bunch
William Bunch Auctions & Appraisals
One Hillman Dr.
Chadds Ford, PA 19317
ph: 610-558-1800
fax: 610-558-0885
whb@williambunchauctions.com
http://www.williambunchauctions.com
 *Specializes in the auction sales of fine
 antiques, silver, decorative objects,
 and fine art.*

Ron & Debra Pook
Pook & Pook, Inc.
P.O. Box 268
Downingtown, PA 19335-0268
ph: 610-269-0695 or 610-269-4040
fax: 610-269-9274
info@pookandpookinc.com
http://www.pookandpookinc.com
 *Auction management and appraisal
 service; catalogued auctions of period
 American, English, Continental
 antiques including 17th to 20th
 century furniture, fine art, folk art,
 ceramics, textiles, metalware, toys,
 decorative accessories.*

Harold & Annette Smith
Smith Auction Company
1415 Horseshoe Pike
Glenmoore, PA 19343
ph: 610-942-2367
auction@chesco.com
http://www.smithauction.com
 *Full service auction company
 specializing in estates, antiques,
 collections, toys, vintage electronics,
 military, sports items, pottery,
 paintings, furniture, jewelry, music
 boxes, Arts & Crafts period items.*

Joyce Ruth
Alderfer Auction Company
501 Fairground Rd.
P.O. Box 640
Hatfield, PA 19440-0640
ph: 215-393-3000
fax: 215-368-9055
info@alderfercompany.com
http://www.alderfercompany.com
 *A full service auction and appraisal
 business, specializing in Pennsylvania
 antiques, fine art, fire arms,
 Americana, and collectibles.*

Edward A. Stinson
Mid-Atlantic Auctions & Appraisals,
 Inc.
P.O. Box 4365
Wilmington, DE 19807-0365
ph: 302-633-9470
fax: 302-633-9478
midatlantic5@aol.com
http://www.mid-atlantic.com
 *Offers auction sales of fine art and
 antiques in the mid-Atlantic region.*

Thomas M. Weschler
Weschler's
909 E St. NW
Washington, DC 20004-2006
ph: 202-628-1281 or 800-331-1430
fax: 202-628-2366
fineart@weschlers.com
http://www.weschlers.com
 *A full service auction service for art,
 antiques, decorative accessories,
 household furnishings, and
 commercial liquidations; also
 specializes in the sale of European
 and American furniture and
 decorative art.*

Gordon Diachenko, VP
Asset Services International Co., Inc.
P.O. Box 40883
Washington, DC 20016
ph: 703-525-0396
fax: 703-243-5562
gd@asset-services.com
http://www.asset-services.com
 *Appraisal, auction, liquidation, sealed
 bid, receiver, trustee, conservator,
 expert witness, replevins, legal/
 litigation support, management
 services, asset recoveries, due
 diligence, monitoring.*

Paula Hantman
Hantman's Auctioneers & Appraisers
P.O. Box 59366
Potomac, MD 20859-9366
ph: 301-770-3720
fax: 301-770-4135
hantman@hantmans.com
http://www.hantmans.com
 *Full service auction firm specializing
 in the sale of fine art and antiques
 with internationally advertised
 catalog auctions; certified appraiser
 for estate, insurance replacement,
 estate planning, family division.*

Robert McArtor
McArtor Auction Gallery
227-K Gateway Dr.
Bel Air, MD 21014
ph: 410-893-1100
 *Estate liquidations, monthly antique/
 estate auctions: antiques, collectibles,
 jewelry, furniture, silver porcelain,
 textiles, art work and more.*

Rick Williams
Williams Auction & Appraisal Service
P.O. Box 381
Forest Hill, MD 21050
ph: 410-836-3031
fax: 410-836-1123
Wilri@erols.com

Richard W. Opfer, Jr.
Richard Opfer Auctioneering, Inc.
1919 Greenspring Dr.
Lutherville Timonium, MD 21093-4113
ph: 410-252-5035
fax: 410-252-5863
info@opferauction.com
http://www.opferauction.com
 *Specializes in auctioning paintings,
 furniture, antiques, toys, dolls, games,
 black memorabilia, and advertising
 items; monthly eclectic collector sales*

feature a wide variety of collectibles;
 weekly auctions include general estate
 merch.

Grant Harding, CAI
Grant Harding Auctioneers
P.O. Box 215
Owings Mills, MD 21117-0215
ph: 410-833-8780
fax: 410-833-2794
jmcx84a@erols.com
 *Licensed and bonded auctioneer/
 appraiser in Maryland and
 Pennsylvania; on premises auctions a
 specialty; providing services to
 private parties and businesses since
 1966.*

Cindy Isennock, CAI
Isennock Auctions & Appraisals, Inc.
4106B Norrisville Rd.
White Hall, MD 21161-9306
ph: 410-557-8052
fax: 410-692-6449
info@isennockauction.com
http://www.isennockauction.com
 *Conducts auction sales of real estate,
 antiques, estates, business liquidations, farms and farm machinery,
 firearms, specialized collectibles.*

Paul R. Cooper
Alex Cooper Auctioneers, Inc.
908 York Rd.
Baltimore, MD 21204
ph: 410-828-4838
fax: 410-828-0875
info@alexcooper.com
http://www.alexcooper.com
 *Auctioneer of antiques, collectibles,
 fine arts, furniture, paintings, Oriental
 rugs and jewelry.*

DeCaro Auction Sales, Inc.
8133 Elliott Rd.
Easton, MD 21601-7184
ph: 410-820-4000
fax: 410-820-4332
info@decaroauctions.com
http://www.decaroauctions.com

Trout Auctioneers Inc.
9801 Hansonville Rd.
Frederick, MD 21702
ph: 301-898-9899
fax: 301-898-3596
troutauct@aol.com
http://www.troutauctions.com
 *In business since 1920; conducts
 gallery on on premises auction sales
 in Maryland, Pennsylvania, and
 Virginia.*

Ed Morris
Morris Auctions Inc.
3607 Buckeystown Pike
P.O. Box 162
Buckeystown, MD 21717
ph: 301-663-8552 or 301-831-8541
fax: 301-663-6522
ed@morrisauctions.com
http://www.morrisauctions.com
 *Full service auction house with focus
 on fine and antique furniture,
 collectibles, real estate, estates,
 decorative and fine arts, jewelry,*

watches, clocks, Civil War, oriental rugs, toys, books, etc.

John D. Compton
J.D. Compton Auctioneering
13833 Rockdale Rd.
Clear Spring, MD 21722
ph: 301-582-0727
fax: 301-582-6114

Matthew Quinn
Quinn's Auction Galleries
431 North Maple Ave.
Falls Church, VA 22046
ph: 703-532-5632
fax: 703-532-4910
matthew.quinn@att.net
http://www.quinnsauction.com
Conducts regular auctions of antiques, collectibles, estates.

Jeffrey Evans
Green Valley Auctions, Inc.
2259 Green Valley Lane
Mount Crawford, VA 22841
ph: 540-434-4260
fax: 540-434-4532
gvai@shentel.net
http://www.greenvalleyauctions.com
Specializing in the auction sale of early American glass, furniture and decorative arts.

David P. Staples, Jr., CAI, ISA
Auction Gallery, The
3140 W. Cary St.
Richmond, VA 23221
ph: 804-358-0500 or 804-359-0688
fax: 804-358-1280
knightm@mindspring.com
Auctions, appraisals, estate services; general interest and specialty collector events; targeted marketing; your site or ours; valuations for all purposes and functions.

Christine N. Corbin, ISA
Motley's Auctions, Inc.
4402 West Broad St.
Richmond, VA 23230
ph: 804-355-2100
fax: 804-359-6954
cncorbin@motleys.com
http://www.motleysgroup.com
Auctioneers and appraisers of furniture, silver, fine art, decorative arts, real estate, general goods and vehicles.

Gail Wolpin, ISA
Phoebus Auction Gallery
14-16 E. Mellen St.
Hampton, VA 23663
ph: 757-722-9210
fax: 757-723-2280
bwelch@phoebusauction.com
http://www.phoebusauction.com
Conducts auctions of antiques, collectibles, estates, furniture, decorative and fine arts, etc.

Mike Bond, Auctioneer
C & M Auctions, Inc.
P.O. Box 12421
Roanoke, VA 24025
ph: 540-992-2410
snoopy@roanoke.infi.net
Professional full auction service with weekly gallery auctions; specializing in on-site estate, furniture and merchandise auctions.

Ken Farmer
Ken Farmer Auctions & Appraisals, LLC
105 Harrison St.
Radford, VA 24141
ph: 540-639-0939
fax: 540-639-1759
ken@kfauctions.com
http://www.kfauctions.com
Specializes in real estate and personal property auctions; also offers appraisals of Southern material culture, American furniture, folk art, decorative arts, collectibles and fine art.

Randy S. Burdette
Riverbend Auction
P.O. Box 800
103 South Monroe St.
Alderson, WV 24910
ph: 304-445-2897 or 800-726-2897
fax: 304-445-2900
rivauction@newwave.net
http://www.riverbendauction.com

Robert Raynor
Historical Collectible Auctions
24 NW Court Sq. #201
Graham, NC 27253
ph: 336-570-2803
fax: 336-570-2748
bids4hca@aol.com
http://www.hcaauctions.com
Specializes in historical Americana: Black Americana, Civil War artifacts and paper items, historic artifacts, Judaica, Indian War, Abraham Lincoln, militaria, photography, political, sports, Western, printed/manuscript Americana.

James McCreery
McCreery Auctions
113 Forest Ave.
Manteo, NC 27954]
ph: 252-473-1872
fax: 252-473-4888
jim@jimmccreery.com
http://www.jimmccreery.com
Specializes in estate auctions.

Robert S. Brunk
Robert S. Brunk Auction Services, Inc.
P.O. Box 2135
Asheville, NC 28802
ph: 828-254-6846
fax: 828-254-6545
auction@brunkauctions.com
http://www.brunkauctions.com
Conducts sales of estates and fine antiques.

Ronald D. Long
Charlton Hall Galleries, Inc.
912 Gervais St.
Columbia, SC 29201
ph: 803-799-5678
fax: 803-733-1701
info@charltonhallauctions.com
http://www.charltonhallauctions.com
Full service auctioneers and appraisers, specializing in 17th, 18th, 19th century American, English, and Continental furniture, paintings and decorative arts.

Gene Patrick
Gene Patrick Auction & Realty
1051 Cooley Bridge Rd.
Belton, SC 29627-9277
ph: 803-243-2394 or 803-338-5720
genepatric@aol.com
http://www.genepatrick.com

Jim Depew
Jim Depew Auctions
1860 Piedmont Rd.
Atlanta, GA 30324-4839
ph: 404-874-2286
fax: 404-874-2285
info@depewauction.com
http://www.depewauction.com
Weekly consignment and estate auctions of antiques and traditional furniture, accessories, porcelains, silver, crystal and jewelry.

Christopher Benjamin
Great American Auction, The
P.O. Box 4020
Saint Augustine, FL 32085-4020
Lists sport and non-sport trading cards, cereal box prizes and premiums, bread end labels, etc. (fee charged.)

Leonard R. Richford
147 Michigan Ave.
Daytona Beach, FL 32114-3297
ph: 386-239-0939
fax: 386-252-1700
srich4d@bellsouth.net

Nancy Bomm
J & N Auctioneers
P.O. Box 656
Clarcona, FL 32710-0656
ph: 407-822-5250
fax: 407-294-7836
jack2741@hotmail.com
http://www.thepotteryexperience.com
Conducts periodic auctions of personal property, antiques & collectibles specializing in pottery.

Ron Kool
A Plus Auctions
3645 N. US 1
Cocoa, FL 32926
ph: 321-639-4440
fax: 321-636-9809
aplus@aplusauctions.com
http://www.aplusauctions.com
Florida-based auction center specializing in fine antique furniture, art glass, pottery, jewelry, estates,

appraisals, liquidations, and bankruptcies.

Harry Stampler, ISA
Stampler Auctions
2801 Evans St.
Hollywood, FL 33020-1119
ph: 954-921-8888
fax: 954-927-2939
hps@stamplerauctions.com
http://www.stamplerauctions.com
Specializes in machinery & equipment appraisals and in business liquidations.

Albert Post, ISA
Albert Post Galleries
2291 Newbury Dr.
West Palm Beach, FL 33414
ph: 561-707-3024
albertpost@aol.com
Accredited Member, International Society of Appraisers; member National Auctioneers Association; auctioneer of fine arts, decorative arts, jewelry, collectibles.

Dawson's
P.O. Box 646
Palm Beach, FL 33480
ph: 561-835-6930
fax: 561-835-8464
info@dawsons.org
http://www.dawsons.org
Specializes in the auction sales of antiques, art, silver, jewelry, toys and collectibles.

Bill Hood
Bill Hood & Sons Art & Antique Auctions
2925 S. Fedearl Hwy.
Delray Beach, FL 33486
ph: 561-278-8996
fax: 561-278-8977
info@hoodauction.com
http://www.hoodauction.com

Jeffrey Burchard
Burchard Galleries/Auctioneers
2528 30th Ave. N.
Saint Petersburg, FL 33713
ph: 727-821-1167 or 727-823-4156
fax: 727-821-1814
mail@burchardgalleries.com
http://www.burchardgalleries.com
Specializes in estate, antiques and fine art auctions; monthly 2-day events with estate merchandise.

Randy Kincaid
Kincaid Auction
3214 E. Hwy. 92
Lakeland, FL 33801
ph: 800-970-1977 or 863-555-1977
kinkaid@kincaid.com
http://www.kincaid.com
On site auction liquidations of antique stores, restaurants, museums, estates, stores and manufacturers.

Private Collections
660 S. Tamiami Trail
Osprey, FL 34229
ph: 941-966-3255 or 888-966-3201
fax: 941-966-7629
auctions4u@privatecollections.net
http://www.privatecollections.net
*Specializes in the auction of fine
quality estates, antiques, art, classic
cars, collectibles, firearms, jewelry.*

Kimball M. Sterling
Kimball M. Sterling Inc.
125 W. Market St.
Johnson City, TN 37601
ph: 423-928-1471 or 423-975-0600
fax: 423-928-8697
kimsold@tricon.net
http://sterlingsold.com

Benny & Ruthie Taylor
Taylor Auction & Realty, Inc.
P.O. Box 357
15229 Hwy. 51 N.
Grenada, MS 38901
ph: 662-226-2080 or 888-526-2080
fax: 662-227-1653
benny@taylorauction.com
http://www.taylorauction.com

Ann Hays, ISA CAPP
Hays & Associates, Inc.
120 South Spring St.
Louisville, KY 40206-1953
ph: 502-584-4297
fax: 502-585-5896
annhays@haysauction.com
http://www.haysauction.com
*Conducts auction sales of toys, dolls,
furniture, ceramics, antique clocks,
music boxes, and silver*

Garth's Auction, Inc.
2690 Stratford Rd.
P.O. Box 369
Delaware, OH 43015
ph: 740-362-4771
fax: 740-363-0164
info@garths.com
http://www.garths.com
*Specializing in Early American,
English, Continental, Oriental
antiques and accessories; paintings,
fine art, folk art, American Indian,
military, jewelry, toys, dolls,
advertising, collectibles.*

Apple Tree Auction Center
1616 West Church St.
Newark, OH 43055
ph: 740-344-4282 or 740-344-4603
fax: 740-366-3673
info@appletreeauction.com
http://www.appletreeauction.com
*Conducts large, quality antique
auctions containing over 3,000 items
every six weeks.*

Mike Clum
Mike Clum, Inc.
7795 Cincinnati Zanesvile Rd.
Rushville, OH 43150
ph: 740-536-7421 or 740-536-9220
fax: 740-536-7242
info@clum.com
http://www.clum.com
*Specializing in auction sales of
antiques and collectibles; over 30
years in business.*

DeFina Auctions
1591 State Route 45
Austinburg, OH 44010
ph: 440-275-6674
fax: 440-275-2028
info@definaauctions.com
http://www.definaauctions.com

John Waldsmith
Collector's Auctioneer, The
P.O. Box 83
Sharon Center, OH 44274
ph: 330-239-1944 or 330-239-2212
vansywalsy@aol.com
http://www.YourAuctionPage.com/
Waldsmith
*Specializes in the auction sale of
personal collections of antiques and
collectibles; licensed and bonded.*

Maggie Beckmeyer, CAI, ISA
Auctions by Maggie, Inc.
P.O. Box 191
North Bend, OH 45052
ph: 513-941-9519
fax: 513-467-1360
avcmag@webtv.net

Shipshewana Auction, Inc.
345 S. Van Buren St.
P.O. Box 185
Shipshewana, IN 46565
ph: 219-768-4129
tradingplace@shipshenet.com
http://www.tradingplaceamerica.com

Phil Wolfe
Wolfe Auction Gallery in partnership
with CatBecca.com
232 W. Van Buren
Columbia City, IN 46725
ph: 260-244-4141 or 260-248-1191
fax: 309-215-5556
webmaster@cwef.com
http://www.catbecca.com
*Conducts live as well as online
auctions; specializing in the auction
sales of glass, pottery, porcelain,
primitives, and antique furniture.*

Michael G. Strawser
Strawser Auctions
200 North Main St.
P.O. Box 332
Wolcottville, IN 46795-0332
ph: 219-854-2859 or 219-854-2235
fax: 219-854-3979
michael@strawserauctions.com
http://www.strawserauctions.com
*Specializes in the auction sale of
Fiesta and other antiques.*

Darin Lawson, CAI
Lawson Auction Service
923 Fourth St.
Columbus, IN 47265
ph: 812-372-2571 or 800-283-4866
dlawson@lawson-auction.com
http://www.lawson-auction.com
*Family-owned auction company
serving southern Indiana with primary
experience in real estate auctions,
estate settlement, antiques, business
liquidations, and farm equipment.*

Don Sohn
Curran Miller Auction & Realty, Inc.
4424 Vogel Rd., Ste. 400
Evansville, IN 47715
ph: 800-264-0601 or 812-474-6100
fax: 812-474-6110
cmar@curranmiller.com
http://www.curranmiller.com
*One of the Midwest's premier auction
companies; specializes in the auction
sale of antiques and collectibles.*

Doug Davies
Davies Auctions
P.O. Box 5542
Lafayette, IN 47903-5542
ph: 765-449-4515
sales@daviesauctions.com
http://www.daviesauctions.com
Specializes in antiques auctions.

Kenny Lindsay
American Eagle Auction & Appraisal
Company
18569 Southampton
Livonia, MI 48152
ph: 248-473-1547
productionline@msn.com
http://www.americaneagleauctions.net
*Specializes in specialty and
fundraising auctioneering along with
estate and business liquidations
through the auction method of
marketing.*

Cedric Ector
ELAC Auctioneers & Appraisers, LLC
18701 Grand River #178
Detroit, MI 48223
ph: 313-534-3522 or 253-663-4915
auction@elac-llc.com
http://www.elac-llc.com
*Full service auctioneering agency
specializing in the liquidation of
personal estates, business inventories,
commercial and residential
properties, and surplus and obsolete
government property.*

Lawrence DuMouchelle
DuMouchelle Art Galleries Co.
409 East Jefferson Ave.
Detroit, MI 48226
ph: 313-963-6255
fax: 313-963-8199
info@dumouchelle.com
http://www.dumouchelles.com
*A fine arts auction house; rugs,
paintings, jewelry, porcelain, silver,
art glass, toys, dolls, furniture, books,
sculpture, etc.*

Joseph DuMouchelle
Joseph DuMouchelle Fine & Estate
Jewelry Auctions
5 Kercheval Ave.
Grosse Pointe Farms, MI 48236
ph: 313-884-4800 or 800-475-4367
fax: 313-884-7662
info@dumouchelleauction.com
http://www.dumouchelleauction.com
*Specializes in the sale of fine and
estate jewelry and small objects of art;
large diamonds and colored stones,
paintings, Oriental rugs, silver,
antique furniture and sculpture,
Russian objects of art.*

Dan & Judy Landino
D & J Auction Services
37037 E. Almont
Sterling Heights, MI 48310
ph: 810-268-8692
djlrest@comcast.net
http://www.dnjauctions.com
*Conducts auctions: antiques, estates,
fund raising, liquidations of business,
CAGA Certified Appraisers;
appraisals for insurance purposes,
estate appraisals, personal property,
divorce settlements, expert witness.*

Tom Terwilliger, CAGA
Pro Auction Company
707 230th St.
Algona, IA 50511
ph: 515-295-7819
fax: 515-295-7742
proauct@ncn.net
http://www.proauctionusa.com
*A complete auction and appraisal
service serving north central Iowa.*

James L. Jackson, ISA
Jackson's Auctioneers & Appraisers
2229 Lincoln St.
P.O. Box 50613
Cedar Falls, IA 50613
ph: 319-277-2256
fax: 319-277-1252
jacksons@jacksonsauction.com
http://www.jacksonsauction.com
*Conducts auction sales of fine arts,
furniture, art pottery, art glass,
porcelain, toys, rugs, etc.*

Jerry Tubaugh
Tubaugh Auctions
1702 8th Ave.
Belle Plaine, IA 52208
ph: 319-444-2413 or 800-368-1292
webmaster@tubaughauctions.com
http://www.tubaughauctions.com
*Specializes in the auction sale of
antiques, collectibles and antique
toys; also estate sales, consignments,
and exotic birds and animals.*

Schrager Auction Galleries, Ltd.
2915 North Sherman Blvd.
P.O. Box 100043
Milwaukee, WI 53210
ph: 414-873-3738
fax: 414-873-5229
askus@schragerauction.com
http://www.schragerauction.com

Kurt R. Krueger
Krueger Auctions
P.O. Box 275
Iola, WI 54945-0275
ph: 715-445-3845
fax: 715-445-4100
Specializing in the mail-bid auction of tokens, advertising, brewery items, Western Americana, postcards, World's Fair & Expo., autographs, sports, coins & currency, pin-backs, military memorabilia, automotive, Disneyana, etc.

Charles Fischer, CAI
Fischer Auction Company
238 Haywire Ave.
P.O. Box 667
Long Lake, SD 57457-0667
ph: 605-577-6600
fax: 605-577-6500
gofish@valleytel.net
http://www.fischerauction.com
Over 40 years in the auction and real estate businesses; auctions medical equipment, antiques, commercial and farm land; complete action service from setup to close.

Doug & Tracy Merfeld
Curt D. Johnson Auction Company
4216 Gateway Dr.
Grand Forks, ND 58203
ph: 701-746-1378 or 888-338-8032
figleo@hotmail.com
http://www.curtdjohnson.com
Over 33 years of auction experience.

Jim & Carol Boshears
CC Selections, Inc.
528 Thomas Rd.
Bolingbrook, IL 60440
ph: 630-783-1639
gondernut@aol.com
Offers general auction services; specialists in American Art Pottery and 20th century collectibles.

William Mastro
MastroNet, Inc.
1515 W. 22nd, Ste. 125
Oak Brook, IL 60523-8412
ph: 630-472-1200
fax: 630-472-1201
info@mastronet.com
http://www.mastronet.com
Conducts auction sales of sports memorabilia, political and campaign material, autographs and manuscripts, animation art, comics, circus and movie posters, classic toys, rock & roll, pop culture, coins, currency, stamps, and more.

Susanin's Auction
900 South Clinton
Chicago, IL 60607
ph: 888-787-2646 or 312-832-9800
fax: 312-832-9311
info@susanins.com
http://www.susaninspremiere.com
One of the Midwest's largest and most innovative auction houses; Web site contains searchable database of past auction results.

Leslie Hindman
Leslie Hindman Auctions
122 North Aberdeen St.
Chicago, IL 60607
ph: 312-280-1212
fax: 312-280-1211
info@Lesliehindman.com
http://www.lesliehindman.com
Fine art auctioneers and appraisers specializing in antique furniture and decorative arts, works of art, jewelry, carpets, books and manuscripts.

John Modica
Direct Auction Galleries
7232 N. Western Ave.
Chicago, IL 60645
ph: 773-465-3300
fax: 773-465-8873
directauc@aol.com
http://www.directauction.com
Antiques & collectibles auctions every 2 weeks; estates and consignments; antique furniture, lighting, jewelry, figurines, porcelain, pottery, glass, toys and more.

Joy Luke
Joy Luke Auction Gallery
300 E. Grove St.
Bloomington, IL 61701-5232
ph: 309-828-5533
fax: 309-829-2266
robert@joyluke.com
http://www.joyluke.com
Conducts regular auctions in fine and decorative arts.

Larry Martin
Martin Auction Co.
Rt. 51 S.
Clinton, IL 61727
ph: 217-935-8211
fax: 217-935-3795
lmcs2000@yahoo.com
http://
    wwww.martinauctioncompany.com

Kurt Aumann
Aumann Auctions Inc.
20114 IL Rt. 16
Nokomis, IL 62075
ph: 217-563-2523
info@aumannauctions.com
http://www.aumannauctions.com
Specializes in the auction sales of estates, antiques and collectibles.

Ivey-Selkirk Auctioneers
7447 Forsyth Blvd.
Saint Louis, MO 63105
ph: 314-726-5515 or 800-728-8002
fax: 314-726-9908
iveyselkirk@iveyselkirk.com
http://www.iveyselkirk.com

Robert Merry
Robert Merry Auction Company
5501 Milburn Rd.
Saint Louis, MO 63129-3514
ph: 314-487-3992 or 314-487-4080
fax: 314-487-4080

Bob Simmons
Simmons & Company Auctioneers
40706 E. 144th St.
Richmond, MO 64085
ph: 816-776-2936 or 800-646-2936
fax: 816-470-5016
bob@simmonsauction.com
http://www.simmonsauction.com
Conducts specialty and general line antiques and collectibles auctions.

Manion's Auction House
P.O. Box 12214
Kansas City, KS 66112-0214
ph: 913-299-6692
fax: 913-299-6792
collecting@manions.com
http://www.manions.com
A mail-bid auction company specializing in militaria from all countries, Scouting memorabilia, toys, antique advertising, and all fine collectibles.

Jason Woody
Woody Auction Company
P.O. Box 618
317 S. Forrest St.
Douglass, KS 67039-9800
ph: 316-747-2694
fax: 316-747-2145
woodyauction@earthlink.net
http://www.woodyauction.com

Larry Frederick
Frederick Auction & Realty Company
232 W. 9th
P.O. Box 1236
Coffeyville, KS 67337
ph: 620-251-5551 or 918-255-6738
fax: 620-251-5553
lfrederick@terraworld.net
http://www.gunslinger.com/
Specializing in the auction sale of antiques and estates in SE Kansas and NE Oklahoma.

Dale Miller
Miller's Auction Service
1808 24000 Rd.
Parsons, KS 67357
ph: 620-421-0753
dsmiller_us@yahoo.com
http://
    www.millersauctionservice.homestead.com/
    auction.html

Neal Auction Co.
4038 Magazine St.
New Orleans, LA 70115
ph: 504-899-5329 or 800-467-5329
fax: 504-897-3808
customerservice@nealauction.com
http://www.nealauction.com
Specializing in antiques and fine art, especially Southern Art, American 19th century furniture, French furniture, and decorative objects.

New Orleans Auction Galleries, Inc.
801 Magazine St.
New Orleans, LA 70130
ph: 504-566-1849 or 800-467-5329
fax: 504-566-1861
info@neworleansauction.com
http://www.neworleansauction.com

Kim Rutledge
Auction Gallery
406 Cresswell Lane
Opelousas, LA 70570
ph: 337-288-0036
fax: 337-406-0306
info@auction-preview.com
http://www.auction-preview.com
Specializing in estate auctions and auction sales of antiques and collectible.

Paul D. Kelly
Kelly Auction Service
3015 Alice Dr.
Batesville, AR 72501
ph: 870-698-0011
info@kellyauction.com
http://www.kellyauction.com

Keith Clanton
C & C Auction Company, The
4801 MacKelman Dr.
Oklahoma City, OK 73135-4135
ph: 405-670-1705
Specializing in the auction sale of antiques and collectibles.

Richard Waskow
HCR 68 Box 745
Vian, OK 74962
ph: 918-489-5164
waskow@ipa.net
Conducts specialty auctions; watches, clocks, Russian items, bronzes.

Jerry W. Holley, VP
Dallas Auction Gallery
1518 Slocum
Dallas, TX 75207
ph: 214-653-3900
fax: 214-653-3912
jwh@dallasauctiongallery.com
http://www.dallasauctiongallery.com
Specializes in the auction sale of antiques and fine art.

Forres L. Meadows, CAI
Forres Meadows Auctioneers
P.O. Box 1287
Boerne, TX 78006-1287
ph: 830-230-5362
fax: 830-816-2311
forres@meadowsauctioneers.com
http://www.meadowsauctioneers.com
Estate and antiques auctioneers; professional auctioneers serving Texas and the Hill Country since 1989.

AUCTION SERVICES

Ross Auction House
109 South Sierra Madre
Colorado Springs, CO 80903
ph: 888-715-4487 or 719-632-6693
fax: 719-632-6694
info@rossauction.com
http://www.rossauction.com
Specializes in the auction sale of antiques, toys, dolls, complete estates.

Warren Anderson
America West Archives
P.O. Box 100
Cedar City, UT 84721-0100
ph: 435-586-9497 or 435-586-7323
awa@netutah.com
http://www.americawestarchives.com
Auction catalogs offer rare & historical documents, letters, photographs, autographs, paper Americana, maps; specializes on Western US, however Eastern material also accepted.

A. N. Abell Auction Co.
2516 Yates Ave.
Los Angeles, CA 90040
ph: 323-724-8102 or 800-404-2235
fax: 323-724-9550
abell@abell.com
http://www.abell.com
Full service auction company.

Bonhams & Butterfields
7601 Sunset Blvd.
Los Angeles, CA 90046-2714
ph: 323-850-7500
fax: 323-850-5843
info@butterfields.com
http://www.butterfields.com

Emilio & Olga Lemeni
Abamex Auction Co.
10050 Via de la Amistad #2452
San Diego, CA 92154-7248
ph: 800-841-3364 or 858-279-2846
fax: 858-576-9577
auctions@abamex.com
http://www.abamex.com
Conducts auctions in Southern CA; real estate, business asset auctions including FF&E, restaurant equipment; also art and collectibles auctions.

G. E. Moore
Mail Bid Auction
P.O. Box 414
Yucca Valley, CA 92286-0414
fax: 619-365-9668
Conducts mail-bid auctions of collectibles: books, coins, medals, Disney, theater, valentines, art, railroad, political, medical/dental, etc.; Continental US only.

Jan Bendis
Bendis Companies, Inc.
3410 La Sierra Ave., Ste. F 123
Riverside, CA 92503
ph: 909-780-4436 or 909-780-3418
fax: 909-780-7384
info@bendisauctions.com
http://www.bendisauctions.com
Auctioneer and appraiser; general

merchandise, vehicles, machinery, electronics, and more.

Joseph M. Kozma
Kozma Auction Service, Inc.
25221 Wagner Way
Hemet, CA 92544-1724
ph: 888-650-6444 or 909-927-0405
fax: 909-927-6806
kaas@pe.net
http://www.kozmaauctions.com
A full service auction and appraisal company for antiques, collectibles and fine arts, both American and European.

Bonhams & Butterfields
220 San Bruno Ave.
San Francisco, CA 94103
ph: 415-861-7500 or 800-223-2854
fax: 415-861-8951
info.US@butterfields.com
http://www.butterfields.com
Auctioneers and appraisers of antiques, fine art and collectibles in all categories; specialty sales include posters, toys, decorative arts, furniture, photography, etc.; the largest full service auction in the West.

Harvey Clars Auction Gallery
5644 Telegraph Ave.
Oakland, CA 94609
ph: 510-428-0100 or 888-339-7600
fax: 510-658-9917
info@harveyclar.com
http://www.harveyclar.com
Auction sales of fine art, paintings, engravings, sculpture, antique and contemporary furniture, porcelains, crystal, ivories, tapestries, rugs, fine jewelry, collectibles, and more.

Ann Sydes
A & A Auction
925a 41St Ave.
Santa Cruz, CA 95062
ph: 831-476-1713
fax: 831-476-1835
webmaster@aaauctions.com
http://www.aaauctions.com
Preview and place bids and/or consign items in upcoming auctions at the Gallery in Santa Cruz.

Mike Vendetti
Auction Center, The
2770B South Bascom Ave.
San Jose, CA 95150
ph: 408-292-6800 or 408-930-1502
fax: 408-292-1792
vendetti@pacbell.net
http://www.vendetti.com
Full service auction company liquidating numerous estates each year.

John Markus
Markus & Markus Auctioneers & Appraisers
P.O. Box 788
Banks, OR 97106
ph: 503-681-0806 or 888-411-8999
fax: 503-693-9159
markus@jps.net
http://www.markusandmarkus.com
Specializes in the auction sale of antiques and collectibles; call for free consultation.

Mike Odell
Mike Odell Auctions & Appraisals
10031 - 240th Place SW
Edmonds, WA 98020
ph: 206-542-4460 or 206-542-5425
fax: 206-542-1445
modell@tradermick.com
http://www.tradermick.com
Conducts live and online auctions, specializing in small collections, estates, and the unusual; Member of the National Auctioneers Association, Auctioneers Association of Canada; Accredited Member of the International Society of Appraisers.

Judith Legat
Dorotheum
Dorotheergasse 17
Vienna, A-1010 Austria
ph: 0431 515 60 x226
fax: 0431 515 60 x489
client.services@dorotheum.at
http://www.dorotheum.com
Specializes in the auction sales of antiques, art, jewelry and collectibles.

Maynards Auctioneers
415 West 2nd Ave.
Vancouver, British Columbia V5Y 1E3 Canada
ph: 604-876-6787 or 604-531-0166
fax: 604-876-2678
antiques@Maynards.com
http://www.maynards.com
Quarterly auctions of Canadian, American & Western European fine art, antiques, silver, jewellery, china, glass, carpets and specialty collectables; Accredited Member of International Society of Appraisers.

Waddington's
111 Bathurst St.
Toronto, Ontario M5V 2R1 Canada
ph: 416-504-9100 or 877-504-5700
fax: 416-504-0033
info@waddingtonsauctions.com
http://www.waddingtonsauctions.com
Canada's oldest and largest auction house specializing in decorative arts, jewelry, antique furniture, Inuit and native Canadian arts, European and Canadian arts, books, militaria, Orientalia, toys, ceramics, etc.

Arthur Clausen & Sons Auctioneers
14504 118 Ave.
Edmonton, Alberta T5L 2H3 Canada
ph: 877-451-4549 or 451-4549
fax: 454-2776
arthur@clausenauction.com
http://www.clausenauction.com
Auction sales of fine art, collectibles, books, jewelry, European and North American antiques, Orientalia, etc.

Ritchie's Auctioneers & Appraisers
288 King St.
Toronto, Ontario M5A 1K4 Canada
ph: 416-3641-1864
fax: 416-364-0704
auction@ritchies.com
http://www.ritchies.com
Fine art and antiques auctioneers and appraisers.

Vintage Auctions of Canada, Ltd.
418 McDermot Ave.
Winnipeg, Manitoba R3A OA9 Canada
ph: 204-783-2262 or 888-560-2277
fax: 204-786-1846
info@VintageAuctions.ca
http://www.VintageAuctions.ca

Norris Auctions
4 Southcott Dr.
Milton, Ontario L9T 2X9 Canada
ph: 905-875-1266
fax: 905-693-1445
mailbag@norrisauction.com
http://www.norrisauction.com
Estate auctioneers specializing in the auction sale of antiques and residential contents.

Etude Tajan
37 Rue des Mathurins
Paris, 75008 France
ph: (+33) 01 53 30 30 30
fax: (+33) 01 53 30 30 31
tajan@worldnet.fr
http://www.tajan.com
A French premier auction house.

Van Ham Kunstauktionen
Schonhauser Str., 10-16
Cologne, D-50968 Germany
ph: 0221 925862-0
fax: 0221 925862-4
info@van-ham.com
http://www.van-ham.com
Specializes in the auctions sales of Old master and 19th century paintings, modern and contemporary art, objets d'Art, furniture, rugs, carpets, bronzes, sculptures, Art Nouveau, jewelry.

Auction Team Breker
Bonner Str. 528-530
Koln, D-50968 Germany
ph: 49 221 387049 or 941-925-0385 (US Rep)
fax: 49 221 374878
auction@breker.com
http://www.breker.com
German auction company specializes in the sale of old office equipment, scientific instruments and devices, photographica, and old technology including toasters, typewriters, sewing

machines, tools, telecommunications, etc.

Nagel Auktionen
Adlerstrasse 31-33
Stuttgart, D-70030 Germany
ph: +49 (711) 649-69-0
fax: +49 (711) 649-69-69
contact@auction.de
http://www.auction.de
Fine German auction house; since 1922.

Michael Pritchard
Christie's London
85 Old Brompton Rd.
London, SW7 3LD U.K.
ph: 020 7930 6074 or 020 7752 3279
fax: 020 7321 3321
info@christies.com
http://www.christies.com
Regular sales of furniture, paintings, silver, jewelry, ceramics, textiles, books and collectibles; free verbal valuations weekdays.

Bonhams 1793
101 New Bond St.
Chelsea
London, W1S 1SR U.K.
ph: +44 20 7629 6602
fax: +44 20 7629 8876
info@bonhams.com
http://www.bonhams.com
Auctioneers and appraisers since 1793.

Bonhams & Brooks
Dowell St.
Honiton, Devonshire EX14 8LX U.K.
ph: 01404 41872
fax: 01404 43137
info@bonhams.com
http://www.bonhams.com
Auctioneers and appraisers since 1793.

Bonhams & Brooks
St. Thomas' Place
Hillgate
Stockport, Cheshire SK1 3TZ U.K.
ph: 0161 429 8283
fax: 0161 429 8285
info@bonhams.com
http://www.bonhams.com
Auctioneers and appraisers since 1793.

Bonhams & Brooks & Martel Maides
Allez St. Auction Rooms
St. Peter Port
Guernsey, Channel Islands GY1 1NG U.K.
ph: 01481 722700
fax: 01481 723306
info@bonhams.com
http://www.bonhams.com
Auctioneers and appraisers since 1793.

Bonhams & Brooks & Langlois
39 Don St.
St. Helier
Jersey, Channel Islands JE2 4TR U.K.
ph: 01534 22441
fax: 01534 59354
info@bonhams.com
http://www.bonhams.com
Auctioneers and appraisers since 1793.

Henry McFadden
Harp Auctioneers & Valuers
29 Broad St.
Northampton, Northamptonshire NN1 2HS U.K.
ph: +44 (0)1604 622333
fax: +44 (0)1604 622333
chief@lotsofinterest.com
http://www.goinggoing.co.uk
Independent provincial auction rooms in the heart of the UK; antiques and general sales, valuation services for insurance, probate, family division; house clearance services.

Clubs/Associations

Joe Keefhaver, Ex. Dir.
National Auctioneers Association
Magazine: Auctioneer, The
8880 Ballentine
Shawnee Mission, KS 66214-1985
ph: 913-541-8084
fax: 913-894-5281
hq@auctioneers.org
http://www.auctioneers.org

Al Briggs, Ex. Dir.
Auctioneers Association of Canada
5240 1A St. S.E., Ste. 100
Calgary, Alberta T2H 1J1 Canada
ph: 403-640-9915 or 866-640-9915
fax: 403-640-9916
aaofc@oanet.com
http://www.auctioneerscanada.com
The national Canadian association for accepted auctioneers who have agreed to meet the Code of Ethics and Conduct as set by the Association's Board of Directors.

Misc. Services

Jodie Benson
Gordon's Art Reference, Inc.
Directory: International Auction House Directory
306 West Coronado Rd.
Phoenix, AZ 85003-1147
ph: 602-253-6948 or 800-892-4622 (orders)
fax: 602-253-2104
office@gordonsart.com
http://www.gordonsart.com
Comprehensive listing of over 5,000 worldwide auction houses including name, address and contact information, key individuals, areas of specialization and three different cross-reference indices.

Ronald P. Hume
Ottawa Valley Auctions
121 Woodbury Circle
Ottawa, Ontario K1G 5C6 Canada
ph: 613-733-0900
fax: 613-733-2728
spider1@capitalnet.com
http://www.capitalnet.com/~spider1/homepage.html
Provides day/date listings of auctions in the Ottawa Valley Region.

Periodicals

David J. Maloney, ISA CAPP
Sales Online Direct, Inc.
Directory: Maloney's Antiques & Collectibles Resource Directory
P.O. Box 2049
Frederick, MD 21702-1049
ph: 301-228-2279
fax: 301-695-6491
dave@maloney.com
http://www.davidmaloney.com/aboutbook.htm
Publishes major resource information source for collectors, sellers, claims adjusters, etc.: includes experts, buyers, clubs, periodicals, repairers, museums/libraries, appraisers, auctioneers, matching services, dealers, etc.

Government Contract

Auction Services

Government Asset Sales
support@financenet.gov
http://www.financenet.gov/sales.htm
A one-stop portal Web site for information on the sale or auction of all manner of public assets and surplus from real property and loans to planes, cars, jewelry.

GSA, Property Management Division, Federal Supply Service
GSAAuctions.NationalCapital@gsa.gov
http://www.gsaauctions.gov
Sells various types of property including cars, vans, trucks, plumbing equipment, heating equipment, paper products, typewriters, computers, other office machines, medical equipment, tools, etc.; expect to pay a fair price.

United States Treasury Auctions Page
c/o Office of Public Correspondence
1500 Pennsylvania Ave., NW
Washington, DC 20220
ph: 202-622-2000
fax: 202-622-6415
http://www.ustreas.gov/auctions
Links to US Customs, IRS, United States Secret Service, US Postal Service unclaimed loose mail, and ATF seized property.

Internet Resources

Buddy Doyle
Government Auction Page
buddy_doyle@yahoo.com
http://www.tgand.com/ainfo/usgovact.htm
Complete, up-to-date information

about Government Federal auctions all over the US.

Government Auctions
usaweb@syspac.com
http://www.usaweb.com/gov.html
Many links to Web sites focusing on government auctions.

Wentworth Publishing, Ltd.
Newsletter: Government Auction News
17 Fleet St.
London, EC4Y 1AA U.K.
ph: 020 7353 6606
fax: 020 7353 6533
wentworth@online.rednet.co.uk
http://www.ganews.co.uk
News in the U.K. about government auctions, buy and sell, deals, tips, advice, reviews, top bargains, etc.

AUDIO EQUIPMENT

(see AUDIO-VISUAL; HI-FI EQUIPMENT)

AUDIO-VISUAL

(see also BROADCASTING; CAMERAS & CAMERA EQUIPMENT; FILMS; GAMES, Video Games; HI-FI EQUIPMENT; MOVIE MEMORABILIA; PHOTOGRAPHS; RADIO SHOWS, Old Time; RADIOS, Vacuum Tubes for; RECORDS; TELEVISION SHOWS & MEMORABILIA)

Appraisers

Steven Smolian
Smolian Sound Preservation Studios
1 Worman's Mill Court #4
Frederick, MD 21701
ph: 301-694-5134
fax: 301-694-5179
smolians@erols.com
http://www.soundsaver.com
Record collections appraised for tax donation, estate & insurance loss purposes; all formats - 78s, 45s, LPs, cylinders, radio disks, etc.; rock, classical, country, old news broadcasts; over 20 years appraising major archives.

Paul Willigan, Pres.
NICE Network, Inc.
2126 Alpine Place
Cincinnati, OH 45206-2603
ph: 513-961-1052 or 800-837-NICE
fax: 513-961-0538
paul@nicenetwork.com
http://www.nicenetwork.com
Appraisers of high tech and high value electronic equipment including computers, PBX telephone systems, medical equipment, copiers, software, film printers, optical jukeboxes, mainframe computers, audio-visual systems, etc.

Dr. Steve Johnson
Behavioral Images, Inc.
Newsletter: Ten Thousands Words
302 Leland St., Ste. 101
Bloomington, IL 61701-5646
ph: 309-829-3931 or 800-988-6427
fax: 309-829-9677
sjohnson@mediavalue.com
http://www.mediavalue.com
Film, video, recordings, photographs, negatives; author of "Appraising Audio-Visual Media; A Guide for Attorneys, Trust Officers, Insurance Professionals, & Archivists" (1993); $34.95 & $3 S&H; publishes newsletter ten times per year.

Misc. Services

Steven Smolian
Smolian Sound Preservation Studios
1 Worman's Mill Court #4
Frederick, MD 21701
ph: 301-694-5134
fax: 301-694-5179
smolians@erols.com
http://www.soundsaver.com
CDs made from old phonograph records of all types, reel-to-reel and cassette tapes, wires and dictation belts; damaged recordings a specialty; 40 years experience.

Repair Services

S.P.E.C.S. Bros. Video Services
P.O. Box 5
Ridgefield Park, NJ 07660
ph: 201-440-6589 or 800-852-7732
fax: 201-440-6588
admin@specsbros.com
http://www.specsbros.com
Offers a videotape rejuvenation and reclamation service; reclaim deteriorating or contaminated video material; optimize tapes for signal retrieval; special fire damage and environmental damage reclamation services.

Analogique Systems Labs
17 West 17th St.
New York, NY 10011
ph: 212-989-4240
fax: 212-633-9389
analogique@earthlink.net
http://www.analogique.com
Factory authorized repair of stereos, hi-fi and audio equipment, video and speaker repair, tube equipment repair, turntables, tape recorders, DAT and VCR repair.

Brent Jessee
Brent Jessee Recording Vacuum Tubes
1655 W. Algonquin Rd., #111
Hoffman Estates, IL 60195
ph: 847-496-4546
brentjes@audiotubes.com
http://www.audiotubes.com
Specializes in the restoration of old sound records: 78 RPM disc, open reel tape and cassette tape recordings can be restored, enhanced, cleaned up and transferred to cassette, CD, or digital tape.

AUTO RACING MEMORABILIA

(see also AUTOMOBILES; AUTOMOBILES, Racing; TOYS, Cars [Racing])

Collectors

George Spruce
33 Washington St.
Sayville, NY 11782-2003
ph: 516-563-4211
Wants Vanderbilt Cup Auto Race Long Island Motor Parkway items and other pre-1917 auto racing memorabilia.

George Koyt
8 Lenora Ave.
Morrisville, PA 19067-1206
ph: 215-295-4908
Wants all types of auto racing items: programs, postcards, books, toys, games, anything auto racing, A to Z, old/new, large or small; will buy one piece or entire collections.

Museums/Libraries

International Motorsports Hall of Fame
3198 Speedway Blvd.
P.O. Box 1018
Talladega, AL 35161
ph: 256-362-5002 or 256-362-5003
fax: 256-362-5684
cbradford@motorsportshalloffame.com
http://www.motorsportshalloffame.com
Preserves the worldwide history of motor sports; over $7M in racing vehicles and memorabilia on display; Hall of Fame.

Indianapolis Motor Speedway Hall of Fame Museum
P.O. Box 24152
Speedway, IN 46224
ph: 317-484-8500
fax: 317-484-6449
imspr@brickyard.com
http://ims.brickyard.com/museum.php

Drag

Museums/Libraries

Don Garlits
Don Garlits Museum of Drag Racing
13700 SW 16th Ave.
Ocala, FL 34473-3970
ph: 352-245-8661
fax: 352-245-6895
info@garlits.com
http://www.garlits.com
Classic car and antique museum encompasses 20,000 square feet of displays, mostly auto related though plenty of old "Americana" as well; adjacent to the Auto Racing Hall of Fame & Museum.

Indy 500

Clubs/Associations

National Indy 500 Collectors Club
Newsletter: Short Chute, The
1920 Patton Dr.
Speedway, IN 46224
ni500cc@ni500cc.com
http://www.ni500cc.com
Goal is to preserve the history of the Indy 500 Mile Race; newsletter has club notes, member spotlight, articles, want, sell, trade, etc.

Collectors

Eric Jungnickel
P.O. Box 4674
Naperville, IL 60567-4674
ph: 630-983-8339
eric@indycollectibles.com
Wants Indy 500 items: auto racing items including felt pennants, programs, posters, tickets, passes, toys, board games, bobbin' head dolls, trophies, any race track; prefers pre-WWII items.

Experts

Jack Mackenzie
6940 Wildridge Rd.
Indianapolis, IN 46256-2132
ph: 317-842-5329
Author of "Indy 500 Buyers Guide."

Museums/Libraries

Indianapolis Motor Speedway Hall of Fame Museum
P.O. Box 24152
Speedway, IN 46224
ph: 317-484-8500
fax: 317-484-6449
imspr@brickyard.com
http://ims.brickyard.com/museum.php

NASCAR

Collectors

John Adipotti
2728 Fifth St.
Monroeville, PA 15146
ph: 412-823-5095
fax: 412-856-3377

Dealers

Alan lowell
T & A Collectables
86 Independence Rd.
Feeding Hills, MA 01030
ph: 413-789-4145 or 413-374-5301
fax: 413-789-7446
alanlowell@hotmail.com
Buys and sells NASCAR die cast collectibles.

Tom & Joanne Schwarz
3125 E. Main St.
EEndwell, NY 13760
ph: 607-785-0707
fax: 607-785-0707
nascartoys@aol.com
http://www.07racingcollectibles.com
Stocks old and new NASCAR related diecast from Action, Revell, Team Caliber, Rousch Authentics, Racing

Champions; on advisory board for "Diecast Digest;" also sells apparel and novelty items.

CJ's Racing Distribution
ph: 570-779-3945
cjracingdiecast@msn.com
http://www.cjsracingdiecast.com
Largest NASCAR specialty store in northeastern PA: apparel, collectibles; Action, RCCA, Revell, Racing Champions, Ertl, Plastic model kits, decals, card supplies, lithographs.

Brickel's Racing Collectibles, Inc.
P.O. Box 205
Leesport, PA 19533-0205
ph: 610-926-6719 or 888-705-0456
fax: 610-926-6977
info@brickelsracing.com
http://www.brickelsracing.com
Stock cars, sprints, late model dirt cars, funny cars, top fuel dragsters, Dually's, 1/18 racer toys, RCCA club pieces, fan fueler items.

Daved Sandefur
Racing Diecast Collecting
P.O. Box 828
Fries, VA 24330
ph: 276-744-2728
davedwrite@aisva.net
http://www.geocities.com/davedwrite/www
Sells NASCAR and other racing diecast collectibles.

Cathy's Racing Collectibles
1829 Old Watkins Rd.
Henderson, NC 27536
ph: 252-438-8614
fax: 252-438-9563
info@CathysRacing.com
http://www.cathysracing.com
Offers a full line of racing souvenirs.

Greg Toney
JSI Motorsports Collectibles
P.O. Box 478
Sandy Springs, SC 29677-0478
ph: 864-231-9491
customerservice@vstore.com
http://jsimotorsports.vstorehobbies.com
Specializes in motorsports collectibles: autographs and rare memorabilia, postcards, trading cards, uniforms, programs.

Thomas Mathews
T & D Toy & Hobby
116 S. Chicago Ave.
Freeport, IL 61032
ph: 815-232-1419 or 815-232-0096
fax: 815-232-0096
tdhobby@aol.com
Dealer of die cast toys, primarily racing memorabilia, but also trains, farm toys, model kits, and other types of toys.

Brent Powell
B & L Racing Collectibles
907 South Memorial Dr.
Tulsa, OK 74112
ph: 800-435-3570 or 918-664-3232
fax: 918-664-7018
brent@nascarshop.com
http://www.nascarshop.com
One of the largest racing collectibles companies in the US; specializes in diecast of all makes; also carries cards and many racing related souvenirs.

Cross RoadsRacing Collectibles
1204 Wadsworth Blvd.
Lakewood, CO 80214
ph: 866-934-2278 or 303-274-0599
fax: 303-278-0586
april@racingstuff.com
http://www.racingstuff.com
NASCAR die cast racing collectibles and merchandise; over 2,000 different race collector toys in stock.

Experts

Whit King
Na-Tex Publishing, Inc.
5620 Concord Parkway S., Ste. 202
Concord, NC 28027
ph: 704-455-1702
fax: 704-455-1707
rcpgdm@aol.com
http://www.racingcollectors.com
Editor-at-large of "Racing Collector's Price Guide."

Internet Resources

Custom & Racing Model Magazine Online
P.O. Box 2037
Garfield, NJ 07026
ph: 973-546-3305
fax: 973-546-7728
editor1@CARmodel.com
http://www.carmodel.com
Covers race cars in all forms: NASCAR, slotcars, diecast, static.

Museums/Libraries

Donna Denardo
North Carolina Auto Racing Hall of Fame
119 Knob Hill Rd.
Mooresville, NC 28117
ph: 704-663-5331
fax: 704-663-6949
donna@ncarhof.com
http://www.ncarhof.com
Features over 30 race cars dedicated to all types of auto racing; racing history films, Indy Simulator, showcases of uniforms, helmets, and photographs.

Hendrick Motorsports Museum & Gift Shop
4400 Papa Joe Hendrick Blvd.
Charlotte, NC 28262
ph: 704-455-0342
fax: 704-455-0341
http://www.hendrickmorotsports.com
25 acre, 200,000 square foot racing

complex; display exhibits, souvenir sales, race shop viewing.

Gloria Durant
NMPA Stock Car Hall of Fame - Joe Weatherly Museum
P.O. Box 500
Darlington, SC 29532
ph: 843-393-2103
Has the largest collection of stock cars in the world; fans can see the pioneers who made the sport of NASCAR what it is today; housed at Darlington Raceway, NASCAR's original Superspeedway.

Periodicals

Alimax Publications & Promotions, Inc.
Magazine: Racing Collector's Price Guide
5620 Concord Parkway South, Ste. 202
Concord, NC 28027
ph: 888-792-RACE or 704-455-1702
fax: 704-455-1707
rcpgdm@aol.com
http://www.racingcollectors.com/main.html
The most thorough price guide on the market for more than 25 racing collectibles categories; listings for diecast, trading cards, postcards, steins, uniforms, programs, knives, models, statues, plates, bottles, posters, and more.

AUTOGRAPHS

(see also ALBUMS, Autograph; BOOKS, Reference [Autographs]; HISTORICAL AMERICANA; MANUSCRIPTS; PAPER COLLECTIBLES; PERSONALITIES; PHOTOGRAPHS, Celebrity; PLAYBOY ITEMS; SPORTS COLLECTIBLES; PERFORMING ARTS)

Appraisers

Brian Kathenes
National Appraisal Consultants, LLC
P.O. Box 482
Hope, NJ 07844-0482
ph: 908-459-5996 or 800-323-5996
fax: 908-459-4899
Brian@nacvalue.com
http://www.nacvalue.com
Specialist Certified Appraiser of Personal Property in Autographs, Manuscripts and Historical Documents; expert appraisal, valuation and consulting services for Hollywood, sports and celebrity memorabilia and collectibles.

Stephen Koschal
P.O. Box 744
Boynton Beach, FL 33425
ph: 561-582-4439
skoschal@aol.com
http://www.stephenkoschal.com
Buys, sells, and appraises autographs, signatures, letters, documents, books, signed photographs or anyone

famous; co-founder IACC/DA; catalogs issued.

Ray Nugent, ASA
Nugent Appraisal Services
P.O. Box 11984
Naples, FL 34101
ph: 888-353-7152 or 941-353-7122
fax: 941-353-8884
renugent@aol.com
http://www.appraisalreferrals.com
ASA senior accredited appraiser of rare books, documents, manuscripts, autographs and antique maps; member of ISA, AAA, AIC, SAA.

Auction Services

Stanley J. Richmond
Daniel F. Kelleher Company, Inc.
24 Farnsworth St., Ste. 605
Boston, MA 02210-1264
ph: 617-443-0033
fax: 617-443-0789
US and BNA stamps at auction; also autographs and documents.

Robert Lifson
Robert Edward Auctions
P.O. Box 7256
Watchung, NJ 07069
ph: 908-226-9900 or 800-766-9324
fax: 908-226-9920
reaauct@aol.com
http://www.robertedwardauctions.com
Specializes in the auction sale of historical Americana, political material, autographs and manuscripts, and original illustration art.

Caroline Birenbaum
Swann Galleries, Inc.
104 E. 25th St.
New York, NY 10010-2977
ph: 212-254-4710
fax: 212-979-1017
swann@swanngalleries.com
http://www.swanngalleries.com
Oldest/largest US auctioneer specializing in rare books, autographs & manuscripts, maps, atlases, photographs, and works of art on paper including vintage posters.

Chris Coover
Christie's
20 Rockefeller Plaza
New York, NY 10020
ph: 212-636-2000
info@christies.com
http://www.christies.com

Robert H. Snyder
Cohasco, Inc.
P.O. Drawer 821
Yonkers, NY 10702-0821
ph: 914-476-8500
fax: 914-476-8573
info@cohascodpc.com
http://www.cohascodpc.com
In business over 55 years, specializing in paper collectibles, autographs, documents, Americana, ephemera, etc.; mail auction catalogs issued; has appeared on PAX TV's "Treasures in Your Home."

Herman Darvick
Herman Darvick Autograph Auctions
P.O. Box 467
Rockville Centre, NY 11571
ph: 516-766-0289
fax: 516-766-7459
Conducts six specialty auctions per year; faxed and mail bids accepted.

Kurt R. Krueger
Krueger Auctions
P.O. Box 275
Iola, WI 54945-0275
ph: 715-445-3845
fax: 715-445-4100
Conducts periodic specialized auction sales of autographs and documents.

Trevor Vennett-Smith
T. Vennett-Smith Auctioneers & Valuers
11 Nottingham Rd.
Gotham, Nottingham NG11 OHE U.K.
ph: +44 (0)115 983 0541
fax: +44 (0)115 983 0114
info@vennett-smith.com
http://www.vennett-smith.com
Great Britain's leading professional autograph auction house, specializing in bi-monthly auctions of fine and varied autographs; also postcards, trade cards, ephemera, sporting memorabilia.

Clubs/Associations

Professional Autograph Dealers Association
P.O. Box 1729
Murray Hill Station
New York, NY 10156
ph: 888-338-4338
padamail@padaweb.org
http://www.padaweb.org
Formed in 1995 to raise the standards of the autograph profession by requiring members to adhere to a strict code of ethics when conducting business with collectors, institutions, and the general public.

Al Wittnebert, Treas.
Universal Autograph Collectors Club
Magazine: Pen & Quill, The
P.O. Box 6181
Washington, DC 20044-6181
ph: 352-383-1958
fax: 352-383-7524
signhere@zoomph.net
http://www.uacc.org
The UACC has over 2,000 members worldwide; offers a bi-monthly magazine with reports on facsimiles, forgeries, authentication, auctions, shows, celebrity addresses, etc.

George Teas, Ex. Dir.
Washington Historical Autograph &
    Certificate Organization (WHACO)
Newsletter: WHACO! News
P.O. Box 2428
Springfield, VA 22152-2428
ph: 703-866-0175
fax: 703-866-0175
gteas@earthlink.net
http://www.whaco.com
    *Formed to bring collectors together to
    promote the hobby of antique stock
    and bond certificates and historical
    autographs; database of prices,
    featured articles, listings of dealers.*

Mike Frost, Treas.
International Autograph Collectors Club
    & Dealers Alliance
P.O. Box 848486
Hollywood, FL 33084
ph: 561-736-8409
fax: 561-736-5902
webmaster@iacc-da.com
http://www.iacc-da.com
    *Largest autograph collectors club in
    the world devoted exclusively to
    autograph collecting.*

David R. Smith, Ex. Dir.
Manuscript Society, The
Magazine: Manuscripts
350 N. Niagara St.
Burbank, CA 91505-3648
manuscrip@aol.com
http://www.manuscript.org
    *An organization of collectors, dealers,
    librarians, archivists, scholars and
    others interested in autographs and
    manuscripts.*

Collectors

Stan Block
128 Cynthia Rd.
Newton, MA 02159
    *Wants autographs, banners, leathers,
    political pins, baseball cards, silks,
    sports memorabilia.*

Kenneth Schwartz
688 Shrewsbury Ave.
Red Bank, NJ 07701
ph: 732-741-6200
fax: 732-450-3749
kenneth@monmouth.com
    *Autograph collector, authenticator,
    expert wants to buy autographs,
    documents, or letters from famous
    people; co-published "The Robot That
    Helped Make a President" with
    Charles Hamilton, a recognized
    authority on autographs.*

Edward Bomsey
Edward N. Bomsey Autographs, Inc.
7317 Farr St.
Annandale, VA 22003-2516
ph: 703-642-2040
fax: 703-642-2040
enbainc@cs.com
http://www.bomsey-autographs.com
    *Sells, buys letters, photographs,
    signatures of personalities in politics,
    military, science, law, history, music,
    arts, etc.*

James Carlson, #73536
Arizona State Prison - Florence
P.O. Box 8400 - South Unit
Florence, AZ 85232-8400
    *Inmate collects autographs in all
    fields; accepts donations of
    autographs only (no money); writes to
    stars and celebrities to obtain
    autographs; member of UACC; has
    had articles written about him; seeks
    penpals with same interests.*

Ralf Mulhern
3710 Alabama St., Apt. 24
San Diego, CA 92104-3344
    *Wants to buy autographs, manu-
    scripts, historical related items; send
    photocopy of items for sale and asking
    price; send lists and auction catalogs
    of items for sale.*

Michael Reese II
P.O. Box 5704
South San Francisco, CA 94083-5704
ph: 415-641-5920
creole@shutmymouth.com
http://www.shutmymouth.com
    *Wants autographs: early aviation
    (1910-1939), letters, Presidents
    letters, any Civil War (Union or
    Confederate); also signed photos,
    California Gold Rush period (1848-
    1851).*

Dealers

Gerald Rubackin
Jerry's Cards & Collectibles
P.O. Box 1271
Framingham, MA 01701-0207
ph: 508-788-0946
fax: 508-788-5197
jermyrauto@att.net
http://www.uacc.org/dealers/
    rubackin.html
    *Buys and sells WWII fighter aces
    autographs and other WWII military
    signatures; also want autographed
    material by the crew of the Enola Gay
    which dropped the first atomic bomb
    on Hiroshima.*

Paul Longo
Paul Longo Americana
P.O. Box 5510
Gloucester, MA 01930-0007
ph: 978-525-2290
    *Wants autographs of Presidents,
    famous athletes, world famous
    inventors, statesmen, actors and
    actresses, etc.*

Mark Vardakis
Mark Vardakis Autographs
P.O. Box 1430
Coventry, RI 02816
ph: 401-823-8440
fax: 401-823-8861
    *Buying and selling autographs:
    presidents, authors, musicians,
    celebrities, scientists, etc.; also
    conducts autograph auctions.*

George & Julie Perron
Old Paperphiles, The
P.O. Box 135
Tiverton, RI 02878-0135
ph: 401-624-9420
opac108@netzero.net
    *Buys and sells paper collectibles:
    autographs, sheet music, postcards,
    photos, stereoviews, documents, old
    letters; sells on eBay, seller name is
    "opac."*

George H. LaBarre
George H. LaBarre Galleries, Inc.
P.O. Box 746
Hollis, NH 03049
ph: 800-717-9529 or 603-882-2411
fax: 603-882-4979
collect@glabarre.com
http://www.glabarre.com
    *Specializes in collectible stocks and
    bonds, autographs, paper money; also
    deals with other areas of Americana;
    retail and wholesale to other dealers
    including large marketing companies;
    inventory includes over 5.7 million
    pieces in stock.*

Bob Eaton
R & R Enterprises
3 Chestnut Dr.
Bedford, NH 03110
ph: 603-471-0808 or 800-973-3880
fax: 603-471-2844
bob@rrauction.com
http://www.rrauction.com
    *Buys and sells photographs,
    signatures, letters and documents
    signed by famous personalities in all
    fields: presidential, historical, sports,
    music, film.*

Scott J. Winslow
Scott J. Winslow Associates, Inc.
P.O. Box 10240
Nashua, NH 03110-0240
ph: 603-641-8292 or 800-225-6233
fax: 603-641-5583
scott@scottwinslow.com
http://www.scottwinslow.com
    *Buys and sells stocks certificates,
    bonds and historical autographs; also
    conducts mail bid auctions of same.*

J.D. Bardwell
J.D. Bardwell Autographs
P.O. Box 324
York, ME 03909
ph: 207-351-3273
fax: 707-897-0652
info@jdbardwell.com
http://www.jdbardwell.com
    *Offers quality autographs at
    wholesale prices; issuing catalogs
    since 1986; specializes in autographs
    from those in the entertainment field;
    author of "In-Person Facsimile Guide
    of Celebrity Autographs."*

Alexander Autographs, Inc.
100 Melrose Ave.
Greenwich, CT 06830
ph: 203-622-8444
fax: 203-622-8765
info@alexautographs.com
http://www.alexautographs.com
    *Conducts mail, phone, fax and
    Internet auctions approximately every
    four months featuring thousands of
    autographs in all fields.*

University Archives
49 Richmondville Ave.
Westport, CT 06880
ph: 800-237-5692 or 203-454-0111
fax: 203-454-3111
john@universityarchives.com
http://www.universityarchives.com
    *Buying and selling fine historical
    autographs, manuscripts, documents,
    autographed books and autographed
    photographs of notable people
    including US presidents, Revolution-
    ary and Civil War, literary, aviation,
    science, art, and music.*

Reggie Turner
P.O. Box 606
Bloomfield, NJ 07003
ph: 973-482-7444
fax: 973-482-7444
singturn@aol.com
http://members.aol.com/singturn
    *Buys, sells authentic autographs, rare
    historical documents and manuscripts,
    autographed sports memorabilia, and
    signed celebrity photographs.*

Marc Zydiak
Star Archives
P.O. Box 285
Westfield, NJ 07091-0285
ph: 908-654-6505
mzunderstood@hotmail.com

Julie A. Baron
Fameabilia Corporation
42 Monmouth St.
Red Bank, NJ 07701
ph: 732-450-8411
fax: 732-450-8413
julie@fameabilia.com
http://www.fameabilia.com
    *Specializes in autographs, sports
    memorabilia, historical documents
    and letters.*

David Lowenherz
Lion Heart Autographs
470 Park Avenue South - Penthouse
New York, NY 10016
ph: 212-779-7050 or 800-969-1310
fax: 212-779-7066
lionheart@lionheartinc.com
http://www.lionheartautographs.com
    *Offers the finest in historical
    autographs and manuscripts in the
    fields of American and world history,
    science, art, literature, and music.*

Kenneth Rendell
Kenneth W. Rendell Gallery, The
989 Madison Ave.
New York, NY 10021
ph: 800-447-1007 or 212-717-1776
fax: 212-717-1492
gallery@kwrendell.com
http://www.kwrendell.com
Leading dealer in historical documents, autographs and manuscripts' author of "Autographs and Manuscripts: A Collector's Manual," "Faking Forgery: The Detection of Fake Letters and Documents," and other books.

Keya Gallery
P.O. Box 7412
New York, NY 10116
ph: 800-906-5392
fax: 212-593-1526
key15@aol.com
http://www.keyagallery.com
One of the world's largest selections of original authentic autographs, letters, and documents of the most famous people in history from 2000 B.C. to Abraham Lincoln; also 19th c. photographs of famous historical people.

Susan Levin Hoffman
North Shore Manuscript Company, Inc.
P.O. Box 458
Roslyn Heights, NY 11577
ph: 516-484-6828
fax: 516-625-3327
nsmc@earthlink.net
http://www.northshoremanuscript.com
Buys and sells historical manuscripts, documents, letters, signatures, and photos in the fields of politics, science, business, art, literature; specializing in Presidents and signers of the Declaration of Independence.

Scott Zellem
Eagle Sports
3280 Sunrise Hwy. #158
Wantagh, NY 11793
ph: 516-623-4530
fax: 516-623-4530
webmaster@eagle-sports.com
http://www.eagle-sports.com
Sells authentic sports, celebrity, and presidential autographs; also promotes celebrity signings and shows.

Jerry Docteur
Pages of History
P.O. Box 2840
Binghamton, NY 13902-2840
ph: 607-724-4943
fax: 607-724-0120
71064.3342@compuserve.com
Wants presidential and other historical autographs and material; buys autographs in all fields; also wants Civil War letters and documents.

James Spence III
James Spence Autographs
1604 Village Rd.
Orwigsburg, PA 17961
ph: 570-366-3138 or 888-947-7788
fax: 570-366-3139
autographs@jspence.com
http://www.jspence.com
Specializes in sports autographs; fourth generation graphophiles; expertise used by law enforcement agencies against forgeries.

James Spence III
James Spence Autographs
130 Brookshire Lane
Orwigsburg, PA 17961
ph: 570-943-7788 or 888-947-7788
fax: 570-943-7790
autographs@jspence.com
http://www.jspence.com
Mail order company specializing in vintage (pre-1975) autographs.

Tom Lingenfelter
Heritage Collectors' Society, Inc.
P.O. Box 2131
Doylestown, PA 18901
ph: 215-235-7955
fax: 215-230-7197
heritagecs@heritagecs.com
http://www.heritagecs.com
Dealers in investment quality historical documents and autographs; in business for over 25 years.

Robert Batchelder
P.O. Box 1779
Ambler, PA 19002-1779
ph: 484-356-0484
fax: 484-356-0485
Wants autograph letters, manuscripts & documents (American & European in all fields): Presidents, historical, literary, musical, etc.; issues periodic catalogs of items for sale.

Steven S. Raab
Steven S. Raab Autographs
P.O. Box 471
Ardmore, PA 19003
ph: 610-446-6193 or 800-977-8333
fax: 610-446-4514
raab@raabautographs.com
http://www.raabautographs.com
Buying and selling autographs, manuscripts, documents and signed photographs in all fields of interest; history is a specialty; issues illustrated catalogs; send for a sample.

Catherine Barnes
Catherine Barnes Autographs
P.O. Box 27782
Philadelphia, PA 19118
ph: 215-247-9240
fax: 215-247-4645
barnes@voicenet.com
Wants autographs, letters, documents, etc. signed by historic individuals, e.g., Presidents, government, science, medicine, the arts, law, etc.

Carmen D. Valentino
Rare Books & Manuscripts
2956 Richmond St., Drawer 19
Philadelphia, PA 19134-5720
ph: 215-739-6056
fax: 215-739-6453
Antiquarian bookseller specializing in autographs and in pre-WWI rare books, manuscripts, documents, early newspapers, handwritten diaries, account books, ledgers, ephemera, broadsides, trade catalogs, pamphlets.

Al Wittnebert
UACC Registered Dealers
Newsletter: Registered Dealer News
P.O. Box 6181
Washington, DC 20044-6181
ph: 352-383-1958
fax: 352-383-7524
signhere@zoomph.net
http://www.uacc.org
Founded in 1997, the UACC Registered Dealer Program is the largest listing of professional autograph dealers in the world; allows dealers to better promote their business as well as shows account-ability and professionalism to collectors.

Nate Dresler
Nate's Autograph Hound
10020 Raynor Rd.
Silver Spring, MD 20901
nate@autograph1.com
http://www.autograph1.com
Carries only authentic autographs form celebrities in rock/pop, movie/TV, political/presidential, space, to name a few; over 300 signed photos, books, cards; some presidential memorabilia, too; member UACC.

Barbara Pengelly
Barb Pengelly, Autographs
13917 No. Meadow Rd.
Hagerstown, MD 21742
ph: 301-733-9070
fax: 301-416-7891
BarbPengly@aol.com
http://www.autographdomain.com
Authenticate, appraise, buy and sell quality autographs, documents, signed photos, letters and diaries; Lifetime UACC registered dealer, also of The Manuscript Society; premium paid for Civil War-related material; references available.

Charles Searle
Searle's Autographs
P.O. Box 2140
Fairview, NC 28730
ph: 828-628-9551
fax: 240-266-3062
au2graph@mindspring.com
http://www.au2graph.com
Regular catalog of celebrity autographs with emphasis on TV, movies, and theatre; also authors, military, aviation, science.

Peter Thurber
Ritzi & Thurber, Inc.
160 S. Beach St.
Daytona Beach, FL 32114
ph: 904-252-2552 or 904-226-8489
fax: 904-226-8490
ritzi1881@earthlink.net
http://www.ritzi-thurber.com
Firm has one of central Florida's largest biographical and historical reference libraries, with over 400 volumes containing 4 million names on the Civil War alone.

Al Wittnebert
Al Wittenbert Autographs, Inc.
140 E. 4th Ave.
Mount Dora, FL 32757
ph: 352-383-1958
fax: 352-383-7524
signhere@zoomph.net
http://www.sign-here.com
Author of "Signature of the Stars" (1989) and "The Study of Star Trek Autographs" (1994); dealer in all fields of autographs with over 40 years experience.

Joseph Rubinfine
505 S. Flagler Dr., Ste. 1301
West Palm Beach, FL 33401-5923
ph: 561-659-7077
joerubinfine@mindspring.com
http://www.joerubinfine.com
Advanced, experienced dealer; catalog of autograph and document offerings available for $5; focuses on 18th century autographs and documents.

Stephen Koschal
P.O. Box 744
Boynton Beach, FL 33425
ph: 561-582-4439
skoschal@aol.com
http://www.stephenkoschal.com
Buys, sells, and appraises autographs, signatures, letters, documents, books, signed photographs or anyone famous; co-founder IACC/DA; catalogs issued.

R. Greg Albach
Sign Here...Autographs
P.O. Box 3777
Plant City, FL 33564
ph: 813-757-0076
fax: 530-348-8194
signhere@autographweb.com
http://www.autographweb.com/signhere
Collector, dealer, expert with online resource for authentic autographs on the Internet; huge selection, secure ordering, monthly auctions.

Ivan Gilbert, MD
Miran Art & Books
2824 Elm Ave.
Columbus, OH 43209
ph: 614-231-3707 or 614-818-3222
fax: 614-818-3223
IGilbert@ahhinc.com
Wants autographs, manuscript materials, letters, note books, documents, etc.

Steve H. Nowlin
History Makers, Inc.
942 Ft. Wayne Ave.
Indianapolis, IN 46202
ph: 800-424-9259 or 317-842-4159
fax: 317-842-4198
Snowlin@indy.rr.com
http://www.rareautograph.com
Wants autographs of heroes, legends, superstars; any famous autographs from 1600 to present; also wants historic documents, rare books, vintage photography, certified rare coins.

Linda Payne
Linda Payne Autographs & Collectibles
P.O. Box 081336
Racine, WI 53408-1336
lindap@wi.net
http://www.lpautographs.com
Buys, sells autographs, antiques, jewelry, collectibles; charter registered dealer of the Universal Autographs Collectors Club (UACC), The Manuscript Society and the Antiques & Collectibles Dealer Association (ACDA).

Thomas J. Joyce
Joyce And Company
400 N. Racine Ave., #103A
Chicago, IL 60622
ph: 312-738-1933
fax: 312-243-6252
tjoyceco@comcast.net
Buys, sells, appraises rare books and manuscripts for over 25 years; members of the Antiquarian Booksellers Association of America & International League of Antiquarian Booksellers; Thomas Joyce appears on HGTV's "The Appraisal Fair."

William Butts
Main St. Fine Books & Manuscripts
206 N. Main St.
Galena, IL 61036-2244
ph: 815-777-3749
fax: 815-777-8950
msfb@galenalink.com
http://www.wcinet.com/msfbooks
Open shop dealing in autographs and out-of-print books in most fields; specializing in all aspects of American history; book and autograph catalogs issued regularly; member of A.B.A.A.; author of "Sign Here" and other autograph columns.

Gateway Stamp Company
P.O. Box D
Florissant, MO 63031-0040
ph: 314-838-7549
fax: 314-838-4106
gatewayco@aol.com
http://www.gatewaystamp.com
Specializes in personally autographed commemorative envelopes.

Classic Rarities & Co.
P.O. Drawer 29109
Lincoln, NE 68529
ph: 402-467-2948
fax: 402-467-3780
http://www.uacc.org/dealers/
classicrarities.html
In business for over 9 years; catalogs feature autographs in the fields of Presidential, Civil Rights Documents, Inventors, Vintage Business and Entertainment.

Larry F. Vrzalik
Lone Star Autographs
P.O. Drawer 10
Kaufman, TX 75142
ph: 972-932-6050
fax: 972-932-6607
mail@lonestarautographs.com
http://www.lonestarautographs.com
Member of the UACC and The Manuscript Society.

Tim Anderson
Autographs of America
P.O. Box 461
Provo, UT 84603-0461
tanders3@autographsofamerica.com
http://www.autographsofamerica.com
Buy, sell, trade autographs: historical, Mormons, sports figures, etc.; specializing in movie stars of the 1930s, '40s and '50s.

Rocky Whitehead
P.O. Box 36561
Tucson, AZ 85740-6561
ph: 520-297-7811
fax: 520-297-7811
aautograph@aol.com
http://www.rockysautogaphs.com
Sells autographs and other memorabilia; also promotes shows.

Todd M. Axelrod
Gallery of History, Inc.
3601 West Sahara Ave.
Promenade Suite
Las Vegas, NV 89102
ph: 800-425-5379 or 702-364-1000
fax: 702-364-1285
TMAxelrod@GalleryofHistory.com
http://www.GalleryofHistory.com
Carries an inventory of 200,000 original pieces including autographs, manuscripts and other historically significant paper.

Joseph Maddalena
Profiles in History
110 North Doheny Dr.
Beverly Hills, CA 90211
ph: 800-942-8856 or 310-859-7701
fax: 310-859-3842
info@profilesinhistory.com
http://www.profilesinhistory.com
Wants original letters, manuscripts, rare books of famous people. Cash paid. Serious inquiries only.

Myron Ross
Heroes & Legends
P.O. Box 9088
Calabasas, CA 91372
ph: 818-346-9220
heroesross@aol.com
http://www.heroesandlegends.net
Wants character memorabilia, books, comic books, Fanzines, movie memorabilia, etc.; science fiction or fantasy, rock 'n' roll, autographs.

Darrell Talbert
Odyssey Publications, a Division of
Collectors Universe
510-A S. Corona Mall
Corona, CA 92879-1420
ph: 909-371-7137 or 800-99-ODYSSEY
fax: 909-371-7139
DBTOGI@aol.com
http://www.odysseygroup.com/
odyssey.htm
One of the world's leading companies in rare autographs and popular culture memorabilia.

Joe Orlando, Ed.
Odyssey Publications, a Division of
Collectors Universe
Magazine: Sports Market Report
510-A S. Corona Mall
Corona, CA 92879-1420
ph: 909-371-7137 or 800-99-ODYSSEY
fax: 909-371-7139
DBTOGI@aol.com
Magazine is the most relied upon twice-monthly price guide in the world; information needed to buy and sell in today's fast moving marketplace; monthly price guides compiled by the industry's top experts on autographs, game-used gear.

Robert A. LeGresley
727 St. John's Mine Rd.
Vallejo, CA 94951
ph: 707-648-9377
rlegres@aol.com
Buys and sells autographs, specializing in historical, scientific, literary, musicians, composers, aviation, Civil War, entertainers, Papal and Saints, William Randolph Hearst.

Bob Blanchard
Antique Access
1010 California Ave.
Klamath Falls, OR 97601
ph: 541-273-1779
bob@cvc.net
Buys and sells autographs and old photographs.

Daniel Cohen
Daniel Cohen Autographs & Memorabilia
P.O. Box 515
Kleinburg, Ontario L0J 1C0 Canada
ph: 905-893-2328
dcohen@danielcohen.com
http://www.danielcohen.com
Specializes in vintage to contemporary celebrity autographs in all fields.

John Wilson
Painswick Lawn
7 Painswick Rd.
Cheltenham, GL50 2EZ U.K.
ph: _44(0)1242 580344
fax: +44(0)1242 580355
web@manuscripts.co.uk
http://www.manuscripts.co.uk
Long-established dealers in the UK specializing in autograph letters, historical documents and textual manuscripts; also signed photographs and other related material having a close association with historical figures in all fields.

Experts

Kenneth Schwartz
c/o World Jeep-Subaru
688 Shrewsbury Ave.
Red Bank, NJ 07701
ph: 732-741-6200
fax: 732-450-3749
kenneth@monmouth.com
Autograph collector, authenticator, expert wants to buy autographs, documents, or letters from famous people; coauthored "The Robot That Helped Make a President" with Charles Hamilton, a recognized authority on autographs.

Helen Sanders
Autograph House
2 Lake Dr.
P.O. Box 658
Enka, NC 28728-0658
ph: 828-667-9835
sanderspg@ioa.com
http://www.autograph-book.com
Co-author with Ralph Roberts of "Collector's Guide to Autographs;" also other books; owns one of the largest and extensive autograph collections; buys, sells, authenticates and appraises autographs.

Al Wittnebert
Al Wittenbert Autographs, Inc.
140 E. 4th Ave.
Mount Dora, FL 32757
ph: 352-383-1958
fax: 352-383-7524
signhere@zoomph.net
http://www.sign-here.com
Author of "Signature of the Stars" (1989) and "The Study of Star Trek Autographs" (1994); dealer in all fields of autographs with over 40 years experience.

Rich Davis
Rich Davis Autograph Authentication &
   Collectible Investments
P.O. Box 563
Kingston, OH 45644
ph: 740-642-2024
prdavis@horizonview.net
http://authenticator.freeservers.com
*Specializes in the authentication and
appraisal of all types of autographs;
expert on sports collectibles, coins &
currency, comic books, and stamps;
also provides services as a research/
grading/appraisal expert.*

Internet Resources

Brent Gutekunst
Autograph Universe
P.O. Box 6289
Newport Beach, CA 92658
ph: 949-567-1234
fax: 949-833-7955
http://www.collectors.com
*Online collector news, buy and sell,
information, auctions, grading &
authentication services.*

Misc. Services

Jim Romeo
Directory: Resource for Autograph
Collectors
1008 Weeping Willow Dr.
Chesapeake, VA 23322-7701
*Publishes a directory of resources for
autograph collectors: dealers, clubs,
associations, auction houses.*

Museums/Libraries

New York Public Library, The
455 5th Ave.
New York, NY 10016-0118
ph: 212-340-0833
branch_web@nypl.org
http://www.nypl.org/branch/
   central_units/mm/midman.html

Periodicals

Christopher C. Jaeckel
Walter R. Benjamin Autographs, Inc.
Magazine: Collector, The
644 Scribner Hollow Rd.
P.O. Box 255
Hunter, NY 12442-0255
ph: 518-263-4133
fax: 518-263-4134
cjaeckel@mhonline.net
http://www.benjaminautographs.com
*One of the oldest autograph firms in
the US; founded in 1887; specializes
in historical, literary, and foreign
material; does not handle sports or
celebrity figures.*

Jeffrey Morey
Newsletter: Autograph Review, The
305 Carlton Rd.
Syracuse, NY 13207-1530
ph: 315-474-3516
*A bi-monthly 24-year publication for
the serious collector; collector growth
oriented: sports, military, actors' and
others addresses, ads, mail-bid
auctions, information and news.
Courtesy sample $1 + LSASE.*

Newspaper: Autograph Times
P.O. Box 5790
Peoria, AZ 85385
ph: 623-544-4037 or 877-860-0349
fax: 623-214-5419
info@autographtimes.net
http://www.autographtimes.net
*News and information on all aspects
of autograph collecting including
historical, space, sports, entertainment and through the mail.*

Darrell Talbert
Odyssey Publications, a Division of
   Collectors Universe
Magazine: Pop Culture Collecting
510-A S. Corona Mall
Corona, CA 91720-1420
ph: 909-371-7137 or 800-99-ODYSSEY
fax: 909-371-7139
DBTOGI@aol.com
http://www.autographs.com/collect.htm
*A monthly magazine focusing on
collecting autographs, movie
memorabilia, movie posters,
television, rock & roll, props,
costumes, sports, space collectibles,
animation art and more.*

Ev Phillips
Odyssey Publications, a Division of
   Collectors Universe
Magazine: Autograph Collector
510-A S. Corona Mall
Corona, CA 92879-1420
ph: 909-371-7137 or 800-99-ODYSSEY
fax: 909-371-7139
DBTOGI@aol.com
http://www.autographs.com/acm.htm
*A bi-monthly magazine covering all
aspects of autograph and historical
document collecting: entertainment,
sports, historical, etc.; for all ages;
sample autographs, free celebrity
addresses, detailed how-to articles,
auctions, ads, etc.*

George Baker
Magazine: Autograph News
P.O. Box 580450
Modesto, CA 95358
ph: 209-537-5221
fax: 209-531-0233
editor@autographnews.com
http://www.autographnews.com
*The first bi-monthly magazine for
autograph collectors in an online
format AND in a print format.*

Astronaut

Dealers

Adam Harwood
Astronaut Autographs
1414 West Aries
Edmond, OK 73003-5826
ph: 405-359-7678
fax: 405-341-8405
75717.1061@compuserve.com
*Over eight years experience buying
and selling astronaut autographs; has
worked with former astronauts and
NASA employees to bring their
collections to the space collectibles
market; writes space memorabilia
column for collectibles mag.*

Celebrity

(see also PHOTOGRAPHS, Celebrity)

Collectors

Josh Kellerman
Josh Kellerman's Celebrity Autograph
   Collecting Page
jmkellerman@cinci.rr.com
http://www.geocities.com/Hollywood/
   Lot/7775/celauto.html
*Web site has tips on collecting,
addressed, images of bad autographs,
images of good autographs, links,
resources; does not buy, sell, or trade.*

Dealers

GalleryofStars.com
14 Holly Circle
Holden, MA 01520
ph: 888-325-3437 or 508-829-2073
fax: 508-829-9352
sales@galleryofstars.com
http://www.galleryofstars.com
*Specializes in signed in-person
celebrity autographs.*

Ed Setfanik
Autographs Plus
P.O. Box 2558
Fall River, MA 02722
ph: 508-674-9090
fax: 508-674-9090
edstef@autographsplus.com
http://www.autographsplus.com
*Buys and sells celebrity autographs
and Sci-fi autographed items; UACC
registered dealer #40.*

Robert Jones
Autograph World
P.O. Box 254
Durham, NH 03824
ph: 603-749-9461
fax: 603-962-2442
jones@autographworld.com
http://www.autographworld.com
*Specializes in the sale of celebrity
autographs; online catalog features
hundreds of stars from vintage
Hollywood through today; every item
in catalog is pictured.*

J.D. Bardwell
J.D. Bardwell Celebrity Autographs
P.O. Box 324
York, ME 03909
ph: 207-351-3273
fax: 707-897-0652
info@jdbardwell.com
http://www.jdbardwell.com
*Offers quality autographs at
wholesale prices; issuing catalogs
since 1986; specializes in autographs
from those in the entertainment field;
author of "In-Person Facsimile Guide
of Celebrity Autographs."*

Jon Allan
Elmer's Nostalgia, Inc.
3 Putnam St.
Sanford, ME 04073-2024
ph: 207-324-2166
elmers@gwi.net
http://www.elmers.net

Doug Wirth
Hummerdude's
P.O. Box 4348
Dunellen, NJ 08812-4348
ph: 732-424-9367
fax: 732-424-1619
sales@hummerdudes.com
http://www.hummerdudes.com
*Celebrity photos, autographs and
collectibles.*

Steve Milwich
Sign of the Times
105 Gilmore Blvd.
Floral Park, NY 11001
fax: 413-473-2063
steve@signofthetimes.com
http://www.signofthetimes.com
*Buys and sells autographs,
autographed photos, sports
memorabilia, and more.*

Arbe Bareis
Safka & Bareis Autographs
P.O. Box 886
Forest Hills, NY 11375
ph: 718-263-2276
fax: 718-263-2276
safkabareis@yahoo.com
http://www.safka-bareis.com
*Collections bought and sold;
specializing in cinema, music, opera
and ballet.*

Charles Searle
Searle's Autographs
P.O. Box 2140
Fairview, NC 28730
ph: 828-628-9551
fax: 240-266-3062
au2graph@mindspring.com
http://www.au2graph.com
*Regular catalog of celebrity
autographs with emphasis on TV,
movies, and theatre; also authors,
military, aviation, science.*

Alan Sherred
Walk of Fame Autographs
P.O. Box 255
Deland, FL 32721-0255
ph: 904-943-9500
fax: 904-943-4115
Buys and sells celebrity autographs: Hollywood, TV, models, political, sports, music, celebrities.

Barbara Meyrowitz
Star-Shots
5389 Bearcup St.
Port Charlotte, FL 33981
ph: 941-697-6935
fax: 941-698-0811
autos@star-shots.com
http://www.star-shots.com
Celebrity autographs and photographs of all kinds; signed photos, 3x5 signature cards, books, T-shirts.

Steve H. Nowlin
History Makers, Inc.
942 Ft. Wayne Ave.
Indianapolis, IN 46202
ph: 800-424-9259 or 317-842-4159
fax: 317-842-4198
Snowlin@indy.rr.com
http://www.rareautograph.com
Buys and sells autographs of Hollywood movie stars.

Gary Price
Autograph Central
P.O. Box 441615
Aurora, CO 80044
webmaster@autographcentral.com
http://www.autographcentral.com
Autograph news, tips on how to collect, free addresses, articles, stories, photo gallery.

Rocky Whitehead
Rocky's Autographs
P.O. Box 91770
Tucson, AZ 85752
ph: 520-572-3712
fax: 520-572-3712
Aautograph@aol.com
http://www.rockysautographs.com
Sells celebrity autographs and memorabilia; member of UACC and IACC/DA.

Golden State Autographs
P.O. Box 14776
Albuquerque, NM 87191
ph: 505-293-7407

Mike Gould
Hollywood Legends Gallery
6621A Hollywood Blvd.
Los Angeles, CA 90028
ph: 323-962-7411
fax: 323-962-6742
hwdbookcity@earthlink.net
http://www.hollywoodbookcity.com
Specializes in signed photographs of contemporary movie stars; also autographs of television stars.

Phil Sears
24592 Via Carissa
Laguna Niguel, CA 92677-7034
ph: 949-643-1477
fax: 949-643-8376
Phil@Phil-Sears.com
http://www.phil-sears.com
Buys and sells 1930-1950 movie star autographs.

Star Struck International
2791 F. North Texas St., Ste. 112
Fairfield, CA 94533
ph: 707-426-0811
fax: 707-426-0811
sales@starcollectibles.com
http://www.starcollectibles.com
Buys and sells memorabilia from TV, film and music: costumes, autographs, memorabilia.

Cindy Starr
Starr Autographs, Inc.
P.O. Box 68618
Portland, OR 97268
ph: 503-659-3333
4collecting@attbi.com
http://www.4collecting.com
Web site has thousands of items for sale with all items pictured; online auctions; certificates of authenticity with every purchase.

Fraser's Autographs
399 Strand
London, WC2E 0LX U.K.
ph: 0207 826 9325 or 0207 836 8444
fax: 0207 836 7342
sales@frasersautographs.co.uk
http://www.frasersautographs.com
Established in 1978; deals with autographed items and celebrity memorabilia; over 60,000 items in stock spanning 500 years: signed photographs, letters, documents relating to film, music, Beatles, history, space, military, art, etc.

Internet Resources

Jane's Celebrity Autographs
jane@icomputerdesigns.com
http://www.janes-autographs.com
Collecting tips, bad addresses, good addresses.

Scott Johnson
Celebrity Locators
P.O. Box 12
North Whitefield, ME 04353
ph: 207-832-6687
fax: 207-832-0546
Scott@CelebrityLocators.com
http://www.CelebrityLocators.com
Specialist in putting fans in contact with celebrities; carries a variety of celebrity-related products; publisher of "The Big Book of Celebrity Addresses," and "The Autograph Collecting News" (a free email newsletter).

Markus Geilfuss
Star Archive, The
Hamsterweg 40
Bad Schwalbach, Hessen 65307
  Germany
webmaster@stararchive.com
http://www.stararchive.com
Great Web site for over 9,000 celebrity addresses, profiles, images, sample autographs of celebrities.

Jewish

Dealers

Ezra M. Holczer
Queen Esther Judaica Autographs
1417 East 28th St.
Brooklyn, NY 11210
ph: 718-253-2581
fax: 718-253-2581
qejudaica@aol.com
http://www.judaicaautographs.com
Deals exclusively in all areas of Judaica autographs; specializes in buying and selling vintage material autographed by American Jews and Zionists.

Music Related

Dealers

Roger Gross
Roger Gross, Ltd.
225 East 57th St.
New York, NY 10022-2822
ph: 212-759-2892
fax: 212-838-5425
rogergross@earthlink.net
http://www.rgrossmusicautograph.com
Buys and sells signed photos of singers, instrumentalists, conductors and composers; letters, musical quotes; classical music and operatic books, memorabilia, ephemera, unsigned photos, etc.

John & Jude Lubrano
J & J Lubrano, Music Antiquarians
351 West Neck Rd.
Huntington, NY 11743
ph: 631-549-0672
fax: 631-421-1677
lubrano2@optonline.net
http://www.bookmarque.net/Lubrano
Buys and sells autograph manuscripts from famous musicals and dance; rare printed music and books about music, musical autographs and manuscripts, rare dance books 16th to 20th centuries; established in 1977; member ABAA, ILAB.

J.B. Muns
Fine Arts Books & Musical Autographs
1162 Shattuck Ave.
Berkeley, CA 94707-2635
ph: 510-525-2420
fax: 510-525-1126
jbmuns@aol.com
Buys and sells musical autographs (classical musicians, composers and singers) as well as books on music.

AUTOMATONS

(see CLOCKS; DOLLS, Automatons; COIN-OPERATED MACHINES; MUSIC BOXES; MUSIC BOXES, Birds & Bird Boxes [Singing]; MUSICAL INSTRUMENTS, Mechanical; TOYS)

AUTOMOBILES

(see also AUTOMOBILIA; BOOKS, Reference [Automobiles]; BUSES; KITS; MILITARIA, Vehicles; MODELS, Cars; AUTO RACING MEMORABILIA; TAXI RELATED COLLECTIBLES; TOYS, Diecast; TRACTORS & RELATED ITEMS; TRAILERS & RVs; TRUCKS; VOLKSWAGEN RELATED ITEMS)

Appraisers

Werner Pfister
Miller Motorcars
342 W. Putnam Ave.
Greenwich, CT 06830
ph: 203-629-3890
fax: 203-629-1621
lorenz50@aol.com
http://www.wpfister.com
Appraises historic sports and racing automobiles, specializing in Ferrari and Corvette.

James Wetzel
Hudson Valley Auto Appraisers, Inc.
40 Plank Rd.
Newburgh, NY 12550
ph: 845-561-1185
fax: 845-561-1745
jim@hvaa.com
http://www.hvaa.com
The source for vehicle appraising; in business for over 30 years and performed over 200,000 appraisals; the Internet source for appraising.

Terry Shaw
Automotive Legal Service
P.O. Box 626
Dresher, PA 19025-0626
ph: 800-487-4947 or 215-659-4947
fax: 215-659-4947
Government licensed appraisers for all appreciable, collectible quality vehicles; specialists in insurance claims, restoration disputes, IRS donations, estate & equity matters, Lemon Law; qualified expert witness; free information.

Edwin W. Baker, Ex. VP
American Society of Appraisers
P.O. Box 17265
Washington, DC 20071
ph: 703-478-2228 or 800-272-8258
fax: 703-742-8471
asainfo@appraisers.org
http://www.appraisers.org
The only appraisal organization in the US representing all the disciplines of appraisal specialists; call 800-ASA-VALU for free referral or membership directory, or visit Web site.

Dorothy Balzer, ISA
Accurate Auto Appraisal
94 Pinewood Rd.
Earleville, MD 21919
ph: 410-275-8287
fax: 410-275-8274
dottie.balzer@dol.net
http://www.autoappraising.com
*Determines value of vehicles for
insurance, estate settlements, etc.;
requires inspection of vehicle; serves
MD, DE, PA, and NJ.*

Larry Batton
Auto Appraisal Group
RR 3 Box 184E
Charlottesville, VA 22903-9322
ph: 800-848-2886 or 804-295-1722
fax: 804-295-7918
AAG@autoappraisal.com
http://www.autoappraisal.com
*Nationwide appraisal service for all
classic and collectible type automobiles: prepurchase inspections,
insurance documentation, property
and divorce settlements, expert
witness testimony; also originality and
historical research.*

Donald R. Peterson
Classic Car Appraisal Service
1400 Lake Ridge Court
Roswell, GA 30076
ph: 770-993-5622
fax: 770-645-9540
wpeterson@carsandparts.com
*One of the largest auto appraisers in
the US; one of three chosen to
appraise the 1,500-car Harrah
collection before it was dispersed;
loss in value, estate, insurance, etc.;
antiques, classics, muscle cars, hot
rods, late models.*

Kruse International
P.O. Box 190
Auburn, IN 46706
ph: 800-968-4444 or 219-925-5600
fax: 219-925-5467
info@kruseinternational.com
http://www.kruseinternational.com
Appraises all collector cars.

Howell Lee Davis
P.O. Box 1420
Brighton, MI 48116-7920
ph: 810-227-5644
fax: 810-227-4809
howell_davis@yahoo.com
*Specializes in the appraisal of special
interest cars, petroliana (glass pump
globes, gas pumps, advertising
signage, promotional items) and
automotive art (original paintings,
signed, numbered or remarqued
prints, bronzes, etc.).*

Al Hagen
Yesterday's Auto
2800 Lyndale Ave. S
Minneapolis, MN 55408-2108
ph: 612-872-9733
fax: 612-872-1386
al@yesterdaysauto.com
http://www.yesterdaysauto.com
*Specializes in the appraisal of antique
and classic cars.*

Carl T. Roedel, Jr., ISA
Automobile Appraisal Service
10097 Manchester
Saint Louis, MO 63122-1828
ph: 314-821-4015
fax: 314-821-4015
*Appraiser of antique, classic and
special interest cars & trucks, both
foreign and late models, sports cars,
muscle cars, street rods, replicas, RVs,
SUVs, motorcycles, boats; also
consignments of collector cars for
sale.*

Danny O'Brien, ISA
Fatdog Auto Appraisal
1816 E. 135th St.
Grandview, MO 64030
ph: 816-763-4741
fatdog_autos@hotmail.com
*Specializes in the appraisal of antique
& classic cars, custom cars,
motorcycles.*

Robert W. Ryan
U.S. Auto Appraisers
5062 S. 108th St., Ste. 225
Omaha, NE 68137-6310
ph: 402-681-2968
fax: 402-861-8772
Bob@usaautoappraisers.com
http://www.usaautoappraisers.com
*Custom and classic auto appraiser;
automotive legal consultant; court-
tested expert witness; prepurchase
inspections, email appraisals; member
NADA classic and collectible advisory
board; 20 years experience; will
return calls.*

Chris M. Zora, ISA, ASA
Automobile Appraisers & Assoc.
P.O. Box 9939
Spring, TX 77380
ph: 281-362-8258 or 800-559-8258
fax: 936-447-4024
autoaprz@txucom.net
http://www.autoappraise.net
*Appraiser of antique, classic, special
interest (cars, trucks and motorcycles,
muscle cars, Corvettes, sports cars
(domestic & foreign), race cars;
insurance, diminished value, product
liability, deceptive trade, Lemon Law,
etc.*

Tiffany Kruse
Dan Kruse Fine Arts & Collectibles
11202 Disco
San Antonio, TX 78216
ph: 210-499-0777 or 210-860-2901
fax: 210-499-4217
tpierce@saami.com
Member of the International Society of

*appraisers; appraises even the rarest
of vehicles.*

Mike Grippo, ISA
M & M Automobile Appraisers, Inc.
584 Broomspun St.
Henderson, NV 89015-6921
ph: 702-568-5120
fax: 702-568-5158
mmautoappr@earthlink.net
http://home.earthlink.net/~mmautoappr
*Special interest, collectible and
antique cars, machinery & equipment;
expert witness, marriage or business
dissolution, loan valuation and
insurance coverage; Accredited
Member, International Society of
Appraisers.*

C. Erik Baltzar
Consulting Distributors
P.O. Box 1331
Palm Desert, CA 92261-1331
ph: 760-346-1984
fax: 760-568-6354
driwasherik@aol.com
Vehicle appraiser.

Dennis Mitosinka
Dennis Mitosinka's Classic Cars
619 E. Fourth St.
Santa Ana, CA 92701-4705
ph: 714-953-5303
fax: 714-953-1810
*Appraises all types of autos from 1900
to present; appraisals accepted by
FBI, IRS, FSLIC and insurance
companies; member of the Inter. Soc.
of Appraisers & the Antique
Appraisers of Amer.*

Randy Hilberg
Collector's Nectar
Box 431
Morro Bay, CA 93443
ph: 805-772-2968
fax: 805-772-2968
gd57@hotmail.com
*Always buying antique cars; offers
complete restoration services;
appraisals; master technician; all
makes and models; no collection too
big or too small to purchase or
restore; the only lifetime guarantee in
the business.*

Roger J. Rapport, ASA
Old Mill Appraisal Company
P.O. Box 646
Mill Valley, CA 94942
ph: 415-388-9420
fax: 415-924-8968
autoappr@aol.com
*Specializes in the appraisal of antique
& classic cars; also residential
contents, small commercial shops.*

International Society of Appraisers
Newsletter: Professional Appraisers
 Information Exchange
1131 SW 7th St., Ste. 105
Renton, WA 98055
ph: 206-241-0359 or 888-472-4732
fax: 206-241-0436
ISA@isa-appraisers.org
http://www.isa-appraisers.org
*Largest assoc. of professional
appraisers devoted solely to personal
property; over 1,300 members
specializing in all areas of antiques &
residential contents, gems & jewelry,
fine art, machinery & equipment;
member directory on Web site.*

Auction Services

Kruse International
P.O. Box 190
Auburn, IN 46706
ph: 800-968-4444 or 219-925-5600
fax: 219-925-5467
info@kruseinternational.com
http://www.kruseinternational.com
*Specializes in auctioning antique,
classic and other special interest
automobiles, planes, motorcycles,
trucks, etc.*

Barrett-Jackson Auction Co., LLC
3020 N. Scottsdale Rd.
Scottsdale, AZ 85251
ph: 480-421-6694
fax: 480-421-6697
econcierge@barrett-jackson.com
http://barrett-jackson.com
*Web site includes comprehensive
searchable database of past sales
prices.*

Steve Barlow
Specialty Sales
4321 First St.
Pleasanton, CA 94566
ph: 925-484-2262 or 800-600-2262
fax: 925-426-8535
info@specialtysales.com
http://www.specialtysales.com
*Auctions antiques, classics, exotics;
largest indoor showroom; ships
overseas.*

Vintage Auctions of Canada, Ltd.
418 McDermot Ave.
Winnipeg, Manitoba R3A OA9 Canada
ph: 204-783-2262 or 888-560-2277
fax: 204-786-1846
info@VintageAuctions.ca
http://www.VintageAuctions.ca
*Conducts specialty automobile
auctions.*

Clubs/Associations

Fred Roth
Milestone Car Society of California, Inc.
ph: 805-241-4606
mcs72roth@aol.com
http://clubs.hemmings.com/
 milestonecarsocietyofcainc
*Focuses on "milestone" cars; certain
club-approved 1946-1974 cars which
are gaining popularity with the*

passage of time; chapters in CA, MN, IN, OH.

Kit Foster
Society of Automotive Historians, Inc.
Magazine: Automotive History Review
1102 Long Cove Rd.
Gales Ferry, CT 06335-1812
foster@netbox.com
http://www.autohistory.org
Interested in the preservation of historically valuable materials.

Ed Hyman
Vintage Sports Car Club of America
116 Sawyer Hill
New Milford, CT 06776
ph: 860-355-1804 or 203-788-3956
edwardh@gullwingsearch.com
http://www.vscca.org
The oldest automotive preservation club in America that offers a complete race program in addition to rally and other automotive conservation events; emphasis is on rare and unusual sports and racing cars up to and including 1959.

West Paterson
Council of Vehicle Associations/Classic Vehicle Advocate Group, Inc.
Newsletter: COVAG/CVAG News
P.O. Box 2136
Little Falls, NJ 07424-3311
ph: 973-208-3259 or 800-227-7166
fax: 973-297-3779
webmaster@covacvag.org
http://www.covacvag.org
Not-for-profit special interest group representing all automotive enthusiasts regarding regulation and legislation potentially contrary to collector interest.

William Schmoll
Fifties Automobile Club of America
(Garden State Auto Club)
1114 Furman Dr.
Linwood, NJ 08234
ph: 609-927-4967
oldiesdj@bellatlantic.net
http://www.classicar.com/clubs/
gardenstate50%27s/home.htm
Purpose of the club is to encourage the restoration, preservation and use of historic, sports and racing cars.

Antique Automobile Club of America
Magazine: Antique Automobile
501 W. Governor Rd.
P.O. Box 417
Hershey, PA 17033
ph: 717-534-1910
fax: 717-534-9101
general@aaca.org
http://www.aaca.org
Dedicated to the history of the automobile; focuses on "antique" cars - (or by state registration a vehicle at least 25 years old); sponsors AACA tours, meets and discussions; regions and chapters across the US.

Vintage Sports Car Drivers Association
3160 Thornapple River Dr.
Grand Rapids, MI 49546
ph: 616-949-8281
fax: 616-949-0191
vscda@iserv.net
http://www.vscda.org
Holds regular wheel-to-wheel racing competitions between vintage sports cars.

James J. Baxter
National Motorists Association
Newsletter: NMA News
402 W. 2nd St.
Waunakee, WI 53597
ph: 608-849-6000
fax: 608-849-8697
nma@motorists.org
http://www.motorists.org
For the protection of the rights of motorists, enhancing personal mobility, encouraging rational traffic laws.

Mike Giel
Perfect "10" Motor Vehicle Club
P.O. Box 1890
Saint Paul, MN 55101
ph: 651-639-1928
tdgiel@aol.com
Vintage and collector automobiles, motorcycles and scooters; runs a small museum/display area; puts on annual car show.

Classic Car Club of America
1645 Des Plaines River Rd., Ste. 7A
Des Plaines, IL 60018
ph: 847-390-0443
fax: 847-390-7118
classiccarclub@aol.com
http://www.classiccarclub.org
For owners of select cars from 1925 through 1948.

Sports Car Club of America, Inc.
Magazine: SportsCar Magazine
P.O. Box 19400
Topeka, KS 66619-0440
ph: 785-357-7222 or 800-770-2055
fax: 785-232-7228
president@scca.org
http://www.scca.org
Sanctions amateur and professional auto sports events throughout the US, and has done so for over 50 years.

Buddy Hoelzeman
Mid-America Old Time Automobile Association, The
Magazine: Antique Car Times
8 Jones Lane
Petit Jean Mountain
Morrilton, AR 72110
ph: 501-727-5427
fax: 501-727-6482
info@motaa.com
http://www.motaa.com
M.O.T.A.A. represents approximately 26 affiliated antique car clubs; "Antique Car Times" filled with articles featuring antique cars; recognizes cars that are 25 years old or older.

Richard Rigby, Sec.
Veteran Motor Car Club of America
Magazine: Bulb Horn
4441 W. Altadena Ave.
Glendale, AZ 85304-3526
ph: 800-428-7327
fax: 602-978-1106
raycw@cvip.net
http://www.vmcca.org
A hobby club organized in 1938 to serve the needs of those interested in the preservation of collector vehicles and related memorabilia.

World Organization of Automotive Hobbyists
P.O. Box 1331
Palm Desert, CA 92261-1331
ph: 619-568-6354
Representing automotive hobbyist interests vis-a-vis regulation and/or legislation.

Todd Miller, Ex. Sec.
Horseless Carriage Club of America
Magazine: Horseless Carriage Gazette
49239 Golden Oak Loop
Oakhurst, CA 93644
ph: 559-658-8800 or 888-832-2374
office@hcca.org
http://www.hcca.org
Interested in pre-1916 brass-era touring cars.

Contemporary Historical Vehicle Association, Inc.
Magazine: Action Era Vehicle
P.O. Box 493398
Redding, CA 96049-3398
chvanatweb@aol.com
http://clubs.hemmings.com/chva
A multi-marque club for cars from 1928 through 1978 and recognized as an important part of our automotive history; magazine published quarterly.

Ralph Linnell
Inliners International
Newsletter: 12 Port News, The
14408 SE 169th
Renton, WA 98058
ph: 425-228-2028
webmaster@inliners.org
http://www.inliners.org
For enthusiasts of all makes, models, years of stock, mild, or racing engines that are 4, 6, or 8 cylinders in-lines.

Earl Clements
Specialty Vehicle Association of Alberta
14621-103 Ave.
Edmonton, Alberta T5N 0T6 Canada
ph: 780-454-5589
ariise2@telusplanet.net
Founded in the late 1970s for anyone who owns or dreams of owning an antique or classic car, any model.

Dealers

Classic Reaction
100 South Locust St.
Dubuque, IA 52003
ph: 319-588-6285
fax: 319-588-2439
classic@mwci.net
http://www.classicreaction.com
Sells vintage stock and custom vehicles on a consignment basis.

Ronnie Craig, Pres.
Duffy's Collectible Cars
250 Classic Car Court S.W.
Cedar Rapids, IA 52404
ph: 319-364-7000
fax: 319-364-4036
sales@duffys.com
http://www.duffys.com
Web site offers nearly 100 restored cars for sale.

Carl T. Roedel, Jr., ISA
Automobile Appraisal Service
10097 Manchester
Saint Louis, MO 63122-1828
ph: 314-821-4015
fax: 314-821-4015
Appraiser of antique, classic and special interest cars & trucks, both foreign and late models, sports cars, muscle cars, street rods, replicas, RVs, SUVs, motorcycles, boats; also consignments of collector cars for sale.

VIP Classics
861 5th Ave.
San Diego, CA 92101
ph: 619-232-6864
fax: 619-232-6849
classics@vipclassics.com
http://www.vipclassics.com
Buys, sells, accepts consignments of all makes of European and American classic and vintage cars.

Fast Cars of California
858 W. 18th St., #B5
Costa Mesa, CA 92627
ph: 949-631-4328
fax: 949-631-4332
bossman@fastcars.net
http://www.vintagesportscars.com
Buys, sells, takes consignments, restores vintage sports cars: Austin Healey, Alfa Romeo, Jaguar, Triumph, MG. Porsche, Mercedes, Maserati, etc.; world wide shipping.

Dennis Mitosinka
Dennis Mitosinka's Classic Cars
619 E. Fourth St.
Santa Ana, CA 92701-4705
ph: 714-953-5303
fax: 714-953-1810
Auto dealer in antique, classic and special interest cars.

Randy Hilberg
Collector's Nectar
Box 431
Morro Bay, CA 93443
ph: 805-772-2968
fax: 805-772-2968
gd57@hotmail.com
Always buying antique cars; offers complete restoration services; appraisals; master technician; all makes and models; no collection too big or too small to purchase or restore; the only lifetime guarantee in the business.

Steve Barlow
Specialty Sales
4321 First St.
Pleasanton, CA 94566
ph: 925-484-2262 or 800-600-2262
fax: 925-426-8535
info@specialtysales.com
http://www.specialtysales.com
For over 20 years a worldwide classic and exotic car dealer selling investment grade Classic, Exotic and European cars.

AP USA - Special Interest Automobiles
1041 Fee Dr.
Sacramento, CA 95815
ph: 916-646-0988
fax: 916-646-0989
bevacqua@pacbell.net
http://www.apusa-sacramento.com
Sells special interest automobiles: classics, customs, street rods, exotics; also motorcycles.

Experts

Tad Burness
Auto Album
P.O. Box 247
Pacific Grove, CA 93950-0247
ph: 831-649-4864
Classic and antique car historian; writes and illustrates syndicated "Auto Album" column for newspapers including "AntiqueWeek;" author of 24 books, most on transportation subjects.

Internet Resources

Auto Restorer Online
autobuff@autorestorer.com
http://www.autorestorer.com
A collection of auto restoration information to help with auto restoration projects and car repair needs.

Edmund's
editor@edmunds.com
http://www.edmunds.com/edweb/used/usedcars.html
Online values (trade in and resale) for used cars; also comprehensive guide to buying and selling used cars; new cars and trucks, consumer advice, vehicle reviews, financial loan calculator.

Hemmings.com
P.O. Box 76
Bennington, VT 05201-0076
ph: 802-442-3101 or 800-227-4373
fax: 802-447-1561
hmnmail@hemmings.com
http://www.hemmings.com/hemmings/htm/clubssearch.cfm
Searchable Web site lists over 9,100 car clubs.

Bob Amott
Horizon Productions Inc.
104 William Howard Taft Rd.
Cincinnati, OH 45219
ph: 513-221-5000
fax: 513-221-0608
info@horizon-productions.com
http://www.horizon-productions.com
Produces a series of videos on car restorations; also Internet resource for all things concerning automotive restoration: tips, links, parts, clubs, and more.

Collector Car TraderOnline.com
360 West Butterfield Rd., Ste. 320
Elmhurst, IL 60126
ph: 630-953-1989
fax: 630-953-8403
csr-chicago@autotrader.com
http://www.collectorcartraderonline.com
The premier online source for enthusiasts of classic, exotic, luxury and sports cars; automotive articles, news, featured marques, directories, auction catalogs, classifieds, advertisements, and other related links.

Kelley Blue Book
Price Guide: Kelley Blue Book
5 Oldfield
Irvine, CA 92618
ph: 949-770-7704
fax: 949-837-1904
kelley@kbb.com
http://www.kbb.com/indexv.html
Web site offers current trade-in values for all makes and model cars for the past 21 years; also publishes printed value guides for cars, RVs, motorcycles, snowmobiles, motor homes, travel trailers, personal watercraft, etc.

Steve Ferguson, Ed.
National Automobile Dealers Association
Price Guide: N.A.D.A. Official Used Car Guide
P.O. Box 7800
Costa Mesa, CA 92628
ph: 800-544-6232 or 714-556-8511
fax: 714-556-8715
info@nadaguides.com
http://www.nada.org
A series of value guides for domestic and foreign cars, trucks, vans, RVs, mobile homes, motorcycles, snowmobiles, and boats, small and large; also Heavy Duty Trucks and Aircraft Book, car clubs & organizations, museums.

Lou Ann Hammond
Car-List
P.O. Box 460070
San Francisco, CA 94146-0070
ph: 530-823-6865
lou@car-list.com
http://www.car-list.com
An online Internet service; Car-List is a used car locating service; you can also get a new car price quote; locate a car club from around the world, or list your car club for free.

ClassicCar.com
1200 Harris Ave., #104
Bellingham, WA 98225
ph: 360-738-7018
fax: 360-738-4815
editor@classiccar.com
http://www.classiccar.com
Premier online source for classic vehicles, automobilia and rare parts, technical information; great Web site for all sorts of classic car information: clubs, chat, swap meet, museums, suppliers, articles, etc.

Bolide
19A Buckingham St.
London, BN1 3LT U.K.
ph: 01273 734451
cars@bolide.co.uk
http://www.bolide.co.uk
U.K. Web site with news, features, events from the world of classic cars.

Misc. Services

Bob Amott
Horizon Productions Inc.
104 William Howard Taft Rd.
Cincinnati, OH 45219
ph: 513-221-5000
fax: 513-221-0608
info@horizon-productions.com
http://www.horizon-productions.com
Produces a series of videos on car restorations; also Internet resource for all things concerning automotive restoration: tips, links, parts, clubs, and more.

Museums/Libraries

James A. Harwick, Cur.
J.K. Lilly III Automobile Museum at Heritage Plantation
P.O. Box 566
Sandwich, MA 02563
ph: 508-888-3300 or 508-888-1222
fax: 508-833-2916
heritage@heritageplantation.org
http://www.heritageplantation.org/autos.htm

Kenneth E. Creed
Auto Museum at Wells, The
1181 Post Rd.
P.O. Box 496
Wells, ME 04090
ph: 207-646-5051 or 207-646-9064
Over 70 vehicles from 1894 to 1963; fine collection of nickelodeons and antique games (all working!).

Antique Automobile Club of America Museum
161 Museum Dr.
Hershey, PA 17033
ph: 717-566-7100
fax: 717-566-7300
general@aaca.org
http://www.aaca.org/museum
Dedicated to the preservation of all forms of historical motor vehicles and related memorabilia.

Sarasota Classic Car Museum, Inc.
5500 North Tamiami Trail
Sarasota, FL 34243-2142
ph: 941-355-6228
fax: 941-358-8065
classiccarmuseum@aol.com
http://www.sarasotacarmuseum.org

Don Garlits
Don Garlits Auto Racing Hall of Fame & Museum
13700 SW 16th Ave.
Ocala, FL 34473-3970
ph: 352-245-8661
fax: 352-245-6895
info@garlits.com
http://www.garlits.com
Classic car and antique museum encompasses 20,000 square feet of displays, mostly auto related though plenty of old "Americana" as well.

Dixie Gun Work's Old Car & Steam Engine Museum
1200 N. Highway 51 S
Union City, TN 38261
ph: 901-885-0700
http://www.dixiegun.com

Charlie Sens Antique Auto Museum
2074 Marion-Mt. Gilead Rd.
Marion, OH 43302
ph: 740-389-4686 or 740-386-2521

Detroit Historical Museum
5401 Woodward Ave.
Detroit, MI 48202-4009
ph: 313-833-1805
fax: 313-833-5342
amy@detroithistorical.org
http://www.detroithistorical.org
Focuses on the 300-year-old cultural heritage of the City of Detroit area including its automotive legacy.

Jim Johnson
Alfred P. Sloan Museum
Newsletter: Sloan News
1221 E. Kearsley St.
Flint, MI 48503
ph: 810-237-3450
fax: 810-237-3451
sloan@flintcultural.org
http://www.sloanmuseum.com
Features vintage automobiles built in Flint, MI; especially Buick and Chevrolet, but also early marques such as Whitney, Mason, Little, Samson, Durant, Dart and others.

Thomas A. Kayser, Ex. Dir.
Gilmore Classic Car Club Museum
6865 Hickory Rd.
Hickory Corners, MI 49060
ph: 616-671-5089
fax: 616-671-5843
gcccam@net-link.net
http://www.gilmorecarmuseum.org
*Over 140 antique, classic and
collector cars are displayed in six
large historic Michigan barns;
exhibits range from a 1899
Locomobile to a Cadillac styling
concept car destined for the year
2002.*

Ronnie Craig, Pres.
Duffy's Collectible Cars
250 Classic Car Court S.W.
Cedar Rapids, IA 52404
ph: 319-364-7000
fax: 319-364-4036
sales@duffys.com
http://www.duffys.com
*A car museum with 100 fully restored
cars from the 1940s through 1960s;
along with other memorabilia from the
eras such as gas pumps, barber poles,
phone booths, wall murals, and a
1950s diner with neon signs.*

Hartford Heritage Auto Museum
147 North Rural St.
Hartford, WI 53027
ph: 414-673-7999
Home of the Kissel.

Greg Grams
Volo Auto Museum
27582 Volo Village Rd.
Round Lake, IL 60073-9613
ph: 815-385-3644
fax: 815-344-0703
http://www.volocars.com
*Nearly 300 collector cars on display;
featuring muscle cars from the '50s to
'70s; one entire building dedicated to
pre-1948 autos; inventory changing
constantly; admission charged.*

Keith R. Gill
Museum of Science & Industry
5700 S. Lake Shore Dr.
Chicago, IL 60637
ph: 773-684-1414
fax: 773-684-0026
msi@msichicago.org
http://www.msichicago.org

Buddy Hoelzeman
Museum of Automobiles, The
8 Jones Lane
Petit Jean Mountain
Morrilton, AR 72110
ph: 501-727-5427
fax: 501-727-6482
info@museumofautos.com
http://www.museumofautos.com
*Founded in 1964 by the late Winthrop
Rockefeller; over 50 cars on display
from 1904 to 1967 models; open year
round 10 a.m. to 5 p.m.; gift shop.*

Hagan Stewart, Dir.
Imperial Palace Auto Collection
3535 Las Vegas Blvd., So.
Las Vegas, NV 89109
ph: 702-794-3174
fax: 702-369-7430
info@autocollections.com
http://www.autocollections.com
*Incredible collection of hundreds of
classic cars: Dusenbergs, Cords,
Auburns, etc.; also celebrity cars:
Elvis, Marilyn Monroe, Steve
McQueen, Al Capone, and presidential cars from Wilson to Nixon.*

National Automobile Museum (The
Harrah Collection)
Newsletter: Precious Metal
10 South Lake St.
Reno, NV 89501-1558
ph: 775-333-9300
fax: 775-333-9309
info@automuseum.org
http://www.automuseum.org
*Museum depicts the history of the
automobile; exhibiting over 220
classic, vintage, and special interest
vehicles; automobile library offering
research by mail; multimedia lecture
hall; educational programs; museum
store.*

Petersen Automotive Museum
6060 Wilshire Blvd.
Los Angeles, CA 90036
ph: 323-930-2277
fax: 323-930-6642
dmyers@petersen.org
http://www.petersen.org
*300,000 square feet showcases over
200 vehicles, from rare to classics.*

Kristin Hartley
Towe Auto Museum
2200 Front St.
Sacramento, CA 95818
ph: 916-442-6802
fax: 916-442-2646
info@toweautomuseum.org
http://www.toweautomuseum.org
*A museum of automobile history,
explaining the impact of the
development of the automobile on our
lives; exhibits are constantly
changing; monthly activities; annual
collector car auction.*

Periodicals

Richard Lentinello, Ed.
Hemmings
Magazine: Special Interest Autos
P.O. Box 196
Bennington, VT 05201-0196
ph: 802-447-9648 or 800-227-4373
fax: 802-447-9542
hmnmail@hemmings.com
http://www.hemmings.com
*A bi-monthly magazine focusing on
special interest vehicles.*

Hemmings
Newsmagazine: Hemmings Motor News
P.O. Box 100
Bennington, VT 05201-5019
ph: 802-442-3101 or 800-227-4373
fax: 802-447-1561
hmnmail@hemmings.com
http://www.hemmings.com
*Newsmagazine for antique and special
interest auto enthusiasts; auctions,
ads, services, insurance, restorations,
etc.*

Eric Lawrence, Pres.
Price Guide: CPI Value Guide
P.O. Box 3190
Laurel, MD 20709-3190
ph: 301-317-4228 or 800-972-5312
Eric.Lawrence@jhu.edu
http://www.cpivalueguide.com
*Published quarterly; covers more than
4,000 collectible and exotic cars and
light trucks made since 1945; current
market values of imported and
domestic collectible, exotic and high-
line cars.*

National Auto Research
Magazine: Black Book Official Auction
Report
2620 Barrett Rd.
P.O. Box 758
Gainesville, GA 30503-0758
ph: 770-532-4111 or 800-367-3759
fax: 770-532-4792
http://www.blackbookguides.com
*Publishes weekly, monthly, bimonthly,
annual guides (Black Books)
containing new and used car and
truck values for the automotive and
finance industries including used and
new car dealers, bankers, wholesale
buyers, credit unions.*

Dan Sage, Mng. Ed.
Path Communications
Magazine: Car Collector
5211 S. Washington Ave.
Titusville, FL 32780
ph: 321-268-5010
fax: 321-267-1894
editorial@carcollector.com
http://www.carcollector.com
*A monthly glossy magazine with
articles about classic, antique and
special interest cars; also ads, parts
sources and restoration services.*

Jeff Broadus
Magazine: Car Collector Magazine
5095 S. Washington Ave., Ste. 207
Titusville, FL 32780
ph: 321-267-8011 or 800-523-6322
fax: 321-269-7004
editorial@carcollector.com
http://www.carcollector.com
*Monthly glossy magazine for the car
collector; restoration tips, museums,
show previews.*

Tim Abbey
Trader Publishing Company
Magazine: Old Car Trader
P.O. Box 9059
Clearwater, FL 34618-9059
ph: 727-712-0035 or 800-548-8889
fax: 727-712-0034
idowu@traderonline.com
http://www.traderonline.com

Magazine: Cars & Parts Magazine
911 Vandemark Rd.
P.O. Box 482
Sidney, OH 45365
ph: 937-498-0877 or 800-613-4519
fax: 937-498-0808
ekaminsky@carsandparts.com
http://www.carsandparts.com
*A monthly magazine founded in 1957;
content is dedicated to the owner,
restorer, and enthusiast who collects
and appreciates vintage American
cars 25 years old and older.*

Gerry Durnell, Editor
Automobile Quarterly, Inc
Magazine: Automobile Quarterly
137 East Market St.
New Albany, IN 47150
ph: 812-948-2886
fax: 812-948-2816
carmaven@aqmagazine.com
http://www.autoquarterly.com
*Hardbound magazine totally without
advertising features in-depth articles
on automotive history, nostalgia, art
and much more for the serious auto
collector and historian; packed with
fine color and rare b&w photographs.*

Stacie Berger
Krause Publications
Newsmagazine: Old Cars
700 E. State St.
Iola, WI 54990-0001
ph: 715-445-2214
fax: 715-445-4087
stacie.berger@fwpubs.com
http://www.krause.com
*Weekly coverage of antique
automobiles of all ages; auction
reports, hobby events, car shows,
swap meets, ads, club activities, etc.*

Stacie Berger
Krause Publications
Magazine: Old Cars Price Guide
700 E. State St.
Iola, WI 54990-0001
ph: 715-445-2214
fax: 715-445-4087
stacie.berger@fwpubs.com
http://www.krause.com
*Bi-monthly lists current values in five
grading categories for all American
cars made from 1901-1989.*

Don Nelson, Ed.
Deals on Wheels Publications
Magazine: Deals on Wheels
P.O. Box 205
Sioux Falls, SD 57101
ph: 605-338-7666 or 800-334-1886
fax: 605-338-5337
dkristja@dealsonwheels.com
http://www.dealsonwheels.com
A comprehensive monthly listing with photo ads of cars for sale nationwide; also classified and display ads for the car enthusiast.

Don Nelson, Ed.
Deals on Wheels Publications
Magazine: Specialty Car Marketplace
P.O. Box 205
Sioux Falls, SD 57101
ph: 605-338-7666 or 800-334-1886
fax: 605-338-5337
dkristja@dealsonwheels.com
http://www.dealsonwheels.com
Photo-ad magazine listing cars and trucks for sale.

Terry Cannon, Ed.
Magazine: Skinned Knuckles
175 May Ave.
Monrovia, CA 91016-2227
ph: 626-358-6255
fax: 626-358-6255
skpubs@earthlink.net
http://www.skinnedknuckles.com
The hobby's premier monthly auto restoration magazine.

Kelley Blue Book
Price Guide: Kelley Blue Book
5 Oldfield
Irvine, CA 92618
ph: 949-770-7704
fax: 949-837-1904
kelley@kbb.com
http://www.kbb.com/indexv.html
Web site offers current trade-in values for all makes and model cars for the past 21 years; also publishes printed value guides for cars, RVs, motorcycles, snowmobiles, motor homes, travel trailers, personal watercraft, etc.

Steve Ferguson, Ed.
National Automobile Dealers Association
Price Guide: N.A.D.A. Official Used Car Guide
P.O. Box 7800
Costa Mesa, CA 92628
ph: 800-544-6232 or 714-556-8511
fax: 714-556-8715
info@nadaguides.com
http://www.nada.org
A series of value guides for domestic and foreign cars, trucks, vans, RVs, mobile homes, motorcycles, snowmobiles, and boats, small and large; also Heavy Duty Trucks and Aircraft Book, car clubs & organizations, museums.

John Hudson
CMM Publications
Magazine: Classic Motor Monthly
P.O. Box 129
Bolton, Lancashire BL3 4YQ U.K.
ph: +44 1204 657212
fax: +44 1204 652764
postmaster@classicmotor.co.uk
http://www.classicmotor.co.uk
One of the UK's leading publications for classic, vintage and veteran auto owners; each issue is packed with ads, events, news and much more; the online version reflects the character of the magazines.

Magazine: Classic American
Optimum House, Clippers Quay
Salford Quays, Manchester M5 2XP U.K.
ph: 0161 8778128
fax: 0161 8726238
clasam@aol.com
http://www.classic-american.com
The U.K.'s leading publication for classic American car enthusiasts.

Repair Services

Back 'N' Time Auto Restoration
57 Cannonball Rd.
Pompton Lakes, NJ 07442
ph: 973-616-6300

Martin Lum
Older Car Restoration
304 S. Main St.
P.O. Box 428
Mont Alto, PA 17237-0428
ph: 717-749-3383 or 717-352-7701
fax: 717-749-3383
marty@oldercar.com
http://www.oldercar.com
Manufactures and sells replacement parts for antique cars; also chrome plating.

Realistic Auto Restorations, Inc.
2519 6th Ave. S.
Saint Petersburg, FL 33712-1640
ph: 727-327-5162 or 727-327-1877
jsamu58686@aol.com
Offers restoration services for antiques, classics, street rods, Corvettes and all sports cars; paint & body, upholstery, mechanics, woodwork, welding, wiring, stainless steel repair; since 1978; many Concours winners.

David Ten Brink
Beckley Auto Restoration Inc.
4405 S.W. Capital Ave.
Battle Creek, MI 49015
ph: 616-979-3013
fax: 616-979-1261
Offers complete classic and antique car restoration.

Dave Lewis
Dave Lewis Restorations
3825 South Second St.
Springfield, IL 62703
ph: 217-529-5290
fax: 217-529-8452
Partial or complete show quality

restorations; over 20 years experience.

Randy Hilberg
Collector's Nectar
Box 431
Morro Bay, CA 93443
ph: 805-772-2968
fax: 805-772-2968
gd57@hotmail.com
Always buying antique cars; offers complete restoration services; appraisals; master technician; all makes and models; no collection too big or too small to purchase or restore; the only lifetime guarantee in the business.

Suppliers

John Kutarna
Wheels of Wood
3235 Hill Ave.
Regina, Saskatchewan S4S 0W5 Canada
ph: 306-586-8658
fax: 306-586-2617
jkutarna@cableregina.com
http://www.wheelsofwood.com
Makes replacement wood spoked wheels for classic automobiles; also rebuilds and restores wood wheels.

Alfa Romeo

Clubs/Associations

Shayna Geller
Alfa Romeo Owners Club - USA
Magazine: Alfa Owner
10 Raskin Rd.
Morristown, NJ 07960
ph: 877-399-2762 or 973-285-9338
fax: 973-285-9343
admin@aroc-usa.org
http://www.aroc-usa.org
National organization with over 40 chapters; membership open to all Alfa Romeo enthusiasts; chapters hold regular meetings, publish newsletters, sponsor technical, competitive and social activities.

AMC

Clubs/Associations

Cheryl Samuel
American Motors Owners Association
Newsletter: American Motoring
523 W. Racine St.
Jefferson, WI 53549
ph: 920-674-2826
sambo@jefnet.com
http://www.amonational.com
Founded in 1974 for AMC enthusiasts to distribute information pertaining to AMC cars and hobby; international convention and several regional meets around the world; for all AMC-built products from 1958 through 1988.

Larry Mitchell
AMC World Clubs
7963 Depew St.
Arvada, CO 80003-2527
ph: 303-428-8760
fax: 303-428-1070
webmaster@amcwc.com
http://www.amcwc.com
For owners of 1955 - 1999 American Motors Corp. automobiles: AMX, Spirit, Eagle, Rebel, Pacer, Marlin, Hornet, Javelin, Classic, Gremlin, Rambler, Matador, AMC/Jeep, Concord, American, Ambassador, Metropolitan.

AMC Pacer

Clubs/Associations

Frank Wrenick
AMC Pacer Club
2628 Queenstown Rd.
Cleveland, OH 44118
ph: 216-371-5946
fax: 216-371-0226
http://clubs.hemmings.com/amcoacer
For those interested in the 1975 through 1980 American Motors Corporation Pacer automobile.

AMC Rambler

Clubs/Associations

Frank Wrenick
AMC Rambler Club
2645 Ashton Rd.
Cleveland, OH 44118
ph: 216-371-5946
fax: 216-371-0226
http://www.amcrc.com

Aston Martin

Clubs/Associations

Jim Whyman, Sec.
Aston Martin Owners Club
1A Hight St.
Sutton
Nr Ely, Cambridgeshire CB6 2RB U.K.
ph: +44 1353 777353
fax: +44 1353 777648
hgstaff@amoc.org
http://www.amoc.org

Auburn-Cord-Duesenberg

Clubs/Associations

Jim Corbin
Auburn-Cord-Duesenberg Club
983 Country Rd., 413
Killen, AL 35645-9801
ph: 205-757-8755

Museums/Libraries

Sheryl Prentice. Dir of Mktg.
Auburn Cord Duesenberg Museum
1600 South Wayne St.
P.O. Box 271
Auburn, IN 46706-0271
ph: 260-925-1444
fax: 260-925-6266
http://www.acdmuseum.org
Preserves and interprets the history of the classic Auburn, Cord and Duesenberg motorcars and their

significance in American history; museum located in the former 1930 Art Deco headquarters of the Auburn Automobile Company.

Austin-Healey

Clubs/Associations

Edie Anderson, Mem.
Austin-Healey Club of America, Inc., The
Magazine: Healey Marque
P.O. Box 3220
Monroe, NC 28111-3220
ph: 877-5-HEALEY
fax: 704-283-7765
membership@healeyclub.org
http://www.healeyclub.org
For owners or those interested in Austin-Healey, Austin-Healey Sprite and other Healey marques; mission is to preserve the Austin-Healey and to maintain the highest standards by sharing technical and mechanical information.

Julie Goldsworth, Mbrship.
Austin-Healey Association
Newsletter: Healey Motor News
20702 Linear Lane
Lake Forest, CA 92630
ph: 979-770-3279
goldjulie@aol.com
Dedicated to the enjoyment of a fine automobile.

Greg Kaufman, Editor
Austin-Healey Club USA
Magazine: Austin-Healey Magazine
P.O. Box 2404
Castro Valley, CA 94546
ph: 888-424-2872 or 510-582-8758
fax: 888-424-2872
editor@healey.org
http://www.healey.org
Established in 1970; members interested in the history, maintenance, restoration and enjoyment of all Austin-Healeys; ownership of an Austin-Healey not required for membership.

Avanti

Clubs/Associations

Total Performance Avanti Club
1511 19th Ave. West
Bradenton, FL 34205

Avanti Owners Association International
Magazine: Avanti Magazine
c/o KRIS Ltd.
Osseo, MN 55311-6743
ph: 763-420-7829
fax: 763-420-7849
kris@tcinternet.net
http://www.classicar.com/clubs/aoai/aoaihome.htm
Open to all Avanti owners; supports the Avanti marque from the 1963 Studebaker Avanti to the 2001 Avanti; ownership not required for membership.

Bentley

Clubs/Associations

Bentley Drivers Club
223 West Malvern
Fullerton, CA 92832
ph: 714-992-2757

Bentley Drivers Club Ltd.
16 Chearsley Rd.
Long Crendon
Aylesbury, Bucks HP18 9AW U.K.
ph: 01844-208233
fax: 01844-208923

BMW

Clubs/Associations

Membership
BMW Car Club of America
Magazine: Roundel
2130 Mass. Ave.
Cambridge, MA 02140-9850
ph: 617-492-2500 or 800-878-9292
fax: 617-876-3424
service@bmwcca.org
http://www.bmwcca.org
Over 50,000 members.

Tom Graham
BMW Vintage Club of America
P.O. Box S
San Rafael, CA 94913-4358
ph: 415-897-0220
fax: 415-898-0831
bmwvintage@arrgh.com
For owners of 1929 through 1965 BMW automobiles.

British

Misc. Services

Karen Miller, Archivist
Jaguar Cars Inc.
555 MacArthur Blvd.
Mahwah, NJ 07430-2326
ph: 201-818-8144 or 845-221-0293
fax: 201-818-0281
A corporate archives offering individual vehicle research from original Jaguar Cars Ltd. build records; verify authenticity of Jaguar and Daimler (from 1960) automobiles.

Repair Services

Ed Miller
Reward Service, Inc.
172 Overhill Rd.
Stormville, NY 12582-5415
ph: 914-227-7647
fax: 914-221-0293
Appraisals, repair & restoration of classic British automobiles by an expert with more than 30 years experience in the field; own research library; family owned and operated.

Bugatti

Clubs/Associations

Paul Simms, Sec.
American Bugatti Club
Magazine: Pur Sang
600 Lakeview Terrace
Glen Ellyn, IL 60137
abcpursang@sbcglobal.net
http://www.americanbugatticlub.org
ph: 617-266-1271
fax: 617-266-8572
Encourages interest in Bugattis and provides network for members whereby they can learn more about each other and their cars; open to Bugatti owners and genuine Bugatti enthusiasts.

Bugatti Owners Club
Prescott Hill, Gottherington
Nr. Cheltenham, Gloucestershire GL52 4RD U.K.
ph: 01242 673136
fax: 011242 677001
club@bugatti.co.uk
http://www.bugatti.co.uk/club/index.html
Founded in 1929, the club has over 1,600 members world wide; any Bugatti enthusiast may apply for membership.

Collectors

Stanley King
260 Fifth Ave.
New York, NY 10001-6408
ph: 212-447-1880
fax: 212-447-0728
Wants to buy anything relating to the Bugatti automobile: car models, posters, auto parts, literature and sales brochures, etc.

Museums/Libraries

Bugatti Trust, The
Prescott Hill, Gottherington
Cheltenham, Gloucestershire GL52 4RD U.K.
ph: +44 (0)1242 677201
fax: +44 (0)1242 674191
trust@bugatti.co.uk
http://www.bugatti.co.uk/trust/index.html
A charitable trust; objectives are to preserve and make available for study the works of Ettore Bugatti; a museum with Bugatti related material.

Buick

Clubs/Associations

Mike & Nancy Book
Buick Club of America
Magazine: Buick Bugle
P.O. Box 360775
Columbus, OH 43236-0775
ph: 614-472-3939
fax: 614-472-3222
BCAOffice@BuickClub.org
http://www.buickclub.org
Over 10,000 members; "Bugle" published monthly; members share an interest in the cars made by the Buick

Motor Division, their restoration, and preservation.

Cadillac

Clubs/Associations

Jay Ann Edmunds, Mem. Sec.
Cadillac-LaSalle Club, Inc.
Magazine: Self-Starter, The
P.O. Box 1916
Lenoir, NC 28645-1916
ph: 828-757-9919
fax: 828-757-0367
membership@cadillaclasalleclub.com
http://www.cadillaclasalleclub.com
Worldwide organization with 6,000+ members; technical service, monthly magazine, annual issue, directory, and annual meet held in various parts of the US.

Wray Tibbs
Cadillac Drivers Club
Newsletter: Leland Letters, The
5825 Vista Ave.
Sacramento, CA 95824-1428
ph: 916-421-3193 or 916-421-3105
fax: 702-972-1726
jbraun6668@aol.com
Keep your Cadillac on the road forever!

Dealers

Frank Corrente's Cadillac Inc.
7614 Sunset Blvd.
Hollywood, CA 90046
ph: 323-850-1881
fax: 323-850-1884
Corrente@ix.netcom.com
http://www.corrente-cadillac.com
Offers Cadillacs from 1938 to 1976 convertibles, coups, sedans, etc.; also other luxury cars including Rolls Royces, Clenets, Zimmers.

Checker

Clubs/Associations

Roy Dickerson, Ed.
Checker Car Club of America
Newsletter: CCCA Newsletter
10530 West Alabama Ave.
Sun City, AZ 85351-3544
ph: 623-974-4987
carclub@get.net
http://clubs.hemmings.com/checkers
Organized to promote interest in and preservation and enjoyment of Checker automobiles from 1922-1982.

Chevrolet

Clubs/Associations

Denny Williams
Bow Tie Chevrolet Association
P.O. Box 607824
Orlando, FL 32860
ph: 407-880-1963 or 800-683-1961
fax: 407-886-7571
info@lategreatchevy.com
http://www.lategreatchevy.com
For 1955 to 1957 Chevys only.

Denny Williams
Late Great Chevrolet Association
P.O. Box 607824
Orlando, FL 32860
ph: 407-880-1963 or 800-683-1961
fax: 407-886-7571
info@lategreatchevy.com
http://www.lategreatchevy.com
For 1958 to 1972 Chevys.

Classic Chevy International
Magazine: Classic Chevy World
P.O. Box 607188
Orlando, FL 32860-7188
ph: 407-880-1505 or 800-456-1957
fax: 407-299-3341
cciworld@aol.com
http://www.classicchevy.com
*108 chapters; and '55 to '57
Chevrolet, including Corvette and
pickup.*

National Chevy Association
Newsletter: Partsline
947 Arcade
Saint Paul, MN 55106-3850
ph: 651-778-9522
fax: 651-778-9686
info@nationalchevyassoc.com
http://www.nationalchevyassoc.com
'49-'54 Chevrolet specialists.

Dennis Fink
Vintage Chevrolet Club of America, Inc.
P.O. Box 5387
Orange, CA 92863-5387
ph: 626-963-CHEV
wtb@swbell.net
http://www.classicar.com/clubs/
  vccaclub/vccaclub.htm

Periodicals

Magazine: Corvette & Chevy Trader
P.O. Box 9059
Clearwater, FL 34618-9059
ph: 727-712-0035 or 800-548-8889
fax: 727-712-0034
idowu@traderonline.com
http://www.traderonline.com

Chevrolet Camaro

Clubs/Associations

Karl Scheffy
American Camaro Association
Magazine: Camaro Review
5786 Buckeye Rd.
Macungie, PA 18062
ph: 610-966-2492
fax: 610-966-2492
karlz28@earthlink.net
http://clubs.hemmings.com/
  americancamaro

International Camaro Club, Inc.
Magazine: In The Fast Lane
2001 Pittson Ave.
Scranton, PA 18505-3233
ph: 570-585-4082
vfitom@aol.com
http://clubs.hemmings.com/
  icccamareoregistry
*Club for all Camaro owners, from the
1967 Classic Collectibles to the
present; bi-monthly magazine has*

*technical tips, trim tag ID, classifieds;
newsletter is an award winning
publication for all Camaro fans!*

Worldwide Camaro Association
Magazine: Camaro World
P.O. Box 607188
Orlando, FL 32860
ph: 407-774-4922 or 800-456-1957
fax: 407-774-0329
info@worldwidecamaro.com
http://www.worldwidecamaro.com

Repair Services

Bob & Cheryl Harris
Camaro Specialists
112 Elm St.
East Aurora, NY 14052-2536

fax: 716-652-2279
sales@camaros.com
http://www.camaros.com
*Parts and restorations for '66-'72 GM
muscle cars; Camaro and Firebird
specialists.*

Chevrolet Chevelle
Clubs/Associations

National Chevelle Owners Association
Newsletter: Chevelle Report, The
7343-J West Friendly Ave.
Greensboro, NC 27410-6209
ph: 336-854-8935
*Focus on interest is on 1964-1987
Chevelle and El Camino; monthly
color magazine featuring members'
cars, tech tips, factory photos,
production information, parts sources,
classified ads, chapter club news; over
6,000 members.*

Chuck Hanson, Pres.
American Chevelle Enthusiasts Society
Newsletter: Chevelle World
4636 Lebanon Pike, Ste. 195
Hermitage, TN 37076-1316
ph: 615-773-2237
admin@chevelles.com
http://www.chevelles.com/aces
*Focuses on Chevelles, Malibus, and El
Caminos from 1964 through 1972.*

Chevrolet Corvette

Appraisers

Werner Pfister
Miller Motorcars
342 W. Putnam Ave.
Greenwich, CT 06830
ph: 203-629-3890
fax: 203-629-1621
lorenz50@aol.com
http://www.wpfister.com
*Appraises historic sports and racing
automobiles, specializing in Ferrari
and Corvette.*

Clubs/Associations

D. Sandoval
National Corvette Owners Association
Newsletter: For Vettes Only
900 So. Washington St., Ste. G-13
Falls Church, VA 22046-4009
ph: 703-533-7222
fax: 703-533-1153
ncoassoc@aol.com
http://www.ncoa-vettes.com
*Dedicated to the concept of uniting all
Corvette enthusiasts with a common
goal, i.e., that of encouraging and
increasing the Corvette enjoyment
among all members.*

Official C5 Registry
P.O. Box 541023
Merritt Island, FL 32954-1023
ph: 407-452-2743
c5Dan@c5registry.com
http://www.c5registry.com
*The C5 is the fifth generation of the
Corvette; the Registry is for C5
owners and enthusiasts.*

Garnett Rogers
Corvette Club of America
Newsletter: Corvette Capers
P.O. Box 9879
Bowling Green, KY 42102
ph: 502-737-6022 or 800-801-7329
fax: 502-737-6022
ccabg@ekx.infi.net
http://www.corvetteclubofamerica.com

Eric Mortimer
National Corvette Restorers Society
Magazine: NCRS Driveline, The
6291 Day Rd.
Cincinnati, OH 45252-1334
ph: 513-385-8526 or 513-385-6367
fax: 513-385-8554
info@ncrs.org
http://www.ncrs.org
*For those interested in the restoration,
preservation, history and enjoyment of
Corvettes for the past 27 years; 36
chapters around the world; 15,000
members.*

Paul Bohannon, Mbrship.
National Council of Corvette Clubs, Inc.
Magazine: Blue Bars
12947 Lillian St.
Omaha, NE 68138
ph: 402-896-1259 or 800-245-VETT
NCCCvpofmem@aol.com
http://www.corvettesnccc.org
*Founded in 1960; 16,000 members,
non-profit, all volunteer national
organization of more that 285 member
clubs that sponsor more than 1,000
competitive events each year;
Concours, wheel-to-wheel drags,
autocrosses, rallies, economy runs.*

Jim VanDorn
Grand Sport Registry
77-700 Enfield Lane
Palm Desert, CA 92211
VanDornJim@aol.com
http://www.grandsportregistry.com
*Formed in 1996 for those interested in
the Corvette Grand Sport.*

American Corvette Association
216 West First St. #D
Brea, CA 92621

Rob Weaver
Western States Corvette Council
Magazine: Redline
15885 Descansa Court
Morgan Hill, CA 95037
ph: 800-409-9722 or 408-778-5164
fax: 408-778-5164
Rob91Vette@aol.com
http://www.wscc.ws

Dealers

Corvette World
219 W. Airport Freeway
Irving, TX 75062
ph: 972-620-8388
fax: 972-620-8388
vetteworldsales@aol.com
http://www.corvetteworlddallas.com
*Has specialized in Corvette sales for
over 20 years; delivered worldwide;
1953 to present.*

Museums/Libraries

Wendell K. Strode, Ex. Dir.
National Corvette Museum
Magazine: America's Sports Car
350 Corvette Dr.
Bowling Green, KY 42102
ph: 800-53V-ETTE or 270-781-7973
fax: 270-781-5286
strode@corvettemuseum.com
http://www.corvettemuseum.com
*A 68,000 sq. ft. building housing more
than 50 Corvette models and one-of-a-
kind concept cars spanning the history
of Corvette; also thousands of
Corvette-related photos, movies,
videos, advertisements, models and
rare memorabilia.*

Periodicals

PRIMEDIA Enthusiast Group
Magazine: Corvette Fever
745 Fifth Ave.
New York, NY 10151
ph: 212-745-0100
fax: 212-745-0121
corvettefever@neodata.com
http://www.corvettefever.com
*For enthusiasts who take the love of
their automobile seriously; do-it-
yourself technical articles, beautiful
color features, advice from top
Corvette industry experts, interesting
news and events listings.*

Magazine: Corvette & Chevy Trader
P.O. Box 9059
Clearwater, FL 34618-9059
ph: 727-712-0035 or 800-548-8889
fax: 727-712-0034
idowu@traderonline.com
http://www.traderonline.com

Magazine: Cars & Parts Corvette
911 Vandemark Rd.
P.O. Box 482
Sidney, OH 45365
ph: 937-498-0877 or 800-613-4519
fax: 937-498-0808
ekaminsky@carsandparts.com
http://www.carsandparts.com
Devoted to lovers of America's premier sports car - the Chevrolet Corvette.

Chevrolet Impala

Clubs/Associations

Dennis Naasz
National Impala Association
Magazine: National Impala Association Magazine
P.O. Box 968
Spearfish, SD 57783-0968
ph: 605-642-5864
fax: 605-642-5868
impala@blackhills.com
http://clubs.hemmings.com/
nationalimpala
Dedicated to the preservation of all full-size Chevrolets from 1958 through 1970; bi-monthly magazine.

Chevrolet Monte Carlo

Clubs/Associations

Larry Ashcraft
National Monte Carlo Owners Association
P.O. Box 187
Independence, KY 41051
ph: 606-491-2378
nmcoa@aol.com
http://www.montecarloclub.com
Dedicated to the preservation and restoration of the Monte Carlo automobile.

Chevrolet Nova

Clubs/Associations

Wayne & Shirley Bushey
National Nostalgic Nova
Magazine: Nova Times
P.O. Box 2344
York, PA 17405
ph: 717-252-4192
fax: 717-252-1666
http://www.nnnova.com
An association of owners and enthusiasts of 1962 through 1979 Chevy II and Novas.

Chrysler

Clubs/Associations

Edward W. Botchie
National Chrysler Products Club
160 Joyce Dr.
Fayetteville, PA 17222
ph: 717-352-7673

Ray Montgomery
Chrysler Product Owners Club, Inc.
Newsletter: Torsion Bar
806 Winhall Way
Silver Spring, MD 20904-2072
ph: 301-622-2962
Club is dedicated to the preservation,

restoration, and enjoyment of all vehicles built by The Chrysler Corporation and its antecedent companies: Plymouth, DeSoto, Imperial, Dodge.

Wendy McKenney
National Hemi Owners Association
1693 S. Reese Rd.
Reese, MI 48757
ph: 517-868-4921
For enthusiasts of hemi-engined Chrysler products.

Ian Smale
Walter P. Chrysler Club, Inc.
Newsmagazine: W.P.C. News
P.O. Box 3504
Kalamazoo, MI 49003-3504
ph: 616-375-5535
fax: 616-375-5535
wpc@pacificcoast.net
http://www.pacificcoast.net/~wpc
Dedicated to the preservation, restoration, enjoyment of Chrysler products: Plymouth, Dodge, DeSoto, Chrysler, Imperial, Jeep, Eagle, and related vehicles including antecedents Maxwell and Chalmers Motor Cars.

Eleanor Riehl
Chrysler 300 Club International, Inc.
Magazine: Club News
4900 Jonesville Rd.
Jonesville, MI 49250-9439
ph: 517-849-2783
fax: 517-849-7445
mayerd@hartwick.edu
http://www.classicar.com/clubs/chrysler/
300club.htm
Of particular interest to owners of Chrysler 300 letter series automobiles.

Periodicals

PRIMEDIA Enthusiast Group
Magazine: Mopar Muscle
745 Fifth Ave.
New York, NY 10151
ph: 212-745-0100
fax: 212-745-0121
moparmuscle@palmcoastd.com
http://www.moparmusclemagazine.com
Covers all aspects of interest to Chrysler-oriented performance car enthusiasts; articles ranging from Concourse-restored cars to all-out Pro St. modifieds to street rods, drag cars, even Chrysler-powered race boats!

Citroen

Clubs/Associations

Citroen Car Club of America
8585 Commerce Ave.
San Diego, CA 92121
ph: 858-566-2860
fax: 858-566-2432
ruudman@citroen-ca.com
http://www.citroen-ca.com

Citroen Car Club
Magazine: Citronenian
P.O. Box 348
Bromely, Kent BR2 8QT U.K.
ph: +44 1689 853999
fax: +44 1689 853999
webmaster@CitroenCarClub.org.uk
http://www.ccc-uk.demon.co.uk
Founded in 1949; now with over 3,000 members worldwide.

Periodicals

Michael Cox, Ed.
Magazine: Citroen Quarterly
P.O. Box 30
Boston, MA 02113
ph: 617-742-6606
citq@aol.com
http://members.aol.com/citq/index.html
The "Citroen Quarterly" contains technical information, Citroen history and events; also publishes "Citroen Quarterly Archives;" sponsors Citroen Rendezvous on Father's Day weekend in Saratoga Springs, NY.

Convertible

Clubs/Associations

Joyce Barrow
National Convertible Association & Registry
1314 Rollins Rd.
Burlingame, CA 94010
ph: 415-348-8269

Crosley

Clubs/Associations

Crosley Automobile Club, Inc.
Newsletter: CAC Newsletter
62 Delphi Dr.
Covington, KY 41018
ph: 859-342-4934
Crosleyhotshot@aol.com
http://www.ggw.org/cac
Primarily for the support of Crosley vehicle owners, but welcomes all that are interested in the products of Powell Crosley.

Customized

Clubs/Associations

National St. Rod Association
4030 Park Ave.
Memphis, TN 38111
ph: 901-452-4030
http://www.nsra-usa.com

Darryl Starbird
National Rod & Custom Car Hall of Fame
Rte. 3, Star Kustom Ave.
Afton, OK 74331
ph: 918-257-4234 or 918-257-8073
fax: 918-257-8224
ldmstar@galstar.com
http://www.darrylstardird.com/
museum.htm
Aims to establish rules for indoor specialty vehicle car shows; national events; the 40,000 sq. ft. facility houses custom-built exotic vehicles by world renowned custom car builder

and designer Darryl Starbird, George Barris, others.

Periodicals

Buckaroo Communications Co.
Magazine: American Rodder
ph: 805-986-0400
info@buckaroocommunications.com
http://www.americanrodder.com
Focuses on latest trends and techniques in the field of street rodding.

Kelsey Publishing Ltd.
Magazine: Custom Car
Cudham Tithe Barn
Berry's Hill
Cudham, Kent TN16 3AG U.K.
ph: 01959 541444
fax: 01959 541400
info@kelsey.co.uk
http://www.kelsey.co.uk
A 68-page monthly British magazine dealing with customization, hot-rodding and cruising, low-riders, lead sleds, drag racing, practical how-tos.

Datsun Roadster

Clubs/Associations

Datsun Roadster Association
Magazine: Datsun Roadster Review
11520 Seahurst Rd.
Richmond, British Columbia V7A 3P2
Canada
ph: 604-271-1902

Datsun/Nissan Z Cars

Clubs/Associations

Mike Willemsen, Pres.
Capital Z of Texas
P.O. Box 80844
Austin, TX 78708-0844
ph: 512-989-3818
mikew@mip.com
http://www.capitalzoftexas.com

DeLorean

Clubs/Associations

John Truscott, Mbrship.
DeLorean Owners Association
Magazine: DeLorean World
879 Randolph Rd.
Santa Barbara, CA 93111-1030
ph: 805-964-5296
fax: 805-964-5296
delorean@impulse.net
http://www.delorean-owners.org

DeSoto

Clubs/Associations

Ray Montgomery
Chrysler Product Owners Club, Inc.
Newsletter: Torsion Bar
806 Winhall Way
Silver Spring, MD 20904-2072
ph: 301-622-2962
Club is dedicated to the preservation, restoration, and enjoyment of all vehicles built by The Chrysler Corporation and its antecedent companies: Plymouth, DeSoto, Imperial, Dodge.

Alan Ralston, Mbrship.
National DeSoto Club, Inc.
Magazine: DeSoto Adventures
P.O. Box 50652
Mendota, MN 55150
desotodriver@cs.com
http://www.desoto.org
Purpose of the club is to promote the restoration, preservation and enjoyment of the DeSoto automobile; non-profit corporation with international membership.

Walter O'Kelly, Editor
DeSoto Club of America
Newsletter: DeSoto Days
403 S. Thornton
Richmond, MO 64085
ph: 816-470-3048 or 816-421-6006
Get information about DeSotos, restoration and locating parts.

DeTomaso

Clubs/Associations

Bill Van Ess
DeTomaso Registry
6780 Kitson NE
Rockford, MI 49341
ph: 616-874-1004
fax: 616-363-2870
billvaness@juno.com
http://clubs.hemmings.com/
detomasoregistry
A registry of all production models from DeTomaso Automobili SpA Moderna including Pantera, Mangusta, Vallelunga, Longchamp, and Deauville.

Dealers

P.I. Motorsports, Inc.
1040 North Batavia, Ste. G
Orange, CA 92867
ph: 714-744-1398
fax: 714-744-1397
pantera@pim.net
http://www.pim.net
One stop shop for all things DeTomaso Pantera.

DeTomaso Pantera

Clubs/Associations

Pantera Owners Club of America
P.O. Box 459
Hadlyme, CT 06439
ph: 860-526-5901
fax: 860-526-4446
webmaster@panteraclub.com
http://www.panteraclub.com
The largest Pantera owners club in America; the only club recognized by the DeTomaso factory in Italy; 15 chapters; produces and participates in racing, Concours, technical and social events; national meeting in Las Vegas each April.

Pantera International Car Club
1040 North Batavia, Ste. F
Huntington Beach, CA 92867
ph: 714-639-8163
fax: 714-288-0378
linda@panteracars.com
http://www.panteracars.com

Dodge

Clubs/Associations

Ray Montgomery
Chrysler Product Owners Club, Inc.
Newsletter: Torsion Bar
806 Winhall Way
Silver Spring, MD 20904-2072
ph: 301-622-2962
Club is dedicated to the preservation, restoration, and enjoyment of all vehicles built by The Chrysler Corporation and its antecedent companies: Plymouth, DeSoto, Imperial, Dodge.

Barry Cogan
Dodge Brothers Club, Inc.
P.O. Box 292
Birmingham, MI 48012-0292
ph: 313-884-4327
info@dodgebrothersclub.org
http://www.dodgebrothersclub.org
Open to anyone interested in 1914 to 1938 Dodge Brothers motor vehicles and Graham Brothers commercial vehicles.

Shelby Dodge Automobile Club
P.O. Box 182072
Utica, MI 48318-2072
ph: 810-759-2072
sdac@sdac.org
http://www.sdac.org
Committed to preserving the history of Shelby-built and inspired Dodge-powered automobiles.

Edsel

Clubs/Associations

Robert Mayer
Edsel Club, Inc., The
Magazine: Edsel World
19296 Tuckaway Ct.
Fort Myers, FL 33903
ph: 941-731-8027
fax: 941-731-8027
edselworld@earthlink.net
http://www.edselworld.com

Lois Barrow, Sec.
International Edsel Club
Newsletter: Edseletter
238 Fairview St.
Paris, TN 38242
ph: 731-642-5356
fax: 731-642-3399
ebarrow@wk.net
http://clubs.hemmings.com/iec
Members interested in Edsel cars and parts as well as in related memorabilia, such as advertisements.

Rodney Seaba
Edsel Owners Club, Inc.
34602 West 86th St.
De Soto, KS 66018-1286
ph: 913-586-1286
eoc@edsel.com
http://www.edsel.com/eoc
Dedicated to the preservation, maintenance and promotion of the Edsel automobile.

Electric

Clubs/Associations

Frank Didik
Electric Car Society
167 Concord St.
Brooklyn, NY 11201
ph: 718-797-0869
fax: 718-596-4852
mail@didik.com
http://www.electriccarsociety.com

Emergency

Clubs/Associations

John Bujosa
Emergency Vehicle Owners & Operators Association
14311 W. Lincoln Rd.
Spokane, WA 99224-9398
ph: 509-244-4062
info@evooa.org
http://www.evooa.org
Formed to unite individuals who are interested in the collection, restoration and preservation of "Emergency" vehicles.

Ferrari

Appraisers

Werner Pfister
Miller Motorcars
342 W. Putnam Ave.
Greenwich, CT 06830
ph: 203-629-3890
fax: 203-629-1621
lorenz50@aol.com
http://www.wpfister.com
Appraises historic sports and racing automobiles, specializing in Ferrari and Corvette.

Clubs/Associations

Ferrari Club of America, Inc.
P.O. Box 720597
Atlanta, GA 30358
ph: 800-328-0444
fax: 770-936-9392
info@ferrariclubofamerica.org
http://www.ferrariclubofamerica.org

Ferrari Owners Club
18000 Studebaker Rd., Ste. 700
Cerritos, CA 90703
ph: 562-467-6957
fax: 562-467-6954
info@ferrariownersclub.org
http://www.ferrariownersclub.org/
menu.htm
The first America Ferrari club.

Fiat

Clubs/Associations

Fiat America
Magazine: FAST
P.O. Box 391068
Mountain View, CA 94039-1068
ph: 408-779-4888
sec@fiatamerica.com
http://www.fiatamerica.com
A race, rally and tour group comprised of enthusiasts and owners of Italian automobiles.

Ford

Clubs/Associations

Barbara Lemaster
Performance Ford Club of America, Inc.
Magazine: Ford Enthusiast Magazine, The
13155 US Route 23
Ashville, OH 43103
ph: 740-983-2273
fax: 740-983-9691
tbolt@bright.net
For all Ford-powered vehicle enthusiasts; hosts car shows, swap meets, and cruise-ins; magazine published bi-monthly.

Toby & Sandy Gorny
Crown Victoria Association
Newsletter: FoMoCo Times
P.O. Box 6
Bryan, OH 43506
ph: 419-636-2475
fax: 419-636-8449
fordpart@bright.net
http://www.classicar.com/clubs/
crownvictoria/index.htm
For owners of all 1954 through 1956 Fords.

Dan Wittern
Early Ford V-8 Club of America
Newsletter: V-8 Times
P.O. Box 2122
San Leandro, CA 94577-2122
ph: 925-443-6534 or 925-606-1925
fax: 925-447-2920
fordv8club@aol.com
http://www.earlyfordv8.org
For 1932 through 1953 V-8 Ford, Mercury, Lincoln owners.

Periodicals

Magazine: Ford & Mustang Trader
P.O. Box 9059
Clearwater, FL 34618-9059
ph: 727-712-0035 or 800-548-8889
fax: 727-712-0034
idowu@traderonline.com
http://www.traderonline.com

Ford Econoline

Clubs/Associations

Jay Long
Econo Club
15039 Costela St.
San Leandro, CA 94579-1524
ph: 919-231-0020
For owners of 1961-1967 Econoline and Falcon vans and pickups.

Ford Escort

Clubs/Associations

Donnie La Curan
Ford Escort Owners Association
10226 La Vine St.
Rancho Cucamonga, CA 91730
don_lacuran@hotmail.com
http://www.feoa.net

Ford Fairlane

Clubs/Associations

Bob Mannel
Fairlane Club of America
Magazine: Fairlaner
340 Clicktown Rd.
Church Hill, TN 37642-6622
ph: 423-245-6678
fax: 423-245-2456
office@fairlaneclubofamerica.com
http://www.fairlaneclubofamerica.com
*For owners of '62 through '76
Fairlanes, Torinos, and Mercury
equivalents; impressive 48-page with
color "Fairlaner" is published six
times per year: restoration tips, how-
tos, ads, color photos.*

Ford Falcon

Clubs/Associations

Falcon Club of America
Newsletter: Falcon News, The
P.O. Box 113
Jacksonville, AR 72078-0113
ph: 501-982-9721
fca@falconclub.com
http://www.falconclub.com
*For owners of 1960 through 1970 1/2
Falcons.*

Ford Galaxie

Clubs/Associations

Mark Reynolds
Ford Galaxie Club of America
Newsletter: Galaxie Gazette
P.O. Box 178
Hollister, MO 65672-0178
galaxieclub@collector.org
http://www.galaxieclub.com
*For owners of 1959 through 1974
Ford Galaxies.*

Ford Model A

Clubs/Associations

Model "A" Restorers Club
Magazine: Model "A" News, The
24800 Michigan Ave.
Dearborn, MI 48124-1713
ph: 313-278-1455
fax: 313-278-2624
talk@ModelaFord.org
http://www.modelaford.org
*To encourage members to acquire,
preserve, restore, exhibit and make
use of Model A Fords (1928-1931);
many regional chapters; articles,
event reviews, lots of ads for parts,
supplies, and services.*

Jerry Wilhelm
Model A Ford Club of America
Magazine: Restorer, The
250 S. Cypress
La Habra, CA 90631-5586
ph: 562-697-2712 or 888-2-MODELA
fax: 562-690-7452
mafcaHQ@aol.com
http://www.mafca.com
*Over 15,000 members; dedicated to
the restoration and preservation of the
1928-1931 Model A Ford.*

Ford Model T

Clubs/Associations

Howard Gustavson, Ex. Sec.
Model T Ford Club International
Magazine: Model-T Times
P.O. Box 276236
Boca Raton, FL 33427-6236
ph: 800-563-4115 or 561-750-7170
hgustav@aol.com
http://www.modelt.org
*Dedicated to the preservation and
enjoyment of the 1909 to 1927 Model
T Ford automobile.*

Jay Klehfoth
Model T Ford Club of America
Magazine: Vintage Ford
P.O. Box 126
Centerville, IN 47330-0126
ph: 765-855-5248
fax: 765-855-3428
jay@mtfca.com
http://www.MTFCA.com
*A non-profit corporation formed to
encourage and promote active interest
in the Model T Ford and its history;
open to all; dedicated to widening the
base of the hobby by providing
information assistance, direction for
interested parties.*

Ford Mustang

Clubs/Associations

Mustang Club of America, Inc.
Magazine: Mustang Times
ph: 770-477-1965
fax: 770-477-1965
robertg@mustang.org
http://www.mustang.org
*An association for the Ford Mustang
and Shelby collector, restorer and
enthusiast.*

Paul McLaughlin, Pres.
Mustang Owners Club International
Newsletter: Pony Express
2720 Tennessee N.E.
Albuquerque, NM 87110-3732
ph: 505-296-2554
For all Mustang enthusiasts.

Vintage Mustang Owners Association
P.O. Box 5772
San Jose, CA 95150-5772
webmaster@vmoa.org
http://www.vmoa.org
*Members interested in 1964 1/2 to
present Ford Mustangs.*

Internet Resources

David & Kathy Bowers
Mustang GT Registry, 1982 - 1993
mustanggt@mustanggt.org
http://www.mustanggt.org
*Dedicated to the documentation and
preservation of the high performance
1982 to 1993 Mustang GT; classifieds,
photo galleries, links, statistics and
more.*

Jim Dingell
Mustang Special Service Registry
info@evooa.org
http://www.intrlink.net/evooa/mssr.htm
*Mission is to promote the popularity
and collectibility of the 1982 - 1993
Special Service Mustang (ex-police
cars).*

Vintage-Mustang.com
bob@vintage-mustang.com
http://www.vintage-mustang.com
*Source of information about 1965-
1973 classic Ford Mustangs: where to
find parts, clubs, discussion area,
links, classifieds, and more.*

John Palmisano
Classic Mustang Analyzer
43 Hunter St.
Lodi, NJ 07644
ph: 973-471-7842
johnpalm@aol.com
http://members.aol.com/johnpalm/
cma.html
*Identify the way a Ford Mustang was
originally built; helps you decode
your VIN number and Warranty Tag
of plate; the numbers and letters will
identify your original body color,
interior, engine, transmission, axle,
assembly plant, etc.*

Periodicals

PRIMEDIA Enthusiast Group
Magazine: Mustang Monthly
745 Fifth Ave.
New York, NY 10151
ph: 212-745-0100
fax: 212-745-0121
mustangmonthly@neodata.com
http://www.mustangmonthly.com
*Dedicated to the entire scope of
Mustang production: repair,
restoration, how-tos, performance
modifications, etc.*

Magazine: Ford & Mustang Trader
P.O. Box 9059
Clearwater, FL 34618-9059
ph: 727-712-0035 or 800-548-8889
fax: 727-712-0034
idowu@traderonline.com
http://www.traderonline.com

Repair Services

Joe Palmere
Garden State Mustang, Inc.
160 Horseneck Rd.
Fairfield, NJ 07004-2328
ph: 201-227-0364
fax: 201-227-0282
*Specializes in restoration and general
service/repairs of Ford Mustangs and*

*Mustang IIs; also supply parts: new,
used, repro, and NOS for same.*

Ford Ranchero

Clubs/Associations

Gene Makrancy
Ranchero Club
Newsletter: Ranchero Courier
1339 Beverly Rd.
Port Vue, PA 15133
ph: 412-678-2670
*For all Ranchero and Courier
enthusiasts.*

Internet Resources

International Ranchero Owners Club
2930 So. 33rd St.
Milwaukee, WI 53215
ranchero_org@worldnet.att.net
http://www.ranchero.org
*An Internet only club for owners of the
Ford Ranchero; if you own one you're
a member; no dues, no meetings; an
electronic meeting place with member
email, listings to share restoration
and modification information,
message board, more.*

Ford Thunderbird

Clubs/Associations

Kitty L. Mummert, Treas.
International Thunderbird Club
Magazine: Thunderbird Script
20 Northview Dr.
Hanover, PA 17331-4521
starbuck@intergrafix.net
http://www.intl-tbirdclub.com
*For those interested in all
Thunderbirds from 1955 to present.*

Heartland Vintage Thunderbird Club of
America
Newsletter: Wings 'N Wheels
6711 Spokane Dr.
Huber Heights, OH 45424
ph: 937-235-9343
fax: 937-235-9343
tbirdclub@aol.com
http://www.tbirdclub.com
*For owners of 1958 to 1971
Thunderbirds.*

Alan Tast Pres.
Vintage Thunderbird Club International
Magazine: Thunderbird Scoop
P.O. Box 2250
Dearborn, MI 48123-2250
ph: 316-390-0439
fax: 913-390-5215
tast@earthlink.net
http://www.classicar.com/clubs/vintbird/
vintbird.htm
*Focuses on vintage Thunderbirds,
1955 to present.*

Classic Thunderbird Club International
Newsletter: Early Bird
1308 E. 29th St.
Signal hill, CA 90806-1842
ph: 562-426-2709
ctci1@msn.com
http://www.ctci.org
For owners and enthusiasts of 1955

through 1957 T-Birds; 110 local chapters.

Hupmobile

Clubs/Associations

Steve Christie
Hupmobile Club
Magazine: Hupp Herald
158 Pond Rd.
North Franklin, CT 06254-1217
ph: 860-642-6997
hupmobil@99main.com
http://clubs.hemings.com/hupmobile
Dedicated to the restoration, preservation and enjoyment of Hupmobiles, RCH and Hupp-Yeats automobiles; worldwide membership in excess of 600; also publishes a bi-monthly parts locator newsletter.

Collectors

L. Robert Hurwitz
4906 Crestwood Lane
Syracuse, NY 13215-1315
ph: 315-468-4281
Wants to buy 1909-1941 Hupmobile related items, literature, dealer giveaways and related collectibles such as factory badges, stickpins, fobs, lapel pins, signs, postcards, trohpies, toys, banners, signs, clocks, etc.

Italian

Clubs/Associations

Italian Car Registry
3305 Valley Vista Rd.
Walnut Creek, CA 94598-3943
ph: 925-458-1163
fax: 925-458-1163
iicar@deboer.net
http://www.iicar.com
Research association devoted to the study of the Italian automobile industry; directory includes information on more than 15,000 limited production automobiles; SASE for details.

Jaguar

Clubs/Associations

Nelson Rath
Jaguar Clubs of North America
1000 Glenbrook
Anchorage, KY 40223
ph: 888-258-2524
nnrath@prodigy.net
http://www.jcna.com
International organization of Jaguar enthusiasts; over 5,000 members; sponsors car shows, Concours D'Elegance, rallies and slaloms.

Dick Strever
Classic Jaguar Association
3530 W. Gary Ave.
Santa Ana, CA 92704
ph: 714-545-1155
cjamail@email.com
http://www.classicjaguar.org

Experts

Karen Miller, Archivist
Jaguar Cars Inc.
555 MacArthur Blvd.
Mahwah, NJ 07430-2326
ph: 201-818-8144 or 845-221-0293
fax: 201-818-0281
Research service; maintains facility housing an extensive photographic collection, technical library, service & parts bulletins, technical bulletins, owner, parts and service manuals, advertising, and paint & upholstery information.

Periodicals

Kelsey Publishing Ltd.
Magazine: Jaguar World
Cudham Tithe Barn
Berry's Hill
Cudham, Kent TN16 3AG U.K.
ph: 01959 541444
fax: 01959 541400
info@kelsey.co.uk
http://www.kelsey.co.uk
A 130-page monthly British magazine for the Jaguar enthusiast covering all aspects of Jaguar ownership from buying to restoration: rallies, projects.

Jeep

Clubs/Associations

Jeff Schwarz
Jeep Registry, Inc., The
172 Long Hill Rd.
Oakland, NJ 07436-3113
ph: 201-405-0480
For 1948 through 1951 Jeeps.

Periodicals

PRIMEDIA Enthusiast Group
Magazine: JP Magazine
745 Fifth Ave.
New York, NY 10151
ph: 212-745-0100
fax: 212-745-0121
jp@neodata.com
http://www.jpmagazine.com
The only all-Jeep periodical about Jeeps and the Jeep lifestyle (no Broncos, Samurais, Explorers, Hummers, Blazers, Scouts, just Jeeps); bi-monthly covering from the first military models to the current TJ Wranglers, Cherokees, etc.

Kit Built

Clubs/Associations

Vintage Kit & Custom Club
1731 Mound Rd.
Jacksonville, IL 62650
ph: 217-245-0020
Dedicated to early kit, coach built and customized autos such as Devin, Glasspar, Kellison, LaDawri, Bocar, Victress, Wildfire, Carson Top cars, Barris, Roth, etc.

Lamborghini

Clubs/Associations

Jim Kaminski
Lamborghini Owners Club
Newsletter: LOC Newsletter
P.O. Box 7214
Saint Petersburg, FL 33734
ph: 727-392-3474
fax: 727-392-3474
Organized in 1978; members in 15 countries; tech tips, services sources, parts information, collectibles, and meeting information.

James Deady
Lamborghini Club of America
1 Northwood Dr.
Orinda, CA 94563-3030
ph: 925-253-9399
heady@eudoramail.com
http://clubs.hemmings.com/
lamborghiniclub

Land Rover

Clubs/Associations

Royal Offroad Vehicle Expedition & Recreational Society
2100 Bulls Sawmill Rd.
Freeland, MD 21053-9411
webviii@earthlink.net
http://www.roversclub.com
Serving the Mid-Atlantic region; membership open to all Land Rover enthusiasts.

Internet Resources

Mark Reid
Colonial Rover
Mreid99@hotmail.com
http://www.colonialrovers.com/links/
links.html
Scores of links to Land Rover related sites.

Lincoln

Clubs/Associations

Jim Griffin
Lincoln Owners Club
Newsletter: Fork & Blade, The
P.O. Box 660
Lake Orion, MI 48361
ph: 715-356-3039
fax: 810-274-1010
friartuck@monmouth.com
http://clubs.hemmings.com/
lincolnowners
Primarily for those interested in Lincolns built between 1921 and 1939.

Lincoln & Continental Owners Club
Magazine: Continental Comments
P.O. Box 1715
Osseo, MN 55311-6715
ph: 763-420-7829 or 800-427-7583
fax: 763-420-7849
lcoc@cornerstonereg.com
http://www.lcoc.org
International club dedicated to the preservation and restoration of all Lincolns, Lincoln Continentals, and Continentals; three national meets

every year; magazine published 7 times per year.

Locomobile

Clubs/Associations

Norm Buckhart
Locomobile Society of America
3165 California St.
San Francisco, CA 94115-2412
ph: 415-563-1771
fax: 415-563-1798
Provides a registry of Locomobiles and owners.

Lotus

Clubs/Associations

Lotus, Limited
Newsletter: LOTUS reMARQUE
P.O. Box L
College Park, MD 20741-3010
ph: 301-982-4054
lotusltd@lotuscarclub.org
http://www.lotuscarclub.org
American's largest Lotus Club, established in 1973.

Maserati

Clubs/Associations

Maserati Club, The
Magazine: Il Tridente
P.O. Box 5300
Somerset, NJ 08875-5300
ph: 732-249-2177
fax: 732-246-7570
email@themaseraticlub.com
http://www.themaseraticlub.com
A nationwide, non-profit member-run club for Maserati enthusiasts with 8 chapters worldwide (4 US, 4 international); together, chapters hold over 50 events a year for Maserati enthusiasts worldwide.

Maserati Owners Club of North America
14220 Saddlebow Ct.
Reno, NV 89511
fax: 702-853-7212
Rileysboss@worldnet.att.net

Maserati Club International
1620 Industry Dr. SW, Ste. F
Auburn, WA 98001
ph: 253-833-2598
fax: 253-735-0946
mci@maseratinet.com
http://www.maseratinet.com
A privately owned subsidiary of MIE Corp.; MIE has the largest, most complete inventory of Maserati parts; the best source for live technical advice in the world devoted exclusively to all Maserati not in current production.

Internet Resources

George Perfect
Maserati Resource Center
P.O. Box 74
Stanley, DH9 0YW U.K.
ph: +44 191 370 3741
georgep@maserati-rc.org
http://www.maserati-rc.org
Provides a central focus for

information about Maserati cars, people and events: technical articles, model information, spare parts, clubs, and more.

Mazda

Clubs/Associations

Mazda Club
P.O. Box 11238
Chicago, IL 60611
ph: 773-769-6262
fax: 773-769-3240
info@mazdaclub.com
http://www.mazdaclub.com
For all Mazdas including the RX-7, Miata, MX-6, 626, MX-3, 424, Millenia, Protege/323, and trucks.

Mercedes-Benz

Clubs/Associations

Mercedes-Benz Club of America
1907 Lelaray St.
Colorado Springs, CO 80909-2872
ph: 800-637-2360
fax: 719-633-9283
info@mbca.org
http://mbca.org

Internet Resources

Stefan Conrady
Mercedes-Benz Classic
R 051
Stuttgart, D-70322 Germany
ph: +49 711/17-83453
fax: +49 711/17-83455
http://www.mercedes-benz.com/e/
   mbclassic
The official Mercedes-Benz Classic Web site: a center for sales, rentals, restorations, parts and accessories; the famous museum collection; clubs around the world; archive of 110 years of automotive tradition; news and reports.

Mercury

Clubs/Associations

Jerry Robbin
International Mercury Owners
   Association
Newsletter: Quicksilver
6445 West Grand Ave.
Chicago, IL 60707-3410
ph: 773-622-6445
fax: 773-622-3602
info@mercuryclub.com
http://www.mercuryclub.com
Open to all Mercury owners (regardless of year or make) and Mercury enthusiasts alike; over 1,200 members.

Mercury Comet

Clubs/Associations

John Howell
Comet Cyclone Registry
6609 Grey Fox Dr.
Springfield, VA 22152
ph: 703-569-0174

Mercury Cougar

Clubs/Associations

Ron & Sally Crouch, Mem.
Cougar Club of America
Magazine: At the Sign of the Cat
1637 Skyline Dr.
Norfolk, VA 23518-4327
membership@cougarclub.org
http://www.cougarclub.org
Dedicated to the preservation of 1967 through 1973 Mercury Cougars.

MG

Clubs/Associations

MG Car Club Ltd., The
Magazine: Safety Fast
Kimber House
P.O. Box 251
Abingdon, Oxfordshire OX14 1FF U.K.
ph: 01235-555552
fax: 01235-533755
robertgammage@mgcc.co.uk
http://www.mgcc.co.uk
Since 1972; for MG enthusiasts of all models, 1923 to present; technical aid, monthly meetings, racing championships, seminars, how-to.

Richard Monk
MG Owners Club, The
Magazine: Enjoying MG
Octagon House
Swavesey, Cambridge CB4 5Qz U.K.
ph: 01954 231125
fax: 01954 232106
mginfo@mgownersclub.co.uk
http://www.mgownersclub.co.uk
Largest single marque car club in the world offering advice, spares, events, camaraderie, accessories, insurance, rallies: everything for the MG owner.

MG A Series

Clubs/Associations

George Merryweather
North American MGA Register
Magazine: MGA!
15 Cimarron Trail
Allen, TX 75002
ph: 972-429-6079
fax: 972-429-6079
namgar@mgcars.org.uk
http://www.mgcars.org.uk/namgar
Register for the English MGA series sports car and variants.

MG B Series

Clubs/Associations

Frank Ochal
American MGB Association
Magazine: Octagon
P.O. Box 11401
Chicago, IL 60611-0401
ph: 800-723-MGMG or 773-878-5055
fax: 773-769-3240
info@mgclub.org
http://www.mgclub.org
Oldest and largest club for all MGBs, MGB-GTs and Midgets; color magazine.

Micro & Mini

Clubs/Associations

Microcar & Minicar Club, The
Magazine: Minutia
P.O. Box 43137
Upper Montclair, NJ 07043-0137
jj@microcar.org
http://www.microcar.org
A club for those interested in small and unusual cars, both foreign and domestic.

Marc Delmont
Micro Car Club
6675 South Sherman St.
Littleton, CO 80121
ph: 303-798-8589

Internet Resources

Rover & Austin Mini Cooper Page
U.K.
mini@minifreak.freeserve.co.uk
http://www.minifreak.freeserve.co.uk
A Web site dedicated to the Mini and Mini Copper automobile.

Muscle Cars

Clubs/Associations

Mike Einwechter
All American Muscle Car Association
216 North Dorset Ave.
Ventnor City, NJ 08406
ph: 609-344-2100
acdntpron6@aol.com
http://clubs.hemmings.com/
   allameriacnmuscle

Alan Scrimager
National Muscle Car Association
Magazine: Muscle Monthly Magazine
3404 Democrat Rd.
Memphis, TN 38118
ph: 901-366-1807
nmca@netten.net
An association whose focus is on grassroots drag racing of street-legal vehicles.

Nash

Clubs/Associations

Jim & Dorothy Bracewell
Nash Car Club of America
Newsletter: Nash Times
1N274 Prarie
Glen Ellyn, IL 60137
bracewell@nashcarclub.org
http://www.nashcarclub.org
A worldwide club over 1,900 strong.

Oldsmobile

Clubs/Associations

Oldsmobile Club of America, Inc.
Magazine: Journey With Olds
P.O. Box 80318
Lansing, MI 48908-0318
ph: 517-663-1811
fax: 517-663-1820
oca@oldsclub.org
http://www.oldsclub.org
For owners and enthusiasts of all Oldsmobile products.

Clay Mollman, Ed.
National Antique Oldsmobile Club, Inc.
Magazine: Runabouts to Rockets
4 Lindworth Dr.
Saint Louis, MO 63124-1454
naoc@mindspring.com
http://www.antiqueolds.org
1897 through 1964 Oldsmobiles only.

Opel

Clubs/Associations

Charles Goin
Opel Association of North America
394 Mystic Lane
Wirtz, VA 24184
ph: 804-379-9737
webmaster@goindesign.com
http://clubs.hemmings.com/oana

Gary Murphy
Opel Motorsport Club
Newsletter: Blitz, The
3824 Franklin St.
La Crescenta, CA 91214
ph: 818-248-5504
president@opelclub.com
http://www.opelclub.com

Packard

Clubs/Associations

Todd Stennis, Mbrship.
Packard Club, The (Packard Automobile
   Classics, Inc.)
Newsletter: Cormorant News Bulletin
420 S. Ludlow St.
Cincinnati, OH 45202
ph: 972-617-8876 or 800-527-3452
fax: 972-617-8371
Senator05@aol.com
http://www.packardclub.org
Worldwide club for fans of the Packard automobile; monthly newsletter and quarterly magazine; national meet for all members.

Richard Hack, Pres.
Packards International Motor Car Club
Magazine: Packards International
   Magazine
302 French St.
Santa Ana, CA 92701-4845
ph: 714-541-8431
rlh@ucicl.eng.uci.edu
http://clubs.hemmings.com/
   packardsinternational
Dedicated to the preservation and driving of the Packard auto; technical information, source of parts, free classified ads for members.

Pierce-Arrow

Clubs/Associations

Charlie Gills, Mbrship.
Pierce-Arrow Society, Inc.
Magazine: Arrow, The
P.O. Box 36637
Richmond, VA 23235-8013
webmaster@pierce-arrow.org
http://www.pierce-arrow.org
Provides technical and historical information on all Pierce vehicles through "The Arrow" magazine, the "Service Bulletin" (technical bulletin)

and "The Emporium" (current events and advertising newsletter.)

Plymouth

Clubs/Associations

Ray Montgomery
Chrysler Product Owners Club, Inc.
Newsletter: Torsion Bar
806 Winhall Way
Silver Spring, MD 20904-2072
ph: 301-622-2962
Club is dedicated to the preservation, restoration, and enjoyment of all vehicles built by The Chrysler Corporation and its antecedent companies: Plymouth, DeSoto, Imperial, Dodge.

Jim Benjaminson, Mem. Sec.
Plymouth Owners Club, Inc.
Magazine: Plymouth Bulletin
P.O. Box 416
Cavalier, ND 58220-0416
ph: 701-549-3746
fax: 701-549-3744
benji@utma.com
http://www.classicar.com/clubs/
 plymouth/home.htm
Recognizes all 4, 6 & V8 powered Plymouth cars, Plymouth trucks and Fargo commercial vehicles built from 1928 through cars over 25 years of age.

Plymouth Barracuda

Clubs/Associations

Ann M. McKnight
Plymouth Barracuda/Cuda Owners Club
Newsletter: PBCOC Bulletin
36 Woodland Rd.
East Greenwich, RI 02818

Police & Sheriff

Clubs/Associations

Sgt. James Post
Police Car Owners of America
15677 Highway 62 West
Eureka Springs, AR 72632
ph: 479-253-4948
fax: 479-253-4949
kopkars@arkansas.net
http://www.policecarowners.com
A club for owners of restored police vehicles - any year and any make; also for collectors of police car models and photographs.

Pontiac

Clubs/Associations

Pete Glinski
Pontiac Owner's Association
1202 Cork Dr.
Papillion, NE 68046
ph: 402-593-1737
pontiac@mitec.net
http://www.geocities.com/poay2k/
 POA.html
A family-oriented club dedicated to the preservation of all Pontiac, Oakland cars and GMC trucks; monthly newsletter, numerous activities, annual show.

Pontiac Fiero

Clubs/Associations

Phil Huff
Fiero Owners Club of America
Magazine: Fiero Owner
1598 S. Anaheim, Unit B
Anaheim, CA 92805
ph: 714-635-0898
fax: 714-635-0898
http://www.fieroownersclub.com
The only Fiero network resource; informational data, historical info, restorative facts and modification upgrades; magazine has articles, car parts for sale.

Pontiac Firebird

Clubs/Associations

Robert Thomas
National Firebird & Trans Am Club
Magazine: Eagle
P.O. Box 11238
Chicago, IL 60611-0238
ph: 773-769-6262
fax: 773-769-3240
info@firebirdtaclub.com
http://www.firebirdtaclub.com
For all Firebirds including the Trans AM Formula and Firehawk.

Pontiac GTO

Clubs/Associations

GTO Association of America
Magazine: Legend, The
5829 Stroebel Rd.
Saginaw, MI 486095249
ph: 800-486-1964 or 989-781-0807
fax: 989-781-4271
gtomaher@worldnet.att.net
http://www.gtoaa.org
Ann international club for Pontiac GTO owners and enthusiasts.

Porsche

Clubs/Associations

Porsche 912 Registry
comments@912registry.org
http://www.912registry.org
For Porsche 912 and 912E enthusiasts.

Porsche Club of America
Magazine: Porsche Panorama
P.O. Box 5900
Springfield, VA 22150
ph: 703-451-9000
admin@pcanational.org
http://www.pca.org
Members must own a Porsche to join; over 50,000 members and 142 chapters across US and Canada; Concours d'Elegance, rallies, autocrosses, and social activities.

Porsche Owners Club, Inc.
Magazine: Velocity
14252 Culver drive #A, PMB 727
Irvine, CA 92604
ph: 760-948-7300
fax: 760-244-1787
officeofpoc@aol.com
http://www.porscheownersclub.org
Offers its members driving schools, races, slaloms, and more.

Collectors

Frank Konisky
People Kars
290 Third Ave. Extension
Rensselaer, NY 12144-5606
ph: 518-465-0477
fax: 518-465-0614
peoplekars@aol.com
http://www.peoplekars.com
Buys, sells, trades anything to do with Volkswagens and Porsche: toys, models, literature, memorabilia.

Preservation

Clubs/Associations

Chris Welborn
Kalamazoo Antique Auto Restorers Club
P.O. Box 532
Oshtemo, MI 49077
ph: 616-624-6757

Paul Gorrell
Black Hawk Auto Restorers
11306 Mill Dam Rd.
Burlington, IA 52601
ph: 319-753-1837

St. Croix Valley Auto Restorers Club
1125 7th St.
Pine City, MN 55063
ph: 320-629-2077

Myra Jongbloedt
Auto Restorers Club of Minnesota
Newsletter: Auto Restorers Club
 Newsletter
P.O. Box 531
Saint Peter, MN 56082
ph: 507-546-3657
snoopy@mnic.net
http://clubs.hemmings.com/autorestorers
Non-profit organization dedicated to the preservation and restoration of antique vehicles through special interest cars; founded in 1961; family-oriented club welcoming all car owners; monthly newsletter,, quarterly meetings; events.

Elaine Jordan
International Society for Vehicle
 Preservation
Magazine: Restoration Magazine
P.O. Box 50046
Tucson, AZ 85703
ph: 520-622-2201
fax: 520-792-8501
isvp@aztexcorp.com
http://www.aztexcorp.com/root/isvp.html
For appreciation, preservation, restoration of self-propelled vehicles; how-to help in restoring, sourcing of materials.

Professional

Clubs/Associations

F. David Petke
Professional Car Society
Magazine: Professional Car, The
5405 Heritage Lane
Kingsport, TN 37664-9506
webmaster@professionalcar.org
http://www.professionalcar.org
For all interested in the preservation of hearses, flower cars, ambulances, limousines, and service cars.

Periodicals

Kelsey Publishing Ltd.
Magazine: Commercial Vehicles
Cudham Tithe Barn
Berry's Hill
Cudham, Kent TN16 3AG U.K.
ph: 01959 541444
fax: 01959 541400
info@kelsey.co.uk
http://www.kelsey.co.uk
A 48-page monthly British magazine dealing with only classic and vintage commercial vehicles: rallies, auctions, restorations.

Racing

Clubs/Associations

Joseph Freeman, Comm. Dir.
National Auto Racing Historical Society
121 Mt. Vernon St.
Boston, MA 02018
ph: 617-723-2661
fax: 617-723-2333
jfreeman@racemaker.com
Shares resources among members, assists publishing and advertising efforts; provides documentation.

Sportscar Vintage Racing Association
Newsletter: Line, The
257 Dekalb Industrial Way
Decatur, GA 30030
ph: 404-298-3323
fax: 404-298-3325
svra1@bellsouth.net
http://www.svra.com

International Hot Rod Association
9 1/2 E. Main St.
Norwalk, OH 44857
ph: 419-663-6666
fax: 419-663-4472
comments@ihra.com
http://www.ihra.com
A sanctioning organization for drag strips and racing events throughout N.A. and Europe; 70 member tracks; produces Snap-on Tools Drag Racing Series of professional and sportsman drag racing.

Vintage Auto Racing Association
Magazine: Vintage Voice
32545B Golden Lantern #480
Dana Point, CA 92629
ph: 800-280-8272 or 949-248-1368
fax: 949-388-8071
vara@msn.com
http://www.vararacing.com
Primary objective of the sport of vintage and historic automobile

racing is to promote the preservation of these cars in a racing format that emphasizes safety.

Renault

Clubs/Associations

Harold Cooke, Mbrship.
Renault Owners Club of North America
Newsletter: Renault Report, The
31218 Stanley
Lucerne Valley, CA 92356
ph: 760-248-2401
webmaster@renaulttownersclub.org
http://www.renaulttownersclub.org

REO

Clubs/Associations

James Neal, Sec.
REO Club of America
Newsletter: REO Echo
1069 Applegate Lane
East Lansing, MI 48823
REOclub@yahoo.com

Rolls-Royce

Clubs/Associations

Rolls-Royce Owners Club
Magazine: Flying Lady, The
191 Hempt Rd.
Mechanicsburg, PA 17055
ph: 717-697-4671 or 800-879-7762
fax: 717-697-7820
rroc@rroc.org
http://www.rroc.org

Silver Ghost Association
191 Hempt Rd.
Mechanicsburg, PA 17055
ph: 717-697-4671
rroc@rroc.org
http://www.rroc.org/regions/sga/sga.htm
Aims to assist, advise and encourage members who own Ghosts to get and keep them on the road.

SAAB

Clubs/Associations

Stephen Goldberger, Pub.
SAAB Club of North America
Magazine: Nines
2389 Chestnut Hill St.
Canton, OH 44720
ph: 330-497-0346
fax: 330-497-5583
nines@neo.rr.com
http://www.saabclub.com
Magazine contains valuable information for owners of all SAAB cars; from 2-stroke through Turbomobiles - tech tips, SAAB news, history, service bulletins, classified ads, and business ads.

Shelby

Clubs/Associations

Rick Kopec
Shelby American Automobile Club
Magazine: Shelby American, The
P.O. Box 788
Sharon, CT 06069-0788
ph: 860-364-0449
fax: 860-364-0769
saac@li.com
http://www.saac.com
SAAC is dedicated to the preservation, care, history and enjoyment of the World Championship cars created by Carroll Shelby from 1962 to present; club in operation since 1975; approx. 5,000 members world wide.

Barry Goodall
Shelby Dodge Automobile Club
P.O. Box 182072
Utica, MI 48318-2072
ph: 810-759-6160
sdac@sdac.org
http://www.sdac.org
For those interested in the Shelby inspired Dodge cars of the mid and late 1980s.

Brock McPherson
Shelby Owners of America, Inc.
P.O. Drawer 1429
Great Bend, KS 67530
ph: 620-793-3420
mcpmcvlaw@carrollsweb.com
http://clubs.hemmings.com/
shelbyowners
Annual convention; bi-monthly newsletter.

Station Wagons

Clubs/Associations

Ken McDaniel
American Station Wagon Owners
  Association
Magazine: Wagon Roundup
8922 Butternut Court
Indianapolis, IN 46260-1525
ph: 317-872-0004
aswoa@aol.com
http://www.stationwagon.com
Dedicated to the preservation of American-built station wagons.

Steam

Clubs/Associations

Tom Kimmel, Pres.
Steam Automobile Club of America
Newsletter: Steam Automobile Bulletin
4669 East Hillcrest Dr.
Berrien Springs, MI 49103
ph: 616-471-7408
fax: 616-471-2495
JReynol@aol.com
http://www.classicar.com/clubs/STEAM/
STEAM.HTM
Encourages the preservation of steam cars and the design of modern ones.

Studebaker

Clubs/Associations

Mark van Deventer
Studebaker Drivers Club
Magazine: Turning Wheels
P.O. Box 1743
Maple Grove, MN 55311
ph: 763-420-7829 or 800-527-3452
fax: 763-420-7849
MarkvanDev@StudebakerClubs.com
http://www.studebakerdriversclub.com

Richard Quinn, Ed.
Antique Studebaker Club
Magazine: Antique Studebaker Review
P.O. Box 28845
Dallas, TX 75228-0845
ph: 972-709-6185 or 800-527-3452
fax: 972-296-7920
rtq11@aol.com
http://www.antiquestudebakerclub.com
For pre-1946 Studebakers.

Museums/Libraries

Studebaker National Museum
525 South Main St.
South Bend, IN 46601-2225
ph: 574-235-9714 or 888-391-5600
info@studebakermuseum.org
http://www.studebakermuseum.org

Stutz

Clubs/Associations

Michael P. Barry
Stutz Club, Inc., The
Magazine: Stutz News
7400 Lantern Rd.
Indianapolis, IN 46256-2120
ph: 330-225-9494
mpbarry@concentric.net
http://www.stutzclub.org

Subaru

Clubs/Associations

Garry Grimes
Subaru Club of America
Newsletter: AnyRoad AnyTime
P.O. Box 84
Camden-Wyoming, DE 19934
ph: 302-399-7519
A little bit of everything related to Subaru.

Ed Parsil
Subaru 360 Drivers' Club
Newsletter: Subaru 360 Drivers' Club
  Newsletter
1421 North Grady Ave.
Tucson, AZ 85715-5013
ph: 520-290-6492
cameach@discovernet.net
http://www.geocities.com/MotorCity/
Garage/5360
All-volunteer association of owners/ drivers of 2-cylinder Subarus.

Sunbeam

Clubs/Associations

Doug Ferrell
Midwest Sunbeam Club
3701 NW Eric Dr.
Topeka, KS 66618-3631
ph: 785-286-2987
midwsunbeam@afo.net
http://clubs.hemmings.com/
frameset.cfm?club=mwsunbeam
For owners of Sunbeam, Hillman, Humber, Singer, Commer, Rootes cars.

Sunbeam Owners Group of San Diego
2250 Rosecrans
San Diego, CA 92106
ph: 619-223-0496
oldealp@aol.com

Triumph

Clubs/Associations

Andrew Mace
Vintage Triumph Register, The
Magazine: Vintage Triumph, The
P.O. Box 655
Howell, MI 48844-0655
ph: 518-766-5413
vtr-www@vtr.org
http://www.vtr.org
Focuses on all Triumphs; magazine published quarterly; also publishes "The English Channel" newsletter; annual convention; nearly 70 local affiliate clubs in the US and Canada.

Melvin S. Merzon, Sec.
Triumph Roadster Club North American
  Affiliate
1002 Hilldale Lane
Buffalo Grove, IL 60089
ph: 630-753-2162 or 847-520-4723
fax: 630-753-2261
melvin.merzon@nav-international.com
http://clubs.hemmings.com/
triumphroadster
For those who appreciate the art and mechanics of the English Triumph Roadster, produced from 1946 to 1949.

Tucker

Clubs/Associations

William E. Pommering
Tucker Automobile Club of America,
  Inc.
Newsletter: Tucker Topics
9509 Hinton Dr.
Santee, CA 92071-2760
ph: 619-596-3028
fax: 815-346-6398
TuckerSite@hotmail.com
http://www.TuckerClub.org

Volkswagen

Clubs/Associations

Peter Cook, Pres.
Vintage Volkswagen Club of America
99 Pine Lane
Westwood, MA 02090-1220
ph: 781-326-7584
bsvwoc@aol.com
http://www.vvwca.com

Volkswagen Club of America
P.O. Box 154
North Aurora, IL 60542-0154
ph: 630-896-2803
info@vwclub.org
http://www.vwclub.org

Collectors

Gary & Gayle Breuilly
Volksgallery Volkswagen Homepage
volksgalny@aol.com
http://www.geocities.com/MotorCity/
4981/vgal.htm
*Wants Volkswagen-related memora-
bilia: advertising, brochures,
accessories, pictures, toys, etc.*

Frank Konisky
People Kars
290 Third Ave. Extension
Rensselaer, NY 12144-5606
ph: 518-465-0477
fax: 518-465-0614
peoplekars@aol.com
http://www.peoplekars.com
*Buys, sells, trades anything to do with
Volkswagens and Porsche: toys,
models, literature, memorabilia.*

Volvo

Clubs/Associations

Gretchen Adams, VP
Volvo Club of America
Magazine: Rolling
P.O. Box 16
Afton, NY 13730-0016
ph: 607-639-2279
fax: 607-639-2279
gretchen@vcoa.org
http://www.vcoa.org

Willys

Clubs/Associations

Ken McIntyre
Mid-America Willys Club
Magazine: Gasser
18222 North 66th Ave.
Glendale, AZ 85308
ph: 602-439-2502
http://www.gasserclub.com
*A nostalgic drag racing enthusiast
group; members love the 1933-1942
Willys and Gasser cars; this is not a
"Jeep" club.*

Woodies

Clubs/Associations

John Lee, Editor
National Woodie Club
Magazine: Woodie Times
P.O. Box 6134
Lincoln, NE 68506-0134
ph: 402-488-0990
woodietimes@nationalwoodieclub.com
http://www.nationalwoodieclub.com
*For restorers and owners of wood-
bodied cars; advice, ads, information,
sources.*

Internet Resources

David Miller
Old Woodies
1706 Cedar Lane
Nashville, TN 37212-5804
ph: 716-292-7470
mail@oldwoodies.com
http://www.oldwoodies.com
*A Web site for enthusiasts of wood-
bodied vehicles.*

AUTOMOBILIA

(see also FARM MACHINERY; GAS
STATION COLLECTIBLES; KEY
CHAINS; LICENSE PLATES;
LICENSES, Driver; MODELS;
MOTORCYCLES; MOTOR
SCOOTERS; TOYS, Cars;
TRANSPORTATION
COLLECTIBLES)

Auction Services

Kruse International
P.O. Box 190
Auburn, IN 46706
ph: 800-968-4444 or 219-925-5600
fax: 219-925-5467
info@kruseinternational.com
http://www.kruseinternational.com

Clubs/Associations

David K. Bausch
Automobile Objects D'Art Club
Newsletter: Automobile Objects D'Art
  Newsletter
252 N. 7th St.
Allentown, PA 18102-4024
ph: 610-432-3355
fax: 610-820-9368
oldtoy@aol.com
http://www.geocities.com/davidkbausch
*A club for collectors interested in
early automobile history as shown
through art and objects of art.*

Collectors

Dave Ogden
P.O. Box 223
Northbrook, IL 60062-5951
ph: 847-564-2893
fax: 847-564-2893
musical@flash.net
http://www.flash.net/~musical
*Wants to buy early automobile lights,
horns, radiator caps, and accessories.*

Dealers

Leila Dunbar
Dunbar's Gallery
76 Haven St.
Milford, MA 01757-3821
ph: 508-634-8697
fax: 508-634-8698
dunbars@dunbarsgallery.com
http://www.dunbarsgallery.com
*Mail order Americana - no reproduc-
tions; buys, sells and specializes in
vintage character and comic toys,
banks, advertising, automobilia, and
Halloween related items.*

Robert H. Snyder
P.O. Drawer 821
Yonkers, NY 10702-0821
ph: 914-476-8500
fax: 914-476-8573
info@cohascodpc.com
http://www.cohascodpc.com
*Wants automobile literature,
materials, periodicals, artifacts &
collectibles of all kinds relating to
autos, trucks, motorcycles, etc.;
collections assembled for institutions
& specialists; also Duryea, Napier/
Edge, pre-war Japanese.*

Frank Konisky
People Kars
290 Third Ave. Extension
Rensselaer, NY 12144
ph: 518-465-0477
fax: 518-465-0614
peoplekars@aol.com
http://www.peoplekars.com
*Buy, sell, trade Volkswagen, Porsche
and select European automobile
models, toys and automobilia.*

Ron & Deb Ladley
1850 Valley Forge Rd.
Lansdale, PA 19446
ph: 610-584-1665
fax: 610-584-8537
*Wants pre-1970 auto, truck and
motorcycle literature, ephemera,
catalogs, brochures, manuals, signs,
dealership items, etc.; any age.*

Bill White
Colonel Bill White Auto Collectibles
HC 88, Box 165
Hudson, KY 40145
ph: 270-257-8642
whiteb@bellsouth.net
*Buys and sells original automobile
literature and collectibles; all years,
most models, especially Ford Motor
Company.*

Experts

David K. Bausch
252 N. 7th St.
Allentown, PA 18102-4024
ph: 610-432-3355
fax: 610-820-9368
oldtoy@aol.com
http://www.geocities.com/davidkbausch
*Author of "The Official Price Guide to
Automobilia."*

Jim & Nancy Schaut
AutoHobbies
7147 W. Angela Dr.
Glendale, AZ 85308-8507
ph: 623-878-4293
fax: 801-697-9381
nancy@autohobbies.com
http://www.autohobbies.com
*Buys, sells; maintains an automobilia
Web site: gas station maps and tins,
automobile dealer advertising signs,
automobile literature, motorcycle
memorabilia, racing; authors of
"American Automobilia," an
illustrated history & price guide.*

Museums/Libraries

Larz Anderson Auto Museum
15 Newton St.
Brookline, MA 02146
ph: 617-522-6547
fax: 617-524-0170
director@mot.org
http://www.mot.org
*The museum collection includes many
unique and remarkable vehicles as
well as many other significant historic
artifacts.*

Patricia B. Swigart, Pres.
Swigart Museum
Rte. 22 E
P.O. Box 214
Huntingdon, PA 16652
ph: 814-643-0885 or 814-643-2024
fax: 814-643-2857
tours@swigartmuseum.com
http://www.swigartmuseum.com
*Cars, toys, lights, license plates,
emblems, bicycles, clothing, and much
more.*

Periodicals

Sue Elliott, Pub.
Challenge Publications, Inc.
Magazine: Car Toy Collectibles
8381 Canoga Ave.
Canoga Park, CA 91304-2605
ph: 818-700-6868 or 800-562-9182
fax: 818-700-6282
office@challengeweb.com
http://www.challengeweb.com/
cartoys.html
*Bi-monthly magazine covers model
cars of all types, sizes, materials, and
vintage; also covers automobilia from
automotive art and racing collectibles
to pedal cars, porcelain signs, neon
clocks, apparel, literature, gas pumps,
etc.*

Buick Related

Collectors

Alvin Heckard
165 Orchard Grove Ave.
Lewistown, PA 17044-7511
ph: 717-248-7071 or 717-248-2816
aheckard@localnet.com
*Wants pre-1965 Buick promotional
items: paperweights, desk sets, ash
trays, key chains, promotional models,
matchbooks, awards, literature, etc.*

Car Club Badges (Grille)

Clubs/Associations

Kayes Chu
Car Badge Collectors' Club of the
  WWW
P.O. Box 105
Taiping, Perak 34000 Malaysia
kayes@pc.jaring.my
http://www.geocities.com/MotorCity/
Downs/2163
*An international online club for
collectors of car grille badges.*

Collectors

Dan Morris
1225 Ramblewood Dr.
Annapolis, MD 21401
ph: 410-757-6430
*Collects European car club badges
and vintage Volkswagon accessories.*

Kayes Chu
P.O. Box 105
Taiping, Perak 34000 Malaysia
kayes@pc.jaring.my
http://www.geocities.com/MotorCity/
Downs/2163
*Has the only online collection of car
grille badges on the Internet.*

Dealers

John A. Boggs, Jr.
2665 Quail Hill Dr.
Pittsburgh, PA 15241
ph: 412-833-6565
boggs@adelphia.net
*Collector, dealer, expert specializing
in automobile badges: AAA, NMA, AA,
RAC, breakdown organizations, clubs,
racing, sports car clubs; specialty is
early badges - radiator cap mount,
brass, enamel; also mascots, radiator
emblems.*

Experts

Raymond A.R.J. Gelder
Duinwetering 29
Noordwijk, 2203 HL The Netherlands
ph: 0031 713618 678
fax: 0031 713618 678
gelder.r.a.r.j@kivi.nl
*Collector of metal car club badges;
national, regional, local, veteran/
vintage car, company, marque clubs;
trades, buys and sells.*

Tony Phillips
UK Car Club Badges
"Lelystad"
22 Gregorys Way
Belper, Derbyshire DE56)HS U.K.
ph: 01773 882717
TonyFanum@lelystad.fsnet.co.uk
*Collector, dealer, expert, appraiser of
AA and associated car club badges
from the UK and overseas; always
interested in exchange or purchase of
interesting badges; can date all UK
AA badges from the badge number.*

Flower Vases

Collectors

Dulce Holt
504 Broadway
Chesterton, IN 46304-2320
ph: 219-926-2838 or 219-926-4170
fax: 219-929-4580
rick@carvase.com
http://www.carvase.com
*Wants to buy 1900-1930 flower vases
(with or without metal attaching
brackets) from old cars; also wants
related information.*

Internet Resources

Dulce Holt
504 Broadway
Chesterton, IN 46304-2320
ph: 219-926-2838 or 219-926-4170
fax: 219-929-4580
rick@carvase.com
http://www.carvase.com
*The Internet site for collectors of car
vases: what they are, photos,
information, movies with vases, how to
fine vases, etc.*

Ford Motor Company

Collectors

Cliff Moebius
484 Winthrop St.
Westbury, NY 11590
ph: 516-333-3797
fax: 516-333-1712
*Wants Ford Motor Co. and Henry
Ford memorabilia: joke books,
postcards, books, photos, Christmas
cards, records, sheet music, script
pens, pins, china, silverware, menus,
sales literature, etc.*

Dealers

Tim O'Callaghan
305 St. Lawrence Blvd.
P.O. Box 512
Northville, MI 48167
ph: 248-449-2652
timothyo@ameritech.net
http://www.hfha.org/fordtrimotor.htm
*Author of numerous articles on Ford
Motor Co.: coins and tokens,
employee longevity, awards and
factory badges, employee tableware,
etc.; Ford aviation historian with
Ford aviation book and video
available for sale; questions
welcomed.*

Hood Ornaments

Collectors

Sy & Ronnie Margolis
17853 Santiago Blvd., #107-210
Villa Park, CA 92861-4113
ph: 714-974-5938
fax: 714-921-0731
smargol@adelphia.net
*Wants pre-WWII hood ornaments,
radiator ornaments, car mascots; also
wants related signs, brochures,
catalogs.*

Dealers

Mike Z. Kleba
P.O. Box 70
Mallorytown, Ontario K0E 1R0 Canada
ph: 613-923-5934
*Wants to buy 1910-1940 hood
ornaments from old cars; good or
broken; metal or glass; one piece or
many; roosters, eagles, aeroplanes,
flying man and lady, Superman, Uncle
Sam, devil, Indian head, etc.*

Hubcaps

Clubs/Associations

Dennis Kuhn
Hubcap Collectors Club
Newsletter: Hubcapper
P.O. Box 54
Buckley, MI 49620
ph: 616-269-3555
Focus on the older threaded hubcaps.

Dealers

Ronald Young, Jr.
Hubcaps on Wheels
P.O. Box 348
Linwood, MA 01525
ph: 401-567-7600 or 508-234-7300
fax: 401-567-7600
HubcapRon@HubcapsOnWheels.com
http://www.HubcapsOnWheels.com
*Over 20,000 new and used wheel
covers, hubcaps, center caps, trim
rings, and chrome wheel skins in
stock; almost 25 years experience in
the field.*

Hubcaps
2825 Selzer
Evansville, IN 47712-3884
*Buys and sells; thousands available
from 1949 through 1982.*

Don Hummel
House of Hubcaps
20052b Pacific Highway South
Seattle, WA 98198
ph: 206-824-5040 or 800-825-9715
fax: 206-824-9780
hubcapcar@aol.com
http://www.houseofhubcaps.com
*Selection starts at the onset of hubcap
manufacturing in the late 1940s to
present.*

Instruments

Repair Services

John Wolf & Co., Inc.
36420 Biltomre Place
Willoughby, OH 44094
ph: 440-942-0083
johnwolfco@aol.com
http://www.tempman.qpg.com
*Provides functional and cosmetic
restoration of gauges and instrumentation; also restores antique auto and
aircraft instruments.*

Literature

Collectors

Walter Miller
6710 Brooklawn Pkwy.
Syracuse, NY 13211-2104
ph: 315-432-8282
fax: 315-432-8256
info@autolit.com
*Buys 1900-1975 automobile sales
brochures, repair manuals, parts
catalogs, showroom items or any
other related literature.*

Bob Olds
364 Vinewood Ave.
Tallmadge, OH 44278
ph: 330-633-5938
*Buys and sell auto, truck, motorcycle,
bicycle sales and dealer literature,
owner's manuals, shop manuals, and
any related memorabilia or scale
model cars.*

Dealers

Bob Johnson
Bob Johnson's Auto Literature
92 Blandin Ave.
Framingham, MA 01702
ph: 508-872-9173 or 800-334-0688
fax: 508-626-0991
bjohnson@autopaper.com
http://www.autopaper.com
*Buying & selling 1900-present auto,
truck, motorcycle, farm, construction,
factory sales brochures, owner &
repair manuals, parts books,
showroom albums, data books, color
& upholstery books, paint chips, auto
dealer promotional items.*

J.B. Hoffert
P.O. Box 801
Reading, PA 19607-0801
ph: 610-777-0105
jhofflit@aol.com
*Buys and sells "original" only
literature for cars, trucks, motorcycles, farm related, construction,
boats, planes, and trains; 1800s
through 1970s.*

Rob & Sharon McLellan
McLellan's Automotive History
9111 Longstaff Dr.
Houston, TX 77031-2711
ph: 713-772-3285
fax: 713-772-3287
Mclellans@MclellansAutomotive.com
http://www.mclellansautomotive.com
*Buys and sells books, sales, literature,
art, programs, magazines and
memorabilia on sport, luxury, classic,
antique and racing cars; over 100,000
items, with detailed descriptions,
photographs and prices listed on Web
site.*

W.R. Sewell
Model Auto
P.O. Box 79253
Houston, TX 77279-9253
ph: 713-467-5899
fax: 713-467-5899
modelaut@ix.netcom.com
http://www.shop-manual.com
*Buys and trades all makes of auto
sales literature: dealer albums,
promotional model cars and old
model car kits, shop manuals.*

Museums/Libraries

Walter Miller
Museum of Automobile History, The
321 Clinton St.
Syracuse, NY 13203
ph: 315-478-CARS
fax: 315-432-8256
info@autolit.com
http://
www.themuseumofautomobilehistory.org
*More than 10,000 items pertaining to
more than 1,000 makes of automobiles, motorcycles and trucks; the first
institution to trace the social effect of
the century's favorite machine; no
cars displayed.*

Model A Advertising

Dealers

Jim Thomas
8165 Glenmill Ct.
Cincinnati, OH 45249
ph: 513-774-0350
*Wants 1928-1931 Ford Model "A"
car and truck advertising, sales
literature, posters, dealer items,
memorabilia; buy/sell/trade.*

Spark Plugs

Clubs/Associations

Chad Windham
Spark Plug Collectors of America
Magazine: Ignitor, The
3401 NE Riverside
Pendleton, OR 97801-3431
ph: 541-276-4069
fax: 541-278-6169
spcoa1@aol.com
*Dedicated to the promotion of spark
plug collecting and research, and the
preservation of spark plug history; the
magazine is published quarterly.*

Collectors

Charles Langley
825 N. Meridian St.
Greentown, IN 46936
ph: 317-628-7579
*Wants to buy antique brand name
spark plugs; also wants related
catalogs and charts, and auto
magazines from 1900 to 1925.*

Bill Bond
P.O. Box 2229
Ann Arbor, MI 48106-2229
ph: 734-646-7735
fax: 734-971-6443
spcoa1@aol.com
*Has a collection of over 2,000 spark
plugs; founded the Spark Plug
Collectors of America in 1975.*

Jeff Bartheld
14018 NE 85th St.
Elk River, MN 55330-6818
ph: 612-441-7059

Chad Windham
3401 NE Riverside
Pendleton, OR 97801-3431
ph: 541-276-4069
fax: 541-278-6169
spcoa1@aol.com

Dealers

Don McKinsey
P.O. Box 94
Wilkinson, IN 46186
ph: 765-785-6284
*Buying and selling obsolete &
collectible spark plugs; 70,000 in
stock; send $2 for price list,
refundable; VHS tape of collector
spark plugs; mail order only; be sure
to include a #10 SASE with inquiries.*

Experts

Cornelius Bergbower
603 Louie Ave.
Bluford, IL 62814
ph: 618-732-6195
*Author of "Spark Collector's Guide,"
available from the author - Vol I $11
ppd., Vol. II $14 ppd.; also wants to
buy spark plugs with odd names and
shapes, especially plugs with priming
cups, gadgets, etc.*

Studebaker Related

Collectors

Paul Straughn
4111 Carnation Dr.
Arlington, TX 76016
ph: 817-572-2817
*Wants Studebaker related memora-
bilia, 1852-1966: car/truck/horse-
drawn items: literature, photographs,
catalogs, signs, sheet music, stock
certificates, pins, badges, promotional
and dealership items, models, china,
banners, etc.*

Barry Mann
10602 Denell Circle
Austin, TX 78753
*Wants anything related to the
Studebaker.*

Stunt/Thrill Show Related

Collectors

Frank E. Richards
43C Canterbury Circle
Reading, PA 19607-3452
ph: 610-796-7486
fax: 610-796-7969
thrilsho@ptd.net
*Wants to buy memorabilia relating to
automotive stunt and thrill shows.*

AVIATION

(see also AIRLINE MEMORABILIA;
AIRPLANES; AIRSHIPS; AVIATION
MEMORABILIA; BOOKS, Reference
[Aviation]; MILITARIA; MODELS,
Aircraft; PERSONALITIES [FAMOUS],
Charles A. Lindbergh; STAMP
COLLECTING, Air Mail Related;
TOYS, Airplane Related)

Clubs/Associations

Maine Aviation Historical Society/Maine
Air Museum
Newsletter: MAHS Newsletter
P.O. Box 2641
Bangor, ME 04402-2641
ph: 207-941-6757 or 877-280-MAHS
townsend@acadia.net
http://www.acadia.net/mahs
*A Historical Society dealing with
aviation in Maine; currently starting
Maine Air Museum in Bangor at
airport.*

American Aviation Historical Society
Magazine: AAHS Journal
2333 Otis St.
Santa Ana, CA 92704-3846
ph: 714-549-4818
fax: 714-549-3657
pres@aahs-online.org
http://www.aahs-online.org
*Provides source of factual historical
data compiled by leading historians;
quarterly newsletter and journal
contain articles on personalities, unit
histories, machines, aviation history,
buy and sell ads, etc.*

Canadian Aviation Historical Society
P.O. Box 224, Station A
Willowdale, Ontario M2N 5S8 Canada
ph: 416-410-9774
fax: 905-294-3525
cahsnatpres@mail.cahs.com
http://www.cahs.com
*Members are writers, photographers,
artists, model builders and others with
an interest in the history of aviation.*

Collectors

Alan C. King
P.O. Box 86
Radnor, OH 43066-0086
ph: 614-595-3332
*Wants aviation related repair
manuals, magazines, handbooks, etc.*

Dealers

Russsell Herron
Galactic Voyager
12335 Kingsride #124
Houston, TX 77024-4116
ph: 713-467-0264
fax: 713-973-0456
contact@galacticvoyager.com
http://www.galacticvoyager.com
*Historic & collectible items from the
history of air & space including
official NASA mission patches & pins,
rare and hard-to-find scale models of
historic spacecraft and aircraft, high
quality diecast models, photos,
commemorative, books.*

Experts

Frank Strand
Aero Collectables
P.O. Box 240
Northport, NY 11768-0240
ph: 516-261-0140
*Wants to buy aviation books and
magazines (Aero Digest, Popular
Aviation, MAN), erection and*

*maintenance manuals, engine
manuals, factory brochures and
drawings, instruments, models, name
plates, photos, memorabilia, etc.*

Jon Aldrich
Pine Mountain Lake Airport
P.O. Box 9
Big Oak Flat, CA 95305-0009
ph: 209-962-6121
fax: 209-962-6121
oldjon@goldrush.com
http://www.aviation-antiques.com
*Long time dealer in vintage
aeronautical memorabilia, both civil
and military; wants to buy aviation
autographs, books, war relics, pilot
memorabilia, airplane parts, aero
nostalgia; please send price and
description; appraisal.*

Internet Resources

Thomas Van Hare
Historic Wings
200 W. Palmetto Park Rd., Ste. 201
Boca Raton, FL 33432
ph: 561-347-0181 or 561-483-7450
fax: 561-347-2240
hw@historicwings.com
http://www.historicwings.com
*An online aviation magazine featuring
stories from the past and present, a
full range of articles and aviation
poetry; download aviation backgrounds for your compute desktop.*

Aviation Home Page, The
12 Sherwood Dr.
Adams, TN 37010
ph: 864-292-2696
http://www.avhome.com
*Airlines and airports, art, photogra-
phy, poetry, weather, meteorology,
academies, universities, flight schools,
classifieds, flight simulation, aviation
news, forums.*

Museums/Libraries

New England Air Museum of the
Connecticut Aeronautical Historical
Assoc.
Bradley International Airport
Windsor Locks, CT 06096
ph: 860-623-3305
fax: 860-627-2820
staff@neam.org
http://www.neam.org

Piper Aviation Museum
One Piper Way
Lock Haven, PA 17745
ph: 717-748-8283
fax: 717-893-8357
piper@cub.kcnet.org
http://www.kcnet.org/~piper

Mid Atlantic Air Museum
11 Museum Dr.
Reading, PA 19605
ph: 610-372-7333
fpierce@avialantic.com
http://www.maam.org

National Air & Space Museum
7th St. & Independence Ave. SW
Washington, DC 20560
ph: 202-357-2700
web@nasm.si.edu
http://www.nasm.si.edu

Experimental Aircraft Association Air
   Adventure Museum
P.O. Box 3065
Oshkosh, WI 54093-3065
ph: 920-426-4818
fax: 920-426-6174
communication@eaa.org
http://www.airventuremuseum.org
   *Collection of over 90 vintage
   airplanes; a gathering place for
   aviation enthusiasts from around the
   world; historical research facilities
   available.*

Keith R. Gill
Museum of Science & Industry
5700 S. Lake Shore Dr.
Chicago, IL 60637
ph: 773-684-1414
fax: 773-684-0026
msi@msichicago.org
http://www.msichicago.org
   *Collections include vintage airplanes,
   Boeing 727.*

Air Museum Planes of Fame - AZ
HCR 34, Box B
Vale-Williams, AZ 86046
ph: 520-635-1000
fly1katana@aol.com
http://www.planesoffame.org
   *One of the first air museums in the
   US; the collection spans from the
   Chanute Hang Glider of 1896 to jet
   fighters of the 1960s.*

Air Museum Planes of Fame - CA
7000 Merrill Ave.
Box 17
Chino, CA 91710
ph: 909-597-3722
fax: 909-597-4755
fly1katana@aol.com
http://www.planesoffame.org

Fiona Hale, Lib.
National Aviation Museum
11 Aviation Parkway, Bldg. 194
P.O. Box 9724, Station T
Ottawa, Ontario K1G 5A3 Canada
ph: 613-993-2010 or 800-463-2038
aviation@nmstc.ca
http://www.aviation.nmstc.ca
   *One of the world's great aeronautical
   collections.*

Periodicals

Hachette Filipacchi Magazines, Inc.
Magazine: Flying Magazine
500 West Putnam Ave.
Greenwich, CT 06830
ph: 203-622-2700
fax: 203-622-2725

Magazine: FlyPast
P.O. Box 100
Avendel, NJ 07001
ph: 800-688-6247
ecm@keypublishing.com
http://www.flypast.com
   Britain's top selling aviation monthly.

PRIMEDIA Enthusiast Group
Magazine: Aviation History
741 Miller Dr., SE, Ste. D-2
Leesburg, VA 20175
ph: 703-779-8318
fax: 703-779-8310
david.masini@primedia.com
http://www.thehistorynet.com/
AviationHistory
   *Offers readers in-depth articles on the
   history of world aviation from its
   earliest beginnings to the present day.*

Ann Lee, Ed.
Magazine: In Flight Aviation News
P.O. Box 620447
Woodside, CA 94062
ph: 650-364-8110
fax: 650-364-1359
editor@inflightusa.com
http://www.inflightusa.com
   *A 120-page newspaper devoted to
   aviation & aviation history; editors
   will answer questions about
   memorabilia and refer sellers to
   buyers.*

Art

Dealers

Jerry Beach
Aeronautical Classics & Fine Arts
1305 King St.
Alexandria, VA 22314-2928
ph: 703-548-7122
fax: 703-548-6414
   *Fine aviation prints, paintings,
   memorabilia, books, desk models,
   propellers, gifts, etc.*

Stephen Remington
AviationArt
1324 De La Vina St
Santa Barbara, CA 93101
ph: 805-560-1323 or 408-828-2810
fax: 805-560-9943
72245.747@compuserve.com
http://www.collectair.com
   *Original aviation art, limited edition
   prints, bronze sculptures, display
   models, aeronautical collectibles,
   aviation books, model airplane
   exhibits, museum.*

Military

Dealers

Bob Von Willer
Exotic Aircraft Company
1719 North Marshall Ave.
El Cajon, CA 92020
ph: 619-562-7467
fax: 619-448-2110
baroness@barnstormers.com
http://www.barnstormers.com
   *Specializes in the restoration and
   marketing of antique aircraft,
   including warbirds; appraiser, dealer,*
expert, collector, and repair services
offered.*

Museums/Libraries

National Warplane Museum, Elmira-
   Corning Regional Airport
17 Aviation Dr.
Horseheads, NY 14845
ph: 607-739-8200
nwm@warplane.org
http://www.warplane.org

U.S. Army Aviation Museum
P.O. Box 620610
Fort Rucker, AL 36362-5134
ph: 334-598-2508
manager@armyavnmuseum.org
http://www.armyavnmuseum.org

Charles Metcalf, Dir.
U.S. Air Force Museum
1100 Spaatz St.
Dayton, OH 45433-7102
ph: 937-255-3286
fax: 937-255-0523
usaf.museum@wpafb.af.mil
http://www.wpafb.af.mil/museum
   *World's largest aviation museum with
   10+ acres of aircraft and other
   exhibits under roof.*

Yankee Air Force Museum
P.O. Box 590
Belleville, MI 48112
ph: 734-483-4030
yankeeairmuseum@provide.net
http://www.yankeeairmuseum.org

Combat Air Museum
Hangars 602-604 "J" St.
P.O. Box 19142
Topeka, KS 66619
ph: 785-862-3303
fax: 785-862-3304
CAMTopeka@aol.com
http://www.combatairmuseum.org

Kevin Raulie, Dir.
Cavanaugh Flight Museum
Addison Airport
4572 Claire Chennault
Addison, TX 75001
ph: 972-380-8800
kevin@cavanaughflightmuseum.com
http://www.cavanaughflightmuseum.com
   *Historic warbirds, trainers, fighters,
   jets and other aircraft chronicle
   heroes, battles and technological
   advances from WWI to present.*

War Eagles Air Museum
8012 Airport Rd.
Santa Teresa, NM 88008
ph: 505-589-2000
information@war-eagles-air-
museum.com
http://www.war-eagles-air-museum.com
   *A non-profit organization dedicated to
   the restoration of vintage WWII and
   Korean War planes.*

Carol Ann Ross, PR
Palm Springs Air Museum
Newsletter: Beacon, The
745 North Gene Autry Trail
Palm Springs, CA 92262
ph: 760-778-6262
fax: 760-320-2548
sales@air-museum.org
http://www.palmspringsairmuseum.org
   *Non-profit educational institution,
   whose mission is to exhibit, educate
   and eternalize the role of the WWII
   combat aircraft and the role the pilots
   and American citizens had in
   achieving this great victory.*

Periodicals

H.G. Frautschy
Experimental Aircraft Association
Magazine: Warbirds Magazine
P.O. Box 3086
Oshkosh, WI 54903-3086
ph: 800-843-3612 or 920-426-4800
fax: 920-426-4828
vintage@eaa.org
http://www.vintageaircraft.org

Magazine: Air Wars
8931 Kittyhawk Ave.
Los Angeles, CA 90045-4128
   *Focuses on the restoration of classic
   (1919-1939) fighter planes; how-to
   articles and photos, museum articles,
   plans for models, etc.*

Erika Daileda
Wise Owl Worldwide Publications
Magazine: Windsock
5150 Candlewood St., Ste. 1
Lakewood, CA 90712-1900
ph: 562-461-7574
fax: 562-461-7212
info@wiseowlmagazines.com
http://www.wiseowlmagazines.com
   *A bi-monthly English publication; the
   journal for WWI aeroplane
   enthusiasts and modelers.*

Challenge Publications, Inc.
Magazine: Air Classics
8381 Canoga Ave.
Canoga Park, CA 91304-2605
ph: 818-760-8983 or 800-562-9182
fax: 818-700-6282
office@challengeweb.com
http://www.challengeweb.com/
airclassics.html
   *Brings you the drama and adventure
   of aviation; read first-hand historical
   accounts by the men who lived them in
   the belly of a B-17 bomber or in the
   cockpit of a P-51 Mustang.*

Magazine: Airpower
P.O. Box 881526
San Diego, CA 92168
aenyedy@millennianet.com
http://www.airpoweronline.com

Magazine: Classic Wings Magazine
P.O. Box 534
Blenheim, New Zealand
admin@classicwings.com
http://classicwings.com
   The only journal dedicated exclusively

to vintage and warbird aeroplanes in
Australia and New Zealand; high
quality publication packed with in-
depth articles, news and superb
photographs.

Races & Meets

Clubs/Associations

Herman Schaub, Sec.
Society of Air Racing Historians
168 Marian Lane
Berea, OH 44017-1566
ph: 440-234-2301
bill@airrace.com
http://www.airrace.com
*Dedicated to preserving air racing
history from 1909 to the present.*

Collectors

Pete Kramer
P.O. Box 52
Glen Ellyn, IL 60138-0052
ph: 630-627-4051
*Wants to buy 1909-1939 aviation meet
and air race programs, posters,
tickets, autographed photos, and
souvenirs.*

AVIATION MEMORABILIA

(see also AIRLINE MEMORABILIA;
AIRPLANES; AVIATION; BADGES;
MILITARIA; MODELS, Aircraft;
POSTCARDS, Aviation Related;
STAMP COLLECTING, Air Mail
Related; TOYS, Airplane Related)

Collectors

Talbert Kanigher
Tal's Nostalgia
P.O. Box 6294
Burbank, CA 91505-6294
ph: 818-848-6469
fax: 818-848-6469
*Collecting aviation memorabilia for
over 30 years: photographs,
programs, autographs, etc.*

Dealers

Tom Heitzman
Stuffinder
P.O. Box 222
Deansboro, NY 13328
ph: 315-841-4444
fax: 315-841-3488
gyro@stuffinder.com
http://www.stuffinder.com
*Buys and sells aviation memorabilia:
original art, scratch-built models,
aircraft/engine sales literature and
photos, postcard, books, magazines
and manuals, airline time tables, crew
insignia, etc., especially pre-1960.*

Frank Cea
Barnstormer Enterprises
3617 Tindall Ct.
Fayetteville, NC 28311
ph: 800-784-1336 pin1999
fax: 910-494-2957
airmodels@barnstormer.net
http://www.barnstormer.net
Buys and sells aviation and model

aircraft items; memorabilia, photos,
magazines, brochures, artifacts,
books, model kits, model motors, race
cars, catalogs, built planes, airline
models and ephemera.

Dan Wells
Dan Wells Antique Toys
P.O. Box 7
Goshen, KY 40026
ph: 502-386-3453
jagdan@aol.com
*Wants to buy all miniature/toy
aircraft, especially travel agency and
factory models.*

Peter DeNevai
20th C. Aviation Collectibles
HC63 Box 5
Duchesne, UT 84021-9701
Pinyon99@yahoo.com
*Buys, sells, trades all manner of
aviation artifacts and publications;
military and civilian; parts,
equipment, uniform items, manuals,
periodicals, books, airline timetables
and handouts, postcards, toys, model
kits, etc.*

Scott Brake
Scott Brake Antiques
17420 Mt. Hermann St., Unit "D"
Fountain Valley, CA 92708
ph: 714-556-8333
fax: 714-556-8333
antiquechi@aol.com
*Specializes in special acquisitions for
entertainment and theme park clients;
prop rentals.*

Experts

Tom Heitzman
Stuffinder
P.O. Box 222
Deansboro, NY 13328
ph: 315-841-4444
fax: 315-841-3488
gyro@stuffinder.com
http://www.stuffinder.com
*Buys and sells aviation memorabilia:
original art, scratch-built models,
aircraft/engine sales literature and
photos, postcard, books, magazines
and manuals, airline time tables, crew
insignia, etc., especially pre-1960.*

Herb Jacobs
P.O. Box 5390
Pompano Beach, FL 33074-5390
ph: 954-943-4213
fax: 954-943-4213
*Buys, sells, appraises and specializes
in aviation memorabilia.*

Russ Huff
P.O. Box 17276
Sarasota, FL 34276-0276
ph: 941-923-3600
russhuff@comcast.net
*Buys, sells and specializes in military
aviation qualification badges of the
world; also other aviation memorabilia.*

Museums/Libraries

Stephen Remington
Museum of Aircraft Recognition
Newsletter: News & Views
1324 De La Vina St
Santa Barbara, CA 93101
ph: 805-560-1323 or 408-828-2810
fax: 805-560-9943
72245.747@compuserve.com
http://www.collectair.com
*Museum dedicated to training aids
used for teaching aircraft identification, primarily during WWII,
including school-built model program.*

Boeing 747

Collectors

Francis Smith
Francis Smith's Boeing 747 Page
213 S. Harrison
Garrett, IN 46738
smitfj01@holmes.ipfw.edu
http://www.geocities.com/
CapeCanaveral/Hangar/4653/
index.htm
*A Boeing 747 enthusiast wants to buy
Boeing 747s memorabilia (especially
the older 747s): 747-related airline
postcards, models, and other
memorabilia (especially from Aer
Lingus, Braniff, Pam Am, and other
old 747 airlines.)*

Civil Air Patrol

Collectors

Andrew Browning
Civil Air Patrol Patch & Insignia
  Collectors Homepage
1622 34St NW
Rochester, MN 55901-1453
http://www.mnwg.cap.gov/cappich
*Collects, trades, buys and sometimes
sells Civil Air Patrol patches and
insignia; will help identify and
research information on Civil Air
Patrol uniform items; can help CAP
patch & insignia collectors get in
contact with each other.*

Helicopters

Collectors

Skip Robinson
18653 Ventura Blvd., #419B
Tarzana, CA 91367
ph: 818-883-9494
*Wants anything related to helicopters:
books, photos, models, manuals, sales
and technical brochures, paper items.*

Military

Clubs/Associations

Steve Eisner
F-4 Phantom II Society
Magazine: Smoke Trails
P.O. Box 8335
Van Nuys, CA 91409-8335
ph: 818-781-9703
fax: 818-781-9618
gibf4@aol.com
http://www.f4phantom.com
Focuses on the F-4 Phantom II;

*"Smoke Trails" is published
quarterly.*

Collectors

David Ostrowski
5411 Masser Lane
Fairfax, VA 22032-3817
ph: 703-323-6674
*Wants to buy military and civilian
aircraft models, ID/recognition
aircraft models, photos/negatives/
slides of military and civilian aircraft.*

Dennis Gordon
1246 N Ave.
Missoula, MT 59801-6602
ph: 406-549-6280
oddpilot@aol.com
*Wants World War I (c. 1914-1918)
aviation items and American
Volunteer items: US and foreign; pilot
log books, I.D. cards, books, photos,
aircraft instruments, souvenir items,
insignia, helmets, uniforms, medals,
documents.*

Dealers

Bob McKowen
215 S. Ace. C
Washington, IA 52353
ph: 319-653-5776
*Specializes in WWII aircraft cockpit
instruments.*

R. "Chad" Le Beau
Aviation Artifacts, Inc.
1213 Sandstone Dr.
Saint Charles, MO 63304-6830
ph: 636-441-2706
fax: 636-447-4071
avnartifacts@mindpsring.com
http://www.aviationartifactsinc.com
*Buys flight gear: flight helmets,
oxygen masks, parachutes, ejection
seats, aircraft parts, instruments.*

Jeff Mark
JMARK
P.O. Box 5178
Santa Monica, CA 90409-5178
ph: 800-644-8537 or 310-396-9767
fax: 310-396-2666
AirForce1944@hotmail.com
*Wants to buy aviation and Air Force
memorabilia 1900-1970: leather
flying, silver wings, medals, helmets,
goggles, documents, photos; also
Wright Brothers, Hindenberg, Amelia
Earhart, Lindbergh, others; all
nations, wars, planes.*

Norm Smith
Aviators World
P.O. Box 608
San Juan Capistrano, CA 92693
ph: 949-240-9606
fax: 949-240-9607
norm@aviatorsworld.com
http://www.aviatorsworld.com
*Buys and sells plane and pilot
collectibles from all eras: air combat,
military, civil, space; issues detailed
illustrated catalog of items for sale
four times each year.*

Military (Nose Art)

(see also PIN-UP ART)

Internet Resources

Gregory David
Bomber Girl
gkd@bombergirl.com
http://www.bombergirl.com
History and many examples of bomber art on this colorful Web site.

Military Insignia

(see also AIRLINE MEMORABILIA, Pilots Wings; MILITARIA; BADGES)

Experts

Russ Huff
P.O. Box 17276
Sarasota, FL 34276-0276
ph: 941-923-3600
russhuff@comcast.net
Buys, sells and specializes in military aviation qualification badges of the world; also other aviation memorabilia.

Models

Dealers

Dixie Aviation Collectibles
P.O. Box 291820
Daytona Beach, FL 32129-1824
ph: 904-763-9994
fax: 904-304-5090
GenDixie@aol.com
http://www.dixieac.com
Sells die-cast, wood, resin & plastic limited edition aircraft models including some hand autographed models; also autographed books specializing in Bob Hoover memorabilia.

Propellers

Dealers

Philip Wallick
Vintage Aeroplane Propellers
P.O. Box 3699
Chico, CA 95927-3699
ph: 530-877-0352
fax: 530-877-0352
wallickphilip@hotmail.com
Buys and sells wooden airplane propellers; original or reconditioned; also offers for sale high quality vintage reproduction propellers for wall decoration and display; write or call for color brochure.

AVON COLLECTIBLES

(see also BOTTLES, Perfume & Scent; CALIFORNIA PERFUME COMPANY)

Clubs/Associations

Connie Clark, Pres.
National Association of Avon Collectors, Inc.
Newsletter: Avon Times
P.O. Box 7006
Kansas City, MO 64113-0006
ph: 816-822-2347
alkmom@msn.com
http://www.icollectavon.com/naac.htm
A national association of Avon collectors; promotes the hobby of Avon collecting; many members clubs throughout the US and Canada; newslettter has buy/sell ads, upcoming shows schedules.

Dealers

Rhonda Schriver
Avon Collector's Lost & Found
7646 Nancy Dr.
Elkridge, MD 21075
ph: 410-799-2881
alkmom@msn.com
http://www.icollectavon.com
Web site where hundreds of collectors gather to buy and sell Avon collectibles.

Anne Thomas
Avon Collectibles
3864 Dollar Circle
Suwanee, GA 30024
ph: 770-271-9492
fax: 770-614-6856
anne@findavon.com
http://www.findavon.com
Great site for Avon collectibles; how to price, NAAV and Avon show information, local Avon collector club info, links to other sites, secure online shopping, free online newsletter; classified ads.

Dwight & Vera Young
P.O. Box 9868
Kansas City, MO 64134-0868
ph: 816-540-3089
fax: 816-540-3089
avontimes@aol.com
http://www.avontimes.com
Buys and sell Avon collectibles.

Vee Manhas
Avon Exclusives
14043 Gulfview Dr.
Nanaimo, BC V9T 6B4 Canada
ph: 800-855-0511 or 250-715-1710
fax: 250-715-1710
avonexclusives6@hotmail.com
http://www.avonexclusives.ontheweb.com
Specializes in vintage and very hard-to-find Avon collectibles; also sells current Avon products.

Experts

Bud Hastin
Hastin Books
P.O. Box 11004
Fort Lauderdale, FL 33339
ph: 954-566-0691
budhastin@hotmail.com
http://www.avonpriceguide.com
Author of "Avon Collectors Encyclopedia - 17th Edition," 640 pages, 6,000 pictures; 1886 to present; lists all Avon products and California Perfume Products (early Avon); all priced with current market value.

Internet Resources

Rhonda Schriver
Avon Collector's Lost & Found
7646 Nancy Dr.
Elkridge, MD 21075
ph: 410-799-2881
alkmom@msn.com
http://www.icollectavon.com
Hundreds of ads from buyers and sellers of all Avon collectibles; browse the ads, contact buyers and sellers online, place your own ad; site updated daily; free current market value look-ups; Avon collectors convention & events information.

Anne Thomas
Avon Collectibles
3864 Dollar Circle
Suwanee, GA 30024
ph: 770-271-9492
fax: 770-614-6856
anne@findavon.com
http://www.findavon.com
Great site for Avon collectibles; how to price, NAAV and Avon show information, local Avon collector club info, links to other sites, secure online shopping, free online newsletter; classified ads.

Periodicals

Dwight & Vera Young
Newsletter: Avon Times
P.O. Box 9868
Kansas City, MO 64134-0868
ph: 816-540-3089
fax: 816-540-3089
avontimes@aol.com
http://www.avontimes.com
A monthly newsletter with international circulation that contains articles, ads, photos, history, convention and show news; buy and sell ads from around the world; devoted strictly to the hobby of Avon collecting.

AWARDS

(see FIREARMS, Shooting Awards; MEDALS, ORDERS & DECORATIONS; PINS, Award)

Here are some tips when contacting someone who is listed in this book:

When requesting information about a particular item, include a description (material, dimensions, maker's mark, model number, etc.) and a photo, sketch, digital image or photocopy of the item in question.

Always ask if there are charges for samples or for the services that you are requesting.

When corresponding by letter, please be sure to include a Large (#10 business size) Self-Addressed and Stamped Envelope (LSASE) if requesting a reply or the return of photographs.

Never call collect unless otherwise directed. When calling, be considerate of time zone differences and always ask if the party you are calling has time to talk. When leaving an answering machine message, always instruct the party to call you back collect.

BABY CARRIAGES

(see CHILDREN'S THINGS; PERAMBULATORS)

BADGES

(see also AUTOMOBILIA; AVIATION MEMORABILIA; FRATERNAL ORGANIZATION ITEMS; MEDALS, ORDERS & DECORATIONS; LAW ENFORCEMENT MEMORABILIA; MILITARIA; AMMUNITION & EXPLOSIVE ORDNANCE, Badges; PATCHES; PINS; SOCIAL CAUSES; TAXI; VETERAN ITEMS)

Collectors

Ken Mitzel
5225 N. George
Manchester, PA 17345-9400
ph: 717-266-2783
Wants to buy Game Warden badges, Fish Warden badges, Forestry badges, Guide badges, Fire Warden badges.

Steve Mizroch
99 Monticello Rd.
San Rafael, CA 94903
Badge collector specializing in California badges: police, fire, taxi, post office, humane society.

Badge Collectors Circle, The
57 Middleton Place
Loughborough
Leicestershire, LE11 2BY U.K.
john@thebadge.co.uk
http://www.thebadge.co.uk
Founded in 1980 for collectors of nonmilitary badges; most members collect enamel and/or button badges.

Chauffeurs

Collectors

George A. Coupe
1243 1st St. S.E.
Washington, DC 20003
ph: 202-554-1000 or 800-368-5466
fax: 202-863-0775
shootthemoonok@webtv.net
Wants to buy chauffeur badges; one or whole collections.

Howard Share
4349 LaVale Ct.
Clemmons, NC 27012-9009
ph: 336-766-6579
fax: 336-766-5445
HowSha43@aol.com
Wants to buy chauffeur or driver license badges, especially from

Southern states and Hawaii; will also trade.

Trent Culp
P.O. Box 550
Misenheimer, NC 28109-0550
ph: 704-463-2857
Collects chauffeurs' badges from all states and all years, especially badges from the Southern states.

Jerome Schaeper, Jr.
365 Meadowlark Dr.
Edgewood, KY 41018-2608
ph: 859-341-3769
Collects and appraises city or state issued driving badges, early Southern badges especially wanted.

Dealers

Walt Feiger
Walt's Antiques
2513 Nelson Rd.
Traverse City, MI 49686-8557
ph: 231-223-7386 or 231-223-4123
feiger@pentel.net
http://www.pentel.net/antiques
Wants to buy Michigan chauffeur badges.

Experts

Dr. Edward H. Miles
888 Eighth Ave.
New York, NY 10019-5704
ph: 212-765-2660
emiles33@aol.com
Editor/publisher "Chauffeurs Badges & Transportation Related Badges of the World" Vol. I N.Y. State & City Badges, Vol. II New England City & State Badges. There is a price guide.

John Connors
3811 Grantley Rd.
Toledo, OH 43613-4218
Author of "Price Guide to American & Canadian Chauffeur Badges."

Employee

Collectors

Gary Wood
733 Myrtle Rd.
North Brunswick, NJ 08902-2549
ph: 732-821-7633
woodrasp@aol.com
Collector seeking "plant badges" with photos; these are pin-back buttons worn by employees; often included a photo of the employee for identification; used primarily 1930s through 1960s; pays $5 to $50 each depending on type.

Douglas W. Tietze
4909 Harter Rd.
Slatington, PA 18080-4318
ph: 610-767-9371
Collects 1920s to 1950s employee badges: oval, round, square; brass, copper, plated steel, plastic; many contain a photograph of the employee.

Federal

Experts

Ken W. Lucas, Sr.
3052 Bel Pre Rd., Apt. 101
Silver Spring, MD 20906-2415
ph: 301-871-0877
Author of "Federal Law Enforcement Badges;" Agriculture, Commerce, Defense, Energy, Health & Human Services, Interior, Park Police, Fish & Wildlife, Indian, Justice, US Marshals, FBI, DEA, Labor, CIA, Postal, Customs, etc.

BAGS

(see AIRLINE MEMORABILIA, Airline Sickness Bags; FEED SACKS; PURSES)

BANANA COLLECTIBLES

Clubs/Associations

L. Ken Bannister, T.B.
International Banana Club
Newsletter: Woddis Newsletter
2524 N. El Molino Ave.
Altadena, CA 91001-2318
ph: 626-798-2272
bananasTB@aol.com
http://www.bananaclub.com
A "fun" humorous club founded in 1972; purpose is to keep people smiling and exercising their sense of humor each day.

Internet Resources

Ann Lovell, Cur.
Banana Museum
ph: 253-833-8043
bananamuseum1@hotmail.com
http://www.bananamuseum.com
Internet virtual museum featuring over 4,000 artifacts representing the world's favorite fruit; includes culture and advertising pieces, original paintings, drawings, photographs and sculptures, antique cookbooks, jewelry, clothing, etc.

Museums/Libraries

L. Ken Bannister, T.B.
International Banana Club Museum
2524 N. El Molino Ave.
Altadena, CA 91001-2318
ph: 626-798-2272
bananasTB@aol.com
http://www.bananaclub.com
More than 17,000 items on display; opened by prearranged appointment only; featured on national TV and magazines.

Stickers

Collectors

George Griffin
P.O. Box 159
Old Town, FL 32680-0159
ph: 352-542-3447
fax: 352-542-3447

BAND ORGANS

(see MUSICAL INSTRUMENTS, Mechanical [Band Organs])

BANKING

(see also COINS & CURRENCY; CREDIT CARDS & CHARGE ITEMS; MONEYCARDS; PAPER COLLECTIBLES; SCRIP; STAMP COLLECTING, Revenue & Tax Stamps; TELEPHONE CARDS; TOKENS; WOODEN MONEY)

Museums/Libraries

Wells Fargo Bank History Museum
2733 San Diego Ave.
San Diego, CA 92110-2731
ph: 619-238-3929
wfh@artmachine.com
http://www.wellsfargohistory.com/museums
Documents the history of Wells Fargo: stories, Western fine art, documents, treasure boxes, stagecoaches, artifacts, early photos, gold coins, mining tools, balance scales, working telegraphs, and more.

Wells Fargo Bank History Museum
420 Montgomery St.
San Francisco, CA 94163
ph: 415-396-2619
wfh@artmachine.com
http://www.wellsfargohistory.com/museums
Documents the history of Wells Fargo: stories, Western fine art, documents, treasure boxes, stagecoaches, artifacts, early photos, gold coins, mining tools, balance scales, working telegraphs, and more.

Bank Checks

Clubs/Associations

Coleman Leifer, Sec.
American Society of Check Collectors
Journal: Check Collector, The
P.O. Box 577
Garrett Park, MD 20896-0577
ph: 301-493-5755
cal493@aol.com
http://members.aol.com/asccinfo
Founded in 1969, ASCC is open to collectors of all types of fiscal paper: engravings, revenue stamps on checks; over 400 members; journal published quarterly.

P. Michael Lord, Esq.
British Cheque Collectors Society
14 Garsdale Rd.
Newsome
Huddersfield, HD4 6QZ U.K.
enquiries@cheque-collectors.co.uk
http://www.cheque-collectors.co.uk
For those interested in collecting classic bank checks.

Collectors

Gary Ronk
6247 Cove Rd.
Roanoke, VA 24019-1715
ph: 540-562-2368
papermemo@aol.com
Wants to buy pre-1900 bank checks, especially those that are illustrated with vignettes or have imprinted revenue stamps.

Dealers

Douglas McDonald
Gypsyfoot Enterprises, Inc.
P.O. Box 5833
Helena, MT 59604
ph: 406-449-8076
gypsyfoot@aol.com
Buys, sells and collects old pre-1902 bank checks, drafts, exchanges, money orders, warrants, etc.; please send photocopies for offer.

Warren Anderson
America West Archives
P.O. Box 100
Cedar City, UT 84721-0100
ph: 435-586-9497 or 435-586-7323
awa@netutah.com
http://www.americawestarchives.com
Buys and sells pre-1910 issued bank checks and other financial papers from the Western US; catalogs issued; author of "Owning Western History."

Periodicals

Stacie Berger
Krause Publications
Newspaper: Bank Note Reporter
700 E. State St.
Iola, WI 54990-0001
ph: 715-445-2214
fax: 715-445-4087
stacie.berger@fwpubs.com
http://www.krause.com
Monthly news source and marketplace for collectors of US and world paper money, notes, checks and related fiscal paper.

BANKS

(see also BANKING; LOCKS; SOUVENIR & COMMEMORATIVE ITEMS, Buildings; STOCKS & BONDS; TOYS)

Appraisers

Diane Patalano
Country Girls Appraisal & Liquidation Service
P.O. Box 376
Saddle River, NJ 07458
ph: 201-327-2499
fax: 20-327-2094
dp@microdsi.net
Bank advisor to "Schroeder's" for over 10 years.

Auction Services

Randy Inman
Randy Inman Auctions, Inc.
P.O. Box 726
West Buxton, ME 04093
ph: 207-872-6900
fax: 207-872-6966
inman@inmanauctions.com
http://www.inmanauctions.com
Conducts specialty auctions for advertising, coin-op, gambling devices, automata, soda pop, Coca Cola, breweriana, robots and space toys, cast iron and tin toys, Disneyana, mechanical music, and mechanical and still banks.

Bertoia Auctions
2141 DeMarco Dr.
Vineland, NJ 08360
ph: 856-692-1881
fax: 856-692-8697
bill@bertoiaauctions.com
http://www.bertoiaauctions.com
Specializing in the auctioning of antique toys, banks, trains, and doorstops; offers online auctions.

Sam Haney
Eden Haney Auction Co.
2686 Green St.
Eden, NY 14057
ph: 716-992-3300
Specializes in the auctioning of toys and banks.

Bob Pierce
Henry Pierce Auctioneers
1525 S. Arcadian Dr.
New Berlin, WI 53151
ph: 262-797-7933
Appraises and auctions still and mechanical banks.

Mike Henry
Henry Pierce Auctioneers
1456 Carson Court
Homewood, IL 60430-4013
ph: 708-798-7508
fax: 708-799-3594
Appraises and auctions still and mechanical banks.

Collectors

George A. Coupe
1243 1st St. S.E.
Washington, DC 20003
ph: 202-554-1000 or 800-368-5466
fax: 202-863-0775
shootthemoonok@webtv.net
Collector looking for old cast iron or tin mechanical banks or toys; will buy one or whole collection; call toll free 24 hours.

Jim Conley
2758 Coventry Lane
Canton, OH 44708-1320
ph: 330-477-7725
fax: 330-879-2950
Very interested in buying mechanical and still banks; OK for sellers to call collect.

Mike Henry
1456 Carson Court
Homewood, IL 60430-4013
ph: 708-798-7508
fax: 708-799-3594
Mechanical and still banks wanted.

Dealers

Bob Brady
Brady Toys & Banks
2341 Woodwick Rd.
Lancaster, PA 17601
ph: 717-569-7408
bobbra@comcast.net
http://www.mechanicalbanks.com
Buys and sells mechanical and still banks; also c. 1900 cast iron toys.

David A. Hull
Small Town Coins & Collectibles
7498 E. Davison Rd.
Davison, MI 48423-2014
ph: 810-658-1992
fax: 810-658-2977
towncoin@small-town.cnchost.com
http://small-town.cnchost.com
Buys and sells still and mechanical cast iron banks.

Experts

Robert L. McCumber
201 Carriage Dr.
Glastonbury, CT 06033-3231
ph: 860-633-4984
Author of several books about toy banks covering repros and fakes, mechanical and still banks, Chein banks, registering banks, building banks, iron safe banks, penny banks, and more.

Sy Schreckinger
P.O. Box 104
East Rockaway, NY 11518-0104
ph: 516-536-4154
fax: 516-596-0004
Buy/sell antique mechanical and still banks: cast iron, tin, wood or lead; also wooden bank shipping boxes, bank trade cards, catalogs, etc.; also wants old photos of children with banks and toys.

Charles Reynolds
Reynolds Toys
2836 Monroe St.
Falls Church, VA 22042-2007
ph: 703-533-1322
reynoldstoys@erols.com
http://www.reynoldstoys.com
Specializes in mechanical and still banks.

Repair Services

Sy Schreckinger
P.O. Box 104
East Rockaway, NY 11518-0104
ph: 516-536-4154
fax: 516-596-0004
Offers professional, museum quality repair, restoration and cleaning of antique iron and tin mechanical and still banks.

Ceramic

Dealers

Carol Silagyi
C.S. Antiques & Jewelry
P.O. Box 151
Wyckoff, NJ 07430
ph: 201-934-6528
csantiques@aol.com
Has collection of over 400 figural ceramic banks; wants to buy cartoon, Disney, ABC, Leeds, McCoy, Japanese, etc.

Glass

Collectors

Jim Crilly
8261 141st St. N.
Seminole, FL 33776-2835
ph: 727-393-7295
jascrilly@aol.com
Wants to buy glass bottle banks - the type with a metal, slotted screw-on cap.

John Honl
P.O. Box 1201
Kailua Kona, HI 96745-1201
ph: 808-325-9905
jhh@kona.net
Wants to buy glass bottle banks including Galaxy Spaceman, Snowcrest seal clown and penguin, administration building, Jumbo peanut butter elephant, Guttuso rabbit, Jocko monkey (prepared mustard), etc.

Experts

Charles Reynolds
Reynolds Toys
2836 Monroe St.
Falls Church, VA 22042-2007
ph: 703-533-1322
reynoldstoys@erols.com
http://www.reynoldstoys.com
Author of "Collector's Guide to Glass Banks - Identification and Values."

Mechanical

Clubs/Associations

Rick Mihlhiem, Sec.
Mechanical Bank Collectors of America
Journal: Mechanical Banker Journal
P.O. Box 13323
Pittsburgh, PA 15234
info@mechanicalbanks.org
http://www.mechanicalbanks.org
For collectors of antique mechanical banks; journal published three times per year.

Dealers

Harry R. McKeon, Jr.
18 Rose Lane
Flourtown, PA 19031-1910
ph: 215-233-4094
toyspost@aol.com
Interested in purchasing mechanical banks; send photo.

Paris Pierce
Mechanical Bank Zone
1701 Addison St.
Philadelphia, PA 19146-1516
ph: 215-546-2017 or 215-557-0400
fax: 215-557-6433
paris@pond.com
http://www.pond.com/~paris/
bankzone.htm
*Collector, dealer, expert in mechanical
banks (1930 to modern); first online
Mechanical Bank Museum and
collectors' Web site.*

Stephen Steckbeck
200 W. Superior St.
Fort Wayne, IN 46802
ph: 219-625-3537
*Buys, sells and appraises old
mechanical banks.*

David Markarian
P.O. Box 2476
Rancho Mirage, CA 92270-1087
ph: 760-202-5000
orion@inland.net
http://www.mechanicalbanks.net
*Wants to buy old cast iron mechanical
banks; member of the Mechanical bank
Collectors of America.*

Experts

Mark Suozzi
P.O. Box 102
Ashfield, MA 01330
ph: 413-628-3241
fax: 413-628-3241
marklyn@valinet.com
http://www.marklynantiques.com
*Antique penny banks, 1-cent arcade
machines, advertising signs, folk art,
political flags 1840 to 1912,
clockwork toys.*

Leon M. Weiss
Gemini Antiques Ltd.
P.O. Box 1752
2418 Montauk Highway
Water Mill, NY 11976
ph: 631-537-4565 or 212-316-6380
fax: 631-726-9366
julgert@geminiantiques.com
http://www.geminiantiques.com
*Buys and sells mechanical still banks,
cast iron toys, door stops, folk art and
more.*

James S. Maxwell, Jr.
P.O. Box 367
Lampeter, PA 17537
ph: 717-464-5573 or 717-464-5572
*Advisor to "Warman's Antiques &
Collectibles Price Guide."*

Paris Pierce
Mechanical Bank Zone
1701 Addison St.
Philadelphia, PA 19146-1516
ph: 215-546-2017 or 215-557-0400
fax: 215-557-6433
paris@pond.com
http://www.pond.com/~paris/
bankzone.htm
*Collector, dealer, expert in mechanical
banks (1930 to modern); first online*

*Mechanical Bank Museum and
collectors' Web site.*

Dr. Greg Zemenick
Dr. "Z"
1350 Kirts, Ste. 160
Troy, MI 48084-4852
ph: 248-642-8129 or 248-244-9430
fax: 248-244-9495
drzzeezz@aol.com
http://www.drzzeezzi.com
*Buys, sells, brokers and specializes in
mechanical banks, any condition or
completeness; wooden or cardboard
packing boxes; trade cards, catalogs;
also bell toys; member ATCA, MBCA,
SBCA and others.*

Repro. Sources

Charles Reynolds
Reynolds Toys
2836 Monroe St.
Falls Church, VA 22042-2007
ph: 703-533-1322
reynoldstoys@erols.com
http://www.reynoldstoys.com
*Offers limited editions of new original
penny banks, of sand-cast aluminum;
political, holiday and event themes;
over 100 editions produced from 1970-
1990.*

Oil Can (Miniature)
Collectors

Peter Capell
1838 West Grace St.
Chicago, IL 60613-2724
ph: 773-871-8735
pcapell@cometlink.com
*Wants tin or tin with paper label
miniature oil can banks produced as
promotional giveaways for gasoline
and motor oil dealers.*

Registering
Collectors

Stanley D. Watson
2959 Hundred Oaks Ave.
Baton Rouge, LA 70808-1536
ph: 225-383-1594
*Collector of antique registering banks
(US mfg. only) by Durable Toy, Hoge,
Kingsbury, Shonk, and other early
manufacturers.*

Experts

Robert L. McCumber
201 Carriage Dr.
Glastonbury, CT 06033-3231
ph: 860-633-4984
*Author of "Registering Banks;"
registering banks (e.g. pocket tube
banks) show amount as coins are
deposit.*

Rocket/Space
Collectors

Anthony Glab
6708 Duluth Ave.
Baltimore, MD 21222-1011
ph: 410-633-5354
z.zz@verizon.net
*Wants to buy rocket/space banks in
mint condition by Astro Mfg.*

Safe Shaped
Collectors

Larry Egelhoff
4175 Millersville Rd.
Indianapolis, IN 46205-2966
ph: 317-846-7228
egelhoffl@juno.com
Collector and appraiser.

Still
Clubs/Associations

Larry Egelhoff, Mem.
Still Bank Collectors Club of America
Newsletter: Penny Bank Post
4175 Millersville Rd.
Indianapolis, IN 46205-2966
ph: 317-846-7228
egelhoffl@juno.com
http://www.stillbankclub.com
*To stimulate knowledge of, interest in,
and the collection of antique and
contemporary still banks and, further,
within the limits of friendly rivalry, to
assist members in adding to and
enhancing the value of their
collections.*

Collectors

Harry Ward
153 Scott Ave.
Bloomsburg, PA 17815-1020
ph: 570-784-3946
hlward@sunlink.net

Tom Kellogg
6125 Rockdale Lane
Sylvania, OH 43560-3644
ph: 419-885-5562
fax: 419-261-1988
ironbanks@aol.com
*Wants to buy still banks in the form of
buildings; also wants other forms of
still and mechanical banks.*

Dealers

Mike Henry
1456 Carson Court
Homewood, IL 60430-4013
ph: 708-798-7508
fax: 708-799-3594
Buys and sells still banks.

Experts

Leon M. Weiss
Gemini Antiques Ltd.
P.O. Box 1752
2418 Montauk Highway
Water Mill, NY 11976
ph: 631-537-4565 or 212-316-6380
fax: 631-726-9366
julgert@geminiantiques.com
http://www.geminiantiques.com
*Buys and sells mechanical still banks,
cast iron toys, door stops, folk art and
more.*

Repro. Sources

Charles Reynolds
Reynolds Toys
2836 Monroe St.
Falls Church, VA 22042-2007
ph: 703-533-1322
reynoldstoys@erols.com
http://www.reynoldstoys.com
*Offers limited editions of new original
still banks of sand-cast aluminum;
political, holiday, and event themes;
flyer on request.*

BANKS (MODERN)

(see also TOYS, Diecast)

Dealers

Kathy & Walter Easterbrook
Eastco Banks & Collectibles
P.O. Box 412
Hancock, NY 13783-0412
ph: 607-467-3040
weastco@hancock.net
http://www.hancock.net/~weastco
*Diecast banks and toys: Ertl, Spec-
Cast, First Gear, plastic gas station
promotions.*

Art & Judy Turner
Homestead Collectibles
P.O. Box 173
Mill Hall, PA 17751
ph: 570-726-3597
jturner@cub.kcnet.org
*Specializing in diecast metal banks
and airplane banks; over 3,200
different banks in stock; send $1 for
price list.*

Toy Collector Club of America
1235 16th Ave. Court SW
Dyersville, IA 52040
ph: 800-452-3303 or 563-875-9263
fax: 563-875-8056
pkerker@speccast.com
http://www.toycollectorclub.com
*For collectors of contemporary diecast
banks and vehicles; gives collectors the
opportunity to purchase diecast metal
banks; newsletter lists what is
available for purchase and discounts
on products; a Spec-Cast company
sponsored club.*

Experts

Richard L. Heuser
Heuser Publishing Div. of Heuser
　Enterprises
508 Clapson Rd.
P.O. Box 300
West Winfield, NY 13491-0300
ph: 315-822-4804
fax: 315-822-4804
toybanks@heuser.com
http://www.heuser.com
　Buys, collects, appraises and
　specializes in modern collectible toy
　banks and diecast toys.

Periodicals

Richard L. Heuser
Heuser Publishing Div. of Heuser
　Enterprises
Price Guide: Heuser's Price Guide to
　Official Collectible Banks
508 Clapson Rd.
P.O. Box 300
West Winfield, NY 13491-0300
ph: 315-822-4804
fax: 315-822-4804
toybanks@heuser.com
http://www.heuser.com
　Quarterly price guide features Ertl,
　First Gear, Liberty Classics, Spec
　Cast, Action Racing Collectibles,
　Gearbox, Crown Premium/Vees
　Collectibles, DG Productions and
　others; listed by name, no., quantity,
　color, year made and value.

Richard L. Heuser
Heuser Publishing Div. of Heuser
　Enterprises
Newsletter: Heuser's Quarterly
　Collectible Diecast Newsletter
508 Clapson Rd.
P.O. Box 300
West Winfield, NY 13491-0300
ph: 315-822-4804
fax: 315-822-4804
toybanks@heuser.com
http://www.heuser.com
　Focuses on modern diecast collectible
　banks and custom imprinted replicas;
　new issues; articles of interest to
　collectors; listing of dealers and
　manufacturers; listing of upcoming toy
　shows.

BAR COLLECTIBLES

(see SALOON & BAR
COLLECTIBLES)

BARBED WIRE

(see also FENCE COLLECTIBLES)

Clubs/Associations

Dan & Nancy Sowle
New Mexico Barbed Wire Collectors
　Association
Newsletter: Wire Barb & Nail
P.O. Box 102
Stanley, NM 87056-0102
ph: 505-832-4339 or 505-832-2552
fax: 505-832-2552
nsowle@aol.com

John Mantz
American Barbed Wire Collectors
　Society
Newsletter: Wire Collector News
1023 Baldwin Rd.
Bakersfield, CA 93304-4203
ph: 805-397-9572
fax: 805-831-3491
　The only national association for
　collectors of barbed wire and
　associated fencing tools.

Collectors

Bill Prain
129 West Homewood Ct.
Genoa, IL 60135-1134
ph: 815-784-2663
billp@tbcnet.com
　Collects, trades barbed wire and
　barbed wire related items including
　barbed wire liniment bottles.

L. W. Love
1520 N. Buckner
Dallas, TX 75218
wirefence@att.net
　Wants advertising, salesman samples,
　and patent models related to barbed
　wire, fence tools and farm gates;
　prefers pre-1900 items.

Experts

Charles & Rosie Dalton
1322 Lark
Lewisville, TX 75067-7606
ph: 972-317-7999
crtoyz@msn.com
　Buys, sells, collects and auctions
　barbed wire; authors of "Pocket Book
　of Wires."

John Mantz
1023 Baldwin Rd.
Bakersfield, CA 93304-4203
ph: 805-397-9572
fax: 805-831-3491

Museums/Libraries

Director
Kansas Barbed Wire Museum
120 West 1st St.
La Crosse, KS 67548
ph: 785-222-9900
rced@gbta.net
http://www.rushcounty.org/
　BarbedWireMuseum
　Exhibit includes thousands of
　examples of barbed wire plus related
　tools.

M.J. VanDeventer
National Cowboy & Western Heritage
　Museum
Magazine: Persimmon Hill
1700 N.E. 63rd St.
Oklahoma City, OK 73111-7906
ph: 405-478-2250
fax: 405-478-4714
info@nationalcowboymuseum.org
http://www.nationalcowboymuseum.org
　Preserves the rich heritage of the Old
　West and honors both deceased and
　living people who have made positive
　contributions to the heritage of the
　West; collections include barbed wire,
　Western art, fashion, guns & gun
　leather, more.

Delbert Trew, Dir.
Devil's Rope Museum
Magazine: Barbed Wire Collector
100 Kingsley St.
P.O. Box 290
Mclean, TX 79057-0290
ph: 806-779-2225 or 806-779-3164
barbwiremuseum@centramedia.net
http://www.barbwiremuseum.com
　Largest barbed wire collection in the
　world; over 14,000 sq. ft. with over
　6,000 artifacts on display; stocks and
　publishes books on barbed wire; hosts
　2-day Barbed Wire Collectors Show
　annually in April.

Barbed Wire Museum
116 S. Cuyler
Pampa, TX 79065
ph: 806-665-5521

BARBERSHOP COLLECTIBLES

(see also BEAUTY SHOP
COLLECTIBLES; BOTTLES, Barber;
HAIRWORK; SHAVING
COLLECTIBLES)

Auction Services

James Hagenbuch
Glass Works Auctions
P.O. Box 180
102 Jefferson St.
East Greenville, PA 18041
ph: 215-679-5849
fax: 215-679-3068
glswrk@enter.net
http://www.glswrk-auction.com
　Specializes in the auction of historical
　flasks, fruit jars, food & milk bottles,
　sodas, poisons, whiskeys, medicines,
　inks, barber bottles, bitters bottles,
　scent bottles, shaving mugs, target &
　range balls, etc.

Tony Nard
Nard Auctions
U.S. Rte. 220
Milan, PA 18831
ph: 570-888-9404
fax: 570-888-7723
　Conducts specialized auctions of
　occupational shaving mugs, barber
　bottles, razors, country store and
　advertising items, etc.

Clubs/Associations

Penny Nader
National Shaving Mug Collectors
　Association
Newsletter: Barbershop Collectibles
　Newsletter
320 S. Glenwood St.
Allentown, PA 18104-6529
ph: 610-437-2534
info@nsmca.org
http://www.nsmca.org
　Mission is to stimulate the study of
　shaving mugs, razors, barber bottles,
　and all related barbering items.

Collectors

Burton Handelsman
18 Hotel Dr.
White Plains, NY 10605-3531
ph: 914-428-4480
fax: 914-428-2145
　Wants to buy shaving mugs,
　personalized barber bottles decorated
　with glass labels, barbershop photos
　and related catalogs.

Mike Griffin
11 Walton Ave.
White Plains, NY 10606-3212
ph: 914-949-7041
　Buys early shaving mugs, occupational
　shaving mugs, barber bottles, signs,
　old barber photos; editor of the
　"National Shaving Mug Collectors
　Association Newsletter."

Bill Campesi
P.O. Box 140
Merrick, NY 11566-0140
ph: 516-546-9630
　Collector of straight razors, especially
　fancy handles; also wants related
　trade catalogs, advertising, show
　cases, postcards, etc.

D. Perkins
6335 W. 62nd St.
Indianapolis, IN 46278-1906
ph: 317-293-9962
　Wants fancy backbars, mugs, cabinets,
　shaving mugs with names and scenes,
　handpainted barber bottles, shave
　paper, vases, signs, shop photos,
　wooden chairs, salesman sample
　chairs, and child chairs, etc.

Dealers

Chris Jones
Barbershop Museum, The
1800 Route 33
Hamilton Square, NJ 08690
ph: 609-261-4258 or 609-584-2600
fax: 609-261-4258
barbrpole@aol.com
　Buys, sells, appraises general
　Barberiana: signs, tools, backbar
　items, bleeding/cupping and leeching
　utensils, furniture, etc.

Sigmund Wohl
Razor's Edge, The
P.O. Box 429
Bronxville, NY 10708-0429
ph: 914-476-5939
fax:914-376-4160
sigwohl@optonline.net
*Buys and sells barber and shaving
collectibles, fancy and unusual razors,
and related advertising.*

Jo Havens-Wright
Wright Enterprises
610 N. Delaware Ave.
Roswell, NM 88201-2135
ph: 505-623-8053
johavens@dfn.com
http://www.dfn.com/~johavens
Collector of barbershop items.

Experts

Chris Jones
Barbershop Museum, The
1800 Route 33
Hamilton Square, NJ 08690
ph: 609-261-4258 or 609-584-2600
fax:609-261-4258
barbrpole@aol.com
*Educational lectures, slide presenta-
tions, stage and movie prop rentals;
also does appraisals of barbershop
and shaving antiques.*

Museums/Libraries

Lester Dequaine, Dir.
National Shaving & Barbershop Museum
39 West Main St.
Meriden, CT 06451-4110
ph: 203-639-9778
fax:203-235-7025
shaving-bshopmuseum@snet.net
*Displays barbershop and shaving
furnishings and artifacts with on-site
theater, sidewalk cafe, and museum
store which buys and sells related
collectibles and books including razor
blade bank price guide.*

Chris Jones
Barbershop Museum, The
1800 Route 33
Hamilton Square, NJ 08690
ph: 609-261-4258 or 609-584-2600
fax:609-261-4258
barbrpole@aol.com
*Over 3,000 items of barbering/shaving
history documenting the subject from
the stone age to present; highlights
include complete, working 1896
barbershop; tours available by
appointment only.*

Edwin Jeffers
Barber Museum, The
2-1/2 S. High St.
Canal Winchester, OH 43110-1213
ph: 614-833-9931
*Collection includes straight razors,
599 shaving mugs, 58 barber poles,
wooden chairs, bloodletting tools, etc.*

Barber Poles
Book Sellers

Robert Marvy
William Marvy Company
1540 St. Clair Ave.
Saint Paul, MN 55105-2344
ph: 651-698-0726 or 800-874-2651
fax: 651-698-4048
scott@wmmarvyco.com
http://www.wmmarvyco.com
*Manufactures barber poles and
replacement parts: domes, motors,
glass and paper cylinders, etc.; also
sells barbershop books.*

Dealers

Mike Pniewski
antiquefreak@socal.rr.com
*Barber pole expert, dealer, collector;
buys, sells, trades barber poles and
parts; incomplete, broken, rusty; also
wants related barber pole catalogs
and photos.*

Suppliers

Robert Marvy
William Marvy Company
1540 St. Clair Ave.
Saint Paul, MN 55105-2344
ph: 651-698-0726 or 800-874-2651
fax: 651-698-4048
scott@wmmarvyco.com
http://www.wmmarvyco.com
*Manufactures barber poles and
replacement parts: domes, motors,
glass and paper cylinders, etc.; also
sells barbershop books.*

Furnishings
Collectors

Joel Scheckner
15 Glendale Dr.
Englishtown, NJ 07726
ph: 732-462-3827
*Wants to buy barbershop contents:
wooden barber chairs, child's chairs,
salesman samples, barber poles, mug
racks, shoeshine stands, backbars, etc.*

Shaving Mugs
Clubs/Associations

Penny Nader
National Shaving Mug Collectors
Association
Newsletter: Barbershop Collectibles
Newsletter
320 S. Glenwood St.
Allentown, PA 18104-6529
ph: 610-437-2534
info@nsmca.org
http://www.nsmca.org
*Mission is to stimulate the study of
shaving mugs, razors, barber bottles,
and all related barbering items.*

Collectors

Lester Dequaine
155 Brewster St.
Bridgeport, CT 06605-3149
ph: 203-335-6833
shaving-bshopmuseum@snet.net
Wants to buy shaving mugs in figural

*shapes of animals, humans, birds;
also shaving brushes with handles in
figural shapes; also early safety
razors, mechanical blade sharpeners,
razor blade banks, and related
advertisements.*

Joseph Albanese
70 Loretta Dr.
Torrington, CT 06790-5914
ph: 860-482-1854
jcl.albanese@juno.com
*Buys, collects shaving mugs:
occupational, fraternal, and
photographical; also wants to buy
interior and exterior photographs of
barbershops.*

Edward J. Meschi
129 Pinyard Rd.
Monroeville, NJ 08343-1870
ph: 856-358-7293
fax: 856-358-7789
ed@meschiarts.com
http://www.meschiarts.com
*Wants to buy occupational shaving
mugs.*

Mike Griffin
11 Walton Ave.
White Plains, NY 10606-3212
ph: 914-949-7041
*Buys early shaving mugs, occupational
shaving mugs, barber bottles, signs,
old barber photos; editor of the
"National Shaving Mug Collectors
Association Newsletter."*

Ralph Nix
P.O. Box 655
Red Bay, AL 35582-0655
ph: 256-356-2997
*Wants old, personalized shaving mugs
including Occupational and Fraternal
mugs.*

Morris Pickerell, Jr.
100 A. Lyon Ave.
Glasgow, KY 42141
ph: 270-678-5848 or 270-783-3124
fax: 270-678-7888
*Wants to buy occupational, fraternal,
and decorative shaving mugs.*

Richard Hebel
233 Dietrich Crescent Dr.
Lawrenceburg, IN 47025-1576
ph: 812-537-0150
bhebel@seidata.com
*Interested in occupational shaving
mugs, especially those that are
railroad related.*

John Bellew
15243 Profit Ave.
Baton Rouge, LA 70817
ph: 225-756-4875 or 225-342-2624
fax: 225-342-5066
framewall@cox.net
http://www.geocities.com/Vienna/9014
*Buys all types of antique shaving
mugs, especially those personalized
with the mug owner's name and/or
pictures, emblems, designs, etc.;
damaged mugs considered.*

Experts

Burton Handelsman
18 Hotel Dr.
White Plains, NY 10605-3531
ph: 914-428-4480
fax:914-428-2145
*Buys and sells occupational shaving
mugs and personalized barber bottles;
author of the "Shaving Mugs" section
in the Time-Life "Encyclopedia of
Collectibles" series.*

Museums/Libraries

Atwater Kent Museum of Philadelphia
15 S. 7th St.
Philadelphia, PA 19106
ph: 215-685-4830
fax:215-685-4937
http://www.philadelphiahistory.org
*Founded in 1938 by radio pioneer A.
Atwater Kent.*

Lightner Museum
P.O. Box 334
75 King St.
Saint Augustine, FL 32085
ph: 904-824-2874
info@lightnermuseum.org
http://www.lightnermuseum.org
*Exhibits relics of America's Gilded
Age: cut glass, Victorian art glass,
stained glass of Tiffany, costumes,
furnishings, mechanical musical
instruments, and other artifacts that
give a glimpse into 19th century daily
life*

BAROMETERS

(see also INSTRUMENTS &
DEVICES, Scientific)

Collectors

Paul H. Hayashi, PE
18 Tarabrook Dr.
Orinda, CA 94563-3121
ph: 925-254-5074 or 925-253-1038
fax: 925-253-0592
Wants to buy old stick barometers.

Dealers

C. Neville Lewis
Neville Antiques
576 Pleasant Pt. Rd.
Cushing, ME 04563
ph: 207-354-8055
fax: 207-354-2687
barometershop@earthlink.net
http://www.barometershop.net
*Sells fully restored and operating
antique English and American
barometers: banjo or wheel, stick,
marine, aneroid, pocket, barographs;
also offers barometer repairs and
restorations.*

Jill & Chuck Probst
Charles Edwin Antiques
P.O. Box 1340
Louisa, VA 23093-1340
ph: 540-967-0416
fax: 540-967-0416
info@charlesedwin.com
http://www.charlesedwin.com
Buys, sells mercury barometers only.

Bob Elsner
Heights Antiques
29 Clubhouse Ln.
Boynton Beach, FL 33436-6056
ph: 561-736-1362
fax: 561-736-1914
rjelsner@aol.com
Barometer expert who buys, sells, appraises and repairs all types of barometers: gimbaled, mercury, aneroid, altimeters, barographs; antique and reproduction.

David Lee
Clockworks, Inc., The
560 N. Western Ave.
Lake Forest, IL 60045-1920
ph: 847-234-7272
fax: 847-234-7286
davidlee@theclockworks.com
http://www.theclockworks.com
Buy, sell, repair, restore clocks, watches, barometers and music boxes.

Don Levison
Don Levison Antiques
P.O. Box 22262
San Francisco, CA 94122
ph: 415-753-0455
fax: 415-753-5206
dlevison@juno.com
http://www.antiquehorology.com
Buys and sells antique and better quality pocket and wrist watches, clocks, music boxes, singing birds, and other small automata; also mercury barometers from the 17th century to present.

Experts

Jill & Chuck Probst
Charles Edwin Antiques
P.O. Box 1340
Louisa, VA 23093-1340
ph: 540-967-0416
fax: 540-967-0416
info@charlesedwin.com
http://www.charlesedwin.com
Buys, sells mercury barometers only.

John Forster
Barometer Fair
P.O. Box 25502
Sarasota, FL 34277
ph: 941-923-6136
fax: 941-923-6136
john@barometerfair.com
Buys, sells, restores all antique barometers; also deals in antique maps, globes, compasses, telescopes and other scientific instruments.

Repair Services

C. Neville Lewis
Neville Antiques
576 Pleasant Pt. Rd.
Cushing, ME 04563
ph: 207-354-8055
fax: 207-354-2687
barometershop@earthlink.net
http://www.barometershop.net
Sells fully restored and operating antique English and American barometers: banjo or wheel, stick, marine, aneroid, pocket, barographs; also offers barometer repairs and restorations.

Jim Mulhern
Medford Clock Shop
3 Union St.
Medford, NJ 08055
ph: 609-953-0014
fax: 609-953-0411
medclock@aol.com
http://www.medfordclock.com
Specializes in the repair of all types of antique clocks; also antique mercury and aneroid barometers repaired and restored; mercury barometer tubes made to fit old barometers.

Bob Elsner
Heights Antiques
29 Clubhouse Ln.
Boynton Beach, FL 33436-6056
ph: 561-736-1362
fax: 561-736-1914
rjelsner@aol.com
Barometer expert who buys, sells, appraises and repairs all types of barometers: gimbaled, mercury, aneroid, altimeters, barographs; antique and reproduction.

David Lee
Clockworks, Inc., The
560 N. Western Ave.
Lake Forest, IL 60045-1920
ph: 847-234-7272
fax: 847-234-7286
davidlee@theclockworks.com
http://www.theclockworks.com
Buy, sell, repair, restore clocks, watches, barometers (mercury and aneroid) and music boxes.

BARS

(see BREWERIANA)

BARWARE

(see SALOON & BAR COLLECTIBLES)

BASEBALL CAPS

(see CAPS)

BASKETS

(see also NATIVE AMERICAN; CRAFTS, Basketry; KITCHEN COLLECTIBLES; REPAIR/ RESTORATION/CONSERVATION, Cane & Basketry)

Internet Resources

WeaveNet
P.O. Box 67
Warner, NH 03278-0067
ph: 603-938-2137
peter@83j.com
http://www.weavenet.com
This Web site provides a complete source of basketry, weaving and caning information; restoration supplies, ash strips, chair cane, dyes, patterns, raffia, seagrass, weaving guilds and associations, etc.

Museums/Libraries

Old Salem Inc.
P.O. Box F
Salem Station
Winston Salem, NC 27108-0346
ph: 336-721-7300 or 888-653-7253
fax: 336-721-7335
webmaster@oldsalem.org
http://www.oldsalem.org
Old Salem, a living history town, is a repository of era baskets and other collection items from the late 1700s and early 1800s.

Repro. Sources

Stephen Zeh
Stephen Zeh, Basketmaker
Newsletter: News From the Basket Shop
P.O. Box 381
Temple, ME 04984-0381
ph: 207-778-2351
fax: 207-778-6439
zehbaskt@somtel.com
Handcrafted brown ash splint baskets in the tradition of Maine woodsmen, Shakers, and the Native American basket makers; portfolio $10.

Darryl & Karen Arawjo
P.O. Box 477
Bushkill, PA 18324-0477
ph: 570-588-6957
Reproduction of Nantucket, Shaker and Appalachian baskets in hand-split white oak; brochure available.

Longaberger

Auction Services

Greg Michael
Craft & Michael Auctioneers
P.O. Box 7
Camden, IN 46917-0007
ph: 219-686-2615 or 219-967-4442
fax: 219-686-9100
Conducts periodic basket auctions.

Internet Resources

Brett Rabideau
Basket Collector's Emporium, The
P.O. Box 16722
West Haven, CT 06516
baskets@basketcollector.com
http://www.basketcollector.com
Secondary market for Longaberger baskets, accessories and pottery; buys, sells, auctions.

Suzy Metzler
Newsletter: Basket Collector's Gazette, The
P.O. Box 100
Pitkin, CO 81241-0100
ph: 970-641-5838
fax: 970-641-2624
suzy@basketlover.com
http://www.basketlover.com
A monthly newsletter designed for avid collectors of Longaberger baskets, ideas, recipes; free Longaberger buy/ sell/swap ads for subscribers; newsletter posted online as well.

Man./Prod./Dist.

Longaberger
webmaster@longaberger.com
http://www.longaberger.com

Periodicals

Suzy Metzler
Newsletter: Basket Collector's Gazette, The
P.O. Box 100
Pitkin, CO 81241-0100
ph: 970-641-5838
fax: 970-641-2624
suzy@basketlover.com
http://www.basketlover.com
A monthly newsletter designed for avid collectors of Longaberger baskets, ideas, recipes; free Longaberger buy/ sell/swap ads for subscribers; newsletter posted online as well.

BATHING BEAUTIES

Nudies & Naughties

(see also EROTICA)

Collectors

Virginia Youngren
111 Temple St.
West Newton, MA 02465-2313
ph: 617-244-6144
fax: 617-244-5689
youngren@earthlink.net
Wants to buy witty Victoria bisque figurines, especially naughties and nudies.

BATHROOM FIXTURES

(see PLUMBING)

BATTERSEA ENAMEL BOXES

(see BOXES, Enamel [Battersea]; ENAMELS)

BAUHAUS

(see MODERNISM)

BAYONETS

(see also ARMS & ARMOR; FIREARMS; MILITARIA; SWORDS; KNIVES; MILITARIA)

Clubs/Associations

John Spangler, Sec.
Society of American Bayonet Collectors, The
P.O. Box 711282
Salt Lake City, UT 84171
ph: 801-947-9442
jmholm@whidbey.com
http://www.amerbayo.org
An organization for collectors of bayonets made or used in the US.

Mery Christian
Association of French Bayonet Collectors
Newsletter: Baionette
France
ph: 03 80 29 82 30
fax: 03 80 29 82 30
christian.mery@wanadoo.fr
http://perso.wanadoo.fr/christian.mery
Web site is in English and French.

Collectors

Derek Complin
ph: 613-547-9595
fax: 613-549-2528
derekc@kingston.net
http://www.cybertap.com/brothers/derek-2.htm
Over 30 years collecting bayonets; interests focus on all British and British Commonwealth bayonets, and plug bayonets from any country; buys, sells and trades.

Shawn K. Gibson
Bayonet Connection, The
1 Gibson Dr.
Graford, TX 76449
ph: 904-779-2461
fax: 940-779-3376
shawn@bayonets.com
http://www.bayonets.com
Buys and sells rare bayonets; collects pre-1850 and toy bayonets from any era.

Jerrey Hayes
12 Crawford Rd.
Hatfield, Hertfordshire AL10 OPG U.K.
ph: 0410 095027
Collector of world bayonets of all types, from plug bayonets to current issue.

Dealers

Ron Riede
Bayonet Trader
841 S. River Rd.
Naperville, IL 60540
ph: 630-357-6779
driver@wideopenwest.com
http://www.bayonetsonline.com
Web site has many bayonets for sale;

also examples of bayonet styles from various periods.

Shawn K. Gibson
Bayonet Connection, The
1 Gibson Dr.
Graford, TX 76449
ph: 904-779-2461
fax: 940-779-3376
shawn@bayonets.com
http://www.bayonets.com
Buys and sells rare bayonets; collects pre-1850 and toy bayonets from any era.

Experts

Jim Maddox
Maddox Collection, The
34 East 50th St.
Savannah, GA 31405
http://www.geocities.com/Pentagon/6591
Bayonet collector for over 38 years; Web site features "The Maddox Collection" and posts six featured bayonets at all times with frequent updates; also Wants List and For Sale List and links; will identify and appraise unknown items.

Internet Resources

Bayonet Collector's Network
mconrad@donet.com
http://www.donet.com/~mconrad/bcn.htm
Comprehensive Web site for collectors of SG 84/98 Mod. III bayonets, German militaria, Imperial, Weimer, and other German era bayonets.

BEADS

(see also NATIVE AMERICAN; GEMS & JEWELRY; PURSES)

Clubs/Associations

Peter Francis, Jr.
Center for Bead Research
Newsletter: Margaretologist, The
4 Essex St.
Lake Placid, NY 12946-1236
ph: 518-523-1794
pfjr@northnet.org
http://www.thebeadsite.com
The New York Times calls Mr. Francis "the world's leading authority on beads." The Center is internationally known for its work: research; publications, workshops, lectures, tours, Web site; devoted to all kinds of beads.

Bead Society of Greater Washington
P.O. Box 70036
Bethesda, MD 20813-0036
ph: 202-462-8933 or 301-656-9255
bsgw@erols.com
http://www.bsgw.org
Monthly meetings featuring slide-illustrated lectures, how-to workshops about beads and related topics; newsletter five times a year with articles on bead research, travel,

collecting, bead bazaars, bead books for sale, etc.

Baltimore Bead Society, The
P.O. Box 311
Riderwood, MD 21139-0311
wheat@craftwolf.com
http://www.craftwolf.com/baltbd01.htm

Michelle Tomaselli
Palm Beach Bead Society
Newsletter: Bead Gazette
5416 Cleveland Rd.
Delray Beach, FL 33484
ph: 561-969-3291
krafty_3@hotmail.com
http://www.gopbi.com/community/groups/pbbeadsociety
Holds monthly meetings; membership includes monthly newsletter, discount at local bead stores; free listing including photos of beadwork and society Web sites.

Judith Schwab
Bead Society of Greater Chicago
Newsletter: BSGC Newsletter
P.O. Box 8103
Wilmette, IL 60091-8103
ph: 312-458-0519 or 847-699-7959
fax: 847-699-7959
info@bsgc.org
http://www.bsgc.org
Offers members monthly slide lectures and workshops.

Chicago Midwest Bead Society
Newsletter: Chicago Midwest Bead Society Newsletter
1511 Sherman Ave.
Evanston, IL 60201-4416
ph: 847-328-4040
info@aylasoriginals.com
http://www.aylasoriginals.com/CMBS.html
Focuses on glass, organic and metal beads and beadwork from ancient to contemporary; workshops, speakers, bazaar.

Austin Bead Society
P.O. Box 656
Austin, TX 78767-0656
info@austinbeadsociety.org
http://www.austinbeadsociety.org
Object of society is to promote education and research regarding beads and bead-related subjects, and to provide support to bead collectors, designers, and enthusiasts.

Kohler Dena
Bead Society of Orange County, The
Bowers Museum of Cultural Art, The
2002 North Main St.
Santa Ana, CA 92706
ph: 714-828-8468
Main goal is to provide an educational resource in the artistic, historical, and intercultural significance of beads; supports The Bowers Museum of Cultural Art, including fund raising and volunteer support of Museum programs.

Northern California Bead Society
Newsletter: Northern California Bead Society Bulletin
P.O. Box 22128
Oakland, CA 94623-2128
ph: 510-869-2723
http://www.norcalbead.org
Dedicated to the study of beads; meetings have lecture slide presentations; members wear beads pertaining to the announced meeting topic; major annual sale open to the public.

Alice Scherer, Dir.
Center for the Study of Beadwork
Newsletter: Notes From a Beadworker's Journal
P.O. Box 13719
Portland, OR 97213-0719
ph: 503-657-0583
fax: 503-657-0583
alice@europa.com
http://www.europa.com/~alice
Purpose is to gather and disseminate information on beadwork; maintains a study collection, library, articles file, and slide bank; quarterly newsletter.

Lester A. Ross
Society of Bead Researchers
Journal: Bead Forum, The
P.O. Box 7304
Eugene, OR 97401
larinc@mindspring.com
http://www.mindspring.com/~larinc/sbr/index
Formed in 1981 to foster research on beads of all materials and periods; membership is open to all.

Dealers

Rita Perloff
Remember When Vintage
355 Summer St.
Bristol, NH 03222
ph: 603-744-2191
rewhen@tias.com
http://www.tias.com/stores/rewhen
Offers a wide selection of vintage Bohemian glass beads and pre-WWII Bohemian pressed glass Egyptian Revival pieces for use in jewelry design.

Barbara VanDusen
Bishop's Gambit
3210 Dover Rd.
Pompano Beach, FL 33062
Makes, collects and sells glass beads and jewelry; collects glass beads and Victorian jewelry; recycles broken necklaces for the glass beads and components; sells beads (vintage and new lampwork), costume jewelry, and buttons.

Ayla's Originals
1511 Sherman Ave.
Evanston, IL 60201-4416
ph: 847-328-4040
info@aylasoriginals.com
http://www.aylasoriginals.com/CMBS.html
Buys and sells a wide selection of beads and components for designing

and collecting; also design and repair of beaded jewelry.

Christina Blessing
Lost Cities
2802 Juan St., #14
San Diego, CA 92110
ph: 800-525-3053 or 619-692-1114
fax: 619-692-0841
Sells old unusual beads: coral, Tibetan, turquoise, amber.

Simma Chester
Simma Chester
805 Fourth St., #2
San Rafael, CA 94901
ph: 415-459-4131
fax: 415-459-4131
simma@simmachester.com
http://www.simmachester.com
Beads, supplies, jewelry; custom design, restringing, knotting.

Experts

Peter Francis, Jr.
Center for Bead Research
4 Essex St.
Lake Placid, NY 12946-1236
ph: 518-523-1794
pfjr@northnet.org
http://www.thebeadsite.com
The New York Times calls Mr. Francis "the world's leading authority on beads."

Judy Kovl
JuDeSigns
P.O. Box 99006
Troy, MI 48099-9066
ph: 248-680-8860
Beadwork expert.

Man./Prod./Dist.

Lucinda Brown
Cindybeads
6240 Everett Court #C
Arvada, CO 80004
ph: 303-423-1616
cindy@cindybeads.com
http://www.cindybeads.com
Makes glass beads lovingly by hand.

Museums/Libraries

Corning Museum of Glass, The
Journal: Journal of Glass Studies
One Museum Way
Corning, NY 14830-2253
ph: 607-937-5371
fax: 607-937-3352
pr@cmog.org
http://www.cmog.org
Over 35,000 glass objects, innovative exhibits, videos, models; glass history, archaeology, and early manufacturing; great Web site with lots of information about glass.

National Museum of the American Indian
470 L'Enfant Plaza, SW, Ste. 7102
Washington, DC 20560
ph: 301-238-6624
NIN@ic.si.edu
http://www.si.edu/nmai
The museum will open on the Mall in Washington, DC, in the year 2002, on a site between the National Air & Space Museum and the US Capitol; will be a center for exhibitions, ceremonies, performances, and educational activities

Bead Museum, The
5754 W. Glenn Dr.
Glendale, AZ 85301
ph: 623-931-2737
fax: 623-930-8561
info@thebeadmuseum.com
http://www.thebeadmuseum.com
Collects, preserves, identifies, documents and exhibits beads, ornaments and related artifacts used in personal adornment from ancient, ethnic and contemporary cultures, covering all periods of history; store features beads, supplies, etc.

Periodicals

Kalmbach Publishing Co.
Magazine: Bead & Button
P.O. Box 1612
21027 Crossroads Circle
Waukesha, WI 53187
ph: 262-796-8776 or 800-446-5489
fax: 262-796-1615
web@beadandbutton.com
http://www2.beadandbutton.com/beadbutton
Dedicated to helping all bead and button enthusiasts with creative projects and providing collectible information; how-to projects, beading tips and techniques, historical articles.

Repair Services

LaVerne Larson, GG (GIA)
Gemological & Appraisal Services
1120 E. Mead Dr.
Chandler, AZ 85249
ph: 480-802-8092
l-m-larson-gg@worldnet.att.net
Restrings pearl and bead jewelry: necklaces, bracelets, etc.

Suppliers

Gampel Supply Corp.
11 West 37th St.
New York, NY 10018-6235
ph: 212-398-9222
fax: 212-575-0931
Bead work and jewelry making supplies.

John & Jaqueline Foutz
550 Silver & Supply
4187 US Highway 64
Kirtland, NM 87417
ph: 505-598-5322
fax: 505-598-0974
sales@beadsource.com
http://www.beadsource.com
Supplies metal and bead crafters with the finest possible jewelry supplies, tools, materials and services: sterling silver, .999 fine silver, silver filled, 14k gold, gold filled, nickel, copper, red and yellow brass, bead supplies, etc.

Barry
Berger Specialty Company
413 E. 8th St.
Los Angeles, CA 90014-2301
ph: 213-627-8785
fax: 213-680-9743
Bergers@earthlink.net
Mail order OK.

BEAM BOTTLES

(see DECANTERS, Figural Whiskey [Beam])

BEATLES

(see PERSONALITIES [MUSICIANS], Beatles)

BEAUTY SHOP COLLECTIBLES

(see also HAIRWORK)

Collectors

Michael Warner
Hair Archives, The
P.O. Box 1003
Portage, MI 49024
mwarner@hairarchives.com
http://www.hairarchives.com
Buys and sells vintage hairdressing collectibles including trade magazines, posters, advertising graphics primarily from the 1920s to 1970s.

BEEKEEPING MEMORABILIA

Collectors

John O. Burgess
10738 Harley Rd.
Lorton, VA 22079-3908
ph: 703-339-5359
Wants to buy beekeeping memorabilia especially glass honey containers.

BEER CAN OPENERS

(see CAN OPENERS)

BEER CANS

(see also BREWERIANA)

Clubs/Associations

Frank Loevi
Gambrinus Stein Club
Newsletter: Gambrinus Gazette
16011 Jerald Rd.
Laurel, MD 20707-2653
fjl@beerstein.net
http://www.beerstein.net/gambrinus/gambrinus.htm
For more than 25 years has been bringing stein collectors from D.C., MD, and VA together; sponsors annual breweriana show; a chapter of Stein Collectors International (SCI).

Don Hicks
Beer Can Collectors of America
Newsletter: Beer Can Collectors News
747 Merus Court
Fenton, MO 63026-2092
ph: 636-343-6486
fax: 636-343-6486
bcca@bcca.com
http://www.bcca.com/index.html
A not-for-profit organization founded in 1974; over 4,000 members worldwide who share an interest in brewery history and/or collect beer cans and other breweriana; also publishes the "BCCA Want Ad Bulletin" newsletter.

Collectors

John Gruskin
P.O. Box 53
Northport, NY 11768
ph: 516-262-0338
jlgruskin@aol.com
http://www.angelfire.com/ny/beerstuff
Beer can collector and expert; has over 10,000 beer cans in his collection.

Frank Munshower
355 W. 8th Ave.
Tarentum, PA 15084
Wants to buy straight steel tab tops, flat tops, and cone tops; member of The Olde Frothingslosh Chapter of the BCCA.

Steve Gordon
P.O. Box 632
Olney, MD 20830-0632
ph: 301-996-4666
fax: 772-264-3292
steve@beercanman.com
http://www.beercanman.com
Wants to buy pre-1960s US cans, especially conetops and flat tops; will answer any letter or call promptly; also will consider other beer-related items such as signs, trays, coasters, etc.; single item or entire collection.

Dick Caughey
324 Fawn Lake Dr.
P.O. Box 607
Millington, TN 38053
ph: 901-876-3117
Wants to buy cone top soda and beer cans; also buying older brewery lithographs and signs.

Jerry Glader
1017 Villa Gran Way
Fenton, MO 63026
ph: 636-343-9433
Collects one beer can from every country and one from every state; also collects one beer label and one beer crown (cap) from every country.

Don Hicks
747 Merus Court
Fenton, MO 63026-2092
ph: 636-343-6486
fax: 636-343-6486
bcca@bcca.com
http://www.bcca.com/index.html

Jim Stille
7463 Augusta Dr.
Boulder, CO 80301
ph: 303-530-4596
Seeks old beer cans that are in good condition: cone tops as well as old flat tops (the ones that need a can opener).

Dealers

Dan Morean
www.breweriana.com
13 Greenleaf St.
Malden, MA 02148
ph: 781-324-3330
danm@breweriana.com
http://www.breweriana.com
Buys, sells, trades old beer cans and brewery advertising.

Paul Ash
Ash's Beer Cans & Breweriana
1295 Caudle St.
Orlando, FL 32828
ph: 407-568-4220
bluesdude@cfl.rr.com
http://www.angelfire.com/biz2/beercans
Appraiser, dealer, collector and specialist in American 12 oz. beer cans; free appraisals; buys and sells better beer can collections; specializes in opening instruction flat top and cone top cans.

Art LaComb
Art's Beer Cans
3208 Parkwood Dr.
Flower Mound, TX 75022
ph: 972-539-9820
jazbo@concentric.net
http://www.concentric.net/~jazbo/beercans.htm
Offers an extensive list of top grade cone top, flat top, and pull tab beer cans; always looking to purchase cone top and flat top beer cans in excellent condition.

Dan Scoglietti
Beer Cans at Canmandanland
7201 Torin Dr. NE
Albuquerque, NM 87122
ph: 505-798-9328
canmandan1@yahoo.com
http://www.usbeercans.com
Wants to buy old beer cans and other breweriana items.

Experts

Allan Aprea
24 Chestnut Rd.
Chatham, NJ 07928-1120
ph: 973-635-6099
ajaprea@pica.army.mil
Collector, appraiser, expert specializing in US and Canadian 12 oz. beer cans as well as other forms of breweriana (signs, lights, etc.) from the G. Krueger Brewery of Newark, NJ and the Trommer's Brewery of Brooklyn, NY & Orange, NJ.

Museums/Libraries

Museum of Beverage Containers & Advertising, The
1055 Ridgecrest Dr.
Goodlettsville, TN 37072
ph: 615-859-5236 or 800-826-4929
fax: 615-859-5238
mbca@gono.com
http://www.gono.com/vir-mus/museum.htm
The largest collection of soda and beer cans in the world; buy, sell, trade beer & soda advertising items; also cleans rust from old beer cans.

Suppliers

Soda Mart - Can World
1055 Ridgecrest Dr.
Goodlettsville, TN 37072
ph: 615-859-5236 or 800-826-4929
fax: 615-859-5238
mbca@gono.com
http://www.gono.com/vir-mus/museum.htm
Sells breweriana books; also cleans and de-rusts on cans, and sells supplies for the beer can collector.

BEER RELATED COLLECTIBLES

(see BEER CANS; BREWERIANA; STEINS)

BEER STEINS

(see STEINS)

BELIEVE IT OR NOT! COLLECTIBLES

(see RIPLEY'S BELIEVE IT OR NOT!)

BELLS

Clubs/Associations

Bob Bamford
American Bell Association
Magazine: Bell Tower, The
P.O. Box 19443
Indianapolis, IN 46219-0443
ph: 210-674-1814
coordinator@americanbell.org
http://www.americanbell.org
Over 1,700 members with 48 chapters worldwide; serves as the primary source for expertise regarding all types of bells, ranging from old to new and large to small; the bimonthly magazine features news, announcements, bell articles.

Collectors

George A. Coupe
1243 1st St. S.E.
Washington, DC 20003
ph: 202-554-1000 or 800-368-5466
fax: 202-863-0775
shootthemoonok@webtv.net
Wants unusual bells, tap bells, figural, but no bells with handles.

Arlene R. Foreman
4841 Springline Dr.
Fort Myers, FL 33919
ph: 239-433-4662
arforeman@comcast.net
Wants to buy brass bells shaped as women with clapper inside skirt area.

Don Mathews
3215 Garner Ave.
Ames, IA 50010-4225
ph: 515-232-0938
Wants to buy metal, figural and figurine bells; needs descriptions, photos and asking price.

Kay Weaver
7210 Bellbrook Dr.
San Antonio, TX 78227-1002
ph: 210-674-1814
aba-kay@earthlink.net
Member of the American Bell Association (ABA), which is composed of over 1,500 bell collectors worldwide.

Dealers

Bob Brosamer
Brosamer's Bells
207 Irwin St.
Brooklyn, MI 49230-9282
ph: 517-592-9030 or 888-592-3557
fax: 517-592-4511
sales@brosamersbells.com
http://www.brosamersbells.com
Advertises as the largest dealer of pre-owned bronze and cast iron bells, mostly from churches, railroads and ships.

Suppliers

Smucker's Harness Shop
2014 Main St.
Narvon, PA 17555
ph: 717-445-5956
fax: 717-445-7752
sales@smuckersharness.com
http://www.smuckersharness.com
Carries complete line of leather working supplies including solid brass and plated brass bells for harnesses and decorative purposes.

BELT BUCKLES

(see also CLOTHING & ACCESSORIES, Vintage; CUFF LINKS)

John Deere

Clubs/Associations

John Cooklin
International Association of John Deere Buckle Collectors
14 Forest Rd.
Rock Island, IL 61201-6140
ph: 309-786-9747
fax: 309-786-0392
jmcooklin@aol.com

Collectors

John Cooklin
14 Forest Rd.
Rock Island, IL 61201-6140
ph: 309-786-9747
fax: 309-786-0392
jmcooklin@aol.com
Primarily involved with John Deere buckles, both issued by Deere and self-designed and self-produced; also other John Deere items.

BERMUDA COLLECTIBLES

Collectors

Ernest M. Roberts
5 Corsa St.
Huntington Station, NY 11746-6607
ph: 631-586-1462
eroberts@optonline.com
Wants pre-1950 postcards, covers, hotel stationery, maps, prints, old books, photographs, and other paper ephemera relating to Bermuda; old plates, mugs, cups, silver spoons and all tourist trinkets from Bermuda.

BIBLES

(see also BOOKS; RELIGIOUS COLLECTIBLES, Holy Cards)

Clubs/Associations

William J. Chamberlin, V.P.
International Society of Bible Collectors
Magazine: Bible Collector's World
6413 Snow Apple Dr.
Clarkston, MI 48346-2455
ph: 248-620-0962
research87@yahoo.com
http://www.abebooks.com/home/BMRFBOOKS

Dealers

Phil Barber
Historic Newspapers & Early Imprints
P.O. Box 8694
Boston, MA 02114-0036
ph: 617-492-4653
fax: 617-868-1534
philb@historicpages.com
http://www.historicpages.com
Buying and selling fine paper collectibles since 1979; specializes in historic newspapers from the period 1775 to 1865; also early Bible leaves, and ephemera dating 1440 to 1940.

Experts

William J. Chamberlin
Bible Museum & Biblical Research
 Foundation
6413 Snow Apple Dr.
Clarkston, MI 48346-2455
ph: 248-620-0962
research87@yahoo.com
http://www.abebooks.com/home/
 BMRFBOOKS
*Considered the Midwest's authority on
English translations of the Bible;
author of "Catalogue of English Bible
Translations" (Westport, Connecticut: Greenwood Press, 1991); still in
print.*

Museums/Libraries

American Bible Society Library
Magazine: Record
1865 Broadway
New York, NY 10023-7505
ph: 800-32-BIBLE
info@americanbible.org
http://www.americanbible.org
*Collection of nearly 50,000 bibles,
testaments, and scripture portions in
approximately 2,000 languages,
dating from the 15th c.*

Repair Services

David Westmoreland
Atwater Book & Bible Repair
1782 McSwain Rd.
Merced, CA 95340
ph: 209-631-6830 or 209-722-9076
atwaterbookandbiblerepair@juno.com
*Specializes in the repair of older
family bibles, both large and small;
also old cookbooks and dictionaries;
all work done by hand and comes with
two year guarantee; in business since
1980.*

BICYCLES & RELATED MEMORABILIA

(see also RIDING TOYS)

Auction Services

Michael Fallon
Copake Auction, Inc.
P.O. Box H, 266 Rt. 7A
Copake, NY 12516
ph: 518-329-1142
fax: 518-329-3369
info@copakeauction.com
http://www.copakeauction.com
*Conducts auctions specializing in the
sale of Americana, period furniture,
folk art, collectibles and classic
bicycles.*

Clubs/Associations

H. Hoene
Wheelmen, The
Magazine: Wheelmen Magazine, The
14 Mulford Lane
Montclair, NJ 07042-1719
heyyou@heyneon.com
http://www.thewheelmen.org
A club with about 800 members

*dedicated to the enjoyment and
preservation of our bicycle heritage.*

Jody Newman, Ex. Dir.
League of American Bicyclists
Magazine: Bicycle USA
1612 K St., NW
Washington, DC 20006
ph: 202-822-1333
fax: 202-822-1334
bikexec@aol.com
http://www.bikeleague.org
*Bicycle advocacy, bicycle safety
promotion, schedules bike events;
many antique bike collectors as well
as replica builders; newsletter has
frequent articles about antique bikes.*

Robert B. Balcomb, Past-Pres.
International Veteran Cycle Association
Newsletter: Veteran Cyclist, The
248 Highland Dr.
Findlay, OH 45840-1207
ph: 419-423-2760
bobalcomb@aol.com
*International umbrella organization
for national clubs of bicycle
collectors, historians, enthusiasts;
promotes the heritage of the bicycle;
focuses on pre-1918 bicycles.*

Scott McCaskey
Vintage Bicycle Club of America
2501 California Lane
Dalworthington Gardens, TX 76015
sm2501@aol.com
http://www.thecabe.com
*Formed to promote the preservation
and restoration of classic and antique
American bicycles made from 1917 to
present.*

Juan DeLeon
Vintage Bicycle Club of Texas
202 Wickhamford Way
Houston, TX 77015
ph: 713-330-9073 or 713-241-0478
vbcoft@argolink.net
http://users.argolink.net/vbcoft
*A club for vintage bicycle collectors
and enthusiasts; monthly newsletter
for members; chapters in Houston and
Arlington.*

Collectors

Wayne R. Batten
303 Landing St.
Lumberton, NJ 08048
ph: 609-267-5953 or 609-714-9495
fax: 609-267-2477
*Serious collector interested in buying
antique bicycles, related memorabilia,
or related items pertaining to antique
bicycles: advertisements, tools, parts,
clocks, trophies, steins, figurines,
photos, lights, etc.*

Eric Berthiaume
Classic Bike Works
14 Independence Row
Stillwater, NY 12170
ph: 518-664-1212
oldbikes@nycap.rr.com
*Buys, sells, restores antique & classic
bicycles from 1870 to 1975; including
Schwinn Stingrays; also wants bicycle*

*related ephemera from 1870s through
1990.*

Ron Klaus
35769 Simon Dr.
Clinton Township, MI 48035
ph: 810-791-5594

Dealers

Donald Paquette
BikeIcons
3 Grove Circle
Saco, ME 04072
ph: 207-282-7336 or 207-282-4910
fax: 207-770-4455
ride@bikeicons.com
http://www.bikeicons.com
*Buys, sells, trades, appraises and
restores antique & classic bicycles;
want to buy old bicycles, parts &
collections.*

Village Schwinn Shop
606 New Rd.
Somers Point, NJ 08244
ph: 609-927-3775

Eric Berthiaume
Classic Bike Works
14 Independence Row
Stillwater, NY 12170
ph: 518-664-1212
oldbikes@nycap.rr.com
*Buys, sells, restores antique & classic
bicycles from 1870 to 1975; including
Schwinn Stingrays; also wants bicycle
related ephemera from 1870s through
1990.*

Jeff Archer
First Flight Bicycles
216 S. Center St.
Statesville, NC 28677
ph: 704-878-9683
fax: 704-878-9689
jeff@firstflightbikes.com
http://www.firstflightbikes.com
*Collector, dealer specializes in the
buying, selling, trading, restoring of
antique and vintage bicycles; bikes as
well as parts are listed on Web site.*

David Waters
Bikes For Us
121 N. Kerns Dr.
Gulfport, MS 39503
ph: 228-832-6333
rdozier@sos.state.ms.us
http://www.angelfire.com/mi/
 antiquebikes
*Specializes in buying, selling and
repairing vintage and classic bicycles.*

Keith Murdock
Keith's Bikes
keithm@boulder.earthnet.net
http://www.keithsbikes.com
*Buys and sells antique bicycles
including Schwinn, Roadmaster,
Shelby, Huffman, Dayton, Elgin,
Sting-Ray and others.*

Rusty Spokes
1344 Garnet Ave.
San Diego, CA 92109
ph: 858-581-1931
fax: 501-421-3124
rustyspokes1@yahoo.com
http://www.rusty-spokes.com
Buys, sells, restores vintage bicycles.

Fat Tire Trading Post
P.O. Box 783
Fairfax, CA 94978
ph: 415-455-9659
*Vintage bicycles for sale, bike repair,
fat tire trading museum, links, and
more.*

Experts

Carl & Clarice Burgwardt
Pedaling History Bicycle Museum
3943 North Buffalo Rd.
Orchard Park, NY 14127-1841
ph: 716-662-3853
fax: 716-662-4594
BicycleMus@aol.com
http://www.pedalinghistory.com
*Experts on vintage American bicycles:
identification, appraisal, restoration,
American bicycle history.*

Lorne Shields
Vintage Cycling
2315 Whirlpool St., Ste. 218
Niagara Falls, NY 14305
ph: 905-886-6911
fax: 905-886-7748
vintage-antique@rogers.com
*Buys, sells, appraises, consults on
cycling and related historical objects;
generally 1817 through 1950s; Expert
for Schroeder's Antiques; bicycles,
related ephemera, memorabilia such
as clocks, trophies, bells, lamps,
parts, books, etc.*

Jerry Peters
Chestnut Hollow, Ltd.
6060 Bordman Rd.
P.O. Box 6
Almont, MI 48003-0006
ph: 810-798-3158
jpeters@expression.org
*Largest collector of classic bicycles in
the US with over 1,000; free museum/
showroom with 300 of rarest and
finest bicycles; issues catalog of parts
and accessories for sale ($6); offers
free bicycle identification service.*

Leon Dixon
P.O. Box 28242
Santa Ana, CA 92799-8242
ph: 714-647-1949
Oldbicycle@aol.com
http://members.aol.com/oldbicycle
*Wants old deluxe, streamlined (1920-
1965) bicycles, bicycle literature,
memorabilia, catalogs, parts, etc.;
curator of the National Bicycle
History Archive; makes personal
appearances with slide shows, old
movies etc. on bicycles.*

Internet Resources

Menotomy Vintage Bicycles
P.O. Box 2864
Acton, MA 01720
Menotomy@aol.com
http://www.oldroads.com
Lots on online information: collector reference books, discussion areas, old maps and pictures, bicycles for sale, parts, literature, etc.

Scott McCaskey
Classic & Antique Bicycle Exchange
2501 California Lane
Dalworthington Gardens, TX 76015
sm2501@aol.com
http://www.thecabe.com
America's largest circulation and longest continually published newsletter for collectors of vintage American-made bicycles.

Museums/Libraries

Carl & Clarice Burgwardt
Pedaling History Bicycle Museum
3943 North Buffalo Rd.
Orchard Park, NY 14127-1841
ph: 716-662-3853
fax: 716-662-4594
BicycleMus@aol.com
http://www.pedalinghistory.com
Contains a sizable collection of bicycles and related items such as carbide & kerosene lamps, photographs, advertising & nearly 100 antique steins; will help with research or appraisals.

Jerry Peters
Chestnut Hollow, Ltd.
6060 Bordman Rd.
P.O. Box 6
Almont, MI 48003-0006
ph: 810-798-3158
jpeters@expression.org
Largest collector of classic bicycles in the US with over 1,000; free museum/ showroom with 300 of rarest and finest bicycles; issues catalog of parts and accessories for sale ($6); offers free bicycle identification service.

Leon Dixon, Curator
National Bicycle History Archive
P.O. Box 28242
Santa Ana, CA 92799-8242
ph: 714-647-1949
Oldbicycle@aol.com
http://members.aol.com/oldbicycle
NBHA performs research on old bicycles and bicycle history; archive includes in excess of 30,000 original catalogs, movies, photos, advertisements, books, etc.; each research based on fee which varies according to services needed.

Periodicals

Scott McCaskey
Directory: N. A. Dir. of Vintage Bicycle
  Dealers & Collectors
2501 California Lane
Dalworthington Gardens, TX 76015
sm2501@aol.com
http://www.thecabe.com
Listing phone numbers and addresses of people in the hobby.

Kevin Barnard, Webmaster
Newsletter: Bicycle Trader, The
510 Frederick
San Francisco, CA 94117
ph: 415-876-1999 or 415-564-2304
fax: 415-876-4507
info@bicycletrader.com
http://www.bicycletrader.com

Repair Services

John Bogan
Bogan Restoration Services
ph: 972-445-4800
fax: 972-445-8207
jbogan@mindspring.com
http://www.mindspring.com/~dagmara/
  deere.html
Buys, sells, restores vintage bicycles, pedal cars, toys and metalware.

Donald Paquette
BikeIcons
3 Grove Circle
Saco, ME 04072
ph: 207-282-7336 or 207-282-4910
fax: 207-770-4455
ride@bikeicons.com
http://www.bikeicons.com
Buys, sells, trades, appraises and restores antique & classic bicycles; wants to buy old bicycles, parts & collections.

David Waters
Bikes For Us
121 N. Kerns Dr.
Gulfport, MS 39503
ph: 228-832-6333
rdozier@sos.state.ms.us
http://www.angelfire.com/mi/
  antiquebikes
Specializes in buying, selling and repairing vintage and classic bicycles.

Juan DeLeon
DeLeon's Restoration
202 Wickhamford Way
Houston, TX 77015
ph: 713-330-9073
juan@bikevato.com
http://www.bikevato.com
Restores vintage bicycles as well as pedal vehicles.

Repro. Sources

Clayton Smith
Aero-Fast Industries
P.O. Box 3812
1730 Westcott St.
Jacksonville, FL 32206
ph: 800-656-2376 or 904-354-3339
fax: 904-354-3488
info@aerofast.com
http://www.aerofast.com
Makes reproductions of vintage bicycles from the 1950s; in the bicycle business since 1944; uses frames, forks, tanks, and chain guards all produced on site and not purchased or imported from other vendors.

Rideable Bicycle Replicas
2329 Eagle Ave.
Alameda, CA 94501
ph: 510-523-2347
hiwheel@barrongroup.com
http://www.hiwheel.com
Makes replica bone shakers and penny farthing bicycles.

Suppliers

Larry Busch
Memory Lane Classics
12551 Jefferson St.
Perrysburg, OH 43551
ph: 419-874-4501
info@memorylane-classics.com
http://www.memorylane-classics.com
Publishes a catalog of old and reproduction parts for sale; also published the "Bicycle Blue Book" which lists current prices for vintage bikes.

Golden Era Bikes
26448 Rialto
Madison Heights, MI 48071
ph: 248-546-0842
Carries a wide variety of reproduction parts for vintage bicycles.

Maple Island Sales
153 SE 1st Lane
Lamar, MO 64759
ph: 417-682-6655
fax: 417-682-6656
sales@mapleislandsales.com
http://www.mapleislandsales.com
Carries a wide variety of reproduction parts for vintage bicycles.

Bikes-R-Us
P.O. Box 5065
Bossier City, LA 71171-5065
Supplier of parts for vintage bicycles; fully illustrated 60-page catalog for $7.50.

License Plates

Collectors

James C. Case
10189 Crane Rd.
Lindley, NY 14858-9719
ph: 607-524-6606
hftlicense@aol.com
http://hometown.aol.com/hftlicense/
  myhomepage/profile.html
Wants pre-1920 sidepath tags (early bike licenses) from all states but especially New York.

Schwinn

Dealers

Tom & Ric Gentilella
Bike Guys, The
29 Ramgren Rd.
Lunenburg, MA 01462
ph: 619-422-2305
fax: 619-422-2305
tombikeguy@net1plus.com
http://www.chulavistaschwinn.com
Collectors, dealers, appraisers, experts in Schwinn bicycles; since 1947.

BILLIARD RELATED ITEMS

Collectors

Tim Lawrence
2489 Bexford Place
Columbus, OH 43209-1710
ph: 614-235-9472
Wants to buy billiard and pool tables, magazines, books, ivory balls, catalogs, art, old prints, billiard cigarette cards and postcards, antique cues and cue racks, and all other billiard related collectibles; pool table expert.

Dealers

Ed Lanza
Lanza Billiard Co.
209 W. Evesham Ave.
Magnolia, NJ 08049-1351
ph: 609-346-0384 or 800-290-7665
fax: 609-346-0048
pal_08086@yahoo.com
http://www.lanzabilliards.com
Antique billiard and pool table accessories.

Paul Giammatteo
Yesteryear Billiards
509 Woodlawn Ave.
Newark, DE 19711-5537
ph: 302-453-8788 or 302-453-8823
fax: 302-454-1550
Dealer and appraiser of antique pool and billiard tables, pool room accessories: cues, chairs, lights, catalogs, trade catalogs, books, ephemera, and related memorabilia; also does restoration of old pool tables.

Brad Morris
New Deco, Inc.
23123 Sunfield Dr.
Boca Raton, FL 33433
ph: 800-543-3326 or 561-488-8841
fax: 561-488-9743
newdeco@mindspring.com
http://www.newdeco.com
Specializes in antique pool and billiard memorabilia including books, advertisements, movie items, pool tables, cue sticks, chalks, billiard catalogs, autographs, postcards, etc.; also sells reproductions including posters, photos, etc.

Mark Stellinga
Flyin' Lion Antiques
416 Sierra Trail
Coralville, IA 52241-1124
ph: 319-354-7287
billiard@avalon.net
http://www.billiard-antiques.com
*Buys, sells, trades Victorian tables,
antique cues, ball racks, lights, ivory
balls, and related collectibles and
accessories; 26 years in business.*

Steven Sawyer
Billiard Warehouse
103 Hardaman Ave.
South Saint Paul, MN 55075
ph: 800-422-7665 or 651-455-1150
fax: 651-455-1150
*Wants pool and billiard items: old
catalogs, books, posters, letterhead,
racks, balls, cues, or anything billiard
related.*

Al Schwinghammer
Antique Billiard Tables & Accessories
3735 18th St. South
Saint Cloud, MN 56301
ph: 320-259-0294
antiquebilliards@msn.com
http://www.AntiqueBilliardTables.com
*Features the finest in antique billiards
restorations; 19th century Brunswick
tables and rare accessories; cue racks,
ball racks, lights, chalk holders, ivory
balls, catalogs, etc.*

Simpson Ltd.
140 S. Seminary St.
Galesburg, IL 61401-4805
ph: 309-342-5800
fax: 309-342-5730
simpsonltd@gallatinriver.net
http://www.simpsonltd.com
*Author of "Blue Book on Pool Cues;"
want to buy old cues, cue racks, pool
tables, old sets of ivory balls in boxes,
old pool hall photos or prints,
billiard trophies and medals -
anything old that relates to pool or
billiards.*

Walt Baxley
Be-Bop Jukeboxes & Gameroom
  Goodies
4804 Mesquite St.
Flowerwood, TX 75028
ph: 972-724-1791
fax: 972-355-1541
wbax1@msn.com
http://www.trinicom.com/bebop
*Southwest's largest retailer of antique
and collectible jukeboxes, pool tables,
and other gameroom items; sales,
service, restoration, and party rentals.*

Dan M. Jacobson
P.O. Box 277101
Sacramento, CA 95827-7101
*Wants to buy pool hall, billiard,
snooker, and related advertising
material.*

Experts

Ken Hash
Classic Billiards
4334 Chapel Rd.
Perry Hall, MD 21128
ph: 410-391-3333
CBilliards@aol.com
http://www.classicpool.com
*Buys, sells, appraises and specializes
in antique pool tables or related
items; also offers repair/restoration/
conservation services.*

Periodicals

Sports Publications Ltd.
Magazine: Pool & Billiard Magazine
810 Travelers Blvd., #D
Summerville, SC 29485
ph: 843-875-5115 or 888-766-5624
fax: 843-875-5171
shari@poolmag.com
http://www.poolmag.com
*Monthly magazine serving the sports
industry and its participants; some
articles feature antique and collectible
tables and other equipment and
related memorabilia.*

Repair Services

Edward O'Connell
Time After Time
5 Padanaran Rd.
Danbury, CT 06811-4835
ph: 203-743-2801
tatpool2@snet.net
http://www.tatpool.com
*Wants pool tables, cues and
accessories; sells museum quality
antique pocket billiard tables;
complete restoration service.*

Al Schwinghammer
Antique Billiard Tables & Accessories
3735 18th St. South
Saint Cloud, MN 56301
ph: 320-259-0294
antiquebilliards@msn.com
http://www.AntiqueBilliardTables.com
*Features the finest in antique billiards
restorations; 19th century Brunswick
tables and rare accessories; cue racks,
ball racks, lights, chalk holders, ivory
balls, catalogs, etc.*

BILLIKENS

Collectors

Belva Green
90 Highland Ave., #1204
Tarpon Springs, FL 34689-5351
ph: 727-942-7354
*Collecting anything Billikens, Royal
Order of Jesters (ROJ): jewelry,
figurines (ivory or other material),
toys; old or new; query with SASE.*

BINOCULARS

(see also OPTICAL ITEMS)

Clubs/Associations

Owen Cashman
International Binocular Collectors
  Association
P.O. Box 601114
San Diego, CA 92160-1114
ph: 619-287-9860
owen@deutscheoptik.com

Experts

William M. Beacom
Quality Binoculars
2423 Jackson St.
Sioux City, IA 51104-3548
ph: 712-255-3412
fax: 712-255-0844
*Wants binoculars of all types, foreign
and domestic; can identify and
appraise; also does repairs on some
models or will buy any and all for
parts.*

BIRD DECOYS

(see DECOYS, Waterfowl)

BIRD'S-EYE-MAPLE

Collectors

Norwood H. Keeney, III
P.O. Box 1026
Georges Mills, NH 03751-1026
ph: 603-763-9157
acer@webryders.com
*Wants items made from bird's-eye-
maple, any period; also wants
information about this wood and its
use; photos encouraged.*

BIRTH RELATED ITEMS

(see also PERSONALITIES
[Famous], Dionne Quintuplets)

Museums/Libraries

"Miss Helen" Kirk
Multiple Birth Museum
P.O. Box 254
Galveston, TX 77553-0254
ph: 409-762-4792
*Interested in anything related to any
multiple births (triplets and above).*

BISQUE

(see CERAMICS, Bisque;
CERAMICS [AMERICAN
PRODUCTION ARTWARE],
American Bisque Company)

BLACK MEMORABILIA

(see also AFRICAN & TRIBAL ART;
ART, African-American;
CHARACTER COLLECTIBLES,
Uncle Remus; CIVIL WAR
ARTIFACTS; COLLECTIBLES
[MODERN], Black Related; DOLLS,
Black; MOVIE MEMORABILIA, Movie
Posters [Black]; SLAVERY ITEMS)

Appraisers

Philip J. Merrill
Nanny Jack & Co., Inc.
5005 Edmondson Ave.
Baltimore, MD 21229
ph: 410-945-8586
fax: 410-945-8595
nannyjack@nannyjack.com
http://www.nannyjack.com
*Specializes in the appraisal of black
memorabilia.*

Mark E. Mitchell
African-American History
3002 Winter Pine Ct.
Fairfax, VA 22031-1125
ph: 703-591-3150
fax: 703-385-3152
info@mitchellarchives.com
http://www.mitchellarchives.com
*Specializes in the appraisal of African
American historical documents, signed
photos, manuscripts, newspapers,
letters and older books; personal
collection will be at the core of the
National Museum of African American
History & Culture.*

Virgil J. Mayberry
V.J.M. Unlimited, Inc.
559 22nd Ave.
Rock Island, IL 61201-4129
ph: 309-786-6595 or 309-912-1571
*Appraises one item or complete
collections for insurance companies,
individuals, and museums; over 30
years experience with black memorabilia; deals only in black memorabilia.*

Clubs/Associations

Black Memorabilia Collector's
  Association
Newsletter: Collecting Our Culture
2482 Devoe Terrace
Bronx, NY 10468
ph: 212-946-1281
*Provides information and promotes
activities that encourage the
collecting, preservation and
documentation of black memorabilia.*

Collectors

Jan Thalberg
23 Mountain View Dr.
Weston, CT 06883-1317
ph: 203-227-8175
janthalberg@yahoo.com
*Wants early rag dolls, greeting cards,
sewing items, children's books, kitchen
items, Aunt Jemima items, playing
cards, games & puzzles, canes,
perfume bottles, mini bronzes, candy
containers; photocopy helpful; please
price & send SASE.*

Ed Natale, Jr.
P.O. Box 222
Wyckoff, NJ 07481-0222
ph: 201-493-7172
jednat@att.net
*Wants to buy black memorabilia:
insulting, exaggerated features; signs,
advertising, tins, etc.; send photo or
photocopy of items.*

Dr. E. Maynard
224 Mine Rd.
Monroe, NY 10950
ph: 914-783-1552
fax: 914-783-2480
emayn37868@aol.com
Wants black American books and memorabilia: history, biography, fiction, non-fiction.

E. Alexander Peters
'Tiques
P.O. Box 3267
Farmingdale, NY 11735-0679
ph: 631-842-9549
Wants documents, pictures, articles and artifacts relating to African-American slavery in the 17th to 19th centuries.

David L. Hartline
P.O. Box 775
Columbus, OH 43085-0775
fax: 614-760-5427
Wants 1860-1950 medals, badges and awards given to Black soldiers; also wants military uniforms from Black regiments; prefers if inscribed; all letters answered; 30 years experience.

Mike Kranz
463 Stage Line Rd.
Hudson, WI 54016-7849
ph: 715-386-7333 or 715-386-9212
Wants Black memorabilia: cookie jars, string holders, toys, salt & peppers, linens, advertising, etc.

John Hamilton
100 Military Rd.
Newport, MN 55055-1572
ph: 651-458-3939
hammer36@webtv.net
Wants to buy black collectibles: quality cookie jars, salt and peppers, humidors, toys, string holders, figures, advertising; wants one piece or entire collection.

Richard Newman
4202 S. MacGregor Way
Houston, TX 77021-1540
ph: 713-747-0804
fax: 713-747-0863
richardnewman0804@msn.com
Wants to buy/trade smoking items, toys, figurines, jewelry.

Esther Roman
6087 Glen Harbor Dr.
San Jose, CA 95123-4321
ph: 916-985-6642
Wants to buy Black memorabilia; available for exhibitions and lectures relating to Afro-American memorabilia and collectibles.

Dealers

Rose Fontanella
324 Ave. F, 2nd Floor
Brooklyn, NY 11218
ph: 718-436-2099
roseyrose2@yahoo.com
Specializes in black memorabilia: books, dolls, toys, jewelry, magazines,
prints, paintings, slave papers, ads, photos, posters, postcards, ceramics, linens, kitchen items; also Outsider art and folk art.*

Mark E. Mitchell
African-American History
3002 Winter Pine Ct.
Fairfax, VA 22031-1125
ph: 703-591-3150
fax: 703-385-3152
info@mitchellarchives.com
http://www.mitchellarchives.com
Buying and selling African-American letters, documents, prints, etc.

Judy Posner
Judy Posner Collectibles
P.O. Box 2194
Englewood, FL 34295
ph: 941-475-1725
fax: 941-475-2645
judyandjef@yahoo.com
http://www.judyposner.com
Wants black Mammy and Chef cookie jars, salt & pepper shakers and kitchen items; buying, selling collecting for over 25 years.

Arnold F. Winfield
Winfield Associates
2640 Summit Dr., Unit 209
Glenview, IL 60025-7630
ph: 847-998-1037
Buys and sells black exonumia including tokens, medals and other unusual collectibles.

Bindy Bitterman
Eureka! Antiques, Nostalgia & Collectibles
705 W. Washington
Evanston, IL 60202-2214
ph: 847-869-9090
rbitt356@aol.com
Wants to buy black memorabilia; everything from kitsch to historical; a small shop - they send no lists but will reply by phone, email or letter; SASEs get first attention.

Experts

Jan Lindenberger
P.O. Box 7224
Colorado Springs, CO 80933
ph: 719-591-9558
fax: 719-591-9558
Buys and sells black memorabilia; author of "Black Memorabilia for the Kitchen - Information and Price Guide" and "Black Memorabilia Around the House - Information & Price Guide" (Schiffer Pub., 1993).

Misc. Services

Lindsey Johnson
Greater Washington, DC Black
   Memorabilia & Collectible Show
P.O. Box 2026
Gaithersburg, MD 20886
ph: 301-216-0876
Ljohnsonshows@aol.com
http://www.johnsonshows.com
Promotes Black Americana collectibles shows.

Esther Roman
6087 Glen Harbor Dr.
San Jose, CA 95123-4321
ph: 916-985-6642
Exhibitions and lectures relating to Black memorabilia; workshops on how to start and build a Black collection.

Museums/Libraries

African American Museum
1765 Crawford Rd.
Cleveland, OH 44106
ph: 216-791-1700
fax: 216-791-1774
ourstory@aamcleveland.org
http://www.aamcleveland.org

Dr. John E. Fleming, Dir.
National Afro-American Museum & Culture Center
1350 Brush Row Rd.
P.O. Box 578
Wilberforce, OH 45384-0578
ph: 937-376-4944 or 800-752-2603
fax: 937-376-2007
naamcc@erinet.com
http://ohiohistory.org/places/afroam
Mission is to educate the public about African American heritage and culture from the African origins to the present by collecting, preserving, and interpreting material evidence of the Black experience.

Museum of African American History
315 E. Warren St.
Detroit, MI 48201
ph: 313-494-5800
fax: 313-494-5855
http://www.maah-detroit.org
Dedicated to the preservation and presentation of African and African American history and culture.

Orans' Black Americana Historical Museum
1240 South 13th St.
Omaha, NE 68108
ph: 402-341-6908
oranz@hotmail.com
http://www.omahalink.org/oma/orans.htm
Preserves and presents Black wax figures, depicts scenes and eras with authentic clothes, uniforms, artifacts; Black memorabilia, Blacks in advertising, Negro League Baseball history, autographs, reference library, and more.

Great Plains Black Museum
2213 Lake St.
Omaha, NE 68110
ph: 402-345-2212
One of 120 American museums belonging to the African American Museum Association; rare photographs, relics and historical displays.

Periodicals

Virgil J. Mayberry
V.J.M. Unlimited, Inc.
Newsletter: Blackin'
559 22nd Ave.
Rock Island, IL 61201-4129
ph: 309-786-6595 or 309-912-1571
Designed to inform subscribers of the different black memorabilia items being bought and sold; send $3 for sample issue.

Postcards (Dance Related)

Collectors

William G. Sommer, MD
9 W. 10th St.
New York, NY 10011-8748
ph: 212-260-0999
wgs2@columbia.edu
Wants postcards depicting African-American dancing, e.g., Cake Walk, Jitterbug; also Waltz, Tango, etc. & dance items in other media.

Sheet Music (Dance Related)

Collectors

William G. Sommer, MD
9 W. 10th St.
New York, NY 10011-8748
ph: 212-260-0999
wgs2@columbia.edu
Wants sheet music depicting African-American dancing, e.g., Cake Walk, Jitterbug; also Waltz, Tango, etc. & dance items in other media.

BLACK POWDER RIFLES

(see FIREARMS, Rifles [Single Shot])

BLACKLIGHTS (UV LAMPS)

Dealers

Rick Morris
Souther Belle Super Antique Mall
P.O. Box 1757
Byron, GA 31008-1757
ph: 912-784-8056
webmaster@southern-belle.com
http://www.southern-belle.com/blacklig.shtml
Detect fakes and reproductions in cut glass, cast iron, paper products, pattern glass, vaseline glass, art glass and more.

Man./Prod./Dist.

A & B Jewels & Tools
350 West Grand River
Williamston, MI 48895
ph: 800-628-6657 or 517-655-4664
fax: 517-655-4665
tooline@voyager.net
http://www.abtool.com
Distributor for all Raytech products including ultraviolet lights, lapidary products, magnetic pin polishers, and glass restoration centers; also sells tools, supplies, equipment to make jewelry items; diamond testers.

UVP Inc.
2066 W. 11th St.
Upland, CA 91786-3509
ph: 909-946-3197 or 800-452-6788
fax: 909-946-3597
uvp@uvp.com
http://www.uvp.com
Manufacturers a wide range of ultraviolet lamps in long wave, shortwave, and midrange UV for brilliant fluorescence of rocks and minerals, and for inspection applications; battery-operated and standard voltage models available.

Don Newsome
UV Systems
16605 127th Ave. SE
Renton, WA 98058
ph: 425-228-9988 or 877-689-5142
fax: 425-793-8712
uvsystems@aol.com
http://www.uvsystems.com
Sells the Superbright 2000SW and 2010LW short wave and long wave ultraviolet lights that are used primarily for mineralogical and geology applications, such as fluorescent minerals; also sells parts and supplies for other UV lights.

Misc. Services

Mark Chervenka
Antique & Collectors Reproduction News
P.O. Box 12130
Des Moines, IA 50312-9403
ph: 515-274-5886 or 800-227-5531
(orders)
fax: 515-255-4530
acrn@repronews.com
http://www.repronews.com
Sells pocket size to professional size models black lights; also invisible marking pens; publishes "Black Light for Antiques & Collectibles," 4th ed., 109 pgs. - book of tests for damages/repairs, fakes, reproductions on glass, etc.

BLACKSMITHING ITEMS

(see also KNIVES; TOOLS)

Collectors

Richard L. Weiss
1885 Klines Mill Rd.
Breinigsville, PA 18031
ph: 610-285-4122
mrsdlw@prodigy.net
Wants rare and unusual blacksmithing tools, literature, advertising signs and related items.

Museums/Libraries

Eugene I. Morris, Dir.
New England Fire & History Museum
Newsletter: Siren Soundings
1439 Main St. (Rte. 6A)
Brewster, MA 02631
ph: 508-896-5711
http://www.nefiremuseum.org
Mr. Morris appraises and has written many articles relating to fire fighting, apothecary and blacksmithing material.

BLIMPS

(see AIRSHIPS)

BLOTTERS

(see also INKWELLS & INKSTANDS; PAPER COLLECTIBLES; PENS)

Collectors

Homer Neel
4213 Westridge Dr.
North Little Rock, AR 72116-8156
ph: 501-753-9468
Wants old advertising ink blotters: all subjects, must be in mint condition.

John E. Kochenburger
1304 Robertson St.
Fort Collins, CO 80524-4258
ph: 304-484-0274
koch@frii.com
Collects a variety of inkstands, inkwells, ink bottles and "go-withs;" also buys and sells.

M. Zweig
P.O. Box 220
Rancho Mirage, CA 92270
ph: 760-328-3090
fax: 760-328-3090
smzrt@aol.com
Wants to buy advertising blotters.

Dealers

Sam Fiorella
Pendemonium
P.O. Box 447
Fort Madison, IA 52627-0447
ph: 888-372-2050 or 319-372-0881
fax: 319-372-0882
sam@pendemonium.com
http://www.pendemonium.com
Buys and sells fountain pens, inkwells, ink bottles, pen stands, blotters, pen catalogs, magazine covers and advertisements.

BLUE JEANS

(see CLOTHING & ACCESSORIES, Denim)

BLUE RIDGE

(see CERAMICS [AMERICAN DINNERWARE], Southern Potteries/Blue Ridge)

BOATS

(see also MODELS; NAUTICAL ANTIQUES; STEAMBOAT COLLECTIBLES; TOYS, Boats & Outboards)

Auction Services

David A. Norton
Norton Auctioneers of Michigan, Inc.
50 W. Pearl St.
Coldwater, MI 49036-1967
ph: 517-279-9063
fax: 517-279-9191
nortonsold@cbpu.com
http://www.nortonauctioneers.com
Conducts specialized auctions for antique, classic and collectible boats.

Clubs/Associations

Antique & Classic Boat Society
Magazine: Rusty Rudder
442 James St.
Clayton, NY 13624
ph: 315-686-2680
hqs@acbs.org
http://www.acbs.org
Has over 40 US and Canadian chapters; not necessary to own a boat in order to be a member.

Collectors

James King
1178 Chillem Dr.
Batavia, IL 60510-3309
ph: 630-879-2263
Wants to buy mahogany boats; inboard launches, runabouts, racers. Chris-Craft, Garwood, Greavette, Century, Streblow, etc.

Dealers

Lou Rauh
Antique Boat Center
5521 Vine St.
Cincinnati, OH 45217
ph: 513-242-0808
fax: 513-242-0555
lou@antiqueboat.com
http://www.antiqueboat.com
Collector, expert, appraiser, buyer, seller, and broker of antique and classic boats; also seller of reproduction wooden boats.

Experts

Wilson W. Wright
217 South Adams St.
Tallahassee, FL 32301-1708
ph: 850-224-2628
fax: 850-224-1033
WWright@nettally.com
http://www.Chris-Craft.org
Specializes in antique boats.

Museums/Libraries

John J. Palmieri, Curator
Herreshoff Marine Museum/America's
  Cup Hall of Fame
One Burnside St.
P.O. Box 450
Bristol, RI 02809-0450
ph: 401-253-5000
fax: 401-253-6222
j.palmieri@herreshoff.org
http://www.herreshoff.org
A tribute to the years of achievement in the creation and development of the boating world by the Herreshoff Manufacturing Co. (1863-1945).

Maine Maritime Museum
Journal: Rumb Line, The
243 Washington St.
Bath, ME 04530
ph: 207-443-1316
fax: 207-443-1665
maritime@bathmaine.com
http://www.bathmaine.com
The repository and exhibition space for the premier collection of objects illustrating Maine's maritime heritage.

Lori Sullivan
Adirondack Museum, The
Rte. 30
P.O. Box 99
Blue Mountain Lake, NY 12812-0099
ph: 518-352-7311
fax: 518-352-7653
lsullivan@adkmuseum.org
http://www.adirondackmuseum.org
The "Smithsonian" of the Adirondacks; 20 outdoor and indoor exhibit buildings; live programming tells the story of the Adirondacks from mid-1800s to present; new Visitors Center with Museum store, magnificent views, landscaped grounds.

Antique Boat Museum
750 Mary St.
Clayton, NY 13624
ph: 315-686-4104
fax: 315-686-2775
info@abm.org
http://www.abm.org
General focus in on freshwater boats and engines: 150 antique and classic boats, 300 engines and related objects; conducts annual boat auction.

Pete Lesher, Cur.
Chesapeake Bay Maritime Museum
Magazine: CBMM Quarterly
P.O. Box 636
St. Michaels, MD 21663-0636
ph: 410-745-2916
fax: 410-745-6088
library@cbmm.org
http://www.cbmm.org
A major regional maritime museum with a 10,000 volume research library; collections include 9,000 objects, 32,000 photos, 1,200 ships' plans, 120 linear feet of manuscripts; decoys, oystering, lighthouses, charts, nautical, tools.

Center for Wooden Boats, The
1010 Valley St.
Seattle, WA 98109-4332
ph: 206-382-2628
fax: 206-382-2699
cwb@cwb.org
http://www.cwb.org
Collection of over 100 historically significant boats; rental fleet; community outreach program.

Periodicals

Bob Hicks
Magazine: Messing About In Boats
29 Burley St.
Wenham, MA 01984
ph: 978-774-0906
http://www.messingaboutinboats.com
Great biweekly magazine about interesting boats & people who design, build, restore and/or use them - sail, oar, antique, steam, etc.

Matt Murphy, Ed.
Magazine: WoodenBoat
P.O. Box 78
Brooklin, ME 04616
ph: 207-359-4651 or 800-877-5284
fax: 207-359-8920
woodenboat@woodenboat.com
http://www.woodenboat.com
A glossy bi-monthly magazine for wooden boat owners, builders, and designers; construction plans and techniques, calendar of events, ads, navigation, wood and other boat building supplies, etc.

Trader Publishing Company
Magazine: Boat Trader
P.O. Box 9059
Clearwater, FL 34618-9059
ph: 727-712-0035 or 800-548-8889
fax: 727-712-0034
idowu@traderonline.com
http://www.traderonline.com
Offers hundreds of boats for sale by both private individuals, brokers and dealers.

Kelley Blue Book
Price Guide: Kelley Blue Book
5 Oldfield
Irvine, CA 92618
ph: 949-770-7704
fax: 949-837-1904
kelley@kbb.com
http://www.kbb.com/indexv.html
Web site offers current trade-in values for all makes and model cars for the past 21 years; also publishes printed value guides for cars, RVs, motorcycles, snowmobiles, motor homes, travel trailers, personal watercraft, etc.

Steve Ferguson, Ed.
National Automobile Dealers Association
Price Guide: N.A.D.A. Official Used Car Guide
P.O. Box 7800
Costa Mesa, CA 92628
ph: 800-544-6232 or 714-556-8511
fax: 714-556-8715
info@nadaguides.com
http://www.nada.org
A series of value guides for domestic and foreign cars, trucks, vans, RVs, mobile homes, motorcycles, snowmobiles, and boats, small and large; also Heavy Duty Trucks and Aircraft Book, car clubs & organizations, museums.

Dan Houston, Ed.
IPC Magazines
Magazine: Classic Boat
Link House, Dingwall Ave.
Croydon, Surrey CR9 2TA U.K.
ph: 0208 774 0882
fax: 0208 774 0943
cb@ipcmedia.com
http://www.classicboat.co.uk
Britain's best selling traditional boat magazine; monthly articles on yachting and work boat histories by leading writers' lively news and opinion pages debating all the current issues in the traditional boat world; restoration tips.

Repair Services

Clawson Classic Instruments
2402 30th St.
Anacortes, WA 98221
ph: 360-299-8636
fax: 360-299-2836
Specializes in the professional restoration of boat gauges and instruments.

Repro. Sources

Lou Rauh
Antique Boat Center
5521 Vine St.
Cincinnati, OH 45217
ph: 513-242-0808
fax: 513-242-0555
lou@antiqueboat.com
http://www.antiqueboat.com
Collector, expert, appraiser, buyer, seller, and broker of antique and classic boats; also seller of reproduction wooden boats.

Canoes

Clubs/Associations

Wooden Canoe Heritage Association, Ltd.
Magazine: Wooden Canoe
P.O. Box 226
Blue Mountain Lake, NY 12812
ph: 803-643-3800
webmaster@wcha.org
http://www.wcha.org
Non-profit association dedicated to preserving, studying, building, restoring and using wooden and birch bark canoes; articles and ads for supplies, restorers, parts, gatherings, etc.; chapters across the US and Canada.

Canadian Recreational Canoeing Association
Magazine: Kanawa
P.O. Box 398
446 Main St. West
Merrickville, Ontario K0G 1N0 Canada
ph: 888-252-6292 or 613-269-2910
fax: 613-269-2908
staff@crca.ca
http://www.crca.ca
The "Voice of Paddling in Canada," 72-page full color magazine covering everything you need to know about canoeing and kayaking.

Experts

Al Bratton
Woodstrip Watercraft Co.
1818 Swamp Pike
Gilbertsville, PA 19525
ph: 610-326-9282
canoeal@aol.com
A wooden canoe historian and expert.

Misc. Services

David Gidmark
Green Leaf Canoes
Box 26
Maniwaki, Quebec J9E 3B3 Canada
Offers course on birch bark canoe building; also sells birch bark canoes from four to eighteen feet in length.

Periodicals

Magazine: Canoe Magazine
P.O. Box 420235
Palm Coast, FL 32142-0235
ph: 800-829-3340
editor@canoemagazine.com
http://www.canoemagazine.com/c
Glossy magazine for the canoe and kayak enthusiast; occasional articles on collectible boats and kayaks.

Repair Services

Rollin Thurlow
Northwoods Canoe Co.
336 Range Rd.
Dover Foxcroft, ME 04426
ph: 207-564-3667
info@woodencanoes.com
http://www.wooden-canoes.com
Restores classic boats and builds custom boats.

McGreivey's Canoe Shop
1379 Old State Rd.
Cato, NY 13033
ph: 315-626-6635
Restorers of classic canoes and guide boats.

Gilbert Cramer
Wooden Canoe Shop, Inc.
03583 RD 13
Bryan, OH 43506-9804
ph: 419-636-1689
gcramer@cityofbryan.net
http://www.wcha.org/builders/wcshop
Repairs and restorations of wood/canvas canoes and boats; buys and sells unrestored canoes and sells restored canoes.

West Coast Canoe Company
P.O. Box 143
Campbell River, British Columbia V9W 5A7 Canada
ph: 250-287-7348 or 800-446-1588
canoes@islandnet.com
http://www.islandnet.com/~canoes
Dedicated to the crafting, restoration and repair of classic cedar canvas canoes.

Chris Crafts

Clubs/Associations

Wilson W. Wright, Ex.Dir.
Chris Craft Antique Boat Club, Inc.
Newsletter: Brass Bell
217 South Adams St.
Tallahassee, FL 32301-1708
ph: 850-224-2628
fax: 850-224-1033
WWright@nettally.com
http://www.Chris-Craft.org
Assists members with collecting, restoring, maintaining vintage Chris Crafts; quarterly newsletter has antique boat show calendar, articles, how-to hints, ads, restorers/boat works, model builders, marine instrument repairs, etc.

Engines

Clubs/Associations

Antique Outboard Motor Club
Magazine: Antique Outboarder
P.O. Box 69
Sussex, WI 53089
webmaster@aomci.org
http://www.aomci.org/aomc.htm

Collectors

Dick Hawkins
Columbia Trading Company
One Barnstable Rd.
Hyannis, MA 02601
ph: 508-778-2929
fax: 508-778-2922
info@columbiatrading.com
http://www.columbiatrading.com
Buys old and antique outboard motors.

Richard Mussehl
Antique Outboard Motor Man
320 W. 20th St.
Erie, PA 16502
ph: 800-354-6089
Wants old rowboat motors by Waterman, Clarke, Amphion, etc.

James King
1178 Chillem Dr.
Batavia, IL 60510-3309
ph: 630-879-2263
Wants to buy old inboard marine engines, one to twelve cylinders. Marinized aero engines, racing engines. Scripps, Kermath, Hisso, Packard, etc.

Dealers

Walter Pawlikowski
Superior Antiques
4022 E. 2nd St.
Superior, WI 54880-4209
ph: 715-398-3665
Buys, collects antique outboards, marine engines, and antique boat equipment or related fishing equipment, boat models and outboard toys literature on pre-1940 items; offers free appraisals on antique outboards; historical writer.

Experts

Walter Pawlikowski
Superior Antiques
4022 E. 2nd St.
Superior, WI 54880-4209
ph: 715-398-3665
*Buys, collects antique outboards,
marine engines, and antique boat
equipment or related fishing
equipment, boat models and outboard
toys literature on pre-1940 items;
offers free appraisals on antique
outboards; historical writer.*

Richard Streater
P.O. Box 393
Mercer Island, WA 98040-0393
ph: 206-232-9060
fax: 206-232-9060
lureguru@aol.com
*Has perhaps the largest collection
hand-cranked and foot-powered
trolling motors (no gas) in the US.*

Internet Resources

Andrew Menkart
OldMarineEngine.com
149 Merion Ave.
Haddonfield, NJ 08033
ph: 856-428-7357
info@OldMarineEngine.com
http://www.OldMarineEngine.com
*A site for the antique marine engine
enthusiast: discussion, research,
classifieds; focus is pre-1940 inboard
marine engines built for motor canoes,
dories, motor launches, skiffs, and
other pleasure or work boats up to
about 30' long.*

Suppliers

Arthur DeKalb
Outboard Engine Catalogs
51 Van Alstyne Dr.
Pulaski, NY 13142
ph: 315-298-3410
adekalb@a-znet.com
http://members.aol.com/ArtDeKalb
*Antique outboard catalogs, parts,
instructions and service manuals for
most brands.*

Model

Clubs/Associations

John Snow
U.S. Vintage Model Yacht Group,
   American Model Yachting Assoc.
Newsletter: Model Yacht, The
78 East Orchard St.
Marblehead, MA 01945
ph: 781-631-4203 or 781-639-0779
usvmyg@amya.org
http://www.amya.org/vintpage.html
*Devoted to preserving, building,
exhibiting, sailing, collecting older
sailing models (pond boats) and to the
study of the history of the sport of
model yachting and all that may
entail; how-to books, videos, design
plans.*

Russell Potts, Ch.
Vintage Model Yacht Group (U.K.)
8 Sherard Rd.
London, SE9 6EP U.K.
ph: +44 (0)20 8850 6805
rpotts@talk21.com
*Members interested in the preserva-
tion, restoration and sailing of older
styles of model yachts.*

Dealers

Susan P. Meisel
Susan P. Meisel Decorative Arts
133 Prince St.
New York, NY 10012
ph: 212-254-0137
fax: 212-533-7340
sue@meisels.com
http://www.liontex.com/spmda
*Wants to buy pond sailboats, big and
small, whole or parts.*

James Tobin
Antique & Classic Boats
12 Carstead Dr.
Slingerlands, NY 12159
ph: 518-439-0477
fax: 518-439-0477
*Buys and sells pond boats - late 19th
and early 20th century sail boats
designed to be sailed on ponds.*

Steam

Collectors

Robin Corsiglia
Toy Steam Engines
5200 NE 9th Lane
Ocala, FL 34470
ph: 352-236-2635 or 352-687-5950
marklinc1@earthlink.net
http://home.earthlink.net/~marklinc1/
   index.html
*Buys, sells and collects toy steam
engines (stationary with real boilers
and flywheels) and tin pop-pop boats,
tin wind up boats, and tin battery
boats; mainly collects buy also buys,
sells, trades and gives out information.*

Tug

Clubs/Associations

Emory Massman
Tugboat Enthusiasts Society of the
   Americas
Magazine: Tug Bitts
420 49th St. E, Lot 127
Palmetto, FL 34221
*Published quarterly; covers steamboat
& inland river history; packed with
news, photos, articles on all types of
tow boats, tugboats (harbor, ocean,
military) and work boat salvage,
restoration and history; a must for
tugboat enthusiasts.*

Yachts

Clubs/Associations

Scottie Dobson
Classic Yacht Association
149-b West Ave. Marquita
San Clemente, CA 92672
fax: 714-366-2987
georgeh@classicyacht.org
http://www.classicyacht.org
*A non-profit organization of
collectors, restorers and skippers of
classic (pre-1942) yachts and boats; a
major influence in growing awareness
and appreciation for the classic.*

Periodicals

Trader Publishing Company
Magazine: Yacht Trader
P.O. Box 9059
Clearwater, FL 34618-9059
ph: 727-712-0035 or 800-548-8889
fax: 727-712-0034
idowu@traderonline.com
http://www.traderonline.com
*Offers hundreds of luxury motor and
sailing yachts for sale by both private
individuals, brokers and dealers.*

BONES

(see ANIMAL TROPHIES;
FURNITURE [ANTIQUE], Antler &
Horn; ODDITIES & THE MORBID;
SKELETONS)

BOOK ARTS

(see also BOOKS, Repair Services
for; PRINTING EQUIPMENT)

Internet Resources

Book Arts Directory, The
P.O. Box 77167
Washington, DC 20013
ph: 800-821-6604
pagetwo@bookarts.com
http://www.bookarts.com
*Purchase the latest directory in book
form or search an online database of
an earlier directory: paper artists,
mills, calligraphers, printmakers,
artist bookmakers, bookbinders/
conservators, book dealers,
periodicals, related services.*

Walter Henry
Conservation OnLine: Resources for
   Conservation Professionals
Stanford University Libraries
Palo Alto, CA 94305-6004
waiscool@palimpsest.stanford.edu
http://palimpsest.stanford.edu/don/toc/
   toc1.html
*A dictionary of descriptive terminology
for bookbinding and the conservation
of books.*

Museums/Libraries

University of California, Special
   Collections Department
P.O. Box 5900
Riverside, CA 92517
ph: 909-787-3233 or 909-784-7324
fax: 909-787-3285
smitch@citrus.ucr.edu
http://lib-www.ucr.edu/spec_coll/
   spec_main.html
*Collection of material on the Book
Arts, especially book binding,
papermaking, fine presses, forgeries,
etc.*

BOOKENDS

Clubs/Associations

Louis Kuritzky
Bookend Collectors Club
Newsletter: Bookend Collectors Club
   Newsletter
4510 N.W. 17th Place
Gainesville, FL 32605-3479
ph: 352-376-3884 or 352-377-3193
fax: 352-377-3193
lkuritzky@aol.com
Color newsletter published quarterly.

Experts

Gerald P. (Jerry) McBride
4005 Dellbrook Dr.
Tampa, FL 33624
ph: 813-264-4005
charlotteweb@earthlink.net
*Specialist in metal bookends; author
of "A Collector's Guide to Cast Metal
Bookends."*

BOOKLETS

(see PAPER COLLECTIBLES)

BOOKMARKS

(see also PAPER CLIPS;
STEVENGRAPHS)

Collectors

Joan L. Huegel
1002 West 25th St.
Erie, PA 16502-2427

Howie Schecter
1704 Harkness St.
Manhattan Beach, CA 90266
ph: 310-379-9761
fax: 310-379-2072
howie@acm.org
http://www.silverbookmarks.com
*Interested mainly in silver bookmarks;
entire collection is displayed on his
Web site.*

Experts

Dr. Judith Ackerman
P.O. Box 354
West Long Branch, NJ 07764-0354
ph: 732-531-3624
fax: 732-222-9214
ackerman1@comcast.net
*Researching and writing about
bookmarks, including all materials,
periods and styles.*

Man./Prod./Dist.

Chuck Thompson
10802 Greencreek Dr., Ste. 203
Houston, TX 77070-5365
ph: 281-970-0479
chilichuck@chilitech.com
*Writer/reviewer specializes in
inspirational bookmarks; has monthly,
syndicated column; useful information
for collectors of old and new
bookmarks; send SASE for reply.*

Periodicals

Joan L. Huegel
Newsletter: Bookmark Collector
1002 West 25th St.
Erie, PA 16502-2427
*A friendly, informative newsletter for
all collectors; for those wanting only
antique as well as those who collect
new and modern bookmarks, too;
published quarterly.*

Notched

Collectors

John T. Ogle
P.O. Box 252
Ocean Springs, MS 39566-0252
*Wants to buy paper clips and notched
bookmarks: antique, foreign, plastic,
novelty, advertising; also wants early
paper clip advertising.*

BOOKPLATES

Clubs/Associations

James P. Keenan
American Society of Bookplate
 Collectors & Designers
Newsletter: Bookplates in the News
P.O. Box 380340
Cambridge, MA 02238-0340
ph: 781-393-9970
fax: 781-393-9972
exlibris@att.net
http://www.bookplate.org
*Organized in 1922; quarterly
newsletter features articles on
contemporary bookplate artists &
collectors, news of exhibitions,
competitions, literature.*

Josef Chalupsky
Association of Collectors & Friends of
 Exlibris
Newsletter: Knizni Znacka (Bookplate)
P.O. Box 645
Praha 1, CZ-111 21 Czech Republic
chalupsk@natur.cuni.cz
http://www.natur.cuni.cz/el/sspeang.htm
Society of about 600 bookplate

*collectors, artists and friends of small
and commemorative graphic works,
particularly book plates (exlibris);
founded in 1918; plays an active role
in the Czech culture.*

Bryan Welch, Sec.
Bookplate Society
Journal: Bookplate Society Journal
11 Nella Rd.
London, W6 9PB U.K.
ph: 0207 385 3099
bryanjwelch@clara.co.uk
http://www.bookplatesociety.org
*Write for details; membership includes
bi-annual journal and quarterly
newsletter, free book and bookplates;
also members only auctions of
bookplates and associated materials.*

Collectors

Lewis Jaffe
1919 Chestnut St., Apt. 1117
Philadelphia, PA 19103-3418
fax: 215-568-6768
bookplatemaven@hotmail.com
*Advanced collector, active buyer of
bookplate (exlibris) collections and
accumulations.*

Dealers

James Wilson
22 Castle St.
Berkhamsted, Hertfordshire HP4 2DW
U.K.
ph: 01442-873396
*Largest dealer in England for
bookplates and books about
bookplates.*

BOOKS

(see also ACCOUNT BOOKS;
ALBUMS, Autograph; ATLASES;
AUCTION CATALOGS; BIBLES;
BOOK ARTS; COMIC BOOKS;
COOKBOOKS; DIARIES;
ILLUSTRATORS; MAPS & CHARTS;
MYSTERY/DETECTIVE ITEMS;
PAPER COLLECTIBLES;
PERSONALITIES [LITERARY];
SCIENCE FICTION)

Appraisers

Ken Gloss
Brattle Book Shop
9 West St.
Boston, MA 02111
ph: 800-447-9595 or 617-542-0210
info@brattlebookshop.com
http://www.brattlebookshop.com
*Specializes in the appraisal of
antiquarian books.*

Richard Austin
327 West 21st St.
New York, NY 10011
ph: 212-741-8133
raustin@rhinoadvisors.com
*Specializing in the appraisal of books
and manuscripts from the 15th to the
20th centuries.*

Stephen C. Massey
108 East 81st St., Apt. 9B
New York, NY 10028
ph: 212-628-6850
fax: 212-327-3934
scmassey@aol.com
*Specialist appraiser of books and
manuscripts.*

Lee Temares
50 Heights Rd.
Plandome, NY 11030-1413
ph: 516-627-8688 or 516-627-2647
fax: 516-627-7822
tembooks@aol.com
*Buys children's series books; must
have dust jackets if they originally had
them; also wants Limited Editions
Club and Heritage Press books, but
must be in very good condition and in
fine boxes; appraises all books except
law & medicine.*

John Schulman
Caliban Books
10 South Craig St.
West Mifflin, PA 15123
ph: 412-681-9111
fax: 412-681-9113
caliban@telerama.com
*Specializes in the appraisal of rare
books.*

Pat & Allen Ahearn
Quill & Brush
1137 Sugarloaf Mountain Rd.
Dickerson, MD 20842
ph: 301-874-3200
fax: 301-874-0824
firsts@qbbooks.com
http://www.qbbooks.com
*Author of "Book Collecting, A
Comprehensive Guide," "Collected
Books, The Guide to Values" and
"Author Price Guides."*

Lynn O'Keefe, ISA
Estate Sales Service
3322 NW 39th Terrace
Gainesville, FL 32606
ph: 352-377-7000 or 352-222-1407
fax: 352-377-7000
ess32606@bellsouth.net
*Specializes in the appraisal of rare,
antique and vintage books;
autographed books authenticated;
children's, historical, sets and others;
also full libraries researched and
documented.*

Ray Nugent, ASA
Nugent Appraisal Services
P.O. Box 11984
Naples, FL 34101
ph: 888-353-7152 or 941-353-7122
fax: 941-353-8884
renugent@aol.com
http://www.appraisalreferrals.com
*ASA senior accredited appraiser of
rare books, documents, manuscripts,
autographs and antique maps; member
of ISA, AAA, AIC, SAA.*

Timmy W. Miller
Flat Signed Rare Books
3415 West End Ave., #1101
Nashville, TN 37203
ph: 615-292-3528
fax: 615-298-2757
timmiller@flatsigned.com
http://www.flatsigned.com
*Appraiser, collector, dealer; one of the
world's largest sellers of rare books,
political memorabilia, and works by
Peter Max.*

Auction Services

Richard & Mary Sykes
New Hampshire Book Auctions
P.O. Box 460
Weare, NH 03281
ph: 603-529-7432
*Specializes in the auction of books,
maps, prints and ephemera.*

Caroline Birenbaum
Swann Galleries, Inc.
104 E. 25th St.
New York, NY 10010-2977
ph: 212-254-4710
fax: 212-979-1017
swann@swanngalleries.com
http://www.swanngalleries.com
*Oldest/largest US auctioneer
specializing in rare books, autographs
& manuscripts, maps, atlases,
photographs, and works of art on
paper including vintage posters.*

Freeman's Auction Gallery
1808 Chestnut St.
Philadelphia, PA 19103
ph: 215-563-9275
fax: 215-563-8236
proberts@freemansauction.com
http://www.freemansauction.com
*America's oldest auction house:
Continental, English and American
furniture, paintings, silver and
decorative arts; Oriental rugs, rare
books, fine jewelry, Orientalia.*

Dale Sorenson
Waverly Auctions, Inc.
4931 Cordell Ave.
Bethesda, MD 20814-2508
ph: 301-951-8883
fax: 301-718-8375
waverly1660@earthlink.net
http://www.waverlyauctions.com
*Specializes in the auction of graphic
art, books, paper, atlases, prints,
postcards, autographs, and other
paper ephemera.*

Chris Bready
Baltimore Book Co., Inc.
2114 N. Charles St.
Baltimore, MD 21218-5765
ph: 410-659-0550
baltobook@comcast.net
*Buys and auctions books, prints,
paintings, autographs, photographs,
and ephemera.*

Stephen Neil Greengard
California Book Auction Galleries
220 San Bruno Ave.
San Francisco, CA 94103
ph: 415-861-7500 or 800-223-2854
fax: 415-861-8951
info.US@butterfields.com
http://www.butterfields.com
Auctioneers and appraisers of antiques, fine art and collectibles in all categories; specialty sales include posters, toys, decorative arts, furniture, photography, etc.; the largest full service auction in the West.

George K. Fox
PBA Galleries
133 Kearny St., 4th Floor
San Francisco, CA 94108-4805
ph: 415-989-2665
fax: 415-989-1664
george@pbagalleries.com
http://www.pbagalleries.com
Conducts numerous auctions each year of rare books, manuscripts, maps, autographs, historical material, early photography, prints, and fine literary property; has online auction operating continually with closings every 10 days.

Clubs/Associations

Antiquarian Booksellers' Association of America (ABAA)
Newsletter: ABAA Newsletter
20 West 44th St., 4th Floor
New York, NY 10036-6604
ph: 212-944-8291
fax: 212-944-8293
inquiries@abaa.org
http://www.abaa.org
A non-profit association; publishes a membership directory and a newsletter; over 330 dealers in rare books, maps and prints available online.

Lee Temares
Long Island Antiquarian Book Dealers Association
Newsletter: LIABDA Newsletter
P.O. Box 42
Manhasset, NY 11030
ph: 516-627-8688 or 516-627-2647
fax: 516-627-7822
liabda@optonline.net
http://www.liabda.com
A professional organization of sellers of rare, out-of-print, and used books; also ephemera, prints, manuscripts, and related materials.

Lee Harrer
Florida Bibliophile Society
Newsletter: FBL Newsletter
1908 Deagull Dr.
Clearwater, FL 34624
ph: 813-536-4029
Newsletter is published monthly.

Antiquarian Booksellers' Association
Sackville House
40 Piccadilly, London W1J ODR U.K.
ph: 44-171-439-3118
fax: 44-171-439-3119
info@aba.org.uk
http://www.ABAinternational.com
Senior trade body for dealers in rare & fine books, manuscripts & allied material in the British Isles & elsewhere; since 1906; the annual "The Handbook of the Antiquarian Booksellers Assoc." contains ABA details & member contact info.

Collectors

Steven N. Jackson
1774 Highway 421 N.
Boone, NC 28607
ph: 828-264-8034
stevejackson@email.com
Wants to buy first edition mystery, suspense, science fiction, pre-1950 baseball and karate hardcover books with dust jackets; include standard bibliographic information along with SASE when writing; extensive want list available.

Tom Rutledge
3015 Bever Ave., SE
Cedar Rapids, IA 52403-3028
ph: 319-399-1427
Wants rare & antiquarian books, manuscripts, autographs, first editions, children's books, fore-edge painted books, illustrated books, Modern Library books, pop-ups, Asian art, and collectible paperbacks.

Dealers

Steve Finer
Steve Finer Rare Books
38 Grinnell St.
Greenfield, MA 01302-3621
ph: 413-773-5811
finerbks@crocker.com

David L. O'Neal
David L. O'Neal Antiquarian Booksellers, Inc.
234 Clarendon St.
Boston, MA 02116
ph: 617-266-5790
fax: 617-266-1089
Buyers and sellers of rare books and manuscripts, 15th to 20th centuries: American, English, travel, French books, fine printing & private press books, early printed books, illustrated books of all periods, etc.

Clare Murphy
Payson Hall Books
50 Watertown St., #202
Belmont, MA 02472
ph: 617-924-8484
fax: 617-923-2258
payson@oldbooks.com
http://www.oldbooks.com
A mail and Internet only company; offers search service and appraisal services; buys books that are out of the ordinary.

Karen & Jim Weyant
Scribe's Perch, The
P.O. Box 3295
Newport, RI 02840-0324
ph: 401-682-1743
fax: 401-682-1752
karen@edgenet.net
Dealers in out-of-print and collectible books; specializing in childrens, Americana, military history, nautical, literature; has searchable database on Web site.

Jon Mayo
Tuttle Antiquarian Books Inc.
28 South Main St.
Rutland, VT 05701
ph: 802-773-8229
fax: 802-773-1493
tuttbook@sover.net
http://www.tuttlebooks.com
Four floors of used books specializing in regional Americana, Orientalia, genealogy, miniature books; welcomes inquiries and quotations concerning books in these subject areas.

Barbara & Richard DePalma
Deer Park Books
609 Kent Rd., Route 7
Gaylordsville, CT 06755
ph: 860-350-4140
deerparkbooks@earthlink.net
http://www.deerparkbooks.com
Fine books bought and sold; antiquarian books, modern first editions, children's and illustrated; also maps, autographs, etc.; all subjects; also wants handwritten diaries, travel journals, scrapbooks, albums.

Ray Boas
Ray Boas, Bookseller
6 Church St.
New Preston, CT 06777
ph: 860-868-9596
ray@rayboasbookseller.com
http://www.rayboasbookseller.com
Founded in 1980; member of the Antiquarian Booksellers Association of America.

Joanmarie Dale
Stray Books
17 Moquis Trail
Oak Ridge, NJ 07438-9804
ph: 973-208-3105
fax: 973-208-3105
JDale@StrayBooks.com
http://www.StrayBooks.com
Specializes in mail order Modern First Editions; offers free book searches.

J.N. Bartfield
J.N. Bartfield Books, Inc.
30 West 57th St.
Third Floor
New York, NY 10019
ph: 212-245-8890
fax: 212-541-4860
bartfield@aol.com
Wants to buy fine books: Americana, atlases, Canadiana, color plate books, fore-edge painting, fine leather bindings, rare books, first editions,

sporting books, autographs, manuscripts, original diaries and journals.

Bibi Mohamed
Imperial Fine Books, Inc.
790 Madison Ave. Ste. 200
New York, NY 10021
ph: 212-861-6620
fax: 212-249-0333
Imperial@dir-dd.com
http://www.dir-dd.com/imperial-fine-books.html
Fine books bought and sold; sets, fine and decorative bindings, first editions, fore-edge paintings, children's & illustrated books, etc.; issues catalogs; bookbinding.

Jon Howell
Factory Books
241 W. 139th St., #2
New York, NY 10030
ph: 917-405-0710
fax: 212-202-4947
jon@factorybooks.com
http://www.factorybooks.com
Specializes in rare and out-of-print books about 20th century art and design.

Antipodean Books, Maps & Prints
P.O. Box 189
Cold Spring, NY 10516
ph: 914-424-3867
fax: 914-424-3617
Antipbooks@highlands.com
http://antipodean.com
Books, maps, prints.

Helen & Marc Younger
Aleph-Bet Books, Inc.
85 Old Mill River Rd.
Pound Ridge, NY 10576
ph: 914-764-7410
fax: 914-764-1356
helen@alephbet.com
http://www.alephbet.com
Specializing in fine first editions of collectible and rare children's and illustrated books; always interested in buying books in fine condition; business established in 1978.

Diana Rudy
Book Look
P.O. Box 450
Warwick, NY 10990
ph: 800-223-0540
fax: 914-651-1233
sales@booklook.com
http://www.booklook.com
Largest out-of-print book search service in the US; any book located.

Daniel Weaver
Book Hound, The
248 Locust Ave.
Amsterdam, NY 12010
ph: 518-842-3498
fax: 775-535-4408
thebookhound@juno.com
http://www.abebooks.com/home/
CAPTAINAHAB
Buys and sells used and out-of-print books in almost all subject areas, but

especially Protestant religion, children's books and books for home schoolers; also offers search service.

Michael Tokman
A-ha! Books, Inc.
17 Railroad St., Ste. #3
Freeville, NY 13068
ph: 607-844-5555
fax: 607-844-5555
info@ahabooks.com
http://www.ahabooks.com
Buys and sells rare, antiquarian and out-of-print books, antiques and collectibles; online catalog.

Stan Modjesky
Bull Moose Books
Antique Center of York
190 East Arsenal Rd.
York, PA 17404
ph: 717-846-1994
bookmisr@valinet.com
Dealer in used, rare and new books; specializes in music, opera, ballet, theatre, motion pictures, history and Americana books.

George S. MacManus Co.
1317 Irving St.
Philadelphia, PA 19107
ph: 215-735-4456
fax: 215-735-3635

Bauman Rare Books
1215 Locust St.
Philadelphia, PA 19107
ph: 215-546-6466
fax: 215-546-9064
brb@baumanrarebooks.com
http://www.baumanrarebooks.com
Rare books and autographs in all fields from the 15th through the 20th centuries, including landmark first editions, inscribed volumes, and leather-bound sets.

David Szewczyk
Philadelphia Rare Books & Manuscripts
  Company
P.O. Box 9536
Philadelphia, PA 19124
ph: 215-744-6734
fax: 215-755-6137
rarebks@prbm.com
http://www.prbm.com
Buying and selling books printed in England from before 1801, on the European continent before 1750, and in the Americas before 1830; all languages, most topics; manuscripts of a substantive nature, not autographs; member ABAA, ILAB.

Carmen D. Valentino
Rare Books & Manuscripts
2956 Richmond St., Drawer 19
Philadelphia, PA 19134-5720
ph: 215-739-6056
fax: 215-739-6453
Antiquarian bookseller specializing in pre-WWI rare books, manuscripts, documents, early newspapers, handwritten diaries, account books, ledgers, ephemera, broadsides, trade

catalogs, pamphlets; collections of old family/business letters.

Bookpress, Ltd., The
P.O. Box KP
Williamsburg, VA 23187
ph: 757-229-1260
fax: 757-229-0498
bookpress@widowmaker.com
http://www.bookpress.com
A rare book service buying and selling fine books, old maps and prints.

Jack Hamilton
Hamilton's Rare Books
ph: 757-220-3000
goodbook@goodbooks.com
http://www.goodbooks.com
Rare books, autographs, documents, ephemera, art, illustrated books, antique maps.

Henry Barnet
Your Town, Inc.
516 Maverick Circle
Spartanburg, SC 29307-3707
ph: 864-579-2112
hbbarnet@cs.com
Buys, sells, appraises rare & collectible books.

Wolf's Head Books, Inc.
48 San Marco Ave.
P.O. Box 3705
Saint Augustine, FL 32085-3705
ph: 904-824-9357
fax: 904-824-2212
wolfhead@aug.com
http://www.wolfsheadbooks.com
Book dealers and appraisers; member of Antiquarian Booksellers' Association of America; specializing in Floridiana, regional Americana, military books and manuals, signed volumes, juveniles & children's series books.

Michael Slicker
Lighthouse Books
1735 First Ave. North
Saint Petersburg, FL 33713
ph: 727-822-3278
lighthousebooks@sprintmail.com
Specializes in books and maps.

Jim Reed
Reed Books/The Museum of Fond
  Memories
107 Twentieth St. South
Birmingham, AL 35233
ph: 205-326-4460
jim@jimreedbooks.com
http://www.jimreedbooks.com
Book dealer, collector, expert; Reed Books is a specialized, international book search company that finds old out-of-print books and magazines.

J. Newcome-Beill
Abstract Eye Books
1517 Vivian Lane
Louisville, KY 40205
abstracteyebooks@cox.net
http://www.abstracteyebooks.com
Buys and sells used and rare photography books, maps, and prints.

Ivan Gilbert, MD
Miran Art & Books
2824 Elm Ave.
Columbus, OH 43209
ph: 614-231-3707 or 614-818-3222
fax: 614-818-3223
IGilbert@ahhinc.com
Specializing in illustrated books, in particular color plates, childrens, medical, photography, erotica, 16th/17th/18th century.

Joe Davidson
Aaron's Archives
5185 Windfall Rd.
Medina, OH 44256-8703
ph: 330-723-7172
Wants to buy pre-1895 books containing color plates, etchings, engravings plus pre-1600 Medieval books and manuscripts.

Richard Titterington
T's Old Things
5562 South M-52
Stockbridge, MI 49285
redileen@dmci.net
http://www.oldthingsandbooks.com
Buys and sells collectible books and magazines; specializes in first editions.

Eldon Bryant
Broken Kettle Books
702 East Madison St.
Fairfield, IA 52556-3649
ph: 641-472-8643
bkettle@kdsi.net
Buys and sells a full line of old books.

Thomas J. Joyce
Joyce And Company
400 N. Racine Ave., #103A
Chicago, IL 60622
ph: 312-738-1933
fax: 312-243-6252
tjoyceco@comcast.net
Buys, sells, appraises rare books and manuscripts for over 25 years; members of the Antiquarian Booksellers Association of America & International League of Antiquarian Booksellers; Thomas Joyce appears on HGTV's "The Appraisal Fair."

Edward Ripp
Edward Ripp Bookseller
6048 N. Washtenaw Ave.
Chicago, IL 60659
ph: 773-764-0201
edwripp@xsite.net
http://www.abebooks.com/home/edwripp
Specializes in illustrated books, woodcut novels, and books related to art history, decorative arts, design, Chicago art & artists, photography, and more.

William Butts
Main St. Fine Books & Manuscripts
206 N. Main St.
Galena, IL 61036-2244
ph: 815-777-3749
fax: 815-777-8950
msfb@galenalink.com
http://www.wcinet.com/msfbooks
Open shop dealing in autographs and out-of-print books in most fields; specializing in all aspects of American history; book and autograph catalogs issued regularly; member of A.B.A.A.; author of "Sign Here" and other autograph columns.

Kent Butterfield
Abba's Books
1170 - 25th St.
Moline, IL 61265
ph: 309-764-6160
http://www.abebooks.com/home/
ABBASBOOKS
Book appraiser and dealer since 1985; specializes in children's books, illustrated books, military books.

Bob & Beverlee Reimers
Peddler's Wagon
P.O. Box 109
Lamar, MO 64759-0109
ph: 417-682-3734
Buys and sells books on quilting, needlework, children's illustrated books, Little Golden books, and series books; mail order only.

Coyote Shadow
A Sentimental Journey
Figger-Dude Rance
4501 Pyeatt
Gladewater, TX 75647-9232
ph: 903-845-6693
fax: 903-845-5621
books@asjourney.com
http://www.asjourney.com
Specializes in fine books and books about religion.

Nita Anderson
2812 Country Rd. 920
Crowley, TX 76036-5732
ph: 817-297-7287

Alcott Books
5909 Darnell
Houston, TX 77074-7719
ph: 713-774-2202
bruppert@earthlink.net
http://www.abebooks.com/home/
ALCOTTBOOKS
Wants any pre-1980 books in dust jackets about Texas and country histories; also children's books, autographed sports books, presidential signed books, books about astronauts, space and NASA.

Barbara Ruppert
Alcott Books
5909 Darnell
Houston, TX 77074-7719
ph: 713-774-2202
bruppert@earthlink.net
http://www.abebooks.com/home/
ALCOTTBOOKS
Wants to buy books: Dick and Jane Readers, first edition mysteries with dust jackets, signed editions, early first editions of Stephen King, books illustrated by Maxfield Parrish, Oz books.

Barrie D. Watson
Barrie D. Watson Bookseller
8760 Grand Ave.
P.O. Box 38
Beulah, CO 81023
ph: 719-485-3136 or 800-785-3136
fax: 719-485-3838

Jim Owens
Thorn Books
5721 N. Killdeer Dr.
Tucson, AZ 85743
ph: 520-743-7773
fax: 520-743-8699
info@thornbooks.com
http://www.thornbooks.com
Offers antiquarian, rare and out-of-print books.

Howard Weetall
Antiquarian Bookworm, The
4562 Skyland Dr.
Las Vegas, NV 89121
ph: 702-898-6764
fax: 702-898-6764
weetall@earthlink.net
http://www.abebooks.com/home/
ABOOKWORM
Buying and selling out-of-print books since 1968; Americana, Civil War, non-fiction, natural History; interested in purchasing good quality books, maps, and prints.

Eric Chaim Kline
P.O. Box 829
Santa Monica, CA 90406
ph: 310-395-4747 or 818-920-9968
fax: 310-395-8825
ecklinebookseller@att.net
Buys, sells, appraises books; member of Antiquarian Booksellers Assoc. of America for over 18 years; maintains inventory of over 50,000 titles: modern photograph, architecture, decorative arts, Judaica, German language, Olympic games.

Art Sowin
Pahaska Books
8436 Samra Dr.
Canoga Park, CA 91304-3214
ph: 818-346-2171
pahaska@pacbell.net
Specializes in books about the old West.

Len Unger
Len Unger Rare Books
P.O. Box 5858
Sherman Oaks, CA 91413
ph: 818-990-7569
fax: 818-905-7909
lenunger@msn.com
http://bookmarque.net/Len.Unger
Specializes in modern first editions, mystery, Western fiction, Zane Grey, signed books, autographs, and books made into movies.

Howard L. Karno
Howard Karno Books, Inc.
P.O. Box 2100
Valley Center, CA 92082
ph: 760-749-2304
fax: 760-749-4390
howard@karnobooks.com
http://www.karnobooks.com
Particular specialty area is in Latin American arts: graphic, architecture, archaeology, dance, music.

Beverly Joy-Karno
Howard Karno Books, Inc.
P.O. Box 2100
Valley Center, CA 92082
ph: 760-749-2304 or 800-345-2766
fax: 760-749-4390
info@karnobooks.com
http://www.karnobooks.com
Book dealer, appraiser, expert; specialists in Latin American subjects, including the Caribbean.

Barbara Gelink
OTENTO Book Search
4756 Terrace Dr.
San Diego, CA 92116-2514
ph: 619-281-8962
Specialist in out-of-print cookbooks and books on food, wine, food history, and related books; also offers a book finder service; showroom has over 5,000 out-of-print and hard-to-find books on all subjects.

Jean Parmer
Parmer Books
7644 Forrestal Rd.
San Diego, CA 92120-2203
ph: 619-287-0693
fax: 619-287-6135
parmerbook@aol.com
http://stairway.org/parmer/index.html
Polar, Arctic, Antarctic, voyages, sail, Pacific, exploration.

Richard Gilbo
Richard Gilbo - Bookseller
P.O. Box 12
Carpinteria, CA 93014-0012
ph: 805-684-2892
Specializes in books about food and drink, cats; also specializes in literature.

David B. Ogle
Antiquarian Archive, The
330 Second St., Ste. 2
Los Altos, CA 94022
ph: 650-949-1593
antarch@earthlink.net
http://www.ippi.com/antiquarian-archive.html
Specialist in Western Americana, railroadiana, nautical & maritime, military history & memoirs, books of the Roycroft printing shop; office hours by appointment only.

Tom Haydon
Wessex Books
558 Santa Cruz Ave.
Menlo Park, CA 94025
ph: 650-321-1333
fax: 650-856-1984
info@wessexbooks.com
http://www.wessexbooks.com
Over 20,000 modern literary first editions, related criticism, and biography for sale: fiction, poetry, University Press titles, Literature in Translation, British and American first editions.

Brick Row Book Shop
49 Geary St. #235
San Francisco, CA 94108-5705
ph: 415-398-0414
fax: 415-398-0435
crichton@brickrow.com
http://www.brickrow.com
Specializes in first editions of English and American literature, especially of the 18th and 19th centuries; over 8,000 titles in stock; want lists accepted; buys fine and rare books.

Alan Bamberger
2510 Bush St.
San Francisco, CA 94115-3002
ph: 415-931-7875
fax: 415-922-3580
alanb@artbusiness.com
http://www.artbusiness.com
Buys and sells rare, out-of-print and collectible reference books on the fine and decorative arts; member Antiquarian Booksellers Association of America, International League of Antiquarian Booksellers.

J.B. Muns
Fine Arts Books & Musical Autographs
1162 Shattuck Ave.
Berkeley, CA 94707-2635
ph: 510-525-2420
fax: 510-525-1126
jbmuns@aol.com
Buys and sells books: art, architecture, dance, photography; member ABAA, Manuscript Society, UACC, PADA; serving libraries, the public and other dealers since 1964; by appointment only.

Steve Mauer
BookMine.com
2775 Cottage Way, Suite 22
Sacramento, CA 95825
916-485-0342 or books@bookmine.com
http://www.bookmine.com
Specializes in rare books: Western Americana, railroading, science & medicine, children's literature, travel & exploration.

Phil Wikelund
Great Northwest Book Store
1234 S.W. Stark St.
Portland, OR 97205-2310
ph: 503-223-8098
fax: 503-223-9747
gnw@greatnorthwestbooks.com
http://www.greatnorthwestbooks.com

David Morrison
David Morrison Books
530 NW 12th
Portland, OR 97209
ph: 503-295-6882
fax: 503-295-6947
One of the largest collection of out-of-print and rare books on the arts in the Northwest; always interested in buying material in these subjects; offers worldwide book search and appraisal service.

Robert Gavora
Robert Gavora, Fine & Rare Books
P.O. Box 448
Talent, OR 97541
ph: 541-512-9000
fax: 541-535-1226
Books@RobertGavora.com
http://www.RobertGavora.com
ABAA member specializing in first and limited editions of science fiction, horror, mystery, Western Americana, railroading; current inventory on the Web site; wants to buy single items or entire collections.

Ed Leimbacher
MisterE Books & Records
1501 Pike Place Market #432
Seattle, WA 98101
ph: 206-622-5182 or 206-463-3986
fax: 206-622-2697
mistere@mistere.com
http://www.wolfenet.com/~mistere
Collector, dealer specializes in mysteries, children's and illustrated books.

Wessel & Lieberman
121 First Ave. S.
Seattle, WA 98104
ph: 206-682-3545
fax: 206-682-2391
read@wlbooks.com
http://www.wlbooks.com

Louis Collins
Louis Collins Books
1211 East Denny Way
Seattle, WA 98122
206-323-3999 orders@collinsbooks.com
http://www.collinsbooks.com
Specializes in all fields of old books with an emphasis on anthropology/

archaeology and American Indian studies; books in all fields are searched rather successfully; no fee or obligation for searches.

Darrel J. Dillon
Stone House Books
8141 Comox Rd.
Blaine, WA 98230
ph: 360-371-2764
webmaster@stonehousebooks.com
http://www.stonehousebooks.com
Dealer in fine used and rare books; specialty is Sci/Fi, Mystery, Horror, and Juvenile; house authors include Edgar Rice Burroughs, Michael Crichton, Stephen King, Douglas Adams, Issac Asimov, Ian Fleming; has over 10,000 books.

Randolph M. Moss
Eclectic Books
9 Clipper Way
Friday Harbor, WA 98250
ph: 360-378-5732
eclecticbk@aol.com
Buys and sells National Geographic: pre-1915 magazines, bound sets, reprint, books; all publications by The National Geographic Society; also non-fiction books such as art, archaeology, anthropology.

Ann Hall
Bridgeburg Bookstore
16 Jarvis St.
Fort Erie, Ontario L2A 2S1 Canada
ph: 905-871-8484
matthews@vaxxine.com
http://www.vaxxine.com/matthews
Carries a very large stock of used and rare books in all fields; specializes in sensational fiction and early fantasy.

Otto Graser
Arlington Books
21 Arlington Ave.
Ottawa, Ontario K2P 1C1 Canada
ph: 613-232-6975
ograser@arlingtonbooks.ca
http://www.arlingtonbooks.ca
Buys and sells modern first editions, nautical, naval, sailing, true crime, biography, occult.

G.V. Barrett
Barrett's Books
Jackson Station
P.O. Box 57165
Hamilton, Ontario L8P 4X1 Canada
ph: 905-560-1741
gbarrett@mountaincable.net
Buys, collects, sells rare books, ephemera, prints, 1st editions.

Jose Fernandez
Libreria Anticuaria Rebel
Avenida De La Constitucion 27 -1,A
Novelda, Alicante 03660 Spain
ph: (34) 965600338
fax: (34) 965600338
jmartine@teleline.es
http://www.sarrias.com
Specializes in old books, paper collectibles, movie posters, fruit crate labels, bookplates.

W.D.J. Bennett
Postaprint
Taidswood House
Iver Heath, Bucks SL0 0PQ U.K.
ph: +44 1 895 833 720
fax: +44 1 895 834 890
sales@postaprint.co.uk
http://www.postaprint.co.uk
Antique maps, prints, historic engravings, antiquarian atlases and books; has an online database of over 200,000 antique maps, steel, copper or wood engravings available for searching; items date from 1550 to 1899.

Nigel P. Burwood
Any Amount of Books
56 Charing Cross Rd.
London, WC2 H0BB U.K.
ph: 00441718363697
fax: 00441712401769
charingx@anyamountofbooks.com
http://www.anyamountofbooks.com
Specializes in selling second hand and rare books.

Experts

Pat & Allen Ahearn
Quill & Brush
1137 Sugarloaf Mountain Rd.
Dickerson, MD 20842
ph: 301-874-3200
fax: 301-874-0824
firsts@qbbooks.com
http://www.qbbooks.com
Authors of "Book Collecting, A Comprehensive Guide," "Collected Books, The Guide to Values" and over 170 "Author Price Guides."

Douglas O'Dell
Chapel Hill Rare Books
P.O. Box 456
Carrboro, NC 27510
ph: 919-929-8351
fax: 919-967-2532
rarebooks@mindspring.com
Fine rare books in all fields, first editions in literature and Americana; inscribe copies, bindings, travels, etc.; author on books.

Ray Walsh
Curious Book Shop
307 E. Grand River
East Lansing, MI 48823-4324
ph: 517-332-0112
fax: 517-332-1915
mmabda@curiousbooks.com
http://www.curiousbooks.com
Dealer/expert; owner of three book shops in Michigan; hosts radio call-in show about books and paper collectibles; writes columns; send a SASE for reply when writing.

Internet Resources

BookSearch, Inc.
ph: 651-292-1842
fax: 651-292-1742
bksearch@bitstream.net
http://www.booksearch.com
An online book search service.

BookFinder.com
ph: 510-841-1384
feedback@bookfinder.com
http://www.bookfinder.com
Lists books being offered online by over 15,000 booksellers; millions of books.

Amazon.com
info@amazon.com
http://www.amazon.com
Search for books in all categories of antiques & collectibles; in print and out-of-print.

Steve Trussel
Books & Book Collecting
steve@trussel.com
http://www.trussel.com/f_books.htm
Massive online resource for book enthusiasts: book associations, bookbinding, book search services, terms, online libraries, valuations, glossaries, author signatures, and much more.

Craig Stark
Bookologist
P.O. Box 668
Natick, MA 01760
ph: 508-655-5697
craig@bookologist.com
http://www.bookologist.com
This site will help you acquire better books, earn higher prices for them, expand and sharpen your knowledge of topics such as book condition, grading, terminology, first edition points, simple repair, hot tips, and more.

Bibliofind, Inc.
875 Massachussets Ave.
Cambridge, MA 02139
info@amazon.com
http://www.bibliofind.com
Bibliofind has combined with Amazon.com to provide millions of rare, used, and out-of-print books.

Barnes & Noble
76 Ninth Ave., 11th Floor
New York, NY 10011
ph: 800-843-2665 or 201-750-4426
fax: 202-414-6150
service@barnesandnoble.com
http://www.barnesandnoble.com
Web site has millions of out-of-print, rare and used books for sale with a searchable database; book sizes & condition, glossary of out-of-print books.

About.com Hobbies
220 East 42nd St.
New York, NY 10017
pr@about-inc.com
http://home.about.com/hobbies
Online source for information about action figures, antiques, book collecting, coin collecting, collectibles, comic books, costume jewelry, dolls, mineral collecting, pin collecting, sports and trading cards, stamps, toy collecting.

Borders
100 Phoenix Dr.
Ann Arbor, MI 48108
ph: 800-770-7811
http://www.borders.com
Search for books in all categories of antiques & collectibles; in print and out-of-print.

Shoshana & Rex Jemison
Shoshana's Books
17019 19th Ave. East
Spanaway, WA 89387
ph: 253-538-6655
ladyemma@qwest.net
http://www.abebooks.com/home/
SHOSHANAJ
Offers a listing of online book search services; also buys and sells medieval books, and books on scientific and technical subjects.

Alibris
1250 45th St., Ste. 100
Emeryville, CA 94608
webmaster@alibris.com
http://www.alibris.com
The electronic marketplace for books; reach more buyers and sellers; select from 2+ million titles offered by booksellers worldwide; book searching; appraisal offerings.

Cathy Waters
Abebooks.com
#4-415 Dunedin St.
Victoria, British Columbia V8T 5GB
Canada
ph: 250-475-6013
fax: 250-475-6014
buyertech@abebooks.com
http://www.abebooks.com
A premier Internet marketplace for out-of-print, used, rare, and antiquarian books; over 25 million of books listed in a searchable database.

Cor Knops
Book Information Website
Rechter Rottekade 171
Rotterdam, 3032 XD The Netherlands
ph: 31 10 4653837
fax: 21 10 4653837
knops@xs4all.nl
http://www.xs4all.nl/~knops/index3.htm
Web site devoted to all aspects of books, bookarts, book history, letterpress printing, fine printing, book schools, paper and paper making, book artists, bookbinding and book binders, antiquarian books, search services, auctions, etc.

Museums/Libraries

Library of Congress
101 Independence Ave. SE
Washington, DC 20540
ph: 202-707-5000 or 202-707-8000
http://www.loc.gov

Consortium of Popular Culture
  Collections
Popular Culture Library
Bowling Green State University
Bowling Green, OH 43403-0001
ph: 419-372-2450
fax: 419-372-7996
atracy@bgnet.bgsu.edu
http://www.bgsu.edu/colleges/library/pcl/
cpccm.html
  *Consortium composed of Bowling
  Green State U., Kent State U.,
  Michigan State U., and Ohio State U.;
  the largest academic library
  collections of primary research
  material in comic art, popular fiction,
  popular music, performing arts.*

Toledo Museum of Art, The
2445 Monroe St.
P.O. Box 1013
Toledo, OH 43697-1013
ph: 419-255-8000 or 800-644-6862
marketing@toledomuseum.org
http://www.toledomuseum.org
  *Internationally recognized collection
  of artist-illustrated books, as well as
  paintings, decorative arts, graphic
  arts, and glass.*

Periodicals

Katharine Kyes Leab, Editor-in-Chief
Bancroft-Parkman, Inc.
Price Guide: American Book Prices
  Current
P.O. Box 1236
Washington, CT 06793
ph: 860-868-7408
fax: 860-868-0080
abpc@snet.net
http://www.bookpricescurrent.com
  *ABPC is published as an annual
  volume listing over 35,000 prices of
  books, serials, autographs &
  manuscripts, broadsides, maps from
  actual auction sales in US & abroad;
  also published on CD-ROM with over
  800K records from 1975 to present.*

Susan Siegel
Book Hunter Press
Directory: Used Book Lover's Guides
P.O. Box 193
Yorktown Heights, NY 10598
ph: 914-245-6608
fax: 914-245-2630
bookhuntpr@aol.com
http://bookhunterpress.com
  *Seven regional directories and a
  searchable online database to 8,000
  used book dealers in the United States
  and Canada.*

John C. Huckans, Ed.
Magazine: Book Source Magazine
2007 Syossett Dr.
P.O. Box 567
Cazenovia, NY 13035-0567
ph: 315-655-8499
fax: 315-655-8499
books@dreamscape.com
http://www.booksourcemagazine.com
  *Book Source Magazine serves both
  members of the antiquarian book trade
  and private collectors; books, paper*

*ephemera; contains book fair
calendar, book auction calendar,
specialists' directories, catalogs
received, open shop guide.*

Doug Watson
Magazine: Paper Collectors' Marketplace
470 Main St.
P.O. Box 128
Scandinavia, WI 54977-0128
ph: 715-467-2379
fax: 715-467-2243
pcmpaper@gglbbs.com
http://www.pcmpaper.com
  *Monthly magazine for collectors of
  autographs, paperbacks, postcards,
  advertising, photographica,
  magazines; all types of paper
  ephemera.*

First Magazine Inc.
Magazine: Firsts: The Book Collector's
  Magazine
P.O. Box 65166
Tucson, AZ 85728-5166
ph: 520-529-1355
fax: 520-529-5847
firstsmag@aol.com
http://www.firsts.com
  *The monthly magazine for book
  collectors: surveys of various
  collecting areas, checklists of authors'
  published works, retail prices for
  collectible books, keys to identification.*

Repair Services

Pamela Talin-Bryant
Talin Bookbindery
947 Rt. 6A, Cranberry Ct.
Yarmouth Port, MA 02675
ph: 508-362-8144
talinbookbindery@yahoo.com
http://www.talinbookbindery.com
  Restorations of old books.

Scott K. Kellar
Bookbinding & Conservation
2650 Montrose Ave.
Chicago, IL 60618
ph: 773-478-2825
  *Rebinding and restoration of rare
  books.*

Don E. Sanders
Don E. Sanders Bookbinder
1116 Pinion Dr.
Austin, TX 78748
ph: 512-282-4774
  *30 years experience; custom binding &
  cases, restoration and repair.*

Peregrine Arts Bookbindery
P.O. Box 1691
Santa Fe, NM 87504
ph: 505-466-0490
fax: 505-466-0490
  Book repair, marbling.

David Westmoreland
Atwater Book & Bible Repair
1782 McSwain Rd.
Merced, CA 95340
ph: 209-631-6830 or 209-722-9076
atwaterbookandbiblerepair@juno.com
  Specializes in the repair of older

*family bibles, both large and small;
also old cookbooks and dictionaries;
all work done by hand and comes with
two year guarantee; in business since
1980.*

Gary D. Muir
Muir's Book Repair
2115 Garden Ave.
Redding, CA 96001-1202
ph: 530-243-3920
  *Repair/restore any and all types of
  books, bibles, cookbooks, newspapers
  and magazines; also other historical
  documents; chewed-up by dog,
  moisture or water damage, fire
  damage, lost spine, lost front or back,
  loose or torn pages.*

Sophia Bogle
Red Branch Book Craftery, The
2305-C Ashland St., #289
Ashland, OR 97520
ph: 541-732-0161
  Repairs and restores old books.

Aviation Related

Collectors

Paul Davis
308 Landsende Rd.
Devon, PA 19333
ph: 610-644-1216
pwbsdavis@msn.com
  *Wants books on general aviation and
  military aviation history, airplanes,
  etc.*

Big Little

Clubs/Associations

Larry Lowery
Big Little Book Collectors Club of
  America
Newsletter: Big Little Times
P.O. Box 1242
Danville, CA 94526-8242
ph: 925-837-2086
larry@sirius-mail.com
http://www.biglittlebooks.com
  *Club provides a conduit among
  collectors and dealers interested in
  Big Little Books and similar books;
  publishes research and other
  information pertaining to Big Little
  Books; bi-monthly newsletter.*

Experts

Larry Lowery
P.O. Box 1242
Danville, CA 94526-8242
ph: 925-837-2086
larry@sirius-mail.com
http://www.biglittlebooks.com
  *Author of "The Collector's Guide to
  Big Little and Similar Books,"
  "Guide to the Tarzan Big Little
  Books," "Guide to the Dick Tracy Big
  Little Books."*

Ken Mitchell
710 Conacher Dr.
Willowdale, Ontario M2M 3N6 Canada
ph: 416-222-5808
  *Buys and sells comic character
  collectibles (comic books, Sunday*

*funnies, "Big Little Books," etc.) and
other nostalgic paper including music
(Pop) magazines and books from 1890
through 1960s.*

Boys'

Collectors

Joseph A. Ruttar
3116 Teesdale St.
Philadelphia, PA 19152-4514
joeruttar@aol.com
  *Wants boys' series books: Andy Blake,
  Trigger Berg, Hal Keen, Conquest of
  US, Sam Steele, Boy Fortune Hunters,
  Jack Race, Jack Straw, Dave Porter
  (no Special Edition), Square Dollar
  Boys, Boys of Liberty.*

British

Clubs/Associations

Ellie Luchinsky, Sec.
Lewis Carroll Society of North America
Newsletter: Knights Letter, The
P.O. Box 204
Napa, CA 94559
webcontact@lewiscarroll.org
http://www.lewiscarroll.org
  *Many members also collect books and
  other Lewis Carroll related materials.*

Children's

(see also BOOKS, Pop-up & Movable)

Collectors

Alan Levine
P.O. Box 1577
Bloomfield, NJ 07003
ph: 973-743-5288
posterking@aol.com

Mary Young
P.O. Box 9244
Dayton, OH 45409-9244
  *Wants to buy children's school
  readers (primarily first and second
  grade readers) from the 1920s to
  1960s, 1930-1960s coloring and
  punch-out books, and girls' series
  books, storybooks by Saalfield,
  Whitman, Beckley Cardy Co.*

Margery Wilder
22 Dungeness Place
Port Townsend, WA 98368
wildem@olympus.net
  *Interested in out-of-print and
  collectible children's books: wants
  Tasha, Tudor, Maurice Sendak and
  various other charming illustrated
  books.*

Dealers

Marion F. Adler
P.O. Box 627
Stockbridge, MA 01262
ph: 413-298-3559
  *Specializing in out-of-print children's
  books.*

Ten Eyck Books
P.O. Box 84
Southborough, MA 01772
ph: 508-481-3517
fax: 508-490-9954
teneyck@ma.ultranet.com
http://www.abebooks.com/home/
  TENEYCK
  *Specializing in out-of-print children's
  books.*

Marnie Bottesch
Snowbound Books
P.O. Box 458
Norridgewock, ME 04957
ph: 207-634-4398
snowbook@kynd.com
  *Primarily mail order and online; open
  by appointment or chance in warm
  weather; unheated 2-floor barn;
  shelved and categorized but mainly
  unpriced; specializes in boy's and
  girl's series books, children's books,
  WWII, Holocaust, Maine.*

Greg Gillert
Justin G. Shiller Ltd.
1270 Avenue of the Americas
Rockefeller Center, Ste. 302
New York, NY 10020
ph: 212-332-7070 or 914-331-3309
fax: 212-332-7028
early@childlit.com
http://www.childlit.com
  *Established in 1959, claims to be the
  oldest antiquarian book firm in the US
  continuously specializing in rare and
  collectible children's books in all
  languages and covering all time
  periods especially 17th to mid-19th
  century.*

Helen & Marc Younger
Aleph-Bet Books, Inc.
85 Old Mill River Rd.
Pound Ridge, NY 10576
ph: 914-764-7410
fax: 914-764-1356
helen@alephbet.com
http://www.alephbet.com
  *Specializing in fine first editions of
  collectible and rare children's and
  illustrated books; always interested in
  buying books in fine condition;
  business established in 1978.*

Lee Temares
50 Heights Rd.
Plandome, NY 11030-1413
ph: 516-627-8688 or 516-627-2647
fax: 516-627-7822
tembooks@aol.com
  *Buys children's series books; must
  have dust jackets if they originally had
  them; also wants Limited Editions
  Club and Heritage Press, but must be
  very good condition and in fine boxes;
  appraises all books except law &
  medicine.*

Jo Ann Reisler
360 Glyndon St., NE
Vienna, VA 22180-3537
ph: 703-938-2967
fax: 703-938-9057
email@joannreisler.com
http://www.joannreisler.com
  *Wants to buy fine and unusual
  children's, illustrated books, and
  illustrative art; issues about four
  color catalogs per year with almost
  all items in stock illustrated; sample
  catalog for $15.*

Daniel Hirsch
Daniel Hirsch - Fine & Rare Books
P.O. Box 5096
Chapel Hill, NC 27514
ph: 919-542-1816
fax: 919-542-1817
rhirsch@interserv.com
http://rarechildrensbooks.homestead.com/
  home.html
  *Wants Dr. Seuss: posters, books,
  dolls, etc.; also wants fairy tale
  books, pop-ups, movable books,
  panoramas and first editions; Hans
  Christian Andersen, Grimm, Perrault,
  Madame D'Aulnoy, Chris Van
  Allsburg, Maurice Sendak, and others.*

Jane & Bill McCullam
Cattermole Books
9880 Fairmont Rd.
Newbury, OH 44065
ph: 216-338-3253
  *Specializes in buying and selling 20th
  century children's books.*

David B. Mischke
ARMS
120 Cedar St.
Ringsted, IA 50578
ph: 712-866-0191
mischke@netins.net
  *Buys, sells, collects late 19th and
  early 20th century children's books as
  well as nonfiction books of the same
  period.*

Dede Kern
Marvelous Books
P.O. Box 170
Rosebud, MO 63091
ph: 573-764-5506
fax: 573-764-5507
  *Buy/sell quality children's books and
  illustrated books; search service
  available; catalogs issued $5; want
  list available; friendly service for 20
  years.*

Richard D. Hendrickson
ArchBooks, Inc.
P.O. Box 140864
Irving, TX 75014
ph: 972-594-6377
archbooks@archbooks.com
http://www.archbooks.com
  *One of the largest inventories of out-
  of-print or hard-to-find children's
  titles in the US; over 55,000 titles in
  stock; in business for over 20 years.*

Alcott Books
5909 Darnell
Houston, TX 77074-7719
ph: 713-774-2202
bruppert@earthlink.net
http://www.abebooks.com/home/
  ALCOTTBOOKS
  *Wants books: Nancy Drew, Hardy
  Boys, Dana Girls, Judy Bolton, Tom
  Swift, Rick Brant, Little Black Sambo,
  Raggedy Ann, Dick and Jane Readers,
  Oz, all children's series books in fine
  conditions, with dust jackets,
  illustrated.*

Jack Hastings
Prince & the Pauper Collectible
  Children's Books
3201 Adams St.
San Diego, CA 92116-1654
ph: 619-283-4380 or 800-454-3726
fax: 619-283-4666
books@adnc.com
http://www.oldkidsbooks.com
  *Largest book store specializing
  exclusively in children's books; 75,000
  out-of-print and collectibles children's
  books; maintains active, long-term
  search service and research library
  related to children's books.*

Experts

E. Lee Baumgarten
718 1/2 W. John St.
Martinsburg, WV 25401-2204
ph: 304-267-2711
  *Compiler of the 2001-2002 edition of
  "Price Guide & Bibliographic
  Checklist for Children's Illustrated
  Books - 1880-1970" featuring over
  17,000 titles; write or call anytime for
  information about the guide and how
  to order.*

Internet Resources

Martha Rasmussen
E-zine: Martha's KidLit Newsletter
P.O. Box 1488
Ames, IA 50014
marti@isunet.net
http://www.kidlitonline.org
  *An online newsletter for children's
  book collectors; news, reviews and
  articles about collectible authors and
  illustrators.*

Museums/Libraries

American Antiquarian Society
185 Salisbury St.
Worcester, MA 01609
ph: 508-755-5221
fax: 508-753-3311
library@mwa.org
  *A learned society founded in 1812;
  maintains a research library of
  American history and culture in order
  to collect, preserve, and make
  available for study the printed record
  of the US; 3 million books, maps,
  pamphlets, etc.*

Free Library of Philadelphia
1901 Vine St.
Philadelphia, PA 19103
ph: 215-686-5322 or 215-686-5416
http://www.library.phila.gov

Lucile Clarke Memorial Children's
  Library
Central Michigan University
Mount Pleasant, MI 48859
ph: 517-774-3197
clarke@cmich.edu
http://www.lib.cmich.edu/clarke

Periodicals

Rebecca Greason
Newspaper: Gold Mine Review, The
P.O. Box 209
Hershey, PA 17033-0209
ph: 717-533-3039
  *For collectors of all children's
  illustrated books from 1900-1970,
  e.g., those published by the Golden
  Book Company.*

Computer Programs For
Man./Prod./Dist.

Niche Software, Inc.
Software: Book, Magazine & Paper
  Collector, The
7118 NW Terrace
Parkland, FL 33076
ph: 954-344-6561
marketing@collectiblessoftware.com
http://www.collectiblessoftware.com
  *Designed for the collector of books,
  magazines, documents, fruit labels,
  etc.*

PrimaSoft PC, Inc.
Software: Book Organizer
P.O. Box 456
Surrey, British Columbia V3T 5B7
Canada
ph: 800-371-7520 or 604-951-1085
fax: 604-951-7797
support@primasoft.com
http://www.primasoft.com
  *A complete program that allows book
  collectors, hobbyists, book clubs,
  small private or public libraries to
  organize, catalog, and manage their
  collections on their computers;
  organize all your information in one
  place; free downloads.*

Dictionaries
Collectors

Edwin A. Miles
2645 Alta Glen Dr.
Birmingham, AL 35243-4509
ph: 205-967-2504
samnoah@aol.com
  *Wants pre-1865 English-language
  dictionaries (including medical,
  scientific, technological, legal,
  musical, fine arts, agricultural,
  commercial, etc.); also works of slang,
  Americanisms, and lexicography.*

Etiquette

Collectors

Maret Webb
5101 E. Monterey Way
Phoenix, AZ 85018-6623
ph: 602-957-0653
fax: 602-957-1631
maret@vehrwebbstudio.com
Wants vintage etiquette books, pre-1875, pretty bindings, gilded edges, "deportment," "decorum," manners.

First Editions

Collectors

Maria E. Raymond
Plow & Pen, Inc.
P.O. Box 758
Knights Landing, CA 95645-0758
ph: 530-735-6596
mariaraymond@afes.com
Wants first editions only: Atwood, Sarton, Plath, Sexton, Duras, Walker, Hurston.

Dealers

Joanmarie Dale
Stray Books
17 Moquis Trail
Oak Ridge, NJ 07438-9804
ph: 973-208-3105
fax: 973-208-3105
JDale@StrayBooks.com
http://www.StrayBooks.com
Online mail order book shop specializing in First Editions, many signed; free book searches.

Ron Lieberman
Family Album, The
4887 Newport Rd.
Kinzers, PA 17535
ph: 717-442-0220
fax: 717-442-7904
rarebooks@POBox.com
http://www.sellbooks.net
Buys, sells and appraises fine books in all fields, specializing in American and European first editions; advisor to "Warman's Antiques & Collectibles Price Guide."

Pat & Allen Ahearn
Quill & Brush
1137 Sugarloaf Mountain Rd.
Dickerson, MD 20842
ph: 301-874-3200
fax: 301-874-0824
firsts@qbbooks.com
http://www.qbbooks.com
Book dealer specializing in 19th & 20th century first editions; members of ABAA (Antiquarian Booksellers' Association of America), and ILBA (International League of Antiquarian Booksellers); also WABA.

Flip

(see BOOKS, Pop-Ups & Movable [Flip])

Fore-Edge Painted

Experts

Ron Lieberman
Family Album, The
4887 Newport Rd.
Kinzers, PA 17535
ph: 717-442-0220
fax: 717-442-7904
rarebooks@POBox.com
http://www.sellbooks.net
Buys and sells fine books in all fields, specializing in American and European first editions; advisor to "Warman's Antiques & Collectibles Price Guide."

German

Collectors

R.L. Rice
612 E. Front St.
Bloomington, IL 61701-5314
Wants oversized illustrated language books and handwritten diaries in German including Bibles, children's, fashion, art; also wants art books and magazines 1830s -1920s.

Dealers

Eric Chaim Kline
P.O. Box 829
Santa Monica, CA 90406
ph: 310-395-4747 or 818-920-9968
fax: 310-395-8825
ecklinebookseller@att.net
Buys, sells, appraises German language and literature from all periods; specializing in illustrated books, exile literature, baroque and scientific literature and Judaica.

Ghosts

Book Sellers

Chris Woodyard
Invisible Ink: Books on Ghosts & Hauntings
1811 Stonewood Dr.
Beavercreek, OH 45432-4002
ph: 937-426-5110
fax: 937-320-1832
invisiblei@aol.com
http://www.invink.com
Collector of nonfiction books on ghosts & hauntings; also dealer in new and paranormal books; founder of Invisible Ink Collection at BGSU Popular Collection Library.

Illustrated

(see also ILLUSTRATORS)

Dealers

Helen & Marc Younger
Aleph-Bet Books, Inc.
85 Old Mill River Rd.
Pound Ridge, NY 10576
ph: 914-764-7410
fax: 914-764-1356
helen@alephbet.com
http://www.alephbet.com
Specializing in fine first editions of collectible and rare children's and

illustrated books; always interested in buying books in fine condition; business established in 1978.

Jo Ann Reisler
360 Glyndon St., NE
Vienna, VA 22180-3537
ph: 703-938-2967
fax: 703-938-9057
email@joannreisler.com
http://www.joannreisler.com
Wants to buy fine and unusual children's, illustrated books, and illustrative art; issues about four color catalogs per year with almost all items in stock illustrated; sample catalog for $15.

Joseph L. Mashburn
Colonial House
P.O. Box 609 - M
Enka, NC 28728-0609
ph: 828-667-1427
fax: 828-667-1111
jmashb0135@aol.com
http://www.postcard-books.com
Wants large gift books with illustrations by Harrison Fisher, Coles Phillips, Clarence Underwood, Henry Hutt, Howard C. Christy, Charles Gibson, Pogany, Dulac, Erte.

Internet Resources

Denis C. Jackson, Ed.
E-zine: Illustrator Collector's News, The
P.O. Box 6433
Kingman, AZ 86401
ticn@olypen.com
http://www.olypen.com/ticn
An online publication for collectors of magazines and other paper illustrations; free classifieds and articles, no charge Web site information; new and old prints.

Jules Verne

Clubs/Associations

Jean-Michel Margot, Pres.
North American Jules Verne Society, Inc.
Newsletter: Extraordinary Voyages
226 Thomas Ruffin St.
Hillsborough, NC 27278-2119
ph: 919-644-1239
info@najvs.org
http://www.najvs.org
Members are interested in the works of Jules Verne including books, stamps comics, movies and other related ephemera.

Collectors

Dana V. Eales
2447 Delta Dr.
Uniontown, OH 44685-8111
ph: 303-699-5341
deals@sssnet.com
Collects French, English and American translations of Jules Verne novels; primarily early editions but also little known or unusual titles.

Dealers

Jack Hastings
Prince & the Pauper Collectible Children's Books
3201 Adams St.
San Diego, CA 92116-1654
ph: 619-283-4380 or 800-454-3726
fax: 619-283-4666
books@adnc.com
http://www.oldkidsbooks.com
Largest book store specializing exclusively in children's books; 75,000 out-of-print and collectibles children's books; maintains active, long-term search service and research library related to children's books.

Internet Resources

Andrew Nash
JulesVerne.ca
U.K.
anash@julesverne.ca
http://www.julesverne.ca
The Jules Verne collecting resource page.

Juvenile Series

Clubs/Associations

Horatio Alger Society
Newsletter: Newsboy, The
P.O. Box 70361
Richmond, VA 23255
has@ihot.com
http://www3.ihot.com/~has
To further the philosophy of Horatio Alger, Jr. and to encourage the spirit of Strive & Succeed.

Collectors

Mike DeBaptiste
4402 Prasse Rd.
Cleveland, OH 44121
ph: 216-381-8092
Mikesbooks@aol.com
Wants Nancy Drew books in dust jackets; also similar series books such as Hardy Boys, Tom Swift, Judy Bolton, Rick Brant, etc.

Jeff Escue
164 Larchmont Ln.
Bloomingdale, IL 60108-1412
ph: 630-307-6415
jsq2@yahoo.com
Buying kids series books: Hardy Boys, Nancy Drew, Rick Brant, Judy Bolton, Tom Swift, Three Investigators, Big Little Books, Ken Holt, Leo Edwards, Hal Keen, Sue Barton, Chip Hilton, etc.

Victoria Broadhurst
P.O. Box 4078
Dana Point, CA 92629
mrscdrew@aol.com
Wants to buy Nancy Drew and Hardy Boys books in dust jackets.

Dealers

David B. Edwards
Book Safari
P.O. Box 8
Trenton, NJ 08640-0008
ph: 856-231-8362
SeriesBks@aol.com
http://www.seriesbooks.com
*Buys and sells vintage children's
books dating from 1870 through 1990;
many one-of-a-kind items: Hardy Boys,
Cherry Ames, Bobbsey Twins.*

Terri Pointon
Two Kids & a Grownup
tmp125@yahoo.com
Sells old juvenile series books.

Jack Hastings
Prince & the Pauper Collectible
   Children's Books
3201 Adams St.
San Diego, CA 92116-1654
ph: 619-283-4380 or 800-454-3726
fax: 619-283-4666
books@adnc.com
http://www.oldkidsbooks.com
*Largest book store specializing
exclusively in children's books; 75,000
out-of-print and collectibles children's
books; maintains active, long-term
search service and research library
related to children's books.*

Gary Nerman
Nerman's Books & Collectibles
721 Osborne St. South
Winnipeg, Manitoba R3L 2C1 Canada
ph: 204-475-1050 or 204-255-2196
fax: 204-947-0753
nerman@mb.sympatico.ca
http://www.abebooks.com/home/nerman
*Publishes a highly informative
catalog; always interested in buying
children and juvenile books; Web site
lists over 40,000 books including
25,000 children's books.*

Experts

Virginia & David Brown
RR 1, Box 73
Machias, ME 04654-9711
ph: 207-255-4223
cybertiques@cybertiques.com
http://www.cybertiques.com
*Buys and sells; newsletter covers all
aspects of collecting, caring for and
enjoying the Whitman Publishing
Company's juvenile books.*

Periodicals

Gil O'Gara
Yellowback Press
Magazine: Yellowback Library
P.O. Box 36172
Des Moines, IA 50315-0310
ph: 515-287-0404
*Focuses on juvenile series books and
dime novels; largest circulation in the
hobby.*

Randy Cox
Journal: Dime Novel Round-Up
P.O. Box 226
Dundas, MN 55019-0226
ph: 507-645-5711
cox@stolaf.edu
http://www.readseries.com
*A magazine devoted to the collecting,
preservation and literature of the old-
time dime and nickel novels and
popular story papers, series books,
and pulp magazine.*

Fred Woodworth, Pub.
Magazine: Mystery & Adventure Series
Review
P.O. Box 3488
Tucson, AZ 85722-3488
*Quarterly magazine devoted to
collecting and preserving c. 1925-1965
series-books, e.g., Hardy Boys, Ken
Holt & Rick Brant.*

Kate Emburg
Society of Phantom Friends, The
Newsletter: Whispered Watchword, The
P.O. Box 1437
North Highlands, CA 95660-1437
ph: 916-331-7435 or 916-331-7352
dolladopt@aol.com
*A club for readers and collectors of
girls' juvenile fiction from 1900 to
present, including but not limited to
Nancy Drew, Judy Bolton, Trixie
Belden, and Beany Malone; books
bought and sold; please send SASE
with inquiries.*

Law Reference

Collectors

Clint Miller
1604 N. Harrison St.
Little Rock, AR 72207-5322
ph: 501-664-8424 or 501-340-6123
*Wants to buy books on legal
reasoning, legal writing, jurispru-
dence, criminal law, American
constitutional law and legal
questions.*

Dealers

Luke Pavone, VP
National Law Resource, Inc.
328 S. Jefferson
Chicago, IL 60661-5605
ph: 800-279-7799 or 800-886-1800
fax: 773-382-0323
lawstuff@aol.com
*Book dealer of up-to-date, excellent
quality, pre-owned law books; carries
inventories of all Federal, National,
Regional and state sets; also tax
libraries, labor law libraries, GPO
titles, bound legal periodicals, ultra-
fiche.*

Little Golden Books

Collectors

Ilene Kayne
1308 S. Charles St.
Baltimore, MD 21230-4219
ph: 410-685-3923
Wants Little Golden Books; especially

*those with dust jackets or in a foreign
language.*

Dealers

Jack Hastings
Prince & the Pauper Collectible
   Children's Books
3201 Adams St.
San Diego, CA 92116-1654
ph: 619-283-4380 or 800-454-3726
fax: 619-283-4666
books@adnc.com
http://www.oldkidsbooks.com
*Largest book store specializing
exclusively in children's books; 75,000
out-of-print and collectibles children's
books; maintains active, long-term
search service and research library
related to children's books.*

Experts

Steve Santi
19626 Ricardo Ave.
Hayward, CA 94541
ph: 510-481-2586
steve@thesantis.com
http://www.thesantis.com/home.htm
*Buys and sells Little Golden Books;
author of "Collecting Little Golden
Books" (Krause).*

Periodicals

Rebecca Greason
Newspaper: Gold Mine Review, The
P.O. Box 209
Hershey, PA 17033-0209
ph: 717-533-3039
*For collectors of all children's
illustrated books from 1900-1970,
e.g., those published by the Golden
Book Company.*

Metaphysics

Dealers

Dennis E. Whelan
Samadhi Books
P.O. Box 609
Melrose, FL 32666
ph: 352-475-9520
fax: 352-475-9520
samadhi@fdt.net
*Collector and seller of metaphysical
books/magazines: esoterica, mysticism,
yoga, astrology, Tibet, Egypt,
Atlantis, herbalism, UFO, tarot,
crystal balls, the unexplained, etc.;
SASE plus $1 for annual catalog; free
search service.*

Military History

(see also MILITARY HISTORY)

Dealers

Paul Hunt
Atlantis Books
3508 W. Magnolia Blvd.
Burbank, CA 91505
ph: 818-556-3441
BuyBook@pacbell.net
http://www.atlantisbookshop.com
Buys and sells books, specialty: back

*issue magazines, and military and
history.*

Miniature

Clubs/Associations

Mark Palkovic, Treas.
Miniature Book Society
Newsletter: Newsletter of the Miniature
   Book Society
620 Clinton Springs Ave.
Cincinnati, OH 45229
ph: 513-556-1964
fax: 513-556-3777
palkovma@ucmail.uc.edu
http://www.mbs.org
*International non-profit organization;
purpose is to sustain an interest in all
phases of miniature book; members
include collectors, book dealers,
bookbinders, book artists and others
interested in books under 3 inches in
size.*

Dealers

Reg & Sally Lombard
Lombard Antiquarian Maps & Prints
P.O. Box 6565
Scarborough, ME 04070
ph: 207-885-9177
fax: 207-885-9575
rtl@lombardmaps.com
http://www.lombardmaps.com
*Specializes in fine maps, charts, fore-
edge-painted books and miniature
books, rare botanical, natural history
and architectural prints; also maps,
prints, and books relating to
Napoleon I.*

Experts

Ron Lieberman
Family Album, The
4887 Newport Rd.
Kinzers, PA 17535
ph: 717-442-0220
fax: 717-442-7904
rarebooks@POBox.com
http://www.sellbooks.net

Modern Library

Periodicals

A. Oestreich
Newsletter: Modern Library Collector,
The
340 Warren Ave.
Cincinnati, OH 45220-1135
*For collectors of "Modern Library"
and "Viking Portable" books;
published twice a year.*

Mountaineering

Book Sellers

Chessler Books
P.O. Box 4359
Kittredge, CO 80457-4359
ph: 800-654-8502 or 303-670-0093
fax: 303-670-9727
chesslerbk@aol.com
http://www.abebooks.com/home/
   CHESSLERBOOKS
Extensive selection of books on

mountaineering, rock climbing,
exploration, guidebooks.

Movable

(see BOOKS, Children's; BOOKS,
Pop-Up & Movable)

Movie & TV Related

Dealers

Paul Hunt
Atlantis Books
3508 W. Magnolia Blvd.
Burbank, CA 91505
ph: 818-556-3441
BuyBook@pacbell.net
http://www.atlantisbookshop.com
Buys and sells books, specialty: back
issue magazines, and military and
history.

Mystery

Collectors

Beverley Furlow-Cleary
2620 Stewart Rd.
Signal Mountain, TN 37377
ph: 423-517-0703
beverleyf@aol.com
http://www.BeverleyFurlowClearly.net
Buys, sells, and appraises collectible
mystery/detective items: books, vintage
clothing and hats.

Dealers

Michael S. Greenbaum
Janus Books, Ltd.
P.O. Box 40787
Tucson, AZ 85717
ph: 520-881-8192 or 800-986-1165
fax: 815-333-2938
mike@janusbooks.com
http://janusbooks.com
Buys and sells first edition of
detective, mystery, and suspense
fiction; related bibliography and
criticism; Sherlock Holmes; catalog
available by snail mail or online.

New York

Collectors

James L. Sedore, Jr. CPA
431 McGrath Blvd.
Fishkill, NY 12524-2831
ph: 845-831-8535
fax: 845-297-1432
91nyg87@worldnet.att.net
Wants to buy books on New York
State; Dutchess City, NY; Hudson
Valley, NY; also of Indians of the
Hudson River Valley; also wants
American history books and books
about the American Revolution.

Paperback

(see also MAGAZINES, Pulp)

Clubs/Associations

Ray Duncan
British Association of Paperback
  Collectors
Newsletter: PBO
21 Wiltshire Close
Bedworth, Warwicks CV12 8EU U.K.
International club interested in vintage
paperback books.

Dealers

Graham Holroyd
Books Are Everything!
31 Lancer Place
Webster, NY 14580
ph: 585-670-9438
fax: 585-670-9704
gholroyd@rochester.rr.com
http://www.booksareeverything.com
Mail-order paperback book company
with over 100,000 vintage paperbacks
in stock.

Jerry Rodnitzky
All America Paper Collectibles
1832 Westcrest Dr.
Arlington, TX 76013
ph: 817-861-8199
jrodprof@yahoo.com
http://www.aapapercollect.com.
Buys and sells vintage paperbacks,
illustrated magazines, movie posters,
sports collectibles, other paper items.

Experts

Gary Lovisi
Gryphon Books
P.O. Box 280209
Brooklyn, NY 11228-0209
ph: 718-646-6126
http://www.gryphonbooks.com
Paperback collector, expert; publisher
of "Paperback Parade," a magazine
for paperback readers and collectors.

Graham Holroyd
Books Are Everything!
31 Lancer Place
Webster, NY 14580
ph: 585-670-9438
fax: 585-670-9704
gholroyd@rochester.rr.com
http://www.booksareeverything.com
Author of "Paperback Prices."

Ray Walsh
Curious Book Shop
307 E. Grand River
East Lansing, MI 48823-4324
ph: 517-332-0112
fax: 517-332-1915
mmabda@curiousbooks.com
http://www.curiousbooks.com
Dealer/expert; owner of three book
shops in Michigan; hosts radio call-in
show about books and paper
collectibles; writes columns; send a
SASE for reply when writing.

Periodicals

Gary Lovisi
Gryphon Books
Magazine: Paperback Parade
P.O. Box 280209
Brooklyn, NY 11228-0209
ph: 718-646-6126
http://www.gryphonbooks.com
A magazine for paperback readers and
collectors; news, articles, lists,
interviews; a hobby publication full of
news and info about paperbacks;
issues are 100+ pages with color
covers; $10 each, subscriptions $35/
year.

Randy Cox
Journal: Dime Novel Round-Up
P.O. Box 226
Dundas, MN 55019-0226
ph: 507-645-5711
cox@stolaf.edu
http://www.readseries.com
A magazine devoted to the collecting,
preservation and literature of the old-
time dime and nickel novels and
popular story papers, series books,
and pulp magazine.

Pocket

Collectors

Bruce Axler
Ansonia Station
P.O. Box 1288
New York, NY 10023-1288
ph: 212-579-0348
Wants to buy pocket books from the
19th century (1800s) that people
carried which were loaded with
information, e.g., dictionaries,
almanacs, encyclopedias, reckoners;
no fiction, religious, poetry, foreign,
speeches, or bio.

Pop-Up & Movable

(see also BOOKS, Children's)

Clubs/Associations

Ann Montanaro
Movable Book Society
Newsletter: Movable Stationery
P.O. Box 11645
New Brunswick, NJ 08906-1645
ph: 732-247-6071 or 732-445-5896
fax: 732-846-7928
montanar@rci.rutgers.edu
http://www.rci.rutgers.edu/~montanar/
  mbs.html
Forum for collectors of pop-up and
movable books to share collecting
resources, research, and questions
about individual titles.

Collectors

Ann Montanaro
P.O. Box 11645
New Brunswick, NJ 08906-1645
ph: 732-247-6071 or 732-445-5896
fax: 732-846-7928
montanar@rci.rutgers.edu
http://www.rci.rutgers.edu/~montanar
Wants to buy pop-up and movable
books.

Margery Wilder
22 Dungeness Place
Port Townsend, WA 98368
wildem@olympus.net
Collecting pop-up, mechanical, fold-
out, unusual children's books.

Dealers

Helen & Marc Younger
Aleph-Bet Books, Inc.
85 Old Mill River Rd.
Pound Ridge, NY 10576
ph: 914-764-7410
fax: 914-764-1356
helen@alephbet.com
http://www.alephbet.com
Specializing in fine first editions of
collectible and rare children's and
illustrated books; always interested in
buying books in fine condition;
business established in 1978.

Ampersand Books
Ludford Mill
Ludlow, Shropshire SY8 1PP U.K.
ph: +44 1584 877813
fax: +44 1584 877519
ampersand.books@mcmail.com
http://
  www.ampersand.books.mcmail.com
Specializes exclusively in dimensional
and interactive books: antiquarian,
rare, second-hand; pop-ups, movables,
children's novelty books, peep show
and tunnel books, panoramas, flicks,
carousels, tab-operated animations,
revolving, etc.

Pop-Up & Movable (Flip)

Collectors

Robin Klein
801 Welington St.
Baltimore, MD 21211-2513
Interested in contacting other
collectors of flip books.

Poultry

Collectors

Clark Kidder
3219 E. County Rd. "N"
Milton, WI 53563
ph: 608-868-4185
fax: 608-868-6808
ckidder@jvlnet.com
http://www.jvlnet.com/marilyn
Expert, collector of pre-1926 books on
fancy show-type poultry that feature
color plates of chickens, ducks, geese,
or turkeys.

Railroad

Experts

Jim Younger
4628 Old Dragon Path
Ellicott City, MD 21042-5970
ph: 410-964-1949
boomer-op@ragingbull.com
Buys, sells, trades out-of-print railroad-themed fiction (novels, short stories, juveniles, poetry, dime novels, paperbacks, etc.) and true stories (autobiographies, biographies, reminiscences of or by railroaders, c. 1830-1990.

Reference (Antiques)

Book Sellers

Amazon.com
info@amazon.com
http://www.amazon.com

Grace Miller Dickinson
Miller's Daughter, The
21 Poplar Hill Rd.
Haydenville, MA 01039-9602
ph: 877-829-9114
Essential reference books on furniture, the decorative arts, tools, antiques, glass and collectibles; appearing at select shows; also by mail order and from the shop.

Joslin Hall Rare Books
P.O. Box 516
Concord, MA 01742
ph: 978-371-3101
fax: 978-371-6445
betty@joslinhall.com
http://www.joslinhall.com
Specialists in rare books on the decorative arts and American fine art.

F. Russack Antiques & Books
20 Beach Plain Rd.
Danville, NH 03819
ph: 603-642-7718
fax: 603-642-7718
info@booksaboutantiques.com
http://www.booksaboutantiques.com
Specializes in out-of-print books about decorative arts, folk art, Americana.

Greg Johnson
Books About Antiques
168 New Milford Tpke.
P.O. Box 2358
New Preston Marble Dale, CT 06777-0358
ph: 860-868-1611
fax: 860-868-1620

Barnes & Noble
76 Ninth Ave., 11th Floor
New York, NY 10011
ph: 800-843-2665 or 201-750-4426
fax: 202-414-6150
service@barnesandnoble.com
http://www.barnesandnoble.com

John-Peter J. Hayden, Jr.
Hayden & Fandetta Rare Books
Radio City Station
P.O. Box 1549
New York, NY 10101-1549
ph: 212-582-2505 or 917-972-6161
Specializes in rare books about antiques, interior design, and gardens and flowers.

Richard & Eileen Dubrow
Richard & Eileen Dubrow Antiques & Books
P.O. Box 128
Flushing, NY 11361-0128
ph: 718-767-9758
fax: 718-767-8172
er4books@aol.com
Sells books (out-of-print and current) about 19th C. furniture and about furniture, fine arts and decorative arts.

Antique Collectors' Club, Ltd.
91 Market St. Industrial Park
Wappingers Falls, NY 12590
ph: 800-247-9955 or 914-297-0003
fax: 914-297-0068
info@antiquecc.com
http://www.antiquecc.com
Carries the best books and price guides on the fine and decorative arts; also on architecture and garden design; retail sales; Mayer's on CD, Gordon's, art books, price guides, furniture, glass, textiles, metalwork, ceramics

Doris Motta
ArtBooks
P.O. Box 745
Cooperstown, NY 13326-0745
ph: 607-547-9748
artbooksdm@aol.com
Books and catalogs on fine and decorative arts; seasonal shop open June through August, Friday, Saturday and Sunday, in the Roseboro Hotel Shop annex in Sharon Springs, NY.

Whitehouse-Books.com
60 East Market St.
Corning, NY 14830
ph: 607-936-8536 or 800-935-8536
fax: 607-936-2465
julia@whitehouse-books.com
http://www.whitehouse-books.com
One of the world's largest selections of new and out-of-print books about glass; also books about ceramics, silver, furniture, jewelry, textiles, and other antiques & collectibles.

William Blystone
Blystone Books
2132 Delaware Ave.
Pittsburgh, PA 15218-1811
ph: 724-371-3511
Sells in print & out-of-print collectibles books by mail; specialty areas are dolls, toys and train books; looking for new book sources.

Donna Stiner
Reference Rack II, Inc., The
P.O. Box 445
Orefield, PA 18069-0445
ph: 800-722-7279 or 610-395-0004
fax: 610-366-0551
dstiner@aol.com
http://www.referencerack.com
New reference books on antiques, art and collectibles.

Schiffer Publishing, Ltd.
4880 Lower Valley Rd.
Atglen, PA 19310-9717
ph: 610-593-1777
fax: 610-593-2002
schifferbk@aol.com
http://www.schifferbooks.com
Carries a line of high quality books focusing on antiques and collectibles.

Winterthur Museum Bookstore
ph: 800-448-3883 or 302-888-4600
webmaster@winterthur.org
http://www.winterthur.org

Edward Johnson
Nancy Antiques & Books
P.O. Box 4894
Lutherville Timonium, MD 21094
ph: 410-683-1519
fax: 410-683-4894
nancyant@erols.com
http://www.bookmallventura.com/nancyantiques.html
Reference books on 20th century design and the decorative arts: antiquarian, in-print, European, Art Deco, Art Nouveau, industrial design, furniture, glass, ceramics, silver, jewelry, fashion, textiles, posters.

Crown Publishers, Inc.
c/o Random House
400 Hahn Rd.
Westminster, MD 21157
ph: 410-848-1900 or 800-733-3000
crownpublicity@randomhouse.com
http://www.randomhouse.com
Offers books about antiques and collectibles.

David & Kathleen Way
Antique Books
P.O. Box 6395
Annapolis, MD 21401-0395
ph: 410-268-0845
fax: 410-268-0845
Sells quality new and out-of-print books about antiques and collectibles.

Perry Franks
Collector's Companion
P.O. Box 935
Mechanicsville, VA 23111-0935
ph: 804-321-9212
bookscc@aol.com
http://www.collectorscompanion.com
Offering over 6,500 different new and out-of-print reference/price guides dealing with antiques and collectibles; exhibits at many Virginia shows; limited book displays at selected Virginia antique malls; mail order available.

Harold Haskins
Southeastern Library Service
P.O. Box 44
Gainesville, FL 32602-0044
ph: 352-372-3823
haskins@gru.net
Sells wholesale to booksellers and libraries; bi-monthly catalogs.

Bill Schroeder
Collector Books
P.O. Box 3009
Paducah, KY 42002-3009
ph: 800-626-5420 or 270-898-6211
fax: 270-898-8890
info@collectorbooks.com
http://www.collectorbooks.com
Publishers of books on antique and collectibles; specializes in full color value guides; since 1970.

Karen Nester
Green Gate Books
P.O. Box 989
Lima, OH 45802-0989
ph: 419-222-3816 or 800-228-3816 orders
fax: 419-227-3816
ggb@greengatebooks.com
http://www.greengatebooks.com
Offers almost 2,000 titles at retail and wholesale on books about antiques, collectibles and related crafts; also carries dealer's stickers, book display racks and plate racks.

L-W Book Sales
P.O. Box 69, Dept. 105
Gas City, IN 46933-0069
ph: 800-777-6450 or 765-674-6450
fax: 765-674-3503
catalogs@lwbooks.com
http://www.lwbooks.com
Distributor of over 1,000 titles of reference books on antiques & collectibles; wholesale and retail; call 1-800-777-6450, Dept. 105 for a FREE catalog.

Borders
100 Phoenix Dr.
Ann Arbor, MI 48108
ph: 800-770-7811
http://www.borders.com
Search for books in all categories of antiques & collectibles; in print and out-of-print.

Nancy Johnson
Library, The
P.O. Box 37
Des Moines, IA 50301-0037
ph: 515-262-6714
fax: 515-263-8116
njohnson@collectorsextravaganza.com
Reference books on antiques, collectibles and the decorative arts; including foreign and private presses; over 7,500 titles in stock; sells at antiques shows in Midwest and West and by mail order.

Mark Chervenka
P.O. Box 12130
Des Moines, IA 50312-9403
ph: 515-274-5886
fax: 515-255-4530
acrn@repronews.com
http://www.repronews.com
Buys and sells used reference books on antiques.

JR's Collector Reference Books, Inc.
P.O. Box 4234
Des Moines, IA 50333
ph: 800-726-5086 or 515-283-0200
fax: 800-836-3243
booksales@jrsbooks.com
http://www.jrsbooks.com
Wholesale mail order source for newly published antiques and collectibles reference books.

Stacie Berger
Antique Trader Books
P.O. Box 1050
Dubuque, IA 52004-1050
ph: 800-334-7165
fax: 800-531-0880
stacie.berger@fwpubs.com
http://www.collect.com
Offers best selling price guides and reference books on nearly every antique and collectible category imaginable; quality purchase discounts available; send or call for free catalog.

Stacie Berger
Krause Publications
700 E. State St.
Iola, WI 54990-0001
ph: 715-445-2214
fax: 715-445-4087
stacie.berger@fwpubs.com
http://www.krause.com
Publisher of a complete line of reference books on antiques and collectibles; more than 700 titles available; call or write for free catalog.

Herzinger & Co., Inc.
P.O. Box 316
Sagle, ID 83860
ph: 800-428-2670
fax: 800-285-1502
books@herzingerco.com
http://www.herzinger.com
Wholesale distributor of reference book & price guides for antiques and collectibles, decor and art; in business for over 20 years; offering over 1,900 titles from Collector Books, Krause, Schiffer, L&W Books, Random House, Charlton, etc.

Mickey Kaz
BooksR4U
P.O. Box 606
Woodland Hills, CA 91365-0606
ph: 818-703-6173
fax: 818-703-6173
mickey@collectibles-unlimited.com
http://www.books4u.net
Specializing in price guides on antiques, collectibles, dolls, toys, jewelry, etc.; online secure shopping cart service, searchable index by keyword; in business since 1977 with over 9,000 titles in stock for shipment worldwide.

Mary M. Claret
Ms. Information
P.O. Box 262
El Granada, CA 94018-0262
ph: 650-726-1367
fax: 650-726-1367
msinfo@mail.coastside.net
http://www.msinfobooks.com
Sells out-of-print, used & new books about antiques & collectibles; Web site has extensive online catalog of books for sale; also provides new (in-print) books and used titles, bibliographical database and free search service.

Paul Brannan
Brannan Books
P.O. Box 475
Garberville, CA 95542
ph: 707-923-3552
fax: 707-923-2560
brannan@humboldt.net
http://www.humboldt.net/~brannan
Stocks out-of-print and rare books and exhibition catalogs on European, American, and Oriental art, artists, and antiques.

Richard J. Perry
Collectors Press, Inc.
P.O. Box 230986
Portland, OR 97281-0986
ph: 503-684-3030 or 800-423-1848
fax: 503-684-3777
rperry@collectorspress.com
http://www.collectorspress.com
Publishes books on nostalgia, art, and collecting; always looking for new book submissions and/or ideas.

Estella Gelder
Estella G. Gelder Books
2728 Iron St.
Bellingham, WA 98225
ph: 360-733-0658
egelder@nas.com
http://www.abebooks.com/home/estellasbooks
Internet online source for books about antiques & collectibles.

W. K. Cross, Pres.
Charlton Press
P.O. Bpx 820
Station Willowdale B
North York, Ontario M2K 2R1 Canada
ph: 800-442-6042 or 416-488-1418
fax: 416-488-4656
chpress@charltonpress.com
http://www.charltonpress.com
Publishes books on Royal Doulton, Beswick, Chintz, Wade, Coalport, Royal Worcester, coins, paper money, country store collectibles.

John Ives
John Ives Antiquarian Books
5 Normanhurst Dr.
Twickenham, Middlesex TW1 1NA
U.K.
ph: 020 8892 6265
fax: 020 8744 3944
jives@btconnect.com
http://www.ukbookworld.com/members/johnives
Supplies specialist reference books on antiques and collecting to customers all over the world; send for free catalog.

Collectors

Karen S. Rabe, ISA CAPP
Appraisal Specialists
P.O. Box 410
Lake Forest, IL 60083
ph: 847-356-2094
fax: 847-356-2139
ksrabe@earthlink.net
Wants to buy out-of-print books about the fine arts and decorative arts, furniture, glass, ceramics, and silver.

Dealers

Wendy Kenney
EphemerArts
229 E. 31st St., #1
New York, NY 10016
ph: 212-481-0138 or 888-518-6610
fax: 212-689-3860
wendy@ephemerarts.com
http://ephemerarts.com
Carries auction catalogs, exhibition catalogs, reference books and out-of-print books on antiques & collectibles; online catalog includes Asian arts, Americana, decorative arts, dolls, pottery, porcelain, glass jewelry, toys, etc.

J. M. Cohen
J. M. Cohen, Rare Books
2 Karin Court
New Paltz, NY 12561
ph: 914-883-9720
fax: 914-883-9142
jmcohen@jmcohenrarebooks.com
http://www.jmcohenrarebooks.com
Specializes in books on the decorative and applied arts, costume and fashion, jewelry, ornament and design.

Internet Resources

Jeff Savage
eCollectica Publishing
ph: 707-824-1711
jsavage@savagesguide.com
http://www.ecollectica.com
Publisher on online ebooks relating to antiques and collectibles.

Reference (Architecture)

Dealers

Arcade Books
P.O. Box 5176
FDR Station
New York, NY 10150-5176
ph: 212-724-5371

Reference (Art)

Book Sellers

Arthur Fraumeni
New England Gallery
367 Gov. Wentworth Hwy.
Wolfeboro, NH 03894-4616
ph: 603-569-3501 or 954-567-7289
fax: 603-569-3358
scollysq@aol.com
http://members.aol.com/scollysq/prof/index.htm
Distributor of "Benezit" Dictionnaire des Peintres, artprice.com International Art Price Annual books and CD-ROM (formerly ADEC) and portable blacklights.

Peter Hastings Falk, Ed.
Falk Art Management, LLC
P.O. Box 833
Madison, CT 06443
ph: 203-245-4761
pfalk@cshore.com
http://www.soundviewpressbooks.com
Researches, writes and publishes books about artists listed in "Who's Who in American Art;" also publishes/sells art reference dictionaries; promotes and manages artist estate collections.

Dealer's Choice Books
P.O. Box 710
Land O Lakes, FL 34639-0710
ph: 813-996-6599 or 800-278-2637
fax: 813-996-5226
orders@dealerschoicebooks.com
http://www.dealerschoicebooks.com
Sells art reference books (new only), e.g., Hislop's "Art Sales Index," "Who Was Who in American Art," "Signatures of American Artists," "Davenport's Art Price Guide," "Benezit," "Meyer's," Falk's "Print Price Index," etc.

Paul Brannan
Brannan Books
P.O. Box 475
Garberville, CA 95542
ph: 707-923-3552
fax: 707-923-2560
brannan@humboldt.net
http://www.humboldt.net/~brannan
Stocks out-of-print and rare books and exhibition catalogs on European, American, and Oriental art, artists, and antiques.

Collectors

Karen S. Rabe, ISA CAPP
Appraisal Specialists
P.O. Box 410
Lake Forest, IL 60083
ph: 847-356-2094
fax: 847-356-2139
ksrabe@earthlink.net
Wants to buy out-of-print books about the fine arts and decorative arts, furniture, glass, ceramics, and silver.

Reference (Art, Asian)

Book Sellers

Jerrold G. Stanoff
Rare Oriental Book Co.
P.O. Box 1599
Aptos, CA 95001-1599
ph: 831-689-0203
fax: 831-689-0204
jgs@rareorientalbooks.com
http://www.rareorientalbooks.com
Sells old, rare choice books on Japan, Korea, China, Tibet, S.E. Asia, Philippines, Hong Kong, Macau, Indonesia, Siam, Malaya, Singapore, Cambodia, Laos, Burma, Vietnam, Mongolia, New Guinea, Central Asia, Indonesia, Bali, etc.

Reference (Automobiles)

Book Sellers

Eric Waiter Associates
205 US Hwy. 22
Dunellen, NJ 08812
ph: 732-424-0200 or 732-424-7811
fax: 732-424-7814
ewa@ewacars.com
http://www.ewacars.com
Carries large selection of automobile related books, magazines and videos; over 1,500 titles on a wide variety of subjects; catalog sent free on request.

MotorLit.com
P.O. Box 4907
Mesa, AZ 85211-4907
ph: 480-969-0102
fax: 413-215-4239
info@motorlit.com
http://www.motorlit.com
Rare and out-of-print automotive books; automobile racing and marquee histories, biographies, yearbooks, programs, ticket stubs, postcards, photos, posters, models, slot cars, and more.

Dennis Mitosinka
Dennis Mitosinka's Classic Cars
619 E. Fourth St.
Santa Ana, CA 92701-4705
ph: 714-953-5303
fax: 714-953-1810
Over 400 titles of car-related out-of-print books including large selection of Clymer books, Indy 500 Year Books, Salt Flat Racing.

Reference (Aviation)

Book Sellers

Historic Aviation
1401 King Wood Rd.
Saint Paul, MN 55122
ph: 800-225-5575 or 612-454-2493
fax: 612-454-8554
Sells aviation related books, videos and prints.

Reference (Breweriana)

Book Sellers

Soda Mart - Can World
1055 Ridgecrest Dr.
Goodlettsville, TN 37072
ph: 615-859-5236 or 800-826-4929
fax: 615-859-5238
mbca@gono.com
http://www.gono.com/vir-mus/museum.htm
Sells breweriana books; also cleans and de-rusts on cans, and sells supplies for the beer can collector.

Reference (Cameras)

Book Sellers

Jim McKeown
Centennial Photo Service
11595 State Route 70
Grantsburg, WI 54840
ph: 715-689-2153
fax: 715-689-2277
mckeown@camera-net.com
http://www.camera-net.com
Publisher of "McKeown's Price Guide to Antique & Classic Cameras," the world's leading camera reference work; over 25,000 different models with values; heavily illustrated; send for details on latest edition; dealer inquiries invited.

William P. Carroll
ACR Books
8500 La Entrada
Whittier, CA 90605
ph: 562-693-8421
fax: 562-945-6011
acrbooks@concentric.net
http://webtch.com/ACRbooks
Antique and classic cameras for sale; offers new and used books on kaleidoscopes, cameras and the history of photography.

Reference (Ceramics)

Book Sellers

Bradshaw & Whelan Ceramic Books
P.O. Box 18521
Asheville, NC 28814
ph: 828-253-1829
fax: 828-281-4798
info@ceramicbooks.com
http://www.ceramicbooks.com
Specializes in out-of-print, used and new ceramic reference books including British, Continental, Oriental, and American pottery and porcelain books; offers a free book search service for ceramics and other decorative arts titles.

David Richardson
Antique Publications
217 Union St.
P.O. Box 553
Marietta, OH 45750-0553
ph: 800-533-3433 or 740-373-6146
fax: 740-373-6917
info@glasscollectingbooks.com
http://www.glasscollectingbooks.com
Offers a wide selection of books about pottery and glass.

Reference (Civil War)

Book Sellers

Jim & Judy McLean
Butternut & Blue
3411 Northwind Rd.
Baltimore, MD 21234
ph: 410-256-9220
bbcwbks@mdo.net
Buys and sells Civil War related books; issues five catalogs per year containing a variety of out-of-print titles as well as in-print selections from almost every publisher of Civil War Books.

Dennis M Gregg
CWBooks.com
P.O. Box 67
Funkstown, MD 21734-0067
ph: 301-714-0005
curator@cwbooks.com
http://www.cwbooks.com
Sells Civil War related reference books; learn what it is and what it is worth; a complete line of books for collectors and dealers.

North South Trader
P.O. Drawer 631
Orange, VA 22960-0370
ph: 540-672-4845
fax: 540-672-5921
publisher@nstcivilwar.com
http://www.nstcivilwar.com
Carries extensive inventory of hardbound and softbound books for Civil War historians, enthusiasts and collectors.

Theodore P. Savas
SAVAS Publishing Company & Consulting Group
P.O. Box 4527
El Dorado Hills, CA 95762
ph: 916-941-6896 or 800-848-6585
fax: 916-941-6895
militarybooks@onemain.com
http://www.savaspublishing.com
Publisher of Civil War books; experienced publishing team assists publishers and independent authors conceive, design, layout, produce, and market their titles.

Reference (Clocks)

Book Sellers

Heart of America Press
55 N. Central
Umatilla, FL 32784
ph: 352-669-4791
fax: 352-669-6969
sales@hoapress.com
http://www.hoapress.com
Issues catalog of horological books and literature.

Tran Duy Ly
Arlington Book Company, Inc.
215 Shadowood Dr.
Johnson City, TN 37604
ph: 423-283-9004
fax: 423-283-9001
tranduyly@aol.com
http://www.arlingtonbooks.com
Carries many books about antique clocks including those by site owner and author Tran Duy Ly.

John Pierson
ClockWorks Press International, Inc.
P.O. Box 1699
Shingle Springs, CA 95682-1699
ph: 530-677-7811 or 800-580-7701
fax: 530-677-7887
info@clockrepair.com
http://www.clockrepair.com
A horological bookseller; carries over 600 titles.

Reference (Coin-Operated)

Book Sellers

Ken Durham
GameRoomAntiques
909 26th St. NW
Washington, DC 20037-2029
durham@gameroomantiques.com
http://www.GameRoomAntiques.com
Sells large selection of books and service manuals about coin-operated machines.

Rosanna Harris
Royal Bell
5815 W. 52nd Ave.
Denver, CO 80212-7503
ph: 303-431-9266
fax: 303-431-6978
info@royalbell.com
http://www.royalbell.com
Carries selection of books and service manuals relating to slot machines.

Peter Movsesian
Coin-Op Classics
17844 Toiyabe St.
Fountain Valley, CA 92708
ph: 714-968-3020
fax: 714-963-1716
Publishes books on vintage coin-operated machines; books include photos, history, original service manuals, schematics, etc.; all books include price guides.

Reference (Coins)

Book Sellers

Bowers & Merena, Inc.
P.O. Box 1224
Wolfeboro, NH 03894-1224
ph: 800-458-4646 or 603-569-5095
fax: 603-569-5319
directsales@Bowersandmerena.com
http://www.bowersandmerena.com
Sells books relating to all areas of the US coin business and hobby; gold, silver, tokens, and all other areas of numismatics including exonumia; member International Association of Professional Numismatists.

George F. Kolbe
Fine Numismatic Books
P.O. Drawer 3100
Crestline, CA 92325-3100
ph: 909-338-6527
fax: 909-338-6980
GFK@numislit.com
http://www.numislit.com
Sells numismatic literature.

Reference (Dolls)

Book Sellers

F. Russack Antiques & Books
20 Beach Plain Rd.
Danville, NH 03819
ph: 603-642-7718
fax: 603-642-7718
info@booksaboutantiques.com
http://www.booksaboutantiques.com

Thomas Farrell
Portfolio Press
130 Wineow St., Ste. 3
Cumberland, MD 21502
ph: 301-724-2795 or 877-737-1200
fax: 301-724-2796
tfarrell@hereintown.net
Specializes in publishing books about collectible dolls and teddy bears.

Jennifer Hare
Hobby House Press, Inc.
One Corporate Dr.
Grantsville, MD 21536
ph: 301-895-3792 or 800-554-1447
fax: 301-895-5029
email@hobbyhouse.com
http://www.hobbyhouse.com
Specializes in books on collectibles, dolls and teddy bears, paper dolls, and vintage clothing; also gift and seasonal books, collectibles organizers and albums; identification and price guides are a specialty.

Reference (Exonumia)

Book Sellers

Rich Hartzog
World Exonumia
P.O. Box 4143CNZ
Rockford, IL 61110-0643
ph: 815-226-0771
hartzog@exonumia.com
http://www.exonumia.com
Carries a large selection of titles relating to tokens, medals, and exonumia.

Reference (Farm Toys)

Book Sellers

Shawn Van Meeuwen
Diamond Enterprises & Book Publishers
P.O. Box 537
Alexandria Bay, NY 13607-0537
ph: 613-475-1771 or 800-481-1353
fax: 613-475-3748
info@yesteryeartoys.com
http://www.yesteryeartoys.com
Offers a complete line of hobby and toy publications; specialty in hobby steam and farm toys including antique tractor books.

Reference (Firearms)

Book Sellers

Stewart Mowbray
Andrew Mowbray Publishing
Magazine: Man at Arms
P.O. Box 460
Lincoln, RI 02865
ph: 800-999-4697 or 401-726-8011
fax: 401-726-8061
stuart@manatarmsbooks.com
http://www.manatarmsbooks.com
Specializes in publishing books about antique and collectible firearms.

Ray Riling
Ray Riling Arms Books Co.
6844 Gorsten St.
Philadelphia, PA 19119
ph: 215-438-2456
larryriling@msn.com
http://www.rayrilingarmsbooks.com
Book dealer in new, used, rare books on firearms, edged weapons, military and related titles; publishes "The American Sword, 1776-1945" by Harold Peterson and "Home Gunsmithing the Colt Single Action Revolvers" by Loran Smith.

Bill Williams
Guncraft Sports Inc.
10737 Dutchtown Rd.
Knoxville, TN 37932-3208
ph: 865-966-4545
fax: 865-966-4500
findit@guncraft.com
http://www.usit.net/hp/guncraft
Serving the shooting public since 1947; a multi-faceted supplier of guns, accessories, appraisal services, training, gunsmithing, gun related books.

Reference (Gems/Jewelry)

Book Sellers

Stuart M. Matlins
GemStone Press
P.O. Box 237
Woodstock, VT 05091-0237
ph: 802-457-4000 or 800-962-4544
fax: 802-457-4004
everyone@longhillpartners.com
http://www.gemstonepress.com
International source for books and gem identification equipment and other items designed to help people in the gem trade and consumers learn more about gems & jewelry.

GIA Gem Instruments
5345 Armada Dr.
Carlsbad, CA 92008
ph: 760-603-4000 or 800-421-7250
fax: 760-603-4266
pr@gia.edu
http://www.gia.edu
Develops quality gemological instruments to help the professional buy, grade, appraise gems; also carries the world's largest selection of gem and jewelry books, along with a wide selection of elegant gift items.

Reference (Glass)

Book Sellers

Whitehouse-Books.com
60 East Market St.
Corning, NY 14830
ph: 607-936-8536 or 800-935-8536
fax: 607-936-2465
julia@whitehouse-books.com
http://www.whitehouse-books.com
Specializes in new and out-of-print books about antique, ancient and contemporary glass.

David Richardson
Antique Publications
217 Union St.
P.O. Box 553
Marietta, OH 45750-0553
ph: 800-533-3433 or 740-373-6146
fax: 740-373-6917
info@glasscollectingbooks.com
http://www.glasscollectingbooks.com
Offers a wide selection of books about pottery and glass.

Ron Lindsey
Lindsey's
2513 Austin Ave.
Pasadena, TX 77502
ph: 713-473-0725
keithlin@swbell.net
http://www.lindseybooks.com
Buys and sells out-of-print reference books on antiques, especially cut glass and art glass.

Reference (Japanese Items)

Book Sellers

Yoneyama
Ginza, "Things Japanese"
1721 Connecticut Ave., NW
Washington, DC 20009-1108
ph: 202-331-7991
fax: 202-265-1319
ginzashop@msn.com
http://www.ginzaonline.com
Carries a wide assortment of Japan related books in English: art, crafts, history, fiction, tea ceremony, Zen, cooking, martial arts, poetry, origami, architecture, interior design, fengshui, etc.

Reference (Japanese Prints)

Book Sellers

G. C. Uhlenbeck
Ukiyo-E Books B.V.
Breestraat 113a
CL Leiden, 23211 The Netherlands
ph: (071) 514 35 52
fax: (071) 514 14 88
ukiyoe@xs4all.nl
http://www.nvva.nl/ukiyoe
Offers largest collection of reference works of Japanese prints, paintings and illustrated books in Japanese and English, German, French and Dutch in the Western world

Reference (Jukeboxes)

Book Sellers

Michael F. Baute
Always Jukin'
404 East Howell, #100
Seattle, WA 98122
ph: 206-652-4005
fax: 206-652-4007
alwaysjuke@aol.com
http://www.alwaysjukin.com
Sells books about jukeboxes, jukebox service manuals and records.

Reference (Knives)

Book Sellers

Knife World Books
P.O. Box 3395
Knoxville, TN 37927-3395
ph: 865-397-1955 or 800-828-7751
fax: 865-397-1969
knifepub@knifeworld.com
http://www.knifeworld.com
Specializes in books about knives.

Louise Weyer
Weyer International - Book Division
2740 Nebraska Ave.
Toledo, OH 43607-3245
ph: 419-534-2020
law-weyerinternational@msn.com
Specializes in books about knives.

Reference (Law Enforcement)

Book Sellers

Matthew G. Forte
Turn of the Century Publishers
P.O. Box 3114
Memorial Station
Montclair, NJ 07043-3114
ph: 973-313-1700
BooksforPolice@aol.com
Publisher of "American Police Collectibles," and "American Police Equipment - A Guide to Early Restraints, Clubs & Lanterns:" billy clubs, nightsticks, handcuffs, mechanical and chain nippers, rattles, bullseye lanterns.

Reference (Maps & Charts)

Misc. Services

Jeremy Pool
MapRecord Publications
60 Shepard St.
Cambridge, MA 02138-1523
ph: 617-661-3718
fax: 617-868-1229
info@MapRecord.com
http://www.maprecord.com
Publisher of the "Antique Map Price Record" CD-ROM; news, comments, recommended references, book reviews, collectors' considerations, glossary of terms, directory of dealers, price listing, title and geographical index, etc.

Reference (Militaria)

Book Sellers

Nate Rind
Antheil Booksellers
2177 Isabelle Court
Bellmore, NY 11710-1599
ph: 516-826-2094
fax: 516-826-3101
antheil231@aol.com
http://www.antheilbooksellers.com
Specializes in naval, maritime, military and aviation books, both new and used; many books from Germany, Great Britain, Japan, and Australia; business done exclusively by mail; 48-page catalog subscription $6 for four catalogs.

Terry Hannon
Phoenix Militaria, Inc. Military Bookstore
116 Lyons Rd.
Mertztown, PA 19539-9801
ph: 610-682-1010 or 800-446-0909
fax: 610-682-1066
TerryHannon@msn.com
http://www.phoenixmilitaria.com
Sells a wide variety of military-related books and publications.

LTC(Ret) Thomas M. Johnson
Johnson Reference Books & Militaria
403 Chatham Square Office Park
Fredericksburg, VA 22405
ph: 540-373-9150 or 540-371-2665
fax: 540-373-0087
ww2daggers@aol.com
http://www.johnsonreferencebooks.com
Wants to buy German War booty; specific interest is in edged weapons (dress swords, daggers, bayonets and other quality items); author of eighteen books about Imperial and Third Reich German edged weapons and militaria.

C. Clayton Thompson
Thompson - Bookseller
584 Briarwood Lane
Boone, NC 28607
ph: 828-265-4970
fax: 828-265-0015
Greatbooks@aol.com
http://members.aol.com/Greatbooks
Specialist in Civil War, World War II and other military books; has one of the largest selections on the Internet and also has an open shop; stock includes new and used regimental and unit histories, rare first editions, reprints, etc.

Nautical & Aviation Publishing Co. of American Inc.
2055 Middleburg Lane
Mount Pleasant, SC 29464
ph: 843-856-0561
fax: 843-856-3164
nauticalaviationpublishing@worldnet.att.net
http://www.nauticalaviation.com
Carries naval, aviation and Civil War military books; many titles are primary sources, i.e., memoirs, biographies, etc.

R. Stephen Dorsey
Collectors' Library
P.O. Box 263
Eugene, OR 97440-0263
ph: 541-937-3348
mail@rsdmilitaria.com
http://www.rsdmilitaria.com
Publisher and book dealer for key reference books and reprints on equipment of the US military; extensive offering in free catalog.

Service Publications
55 Abingdon Dr.
Nepean, Ontario K2H 7M5 Canada
ph: 613-820-7350
fax: 613-820-1288
sales@servicepub.com
http://www.servicepub.com
Specializes in publishing books about firearms and collectible military artifacts.

Dealers

Last Square, The
5944 Odana Rd.
Madison, WI 53719
ph: 800-750-4401 or 608-278-4401
fax: 608-278-4402
orders@lastsquare.com
http://www.lastsquare.com
A military/militaria art & books/ historical miniatures dealer catering to all aspects of the military history hobby; from collectible art to large-scale hand-painted figures to wargaming miniatures.

Reference (Music)

Book Sellers

Linda Osborne
Jellyroll Productions
P.O. Box 255
Port Townsend, WA 98368
ph: 360-385-1200
fax: 360-385-6572
jpo@olympus.net
http://www.jerryosborne.com
Specializes in books relating to the hobby of music & music memorabilia collecting; artists, titles, price guides, etc.

Reference (Native American)

Book Sellers

Lar Hothem
Hothem House
P.O. Box 458
Lancaster, OH 43130-0458
ph: 740-653-9030
shothem@greenapple.com
http://www.HothemHouse.com
Buys and sells Indian related books covering archaeology, artifacts, earthworks, US prehistory; free catalog of books on Indian artifacts.

Reference (Natural History)

Book Sellers

Leslie Kostrich
minniesland.com, LLC
P.O Box 16380
Alexandria, VA 22302
ph: 703-823-7436
leslie@minniesland.com
http://www.minniesland.com
Specializes in original color-plate books by Audubon & other natural history artists; offers good selection of reference books reference books; Web site has detailed information on all major Audubon editions including authentication tips.

Donald E. Hahn
Natural History Books
P.O. Box 1004
Cottonwood, AZ 86326-1004
ph: 520-634-5016 or 520-634-1217
fax: 520-634-1217
Offers technical publications about earth, biological sciences, and meteorites.

Reference (Nautical)

Book Sellers

Dick Hawkins
Columbia Trading Company
One Barnstable Rd.
Hyannis, MA 02601
ph: 508-778-2929
fax: 508-778-2922
info@columbiatrading.com
http://www.columbiatrading.com
Issues 6 catalogs a year each offering 600 nautical, boating, and naval books, magazines and ephemera for sale; has an open shop in Hyannis with about 7,000 nautical and maritime books as well as ships models, marine art, antiques, and more.

Reference (Orientalia)

Book Sellers

Paragon Book Gallery, Inc.
1507 S. Michigan Ave.
Chicago, IL 60605-2812
ph: 312-663-5155
fax: 312-663-5177
paragon@paragonbook.com
http://www.paragonbook.com
Carries rare, out-of-print, and scholarly books on Asia; specializes in books on Asian arts and Asian studies; new and out-of-print.

Jerrold G. Stanoff
Rare Oriental Book Co.
P.O. Box 1599
Aptos, CA 95001-1599
ph: 831-689-0203
fax: 831-689-0204
jgs@rareorientalbooks.com
http://www.rareorientalbooks.com
Sells old, rare choice books on Japan, Korea, China, Tibet, S.E. Asia, Philippines, Indonesia, Siam, Malaya, Singapore, Cambodia, Laos, Burma, Vietnam, Mongolia, New Guinea, Bali, etc.

Reference (Paperweights)

Book Sellers

Paul H. Dunlop
Papier Presse
P.O. Box 6269
Statesville, NC 28687-6269
ph: 800-227-1996 or 704-871-2626
fax: 704-871-2329
"Paperweights of the 19th & 20th Centuries," (Paul Jokelson & Gerald Ingold); "Old Glass Paperweights of Southern New Jersey," (Clarence Newell), "The Jokelson Collection of Antique Cameo Incrustation," (Paul H. Dunlop).

Betty & Larry Schwab
Paperweight Shoppe, The
2507 Newport Dr.
Bloomington, IL 61704-4525
ph: 309-662-1956 or 877-517-6518
mail@thepaperweightshoppe.com
http://www.thepaperweightshoppe.com
Sells paperweight reference books.

Lawrence H. Selman
L.H. Selman, Ltd.
123 Locust St.
Santa Cruz, CA 95060
ph: 800-538-0766 or 831-427-1177
fax: 831-427-0111
lselman@got.net
http://www.paperweight.com
Carries over 50 books about paperweights.

Reference (Phonographs)

Book Sellers

Allen Koenigsberg
502 E. 17th St.
Brooklyn, NY 11226-6606
ph: 718-941-6835
AllenAmet@aol.com
http://www.PhonoBooks.com
Carries the most complete list of phonograph related books, catalogs, manuals, discographies, posters and magazines; "The Antique Phonograph Monthly" available for $15 per volume, or sample for $3 in stamps.

Reference (Postcards)

Book Sellers

Dr. James Lewis Lowe, Dir.
Deltiologists of America
P.O. Box 8
Norwood, PA 19074
ph: 610-485-8572
PostcardClassics@juno.com
http://www.Deltiologists-America.com
International postcard society for collectors, dealers, librarians, and archivist; offers several postcard related books for sale.

Reference (Quilts)
Book Sellers

Kris Driessen
Hickory Hill Antique Quilts
P.O. Box 273
Esperance, NY 12066
ph: 518-875-6133 or 888-817-6577
fax: 518-875-9141
krisdriessen@yahoo.com
http://www.HickoryHillQuilts.com
Offers antique quilt tops, blocks by catalog; also offers vintage and reproduction fabrics, as well as restoration supplies and Quilt Heritage reference books.

Reference (Radios)
Book Sellers

Tom French
Artifax Books
151 Barton Rd.
Stow, MA 01775
ph: 978-562-5573
artifaxbooks@yahoo.com
http://www.artifaxbooks.com
Sells books for communications historians and collectors, including telegraph instruments, telephone, early radio, and reprints of early books on telegraphy; send SASE for list.

Mark Stein, Publisher
Radiomania(R) Books
3100 Falls Cliff Rd., Ste. 6
Baltimore, MD 21211
ph: 410-366-3993
fax: 800-891-4484
rpbook@bellatlantic.net
http://www.radiomania.com
Publisher of "The Complete Price Guide to Antique Radios" series which picture over 13,000 table radios and 3,500 consoles; largest radio publisher in US; Web site offers books as well as vintage radios and related items.

Reference (Railroads)
Book Sellers

Harold H. Carstens
Carstens Publications
108 Phil Hardin Rd.
P.O. Box 700
Newton, NJ 07860-0700
ph: 973-383-3355 or 800-474-6995
fax: 973-383-4064
carstens@carstens-publications.com
http://www.carstens-publications.com
Carries large line of books about railroads.

Richard C. Barrett
Railroad Research Publications
3400 Ridge Rd. West, Ste. 5-266
Rochester, NY 14626-3458
ph: 716-227-6903
rrpubl@frontiernet.net
Publishes and sells books on railroad collectibles and railroad history; send SASE for catalog.

Reference (Records)
Book Sellers

Linda Osborne
Jellyroll Productions
P.O. Box 255
Port Townsend, WA 98368
ph: 360-385-1200
fax: 360-385-6572
jpo@olympus.net
http://www.jerryosborne.com
Offers an assortment of publications for the record collector.

Reference (Reptile/Amphibians)
Book Sellers

Mark F. Miller
Herpetology.com
P.O. Box 52261
Philadelphia, PA 19115-7261
ph: 215-464-3561
fax: 215-464-3561
reptiles@earthling.net
http://www.herpetology.com
Buys reptile or amphibian books, serials, monographs, PH.D. thesis, etc.; please quote anytime; do not send books or other items unless instructed; send only descriptions and photos; DO NOT send items on approval.

Reference (Space Collectibles)
Book Sellers

Richard H. Jackson
Missile, Space or Rocket Used Books
P.O. Box 93
Mount Vernon, VA 22121-0093
ph: 703-360-7677
fax: 703-360-2886
jackson@usedspacebooks.com
http://www.usedspacebooks.com
Buys and sells used books about missile, space or rockets; mail order; quarterly price lists.

Reference (Stamps)
Book Sellers

Leonard H. Hartmann
Philatelic Bibliophile
P.O. Box 36006
Louisville, KY 40233-6006
ph: 502-451-8538
fax: 502-459-8538
Leonard@pbbooks.net
http://www.pbbooks.com
Sells new and used stamp books (no annual catalogs such as Scott's, S.G., Minkus, Yvert) stocked from over 100 publishers; does not drop ship; check out Web site that has over 1,000 pages online.

Newspaper: Linn's Stamp News
P.O. Box 29
Sidney, OH 45365-0029
ph: 937-498-0801 or 800-448-7293
fax: 800-340-9501
linns@linns.com
http://www.linns.com
World's largest stamp marketplace with up-to-the-minute hobby news, reports on topics from trends in values, special interest collections to under-collected stamps; well-respected in the hobby; indispensable for the stamp collector.

Reference (Teddy Bears)
Book Sellers

Thomas Farrell
Portfolio Press
130 Wineow St., Ste. 3
Cumberland, MD 21502
ph: 301-724-2795 or 877-737-1200
fax: 301-724-2796
tfarrell@hereintown.net
Specializes in publishing books about collectible dolls and teddy bears.

Jennifer Hare
Hobby House Press, Inc.
One Corporate Dr.
Grantsville, MD 21536
ph: 301-895-3792 or 800-554-1447
fax: 301-895-5029
email@hobbyhouse.com
http://www.hobbyhouse.com
Specializes in books on collectibles, dolls and teddy bears, paper dolls, and vintage clothing; also gift and seasonal books, collectibles organizers and albums; identification and price guides are a specialty.

Reference (Telegraph Items)
Book Sellers

Tom French
Artifax Books
151 Barton Rd.
Stow, MA 01775
ph: 978-562-5573
artifaxbooks@yahoo.com
http://www.artifaxbooks.com
Sells books for communications historians and collectors, including telegraph instruments, telephone, early radio, and reprints of early books on telegraphy; send SASE for list.

Reference (Textiles)
Book Sellers

Mary Chapman
Mary Chapman, Booksellers
P.O. Box 304
College Park, MD 20741-0304
ph: 301-490-0400
MChapmanbooks@aol.com
Specialists in out-of-print books on all textile and needle arts; mail order only; catalogs issued; want lists solicited.

Fred Struthers
R. L. Shep Publications
P.O. Box 2706
Fort Bragg, CA 95437-2706
ph: 707-964-8662
fsbks@mcn.org
http://www.rlshep.com
An important source to collectors and researchers for hard-to-find and out-of-print books on costume, textiles, tailoring; carries period sewing and etiquette books and periodicals; publishes two catalogs per year for $2.50.

Reference (Tiles)
Book Sellers

Joseph Taylor
Tile Heritage Foundation
P.O. Box 1850
Healdsburg, CA 95448
ph: 707-431-8453
fax: 707-431-8455
foundation@tileheritage.org
http://www.tiles.org/pages/tileorgs/thfinfo.htm
Offers a selection of books about tiles, historic and contemporary; terracotta, foreign, decorated, Delftware, English medieval, Victorian tiles, etc.; also offers bound photocopies of more than 70 historic tile catalogs, many with color.

Chris Blanchett
Buckland Books
Holly Tree House
18 Woodlands Rd.
Littlehampton, West Sussex BN17 5PP
U.K.
ph: (+44) 1903 717648
fax: (+44) 1903 717648
cblanchett@lineone.net
http://www.tiles.org/pages/bookshlf/BUCKLAND_BOOKS.html
A mail-order service selling new and secondhand books about tiles and associated subjects such as architecture, bricks, terracotta & mosaics; publishes six monthly book lists.

Reference (Tools)
Book Sellers

Lisa J. Pollak
Astragal Press, The
5 Cold Hill Rd., S., Ste. 12
P.O. Box 239
Mendham, NJ 07945-0239
ph: 973-543-3045
fax: 973-543-3044
astragalpress@attglobal.net
http://www.astragalpress.com
Publishes and distributes books on early tools, trades, and technology including books on woodworking tools, metalworking, scientific instruments, architecture, wood turning, machinists' tools, and reprints of early trade catalogs.

Martin J. Donnelly
Martin J. Donnelly Antique Tools
P.O. Box 281
Bath, NY 14810-0281
ph: 800-869-0695 or 607-566-2617
fax: 607-566-2575
mjd@mjdtools.com
http://www.mjdtools.com
Web site offers a long list of books about tools for sale.

Bob Finch
Glen Moor Press
1864 Glen Moore Dr.
Lakewood, CO 80215-3038
ph: 303-232-1932
fax: 303-232-4724
rffinch@aol.com
Published reprint "Woodworking Machinery - Its Rise, Progress, and Construction - 1800 - 1880," illustrated; 400 pp.; $12.

Reference (Toys)
Book Sellers

F. Russack Antiques & Books
20 Beach Plain Rd.
Danville, NH 03819
ph: 603-642-7718
fax: 603-642-7718
info@booksaboutantiques.com
http://www.booksaboutantiques.com

Reference (Vintage Clothing)
Book Sellers

Jennifer Hare
Hobby House Press, Inc.
One Corporate Dr.
Grantsville, MD 21536
ph: 301-895-3792 or 800-554-1447
fax: 301-895-5029
email@hobbyhouse.com
http://www.hobbyhouse.com
Specializes in books on collectibles, dolls and teddy bears, paper dolls, and vintage clothing; also gift and seasonal books, collectibles organizers and albums; identification and price guides are a specialty.

Wooden Porch Books
Rte. 1 Box 262
Middlebourne, WV 26149-9748
ph: 304-386-4434
fax: 304-386-4868
books@woodenporch.com
http://www.woodenporch.com
6 catalogs per year listing approximately 2,400 out-of-print books and magazines on the fiber arts and kindred subjects.

Fred Struthers
R.L. Shep Publications
P.O. Box 2706
Fort Bragg, CA 95437
ph: 707-964-8662
fax: 707-964-8662
fsbks@mcn.org
http://www.rlshep.com
Reprints of Victorian and Edwardian costume books stressing patterns, instructions, embroidery, etc.; women and men; practical manuals; also Civil War books about women's activities.

Patrick Pasky
Toy Book Shop
13 rue de la Courtine
Remiremont, 88200 France
ph: 33 329 62 10 31
paskytoy@wanadoo.fr
http://www.toybookshop.net
Specializes in books dealing with antique toys and the collecting hobby: out-of-print books, trade catalogs, and hard-to-find books; site in French and English.

Reference (Watches)
Book Sellers

Heart of America Press
55 N. Central
Umatilla, FL 32784
ph: 352-669-4791
fax: 352-669-6969
sales@hoapress.com
http://www.hoapress.com
Issues catalog of horological books and literature.

Reference (Western Americana)
Book Sellers

Early West, The
P.O. Box 9292
College Station, TX 77842-9292
ph: 800-245-5841 or 409-775-6047
fax: 979-764-7758
Sells, buys and trades non-fiction books on the old west: outlaws, lawmen, towns, areas.

Bill Mackin
1137 Washington St.
Craig, CO 81625-1613
ph: 970-824-6717 or 970-824-6360
fax: 970-824-7175
Sells books and reprinted catalogs for Old West and cowboy collectors; over 50 titles including his own "Cowboy and Gunfighter Collectibles" with updated prices; $25 plus $3 postage.

Kenneth Asher
Maverick Publications, Inc.
P.O. Box 5007
Bend, OR 97708
ph: 541-382-6978 or 800-800-4831
fax: 541-382-4831
information@mavbooks.com
http://www.mavbooks.com
Sells Western Americana books: Indian art & artifacts, bottles, cowboy & horse collectibles, fruit jars, railroad, logging, fur trade, history. etc.

Roycroft
Dealers

David B. Ogle
Antiquarian Archive, The
330 Second St., Ste. 2
Los Altos, CA 94022
ph: 650-949-1593
antarch@earthlink.net
http://www.ippi.com/antiquarian-archive.html
Specialist in Western Americana,

railroadiana, nautical & maritime, military history & memoirs, books of the Roycroft printing shop; office hours by appointment only.

Scottish
Periodicals

Jennie Renton
Magazine: Scottish Book Collector
8 Lauriston Street
Edinburgh, Scotland EH3 9DJ U.K.
phone: +44 (0) 131 228 4837
jennie@essbc.demon.co.uk
http://www.essbc.demon.co.uk/subs.htm
A quarterly magazine that specializes in in-depth features about collectible, old and rare Scottish books alongside profiles of contemporary Scottish writers and publishers.

Sports
Collectors

John Buonaguidi
540 Reeside Ave.
Monterey, CA 93940-1828
ph: 831-375-7345
sportmsm@redshift.com
Wants 19th century non-fiction books about baseball, football, or boxing.

Yearbooks
Appraisers

Seth & Danine Poppel
Yearbook Library
38 Range Dr.
Merrick, NY 11566
ph: 516-867-6280
fax: 516-546-4128
Sethpoppel@aol.com
http://members.ebay.com/aboutme/sethpoppel@aol.com
Appraises high school yearbooks that feature the senior pictures of famous and infamous people; if you don't know whether there is a famous person in the yearbook just email, mail or fax year, school, city and state.

Dealers

Seth & Danine Poppel
Yearbook Library
38 Range Dr.
Merrick, NY 11566
ph: 516-867-6280
fax: 516-546-4128
Sethpoppel@aol.com
http://members.ebay.com/aboutme/sethpoppel@aol.com
Always eager to buy high school yearbooks that feature the senior pictures of famous and infamous people; if you don't know whether there is a famous person in the yearbook just email, mail or fax year, school, city and state.

Experts

Mitchell Moore
Bygone Era
5203 16th St.
Lubbock, TX 79416
ph: 806-785-1823
Specializing in all sections of both high school and college yearbooks spanning over 120 years; call for specifics or general yearbook trends over the years; also searching for additional copies.

BOSSONS
Clubs/Associations

John J. Cassidy, Pres/ExDir
International Bossons Collectors Society, Inc.
Newsletter: Bossons Briefs
1317 N. San Fernando Blvd., Ste. #325
Burbank, CA 91504-4272
ph: 661-250-2664 or 818-522-0727
fax: 661-250-7166
Director@bossons.org
http://www.bossons.org
Founded in 1981 with now over 3,600 members worldwide; members are collectors of Bossons character heads or figurines; newsletter includes new discoveries, articles and stories about rare finds, member profiles, sell/swap columns, and more.

Dealers

Bruce Bleier
73 Riverdale Rd.
Valley Stream, NY 11581
ph: 516-791-4353
fax: 516-792-0519
emeralite@aol.com
Collects, buys and sells Bossons artware including faces, animals and plaques; member of The International Bossons Collectors Society.

Donald M. Hardisty
Don's Collectibles
3020 E. Majestic Ridge
Las Cruces, NM 88011
ph: 505-522-3721
fax: 505-522-7909
don@donsbossons.com
http://www.donsbossons.com
Internationally recognized expert, collector, supplier, appraiser, and restoration artist recommended by Bossons; member Inter. Bossons Collectors Society.

Experts

Dr. Robert E. Davis
1787 Morgan Valley Rd.
Rockmart, GA 30153
ph: 770-684-4625
bossonsbooks@att.net
Author of "The Imagical World of Bossons" and "The Imagical World of Bossons - Book II."

Donald M. Hardisty
Don's Collectibles
3020 E. Majestic Ridge
Las Cruces, NM 88011
ph: 505-522-3721
fax: 505-522-7909
don@donsbossons.com
http://www.donsbossons.com
Internationally recognized expert, collector, supplier, appraiser, and restoration artist recommended by Bossons; member Inter. Bossons Collectors Society.

John & Joanna Cassidy
Ultimate Bosson Website, The
1317 N. San Fernando Blvd., Ste. #325
Burbank, CA 91504-4272
ph: 661-250-2664 or 818-522-0727
fax: 661-250-7166
bossonsman@aol.com
http://www.bossons.com
Online resource for Bossons artware; information and photos of the character wall masks, figurines, and many other items produced by the W.H. Bossons, Co., of Congleton, England; offers Bossons books.

Internet Resources

John & Barb Spinner
Bossons
johnspinner@fuse.net
http://home.fuse.net/johnspinner

BOTTLE CAPS

(see also BOTTLES, Milk;
BREWERIANA; DAIRY
COLLECTIBLES; SOFT DRINK
COLLECTIBLES)

Crown

Clubs/Associations

John Vetter
Crown Collectors Society International
Newsletter: Crown Cappers Exchange
4300 San Juan Dr.
Fairfax, VA 22030-5351
ph: 703-591-3060
fax: 703-591-3197
crownking@erols.com
A collector's organization dedicated to helping those interested in collecting and working to preserve the rich colorful history of the bottle crown closure as used for beer, soda, mineral water, etc. bottles.

Collectors

Barry Oremland
1260 Washington St.
Walpole, MA 02081-3116
ph: 508-688-9086 or 617-864-0161
fax: 617-864-4422
crownclctr@rcn.com
Collects, trades, buys, sells crown caps of all types; all origins, and all reasonable conditions; also wants crown industry material, reseal caps, signs, pictures, articles, letters, etc. depicting or mentioning crown caps.

Christopher Leppek
1016 S. Washington St.
Denver, CO 80209-4318
ph: 303-744-8385
redraven75@aol.com
Buys, sells and trades crowns (bottle caps); vintages, nationalities of all types - beers, sodas, waters, oddball. Will buy loners, groups or entire collections.

David Friedman
11129 Barman Ave.
Culver City, CA 90230-4208
ph: 310-837-3089
Buys collections of old bottle caps: beer and soda bottle caps; also Crown bottle cap industry literature, advertising, and historical items.

Konstantin Levochkin
Kievskaya ul 16-7
Moscow, 121151 Russia
kostya@invsbank.glasnet.ru
http://www.geocities.com/NapaValley/2544
A beer cap collector from Moscow; wants to trade with other collectors.

Edward Veld
Verschoorstraat 25 B
Rotterdam, 3081 JT The Netherlands
tcgb@crowncap.demon.nl
http://www.crowncap.demon.nl
Collector of crown bottle caps; Web site is for collectors of Williams Painters crown bottle caps.

Experts

Robert Walters
RTW Services
63 Mount Batten St.
Rochester, NY 14623
ph: 716-359-4917
fax: 716-359-4917
Historian, collector, dealer of beer crowns from US breweries; knowledgeable in grading and valuation of all US beer crowns; Web site has member listings, crowns for sale, convention information, buy-sell-trade ads, links.

Internet Resources

Eric Budesheim
Bottle Caps Via the Internet
buda@global2000.net
http://members.global2000.net/~buda

Algis Kibirkstis
Beer Cap Page, The
Canada
kibi@cam.org
http://www.cam.org/~kibi/TBCP
A forum for those interested in the hobby of collecting beer crown caps.

Edward Veld
Verschoorstraat 25 B
Rotterdam, 3081 JT The Netherlands
tcgb@crowncap.demon.nl
http://www.crowncap.demon.nl
Online resources for crown cap collecting on the Internet.

Milk

Collectors

Nick Dudek
425 Madison St.
Ravenna, OH 44266
ph: 330-296-0140
ohiomilkcaps@neo.rr.com
Serious dairy collector and dealer buying dairy collectibles including milk caps and milk bottles; specializes in Ohio milk caps; eBay seller name is "milkdude."

Dealers

Debbie Gillette
Debbie's Milk Bottles
116 E. Division St.
Watertown, NY 13601
ph: 315-788-0587
ilovemilkbottles@yahoo.com
http://milkbottle.cjb.net
Collector, dealer, expert specializing in dairy collectibles and milk bottles.

Experts

Dan Ryan
45 Sunnyside Ave.
Putnam, CT 06260-1830
ph: 860-928-5014
milkcaps@worldnet.att.net
http://home.att.net/~milkcaps
Writes "Covering Caps" column for "The Milk Route," newsletter of The National Association of Milk Bottle Collectors.

BOTTLE OPENERS

Figural

(see also BREWERIANA; CAN
OPENERS; CORKSCREWS)

Clubs/Associations

John T. Fitzsimmons
Figural Bottle Opener Collectors Club
Newsletter: Opener, The
9697 Gwynn Park Dr.
Ellicott City, MD 21042
johnf129@aol.com
http://www.dol.net/~c-llesser
Formed to promote interest in and knowledge about figural bottle openers.

John Stanley
Just for Openers
Newsletter: Just for Openers Newsletter
P.O. Box 64
Chapel Hill, NC 27514
ph: 919-419-1546 or 919-966-5794
jfo@mindspring.com
http://www.just-for-openers.org
Just for Openers is a club for bottle and corkscrew collectors; quarterly newsletter.

Collectors

John Stanley
P.O. Box 64
Chapel Hill, NC 27514
ph: 919-419-1546 or 919-966-5794
jfo@mindspring.com
http://www.just-for-openers.org
Wants any bottle opener or corkscrew from the Southeast US; also wants to buy any beer advertising items.

Marc Benjamin
167 Nixon Beach Rd.
Edenton, NC 27932
ph: 252-482-2099
Wants flat figural bottle openers; beer and non-beer.

Kurt Bachmann
57883 Hanover Rd.
Washington, MI 48094
ph: 810-677-3284
fax: 248-745-1221
Dealing with all types of breweriana advertising including, but not limited to, beer advertising bottle openers.

Kelly C. Devlin
455 Commercial Park Rd.
Wahoo, NE 68066-9730
ph: 402-443-4305
fax: 402-443-4849
kd31202@alltel.net
Wants to buy figural bottle openers.

Experts

Charles Reynolds
Reynolds Toys
2836 Monroe St.
Falls Church, VA 22042-2007
ph: 703-533-1322
reynoldstoys@erols.com
http://www.reynoldstoys.com
An advanced collector paying top dollar for openers, e.g., wall mount boy winking, Amish Man, Skull, Coyote, Bear, Eagle, Standing College Figures, etc.

Phyllis Eisenach
3759 SW Whispering Sound Dr.
Palm City, FL 34990-7735
ph: 561-223-8275
eisenach@webtv.net
Interested in figural (three-dimensional) bottle openers; 18 years collecting; member of the Figural Bottle Opener Collectors Club; prefers iron or other metal openers.

Repro. Sources

Charles Reynolds
Reynolds Toys
2836 Monroe St.
Falls Church, VA 22042-2007
ph: 703-533-1322
reynoldstoys@erols.com
http://www.reynoldstoys.com
Offers limited editions of new original figural bottle openers of sand-cast aluminum; flyer on request.

BOTTLES

(see also BOTTLE CAPS;
BREWERIANA; DAIRY
COLLECTIBLES; DECANTERS,
Figural Whiskey; FRUIT JARS;
INFANT FEEDERS; INKWELLS &
INKSTANDS; INSULATORS;
SALOON & BAR COLLECTIBLES;
SODA FOUNTAIN COLLECTIBLES;
SOFT DRINK COLLECTIBLES;
TREASURE HUNTING)

Appraisers

David Robinson
Antique Bottle Collectors
W142 N4896 Fieldcrest Court
Menomonee Falls, WI 53051
ph: 262-790-1871

Auction Services

Stephen Fletcher
Skinner, Inc.
63 Park Plaza
The Heritage on the Garden
Boston, MA 02116
ph: 617-350-5400
fax: 617-350-5429
info@skinnerinc.com
http://www.skinnerinc.com
*Established in 1971, Skinner Inc. is
the fourth largest auction house in the
US; has offices in Boston and Bolton,
MA.*

Norman C. Heckler
Norman C. Heckler & Company
79 Bradford Corner Rd.
Woodstock Valley, CT 06282-2002
ph: 860-974-1634
fax: 860-974-2003
info@heckleratuction.com
http://www.heckleratuction.com
*Specializes in the sale of early glass
and bottles; Heckler & Co. sold a
single bottle for $66,000 at auction in
1993.*

James Hagenbuch
Glass Works Auctions
P.O. Box 180
102 Jefferson St.
East Greenville, PA 18041
ph: 215-679-5849
fax: 215-679-3068
glswrk@enter.net
http://www.glswrk-auction.com
*Specializes in the auction of historical
flasks, fruit jars, food & milk bottles,
sodas, poisons, whiskeys, medicines,
inks, barber bottles, bitters bottles,
scent bottles, shaving mugs, target &
range balls, etc.*

Pacific Glass Auctions
1507 21st St., Ste. 203
Sacramento, CA 95814
ph: 916-443-3296 or 916-443-3210
fax: 916-443-3199
info@pacglass.com
http://www.pacglass.com
*The largest antique bottle auction
house currently on the Internet.*

Alan R. Blakeman
B.B.R. Auctions
Elsecar Heritage Centre
Nr Barnsley, South Yorks S74 8HJ U.K.
ph: 01226 745156
fax: 01226 361561
sales@onlinebbr.com
http://www.onlinebbr.com
*England's leading specialists and
auction house for antique bottles, pot
lids and related advertising material.*

Clubs/Associations

Steve Berquist, Treas.
Little Rhody Bottle Club
dandrews@littlerhodybottleclub.org
http://www.littlerhodybottleclub.org
*Strives to promote the hobby of
antique bottle collecting through the
preservation of antique bottles and
education through research relative to
the companies those bottles represent.*

Philip R. Donovan
New England Antique Bottle Club
Newsletter: NEABC News
120 Commonwealth Rd.
Lynn, MA 01904
*Membership throughout New England;
meets 2nd Sunday of each month
(except July & August) in Kennebunk,
ME; newsletter published 10 times per
year; for club information pack or
bottle related questions please send
SASE.*

Creighton Hall
Yankee Bottle Club
382 Court St.
Keene, NH 03431
ph: 603-352-2959
fax: 603-352-7919

Joe Maggi
North Jersey Antique Bottle Collectors
Association
117 Lincoln Place
Waldwick, NJ 07463-2114
ph: 201-445-9079 or 201-294-0878

Dave Tripet
Jersey Shore Bottle Club
P.O. Box 995
Toms River, NJ 08754-0649
dtripet@comcast.net
http://www.geocities.com/dtripet2000/
jsbc/jsbc.html
*Members are dedicated to collecting
bottles and other related items of
interest; sample newsletter sent on
request.*

Kevin Lawless, VP
Capital Region Antique Bottle &
Insulator Club
Newsletter: Watercloset Gazette, The
3363 Guilderland Ave., Apt. 3
Schenectady, NY 12306-1820
ph: 518-357-2333
fax: 518-344-7485
kflbostons@aol.com
*Club for collectors of antique bottles
and electrical insulators; membership
based in Northeast US; annual show;
regular club swaps and meetings.*

Kim Bloomer
Hudson Valley Antique Bottle Club
6 Columbus Ave.
Cornwall On Hudson, NY 12520

Bruce Babcock, Show Ch.
Empire State Bottle Collectors
Association
Newsletter: ESBCA Newsletter
115 Marshia Ave.
North Syracuse, NY 13212
ph: 315-458-3627

Genessee Valley Bottle Collectors
Association
P.O. Box 15528
Rochester, NY 14615
barthology@aol.com
http://www.gvbca.org
*Founded in 1969 for those having a
common interest old bottles.*

Engvard Johnson
Pittsburgh Antique Bottle Club
650 Hood School Rd.
Indiana, PA 15701
ph: 724-465-8287

Pennsylvania Bottle Collector's
Association
Newsletter: Dirty Bottle, The
251 Eastland Ave.
York, PA 17402-1105
ph: 717-854-4965
*Members collect or are interested in
antique bottles and are from various
states with the majority of members
from the York-Lancaster-Harrisburg
area.*

Bill Hegedus
Forks of the Delaware Bottle Collectors
Association
20 Cambridge Place
Catasauqua, PA 18032
ph: 610-264-5945

Bill Baumgardner
Delmarva Antique Bottle Club
57 Lakewood Dr.
Lewes, DE 19958
ph: 302-945-2025

Steve Charing
Baltimore Antique Bottle Club
Newsletter: Baltimore Bottle Digger
P.O. Box 36061
Towson, MD 21286-6061
ph: 410-531-9459
baltimore@antiquebottles.com
http://www.antiquebottles.com/baltimore
*Monthly meetings include displays,
selling/trading, speaker programs
about bottles & related items: jugs,
fruit jars, etc.; sponsors largest one-
day bottle show in the world each
March where free bottle appraisals
are available to public.*

Ken Anderson
Potomac Bottle Collectors
Newsletter: Potomac Pontil, The
4028 Williamsburg Court
Fairfax, VA 22032-1139
ph: 703-273-7415
fax: 703-385-7330
kaajws@aol.com
http://members.aol.com/potomacbtl/
bottle2.htm
*Club serves the metropolitan
Washington, D.C. area; provides a
monthly meeting with educational
programs, library, public speakers,
annual bottle show, and other services
of interest to collectors of antique
bottles and jars.*

Ken Anderson
Potomac Bottle Collectors
4028 Williamsburg Court
Fairfax, VA 22032-1139
ph: 703-273-7415 or 703-360-8181
fax: 703-385-7330
pehraug@aol.com
http://members.aol.com/potomacbtl/
bottle2.htm
*Club serves the metropolitan
Washington, D.C. area; provides a
monthly meeting with educational
programs; also a library, public
speakers, annual bottle show, and
other services of interest to collectors
of antique bottles and jars.*

Frank Kowalski
Apple Valley Bottle Collectors Club
Newsletter: Bottle Worm, The
3015 Northwestern Pike
Winchester, VA 22603-3825
ph: 540-877-1093
polishbn@shentel.net
http://www.antiquebottles.com/apple
*Members are interested in antique
bottles: bitters, whiskeys, beers,
mineral waters, White House
vinegars, milks, medicines, cures,
Depression glassware, local pottery,
postcards and milk glass; annual
show in Winchester.*

Historical Bottle Diggers of Virginia,
The
Newsletter: HBDV Newsletter
242 E. Grattan St.
Harrisonburg, VA 22801
*Member of National Federation of
Historical Bottle Collectors;
newsletter published bi-monthly.*

Ed Faulkner
Richmond Area Bottle Collectors
Association
4718 Kyloe Lane
Moseley, VA 23120
ph: 804-739-2951
faulkner@antiquebottles.com
http://mywebpages.comcast.net/
edandlucy1
*An active club of bottle enthusiasts
that has been meeting since 1970.*

Reggie Lynch
Raleigh Bottle Club
P.O. Box 13736
Durham, NC 27709
ph: 919-789-4545
rlynch@antiquebottles.com
http://www.antiquebottles.com/raleigh

Reggie Lynch
Southeast Bottle Club
P.O. Box 13736
Durham, NC 27709
ph: 919-789-4545
fax: 561-760-6246
southeast@antiquebottles.com
http://www.antiquebottles.com/southeast
Holds monthly meetings and an annual "Bottle Show & Auction" each year in April; all are welcome to join.

Ed Herrold
Sarasota-Manatee Antique Bottle
Collectors Association
P.O. Box 3105
Sarasota, FL 34230-3105
ph: 941-923-6550
Networking for education and pleasure of antique bottle, insulator, and fruit jar collectors; only interested in 19th century and earlier; no Jim Beam bottles or Avon bottles.

Nancy Pennington
Middle Tennessee Bottle & Collector's
Club
Newsletter: MTBCC Newsletter
1750 Keyes Rd.
Greenbrier, TN 37073
ph: 615-643-0290
fax: 615-643-0290

East Tennessee Antique Bottle &
Collectibles Society
Newsletter: ETABCS Newsletter
220 N. Carter School Rd.
Straw Plains, TN 37871-1237
ph: 865-933-2333
etabcs@korrnet.org
http://www.korrnet.org/etabcs
Newsletter published bi-monthly; club sponsors annual antique bottle, advertising and collectibles show on 2nd Saturday in June at Knoxville Convention Center, Knoxville, TN; largest show of its kind in the country.

Terri Grove, Ed.
Ohio Bottle Club
Newsletter: Ohio Swirl
7126 12th St.
Minerva, OH 44657
dgrove@valkyrie.net
http://
www.ohiobottles.freehomepage.com
One of the largest bottle clubs in the country.

Norman & Junne Barnett
Midwest Antique Fruit Jar & Bottle
Club
Newsletter: Midwest Glass Chatter, The
P.O. Box 38
Flat Rock, IN 47234
ph: 812-587-5560
thebarnetts@lightbound.com
http://www.fruitjar.org
An organization for those interested in collecting and learning about fruit jars and bottles; sponsors two fruit and bottle shows each year in Indianapolis.

Shaun Kotlarsky
Huron Valley Antique Bottle & Insulator
Club
2475 West Walton Blvd.
Waterford, MI 48329-4435
ph: 248-673-1650
hvbic@clubs.insulators.com
http://www.insulators.com/clubs/
hvbic.htm

Doug Shilson
North Star Historical Bottle Association,
Inc.
Newsletter: North Star Bottle News
3308 32 Ave. South
Minneapolis, MN 55406-2015
ph: 612-721-4165
bittersdug@aol.com
Largest historical bottle club in the Upper Midwest; meets 3rd Sunday each month, except for June, July and August; President and Editor.

Glenn Poch
Antique Bottle Club of Northern Illinois
667 White Birch Lane
Lake Zurich, IL 60047
ph: 847-726-6044
oldbottles@yahoo.com
http://www.antiquebottles.com/poch

John E. Panek
First Chicago Bottle Club
Newsletter: Midwest Bottle News, The
P.O. Box A3382
Chicago, IL 60690
ph: 847-945-5493
Organization of antique bottle and stoneware collectors who research, educate, buy and sell at monthly meetings, annual shows, and annual auctions.

Federation of Historical Bottle
Collectors, Inc.
Magazine: Bottles & Extras
401 Johnston Court
Raymore, MO 64083
ph: 816-318-0160
osubuckeyes71@aol.com
http://www.fohbc.com
"Bottles & Extras" contains articles, pictures, letters, show dates, and show and auction reports in the field of antique bottles, insulators, fruit jars and associated items; check Web site for list of scores of clubs by region.

J. D. Moore
Antique Bottles & Old Jugs Association
ph: 870-931-3772
bottle40@yahoo.com
A club for collectors of old bottles, jugs, coins, and marbles; Web site has message board, chat, list of USA bottle clubs, and more.

Tino Romero
New Mexico Historical Bottle Society
3256 c/s
Socorro, NM 87801
ph: 505-838-1636
tromero@nmt.edu
http://www.nmt.edu/~tromero/
nmhbs.html
Focus in on the education preservation, and history of historical bottles.

Peter Sidlow
Las Vegas Antique Bottle & Collectibles
Club
Newsletter: Punkin Seed, The
5895 Duneville St.
Las Vegas, NV 89118
ph: 702-257-9692
Members promote the hobby of collecting, researching, displaying and trading of antique bottles and collectibles; sponsors an annual collectibles show and sale in February of each year.

Willy Young
Antique Bottle & Collectibles Club
P.O. Box 1061
Verdi, NV 89439
ph: 775-746-0922

Gaery Johnston
San Bernardino County Historical Bottle
& Collectible Club
22853 DeBerry
Grand Terrace, CA 92313
ph: 909-783-4101

San Jose Antique Bottle Collectors
Association
P.O. Box 5432
San Jose, CA 95150-5432

Collectors

Leo A. Bedard
968 Lyon St.
Ludlow, MA 01056-1142
ph: 413-583-5746
Collects antique bottles, specializing in embossed, strapsided, and coffin flasks.

Philip R. Donovan
120 Commonwealth Rd.
Lynn, MA 01904
Collect/buy/trade 1870s to 1920s bottles: medicine, soda, milk; will buy collections of dug bottles of all types; purchases labeled embossed 1800s-1910s medicines, sodas, beers, foods, etc. for personal collection; also digs.

Ed & Kathy Gray
GreatAntiqueBottles.com
1049 Eigth Ave.
Brockway, PA 15824
ph: 814-268-4503
edgray@penn.com
http://www.greatantiquebottles.com
Collectors of antique bottles including historical flasks, bitters bottles, fruit jars, medicine bottles, barber bottles, whiskey bottles, inkwells, and pickle jars.

Douglas Anderson
112 S. Commerce St.
Centreville, MD 21617-1116
ph: 410-758-3278

Ed Faulkner
4718 Kyloe Lane
Moseley, VA 23120
ph: 804-739-2951
faulkner@antiquebottles.com
http://mywebpages.comcast.net/
edandlucy1
Collecting bottles for over 10 years; specializes in ink bottles, VA bottles, and bottles with marks from early glass works; will evaluate and purchase small collections that are for sale.

Dan Argentati
61342 Creekview Dr.
South Lyon, MI 48178
ph: 248-437-6104
Collector of antique bottles, specializing in bitters bottles and any bottles from Michigan cities.

Mark S. McNee
1009 Vassar Dr.
Kalamazoo, MI 49001-4483
ph: 269-343-8393
nostrums@chartermi.net
Wants to buy early American bottles of all types including bitters, poisons, historical flasks, and medicines.

Steve Ketcham
P.O. Box 24114
Minneapolis, MN 55424-0114
ph: 952-920-4205
s.ketcham@unique-software.com
Wants to buy early American bitters bottles, flasks with pictures, inks, barber bottles, patent medicine bottles, and figural bottles.

John E. Panek
P.O. Box A3382
Chicago, IL 60690
ph: 847-945-5493
Specialists in historical flasks, bitters, sodas and Chicago bottles and stoneware.

Tino Romero
3256 c/s
Socorro, NM 87801
ph: 505-838-1636
tromero@nmt.edu
http://www.nmt.edu/~tromero/
nmhbs.html
Specializes in New Mexico bottles, Dr.

Kilmer, embalming fluids, poisons and narcotic bottles.

Kitty & Russell Umbraco
P.O. Box 5331
Richmond, CA 94805-0331
ph: 510-235-1656
fax: 510-237-6019
russellu1@juno.com
Wants to buy Western bottles, especially Nevada, San Francisco and related advertising.

John Goetz
P.O. Box 1570
Cedar Ridge, CA 95924
ph: 530-272-4644
Buying pre-1920 embossed glass bottles: bitters, fifths, flasks, mineral water, beer, California bottles.

Scott Grandstaff
63742 Applegate Dr.
P.O. Box 409
Happy Camp, CA 96039
ph: 530-493-2032
scottg@snowcrest.net
Past-Publisher of "Bottles & Extras" magazine; casual appraisals done free; detailed appraisals and professional consulting are available for a fee.

Dealers

John Brandt
Historic Glasshouse
157 Fairgrounds Rd.
Plymouth, NH 03264-3326
ph: 516-759-6744 or 603-536-3137
fax: 509-461-1572
john@antiquebottles-glass.com
http://www.antiquebottles-glass.net
One of the largest dealers in 17th - 19th century antique bottles and glass; Web site lists a wide variety of fine quality items for sale; professionally cleans staining on glass items; will search for specific items; also appraises.

Jack Pelletier
211 Main St.
Gorham, ME 04038
ph: 207-839-4389
Buying and selling antique bottles for over 30 years; expert on Bininger bottles.

John Crary
North Country Bottle Shop
P.O. Box 417
Canton, NY 13617
ph: 315-386-8715
crary@northnet.org
http://www.northnet.org/ncbshome/
salesbottles.html
Buys and sells bottles, insulators and go withs.

Kevin A. Sives
Kevin A. Sives, Antiques
1485 Buck Hill Dr.
Southampton, PA 18966
ph: 215-953-1686
sives@antiquez.com
Collects, buys and sells antique blown glass, bottles, and flasks.

Frank Kowalski
Polish Barn Antiques, The
3015 Northwestern Pike
Winchester, VA 22603-3825
ph: 540-877-1881 or 540-877-1093
polishbn@shentel.net
Bottle collector, dealer, appraiser; interested in Winchester VA antique bottles: bitters, whiskeys, beers, mineral waters, White House vinegars, milks, medicines, cures, Depression glassware, local pottery, postcards and milk glass.

Duane Combs
Mountain State Bottle Exchange
P.O. Box 181
Burlington, WV 26710
ph: 304-788-5517
fax: 304-788-5517
Buys, sells, trades old bottles: bitters, medicines, poisons, flasks, White House vinegars, early sodas, Warner Safe Cures, etc.

Earl's Bottles
108 Crystal Lane
Aurora, OH 44202

Don Dzuro
Antique of Copley
1442 St. Michaels Ave.
Akron, OH 44320-3236
ph: 330-867-8024
Buys, sells and trades bottles, jars and pottery; author of "Ohio Bottles."

David Robinson
Antique Bottle Collectors
W142 N4896 Fieldcrest Court
Menomonee Falls, WI 53051
ph: 262-790-1871

Glenn Poch
667 White Birch Lane
Lake Zurich, IL 60047
ph: 847-726-6044
oldbottles@yahoo.com
http://www.antiquebottles.com/poch
Appraises, buys, sells, collects, repairs antique bottles; specializes in pre-1900 bottles, flasks, bitters, medicines, inks, scents, etc.

Keith Lunt
Antique Bottle Trader
2668 Montara Dr.
Medford, OR 97504
ph: 541-773-2404
fax: 541-772-1515
keith@antiquebottletrader.com
http://www.antiquebottletrader.com
Avid antique bottle collector, dealer, trader, and appraiser for over 25 years; member of The Oregon Bottle Collectors Association and The

Antique Poison Bottle Collectors Association; also a bottle show promoter.

Rob Sturrock
Old Bottles from British Columbia
Canada
ph: 604-980-3679
primex@portal.ca
http://www.geocities.com/Eureka/
Promenade/4600
Buys, sells, trades bottles: sodas, ginger beers, milks, poisons, fruit jars, etc.

Mike Sheridan
30 Brabant Rd.
Cheadle Hulme
Cheadle, Cheshire SK8 7AU U.K.
ph: 011 44 7931 812156
fax: 011 44 7931 812156
bygonz@yahoo.com
http://members.tripod.co.uk/
~MikeSheridan
English dealer/collector seeks old English bottles now resident in the US: stenciled Scots/Irish whiskeys, pontiled medicine, including Turlingtons, old stoneware bottles, highly pictorial and colorful old labels of all types.

Experts

Reggie Lynch
P.O. Box 13736
Durham, NC 27709
ph: 919-789-4545
fax: 561-760-6246
rlynch@antiquebottles.com
http://www.antiquebottles.com
Buys, sells, collects and specializes in antique bottles such as inks, medicine and Coke.

Mike Jordan
M & B Antiques
310 SW 35 St.
Ocala, FL 34474
ph: 352-291-1024
bjordan850@aol.com
http://members.aol.com/Potomacbtl/
bottle2.htm
Buy, sells, appraises and specializes in rare, early American bottles.

Jamie Houdeshell
16255 Normandy South
Perrysburg, OH 43551
ph: 419-872-1966
Buys, sells, appraises and specializes in antique bottles and early American glass.

Doug Shilson
3308 32 Ave. South
Minneapolis, MN 55406-2015
ph: 612-721-4165
bittersdug@aol.com
Bottle collector, appraiser, expert, dealer; founded North Star Historical Bottle Assn., Inc.; runs yearly bottle show; contributor to several bottle books; has been collecting bottles and bottle advertising since 1961.

Scott Grandstaff
63742 Applegate Dr.
P.O. Box 409
Happy Camp, CA 96039
ph: 530-493-2032
scottg@snowcrest.net
Past-Publisher of "Bottles & Extras" magazine; casual appraisals done free; detailed appraisals and professional consulting are available for a fee; extensive expertise in all pre-1900 American bottles; has contacts around the world.

Keith Lunt
Antique Bottle Trader
2668 Montara Dr.
Medford, OR 97504
ph: 541-773-2404
fax: 541-772-1515
keith@antiquebottletrader.com
http://www.antiquebottletrader.com
Avid antique bottle collector, dealer, trader, and appraiser for over 25 years; member of The Oregon Bottle Collectors Association and The Antique Poison Bottle Collectors Association; also a bottle show promoter.

Internet Resources

Reggie Lynch
Antique Bottle Collectors Haven
P.O. Box 13736
Durham, NC 27709
ph: 919-789-4545
fax: 561-760-6246
rlynch@antiquebottles.com
http://www.antiquebottles.com
Web site is a haven for antique bottle collectors: information on clubs, shows, books, magazines, newsletters, newsgroups, for sale, auctions, want to buy, questions, etc.

Mike Sheridan
World of Bottles & Bygones
30 Brabant Rd.
Cheadle Hulme
Cheadle, Cheshire SK8 7AU U.K.
ph: 011 44 7931 812156
fax: 011 44 7931 812156
bygonz@yahoo.com
http://members.tripod.co.uk/
~MikeSheridan
Britain's biggest and busiest Internet site relating to old bottles, pot lids and old advertising.

Antique-Bottles.Net
U.K.
roger@antique-bottles.net
http://www.antique-bottles.net
An online forum for antique bottle collectors: identification, cleaning, finding, photographing, events, etc.

Misc. Services

R. Wayne Lowry
Jar Doctor
401 Johnston Ct.
Raymore, MO 64083
ph: 816-318-0161
fax: 816-318-0162
Jardoctor@aol.com
http://www.jardoctor.com
*Manufacturers a bottle and jar
cleaning system; also manufactures
glass cleaning equipment for
insulators, marbles as well - any
antique glass.*

Museums/Libraries

Jan Rutland, Dir.
National Bottle Museum
Newsletter: Bottle Muse, The
76 Milton Ave.
Ballston Spa, NY 12020-1405
ph: 518-885-7589
fax: 518-885-0317
nbm@crisny.org
http://family.knick.net/nbm
*Open year round; exhibits, videos and
library deal with the history and
beauty of 18th and 19th century
bottles manufactured with hand tools
and lung power; artifacts represent an
industry and way of life that has
vanished.*

Hawaii Bottle Museum
Newsletter: Hawaii Bottle Museum News
27 Kalopa Mauka Rd.
P.O. Box 1635
Honokaa, HI 96727-1635
ph: 808-775-0411
*Collection contains bottles from 1776
to 1900.*

Alan R. Blakeman
National Bottle Museum
Elsecar Heritage Centre
Nr Barnsley, South Yorks S74 8HJ U.K.
ph: 01226 745156
fax: 01226 361561
sales@onlinebbr.com
http://www.onlinebbr.com
*Specialist museum covering all areas
of bottles: wines, medicines, inks,
brewery, etc.*

Periodicals

James Hagenbuch
Magazine: Antique Bottle & Glass
  Collector
P.O. Box 180
102 Jefferson St.
East Greenville, PA 18041
ph: 215-679-5849
fax: 215-679-3068
glswrk@enter.net
http://www.glswrk-auction.com
*A monthly magazine for the glass and
bottle collector.*

Glenn Poch
Newsletter: Glenn Poch's Bottle
  Collecting Newsletter
667 White Birch Lane
Lake Zurich, IL 60047
ph: 847-726-6044
oldbottles@yahoo.com
http://www.antiquebottles.com/poch

Alan R. Blakeman
B.B.R. Publishing
Magazine: British Bottle Review &
  Collectors Mart
Elsecar Heritage Centre
Nr Barnsley, South Yorks S74 8HJ U.K.
ph: 01226 745156
fax: 01226 361561
sales@onlinebbr.com
http://www.onlinebbr.com
*Published for over 22 years; full color
magazine; the world's longest
continuous running publication
covering the multitudinous areas of
antique bottles; including world news;
published quarterly.*

Mike Sheridan
Magazine: Bygones
30 Brabant Rd.
Cheadle Hulme
Cheadle, Cheshire SK8 7AU U.K.
ph: 011 44 7931 812156
fax: 011 44 7931 812156
bygonz@yahoo.com
http://members.tripod.co.uk/
  ~MikeSheridan
*Magazine loaded with articles and
photos about glass and stoneware
bottles and related items; published
quarterly; Britain's most informative
bottle magazine; company histories,
new discoveries, digging articles;
great source for info!*

Barber

(see also BARBERSHOP
COLLECTIBLES)

Collectors

George A. Coupe
1243 1st St. S.E.
Washington, DC 20003
ph: 202-554-1000 or 800-368-5466
fax: 202-863-0775
shootthemoonok@webtv.net
*Wants barber bottles; must be in good
condition.*

Bitters

Experts

Robert Daly
10341 Jewell Lake Ct.
Fenton, MI 48430-2418
ph: 810-629-4934
fax: 810-714-1009
Ldaly1@aol.com
http://www.dalys-historic-lighting.com
*Serious collector wants old colored
bottles, hand blown in shapes; must
have a "pontil" mark (a rough break-
off) on the bottom of the bottle.*

Doug Shilson
3308 32 Ave. South
Minneapolis, MN 55406-2015
ph: 612-721-4165
bittersdug@aol.com
*Bottle collector, appraiser, expert,
dealer; has over 1,200 bitters bottles
and related advertising of all kinds;
has been collecting bottles and bottle
advertising since 1961.*

Bubble Bath

Collectors

Pete Nowicki
1531 39th Ave.
San Francisco, CA 94122-3015
ph: 415-566-7506
portfire86@aol.com
*Collects plastic Soaky and Purex
containers which came in the shape of
figures such as Donald Duck, Batman,
Mr. Magoo; were filled with soap to
get kids clean; when empty they
became a new toy.*

Cappers

Collectors

Robert Rauhauser
P.O. Box 324
Thomasville, PA 17364-0324
ph: 717-792-0278
*Wants bottle cappers: free standing,
table mounted, wall mounted, hand
held.*

Computer Programs For

Man./Prod./Dist.

Niche Software, Inc.
Software: Antique Bottle & Glass
  Collector, The
7118 NW Terrace
Parkland, FL 33076
ph: 954-344-6561
marketing@collectiblessoftware.com
http://www.collectiblessoftware.com
*Designed for the collector of antique
bottles, glass, insulators and any type
of glass collectible.*

Ginger Beer

Collectors

Keith Roloson
6220 Carriage Ct.
Cumming, GA 30040-9111
ph: 770-781-5021 or 770-750-6429
kroloson@mindspring.com
http://www.insulators.com/clubs/
  djic.htm
*Wants to buy American, Canadian,
South African, Australian, and other
stone ginger beer bottles with
pictorials.*

Historical Flasks

Experts

John Crary
North Country Bottle Shop
P.O. Box 417
Canton, NY 13617
ph: 315-386-8715
crary@northnet.org
http://www.northnet.org/ncbshome/
  salesbottles.html
*Author of "Guide to the Value of
Historical Flasks."*

Robert Daly
10341 Jewell Lake Ct.
Fenton, MI 48430-2418
ph: 810-629-4934
fax: 810-714-1009
Ldaly1@aol.com
http://www.dalys-historic-lighting.com
*Serious collector wants old colored
bottles, hand blown in shapes; must
have a "pontil" mark (a rough break-
off) on the bottom of the bottle.*

Japanese

Collectors

Al Sparacino
743 La Huerta Way
San Diego, CA 92154-2656
ph: 619-690-3632
*Buys, sells, trades Japanese figural
sake, wine, liquor bottles: House of
Koshu, Kikukawa, Kamotsuru,
Kikkoman, Sasaiti Shuzo, Okura
Shuzu, etc.*

Japanese/German Giveaway

Collectors

Paul Stookey
24724 Brightwater Ct.
Leesburg, FL 34748
ph: 352-435-6169
stock22@aol.com
*Wants Japanese and German giveaway
bottles - "nippers."*

Milk

(see also BOTTLE CAPS, Milk;
DAIRY COLLECTIBLES)

Clubs/Associations

Julian Gottlieb
National Association of Milk Bottle
  Collectors, Inc.
Newsletter: Milk Route, The
18 Pond Place
Cos Cob, CT 06807
ph: 203-869-8411
fax: 203-869-1625
gottmilk@msn.com
http://www.milkroute.org
*Focuses on milk and dairy history and
related memorabilia; membership
includes the newsletter and directory
of members; newsletter has articles,
ads, show dates, information
exchange, patents, events, etc.*

Collectors

Nick Dudek
425 Madison St.
Ravenna, OH 44266
ph: 330-296-0140
ohiomilkcaps@neo.rr.com
*Serious dairy collector and dealer
buying dairy collectibles including
milk caps and milk bottles; specializes
in Ohio milk caps; eBay seller name is
"milkdude."*

Ralph & Bonnie Kipp
836 Lehman Dr.
Chester, IL 62233
ph: 618-826-2534
kippsfam@egyptian.net
http://www.kippfamily.com/bottles
*Milk bottle collector; Styrofoam milk
bottle fill available.*

Larry Berndt
3815 Avocet Ct.
Reno, NV 89506
ph: 775-677-0998
fax: 775-306-6914
nevadamilk@juno.com
http://www.angelfire.com/mi/bottle/
index.html
Buys, sells milk bottles and caps.

Dealers

Debbie Gillette
Debbie's Milk Bottles
116 E. Division St.
Watertown, NY 13601
ph: 315-788-0587
ilovemilkbottles@yahoo.com
http://milkbottle.cjb.net
*Collector, dealer, expert specializing
in dairy collectibles and milk bottles.*

O. B. Lund
13009 So. 42nd St.
Phoenix, AZ 85044-3917
ph: 480-893-3567
*Buy, sell, trade milk bottles; round,
long neck bottles only, in good
condition; bottles must have name of
dairy, city and state; they may be
embossed or painted (pyro-glazed).*

Experts

Julian Gottlieb
18 Pond Place
Cos Cob, CT 06807
ph: 203-869-8411
fax: 203-869-1625
gottmilk@msn.com
*Appraiser, dealer, expert in dairy
collectibles.*

David Whitehead
47 Abbott Ave.
Danbury, CT 06810-5311
ph: 203-743-9803
udderlywonerful@aol.com
*Appraiser, dealer, expert in dairy
collectibles.*

Ralph Riovo
Purple Cow, The
686 Franklin St.
Alburtis, PA 18011-9578
ph: 610-966-2536
fax: 610-966-0368
thepurplecow@erols.com
http://www.papurplecow.com
*Buying and selling milk and dairy
items since 1972; wants milk bottles
with Hopalong Cassidy, Annie Oakley,
Disney characters, etc.*

John Tutton
Early American Workshop
1967 Ridgeway Rd.
Front Royal, VA 22630-8652
ph: 540-635-7058 or 540-635-6141
jtutton@rmaonline.net
http://www.earlyamericanworkshop.com
*Involved in milk bottles for 23 years;
covering collecting, buying and
selling; lecturer and author of three
books on milk bottles; author of
"Udderly Beautiful" and "Udderly
Splendid."*

Periodicals

Mike & Naomi Hull
Newsletter: Milk Bottle News
Stonemasons
Burleigh
Stroud, Gloucester GL5 2PJ U.K.
ph: 01453 884922
info@milkbottlenews.org.uk
http://www.milkbottlenews.org.uk
*A British newsletter for collectors of
milk bottles and dairy related
memorabilia.*

Miniature

Clubs/Associations

Midwest Miniature Bottle Collector
Newsletter: MMBC
P.O. Box 240388
Apple Valley, MN 55124-0388
sajwife@aol.com
*20 year old club with over 400
members in 10 countries; quarterly
newsletter.*

Collectors

Butch Jones
P.O. Box 240388
Apple Valley, MN 55124-0388
sajwife@aol.com

Lee Weiss
5626 Corning Ave.
Los Angeles, CA 90056-1305
ph: 310-534-4943 or 323-294-3231
*Buys, trades miniature bottles such as
whiskey, beer, liquor and pop
containers.*

Harry Ford
54 Village Circle
Manhattan Beach, CA 90266-7222

Periodicals

David Spaid
Briscoe Publications
Magazine: Miniature Bottle Collector,
The
P.O. Box 2161
Palos Verdes Peninsula, CA 90274-8161
ph: 310-534-4943
fax: 310-534-8437
editor@bottlecollecting.com
http://www.bottlecollecting.com
*For collectors of modern or old
miniature bottles; published six times
per year.*

Miniature Beer & Soda

Dealers

Alexander Mullin
Miscellanea
331 North Lehigh Circle
Swarthmore, PA 19081
ph: 610-328-7381
*Wants American and foreign
MINIATURE beer bottles (3"-6" high),
1880-1960; bottles may be embossed;
most will have paper, decal, or foil
labels; labels must be in good
condition; small breweries bring
premium; describe, especially label.*

Miniature Liquor

Clubs/Associations

Wayne L. Full
Western New York Miniature Liquor
Bottle Club
Newsletter: How Little We Know About
Bottles
P.O. Box 182
Cheektowaga, NY 14225-0182
ph: 716-683-8939

Norm Luber
Del-Val Miniature Bottle Club
Newsletter: It's A Small World
57104 Del Aire Landing Rd.
Philadelphia, PA 19114
*Members show and exchange
information on miniature liquor
bottles; club meets every other month;
two shows every year.*

Paul M. Murray
Great Lakes Miniature Bottle Club
Newsletter: GLMBC Newsletter
19745 Woodmont
Harper Woods, MI 48225-1873
ph: 313-882-8917
*Club is devoted to collecting miniature
liquor bottles and related items such
as giveaways and mini beers; all are
welcome.*

Harry Ford, Treas.
Lilliputian Bottle Club, The
Newsletter: Gulliver's Gazette
54 Village Circle
Manhattan Beach, CA 90266-7222
*215 member club is 20 years old and
very active; meets monthly, sponsors a
mini-bottle show and sale each
October.*

David Smith
Port Nicholson Miniature Bottle Club
Newsletter: miNiZ
P.O. Box 384
Wellington, Wellington 6006 New
Zealand
ph: 64-4-239 9536 or 64-4-478 4391
fax: 64-4-914 2829
minibottles@xtra.co.nz
http://minibottles.artshost.com/mini-
bottle-club-site1.htm
*New Zealand's only miniature bottle
collectors club; members throughout
the world.*

Mini Bottle Club, The
Newsletter: Mini Bottle Club Newsletter
47 Burradon Rd.
Burradon
Cramlington, Northumberland NE23
7NF U.K.
ph: 0191 2686561
fax: 0191 2160787
minibottleclub@aol.com
http://www.minibottleclub.co.uk
*Large bi-monthly newsletter with
latest information on old & new
miniatures as well as members' buy/
sell ads, feature articles, and bottle
outlets; primarily scotch whisky but
also gins, cognacs, rums, vodkas,
liquors, and ceramics.*

Collectors

Dr. Dana Cable
8605 Pinecliff Dr.
Frederick, MD 21704
ph: 301-694-9297
fax: 301-694-3539
danagcable@adelphia.net
*Buys and sells miniature liquor
bottles; interested in purchase of
individual bottles; send description
and price.*

Paul Stookey
24724 Brightwater Ct.
Leesburg, FL 34748
ph: 352-435-6169
stock22@aol.com
*Buys, sells, trades miniature whiskey
jugs and older miniature whiskey
bottles.*

M.L. Trangmoe
Roscoes Restaurant
22746 Roscoe Blvd.
Canoga Park, CA 91304-3350
ph: 818-883-5597
fax: 818-883-5541
Has 1,000s of minis on display.

Fred Hawley
1311 Montero Ave.
Burlingame, CA 94010
ph: 650-342-7085
*Collector of miniature liquor bottles
wants minis with labels from pre-
prohibition through the 1950s;
especially interested in 1930s minis
from California.*

Perfume & Scent

(see also AVON COLLECTIBLES;
PERFUME LAMPS)

Appraisers

Kathy Finch, ISA
5815 La Vista Court
Dallas, TX 75206
ph: 214-824-4684
klfelvis@aol.com
Accredited member of the International Society of Appraisers; appraises and collects perfume bottles.

Auction Services

Randy Monsen
Monsen & Baer Inc.
P.O. Box 529
Vienna, VA 22183-0529
ph: 703-938-2129
fax: 703-242-1357
monsenbaer@erols.com
Cataloged auctions of perfume bottles: commercial, Czechoslovakian, Lalique, Baccarat, Victorian, Crown Top, factices (perfume display bottles), miniatures.

Clubs/Associations

ElsaBeth Crohn, Pres.
International Perfume Bottle Association
Newsletter: Perfume Bottle Quarterly
1789 Maryland Ave. N.
Minneapolis, MN 55427
ph: 763-544-5038
scentbottlelsab@attbi.com
http://www.perfumebottles.org
Largest organization worldwide of collectors and dealers in perfume bottles: commercials, atomizers, art glass, Czech, minis, etc.; informative quarterly newsletter, annual meeting, membership directory, special programs for members.

Sandy Katz-Leegood
Lone Star Chapter of the International Perfume Bottle Association
Newsletter: Lone Star Scents
P.O. Box 596553
Dallas, TX 75227-1429
ph: 214-275-4370
jleegood@yahoo.com
Members receive two newsletters, regional meetings and opportunities to participate in Annual Vintage Vanity Convention featuring all ladies vanity items: perfumes, compacts, vintage purses, powders, hatpins, combs, etc.

Linda Brine
UK Perfume Bottle Collectors' Club
England, U.K.
pamela.taylor@ipba-uk.co.uk
http://www.ipba-uk.co.uk

Collectors

Arielle Hart
PMB 421 Ste. 104
4044 W. Lake Mary Blvd.
Longwood, FL 32779
ph: 407-833-9234
fax: 407-833-9235
aaahart@earthlink.net
Collector of commercial perfume bottles; would enjoy hearing from anyone who would like to sell or trade; or anyone who would just like to chat about perfumes.

Jeane Parris
Sugarplums, etc.
2022 E. Charleston Blvd.
Las Vegas, NV 89104-2018
ph: 702-385-6059
fax: 702-388-1202

Beverly Nelson
1010 Lorna St.
Corona, CA 92882-4066
ph: 909-737-0977
Specializes in perfume bottles, sets, compacts, lipsticks, and counter displays from the Bourjois Co. (makers of Evening in Paris, Mais Oui, Kobako) and Woodworth Co. (makers of Karess, Viegay, Fiancee); price guide available for $15.

Dealers

Ken Leach
Gallery #47
1050 2nd Ave.
New York, NY 10022
ph: 800-942-0550 or 212-888-0165
fax: 212-355-4403
kenleach47@aol.com
http://www.gallery47.com
Buys and sells commercial and Czechoslovakian perfume bottles.

Christie Mayer Lefkowith
Christie Mayer, Inc.
FDR Station
P.O. Box 5200
New York, NY 10150-5200
ph: 212-838-2932 or 212-758-8550
fax: 212-688-9313
mayerlef@panix.com
http://www.mayerlef.com
Buys and sells all sizes of commercial perfume bottles, preferably with boxes: Lalique, Viard and other glass artists, Baccarat, Brosse, Pochet & du Courval, and other crystal works by the European Chamber of Art Experts.

Kathy Burch
Tri-State Antique Center
47 W. Pike
Canonsburg, PA 15317
ph: 724-745-9116
fax: 412-291-1367
kathy&ed@tri-stateantiques.com
http://tri-stateantiques.com
Specializes in lady's beaded and mesh purses, Lucite purses, chatelaines, compacts, and other ladies vanity items.

Randy Monsen
Monsen & Baer Inc.
P.O. Box 529
Vienna, VA 22183-0529
ph: 703-938-2129
fax: 703-242-1357
monsenbaer@erols.com
Wants commercial perfume bottles, especially with original boxes: by Guerlain, Coty, Nina Ricci, Dior, Corday, Lalique, etc.

Myra Jaffe
Oldies But Goodies
P.O. Box 880244
Port Saint Lucie, FL 34986
ph: 561-873-0968
fax: 561-873-0968
email@oldgood.com
http://www.oldgood.com
Buys, sells perfume bottles (Czech, DeVilbiss, R. Lalique, crown tops, etc.).

Janice Holton
Passion for Perfume
14251 Frost Rd.
Caldwell, ID 83607
ph: 208-454-8876
janice@micron.net
http://passionforperfume.com
Collectible bottles in many categories including commercial, miniature, Czech, atomizers, factices (perfume display bottles), novelties, figurals, perfume solids, Victorian, and much more.

Tina Schaare
2331 D2 E Ave. S, #275
Palmdale, CA 93550
fax: 661-538-9240
crowns97@aol.com
http://home.earthlink.net/~schaare4
Buy, sell, trade high quality commercial perfume bottles; specializing in minis, samplers and testers, solid perfume compacts.

Experts

Ken Leach
Gallery #47
1050 2nd Ave.
New York, NY 10022
ph: 800-942-0550 or 212-888-0165
fax: 212-355-4403
kenleach47@aol.com
http://www.gallery47.com
Internationally known commercial perfume bottle collector/dealer; author of "Perfume Presentation - 100 Years of Artistry."

Christie Mayer Lefkowith
Christie Mayer, Inc.
FDR Station
P.O. Box 5200
New York, NY 10150-5200
ph: 212-838-2932 or 212-758-8550
fax: 212-688-9313
mayerlef@panix.com
http://www.mayerlef.com
Buys all sizes of commercial perfume bottles, preferably with boxes: Lalique, Baccarat, and others from 1850 to 1960; author of "The Art of Perfume, Discovering and Collecting Perfume Bottles," and "Masterpieces of the Perfume Industry."

Internet Resources

Montage
montage@cicat.com
http://www.cicat.com/montage
Perfume bottle information center.

Janice Holton
Passion for Perfume
14251 Frost Rd.
Caldwell, ID 83607
ph: 208-454-8876
janice@micron.net
http://passionforperfume.com
Web site has everything you can think of that is perfume related plus places to list wants or advertise for missing parts; list of good perfume bottle shopping places, and perfume bottle books for sale.

Steph Burton
Javaslublu Perfume Encyclopedia
14 Shepherds Close
Ringmer
East Sussex, BN8 5LU U.K.
javaslublu@btinternet.com
http://www.javaslublu.com
A comprehensive gathering of perfume and perfume bottle information: images, identification service, auction results, values, articles, perfume names and release dates, and more.

Periodicals

Christie Mayer Lefkowith
Newsletter: Art & Fragrances Perfume Presentations
FDR Station
P.O. Box 5200
New York, NY 10150-5200
ph: 212-838-2932 or 212-758-8550
fax: 212-688-9313
mayerlef@panix.com
http://www.mayerlef.com
An annual review of specialty perfume bottle auctions at Art & Fragrances Auctions in Geneva, Switzerland, along with pre-sale auction estimates and actual prices realized.

Repair Services

Myra Jaffe
Oldies But Goodies
P.O. Box 880244
Port Saint Lucie, FL 34986
ph: 561-873-0968
fax: 561-873-0968
email@oldgood.com
http://www.oldgood.com
Will custom fit their atomizer perfume parts onto your bottle or top; send SASE for information.

Shari Hopper
Paradise & Co.
2902 Neal Rd.
Paradise, CA 95969-6169
ph: 530-872-5020
fax: 530-872-5052
paradise@sunset.net
http://www.paradise-co.com
Replacement parts for atomizers: cords, balls, tassels; metal sprayer tops and collars; glass siphon tubing and daubers; also repairs, restoration and conservation available for perfume bottles.

Suppliers

Shari Hopper
Paradise & Co.
2902 Neal Rd.
Paradise, CA 95969-6169
ph: 530-872-5020
fax: 530-872-5052
paradise@sunset.net
http://www.paradise-co.com
Replacement parts for atomizers: cords, balls, tassels; metal sprayer tops and collars; glass siphon tubing and daubers; also repairs, restoration and conservation available for perfume bottles.

Perfume & Scent (Miniature)

Clubs/Associations

Melinda Churchfield
Miniature Perfume Bottle Collectors
Newsletter: Mini-Scents
28227 Paseo El Siena
Laguna Niguel, CA 92677-4500
ph: 949-364-9510
For collectors of miniature perfume bottles; newsletter includes what's new, history of perfume houses, different versions and a color center page.

Collectors

Arielle Hart
PMB 421 Ste. 104
4044 W. Lake Mary Blvd.
Longwood, FL 32779
ph: 407-833-9234
fax: 407-833-9235
aaahart@earthlink.net
Collector of commercial perfume bottles; would enjoy hearing from anyone who would like to sell or trade; or anyone who would just like to chat about perfumes.

Dealers

Eric Lipson
1700 University Dr., Ste. 205
Pompano Beach, FL 33071
ph: 877-755-2805 or 954-340-9400
fax: 954-755-3061
perfumedad@aol.com
Appraiser, dealer, collector specializes in vintage miniature perfume samples and commercial perfume bottles; reseller of fine perfume display bottles (factices).

Melinda Churchfield
My Mom & Me
28227 Paseo El Siena
Laguna Niguel, CA 92677-4500
ph: 949-364-9510
Collector, dealer of commercial miniature/sample perfume bottles; in business for over 12 years.

Poison

Clubs/Associations

Joan Cabaniss
Antique Poison Bottle Collectors Association
312 Summer Lane
Huddleston, VA 24104
Jjcab@aol.com
http://antique.poisonbottle.com
Purpose of the club is unite poison bottle collectors and to promote, foster, and encourage the betterment of their collections; encourages the exchange of information about collecting, displaying, researching poison bottles.

Collectors

Mary Riggin
Rt. 617
Marionville, VA 23408
ph: 757-442-5321 or 757-442-2179
fax: 757-442-5321
Collector wants to buy old poison bottles.

Puzzle

Collectors

Alvin Schenk
5728 Pimlico Rd.
Baltimore, MD 21209
ph: 410-367-4371
Collects puzzle bottles - small, handcarved curiosities placed in bottles with small openings.

Soda

(see also SODA FOUNTAIN COLLECTIBLES; SOFT DRINK COLLECTIBLES)

Experts

Paul & Karen Bates
Interactive Publishers
1055 Ridgecrest Dr.
Goodlettsville, TN 37072
ph: 615-859-5236 or 800-826-4929
fax: 615-859-5238
mbca@gono.com
http://www.gono.com/vir-mus/museum.htm
Publishes always-current price updates to earlier soda bottle books.

Ron Fowler
Seattle History Company
4518 35th Ave. NE
Seattle, WA 98105-3002
ph: 206-525-1050
SodaBottles@yahoo.com
http://members.tripod.com/~SodaBottles
Author of "Ice-Cold Soda Pop 5 Cents," "Washington Sodas," "The Bottler's Helper," and "An Introduction to Collecting Soda Pop Bottles."

Violin

Clubs/Associations

Peggy Sweet
Violin Bottle Collectors Association
158 Rosamond St.
Carleton Place, Ontario K7C 1V2
Canada
Peggy.Sweet@jus.gov.on.ca
http://viobot.tripod.com

Western Whiskey

Clubs/Associations

49'er Historical Bottle Club
P.O. Box 561
Penryn, CA 95663
Always glad to provide information on West Coast bottles or on club membership.

Experts

Bob Barnett
P.O. Box 109
Lakeview, OR 97630
ph: 541-947-2415
fax: 541-947-2642
Author of "Western Whiskey Bottles."

BOW HUNTING

(see SPORTING COLLECTIBLES, Archery)

BOXES

(see also ADVERTISING COLLECTIBLES; CEREAL BOXES; CIGAR BOXES, LABELS & BANDS; ENAMELS; ORIENTALIA; PLASTIC COLLECTIBLES, Celluloid; RUSSIAN ITEMS; SMOKING COLLECTIBLES, Snuff Boxes)

Dealers

Sally Kaltman
Sallea Antiques
66 Elm St.
New Canaan, CT 06840
ph: 203-972-1050
fax: 203-972-1567
Buys, sells and specializes in distinctive antique boxes; all shapes, styles, materials and sizes.

Rob Hanson
BoxCollector.com
8581 Santa Monica Blvd. #702
West Hollywood, CA 90069
ph: 323-512-0206
rob@boxcollector.com
http://www.boxcollector.com
Buys and sells quality art, antique, and import boxes including kuduo boxes, antique Ghanian British Colonial mahogany chests, exotic wood boxes, carved boxes, lacquer boxes, etc.

June & Tony Stone
June & Tony Stone Fine Antique Boxes
5 Burlington Arcade
Bond St.
Peacehaven, East Sussex W1J 0PD U.K.
ph: 44 (0) 1273 579 333
fax: 44 (0) 1273 588 908
jts@boxes.co.uk
http://www.boxes.co.uk
Specialists in high quality and rare antique boxes of the 18th and 19th century: tea caddies, snuff boxes, humidors, knife boxes, games boxes, drinks boxes, jewel boxes, etc.; 44-page color catalog sent on request; large Web site.

Antique Boxes
2 Middleton Rd.
London, E8 4BL U.K.
ph: 00 44 (0)20 7254 7074
fax: 00 44 (0)870 1257669
boxes@hygra.com
http://www.hygra.com
Specializes in boxes from the 18th and 19th century: tea caddies, sewing boxes, jewellery boxes, writing boxes, lap desks, fitted dressing boxes, snuff boxes, patch boxes; of wood, tortoise shell, ivory, papier-mâché, etc.

Experts

Janice & Richard Vogel
8420 SW 92nd St., Unit B
Ocala, FL 34481-9317
ph: 352-854-0799
fax: 352-854-0799
vogels@contaandboehme.com
http://www.contaandboehme.com
Authors of "Victorian Trinket Boxes," a handbook with price guide for the porcelain trinket box collector.

Enamel

Dealers

Bob Smith
Cameron & Smith Ltd.
P.O. Box 637
Vero Beach, FL 32961-0637
ph: 800-472-9862 or 772-778-7862
fax: 772-794-0544
enamels@cameronsmith.com
http://www.cameronsmith.com
Buys, sells enamel boxes: Halcyon Days, Marshall Enamels, McLaughlin Enamels, Staffordshire, Crummles, Moorcroft, Bilston, Battersea, etc.; specializing in retired limited editions Beatrix Potter enamels and any Royalty enamels.

Taylor B. Williams
Taylor B. Williams Antiques LLC
P.O. Box 11297
Chicago, IL 60611
ph: 312-266-0908
fax: 312-266-0995
TaylorBWms@aol.com
http://www.TaylorBWilliams.com
A specialist in American and English furniture, decorative accessories and enamel boxes.

Enamel (Battersea)

Experts

Mel & Barbara Alpren
14 Carter Rd.
West Orange, NJ 07052-4612
ph: 973-731-9427
*Advisor to "Warman's Antiques &
Collectibles Price Guide."*

Enamel (Halcyon)

Man./Prod./Dist.

Halcyon Days Enamels
14-16 Barton Park Mount Pleasant
Bilston, West Midlands WV14 7LH
U.K.
ph: 011 44 1902 408440
fax: 011 44 1902 498008

BOY SCOUT MEMORABILIA

(see also CAMPING EQUIPMENT;
GIRL SCOUT MEMORABILIA; LONE
SCOUT MEMORABILIA; STAMP
COLLECTING, Boy Scouting)

Appraisers

Brill Lee
Brill Lee Appraisal Services
P.O. Box 244
Bellevue, WA 98009-0244
ph: 425-885-4518
fax: 425-895-1022
brilllee@hotmail.com
*Active Boy Scout for over 40 years;
Eagle Scout, Silver Explorer,
Woodbadge; has appraised, bought,
sold, collected vintage Boy Scout
equipment, uniforms, awards,
handbooks etc., for over 20 years; also
will sell on consignment for clients.*

Book Sellers

Doug Bearce
Scouting Collectables
P.O. Box 4742
Salem, OR 97302-8742
ph: 503-399-9872
fax: 503-399-0559
bearce@prodigy.net
http://www.scouting-collectables.com
*Publishes and sells books on
collecting Boy Scout items.*

Clubs/Associations

Ron Aldridge, Ch.
International Scouting Collectors
    Association, Inc.
Journal: ISCA Journal
250 Canyon Oaks Dr.
Argyle, TX 76226
ph: 940-455-2519
noacman@aol.com
http://www.scouttrader.org
*A non-profit organization that
promotes education regarding the
history of the Scouting Movement
through the collecting and trading of
Scouting Memorabilia.*

Michelle Iddon
International Badgers Club
21 Lynfield Rd.
Great Harwood
Blackburn, Lancashire 37803 U.K.
webmaster@IntBC.org
http://www.intbc.org
*Members interested in collecting Scout
and Guide badges of the entire world;
an international organization with
representatives all around the world.*

Collectors

Norm Sapolnick
P.O. Box 5
Hillside, NJ 07205-0005
ph: 908-687-3920
fax: 908-687-6300
Wants to buy Boy Scout memorabilia.

Bruce J. White
3 Woodfern Ave.
Trenton, NJ 08628-1537
ph: 609-882-5584
boyscout08628@aol.com
*Wants Boy Scouts of America patches,
pins, literature, WWW items,
jamboree, etc.*

John Burch
173 Hutton Dr.
Williamsburg, KY 40769
ph: 606-539-4160

Mike Wroblewski
5526 E. County Rd. 100 N.
Greensburg, IN 47240-8805
ph: 812-663-9403
bwrob00@hsonline.net
*Wants all Boy Scout related
memorabilia: special interest in all
War Service related Scouting items
(WWI and WWII).*

Dr. Larry Ruehlen, Sr.
21124 Hoffman St.
Saint Clair Shores, MI 48082-1517
ph: 248-964-0530
*Wants Scout rings, square merit
badges and ranks, Air Scout items,
Eagle items, OA vigil items.*

Billie Lee
806 E. Scott St.
Tuscola, IL 61953-1726
ph: 217-253-3243

Jody Tucker
1627 Main St., Ste. 100
Kansas City, MO 64108
ph: 913-927-5074 or 816-471-3333 x223
fax: 816-471-3010
jody@cytekcorp.com
http://www.boyscoutwanted.com
*Collector, expert buying Boy Scout
Memorabilia: pins, patches, uniforms,
pictures, medals, books, etc.; single
item or entire collection*

Robert N. Hightower
1141 A.C.R. 378
Palestine, TX 75801
ph: 903-723-0418
hightower@risecom.net
Buys Boy Scout and Order of the

*Arrow items: patches, pins, books,
uniforms, medals, equipment, etc.;
displays Boy Scout and Order of the
Arrow items in mobile museum.*

John C. Williams
Heart O' Texas Trader
P.O. Box 23374
Waco, TX 76702-3374
ph: 254-772-1106
fax: 254-741-9715
jconleywilliams@prodigy.net
http://www.hottrader.com
*Dealer, collector, appraiser, online
resource specializing in Boy Scouting;
wants to buy Boy Scout patches: Order
of the Arrow (WWW), Philmont, High
Adventure, Jamboree; also wants other
Boy Scout related memorabilia.*

Dealers

Richard Shields
Carolina Trader, The
P.O. Box 769
Monroe, NC 28111-0769
ph: 704-282-1339 or 704-289-1604
carotrader@trellis.net
http://www.TheCarolinaTrader.com
*Buys anything associated with the Boy
Scouts of America; author of "Patrol
Yell - History of the Patrol Medallions
of the BSA;" publishes large catalog
of BSA items for sale.*

Roland Sayers
Southeastern Antiques & Collectibles
P.O. Box 629
Brevard, NC 28712
ph: 828-883-9562
*Wants to buy pre-1960 Boy and Girl
Scout collectibles.*

Darrell Wessinger
dwessinger.com
1036 Two Notch Rd.
Lexington, SC 29073-8953
ph: 803-359-6752
darrell@dwessinger.com
http://www.dwessinger.com
*Dealer, collector, expert with over 35
years specializing in Boy Scout and
Girl Scout memorabilia; buys all kinds
of scouting memorabilia; collections
bought and sold.*

Chris R. Jensen
Streamwood, Inc.
Newsletter: Scout Stuff
121 Gulf St.
P.O. Box 1841
Easley, SC 29641-1841
ph: 864-859-2915
fax: 800-453-0398
cjensen@streamwood.net
http://www.streamwood.net
*Wants Boy Scout memorabilia: pre-
1936 handbooks, Order of the Arrow
(WWW), merit badges, jamboree,*

medals, patches, insignia, uniforms; publishes extensive catalog four/five times a year; 40-page tabloid paper; send for free sample.

Randall M. MacDonald
Suncoast Patch Supply
P.O. Box 2501
Lakeland, FL 33806-2501
ph: 941-644-4177
macdonr@tfn.net
http://www.angelfire.com/fl/thetrader/
   index.html
Avid collector and dealer of Boy Scout patches since 1973; also wants patches and memorabilia from Philmont Scout Ranch in Cimarron, NM.

Nancy & Glenn Darst
Boston Store, The
P.O. Box 190394
Mobile, AL 36619
ph: 334-666-9265 or 334-666-2079
gdarst@zebra.net
Buys and sells fishing and hunting collectibles from 1800s to 1950s: Girl Scout and Boy Scout knives, hatchets, axes; also landing & trout nets, backpacks, lures, bobbers, knives, creels, pack baskets, fishing catalogs, pre-1950 LL Bean.

Mark Browning
Ploughshare Trades
12300 E. 5th St.
Kansas City, MO 64133
ph: 816-353-2876
mbrownin@jccc.net
Buys and sells all sorts of Boy Scout collectibles; specializes in Order of the Arrow and Council Shoulder patches.

Jeff Feldman
P.O. Box 9153
Calabasas, CA 91302
ph: 818-883-4720 or 818-535-9494
fax: 818-883-2220
jfbf@ix.netcom.com
Collects and sells Buy and Girl Scout memorabilia of all kinds: patches, pins, medals, books, pictures, periodicals, Eagle Scout, cards, etc.

Doug Bearce
P.O. Box 4742
Salem, OR 97302-8742
ph: 503-399-9872
fax: 503-399-0559
bearce@prodigy.net
http://www.scouting-collectables.com
Buys and sells Boy Scout & Girl Scout items: books, uniforms, patches, pins, Order of the Arrow items, Jamboree, etc.

Experts

Chris R. Jensen
Streamwood, Inc.
121 Gulf St.
P.O. Box 1841
Easley, SC 29641-1841
ph: 864-859-2915
fax: 800-453-0398
cjensen@streamwood.net
http://www.streamwood.net
30 years experience as dealer/ collector/appraiser; largest sale list of exclusive Scouting items in the world; largest inventory of Scout collecting guide books available anywhere; author of 7 Scout collecting books and price guides.

Roy More
Scout Patch Auction
2484 Dundee
Ann Arbor, MI 48103
ph: 734-663-6203
fax: 734-663-7227
spa@msen.com
http://www.tspa.com
Collector, dealer, appraiser expert in Boy Scout memorabilia.

Jim & Bea Stevenson
Stevensons, The
316 Sage Lane
Euless, TX 76039-7906
ph: 817-354-8903
fax: 817-354-9382
thestevensons@airmail.net
http://www.thestevensons.com
Wants Boy Scout handbooks, paper items, Jamboree items, uniforms, insignia, Sea Scouts, Skippers, Order of the Arrow, etc.; all catalogs are sent via Email.

John C. Williams
Heart O' Texas Trader
P.O. Box 23374
Waco, TX 76702-3374
ph: 254-772-1106
fax: 254-741-9715
jconleywilliams@prodigy.net
http://www.hottrader.com
Dealer, collector, appraiser, online resource specializing in Boy Scouting; wants to buy Boy Scout patches: Order of the Arrow (WWW), Philmont, High Adventure, Jamboree; also wants other Boy Scout related memorabilia.

Internet Resources

Glenn Chase
Scout Patch Collector, The
2604 Rock Terrace Dr.
Austin, TX 78704-3842
spanky@mac.com
http://www.patchcamp.com
Premiere Internet directory of online resources related to trading, collecting, displaying, and preserving Scout memorabilia; over 80 helpful links; promotes teamwork to help preserve the heritage of Scouting.

Ken Wiltz
World of Scouting, The
126 Seagull Row
Novato, CA 94945-4515
ph: 415-892-5977
fax: 415-892-5977
kenwiltzCA@juno.com
http://n2zgu.topcities.com
Great source for Scouting information; includes online version of former Fleur-de-lis magazine.

Museums/Libraries

Edward Rowan
Lawrence L. Lee Scout Museum & Max I. Silber Scouting Library
Magazine: Scout Memorabilia
P.O. Box 1121
Manchester, NH 03105-1121
ph: 603-627-1492 or 603-669-8919
fax: 603-641-6436
administrator@scoutingmuseum.org
http://www.scoutingmuseum.org
Home to one of the finest collections of Boy Scout memorabilia; "Scout Memorabilia" has insert listing sales, auctions, ads, etc.

Mollie Perrot, Ex. Dir.
Ottawa Scouting Museum
1100 Canal St.
P.O. Box 2241
Ottawa, IL 61350
ph: 815-431-9353
scouter@theramp.net
http://osm.hypermart.net
Houses the Zitelman Collection of Rockford, the Sullivan Collection of Friendship Village, and memorabilia from local donors: covers Boy Scouting, Girl Scouting, and Camp Fire; does not do appraisals.

Ed W. Hillenberg, Curator
Hillenberg Scout Museum
123 Beard St.
Danville, IL 61832-6009
ph: 217-442-6678

Periodicals

Edward Rowan
Lawrence L. Lee Scout Museum & Max I. Silber Scouting Library
Magazine: Scout Memorabilia
P.O. Box 1121
Manchester, NH 03105-1121
ph: 603-627-1492 or 603-669-8919
fax: 603-641-6436
administrator@scoutingmuseum.org
http://www.scoutingmuseum.org
Home to one of the finest collections of Boy Scout memorabilia; "Scout Memorabilia" has insert listing sales, auctions, ads, etc.

Camps

Periodicals

David Minnihan
Newsletter: Camp Patch Collector, The
P.O. Box 210013
San Francisco, CA 94121-0013
ph: 714-641-4845
asta@scouter.org
Newsletter dealing with history and memorabilia of Boy Scout Camps.

Neckerchief Slides

Collectors

John Koppen
12705 N.W. Puddy Gulch Rd.
Yamhill, OR 97148-8020
ph: 503-662-3953
mrncslide@netscape.net

Order Of The Arrow

Collectors

Paul Judge
4 Winthhrop Place
Maplewood, NJ 07040
Collector and expert who specializes in collecting and trading Order of the Arrow Boy Scout patches, especially OA flap patches from past and present New Jersey Lodges.

Greg Souchik
P.O. Box 161
Custer City, PA 16725-0161
ph: 814-362-2642
fax: 814-362-7356
Mg34@mg34.com
http://www.mg34.com
Wants to buy "Order of the Arrow" embroidered patches; may have "W.W.W.," "Lodge," or "O.A." on them; will pay up to $1,000 for some patches; send photos or photocopies.

John E. Pannell
600-C Tracy Dr.
Burlington, NC 27215
jpannell@triad.rr.com
http://www.oaimages.com

Internet Resources

John E. Pannell
Internet Guide to Order of the Arrow Insignia
600-C Tracy Dr.
Burlington, NC 27215
jpannell@triad.rr.com
http://www.oaimages.com
The Internet's largest collection of Order of the Arrow insignia; with over 33,325 images from 766 lodges.

Seals

Clubs/Associations

Murray Fried
World Scout Sealers
Newsletter: World Scout Sealers Newsletter
509-11 Margaret Ave.
Kitchener, Ontario N2H 6M4 Canada
ph: 519-745-7947
murryfried@golden.net
Members buy, sell and trade Scout

seals, decals and other Boy Scout memorabilia; publishes an 8-page newsletter twice a year; eBay ID is "drift4."

BRASS ITEMS

(see also BELLS; CANDLEHOLDERS; FIREPLACE ITEMS; INSTRUMENTS & DEVICES; LAMPS & LIGHTING; MEDICAL, DENTAL & PHARMACEUTICAL; REPAIR/RESTORATION/ CONSERVATION, Metal Items; TRENCH ART)

Experts

Eve Stone
Eve Stone Antiques, Ltd.
22 Selden St.
Woodbridge, CT 06525
ph: 203-389-6665 or 800-833-1665
fax: 203-389-6103
info@evestoneantiques.com
http://www.evestoneantiques.com
Specializes in period brass and copper French and English antiques; a nationally known expert in copper and brass.

Repair Services

Don L. Reedy
Brass & Copper Polishing Shop
13 South Carroll St.
Frederick, MD 21701-5606
ph: 301-663-4240
fax: 301-694-9190
shineit4u@aol.com
http://www.frederickcouonty.com/
    antiques/brass.htm
Repairs and polishes or lacquers brass and copper items.

D & E Brass Buffing
101 Wagonsheel Lane
Rowlett, TX 75088
ph: 972-412-2260
fax: 972-527-5373
Professional polishing, lacquering and antique restoration of anything brass.

Repro. Sources

Virginia Metalcrafters
1010 East Main St.
Waynesboro, VA 22980-5855
ph: 540-949-9400 or 800-368-1002
fax: 540-949-9446
wcs@netlos.net
http://www.vametal.com
Makes and sells andirons, fireplace tools and fenders, chandeliers, candlesticks, sconces, garden sculpture.

BREWERIANA

(see also ADVERTISING COLLECTIBLES; BEER CANS; BOTTLES; BOTTLE CAPS; BOTTLE OPENERS; COLLECTIBLES [MODERN], Steins; CORKSCREWS; GLASSES, Drinking; NEON; PAPER COLLECTIBLES; PROHIBITION ITEMS; SALOON & BAR COLLECTIBLES; STEINS)

Appraisers

Judy Owen, ISA
Antique Appraisers - Grand Traverse
10332 Stoneybeach Pointe
Traverse City, MI 49686-8584
ph: 231-946-2534
fax: 231-946-2573
judy@antiqueappraisers.com
http://www.antiqueappraisers.com
Collects, specializes in, and appraises breweriana: Strohs, Goebels, all Michigan breweries, pre-prohibition trays and signs, etched glasses, bottle-shaped openers, etc.

Lynn Geyer
300 Trail Ridge
Silver City, NM 88061-6071
ph: 505-538-2341
fax: 505-388-3493
Appraiser, expert specializes in all aspects of breweriana and soda-pop; also contemporary steins, mugs & drinking glasses; advertising trays, advertising signs, tap knobs; member of Certified Appraiser Guild of America.

Auction Services

Lynn Geyer
Lynn Geyer Advertising Auctions
300 Trail Ridge
Silver City, NM 88061-6071
ph: 505-538-2341
fax: 505-388-3493
Conducts semi-annual mail/phone bid specialized auctions on all aspects of breweriana and soda-pop; also contemporary steins, mugs & drinking glasses; advertising trays, advertising signs, tap knobs.

Clubs/Associations

Chris & Roger Levesque
Microbes
Newsletter: Micro Connection, The
P.O. Box 826
South Windsor, CT 06074
ph: 860-644-9582
chris.roger@snet.net
Focuses on collecting breweriana relating to micro breweries.

John Stanley
East Coast Breweriana Association
Newsletter: Keg, The
P.O. Box 64
Chapel Hill, NC 27514
ph: 919-419-1546 or 919-966-5794
jfo@mindspring.com
http://www.eastcoastbrew.com
The oldest breweriana collectors organization; serving collectors of all

types of brewery advertising; emphasis on Eastern US; write and request a membership application.

Kurt Bachmann
Dog Gone Good
Newsletter: Dog Gone Good Dispatch
57883 Hanover Rd.
Washington, MI 48094
ph: 810-677-3284
fax: 248-745-1221
Dealing with all types of breweriana advertising including, but not limited to, beer advertising bottle openers; official chapter of the National Association of Breweriana Advertising dedicated to breweriana history and collecting.

Ray Capek
Westmont Strohs Chapter of the Beer Can Collectors of America
Newsletter: Westmont Strohs Streaker
3051 Ridgeland Ave.
Lisle, IL 60532
ph: 630-778-1482
fax: 630-778-1482
rbcapek@aol.com
A chapter of the Beer Can Collectors of America; based in the Chicago area; shows held twice a year in April and October; over 100 active members; members collect all types of breweriana (beer cans, beer signs, etc.).

Keith Ajayan
Beer Can & Breweriana Collectors of America, Mile High Chapter
414 Wright St. #107
Lakewood, CO 80228
ph: 303-763-5811
beerstuff@aol.com

Christine Galloway, Ex. Dir.
American Breweriana Association, Inc.
Journal: American Breweriana Journal
P.O. Box 11157
Pueblo, CO 81001-0157
ph: 719-544-9267
fax: 719-544-4289
breweriana1@earthlink.net
http://
    www.americanxs4all.ntbreweriana.org
Association of brewery historians and collectors of beer advertising and collectibles; offers seven free exchange services for collectors, Lending Library, and annual meeting for members to buy/sell/trade breweriana; 3,300 members.

Andy Reiner
Canadian Brewerianist, The
19 Lambert Rd.
Thornhill, Ontario L3T 7E6 Canada

Mike Peterson
Association of Bottled Beer Collectors
Newsletter: What's Bottling
28 Parklands
Kidsgrove, Stoke-on-Trent ST7 4US
U.K.
ph: +44 1782 761048
michael.peterson@ntlworld.com
http://www.abbc.org.uk
Collectors of (mainly) British

commemorative bottled beers, beer labels and other breweriana.

Collectors

Ed Natale, Jr.
P.O. Box 222
Wyckoff, NJ 07481-0222
ph: 201-493-7172
jednat@att.net
Wants to buy beer trays with brewery scenes, women, dogs, children; foam scrapers, NJ & NYC brewery items, painted label bottles, punch-top and spout-top cans, signs; photos helpful.

Ron Gavin
1721 Depot Rd.
Duanesburg, NY 12056
ph: 518-895-8165
hopps53@capital.net
Wants breweriana items; specializes in trays, signs, bottles, and coasters; wants items from upstate New York cities such as Albany, Troy, Schenectady, Amsterdam, Utica, Rome, Cohoes, Hudson, and Binghamton.

Steve Gordon
P.O. Box 632
Olney, MD 20830-0632
ph: 301-996-4666
fax: 772-264-3292
steve@beercanman.com
http://www.beercanman.com
Wants to buy pre-1960s US cans, especially conetops and flat tops; will answer any letter or call promptly; also will consider other beer-related items such as signs, trays, coasters, etc.; single item or entire collection.

Kurt Bachmann
57883 Hanover Rd.
Washington, MI 48094
ph: 810-677-3284
fax: 248-745-1221
Dealing with all types of breweriana advertising including, but not limited to, beer advertising bottle openers.

Mike England
718 NW Scott St.
Ankeny, IA 50021-2267
ph: 515-965-2448
Mike.England@bcca.com
http://www.angelfire.com/ia/england3260
Want old cone top & flat top beer & soda cans; also breweriana (beer advertising) items; especially interested in pre-prohibition era, anything from Iowa breweries, Dr. Pepper, etc.; look in crawl spaces, attics, walls, under stoop.

Steve Ketcham
P.O. Box 24114
Minneapolis, MN 55424-0114
ph: 952-920-4205
s.ketcham@unique-software.com
Wants pre-prohibition brewery memorabilia: calendars, publications, brewery signs, trays, glasses, posters, pocket mirrors, steins, etc.; please send SASE with inquiries.

Dale Schmidt
610 Howell Prairie Rd. SE
Salem, OR 97301-9097
ph: 503-364-0499
fax: 503-585-3071
jschm62655@aol.com
Wants anything pre-Prohibition that is related to beer and/or breweries.

Mike Peterson
28 Parklands
Kidsgrove, Stoke-on-Trent ST7 4US
U.K.
ph: +44 1782 761048
michael.peterson@ntlworld.com
http://www.mpeterson.co.uk
Collector of UK commemorative bottled beers, brewery jugs, mirrors and advertising, brewery histories, stout labels pre-1965, as well as Guinness miniatures from all over the world; offers an appraisal service via his Web site.

Dealers

Dan Morean
www.breweriana.com
13 Greenleaf St.
Malden, MA 02148
ph: 781-324-3330
danm@breweriana.com
http://www.breweriana.com
Collects MA breweriana, buys and sells all other breweriana items; specializes in pre-prohibition brewery advertising, beer cans, bottles, trays, lithographs, trade cards, openers, matchbooks, labels; also soda collectibles.

Bob Lucian
33 Merritts Rd.
Farmingdale, NY 11735-1820
ph: 516-293-3927
bbluc@optonline.net
Buys and sells old pre-prohibition American beer items: mugs, steins, advertising signs, bottle openers, match safes, glasses, "giveaways," etc.; prefers items from the NYC and L.I. area; also wants prohibition items; call collect.

John Gruskin
P.O. Box 53
Northport, NY 11768
ph: 516-262-0338
jlgruskin@aol.com
http://www.angelfire.com/ny/beerstuff
Buys and sells beer cans, trays, steins, advertising.

Don Fink
108 E. Seventh St.
Lansdale, PA 19446-2622
ph: 215-855-9732
fax: 215-855-6325
lansbeer@finksauctions.com
http://www.finksauctions.com
Deals in a wide range of brewery collectibles.

Mike Hennech
Ale Publishing Co.
P.O. Box 1396
Alto, NM 88312-1396
ph: 505-336-1698
Buys, sells, appraises collectibles relating to US breweries: beer business cards, bottles, cans, trays, matchcovers, coasters, labels, glasses, etc.

Paul Jarmusz
Vintage Original Fruit Crate Labels
2845 D St. N.E.
Salem, OR 97301-1600
ph: 503-371-0868
fax: 503-371-0868
mikajz@attbi.com
http://www.labelcollector.com
Buys and sells old can labels, beer labels, soda labels; unused stock found from breweries, old packing houses, canneries, produce businesses.

Bill Mugrage
Pacific Coast Breweriana
3819 190th Place S.W.
Lynnwood, WA 98036
ph: 425-774-9849
premium@pc-breweriana.com
http://www.pc-breweriana.com
Dealing in all aspects of US breweriana; buys, sells, trades all forms of beer advertising; free appraisals; inquiries promptly answered.

Experts

Tom Terwilliger, CAGA
Pro Auction Company
707 230th St.
Algona, IA 50511
ph: 515-295-7819
fax: 515-295-7742
proauct@ncn.net
http://www.proactionusa.com
Collects and specializes in breweriana.

Pete Kroll
P.O. Box 207
Sun Prairie, WI 53590-0207
ph: 608-837-4818
fax: 608-825-4205
pkroll@chorus.net
http://www.gmskroll.com
Buys and sells collectible advertising glasses, mugs, & steins.

Bill Mugrage
Pacific Coast Breweriana
3819 190th Place S.W.
Lynnwood, WA 98036
ph: 425-774-9849
premium@pc-breweriana.com
http://www.pc-breweriana.com
Dealing in all aspects of US breweriana; buys, sells, trades all forms of beer advertising; free appraisals; inquiries promptly answered.

Internet Resources

Louis DiDona
BeerAuctions.com
623 Center St.
Bethlehem, PA 18018-4035
ph: 610-866-2373
fax: 610-866-2373
info@beerauctions.com
http://www.beerauctions.com
Buy, sell beer cans and breweriana; Web site also has a huge selection of collectors supplies, information, and reference guides.

Museums/Libraries

American Museum of Brewing History &
  Arts, Oldenberg Brewing Company
400 Buttermilk Pike Exit
Ft. Mitchell, KY 41017
ph: 606-341-7223
fax: 606-341-0580
World's largest collection of breweriana: tens of thousands of labels, coasters, bottles, cans, match boxes, signs, foam scrapers, etc.

Periodicals

Julie Bradford
Magazine: All About Beer
501 H Washington St.
Durham, NC 27701
ph: 800-977-2337
fax: 919-530-8160
editor@allaboutbeer.com
http://www.allaboutbeer.com
For over 23 years the voice of beer lovers; brew pub finder, home brewing, beer links, some discussion of beer collectibles, calendar of events, beer & food, beer travelers, beer talk.

Alan R. Blakeman
B.B.R. Publishing
Magazine: British Bottle Review &
  Collectors Mart
Elsecar Heritage Centre
Nr Barnsley, South Yorks S74 8HJ U.K.
ph: 01226 745156
fax: 01226 361561
sales@onlinebbr.com
http://www.onlinebbr.com
Published for over 22 years; full color magazine; the world's longest continuous running publication covering the multitudinous areas of antique bottles; including world news; published quarterly.

Advertising

Clubs/Associations

John Stanley
National Association of Breweriana
  Advertising
Newsletter: Breweriana Collector, The
P.O. Box 64
Chapel Hill, NC 27514
ph: 919-419-1546 or 919-966-5794
naba@mindspring.com
http://www.nababrew.org
Focuses on anything with the word "Beer" or "Brewery" on it; encourage the collection, preservation and study of American brewery

advertising on a national level; membership directory and annual convention; 4 newsletters per year.

Collectors

David Donovan, Sr.
129 S. Linwood Ave.
Baltimore, MD 21224-2246
ph: 410-276-7577 or 410-732-2778
bowery@erols.com
Interested in all types of advertising from any Baltimore or Maryland brewery, especially pre-prohibition.

Robert E. Jaeger
2343 Met-To-Wee Lane
Milwaukee, WI 53226-1612
ph: 414-257-0158
Wants any advertising item with the word "Beer" or "Brewery" on it.

Anheuser-Busch

Dealers

Steinland
14N 679 Route 25, Ste. A
Dundee, IL 60118
ph: 847-428-3150 or 800-498-3215
fax: 847-428-3170
information@steinland.com
http://www.steinland.com
Carries an extensive collection of Budweiser beer steins, Anheuser-Busch and Ceramarte beer steins; also Coors, Corona, Hamms, Holiday, Miller, and related plates and figurines.

Internet Resources

Stein Site, The
info@thesteinsite.com
http://www.thesteinsite.com
The ultimate Budweiser stein reference site.

Man./Prod./Dist.

Anheuser-Busch Gifts & Merchandise
  Online Catalog
P.O. Box 503015
Saint Louis, MO 63150
ph: 800-742-5283
fax: 618-241-7602
budshop@anheuser-busch.com
http://www.budshop.com
Source for contemporary Anheuser-Busch brand logoed gifts: steins, sweatshirts, hats, T-shirts, collectibles, Clydesdales merchandise, beer signs, glassware, and other items with the Budweiser, Bud Light, Michelob, O'Doul's logos.

Apache

Collectors

Bob Temarantz
2824 N. Bentley Ave.
Tucson, AZ 85716-5513
ph: 520-326-6704 or 520-741-9751
fax: 520-294-6052
azsnipe@hotmail.com
Wants to buy Apache beer brand memorabilia: tip trays, ashtrays, matchcovers, serving trays, beer cans, anything associated with Apache beer.

Back Bar Statues
Experts
George Baley
1585 Tiffany Woods
La Porte, IN 46350-7599
Author of "Back Bar Breweriana."

Blatz
Collectors
Jim Welytok
W241 N8938 Penny Lane
Sussex, WI 53089
ph: 262-246-7171
unievents@aol.com
Has one of the most extensive Blatz beer advertising collections in the country; wants to buy any Blatz related advertising items.

Canadian
Dealers
Phil Greenwood
6 Wildrose Place
Sherwood Park, Alberta T8H 1H1
Canada
ph: 780-449-7048
Collects, buys and sells Canadian breweriana: cans, trays, signs, calendars, labels, crowns, etc.; welcomes contact with others who might have questions about Canadian breweriana.

Coasters
Clubs/Associations
Tony Matthews
British Beermat Collectors' Society
69 Dunnington Ave.
Kidderminster, Worcestershire DY10 2YT U.K.
tony.peach@lineone.net
http://website.lineone.net/~tony.peach/BBCSIndex.html
Aim is to further and encourage the interests, knowledge and activities of Tegestologists (beermat collectors).

Collectors
Steve Barile
Stogie Steve
1905 Hunter Lane
Brandon, FL 33510
SEBDGB@aol.com
http://members.aol.com/sebdgb/collect
Wants to buy beer mats (beer coasters); trade or purchase.

Ken Kositzke
1623 N. Linwood Ave.
Appleton, WI 54914-2408
Runs the ABA Coaster Exchange.

Scott deMasi
5610 Kiowa Timbers Dr.
Humble, TX 77346-1929
ph: 281-852-0077
demasi@flash.net

Earl S. Pykett
1280 Rider Ave., #38
Salinas, CA 93905
ph: 831-424-6601
Collector of domestic, international, European, Asian beer coasters.

Dealers
George Barone
94 Ridgeview Place
Cheshire, CT 06410
ph: 203-272-2656
geobaron@ix.netcom.com
http://members.aol.com/gbarone
Coaster collector, dealer, and expert.

Vic Kroll
Kroll's Kollectibles
3451 Nighthawk Ct.
Punta Gorda, FL 33950-6675
ph: 941-575-0303
beer104@comcast.net
Buys, sells, trades US brewery coasters, postcards, letterheads, tokens, stock certificates and other advertising items.

Experts
George Barone
94 Ridgeview Place
Cheshire, CT 06410
ph: 203-272-2656
geobaron@ix.netcom.com
http://members.aol.com/gbarone
Coaster collector, dealer, and expert; author of "Coasters of New England."

Internet Resources
George Barone
Beer Coaster Mania
94 Ridgeview Place
Cheshire, CT 06410
ph: 203-272-2656
geobaron@ix.netcom.com
http://members.aol.com/gbarone
Web site has all the information you need on collecting beer coasters: mystery coasters, rare new finds, trade lists, coaster guides, recent news, and more.

George Klann
George's Tegestology Page
2316 Telemark Ln., N.W.
Rochester, MN 55901
klann.george@mayo.edu
Beer coaster collecting is known as tegestology.

Guinness
Clubs/Associations
Nick Fairall
Guiness Collectors Club
U.K.
admin@guinntiques.com
http://www.guinntiques.com
The official site for collectors of Guinness memorabilia.

Hamm's Beer
Collectors
Jim Welytok
W241 N8938 Penny Lane
Sussex, WI 53089
ph: 262-246-7171
unievents@aol.com
Wants 1954-1968 Hamm's Beer items: animated moving store displays, statues, artwork, advertising, signs, etc.

Rich Wojcik
2461 Brenner Ave. E.
Maplewood, MN 55109
ph: 651-773-7953
rjw2461@cs.com
Wants to buy Hamm's Beer items or complete collections; especially wants pre-1968 items; salesman's items the most desirable; also jewelry, sales awards, Red Wing pottery, sales catalogs, motion signs, point of purchase displays.

Craig Ventzke
1837 Park Blvd.
Fargo, ND 58103-4735
ph: 701-293-1547
kicrvi@aol.com
Looking for Hamm's Beer signs, point of sale displays, neon signs, old grain belt signs; pre-prohibition items.

Pete Nowicki
1531 39th Ave.
San Francisco, CA 94122-3015
ph: 415-566-7506
portfire86@aol.com
Collector desires to obtain older Hamm's Beer advertising: glasses, signs, neons, etc.; the older the better.

Heineken
Collectors
Jan Stabij
Suideinde 382
Amsterdam, NH 1035 PP Holland
ph: +31206332257
stabij@excite.com
http://angelfire.com/ns/stabij
Collects anything from the Heineken beer company, especially advertising items.

Peter van Otterloo
Libanonstraat 12
Delft HS, 2622 The Netherlands
ph: 015-2564580
Collects all kind of items of Heineken beer, especially pre-1950 glasses and mugs from all countries of the world.

Labels
Collectors
Pat Wheeler
4330 W. 152nd St.
Cleveland, OH 44135-1367
abalabex@aol.com
http://members.aol.com/abalabex/labex.htm
Trade, sell labels; Webmaster of http://www.americanbreweriana.org.

Petr Vaverka
Labolog Club
Palackeho 13
Litomerice, 4120 Czech Republic
petr.vaverka@zero.cz
http://labolog.zero.cz
Largest beer label collection on the Internet.

Dealers
Adrian Angleton
1303 Main
South Roxana, IL 62087
ph: 618-254-0401

Lexington Brewery
Collectors
Thom
1389 Alexandria Dr., Ste. #7
Lexington, KY 40504-1777
ph: 859-255-2727 or 859-873-8787
fax: 859-255-2727
Collector of memorabilia of the Lexington Brewing Company, Lexington, KY; pre-prohibition brewery, Dixie Beer, openers, trams, pocket mirrors, advertisements, letterheads, anything relevant to this company.

Napkins
Collectors
Duane C. Gutterud
2509 N. Campbell, PMB 375
Tucson, AZ 85719
Runs the ABA Napkin Exchange.

Openers
(see also BOTTLE OPENERS)

Collectors
Lawrence Biehl
448 Crandon
Calumet City, IL 60449
ph: 708-891-4269
Wants to buy beer can, bottle or cork openers that have name of brewery on them.

Schlitz
Collectors
Larry Barnett
10322 Mawman Ave.
Waukegan, IL 60087
ph: 847-244-2030
fax: 847-244-8231
schlitzerland@prodigy.net
Advanced collector of Schlitz Brewery advertising; wants older, prohibition, and pre-prohibition items.

BREYER HORSE MODELS
(see ANIMAL COLLECTIBLES, Horses [Models/Breyer])

BRICKS

Clubs/Associations

Ken Jones
International Brick Collectors Association
Journal: International Brick Collectors
    Association Journal
100 Manor Dr.
Columbia, MO 65203
ph: 573-445-7171
nanken@mchsi.com
http://www.msinter.net/tweety
*Organization trades bricks at swap
meets.*

Collectors

Bill & Barb Brownlee
80 E. 106th Terrace
Kansas City, MO 64114-5080
fax: 816-941-7472
bbrownlee@everestkc.net

Ken Jones
100 Manor Dr.
Columbia, MO 65203
ph: 573-445-7171
nanken@mchsi.com
http://www.msinter.net/tweety

Betty & Norman Roller
4034 Brown Rd., Rt. 2
Coffeyville, KS 67337
ph: 620-251-2647
tweety@msinter.net
http://www.msinter.net/tweety
*Collects and swaps bricks; has three
brick swaps a year.*

Museums/Libraries

General Shale Museum of Ancient Brick
3211 North Roan St.
P.O. Box 3547
Johnson City, TN 37602
ph: 423-282-4661
fax: 423-828-0491

BRIDAL COLLECTIBLES

Collectors

Jeannie Greenfield
310 Parker Rd.
Stoneboro, PA 16153-2810
ph: 724-376-2584
dlg3684@yahoo.com
*Wants pre-1950 cake toppers, any
condition; also wants related pre-
1950s wedding memorabilia.*

Experts

Ann C. Bergin
P.O. Box 105
Amherst, NH 03031-0105
fax: 978-649-6807
acbergin@aol.com
*Wants preferably old wedding
programs, invitations, bridal
magazines and books, etc.; no cake
toppers.*

Periodicals

Ann C. Bergin
Newsletter: Bridal Collector's Roster
P.O. Box 105
Amherst, NH 03031-0105
fax: 978-649-6807
acbergin@aol.com
*Wants wedding and bride related
pictorial books, dolls, music boxes,
etc.; also first communions,
Christenings, "rites" of passage.*

Cake Toppers

Collectors

Jeannie Greenfield
310 Parker Rd.
Stoneboro, PA 16153-2810
ph: 724-376-2584
dlg3684@yahoo.com
*Wants pre-1950 cake toppers, any
condition; also wants related pre-
1950s wedding memorabilia.*

Experts

Cathy Cook
10 E. 13th St., #2D
New York, NY 10003-4467
ph: 212-691-2406
fax: 212-691-2406
ccook710@aol.com
*Collector always looking for
historical information on bride-and-
groom cake toppers; also wants to buy
vintage toppers.*

Wedding Gowns

Dealers

Gayle Wilson
Gayle's Vintage Clothing & Accessories
3742 Kellogg Ave.
c/o Ferguson Antiques Mall
Cincinnati, OH 45226
ph: 513-271-3722
*Carries a wide selection of vintage
wedding gowns from the 1930s
through the 1950s.*

Lauren Lavonne Pritchett
Gulden & Brown Antique Wedding
    Gowns
1144 Koko Head Ave., Ste. 233
Honolulu, HI 96816
ph: 808-349-2214
gulden_brown@worldnet.att.net
http://www.vintagegown.com
*Carries everything for the vintage
wedding: a large assortment of
antique vintage wedding gowns and
dresses, wax blossom headpieces,
veils, and vintage bridal handbags
from the '30s; specializes in evening
gowns from the '30s and '40s.*

BRIDGE

(see also PLAYING CARDS)

Dealers

Bill Sachen
Waukegan Bridge Center
1075 Victory Dr., Apt. 227
Lindenhurst, IL 60046
ph: 847-265-3573
futilewill@aol.com
http://members.aol.com/FutileWill
*Buys and sells items relating to bridge
and other indoor games as well as
playing cards; many books in foreign
languages.*

Periodicals

Magazine: Bridge Buff's Bulletin
1075 Victory Dr., Apt. 227
Lindenhurst, IL 60046
ph: 847-265-3573
futilewill@aol.com
http://members.aol.com/FutileWill
*A quarterly publication for collectors
of bridge books and periodicals.*

BROADCASTING

(see also AUDIO-VISUAL; FILMS;
MOVIE MEMORABILIA; RADIO
SHOWS, Old Time; RADIOS;
TELEVISION SHOWS &
MEMORABILIA; TELEVISIONS;
TELEGRAPH ITEMS)

Experts

Mike Adams
112 Crescent Ct.
Scotts Valley, CA 95066-2815
ph: 408-924-4545
fax: 408-924-4543
adams@email.sjsu.edu
http://www.mikeadams.org
*Specialty area is radio and broadcast
history; produced "Radio Collector"
series for PBS TV; writes for
"Antique Radio Classified."*

Museums/Libraries

Steve Raymer
Pavek Museum of Broadcasting
3515 Raleigh Ave.
Minneapolis, MN 55416
ph: 952-926-8198
fax: 952-929-6105
sraymer@pavekmuseum.org
http://www.MuseumofBroadcasting.com
*Houses one of the world's finest
collections of antique radio,
television, and broadcast equipment.*

Military

Collectors

Bob Putnam
9129 Lake Braddock Dr.
Springfield, VA 22153
ph: 703-644-9711
putmanb@email.msn.com
*Serious collector wants all items,
transcripts, pictures, etc. concerning
military broadcasters who served in
WWII, Korea and Vietnam as well as
in all other military campaigns.*

BROADSIDES

(see PAPER COLLECTIBLES;
POSTERS)

BRONZES

(see also ART; COLLECTIBLES
[MODERN], Sculptures;
ORIENTALIA; SCULPTURE)

Appraisers

Jerry Bengis, ISA
Bengis Fine Art
1440 Coral Ridge Dr., #166
Pompano Beach, FL 33071
ph: 954-757-2444
fax: 954-757-6222
yascha7@netrox.net
http://www.bengisfineart.com
*Fine art appraiser specializing in
prints (especially Salvador Dali),
graphics (Miro, Chagall, Picasso,
Warhol), etchings, engravings, prints,
bronzes.*

William Lavendusky, M.S., ISA
William Lavendusky, Fine Art
3345 So. Harvard, Bldg. 100
Tulsa, OK 74135
ph: 918-747-5336
fax: 918-742-3425
*Dealer and appraiser of paintings and
sculpture; specialist in 19th century
French animal bronzes.*

Jane C. Brennom
Zaisan Enterprises, Inc.
3240 Las Palmas
Houston, TX 77027-0184
ph: 713-527-0124
fax: 713-527-0124
brennom@sbcglobal.net
*Specializes in the appraisal of bronze
sculptures; also other decorative arts
and furniture.*

Dealers

Bronze Gallery
webmaster@bronze-gallery.com
http://www.bronze-gallery.com
*Web site has hundreds of 19th and
20th century French and American
bronze sculptures for sale.*

James Graham & Sons Gallery
1014 Madison Ave. at 78th
New York, NY 10021-0103
ph: 212-535-5767
fax: 212-794-2454
info@jamesgrahamandsons.com
http://www.jamesgrahamandsons.com
*Specializes in late 19th and early 20th
century European and American
sculpture as well as contemporary
bronzes: French Animalier school,
American Western and wildlife,
figurative, Neoclassical marbles,
historical subjects, etc.*

David E. Newman
Newman & Assoc.
2476 Bolsover, #504
Houston, TX 77005-2518
ph: 713-521-7044
newmanasoc@aol.com
*Specializes in buying, selling,
authenticating and appraising vintage
bronze sculptures.*

Repair Services

Howard & Mary Newman
Newmans Ltd.
55 Farewell St.
Newport, RI 02840
ph: 401-846-4784 or 401-847-8557
fax: 401-849-0611
newmansltd@cox.net
http://www.newmansltd.com
*Fine metal restoration and conserva-
tion; master silversmith, specialist in
bronze finishing and patination;
trained at RI School of Design & in
Italy; conservation & restoration of
personal items & museum works; can
ship anywhere.*

Repro. Sources

Jim Solk
Solk Enterprises, Inc.
4073 Glencoe Ave.
Marina Del Rey, CA 90292
ph: 310-448-4433 or 800-835-3600
fax: 310-448-4435
solk2002@hotmail.com
http://www.eastwestbronze.com
*A bronze foundry for manufacturing of
antique reproduction statues; over 300
statues in their online catalog.*

EMI
401 E. Cypress
Visalia, CA 93277-2834
ph: 559-732-8126 or 800-777-8126
fax: 559-732-5961
info@artbronze.com
http://www.artbronze.com
*Buy foundry direct bronze sculptures
by Remington, Russell, Mene,
Bonhuer; over 300 quality "lost wax"
bronze reproductions; send $10 for
56-page full-color catalog.*

Foundry

Man./Prod./Dist.

Mike Petrucci
Fine Arts Sculpture Centre, Inc.
4975 Waldon Rd.
Clarkston, MI 48348
ph: 810-391-3010 or 810-391-4093
*A foundry offering mold-making, lost-
wax shell casting, sand casting, repair
& restoration, patina application,
installation.*

Ed Pogue
Pogue Sculpture
205 East Normal
Lindsborg, KS 67456
ph: 785-227-3380
poguee@bethanylb.edu
http://www.poguesculpture.com
*Specializing in all types of metal
casting with specific expertise in the*

*lost wax, ceramic shell, and resin
bonded sand mold casting processes
for non-ferrous metals.*

John Branstetter
John Branstetter Studion
83810 Vin Deo CIrcle, #103
Indio, CA 92201
ph: 760-342-5517 or 760-408-2105
fax: 760-342-5517
bronzjon@yahoo.com
*Complete sculpture services,
specializing in bronze casting,
fabrication, patination and
restoration; established sculptor with
over 22 years of experience.*

Vince Maggiore
Bronze Works, The
50 W. Fredson Rd.
Shelton, WA 98584
ph: 360-427-3857 or 888-821-0372
fax: 360-427-9464
info@thebronzeworks.com
http://www.nwwebessentials.com/
  bronzeworks
*A full service sculpture foundry
specializing in fine art; can also
repair, recondition, or reproduce
metal sculpture or artifacts; also
offers sculpting classes.*

Remington

Repro. Sources

Manny Shaool
Manny's Oriental Rugs
72 W. Washington St.
Hagerstown, MD 21740
ph: 301-797-7434
*Importer of Oriental ivory, porcelain,
reverse paintings, rugs; also
Remington recast bronzes, clocks,
lacquered furniture.*

BROWNIES

(see ELVES; ILLUSTRATORS,
Palmer Cox)

BUBBLE GUM & CANDY WRAPPERS

Collectors

David Welch
P.O. Box 714
Murphysboro, IL 62966-0714
ph: 618-687-2282
fax: 618-684-2243
PEZDude1@aol.com
http://www.pezheads.net/dwelch
*Wants pre 1970 chewing gum items:
Wrigleys, Beechnut, Adams, Clarks,
etc.; wrappers, packages, advertising
(no magazine ads), displays, boxes,
etc.; especially wants gum/candy items
with cartoon, TV, movie character tie-
ins.*

Carl Lepiane
104 Karina Ct.
San Jose, CA 95131
ph: 408-356-1922
Wants old chewing gum: pre-1950s

*tins, full boxes, packs, sticks, or
wrappers; also gum cases, store
displays and advertising.*

Experts

John Neuner
2189 Llewellyn Pkwy.
Forked River, NJ 08731-3704
gpnoons@bellatlantic.net
*Author of "Non-Sport Wrapper
Checklist and Price Guide."*

Periodicals

Craig Willardson
Newsletter: Chewing Gum Times
P.O. Box 8296
Spokane, WA 99203-0296
ph: 509-624-0772
cwillardsn@aol.com
*Semi-annual newsletter for collectors
of early chewing gum packs, sticks,
wrappers, displays and related
advertising; classified and display ad
space available; published in April
and November.*

BUBBLE GUM CARDS

(see TRADING CARDS, Non-Sport)

BUCKLES

(see BELT BUCKLES; CLOTHING &
ACCESSORIES, Vintage)

BUGGIES

(see HORSE-DRAWN VEHICLES,
Carriages)

BUILDERS ITEMS

(see ARCHITECTURE & RELATED
ITEMS)

BUILDING BLOCKS

(see TOYS, Construction Sets)

BUILDING REPLICAS

(see SOUVENIR &
COMMEMORATIVE ITEMS, Buildings)

BULLION

(see GOLD; PLATINUM; SILVER)

BURLESQUE

(see STRIPTEASE)

BURMA SHAVE COLLECTIBLES

Collectors

Steve Soelberg
29126 Laro Dr.
Agoura Hills, CA 91301-1635
ph: 818-889-9909
*Burma Shave collectibles bought and
sold, especially road signs; write with
complete description and price; sorry,
no list available; world's largest
Burma Shave collector.*

Internet Resources

Dan Gookin
Burma Shave Slogans
http://www.nidlink.com/~dgookin/
  burma_shave
*Burma Shave signs from 1927 to
1963.*

BURNT WOOD COLLECTIBLES

(see PYROGRAPHY ITEMS)

BUS LINE COLLECTIBLES

(see also TRANSPORTATION
COLLECTIBLES)

Collectors

Bernard F. Lopez
Bernie's Model & Classic Bus Depot
P.O. Box 1713
Bayonne, NJ 07002-6713
bflop@earthlink.net
http://home.earthlink.net/~bflop

Charles Wotring
Royal Coach
911 Conley Dr.
Mechanicsburg, PA 17055-5159
ph: 717-691-1147
fax: 717-691-6623
royal.coach@worldnet.att.net
http://www.royalcoachbuses.com
*Wants to buy bus-related memorabilia
from models to paper ephemera; also
sells promotional bus banks.*

Internet Resources

Bernard F. Lopez
Bernie's Model & Classic Bus Depot
P.O. Box 1713
Bayonne, NJ 07002-6713
bflop@earthlink.net
http://home.earthlink.net/~bflop
*Internet resource for model, toy and
classic bus collectors and enthusiasts;
lots of photos.*

BUSES

Clubs/Associations

Motor Bus Society
Magazine: Motor Coach Age
P.O. Box 251
Paramus, NJ 07653-0251
motorbussociety@yahoo.com
http://www.motorbussociety.org
*Publishes "Motor Coach Age" which
emphasizes history and "Motor Coach*

Today" which provides fresh coverage of ever-changing bus fleets from charter operators to transit to over-the-road companies.

Robert B. Redden, Sr.
International Bus Collectors Club
Newsletter: IBCC Newsletter
12 Gunnells St.
Goose Creek, SC 29445
ph: 843-863-0412
nightbus@worldnet.att.net
The definitive bus club in the US; work as consultants to the movie industry and media; produces the only American line of bus models; 20+ original video productions available; send for catalog.

Bernard Drovillard
Bus History Association
Magazine: Bus Industry Magazine
965 McEwan
Windsor, Ontario N9B 2G1 Canada
ph: 519-977-0664
Founded to preserve and record data, information and other materials related to the bus industry in North America and worldwide.

Collectors

Eugene R. Farha
P.O. Box 633
Cedar Grove, WV 25039-0633
ph: 304-340-3229 or 304-595-2296
fax: 304-340-3315
farha@mail.wvnet.edu
Wants Greyhound and Trailways memorabilia: 10-yr. and 20-yr. service watch, years-of-service pins, match covers, Greyhound Bus Depot sign with dog; also wants Trailways items and Greyhound data, Greyhound Bus Lines rings.

Steve Wessing
P.O. Box 3050
Madison, WI 53704
Wants to buy bus items: tokens, passes, tickets, maps, schedules, advertising, promo items, bus driver hats, uniforms, badges, bus toys, signs, photos, postcards with bus station or buses, bus company items, etc.

Internet Resources

Bernard F. Lopez
Bernie's Model Bus Depot
P.O. Box 1713
Bayonne, NJ 07002-6713
bernie@discomusic.com
http://home.earthlink.net/~bflop/
A Web site for those interested in old buses, bus models, bus photographs.

Museums/Libraries

Museum of Bus Transportation, The
426 South Third St., Ste. 201
Lemoyne, PA 17043
ph: 717-774-4848 or 717-566-7100
fax: 717-774-4854
bus@busmuseum.org
http://www.busmuseum.org
An archive of the people, companies

and photographs of the bus transportation industry; the above is the business office; the museum is located in the Antique Automobile Car Association museum, 161 Museum Dr., Hershey, PA 17033.

Ron Medaglia
Pacific Bus Museum
P.O. Box 91
San Anselmo, CA 94979-0091
ph: 415-458-2877
info@pacbus.org
http://www.pacbus.org/index.html
An active organization of bus enthusiasts dedicated to honoring the history of bus transportation; has collection of buses, bus artifacts and related memorabilia.

Periodicals

Kelsey Publishing Ltd.
Magazine: Bus & Coach Preservation
Cudham Tithe Barn
Berry's Hill
Cudham, Kent TN16 3AG U.K.
ph: 01959 541444
fax: 01959 541400
info@kelsey.co.uk
http://www.kelsey.co.uk
A 56-page monthly British magazine dealing with British bus and coach preservation and restoration.

BUSINESS CARD HOLDERS

Collectors

Stephen Seltzer
7912 Georgia Ave.
Silver Spring, MD 20910-4837
ph: 301-565-2444 or 301-565-3339
fax: 301-565-2228
eseltzer@aol.com
Wants to buy business cards and wallets - any material.

BUSINESS CARDS

(see also CARDS; PAPER COLLECTIBLES)

Clubs/Associations

Suzanne McCartney
International Business Card Collectors
588 Lee Rd.
Hartselle, AL 35640
ibcc@ibccsite.com
http://www.ibccsite.com
Goal is to bring business card collectors together, to educated and to entertain; membership is free but requires joining an online mailing list.

Steve Patterson
Tennessee Business Card Club
P.O. Box 27840
Knoxville, TN 37927-7840
ph: 865-540-8388
fax: 775-242-4178
stevezdesignz@usexpress.net
http://www.geocities.com/
  businesscardcollecting/tbcc.htm
A club for those interested in collecting business cards.

Avery Pitzak
American Business Card Club
Newsletter: Card Talk
P.O. Box 460297
Aurora, CO 80046-0297
The American Business Card Club is a unique resource for business people and collectors alike; please provide SASE with inquiries.

Collectors

Mark S. Waskow
95 St. Paul St., Ste. 440
Burlington, VT 05401
ph: 802-660-9522
fax: 802-862-8652
waskowgp@charter.net
Wants business cards that are antique, from celebrities, made of materials other than paper, large, small, unusual shapes, die-cut, etc.

Stephen Seltzer
7912 Georgia Ave.
Silver Spring, MD 20910-4837
ph: 301-565-2444 or 301-565-3339
fax: 301-565-2228
eseltzer@aol.com
Wants to buy unusual business cards.

Suzanne McCartney
588 Lee Rd.
Hartselle, AL 35640
ph: 256-784-6300
fax: 775-305-8287
suz@suzykat.com
http://expage.com/page/
  businesscardcollecting
Looking for unusual or unique business cards of any era.

Steve Patterson
P.O. Box 27840
Knoxville, TN 37927-7840
ph: 865-540-8388
fax: 775-242-4178
stevezdesignz@usexpress.net
http://www.geocities.com/
  businesscardcollecting
Serious collector has a collection of over 18,700 business cards; site shows cards having same name as Steve Patterson; also famous and autographed business cards and more.

Jack Gurner
116 Dupuy St.
Water Valley, MS 38965-2901
ph: 662-473-1154
jgurner@watervalley.net
http://www.watervalley.net/users/jgurner/
  bizcard.htm
Wants to buy OLD business cards;

also wants some trade cards related to photographers and newspapers; main interest is in illustrated, odd or unusual; inquire first or send photocopy; always include SASE.

Experts

Avery N. Pitzak
P.O. Box 460297
Aurora, CO 80046-0297
Author of "Make Your Business Cards INCREDIBLY EFFECTIVE!"

Internet Resources

Terry Stewart
Collector Link
71 John St. East
Waterloo, Ontario N2J 1G2 Canada
ph: 519-745-1745
stewart@collector-link.com
http://www.collector-link.com
Catalogs over 2,000 trading card related Web sites for: baseball, hockey, basketball, football, other sports, non-sports, phone cards, credit-debit cards, business cards, postcards.

BUTTER PATS

Clubs/Associations

Mary Dessoie
Butter Pat Patter Association
Newsletter: Patter, The
265 Eagle Bend Dr.
Bigfork, MT 59911-6235
montanasteve@centurytel.net
Association is for the serious collector of Victorian-era 3 inch butter pats and 19th century to modern day hotel and transportation pats; monthly newsletter with research, buy and sell ads, and butter pat values: $3 & LSASE for sample.

Collectors

Fred & Lila Schrader
2025 Highway 199
Crescent City, CA 95531
ph: 707-458-3525

Experts

Mary Dessoie
265 Eagle Bend Dr.
Bigfork, MT 59911-6235
montanasteve@centurytel.net
Buys, sells, collects, appraises and specializes in butter pats; nationally published author and expert on butter pats; has written feature articles for AntiqueWeek, American Country Collectibles, Victorian Homes and others.

BUTTON COVERS

(see CLOTHING & ACCESSORIES, Vintage; CUFF LINKS)

BUTTONHOOKS

Clubs/Associations

Buttonhook Society, The
<u>Newsletter: Boutonneur, The</u>
2 Romney Place
Maidstone, Kent ME15 6LE U.K.
ph: 01622 752949
http://www.thebuttonhooksociety.com
*To promote interest and research in
the history, origins, uses and the
collecting of buttonhooks; newsletters,
exhibitions; new American point of
contact: Priscilla Stoffel, Box 287,
White Marsh, MD 21162-0287.*

Collectors

Richard Mathes
P.O. Box 1408
Springfield, OH 45501-1408
*Wants unusual types of buttonhooks to
add to substantial collection; boot/
shoe hooks, glove hooks, loop
buttoners, or collar buttoners.*

Paul Moorehead
2 Romney Place
Maidstone, Kent ME15 6LE U.K.
ph: 01622 752949
http://www.thebuttonhooksociety.com
*Seeks unusual buttonhooks singles or
in sets.*

BUTTONS

(see also CUFF LINKS; SEWING
ITEMS & GO-WITHS)

Appraisers

Lisa Schulz
Button Images
1317 Lynndale Rd.
Madison, WI 53711-3370
ph: 608-271-4566
fax: 608-271-4566
buttonldy@aol.com
http://www.buttonimages.com
*Collectible clothing buttons
appraised, bought and sold; also sells
button collecting products (mounting
cards and wire, storage envelopes);
catalog on request.*

Julie Dearman, ISA
Boulevard Appraisals
2907 North Monroe St.
Spokane, WA 99205
ph: 509-324-2018 or 509-323-9200
fax: 509-323-9082
jubutton@aol.com
*Button expert, collector, dealer,
specializes in the appraisal of clothing
buttons and sewing go-withs;
Accredited Member of the International Society of Appraisers.*

Clubs/Associations

Lois Pool, Sec.
National Button Society
<u>Newsletter: National Button Bulletin</u>
2733 Juno Place, Apt. 4
Akron, OH 44313-4137
ph: 330-864-3296
Over 4,000 members worldwide;

*focuses on preserving buttons and
learning button history; one national
show each year.*

Gwendolyn Niemisto
Michigan Button Society
<u>Newsletter: Michigan Button Society
Bulletin</u>
P.O. Box 2006
Gaylord, MI 49734
http://www.iserv.net/~dbuttons/
clubs.htm

Barbara Reiter
Colorado State Button Society
<u>Newsletter: Colorado State Button
Bulletin</u>
779 Alkire St.
Golden, CO 80401-4650
ph: 303-237-5142
berei1@aol.com
*Members are interested in all types of
buttons and all button materials; six
clubs in the Metro Denver area.*

California State Button Society
<u>Newsletter: California Button Brief</u>
P.O. Box 3084
Grass Valley, CA 95945-3084
http://members.aol.com/csbsweb

British Button Society
Jersey Cottage Parklands Rd.
Bower, Ashton
Bristol, BS3 2JR U.K.

Collectors

Warren K. Tice
W. Tice & Company
8 Orchard Terrace
Essex Junction, VT 05452-3501
ph: 802-878-3835
*Wants to purchase decorative ladies
buttons.*

Barbara Reiter
779 Alkire St.
Golden, CO 80401-4650
ph: 303-237-5142
berei1@aol.com
*VP of Colorado State Button Society;
would be happy to share information
about button collecting with others.*

Dealers

Jerry's Buttons
jerry@jerrysbuttons.com
http://www.jerrysbuttons.com
*Site devoted to the hobby of collecting
antique and vintage clothing buttons.*

Debbie Woolley
Favorite Past-Times Antiques
6 Main Hill
Bridgton, ME 04009
ph: 207-647-4486
info@maine-antiques.com
http://www.maine-antiques.com/fpt/Index
*Buys and sells antique buttons and
button collections.*

Gail Busche
Archangel Antiques
334 East Ninth St.
New York, NY 10003-7924
ph: 212-260-9313
richgail38@aol.com
*Specializes in vintage and antique
clothing buttons, cufflinks, eyewear,
lighters, and home furnishings; also
Art Deco and Art Nouveau, and
classic 1950s and 1960s home
furnishings and decorative items.*

Millicent Safro
Tender Buttons
143 East 62nd St.
New York, NY 10021
ph: 212-758-7004 or 212-980-3540
fax: 212-319-8474
*Has the largest collection of antique
buttons in America for both the
collector and the wholesale dealers;
also carries out-of-print books on
buttons; co-author with Diana Epstein
of "Buttons."*

Gale VerHague
Gale's Gallery
2646 Mezzio Rd.
Forestville, NY 14062

Ann Olson
Perennial Buttons
2025 Ashmore Dr.
Ames, IA 50014
ph: 515-292-0929
perbuttons@aol.com
*Button appraiser, dealer, expert;
member of National Button Society for
over 25 years.*

Lisa Schulz
Button Images
1317 Lynndale Rd.
Madison, WI 53711-3316
ph: 608-271-4566
fax: 608-271-4566
buttonldy@aol.com
http://www.buttonimages.com
*Buys, sells, collects collectible
clothing buttons and button display
products; buttons can be shipped on
approval; $25 minimum purchase.*

Gwen Daniel
18 Belleau Lake Ct.
O Fallon, MO 63366-3144
ph: 636-978-3190
SimGirl200@aol.com
*Buys and sells old interesting sewing
buttons (picture buttons, Oriental
buttons, carved Bakelite buttons) and
related items.*

Buttons, Etc.
P.O. Box 7572
Dallas, TX 75209
buttons@ont.com
http://www.OnlineToday.Com/users/
buttons

Carol Cienna
3444 Garden Ave.
Los Angeles, CA 90039-1942
ph: 323-662-6944
carolc@vintagebuttons.net
http://www.vintagecuttons.net
*Experienced button collector, dealer,
appraiser; specializes in clothing as
well as military buttons; active seller
on eBay with username "svengali."*

Jude Seyk
Vintage Collection
356 Main St.
Half Moon Bay, CA 94019-1724
ph: 650-712-0366
fax: 650-726-545
vintgecol@aol.com
http://www.vintagecollection.net
*Appraises, buys and sells linen and
lace; also old yardage, buttons, quilts,
sewing implements, sewing machines
and miniature sewing machines.*

Eureka, I Found It! Antiques &
Collectibles
P.O. Box 2192
Petaluma, CA 94953-2192
eureka@eureka-i-found-it.com
http://www.eureka-i-found-it.com
*An online dealer specializing in
vintage textiles and clothing, toy and
model steam engines, buttons, fans,
Art Deco, costume jewelry, toy sewing
machines.*

Veronica Wexler
Button Bytes
rwexler@tias.com
http://www.tias.com/lists/buttons.shtml
*Collector, dealer specializing in
collectible clothing buttons; moderates
a button chat list; also moderates a
military/livery/uniform button chat list
at http://www.tias.com/lists/
milbuttons.shtml.*

Georgia Fox
Foxes' Den Antiques
P.O. Box 846
Sutter Creek, CA 95685-0846
ph: 209-267-0774
*Wants antique clothing buttons:
porcelain, metal, gilt and Satsuma
buttons with pictures, fables,
buildings, and heads of famous
people.*

Experts

Millicent Safro
Tender Buttons
143 East 62nd St.
New York, NY 10021
ph: 212-758-7004 or 212-980-3540
fax: 212-319-8474
*Has the largest collection of antique
buttons in America for both the
collector and the wholesale dealers;
also carries out-of-print books on
buttons; co-author with Diana Epstein
of "Buttons."*

Lois Pool
2733 Juno Place, Apt. 4
Akron, OH 44313-4137
ph: 330-864-3296

Debra J. Wisniewski
410 E. Bond St.
Hastings, MI 49058
dbuttons@iserv.net
http://www.iserv.net/~dbuttons
Author of "Antique & Collectible
Buttons."

Kathy Hoppe
O'gosh Buttons
2411 Doty St.
Oshkosh, WI 54902
ph: 920-231-6477
fax: 920-231-6477
button@ohgosh-buttons.com
http://www.ohgosh-buttons.com
Dealer, expert, collector, appraiser
specializing in antique and vintage
collectible clothing buttons only.

Internet Resources

Debra J. Wisniewski
Button Bug
410 E. Bond St.
Hastings, MI 49058
dbuttons@iserv.net
http://www.iserv.net/~dbuttons
Learn more about the world of button
collecting: button book info, shows,
buttons for sale, related links.

Linda Stark
Our Button Box
1113 Wheelis Rd.
Wylie, TX 75098
ph: 972-442-1410
LL2Starks@aol.com
http://members.aol.com/LL2Starks/
index.htm
A Web site for button lovers; links to
dozens of button dealers, informative
sites, a pictorial glossary of button
terms, club listings, and more.

Museums/Libraries

Jennifer Jacobs
Buttonarium Button Museum
P.O. Box 577428
Chicago, IL 60657-7428
ph: 773-296-0733
fax: 773-296-0793
buttonarium@aol.com
http://www.buttonarium.com

Suppliers

Lisa Schulz
1317 Lynndale Rd.
Madison, WI 53711-3370
ph: 608-271-4566
fax: 608-271-4566
buttonldy@aol.com
http://www.buttonimages.com
Collectible clothing buttons
appraised, bought and sold; also sells
button collecting products (mounting
cards and wire, storage envelopes);
catalog on request.

Military (American)

Collectors

Warren K. Tice
W. Tice & Company
8 Orchard Terrace
Essex Junction, VT 05452-3501
ph: 802-878-3835
Wants to purchase US Military,
Confederate, and high quality
decorative buttons; also wants to buy
military antiques.

Experts

Daniel J. Binder
927 20th St.
Rockford, IL 61104-3508
ph: 815-226-9056
Wants 1812-1865 US military buttons,
especially Confederate States,
Southern State seals, and Southern
military school buttons.

Pin-Back

(see also PINS; POLITICAL
COLLECTIBLES)

Collectors

Bob Cereghino
6400 Baltimore National Pike, Ste.
170A-319
Baltimore, MD 21228-3914
ph: 410-766-7593
jwbc@juno.com
Wants advertising, entertainment and
political pin-back buttons.

Lon Ellis
P.O. Box 99123
Raleigh, NC 27624
ph: 919-844-9962
fax: 919-844-9962
lellis@rocksolid.com
Active collector of pre-1960 political
campaign pin-back buttons and other
political campaign memorabilia
including ribbons, badges, posters,
postcards, banners, etc.

Scott Weiss
1158 26th St., #489
Santa Monica, CA 90403
ph: 310-264-7202
fax: 310-264-7203
sweiss5905@aol.com
Wants to buy TV and movie pin-back
buttons, pins, badges, and ribbons;
promotional, licensed, product tie-ins,
prop or cast and crew; wants from all
years.

Experts

Ted Hake
Hake's Americana & Collectibles
Auction
P.O. Box 1444
York, PA 17405-1444
ph: 717-848-1333
Ted@hakes.com
http://www.hakes.com
Author of "Hake's Guide to TV
Collectibles" and several other books
on collectibles; always purchasing
items for mail-bid auctions of

Disneyana, historical Americana, toys,
premiums, political items, character
and other collectibles.

Pin-Back (Advertising)

Dealers

Dave Beck
P.O. Box 435
Mediapolis, IA 52637-0435
ph: 319-394-3943
fax: 319-394-3943
adman@mepotelco.net
Buys and sells advertising watch fobs,
mirrors and pin-backs; send stamp for
illustrated mail auction catalog.

Pin-Back (Character/Comic)

Collectors

Walter Koenig
P.O. Box 4395
North Hollywood, CA 91617-0395
gineokw@aol.com
Wants to buy comic (strip kind) pin-
back buttons 1890s-1960s; no pep
cereal buttons.

Transportation Employees'

Book Sellers

Donald P. Van Court
41 Hillcrest Rd.
Madison, NJ 07940-2559
ph: 973-377-2676
dpvancourt@aol.com
Sells books, including his own,
focusing on railroad, transit,
maritime and aviation uniform
buttons.

Experts

Donald P. Van Court
41 Hillcrest Rd.
Madison, NJ 07940-2559
ph: 973-377-2676
dpvancourt@aol.com
Author of books illustrating the
monograms, sets of initials, trade
marks and designs on uniform
buttons; historical notes on companies
(land, sea and air) for which uniform
button designs were created; also sells
own book.

BUYING TRIPS

(see TOURS/BUYING TRIPS)

Here are some tips when contacting someone who is listed in this book:

When requesting information about a particular item, include a description (material, dimensions, maker's mark, model number, etc.) and a photo, sketch, digital image or photocopy of the item in question.

Always ask if there are charges for samples or for the services that you are requesting.

When corresponding by letter, please be sure to include a Large (#10 business size) Self-Addressed and Stamped Envelope (LSASE) if requesting a reply or the return of photographs.

Never call collect unless otherwise directed. When calling, be considerate of time zone differences and always ask if the party you are calling has time to talk. When leaving an answering machine message, always instruct the party to call you back collect.

CABINET CARDS

(see PHOTOGRAPHS)

CALCULATORS

(see also ADDING MACHINES;
COMPUTERS; OFFICE
EQUIPMENT; SLIDE RULES;
TYPEWRITERS)

Auction Services

Auction Team Breker
Bonner Str. 528-530
Koln, D-50968 Germany
ph: 49 221 387049 or 941-925-0385 (US Rep)
fax: 49 221 374878
auction@breker.com
http://www.breker.com
German auction company specializes in the sale of old office equipment, scientific instruments and devices, photographica, and old technology including toasters, typewriters, sewing machines, tools, telecommunications, etc.

Clubs/Associations

Guy Ball
International Association of Calculator Collectors
Newsletter: International Calculator Collector, The
P.O. Box 345
Tustin, CA 92781-0345
ph: 714-730-6140
fax: 714-730-6140
mrcalc@usa.net
http://www.oldcalcs.com
Informative quarterly newsletter about collecting calculators from the "golden years" (1971-1978); send SASE for more information.

Collectors

Peter Frei
P.O. Box 500
Brimfield, MA 01010-0500
ph: 413-245-4660
peterfrei@prodigy.net
Wants to buy handpowered vacuum cleaners, pre-1875 sewing machines, typewriters, calculators, and adding machines.

Bill Wood
8 Oregon Place
Buffalo, NY 14207-1522
ph: 716-875-9874345
fax: 716-874-6724
merlin206@adelphia.net
Collects pocket calculators and will

answer questions to help other collectors.

John E. Kendall
P.O. Box 436
Fallston, MD 21047-0436
maloney@vintage-electronics.com
http://www.vintage-electronics.com
Wants to buy Victor 3900, Philco 3900 and Philco 2400 electronic desktop calculators; also any advertising, service manuals, parts or anything pertaining to these calculators.

Arthur Cheslock
514 St. Paul St.
Baltimore, MD 21202
ph: 410-962-8580
fax: 410-752-8112
Wants pre-1945 calculators, adding machines and scientific instruments; also wants related literature.

Dale R. Beeks
Perceptions Scientifica
P.O. Box 117
Mount Vernon, IA 52314-0117
ph: 800-880-5178 or 319-895-0506
dbeeksci@aol.com
Wants to buy pre-1960 pocket-sized adders and slide rules; also any in unusual forms.

Robert Otnes
2160 Middlefield Rd.
Palo Alto, CA 94301-4022
ph: 650-324-1821
botnes@pacbell.net
A leading collector of calculating machines and slide rules.

Robert De Cesaris
7429 Bree Ann Ct.
Citrus Heights, CA 95610-2455
ph: 916-356-5769
rdecesar@pcocd2.intel.com
Very serious collector of mechanical calculators, early adders, and slide rules; seeking lever-set (Marchant, Brunsviga, Odhner, etc.), Arithometers, small adders (Calcumeter, Webb, Stephenson, etc.), Curta calculators, and others.

Erez Kaplan
Calculating Machines Website
5 Baytar St.
Hertzelia, 46432 Israel
ph: 972 99 509 663
fax: 972 99 509 663
calcmach@actcom.net.il
http://www.webcom.com/calc
Interested in collecting mechanical calculating machines (non-electrical) dating from 1642 through 1965.

Experts

Darryl Rehr
P.O. Box 641824
Los Angeles, CA 90064-6824
ph: 310-477-5229
fax: 310-268-8420
dcrehr@earthlink.net
Wants early calculators (they subtract, multiply, divide and add)

such as the "Comptometer", "Curta", and "Millionaire."

Guy Ball
P.O. Box 345
Tustin, CA 92781-0345
ph: 714-730-6140
fax: 714-730-6140
mrcalc@usa.net
http://www.oldcalcs.com
Recognized authority on early, electronic, pocket calculators; co-author of "Collector's Guide to Pocket Calculators" (1997); producer of "Collecting Calculators" video; send SASE with requests for rarity and/or pricing information.

Internet Resources

Rick Furr
Calculator Reference, The
rfurr@vcalc.net
http://www.vcalc.net
Lots of information about HP and TI pocket calculators.

Vintage Calculators
vintage@dotpoint.com
http://www.dotpoint.com/xnumber/vintage.htm
Lots of historical data about calculators, mechanical and electronic.

Brooke W. Boering
Comptometer
vagabond@cruzio.com
http://www2.cruzio.com/~vagabond/Compthome.html
A site dedicated to the Comptometer - its inventor, the company, schools for operators, and competitors.

Rick Bensene
Old Calculator Web Museum, The
oldcalc@bensene.com
http://www.oldcalculatormuseum.com
Site devoted to preserving, documenting, and sharing the technology of desktop automatic calculating machines; from the electro-mechanical calculators of the 1950s and 1960s to the desktop computer of the 1970s and 1980s.

Guy Ball
Collecting Calculators Website
P.O. Box 345
Tustin, CA 92781-0345
ph: 714-730-6140
fax: 714-730-6140
mrcalc@usa.net
http://www.oldcalcs.com
This site contains historical and collectible information for calculator collectors; focus is on early electronic calculators of the 1960s and 1970s, but also covers the older and larger electro-mechanical "monsters."

Gerhard Wenzel
Museum of Pocket Calculating Devices
Germany
wenzel@calculators.de
http://www.calculators.de
Pocket calculators, special calcula-

tors, addiators, slide rules, abacuses, pocket computers, mechanical calculators, counting frames, Napiers bones, other pocket devices.

Erez Kaplan
5 Baytar St.
Hertzelia, 46432 Israel
ph: 972 99 509 663
fax: 972 99 509 663
calcmach@actcom.net.il
http://www.webcom.com/calc
Pictorial views of calculators, old ads, related links, magazines, organizations, other sites of interest; covers all aspects of mechanical calculating machines.

Hewlett-Packard

Museums/Libraries

Dave Hicks
Museum of HP Calculators
dgh@hpmuseum.org
http://www.hpmuseum.org
Displays and describes Hewlett-Packard calculators introduced from 1968 to 1986 plus a few interesting later models; also sections on calculating machines and slide rules; plus sections for buying and selling HP calculators.

CALENDAR PLATES

Clubs/Associations

Alan Gumtow
Calendar Plate Collectors Club
Newsletter: Calendar, The
710 N. Lake Shore Dr.
Tower Lakes, IL 60010-1277
ph: 847-526-5319
agumtow@aol.com
Publishes a quarterly newsletter for collectors and dealers of old calendar plates from 1880-1949.

Collectors

Carole Melfi
Carole Melfi's Calendar Plates
1764 Wellington Dr.
Langhorne, PA 19047
cmelfi@jersey.net
http://www.welcome.to/calendarplates
Has a Web site devoted to her calendar plate collection; site features the history of calendar plates, images, and links to related sites.

Jane M. Cummings
37943 Wright St.
Willoughby, OH 44094-5851
ph: 440-946-2174
Wants any '20s, '30s & '40s or earlier calendar plates, especially the unusual or pre-1906.

James Lambert
14 Whitby Ct.
Lincolnshire, IL 60069
ph: 847-945-7023
fax: 847-945-5180
mijlamb@attbi.com
*Specializes in collecting calendar
plates from 1950 to present.*

Dealers

Alan Gumtow
Odd Things
710 N. Lake Shore Dr.
Tower Lakes, IL 60010-1277
ph: 847-526-5319
agumtow@aol.com
*Buys and sells 1880-1933 calendar
plates with or without store, town or
person on it, old giveaways.*

CALENDARS

(see also ADVERTISING
COLLECTIBLES; ILLUSTRATORS;
PAPER COLLECTIBLES)

Clubs/Associations

Larry L. Krug
Calendar Collector Society
E-zine: Calendar & Paper Collectors
eNews
18222 Flower Hill Way, #299
Gaithersburg, MD 20879-5300
ph: 301-926-8663
fax: 301-926-7648
info@calendarcollectors.org
http://www.calendarcollectors.org
*Electronic newsletter goes to over 600
collectors.*

Dealers

Mary Ann Hahn
Second Hand Mary Ann's
103 Ocean Point Rd.
Boothbay Harbor, ME 04538
ph: 207-633-2426
fax: 207-633-2586
maryann@gwi.net
*Wants to buy calendars of all kinds
and categories: pin-up, scenics,
hunting & fishing, children's
illustrators, advertising, auto, Coca-
Cola.*

Firearms Related

Collectors

Bill Bramlett
P.O. Box 12600
Florence, SC 29504-1965
ph: 843-629-1965 or 843-662-0702 x102
BillBramlett@webtv.net
*Wants to buy 1897-1927 calendars,
posters and signs advertising shotgun
shells and cartridges from companies
such as Peters, Austin Cartridge Co.,
Remington-UMC, Selby shells, Union
Metallic Cartridge Co., Western,
Winchester.*

CALIFORNIA PERFUME COMPANY

(see also AVON COLLECTIBLES;
BOTTLES, Perfume & Scent)

Collectors

Patrick Brady
210 Fulton St.
Elmira, NY 14904-1215
ph: 607-732-2894
*Wants CPC paper, tins, bottles,
anything.*

Experts

Dick Pardini
3107 N. El Dorado St.
Dept. M
Stockton, CA 95204-3412
ph: 209-466-5550
*Wants certain boxed CPC items (1886
to 1929); no AVON please; will help
with CPC prices and identification;
enclose LSASE for information;
LSASE NOT necessary when offering
items for sale.*

CALLING CARDS

(see BUSINESS CARDS)

CALLIOPES

(see CAROUSELS & CAROUSEL
FIGURES; MUSICAL
INSTRUMENTS, Mechanical [Band
Organs])

CALLS

(see SPORTING COLLECTIBLES,
Game Calls)

CAMERAS & CAMERA EQUIPMENT

(see also BOOKS, Reference
[Cameras]; 3-D PHOTOGRAPHICA;
MAGIC LANTERNS;
PHOTOGRAPHS; PHOTOGRAPHY;
SPY EQUIPMENT; STEREO
VIEWERS & STEREOVIEWS; TOYS,
Optical)

Auction Services

Bryan W. Ginns
2109 Cty. Rte. 21
Valatie, NY 12184-6001
ph: 518-392-5805
fax: 518-392-7925
the3dman@aol.com
*Conducts mail sales specializing in
optical items such as cameras, magic
lantern slide projectors,
stereographica, polyorama
pantoptiques, praxinoscopes,
zeotropes, kinoras, coin-operated
mutoscopes, etc.*

Auction Team Breker
Bonner Str. 528-530
Koln, D-50968 Germany
ph: 49 221 387049 or 941-925-0385 (US
Rep)
fax: 49 221 374878
auction@breker.com
http://www.breker.com
*German auction company specializes
in the sale of old office equipment,
scientific instruments and devices,
photographica, and old technology
including toasters, typewriters, sewing
machines, tools, telecommunications,
etc.*

Michael Pritchard
Christie's South Kensington, Ltd.
85 Old Brompton Rd.
London, SW7 3LD U.K.
ph: 020 7930 6074 or 020 7752 3279
fax: 020 7321 3321
info@christies.com
http://www.christies.com
*An international auction house
specializing in the sale of rare and
collectible cameras, photographic
equipment and optical toys.*

Clubs/Associations

Gerald Fine
American Photographic Historical
Society, Inc.
Magazine: Photographica
1150 Avenue of the Americas
New York, NY 10036
ph: 212-575-0483 or 732-617-3142
fax: 732-617-1360
*International organization with
educational meetings six times each
year in NYC; conducts two fairs for
the selling of antique cameras,
equipment & photos; publishes
"Photographica" quarterly and a
monthly newsletter, "In Focus."*

Paul K. Kirchner
Camera & Memorabilia Enthusiasts
Regional Association (C.A.M.E.R.A.)
103 Greenwich Dr.
Albany, NY 12203

Pennsylvania Photographic Historical
Society, Inc.
P.O. Box 862
Beaver Falls, PA 15010-0862
ph: 724-843-5688

John Durand
Ohio Camera Collectors Society, The
Newsletter: Developments, The Members
Memo
P.O. Box 282
Columbus, OH 43216-0282
ph: 614-885-3224
*Focuses on cameras, camera
equipment, images and photographic
history; holds annual show, sale,
auction, guest speakers on Memorial
Day weekend; various members have
considerable camera expertise about
cameras and makers; annual auction.*

William S. Nehez, Mem. Ch.
Photographic Historical Society of the
Western Reserve
Newsletter: Collector, The
P.O. Box 25663
Cleveland, OH 44125
ph: 216-382-6727
*To further advance the collection and
preservation of historical photo-
graphic material; for those with an
interest in photography and
photographic equipment; bi-monthly
newsletter; holds annual Photographic
Flea Market.*

Bill Bond, Pres.
Tri-State Photographic Collectors
Society
8910 Cherry St.
Blue Ash, OH 45242
ph: 513-891-5266
*Collectors of cameras and various
photographic equipment, prints, books
and anything related to photography.*

Michigan Photographic Historical
Society
Newsletter: Photogram, The
P.O. Box 2278
Birmingham, MI 48012-2278
ph: 313-882-1113 or 245-549-6026
pmotz@worldnet.att.net

Marv B. Chait, Pres.
Chicago Photographic Collectors Society
Newsletter: CPCS Bulletin
P.O. Box 1979
Evanston, IL 60204-1979
ph: 847-223-4348
info@chicagophotographic.org
http://www.chicagophotographic.org
*A non-profit organization since 1971;
over 200 US and foreign members;
sponsors two trade shows a year in
the Chicago area; "CPCS Bulletin" is
published monthly; also publishes the
journal "By Daylight" periodically.*

Betty Graham
Vintage Camera Club
2562 Victoria St.
Wichita, KS 67216
ph: 316-265-0393
*For collectors of vintage cameras;
also stereo cameras and stereo
images.*

Photographic Collectors of Houston
1201 McDuffie #104
Houston, TX 77019
jdunn@pop3.wt.net
http://web.wt.net/~jdunn

Tom Kowach
Historic Camera Collectors Club
ph: 310-645-3767
tomko@earthlink.net
http://www.historiccamera.com/
club.html
*An international club bringing
together camera collectors, photograph collectors, and photography
historians via the Internet; club
provides various information and Web*

site resources; share collections, information, answer questions.

David Silver
Bay Area Photographica Association
Newsletter: BAPA News
2538 34th Ave.
San Francisco, CA 94116-2801
ph: 415-664-6498 or 415-681-4356
silver@well.com
http://www.well.com/user/silver/
  bapahome.html
A collectors' group specializing in cameras, photographs and related materials; members buy, sell and trade collectibles as well as share information on the field of photo-history.

Shirley Sparrow
Puget Sound Photographic Collectors
  Society
Newsletter: Bellows
300 Pease Rd.
Cle Elum, WA 98922
ph: 509-647-1916
mvmmvm@gte.net
http://www.geocities.com/Eureka/Park/
  3740
Dedicated to the collection and preservation of historical photographica; holds monthly meetings, sponsors annual camera show, publishes monthly newsletter.

Rolf Eipper, Pres.
Western Canada Photographic Historical
  Association
P.O. Box 78082
2606 Commercial Dr.
Vancouver, British Columbia V5N 5W1
  Canada
ph: 604-254-6778
fax: 604-254-6774
rolfs-3d-@collector.org
Conducts camera shows each spring and fall; for more info contact show coordinator Siggi Rohde at 604-941-0330.

Michael Pritchard, Editor
Photographic Collectors Club of Great
  Britain
Magazine: Photographica World
5 Buntingford Rd.
Puckeridge
Ware, SG11 1RT U.K.
ph: (0044) (0)929 821611
info@pccgb.org
http://www.pccgb.org
Club aims to promote the study and collection of photographic equipment and images by publications, meetings, auctions and shows; covers cameras, lenses, photographers, optical toys, stereoscopes, magic lanterns, and related areas.

Collectors

Dan Colucci
Antique & Classic Camera Web Site
ph: 978-808-9906
DColucci@aol.com
http://members.aol.com/dcolucci
Collector of pre-1900 wood and brass cameras, brass lenses, shutters,

catalogs, photography books and related photographica.

Dan Colucci
Antique & Classic Camera Web Site
82 Brick Kiln Rd.
Chelmsford, MA 01824
ph: 617-790-4915
DColucci@aol.com
http://members.aol.com/dcolucci
Collector of 19th century American wood and brass cameras, lenses, shutters and related ephemera: American Optical, Anthony, Scovill, Rochester Optical and others.

Norman D. Leckert
P.O. Box 363
Bethel, VT 05032-0363
ph: 802-234-5657 or 800-717-2021
fax: 802-234-6104
Wants to buy old cameras, lenses and accessories; any age, type or condition.

Harry Poster
P.O. Box 1883
South Hackensack, NJ 07606-0483
ph: 201-794-9606
fax: 201-794-9553
hposter@att.net
http://www.harryposter.com
Wants early wooden cameras and lenses; stereo 3-D cameras, viewers, projectors; Pathe and 16mm movie cameras and projectors; Polaroid models 180, 185, 190, 195 only; old film, accessories, flash units; press cameras; buys camera shops.

Fred Spira
158-17 Riverside Dr.
Flushing, NY 11357-1341
ph: 718-767-6761 or 718-767-5297
Private collector buys early (Daguerreian, wet-plate), color, detective and other rare and unusual cameras and camera accessories; single items or entire collections; also pre-1900 photographic images and photo albums.

Bob Coyle
1006 Lincoln
Dubuque, IA 52001-3457
ph: 563-588-9464
fax: 563-583-9083
Private camera collector wants to buy most all types and brands of collectible cameras, lenses, accessories: Leica/Leitz items; also collects interchangeable camera view finders; contact with details and asking prices.

Kirk Kekatos
P.O. Box 303
Grayslake, IL 60030-0303
ph: 847-223-4348
kekfoto@aol.com
Information officer for the Chicago Photographic Collectors Society.

Marv B. Chait
P.O. Box 1979
Evanston, IL 60204-1979
ph: 847-853-8521
Marv5555@aol.com

Richard Ogden
Exotic Camera
P.O. Box 210
Chapman, NE 68827-0210
ph: 308-986-2247
Wants exotic cameras: such as cameras that look like machine guns, aerials, military, medical, concealed, special purpose, swinging lens, Cirkuts, subminiature cameras, beverage can shaped cameras and others that are odd or unusual.

Charles R. Scribner
555 Sherwood Lane
Muskogee, OK 74403-8300
ph: 918-687-9639
scrib@azalea.net
http://www.scrib.net
Private collector who enjoys sharing information about cameras.

Dave Gorski
21045 N. 124th Ave.
Sun City West, AZ 85375
ph: 623-975-4061
fax: 623-975-4061
davegorski@yahoo.com
http://www.davegorski.com
Wants to buy stereo cameras, wood cameras with two or more lenses, folding or box cameras, any multi-lens camera, 1920s movie cameras or projectors; also cameras by Canon, Nikon, Leica, Zeiss, Voightlander, Alpa, Ernemann.

Mike Kramer
P.O. Box 3257
Vallejo, CA 94590-0676
ph: 800-568-8883 or 800-446-6581
fax: 707-642-2456
Collector wants to buy pre-1960 range-finder cameras such as Nikon, Canon, Leica, Zeiss plus all stereo, subminiature and colored cameras.

Henk van Roy
235 Kelvin Grove Rd.
Kelvin Grove
Brisbane, Queensland 4059 Australia
ph: +61 7 3856 4757
fax: +61 7 3856 4790
freeplan@bigpond.net.au
http://www.freeman.powerup.com.au
Collector and appraiser of cameras of yesteryear; buy, sell, swap.

Dealers

Gary Dicker
Photon Enterprises
173 Park St.
Putnam, CT 06260
ph: 860-928-2615
Buys, sells, trades cameras and related equipment - one item of a whole collection; provides accurate and honest evaluations of your vintage

or modern camera equipment; years of experience.

John S. Craig
Craig Camera
P.O. Box 1637
Torrington, CT 06790
ph: 860-496-9791
fax: 860-496-0664
john@craigcamera.com
http://www.craigcamera.com
Buys and sells antique and collectible photographica: cameras, daguerreo-types, stereos, literature.

Allen & Hilary Weiner
80 Central Park West
New York, NY 10023-5204
ph: 212-787-8357
fax: 212-496-6502
amwcameras@msn.com
Well-established and respected dealers who are always interested in buying entire collections or fine individual items.

Konny Lang, Pres.
Atlantic Camera Repair
276 Higbie Lane
West Islip, NY 11795-2822
ph: 516-587-7959
fax: 516-587-7750
Buys and sells cameras and photographic equipment.

Bryan W. Ginns
2109 Cty. Rte. 21
Valatie, NY 12184-6001
ph: 518-392-5805
fax: 518-392-7925
the3dman@aol.com
Wants large collections of stereo views, old cameras, daguerreotypes, magic lanterns, optical toys; anything relating to photographics.

Jim O'Neil
Fredonia Camera Exchange
60 West Main St.
Fredonia, NY 14063
ph: 716-679-4582
fax: 716-215-6239
http://www.camerex.com
Buying Leica, Nikon, Minox, Super Ikonta, Unhof, Stereo Realist, Rolleiflex, Contarex, Hasselblad, Retina, Voigtlander, Plaubel, and many others.

Bruce Walker
CameraWeb
2347 E. Lincoln Highway
Coatesville, PA 19320
ph: 610-383-7094
fax: 610-383-7240
A great place to buy, sell, trade cameras and camera equipment; free online ads; free photographic tips.

Bill Green
Classic & Used Cameras
3735 Franklin Rd., #191
Roanoke, VA 24014
ph: 540-725-4351 or 888-246-3686
fax: 540-725-4359
bill@classic-cameras.com
http://www.classic-cameras.com
*Buys, sells, trades, classic Leicas,
Cannons, Nikons, Rollei, etc.;
anything useable; also repairs classic
and used cameras.*

Robert L. Johnson
North Georgia Graphics
P.O. Box 309
Chickamauga, GA 30707-0309
ph: 706-375-4326
oldgoat@voy.net
*Specializing in large-format (view and
studio) cameras, panoramic and
banquet cameras and enlargers,
lenses, accessories, books on
photography history, collectible
cameras.*

Eric Mehl
Columbus Camera Group, Inc.
55 East Blake Ave.
Columbus, OH 43202-2905
ph: 614-267-0686
fax: 614-267-5526
colscamr@infinet.com
http://www.columbuscamera.com
*Buys and sells all photographic
equipment new and old; Nikon, Stereo,
Rollei, Linhof, Canon, Leica, Pentax,
Zeiss; appraises estates; also buy
current equipment as well as photos
and darkrooms.*

T.K. Treadwell
4201 Nagle Rd.
Bryan, TX 77801-3938
ph: 409-846-0209
71222.1571@compuserve.com

Brian P. Wolfe
BPW Limited Photographic
10870 W. Washington Blvd.
Culver City, CA 90232-3610
ph: 310-202-0816
fax: 310-202-0817
cameras@bpwltd.com
http://www.bpwltd.com
*Used and collectible cameras, lenses
and accessories; buy, sell, trade,
repair and restore all types of
photographic equipment; also rents
photo equipment to film makers:
Hasselblad, Rolleiflex, Nikon,
Japanese, German, Russian, etc.*

William P. Carroll
ACR Books
8500 La Entrada
Whittier, CA 90605
ph: 562-693-8421
fax: 562-945-6011
acrbooks@concentric.net
http://webtch.com/ACRbooks
*Antique and classic cameras for sale;
offers new and used books on
kaleidoscopes, cameras and the history
of photography.*

Alex Beringer
Online Camera Exchange
P.O. Box 1711
Imperial Beach, CA 91933
ph: 760-739-7601
fax: 760-739-7601
alex@tfb.com
http://www.tfb.com/oce/oce.htm
*Buys and sells fine used and
collectible cameras; specialty is
wooden cameras, spy cameras, 1950s-
1960s rangefinder cameras, military
cameras and other unusual equipment.*

Roger Kasner
NW Camera
503-684-6297
Portland, OR 97224
ph: 503-684-6297
nwcamera1@nwcamera.com
http://www.nwcamera.com
*Dealers in all kinds of interesting
photographic equipment; from early
box cameras to modern SLR and
medium format equipment; specializes
in post-war German and Japanese
35mm and 120 cameras, lenses, and
accessories.*

Dale Lampson
Pacific Rim Camera
1965 Davcor St., SE
Salem, OR 97302
ph: 503-370-7461
fax: 503-370-8301
staff@pacificrimcamera.com
http://www.pacificrimcamera.com
*Collector, appraiser, expert, dealer in
collectible cameras since 1986;
handles a wide variety of
photographica; specializes in cameras
from the 1930s through the 1960s;
over 10,000 items in stock; member
Nikon Historical Society.*

F. & S. Marriott
59 Rustic Gallery
Piece Hall
Halifax, HX1 1RE U.K.
photo@marriott.u-net.com
http://www.marriott.u-net.com
*Specializes in classic still and movie
cameras and related equipment, books
and accessories.*

Experts

Fred Waterman
1704 Valencia Dr.
Rockford, IL 61114-6107
ph: 815-639-9986
*Buys and specializes in novel cameras
with unusual devices or appearances;
also in camera accessories such as
meters, exposure guides, darkroom
equipment, etc.*

William P. Carroll
ACR Books
8500 La Entrada
Whittier, CA 90605
ph: 562-693-8421
fax: 562-945-6011
acrbooks@concentric.net
http://webtch.com/ACRbooks
Buys, specializes in early shutters,

*small format roll-film cameras,
mechanically complex cameras (built-
in motor drives or other unusual
features); also wants camera look-
alikes (flasks, compacts, etc.).*

Mike & Gladys Kessler
25749 Anchor Circle
San Juan Capistrano, CA 92675-4002
ph: 949-661-3320
*Buys and specializes in unusual 1880-
1890s disguised or detective cameras;
also Simon Wing cameras.*

Internet Resources

Rob Niederman
rniederman@usinternet.com
http://www.antiquewoodcameras.com/
*Camera collector with Web site
displaying and describing wood and
brass cameras made before 1900;
includes related history and 19th
century advertisements.*

Camprice.com
info@camprice.com
http://www.camprice.com
*An subscription-based online camera
price guide for those in the camera
collecting community.*

Dan Colucci
Antique & Classic Camera Web Site
82 Brick Kiln Rd.
Chelmsford, MA 01824
ph: 617-790-4915
DColucci@aol.com
http://members.aol.com/dcolucci
*A collectors Web site devoted to
antique and classic collectors; site
contains links, photographs and
information about pre-1900
photographica as well as classic
cameras.*

Museums/Libraries

Jack Naylor
Naylor Museum of Photographic History
ph: 617-731-6603
fax: 617-277-7878
jacknaylor@aol.com
*A private museum with photographic
exhibitions for collectors and
historians; pre-photography, the first
photograph, wet and dry plate, roll
film, research library; by appointment
only.*

Fleetwood Museum of Art &
Photographica
614 Greenbrook Rd.
North Plainfield, NJ 07063
ph: 908-757-5507
*Exhibits a collection of vintage
cameras and images; maintains a
photo-techniques and photo-history
library.*

Periodicals

Newspaper: CameraShopper
P.O. Box 1086
New Canaan, CT 06840
ph: 203-972-5700
fax: 203-972-5702
editor@camera-shopper.com
http://www.camera-shopper.com
*A worldwide buy, sell, trade
publication for photographic
equipment and images.*

Bonnie Paulk, Ed. Dir.
PRIMEDIA Enthusiast Group
Magazine: Shutterbug
5211 S. Washington Ave.
Titusville, FL 32780
ph: 321-269-3212
fax: 321-267-2894
editorial@shutterbug.net
http://www.shutterbug.net
*Geared to the advanced to profes-
sional photographer; articles about
new/old equip. & access., collectibles
and new products; many ads.*

Fred & Stephanie Marriott
Magazine: Classic Camera Magazine
59 Rustic Gallery
Piece Hall
Halifax, West Yorkshire HX1 1RE U.K.
ph: 01484-713992
photo@marriott.u-net.com
http://www.marriott.u-net.com/ccm.htm
*Occasional magazine devoted to
classic still and cine equipment.*

Repair Services

Konny Lang, Pres.
Atlantic Camera Repair
276 Higbie Lane
West Islip, NY 11795-2822
ph: 516-587-7959
fax: 516-587-7750
*Repairs cameras, studio equipment,
35mm SLRs, video and movie cameras,
VCRs, meters, graphic art lenses,
projectors, electronic strobes,
surveillance equipment, underwater
cameras; also modifies or restores
cameras including antique.*

Ed Romney
Romney Publishing
P.O. Box 487
Drayton, SC 29333
ph: 864-597-1882
ed@edromney.com
http://www.edromney.com
*Fix your own cameras! Romney offers
camera repair manuals, courses, tools
and restoration supplies for most
cameras, old or new: Leica Graflex,
Rolleiflex, Nikon, Canon and many
more; also books on repairing old
radios.*

Ken Ruth
Photography on Bald Mountain
113 Bald Mountain
Davenport, CA 95017-0113
ph: 831-423-4465
baldmtn@pacbell.net
http://home.pacbell.net/baldmtn
Repairs only older and classic

mechanical cameras; parts fabrication, modifications, adaptations.

Suppliers

Ed Romney
Romney Publishing
P.O. Box 487
Drayton, SC 29333
ph: 864-597-1882
ed@edromney.com
http://www.edromney.com
*Fix your own cameras! Romney offers
camera repair manuals, courses, tools
and restoration supplies for most
cameras, old or new: Leica Graflex,
Rolleiflex, Nikon, Canon and many
more; also books on repairing old
radios.*

Exakta

Clubs/Associations

Maruizio Frizziero
Exakta Circle
via De Gaspari 1
Genova, 16146 Italy
ph: +3910365999 or +3910365996
fax: +3919364316
mfrizzi@tin.it
http://www.exakta.org
*The Exakta camera was the first 35mm
SLR in the world; the Web site offers
lots of information about this camera.*

Film

Suppliers

Dick Haviland
Film for Classics
P.O. Box 486
Honeoye Falls, NY 14472
ph: 716-624-4945
fax: 716-624-5651
joan@filmforclassics.com
http://www.filmforclassics.com
*Provides film for collectors/users of
classic and antique cameras all over
the world.*

Kodak

Clubs/Associations

Dr. George Layne
International Kodak Historical Society
P.O. Box 21
Paoli, PA 19301-0021
Georgelayne@aol.com

Dr. David L. Jentz
Historical Society for Retina Cameras
50695 Ridgemoor Way
Granger, IN 46530-6945
ph: 219-272-4193
fax: 219-232-2162
retinacam@msn.com
*The Kodak Retina was first introduced
in 1934; it featured the new
development of a daylight loading 35
mm format film cartridge that made
quality cameras and pictures available
to the ordinary person.*

Collectors

Frank T. Storey
194 School Lane
Linthicum Heights, MD 21090-2528
ph: 410-850-5728 or 410-691-6373
fax: 410-850-5728
itbalto@aol.com
http://frankstorey.netfirms.com
*Collects Kodak cameras in excellent
condition; also wants any Kodak
advertising items such as signs, ads,
trucks, plates, glasses, stuffed
animals, pins, pens, etc.*

Greg Milneck
9146 Jefferson Hwy.
Baton Rouge, LA 70809
ph: 225-928-4814
camcollect@aol.com
http://www.digitalfxinc.com/kodak
*Wants to buy Kodak cameras in mint
condition; from 1928-1933 Kodak
made several colored and deco-style
cameras designed for women: Beau
Brownie, Bantam, Special, Coquette,
Ensemble, Vanity Ensemble, Petites,
and Vanity.*

Walker Mangum
Kodak Collector's Page
15910 Laurelfield Dr.
Houston, TX 77059-6432
kodak@nwmangum.com
http://www.nwmangum.com/Kodak/
index.html
*Private collector with comprehensive
online collection of Eastman Kodak
cameras and collectibles with
information about each.*

Joe Fix
10315 Timberloch
Houston, TX 77070
jdfix@thompson-grp.com
http://www.thompson-grp.com/fix/
images/instamatic.htm
*Specializes in Kodak Instamatic
cameras.*

Chris Eve
Flat 2 The Elms
Rue Des Cosnets
St. Ouen, Jersey JE3 2BJ U.K.
kypfer@psilink.co.je
http://www.toptown.com/nowhere/kypfer
*Web site contains a private collection
in virtual museum format of about 500
Kodak cameras, including Box
cameras, Brownie cameras, Instamatic
cameras, Instant Picture cameras,
Retina and Retinette cameras.*

Kodak Brownie

Internet Resources

Jeff Jost
Brownie Camera Discussion Group
23705 Vanowen St., Ste. 288
West Hills, CA 91307
ph: 818-704-5731
fax: 818-702-6824
brownielover@westval.com
http://westval.com/brownie
*Discussion group and mailing list of
hundreds of Kodak Brownie camera
collectors; join now for free and have*

access to these experts for your
Brownie camera questions.

Chuck Baker
Brownie Camera Page, The
Voorstadslaan 69
SJ Nijmegen, 6541 The Netherlands
chuck@browniecamera.com
http://www.browniecamera.com
*An information Web site about Kodak
Brownie and Kodak cameras; there is
an interactive forum, a submittable art
gallery and a photography-related
store among other features.*

Leica

Clubs/Associations

Sean Allen
Leica Historical Society of America
Journal: Viewfinder, The
60 Revere Dr., Ste. 500
Northbrook, IL 60062
ph: 847-564-2181
fax: 847-480-9282
lhsa@lhsa.org
http://www.lhsa.org
*An international group of photogra-
phers, collectors, enthusiasts and
historians dedicated to the use of the
Leica system and the preservation of
its heritage.*

Dealers

Don Chatterton
Don Chatterton International
ph: 253-549-7900
fax: 253-549-7771
leica@qwest.net
http://www.donchatterton.com
*Leica specialist; Web site has
information on R, M, and screw
mount Leica cameras.*

Military

Collectors

Richard J. Kimmel
P.O. Box 19
Bayville, NJ 08721-1412
ph: 732-269-8581
*Wants WWII combat cameras:
military versions with subdued olive
drab and black finish only.*

Dealers

Brian P. Wolfe
BPW Limited Photographic
10870 W. Washington Blvd.
Culver City, CA 90232-3610
ph: 310-202-0816
fax: 310-202-0817
cameras@bpwltd.com
http://www.bpwltd.com
*Used and collectible cameras, lenses
and accessories; buy, sell, trade,
repair and restore all types of
photographic equipment; also rents
photo equipment to film makers:
Hasselblad, Rolleiflex, Nikon,
Japanese, German, Russian, etc.*

Movie

(see also MOVIE PROJECTORS)

Clubs/Associations

Paul Pottash, Sec. Treas.
Movie Machine Society, The
Newsletter: Sixteen Frames
P.O. Box 94
Oley, PA 19547-0094
ph: 610-689-9279
movmacso@satx.net
http://members.tripod.com/moviems
*Devoted to the exchange of informa-
tion among those interested in the
technical history of all kinds of
apparatus designed to create a moving
image, from Arriflexes to
Zoopraxiscopes.*

Collectors

Alan Kattelle
50 Old Country Rd.
Hudson, MA 01749-3026
ph: 978-562-9184
alankatt@aol.com
http://www.homemoviehistory.com
*Wants unusual amateur movie
cameras & projectors: Devry 16
Deluxe, Pathe KOK Projector,
"Wedding Brownie" movie camera,
Duplex 11mm camera and projector,
and Victor Cine cameras &
projectors.*

David Hale
17 West Broad St.
Hazleton, PA 18201
ph: 570-459-7049
*Wants hand crank movie cameras and
hand crank movie projectors from the
1940s through 1960s; any condition.*

Gregory J. Vonderheide
29032 Rivergate Run
Zephyrhills, FL 33543-6544
ph: 813-907-9291
fax: 813-994-0500
gvondo1@aol.com
*Wants to buy wind-up movie cameras;
all mm, prefer pre-1940; must be
working.*

Alan Heim
8007 West 4th St.
Los Angeles, CA 90048-4414
ph: 213-935-0865
fax: 213-931-9549
*Collector and sometimes trader of all
forms of early film equipment with a
focus on editing equipment; movie
cameras, magic lanterns, pre-cinema.*

Michael Rogge
The Netherlands
wichm@xs4all.nl
http://www.xs4all.nl/~wichm/
cinemat.html
*Buys, sells rare vintage movie
equipment; Web site contains
information on collecting vintage
movie equipment; links to other
cinematrographica sites, an article
"100 Years of Film Sizes;" list of
3000 vintage movie cameras &
projectors.*

Dealers

International Cinema Equipment
  Company, Inc.
100 NE 39th St.
Miami, FL 33137
ph: 305-573-7339
fax: 305-573-8101
sales@iceco.com
http://www.iceco.com
  *Sells pre-owned, rebuilt, refurbished,
  and secondhand professional cinema
  equipment.*

Randy Donley
Donley's Wild West Town & Museum
8512 S. Union Rd.
Union, IL 60180-9661
ph: 815-923-9000
fax: 815-923-2253
mdonley@dls.net
http://www.wildwesttown.com
  *Wants pre-1930 34mm hand-crank
  movie projectors and cameras.*

Larry Urbanski
Urbanski Film
P.O. Box 438
Orland Park, IL 60462-0438
ph: 708-460-9082
fax: 708-460-9099
info@urbanskifilm.com
http://www.urbanskifilm.com
  *Buys and sells 16mm, 8mm, 35mm
  film and equipment; specializing in
  cartoons, educational, features, TV
  shows, and shorts; archival cans,
  reels, film cleaner; also buys same;
  send two stamps for list of wants.*

Experts

Alan Kattelle
50 Old Country Rd.
Hudson, MA 01749-3026
ph: 978-562-9184
alankatt@aol.com
http://www.homemoviehistory.com
  *Author of "HOME MOVIES, A
  History of the American Industry 1897
  - 1979;" available from author.*

Internet Resources

Michael Rogge
The Netherlands
wichm@xs4all.nl
http://www.xs4all.nl/~wichm/
  cinemat.html
  *Web site contains information on
  collecting vintage movie equipment;
  links to other cinemotographica sites,
  an article "100 Years of Film Sizes;"
  list of 3000 vintage movie cameras &
  projectors.*

Periodicals

Stacie Berger
Antique Trader Publications, Inc.
Magazine: Big Reel
P.O. Box 1050
Dubuque, IA 52004-1050
ph: 800-334-7165 or 800-482-4155
fax: 800-531-0880
stacie.berger@fwpubs.com
http://www.bigreel.com
  A monthly tabloid for movie and
television memorabilia collectors and
fans: ads, news, current & nostalgic
feature articles, obits, etc.

Nikon

Clubs/Associations

Robert J. Rotoloni
Nikon Historical Society
Magazine: Nikon Journal, The
P.O. Box 3213
Munster, IN 46321-0213
ph: 219-322-9966
fax: 219-322-9977
rotoloni@msn.com
http://www.nikonhs.org
  *Focuses on the history of Nikon
  cameras; magazine contains articles
  and ads for the Nikon collector.*

Collectors

Harry Poster
P.O. Box 1883
South Hackensack, NJ 07606-0483
ph: 201-794-9606
fax: 201-794-9553
hposter@att.net
http://www.harryposter.com
  *Wants early Nikons and Nikon
  accessories.*

Experts

Robert J. Rotoloni
P.O. Box 3213
Munster, IN 46321-0213
ph: 219-322-9966
fax: 219-322-9977
rotoloni@msn.com
http://www.nikonhs.org
  *Author of "The Nikon..An Illustrated
  History of the Nikon Camera",
  founder of the Nikon Historical
  Society.*

Stereo Cameras

(see also STEREOVIEWERS &
STEREOGRAPHS)

Clubs/Associations

Betty Graham
Vintage Camera Club
2562 Victoria St.
Wichita, KS 67216
ph: 316-265-0393
  *For collectors of vintage cameras;
  also stereo cameras and stereo
  images.*

Dealers

Harry Poster
P.O. Box 1883
South Hackensack, NJ 07606-0483
ph: 201-794-9606
fax: 201-794-9553
hposter@att.net
http://www.harryposter.com
  *Since 1979; wants 3-D stereo cameras
  and accessories including Macro
  Realist and Donaldson, Belplasca,
  Verascope f40, Realist, Wollensak,
  TDC, Realist, Kodak, Delta, Sputnik,
  plus other stereoscope cameras,
  viewers, projectors, etc.*

Subminiature

(see also SPY EQUIPMENT)

Collectors

Dave Gorski
21045 N. 124th Ave.
Sun City West, AZ 85375
ph: 623-975-4061
fax: 623-975-4061
davegorski@yahoo.com
http://www.davegorski.com
  *Wants to buy cameras disguised in
  hats, binoculars, canes, guns,
  lighters, purses, pens or watches; or
  just very tiny cameras.*

Internet Resources

Joe McGloin
Sub Club, The
3271 S. Clay St.
Sheridan, CO 80110
xkaes@aol.com
http://www.subclub.org
  *A Web site that covers all aspects of
  subminiature photography; various
  resources such as descriptions of all
  subminiature cameras (half-frame and
  smaller), lists of books and articles,
  how to use, processing film, photo
  gallery, etc.*

Zeiss

Clubs/Associations

Zeiss Historica Society
Journal: Zeiss Historica Society Journal
300 Waxwing Dr.
Cranbury, NJ 08512
ph: 540-981-1036
msmall@roanoke.infi.net
http://showcase.netins.net/web/crye/zi-
  hist.htm
  *Dedicated to the study & exchange of
  information on the history of Carl
  Zeiss Optical Co. and Zeiss-Ikon, its
  people and products (cameras,
  accessories, and optical equipment of
  all types) from 1846 to present; semi-
  annual journal.*

Internet Resources

Greg Bedore
Something Zeiss to Say
3611 8th St. N.
Saint Petersburg, FL 33704
zeisser1@aol.com
http://www.netcontax.com
  *A Web site dedicated to classic and
  collectible cameras and photographic
  products manufactured by Zeiss Ikon
  and the Zeiss companies.*

CAMPBELL SOUP COLLECTIBLES

Clubs/Associations

Penny Weaver
CC International Ltd.
P.O. Box 208
Union City, OH 45390-0208
ph: 937-833-5300
fax: 937-833-0123
wbrkv@aol.com
http://www.soupclan.com
  *Collectors of Campbell Soup
  memorabilia; has worldwide
  membership; convention held every two
  years; the "Kids" are the most highly
  sought after items, but members also
  want paper items, trucks, dolls,
  cookware, glassware, etc.*

David R. Young
Soup Collectors Club, The
Newsletter: Soup Collector, The
414 Country Lane Ct.
Wauconda, IL 60084
ph: 847-487-4917
soupclub@yahoo.com
http://clubs.yahoo.com/clubs/
  campbellssoupcollectorclub
  *Networking; quarterly newsletter
  features articles and classified ads;
  write for more information.*

Experts

Mary Jane Lamphier
Quilted Keepsakes & Unique Dolls
  Exhibit
577 Main St.
Arlington, IA 50606-9712
ph: 319-633-5885
  *Specializes in Campbell's Soup Kids;
  please include a SASE if requesting a
  reply or the return of photos.*

David R. Young
414 Country Lane Ct.
Wauconda, IL 60084
ph: 847-487-4917
soupclub@yahoo.com
http://clubs.yahoo.com/clubs/
  campbellssoupcollectorclub
  *Author of "Campbell Soup Col-
  lectibles."*

Man./Prod./Dist.

Campbell's Shop, Campbell Soup
  Company
http://www.campbellshop.com
  *For collectors of contemporary
  Campbell Soup memorabilia: dolls,
  vehicles, kitchen, porcelains, etc.; a
  Campbell Company sponsored Web
  site.*

CAMPING EQUIPMENT

(see also BOY SCOUT
MEMORABILIA; SPORTING
COLLECTIBLES; TRAILERS & RVs)

154

Coleman
Clubs/Associations

International Coleman Collectors Club
Newsletter: Coleman Collector, The
7472 Dumosa Ave.
Yucca Valley, CA 92284
webmaster@colemancollectorsclub.com
http://www.colemancollectorsclub.com
*For collectors of any Coleman
products such as lamps, lanterns,
irons, camp stoves and other
pressurized liquid fuel appliances;
also literature, old repair manuals,
sales samples.*

Collectors

Bud Michael
P.O. Box 1236
Lincolnton, NC 28093-1236
ph: 704-735-8643
bud@vnet.net

Jim Adkins
808 Turner Rd.
Independence, MO 64056
ph: 816-796-9205

Jay Poirier
5964 S. Lee Way
Littleton, CO 80127
ph: 303-973-4255
fax: 303-288-1790
*Wants Coleman items: lamps,
lanterns, stoves, parts, irons, sales
catalogs, advertising, military.*

Man./Prod./Dist.

Coleman Company, The
P.O. Box 2931
Wichita, KS 67201
ph: 316-261-3211
http://www.coleman.com
*Manufacturer of quality sporting and
camping equipment.*

CAN OPENERS
Collectors

Stan Dickinson
307 1/2 E. Lake St., Apt. B
Petoskey, MI 49770-2417
ph: 231-347-1022
*Have about 225 different can openers;
all for sale.*

Joe Young
P.O. Box 587
Elgin, IL 60121-0587
ph: 847-695-0108
istamp2@aol.com
*Wants to buy unusual can openers;
also interested in combination tools
with can openers; all correspondence
answered.*

CAN-CAN
Collectors

Taylor Warren
P.O. Box 1802
Williamsburg, VA 23187-1802
Wants stills and clippings of can-can

*dancers; wants girls wearing skirts,
especially Las Vegas can-can
programs and can-can items from the
movies.*

CANAL COLLECTIBLES
Clubs/Associations

Canal Society of New Jersey
P.O. Box 737
Morristown, NJ 07963-0737
ph: 908-722-9556
fax: 908-722-9556
canalsocietynj@yahoogroups.com
http://www.canalsocietynj.org
*Group fosters the study of the history
of NJ's two towpath canals; preserves
and restores canal remains and
artifacts.*

Charles W. Derr, Treas.
American Canal Society, Inc.
Newsletter: American Canals
117 Main St.
Freemansburg, PA 18017
ph: 610-691-0956
deruls@aol.com
http://www.americancanalsociety.org
*Focuses on the preservation,
restoration, interpretation and use of
the historic navigational canals of the
Americas.*

Lynn Howlett, Corr. Sec.
Virginia Canals & Navigations Society
Newsletter: Tiller, The
6826 Rosemont Dr.
Mc Lean, VA 22101
alhowlett@juno.com
http://organizations.rockbridge.net/canal
*Formed in 1977 to preserve and
enhance Virginia's rich inland
waterways heritage in all its aspects:
history, exploration, archaeology,
modeling, local lore and legend,
restoration, preservation, park and
trail, development, etc.*

Canadian Canal Society
P.O. Box 23016, Midtown P.O.
124 Welland Ave.
St. Catharines, Ontario L2R 7P6 Canada
ccs@becon.org
http://people.becon.org/~ccs
*A non-profit, educational, scientific
and historical organization dedicated
to the preservation of canal heritage
in Canada.*

Collectors

Harry L. Rinker
5093 Vera Cruz Rd.
Emmaus, PA 18049-9554
ph: 610-965-1122
fax: 610-965-1124
rinkeron@fast.net
http://www.harryrinker.com
*Seeks artifacts, books, paper ephemera
and commemorative objects associated
with America's mule-drawn canal era.*

Museums/Libraries

Erie Canal Museum
Newsletter: Canal Packet, The
318 Erie Blvd.
Syracuse, NY 13202
ph: 315-471-0593
contactus@eriecanalmuseum.org
http://www.eriecanalmuseum.org

National Canal Museum & Hugh Moore
  Historical Park & Museums, Inc.
30 Centre Square
Easton, PA 18042-7743
ph: 610-559-6613
ncm@canals.org
http://canals.org

Erie Canal
Collectors

Robert Preston
8 Newman St.
Gloversville, NY 12078
ph: 518-725-8214

Panama Canal
Collectors

Frederick Lingenfelser
814 Byram St.
Reading, PA 19606-1446
lingy@afo.net
*Collecting anything related to the
construction of the Panama Canal,
1870-1914, the French or American
effort: maps, letters, photographs,
books, autographs, diaries, etc.*

CANCELLATIONS
Postal

(see STAMP COLLECTING, Cancels)

CANDY

(see also BOXES, Candy; BUBBLE
GUM & CANDY WRAPPERS;
MOLDS, Candy; PEZ)

Museums/Libraries

Michelle Havrilla
Wilbur Chocolate's Candy Americana
Museum
48 N. Broad St.
Lititz, PA 17543-1026
ph: 717-626-3249 or 888-294-5287
http://www.wilburbuds.com
*Collection of the making of candy:
antique novelty candy containers,
cocoa tins, chocolate molds.*

CANDY BARS

(see BUBBLE GUM & CANDY
WRAPPERS; CANDY)

CANDY CONTAINERS

(see also BUBBLE GUM & CANDY
WRAPPERS; CANDY; PEZ)

Clubs/Associations

Mike & Jo Baldwin, Mem. Ch.
Candy Container Collectors of America
Newsletter: Candy Gram, The
P.O. Box 2971
Anderson, IN 46018-2971
ph: 765-643-7065
gmja59@insoghtbb.com
http://www.candycontainer.org
*Dedicated to promoting the collecting
of antique candy containers.*

Collectors

Douglas Dezso
864 Paterson Ave.
Maywood, NJ 07607
ph: 201-845-7707

Jim Olean
115 MacBeth Dr.
Lower Burrell, PA 15068-2628
candy46man@aol.com
*Avid collector of tire ashtrays, toy
candy containers and American glass
target balls.*

Terry Whitmeyer
88 Woodbine Dr.
Hershey, PA 17033-2668
ph: 717-533-3716

Dealers

Kit Carter Weilage
506 Briar Hill Rd.
Louisville, KY 40206
ph: 502-561-5030
kit1@bellsouth.net
*Buys and sells Christmas collectibles,
specializing in German-made Santa
candy containers.*

Paul W. Schofield
Lion's Den Antiques
7988 Bethel Burley Rd. SE
Port Orchard, WA 98366
ph: 360-876-3364
fax: 360-876-5421
*Buys, sells, appraises, and specializes
in old Santas, candy containers,
Halloween, Easter, Christmas, Easter,
Dresden, figural lights.*

Experts

Jack Bush
3300 Robinson Creek Rd.
Ukiah, CA 95482
ph: 707-462-0851
jpbrush@saber.net
http://www.candyfilledtoys.com
*Co-author of "Modern Candy
Containers;" over 500 full-color
pictures, brief history of candy
containers, candy container
manufacturers.*

Suppliers

Bob & Linda Keimig
3016 Montrose Dr.
Bartlesville, OK 74005
ph: 918-335-3265
*Supplies replacement paper closures
for candy containers; also tin and
other paper parts.*

Jars

Collectors

Tom "The Jar Man"
421 De La Vina
Santa Barbara, CA 93101
ph: 805-966-3076
Wants pedestal candy jars, any size or condition.

CANES & WALKING STICKS

(see also PIPES)

Appraisers

Henry Taron
Tradewinds Antiques & Auctions
24 Magnolia Ave.
P.O. Box 249
Manchester, MA 01944
ph: 978-526-4085
fax: 978-526-3088
taron@tradewindsantiques.com
http://www.tradewindsantiques.com
A premier antique all-cane auction house sells live twice a year and additionally has four online events; sells highest quality examples in carved ivory, folk art, nautical, decorative, historical, political, gadget, etc.

Auction Services

Henry Taron
Tradewinds Antiques & Auctions
24 Magnolia Ave.
P.O. Box 249
Manchester, MA 01944
ph: 978-526-4085
fax: 978-526-3088
taron@tradewindsantiques.com
http://www.tradewindsantiques.com
A premier antique all-cane auction house sells live twice a year and additionally has four online events; sells highest quality examples in carved ivory, folk art, nautical, decorative, historical, political, gadget, etc.

Joel & Michael Malter
Malter Galleries, Inc.
17003 Ventura Blvd., Ste. 205
Encino, CA 91316
ph: 818-784-7772 or 888-784-2131
fax: 818-784-4726
mike@maltergalleries.com
http://www.maltergalleries.com
Conducts periodic auction sales of canes and walking sticks.

Clubs/Associations

Cane Collectors Club of America
Newsletter: Cane Collectors Chronicle
2 Horizon Rd., Ste. G18
Fort Lee, NJ 07024
ph: 201-969-1824
bnelson@bellatlantic.net
For those interested in old or antique walking sticks.

Collectors

Sherlock S. Holmes, D.D.
P.O. Box 3
Worcester, MA 01613-0003
ph: 888-651-0421
fax: 888-651-0421
mail@SherlockHolmes.com
http://www.Sherlock.Holmes.Name
Wants to buy pre-1940 walking sticks (or rare canes); especially interested in walking sticks with guns, swords or other items hidden inside.

Bruce Thalberg
23 Mountain View Dr.
Weston, CT 06883-1317
ph: 203-227-8175
gortoh@yahoo.com
Wants to buy canes: carved wood, ivory and bone figural handles and knobs, container and gadget canes; handles without shafts are acceptable; photocopy helpful; please price items & send SASE.

Barry Koffman
1 Vincent St.
Binghamton, NY 13905
ph: 607-723-5167
fax: 607-797-6959
caneman94@aol.com
Specializes in carved folk art canes.

Howard Frank Glazer
20 Windermere Court
Downingtown, PA 19335-1113
ph: 610-269-9698 or 610-269-9698
hglazer@nni.com
Collector of antique walking canes, including glass walking canes.

Arnold Scher
Beaver Bros. Antiques
1637 Market St.
San Francisco, CA 94103-1217
ph: 415-863-4344
fax: 415-863-4399
beaverprop@aol.com
Wants dual purpose, container, weapon, gadget, fancy carved ivory, gold or silver canes; also wants carved folk art canes.

Dealers

Henry Taron
Tradewinds Antiques & Auctions
24 Magnolia Ave.
P.O. Box 249
Manchester, MA 01944
ph: 978-526-4085
fax: 978-526-3088
taron@tradewindsantiques.com
http://www.tradewindsantiques.com
A premier antique all-cane auction house sells live twice a year and additionally has four online events; sells highest quality examples in carved ivory, folk art, nautical, decorative, historical, political, gadget, etc.

Brian J. Kiracofe
Newport Scrimshander, The
14 Bowen's Wharf
Newport, RI 02840
ph: 401-849-5680 or 800-635-5234
fax: 401-849-9306
newportscrimshaw@juno.com
http://www.scrimshanders.com
Carries an extensive collection of canes and walking sticks; mostly ivory handles.

Liela Nelson
World of the Walking Stick, The
P.O. Box 1004
Englewood Cliffs, NJ 07632
ph: 201-886-8826 or 800-442-2637
fax: 201-886-9543
liela@walkingstickworld.com
http://www.walkingstickworld.com
Specializes exclusively in old and antique walking sticks.

Kim Robertson
Robertsons
6365 Greenhill Rd.
New Hope, PA 18938
ph: 215-297-5068
fax: 215-297-5669
Buys and sells walking sticks, especially quality decorative, ivory, system and defense walking sticks.

C.B. Grissom
Cane Man, The
2180 Stephens Lane
Lexington, KY 40504-3020
ph: 606-277-7665
Wants to buy antique canes, walking sticks, umbrella handles; karat gold, sterling, ivory, V.I.P., container, watch.

Rick Berkoff
Rick's Sticks
P.O. Box 226
New Buffalo, MI 49117
ph: 616-469-3380
ricksticks@attbi.com
Buys and sells antique canes and walking sticks.

Keil's Antiques
325 Royal St.
New Orleans, LA 70130
ph: 504-522-4552
fax: 504-522-8754
info@mcgrewmcdaniel.com
http://www.keilsantiques.com
Specializes in walking and "system" sticks: shaving knife & brush, sewing kits, animal sticks, flask sticks, sword and dagger sticks, camera and opium pipe sticks, gaming and writing canes, etc.; since 1899

M.S. Rau Antiques
630 Royal St.
New Orleans, LA 70130
ph: 504-523-5660 or 800-544-9440
fax: 504-566-0057
info@rauantiques.com
http://www.rauantiques.com
Specializes in fine canes and walking sticks.

Gary Wiley
Antique Cane Trader, The
P.O. Box 372
Krum, TX 76249
ph: 940-482-5933
canetrader@canetrader.com
http://www.canetrader.com
Avid collector and reseller of only fine and collectible antique walking canes: ivory and bond handles, gadget sticks, folk art carved canes, weapon canes, etc.; will broker your canes; does research on historical items; appraises.

Marvin & Donna Stewart
Mardon Collectibles
P.O. Box 6385
Oceanside, CA 92052
mardon_collect@yahoo.com
Collects, buys and sells unusual canes/walking sticks.

Experts

George H. Meyer
100 West Long Lake Rd., Ste. 100
Bloomfield Hills, MI 48304
ph: 248-646-2907
fax: 248-647-5079
gmeyer@meyerkirk.com
Author of "American Folk Art Canes - Personal Sculpture."

Museums/Libraries

Peabody Essex Museum
Essex & Libert Sts.
Salem, MA 01970
ph: 978-745-9500 or 800-745-4054
pem@pem.org
http://www.pem.org

Curator
Fairfield Historical Society
636 Old Post Rd.
Fairfield, CT 06430-6647
ph: 203-259-1598
fax: 203-255-2716
info@fairfieldhs.org
http://www.fairfieldhistoricalsociety.org

Remington Firearms Museum
P.O. Box 179
Ilion, NY 13357-0179
ph: 315-895-3200
fax: 315-895-3237
webmaster@remington.com
http://www.remington.com
Affiliated with the Remington Arms Company, Inc.

Periodicals

Patrick Arthur
Newsletter: Cane Collector's Chronicle, The
P.O. Box 271668
Houston, TX 77277-1668
ph: 713-669-9810
fax: 713-662-2797
pwarthur@hal-pc.org
A color quarterly newsletter for the collector of antique walking sticks: articles, ads, photographs, auction results, book reviews, Q&A, etc.

Repair Services

Gilbert Center
81-83 Seaman Ave., #D
New York, NY 10034
ph: 212-304-2309 or 800-994-2594
fax: 212-304-9106
gilcenter@aol.com
http://www.umbrellarepair.com
Repairs and restores canes and umbrellas.

Political

Collectors

Jim Gifford
P.O. Box 51
Bath, OH 44210-0051
ph: 330-666-3692
Specializes in collecting canes that have a political theme or motif.

CANNING JARS

(see BOTTLES; FRUIT JARS; JELLY CONTAINERS)

CANNONS

(see also ARMS & ARMOR; CIVIL WAR ARTIFACTS; FIREWORKS MEMORABILIA; MILITARIA: AMMUNITION & EXPLOSIVE ORDNANCE; TOYS, Cannons; TOY GUNS)

Collectors

Charles G. Kratz, Jr.
17821 Golfview
Homewood, IL 60430-1210
ph: 708-799-8478 or 312-951-0336
Wants old muzzle loading military cannons (only full-size, authentic type) in any condition; also want US artillery clothing and equipment such as wooden artillery carriages and ammunition chests.

Man./Prod./Dist.

Marshall Steen
Steen Cannons
520 13th St.
Ashland, KY 41102
ph: 606-329-2477
steencannons@wwd.net
http://www.wwd.net/steen
Manufacturer of Civil War period artillery, carriages, and limbers.

South Bend Replicas, Inc.
61650 Oak Rd.
South Bend, IN 46614
ph: 574-289-4500
http://www.southbendreplicas.com
Manufactures reproductions of muzzle loading cannons.

Starter

Man./Prod./Dist.

Robert B. George
R.B.G. Cannons
20 Amber Trail
Madison, CT 06443-2037
ph: 203-245-1216 or 800-327-2193
fax: 860-669-6982
Cannon manufacturers for over 35 years; most cannons are scale reproductions, meticulously finished with special attention to details; used as starting cannons and trophies; units fire black powder or 10 ga. black powder shells.

CANS

(see ADVERTISING COLLECTIBLES; BEER CANS; BREWERIANA; OYSTER RELATED COLLECTIBLES; SOFT DRINK COLLECTIBLES, Soft Drink Cans)

CANTON

(see CERAMICS [ORIENTAL], Chinese Export Porcelain)

CAP PISTOLS

(see TOY GUNS)

CAPS

(see also BOTTLE CAPS)

Clubs/Associations

Gene Dittman
National Cap Association
Newsletter: NCPA Newsletter
P.O. Box 2216
Deer Park, WI 54007
Members collect baseball-style caps with logos on them; quarterly newsletter, members receive annual cap printed with the year and different logo.

CARDS

(see also ADVERTISING COLLECTIBLES, Trade Cards; BUBBLE GUM CARDS; BUSINESS CARDS; CREDIT CARDS & CHARGE ITEMS; HOLIDAY COLLECTIBLES; GAMES, Cards; PLAYING CARDS; RELIGIOUS COLLECTIBLES, Holy Cards; SPORTS COLLECTIBLES; TRADING CARDS, Non-Sport)

Clubs/Associations

John W. Townsend
MICE - Modern Information Collectors Exchange - Free Card Guild
Newsletter: Mice Tales
4 Stiles Ave.
Marple
Stockport, Cheshire SK6 6LR U.K.
fax: +44 (0) 161-427-1030
miceclub@hotmail.com
http://www.micefreecardclub.co.uk
For collectors of pictorial non-insert advertising/publicity cards which are given away free: postcards, bookmarks, tourist information cards, radio/TV presenter cards, recipe cards, telephone publicity cards, pocket calendars, etc.

Tarot

Collectors

Joan Iris Eisenberg
176 East 77th St., Apt. #2F
New York, NY 10021-1909
ph: 212-879-9013
fax: 603-288-0429
Joaniris@aol.com
Wants to buy unusual and quality fortune telling cards and tarot cards.

Dealers

Jeannette Roth
Tarot Garden, The
1304 20th St.
West Des Moines, IA 50265-2211
ph: 515-224-7654
info@tarotgarden.com
http://www.tarotgarden.com
Specialists in imported, unusual, hard-to-find, out-of-print, and rare collectible tarots; buys, sells, trades; free search service available.

CARNEGIE HALL ITEMS

Collectors

Gino Francesconi
Carnegie Hall Corporation
881 Seventh Ave.
New York, NY 10019-3210
ph: 212-903-9629
fax: 212-424-2026
gfrancesconi@carnegiehall.org
http://www.carnegiehall.org
Wants house programs, stagebills, photographs of building, posters of events, other early memorabilia.

CARNIVAL ITEMS

(see also AMUSEMENT PARK ITEMS; CAROUSELS & CAROUSEL FIGURES)

Collectors

David Gaylin
P.O. Box 9686
Baltimore, MD 21237
ph: 410-665-6295
Always seeking carnival-related advertising, posters, promotional items, literature, ride manufacturers' literature, games, etc.

Allen Franklin
Rt. 2, Box 470
Farmville, VA 23901
ph: 804-392-6578
Wants to buy Carnival & Fair prizes from the 1940s through the 1960s: chalkware, dolly canes, fur monkeys, china cane tops, dolls with feathers; games of skill pieces such as knock-down cats & clowns, bottles, and rings from toss games.

Chalkware

Experts

Cathy Cook
10 E. 13th St., #2D
New York, NY 10003-4467
ph: 212-691-2406
fax: 212-691-2406
ccook710@aol.com
Interested in historical information about carnival chalkware and carnivals in general.

Thomas G. Morris
Prize Publishers
P.O. Box 8307
Medford, OR 97504-0307
chalkman@cdsnet.net
http://chalkman.homestead.com
Buys, sells and specializes in carnival chalkware figures; author of "The Carnival Chalk Prize" Vol. I and Vol. II; will assist with information or appraisals on the subject; SASE for info.

Periodicals

John & Cathy Daniel
Newsletter: Chalk Talk
720 Mission St.
South Pasadena, CA 91030
ph: 323-682-3557
jadsden1@aol.com

Repro. Sources

Peg McCormack
Folkwerks
121 S Main St.
Alburtis, PA 18011
ph: 610-965-1432
fax: 610-965-1432
folkwerks@aol.com
http://members.aol.com/folkwerks
Sculpts original pieces in earth clay; a mold is made, each piece is cast, handpainted, signed, dated, and numbered.

CAROUSELS & CAROUSEL FIGURES

(see also AMUSEMENT PARK ITEMS; CARNIVAL ITEMS; COLLECTIBLES [MODERN], Figurines [Carousels]; FOLK ART; MUSICAL BOXES; MUSICAL INSTRUMENTS, Mechanical [Band Organs])

Appraisers

Ken Weaver
Weavers Antiques
7 Cooks Glen Rd.
Spring City, PA 19475-3303
ph: 610-469-6331
fax: 610-469-6845
BarbMGR@aol.com
Auctions, buys, sells, restores and appraises carousel figures.

Mary Jenkins
3845 Telegraph Rd.
Elkton, MD 21921-2442
ph: 410-392-4289
fax: 410-392-6129
jenkinsm@zoominternet.net
http://www.carousels.com/acs.htm
Collects, appraises and specializes in carousels and carousel art; Executive Secretary of the American Carousel Society.

John & Cathy Daniel
720 Mission St.
South Pasadena, CA 91030
ph: 323-682-3557
jadsden1@aol.com
Collects, restores, appraises carousel animals; also supplies twisty brass tubing and carousel stands for collectors.

Auction Services

Arlan Ettinger
Guernsey's Auction
108 East 73rd St.
New York, NY 10021
ph: 212-794-2280
fax: 212-744-3638
auctions@guernseys.com
http://www.guernseys.com
Specializes in the sale of carousel figures.

Gordon Riewe
2287 Millville Rd.
Lapeer, MI 48446
ph: 810-664-5648
fax: 810-664-7141
Dealer of carousel horses; carousel auctions.

David A. Norton
Norton Auctioneers of Michigan, Inc.
50 W. Pearl St.
Coldwater, MI 49036-1967
ph: 517-279-9063
fax: 517-279-9191
nortonsold@cbpu.com
http://www.nortonauctioneers.com
Specializing in the auctioning of amusement rides, carousels, amusement parks, arcades, museums, etc.

Clubs/Associations

Mary Jenkins, Ex. Sec.
American Carousel Society
Newsletter: Rounding Board, The
3845 Telegraph Rd.
Elkton, MD 21921-2442
ph: 410-392-4289
fax: 410-392-6129
jenkinsm@zoominternet.net
http://www.carousels.com/acs.htm
The goal of the ACS is to preserve operating carousels and carousel art; please send SASE for information.

Edward F. Gallenstein
National Wood Carvers Association
Magazine: Chip Chats
P.O. Box 43218
Cincinnati, OH 45243
ph: 513-561-0627 or 513-561-9051
fax: 513-561-0627
nwca@chipchats.org
http://www.chipchats.org
NWCA's aims are to promote woodcarving and fellowship among members; encourage exhibitions; list tool and wood suppliers, and find markets for those who sell their work - in short, anything that aids the carver and/or whittler.

Terry Blake, ExSec.
National Carousel Association
Magazine: Merry-Go-Roundup
P.O. Box 4333
Evansville, IN 47724-0333
ph: 812-428-3675
terrybnca@juno.com
http://www.nca-usa.org
Primary goal is to protect existing wooden operating carousels; please send SASE for information.

Jean Martell
Colorado Carousel Society
6651 Metropolitan
Colorado Springs, CO 80911
ph: 719-392-9826

Collectors

Tommy Sciortino
3723 Nebraska Ave.
Tampa, FL 33603
ph: 813-248-9911
fax: 813-247-6369
tommyintpa@aol.com
Restores antique carousels; buys and sells whole carousels, horses, chariots, parts, etc.

Dealers

Bruce Zubee
Carousels.com
13 Argonne Terrace
Seymour, CT 06483
webmaster@carousels.com
http://www.carousels.com
Wants to buy any old wooden carousel horses or menagerie figures in any condition; also buying band organs, carousel scenery panels and rounding boards, etc.; sales, purchases, museum quality restorations, worldwide service.

Ken Weaver
Weavers Antiques
7 Cooks Glen Rd.
Spring City, PA 19475-3303
ph: 610-469-6331
fax: 610-469-6845
BarbMGR@aol.com
Auctions, buys, sells, restores and appraises carousel figures.

Steve Crescenze
Restorations by Wolf
8480 Gunston Rd.
Welcome, MD 20693-3213
ph: 301-932-2734
wolfrestorations@aol.com
http://www.carouselrestorations.com
Buys, sells, trades carousel figures (one to a whole carousel); professional restoration services with photo documentation of each figure.

Sandy & Gary Franklin
Antique Carousel Figures
3818 South 9th St.
Arlington, VA 22204-1530
ph: 703-892-8666 or 703-624-2981
mycarousel@mycarousel.com
http://www.mycarousel.com
Carries large selection of antique carousel animals, figures and trim on the Internet; buys, sells, trades; museum quality restorations; broker service.

Craig Swanson
Midwest Carousel Organization
1952 Lake Dr.
Independence, MO 64055-1863
ph: 816-685-6602 or 800-896-9661
extra@finest1.com
http://www.finest1.com/hand
World famous woodcarver, professional animal restorations; also buys, sells, and trades.

Don Snider
Merry-Go-Art
2606 Jefferson
Joplin, MO 64804
ph: 417-624-7281
hsnider@joplin.com
http://www.joplin.com/~hsnider
Buys and sells carousel figures, and video tapes of antique carousels.

John & June Reely
Flying Tails
1209 Indiana Ave.
South Pasadena, CA 91030-3611
ph: 223-256-8657
Send 2 stamp SASE for catalog of carousel figures hair tails.

Danie Horenberger
Brass Ring Entertainment
11001 Peoria St.
Sun Valley, CA 91352
ph: 818-394-0028
fax: 818-394-0062
sales@carousell.com
http://www.carousell.com
20 years experience, sales, restoration, parts, service.

Experts

Sandy & Gary Franklin
Antique Carousel Figures
3818 South 9th St.
Arlington, VA 22204-1530
ph: 703-892-8666 or 703-624-2981
mycarousel@mycarousel.com
http://www.mycarousel.com
Carries large selection of antique carousel animals, figures and trim on the Internet; buys, sells, trades; museum quality restorations; broker service.

William Manns
P.O. Box 6459
Santa Fe, NM 87502-6459
ph: 505-995-0102
fax: 505-995-0103
zon@nets.com
Author of "Painted Ponies, American Carousel Art." Send photo and request for information about your carving and its authenticity.

Marianne Stevens
Wooden Horse, The
920 W. Mescalero Rd.
Roswell, NM 88201
ph: 505-622-7397
fax: 505-622-7397
Buys, sells, trades, brokers, and appraises carousel figures.

Internet Resources

Bruce Zubee
Carousels.com
13 Argonne Terrace
Seymour, CT 06483
webmaster@carousels.com
http://www.carousels.com
The "World's Source" for the collector of antique carousel figures and related collectibles.

Man./Prod./Dist.

Bill Dentzel
Dentzel Carousel Company
843 53rd St.
Port Townsend, WA 98368
ph: 360-385-0304
fax: 360-385-1067
bill@dentzel.com
http://www.dentzel.com
Makes small wooden carousels, offers classes teaching those skills, hosts a museum and other educational programs.

Misc. Services

Tommy Sciortino
American Carousel & Novelty
3723 Nebraska Ave.
Tampa, FL 33603
ph: 813-248-9911
fax: 813-247-6369
tommyintpa@aol.com
Experienced in relocation, setup and dismantling of carousels.

Museums/Libraries

Heritage Plantation of Sandwich
P.O. Box 566
Sandwich, MA 02563
ph: 508-888-3300 or 508-888-1222
fax: 508-833-2916
heritage@heritageplantation.org
http://www.heritageplantation.org/autos.htm

Louise L. DeMars, Ex. Dir.
New England Carousel Museum, Inc.
Newsletter: Carousel, The
95 Riverside Ave.
Bristol, CT 06010
ph: 860-585-5411
fax: 860-314-0483
info@thecarouselmuseum.com
http://www.thecarouselmuseum.com
One of the nation's largest collections of historic carousel art, figurines and memorabilia.

Elizabeth Brick, Dir.
Herschell Carousel Factory Museum
Newsletter: Carousel Newsletter
180 Thompson St.
P.O. Box 672
North Tonawanda, NY 14120-0672
ph: 716-693-1885
fax: 716-743-9018
info@carouselmuseum.org
http://www.carouselmuseum.org
Allen Herschell wooden carousel c. 1916 (wood), a metal children's carousel c. 1946, and original Allan Herschell factory site; exhibit on history of Herschell Co., carousels, amusement rides, and band organs.

Merry-Go-Round Museum
301 Jackson St.
Sandusky, OH 44870
ph: 419-626-6111 or 419-626-6527
fax: 419-626-1297
MerryGoR@aol.com
http://www.merrygoroundmuseum.org
Features a working carousel, and master carver Gustav Dentzel's 19th century carving shop; carving & restoration demonstrations of carousel animals & band organs.

Charylene Brombaugh
Children's Museum of Indianapolis, The
3000 N. Meridian St.
Indianapolis, IN 46208-4716
ph: 317-334-3322 or 317-334-4000
fax: 317-921-4019
communic@childrensmuseum.org
http://www.childrensmuseum.org
The museum's carousel was originally installed at White City Park (now called Broad Ripple Park) in 1917.

Carol Perron
International Museum of Carousel Art
P.O. Box 1522
304 Oak St.
Hood River, OR 97031
ph: 541-387-2979
mail@carouselmuseum.com
http://www.carouselmuseum.com
Historical museum dedicated to preserving the carousel.

Periodicals

Magazine: Carnival Magazine
P.O. Box 4165
Salisbury, NC 28145-4138
ph: 704-636-0841
fax: 704-636-1051
http://www.carnivalmag.com
A quality monthly publication for the amusement industry: articles about current carnival activities, midway talk and personalities, manufacturers' showcase, rides of the past, carnival modeling of miniature creations.

Walter Loucks
Magazine: Carousel News & Trader, The
87 Park Ave. West, Ste. 206
Mansfield, OH 44902-162
ph: 419-529-4999
fax: 419-529-2321
cnsam@aol.com
http://www.carouseltrader.com
Monthly magazine serving the carousel enthusiast since 1985; color photos, ads, stories, auctions, restoring, events, etc.

William Manns
Zon International Publishing
Directory: Carousel Shopper
P.O. Box 6459
Santa Fe, NM 87502-6459
ph: 505-995-0102
fax: 505-995-0103
zon@nets.com
A carousel resource directory: suppliers, museums, carousel events, shows, restorers, auctions, reproductions, cards, posters, etc.

Repair Services

Steve Crescenze
Restorations by Wolf
8480 Gunston Rd.
Welcome, MD 20693-3213
ph: 301-932-2734
wolfrestorations@aol.com
http://www.carouselrestorations.com
Buys, sells, trades carousel figures (one to a whole carousel); professional restoration services with photo documentation of each figure.

Sandy & Gary Franklin
Antique Carousel Figures
3818 South 9th St.
Arlington, VA 22204-1530
ph: 703-892-8666 or 703-624-2981
mycarousel@mycarousel.com
http://www.mycarousel.com
Carries large selection of antique carousel animals, figures and trim on the Internet; buys, sells, trades; museum quality restorations; broker service.

Marsha A. Schloesser
Carousel Workshop, The
29915 Fullerville Rd.
Deland, FL 32720-5704
ph: 352-669-6449
fax: 352-669-5573
carouselworkshop@yahoo.com
http://www.carouselworkshop.com
Dealer and lecturer; buys, sells,
restores carousel figures; also gliding & rocking horses; antique and reproduction carousel figures.

Sherrell Anderson
Carousel Magic!
P.O. Box 1466
Mansfield, OH 44901-1466
ph: 419-526-4009
fax: 419-526-4561
carmagic@richnet.net
http://carouselmagic.com
Highest quality custom made full size carousels, individual animals, restorations, carving classes and carving kits.

Dan & Judy Landino
D & J Restorations
37037 E. Almont
Sterling Heights, MI 48310
ph: 810-268-8692
djlrest@comcast.net
http://www.dnjauctions.com
Over 35 years experience in restoration of antiques: from carousel figures and antique furniture to soda machines and license plates.

Craig Swanson
Midwest Carousel Organization
1952 Lake Dr.
Independence, MO 64055-1863
ph: 816-685-6602 or 800-896-9661
extra@finest1.com
http://www.finest1.com/hand
World famous woodcarver, professional animal restorations; also buys, sells, and trades.

Marlene Irvin
Custom Carving & Restoration
P.O. Box 771331
454 Acadia
Wichita, KS 67212
ph: 316-722-1872
ccrmar@att.net
http://home.att.net/~ccrmar
Carves and restores carousel figures; experienced in antique wood, new wood, metal and fiberglass; has access to fiberglass for custom-made, one-of-a-kind horses; does restorations for home and commercial use.

John & Cathy Daniel
720 Mission St.
South Pasadena, CA 91030
ph: 323-682-3557
jadsden1@aol.com
Collects, restores, appraises carousel animals; also supplies twisty brass tubing and carousel stands for collectors.

Pam Hessey
Hawk's Eye Studio
145 Hillside Lane
Martinez, CA 94553
ph: 925-228-7309
pam@hawkseyestudio.com
http://www.hawkseyestudio.com
Professional restoration of classic carousel horses and other figures.

Bill Hughes
Hughes Carousel Restoration
10325 Dougherty Ave.
Morgan Hill, CA 95037-9241
ph: 408-778-5077
Museum quality restorations.

Repro. Sources

Bob Morris
Wooden Horse Studio, The
11152 Kootenay Path
Lakeview, OH 43331
ph: 937-843-3346
http://www.woodenhorsestudio.com
Contemporary carvings; does not do reproductions.

Joe & Susan Leonard
Custom Woodcarving
12107 St. Rt. 88
Garrettsville, OH 44231
ph: 330-527-2307
Specializing in restoring and carving carousel figures.

Sherrell Anderson
Carousel Magic!
P.O. Box 1466
Mansfield, OH 44901-1466
ph: 419-526-4009
fax: 419-526-4561
carmagic@richnet.net
http://carouselmagic.com
Highest quality custom made full size carousels, individual animals, restorations, carving classes and carving kits.

Suppliers

Sally Craig
Nostalgia
336 W. High St.
Elizabethtown, PA 17022-2140
ph: 717-295-9188
Reins, horse hair tails, stirrups, jewels, twisted brass; send SASE for list; also sells antique carousel horses and other figures.

Marsha A. Schloesser
Carousel Workshop, The
29915 Fullerville Rd.
Deland, FL 32720-5704
ph: 352-669-6449
fax: 352-669-5573
carouselworkshop@yahoo.com
http://www.carouselworkshop.com
Sells carousel supplies: cast iron and wood bases, brass poles, glass eyes, reins, stirrups, jewels.

Miniature

Clubs/Associations

Jerry Defenderfer
Miniature Carousel Builders, Inc.
2746 Warmspring Rd.
Chambersburg, PA 17201
ph: 717-375-4256

Patrick Wentzel
Carousel Modelers & Miniatures
  Association
Magazine: Horse Tales
2310 Highland Ave.
Parkersburg, WV 26101-2920
ph: 304-428-3544
  *Formed in 1986 for those interested in
  the building miniature carousels and
  related items.*

Collectors

Patrick Wentzel
2310 Highland Ave.
Parkersburg, WV 26101-2920
ph: 304-428-3544
  *Wants to buy carousel, carnival,
  amusement park, and circus items
  including photographs, miniature
  carvings, books, and related articles.*

Suppliers

Patrick Wentzel
2310 Highland Ave.
Parkersburg, WV 26101-2920
ph: 304-428-3544
  *Sells scale wood carving kits in 1", 1-
  1/2", and 2" scales; over 50 different
  kits available.*

CARPENTER ITEMS

(see ARCHITECTURE & RELATED
ITEMS)

CARPET SWEEPERS

(see VACUUM CLEANERS)

CARRIAGES

(see HORSE-DRAWN VEHICLES,
Carriages)

CARS

(see AUTOMOBILES; AUTOMOBILIA;
AUTO RACING MEMORABILIA;
KITS; MILITARIA, Vehicles;
MODELS, Cars; TOYS, Diecast;
TRAILERS & RVs)

CARTE-DE-VISITES

(see CIVIL WAR ARTIFACTS,
Photographs; PHOTOGRAPHS)

CARTOON ART

(see also ANIMATION FILM ART;
CHARACTER COLLECTIBLES;
COMIC BOOKS; COMIC STRIPS,
Sunday Newspaper; POLITICAL
COLLECTIBLES, Nast Cartoons;
POPULAR CULTURE; POSTERS,
Cartoon; SCIENCE FICTION)

Clubs/Associations

National Cartoonists Society
Magazine: Cartoonist, The
Columbus Circle Station
P.O. Box 20267
New York, NY 10023
http://www.reuben.org
  *World's largest and most prestigious
  organization of professional
  cartoonists.*

Collectors

Timothy F. Isaacson
1002 Clinton
Oak Park, IL 60304
ph: 708-383-5646
moeknows1007@msn.com
  *Wants to buy original (cover)
  paintings; paintings that were used
  for the cover art for pulps, magazines,
  paperback and digest books, and
  movie posters: lurid, sleazy dames,
  hard boiled detective action, sexy gals,
  monsters, sci-fi, etc.*

Bill Bush
P.O. Box 61868
Houston, TX 77208-1868
  *Wants to buy original cartoons and
  comic art by Caniff, Baker, Eisner,
  Interlandi, Kaufman, Kremos, Lichty,
  Machamer, Priscilla, Rayon, Ross,
  Ben Roth, Shermund, Simms
  Campbell, Troop, Wenzel, Wood, and
  Wolfe.*

Lee Aronsohn
16430 Westfall Place
Encino, CA 91436
ph: 818-905-0225
fax: 818-905-6334
overpaid@metawire.com
  *Collects material relating to
  cartoonist Gary Trudeau and the
  "Doonesbury" comic strip; also wants
  humorous 3-D postcards marked
  "Eden Plastics," "Postplax," or
  "Cardell."*

Dealers

Bill & Joanne Bruegman
Toy Scouts, Inc.
137 Casterton Ave.
Akron, OH 44303-1543
ph: 330-836-0668
orders@toyscouts.com
http://www.toyscouts.com
  *Wants to buy original artwork from
  comic books, especially super hero;
  artists such as Jack Kirby, Steve
  Ditko, Will Eisner, John Comita.*

Robert A. LeGresley
727 St. John's Mine Rd.
Vallejo, CA 94951
ph: 707-648-9377
rlegres@aol.com
  Buys and sells original comic art.

Bill Asprey
Cartoon World
P.O. Box 14384
London, NW11 6WS U.K.
ph: 020 8455 3906
fax: 020 8455 3906
info@cartoonworld.org
http://www.cartoonworld.org
  *Buys and sells original cartoons,
  comic strips, and political cartoons.*

Experts

Frederick P. Dose, Jr.
Frederick Dose Appraisals Ltd.
778 Pleasant Ave.
Highland Park, IL 60035-4613
ph: 847-433-7870 or 847-433-1090
fdoseappraisals@comcast.net
  *Has verified and valued over 60,000
  original gag and political cartoons
  for the Cartoon Museum of Ohio State
  University, plus 5,000 Chester Gould
  Dick Tracy and Gravies strips.*

Museums/Libraries

International Museum of Cartoon Art
201 Plaza Real
Boca Raton, FL 33432
ph: 561-391-2200
fax: 561-391-2721
correspondence@cartoon.org
http://www.cartoon.org

Curator
Cartoon Research Library, University of
  Ohio
023L Wexner
27 West 17 Avenue Mall
Columbus, OH 43210-1393
ph: 614-292-0538
fax: 614-292-9101
cartoons@osu.edu
http://www.lib.ohio-state.edu
  *Houses more than 200,000 original
  cartoons including editorial cartoons,
  comic strips, sports cartoons,
  magazine cartoons, and comic book
  art; several hundred cartoonists are
  represented including Milton Caniff
  and Walt Kelly.*

Consortium of Popular Culture
  Collections
Popular Culture Library
Bowling Green State University
Bowling Green, OH 43403-0001
ph: 419-372-2450
fax: 419-372-7996
atracy@bgnet.bgsu.edu
http://www.bgsu.edu/colleges/library/pcl/
cpccm.html
  *Consortium composed of Bowling
  Green State U., Kent State U.,
  Michigan State U., and Ohio State U.;
  the largest academic library
  collections of primary research
  material in comic art, popular fiction,
  popular music, performing arts.*

Cartoon Art Museum, The
Newsletter: Cartoon Times
655 Mission St.
San Francisco, CA 94105
ph: 415-227-8666
fax: 415-243-8666
office@cartoonart.org
http://www.cartoonart.org
  *Exhibits, collects and studies original
  cartoon art from comic strips, comic
  books, animation, magazines and
  editorial cartoons; galleries contain
  an overview of cartoon art in all
  forms and features rotating
  exhibitions; bookstore.*

San Francisco Academy of Comic Art
170 W. Cliff Dr., #15
Santa Cruz, CA 95060-5432
ph: 831-427-1737
fax: 831-427-1737
  *Millions of newspaper strips, bound
  files, major dailies from 1890-1960,
  pulps, all science fiction, crime
  fiction, film history, children's books,
  comic books; excellent copies made of
  all graphic material; dup material for
  trade.*

Comics

Collectors

John S. Fawcett
P.O. Box 1156
Waldoboro, ME 04572-1156
ph: 207-832-7398
fawcetoy@gwi.net
http://home.gwi.net/~fawcetoy
  *Wants to buy original comic art:
  wants original Krazy Kat by George
  Herriman, original Lone Ranger art
  and pulp cover paintings of Lone
  Ranger; also Pogo originals by Walt
  Kelly.*

Dealers

Jack Gilbert
P.O. Box 122
New York, NY 10014
ph: 212-242-5535
fax: 212-242-5536
  *Specializes in original classic comic
  strip art.*

Milton Caniff

Collectors

Bill Bush
P.O. Box 61868
Houston, TX 77208-1868
  *Wants to buy Milton Caniff sketches,
  color guides and proofs, letters,
  photos, audios, VHS videos and other
  ephemera.*

Periodicals

Journal: Caniffites Journal
P.O. Box 32
Manitou Springs, CO 80829 Canada
specproductions@msn.com
http://www.specproductions.com
  *Members focus on the works of Milton
  Caniff - original art or Sunday comic
  strips: Terry and the Pirates, Steve*

Canyon, etc.; newsletter published 4 times a year.

Walt Kelly

Experts

Steve Thompson
6908 Wentworth Ave. South
Minneapolis, MN 55423-2363
ph: 612-869-6320
thomp034@tc.umn.edu
Internationally-known bibliographer and biographer of Walt Kelly and "Pogo;" active collector of unusual and esoteric Kellyana.

CARTRIDGES

(see AMMUNITION & EXPLOSIVE ORDNANCE)

CARTS

(see RIDING TOYS)

CASH REGISTERS

Clubs/Associations

Mike Hennessey
Cash Register Collectors Club
Newsletter: Bronze Idol
P.O. Box 20534
Dayton, OH 45420-0534
ph: 937-433-3529

Collectors

Hayne Dominick
8300 Highgrove Circle
White Plains, MD 20695
ph: 301-638-1969
fax: 301-638-1969
domndom@aol.com
Buying early and unusual cash registers; specializing in antique wooden and brass National Cash Registers, related memorabilia & advertising; sales, repairs and restorations.

Lewis
18915 Los Palominos Dr.
Yorba Linda, CA 92886-2649
ph: 714-970-8390
BookEmDano@webtv.net
Wants to buy cash registers and related items, especially small wooden, figural, ornate, unusual machines.

Dealers

Bill Heuring
Hickory Bend Antiques & Collectibles
2995 Drake Hill Rd.
Jasper, NY 14855-9715
ph: 607-792-3343
fax: 607-792-3309
Cash registers bought and sold; professional restoration and repair; also sells parts.

Hayne Dominick
8300 Highgrove Circle
White Plains, MD 20695
ph: 301-638-1969
fax: 301-638-1969
domndom@aol.com
Buying early and unusual cash registers; specializing in antique wooden and brass National Cash Registers, related memorabilia & advertising; sales, repairs and restorations.

Brass Cash Register Shoppe
P.O. Box 2176
Mishawaka, IN 46544
ph: 219-255-7977
fax: 219-258-9796
hallwood@worldnet.att.net
http://www.brasscashregisters.com
Specializes in parts, professional repair and restoration of antique fancy brass or wood case cash registers; free appraisals.

Experts

John Gillman
2125 Seneca St.
Kingman, AZ 86401
ph: 520-753-1192
Buys, sells, repairs and completely restores NCR cash registers for customers throughout the US.

Henry Bartsch
Antique Registers
P.O. Box 444
Rockaway Beach, OR 97136-0444
ph: 503-355-2932
Author of "Antique Cash Registers 1880-1920;" offers antique cash register sales and service.

Repair Services

Bill Heuring
Hickory Bend Antiques & Collectibles
2995 Drake Hill Rd.
Jasper, NY 14855-9715
ph: 607-792-3343
fax: 607-792-3309
Cash registers bought and sold; professional restoration and repair; also sells parts.

Andy Karaffa
1875 S. Pearl St.
Denver, CO 80210
ph: 303-744-1615
akaraffa@aol.com
Repairs antique brass cash registers.

CASINO COLLECTIBLES

(see ASHTRAYS, Casino; GAMBLING COLLECTIBLES; GAMBLING COLLECTIBLES, Gambling Chips & Gaming Tokens; MATCHCOVERS, Casino)

CAST IRON ITEMS

(see also BANKS; FARM COLLECTIBLES, Cast Iron Seats; FIREPLACE ITEMS; GARDEN FURNITURE; KITCHEN COLLECTIBLES; METAL ITEMS; PAPERWEIGHTS, Cast Iron; STOVES; TARGETS; TOYS; WINDMILL COLLECTIBLES, Weights)

Collectors

Dave Johnson
113 Hix Ave.
Rye, NY 10580
ph: 914-967-4809
mrmunelite@aol.com
Wants cast iron match holders, string holders, etc.

Craig Dinner
P.O. Box 4399
Long Island City, NY 11104-0399
ph: 718-729-3850
ferrouswheel123@aol.com

Dealers

John & Nancy Smith
American Sampler
P.O. Box 371
Barnesville, MD 20838-0371
ph: 301-972-6250
Wants cast iron doorstops, figural bottle openers, doorknockers, paperweights, banks, bookends, etc.

Louis Picek
Main St. Antiques & Art
110 West Main
P.O. Box 340
West Branch, IA 52358-0340
ph: 319-643-2065
msantiques@bigplanet.com
Buys and sells figural iron of all types; offers a monthly list of items for sale.

Experts

Craig Dinner
P.O. Box 4399
Long Island City, NY 11104-0399
ph: 718-729-3850
ferrouswheel123@aol.com
Wants cast iron doorstops, figural bottle openers, doorknockers, paperweights, lawn sprinklers, shooting gallery targets, architectural items, etc.

Richard Tucker
Argyle Antiques
P.O. Box 262
Argyle, TX 76226-0262
ph: 940-464-3752
fax: 940-464-7293
lead1234@gte.net

Museums/Libraries

Birmingham Museum of Art
2000 8th Ave. N.
Birmingham, AL 35203
ph: 205-254-2566
fax: 205-254-2714
http://www.artsbma.org
Holds the Lamprecht Collection of decorative cast iron, the largest in the world.

Repair Services

Rocco V. DeAngelo
Antique Cast Iron
425 Hoose Rd.
Cherry Valley, NY 13320
ph: 607-264-3607
fax: 607-264-3607
Quality restoration of antique cast iron; sandblasting, painting, repair, fabrication of parts; garden furniture, urns, fences installed, handwrought iron, brass & iron beds, etc.

Cookware

Clubs/Associations

Gregory L. Stahl, Pres.
Wagner & Griswold Society
290 Chestnut St.
Clinton, MA 01510
ph: 978-368-6646
fax: 617-730-2819
webmaster@wag-society.org
http://www.wag-society.org
Community for collectors of cast iron and aluminum cookware.

Collectors

Jim Bell
P.O. Box 355
Swainsboro, GA 30401
ph: 912-237-7815
Wants to buy old cast iron cookware.

Patrick Bedwell
4200 Bohannon Dr.
Menlo Park, CA 94025
ph: 650-473-2456
Collector of cast iron cookware from manufacturers such as Griswold, Wagner, Wapak, Favorite, and Filley; Web site has historical information about these companies and lots of images of skillets, muffin pans, waffle irons, etc.

Steve Stephens
28 Angela Ave.
San Anselmo, CA 94960
ph: 415-453-7790
mcstevestephens@yahoo.com
Best to call early morning or late evening Pacific time.

Dealers

David G. Smith
Pan Man, The
P.O. Box 247
Perrysburg, NY 14129
ph: 716-532-5154
panman@panman.com
http://www.panman.com
Cast iron collector specializing in cast

iron muffin pans and broilers; has over 250 different patterns and/or variations; buys, sells and trades cast iron cookware; author of new "The Book of Griswold & Wagner."

LaVon Deatsman
609 1st St.
Lake Odessa, MI 48849
ph: 616-374-5482
Buys and sells Griswold and Wagner cast iron cookware items.

Bernie Ver Hey
623 Watkins Glen
Saint Charles, MO 63304-7905
ph: 636-922-3580
weehu@yahoo.com
http://verhey.tripod.com/mywebpage
Buys and sells Griswold, Wagner, Erie, Wapak, G.F. Filley, Favorite cast iron cookware.

Experts

David G. Smith
Pan Man, The
P.O. Box 247
Perrysburg, NY 14129
ph: 716-532-5154
panman@panman.com
http://www.panman.com
Cast iron collector specializing in cast iron muffin pans and broilers; has over 250 different patterns and/or variations; buys, sells and trades cast iron cookware; author of new "The Book of Griswold & Wagner."

Periodicals

David G. Smith, Ed.
Newsletter: Kettles 'n' Cookware
P.O. Box 247
Perrysburg, NY 14129
ph: 716-532-5154
panman@panman.com
http://www.panman.com
Focuses on cast iron, aluminum, tin and other items made by the Griswold and other manufacturers.

Cookware (Griswold)

Clubs/Associations

Griswold & Cast Iron Cookware Association
Newsletter: Pan Handler, The
P.O. Box 552
Saegertown, PA 16433
ph: 814-763-4819
fax: 814-763-1567
dmosier@griswoldcookware.com
http://www.gcica.org
The first national organization for collectors of fine cast iron cookware; members interested in cast iron and aluminum by makers such as Wagner, Favorite, Martin, Filley, etc; educates and shares information; regional chapters.

Collectors

Sally Swanson
562 Shady Brook Circle W.
Girard, PA 16417
ph: 814-774-2166
Wants to buy cast iron items made by the Griswold Manufacturing Co.

Joe Noto
54 Macon Ave.
Asheville, NC 28801
ph: 828-258-0077
fax: 828-258-0077
drjono@aol.com
Past president of Griswold & Cast Iron Cookware Association; publisher of the G&CICA national newsletter, "The Pan Handler."

Dealers

Scott Lamb
1550 Kennelworth Court
State College, PA 16801
ph: 814-237-3303
Buys, sells, trades Griswold cast iron cookware.

Larry & Sue Foxx
400 Creek Rd.
Carlisle, PA 17013-9645
ph: 717-243-9231
Interested in collecting cast iron, aluminum, tin and other items made by the Griswold Manufacturing Co., Erie, PA; also wants items marked Selden & Griswold and Erie.

Cookware (Wagner)

Collectors

Joe Noto
54 Macon Ave.
Asheville, NC 28801
ph: 828-258-0077
fax: 828-258-0077
drjono@aol.com
Past president of Griswold & Cast Iron Cookware Association; publisher of the G&CICA national newsletter, "The Pan Handler."

CATALOGS

(see also ADVERTISING COLLECTIBLES; AUCTION CATALOGS; HARDWARE; MACHINERY & EQUIPMENT, Catalogs; MAGAZINES; PAPER COLLECTIBLES; PLUMBING; SEEDS)

Christmas

Dealers

Christmas Catalog Collector, The
175 East Delaware, #7403
Chicago, IL 60611-1731
ph: 800-879-6948 or 312-337-3123
fax: 312-266-7982
Seeks toy and Christmas catalogs and flyers from Sears, Wards, all retailers, wholesalers and manufacturers; also buying toy magazines and

general merchandise catalogs if containing many toys.

Mail Order

Dealers

Judith J. Hesson
Hesson Collectables
1261 S. Lloyd
Lombard, IL 60148-4234
ph: 630-627-3298
Buys & sells original mail order catalogs: Sears, Montgomery Ward, Penny, Aldens, Spiegel: 1900-1990; also other catalogs; send $4 for list of 2000 for sale.

Trade

(see also ADVERTISING COLLECTIBLES; MACHINERY & EQUIPMENT, Catalogs; MAGAZINES)

Collectors

Tom Rutledge
3015 Bever Ave., SE
Cedar Rapids, IA 52403-3028
ph: 319-399-1427
Wants to buy old trade catalogs and flyers; all companies desired; all retailers, wholesalers, manufacturers, distributors, etc.

Don Hooper
Vintage Plumbing Bathroom Antiques
9645 Sylvia Ave.
Northridge, CA 91324-1756
ph: 818-772-1721
fax: 818-772-4647
vintageplumbing@juno.com
http://www.vintageplumbing.com
Wants early pre-1910 plumbing trade catalogs showing ornamental bath fixtures.

Peter Morris
2 Lisa Court
Hammonds Plains, NS B4B 1K4 Canada
ph: 902-835-7692
Wants to buy all Canadian horse-drawn vehicle trade catalogs, very early (c. 1860s) American horse-drawn vehicle trade catalogs, and other very early trade catalogs.

Dealers

Steve Finer
38 Grinnell St.
Greenfield, MA 01302-3621
ph: 413-773-5811
finerbks@crocker.com

Joseph F. Loccisano
Historic Photographs & Paper Americana
2264 Nicholson Square Dr.
Lancaster, PA 17601-3966
ph: 717-560-5182
always_buying@yahoo.com
http://www.always-buying.com
Wants to buy early high quality trade catalogs illustrating hardware specialties, cast iron toys, architecturals, garden ornaments, hitching posts, stable fixtures,

occupational supplies, millwork, stained glass windows, etc.

Kenneth Schneringer
Old-Paper.Com
271 Sabrina Ct.
Woodstock, GA 30188-4228
ph: 770-926-9383
trademan68@aol.com
http://www.old-paper.com
Buys and sells trade catalogs, old paper and other ephemera.

Judith J. Hesson
Hesson Collectables
1261 S. Lloyd
Lombard, IL 60148-4234
ph: 630-627-3298
Buys and sells trade catalogs: sports, fashion, hardware, architectural, wholesale, retail; send $4 for list of 900 for sale.

Trade (Furniture)

Museums/Libraries

Christian G. Carron
Grand Rapids Public Museum
272 Pearl St. NW
Grand Rapids, MI 49504-5371
ph: 616-456-3977
fax: 616-456-3873
staff@grmuseum.org
http://www.grmuseum.org
Large collection of 20th century furniture and furniture manufacturing trade catalogs.

Trade (Homebuilding)

Collectors

Charles W. Wardell
P.O. Box 195
Trinity, NC 27370-0195
ph: 336-434-1145
Wants early (1870-1910) manufacturers' catalogs of ornate builders' hardware such as doorknobs, escutcheon plates, doorknobs, store door handles, etc.

Jerry L. Wilson
1002 E. Main St.
P.O. Box 220
Cherryvale, KS 67335-0220
ph: 620-336-2495
ringstaff@cox.net
Wants to buy millwork or sash & door company catalogs from the 1800s to 1920; also wants any other building related catalogs such as stained glass, paint, general hardware, metal ceilings, etc. from the same era.

Trade (Kitchen Collectibles)

Collectors

Reid Cooper
32942 Josheroo Ct.
Temecula, CA 92592
ph: 909-302-3348
res20rs2@verizon.net
Advanced collector/researcher wants to buy pre-1920 trade catalogs of kitchen implements, gadgets,

eggbeaters, etc.; also interested in old advertising, billheads, and trade cards that relate to same; send price, sample photocopy.

CAVE RELATED ITEMS

Collectors

Jack Speece
711 East Atlantic Ave.
Altoona, PA 16602-5405
ph: 814-946-3155 or 814-342-0470
fax: 814-342-5660
Wants items pertaining to caves, caverns, speleo history and folklore.

Bert Ashbrook
Cave Investigation & Exploration
1257 Lehigh Parkway South
Allentown, PA 18103-3875
ph: 610-797-3981
Collects books, ephemera, antiques, and memorabilia related to caves, commercial caverns, wild caves, cave history, and cave science.

Anthony Glab
6708 Duluth Ave.
Baltimore, MD 21222-1011
ph: 410-633-5354
z.zz@verizon.net
Wants to buy cave memorabilia such as paperweights, signs, souvenirs, etc.

Gordon Smith
P.O. Box 217
Marengo, IN 47140-0217
ph: 812-945-5721
CaveMuseum@aol.com
Wants items pertaining to caves and caverns: books, pamphlets, brochures, photos, souvenir plates and spoons, stereo views, sheet music, etc.

CELEBRITIES

(see AUTOGRAPHS; MOVIE MEMORABILIA; PERSONALITIES; PHOTOGRAPHS, Celebrity; TELEVISION SHOWS & MEMORABILIA)

CELLULOID ITEMS

(see also ALBUMS)

Auction Services

Kurt R. Krueger
Krueger Auctions
P.O. Box 275
Iola, WI 54945-0275
ph: 715-445-3845
fax: 715-445-4100

Collectors

John Andreae
P.O. Box 156
Granger, IN 46530-0156
ph: 219-675-9960
fax: 219-675-9961
jkandreae@aol.com
Wants celluloid pieces with advertising on them: pocket mirrors,

pin-back buttons, bookmarks and blotters; anything that is made of celluloid and that has advertising on it.

Andra Behrendt
P.O. Box 217
Western Springs, IL 60558
ph: 708-246-2676
andra@lady-a.com
http://www.lady-a.com
Collects decorative Celluloid glove, collar, trinket, dresser set boxes and celluloid autograph albums; must be in mint condition; also wants 1895-1910 catalogs that advertise these items.

Sherry & Mike Miller
303 Holiday Dr. #130
Tuscola, IL 61953-2118
ph: 217-253-4991
miller1@net66.com
Wants to buy Victorian era boxes which held collars/cuffs, gloves, neckties, shaving sets, etc.; also photograph albums and autograph albums; must have lithograph prints of scenes or people; all covered in thin layer of clear Celluloid.

Dealers

Judith Rubin
This Time Around Antiques
9226 Cynthia St.
Manassas Park, VA 20111
ph: 703-330-8167
Buys and sells Victorian (1895-1910) celluloid boxes (collar/cuff, vanity, etc.), photo albums, autograph albums, 3-way shaving mirrors; excellent condition only; contents not necessary in boxes or albums; no ivorine, or French ivory.

Andra Behrendt
Lady A Antiques
P.O. Box 217
Western Springs, IL 60558
ph: 708-246-2676
andra@lady-a.com
http://www.lady-a.com
Buys, sells and collects decorative Celluloid glove, collar, trinket, dresser set boxes and celluloid autograph and photograph albums; must be in mint condition; also wants 1893-1910 catalogs that advertise these items.

Experts

Julie P. Robinson
P.O. Box 117
Upper Jay, NY 12987
ph: 518-946-7753
celuloid@frontiernet.net
Identification of natural and synthetic moldable materials: Gutta Percha, Vulcanite, Horn, Tortoise shell, Ivory imitations, Celluloid, Casine, bakelite, Beetleware, Acrylic, Acetate, and early poly plastics; written extensively.

Museums/Libraries

National Plastics Center & Museum
210 Lancaster St.
Leominster, MA 01453
ph: 978-537-9529
fax: 978-537-3220
npcm@plasticsmuseum.org
http://www.plasticsmuseum.org
Follow the history of plastic from Egypt into the Millennium; see exhibits of celluloid toys and turn of the century combs.

CELS

(see ANIMATION FILM ART; AUDIO-VISUAL)

CERAMICS

(see also CALENDAR PLATES; COOKIE JARS; DINNERWARE; FAIRINGS; FIGURINES; HOWARD HOLT; OINTMENT POTS & POT LIDS; PRECOLUMBIAN; REPAIR/ RESTORATION/CONSERVATION; RAILROAD COLLECTIBLES, China; RESTAURANT COLLECTIBLES; STEINS; TILES)

Appraisers

David J. LeBeau
David J. LeBeau Appraisal Services
119 South Main St.
Sheffield, MA 01257
ph: 413-229-3445
djlebeau@rcn.com
http://www.appraisalbylebeau.com
Specializes in the appraisal of furniture, silver, ceramics and decorative arts; former ASA (1974-99) & Past Pres. NY Chapter ASA; retired Asst. Prof. Appraisal Studies NYU, founding faculty of Appraisal Studies program Yeshiva U.

Lynn Magnusson, AM
Personal Property Consultants, Inc.
271 Parsippany Rd.
Parsippany, NJ 07054
ph: 973-884-2466
fax: 973-884-1781
info@ppcappraisals.com
http://www.ppcappraisals.com
Specializes in the appraisal of furniture, ceramics, silver and other residential contents for insurance, equitable distribution, donation, matrimonial; offers expert witness and litigation services; appraisals comply with USPAP.

Karen J. Russo, G.G., ISA
Karen Jocelyn, Inc.
792 Partridge Dr.
P.O. Box 6795
Bridgewater, NJ 08807
ph: 908-526-8440
fax: 908-526-8348
Specializing in 19th and 20th century ceramics; has constant contact with metropolitan area galleries that

specialize in this area; appraisal, photography, market research.

Barbara M. Lessig, ISA CAPP
Pleasant Valley Antiques
21000 Georgia Ave.
Brookeville, MD 20833-1138
ph: 301-924-2293
fax: 301-570-1625
bmlessig@aol.com
http://www.lessigs.com
Specializes in the appraisal of glass, ceramics, silver, furniture, and household contents.

Paula Hantman, ASA
Hantman's Auctioneers & Appraisers
P.O. Box 59366
Potomac, MD 20859-9366
ph: 301-770-3720
fax: 301-770-4135
hantman@hantmans.com
http://www.hantmans.com
American, European and Asian antiques (furniture, porcelain, silver, decorative arts, Americana), collectibles, residential contents; estates; insurance replacement and damage claims; estate planning; family division; also auctioneer.

Christine N. Corbin, ISA
Motley's Auctions, Inc.
4402 West Broad St.
Richmond, VA 23230
ph: 804-355-2100
fax: 804-359-6954
cncorbin@motleys.com
http://www.motleysgroup.com
Auctioneers and appraisers of furniture, silver, fine art, decorative arts, real estate, general goods and vehicles.

Louise Phillips
Alexander Appraisal Service
3116 Weddington Rd. #900 PMB 190
Matthews, NC 28105
ph: 704-849-7352
flownlogic@aol.com
Specializes in appraising furniture, silver, ceramics as well as antiques & residential contents for insurance, liquidation, marital dissolution; also consulting services for clients wishing to sell their items in the highest, best market.

Caroline T. Gray, ISA CAPP
Thistle, The
P.O. Box 220064
Charlotte, NC 28222-0064
ph: 704-365-4539
fax: 704-365-4539
cgray@carolina.rr.com
Certified Appraiser of Personal Property with the International Society of Appraisers; specializes in the appraisal of furniture, ceramics and silver.

Louis Craig
Craig Southeastern Appraisal Company
4714 Rosewll Rd.
Bldg 0, Ste. 2
Atlanta, GA 30342
ph: 404-254-1777
lcraig1122@aol.com
*Specializes in the appraisal and
restoration of porcelain, pottery and
fired objects; also appraisals of
residential contents for estates,
divorce, gift, insurance, loss.*

Judy L. Campbell
Judy L. Campbell Appraisal & Estate
Sales
5500 Summerset Dr.
Midland, MI 48640-2931
ph: 989-631-9263 or 989-631-4874
fax: 989-631-4874
go4nteks@aol.com
http://www.judycampbell.com
*Appraiser of antique furniture, fine &
decorative arts, American & European
paintings and sculpture, American and
European ceramics, antiques & 20th
century collectibles; also other
personal property.*

Patricia M. Knight
Finetooth Comb Antiques Research &
Appraisal Service
P.O. Box 1177
Ames, IA 50014-1177
ph: 515-292-9028
ftcres@aol.com
*Consultant and qualified appraiser of
ceramics of Oriental, European,
English and American origin or style,
including "American Satsuma;"
please send SASE for reply; does not
purchase; send SASE if requesting
return of photos.*

Sharon Niles
Carousel, Inc.
14409 Manchester Rd.
Ballwin, MO 63011
ph: 636-391-4900
fax: 636-391-3993
carouselinc@hotmail.com
*Specializes in the appraisal,
conservation and restoration of fine
porcelains.*

Linda H. Richard, ISA
Cajun Collection
3308 White Oak
Temple, TX 76502-3028
ph: 254-774-8608
cajun@vvm.com
http://www.vvm.com/~cajun
*Specializing in pottery, porcelain,
with emphasis on American &
European pottery.*

David Lackey
David Lackey Antiques
2311 Westheimer
Houston, TX 77098
ph: 713-942-7171
fax: 713-521-2546
davidlackey@earthlink.net
*Specialist in the appraisal of
ceramics, with a focus on Spode.*

Nancy Alison Martin, ASA
Nancy Martin Appraisals
ph: 626-304-0900
fax: 626-304-0928
namartin@pacbell.net
http://www.nancymartinappraisals.com
*Carefully researched and well
documented appraisals of antiques,
furniture, silver, ceramics, glass and
residential contents for litigation
support, compensation, insurance,
dissolution, estates, fraud and
charitable contribution.*

Kathryn Wolk, ISA
Antique Appraisal Services
P.O. Box 1834
Fallbrook, CA 92088
ph: 760-728-2346 or 760-505-7654
aprazit@earthlink.net
*Specializes in the appraisal of
ceramics, Orientalia, and furniture;
Accredited member of the International
Society of Appraisers and the
Appraisers National Association.*

Kathleen M. Bailey, AAA, ISA CAPP
Antique Appraisal & Estate Sale Service
- the Original
160 NW Gilman Blvd., Ste. #1
Issaquah, WA 98027
ph: 425-746-2777
fax: 425-746-3793
antiquabailey@aol.com
*Antiques specialist since 1973;
Certified ISA CAPP and AAA; estate
sales specialist; specialist in
American, English and Continental
furniture of the 18th and 19th
centuries, silver, glass, china,
enamels, decorative arts, Victoriana.*

Robert G. Jason-Ickes
3600 14th Ave., SE #19-201
Olympia, WA 98501
ph: 360-455-9914
fax: 360-459-7154
r.jason-ickes@attbi.com
*Specializes in American ceramics and
American art pottery; also lectures.*

Auction Services

Tom Harris Auction Center
203 South 18th Ave.
Marshalltown, IA 50158
ph: 641-754-4890
tomharris@tomharrisauctions.com
http://www.tomharrisauctions.com
*Specialized auctions of flint glass,
Sandwich, carnival, Pittsburgh; also
ceramics such as transferware, lustre,
historical Staffordshire, etc.*

Bonhams & Butterfields
7601 Sunset Blvd.
Los Angeles, CA 90046-2714
ph: 323-850-7500
fax: 323-850-5843
info@butterfields.com
http://www.butterfields.com

Clubs/Associations

Nancy K. Lester, Ex. Dir.
American Ceramic Circle
Journal: American Ceramic Circle
Journal
520 16th St.
Brooklyn, NY 11215
fax: 718-832-5446
nlester@earthlink.net
*Founded in 1970, a nonprofit
organization that promotes
scholarship and research in the
history, use, and preservation of
ceramics of all kinds, periods, and
origins; membership restricted;
Journal available for purchase by
public.*

San Francisco Ceramic Circle
P.O. Box 15163
San Francisco, CA 94115
ph: 415-752-3830
info@patricianantiques.com
http://www.patricianantiques.com/
sfcc.html
*Monthly lectures with lectures by
internationally renowned experts -
programs on Web site; affiliated with
the Fine Arts Museum of San
Francisco; a valuable resource for
anyone with an interest in antique
ceramics or ceramic art.*

FUSION: Ontario Clay & Glass
Association, The
Magazine: Fusion Magazine
225 Confederation Dr.
Toronto, Ontario M1G 1B2 Canada
ph: 416-438-8946
fax: 416-438-0192
2fusion@interlog.com
http://www.clayandglass.on.ca
*An arts organization dedicated solely
to makers and collectors of handmade
clay and glass; focuses on contemporary potters, glassmakers and their
products and techniques.*

Collectors

Shirley Vickers
Shirley Vickers School of China
Restoration
P.O. Box 688
Pine, AZ 85544-0688
ph: 928-476-3703
fax: 928-476-3703
shirley@shirleyvickers.com
http://www.shirleyvickers.com
*Will buy damaged pottery of any kind;
call or fax or write with descriptions
of damage and price.*

Dealers

Pat Dillon
Antique Legacy
P.O. Box 12
Portville, NY 14770
ph: 716-928-2334
info@etalinc.com
http://www.antiquelegacy.com
*Buys and sells hand painted china,
Limoges, Bavaria, Staffordshire,
majolica, etc.*

George Kamm
George Kamm's 20th Century Glass,
Pottery, Etc.
23 Phillip Dr.
Kirkwood, PA 17536-9511
ph: 717-529-3741
fax: 717-529-2042
gkamm@earthlink.net
http://www.artglass-pottery.com
*Sells contemporary art glass,
paperweights, pottery, Raku, animal
and bird figurines, and more.*

Kathy Hughes
Tudor House Galleries
4126 Park Rd., Ste. E.
Charlotte, NC 28209
ph: 704-676-4871 or 704-676-4872
fax: 704-676-5197
tudorhouse@aol.com
http://www.tudorhouse.com
*Buys, sells and appraises 18th and
19th century ceramics; Accredited
Member, International Society of
Appraisers.*

Karen M. Guido
Karen Michelle Antique Tiles
1835 US 1 South #119, PMB 243
Saint Augustine, FL 32084
ph: 904-471-3226
karen@antiquetiles.com
http://www.antiquetiles.com
*Specializing in American & English
tiles mostly from 1870 to 1950; pre-
Victorian, Aesthetic Movement, Art
Nouveau, Arts & Crafts, Art Deco,
Moderne; stock includes studio
potters, terracotta, hand painted,
majolica, molded, and more.*

Arthur Tedeschi
Premium Resale Investments
P.O. Box 763699
Dallas, TX 75376
ph: 972-709-5400
ecollectics@aol.com
http://www.rubylane.com/shops/
ecollectics
*Specializes in Nippon, Noritake,
Limoges, and Pickard hand painted
porcelain.*

Beth Marshall
Marshall's Brocante
8505 Broadway
San Antonio, TX 78217
ph: 210-804-6320
fax: 210-804-6321
info@marshallsbrocante.com
http://www.marshallsbrocante.com
*Carries large inventory of porcelain:
Royal Worcester, Meissen, Severs,
R.S. Prussia, Nippon, Dresden and
flow blue; also Harding Black
porcelain (from San Antonio, one of
America's best ceramic artists)*

Kathleen M. Bailey, AAA, ISA CAPP
Antique Appraisal & Estate Sale Service
 - the Original
160 NW Gilman Blvd., Ste. #1
Issaquah, WA 98027
ph: 425-746-2777
fax: 425-746-3793
antiquabailey@aol.com
Specialist in American, English, German, Continental ceramics, furniture, silver, glass, enamels, Victoriana and decorative arts of the 18th to 20th centuries; full service appraiser & estate sales since 1973.

Experts

Susan & Jim Harran
Moment In Time, A
208 Hemlock Dr.
Neptune, NJ 07753
antique208@msn.com
http://www.tias.com/stores/amit
Specializes in porcelains; authors of "World of Ceramics" column and the book "Dresden Porcelain Studios."

Allen Bagdade
Country Peasants, The
1325 North State Parkway, Apt. 15A
Chicago, IL 60610
ph: 312-397-1321
fax: 847-392-5848
ADBSDB@aol.com
Authors of "Warman's American Pottery & Porcelain" (Krause).

Dr. Dorothy I. Godfrey-Smith
TOSL Research Laboratory
Department of Earth Sciences
Dalhousie University
Halifax, Novia Scotia B3H 3J5 Canada
ph: 902-494-1451 or 902-494-2358
fax: 902-494-6889
digs@is.dal.ca
Offers an analytical service using thermoluminescence to analyze ceramic artifacts and art objects; used by museums, art galleries, private collectors and estate appraisers wishing to ensure authenticity of ceramic objects.

Man./Prod./Dist.

Dona Danziger
Clay Werks, Ltd.
4058 S. Main St.
P.O. Box 352
Exmore, VA 23350
ph: 757-414-0567
fax: 757-414-0571
info@claywerksltd.com
http://www.claywerksltd.com
Hand painted pottery and art tiles in current studio productions; brochures and shipping available.

Museums/Libraries

Schein-Joseph International Museum of
 Ceramic Art
New York College of Ceramics
Alfred University
Alfred, NY 14802
ph: 607-871-2421
fax: 607-871-2476
ceramicsmuseum@alfred.edu
http://www.ceramicsmuseum.alfred.edu
Permanent collection includes works by internationally recognized ceramic artists such as Rosanjin Kitaoji, Bernard Leach, Shoji Hamada, Lucie Rie; also Chinese funerary jars & tomb sculptures, Roman & Byzantine, European, American wares.

National Museum of American History
14th & Constitution Ave. NW
Washington, DC 20560
ph: 202-357-2700
webmaster@si.edu
http://www.si.edu/organiza/museums/
 nmah/nmah.htm

Houston Museum of Decorative Arts,
 The
201 High St.
Chattanooga, TN 37403
ph: 423-267-7176
houston@chattanooga.net
http://www.chattanooga.net/houston
Contains one of the world's finest collections of antique glass, furniture, and ceramics.

Ohio Ceramic Center, The Ohio
 Historical Society
P.O. Box 200
Crooksville, OH 43731
ph: 740-697-7021 or 800-752-2604
Devoted to the display of ceramic wares produced in east central Ohio.

George Gardiner Museum of Ceramic Art
111 Queen's Park
Toronto, Ontario M5S 2C7 Canada
ph: 416-586-8080
fax: 416-586-8085
mail@gardinermuseum.on.ca
http://www.gardinermuseum.on.ca
The only specialized museum of its kind in North America; internationally-renowned collection of ceramics ranging from Precolumbian artifacts of 3,000 BC to 20th-century wares from around the world including Europe and South America.

Periodicals

Lladro USA, Inc.
Newsletter: Lladro Antique News
1 Lladro Dr.
Moonachie, NJ 07074
ph: 201-807-1177 or 800-634-9088
fax: 201-807-1168
http://www.lladro.com
Focuses on the current secondary market values of Lladro's 3,000 hard-paste porcelain figurines produced since 1941; also covers history of hard-paste porcelain (1000 AD to present) such as Meissen, Sevres, Nymphenburg, etc.

Magazine: Ceramics Monthly
735 Ceramic Place
Westerville, OH 43081
ph: 614-523-1660
fax: 614-891-8960
editorial@ceramicsmonthly.org
http://www.ceramicsmonthly.org
Founded in 1953, has international distribution; articles on potters and ceramics artists worldwide, exhibitions, production processes, critical commentary, book & video reviews, clay & glaze recipes, kiln design, advice from experts.

Scott Publications
Magazine: Fired Arts & Crafts
P.O. Box 5000
Iola, WI 54945
ph: 715-445-5000 or 800-331-0038
fax: 715-445-4053
jonespub@jonespublishing.com
http://www.jonespublishing.com/
 magazine.htm
The "Bible" for the ceramic hobbyist since 1955; each monthly issue filled with projects and patterns, celebrity clips, new products, show listings, industry news, shoppers guides, book reviews, ads and classifieds.

Paradise Publications
Newsletter: Pottery Collectors Express,
 The
P.O. Box 221
Mayview, MO 64071-0221
ph: 816-584-6309

ABC Plates

Clubs/Associations

Dr. Joan M. George
ABC Collectors' Circle
Newsletter: ABC Collectors' Circle
 Newsletter
67 Stevens Ave.
Old Bridge, NJ 08857-2244
ph: 732-679-8924
fax: 732-679-6102
drjgeorge@nac.net
Collectors of educational plates and mugs in china, tin and glass; many collect only those with alphabet displayed; most prefer 19th century items; buy, sell, trade through quarterly newsletter.

Belleek

Clubs/Associations

Belleek Collectors' International Society
 (USA), The
Newsletter: Belleek Collector, The
9893 Georgetown Pike, Ste. 525
Great Falls, VA 22066
ph: 800-235-5335 or 703-847-6207
fax: 703-847-6201
visitorcentre@belleek.ie
http://www.belleek.ie/collectors1.htm
Membership of over 5,000; biennial conferences; for collectors of new or antique Belleek.

Jan Golaszewski
Belleek Collectors Group (UK)
5 Waterhall Ave.
Chingford
London, E4 6NB U.K.
ph: 020 8529 0510
jangolly@hotmail.com
For collectors of Irish Belleek; 4 gatherings per year spread across England; 2 newsletters per year.

Belleek Collectors' International Society
 (UK), The
Newsletter: Belleek Collector, The
21 Daleview Ave.
Chingford
London, C4B 6PJ U.K.
ph: 011 44 181 524 3279
visitorcentre@belleek.ie
http://www.belleek.ie/collectors2.htm
Membership of over 5,000; biennial conferences; for collectors of new or antique Belleek.

Collectors

Del E. Domke
16142 N.E. 15th St.
Bellevue, WA 98008-2711
ph: 425-643-3359
fax: 425-746-6363
delyicious@aol.com
http://hometown.aol.com/delyicious/
 index.html
Belleek collector, appraiser, expert; Web site dedicated to all Belleek china.

Dealers

Andrew Boyd
IBgifts
232 Frocess Rd.
Cloughmills, County Antim BT44 9PX
 Northern Ireland
ph: 0044 28 2763 8314
enquiry@ibgifts.com
http://www.ibgifts.com
Carries a full line of contemporary Belleek shipped direct from Ireland.

Experts

Miriam & Aaron Levine
Miriam & Aaron Levine Antiques
881 Whalley Ave.
New Haven, CT 06515
ph: 203-389-5440
fax: 203-387-3939
chivas1@prodigy.net

Jack Mulhern
3212 Winterset Dr.
Dayton, OH 45440-3630
ph: 937-426-2592
Collector specializes in Irish Belleek.

Kathleen Mitchell
Old Pump Antiques
P.O. Box 774
San Bruno, CA 94066-0774
ph: 650-588-9514 or 650-588-4894
fax: 650-875-7556
Buys, sells, appraises and specializes in 18th and 19th century porcelain including black mark Irish Belleek,

Dresden, and Meissen; also specializes in Irish Belleek stoneware.

Marion Langham
Irish Belleek Porcelain
Claranagh
Tempo
County Fermanagh, Northern Ireland
BT94 3FJ U.K.
ph: (44) 28 895 41247
fax: (44) 28 895 41 690
belleek@ladymarion.co.uk
http://www.ladymarion.co.uk
Author of "Irish Porcelain" and "Encyclopedia of Belleek Flower Holders;" great Web site about antique and contemporary Belleek; includes a price guide, marks, numbering system, and more.

Internet Resources

Del E. Domke
16142 N.E. 15th St.
Bellevue, WA 98008-2711
ph: 425-643-3359
fax: 425-746-6363
delyicious@aol.com
http://hometown.aol.com/delyicious/index.html
Web site has links to Belleek marks, Belleek for sale, other collector pages.

Brian Graham
Canada
bjgcelt@telus.net
http://www3.telus.net/bjgcelt
Lots of Belleek related information: identification, clubs, events.

Marion Langham
Irish Belleek Porcelain
Claranagh
Tempo
County Fermanagh, Northern Ireland
BT94 3FJ U.K.
ph: (44) 28 895 41247
fax: (44) 28 895 41 690
belleek@ladymarion.co.uk
http://www.ladymarion.co.uk
Author of "Irish Porcelain" and "Encyclopedia of Belleek Flower Holders;" great Web site about antique and contemporary Belleek; includes a price guide, marks, numbering system, and more.

Museums/Libraries

Museum of Ceramics at East Liverpool
400 E. 5th St.
East Liverpool, OH 43920-3134
ph: 330-386-6001 or 800-600-7180
webmaster@ohiohistory.org
http://www.ohiohistory.org/places/ceramics
Detailed exhibit of the local ceramic industry; "The East Liverpool, Ohio Pottery District: Identification of Manufacturers & Marks" by Wm. Gates, Jr. and Dana Ormerod can be obtained by contacting the museum.

Belleek (American)

Appraisers

Peggy Sebek, ISA, AAA
Century Antiques & Appraisals, Inc.
3255 Glencairn Rd.
Shaker Heights, OH 44122-3407
ph: 216-991-2356 or 216-533-5874
fax: 216-991-2935
peggys@hpyday.com
Specializes in and appraises American Belleek; also residential contents, Victorian furniture, and silver; Accredited Member of the International Society of Appraisers, Member of the Appraisers Association of America.

Blue & White Pottery

Clubs/Associations

Howard Gardner
Blue & White Pottery Club
Newsletter: Blue & White Pottery Club Newsletter
224 12th St. NW
Cedar Rapids, IA 52405-3913
ph: 319-362-8116
For collectors of blue and white stoneware, blue and white spongeware, and related blue stoneware; annual convention for members only; 650 members.

Dealers

Susan Lengyel
Dinnerware & More
P.O. Box 1402
Carmichael, CA 95609-1402
ph: 916-207-9983
TheFourLs@aol.com
http://members.aol.com/LIBBLU/homepage.htm
Appraiser, dealer, collector, expert in blue and white pottery; replacements for discontinued Staffordshire patterns such as Liberty Blue, Blue Danube.

Experts

Gregg Ellington
Upper Loft Antiques
47 Columbus St.
Wilmington, OH 45177
ph: 937-382-4311
Buys, sells, trades and collects graniteware and American ceramics including mochaware, yellowware, spatterware, spongeware, etc.; appraisals provided for a small fee; if writing, enclose SASE for reply.

Blue Willow

(see CERAMICS, Willow Pattern)

Borghese

Collectors

Chris Stanton
1126 Old Military Rd.
Arkadelphia, AR 71923
ph: 870-236-2411 x125 or 870-246-5317
fax: 870-246-5400
stanton@iosa.com
Wants to buy Borghese (a Washing-

ton, DC based company, 1912-1976) works of art and decorative accessories: lamps, figurines (especially animals), vases, bookends, framed pictures; must have original Borghese sticker on them.

Chalkware

Collectors

Joann Munson
4703 18th Ave. Ct.
Moline, IL 61265
ph: 309-764-3050
prizelady@qconline.com
Interested in communicating with other carnival chalkware collectors; has collected for over 17 years; collection of over 450 pieces.

Chintz

(see also CERAMICS [ENGLISH], Royal Winton)

Clubs/Associations

Chintz Connection
Newsletter: Chintz Connection Newsletter
P.O. Box 222
Riverdale, MD 20738-0222
ph: 301-937-8270
welshjo@webtv.net

Collectors

Bruce E. Thulin
69 Hanson's Landing Rd.
Ellsworth, ME 04605
ph: 207-667-5225
thulin@acadia.net
Wants floral pattern chintz ceramics with all over decoration: Royal Winton, Shelley, Lord Nelson, James Kent, Crown Ducal, Midwinter; teapots, plates, stacking teapots, cups, etc.

Dealers

Joyce Settel
Joyce Settel Ltd.
P.O. Box 94
Quogue, NY 11959-0094
ph: 516-288-0436
Specializes in English porcelain, Chintz, Royal Winton, James Kent, Lord Nelson, Crown Ducal.

Nancy Grigsby
Chintz Bug Antiques, The
2222 Highway 66, #10
Estes Park, CO 80517-8358
ph: 970-586-3161
fax: 970-586-2679
njghsl@frii.com
Partners with Harry Lipscomb.

Jane Fehrenbacher
Chintz Central
P.O. Box 50888
Pasadena, CA 91115
ph: 626-441-2490
fax: 626-441-4122
chintz4u@aol.com
http://www.chintznet.com
Buying and selling chintz; specializing

in English Chintz china, primarily Royal Winton, James Kent, Lord Nelson, and Crown Ducal; US agent for Chintz World International.

Dianne Brackett
Yesteryears Antiques
7780 Sierra Dr.
Granite Bay, CA 95746
ph: 916-797-7664 or 916-797-7663
deb1117@aol.com
http://www.chintznet.com/yesteryears
Buys and sells chintz by Royal Winton, James Kent, Lord Nelson, and Shelley.

Dianne Howerton
Royal Pair Antiques, The
105 Turnagain Place
Sequim, WA 98382-9360
ph: 360-582-3788
fax: 360-582-3790
dianne@olympus.net
Buys and sells English semi-porcelain chintzware in Royal Winton, Lord Nelson, James Kent, Midwinter, Myott, Crown Ducal, Ridgeway, Shelley, Wood & Sons and Empire Porcelain Co. patterns.

Dave Timney
2362 Meadowlark
Nanaimo, British Columbia V9T 3P1
Canada
ph: 250-758-4728
fax: 250-758-4728
dave@chintzchina.com
http://www.chintzchina.com
A weekly mailed newsletter that gives information about all of the currently available pictorial postmarks used by the United States Postal Service.

Experts

Susan Scott
882 Queen St. West
Toronto, Ontario M6J 1G3 Canada
ph: 416-538-8536
fax: 416-534-4814
SusanScottCA@aol.com
http://www.chintznet.com/susan
Specializing in chintz ceramics, especially by Royal Winton, Crown Ducal, James, Kent, Elijah Cotton; author of "Charlton Standard Catalogue of Chintz, 3rd Edition" (1999).

Internet Resources

Jane Fehrenbacher
ChintzNet
P.O. Box 50888
Pasadena, CA 91115
ph: 626-441-2490
fax: 626-441-4122
chintz4u@aol.com
http://www.chintznet.com
Chintz sellers ads, Chintz conventions.

Clay Art

Man./Prod./Dist.

Clay Art, Inc.
239 Utah Ave.
South San Francisco, CA 94080-6802
ph: 650-244-4970
fax: 650-244-4979
Specializes in collectible giftware and tabletop accessories; handcrafted ceramic masks, salt & peppers, cookie jars, creamers & sugars, mugs, plates, and more designed with a unique and whimsical nature.

Cups & Saucers

Experts

Susan & Jim Harran
Moment In Time, A
208 Hemlock Dr.
Neptune, NJ 07753
antique208@msn.com
http://www.tias.com/stores/amit
Authors of "Collectible Cups & Saucers," Books I, II, III; over 800 full color photos in Book II; history, dates, sizes, illustrations of shapes and handles, makers, prices, marks, catalog pages.

Don Winton

Clubs/Associations

Michael L. Ellis
Twin Winton Collector Club
266 Rose Lane
Costa Mesa, CA 92627
ph: 949-646-7112
fax: 949-645-4919
ellis5@pacbell.net
http://www.twinwinton.com

Elfinware

Dealers

Nadine Ketchum
Tulsa Antique Mall
7142 S. Memorial Dr.
Tulsa, OK 74133
ph: 918-252-4477
denny@cottagesoft.com
http://www.tulsaantiquemall.com

Roy M. Smith
Smith Place, The
16401 Redlands Lane
Huntington Beach, CA 92647-4042
ph: 714-842-8315
Elfinware is a mark found on Dresden-like porcelain that was sold in dime stores and gift shops; many pieces were decorated with raised flowers.

Flow Blue

Appraisers

Edward Tuten
Team Estate Sale & Appraisal
7007 McVay Place Dr.
Memphis, TN 38119
ph: 901-758-2659
fax: 901-758-2659
etuten551@aol.com
http://www.teamestatesales.com
Specializes in the appraisal of Flow Blue but also offers complete appraisal services for Memphis and the mid-South.

Robert G. Jason-Ickes
3600 14th Ave., SE #19-201
Olympia, WA 98501
ph: 360-455-9914
fax: 360-459-7154
r.jason-ickes@attbi.com

Clubs/Associations

James Swan, Mem.
Flow Blue International Collectors' Club, Inc.
Newsletter: Blue Berry Notes
P.O. Box 6664
Leawood, KS 66206
jswan@kc.rr.com
http://www.flowblue.org
For those interested in flow blue china; membership includes newsletter, regional meetings, sharing information with fellow collectors of Flow Blue and Mulberry china.

Judie Siddall
Transferware Collector's Club
734 Torreya Court
Palo Alto, CA 94303
ph: 650-494-7920
info@merlinantiques.com
http://www.transcollectorsclub.org
An organization of collectors, dealers and museum personnel interested in English transferware, c. 1760-1880.

Dealers

John Bove
Pedigree Antiques
61 West Shore Rd.
Bristol, NH 03222
ph: 603-744-5346
http://angelfire.com/nh/pedigreeantiques
Large selection of Flow Blue; also Roseville, Lundberg Art Glass, Majolica.

Anne & Dave Middleton
Pot O Gold Antiques
P.O. Box 124
Allenwood, NJ 08720-0124
ph: 732-528-6648
fax: 732-528-6648
anne@potogoldantiques.com
http://www.potogoldantiques.com
Interested in flow blue china, epergnes, and Historical Staffordshire.

Carl McCann
Troy & Black, Inc.
P.O. Box 228
Red Creek, NY 13143-0228
ph: 315-754-8115
Buys and sells high quality flow blue, Staffordshire figurines, American painted furniture, stoneware, redware, coverlets, samplers, and other American textiles, folk art, etc.

Louise M. Loehr
Louise's Old Things
131 Virginville Rd.
Kutztown, PA 19530-8862
ph: 610-683-6388
fax: 610-683-6865
louises@bellatlantic.net
http://www.louisesoldthings.com
Co-author of "Willow Pattern China." Specializing in willow, flow blue, and early children's china. Wants one piece or collections.

Experts

Mary Frank Gaston
P.O. Box 342
Bryan, TX 77806
Author of "Collector's Encyclopedia of Flow Blue China."

John W. Humphries
P.O. Box 965
Los Molinos, CA 96055-0965
jhantiques@hotmail.com
Author of "The Professionals Price Guide to Flow Blue."

Gaudy

Dealers

Luke Surrey
Glamorgan Antiques
Dysnni
Cardiff, Wales CF40 U.K.
luke@glamorganantiques.co.uk
http://www.glamorganantiques.co.uk
Quality British Web site offering genuine antique ceramics; specialist in Gaudy Welch and Swansea pottery; also glassware, silver, Art Deco.

Experts

John D. Querry
137B RR 2
Martinsburg, PA 16662
ph: 814-793-3185 or 814-693-7985
fax: 814-793-3802
jdquerryantiques@aol.com
Specializes in Gaudy Dutch; advisor to "Warman's Antiques & Collectibles Price Guide."

Handpainted

Clubs/Associations

World Organization of China Painters, The
Magazine: China Painter, The
2641 N.W. 10th St.
Oklahoma City, OK 73107-5407
ph: 405-521-1234
fax: 405-521-1265
wocporg@theshop.net
http://www.theshop.net/wocporg
Organization with 7000 members; online museum dedicated to handpainted china; seminars, courses, library.

Experts

Dorothy Kamm
P.O. Box 7460
Port Saint Lucie, FL 34985-7460
ph: 772-465-4008
dorothykamm@adelphia.net
Author of "American Painted Porcelain: Collector's Identification & Value Guide," "Antique Trader's Comprehensive Guide to American Painted Porcelain," and "Painted Porcelain Jewelry and Buttons: Identification and Value Guide."

Museums/Libraries

World Organization of China Painters, The
Magazine: China Painter, The
2641 N.W. 10th St.
Oklahoma City, OK 73107-5407
ph: 405-521-1234
fax: 405-521-1265
wocporg@theshop.net
http://www.theshop.net/wocporg
Museum houses examples of handpainted porcelain from all over the US and from several foreign countries.

Head Vase Planters

Clubs/Associations

Maddy Gordon
Head Vase Convention
Newsletter: Head Hunters Newsletter
P.O. Box 83H
Scarsdale, NY 10583-8583
ph: 914-472-0200 or 914-472-0227
maddy.Gordon@worldnet.att.net
Annual gathering of head vase collectors.

Collectors

Dan Morphy
121 Moorland Ct.
Lititz, PA 17543-8016
ph: 717-627-7270
Top dollar paid for Disney, Marilyn Monroe, unusual lady head vases.

Judi Crabb
412 Palmerland Dr.
Hope Mills, NC 28348
ph: 910-424-1560
jcrabb@nc.rr.com
Wants to buy head vase planters.

Dealers

Millie Miller
1027 Emory Lane
Indianapolis, IN 46241
ph: 317-241-4123
Buys, sells, or trades head vases.

Lois & Ralph Behm
Lois' Collectibles of Antique Market III
413 W. Main St.
Saint Charles, IL 60174-1815
ph: 630-377-5599 or 847-831-5997
fax: 847-831-5998
Buys and sells lady head vases; will buy entire collections.

Christina Stelzer
Chrissy's Lady Head Vases
10300 Grand Oak Dr.
Austin, TX 78750
ph: 512-918-2576
chrissy@chrissy.com
http://www.chrissy.com/heads.html
Offers a huge selection of Limoges and porcelain hinged boxes, Halcyon Days enamels, and Lady Head Vases.

Jennifer Sykes
Jennifer Sykes Antiques
9018 Balboa Blvd. #595
Northridge, CA 91325-2610
ph: 818-993-1916
fax: 818-993-7612
Veeda10@aol.com
Buys, sells Lady Head vases, especially those over 7" tall; also buying Head Vases by Betty Lou Nichols.

Experts

Maddy Gordon
P.O. Box 83H
Scarsdale, NY 10583-8583
ph: 914-472-0200 or 914-472-0227
maddy.Gordon@worldnet.att.net
Head vase collector, dealer and expert.

David L. Barron
Head Vase Collectors Corner
P.O. Box 7901
Columbus, MS 39705-7901
dlb@ebicom.net
http://www.ebicom.net/~dlb/heads.htm
Author of "Head Vases by Numbers 2001 Price Guide."

Mike Posgay
Mianco Partners
499 Main St. South
P.O. Box 93022
Brampton, Ontario L6Y 4V8 Canada
ph: 905-453-9074
Specializes in head-vase planters; co-author with Ian Warner of "Head Vases Identification and Values."

Ironstone (Mason's)

Clubs/Associations

Gerard Larkin Haverstock Esq.
Mason's Ironstone China Society
Glendermont House
109 Noble Ave.
Winnipeg, Manitoba R2L 0J5 Canada
ph: 204-667-3248 or 204-663-1151
fax: 204-667-3248
Non-profit society open to all; Purpose is to propagate the study and appreciation of the pottery and porcelain manufactured by Mason's Ironstone China Company of England; info as to patterns and marks; late 18th century to present.

Mason's Ironstone Collectors' Club
Newsletter: MICC Newsletter
c/o City Museum & Art Gallery
Stoke-on-Trent, ST1 3DW U.K.

Ironstone (Tea Leaf)

Clubs/Associations

Tea Leaf Club International
Newsletter: Tea Leaf Readings
P.O. Box 377
Belton, MO 64012
TeaLeafClubIntl@cs.com
http://www.tealeafclub.com
Purpose is to inform membership about Tea Leaf Ironstone and its copper lustre variants.

Collectors

Sheree Baker
1201 N. Garfield Ave.
Sand Springs, OK 74063
Sheree.Baker@att.net

Experts

Julie Rich
411 Kinross Dr.
Newark, DE 19711-1535
ph: 302-456-5769
fax: 302-454-8538
RRich411@aol.com
Buys, sells, collects and specializes in Tea Leaf & White Ironstone; writes and lectures on American ironstone, especially Tea Leaf.

Dale Abrams
Tea Leaf Ironstone China Home Page
960 Bryden Rd.
Columbus, OH 43205-1809
ph: 614-258-5258
fax: 614-258-6663
TLAntiques@aol.com
http://ourworld.cs/TeaLeafIronstone
Buys and sells quality Tea Leaf and Teaberry ironstone china and other white ironstone decorated with copper lustre motifs.

Ironstone (White)

Clubs/Associations

Diane Dorman, Mem.
White Ironstone China Association, Inc.
Newsletter: White Ironstone Notes
P.O. Box 855
Fairport, NY 14450-0855
Dieringer1@aol.com
http://www.whiteironstonechina.com

Collectors

Ernie & Bev Dieringer
Dieringer's Antiques
P.O. Box 536
Redding Ridge, CT 06876
fax: 203-938-8378
Dieringer1@aol.com
Editors of "White Ironstone Notes," newsletter for The White Ironstone China Association, Inc.; send email for membership information; ask about the Web site under construction; visit WICA's Web site at www.whiteironstonechina.com.

Rick Nielsen, ISA
Fleur-De-Lis Appraisals
1132 Westmoor Place
Saint Louis, MO 63131
ph: 314-997-7963
fax: 801-858-2907
rn1132@earthlink.net
http://home.earthlink.net/~rn1132a/harmonicas

Dealers

Dale Abrams
960 Bryden Rd.
Columbus, OH 43205-1809
ph: 614-258-5258
fax: 614-258-6663
TLAntiques@aol.com
http://ourworld.cs.com/TeaLeafIronstone
Expert and dealer buys and sells quality Tea Leaf and white ironstone china.

Experts

Julie Rich
411 Kinross Dr.
Newark, DE 19711-1535
ph: 302-456-5769
fax: 302-454-8538
RRich411@aol.com
Buys, sells, collects and specializes in Tea Leaf & White Ironstone; writes and lectures on American ironstone, especially Tea Leaf.

Jean Wetherbee
1415FF RR 2
Crescent City, FL 32112
ph: 386-698-0887
Author of "A Look at White Ironstone," "A Second Look at White Ironstone," and "White Ironstone: A Collector's Guide."

Jugs (Molded)

Experts

Kathy Hughes
Tudor House Galleries
4126 Park Rd., Ste. E.
Charlotte, NC 28209
ph: 704-676-4871 or 704-676-4872
fax: 704-676-5197
tudorhouse@aol.com
http://www.tudorhouse.com
Specializes in 19th century relief-molded jugs (pitchers); author of "A Collector's Guide to 19th Century Jugs" Vol. I and Vol. II.

Jugs (Puzzle)

Collectors

Don Berey
151 Prospect Ave., Ste. 7A
Hackensack, NJ 07601
ph: 201-498-0944
fax: 201-498-0988
Wants to buy puzzle jugs.

Kutani

Internet Resources

Georges Bouvier
Kutani Forum
France
mail@gbouvier.com
http://www.gbouvier.com
Kutani ceramics homepage; history of Kutani kilns from the origin to present; the site includes a virtual library and a virtual museum focusing on Kutani; comprehensive list of Kutani seals and marking; Kutani forum discussion group.

Lefton

Clubs/Associations

Loretta DeLozier
National Society of Lefton Collectors
Newsletter: Lefton Collector
P.O. Box 50201
Knoxville, TN 37950-0201
Members are interested in dinnerware and figurines made by Lefton.

Collectors

Loretta DeLozier
P.O. Box 50201
Knoxville, TN 37950-0201
Wants to buy Lefton porcelain dinnerware and figurines.

Experts

Karen Barton
14660 Sherwood Place
Burnsville, MN 55309
jbarton@frontiernet.net
http://members.ebay.com/aboutme/20thcenturylefton/
Author of "20th Century Lefton China & Collectibles."

Man./Prod./Dist.

John Lefton
Lefton Company, The
5750 McDermott Dr.
Berkeley, IL 60163
ph: 800-938-1800
fax: 888-609-8774
jlefton@leftonco.com
http://www.leftonco.com
The company was founded in 1941 by Hungarian immigrant George Zoltan Lefton.

Majolica

Auction Services

Amory Spizzirri, Client Svc.
William Doyle Galleries
175 E. 87th St.
New York, NY 10128-2205
ph: 212-427-2730
fax: 212-369-0892
info@doylegalleries.com
http://www.doylegalleries.com
Holds over 50 auctions annually of furniture and decorations, paintings and sculpture, jewelry, books and prints, couture and textiles, 20th century art & design, majolica, Lalique, Asian works of art and other specialty categories.

Michael G. Strawser
Majolica Auctions
200 North Main St.
P.O. Box 332
Wolcottville, IN 46795-0332
ph: 219-854-2859 or 219-854-2235
fax: 219-854-3979
michael@strawserauctions.com
http://www.strawserauctions.com
Specializing in majolica auctions in the US.

Clubs/Associations

Majolica International Society
Newsletter: Majolica Matters
1275 First Ave., PBO 103
New York, NY 10021-5601
ph: 212-969-0025
fax: 212-744-1124
secretary@majolicasociety.hypermart.net
http://www.majolicasociety.com
Conventions held in April/May each year with international speakers and show/sale; members are collectors, dealers, experts.

Debora Lamm
Pacific Northwest Majolica Club
Newsletter: Majolica Madness
16302 - 34th St. NE
Snohomish, WA 98290
ph: 425-334-6585
danes90@aol.com
http://members.aol.com/danes90/
homepage3.html

Collectors

Michael G. Strawser
200 North Main St.
P.O. Box 332
Wolcottville, IN 46795-0332
ph: 219-854-2859 or 219-854-2235
fax: 219-854-3979
michael@strawserauctions.com
http://www.strawserauctions.com

Dealers

Nancy Kramer
Sparrows Inc.
4115 Howard Ave.
Kensington, MD 20895-2417
ph: 301-530-0175 or 888-800-1235
fax: 301-530-0189
sparrows@sparrows.com
http://www.sparrows.com
Specializes in mid-19th through mid 20th century French majolica.

Hardy Hudson
Our Antiques Market
5453 Lake Howell Rd.
Winter Park, FL 32792-1033
ph: 407-657-2100 or 407-444-9009
todiefor@mindspring.com
Serious buyer of majolica by Minton, George Jones, Holdcroft, Wedgwood, Fielding, Copeland, Etruscan, James Carr, Royal Worcester, and Brown, Westhead & Moore; majolica oyster plates.

Experts

Nicholas Dawes
67 East 11th St.
New York, NY 10003-4613
ph: 212-473-5111
fax: 212-353-3845
nmdawes@aol.com
Buys, sells and specializes in Victorian majolica; author of "Majolica" (Crown Publishers, 1989).

Linda Ketterling
Linda Ketterling Antiques
3202 E. Lincolnshire Blvd.
Toledo, OH 43606-1207
ph: 419-536-5531
Buys & sells 19th century majolica, with emphasis on English, but including good quality pieces from many countries.

Brenda Wilson
2720 N. 45th Rd.
Manton, MI 49663
ph: 616-824-3043
fax: 616-824-9357
Will answer collectors questions to help identify majolica; please include SASE for reply.

Majolica (Palissy Ware)

Experts

Marshall P. Katz
Gateway Towers, Ste. 24A
Pittsburgh, PA 15222
ph: 412-471-1600
fax: 412-471-0250
palissy@usaor.net
http://www.palissy.com
Co-author with Robert Lehr of "Palissy Ware: Nineteenth Century French Ceramists From Avisseau to Renoleau" and "Portuguese Palissy Ware: A Survey of Ceramics From Caldas da Rainha;" write for list of dealers specializing Palissy ware.

Mexican

Collectors

Kier Linn
P.O. Box 641824
Los Angeles, CA 90064
ph: 310-477-5229
fax: 310-313-4738
dcrehr@earthlink.net
Seeking Mexican pottery sold to tourists from the 1930s to 1960s; of particular interest are large pieces, and those with black backgrounds in design.

Military Related

Collectors

Rex Stark
P.O. Box 1029
Gardner, MA 01440-6029
ph: 978-630-3237
fax: 978-630-2388
rexstark@yahoo.com
Wants to buy china with American political and military portraits or scenes; Liverpool, lustreware, parian ware, Staffordshire, etc.

Mochaware

Experts

Gregg Ellington
Upper Loft Antiques
47 Columbus St.
Wilmington, OH 45177
ph: 937-382-4311
Buys, sells, trades and collects graniteware and American ceramics including mochaware, yellowware, spatterware, spongeware, etc.; appraisals provided for a small fee; if writing, enclose SASE for reply.

Picasso Editions

Collectors

Albert Merola
Universal Fine Objects, Inc.
424 Commercial St.
Provincetown, MA 02657
ph: 508-487-4424
fax: 508-487-4743
ufoarts@attbi.com
http://www.universalfineobjects.com
Fine art dealer in contemporary prints, paintings, and ceramic;

primary interest is Picasso ceramic editions and other Madoura ceramics.

Brian Hourican
33347 MartinLuther King, Jr. Way
Berkeley, CA 94703
ph: 510-658-9050

Pixieware

(see also HOLT HOWARD)

Collectors

Walter Dworkin
8 Rugby Rd.
Westbury, NY 11590
ph: 516-334-4674
Collects Pixieware - those oh-so-cute ceramic containers for condiments, liquor, hor d'oeuvres, salt and pepper, and oil and vinegar bade by the Holt-Howard company of Stamford, CT from 1958 to the early 1960s.

Carol Power
1014 E. Park Ave.
Riverton, WY 82501
ph: 307-857-2404
http://www.cmpjewelry.com/Pixies/
Main.htm

Internet Resources

Carol Power
Pixie Watch
1014 E. Park Ave.
Riverton, WY 82501
ph: 307-857-2404
http://www.cmpjewelry.com/Pixies/
Main.htm
Web site for collectors of Pixies from the 1950s and 1960s; information on manufacturers, tips on collecting, and lots of pictures.

Planters

Experts

Bill & Betty Newbound
4567 Chadsworth
Commerce, MI 48382
Authors of "Collector's Encyclopedia of Figural Planters & Vases."

Political Related

Collectors

Rex Stark
P.O. Box 1029
Gardner, MA 01440-6029
ph: 978-630-3237
fax: 978-630-2388
rexstark@yahoo.com
Wants to buy china with American political and military portraits or scenes; Liverpool, lustreware, parian ware, Staffordshire, etc.

Redware

Dealers

Richard Hume
Liberty Forever Auctioneers
P.O. Box 281
Bay Head, NJ 08742
ph: 732-899-8707 or 732-244-7007
libertyforever76@hotmail.com
*Collects, appraises, buys, sells,
auctions American decorated
stoneware: jugs, crocks, etc.; also
Southern pottery, American redware,
folk pots, etc.; conducts auctions twice
a year.*

Carl McCann
Troy & Black, Inc.
P.O. Box 228
Red Creek, NY 13143-0228
ph: 315-754-8115
*Buys and sells high quality flow blue,
Staffordshire figurines, American
painted furniture, stoneware, redware,
coverlets, samplers, and other
American textiles, folk art, etc.*

Repro. Sources

James Nyeste
3717 Green Valley Rd.
Seven Valleys, PA 17360-8609
ph: 717-428-3314
*Makes figural redware sculptures:
animals and figures in the Pennsylvania and Shenandoah Valley traditions.*

Lester Breininger
Breininger Pottery
176 S. Church St.
Robesonia, PA 19551
ph: 610-693-5344
*Producing Pennsylvania-German style
redware since 1965.*

Rockingham

Experts

George Eck
1987 Limewood Dr.
San Jose, CA 95132
*Collector and expert who has been
specializing in Rockingham for 10
years; has researched every US and
English museum that has a ceramics
collection.*

Southern Folk Pottery

Museums/Libraries

Museum of Southern Stoneware
River Market Antiques Mall
3226 Hamilton Rd.
Columbus, GA 31904
ph: 706-653-6240
fax: 706-221-4658
webmaster@rivermarketantiques.com
http://www.rivermarketantiques.com
*Over 1,000 pieces of pottery from
Georgia, Alabama, South Carolina,
North Carolina, Tennessee,
Mississippi, and Florida are on
display.*

Souvenir & Commemorative

(see also SOUVENIR &
COMMEMORATIVE ITEMS)

Spatterware

Appraisers

Diane Patalano
Country Girls Appraisal & Liquidation
  Service
P.O. Box 376
Saddle River, NJ 07458
ph: 201-327-2499
fax: 20-327-2094
dp@microdsi.net
*Spatterware advisor to "Schroeder's"
for over 10 years.*

Experts

Gregg Ellington
Upper Loft Antiques
47 Columbus St.
Wilmington, OH 45177
ph: 937-382-4311
*Buys, sells, trades and collects
graniteware and American ceramics
including mochaware, yellowware,
spatterware, spongeware, etc.;
appraisals provided for a small fee; if
writing, enclose SASE for reply.*

Spongeware

Experts

Gregg Ellington
Upper Loft Antiques
47 Columbus St.
Wilmington, OH 45177
ph: 937-382-4311
*Buys, sells, trades and collects
graniteware and American ceramics
including mochaware, yellowware,
spatterware, spongeware, etc.;
appraisals provided for a small fee; if
writing, enclose SASE for reply.*

Studio Ceramic Art

Dealers

Joseph Belperio
1303 Hawthorne Ct.
Sewell, NJ 08080-3511
ph: 8569-256-0791 or 856-782-7884
fax: 856-256-0791
shimazu@worldnet.att.net
*Specializes in fine quality Japanese
Satsuma, cloisonne, and studio
ceramics.*

Experts

Jim Messineo
JMW Gallery
144 Lincoln St.
Boston, MA 02111-2523
ph: 617-338-9097
fax: 617-338-7636
mail@jmwgallery.com
http://www.jmwgallery.com
*Buys, sells and specializes along with
co-owner Mike Witt in the Arts &
Crafts movement. Mission furniture:
Lifetime, Limbert, Stickley; American
Art Pottery 1875 to 1950s: Grueby,*

*Newcomb, Marblehead, etc.;
metalwork, Roycroft.*

Elinor Racine
Racine & Racine Inc.
175 Bessborough Dr.
Toronto, Ontario M4G 3J8 Canada
ph: 416-483-8675
fax: 416-483-2805
elinoraracine@sympatico.ca
*Specialist in American, Canadian,
British, Eurpoean and Japanese
Studio Ceramics Art.*

Terra Cotta

Clubs/Associations

Susan Tunick
Friends of Terra Cotta
c/o Tunick 771
771 West End Ave., #10E
New York, NY 10025-5539
ph: 212-932-1750
fax: 212-662-0768
http://www.preserve.org/fotc
*Formed to promote and educate and
research architectural terracotta and
related ceramic materials.*

Dealers

Karen M. Guido
Karen Michelle Antique Tiles
1835 US 1 South #119, PMB 243
Saint Augustine, FL 32084
ph: 904-471-3226
karen@antiquetiles.com
http://www.antiquetiles.com
*Specializing in antique & collectible
tiles from 1860 through 1960:
terracotta companies, studio pottery
(in terracotta), smaller architectural
works by Rookwood and other
manufacturers, and advertising items
for terracotta companies.*

Texas

Collectors

James E. Kattner
P.O. Box 11132
Spring, TX 77391-1132
ph: 281-376-4826
victorio1sw@yahoo.com
*Wants to buy Texas whiskey jugs
which display the merchant's name
and town; some may display saloon
name and town; especially want Texas
jugs, but will pay equally well for
same from other Southern and
Western states.*

Willow Pattern

Clubs/Associations

International Willow Collectors
503 Chestnut St.
Perkasie, PA 18944
willowpd@enter.net
http://www.willowcollectors.org
*Members interested in collecting and
studying of ceramics and other
materials decorated with the willow
pattern.*

J. Hightower
Ohio Willow Society
1232 Anthony Trace
Waynesville, OH 45068

Collectors

Jeff Siptak
P.O. Box 41312
Nashville, TN 37204
ph: 615-269-6833
fax: 615-269-7123
WillowWare@aol.com
*Buys, sell, trade unusual willow-
pattern items.*

Joyce LaFont
331 Edenwood
Jackson, TN 38301
ph: 901-668-5974
jlafont@aeneas.net
*Buys and sells Willow Pattern
ceramics.*

Al Little
151 Highway 173
Antioch, IL 60002
ph: 847-395-7752
fax: 847-395-7703
*Buy, sells and trades Blue Willow
china.*

Dealers

Louise M. Loehr
Louise's Old Things
131 Virginville Rd.
Kutztown, PA 19530-8862
ph: 610-683-6388
fax: 610-683-6865
louises@bellatlantic.net
http://www.louisesoldthings.com
*Co-author of "Willow Pattern
China." Specializing in willow, flow
blue, and early children's china.
Wants one piece or collections.*

Experts

Connie Rogers
309 Fleming Rd.
Cincinnati, OH 45215
ph: 513-761-5558
con1733@fuse.net
*Editor of "American Willow Report"
7/87 through 5/90; consultant to "The
Official Price Guide to Pottery &
Porcelain;" author of "Willow Ware
Made in the USA," available from
author, "Illustrated Encyclopedia of
British Willow" (2004).*

Mary Frank Gaston
P.O. Box 342
Bryan, TX 77806
*Author of "Blue Willow: An
Identification & Value Guide."*

Periodicals

Jeff Siptak, Pub.
Newsletter: Willow Review, The
P.O. Box 41312
Nashville, TN 37204
ph: 615-269-6833
fax: 615-269-7123
WillowWare@aol.com
The only international newsletter

devoted to collecting and enjoying willow pattern china and collectibles; quarterly issues featuring photos, prices, trends in collecting, articles on a wide variety of subjects, and more.

Yellowware

Experts

Gregg Ellington
Upper Loft Antiques
47 Columbus St.
Wilmington, OH 45177
ph: 937-382-4311
Buys, sells, trades and collects graniteware and American ceramics including mochaware, yellowware, spatterware, spongeware, etc.; appraisals provided for a small fee; if writing, enclose SASE for reply.

CERAMICS (AMERICAN)

Auction Services

Vicki & Bruce Waasdorp
American Pottery Auction
10931 Main St.
P.O. Box 434
Clarence, NY 14031
ph: 716-759-2361
fax: 716-759-2397
waasdrop@antiques-stoneware.com
http://www.antiques-stoneware.com
Provides a mail and phone bid auction service for both collectors and dealers of antique American pottery, stoneware, spongeware, yellowware; also appraisals, category history, and pertinent information on request; consignments accepted.

Clubs/Associations

Wisconsin Pottery Association
P.O. Box 8213
Madison, WI 53708-8213
ph: 608-301-0185 or 608-241-9138
fax: 608-241-8770
president@wisconsinpottery.org
http://www.wisconsinpottery.org
Club meets monthly; meetings include guest speakers on featured pottery or various lines of vintage pottery; affiliated with the State Historical Society of Wisconsin.

Dealers

Karen M. Guido
Karen Michelle Antique Tiles
1835 US 1 South #119, PMB 243
Saint Augustine, FL 32084
ph: 904-471-3226
karen@antiquetiles.com
http://www.antiquetiles.com
Specializing in American & English tiles mostly from 1870 to 1950; always has an abundance of tiles in stock: American Encaustic, Mosaic Tile Company, J & JG Low, Hamilton, Pewabic, Mueller, Arthur Osborne, Isaac Broome, Harris Strong.

Experts

Brian Cullity
18 Pleasant St.
P.O. Box 595
Sagamore, MA 02561
ph: 508-888-8409
bcullity@adelphia.net
Dealer, appraiser, expert specializing in American ceramics; also decorative arts consultant with over ten years experience as museum curator and over 35 years experience in the antiques field.

Harvey Duke
577 Ave. Y
Brooklyn, NY 11235
Author of "Price Guide to Pottery and Porcelain;" covering 90 collectible American potteries with 22,000 items priced; $15 + P&H, call 800-726-0600; specializes in Ohio and West Virginia dinnerware made from the 1890s to 1950s.

Lorrie Kitchen
Lorrie Kitchen Antiques
ph: 419-475-1759
lorrie@kitchenantiques.com
http://www.kitchenantiques.com
Specializes in American dinnerware such as Hall China, Fiesta, Blue Ridge and Shawnee; sells labels for Anchor Hocking or Owens Illinois glass kitchen canisters.

George H. Meyer
100 West Long Lake Rd., Ste. 100
Bloomfield Hills, MI 48304
ph: 248-646-2907
fax: 248-647-5079
gmeyer@meyerkirk.com
Collector and expert wants to purchase early American face jugs, snake jugs, and other figural American pottery.

Allen Bagdade
Country Peasants, The
1325 North State Parkway, Apt. 15A
Chicago, IL 60610
ph: 312-397-1321
fax: 847-392-5848
ADBSDB@aol.com
Author of "Warman's American Pottery & Porcelain" (Krause).

Museums/Libraries

Sandra Trop
Everson Museum of Art
401 Harrison St.
Syracuse, NY 13202-3019
ph: 315-474-6064
fax: 315-474-6943
everson@everson.org
http://www.everson.org
Contains one of the most important collections of American ceramics.

Museum of Ceramics at East Liverpool
400 E. 5th St.
East Liverpool, OH 43920-3134
ph: 330-386-6001 or 800-600-7180
webmaster@ohiohistory.org
http://www.ohiohistory.org/places/ceramics
Detailed exhibit of the local ceramic industry; "The East Liverpool, Ohio Pottery District: Identification of Manufacturers & Marks" by Wm. Gates, Jr. and Dana Ormerod can be obtained by contacting the museum.

Art Deco

Dealers

David Fein
South Beach Antiques
736-13th St., #102
Miami Beach, FL 33139-4418
ph: 305-673-8044
dbf57@hotmail.com
http://www.angelfire.com/art/antiquepottery
Appraiser, dealer, collector specializes in Art Deco, Arts & Crafts, Art Nouveau and European Art Pottery: Czech, Gouda, and English; Ditmar Urbach, Grays, PZH, Regina, Zenith.

Bennington

(see also CERAMICS [AMERICAN], Stoneware)

Experts

Gregg Ellington
Upper Loft Antiques
47 Columbus St.
Wilmington, OH 45177
ph: 937-382-4311
Buys, sells, trades and collects graniteware and American ceramics including mochaware, yellowware, spatterware, spongeware, etc.; appraisals provided for a small fee; if writing, enclose SASE for reply.

Museums/Libraries

Bennington Museum, The
West Main St.
Bennington, VT 05201
ph: 802-447-1571
fax: 802-442-8305
bennmuse@sover.net
http://www.benningtonmuseum.com
One of the finest regional art history museums in the country; works by Grandma Moses, American glass, VT furniture, Bennington pottery, the oldest Stars & Stripes in existence, the 1925 luxury touring car "The Wasp", and much more.

Bybee

Man./Prod./Dist.

Bybee Pottery
P.O. Box 555
610 Waco Loop
Waco, KY 40385
ph: 606-369-5350
In business since the early 19th century.

George Ohr

Experts

Dr. Eugene Hecht
Adelphi University Physics Department
Adelphi University
Garden City, NY 11530
genehecht@aol.com
Is available by mail to help authenticate George Ohr pottery; send SASE with inquiry; this is not an appraisal service.

Museums/Libraries

Ohr/O'Keefe Museum of Art, The
136 G. E. Ohr St.
Biloxi, MS 39530
ph: 228-374-5547
fax: 228-436-3641
marjie@georgeohr.org
http://www.georgeohr.org
Exhibits over 250 works by the potter George Ohr.

Harding Black

Dealers

Beth Marshall
Marshall's Brocante
8505 Broadway
San Antonio, TX 78217
ph: 210-804-6320
fax: 210-804-6321
info@marshallsbrocante.com
http://www.marshallsbrocante.com
Carries large inventory of porcelain: Royal Worcester, Meissen, Severs, R.S. Prussia, Nippon, Dresden and flow blue; also Harding Black porcelain (from San Antonio, one of America's best ceramic artists)

Illinois

Clubs/Associations

Collectors of Illinois Pottery & Stoneware
Newsletter: Collectors of Ill. Pottery & Stoneware Newsletter
308 N. Jackson St.
Clinton, IL 61727-1320
ph: 217-935-6825
samsjrn@onemain.com
An organization for persons interested in collecting Illinois pottery; quarterly newsletter features photos and information.

Lewistown Pottery

Collectors

Scott Armstrong
458 Three Locks Rd.
Lewistown, PA 17044
ph: 717-248-1535
Wants pieces marked Lewistown Pottery.

Russel Wright Designs

(see also RUSSEL WRIGHT)

Collectors

Chad Sutton
1344 N. Westview
Derby, KS 67037
ph: 316-788-8916
chadsutton@cox.net
*Collector of Iroquois and early metal
objects designed by Russel Wright;
knowledgeable on many Wright topics.*

Chad Sutton
1344 N. Westview
Derby, KS 67037
ph: 316-788-8916
chadsutton@cox.net

Dealers

Robert & Nancy Perzel
Popkorn Antiques
P.O. Box 1057
Flemington, NJ 08822
ph: 908-782-9631
*Buys and sells American ceramics
including Franciscan Apple, Dessert
Rose, Metlox, Vernon plaids, Currier
& Ives, Pennsbury, Purinton, Russel
Wright designs, Stangl, Fulper,
Homer Laughlin Fiesta.*

Kathryn Wiese
Retrospective Modern Designs
P.O. Box 305
Manning, IA 51455
ph: 712-653-3678 or 888-301-6829
fax: 712-653-3027
inquire@retrospective.net
http://www.retrospective.net
*Russel Wright, Eva Zeisel, Ben Seibel
and other mid-century modern
dinnerware sold exclusively on the
Internet and by phone; featuring
American Modern, Casual by
Iroquois, Hallcraft and more; no
storefront sales.*

Southern Folk Pottery

Auction Services

Billy Ray & Susan Hussey
Southern Folk Pottery Collectors Society
Catalog: SFPCS Auction Catalog
220 Washington St.
Bennett, NC 27208
ph: 336-581-4246
fax: 336-581-4247
sfpcs@rtmc.net
*Conducts periodic auction of pottery
made by self-taught Southern folk
potters of the 18th and 19th centuries
and today; holds two absentee
auctions per year; each auction
catalog includes extensive research
data, photos, post sale results.*

Steve Slotin
Slotin Folk Art Auction House
5967 Blackberry Lane
Buford, GA 30518
ph: 770-932-1000
fax: 770-932-0506
folkfest@bellsouth.net
http://www.slotinfolkart.com
*Leading venue for self-taught,
Outsider, Folk Art and Southern folk
pottery.*

Clubs/Associations

Billy Ray & Susan Hussey
Southern Folk Pottery Collectors Society
Newsletter: SFPCS Newsletter
220 Washington St.
Bennett, NC 27208
ph: 336-581-4246
fax: 336-581-4247
sfpcs@rtmc.net
*Formed for the purpose of educating
and continuing the role of the self-
taught Southern folk potter of the 18th
and 19th centuries and today; holds
two absentee auctions per year.*

Museums/Libraries

Billy Ray & Susan Hussey
Southern Folk Pottery Collectors Society
Shop/Museum
Newsletter: SFPCS Newsletter
220 Washington St.
Bennett, NC 27208
ph: 336-581-4246
fax: 336-581-4247
sfpcs@rtmc.net
*Formed for the purpose of educating
and continuing the role of the self-
taught Southern folk potter of the 18th
and 19th centuries and today.*

Stoneware

Auction Services

Richard Hume
Liberty Forever Auctioneers
P.O. Box 281
Bay Head, NJ 08742
ph: 732-899-8707 or 732-244-7007
libertyforever76@hotmail.com
*Collects, appraises, buys, sells,
auctions American decorated
stoneware: jugs, crocks, etc.; also
Southern pottery, American redware,
folk pots, etc.; conducts auctions twice
a year in April and October.*

Vicki & Bruce Waasdorp
American Pottery Auction
10931 Main St.
P.O. Box 434
Clarence, NY 14031
ph: 716-759-2361
fax: 716-759-2397
waasdrop@antiques-stoneware.com
http://www.antiques-stoneware.com
*Provides a mail and phone bid auction
service for both collectors and dealers
of antique American pottery,
stoneware, spongeware, yellowware;
also appraisals, category history, and
pertinent information on request;
consignments accepted.*

Wayne Arthur
Arthur Auctioneering
563 Reed Rd.
Hughesville, PA 17737
ph: 570-584-3697 or 800-278-4873
*Conducts specialized sales of
decorated stoneware.*

Clubs/Associations

Richard Hume
American Stoneware Collectors Society
Newsletter: ASCC Newsletter
P.O. Box 281
Bay Head, NJ 08742
ph: 732-899-8707 or 732-244-7007
libertyforever76@hotmail.com
*A growing society of stoneware
collectors; call or write for more
information.*

Collectors

Dr. Fred Cesana
49 E. Main St.
Plainville, CT 06062
ph: 860-747-2759 or 860-379-0054
fax: 860-793-6019
*Wants to buy stoneware crocks and
jugs from Bennington, VT and
Rochester, NY with elaborate
decorations of animals and birds.*

Ivy & Geoff Bean
8200 Mountain Laurel Ln.
Gaithersburg, MD 20879-1558
ph: 301-963-7469
gibpbean@msn.com
*Wants blue decorated American
stoneware: crocks, jugs, jars, etc.;
specific interest is in Western
Pennsylvania region; buys, sells,
trades all regions and areas.*

Ed McDermott
1415 McKendree
Kevil, KY 42053
ph: 270-488-3420
emcdermott@brtc.net
*Wants stencil or scratch advertising
stoneware from pre-1920 grocery and
whiskey firms; especially wants
whiskey jugs from small towns located
in Southern and Western states; pays
premium for saloon whiskey jugs.*

Steve Ketcham
P.O. Box 24114
Minneapolis, MN 55424-0114
ph: 952-920-4205
s.ketcham@unique-software.com
*Primarily interested in crocks, jugs,
etc. which carry name of product or
advertising such as liquor dealers,
medicines, etc.; especially wants Red
Wing stoneware; please send SASE
with all inquiries.*

James E. Kattner
P.O. Box 11132
Spring, TX 77391-1132
ph: 281-376-4826
victorio1sw@yahoo.com
*Wants to buy Texas whiskey jugs
which display the merchant's name
and town; some may display saloon
name and town; especially want Texas
jugs, but will pay equally well for
same from other Southern and
Western states.*

Bruce & Nada Ferris
Ev'ry Nook & Cranny
3094 Oakes Dr.
Hayward, CA 94542-1234
ph: 510-581-5285
fax: 510-581-4469
Nada.Ferris@ncal.kaiperm.org
*Wants mini advertising jugs,
advertising 7" spongeband pitcher,
advertising spongeware bowls,
dometop stoneware jars; Ferris jugs
from NY; any dated or holiday mini
advertising jugs.*

Scott Grandstaff
63742 Applegate Dr.
P.O. Box 409
Happy Camp, CA 96039
ph: 530-493-2032
scottg@snowcrest.net
*Past-Publisher of "Bottles & Extras"
magazine; casual appraisals done
free; detailed appraisals and
professional consulting are available
for a fee.*

Dealers

Richard Hume
Liberty Forever Auctioneers
P.O. Box 281
Bay Head, NJ 08742
ph: 732-899-8707 or 732-244-7007
libertyforever76@hotmail.com
*Collects, appraises, buys, sells,
auctions American decorated
stoneware: jugs, crocks, etc.; also
Southern pottery, American redware,
folk pots, etc.; conducts auctions twice
a year.*

Greg Walsh
32 River View Lane
P.O. Box 747
Potsdam, NY 13676-0747
ph: 315-265-9111
fax: 315-265-9222
gwalsh@twcny.rr.com
http://www.walshauction.com
*Stoneware dealer since 1979 wants to
buy blue decorated stoneware of
exceptional quality; also appraises.*

Anthony & Barb Zipp
Anthony & Barbara Zipp Antiques
P.O. Box 725
Riderwood, MD 21139-0725
ph: 410-337-5090
*Buys and sells quality, 19th century,
blue decorated stoneware.*

Experts

Vicki & Bruce Waasdorp
Antiques & Americana
10931 Main St.
P.O. Box 434
Clarence, NY 14031
ph: 716-759-2361
fax: 716-759-2397
waasdrop@antiques-stoneware.com
http://www.antiques-stoneware.com
*Provides a mail and phone bid auction
service for both collectors and dealers
of Decorated American Stoneware;
also buys, sells, appraisals, category*

history, and pertinent information on request.

Museums/Libraries

Museum of Ceramics at East Liverpool
400 E. 5th St.
East Liverpool, OH 43920-3134
ph: 330-386-6001 or 800-600-7180
webmaster@ohiohistory.org
http://www.ohiohistory.org/places/
ceramics
Detailed exhibit of the local ceramic industry; "The East Liverpool, Ohio Pottery District: Identification of Manufacturers & Marks" by Wm. Gates, Jr. and Dana Ormerod can be obtained by contacting the museum.

Repro. Sources

Rowe Pottery Works
404 England St.
Cambridge, WI 53523
ph: 608-423-3363 or 800-356-5003
fax: 608-423-4273
sales@rowepottery.com
http://www.rowepottery.com
Produces authentic reproductions of 19th century salt-glaze stoneware plates, figurines, and steins; also wrought iron.

Stoneware (Red Wing Pottery)

Clubs/Associations

Kay Wilshusen, Bus. Mngr.
Red Wing Collectors Society, Inc.
Newsletter: Red Wing Collectors
  Newsletter
2000 West Main St., Ste. 300
P.O. Box 50
Red Wing, MN 55066
ph: 800-977-7927 or 651-388-4004
rwcs1@redwing.net
http://www.redwingcollectors.org
Dedicated to the preservation of Red Wing and American pottery.

Collectors

David Lenling
108A Chancellors Hall
820 University Dr.
Eau Claire, WI 54701
ph: 952-447-8213
lenlinde@uwec.edu
http://www.RedWingNet.com
Seeking Red Wing pottery water coolers, salt glazed items, butter churns, crocks, advertising ware, jugs, crocks, beater jars, bowls, and any other type of Red Wing stoneware; please no wing-decorated crocks unless at least 40 gallons.

Peter M. Naysmith
Mounted Rte. Box 444
Two Harbors, MN 55616
ph: 218-834-4770
Collector of Red Wing stoneware always looking for advertising pieces including moonshine jugs; will pay up to $50 for stoneware (jugs preferred) with advertising on the side and the name of the pottery on the bottom.

Charles W. Casad
801 Tyler Ct.
Monticello, IL 61856-2246
ph: 217-762-2303
Wants Red Wing crocks, beehive jugs, shoulder jugs, water coolers, commemorative pieces, Red Wing advertising pieces and any other unusual Red Wing pieces; mint or near-mint only, please.

Dealers

Byron Bush
Unit 23809
Apo, AE 09034-3809
Experts specializing, buying and selling Red Wing ceramics.

Pat Puckett
Teacherage, The
1583 Ranch Rd.
San Bernardino, CA 92407
ph: 909-887-8383
fax: 909-887-8383
tcherage@aol.com
http://members.aol.com/tcherage/
index.html
Specializes in Red Wing and RumRill art pottery, stoneware and ephemera; visitors may post want ads or items for sale at no charge; also trades.

Internet Resources

David Lenling
Wing Tips
108A Chancellors Hall
820 University Dr.
Eau Claire, WI 54701
ph: 952-447-8213
lenlinde@uwec.edu
http://www.RedWingNet.com
This site is committed to antique Red Wing artware; pottery, dinnerware, stoneware, crocks/crockery and anything else associated with Red Wing.

CERAMICS (AMERICAN ART POTTERY)

Appraisers

Paul Royka
AppraisalDay.com
210 Park Avenue, #295
Worcester, MA 01609
ph: 978-582-8207
fax: 978-582-8207
appraisalday@aol.com
http://www.appraisalday.com
Expert, author and appraiser of American art pottery.

Tony McCormack
McCormack & Company
P.O. Box 49093
Sarasota, FL 34320
ph: 941-952-1244 or 941-350-2785
birdkey@aol.com
http://www.birdkey.net
Dealer, expert appraiser specializing in American art pottery and the Arts & Crafts Movement; always buying Rookwood, Grueby, Newcomb

College, Teco, Marblehead, Overbeck; dated Van Briggle, George Ohr, Weller & Roseville pottery; member ISA.

James S. Harriss
James S. Harris Antiques & Appraisals
P.O. Box 672
Richmond, KY 40475
ph: 859-623-9100
jimant@ipro.net
Specializes in the appraisal of coin and English hallmarked silver, American art pottery, stevengraphs, and English watercolors.

Sylvia Fitzgerald, ISA
A.A.E.S.
P.O. Box 2509
Sacramento, CA 95812
ph: 800-471-9841 or 916-448-2428
sylfitz@compuserve.com
Accredited ISA appraiser specializing in Art Nouveau, Art Deco, Arts & Crafts, art glass, art pottery, and fine porcelains.

Auction Services

Jane Prentiss
Skinner, Inc.
63 Park Plaza
The Heritage on the Garden
Boston, MA 02116
ph: 617-350-5400
fax: 617-350-5429
info@skinnerinc.com
http://www.skinnerinc.com
Established in 1971, Skinner Inc. is the fourth largest auction house in the US; has offices in Boston and Bolton, MA.

Barry Brooks
PotteryAuction.com
P.O. Box 224
Winter Park, FL 32790-0224
ph: 407-740-8260
admin@potteryauction.com
http://www.potteryauction.com
An online person-to-person auction specializing in pottery.

Mike Clum
Mike Clum, Inc.
7795 Cincinnati Zanesvile Rd.
Rushville, OH 43150
ph: 740-536-7421 or 740-536-9220
fax: 740-536-7242
info@clum.com
http://www.clum.com
Conducts periodic auctions specializing in American art pottery.

Riley Humler
Cincinnati Art Galleries
225 East 6th St.
Cincinnati, OH 45202
ph: 513-381-2128
fax: 513-381-7527
info@cincinnatiartgalleries.com
http://www.cincinnatiartgalleries.com
Conducts specialty auctions of American art pottery including Rookwood, Van Briggle, Newcomb, Grueby, etc.

Don Treadway
Treadway Auctions
2029 Madison Rd.
Cincinnati, OH 45208
ph: 513-321-6742
fax: 513-871-7722
treadway2029@earthlink.net
http://www.treadwaygallery.com
Specializes in the sale of Arts and Crafts pottery: Grueby, Teco, Newcomb, Van Briggle, Marblehead.

Jon Crisman, ISA
Jackson's Auctioneers & Appraisers
2229 Lincoln St.
P.O. Box 50613
Cedar Falls, IA 50613
ph: 319-277-2256
fax: 319-277-1252
jacksons@jacksonsauction.com
http://www.jacksonsauction.com
Conducts specialty auctions of art pottery including Rookwood, Van Briggle, Roseville, Weller, Grueby, Teco, etc.

Clubs/Associations

Patti Bourgeois, Sec.
American Art Pottery Association
Magazine: Journal of the AAPA
P.O. Box 834
Westport, MA 02790-0697
patspots@ma.ultranet.com
http://www.amartpot.org
Content heavy information site for lovers of American art pottery including Mystery pot ID, "fakes" information, pottery events calendar, hundreds of selected hot links, and more.

Jen & John Stofft
Pottery Lovers Reunion
Newsletter: Pottery Lovers Newsletter
45 12th St.
Tell City, IN 47586
ph: 812-547-5707
showandsale@potterylovers.org
http://www.potterylovers.org
Publishes a quarterly newsletter describing activities and plans for the upcoming Pottery Lovers Reunion and show.

Gordon Hoppe
Minnesota Art Pottery Association
10120 32nd Ave.
Minneapolis, MN 55441
ph: 612-724-1734

Collectors

Bruce E. Thulin
69 Hanson's Landing Rd.
Ellsworth, ME 04605
ph: 207-667-5225
thulin@acadia.net
Wants to buy pottery signed Grand Feu Pottery, Flame, Losanti, Pauleo, W J W, Fulper, S.E.G., overlapping "LCT", N encircled by a C, M P with a front view ship in between; Moorcroft, Scheier, Dedham, Alberhill, and others.

Bob Hut
P.O. Box 1495
Grand Central Station
New York, NY 10163-1495
ph: 800-321-7687
Wants to buy dated Van Briggle, artist-signed Rookwood, decorated Marblehead and Grueby; also any and all unusual pre-1930 high quality American and French Art Nouveau and Art Deco pottery (no Roseville, Fulper, Hull, McCoy).

Nancy Bomm
P.O. Box 656
Clarcona, FL 32710-0656
ph: 407-822-5250
fax: 407-294-7836
jack2741@hotmail.com
http://www.thepotteryexperience.com
Specializing in Roseville pottery and all types of antique American art pottery.

Larry Crawford
313 12 Ave. SW
Minot, ND 58701
ph: 701-838-5876
digitim@minot.ndak.net
Collects most art pottery including Roseville, Hull, Weller, UND, Rosemeade.

Richard L. Sasicki
P.O. Box 3113
Glen Ellyn, IL 60138-3113
ph: 630-682-8706
artware@sprynet.com
http://home.sprynet.com/~artware
Wants to buy Van Briggle, Pine Ridge, Broadmoor, Coors Pottery, Teco, Grueby, Fulper, Newcomb, Arts & Crafts style and other American Art pottery; author of "The Collector's Encyclopedia of Van Briggle Art Pottery."

Dealers

Jim Messineo
JMW Gallery
144 Lincoln St.
Boston, MA 02111-2523
ph: 617-338-9097
fax: 617-338-7636
mail@jmwgallery.com
http://www.jmwgallery.com
Buys, sells and specializes along with co-owner Mike Witt in the Arts & Crafts movement. Mission furniture: Lifetime, Limbert, Stickley; American Art Pottery 1875 to 1950s: Grueby, Newcomb, Marblehead, etc.; metalwork, Roycroft.

Pat Bourgeois
Patti's Past Perfect Pottery
P.O. Box 1226
Westport, MA 02790
ph: 508-679-5910
patspots@ma.ultranet.com
http://www.antiqnet.com/patspots
Specializes in American Art Pottery made in the US from the late 1800s to the present.

Marvin McKee
104 Jackson St.
Bangor, ME 04401
ph: 207-945-3450
mcmckee@adelphia.net
http://www.tias.com/stores/amaine
Buys and sells American art pottery, especially Roseville.

Valerie Sevene
Route 7 Antiques & Treasures
388 Shelburne Rd.
Burlington, VT 05401
ph: 802-859-0917
sevene@together.net
Wants to buy Brush McCoy, Niloak, Rumrill, McCoy and Roseville art pottery.

Edward E. Stump
Raccoon's Tale
6 High St.
Mullica Hill, NJ 08062-9540
ph: 609-478-4488
ractale@fast.net
Wants Roseville and Weller art pottery.

David Rago
Perrault Rago Gallery
117 South Main St.
Lambertville, NJ 08530
ph: 609-397-1802
fax: 609-397-5543
perraggal@ragoarts.com
http://www.ragoarts.com
Wants American art pottery, and Arts and Crafts items such as furniture and metal items by Stickley, Rohlfs, Wright, Roycroft, etc.

Bob Berman
441 S. Jackson St.
Media, PA 19063-3715
ph: 610-566-1516 or 888-784-2554
ber441@aol.com
http://www.bermangallery.com
Wants to buy American art pottery by Teco, Rookwood, George Ohr, Van Briggle, Cowan, Newcomb College, Fulper, Grueby, etc.

Caren Fine
11603 Gowrie Ct.
Potomac, MD 20854-3623
ph: 301-299-6886 or 301-854-6262
fine2beme@aol.com
Buys, sells, trades art pottery: Overbeck, Newcomb College, Van Briggle, Grueby, Teco, Roseville, Marblehead, SEG, Ohr, Paul Revere, North Dakota School of Mines, Walrath, Tiffany, Robineau, Redlands, Arequipa, Cowan, sculptures.

Ken Forster
5501 Seminary Rd., Ste. 1311 South
Falls Church, VA 22041-3907
ph: 703-379-1142
kencforster@aol.com
Dealer in American art pottery and tiles, specializing in American tiles from 1860 to 1940; also Art Nouveau,

Art Deco, Georg Jensen silver, and American Modernism.

Mike & Renee Aschkenas
Renee's Racket
P.O. Box 8641
Virginia Beach, VA 23450
ph: 757-463-6941
rracket@aol.com
Buys and sells American art pottery, cookie jars, glassware, Hummels, and Roseville.

Stephanie Hull Winters
Classic Treasures
3232 Morgan Rd.
Temple, GA 30179
ph: 770-562-1332
swinters@bellsouth.net
Buys, sells, collects American art pottery including Hull, McCoy, Shawnee, Stangl, Royal Copley, Red Wing, Frankoma, Haeger, Niloak, Weller, etc.

Karen M. Guido
Karen Michelle Antique Tiles
1835 US 1 South #119, PMB 243
Saint Augustine, FL 32084
ph: 904-471-3226
karen@antiquetiles.com
http://www.antiquetiles.com
Specializing in American & English tiles mostly from 1870 to 1950; California A&C tile makers and potteries: Batchelder, Claycraft, Taylor, California Art Tile, Solon & Schemmel, Rookwood, Wheatley, Grueby, Flint Faience, Moravian, etc.

Hardy Hudson
Our Antiques Market
5453 Lake Howell Rd.
Winter Park, FL 32792-1033
ph: 407-657-2100 or 407-444-9009
todiefor@mindspring.com
Serious buyer of Grueby, Newcomb, Ohr, Weller animals/birds/garden ornaments, Roseville, Teco, Cowan figurals, Overbeck, S.E.G., Marblehead, Fulper, Arequipa, Owens, Clifton, Avon, Niloak Swirl, Kay Finch, Dedham, Rookwood, Pewabic.

Steve Traband
P.O. Box 7064
Saint Petersburg, FL 33734-7064
ph: 813-896-2308
Buys and sells American Art Pottery: Rookwood, Grueby, Newcomb, Teco, Marblehead, Fulper, Dedham, Hampshire, S.E.G.-O.B.K., early Van Briggle, etc.

Tony McCormack
McCormack & Company
P.O. Box 49093
Sarasota, FL 34320
ph: 941-952-1244 or 941-350-2785
birdkey@aol.com
http://www.birdkey.net
Dealer, expert appraiser specializing in American art pottery and the Arts & Crafts Movement; always buying Rookwood, Grueby, Newcomb

College, Teco, Marblehead, Overbeck; dated Van Briggle, George Ohr, Weller & Roseville pottery; member ISA.

Tina & Mark Richey
Spotted Horse Collectibles
12141 Couch Mill Rd.
Knoxville, TN 37932-1102
shcollect@aol.com
http://members.aol.com/shcollect/ homepage.html
Collectors and dealers of American Art Pottery including Rookwood, Fulper, Niloak, Missionware, Cowan, Van Briggle, Weller.

Betty Powell
Pottery Place, The
P.O. Box 571
Columbus, OH 43085-0571
ph: 614-885-1962
fax: 614-885-1962
Buys and sells American art pottery, specializing in Rookwood, Roseville, Arts & Crafts style.

Don Treadway
Treadway Gallery, Inc.
2029 Madison Rd.
Cincinnati, OH 45208
ph: 513-321-6742
fax: 513-871-7722
treadway2029@earthlink.net
http://www.treadwaygallery.com

Connie Zeigler
Durwyn Smedley Antiques
431 Massachusetts Ave.
Indianapolis, IN 46204
ph: 317-822-0102
Buys and sells 20th century design: Arts & Crafts era, Art Deco, Mid-Century Modern, upscale '50s; art pottery from all eras and designer dinnerware; the first Indiana antique shop in the World Wide Web.

Greg & Lana Myroth
JustArtPottery.com
6606 N. Rustic Oak Ct.
Peoria, IL 61614
ph: 309-690-7966
gregmy@justartpottery.com
http://www.justartpottery.com
Specializes in American art pottery: Roseville, Weller, Van Briggle, Rookwood, etc.

Gary Moore
Arkansas Pottery Exchange, The
2006 Beckenham Cove
Little Rock, AR 72212
info@moorecsi.net
http://home.flash.net/~gemoore/ nsapc.htm
Collector of Camark pottery, dealer in American art pottery, publisher of the National Association of Arkansas Pottery Collector's newsletter.

Alan Phair
Alan's Antiques
P.O. Box 30373
Long Beach, CA 90853-0373
ph: 562-983-7020
AlanPhair@aol.com
Buys pieces marked "Catalina Pottery" made by Gladding-McBean; shells and some pieces marked with blue ink stamp "MADE IN U.S.A.;" G.M.B., Franciscan and Catalina Pottery advertising items and price lists; Franciscan, all Art Pottery.

Kathy Flynn
Art Pottery Exchange
200 A Ave.
Coronado, CA 92118
ph: 619-435-4350

Barry & Donna Williams
300 San Antonio Rd.
Santa Barbara, CA 93110-1316
ph: 805-964-4820
Special interest in Walrath, Newcomb, and Rhead pottery.

Bill Warmboe
1003 California Dr.
Burlingame, CA 94010
ph: 650-579-7908
Buys and sells art pottery: Catalina Island, Bauer, Roseville, Batchelder, Rookwood, Arequipa, Van Briggle, Fiesta, Weller, Teco, Rhead, Robertson, McCoy, Newcomb College, California Faience, Peters & Reed, Vernon Kilns.

Mr. Naomi Murdach
Naomi's Antiques To Go
1817 Polk St.
San Francisco, CA 94109-3003
ph: 415-775-1207
Buys/sells American dinnerware and art pottery: Hall, Bauer, Tepco, Wallace, Coors, Autumn Leaf, Russel Wright, American Modern, Iroquois, Roseville, Weller, Catalina, and Art Pottery.

Patricia Huerta
Another Man's Treasure
45 Palm Dr.
Union City, CA 94587
ph: 510-487-5330

Charles Wollitz
Arts & Crafts, etc.
P.O. Box 2958
Clackamas, OR 97015
ph: 503-558-0838
cwollitz@attbi.com
http://www.oldpottery.com
Buys and sells quality American Art Pottery including Weller, Roseville, Rookwood, Fulper and others.

Michael Lindsey
Vintage American Pottery
116 S. Washington St.
Seattle, WA 98104-2522
ph: 206-682-6162
fax: 206-405-3561
oiljars@aol.com
http://www.lagunapottery.com
Wants collectible and discontinued American dinnerware and art pottery by Franciscan, Metlox, Heath, Fiesta, Russel Wright, Vernon, Roseville, Rookwood, Grueby, Teco, Weller, Catalina, Newcomb, Owens, Voulkos and many others.

Experts

Jim & Ellen Tyne
American Pottery, Earthenware & China
ph: 815-758-7829
jtyne@niu.edu
Owns and manages the APEC (American Pottery, Earthenware & China) Show and Sale held annually in Springfield, IL in late summer.

Gerald Schultz
Antique Gallery, The
8523 Germantown Ave.
Philadelphia, PA 19118-3316
ph: 215-248-1700
fax: 215-247-8411
geraldluv@aol.com
Buys, sells, and specializes in Weller, Sicard, Roseville, Fulper, Cowan, Matt Morgan, Rookwood, Grueby, Pillin, California - all American art pottery.

A. Everette James, Jr.
St. James Place
205 New Castle Place
Chapel Hill, NC 27514
ph: 919-933-6853
fax: 919-942-0437
everette@nc.rr.com
Author of "North Carolina Art Pottery, 1900-1960."

Mark Bassett
P.O. Box 77123
Lakewood, OH 44107
ph: 216-221-6025
mark@markbassett.com
http://www.markbassett.com
Author of books on American art pottery including "Cowan Pottery and the Cleveland School," "Introducing Roseville Pottery," "Bassett's Roseville Prices," "Understanding Roseville Pottery;" Web site contains art pottery information.

Riley Humler
Cincinnati Art Galleries
225 East 6th St.
Cincinnati, OH 45202
ph: 513-381-2128
fax: 513-381-7527
info@cincinnatiartgalleries.com
http://www.cincinnatiartgalleries.com
Rookwood is their specialty; also want Van Briggle, Newcomb, Grueby, etc.

Jim & Carol Boshears
CC Selections, Inc.
528 Thomas Rd.
Bolingbrook, IL 60440
ph: 630-783-1639
gondernut@aol.com
Expert in American Art Pottery; also Gonder appraiser, collector, dealer and expert; author of "Gonder Ceramic Arts, A Comprehensive Guide;" also publishes "The Gonder Collector" newsletter.

Museums/Libraries

Sandra Trop
Everson Museum of Art
401 Harrison St.
Syracuse, NY 13202-3019
ph: 315-474-6064
fax: 315-474-6943
everson@everson.org
http://www.everson.org

Zanesville Art Center
620 Military Rd.
Zanesville, OH 43701
ph: 740-452-0741
fax: 740-452-0797
info@zanesvilleartcenter.org
http://www.zanesvilleartcenter.org

Cincinnati Art Museum
Eden Park
Cincinnati, OH 45202
ph: 513-639-2995
information@cincyart.org
http://www.cincinnatiartmuseum.com

Newcomb Art Gallery
1229 Broadway
New Orleans, LA 70118
ph: 504-865-5327
webmaster@tulane.edu
http://www.newcomb.tulane.edu/
    newcomb_art_gallery.htm

American Art Clay Co.

Experts

Virginia Heiss
7777 N. Alton Ave.
Indianapolis, IN 46268-7901
ph: 317-875-6797
Specializes in pottery made by the American Art Clay Co., Indianapolis, IN.

Clewell Pottery

Museums/Libraries

Jesse Besser Museum
491 Johnson St.
Alpena, MI 49707
ph: 989-356-2202
fax: 989-356-3133
jbmuseum@northland.lib.mi.us
http://www.ogdennews.com/upnorth/
    museum/home.html
Owns a large and important collection of Clewell Pottery.

Cowan Pottery Co.

Experts

Timothy & Jamie Saloff
P.O. Box 339
Edinboro, PA 16412
ph: 814-734-5189
fax: 814-734-7162
jlsaloff@erie.net
http://www.saloff.com/cowan
Authors of "The Collectors Encyclopedia of Cowan Pottery."

Mark Bassett
P.O. Box 77123
Lakewood, OH 44107
ph: 216-221-6025
mark@markbassett.com
http://www.markbassett.com
Author of books on American art pottery including "Cowan Pottery and the Cleveland School," "Introducing Roseville Pottery," "Bassett's Roseville Prices," "Understanding Roseville Pottery;" Web site contains art pottery information.

Museums/Libraries

Cowan Pottery Museum, Rocky River Public Library
Journal: Cowan Pottery Journal
1600 Hampton Rd.
Rocky River, OH 44116-2699
ph: 440-333-7610
webmaster@rrpl.org
http://www.rrpl.org/rrpl_cowan.stm
Features a collection of over 700 pieces by the artists of the Cowan Pottery Studio of Lakewood and Rocky River, Ohio, 1912-1932.

Dedham Pottery Co.

Clubs/Associations

Jim Kaufman
Dedham Pottery Collectors Society
Newsletter: Dedham Pottery Collectors Society Newsletter
248 Highland St.
Dedham, MA 02026-5833
ph: 800-283-8070 or 781-329-8070
fax: 781-329-9538
dpcurator@aol.com
http://www.dedhampottery.com
Devoted to the history and study of Dedham and Chelsea Keramic Art Works pottery; published by Jim Kaufman, curator for Dedham pottery at the Dedham Historical Society, Dedham, MA; quarterly newsletter.

Collectors

Jane Lee
P.O. Box 134
Monmouth Junction, NJ 08852-0134
ph: 201-429-1531
Wants to buy Dedham dinnerware and service pieces produced in the late 1800s and early 1900s in Massachusetts; "Bunny" items preferred.

Dealers

Jim Kaufman
248 Highland St.
Dedham, MA 02026-5833
ph: 800-283-8070
dpcurator@aol.com
http://www.dedhampottery.com
*Wants to buy Dedham pottery and
Chelsea Keramic Art Works pottery
and related papers or other historical
information; all calls are welcome.*

Experts

Jim Kaufman
248 Highland St.
Dedham, MA 02026-5833
ph: 800-283-8070 or 781-329-8070
fax: 781-329-9538
dpcurator@aol.com
http://www.dedhampottery.com
*Wants to buy Dedham pottery and
Chelsea Keramic Art Works pottery
and related papers or other historical
information; all calls are welcome.*

Museums/Libraries

Ron Frazier
Dedham Historical Society
612 High St.
P.O. Box 215
Dedham, MA 02027-0215
ph: 781-326-1385
fax: 781-326-5762
Society@DedhamHistorical.org
http://www.dedhamhistorical.org
*The Society's museum displays the
largest public collection of Dedham
pottery as well as Chelsea Keramic
Art Works pottery.*

Repro. Sources

Potting Shed Inc., The
43 Bradford St.
P.O. Box 1287
Concord, MA 10742
ph: 978-369-1382 or 800-722-2487
fax: 978-369-1416
info@harelooms.com
http://www.harelooms.com
*Hand made Dedham reproduction
pottery; each piece signed by the
artist.*

Fulper Pottery Co.

Clubs/Associations

Jonathan Nielsen
Stangl Fulper Collectors Club
Newsletter: Stangl Fulper Collectors
Club Newsletter
P.O. Box 538
Flemington, NJ 08822
ph: 908-995-2696 or 908-782-9631
jonathannielsen@stanglfulper.com
http://www.stanglfulper.com
*Promotes Stangl/Fulper pottery,
dinnerware, birds, animals; holds an
annual auction in June and a Pottery
show/convention in October.*

Dealers

David Rago
Perrault Rago Gallery
117 South Main St.
Lambertville, NJ 08530
ph: 609-397-1802
fax: 609-397-5543
perraggal@ragoarts.com
http://www.ragoarts.com

Robert & Nancy Perzel
Popkorn Antiques
P.O. Box 1057
Flemington, NJ 08822
ph: 908-782-9631
*Buys and sells American ceramics
including Franciscan Apple, Dessert
Rose, Metlox, Vernon plaids, Currier
& Ives, Pennsbury, Purintan, Russel
Wright designs, Stangl, Fulper,
Homer Laughlin Fiesta.*

Robert & Diana Runge
Hill-Fulper-Stangl Pottery Museum
P.O. Box 5427
Somerset, NJ 08875
ph: 732-846-1368
robrunge@stanglpottery.org
http://www.stanglpottery.org
*Owners/directors of the Hill-Fulper-
Stangl Pottery Museum located in the
original Stangl factory outlet on Mine
St., Flemington, NJ; also authors of
three books on Stangle Dinnerware,
Artware and Fulper Pottery; buys,
sells, appraises.*

Experts

Robert & Diana Runge
Hill-Fulper-Stangl Pottery Museum
P.O. Box 5427
Somerset, NJ 08875
ph: 732-846-1368
robrunge@stanglpottery.org
http://www.stanglpottery.org
*Owners/directors of the Hill-Fulper-
Stangl Pottery Museum located in the
original Stangl factory outlet on Mine
St., Flemington, NJ; also authors of
three books on Stangle Dinnerware,
Artware and Fulper Pottery; buys,
sells, appraises.*

Douglass White
Classic Interiors & Antiques
2042 N. Rio Grande Ave., Ste. E
Orlando, FL 32804-5644
ph: 407-839-0004

Gonder Pottery

Clubs/Associations

Jim & Carol Boshears
Gonder Collectors Club
Newsletter: Gonder Collector
528 Thomas Rd.
Bolingbrook, IL 60440
ph: 630-783-1639
gondernut@aol.com
http://www.happysempoprium.com/
gonder_collector_club.htm

Collectors

Jim & Pat Persinger
Gonder Museum, The
115 W. Third St.
Ayden, NC 28513
persinger@starfishnet.com
http://www.happysemporium.com/
gonderMuseum.htm

Dealers

Mike Landis
P.O. Box 814
Adamstown, PA 19501
ph: 888-248-2291
landis2@ptd.net
*Buys and sells Gonder pottery;
especially interested in larger pieces,
pieces in gold crackle glaze, other
crackle glazes, or red flambe.*

Jim & Carol Boshears
528 Thomas Rd.
Bolingbrook, IL 60440
ph: 630-783-1639
gondernut@aol.com
*Gonder appraiser, collector, dealer
and expert; author of "Gonder
Ceramic Arts, A Comprehensive
Guide;" also publishes "The Gonder
Collector" newsletter.*

Experts

Jim & Carol Boshears
528 Thomas Rd.
Bolingbrook, IL 60440
ph: 630-783-1639
gondernut@aol.com
*Gonder appraiser, collector, dealer
and expert; author of "Gonder
Ceramic Arts, A Comprehensive
Guide;" also publishes "The Gonder
Collector" newsletter.*

John & Marilyn McCormick
6400 Payne St.
Shawnee Mission, KS 66226
*Buys and sells; consultant to "The
Official Price Guide to Pottery and
Porcelain."*

Internet Resources

Jim & Pat Persinger
Gonder Museum, The
115 W. Third St.
Ayden, NC 28513
persinger@starfishnet.com
http://www.happysemporium.com/
gonderMuseum.htm
*Great Web site for the Gonder
collector; history, images, reproductions, etc.*

Houghton/Dalton

Experts

Jim & Mira Houdeshell
Houdeshell's Antiques Center
1610 South Main St.
Findlay, OH 45840
ph: 419-423-2895 or 419-434-4551
fax: 419-434-6974
houdeshell@findlay.edu
*Author of "Houghton and Dalton
Pottery."*

Newcomb College

Dealers

David Rago
Perrault Rago Gallery
117 South Main St.
Lambertville, NJ 08530
ph: 609-397-1802
fax: 609-397-5543
perraggal@ragoarts.com
http://www.ragoarts.com
*Wants American art pottery, and Arts
and Crafts items such as furniture and
metal items by Stickley, Rohlfs,
Wright, Roycroft, etc.*

Clifford P. Catania
Joshua's Attic
518 Kimberton Rd.
Phoenixville, PA 19460-4737
ph: 610-917-1167
clifford@joshuasattic.com
http://www.davidchasegallery.com
*Buy and sell Newcomb pottery; special
interest in early, high-glaze pieces.*

Caren Fine
11603 Gowrie Ct.
Potomac, MD 20854-3623
ph: 301-299-6886 or 301-854-6262
fine2beme@aol.com
*Buys, sells, trades all decorated
pieces, vases, plaques, lamps,
jardiniers; special interest in large
pieces, even if not perfect; all
Newcomb College arts and crafts
objects.*

North Dakota

Clubs/Associations

Sandy Short, Mem. Ch.
North Dakota Pottery Collectors Society
Newsletter: North Dakota Pottery
Collectors Society Newsletter
P.O. Box 14
Beach, ND 58621-0014
ph: 701-872-3236
fax: 701-872-3236
csshortnd@mcn.net
*Focuses on North Dakota potteries,
e.g. Rosemeade (Wahpeton Pottery
Co.), WPA, Dakota, UND School of
Mines.*

Owens Pottery Co.

Experts

Frank L. Hahn
P.O. Box 934
Lima, OH 45802-0934
ph: 419-225-3816 or 419-222-3816
fax: 419-227-3816
ggb@wcoil.com
*Expert and avid collector of J.B.
Owens Pottery of Zanesville, OH; also
buys, sells and appraises; has
published a book on Owens Pottery.*

Jeanette Stofft
ph: 812-547-5707
5thwheel@swindiana.net
*Manager of the Pottery Lovers
American Art Pottery Show and Sale;
author of "Owens Pottery Un-
earthed."*

Pisgah Forest

Collectors

Roland Sayers
P.O. Box 629
Brevard, NC 28712
ph: 828-883-9562
*Wants to buy Pisgah Forest and
Nonconnah Pottery, most are dated;
also wants Pisgah Forest cameo
pieces with designs.*

Red Wing

Collectors

Ray Reiss
2144 North Leavitt
Chicago, IL 60647
ph: 773-384-3245 or 800-355-2324
fax: 773-384-3252
ray@rayreiss.com
http://www.rayreiss.com
*Author of "Red Wing Art Pottery, I &
II" (including pottery made for
RumRill), classic American pottery
from the 1930s through 1960s;
interested in buying Red Wing art
pottery; published Red Wing
dinnerware price & identification
guide.*

Experts

Roger & Brenda Dollen
214 N. Elm
P.O. Box 386
Avoca, IA 51521
ph: 712-343-6006
*Authors of "Red Wing Art Pottery
Identification & Value Guide;"
appeared on PAX TV's "Treasures in
Your Home."*

Ron Linde
500 South Water St.
Northfield, MN 55057-2060
ph: 507-645-6946
*Collects and consultant to "The
Official Price Guide to Pottery and
Porcelain."*

Ray Reiss
2144 North Leavitt
Chicago, IL 60647
ph: 773-384-3245 or 800-355-2324
fax: 773-384-3252
ray@rayreiss.com
http://www.rayreiss.com
*Author, publisher of "Red Wing Art
Pottery" (including pottery made for
RumRill), classic American pottery
from the 1930s through 1960s; also
author of "Red Wing Pottery Two"
and "Red Wing Dinnerware Price &
Identification Guide."*

Rookwood Pottery Co.

Appraisers

Riley Humler
Cincinnati Art Galleries
225 East 6th St.
Cincinnati, OH 45202
ph: 513-381-2128
fax: 513-381-7527
info@cincinnatiartgalleries.com
http://www.cincinnatiartgalleries.com
*Rookwood is their specialty; also want
Van Briggle, Newcomb, Grueby, etc.*

Auction Services

Don Treadway
Treadway Auctions
2029 Madison Rd.
Cincinnati, OH 45208
ph: 513-321-6742
fax: 513-871-7722
treadway2029@earthlink.net
http://www.treadwaygallery.com
*Specializes in the sale of Arts and
Crafts pottery.*

Collectors

Bob Hut
P.O. Box 1495
Grand Central Station
New York, NY 10163-1495
ph: 800-321-7687
*Wants to buy Rookwood pottery, artist
signed by Schmidt, Valentine, Daly,
Toohey, Horsfall, McDonald,
Laurence, Nichols, Wilcox, Storer,
Wareham, Hurley, Shirayamadani,
Artus Van Briggle, Conant, Robineau,
Losanti, Natzler.*

Man./Prod./Dist.

Art Townley
Rookwood Pottery Co.
10696 Hewitt Rd.
Brooklyn, MI 49230-9760
ph: 517-592-2169
Company makes new pottery.

Roseville Pottery Co.

Clubs/Associations

Roseville Historical Society
91 Main St.
Roseville, OH 43777
ph: 740-697-7127
pchs@netpluscom.com
http://www.netpluscom.com/~pchs/
rosevill.htm

Andrew E. Thomas, Pres.
Valley of the Sun Roseville Collectors
Club
Newsletter: Chasing the Clay
4681 North 84th Way
Scottsdale, AZ 85251-1864
ph: 888-255-0664 or 480-947-5693
fax: 480-994-4382
andrew-thomas@qwest.net
*Meets quarterly in collectors' homes
or local restaurants; purpose is to
increase level of knowledge regarding
Roseville; welcomes collectors, dealers
and all Roseville enthusiasts.*

Collectors

John Hollcraft
15 Smithfield Lane
Bedford, NH 03110
ph: 603-759-0217
john@hollcraft.ws
http://groups.msn.com/
rosevillepotteryexchange
*Roseville collector seeking other like
minded collectors to share information.*

Todd P. Violette
P.O. Box 2594
Waterville, ME 04901-2594
ph: 207-873-8898
antiques@gwi.net
*Wants Roseville Pottery pieces: vases,
umbrella stands, pedestals.*

Nancy Bomm
P.O. Box 656
Clarcona, FL 32710-0656
ph: 407-822-5250
fax: 407-294-7836
jack2741@hotmail.com
http://www.thepotteryexperience.com
*Specializing in Roseville pottery and
all types of antique American art
pottery.*

Andrew E. Thomas
Chasing the Clay
4681 North 84th Way
Scottsdale, AZ 85251-1864
ph: 888-255-0664 or 480-947-5693
fax: 480-994-4382
andrew-thomas@qwest.net
*Buys, sells, trades all patterns of
Roseville pottery from Apple Blossom
to Zephyr Lily; any condition from
mint to severely damaged; the larger
and older the better.*

Dealers

Debbie Woolley
Favorite Past-Times Antiques
6 Main Hill
Bridgton, ME 04009
ph: 207-647-4486
info@maine-antiques.com
http://www.maine-antiques.com/fpt/Index
*Buys and sells authentic Roseville
pottery.*

Marvin McKee
104 Jackson St.
Bangor, ME 04401
ph: 207-945-3450
mcmckee@adelphia.net
http://www.tias.com/stores/amaine
*Buys and sells American art pottery,
especially Roseville.*

David Rago
Perrault Rago Gallery
117 South Main St.
Lambertville, NJ 08530
ph: 609-397-1802
fax: 609-397-5543
perraggal@ragoarts.com
http://www.ragoarts.com

Randy Monsen
Monsen & Baer Inc.
P.O. Box 529
Vienna, VA 22183-0529
ph: 703-938-2129
fax: 703-242-1357
monsenbaer@erols.com

Gary Lickver
P.O. Box 1778
San Marcos, CA 92079-1778
ph: 760-744-5686 or 760-803-0927
*Dealer/collector specializes in
Roseville pottery.*

Experts

Nancy Bomm
P.O. Box 656
Clarcona, FL 32710-0656
ph: 407-822-5250
fax: 407-294-7836
jack2741@hotmail.com
http://www.thepotteryexperience.com
*Authors of "Roseville in All its
Splendor," and "Exclusively
Roseville."*

Mark Bassett
P.O. Box 77123
Lakewood, OH 44107
ph: 216-221-6025
mark@markbassett.com
http://www.markbassett.com
*Author of books on American art
pottery including "Cowan Pottery and
the Cleveland School," "Introducing
Roseville Pottery," "Bassett's
Roseville Prices," "Understanding
Roseville Pottery;" Web site contains
art pottery information.*

Gordon Hoppe
10120 32nd Ave.
Minneapolis, MN 55441
ph: 612-724-1734
*Buys and sells; consultant to "The
Official Price Guide to Pottery and
Porcelain."*

John W. Humphries
P.O. Box 965
Los Molinos, CA 96055-0965
jhantiques@hotmail.com
*Author of "A Price Guide to Roseville
Pottery by the Numbers;" does radio
talk shows.*

Internet Resources

Karen Teneyck
karen@teneyck.com
http://www.inch.com/~kteneyck/
roseville.html
*Great Web site to learn how to tell
fake from original Roseville.*

San Jose Pottery

Experts

Susan Frost
San Jose Tiles & Pottery
806 Rosedale Terrace
Austin, TX 78704-3159
ph: 512-447-2575 or 512-447-0407
fax: 512-447-2575
sfrost@austin.rr.com
http://www.io.com/~reuter
Researches and collects San Jose Pottery, San Jose Mission Crafts, Mexican Arts & Crafts, Inc., and other related San Antonio pottery and tiles.

Van Briggle Pottery Co.

Clubs/Associations

Van Briggle Collectors Society
600 S. 21st St.
Colorado Springs, CO 80901
ph: 719-633-7729 or 800-847-6341
fax: 719-633-7720
VANpottery@aol.com
http://www.vanbriggle.com
A company sponsored club; members receive quarterly newsletter, logo tile, product catalog.

Dealers

Gary Lickver
P.O. Box 1778
San Marcos, CA 92079-1778
ph: 760-744-5686 or 760-803-0927
Collector/dealer buys, sells, collects 1901-1940 Van Briggle art pottery; at most quality indoor antique shows in California.

Experts

Scott Nelson
1636 Nicholson St. NW
Washington, DC 20011
ph: 202-726-6003
Wants early and dated Van Briggle, decorated North Dakota, Hylong, and any fine pottery, damage OK if priced accordingly; consultant to "The Official Price Guide to Pottery and Porcelain," author of book on Van Briggle.

Richard L. Sasicki
P.O. Box 3113
Glen Ellyn, IL 60138-3113
ph: 630-682-8706
artware@sprynet.com
http://home.sprynet.com/~artware
Author of "The Collector's Encyclopedia of Van Briggle Art Pottery."

Man./Prod./Dist.

Van Briggle Pottery Co.
600 S. 21st St.
Colorado Springs, CO 80901
ph: 719-633-7729 or 800-847-6341
fax: 719-633-7720
VANpottery@aol.com
http://www.vanbriggle.com
In continuous operation since 1899. Free tour through production facility.

Showroom for retail sales of beautiful pottery figurines and tiles.

Weller Pottery Co.

Experts

Mark Bassett
P.O. Box 77123
Lakewood, OH 44107
ph: 216-221-6025
mark@markbassett.com
http://www.markbassett.com
Author of books on American art pottery including "Cowan Pottery and the Cleveland School," "Introducing Roseville Pottery," "Bassett's Roseville Prices," "Understanding Roseville Pottery;" Web site contains art pottery information.

CERAMICS (AMERICAN DINNERWARE)

(see also DINNERWARE; MODERNISM)

Collectors

Dave Folckemer
1671 Bellmead Dr.
Altoona, PA 16602
ph: 814-941-3417
mcfol@nb.net
Advisor to "Warman's" for Royal China.

Dealers

Karin Stafford
Great American Dinnerware
kstafford@greatamericandinnerware.com
http://www.greatamericandinnerware.com
Collector, dealer specializing in vintage American dinnerware and kitchenware; buying and selling Homer Laughlin, Taylor Smith & Taylor, Gladding McBean/Franciscan, and others; offers a pattern locating service.

Carolyn Brooks
Neat Stuff
6839 Stefani Dr.
Dallas, TX 75225-2727
ph: 214-696-1803
fax: 214-706-9152
carolyn@neatstuff2.com
http://www.neatstuff2.com
Specializes in Franciscan handpainted dinnerware, Fiestaware, Coors Rosebud.

Joanne Jasper
28005 Balkins Dr.
Agoura Hills, CA 91301
ph: 818-597-0234
fax: 818-597-9503
Author of "The Collectors Encyclopedia of Homer Laughlin China" (Collector Books); autographed copies available; buys and sells Home Laughlin Decorated china and turn of the century American china.

Mr. Naomi Murdach
Naomi's Antiques To Go
1817 Polk St.
San Francisco, CA 94109-3003
ph: 415-775-1207
Buys/sells American dinnerware and art pottery: Hall, Bauer, Tepco, Wallace, Coors, Autumn Leaf, Russel Wright, American Modern, Iroquois, Roseville, Weller, Catalina, and Art Pottery.

Experts

Mark Gonzalez
markgon@bellsouth.net
http://www.ohioriverpottery.com
Author of "Collecting Fiesta, Lu-Ray and Other Colorware;" Web site has dinnerware makers, patterns, images and makers' marks.

Harvey Duke
577 Ave. Y
Brooklyn, NY 11235
Author of "Price Guide to Pottery and Porcelain;" covering 90 collectible American potteries with 22,000 items priced; $15 + P&H, call 800-726-0600; specializes in Ohio and West Virginia dinnerware made from the 1890s to 1950s.

Jo Cunningham
535 E. Normal
Springfield, MO 65807-1659
ph: 417-831-1320
Hlresearcher@aol.com
Author of "The Best Collectible Dinnerware."

Internet Resources

Mark Gonzalez
markgon@bellsouth.net
http://www.ohioriverpottery.com
Author of "Collecting Fiesta, Lu-Ray and Other Colorware;" Web site has dinnerware makers, patterns, images and makers' marks

Blair Ceramics

Collectors

Lori Hinterleiter
43597 Emerald Dunes Place
Leesburg, VA 20176
lhinterl@aol.com
Wants to buy Blair Ceramics in all patterns.

Buffalo Pottery Co.

Collectors

Fred & Lila Schrader
2025 Highway 199
Crescent City, CA 95531
ph: 707-458-3525
Wants to buy Buffalo pottery: Deldare, Blue Willow, jugs and pitchers, game and fish sets.

Experts

Phillip M. Sullivan
580 S. Orleans Rd.
P.O. Box 69
South Orleans, MA 02662-0069
ph: 508-255-8495
fax: 5080-240-1665
Collector and consultant to "The Official Price Guide to Pottery and Porcelain," and "The Antique Trader Price Guide, Pottery."

Vi & Si Altman
Vi & Si's Antiques
39 Spice Bush
Williamsville, NY 14221
ph: 716-688-6925
Buys, sells, appraises and specializes in all ceramic items marked Buffalo Pottery Co. and Buffalo China; authors of "The Book of Buffalo Pottery," $30.50 ppd.

Man./Prod./Dist.

Buffalo China, Inc./Oneida Food Service
500 Bailey Ave.
Buffalo, NY 14210-1733
ph: 716-824-8515 or 800-828-7033

Coors Porcelain Co.

Collectors

Derek Urbaniak
Coors Rosebud Home, The
7509 Orrick
Austin, TX 78749
ph: 512-301-6938
fax: 512-301-6938
admin@potterygallery.com
http://www.potterygallery.com
Interested in buying rare pieces of Coors Rosebud, Coors Decalcomania, and Coors Corrado dinnerware; Web site provides online information for Coors Rosebud collectors.

Jo Ellen Winther
8449 W. 75th Way
Arvada, CO 80005-4533
ph: 800-872-2345 or 303-421-2371
fax: 303-431-5350
repofam@aol.com
Collects Coors Rosebud and other items made by the Coors Porcelain/ Pottery Company of Golden, Colorado.

Gladding-McBean/Franciscan

Clubs/Associations

James Elliot
Franciscan Pottery Collectors Society
Newsletter: Franciscan Newsletter
500 South Farrell Dr., #s-114
Palm Springs, CA 92264
ph: 760-416-6381
gmcb@ix.netcom.com
http://www.gmcb.com/franciscan
Club is devoted to the preservation of the history of Gladding McBean and Franciscan Ware.

Dealers

Karin Stafford
Great American Dinnerware
kstafford@greatamericandinnerware.com
http://www.greatamericandinnerware.com
Collector, dealer specializing in vintage American dinnerware and kitchenware; buying and selling Homer Laughlin, Taylor Smith & Taylor, Gladding McBean/Franciscan, and others; offers a pattern locating service.

Alan Phair
Alan's Antiques
P.O. Box 30373
Long Beach, CA 90853-0373
ph: 562-983-7020
AlanPhair@aol.com
Buys pieces marked "Catalina Pottery" made by Gladding-McBean; shells and some pieces marked with blue ink stamp "MADE IN U.S.A.;" G.M.B., Franciscan and Catalina Pottery advertising items and price lists; also Franciscan dinnerware.

Experts

Mick & Lorna Chase
Fiesta Plus
380 Hawkins Crawford Rd.
Cookeville, TN 38501-6658
ph: 931-372-8333
fiestaplus@yahoo.com
http://www.fiestaplus.com
Advisors on Franciscan to Schroeder's Antiques Price Guide.

James Elliot
500 South Farrell Dr., #s-114
Palm Springs, CA 92264
ph: 760-416-6381
gmcb@ix.netcom.com
http://www.gmcb.com/franciscan
Buys and sells; consultant to "The Official Price Guide to Pottery and Porcelain;" author of "Franciscan, Catalina, and other Gladding, McBean Wares."

Matching Services

Delleen Enge
Franciscan Dinnerware Matching
323 E. Matilija, Ste. 112
Ojai, CA 93023-2775
fax: 805-646-0927
Specializing in mail order sales of Franciscan (trade name used by Gladding McBean and Co.) china, earthenware, and stoneware; large inventory in stock; author of "Franciscan Ware" and "Embossed and Handpainted Franciscan."

Gorham

Man./Prod./Dist.

Gorham, Inc.
100 Lenox Dr.
Lawrenceville, NJ 08648
ph: 609-896-2800 or 800-635-3669
http://www.lenox.com
Sterling and stainless steel flatware, sterling and silverplated hollowware;

fine china, crystal stemware, giftware and dolls; a division of Lenox Brands.

Hall China Co.

Clubs/Associations

Virginia Lee
Hall China Collector's Club
Newsletter: Hall China Collector's Club Newsletter
P.O. Box 360488
Cleveland, OH 44136-0488
ph: 330-220-7456
http://www.chinaspecialties.com/hallnews.html
Association commissions Hall China to produce unique, limited edition items in the Autumn Leaf, Silhouette, Red Poppy, crocus and other patterns; newsletter published yearly; 2000+ members; send SASE for free information.

Dealers

Sue Cross
1603 Madison Ave.
Edwardsville, IL 62025-2514
ph: 618-656-7253
jeweltea@charter.net
http://autumnleaf.freeyellow.com
Buy, sell, trade Hall China patterns: Red Poppy, Cameo Rose, Autumn Leaf; specializes in Autumn Leaf and other items from the Jewel Tea Company.

Experts

Fred Squicciarini
3360 Culver Rd.
Rochester, NY 14622
ph: 716-336-9294
Expert, collector of Hall China Co. Refrigerator Ware and china.

Steve Cagle
With Dave Periord collects Hall China teapots, coffee pots, kitchenware, dinnerware, advertising, early Hall production ware; always willing to answer questions, but please no appraisal requests.

Jane & Don Warner-Smith
Hallway, The
28314 E. 1st Rd.
Farmersville, IL 62533
ph: 217-227-4194 or 941-629-9601 (winter)
Buys and sells; consultant to "The Official Price Guide to Pottery and Porcelain;" has no shop, but does major antique-only shows across the country.

Internet Resources

Marty Kennedy
Hall China Collectors Home Page
4711 SW Brentwood Rd.
Topeka, KS 66606
ph: 785-554-5837
martykennedy@cox.net
http://www.inter-services.com/HallChina
Comprehensive services for Hall China collectors and dealers; site includes items for sale, bulletin board,

classified ads, item identification services, historical information.

Hall China Co./Autumn Leaf

Clubs/Associations

Dianna Kowallis
National Autumn Leaf Collectors Club
Newsletter: NALCC News
P.O. Box 7929
Moreno Valley, CA 92552-7929
ph: 909-653-6308
fax: 909-653-6637
bescom2@nalcc.org
http://www.nalcc.org
Purpose is to broaden collector knowledge of Autumn Leaf dinnerware and accessory pieces to further the enjoyment and pleasure of collecting.

Dealers

Virginia Lee
China Specialties, Inc.
P.O. Box 361280
Strongsville, OH 44136-1280
ph: 330-220-7456
http://www.chinaspecialties.com
Specializes in the Autumn Leaf pattern.

Experts

Harvey Duke
577 Ave. Y
Brooklyn, NY 11235
Author of "Superior Quality Hall China" and "Hall 2", the authoritative books on the Hall China Company; each is $16.95 ppd.; Price Update is $8.50 ppd.

Margaret & Kenn Whitmyer
K & M Antiques
P.O. Box 30806
Columbus, OH 43230
junquer9@columbus.rr.com
http://www.kandmantiques.com
Author of "The Collector's Guide to Hall China."

Ben Moulton
300 West York Dr.
Terre Haute, IN 47802-4492
ph: 812-234-3870
Specializes in Hall China: refrigerator ware, kitchenware, dinnerware, novelties, tea pots, etc.

Jo Cunningham
535 E. Normal
Springfield, MO 65807-1659
ph: 417-831-1320
Hlresearcher@aol.com
Author of "The Autumn Leaf Story," "The Collectors' Encyclopedia of American Dinnerware," and "The Best of Collectible Dinnerware."

Man./Prod./Dist.

Hall China Company, The
1 Anna St.
East Liverpool, OH 43920
ph: 330-385-2900 or 800-445-4255
fax: 330-385-6185
custserv@hallchina.com
http://www.hallchina.com
Maker of Hall China since 1903.

Homer Laughlin China Co.

Clubs/Associations

Nancy May
Homer Laughlin China Collectors Association
Magazine: Dish, The
P.O. Box 1093
Corbin, KY 40702-1093
ph: 877-874-5222
info@hlcca.org
http://www.hlcca.org
For collectors of Homer Laughlin China Company dinnerware including Fiestaware; provides educational material and resources to collectors, dealers, museums, and other interested parties; quarterly magazine.

Dealers

Karin Stafford
Great American Dinnerware
kstafford@greatamericandinnerware.com
http://www.greatamericandinnerware.com
Collector, dealer specializing in vintage American dinnerware and kitchenware; buying and selling Homer Laughlin, Taylor Smith & Taylor, Gladding McBean/Franciscan, and others; offers a pattern locating service.

Edward E. Stump
Raccoon's Tale
6 High St.
Mullica Hill, NJ 08062-9540
ph: 609-478-4488
ractale@fast.net
Specializes in Homer Laughlin China Company's Fiesta, Harlequin and Riviera patterns; buying and selling.

Heather Crossland
Heather's Place
2 North Fordham
Perryton, TX 79070
ph: 806-434-2201
information@heathers-place.net
http://www.heathers-place.net
Specializes in vintage, decorated Homer Laughlin dinnerware.

Kelley Dingess
Missing Piece, The
ph: 253-538-6822
findit@missing-piece.com
http://www.missing-piece.com
Internet-only store specializing in pre-1960 Homer Laughlin decorated dinnerware; offers only the finest HLC dinnerware replacements; pattern ID and locating services available; no Fiesta, Harlequin, Riviera or Restaurant ware.

Experts

Michael Haas
Rte. 46E Box 106
Buttzville, NJ 07829
ph: 908-453-2918
mikeh@nac.net
Buys and sells; consultant to "The Official Price Guide to Pottery and Porcelain."

Matthew Whalen
P.O. Box 26021
Arlington, VA 22215-6201
http://www.mediumgreen.com
Specialist in dinnerware made by the Homer Laughlin China Company.

Richard Racheter
1270 63rd Terrace So.
Saint Petersburg, FL 33705-5842
ph: 727-867-3982
fax: 727-867-3982
Author of "Collector's Guide to Homer Laughlin's Virginia Rose Identification & Values."

Jo Cunningham
535 E. Normal
Springfield, MO 65807-1659
ph: 417-831-1320
Hlresearcher@aol.com
Author of "Homer Laughlin China - A Giant Among Dishes 1873-1939," and "Homer Laughlin, 1940s and 1950s" (Schiffer); co-author with Darlene Nossaman of "Homer Laughlin China - Guide to Shapes and Patterns."

Darlene Nossaman
5419 Lake Charles
Waco, TX 76710
Co-author with Jo Cunningham of "Homer Laughlin China Identification...Shapes and Decorations."

Joanne Jasper
28005 Balkins Dr.
Agoura Hills, CA 91301
ph: 818-597-0234
fax: 818-597-9503
Author of "The Collectors Encyclopedia of Homer Laughlin China" (Collector Books); autographed copies available; buys and sells Home Laughlin Decorated china and turn of the century American china.

Man./Prod./Dist.

Homer Laughlin Co., The
6th & Harrison Sts.
Newell, WV 26050
ph: 304-387-1300 or 800-452-4462
fax: 304-387-0593
hlc@hlchina.com
http://www.hlchina.com
Vitrified china and ironstone dinnerware; Web site has a page for collectors.

Periodicals

Kelley Dingess
Missing Piece, The
Newsletter: Laughlin Eagle, The
ph: 253-538-6822
findit@missing-piece.com
http://www.missing-piece.com

Homer Laughlin/Fiesta

Clubs/Associations

Virginia Lee
Fiesta Collectors Club
Newsletter: Fiesta Collectors Quarterly
P.O. Box 471
Valley City, OH 44280-0471
ph: 330-220-7456
http://www.chinaspecialties.com/fiesta.html
The original association for Fiesta Collectors, now in its tenth year; newsletter dedicated to Fiesta, Harlequin Riviera and other 1930s to 1970s solid-glazed dinnerware from the Newell/East Liverpool region; buy and sell ads.

Dealers

Fred & Linda Suzman
Suzman's Antiques
P.O. Box 301
Rehoboth, MA 02769
ph: 508-252-5729
suzmanf@ride.ri.net
Buys and sells Depression glass and Fiestaware.

Larry Sherman
Fiesta Dish
12 Skip Lane
Burlington, CT 06013
ph: 860-675-3159
Buys and sells original 1950s colors of Fiesta; Web site has a listing and prices of pieces for sale; mail order only.

Gus Gustafson
Buttzville Center
Rte. 46E Box 106
Buttzville, NJ 07829-9999
ph: 908-453-2918
Buys and sells, specializes in Homer Laughlin China Company's Fiesta pattern; consultant to "The Official Price Guide to Pottery and Porcelain."

Robert & Nancy Perzel
Popkorn Antiques
P.O. Box 1057
Flemington, NJ 08822
ph: 908-782-9631
Buys and sells American ceramics including Franciscan Apple, Dessert Rose, Metlox, Vernon plaids, Currier & Ives, Pennsbury, Puritan, Russel Wright designs, Stangl, Fulper, Homer Laughlin Fiesta.

Liz Kramar
Kramar's Kollectible Korner
P.O. Box 30
Elk Mills, MD 21920-0030
ph: 410-398-0105
wildwedge@comcast.net

Mick & Lorna Chase
Fiesta Plus
380 Hawkins Crawford Rd.
Cookeville, TN 38501-6658
ph: 931-372-8333
fiestaplus@yahoo.com
http://www.fiestaplus.com
Buys and sells Fiesta, Franciscan USA, Metlox, Lu Ray, Vernon Kilns, Harlequin, Riviera, Kitchen Kraft, Spode Christmas Tree pattern; ships anywhere; ironclad money back guarantee; credit cards welcome.

Virginia Lee
China Specialties, Inc.
P.O. Box 361280
Strongsville, OH 44136-1280
ph: 330-220-7456
http://www.chinaspecialties.com
Buys and sells Fiesta, all colors and all pieces; carries full line of new Fiesta as well.

Internet Resources

Candy Fagerlin
Fiesta Fanatic @ Work
c/o QL Capital
5161 "C" CLayton Rd.
Concord, CA 94521
fiestafanatic@fiestafanatic.com
http://www.fiestafanatic.com
A Web site devoted to vintage and reissue Fiesta dinnerware produced by Homer Laughlin China Co; up-to-the-minute news of soon-to-be released additions to the Fiesta line, photos, updated daily with answers on "How to Find Fiesta."

Iroquois China Co.

Experts

Paul Beedenbender
1203 East Paris St.
Tampa, FL 33604
Collects and consultant to "The Official Price Guide to Pottery and Porcelain."

Metlox Potteries

Collectors

Rhea & Gene Evanson
Metlox Nuts, The
ge1228@earthlink.net
http://home.earthlink.net/~ge1228
Long-time collectors of California's Metlox Potteries Dinner ware and Art ware.

Experts

Carl Gibbs, Jr.
P.O. Box 131584
Houston, TX 77219-1584
ph: 713-521-9661
Author of "Collector's Encyclopedia

of Metlox Potteries;" autographed copies for $24.95 plus $3 postage.

Pennsbury Pottery Co.

Collectors

Mark & Ellen Supnick
Collectibles R US Inc.
2623 Center Court Dr.
Fort Lauderdale, FL 33332
ph: 954-727-9770
ellen@sunshinejars.com
http://www.sunshinejars.com
Author of "Shawnee Pottery", and "Collecting Hull's Little Red Riding Hood."

Pfaltzgraff Pottery Co.

Clubs/Associations

Vicki Quint
Pfaltzgraff America Collectors Club
Newsletter: America Messenger, The
821 Briar Court
Watertown, WI 53094
ph: 920-206-0954
vquint@charter.net
http://groups.yahoo.com/pfaltzgraffamericacollectors
Members interested in the "America" or "Americana" pattern of Pfaltzgraff dinnerware (made from 1983 to 1989.)

Sandy Anderson
Pfaltzgraff Folk Art Collectors Club
E-zine: Folk Art News
RT 1, Box 328A
Edwards, MO 65326
ph: 573-347-2733
fax: 573-347-2737
acgraph@aroundthelake.com
http://www.aroundthelake.com/pfaltzgraff
Members are interested in the discontinued "Folk Art" pattern of Pfaltzgraff dinnerware.

Collectors

Denise Brown
P.O. Box 648
Columbus, IN 47202
ph: 812-379-2201
fax: 812-379-4306
zubba@iquest.net
http://groups.yahoo.com/pfaltzgraffamericacollectors
Past-membership chairman for the Pfaltzgraff America Collectors Club; contact for info regarding the club.

Vicki Quint
821 Briar Court
Watertown, WI 53094
ph: 920-206-0954
vquint@charter.net
http://clubs.yahoo.com/clubs/pfaltzgraffamericacollectors

Sandy Anderson
RT 1, Box 328A
Edwards, MO 65326
ph: 573-347-2733
fax: 573-347-2737
acgraph@aroundthelake.com
http://www.aroundthelake.com/pfaltzgraff
*Wants to buy Pfaltzgraff dinnerware
in the "Folk Art" pattern.*

Marie Fibelstad
324 E. Lincoln St.
Derby, KS 67037
ph: 316-788-0415
Collects American Pfaltzgraff dishes.

Experts

David Zeiger
P.O. Box 105
Spring Grove, PA 17362
ph: 717-632-5912
*Buys and sells anything "Pfaltzgraff":
Salt, Albany, and Bristle glazed
stoneware Art Pottery, dinner ware
patterns, old brochures and catalogs,
etc.; consultant to "The Official Price
Guide to Pottery and Porcelain."*

Teresa Streacher
ttales@bright.net

Man./Prod./Dist.

Dave Walsh
Pfaltzgraff Co., The
140 East Market
York, PA 17401
ph: 717-848-5500 or 800-999-2811
fax: 717-846-1133
consumer.service@pfz.com
http://www.pfaltzgraff.com
*Begun in 1811 in York, PA,
Pfaltzgraff manufactured cobalt-
decorated salt-glazed stoneware,
Bristol-glazed ware, blue sponge,
yellowware, Art Pottery, kitchen and
ovenware, etc.; today a leading
manufacturer of ceramic dinnerware.*

Matching Services

David Zeiger
P.O. Box 105
Spring Grove, PA 17362
ph: 717-632-5912
*Matching and/or replacements for old
and new Pfaltzgraff dinner ware
patterns; also others upon request.*

Pickard

Auction Services

Joy Luke
Joy Luke Auction Gallery
300 E. Grove St.
Bloomington, IL 61701-5232
ph: 309-828-5533
fax: 309-829-2266
robert@joyluke.com
http://www.joyluke.com
*Conducts periodic auctions
specializing in the sale of toys, banks,
trains and dolls.*

Clubs/Associations

Jackie Pope
Pickard Collectors Club
Newsletter: Pickard Collectors Club
Newsletter
300 E. Grove St.
Bloomington, IL 61701-5232
ph: 309-828-5533
fax: 309-829-2266
joyluke@aol.com
*Organized to advance the knowledge
of collectors and dealers about this
fine porcelain hand decorated in
America.*

Dealers

Glenda Ridgway
P.O. Box 231
Anna, IL 62906
ph: 618-833-7971
*Charter member, Pickard Collectors
Club.*

Man./Prod./Dist.

Pickard China Co.
782 Pickard Ave.
Antioch, IL 60002
ph: 847-395-3800
fax: 847-395-3827
Finest@pickardchina.com
http://www.pickardchina.com
*Fine china dinnerware and giftware;
limited edition plates.*

Porcelier

Clubs/Associations

Shirley Hall
Porcelier Collectors Club
Newsletter: Porcelier Paper, The
21 Tamarac Swamp Rd.
Wallingford, CT 06492-5529
ph: 203-265-5791
ThePPLady@aol.com
*For collectors of Porcelier dinner-
ware, service pieces and all-ceramic
small electrical kitchen appliances; bi-
monthly newsletter features
information and pictures of patterns,
new finds, and research; free ads for
members.*

Collectors

Shirley Hall
21 Tamarac Swamp Rd.
Wallingford, CT 06492-5529
ph: 203-265-5791
ThePPLady@aol.com
*Collectors of Porcelier china, coffee
pots, teapots, service pieces and all-
ceramic small electrical kitchen
appliances.*

Experts

Susan E. Grindberg-Lynn
Porcelier Connection, The
1412 Pathfinder Rd.
Henderson, NV 89014
ph: 702-898-7535
*Author of "Collector's Guide to
Porcelier China;" buys and sells
Porcelier china; especially interested*

*in toasters, waffle irons, sandwich
grills and percolators.*

Red Wing

Collectors

Doug Way
1215 Packard
Ann Arbor, MI 48104
dway@mat.net
http://www.mindspring.com/~dway/
town.html
*Specializes in the Town & Country
pattern dinnerware designed by Eva
Zeisel for Red Wing Pottery.*

Experts

Monna Erickson
1712 Harrison Court
Northfield, MN 55057
*Collects and consultant to "The
Official Price Guide to Pottery and
Porcelain;" specializing in Red Wing
hand-painted dinnerware.*

Reed & Barton

Man./Prod./Dist.

Reed & Barton
144 W. Britannia St.
Taunton, MA 02780
ph: 508-824-6611 or 800-822-1824
fax: 508-822-7269
information@reedbarton.com
http://www.reedbarton.com
*Produces china, crystal, silver,
silverplate, and stainless flatware,
collectible plates, bells, dolls,
ornaments and accessories.*

Royal China Co./Currier & Ives

Clubs/Associations

Eldon R. "Bud" Aupperle
Currier & Ives Dinnerware Collectors
Club
Newsletter: Currier & Ives Collectors'
Newsletter
29470 Saxon Rd.
Toulon, IL 61483-9205
ph: 309-896-3331
fax: 309-856-6005
Aupperlee@bhc.edu
http://www.royalchinaclub.com
*For collectors all items made by the
Royal China Co. of Sebring, OH,
including Currier & Ives dinnerware.*

Collectors

Kory McMahon
8521 Cazenovia Rd.
Manlius, NY 13104
kjm_kdb@a-znet.com
*Avid collector of pink and blue
Currier and Ives Royal China and
Memory Lane Royal China.*

Dave Folckemer
1671 Bellmead Dr.
Altoona, PA 16602
ph: 814-941-3417
mcfol@nb.net
*Advisor to "Warman's" for Royal
China.*

Duaine Goodno
104 Esworthy Place
Gaithersburg, MD 20878
ph: 301-208-0464
royalchina@collector.org
*Collects Royal China Co.'s Currier &
Ives dinnerware.*

Eldon R. "Bud" Aupperle
29470 Saxon Rd.
Toulon, IL 61483-9205
ph: 309-896-3331
fax: 309-856-6005
Aupperlee@bhc.edu
*Author of "A Collector's Guide for
Currier & Ives Dinnerware by Royal
China Co."*

Patti St.
3108 SE Quaker Rd.
Columbus, KS 66725
ph: 316-848-3529
*A newsletter especially for enthusiasts
of Currier & Ives china by the Royal
China Co. of Sebring, OH; also
covers other china patterns by Royal
China Co. as well as other Currier &
Ives collectibles.*

Experts

Eldon R. "Bud" Aupperle
29470 Saxon Rd.
Toulon, IL 61483-9205
ph: 309-896-3331
fax: 309-856-6005
Aupperlee@bhc.edu
*Author of "A Collector's Guide for
Currier & Ives Dinnerware by Royal
China Co."*

Scio Pottery

Man./Prod./Dist.

Scio Pottery Museum
38500 Crimm Rd.
P.O. Box 565
Scio, OH 43988
ph: 740-945-3111 or 740-945-3121
fax: 740-945-1575
sciopackage@eohio.net
*Antique dinnerware made by the Scio
Pottery Company.*

Southern Potteries/Blue Ridge

Clubs/Associations

Wanda Hashe
Blue Ridge Collectors Club
208 Harris St.
Erwin, TN 37650
ph: 423-743-9337
fax: 423-743-4629

Dealers

Diana E. Bullock
Bullock Antiques
P.O. Box 5427
Somerset, NJ 08875
ph: 732-846-1368
*Buys and sells Blue Ridge/Southern
Pottery dinnerware and Stangl
dinnerware.*

Wanda Hashe
208 Harris St.
Erwin, TN 37650
ph: 423-743-9337
fax: 423-743-4629

Experts

Norma Lilly
144 Highland Dr.
Blountville, TN 37617-5404
ph: 423-323-5247
Dealer, collector, expert wants Blue Ridge china made by Southern Potteries, Inc.; any unusual form or pattern.

Susan Moore
51803 Windyridge Dr.
South Bend, IN 46628-9290
Collects and consultant to "The Official Price Guide to Pottery and Porcelain."

Bill & Betty Newbound
4567 Chadsworth
Commerce, MI 48382
Authors of "Collector's Encyclopedia of Blue Ridge Dinnerware."

Periodicals

Norma Lilly
Newsletter: National Blue Ridge Newsletter
144 Highland Dr.
Blountville, TN 37617-5404
ph: 423-323-5247
10 pre-punched pages; Q&A up-date, articles, new patterns, readers comment section; published bi-monthly; published since 1980.

Stangl Pottery Co.

(see also CERAMICS [AMERICAN FIGURES], Stangl Pottery Co.)

Dealers

Diana E. Bullock
Bullock Antiques
P.O. Box 5427
Somerset, NJ 08875
ph: 732-846-1368
Buys and sells Blue Ridge/Southern Pottery dinnerware and Stangl dinnerware.

Robert & Diana Runge
Hill-Fulper-Stangl Pottery Museum
P.O. Box 5427
Somerset, NJ 08875
ph: 732-846-1368
robrunge@stanglpottery.org
http://www.stanglpottery.org
Owners/directors of the Hill-Fulper-Stangl Pottery Museum located in the original Stangl factory outlet on Mine St., Flemington, NJ; also authors of three books on Stangle Dinnerware, Artware and Fulper Pottery; buys, sells, appraises.

Experts

Robert & Nancy Perzel
Popkorn Antiques
P.O. Box 1057
Flemington, NJ 08822
ph: 908-782-9631
Offers a Stangl Pottery dinner matching service; also Stangl birds and Artware; consultant to "The Official Price Guide to Pottery and Porcelain," "Schroeder's," and "Warman's."

Robert & Diana Runge
Hill-Fulper-Stangl Pottery Museum
P.O. Box 5427
Somerset, NJ 08875
ph: 732-846-1368
robrunge@stanglpottery.org
http://www.stanglpottery.org
Owners/directors of the Hill-Fulper-Stangl Pottery Museum located in the original Stangl factory outlet on Mine St., Flemington, NJ; also authors of three books on Stangle Dinnerware, Artware and Fulper Pottery; buys, sells, appraises.

Taylor, Smith & Taylor/LuRay

Collectors

Joe Zacharias
P.O. Box 99516
Raleigh, NC 27624-9516
ph: 919-848-6966
IBUYLURAY2@aol.com
Wants LuRay PASTELS: chocolate/straight-sided A/D pots, sugars, creamers; blue/green - 7" mini-platters; grey 36's bowls, chop plate; 8", 9", 10" LuRay Calendar plates; decalled LuRay items; also any Taylor, Smith & Taylor ads, brochures.

Dealers

Karin Stafford
Great American Dinnerware
kstafford@greatamericandinnerware.com
http://www.greatamericandinnerware.com
Collector, dealer specializing in vintage American dinnerware and kitchenware; buying and selling Homer Laughlin, Taylor Smith & Taylor, Gladding McBean/Franciscan, and others; offers a pattern locating service.

Edward E. Stump
Raccoon's Tale
6 High St.
Mullica Hill, NJ 08062-9540
ph: 609-478-4488
ractale@fast.net
Specializes in Taylor, Smith and Taylor Company's LuRay Pastels line.

Experts

Bill & Kathy Meehan
P.O. Box 2054
Haddonfield, NJ 08033
Authors of "Collector's Guide to LuRay Pastels: Identification & Values."

Ray & Virginia Cramble
Antiques From Memory Lane
7340 Memory Lane Lane NE
Minneapolis, MN 55432-3217
Buys, sells, collects and appraises almost all Abingdon and rare LuRay.

Vernon Kilns

Collectors

Bill Stern
361 North Orange Dr.
Los Angeles, CA 90036
ph: 323-965-0371
wbstern@aol.com
http://www.mocad.org
Author of "California Pottery: From Missions to Modernism" (Chronicle Books, 2001).

Dealers

Judi & Dave Thompson
1668 Melissa Way
Anaheim, CA 92802
ph: 714-520-0050

Tim & Linda Colling
TLC*Antiques
P.O. Box 110605
Campbell, CA 95011-0605
ph: 408-761-4145
tim@colling.com
http://www.vernonware.com
A Web site for collectors of Vernonware - art pottery and dinnerware made by Vernon Kilns in Los Angeles during the 1930s through the 1950s; buys and sells.

Experts

Harold Mathews
24 Church St.
Honeoye, NY 14471
Consultant to "The Official Price Guide to Pottery and Porcelain."

Maxine Nelson
7657 E. Hazelwood St.
Scottsdale, AZ 85251-1510
Author of "Collectible Vernon Kilns," 2nd Edition (2003).

Bess Christensen
1313 East Locust Ave.
Lompoc, CA 93436-7442
ph: 805-736-7248
Consultant to "The Official Price Guide to Pottery and Porcelain."

Internet Resources

Tim & Linda Colling
Vernon Kilns Website
P.O. Box 110605
Campbell, CA 95011-0605
ph: 408-761-4145
tim@colling.com
http://www.vernonware.com
An information site for Vernon Kilns collectors: buy, learn, identify, chat, post; offers a free email list dedicated to Vernonware collecting.

Periodicals

Newsletter: Vernon Views
P.O. Box 24234
Tempe, AZ 85285
The newsletter for collectors of Vernon Kilns pottery; recent finds, free ads, interesting articles.

Wallace China Co.

Collectors

Terry Ahlberg
1000 Irvine Blvd.
Tustin, CA 92780-3527
ph: 714-730-1000 or 949-856-9395
fax: 714-730-1752
emailit@earthlink.net
Wants the Westward Ho series in the following pattern: Rodeo, Pioneer Trails, Boots & Saddle, Longhorn, Little Buckaroo.

Warwick China Co.

Experts

Donald C. Hoffmann, Sr.
1291 N. Elmwood Dr.
Aurora, IL 60506
ph: 630-859-3435
Author of "Why Not Warwick," and "Warwick A to W;" also advisor to Schroeder's Price Guide.

Watt Pottery Co.

Clubs/Associations

Watt Collectors Association
Newsletter: Watt's News
1431 4th St. SW
P.M.B. 221
Mason City, IA 50401
wattcollectors@yahoo.com
http://server34.hypermart.net/wattcollectors/watt.htm
A non-profit educational organization dedicated to the study and preservation of this unique segment of the pottery world.

Dealers

Henry & Ashley Higham
Higham Enterprise, Inc.
P.O. Box 8183
Dothan, AL 36304
ph: 334-678-6331
info@wattpottery.com
http://www.wattpottery.com
Buy and sell Watt Pottery.

Experts

Dennis Thompson
P.O. Box 26067
Cleveland, OH 44126-0067
ph: 216-235-8548
dennis.thompson@lerc.nasa.gov
http://www.execpc.com/~wmhill/wpcusa2.html
Author of "Watt Pottery, a Collectors Reference with Price Guide" (Schiffer, 1994); 240 pages; 800 color photos; $43ppd from author; consultant to "The Official Price Guide to Pottery and Porcelain."

CERAMICS (AMERICAN FIGURES)

Ceramic Arts Studio

Clubs/Associations

Jim Petzold
Ceramic Arts Studio Collectors
Association
Newsletter: CAS Collector
P.O. Box 46
Madison, WI 53701-0046
ph: 608-241-9138
fax: 608-241-8770
cas@ceramicartsstudio.com
http://www.ceramicartsstudio.com
Provides accurate information on authentic Ceramic Arts Studio (Madison, WI) works; quarterly newsletter with stories and memories of the Studio and the collecting experience; "Inventory Record & Price Guide" lists 800+ works; conventions.

Collectors

Tim Holthaus
P.O. Box 46
Madison, WI 53701-0046
ph: 608-241-9138
fax: 608-241-8770
cas@ceramicartsstudio.com
http://www.ceramicartsstudio.com
Co-editor with of "CAS Collector;" wants to buy all Ceramic Arts Studio & Royal Copley creations including shakers, figurines, dolls, lamps, and metal art.

Experts

Jim Petzold
P.O. Box 46
Madison, WI 53701-0046
ph: 608-241-9138
fax: 608-241-8770
cas@ceramicartsstudio.com
http://www.ceramicartsstudio.com
Co-editor with of "CAS Collector;" wants to buy all Ceramic Arts Studio & Royal Copley creations including shakers, figurines, dolls, lamps, and metal art.

Florence

Clubs/Associations

David Miller, Pres.
Florence Ceramics Collectors Society
1971 Blue Fox Dr.
Lansdale, PA 19446
FlorenceCeramics@aol.com
Publishes quarterly color newsletter.

Dealers

Florence Showcase
P.O. Box 468
Bennington, VT 05201-0468
ph: 802-442-3336
floshow@sweetpea.net
http://www.sweetpea.net/floshow/
  default.asp
Large selection of Florence figurines: ladies, gentlemen, pairs and sets, children, young adults, artware, seated figures; also reference information.

Mike & Bev
637 E. Main St.
Cottage Grove, OR 97424-2039
ph: 541-942-3664

Experts

Sue & Jerry Kline
Sweetpea Antiques & Collectibles
1265 S Route 7
Bennington, VT 05201
ph: 802-442-3336
floshow@sweetpea.net
http://www.sweetpea.net
Buys and sells; co-authors with Margaret Wehrspaun of "Florence Ceramics A Labor of Love;" consultant to "The Official Price Guide to Pottery and Porcelain" and "Schroeder's."

Jeanne Fredericks
12364 Downey Ave.
Downey, CA 90242-3556
ph: 562-861-4781
jeenrob@aol.com
Collector and consultant to "The Official Price Guide to Pottery and Porcelain" and "The Florence Collectibles - An Era of Elegance" by Doug Foland.

Rita Bee
6960 Abel Stearns Ave.
Riverside, CA 92509
ph: 909-683-1485
AR2Bee@aol.com
Editor of the "Florence Collector's Club Newsletter."

Doug Foland
6203 SE 92nd
Portland, OR 97266
ph: 503-772-0471
floc69@aol.com
Florence advisor to "Schroeder's Price Guide."

Kay Finch

Experts

Frances Finch Webb
1589 Gretel Lane
Mountain View, CA 94040-3704
ph: 650-968-0739
Author of "The New Kay Finch Field Identification Guide," available from author; keeper of FINCH archival and historic records; research consultant for other authors on Kay Finch.

Stangl Pottery Co.

(see also CERAMICS [AMERICAN DINNERWARE], Stangl Pottery Co.)

Clubs/Associations

Jonathan Nielsen
Stangl Fulper Collectors Club
Newsletter: Stangl Fulper Collectors
  Club Newsletter
P.O. Box 538
Flemington, NJ 08822
ph: 908-995-2696 or 908-782-9631
jonathannielsen@stanglfulper.com
http://www.stanglfulper.com
Promotes Stangl/Fulper pottery, dinnerware, birds, animals; holds an annual auction in June and a Pottery show/convention in October.

Dennis Barone
Stangl Bird Collectors Club
P.O. Box 3146
Patchogue, NY 11772
ph: 631-654-9386 or 631-475-6537
fax: 631-475-0315
stangl.bird@verizon.net
http://members.bellatlantic.net?~ljsdavis
A cyber based club with monthly email newsletter focusing on Stangl birds.

Dealers

Liz Kramar
Kramar's Kollectible Korner
P.O. Box 30
Elk Mills, MD 21920-0030
ph: 410-398-0105
wildwedge@comcast.net
Buying and selling Stangl birds.

Experts

Harvey Duke
577 Ave. Y
Brooklyn, NY 11235
Author of "Stangl Pottery", the most comprehensive and authoritative price and identification guide on Stangl; $22.45 ppd.

CERAMICS (AMERICAN PRODUCTION ARTWARE)

(see also COOKIE JARS; MODERNISM)

Auction Services

Michael Verlangieri
Verlangieri Gallery
P.O. Box 844
Cambria, CA 93428-0844
ph: 805-927-4428
fax: 805-924-0110
michael@calpots.com
http://www.calpots.com
Periodic auctions of Bauer, Russel Wright, Gladding McBean, Catalina Island, Pacific, Sascha Brastoff, Matthew Addame, Metlox, Vernon Kilns, Franciscan, Modglins, Halderman, Camark, Brayton Laguna, Batchelder, and more.

Dealers

Karen M. Guido
Karen Michelle Antique Tiles
1835 US 1 South #119, PMB 243
Saint Augustine, FL 32084
ph: 904-471-3226
karen@antiquetiles.com
http://www.antiquetiles.com
Specializing in American & English tiles mostly from 1870 to 1950; American Encaustic (Los Angeles), Catalina Island, Tropico, Gladding McBean, California potteries, and pottery by tile manufacturers.

Dave DeWitt
Mad Dog Pottery
8712 N. Eastern Ave.
Oklahoma City, OK 73131
ph: 405-478-1725
http://members.aol.com/ddewitt506
Buys and sells Frankoma pottery; Web site updated weekly with new products.

Susan & Mark Wiskow
5214 F Diamond Heights #302
San Francisco, CA 94131
ph: 415-587-9133
fax: 415-239-5148
Buys and sells American-made pottery and glass figurines from the period 1920 to 1950.

Internet Resources

Ohiopottery.com
webmaster@ohiopottery.com
http://www.ohiopottery.com
Where collectors of Ohio pottery come together; cookie jars, vases & planters, reproductions, reference books, for sale, wanteds, upcoming events, etc.; Goner, hull, McCoy, Robinson Ransbottom, Roseville, Shawnee, Watt, Weller.

Abingdon

Clubs/Associations

Elaine Westover
Abingdon Pottery Collectors Club
Newsletter: Abingdon Pottery Collectors
  Newsletter
210 Knox Hwy. 5
Abingdon, IL 61410-9332
ph: 309-462-3267
Sponsors annual show and flea market on the 3rd Saturday in August of every year.

Collectors

Don King
7474 Jason Ave. NE
Monticello, MN 55362-3000
ph: 612-295-8405
Wants Abingdon Pottery decorated pieces, tableware, salesman samples, cookie jars.

Dealers

Barbara Stevens
Some Where in Time Antiques
3448 S. Hagadorn Rd.
Okemos, MI 48864
ph: 517-699-8372 or 517-337-4988
fax: 517-337-4560
stevensg44@aol.com
Buys and sells Abingdon pottery.

Vicki Quint
Quintiques
821 Criar Court
Watertown, WI
ph: 920-206-0954
vquint@charter.net
http://clubs.yahoo.com/clubs/
pfaltzgraffamericacollectors
Buys and sells Abingdon pottery.

Experts

Ray & Virginia Cramble
Antiques From Memory Lane
7340 Memory Lane Lane NE
Minneapolis, MN 55432-3217
Buys, sells, collects and appraises almost all Abingdon and rare LuRay.

Robert Rush
210 North Main St.
Abingdon, IL 61410-1443
ph: 309-462-2423
Collects and consultant to "The Official Price Guide to Pottery and Porcelain."

Elaine Westover
210 Knox Hwy. 5
Abingdon, IL 61410-9332
ph: 309-462-3267
Collects and consultant to "The Official Price Guide to Pottery and Porcelain."

American Bisque Company

Experts

Joyce Roerig
1501 Maple Ridge Rd.
Walterboro, SC 29488-9278
ph: 843-538-2487
fax: 843-538-4263
Buys and sells; consultant to "Official Price Guide to Pottery & Porcelain;" founded in 1919, American Bisque Company produced florist ware, kitchenware, and cookie jars.

Arkansas Potteries

Clubs/Associations

Gary Moore, Pub.
National Association of Arkansas Pottery Collectors
Newsletter: Arkansas Pottery Exchange
2006 Beckenham Cove
Little Rock, AR 72212
info@moorecsi.net
http://home.flash.net/~gemoore/
nsapc.htm
Will answer questions about Arkansas pottery such as Camark, Niloak and Ouchita pottery; please include LSASE with questions.

Bauer

Collectors

Ed McDermott
1415 McKendree
Kevil, KY 42053
ph: 270-488-3420
emcdermott@brtc.net
Wants to buy any marked stoneware or advertising paper from J.A. Bauer Pottery when they were located in Paducah, KY.

Tim & Paul
P.O. Box 2524
Berkeley, CA 94702-0524
ph: 510-540-8960
bauerpot@ix.netcom.com
Former editors of the "Bauer Quarterly" newsletter.

James L. Harmon
P.O. Box 25
Banks, OR 97106
ph: 503-324-9099
Wants to buy Bauer; Bauer ringware wanted in all colors; top dollar paid for black; bowls especially wanted.

Experts

Jack Chipman
P.O. Box 1079
Venice, CA 90294-1079
ph: 310-396-5320
jchipman@amerimail.net
http://www.jackchipman.com
Buys and sells; consultant to "The Official Price Guide to Pottery and Porcelain" (1992) and "Schroeder's Antiques Price Guide", author of "Collector's Guide to Bauer Pottery" (1997).

Internet Resources

Bauer Pottery Page, The
DMagnon@aol.com
http://users.aol.com/Stadelbach/
BauerPottery.htm

Debra Zeller
Bauer Pottery
info@bauerpottery.com
http://www.bauerpottery.com
Bauer publications, Bauer talk, displays, other Bauer info; does not provide appraisals.

Brush-McCoy Pottery

Experts

Martha & Steve Sanford
230 Harrison Ave.
Campbell, CA 95008
ph: 408-978-8408
info@sanfords.com
http://www.sanfords.com
Authors of eight books on pottery including "SanfordS Guide to Brush-McCoy Pottery," "SanfordS Guide to McCoy Pottery," and "SanfordS Guide to Peters & Reed and The Zane Pottery Company."

California Potteries

(see also CERAMICS [AMER. PROD. ARTWARE], Bauer; CERAMICS [AMER. PROD. ARTWARE], Catalina Island Pottery; CERAMICS [AMER. PROD. ARTWARE], deLee; CERAMICS [AMER. PROD. ARTWARE], Hedi Schoop; CERAMICS [AMER. PROD. ARTWARE], Sascha Brastoff)

Dealers

Rick & Sharon Blumenthal
California Dreamin'
5436 Matilija Ave.
Van Nuys, CA 91401
ph: 818-781-7589
Buys, collects and sells Catalina, Howard Pierce, Roselane, Kay Finch, Hedi Schoop.

Experts

Bill Stern
361 North Orange Dr.
Los Angeles, CA 90036
ph: 323-965-0371
wbstern@aol.com
http://www.mocad.org
Author of "California Pottery: From Missions to Modernism" (Chronicle Books, 2001).

Jack Chipman
P.O. Box 1079
Venice, CA 90294-1079
ph: 310-396-5320
jchipman@amerimail.net
http://www.jackchipman.com
Buys and sells; consultant to "The Official Price Guide to Pottery and Porcelain" (1992), author of "Collector's Encyclopedia of California Pottery, 2nd Edition" (1999)

Susan Cox
800 Murray Dr.
El Cajon, CA 92020
ph: 619-697-5922
antiqfever@aol.com

Internet Resources

Michael Verlangieri
Verlangieri Gallery
P.O. Box 844
Cambria, CA 93428-0844
ph: 805-927-4428
fax: 805-924-0110
michael@calpots.com
http://www.calpots.com
Features dealer ads, pottery news, pottery show coverage, and books on California pottery.

Museums/Libraries

Catalina Island Museum
P.O. Box 366
Avalon, CA 90704
ph: 310-510-2414
fax: 310-510-2780
catalinaislmuseum@catalinaisp.com
http://www.catalina.com/museum.html
Dedicated to collecting, preserving, exhibiting Santa Catalina Island's rich and unique historical and cultural heritage including tile and pottery manufactured on the Island from 1927 to 1937.

Camark Pottery Co.

Collectors

Gary Moore
2006 Beckenham Cove
Little Rock, AR 72212
info@moorecsi.net
http://home.flash.net/~gemoore/
nsapc.htm
Collector of Camark pottery, dealer in American art pottery, publisher of the National Association of Arkansas Pottery Collector's newsletter.

Experts

Letitia Landers
Colony Publishing
P.O. Box 203
Camden, AR 71711
ph: 870-231-6861 or 870-836-3022
fax: 870-836-0127
camark@cei.net
http://www.camark.com
Expert, collector, author on Camark pottery which was made in Camden, AR from 1920s through 1960s; "Camark Pottery, An Identification and Value Reference," Vol. 1 & 2, price guide, photographs, catalog pages; $24.90 ea.

David Gifford
P.O. Box 7617
Little Rock, AR 72212
Buys and sells; consultant to "The Official Price Guide to Pottery and Porcelain."

Catalina Island Pottery

Collectors

Walter S. Sanford
Sanford Systems & Strategies
559 S. Washington Ave.
Kankakee, IL 60901
ph: 815-592-9258
fax: 815-929-9200
walter@waltersanford.com
http://www.waltersanford.com
Buy, sells and specializes in ceramics produced by the Catalina Island Pottery from 1927 through 1937.

Steven Hoefs
P.O. Box 1024
Avalon, CA 90704
ph: 310-510-2623
shoefs@catalinaisp.com
Wants to buy Catalina Island Pottery.

Dealers

Alan Phair
Alan's Antiques
P.O. Box 30373
Long Beach, CA 90853-0373
ph: 562-983-7020
AlanPhair@aol.com
Buys pieces marked "Catalina Pottery" made by Gladding-McBean; shells and some pieces marked with

blue ink stamp "MADE IN U.S.A.;"
G.M.B., Franciscan and Catalina
Pottery advertising items and price
lists; also Franciscan dinnerware.

Experts

Steve Soukup
California Crazed
P.O. Box 7662
Van Nuys, CA 91409-7662
ph: 818-787-5990 or 818-781-9262
soukup@dfhaia.com
Collects, buys and sells Catalina
Island pottery and tiles.

Cliftwood

Experts

Doris & Burdell Hall
B & B Antiques
210 West Sassafras Dr.
Morton, IL 61550-1254
ph: 309-263-2988
bnbhall@mtco.com
http://www.mtco.com/~bnbhall
Buys and sells; specializing in Morton
potteries including Cliftwood Art
Potteries Inc (Midwest Potteries Inc.),
and American dinnerware.

deLee

Collectors

Nancy M. Franz
499 Lexington Circle
Oceanside, CA 92057
fax: 760-757-9419
WiseTulip@aol.com
DeLee figures were made in
California in the 1940s; usually a boy
or girl figurine made of pottery with
eyes closed, long eye lashes and most
had planters attached.

Experts

Joanne Schaefer
S & S Publishing
3184 Williams Rd.
Butte Valley, CA 95965-8300
jschaefer@sunset.net
Co-author with John Humphries of
"deLee Art - The Pictorial History -
1937-1958" including price guide.

Dryden Pottery

Man./Prod./Dist.

Zack Dryden
Dryden Pottery
341 Whittington Ave.
Hot Springs National Park, AR 71901
ph: 501-623-4201
zdryden@excite.net
http://www.drydenpottery.com
Dryden Pottery has been producing
collectible pottery for over 57 years; a
family owned and operated business
for three generations.

Eva Zeisel

Clubs/Associations

Pat Moore, Pres.
Eva Zeisel Collectors Club
Newsletter: Eva Zeisel Times
695 Monterey Blvd., #203
San Francisco, CA 94127
ph: 415-587-6725
patmoore@evazeisel.org
http://www.evazeisel.org
Dedicated to the exchange of
information, conducting research and
disseminating information about the
work of contemporary designer, Eva
Zeisel.

Experts

Pat & Gene Moore
Zeisel, Mostly
695 Monterey Blvd., #203
San Francisco, CA 94127
ph: 415-587-6725
Zeiselmostly@pacbell.net
http://www.zeiselmostly.com
Can put buyers in touch with sellers
of Eva Zeisel-designed china by Hall,
Red Wing, Castleton, Schmid, Johann
Haviland, Rosenthal, Federal Glass,
Monmouth Stoneware, Schramberg,
and Stratoware.

Frankoma Pottery Co.

Clubs/Associations

Nancy Littrell, Treas.
Frankoma Family Collectors Association
Magazine: Pot & Puma
P.O. Box 32571
Oklahoma City, OK 73123-0771
ph: 405-722-2941 or 918-224-6610
fax: 405-728-3332
ffca4nancy@aol.com
http://www.frankoma.org
A national non-profit organization
dedicated to the appreciation,
preservation and promotion of
Frankoma Pottery as a collectible;
quarterly journal and Trader; annual
show and auction; complete resource
for the dedicated collector.

Collectors

Steve & Nancy Littrell
P.O. Box 32571
Oklahoma City, OK 73123-0771
ph: 405-722-2941
fax: 405-728-3332
stevelittrell@aol.com
http://www.frankoma.net
Major collectors of Frankoma.

Donna Frank
1300 Luker Lane
Sapulpa, OK 74066-6024
ph: 918-224-6610
ffca4donna@aol.com
Author of "Clay in the Master's
Hands," a history of Frankoma
founder and artist John Frank, his
family and Frankoma Pottery; a must
for all Frankoma collectors; details
evolution of ceramics in American
Southwest.

Dealers

Homespun Treasures Antiquity
209 E. Dewey Ave.
Sapulpa, OK 74066
ph: 918-227-4508

Experts

Ray Stoll
4618 NW 34th St.
Oklahoma City, OK 73122-1330
ph: 405-947-8505
fax: 405-947-8505
ffca4ray@aol.com
Specializes in Frankoma and
Gracetone pottery, most other
Oklahoma potteries; also elephants of
all kinds, particularly Disney Dumbos.

Gary V. Schaum
P.O. Box 303
Mounds, OK 74047-0303
ph: 918-827-6455
Author of "Collector's Guide to
Frankoma Pottery."

Tom & Phyllis Bess
14535 East 13th St.
Tulsa, OK 74108-4527
ph: 918-437-7776
Buys and sells; authors of "Frankoma
Treasurers" with price guide; $24
postpaid; consultant to "The Official
Price Guide to Pottery and Porce-
lain."

Susan Cox
800 Murray Dr.
El Cajon, CA 92020
ph: 619-697-5922
antiqfever@aol.com
Author of "The Collectors Guide to
Frankoma, Book 2," "How to
Successfully Own a Booth in a Mart,"
Antique Trader's "20th Century
American Ceramics;" columnist for
"The Antique Trader Weekly" and
"The Collector."

Internet Resources

Nancy Littrell, Treas.
Frankoma Family Collectors Association
P.O. Box 32571
Oklahoma City, OK 73123-0771
ph: 405-722-2941 or 918-224-6610
fax: 405-728-3332
ffca4nancy@aol.com
http://www.frankoma.org
Club Web site has value guides, glaze
& color guide, reproduction alerts,
books and videos, pictorial library,
Frankoma FAQs, history, articles,
classifieds, upcoming events, and
more.

Man./Prod./Dist.

Frankoma Pottery, Inc.
2400 Frankoma Rd.
P.O. Box 789
Sapulpa, OK 74067
ph: 918-224-5511 or 800-331-3650
fax: 918-227-3117
frankoma@frankoma.com
http://www.frankoma.com
Earthenware dinnerware, serving
accessories, floral containers.

Haeger/Royal Haeger

Clubs/Associations

Dennis & Lanette Clarke
Haeger Pottery Collectors of America
Newsletter: HPCA Newsletter
5021 Toyon Way
Antioch, CA 94509-8426
ph: 510-776-7784

Dealers

Mike Landis
P.O. Box 814
Adamstown, PA 19501
ph: 888-248-2291
landis2@ptd.net
Buys and sells Royal Haeger, Haeger,
Royal Hickman pottery; especially
interested in pieces marked "Royal
Haeger by Royal Hickman."

Dennis & Lanette Clarke
5021 Toyon Way
Antioch, CA 94509-8426
ph: 510-776-7784
Collectors, dealers, appraisers
specializing in Haeger pottery.

Experts

David D. Dilley
312 W. Weber Dr.
Muncie, IN 47303
ph: 765-284-7443
advertising@lwbooks.com
Author of "Haeger Potteries -
Through the Years;" collects Haeger
in these glazes: anything purple,
Mandarin Orange, Pearl Shell, Ebony,
Lilac, Turquoise-Blue, Black Mystique
and others; planters, bowls, figurals,
wall pockets, lamps, etc.

Man./Prod./Dist.

Haeger Potteries
7 Maiden Lane
Dundee, IL 60118-2307
ph: 847-783-5420
fax: 847-783-5438
customerservice@haegerpotteries.com
http://www.haegerpotteries.com

Museums/Libraries

Gene D'Amico
Haeger Potteries
7 Maiden Lane
Dundee, IL 60118-2307
ph: 847-783-5420
fax: 847-783-5438
customerservice@haegerpotteries.com
http://www.haegerpotteries.com

Harker

Experts

Neva Colbert
69565 Crescent Rd.
Saint Clairsville, OH 43950-9350
ph: 740-695-2355
colbert@1st.net
http://www.1st.net/colbert/harker
Author of "The Collector's Guide to Harker Pottery;" writes and distributes "The Harker Arrow", a newsletter about cameoware and other Harker pottery; also is a contributor to "American Country Collectibles" magazine.

Jane & Don Warner-Smith
Hallway, The
28314 E. 1st Rd.
Farmersville, IL 62533
ph: 217-227-4194 or 941-629-9601 (winter)
Buys and sells; consultant to "The Official Price Guide to Pottery and Porcelain;" has no shop, but does major antique-only shows across the country.

Periodicals

Neva Colbert
Newsletter: Harker Arrow, The
69565 Crescent Rd.
Saint Clairsville, OH 43950-9350
ph: 740-695-2355
colbert@1st.net
http://www.1st.net/colbert/harker

Hull Pottery

Clubs/Associations

Hull Pottery Association
112 Park DeVille Dr.
Columbia, MO 65203
ph: 573-445-6583
http://www.hullpotteryassociation.org
Goal is to preserve, educate and promote Hull Pottery, its collectors and its heritage.

Collectors

Joe & Betty Yonis
11023 Tunnell Hill NE
New Lexington, OH 43764
ph: 740-982-6763

Marilyn Felkins
P.O. Box 221
Atlanta, TX 75551
ph: 903-796-6055
Mfelkins@aol.com
Wants to buy Hull pottery pieces in the white gloss water lily pattern.

Dealers

Cathlyne McKay
www.HullDinnerware.com
P.O. Box 2022
Imperial Beach, CA 91932
ph: 619-429-0086
fax: 413-556-6865
owner@hulldinnerware.com
http://www.HullDinnerware.com
Online source for buying Hull pottery;

for non-Internet customers send $15 by money order for a full-color catalog.

Experts

Barbara Burke
4028 Palo Alto Ct.
Orlando, FL 32817-3803
ph: 407-677-9097
Author of "Hull Pottery, The Dinnerware Lines."

Joan Gray Hull
1376 Nevada S.W.
Huron, SD 57350-3135
ph: 605-352-1685
Author of "Hull - The Heavenly Pottery", an alphabetized, numerical, pictorial, pocket size price guide; all newly revised 6th edition with updated prices; advisor to "Warman's Antiques & Collectibles Price Guide", $24 ppd.

Brenda Roberts
Country Side Antiques
RR 2, Box 14-B
Marshall, MO 65340-9802
ph: 660-886-8888
Author of "The Collector's Encyclopedia of Hull Pottery", "Roberts' Ultimate Encyclopedia of Hull Pottery" and "The Companion Guide to Roberts' Ultimate Encyclopedia of Hull Pottery."

Hull Pottery/Red Riding Hood

Experts

Mark & Ellen Supnick
Collectibles R US Inc.
2623 Center Court Dr.
Fort Lauderdale, FL 33332
ph: 954-727-9770
ellen@sunshinejars.com
http://www.sunshinejars.com
Author of "Shawnee Pottery", and "Collecting Hull's Little Red Riding Hood."

Kreiss

Collectors

Michells & Mike King
P.O. Box 3519
Alliance, OH 44601

Barb & Russ Vandervate
1430 Oak Court
Lafayette, IN 47905-2115

Pat & Larry Aikins
P & L Collectibles
101 Trail Ridge Rd.
Athens, TX 75751
ph: 903-675-3765
fax: 903-677-3643
Authors of "The World of Kreiss Ceramics" price guide covering the Kreiss Psuchoss, Elegant Heirs, Napkin Ladies, and salt & pepper shakers.

James Casey
8004 Gault St. #A
Austin, TX 78757-8413

Carol & Mike Shong
2500 S. 370th #265
Federal Way, WA 98003

McCoy Pottery Co.

Clubs/Associations

Frank Poolas
McCoy Pottery Collectors' Society
Journal: Journal of the McCoy Pottery Collectors' Society
14 North Morris St.
Dover, NJ 07801
ph: 973-989-4412
mcflo@nac.net
http://
www.mccoypotterycollectorssociety.org
Non-profit organization devoted to the promotion and enhancement of the study of McCoy pottery for the advancement of knowledge relating to all facets of the pottery; provides assistance and support for McCoy researchers and collectors.

Collectors

Laura Simecek
McCoy Pottery Collectors Connection
2210 Sherwin Dr.
Twinsburg, OH 44087
ph: 330-963-1096
Nuts4McCoy@aol.com
http://www.ohiopottery.com/mccoy
Collecting McCoy since 1993; always looking for maroon and cobalt colored pieces; Web site is an Internet resource for all McCoy collectors; links to anything and everything McCoy.

Carol Seman
8934 Brecksville Rd.
Brecksville, OH 44141-2318
ph: 440-526-2094
fax: 440-526-2094
McCjs@aol.com
http://www.mccoylovers.com
Editor of "The NM Express" McCoy newsletter.

Dealers

Ruth Weeks
Borrowed Time
Uniontown Rd.
Phillipsburg, NJ 08865
ph: 908-859-0097
Wants to buy McCoy pottery from the 1930s and 1940s; prefers decorative vases in matte glazes and animal figures and planters, especially animal-form pitchers.

Amy Musher
Mostly McCoy
39 Walbrooke Rd.
Scarsdale, NY 10583
om108@aol.com
http://www.mostlymccoy.com
Offers a large varied sample of high quality McCoy pottery and other pieces of the same vintage.

Sandy & Ed Seward
Vintage Collectibles
6601 17th Lane, N.
Saint Petersburg, FL 33702
ph: 727-522-9918
fax: 727-525-6285
vintage@tias.com
http://www.tias.com/stores/vintage
Offers large collection of McCoy and other ceramics.

Ron McCoy
131 E. 57 St.
Tulsa, OK 74105-7714
ph: 918-747-1344
ronmccoy@cox.net
http://www.collectingbuzz.com
Buys and sells McCoy pottery.

John Marshall
For Love or Money
16693 NW Meadowgrass Ct.
Beaverton, OR 97006
john@europa.com
http://home.europa.com/~john
Buys and sells all types of McCoy pottery.

JoAnn Griffin
Canada
mcjode@sympatico.ca
http://www3.sympatico.ca/mcjode
Buys and sells a large section of vintage pottery, mainly McCoy.

Experts

Chiquita Prestwood
Chiquita's McCoy Pottery
P.O. Box 402
Lenoir, NC 28645-0402
McQuita@aol.com
http;//www.quita.net
Buys and sells; consultant to "The Official Price Guide to Pottery and Porcelain."

Craig Nissen
P.O. Box 223
Grafton, WI 53024-0223
ph: 262-377-7932
McCoyCN@aol.com
Co-author with Bob & Margaret Hanson of "McCoy Pottery Collectors' Reference & Value Guide," Vols. I, II & III.

Bob Hanson
P.O. Box 1945
Woodinville, WA 98072-1945
hnh4two@msn.com
Co-authors with Craig Nissen of "McCoy Pottery Collectors' Reference & Value Guide," Vols. I, II & III.

Periodicals

Carol Seman
Newsletter: McCoy Lovers' NMXpress, The
8934 Brecksville Rd.
Brecksville, OH 44141-2318
ph: 440-526-2094
fax: 440-526-2094
McCjs@aol.com
http://www.mccoylovers.com
Monthly newsletter "for, by and about

McCoy lovers everywhere;" read about rare finds, meet fellow collectors, stay abreast of McCoy pottery and cookie jar sales, shows and auctions; free classifieds for all subscribers.

Morton Potteries

Experts

Doris & Burdell Hall
B & B Antiques
210 West Sassafras Dr.
Morton, IL 61550-1254
ph: 309-263-2988
bnbhall@mtco.com
http://www.mtco.com/~bnbhall
Buys and sells; specializing in Morton pottery and American dinnerware; author of "Morton's Potteries: 99 Years."

Muncie Pottery Co.

Collectors

Barbara Norman Milin
ph: 561-995-7300
fax: 561-995-0096
bamilin@aol.com
Wants to buy Muncie Ruba Rombic pottery.

Paul Galli
ph: 408-730-4010
eichlerera1@comcast.net
Wants to buy or trade Muncie Pottery, Ruba Rombic line.

Experts

Virginia Heiss
7777 N. Alton Ave.
Indianapolis, IN 46268-7901
ph: 317-875-6797
Specializes in pottery made by the Muncie Clay Products Co., of Muncie, IN.

Brent & Donna Holloway
2006 S. Spruce St.
Muncie, IN 47302-1929
ph: 765-282-3772
http://members.aol.com/gillclay
An advanced collector of Muncie pottery for over ten years; always buying including entire collections; can advise on current market prices and trends.

Jack D. Wilson
1514 Eagle Ridge Rd.
Prescott, AZ 86301-5418
ph: 520-445-5137
jdwilson1@earthlink.net
http://home.earthlink.net/~jdwilson1
See Web site for information on this company.

Nemadji Tile & Pottery Co.

Clubs/Associations

Michelle Lee
Nemadji Pottery Collectors Club
Newsletter: Left Hand Gazette
P.O. Box 95
Moose Lake, MN 55767
ph: 218-485-8173
nemadji@computerpro.com
http://www.computerpro.com/~nemadji
Members share information about this swirl pottery made in Moose Lake, MN; while not made by Native Americans, Nemadji pottery is often referred to as "Indian" pottery; newsletter published quarterly; free sample newsletter with SASE.

Collectors

Michelle Lee
P.O. Box 95
Moose Lake, MN 55767
ph: 218-485-8173
nemadji@computerpro.com
http://www.computerpro.com/~nemadji
Specializes in Nemadjy pottery, "Indian" pottery, and tiles; Nemadji is a hand painted, swirl pottery made in Moose Lake, MN, from 1923 to 1972; since 1972 it has been produced in Kettle River, MN.

Niloak Pottery

Experts

David Gifford
P.O. Box 7617
Little Rock, AR 72212
Author of "Collector's Encyclopedia of Niloak Pottery."

Overbeck

Museums/Libraries

Museum of Overbeck Art Pottery
33 West Main St.
Cambridge City, IN 47327
ph: 765-478-3335
fax: 765-962-1318
jane@waynet.org
http://www.waynet.org/nonprofit/overbeck.htm
Overbeck pottery was produced between 1911 and 1955 in Cambridge City, IN.

Pewabic Pottery

Clubs/Associations

Pewabic Pottery
10125 East Jeferson Ave.
Detroit, MI 48214
ph: 313-823-0954
fax: 313-822-6266
pewabic@pewabic.com
http://www.pewabic.com
Founded in 1903, Pewabic Pottery is today a non-profit organization dedicated to the preservation of the Arts & Crafts ideals while advancing contemporary ceramic arts through educational programs, support of artists, community outreach.

Purinton

Collectors

Lori Hinterleiter
43597 Emerald Dunes Place
Leesburg, VA 20176
lhinterl@aol.com

Periodicals

Joseph McManus, Editor
Newsletter: Purinton News & Views
P.O. Box 153
Connellsville, PA 15425
ph: 724-628-4409
jmcmanus@hhs.net
Quarterly newsletter for collectors of Purinton Pottery and Blair Ceramics; current values, historical information, collector comments; sponsors annual Purinton Pottery Get Together.

Ransburg

Experts

Jo Lauderdale
2014 Richmond Rd.
Decatur, IL 62521
Collects and consultant to "The Official Price Guide to Pottery and Porcelain."

Regal China Corp.

Experts

Judy Posner
Judy Posner Collectibles
P.O. Box 2194
Englewood, FL 34295
ph: 941-475-1725
fax: 941-475-2645
judyandjef@yahoo.com
http://www.judyposner.com
Collects and consultant to "The Official Price Guide to Pottery and Porcelain;" buying, selling collecting for over 25 years.

Robinson Ransbottom

Man./Prod./Dist.

Robinson Ransbottom Pottery
P.O. Box 7
Roseville, OH 43777
ph: 740-697-7355
fax: 740-697-0475
info@ransbottompottery.com
http://www.ransbottompottery.com
Newcomb Pottery history, artists, Newcomb Pottery today, pottery links.

Rumrill Pottery Co.

Clubs/Associations

Francesca Malone-Gern
Rumrill Society, The
Newsletter: Rumrill Society Newsletter, The
P.O. Box 2161
Hudson, OH 44236-0161
ph: 330-655-9325
fax: 330-655-9347
rumrill2@aol.com
Quarterly newsletter discusses RumRill art pottery and post Redwing RumRill art pottery; offers free appraisals of your RumRill pottery;

please send photo and be sure to include a self-addressed, stamped envelope.

Dealers

Pat Puckett
Teacherage, The
1583 Ranch Rd.
San Bernardino, CA 92407
ph: 909-887-8383
fax: 909-887-8383
tcherage@aol.com
http://members.aol.com/tcherage/index.html
Specializes in Red Wing and RumRill art pottery, stoneware and ephemera; visitors may post want ads or items for sale at no charge; also trades.

Experts

Francesca Gern
P.O. Box 2161
Hudson, OH 44236-0161
ph: 330-655-9325
fax: 330-655-9347
rumrill2@aol.com
Expert and avid collector of Rumrill pottery; also buys and sells and appraises; publisher of "The Rumrill Society Newsletter."

Mike Zaeske
1796 North 9th St.
Kalamazoo, MI 49099
zaeskem@net-link.net
Collects and consultant to "The Official Price Guide to Pottery and Porcelain."

Ron Linde
500 South Water St.
Northfield, MN 55057-2060
ph: 507-645-6946
Collects and consultant to "The Official Price Guide to Pottery and Porcelain."

Shawnee Pottery Co.

Collectors

Pamela D. Curran
P.O. Box 713
New Smyrna Beach, FL 32170-0713
ph: 386-760-6600
fax: 386-760-5004
gramiepam2002@yahoo.com
Buys, collects, and specializes in Shawnee Pottery; interested in purchasing all Shawnee Pottery including cookie jars, Valencia, salt & pepper shakers, miniatures, lamps, and most gold-trimmed planters.

Experts

Pamela D. Curran
P.O. Box 713
New Smyrna Beach, FL 32170-0713
ph: 386-760-6600
fax: 386-760-5004
gramiepam2002@yahoo.com
Author of "Shawnee Pottery, The Full Encyclopedia;" publishes the Shawnee newsletter, "Exclusively Shawnee."

Mark & Ellen Supnick
Collectibles R US Inc.
2623 Center Court Dr.
Fort Lauderdale, FL 33332
ph: 954-727-9770
ellen@sunshinejars.com
http://www.sunshinejars.com
Author of "Shawnee Pottery", and
"Collecting Hull's Little Red Riding
Hood."

Bev & Jim Mangus
5147 Broadway Ave.
Louisville, OH 44641-8869
ph: 330-455-8785
Collects and consultant to "The
Official Price Guide to Pottery and
Porcelain."

Duane & Janice Vanderbilt
6038 E. Country Rd. 800 N
Brownsburg, IN 46112-8820
ph: 317-892-5797
Collects and consultant to "The
Official Price Guide to Pottery and
Porcelain."

Periodicals

Pamela D. Curran
Newsletter: Exclusively Shawnee
P.O. Box 713
New Smyrna Beach, FL 32170-0713
ph: 386-760-6600
fax: 386-760-5004
gramiepam2002@yahoo.com
A newsletter for Shawnee Pottery
(made in Zanesville until 1961)
collectors and enthusiasts; send
LSASE for information; has plenty of
pictures, letters, buy/sell classifieds,
and new discoveries.

Spaulding China/Royal Copley

Collectors

Barbara Burke
4028 Palo Alto Ct.
Orlando, FL 32817-3803
ph: 407-677-9097

Dealers

Dan Benton
1639 N. Catalina St.
Burbank, CA 91505-1605
ph: 818-848-6541
copleydb1@aol.com
Buys and sells Royal Copley china
which was made by Spaulding China
of Sebring, OH (1942-1957).

Experts

Joe Devine
1411 3rd St.
Council Bluffs, IA 51503
Collects and consultant to "The
Official Price Guide to Pottery and
Porcelain."

Jim Petzold
P.O. Box 46
Madison, WI 53701-0046
ph: 608-241-9138
fax: 608-241-8770
cas@ceramicartsstudio.com
http://www.ceramicartsstudio.com
Co-editor with of "CAS Collector;"
wants to buy all Ceramic Arts Studio
& Royal Copley creations including
shakers, figurines, dolls, lamps, and
metal art.

Stanford Pottery

Experts

Kathy Kimball
140 Linnell Rd.
Grand Marais, MN 55604-2121
circlek@boreal.org
Collects and consultant to "The
Official Price Guide to Pottery and
Porcelain."

Tamac Pottery

Experts

Kelly Alworth
415 NW 8th
Oklahoma City, OK 73102
ph: 405-272-0773
Appraiser, collector, dealer, expert in
Tamac pottery.

Tom & Phyllis Bess
14535 East 13th St.
Tulsa, OK 74108-4527
ph: 918-437-7776
Buys and sells; consultant to "The
Official Price Guide to Pottery and
Porcelain."

Treasure Craft Pottery

Appraisers

George Higby
20th Century Ltd
Sutton Palce #205
1221 Minor Ave.
Seattle, WA 98101
ph: 206-682-7288
geoahigby@hotmail.com
Author, researcher, expert, appraiser
of Treasure Craft Pottery.

Experts

Joyce Roerig
1501 Maple Ridge Rd.
Walterboro, SC 29488-9278
ph: 843-538-2487
fax: 843-538-4263
Buys and sells; consultant to "Official
Price Guide to Pottery & Porcelain."

Twin Winton

Experts

Joyce Roerig
1501 Maple Ridge Rd.
Walterboro, SC 29488-9278
ph: 843-538-2487
fax: 843-538-4263
Buys and sells; consultant to "Official
Price Guide to Pottery & Porcelain."

Uhl Pottery Co.

Clubs/Associations

Uhl Collectors Society, Inc.
Newsletter: Uhl Family Happenings
3704 W. Old Rd. 64
Huntingburg, IN 47542
tbaugh@dmrtc.net
http://www.uhlcollectors.org
Purpose is the preservation and
sharing of information relating to the
production of Uhl pottery; production
dates back to 1849 and ran through
the mid-1940s when the company
ceased operation.

Collectors

Tom & Donna Uebelhor
233 E. Timberlin Lane
Jasper, IN 47546-7303
ph: 812-482-9575
Lives in the area where Uhl pottery
was made.

Joseph Erbacher
P.O. Box 98
St. Anthony, IN 47565-0098
ph: 812-326-2777
President of Uhl Collectors Society;
membership info sent on request;
annual convention.

Jerry & Patty Schurz
5150 S 400 W
Huntingburg, IN 47542
ph: 812-683-4335
jschurz@msn.com
Specializes in collecting Uhl pottery.

Dave & Donna Swick
506 Martin St.
Newton, IL 62448-1340
ph: 618-783-3455
ddswick@psbnewton.com
Publish the Uhl Pottery Newsletter for
the Uhl Collectors Society.

Dealers

Don Schwartz
3704 W. Old Rd. 64
Huntingburg, IN 47542
tbaugh@dmrtc.net
http://www.uhlcollectors.org

Experts

Tim Hodges
1378 West Andrew Lane
Jasper, IN 47546
Consultant to "The Official Price
Guide to Pottery and Porcelain."

CERAMICS (CONTINENTAL)

(see also DINNERWARE)

Appraisers

Farhad Radfar, ISA
MIR Appraisal Services, Inc.
307 N. Michigan Ave., Ste. 308
Chicago, IL 60601
ph: 312-814-8510
fax: 312-814-8511
appraisers@mirgallery.com
http://www.mirgallery.com
Specializing in Meissen, KPM and
Vienna porcelain; offers expert
appraisals of personal property
including Continental ceramics, furs,
fine art, antiques, jewelry, furniture,
silver, porcelain, rugs, marble,
bronze, and other fine items.

Michael Sassoon
Arte Gallery
9000 Wilshire Blvd.
Beverly Hills, CA 90211
ph: 310-858-7666
fax: 310-858-0525
artela@aol.com
Specializes in the appraisal of 18th
through 20th century antique furniture
and Continental ceramics as well as
other antiques, collectibles, and
household contents.

Keith De Long
Keith C. De Long & Associates
Appraisal Service
32031 4th Ave. SW
Federal Way, WA 98023
ph: 253-874-6088
delong99@hotmail.com
Has 40 years experience in appraising
Continental and English ceramics.

Auction Services

Christie's
20 Rockefeller Plaza
New York, NY 10020
ph: 212-636-2000
info@christies.com
http://www.christies.com

Collectors

John Coates
324 Woodland Dr.
Stevens Point, WI 54481-9285
ph: 715-341-6113
Especially interested in Boch Feres/
Keramis Belgium art pottery depicting
animals or birds, and those pieces
with strong Art Deco design.

Dealers

Gerald Schultz
Antique Gallery, The
8523 Germantown Ave.
Philadelphia, PA 19118-3316
ph: 215-248-1700
fax: 215-247-8411
geraldluv@aol.com
18th century Sevres, Coalport,
Worcester, Meissen, Bow, Chelsea.

Karen M. Guido
Karen Michelle Antique Tiles
1835 US 1 South #119, PMB 243
Saint Augustine, FL 32084
ph: 904-471-3226
karen@antiquetiles.com
http://www.antiquetiles.com
*Specializing in antique & collectible
tiles from 1860 through 1960: French,
Italian, Royal Delft, Villeroy & Boch,
German, Portuguese, and Mexican
tiles.*

Farhad Radfar, ISA
MIR International Gallery, Inc.
307 N. Michigan Ave., Ste. 308
Chicago, IL 60601
ph: 312-814-8510
fax: 312-814-8511
mirgallery@aol.com
http://www.mirgallery.com
*Specializing in Meissen, KPM and
Vienna porcelain.*

Experts

Gerald Schultz
Antique Gallery, The
8523 Germantown Ave.
Philadelphia, PA 19118-3316
ph: 215-248-1700
fax: 215-247-8411
geraldluv@aol.com
*Buys, sells and specializes in 18th
century Delft, Sevres, Meissen,
Longwy, Galle, Massier, Quimper,
Doat, Boch, etc.*

Allen Bagdade
Country Peasants, The
1325 North State Parkway, Apt. 15A
Chicago, IL 60610
ph: 312-397-1321
fax: 847-392-5848
ADBSDB@aol.com
*Author of "Warman's English &
Continental Pottery & Porcelain"
(Krause); advisor to "Warman's
Antiques & Collectibles Price Guide."*

Museums/Libraries

Wadsworth Atheneum Museum of Art
600 Main St.
Hartford, CT 06103
ph: 860-278-2670
fax: 860-527-0803
info@wadsworthatheneum.org
http://www.wadsworthatheneum.org
*Featured displays include the Harold
& Wendy Newman Collection of
Veilleuses, the J. Pierpont Morgan
Collection of Meissen & Sevres
Porcelain, and other diverse examples
of fine European ceramics.*

Amphora
Clubs/Associations

Wilf Pegg
Amphora Collectors Club
Newsletter: Amphora Files
129 Bathurst St.
Toronto, Ontario M5V 2R2 Canada
ph: 416-703-0338
fax: 416-703-1330
amphora@idirect.com
*Newsletter is published quarterly;
articles about Amphora and related
wares (particularly Austrian);
articles, photos, reader exchanges.*

Collectors

John Cobabe
800 South Pacific Hwy., Ste. 8-301
Redondo Beach, CA 90277
ph: 310-544-8790
johncobabe@aol.com
*Wants to buy Amphora; send photo,
size and price.*

Experts

Les & Irene Cohen
P.O. Box 17001
Pittsburgh, PA 15235-0001
ph: 412-793-0222 or 412-795-3030
fax: 412-793-0222
am4ah@yahoo.com
*Buys, collects and specializes in
Austrian Amphora art pottery; prefers
vases.*

Jack Gunsaulus
Gray's Gallery
583 W. Ann Arbor Trail
Plymouth, MI 48170-1627
ph: 734-455-2373
*Buys and sells Teplitz-Turn art
pottery, e.g. items made by the
Amphora Porcelain Works and
Alexandra Works.*

Art Pottery
Dealers

Gerald Schultz
Antique Gallery, The
8523 Germantown Ave.
Philadelphia, PA 19118-3316
ph: 215-248-1700
fax: 215-247-8411
geraldluv@aol.com
*Boch, Pilkington, B. Moore, Martin
Bros., Moorecroft, DeMorgan,
Amphora, Wedgwood, Crimson, B.
Leach, Doulton, Rambervillers, T.
Deck, T. Doat, Clarice Cliff, S.
Cooper, Carltonware, Longwy,
Torquay.*

Alain Fournier
La Verrerie D'Art
P.O. Box 757
Bowie, MD 20718-0757
ph: 301-464-3251
Mail@decoesque.com
http://www.decoesque.com
*Buys, sells, specializes in European
art pottery from the Art Nouveau and
Art Deco eras; C. Catteau, Dage,*

*Amphora, early Sarraguemine, Czech,
Austrian, French, Belgian.*

Capodimonte

(see also COLLECTIBLES
[MODERN], Flowers [Capodimonte])

Dealers

James R. Highfield
Diamonds & Gold
6301 D University Commons
South Bend, IN 46635
ph: 219-272-4200
diamondjrh@aol.com
http://www.diamondsandgold.net
*Wants old blue crown N relief style
capodimonte to purchase; please send
picture and price; also need pictures
and information for upcoming book.*

Conta & Boehme
Experts

Janice & Richard Vogel
8420 SW 92nd St., Unit B
Ocala, FL 34481-9317
ph: 352-854-0799
fax: 352-854-0799
vogels@contaandboehme.com
http://www.contaandboehme.com
*Authors of "Conta & Boehme
Porcelain with value Guide," a
complete history of the company with
over 1,000 color photos; also
reproduced "Conta & Boehme
Product Catalog" (1914-1918) with
over 850 items being sold at that time
pictured.*

Ray Begley
2 Lydiate Ash Rd.
Bromsgrove, Worcestershire B61 OHU
U.K.
ph: (44) 121 457 9181
fax: (44) 121 457 9212
*Collector and expert in Conta &
Boehme fairings and match holders/
strikers.*

Czechoslovakian
Clubs/Associations

Cheryl Goyda, Pres.
Czechoslovakian Collectors Association
Magazine: Journal of Czech Decorative
Arts
P.O. Box 137
Hopeland, PA 17533
ph: 717-738-2678
fax: 717-738-3413
MzCzech@aol.com
http://www.czechcollectors.org
*A non-profit association organized to
foster the collection and aesthetic
appreciation of the art glass, ceramics
and other decorative arts of Austria,
Bohemia, and Czechoslovakia from the
years 1850 to 1940.*

Collectors

Burt Smith
2000 Commonwealth Ave.
Brighton, MA 02135
ph: 617-787-6336
Wants large unusual pieces of Czech

*porcelain with dime-size round label
marked "Made in Czechoslovakia;"
figurals of birds, animals, people;
also wants pitchers, urns, vases.*

Cheryl Goyda
P.O. Box 137
Hopeland, PA 17533
ph: 717-738-2678
fax: 717-738-3413
MzCzech@aol.com
Wants to buy Czech pottery.

Dealers

David Fein
South Beach Antiques
736-13th St., #102
Miami Beach, FL 33139-4418
ph: 305-673-8044
dbf57@hotmail.com
http://www.angelfire.com/art/
antiquepottery
*Appraiser, dealer, collector specializes
in Art Deco, Arts & Crafts, Art
Nouveau and European Art Pottery:
Czech, Gouda, and English; Ditmar
Urbach, Grays, PZH, Regina, Zenith.*

R. Snaith
8446 W. 3rd St.
Los Angeles, CA 90048
ph: 323-930-2930
Buys, sells, trades Czech pottery.

Museums/Libraries

National Czech & Slovak Museum &
Library
30 16th Ave. SW
Cedar Rapids, IA 52404-5904
ph: 319-362-8500
fax: 319-363-2209
dmuhlena@ncsml.org
http://www.ncsml.org
*Serves as a clearing house for
information for Czech cultural
organizations active in the US.*

Danish
Dealers

Phil Anderson
Anderson & Associates
2147 W. Farwell
Chicago, IL 60645-4900
ph: 773-338-1758
fax: 773-338-1758
*Buys and sells porcelain figurines and
vases from the Denmark, especially
Royal Copenhagen, Bing & Grondahl,
and Dahl Jensen; also collects
Scandinavian wood carvings especially
those signed Trygg and/or
Gunnarsson.*

Delft

Clubs/Associations

Ed Goldgehn
Delftware Collectors Association
P.O. Box 670673
Marietta, GA 30066
ph: 770-499-8515
fax: 770-514-6398
comments@delftware.org
http://www.delftware.org
An association for collectors of Dutch Delftware and Gouda Pottery.

Dealers

Ed Goldgehn
Delft Wares, Inc.
26 Winters St.
Marietta, GA 30066
ph: 404-592-5019
fax: 404-592-5019
info@delftwares.com
http://www.delftwares.com
Specializes in modern Dutch delftware and Gouda pottery articles that can be dated based on the factory and artist mark; FREE Internet appraisals of modern Dutch Delftware and Gouda Pottery also provided.

Experts

Martin Wittenbols
Martin Wittenbols' Dutch Pottery
320 Hamers Rd.
Brooklin, Ontario L1M 2A3 Canada
ph: 905-655-9010
imonfi@myexcel.ca
Expert in Dutch Art Nouveau, Art Deco pottery and ceramics including Rozenburg, Purmerend, Amstelhoek, Gouda, Amphora, De Distel, Velsen, Arnhem, Ram, Ultrecht, etc.

French

Dealers

Cascade Antique Gallery
318 Grove St.
New Castle, PA 16101
ph: 724-657-6888
fax: 724-657-3391
Specializes in fine French antique furniture and French Quimper ceramics.

Gouda

Clubs/Associations

Ed Goldgehn
Delftware Collectors Association
P.O. Box 670673
Marietta, GA 30066
ph: 770-499-8515
fax: 770-514-6398
comments@delftware.org
http://www.delftware.org
An association for collectors of Dutch Delftware and Gouda Pottery.

Collectors

Jareth Holub
Ceramic Restorations, Inc.
224 W. 29th St., 12th Floor
New York, NY 10001
ph: 212-564-8669
fax: 212-843-3742
DMarekJHolub@netzero.net
Collector of 20th century Dutch Art Nouveau ceramics: Rosenburg, Gouda, Saint Lukas, Distel, Brouwer, Holland Utrecht, etc.

Dealers

Ed Goldgehn
Delft Wares, Inc.
26 Winters St.
Marietta, GA 30066
ph: 404-592-5019
fax: 404-592-5019
info@delftwares.com
http://www.delftwares.com
Specializes in modern Dutch delftware and Gouda pottery articles that can be dated based on the factory and artist mark; FREE Internet appraisals of modern Dutch Delftware and Gouda Pottery also provided.

David Fein
South Beach Antiques
736-13th St., #102
Miami Beach, FL 33139-4418
ph: 305-673-8044
dbf57@hotmail.com
http://www.angelfire.com/art/antiquepottery
Appraiser, dealer, collector specializes in Art Deco, Arts & Crafts, Art Nouveau and European Art Pottery: Czech, Gouda, and English; Ditmar Urbach, Grays, PZH, Regina, Zenith.

Dutch Pottery Portal
The Netherlands
c.engelen@quicknet.nl
http://www.geocities.com/dutchpottery
Buys and sells old and new Gouda pottery from Holland.

Experts

Phyllis Ritvo
World of Gouda Pottery, The
P.O. Box 95
Weston, MA 02493
ph: 781-899-2464 or 781-899-2449
fax: 781-788-9643
Gene_Ritvo@msn.com
http://www.goudapottery.com
Author of "The World of Gouda Pottery."

Martin Wittenbols
Martin Wittenbols' Dutch Pottery
320 Hamers Rd.
Brooklin, Ontario L1M 2A3 Canada
ph: 905-655-9010
imonfi@myexcel.ca
Expert in Dutch Art Nouveau, Art Deco pottery and ceramics including Gouda, Rozenburg, Permerend, Distel, Holland, Utrecht, etc.

Haviland

(see also CERAMICS [CONTINENTAL], Limoges; DINNERWARE, Haviland)

Clubs/Associations

Haviland Collectors International Foundation
Newsletter: HCIF Newsletter
P.O. Box 271383
Fort Collins, CO 80527
haviland@aeroinc.net
http://www.havilandcollectors.com
An organization dedicated to the study and promotion of porcelain and pottery made by the Haviland companies of France and America; newsletter published quarterly.

Dealers

Susan & Kevin Keeney
Porcelain Pond, The
P.O. Box 1108
Kenbridge, VA 23944
ph: 703-777-5603
fax: 703-777-5637
info2003@porcelainpond.com
http://www.porcelainpond.com
Specializes in French Haviland porcelain.

Grace Graves
Haviland Matching Service, Ltd.
219 N. Milwaukee St.
Milwaukee, WI 53202-5818
ph: 414-291-9111
fax: 414-291-9018
hmsgraves@aol.com
http://www.graveshaviland.com
Collector, dealer in porcelains and pottery by the Haviland families of Limoges, France; specialists in identifying and locating French & American Haviland patterns; use Schleiger number or send photocopy for pattern identification.

Experts

Dee Hooks
13050 Blackstump Rd.
Percy, IL 62272-1104
ph: 618-965-3832
dhooks@egyptian.net

Dick & Dona Schleiger
1626 Crestview Rd.
Redlands, CA 92374-6460
ph: 909-798-0412
davidaschleiger@hotmail.com
http://www.schleigerbooks.com
Son and daughter-in-law of Arlene & Dick Haviland, original authors of Haviland pattern books and developers of the "Schleiger" numbers for Haviland identification; currently authors of more recent Haviland pattern books.

Internet Resources

Cathy Grammer-Margolin
Haviland Online
P.O. Box 1965
Newport Beach, CA 92659
ph: 949-645-5950
webmaster@HavilandOnline.com
http://www.havilandonline.com
A wealth of Haviland related information is available on this Web site: identification tips, backmarks, Haviland dealers, related books, history, sample images, pattern matching, china locating services.

Matching Services

Jan Cruikshank
Coleman's Antiques
3313 N. Sepulveda Blvd.
Manhattan Beach, CA 90266-3626
ph: 888-458-4988 or 310-545-6699
fax: 310-545-6699
jcruikshank@earthlink.net
http://www.colemansantiques.com
Has been in business for 50 years; specializes in pre-1930 French Haviland; also sells English, German, Bohemian and Delft porcelain, silver and glassware; send Schleiger number or photocopy for Haviland matching.

Herend

Dealers

Robert Edwards
Rumson China & Glass Shop
125 East River Rd.
Rumson, NJ 07760
ph: 732-842-2322 or 888-800-0020
redwards@rumsonchina.com
http://www.rumsonchina.com
Sells Herend porcelain, Waterford crystal, Lynn Chase Designs, Mottahedeh, Vietri, Yeoward Crystal, Agresti, Orrefors, Casafina, Buccellati, Lalique, Laura Slatkin, Christian Tortu, Chelsea clocks, and more.

Scully & Scully
504 Park Ave.
New York, NY 10022
ph: 212-755-2590 or 800-223-3717
customerservice@scullyandscully.com
http://www.scullyandscully.com
Offering distinctive gifts since 1934: Herend porcelain, Limoges & Halcyon Days, Murano glass.

Museums/Libraries

Herend Porcelain Museum
Kossuth L. u. 140
Herend, 8440 Hungary
ph: +36 88 523 197
museum@herend.com
http://www.museum.herend.com

Hutschenreuther

Experts

Jack Gunsaulus
Gray's Gallery
583 W. Ann Arbor Trail
Plymouth, MI 48170-1627
ph: 734-455-2373

Italian

Dealers

Kenneth P. Lesko
Kenneth Paul Lesko 20th Century
   Decorative Arts
P.O. Box 16099
Rocky River, OH 44116-0099
ph: 440-356-0275
fax: 440-331-1280
kplesko@aol.com
http://members.aol.com/kplesko/
kplesko.html
*Specialist in Italian ceramics 1900-
1970; wants to buy ADCF/Firenze,
Albisola, G. Andloviz, Baldelli,
Bassanelli, Roberto Bertagnin,
Bertetti, R. Bevilacqua, Biancini, B.
Brunetti, A Bucci/Faenza, C.A.S., CD
or DC, and all others.*

Shaw
P.O. Box 5096
Southfield, MI 48086
*Wants to buy Italian ceramics:
Gamboni, Fantoni, Melotti, Gratti,
Melandri, Campi, Ginori, Garaboldi,
Mazzotti, Albisola, Fabbari, Tasca,
Fontana, Patrinini, Arte Della
Ceramica, etc.*

Limoges

Dealers

Debby DuBay
Limoges Antiques
20 Post Office Ave.
Andover, MA 01810
ph: 978-470-8773
dlimoges@flash.net
http://www.limogesantiques.com
*Dealer, expert specializes in 19th
century Limoges hand painted
porcelain including vases, jardiniers,
punch bowls, etc.; a 27+ year
collector of Limoges and other fine
porcelains such as American Belleek,
Sevres, Paris porcelain.*

Susan Leite
44 Glenwood Rd.
Brewster, MA 02631-2202
ph: 508-385-4905
*Wants to buy undamaged Limoges
items.*

Experts

Debby DuBay
Limoges Antiques
20 Post Office Ave.
Andover, MA 01810
ph: 978-470-8773
dlimoges@flash.net
http://www.limogesantiques.com
*Author of "Living With Limoges," a
unique collector's book with
professional photographs of Limoges*

collections; contributed to the 3rd
"Encyclopedia of Limoges" by Mary
Frank Gaston and "Limoges Boxes"
by Faye Strumpf.*

Massier

Collectors

John Cobabe
800 South Pacific Hwy., Ste. 8-301
Redondo Beach, CA 90277
ph: 310-544-8790
johncobabe@aol.com

Meissen

Dealers

Martin & Helene Schwalberg
Meissen Shop, The
329 Worth Ave.
Palm Beach, FL 33480-6012
ph: 561-832-2504
fax: 561-833-4171
*Devoted exclusively to antique Meissen
porcelain.*

Experts

Mimi Levine
Mimi & Steve Levine Antiques, Inc.
6205 Marilyn Dr.
Alexandria, VA 22310
ph: 703-971-3941
mimilev@erols.com
*Buys and sells pre-1900 English,
American, and German porcelains and
English pottery: Meissen, Wedgwood,
Worcester, Minton, and other excellent
companies; also appraises and
lectures.*

Mottahedeh

Man./Prod./Dist.

Mottahedeh & Co.
225 Fifth Ave.
New York, NY 10010
ph: 212-685-3050 or 800-242-3050
fax: 212-889-9483
http://www.mottahedeh.com
*Porcelain, pottery, glassware,
brassware; antique reproductions,
metal and wood and ceramics; china
dinnerware.*

Old Ivory

Clubs/Associations

Society for Old Ivory & Ohme Porcelains
Newsletter: Elegance of Old Ivory, The
700 High St.
Hicksville, OH 43526
research@soiop.org
http://www.soiop.org
*Members interested in a wide variety
of Hermann Ohme porcelains,
including Old Ivory; newsletter focuses
on the Old Ivory (Silesia) patterns of
porcelain dinnerware produced in
Germany during the late 1800s by the
Ohme factory.*

Collectors

Jeff Gerbacht
jgerbman@yahoo.com
*Specializes in collecting Hermann
Ohme Porcelains, including Old Ivory.*

John Harms
P.O. Box 326
Osage, IA 50461
ph: 641-732-3872

Pat Fitzwater
28101 SW Petes Mountain Rd.
West Linn, OR 97068-9537
ftzh20@attbi.com
*Long time Old Ivory collector; former
publisher of "The Elegance of Old
Ivory" newsletter.*

Dealers

Eleanor Callanan
Old Ivory China
90 Riverwood Dr.
York, ME 03909
ph: 207-363-7117

Experts

Alma Hillman
362 East Main St.
Searsport, ME 04974-3103
ph: 207-548-6658
alma@oldivorychina.com
http://www.oldivorychina.com
*Buys and sells Old Ivory china; co-
author with David Goldschmitt of
"Collector's Encyclopedia of Old
Ivory China;" author of "Painted
Porcelain: Collector's Identification
& Value Guide."*

Portuguese

Dealers

Tucha Gift Shop, Inc.
110 Ferry St.
Newark, NJ 07105
ph: 973-589-3681 or 973-589-6672
fax: 973-589-8284
*Carries a large line of contemporary
items made in Portugal, especially
handpainted ceramics.*

Quimper

Auction Services

Sandra Bondhus
New England Absentee Auctions LLC
16 Sixth St.
Stamford, CT 06905
ph: 203-975-9055
fax: 203-323-6407
neaauction@aol.com
http://members.tripod.com/~bondhus
*Specializing in the auctions of
Quimper Pottery; accepts Quimper and
related accessories for consignment;
two or three sales per year.*

Clubs/Associations

Diane Robinson, Treas.
Quimper Club International
Newsletter: Quimper Club International
Newsletter
5316 Seascape Lane
Plano, TX 75093
ph: 942-867-7839
dianerobinson@quimperclub.org
http://www.quimperclub.org
*Dedicated to collectors of Quimper, a
beautiful, tin-glazed earthenware from
the Brittany region of France.*

Dealers

Gerald Schultz
Antique Gallery, The
8523 Germantown Ave.
Philadelphia, PA 19118-3316
ph: 215-248-1700
fax: 215-247-8411
geraldluv@aol.com

Experts

Millicent S. Mali
P.O. Box 377
East Greenwich, RI 02818-2916
ph: 401-884-6461
*Author of "French Faience of the 19th
and 20th Centuries," and "CA, A
French Faience Breakthrough," editor
of "Old Quimper Review;" buys and
sells vintage Quimper.*

Sandra Bondhus
P.O. Box 100
Unionville, CT 06085-0100
ph: 860-678-1808
*Author of "Quimper Pottery;"
specializes in 19th & 20th century
Quimper of fine artistic merit; always
buying and selling Quimper.*

Noelle B. Beatty
Old Quimper Pottery
3438 34th Place, NW
Washington, DC 20016-3136
ph: 202-537-0855
fax: 202-537-1609
beatty@oldquimperpottery.com
http://www.oldquimperpottery.com
*Buys, sells, specializes in Quimper;
wide variety of 19th and 20th century
Quimper for sale; will answer
collectors' questions about old
Quimper.*

Joan Datesman
Merry Walk Antiques
105 Market St.
Annapolis, MD 21401-1628
ph: 410-268-6233
fax: 410-268-3061
*Author of "Collecting Quimper;
Quimper Collections;" trips to France
maintains large 1860-1930 inventory;
rustic to elaborate designs.*

Allen Bagdade
Country Peasants, The
1325 North State Parkway, Apt. 15A
Chicago, IL 60610
ph: 312-397-1321
fax: 847-392-5848
ADBSDB@aol.com
Buys and sells Quimper pottery, especially unusual pieces: figures and early decorative examples; authors, lecturers, staff writers.

Internet Resources

Adela Meadows
Meadows Collection, The
P.O. Box 819
Carnelian Bay, CA 96140
ph: 530-546-5516
meadows@meadowscollection.com
http://www.oldquimper.com
Publishes an E-zine for those interested in old Quimper ceramics.

Man./Prod./Dist.

Quimper Faience
Newsletter: Le Monde de Quimper
141 Water St.
Stonington, CT 06378-1323
ph: 860-535-1712
fax: 860-535-3509
mail@quimperfaience.com
http://www.quimperfaience.com
The American branch of the French Quimper factory; retail mail order available; publishes newsletter twice a year; newsletter includes topics of interest to the Quimper collector including articles about Brittany.

Periodicals

Millicent S. Mali
Newsletter: Old Quimper Review
P.O. Box 377
East Greenwich, RI 02818-2916
ph: 401-884-6461
Semi-annual, 12-page periodical with color photos featuring articles on the history and production of different factories in Quimper, France; contains advertisements by leading Quimper dealers.

R.S. Prussia

Auction Services

Jim Wroda
Jim Wroda Auctions
P.O. Box 111
Gettysburg, OH 45328
ph: 937-447-8909 or 937-447-8909
jwrodamidwest@earthlink.net
http://www.jimwrodaauction.com
Specializes in the auction sale of R.S. Prussia and Carnival Glass.

Clubs/Associations

Linn Schultz
International Association of R.S. Prussia Collectors Inc.
Newsletter: IARSPC Newsletter
P.O. Box 185
Lost Nation, IA 52254
lschultz@netins.net
http://www.rsprussia.com

Dealers

Mary McCaslin
6887 Black Oak Court East
Avon, IN 46123
ph: 317-272-7776
fax: 317-272-7776
Author of "Royal Bayreuth: A Collector's Guide", past-president of International Assoc. of RS Prussia Collectors and the Royal Bayreuth Collectors Club.

Experts

Mary McCaslin
6887 Black Oak Court East
Avon, IN 46123
ph: 317-272-7776
fax: 317-272-7776
Author of "Royal Bayreuth: A Collector's Guide - Books I & II", past-president of International Assoc. of RS Prussia Collectors and the Royal Bayreuth Collectors Club.

Dee Hooks
13050 Blackstump Rd.
Percy, IL 62272-1104
ph: 618-965-3832
dhooks@egyptian.net
Has been buying and selling R.S. Prussia for 20 years.

Mary Frank Gaston
P.O. Box 342
Bryan, TX 77806
Author of "The Collector's Encyclopedia of R.S. Prussia."

Rosenthal

Man./Prod./Dist.

Rosenthal USA Limited
355 Michele Place
Carlstadt, NJ 07072-2304
ph: 201-804-8000 or 800-804-8070
info@rosenthalchina.com
http://www.rosenthalchina.com
Glassware, giftware, flatware, dinnerware, china and stoneware, stemware, silverplate, stainless steel, figurines, ceramic, glass, wood serving accessories.

Royal Bayreuth

Appraisers

Larry Brenner
L. Brenner Antiques
1005 Chestnut St.
Manchester, NH 03104
ph: 603-625-8203
elberenee@aol.com
Royal Bayreuth advisor to Schroeder's

Price Guide; charter member of Royal Bayreuth Collectors Club.

Clubs/Associations

Howard & Sarah Wade
Royal Bayreuth International Collectors' Society
Newsletter: RBICS Newsletter
P.O. Box 325
Orrville, OH 44667-0325
ph: 330-682-8551
fax: 330-682-3655
RBCollectr@aol.com
Bi-monthly newsletter with information on members' collections, new finds, price trends across the country and classified ads.

Mary McCaslin, Sec.
Royal Bayreuth Collectors' Club
6887 Black Oak Court East
Avon, IN 46123
ph: 317-272-7776
fax: 317-272-7776

Collectors

Eric Sidman
Eric's Antiques
381 Elliot St.
Milton, MA 02186-1748
ph: 617-332-3744
Wants old blue mark Royal Bayreuth items; all figurals but especially Santa Claus, Tiger, Squirrel, Rabbit, etc.; Rose Tapestry items, Sunbonnets, Snow Babies, Beach Babies; any unusual or rare items; will pay for photos; prompt reply.

Howard & Sarah Wade
P.O. Box 325
Orrville, OH 44667-0325
ph: 330-682-8551
fax: 330-682-3655
RBCollectr@aol.com

Judith White
926 Essex Circle
Kalamazoo, MI 49008
ph: 616-343-6066
judykazoo@aol.com

Dealers

Larry Brenner
L. Brenner Antiques
1005 Chestnut St.
Manchester, NH 03104
ph: 603-625-8203
elberenee@aol.com
Buys and sells Royal Bayreuth.

Mary McCaslin
6887 Black Oak Court East
Avon, IN 46123
ph: 317-272-7776
fax: 317-272-7776
Author of "Royal Bayreuth: A Collector's Guide", past-president of International Assoc. of RS Prussia Collectors and the Royal Bayreuth Collectors Club.

Experts

Mary McCaslin
6887 Black Oak Court East
Avon, IN 46123
ph: 317-272-7776
fax: 317-272-7776
Author of "Royal Bayreuth: A Collector's Guide", past-president of International Assoc. of RS Prussia Collectors and the Royal Bayreuth Collectors Club.

Dee Hooks
13050 Blackstump Rd.
Percy, IL 62272-1104
ph: 618-965-3832
dhooks@egyptian.net

Royal Copenhagen

Dealers

Pat Owen
Viking Import House, Inc.
1516 South Federal Highway
Fort Lauderdale, FL 33316
ph: 954-763-3388 or 800-327-2297
fax: 954-462-2317
vikingimp@aol.com
http://www.vikingimporthouse.com
Operates the VIDEX, a buy/sell service for any and all Royal Copenhagen and Bing & Grondahl collectibles; also Rorstrand, Porsgrund, Svend Jensen, and Berlin Design Christmas plates.

Royal Copenhagen/Flora Danica

Dealers

Jeffrey E. Purtell
P.O. Box 28
Amherst, NH 03031-0028
ph: 603-673-4331 or 800-973-4331
fax: 603-673-1525
jfpurtell@steubenpurtell.com
http://www.steubenpurtell.com
Specializes in Royal Copenhagen Flora Danica.

Scandinavian

Dealers

Anita L. Grashof
Gallerie Antiques
Stage House Village
366 Park Ave.
Scotch Plains, NJ 07076-1121
ph: 908-322-4600
Buys, sells, appraises Swedish art pottery such as Argenta by Kage, Gustavsberg, Rorstrand; also Finnish Arabia pottery.

Schlegelmilch

(see CERAMICS [CONTINENTAL], R.S. Prussia)

Sevres

Experts

Ann Friedman
Meadow Brook Hall
Oakland University
Rochester, MI 48309

Sitzendorf

Man./Prod./Dist.

Sitzendorfer Porzellanmanufaktur
Hautstrade 26
Sitzendorfe, D-07429 Germany
ph: +49 367 30 3660
fax: +49 367 30 22233
info@sitzendorf-porzellan.de
http://www.sitzendorf-porzellan.de/en/
index.html
The Sitzendorfer porcelain manufactory was founded in 1850.

Teplitz-Turn

Experts

Les & Irene Cohen
P.O. Box 17001
Pittsburgh, PA 15235-0001
ph: 412-793-0222 or 412-795-3030
fax: 412-793-0222
am4ah@yahoo.com
Buys, collects and specializes in Teplitz-Turn art pottery such as Amphora Porcelain Works, Alexandra Works, Heliosine Ware, "PD" marked Teplitz; prefers vases.

Jack Gunsaulus
Gray's Gallery
583 W. Ann Arbor Trail
Plymouth, MI 48170-1627
ph: 734-455-2373
Buys and sells Teplitz-Turn art pottery, e.g. items made by the Amphora Porcelain Works and Alexandra Works.

Villeroy & Boch

Collectors

Steve Elliott
1600 Tennessee St.
Vallejo, CA 94590-4629
ph: 707-552-8400 or 707-642-1949
fax: 707-552-0881
Wants antique Villeroy & Boch Mettlach items.

Man./Prod./Dist.

Villeroy & Boch (USA), Inc.
5 Vaugh Dr., Ste. 307
Princeton, NJ 08540
ph: 609-419-4110
fax: 609-419-4148
info@villeroy-boch-usa.com
Imported dinnerware, glassware.

Museums/Libraries

Ceramic Museum Westerwald
Schloss Ziegelberg
Mettlach/Saar, 66693 Germany
ph: 0 26 2494 6010
fax: 0 26 2494 60120
info@keramikmuseum.de
http://www.keramikmuseum.de
Collection includes historical and contemporary ceramics.

Zsolnay

Collectors

John Cobabe
800 South Pacific Hwy., Ste. 8-301
Redondo Beach, CA 90277
ph: 310-544-8790
johncobabe@aol.com

Dealers

Federico Santi
Zsolnay Store, The
152 Spring St.
Newport, RI 02840-6806
ph: 401-841-5060
fax: 401-848-0953
zsolnay@drawrm.com
http://www.drawrm.com
Buys and sells Hungarian Zsolnay and Eastern European pottery; interested in Zsolnay, Amphora, Turin-Tepliz art pottery; send photos and price; can buy from photo; Web site has virtual museum of Zsolnay ceramics.

Experts

John Gacher
Zsolnay Store, The
152 Spring St.
Newport, RI 02840-6806
ph: 401-841-5060
fax: 401-848-0953
zsolnay@drawrm.com
http://www.drawrm.com
Author of "Zsolnay: Collecting a Culture;" wants to buy fine examples of Zsolnay pottery; will purchase from photo.

Laszlo Gyugyi
P.O. Box 17329
Pittsburgh, PA 15235-0329
ph: 412-256-2300 or 412-731-1753
fax: 412-256-2223
Collector wants to buy quality Zsolnay pieces from the Art Nouveau period and from the preceding classical periods; quality more important than price; send photo and/or description; all letters answered; information seekers welcome.

Misc. Services

American Hungarian Foundation, The
300 Somerset St.
P.O. Box 1084
New Brunswick, NJ 08903
ph: 732-846-5777
fax: 732-249-7033
info@ahfoundation.org
http://www.ahfoundation.org
Devoted to furthering the understanding and appreciation of the Hungarian cultural and historical heritage in US; held exhibit of art pottery from the factory of Vilmos Zsolnay in Pecs, Hungary.

CERAMICS (ENGLISH)

(see also DINNERWARE)

Appraisers

Paul G. Bailey, ISA
Antique Appraisal & Estate Services
12819 SE 38th St., PMB 320
Bellevue, WA 98006-1395
ph: 425-746-2777
fax: 425-746-3793
antiquabailey@aol.com
30 years experience in appraising English ceramics and porcelains, 18th through 20 centuries.

Keith De Long
Keith C. De Long & Associates
Appraisal Service
32031 4th Ave. SW
Federal Way, WA 98023
ph: 253-874-6088
delong99@hotmail.com
Has 40 years experience in appraising Continental and English ceramics.

Auction Services

Stuart Slavid
Skinner, Inc.
63 Park Plaza
The Heritage on the Garden
Boston, MA 02116
ph: 617-350-5400
fax: 617-350-5429
info@skinnerinc.com
http://www.skinnerinc.com
Established in 1971, Skinner Inc. is the fourth largest auction house in the US; has offices in Boston and Bolton, MA.

W. Buckley
Potteries Antique Centre Auctions
271 Waterloo Rd.
Cobridge
Stoke on Trent, Staffordshire ST6 3HR
U.K.
ph: 01782-201455
fax: 01782-201518
potteriesantiquecentre@compuserve.com
http://www.potteriesantiquecentre.com
Conducts three specialized British pottery auctions each year.

Clubs/Associations

Dr. Keith McLeod
Wedgwood International Seminar
Newsletter: WIS Proceedings
22 DeSavry Crescent
Toronto, Ontario M4S 2L2 Canada
ph: 416-978-7011
fax: 416-489-4089
wis@w-i-s.org
http://www.w-i-s.org
An educational association sharing the latest information on Wedgwood and in the field of English ceramics; also publishes the "Annual Proceedings;" offers lectures and annual conference.

Dealers

McKenzie
James Graham & Sons Gallery
1014 Madison Ave. at 78th
New York, NY 10021-0103
ph: 212-535-5767
fax: 212-794-2454
info@jamesgrahamandsons.com
http://www.jamesgrahamandsons.com
Has been exhibiting the work of modern British ceramists since 1977 in both group and one-person exhibitions including Vivienne Foley, Peter Hayes, Jennifer Price, Dame Lucie Rie, Geoffrey Swindell, Angela Verdon, John Ward and others.

Leo Kaplan
Leo Kaplan, Ltd.
114 East 57th St.
New York, NY 10022
ph: 212-355-7212
fax: 212-355-7209
leokaplan@mindspring.com
http://www.leokaplan.com
Specializes in early English pottery and porcelain; also antique and contemporary glass paperweights.

Mimi Levine
Mimi & Steve Levine Antiques, Inc.
6205 Marilyn Dr.
Alexandria, VA 22310
ph: 703-971-3941
mimilev@erols.com
Buys and sells pre-1900 English, American, and German porcelains and English pottery: Meissen, Wedgwood, Worcester, Minton, and other excellent companies; also appraises and lectures.

Karen M. Guido
Karen Michelle Antique Tiles
1835 US 1 South #119, PMB 243
Saint Augustine, FL 32084
ph: 904-471-3226
karen@antiquetiles.com
http://www.antiquetiles.com
Specializing in American & English tiles mostly from 1870 to 1950; always has an abundance of tiles in stock: Wedgwood, Minton China Works, Minton, Maw, Dresser, Minton Hollins, J. Moyr Smith, William Wise; series tiles, encaustics, etc.

Merlin Antiques
734 Torreya Court
Palo Alto, CA 94303
ph: 650-494-7920
fax: 650-494-2515
merlinbl@pacbell.net
http://www.merlnantiques.com
Specializes in English pottery and other ceramics: transferware, Staffordshire figures, Gaudy Welsh, lustreware, Prattware, children's plates, Spode, Clews, Enoch Wood, etc.

W. Buckley
Potteries Antique Center Auctions
271 Waterloo Rd.
Cobridge
Stoke on Trent, Staffordshire ST6 3HR
U.K.
ph: 01782-201455
fax: 01782-201518
potteriesantiquecentre@compuserve.com
http://www.potteriesantiquecentre.com
Antique store with large stocks of British pottery from the 19th and 20th centuries.

Experts

Stuart Slavid
9 Gryzboska Circle
Framingham, MA 01702-5519
ph: 508-620-2531
wedghead@rcn.com
Specializes in Wedgwood, Staffordshire, and Royal Worcester.

Linda Arman
P.O. Box 39
Portsmouth, RI 02871-0039
ph: 401-841-8403
fax: 401-841-8403
ldarman@msn.com
Expert, dealer, auction sales; monthly sales of Historical Staffordshire, Liverpool, and War of 1812 ceramics; also sales of American glass and references dealing with English ceramics and American glass.

Gerald Schultz
Antique Gallery, The
8523 Germantown Ave.
Philadelphia, PA 19118-3316
ph: 215-248-1700
fax: 215-247-8411
geraldluv@aol.com
Buys, sells and specializes in English ceramics: Coalport, Worcester, Bow, Chelsea, Davenport, Doulton.

Allen Bagdade
Country Peasants, The
1325 North State Parkway, Apt. 15A
Chicago, IL 60610
ph: 312-397-1321
fax: 847-392-5848
ADBSDB@aol.com
Author of "Warman's English & Continental Pottery & Porcelain" (Krause); advisor to "Warman's Antiques & Collectibles Price Guide."

Susan Scott
882 Queen St. West
Toronto, Ontario M6J 1G3 Canada
ph: 416-538-8536
fax: 416-534-4814
SusanScottCA@aol.com
http://www.chintznet.com/susan
Specializes in 20th century English ceramics.

Internet Resources

Graham
Antique British Ceramics Information
　Resource
U.K.
graham@abcir.org
http://www.abcir.org
Abcir.org holds an extensive information base on British potteries, their products and their work force.

Art Pottery

Experts

Gerald Schultz
Antique Gallery, The
8523 Germantown Ave.
Philadelphia, PA 19118-3316
ph: 215-248-1700
fax: 215-247-8411
geraldluv@aol.com
Buys, sells and specializes in Bernard Moore, Doulton, Pilkington, Clarice Cliff, Susie Cooper, Moorcroft, Roole, Minton, Carlton Ware.

Beswick

Clubs/Associations

Frank Salmon
Beswick Collectors Club
5 Southbrook Mews
Southbrook Rd.
London, SE12 8LG U.K.
ph: 0181 318 9580
frank.salmon@carltonware.co.uk
http://www.collectingdoulton.com

Dealers

Box of Porcelain
51d Icen Way
Dorchester, Dorset DT1 1EW U.K.
ph: +44(0) 1305 267110
fax: +44(0) 1305 263201
rlunn@boxofporcelain.net
http://www.boxofporcelain.net
Specializes in Beswick, Royal Doulton, Beatrix Potter, Royal Worcester, and Spode.

Internet Resources

Ron Heath
Search4Doulton.com
P.O. Box 64
Longwell Green
Kingswood, Bristol BS30 9ZT U.K.
ph: 0117 932 5852
fax: 0117 904 9994
enquiries@search4doulton.com
http://www.search4doulton.com
Essential resources for collectors of discontinued Royal Doulton, Beswick, Royal Crown Derby; dealer sales, free message board, events, worldwide dealers.

Periodicals

Laura J. Rock-Smith
Newsletter: Beswick Quarterly
10 Holmes Court
Sayville, NY 11782-2408
ph: 631-589-9027
fax: 631-589-9027
beswickquarterly@yahoo.com
http://members.tripod.com/
　~BeswickQuarterly
A quarterly newsletter for Beswick collectors: photographs, columns, articles, up-to-date information on Beswick, for sale and wanted ads.

Bunnykins

Dealers

Wendy Link
Pascoe & Company
101 Alameria Ave.
Coral Gables, FL 33134
ph: 800-872-0195 or 305-445-3229
fax: 305-445-3305
webmaster@pascoeandcompany.com
http://www.pascoeandcompany.com
Buying Royal Doulton figurines, character jugs, and coaching ware; carries large inventory for sale.

Burleigh Ware

Clubs/Associations

Julie Glover
Burleigh Ware International Collectors'
　Club
2 Braunston Rd., Knossignton
Oakham
Rutland, LE15 8LN U.K.
ph: 01664 454570
fax: -1664 454115
thebicc@aol.com

Dealers

Julie Glover
House of Burleigh
2 Braunston Rd., Knossignton
Oakham
Rutland, LE15 8LN U.K.
ph: 01664 454570
fax: -1664 454115
thebicc@aol.com
Publisher of two comprehensive guides on Burleigh Ware.

Carlton Ware

Clubs/Associations

Helen & Keith Martin
Carlton Ware Collectors International
Newsletter: Carlton Times
P.O. Box 161
Sevenoaks, Kent TN15 6GA U.K.
ph: 01474 853630 or 01374-147197
fax: 01474 854385
cwciclub@aol.com
http://www.lattimore.co.uk/deco/
　carlton.htm
Leading Carlton Ware club.

Dealers

Helen & Keith Martin
P.O. Box 161
Sevenoaks, Kent TN15 6GA U.K.
ph: 01474 853630 or 01374-147197
fax: 01474 854385
cwciclub@aol.com
http://www.lattimore.co.uk/deco/
　carlton.htm
World's leading Carlton Ware specialists.

Chelsea Ware

Experts

Stephanie M. Schnatz
17 Tallow Ct.
Baltimore, MD 21244-2516
ph: 410-944-0819
chelsealady@hotmail.com
http://www.geocities.com/Paris/Palais/
　7498
Buying applied sprig ware called Chelsea or Grandmother's Ware; willing to buy any motif in lavender on white china, or white motifs/ decorations on lavender china: jugs, foot bath, soup tureen, miniatures, toast rack, creamers, etc.

Clarice Cliff

Clubs/Associations

Clarice Cliff Collector's Club
Fantasque House
Tennis Dr.
The Park, Nottingham NG7 1AE U.K.
ph: +44(0) 870 0522365
webmaster@claricecliff.com
http://www.claricecliff.com
The "Official" Web site for collectors of Clarice Cliff pottery - Art Deco "masterpieces" from the 1920s and 1930s.

Collectors

Darryl Rehr
P.O. Box 641824
Los Angeles, CA 90064-6824
ph: 310-477-5229
fax: 310-268-8420
dcrehr@earthlink.net
Wants handpainted "Bizarre-Ware" only; many patterns including "Fantasque", "Cruise Ware" and others; please send photos.

Experts

Carole A. Berk
Carole A. Berk, Ltd.
4913 Hampden Lane
Bethesda, MD 20814
ph: 301-365-3400
fax: 301-365-8837
cab@caroleberk.com
http://www.caroleberk.com
Specializes in 20th century decorative art: Clarice Cliff, Keith Murray, Charlotte Rhead, Mexican silver, Bakelite, and costume jewelry; co-author of "Mexican Silver."

Susan Scott
882 Queen St. West
Toronto, Ontario M6J 1G3 Canada
ph: 416-538-8536
fax: 416-534-4814
SusanScottCA@aol.com
http://www.chintznet.com/susan

Cornish Ware

Clubs/Associations

Janet Winterbottom
Cornish Collectors' Club, The
Newsletter: Cornish Pixie
P.O. Box 58
Buxton
Derbyshire, SK17 0FH U.K.
ph: 01298 687070
fax: 01298 687071
cornish@btconnect.com
For collectors of T.G. Green's blue-banded Cornish Ware kitchen ceramics.

Dealers

Dave Simmons
1242 Ontario St.
Cobourg, Ontario K9A 3CP Canada
ph: 905-372-4147
simwhit@eagle.ca
Buys and sells vintage cornish kitchen ware.

Marilyn Gentry
Gentry Antiques
Rod & Line Shop
Little Green
Polperro, Cornwall PL13 2RF U.K.
ph: 0207 792 1402
fax: 0207 792 6958
info@cornishwarecollector.co.uk
http://www.cornishwarecollector.co.uk

Susan Glover
Cornish Ware Search
8 St.James Meadow Rd.
Leamington Spa
Warwickshire, CV32 6BZ U.K.
ph: 01926 427069
sue@cornishwaresearch.freeserve.co.uk
http://www.cornishwaresearch.co.uk
Buys and sells Cornish Ware as well as Domino Ware.

Derby

Clubs/Associations

Derby Porcelain International Society
Box 6997
Coleshill
Warwickshire, B46 2LF U.K.
derby118@onetel.net.uk
http://www.derby-porcelain.org.uk
For those interested in Derby porcelain and Derbyshire ceramics.

Doulton

(see also CERAMICS [ENGLISH],
Royal Doulton; COLLECTIBLES
[MODERN], Royal Doulton)

Dealers

Arnie Berger
Yesterdays South, Inc.
P.O. Box 565097
Miami, FL 33256
ph: 800-368-5866 or 305-251-1988
fax: 305-254-5977
arnieb@bellsouth.net
http://www.yesterdayssouth.com
Send SASE for list of almost 1,000 Doultons, Hummels, and Lladros for sale.

Tom Power
Tablewhere London Limited
4 Queens Parade Close
London, N11 3FY U.K.
ph: +44 0208 361 7787 or 800-514-8176
fax: +44 0208 361 4143
tpower@globalnet.co.uk
http://www.tablewhere.co.uk
Specialist dealer in modern collectibles such as Doulton, Coalport, Moorcroft; Beswick, David Winter, Lilliput Lane; call 800-514-8176.

Periodicals

Frank Salmon
Magazine: Collecting Doulton
5 Southbrook Mews
Southbrook Rd.
London, SE12 8LG U.K.
ph: 0181 318 9580
frank.salmon@carltonware.co.uk
http://www.collectingdoulton.com

Goss China/Crested Ware

Collectors

Jeanne Goss Spaulding
1325 West Ave.
Hilton, NY 14468
ph: 716-392-2706
Only wants pieces marked "W.H. Goss;" pictorials, parian busts, cottages, monuments, and animals preferred.

Frank Owen
28, Urswick Rd.
Becontree
Dagenham, Essex RM9 6EA U.K.
ph: +44 0181 491 4035
fax: +44 0181 262 9713
info@gosscrestedchina.demon.co.uk
http://
www.gosscrestedchina.demon.co.uk
Has a Web site that gives free advice to collectors of Goss and Crested china.

Dealers

Lynda Pine
Goss & Crested China Club
62 Murray Rd.
Horndean
Waterlooville, Hants P08 9JL U.K.
ph: (011 44 23) 92597440
fax: (011 44 23) 92591975
info@gosschinaclub.demon.co.uk
http://www.gosscrestedchina.com/
Club.html
Dealers for over 25 years in Goss and all Crested china made from 1857 to
1939; has a showroom and a free museum; offers mail order catalog; writes the definitive price guide and other books on Goss & crested ware.

Internet Resources

Frank Owen
28, Urswick Rd.
Becontree
Dagenham, Essex RM9 6EA U.K.
ph: +44 0181 491 4035
fax: +44 0181 262 9713
info@gosscrestedchina.demon.co.uk
http://
www.gosscrestedchina.demon.co.uk
Offers information for collectors of Goss and Crested china.

Man./Prod./Dist.

Mike Wallington
Sixpenny Pig, The
75 Cannon Grove
Fetcham
Leatherhead, Surrey KT22 9LP U.K.
ph: 01372-376612
A Goss and Crested China Company.

Honiton

Clubs/Associations

David Curtis
Honiton Pottery Collectors' Society
66B Hillfield Ave.
Crouch End
London, N8 7DN U.K.
hpcs@moshpit.cix.co.uk
http://www.cix.co.uk/~moshpit/hpcs
A society for collectors interested in Honiton and Crown Dorset pottery and in particular the work of Charles Collard.

Hornsea

Clubs/Associations

Peter Tennant
Hornsea Pottery Collectors & Research Society
Journal: Hornsea
128 Devonshire St.
Keighley, West Yorkshire BD21 2QJ U.K.
hornsea@pdtennant.fsnet.co.uk
Exists to promote the collecting of Hornsea pottery and to research the history of the pottery and its products from its beginnings in 1949 to present; holds 4 to 6 meetings a year.

Matching Services

Hornsea Pottery Matching Service
U.K.
ph: 44 (0) 1482 715596
fax: 44 (0) 1964 650092
sales@hornseamatchingservice.fsbusiness.co.uk
http://
www.hornseamatchingservice.fsbusiness.co.uk
Specializes in matching Hornsea, Denby, Marks & Spencer, BHS, Books, Adams, Johnson Brothers, Royal Albert, Royal Doulton; also carries early Hornsea collectables.

Langley Ware

Clubs/Associations

Jenifer Giblin, Sec.
Langley Mill Pottery Collectors' Society
64 Hands Rd.
Heanor, Derbyshire DE75 7HB U.K.
ph: 01773 716847
langleymill.society@btinternet.com
http://www.langleypotterysociety.co.uk
A society for collectors of all ware made at the Langley Mill Pottery from 1865 to 1982; monthly meetings held in Heanor, Derbyshire, U.K.

Maling

Clubs/Associations

David Holmes, Sec.
Maling Collectors' Society
Newsletter: Maling News
P.O. Box 1762
North Shields, NE30 4YJ U.K.
info@maling-pottery.org.uk
http://www.maling-pottery.org.uk
For those interested in ceramics manufactured by the C.T. Maling company, England.

Moorcroft

Appraisers

Brill Lee
Brill Lee Appraisal Services
P.O. Box 244
Bellevue, WA 98009-0244
ph: 425-885-4518
fax: 425-895-1022
brilllee@hotmail.com
Specializes in the appraisal of Moorcroft and Hjorth Danish art pottery.

Clubs/Associations

Moorcroft Collectors Club
c/o W. Moorcroft PLC
Sandbach Rd.
Burslem, Stoke-on-Trent ST6 2DG U.K.
ph: 01782 820500
fax: 01782 820501
oberon@globalnet.co.uk
http://www.moorcroft.com

Collectors

Leo & Susan Poole
P.O. Box 692
Mill City, OR 97360
ph: 503-897-2625
susita@wvi.com

Man./Prod./Dist.

W. Moorcroft PLC
Sandbach Rd.
Burslem, Stoke-on-Trent ST6 2DQ U.K.
ph: 01782 820500
fax: 01782 820501
oberon@globalnet.co.uk
http://www.moorcroft.com

Museums/Libraries

Moorcroft Museum
c/o W. Moorcroft PLC
Sandbach Rd.
Burslem, Stoke-on-Trent ST6 2DQ U.K.
ph: 01782 820500
fax: 01782 820501
kimt@moorcroft.co.uk
http://www.moorcroft.com
For more than a century Moorcroft has produced handmade decorated collectible giftware; using a totally unique decorating process, Moorcroft pottery is highly sought after by collectors around the world.

Pilkington

Clubs/Associations

Wendy Stock
Pilkington's Lancastrian Pottery Society
Sullom Side Barnacre
Garstang
Preston, Lancashire PT3 1GH U.K.
ph: 01995 603427
barry@pilkpotsoc.freeserve.co.uk
http://www.pilkpotsoc.freeserve.co.uk

Pinxton

Clubs/Associations

Mavis Sheppard
Pinxton Porcelain Society
Hurst Lodge, 73 Chesterfield Rd.
Tibshelf
Derbys, DE55 5NJ U.K.
ph: 01773 872419

Poole Pottery

Clubs/Associations

Peter Mills, Sec.
Poole Pottery Collectors Club
The Quay
Poole, Dorset BH15 1RF U.K.
ph: 1202 666200
fax: 1202 682894
sales@poolepottery.co.uk
http://www.poolepottery.co.uk
A company sponsored club for collectors of Poole Pottery hand painted and decorative ware which has been produced in the U.K. for over one hundred years.

Man./Prod./Dist.

Poole Pottery
The Quay
Poole, Dorset BH15 1RF U.K.
ph: 1202 666200
fax: 1202 682894
sales@poolepottery.co.uk
http://www.poolepottery.co.uk
Poole Pottery has been produced in the U.K. for over one hundred years.

Rabbitware

Collectors

William F. Oliver, Jr.
P.O. Box 886
Fernandina Beach, FL 32035-0886
ph: 904-261-5328
Wants to buy rabbitware - a colorful Staffordshire ceramic; comes in four

patterns: *Virginia Rose, Single Rose, Adams Rose and Bullseye, with rabbits around the rim or in the center; usually in form of plates, platters, mugs, chargers.*

Royal Crown Derby

Internet Resources

Ron Heath
Search4Doulton.com
P.O. Box 64
Longwell Green
Kingswood, Bristol BS30 9ZT U.K.
ph: 0117 932 5852
fax: 0117 904 9994
enquiries@search4doulton.com
http://www.search4doulton.com
Essential resources for collectors of discontinued Royal Doulton, Beswick, Royal Crown Derby; dealer sales, free message board, events, worldwide dealers.

Royal Doulton

(see also CERAMICS [ENGLISH], Doulton; COLLECTIBLES [MODERN], Royal Doulton)

Clubs/Associations

Ed & Roxana Khachadourian
Northern California Doulton Collectors' Club
P.O. Box 214
Moraga, CA 94556
ph: 925-376-2221
royaldoultonwest@yahoo.com
http://www.royaldoultonwest.com
A club in Northern California for Royal Doulton collectors: character jugs, Tobies, Bunnykins, Beatrix Potter, Flambe, Beswick, Kingsware, loving cups, character figures, seriesware, Dickensware, etc.

Dealers

Peggy Guy
Happy Pastime
10114 Frederick Rd.
Ellicott City, MD 21042
ph: 410-480-8119 or 410-203-1101
sales@happypastime.com
http://www.happypastime.com
Buys and sells; specializes in carnival glass, Royal Doulton, M.I. Hummel, Royal Copenhagen, Bing & Grondahl, Lladro, Goebel, Beswick, Royal Worcester.

Jean-Paul Iannantuoni
455 Concord Parkway N., #5500
Dept. CIC
Concord, NC 28027-6736
ph: 704-786-7758
fax: 704-795-7975
dinnerware.search@bigfoot.com
Buys and sells Doulton and Royal Doulton character jugs, figurines and series ware; dinnerware search service for all manufacturers; send; send $2 for current price list; appraisals by fee only.

Wendy Link
Pascoe & Company
101 Alameria Ave.
Coral Gables, FL 33134
ph: 800-872-0195 or 305-445-3229
fax: 305-445-3305
webmaster@pascoeandcompany.com
http://www.pascoeandcompany.com
Buying Royal Doulton figurines, character jugs, and coaching ware; carries large inventory for sale.

Stan Worrey
Colonial House Antiques
182 Front St.
Berea, OH 44017-1920
ph: 440-826-4169 or 800-344-9299
fax: 440-826-0839
Specializes in old and new Royal Doulton figurines and character jugs; mail lists on request.

Mary Pole
Seaway China
135 Broadway
Marine City, MI 48039-1607
ph: 800-968-2424
fax: 800-968-9005
sales@seawaychina.com
http://www.collectoronline.com/booth-5.html
Specialists in both new and discontinued Royal Doulton including character jugs; also offers a full line of new Bunnykins and Beatrix Potter figurines as well as hundreds of discontinued figurines.

Carol Payne
Carol's Antique Gallery
14455 Big Basin Way
Saratoga, CA 95070-6008
ph: 408-867-7055
Wants to buy animal figurines; will also consider lady figurines, series ware (teapots, or plates with scenes, etc.), stoneware, teapots and cups.

David Harcourt
Thorndon Antiques & Collectibles
P.O. Box 12076
Thorndon
Wellington, 6000 New Zealand
ph: 64-4-4730173 or 64-4-4733560
thorndon@paradise.net.nz
http://www.thorndon.co.nz
Dealer, expert, appraiser specializes in Shelley, Lilliput Lane, and Royal Doulton.

Man./Prod./Dist.

Customer Service
Royal Doulton USA Inc.
701 Cottontail Lane
Somerset, NJ 08873
ph: 732-356-7880 or 800-682-4462
fax: 732-764-4974
usa@royal-doulton.com
http://www.royal-doulton.com
China, dinnerware; cups and saucers, figurines, crystal giftware and stemware; US offices.

Museums/Libraries

Yvonne Wood, Manager
Royal Doulton Museum, Royal Doulton Visitor Centre
Nile St.
Burslem
Stoke-on-Trent, Staffordshire ST6 2AJ U.K.
ph: (01782) 292434 or (01782) 291770
fax: (01782) 292424
visitor@royal-doulton.com
http://www.royal-doulton.com/rd/visitors
Home of the Royal Doulton Figure; located within the original factory building; contains the world's largest public display of figures past and present; also the Sir Henry Doulton Gallery, displaying pieces dating from 1815.

Periodicals

Alan R. Blakeman
B.B.R. Publishing
Magazine: British Bottle Review & Collectors Mart
Elsecar Heritage Centre
Nr Barnsley, South Yorks S74 8HJ U.K.
ph: 01226 745156
fax: 01226 361561
sales@onlinebbr.com
http://www.onlinebbr.com
Published for over 22 years; full color magazine; the world's longest continuous running publication covering the multitudinous areas of antique bottles; including world news; published quarterly.

Royal Winton

Clubs/Associations

Sheryl Vogt
Royal Winton Collectors' Club
Newsletter: RWCC Newsletter
2 Kareela Rd.
Baulkham Hills, New South Wales 2153 Australia
ph: (61-2) 9686 1416
fax: (61-2) 9686 4246
s_winton@zipworld.com.au
http://www.royalwintoncollectors.com
Provides information on Royal Winton and on vintage chintz of all makes; relief ware, pastel ware, musical jugs/tankards, cottage ware; newsletter published five times each year.

Man./Prod./Dist.

Royal Winton
Unit 1, Lonpark Industrial Estate
Chadwick St., Longton
Stoke on Trent, Staffordshire ST3 1PJ U.K.
ph: 01782 598811
fax: 01782 342737
rwccc@royalwinton.co.uk
http://www.royalwinton.co.uk

Royal Worcester

Dealers

Peg Zurkowski
Becker Brooks Antiques
8027 Ellingson Dr.
Chevy Chase, MD 20815-3029
ph: 301-588-8558
fax: 301-608-2167
pegbeckz@aol.com

Gwendolyn R. Reasoner, Ph.D.
Re Vann Galleries
125 Arthur Lane
Hackberry, LA 70645-3001
ph: 337-762-4280 or 800-821-4278
revanngal@aol.com
*Largest Boehm dealer in the US;
specializes in the Boehm secondary
market; also Cybis, Royal Worcester,
Erte; also appraises.*

Man./Prod./Dist.

Royal Worcester Limited
Severn St.
Worcester, Worcestshire WR1 2NE U.K.
ph: +44 (0) 1905 746000
fax: +44 (0) 1905 23601
rwgeneral@royal-worcester.co.uk
http://www.royal-worcester.co.uk
*Plates, figurines, giftware, tableware;
Visitor Canter, factory tours.*

Museums/Libraries

Museum of Worcester Porcelain, The
Severn St.
Worcester, Worcestshire WR1 2NE U.K.
ph: +44 (0) 1905 746000
fax: +44 (0) 1905 23601
rwgeneral@royal-worcester.co.uk
http://www.royal-worcester.co.uk
*The largest and most comprehensive
collection of Worcester porcelain in
the world, 1751-2000; situated on the
factory site; tours available seven days
a week.*

Seacombe

Experts

Peter Blundell
P.O. Box 6
Vernon, British Columbia V1T 6M1
  Canada
ph: 250-542-4540
petersblundell@shaw.ca
*English-born collector, born where
this pottery existed in the 1850s near
Liverpool; has researched extensively
this type of pottery (mostly transfer
decorated earthenware).*

Shelley Potteries

Clubs/Associations

Rochelle Hart, Treas.
National Shelley China Club
Newsletter: NSCC Newsletter
591 West 67th Ave.
Anchorage, AK 99518-1555
ph: 907-562-2124
imahart@alaska.net
http://www.nationalshelleychinaclub.com
*Over 550 members world-wide;
provides information and services to
member and regional units; holds
national conferences; quarterly color
newsletter with listed Shelley pubs and
ads.*

Trevor Shelley, Publicity
Shelley Group
Newsletter: Shelley Group Newsletter
15 Frolesworth Lane
Claybrooke Magna
Lutterworth, Leicestershire LE17 5AS
  U.K.
ph: 01455 202164
shelley.group@shelley.co.uk
http://www.shelley.co.uk

Collectors

Curtis Leiser
12010 38th Ave. NE
Seattle, WA 98125
ph: 206-362-7136
fax: 206-362-7136
curtispleiser@cs.com
*Shelley Potteries collector, appraiser,
expert; writer/editor for the National
Shelley China Club newsletter.*

Experts

Phyllis Osjecki
Phyllis'
P.O. Box 792
Canyonville, OR 97417
ph: 541-839-4135 or 541-839-6151
*Buys, sells, and appraises Shelley
china.*

Curtis Leiser
12010 38th Ave. NE
Seattle, WA 98125
ph: 206-362-7136
fax: 206-362-7136
curtispleiser@cs.com
*Shelley Potteries collector, appraiser,
expert; writer/editor for the National
Shelley China Club newsletter.*

Spode

Clubs/Associations

Rosalind Pulver, Mem.
Spode Society, The
Newsletter: Review
P.O. Box 1812
London, NW4 4NW U.K.
ph: 0181 203 1769
spodemuseum@spode.co.uk
http://www.spode.co.uk/history/
  history_society.html
*Brings together collectors and lovers
of Spode to increase knowledge of the
Spode/Copeland families, the factory
and its wares; founded in 1986.*

Dealers

Carol Payne
Carol's Antique Gallery
14455 Big Basin Way
Saratoga, CA 95070-6008
ph: 408-867-7055
*Wants to purchase any pre-1975
Spode; one item or sets; must be in
perfect condition; especially likes the
"Mayfair," "Maritime," and "Rose"
patterns.*

Don Haase
Mr. Spode - D & D Antiques
P.O. Box 818
Mukilteo, WA 98275-0818
ph: 425-348-7443
mrspode@aol.com
http://www.mrspode.com
*Spode/Copeland appraiser, dealer,
expert; offers pattern matching service
for Spode/Copeland china from 1770
to present.*

Man./Prod./Dist.

Spode
Church St.
Stoke-on-Trent, Staffordshire ST4 1BX
  U.K.
ph: 01782 744011
fax: 01782 744220
spode@spode.co.uk
http://www.spode.co.uk
*Will answer questions about Spode
and Copeland factory wares.*

Museums/Libraries

Curator
Spode Museum
Church St.
Stoke-on-Trent, Staffordshire ST4 1BX
  U.K.
ph: 01782 744011
fax: 01782 744220
spode@spode.co.uk
http://www.spode.co.uk

Staffordshire

Appraisers

Jesse Bannister
Koch & Associates Consulting
2306 Main St.
Newberry, SC 29108
ph: 803-321-9246 or 877-488-4730
fax: 803-345-9794
daguys@backroads.net
http://kochappraisal.hypermart.net
*Buyers of English Staffordshire
transferware, old blue and colors;
specializes in the Adams potteries.*

Auction Services

Joseph Arman
Collector's Sales & Services
P.O. Box 6
Pomfret Center, CT 06259
ph: 860-974-7008 or 860-974-7009
*Specialize in mail-bid auctions for
historical Staffordshire, Quimper,
American glass, paperweights, bottles,
etc.*

Dealers

Anita L. Grashof
Gallerie Ani'tiques
Stage House Village
366 Park Ave.
Scotch Plains, NJ 07076-1121
ph: 908-322-4600
*Buys, sells and appraises 19th century
English figurines and dogs; royalty,
theater, naval and army, sports and
miscellaneous groups; also all
animals and breeds of dogs in pairs.*

Anne & Dave Middleton
Pot O Gold Antiques
P.O. Box 124
Allenwood, NJ 08720-0124
ph: 732-528-6648
fax: 732-528-6648
anne@potogoldantiques.com
http://www.potogoldantiques.com
*Interested in flow blue china,
epergnes, and Historical Staffordshire.*

Elinor Penna
P.O. Box 324
Old Westbury, NY 11568
ph: 800-294-0324 or 516-294-4668
fax: 516-294-4923
elpen@aol.com
http://www.elinorpenna.com
*Specializes in Staffordshire pottery:
antique animals, cottages, historical
figures.*

Carl McCann
Troy & Black, Inc.
P.O. Box 228
Red Creek, NY 13143-0228
ph: 315-754-8115
*Buys and sells high quality flow blue,
Staffordshire figurines, American
painted furniture, stoneware, redware,
coverlets, samplers, and other
American textiles, folk art, etc.*

Andrew J. Pye
Lovers of Blue & White
Steeple Morden
Royston, Hertfordshire SG8 0RN U.K.
ph: +44 1763 853 800
fax: +44 1763 853 700
andrew@blueandwhite.com
http://www.blueandwhite.com
*Web site dedicated to "Asiatic
Pheasants," the most popular English
Blue transferware pattern of the
Victorian era; articles on history,
index of makers to assist with
identification and dating, tips on
buying and selling.*

Experts

Adele Kenny
c/o Schiffer Publishing, Ltd.
77 Lower Valley Rd.
Atglen, PA 19310
ph: 908-889-7223
amkenny@worldnet.att.net
http://home.att.net/~yorkshirehouse/
*Author of "Staffordshire Spaniels: A
Collector's Guide to History, Styles &
Values," and "Staffordshire
Animals;" contributing editor to "The
Antiques News;" interested in buying
& trading all types of Staffordshire
figures 1740-1900.*

Peter Blundell
P.O. Box 6
Vernon, British Columbia V1T 6M1
  Canada
ph: 250-542-4540
petersblundell@shaw.ca
*Staffordshire collector, appraiser and
expert; has a teaching collection of
brown transfer printed earthenware*

from Britain; holds two-day antiques courses where needed.

Staffordshire (Historical)

Dealers

Anne & Dave Middleton
Pot O Gold Antiques
P.O. Box 124
Allenwood, NJ 08720-0124
ph: 732-528-6648
fax: 732-528-6648
anne@potogoldantiques.com
http://www.potogoldantiques.com
Interested in flow blue china, epergnes, and Historical Stafford-shire.

William & Teresa Kurau
P.O. Box 457
Lampeter, PA 17537
ph: 717-464-0731
fax: 717-464-0590
lampeter@epix.net
http://www.historicalchina.com
Wants dark blue and lighter colors; Arms of the States by Mayer; Erie Canal and Liverpool pitchers; will buy one piece or entire collection of historical Staffordshire, Landing of Lafayette, American & English views, War of 1812.

Norman Wolfe
Flo Boo - Staffordshire Plus Antiques
734 Torreya Court
Palo Alto, CA 94303
floboo@earthlink.net
Specializes in flow blue, Mulberry ironstone, all colors of transferware, Historical Staffordshire, cup plates and child's dishes.

Staffordshire (Romantic)

Dealers

Mary E. Thompson
21 McCall Rd.
Lebanon, CT 06249
ph: 860-642-6804
fax: 860-642-6466
chinadish@earthlink.net
Specializes in romantic transferware, Staffordshire prior to 1850.

Experts

Mark Brown
Seekers Antiques
P.O. Box 10083
Columbus, OH 43201
ph: 614-291-2203
Advisor to "Warman's Antiques & Collectibles Price Guide."

Tim Sublette
Seekers Antiques
P.O. Box 10083
Columbus, OH 43201
ph: 614-291-2203
Advisor to "Warman's Antiques & Collectibles Price Guide."

Susie Cooper China Ltd.

Clubs/Associations

Susie Cooper Collectors Group
Newsletter: Susie Cooper Collectors Group Newsletter
18 Oaklea Mews
Aycliffe Village
London, DL5 6JP U.K.
ph: +44 (07092) 334451
enquiries@susiecooper.co.uk
http://www.susiecooper.co.uk
An international organization for collectors of Susie Cooper ceramics; quarterly newsletter with news, buy/ sell ads, auctions, etc.; please send SASE with inquiries.

Collectors

Darryl Rehr
P.O. Box 641824
Los Angeles, CA 90064-6824
ph: 310-477-5229
fax: 310-268-8420
dcrehr@earthlink.net
Wants Art Deco style patterns and shapes; please send photo and SASE for guaranteed reply.

Experts

Susan Scott
882 Queen St. West
Toronto, Ontario M6J 1G3 Canada
ph: 416-538-8536
fax: 416-534-4814
SusanScottCA@aol.com
http://www.chintznet.com/susan

Sylvac

Clubs/Associations

SylvaC Collectors' Circle
174 Portsmouth Rd.
Horndean
Waterlooville, Hants PO8 9HP U.K.
admin@sylvacclub.com
http://www.sylvacclub.com
A club for collectors of Shaw & Copestake pottery and SylvaC Ware.

Torquay

Clubs/Associations

Marlene Graham
North American Torquay Society
Magazine: Torquay Collector, The
214 N. Ronda Rd.
Mc Henry, IL 60050
rxmanlee@mc.net
http://www.torquayus.org
For the enhancement of knowledge and enjoyment of Torquay pottery; magazine offers articles, ads, convention news; magazine published quarterly; send LSASE for membership form.

Torquay Pottery Collectors Society
Magazine: Scandy
Torre Abbey
The Kings Dr.
Torquay, Devon TQ2 5JX U.K.
torquaypottery@aol.com
http://www.torquaypottery.com
Founded in 1976 to stimulate interest in the history of the old South Devon potteries, and to bring together the collectors of Torquay in a common aim of research; publishes books on Torquay; three national meetings each year in England.

Collectors

Gerry & Jerry Kline
604 Orchard View Dr.
Maumee, OH 43537-2982
ph: 419-893-1226
klinegerry@msn.com
Members of the North American Torquay Society and the Torquay Pottery Collectors' Society; during winter months contact at 26485 Rampart Blvd., Pt. Charles, FL 33983, phone 941-764-9546.

Experts

Cynthia Holt
9067 Duarte Rd.
San Gabriel, CA 91775-2011
ph: 626-309-1454 or 626-286-6223
libragem@copper.net
Collector of a wide range of Torquay pottery; especially interested in Longpark art "rustic ware," personalized pieces with actual names and dates, and renditions of historical sites by Longpark/Watcombe ("faience ware").

Transferware

(see also CERAMICS, Ironstone; CERAMICS [ENGLISH], Staffordshire)

Clubs/Associations

Judie Siddall
Transferware Collector's Club
734 Torreya Court
Palo Alto, CA 94303
ph: 650-494-7920
info@merlinantiques.com
http://www.transcollectorsclub.org
An organization of collectors, dealers and museum personnel interested in English transferware, c. 1760-1880.

Arthur Roberts, Sec.
Friends of Blue Society
P.O. Box 122
Didcot
S. Oxfordshire, OX11 0YN U.K.
ph: 44 1235 816266
grledger@fob.org.uk
http://www.fob.org.uk
Founded in 1973, the club exists to study underglaze blue decoration using a transfer print, a technique developed in Britain during the last two decades of the 18th century

Dealers

Alvin & Rose Mary Harper
Harpers Antiques & Interiors
236 Second St.
Lewes, DE 19958-1326
ph: 302-645-9750
Specializes in English transferwares, European children's tea sets and furniture, and sterling and silver plate items; member of the Transferware Collectors Club.

Judie Siddall
Merlin Antiques
734 Torreya Court
Palo Alto, CA 94303
ph: 650-494-7920
info@merlinantiques.com
http://www.merlinantiques.com
Specializes in 19th century English pottery with a focus on Blue and White Transferware as well as transferware in other colors; also Staffordshire figures, Gaudy Welch china, Lustreware, Pot Lids, Aesthetic Movement pottery, Pearlware.

Wade

Clubs/Associations

Wade Watch, Ltd.
Newsletter: Wade Watch Newsletter
8199 Pierson Ct.
Arvada, CO 80005
ph: 303-421-9655 or 303-424-4401
fax: 303-421-0317
webmaster@wadewatch.com
http://www.wadewatch.com
Founded in 1983.

Official International Wade Collectors Club
Royal Victorian Pottery
Westport Rd.
Burslem, Stoke-on-Trent ST6 4AG U.K.
ph: 01782 255 255
fax: 01782 575 195
club@wade.co.uk
http://www.wade.co.uk
A company-sponsored collectors' club.

Dealers

Patty Keenan
Keenan Antiques
P.O. Box 111
Dover, PA 17315
ph: 717-292-4820
fax: 717-292-4664
keenan@blazenet.net
Dealer in commissioned Christmas ornaments from Wade; major dealer in English/Irish Wade.

Liz Kramar
Kramar's Kollectible Korner
P.O. Box 30
Elk Mills, MD 21920-0030
ph: 410-398-0105
wildwedge@comcast.net
Wants to buy English/Irish Wade.

Experts

Ian Warner
Mianco Partners
499 Main St. South
P.O. Box 93022
Brampton, Ontario L6Y 4V8 Canada
ph: 905-453-9074
Co-author with Mike Posgay of "The World of Wade," "The World of Wade Book 2," and "Wade Price Trends First Edition."

Man./Prod./Dist.

Jenny Wright
Wade Ceramics Limited
Royal Victorian Pottery
Westport Rd.
Burslem, Stoke-on-Trent ST6 4AG U.K.
ph: 01782 255 255
fax: 01782 575 195
club@wade.co.uk
http://www.wade.co.uk
*Manufacturer of highly collectible
ceramic figurines made in the heart of
the Potteries in England; operates a
very active collectors club with
members worldwide.*

Wedgwood

Clubs/Associations

Ronald F. Frazier
Wedgwood Society of Boston, Inc.
Newsletter: WSB Newsletter
Frazier at D.H.S./Wedgwood
P.O. Box 215
Dedham, MA 02027-0215
ph: 781-843-5091
wedgwood@hotmail.com
http://www.angelfire.com/ma/wsb
*Publishes regular newsletter with in-
depth articles on Wedgwood; holds
regular meetings with speakers on
Wedgwood.*

Wedgwood Society of New York
Magazine: ARS Ceramica
5 Dogwood Ct.
Glen Head, NY 11545-2740
ph: 516-626-3427
fax: 516-626-3430
www@wsny.org
http://www.wsny.org
*An annual publication with in-depth
articles about Wedgwood and other
English ceramics, ads and auctions;
also publishes a bi-monthly
newsletter.*

Wedgwood Society of Washington,
D.C., The
3505 Stringfellow Ct.
Fairfax, VA 22033
fax: 703-435-7533
WSofWDC@aol.com
*Dedicated to the study and enjoyment
of Wedgwood.*

Dr. Keith McLeod
Wedgwood International Seminar
Newsletter: WIS Proceedings
22 DeSavry Crescent
Toronto, Ontario M4S 2L2 Canada
ph: 416-978-7011
fax: 416-489-4089
wis@w-i-s.org
http://www.w-i-s.org
*An educational association sharing
the latest information on Wedgwood
and in the field of English ceramics;
also publishes the "Annual
Proceedings;" offers lectures and
annual conference.*

Wedgwood Society of Great Britain
Newsletter: Proceedings of the
Wedgwood Society, The
89 Andrewes House
Barbican
London, ECY 8AY U.K.
http://www.geocities.com/Heartland/
3203/WSGB.html
*A learned society studying 18th
through 20th century Wedgwood
including 20th century Wedgwood
studio glass.*

Collectors

Stuart Slavid
9 Gryzboska Circle
Framingham, MA 01702-5519
ph: 508-620-2531
wedghead@rcn.com
*Wants to buy old Wedgwood; one
piece or entire collections.*

Bernard Starr
5 Dogwood Ct.
Glen Head, NY 11545-2740
ph: 516-626-3427
fax: 516-626-3430
bstarr1264@aol.com
*Specializes in Wedgwood and other
English ceramics.*

K. Paterson
2772 Windmill View Rd.
El Cajon, CA 92020
ph: 619-562-4136
*Collecting Wedgwood Jasperware
boxes and jars; send email with
information on ones for sale; also
wants out-of-print books on
Wedgwood.*

Karen Patterson
2772 Windmill View Rd.
El Cajon, CA 92020
ph: 619-581-9844
*Wants to buy Wedgwood Jasperware
boxes; also Queensware dishes, cream-
on-cream of cream-on-lavender.*

Dealers

Benton & Beverly Rosen
Mansion House, Inc.
9 Kenilworth Way
Pawtucket, RI 02860-5607
ph: 401-722-2927 or 508-759-4303
bevnbent@aol.com
*Dealers and collectors; want to buy
Wedgwood transfer print decorated
commemorative items.*

Eric H. Granberg
Deja Vue Antiques
428 Branch Ave.
Providence, RI 02904
ph: 401-521-0872 or 508-226-1816
fax: 401-272-8446
*Specialist in Wedgwood; also buys
complete or partial dinnerware sets.*

Howard Lewis
Howard Lewis Antiques
P.O. Box 5911
Wilmington, DE 19808-0911
ph: 302-731-5597
Buying and selling 18th, 19th and

collectible 20th century Wedgwood:
Jasper, Basalt, Caneware, Rosso
Antico, Drabware, etc.; also buying
and selling Embossed Queensware
patterns of dinnerware by Wedgwood.

Collector's Wedgwood
P.O. Box 462
Newbury Park, CA 91319-0462
*Specializes in antique and collectors'
Jasper, Fairyland, Creamware,
Basalts, Dry Bodies, Majolica; all
shapes; no dinnerware, please; send
SASE for list.*

Experts

Ronald F. Frazier
Frazier at D.H.S./Wedgwood
P.O. Box 215
Dedham, MA 02027-0215
ph: 781-843-5091
wedgwood@hotmail.com
http://www.angelfire.com/ma/wsb
*Collects and lectures on Wedgwood;
freelance writer/contributor for
periodicals' member of most major
Wedgwood collector organizations.*

Miriam & Aaron Levin
881 Whalley Ave.
New Haven, CT 06515
ph: 203-389-5440
fax: 203-387-3939
chivas1@prodigy.net

Muriel Polikoff
Muriel Polikoff Antiques
7708 Woodlawn Ave.
Elkins Park, PA 19027-2915
ph: 215-635-4948
fax: 215-635-5721
vicpol@aol.com
*Wedgwood specialty dealer for 35
years; Curator, Buten Museum of
Wedgwood for over 20 years;
President Wedgwood International
Seminar; published author and well
known lecturer.*

Leslie V. Canavan
Alexis Antiques
7576 Clayton Rd.
Saint Louis, MO 63117
ph: 314-647-7986 or 877-WEDGWOOD
wedgwood@alexisantiques.com
http://www.alexisantiques.com
*Appraiser, dealer, collector
specializing in Wedgwood products of
all types and eras; china matching,
giftware; college, commemorative &
historical plates; appraisals.*

Christopher Kenward
Christopher's
P.O. Box 7034
Redwood City, CA 94063-7034
ph: 650-364-7183
acoolman@excite.com
*Appraiser and dealer who specializes
in fine Wedgwood from the 18th, 19th
and early 20th centuries.*

Man./Prod./Dist.

Waterford/Wedgwood USA Inc.
P.O. Box 1276
Wall, NJ 07719
ph: 732-938-5800 or 800-444-1997
fax: 732-938-6915
feedback@wedgwood.com
http://www.wedgwood.com
Bone china and earthenware.

Museums/Libraries

Birmingham Museum of Art
2000 8th Ave. N.
Birmingham, AL 35203
ph: 205-254-2566
fax: 205-254-2714
http://www.artsbma.org
*Holds the Beeson Collection of
Wedgwood, the largest and finest
outside England.*

Wedgwood Visitor Center & Museum
Barlaston
Stoke-on-Trent, ST12 9ES U.K.
ph: 01782-204218
fax: 01782-374083
feedback@wedgwood.com
http://www.wedgwood.com

Worcester

Internet Resources

Graham
Antique Worcester Porcelain Internet
 Archives, The
U.K.
graham@tawpia.org
http://www.tawpia.org
*This site contains Worcester marks,
date codes, history, patterns, shape
numbers, the painters, the modelers,
and related articles.*

CERAMICS (ORIENTAL)

(see also DINNERWARE;
ORIENTALIA)

Clubs/Associations

Jean Martin, Sec.
Oriental Ceramics Society
30b Torrington Square
London, WC1E 7JL U.K.
ph: 0171 636 7985
*For those interested in the arts of
Asia, particularly ceramics.*

Periodicals

Chinese Ceramic Art Council, USA
Newsletter: Chinese Clayart
P.O. Box 1733
Cupertino, CA 95015
ph: 408-245-6271
fax: 408-245-8756
chineseclayart@hotmail.com
http://www.chineseclayart.com
*Bi-monthly newsletter for professional
artists, curators, collectors, writers,
experts, educators and students in the
field of ceramics; focuses on ceramic
art in China and related issues.*

Chinese Export Porcelain

Appraisers

Patricia M. Knight
Finetooth Comb Antiques Research &
Appraisal Service
P.O. Box 1177
Ames, IA 50014-1177
ph: 515-292-9028
ftcres@aol.com
*Consultant and qualified appraiser
and lecturer on Chinese export
porcelains; please send SASE for
reply; does not purchase; send SASE if
requesting return of photos.*

Dealers

Arttiques
235 East River Dr., Ste. 605
East Hartford, CT 06108
ph: 860-291-8151
fax: 860-282-6161
info@arttiques.com
http://www.arttiques.com
*Specializing in authentic and
reproduction Chinese export
porcelain; Web site offers historical
information about Chinese porcelain
as well as about porcelain making
techniques and styles.*

Experts

Stuart Slavid
9 Gryzboska Circle
Framingham, MA 01702-5519
ph: 508-620-2531
wedghead@rcn.com

Hobart D. Van Deusen
15 Belgo Rd.
Lakeville, CT 06039
ph: 860-435-0088
rtn.hoby@snet.net
*Wants to buy rare & unusual forms of
blue & white Canton; willing to
assist others in identifying and pricing
their Canton.*

Elinor Gordon
Elinor Gordon Gallery
P.O. Box 211
Villanova, PA 19085
ph: 610-525-0981
fax: 610-525-1451

Museums/Libraries

Peabody Essex Museum
Essex & Libert Sts.
Salem, MA 01970
ph: 978-745-9500 or 800-745-4054
pem@pem.org
http://www.pem.org

Christine M. Sullivan
Captain Forbes House
215 Adams St.
Milton, MA 02186-4215
ph: 617-696-1815
fax: 617-696-1815
fhm@gis.net
http://www.key-biz.com/ssn/Milton/
forbes.html
*A Boston China trade merchant
family's country mansion; 19th century
furnishings, American and Chinese*

export porcelain, prints, paintings,
furniture; also Abraham Lincoln and
Civil War memorabilia.

Dragonware

Collectors

Rick Penley
6438 Old Hanover Rd.
Hanover, PA 17331
ph: 717-225-3241
penley10@yahoo.com

Paul Kemske
P & S Collectables
5 Furman Ct.
Newark, DE 19713
ph: 302-368-3708
paulkee1@earthlink.net
http://home.earthlink.net/~paulkee1
*Avid collector of Dragonware since
the early 80s; over 500 pieces in
collection; from the Nippon era to
WWII; also over 100 pieces of
miniature Dragonware.*

Joyce Lynn
3201 Miami
Wichita Falls, TX 76309
ph: 940-696-1930
drgnlady@wf.quik.com
*Dragonware expert has been collecting
dragonware ceramics for 30 years.*

Internet Resources

John Falkenberg
jrfjr53@aol.com
http://www.dragonware.com
*Great site for information on moriage,
lithophane and dragonware -
porcelain items with a raised
decoration which depicts an Oriental
dragon; produced from the late 1800s
to the mid 1900s.*

Geisha Girl Porcelain

Experts

Elyce Litts
Happy Memories Antiques & Col-
lectibles
P.O. Box 394
Morris Plains, NJ 07950-0394
ph: 973-361-4087
happy-memories@worldnet.att.net
http://home.att.net/~happy-memories
*Author, dealer, collector buys and
sells Geisha Girl porcelain; author of
"The Collector's Encyclopedia of
Geisha Girl Porcelain."*

Nippon

Auction Services

James W. Breadmore, Sr.
J. Breadmore & Co.
ph: 978-682-0705
breadmor@aol.com

Jon Crisman, ISA
Jackson's Auctioneers & Appraisers
2229 Lincoln St.
P.O. Box 50613
Cedar Falls, IA 50613
ph: 319-277-2256
fax: 319-277-1252
jacksons@jacksonsauction.com
http://www.jacksonsauction.com
Specializes in Nippon.

Clubs/Associations

Janice C. Eldridge
New England Nippon Collectors Club
64 Burt Rd.
Springfield, MA 01118-1848
ph: 413-783-4629
*Regional chapter of the International
Nippon Collectors' Club.*

Anne Dickinson
Sunshine State Nippon Collectors' Club
P.O. Box 425
Frostproof, FL 33843-0425
ph: 941-635-4866 or 941-635-4121
fax: 941-635-4866
*Regional chapter of the International
Nippon Collectors' Club.*

Gerry Goldsmith
International Nippon Collectors' Club
Magazine: INCC Journal
1387 Lance Court
Carol Stream, IL 60188
info@nipponcollectorsclub.com
http://www.nipponcollectorsclub.com
*Fun club specializing in Nippon
porcelain; annual convention with
seminars, in-room selling, auction,
etc.; focusing now on education
regarding danger of reproduction
items; "INCC Journal" 3 times a
year; "INCC Newsletter" 3 times a
year.*

Kathy Wojciechowski
Lakes & Plains Nippon Collectors Club
P.O. Box 230
Peotone, IL 60468-0230
ph: 708-258-6105
fax: 708-258-6105
val7k@aol.com
*Please include a LSASE when
requesting a reply; regional chapter of
the International Nippon Collectors'
Club.*

Collectors

Yvonne Matlosz
9101 Sulkirk Dr.
Raleigh, NC 27613
ph: 941-278-4239

Mark Griffin
1417 Steele St.
Fort Myers, FL 33901-8431
ph: 800-726-1489
nippononly@aol.com
*Buys quality Nippon: chocolate & tea
sets, molded, portraits, wall plaques,
coralene, urns, jugs, moriage, figural,
Deco Noritake.*

Debra Tuttle
112 Ascot Dr.
Southlake, TX 76092-5117
ph: 817-481-4129 or 972-242-2160
fax: 972-466-0532

Dealers

Janice C. Eldridge
64 Burt Rd.
Springfield, MA 01118-1848
ph: 413-783-4629
*Wants to buy Nippon - moriage,
coralene, high quality vases, urns,
etc..*

Susan Leite
44 Glenwood Rd.
Brewster, MA 02631-2202
ph: 508-385-4905
*Wants to buy undamaged Nippon
items.*

Jacque Merritt
Jacque's Online Service
4104 Arrowbend Dr.
Williamson, NY 14589
ph: 315-589-4824
djmer@yahoo.com
http://sites.netscape.net/djmer/homepage
*Antique dealer for over 20 years and
Nippon collector for over 10 years.*

Alison Libby
Nippon Collection, The
ph: 616-895-6445
auntieal@aol.com
http://members.aol.com/AuntieAl/
index.html
*Collector and dealer of authentic,
quality Nippon antique porcelain
items; Internet Web site has photos
and descriptions of items for sale.*

Experts

Jacque Merrit
Jacque's Online Service
4104 Arrowbend Dr.
Williamson, NY 14589
ph: 315-589-4824
djmer@yahoo.com
http://sites.netscape.net/djmer/homepage
*Dealer, expert and researcher on
Nippon.*

Kathy Wojciechowski
Quality Nippon
P.O. Box 230
Peotone, IL 60468-0230
ph: 708-258-6105
fax: 708-258-6105
val7k@aol.com
*Pays top dollar for high quality
undamaged Nippon: large vases, urns,
portraits, moriage, coralene, tapestry,
dresser sets, dolls, etc.; author of
"The Wonderful World of Nippon
Porcelain (1891-1921)", appraiser,
lecturer on Nippon.*

Wilf Pegg
129 Bathurst St.
Toronto, Ontario M5V 2R2 Canada
ph: 416-703-0338
fax: 416-703-1330
amphora@idirect.com
Advanced collector specializing in early "blown-out" or relief-molded Nippon (1891-1921); features animals, birds and humans in relief.

Noritake

Clubs/Associations

David H. Spain, Editor
Noritake Collectors' Society
Newsletter: Noritake News
1237 Federal Ave. E.
Seattle, WA 98102-4329
ph: 206-323-8102
spain1237@yahoo.com
http://www.noritakecollectors.com
Art Deco, 1920s through 1940s Noritake Lustreware, excluding dinnerware; quarterly newsletter, holds annual convention.

Collectors

Tim Trapani
145 Andover Place
West Hempstead, NY 11552-1603
ph: 516-292-8355 or 718-464-9009
fax: 718-464-8448
Wants to buy Art Deco Noritake, especially women and men figurals; no dinnerware, please.

Adrienne Leff
1550 S Dixie Hwy. #210
Coral Gables, FL 33146-3034
ph: 305-667-4214
fax: 305-668-2592
Buys, sells, collects Art Deco Noritake, hand painted ladies, clowns, figural ladies and clowns, and strong geometric designs.

Mark Griffin
1417 Steele St.
Fort Myers, FL 33901-8431
ph: 800-726-1489
nippononly@aol.com
Wants to buy Noritake Art Deco men and women, also figural and Deco floral decors.

Dealers

Gloria Munsell
Allenwood Americana Antiques
P.O. Box 116
Allenwood, PA 17810-0116
ph: 570-538-1440 or 570-538-1932
fax: 570-538-1932
kwkipp@ptd.net
Wants the Azalea pattern & scenic Noritake (Tree-in-The-Meadow) china only; largest dealer of these patterns in the country; over 20 years experience; always buying & selling.

Gloria Munsell
P.O. Box 116
Allenwood, PA 17810-0116
ph: 570-538-1440 or 570-538-1932
fax: 570-538-1932
kwkipp@ptd.net
A leading dealer in two Noritake patterns: Azalea and Tree-in-the-Meadow (Scenic).

Experts

David H. Spain
1237 Federal Ave. E.
Seattle, WA 98102-4329
ph: 206-323-8102
spain1237@yahoo.com
Collector and expert publishes books and lectures on Art Deco NON-dinnerware "fancy" Noritake from the 1920s and 1920s; for 15 years has been the editor of "Noritake News," the official publication of the Noritake Collectors Society.

Phoenix Bird Pattern

Clubs/Associations

Joan Oates
Phoenix Bird Collectors of America
Newsletter: Phoenix Bird Discoveries
685 S. Washington
Constantine, MI 49042-1407
ph: 269-435-8353
koates120@earthlink.net
Members interested in ceramics decorated in the blue-and-white Phoenix Bird pattern and variants; advisor to "Warman's Antiques & Collectibles Price Guide," "Schroeder's Price Guide," and to "Garage Sale & Flea Market Annual."

Collectors

Dalen Whitt
Rte. 6, Box 356
Lewisburg, WV 24901
ph: 304-497-2425
mrphoenixbird@hotmail.com
Wants to buy rare items in Phoenix Bird China (spots on breast of bird); also Jadite kitchenware by McKee, Noritake HOWO China, and Delphite kitchenware.

Dealers

Seth Price
Antiques Nook, The
402 Benfield Rd.
Severna Park, MD 21146
ph: 410-544-5607
theprices@telocity.com
http://www.antiquesnook.com
Buys and sells Phoenix Bird china; mail order or Internet sales; no shop.

Carleton L. Cotting
1441 Crowell Rd.
Vienna, VA 22182-1512
ph: 703-759-5646
Collects, buys and sells Phoenix Bird pattern china.

Experts

Joan Oates
685 S. Washington
Constantine, MI 49042-1407
ph: 269-435-8353
koates120@earthlink.net
Collector, historian, consultant wants blue & white Phoenix Bird dinnerware; author of "Phoenix Bird Chinaware" Books I, II, III, IV, V; available from the author; specializes in the Flying Turkey pattern variant.

Satsuma

Dealers

Joseph Belperio
1303 Hawthorne Ct.
Sewell, NJ 08080-3511
ph: 8569-256-0791 or 856-782-7884
fax: 856-256-0791
shimazu@worldnet.att.net
Specializes in fine quality Japanese Satsuma, cloisonne, and studio ceramics.

Bill Eberhardt
Harry A. Eberhardt & Son
2010 Walnut St.
Philadelphia, PA 19103-5608
ph: 215-568-4144
artfix@magpage.com
http://www.eberhardts.com
Specializes in Japanese cloisonne and fine Satsuma.

CEREAL BOXES

(see also PAPER COLLECTIBLES; PREMIUMS, Cereal Boxes)

Collectors

John S. Fawcett
P.O. Box 1156
Waldoboro, ME 04572-1156
ph: 207-832-7398
fawcetoy@gwi.net
http://home.gwi.net/~fawcetoy
Wants complete 1930s through 1950s cereal boxes showing Disney, Lone Ranger, Tom Mix, Roy Rogers, Gene Autry, Sgt. Preston, Straight Arrow, radio premiums, rings, decoders, Bugs Bunny, etc.

Dan Goodsell
Tick Tock Toys
P.O. Box 48021
Los Angeles, CA 90048
grickily@aol.com
http://www.theimaginaryworld.com/page4.html
Interested in all 1940s to 1970s kid's food packaging and premiums such as cereal boxes and cereal box prizes.

Dealers

Ron Davison
TV Toy Memories
618 South Northwest Hwy. #179
Barrington, IL 60010
ph: 847-542-7473
cerealboxman@yahoo.com
http://www.tvtoymemories.com
Buys and sells 1950s through 1990s TV related memorabilia: toys, coloring books, advertising memorabilia, paper dolls, cereal dolls; most items are unused and many are autographed by the TV celebrity.

Experts

David Welch
P.O. Box 714
Murphysboro, IL 62966-0714
ph: 618-687-2282
fax: 618-684-2243
PEZDude1@aol.com
http://www.pezheads.net/dwelch
Wants pre-1975 food or household product boxes showing TV, movie, cartoon, sports, or comic characters or premium offers, especially super heroes; up to $1500 for 1940s-1950s Batman or Superman.

Internet Resources

Steve Wronker
Wheaties & the Hobby of Collecting Sport Themed Cereal Boxes
39 Boswell Rd.
West Hartford, CT 06107
ph: 860-561-8910
fax: 860-561-8910
FunnyBusiness3@prodigy.net
http://pages.prodigy.net/funnybusiness3/cbox.htm
This Web site is the ultimate source about collectors of sport Wheaties cereal boxes; a collector for over 10 years; writes a column about sports related cereal boxes in Beckett Publications and is considered an expert in the field.

Topher's Breakfast Cereal Character Guide
toph@carolina.rr.com
http://www.lavasurfer.com/cereal-guide.html
A complete reference guide to all your favorite cereal box characters from the early 1900s to present; publishes a cereal netletter, "The Boxtop."

Periodicals

Kevin Meisner
Magazine: Freakie Magnet, The
5400 Cheshire Meadows Way
Fairfax, VA 22032-3216
ph: 703-527-3485
Meisner65@aol.com
http://members.tripod.com/~Meisner65
High-quality magazine for cereal box and cereal box prize collectors; articles, photos, artwork featuring cereals from 1960s to present; buy/sell cereal boxes, prizes, cereal art.

John Cahill
Newsletter: Crunch Newsletter
9 Weald Rise, Tilehurst
Reading
Berks., RG30 6XB U.K.
ph: 0118 942 7291

Oats

Collectors

Mike Boggs
2075 Beaver Valley Rd.
Dayton, OH 45434-6987
ph: 937-426-2171
fax: 937-426-3063
oatbox@erinet.com
Wants pre-1965 oat boxes; either round or rectangular; Rolled Oats or Quick Oats; such brands as Kamo, Friends, Purity, etc.; any oat boxes with pictures or early artwork.

Sports Related

Experts

Steve Wronker
Wheaties & the Hobby of Collecting Sport Themed Cereal Boxes
39 Boswell Rd.
West Hartford, CT 06107
ph: 860-561-8910
fax: 860-561-8910
FunnyBusiness3@prodigy.net
http://pages.prodigy.net/funnybusiness3/cbox.htm
This Web site is the ultimate source about collectors of sport Wheaties cereal boxes; a collector for over 10 years; writes a column about sports related cereal boxes in Beckett Publications and is considered an expert in the field.

Internet Resources

Steve Wronker
Wheaties & the Hobby of Collecting Sport Themed Cereal Boxes
39 Boswell Rd.
West Hartford, CT 06107
ph: 860-561-8910
fax: 860-561-8910
FunnyBusiness3@prodigy.net
http://pages.prodigy.net/funnybusiness3/cbox.htm
This Web site is the ultimate source about collectors of sport Wheaties cereal boxes; a collector for over 10 years; writes a column about sports related cereal boxes in Beckett Publications and is considered an expert in the field.

CHARACTER COLLECTIBLES

(see also COMIC BOOKS; COMIC COLL.; COMIC STRIPS; COWBOY HEROES; DISNEY COLLECTIBLES; FAN CLUBS; MOVIE MEMORABILIA; POPULAR CULTURE; PREMIUMS; TELEVISION SHOWS & MEMORABILIA; TOYS, Character; WATCHES, Character/Comic)

Appraisers

Richard Olson
103 Doubloon Dr.
Slidell, LA 70461-2715
ph: 504-641-5173 or 504-280-6778
fax: 504-280-6049
http://www.neponset.com/yellowkid
Appraises all forms of pre-1950 comic character memorabilia: art, books, comic books, games, pin-backs, posters, sheet music, and toys.

Collectors

Warren Dotz
2999 Regent St., Ste. 300
Berkeley, CA 94705-2118
ph: 510-652-1159
fax: 510-540-0325
wellipsis@aol.com
Wants to buy advertising trademark character figures in the form of store displays, banks, statuettes, premiums and dolls; characters include Speedy Alka-Seltzer, PEP Boys, Reddy Kilowatt, Mido Watch Robot, Elsie the Cow, etc.

Dealers

Bob Gobeil
Bobby's Toys & Collectibles
P.O. Box 1416
Biddeford, ME 04005
bob@bobbystoys.com
http://www.bobbystoys.com
Offers character toys from the 1970s and 1980s from Alfs to Wuzzles; also TV and movie memorabilia, cereal premiums, fast food collectibles.

Greg Quire
Cool Toy Shop, The
1008 Fairview St.
Stroudsburg, PA 18360
ph: 570-424-0354
cooltoys@cooltoys.com
http://www.cooltoys.com
Featuring over 5,000 collectible toys from the 1970s to present; action figures, Barbie, Hot Wheels, Cabbage Patch, California Raisins, character glasses, Disney, Looney Tunes, PEZ, Snoopy, Smurfs, McDonald's, 101 Dalmatians, etc.

Charles Reagle
Collectibles Shop
600 Eaglenook Way
Osprey, FL 34229
ph: 941-966-6816
collectibles_shop@despammed.com
http://collectibleshop.tripod.com
Specializes in character collectibles, post-1960s comic books, Star Trek, Star Wars, other sci-fi, character watches; also Hallmark ornaments.

Rod W. Carnahan
Classic Antiques-Toys
537 El Paso St.
Jacksonville, TX 75766
ph: 903-586-1355
rodcarnahan_toys@tyler.net
http://www.antique-center.com/classic.htm

Experts

John Marshall
Toyzilla Enterprises
P.O. Box 340
Rancocas, NJ 08073-0340
jm@jmuniverse.com
http://www.jmuniverse.com
Author, expert buys and sells action figures and character collectibles from 1950s to present.

Doug & Pat Wengel
P.O. Box 305
Skillman, NJ 08558-0305
ph: 609-466-2461
fax: 609-466-8911
wengel@njcc.com
http://pluto.njcc.com/~wengel
Buys, sells and specializes in vintage character collectibles, especially those with early images of Disney characters Mickey, Minnie, Horace and Clarabelle.

Judith Katz-Schwartz
Twin Brooks Antiques & Collectibles
E-zine: Antiques & Collectibles Newsletter
P.O. Box 6572
New York, NY 10128-0006
ph: 212-876-3512
fax: 212-876-3512
twinb@msjudith.net
http://www.msjudith.net
Buys, sells, appraises vintage character items, especially early Disneyana, Popeye, Betty Boop, Felix, G.I Joe, Howdy Dowdy, etc.; member Assoc. of Online Appraisers (AOA) & Inter. Soc. of Appraisers; free online newsletter.

Mary Jane Lamphier
Quilted Keepsakes & Unique Dolls Exhibit
577 Main St.
Arlington, IA 50606-9712
ph: 319-633-5885
Buys, sells and trades advertising dolls and characters such as Jolly Green Giant, the Ronald McDonald collection, Campbell Soup Kids, etc.; author of "Zany Characters of the Ad World" (Collector Books, 1995).

Warren Dotz
2999 Regent St., Ste. 300
Berkeley, CA 94705-2118
ph: 510-652-1159
fax: 510-540-0325
wellipsis@aol.com
Buys & specializes in advertising character figures including statuettes, banks, store displays, vinyl dolls, cartoonish trademark figurals (Speedy, Alka-Seltzer, Reddy Kilowatt, Mr. Clean, etc.); author of books on the subject.

Museums/Libraries

Herb Barker
Barker Character, Comic & Cartoon Museum
1188 Highland Ave.
Cheshire, CT 06410-1624
ph: 800-227-5372 or 800-995-2357
fax: 203-699-1188
fun@barkeranimation.com
http://www.BarkerAnimation.com
Features comic character collectibles, television collectibles, cartoon character collectibles, toys, and comic memorabilia.

Alice In Wonderland

Clubs/Associations

Joel Birenbaum
Alice in Wonderland Collectors Network
Newsletter: Alice in Wonderland Collectors Network Newsletter
2765 Shellingham Dr.
Lisle, IL 60532-4245
ph: 630-637-8530
collectalice@att.net
http://collectalice.home.att.net
An organization of collectors, buyers and sellers of Alice In Wonderland and Lewis Carroll items.

Lewis Carroll Society of North America
Newsletter: Knights Letter, The
P.O. Box 204
Napa, CA 94559
webcontact@lewiscarroll.org
http://www.lewiscarroll.org
Many members also collect books and other Lewis Carroll related materials.

Collectors

Alice Berkey
127 Alleyne Dr.
Pittsburgh, PA 15215-1401
ph: 412-782-2686
Wants old Alice in Wonderland items: Alice dolls, toys, figurines, books (especially translations into foreign languages), etc.; anything Alice! Complete and original only, please.

Joel Birenbaum
2765 Shellingham Dr.
Lisle, IL 60532-4245
ph: 630-637-8530
collectalice@att.net
http://collectalice.home.att.net

Betty Boop

Clubs/Associations

Kim Gordon
Betty Boop Fan Club
P.O. Box 42
Moorhead, MN 56561
BBoopClub@aol.com
http://hometown.aol.com/bboopclub/BBoopClub.html

Barbara West
Official Betty Boop Fan Club, The
Newsletter: Betty Boop Fan Club
 Newsletter
10550 Western Ave., #133
Stanton, CA 90680
ph: 714-816-0717
bboopfans@aol.com
http://www.geocities.com/drsdune/betty
 *Publishes places to find Betty Boop
 items, special stories about members,
 pictures for members to use, stories
 about Betty's past and old
 "Boopabelia;" newsletter published
 quarterly.*

Collectors

Gene King
2307 W. Dearfield Rd.
Mount Pleasant, MI 48858
ph: 517-772-4625

Dealers

Barbara West
10550 Western Ave., #133
Stanton, CA 90680
ph: 714-816-0717
bboopfans@aol.com
http://pw1.netcom.com/~dself/
 boopfan.html
 *Buys and sells "Betty Boop"-a-bilia,
 both new and old; will buy collections
 or will sell collections on consignment; send LSASE for latest catalog.*

Man./Prod./Dist.

Connie Bingaman
P.O. Box 370
Brownstown, IL 62418
ph: 618-427-2761
fax: 314-230-9559
mr356@aol.com
 *Sells many new different Betty Boop
 collectible items; send SASE for list.*

California Raisins

Collectors

Ken Alexander
415 Morgan St.
Elgin, IL 60123-7537
ph: 847-931-0174
 *Wants to buy items relating to the
 California Raisins.*

Experts

Larry DeAngelo
516 King Arthur Dr.
Virginia Beach, VA 23464-2236
ph: 757-424-1691
 *Wants to buy or trade California
 Raisin figurines: surfboards,
 tambourines, Mom, AC, Graduates,
 Leonard and Cecil; buys old store
 stock and closeouts; has appeared on
 the TV shoe "Collecting Across
 America" his with extensive collection.*

George & Pam Curran
P.O. Box 713
New Smyrna Beach, FL 32170-0713
ph: 386-760-6600
fax: 386-760-5004
gramiepam2002@yahoo.com
 *Advanced collector looking for PVC
 characters and any of the related
 California Raisins products; prefers
 mint in box, but will consider rarity of
 item; author of "Collectible
 California Raisins."*

Cartoon & Comic

(see also ANIMATION FILM ART;
COMIC BOOKS; COMIC STRIPS,
Sunday Newspaper; POLITICAL
COLLECTIBLES, Nast Cartoons;
POSTERS, Cartoon; SCIENCE
FICTION)

Museums/Libraries

Cartoon Art Museum, The
Newsletter: Cartoon Times
655 Mission St.
San Francisco, CA 94105
ph: 415-227-8666
fax: 415-243-8666
office@cartoonart.org
http://www.cartoonart.org
 *Exhibits, collects and studies original
 cartoon art from comic strips, comic
 books, animation, magazines and
 editorial cartoons; galleries contain
 an overview of cartoon art in all
 forms and features rotating
 exhibitions; bookstore.*

Dagwood-Blondie

Collectors

Rod W. Carnahan
537 El Paso St.
Jacksonville, TX 75766
ph: 903-586-1355
rodcarnahan_toys@tyler.net
http://www.antique-center.com/
 classic.htm
 *Wants to buy Dagwood and Blondie
 collectibles.*

Davy Crockett

Collectors

Gary Pimenta
64 Lakeside Dr.
Tiverton, RI 02878-3111
 *Wants to buy Davy Crockett, The
 Alamo, and Zorro character
 collectibles including toys, banks,
 magazines, comic books, trading
 cards, records, etc.; send photos and
 asking prices.*

Experts

Howard Bender
Crocket Craze
515 Buxton Rd.
Toms River, NJ 08755
croktcraze@aol.com
http://www.geocities.com/
 TelevisionCity/Set/1486
 Appraises, buys, sells, collects and

*specializes in memorabilia related to
Davy Crockett.*

Dick Tracy

Experts

Larry Doucet
2351 Sultana Dr.
Yorktown Heights, NY 10598-3706
ph: 914-245-1320
fax: 914-739-9094
 *Buys, sells, appraises, Dick Tracy; co-
 author of "The Authorized Guide to
 Dick Tracy Collectibles;" will
 appraise Dick Tracy collectibles and
 memorabilia free of charge; wants to
 buy anything from premiums and toys
 to ephemera and art.*

Felix The Cat

Dealers

Jan Wachtel
Dr. Jan's Cartoon Cat House
316 Midvalley Center #115
Carmel, CA 93923
ph: 831-624-4906
fax: 831-622-0225
drjan@cartooncat.com
http://www.cartooncat.com
 *Specializes in Felix the Cat
 collectibles of all vintages; antique
 Felix as well as newer collectibles
 including figures, plushes, jewelry,
 watches, toys, clothing, etc.*

Garfield

Clubs/Associations

Denise Karl
Garfield Connection, The
Newsletter: Garfield Connection
 Newsletter
2 Lyons Rd.
Armonk, NY 10504-2224
ph: 914-273-3575
garfconect@aol.com

Collectors

Adrienne Warren
1032 Feather Bed Lane
Edison, NJ 08820
ph: 732-381-7083
 *Wants Garfield items: ceramics,
 figurines, banks, water domes,
 musicals, plush, promotional items,
 displays, European items.*

Sandy Getz
93776 Hidden Spring Dr.
Manassas, VA 20112
ph: 703-330-2763 or 703-369-6167
fax: 703-369-5124
 *Collects all types of Garfield items:
 plush, ceramic figurines, music boxes,
 etc.*

Dealers

Denise Karl
2 Lyons Rd.
Armonk, NY 10504-2224
ph: 914-273-3575
garfconect@aol.com
 *Buys, sells, trades Garfield
 collectibles; entire collections wanted.*

Grinch

Collectors

Robin Brickell
952 North Oriole
Virginia Beach, VA 23451
ph: 757-490-1111
rbrickell@cfmc.net

Gumby

Internet Resources

Gumby World
sybilcasey@earthlink.net
http://www.gumbyworld.com
 *Shop for unique and eclectic Gumby
 and friends toys and products.*

Hanna-Barbera

Collectors

John Krupienski
5200 Hilltop Dr.
P.O. Box AA6
Brookhaven, PA 19015-1200
ph: 610-874-3003
 *Collector specializing in Hanna-
 Barbera character collectibles:
 Flintstones, Jetsons, Huckleberry
 Hound, Pixie and Dixie, Quick Draw
 McGraw, Yogi Bear and Top Cat.*

Howdy Doody

Clubs/Associations

Jeff Judson
Howdy Doody Memorabilia Collectors
 Club
Newsletter: Howdy Doody Times
8 Hunt Court
Flemington, NJ 08822-3349
ph: 908-782-1159
fax: 908-782-0188
jjudson@ptd.net
 *Members are interested in anything
 related to Howdy Doody - old or new;
 also known as the Doodyville
 Historical Society.*

Collectors

Chris Swain
P.O. Box 513
Williamsburg, MA 01096
ph: 413-628-3213
Bluejettoy@aol.com
 Wants Howdy Doody memorabilia.

Jeff Judson
8 Hunt Court
Flemington, NJ 08822-3349
ph: 908-782-1159
fax: 908-782-0188
jjudson@ptd.net
 *World's foremost Howdy Doody
 collector.*

Christmas Catalog Collector, The
175 East Delaware, #7403
Chicago, IL 60611-1731
ph: 800-879-6948 or 312-337-3123
fax: 312-266-7982
 *Major and enthusiastic collector
 wants more Howdy Doody toys and
 other Howdy items; also wants all
 pre-1985 toy/Christmas catalogs.*

Experts

Jack Koch
P.O. Box 428
Morrisville, PA 19067
Author of "Howdy Doody Collector's Reference and Trivia Guide."

Humpty Dumpty

Clubs/Associations

Dee Sharp
Humpty Dumpty Club, The
P.O. Box 328
Fairview, NC 28730
ph: 828-628-0520
humptyclub@aol.com
http://members.aol.com/humptyclub
Club for Humpty Dumpty collectors and enthusiasts; free membership.

Collectors

Dee Sharp
P.O. Box 328
Fairview, NC 28730
ph: 828-628-0520
humptyclub@aol.com
http://members.aol.com/humptyclub
Wants old Humpty Dumpty related items: paper, wooden, metal, figurines, etc.

Li'l Abner

Dealers

Wilma Schiebel
No Place Like Home Collectibles
2200 S. Hwy 62-65
Harrison, AR 72601
ph: 870-741-9494
nplhc@alltel.net
Wants any souvenir related to Dogpatch USA Theme Park; also wants anything related to Li'l Abner such as books, snowdomes, Schmoo, Mammy & Pappy Yokum, etc.

Mystery Science Theater 3000

Clubs/Associations

MST3K Information Club
P.O. Box 5325
Hopkins, MN 55343
juliewa@aol.com
Interested in the low-budget cable show featuring Tom Servo, Mike Nelson, and Crow T. Robot.

Peanuts Characters

Clubs/Associations

Andrea Podley
Peanuts Collector Club, Inc.
Newsletter: Peanuts Collector Club Newsletter
539 Sudden Valley
Bellingham, WA 98226-4811
ph: 360-733-5209
fax: 360-733-5239
bang@dcn.davis.ca.us
http://www.peanutscollectorclub.com
A privately-owned club dedicated to the art & memorabilia associated with "Peanuts" and with its creator, Charles M. Schulz; also interested in memorabilia associated with the related characters in the "Peanuts" strip.

Experts

Freddi Karin Margolin
12 Lawrence Lane
Bay Shore, NY 11706
ph: 516-666-6861
fax: 516-665-7986
Wants to buy Snoopy/Peanuts character items; especially wants older wooden music musicals, ephemera, old catalogs from 1967 through the '70s showing Peanuts items; author of "Peanuts ... The Home Collection."

Andrea Podley
539 Sudden Valley
Bellingham, WA 98226-4811
ph: 360-733-5209
fax: 360-733-5239
acpodley@nas.com
Co-author with Derrick Bang of "Peanuts Collectibles Identification & Value Guide", available from author.

Museums/Libraries

Begell, Dir.
Charles M. Schulz Museum
2301 Hardies Lane
Santa Rosa, CA 95403
ph: 707-579-4452
fax: 707-579-4436
inquiries@schulzmuseum.org
http://www.schulzmuseum.org
Archives the work of artist Charles Schulz and chronicles his life; does not offer authentication or appraisal services.

Pink Panther

Collectors

Cheryl Dickinson
P.O. Box 36
Montague, MA 01351
ph: 413-367-9389
pinky@massed.net
Wants all Pink Panther collectibles: toys, ceramics, books, and ephemera; US or foreign.

Pogo

Clubs/Associations

Steve Thompson
Pogo Fan Club
Magazine: Fort Mudge Most, The
6908 Wentworth Ave. South
Minneapolis, MN 55423-2363
ph: 612-869-6320
thomp034@tc.umn.edu
International club explores all aspects of Walt Kelly's career; magazine reprints scarce and unpublished Kellyana, ads, letters, strip; magazine published bi-monthly.

Dealers

Marilyn White
14099 Lakeshore Dr.
Nampa, ID 83686
ph: 208-466-1746
mizbeaver@igopogo.com
http://www.igopogo.com
Long time collector and active buyer of rarer Pogo and Walt Kelly items; offers list of Pogo items for sale by mail or on Internet.

Experts

Steve Thompson
6908 Wentworth Ave. South
Minneapolis, MN 55423-2363
ph: 612-869-6320
thomp034@tc.umn.edu
Author of "The Walt Kelly Collector's Guide: A Bibliography and Price Guide."

Marilyn White
14099 Lakeshore Dr.
Nampa, ID 83686
ph: 208-466-1746
mizbeaver@igopogo.com
http://www.igopogo.com
Long time collector and active buyer of rarer Pogo and Walt Kelly items.

Popeye

Clubs/Associations

Official Popeye Fan Club
Newsletter: Popeye Fan Club Newsletter
1001 State St.
Chester, IL 62233
ph: 618-826-4567
fax: 618-826-2809
spinach@midwest.net
http://www.popeyethesailor.com
Specializes in Popeye related collectibles; quarterly newsletter.

Collectors

Patricia L. Norberg
1135 W. 18th Ave.
Eugene, OR 97402-3951
ph: 541-345-9409
Collects Popeye the Sailor Man toys, art and other related collectibles.

Dealers

Spinach Can Collectibles
1001 State St.
Chester, IL 62233
ph: 618-826-4567
fax: 618-826-2809
spinach@midwest.net
http://www.popeyethesailor.com
Buys, sells, appraises Popeye related items, old and new.

Museums/Libraries

Popeye Museum
1001 State St.
Chester, IL 62233
ph: 618-826-4567
fax: 618-826-2809
spinach@midwest.net
http://www.popeyethesailor.com
Hundreds of Popeye related collectibles dating from 1930s to 1990s are on display; also buys, sells, appraises Popeye items.

Punch & Judy

Dealers

Jonathan & Lisa Reynolds
Dramatis Personae - Booksellers
P.O. Box 1070
Sheffield, MA 01257-1070
ph: 413-229-7735
fax: 413-229-7735
books@dramatispersonae.com
http://www.bibliocity.com/home/DP
Wants to buy pre-1890 Punch and Judy books, prints, ephemera, puppets, pottery, memorabilia, etc.

Red Riding Hood

Clubs/Associations

Ann C. Bergin
Red Riding Hood!
Newsletter: Red Riding Hood Network
P.O. Box 105
Amherst, NH 03031-0105
fax: 978-649-6807
acbergin@aol.com
For collectors of (Little) Red Riding Hood; focus is not Hull and McCoy pieces, but rather on general Red Riding Hood collectibles.

Rocky & Bullwinkle

Dealers

Dudley Do-Right's Emporium
8200 Sunset Blvd.
Los Angeles, CA 90046
ph: 323-656-6550 or 323-654-3050
fax: 323-650-2940
dorightemporium@aol.com
http://www.designtrain.com/jayward
Filled with T-shirts, keychains, charms, pictures, Wossammatta U sweatshirts, and many other types of merchandise, all related to the Jay Ward characters; mail order also.

Periodicals

Gary David
Newsletter: Frostbite Falls Far-Flung Flier
P.O. Box 39
Macedonia, OH 44056-0039
ph: 330-467-1074
fax: 330-468-6936
gdcomputer@aol.com
http://members.shaw.ca/fffff/back.html
Focuses on Rocky & Bullwinkle and Jay Ward cartoons.

Sherlock Holmes

(see also BOOKS, Mystery; MAGAZINES, Mystery; MYSTERY/DETECTIVE ITEMS; PIPES; SMOKING COLLECTIBLES)

Collectors

Sherlock S. Holmes, D.D.
P.O. Box 3
Worcester, MA 01613-0003
ph: 888-651-0421
fax: 888-651-0421
mail@SherlockHolmes.com
http://www.Sherlock.Holmes.Name
Collects Sherlockiana; wants items relating to, covering, showing, the great detective Sherlock Holmes and/or Dr. John H. Watson: books, memorabilia, cups, magazines, videos, etc.; contact if you are unsure.

Robert C. Hess
559 Potter Blvd.
Brightwaters, NY 11718-1615
ph: 516-665-8365
hessmudlark@aol.com
Wants Sherlock Holmes/Sir Arthur Conan Doyle items: figurines, sculpture, statuary, dolls, original artwork, illustrations, etc.

Jerry Margolin
10007 SW Quail Post Rd.
Portland, OR 97219-6368
ph: 503-293-7274
Wants to buy and and all things relating to Sherlock Holmes.

Dealers

Chuck Haley
Sherlock's
13926 Double Girth Ct.
Matthews, NC 28105-4068
ph: 704-847-5480
mirepoix2@aol.com
Interested on all things Sherlockian.

Michael S. Greenbaum
Janus Books, Ltd.
P.O. Box 40787
Tucson, AZ 85717
ph: 520-881-8192 or 800-986-1165
fax: 815-333-2938
mike@janusbooks.com
http://janusbooks.com
Buys and sells first edition of detective, mystery, and suspense fiction; related bibliography and criticism; Sherlock Holmes; catalog available by snail mail or online.

Simpsons

Collectors

William LaRue
P.O. Box 292
Liverpool, NY 13088
ph: 315-451-0113
fax: 315-451-0113
BartFan@aol.com
http://www.bartfan.com
Web site contains an online price guide for Simpson collectibles.

Jay Shearer
2325 Middleton Dr.
North Little Rock, AR 72116
ph: 501-758-2617
shearer100@hotmail.com
Wants Bart Simpson memorabilia.

Dealers

Scott Carruthers
Scott's Simpsons Merchandise Page
10507 NE 269th St.
Battle Ground, WA 98604
carrwash@prodigy.net
http://www.geocities.com/
TelevisionCity/Studio/2930/
merchandise.html
Sells rare and new Simpsons merchandise.

Internet Resources

William LaRue
Collecting Simpsons!
P.O. Box 292
Liverpool, NY 13088
ph: 315-451-0113
fax: 315-451-0113
BartFan@aol.com
http://www.bartfan.com
A comprehensive online resource to collecting licensed merchandise from Fox's "The Simpsons."

Smurf

Collectors

Peter Caparelli
3528 204th St.
Bayside, NY 11361-1232
ph: 718-352-9010
fax: 413-683-7483
prc@landofmarbles.com
http://www.mushroomvillage.com
Collector of Smurf related items.

Isabel Haecker
160 Main St. S.
P.O. Box 92508
Brampton, Ontario L6W 2G0 Canada
astro@websmurfclub.org
http://www.websmurfclub.org
Collector and expert who wants to buy Smurf collectibles.

Dealers

Colleen Lewis
Buffalo Rd. Hobby
10120 Main St.
Clarence, NY 14031-2049
ph: 716-741-8399
fax: 716-759-7462
bripvc@toyline.com
http://www.toyline.com/clubs/pcc
Carries complete line of Smurfs, including figures, supers, playsets, super playsets, cottages, castle, displays, key chains, mugs, jewelry, toys, etc.; $3 for catalog; collections sought to buy.

Experts

Greg Quire
Cool Toy Shop, The
1008 Fairview St.
Stroudsburg, PA 18360
ph: 570-424-0354
cooltoys@cooltoys.com
http://www.cooltoys.com
World's largest Smurf reseller featuring over 400 Smurfs and Smurfy items.

Internet Resources

Peter Caparelli
MushroomVillage.com
E-zine: Smurfy News
3528 204th St.
Bayside, NY 11361-1232
ph: 718-352-9010
fax: 413-683-7483
prc@landofmarbles.com
http://www.mushroomvillage.com
Oldest and largest world-wide Smurf collectors club is now free to join; Web site offers ID and price guide, collector checklists, library of articles, community bulletin boards (learn, chat, buy, sell, trade) and more.

Isabel Haecker
Ultimate Web Smurf Club
160 Main St. S.
P.O. Box 92508
Brampton, Ontario L6W 2G0 Canada
astro@websmurfclub.org
http://www.websmurfclub.org
Free online collectors club with worldwide connections; the latest information on Smurf figurines and other collectibles; the place to buy, sell and trade Smurf items; free membership entitles you to free ads.

Periodicals

Alan G. Rennard
Newsletter: Smurfing Times
3 Indian Lane
Burlington, NJ 08016-5123
ph: 609-386-8186
fax: 609-386-8186
A bi-monthly newsletter dedicated to creating a worldwide Smurf collectors network.

Snoopy

(see CHARACTER COLLECTIBLES, Peanuts Characters)

Soupy Sales

Collectors

Bob Averill
1942 W. Market St.
Pottsville, PA 17901-2043
ph: 570-628-3084
Wants Soupy Sales collectibles: board games, dolls, pencil cases, cards, pencils, pens, cereal boxes, books, clothing, anything Soupy.

Spy Memorabilia

Clubs/Associations

Charles Helfenstein
Secret Agent Fan Club
Newsletter: Spies
P.O. Box 476
Frederick, MD 21705-0476
ph: 301-695-4367
ohmss@erols.com
Spies, 007, Avengers, Mission Impossible, Man from U.N.C.L.E.

Dealers

Spy Guise, Inc.
P.O. Box 7013
Jersey City, NJ 07307
ph: 201-653-7395
spyguise@msn.com
http://www.spyguise.com
Buys, sells, trades; world's largest dealer of spy memorabilia: James Bond 007, Our Man Flint, Man From U.N.C.L.E., I Spy, Avengers; toys, games, novelties, records, lobby cards, posters from around the world.

Spy Memorabilia (James Bond)

Clubs/Associations

Graham Rye
James Bond 007 International Fan Club
& Archive, The
Magazine: 007 Magazine
P.O. Box 007
Addlestone, Surrey KT15 1DY U.K.
ph: 01483-756007
fax: 01483-756007
jbifc@jb007.net
http://www.thejamesbondfanclub.com
Focuses on James Bond; publishes "007 Magazine" (glossy, professionally produced, many never-before-seen photographs) 3 timer per year, and "007 Newsletter" newsletter (James Bond news worldwide) twice each year.

Collectors

Gary Pimenta
64 Lakeside Dr.
Tiverton, RI 02878-3111
Wants to buy James Bond 007 related toys, clothes, posters, etc.; send photos and asking prices.

Internet Resources

Matt Sherman
Not Stirred Collectors
2711 NW 42 Pl
Gainesville, FL 32605
ph: 352-372-5094
ms@007forever.com
http://www.007forever.com
Premiere group serving James Bond 007 collectors worldwide with a large online presence and annual collectors' events featuring celebrities, exotic locations and more.

Tarzan

(see also PERSONALITIES [LITERARY], Edgar Rice Burroughs)

Collectors

Jim Gerlach
2206 Greenbrier Dr.
Irving, TX 75060
ph: 972-790-0922

Three Stooges

Clubs/Associations

Gary Lassin
Three Stooges Fan Club
Newsletter: Three Stooges Journal
P.O. Box 747
Gwynedd Valley, PA 19437-0747
ph: 215-654-9466
fax: 215-368-3595
garystooge@aol.com

Collectors

Frank R. Levine
393 Charles St.
Malden, MA 02148-6318
ph: 781-321-0639
*Buys, sells, trades 3 Stooges
memorabilia.*

John Krupienski
5200 Hilltop Dr.
P.O. Box AA6
Brookhaven, PA 19015-1200
ph: 610-874-3003

Gary Lassin
P.O. Box 747
Gwynedd Valley, PA 19437-0747
ph: 215-654-9466
fax: 215-368-3595
garystooge@aol.com
*Wants 3 Stooges memorabilia; toys,
games, posters, stills, anything.*

Knuckleheads, Inc.
P.O. Box 10666
Glendale, CA 91209
ph: 800-500-4001
fax: 800-500-7494
custserv@threestooges.com
http://www.goknuckleheads.com
*Wants to buy Three Stooges toys,
games, original movie posters, props,
autographs, autographs, and more!*

Mark Lyons
6020 Paseo Del Norte, Ste. B
Carlsbad, CA 92009
ph: 760-431-5397
fax: 760-607-3299
cuffsandstuff@sbcglobal.net
*Wants pre-1970 Three Stooges toys,
games, puppets, promotional items,
autographs; also wants newer
advertising tie-ins.*

Neil J. Teizeira
P.O. Box 20812
Piedmont, CA 94620-0812
ph: 510-658-9938
fax: 510-658-8757
n.teixeira@worldnet.att.net
*Wants anything related to The Three
Stooges: posters, lobby cards, toys,
memorabilia, promotional items.*

Neal Austinson
P.O. Box 1691
Windsor, CA 95492-1691
ph: 707-838-9015
*Wants to buy Three Stooges 1930s
composition head hand puppets, toys,
etc.*

Internet Resources

Three Stooges Official Website, The
P.O. Box 10666
Glendale, CA 91206-3666
webmaster@threestooges.com
http://www.threestooges.com

Man./Prod./Dist.

Knuckleheads, Inc.
P.O. Box 10666
Glendale, CA 91209
ph: 800-500-4001
fax: 800-500-7494
custserv@threestooges.com
http://www.goknuckleheads.com
*Catalog of new Three Stooges gifts -
dolls, books, videos, posters, T-shirts,
watches, ties, magnets, comics,
photos, clocks, etc.; send for quarterly
"Soitenly Stooges" catalog.*

Uncle Remus

Museums/Libraries

Uncle Remus Museum
P.O. Box 3184
Highway 441 S.
Eatonton, GA 31024
ph: 706-485-6856
epchamber@eatonton.com
http://www.eatonton.com/remus.html
*Collection of items related to Joel
Chandler Harris, author of the fables
of Br'er Rabbit and Br'er Fox.*

Uncle Wiggily

Collectors

Martin McCaw
P.O. Box 9
Prescott, WA 99348
ph: 800-451-9755
*Wants to buy Uncle Wiggly items
including puzzles, books, Sunday
comics, candy tins, cloth dolls (Nurse
Jane, too), animal cracker box, all
dishes, advertising items, etc.; call toll
free about anything Uncle Wiggily;
finder's fees paid.*

Yellow Kid

Clubs/Associations

Richard Olson
R.F. Outcault Society
Newsletter: R.F. Outcault Reader, The
103 Doubloon Dr.
Slidell, LA 70461-2715
ph: 504-641-5173 or 504-280-6778
fax: 504-280-6049
http://www.neponset.com/yellowkid
*Members collect the art and history of
Richard F. Outcault, creator of The
Yellow Kid, Buster Brown, and Poor
Li'l Mose.*

Collectors

William Nielsen
1379 Main St.
Brewster, MA 02631-1723
ph: 508-385-9247
Wants Yellow Kid items.

Marty Goldman
5 East Genesee St.
Auburn, NY 13021
ph: 315-253-0236
yellowkid@tds.net
*Advanced collector of all pre-1920
Buster Brown memorabilia; always
looking for paper to pin-backs; also
Yellow Kid.*

Richard Olson
103 Doubloon Dr.
Slidell, LA 70461-2715
ph: 504-641-5173 or 504-280-6778
fax: 504-280-6049
http://www.neponset.com/yellowkid
*Wants all Yellow Kid items including
pin-backs, gum cards, toys, ads,
magazines, comic supplements, etc.*

CHARACTER JUGS

(see CERAMICS [ENGLISH], Royal
Doulton; COLLECTIBLES
[MODERN], Toby Jugs)

CHARGE CARDS

(see CREDIT CARDS & CHARGE
ITEMS)

CHARLIE TUNA

(see ADVERTISING COLLECTIBLES,
Figures [Charlie Tuna])

CHARMS

(see also PLASTIC COLLECTIBLES)

Clubs/Associations

Maureen McCaffrey
Bubble-Gum Charm Collector's Club
Newsletter: Charmed I'm Sure!
24 Seafoam St.
Staten Island, NY 10306-5770
ph: 718-979-8496
zacherly@earthlink.net

Plastic

Collectors

Jeffrey Maxwell
Alphabet26 Web Site
213 East Wells Blvd.
Sapulpa, OK 74066-6439
ph: 918-227-0657 or 918-594-8280
fax: 918-594-8281
alphabet26@aol.com
http://members.aol.com/Alphabet26
*A Web site dedicated to the study of
1940 to 1960s plastic prizes from gum
machines and Cracker Jacks with an
alphabet theme.*

Leo & Susan Poole
P.O. Box 692
Mill City, OR 97360
ph: 503-897-2625
susita@wvi.com
Wants older plastic charms.

CHARTS

(see MAPS & CHARTS)

CHECKS

(see BANKING, Bank Checks;
COINS & CURRENCY)

CHESS SETS

(see also GAMES)

Appraisers

Jeffrey Litwin
Litwin Antiques
P.O. Box 494
Princeton Junction, NJ 08550-5225
ph: 609-275-1427 or 609-275-0996
fax: 609-275-1427
jsl58@comcast.net
*Buys, sells and appraises chess sets,
chess books, chess art and chess
ephemera. Please send description
and/or photo of items for sale.*

Clubs/Associations

Dr. Thomas Thomsen
Chess Collectors International
Newsletter: Chess Collector, The
P.O. Box 166
Commack, NY 11725-0166
ph: 631-543-1330
fax: 631-543-7901
lichess@aol.com
http://www.chesscollectors.com
*International membership interested in
collecting chess sets, chess stamps,
chess books, chess art, and other chess
related items; meetings held biennially
in the even numbered years.*

Collectors

Jeffrey Litwin
Litwin Antiques
P.O. Box 494
Princeton Junction, NJ 08550-5225
ph: 609-275-1427 or 609-275-0996
fax: 609-275-1427
jsl58@comcast.net
*Buys, sells and appraises chess sets,
chess books, chess art and chess
ephemera. Please send description
and/or photo of items for sale.*

Jim Stephens
10906 Watermill Ct.
Oakton, VA 22124-1024
ph: 703-620-2031
*Wants chess sets and related books,
pictures, catalogs, etc.; fabricates
decorated chess sets from molds;
member of Chess Collectors
International.*

Dennis Horwitz
P.O. Box 301
Topanga, CA 90290-0301
ph: 310-202-7393
*Collects antique or unusual chess sets,
especially figural sets based on
themes; describe condition and
composition of set; height of pawn*

and king; date, location and price of purchase; board or box; include SASE and photo for reply.

Experts

Floyd Sarisohn
P.O. Box 166
Commack, NY 11725-0166
ph: 631-543-1330
fax: 631-543-7901
lichess@aol.com
http://www.chesscollectors.com
Collector and expert in antique and collectible chess sets.

Ray Alexis
608 Emery St.
Longmont, CO 80501
ph: 303-776-8892
chessstuff911459@aol.com
http://members.ebay.com/aboutme/
  chessstuff911459@aol.com
Chess collector, dealer, expert: chess memorabilia, chess sets, chess art, chess on stamps, chess in comic books and on money, chess in stereoviews and in the cinema; member of Chess Collectors International, editor of "The CCI-USA News."

Museums/Libraries

Bernice & Floyd Sarisohn
Long Island Chess Museum
P.O. Box 166
Commack, NY 11725-0166
ph: 631-543-1330
fax: 631-543-7901
lichess@aol.com
http://www.chesscollectors.com
Private museum of over 900 chess sets and chess related art and collectibles; viewing by appointment only.

Maryhill Museum of Art
35 Maryhill Museum Dr.
Goldendale, WA 98620-4601
ph: 509-773-3733
fax: 509-773-6138
MaryHill@gorge.net
http://www.maryhillmuseum.org
Collection contains over 200 antique and unusual sets from around the world.

CHILDREN'S THINGS

(see also BOOKS; CERAMICS, ABC Plates; DOLLS; DOLL HOUSES & FURNISHINGS; DR. SEUSS ITEMS; HANDKERCHIEFS, Children's; MINIATURES; PERAMBULATORS; RIDING TOYS; TOYS)

Auction Services

Shari McMasters
McMasters Harris Doll Auctions
5855 John Glenn Hwy.
P.O. Box 1755
Cambridge, OH 43725
ph: 800-842-3526 or 740-432-7400
fax: 740-432-3191
info@mcmastersharris.com
http://www.mcmastersharris.com
Specializes in auctioning antique and

collectible dolls and doll related items such as teddy bears, children's dishes, toys, children's books, etc.

Clubs/Associations

Lorraine Punchard, Treas.
Treasures for Little Children
Newsletter: Tiny Times
8201 Pleasant Ave. S.
Minneapolis, MN 55420
webmaster@treasuresforlittlechildren.com
http://www.treasuresforlittlechildren.com
A club for collectors of children's toy dishes, toy glass, miniature furniture, doll houses, salesman's samples, miniature stoves, doll accessories, and related toys.

Collectors

Mary Young
P.O. Box 9244
Dayton, OH 45409-9244
Wants to buy children's tin tea sets from Ohio Art and Wolverine, school readers (primarily first and second grade readers) from the 1920s to 1960s, 1930-1960s coloring and punch-out books.

Dealers

Marjorie Jeffreys
Going to Pieces
P.O. Box 390
Cibolo, TX 78108
ph: 210-659-2458
Buys and sells old games, toys, blocks and children's dishes and children's baking items.

Baby Rattles

Dealers

Jennifer Sykes
Jennifer Sykes Antiques
9018 Balboa Blvd. #595
Northridge, CA 91325-2610
ph: 818-993-1916
fax: 818-993-7612
Veeda10@aol.com
Wants to buy Bakelite crib toys, pre-1970 sterling/celluloid/tin antique baby rattles, boudoir dolls.

Cups

Collectors

Deborah Gillham
47 Midline Ct.
Gaithersburg, MD 20878-1996
ph: 301-977-5727
reamers@erols.com
http://www.reamers.org
Wants whimsical children's cups with whistles or figurals on handles or with writing and child illustrations on cup.

Dishes

Clubs/Associations

Lorraine Punchard
Treasures of Little Children
Newsletter: Tiny Times, The
8201 Pleasant Ave. So.
Minneapolis, MN 55420
rainyp@earthlink.net
http://www.treasuresforlittlechildren.com
A club for collectors of children's dishes, toy glass, toy graniteware, tin tea sets, miniature furniture, doll houses, kitchen doll accessories, and related toys.

Collectors

Mary Young
P.O. Box 9244
Dayton, OH 45409-9244
Wants to buy children's tin tea sets from Ohio Art and Wolverine.

Doris M. Diabo
19953 Great Oaks Circle S.
Clinton Township, MI 48036-2440
ph: 810-463-5651
Wants to buy children's tea sets, especially Majolica; also R.S. Prussia, Wedgwood, Royal Doulton, Royal Rudolstadt, and other quality makers; send photo or photocopy of pattern & markings with price, # of pieces, condition and SASE.

F.J. Steffen
9705 Mill Creek Dr.
Eden Prairie, MN 55347
ph: 952-944-1041
Wants to buy children's dishes, doll houses, furniture, kitchen and shops, etc.

Patrick Batzler
8118 Virginia Circle North
St. Louis Park, MN 55426
ph: 952-525-9590
fax: 952-545-7662
patrickbatzler@aol.com
Wants to buy children's dishes: breakfast sets, whistle cups, etc.

Dealers

Shelley Smith
P.O. Box 159
Bethlehem, CT 06751-0159
ph: 203-266-7496
Buys and sells toys, doll houses and miniatures, Steiff, children's collectibles, and country smalls.

Abbie Kelly
5196 Onondaga Rd.
Syracuse, NY 13215
ph: 315-487-7451
Buys and sells doll dishes, toy glass, toy tea sets, doll furniture.

Anna Green
P.O. Box 92
Effort, PA 18330-0092
ph: 570-992-4566
Buys and sells children's dishes in pressed glass, Akro Agate, and

Depression glass; also china, tin litho, sets or individual pieces.

Louise M. Loehr
Louise's Old Things
131 Virginville Rd.
Kutztown, PA 19530-8862
ph: 610-683-6388
fax: 610-683-6865
louises@bellatlantic.net
http://www.louisesoldthings.com
Co-author of "Willow Pattern China." Specializing in willow, flow blue, and early children's china. Wants one piece or collections.

Experts

Cathy Cook
10 E. 13th St., #2D
New York, NY 10003-4467
ph: 212-691-2406
fax: 212-691-2406
ccook710@aol.com
Collector, author, expert always looking for early 20th century tin litho dishes including those by Ohio Art, Chein Wolverine, etc.

Lorraine Punchard
8201 Pleasant Ave. So.
Minneapolis, MN 55420-2264
ph: 952-888-1079
fax: 952-888-8527
rainyp@earthlink.net
Author of "Playtime Pottery & Porcelain from the United Kingdom and the US" (1996), and "Playtime Pottery & Porcelain from Europe and Asia" (1996), "200 Years of Playtime Pottery & Porcelain" (2003), and other books.

Ellen Charland, ANA, MCPA
1407 Foothill Blvd., #19
La Verne, CA 91750
ph: 909-592-0101 or 626-963-7695
fax: 626-335-6651
antiquetea@aol.com
http://members.tripod.com/~antiquetalk/
  index-4.html
Specializes in children's tea sets; offers online appraisals.

Handkerchiefs

Collectors

J.J. Murphy
310 Vista Rd.
Madison, WI 53726
ph: 608-238-3378
jjmurphy@wisc.edu
Collector seeks 19th century printed children's kerchiefs and bandannas; special interest in moralistic, religious, instructional and black related examples (e.g. Uncle Tom's Cabin); condition important; serious sellers only, please.

CHINA

(see CERAMICS; DINNERWARE; RESTAURANT COLLECTIBLES)

CHINESE ITEMS

(see FURNITURE [ANTIQUE], Chinese; ORIENTALIA)

CHIPS

(see GAMBLING COLLECTIBLES, Gambling Chips & Gaming Tokens)

CHRISTMAS COLLECTIBLES

(see also CATALOGS, Christmas; COLLECTIBLES [MODERN], Ornaments; COLLECTIBLES [MODERN], Christmas; ELVES; GEMS & JEWELRY, Christmas; HOLIDAY COLLECTIBLES; LIGHT BULBS)

Auction Services

Robert J. Connelly, ASA
Bob & Sallie Connelly Auctions
666 Chenango St.
Binghamton, NY 13901-2015
ph: 607-722-9593 or 607-722-3555
fax: 607-722-1266
connelly@clarityconnect.com
Conducts specialty Christmas sales.

Clubs/Associations

Rita B. Bocher
Friends of the Creche Society
Newsletter: Creche Herald
117 Crosshill Rd.
Wynnewood, PA 19096-3511
ph: 610-649-7520
fax: 610-649-5782
crecher@op.net
http://www.op.net/~bocassoc
A society for all who love, own or collect creches; Christmas events, art, collections, products; creche competitions, exchange for trading, selling, buying creches, figurines.

Golden Glow of Christmas Past
Newsletter: Golden Glow of Christmas Past Newsletter
6401 Winsdale St.
Minneapolis, MN 55427-4250
ph: 612-544-8933
snowbaby@marymorrison.org
http://www.goldenglow.org
Network of Christmas antique collectors focusing on 1870-1950; annual convention.

Collectors

Bob Merck
44 Newtown Turnpike
Weston, CT 06883-2118
fax: 203-761-8777
santa@optonline.net
Wants pre-1940 figural glass, cotton and cardboard/paper Christmas ornaments, Santa Claus figures, Santa blocks & games, holly pattern china, children's Christmas theme dishes, figural glass light bulbs (need not work.)

Greg Spatafore
132105 Old Hanover Rd.
Reisterstown, MD 21136
ph: 410-526-2724
mrgoodlite@aol.com
Wants to buy old Christmas lighted decorations: bubble lights, candelabras, matchless stars, lighted plaques, unusual bulbs, etc.

Coleen Detzel
28 Lacresta Dr.
Florence, KY 41042-9663
ph: 606-647-6156
Wants older blown glass ornaments, older Santas; also any Christmas related items from the 1940s and 1950s.

J. W. & Treva Courter
3935 Kelley Rd.
Kevil, KY 42053-9431
ph: 270-488-2116
fax: 270-488-2055
brtknight@aol.com
http://www.aladdinknights.org
Wants German Christmas glass figural ornaments, old Father Christmas and matchless Wonder Stars.

Linda L. Vines
2911 4th St., #112
Santa Monica, CA 90405
ph: 310-314-0402
lleigh2000@hotmail.com
Wants to buy 1880-1940 German Santas, candy containers, glass and paper ornaments, early Christmas books, Snow Babies.

Susan Murphy
29668 Orinda Rd.
San Juan Capistrano, CA 92675-1211
ph: 949-364-4333
Wants to buy pre 1940s Christmas collectibles: Santa Claus, all ornaments, nativity sets, animals, celluloid toys, candy containers, etc.; please enclose SASE.

Sally Kimmel
1471 Lark Lane
Concord, CA 94521-2942
ph: 925-689-4138
sallyraek@yahoo.com
Wants to buy elves, Santas, snowmen, angels, reindeer, toy soldiers, etc.; ornaments and decorations made out of plastic, paper cardboard, etc. made during the 1930s to 1970s; also wants Nativity scenes, sets and mangers.

Dealers

Georgeann High
Yesterday's Memories & More
4618 Liberty Ave.
Pittsburgh, PA 15224
ph: 412-683-1103 or 724-239-6000
fax: 724-239-6011
yestrday@bentcom.net
Buys and sells Christmas ornaments: Hallmark, Enesco, German, Czech, early 20th century, handmade; Christmas lights and displays from the early 1900s through 1950s; also a traditional antique shop with 19th and 20th century antiques.

Bettie Petzoldt
178 Woolen Mill Rd.
New Park, PA 17352
ph: 717-382-1416
bpetzoldt@supernet.com
http://www.mindyourbusiness.com/ornaments
Collect/buy/sell early German Christmas ornaments: glass, diecut, Dresden, cotton, snow babies, lights, Santas; free monthly illustrated sales list available.

George Johnson
Agent Stag Enterprises
18 E. Hunter St.
Logan, OH 43138-1217
ph: 740-385-4845
Appraises Christmas ornaments; also buys and sells; author of "Christmas Ornaments, Lights, and Decorations Vols., I, II, and III."

Jenny Tarrant
Holly Daze Antiques
4 Gardenview Dr.
Saint Peters, MO 63376-3507
ph: 314-397-1763
jennyjol@aol.com
http://www.holly-days.com
Wants German Santas, Japan Santas, early Christmas candy containers, German woolly sheep, German animals, and old snowmen candy containers.

Mary Lou Holt
12510 Jackson
Grandview, MO 64030
ph: 816-761-5479

Paul W. Schofield
Lion's Den Antiques
7988 Bethel Burley Rd. SE
Port Orchard, WA 98366
ph: 360-876-3364
fax: 360-876-5421
Buys, sells, appraises, and specializes in old Santas, candy containers, Halloween, Easter, Christmas, Easter, Dresden, figural lights.

Experts

George Johnson
Agent Stag Enterprises
18 E. Hunter St.
Logan, OH 43138-1217
ph: 740-385-4845
Appraises Christmas ornaments; also buys and sells; author of "Christmas Ornaments, Lights, and Decorations Vols., I, II, and III."

Margaret & Kenn Whitmyer
K & M Antiques
P.O. Box 30806
Columbus, OH 43230
junquer9@columbus.rr.com
http://www.kandmantiques.com
Author of "Christmas Collectibles."

Dave Eppelheimer
47 Union Ave., SE
Grand Rapids, MI 49503
ph: 616-459-0474

Creches

Clubs/Associations

Rita B. Bocher
Friends of the Creche Society
Newsletter: Creche Herald
117 Crosshill Rd.
Wynnewood, PA 19096-3511
ph: 610-649-7520
fax: 610-649-5782
crecher@op.net
http://www.op.net/~bocassoc
A society for all who love, own or collect creches; Christmas events, art, collections, products; creche competitions, exchange for trading, selling, buying creches, figurines.

Collectors

Rita B. Bocher
117 Crosshill Rd.
Wynnewood, PA 19096-3511
ph: 610-649-7520
fax: 610-649-5782
crecher@op.net
http://www.op.net/~bocassoc

Feather Trees

Repro. Sources

Karen Shields
Twins Feather Trees & Holiday Collectibles
1543 Pullan Ave.
Cincinnati, OH 45223-2164
ph: 513-681-9357
fax: 513-681-9357
twinsfeathertree@mindspring.com
http://www.twinsfeathertrees.com
Limited productions of quality reproductions of feather trees and other Christmas items; Santa figures, Putz animals, fences; also Easter and Halloween; offers antique feather repair and restoration.

Mail Order Catalogs

Dealers

Judith J. Hesson
Hesson Collectables
1261 S. Lloyd
Lombard, IL 60148-4234
ph: 630-627-3298
Buys & sells Christmas mail order catalogs: Sears, Montgomery Ward, Penny, Aldens, Spiegel: 1900-1990; also other catalogs featuring toys; send $2 for 10-page listing.

Mexican

Dealers

Ed Barry
Shop - A Christmas Store, The
116 E. Palace Ave.
Santa Fe, NM 87501-2011
ph: 505-983-4823 or 800-525-5764
fax: 505-983-1630
theshopchristmas@uswest.net
http://www.theshopchristmas.com
Specializes in Mexican Christmas items including Nativities, many exclusively crafted for The Christmas Shop; also carries Steinbach, Polonaise, Dept. 56.

Santa Claus

Collectors

Douglas M. Singleton
P.O. Box 416
Westmoreland, NY 13490-0416
ph: 315-336-7792
archaic123@aol.com
Wants to buy Santa Claus pin-back buttons from Department stores, banks, advertising products, etc.; also wants Santa pocket mirrors, whistles, spinners, etc.

Craig Emerson
101 Wintergreen Lane
Stafford, VA 22554
ph: 540-659-5327
fax: 540-657-8361
etc@tidalwave.net
Collects vintage lead and cast iron Santa figures.

Jim Abicht
131 Main St.
P.O. Box 157
Smithfield, VA 23431
ph: 757-365-0223
bobani@visi.net
Specializes in mechanical Santas powered by clockwork or spring driven mechanisms.

Martha Tucker
21 Briar Hollow #803
Houston, TX 77027
ph: 713-877-1133
Has an extensive collection of over 2,500 Santas.

CHRONOMETERS

(see CLOCKS; CLOCKS, Marine Chronometers; WATCHES)

CIGAR BOXES, LABELS & BANDS

(see also CIGAR STORE COLLECTIBLES; LABELS; PAPER COLLECTIBLES; SMOKING COLLECTIBLES; TOBACCO COLLECTIBLES)

Collectors

David & Barbara Freiberg
Cerebro
P.O. Box 327
East Prospect, PA 17317-0327
ph: 717-252-2400 or 800-69L-ABEL
fax: 717-252-3685
cerebro@cerebro.com
http://www.cerebro.com
Wants cigar boxes, cigar bands, old advertising labels: fire cracker labels, baggage labels, US cigarette cards, sample books of labels.

Joseph Hruby
1511 Lyndhurst Rd.
Cleveland, OH 44124-2857
ph: 440-449-0977
Wants old cigar band collections in good condition.

Margo Toth
Up Down Tobacco Shop
1550 N. Wells St.
Chicago, IL 60610
ph: 312-337-8505
info@updowncigar.com
http://www.updowncigar.com
Wants to buy cigar store artifacts and related memorabilia.

Mike Bianco
InStone, Inc.
P.O. Box 231878
Encinitas, CA 92023
ph: 760-436-3637
fax: 760-436-3784
instone@pacbell.net
http://www.instoneinc.com
Buys and sells quality cigar box labels, samples, proofs and sample books, especially mining, frogs, Indians, sports; over 2,800 labels in stock.

Dr. Tony Hyman
Treasure Hunt Publications
P.O. Box 3028
Pismo Beach, CA 93448-3028
ph: 805-773-6777 or 805-773-0117
fax: 805-773-8436
thyman@fix.net
http://www.tobacciana.com
Collector, expert, author; wants pre-1920 cigar box labels, cans, photos, pamphlets, documents, trade cards, postcards, etc; author of "Handbook of Cigar Boxes", writing on tobacco collectibles since mid 1970s.

Dealers

Steven Gilbert
230 Forge Hill Rd.
Wrightsville, PA 17368
ph: 717-252-2023
sgil2001@aol.com
http://members.aol.com/sgil2001
Collector and dealer of cigar box labels.

Jerry L. Striker
P.O. Box 372
Lititz, PA 17543-0372
ph: 717-625-2031
fax: 717-625-4314
Wants to buy antique lithographed cigar box labels, cigar sample books, and other cigar related advertising.

David M. Beach
Paper Americana
P.O. Box 471356
Lake Monroe, FL 32747
ph: 407-688-7403
fax: 407-688-7495
dbeach@cigarboxlabels.com
http://www.cigarboxlabels.com
Wants to buy old cigar box labels.

Joe Davidson
Aaron's Archives
5185 Windfall Rd.
Medina, OH 44256-8703
ph: 330-723-7172
Buys and sells rare cigar labels.

InStone, Inc.
P.O. Box 231878
Encinitas, CA 92023
ph: 760-436-3637
fax: 760-436-3784
instone@pacbell.net
http://www.instoneinc.com
Buys and sells quality cigar box labels, samples, proofs and sample books, especially mining, frogs, Indians, sports; over 2,800 labels in stock.

Silas W. Bass
788 Cuchillo St.
Oceanside, CA 92057-6347
ph: 760-726-9937
Wants to buy cigar labels; co-author of "Patriotic Cigar-Label Art."

Wayne Dunn
Cigar Label Art
P.O. Box 3902
Mission Viejo, CA 92691
ph: 949-582-7686
fax: 949-582-7947
wayne@cigarlabelart.com
http://www.cigarlabelart.com
Buys, sells, collects, appraises, trades cigar labels; has over 1,300 in stock; sells "Cigar Label Art Price Guide" and other cigar art books, also Cigar Label Art CD-ROM with 18,000 labels in full 24 bit color.

Experts

Stephen C. Jones
P.O. Box 267
Homer, NY 13077-0267
ph: 607-753-8822
Buy, sells, collects and specializes in cigar box labels; cigar box sample books, sample labels & proofs; also wants pre-1900 trade cards, cigarette cards, business cards, billheads, letterheads illustrating products sold; no cigar bands.

Joe & Sue Davidson
Aaron's Archives
5185 Windfall Rd.
Medina, OH 44256-8703
ph: 330-723-7172
Author and expert specializing in stone lithography especially cigar box labels; author of "The Art of the Cigar Label," "Smoker's Art."

Wayne Dunn
Cigar Label Art
P.O. Box 3902
Mission Viejo, CA 92691
ph: 949-582-7686
fax: 949-582-7947
wayne@cigarlabelart.com
http://www.cigarlabelart.com
Buys, sells, collects, appraises, trades cigar labels; has over 1,300 in stock; sells "Cigar Label Art Price Guide" and other cigar art books, also Cigar Label Art CD-ROM with 18,000 labels in full 24 bit color.

Dr. Tony Hyman
Treasure Hunt Publications
P.O. Box 3028
Pismo Beach, CA 93448-3028
ph: 805-773-6777 or 805-773-0117
fax: 805-773-8436
thyman@fix.net
http://www.tobacciana.com
Collector, expert, author; wants pre-1920 cigar box labels, cans, photos, pamphlets, documents, trade cards, postcards, etc; author of "Handbook of Cigar Boxes", writing on tobacco collectibles since mid 1970s.

Internet Resources

"Up-in-Smoke" Cigar Band Museum
whizstrt@pop.ripco.com
http://pages.ripco.net/~whizstrt/
cigar.html
Online museum exhibiting over 800 different vintage cigar bands from the period of 1890s through the 1920s.

Terry Celano
ASTRAL, Inc
128 W. Main
Brighton, MI 48116
ph: 810-494-2000
fax: 810-227-2450
tcelano@ismi.net
http://www.astralinc.com
A community Web site where hundreds of people buy and sell antique cigar box labels, cigar boxes, and fruit crate labels.

Museums/Libraries

Dr. Tony Hyman
National Cigar Museum
P.O. Box 3000
Pismo Beach, CA 93448-3028
ph: 805-773-6777 or 805-773-0117
fax: 805-773-8436
cigarmuseum@tobacciana.com
http://www.cigarnexus.com/
nationalcigarmuseum
Seeks fine condition cigar boxes and labels (no bands) from before 1940,

and especially from before 1920; labels in sample books only, please.

Periodicals

Ed Barnes
Newsletter: Cigar Label Gazette, The
P.O. Box 3
Lake Forest, CA 92609-0003
ph: 949-457-0737
editor@cigarlabelgazette.com
http://www.cigarlabelgazette.com
A bi-monthly newsletter specializing in collecting cigar label art; lists and reviews cigar label auctions; articles, terminology, book reviews, advertisements.

CIGAR STORE COLLECTIBLES

(see also CIGAR BOXES, LABELS & BANDS; SMOKING COLLECTIBLES; TOBACCO COLLECTIBLES)

Collectors

Dr. Greg Zemenick
Dr. "Z"
1350 Kirts, Ste. 160
Troy, MI 48084-4852
ph: 248-642-8129 or 248-244-9430
fax: 248-244-9495
drzzeezz@aol.com
http://www.drzzeezzi.com
Wants cigar store items: Indians, figures, cigar cutters, lighters, photos, blinking eye clocks, cast iron items: anything cigar store.

Mike Schwimmer
325 East Blodgett
Lake Bluff, IL 60044-2112
ph: 847-295-1901
Collector of cigar memorabilia; dealer in all forms of vintage advertising; buys and sells.

Russell Barnes
P.O. Box 141994
Austin, TX 78714-1994
ph: 512-799-6076
fax: 512-835-9510
csindian@flash.net
http://www.cigarstorefigure.com
Wants to buy pre-1910 cigar store Indians and other figures; wood or metal; also wants original pictures of cigar store Indians; willing to travel; please call collect; pays finders fees.

Museums/Libraries

New York Public Library, Arents Collections, The
455 5th Ave.
New York, NY 10016-0118
ph: 212-340-0833
branch_web@nypl.org
http://www.nypl.org/branch/central_units/mm/midman.html

Cigar Cutters
Collectors

Howie Gross
407 Lincoln Rd.
Miami Beach, FL 33139
ph: 305-534-4757
fax: 305-538-5504
cowboyjudg@aol.com
Wants to buy cigar cutters: desk, pocket, figural, counter advertising.

CIGARETTE COLLECTIBLES

(see also ADVERTISING COLLECTIBLES, Trade Cards [Tobacco]; ADVERTISING COLLECTIBLES, Lucky Strike; ADVERTISING COLLECTIBLES, Philip Morris; LIGHTERS; MATCHCOVERS; MATCHBOXES & LABELS; MATCH SAFES; SMOKING COLLECTIBLES; TOBACCO COLLECTIBLES)

Collectors

Jim Cawthorn
1021 Spitz Kagel View Dr.
Canyon Lake, TX 78130
Collector of cigarette collectibles including rolling papers and smoking tobacco packages.

Michael Foster
School House, Church St.
Ticehurst
Wadhurst, East Sussex TN5 7DL U.K.
ph: 01580200967
mike@upinsmoke.freeserve.co.uk
Collector of live cigarette packets (complete with contents) and empty packets issued in the U.K.; also wants related tobacco items; possibly the only Web site in the UK specializing in R.J. Lea Tobacco Co. of Manchester & Stockport.

Cards

(see ADVERTISING COLLECTIBLES, Trade Cards [Tobacco])

Cigarette Boxes
Dealers

Lenore Monleon
33 Fifth Ave.
New York, NY 10003-4338
ph: 212-475-7871 or 212-675-7771
Wants enamel and sterling match safes and cigarette boxes.

Packs
Clubs/Associations

Richard Elliott
Cigarette Pack Collectors' Association
Newsletter: Brandstand
61 Searle St.
Georgetown, MA 01833-2213
ph: 978-352-7377
cigpack@aol.com
http://hometown.aol.com/cigpack/index.html
For those interested in cigarette packs,

tins, boxes and related advertising items; especially obsolete US brands.

Barry Russell
Cigarette Packet Collectors Club of Great Britain
Talisker
Vines Cross Rd., Horam
Heathfield, East Sussex TN21 0HF U.K.
mike@upinsmoke.freeserve.co.uk
http://www.cpcc-bg.34sp.com

Collectors

Richard Elliott
61 Searle St.
Georgetown, MA 01833-2213
ph: 978-352-7377
cigpack@aol.com
http://hometown.aol.com/cigpack/index.html
Interested primarily in old US brands of cigarettes; wants both packages as well as advertising items.

Roll-Your-Own Papers
Collectors

Paul Scheuer
6753 Humbolt Ave.
Minneapolis, MN 55430-1533
ph: 763-561-7321
Collects Roll-Your-Own cigarette paper packets and related memorabilia; also wants old pipe cleaner containers.

Silks
Collectors

William Nielsen
1379 Main St.
Brewster, MA 02631-1723
ph: 508-385-9247
Wants US cigarette silks, leathers, and inserts.

CIGARS

(see ADVERTISING COLLECTIBLES, Trade Cards [Tobacco]; CIGAR BOXES, LABELS & BANDS; CIGARETTE COLLECTIBLES; CIGAR STORE COLLECTIBLES; LIGHTERS; MATCHBOXES & LABELS; MATCHCOVERS; MATCH SAFES; PIPES; TOBACCO COLLECTIBLES)

CIPHER MACHINES

(see SPY EQUIPMENT)

CIRCUS COLLECTIBLES

(see also CIRCUS EQUIPMENT, Miniature Models of; CLOWN COLLECTIBLES; PERFORMING ARTS)

Clubs/Associations

Dave Price, Sec. Treas.
Circus Historical Society
Magazine: Bandwagon, The
1075 West Fifth Ave.
Columbus, OH 43212
Members interested in the circus, past and present.

Cheryl Deptula, Sec.
Circus Fans Association of America
Magazine: White Tops, The
2704 Marshall Ave.
Lorain, OH 44052-4315
deptulascircus@centurytel.net
http://www.circusfans.org
Focuses on circus history, current acts and activities, reviews of books about the circus, circus bands, etc.

Collectors

Irvin C. Mohler
6 Stratton Court
Potomac, MD 20859
ph: 301-762-8272
mohlerbros@aol.com
Wants to buy books on circus history and logistics, circus programs and other circus related collectibles including miniature circus items in 1/4" scale.

Tommy Sciortino
3723 Nebraska Ave.
Tampa, FL 33603
ph: 813-248-9911
fax: 813-247-6369
tommyintpa@aol.com
Circus equipment and memorabilia, carousels, amusement devices, coin-ops; no circus toys.

Museums/Libraries

Barbara Kram, Ex. Dir.
Barnum Museum, The
Newsletter: Barnum Herald
820 Main St.
Bridgeport, CT 06604
ph: 203-331-1104
fax: 203-339-4341
awestmoreland@barnum-museum.org
http://www.barnum-museum.org
Preserves and perpetuates the life and times of P.T. Barnum, museum circus owner and entrepreneur, one-time mayor of Bridgeport, CT, founder of "The Greatest Show on Earth", promoter of General Tom Thumb, Jenny Lind.

Ringling Museum of The Circus, The
John & Mable Ringling Museum of Art
5401 Bayshore Rd.
Sarasota, FL 34243
ph: 941-359-5371
fax: 941-359-5744
circusmuseum@ringling.org
http://www.ringling.org
Complex encompasses an internationally recognized museum of Western European and American art, a Museum of the Circus, the RInglings; 32-room mansion, the historic Asolo

*theater from Venice, and over 60 acres
of landscaped grounds.*

Circus City Festival Museum
154 North Broadway
Peru, IN 46970-2234
ph: 765-472-3918
fax: 765-472-2826
perucirc@perucircus.com
http://www.perucircus.com/info.htm
*Filled with photos, miniatures and
displays.*

Fred Dahlinger, Dir. Coll.
Circus World Museum
550 Water St.
Baraboo, WI 53913-2597
ph: 608-356-8342 x3282 or 608-356-
   8341
fax: 608-355-7959
fdahlinger.cwm@baraboo.com
http://www.circusworldmuseum.com
*The Museum collects all forms of
circus ephemera, documentation,
photography and sound recordings;
particularly desirable are pre-1900
examples of posters, photographs,
correspondence and business records.*

Emmett Kelly Historical Museum
202 E. Main
Sedan, KS 67361-1629
ph: 316-725-3470
stettler@kans.com
http://skyways.lib.ks.us/kansas/towns/
Sedan/museum.html
*This museum honors a native son, the
famous clown Emmett Kelly (1898-
1979) and his sad-faced character
"Willie;" collection includes
memorabilia of his circus career as
well as many items related to local
history.*

Hertzberg Circus Museum
210 W. Market St.
San Antonio, TX 78205-2628
ph: 210-207-7819
*Collection and library contains
thousands or circus related artifacts
including posters, books, Tom Thumb,
etc.*

Periodicals

Don Marcks
Newsletter: Circus Report
525 Oak St.
El Cerrito, CA 94530-3620
ph: 510-525-3332
circusreport@earthlink.net
*A weekly newsletter devoted to the
circus business.*

Ricketts Circus
Collectors

Bill Ricketts
P.O. Box 9605
Asheville, NC 28805-0605
ph: 828-669-2205 or 828-669-2668
fax: 828-669-2205
*Wants to buy any posters, newspaper
ads, etc. which advertise the Ricketts
Circus (first circus in the US - Phila.,
PA.)*

CIVIL RIGHTS

(see BLACK MEMORABILIA; PAPER
COLLECTIBLES; POLITICAL
COLLECTIBLES; SLAVERY ITEMS;
SOCIAL CAUSES)

CIVIL WAR ARTIFACTS

(see also AMMUNITION &
EXPLOSIVE ORDNANCE; BLACK
MEMORABILIA; BOOKS, Reference
[Civil War]; CIVIL WAR HISTORY;
MEDICAL, DENTAL &
PHARMACEUTICAL, Civil War;
MILITARIA; PERSONALITIES
[HISTORICAL], Abraham Lincoln;
TREASURE HUNTING)

Appraisers

Courtney Wilson
American Military Antiques
8398 Court Ave.
Ellicott City, MD 21043-4514
ph: 410-465-6827
fax: 410-461-6820
*Military antiques 1700-1900:
appraiser, consultant, broker, dealer;
arms, uniforms, equipment,
memorabilia - especially Civil War.*

Ronald R. Seagrave, CEO
Sergeant Kirkland's Museum &
   Historical Society, Inc.
8 Yakama Trail
Spotsylvania, VA 22553
ph: 540-582-6296
fax: 540-582-8312
*Appraiser, consultant: autographs,
documents, books, photographs;
specializes in early Southern book and
document collections: Civil War,
slavery, and Black Memorabilia.*

Will Gorges
Battleground Antiques, Inc.
3910 US Highway 70 East
New Bern, NC 28560
ph: 252-636-3039 or 252-636-5445
fax: 252-637-1862
rebel@civilwarantiques.com
http://www.civilwarshop.com
*Civil War expert, appraiser, dealer,
auctioneer; swords, muskets, guns,
flags, uniforms, etc; Associate Member
of the International Society of
Appraisers and Association of Online
Appraisers; over 28 years experience.*

John Sexton
Stone Mountain Relics, Inc.
1551 Annapolis Way
Stone Mountain, GA 30017
ph: 770-329-4984
fax: 770-972-1953
john@civilwardealer.com
http://www.civilwardealer.com
*Specializes in appraising Civil War
artifacts; well known and respected
expert in the field of Civil War
memorabilia, including anything
related to the American Civil War,
especially Confederate items.*

Rafael N. Eledge
Shiloh Civil War Relics
4730 Hwy. 22
Shiloh, TN 38376
ph: 731-689-4114
rafael@shilohrelics.com
http://www.ShilohRelics.com
*A 2300 square foot relic shop next to
Shiloh National Park in West TN;
buys, sells, trades on everything from
bullets to full size cannons; also
appraises.*

Brill Lee
Brill Lee Appraisal Services
P.O. Box 244
Bellevue, WA 98009-0244
ph: 425-885-4518
fax: 425-895-1022
brilllee@hotmail.com
*Appraises Civil War and Indian Wars
military items including weapons
(knives, swords, firearms), clothing,
horse gear and related items.*

Auction Services

Ron Meininger
Antebellum Covers
P.O. Box 3494
Gaithersburg, MD 20885
ph: 888-268-3235 or 240-498-3535
fax: 301-869-2623
antebell@antebellumcovers.com
http://www.antebellumcovers.com
*Offers Civil War and 19th century
American paper for sale through
monthly auctions, net price lists and
private treaty: soldier's letters,
autographs, images, engravings,
patriotic envelopes, images, general
orders, slavery items.*

Carson G. Jenkins, Jr.
RelicAuction.com, Inc.
6178 Forest Creek Ct.
Springfield, VA 22152
ph: 703-587-8365
auctioneer@relicauction.com
http://www.relicaucion.com
*Online source for buying and selling
high quality Civil War and military
artifacts; a vetting staff examines each
post to weed out fakes,
misidentifications and other obvious
errors.*

Kurt R. Krueger
Krueger Auctions
P.O. Box 275
Iola, WI 54945-0275
ph: 715-445-3845
fax: 715-445-4100

Clubs/Associations

Civil War Artifact Forum, The
95 Briarwood Dr.
Holland, PA 18966
info@artifactforum.com
http://www.artifactforum.com
*Organized for the purpose of
promoting research about, and
preservation of, Civil War artifacts,
in private and public collections;*

*promotes these goals through events
and publications.*

Karen Eubanks, Sec.
Northern Virginia Relic Hunters
   Association
P.O. Box 5257
Fredericksburg, VA 22403
contact@nvrha.com
http://www.nvrha.com
*Organized to promote the study and
preservation of American history
through the location, identification
and preservation of military and relate
historical artifacts; neither encourages
nor supports procuring artifacts from
public lands.*

Rob Morgan
Civil War Collectors Society & the
   American Militaria Exchange
5970 Toylor Ridge Dr.
West Chester, OH 45069
ph: 513-874-0483
RWMorgan@jackrouse.com
http://www.civilwar-collectors.com
*Established to promote the preserva-
tion and collecting of material
relating to our nation's rich military
heritage, from pre-Revolutionary times
to present day.*

Collectors

Warren K. Tice
W. Tice & Company
8 Orchard Terrace
Essex Junction, VT 05452-3501
ph: 802-878-3835
*Wants to purchase US Military,
Confederate, and high quality
decorative buttons; also wants to buy
military antiques.*

E. Alexander Peters
'Tiques
P.O. Box 3267
Farmingdale, NY 11735-0679
ph: 631-842-9549
*Wants documents, pictures, articles
and artifacts relating to the African-
Americans during the Civil War,
including slavery and reconstruction.*

Julie Brighenti
1036 Rostraver Rd.
Belle Vernon, PA 15012
ph: 724-929-7311
*Wants to buy Civil War memorabilia:
swords, belt buckles, medals, badges,
etc.*

Ken Turner
Ken Turner's Civil War
P.O. Box 911
Ellwood City, PA 16117
*Civil War collector and historian,
also some items for sale.*

Gil Barrett
8322 Sperry Court
Laurel, MD 20723-1184
ph: 301-498-1412
*Wants Civil War photos and
memorabilia particularly Maryland*

Union, 6th and 8th Mass. Infantry, and Boston Light Artillery.

Barry Smith
P.O. Box 38306
Greensboro, NC 27438-8306
ph: 336-294-3262
fax: 336-299-3182
bsmith1707@aol.com
Wants Union or Confederate Civil War memorabilia: letters, documents, autographs, photos, etc.

Lewis McSwain
1512 Carlson Ct.
Marietta, GA 30064
Specializes in excavated Civil War relics: buckles, plates, buttons, artillery and similar items.

Dean Roath
3050 Winnipeg Dr.
Baton Rouge, LA 70819
Collector of Civil War relics.

James Carlson, #73536
Arizona State Prison - Florence
P.O. Box 8400 - South Unit
Florence, AZ 85232-8400
Inmate collects Civil War autographs and letters accepts donations of autographs only (no money); writes to stars and celebrities to obtain autographs; member of UACC; seeks penpals with similar interests.

Dealers

Bedford & Janet Hayes
Gunsight Antiques
P.O. Box 687
Standish, ME 04084-0687
ph: 207-839-3825
info@gunsightantiques.com
http://www.gunsightantiques.com
Specializing in quality items of the Civil War era; especially wants

significant items belonging to Civil War soldiers from Maine.

Dale C. Anderson Co.
P.O. Box 3516
Gettysburg, PA 17325
http://www.andersonmilitaria.com
Sells antique firearms, swords, uniforms, headgear, accouterments, and more from the period 1775 to 1945; US and foreign; emphasis on 1860 to 1900 era; 40-page bimonthly catalog $12/yr and by Web site; since 1961.

Herbert Brown
Fields of Glory
55 York St.
Gettysburg, PA 17325
ph: 717-337-2837
foglory@cvn.net
http://www.fieldsofglory.com
Specializes in original, authentic Civil War antiques; also carries Civil War related books, prints, reproduction accouterments, and souvenirs.

Sam Small
Horse Soldier, The
777 Baltimore St.
Gettysburg, PA 17325
ph: 717-334-0347
fax: 717-334-5016
info@horsesoldier.com
http://www.horsesoldier.com
Specializing in the sale of fine Civil War military antiques: firearms, edged weapons, photographs, documents, battlefield relics and more; all items backed by unconditional guarantee; appraisal and soldier research services available.

Clifford P. Catania
Joshua's Attic
518 Kimberton Rd.
Phoenixville, PA 19460-4737
ph: 610-917-1167
clifford@joshuasattic.com
http://www.joshuasattic.com
Specializes in Civil war artifacts and dug relics.

Bill & Anne Shaner
Shaner's Antiques & Collectibles
403 N. Charlotte St.
Pottstown, PA 19464-5311
ph: 610-326-0165
Wants Civil War photographs, uniforms, equipment.

Bob Buttafuso
Centreville Electronics
13810B Braddock Rd.
Centreville, VA 20121
ph: 703-631-0202
fax: 703-222-8625
centelec@erols.com
http://www.cwrelics.com
Buys, sells, collects and specializes in dug Civil War relics including bullets, buckles, buttons, shells, fuses, spurs, etc.; all guaranteed to be authentic.

Ron Meininger
Antebellum Covers
P.O. Box 3494
Gaithersburg, MD 20885
ph: 888-268-3235 or 240-498-3535
fax: 301-869-2623
antebell@antebellumcovers.com
http://www.antebellumcovers.com
Offers Civil War and 19th century American paper for sale through monthly auctions, net price lists and private treaty: soldier's letters, autographs, images, engravings,

patriotic envelopes, images, general orders, slavery items.

Barbara Pengelly
Barb Pengelly, Autographs
13917 No. Meadow Rd.
Hagerstown, MD 21742
ph: 301-733-9070
fax: 301-416-7891
BarbPengly@aol.com
http://www.autographdomain.com
Authenticate, appraise, buy and sell Civil War documents, letters, diaries, autographs, photos, imprints; member of UACC and of The Manuscript Society; premium paid for Civil War-related material; references available.

Picket Post, The
602 Caroline St.
Fredericksburg, VA 22401
ph: 540-371-7703
email@picketPost.com
http://www.picketpost.com
Caries a complete line of authentic Civil War memorabilia and metal detectors.

Rick Burton
Carolina Collectors Civil War Relics
P.O. Box 1177
Kernersville, NC 27285
ph: 336-771-0346
ccrelics@collectorsnet.com
http://www.collectorsnet.com/ccrelics
Collector and dealer specializes in authentic Civil War items including buttons, buckles, bullets and other Civil War artifacts; Web site has photo illustrated catalog online.

Brian & Maria Green
Brian & Maria Green, Inc.
P.O. Box 1816
Kernersville, NC 27285-1816
ph: 336-993-5100
fax: 336-993-1801
bmgcivilwar@triad.rr.com
http://www.bmgcivilwar.com
Buy & sell Confederate States and Union autographs, letters and documents, especially military related; also photos, CDVs and other memorabilia.

R. Douglas Sanders
McGowan Book Company
P.O. Box 4226
Chapel Hill, NC 27515-4226
ph: 800-449-8406 or 919-968-1121
fax: 919-968-1644
mcgowanbooks@mindspring.com
http://www.mcgowanbooks.com
Specializes in Abraham Lincoln and the American Civil War: books, autographs, photographs, and objects of the period.

Will Gorges
Battleground Antiques, Inc.
3910 US Highway 70 East
New Bern, NC 28560
ph: 252-636-3039 or 252-636-5445
fax: 252-637-1862
rebel@civilwarantiques.com
http://www.civilwarshop.com
Full time dealer buys, sells, collects and appraises authentic Civil War artifacts: firearms, accouterments, edged weapons, dug items, documents, uniforms, coins, etc.; catalog available.

John Sexton
CivilWarDealer.com
1551 Annapolis Way
Stone Mountain, GA 30017
ph: 770-329-4984
fax: 770-972-1953
john@civilwardealer.com
http://www.civilwardealer.com
Offers authentic Civil War memorabilia and collectibles; Confederate items a specialty.

Civil War Outpost, The
800 Wyntuck Dirve
Kennesaw, GA 30152
ph: 770-514-7720
civilwar@mindspring.com
http://www.civilwaroutpost.com
Specializing in Civil War relics and related memorabilia for over 10 years.

William Skelton
Highland's Vault
P.O. Box 55448
Birmingham, AL 35255-5548
ph: 205-939-1178 or 205-939-3166
fax: 205-939-3166
Buys and sells Civil War paper items: newspapers (North and South), letters, photos, books, documents, reunion ribbons and medals.

Christopher Mitchell
P.O. Box 9
Point Clear, AL 36564
ph: 334-928-5007
jcmantq@gulftel.com
Specializes in Civil War era guns and swords.

James Mitchell
Ye Old Post Office Antiques & Militaria
P.O. Box 9
17070 Scenic Highway 98
Point Clear, AL 36564-0009
ph: 334-928-0108
jim@confederateordinance.com
http://www.confederateordinance.com
Specializes in Civil War arms, accessories, books, etc.

Larry & Debbie Hicklen
Yesteryear Civil War Relics
3511 Old Nashville Highway
Murfreesboro, TN 37129-3094
ph: 615-893-3470
DebHicklen@comcast.net
http://www.midtenrelics.com
Buys & sells CW muskets, pistols, sabers, buckles, buttons, letters, etc.

Paul & Linda Gibson
Gibson's Civil War Newspapers
P.O. Box 948
Bristol, TN 37621-0948
ph: 423-323-2427
fax: 423-323-8123
gcivilwar@aol.com
Buys and sells Civil War era (1861-1865) newspapers as well as Civil War related letters, diaries, flags, uniforms, photos; CSA bonds, currency and interim deposit slips; slavery items.

Miles Huskey
Miles of History
P.O. Box 599
Sweetwater, TN 37874
ph: 423-337-2540
milesofhistory@charter.net
http://www.milesofhistory.com
Collector, dealer and expert in Civil War items.

Rafael & Lori Eledge
Shiloh Civil War Relics
4730 Hwy. 22
Shiloh, TN 38376
ph: 731-689-4114
rafael@shilohrelics.com
http://www.ShilohRelics.com
A 2300 square foot relic shop next to Shiloh National Park in West TN; buys, sells, trades on everything from bullets to full size cannons; also appraises.

Barry Anderson
Barry'd Treasure - Civil War Relics
P.O. Box 40256
Louisville, KY 40256
ph: 502-448-8772
btreasur@iglou.com
http://www.iglou.com/btreasure
Collector and dealer in authentic Civil War relics and related items; online catalog.

Ted & Sallie Caldwell
Caldwell & Co. Civil War Antiques
816 Pleasant St.
Lebanon, IN 46052
ph: 765-482-0292 or 765-482-6280
civilwr@in-motion.net
http://www.caldwellandcompany.net
Actively buy, sell, trade all military items from Revolutionary War through Indian War era; also rewraps leather grips on swords and sabers.

Karl Sundstrom
2512 2nd Ave.
Riverside, IL 60546-1313
ph: 708-447-8673
sndstrm68@aol.com
Wants to buy all Civil War photographs especially CDVs, albumens, tintypes, ambrotypes, military daguerreotypes; also wants Corps unit badges, paper items, books, personal items; issues photo catalog 3 times per year.

William Butts
Main St. Fine Books & Manuscripts
206 N. Main St.
Galena, IL 61036-2244
ph: 815-777-3749
fax: 815-777-8950
msfb@galenalink.com
http://www.wcinet.com/msfbooks
Open shop dealing in autographs and out-of-print books in most fields; specializing in all aspects of American history; book and autograph catalogs issued regularly; member of A.B.A.A.; author of "Sign Here" and other autograph columns.

Alex Peck
Antique Scientifica
P.O. Box 710
Charleston, IL 61920-0710
ph: 217-348-1009
antiques@advant.net
http://antiquescientifica.com
Wants uniforms, insignia, guns, swords, diaries, photos, Corps badges, Bowie knives, medical instruments, hats, medals, belt plates, tokens, autographs, Lincoln items.

Charles Brecheisen
Trans-Mississippi Militaria
1004 Simon Dr.
Plano, TX 75025-2501
ph: 972-517-8111
fax: 972-517-8111
Buys, sells, trades anything to do with the Civil War, with a specialty in Civil War medical items: UCV, GAR, reunion items, paper, relics, photographs.

Experts

Ken & Jean Owings
Americana
P.O. Box 561
North Dighton, MA 02764
ph: 508-880-7362
fax: 508-977-0763
kcojco@attbi.com
Over 25 years in business; Civil War, Colonial American documents, books, autographs and related collectibles.

Mike Woshner
2306 Spokane Ave.
Pittsburgh, PA 15210-4414
ph: 412-884-9299
mwoshner@bellatlantic.net
Collects India-rubber and gutta-percha military and civilian artifacts; conducts patent research, publishes articles, displays artifacts and delivers presentations.

Robert P. Broadwater
ph: 814-684-0385
Author of books about the Civil War; contributor to "North South Trader's Civil War Collector's Price Guide."

Lewis Leigh, Jr.
38785 Leighfield Ln.
Leesburg, VA 20175-6810
ph: 703-771-3081
fax: 703-771-1432
Wants to buy Confederate & Union uniforms, swords, buttons, weapons, belts, soldiers' letters & diaries, hats and related items.

Courtney Wilson
American Military Antiques
8398 Court Ave.
Ellicott City, MD 21043-4514
ph: 410-465-6827
fax: 410-461-6820
Military antiques 1700-1900: appraiser, consultant, broker, dealer; arms, uniforms, equipment, memorabilia - especially Civil War.

Craig Wofford
723 Mount Vernon St.
Orlando, FL 32803
ph: 407-873-2639
Collects, appraises and specializes in Civil War memorabilia, Union or Confederate: photographs, letters, documents, diaries, uniforms, canteens, etc.; 25 years experience; free appraisals with SASE; references available.

Internet Resources

C. Clayton Thompson
Civil War Mall, The
584 Briarwood Lane
Boone, NC 28607
ph: 828-265-4970
fax: 828-265-0015
Greatbooks@aol.com
http://www.civilwarmall.com
An online marketplace for buyers and sellers of Civil War books, prints, maps. ephemera, artifacts and collectibles.

Dean Roath
3050 Winnipeg Dr.
Baton Rouge, LA 70819
Web site is dedicated to the detection, recovery, cleaning, and preservation of metallic artifacts from the American Civil War.

Robert Weaver
ValueTrac
P.O. Box 5
Sandpoint, ID 83864
ph: 208-255-4280
fax: 208-263-2978
info@valuetrac.com
http://www.valuetrac.com
Online database providing the current market values for thousands of both common and unique Civil War collectibles; updated daily; $29.95 for annual subscription.

Museums/Libraries

Grand Army of the Republic Civil War
   Museum & Library
4278 Griscom St.
Philadelphia, PA 19124-3954
ph: 215-289-6484
garmuslib@aol.com
http://suvcw.org/garmus.htm
   *Civil War Museum & Library;
   artifacts, personal memorabilia,
   paintings, G.A.R. & S.U.V.C.W.
   records; open first Sunday or by appt.*

Museum of the Confederacy, The
1201 East Clay St.
Richmond, VA 23219
ph: 804-644-7150
info@moc.org
http://www.moc.org
   *One of the largest and most
   comprehensive collections of
   Confederate art, artifacts, and
   memorabilia.*

Will Gorges, Dir.
New Bern Civil War Museum
3910 US Highway 70 East
New Bern, NC 28560
ph: 252-636-3039 or 252-636-5445
fax: 252-637-1862
rebel@civilwarantiques.com
http://www.civilwarshop.com
   *Largest inventory of authentic Civil
   War items in the Southern US; on-site
   museum and textile conservation
   studio; full appraisal services; large
   selection of historical reference books;
   full authentication services available.*

Civil War Soldiers Museum
108 South Palafox Place
Pensacola, FL 32501
ph: 850-469-1900
fax: 850-469-9328
info@cwmuseum.org
http://www.cwmuseum.org
   *Provides an accurate, in-depth and
   enjoyable trip back to the Civil War
   through a diverse collection of
   artifacts, music, art, handcrafted
   figurines, and life-size camp scenes.*

Dr. B.D. Patterson
Confederate Research Center, The Harold
   B. Simpson
P.O. Box 619
Hillsboro, TX 76645
ph: 817-582-2555
   *Large collection of Civil War
   artifacts; museum provides information about Confederate soldiers &
   capsule histories of Confederate
   regiments.*

Periodicals

Stacie Berger
Antique Trader Publications, Inc.
Magazine: Military Trader
P.O. Box 1050
Dubuque, IA 52004-1050
ph: 800-334-7165 or 800-482-4155
fax: 800-531-0880
stacie.berger@fwpubs.com
http://www.militarytrader.com
   Monthly publication focusing on

*military collectibles: articles,
collecting, interviews with dealers,
military toy column, book reviews,
collectibles for sale, espionage.*

Repair Services

Lynn Gorges
Historic Textiles Studio
3910 US Highway 70 East
New Bern, NC 28560
ph: 252-636-3039 or 252-636-5445
fax: 252-637-1862
palampore@aol.com
http://www.textilepreservation.com
   *Specializes in the restoration,
   conservation, appraisal, evaluation of
   military uniforms, including Civil
   War uniforms and Civil War flags.*

Artillery

Dealers

Jack Melton
JWMelton.Company
ph: 770-424-5225
jack@jwmelton.com
http://www.civilwarartillery.com
   *Collects, buys, sells, specializes in
   Civil War artillery; Web site has
   hundreds of photos and descriptions
   of American Civil War artillery
   projectiles, fuses; also glossary, cross-
   sectional views.*

Experts

Jack Melton
Civil War Artillery
ph: 770-424-5225
jack@jwmelton.com
http://www.civilwarartillery.com
   *With Lawrence E. Paul co-authored
   "Guide to Civil War Artillery
   Projectiles;" Web site has hundreds of
   photos and descriptions of American
   Civil War artillery projectiles, fuses;
   also glossary, cross-sectional views.*

Internet Resources

Jack Melton
Civil War Artillery
ph: 770-424-5225
jack@jwmelton.com
http://www.civilwarartillery.com
   *A specialized Civil War artillery site:
   introduction to artillery, projectiles
   and fuses, technical information,
   artillery sounds, historical documents,
   cannons and forts, items for sale.*

Bullets

Clubs/Associations

Charles Haislip
Civil War Bullet Collecting Association,
   The
Newsletter: CWBCA Newsletter
1420 Champions Pines Lane
Augusta, GA 30909
cwbulle@cwbullet.com
http://www.cwbullet.com
   *A nonprofit organization to promote
   the hobby and education about
   collecting Civil War ammunition.*

Experts

Charles Haislip
1420 Champions Pines Lane
Augusta, GA 30909
cwbulle@cwbullet.com
http://www.cwbullet.com
   *Expert, collector, appraiser of Civil
   War bullets.*

Computer Programs For

Man./Prod./Dist.

Niche Software, Inc.
Software: Civil War Relic Collector, The
7118 NW Terrace
Parkland, FL 33076
ph: 954-344-6561
marketing@collectiblessoftware.com
http://www.collectiblessoftware.com
   *Designed for the collector of Civil
   War relics, or any relics from any war
   or battle and reenactment equipment.*

Confederate

Dealers

Will Gorges
Battleground Antiques, Inc.
3910 US Highway 70 East
New Bern, NC 28560
ph: 252-636-3039 or 252-636-5445
fax: 252-637-1862
rebel@civilwarantiques.com
http://www.civilwarshop.com
   *Full time dealer buys, sells, collects
   and appraises authentic Civil War
   artifacts: firearms, accouterments,
   edged weapons, dug items, documents,
   uniforms, coins, etc.; catalog
   available.*

John Sexton
Stone Mountain Relics, Inc.
1551 Annapolis Way
Stone Mountain, GA 30017
ph: 770-329-4984
fax: 770-972-1953
john@civilwardealer.com
http://www.civilwardealer.com
   *Offers authentic Civil War memora-
   bilia and collectibles; Confederate
   items a specialty.*

Confederate Bonds

Dealers

William Skelton
Highland's Vault
P.O. Box 55448
Birmingham, AL 35255-5548
ph: 205-939-1178 or 205-939-3166
fax: 205-939-3166
   *Wants all US currency before 1929
   and all Confederate States of America
   currency and coins; also CSA bonds.*

Paul & Linda Gibson
Gibson's Civil War Newspapers
P.O. Box 948
Bristol, TN 37621-0948
ph: 423-323-2427
fax: 423-323-8123
gcivilwar@aol.com
   *Buys and sells Civil War era (1861-
   1865) newspapers as well as Civil
   War related letters, diaries, flags,*

*uniforms, photos; CSA bonds,
currency and interim deposit slips;
slavery items.*

Pierre Bonneau, CEO
Stock Search International, Inc.
4761 W. Waterbuck Dr.
Tucson, AZ 85742
ph: 800-537-4523 or 520-579-5635
fax: 520-579-5639
ssi@stocksearchintl.com
http://www.stocksearchintl.com
   *Buys and sells quality Confederate
   bonds issued between 1861 and 1865;
   sells through a regular price list or a
   bi-annual Mail Bid auction.*

Confederate Swords

Collectors

Steve Hess
P.O. Box 1747
Deland, FL 32720-1747
ph: 386-736-1067

Currency

Dealers

William Skelton
Highland's Vault
P.O. Box 55448
Birmingham, AL 35255-5548
ph: 205-939-1178 or 205-939-3166
fax: 205-939-3166
   *Wants all US currency before 1929
   and all Confederate States of America
   currency and coins; also CSA bonds.*

Medical

Museums/Libraries

National Museum of Civil War Medicine
Newsletter: Surgeon's Call
P.O. Box 470
Frederick, MD 21705-0470
ph: 301-695-1864
fax: 301-695-6823
museum@civilwarmed.org
http://www.civilwarmed.org
   *Contains the Gordon E. Dammann
   Collection which includes the only
   surviving Civil War surgeon's tent,
   medical chests, uniforms, stretchers,
   medical instruments, swords, books
   and personal effects.*

Paper Items

Collectors

Jack Donahue
P.O. Box 610123
Flushing, NY 11361-0123
ph: 718-225-0446 or 800-248-5927
fax: 718-225-4067
jvdonahue@yahoo.com
   *Wants Civil War autographs, letters,
   diaries, arms; also daguerreotypes,
   ambrotypes, tintypes, carte-de-visites;
   North and South.*

Dealers

Bob & Pat Bartosz
P.O. Box 226
Wenonah, NJ 08090-0226
ph: 856-468-0866
civilwarbnp@snip.net
*Wants Civil War paper items, e.g.
letters, diaries, bank checks, fire
department items, early baseball, slave
papers. Author of "The Civil War
Letter of George R. White 19th Mass.
Vol."*

Photographs

Collectors

Peter Hastings Falk
P.O. Box 833
Madison, CT 06443
ph: 203-245-4761
pfalk@cshore.com
http://www.soundviewpressbooks.com
*Wants important vintage Civil War
photographs, especially of notable
figures such as Abraham Lincoln,
Grant, Lee, etc.*

David Cress
Images, Inc.
P.O. Box 21036
Charlotte, NC 28277
ph: 704-849-0740
dcress@carolina.rr.com
Collector of Civil War images.

Tom Molocea
P.O. Box 100
North Lima, OH 44452-0100
ph: 330-549-3245 or 330-629-1864
*Wants to buy vintage Civil War
photographs in any format; will buy
single image or entire collection.*

Dealers

Henry Deeks
39 Nason St.
Maynard, MA 01754
ph: 978-897-8994
fax: 978-263-1861
kate@henrydeeks.com
http://www.henrydeeks.com
*Buys and sells Civil War photo-
graphs; issues a sales catalog twice a
year.*

Herbert Brown
Fields of Glory
55 York St.
Gettysburg, PA 17325
ph: 717-337-2837
foglory@cvn.net
http://www.fieldsofglory.com
*Specializes in original, authentic Civil
War antiques; also carries Civil War
related books, prints, reproduction
accouterments, and souvenirs.*

Karl Sundstrom
2512 2nd Ave.
Riverside, IL 60546-1313
ph: 708-447-8673
sndstrm68@aol.com
*Wants to buy all Civil War
photographs especially CDVs,
albumens, tintypes, ambrotypes,*
*military daguerreotypes; also wants
Corps unit badges, paper items,
books, personal items; issues photo
catalog 3 times per year.*

Dan Furtak
Shades of Blue & Gray
3543 S. Ferguson
Springfield, MO 65807
ph: 417-887-0009
dugspring@mchsi.com
http://home.mchsi.com/~dugspring/
Dan.html
*Appraiser, collector, dealer in Civil
War photography & ephemera; has
over 150 Civil War images for sale,
trade; always looking to buy Civil
War photographs, especially of
identified soldiers from MO, KS, AR;
also wants CW autography.*

Swords

Dealers

Will Gorges
Battleground Antiques, Inc.
3910 US Highway 70 East
New Bern, NC 28560
ph: 252-636-3039 or 252-636-5445
fax: 252-637-1862
rebel@civilwarantiques.com
http://www.civilwarshop.com
*Full time dealer buys, sells, collects
and appraises authentic Civil War
artifacts: firearms, accouterments,
edged weapons, dug items, documents,
uniforms, coins, etc.; catalog
available.*

John Sexton
CivilWarDealer.com
1551 Annapolis Way
Stone Mountain, GA 30017
ph: 770-329-4984
fax: 770-972-1953
john@civilwardealer.com
http://www.civilwardealer.com
*Offers authentic Civil War memora-
bilia and collectibles; Confederate
items a specialty.*

Repro. Sources

Sudha Gupta
Legendary Arms, Inc.
P.O. Box 197
Califon, NJ 07830
ph: 800-528-2767 or 908-832-0185
fax: 908-832-0812
sales@legendaryarms.com
http://www.legendaryarms.com
*Offers Union and Confederate
reproduction edged weapons,
uniforms, leather goods, etc.; also
medieval swords.*

Tokens

Clubs/Associations

Dale Cade
Civil War Token Society
Journal: Civil War Token Journal
26548 Mazur Dr.
Rancho Palos Verdes, CA 90274
ph: 310-378-4182
TC38thark@worldnet.att.net
http://home.att.net/~cwts/cwts.htm
*Purpose is to promote the study of
Civil War tokens along educational,
historic and scientific lines.*

Veterans

(see VETERAN ITEMS, Civil War)

CIVIL WAR HISTORY

(see also CIVIL WAR ARTIFACTS;
LIVING HISTORY, Civil War)

Clubs/Associations

Pepper Zenger, Registrar
Chicago Civil War Round Table, The
Newsletter: Civil War Roundtable
Newsletter
4332 West 109th St.
Oak Lawn, IL 60453-5358
http://www.thecwrt.org
*The nation's leading organization
dedicated to the study of Civil War
history.*

Jerry L. Russell
Heritagepac
P.O. Box 7388
Little Rock, AR 72217
ph: 501-225-3996
milhistory@aristotle.net
http://www.civilwarbuff.org
*The nation's leading battlefield
preservation organization.*

Jerry L. Russell, NatCh.
Civil War Round Table Associates
Newsletter: Civil War Round Table
Digest
P.O. Box 7388
Little Rock, AR 72217
ph: 501-225-3996
milhistory@aristotle.net
http://www.civilwarbuff.org
*The nation's leading battlefield
preservation organization.*

Jerry L. Russell
Confederate Historical Institute, The
Newsletter: CHI Dispatch
P.O. Box 7388
Little Rock, AR 72217
ph: 501-225-3996
milhistory@aristotle.net
http://www.civilwarbuff.org
*The only organization devoted to the
study of the history of The Confederate States of America.*

Dr. Stephen Engle
Society of Civil War Historians, The
Newsletter: SCWH Newsletter
P.O. Box 7388
Little Rock, AR 72217
ph: 501-225-3996
milhistory@aristotle.net
http://www.civilwarbuff.org
*The only organization for the teachers
of Civil War history; Dr. Engle can be
emailed at engle@acc.fau.edu.*

Internet Resources

George H. Hoemann
American Civil War Homepage, The
719 Luttrell
Knoxville, TN 37920
ph: 423-974-5917
fax: 423-546-3182
hoemann@utk.edu
*Gathers together in one place
hypertext links to the most useful
identified electronic files about the
American Civil War.*

Leah Jewett, Dir.
U.S. Civil War Center
Journal: Civil War Book Review
Louisiana State University
Raphael Semmes Dr.
Baton Rouge, LA 70803
ph: 225-578-3151
fax: 225-578-4876
lwood@lsu.edu
http://www.cwc.lsu.edu
*Mission is to promote the study of the
war from perspectives of all
professions, occupations, and
academic disciplines; Web site
features links to 6000 Civil War
related sites, including sites dealing
with collectibles & antiques.*

Misc. Services

American Civil War Research Database
P.O. Box 35
Duxbury, MA 02331
ph: 800-244-3446
civilwardata@sprynet.com
http://www.civilwardata.com
*Contains the military records of 2.6M
soldiers: battle synopses, regimental
chronicles, soldier records, regimental
rosters, officer profiles; free demo
available; annual fee.*

National Archives & Records Administration
700 Pennsylvania Ave. NW
Washington, DC 20408
ph: 202-501-5403
inquire@nara.gov
http://www.nara.gov
*For locating military records of Civil
War veterans; regional offices located
across the country; check out their
exhibit hall at http://www.nara.gov/
exhall/.*

Department of Veteran Affairs, National
Cemetery Administration
810 Vermont Ave. NW
Washington, DC 20420
http://www.cem.va.gov
Contact to find out where a Civil War

ancestor was buried during or after the Civil War.

Marie Varrelman Melchiori, CGRS, CGL
121 Tapawingo Rd. SW
Vienna, VA 22180-5964
ph: 703-938-8103
fax: 703-938-7279
mvmcgrs@aol.com
http://www.ancestordetective.com/speakers/melchiori.htm
Certified Genealogical Record Specialist in Civil War research; will help identify owners of historical items; will assist members of the legal profession locate missing heirs.

Periodicals

Newspaper: Civil War News, The
234 Monarch Hill Rd.
Tunbridge, VT 05077
ph: 802-889-3500 or 800-777-1862
fax: 802-889-5627
mail@civilwarnews.com
http://www.civilwarnews.com
A current events newspaper published eleven times per year for people with an active interest in Civil War history: coming events, book reviews, columns, ads, news, features, photos.

PRIMEDIA Enthusiast Group
Magazine: Civil War Times
741 Miller Dr., SE, Ste. D-2
Leesburg, VA 20175
ph: 703-779-8318
fax: 703-779-8310
david.masini@primedia.com
http://www.thehistorynet.com/CivilWarTimes
A bi-monthly magazine focusing on the historical aspects of the great conflict; a general interest magazine examining all aspects of the Civil War era, including personalities, battles, travel, art, artifacts and politics; bi-monthly.

PRIMEDIA Enthusiast Group
Magazine: America's Civil War
741 Miller Dr., SE, Ste. D-2
Leesburg, VA 20175
ph: 703-779-8318
fax: 703-779-8310
david.masini@primedia.com
http://www.thehistorynet.com/AmericasCivilWar
A bi-monthly magazine with colorful articles on Civil War battles, personalities, units; also ads for Civil War related products, prints, books, models, etc.

Magazine: North South Trader's Civil War
P.O. Drawer 631
Orange, VA 22960-0370
ph: 540-672-4845
fax: 540-672-5921
publisher@nstcivilwar.com
http://www.nstcivilwar.com
Bi-monthly magazine for Civil War relic hunters, collectors, reenactors & historians.

Reece Sexton
Lakeway Publishers, Inc.
Newspaper: Civil War Courier, The
P.O. Box 625
Morristown, TN 37814
ph: 423-581-5630 or 800-624-0281
fax: 423-581-3061
cwc1861@lcs.net
http://www.civilwarcourier.com
A monthly newspaper containing classified ads, articles, events, calendar, book reviews, reenactors, and goods/services for Civil War buffs.

Magazine: Blue & Gray Magazine
P.O. Box 28685
Columbus, OH 43228
ph: 800-248-4592 or 614-870-1861
fax: 614-870-7881
AdvRep@aol.com
http://www.bluegraymagazine.com
A bi-monthly full-color magazine focusing on the Civil War.

Theodore P. Savas
SAVAS Publishing Company & Consulting Group
Journal: Civil War Regiments
P.O. Box 4527
El Dorado Hills, CA 95762
ph: 916-941-6896 or 800-848-6585
fax: 916-941-6895
militarybooks@onemain.com
http://www.savaspublishing.com
A quarterly journal of the American Civil War; book reviews, The Preservation Report and The Regimental Bookshelf, unit-related articles.

Cavalry

Experts

Nick Nichols
Heartland House
P.O. Box 63
Rochelle, VA 22738
heartlandhouse@hotmail.com
Over 30 years of research & scholarship in Civil War history; special emphasis on cavalry themes; extensive background in material culture, tactics, period horsemanship, etc.; references provided; buys & collects cavalry-related artifacts.

CIVILIAN CONSERVATION CORPS ITEMS

Clubs/Associations

Association of Civilian Conservation Corps Alumni
P.O. Box 16429
Saint Louis, MO 63125
ph: 314-487-8666
fax: 314-487-9488
nacca@aol.com
A group of over 10,000 members who served in the CCC from 1933 to 1942.

Collectors

Jake Eckenrode
310 Wallace Rd.
Bellefonte, PA 16823
ph: 814-355-8769
Wants CCC items from the 1930s.

Robert A. Fratkin
1650 Tysons Blvd., 10th Floor
Mc Lean, VA 22102
ph: 703-556-8108 or 703-629-1941
fax: 703-356-6492
coxfdr@erols.com
Wants all CCC issued items.

Larry Jarvinen
313 Condon Rd.
Manistee, MI 49660-1008
ph: 231-723-5063
Wants CCC or WPA marked items and early forestry or conservation related items; also wants USFS, FSR, FSF, and US marked items.

Thomas W. Pooler
Timber Groves
P.O. Box 1861
Grass Valley, CA 95945-1861
ph: 530-268-1338
Wants all CCC material: medals, flags, rings, tokens, insignia (especially numbered company patches - will pay $25 for each numbered Unit sleeve patch.) Send description AND price.

Dealers

Ken Kipp
Allenwood Americana Antiques
P.O. Box 116
Allenwood, PA 17810-0116
ph: 570-538-1440 or 570-538-1932
fax: 570-538-1932
kwkipp@ptd.net
Wants 1933-1942 Civilian Conservation Corps items: uniforms, souvenirs, awards, crafts, china, photos, tokens, script, equipment, tools.

Museums/Libraries

Civilian Conservation Corps Museum
North Higgins Lake State Park
11747 N. Higgins Lake Dr.
Roscommon, MI 48653
ph: 517-821-6374
webspinners@state.mi.us
http://www.sos.state.mi.us/history/museum/museccc
Accepts donations of Michigan-related and Michigan-made artifacts, subject to review and approval; persons wishing tax deductions must provide own appraisal for tax purposes.

CLOCKS

(see also ART DECO; BOOKS, Reference [Clocks]; GLASS, Domes; INSTRUMENTS & DEVICES, Scientific; NAUTICAL ANTIQUES, Marine Chronometers; NEON, Clocks; WATCHES)

Appraisers

Jonathan Snellenburg
Jonathan Snellenburg Antiques, Inc.
594 Broadway, Ste. 507
New York, NY 10012
ph: 212-334-7270
fax: 212-334-7761
writeme@snellenburg.com
http://www.snellenburg.com
Specializes in the appraisal of vintage clocks, pocket watches, and scientific instruments.

Robert J. Connelly, ASA
Bob & Sallie Connelly Auctions
666 Chenango St.
Binghamton, NY 13901-2015
ph: 607-722-9593 or 607-722-3555
fax: 607-722-1266
connelly@clarityconnect.com
Appraisers and brokers of American & European clocks.

Walter A. Dayett
Dayett's Clock Repair & Appraisals
75 Study Rd.
Littlestown, PA 17340-9746
ph: 717-359-4850
fax: 717-359-4850
ldayett@superpa.net
Specializes in antique and contemporary clock sales and repair, primarily weight and spring driven movements; also specializes in clock appraisals.

William Bunch
William Bunch Auctions & Appraisals
One Hillman Dr.
Chadds Ford, PA 19317
ph: 610-558-1800
fax: 610-558-0885
whb@williambunchauctions.com
http://www.williambunchauctions.com
Specializes in the appraisal of antique clocks, music boxes, silver, paintings and other decorative objects.

Olivier Perrault
ClockWorld
3330 Pacific Ave., Ste. 404
Virginia Beach, VA 23451
ph: 757-428-8180
fax: 757-428-6253
olivier@imsnews.com
http://www.clockworld.com
Appraises, repairs, buys and sells clocks; specializes in European clocks, cuckoo clocks, Trumpeter clocks, and Atmos clocks.

Gregory L. Minuskin
Time on Your Hands
P.O. Box 538
Tustin, CA 92781
ph: 310-358-9006
chronofix@cs.com
Specializes in the appraisal of vintage clocks and watches.

Jim Erickson
1992 Waycross Rd.
Fremont, CA 94539
Collects, repairs, sells, appraises American clocks; Web site has a significant amount of information about the Attleboro Clock Co.

including a clock database and images.

Auction Services

George Horan
Jones & Horan Auction Team
453 Mast Rd.
Goffstown, NH 03045
ph: 603-623-5314
fax: 603-623-5314
pat@jones-horan.com
http://www.jones-horan.com
Specializes in horological artifacts and timepieces.

Robert Schmitt
R. O. Schmitt Fine Arts
P.O. Box 1941
Salem, NH 03079
ph: 603-893-5915
fax: 603-893-9777
bob@roschmittfinearts.com
http://www.roschmittfinearts.com
Two antique clock auctions per year.

John McClain
York Town Auction Inc.
1625 Haviland Rd.
York, PA 17404
ph: 717-751-0211
fax: 717-767-7729
info@yorktownauction.com
http://www.yorktownauction.com
Antique & specialty auctions, lecture & appraisal services; antiques also purchased; American & English furniture, related specialties & accessories, Americana, folk art, jewelry, art, clocks & watches, militaria, steins, Oriental rugs.

Clubs/Associations

Caroline M. Stuckert, PhD
National Association of Watch & Clock
   Collectors, Inc.
Magazine: Bulletin of the NAWCC
514 Poplar St.
Columbia, PA 17512-2130
ph: 717-684-8261
fax: 717-684-0878
jbland@nawcc.org
http://www.nawcc.org
The NAWCC is a non-profit and scientific-driven association founded in 1943 and now serving the horological interests of 38,000 members worldwide.

American Watchmakers-Clockmakers
   Institute
Magazine: Horological Times
701 Enterprise Dr.
Harrison, OH 45030-1696
ph: 513-367-9800
fax: 513-367-1414
awi-info@awi-net.org
http://www.awi-net.org
For those interested in horology as a profession or avocation; monthly technical magazine, technical bulletins, training, public relations, networking.

Doug Cowan
British Horology, Chapter #159
   NAWCC
110 Central Terrace
Cincinnati, OH 45215

Debbie Andrle
Southwestern Chapter #15, National
   Association of Watch & Clock
   Collectors
P.O. Box 99
Ross, TX 76684-0099
One of the oldest chapters of the National Association of Watch & Clock Collectors.

John Hubby, Sec.
National 400-Day Clock Chapter #168
   NAWCC
28 Red Sable Place
The Woodlands, TX 77380-2643

George Chistensen
South Oregon Watch & Clock Collectors
P.O. Box 562
Gold Hill, OR 97525
ph: 541-855-7215

Wendy B. Barr, Sec.
Antiquarian Horological Society, The
Magazine: Antiquarian Horology
New House, High St.
Ticehurst, East Sussex TN5 7AL U.K.
ph: 01580-200155
fax: 01580-201323
secretary@ahsoc.demon.co.uk
http://www.ahsoc.demon.co.uk
The world's leading organization in this field; the Society's aim is to serve all those interested in antique clocks, watches and other time-measuring instruments; publishes the quarterly journal, books, and monographs.

British Horological Institute
Upton Hall, Upton
Newark, Nottingham NG23 5TE U.K.
ph: (01636) 813795
fax: (01636) 812258
info@bhi.co.uk
http://www.bhi.co.uk
Education is a major part of the BHI; strong ties with institutions offering horological training; members have access to museum collection for study; membership open to anyone with an interest in timekeeping.

Collectors

Jerry Boxenhorn
Clock Exchange, The
2045 Legion St.
Bellmore, NY 11710-4914
ph: 516-221-2723
clockpin@optonline.net
Wants to buy one clock or entire collections; also movements, parts, and all clock related items; especially wants Ansonia statue clocks, Ansonia Royal Bonn clocks, French bronze clocks, and any animated or unusual clocks.

Howard Prince
ph: 540-752-2783
ecnir@erols.com
Buys and sells American antique clocks.

Larry Spilkin
P.O. Box 5039
Southfield, MI 48086-5039
ph: 248-642-3722
Wants Lawson, Herman-Miller, Howard-Miller clocks.

Paul H. Hayashi, PE
18 Tarabrook Dr.
Orinda, CA 94563-3121
ph: 925-254-5074 or 925-253-1038
fax: 925-253-0592
Wants to buy precision wall regulators with different escapments.

Dealers

Robert C. Cheney
Robert C. Cheney Fine Antique Clocks
19 Brookfield Rd.
Brimfield, MA 01010
ph: 413-245-7017
Since 1900 the Cheney clock makers have provided consulting services, restoration, appraisals, and sales of fine antique clocks; by appointment.

John Delaney
Delaney's Antique Clocks
435 Main St., Route 119
Townsend, MA 01474
ph: 978-597-2231 or 978-597-1340
delaney@net1plus.com
http://www.delaneyantiqueclocks.com
In business for over 30 years; carries extensive selection of American tall case as well as antique wall and shelf clocks; located 50 miles northwest of Boston.

Bob Frishman
Bell-Time Clocks
53 Poor St.
Andover, MA 01810-2501
ph: 978-475-5001
rjfjs@attbi.com
http://www.bell-time.com
Buys and sells clocks of all styles, ages, sizes and nationalities; also repairs and restores clocks.

Howard Zimmerman
Internet Clock Shop
ph: 978-462-5311
howard@antiqueclocks.com
http://www.antiqueclocks.com
Buys and sells American and European antique clocks, early American tallcase, mantel and wall clocks; also French antique marble, steeple, calendar, Ansonia, Chelsea, Waterbury, Gilbert, Seth Thomas, Japy Freres clocks.

Mounir Mazzawi
Oakshadows Hour
105 Plimpton St.
Walpole, MA 02081
mounir.mazzawi@verizon.net
http://www.oakshadows.com
Buys and sells antique clocks: American, English, French, and others.

Adam Schoolsky
P.O. Box 95
Nashua, NH 03061
ph: 603-883-7931
fax: 603-882-3781
adam@ArtDeco.com
Buying one item or entire collections or estates; specializing in clocks with Art Deco styling, American weight regulators, complicated musical clocks; also buys clock/watch related advertising signs; expert clock restorations.

Debbie Woolley
Favorite Past-Times Antiques
6 Main Hill
Bridgton, ME 04009
ph: 207-647-4486
info@maine-antiques.com
http://www.maine-antiques.com/fpt/Index
Buys and sells keywind American mantle and kitchen clocks; will buy even if not working.

James Taylor
Taylor Time
P.O. Box 311
Woodstock, VT 05091
ph: 802-457-3757
fax: 802-457-3757
taylor.time@taylor-time.com
http://www.taylor-time.com
Working with Bill Mather, has 40 years experience supplying rare quality antique clocks and reliable service; cleaning, bushing, overhaul of case and movement.

Lindy Larson
Larson's Clock Shop
P.O. Box 144
Westminster, VT 05158
ph: 802-722-4203
lindyl@sover.net
http://www.larsonsclocks.com
Issues large catalog of clocks for sale including ships, novelty, carriage, shelf, wall, and tallcase clocks; in business for over 30 years.

Ed Kazemekas
35 Riverview Circle
Wolcott, CT 06716
ph: 203-879-1814
Buy, sell, restores American clocks; specializes in Lux pendulettes, novelty and alarm clocks.

Kathleen Carroll
About Time Clock Company
1411 Wickapecko Dr.
Asbury Park, NJ 07712
ph: 732-775-4650
fax: 732-775-4684
about_time@msn.com
http://www.abtime.com
Sales and restoration of antique clocks; French clock specialist.

G & R Clocks
27 Division St.
Somerville, NJ 08876
ph: 908-685-2207
fax: 908-722-2862
Buys and sells antique clocks; also offers expert clock and watch repair and restoration.

Charles F. Breuel
Charles Breuel Antiques
P.O. Box 261
Glenmont, NY 12077
ph: 518-439-6717
cfbclock@msn.com
Specializing in American time pieces, furniture, unusual accessories; shows only.

Bruce A. Austin
c/o RIT/College Liberal Arts
92 Lomb Memorial Dr.
Rochester, NY 14623-5604
ph: 585-475-2879 or 585-387-9820
fax: 585-475-7732
baagll@rit.edu
Buying American clocks manufactured between 1800 - 1915; especially interested in wall regulators.

Ken Markley
Old Timers Antique Clocks
P.O. Box 392
Camp Hill, PA 17001-0392
ph: 717-761-1908
fax: 717-761-7446
anytime@prodigy.net
http://www.oldtimersclocks.com
Buys and sells antique clocks; must be at least 100 years old, no reproductions, electrics or cuckoos; if selling, seller must send clear photos and asking for each clock; in business for over 50 years; Life Member NAWCC.

Walter A. Dayett
Dayett's Clock Repair & Appraisals
75 Study Rd.
Littlestown, PA 17340-9746
ph: 717-359-4850
fax: 717-359-4850
ldayett@superpa.net
Specializes in antique and contemporary clock sales and repair, primarily weight and spring driven movements; also specializes in clock appraisals.

Paul D. Phillips
Paul Phillips Antiques
P.O. Box 147
Bryn Mawr, PA 19010
ph: 610-527-3571
fax: 610-527-4577
paul@paulphillipsantiques.com
http://www.paulphillipsantiques.com
Buys, sells and appraises fine examples of American clocks from the 18th to 19th centuries; also sells period American furniture and works of art.

Gordon S. Converse
Gordon S. Converse & Co.
503 W. Lancaster Ave.
Strafford, PA 19087
ph: 610-964-7632 or 800-789-1001
fax: 610-964-1181
email@converseclocks.com
http://www.converseclocks.com
Specializes in fine antique clocks including American, French, English, porcelain, banjo, Vienna regulators, ships clocks, skeleton clocks, mantel and tallcase; high quality color catalog issued periodically.

Douglas Whitesell
P.O. Box 1805
Middleburg, VA 20118
ph: 540-687-5550
Buys, sells and repairs clocks; does resilvering of dials.

N. Kenzie Smith
Clock Shop, The
119 East St.
Frederick, MD 21701
ph: 301-698-8252
http://www.frederickcounty.com/antiques/clock.htm
Sells, repairs and restores all mechanical clocks and watches; references upon request.

Jill & Chuck Probst
Charles Edwin Antiques
P.O. Box 1340
Louisa, VA 23093-1340
ph: 540-967-0416
fax: 540-967-0416
info@charlesedwin.com
http://www.charlesedwin.com
Buys and sells long case clocks.

Olivier Perrault
ClockWorld
3330 Pacific Ave., Ste. 404
Virginia Beach, VA 23451
ph: 757-428-8180
fax: 757-428-6253
olivier@imsnews.com
http://www.clockworld.com
Appraises, repairs, buys and sells clocks; specializes in European clocks, cuckoo clocks, Trumpeter clocks, and Atmos clocks.

Kathy Thomas
Antique Clock Shop
200 Federal St.
Bluefield, WV 24701
ph: 304-327-9686
clocks@antiqueclockshop.com
http://www.antiqueclockshop.com
Buys and sells antique clocks.

Lee Yelvington
It's About Time
Antiques Emporium
2060 Clark Ave.
Raleigh, NC 27605-1604
ph: 919-834-7250 or 919-851-3073
fax: 919-851-5017
itsabouttime@mindspring.com
http://www.itsabouttime-clocks.com
In business for over 14 years; carries an assortment of fine American clocks including tall case clocks.

Larry Davenport
Roswell Clock & Antique Co.
955 Canton St.
Roswell, GA 30075
ph: 770-992-5232
fax: 770-587-4597
roswellclock@mindspring.com
http://www.rosewellclockandantique.com
Carries large selection of antique clocks.

L.J. & Joanie Latorre
Albert's Antique Clocks
1808-B Ridgewood Ave.
Holly Hill, FL 32117
ph: 386-673-4822
time1@bellsouth.net
http://www.albertsantiqueclocks.com
Repairs, buys, sells all foreign and domestic clocks and watches, antique and new; huge showroom of wall, mantel, floor clocks as well as the areas largest selection of cuckoo clocks; free in-shop estimates.

Mark Peer
Mark of Time
1128 8th Ave.
Palmetto, FL 34221
ph: 800-277-5275 or 941-721-1801
fax: 941-955-3211
Mailbox@markoftime.com
http://www.markoftime.com
Buys and sells antique clocks and entire clock collections.

Mark Russell
Clock Exchange, The
c/o Mentzer's Antique Mall
132 Tarpon Ave. East
Tarpon Springs, FL 34689
ph: 727-692-8361
fax: 727-938-2986
clock_exchange@verizon.net
http://www.nvo.com/clock_exchange/door
Buys, sells, restores antique American clocks; specializes in wall regulators, double dial calendar clocks, early shelf clocks and industrial time clocks; also sells new and used clock books.

Robert Crowder
Professional Clockery, Inc.
7600 Hamilton Ave.
Cincinnati, OH 45231
ph: 513-931-8463
fax: 513-755-3761
bob@proclocks.com
http://www.proclocks.com
Buys, sells, restores antique clocks.

Norm Koloski
About Time Clock Repair
ph: 734-953-0586
abouttime@adni.net
http://www.abouttimes.com
Buys, sells, repairs, restores antique clocks.

David Lee
Clockworks, Inc., The
560 N. Western Ave.
Lake Forest, IL 60045-1920
ph: 847-234-7272
fax: 847-234-7286
davidlee@theclockworks.com
http://www.theclockworks.com
Buy, sell, repair, restore clocks, watches, barometers and music boxes.

Rick Chandler
Attic Antiques
P.O. Box 131
Algonquin, IL 60102
ph: 847-658-1433
ticktockchandler@earthlink.net
http://www.attic-antiques.net
Specializes in clocks, and wrist and pocket watches; over 35 years experience; 17th century to present; will answer questions about values and makers.

Bruce Hannon
Investor's Antiques
1208 W. Union St.
Champaign, IL 61821
b-hannon@uiuc.edu
http://www.shout.net/~smgorman/bruce
Selling and repairing clocks since 1969; everything from tower clocks to pocket watches.

Tim Sweet
M.O.S.T. Watch & Clock Co.
3010 Forest Trail
San Angelo, TX 76904
ph: 915-947-8196
timsweet@cox.net
Dealer, collector, expert, auction and repair services, appraiser offering all aspects of antique clock and watch services; Web site has an Internet Horology Club.

Carl E. Schmeig
Carl's Clocks
Antique Center of Texas
1001 West Loop North
Houston, TX 77055
ph: 281-296-7256 or 713-684-4644
cclocks@infohwy.com
http://www.carlsclocks.com
Antique American and European clocks; has over 400 antique clocks in inventory at all times: mantle, wall, tallcase clocks dating from 1750 to

1900; also offers repair and restoration of all clocks.

Richard W. Oliver, Jr.
Clock Guy Antique Brokerage, The
ph: 760-604-0262
fax: 760-598-0327
theclockguy@clockguy.com
http://www.clockguy.com
Largest broker of antique clocks in North America; represents collectors, estates and those down-sizing; also brokers mechanical music devices; their extensive search database helps in locating specific items for their clients.

Don Levison
Don Levison Antiques
P.O. Box 22262
San Francisco, CA 94122
ph: 415-753-0455
fax: 415-753-5206
dlevison@juno.com
http://www.antiquehorology.com
Buys and sells antique and better quality pocket and wrist watches, clocks, music boxes, singing birds, and other small automata; also mercury barometers from the 17th century to present.

Steve Bogoff
Bogoff Antique Timepieces
P.O. Box 408
Mill Valley, CA 94942
ph: 415-383-8100
fax: 415-383-8112
info@bogoff.com
http://www.bogoff.com
Buys, sells, appraises and has online catalog of complicated, rare, early, unusual, beautiful pocket watches, vintage wrist watches, small clocks, singing bird boxes and more.

Bob Setnik
Setniks In Time Again
815 Sutter St., Ste. 2
Folsom, CA 95630
ph: 916-985-2390 or 888-333-1715
info@setniksintimeagain.com
http://www.setniksintimeagain.com
Over 35 years in service; sells thoroughly and properly restored American Victorian antique furniture and antique clocks; ships worldwide.

James Poag, GG, ISA CAPP
James O. Poag Jewellers, Ltd.
94 Frank St.
P.O. Box 39
Strathroy, Ontario N7G 3J1 Canada
ph: 519-245-1040 or 519-245-1580
fax: 519-245-6073
james@poags.com
http://www.poags.com
Retail clock, jewellery, china and gift stores; staff includes 3 goldsmiths, 2 stone setters, watchmaker, clockmaker and ISA Certified Appraiser; largest selection of clocks in Ontario; in business since 1959.

Jacques Duvoisin
Pendulantic
Neuchatel 2
BP 142
Saint-Blaise, CH-2072 Switzerland
ph: +41 3275 33019 or +41 7860 63019
fax: +41 3274 33019
duvoisin@pendulantic.com
http://www.pendulantic.com
Antique clock dealer and restorer; Swiss clockmaker specializes in wall clocks, mantel clocks, bracket and carriage clocks, fine antique clocks and longcase clocks.

Experts

Robert W.D. Ball
26 Byron Dr.
Avon, CT 06001-4507
Author of "American Shelf and Wall Clocks, A Pictorial History For Collectors."

Eric Chandlee Wilson
16 Bondsville Rd.
P.O. Box 102
Thorndale, PA 19372
ph: 610-383-5597
Tallcase clock dealer specializing in English and American tall case clocks; special interest in Chester County, PA clocks and in clocks by the Chandlee's.

Julian Gibbard
P.O. Box 1092
Harpers Ferry, WV 25425
ph: 304-725-2035
fax: 304-725-2035
Specialist in long case clocks and barometers.

Joe Cohen
3090 North Couse Dr., Apt. #107
Pompano Beach, FL 33069
ph: 954-917-4676
jccohen3@attbi.com
Specializing in 17th, 18th, and 19th century clocks and watches; teaches course in identifying and researching antique clocks and watches.

Tran Duy Ly
215 Shadowood Dr.
Johnson City, TN 37604
ph: 423-283-9004
fax: 423-283-9001
tranduyly@aol.com
http://www.arlingtonbooks.com
Author of several books about antique clocks.

Internet Resources

Horological Foundation, The
mail@antique-horology.org
http://www.antique-horology.org
A meeting and trading place for all those devoted to fine antique clocks, watches, barometers and instruments.

Fortunat Mueller-Maerki
Horology - The Index
350 Park Ave.
New York, NY 10022
horology@horology.com
http://www.horology.com
A comprehensive resource guide to clock, watch, horology, and timekeeping related sites on the Internet; 100 pages with 3000 links to dealers, brands, repair tips, museums, schools, periodicals, organizations, related people.

Jeff Savage
Price Guide: Antique Clocks Identification & Price Guide Online
ph: 707-824-1711
jsavage@savagesguide.com
http://www.antiqueclockspriceguide.com
Fee-based online eBook clock price guide with values, descriptions and photos for more than 4,000 antique and collectibles clocks; American and European models of all types and makers; illustrated glossary; wood ID type, valuing tips.

British Horological Institute Workshop Hints & Tips
Upton Hall, Upton
Newark, Nottingham NG23 5TE U.K.
ph: (01636) 813795
fax: (01636) 812258
info@bhi.co.uk
http://www.bhi.co.uk/hints
Web site contains details and practical hints and tips for clocks, watches, and barometers.

Misc. Services

Joe Cohen
3090 North Couse Dr., Apt. #107
Pompano Beach, FL 33069
ph: 954-917-4676
jccohen3@attbi.com
Teaches course in identifying and researching antique clocks and watches.

Museums/Libraries

American Clock & Watch Museum
Journal: Timepiece Journal
100 Maple St.
Bristol, CT 06010-5034
ph: 860-583-6070
fax: 860-583-1862
info@clockmuseum.org
http://www.clockmuseum.org
Preserves the history of American horology, especially Connecticut and Bristol's role; large displays of clocks & watches.

Caroline M. Stuckert, PhD
National Association of Watch & Clock Collectors Museum, Inc., The
514 Poplar St.
Columbia, PA 17512-2130
ph: 717-684-8261
fax: 717-684-0878
jbland@nawcc.org
http://www.nawcc.org
The National Watch & Clock Museum of the National Assoc. of Watch &

Clock Collectors, documents the evolution of timekeeping around the world - from early sundials to atomic clocks with a collection of over 12,000 horological timepieces.

National Museum of American History
14th & Constitution Ave. NW
Washington, DC 20560
ph: 202-357-2700
webmaster@si.edu
http://www.si.edu/organiza/museums/nmah/nmah.htm

Carol Riehle
Bily Clock Exhibit/Antonin Dvorak Exhibit
323 Main St.
P.O. Box 258
Spillville, IA 52168-0258
ph: 319-562-3569 or 319-562-3457
fax: 319-562-4373
bily@oneota.net
http://www.bilyclocks.org
One-of-a-kind exhibit displaying clocks by the two Bily brothers; historical and educational display of handcarved clocks; housed in the building famous composer Antonin Dvorak lived in during his stay in 1893.

Allan Symons, Manager
Canadian Clock Museum, The
P.O. Box 1684
60 James St.
Deep River, Ontario K0J 1P0 Canada
ph: 613-584-9687
enquiries@canclockmuseum.ca
http://www.canclockmuseum.ca
Focuses on 1800 to 2000 Canadian clock sellers and clock makers.

Wichterheer Museum of Timepieces & Mechanical Music
Stattsstrasse 18
Oberhofen am Thunersee, CH 3853 Switzerland
ph: +41 33 243 4377
horology@horology.com

Periodicals

Alan
Clock Cellar, The
ph: 856-546-5646
Alan@clockcellar.com
http://www.clockcellar.com
Repair and setup of antique and modern clocks in the Delaware Valley area; specializes in grandfather clocks.

Steven G. Conover, Ed.
Newsletter: Clockmakers Newsletter
203 John Glenn Ave.
Reading, PA 19607
ph: 610-796-0969
editor@clockmakersnewsletter.com
http://www.clockmakersnewsletter.com
Published since 1987; an 8-page, clocks-only newsletter for repairers and for collectors who restore their own clocks, old and new; photos, drawings, free classifieds; emphasis is on practical repairs rather than on theory.

Magazine: Watch & Clock Review
2403 Champa St.
Denver, CO 80205-9903
ph: 303-296-1600
fax: 303-295-2159
print@goldenbellpress.com
http://www.goldenbellpress.com
Monthly magazine primarily for new and vintage watch and clock retailers; features articles on watches, clocks and shops; also ads for buyers, sellers, and restorers.

Erika Daileda
Wise Owl Worldwide Publications
Magazine: Clocks
5150 Candlewood St., Ste. 1
Lakewood, CA 90712-1900
ph: 562-461-7574
fax: 562-461-7212
info@wiseowlmagazines.com
http://www.wiseowlmagazines.com
A monthly English publication; the international monthly magazine for clock enthusiasts; feature articles on clock history and restoration from all over the world; horological news and views; clock questions and answers; great photos!

John Hunter
Splat Publishing Ltd.
Magazine: Clocks Magazine
28 Gillespie Crescent
Edinburgh, Scotland EH10 4HU U.K.
ph: 0131 228 6638
fax: 0131 229 5550
editor@clocksmagazine.com
http://www.clocksmagazine.com/
   homepage.html
The international monthly magazine for clock enthusiasts; feature articles on clock history and restoration from all over the world; horological news and views; clock questions and answers.

Repair Services

Bob Frishman
Bell-Time Clocks
53 Poor St.
Andover, MA 01810-2501
ph: 978-475-5001
rjfjs@attbi.com
http://www.bell-time.com
Buys and sells clocks of all styles, ages, sizes and nationalities; also repairs and restores clocks.

Leon Trefler
Trefler & Sons Antique Restoring
   Studio, Inc.
99 Cabot St.
Needham, MA 02494
ph: 781-444-2685
fax: 781-444-0659
trefler@trefler.com
http://www.trefler.com
Restoration of porcelain and painted faces as well as porcelain and wood clock cases.

James Taylor
Taylor Time
P.O. Box 311
Woodstock, VT 05091
ph: 802-457-3757
fax: 802-457-3757
taylor.time@taylor-time.com
http://www.taylor-time.com
Working with Bill Mather, has 40 years experience supplying rare quality antique clocks and reliable service; cleaning, bushing, overhaul of case and movement.

Jim Mulhern
Medford Clock Shop
3 Union St.
Medford, NJ 08055
ph: 609-953-0014
fax: 609-953-0411
medclock@aol.com
http://www.medfordclock.com
Specializes in the repair of all types of antique clocks; also antique mercury and aneroid barometers repaired and restored; mercury barometer tubes made to fit old barometers.

Garrett Moore
Garrett's Clock Sales & Repair
24 Main St.
Clinton, NJ 08809
ph: 908-735-0496
fax: 908-231-9231
garrett@officeclocks.com
http://www.officeclocks.com
Buys, sells and restores clocks - new and old.

Philip M. Poniz
European Watch & Casemakers, Ltd.
P.O. Box 1314
Highland Park, NJ 08904-1314
ph: 732-777-0111
fax: 732-777-0118
horology@webspan.net
Restoration of watches, clocks, and music boxes; museum experience; can make any part and restore any watch; clients include Sotheby's, Cartier, collectors in USA, Asia and Europe; appraises, researches, lectures on watch making, fakes.

Roger Gordon
Gordon's Gallery of Clocks
223 Chestnue St.
Meadville, PA 16335
ph: 814-337-6843
fax: 814-337-0686
Authentic antique clock restorations and repair; 20 years experience; uses only the highest quality standards in restoring heirloom clock movements.

Walter A. Dayett
Dayett's Clock Repair & Appraisals
75 Study Rd.
Littlestown, PA 17340-9746
ph: 717-359-4850
fax: 717-359-4850
ldayett@superpa.net
Specializes in antique and contemporary clock sales and repair, primarily

weight and spring driven movements; also specializes in clock appraisals.

Joel J. Lynn
Joel Lynn, Clock Repair & Restoration
4100 W St. NW
Washington, DC 20007
ph: 202-333-5541
jlynn43375@aol.com
Complete clock restoration including parts fabrication; offers in-home service.

Douglas Whitesell
P.O. Box 1805
Middleburg, VA 20118
ph: 540-687-5550
Buys, sells and repairs clocks; does resilvering of dials.

Andre Walliman
Antique Clock Repair
1612 LeFrak Ct.
Herndon, VA 20170
ph: 703-318-6292
clockman@atmosclocks.com
http://www.atmosclocks.com
Specializes in the repair of electric Atmos clocks.

James Horner
Horner Clock Services
310-C East Market St.
Leesburg, VA 20176
ph: 703-771-4636
Repair to complete restoration of clocks from the 17th century to present.

Joel Vernick
Antique Clock Repair
10807 Kenilworth Ave.
P.O. Box 81
Garrett Park, MD 20896-0081
ph: 301-933-0654 or 301-933-4689
fax: 301-933-4689
Over 30 years experience in clock repair.

Harvey Flemister
512 Highgate Terrace
Silver Spring, MD 20904-6314
ph: 301-622-3686
Many years experience in the repair, service and restoration of antique clocks.

John Stephens
Stephens & Stephens Horologists
429 St. Johns St.
Havre De Grace, MD 21078-2818
ph: 410-939-3334
Jstep880@aol.com
http://www.clockology.com
Area's largest selection of antique clocks; also offers on-site repair facility.

N. Kenzie Smith
Clock Shop, The
119 East St.
Frederick, MD 21701
ph: 301-698-8252
http://www.frederickcounty.com/
   antiques/clock.htm
Repairs and restores all mechanical

clocks and watches; references upon request.

Olivier Perrault
ClockWorld
3330 Pacific Ave., Ste. 404
Virginia Beach, VA 23451
ph: 757-428-8180
fax: 757-428-6253
olivier@imsnews.com
http://www.clockworld.com
Repairs, buys and sells clocks; specializes in European clocks, cuckoo clocks, Trumpeter clocks, and Atmos clocks.

Julian Gibbard
P.O. Box 1092
Harpers Ferry, WV 25425
ph: 304-725-2035
fax: 304-725-2035
Specialist in long case clocks and barometers.

Dennis Kaye
Advanced Clock Service
117 Luxon Place
Cary, NC 27513
ph: 919-465-9800
fax: 919-465-7363
clocks@dwk.org
http://clocks.dwk.org
Clock dealer, expert and appraiser; repair and restoration of any type clock including Atmos and 400 day clocks; especially wants any item marked "Tiffany."

Len Hambleton
Reversen Time Inc.
6005 Bunchberry Court
Raleigh, NC 27616-5454
ph: 919-981-7323
hamblesl@mindspring.com
http://www.mindspring.com/~hamblesl/
   index.html
Specializes in wooden clock case restoration, reviving and cleaning original finish, carving, scroll work, turnings or missing elements; museum objects conservator/cabinetmaker; please call after 6 PM EST.

David Pendley
Pendley Clock Repair
181 23rd St. NW
Hickory, NC 28601
ph: 828-324-5193
dbpendley@dbpendley.com
http://www.dbpendley.com
Repairs, restores, antique clocks; member of NAWCC, AWI, Clocksmiths; Certified Clockmaker; Howard Miller and Sligh authorized service.

L.J. & Joanie Latorre
Albert's Antique Clocks
1808-B Ridgewood Ave.
Holly Hill, FL 32117
ph: 386-673-4822
time1@bellsouth.net
http://www.albertsantiqueclocks.com
Repairs, buys, sells all foreign and domestic clocks and watches, antique and new; huge showroom of wall,

mantel, floor clocks as well as the
areas largest selection of cuckoo
clocks; free in-shop estimates.

Robert Terwilliger
2963 Bird Ave.
Miami, FL 33133-4501
ph: 305-447-4619
robert@twigsdigs.com
http://www.shadow.net/~bobt
*Certified as a Master Clockmaker by
the American Clock & Watchmaker's
Institute.*

Norm Koloski
About Time Clock Repair
ph: 734-953-0586
aboutime@adni.net
http://www.aboutimes.com
*Buys, sells, repairs, restores antique
clocks.*

Ron Hughes
Main St. Clock Repair
4923 Main St.
Downers Grove, IL 60515
ph: 630-810-1366
clockmd@clockmd.com
http://www.clockmd.com
*Expert repair of modern and antique
clocks.*

Bruce Hannon
Investor's Antiques
1208 West Union St.
Champaign, IL 61821
ph: 217-333-0348
fax: 217-244-1785
b-hannon@uiuc.edu
http://www.shout.net/~smgorman/bruce
*Has been repairing American and
foreign clocks since 1970; NAWCC
#41581.*

Bill Tosh
B & L Associates
Rt. 1, Box 118-b
Rusk, TX 75785
ph: 903-743-5555
fax: 903-743-5556
*Specializes in the fabrication of finials
and other custom woodwork.*

Carl E. Schmeig
Carl's Clocks
Antique Center of Texas
1001 West Loop North
Houston, TX 77055
ph: 281-296-7256 or 713-684-4644
cclocks@infohwy.com
http://www.carlsclocks.com
*Antique American and European
clocks; has over 400 antique clocks in
inventory at all times: mantle, wall,
tallcase clocks dating from 1750 to
1900; also offers repair and
restoration of all clocks.*

Bill Gesswein
Clock Doctor, Inc., The
10610 N. 71st Place
Scottsdale, AZ 85254
ph: 888-256-2537
clockdr@clockdr.com
http://www.clockdr.com
Sells and repairs wall, mantel,

grandfather, cuckoo clocks; also music
boxes.

John H. Pohlpeter
Another Time Restorations
502 4th Ave.
Oregon City, OR 97045-3100
ph: 503-656-9757 or 503-656-9757
*Buys, sells, restores clocks, player
pianos, band organs and orchestrions,
pump and reed organs.*

Lowell & Nora Fronek
L. C. Antiques Antiques in Time
2316 Poplar Dr.
Medford, OR 97504
ph: 541-779-1115 or 800-866-8310
lcf1115@cdsnet.net
http://www.lcantiques.com
Antique and modern clock repair.

John & Susan Olivo
Perfect Time Watch & Clock Shop
1720 Redwood Ave #E
Grants Pass, OR 97527
ph: 541-471-1159
Watch and clock repair and sales.

James Poag, GG, ISA CAPP
James O. Poag Jewellers, Ltd.
94 Frank St.
P.O. Box 39
Strathroy, Ontario N7G 3J1 Canada
ph: 519-245-1040 or 519-245-1580
fax: 519-245-6073
james@poags.com
http://www.poags.com
*Retail clock, jewellery, china and gift
stores; staff includes 3 goldsmiths, 2
stone setters, watchmaker, clockmaker
and ISA Certified Appraiser; largest
selection of clocks in Ontario; in
business since 1959.*

Repro. Sources

Edward Jorgensen
P.O. Box 892
Buellton, CA 93427
ph: 805-686-2070
fax: 805-693-8031
bluestar@syv.com
http://www.jorgensencollection.com
*A unique furniture design studio that
specializes in the manufacture of
clocks and clock cases; can restore or
reproduce American styles.*

Suppliers

S. LaRose, Inc.
3223 Yanceyville St.
P.O. Box 21208
Greensboro, NC 27420-1208
ph: 336-621-1936
fax: 336-621-0706
info@slarose.com
http://www.slarose.com
Supplier of clock and watch parts.

Butterworth Clocks, Inc.
1715 Pearlview Ct.
Muscatine, IA 52761
ph: 563-263-0047 or 800-258-5418
fax: 888-599-8463
bci@muscanet.com
Clock MOVEMENTS only; largest

distributor of mechanical clock
movements in the US; grandfather
units, wall and mantle units, Hermle
movements, Kieninger, German
movements.

KLOCKIT
N3211 Country Rd. H
P.O. Box 636
Lake Geneva, WI 53147
ph: 800-556-2548
fax: 414-248-9899
klockit@klockit.com
http://www.klockit.com
*Mail order source for clock
movements, hands, faces, hardware,
music boxes, barometers, parts, tools,
etc.*

Turncraft Clocks Inc.
P.O. Box 100
Mound, MN 55364-0100
ph: 800-544-1711 or 612-471-9573
fax: 612-471-8579
*Mail order source of fine clock
movements, kits, parts and supplies.*

Southwest Clock Supply
P.O. Box 394
Carthage, MO 64836-0394
ph: 417-358-1865 or 800-654-8629
fax: 417-358-7446

Steven Berger
Timesavers
7745 East Redfield Rd., Ste. 500
Scottsdale, AZ 85267
ph: 480-483-3711 or 800-552-1520
fax: 480-483-6116
info@timesavers.com
http://www.timesavers.com
*Sells new clock parts, tools, books and
kits; inventories 1,000s of keys,
pendulums, dials, hands, ultrasonic
cleaners, springs, quartz and
mechanical movements, tools, cleaning
solutions and lubricants.*

Alarm

Clubs/Associations

Howard Banta, Pres.
Alarm Clock, Chapter #178 NAWCC
18631 Vincennes
Northridge, CA 91324
hbanta@socal.rr.com
http://www.alarmcloxchapter.com
*Dedicated to the collecting, research
and study of alarm clocks and their
manufacturing.*

Anniversary (400-Day)

Clubs/Associations

John Connolly
International 400-Day Clock Chapter,
 Chapter #168 NAWCC
6051 Sunwood Dr.
Delta, British Columbia V4E 2X5
Canada

Repair Services

Michael P. Murray
Mike's Clock Clinic
17000 S. Western Ave., #7
Gardena, CA 90247-5262
ph: 310-225-5646 or 877-286-6762
mike@atmos-man.com
http://www.atmos-man.com
*Specializing in the repair and dating
of Atmos, 400 day (anniversary), and
plug-in electric clocks.*

Art Deco

Dealers

John Sakas
P.O. Box 4124
South Hackensack, NJ 07606-4124
ph: 201-794-0437
fax: 201-794-8359
*Specializing in Catalin, Deco, mirror
radios; also in Art Deco clocks.*

Experts

Ira Raskin
Try To Remember
5120 Wilson Ln.
Bethesda, MD 20814-2436
ph: 301-652-1695
fax: 301-986-4528
ieraskin@aol.com
*Buys and sells Art Deco radios and
clocks of the 1920s to 1950s; also
repairs electric clocks.*

Mark Stein
Radiomania(R)
3100 Falls Cliff Rd., Ste. 6
Baltimore, MD 21211
ph: 410-366-3993
fax: 800-891-4484
rpbook@bellatlantic.net
http://www.radiomania.com
*Publisher of radio identification price
guides: "Complete Price Guide to
Antique Radios Series," "Tabletop
Radios" (4 vols), "Pre-War
Consoles," "Sears Silvertone
Catalogs."*

Character/Comic

Collectors

David Welch
P.O. Box 714
Murphysboro, IL 62966-0714
ph: 618-687-2282
fax: 618-684-2243
PEZDude1@aol.com
http://www.pezheads.net/dwelch
*Wants pre-1980 watches/clocks
relating to sports, TV, cartoon, comic,
movie characters with original boxes
ONLY; also wants empty boxes; no
political, please.*

Computer Programs For

Man./Prod./Dist.

John Christians
Software: ClockWare
4130 Terrace Dr.
Anchorage, AK 99502
ph: 907-243-8894
watch@watchware.net
http://www.watchware.org
Horological software for collectors or businesses; keep track of your collections with easy-to-use software; print reports for quick reference.

Cuckoo

Collectors

Steve Elliott
1600 Tennessee St.
Vallejo, CA 94590-4629
ph: 707-552-8400 or 707-642-1949
fax: 707-552-0881
Wants to buy carved wooden cuckoo clocks.

Dealers

DV Marketing
Buchenweg 39
Rheinstetten, D-76287 Germany
ph: +44 721 9513301
fax: +44 721-9513309
info@black-forest-shop.de
http://www.black-forest-shop.de
Specializes in Black Forest cuckoo clocks; hand carved and hand painted; some with music and dancing figurines.

Dials

Repair Services

Dennis Kaye
Advanced Clock Service
117 Luxon Place
Cary, NC 27513
ph: 919-465-9800
fax: 919-465-7363
clocks@dwk.org
http://clocks.dwk.org
Clock dealer, expert and appraiser; repair and restoration of any type clock including Atmos and 400 day clocks; especially wants any item marked "Tiffany;" specializes in porcelain and enamel dial repair.

Martha Smallwood
Dial House, The
3971 Buchanan Highway
Dallas, GA 30157-7755
ph: 770-445-2877
fax: 770-443-5426
dial_house@juno.com
Antique clock dials only; preserved, restored or replaced; call or write before shipping.

Robert Crowder
Professional Clockery, Inc.
7600 Hamilton Ave.
Cincinnati, OH 45231
ph: 513-931-8463
fax: 513-755-3761
bob@proclocks.com
http://www.proclocks.com
Buys, sells, restores antique clocks; specializes in manufacturing porcelain dials.

Repro. Sources

Larry Petro
Old Times Clock Dials
ph: 770-425-2544
info@clockdials.com
http://www.clockdials.com
Manufactures authentic, high quality replacement dials for antique clocks.

Electric

Clubs/Associations

Harvey Schmidt
Electric Horology Society, Chapter #78 NAWCC
Journal: Electric Horology Society Journal
75-80 179 St.
Flushing, NY 11366
ph: 732-350-2084
wwlathlot@aol.com
A specialty chapter within the National Association of Watch & Clock Collectors, Inc.; purpose is to inform members of the various types of battery/electrical clocks from the earliest inception to present.

Elmer G. Crum, FNAWCC
Midwest Electric Horology Group, Chapter #125 NAWCC
18220 Oak Way Dr.
Hudson, FL 34667-6333
ph: 727-868-0181
electrichorology@juno.com
A specialty chapter within the National Association of Watch & Clock Collectors, Inc.; purpose is to inform members of the various types of battery/electrical clocks from the earliest inception to present.

Jat McAlister, Sec.
Western Electrics, Chapter #133 NAWCC
P.O. Box 1889
Costa Mesa, CA 92628
A specialty chapter within the National Association of Watch & Clock Collectors, Inc.; purpose is to inform members of the various types of battery/electrical clocks from the earliest inception to present.

Experts

Elmer G. Crum, FNAWCC
18220 Oak Way Dr.
Hudson, FL 34667-6333
ph: 727-868-0181
electrichorology@juno.com
Collects, repairs, appraises and specializes in early battery and electric clocks; from time of their inception to

present including watches; lectures on electric horology; a Fellow of the NAWCC.

Michael P. Murray
Mike's Clock Clinic
17000 S. Western Ave., #7
Gardena, CA 90247-5262
ph: 310-225-5646 or 877-286-6762
mike@atmos-man.com
http://www.atmos-man.com
Specializing in the repair and dating of Atmos, 400 day (anniversary), and plug-in electric clocks.

Internet Resources

Martin Ridout
Electrical Horology
U.K.
martin@mridout.force9.co.uk
http://www.mridout.freeserve.co.uk
Informative Web site about electric clocks.

Repair Services

Michael P. Murray
Mike's Clock Clinic
17000 S. Western Ave., #7
Gardena, CA 90247-5262
ph: 310-225-5646 or 877-286-6762
mike@atmos-man.com
http://www.atmos-man.com
Specializing in the repair and dating of Atmos, 400 day (anniversary), and plug-in electric clocks.

Electric (Atmos)

Experts

Michael P. Murray
Mike's Clock Clinic
17000 S. Western Ave., #7
Gardena, CA 90247-5262
ph: 310-225-5646 or 877-286-6762
mike@atmos-man.com
http://www.atmos-man.com
Specializing in the repair and dating of Atmos, 400 day (anniversary), and plug-in electric clocks.

Repair Services

Andre Walliman
Antique Clock Repair
1612 LeFrak Ct.
Herndon, VA 20170
ph: 703-318-6292
clockman@atmosclocks.com
http://www.atmosclocks.com
Specializes in the repair of electric Atmos clocks.

European (French)

Dealers

Robert Beaver
Classic Touch Antiques
P.O. Box 27
Newport, RI 02840-0001
ph: 401-849-1717 or 401-846-9663
fax: 401-849-1717
Buys and sells all types of French and English clocks, including clock movements, cases, etc.

Kathleen Carroll
About Time Clock Company
1411 Wickapecko Dr.
Asbury Park, NJ 07712
ph: 732-775-4650
fax: 732-775-4684
about_time@msn.com
http://www.abtime.com
Sales and restoration of antique clocks; French clock specialist.

Alfred L. Chatelain
L'Epoque Romantique/Antique Quest
P.O. Box 4080
Queensbury, NY 12804
ph: 518-743-8653
fax: 518-743-8653
nracnyfr@albany.net
http://www.albany.net/~nracnyfr
Dealers and collectors of quality French clocks; also barometers, 19th century oil paintings, and porcelain.

Military

Clubs/Associations

William R. Bricker
Society of Military Horologists, Chapter #143 NAWCC
4 Hull Cove
Jamestown, RI 02835
A specialty chapter within the National Association of Watch & Clock Collectors, Inc.; focuses on time keeping devices as applied to military use.

Neon

Experts

Fred Kearney
735 Robinwood Dr.
Troy, MI 48083-1823
ph: 248-689-6997 or 248-207-0778
L35kearney@aol.com
Always interested in buying, trading, selling original neon clocks: Electric Neon Clock Co., and Federal & Neon Time Corp, Cleveland Ohio.

Novelty Animated

Collectors

Carole Kaifer
P.O. Box 232
Bethania, NC 27010-0232
ph: 336-924-9672
kaifer@earthlink.net
Novelty clocks are spring-powered and pendulum operated from 1930s to 1950s; wants to buy clocks by Lux, Keebler, Westclox, Columbia Time, Oswald, and Mi-Ken.

Dealers

Ed Kazemekas
35 Riverview Circle
Wolcott, CT 06716
ph: 203-879-1814
Buy, sell, restores American clocks; specializes in Lux pendulettes, novelty and alarm clocks.

Experts

Sam & Anna Samuelian
SMS Noveltiques
P.O. Box 504
Edgemont, PA 19028-0504
ph: 610-566-7248
fax: 610-566-7285
sms@bee.net
http://www.motionlamp.com
*Buys, sells, restores novelty electric
animated clocks; leading buyers and
sellers with largest collection in the
world from 1920s-1980s; can
reproduce parts.*

Sundials

Clubs/Associations

Fred Sawyer, Pres.
North American Sundial Society
Journal: Compendium
8 Sachem Dr.
Glastonbury, CT 06033
fwsawyer@aya.yale.edu
http://www.sundials.org
*An international association of people
from a wide variety of disciplines who
are interested in the study, development, history and preservation of
sundials and the art of dialing.*

Robert B. Sylvester, Mem. Sec.
British Sundial Society
Windycroft
Alexander Place
Askam-in-Furness, Cumbria LA16 7BT
U.K.
ph: 01229 465536
bss@exford.co.uk
http://www.sundialsoc.org.uk
*Members include professional
scientists, artists in stone and metal,
historians and designers, and other
sundial enthusiasts; Web site has
sundial glossary, dial of the month,
activities, and more.*

Dealers

David & Yola Coffeen
Tesseract
P.O. Box 151
Hastings On Hudson, NY 10706-0151
ph: 914-478-2594
fax: 914-478-5473
coffeen@aol.com
http://www.etesseract.com
*Issues a series of well illustrated
catalogs of early scientific instruments: astronomy, microscopy,
sundials, surveying, calculation,
demonstration, medical, surgical,
navigation, etc.; interested in buying
single items of collections.*

R.C. & Faye Blankenhorn
Gemmary, The
P.O. Box 2560
Fallbrook, CA 92088
ph: 760-728-3321
fax: 760-728-3322
rcb@gemmary.com
http://www.gemmary.com/rcb
*Antique scientific instruments: 18th &
19th C. mathematical, philosophical,
optical instruments, microscopes,*

*telescopes, globes, orreries, sundials,
compasses, surveying, navigating,
drawing, medical, laboratory.*

Internet Resources

Sundials on the Internet
P.O. Box 292
Epsom, KT17 4LQ U.K.
ph: +44 1 372 747 767
sundiweb@aol.com
http://www.sundials.co.uk
*The leading world Internet site for
information about all aspects of
sundials including projects, books,
national societies, pictures, and
sundials for sale.*

Man./Prod./Dist.

Robert Terwilliger
2963 Bird Ave.
Miami, FL 33133-4501
ph: 305-447-4619
robert@twigsdigs.com
http://www.shadow.net/~bobt
*Makes unique one-of-a-kind, custom-
designed, exceptional, uncommon, and
site-specific sundials.*

Tower

Clubs/Associations

Donn Lathrop, Webmaster
Tower Clock, Chapter #134 NAWCC
P.O. Box 552
Lyndon Center, VT 05850
ph: 802-626-1094
fax: 815-371-3312
Donnl@sover.net
http://members.aol.com/indexnawcc/
134.html
*A specialty chapter within the
National Association of Watch &
Clock Collectors, Inc.; focusing on
tower clocks.*

Repair Services

Steve Callihan
Another Time
P.O. Box 10680
Pittsburgh, PA 15235-0680
ph: 412-795-2358
fax: 412-798-3836
http://www.towerclockrestore.com
*Specializes in the repair and
restoration of mechanical tower
clocks.*

Willard

Museums/Libraries

John R. Stephens, Curator
Willard House & Clock Museum, Inc.
11 Willard St.
North Grafton, MA 01536-2011
ph: 508-839-3500
willardhouse@erols.com
http://www.nawcc.org/museum/willard/
willard.htm
*With over 70 Willard clocks, this is
the largest known collection of
Willard clocks and memorabilia;
styles of clocks include Turret,
Gallery, Skeleton, Tall Case,*

*Regulator, Eddystone Lighthouse, Act
of Parliament, Lyre, Shelf, others.*

CLOISONNE

(see also ORIENTALIA)

Dealers

Joseph Belperio
1303 Hawthorne Ct.
Sewell, NJ 08080-3511
ph: 8569-256-0791 or 856-782-7884
fax: 856-256-0791
shimazu@worldnet.att.net
*Specializes in fine quality Japanese
Satsuma, cloisonne, and studio
ceramics.*

Bill Eberhardt
Harry A. Eberhardt & Son
2010 Walnut St.
Philadelphia, PA 19103-5608
ph: 215-568-4144
artfix@magpage.com
http://www.eberhardts.com
*Specializes in Japanese cloisonne and
fine Satsuma.*

Museums/Libraries

George Walter Vincent Smith Art
Museum
220 State St.
Springfield, MA 01103-1703
ph: 413-263-6800
fax: 413-263-6889
info@spfldlibmus.org
http://www.quadrangle.org/GWVS.htm
*Recognized collections of American
paintings; Orientalia including
Japanese arms & armor, screens,
lacquers, textiles and ceramics;
Islamic rugs; and the largest
collection of Chinese cloisonne in the
Western world.*

CLOTHES SPRINKLERS

Collectors

Phyllis Burt
P.O. Box 681
New Canaan, CT 06840-0681
ph: 203-798-2763
themmojos@aol.com
*Wants to buy ceramic clothes
(laundry) sprinklers.*

Bobbie & Alan Bryson
1 St. Eleanoras Ln.
Tuckahoe, NY 10707-1307
ph: 914-779-1405
napkindoll@aol.com
*Dealer and collector wants to buy
vintage laundry sprinklers.*

Craig Dinner
P.O. Box 4399
Long Island City, NY 11104-0399
ph: 718-729-3850
ferrouswheel123@aol.com
*Wants to buy ceramic laundry
sprinkler bottles.*

Emma Kretchek
5726 Terrace Park Dr.
Dayton, OH 45429-6048
ph: 937-434-9126

Al Little
151 Highway 173
Antioch, IL 60002
ph: 847-395-7752
fax: 847-395-7703
*Buy, sells and trades laundry sprinkle
bottles.*

Dealers

Carol Silagyi
C.S. Antiques & Jewelry
P.O. Box 151
Wyckoff, NJ 07430
ph: 201-934-6528
csantiques@aol.com
*Wants figural ceramic clothes
sprinklers; Cardinal, American
bisques, Japanese, etc.*

Bobbie & Alan Bryson
1 St. Eleanoras Ln.
Tuckahoe, NY 10707-1307
ph: 914-779-1405
napkindoll@aol.com
*Dealer and collector wants to buy
vintage laundry sprinklers.*

CLOTHING & ACCESSORIES

(see also BRIDAL COLLECTIBLES;
BUTTONS; BUTTON HOOKS;
CLOTHES SPRINKLERS;
COMPACTS; COMBS & HAIR
ACCESSORIES; CUFF LINKS;
DRESSER ITEMS; LIVING
HISTORY; LUGGAGE; PURSES;
REPAIR/RESTORATION/
CONSERVATION, Textiles; SEWING
ITEMS & GO-WITHS; TEXTILES)

Dealers

Jeannine Yeager
American Vintage Blues
P.O. Box 3462
Rock Island, IL 61204-3462
ph: 309-721-8949
jen@vintageblues.com
http://www.vintageblues.com
*Specializing in vintage denim and
other vintage clothing, new/old stock,
recycled Levi's.*

Experts

Sid Warshafsky
240 Overlook Rd. (new 4 Corners)
Woodstock, NY 12498-2212
ph: 845-246-9363
fax: 845-246-9363
maimayo@hotmail.com
*Vintage clothes dealer, collector,
expert and designer; focuses on all
items Victorian and Edwardian.*

Periodicals

Ornament, Inc.
Magazine: Ornament
P.O. Box 2349
San Marcos, CA 92079-2349
ph: 760-599-0222
fax: 760-599-0228
ornament@cts.com
http://www.ornamentmagazine.com
A quarterly magazine focusing on craft and art items of personal adornment in any media or form: fiber, glass, metal, ancient historic/ ethnic ornament; ethnographic and tribal jewelry; also reviews of museum exhibits and publications.

Repair Services

Lynn Gorges
Historic Textiles Studio
3910 US Highway 70 East
New Bern, NC 28560
ph: 252-636-3039 or 252-636-5445
fax: 252-637-1862
palampore@aol.com
http://www.textilepreservation.com
Specializes in the restoration, conservation, appraisal, evaluation of vintage clothing.

Janyce Engan
Vintage Pattern Lending Library
1617 Ashby Ave.
Berkeley, CA 94703
ph: 510-843-3071
ladyejan@aol.com
http://www.vpll.org/index.html
Provides member copies (loan or purchase) of rare, antique, vintage sewing patterns and related fashion items; site has fashion history and other info of interest to reenactors and those researching fashion history.

1960s & 1970s

Collectors

Steve Hannan
141 East Central St.
Natick, MA 01760-3625
Wants to buy 1960s leather clothing, mini-skirts, micro-skirts, and hotpants; no suede, please; also wants leather clothing from 1970 to present, including dresses and lingerie.

Dealers

Lanajean Vecchione
Groovy Juice
P.O. Box 138
San Mateo, CA 94401
ph: 650-344-6977
lanajean@groovyjuice.com
http://www.groovyjuice.com
Specializes in vintage clothing and sewing patterns from the 1960s and 1970s.

Internet Resources

Lanajean Vecchione
Fashion-Flashbacks/Exploring Retro Style
Newsletter: Fashion Flashbacks
P.O. Box 138
San Mateo, CA 94401
ph: 650-344-6977
lanajean@fashion-flashbacks.com
http://www.fashion-flashbaks.com
Provides resources to vintage fashion consumers while promoting original retro artifacts from the 1960s and 1970s; clearinghouse for vintage fashion including where to study, research, read about, view, purchase and sell older styles.

Boots

Collectors

D. Seagraves
P.O. Box 23988
Pleasant Hill, CA 94523
ph: 925-934-4848
Wants to buy 1950s women's rubber boots.

Collars & Cuffs

(see CUFF LINKS)

Costumes (Historical)

(see also CLOTHING & ACCESSORIES, Costumes; CLOTHING & ACCESSORIES, Vintage; MOVIE MEMORABILIA; LIVING HISTORY; SCIENCE FICTION, Costuming)

Clubs/Associations

Costume Society of America, The
Newsletter: CSA News
55 Edgewater Dr.
P.O. Box 73
Earleville, MD 21919-0073
ph: 410-275-1619x or 800-CSA-9447
fax: 410-275-8936
webmaster@costumesocietyamerica.com
http://www.costumesocietyamerica.com
Dedicated to advancing the global understanding of all aspects of dress and appearance; also publishes the journal "Dress."

Pat Poppy, Mbrship.
Costume Society of Great Britain, The
Journal: Costume
56 Wareham Rd.
Lytchett Matravers
Poole, Dorset BH16 6DS U.K.
http://www.costumesociety.org.uk
Formed to promote the study and preservation of significant examples of costume history and development; publishes an illustrated journal and newsletters; organizes an annual symposium; visits collections; study days.

Marion Byott, Mem. Sec.
Costume Guild of UK
Newsletter: Cutting Edge
6 Blacksmiths Meadow
Oak Leys
Oxford, Oxforshire OX4 5YF U.K.
Lorloth@aol.com
http://www.ireadh.demon.co.uk/cguk/index.html
"Cutting Edge" features forthcoming events and items of special interest including other recommended societies or suppliers; also publishes the magazine "The Mantle."

Internet Resources

Costumer's Manifesto, The
Tara@costumes.org
http://www.costumes.org
Amazing costume resource Web site: discussion lists, history of fashion and dress, wigs, timeline of costume history with images from ancient Babylon to modern, costume links, makeup classes, costume shops on the Web, supplies, and more.

Man./Prod./Dist.

Time Warp Custom & Vintage Attire
P.O. Box 9186
Schenectady, NY 12305-0186
ph: 518-347-1126
fax: 518-347-1126
timewarp@timewarp.com
http://www.timewarp.com
Buys/sells/appraises vintage clothing, jewelry, accessories; reproduces vintage and historical clothing for museums, reenactment, theater, ballroom dancing, etc.; also restores, repairs and alters clothing, textiles and costume jewelry.

Kelle Vogel
Kelle's Kreations
P.O. Box 2452
Silver Spring, MD 20915-2452
ph: 301-942-5178
KellesKreations@aol.com
Expert seamstress and costume technologist: costumes, uniforms, period garments & accessories, wigs, makeup, hat sculptures, theatrical stylist.

Kathi Reynolds
Creative Clothes
330 N. Church St.
Thurmont, MD 21788-1640
ph: 301-695-5340
ksrcreate@earthlink.net
Researches, designs, creates clothing for men, women, and children; especially 18th and 19th century historical costumes, uniforms, great coats.

Saundra Ros Altman
Past Patterns
P.O. Box 2446
Richmond, IN 47375-2446
ph: 765-962-3333 or 866-738-8426
fax: 765-962-3773
merchant@pastpatterns.com
http://www.pastpatterns.com
Sells clothing patterns from the years 1830-1949 in woman's sizes 8-20; also men and children's patterns available; free information.

Sarah Fox
Somewhere in Time
P.O. Box 263
Breaux Bridge, LA 70517
ph: 318-983-9364 or 318-893-7824
fax: 318-232-3001
Costume design, period and contemporary; research, sketches, swatches, construction; offers clothing and accessories 1850-1960; wants handbags, jewelry, buttons; supplier/ stylist/costumer for film, television, videos.

Heidi Marsh
Heidi Marsh Patterns
3494 N. Valley Rd.
Greenville, CA 95947-9604
Men's, women's, and children's patterns from the Civil War era; many taken from Godey's Lady Book diagrams and patterns; catalog $3.

Denim

Dealers

Marc Luers
Tatters
2928 Lyndale Ave. South
Minneapolis, MN 55408-2110
ph: 612-823-5285
fax: 612-823-6887
Wants old denim as well as pre-1960 Japanese, Korean, and European satin and velveteen reversible souvenir jackets; also buys any other interesting vintage clothing.

Jeannine Yeager
American Vintage Blues
P.O. Box 3462
Rock Island, IL 61204-3462
ph: 309-721-8949
jen@vintageblues.com
http://www.vintageblues.com
Specializing in vintage denim and other vintage clothing, new/old stock, recycled Levi's.

Dan Kelley
Experienced Denim
P.O. Box 239
Fayetteville, AR 72702-0239
ph: 501-444-7541 or 800-336-4694
fax: 501-521-8331
exd@edenim.com
http://www.edenim.com
Wants '30s-'50s Levis, denim wear of all types, '40s-'50s gabardine shirts & jackets, Hawaiian and bowling shirts; also vintage fabrics, textiles, bedspreads, tablecloths with Western

or Mexican theme; vintage mens wear, casual clothing.

Kurt Watson
Blue Denim Clothing Co.
3213 Jeannie Ln.
Muskogee, OK 74403-7775
ph: 918-683-1589 or 918-230-6116
fax: 918-683-6293
kurt@intellex.com
Wants to buy vintage Levis, Lee, Wrangler: jeans, jackets, men's 501 Blue Jeans, vintage workwear advertising, pre-1960 sweatshirts, vintage Air Jordans and pre-1980 Nike shoes, Buddy Lee Dolls, banners, denim shirts, etc.

Avenue 13 Five & Dime Vintage
606 East 13th Ave.
Denver, CO 80206
ph: 303-818-8107
info@510vintage.com
http://www.510vintage.com
Buys and sells vintage clothing, used and vintage Levi's jeans, wearable retro fashions from the 1940s through 1970s.

Jeff Mark
JMARK
P.O. Box 5178
Santa Monica, CA 90409-5178
ph: 800-644-8537
fax: 310-396-2666
bigjoho@hotmail.com
America's largest buyer of and leading authority on Levi & Lee brand and other brands of blue jeans, jackets, old work clothing, and advertising display materials; wants items dating 1850 to 1960.

David Bailey
Bailey's Antiques & Aloha Shirts
517 Kapahulu Ave.
Honolulu, HI 96815-3854
ph: 808-734-7628
baileysantiques@webtv.net
Buys and appraises pre-1960 Levis, pre-1960 Aloha shirts, and Hawaiiana; pre-1960 Levis have a capital "E", hence "Big E" on small red tag at side of left breast pocket (jackets) and right rear pocket (pants).

Larry McKaugham
Heller's Far West Clothing
1000 Lenora, Ste. 116
Seattle, WA 98121
ph: 206-233-9014 or 800-328-5384
hellers@halcyon.com
http://www.hellerscafe.com
Wants to buy 1930s and 1940s denim buckleback pants, vintage running and basketball shoes from 1970s and 1980s.

Husky Boy Vintage
4441 S. Meridian, Ste. 471
Puyallup, WA 98373-5959
ph: 800-HUSKY-BO or 253-472-6341
steve@huskyboy.com
Wants to buy Nike Air Jordan 1985-1991 and 1970s-1980s Nike shoes and sportswear; also buying vintage denim

workwear, i.e., Levi's, Lee, etc. and vintage military flight jackets.

Museums/Libraries

Levi Strauss & Co. Museum
250 Valencia St.
San Francisco, CA 94103
ph: 415-565-9159
Open by appointment; located in the oldest jeans factory still in operation.

Hats

Collectors

Daniell Ware
1199 S. Main Rd.
Vineland, NJ 08360-6538
ph: 856-794-8300
fax: 856-794-8300
Long time collector wants to buy millinery items: hat stands, hat blocks, signs, trade cards, ladies hats, hat boxes, beaded and mesh purses from 1800s to 1940s.

Museums/Libraries

Colonial Williamsburg Millinery Shop
P.O. Box 1776
Williamsburg, VA 23187-1776
ph: 757-229-1000 x8540 or 800-HISTORY
mmartin@cwf.org
http://www.history.org

Suppliers

Manny's Millinery
26 W. 38th St.
New York, NY 10018-6227
ph: 212-840-2235 or 212-840-2236
Sells hatmaking supplies in small quantities for refurbishing old ones or making new hats.

Lingerie

Museums/Libraries

Frederick's of Hollywood Lingerie Museum & Celebrity Lingerie Hall of Fame
6608 Hollywood Blvd.
Los Angeles, CA 90028
ph: 213-466-8506
Contains famous underfashions beginning with lingerie and bras from 1946.

Mannequins

Collectors

Gwen Daniel
18 Belleau Lake Ct.
O Fallon, MO 63366-3144
ph: 636-978-3190
SimGirl200@aol.com
Wants Victorian through 1950s mannequins; heads only or full mannequins; send photos first if possible.

Suppliers

Mark Goldsmith
Goldsmith, Inc.
10-09 43rd Ave.
Long Island City, NY 11101
ph: 718-937-8476
fax: 718-937-4525
manic2@mindspring.com
http://www.goldsmith-inc.com
Manufacturers and sells Victorian and Edwardian mannequins; also other mannequins, display forms, fixtures, props, furniture, custom moldings.

Neckties

Clubs/Associations

Barry Hautala
Kollectors of Nasty Old Ties (K.N.O.T.)
1860 Greentree Dr.
Plover, WI 54467
ph: 715-344-4779
baha@charter.net
http://www.geocities.com/knot.geo
A place for accumulators and enthusiasts of vintage neckties; specializing in the colorful and unusual tie designs of the late 1940s and early 1950s; buy, sell or trade ties at the "Trading Post."

Collectors

Al Guerra
162 Dover Parkway
Stewart Manor, NY 11530
mufsoir@aol.com
Collector of vintage ties; specializes in rare 1940s-1950s hand-painted men's neckties; also other '40s and '50s souvenir/commemorative ties such as political, World's Fair, fraternal, advertising, pin-up, cowboy/western; include SASE for reply.

Barry Hautala
1860 Greentree Dr.
Plover, WI 54467
ph: 715-344-4779
baha@charter.net
http://www.geocities.com/knot.geo
Collector of vintage neckties; specializing in the colorful and unusual tie designs of the late 1940s and early 1950s.

Dealers

John Marshall
For Love or Money
16693 NW Meadowgrass Ct.
Beaverton, OR 97006
john@europa.com
http://home.europa.com/~john
Buys and sells vintage neck ties.

Experts

Dr. Ron Spark
P.O. Box 43414
Tucson, AZ 85733-3414
ph: 520-323-8714 or 520-324-5332
fax: 520-324-5341
Ron.Spark@tmcaz.com
Author of "Fit-To-Be-Tied" (Abbeville, 1988) specializes in 1940s

and early 1950s neckties and bow ties; inquiries always invited.

Parasols

Repair Services

Abbie Orem
265 N. Union St.
Russianville, IN 46979-9602
ph: 765-883-5108
Recovers parasols; call first to discuss the project.

Patterns

Book Sellers

Fred Struthers
R.L. Shep Publications
P.O. Box 2706
Fort Bragg, CA 95437
ph: 707-964-8662
fax: 707-964-8662
fsbks@mcn.org
http://www.rlshep.com
Publishes reprints of dressmaking/ tailoring manuals and needlework books.

Collectors

Joy Emery
Commercial Pattern Archive
URI Library Special Collections
15 Lippti Rd.
Kingston, RI 02881
ph: 401-874-2713
fax: 401-874-4608
jemery@uri.edu
Devoted collector who is compiling a complete database of tissue patterns.

Dealers

Bette S. Feinstein
Hard-to-Find Needlework Books
96 Roundwood Rd.
Newton, MA 02164-1217
ph: 617-969-0942
fax: 617-969-0942
hardtofind@needleworkbooks.com
http://www.needleworkbooks.com
Buys and sells vintage fashion magazines, old and new books on many types of needlework.

Saundra Ros Altman
Past Patterns
P.O. Box 2446
Richmond, IN 47375-2446
ph: 765-962-3333 or 866-738-8426
fax: 765-962-3773
merchant@pastpatterns.com
http://www.pastpatterns.com
Carries a large selection of copies of sewing patterns from 1900 to 1950 in original sizes.

Shoes

Dealers

Wishing Corner, The
9201 S.E. Foster Rd.
Portland, OR 97266
ph: 503-771-1549
diane777@teleport.com
http://www.hilndr.com/wishing
Huge stock of over 10,000 pairs of

vintage shoes from 1940s to 1970s; never ben worn; '40s pumps and granny shoes, '70s platforms, '60s slings, '50s saddles, etc.

Museums/Libraries

Brockton Shoe Museum
216 No. Pearl St.
Brockton, MA 02401
ph: 508-583-1039
gerryb@brocktonma.com
http://www.brocktonma.com/bhs/shoe.html
Claims to be the only authentic shoe museum in America.

Shoe Museum, Temple University
School of Podiatric Medicine
8th & Race Sts.
Philadelphia, PA 19107
ph: 215-629-0300
webmaster@tuspm.temple.edu
http://podiatry.temple.edu/shoe_museum/shoe_museum.html
Collection contains over 700 examples of shoes, dating back to Egyptian burial sandals c. 2000 B.C.

Bata Shoe Museum
327 Bloor St. West
Toronto, Ontario M5S 1W7 Canada
ph: 416-979-7799
fax: 416-979-0078
http://www.batashoemuseum.ca
A five-story building with over 130,000 visitors each year; collection includes more than 10,000 pieces of footwear and related artifacts spanning 4,500 years and representing every culture in the world.

Shoes (Oversize)
Clubs/Associations

Danny Eskenazi, Pres.
Society for Preservation of Oversize
Footwear (SPOOF)
ph: 206-679-5777
desk@nwlink.com
Wants to buy big display shoes; curator of the Giant Shoe Museum.

T-shirts
Collectors

Rich Cacioppo
44 Brookside Terrace
North Caldwell, NJ 07006
ph: 973-364-1765
fax: 973-364-1766
Interested in the history of imprinted T-shirts.

Vintage

(see also BRIDAL COLLECTIBLES; BUTTONS; BUTTON HOOKS; CLOTHES SPRINKLERS; COMPACTS; COMBS & HAIR ACCESSORIES; CUFF LINKS; DRESSER ITEMS; LIVING HISTORY; LUGGAGE; PURSES; REPAIR/RESTORATION/CONSERVATION, Textiles; SEWING ITEMS & GO-WITHS; TEXTILES)

Appraisers

Leon Castner, ISA CAPP
National Appraisal Consultants
P.O. Box 482
Hope, NJ 07844
ph: 800-323-5996 or 908-459-5996
fax: 908-459-4899
castner@garden.net
http://www.nacvalue.com
Expert witness on several high level fashion claims including insurance loss, fair market value; has written articles regarding collectible fashion clothing.

Laura "Miss Kitty" Millin
Cats Pajamas, The
335 Maynard St.
Williamsport, PA 17701
ph: 570-322-5580
kitty@catspajamas.com
http://www.catspajamas.com
Vintage clothing appraiser, collector, dealer; one of the most comprehensive online vintage clothing supplier; carries mens, womens, some childrens from Victorian through 1970s; can supply costumers and individuals.

Genae Fields, ISA
Image One International
16126 Rainbow Lake Rd.
Houston, TX 77095-4053
ph: 281-856-8866
fax: 281-550-8618
gfields@imageoneinternational.com
http://www.imageoneinternational.com
Specializes in the appraisal of vintage clothing.

Auction Services

Amory Spizzirri, Client Svc.
William Doyle Galleries
175 E. 87th St.
New York, NY 10128-2205
ph: 212-427-2730
fax: 212-369-0892
info@doylegalleries.com
http://www.doylegalleries.com
Holds over 50 auctions annually of furniture and decorations, paintings and sculpture, jewelry, books and prints, couture and textiles, 20th century art & design, majolica, Lalique, Asian works of art and other specialty categories.

Robert J. Connelly, ASA
Bob & Sallie Connelly Auctions
666 Chenango St.
Binghamton, NY 13901-2015
ph: 607-722-9593 or 607-722-3555
fax: 607-722-1266
connelly@clarityconnect.com
Conducts specialty vintage clothing and fabric auctions.

Clubs/Associations

Bill Carmody
Petticoats Remembered
976 Sunrise Highway
West Babylon, NY 11704
ph: 607-733-9311 or 631-661-6177
taffetaslips@hotmail.com
Members are collectors of slips and

miscellaneous lingerie; primarily collectors of taffeta and nylon satin slips.

Collectors

Jeannette Schoolsky
P.O. Box 95
Nashua, NH 03061
ph: 603-883-7931
fax: 603-882-3781
Purses@ArtDeco.com
Advanced collector seeks stylish women's (sizes 10-14) 1920s-1940s clothing in excellent condition; also accessories: Victorian umbrellas, ladies hats, compacts, mesh & glass beaded purses; also wants men's fashion from 1920s to 1940s.

Lydia M. Jackson-Fryer
608 Winans Way
Baltimore, MD 21229-1430
ph: 410-233-6231
fax: 410-233-6231
ljackson@umbc.edu
Wants to buy vintage clothing female size 18 or plus size; also male 44 regular.

Cheryl Melnick
P.O. Box 790
Cupertino, CA 95015
ph: 408-559-7799 x222
webmistress@hand-fan.org
http://www.hand-fan.org
Serious collector wants to buy vintage clothing and accessories for personal collection and for reenacting to teach living history to others as a volunteer: clothing, parasols, hand-held fans, hats, accessories.

Dealers

Daveda Howe
Davenport & Co.
146 Bowdoin St.
Springfield, MA 01109
ph: 413-781-1505
dee@davenportandco.com
http://www.davenportandco.com
Buys and sells fine vintage clothing from the 1840s to 1960s.

Deborah Burke
Antique & Vintage Dress Gallery
P.O. Box 600353
Newtonville, MA 02460-0003
ph: 781-891-9659
antiquedress@attbi.com
http://www.antiquedress.com
A constantly changing gallery of clothing and accessories for sale featuring the elegance of original clothing from the 1800s to present; Victorian ensembles, Edwardian whites, 1920s beaded dresses, bridal gowns, hats, purses, etc.

Linda Dalenberg
Timeless Pieces
246 West Main St.
Hillsboro, NH 03244-5239
ph: 603-464-5621 or 603-464-6747
Wants to buy antique dolls, doll clothes, and doll accessories; also

wants adult and children's vintage clothing, estate linens, and pre WWII toys.

Fay Knicely
Antique Apparel
P.O. Box 1
Acworth, NH 03601-0001
ph: 603-835-2295
fax: 603-835-2295
fay@sover.net
Over 30 years buying and selling a wide range of antique and vintage clothing, accessories, and related goods; open by appointment.

Judith A. Young
Yesterday's Threads
206 Meadow St.
Branford, CT 06405-3634
ph: 203-481-6452
fax: 203-483-7550
Buys and sells women's, men's and children's clothing and accessories from mid-1800s through 1960s; call for information about upcoming vintage clothing shows; in business over 25 years.

Pahaka September
Pahaka
19 Fox Hill
Upper Saddle River, NJ 07458-1314
ph: 201-327-1464
pahakasept@aol.com
Buys and sells women's, men's and children's clothing 1800s-1950s; also jewelry, hats, shoes, fashion accessories, and patterns; by appointment or mail order; sorry, no catalog; in business for over 25 years.

Sid Warshafsky
240 Overlook Rd. (new 4 Corners)
Woodstock, NY 12498-2212
ph: 845-246-9363
fax: 845-246-9363
maimayo@hotmail.com
Wants to buy vintage clothing, watches, jewelry, lace, hats, accessories: Christian Dior, Chanel, Yves St. Laurant, Gucci, Hermes, Louis Vuitton, Pucci, Fortuny, Halston, etc.; veils, collars, umbrellas, curtains, shawls.

Laura "Miss Kitty" Millin
Cats Pajamas, The
335 Maynard St.
Williamsport, PA 17701
ph: 570-322-5580
kitty@catspajamas.com
http://www.catspajamas.com
One of the most comprehensive online vintage clothing supplier; carries mens, womens, some childrens from Victorian through 1970s; can supply costumers and individuals; also carries all accessories including jewelry and some home decor.

Dottie Wordell
30-A Trolley Sq.
Wilmington, DE 19806
ph: 302-651-9331
fax: 302-429-8491
Davidam@dca.net
*Appraiser, dealer, collector and expert
in vintage clothing and jewelry; see
Web site for online catalog.*

Kathleen Flynn
Carriage House Antiques
4212 Gallatin St.
Hyattsville, MD 20781-2049
ph: 301-779-3696 or 301-220-1451
kathleenbflynn@hotmail.com
*Always buying vintage fashions,
accessories and jewelry; prefers
Victorian though 1950s; especially
wants antique purses, compacts, silver
smalls, and costume jewelry.*

Yvonne D. Smith
Yvon's Vintage Chic
7 North Court St.
Frederick, MD 21701-5413
ph: 301-694-5500
*Wants pre-1950 vintage clothing,
accessories, and jewelry; vintage
bridal gowns, silk shawls, beaded and
mesh purses, fine wearable vintage
apparel, antique jewelry, vintage gifts.*

Joyce McCandless
Krazy Cat Collectibles
P.O. Box 1192
Emmitsburg, MD 21727
ph: 301-271-9851
KrazyCatCo@aol.com
http://www.krazycatcollectibles.com
*Buys and sells exceptional quality
vintage ladies accessories and jewelry:
Lucite purses, vintage beaded bags,
enamel compacts, etc.*

Evie Myatt
Echoes of Time
700 Norfolk Ave.
Virginia Beach, VA 23451
ph: 757-428-2332
fax: 757-428-8099
eechoes@msn.com
http://www.echoes-of-time.com
*Specializes in vintage clothing,
costume, jewelry from the 1920s
through 1970s.*

Vintageous Vintage Clothing
P.O. Box 11111
Norfolk, VA 23517
webmaster@vintageous.com
http://www.vintageous.com
*Buys and sells vintage clothing:
evening gowns, vintage suits and
dresses, purses and eyewear from the
1920s to 1960s including designer
pieces by Dior, Lilli Ann, etc.*

Susan M. Black
Susan's Vintage Boutique
120 Mopar Lane
West End, NC 27376
ph: 910-295-6575
fax: 910-295-9109
susans@tias.com
http://www.tias.com/stores/susans
*In business since 1984; specializes in
vintage clothing and jewelry, 1800s
and 1900s.*

Donna Barr
Victorian Elegance, A
P.O. Box 2091
Plant City, FL 33564-2091
ph: 813-719-8392
designs@gator.net
http://victorianelegance.com
*Specializing in vintage clothing and
accessories, vintage jewelry, and
vintage wedding gowns from the
1800s to 1970s; carries a full line of
hats, shoes and accessories.*

Sherry King
Yester DAZE
1908 S. MacDill Ave.
Tampa, FL 33629
ph: 813-258-2388
sherrysyesterdaze@ij.net
Specializes in vintage clothes.

Maryce Garber
Antique Addict
1234 Grove St.
Clearwater, FL 33755
ph: 727-449-8336 or 727-464-2499
*Carries male and female attire,
accessories, costume jewelry, swing
clothes; shop located at Oldsmar Flea
Market, 180 Race Track, Oldsmar,
FL.*

Joan M. Redden
Joan's Jewels & Collectibles
P.O. Box 462
Tallevast, FL 34270-0462
ph: 941-355-9171
fax: 941-355-9171
jmrrar@comcast.net
http://
www.joansjewelsandcollectibles.com
*Buys and sells costume jewelry from
antique to contemporary; also vintage
clothing, purses, shoes, men's jewelry,
compacts; designs one-of-a-kind
jewelry predominantly made from
vintage jewelry components; will
design to order.*

Joanne Haug
Reflections of the Past
P.O. Box 910037
Lexington, KY 40513
ph: 859-219-1393
antiques@victoriana.com
http://www.victoriana.com/antique-
marketplace
*Buys and sells antique and vintage
clothing (1770-1930): bridal gowns,
Civil War era dresser, christening
gowns, Victorian corsets, hats,
purses, parasols, shoes, hand-held
fans; also bed and table linen.*

Gayle Wilson
Gayle's Vintage Clothing & Accessories
3742 Kellogg Ave.
c/o Ferguson Antiques Mall
Cincinnati, OH 45226
ph: 513-271-3722
*Buys and sells vintage clothing; men's,
women's, children's, wedding gowns;
also costume jewelry.*

Sharon Kanko
Antiques to Cherish
P.O. Box 752263
Dayton, OH 45475-2263
ph: 937-436-3677
sharon@victiques.com
http://www.victiques.com
*Specializes in antique clothing from
the Victorian and Edwardian eras,
Victorian and Art Deco jewelry,
compacts, perfume bottles, beaded
mesh and tapestry purses, antique and
collectible buttons, fancy hankies,
cookbooks.*

Ann Mills
Collections by Ann: Vintage Jewelry &
Accessories
P.O. Box 102
Clawson, MI 48017
ph: 248-588-7232
amills@annscollection.com
http://www.annscollection.com
*Specializing in quality vintage jewelry,
Bakelite, sterling sliver, and glittering
evening bags.*

Barbara Stevens
Rare Wear at Farm Village Antique Mall
3448 S. Hagadorn Rd.
Okemos, MI 48864
ph: 517-699-8372 or 517-337-4988
fax: 517-337-4560
stevensg44@aol.com

Patricia O'Brien
Flapper Alley Ltd.
1518 North Farwell Ave.
Milwaukee, WI 53202
ph: 414-276-6252 or 414-332-3618
*Wants to buy antique clothing and
textiles from the 1920s and earlier;
also fancy beaded bags; appraisal
services available.*

Barbara Nell
Daisy Shop, Women's Couture Resale
E-zine: Perspicacios Woman OnLine
67 East Oak, 6th Floor
Chicago, IL 60611
ph: 312-943-8880
fax: 312-943-6660
daisyshop@aol.com
http://www.daisyshop.com
*Carries an excellent selection of
women's vintage couture daywear,
evening wear, and accessories in
pristine condition; well regarded
locally and internationally as dealer
of authentic vintage couture clothing
and accessories.*

Carrie Homann
Carrie's Vintage Clothing
204 N. Neil
Champaign, IL 61820
ph: 217-352-3231
carries@advancenet.net
http://www.advancenet.net/~carries
*A complete range of 20th century stock
through the 1970s.*

Diane McGee
Diane McGee Estate Clothing Company
5225 Jackson
Omaha, NE 68106-1331
ph: 402-551-0727
*Mail order only; complete line from
1850s to 1960s.*

Sarah Fox
Somewhere in Time
P.O. Box 263
Breaux Bridge, LA 70517
ph: 318-983-9364 or 318-893-7824
fax: 318-232-3001
*Costume design, period and
contemporary; research, sketches,
swatches, construction; offers clothing
and accessories 1850-1960; wants
handbags, jewelry, buttons; supplier/
stylist/costumer for film, television,
videos.*

Jeanne Little
Little Treasures Antiques
6351 Cantel St.
Long Beach, CA 90815
ph: 562-598-1423
liltreasures@earthlink.net
http://www.littletreasures.net
*Specializes in vintage clothing and
accessories, costume jewelry,
compacts, and vanity items; does a
number of vintage clothing shows
throughout the year - see Web site for
schedule.*

Janene & Art Fawcett
Vintage Silhouettes
190 Parker Ave.
Rodeo, CA 94572
ph: 510-245-2443 or 800-636-1410
stone@vintagesilhouettes.com
http://www.vintagesilhouettes.com
*Specializes in men's and women's
vintage fashion.*

Jules Kliot
Lacis
3163 Adeline St.
Berkeley, CA 94703-2401
ph: 510-843-7178
fax: 510-843-5018
staff@lacis.com
http://www.lacis.com
*Antique & historic textiles, lace from
the 16th century, vintage garments and
accessories; sells books and supplies
for costume, lace and embroidery; also
offers repairs and conservation
services.*

Eureka, I Found It! Antiques &
  Collectibles
P.O. Box 2192
Petaluma, CA 94953-2192
eureka@eureka-i-found-it.com
http://www.eureka-i-found-it.com
*An online dealer specializing in
vintage textiles and clothing, toy and
model steam engines, buttons, fans,
Art Deco, costume jewelry, toy sewing
machines.*

Reed Wetter
Moon Zooom
813 Pacific Ave.
Santa Cruz, CA 95060-4433
ph: 831-423-8500
*Specializes in clothing from the 1960s
and 1970s: go-go boots, girly dresses,
bowling shirts, polyester, Brady
Bunch styles.*

Rob & Jen Chadwick
RustyZipper.com Vintage Clothing
P.O. Box 700547
San Jose, CA 95170-0547
ph: 800-816-4699 or 503-909-0358
jen@rustyzipper.com
http://www.rustyzipper.com
*An online vintage clothing store;
specializes in 1940s through 1970s
vintage clothing, patterns, books and
accessories.*

Lora Jabot
Jabot's Vintage Boutique
P.O. Box 3394
Eureka, CA 95501
ph: 707-445-8220 or 707-445-8344
jabotsboutiques@aol.com
http://www.jabotsboutique.com
*Authentic vintage apparel for men and
women; Victorian through the 1970s
including hats, shoes, purses, and
accessories.*

Sandy Thornton
Velvet Moon Designs
P.O. Box 5512
Salem, OR 97304
velvetrhiannon@attbi.com
http://www.velvetmoondesigns.com
*Online shop carries hip retro wear
from the 1960s and 1970s with other
vintage clothing from 1920s through
1980s: Gunne Sax, McClintock,
Valentino, Nordstroms, and many
more.*

Meg Andrews
Meg Andrews, Costumes & Textiles
U.K.
ph: +44 1582 460107
fax: +44 1582 461112
meg.andrews@cwcom.net
http://www.meg-andrews.com
*Specializes in 18th/19th c. English
costumes & accessories, 19th c.
paisley shawls, Arts & Crafts textiles
including William Morris, Chinese
court costumes and textiles, worldwide
hangings, 18th/19th c. samplers.*

Margaret Bolger
Artizania
16 Hale Rd.
Wallasey, Wirral CH45 7QU U.K.
ph: +44(0) 151 639 4920
fax: +44(0) 151 639 4920
artizania@artizania.co.uk
http://www.artizania.co.uk
*Carries a wide range of antique &
vintage costumes, accessories, textiles,
lace, shoes, hats, etc.; Web site also
offers a listing of specialist antique
costume and textile shows and tours
across the U.K.; promotes textile
shows.*

Experts

Evelyn Kennedy
Sewtique, Inc.
391 Long Hill Rd.
P.O. Box 1293
Groton, CT 06340-1293
ph: 860-445-7320 or 800-332-9122
fax: 860-445-1448
sewtique@aol.com
http://www.sewtiqueonline.com
*Specialist in restoration, preservation
& conservation of apparel and
textiles; full service by mail/phone or
appt.; appraises textiles, laces,
tapestries, etc.; removes spots &
stains; teaches textile appraisal &
restoration workshops.*

Elizabeth S. Brown
45 Whippoorwill Way
Belle Mead, NJ 08502-5827
ph: 908-359-3395
fax: 908-874-7590
ebrown@nerc.com
*Lecturer, appraiser & costume
consultant on various aspects of
historic clothing collecting &
conservinguses own collection for
lectures; specializes in old patterns
and garment drafting tools and/or
systems.*

Time Warp Custom & Vintage Attire
P.O. Box 9186
Schenectady, NY 12305-0186
ph: 518-347-1126
fax: 518-347-1126
timewarp@timewarp.com
http://www.timewarp.com
*Buys/sells/appraises vintage clothing,
jewelry, accessories; reproduces
vintage and historical clothing for
museums, reenactment, theater,
ballroom dancing, etc.; also restores,
repairs and alters clothing, textiles
and costume jewelry.*

Roseann Ettinger
Remember When
21-23 W. Broad St.
Hazleton, PA 18201
ph: 570-454-8465 or 570-450-5542
popgems2001@hotmail.com
*Author of "50's Popular Fashions,"
"Fifties Forever," and "Twentieth
Century Neckties," "Psychedelic
Chic."*

Barbara Nell
Daisy Shop, Women's Couture Resale
E-zine: Perspicacios Woman OnLine
67 East Oak, 6th Floor
Chicago, IL 60611
ph: 312-943-8880
fax: 312-943-6660
daisyshop@aol.com
http://www.daisyshop.com
*Carries an excellent selection of
women's vintage couture daywear,
evening wear, and accessories in
pristine condition; well regarded
locally and internationally as dealer
of authentic vintage couture clothing
and accessories.*

Diane McGee
5225 Jackson
Omaha, NE 68106-1331
ph: 402-551-0727
*Author of "A Passion for Fashion:
Antique, Collectible, & Retro Clothes
1850-1950;" 200 pgs., over 190
photos; send $24.95 + $2 UPS.*

Frances Grimble
Lavolta Press
20 Meadowbrook Dr.
San Francisco, CA 94132
ph: 415-566-6259
lavolta@best.com
http://www.lavoltapress.com
*Lavolta Press has published "After a
Fashion," "The Edwardian Modiste,"
and "The Voice of Fashion;" Frances
Grimble collects pre-1930 clothing,
books and magazines with clothing
patterns, and books and mags with
dance instruction.*

Kristina Harris
Vintage Connection
1205 S. 8th St.
Cottage Grove, OR 97424
kriswrite@aol.com
http://www.geocities.com/
  vintageconnection
*Lectures on collectible clothing and
historical fashion; author of twelve
books on the subject, including
"Victorian & Edwardian Fashions
For Women: 1840-1919," and
"Collector's Guide to Vintage
Fashions."*

Terry McCormick
2009 23rd Ave. W, Apt 2
Seattle, WA 99899-4145
ph: 206-545-2945
*Gives workshops on vintage clothing
and hats.*

Internet Resources

Kristina Harris, Editor
Vintage Connection
kriswrite@aol.com
http://www.geocities.com/
  vintageconnection
*Offers a free online newsletter for
collectors of vintage and antique
fashions; covers specific areas of the
19th and 20th centuries; reproductions, sources, dealers, how-to
articles.*

Leila Hidic
Corsets & Crinolines
29 Lansdowne Grove
Wigston, Leicestershire LE18 4LU U.K.
ph: 0116 224 5361
crinolinegirl@corsetsandcrinolines.com
http://www.corsetsandcrinolines.com
*A resource center devoted to Victorian
and Edwardian costume and corsetry;
features a discussion area, links,
education, items for sale.*

Misc. Services

Lauriann Greene
Vintage Clothing Shopping Tours
1122 E. Pike St., Ste. 609
Seattle, WA 98122
ph: 206-324-8139 or 877-261-1500
info@gildedagetours.com
http://www.gildedagetours.com
*Offers vintage clothing shopping tours
of France and England; small group,
bilingual tour escort is vintage
clothing expert; also lace tours of
England, France and Belgium.*

Museums/Libraries

Museum of Fine Arts, Boston
465 Huntington Ave.
Boston, MA 02115-5523
ph: 617-267-9300
webmaster@mfa.org
http://www.mfa.org

Rhode Island School of Design Museum
224 Benefit St.
Providence, RI 02903-2723
ph: 401-454-6500
fax: 401-454-6556
mshaw@risd.edu
http://www.risd.edu/museum.cfm
*Apparel, architecture, furniture,
graphic design, industrial design,
interior architecture, landscape
architecture.*

Wadsworth Atheneum Museum of Art
600 Main St.
Hartford, CT 06103
ph: 860-278-2670
fax: 860-527-0803
info@wadsworthatheneum.org
http://www.wadsworthatheneum.org
*Regularly changing themed exhibitions
display and interpret selections from
an extensive collection of historic
costumes and textiles.*

Museum at The Fashion Institute of
  Technology
Seventh Ave. at 27th St.
New York, NY 10001-5992
ph: 212-217-5800 or 212-217-7970
musinfo@fitsuny.edu
http://www.fitnyc.edu/museum
*Founded in 1967, MFIT is the
repository for one of the world's
largest and most important collections
of clothing, textiles and accessories;
temporary exhibitions explore
creativity and culture in design, art,
fashion; free admission.*

Metropolitan Museum of Art, The
   Costume Institute
1000 Fifth Ave.
New York, NY 10028-0198
ph: 212-535-7710
fax: 212-794-9316
http://www.metmuseum.org

Phyllis Magidson
Museum of the City of New York
1220 5th Ave. at 103rd St.
New York, NY 10029-5221
ph: 212-534-1672
fax: 212-534-5974
http://www.mcny.org
   *Specializes in street and theatrical
   costumes; access by appointment;
   research fee charged.*

Long Island Museum of American Art,
   History & Carriages
Newsletter: News & Events
1200 Route 25A
Stony Brook, NY 11790-1992
ph: 631-751-0066
fax: 631-751-0353
mail@longislandmuseum.org
http://www.longislandmuseum.org
   *Large collection of American Art,
   decoys, horse-drawn vehicles,
   costumes, and miniature period
   rooms; museum shop.*

Hilary Jay, Dir.
Philadelphia University, The Goldey
   Paley Design Center
4200 Henry Ave.
Philadelphia, PA 19144
ph: 215-951-2860
fax: 215-951-2662
JayH@philau.edu
http://www.whatisdesigntoday.com
   *A repository for over 200,000
   historical textiles and textile-related
   artifacts; serves as an educational
   resource for students, faculty,
   researchers, and the general public;
   invites public to engage in learning
   about contemporary design.*

National Museum of American History
14th & Constitution Ave. NW
Washington, DC 20560
ph: 202-357-2700
webmaster@si.edu
http://www.si.edu/organiza/museums/
   nmah/nmah.htm

Colleen Callahan
Valentine Richmond History Center
1015 E. Clay St.
Richmond, VA 23219
ph: 804-649-0711
fax: 804-643-3510
info@richmondhistorycenter.com
www.RichmondHistoryCenter.com
   *Largest costume and textile collection
   in the South.*

Western Reserve Historical Society
10825 East Blvd.
Cleveland, OH 44106-1703
ph: 216-721-5722
fax: 216-721-0645
webmaster@wrhs.org
http://www.wrhs.org
   *Oldest cultural institution in
   Cleveland, with a research/
   genealogical library, costume wing,
   auto & aviation museum and restored
   mansion under one roof; special
   interest area in costume and textiles.*

Indianapolis Museum of Art, Indiana
   Fashion Design Collection
1200 W. 38th St.
Indianapolis, IN 46208
ph: 317-923-1331
ima@ima-art.org
http://www.ima-art.org/collections/
   textiles.html

Detroit Historical Museum
5401 Woodward Ave.
Detroit, MI 48202-4009
ph: 313-833-1805
fax: 313-833-5342
amy@detroithistorical.org
http://www.detroithistorical.org
   *Focuses on the 300-year-old cultural
   heritage of the City of Detroit area
   including its automotive legacy.*

Douglas Greenberg, Dir.
Chicago Historical Society
Clark St. at North Ave.
Chicago, IL 60614-6099
ph: 312-642-4600
fax: 312-266-2077
http://www.chicagohs.org

Missouri Historical Society
P.O. Box 11940
Saint Louis, MO 63112-0040
ph: 314-746-3150
fax: 314-746-4548
library@mohistory.org
http://www.mohistory.org

Patricia L. McClain, Cur.
Museum of Vintage Fashion, Inc.
708 Yerington Ct.
Lincoln, CA 95648
ph: 916-408-3737
   *Research center; collects and preserves
   historical and vintage clothing (1700-
   2000) for men, women, children;
   library; terrace tea room and garden;
   ongoing exhibitions on and off site;
   tours by appointment.*

Museum of Costume
Assembly Rooms
Bennett St.
Batt, Somerset BA1 2QH U.K.
ph: 0122-5477789 or 0122-5477752
fax: 0122-5444793
costume_enquiries@bathnes.gov.uk
http://www.museumofcostume.co.uk
   *The museum's collection includes all
   aspects of fashion from the 16th
   century to the present - handmade,
   ready-to-wear and designer.*

Periodicals

Molly Turner
Molly's Vintage Promotions
Newsletter: Vintage Gazette, The
194 Amity St.
Amherst, MA 01002-2201
ph: 413-549-6446
merrylees@aol.com
   *Quarterly newsletter focusing on
   vintage clothing.*

Elyse Zorn Karlin, Ed.
Newsletter: Adornment
1333A North Ave., Box 103
New Rochelle, NY 10804
ph: 914-235-0983
fax: 914-235-0983
info@jewelryhistorians.com
http://www.jewelryhistorians.com
   *Quarterly newsletter covering ancient,
   antique, contemporary studio, costume
   and vintage jewelry, historic costume,
   antique buttons and beads; contains
   articles, book reviews, terminology,
   extensive calendar, and more.*

Repair Services

Time Warp Custom & Vintage Attire
P.O. Box 9186
Schenectady, NY 12305-0186
ph: 518-347-1126
fax: 518-347-1126
timewarp@timewarp.com
http://www.timewarp.com
   *Buys/sells/appraises vintage clothing,
   jewelry, accessories; reproduces
   vintage and historical clothing for
   museums, reenactment, theater,
   ballroom dancing, etc.; also restores,
   repairs and alters clothing, textiles
   and costume jewelry.*

Suppliers

Greenburg & Hammer, Inc.
24 W. 57th St.
New York, NY 10019-3918
ph: 800-955-5135
fax: 212-765-8475
   *Supplier of mounting and displaying
   products for clothing: silk thread,
   hangers, ready-made torsos, steamers,
   Kraft wrapping paper.*

Rita Marx
Cherish
205 W. 86th St.
New York, NY 10024-3327
ph: 212-724-1748
smarx@i2000.com
   *Carries Orvus and other conservation
   supplies for the storage, cleaning and
   displaying of vintage textiles and
   clothing.*

Baltimore Display
1900 Bayard St.
Baltimore, MD 21230
ph: 800-638-3764 or 410-685-3393
fax: 410-685-6877
   *A clothing store supply company
   selling display cases, racks, etc.; also
   sells "poly forms" for the display of
   vintage clothing.*

Vintage (Black)

Museums/Libraries

Joyce Bailey, Ex. Dir.
Black Fashion Museum, The
Newsletter: BFM Newsletter
2007 Vermont Ave. NW
Washington, DC 20001-4029
ph: 202-667-0744
fax: 202-667-4379
bfmdc@aol.com
http://www.bfmdc.org
   *Mission is to identify, acknowledge
   and spotlight the achievements and
   contributions of people of African
   descent to the fashion industry.*

Wearable Art

Appraisers

Phyllis Twigg
2775 Gingerview Lane
Annapolis, MD 21401
ph: 410-571-8847
ptwigg@radix.net
http://www.quilt-appraiser.com
   *Qualified to appraise both antique
   and new quilts, tops, blocks, and
   quilted wearable art in all traditional,
   contemporary, and innovative styles;
   offers hands-on fabric dating
   workshops, lectures, appraisal
   sessions at quilt shows.*

Sally A. Ambrose, ISA CAPP
Ambrose Appraisal Service
P.O. Box 536
11156 North Rd.
Leavenworth, WA 98826-9512
ph: 509-548-7472
fax: 509-548-0240
sally@televar.com
   *Specializes in the appraising of
   antique and contemporary American
   quilted textiles, contemporary
   wearable art, and residential contents;
   ASA accredited Senior Appraiser,
   American Quilt Society Certified
   Appraiser of Quilted Textiles.*

CLOWN COLLECTIBLES

(see also CIRCUS COLLECTIBLES;
COLLECTIBLES [MODERN], Clowns;
COLLECTIBLES [MODERN],
Figurines [Emmett Kelly, Jr.])

Collectors

G. Konok
4136 Elliot Ave. S.
Minneapolis, MN 55407-3149
   *Wants clowns and related memora-
   bilia: figurines, musicals, banks,
   paintings, pictures, dolls and circus
   related.*

Emmett Kelly

Collectors

N.W. Neill, Jr.
P.O. Box 38
Ennice, NC 28623-0038
fax: 336-657-8084
saddlemtn@skybest.com
   Wants to buy Emmett Kelly SR/JR

pieces, dolls, Circus items, books, photos; anything related to Emmett Kelly Senior or Junior.

Museums/Libraries

Emmett Kelly Historical Museum
202 E. Main
Sedan, KS 67361-1629
ph: 316-725-3470
stettler@kans.com
http://skyways.lib.ks.us/kansas/towns/
Sedan/museum.html

COAST GUARD

(see also NAUTICAL ANTIQUES;
NAUTICAL ANTIQUES, Lighthouses)

Collectors

Dick Hawkins
Columbia Trading Company
One Barnstable Rd.
Hyannis, MA 02601
ph: 508-778-2929
fax: 508-778-2922
info@columbiatrading.com
http://www.columbiatrading.com

Rex M. "Wess" Wessling
15706 North East 56th Way
Redmond, WA 98052
ph: 425-497-1480
wwesslin@ix.netcom.com
http://www.rexmwess.com
Collects, buys, sells, trades, documents US Coast Guard patches; Web site has 200-400 patches available for sale; also illustrations of several hundred C.G. patches and books for sale regarding C.G. patches and history.

Dealers

James W. Claflin
Kenrick A. Claflin & Son Nautical
  Antiques
30 Hudson St.
Northborough, MA 01532
ph: 508-869-6955
jclaflin@ma.ultranet.com
http://www.ultranet.com/~jclaflin
Collectors and dealers in fine nautical antiques; specializing in US Lighthouse Service, US Lifesaving Service, US Revenue Cutter Service, US Coast Guard.

Adin Otto
253 Bonnybrook Rd.
Carlisle Barracks, PA 17013
Wants to buy US Lifesaving Service, Lighthouse Service, Revenue Cutter Service, and Coast Guard items: photographs, uniforms, china, annual reports, etc.

Museums/Libraries

Ken Black, Dir.
Shore Village Museum
<u>Newsletter: Shore Village Museum Newsletter</u>
104 Limerock St.
Rockland, ME 04841-2945
ph: 207-594-0311 or 207-236-3206
fax: 207-594-9481
kenblack@midcoast.com
http://www.lighthouse.cc/shorevillage
Largest collection of lighthouse and Coast Guard artifacts in the US; navigation instruments, ship models, scrimshaw, lighthouse models, and 5,000 lighthouse postcards from around the world; also lighthouses, Civil War, navigation, GAR.

Cindee Herrick, Curator
U.S. Coast Guard Museum
U.S. Coast Guard Academy
15 Mohegan Ave.
New London, CT 06320-4195
ph: 860-444-8511
CHerrick@cga.uscg.mil
http://www.uscg.mil/hq/g-cp/museum/
MuseumIndex.html
History of the US Coast Guard including the Lifesaving Service, Lighthouse Service, and Revenue Cutter Service.

Port Orford Lifeboat Station Museum
P.O. Box 1132
Port Orford, OR 97465
ph: 541-332-1502
rubarb@harborside.com
http://www.portorfordlifeboatstation.org
Seeks to buy WWII Navy sextant used by the Coast Guard, clock with a paper dial used by the CG on watch, WWII marine radio used by the CG, WWII teletype machine used by the CG, old black wall telephone c. 1934-1945.

U.S. Life-Saving Service

Clubs/Associations

Maurice E. Gibbs
U.S. Life-Saving Service Heritage
  Association, The
<u>Journal: Wreck & Rescue</u>
P.O. Box 75
Caledonia, MI 49316-0075
mo72506@nantucket.net
http://www.uslife-savingservice.org
Quarterly magazine on the Life-Saving Service and the Coast Guard, historic preservation activities, station tours, learn about shipwrecks, rescues and maritime history.

Collectors

Mark Burchill
25 E. 10th St., #7B
New York, NY 10003
ph: 212-529-3666
Owns a former US Life-Saving Service station in Quogue, NY; interested in buying items relating to the US LSS, especially items relating to station #74.

Dealers

James W. Claflin
Kenrick A. Claflin & Son Nautical
  Antiques
30 Hudson St.
Northborough, MA 01532
ph: 508-869-6955
jclaflin@ma.ultranet.com
http://www.ultranet.com/~jclaflin
Collectors and dealers in fine nautical antiques; specializing in US Lighthouse Service, US Lifesaving Service, US Revenue Cutter Service, US Coast Guard.

Jacques Noel Jacobsen, Jr.
Collector's Antiquities
60 Manor Rd.
Staten Island, NY 10310-2698
ph: 718-981-0973
jnjacobsen@mail.volusiacable.com
http://home.fiam.net/milantique
Buys and sells US Lifesaving Service, US Lighthouse Service, and lighthouse artifacts, photographs, books and ephemera; American military antiques 1840-1940 large illustrated catalog, 3 issues for $12 ($15 overseas).

U.S. Lighthouse Service

Collectors

Timothy Harrison
P.O. Box 1690
Wells, ME 04090
ph: 800-758-1444 or 207-646-0515
fax: 207-646-0516
timh@lhdigest.com
http://www.lhdigest.com
Wants to buy memorabilia from US Lighthouse Service (USLHS) or US Lighthouse Establishment (USLHE): badges, flags, dinnerware, buttons, uniforms, old photographs of keepers and their families, postcards, newspaper stories.

Dealers

James W. Claflin
Kenrick A. Claflin & Son Nautical
  Antiques
30 Hudson St.
Northborough, MA 01532
ph: 508-869-6955
jclaflin@ma.ultranet.com
http://www.ultranet.com/~jclaflin
Collectors and dealers in fine nautical antiques; specializing in US Lighthouse Service, US Lifesaving Service, US Revenue Cutter Service, US Coast Guard.

U.S. Revenue Cutter Service

Dealers

James W. Claflin
Kenrick A. Claflin & Son Nautical
  Antiques
30 Hudson St.
Northborough, MA 01532
ph: 508-869-6955
jclaflin@ma.ultranet.com
http://www.ultranet.com/~jclaflin
Collectors and dealers in fine nautical antiques; specializing in US Lighthouse Service, US Lifesaving Service, US Revenue Cutter Service, US Coast Guard.

COAT OF ARMS

(see BOOKS, Heraldry; HERALDRY)

COCA-COLA COLLECTIBLES

(see SOFT DRINK COLLECTIBLES, Coca-Cola)

CODE MACHINES

(see SPY EQUIPMENT)

COFFEE

(see also ELECTRICITY RELATED ITEMS, Appliances [Coffee Pots])

Collectors

Bill Park
12312 Starlight Lane
Bowie, MD 20715-2138
ph: 301-464-1608
coffee5@erols.com
Wants to buy coffee containers of all types (condition important), but prefers 1-lb. screw-top and sample sizes; also wants other types of coffee memorabilia.

Nancy Pennington
1750 Keyes Rd.
Greenbrier, TN 37073
ph: 615-643-0290
fax: 615-643-0290
Wants coffee related collectibles such as coffee jars.

Arbuckles Bros. Coffee Co.

Collectors

Herb Arbuckle
herb@elpaso.net
http://server.elpaso.net/~herb/collect.html
Wants to buy Arbuckles Coffee memorabilia" trade cards, extract bottles, paper advertising, spice tins, tea tins, spice/coffee scoops, metal signs, etc.

Al Kruse
2536 Teslin St.
Juneau, AK 99801
ph: 907-789-1817
Wants to buy memorabilia relating to Arbuckles Bros. Coffee Company.

Experts

Greg Q. ArBuckle
Arbuckles' Coffee Museum
97 16th Ave. SW
Cedar Rapids, IA 52404-5948
ph: 319-363-1242
fax: 319-365-5115
stran@inav.net
Wants to buy memorabilia relating to Arbuckles Bros. Coffee Company.

Internet Resources

Herb Arbuckle
Arbuckles' Coffee Collectors
herb@elpaso.net
http://server.elpaso.net/~herb/collect.html
A Web site dedicated to all collectors of Arbuckles' Coffee memorabilia - the coffee that won the West.

Museums/Libraries

Greg Q. ArBuckle
Arbuckles' Coffee Museum
97 16th Ave. SW
Cedar Rapids, IA 52404-5948
ph: 319-363-1242
fax: 319-365-5115
stran@inav.net
Large displayed collection of Arbuckles Bros. Co. products: coffee tins, spice tins, tea tins, trade cards, company documents, billings, letters, covers, bottles, banners, signs, counter displays, magazine ads.

Mills & Grinders

Clubs/Associations

Judith A. Sivonda, Sec.
Association of Coffee Mill Enthusiasts
Newsletter: Grinder Finder
375 Congdon St.
Middletown, CT 06457
ph: 860-346-9356
millmania@att.net
http://www.millmania.com
An organization for coffee grinder enthusiasts; newsletter published quarterly; annual convention; focuses on coffee mills and their manufacturers, restoration tips, sale and auctions of mills and coffee related items.

Collectors

Terry Friend
839 Glendale Rd.
Galax, VA 24333
ph: 540-236-9027

Lucy Fullinwider
P.O. Box 5761
Midland, TX 79704
ph: 915-684-4800
msenterprz@aol.com

Andrew E. Thomas
4681 North 84th Way
Scottsdale, AZ 85251-1864
ph: 888-255-0664 or 480-947-5693
fax: 480-994-4382
andrew-thomas@qwest.net
Wants coffee grinders.

Experts

Judith A. Sivonda
Millmania
375 Congdon St.
Middletown, CT 06457
ph: 860-346-9356
millmania@att.net
http://www.millmania.com
Collector, dealer, expert; does not offer appraisals or valuations, but can help identify or authenticate coffee mills.

Judith A. Sivonda
375 Congdon St.
Middletown, CT 06457
ph: 860-346-9356
millmania@att.net
http://www.millmania.com
Co-author of "Antique Coffee Grinders: American, English & European," available from author.

Joe MacMillan
657 Old Mountain Rd.
Marietta, GA 30064-1339
ph: 770-427-6434
fax: 770-422-8807
info@cumberlandgeneral.com
http://www.cumberlandgeneral.com
Coffee mill collector and expert; author of "The MacMillan Index of Antique Coffee Mills."

Mike White
P.O. Box 483
Fraser, CO 80442
ph: 970-726-0448
mwhite483@rkymtnhi.com
http://rkymtnhi.com/grinder
Co-author with Derek White of "Early American Coffee Mills."

Repair Services

Joe MacMillan
657 Old Mountain Rd.
Marietta, GA 30064-1339
ph: 770-427-6434
fax: 770-422-8807
info@cumberlandgeneral.com
http://www.cumberlandgeneral.com
Repair and restoration of old coffee mills and grinders.

Tins

Collectors

Hugh Pinney
1387 Madison St.
Santa Clara, CA 95050-4758
ph: 408-241-5417
Buys keywind coffee tins which are unopened, mint or near mint, and free of rust.

Dealers

Timothy R. Schweighart
1123 Santa Luisa Dr.
Solana Beach, CA 92075-1614
ph: 858-481-8315
fax: 858-481-5699
Collector, appraiser, and dealer of coffee tins.

COFFINS

(see FUNERAL ITEMS)

COIN-OPERATED MACHINES

(see also AMUSEMENT PARK ITEMS; BOOKS, Reference [Coin-Operated]; GAMBLING COLLECTIBLES, Punchboards; POPULAR CULTURE; REPAIR/ RESTORATION/CONSERVATION, Metal Items; SCALES; SOFT DRINK COLLECTIBLES, Soda Machines)

Auction Services

Randy Inman
Randy Inman Auctions, Inc.
P.O. Box 726
West Buxton, ME 04093
ph: 207-872-6900
fax: 207-872-6966
inman@inmanauctions.com
http://www.inmanauctions.com
Conducts specialty auctions for advertising, coin-op, gambling devices, automata, soda pop, Coca Cola, breweriana, robots and space toys, cast iron and tin toys, Disneyana, mechanical music, and mechanical and still banks.

Clubs/Associations

Paul Hindin
Coin Operated Collectors Association
Newsletter: C.O.C.A. Newsletter
3712 W. Scenic Ave.
Thiensville, WI 53092
ph: 262-242-3131
bedvibr8or@aol.com
Publishes a quarterly newsletter for collectors of gambling, penny arcade and vending machines.

Collectors

Andy Rudoff
P.O. Box 111
Oceanport, NJ 07757-0111
ph: 732-542-3712
fax: 732-542-3712
shoreguy@comcast.net
Wants pre-1945 coin operated machines: arcade machines, vending, slots, trade stimulators, and games; send description and price; photos very helpful.

Richard O. Gates
P.O. Box 187
Chesterfield, VA 23832-0187
ph: 804-748-0382 or 804-794-5146
fax: 804-748-6349
rogates@mindspring.com
Wants coin-operated machines including jukeboxes, pinballs, trade stimulators, slot machines, old gumball machines, Coca-Cola, Pepsi, R.C., Dr. Pepper machines and any signs or literature related to any of the above.

Mike Gorski
1770 Dover Rd.
Westlake, OH 44145
ph: 440-871-6071
Slot machines, old penny arcade machines; Wurlitzer 78 RPM jukeboxes, odd vending machines;

Regina musical boxes, old coin-operated machines.

Frank DeMayo
1511 Holliston Trail
Fort Wayne, IN 46825
ph: 219-489-0053 or 800-258-8243
fax: 219-484-8605
seeburgh@aol.com
Wants coin-operated slot, gum, card, dice machines; also wants to buy automatons and key wound figures.

Richard Trautwein
Toys N Such
437 Dawson St.
Sault Sainte Marie, MI 49783-2119
ph: 906-635-0356
Collector, dealer wants to buy coin-op machines such as slot machines, scales, gumball and other vending machines; also wants arcade games such as strength tester games and games of skill, etc.

Jim Welytok
W241 N8938 Penny Lane
Sussex, WI 53089
ph: 262-246-7171
unievents@aol.com
Collects 1920s to 1970s arcade games, pinball machines, jukeboxes.

Dave Ogden
P.O. Box 223
Northbrook, IL 60062-5951
ph: 847-564-2893
fax: 847-564-2893
musical@flash.net
http://www.flash.net/~musical
Wants to buy early coin-operated machines, gambling and slot machines.

Dealers

John S. Zuk
Collector Technologies
106 Orchard St.
Belmont, MA 02478-2940
ph: 617-484-4800 or 617-588-5709
fax: 810-283-5371
Buys, sells and repairs slot machines, jukeboxes, arcade machines, gumballs, neon clocks, etc.

Chick Darrow
Darrow's Fun Antiques
1101 1st Ave.
New York, NY 10021-8737
ph: 212-838-0730 or 888-DARROWS
fax: 212-838-3617
george@fun-antiques.com
http://www.fun-antiques.com
Buys & sells antique games, toys, ad signs, animated art, jukeboxes, slot machines, comic watches, bicycles & memorabilia of all types; also prop rentals.

John T. Johnston
John T. Johnston's Jukebox Classics &
  Vintage Slot Machines, Inc.
6742 Fifth Ave.
Brooklyn, NY 11220-5418
ph: 718-833-8455
fax: 718-833-0560
*Buys, sells, rents, trades and repairs
slot and jukeboxes; wants to buy old
jukeboxes, slot machines, vending,
arcade, old gambling items, neons,
cash registers, music boxes,
phonographs, syrup dispensers.*

Steve Wager
Pennsylvania Gameroom Warehouse
520 Lehman St.
Lebanon, PA 17042
ph: 717-272-7052 or 888-443-4837
gameroom@gameroomwarehouse.com
http://gameroomwarehouse.com
*Buys and sells arcade amusements that
have been fully-reconditioned for home
or commercial use; full-color online
catalog; two central-PA retail
locations.*

Ken Durham
GameRoomAntiques
909 26th St. NW
Washington, DC 20037-2029
durham@gameroomantics.com
http://www.GameRoomAntiques.com
*Buy and sell gameroom collectibles
including slots, jukeboxes, pinballs,
soda machines, gumballs, trade
stimulators, popcorn machines,
pachinko and pachislos; service
manuals also available; Web site has
over 100 pages.*

Lloyd Thoburn
CoinOpWarehouse.
727 N. Mulberry St.
Hagerstown, MD 21740
ph: 703-801-1459
lloyd@coinopwarehouse.com
http://www.coinopwarehouse.com
*Buys and sells coin-operated machines
such as pinballs, jukeboxes, slot
machines, soda machines, etc.*

Harold Daniel
Quicksilver Oddities Antique Coin-Ops
  & Collectibles
2500 E. Grann Blanc Rd.
Grand Blanc, MI 48439
ph: 810-694-0787
*With Greg Young wants slot machines
25 yrs. old or older; also antique
coin-operated gaming devices, trade
stimulators, vending machines, arcade
games, and items with sports themes.*

Jack Freund
Slots of Fun
P.O. Box 4
Springfield, WI 53176-0004
ph: 262-642-3655
jbgum@msn.com
*Buys and sells counter top gum or nut
machines, early cigar store trade
stimulators, and cigar nippers; any
coin operated game or machine; 25
years experience in the field; can*

*identify and appraise old coin
operated machines.*

John Adorjan
Amusing Devices
1505 Highland Park
Highland Park, IL 60035
ph: 847-274-3759
fax: 847-836-0104
*Specializes in any machine that takes a
coin from 1899 to present: video
games, pinball, bowling, mechanical,
antique and more; sell, services, buys,
trades.*

Allan B. Pall
1118 North Harlem Ave.
River Forest, IL 60305
ph: 708-771-7446
*Wants to buy coin-operated machines:
gambling, trade stimulators, vending
machines, arcade games, automatons,
bird boxes, music boxes, nickelodeons,
etc.*

Home Arcade Corp.
4611 Main St.
Lisle, IL 60532
ph: 630-964-2555
fax: 630-964-9367
arcadehom@aol.com
http://www.homearcadecorp.com
*Sells restored vintage Coke machines;
also juke boxes, phone booths, beer
signs, tavern items, barber poles and
other '50s memorabilia; send $5 for
Coke Restoration Parts Catalog.*

Larry Lubliner
Avant Carde
3814 N. Fremont #3
Chicago, IL 60613-9998
ph: 773-883-0073
fax: 773-883-1199
joker1854@aol.com
http://www.avantcarde.com
*Buys and sells gambling collectibles,
poker chips, playing cards, coin-
operated gambling machines.*

Walt Baxley
Be-Bop Jukeboxes & Gameroom
  Goodies
4804 Mesquite St.
Flowerwood, TX 75028
ph: 972-724-1791
fax: 972-355-1541
wbax1@msn.com
http://www.trinicom.com/bebop
*Southwest's largest retailer of antique
and collectible jukeboxes, pool tables,
and other gameroom items; sales,
service, restoration, and party rentals.*

Rosanna Harris
Royal Bell
5815 W. 52nd Ave.
Denver, CO 80212-7503
ph: 303-431-9266
fax: 303-431-6978
info@royalbell.com
http://www.royalbell.com
*Sells home use slot machines, poke
machines, stands, game room
accessories, and related books.*

Daina Pettit
Mr. Pinball
4805 Marabow Circle
Salt Lake City, UT 84117-5419
ph: 801-277-6296 or 801-277-0888
fax: 801-277-0888
daina@mrpinball.com
http://www.xmission.com/~daina/
  pinball.html
*Pinball machine collector, dealer,
expert and restorer.*

Dennis Clark
Off the Wall Antiques, Inc.
7325 Melrose Ave.
Los Angeles, CA 90046
ph: 323-930-1185
fax: 323-930-1595
weirdstuff@earthlink.net
http://www.offthewallantiques.com

Herb Silvers
Fabulous Fantasies
12455 Branford, Unit #3
Arleta, CA 91331
ph: 818-761-2255
fax: 818-834-1950
pinball@fabulousfantasies.com
http://www.fabulousfantasies.com
*Sells and restores vintage pinball and
arcade games and all Gameroom
furnishings; also reproduces many
pinball machine backglass art and
video game overlays; can also create
custom upholstered pieces; offers
gameroom design assistance.*

Randy Hilberg
Collector's Nectar
Box 431
Morro Bay, CA 93443
ph: 805-772-2968
fax: 805-772-2968
gd57@hotmail.com
*Always buying coin-operated devices;
offers complete restoration services;
appraisals; no collection too big or
too small to purchase or restore; the
only lifetime guarantee in the
business.*

Mike Harrod
Trailside Treasures
365 Victor St. "S"
Salinas, CA 93907
*Buy, sells and trades coin-operated
machines; many coin-ops, plastic
radios and other gameroom
collectibles in stock.*

John Robertson
John's Jukes Ltd.
2343 Main St.
Vancouver, British Columbia V5T 3C9
  Canada
ph: 604-872-5757
fax: 604-872-2010
JRR@flippers.com
http://www.flippers.com
*Sales and service of pinball, video
games and jukeboxes; parts and
schematics available; shop service for
game boards; call about shipping for
repair.*

Experts

Bob Levy
Unique One, The
2802 Centre St.
Pennsauken, NJ 08109-5304
ph: 856-663-2554
antiqueslotmachines@yahoo.com
http://www.antiqueslotmachines.com
*Buys and sells coin-operated machines
including slot machines and arcade
games; advisor to "Warman's
Antiques & Collectibles Price Guide."*

Bill Nesnay
P.O. Box 2
Pine Beach, NJ 08741-0002
ph: 732-341-2622
coinop@prodigy.net
*Specializes in and wants to buy
baseball related coin-op machines:
gumball, pinball, arcade, vending,
and trade stimulators; please no calls
after 10 pm EST.*

Joseph S. Jancuska
619 Miller St.
Luzerne, PA 18709-1307
ph: 570-287-3478
*Buys, sells, repairs and appraises slot
machines, trade stimulators, gum &
nut machines & other coin-operated
machines.*

Bill Enes
8520 Lewis Dr.
Shawnee Mission, KS 66227-3277
ph: 913-441-1492 or 913-441-1502
fax: 913-441-1502
*Author of "Silent Salesmen - an
Encyclopedia of Collectible Gum,
Candy & Nut Machines."*

Internet Resources

Ken Durham
GameRoomAntiques
909 26th St. NW
Washington, DC 20037-2029
durham@gameroomantics.com
http://www.GameRoomAntiques.com
*A World Wide Web site dedicated to
game room collecting: pinball
machines, juke boxes, Coke machines,
etc.; monthly feature articles, book
reviews, links to other game room
resources; site has over 100 pages.*

Roy Baker
Coin-Op Connection
10132 Brentridge Court
Dallas, TX 75243
ph: 972-783-0767
fax: 972-783-0705
roy@2nd-sight.com
http://2nd-sight.com/coin-op
*An Internet resource for collectors,
dealers and gameroom owners; focus
is in jukeboxes and related items, but
also covers advertising, salesman
samples, pinballs, slot machines, etc.*

Museums/Libraries

Marvin Yagoda
Marvin's Marvelous Mechanical
  Museum
31005 Orchard Rd.
Farmington, MI 48334
ph: 248-626-5020
fax: 248-626-7945
adamant726@aol.com
http://www.marvin3m.com

Periodicals

Tim Ferrante
Magazine: Gameroom Magazine
P.O. Box 41
Keyport, NJ 07735-0041
ph: 732-739-1955
fax: 732-739-2834
coinop@gameroommagazine.com
http://www.gameroommagazine.com
  *A great source of information for the
  collector and dealer of jukeboxes,
  pinballs, slot machines, Coke and
  other soda machines, arcade games,
  classic arcade video, and other
  gameroom collectibles.*

Rosanna Harris
Newspaper: Coin Drop International
5815 West 52nd Ave.
Denver, CO 80212
ph: 303-431-9266
fax: 303-431-6978
info@royalbell.com
  *A newspaper style publication
  published 6 times a year covering
  coin-operated machine collections;
  primary focus in slot machines, but
  also pinballs, jukeboxes, and other
  arcade machines.*

Chris Murphy, Ed.
Magazine: Coin Slot International
P.O. Box 53
2 Daltry St.
Oldham, Manchester OL1 4BB U.K.
ph: 01204 388007
fax: 01273 204827
cm@sjc.co.uk
http://www.coinslot.co.uk
  *The U.K.'s premier weekly magazine
  for the coin-op industry.*

Steve Hunt, Ed.
Antique Amusement Co.
Magazine: Antique Amusements
  Magazine
Mill Lane
Swaffham Bulbeck
Cambridge, CB5 0NF U.K.
ph: 01223 813041
post@aamag.co.uk
http://www.aamag.co.uk
  *A monthly published in the U.K.:
  articles, photos, ads.*

Repair Services

Tony DeLucia
Antique Amusement Service
765 Shephard Ave.
Hamden, CT 06514
ph: 203-288-3797
AntAmuSvc@webtv.net
  *Restoration and repair of jukeboxes,
  pinball machines, and other 1930s*

*through 1960s coin-operated
machines; over 20 years experience;
large selection of restored machines
always on hand.*

Gary Taplin
Penny Arcade Restorations
28 Southfield Ave.
Stamford, CT 06902-7232
ph: 203-357-1913
fax: 203-357-1913
gtaplin@cloud9.net
  *Restores all kinds of coin-operated
  machines: mechanical, electro-
  mechanical, pneumatics, part
  fabrication, cabinetry refinishing,
  marbleizing, graphics, marquees,
  papier mache, glass, carving,
  castings, polishing, plating.*

Tony Miklos
Pinball Paramedic Repair Service
1372 Targat Rd.
East Greenville, PA 18041
ph: 215-541-4167
tmiklos@netcarrier.com
  *Serving Eastern Pennsylvania from
  Allentown to Philadelphia; repairs
  pinballs, jukeboxes, slot machines,
  shuffle alleys, etc.; from antique to
  state-of-the-art; in business since
  1979; no retail parts for sale.*

Joseph S. Jancuska
619 Miller St.
Luzerne, PA 18709-1307
ph: 570-287-3478
  *Buys, sells, repairs and appraises slot
  machines, trade stimulators, gum &
  nut machines & other coin-operated
  machines.*

John Adorjan
Amusing Devices
1505 Highland Park
Highland Park, IL 60035
ph: 847-274-3759
fax: 847-836-0104
  *Specializes in any machine that takes a
  coin from 1899 to present: video
  games, pinball, bowling, mechanical,
  antique and more; sell, services, buys,
  trades.*

Dennis & Vicky Hartwig
Lost in the 50's
4650 Whistler Ave.
Santa Rosa, CA 95407
ph: 707-584-1972
dvhartwig@aol.com
  *Repairs/restores coin-operated
  machines; also buys and sells.*

John Robertson
John's Jukes Ltd.
2343 Main St.
Vancouver, British Columbia V5T 3C9
  Canada
ph: 604-872-5757
fax: 604-872-2010
JRR@flippers.com
http://www.flippers.com
  *Sales and service of pinball, video
  games and jukeboxes; parts and
  schematics available; shop service for*

*game boards; call about shipping for
repair.*

Repro. Sources

Steve Gronowski
Mechanical Antiques & Amusements
  Co.
363-A Bateman Circle
Barrington, IL 60010
ph: 847-381-1234
coinopsteve@aol.com
  *Buy and sell antique penny arcade
  machines; manufactures reproduction
  arcade machines such as Love Testers
  and Grandma Fortune Tellers.*

Suppliers

Rick Frink
2977 Eager
Howell, MI 48843-6711
  *Supplies reelstrips, pay cards, decals,
  instruction sheets, and mint wrappers
  for antique slot machines and some
  trade stimulators; send eight 1st class
  postage stamps for catalog; also buys
  and repairs antique machines.*

Arcade Games

Dealers

Joe Iozzia
Chameleon Collectibles
P.O. Box 1005
Pomona, NJ 08240-1005
ph: 609-652-8504
pinflyers@aol.com
http://members.aol.com/Pinflyers/
  flyer.html
  *Collector, dealer, expert buys and
  sells vintage coin operated pinball
  machines by Gottlieb, Williams, Bally
  and others; also wants arcade game
  advertising flyers and brochures.*

TNT Amusements
1028 Shade Lane Rd.
Columbus, OH 43227
ph: 614-577-0111
tntgame@netwalk.com
http://www.tntgame.com
  *Specializes in quality arcade video
  games, pinball machines, jukeboxes.*

Gumball Machines

Collectors

Don L. Reedy
13 South Carroll St.
Frederick, MD 21701-5606
ph: 301-663-4240
fax: 301-694-9190
shineit4u@aol.com
http://www.frederickcouonty.com/
  antiques/brass.htm
  *Buying pre-1940 cast iron or
  porcelain gumball and peanut vending
  machines and parts.*

Robert Couch
Mr. Gumball
6321 West Fletcher St.
Chicago, IL 60634
ph: 773-889-3115
  *Wants gumball and peanut machines
  from 1890 to 1960.*

Dealers

Rich Brinkos
Antique Gumball Machines
948 Clyde Lane
Philadelphia, PA 19128-1136
ph: 215-482-1429 or 215-482-9099
thegumballguy@aol.com
http://www.thegumballguy.com
  *Sells, restores, repairs and services
  gumball and peanut machines; globes,
  parts, vending products, stands;
  anything required to make a fully
  authentic period vending machine.*

John S. Carini
1501 Blakewood Court
South Milwaukee, WI 53172
ph: 414-768-1076
jscarini@execpc.com
  *Buys and sells gumball machines,
  peanut machines, novelty machines.*

Richard Ackerberg
American Gumball Machine Co.
13900 Tahiti Way, #112
Marina Del Rey, CA 90292
ph: 800-779-2764 or 310-823-7818
fax: 310-823-6932
gumballmachines@aol.com
http://www.antiquegumball.com
  *Buys and sells antique and contempo-
  rary gumball machines.*

Repair Services

Rich Brinkos
Antique Gumball Machines
948 Clyde Lane
Philadelphia, PA 19128-1136
ph: 215-482-1429 or 215-482-9099
thegumballguy@aol.com
http://www.thegumballguy.com
  *Sells, restores, repairs and services
  gumball and peanut machines; globes,
  parts, vending products, stands;
  anything required to make a fully
  authentic period vending machine.*

Jukeboxes

(see also BOOKS, Reference
[Jukeboxes])

Collectors

Joe Weber
604 Centre St.
Ashland, PA 17921-1332
ph: 570-875-4787 or 570-875-4401
  *Wants early Capehart & Wurlitzer
  jukeboxes which play 78 rpm records;
  will arrange pickup; all letters
  answered; will offer advise.*

Mike Gorski
1770 Dover Rd.
Westlake, OH 44145
ph: 440-871-6071
  *Slot machines, old penny arcade
  machines; Wurlitzer 78 RPM
  jukeboxes, odd vending machines;
  Regina musical boxes, old coin-
  operated machines.*

Roark Vane
6839 Havenside Dr.
Sacramento, CA 95831-2168
ph: 916-392-3864
neonclock@aol.com
Wants to buy Wurlitzer, Rock-Ola or other 1929-1948 jukeboxes; also wants jukebox related accessories or related advertising items.

Dealers

John T. Johnston
John T. Johnston's Jukebox Classics & Vintage Slot Machines, Inc.
6742 Fifth Ave.
Brooklyn, NY 11220-5418
ph: 718-833-8455
fax: 718-833-0560
Buys, sells, rents, trades and repairs slot and jukeboxes; wants to buy old jukeboxes, slot machines, vending, arcade, old gambling items, neons, cash registers, music boxes, phonographs, syrup dispensers.

Lloyd Thoburn
CoinOpWarehouse
727 N. Mulberry St.
Hagerstown, MD 21740
ph: 703-801-1459
lloyd@coinopwarehouse.com
http://www.coinopwarehouse.com
Buys and sells coin-operated machines such as pinballs, jukeboxes, slot machines, soda machines, etc.

TNT Amusements
1028 Shade Lane Rd.
Columbus, OH 43227
ph: 614-577-0111
tntgame@netwalk.com
http://www.tntgame.com
Specializes in buying, selling, restoring quality arcade video games, pinball machines, jukeboxes.

David Reed
Jukebox Central
841 West Main St.
Madison, OH 44057-9763
ph: 440-428-6666
Buys, sells, collects and repairs jukeboxes and other coin-op equipment; also sells jukebox accessory equipment and parts.

Walt Baxley
Be-Bop Jukeboxes & Gameroom Goodies
4804 Mesquite St.
Flowerwood, TX 75028
ph: 972-724-1791
fax: 972-355-1541
wbax1@msn.com
http://www.trinicom.com/bebop
Southwest's largest retailer of antique and collectible jukeboxes, pool tables, and other gameroom items; sales, service, restoration, and party rentals.

Tony Duran
Nostalgia Warehouse LLC
7801 US Hwy 287
Arlington, TX 76001
ph: 817-572-5012
fax: 817-563-0572
tonyduran@nostalgiawarehouse.com
http://www.nostalgiawarehouse.com
Buy/sell/restore jukeboxes, coke machines, radios, gas pumps, pedal cars, neon signs, and more; an authorized distributor for Wurlitzer and Crosley Radio products.

Randy Hilberg
Collector's Nectar
Box 431
Morro Bay, CA 93443
ph: 805-772-2968
fax: 805-772-2968
gd57@hotmail.com
Always buying jukeboxes; offers complete restoration services; appraisals; no collection too big or too small to purchase or restore; the only lifetime guarantee in the business.

Experts

Rick Botts
2545 SE 60th Ct.
Des Moines, IA 50317-5049
ph: 515-265-8324
fax: 515-265-1980
jukeboxmagazine@att.net

Frank Zygmunt
Illinois Slot Machine Company
P.O. Box 542
Westmont, IL 60559-0542
ph: 630-985-2742 or 630-971-1015
fax: 630-985-5151
zygm1015@aol.com
Buys and sells slot machines and jukeboxes; 200-300 slot machines & Wurlitzer jukeboxes in stock; also Wurlitzer One More Time distributor; also interested in music boxes, nickelodeons, and Coke machines.

Man./Prod./Dist.

Joseph Pankus
Wurlitzer Jukebox Company
1318 Estes St.
Gurnee, IL 60031
ph: 800-987-5480 or 847-662-1700
fax: 847-662-1212
bubbles@wurlitzer-jukebox.com
http://www.wurlitzer-jukebox.com
Web site contains a historical account of Wurlitzer, recent news stories, displaying old and current jukebox models, offering licensed products to be purchased, on line price guide.

Periodicals

Ken Durham
GameRoomAntiques
Newspaper: Antique Amusements, Slot Machine & Jukebox Gazette
909 26th St. NW
Washington, DC 20037-2029
durham@gameroomantiques.com
http://www.GameRoomAntiques.com/GAZ.HTM
Semi-annual newspaper focusing on slot machines and jukeboxes; lots of ads, articles, shows, auctions; send $10 for sample or subscribe for $30 for two years.

Rick Botts
Magazine: Jukebox Collector
2545 SE 60th Ct.
Des Moines, IA 50317-5049
ph: 515-265-8324
fax: 515-265-1980
jukeboxmagazine@att.net
http://www.jukeboxmagazine.com
A monthly magazine with large classified ad department, articles, repair information, shows, auctions, etc.

Michael F. Baute
Magazine: Always Jukin'
404 East Howell, #100
Seattle, WA 98122
ph: 206-652-4005
fax: 206-652-4007
alwaysjuke@aol.com
http://www.alwaysjukin.com
Largest circulation monthly jukebox publication; photos, show reports, ads, new products, restoring guides, etc.

Repair Services

David Adamitis
Antique Musical Machines
RR #5, Box 5295
Moscow, PA 18444
ph: 570-689-7263
fax: 570-689-3703
davediane@ezaccess.net
http://www.antiqnet.com/antiquemusicalmachines
Sells, services, restores music boxes, phonographs, band organs, nickelodeons, violanos, barrel pianos, orchestrions, jukeboxes; anything that plays music automatically.

Chance Tess
Pinball Wizard Sales & Service
39425 Atkinson Dr.
Sterling Heights, MI 48313-5018
ph: 810-978-0393
fax: 313-369-6377
Restores '50s and '60s Seeburg & Wurlitzer juke boxes.

David Headley
DH Distributors
651 S. Yale St.
Wichita, KS 67218-2043
ph: 316-684-0050 or 888-684-0050
Repairs and restores jukebox amplifiers; sells filer capacitor cans for jukebox amplifiers.

Electrons Past Vintage Electronics
ph: 801-262-3903
fax: 801-262-3903
sales@jukin.com
http://www.jukin.com
Repairs old jukeboxes and radios.

Jukeboxes (Film)

Experts

Fred Bingaman
P.O. Box 370
Brownstown, IL 62418
ph: 618-427-2761
fax: 314-230-9559
mr356@aol.com
Wants audio visual (film) jukeboxes (scopitones), and related advertising items, films, spare parts, etc.

Periodicals

Fred Bingaman
Newsletter: Scopitone Newsletter, The
P.O. Box 370
Brownstown, IL 62418
ph: 618-427-2761
fax: 314-230-9559
mr356@aol.com

Parking Meters

Dealers

Ron Rogers
Gas Pumps & Parking Meters
ph: 418-673-1067
impala1@bright.net
http://www.bright.net/~impala1
Specializes in buying, selling and restoring old gas pumps and parking meters; also other gas station memorabilia such as oil cans, porcelain and tin signs; pedal cars, too.

Pinball Machines

Appraisers

Amy D. Moore
Thundercade, Inc.
RR1 Box 290
Pownal, VT 05261
ph: 802-823-0215 or 802-447-8558
amoore@thundercade.com
http://www.thundercade.com
Appraiser, dealer, repairer of pinballs and other coin-operated machines.

Clubs/Associations

David Blake
Pinball Owners Association
P.O. Box 122
Cambridge, Cambridgeshire CB1 8AH U.K.
ph: 01223 251477
fax: 01233 351730
dmbl@pcmail.nerc-bas.ac.uk
http://ds.dial.pipex.com/poa
500 members; over 20 years old; promotes the owning, restoration and playing of pinball machines; produces a magazine, organizes an annual convention and sells spares and collectibles; pinball ownership not necessary to join.

Collectors

Bill Cowles
Vintage Pinballs
4255 Green Ave.
Los Alamitos, CA 90720
ph: 562-594-6489
pbartist@aol.com

Dealers

Joe Iozzia
Chameleon Collectibles
P.O. Box 1005
Pomona, NJ 08240-1005
ph: 609-652-8504
pinflyers@aol.com
http://members.aol.com/Pinflyers/
　pinball.html
*Collector, dealer, expert buys and
sells vintage coin operated pinball
machines by Gottlieb, Williams, Bally
and others; also wants arcade game
advertising flyers and brochures.*

PinballSales.com
1915 Swarthmore Ave.
Lakewood, NJ 08701
ph: 732-364-9900
fax: 732-364-7949
pinballsales@aol.com
http://www.pinballsales.com
*In the coin-op amusement industry
since 1975; buys, sells, trades,
services all types of coin operated
games and jukeboxes.*

Steve Young
Pinball Resource, The
8 Commerce St.
Poughkeepsie, NY 12603
ph: 845-473-7114
fax: 845-473-7116
PBResource@idsi.net
*Source for maintenance manuals,
schematics, replacement parts and
supplies to restore and maintain
vintage pinball machines; manufacturer of replacement parts; sells
pinball books and price guides.*

Lloyd Thoburn
CoinOpWarehouse
727 N. Mulberry St.
Hagerstown, MD 21740
ph: 703-801-1459
lloyd@coinopwarehouse.com
http://www.coinopwarehouse.com
*Buys and sells coin-operated machines
such as pinballs, jukeboxes, slot
machines, soda machines, etc.*

Marc Mandeltort
Macro Specialties, Inc.
5290 Platt Springs Rd.
Lexington, SC 29073-9252
ph: 803-957-5500
fax: 803-957-6974
support@marcospec.com
http://www.marcospec.com
*Provides books, parts, supplies,
manuals, schematics, etc. for pinball
machine owners.*

TNT Amusements
1028 Shade Lane Rd.
Columbus, OH 43227
ph: 614-577-0111
tntgame@netwalk.com
http://www.tntgame.com
*Specializes in buying, selling,
restoring quality arcade video games,
pinball machines, jukeboxes.*

Chance Tess
Pinball Wizard Sales & Service
39425 Atkinson Dr.
Sterling Heights, MI 48313-5018
ph: 810-978-0393
fax: 313-369-6377
*Pinball machine expert; buys, sells,
trades and restores all makes and
models of pinball machines; also
repairs '50s and '60s Seeburg &
Wurlitzer juke boxes.*

Herb Silvers
Fabulous Fantasies
12455 Branford, Unit #3
Arleta, CA 91331
ph: 818-761-2255
fax: 818-834-1950
pinball@fabulousfantasies.com
http://www.fabulousfantasies.com
*Sells and restores vintage pinball and
arcade games and all Gameroom
furnishings; also reproduces many
pinball machine backglass art and
video game overlays; can also create
custom upholstered pieces; offers
gameroom design assistance.*

Kent Tieche
Game Doc, The
8000 Wheatland Ave. #B
Sun Valley, CA 91352
ph: 800-766-3166 or 818-504-0440
fax: 818-504-1153
KTieche@gamedoc.com
http://www.gamedoc.com
*Sales, service and rentals of classic to
new video games and pinball
machines.*

Bell Springs Repair
P.O. Box 1240
Willits, CA 95490
ph: 707-459-6372 or 800-515-8050
fax: 707-459-8614
bellsprings@saber.net
http://www.aboutpinball.com
*Pinball machine care and mainte-
nance: how to purchase, maintain,
adjust, repair your machine.*

Harold Balde
Fungus Amungus
21 Wellington St.
Orangeville, Ontario L9W 2L2 Canada
ph: 519-938-8808
boardwalk12345@yahoo.com
http://www.fungus-amungus.com
*Collector and dealer of coin-operated
machines, mostly pinballs but can also
help with other coin-ops; will help
new collectors with pricing and
general info.*

Experts

Steve Orringer
Silverball Amusements
105 Sandlebrook Dr.
Clayton, NC 27520
ph: 919-553-8891
silverballwiz@aol.com
http://www.silverballamusements.com
*Sells and repairs coin-operated
equipment; also has a full line of 45
rpm records.*

Marc Mandeltort
Macro Specialties, Inc.
5290 Platt Springs Rd.
Lexington, SC 29073-9252
ph: 803-957-5500
fax: 803-957-6974
support@marcospec.com
http://www.marcospec.com
*Provides books, parts, supplies,
manuals, schematics, etc. for pinball
machine owners.*

Internet Resources

Ron Maxwell
NYC Pinball
808 West End Ave., #106
New York, NY 10025
ph: 212-662-5104
rmaxwell@nycpinball.com
http://www.nycpinball.com
*Resource for pinball collectors and
players in the Tri-State area: home of
NYCPPOA, Metro Guide listing where
to play pinball, current news, links to
repairers, collectors' pages, pinball
discussion group.*

Daina Pettit
Mr. Pinball
4805 Marabow Circle
Salt Lake City, UT 84117-5419
ph: 801-277-6296 or 801-277-0888
fax: 801-277-0888
daina@mrpinball.com
http://www.xmission.com/~daina/
　pinball.html
*Web site contains large pinball-
related classifieds as well as hundreds
of repair tips; also "The Pinball
Collector Register" - over 1,500
pinball collectors around the world
that help, buy, sell, trade, repair.*

Periodicals

Jim Schelberg, Ed.
Journal: pinGame journal
31937 Olde Franklin Dr.
Farmington, MI 48334-1731
ph: 248-626-5203
fax: 248-626-5203
jim@pingamejournal.com
http://www.pingamejournal.com
*Focuses on old as well as new pinball
machines; articles on game development, repair and play; lots of buy and
sell ads.*

Repair Services

Bob Thurman
Bob's Servicing
494 Cameron St.
Elmont, NY 11003-3818
ph: 516-354-7737
Big7pinwiz@aol.com
*Repair of coin-operated, flipper
pinball machines; over 26 years
experience; electro-mechanical pinballs
our specialty; rates determined by
travel from the New York City/Long
Island, NY area.*

Steve Engel
Mayfair Amusement Company
60-41 Woodbine St.
Flushing, NY 11385-3234
ph: 718-417-5050
fax: 718-386-9049
info@mayfairamusement.com
http://www.mayfairamusement.com
*Repair or replace most Bally and
Williams circuit boards.*

Bob Graham
Bob G.'s Pinball
bobgspinball@aol.com
http://hometown.aol.com/bobgspinball
*Repairs pinball machines; buys and
sells pinball games also.*

Don Bryant
Bryant Antique Players
4819 Stallcup
Mesquite, TX 75150-1143
ph: 972-270-0135
fax: 972-613-1627
aplayr@airmail.net
http://www.bryanantiques.net
*Sales, service and rebuilding of player
pianos, pump organs, reproducing &
coin-operated instruments, pin balls,
& game room equipment; since 1975.*

Bill Cowles
Vintage Pinballs
4255 Green Ave.
Los Alamitos, CA 90720
ph: 562-594-6489
pbartist@aol.com
*Restores the old-style vintage pinball
machines.*

Kent Tieche
Game Doc, The
8000 Wheatland Ave. #B
Sun Valley, CA 91352
ph: 800-766-3166 or 818-504-0440
fax: 818-504-1153
KTieche@gamedoc.com
http://www.gamedoc.com
*Sales, service and rentals of classic to
new video games and pinball
machines.*

Suppliers

Steve Engel
Mayfair Amusement Company
60-41 Woodbine St.
Flushing, NY 11385-3234
ph: 718-417-5050
fax: 718-386-9049
info@mayfairamusement.com
http://www.mayfairamusement.com
Source for over 6,000 backglasses in stock.

Marc Mandeltort
Macro Specialties, Inc.
5290 Platt Springs Rd.
Lexington, SC 29073-9252
ph: 803-957-5500
fax: 803-957-6974
support@marcospec.com
http://www.marcospec.com
Provides books, parts, supplies, manuals, schematics, etc. for pinball machine owners.

Tim Nabours
Nabours Novelty Inc.
320 Hwy. 55 West
P.O. Box 204
Maple Lake, MN 55358-0204
ph: 320-963-5953 or 800-657-4657
fax: 320-963-5953
nabours@lkddlink.net
http://www.pinballplace.com
Parts for Foosball and Pinball machines: rubber rings, coils, flipper rings, rebound rubbers, plastic pins, etc.; for Atari, Bally, Chicago Coin, Gottlieb, Game Plan, Williams, Stern, etc.; also carries complete pinballs and jukeboxes.

Scales

Dealers

Bill & Jan Berning
135 W. Main St.
Genoa, IL 60135-1101
ph: 815-784-3134
fax: 815-784-3134
iweighu@yahoo.com
http://www.PennyScale.com
Buys, sell, repair, restore, collect, trade and operate coin-operated scales and most other scales; also sells original and reproduction parts; free parts catalog and adjustment information.

Repair Services

Bill & Jan Berning
135 W. Main St.
Genoa, IL 60135-1101
ph: 815-784-3134
fax: 815-784-3134
iweighu@yahoo.com
http://www.PennyScale.com
Buys, sell, repair, restore, collect, trade and operate coin-operated scales and most other scales; also sells original and reproduction parts; free parts catalog and adjustment information.

Slot Machines

Collectors

Mike Gorski
1770 Dover Rd.
Westlake, OH 44145
ph: 440-871-6071
Slot machines, old penny arcade machines; Wurlitzer 78 RPM jukeboxes, odd vending machines; Regina musical boxes, old coin-operated machines.

Scott Fawcett
3835 Birch St.
Newport Beach, CA 92660-2616
ph: 949-756-8677 or 714-968-5000
fax: 949-756-8436
Collector wants to buy unusual slot machines including Watling Rol-A-Top and other slot machines in tall floor model console stands; also wants Silver Dollar slot machines including Fey.

Bill Whelan
Slot Dynasty Restorations
P.O. Box 617
Daly City, CA 94017-0617
ph: 650-756-1189
fax: 650-756-4772
slotdynasty@earthlink.net
Wants early slot machines from 1890s to 1930s, especially Victorian uprights in oak cabinets; cast iron slot & trade stimulators; any payout, or non-payout dice machines; any 2,3,4,5, or 7 jackpot pinboard machines; target games, ads, etc.

Fred & Marjie Ryan
Slot Closet
P.O. Box 83135
Portland, OR 97283-0135
ph: 503-286-3597 or 503-235-9559
Wants slot machines and related literature and advertisements.

Dealers

John T. Johnston
Jukebox Classics & Vintage Slot Machines, Inc.
6742 Fifth Ave.
Brooklyn, NY 11220-5418
ph: 718-833-8455
fax: 718-833-0560
Buys, sells, rents, trades and repairs slot and jukeboxes; wants to buy old jukeboxes, slot machines, vending, arcade, old gambling items, neons, cash registers, music boxes, phonographs, syrup dispensers.

David Claxton
2952 Lynn Ave.
Billings, MT 59102-6640
ph: 406-656-0949
Buys, sells and trades slot machines; specializes in the repair and restoration of Mills, Jennings, and Pace slot machines.

Alan D. Sax
Nationwide Amusement/Slot Machine Brokers, Inc.
3239 R.F.D.
Long Grove, IL 60047
ph: 847-438-5900
slots4you@aol.com

Tom Kolbrener
St. Louis Slot Machine Company
2366 Schuetz Rd.
Saint Louis, MO 63146
ph: 314-432-1699
stlslot@earthlink.net
In business for over 20 years; buys, sells, repairs and restores the finest quality antique slot machines; offers lifetime guarantee; authentic restorations of your machines or theirs.

Don Creekmore
Nations Attic, The
ph: 316-371-1828
dcreekmore@cox.net
http://www.nationsattic.com
Wants to buy vintage, pre-1970 slot machines; wants single machine or entire collections.

Royal Bell, Ltd.
5815 W. 52nd Ave.
Denver, CO 80212-7503
ph: 303-431-9266
fax: 303-431-6978
info@royalbell.com
http://www.royalbell.com
Specializes in vintage, remanufactured and new slot machines.

Slot Shop, The
1184 Hwy. 95
Bullhead City, AZ 86429
ph: 520-754-1122
Since 1985; buys, sells and trades antique slot machines.

Randy Hilberg
Collector's Nectar
Box 431
Morro Bay, CA 93443
ph: 805-772-2968
fax: 805-772-2968
gd57@hotmail.com
Always buying slot machines; offers complete restoration services; appraisals; no collection too big or too small to purchase or restore; the only lifetime guarantee in the business.

Experts

Bob Levy
Unique One, The
2802 Centre St.
Pennsauken, NJ 08109-5304
ph: 856-663-2554
antiqueslotmachines@yahoo.com
http://www.antiqueslotmachines.com
Buys and sells coin-operated machines including slot machines and arcade games; advisor to "Warman's Antiques & Collectibles Price Guide."

Richard Reddock
914 Isle Ct.
Bellmore, NY 11710-1545
ph: 516-826-2032 or 800-223-PNUT
pnutfanclb@aol.com
Buys, sells, restores slot machines; author of "Price Guide to Antique Slot Machines."

Frank Zygmunt
Illinois Slot Machine Company
P.O. Box 542
Westmont, IL 60559-0542
ph: 630-985-2742 or 630-971-1015
fax: 630-985-5151
zygm1015@aol.com
Buys and sells slot machines and jukeboxes; 150-200 slot machines & Wurlitzer jukeboxes in stock; also Wurlitzer One More Time distributor; also interested in music boxes, nickelodeons, and Coke machines.

Clark Phelps
Amusement Sales Co.
7610 Main St.
Midvale, UT 84047-7106
ph: 801-255-4731
clarkp@aros.net

Marshall Fey
Liberty Belle Saloon Saloon & Restaurant
4250 South Virginia St.
Reno, NV 89502-6011
ph: 775-826-2607 or 775-825-1776
fax: 775-826-7411
libbelbks@aol.com
http://www.libertybellereno.com
Collector of antique slot machines for 38 years; author of "Slot Machines - A Pictorial History of the First 100 Years" and "Slot Machines: America's Favorite Gaming Device", 6th edition.

Bill Whelan
Slot Dynasty Restorations
P.O. Box 617
Daly City, CA 94017-0617
ph: 650-756-1189
fax: 650-756-4772
slotdynasty@earthlink.net
Expert in slot machines and trade stimulators; has studied the history for over 30 years and has written many articles on the subject for trade magazines; has also helped other authors by supplying information and photos for their books.

Museums/Libraries

Marshall Fey
Liberty Belle Saloon & Slot Machine Collection
4250 South Virginia St.
Reno, NV 89502-6011
ph: 775-826-2607 or 775-825-1776
fax: 775-826-7411
libbelbks@aol.com
http://www.libertybellereno.com
Nations largest display of antique slot machines; also other antiques; free admission.

Periodicals

Ken Durham
GameRoomAntiques
Newspaper: Antique Amusements, Slot
 Machine & Jukebox Gazette
909 26th St. NW
Washington, DC 20037-2029
durham@gameroomantiques.com
http://www.GameRoomAntiques.com/
GAZ.HTM
*Semi-annual newspaper focusing on
slot machines and jukeboxes; lots of
ads, articles, shows, auctions; send
$10 for sample or subscribe for $30
for two years.*

Repair Services

David Claxton
2952 Lynn Ave.
Billings, MT 59102-6640
ph: 406-656-0949
*Buys, sells and trades slot machines;
specializes in the repair and
restoration of Mills, Jennings, and
Pace slot machines.*

Bill Whelan
Slot Dynasty Restorations
P.O. Box 617
Daly City, CA 94017-0617
ph: 650-756-1189
fax: 650-756-4772
slotdynasty@earthlink.net
*Specializes in the repair & restoration
of antique slot machines as well as all
other types of coin-operated gaming
machines such as trade stimulators,
arcade games & vending machines;
also buys/sells/trades coin-operated
gaming machines.*

Suppliers

Tom Krahl
Antique Slot Machine Part Co.
140 N. Western Ave.
Carpentersville, IL 60110
ph: 847-428-8476
fax: 847-428-4471
*Publishes a catalog of reproduction
slot machine parts; also repairs.*

Bernie Berten
9420 S. Trumbull Ave.
Evergreen Park, IL 60642-2224
ph: 708-499-0688
fax: 708-499-5797
*Carries just about every spring needed
by coin machines; also castings for
antique slot machines.*

Bill Whelan
Slot Dynasty Restorations
P.O. Box 617
Daly City, CA 94017-0617
ph: 650-756-1189
fax: 650-756-4772
slotdynasty@earthlink.net
*Sells reel strips, award cards, and
instruction cards for trade stimulators, counter skill games, and vendors;
send $1 postage for 13-page catalog,
or can send catalog via email in
Microsoft Word format.*

Trade Stimulators

Experts

Bill Whelan
Slot Dynasty Restorations
P.O. Box 617
Daly City, CA 94017-0617
ph: 650-756-1189
fax: 650-756-4772
slotdynasty@earthlink.net
*Expert in slot machines and trade
stimulators; has studied the history
for over 30 years and has written
many articles on the subject for trade
magazines; has also helped other
authors by supplying information and
photos for their books.*

Vending Machines

(see also SOFT DRINK
COLLECTIBLES, Soda Machines)

Collectors

Don L. Reedy
13 South Carroll St.
Frederick, MD 21701-5606
ph: 301-663-4240
fax: 301-694-9190
shineit4u@aol.com
http://www.frederickcouonty.com/
 antiques/brass.htm
*Buy, sell, trade gumball and peanut
machines; also Coca-Cola advertising.*

Mike Gorski
1770 Dover Rd.
Westlake, OH 44145
ph: 440-871-6071
*Slot machines, old penny arcade
machines; Wurlitzer 78 RPM
jukeboxes, odd vending machines;
Regina musical boxes, coin-operated
machines.*

Steve Perry
593 Lavina
Hemet, CA 92544
ph: 909-658-4620
*Wants to buy old gum, peanut, and
candy machines; even if incomplete or
not working.*

Dealers

Vintage Vending, Inc.
68 Stiles Rd., Unit C
Salem, NH 03079
ph: 603-898-7676 or 888-242-6633
fax: 603-898-2080
memories@vintagevending.com
http://www.vintagevending.com
*Specializes in the sale of restored
1950s vending machines: soda, candy,
Coke; also neon clocks and signs,
soda bars, fountain dispensers, picnic
coolers, gas pumps, pedal cars, juke
boxes, bar stools, and other game
room items.*

Rich Brinkos
Antique Gumball Machines
948 Clyde Lane
Philadelphia, PA 19128-1136
ph: 215-482-1429 or 215-482-9099
thegumballguy@aol.com
http://www.thegumballguy.com
*Sells, restores, repairs and services
gumball and peanut machines; globes,
parts, vending products, stands;
anything required to make a fully
authentic period vending machine.*

Craig Willardson
P.O. Box 8296
Spokane, WA 99203-0296
ph: 509-624-0772
cwillardsn@aol.com
*Collector, dealer and expert in early
gum and peanut vending machines;
will buy one machine of an entire
collection; also interested in parts,
broken and incomplete machines, and
related literature.*

Experts

Bill Enes
8520 Lewis Dr.
Shawnee Mission, KS 66227-3277
ph: 913-441-1492 or 913-441-1502
fax: 913-441-1502
*Author of "Silent Salesmen -
Encyclopedia of Collectible Gum,
Candy, and Nut Machines;" buys and
sells.*

Repair Services

Rich Brinkos
Antique Gumball Machines
948 Clyde Lane
Philadelphia, PA 19128-1136
ph: 215-482-1429 or 215-482-9099
thegumballguy@aol.com
http://www.thegumballguy.com
*Sells, restores, repairs and services
gumball and peanut machines; globes,
parts, vending products, stands;
anything required to make a fully
authentic period vending machine.*

COINS & CURRENCY

(see also ANTIQUITIES; BANKING,
Bank Checks; BOOKS, Reference
[Coins]; CIVIL WAR ARTIFACTS,
Currency; CREDIT CARDS &
CHARGE ITEMS; ELONGATED
COINS; GOLD; MACERATED
CURRENCY ITEMS; SILVER;
STOCKS & BONDS; TOKENS;
WOODEN MONEY)

Appraisers

Dr. Spencer Peck
Spencer Peck Numismatist
P.O. Box 526
Oldwick, NJ 08858-0526
ph: 908-236-2880
spencerpeck@earthlink.net
http://www.spencerpeck.com
*One of only nine ASA accredited
appraisers of rare coins, currency,
tokens and medals for IRS, estate,
insurance, trust, liquidation and
equitable distribution purposes in the
US; collections liquidated on your
behalf.*

Charles R. Hoskins
International Numismatic Society
P.O. Box 2091
Aston, PA 19014
ph: 610-494-2880
fax: 610-494-2270
*Specializes in and appraises rare
coins and currency.*

Thomas J. Terpilak, GG, ASA, AAA
Metro Gem Consultants
7315 Wisconsin Ave.
Bethesda, MD 20814-3202
ph: 301-654-0838 or 301-654-8678
*Professional numismatist and
numismatic appraiser.*

Dave Cunningham
5 Waterberry Circle
Ormond Beach, FL 32174
cunn5393@bellsouth.net

Steven Schor
5029 NW 11th Ave.
Pompano Beach, FL 33064
ph: 954-571-8510
lhnumis@gate.net

Terry L. Smith
Ter Den Enterprises
300 N. Michigan St. Box 9
South Bend, IN 46601
ph: 219-289-3349
Ter_Den@hotmail.com
Buys, sells, appraises coins.

John L. Frank
John Frank Rare Coins
725 South Adams, Ste. 21
Birmingham, MI 48009-6916
ph: 248-644-8818
fax: 248-258-1669
*Buys, sells, appraises rare coin &
currency collections; liquidates for
maximum value; certified in rare coin
grading by Adelphi University Institute
of Numismatics & Philatelic Studies;
source for Morgan Carson City silver
dollars.*

Margaret A. Olsen, ASA
Westminster Coin, Jewelry & Sports
P.O. Box 276
Westminster, CO 80036-0276
ph: 303-428-9175
fax: 303-428-1842
marg@mysportsappraiser.com
http://www.4preciousmetals.com
*Specializes in the appraisal of sports
memorabilia and coins.*

Auction Services

Bowers & Merena, Inc.
P.O. Box 1224
Wolfeboro, NH 03894-1224
ph: 800-458-4646 or 603-569-5095
fax: 603-569-5319
directsales@Bowersandmerena.com
http://www.bowersandmerena.com
*Specializes in coin auctions; member
International Association of
Professional Numismatists.*

Lawrence Stack
Stack's Coin Galleries
123 West 57th St.
New York, NY 10019-2280
ph: 212-582-2580
fax: 212-245-5018
info@stacks.com
http://www.stacks.com
*Specializes in the auctions of coins,
medals, tokens, silver, paper currency.*

Christie's
20 Rockefeller Plaza
New York, NY 10020
ph: 212-636-2000
info@christies.com
http://www.christies.com

Teletrade Certified Coin Auctions
27 Main St.
Kingston, NY 12401-3853
ph: 800-232-1132 or 845-339-2900
fax: 845-339-3288
cust@teletrade.com
http://www.teletrade.com
*Conducts three certified coin auctions
each week.*

John D. Compton
J.D. Compton Auctioneering
13833 Rockdale Rd.
Clear Spring, MD 21722
ph: 301-582-0727
fax: 301-582-6114
*Specializes in the auction sale of US
coins and currency; call toll-free in the
US 1-800-66-AUCTION.*

Kurt R. Krueger
Krueger Auctions
P.O. Box 275
Iola, WI 54945-0275
ph: 715-445-3845
fax: 715-445-4100
*Specializing in the mail-bid auction of
tokens, advertising, brewery items,
Western Americana, postcards,
World's Fair & Expo., autographs,
sports, coins & currency, pin-backs,
military memorabilia, automotive,
Disneyana, etc.*

James Halperin
Heritage Numismatic Auctions
Dallas, TX 75219
ph: 800-872-6467 or 214-528-3500
fax: 214-520-7108
auctions@HeritageCoin.com
http://www.HeritageCoin.com
*Rare coin auctioneer; over $75M sold
in 2002; official public auctions held
at every major coin show; takes your*

*coins to the buyers; also weekly
Internet auctions of NGC, ANACS,
and PCGS certified coins; free online
community.*

Joe Stephens
CCE-Auction
10681 Haddington #100
Houston, TX 77279
ph: 713-973-1616
joe@atchou.com
http://www.cce-auction.com
*U.S. rare coin auction service via the
Internet.*

Dennis R. Baker
NumisMedia Online Auctions
26895 Aliso Creek Rd., Ste. B #327
Aliso Viejo, CA 92656
ph: 949-362-3786
info@numismedia.com
http://www.numismedia.com
Online coin auctions.

Julia Walker
Spink & Son, Ltd.
69 Southampton Row
Bloomsbury
London, WC1B 4ET U.K.
ph: +44 (0) 20 7563 4000
fax: +44 (0) 20 7563 4066
info@spinkandson.com
http://www.spink-online.com
*Auctioneers and dealers of coins
(ancient to present), banknotes,
medals, orders, tokens, decorations
and other numismatic items; also
stamps and postal history as well as
fine European, Indian and Islamic art.*

Clubs/Associations

Young Numismatists of America
Newsletter: Young Numismatists Digest
2315 Poplar Lane
Anderson, SC 29621-3247
ph: 864-224-2084
John536693@aol.com
http://members.aol.com/TheYNA
*Only nationwide club dedicated
specifically to young numismatists.*

Bradley S. Karoleff, Co.-Ed.
John Reich Collectors Society
Journal: John Reich Journal
P.O. Box 135
Harrison, OH 45030-0135
Karoleffs4@aol.com
http://www.logan.com/jrcs
*The purpose of the JRCS is to
encourage the study of numismatics,
particularly US gold and silver coins
minted before 1838.*

Bloomington Coin Club
P.O. Box 5906
Bloomington, IN 47407-5906
coincollec@aol.com
*Meets the 3rd Thursday of each month
at Ellettesville Branch of the Monroe
County Library at 7 pm; meetings
have auction, lectures, door prizes.*

Christopher Cipoletti, Ex. Dir.
American Numismatic Association
Magazine: Numismatist, The
818 N. Cascade Ave.
Colorado Springs, CO 80903-3279
ph: 719-632-2646 or 800-367-9723
fax: 719-634-4085
ana@money.org
http://www.money.org
*Worldwide nonprofit assoc. chartered
by US Congress to promote the study
and collection of money including
coins, tokens, paper currency, for
research, interpretation, preservation
of history and culture from ancient
time to present.*

Israel I. Bick, Ex. Dir.
International Coin & Stamp Collectors
Society
Newsletter: Interstamps
P.O. Box 854
Van Nuys, CA 91408-0854
ph: 818-997-6496
fax: 818-988-4337
iibick@aol.com
http://www.bick.net
*Promoting understanding in the world
through coin & stamp collecting.*

Robert Brueggeman, Ex. Dir.
Professional Numismatists Guild
3950 Concordia Lane
Fallbrook, CA 92028
ph: 760-728-1300
fax: 760-728-8507
info@pngdealers.com
http://www.pngdealers.com
*Send for free copy of "The Pleasure of
Coin Collecting." Founded in 1955,
the P.N.G. has more than 300
members in 35 states. Directory lists
professional member numismatists
who possess knowledge, responsibil-
ity, and integrity.*

Bill Grant
San Bernardino County Coin Club
Newsletter: Coin Press, The
P.O. Box 295
Patton, CA 92369-0295
ph: 909-864-7617
mesared@aol.com
*Program speakers, auctions, short
general meeting; meets monthly at the
San Bernadino County Museum, 2024
Orange Tree Lane in Redlands, CA;
annual coin show.*

Pacific Coast Numismatic Society
P.O. Box 194271
San Francisco, CA 94119-4271
http://www.pcns.org
*Since 1915 has promoted the many
facets of numismatics; fosters strong
tradition of research and literary
publication; regular monthly meetings
with presentations on a wide variety
of numismatic topics.*

International Association of Professional
  Numismatists
14, Rue de la Bourse
Brussels, B-1000 Belgium
ph: +32-2-513-3400
fax:+32-2-512-2528
iapnsecret@compuserve.com
http://www.iapn.ch
  *Object is to develop a healthy and
  prosperous numismatic trade
  conducted according to the highest
  ethical standards; membership limited
  to firms or departments of commercial
  institutions; all sales by members are
  fully guaranteed.*

Kenneth B. Prophet, Ex. Sec.
Canadian Numismatic Association
Journal: Canadian Numismatic Journal
P.O. Box 226
Barrie, Ontario L4M 4T2 Canada
ph: 705-737-0845
fax: 705-737-0293
cdn.numismatic@on.aibn.com
http://www.nunetcan.net/cna.htm
  *The national numismatic organization
  of Canada.*

British Numismatic Society
c/o The Warburg Institute
Woburn Square
London, WC1H 0AB U.K.
http://www.britnumsoc.org
  *Founded in 1903 to encourage and
  promote numismatic science,
  particularly through the study of
  coins, medals, tokens, and banknotes
  of the British Isles and Commonwealth, and territories that at any
  time were under British jurisdiction.*

Royal Numismatic Society, c/o The
  British Museum
Department of Coins & Medals
Great Russell St.
London, WC1 3DG U.K.
ph: 020 76361555
RNS@dircon.co.uk
http://www.users.dircon.co.uk/~rns/
  index.html
  *Founded in 1836, the RNS lectures
  and publications deal with classical,
  Asian, medieval and modern coins,
  paper money, tokens and medals.*

Collectors

Wayne K. Homren
Coin Library, The
1810 Antietam St.
Pittsburgh, PA 15206
whomren@coinlibrary.com
http://www.coinlibrary.com
  *Buying books, periodicals, auction
  catalogs, and ephemera relating to
  coins, medals, tokens, or paper money.*

Frederick Lingenfelser
814 Byram St.
Reading, PA 19606-1446
lingy@afo.net
  *Wants pre-1950 coin auction catalogs,
  books, price lists, photographic plates
  of coins, and signed letters from coin
  dealers of yesteryear; also wants to*

*buy any undamaged US coins dated
before 1816.*

John & Nancy Wilson
Wilson's Syngraphics
9353 SW 92nd Place Rd.
Ocala, FL 34481-6502
ph: 352-291-0775
fax: 352-291-0776
johnancyw@aol.com
http://www.johnnancywilson.com
  *Wants any pre-1929 paper money or
  advertising notes along with old pre-
  1910 postcards depicting banks.*

Dealers

BRM Coin Gallery
P.O. Box 261
Southborough, MA 01772
ph: 508-480-9748
fax: 508-480-9748
brmcoin@aol.com

Michael Sachar
B & M Coin Company
P.O. Box 4007
Peabody, MA 01961-4007
ph: 978-538-3183
  *Collector, dealer, appraiser; buys and
  sells RARE coins only.*

Rare Coins of New Hampshire
P.O. Box 720
28 Jones Rd., Ste. #1
Milford, NH 03055
ph: 603-673-9311 or 800-225-7264
fax: 603-673-9539
rcnh@ix.netcom.com

Jeff Kierstead
Jeff Kierstead Rare Coins
P.O. Box 425
New Boston, NH 03070
ph: 800-882-2646
fax: 603-487-2802
jkrccoin@gsinet.net

Branch Mint
64 Laval St.
Manchester, NH 03102
ph: 603-623-7061
leayer@aol.com
  Buys and sells all types of US coins.

Bowers & Merena, Inc.
Magazine: Rare Coin Review
P.O. Box 1224
Wolfeboro, NH 03894-1224
ph: 800-458-4646 or 603-569-5095
fax: 603-569-5319
directsales@Bowersandmerena.com
http://www.bowersandmerena.com
  *Buys and sells US coins and currency;
  publishes Rare Coin Review bi-
  monthly, includes articles, price lists,
  coins for sale; member International
  Association of Professional
  Numismatists.*

Jim Fehr
Ellesmere Numismatics
P.O. Box 402
Brookfield, CT 06804
ph: 203-740-8223 or 800-426-3343
fax: 203-740-7833
ellesmerecoin@ellesmerecoin.com
http://www.ellesmerecoin.com
  *Buys and sells PCGS and NGC
  certified US coins; also publishes
  "The Winning Edge" every three
  weeks (call for free copy) which
  contains current market information
  as well as a listing of certified coins
  for sale.*

Allen G. Berman
Allen G. Berman Professional
  Numismatist
P.O. Box 605
Fairfield, CT 06824-0605
ph: 845-434-6090 or 845-434-6079
fax: 845-434-6079
agberman@aol.com
http://www.bermania.com
  *Buying, selling and appraising
  foreign, ancient, medieval and rare US
  coins since 1973; extensively
  published; consultant to auction
  houses; will consider purchase of
  items too early or esoteric for smaller
  "main line" dealers.*

Arthur & Ira Friedberg
Coin & Currency Institute, Inc.
P.O. Box 1057
Clifton, NJ 07014
ph: 9731-471-1441
fax: 973-471-1062
coincurin@aol.com
http://www.coin-currency.com
  *Member International Association of
  Professional Numismatists.*

Anthony's
P.O. Box 1523
Englewood Cliffs, NJ 07632
ph: 800-451-9645 or 201-871-3705
manth@astampcoin.com
http://www.astampcoin.com
  *Buying and selling collections of
  coins, stamps, paper money since
  1958.*

Nathan Sonnheim
ph: 856-667-3796
fax: 856-667-9705
  *Buys coins & paper money; American
  & foreign; calls welcome.*

Gary Curto
Clocks, Coins & Collectibles
226 19th Ave.
Brick, NJ 08724-4324
ph: 732-840-4324
garyc732@yahoo.com
  Buys, sells and appraises coins.

Seaport Coins
2 Washington St.
Toms River, NJ 08753
ph: 732-341-0900
http://www.seaportcoins.com
  *Offers accurately graded high end
  coins and US paper currency.*

Harvey Stack
Stack's Coin Galleries
123 West 57th St.
New York, NY 10019-2280
ph: 212-582-2580
fax: 212-245-5018
info@stacks.com
http://www.stacks.com
  *United States, European, ancient,
  medieval coins; member International
  Association of Professional
  Numismatists.*

Coin Dealers Inc.
15 West 47th St., #12
New York, NY 10036
ph: 212-768-7297
fax: 212-768-7299
coindealer@mindspring.com
http://www.coindealers.com
  *Buys, sells, appraises rare foreign,
  US, gold coins, silver coins, certified
  and proof coins, bullion, currency,
  paper money, and collections.*

Wade Hinderling
P.O. Box 606
Manhasset, NY 11030
ph: 516-365-3729
fax: 516-365-3729
  *Buys and sells coins of the US and
  France; member International
  Association of Professional
  Numismatists.*

American Coin & Stamp Brokerage, Inc.
30 Merrick Ave.
Merrick, NY 11566
ph: 516-546-2300 or 800-682-2272
fax: 516-546-2315
acsb@acsb.com
http://www.wid.com/coin

Michael Teitelbaum
Advantage Associates, Inc.
P.O. Box 469
Plainview, NY 11803
ph: 516-692-0557 or 888-771-4322
fax: 516-692-0557
  *Specializes in high quality stamps and
  coins; buys and sells.*

William S. Panitch
William S. Panitch, Inc.
855 Central Ave., Ste. #103
Albany, NY 12206
ph: 518-489-4400
fax: 518-489-2776
wpanitch@aol.com
  *Dealers, appraisers, consultants for
  US and foreign coins, paper money;
  free brochure.*

Bill Blair
Blair Collectibles
P.O. Box 655
Pine Hill, NY 12465
ph: 845-254-4717
blaircol@aol.com
http://www.collectoronline.com/booths/
  booth-50
  *Buys, sells, appraises coins and
  currency; US or foreign; in business
  since 1968.*

Brad Shiff
Cybercoins, net, Inc.
1000 Greentree Rd.
Pittsburgh, PA 15220
ph: 412-937-1999 or 412-937-9990
cybercoins@aol.com
http://www.cybercoins.net
*Shows you exactly what you are
purchasing; carries coins (B.C. to
modern US and World), stamps (US
and World, currency (US and World),
medals, tokens, newspapers from the
1700s; also does appraisals.*

Jack L. Dempsey
Dempsey & Baster
1009 East 38th St.
Erie, PA 16504
ph: 814-825-7690 or 814-825-6381
info@dempseyandbaxter.com
http://www.dempseyandbaxter.com
*Owns the only one-of-a-kind American
coin in existence - the 11-cent coin;
buys coins and currency; also tin toys,
paper ephemera, fine estate jewelry.*

James J. Reeves
James J. Reeves, Inc.
P.O. Box 219
Huntingdon, PA 16652-0219
ph: 800-364-2948 or 814-643-5497
fax: 814-641-2600
comments@jamesjreeves.com
http://www.jamesjreeves.com
*Buys and sells stamps, coins,
currency, railroad, sportscards,
comics, paper and nostalgic
memorabilia; in business for over 25
years.*

Catherine E. Bullowa
Coinhunter
1616 Walnut St., Ste. 2112
Philadelphia, PA 19103-5364
ph: 215-735-5517
fax: 215-735-5517
*Buys and sells US, ancient and foreign
coins and books; appraisals; member
International Association of
Professional Numismatists.*

Ken Pine
Coast to Coast Coins
9365 Gerwig Lane
Columbia, MD 21046
ph: 800-638-8869 or 410-309-1622
fax: 410-309-1626
info@coastcoin.com
http://www.coastcoin.com
*Specializes in rare coins, ancient
coins, US coins and currency.*

Milton O. Lynn
Harford Coin Co.
2160 E. Joppa Rd., Ste. 101
Baltimore, MD 21234
ph: 410-665-1814 or 410-665-1815
fax: 410-665-1815
oldtenor@erols.com
http://209.130.65.234/shophc
*Dealer, appraiser, expert in rare
coins, currency, tokens and medals
through 20th century; offers online
appraisal services.*

Robert Lehmann
Reeded Edge, The
113-115 Baltimore St.
Cumberland, MD 21502
ph: 301-724-0400
fax: 301-724-0478
mail@reedededge.com
http://www.reedededge.com
*Appraises, collects, buys and sells all
rare US coins and currency; PCGS
authorized submission center; Life
Member of A.N.A.*

Burton's Coins & Cards
5831 Buckeystown Pike
Frederick, MD 21701
ph: 301-663-3223
fax: 3910663-3262
burtons@erols.com
http://www.collectingexchange.com/
dealers/burtons
*Carries sports cards (baseball,
football, basketball, hockey),
memorabilia (bobbing heads, mini-
helmets, jerseys), and coins (silver
dollars, Peace dollars, proof sets).*

Mark E. Mitchell
Rare Coins & Antique Newspapers
3002 Winter Pine Ct.
Fairfax, VA 22031-1125
ph: 703-591-3150
fax: 703-385-3152
info@mitchellarchives.com
http://www.mitchellarchives.com
*Buying and selling coin collections
and accumulations.*

Will Gorges
Battleground Antiques, Inc.
3910 US Highway 70 East
New Bern, NC 28560
ph: 252-636-3039 or 252-636-5445
fax: 252-637-1862
rebel@civilwarantiques.com
http://www.civilwarshop.com
*Specializes in buying, selling,
appraising coins.*

Carolina Gold & Silver
8502-A Two Notch Rd.
Columbia, SC 29223
ph: 803-736-0540
kathy3@mindspring.com
http://www.carolinacoin.com
*Specializing in US coins and currency
since 1974.*

Thomas Flowers
Mintmark Numismatics
P.O. Box 48
Ortega Station 172
Jacksonville, FL 32210-0048
ph: 877-443-9147
currency@mintmark.com
http://www.mintmark.com
*Buys and sells numismatic specimens
in all price ranges; also sells related
books.*

Ron Gordon
San Juan Precious Metals Corp.
4818 San Juan Ave.
Jacksonville, FL 32210-3232
ph: 904-387-3466
fax: 904-387-5166
sjpm@bigfoot.com
http://www.ejewelry.com/sjpm
*Buys and sells all US and foreign
coins and currency.*

Dwight Morrow
DeLand Coins & Collectibles
109 W. Indiana Ave.
Deland, FL 32720
ph: 904-738-5472
delandcoins@hotmail.com
http://www.stores.ebay.com/
delandcoinsandcollectibles
*Specializes in ancient, foreign and US
coins.*

Ed Kuszmar
Florida Currency & Coins
P.O. Box 4049
Boca Raton, FL 33429-4049
ph: 561-392-8551
fax: 561-392-8583
*Buys and sells coins, currency, paper
Americana, ephemera, and 1893
Columbia Exposition items;
specializes in Confederate and
obsolete currency; large and small size
nationals, Colonial, fractional, error
notes, precious metals, etc.*

William Youngerman
William Youngerman, Inc.
95 South Federal Hwy., Ste. 203
Boca Raton, FL 33432
ph: 800-327-5010
wymoney@aol.com
http://www.williamyoungerman.com
*Specializing in hometown currency,
national bank notes, national
currency.*

Jeff Z. Means
Enterprise Coins
P.O. Box 2338
Lutz, FL 33549
ph: 813-948-2505
fax: 813-948-2305
coin_request_2002@coach.net
http://www.coach.net/coins
*Dealer, collector, appraiser;
specializes in purchasing and selling
foreign coins.*

Carlos A. Amaro
COINS et cetera
P.O. Box 76232
Ocala, FL 34481
ph: 352-854-4513
c.etc@atlantic.net
http://www.atlantic.net/~c.etc
*Buys and sells US coins (certified and
raw), collectible newspapers and
financial documents such as checks,
bonds, and stock certificates.*

Kenneth Dittman
Azmus Coins & Jewelry
1001-1 South 14th St.
Leesburg, FL 34748
ph: 352-787-7500
azmus@lsbg.net
http://www.azmus.com
*Buys and sells coins and currency;
member ANA, FUN, CPCC, BRNA.*

William Skelton
Highland's Vault
P.O. Box 55448
Birmingham, AL 35255-5548
ph: 205-939-1178 or 205-939-3166
fax: 205-939-3166
*Wants all US currency before 1929
and all Confederate States of America
currency and coins; also CSA bonds.*

Abbott's Corporation
33700 S. Woodward Ave.
Birmingham, MI 48009
ph: 248-644-8565
fax: 248-644-7038
sales@abbottscorp.com
http://www.abbottscorp.com
*Buys and sells rare coins and precious
metals.*

Kent Froseth
K.M. Froseth, Inc.
P.O. Box 23116
Minneapolis, MN 55423-0116
ph: 952-831-9550 or 800-648-7662
fax: 952-835-3903
fm26@uswest.net
*US, foreign gold and silver coins;
member Professional Numismatists
Guild, International Association
Professional Numismatists; also life
member of ANA and CNA.*

Jeff Munger
National Coin
P.O. Box 385502
Minneapolis, MN 55438-5502
ph: 612-861-3836 or 800-657-8942
fax: 952-820-0786
natlcoin@aol.com
http://www.coinworld.com/nationalcoin

Gary Adkins
MGS & NSI
5599 W. 78th St.
Minneapolis, MN 55439
ph: 800-653-615 or 952-946-8877
fax: 952-946-8944
gary@coindeals.com
http://www.coindeals.com
*Appraises, buys, sells all US collector
coins and paper money; member of
ANA, PNG, ISA; over 35 years in
business.*

Edward Milas
Rare Coin Company of America, Inc.
6262 South Rte. 83, Ste. 102
Willowbrook, IL 60514
ph: 630-654-2580 or 800-774-2580
fax: 630-654-3556
wmilas@rarcoa.com
http://www.rarcoa.com
*U.S., foreign type coins and paper
money; member International*

Association of Professional Numismatists.

Harlan Berk
Harlan J. Berk, Ltd.
31 North Clark St.
Chicago, IL 60602
ph: 312-609-0016
fax: 312-609-1309
info@harlanjberk.com
http://www.harlanjberk.com
Buys and sells all coins 700 BC to present; classical antiquities; member International Association of Professional Numismatists.

John G. Ross
John G. Ross, Inc.
55 West Monroe St., Ste. 1070
Chicago, IL 60603
ph: 312-236-4088
fax: 312-236-6839
U.S. coins, coins of the world; member International Association of Professional Numismatists.

Dr. Robert A. Hiett
Maple City Coin
P.O. Drawer 47
Monmouth, IL 61462-0047
ph: 309-734-3212
fax: 309-734-8083
hiett@gallatinriver.net
Buys and sells all coins and numismatic items; also knives, Indian artifacts, fishing lures, old pens, and many other miscellaneous items.

Art's Coin City
525 St. Francois St., Ste. 4
Florissant, MO 63031-5036
ph: 314-838-2824
fax: 314-830-2980
artscoin@swbell.net
http://209.130.65.234/shopart

Marek Mamelian
Scotsman Coin & Jewelry
11262 Olive Blvd.
Saint Louis, MO 63141
ph: 314-692-2646 or 800-642-4305
fax: 314-692-0410
mark@scoins.com
http://www.scoins.com
Buys, sells US and foreign currency and coins; also gives free verbal appraisals.

Blanchard & Co.
P.O. Box 61740
New Orleans, LA 70161-1740
ph: 888-524-2646
fax: 504-837-4884
info@blanchardonline.com
http://www.blanchardonline.com
Dealers in rare coins and precious metals.

Coinwire.com
P.O. Box 218
Ada, OK 74820
ph: 510-310-9100
fax: 580-332-9034
sales@coinwire.com
http://www.coinwire.com
Sales of US coins, statehood quarters,

American Silver Eagles, gold and silver coins of the world, and coin supplies at discounted prices.

Douglas Winter
Douglas Winter Numismatics
P.O. Box 7828
Dallas, TX 75209
ph: 214-654-9905
fax: 214-654-9906
dwn@ont.com
http://www.raregoldcoins.com
Founded in 1985, specializes in choice and rare 18th and 19th century US gold coins with emphasis on branch mint issues struck at Carson City, Charlotte, Dahlonega, and New Orleans mints.

James Halperin
Heritage Galleries & Auctioneers
Dallas, TX 75219
ph: 800-872-6467 or 214-528-3500
fax: 214-520-7108
auctions@HeritageCoin.com
http://www.HeritageCoin.com
One of the world's largest numismatic firms offering rare coins and currency; free automated want-list notification.

Robert P. Hoover, ISA
Rice Coin & Stamp Co., Inc.
9440 Old Katy Rd., Ste., 121
Houston, TX 77055-6363
ph: 713-973-0030
Buying, selling, appraising coins, stamps, paper money, tokens; US and worldwide 1600 to present; member of ANA, APS, GHCC, TSDA, and NGC.

Joe Stephens
Archives Coins
P.O. Box 79682
Houston, TX 77279
ph: 281-216-0359
joe@rummelcreek.com
Buys and sells quality rare US coins.

Robert L. Astrich
Robert L. Astrich Rare Coin Company
P.O. Box 981
Hempstead, TX 77445
ph: 979-826-2221
fax: 979-826-6566
rastrich@direcway.com
http://www.bobastrich.com
Active buyer of large coin collections and estates.

Chuck D'Ambra
Chuck D'Ambra Coins
P.O. Box 523
Castle Rock, CO 80104
ph: 303-681-2261
chuckd@telesphere.com
http://www.telesphere.com/ts/coins
Buys and sells collectible coins and paper money; Web site has been a favorite Internet resource for coin collectors since 1993; lots of hobby info including extensive Coin Collecting FAQ; also large selection of quality US coins for sale.

David Olmstead
Alpine Numismatics, Inc.
P.O. Box 532
Franktown, CO 80116
ph: 303-660-2219 or 800-654-9599
fax: 303-660-5872
alpinenum@aol.com
Coin dealer buying and selling Colonial, commemoratives, Morgans, Barbers, Walking Liberty, Peace dollars, etc.

Klaus J. Degler
Rocky Mountain Coin, Inc.
538 S. Broadway
Denver, CO 80209-4002
ph: 800-781-4653 or 307-777-4653
fax: 303-733-4946
rmcoin@uswest.net
http://www.rmcoin.com
Appraises, buys, sells, collects and specializes in coins and currency.

American Rarities
P.O. Box 11277
Boulder, CO 80301
ph: 800-622-5680 or 303-530-0425
fax: 303-530-0423
staff@americanrarities.com
http://www.americanrarities.com
Buys and sells quality coins.

American Bullion & Coin co.
P.O. Box 2938
Flagstaff, AZ 86003
ph: 800-897-9817 or 520-527-0047
fax: 520-527-0051
amerbc@infomagic.com
http://www.americancoins.com
Dealer in rare and certified gold, silver and platinum coin and bullion.

Donald M. Hardisty
Don's Collectibles
3020 E. Majestic Ridge
Las Cruces, NM 88011
ph: 505-522-3721
fax: 505-522-7909
don@donsbossons.com
http://www.donsbossons.com
Mainly deals in Morgan dollars and in certified coins including early yearly issues from the US Mints.

Washington Rare Coin Center
P.O. Box 370940
Las Vegas, NV 89137
ph: 800-553-1505
coinguys@coinbuyers.com
http://www.coinbuyers.com
Consignment program, rare coil loans, collection building advice.

Superior Galleries
9478 West Olympic Blvd.
Beverly Hills, CA 90212-4246
ph: 310-203-9855 or 800-421-0754
fax: 310-203-0496
superior@superiorgalleries.com
http://www.superiorgalleries.com
Has been a retail and auction source for dealers and collectors for over 70 years; specializes in stamps, coins, sports memorabilia and other collectibles.

L & C Coins
3700 Katella Ave., Ste. D
Los Alamitos, CA 90720
ph: 562-795-0560
fax: 562-596-2498
lccoins@lccoins.com
http://www.lccoins.com/contact.htm

Teller Numismatic Enterprises
16055 Ventura Blvd., Ste. 635
Encino, CA 91436
ph: 818-783-8545 or 818-835-5279
fax: 818-783-9083
mlt@tellercoins.com
http://www.tellercoins.com
Gold and silver coins of the World; specialist in Russia, China, 19th century Oriental coins, and choice foreign paper money; member International Association of Professional Numismatists (IAPN), PNG, ANA.

Neil Osina
Best Variety Sports Cards & Coins
358 W. Foothill Blvd.
Glendora, CA 91741
ph: 626-914-2273
bestvariety@hotmail.com
http://home.earthlink.net/~nosina
Wants to buy USA coins from the period 1792 through 1885; Life Member of all major associations; over 38 years experience.

Karl Stephens
Karl Stephens, Inc.
P.O. Box 3038
Fallbrook, CA 92088
ph: 760-731-6138
fax: 760-731-9132
Foreign coins, medals, tokens, eastern Europe, US type and copper coins; member International Association of Professional Numismatists.

Richard Ponterio
Ponterio & Associates, Inc.
1818 Robinson Ave.
San Diego, CA 92103-4606
ph: 800-854-2888 or 619-299-0400
fax: 619-299-6952
coins@ponterio.com
http://www.ponterio.com
Coins, medals and banknotes of Mexico and Latin America, World paper money, gold coins and crowns, Ancient coins; member International Association of Professional Numismatists, Professional Numismatists Guild.

Howard Markham
Howard Markham Professional Numismatist
5225 Canyon Crest Dr., Ste. 20
Riverside, CA 92507-6319
ph: 909-686-2122 or 800-953-3027
Buys all US coins, gold coins, collections and accumulations; nationally recognized numismatist; will pay top dollar for rare coins; will travel to buy larger collections.

Albany Coin Exchange
1107 Solano Ave.
Albany, CA 94706
ph: 510-526-4791
info@albanycoin.com
http://www.albanycoin.com
A leading coin and bullion dealer in Northern California.

Freeman Craig
P.O. Box 4176
San Rafael, CA 94913-4176
ph: 415-883-5336
fax: 415-382-1008
monedas@aol.com
Expert in Latin American coinage in gold, silver and minor metals from 1536-1950 including medals; member International Association of Professional Numismatists.

Kagins
98 Main St., #201
Belvedere Tiburon, CA 94920
ph: 888-8KAGINS or 415-435-2601
kagins@earthlink.net
http://www.kagins.com
Specializes in early and rare US copper, gold and silver coins; US Colonials, patterns, paper currency, California fractional coinage, pioneer gold and patterns.

James F. Elmen
World-Wide Coins of California
P.O. Box 3684
Santa Rosa, CA 95402
ph: 707-527-1007
fax: 707-527-1204
elmen@sonic.net
Specializes in world coins and medals from 1500 to present.

Steve Estes
Steve Estes, P.N., Inc.
P.O. Box 25509
Portland, OR 97298
ph: 800-705-5057 or 503-244-5057
fax: 503-244-6015
estes@steveestes.com
http://www.steveestes.com
Professional numismatist and coin dealer since 1963 specializes in buying and selling certified and raw US coins; offers secure online coin sales, numismatic studies, and reference material.

Alex Pancheco
Tipsico Coin LLC
P.O. Box 2067
Corvallis, OR 97339-2067
ph: 541-343-0091
tipsico@qwest.net
Appraises, sells and buys all US and world coins, currency, tokens, medals, gold & silver bullion; bimonthly catalog; complete range of collector coin and stamp supplies and albums.

Pinnacle Rarities
1142 Broadway #130
Ronald, WA 989402
ph: 800-432-6467 or 253-272-7300
fax: 253-272-7322
inquire@pinnacle-rarities.com
http://pinnacle-rarities.com
Offers the finest in certified rare coins, market resources and information.

Erik Kafrissen
Perth Numismatics
R.R. #3
Lanark, Ontario K0G 1K0 Canada
ph: 888-737-8410 or 401-743-8166
info@perthmoney.com
http://www.perthmoney.com
A dealer in rare foreign currency Antarctic to Zimbabwe; full online service including a full inventory of banknotes, weekly specials, hard-to-find books, online banknote appraisals; offers online appraisals of paper money.

Experts

Allen G. Berman
Allen G. Berman Professional Numismatist
P.O. Box 605
Fairfield, CT 06824-0605
ph: 845-434-6090 or 845-434-6079
fax: 845-434-6079
agberman@aol.com
http://www.bermania.com
Author of "Warman's Coins and Paper Money;" author/editor of numerous books and articles on early coinage; leading authority on coins of Middle Ages and Papacy; recognized authority by periodicals & auction houses; ANA instructor.

Scott A. Travers
Scott Travers Rare Coin Galleries, Inc.
P.O. Box 171
F.D.R. Station
New York, NY 10150-1711
ph: 212-535-9135
travers@inch.com
http://www.inch.com/~travers/travers3.htm
Author of "How to Make Money in Coins Right Now."

Rich Davis
Rich Davis Autograph Authentication & Collectible Investments
P.O. Box 563
Kingston, OH 45644
ph: 740-642-2024
prdavis@horizonview.net
http://authenticator.freeservers.com
Specializes in the authentication and appraisal of all types of autographs; expert on sports collectibles, coins & currency, comic books, and stamps; also provides services as a research/grading/appraisal expert.

Douglas Winter
Douglas Winter Numismatics
P.O. Box 7828
Dallas, TX 75209
ph: 214-654-9905
fax: 214-654-9906
dwn@ont.com
http://www.raregoldcoins.com
Has written seven references on US gold coins and is a widely recognized expert in the field.

W. Crutchfield Williams, II
Crutchfield's Currency
P.O. Box 521
Kemah, TX 77565
ph: 281-334-3297
CrutchfieldWilliams-CSA@worldnet.att.net
http://www.CrutchWilliams.com
Buys, sells, appraises Confederate States of America and Southern state currency, broken bank notes, Republic of Texas collectibles (TEXANA), US Federal issues, coins, tokens, and other related material; life member ANA, SPMC, IBNS.

Klaus J. Degler
Rocky Mountain Coin, Inc.
538 S. Broadway
Denver, CO 80209-4002
ph: 800-781-4653 or 307-777-4653
fax: 303-733-4946
rmcoin@uswest.net
http://www.rmcoin.com
Professional Numismatist Guild #463, American Numismatic Assoc. Life Member, Industry Council for Tangible Assets, consultant to the American Numismatic Assoc., Colorado Professional Numismatic Assoc. Pres.; expert witness experience.

Kelly Anderson
American Coin Online
P.O. Box 51432
Provo, UT 84605
kelly@acoin.com
http://www.acoin.com
Collector and dealer in US coins; runs a large mailing list on the subject; specialties include early dimes; does not have experience in paper money, only coins.

Internet Resources

Numismatica
ltleelim@mail.limunltd.com
http://www.limunltd.com/numismatica
A site dedicated to providing information about numismatics - the study and collecting of coins, paper money, tokens, medals, and other similar objects: FAQ's, glossaries, biographies, news, articles, stories, reviews, trivia, etc.

CoinLink
coinlink@coinlink.com
http://www.coinlink.com
Web site listing coin related associations, auctions, books, bullion prices, bulletin boards, clubs,
classified ads, coin facts, coin grading, collector sites, dealers, news, articles, products, services, resources, and lots more.

About.com Hobbies
220 East 42nd St.
New York, NY 10017
pr@about-inc.com
http://home.about.com/hobbies
Online source for information about action figures, antiques, book collecting, coin collecting, collectibles, comic books, costume jewelry, dolls, mineral collecting, pin collecting, sports and trading cards, stamps, toy collecting.

Wayne K. Homren
Coin Library, The
1810 Antietam St.
Pittsburgh, PA 15206
whomren@coinlibrary.com
http://www.coinlibrary.com
An online resource for information about numismatics, the study of coins, tokens, medals, and paper money; basic information for students and researchers interested in learning more about the subject.

Roxanne Goldberg
CoinMasters
P.O. Box 0116
Wyncote, PA 19095-0116
gregg@epicsoftware.net
http://www.coinmasters.org
An Internet club built by coin collectors for coin collectors; CM is a world-wide online interactive clubhouse which focuses on ALL aspects of coin collecting; Web site is a huge source of numismatic information contributed by members.

U.S. Mint
801 9th St. NW
Washington, DC 20220
ph: 202-283-2646
http://www.usmint.gov
How coins are made, fun facts, history of the Mint, paper money, tour information,

Stan Klein
Coin Site, The
1712 SE 13th St.
Fort Lauderdale, FL 33316
ph: 954-954-0770
info@coinsite.com
http://www.coinsite.com
A most informative Web site for coins and paper money: images, The Coin Doctor, articles about coins, list coins to buy/sell/trade in The Trading Room; links to research sites, coin dealers, etc.

Stan Kline
Coin Site Collectors' Showcase
1712 SE 13th St.
Fort Lauderdale, FL 33316
ph: 954-954-0770
info@coinsite.com
http://www.coinsite.com
The easiest, most effective way to buy

and sell coins and currency on the
Web; see what others are asking for
US coins, world coins, ancient coins,
US currency, world currency,
exonumia.

Coin World Online
P.O. Box 150
Sidney, OH 45365-0150
ph: 800-673-8311 or 937-498-0800
fax: 937-498-0812
webmaster@coinworld.com
http://www.coinworld.com
*The weekly newspaper for the entire
numismatic field; articles, ads, paper
money, foreign and ancient coins,
auctions, value guides, grading, etc.*

Deven
Penny Lane
deven@bright.net
http://www.bright.net/~deven/
pennylane.htm
*Lots of links to coin Web sites and
resources worldwide.*

Coin Shop's Coin Collecting
Homepage, The
4710 W. 34th St.
Indianapolis, IN 46222
ph: 317-291-1930
mikec@iquest.net
http://emporium.turnpike.net/M/mikec
*Buys and sells, also provides grading
services.*

ICG Coin Club
7901 East Belleview Ave., Ste. 50
Englewood, CO 80111
ph: 877-221-4424 or 303-221-4424
fax: 303-221-5524
customersatisfaction@icgcoin.com
http://www.coinclub.com
*A site for Coin Clubs everywhere;
dedicated to promoting the hobby of
coin collecting; find access to
community coin clubs and numismatic
organizations, shows, auctions,
dealers, news, reference library,
grading information, coin values.*

Museum of the American Numismatic
Association
818 N. Cascade Ave.
Colorado Springs, CO 80903-3279
ph: 719-632-2646 or 800-367-9723
fax: 719-634-4085
ana@money.org
http://www.money.org
*Money museum, club listings,
educational programs, events, links,
marketplace directory.*

Coin Gallery Online
P.O. Box 8123
Colorado Springs, CO 80933
ph: 719-596-1651
info@coin-gallery.com
http://www.coin-gallery.com
*Online coin collecting guide: dealers,
auctions, books & periodicals, clubs,
organizations, collecting supplies,
educational resources, grading
services, major coin shows, articles,
glossary, exhibits, etc.*

Kelly Anderson
American Coin Online
P.O. Box 51432
Provo, UT 84605
kelly@acoin.com
http://www.acoin.com
*Goal is to help learn about buying,
selling, trading American coins; coin
identification, what are coins worth,
coin school, cleaning coins, coins as
an investment, mint marks.*

Robert Johnson
COINSHEET Numismatic Directory
5560 Shasta Lane, Ste. 3
La Mesa, CA 91942-4402
ph: 619-697-8541
rjohnson@coinsheetlinks.com
http://www.coinsheetlinks.com
*Comprehensive directory of Internet
numismatic resources, bullion spot
prices, coin supplies.*

Ron Guth
CoinFacts.com, Inc.
P.O. Box 90037
San Diego, CA 92169
ph: 619-972-9449
fax: 419-710-7699
ron@coinfacts.com
http://www.coinfacts.com
*An Internet encyclopedia and price
guide of US coins: free information
and thousands of enlarged, full color
images of rare US coins.*

NumisMedia Price Guide
26895 Aliso Creek Rd., Ste. B #327
Aliso Viejo, CA 92656
ph: 949-362-3786
info@numismedia.com
http://www.numismedia.com
Online price guide for US coins.

Brent Gutekunst
Coins Universe
P.O. Box 6289
Newport Beach, CA 92658
ph: 949-567-1234
fax: 949-833-7955
http://www.collectors.com
*Online collector news, buy and sell,
information, auctions, grading &
authentication services.*

Brent Gutekunst
Currency Universe
P.O. Box 6289
Newport Beach, CA 92658
ph: 949-567-1234
fax: 949-833-7955
http://www.collectors.com
*Online collector news, buy and sell,
information, auctions, grading &
authentication services.*

Brian R. Smith
Canadian Coin Reference Site, The
110 The Esplanade, Ste. 521
Toronto, Ontario M5E 1X9 Canada
ph: 416-861-9523
torexcoinshow@yahoo.com
http://www.canadiancoin.com
*Web site created primarily for the
novice and intermediate coin
enthusiast; Web site includes*

*important numismatic reference
material.*

Graham Dyer
British Royal Mint
U.K.
ph: 01443 623004
fax: 01443 623190
graham.dyer@royalmint.gov.uk
http://www.royalmint.com
*Web site contains information about
coins and coin-making from the past
to present; Mint's history and current
activities.*

Man./Prod./Dist.

Kennedy Mint, Inc., The
12102 Pearl Rd.
Strongsville, OH 44136-3398
ph: 800-442-6468
fax: 440-572-3692
support@kennedymint.com
http://www.kennedymint.com
*Sells individual and proof sets of early
and new commemorative US coins;
write for catalog - in addition to coins
and coin sets for sale, it contains
tools and storage devices for coin
collectors.*

Misc. Services

Numismatic Guaranty Corporation of
America (NGC)
P.O. Box 1776
Parsippany, NJ 07054
ph: 973-984-6222
info@ngccoin.com
http://www.ngccoin.com/home.cfm
*Grades coins and issues a guarantee
of authenticity; submit coins for
grading through an authorized NGC
member/dealer.*

Charles R. Hoskins
International Numismatic Society
Newsletter: Numorum
P.O. Box 2091
Aston, PA 19014
ph: 610-494-2880
fax: 610-494-2270
*The INS offers authentication and
grading of rare coins and paper
money to the public for a nominal fee.*

John M. McDonough
ANACS
P.O. Box 182141
Columbus, OH 43218-2141
ph: 800-888-1861 or 614-791-8704
fax: 614-791-9103
webmaster@webplex.net
http://www.anacs.com
*Authenticates, grades and encapsu-
lates US and World coins; accepts
error and variety coins plus cleaned,
damaged and repaired coins.*

James Taylor, Pres.
ICG - Independent Coin Grading
7901 East Belleview Ave., Ste. 50
Englewood, CO 80111
ph: 877-221-4424 x203 or 303-221-4424
fax: 303-221-5524
gamestaylor@icgcoin.com
http://www.icgcoin.com
*Offers absolute unbiased grading of
coins.*

Brian A. Silliman
American Numismatic Association
Authentication Bureau (ANAAB)
818 N. Cascade Ave.
Colorado Springs, CO 80903-3279
ph: 719-632-2646 or 800-467-5725
fax: 719-634-4085
anaab@money.org
http://www.money.org
*Offers independent, unbiased,
professional opinions about the
attribution & authenticity of all coins,
medals, tokens, paper money;
determinations are made by
experienced numismatists using the
most accurate information &
techniques.*

Professional Coin Grading Service
(PCGS)
P.O. Box 9458
Newport Beach, CA 92658-9458
ph: 800-447-8848
feedback@pcgs.com
http://www.pcgs.com
*Grades coins and issues a guarantee
of authenticity.*

Museums/Libraries

Newark Museum, The
49 Washington St.
Newark, NJ 07101
ph: 973-596-6550 or 800-7-MUSEUM
fax: 973-642-0459
webmaster@newarkmuseum.org
http://www.newarkmuseum.org
*The Numismatic Collection emerged in
1911 and includes coins and paper
currency from around the world, as
well as other objects relating to
finance, such as bonds and bullion,
medals, badges and decorations.*

Dr. Ute Wartenberg, Ex. Dir.
American Numismatic Society, The
Magazine: American Numismatic Society
Magazine, The
Broadway at 155th St.
New York, NY 10032
ph: 212-234-3130
fax: 212-234-3381
info@amnumsoc.org
http://www.amnumsoc.org
*Has a major collection of American
coins in addition to major and
important collections of ancient, Latin
American, Islamic, European, and
other material; also publishes
"American Journal of Numismatics"
and "Numismatic Literature."*

National Museum of American History,
  National Numismatic Collection
14th & Constitution Ave. NW
Washington, DC 20560
ph: 202-357-2700
webmaster@si.edu
http://www.si.edu/organiza/museums/
  nmah/nmah.htm
The Hall of Monetary History and
Medallic Art exhibits an amazing
number of US and foreign coins,
tokens, medals, and paper money from
earliest times to the present; the finest
coin collection in the world.

Money Museum, Federal Reserve Bank
  of Richmond
701 East Byrd St.
Richmond, VA 23219
ph: 804-697-8108
fax: 804-697-8123
fedbalt@rich.frb.org
http://www.rich.frb.org/generalinfo/
  richmond/tour.html
Primitive monies, ancient coins,
Colonial money, US coins and paper
money, Confederate currency, and US
commemorative coins are on display.

Museum of the American Numismatic
  Association
818 N. Cascade Ave.
Colorado Springs, CO 80903-3279
ph: 719-632-2646 or 800-367-9723
fax: 719-634-4085
ana@money.org
http://www.money.org
A museum collection 400,000 items
including American, ancient, Latin
American, Islamic, European, and
other coins; largest numismatic
circulating library with books and A/V
material free to members.

American Numismatic Association
  Money Museum
818 N. Cascade Ave.
Colorado Springs, CO 80903-3279
ph: 719-632-2646 or 800-467-5724
fax: 719-634-4085
museum@money.org
http://www.money.org
One of the largest collections of coins,
paper money, tokens and medals -
everything from a half-cent to a
hundred-grand; from 3,000-year-old
coins to a nickel worth $1,000,000;
see virtual exhibits on Web site; free
to the public.

Bank of Canada Currency Museum
245 Sparks St.
Ottawa, Ontario K1A 0G9 Canada
ph: 613-782-8914
museum-musee@bank-banque-canada.ca
http://www.bank-banque-canada.ca
Eight galleries trace the history of
money from barter to modern
currency, with emphasis on Canada's
monetary history; impressive coin and
paper money exhibits.

Periodicals

Newsletter: Trader's Horn
P.O. Box 2781
Henderson, NC 27536
thorn@gloryroad.net
A monthly newsletter serving the small
to intermediate collector of coins,
paper money, stamps, lottery tickets,
tokens and other collecting area.

Newsletter: Silver & Gold Report
P.O. Box 109665
West Palm Beach, FL 33410
ph: 800-289-9222 or 561-627-3300
fax: 561-625-6685
sgr@weissinc.com
Financial advice newsletter in
precious medals, and gold & silver
bullion and coins.

Amos Press, Inc.
Newspaper: Coin World
P.O. Box 150
Sidney, OH 45365-0150
ph: 800-673-8311 or 937-498-0800
fax: 937-498-0812
webmaster@coinworld.com
http://www.coinworld.com
The weekly newspaper for the entire
numismatic field; articles, ads, paper
money, foreign and ancient coins,
auctions, value guides, grading, etc.

Stacie Berger
Krause Publications
Magazine: Coin Prices
700 E. State St.
Iola, WI 54990-0001
ph: 715-445-2214
fax: 715-445-4087
stacie.berger@fwpubs.com
http://www.krause.com
Provides complete current market
prices for US coins; values listed for
up to 12 grades of preservation;
frequently updated pricings; bi-
monthly.

Stacie Berger
Krause Publications
Magazine: Coins
700 E. State St.
Iola, WI 54990-0001
ph: 715-445-2214
fax: 715-445-4087
stacie.berger@fwpubs.com
http://www.krause.com
Leading monthly newsstand magazine
provides in-depth features on US coins
with color photos; collector columns,
articles, values, ads; the complete
magazine for collectors.

Stacie Berger
Krause Publications
Magazine: Numismatic News
700 E. State St.
Iola, WI 54990-0001
ph: 715-445-2214
fax: 715-445-4087
stacie.berger@fwpubs.com
http://www.krause.com
A weekly guide to the coin collecting
hobby serving active collectors of US

coins with timely news; values, ads,
calendar.

Stacie Berger
Krause Publications
Magazine: World Coin News
700 E. State St.
Iola, WI 54990-0001
ph: 715-445-2214
fax: 715-445-4087
stacie.berger@fwpubs.com
http://www.krause.com
Monthly guide serving world coin
collectors; news, historical features,
huge ad section, coin values, show
calendar.

CDN Publications
Newsletter: Certified Coin Dealer
  Newsletter (The "Bluesheet")
P.O. Box 7939
Torrance, CA 90504
ph: 310-515-7369
fax: 310-515-7534
cdn@greysheet.com
http://www.greysheet.com
A weekly report on the certified coin
market; unbiased wholesale
information on rare coins for the coin
hobby and business.

CDN Publications
Newsletter: Coin Dealer Newsletter (The
  "Greysheet")
P.O. Box 7939
Torrance, CA 90504
ph: 310-515-7369
fax: 310-515-7534
cdn@greysheet.com
http://www.greysheet.com
A weekly report on the certified coin
market; unbiased wholesale
information on rare coins for the coin
hobby and business.

CDN Publications
Newsletter: Currency Dealer Newsletter,
  The (The "Greensheet")
P.O. Box 7939
Torrance, CA 90504
ph: 310-515-7369
fax: 310-515-7534
cdn@greysheet.com
http://www.greysheet.com
A monthly newsletter reporting on the
currency market.

Barry Stuppler, Pub.
Magazine: Coin Connoisseur
P.O. Box 6494
Woodland Hills, CA 91365
ph: 888-264-6624 or 818-592-2800
fax: 818-594-8599
barry@coinmag.com
http://www.coinmag.com
The international magazine for coin
collectors and investors.

Miller Magazines, Inc.
Magazine: COINage
4880 Market St.
Ventura, CA 93003-7783
ph: 805-644-3824
coinmag2@aol.com
http://www.coinagemag.com

Trajan Publishing Corporation
Newspaper: Canadian Coin News
103 Lakeshore Rd., Ste. 202
St. Catharines, Ontario L2N 2T6 Canada
ph: 905-646-7744
fax: 905-646-0995
rscott@trajan.com
http://www.tarjan.com
All the news on Canadian coin
collecting.

Repro. Sources

Ron Landis
Gallery Mint Museum
Newsletter: Gallery Mint Report
P.O. Box 706
Eureka Springs, AR 72632
ph: 501-253-5055 or 888-558-MINT
fax: 501-253-5056
gmm@arkansas.net
http://www.coin-gallery.com/gmm
A mint and museum; reproductions of
early American coins and commemora-
tive medals, hobo nickels and tokens
for collectors; preserves numismatic
arts and coin-making techniques.

Suppliers

James Moran
Telequest
1566 W. Algonquin, #165
Hoffman Estates, IL 60195-1575
ph: 847-991-1228
telequest@usa.net
http://www.telequest.biz
Authorized dealer for Eagle and SAFE
storage supplies: albums, binders,
pages, holders, magnifiers, lamps,
humidity control; for coins, currency,
phone/moneycards, casino chips and
other collectibles.

Chinese

Collectors

Chris Krubel
1405 Beaver Ruin Rd., Apt. 608
Norcross, GA 30093
ph: 770-923-9221
Specializes in Chinese cash coins, i.e.,
the old round ones with a square hole;
usually containing 4 characters on the
front, maybe on reverse, too; also
collects coins from India: British
Regal Era and native coinage.

Coins (Ancient)

(see also ANTIQUITIES)

Auction Services

Alex G. Malloy
Alex G. Malloy, Inc.
P.O. Box 38
South Salem, NY 10590-0038
ph: 203-438-0396 or 203-438-9652
fax: 203-438-6744
alexmalloy@aol.com
http://members.aol.com/AlexMalloy/
  agmalloy.htm
Issues fixed price lists and mail bid
sales of ancient and medieval coinage,
and of ancient art and antiquities for
sale; co-author of "Warman's Coins

& Currency" (1994 Wallace-
Homestead).

Clubs/Associations

Barry Rightman
Ancient Coin Club of Los Angeles
P.O. Box 227
Canoga Park, CA 91305-0227

Bill McDonald, Exec. Sec.
Classical & Medieval Numismatic
  Society
Journal: Journal of the CMNS
P.O. Box 956
Station B
Willowdale, Ontario M2K 2T6 Canada
ph: 416-490-8659
fax: 416-490-6452
billmcdo@idirect.com
http://www.cmns.ca
  *A non-profit educational society for
  anyone interested in ancient and
  medieval coinage and history;
  quarterly Journal of 50+ pages
  contains articles on ancient and
  medieval coinage.*

Dealers

Jan Blamberg
Stack's Coin Galleries
123 West 57th St.
New York, NY 10019-2280
ph: 212-582-2580
fax: 212-245-5018
info@stacks.com
http://www.stacks.com
  *Buys and sells European, ancient,
  medieval coins; member International
  Association of Professional
  Numismatists.*

Alex G. Malloy
Alex G. Malloy, Inc.
P.O. Box 38
South Salem, NY 10590-0038
ph: 203-438-0396 or 203-438-9652
fax: 203-438-6744
alexmalloy@aol.com
http://members.aol.com/AlexMalloy/
  agmalloy.htm
  *Issues fixed price lists and mail bid
  sales of ancient and medieval coinage,
  and of ancient art and antiquities for
  sale; co-author of "Warman's Coins
  & Currency" (1994 Wallace-
  Homestead).*

Edward J. Waddell, Jr.
Edward J. Waddell, Ltd.
P.O. Box 3759
Frederick, MD 21705-3759
ph: 301-473-8600 or 800-381-6396
fax: 301-473-8716
sales@coin.com
http://www.coin.com
  *Greek, Roman, Byzantine and
  Medieval coins, antiquities and
  numismatic literature; member
  International Association of
  Professional Numismatists.*

Ancient Coin Company
P.O. Box 3015
Chesapeake, VA 23327
ph: 800-896-1748
fax: 800-896-1748
  *Specializing in ancient coins and
  antiquities.*

Carl & Jon Subak
Subak Inc.
22 West Monroe St.
Room 1506
Chicago, IL 60603
ph: 312-346-0609 or 312-346-0673
fax: 312-346-0150
subakinc@interlync.com
  *Roman, Byzantine, medieval coins;
  member International Association of
  Professional Numismatists.*

Wayne Sales
Wayne G. Sayles, Antiquarian
P.O. Box 911
Gainesville, MO 65655
ph: 417-679-2142
wayne@ancientcoincollecting.com
http://www.ancientcoincollecting.com
  *Buys and sells ancient Greek, Roman,
  Byzantine, Islamic and related coins;
  authenticity guaranteed without
  limitation; 32 years experience in the
  field.*

Jim Mason
Jim's Medieval Coins
4080 S. 570 E.
Salt Lake City, UT 84107
ph: 801-263-2350
jimbomason@lycos.com
http://members.tripod.com/
  ~Charlemagne64/medieval.html
  *Specializes in medieval European
  coins, with an emphasis on Royal and
  Feudal French denier from the 8th to
  the 14th century.*

Joel & Michael Malter
Malter Galleries, Inc.
17003 Ventura Blvd., Ste. 205
Encino, CA 91316
ph: 818-784-7772 or 888-784-2131
fax: 818-784-4726
mike@maltergalleries.com
http://www.maltergalleries.com
  *Specializing in ancient coins since the
  1960s; buys and sells ancient and
  medieval coins, classical antiquities,
  numismatic books and literature;
  member International Association of
  Professional Numismatists.*

Dr. Geoffrey A. Smith
Antiquities in Design - CoinSold
P.O. Box 1004
Redlands, CA 92373
ph: 858-442-7835
fax: 858-759-7835
coinsold@aol.com
http://hometown.aol.com/coinsold
  *Buys, sells, appraises and specializes
  in ancient coins, jewelry and artifacts;
  GIA trained and certified in gemology
  - ancient and modern gems, metals,
  and jewelry; has up-to-date CEU and
  forensics certification.*

Frank L. Kovacs
P.O. Box 25300
San Mateo, CA 94402
ph: 650-574-2028
fax: 650-574-1995
frank@frankkovacs.com
http://www.frankkovacs.com
  *Buys and sells ancient and Byzantine
  coins and antiquities; member
  International Association of
  Professional Numismatists.*

A. G. & S. Gillis Ancient Coins &
  Antiquities
20 Howard St.
Darfield
Barnsley, South Yorkshire S73 9JD
  U.K.
ph: 01226 750371
fax: 01226 750371
agillis@gilliscoins.com
http://www.gilliscoins.com
  *Specializing in ancient coins and
  antiquities.*

Periodicals

Kerry K. Wetterstrom, Ed./Pub.
Magazine: Celator, The
P.O. Box 839
Lancaster, PA 17608-0839
ph: 717-656-8557
fax: 717-656-8557
kerry@celator.com
http://www.celator.com
  *A monthly magazine focusing on
  ancient Greek, Roman and Byzantine
  coins: ads, articles, auction reports,
  etc.*

Coins (Copper)

Clubs/Associations

Rod Burress
Early American Coppers
Newsletter: Penny-Wise
P.O. Box 15782
Cincinnati, OH 45215
info@eacs.org
http://www.eacs.org
  *Interested in early American copper
  coinage.*

Internet Resources

H. Craig Hamling
USCents.com
consign@uscents.com
http://www.uscents.com
  *Auctions of copper coins, feature
  articles, photo library, chat room,
  copper grading guide, rarity guide,
  glossary of copper terms, copper
  checklist, etc.*

Coins (World Proof)

Clubs/Associations

Edward J. Moschetti, Pres.
World Proof Numismatic Association
Newsletter: Proof Collectors Corner
P.O. Box 4094
Pittsburgh, PA 15201-0094
ph: 412-782-4477
fax: 412-782-0227
  *WPNA is dedicated to the collector of
  proof and BU coinage; purpose is to*

bring forth the latest news on new
coin issues, medals and books, etc.;
special Master Price List is mailed out
to all members containing over 1,000
proof coins.

Dealers

Edward J. Moschetti
Treasures of the World
P.O. Box 4094
Pittsburgh, PA 15201-0094
ph: 412-782-4477
fax: 412-782-0227
  *Medals in silver and gold proof
  condition; offering the Rarities Mint
  issues, plus Batman, Bugs Bunny, etc.*

Commemorative Coins

Clubs/Associations

Society for U.S. Commemorative Coins
P.O. Box 302
Huntington Beach, CA 92648-0302
ph: 714-847-3495
fax: 714-847-3495
hcarmody@money.org
http://www.money.org/sum-
  carmody.html
  *Members dedicated to sharing the
  knowledge and enjoyment of collecting
  US commemorative coins.*

Computer Programs For

Man./Prod./Dist.

Software: CoinWorks
sgeosits@rcn.com
http://members.aol.com/sgeosits/
  CoinWorks/cwmain.htm
  *An inventory software program for
  coin collectors.*

Tom Bilotta
Carlisle Development Corp.
Software: Coin Collectors Assistant
P.O. Box 291
Carlisle, MA 01741-0291
ph: 800-219-0257
carlisleDC@aol.com
http://www.carlisledevelopment.com
  *Coin Collectors Assistant is a
  collection management software
  program for coin collectors; linked
  automatically to "Coin World" values
  price database.*

Niche Software, Inc.
Software: Coin Collector, The
7118 NW Terrace
Parkland, FL 33076
ph: 954-344-6561
marketing@collectiblessoftware.com
http://www.collectiblessoftware.com
  *Collection management software
  program for any type of coin or token;
  US or foreign.*

PrimaSoft PC, Inc.
Software: Coin Organizer
P.O. Box 456
Surrey, British Columbia V3T 5B7
    Canada
ph: 800-371-7520 or 604-951-1085
fax: 604-951-7797
support@primasoft.com
http://www.primasoft.com
    *A complete program that allows coin
    collectors, hobbyists, and clubs to
    organize, catalog, and manage their
    collections on their PCs.*

Liberty St. Software
Software: CoinManage
3126 Lendnier Software
Mississauga, Ontario L4Y 4A1 Canada
ph: 905-566-5314 or 888-282-5887
fax: 905-566-5314
info@libertystreet.com
http://www.libertystreet.com
    *A program to manage your coin
    collection.*

Liberty St. Software
Software: CurrencyManage
3126 Lendnier Software
Mississauga, Ontario L4Y 4A1 Canada
ph: 905-566-5314 or 888-282-5887
fax: 905-566-5314
info@libertystreet.com
http://www.libertystreet.com
    *A program to manage your collection
    of bank notes.*

Croatian

Clubs/Associations

Eck Spahich, Ed.
Croatian Philatelic Society
Journal: Trumpeter, The
P.O. Box 696
Fritch, TX 79036-0696
ph: 806-857-0129
ou812@arn.net
http://www.croatianmall.com/cps
    *Focuses on the history of the stamps
    and numismatic items of all the
    Balkan states, past and present.*

Errors

Clubs/Associations

Paul Funaiole
Combined Organizations of Numismatic
    Error Collectors of America
Newsletter: Errorscope
35 Leavitt Lane
Bangor, ME 04401-1013
pfunny@telplus.net
http://hermes.csd.net/~coneca
    *The only national numismatic
    organization devoted exclusively to the
    study of error and variety coinage;
    newsletter contains informative
    articles and a 16-page auction.*

Dealers

Michael Ellis
Rt. 2, Box HI 504
Donalsonville, GA 31745
ph: 912-861-2089
fax: 912-861-2089
    Numismatic collector/dealer since

*1968; has specialized in error/variety
coinage since 1987; recognized as an
authority in the field; author of the
column "The Error Chronicles" for
"Numismatic News," the hobby's
leading weekly paper.*

Randy L. Camper
Modern Rarities
P.O. Box 1875
Lima, OH 45802
ph: 888-662-3258
fax: 419-222-8234
ran10@wcoil.com
http://www.modernrarities.com
    *Specializing in 20th century coinage
    and die varieties from inexpensive
    RPM's to very rare doubled dies.*

Neil Osina
Best Variety Sports Cards & Coins
358 W. Foothill Blvd.
Glendora, CA 91741
ph: 626-914-2273
bestvariety@hotmail.com
http://home.earthlink.net/~nosina
    *Wants to buy coin errors; Life
    Member of all major associations;
    over 38 years experience; if writing,
    please include SASE if you want a
    reply.*

Experts

Michael Ellis
Rt. 2, Box HI 504
Donalsonville, GA 31745
ph: 912-861-2089
fax: 912-861-2089
    *Numismatic collector/dealer since
    1968; has specialized in error/variety
    coinage since 1987; recognized as an
    authority in the field; author of the
    column "The Error Chronicles" for
    "Numismatic News," the hobby's
    leading weekly paper.*

Stephen M. Sullivan
Capital Currency, Incorporated
P.O. Box 361632
Melbourne, FL 32936-1632
ph: 321-773-5305
errors@capcurr.com
http://www.capcurr.com
    *Appraiser, auctioneer, collector,
    dealer, expert in US currency; full
    service dealer for rare US currency;
    author of "The US Error Note
    Encyclopedia."*

Periodicals

Arnold Margolis
Magazine: Error Trends Coin Magazine
P.O. Box 158
Oceanside, NY 11572-0158
ph: 516-764-8063
etcmman@aol.com
http://www.etcmmag.com
    *A monthly magazine focusing on coin
    errors.*

Lincoln Cent

Clubs/Associations

Lincoln Cent Society
Newsletter: Centinel, The
P.O. Box 113
Winfield, IL 60190
ph: 630-462-8654
    *Dedicated to the study of the Lincoln
    cent.*

Medieval

(see ANTIQUITIES; COINS &
CURRENCY, Coins [Ancient])

Oriental

Clubs/Associations

Jan Lingen, Reg. Sec.
Oriental Numismatic Society
Newsletter: ONS Newsletter
Dr. A Schweitberstraat 29
Bergmanbacht, 2861 XZ The
    Netherlands
ph: +(31) 182-357092
fax: +(31) 182-357093
eu@onsnumis.org
http://www.onsnumis.org
    *Promotes the systematic study of
    coins, medals and currency, both
    ancient and modern, of India, the Far
    East, the Islamic countries and their
    non-Western predecessors; founded in
    1970.*

Paper Money

Auction Services

R.M. Smythe & Company
26 Broadway, Ste. 271
New York, NY 10004-1701
ph: 212-943-1880 or 800-622-1880
fax: 212-908-4670
info@smytheonline.com
http://www.smytheonline.com
    *Conducts auctions of Colonial
    currency, Confederate currency,
    federal essay notes, proof vignettes,
    fractional and obsolete currency,
    stocks, bonds, coins and autographs.*

James Halperin
Heritage Galleries & Auctioneers
Dallas, TX 75219
ph: 800-872-6467 or 214-528-3500
fax: 214-520-7108
auctions@HeritageCoin.com
http://www.CurrencyAuction.com
    *A Web site dedicated exclusively to
    auctioning of rare currency; twice-
    monthly currency auctions.*

Clubs/Associations

Arthur C. Matz
Latin American Paper Money Society
Newsletter: LANSA
3304 Milford Mill Rd.
Baltimore, MD 21244-2041
ph: 410-655-3109
    *A booklet issued three times a year for
    those interested in Latin American and
    Iberia paper money.*

Milan Alusic, Gen. Sec.
International Bank Note Society
Journal: International Bank Note Society
    Journal
P.O. Box 1642
Racine, WI 53401-1642
ph: 262-554-6255
milana@wi.net
http://www.syngraphics.net/ibns/
    index.htm
    *Members interested in worldwide bank
    notes and paper currencies; journal
    published quarterly with articles, ads,
    etc.*

James Simek
Professional Currency Dealers Associa-
    tion
P.O. Box 7157
Westchester, IL 60154
ph: 630-889-8207
    *This organization is just for dealers,
    but send a SASE for a free list of
    respectable dealers; also send 59 cents
    for the booklet "How to Collect Paper
    Money."*

Frank Clark, Mem.
Society of Paper Money Collectors, Inc.
Journal: Paper Money
P.O. Box 117060
Carrollton, TX 75011
webmaster@spmc.org
http://www.spmc.org
    *Interested in all aspects of collecting
    paper currency; welcomes opportunity
    to help non-collectors, but PLEASE
    send SASE for reply.*

Paul Willis
Canadian Paper Money Society
P.O. Box 562
Pickering, Ontario L1V 2R7 Canada
ph: 905-509-1146
admin@CdnPaperMoney.com
http://www.cdnpapermoney.com
    *A resource for those interested in
    Canadian paper money issued by the
    Bank of Canada since its first issue in
    1935.*

Collectors

Bob Cochran
P.O. Box 1085
Florissant, MO 63031-0085
bob@spmc.org
    *Collector of US paper money; also
    banking history.*

Dealers

Jim Sciuto
GoldTek
P.O. Box 128
Methuen, MA 01844
ph: 978-374-2254 or 603-645-4717
fax: 978-373-1088
    *Wants old paper money: gold
    certificates, silver certificates, errors,
    star notes, red seals, etc.*

■

246

Denly's of Boston
P.O. Box 1010
Boston, MA 02205
ph: 617-482-8477
fax: 617-357-8163
info@denlys.com
http://www.denlys.com
Buys and sells national currency, banknotes, fractional and Colonial currency.

George H. LaBarre
George H. LaBarre Galleries, Inc.
P.O. Box 746
Hollis, NH 03049
ph: 800-717-9529 or 603-882-2411
fax: 603-882-4979
collect@glabarre.com
http://www.glabarre.com
Specializes in collectible stocks and bonds, autographs, paper money; also deals with other areas of Americana; retail and wholesale to other dealers including large marketing companies; inventory includes over 5.7 million pieces in stock.

Glen Johnson
Glen Johnson United States Currency
P.O. Box 3260
West Orange, NJ 07052
info@uspapermoney.com
http://www.uspapermoney.com
Specializes in US paper money; auctions, images, info.

Russell Kaye
P.O. Box 635
Shrub Oak, NY 10588
ph: 914-528-1496
rkaye@sellitstore.com
http://www.sellitstore.com
Buys and sells old US currency, 1700s through 1929; send photocopy or email of items for sale; especially interested in large size notes, National currency, broken banknotes and scrip.

William S. Panitch
William S. Panitch, Inc.
855 Central Ave., Ste. #103
Albany, NY 12206
ph: 518-489-4400
fax: 518-489-2776
wpanitch@aol.com
Dealers, appraisers, consultants for US and foreign coins, paper money; free brochure.

Art Leister
Commercial Coin Co.
1611 Market St.
P.O. Box 607
Camp Hill, PA 17001-0607
ph: 717-737-8981 or 717-761-8264
Buys and sells national banknotes.

James Miller
DeucemanCurrency.com
P.O. Box 2094
Waycross, GA 31502-2094
ph: 912-338-0190 or 912-614-4980
jwmiller11@aol.com
http://www.DeucemanCurrecny.com
Buys, sells, appraises all types of US currency with an emphasis on

obsolete/broken bank notes; member of PCDA and SPMC.

Stephen M. Sullivan
Capital Currency, Incorporated
P.O. Box 361632
Melbourne, FL 32936-1632
ph: 321-773-5305
errors@capcurr.com
http://www.capcurr.com
Appraiser, auctioneer, collector, dealer, expert in US currency; full service dealer for rare US currency; author of "The US Error Note Encyclopedia."

Donald C. Kelly
P.O. Box 85
Oxford, OH 45056
ph: 513-523-6861
don@donckelly.com
http://www.donckelly.com
Specializes in paper money from Continental Currency to National Bank Notes.

Gary Adkins
MGS & NSI
5599 W. 78th St.
Minneapolis, MN 55439
ph: 800-653-615 or 952-946-8877
fax: 952-946-8944
gary@coindeals.com
http://www.coindeals.com
Appraises, buys, sells all US collector coins and paper money; member of ANA, PNG, ISA; over 35 years in business.

Tom Sluszkiewicz
ATS Numismatics
P.O. Box 54521
Burnaby, British Columbia V5E 4J6 Canada
ats@atsnotes.com
http://www.atsnotes.com
Buys and sells numismatic world banknotes, local and private paper money, collectibles bonds and stock certificates.

Experts

Ken D. Tanaka
Nova Online, Inc.
P.O. Box 231028
Portland, OR 97281-1028
ph: 503-670-9855
fax: 503-670-9855
ken@novacoins.com
http://www.novacoins.com
Specialist in all forms of paper money; offering evaluations and appraisals; also buys and sells paper money.

Internet Resources

Ron Wise
Ron Wise's World Paper Money Homepage
425 University Blvd., Room 001E
Indianapolis, IN 46202
rjwise1@iupui.edu
http://www.banknoteworld.com
The largest collection of currency images on the Internet; over 4,000.

Cael Chappell
CollectPaperMoney.com
504 Jenifer Court
Santa Rosa, CA 95404
cael@collectpapermoney.com
http://www.collectpapermoney.com
Banknote features, collector tips, currency identifiers, reference books, Q&A, lots of related links.

Misc. Services

Currency Grading & Authentication, Inc.
P.O. Box 418
Three Bridges, NJ 08887
ph: 908-788-8866
fax: 908-788-1677

Periodicals

Stacie Berger
Krause Publications
Newspaper: Bank Note Reporter
700 E. State St.
Iola, WI 54990-0001
ph: 715-445-2214
fax: 715-445-4087
stacie.berger@fwpubs.com
http://www.krause.com
Monthly news source and marketplace for collectors of US and world paper money, notes, checks and related fiscal paper.

Token Publishing, Ltd.
Magazine: Coin News
Orchard House
Duchy Rd., Heathpark
Honiton, Devon EX14 1YD U.K.
ph: +44 1404 46972
fax: +44 1404 44788
info@coin-news.com
http://www.coin-news.com
A monthly English publication focusing on coins and paper money.

Paper Money (World)
Clubs/Associations

Milan Alusic
International Bank Note Society (USA)
P.O. Box 1642
Racine, WI 53401
Formed in 1961 for collectors of world paper money; USA office.

International Bank Note Society (UK)
36B Dartmouth Park Hill
Tufnell Park
London, NW5 1HN U.K.
ph: 0171 281 0839
Formed in 1961 for collectors of world paper money; U.K. office.

Dealers

Donald Arnone
P.O. Box 240
Bohemia, NY 11716-0240
On this Web site you will find some good information on collecting and grading paper money; member IBNS and the ANA.

Steve Eyer
P.O. Box 123 -MAC
Mount Zion, IL 62549-0123
ph: 217-864-4321
fax: 217-864-3021
steve@eyersworld.com
http://www.eyersworld.com
Specializes in World Paper Money, and issues weekly price lists and newsletters; write to subscribe at no charge.

Gary Snover
P.O. Box 9696
San Bernardino, CA 92427-0696
ph: 909-883-5849
fax: 909-886-6874
garysnover@cs.com
http://www.coinmall.com/snover
Buys and sells world banknotes; send for free catalog; active buyer of all world paper money.

Peter Hill
Classy Collectables
P.O. Box 521
Morwell, Victoria 3840 Australia
ph: 03 5134 2698
fax: 03 5134 2348
p+whill@sympac.com.au
http://www.classycollectables.com.au
Dealer in World Banknotes for the beginner to the serious collector/ investor.

Kristian Chiduch
Worldbanknotes
C/. Escultor Alfonso Gabino, 7
Valencia, 46022 Spain
ph: 96 332 08 35
fax: 96 332 08 35
banknote@mail.ono.es
http://www.geocities.com/ billetes_y_monedas/pagina1.htm
Offers one of the largest stocks of world banknotes on the Internet; instructions to collecting paper money; extensive price list; Web site in English, Spanish and German.

Yasha Beresiner
InterCol Gallery
43 Templars Crescent
London, N3 3QR U.K.
ph: (00 44) 208349 2207 or (00 44) 207354 2599
fax: (00 44) 208346 9539
yasha@compuserve.com
http://www.intercol.co.uk
Buys and sells world banknotes, all playing cards, old maps, related books on Free Masonry.

Experts

Neil Shafer
P.O. Box 170138
Milwaukee, WI 53217
ph: 414-352-5962
fax: 414-352-5974
nelsshaf@aol.com
Editor of "Standard Catalog of World Paper Money."

Play Money

Clubs/Associations

Jack Phillips
American Play Money Society
Newsletter: Fun Money
2044 Pine Lake Trail, NW
Arab, AL 35016
japhillips@mindspring.com
http://members.theglobe.com/japhillips/
play/home.html
*Dedicated to the promotion and
research of play money and related
exonumia.*

Collectors

Richard & Wendy Clothier
881 S. Washington State Rd.
Becket, MA 01223
ph: 413-623-8866 or 413-558-9203
clothier@prodigy.net
http://www.geocities.com/Athens/
Parthenon/7338
*Author of "Play Money of American
Children;" member of American Play
Money Society.*

Jack Phillips
2044 Pine Lake Trail, NW
Arab, AL 35016
japhillips@mindspring.com
http://members.theglobe.com/japhillips/
play/home.html
*Interested in learning about all types
of play money including coins and
currency in all types of materials
including plastic, metal, cardboard,
and paper.*

Russian

Internet Resources

Brent Frampton
Russian Coin World
Russiancoinworld@juno.com
http://www.russiancoinworld.com
*Web site for Russian numismatics;
features virtual coin museum, glossary
and coin identification information.*

Silver Dollars

Clubs/Associations

Jeff Oxman, Ed.
Society of Silver Dollar Collectors
Journal: S.S.D.C. Journal
P.O. Box 2123
North Hills, CA 91393
jeffssdc@aol.com
http://www.vamlink.com
*Club's Web site dedicated to Morgan
and Peace silver dollars: updates,
lists, pricing, articles, books, for sale.*

Souvenir Cards

Clubs/Associations

Souvenir Card Collectors Society
Journal: Souvenir Card Journal
P.O. Box 4155
Tulsa, OK 74159-0155
ph: 918-664-6724
dmarr5569@aol.com
*Souvenir cards are 8-1/2" x 11" cards
with engraved reproductions of*

*philatelic or numismatic designs from
original plates.*

Supplies For

Suppliers

Lighthouse Publications
P.O. Box 705
Hackensack, NJ 07602-0705
ph: 201-342-1513 or 888-269-1513
fax: 201-342-7142
info@usa.leuchtturm.com
http://www.leuchtturm.com/us
*Carries full line of products for the
coin and stamp collector: albums,
binders, blank pages, magnifiers,
tongs, UV lamps.*

Brooklyn Gallery Coin & Stamp
8725 Fourth Ave.
P.O. Box 146
Brooklyn, NY 11209-0146
ph: 718-745-5701
fax: 718-745-2775
info@brooklyngallery.com
http://www.brooklyngallery.com
Send $1.50 for 100+ page catalog.

COLLAR BUTTONS & PINS

(see CLOTHING & ACCESSORIES,
Vintage; CUFF LINKS)

COLLECTIBLES

(see ANTIQUES & COLLECTIBLES;
COLLECTIBLES [MODERN])

COLLECTIBLES (MODERN)

(see also ANIMATION FILM ART;
DOLLS; ENESCO; FIGURINES;
MINIATURES, Sculptures; PRINTS
[MODERN]; STEIFF)

Clubs/Associations

Ann Marie Smith, Dir.
National Association of Limited Edition
Dealers
236 Route 38 West, Ste. 100
Moorestown, NJ 08057
ph: 800-446-2533 or 312-782-5252
fax: 312-236-1140
asmith@ahint.com
http://www.naled.com
*An association of retailers of artwork
and collectibles including figurines,
Christmas ornaments, dolls, plates,
crystal, prints, houses, plush,
miniatures, and musicals.*

Cowboy Collector Society, c/o Shade
Tree Creations, Inc.
4248 Burningtown Rd.
Franklin, NC 28734
ph: 800-327-6923 or 828-524-0863
fax: 704-349-3253
billvernon@hotmail.com
http://www.billvernon.com

Karen Feil, Mng. Dir.
Gifts & Collectibles Guild
77 W. Washington St., Ste. 1716
Chicago, IL 60602
ph: 312-379-2935
fax: 312-379-2939
cggnews@aol.com
http://www.giftguild.org
*Trade association of the leading
producers of contemporary limited
editions and collectibles ranging from
art prints to porcelain figures, dolls,
plates, diecast, and more.*

Dealers

Jim Darwiche
Touch of Class, A
ph: 800-726-1803
touchoclass@wyoming.com
http://www.topgifts.com
*Specializes in G. Armani, Disney,
Lladro, Lladro Goyescas, Legend,
Swarovski, Wee Forest, and other
contemporary collectibles.*

Bob Dorman
New England Collectibles Exchange
201 Pine Ave.
Clarksburg, MA 01247-4640
ph: 413-663-3643
fax: 413-663-5140
nece@collectiblesbroker.com
http://www.collectiblesbroker.com
*Lists, buys, sells or trades limited
editions and retired pieces; Boyds
Bears, Cherished Teddies, Harbour
Lights, Harmony Kingdom, Cat's
Meow, Dept. 56, Shelia's, Hummel,
Swarovski, Disney Classics, Tom
Clark Gnomes, Boyds Bears, others.*

Mary Gavrilles
Collector's Cabinet
293 Turnpike Rd., #722
Westborough, MA 01581
ph: 800-847-5283
collector@collectors-cabinet.com
http://www.collectors-cabinet.com
*Online collectibles super store: limited
edition plates, figurines, dolls,
ornaments, lithographs, and more;
over 1800 items pictured: Disney
Classics, Hummels, Hibel, David
Winter, Sandra Kuck, DeGrazia,
Titanic, Bradford, etc.*

Linda's Originals & The Yankee
Craftsmen
220 Rt. 6A
Brewster, MA 02631
ph: 800-385-4758
collects@tiac.net
http://www.my-collectibles.com
*All God's Children, Armani, Annalee
Dolls, Byers Choice, Cat's Meow,
Cherished Teddies, Dept. 56, Harbour
Lights, Hummel, Krystonia, Lilliput
Lane, Shelia's, Steinbeck, and more.*

Elissa Cohen ISA CAPP, GG
Suburban Jewelers
126 East Front St.
Plainfield, NJ 07060-1202
ph: 908-756-1774 or 800-272-1315
fax: 908-756-6596
lisa@suburbanjewelers.com
http://www.suburbanjewelers.com
*Authorized dealer of Lladro, Hummel,
Precious Moments, Swarovski, All
God's Children, Sarah's Attic, G.
Armani, Miss Martha, Ebony Visions,
Tom Clark, and other modern
collectibles; buys, sells, trades.*

Jerry Ellner
Someone Special
1830 Route 70 East
Cherry Hill, NJ 08003
ph: 609-424-1914 or 800-237-7656
info@someonespecial.com
http://www.someonespecial.com
*Web site has over 9,000 items, over
8,500 images, and over 1,300 pages:
Armani, Boehm, Belleek, Cardew
teapots, Chilmark pewter, Lowell
Davis, Emmett Kelly Jr., Forma
Vitrum, Hummels, Harbour Lights,
Hibel, Maruri, Olszewski and more.*

Andy Halapin
European Treasures
4201 Murray Ave.
Pittsburgh, PA 15217
ph: 412-421-8660 or 800-561-8660
fax: 412-421-3575
info@eurotreas.com
http://www.eurotreas.com
*Specializes in fine collectibles by
David Winter, Fontanini, Franklin
Mint, Armani, Harmony Kingdom,
Lenox, Paper Weights, Radko,
Swarovski, Disney and many more.*

Irv Losman
Tiara Galleries & Gifts
1675 Rockville Pike
Congressional Plaza
Rockville, MD 20852
ph: 301-468-1122 or 800-748-4272
fax: 301-468-1481
tiara@tiatagalleries.com
http://www.tiaragalleries.com
*Carries Armani, Lladro, Herend,
Waterford, Swarovski, Hummel, Dept.
56, Thomas Kinkade, Harmony
Kingdom, Brighton Leather &
Jewelry, Vera Bradley, and others.*

Donny Biggs
Biggs Limited Editions
10101 Brook Rd., Ste. 604
Glen Allen, VA 23059
ph: 804-553-1800 or 800-362-0677
fax: 804-553-1520
sales@biggsltd.com
http://www.biggsltd.com
*Carries lots of limited edition dolls
(Ashton Drake dealer of the year);
also Chilmark, Hummel, David
Winter, Lladro, Jan Hagara, Lowell
Davis, Maud Humphrey, Swarovski,
etc.*

Linda Ross Hughes
Best Collectibles
16151 Morganton Highway
P.O. Box 152
Morganton, GA 30560-0152
ph: 706-838-5920
fax: 706-838-4008
bestcollectibles@tds.net
http://www.bestcollectibles.com
*A secondary market for retired and
limited edition collectibles featuring
Byers' Choice, Dept. 56, Lefton,
Cherished Teddies, Charming Tails,
Dreamsicles, NASCAR, Walt Disney
Classics and many others.*

Mary Ann Lowery
Crystal Corner, Inc., The
317 Billy Dyar Blvd.
P.O. Box 756
Boaz, AL 35957-0756
ph: 256-593-6169
fax: 256-593-6560
ccorner@hiwaay.net
http://www.crystalcorner.com
*Carries Boyd's Bears, Cherished
Teddies, Bradford collectible plates,
Hawthorne Villages, Ashton Drake
dolls, etc.*

Graham's Crackers Inc.
5981 E. 86th St.
Indianapolis, IN 46250
ph: 317-842-5727 or 800-442-5727
fax: 317-577-7777
info@grahamscrackers.com
http://www.grahamscrackers.com
*Christopher Radko, Department 56,
Fontanini, Steinbach and Ulbricht
nutcrackers, Beyer's Choice.*

Tom Fritz
Fritz Gifts & Collectibles
1325 N. Telegraph Rd.
Monroe, MI 48162
ph: 734-241-6760
fax: 734-241-6768
tom@fritzgifts.com
http://www.fritzgifts.com
*Has over 13 years experience in gifts
and collectibles; information about
thousands of the most popular
collectibles available.*

British Collectibles
917 Chicago Ave.
Evanston, IL 60202
ph: 800-634-0431 or 847-570-4867
fax: 847-570-4871
Britcol@msn.com
http://www.britishcollectibles.com
*Produces Toby Jugs designed by
Francis Salmon and Kevin Pearson;
carries a wide assortment of modern
collectibles, focusing on British.*

Ken Armke
OHI Exchange
Newsletter: OHI Exchange Newsletter
553 Landa St.
New Braunfels, TX 78130
ph: 830-629-1191
fax: 830-606-1118
Comments@OHIExchange.com
http://www.ohioexchange.com/steins
Acts as broker to match buyers and

*sellers of all limited edition
collectibles such as collector plates,
figurines, bells, ornaments, dolls, etc.;
Dept. 56, David Winter, Lowell
Davis, Hummel, Duncan Royale, etc.*

Genevra Fox
Fox's Gifts & Collectables
7030 5th Ave.
Scottsdale, AZ 85251
ph: 602-947-0560 or 800-592-2555
*Specializes in modern collectibles by
Ted DeGrazia, Cat's Meow, J.
Hagara, Dept. 56, and Bradford
plates.*

Mickey Kaz
Collectibles Unlimited
P.O. Box 606
Woodland Hills, CA 91365-0606
ph: 818-703-6173
fax: 818-703-6173
mickey@collectibles-unlimited.com
http://www.collectibles-unlimited.com
*Specializes in contemporary collectible
plates, figurines, dolls, and more.*

Aine Dugan
Holiday Gift & Craft Shop
526 19th Ave. E
Seattle, WA 98112
ph: 206-328-7158
fax: 206-325-4030
ainedugan@earthlink.net
http://www.holidaygift-craftshop.com
*Carries Just The Right Shoe, Take A
Seat, Daddy's Long Legs, Van Mark,
Snowbabies, Boyds Collection, Harry
Potter, Snowbunnies, Lord of the
Rings, Flower Fairies Collection,
Pooh & Friends, etc.*

Eva Flynn
Eva Flynn Collectibles & Antiques
P.O. Box 1011
Carlsborg, WA 98324-1011
ph: 360-683-7725
evaflynn@tenforward.com
http://www.isnbiz.com/evaflynn
*Specializes in B&G/RC Christmas
plates; search service for back issues
for most major collectibles including
Disney, Raggedy Ann, Peanuts,
Rockwell, Hummels, Royal Doulton,
doll plates, Ferrandiz, Veneto Flair,
Rosenthal; send SASE.*

Lynn Hamilton
Over The Rainbow Collectables
1711-714 The West Mall
Toronto, ON M9C 4X1 Canada
ph: 416-622-6835
otrcollectables@netscape.net
*Carries a large selection of David
Winter, plates, figurines, Bradford,
Reco, Hamilton, Enesco, Precious
Moments, etc.*

Russell Schooley
C&S Collectables Direct
Ford Lane
Arundel, West Sussex BN18 0EF U.K.
ph: (01144) (0) 1243 555371
fax: (01144) (0) 1243 554981
enquiries@cscollectables.co.uk
http://www.cscollectables.co.uk
*Wade limited editions, official Wade
Collectors' Centre, licensed Betty
Boop, Peanuts, Thomas the tank,
Snoopy, Disney, Garfield, Arthur
Hare, Wedgwood, Warner Bros.,
Hagen Renaker Official UK
Collectors' Centre.*

Experts

Karen Feil, Ex. Dir.
Collectors' Information Bureau
Newsletter: C.I.B. Report & Showcase,
The
77 W. Washington St., Ste. 1716
Chicago, IL 60602
ph: 312-379-2940
fax: 312-379-2939
CIBnews@aol.com
http://www.collectorsinfo.com
*CIB provides collectors with the most
accurate and up-to-date information
on limited edition plates, figurines,
bells, graphics, ornaments, and dolls;
publishes an annual "Collectibles
Price Guide" and a quarterly
newsletter.*

Internet Resources

Karen Feil, Ex. Dir.
Collectors' Information Bureau
Directory: Directory to Secondary Market
Retailers
77 W. Washington St., Ste. 1716
Chicago, IL 60602
ph: 312-379-2940
fax: 312-379-2939
CIBnews@aol.com
http://www.collectorsinfo.com
*Your complete source for the latest
information about Limited Edition
Collectibles; collectibles reports, price
guides, manufacturers, dealer search,
clubs, tours, and lots more.*

Darryl Kirk
World Collectors Net
8 Aldous Court, Clifton Rd.
Kingston-upon-Thames, Surrey KT2
6PH U.K.
ph: 011 44 7071 225 404
fax: 011 44 7071 225 404
info@worldcollectorsnet.com
http://www.worldcollectorsnet.com
*An online resource that provides news,
information, message boards, and
chat rooms for a number of
collectibles; also a free online
Collectors Magazine featuring
articles, clubs and magazines from
around the world.*

Man./Prod./Dist.

American Artists
P.O. Box 536
Cold Spring Harbor, NY 11724
ph: 800-828-0086
AmericanArt1@aol.com
*Manufactures and distributes limited
edition plates, figurines and prints by
artists such as Fred Stone, Donald
Zolan and Susan Leigh.*

Anna-Perenna, Inc.
35 River St.
New Rochelle, NY 10801
ph: 914-633-3777 or 800-627-2550
fax: 914-633-8727
*Manufactures and publishes limited
edition figurines, sculpture and plates
by artists such as P. Buckley Moss.*

Heio Reich
Reco International Corp.
138 Haven Ave.
Port Washington, NY 11050
ph: 516-767-2400 or 800-221-5356
fax: 516-767-2409
customerservice@buylink.com
http://www.reco.buylink.com
*Distributor of collector plates, bells,
Christmas ornaments, dolls,
handpainted 3-dimentional plates,
figurines and graphics based in
designs by noted artists such as John
McClelland, Greg Perillo, Sandra
Kuck, Guy Buffet & others.*

United States Historical Society
25 E. Main St.
Richmond, VA 23219
ph: 804-648-4736 or 800-788-4478
fax: 804-648-0002
dolls@ushsdolls.com
http://www.ushsdolls.com
*Direct mail marketer of plates,
figurines, dolls and Christmas
ornaments in stained glass, pewter,
porcelain and other materials.*

James Measell
Fenton Art Glass Company, The
Newsletter: Glass Messenger
700 Elizabeth St.
Williamstown, WV 26187-1028
ph: 304-375-6122 or 800-249-4527
fax: 304-375-7833
askfenton@fentonartglass.com
http://www.fentonartglass.com
*Manufactures collectible plates,
figurines and bells.*

Cavanagh Group International
1665 Bluegrass Lakes Pkwy.
Alpharetta, GA 30004-7757
ph: 678-366-2800
fax: 678-366-2801
info@cavanaghgrp.com
http://www.cavanaghgrp.com
*Manufacturer of high-quality
porcelain buildings, ornaments and
figurines.*

Flambro Imports, Inc.
1530 Ellsworth Industrial Dr.
Atlanta, GA 30318-3752
ph: 800-352-6276 or 404-352-1381
fax: 404-352-2150
flambro@flambro.com
http://www.flambro.com
Importer of collectible clowns (Emmett Kelly, Jr.) and circus-related items, plates, ornaments, figurines and miniatures.

Niche Software, Inc.
Software: Doll & Figurine Collector, The
7118 NW Terrace
Parkland, FL 33076
ph: 954-344-6561
marketing@collectiblessoftware.com
http://www.collectiblessoftware.com
Designed for the collector of dolls, figurines, and accessories.

American Greetings Corp.
One American Rd.
Cleveland, OH 44144
ph: 216-252-7300 or 800-321-3040
fax: 216-252-6777
http://www.corporate.americangreetings.com
World's largest manufacturer of greeting cards and social expression products, gift wrap and accessories, Christmas ornaments, collector plates, etc.; licenses Holly Hobbie, Strawberry Shortcake, and the Care Bears.

Midwest of Cannon Falls, Inc.
32067 64th Ave.
P.O. Box 20
Cannon Falls, MN 55009-0020
ph: 507-263-4261 or 800-776-2075
fax: 507-263-7752
webmaster@mcfcannon.com
http://www.midwestofcannonfalls.com
Imports and wholesales unique seasonal decor items and gifts from around the world - bells, paperweights, dolls, ornaments, figurines, German nutcrackers, etc.; for Christmas, Fall/Halloween, Thanksgiving, Spring/Easter.

ENESCO Corp.
225 Windsor Dr.
Itasca, IL 60143
ph: 630-875-5300 or 800-436-3726
fax: 630-875-5359
caffairs@enesco.com
http://www.enesco.com
Giftware company produces/designs fine gifts & collectibles: figurines, musicals, waterballs, etc. by Precious Moments and others.

Hamilton Collection, The
9307 N. Milwaukee Ave.
Niles, IL 60714-1381
ph: 877-268-6638 or 847-581-8452
fax: 847-966-2875
http://www.collectiblestoday.com
Formerly The Hamilton Mint now a division of the Bradford Exchange; produces collectible plates, die cast,

dolls, prints, boxes, figurines and dolls.

Dave Grossman Creations
1608 N. Warson Rd.
Saint Louis, MO 63132
ph: 314-423-5600 or 800-325-1655
fax: 314-423-7620
dgcrea@aol.com
Producer of collectible plates, ornaments and figurines including Rockwell, Gone With the Wind, Wizard of Oz, and Emmett Kelly, Sr.

Robert M. Ready
World of Products
1410 Oak Tree Dr.
Houston, TX 77055-4316
Colorful catalog full of modern collectibles, knickknacks, curios: figurines, lit cottages, night lights, miniature furniture, carousel horses, frames, wall decor, music boxes, brass and wood sculptures, music boxes, "Mandarin" ivory.

Willitts Designs
1129 Industrial Ave.
P.O. Box 750009
Petaluma, CA 94975
ph: 877-587-5877 or 707-778-7211
fax: 707-769-0304
jtrc@willitts.com
http://www.willitts.com
Produces The American Carousel limited edition collections by Tobin Fraley; also other collectibles including plates, figurines, and Just The Right Shoe miniature shoes.

Misc. Services

Unity Marketing
Newsletter: Collectibles Business
188 Cocalico Creek Rd.
Stevens, PA 17578
ph: 717-336-1600
fax: 717-336-1601
mail@unitymarketingonline.com
http://www.unitymarketingonline.com
Specializes in tracking the contemporary collectibles marketplace and in publishing market research studies.

Pam Danziger
Unity Marketing
Newsletter: Collectibles Business
188 Cocalico Creek Rd.
Stevens, PA 17578
ph: 717-336-1600
fax: 717-336-1601
mail@unitymarketingonline.com
http://www.unitymarketingonline.com
Specializes in tracking the contemporary collectibles marketplace and in publishing market research studies.

Periodicals

Geyer-McAllister Publications, Inc.
Magazine: Gifts & Decorative Accessories
345 Hudson St., 4th Floor
New York, NY 10014
ph: 212-519-7200
fax: 212-519-7431
Trade magazine for new gifts,

decorative accessories, collectibles, stationery, gift baskets, and tabletop wares; buyer's resource directory guide available with subscription.

David J. Maloney, ISA CAPP
Sales Online Direct, Inc.
Directory: Maloney's Antiques & Collectibles Resource Directory
P.O. Box 2049
Frederick, MD 21702-1049
ph: 301-228-2279
fax: 301-695-6491
dave@maloney.com
http://www.davidmaloney.com/aboutbook.htm
Publishes major resource information source for collectors, sellers, claims adjusters, etc.: includes experts, buyers, clubs, periodicals, repairers, museums/libraries, appraisers, auctioneers, matching services, dealers, etc.

Linda Kruger, Ed.
Pioneer Communications, Inc.
Magazine: Collectors News
506 Second St.
P.O. Box 306
Grundy Center, IA 50638
ph: 319-824-6981 or 800-352-8039
fax: 319-824-3414
collectors@collectors-news.com
http://www.collectors-news.com
The monthly publication for antiquers & collectors; complete show & sale calendar, articles, expert advice, values, etc.; a special emphasis is always given to contemporary limited edition collectibles: what's new, artists, events.

Linda Kruger, Ed.
Pioneer Communications, Inc.
Magazine: Collector Editions
506 Second St.
P.O. Box 306
Grundy Center, IA 50638
ph: 319-824-6981 or 800-352-8039
fax: 319-824-3414
lkruger@thepioneergroup.com
http://www.collectoreditions.com
A biweekly consumer magazine covering contemporary collector plates, figurines, prints and glass objects; companies, artists, etc.

Stacie Berger
Krause Publications
Magazine: Collector's Mart
700 E. State St.
Iola, WI 54990-0001
ph: 715-445-2214
fax: 715-445-4087
stacie.berger@fwpubs.com
http://www.krause.com
Bi-monthly magazine for limited edition art and collectibles: classifieds, articles, dealers ads, club notices, etc.

Karen Feil, Ex. Dir.
Collectors' Information Bureau
Directory: Directory to Secondary Market Retailers
77 W. Washington St., Ste. 1716
Chicago, IL 60602
ph: 312-379-2940
fax: 312-379-2939
CIBnews@aol.com
http://www.collectorsinfo.com
Lists scores of dealers and exchanges to assist in liquidating, buying, locating, or trading your contemporary limited edition artwork: prints, figurines, plates, bells, ornaments, etc.

Bing & Grondahl

Dealers

Pat Owen
Viking Import House, Inc.
1516 South Federal Highway
Fort Lauderdale, FL 33316
ph: 954-763-3388 or 800-327-2297
fax: 954-462-2317
vikingimp@aol.com
http://www.vikingimporthouse.com
Operates the VIDEX, a buy/sell service for any and all Royal Copenhagen and Bing & Grondahl collectibles; also Rorstrand, Porsgrund, Svend Jensen, and Berlin Design Christmas plates.

Man./Prod./Dist.

Royal Scandinavian, Inc.
140 Bradford Dr.
West Berlin, NJ 08091
ph: 609-768-5400 or 800-431-1992
fax: 800-448-7553
http://www.royalscandinavia.com
Royal Copenhagen, Bing & Grondahl, Holmegaard, and Georg Jensen are the best of Scandinavian collectibles; manufactures dinnerware, cobalt blue underglaze collector plates, figurines, bells, dolls, ornaments and gift accessories.

Buildings

(see also COLLECTIBLES [MODERN], Cottages)

Buildings (Brandywine)

Clubs/Associations

Truman Whiting
Brandywine Neighborhood Association
104 Greene Dr.
Yorktown, VA 23692-4800
ph: 800-336-5031 or 757-898-5031
fax: 757-898-6895
heartbwine@aol.com
http://www.brandywinecollectibles.com
A company sponsored collectors club.

Man./Prod./Dist.

Truman Whiting
Brandywine Woodcrafts Inc.
104 Greene Dr.
Yorktown, VA 23692-4800
ph: 800-336-5031 or 757-898-5031
fax: 757-898-6895
heartbwine@aol.com
http://www.brandywinecollectibles.com
*Manufactures three types of miniature
collectible houses and accessories in
hand painted cast resin and full color
prints on wood; all buildings can be
personalizes with your choice of name
on sign.*

Buildings (Brian Baker)

Clubs/Associations

Brian Baker Collectors' Club
Newsletter: Brian's Backyard
P.O. Box 290682
Tampa, FL 33617
ph: 888-619-9700 or 813-985-8712
fax: 813-985-8530
info@bumbershootstudios.com
http://www.brianbakercollection.com
*A club for collector's of Brian Baker's
architectually-inspired wall
sculptures.*

Man./Prod./Dist.

Giftstar
P.O. Box 290682
Tampa, FL 33617
ph: 888-619-9700 or 813-985-8712
fax: 813-985-8530
info@bumbershootstudios.com
http://www.brianbakercollection.com
*Produces Brian Baker's architectually-
inspired wall sculptures.*

Buildings (Cat's Meow)

Clubs/Associations

Cat's Meow Collectors Club
Newsletter: Village Mews, The
2163 Great Trails Dr.
Wooster, OH 44691-3738
ph: 330-264-1377
fax: 330-263-0219
cmv@fjdesign.com
http://www.catsmeow.com
*For collectors of the Cat's Meow
Village, a product line of two-
dimensional miniature historical
buildings and accessories.*

Man./Prod./Dist.

F.J. Designs, Inc./The Cat's Meow
  Village
2163 Great Trails Dr.
Wooster, OH 44691-3738
ph: 330-264-1377
fax: 330-263-0219
cmv@fjdesign.com
http://www.catsmeow.com
*Manufacturer of the Cat's Meow
Village, a product line of two-
dimensional miniature historical
buildings and accessories.*

Buildings (My Friends & Me)

Man./Prod./Dist.

My Friends & Me
P.O. Box 8000
Spokane, WA 99203
tedebear@erols.com
*4" to 6" hand-cast reproductions of
historic homes.*

Buildings (Shelia's)

Clubs/Associations

Shelia's Collectors Society
Newsletter: Our House
1856 Belgrade Ave.
Charleston, SC 29407
ph: 843-766-0485 or 800-227-6564
fax: 843-556-0040
feedback@shelias.com
http://www.shelias.com
*Miniature handpainted two-
dimensional houses made of wood.*

Man./Prod./Dist.

Shelia's Collectibles
1856 Belgrade Ave.
Charleston, SC 29407
ph: 843-766-0485 or 800-227-6564
fax: 843-556-0040
feedback@shelias.com
http://www.shelias.com
*Miniature handpainted two-
dimensional houses made of wood.*

Buildings (Town Square)

Man./Prod./Dist.

Cavanagh Group International
1665 Bluegrass Lakes Pkwy.
Alpharetta, GA 30004-7757
ph: 678-366-2800
fax: 678-366-2801
info@cavanaghgrp.com
http://www.cavanaghgrp.com
*Manufacturer of high-quality
porcelain buildings, ornaments and
figurines.*

Christmas

Clubs/Associations

Cavanaugh's Coca-Cola Christmas
  Collectors' Society
1665 Bluegrass Lakes Pkwy.
Alpharetta, GA 30004-7757
ph: 678-366-2800
fax: 678-366-2801
info@cavanaghgrp.com
http://www.cavanaghgrp.com
*Sells modern Coca-Cola collectibles
with a Christmas theme.*

Man./Prod./Dist.

Kurt S. Adler
Kurt S. Adler, Inc.
1107 Broadway
New York, NY 10010
ph: 212-924-0900 or 800-243-9627
fax: 212-807-0575
info@kurtadler.com
http://www.kurtadler.com
*The nations leading importer,
designer and supplier of Christmas
ornaments, decorations and
accessories.*

Bob McAdams
Knobstone Studio
5809 West Oak Hill Rd.
Scottsburg, IN 47170
ph: 812-752-7022
fax: 812-752-7022
*Produces collectible old world Santas;
each face is an original (not molded
or cast), bodies are soft sculpture.*

Dan Sherman
Great American Holiday Collectibles
  Company
10567 SW Coleman Loop N.
Wilsonville, OR 97070
ph: 877-399-3111
fax: 815-327-1238
email@dansherman.com
http://www.greatamericancollectibles.net
Manufacturer of old world Santas.

Christmas (Clothtique)

Clubs/Associations

Santa Claus Network
Newsletter: Santa Claus Network
  Newsletter
6 Perry Dr.
Foxboro, MA 02035-1051
ph: 508-543-6667 or 508-543-5412
fax: 508-543-4255
info@possibledreams.com
http://www.possibledreams.com
*Members receive free Possible Dreams
Clothique (stiffened cloth) Santa and
more.*

Possible Dreams Limited
6 Perry Dr.
Foxboro, MA 02035-1051
ph: 508-543-6667 or 508-543-5412
fax: 508-543-4255
info@possibledreams.com
http://www.possibledreams.com
*Manufacturer of the Clothique (uses a
centuries-old method of stiffening
cloth) line of collectible Christmas
ornaments and figurines such as
angels and Santa Claus.*

Clarissa Johnson

Man./Prod./Dist.

Clarissa Johnson
Clarissa's Creations
18111 Meyers
Detroit, MI 48235
ph: 313-341-7762
*Produces original Afro American
artwork: prints, collector plates, and
note and greeting cards designed by
Clarissa Johnson.*

Clowns (Ron Lee)

Clubs/Associations

Ron Lee's Greatest Clown Collector's
  Club
Newsletter: Collectible News From Ron
  Lee
330 Carousel Parkway
Henderson, NV 89014
ph: 800-829-3928 or 702-434-1700
fax: 702-434-4310
info@ronlee.com
http://www.ronlee.com
*For collectors of Ron Lee's fine white
metal or pewter figurines with 24-
karat gold plating and hand painting;
on hand-cut onyx bases with gold
beading.*

Man./Prod./Dist.

Ron Lee's World of Clowns
330 Carousel Parkway
Henderson, NV 89014
ph: 800-829-3928 or 702-434-1700
fax: 702-434-4310
info@ronlee.com
http://www.ronlee.com
*Manufacturer and sculpture of clown
and circus-theme collectibles; fine
white metal or pewter figurines with
24-karat gold plating and hand
painting; on hand-cut onyx bases with
gold beading.*

Computer Programs For

Man./Prod./Dist.

Russ Wood
Collector's Marketplace
Software: Intelligent Collector Software
RD 1 Box 213B
Montrose, PA 18801-9779
ph: 570-278-2099
cmonline@epix.net
*Lists secondary market products,
mainly Dept. 56; also David Winter,
Lilliput Lane, Swarovski, Lladro,
Precious Moments, Barbie, Disney
Classics, Harbour Lights, Radko, and
others; developer of Windows
software for collectors.*

J. Phillip, Inc.
Software: Collectibles Database for
  Collectors
5870 Zarley St., Ste. C
New Albany, OH 43054
ph: 800-407-4147 or 614-933-0887
fax: 614-855-7893
info@collectiblesdatabase.com
http://www.msdatabase.com
*Program includes one price guide;
purchase additional price guides for:
Longaberger baskets, Precious
Moments, Hallmark, Harbour Lights,
Boyds Bears, Christopher Radko,
Dept. 56, Disney Classics, Forma
Vitrum, Cherished Teddies and more.*

Cottages

(see also COLLECTIBLES
[MODERN], Buildings;
COLLECTIBLES [MODERN], Dept.
65)

Man./Prod./Dist.

Department 56, Inc.
Magazine: Celebration
P.O. Box 44456
Eden Prairie, MN 55344-1056
ph: 800-548-8696
fax: 612-943-4500
Mslittown@dept56.com
http://www.department56.com/
home.html
*Produces "Snow Village", "Dickens'
Village" and other lighted houses and
accessories.*

Cottages (David Winter)

Appraisers

Sherry Greener
Greener Collectibles
8697 Diablo View Lane
Winters, CA 95694
ph: 530-795-3710
fax: 530-795-3815
sheg621@aol.com
*Certified appraiser of David Winter
Cottages through the International
Society of Appraisers; is considered an
expert by collectors worldwide.*

Clubs/Associations

Enesco David Winter Cottages
Collectors Guild
Magazine: Cottage Country
225 Windsor Dr.
Itasca, IL 60143
ph: 630-875-5300 or 800-436-3726
fax: 630-875-5359
caffairs@enesco.com
http://www.enesco.com
*For David Winter Cottage collectors;
membership includes "Cottage
Country" magazine plus the "Squeek"
& "Studio News" newsletters,
members-only pieces, complimentary
gift from David Winter.*

Dealers

Stan Worrey
Colonial House Antiques
182 Front St.
Berea, OH 44017-1920
ph: 440-826-4169 or 800-344-9299
fax: 440-826-0839
*Specializes in David Winter and
Lilliput Lane cottages; mail lists on
request.*

Cottages (Forma Vitrum)

Man./Prod./Dist.

Forma Vitrum
Newsletter: Vitreville Voice
1665 Bluegrass Lakes Pkwy, St. 100
Roswell, GA 30004-7757
ph: 770-643-1175 or 800-537-7899
fax: 770-643-1172
formavit@aol.com
http://www.formavit.com
*Manufacturer of collectible lit glass
cottages handcrafted by artist Bill
Job.*

Cottages (Hawthorne)

Man./Prod./Dist.

Hawthorne Villages
9307 N. Milwaukee Ave.
Niles, IL 60714-1381
ph: 877-268-6638 (US) or 800-265-1027
(Canada)
http://www.hawthorne.com
*A leading marketer of highly detailed
architectural miniatures with an
emphasis on sculptures inspired by
traditional architecture.*

Cottages (Lemax)

Clubs/Associations

Gaston Lee
Lemax Collectors Club
Newsletter: Collector's Club Journal
25 Pequot Way
Canton, MA 02021-2354
ph: 888-536-2988 or 781-821-4555
fax: 781-821-4455
lemax@earthlink.net
A company-sponsored collectors' club.

Man./Prod./Dist.

Gaston Lee
Lemax, Inc.
25 Pequot Way
Canton, MA 02021-2354
ph: 888-536-2988 or 781-821-4555
fax: 781-821-4455
lemax@earthlink.net
*Produces the Lemax Dickensvale
Collectible line of fine handcrafted
porcelain cathedrals, quaint cottages,
and accessories.*

Cottages (Liberty Falls)

Clubs/Associations

Robyn Rosenberg
Liberty Falls Collectors Club
60 Revere Dr., Ste. 725
Northbrook, IL 60062
ph: 847-291-0282
LibertyFalls@ameritech.net
http://www.libertyfalls.com/libertyfalls
*Collectors of a line of resin molded
miniature cottages based on a
fictitious late 1800s Colorado mining
town.*

Cottages (Lilliput Lane)

Clubs/Associations

Enesco Lilliput Lane Collectors' Club
225 Windsor Dr.
Itasca, IL 60143
ph: 630-875-5300 or 800-436-3726
fax: 630-875-5359
caffairs@enesco.com
http://www.enesco.com
*For collectors of Lilliput Lane
miniature cottages.*

Experts

Annette Power
4 Queens Parade Close
London, N11 3FY U.K.
ph: +44 0208 361 7787 or 800-514-8176
fax: +44 0208 361 4143
tpower@globalnet.co.uk
http://www.tablewhere.co.uk
*Author of "The Collector's Handbook
of Lilliput Lane Cottages."*

Man./Prod./Dist.

ENESCO Corp.
225 Windsor Dr.
Itasca, IL 60143
ph: 630-875-5300 or 800-436-3726
fax: 630-875-5359
caffairs@enesco.com
http://www.enesco.com

Cottages (Pleasantville)

Clubs/Associations

Mary Lee Graham
Pleasantville 1893 Historical Preservation Society, c/o Flambro
Newsletter: Pleasantville Gazette
1530 Ellsworth Industrial Dr.
Atlanta, GA 30318-3752
ph: 800-355-2582 or 404-352-1381
fax: 404-352-2150
flambro@flambro.com
http://www.flambro.com
*Bisque porcelain village figurines by
Joan Berg Victor; sponsored by
Flambro, Inc; gazette, Pleasantville
Gazette lighted building, lapel pin,
and retailer listing.*

Cottages (Windy Meadows)

Clubs/Associations

Jan Richardson
Windy Meadows Pottery Collector Club,
c/o Windy Meadows Pottery
1036 Valley Rd.
Knoxville, MD 21758
ph: 301-834-8857 or 800-527-6274
fax: 301-663-0612
info@windymeadowspottery.com
http://www.windymeadowspottery.com
*Specializes in the original hand-
constructed stoneware Windy
Meadows candlehouses & cottages
designed by Jan Richardson. A
company-sponsored club.*

Man./Prod./Dist.

Jan Richardson
Windy Meadows Pottery
1036 Valley Rd.
Knoxville, MD 21758
ph: 301-834-8857 or 800-527-6274
fax: 301-663-0612
info@windymeadowspottery.com
http://www.windymeadowspottery.com

Crystal

Man./Prod./Dist.

Crystallite
963 Transport Way
Petaluma, CA 94954
ph: 800-999-9856 or 707-765-0500
fax: 707-765-0600
*Distributes Austrian crystal figurines
by Charles Castelli and cold-cast
porcelain fantasy figurines by Mark
Newman and Randy Bowen.*

Repair Services

Allan B. Mittelmark
366 Clinton Ave.
Cedarhurst, NY 11516
ph: 516-569-2000
fax: 516-569-2001
*Crystal repair including lead crystal
and Swarovski crystal.*

Crystal (Crystal Reflection)

Man./Prod./Dist.

Crystal Reflection
201 South Hill Drive
Brisbane, CA 94005
ph: 415-468-2520 or 800-255-3536
fax: 415-468-6368
tecno@tecnodisplay.com
http://www.tecnodisplay.com
*A leader in the design and production
of 32% Austrian lead crystal
collectibles.*

Crystal (Crystal World)

Man./Prod./Dist.

Crystal World Co., The
89 Leuning St., Unit A-2
South Hackensack, NJ 07606
ph: 201-488-0909 or 800-445-4251
fax: 201-488-7447
trinaw@crystalworld.com
http://www.crystalworld.com
*America's premier producer of full-
cut, faceted crystal figurines; offers a
wide selection of award-winning
crystal gifts and collectibles, including
Disney Showcase Collection, wildlife
figures, Teddy Bears, famous
buildings, etc.*

Crystal (Silver Deer)

Clubs/Associations

Silver Deer Collectors' Club
963 Transport Way
Petaluma, CA 94954
ph: 707-765-8311 or 800-729-3337
fax: 707-765-0770
ambcrystallite@att.net
*A manufacturer-sponsored club
offering members-only figurines,
special club activities and promotions,
and a quarterly newsletter with
information about designers, product
retirements and upcoming events.*

Man./Prod./Dist.

Silver Deer, Ltd.
963 Transport Way
Petaluma, CA 94954
ph: 707-765-8311 or 800-729-3337
fax: 707-765-0770
ambcrystallite@att.net
Designs, manufactures and distributes limited edition crystal figurines and other giftware.

Crystal (Swarovski)

Appraisers

Jane Warner, ISA
Warner's Books
7613 W. Frederick-Garland Rd.
Union, OH 45322-9621
ph: 937-698-4508
fax: 937-698-5408
jane@wbrb.com
http://www.wbrb.com
Appraises crystal and specializes in Swarovski crystal.

Clubs/Associations

Swarovski Collectors Society, c/o
Swarovski America, Ltd.
Newsletter: Swarovski Collector
1 Kenney Dr.
Cranston, RI 02920
ph: 800-289-4900
fax: 401-463-8459
manuela.sieberer@swarovski.com
http://www.swarovski.com
Focuses on Austrian Swarovski crystal figurines and giftware. Sponsored by Swarovski America, Ltd.

Pat King
Crystal Fanatics Club for Collectors of
Swarovski Crystal
4100 No. Hwy. A1A, #323
Fort Pierce, FL 34949-8345
pat@crystalfanaticsclub.com
http://www.CrystalFanaticsClub.com
Web site/club expressly for collectors of Swarovski Crystal from around the world; lots of useful information, message boards, evening chats, photo galleries, and links for the avid collector.

Collectors

Jimer DeVries
9740 Campo Rd., #134
Spring Valley, CA 91977-1415
ph: 619-462-2333
fax: 619-462-5517
JimerD@swanseekers.com
http://www.swanseekers.com
A long-time Swarovski collector; knowledgeable about manufacturing variations and values of current and retired Swarovski Silver Crystal including items not available at retail in USA.

Dealers

Cindy Morton
Morton's Crystal
600 Harbor Blvd.
Union City, NJ 07087
ph: 201-865-7777
fax: 201-865-7777
mail@mortonscrystal.com
http://www.mortonscrystal.com

Gregg Shienbaum
Lladro Connection, A
30 NE 1st St.
Miami, FL 33132
ph: 800-984-5586
illum1@aol.com
http://www.illumcollectibles.com
Specializing in current and retired Swarovski and Lladro; also carries a complete line of Lalique and Kosta Boda.

Cindy Morton
Morton's Crystal, Inc.
8112 Lone Tree Glen
Bradenton, FL 34202-2414
ph: 941-907-9892
mail@mortonscrystal.com
http://www.mortonscrystal.com
An exclusive secondary market service for retired and limited edition Swarovski crystal and unique items made by Swarovski; will provide information on value; buys, sells, auctions Swarovski crystal.

David & Angie McIntosh
Crystal Exchange America
6505 Browns Run Rd.
Middletown, OH 45042
ph: 513-423-5272
fax: 513-423-8318
angie@crystalexchange.com
http://www.crystalexchange.com
Swarovski secondary market specialists; brokerage service for buying and selling retired and limited edition Swarovski; current product offerings available at the Web site.

Robert Gilson
Always Crystal
Kenwood Towne Centre #93
7875 Montgomery Rd.
Cincinnati, OH 45236
ph: 513-891-0730 or 800-906-7654
fax: 513-891-0751
customerservice@alwayscrystal.com
http://www.alwayscrystal.com
A premiere Swarovski crystal dealer; offers fine crystal collectibles by Swarovski and Waterford.

Robin Yaw
Crystal Connection, The
Newsletter: Crystal News
8510 N. Knoxville Ave. #218
Peoria, IL 61615-2034
ph: 309-692-2221 or 800-692-0708
fax: 309-692-2221
crystalconnection@att.net
http://www.crystal.org
A comprehensive listing service for collectors worldwide interested in buying, selling, trading retired

Swarovski crystal on the secondary market; free listings, registration, search, courier delivery and appraisal services; member ISA.

Clark Sanchez
Sanchez Collectibles
1555 East Glendale Ave.
Phoenix, AZ 85020
ph: 602-395-9974 or 602-277-1661
fax: 602-241-0702
Buys, sells, appraises Swarovski crystal; does not sell new pieces, only pre-owned pieces no longer being manufactured; list available for free by snail mail if a mailing address is provided.

Ben Swan
Golden Swan Collectibles
881 Lincoln Way
Auburn, CA 95603
ph: 530-823-7926 or 800-231-9055
fax: 530-823-1945
Offers a "search and find" and a listing service to collectors, buyers and sellers of Lladro figurines; also for Swarovski, Walt Disney Classics, and Disneyana Convention figurines.

Experts

Jane Warner, ISA
Warner's Books
7613 W. Frederick-Garland Rd.
Union, OH 45322-9621
ph: 937-698-4508
fax: 937-698-5408
jane@wbrb.com
http://www.wbrb.com
Appraises and specializes in Swarovski crystal; author of four Warner books now available: "Warner's Blue Ribbon Book on Swarovski Silver Crystal" (plus Companion) and "Warner's Blue Ribbon Book on Swarovski" (plus Companion).

Robin Yaw
Crystal Connection, The
Newsletter: Crystal News
8510 N. Knoxville Ave. #218
Peoria, IL 61615-2034
ph: 309-692-2221 or 800-692-0708
fax: 309-692-2221
crystalconnection@att.net
http://www.crystal.org
Buy, sell, trade appraises retired Swarovski crystal on the secondary market; free listings, registration, search, courier delivery and appraisal services; Accredited Member ISA.

Clark Sanchez
Sanchez Collectibles
1555 East Glendale Ave.
Phoenix, AZ 85020
ph: 602-395-9974 or 602-277-1661
fax: 602-241-0702
Buys, sells, appraises Swarovski crystal; does not sell new pieces, only pre-owned pieces no longer being manufactured; list available for free by snail mail if a mailing address is provided.

Jimer DeVries
Swan Seekers Network
9740 Campo Rd., #134
Spring Valley, CA 91977-1415
ph: 619-462-2333
fax: 619-462-5517
JimerD@swanseekers.com
http://www.swanseekers.com
A long-time Swarovski collector; knowledgeable about manufacturing variations and values of current and retired Swarovski Silver Crystal including items not available at retail in USA.

Internet Resources

Cindy Morton
Morton's Crystal
600 Harbor Blvd.
Union City, NJ 07087
ph: 201-865-7777
fax: 201-865-7777
mail@mortonscrystal.com
http://www.mortonscrystal.com
Extensive informational Web site for collectors of Swarovski crystal; includes many items for sale.

David & Angie McIntosh
Crystal Exchange America
6505 Browns Run Rd.
Middletown, OH 45042
ph: 513-423-5272
fax: 513-423-8318
angie@crystalexchange.com
http://www.crystalexchange.com
Swarovski secondary market specialists; brokerage service for buying and selling retired and limited edition Swarovski; current product offerings available at the Web site.

Man./Prod./Dist.

Swarovski America Ltd.
1 Kenney Dr.
Cranston, RI 02920
ph: 800-289-4900
fax: 401-463-8459
manuela.sieberer@swarovski.com
http://www.swarovski.com

Matching Services

Jimer DeVries
Swan Seekers Network
9740 Campo Rd., #134
Spring Valley, CA 91977-1415
ph: 619-462-2333
fax: 619-462-5517
JimerD@swanseekers.com
http://www.swanseekers.com
Dedicated strictly to the Swarovski secondary market; buy, sell, trade or information about retired and current Swarovski Silver Crystal for collectors in USA and 38 other countries; over 6500 retired items listed.

Periodicals

Dean A. Genth
Newsletter: Crystal Report, The
500 Hallmark Dr.
Eaton, OH 45320
ph: 937-472-4072
fax: 937-472-4081
dean@millershallmark.com
http://www.millershallmark.com
The international forum for collectors of retired Swarovski silver crystal: histories, secondary market reports and prices, information on variations, collector questions and answers, classified ads.

Repair Services

McHugh's Restoration Inc.
3461 W. Cary St.
Richmond, VA 232221
ph: 804-353-9596 or 804-353-9412
mchughs@aol.com
China mending and restoration service; repairs chips, cracks, and fabricates missing pieces; Boehm restorer; official Lladro and Hummel restorer; also official restorers of Swarovski Crystal & Thomas Blackshear pieces produced by Willits.

Tomas Maebrae
Crystal Beaver Collectibles
13 Cardinal Crescent
Petawawa, Ontario K8H 3N9 Canada
ph: 613-687-8667
fax: 613-687-1555
crystalbeaver@sympatico.ca
Repair and restoration of Swarovski crystal items; please contact via email or phone before sending any Swarovski crystal pieces for restoration or repair.

Danbury Mint

Collectors

Jim Crane
15 Clemson Ct.
Newark, DE 19711-4301
ph: 302-738-6031
spcjpc@earthlink.net
Wants Danbury Mint diecast cars as well as other Franklin Mint items such as books and ads.

Man./Prod./Dist.

Danbury Mint, The
47 Richards Ave.
Norwalk, CT 06857
ph: 203-853-2000 or 800-243-4664
fax: 203-847-5251
customerservice@danburymint.com
http://www.danburymintsports.com
A direct mail marketer of collector plates. Also produces miniatures, dolls, figurines and other collectibles.

Dept. 56

Collectors

Sue Coffee
10 Saunders Hollow Rd.
Old Lyme, CT 06371-1126
ph: 860-434-5641
fax: 860-434-3640
SueCoffee@aol.com
http://www.suecoffee.com
Buys and sells retired Dept. 56 snowbabies.

Dealers

Tim Stephenson
Pretty Petals
303 Jefferson Dr.
Smithfield, VA 23430
ph: 757-357-9136
Pretty@visi.net
http://www.pretty-petals.com
Collector and dealer of Dept.56 flowers, landscaping and accessories for all Department 56 villages.

Becky Carter
Becky Carter, Inc.
9605 Red Bird Lane
Alpharetta, GA 30022-8493
ph: 770-475-8138
fax: 770-475-0211
D564U2@aol.com
Department 56: all villages, accessories, snowglobes, miniature snowbabies, ornaments; also handles limited quantities of Hallmark ornaments and WDCC.

Linda Ross Hughes
Best Collectibles
16151 Morganton Highway
P.O. Box 152
Morganton, GA 30560-0152
ph: 706-838-5920
fax: 706-838-4008
bestcollectibles@tds.net
http://www.bestcollectibles.com
An independent exchange service specializing in listing and selling retired and limited edition collectibles for most major collectible lines.

Marilyn & Cecil
Villages Revisited
ph: 850-897-9326
fax: 850-897-2369
villagesrevisited@cox.net
http://www.villagesrevisited.com
Specializes in retired Dept. 56 Snow Village, Dickens, Christmas In The City, North Pole, New England, Alpine, Storybook buildings and accessories in excellent condition with box and sleeve.

Partridge Christmas Shop, The
105 Riverwalk
New Orleans, LA 70130
ph: 504-566-0149
info@thepartridge.com
http://www.thepartridge.com
Sells Heritage Village, Snow Village, Disney Parks Village.

Experts

Peter & Jeanne George
Collectible Source, Inc., The
757 Park Ave.
Cranston, RI 02910-2137
ph: 401-467-9343 or 877-212-4356
fax: 401-467-9359
d56er@aol.com
http://www.villagechronicle.com
Publishers of "The Village Chronicle."

Linda Harlan
4920 Franklin Rd.
Nashville, TN 37210-2834
ph: 800-388-2556 or 615-832-0564
fax: 615-244-1553
http://www.quackin.com/HVY-DUTY
Collector specializing in Dept. 56 ceramic cottages and other Dept. 56 collectibles.

Man./Prod./Dist.

Department 56, Inc.
Magazine: Celebrations
P.O. Box 44456
Eden Prairie, MN 55344-1056
ph: 800-548-8696
fax: 612-943-4500
Mslittown@dept56.com
http://www.department56.com/
home.html
Produces "Snow Village", "Dickens' Village" and other lighted houses and accessories.

Misc. Services

Weishair Custom Software
Software: Village Collector
P.O. Box 717
Albany, MN 56307-0717
ph: 888-745-7031 or 320-845-7031
fax: 320-845-7306
info@villagecollector.com
http://www.villagecollector.com
Software program designed to make keeping track of village collections; pre-loaded with Department 56, Snowbabies, Merry Makers, All Through the House, Winter Silhouette, and others.

Periodicals

Peter & Jeanne George
Collectible Source, Inc., The
Magazine: Village Chronicle, The
757 Park Ave.
Cranston, RI 02910-2137
ph: 401-467-9343 or 877-212-4356
fax: 401-467-9359
d56er@aol.com
http://www.villagechronicle.com
The largest independent publication for Department 56 collectors; the latest news, tips, information, display ideas, informative articles; "All the News that's Lit to Print!"

Linda Harlan
Newsletter: Snowflake News
4920 Franklin Rd.
Nashville, TN 37210-2834
ph: 800-388-2556 or 615-832-0564
fax: 615-244-1553
http://www.quackin.com/HVY-DUTY
A newsletter for Dept. 56 collectors: published bi-monthly, photos, club activities, upcoming activities, collector profiles.

Dolls

(see also DOLLS; DOLLS, Artist)

Auction Services

Nancy Farley
Auctions by Nancy
505 Trelawney Lane
Apex, NC 27502
ph: 919-362-7235
info@auctionsbynancy.com
http://www.auctionsbynancy.com
Conducts auction sales of collectible dolls.

Book Sellers

Scott Publications
30595 Eight Mile
Livonia, MI 48152-1798
ph: 800-458-8237 or 248-477-6650
fax: 248-477-6795
concatus@scottpublications.com
http://www.scottpublications.com
Published two catalogs of books offered: one for the person who does hobby ceramics and another for those interested in dolls (making and collecting).

Clubs/Associations

Jeanne Niswonger
Modern Doll Club
Journal: Modern Doll Club Journal
305 West Beacon Rd.
Lakeland, FL 33803-7248
ph: 863-682-8484
A corresponding club for doll collectors; members receive illustrated journal featuring research articles, doll stories, craft ideas for dolls, patterns, paper dolls, photos, etc.

Shelley Thornton, Sec.
National Institute of American Doll Artists
1600 South 22nd St.
Lincoln, NE 68502
ph: 402-474-7948
shelley@forus.com
http://www.niada.org
An organization of doll artists and supportive patrons whose purpose is to promote the art of the original, handmade doll.

Dealers

Nancie Mann
Mann Gallery - Art of the Doll
P.O. Box 1106
Boston, MA 02117
ph: 617-266-6266
fax: 617-696-6667
artmann@worldnet.att.net
http://www.manngallery.com
Deals in one-of-a-kind and very small editions of dolls created by doll artists; Web site also has lots of fun pages for the artist and collector alike.

Doll Menagerie, The
127-6 Rouote 23
Hamburg, NJ 07419
ph: 973-209-2828
fax: 973-209-2030
menagere@warwick.net
http://www.dollmenagerie.com
Specializing in collectible dolls from the finest artists and companies in the world; online catalog features over 60 of these artists and companies.

Nancy Pelham
Homestead Gift Shop
4 Hillwood Lane
Catskill, NY 12414
ph: 518-943-4371
fluffy@capital.net
http://www.homestead-gift-shop.com
Sells new manufactured dolls from Hamilton, Georgetown, Daddy's Long Legs, Kingstate, Seymour Mann and others; also doll furniture.

Doll Market, The
4215 Highpoint Rd.
Greensboro, NC 27407
ph: 336-632-4600 or 800-432-DOLL
fax: 336-632-4466
Carries limited edition and collector dolls from scores of artists.

Jean's Dolls
1818 Augusta Rd.
West Columbia, SC 29169
ph: 803-791-7421
fax: 803-791-1646
JeansDolls@aol.com
http://www.jeansdolls.com
Sells wide range of contemporary artists dolls: Robert Tonner, Gene, Ashton Drake, Madame Alexander.

Littlest Princess Doll Shoppe, The
6365 Spalding Dr.
Norcross, GA 30092
ph: 770-446-8909
fax: 770-446-7103
Disney, Gunzel, limited editions, Alexander, Zook, Barbie, Annalee, Gotz, Royal, Susan Wakeen.

Celia's & Susan's Dolls & Collectibles
788 East Hallandale Beach Blvd.
Hallandale, FL 33009
ph: 954-458-0661
fax: 954-458-5609
info@celiasandsusansdolls.com
http://www.celiasandsusansdolls.com
Barbie, Lee Middleton, Susan Wakeen, Effanbee, Connie Walser Derek, Robin Woods, Madame Alexander, Gotz, R. John Wright, Julie Good-Kruger, Georgetown, Turner, Gunzel, Wendy Lawton, Fayzah Spanos, Zook, Himstedt, Steiff, etc.

Mary Grettenberger
Doll Lady, The
11902 Ft. King Hwy.
Thonotosassa, FL 33592
ph: 813-982-9076
fax: 813-986-3708
mcb11902@aol.com
http://www.thedolllady.com
Carries many lines of modern dolls, plush, Teddy Bears, and Raggedy Ann & Andy.

Beckett's Doll House
646 High St.
Columbus, OH 43085-4106
ph: 614-848-9636
Madame Alexander, Annette Himstedt, Barbie, Effanbee, Pfaltzgraff, Ginny.

Lots of Dolls
215 Garfield Ave.
Milford, OH 45150
ph: 513-248-2151 or 800-755-6402
Sells older and contemporary artists dolls; Barbies, Robin Wood, Ashton Drake, Annalees, Steiff, Alexanders, Wendy Lawton, Annette Himstedt, Hartman, etc.

Joe Schulte
Gift Music Book & Collectibles
420 Wallace St.
Chicago Heights, IL 60411
ph: 708-877-7099 or 708-755-7622
fax: 208-275-5014
jntschulte@rocketmail.com
http://www.tias.com/stores/gift
In stock or free search for retired: Hamilton, Ashton Drake, Madame Alexander, Phyllis Parkins, I Love Lucy, Little Rascals, Brides, Musicians, Religious, etc.; a non-profit music group.

Joyce Hoover
Doll and Gift Gallery
2301 West Walnut St., Ste. 2
Rogers, AR 72756
ph: 501-631-4120
fax: 501-631-4120
jhoover501@aol.com
http://www.dollandgift.com
Sells Lee Middleton, Ginny Dolls, Effanbee Dolls, Susan Wakeen, Ashton Drake Precious Moments dolls, Boyd's dolls, Raggedy Ann & Andy, Seraphim Angels, and other modern dolls.

Darlene Simpson
Simpsons, The
4628 Morris Ave. S
Renton, WA 98055
ph: 524-277-0819 or 206-369-1869
fax: 425-277-0821
thesimpsons1@attbi.com
http://www.simpsonscollect.com
Sells Ashton Drake, Danbury Mint, Effanbee, Madame Alexander, Goebel, Ideal, Mattel, Seymour Mann, Special Edition Barbies, and other.

Dixie Sieverson
Doll Cellar, The
1024 1st St., Ste. LL#1
Snohomish, WA 98290
ph: 360-563-2716
dollied123@aol.com
http://dollsnw.com/dollcellar
Buys, sells, specializes in modern dolls; also sells doll-related books: Barbie, Gene, Ginny, Effanbee Storybook Dolls, Brenda Starr, Georgetown, Ashton-Drake, Marie Osmond, Raggedy Ann, Robert Tonner, Susan Wakeen, and more.

Internet Resources

Don Thompson
Vintage Toy Encyclopedia, The
P.O. Box 8701
Kansas City, MO 64114
http://www.toynfo.com
Great Web site with informative articles about scores and scores of action figures, dolls, toys and other collectibles.

Flossy Eddy
Flossy's Dolls & Collectibles
153 Sundance Dr.
Grand Junction, CO 81503
ph: 970-242-1358
flossysdolls@youfoundme.com
http://www.youfoundme.com/dollarea.htm
Large online Web site for doll enthusiasts: Barbie, fast food toys, Beanie Babies, doll tips and terms, collectible dolls chat room, and more; dolls, free classifieds, collector books.

Periodicals

Scott Publications
Magazine: Contemporary Doll Collector
30595 Eight Mile
Livonia, MI 48152-1798
ph: 800-458-8237 or 248-477-6650
fax: 248-477-6795
concatus@scottpublications.com
http://www.scottpublications.com
Award-winning magazine covers the vast doll market for doll lovers; how-to collect, where to buy, restoring your dolls and display ideas; published bi-monthly; breathtaking color photos of dolls.

Scott Publications
Magazine: Ceramic Arts & Crafts
30595 Eight Mile
Livonia, MI 48152-1798
ph: 800-458-8237 or 248-477-6650
fax: 248-477-6795
concatus@scottpublications.com
http://www.scottpublications.com
The "Bible" for the ceramic hobbyist since 1955; each monthly issue filled with projects and patterns, celebrity clips, new products, show listings, industry news, shoppers guides, book reviews, ads and classifieds.

Joe Jones
Jones Publishing, Inc.
Magazine: Dollmaking
P.O. Box 5000
Iola, WI 54945
ph: 715-445-5000 or 800-331-0038
fax: 715-445-4053
jonespub@jonespublishing.com
http://www.jonespublishing.com/magazine.htm
A bi-monthly magazine of dollmaking projects and plans for makers of porcelain and sculpted modern dolls; beautifully and lavishly illustrated.

Joe Jones
Jones Publishing, Inc.
Magazine: Doll Artisan
P.O. Box 5000
Iola, WI 54945
ph: 715-445-5000 or 800-331-0038
fax: 715-445-4053
jonespub@jonespublishing.com
http://www.jonespublishing.com/magazine.htm
A bi-monthly publication of reproduction porcelain dollmaking, projects, and plans illustrated with photos of antique and reproduction dolls.

Jones Publishing, Inc.
Magazine: Doll Crafter
P.O. Box 5000
Iola, WI 54945
ph: 715-445-5000 or 800-331-0038
fax: 715-445-4053
jonespub@jonespublishing.com
http://www.jonespublishing.com/magazine.htm
Most complete magazine for creating and collecting beautiful dolls; filled with beautiful color photos of antique reproduction and modern dolls, patterns; informative articles by experts on how-to make, collect, costume and sculpt dolls.

Jones Publishing, Inc.
Magazine: Dolls Magazine
P.O. Box 5000
Iola, WI 54945
ph: 715-445-5000 or 800-331-0038
fax: 715-445-4053
jonespub@jonespublishing.com
http://www.dollsmagazine.com
Information and feature articles from the doll world's most renowned professionals: collecting values, new issues, limited edition pieces, restoration, costuming; hints & tricks, latest artist designs, contests.

Jones Publishing, Inc.
Magazine: Doll Costuming
P.O. Box 5000
Iola, WI 54945
ph: 715-445-5000 or 800-331-0038
fax: 715-445-4053
jonespub@jonespublishing.com
http://www.jonespublishing.com/magazine.htm
Dedicated to discerning doll artists whose mission is to create beautiful, unique, authentic and exciting doll

fashions: pull-out patterns, doll costumer profiles, Q&A, national show calendar.

Brian Savage
Fun Publications
Newspaper: Master Collector
225 Cattle Baron Parc Dr.
Fort Worth, TX 76108
ph: 800-772-6673 or 817-448-9863
fax: 817-448-9843
brian@mastercollector.com
http://www.mastercollector.com
Ads-only newspaper; dolls (antique and modern collectible), toys, banks, models, cars, Matchbox, monsters, puzzles, political, toy trains, etc.; subscribers receive free 30-word ad each month; published monthly; reaches 20,000.

Dolls (American Girl)
Clubs/Associations

American Girls Club, The
8400 Fairway Place
Middleton, WI 53562
ph: 800-845-0005
im_cs@americangirl.com
http://www.americangirl.com
A company-sponsored collector's club.

Man./Prod./Dist.

American Girl/Pleasant Company
8400 Fairway Place
Middleton, WI 53562
ph: 800-845-0005
im_cs@americangirl.com
http://www.americangirl.com
The "Fun For Girls" section of the American Girl Web site features activities, games, puzzles, polls, advice, and more based on the American Girls Collection and American Girl magazine; Web site intended for girls ages 8 and older.

Dolls (Annette Himstedt)
Clubs/Associations

Annette Himstedt Collector Club
Karl Schurz Strasse 27
Paderborn, D-33110 Germany
ph: +49 (0) 5251 521717
fax: +49 (0) 5251 521730
annette.himstedt@owl-online.de
http://www.annettehimstedt.com
Original artist dolls by Annette Himstedt.

Dolls (Ashton-Drake)
Clubs/Associations

K. Darden
Tennessee Internet Gene Group
Newsletter: Tennessee Doll
P.O. Box 210182
Nashville, TN 37221-0182
ph: 615-662-6212
barbieintn@yahoo.com
http://www.geocities.com/
FashionAvenue/6487/tiggers.html
An Internet club for Gene and Tyler collectors.

Dealers

Bobbi Stavros
12 Arlington Rd.
Burlington, MA 01803
ph: 781-273-0293
Specializing in Gene/Ashton Drake, current and discontinued.

Man./Prod./Dist.

Laura Kazimier
Ashton-Drake Galleries, The
9307 N. Milwaukee Ave.
Niles, IL 60714-1381
ph: 877-268-6638 or 847-581-8452
fax: 847-966-2875
http://www.collectiblestoday.com
Direct mail marketer of dolls by various designers such as Yolando Bello, Dianna Effner, Cindy M. McClure, and Kathy Hippensteel.

Dolls (Attic Babies)
Clubs/Associations

Attic Babies Collectors Club
P.O. Box 2475
Stillwater, OK 74076
ph: 888-622-2437
fax: 405-372-3878

Man./Prod./Dist.

Attic Babies
P.O. Box 2475
Stillwater, OK 74076
ph: 888-622-2437
fax: 405-372-3878
Manufacturer of Attic Babies dolls.

Dolls (Daddy's Long Legs)
Clubs/Associations

Daddy's Long Legs Collector's Club
Newsletter: Daddy's Long Legs
Newsletter
300 Bank St.
Southlake, TX 76092-9972
ph: 817-488-4644 or 888-2-DADDYS
A club sponsored by the manufacturer, KVC, Inc.

Man./Prod./Dist.

KVC, Inc.
300 Bank St.
Southlake, TX 76092-9972
ph: 817-488-4644 or 888-2-DADDYS
Produces Daddy's Long Legs dolls.

Dolls (Effanbee)
Man./Prod./Dist.

Effanbee Doll Company
459 Hurley Ave.
Hurley, NY 12443
ph: 845-339-9537
fax: 845-339-1259
customerservice@tonnerdoll.com
http://www.effanbeedoll.com
Founded in 1910, Effanbee Soll Company was bought by Tonner Doll Company, Inc. in 2002.

Dolls (Federica Kasabasic)
Man./Prod./Dist.

Federica Dolls of Fine Art
4501 West Highland Rd.
Milford, MI 48380
ph: 800-421-3655 or 248-887-9575
fax: 248-887-9575
Produces dolls in the highest quality vinyl and porcelain.

Dolls (Lee Middleton)
Clubs/Associations

Our Doll Family, Lee Middleton
Original Dolls
Newsletter: Our Doll family
480 Olde Worthington Dr., Ste. 110
Westerville, OH 43082
ph: 614-901-0604 or 614-901-0550
fax: 614-901-0517
club@leemiddleton.com
http://www.leemiddleton.com
For collectors of original porcelain and vinyl dolls designed by artists Lee Middleton and Reva Schick.

Experts

Larry Koon
P.O. Box 808
Belpre, OH 45714-0808
Author of "Lee Middleton Original Dolls Price Guide."

Man./Prod./Dist.

Becky Richardson
Lee Middleton Original Dolls, Inc.
480 Olde Worthington Dr., Ste. 110
Westerville, OH 43082
ph: 614-901-0604 or 614-901-0550
fax: 614-901-0517
club@leemiddleton.com
http://www.leemiddleton.com
The sole manufacturer and producer of original porcelain and vinyl dolls designed by artists Lee Middleton and Reva Schick.

Dolls (Lenox)
Man./Prod./Dist.

Lenox Collections/Gorham
900 Wheeler Way
Langhorne, PA 19047
ph: 215-750-6900 or 800-223-4311
fax: 215-750-7362
Lenox_Collections@lenox.com
http://www.lenoxcollections.com
Producers of the Lenox Collection/ Gorham line of collectible porcelain dolls.

Dolls (Lizzie High)
Clubs/Associations

Lizzie High Society
Newsletter: Lizzie High Notebook
220 North Main St.
Sellersville, PA 18960
ph: 215-453-8200 or 800-763-6557
fax: 215-453-8155
lizzie1@bellatlantic.net
http://www.lizziehigh.com
Wooden folk art dolls by husband and

wife Peter Wisber and Barbara Kafka Wisber.

Man./Prod./Dist.

Ladie & Friends
220 North Main St.
Sellersville, PA 18960
ph: 215-453-8200 or 800-763-6557
fax: 215-453-8155
lizzie1@bellatlantic.net
http://www.lizziehigh.com
Producers of the Lizzie High doll collection.

Dolls (Madame Alexander)
Clubs/Associations

Madame Alexander Doll Club
Newsletter: Review
P.O. Box 330
Mundeline, IL 60060
ph: 847-949-9200
fax: 847-949-9201
office@madc.org
http://www.madc.org
Members receive the "Madame Alexander Shopper" which is devoted to buying and selling Madame Alexander dolls and accessories.

Collectors

Elaine DeVylder
2 Weed Circle
Stamford, CT 06902-4414

Experts

Jane Sarasohn-Kahn
125 Shelbourne Lane
Phoenixville, PA 19460-5710
ph: 610-933-5710
fax: 610-933-5636
jskahn@aol.com
http://www.dollreport.com
Author of "Contemporary Barbie 1980 to Present," "Contemporary Barbie, 1998 Edition" (2nd edition), and "Notes From a Friend of the Barbie Doll" and "Regarding the Doll" monthly columns.

Internet Resources

Milton & Gayle Shaw
Madame Alexander Collector Values & Reference Database
518 North Indian Rocks Rd.
Bellair Bluffs, FL 33770
ph: 727-584-7277
mshaw1@tampabay.rr.com
http://www.dollvalues.com
History and values for Madame Alexander dolls.

Man./Prod./Dist.

Alexander Doll Company, Inc.
615 West 131 St.
New York, NY 10027
ph: 212-283-5900
fax: 212-283-4901
http://www.alexanderdoll.com
Manufactures, produces and/or distributes Madame Alexander dolls.

Dolls (Marie Osmond)

Man./Prod./Dist.

Marian, LLC
30055 Comercio Rancho
Rancho Santa Margarita, CA 92688
ph: 800-779-5335
http://www.marianllc.com

Dolls (Naber)

Man./Prod./Dist.

Naber Gestalt Corp.
8915 S. Suncoast Blvd.
Homosassa, FL 34446
ph: 352-382-1001
fax: 352-382-1002
hnaber@naberkids.com
http://www.naberkids.com
Monthly newsletter containing information for doll collectors and enthusiasts alike; focuses on Naber dolls.

Dolls (Phyllis Parkins)

Clubs/Associations

Phyllis Parkins
Phyllis' Collectors Club
Newsletter: PCC Newsletter
2301 Old St. James Rd.
Rolla, MO 65401
ph: 573-364-7849 or 800-874-7120
fax: 573-364-2448
mail@thecollectables.com
http://www.thecollectables.com
Focuses on the Phyllis Parkins' collectible dolls, treetop angels, and a line of Victorian jewelry and frames. Sponsored by The Collectables, Inc.

Man./Prod./Dist.

Collectables, The
2301 Old St. James Rd.
Rolla, MO 65401
ph: 573-364-7849 or 800-874-7120
fax: 573-364-2448
mail@thecollectables.com
http://www.thecollectables.com
Produces Phyllis Parkins' collectible dolls, treetop angels, and a line of Victorian jewelry and frames.

Dolls (Robin Woods)

Collectors

Elaine DeVylder
2 Weed Circle
Stamford, CT 06902-4414
Wants cloth or vinyl "Robin Woods" dolls.

Dolls (Seymour Mann)

Clubs/Associations

Seymour Mann Collectible Doll Club
230 Fifth Ave., Rm. 102
New York, NY 10010
ph: 212-683-7262
fax: 212-213-4920
smanninc@aol.com
http://www.seymourmann.com
For collectors of the Seymour Mann Signature Collection of collectible dolls.

Man./Prod./Dist.

Seymour Mann, Inc.
230 Fifth Ave., Rm. 102
New York, NY 10010
ph: 212-683-7262
fax: 212-213-4920
smanninc@aol.com
http://www.seymourmann.com
Produces the Seymour Mann Signature Collection of collectible dolls, as well as a cat musical collection featuring cats in whimsical settings accompanied by popular tunes; also unique collectible teapots.

Dolls (Susan Wakeen)

Man./Prod./Dist.

Susan Wakeen Doll Company, Inc.
P.O. Box 1321
Litchfield, CT 06759-1321
ph: 860-567-0007
fax: 860-567-5334
info@susanwakeendolls.com
http://www.susanwakeendolls.com
Manufactures collectible vinyl and porcelain dolls designed by Susan Wakeen.

Dolls (Terri Lee)

Clubs/Associations

Susan Girardot
Terri Lee Collectors Club
Newsletter: TL Love of a Lifetime
05432 State Route 119
Minster, OH 45865
ph: 419-628-3405
gdot@bright.net
http://www.mt-healthy-toy.com/terrilee.html
A newsletter for Terri Lee collectors; annual convention.

Collectors

Lois Burger
2323 Lincoln
Beatrice, NE 68310-3306
ph: 402-228-2797
BarbieLJB@yahoo.com
Wants pre-1966 Barbie clothes, accessories, Ken, Midge, Skipper & their clothes; also anything Barbie related such as comics, cars; also Terri Lee dolls.

Terry Bukowski
271 Kittyhawk #49
Universal City, TX 78148
terrileedolls@earthlink.net
http://www.ericsilva.org/daisychain
Collector of Terri Lee dolls.

Dealers

Rosalee Rainbolt
Rosalee's Terri Lee Gallery & Hospital
986 E. 1587 Rd.
Lawrence, KS 66046
ph: 785-842-9799
rose@sunflower.com
http://www.sunflower.com/~rose/index.html
Buys, sells, restores Terri Lee dolls; specializes in Terri Lee repair,
restyling hair, wig making, repairing slits, face paint touch-up.

Experts

Peggy Wiedman Casper
314 South 93rd St.
Omaha, NE 68114
peggyWC@aol.com
Author of "Fashionable Terri Lee Dolls," and "Terri Lee Identification and Price Guide."

Man./Prod./Dist.

Terri Lee Associates
One Galleria Tower, Ste. 1315
Dallas, TX 75240-6603
ph: 888-837-7450
domreg@hosting.netcom.com
http://www.terrilee.com
The official homepage for Terri Lee dolls; company formed to perpetuate and enhance the Terri Lee line.

Periodicals

Terry Bukowski
Newsletter: Daisy Chain Newsletter
271 Kittyhawk #49
Universal City, TX 78148
terrileedolls@earthlink.net
http://www.ericsilva.org/daisychain
A quarterly newsletter about Terri Lee dolls: color photos, articles, want and for sale ads, birthday club, and a Christmas card.

Repair Services

Rosalee Rainbolt
Rosalee's Terri Lee Gallery & Hospital
986 E. 1587 Rd.
Lawrence, KS 66046
ph: 785-842-9799
rose@sunflower.com
http://www.sunflower.com/~rose/index.html
Buys, sells, restores Terri Lee dolls; specializes in Terri Lee repair, restyling hair, wig making, repairing slits, face paint touch-up.

Dolls (Wendy Lawton)

Clubs/Associations

Lawton Collectors Guild
Newsletter: Lawton Collectors Guild Newsletter
548 North First St.
Turlock, CA 95380
ph: 209-632-3655
fax: 209-632-6788
Guild@lawtondolls.com
http://www.lawtondolls.com/Guild.htm
Original artist dolls by artist Wendy Lawton.

Man./Prod./Dist.

Lawton Doll Company
548 North First St.
Turlock, CA 95380-3804
ph: 209-632-3655
fax: 209-632-6788
customerservice@lawtondolls.com
http://www.lawtondolls.com
Original artist dolls by artist Wendy Lawton.

Dolls (Wimbledon)

Man./Prod./Dist.

Wimbledon Collection at The Stone Fence
P.O. Box 22702
Lexington, KY 40522-2702
ph: 606-275-1962 or 800-695-3590
fax: 606-277-9231
gustavwolf@aol.com
http://www.cetehbis.com/STONEFEN/STONEFEN
All dolls are original sculptures of award winning artist Gustave F. Wolff; each doll is signed and numbers and comes with a certificate of authenticity.

Dolls (Xavier Roberts)

(see DOLLS, Cabbage Patch Kids)

Donald Zolan

Collectors

Jo Hancock
Jo's Antiques & Collectibles
621 S. Main St.
Nashville, AR 71852-2707
ph: 870-845-1070
Sells Donald Zolan items, also Lenox collectibles, Cybis figurines, Pickard, Royal Bonn, and Art Glass by Moser, Loetz, Webb, etc.

Eggs

Internet Resources

Tom Yanez
Creative Side, The
126 W. High St.
Hicksville, OH 43526
ph: 419-542-9533
Great online resource for those interested in making or collecting collectible eggs; egger supplies, techniques, auctions, awards.

Man./Prod./Dist.

eggspressions!
1635 Deadwood Ave.
Rapid City, SD 57702-0353
ph: 800-551-9138 or 605-342-4268
fax: 605-342-8699
Manufacturer of decorated porcelain eggs containing jewels, cute bunnies, foliage or other decorations.

Figurines

Dealers

Peggy Guy
Happy Pastime
10114 Frederick Rd.
Ellicott City, MD 21042
ph: 410-480-8119 or 410-203-1101
sales@happypastime.com
http://www.happypastime.com
Buys and sells; specializes in carnival glass, Royal Doulton, M.I. Hummel, Royal Copenhagen, Bing & Grondahl, Lladro, Goebel, Beswick, Royal Worcester.

Robert Goins
Replacements Ltd.
P.O. Box 26029
1089 Knox Rd.
Greensboro, NC 27420
ph: 800-737-5223 or 336-697-3000
fax: 336-697-3100
inquire@replacements.com
http://www.replacements.com
Carries post-1960 limited edition figurines in addition to china, crystal and flatware (obsolete, active and inactive.)

Stan Worrey
Colonial House Antiques
182 Front St.
Berea, OH 44017-1920
ph: 440-826-4169 or 800-344-9299
fax: 440-826-0839
Specializes in old Royal Doultons, Hummels, David Winter & Lilliput Lane Cottages; mail list on request.

Joe Schulte
Gift Music Book & Collectibles
420 Wallace St.
Chicago Heights, IL 60411
ph: 708-877-7099 or 708-755-7622
fax: 208-275-5014
jntschulte@rocketmail.com
http://www.tias.com/stores/gift
In stock or free search for retired: Seraphim Angels, Swarovski, Precious Moments, Hamilton Collection, ANRI, Cherished Teddies, Fontanini, Lladro, Hummel, Sports Impressions, D56, EKJ, Rockwell, etc.; a non-profit music group.

Man./Prod./Dist.

H & G Studios, Inc.
1490 S. Military Trail, Ste. n.3
West Palm Beach, FL 33415
ph: 561-649-3140
fax: 561-649-3141
http://www.hgstudios.com
Produces collectible plates, figurines, dolls and graphics by leading artists; exclusive distributor of M.I. Hummel music boxes in North America.

David Grossman Creations, Inc.
1608 North Warson Rd.
Saint Louis, MO 63132-1028
ph: 314-423-5600
fax: 314-423-7620
dgcrea@aol.com
Creates and markets resin/porcelain sculptures and other collectible art.

Donna Lamb
United Design Corp.
P.O. Box 1200
Noble, OK 73068-1200
ph: 800-727-4883 or 405-872-3468
fax: 405-360-4442
cservice@united-design.com
http://www.united-design.com
A leading manufacturer/distributor of fine figurines and collectibles.

Periodicals

Scott Publishing
Magazine: Figurines & Collectibles
P.O. Box 9707
Kalispell, MT 59904
ph: 406-755-0099 or 800-628-0212
fax: 406-756-0098
scottpub@digisys.net
A vehicle for both the advertiser and the reader to sell and buy figurines; covers porcelain, resin, crystal, and pewter figurines - both new and old; secondary market information.

Figurines (All God's Children)

Clubs/Associations

Kathy Martin, Dir.
All God's Children Collector's Club
Magazine: All God's Children Collector's Edition
P.O. Box 5038
Gadsden, AL 35905-0038
ph: 256-492-0221
fax: 256-492-0261
info@missmarthaoriginals.com
http://www.missmarthaoriginals.com
Focuses on All God's Children figurines; offers members personal checklist and the opportunity to purchase members-only figurines.

Man./Prod./Dist.

Miss Martha Originals, Inc.
P.O. Box 5038
Gadsden, AL 35905-0038
ph: 256-492-0221
fax: 256-492-0261
info@missmarthaoriginals.com
http://www.missmarthaoriginals.com
Manufacturer of nostalgic figurines cast from original sculptures by Martha Holocombe.

Figurines (Andrea by Sadek)

Dealers

Jerry Pope
West Alabama Collectibles
12339 Lakeview Manor Dr.
Northport, AL 35475
ph: 205-339-5075
ordermanporcelain@hotmail.com
http://www.porcelain-collectibles.com
Specialists in Andrea by Sadek birds, wildlife, and flower figurines and other fine porcelain.

Figurines (Anri)

Clubs/Associations

Thomas Riffeser, Mng. Dir.
ANRI Collectors Society
Newsletter: ANRI Collector Society Newsletter
Plan da Tieja 67
Wolkenstein, 39048 Italy
ph: 800-498-4894
fax: 800-498-5132
info@anri.com
http://www.anri.com
A company-sponsored club for Anri collectors; information on new products, exclusive figures for purchase, limited research on old pieces.

Dealers

Joe Iozzia
Chameleon Collectibles
P.O. Box 1005
Pomona, NJ 08240-1005
ph: 609-652-8504
pinflyers@aol.com
http://members.aol.com/Pinflyers/anri.html
Buys and sells vintage Anri handcarved items made in Italy; buys entire collections; also bottle stoppers, nutcrackers, humidors, napkin rings, bar sets and more; only wants carved figural items from Italy.

Experts

Philly Rains
1401 Brentwood Dr.
Harrison, AR 72601
ph: 870-743-2040
fax: 419-735-0610
phillyr@anricarvings.com
http://www.anricarvings.com
Expert in antique ANRI Italian wood carvings, 1912 through 1960s; bottle stoppers, corkscrews, nutcrackers, bar sets, figurines, napkin rings, smoking accessories, and more; appraisals upon request; coauthor of book on subject.

Man./Prod./Dist.

Thomas Riffeser, Mng. Dir.
ANRI Art GmbH
Plan da Tieja 67
Wolkenstein, 39048 Italy
ph: 800-498-4894
fax: 800-498-5132
info@anri.com
http://www.anri.com
Import and distribution of high-end collectible ANRI wooden hand carved maple figurines; emphasis on Nativity sets and religious items, also animals, children, and chess sets.

Figurines (Armani)

Clubs/Associations

Society of Giuseppe Armani Art, The
Newsletter: Society Newsletter, The
300 Mac Lane
Keasbey, NJ 08832-1200
ph: 732-417-0330 or 800-3-ARMANI
fax: 732-417-0031
society202@aol.com
http://www.the-society.com
For fans and collectors of the cold cast porcelain figurines of master sculptor Giuseppe Armani.

Dealers

Allan & Pat Clay
Clemons-Eicken Fine European Imports
6166 N. Scottsdale Rd., #204
Scottsdale, AZ 85253
ph: 602-998-9042 or 800-250-5423
fax: 602-998-3755
Carries Lladro, Armani, Boehm, Lalique, Cybis.

Experts

Herb Miller
Miller Import Co.
300 Mac Lane
Keasbey, NJ 08832-1200
ph: 732-417-0330 or 800-3-ARMANI
fax: 732-417-0031
society202@aol.com
http://www.the-society.com

Sid Perkins
Roberta's Collectible Showcase
4972 North Pine Rd.
Fort Lauderdale, FL 33351
ph: 800-514-1114
service@robertascollectibles.com
http://www.robertascollectibles.com
Caries a full line of fine collectibles, figurines and art: Armani, Cybis, Disney, E. Kelly, Jr., Melody in Motion, Precious Moments, Ron Lee, Swarovski, Harmony Kingdom, etc.

Figurines (Byers)

Clubs/Associations

Caroler Chronicle, The
4355 County Line Rd.
P.O. Box 158
Chalfont, PA 18914
ph: 215-822-6700
fax: 215-822-3847
support@byerschoice.com
http://www.byerschoice.com
For collectors of Byers caroling figurines.

Dealers

Linda's Originals & The Yankee
　Craftsmen
220 Rt. 6A
Brewster, MA 02631
ph: 800-385-4758
collects@tiac.net
http://www.my-collectibles.com
　*Buy and sell new and old Byers
　Choice Carolers dolls.*

Linda Ross Hughes
Best Collectibles
16151 Morganton Highway
P.O. Box 152
Morganton, GA 30560-0152
ph: 706-838-5920
fax: 706-838-4008
bestcollectibles@tds.net
http://www.bestcollectibles.com
　*A secondary market for retired and
　limited edition collectibles featuring
　Byers' Choice, Dept. 56, Lefton,
　Cherished Teddies, Charming Tails,
　Dreamsicles, NASCAR, Walt Disney
　Classics and many others.*

Man./Prod./Dist.

Byers' Choice Ltd.
4355 County Line Rd.
P.O. Box 158
Chalfont, PA 18914
ph: 215-822-6700
fax: 215-822-3847
support@byerschoice.com
http://www.byerschoice.com
　*Manufacturer of caroling figurines
　reminiscent of the 19th century.*

Museums/Libraries

Byers' Choice Museum
Wayside Country Store
1015 Boston Post Rd.
Marlboro, MA 01752
ph: 508-481-3458
fax: 508-485-4978
comments@waysidecountrystore.com
http://waysidecountrystore.com/
　byers.htm

Figurines (Cairn)

Clubs/Associations

Cairn Collector Society, The
Newsletter: Cairn Collector Society
　Newsletter
P.O. Box 400
Davidson, NC 28036
ph: 704-892-5859
info@cairnstudio.com
http://www.cairnstudio.com
　*Focuses on collectible figurines such
　as Dr. Tom Clark's Gnomes issued by
　Cairn Studio Ltd. Sponsored by
　Cairn Studio, Ltd.*

Man./Prod./Dist.

Cairn Studio Ltd.
P.O. Box 400
Davidson, NC 28036
ph: 704-892-5859
info@cairnstudio.com
http://www.cairnstudio.com
　Manufactures gnomes and other

*character figurines by artist Dr. Tom
Clark.*

Museums/Libraries

Tom Clark Museum
P.O. Box 400
Davidson, NC 28036
ph: 704-892-5859
info@cairnstudio.com
http://www.cairnstudio.com
　*Large collection of sculptures by noted
　artist, Dr. Tom Clark.*

Figurines (Carousels)

Dealers

Melody in Motion
c/o Desert Specialties
6280 S. Valley View, Ste. 404
Las Vegas, NV 89118
ph: 702-253-0450 or 888-894-2417
fax: 702-253-1871
103067.2265@compuserve.com
http://www.melodyinmotion.com
　*Buys and sells retired Melody in
　Motion carousel figurines: Santas,
　Clowns, Madames, Willies.*

Figurines (Cherished Teddies)

Clubs/Associations

Enesco Cherished Teddies Collectors
　Club
P.O. Box 99
Itasca, IL 60143-0099
ph: 630-875-5300 or 800-436-3726
fax: 630-875-5359
caffairs@enesco.com
http://www.enesco.com
　*For collectors of Cherished Teddies
　resin figurines.*

Internet Resources

Vivienne Wiltberger
Teddies Trader, The
vivienne@theteddiestrader.com
http://www.theteddiestrader.com
　*Internet club for Cherished Teddie
　collectors: news, events, contests,
　Teddie facts and information, trading
　post, and more.*

Figurines (Disney)

Clubs/Associations

Walt Disney Collectors Society, The
Magazine: Sketches
500 South Buena Vista St.
Burbank, CA 91521
ph: 818-567-5500 or 800-932-5749
http://disney.go.com/disneyartclassics/
　collectorssociety
　*For Disney collectors around the
　world; members get free animation
　sculpture, quarterly magazine,
　opportunity to buy "member only"
　figurines, and advance notice of new
　releases; for Walt Disney Classics call
　800-WD-CLSIX.*

Dealers

Ben Swan
Golden Swan Collectibles
881 Lincoln Way
Auburn, CA 95603
ph: 530-823-7926 or 800-231-9055
fax: 530-823-1945
　*Offers a "search and find" and a
　listing service to collectors, buyers
　and sellers of Lladro figurines; also
　for Swarovski, Walt Disney Classics,
　and Disneyana Convention figurines.*

Figurines (Dreamsicles)

Clubs/Associations

James Farrell
Dreamsicles Collectors' Club
Newsletter: ClubHouse
1120 California Ave.
Corona, CA 92881-3324
ph: 800-437-5818 or 909-371-3025
fax: 909-371-0674
info@dreamsiclesclub.com
http://www.dreamsiclesclub.com
　*A company-sponsored club for
　collectors of Dreamsicles collectible
　cherubs and animals; also sells
　Bumpkins and Ivy & Innocence
　figurines.*

Man./Prod./Dist.

Cast Art Industries, Inc.
1120 California Ave.
Corona, CA 92881-3324
ph: 800-437-5818 or 909-371-3025
fax: 909-371-0674
　*Architectural miniatures, figurines,
　sculpture, ornaments.*

Figurines (Emmett Kelly, Jr.)

(see also CLOWN COLLECTIBLES)

Clubs/Associations

Mary Lee Graham
Emmett Kelly, Jr. Collectors' Society
c/o Flambro
Journal: EK Journal
1530 Ellsworth Industrial Dr.
Atlanta, GA 30318-3752
ph: 800-355-2582 or 404-352-1381
fax: 404-352-2150
flambro@flambro.com
http://www.flambro.com
　*Focuses on the Emmett Kelly, Jr.
　clown figurines. Sponsored by
　Flambro Imports, Inc.; journal,
　binder, pin, "members only" plaque;
　enrollment includes member's plaque,
　newsletter, lapel pin, registry,
　member's-only redemption coupon.*

Emmett's Friends, c/o Frankenmuth
　Gallery
568 South Main St.
Frankenmuth, MI 48734
ph: 800-344-2917
gallery@tir.com
http://www.frankenmuthgallery.com
　*Focuses on the clown figurines issued
　by Flambro Imports, Inc.; also Gantz,
　Snoopy, Armani, Pocket Dragons,
　Lenox, Thomas Kinkade.*

Collectors

N.W. Neill, Jr.
P.O. Box 38
Ennice, NC 28623-0038
fax: 336-657-8084
saddlemtn@skybest.com
　*Wants anything related to Emmett
　Kelly, Jr. or Emmett Kelly, Sr.:
　advertising, postcards, Flambro
　pieces, dolls, etc.*

Figurines (Enchanted Kingdom)

Clubs/Associations

Victoria Rangel, Dir.
Enchanted Kingdom Collector's Club
Newsletter: Enchanted Times
347 W. Sierra Madre Blvd.
Sierra Madre, CA 91024
ph: 818-355-1813
fax: 818-355-1982
　For fantasy and castle enthusiasts.

Figurines (Fontanini)

Clubs/Associations

Liezl Bowman
Fontanini Collectors' Club
Newsletter: Fontanini Collector
555 Lawrence Ave.
Roselle, IL 60172-1599
ph: 630-529-3000 or 800-729-7662
fax: 630-529-1121
liezlb@roman.com
http://www.roman.com
　*For collectors of Fontanini nativity
　sets and figurines including angels,
　stables, and village buildings;
　sponsored by Roman, Inc.*

Man./Prod./Dist.

Liezl Bowman
Roman, Inc.
555 Lawrence Ave.
Roselle, IL 60172-1599
ph: 630-529-3000 or 800-729-7662
fax: 630-529-1121
liezlb@roman.com
http://www.roman.com
　*Produces figurines, plates, litho-
　graphs, bells, dolls, music boxes, etc.
　Exclusive importer of Fontanini
　nativity sets and plates.*

Figurines (Goebel)

Clubs/Associations

Goebel Networkers
P.O. Box 355
Hamburg, PA 19526
　*A club that focuses on non-Hummel
　Goebel figurines.*

Dealers

Lois & Ralph Behm
Lois' Collectibles of Antique Market III
413 W. Main St.
Saint Charles, IL 60174-1815
ph: 630-377-5599 or 847-831-5997
fax: 847-831-5998
　*Buys and sells Goebel figurines Friar
　Tuck, Cardinal Tuck, and Redheads;
　will buy entire collections.*

Man./Prod./Dist.

Goebel United States
P.O. Box 10
Pennington, NJ 08534-0010
ph: 609-737-8700 or 800-366-4632
fax: 609-737-8685
memsrv@mihummel.com
http://www.mihummel.com
Distributors of Goebel and other figurines; Web site has glossary of terms, tips on appraising, cleaning, marks of authenticity.

Figurines (Goebel-Charlot Byj)

Experts

Rocky Rockholt
2678 Sumac Ridge
Saint Paul, MN 55110-5646
ph: 651-777-9000 or 651-503-3306
fax: 651-777-9000
rockyrockholt@email.msn.com
Author of the full color 144-page book regarding the figurines and other items designed by Charlot Byj and produced by the Goebel Co.

Figurines (Goebel-Friar Tuck)

Clubs/Associations

Carol Skaggs-Austin
Friar Tuck Collectors Club
Newsletter: FTCC Newsletter
1076 Grays Creek Church Rd.
Rutherfordton, NC 28139
ph: 828-248-3984
friartuckcollectorclub@webtv.net
Established in 1994 for the purpose of exchanging information on collecting Friar and Cardinal Tucks figurines by Goebel; newsletter published four times per year.

Figurines (Goebel-Miniatures)

Experts

Dick Hunt
Hunt's Collectibles
114 Scenic Dr.
Flat Rock, NC 28731-9522
ph: 828-693-6150 or 800-621-8112
fax: 828-693-6150
micro@miniature.com
http://www.miniature.com
Specializes in buying and selling Goebel Miniatures by Robert Olszewski; also author of "The Goebel Miniatures of Robert Olszewski."

Man./Prod./Dist.

Goebel Miniatures
P.O. Box 10
Pennington, NJ 08534-0010
ph: 609-737-8700 or 800-366-4632
fax: 609-737-8685
memsrv@mihummel.com
http://www.mihummel.com
Produces fine handpainted limited edition Goebel miniature figurines.

Figurines (Great American)

Clubs/Associations

Dan Sherman
Great American Collector's Club
Newsletter: Old World Santa News
10567 SW Coleman Loop N.
Wilsonville, OR 97070
ph: 877-399-3111
fax: 815-327-1238
email@dansherman.com
http://www.greatamericancollectibles.net
Wood carving reproductions of Old World Santas and houses; made of resin.

Figurines (Janco Studio)

Man./Prod./Dist.

Bert Anderson
Janco Studio
P.O. Box 30012
Lincoln, NE 68503
ph: 402-435-1430 or 800-490-1430
janco11111@aol.com
http://www.jancostudio.com
Produce very detailed figurines and Christmas ornaments.

Figurines (June McKenna)

Dealers

Brenda Higgins
Handmaiden, The
P.O. Box 392
Fiskdale, MA 01518
ph: 508-347-7757
Specializes in buying and selling works by artist June McKenna.

Man./Prod./Dist.

June McKenna Collectibles, LLC
P.O. Box 846
205 Haley Rd.
Ashland, VA 23005
ph: 804-798-2024
JunMcKenna@aol.com
http://www.junemckenna.com
Designs, manufactures and distributes three dimensional highly detailed limited edition figurines including Black Folk Art figurines and Christmas/Santa figurines, and one-of-a-kind animated Santa dolls designed by June McKenna.

Figurines (Krystonia)

Clubs/Associations

Krystonia Collectors Club
Newsletter: Phargol Horn
100 W. Ellsworth Rd.
Ann Arbor, MI 48108
ph: 313-677-3411
fax: 313-677-3412
Focuses on the collectible Krystonia dragons, wizards, and storybooks. Sponsored by Precious Art/Panton, Inc.; "members' only" pieces available.

Man./Prod./Dist.

Precious Art/Panton Inter.
100 W. Ellsworth Rd.
Ann Arbor, MI 48108
ph: 313-677-3411
fax: 313-677-3412
Manufacturer of make-believe collectible Krystonia dragons, wizards, and storybooks.

Figurines (Lighthouses)

Clubs/Associations

Harbour Lights Collectors' Society
Newsletter: Lighthouse Legacy
1000 N. Johnson Ave.
El Cajon, CA 92020
ph: 800-365-1219 or 619-579-1820
fax: 619-579-1911
HarbourLights@HarbourLights.com
http://www.harbourlights.com
For collectors of Harbour Lights Hydrostone lighthouses.

Man./Prod./Dist.

Cheryl Spencer Collin Studio
2 Government St.
Kittery, ME 03904
ph: 207-439-6016
fax: 207-439-5787
Produces exquisite lighthouse recreations of incredible detail.

Bill Younger
Harbour Lights
1000 N. Johnson Ave.
El Cajon, CA 92020
ph: 800-365-1219 or 619-579-1820
fax: 619-579-1911
HarbourLights@HarbourLights.com
http://www.harbourlights.com
Manufacturer of Hydrostone lighthouses and a full line of lighthouse collectibles.

Figurines (Margaret Furlong)

Clubs/Associations

Margaret Furlong Collectors Club
210 State St.
Salem, OR 97301-3444
http://www.margaretfurlong.com
A company-sponsored collectors club.

Man./Prod./Dist.

Margaret Furlong Designs
210 State St.
Salem, OR 97301-3444
http://www.margaretfurlong.com
Produces white-on-white porcelain angels, shell stars, hearts, snowflakes, wreaths, and home decor and wedding line products.

Figurines (Maruri)

Man./Prod./Dist.

Maruri USA
21510 Gledhill St.
Chatsworth, CA 91311-5878
ph: 818-717-9900 or 800-562-7874
fax: 818-717-9901
maruriUS@pacbell.net
Producer and distributor of high quality porcelain plates and figurines.

Figurines (Maud Humphrey)

Clubs/Associations

Barbara Schrage
Maud Humphrey Bogart Collectors' Club
Newsletter: Victorian Times
225 Windsor Dr.
Itasca, IL 60143
ph: 630-875-5300 or 800-436-3726
fax: 630-875-5359
caffairs@enesco.com
http://www.enesco.com
Members receive symbol of membership figurine, quarterly newsletter, membership card, members' only offering, collection registry, catalog.

Figurines (Memories Of Yesdy')

Clubs/Associations

Enesco Memories of Yesterday
Collectors' Society
Newsletter: Sharing Memories...
225 Windsor Dr.
Itasca, IL 60143
ph: 630-875-5300 or 800-436-3726
fax: 630-875-5359
caffairs@enesco.com
http://www.enesco.com
Members receive symbol of membership figurine, club newsletter, membership card, members' only offering, club binder.

Figurines (Michael Garman)

Man./Prod./Dist.

Michael Garman Productions, Inc.
2418 W. Colorado Ave.
Colorado Springs, CO 80904
ph: 800-731-3908 or 719-471-9391
info@chest.com
http://www.michaelgarman.com
Manufactures three-dimensional sculptures of people who have shaped America: cowboys, aviators, soldiers, policemen, wino, heroes, etc.

Figurines (Myth & Magic)

Clubs/Associations

Myth & Magic Collectors Club
55-E East Beaver Creek Rd.
Richmond Hill, Ontario L4B 1EB
  Canada
ph: 905-731-3232
fax: 905-731-0872
contactus@samacotrading.com

Myth & Magic Collectors Club
Vulcan Rd.
Solihull
West Midlands, B91 2JY U.K.
ph: (0121) 7114128
fax: (0121) 7111086
  *For collectors of Olde English pewter
  figurines, each of which incorporates
  a piece of Swarovski Crystal.*

Figurines (Patchville)

Man./Prod./Dist.

MCK Gifts, Inc.
P.O. Box 621848
Littleton, CO 80162-1848
ph: 800-755-6254
fax: 303-789-9379
mckgifts@sprintmail.com
http://www.mckgifts.com
  *Produces the world of Patchville -
  individually cast and delicately
  handpainted whimsical, lop-eared
  bunnie figurines.*

Figurines (PenDelfin)

Clubs/Associations

Susan Beard
PenDelfin Family Circle
Newsletter: PenDelfin Times, The
Atlanta Gift Mart
230 Spring St. MW, Ste. 1238
Atlanta, GA 30303-1063
ph: 800-872-4876 or 404-523-3380
boswell@pendelfin.co.uk
http://www.pendelfin.co.uk/family.htm
  *For collectors of PenDelfin miniature
  stoneware handpainted Rabbit Family
  members backdrop cottages, shops and
  landmarks.*

Man./Prod./Dist.

PenDelfin Sales Inc.
Cameron Mill
Hoswin St.
Burnley, Lancashire BB10 1PP U.K.
ph: 01282 432301
fax: 01282 459464
boswell@pendelfin.co.uk
http://www.pendelfin.co.uk
  *Manufacturer of PenDelfin miniature
  stoneware handpainted Rabbit Family
  members backdrop cottages, shops and
  landmarks.*

Figurines (Pocket Dragons)

Clubs/Associations

Pocket Dragons & Friends Collectors
  Club, c/o Flambro
Newsletter: Pocket Dragon Gazette
1530 Ellsworth Industrial Dr.
Atlanta, GA 30318-3752
ph: 800-355-2582 or 404-352-1381
fax: 404-352-2150
flambro@flambro.com
http://www.flambro.com
  *Members get Membership card,
  newsletter, lapel pin, exclusive
  members-only figurines, club-
  sponsored events.*

Figurines (Red Mill)

Clubs/Associations

Karen S. McClung
Red Mill Collectors Society
Newsletter: RMCS Newsletter
One Hunters Ridge
Summersville, WV 26651
ph: 304-872-5237
fax: 304-872-5234
  *A manufacturer-sponsored club for
  collectors of Red Mill figurines made
  from crushed pecan shells.*

Man./Prod./Dist.

Red Mill Mfg.
P.O. Box 252
Marlboro, NJ 07746
ph: 732-409-7174 or 800-624-8280
fax: 732-409-6129
sales@red-mill.com
http://www.red-mill.com
  *Manufactures Red Mill figurines made
  from crushed pecan shells.*

Figurines (Ron Lee)

Man./Prod./Dist.

Ron Lee's World of Clowns
330 Carousel Parkway
Henderson, NV 89014
ph: 800-829-3928 or 702-434-1700
fax: 702-434-4310
info@ronlee.com
http://www.ronlee.com

Figurines (Sarah Schultz)

Man./Prod./Dist.

Sarah's Attic
126 1/2 W. Broad
P.O. Box 448
Chesaning, MI 48616
ph: 989-845-3990 or 800-437-4363
fax: 989-845-3477
info@sarahsattic.com
http://www.sarahsattic.com
  *Manufactures collectible figurines
  designed by Sarah Schultz.*

Figurines (Sebastian)

Clubs/Associations

Cyndi Gavin McNally, Dir.
Sebastian Miniatures Collectors Society
Newsletter: Sebastian Miniatures
  Collectors Society News
111 Island St.
Stoughton, MA 02072-1401
ph: 508-568-1401
fax: 508-568-8741
  *Focuses on the Sebastian collectible
  figurines; members receive free
  miniature, annual value guide; also
  distributes the "Sebastian Exchange
  Quarterly" newsletter for secondary
  market information.*

Dealers

James Waite
Blossom Shop Collectibles
308 S. Main, Ste. B
Farmer City, IL 61842-0025
ph: 309-928-3222 or 800-842-2593
bigjim@farmwagon.com
http://homepage.mac.com/matscherz/
  blossom/main.html
  *Buys and sells old and new Sebastian
  miniatures by P.W. and "Woody"
  Baston, private issues, commercial &
  Marblehead, MA; sponsors Midwest
  Sebastian fair which each October
  includes an auction of hard-to-find
  pieces.*

Experts

Robert Edmunds
Sebastianworld, Inc.
11 Cochituate Rd.
Wayland, MA 01778
ph: 508-668-4212
fax: 508-668-7553
webmaster@sebastianworld.com
http://www.sebastianworld.com
  *Collector, expert, appraiser of
  Sebastian miniatures.*

Internet Resources

Robert Edmunds
Sebastianworld, Inc.
11 Cochituate Rd.
Wayland, MA 01778
ph: 508-668-4212
fax: 508-668-7553
webmaster@sebastianworld.com
http://www.sebastianworld.com
  *Web site brings together those with an
  interest in Sebastian Miniatures
  created by Prescott W. Baston and his
  son "Woody" Baston: announcements,
  listing of all known figurines, each
  pictured and valued, products and
  services, and more.*

Figurines (Second Nature)

Man./Prod./Dist.

Second Nature Design
P.O. Box 50624
Phoenix, AZ 85076
ph: 480-961-3963 or 800-939-3963
fax: 480-961-4178
  *Creates affordable wildlife collectible
  figurines.*

Figurines (Seraphim Classics)

Clubs/Associations

Liezl Bowman
Seraphim Classics Collectors Club
Newsletter: Seraphim Classics Herald
555 Lawrence Ave.
Roselle, IL 60172-1599
ph: 630-529-3000 or 800-729-7662
fax: 630-529-1121
liezlb@roman.com
http://www.roman.com
  *For collectors of Seraphim Classics
  angel figurines; sponsored by Roman,
  Inc.*

Figurines (Shade Tree)

Clubs/Associations

Shade Tree Cowboy Collector Society
Newsletter: Cowboy Times
4248 Burningtown Rd.
Franklin, NC 28734
ph: 800-327-6923 or 828-524-0863
fax: 704-349-3253
billvernon@hotmail.com
http://www.billvernon.com
  *For collectors of Bill Vernon's
  humorous cowboy figurines; wildlife
  images which seem to "evolve" from
  twisted pieces of driftwood.*

Man./Prod./Dist.

Shade Tree Creations
4248 Burningtown Rd.
Franklin, NC 28734
ph: 800-327-6923 or 828-524-0863
fax: 704-349-3253
billvernon@hotmail.com
http://www.billvernon.com
  *Creators of sculptures designed by
  artists including Bill Vernon:
  dragons, road kill, Shade Tree
  Cowboys, Treeples, Mini Nuts, The
  Series of Evolution.*

Figurines (Silver Deer)

Clubs/Associations

Silver Deer Collectors' Club
963 Transport Way
Petaluma, CA 94954
ph: 707-765-8311 or 800-729-3337
fax: 707-765-0770
ambcrystallite@att.net
  *A manufacturer-sponsored club for
  collectors of cold-cast figurines;
  special club activities/promotions,
  members-only figurines, and a
  quarterly newsletter with information
  about designers, product retirements
  and upcoming events.*

Man./Prod./Dist.

Silver Deer, Ltd.
963 Transport Way
Petaluma, CA 94954
ph: 707-765-8311 or 800-729-3337
fax: 707-765-0770
ambcrystallite@att.net
  *Designs, manufactures and distributes
  limited edition crystal figurines and
  other giftware.*

Figurines (VickiLane)

Clubs/Associations

VickiLane Collectors Club
3233 NE Cadet Ave.
Portland, OR 97220-3601
ph: 503-257-4664
fax: 503-251-5916
netsales@vikilane.com
http://www.vikilane.com
Focuses on collectible figurines designed by Vicki Anderson and others at VivkiLane.

Figurines (Wee Forest Folk)

Clubs/Associations

Wee Forest Folk Collector's Club
Newsletter: Folktales
2605 Hospital Rd.
Saginaw, MI 48603-2611
ph: 517-792-8478
fax: 517-792-8478
wffcclady1@aol.com
http://www.weeforestfolkclub.org
Club provides information about Wee Forest Folk figurines, past and present; helps locate figurines from 1978 to present.

Collectors

Ann Brogley
P.O. Box 16033
Philadelphia, PA 19114-0033
ph: 215-824-4698 or 215-824-2350
fax: 215-824-4698
mostprod@erols.com
http://www.geocities.com/Heartland/
Hills/2081
Wants to buy Wee Forest Folks brochures, advertising, display items.

Jeanne Fredericks
12364 Downey Ave.
Downey, CA 90242-3556
ph: 562-861-4781
jeenrob@aol.com
Collector wants older, retired Wee Forest Folk figurines created by the Peterson family.

Dealers

Creative Hands
243 R.P. Coffin Rd.
Long Grove, IL 60047
ph: 847-634-0545
creativehands1@aol.com
http://www.creative-hands.com
Specializes in the endearing miniature figurines sculpted by Annette Peterson of Wee Forest Folk.

Dan Thompson
Thompson Studios
1414 W. Central, Ste. 24
Brea, CA 92821
ph: 714-749-2858
habitat-hideaway@cybercitymall.com
http://www.cybercitymall.com/habitat-hideaway
The Habitat Hideaway collection are exquisitely sculpted, hand cast and hand painted nature scenes designed to accessorize and display a collection of Wee Forest Folk.

Internet Resources

Bill Montague
Wee Forest Folk news - The Monthly Squeak
ph: 978-287-4800
fax: 978-287-4240
Bill@concordmousetrap.com
http://concordmousetrap.com/
squeak.html
Online newsletter for collectors of Wee Forest Folk.

GeoffLee
Nu Insight/WFF Resource Information
wff_collector@yahoo.com
http://www.neu-insight.com/cgi-bin/wff/
buzz.cgi
Information resource listings for Wee Forest Folk: shops, pricing guides, want ads, pieces for sale.

Figurines (Wizards & Dragons)

Clubs/Associations

Mary Lee Graham
Wizards & Dragons Collectors Club, c/o Flambro
Newsletter: Land of Legend
1530 Ellsworth Industrial Dr.
Atlanta, GA 30318-3752
ph: 800-355-2582 or 404-352-1381
fax: 404-352-2150
flambro@flambro.com
http://www.flambro.com
Figurines of amazingly detailed dragons and wizards with splendid coloring and stones; designed by international artist Hap Henrikson.

Flowers (Capodimonte)

Man./Prod./Dist.

Napoleon U.S.A.
P.O. Box 860
Oaks, PA 19456-0860
ph: 610-666-1650 or 800-548-2661
fax: 610-666-1379
napusa@aol.com
U.S. distributor for Napoleon Capodimonte flowers with the crown/ "N" mark from Italy.

Folk Art

Man./Prod./Dist.

Vaillancourt Folk Art
145 Armsby Rd.
Sutton, MA 01590
ph: 508-865-9183
fax: 508-865-4140
valfa@valfa.com
http://www.valfa.com
Creates limited edition chalkware replicas cast from antique chocolate molds and ice cream forms.

Franklin Mint

Collectors

Jim Crane
15 Clemson Ct.
Newark, DE 19711-4301
ph: 302-738-6031
spcjpc@earthlink.net
Wants Franklin Mint diecast cars as well as other Franklin Mint items such as books and ads.

Man./Prod./Dist.

Customer Service
Franklin Mint, The
U.S. Route 1
Franklin Center, PA 19091-0001
ph: 877-843-6468 or 610-459-6480
fax: 610-459-6880
http://www.franklinmint.com
Designs, manufactures and markets collectibles including jewelry, sculpture, dolls, figurines, bells, ornaments, arms replicas, etc.

Holly Hobbie

Collectors

Mary Winfrey
3202 Kilgrennan Ct.
Herndon, VA 22071
ph: 703-435-3788
fax: 703-435-2805
Wants to buy pre-1990 adult luncheon and dinner sets, fabric, playing cards, adult tea sets, bicentennial glasses, Holly Hobbie porcelain dolls, music boxes, figurines, sterling silver plates, and Christmas tree ornaments.

Dealers

Wilma Schiebel
No Place Like Home Collectibles
2200 S. Hwy 62-65
Harrison, AR 72601
ph: 870-741-9494
nplhc@alltel.net
Buys and sells anything Holly Hobbie: prefer luncheon plates, bisque figurines, vases, cookie jars, ginger jars, tea sets, banks, eggs, lunch boxes, jewelry, etc.; NO plates or dolls.

Man./Prod./Dist.

Sue Holiday
American Greetings Corp.
One American Rd.
Cleveland, OH 44144
ph: 216-252-7300 or 800-321-3040
fax: 216-252-6777
http://
www.corporate.americangreetings.com
American Greetings produced Holly Hobbie items - including figurines, plates, bells, etc. - from 1974 through 1986. Items were reintroduced through the Summit Corp. in 1990-91; the "Summit" figurines have also now been retired.

Periodicals

Donna Stultz
Newsletter: Holly Hobbie Collectors Gazette
1455 Otterdale Mill Rd.
Taneytown, MD 21787-3032
ph: 410-775-2570
hhgazette@hotmail.com
For the enthusiast of Holly Hobbie memorabilia; the bi-monthly newsletter has articles, information, free buy/sell/trade ads with subscription; holds annual convention for Holly Hobbie collectors; send SASE to join; $25 per year.

Jan Hagara

Clubs/Associations

Jan Hagara Collectors' Club/Jan Hagara Collectables
Newsletter: Official Jan Hagara Collectors' Club Newsletter
40114 Industrial Park
Georgetown, TX 78626-4704
ph: 512-863-9499 or 800-722-3996
fax: 512-869-2093
info@hagaradolls.com
http://www.hagaradolls.com/club/
index.html
For collectors of Hagara prints, figurines, porcelain dolls, miniatures. Sponsored by Jan Hagara Collectables, Inc.

Dealers

Mary Sower
Card Cupboard, The
116 W. Main St.
Coldwater, OH 45828-1773
ph: 419-678-2417
Maintains a price list for Jan Hagara collectibles; will try to find any retired Jan Hagara item for customers.

Man./Prod./Dist.

B & J Company, The
P.O. Box 67
Georgetown, TX 78627
ph: 512-863-8318 or 800-722-3996
fax: 512-863-0833
info@hagaradolls.com
http://www.hagaradolls.com
Produces and distributes prints, porcelain dolls, cards and collector plates by Jan Hagara.

Lenox

Man./Prod./Dist.

Lenox Collections
900 Wheeler Way
Langhorne, PA 19047
ph: 215-750-6900 or 800-223-4311
fax: 215-750-7362
Lenox_Collections@lenox.com
http://www.lenoxcollections.com
Direct mail marketing division of Lenox Corp. selling doll, ornament, figurines and giftware collectibles issued by Lenox.

Lithophanes

Man./Prod./Dist.

David N. Failing
Schmidt-Failing, Ltd.
10579 Miller Rd.
Utica, NY 13502-7005
ph: 315-724-1139 or 800-498-5866
fax: 315-724-0496
David Failing is the only American artist skilled in the creation of original porcelain lithophanes; all are signed, numbered & limited.

Lowell Davis

Clubs/Associations

Lowell Davis Farm Club
Newsletter: Lowell Davis Farm Club
　Gazette
55 Pacella Park Dr.
Randolph, MA 02368
ph: 617-961-3000
fax: 617-986-8168
　Focuses on the collectible plates and
　figurines designed by artist Lowell
　Davis. Sponsored by Schmid Co.

Music Boxes

Man./Prod./Dist.

Splendid Music Box Co.
225 Fifth Ave.
New York, NY 10010-1102
ph: 212-532-9304
fax: 212-532-9334
　Imports over 1,000 types of music
　boxes from all over the world.

H & G Studios, Inc.
1490 S. Military Trail, Ste. n.3
West Palm Beach, FL 33415
ph: 561-649-3140
fax: 561-649-3141
http://www.hgstudios.com
　Sells Italian-made, wooden music
　boxes; containing images of exclusive
　original art; have Swiss Reuge
　musical movements.

Norman Rockwell

(see also ILLUSTRATORS, Norman
Rockwell)

Experts

Mary Moline
P.O. Box 1-4444
South Lake Tahoe, CA 96151
ph: 530-543-1414
fax: 530-543-1414
RockwellArt@aol.com
http://www.RockwellArt.com
　World authority on original Norman
　Rockwell art; author of "Norman
　Rockwell Collectibles Values Guide,"
　"Norman Rockwell Encyclopedia" as
　well as six other books on the subject.

Ornaments

(see also CHRISTMAS
COLLECTIBLES; HOLIDAY
COLLECTIBLES)

Collectors

Maret Webb
5101 E. Monterey Way
Phoenix, AZ 85018-6623
ph: 602-957-0653
fax: 602-957-1631
maret@vehrwebbstudio.com
　Wants Biederman brass ornaments;
　also wants Swarovski and Trimlite
　ornaments.

Dealers

Kathy Parrott
Christmas in Vermont
51 Jalbert Rd.
Barre, VT 05641
ph: 802-479-2024
katparrott@aol.com
　Specializes in mail order Barbie dolls,
　Hallmark Christmas ornaments,
　Kiddie Car classics, Merry Miniatures
　and other Hallmark collectibles;
　serving collectors worldwide since
　1988; catalog 4 times per year, send
　$5 for copy.

Alice Korman
Alice's Past & Presents Replacements
P.O. Box 465
Merrick, NY 11566-0465
ph: 516-379-1352
fax: 516-379-7302
alicechina@aol.com
http://hometown.aol.com/alicechina/
　myhomepage/business.html
　Specializes in Lenox, Gorham, Towle
　and other Christmas ornaments.

Joe Schulte
Gift Music Book & Collectibles
420 Wallace St.
Chicago Heights, IL 60411
ph: 708-877-7099 or 708-755-7622
fax: 208-275-5014
jntschulte@rocketmail.com
http://www.tias.com/stores/gift
　In stock or free search for retired:
　Swarovski, Radko, Wedgwood,
　Carlton, Hallmark, Enesco, Roman,
　Hummel, Precious Moments, Schmid,
　B & G, ANRI, Goebel, Grossman,
　Rockwell, Hibel, D56, etc.; a non-
　profit music group.

Misc. Services

Duck Software, Inc.
Software: Ornament Organizer
4015 Sunridge Rd.
Raleigh, NC　27613
mail@ducksoftware.com
http://www.ducksoftware.com
　Catalog all your Christmas ornaments
　with 16 different fields including
　name, category, series, series number,
　value, manufacturer, year made,
　artist, purchase price, date purchased,
　condition, and more.

TOdd Ray
YuleLog Ornament Collection Database
Software: YuleLog Software
4390 Jessica Dr.
Southaven, MS 38672
ph: 601-895-0053 or 800-243-1515 x110
todd@yulelog.com
http://www.yulelog.com
　Form your personal list of ornaments
　from this ornament database; market
　prices inserted automatically; program
　is rich in features.

Periodicals

Newsletter: Christmas Times
1024 N. Hamilton Ave.
Lindenhurst, NY 11757
voesack@interport.net
　Monthly buy-sell publication.

Ornaments (Buccellati)

Man./Prod./Dist.

Buccellati, Inc.
46 East 57th St.
New York, NY 10022
ph: 212-308-2900 or 800-223-7885
fax: 212-750-1323
http://www.buccellati.com
　Produces hundreds of entirely
　handmade ornaments annually using
　classical and baroque influences,
　gold, silver, precious and semi-
　precious stones

Ornaments (Carlton Cards)

Man./Prod./Dist.

Carlton Cards
One American Rd.
Cleveland, OH 44144
ph: 216-252-7300 or 800-679-8343
fax: 216-252-6777
linda.orient@amgreetings.com
http://www.carltoncards.com
　Offers many ornaments including Jim
　Hensen's Muppets and lighted
　ornaments.

Ornaments (Cazenovia Abroad)

Man./Prod./Dist.

Glen Trush
Cazenovia Abroad, Ltd.
67 Albany St.
Cazenovia, NY 13035-1219
ph: 315-655-3433 or 800-722-4327
fax: 315-655-4249
dtrush@dreamscape.com
http://www.cazenoviaabroad.com
　Offers a collection of over 50 full-size
　ornaments and almost as many
　miniature ornaments; also offers
　limited edition carousel figurines.

Ornaments (Christopher Radko)

Clubs/Associations

Christopher Radko Starlight Family of
Collectors
Magazine: Starlight
P.O. Box 775249
Saint Louis, MO 63177-2356
ph: 800-717-RADKO or 516-742-7616
support@christopherradko.com
http://www.christopherradko.com
　For Christopher Radko collectors;
　membership includes an ornament
　exclusive to members, a quarterly full-
　color magazine, mailings on upcoming
　appearances, new products, plus a full
　compliment of Christopher Radko
　catalogs for the year.

Dealers

Captain Jack
2866 NW 82nd Ave.
Ankeny, IA 50021
ph: 515-964-8500
captain@captainjack.com
http://www.radko.org
　Web site has images and prices for
　over 3000 Christopher Radko
　ornaments.

Experts

David Williams
Williams Nursery & The Gift House
524 Springfield Ave.
Westfield, NJ 07090
ph: 888-88R-ADKO or 908-232-4076
fax: 908-232-0079
dave@williamsnursery.com
http://www.radkoshop.com
　A Christopher Radko Rising Star
　store; large selection of Radko
　ornaments; visit Web site for live
　ornament chat, bulletin board, and
　current inventory.

Ornaments (Danforth)

Man./Prod./Dist.

Danforth Pewterers
P.O. Box 828
Middlebury, VT 05753
ph: 877-326-3678
fax: 802-388-0099
info@danforthpewter.com
http://www.danforthpewter.com
　Specializes in Christmas ornaments;
　also original Danforth Pewter
　holloware.

Ornaments (Enesco)

Clubs/Associations

Enesco Treasury of Christmas Ornaments
Collectors' Club
Newsletter: Treasury Trimmings
P.O. Box 277
Itasca, IL 60143-0277
ph: 630-875-5300 or 800-436-3726
fax: 630-875-5359
http://www.enesco.com
　Members receive symbol of member-
　ship ornament, membership card, club
　newsletter, subscription to Treasury
　Trimmings, collector's guide, list of
　dealers.

Ornaments (Hallmark)

Clubs/Associations

California Ornament Collectors Club
Newsletter: California Ornament
　Collectors Newsletter
105 Halstead Rd.
Marietta, OH 45750-1218
ph: 740-373-3114
jarvises@juno.com
　The original club for Hallmark
　Ornament collectors; offers answers to
　your questions.

Nancy M. Soddy
Central Wisconsin Ornament Collectors
　Club
401 Novak St.
Mosinee, WI 54455-2030
ph: 715-693-4135
　*Members interested primarily in
　collecting Hallmark Christmas
　ornaments; some members have other
　areas of interest as well.*

Hallmark Keepsake Ornament Collectors
　Club
Newsletter: Collector's Courier
P.O. Box 419034
Kansas City, MO 64141-6034
ph: 816-274-4000 or 800-523-5839
fax: 816-274-5061
　*Focuses on Hallmark Ornaments made
　of wood, acrylic, bone china,
　porcelain. A manufacturer-sponsored
　club.*

Dealers

Kathy Parrott
Christmas in Vermont
51 Jalbert Rd.
Barre, VT 05641
ph: 802-479-2024
katparrott@aol.com
　*Specializes in mail order Barbie dolls,
　Hallmark Christmas ornaments,
　Kiddie Car classics, Merry Miniatures
　and other Hallmark collectibles;
　serving collectors worldwide since
　1988; catalog 4 times per year, send
　$5 for copy.*

Joan Ketterer
Joan Ketterer Ornaments
P.O. Box 97172
Pittsburgh, PA 15229
ph: 412-367-2352
　Buys and sells Hallmark ornaments.

Experts

Kathy Parrott
Christmas in Vermont
51 Jalbert Rd.
Barre, VT 05641
ph: 802-479-2024
katparrott@aol.com
　*Specializes in mail order Barbie dolls,
　Hallmark Christmas ornaments,
　Kiddie Car classics, Merry Miniatures
　and other Hallmark collectibles;
　serving collectors worldwide since
　1988; catalog 4 times per year, send
　$5 for copy.*

Internet Resources

Susan Marr
Collecting Ornaments On Line (COOL)
1750 North Main St.
Terre Haute, IN 47803
smarr@abcs.com
http://www.daffodilgifts.com/club/
　cool.html
　*A not-for-profit online collectors club
　designed to bring together collectors
　of Hallmark Keepsake Ornaments, to
　provide a "club" experience for all
　collectors, and to support a charity.*

Man./Prod./Dist.

Hallmark Cards, Inc.
Consumer Affairs #216
P.O. Box 419034
Kansas City, MO 64141-6034
ph: 800-425-5627
http://www.hallmark.com
　*Producer of Christmas ornaments and
　figurines.*

Museums/Libraries

Prudencio/Hamrick Hallmark Ornament
　Museum
c/o The Party Shop
3418 Lake City Hwy.
Warsaw, IN 46580
ph: 219-267-8787
david@thepartyshop.com
http://www.thepartyshop.com/
　museum.html
　*Displays over 2,800 Hallmark
　ornaments - one of every design
　produced since Hallmark debuted its
　line of Keepsake Ornaments in 1973.*

Hallmark Visitors Center
P.O. Box 419580
Mail Drop 132
Kansas City, MO 64141-6580
ph: 816-274-5672 or 800-425-5627
http://www.hallmark.com

Periodicals

Joan Ketterer
Newsletter: Twelve Months of Christmas
P.O. Box 97172
Pittsburgh, PA 15229
ph: 412-367-2352
　*A biweekly newsletter for new and
　long-time Hallmark collectors.*

Ornaments (Old World)

Clubs/Associations

Old World Christmas Collectors' Club
Newsletter: Old World Christmas Star
　Gazette
P.O. Box 8000
Spokane, WA 99203-0030
ph: 800-962-7669 or 509-534-9000
fax: 509-534-9098
customerservice@oldworldchristmas.com
http://www.oldworldchristmas.com
　*Club members can purchase exclusive
　German holiday collectibles made of
　wood or glass.*

Man./Prod./Dist.

Old World Christmas Collectors' Club
P.O. Box 8000
Spokane, WA 99203-0030
ph: 800-962-7669 or 509-534-9000
fax: 509-534-9098
customerservice@oldworldchristmas.com
http://www.oldworldchristmas.com
　*Distributes high-quality, collectible
　Christmas collectibles and decora-
　tions.*

Ornaments (Sterling Silver)

Clubs/Associations

Hand & Hammer Collectors Club
Newsletter: Silver Tidings
2610 Morse Lane
Woodbridge, VA 22192
ph: 703-491-4866 or 800-SIL-VERY
fax: 703-491-2031
deChip@hand-hammer.com
http://www.hand-hammer.com
　*Focuses on the sterling silver
　collectibles designed by Chip
　deMatteo. Sponsored by Hand &
　Hammer, Co.*

Peggy Hart
Sterling Ornament Collectors
33 Ruffian Dr.
Stafford, VA 22554
ph: 540-286-3676
peggyphd@peggyhart.com
http://www.peggyhart.com
　*An association for sterling silver
　Christmas ornament collectors,
　designers, manufacturers, and other
　sterling silver ornament enthusiasts.*

Collectors

Kimlie Fox
525 2nd Ave. NW
Hickory, NC 28601
ph: 828-322-6326
foxden@conninc.com
　*Specializes in silver Christmas
　ornaments.*

Betty Overton
200 Avenida Santa Margarita
San Clemente, CA 92672
ph: 949-498-5330 or 949-498-4027
fax: 949-498-5330
edwhiffen@aol.com
　*Wants sterling and silverplated
　Christmas ornaments which have been
　made by many silver companies since
　1970.*

Dealers

Gary Niederkorn
Niederkorn Silver
Newspaper: Silver Edition
2005 Locust St.
Philadelphia, PA 19103-5606
ph: 215-567-2606
fax: 215-567-2606
niederkornsilver@aol.com
　*Specializes in 19th and 20th c. silver
　novelties, Christmas ornaments,
　napkin rings, Judaica, picture frames,
　etc.; also Tiffany, Jensen, Mexican.*

Peg Zurkowski
Becker Brooks Antiques
8027 Ellingson Dr.
Chevy Chase, MD 20815-3029
ph: 301-588-8558
fax: 301-608-2167
pegbeckz@aol.com
　*Specializing in out-of-production
　sterling ornaments.*

Experts

Peggy Hart
Christmas Editions
33 Ruffian Dr.
Stafford, VA 22554
ph: 540-286-3676
peggyphd@peggyhart.com
http://www.peggyhart.com
　*Experts on sterling silver Christmas
　ornaments and co-authors of "Sterling
　Ornaments, 2002", the only complete
　guide for collectors of sterling silver
　Christmas ornaments; much of it in
　color; available through author.*

Man./Prod./Dist.

Hand & Hammer Silversmiths
Newsletter: Silver Tidings
2610 Morse Lane
Woodbridge, VA 22192
ph: 703-491-4866 or 800-SIL-VERY
fax: 703-491-2031
deChip@hand-hammer.com
http://www.hand-hammer.com
　*Manufacturer of sterling silver
　Christmas ornaments.*

P. Buckley Moss

Clubs/Associations

P. Buckley Moss Society
Newsletter: Sentinel
601 Shenandoah Village Dr., Ste. 1C
Waynesboro, VA 22980
ph: 540-943-5678 or 804-725-7378
fax: 540-949-8408
society@mosssociety.org
http://www.MossSociety.org
　*The Society was established to foster
　an awareness of the art of P. Buckley
　Moss and to promote charitable
　endeavors consistent with her ideals;
　society administers an exclusive
　members-only benefits program.*

Man./Prod./Dist.

Moss Portfolio, The
HC69 Box 17118
Mathews, VA 23109
ph: 804-725-7378
fax: 804-725-3040
mossportfolio@ccsinc.com
http://www.p-buckley-moss.com
　*Publisher and distributor of
　watercolors, original prints, offset
　lithographs, plates, dolls, and
　figurines by P. Buckley Moss.*

Penni Anne Cross

Man./Prod./Dist.

Cross Gallery, Inc.
P.O. Box 990
Willow, AK 99688
ph: 907-495-6472
fax: 907-495-6473
pacross@mtaonline.net
　*Offers plates, figurines, dolls,
　Christmas ornaments, and graphics
　designed by Penni Anne Cross.*

Pickard

Man./Prod./Dist.

Pickard China Co.
782 Pickard Ave.
Antioch, IL 60002
ph: 847-395-3800
fax: 847-395-3827
Finest@pickardchina.com
http://www.pickardchina.com
In addition to dinnerware, manufactures collectible plates, bells, ornaments, steins and bowls.

Plates

(see also PLATES)

Clubs/Associations

Karen Feil, Mng. Dir.
Gifts & Collectibles Guild
77 W. Washington St., Ste. 1716
Chicago, IL 60602
ph: 312-379-2935
fax: 312-379-2939
cggnews@aol.com
http://www.giftguild.org
Trade association of the leading producers of contemporary limited editions and collectibles ranging from art prints to porcelain figures, dolls, plates, diecast, and more.

International Collectors Guild
Newsletter: Platter Platter
P.O. Box 487
Artesia, CA 90702-0487
ph: 562-694-4007
A monthly newsletter for collectors of limited edition plates.

Dealers

Nancy Pelham
Homestead Gift Shop
4 Hillwood Lane
Catskill, NY 12414
ph: 518-943-4371
fluffy@capital.net
http://www.homestead-gift-shop.com
Carries a variety of collector plates by several manufacturers as well as display easels and frames.

Village Plate Collector, The
120 Forrest Ave.
Cocoa, FL 32922
ph: 800-511-2935
fax: 407-636-0929
loisvpc@aol.com
http://collectibles.net/naled/villageplate

Joe Schulte
Gift Music Book & Collectibles
420 Wallace St.
Chicago Heights, IL 60411
ph: 708-877-7099 or 708-755-7622
fax: 208-275-5014
jntschulte@rocketmail.com
http://www.tias.com/stores/gift
In stock or free search for retired: Hamilton, Wedgwood, Roman, ANRI, Bradford, Hummel, Reco, Knowles, B & G, RD, Perillo, DeGrazia, Gorham, Rockwell, Royal

Copenhagen, D56, etc.; a non-profit music group.

Laura Kazimier
Bradford Exchange Trading Center, The
9307 N. Milwaukee Ave.
Niles, IL 60714-1381
ph: 877-268-6638 or 847-581-8452
fax: 847-966-2875
http://www.collectiblestoday.com
A brokerage service to match secondary market buyers and sellers of collector plates that are no longer in production.

Mickey Kaz
Collectibles Unlimited
P.O. Box 606
Woodland Hills, CA 91365-0606
ph: 818-703-6173
fax: 818-703-6173
mickey@collectibles-unlimited.com
http://www.collectibles-unlimited.com
Serving the world of plate collectors since 1977: plates, plate frames, stands, easels.

Experts

Ross Ernst
Collectors Plates
7308 Izard
Omaha, NE 68114-3237
ph: 402-391-3469
Buys and sells Bradford plates, Royal Copenhagen (RC), Bing & Grondahl (B/G), P. Buckley Moss plates, Perillo, M.I. Hummel, Duncan Royale, Lilliput Lane, Hamilton Dolls, Ashton Drake Dolls, and old estate RC & B/G plates.

Man./Prod./Dist.

Laura Kazimier
Bradford Exchange, The
9307 N. Milwaukee Ave.
Niles, IL 60714-1381
ph: 877-268-6638 or 847-581-8452
fax: 847-966-2875
http://www.collectiblestoday.com
Pioneered direct mail marketing of collector plates and created an organized secondary market trading exchange for collector plates.

Matching Services

Robert Goins
Replacements Ltd.
P.O. Box 26029
1089 Knox Rd.
Greensboro, NC 27420
ph: 800-737-5223 or 336-697-3000
fax: 336-697-3100
inquire@replacements.com
http://www.replacements.com
Carries collector plates in addition to china, crystal and flatware (obsolete, active and inactive.)

Museums/Libraries

Laura Kazimier
Bradford Museum of Collector's Plates, The
9307 N. Milwaukee Ave.
Niles, IL 60714-1381
ph: 877-268-6638 or 847-581-8452
fax: 847-966-2875
http://www.collectiblestoday.com

Plates (Rockwell)

Clubs/Associations

Michael J.P. Collins, Pres.
Rockwell Society of America
Newsletter: Rockwell Society of America Newsletter
P.O. Box 705
Ardsley, NY 10502-0705
Founded in 1974 and dedicated to the appreciation of America's most famous artist, Norman Rockwell; specializing in original paintings, drawings, collectibles, e.g. Saturday Evening Post covers/magazines, illustrated books, etc.

Prayer Ladies

Experts

April M. Tvorak
P.O. Box 94
Warren Center, PA 18851
Wants to buy Mother-in-the-Kitchen (Prayer Ladies) ceramic figurines and accessories; imported in the 1960s by ENESCO; typically decorated with a motif of an older woman with hair in bun, head bowed, hands in prayer, and prayer on apron.

Steven C. Johnson
4003 Jefferson St.
Sioux City, IA 51108
ph: 712-239-5188
Collector and consultant to "The Official Price Guide to Pottery and Porcelain."

Precious Moments

Clubs/Associations

Enesco Precious Moments Collectors' Club
Newsletter: Goodnewsletter
P.O. Box 99
Itasca, IL 60143-0099
ph: 630-875-5300 or 800-436-3726
fax: 630-875-5359
caffairs@enesco.com
http://www.enesco.com
Members receive symbol of membership figurine, quarterly newsletter, membership card, members' only offerings, gift registry, club binder, annual local chapter national convention, Orient tour.

Enesco Precious Moments Birthday Club
Newsletter: Good News Parade
P.O. Box 689
Itasca, IL 60143-0689
ph: 630-875-5300 or 800-436-3726
fax: 630-875-5359
http://www.enesco.com
For young collectors; this category of

Precious Moments figurines feature animals and circus themes; members receive symbol of membership figurine, club newsletter, membership certificate, members' only offerings, birthday card.

Dealers

Limited Edition, The
2170 Sunrise Highway
Merrick, NY 11566
ph: 516-623-4400 or 800-645-2864
fax: 516-867-3701
gifts@thelimitededition.com
http://www.thelimitededition.com
Specializes in suspended and retired Precious Moments, Cherished Teddies, Department 56, Harmony Kingdom, Charming Tales, and Walt Disney CLassics.

Experts

Kristi Schult
7601-E Nehe St.
Honolulu, HI 96818
ph: 808-421-0747 or 808-277-9940
fax: 208-955-7715
KristiS@preciousmomentscommunity.com
Precious Moments collector and dealer; author of "2003 Kristi's Guide to the World of Precious Moments."

Internet Resources

Hans J. Schindhelm
M.I. Hummel & Precious Moments Internet Sites Directory
8 John Walsh Blvd., Ste. 412
Peekskill, NY 10566
ph: 914-734-8410
fax: 914-762-1719
siegmar@aol.com
http://members.aol.com/hummel2001
Free online directory of Web pages and Internet sites relating to M.I. Hummel and Precious Moments collectibles.

Kristi Schult
Precious Moments Community
7601-E Nehe St.
Honolulu, HI 96818
ph: 808-421-0747 or 808-277-9940
fax: 208-955-7715
KristiS@preciousmomentscommunity.com
http://
www.preciousmomentscommunity.com
The only Precious Moments licensed community on the Internet; provides a wealth of information about Precious Moments; members get exclusive news, classified ads, e-cards, PM Museum and more.

Repair Services

Hans J. Schindhelm
Ceramic Restorations of Westchester, Inc.
8 John Walsh Blvd., Ste. 412
Peekskill, NY 10566
ph: 914-734-8410
fax: 914-762-1719
siegmar@aol.com
http://www.swiftsite.com/hummel-preciousmoments/repair.html
Repair and restoration service for any brand of porcelain and ceramic collectibles, antiques and art objects; specializing in Precious Moments and Hummels; also Disney, Cybis, Boehm, Hutschenreuther, Rosenthal and others.

Precious Moments (Musicals)

Clubs/Associations

Enesco Musical Society
Newsletter: Musical Notes
225 Windsor Dr.
Itasca, IL 60143
ph: 630-875-5300 or 800-436-3726
fax: 630-875-5359
caffairs@enesco.com
http://www.enesco.com
For collectors of Enesco's musical collectibles; members receive color calendar, quarterly newsletter, membership certificate, members' only offering.

Reed & Barton

Man./Prod./Dist.

Reed & Barton
144 W. Britannia St.
Taunton, MA 02780
ph: 508-824-6611 or 800-822-1824
fax: 508-822-7269
information@reedbarton.com
http://www.reedbarton.com
Produces china, crystal, silver, silverplate, and stainless flatware, collectible plates, bells, dolls, ornaments and accessories.

Royal Copenhagen

Man./Prod./Dist.

Royal Scandinavian, Inc.
140 Bradford Dr.
West Berlin, NJ 08091
ph: 609-768-5400 or 800-431-1992
fax: 800-448-7553
http://www.royalscandinavia.com
Royal Copenhagen, Bing & Grondahl, Holmegaard, and Georg Jensen are the best of Scandinavian collectibles; manufactures dinnerware, cobalt blue underglaze collector plates, figurines, bells, dolls, ornaments and gift accessories.

Royal Doulton

(see also CERAMICS [ENGLISH], Doulton; CERAMICS [ENGLISH], Royal Doulton)

Clubs/Associations

Royal Doulton International Collectors Club
Magazine: Gallery
701 Cottontail Lane
Somerset, NJ 08873
ph: 732-356-7880 or 800-682-4462
fax: 732-764-4974
usa@royal-doulton.com
http://www.royal-doulton.com
Focuses on the Royal Doulton collectibles; members entitled to purchase "member only" figurines or character and Toby jugs; advance notice of introductions and withdrawals; a newsletter has free buy/sell ads for members.

Valerie Baynton
Royal Doulton International Collectors Club
Magazine: Gallery
Minton House
London Rd.
Stoke-on-Trent, Staffordshire ST4 7QD U.K.
ph: (01782) 292127 or (01782) 292292
fax: (01782) 292099
icc@royal-doulton.com
http://www.royal-doulton.com
Focuses on the Royal Doulton collectibles; members entitled to purchase "member only" figurines or character and Toby jugs; advance notice of introductions and withdrawals; a newsletter has free buy/sell ads for members.

Dealers

Recollections by Arlene & Barry
3823 Oceanside Rd. East
Oceanside, NY 11572
ph: 516-678-4652
fax: 516-536-1804
recollects@usa.net
http://www.recollects.com
Collectors of Royal Doulton for over 30 years: Character and Toby jugs, Bunnykins, Beatrix Potter, Flambe, Doulton Lambeth, Doulton Burslem.

Sandy & Ed Seward
Vintage Collectibles
6601 17th Lane, N.
Saint Petersburg, FL 33702
ph: 727-522-9918
fax: 727-525-6285
vintage@tias.com
http://www.tias.com/stores/vintage
Specializes in Royal Doulton collectibles: rare vintage figurines, character and Toby jugs, Beatrix Potter, Bunnykins, Branbly Hedge, Minton, Royal Crown Derby, Royal Albert, etc.

Internet Resources

Ron Heath
Search4Doulton.com
P.O. Box 64
Longwell Green
Kingswood, Bristol BS30 9ZT U.K.
ph: 0117 932 5852
fax: 0117 904 9994
enquiries@search4doulton.com
http://www.search4doulton.com
Essential resources for collectors of discontinued Royal Doulton, Beswick, Royal Crown Derby; dealer sales, free message board, events, worldwide dealers.

Matching Services

Michael Negrotti
Tabletop Designs
P.O. Box 448
Cheshire, CT 06410
ph: 800-801-4084
lenox@ntplx.net
http://www.tabletopdesigns.com
A small, personal matching service with a constantly changing inventory; want lists are kept; send photocopy or photo when unsure of pattern name; specializes in Lenox.

Russian

(see also RUSSIAN ITEMS)

Dealers

Walton Conway
Golden Cockerel
4697 Rich Mountain Rd.
Boone, NC 28607
ph: 828-297-4653
goldencc@boone.net
http://www.goldencockerel.com
Designer, producer, direct importer, wholesaler, retailer of Russian applied arts and folk crafts.

Natalie Bell
Open House Miniatures
402 Railroad Ave. W.
Allendale, SC 29810
Carries highest quality Russian miniatures available; also painted eggs, matreshkas (nesting dolls), icons, and Palekh boxes made by the Russian Association of Dollhouse & Miniature Masters (see examples at http://www.aha.ru/~vladin/).

Vitaly Shukin
Russian Shop, The
1720 Ogden Ave.
Lisle, IL 60532-1230
ph: 630-963-5160 or 800-778-9404
fax: 630-963-5170
mail@TheRussianShop.com
http://www.TheRussianShop.com
Imports unusual Russian gifts and collectibles; experts in identifying authentic Russian lacquer boxes and nesting dolls; dealer in contemporary Russian porcelain; free catalog; family business for over 25 years.

Paul Tyutin
Russian Sunbirds, Inc.
3780 Hancock St., Ste. E
San Diego, CA 92110
ph: 619-220-7172
fax: 619-220-7175
sales@sunbirds.com
http://www.sunbirds.com
Carries exquisite Russian lacquer art, featuring unique works by artists from Fedoskino, Palekh, Khuloy and Mstera; Web site contains a vast artist database, an extensive readings section, and a detailed FAQ; searchable inventory.

Natasha Soboleva
Russian Treasure
2801 Leavenworth St.
San Francisco, CA 94133
ph: 415-346-1104
fax: 415-664-6561
natasha@russiantreasure.com
http://www.russiantreasure.com
Sells contemporary Russian items: matreshkas-babushka (nesting dolls), original Palekh, Fedoskino, Mstera lacquered papier-mâché boxes, Faberge eggs, Baltic amber, chess sets.

Matvei Finkel
Siberian Wild Products
325 W. Brierwood Ave.
Spokane, WA 99218
ph: 509-467-5562
fax: 509-468-2184
mfinkel@cet.com
http://www.russianmade.com/temp
Sells hand crafted items from Siberia, the Russian Far East, and also from many parts of Moscow and Western Russia; nesting dolls, eggs, icons, lacquered boxes.

Man./Prod./Dist.

Marina's Russian Collection
900 N.. Michigan Ave., 5th Floor
Chicago, IL 60611
ph: 312-664-7596
Distributes Russian matryoshka (nesting dolls) and lacquered boxes.

Sculptures (Cain)

Clubs/Associations

Mike Kemp
Cain Studios Collectors Guild
Newsletter: Rick Cain Studios' Collectors Guild News
3500 NE Waldo Rd.
Gainesville, FL 32609
ph: 800-535-3949 or 352-377-7657
fax: 352-377-7038
A club for fans of artist Rick Cain; members receive free membership sculpture, redemption coupons, members-only sculptures, and more.

Sculptures (Chilmark)

Clubs/Associations

Jim Swieznski, Dir.
Chilmark Gallery
Newsletter: Chilmark Report
111 Island St.
Stoughton, MA 02072-1401
ph: 508-568-1401
fax: 508-568-8741
Focuses on Chilmark pewter sculptures; "Chilmark Report" reports on new editions and artist appearances. "The Observer" keeps collectors up-to-date on secondary markets and values.

Repair Services

Isaura
CRC Workshop
5 Birch Hill Rd.
Pepperell, MA 01463-1286
ph: 978-448-5252
Specializes in the complete restoration of Chilmark pewters made by the Lance Corp.; extremely knowledgeable about Lance materials, processes and techniques.

Sculptures (CPSmithshire)

Clubs/Associations

Jim Swiezynski, Dir.
Pangaean Society, The
Newsletter: Shirespeak
111 Island St.
Stoughton, MA 02072-1401
ph: 508-568-1401
fax: 508-568-8741
Focuses on Cindy Smity's collection of Shireling Figurines.

Sculptures (Don Polland)

Clubs/Associations

Polland Collectors Society, c/o Polland
  Studios
Newsletter: Collectors Review
P.O. Box 2468
Prescott, AZ 86302
ph: 520-778-1900 or 800-553-0671
fax: 520-778-4034
Focuses on Don Polland's pewter sculpture collectible figurines. Sponsored by Polland Studios.

Man./Prod./Dist.

Donald J. Polland
Polland Studios
P.O. Box 2468
Prescott, AZ 86302
ph: 520-778-1900 or 800-553-0671
fax: 520-778-4034
Focuses on Don Polland's pewter sculpture collectible figurines. Sponsored by Polland Studios (Gerard Corp.)

Sculptures (LEGENDS)

Clubs/Associations

Starlite Collectors Society
11908 Ventura Blvd.
Studio City, CA 91604
ph: 800-726-9660 or 818-761-7779
fax: 818-761-8889
legends1@aol.com
http://www.legends4you.com
Collectors of art sculptures in mixed media such as bronze, fine pewter and 24 karat gold vermeil made by Legends. A manufacturer-sponsored collector's club.

Man./Prod./Dist.

LEGENDS
11908 Ventura Blvd.
Studio City, CA 91604
ph: 800-726-9660 or 818-761-7779
fax: 818-761-8889
legends1@aol.com
http://www.legends4you.com
Producers of art sculptures in mixed media such as bronze, fine pewter and 24 karat gold vermeil.

Sculptures (Mark Hopkins)

Clubs/Associations

L. Susan Fife
Mark Hopkins Bronze Guild
Newsletter: Bronzeworks
21 Shorter Industrial Blvd.
Rome, GA 30165-1838
ph: 800-678-6564 or 706-235-8773
fax: 706-235-2814
Focuses on bronze castings by Mark Hopkins.

Man./Prod./Dist.

Russell Bower
Mark Hopkins Bronze Guild
21 Shorter Industrial Blvd.
Rome, GA 30165-1838
ph: 800-678-6564 or 706-235-8773
fax: 706-235-2814
Produces and sells fine bronze sculptures.

Sculptures (Rawcliffe)

Man./Prod./Dist.

Rawcliffe Corp.
175 Dupont Circle
Providence, RI 02907
ph: 401-331-1645 or 800-343-1811
info@rawcliffe.com
http://www.rawcliffe.com
Manufactures giftware and collectibles in fine pewter.

Sculptures (Sandicast)

Clubs/Associations

Steve Yaptangco
Sandicast Collectors Guild
Newsletter: Paw Press
P.O. Box 910079
San Diego, CA 92191-0079
ph: 858-695-9611 or 800-722-3316
fax: 858-695-0615
guild@sandicast.com
http://www.sandicast.com
For collectors of animal sculptures noted for their lifelike appearance and designed by artist Sandra A. Brue; annual members-only piece not available to the general public.

Man./Prod./Dist.

Steve Yaptangco
Sandicast, Inc.
P.O. Box 910079
San Diego, CA 92191-0079
ph: 858-695-9611 or 800-722-3316
fax: 858-695-0615
guild@sandicast.com
http://www.sandicast.com
Manufacturer of handcast and handpainted animal sculptures noted for their lifelike appearance and designed by artist Sandra A. Brue; Paw Press published semiannually.

Sculptures (Tom Clark)

(see also GNOMES)

Man./Prod./Dist.

Cairn Studio Ltd.
P.O. Box 400
Davidson, NC 28036
ph: 704-892-5859
info@cairnstudio.com
http://www.cairnstudio.com
Manufactures gnomes and other character figurines by artist Dr. Tom Clark.

Shoes (Miniature)

Clubs/Associations

Just The Right Club
Magazine: inStep
1129 Industrial Ave.
P.O. Box 750009
Petaluma, CA 94975
ph: 877-587-5877 or 707-778-7211
fax: 707-769-0304
jtrc@willitts.com
http://www.willitts.com
For collectors of miniature shoes designed by Raine.

Skippy

Clubs/Associations

Joan Crosby Tibbetts, Pres.
Skippy Collectors Club, c/o Skippy, Inc.
8304 Tobin Rd., #14
Annandale, VA 22003
ph: 703-698-4346
fax: 703-698-4346
JCTSkippy@aol.com
http://www.skippy.com
Focuses on the Skippy print and doll collectibles. Sponsored by Skippy, Inc.

Spangler's Realm

Man./Prod./Dist.

Spangler's Realm Collectors Club, c/o
  Realms, Inc.
11733 Lackland Rd.
Maryland Heights, MO 63146
ph: 314-991-0793
fax: 314-991-0958
Focuses on the Spangler's Realm line of figurines, bells, ornaments and prints. Sponsored by Realms, Inc.

Sports Related

(see also SPORTS COLLECTIBLES)

Sports Related (Gartlan)

Clubs/Associations

Tom Nardi
Collectors' League
Newsletter: Collectors' Quarterly
575 Hwy. 73 North, Ste. A-6
West Berlin, NJ 08091-2440
ph: 856-753-9229
fax: 856-753-9280
info@gartlanusa.com
http://www.gartlanusa.com
Focuses on the Gartlan sports and entertainment collectibles; sponsored by Gartlan USA.

Man./Prod./Dist.

Tom Nardi
Gartlan USA
575 Hwy. 73 North, Ste. A-6
West Berlin, NJ 08091-2440
ph: 856-753-9229
fax: 856-753-9280
info@gartlanusa.com
http://www.gartlanusa.com
Produces sports and entertainment collectibles including plates, figurines, graphics, ornaments, and baseballs.

Sports Related (Sports Imp.)

Man./Prod./Dist.

ENESCO Corp.
225 Windsor Dr.
Itasca, IL 60143
ph: 630-875-5300 or 800-436-3726
fax: 630-875-5359
caffairs@enesco.com
http://www.enesco.com
Distributor of Sports Impressions.

Sports Related (Start. Lineup)

Dealers

Minnesota Connection, The
8393 213th St. West
Lakeville, MN 55044
ph: 612-469-1321
fax: 612-469-4477
mnconn@mninter.net
http://www.mnconn.com
Large dealer in Kenner's Starting Lineup figures.

Steins

(see also GLASSES, Drinking)

Clubs/Associations

Joyce M. Reyhons, Pres.
Advertising Cup & Mug Collectors of America
Newsletter: Cupletter, The
P.O. Box 680
Solon, IA 52333
ph: 319-644-3636
For collectors of special custom-made ceramic or plastic mugs, cups, and steins from advertisers, fund raisers, shows, conventions, or promotions; quarterly newsletter; send $2 plus LSASE for sample.

Anheuser-Busch Collectors Club
P.O. Box 503015
Saint Louis, MO 63150
ph: 800-742-5283
fax: 618-241-7602
budshop@anheuser-busch.com
http://www.budshop.com
For collectors of Anheuser-Busch steins and related collectibles.

Dealers

Sam & Samantha May
Sam's Steins & Collectibles
2207 Lincoln Highway East
Lancaster, PA 17602-1111
ph: 717-394-6404 or 888-442-5726 (orders)
fax: 717-394-6427
info@samssteins.com
http://www.samssteins.com
For the collector of mugs and steins: Anheuser Busch, Strohs, Coors, Miller, Hamm's, Pabst, Yuengling, etc.; also German steins, Cavanaugh Coca-Cola bear figurines; send two first class stamps for list.

Bob Lamson
Bob Lamson Beer Steins, Inc.
509 N. 22nd St.
Allentown, PA 18104-4305
ph: 610-435-8611 or 800-435-8611

Wally Karutz
Great American Brewery Shoppe, The
128 N.Main St.
P.O. Box 4417
Salisbury, NC 28145-4417
ph: 704-642-1345 or 800-223-8197
fax: 704-642-1377
wallyworld@collectorsteins.com
http://www.geocities.com/Eureka/Plaza/3544
Carries large selection of Budweiser and other brewery steins and collectibles.

Larry Meyer
Kaiser Bill's
P.O. Box 177
Helen, GA 30545
ph: 800-922-2182 or 706-878-1408
fax: 706-878-1409
kaiserbills@alltel.net
http://www.kaiserbills.com
Displays over 1500 different beer steins including Budweiser, German, Coke, Civil War, wooden, and NASCAR steins; 1995's largest Anheuser-Busch dealer in the country.

Roy & Cordie Willis
Heartland of Kentucky Decanters & Steins
P.O. Box 428
Lebanon Junction, KY 40150
ph: 502-833-2827
fax: 502-833-3480
heartland@decantersandsteins.com
http://www.decantersandsteins.com
Hundreds of steins available: Budweiser, Corona and German figural and commemorative steins; also decanters by Jim Beam, and others; call ONLY 10-6 Eastern time, Monday through Saturday.

Bill Cress
P.O. Box 989
Alton, IL 62002-0989
ph: 618-466-3513
williambud@webtv.net
Buys and sells all of the new and lots of the old steins; quarterly lists of modern steins and mugs for sale.

Doug & Natalie Marks
Flash Collectibles
PMB 287
560 N. Moorpark Rd.
Thousand Oaks, CA 91360
ph: 805-499-9222
fax: 805-376-5541
flashcoll@aol.com
http://members.aol.com/flashcoll
Buys and sells contemporary beer steins by mail order; specializes in American beer brands, Budweiser, Miller, Coors, Hamms, Pabst, Old Style, etc.

Jim & Linda Cheely
These Steins of Mine
2449 Hugo Rd.
Merlin, OR 97532
ph: 541-479-1971
lcheely@cpros.com
http://www.cpros.com/~lcheely
Buys, sells, trades Anheuser Busch

Budweiser steins in the secondary market worldwide over the Internet.

Man./Prod./Dist.

Anheuser-Busch, Inc.
P.O. Box 503015
Saint Louis, MO 63150
ph: 800-742-5283
fax: 618-241-7602
budshop@anheuser-busch.com
http://www.budshop.com
Creates collector steins and plates of character and celebration, with classic and contemporary themes and styles.

Ken Armke
OHI Exchange
553 Landa St.
New Braunfels, TX 78130
ph: 830-629-1191
fax: 830-606-1118
Comments@OHIExchange.com
http://www.ohioexchange.com/steins
OHI offers exclusive limited edition steins and mugs for the discerning collector.

Misc. Services

Weishair Custom Software
Software: Beer Stein Collector
P.O. Box 717
Albany, MN 56307-0717
ph: 888-745-7031 or 320-845-7031
fax: 320-845-7306
info@villagecollector.com
http://www.villagecollector.com
Software program designed to make keeping track of your collectibles fun and easy; pre-loaded databases include Anheuser-Busch beer steins, plates, banks, Miller steins, and other steins.

Ted DeGrazia

Man./Prod./Dist.

Artists of the World
2915 N. 67th Place
Scottsdale, AZ 85251-6001
ph: 602-946-6361
fax: 602-941-8918
a-o-w@primenet.com
http://www.a-o-w.com
Produces collector plates, figurines, ornaments and miniatures based on the work of Ted DeGrazia.

Toby Jugs (Kevin Francis)

Clubs/Associations

Kevin Francis Toby Jug Collectors Guild
917 Chicago Ave.
Evanston, IL 60202
ph: 800-634-0431 or 847-570-4867
fax: 847-570-4871
Britcol@msn.com
http://www.britishcollectibles.com
Produces Toby Jugs designed by Francis Salmon and Kevin Pearson.

COLLEGE COLLECTIBLES

Humor Magazines

Collectors

Michael Gessel
P.O. Box 748
Arlington, VA 22216-0748
ph: 703-524-0462
mgessel@cheerful.com
Wants magazines (bound or individual copies); also posters and anthologies.

COMBS & HAIR ACCESSORIES

(see also BARBERSHOP COLLECTIBLES; BEAUTY SHOP COLLECTIBLES; CLOTHING & ACCESSORIES, Vintage; DRESSER ITEMS, Hatpins & Hatpin Holders; HAIRWORK; GEMS & JEWELRY; SHAVING COLLECTIBLES)

Clubs/Associations

Theresa Bagasra
Antique Comb Collectors Club International
Newsletter: Antique Comb Collector
205 Hawk Chase Dr.
Orangeburg, SC 29118
ph: 803-516-9758
fax: 803-516-9758
trb@sc.rr.com
http://www.geocities.com/heartland/pointe/5350
Organization dedicated to sharing research and information about antique and ornamental accessories for the hair from any culture; offers research, networking, networking, bi-annual convention.

Collectors

Linda Shapiro
8712 Pleasant View Rd.
Bangor, PA 18013

Belva Green
90 Highland Ave., #1204
Tarpon Springs, FL 34689-5351
ph: 727-942-7354
belva.green@verizon.net
Serious comb collector; active in Antique Comb Collector's Club.

Mary Bachman
4901 Grandview
Ypsilanti, MI 48197-3762
ph: 734-434-2045
bachman@provide.net
Author of "Collectors Guide to Hair Combs" (Collector Books).

Glenn L. Beall
32981 N. River Rd.
Libertyville, IL 60048-4259
ph: 847-549-9970
fax: 847-549-9935

Experts

Belva Green
90 Highland Ave., #1204
Tarpon Springs, FL 34689-5351
ph: 727-942-7354
Collector, historian, researcher, writer, lecturer on combs, jewelry and accessories for the hair; travelling exhibits; editor for Antique Comb Collector Club International newsletter; manuscripts welcome; query with SASE.

Museums/Libraries

Leominster Historical Society, Field School Museum
17 School St.
Leominster, MA 01453
ph: 978-534-5375
Lcris5745@aol.com
http://hometown.aol.com/
 Leominster476/Historical.html
One of the best comb collections in the US.

COMIC ART

(see CARTOON ART)

COMIC BOOKS

(see also CARTOON ART;
CHARACTER COLLECTIBLES;
COMIC ART; COMIC
COLLECTIBLES; COWBOY
HEROES; DISNEY COLLECTIBLES;
FAN CLUBS; PREMIUMS; SCIENCE
FICTION; SUPER HEROES;
TRADING CARDS, Non-Sport)

Appraisers

Thomas Bauer
Nonstop Collectibles
6152 Terrebonne
Montreal, Quebec H4B 1A3 Canada
ph: 514-489-5499
thomasbauer@sympatico.ca
http://www.thomasbauer.ca
Internet sales consultant and broker since 1993; active in online sales and marketing of comic books and other collectibles; will do qualified evaluations of your collection; list items for sale for 20% commission; good comic info.

Auction Services

John Petty
Heritage Comics Auctions
100 Highland Park Village, 2nd Fl.
Heritage Plaze
Dallas, TX 75205-2788
ph: 800-872-6467 or 214-528-3500
fax: 214-520-6968
JPetty@heritagecomics.com
http://www.heritagecomics.com
Specializes in the auction sale of comic books; also buys and sells.

James Halperin
Heritage Galleries & Auctioneers
Dallas, TX 75219
ph: 800-872-6467 or 214-528-3500
fax: 214-520-7108
auctions@HeritageComics.com
http://www.HeritageComics.com
Free online community of over 13,000 popular culture bidder-members; specializes in comic books, comic art, memorabilia, character toys; quarterly multi-million dollar Signature auctions; over $17M in comics/comic art sold in 2002.

Collectors

Gary Pimenta
64 Lakeside Dr.
Tiverton, RI 02878-3111
Wants to buy comic books based on TV shows and theatrical movies; send photos and asking prices.

Steve A. Geppi
Diamond Comic Distributors, Inc.
1966 Greenspring Dr., Ste. 300
Lutherville Timonium, MD 21093-4161
ph: 410-560-7100
webmaster@diamondcomics.com
http://www.diamondcomics.com
Golden Age, DC's, Timelys, Marvels, all 10-cent and 12-cent comics pre-1968; also baseball cards or related items.

Dealers

Northeast Comics/Action Figures
gtalon@hotmail.com
http://members.tripod.com/~gtalon/
 index.html
Over 10,000 Silver Age comics; also hundreds of action figures.

Joshua Nathanson
ComicLink: The Internet Comic Book
 Exchange
4842 Glenwood St.
Flushing, NY 11363-0299
ph: 718-423-6079
fax: 718-423-9801
buysell@comiclink.com
http://www.comiclink.com

Richard Semowich
56 John Smith Rd.
Binghamton, NY 13901
ph: 607-648-4025
Wants old comic books from 1933 to 1970; buying any size collection; contact for the best price.

Jon Warren
Iguide Media Inc.
2401 Broad St.
Chattanooga, TN 37408
ph: 423-265-5515
fax: 423-265-5515
jon@iguide.net
http://www.iguide.net
Wants comics, also wants cartoon art, Disney, Big Little Books, Pulp Magazines, Baseball and Non-Sport Cards.

Bill & Joanne Bruegman
Toy Scouts, Inc.
137 Casterton Ave.
Akron, OH 44303-1543
ph: 330-836-0668
orders@toyscouts.com
http://www.toyscouts.com
Wants to buy 1935-1965 super hero, horror, etc. 10-cent and 12-cent comics.

Cashman Comics
1018 S. Madison
Bay City, MI 48708
ph: 989-895-1113
cashmanscomics@aol.com
http://members.aol.com/Paralax
Features new releases that ship weekly; also extensive Silver Age and Golden Age back issues.

John Kula
Goldmine Collectibles
65 54th St. SW
Grand Rapids, MI 49548
ph: 616-534-7227 or 616-361-2352
fax: 616-534-0009
comicman@grnet.com
http://www.GoldmineComics.com
Collector and expert buys, sells, trades comic, toys and other collectibles pertaining to Star Wars, Spawn, GI Joe, Transformers, X-Files,

Babylon V, and other science fiction shows or movies.

Carl Bonasera
All American Comic Shops, Ltd.
3514 W. 95th St.
Evergreen Park, IL 60805
ph: 708-425-7555
alamcarl@ameritech.net
Advisor to Alex Malloy's "Comic Values Annual;" specializes in 1950s-1990s comic books, magazines, science fiction digests and pulps.

Mark Farace
All American Collectibles
6510 Chippewa St.
Saint Louis, MO 63109-4107
ph: 314-353-9500 or 314-352-7700
mf@aac-mo.com
http://www.aac-mo.com

Stan Gold
As Time Goes By
7042 Dartbrook Dr.
Dallas, TX 75240
ph: 972-239-8621 or 972-352-2765
fax: 972-239-9622
record@astimegoesby.com
http://www.astimegoesby.com
Wants to buy Golden Age, Silver Age, 1940s and 1950s horror/humor/war comic books, TV related and Western comics; also wants vintage comic

related puzzles, books, records and toys.

Michael Dice
309 S Washington
Cortez, CO 81321
ph: 970-564-9018
Buys, sells, trades comic strips from Sunday papers, especially from bound newspapers; also wants pre-1955 comic books.

Pacific Comics Exchange, Inc.
P.O. Box 2629
Palos Verdes Peninsula, CA 90274
ph: 310-544-4936
fax: 310-544-4900
sales@pcei.com
http://www.pcei.com
Over 50 years experience with comic books.

Dennis Schamp
Comic Gallery, The
4224 Balboa Ave.
San Diego, CA 92117-5508
ph: 858-483-4853
comicgallerysd@hotmail.com
Advisor to Alex Malloy's "Comic Values Annual;" 5 star comic book expert on Yahoo!; since 1980.

David Smith
Rocket Comics
P.O. Box 30183
Seattle, WA 98103
ph: 206-784-7300
fax: 206-782-2844
rocket@jetcity.com
http://www.jetcity.com/~rocket
Dealer/expert buying and selling vintage comic books and pulp magazines since 1969; store has 2,500 sq. ft. of vintage comic books, pulp magazines, mass market magazines and paper books, and related paper collectibles.

Thomas Bauer
Nonstop Collectibles
6152 Terrebonne
Montreal, Quebec H4B 1A3 Canada
ph: 514-489-5499
thomasbauer@sympatico.ca
http://www.thomasbauer.ca
Internet sales consultant and broker since 1993; active in online sales and marketing of comic books and other collectibles; will do qualified evaluations of your collection; list items for sale for 20% commission; good comic info.

Vintage Magazines & Paper Ephemera
Mare St. Studios
203-213 Mare St.
London, E8 3QE U.K.
ph: 020-8533-7588
fax: 020-8533-7283
thearchive@ndirect.co.uk
http://www.vinmag.com
Specializes in comics and magazines covering fashion, science fiction, movies, pulp fiction, glamour, social history and more; buys and sells.

Experts

Alex G. Malloy
Alex G. Malloy, Inc.
P.O. Box 38
South Salem, NY 10590-0038
ph: 203-438-0396 or 203-438-9652
fax: 203-438-6744
alexmalloy@aol.com
http://members.aol.com/AlexMalloy/agmalloy.htm
Specialist in comic books and comic related collectibles; author of "Comics Values Annual" (Krause).

Robert Overstreet
Gemstone Publishing, Inc.
1966 Greenspring Dr.
Lutherville Timonium, MD 21093
ph: 888-375-9800 or 410-560-5806
fax: 410-560-6107
obob@gemstonepub.com
http://www.gemstonepub.com
Author of "The Overstreet Comic Book Price Guide."

Rich Davis
Rich Davis Autograph Authentication & Collectible Investments
P.O. Box 563
Kingston, OH 45644
ph: 740-642-2024
prdavis@horizonview.net
http://authenticator.freeservers.com
Specializes in the authentication and appraisal of all types of autographs; expert on sports collectibles, coins & currency, comic books, and stamps; also provides services as a research/grading/appraisal expert.

Ernst Gerber
Gerber Publishing
P.O. Box 201
Glenbrook, NV 89413
ph: 775-883-4100
fax: 775-887-1000
Author of "The Photo-Journal Guide to Comic Books."

Ken Mitchell
710 Conacher Dr.
Willowdale, Ontario M2M 3N6 Canada
ph: 416-222-5808
Buys and sells comic character collectibles (comic books, Sunday funnies, "Big Little Books", etc.) and other nostalgic paper including music (Pop) magazines and books from 1890 through 1960s.

Internet Resources

Tony Rose
Grand Comicbook Database
tonyrose@cei.net
http://www.comics.org
A simple database listing all the comic books ever written: information about the creator, story details, and other information useful to the comic book reader and fan.

About.com Hobbies
220 East 42nd St.
New York, NY 10017
pr@about-inc.com
http://home.about.com/hobbies
Online source for information about action figures, antiques, book collecting, coin collecting, collectibles, comic books, costume jewelry, dolls, mineral collecting, pin collecting, sports and trading cards, stamps, toy collecting.

Joshua Nathanson
ComicLink: The Internet Comic Book Exchange
4842 Glenwood St.
Flushing, NY 11363-0299
ph: 718-423-6079
fax: 718-423-9801
buysell@comiclink.com
http://www.comiclink.com
High quality comic book exchange where dealers and collectors buy and sell pre-1980 comic books, collections, original comic art and related items; wide selection of Golden and Silver Age comics including some of the most valuable.

ComicWeb, The
P.O. Box 3416
Silver Spring, MD 20918-3416
editor@comicweb.com
http://www.comicweb.com

Charles S. LePage
New Comic Book Resource List
ph: 904-374-1648
chuck@comiclist.com
http://www.comiclist.com
For those interested in new comic book releases: find out which comics came out this week, which ones came out last week, which ones were late or cancelled, who publishes them, who creates them, etc.

Bryan Neely
ComicsPriceGuide.com
contact@comicspriceguide.com
http://www.comicspriceguide.com
Online price guide for may categories of comics.

Jonah Weiland
Comic Book Resources
10153 1/2 Riverside Dr., Ste. #604
North Hollywood, CA 91602
ph: 818-9895-6688
fax: 818-985-6668
jonah@comicbookresources.com
http://www.comicbookresources.com
The Web site for comic book fans: news, interviews, commentary, discussions.

Museums/Libraries

Randall W. Scott
Russel B. Nye Popular Culture Collection, Michigan State University Libraries
Michigan State Univ. Libraries
Special Collections
East Lansing, MI 48824-1048
ph: 517-355-3770
fax: 517-353-5069
scottr@pilot.msu.edu
http://www.lib.msu.edu/coll/main/spec_col/nye
Includes a popular culture vertical file of related ephemera; also has the world's largest comic book collection (150,000 items) plus large collections of science fiction, mysteries, romances, girls' and boys' series books, Westerns.

Periodicals

Gary M. Carter
Gemstone Publishing, Inc.
Magazine: Overstreet's Comic Book Marketplace
1996 Greenspring Dr., Ste. 405
Lutherville Timonium, MD 21093-4117
ph: 888-375-9800 x249
fax: 410-560-6107
vjeff@gemstonepub.com
http://www.fanuniverse.com
Monthly comic book price guide; values, latest hot titles, regional market reports, fully illustrated; full color, 130-150 pgs.

Gary M. Carter
Gemstone Publishing, Inc.
Magazine: Overstreet's Advanced Collector
1996 Greenspring Dr., Ste. 405
Lutherville Timonium, MD 21093-4117
ph: 888-375-9800 x249
fax: 410-560-6107
vjeff@gemstonepub.com
http://www.fanuniverse.com
Quarterly magazine the specifically focuses on Golden Age & Silver Age comic books & collectibles.

Stacie Berger
Krause Publications
Magazine: Comics Buyer's Guide
700 E. State St.
Iola, WI 54990-0001
ph: 715-445-2214
fax: 715-445-4087
stacie.berger@fwpubs.com
http://www.krause.com
Only weekly newspaper serving comic fans, collectors & the entire comics industry; articles on comics of the past & present, news, columns by top writers, comics show calendar, monthly price guide supplements on comics & trading cards.

Stacie Berger
Krause Publications
Magazine: Comics Retailer
700 E. State St.
Iola, WI 54990-0001
ph: 715-445-2214
fax: 715-445-4087
stacie.berger@fwpubs.com
http://www.krause.com
Contains business-related editorial to help retailers become more profitable; covers comics, games, video, books, toys, trading cars; columns written by retailers and business experts.

Dana Gabbard
Magazine: Duckburg Times
3010 Wilshire Blvd. #362
Los Angeles, CA 90010-1146
ph: 213-388-2364
Focuses on comics based on Walt Disney characters.

Magazine: Comic Book Marketplace
P.O. Box 180700
Coronado, CA 92178
ph: 619-437-1996
cbm@gemstonepub.com
http://www.gemstonepub.com

Fantagraphics Books
Magazine: Comics Journal, The
7563 Lake City Way
Seattle, WA 98115
ph: 206-524-1967
fax: 206-524-2104
milo@tcj.com
http://www.tcj.com
Monthly magazine for the comic book industry: news, interviews, comic reviews, etc.

Ken Mitchell
Newsletter: Comic Buyers Guide
710 Conacher Dr.
Willowdale, Ontario M2M 3N6 Canada
ph: 416-222-5808
A weekly publication.

Computer Programs For
Man./Prod./Dist.

Niche Software, Inc.
Software: Doll & Figurine Collector, The
7118 NW Terrace
Parkland, FL 33076
ph: 954-344-6561
marketing@collectiblessoftware.com
http://www.collectiblessoftware.com
Designed for the collector of comic books.

Todd VerBeek
Radio Zero
Software: cDATA2000
1311 Lake Dr., #2
Grand Rapids, MI 49506
TVerBeek@RZero.com
http://www.rzero.com/soft
A database for comic book collectors.

Fawcett
Clubs/Associations

P.S. Hamerlinck
Fawcett Collectors of America
P.O. Box 24751
Minneapolis, MN 55424-0751
WaltGrogan@aol.com
http://shazam.imginc.com/fca
For collectors of Fawcett comics and Magazine Enterprise comics.

Magazine Enterprise
Clubs/Associations

P.S. Hamerlinck
Fawcett Collectors of America
P.O. Box 24751
Minneapolis, MN 55424-0751
WaltGrogan@aol.com
http://shazam.imginc.com/fca
For collectors of Fawcett comics and Magazine Enterprise comics.

Super Heroes
Dealers

Anton Kawasaki
Adventure Ink
475 Bedford Rd.
Pleasantville, NY 10570
ph: 914-741-2510
fax: 914-741-2510
Interested in super hero comic books.

COMIC COLLECTIBLES

(see CARTOON ART; CHARACTER COLLECTIBLES; COMIC ART; COMIC BOOKS; COWBOY HEROES; DISNEY COLLECTIBLES; FAN CLUBS; PREMIUMS; SCIENCE FICTION; SUPER HEROES)

COMIC STRIPS
Sunday Newspaper

(see also CARTOON ART; CHARACTER COLLECTIBLES; ELVES)

Dealers

Claude Held
Claude Held Collectibles
P.O. Box 515
Cheektowaga, NY 14225-0515
ph: 716-634-4842
Wants to buy pre-1960 Sunday comic sections; also pulp magazines before 1950 (horror, spicy, science fiction, weird types), and pre-1950 E.R. Burroughs books with dust jackets.

John Cosgriff
American Illustration
204 Wickham Dr.
Schaumburg, IL 60194
ph: 847-882-0839
fax: 847-882-1245
pulpmonger@aol.com
Buys and sells original artwork done for magazines, books, advertising, and comic strips; also buys and sells illustrated books, magazines, newspapers, comic strips and comic books; over 25 years experience selling ephemera.

Michael Dice
309 S Washington
Cortez, CO 81321
ph: 970-564-9018
Buys, sells, trades comic strips from Sunday papers, especially from bound newspapers; also wants pre-1955 comic books.

Experts

Ken Mitchell
710 Conacher Dr.
Willowdale, Ontario M2M 3N6 Canada
ph: 416-222-5808
Buys and sells comic character collectibles (comic books, Sunday funnies, "Big Little Books", etc.) and other nostalgic paper including music (Pop) magazines and books from 1890 through 1960s.

Internet Resources

Stu's Comic Strip Connection
stu@stus.com
http://www.stus.com
You gateway to 1,000+ comic strip resources on the Internet: funnies pages, search tools, original content, descriptions of over 1,300 online cartoons.

Museums/Libraries

San Francisco Academy of Comic Art
170 W. Cliff Dr., #15
Santa Cruz, CA 95060-5432
ph: 831-427-1737
fax: 831-427-1737
Millions of newspaper strips, bound files, major dailies from 1890-1960, pulps, all science fiction, crime fiction, film history, children's books, comic books; excellent copies made of all graphic material; dup material for trade.

Periodicals

Tom Heintjes, Ed.
Bull Moose Publishing Co.
Magazine: Hogan's Alley
P.O. Box 47684
Atlanta, GA 30362-0684
ph: 770-458-2624
fax: 815-328-0889
HoganLetters@aol.com
http://www.hoganmag.com
Contains coverage of comic strips, comic books, animation, political cartooning, gag cartooning, illustration, children's books, and more.

COMMEMORATIVE ITEMS

(see ROYALTY COLLECTIBLES; SOUVENIR & COMMEMORATIVE ITEMS)

COMMUNISM

(see SOCIAL CAUSES)

COMPACT DISCS

(see also RECORDS)

Dealers

Princeton Record Exchange
20 S. Tulane St.
Princeton, NJ 08542
ph: 609-921-0881
info@prex.com
http://www.prex.com
Buys and sells new and used CDs, LPs, and tapes: rock, jazz, alternative, imports, oldies, hip hop, soul, funk, new releases, classical, opera, etc.

Record Setter, The
742 Rt. 18
East Brunswick, NJ 08816-4906
ph: 732-257-3888
fax: 732-257-2366
recsetter@aol.com
http://www.recordsetter.com
Specializing in used CDs and out-of-print albums; promoters of largest record collectors convention in the US.

Paul C. Mawhinney
Record-Rama Sound Archives
1130 Perry Highway
Pines Plaza
Pittsburgh, PA 15237-2132
ph: 412-367-7330
fax: 412-367-7388
recrama@recordrama.com
http://www.recordrama.com
Carries over 2,500,000 vinyl sound recordings and over 200,000 compact discs; orders by phone.

Jay Notartomaso
Musical Energi
59 N. Main St.
Wilkes Barre, PA 18701
ph: 570-829-2929
fax: 570-829-2929
orders@musicalenergi.com
http://www.musicalenergi.com
Buys and sells CDs, records, tapes, videos, DVDs, and computer games; also large selection of gifts.

Mike Hawkinson
Disc Collector
P.O. Box 4000
Parker, CO 80134
ph: 303-841-3000 or 303-841-1118
fax: 303-840-9373
cd@discol.com
http://www.discol.com
Specializing in oldies from the '50s to '70s; one of the world's largest selections.

COMPACT DISCS

Experts

Paul Bergquist
1800 S. Robertson Blvd., #279
Los Angeles, CA 90035
ph: 310-275-1444
paul@vinylvendors.com
http://www.vinylvendors.com
Co-author with Jerry Osborne of "The Official Price Guide to Compact Discs" (House of Collectibles, 1994).

Jerry Osborne
P.O. Box 255
Port Townsend, WA 98368
ph: 360-385-1200
fax: 360-385-6572
jpo@olympus.net
http://www.jerryosborne.com
Co-author with Paul Bergquist of "The Official Price Guide to Compact Discs" (House of Collectibles, 1994).

Periodicals

Peter Howard, Pub.
Howard Communications Inc.
Magazine: ICE Magazine
P.O. Box 3043
Santa Monica, CA 90408-3043
ph: 310-829-1291
fax: 310-829-2979
emailice@aol.com
http://www.icemagazine.com
ICE provides collectors and enthusiasts a monthly dose of unrivaled CD coverage: release schedules, first word on new albums, upcoming box sets, reissues, and industry news; published monthly.

COMPACTS

(see also CLOTHING & ACCESSORIES, Vintage; DRESSER ITEMS; PURSES)

Clubs/Associations

Roselyn Gerson
Compact Collectors Club
Newsletter: Powder Puff
P.O. Box 40
Lynbrook, NY 11563-0040
ph: 516-593-8746
fax: 516-593-0611
compactldy@aol.com
An international club whose members collect compacts, vanities, necessaires, etc.; newsletter contains articles, buy/sell ads, etc.

Juliette Edwards
British Compact Collectors' Society
Newsletter: Face Facts
P.O. Box 131
Woking, Surrey GU24 9YR U.K.
janwest24@hotmail.com
http://www.thebccs.org.uk
For compact collectors and enthusiasts.

Collectors

Sherry & Mike Miller
303 Holiday Dr. #130
Tuscola, IL 61953-2118
ph: 217-253-4991
miller1@net66.com
Wants ladies powder compacts in shape of objects (figural compacts), e.g. shaped like a bird, a guitar, or a padlock; many made from 1920s through early 1960s by companies like Volupte, Zell, and Elgin.

Lori Landgrebe
2331 E. Main St.
Decatur, IL 62521-2263
ph: 217-423-2254
Wants to buy ladies' compacts and compact purses; buying any colorful, Art Deco, enamel novelty and figural compacts; must be in good to mint condition.

Jette Bellew
15243 Profit Ave.
Baton Rouge, LA 70817
ph: 225-756-4875
framewall@cox.net
http://www.geocities.com/Vienna/9014/jette.html
Wants to buy antique and vintage ladies' powder compacts, carryalls, mesh purses and accessories of all types from 1890 to the 1950 era.

Susan Murphy
29668 Orinda Rd.
San Juan Capistrano, CA 92675-1211
ph: 949-364-4333
Wants to buy older powder compacts and anything with a compact in it or a part of it such as purses, lighters; please enclose SASE.

Dealers

Kathy Burch
Tri-State Antique Center
47 W. Pike
Canonsburg, PA 15317
ph: 724-745-9116
fax: 412-291-1367
kathy&ed@tri-stateantiques.com
http://tri-stateantiques.com
Specializes in lady's beaded and mesh purses, Lucite purses, chatelaines, compacts, and other ladies vanity items.

Andra Behrendt
Lady A Antiques
P.O. Box 217
Western Springs, IL 60558
ph: 708-246-2676
andra@lady-a.com
http://www.lady-a.com
Dealer specializing in ladies' accessory items including a large variety of compacts and mesh/beaded purses.

Susan Murphy
29668 Orinda Rd.
San Juan Capistrano, CA 92675-1211
ph: 949-364-4333
Buys and sells ladies powder compacts, any and all that are in good to mint condition; please enclose SASE.

Experts

Roselyn Gerson
P.O. Box 100
Malverne, NY 11565
ph: 516-593-8746
fax: 516-593-0611
Wants unusual gadget compacts: cane/compact, hatpin/compact, gun/compact; also compact advertising; author of "Ladies' Compacts of the 19th & 20th Centuries", a fully-illustrated identification & value guide.

Roseann Ettinger
Remember When
21-23 W. Broad St.
Hazleton, PA 18201
ph: 570-454-8465 or 570-450-5542
popgems2001@hotmail.com
Author of "Compacts and Smoking Accessories."

Leslie Scatch
664 Milwood Ave.
Venice, CA 90291
ph: 310-821-8011
fax: 310-837-6109
vintagevamp@sprynet.com
Vintage compact, face powder boxes and vanity items collector and expert.

Repair Services

A. Laub Glass Corp.
1873 Second Ave.
New York, NY 10029-7453
ph: 212-734-4270 or 718-430-1901
Installation, beveling and resilvering of glass mirrors including the especially thin mirrors required for compacts.

COMPUTERS

(see also ANTIQUES DEALERS & COLLECTORS, Computer Programs For; CALCULATORS; SLIDE RULES)

Appraisers

Paul Willigan, Pres.
NICE Network, Inc.
2126 Alpine Place
Cincinnati, OH 45206-2603
ph: 513-961-1052 or 800-837-NICE
fax: 513-961-0538
paul@nicenetwork.com
http://www.nicenetwork.com
Appraisers of high tech and high value electronic equipment including computers, PBX telephone systems, medical equipment, copiers, software, film printers, optical jukeboxes, mainframe computers, audio-visual systems, etc.

Clubs/Associations

David Greelish
1 Oakleigh Ct.
Richmond, VA 23233-3125
ph: 804-754-1951
Collector of classic computers and related memorabilia.

Computer History Association of California
Newsletter: Analytical Engine, The
4159-C El Camino Way
Palo Alto, CA 94306-4010
ph: 650-856-9915
fax: 650-856-9914
engine@chac.org
http://www.chac.org
Focuses on the history of computers and the computer industry in California.

Collectors

Tom Copper
Tom's Classic Computers
1416 Ralapen St.
Roxboro, NC 27573-4232
ph: 336-599-6908
tcopper@person.net
http://members.person.net/~tcopper/index.html
Collector of obsolete personal computers, peripherals, software, manuals and literature for same; offers support for people still using older computers.

Paul Pierce
2933 NE 17th Ave.
Portland, OR 97212
ph: 503-281-6995
Specializes in older mainframes, minis, and representative examples of other types of computers.

Experts

Thomas F. Haddock
P.O. Box 2626
Ann Arbor, MI 48106
Author of "A Collector's Guide to Personal Computers and Pocket Calculators: A Historical, Rarity, and Value Guide" (Books Americana, 1993).

Kevin Stumpf
Nostalgic Technophile
220 Samuel St.
Kitchener, Ontario N2H 1R6 Canada
ph: 519-744-2900
kstumpf@nostalgictechnophile.com
http://www.nostalgictechnophile.com
Author of "A Guide to Collecting Computers & Computer Collectibles: History, Practice, and Technique," and magazine column, "Nostalgic Technophile."

Internet Resources

Tom Carlson
Obsolete Computer Museum
Nat. Center for State Courts, Court Tech
  Lab
300 Newport Ave.
Williamsburg, VA 23185
tcarlson@ncsc.dni.us
http://
  www.obsoletecomputermuseum.org
  *Images of obsolete computers, latest
  news.*

Michele Perini
Ancient Computer Community
Italy
michele.perini@aceadvanced.com
http://www.ancientcomputer.com
  *A Web site dedicated to the history of
  computers and computer science: news
  articles, images, curiosities.*

Museums/Libraries

Steve Plotkin
Real World Computer Museum
303 Cayuga Rd.
Cheektowaga, NY 14225-1960
ph: 610-494-9000
fax: 610-494-2090
  *A regional computer museum
  dedicated to preserving and displaying
  computing and allied technologies,
  storage devices, semiconductor
  technology, computer art; seeking old
  computers and electronic relics,
  devices and related memorabilia.*

George Keremedjiev, Dir.
American Computer Museum
234 East Babcock St.
Bozeman, MT 59715-4765
ph: 406-587-7545
fax: 406-587-9620
bitenbyte@aol.com
http://www.compustory.com
  *Comprehensive display of calculation
  devices spanning 4,000 years of
  history; from slide rules to micro
  chips.*

David Weil, Cur.
Computer Museum of America at
  Coleman College
Newsletter: Circuit, The
640 C St.
San Diego, CA 92101
ph: 619-235-8222
fax: 619-235-8220
dweil@computer-museum.org
http://www.computer-museum.org
  *Computer and data processing related
  exhibits chronicling the history of the
  modern computer over the past
  century.*

Commodore

Collectors

Bo Zimmerman
Bo Zimmerman's Collection of
  Commodore Computers
bo@zimmers.net
http://www.zimmers.net/cbmpics
  *Has the largest collection of
  Commodore Business Machines (1954-*

*1994) computers, accessories and
peripherals.*

CONDOM TINS

(see PROPHYLACTICS, Tins)

CONJURING

(see MAGICIANS PARAPHERNALIA)

CONSERVATION

(see also REPAIR/RESTORATION/
CONSERVATION)

Museums/Libraries

American Association of State & Local
  History
Newsletter: History News Dispatch
1717 Church St.
Nashville, TN 37203-2991
ph: 615-320-3203
fax: 615-327-9013
history@aaslh.org
http://www.aaslh.org
  *Supplies technical leaflets on such
  things as proper lighting techniques
  for collectors & small museums; write
  for list of leaflets and books on
  similar subjects that are offered for
  sale; the "Dispatch" monthly,
  "History News" bi-monthly.*

CONSERVATORS

(see REPAIR/RESTORATION/
CONSERVATION)

CONSTRUCTION EQUIPMENT

(see INDUSTRY RELATED ITEMS;
MACHINERY & EQUIPMENT)

COOKBOOKS

(see also BOOKS; COOKIES &
COOKIE SHAPING; FOOD
COLLECTIBLES; KITCHEN
COLLECTIBLES; MENUS)

Clubs/Associations

Bob & Jo Ellen Allen
Cook Book Collectors Club of America,
  Inc.
Newsletter: Cook Book Gossip
P.O. Box 56
Saint James, MO 65559-0056
ph: 573-265-8296
  *Focuses on cookbooks & advertising
  cook books and recipe publications by
  many companies such as Jell-O,
  Pillsbury, Betty Crocker, etc.*

Barbara Gelink
Cook Book Collector's Club
Newsletter: Cook Book Collector's Club
  Newsletter
4756 Terrace Dr.
San Diego, CA 92116-2514
ph: 619-281-8962
  *Membership includes 12 newsletters,
  local field trips and quest speakers;
  club has nationwide membership;
  newsletter reports on cookbook
  auction results, list of cookbooks for
  sale each month; send SASE for info.*

Collectors

Steve Armstrong
P.O. Box 1409
Florence, AL 35631-1409
  *Wants pre-1940 soft bound cookbooks,
  booklets, advertising recipe
  publications such as baking powder,
  JELL-O, flour, etc.; send complete
  description and price.*

Dealers

Louise Pennisi
Around the Kitchen
P.O. Box 840
Georgetown, CT 06829
ph: 203-438-2338
  *Buying and selling collectible
  cookbooks (19th & 20th century),
  cookery booklets (Pillsbury, Baker's
  Chocolate, Jell-O, etc.), antique
  kitchen instruction & recipe
  pamphlets; issues catalogs of items for
  sale.*

Mary Barile
Heritage Publications
P.O. Box 335
Arkville, NY 12406
ph: 914-586-3810
fax: 914-586-2797
  *Offers out-of-print and rare
  cookbooks; also "Cookbooks Worth
  Collecting", an illustrated history and
  guide with prices to the world of
  American cookbooks; for collectors,
  dealers, sellers, etc.; send SASE for
  information.*

Susan B. Jimenez
Vintage Bookbookery, The
P.O. Box 3943
Albuquerque, NM 87190-3943
ph: 505-837-2569
fax: 505-872-0851
kalesija@aol.com
http://www.bibliofind.com/
  vintagecookbookery.htm
  *Buys and sells vintage, collectible, and
  classic cookbooks, cooking pamphlets,
  and advertising recipe booklets.*

Vintage Cookbookery
P.O. Box 3943
Albuquerque, NM 87190-3943
ph: 505-837-2569
kalesija@aol.com
http://www.bibliofind.com/
  vintagecookbookery.htm

Janet Jarvits
Janet Jarvits, Bookseller
1388 E. Washington Blvd.
Pasadena, CA 91104
ph: 626-296-1638
fax: 626-296-3231
cookbkjj@cookbkjj.com
http://www.cookbkjj.com
  *Sells out-of-print cookbooks, books on
  wine and beverages, and related
  magazines, ephemera, etc.; issues
  periodic catalogs listing items for
  sale; want list is available upon
  request; mail order.*

Barbara Gelink
OTENTO Book Search
Newsletter: Old Cookbook News &
  Views
4756 Terrace Dr.
San Diego, CA 92116-2514
ph: 619-281-8962
  *Specialist in out-of-print cookbooks
  and books on food, wine, food history,
  and related books; also offers a book
  finder service; showroom has over
  5,000 out-of-print and hard-to-find
  books on all subjects.*

Museums/Libraries

Conrad N. Hilton Library at the Culinary
  Institute of America
1946 Campus Dr.
Hyde Park, NY 12538
ph: 845-452-9600
d_white@culinary.edu
http://www.ciachef.edu/Library/
  lwelcome.html
  *Large cookbook collection including
  many hard-to-find modern cookbooks
  and videos.*

Library of Congress, Rare Books &
  Special Collections Division
101 Independence Ave. SE
Washington, DC 20540-4640
ph: 202-707-3448
fax: 202-707-4142
rbsc@loc.gov
http://www.loc.gov
  *Houses the Katherine Bitting and
  Elizabeth Pennell collections of
  gastronomy and culinary publications
  including the musical cookbook in
  which recipes may be sung.*

COOKIE JARS

(see also CERAMICS [AMERICAN
PRODUCTION ARTWARE])

Clubs/Associations

Barbara Crews
American Cookie Jar Association
4005 Spyglass Lane
Bethany, OK 73008
barbc@thecookiejar.net
http://www.cookiejarclub.com
  *An online club for cookie jar
  collectors; over 200 members.*

Collectors

John Krupienski
5200 Hilltop Dr.
P.O. Box AA6
Brookhaven, PA 19015-1200
ph: 610-874-3003
Wants to buy character shaped cookie jars.

Mark & Ellen Supnick
Collectibles R US Inc.
2623 Center Court Dr.
Fort Lauderdale, FL 33332
ph: 954-727-9770
ellen@sunshinejars.com
http://www.sunshinejars.com
Wants to buy figural cookie jars; Web site has lots of cookie jars listed for sale by various manufacturers; also salt shakers and banks.

Dealers

Carol Silagyi
C.S. Antiques & Jewelry
P.O. Box 151
Wyckoff, NJ 07430
ph: 201-934-6528
csantiques@aol.com
Buys and sells cartoon, Storybook, etc. cookie jars by Abingdon, Brush, McCoy, RRP, Shawnee, Regal, etc.; also collects head/faces cookie jars - over 200 in collection.

Mark McMahon
Cookie Jars, Etc.
806 Sixth Ave.
Asbury Park, NJ 07712
ph: 732-776-9216
peter@peterandmark.com
http://www.peterandmark.com
Buy, sell, trade cookie jars, banks, salt & peppers and PEZ; in partnership with Peter Linski.

Martin C. Sobin
Ye Olde Cookie Jar Trader
91 Fox Hollow Rd.
Sparta, NJ 07871-1107
ph: 201-729-9492
Wants to buy figural cookie jars in very good or better condition, especially interested in cookie jars made by Abingdon, Brush, and Shawnee.

Mel Cohen
Cooki-Jar
P.O. Box 700
Pomona, NY 10970-0700
ph: 914-354-8707
Serious cookie jar collector.

Joyce McCandless
Krazy Cat Collectibles
P.O. Box 1192
Emmitsburg, MD 21727
ph: 301-271-9851
KrazyCatCo@aol.com
http://www.krazycatcollectibles.com
Large selection of cookie jars from McCoy, American Bisque, Treasure Craft, Twin Winton, Doranne of California, Red Wing, Shawnee,

Purinton Potteries, Ramsburg, Vandor, Clay Art, and foreign.

Olga Andreu
Extinct Collectibles
2376 SW 25 Ave.
Miami, FL 33145
ph: 305-857-3440
oandreu@aol.com
http://www.extinctcollectibles.com
Buys and sells quality ceramic and glass collectibles including Cookie Jars; also Czech art glass, character collectibles, Betty Boop, Simpsons, Peanuts, Fitz & Floyd, salt & pepper sets, teapots and Christmas ornaments.

Judy Posner
Judy Posner Collectibles
P.O. Box 2194
Englewood, FL 34295
ph: 941-475-1725
fax: 941-475-2645
judyandjef@yahoo.com
http://www.judyposner.com
Wants FIGURAL cookie jars: comic characters, Disney, Black Mammys, Chefs, Butlers, etc.; buying, selling collecting for over 25 years.

Lois & Ralph Behm
Lois' Collectibles of Antique Market III
413 W. Main St.
Saint Charles, IL 60174-1815
ph: 630-377-5599 or 847-831-5997
fax: 847-831-5998
Buys and sells cookie jars; will buy entire collections.

Mercedes DiRenzo
Jazz'e Junque
4107 N. Pulaski Rd.
Chicago, IL 60641
ph: 773-463-3687
fax: 773-463-3687
cookejarlayde@aol.com
Buys and sells vintage and new cookie jars.

Jennifer & Co. Antiques & Fine Gifts
18744 Main St.
P.O. Box 884
Groveland, CA 95321-0884
ph: 209-962-7112
jennifer@jenniferandcompany.com
http://www.jenniferandcompany.com
Specializes in much-sought-after kitchen collectibles and cookie jars.

Neil Wegner
Have Treasure Will Travel
5737 35 St.
Red Deer, Alberta T4N 0S5 Canada
ph: 403-346-9706
Sells vintage character, advertising and figural cookie jars; also related "go-withs."

Experts

Fred & Joyce Roerig
1501 Maple Ridge Rd.
Walterboro, SC 29488-9278
ph: 843-538-2487
fax: 843-538-4263
Buys/sells/collects cookie jars; 20+

years experience; wants figural cookie jars not in books: Metlox, Twin Winton Jars & accessories, black Americana, ND School of Mines Mammy; author of "The Collector's Encyclopedia of Cookie Jars."

Mark & Ellen Supnick
Collectibles R US Inc.
2623 Center Court Dr.
Fort Lauderdale, FL 33332
ph: 954-727-9770
ellen@sunshinejars.com
http://www.sunshinejars.com
Authors of three books on cookie jar and pottery collecting.

John W. Humphries
P.O. Box 965
Los Molinos, CA 96055-0965
jhantiques@hotmail.com
Author of "The Professionals Price Guide to Cookie Jars."

Internet Resources

Barbara Crews
About.com - Cookie Jars
E-zine: Cookie Jar Digest, The
4005 Spyglass Lane
Bethany, OK 73008
collectibles.guide@about.com
http://collectibles.about.com
The complete Internet resource for cookie jar collecting; over 100 cookie jar Web sites; weekly feature on different aspects of cookie jar collecting.

Misc. Services

Bill Kasting
Cookie Jar Matchmaker
P.O. Box 96
Kelso, MO 63758
kazz@cookiejarmatchmaker.com
http://www.cookiejarmatchmaker.com
A Web site dedicated to "matching" cookie jar lids and bases.

Museums/Libraries

Lucille Bromberek
Cookie Jar Museum, The
111 Stephen St.
Lemont, IL 60439
ph: 630-257-5012
Only Cookie Jar Museum in the world; over 2000 jars from US and all over the world; also buys and sells.

Periodicals

Joyce Roerig
Newsletter: Cookie Jarrin'
1501 Maple Ridge Rd.
Walterboro, SC 29488-9278
ph: 843-538-2487
fax: 843-538-4263
A bi-monthly newsletter with new information, current pricing, exciting discoveries, lots of photos; carefully researched for accuracy providing collectors and dealers with an unequaled professional quality newsletter.

COOKIES & COOKIE SHAPING

(see also COOKBOOKS; COOKIE JARS; KITCHEN COLLECTIBLES)

Clubs/Associations

Joyce Moorhouse
Cookie Cutter Collectors Club
Newsletter: Cookie Crumbs
2763 - 310th St.
Cannon Falls, MN 55009
Focusing on cookie cutters, boards and rollers.

Collectors

Milli Simerl
508 N. Clinton
Defiance, OH 43512-1607
ph: 419-784-1545

Joyce Moorhouse
2763 - 310th St.
Cannon Falls, MN 55009

Priscilla Hinners
2711 Jaynia Place
Lemon Grove, CA 91945-1319
ph: 619-265-1046
phinners@yahoo.com
Wants cookie/cake boards, cookie molds, multiple cutters, springerle, rollers.

Experts

Rosemary Henry
9610 Greenview Lane
Manassas, VA 20109-3320
ph: 703-361-5898
fax: 703-361-5898
editor@cookiesnewsletter.com
http://www.cookiesnewsletter.com
Buys/collects cookie shaping items and anything related to cookies: cutters, molds, presses, irons, photographs, postcards, ads, etc.

Periodicals

Rosemary Henry
Newsletter: Cookies Newsletter
9610 Greenview Lane
Manassas, VA 20109-3320
ph: 703-361-5898
fax: 703-361-5898
editor@cookiesnewsletter.com
http://www.cookiesnewsletter.com
For over 25 years, "Cookies" contains historical information about the shaping of cookies: flea market finds, new and old cutters, molds and stamps, tinsmiths, irons, presses, etc.; bi-monthly.

COPPER ITEMS

(see also ARTS & CRAFTS, Roycroft)

Experts

Eve Stone
Eve Stone Antiques, Ltd.
22 Selden St.
Woodbridge, CT 06525
ph: 203-389-6665 or 800-833-1665
fax: 203-389-6103
info@evestoneantiques.com
http://www.evestoneantiques.com
Specializes in period brass and copper French and English antiques; a nationally known expert in copper and brass.

Repro. Sources

Steve Kayne
Kayne & Son Custom Forged Hardware
100 Daniel Ridge Rd.
Candler, NC 28715-9434
ph: 828-667-8868 or 828-665-1988
fax: 828-665-8303
kaynehdwe@charter.net
http://www.customforgedhardware.com
Steel, brass, bronze reproductions of locks, pulls, thumb latches, furniture & interior/exterior hardware, fireplace tools & accessories, lighting, kitchen utensils, etc.; also does repairs, restoration & conservation; $5 for two catalogs.

CORKPULLERS

(see CORKSCREWS)

CORKSCREWS

(see also BOTTLE OPENERS, Figural; WINES & WINE RELATED ITEMS)

Clubs/Associations

Milt Becker
Canadian Corkscrew Collectors Club
Newsletter: Quarterly Worm, The
One Madison St.
East Rutherford, NJ 07073
ph: 973-773-9224
ccccdues@aol.com
http://www.corkscrewnet.com/cccc.htm
Worldwide membership; write for application form.

Bert Giulian
International Correspondence of Corkscrew Addicts
Newsletter: Bottle Scrue Times
649 Johns Dr.
Camp Hill, PA 17011
ph: 717-737-5828
giulian@kp.net
http://www.corkscrewnet.com/icca.htm
Membership limited to 50; members interested in corkscrews and all related item such as decanters, wine strainers, funnels, etc.; most of the existing books and literature on corkscrews were authored by members of ICCA.

John Stanley
Just for Openers
Newsletter: Just for Openers Newsletter
P.O. Box 64
Chapel Hill, NC 27514
ph: 919-419-1546 or 919-966-5794
jfo@mindspring.com
http://www.just-for-openers.org
Just for Openers is a club for bottle and corkscrew collectors; quarterly newsletter.

Collectors

Milt Becker
One Madison St.
East Rutherford, NJ 07073
ph: 973-773-9224
ccccdues@aol.com
http://www.corkscrewnet.com/cccc.htm
Wants any corkscrew or corkpuller; buys single items or entire collections; send photocopy of item and price.

Donald A. Bull
P.O. Box 596
Wirtz, VA 24184
ph: 540-721-1128
fax: 540-721-5468
corkscrew@bullworks.net
http://www.bullworks.net
Buys corkscrews or anything picturing corkscrews; author of "A Price Guide to Beer Advertising Openers and Corkscrews."

Joe Young
P.O. Box 587
Elgin, IL 60121-0587
ph: 847-695-0108
istamp2@aol.com
Wants to buy unusual corkscrews; also interested in combination tools with corkscrews; all correspondence answered.

Bob Anthony
222 West 68 Terrace
Kansas City, MO 64113
ph: 816-361-1825 or 800-821-2002
corkscrew@juno.com
Corkscrew expert and collector wants to buy rare and unusual antique corkscrews; no collection too small or too large; offers free appraisals.

Raj & Justine Kanodia
Corkscrew.Com
3717 Ortega Court
Palo Alto, CA 94303
corky@corkscrew.com
http://www.corkscrew.com
Web site has some great corkscrew information and photographs.

Dealers

Mike Gordon
M & R Gordon
57 Bundy Lane
Storrs, CT 06268
ph: 860-429-3834
fax: 860-429-3834
Wants to buy any old or unusual corkscrew; please photocopy.

Paul P. Luchsinger
1126 Wishart St.
Hermitage, PA 16148-4410
ph: 724-346-2331
fax: 724-346-2331
ppl@infonline.net
Buys, sells, collects old and unusual corkscrews as well as other wine related items.

Derek White
10 Spring Dr.
Newtown, PA 18940
ph: 215-504-5552
dswhite@360youth.com
Active collector and dealer of antique corkscrews; specialty is rare, unusual mechanical and pocket figural corkscrews; will buy single items as well s entire collections; also wants wine-related items: funnels, bin labels, etc.

Dean Walters
Vintage Antiques
P.O. Box 717
San Anselmo, CA 94979
ph: 415-459-6393
fax: 415-459-6317
dean_w@pacbell.net
http://home.pacbell.net/dean_w
Since 1983 buying, selling, trading, appraising collectible corkscrews; online catalog changes four timer each year.

Joseph C. Paradi
670 Meadow Wood Rd.
Mississauga, Ontario L5J 2S6 Canada
ph: 905-823-3754 or 416-978-6924 x210
fax: 905-823-3775
paradi@mie.utoronto.ca
http://www.corkscrewnet.com
Will trade, buy or sell hand held corkscrews of any type, champagne taps, bar screws, cork pullers, corkers; also ladies' kits, necessaires, camping kits, cocktail shakers, etc. containing corkscrews; plus related ephemera.

Experts

Donald A. Bull
P.O. Box 596
Wirtz, VA 24184
ph: 540-721-1128
fax: 540-721-5468
corkscrew@bullworks.net
http://www.bullworks.net
Buys corkscrews or anything picturing corkscrews; author of "A Price Guide to Beer Advertising Openers and Corkscrews" along with several other books related to corkscrews.

Mark Barlow
Winetiques
3107A Medlock Bridge Rd.
Norcross, GA 30071-1423
ph: 770-449-7610
fax: 770-449-1839
sales@wineaccessoriesmart.com
http://www.wineaccessoriesmart.com
Buys, sells and specializes in

corkscrews and all wine related items; from basic to unique patents.

Roger V. Baker
Baker's Lady Luck Emporium
P.O. Box 620417
Redwood City, CA 94062-0417
ph: 650-851-7188
fax: 650-851-7188
Specializing in saloon collectibles: gambling, bar bottles, shaving mugs, razors, Bowie knives, daggers, barber items, match safes.

Joseph C. Paradi
670 Meadow Wood Rd.
Mississauga, Ontario L5J 2S6 Canada
ph: 905-823-3754 or 416-978-6924 x210
fax: 905-823-3775
paradi@mie.utoronto.ca
http://www.corkscrewnet.com
Corkscrew dealer, expert, collector and appraiser.

Internet Resources

Donald A. Bull
Virtual Corkscrew Museum
P.O. Box 596
Wirtz, VA 24184
ph: 540-721-1128
fax: 540-721-5468
corkscrew@bullworks.net
http://www.corkscrewmuseum.com
An online corkscrew museum containing over 2500 pictures and 500 pages of information.

Raj & Justine Kanodia
Corkscrew.Com
3717 Ortega Court
Palo Alto, CA 94303
corky@corkscrew.com
http://www.corkscrew.com
Learn all about corkscrews: history, patents, functionality; over 150 photos with text; New York Times calls this "a fascinating site built by a dedicated San Francisco Bar area couple's 20-year passion for collecting corkscrews."

CORN COLLECTIBLES

Clubs/Associations

Robert S. Chamberlain, Ed.
Corn Items Collectors Association Inc.
Newsletter: Bang Board, The
9288 Poland Rd.
Warrensburg, IL 62573-2062
ph: 217-674-3334
fax: 217-674-3334
lain@frontiernet.net
Association collecting and studying anything having to do with corn, i.e., inventions, corn collectibles, etc.; large format newsletter with lots of pictures and articles.

Corn Shellers

Collectors

Robert Rauhauser
P.O. Box 324
Thomasville, PA 17364-0324
ph: 717-792-0278
Wants corn shellers: handheld, table mounted, box mounted; any unusual corn shellers; also popcorn shellers.

CORONATION MEMORABILIA

(see POSTCARDS, Royalty Related; ROYALTY COLLECTIBLES, British)

COUNTERFEIT DETECTING ITEMS

Collectors

Donald Gorlick
P.O. Box 24541
Seattle, WA 98124-0541
ph: 206-824-0508
Wants counterfeit currency detectors, coin testers, scales, scanners, grids, books, reporters, recorders, magnifiers, Detectographs, etc.

COUNTRY STORE COLLECTIBLES

(see ADVERTISING COLLECTIBLES; BOTTLES; CIGAR BOXES, LABELS & BANDS; FARM COLLECTIBLES; LABELS; STRING HOLDERS; TIN CONTAINERS)

COVERED BRIDGES

Clubs/Associations

Russell J. Holmes
Theodore Burr Covered Bridge Society of Pennsylvania, Inc.
Magazine: Wooden Covered Spans
P.O. Box 2382
Lancaster, PA 17606-2382
ph: 717-428-1006
rusholmes@worldnet.att.net
http://www.tbcbspa.com
Society is committed to saving and preserving covered bridges; monthly meeting held for collectors of bridge related material; also publishes the newsletter "Pennsylvania Crossings."

Collectors

Marie Ward
2461 E. High St.
Pottstown, PA 19464-3189
ph: 610-970-6299
kunmingcbi@aol.com
Wants items relating to covered bridges.

COVERLETS

(see also FOLK ART; REPAIR/ RESTORATION/CONSERVATION, Textiles; TEXTILES)

Clubs/Associations

Barbara Frisbie
Colonial Coverlet Guild of America
Newsletter: CCGA Newsletter
5617 Blackstone
La Grange, IL 60525-3420
ph: 708-352-3812
Members are interested in coverlets or antique textiles, their preservation and in the present revival of weaving.

Dealers

Carl McCann
Troy & Black, Inc.
P.O. Box 228
Red Creek, NY 13143-0228
ph: 315-754-8115
Buys and sells high quality flow blue, Staffordshire figurines, American painted furniture, stoneware, redware, coverlets, samplers, and other American textiles, folk art, etc.

Misc. Services

Barbara Luck
Abby Aldrich Rockefeller Folk Art Center
P.O. Box 1776
Williamsburg, VA 23187
Will assist in identifying an unknown coverlet weaver.

Museums/Libraries

American Textile History Museum
491 Dutton St.
Lowell, MA 01854-4221
ph: 978-441-0400
fax: 978-441-1412
espear@athm.org
http://www.athm.org
Outstanding collection of textiles and textile making machinery and equipment; tools, machines, prints, photographs, business records, industry periodicals, textiles, swatches, sample books, trade catalogs, etc.

DuPage County Illinois Historical Museum
102 E. Wesley St.
Wheaton, IL 60187
ph: 630-682-7343
historical.museum@dupageco.org
http://www.dupageco.org/museum
Collection includes 103 loom-woven coverlets donated by the Colonial Coverlet Guild of America.

Repro. Sources

David C. Kline
Family Heir-Loom Weavers
775 Meadowview Dr.
Red Lion, PA 17356-8608
ph: 717-246-2431 or 717-246-2431
fax: 717-246-7439
PatKline@familyheirloomweavers.com
http://www.familyheirloomweavers.com
Makers of fancy jacquard coverlets, ingrain carpets & other historic textiles; send $4.00 for brochure.

COWBOY HEROES

(see also CHARACTER COLLECTIBLES; COMIC BOOKS, Super Heroes; MOVIE MEMORABILIA, Westerns; POPULAR CULTURE; PREMIUMS; TELEVISION SHOWS & MEMORABILIA, Westerns; TOY GUNS; WESTERN AMERICANA)

Appraisers

Brill Lee
Brill Lee Appraisal Services
P.O. Box 244
Bellevue, WA 98009-0244
ph: 425-885-4518
fax: 425-895-1022
brilllee@hotmail.com
Appraises children's cowboy and cowgirl memorabilia including clothing, boots, hats, costumes, cap guns, games and related items.

Clubs/Associations

Norman Kietzer
Westerns & Serials Fan Club
Magazine: Westerns & Serials
527 S. Front St.
Mankato, MN 56001-3718
ph: 507-344-8913
fax: 507-344-0255
kietzer@mctcnet.net
http://www.angelfire.com/biz2/ normankietzerpubs
A club for collectors as well as non-collectors interested in westerns and serials of the silver screen; also interested in related memorabilia.

Collectors

Jim Babchak
313 East 85 #4B
New York, NY 10028
ph: 212-861-1356
Wants to buy old cowboy stuff including cowboy boots, shirts, horsehair bridles, spurs, chaps, children's costumes from the 1940s and 1950s, anything Roy Rogers, Hopalong Cassidy or Gene Autry.

Dealers

Terri Mardis-Ivers
Terri's Toys & Nostalgia
114 Whitworth Ave.
Ponca City, OK 74601-3438
ph: 580-762-8697
toylady@cableone.net
Wants to buy Western character items: Roy Rogers, Gene Autry, Hopalong Cassidy, Bonanza, Maverick, Lone Ranger, Gunsmoke, others; cap guns, holsters, lunch boxes, Hartland, Breyer plastic horses/animals, Western dolls, figures and clothing.

Jim & Shirley's Antiques
2245 Faust Ave.
Long Beach, CA 90815-3354
ph: 562-598-1914
jimandshirley@webtv.net
Specializes in Hopalong Cassidy, and

Roy Rogers and Dale Evans memorabilia.

Experts

Mario De Marco
152 Maple St.
West Boylston, MA 01583-1825
ph: 508-835-4085
Author and publisher of books on Charles Starrett, George "Gabby" Hayes, Tom Mix, Horse Bits and B Westerns, John Wayne, Don Barry, Tex Ritter and Fred Scott, Sagebrush heroes, William "Hoppy" Boyd, and others.

Rudy D'Angelo
P.O. Box 350
Farmington, CT 06034-0350
ph: 860-674-9422
fax: 860-677-7433
radpiimc44@aol.com
http://members.tripod.com/rudydangelo
Author of "Television's Cowboys Gunfighters & Cap Pistols."

Ted Hake
Hake's Americana & Collectibles Auction
P.O. Box 1444
York, PA 17405-1444
ph: 717-848-1333
Ted@hakes.com
http://www.hakes.com
Author of "Hake's Guide to TV Collectibles" and several other books on collectibles; always purchasing items for mail-bid auctions of Disneyana, historical Americana, toys, premiums, political items, character and other collectibles.

Internet Resources

CowboyPal Round-Up Time in Texas
konnyu@fc.net
http://www.cowboypal.com
Devoted to Hollywood cowboy heroes of the 1930s through 1950s including Gene Autry, Roy Rogers, Hopalong Cassidy, Tom Mix; radio shows, movie clips, history and more.

Periodicals

Joseph Caro
Newsletter: Cowboy Collector Network, The
P.O. Box 7486
Long Beach, CA 90807-0486
ph: 714-840-3942
hoppyccn@aol.com
Articles and collector values on Hopalong Cassidy, Gene Autry, Roy Rogers, The Lone Ranger, etc.

Gene Autry

Museums/Libraries

Elvin Sweeten
Gene Autry Oklahoma Museum
Newspaper: Gene Autry Star Telegram
P.O. Box 67
Gene Autry, OK 73436
ph: 580-389-5335 or 580-294-3047
fax: 580-389-5139
esweeten@brightok.net
http://www.cow-boy.com/museum.htm
Museum of Gene Autry memorabilia including photos, posters, etc.; also local memorabilia; the newspaper is an annual to promote the community & the man; very big with collectors world over; includes photos & stories relating to both.

Autry Museum of Western Heritage
Magazine: Spur
4700 Western Heritage Way
Los Angeles, CA 90027-1462
ph: 323-667-2000
fax: 323-660-5721
tbailey@autry-museum.org
http://www.autry-museum.org
Explores, collects, and preserves objects and art relating to the mythology and history of the American West.

Hopalong Cassidy

Clubs/Associations

Laura Bates
Friends of Hopalong Cassidy International Fan Club
Newsletter: Hoppy Talk
6310 Friendship Dr.
New Concord, OH 43762-9708
ph: 740-826-4850
fax: 740-826-1219
LBates1205@cs.com
http://www.hopalong.com/f_friends.asp
Club organized to establish a museum in Cambridge, OH (boyhood home of William Boyd); newsletter contains, articles, buy/sell ads, etc.; newsletter published quarterly.

Collectors

Chris Swain
P.O. Box 513
Williamsburg, MA 01096
ph: 413-628-3213
Bluejettoy@aol.com
Wants items relating to Hopalong Cassidy and Roy Rogers.

Harry L. Rinker
5093 Vera Cruz Rd.
Emmaus, PA 18049-9554
ph: 610-965-1122
fax: 610-965-1124
rinkeron@fast.net
http://www.harryrinker.com
Seeking Hopalong Cassidy memorabilia.

Ron Pieczkowski
1707 Orange Hill Dr.
Brandon, FL 33510-2632
ph: 813-685-2338
Wants to buy Hopalong Cassidy collectibles; single items or entire collections.

Laura Bates
6310 Friendship Dr.
New Concord, OH 43762-9708
ph: 740-826-4850
fax: 740-826-1219
LBates1205@cs.com
Editor of "Hoppy Talk", the newsletter of the Friends of Hopalong Cassidy International Fan Club; coordinator of Hopalong Cassidy festival held each May in Cambridge, OH; curator of Hopalong Cassidy Museum.

Dealers

Howard R. Cherry
10th St. Antique Mall
127 South 10th St.
Cambridge, OH 43725
ph: 740-432-3364
hcherry@cambridgeoh.com
http://www.hcherry.com
Wants to buy Cowboy memorabilia: Roy Rogers, Gene Autry, Hopalong Cassidy.

Experts

Joseph Caro
P.O. Box 7486
Long Beach, CA 90807-0486
ph: 714-840-3942
hoppyccn@aol.com
Leading expert on Hoppy memorabilia; author of "Collectors Guide to Hopalong Cassidy Memorabilia" (1992) and "Hopalong Cassidy Collectibles" (1997); available from author.

Jerry Rosenthal
Hopalong Cassidy Enterprises
P.O. Box 572063
Tarzana, CA 91357
ph: 818-881-2081 or 800-711-4677
fax: 818-881-4557
jerry@hopalong.com
http://www.hopalong.com
Restoration of 66 Hopalong Cassidy motion pictures; new Hoppy collectibles.

Lone Ranger

Clubs/Associations

Joe Southern
Lone Ranger Fan Club
Newsletter: Silver Bullet, The
P.O. Box 1493
Longmont, CO 80502
ph: 303-485-9997
fax: 303-485-9997
theloneranger@worldnet.att.net
http://www.lonerangerfanclub.com
The official Lone Ranger Fan Club, featuring "The Silver Bullet", a quarterly newsletter for Lone Ranger enthusiasts and collectors; publishing since 1988; will reply if SASE is enclosed.

John Samorajczyk
Lone Ranger Fan Club
Newsletter: Pictorial Scrapbook
19205 Seneca Ridge Court
Gaithersburg, MD 20879-3135
ph: 301-869-1755
rasamora@aol.com

Collectors

John S. Fawcett
P.O. Box 1156
Waldoboro, ME 04572-1156
ph: 207-832-7398
fawcetoy@gwi.net
http://home.gwi.net/~fawcetoy
Wants to buy 1930s to 1950s Lone Ranger items; wants everything.

Karl L. Rommel
1377 Cloverleaf Rd.
Lansing, MI 48906
ph: 517-484-7865
Wants all 1933-1955 "Lone Ranger" memorabilia; especially wants anything related to radio's Lone Ranger, Brace Beemer, and any sponsor items of the radio show.

Experts

Terry & Kay Klepey
P.O. Box 553
Forks, WA 98331-0553
ph: 360-327-3726 or 360-374-5717
slvrbllt@olypen.com
http://www.olypen.com/slvrbllt
Collector, dealer expert; buys, sells and collects Lone Ranger and related items: comics, toys, books, dolls, etc.; also interested in other 1950s Westerns.

Richard Dix

Internet Resources

Glenn Taranto
Dix Archives
info@richarddix.com
http://www.richarddix.com
The goal of the Dix Archives is to preserve the memory and celebrate the film career of Richard Dix by collecting movie paper for all 100 of his films and to present them in an informative and entertaining fashion on his fan Web site.

Roy Rogers & Dale Evans

Clubs/Associations

Nancy Horsley, ExSec
Roy Rogers - Dale Evans Collectors Association
Newsletter: RRDECA Newsletter
P.O. Box 1166
Portsmouth, OH 45662-1166
ph: 740-353-0900 or 740-353-4002
Organized as a part of the Portsmouth Area Community Exhibits which maintains the Roy Rogers Hometown Exhibit in Portsmouth, Roy's boyhood hometown.

Collectors

Chris Swain
P.O. Box 513
Williamsburg, MA 01096
ph: 413-628-3213
Bluejettoy@aol.com
Wants items relating to Hopalong Cassidy and Roy Rogers.

Laura Lee Gwaltney
3104 East 5th St.
Anderson, IN 46012-3814
ph: 765-642-6318
Especially interested in Western paper items, but also collects anything to do with Roy Rogers & his family.

Don Mabbitt
P.O. Box 114
Sheldon, IL 60966-0114
ph: 815-429-3671
Wants to buy Roy Rogers and Dale Evans collectibles: cap guns, toys, and other memorabilia.

Linda Burke
24430 Alcarol Dr.
Fenton, MO 63026
ph: 636-225-7790
fax: 636-225-7838
linroda@aol.com
Wants to buy Roy & Dale memorabilia.

Museums/Libraries

Roy Rogers Hometown Exhibit, c/o Chamber of Commerce
P.O. Box 509
Portsmouth, OH 45662
ph: 740-353-1116
Located in downtown Portsmouth, OH; displays western film memorabilia of Roy Rogers and other Western stars.

Roy Rogers - Dale Evans Museum & Happy Trails Theater, The
Newsletter: Roy Rogers Riders Club Newsletter
3950 Green Mountain Dr.
Branson, MO 65616
ph: 417-339-1900
administrator@royrogers.com
http://www.royrogers.com
Museum now offers a 308 seat theater with live music to enjoy.

Tom Mix

Clubs/Associations

John Samorajczyk
Tom Mix Fan Club
19205 Seneca Ridge Court
Gaithersburg, MD 20879-3135
ph: 301-869-1755
rasamora@aol.com
An online club for Tom Mix fans; members receive a membership kit.

Dealers

Paul E. Mix
P.O. Box 180182
Austin, TX 78718-0182
ph: 512-836-8005
fax: 512-835-1708
Sells Tom Mix related booklets and photo catalogs; also collects, buys and sells Tom Mix memorabilia.

Experts

Mario De Marco
152 Maple St.
West Boylston, MA 01583-1825
ph: 508-835-4085
Author of "Photostory of The Screen's Greatest Cowboy - Tom Mix;" one of the very early publications on Tom Mix, soft cover, 100+ pages, loaded with rare photos and bio of Tom and some of the other associated stars; $10.50 ppd.

M.G. "Bud" Norris
1324 N. Hague Ave.
Columbus, OH 43204-2108
ph: 614-274-4646
Buys Tom Mix memorabilia; author of "The Tom Mix Book;" publicity director of the International Tom Mix Festival; consultant to the Tom Mix Museum, Dewey, OK.

Museums/Libraries

Tom Mix Museum
721 North Delaware
P.O. Box 190
Dewey, OK 74029-0190
ph: 918-534-1555
http://www.ok-history.mus.ok.us/mus-sites/masnum31.htm

COWBOY/COWGIRL COLLECTIBLES

(see COWBOY HEROES; WESTERN AMERICANA)

CRACKER JACK COLLECTIBLES

Clubs/Associations

Theresa Richter, Mem.
Cracker Jack Collectors Association
Newsletter: Prize Insider, The
5469 S. Dorchester Ave.
Chicago, IL 60615
WaddyTMR@aol.com
http://www.collectoronline.com/CJCA
A nonprofit association dedicated to the collector of Cracker Jack and related memorabilia; share knowledge and correspondence; membership includes newsletter and membership card; holds annual convention.

Collectors

Larry White
108 Central St.
Rowley, MA 01969
ph: 978-948-8187
larrydw@erols.com
http://www.erols.com/larrydw
Buys and sells Cracker jack toys; author of two books on Cracker Jacks.

Ann Brogley
P.O. Box 16033
Philadelphia, PA 19114-0033
ph: 215-824-4698 or 215-824-2350
fax: 215-824-4698
mostprod@erols.com
http://www.geocities.com/Heartland/Hills/2081
Founder of Cracker Jack Collectors Association; avid collector wants to buy Cracker Jack items; one item or entire collections; all letters answered.

Wes Johnson
RFD
Glenview, KY 40025
Advanced collector wants tin, cast metal, plastic toy prizes, old paper items; also ANGELUS Marshmallows, CHECKERS Confection items.

Edwin Snyder
P.O. Box 156
Lancaster, KY 40444-0156
ph: 606-792-4816
Wants to buy Cracker Jack, Checkers Confections, Chums, and related items, prizes and advertising.

Barry Brandon
651 Linda Ln.
Bonner Springs, KS 66012-1809
ph: 913-441-8663
barry@cameragrafx.com
Wants Cracker Jack prizes: tin, cast metal, plastic and paper; also collects Angelus, Checkers, Reliable Confections.

Jeffrey Maxwell
Alphabet26 Web Site
213 East Wells Blvd.
Sapulpa, OK 74066-6439
ph: 918-227-0657 or 918-594-8280
fax: 918-594-8281
alphabet26@aol.com
http://members.aol.com/Alphabet26
A Web site dedicated to the study of 1940 to 1960s plastic prizes from gum machines and Cracker Jacks with an alphabet theme.

Experts

Ron Toth, Jr.
72 Charles St.
Rochester, NH 03867-3413
ph: 603-335-2062
ron@timepassagesnostalgia.com
http://www.timepassagesnostalgia.com
Collects and specializes in Cracker Jack memorabilia; historian, advisor, and artist for Cracker Jack; First VP and current Director for the Cracker Jack Collectors Association; member of the Cracker Jack Advisory Board.

Jim Davis
Cracker Jack Box, The
135 Jefferson Heights Ave.
New Orleans, LA 70121-3207
ph: 504-733-3619
jeepers@ix.netcom.com
http://pw2.netcom.com/~jeepers/CrackerJackBox.html
Collects all types of Cracker Jack prizes and related Cracker jack items; has served on the Cracker Jack Collectors Assoc. Board of Directors; maintains updated Web site dedicated to Cracker Jacks.

Internet Resources

Jim Davis
Cracker Jack Box, The
135 Jefferson Heights Ave.
New Orleans, LA 70121-3207
ph: 504-733-3619
jeepers@ix.netcom.com
http://pw2.netcom.com/~jeepers/CrackerJackBox.html
This site is dedicated to Cracker Jack collecting: prizes, ads, mail-in and point-of-sale premiums, etc,; also includes history and other related information along with Cracker Jack resources and links.

CRAFTS

(see also BASKETS; LAPIDARY; RUGS, Hooked; REPAIR/RESTORATION/CONSERVATION, Woodworking [Suppliers]; STAINED GLASS)

Clubs/Associations

American Craft Council
21 South Eltings Corner Rd.
Highland, NY 12528-2805
ph: 800-836-3470 or 845-883-6100
fax: 845-883-6130
shows@craftcouncil.org
http://www.craftcouncil.org
An association offering trade and professional services to craft persons and craft retailers; produce craft shows in Baltimore, Atlanta, St. Paul, Chicago, San Francisco, Sarasota, and Charlotte.

National Crafts Association
1945 E. Ridge Rd., Ste. 5178
Rochester, NY 14622-2467
ph: 800-715-9594 or 716-266-5472
fax: 716-785-3231
nca@craftsassoc.com
http://www.craftsassoc.com
Information source for the professional arts & crafts industry.

Fred Bair, Jr.
Society of Workers in Early Arts & Trades
Newsletter: Sweat Rag, The
606 Lake Lena Blvd.
Auburndale, FL 33823-2937
ph: 813-967-3262
fax: 813-967-3262
Members are largely those who do public demonstrations of early crafts, but membership is open to anyone; exchange knowledge of practices in crafts; promotes the finding, making and exchange of tools; annual directory.

Internet Resources

World Wide Arts Resource
761 Franklin Ave.
Columbus, OH 43205
ph: 614-221-7661
fax: 614-221-1933
contact@wwar.com
http://www.wwar.com
Online crafts resources: baskets, ceramics, costumes, dolls, embroidery, furniture, instruments, jewelry, miniatures, pottery, quilts, textiles, wood carving.

Misc. Services

Linda Gibbs
Victorian - An Era of the Past
10380 Miranda Ave.
Buena Park, CA 90620-4447
ph: 714-827-6488
Offers classes in the lost Victorian arts & crafts; ribbon embroidery, hearts, flowers, a touch of lace create old fashioned delights, one-of-a-kind items that will become your heirloom keepsakes; send SASE for info.

Museums/Libraries

American Craft Museum
40 West 53rd St.
New York, NY 10019
ph: 212-956-3535
fax: 212-459-0926
http://www.americancraftmuseum.org

Periodicals

American Craft Council
Magazine: American Craft
21 S. Eltings Courner Rd.
Highland, NY 12528
ph: 845-883-6100 or 800-836-3470
fax: 845-883-6130
council@craftcouncil.org
http://www.craftcouncil.org
Non-profit educational organization founded in 1943; offers juried craft fairs, maintains special library of 20th century crafts; offers seminars and services to professional crafts people; membership open to all.

Magazine: Crafts Report, The
P.O. Box 1992
Wilmington, DE 19899-1992
ph: 302-656-2209 or 800-777-7098
fax: 302-656-4894
webeditor@craftsreport.com
http://www.craftsreport.com
The business journal for the crafts industry.

Palm House Publishing
Magazine: Sunshine Artist
3210 Dade Ave
Orlando, FL 32804
ph: 407-228-9772
fax: 407-228-9862
business@sunshineartist.com
http://www.sunshineartist.com
Covering the art and craft event marketplace for more than 25 years; show listings, reviews, entry information, articles, suppliers.

Scott Publications
Magazine: Stamping Arts & Crafts
30595 Eight Mile
Livonia, MI 48152-1798
ph: 800-458-8237 or 248-477-6650
fax: 248-477-6795
concatus@scottpublications.com
http://www.scottpublications.com
Includes a variety of full-length articles covering everything from stamping on paper, walls, fabric, furniture and polymer clay; for the beginner to advanced stamper.

Ornament, Inc.
Magazine: Ornament
P.O. Box 2349
San Marcos, CA 92079-2349
ph: 760-599-0222
fax: 760-599-0228
ornament@cts.com
http://www.ornamentmagazine.com
A quarterly magazine focusing on craft and art items of personal adornment in any media or form: fiber, glass, metal, ancient historic/ethnic ornament; ethnographic and tribal jewelry; also reviews of museum exhibits and publications.

Basketry

(see also BASKETS)

Internet Resources

Alan Beebe
Basketry Information
277 Raplh Vedder Rd.
Saugerties, NY 12477
abeebe@ulster.net
http://www.ulster.net/~abeebe/basket.html
Online resource containing books, magazines & newsletters, sources of materials, associations and guilds, classes, conventions and meetings, basketmakers' Web pages, related Web links, basketmakers' email addresses.

Periodicals

Magazine: Fiberarts
50 College St.
Asheville, NC 28801-2818
Focuses on contemporary fiber arts and artists.

Sheri L. Van Duyn
Magazine: Just Patterns
18784 North Fruitport Rd.
Spring Lake, MI 49456
ph: 616-846-7926
sheri@justpatterns.com
http://www.justpatterns.com/index.html
The Idea Magazine for basketmakers: published quarterly; now featuring 5 or more patterns in each issue, suppliers, weavers, Devotional, etc.

Sandy Heried
Basket Publications, Etc.
Magazine: Basket Bits
3201 County Rd. H
Sturtevant, WI 53177-2301
ph: 262-886-8651
fax: 262-886-5184
basketbitsmag@aol.com
http://www.basketbits.com
A magazine for basket makers.

Glass

(see also GLASS; STAINED GLASS)

Periodicals

Jim Thingwold, Ed.
Magazine: Glass Line
120 S. Kroeger St.
Anaheim, CA 92805-4011
ph: 714-520-0121
fax: 714-520-4370
info@hotglass.com
http://www.hotglass.com
Bi-monthly; glass working information, supplies, etc.; the number one publication for the hot glass artists; beads, hobby, glass art, sculptures, supplies, equipment, collectors.

Jewelry

(see also GEMS & JEWELRY)

Appraisers

Daloma Armentrout
Armentrout-Hawken Appraisal Associates
P.O. Box 160906
Austin, TX 78716-0906
ph: 512-328-9411
agx@earthlink.net
Expert specializing in the appraisal of fine contemporary art jewelry and art metals crafts; author of "Art Jewelry & Metals - Makers, Markets, Meaning;" also collection consultant, and educator.

Metal

Clubs/Associations

Dana Singer, Ex. Dir.
Society of North American Goldsmiths
Journal: Metalsmith
710 East Ogden Ave., Ste. 600
Naperville, IL 60563-8603
ph: 630-579-3272
fax: 630-369-2488
DSinger@SNAGmetalsmith.org
http://www.snagmetalsmith.org
An association for jewelers and metal artisans; quarterly magazine devoted to the development and appreciation

for the craft of fine metalsmithing: jewelry, decorative art, etc.

CRANBERRY INDUSTRY ITEMS

Collectors

Peter K. Meier
136 Hayward St.
Halifax, MA 02338-1804
ph: 781-293-3218
Wants to buy cranberry scoops and related items; paper goods, tools and implements related to the cranberry growing industry.

CREDIT CARDS & CHARGE ITEMS

(see also BANKING; CIVIL WAR ARTIFACTS, Currency; COINS & CURRENCY; MONEYCARDS; TELEPHONE CARDS; WOODEN MONEY)

Clubs/Associations

Bill Wieland, Pres.
American Credit Card Collectors Society
Journal: Charge
P.O. Box 2465
Midland, MI 48640
ph: 517-839-2026
fax: 517-839-2026
Members interested in credit cards and charge coins.

Collectors

Gary Olsen
HPDRI Book Traders
505 S. Royal Ave.
Front Royal, VA 22630
ph: 540-635-7157 or 800-954-7374
fax: 540-635-1818
olsenhp@hpfri.com
http://www.hpfri.com
Collecting since 1960s; will pay $1 each plus postage for any age, quantity or condition of expired credit cards; plastic, paper, metal.

Jerry Ballard
4016 Poplar Grove Rd.
Midlothian, VA 23112-4735
ph: 804-744-7700
fax: 804-744-6600
cbballard@aol.com
Wants credit cards and charge coins; will pay $1 to $5 for each pre-1985 card; send photocopy or cards.

Jose Moreira
4450 East 8 Lane
Miami Beach, FL 33013
jmoreira@attbi.com
Wants old, expired, obsolete charge or credit cards; from anywhere, any vintage, any quantity; free appraisals, send photocopies of front and back.

Bo Buchanan
P.O. Box 188
Yorkville, IL 60560
ph: 630-846-4663
fax: 425-732-1996
merlin@galahads.com
Wants to buy credit cards, gift cards, debit cards Visa cash, Monex; cards of all kinds: gas station, department store, Visa, AMEX, Diners Club; paper, plastic, charge plates, and charge coins; will buy collections; $1 per card unseen.

T.L. Helgeson
Credit Card Collector, The
1791 W. Tennyson Dr.
Tucson, AZ 85746-1381
ph: 520-294-6865
fax: 520-573-1509
cctuc@yahoo.com
Wants to buy all types of credit and charge items: paper, plastic, metal, and celluloid from the late 1800s to 1990s; expired/closed account items only; send photocopy and description of what you have.

Cards

Internet Resources

Terry Stewart
Collector Link
71 John St. East
Waterloo, Ontario N2J 1G2 Canada
ph: 519-745-1745
stewart@collector-link.com
http://www.collector-link.com
Catalogs over 2,000 trading card related Web sites for: baseball, hockey, basketball, football, other sports, non-sports, phone cards, credit-debit cards, business cards, postcards.

CRESTED WARE

(see CERAMICS [ENGLISH], Goss Pottery/Crested Ware)

CRIME

(see LAW ENFORCEMENT MEMORABILIA; MYSTERY/DETECTIVE ITEMS; OUTLAWS & LAWMEN; PERSONALITIES [CRIMINALS])

CRUCIFIXES

(see RELIGIOUS COLLECTIBLES, Crosses)

CRUETS

(see also GLASS, Pattern; GLASS, Art)

Experts

Elaine Ezell
Cruets, Cruets, Cruets
P.O. Box 1609
Pasadena, MD 21122-1609
ph: 410-255-6777 or 410-551-4101
fax: 410-551-3575
aaaantiquesmall@earthlink.net
Advanced collector and co-author with George Newhouse of "Cruets, Cruets, Cruets" (Vol I $29.95 and Vol II $32.95 from author); buys/sells art glass and colored Victorian cruets.

CRUISE SHIP ITEMS

(see OCEAN LINER COLLECTIBLES)

CRYPTOGRAPHIC DEVICES

(see SPY EQUIPMENT)

CRYSTAL

(see GLASS, Crystal; TABLEWARE)

CRYSTAL BALLS

(see UFOs & UNEXPLAINED PHENOMENA)

CUBAN COLLECTIBLES

Dealers

Gerardo Chavez
Cuba Collectibles, Inc.
P.O. Box 832782
Miami, FL 33283
ph: 305-753-8610
fax: 305-225-0286
Gerardo_Chavez@cubacollectibles.com
http://www.cubacollectibles.com
Specializes in Cuban collectibles and memorabilia.

CUFF LINKS

(see also BELT BUCKLES; CLOTHING & ACCESSORIES, Vintage; GEMS & JEWELRY; TIE BARS, CLIPS & TACKS)

Clubs/Associations

National Cuff Link Society
P.O. Box 58328
New Orleans, LA 70158-8328
ph: 504-524-2233
fax: 504-525-9327
ncls@bellsouth.net
http://www.cufflink.com
Web site has information for collectors of cuff links, tie bars, tie tacks, collar buttons, collar pins, shirt studs, stick pins, money clips, vintage collars/cuffs, belt buckles, and button covers.

Collectors

Claude Jeanloz
Yield House Industries, Inc.
71 Hobbs St.
P.O. Box 2525
Conway, NH 03818
ph: 413-659-3109
Wants all types of cull links for cuff link museum: cuff links, cuff buttons, cuff jewelry, and cuff link memorabilia.

James S. McCormick
476 Windswept Dr.
Asheville, NC 28801
ph: 828-253-2660 or 828-254-0071

Dealers

Gail Busche
Archangel Antiques
334 East Ninth St.
New York, NY 10003-7924
ph: 212-260-9313
richgail38@aol.com
Specializes in vintage and antique clothing buttons, cufflinks, eyewear, lighters, and home furnishings; also Art Deco and Art Nouveau, and classic 1950s and 1960s home furnishings and decorative items.

Michael A. Pratt, Sr.
Off the Cuff
512 North Spruce St.
Valley, NE 68064-9670
ph: 402-359-5539
fax: 402-359-5539
sales@usadisplay.net
http://www.usadisplay.net
Buys and sells unique cuff links of all kinds; also sells display cases for cuff links and collectibles of all types.

Experts

Eugene R. Klompus
P.O. Box 5970
Vernon Hills, IL 60061
ph: 847-816-0035
fax: 847-816-0035
genek@cufflinksrus.com
http://www.cufflinksrus.com
Buys, sells, collects, appraises cuff links; author of "Collectors Guide to Cuff Link Collecting;" expert spokesperson on cuff links and related miscellaneous jewelry; authority and source for Presidential and political cuff links.

Museums/Libraries

Claude Jeanloz
Cuff Link Museum
71 Hobbs St.
P.O. Box 2525
Conway, NH 03818
ph: 413-659-3109
The world's largest collection of cuff links includes more than 50,000 pairs in every shape, size, and material imaginable.

Enamel

Dealers

Derek Anastasia
Anastasia, Ltd.
P.O. Box 2094
Fort Lauderdale, FL 33303
ph: 954-520-8066
DerekAnast@aol.com
http://www.EnamelCuffLinks.com
Appraises, collects, writes, lectures; specializes in antique/vintage enameled cuff links; has thousands of sets; appeared on PAX TV's "Treasures in Your Home" and FOX TV's "personal FX;" publishes online Enamel Cuff Links Newsletter.

Experts

Derek Anastasia
Anastasia, Ltd.
P.O. Box 2094
Fort Lauderdale, FL 33303
ph: 954-520-8066
DerekAnast@aol.com
http://www.EnamelCuffLinks.com
Appraises, collects, writes, lectures; specializes in antique/vintage enameled cuff links; has thousands of sets; appeared on PAX TV's "Treasures in Your Home" and FOX TV's "personal FX;" publishes online Enamel Cuff Links Newsletter.

CUP PLATES

(see also CERAMICS, Cups & Saucers; GLASS)

Experts

John E. Bilane
2065 Morris Ave., Apt. 109
Union, NJ 07083-6015
ph: 908-686-3060
Buys and sells antique glass cup plates.

CURRENCY

(see COINS & CURRENCY)

CUTLERY

(see DIAMOND EDGE; KEEN KUTTER; KNIVES)

Here are some tips when contacting someone who is listed in this book:

When requesting information about a particular item, include a description (material, dimensions, maker's mark, model number, etc.) and a photo, sketch, digital image or photocopy of the item in question.

Always ask if there are charges for samples or for the services that you are requesting.

When corresponding by letter, please be sure to include a Large (#10 business size) Self-Addressed and Stamped Envelope (LSASE) if requesting a reply or the return of photographs.

Never call collect unless otherwise directed. When calling, be considerate of time zone differences and always ask if the party you are calling has time to talk. When leaving an answering machine message, always instruct the party to call you back collect.

DAGUERREOTYPES

(see PHOTOGRAPHS, Daguerreotypes)

DAIRY COLLECTIBLES

(see also ANIMAL COLLECTIBLES, Cows; BOTTLE CAPS, Milk; BOTTLES, Milk; ELSIE THE BORDEN COW ITEMS; FARM COLLECTIBLES; KITCHEN COLLECTIBLES)

Clubs/Associations

Julian Gottlieb
National Association of Milk Bottle Collectors, Inc.
Newsletter: Milk Route, The
18 Pond Place
Cos Cob, CT 06807
ph: 203-869-8411
fax: 203-869-1625
gottmilk@msn.com
http://www.milkroute.org
Focuses on milk and dairy history and related memorabilia; membership includes the newsletter and directory of members; newsletter has articles, ads, show dates, information exchange, patents, events, etc.

Collectors

Stephen Foster
94 Knobb Hill Rd.
Milford, CT 06460-7245
ph: 203-877-5802
Wants to buy milk bottles and "udder" dairy items.

Sam A. Stephens
319 Juniper St.
Warminster, PA 18974-4720
ph: 215-672-4814 or 215-443-4173
sharplesam@aol.com
Collector of advertising items relating to cream separators and the dairy industry; member of the Board of Directors of the North American Dairy Foundation.

Jar Nut
412 South Baldwin Ave.
Spencer, NC 28159
ph: 704-636-9510
ncmilks@carolina.rr.com
Buys, sells, trades embossed milk bottles (pyro-glazed), milk bottle caps, dairy advertisements, signs, clocks, and thermometers.

Nancy Pennington
1750 Keyes Rd.
Greenbrier, TN 37073
ph: 615-643-0290
fax: 615-643-0290
Wants to buy dairy items such as milk bottles, advertising, cow pitchers, and ice cream items.

Nick Dudek
425 Madison St.
Ravenna, OH 44266
ph: 330-296-0140
ohiomilkcaps@neo.rr.com
Serious dairy collector and dealer buying dairy collectibles including milk caps and milk bottles; specializes in Ohio milk caps; eBay seller name is "milkdude."

Dealers

Debbie Gillete
116 E. Division St.
Watertown, NY 13601
ph: 315-788-0587
dgillett@twcny.rr.com
http://home.twcny.rr.com/dgillett
A milk bottle and dairy memorabilia collector specializing in pyro (painted label) bottles and other dairy collectibles and go-withs.

Debbie Gillette
Debbie's Milk Bottles
116 E. Division St.
Watertown, NY 13601
ph: 315-788-0587
ilovemilkbottles@yahoo.com
http://milkbottle.cjb.net
Collector, dealer, expert specializing in dairy collectibles and milk bottles.

Ralph Riovo
Purple Cow, The
686 Franklin St.
Alburtis, PA 18011-9578
ph: 610-966-2536
fax: 610-966-0368
thepurplecow@erols.com
http://www.papurplecow.com
Adlactilist and dealer in milk and dairy memorabilia; wants milk bottles, dairy advertising and related memorabilia.

Experts

Julian Gottlieb
18 Pond Place
Cos Cob, CT 06807
ph: 203-869-8411
fax: 203-869-1625
gottmilk@msn.com
Appraiser, dealer, expert in dairy collectibles.

David Whitehead
47 Abbott Ave.
Danbury, CT 06810-5311
ph: 203-743-9803
udderlywonerful@aol.com
Appraiser, dealer, expert in dairy collectibles.

Leigh Giarde
LG Enterprises
P.O. Box 2243
Redlands, CA 92373-0741
ph: 909-792-8681
fax: 909-792-8681
onlyleigh@cpl.net
Mail order sales and purchases of milk bottles and go-withs; author of "Glass Milk Bottles: Their Makers and Marks."

Museums/Libraries

New York State Historical Association & The Farmers' Museum, Inc., The
P.O. Box 800
Lake Rd., State Highway 80
Cooperstown, NY 13326
ph: 607-547-1400 or 888-547-1450
cliggio@nysha.org
http://www.nysha.org

Periodicals

Dr. Paul Dettloff, Ed.
Newsletter: Cream Separator & Dairy Newsletter
W 20876 State Rd. 95
Arcadia, WI 54612
ph: 608-323-7470
fax: 608-323-3310
For those interested in cream separators and other dairy items; newsletter contains articles, free ads for subscribers, photos, etc.

Mike & Naomi Hull
Newsletter: Milk Bottle News
Stonemasons
Burleigh
Stroud, Gloucester GL5 2PJ U.K.
ph: 01453 884922
info@milkbottlenews.org.uk
http://www.milkbottlenews.org.uk
A British newsletter for collectors of milk bottles and dairy related memorabilia.

Cream Separators

Collectors

Sam A. Stephens
319 Juniper St.
Warminster, PA 18974-4720
ph: 215-672-4814 or 215-443-4173
sharplesam@aol.com
Collector of advertising items relating to cream separators and the dairy industry; member of the Board of Directors of the North American Dairy Foundation.

Dave Ogle
954 W. Monroe
Jackson, MI 49202-2036
ph: 517-688-4561
Wants to buy DeLaval, Sharples, or other cream separator advertising: calendars, signs, trays, match holders, fobs, etc.

Dealers

Bill Heuring
Hickory Bend Antiques & Collectibles
2995 Drake Hill Rd.
Jasper, NY 14855-9715
ph: 607-792-3343
fax: 607-792-3309
Cream separators and related dairy collectibles bought and sold.

Periodicals

Dr. Paul Dettloff, Ed.
Newsletter: Cream Separator & Dairy Newsletter
W 20876 State Rd. 95
Arcadia, WI 54612
ph: 608-323-7470
fax: 608-323-3310
For those interested in cream separators and other dairy items; newsletter contains articles, free ads for subscribers, photos, etc.

Creamers

Collectors

Toni & Michael Fusco
2629 Oneida St.
Utica, NY 13501
ph: 315-724-8773

Dealers

Ken Clee
P.O. Box 11412
Philadelphia, PA 19111-0412
ph: 215-722-1979
waxntoys@aol.com
http://members.aol.com/waxntoys/main/kidsmeal.htm
Wants to buy glass dairy creamers with names printed on creamers; will buy one or an entire collection.

Experts

Lloyd Bindscheattle
P.O. Box 11
Lake Villa, IL 60046-0011
Collector and expert on dairy creamers.

Periodicals

Lloyd Bindscheattle
Newsletter: Creamers
P.O. Box 11
Lake Villa, IL 60046-0011
A quarterly, 16-page newsletter dealing with glass, advertising, individual, dairy, coffee creamers; free ads.

Milk Cartons

Collectors

Paul Jarmusz
2845 D St. N.E.
Salem, OR 97301-1600
ph: 503-371-0868
fax: 503-371-0868
mikajz@attbi.com
http://www.labelcollector.com
Wants to buy flat top waxed milk cartons with pull tab from the 1930s to the 1960s; found in 5 sizes; has

collection of over 100; see Web site for images.

DATE NAILS

Clubs/Associations

Charles Sebesta, Ed.
Texas Date Nail Collectors Association
Newsletter: Nailer News
P.O. Box 580
Caldwell, TX 77836
ph: 979-567-3764
csebesta@alpha1.net
Date nails are 1" to 2" long; dime-size heads are marked with number on top to show the year installed; driven into railroad ties, telephone poles, or other wood products; shows the year put in service; collect by years or sets.

Collectors

Bob Schneider
2321 Londale Court
Virginia Beach, VA 23456
ph: 757-471-7433
fax: 757-200-3900
mykidsplay@aol.com
http://www.fantasticprices.com

Jerry Waits
501 W. Horton No. 10
Brenham, TX 77833-2357
ph: 979-830-1495

Experts

John Hoffmann
8334 Heron Circle
Ooltewah, TN 37363-9794
Expert on railroad tie date nails and transportation tokens.

Jeff Oaks
Newsletter: Nail Notes
Dept. of Mathematics, Univ. of
 Indianapolis
1400 E. Hanna Ave.
Indianapolis, IN 46227
ph: 317-788-3454
fax: 317-788-3569
oaks@uindy.edu
http://facstaff.uindy.edu/~oaks/
 DateNailInfo.htm
Comprehensive, illustrated Web site on date nails and the history of railroad tie preservation; introduction to date nails, history, FAQ, info about the book & club, images, etc.; author of the book "Date Nails & Railroad Tie Preservation."

Internet Resources

Nailhunter
nailhunter@yahoo.com
http://web7.wt.net/~doomster
Web site contains a pictorial guide to date nails.

Repair Services

Jeff Oaks
Dept. of Mathematics, Univ. of
 Indianapolis
1400 E. Hanna Ave.
Indianapolis, IN 46227
ph: 317-788-3454
fax: 317-788-3569
oaks@uindy.edu
http://facstaff.uindy.edu/~oaks/
 DateNailInfo.htm
Comprehensive, illustrated Web site on date nails and the history of railroad tie preservation; introduction to date nails, history, FAQ, info about the book & club, images, etc.; author of the book "Date Nails & Railroad Tie Preservation."

DAY BOOKS

(see ACCOUNT BOOKS; PAPER COLLECTIBLES)

DEALERS

(see ANTIQUES DEALERS & COLLECTORS)

DECANTERS

Figural Whiskey

(see also BOTTLES)

Collectors

Patrick Batzler
8118 Virginia Circle North
St. Louis Park, MN 55426
ph: 952-525-9590
fax: 952-545-7662
patrickbatzler@aol.com
Wants to buy figural liquor decanters from the 1950s and 1960s.

Dealers

Rick Williams
Burgerjane's Cyber Saloon
Burgerjane@aol.com
http://members.aol.com/burgerjane/
 home.html

Roy & Cordie Willis
Heartland of Kentucky Decanters &
 Steins
P.O. Box 428
Lebanon Junction, KY 40150
ph: 502-833-2827
fax: 502-833-3480
heartland@decantersandsteins.com
http://www.decantersandsteins.com
Hundreds of whiskey decanters by Jim Beam, Wild Turkey, Ski Country, McCormick and others; also beer steins, Budweiser and others; call ONLY 10-6 eastern time, Monday through Saturday.

PRC Associates, Inc.
P.O. Box 611
Alliance, NE 69301
ph: 308-762-1935
info@prcassociates.com
http://www.prcassociates.com
Specializes in Ezra Brooks, McCormack, Beam, Ski Country and other makers of decanters; does not provide private decanter valuations, but Web site offers a decanter price guide for sale.

Experts

PRC Associates, Inc.
P.O. Box 611
Alliance, NE 69301
ph: 308-762-1935
info@prcassociates.com
http://www.prcassociates.com
Author of "The Decanter Collector Price Guide;" does not provide private decanter valuations, but Web site offers a decanter price guide for sale.

Internet Resources

Tom Dunn
Decanter Collectors
519 NE 165th
Seattle, WA 98155
ph: 206-364-1155
fax: 206-364-1023
motnud@aol.com
http://www.decantercollectors.com
Online auction service for decanters and other fine breweriana collectibles.

Figural Whiskey (Beam)

Clubs/Associations

Shirley Sumbles
International Association of Jim Beam
 Bottle & Specialties Club
Newsletter: Beam Around the World
P.O. Box 486
Kewanee, IL 61443-0486
ph: 309-853-3370
fax: 309-852-5174
pbiba@charter.net
http://www.jimbeamclubs.com
A group of collectors world wide with clubs in most states in the US as well as in New Zealand, Japan and Germany; annual international convention.

Cheryl Hendrix
Evergreen Beam Bottle & Specialties
 Club
519 NE 165th
Seattle, WA 98155
ph: 206-364-1155
beamclub@aol.com
http://www.JimBeamClub.com
Focuses on the hobby of collecting Jim Beam and other ceramics decanters; new members always welcome; Web site offers buy and sell board, bottle store, online auctions, pictorials of over 5,000 decanters, bottle collecting FAQs.

Experts

Bernie V. Durance
B.V.D. on Bottles
1008 North Star Dr.
Colorado Springs, CO 80906
ph: 719-577-9033
fax: 719-226-0731
bvd30@hotmail.com
http://www.worldcollectorsnet.com/
 jimbeam/berniesbeam.html
Expert, dealer, collector of Jim Beam and other whiskey decanters; appraisals, identification, buy, sell, trade; writes monthly column.

Figural Whiskey (Bell)

Clubs/Associations

Bells' Decanter Registry, The
U.K.
info@bellsdecanters.co.uk
http://www.bellsdecanters.co.uk
For collectors of Arthur Bell & Sons figural whiskey decanter bottles (1920s to present.)

Figural Whiskey (Ski Country)

Clubs/Associations

Frank & Jacque Willburn
Ski Country Club
Newsletter: Ski Country Club Newsletter
302 Rancho Trail
Amarillo, TX 79108
ph: 806-383-3788
jmwillburn@aol.com
http://www.skicountrydecanters.com
Web site includes images and values for Ski Country figural decanters.

Experts

Frank & Jacque Willburn
302 Rancho Trail
Amarillo, TX 79108
ph: 806-383-3788
jmwillburn@aol.com
http://www.skicountrydecanters.com
Ski Country collectors for over 30 years; authors of "Ski Country Price Guide."

DECORATED OBJECTS

(see FOLK ART; FURNITURE [ANTIQUE], Painted)

DECORATIVE ARTS

(see also Appraisers listed under specific categories throughout this Directory.)

Clubs/Associations

Gerald Ward, Pres.
Museum of Fine Arts, Boston
Newsletter: Decorative Arts Society
 Newsletter
465 Huntington Ave.
Boston, MA 02115-5523
ph: 617-267-9300
webmaster@mfa.org
http://www.mfa.org

Museums/Libraries

Deborah Waters
Museum of the City of New York
1220 5th Ave. at 103rd St.
New York, NY 10029-5221
ph: 212-534-1672
fax: 212-534-5974
http://www.mcny.org
Access by appointment; research fee charged.

Daughters of the American Revolution Museum
1776 D St. NW
Washington, DC 20006-5392
ph: 202-879-3241 or 202-879-3208
fax: 202-628-0820
museum@dar.org
http://www.dar.org/museum
Washington DC's only American Decorative Arts collection; 33,000 objects made or used in America prior to 1840 are exhibited in 33 period rooms and two galleries.

Sally Gant
Museum of Early Southern Decorative Arts
Journal: Journal of the Early Southern Decorative Arts
P.O. Box 10310
Winston Salem, NC 27108-0310
ph: 336-721-7360 or 888-653-7253
fax: 336-721-7367
webmaster@oldsalem.org
http://www.mesda.org
Focuses on Southern decorative arts; has Research Center, Catalog of Early Southern Decorative Arts, and Index of Southern Artists.

Victoria & Albert Museum
Cromwell Rd.
South Kensington
London, SW7 2RL U.K.
ph: +44 (0)20 7942 2000
fax: +44 (0)20 7942 2266
vanda@vam.ac.uk
http://www.vam.ac.uk
The V&A is Britain's national museum of art and design; houses many of the world's greatest decorative art treasures from priceless Oriental carpets to Italian sculpture.

Periodicals

Decorative Arts Trust
Newsletter: Decorative Arts Trust Newsletter
106 Bainbridge St.
Philadelphia, PA 19147-2402
ph: 215-627-2859
fax: 215-925-1144
Study and preservation of American decorative arts; features private collections, museums, restorations, and preservation; Spring and Fall symposiums each year held at various, rich historic sites throughout the US; a non-profit group.

Paula Chamblee
Museum of Early Southern Decorative Arts
Journal: Journal of the Early Southern Decorative Arts
P.O. Box 10310
Winston Salem, NC 27108-0310
ph: 336-721-7360 or 888-653-7253
fax: 336-721-7367
webmaster@oldsalem.org
http://www.mesda.org
Focuses on Southern decorative arts; has Research Center, Catalog of Early Southern Decorative Arts, and Index of Southern Artists.

DECOYS

(see also ART, Wildlife; FISHING COLLECTIBLES; FOLK ART; SPORTING COLLECTIBLES)

Book Sellers

Dean Dashner
Hunting Rig Books
349 S. Green Bay Rd.
Neenah, WI 54956
ph: 920-725-4350 or 920-725-4421
dashners@athenet.net
http://www.huntingrigbooks.com
Buys and sells decoys, duck calls, Ducks Unlimited pin-backs, sporting books, old sporting magazines.

Experts

A. Everette James, Jr.
St. James Place
205 New Castle Place
Chapel Hill, NC 27514
ph: 919-933-6853
fax: 919-942-0437
everette@nc.rr.com
Decoy collector, writer, historian.

Internet Resources

Joseph & Donna M. Tonelli
E Decoy Online Magazine
E-zine: E Decoy Online Magazine
29046 377th Ave.
P.O. Box 459
Lake Andes, SD 57356
ph: 605-337-2301 or 815-664-4580
tonelli47@hotmail.com
http://www.edecoy.com
Online magazine for collectors of duck and fish decoys: message board, directory, calendar auction and show reports, articles, auctions.

Canadian

Experts

Bernie Gates
30 D Chambers St.
P.O. Box 653
Smiths Falls, Ontario K7A 5B8 Canada
ph: 613-283-1168
fax: 613-283-1345
uppercanadian@recorder.ca
http://www.uppercanadian.com
Author of "Ontario Decoys III;" $23.95 Canadian.

Factory

Experts

Henry A. Fleckenstein
P.O. Box 577
Cambridge, MD 21613
ph: 410-221-0076
Appraiser, consultant, agent, author of "American Factory Decoys," "Decoys of the Mid-Atlantic Region," "Southern Decoys of Virginia & the Carolinas," "Shorebird Decoys," and "New Jersey Decoys."

Fish

Clubs/Associations

Frank R. Baron, Sec.
Great Lakes Fish Decoy Collectors & Carvers Association
35824 West Chicago
Livonia, MI 48150-2522
ph: 734-427-7768
Regular meetings and newsletter; long range goal is to establish a permanent display of spearfishing artifacts.

John E. Shoffner
American Fish Decoy Association
Newsletter: American Fish Decoy Forum, The
624 Merritt St.
Fife Lake, MI 49633-9142
ph: 231-879-3912
The largest fish decoy collectors association with approx. 160 members; newsletter has color photos; since 1993.

Collectors

Derald Radtke
195 New Boston Rd.
Francestown, NH 03043
ph: 603-547-2050
millvill@monad.net
http://www.millvillageantiques.com/pages/decoy.html

Art Pietraszewski
60 Grant St.
Depew, NY 14043
ph: 716-681-2339
pie48@hotmail.com
Fish decoy collector buys folk art: wooden decoys, bird carvings, folk art of any type of condition, including damaged or separate heads, bodies, parts; send close up images or photos.

Dealers

Ronald & Kathy Fritz
Fritz Antiques
P.O. Box 575
Zephyrhills, FL 33539
ph: 813-788-2312
fritzantiques@earthlink.net
http://www.fritzantiques.com
Buying and selling old working fish decoys by carvers from Michigan, New York as well as from other areas.

Frank R. Baron
Great Lakes Ice Decoys
35824 West Chicago
Livonia, MI 48150-2522
ph: 734-427-7768
Buys, sells, trades fish decoys; quarterly list of decoys for sale; author of "Bud Stewart, Michigan's Legendary Lure Maker."

John E. Shoffner
624 Merritt St.
Fife Lake, MI 49633-9142
ph: 231-879-3912
Issues 6 lists a year with approx. 600 fish decoys and antique fishing tackle items for sale.

John Cook
Peace Antiques
HC 3 Box 13A
Remer, MN 56672-9602
ph: 218-566-2793
Has specialized in buying and selling fish and duck decoys for 20 years.

Experts

Ronald & Kathy Fritz
Fritz Antiques
P.O. Box 575
Zephyrhills, FL 33539
ph: 813-788-2312
fritzantiques@earthlink.net
http://www.fritzantiques.com
Specialist in the fish decoy carvings of Michigan carvers Peterson, Nelson, Ramey, Hulbert & Bruning; author of book on subject.

Man./Prod./Dist.

Mikko
Mikko's Bait Shop
P.O. Box 100
Osakis, MN 56360-0100
ph: 800-252-1186
Wholesale fish decoys to dealers only.

Waterfowl

Auction Services

Ted Harmon
Decoys Unlimited, Inc.
2320 Main St.
P.O. Box 206
West Barnstable, MA 02668
ph: 508-362-2766
fax: 508-362-2766
tsharmon@attbi.com
http://www.decoysunlimitedinc.com
Periodic auction sales of decoys and related items including prints, paintings, hunting and sporting paraphernalia, etc.

Frank M. Schmidt
Guyette & Schmidt, Inc.
P.O. Box 522
West Farmington, ME 04992
ph: 207-778-6256
fax: 207-778-6501
decoys@guyetteandschmidt.com
http://www.guyetteandschmidt.com
The world's largest decoy auction

firm; please note that an alternate fax number is 207-625-4742.

Frank & Frank Sporting Collectibles
422 Lakewood-Farmingdale Rd.
Howell, NJ 07731
ph: 732-938-2988
fax: 732-938-2988
afrank1807rh@cs.com
http://www.frankandfrankdecoys.com
Auctions, buys and sells decoys, sporting collectibles, wildlife/sporting art.

Clubs/Associations

Ted Harmon
New England Decoy Collectors
  Association
2320 Main St.
P.O. Box 206
West Barnstable, MA 02668
ph: 508-362-2766
fax: 508-362-2766
tsharmon@attbi.com
http://www.decoysunlimitedinc.com

John L. Clayton, Jr.
New Jersey Decoy Collectors Association
1745 Silverton Rd.
Toms River, NJ 08753
ph: 732-255-6291

Nat Glanz
Long Island Decoy Collectors
  Association
P.O. Box 807
Smithtown, NY 11787
ph: 516-537-0153
One of the oldest decoy collecting clubs in the country.

Jim Trimble, Sec./Treas.
East Coast Decoy Collectors Association
P.O. Box 305
Camden, DE 19934
ph: 703-768-7264
potomacduck@cox.net
An organization to promote decoy collecting, the history of decoys, their makers, and related waterfowling interests.

Chad Tragacis
Potomac Decoy Collectors Association
6813 Moon Rock Court
Alexandria, VA 22306
ph: 703-768-2949
potomacduck@cox.net
http://hometown.aol.com/potomacduck/
  myhomepage/club.html
Explores the history of duck, goose, and shorebird decoys, the identification and background of their makers; members also collect related waterfowl items of interest.

Carolina Decoy Collectors Association
4 St. Mary's Place
Wilmington, NC 28403

Duane Ganser
Ohio Decoy Collectors & Carvers
  Association
Newsletter: ODCCA Newsletter
P.O. Box 499
Richfield, OH 44286
webmaster@odcca.org
http://www.odcca.org
Focuses on both vintage and contemporary decoys and their makers.

Midwest Decoy Collectors Association
6 E. Scott St.
Chicago, IL 60610
ph: 312-337-7957
fax: 312-337-9679
mdc@midwestdecoy.org
http://www.midwestdecoy.org
Sponsors annual National Decoy & Sporting Collectibles Show in the Chicago area.

Bryn Watson, Treas.
International Waterfowl Carvers
  Association
P.O. Box 877
Bonsall, CA 92003
ph: 760-731-9717
secretary@iwfca.com
http://www.iwfca.com
Promotes carving by standardizing show rules to ensure fairness, establishing standards for judging and carver advancement, promoting and motivating novice and intermediate carvers, sponsoring contests, etc.

Jim Patrick
Decoy & Wildfowl Carvers Association
18450 Gentian
Riverside, CA 92508
jpatr2562@msn.com
http://www.dwca.net
Created to promote and encourage bird carving in Southern California; new members always welcome; providing free instruction in woodcarving and painting techniques in a major objective of the association.

Collectors

Art Pietraszewski
60 Grant St.
Depew, NY 14043
ph: 716-681-2339
pie48@hotmail.com
Waterfowl decoy collector buys folk art: wooden decoys, bird carvings, folk art of any type of condition, including damaged or separate heads, bodies, parts; send close up images or photos.

David A. Galliher
2500 W. Berwyn Rd.
Muncie, IN 47304-5113
ph: 317-289-2233 or 317-284-6668
fax: 317-289-2376
Wants to buy antique or old decoys from the Midwest area, especially by the carver Charles Perdew (deceased) from Henry, IL; publishing a book on Charles Perdew; 295 pgs, 400

illustrations, color, museum quality printing and binding.

Dealers

Gene & Linda Kangas
Creekside Art Gallery
Kangas@CreeksideArtGallery.com
http://www.creeksideartgallery.com
Dealers in folk art and hunting decoys.

Stephen B. O'Brien, Jr.
268 Newbury St.
Boston, MA 02116
ph: 617-536-0536
fax: 617-536-2238
info@americansportingart.com
http://www.americansportingart.com
Buys and sells quality antique decoys; also folk art, and American paintings; offers appraisals, auction representation, brokerage, and collections management services.

Russ & Karen Goldberger
RJG Antiques
P.O. Box 60
Rye, NH 03870
ph: 603-433-1770
fax: 603-433-3937
decoys@rjgantiques.com
http://www.rjgantiques.com
Dealers, appraisers, experts in waterfowl decoys; specializes in quality working decoys, folk art, and American furniture and accessories in their original painted surfaces.

Alan G. Haid
P. O. Box 1211
Darien, CT 06820
ph: 203-655-5188
clasdecoys@aol.com
http://www.decoymag.com/haid
Specializes in classic old decoys.

Lisa Trayer
Brickerville Antiques & Decoys
117 E. 28th Div. Hwy (Rte. 322)
Lititz, PA 17543
ph: 717-627-2466
Specializes in old factory and working decoys; also sporting antiques related to hunting and fishing; buy/sell/trade old decoys, creels, fishing tackle, eel traps, gigs, old advertising, salesman sample decoys, shell boxes, shorebirds.

Herbert & Joyce Windle
Windle's Antiques
5716 Kennett Pike
Centreville, DE 19807
ph: 302-651-9222
herbnjoyce@netzero.net
Specializes in the appraisal of antique American furniture; also carries a large inventory of decoys from the St. Lawrence areas - both from NY and Ontario sides, early lighting and fireplace cooking equipment.

Henry H. Stansbury
939 Elkridge Landing Rd.
Linthicum Heights, MD 21090
ph: 410-691-9120 or 410-744-8376
henry@asionline.com

Andrea J. Shreiner
Initialed Duck Antiques & Collectibles
3812 Hamilton Ave.
Baltimore, MD 21206-3505
ph: 410-319-7529
Buys, sells and collects waterfowl decoys.

Dick McIntyre
Collectable Old Decoys
1054 Otter Circle
Beaufort, SC 29902-5864
ph: 843-524-0250
decoyczar@charter.net
Decoy dealer and auctioneer; appraiser, expert in American antique decoys; staff writer for "Decoy Magazine," over 30 years in the field; specialist in South Carolina decoys.

John Cook
Peace Antiques
HC 3 Box 13A
Remer, MN 56672-9602
ph: 218-566-2793
Has specialized in buying and selling fish and duck decoys for 20 years.

Experts

Dick McIntyre
Collectable Old Decoys
1054 Otter Circle
Beaufort, SC 29902-5864
ph: 843-524-0250
decoyczar@charter.net
Decoy dealer and auctioneer; appraiser, expert in American antique decoys; staff writer for "Decoy Magazine," over 30 years in the field; specialist in South Carolina decoys.

Museums/Libraries

Peabody Essex Museum
Essex & Libert Sts.
Salem, MA 01970
ph: 978-745-9500 or 800-745-4054
pem@pem.org
http://www.pem.org

Heritage Plantation of Sandwich
P.O. Box 566
Sandwich, MA 02563
ph: 508-888-3300 or 508-888-1222
fax: 508-833-2916
heritage@heritageplantation.org
http://www.heritageplantation.org/
  autos.htm
Contains an outstanding exhibit of decoys by carvers including Elmer Crowell and his memorabilia.

Shelburne Museum, Inc.
P.O. Box 10
Shelburne, VT 05482-0010
ph: 802-985-3346 or 802-985-3348
fax: 802-985-2331
info@shelburnemuseum.org
http://www.shelburnemuseum.org
37 historic structures and exhibit

buildings; diverse collection of
American folk, fine, decorative and
utilitarian art.

Long Island Museum of American Art,
  History & Carriages
Newsletter: News & Events
1200 Route 25A
Stony Brook, NY 11790-1992
ph: 631-751-0066
fax: 631-751-0353
mail@longislandmuseum.org
http://www.longislandmuseum.org
  *Large collection of American Art,
  decoys, horse-drawn vehicles,
  costumes, and miniature period
  rooms; museum shop.*

Jennifer Jones, Ex. Dir.
Havre de Grace Decoy Museum
Magazine: Canvasback, The
215 Giles St.
Havre De Grace, MD 21078
ph: 410-939-3739
fax: 410-939-3775
decoymuseum@aol.com
http://www.decoymuseum.com
  *Privately funded, non-profit
  organization for the documentation
  and interpretation of waterfowl decoys
  as a uniquely American folk art.*

Pete Lesher, Cur.
Chesapeake Bay Maritime Museum
Magazine: CBMM Quarterly
P.O. Box 636
St. Michaels, MD 21663-0636
ph: 410-745-2916
fax: 410-745-6088
library@cbmm.org
http://www.cbmm.org
  *A major regional maritime museum
  with a 10,000 volume research
  library; collections include 9,000
  objects, 32,000 photos, 1,200 ships'
  plans, 120 linear feet of manuscripts;
  decoys, oystering, lighthouses, charts,
  nautical, tools.*

Ward Museum of Wildfowl Art (Ward
  Foundation)
Magazine: Wildfowl Art
909 S. Schumaker Dr.
Salisbury, MD 21804
ph: 410-742-4988
fax: 410-742-3107
ward@wardmuseum.org
http://www.wardmuseum.org
  *Conducts seminars on carving and
  painting decoys; holds the Ward
  Championship Wildfowl Carving
  Competition each April and the
  Chesapeake Wildfowl Expo each
  October.*

Refuge Waterfowl Museum
7059 Maddox Blvd.
P.O. Box 272
Chincoteague, VA 23336
ph: 757-336-5800

Periodicals

Candi Derr, Ed.
Stackpole, Inc.
Magazine: Wildfowl Carving Magazine
1300 Market St., Ste. 202
Lemoyne, PA 17043-1420
ph: 717-234-5091 or 800-233-9015
fax: 717-234-1359
editor@wildfowl-carving.com
http://www.wildfowl-carving.com
  *Quarterly magazine devoted exclusively
  to bird carving; complete "how-to"
  and reference information for
  professional and amateur carvers
  alike; ads, articles, competition
  photos, special annual "Competition"
  issue.*

Joe Engers
Magazine: Decoy Magazine
P.O. Box 787
Lewes, DE 19958
ph: 302-644-9001
fax: 302-644-9003
DecoyMag@aol.com
http://www.DecoyMag.com
  *Only bi-monthly magazine serving the
  decoy collecting market; classifieds,
  calendar, auction news, carver
  profiles, full color.*

Repro. Sources

Duane Sylor
49 Horner Rd.
Angelica, NY 14709-8780
ph: 716-466-7700
  *Make and sells handcarved and
  painted duck and shorebird decoys;
  copies of original working decoys.*

Waterfowl (Mason)

Experts

Russ Goldberger
RJG Antiques
P.O. Box 60
Rye, NH 03870
ph: 603-433-1770
fax: 603-433-3937
decoys@rjgantiques.com
http://www.rjgantiques.com
  *Specializes in quality working decoys,
  folk art, and American furniture and
  accessories in their original painted
  surfaces; co-author with Alan G. Haid
  of "Mason Decoys, A Complete
  Pictorial Guide."*

DENTAL

(see MEDICAL, DENTAL &
PHARMACEUTICAL, Dental)

DESERT STORM

Collectors

Carl F. Planzer
205 US Hwy. 22
Green Brook, NJ 08812
ph: 732-424-7811
fax: 732-424-7814
ewa@ewacars.com
http://www.ewacars.com
  *Wants Desert Storm memorabilia:
  Marx Playsets, trading cards, games,
  propaganda, etc.*

DETECTIVE ITEMS

(see BOOKS, Mystery; CHARACTER
COLLECTIBLES, Sherlock Holmes;
MAGAZINES, Mystery; MYSTERY/
DETECTIVE ITEMS)

DIAMOND EDGE (SHAPLEIGH
HARDWARE)

(see also HARDWARE; KEEN
KUTTER [SIMMONS HARDWARE];
KNIVES; TOOLS; WINCHESTER
COLLECTIBLES)

Auction Services

Bob Simmons
Simmons & Company Auctioneers
40706 E. 144th St.
Richmond, MO 64085
ph: 816-776-2936 or 800-646-2936
fax: 816-470-5016
bob@simmonsauction.com
http://www.simmonsauction.com
  *Conducts annual specialty auctions of
  Winchester, Keen Kutter (E.C.
  Simmons Hardware) and Diamond
  Edge (Shapleigh Hardware)
  collectibles; has a well-established
  reputation for expertise and high
  quality merchandise.*

Clubs/Associations

Barbara Huhn, Mem.
Hardware Companies Kollectors' Klub,
  The
Newsletter: Winchester Keen Kutter
  Diamond Edge Chronicles
432 S. Gore St.
Saint Louis, MO 63119
ph: 314-968-0304
dhuhn@earthlink.net
http://www.thckk.org
  *A non-profit organization to serve as
  an interactive information distribution
  center for collectors of E.C. Simmons/
  Keen Kutter, Winchester Store (non-
  gun), A.F. Shapleigh/Diamond Edge,
  Hibbard, and other hardware store
  brands.*

Experts

Bob Simmons
40706 E. 144th St.
Richmond, MO 64085
ph: 816-776-2936 or 800-646-2936
fax: 816-470-5016
bob@simmonsauction.com
http://www.simmonsauction.com
  *Collects and specializes in Diamond
  Edge (Shapleigh Hardware) items
  especially advertising, catalogs, store
  signs and displays, promotions,
  sporting goods, and household items
  made for this St. Louis firm from the
  late 1800s to 1940.*

DIARIES

Collectors

Roy C. Kulp
P.O. Box 264
Hatfield, PA 19440-0264
ph: 215-362-0732
  *Wants to buy account books and day
  books by farmers, carpenters,
  blacksmiths, coffin & carriage
  makers, and weavers; also wants pre-
  1890 handwritten travel diaries.*

Dealers

Barbara & Richard DePalma
Deer Park Books
609 Kent Rd., Route 7
Gaylordsville, CT 06755
ph: 860-350-4140
deerparkbooks@earthlink.net
http://www.deerparkbooks.com
  *Fine books bought and sold;
  antiquarian books, modern first
  editions, children's and illustrated;
  also maps, autographs, etc.; all
  subjects; also wants handwritten
  diaries, travel journals, scrapbooks,
  albums.*

DICE

(see also GAMBLING
COLLECTIBLES)

Collectors

Jeff Lauderman
Diceman, The
P.O. Box 9293
Canoga Park, CA 91309
  *Buys and sells; has collection of over
  5,000 pairs of casino dice.*

Bill Whelan
P.O. Box 617
Daly City, CA 94017-0617
ph: 650-756-1189
fax: 650-756-4772
slotdynasty@earthlink.net
  *Wants to buy dice with Casino or
  private club imprints, US and
  Foreign; also from gambling ships,
  riverboats, and Indian casinos; also
  color variations, shapes and sizes; any
  type of dice, and old dice related
  items.*

Dealers

Steve Lerner
42 Barefoot Hill Rd.
Sharon, MA 02067
ph: 781-784-2286
slerner@attbi.com
http://www.gamblingcollectibles.com
Buys and sells dice, punchcards, and gaffed gambling items and equipment.

DIECUTS

(see PAPER COLLECTIBLES)

DIME NOVELS

(see BOOKS, Paperback)

DIMESTORE SOLDIERS

(see SOLDIERS, Toy)

DINERS & RELATED ITEMS

(see also RESTAURANT COLLECTIBLES)

Collectors

Daniel Zilka
P.O. Box 885
Providence, RI 02901
ph: 401-331-8575 x102 or 401-461-7932
fax: 401-351-0127
dzilka@faithinphysics.com
http://www.dinermuseum.org
Wants to buy diner photographs, postcards, matchbook covers, diner magazines, diner stools, coffee urns, vintage restaurant equipment.

John Richard Shoaf
2173 Smithtown Rd.
Morgantown, WV 26508-2482
ph: 304-292-4837
jshoaf@access.k12.wv.us
DINERholic doing research on diners; charter member of the American Diner Museum.

Steve Harwin
Diversified Diners
2043 Random Rd. #302
Cleveland, OH 44106-5916
ph: 216-229-4003
fax: 216-229-4005
diners@usa.com
http://www.oh-diners.com
Buys and sells diner parts such as stools, booths, counter tops, fixtures, laminates; also wants diner-related menus, ashtrays, signs, etc.

Larry Spilkin
P.O. Box 5039
Southfield, MI 48086-5039
ph: 248-642-3722
Wants postcards and matchbook covers of drive-ins, diners, cafes, gas stations and 1930s-1950s motels, restaurant/bar, cabins and Art Deco streamline hotels.

Museums/Libraries

Daniel Zilka
American Diner Museum
P.O. Box 885
Providence, RI 02901
ph: 401-331-8575 x102 or 401-461-7932
fax: 401-351-0127
dzilka@faithinphysics.com
http://www.dinermuseum.org
A museum showcasing numerous manufacturers and various aspects of the diner industry; extensive photograph and artifact collection and reference library; wants photos and other items relating to diner history.

Periodicals

Coffee Cup Publications
Magazine: Roadside
P.O. Box 652
West Side Station
Worcester, MA 01602
ph: 508-791-1838
fax: 508-755-5319
http://www.roadage.com/roadside
A quarterly journal for the diner owner; the only publication devoted to the appreciation and preservation of the American Diner.

Repair Services

Daniel Zilka
P.O. Box 885
Providence, RI 02901
ph: 401-331-8575 x102 or 401-461-7932
fax: 401-351-0127
dzilka@faithinphysics.com
http://www.dinermuseum.org
Performs restoration work on historic diners.

Steve Harwin
Diversified Diners
2043 Random Rd. #302
Cleveland, OH 44106-5916
ph: 216-229-4003
fax: 216-229-4005
diners@usa.com
http://www.oh-diners.com
Buys, sells and restores diners and related items; diner restoration consultant; also buys diner related memorabilia.

Suppliers

Bill Raymer
Restoration Resources
31 Thayer St.
Roxbury, MA 02118
ph: 617-542-3033
fax: 617-542-3034
wcrres@aol.com
http://members.aol.com/wcrres/
 index.htm
Supplies vintage parts for diners: stools, jukeboxes, etc.

DINNERWARE

(see also CERAMICS; CERAMICS [AMERICAN DINNERWARE]; CERAMICS [CONTINENTAL]; CERAMICS [ENGLISH]; CERAMICS [ORIENTAL]; FLATWARE; GLASS, Elegant; GLASS, Crystal; MODERNISM; REPAIR/ RESTORATION/CONSERVATION; TABLEWARE)

Clubs/Associations

International Association of Dinnerware Matchers
info@dinnerwarematchers.org
http://www.dinnerwarematchers.org
IADM is a group of independent dinnerware matchers (china, crystal, and flatware) in the US & Canada organized to promote honesty and integrity within the profession; printable Directory of Members on Web site as well as links and search.

Collectors

Deborah G. Taylor
Bluegrass Rainbow Collection
229 Boiling Springs Dr.
Lexington, KY 40511-2103
ph: 859-254-2299
bluegrassrainbow@att.net
http://home.att.net/~stefan.kwiatkowski/
 icons.index.htm
Collector of fine European dinnerware: RS Prussia, RS Tillowitz, Limoges, Meissen, Royal Copenhagen, etc.

Matching Services

J.P. Faddoul Company, Inc.
115 Boston Turnpike
Shrewsbury, MA 01545
ph: 508-755-5505
inquire@jpfaddoul.com
http://www.jpfaddoul.com
Carries discontinued and active china, crystal, and flatware; all merchandise is new, first quality and was purchased directly from the manufacturers.

Network Pattern Matching
618 Main St.
Winchester, MA 01890
ph: 781-729-8400
service@patternmatching.net
http://www.networkpatternmatching.com
NPM is a network of more than 300 fine china dealers who have combined their inventories into a listing of more than 53,000 patterns, with a comprehensive selection of pieces, prices and pictures on the site; easy and free searches.

Ross-Simons
#9 Ross-Simmons Dr.
Cranston, RI 02920-4476
ph: 800-521-7677 or 800-835-0919
fax: 800-896-9191
customerservice@ross-simons.com
http://www.ross-simons.com
Sells new, active patterns of Royal Doulton, Minton, Wedgwood,

Noritake, Villeroy & Boch, Royal Worcester, Lenox, etc.; several outlets on East Coast.

Michael Negrotti
Tabletop Designs
P.O. Box 448
Cheshire, CT 06410
ph: 800-801-4084
lenox@ntplx.net
http://www.tabletopdesigns.com
A small, personal matching service with a constantly changing inventory; want lists are kept; send photocopy or photo when unsure of pattern name; specializes in Lenox.

Paul & Pearl Hoffman
China Brokers, Ltd.
11 Westgate Ct.
Colts Neck, NJ 07722-1650
ph: 732-780-5062
chinabrokers@worldnet.att.net
Over 40,000 dinnerware patterns in stock; obsolete, inactive, active.

Alice Korman
Alice's Past & Presents Replacements
P.O. Box 465
Merrick, NY 11566-0465
ph: 516-379-1352
fax: 516-379-7302
alicechina@aol.com
http://hometown.aol.com/alicechina/
 myhomepage/business.html
Matching and locating service for Lenox, Oxford, Chinastone, Temperware, Gorham, Dansk, Denby, Wedgwood, Adams, Midwinter, Coalport, Fitz & Floyd, Christian Dior, Mikasa, Noritake, Royal Doulton, Minton, Royal Worcester, Spode, others.

Pattern Finders, A
P.O. Box 206
Port Jefferson Station, NY 11776-0206
ph: 631-928-5158 or 800-216-2446
fax: 631-928-5170
apattern@aol.com
http://www.patternfinders.com
Adams, Arabia, Aynsley, Castleton, Coalport, Denby, Enoch, Franciscan, Gorham, Haviland, Johnson Brothers, Lenox, Mikasa, Minton, Noritake, Oxford, Rosenthal, Royal Doulton, Royal Worcester, Spode, Syracuse, Wedgwood.

Sophia Papapanu
Sophia's China & Crystal
141 Sedgwick Rd.
Syracuse, NY 13203-1136
ph: 315-472-6834
sophia@sophiaschina-crystal.com
http://www.sophiaschina-crystal.com
Discontinued china and crystal patterns; over 22 years service; American, English, and other manufacturers; mail order or by special appointment; email or please send SASE with requests for information

Constance Stolz
China Match & Crystal Match
72 Longacre Rd.
Rochester, NY 14621-1019
ph: 585-338-3781
chinamat@frontiernet.net
Replacements of discontinued china and stoneware; Fitz & Floyd, Royal Doulton, Royal Worcester, Spode, Wedgwood; buy and sell.

Dick & Rosemarie Lewis
Dining Antiques
#6 Market Plaza
Reinholds, PA 17569
ph: 888-346-4642 or 717-484-0661
diningan@ptdprolog.net
Specializes in matching Syracuse china, 9,000 pieces and 80 patterns in stock.

Michael Round Fine China & Crystal, Inc.
7845 Wisconsin Ave.
Bethesda, MD 20814
ph: 301-656-2626 or 800-467-6863
fax: 703-550-7881
feedback@Mround.com
http://www.michaelround.com
Impressive Web site for matching china, crystal or flatware.

Cee Cee China
3904 Parsons Rd.
Chevy Chase, MD 20815
ph: 301-652-6226 or 800-619-6226
ceeceechina@aol.com
http://www.ceeceechina.com
Buys, sells and locates; specializing in discontinued Lenox, Oxford, and Syracuse china only.

Armand Shank
China Lane
75 W. Timonium Rd.
Lutherville Timonium, MD 21093
ph: 888-737-5283 or 410-252-9061
fax: 410-252-9426
info@chinalane.com
http://www.chinalane.com
Fine china and dinnerware bought, sold and located; full service registration and pattern search provided.

Thurber's
2256C Dabeny Rd.
Richmond, VA 23230-3342
ph: 804-278-9080 or 800-848-7237
fax: 804-278-9480
Carries only active patterns; will locate old patterns.

Randy Foster
Replacements Ltd.
P.O. Box 26029
1089 Knox Rd.
Greensboro, NC 27420
ph: 800-737-5223 or 336-697-3000
fax: 336-697-3100
inquire@replacements.com
http://www.replacements.com
China, crystal and flatware (obsolete, active and inactive.)

D & J Locations
1601 E. Canal St.
Tarboro, NC 27886
ph: 252-823-5333 or 800-818-5565
Discontinued china: Gorham, Haviland, Lenox, Metlox, Mikasa, Minton, Noritake, Pickard, Royal Doulton, Spode, Wedgwood, and other major brands; buys, sells, locates.

Jean-Paul Iannantuoni
455 Concord Parkway N., #5500
Dept. CIC
Concord, NC 28027-6736
ph: 704-786-7758
fax: 704-795-7975
dinnerware.search@bigfoot.com
Dinnerware search service for all manufacturers but specializes in Arabia, Block China, Boda Nova, Christopher Stuart, Epoch, Gibson, International China, Longchamp, Midwinter, Monton, Newcor, Nikko, Murifield; appraisals by fee only.

China Cabinet, The
214 Hillside Dr.
P.O. Box 426
Clearwater, SC 29822-0426
ph: 803-593-9655 or 800-787-1605
fax: 803-593-9655
thechinacabinet@aol.com
Discontinued patterns in: Adams, Franconia, Franciscan, Lenox, Oxford, Noritake, Mikasa, Royal Doulton, Royal Worcester, Spode, Wedgwood, Fostoria, Gorham, Glastonbury.

China & Crystal Matchers, Inc.
2379 John Glenn Dr., Ste. #108-M
Atlanta, GA 30341-1924
ph: 770-455-1162 or 800-286-1107
fax: 770-452-8616
chinacmi@bellsouth.net
http://www.chinaandcrystal.com
All manufacturers; buys, sells, locates; member of the International Association of Dinnerware Matchers.

Harry Weitkemper
China Finders
2823 Central Ave.
St. Petersburg, FL 33781
ph: 888-244-6239 or 800-900-2557
fax: 727-321-3868
ChinaFinders@aol.com
http://www.chinafinders.com
Buys and sells Castleton, Lenox, Doulton, Franciscan, Haviland, Spode, Wedgwood, Shelley, Minton, Noritake, Adams, Metlox, Vernon Kilns, and most major manufacturers.

Paul Church
Replacement Service, A
500 Oregon Ave.
Saint Cloud, FL 34769
ph: 407-957-1719 or 800-337-9075
fax: 649-915-2469
chinacrystal@juno.com
http://www.chinacrystalandmore.com
Buys, sells, locates Lenox, Oxford,

Temperware, Castleton, Franciscan fine china and earthenware.

Mary Ann Lowery
Crystal Corner, Inc., The
317 Billy Dyar Blvd.
P.O. Box 756
Boaz, AL 35957-0756
ph: 256-593-6169
fax: 256-593-6560
ccorner@hiwaay.net
http://www.crystalcorner.com
Royal Doulton, Fitz & Floyd, Gorham, Noritake, Mikasa, Haviland, etc.

Mara F. Sprott
Fulbreit China Locators
607 Center Dr.
Memphis, TN 38112-1701
ph: 901-327-3725 or 901-346-7357
fax: 901-346-7416
chinas@midsouth.rr.com
http://www.fulbreitchina.com
Carries Fiesta, Haviland & Co., Theodore Haviland, American and French Haviland, Johann Haviland, Charles Field Haviland, Homer Laughlin, Metlox; want lists maintained; shipment by UPS; send photocopy of front and back.

Joan Wurmbrand
Good Buy Girls
2691 East Main St., Ste. 102
Bexley, OH 43209
ph: 614-231-0437 or 866-886-0467
fax: 614-231-3140
goodbuygirls@tias.com
http://www.goodbuygirls.com
Buys and sells Desert Rose, Apple, Coronado, Franciscan.

Barron's
P.O. Box 994
Novi, MI 48376
ph: 800-538-6340
fax: 800-523-4456
barronsdw@aol.com
http://www.barronsdinnerware.com
Carries only active patterns.

Colleen Becker
Heritage China of Iowa
P.O. Box 244
Palo, IA 52324
ph: 888-416-1595 or 319-227-3688
fax: 319-227-7781
dischina@aol.com
http://www.dish-china.com
Large inventory of china and crystal; buys and sells discontinued china: Dansk, Denby, Franciscan, Haviland, Homer Laughlin, Mikasa, Minton, Noritake, Royal Doulton, Sango, Wedgwood, Japanese patterns, etc.

Jacquelynn Ives
Jacquelynn's China Matching Service
219 N. Milwaukee St.
Milwaukee, WI 53202-5818
ph: 414-272-8880 or 800-482-8287
fax: 414-272-0361
jchinams@aero.net
http://www.jchinareplacements.com
English/American exclusively;

discontinued Coalport, Castleton, Franciscan, Lenox, Minton, Spode, Royal Doulton, Wedgwood, Flintridge/Gorham, Royal Crown Derby, Royal Worcester, Pickard, Royal Winton, Royal Albert, etc.

China & Crystal Replacements
P.O. Box 187
5613 Country Rd. 19
Excelsior, MN 55331
ph: 612-474-6418 or 800-432-4448
Discontinued and active china, dinnerware and crystal bought and sold.

China Replacements
P.O. Box 508
High Ridge, MO 63049
ph: 800-562-2655 or 636-677-5577
fax: 636-376-6319
chinarep@swbell.net
http://www.chinareplacements.com
Buys, sells, and locates all major brands of china; Lenox/Oxford, Royal Doulton, Royal Worcester/Spode, Denby, Castleton, Syracuse, Franciscan, Wedgwood, Noritake, Mikasa and many others.

Dining Elegance, Ltd.
P.O. Box 4203
Saint Louis, MO 63163
ph: 314-865-1408
de-3@earthlink.net
http://www.diningelegance.com
American Lenox/Oxford; most English manufacturers; French & American Haviland; French Ceralene-Raynaud.

Barbara Coleman
Finders Keepers China Lady
1537 Metairie Rd.
Metairie, LA 70005-3938
ph: 504-455-1530 or 504-831-4514
fax: 504-885-2512
Stock or locate Doulton, Lenox/ Oxford, Minton, Noritake, Pickard, Spode, Wedgwood; also other china and crystal.

Jo Hancock
Jo's Antiques & Collectibles
621 S. Main St.
Nashville, AR 71852-2707
ph: 870-845-1070
China and crystal matching; Lenox and other fine brands; 35 years experience collecting and selling Lenox items.

Jennifer Marcel
Dishes From the Past
3701 Lovell Ave.
Fort Worth, TX 76107
ph: 800-984-8801 or 817-737-6390
fax: 817-737-7728
dishesfrompast@aol.com
http://www.dishesfromthepast.com

Teri Read
China Teacup, The
509 East Texas Ave.
Mart, TX 76664
ph: 254-876-3453
fax: 254-876-3533
teacup@flash.net
*All major brands: Castleton, Denby,
Franciscan, Lenox, Gorham, Mikasa,
Royal Doulton, Noritake, Spode,
Syracuse, Wedgwood, etc.; buys and
sells.*

edish, inc.
2311 Westheimer
Houston, TX 77098
ph: 713-942-7171
fax: 713-521-2546
questions@edish.com
http://www.edish.com
*Browse the online inventory of
discontinued and current china,
crystal, dinnerware.*

John & Andrea McDonald
DishMatchers
P.O. Box 142284
Austin, TX 78714
ph: 866-503-3474 or 512-264-2467
fax: 512-264-2727
match@dishmatchers.com
http://www.dishmatchers.com
*Carries thousands of pottery and
china patterns for replacement:
Noritake, Mikasa, Franciscan,
Pfaltzgraff, Royal Doulton, Lenox,
International, and many more.*

Larry McDonald
A & A Dinnerware Locators
P.O. Box 50222
Austin, TX 78763-0222
ph: 512-264-1054 or 888-898-4202
info@aadinnerware.com
http://www.aadinnerware.com
*Locate/match discontinued china,
earthenware, etc.; all major
manufacturers: American, European,
Japanese: Castleton, Adams, Doulton,
Franciscan, Gorham, Lenox, Metlox,
Mikasa, Noritake, Spode, Worcester;
primarily mail order.*

edish, inc.
815 East 2100 South
Salt Lake City, UT 84106
ph: 801-486-8282 or 888-767-8282
fax: 801-485-7644
questions@edish.com
http://www.edish.com
*Buys and sells major brands: Lenox,
Castleton, Wedgwood, Noritake,
Franciscan, Haviland, Spode, Royal
Doulton.*

Olympus Cove Antiques & China
Matching
179 E. 300 St.
Salt Lake City, UT 84111
ph: 800-284-8046 or 801-532-0431
olympuscove@uswest.net
http://www.olympuscove.com
Buys and sells discontinued china:

*Syracuse, Spode, Lenox, Franciscan,
Castleton, Haviland, and much more.*

Beverly Hills Pattern Matching Service
270 N. Canon Dr., #1419
Beverly Hills, CA 90210
ph: 800-443-1122
fax: 818-707-0425
*Discontinued patterns of china:
Gorham, Lenox, Pickard, Royal
Doulton, Minton, Royal Worcester-
Spode, Sango.*

Carol Ulrey
Unique Antiques
P.O. Box 15815
San Diego, CA 92175-5815
ph: 619-281-8650
fax: 619-282-8407
culrey@webcc.net
*Specializing in china matching:
Haviland, old French and American;
also Lenox china and crystal;
publishes booklet "Matching Services
for Haviland China," updated yearly
and lists matching services in 24
states & Canada, cost is $4 ppd.*

Joanne Cone
Joanne Cone Matching Service
34 Silverwood
Irvine, CA 92604
ph: 949-551-3173
jochina@aol.com
*Buys, sells, locates all major
manufacturers (Mikasa specialist):
Mikasa, Castleton, Denby,
Franciscan, Johnson, Lenox, Metlox,
Noritake, Royal Doulton, Spode,
Syracuse, Wedgwood, etc.*

Joan Martin
China Traders Replacement Service
310-C Easy St.
Simi Valley, CA 93065
ph: 805-578-3800 or 800-244-6248
fax: 805-578-3803
info@chinatraders.com
http://www.chinatraders.com
*Totally computerized discontinued
china matching service; all major
patterns; large inventory; friendly and
knowledgeable staff.*

Past & Present
14851 Ave. 360
Visalia, CA 93292
ph: 559-798-0029
fax: 559-798-1415
info@china-crystal-flatware.com
http://www.pastpresent.net
*Formal and casual: Castleton,
Community, Denby, Doulton,
Flintridge, Franciscan, Gorham, Hall,
Haviland, Johnson Bros., Lenox,
Mason's, Metlox, Mikasa, Noritake,
Redwing, Rosenthal, Spode, Syracuse,
Wedgwood, etc.*

Silver Lane Antiques
P.O. Box 322
San Leandro, CA 94577-0032
ph: 510-483-0632
*Buys and sells discontinued patterns
by major American and English china
and earthenware companies; Lenox,*

*Spode, Minton, Franciscan, Syracuse,
Wedgwood, Royal Copenhagen,
Doulton, Ceralene, American
Haviland, Rosenthal, Castleton, etc.*

B. Diane Ayers
5th Generation Antiques
124 W. 8th Ave.
Chico, CA 95926-3240
ph: 530-895-0813
fax: 530-895-0813
diane5thgen@webtv.net
*Specializes in Haviland and other
china matching and in stemware
matching.*

Michael Lindsey
Laguna: Vintage American Pottery
116 S. Washington St.
Seattle, WA 98104-2522
ph: 206-682-6162
fax: 206-405-3561
oiljars@aol.com
http://www.lagunapottery.com
*Specializes in American made
collectible and discontinued
dinnerware only: Bauer, Franciscan,
Hall, Heath, Metlox, Russel Wright,
Red Wing, Vernon, Winfield, and
many others.*

Warren & Betty Roundhill
Patterns Unlimited International
Dept. CIC
P.O. Box 15238
Seattle, WA 98115-0238
ph: 206-523-9710
fax: 206-524-1252
*Buy and sell china from England,
France and USA; also appraises
discontinued tableware patterns of all
china, silver and glass.*

Old China Patterns Ltd.
1560 Brimley Rd.
Scarborough, Ontario M1P 3G9 Canada
ph: 800-663-4533 or 416-299-8880
fax: 416-299-4721
ocp@chinapatterns.com
http://www.chinapatterns.com
*Canada's largest matching service;
buys and sells internationally; since
1966; specializing in English china
and crystal; charter member
International Association of
Dinnerware Matchers.*

Echo's Discontinued China & Silver
Lonsdale Court #121
1433 Lonsdale Ave.
North Vancouver, British Columbia
V7M 2H9 Canada
ph: 800-663-6004 or 604-980-8011
fax: 604-988-3611
info@echoschina.com
http://www.echoschina.com
*Buys and sells discontinued china and
silver tableware.*

Janice Howard
Missing Pieces
1730 Taylor Ave., Unit #1
Winnipeg, Manitoba R3N 0N8 Canada
misspcs@mts.net
http://www.missingpieces.com
Specializes in Aynsley, Coalport,

*Denby, Hutschenreuther, Johnson
Bros., Midwinter, Mikasa, Minton,
Noritake, Paragon, Royal Albert,
Royal Doulton, Royal Worcester,
Spode, Wedgwood, and others.*

Lea Shaw
China Cupboard, The
1507 Wilmot Place
Victoria, British Columbia V8R 5S3
Canada
ph: 800-598-3858
fax: 250-598-4585
shop@thechinacupboard.com
http://www.thechinacupboard.com
*Specializes in discontinued English
china, earthenware, ironstone
dinnerware.*

Tom Power
Tablewhere London Limited
4 Queens Parade Close
London, N11 3FY U.K.
ph: +44 0208 361 7787 or 800-514-8176
fax: +44 0208 361 4143
tpower@globalnet.co.uk
http://www.tablewhere.co.uk
*Specializing in discontinued tableware
of most British manufacturers from
1900 to the present day; also carries
some foreign manufacturers;
worldwide mail order service; VISA/
MC/AMEX.*

Periodicals

Cleo Kapilla
Joyful Ventures
Directory: Directory of Discontinued
Tableware Services
P.O. Box 5297
Ocala, FL 34478-5297
ph: 352-622-4077
*Publishes biennial directory listing
over 50 matching services that sell and
search for discontinued tableware
items - china, crystal, and flatware.*

Susan Ranta
Ranta Enterprises
Directory: Set Your Table Discontinued
Tableware Dealers
P.O. Box 22481
Lincoln, NE 68542-2481
ph: 800-600-2127 or 402-423-4865
fax: 402-423-4865
sranta@setyourtable.com
http://www.setyourtable.com
*Whether its pottery, stoneware or
china, "Set Your Table" has a
growing list of dealers who can help
you find your missing pieces; dealer
listings are indexed by manufacturer;
Web site is always up to date.*

Haviland

(see also CERAMICS
[CONTINENTAL], Haviland)

Appraisers

Virginia Cannon, ISA CAPP
China House, The
801 W. Eldorado
Decatur, IL 62522
ph: 217-428-7212
fax: 217-864-4852
apprreant@aol.com
   *Matches, specializes in, and appraises
   French & American; carries large
   selection of Haviland patterns for sale
   by mail order or from the shop.*

Dealers

Frances M. Jepson
Jepson Haviland China
13211 Redhills Rd.
P.O. Box 295
Chinese Camp, CA 95309-0295
ph: 209-984-4432
   *Experienced, buys, sells, does
   identification; send photocopy of front
   and back of plate, color and
   description plus $7.50 and SASE; will
   refund if cannot identify; appraisals
   $75; member International Haviland
   Collectors Association.*

Experts

Nora Travis
Haviland China Replacements
P.O. Box 6008-161
Cerritos, CA 90701
ph: 714-521-9283
fax: 714-521-9283
travishrs@aol.com
http://www.havilandchinareplace.com
   *Author of "Evolution of Haviland
   China Design."*

Matching Services

Sailor's Wife, The
6 Berry Rd.
Buxton, ME 04093
ph: 207-929-3009
afearing@sacoriver.net
   *Specializing in old French Haviland;
   matching service for Haviland & Co.,
   Theodore Haviland and C.F.H.
   backmarks; some American Haviland;
   send Schleiger number or photocopy
   for identification.*

Jan Fenger
Presence of the Past
488 Main St.
Old Saybrook, CT 06475-2530
ph: 860-388-9021
fax: 860-388-2025
presencepast13@aol.com
   *Haviland, Noritake; send Schleiger
   number or sample saucer with SASE.*

Linda Kinnett
Kinnett Antiques
110 Lake Terrace Ct.
Hendersonville, TN 37075-5101
ph: 615-824-5987
fax: 615-264-8751
   *A Haviland matching service with
   hundreds of patterns in stock; member
   of A.A.D.A.; in business for over 30
   years.*

Mara F. Sprott
Fulbreit China Locators
607 Center Dr.
Memphis, TN 38112-1701
ph: 901-327-3725 or 901-346-7357
fax: 901-346-7416
chinas@midsouth.rr.com
http://www.fulbreitchina.com
   *Carries Fiesta, Haviland & Co.,
   Theodore Haviland, American and
   French Haviland, Johann Haviland,
   Charles Field Haviland, Homer
   Laughlin, Metlox; want lists
   maintained; shipment by UPS; send
   photocopy of front and back.*

Everett Scott
Scott's Haviland Matching Service
1911 Leland Ave.
Des Moines, IA 50315-4952
ph: 800-952-7857 or 515-285-2739
fax: 515-285-0744
scottshaviland@worldnet.att.net
http://www.havilandchinabyscotts.com
   *Specializing in French, American,
   Bavarian, Charles Field, (Johann)
   Haviland; buy, sell, and identify;
   brides; send Schleiger number or
   photocopy of front and of backstamp;
   enclose phone number or fax number
   to which you would like a reply.*

Grace Graves
Haviland Matching Service, Ltd.
219 N. Milwaukee St.
Milwaukee, WI 53202-5818
ph: 414-291-9111
fax: 414-291-9018
hmsgraves@aol.com
http://www.graveshaviland.com
   *Collector, dealer in porcelains and
   pottery by the Haviland families of
   Limoges, France; specialists in
   identifying and locating French &
   American Haviland patterns; use
   Schleiger number or send photocopy
   for pattern identification.*

Al & Jeanne Hines
Haviland Matching Service of Winona
476 East 5th St.
Winona, MN 55987-3923
ph: 507-454-3283
china@havilandmatching.com
http://www.havilandmatching.com
   *Identifying and locating French &
   American Haviland patterns; use
   Schleiger number or send photocopy of
   saucer for pattern identification.*

Mary Jane Jurgens
2330 DuClaire Rd.
Decatur, IL 62521
ph: 217-423-8303
jurgens@springnet1.com
   *Sells and appraises dinnerware with a
   specialty in Haviland.*

Virginia Cannon, ISA CAPP
China House, The
801 W. Eldorado
Decatur, IL 62522
ph: 217-428-7212
fax: 217-864-4852
apprreant@aol.com
   Matches, specializes in, and appraises

*French & American; carries large
selection of Haviland patterns for sale
by mail order or from the shop.*

Herbert Crosson
Crosson Antiques
835 N. 3rd Ave.
Minneapolis, KS 67467
ph: 785-392-2810
   Specializes in Haviland china.

Nora Travis
Haviland China Replacements
P.O. Box 6008-161
Cerritos, CA 90701
ph: 714-521-9283
fax: 714-521-9283
travishrs@aol.com
http://www.havilandchinareplace.com
   *Specializing in French and American
   Haviland; will identify and locate your
   pattern if possible; large inventory;
   send Schleiger number or photocopy of
   your pattern; author of "Haviland
   China - Age of Elegance" (Schiffer).*

Carol Ulrey
Unique Antiques
P.O. Box 15815
San Diego, CA 92175-5815
ph: 619-281-8650
fax: 619-282-8407
culrey@webcc.net
   *Specializing in china matching:
   Haviland, old French and American;
   also Lenox china and crystal;
   publishes booklet "Matching Services
   for Haviland China," updated yearly
   and lists matching services in 24
   states & Canada, cost is $4 ppd.*

Carol Williams
Lillian Johnson Antiques
405 Third St.
P.O. Box 1207
San Juan Bautista, CA 95045
ph: 831-623-4381
fax: 831-623-4381
cwilly@hollinet.com
   *Well-established French and American
   Haviland matching service; pattern
   predominantly from the WWI era;
   buys, sells, appraises.*

Frances M. Jepson
Jepson Haviland China
13211 Redhills Rd.
P.O. Box 295
Chinese Camp, CA 95309-0295
ph: 209-984-4432
   *Buys and sells Haviland & Co.,
   American Haviland, French Haviland,
   Theodore Haviland, Charles Field
   Haviland.*

Holly Krieg
Auld Lang Syne
6321 Delta Ct.
Magalia, CA 95954-9535
ph: 530-873-0693
hollyzhit@aol.com
   *Over 30,000 patterns of Haviland;
   send photocopy of front and back,
   color and description plus SASE and
   $7.50 for identification.*

Johnson Bros.

Matching Services

Mary J. Finegan
Marfine Antiques
P.O. Box 3618
Boone, NC 28607-8911
ph: 828-262-3441
   *Johnson Brothers dinnerware
   exclusively.*

Lenox

Man./Prod./Dist.

Lenox China Shop
53 Commerce Dr.
Cranberry, NJ 08512
ph: 609-395-8054 or 800-367-7467
   *Retail showroom selling open stock on
   current stemware, dinnerware, and
   giftware patterns.*

Lenox China & Crystal Consumer
Service
100 Lenox Dr.
Lawrenceville, NJ 08648
ph: 609-896-2800 or 800-635-3669
http://www.lenox.com
   *Offers Matching Services List of
   dealers who offer replacements for
   current of discontinued Lenox items;
   also gives insurance estimates.*

Matching Services

Michael Negrotti
Tabletop Designs
P.O. Box 448
Cheshire, CT 06410
ph: 800-801-4084
lenox@ntplx.net
http://www.tabletopdesigns.com
   *A small, personal matching service
   with a constantly changing inventory;
   want lists are kept; send photocopy or
   photo when unsure of pattern name;
   specializes in Lenox.*

Jo Hancock
Jo's Antiques & Collectibles
621 S. Main St.
Nashville, AR 71852-2707
ph: 870-845-1070
   *China and crystal matching; Lenox
   and other fine brands; 35 years
   experience collecting and selling Lenox
   items.*

Carol Ulrey
Unique Antiques
P.O. Box 15815
San Diego, CA 92175-5815
ph: 619-281-8650
fax: 619-282-8407
culrey@webcc.net
   *Specializing in china matching:
   Haviland, old French and American;
   also Lenox china and crystal;
   publishes booklet "Matching Services
   for Haviland China," updated yearly
   and lists matching services in 24
   states & Canada, cost is $4 ppd.*

Forget-Me-Not China
17255 SE Licorice Way
Renton, WA 98059
ph: 425-254-0200 or 800-553-6693
fax: 425-254-0239
info@forgetmenotchina.com
http://www.forgetmenotchina.com
*Lenox only; extensive inventory of
discontinued Lenox Fine China and
Lenox casual chinas; mail or phone
inquiries welcomed.*

Mikasa

Man./Prod./Dist.

Mikasa
1 Mikasa Dr.
Secaucus, NJ 07096
ph: 201-867-9210 or 866-645-2721
fax: 201-867-0457
http://www.mikasa.com
*Dinnerware, crystal giftware,
flatware, linens; call for location of
nearest Mikasa factory store.*

Matching Services

Cleo Kapilla
CK's China Trade
P.O. Box 5297
Ocala, FL 34478-5297
ph: 352-622-4077
*A matching service for thousands of
fine & casual discontinued pieces of
Mikasa dinnerware; buys, sells,
locates.*

Noritake

Matching Services

R.L. Watson
Matchers, The
181 Belle Meade
Memphis, TN 38117-3017
ph: 901-683-1337
fax: 901-682-9491
chinalady@earthlink.net
*Noritake specialists; also Lenox,
Royal Doulton, American Haviland,
Oxford, Wedgwood, Franciscan, and
other major factories; best to phone.*

Noritake Co., Inc.
2635 Clearbrook Dr.
Arlington Heights, IL 60005
ph: 800-562-1991
fax: 847-228-5104
servicecenter@noritakechina.com
http://www.noritakechina.com
*Sells formal china, casual dinnerware,
crystal, glassware, giftware from
around the world.*

Ms. China
P.O. Box 229
Monterey, CA 93942
ph: 800-688-6807 or 831-655-9984
fax: 831-655-0198
info@ms-china.com
http://www.ms-china.com
*Noritake only; pre-war and newly
discontinued china identification and
matching service.*

Wedgwood

Matching Services

Howard Lewis
Howard Lewis Antiques
P.O. Box 5911
Wilmington, DE 19808-0911
ph: 302-731-5597
*Buying and selling 18th, 19th and
collectible 20th century Wedgwood:
Jasper, Basalt, Caneware, Rosso
Antico, Drabware, etc.; also buying
and selling Embossed Queensware
patterns of dinnerware by Wedgwood.*

DINOSAURS

Clubs/Associations

Mike Fredericks
Prehistoric Times, The
Newsletter: Prehistoric Times Newsletter
145 Bayline Circle
Folsom, CA 95630-8077
ph: 916-985-7986 or 916-985-2481
fax: 916-985-2481
pretimes@aol.com
http://members.aol.com/pretimes
*The Prehistoric Times is a fanzine
dedicated to dinosaur collectors and
enthusiasts, including info on all
manner of collectibles and other items
of interest for Dinophiles everywhere;
48+ pages; bi-monthly; nothing like
it!*

Museums/Libraries

Museum of Western Colorado Dinosaur
Journey
550 Jurassic Ct.
Fruita, CO 81521
ph: 970-858-1307 or 888-488-3466
mstricklan@westcomuseum.org
http://www.dinosaurjourney.org
*Museum features the latest exhibits
and information about dinosaur
excavations, realistic robotic
dinosaurs, and a working paleontology lab.*

BYU Earth Science Museum
1683 North Canyon Rd.
P.O. Box 23300
Provo, UT 84602-3300
ph: 801-378-3680
fax: 801-378-7919
*Features mounted dinosaur skeletons,
a fossil touch table, a mural of the
Jurassic period, and a working
paleontology lab.*

DIPPERS

(see ICE CREAM COLLECTIBLES,
Dippers)

DIRECTORIES

(see ANTIQUES SHOP
DIRECTORIES; FLEA MARKETS,
Directories; TOURS/BUYING TRIPS)

DIRIGIBLES

(see AIRSHIPS)

DIRILYTE FLATWARE

(see FLATWARE)

DIRT

(see also SAND)

Museums/Libraries

Glenn Johansen
Museum of Dirt
36 Drydock Ave.
Boston, MA 02210
ph: 617-574-4800
http://www.planet.com/dirtweb/dirt.html
*A virtual museum of dirt, some with
celebrity associations.*

DISCONTINUED TABLEWARE PATTERNS

(see FLATWARE; DINNERWARE;
GLASS, Elegant; GLASS, Crystal)

DISNEY COLLECTIBLES

(see also CHARACTER
COLLECTIBLES; COLLECTIBLES
[MODERN]; POPULAR CULTURE;
POSTCARDS, Disney)

Appraisers

Doug & Pat Wengel
P.O. Box 305
Skillman, NJ 08558-0305
ph: 609-466-2461
fax: 609-466-8911
wengel@njcc.com
http://pluto.njcc.com/~wengel
*Experienced appraisers of pre-1950s
vintage Disneyana; no animation art,
please.*

Joel J. Cohen, ISA
Cohen Books & Collectibles
P.O. Box 810310
Boca Raton, FL 33481-0310
ph: 561-487-7888
fax: 561-487-3117
joel@disneycohen.com
http://www.disneycohen.com
*Walt Disney specialist for over 30
years; Accredited Member of the
International Society of Appraisers;
buys, sells, appraises Disneyana: from
Mickey Mouse and Snow White to
present; vintage as well as limited
edition items.*

Robert G. Jason-Ickes
3600 14th Ave., SE #19-201
Olympia, WA 98501
ph: 360-455-9914
fax: 360-459-7154
r.jason-ickes@attbi.com
*Specializes in pre-1950 Disney
collectibles; also lectures.*

Clubs/Associations

Robert Crooker
Mouse Club East
Newsletter: Mouse Club East Newsletter
11 Turnbull Ave.
Wakefield, MA 01880
ph: 781-775-1590
mouse-man@rcn.com
http://www.mouseman.com
*Interested in Disney related
collectibles.*

National Fantasy Fan Club for Disneyana
Collectors & Enthusiasts, Studio
Chapt.
Newsletter: Star News
P.O. Box 280681
Northridge, CA 91328
studiochapter@yahoo.com
http://www.geocities.com/Studiochapter
*Web site includes club and meeting
information, event schedule,
photographs, and membership
application.*

Louis Boish
National Fantasy Fan Club for Disneyana
Collectors & Enthusiasts
Journal: Fantasyline Express
P.O. Box 19212
Irvine, CA 92713-9212
ph: 714-731-4705
membership@nffc.org
http://www.nffc.org
*To preserve the legacy of Walt Disney
through collecting and preserving of
Disney memorabilia, research and
sharing of information; a monthly
newsletter.*

Collectors

John S. Fawcett
P.O. Box 1156
Waldoboro, ME 04572-1156
ph: 207-832-7398
fawcetoy@gwi.net
http://home.gwi.net/~fawcetoy
*Collects 1930s comic character items,
Post Toasties Disney cereal boxes &
other old Disneyana.*

Bob Havey
P.O. Box 183
North Sullivan, ME 04664-0183
ph: 207-422-3083
fax: 207-422-3430
*Disney collector buys all nice 1930s/
40s items; excellent prices paid.*

Dan Calandriello
10 Weston Place
Eatontown, NJ 07724
ph: 732-542-4770
danster-nj@comcast.net
*Wants 1930s to 1950s Disney
collectibles: poster ads, cards,
albums, games, etc.*

Charles Sanna
P.O. Box 27
Brooklyn, NY 11231
ph: 718-448-7528
fax: 718-625-2895
*Wants to buy all types of early Disney
and comic collectibles.*

Jim Conley
2758 Coventry Lane
Canton, OH 44708-1320
ph: 330-477-7725
fax: 330-879-2950
Very interested in early Disney.

Dan Goodsell
Tick Tock Toys
P.O. Box 48021
Los Angeles, CA 90048
grickily@aol.com
http://www.theimaginaryworld.com/
page4.html
*Wants to buy vintage (1950s and
1960s) Disneyland memorabilia
especially guide books, maps,
souvenirs, toys, model kits, brochures,
etc.*

Linda Trew Ahlfield-Bruhn
Divine Inc.
4441-C Mohala Place
Wahiawa, HI 96786
kagneys@aol.com
*Wants to buy Mickey Mouse
memorabilia; no records, please;
include asking price.*

Dealers

Robert Crooker
Mouse Man Ink, The
11 Turnbull Ave.
Wakefield, MA 01880
ph: 781-775-1590
mouse-man@rcn.com
http://www.mouseman.com
Sells vintage Disney, 1930s to 1970s.

Jane & John Carroll
2894 John Tyler Highway
Williamsburg, VA 23185-1335
ph: 757-258-9322
fax: 757-258-9552
carroll@visi.net
Buys and sells Disneyana.

Joel J. Cohen, ISA
Cohen Books & Collectibles
P.O. Box 810310
Boca Raton, FL 33481-0310
ph: 561-487-7888
fax: 561-487-3117
joel@disneycohen.com
http://www.disneycohen.com
*Walt Disney specialist and collector
for over 30 years; buys, sells,
appraises Disneyana from Mickey
Mouse to Snow White to Bambi to
present; vintage as well as limited
edition items, animation art, books,
figurines, toys, etc.*

Bob Molinari
Fantasies Come True
8012 Melrose Ave.
Los Angeles, CA 90046
ph: 323-655-2636 or 800-579-0303
fax: 323-655-2636
inquiries@fantasiescometrue.com
http://www.fantasiescometrue.com
*Top-notch Walt Disney memorabilia
for the fan or collector.*

Thomas Bauer
Nonstop Collectibles
6152 Terrebonne
Montreal, Quebec H4B 1A3 Canada
ph: 514-489-5499
thomasbauer@sympatico.ca
http://www.thomasbauer.ca
*Internet sales consultant and broker
since 1993; active in online sales and
marketing of Disneyana, other
collectibles; will do qualified
evaluations of your collection; list
items for sale for 20% commission;
good comic info.*

Experts

Doug & Pat Wengel
P.O. Box 305
Skillman, NJ 08558-0305
ph: 609-466-2461
fax: 609-466-8911
wengel@njcc.com
http://pluto.njcc.com/~wengel
*Buys, sells and specializes in vintage
character collectibles, especially those
with early images of Disney characters
Mickey, Minnie, Horace and
Clarabelle; offers matching service for
Disney china dishes - Japanese,
Bavarian, Paragon.*

Ted Hake
Hake's Americana & Collectibles
  Auction
P.O. Box 1444
York, PA 17405-1444
ph: 717-848-1333
Ted@hakes.com
http://www.hakes.com
*Author of "Hake's Guide to TV
Collectibles" and several other books
on collectibles; always purchasing
items for mail-bid auctions of
Disneyana, historical Americana, toys,
premiums, political items, character
and other collectibles.*

Joel J. Cohen, ISA
Cohen Books & Collectibles
P.O. Box 810310
Boca Raton, FL 33481-0310
ph: 561-487-7888
fax: 561-487-3117
joel@disneycohen.com
http://www.disneycohen.com
*Walt Disney specialist and collector
for over 30 years; buys, sells,
appraises Disneyana from Mickey
Mouse to Snow White to Bambi to
present; vintage as well as limited
edition items, animation art, books,
figurines, toys, etc.*

Tom Tumbusch
Tomart Publications
3300 Encrete Lane
Dayton, OH 45439-1944
ph: 937-294-2250
fax: 937-294-1024
office@tomart.com
http://www.tomart.com
*Buys Disneyana items; author of
"Tomart's Illustrated Disneyana
Catalog and Price Guide" series
depicting 20,000 items in color.*

Paul F. Anderson
2250 E. High Mountain Dr.
Salt Lake City, UT 84092-5509
ph: 801-523-0888
fax: 801-523-0889
pov@aros.net
http://www.disneypov.com
*Collector, dealer and expert on Disney
collectibles.*

Phil Sears
24592 Via Carissa
Laguna Niguel, CA 92677-7034
ph: 949-643-1477
fax: 949-643-8376
Phil@Phil-Sears.com
http://www.phil-sears.com
*Buys and sells vintage Walt Disney
memorabilia, including Disneyland
and Disney Studio collectibles; Walt
Disney autograph specialist.*

Periodicals

Tom Tumbusch
Tomart Publications
Magazine: Tomart's Disneyana Digest
3300 Encrete Lane
Dayton, OH 45439-1944
ph: 937-294-2250
fax: 937-294-1024
office@tomart.com
http://www.tomart.com
Published quarterly.

Paul F. Anderson
Persistence of Vision Publishing
Journal: Persistence of Vision
2250 E. High Mountain Dr.
Salt Lake City, UT 84092-5509
ph: 801-523-0888
fax: 801-523-0889
pov@aros.net
http://www.disneypov.com
*Filled with rare and unusual Disney
items, most with an historical slant;
an unofficial journal celebrating the
creative legacy of Walt Disney
featuring articles on Disneyana, Walt
Disney, the Theme Parks, films and
collectibles.*

Paul F. Anderson
Persistence of Vision Publishing
Newsletter: Disneyana Times, The
2250 E. High Mountain Dr.
Salt Lake City, UT 84092-5509
ph: 801-523-0888
fax: 801-523-0889
pov@aros.net
http://www.disneypov.com
*Each issue features thousands of
Disney collectibles.*

Magazine: E Ticket
P.O. Box 800800
Santa Clarita, CA 91380-0880
fax: 818-368-8701
etick@earthlink.net
http://www.the-e-ticket.com
*Collecting theme park memories; for
those interested in Disneyland, Walt
Disney, Disney artists, rides and
attractions at Disneyland, and Disney
collectibles.*

Ceramics

Dealers

Calvin L. Hackeman
8865 Olde Mill Run
Washington, DC 20010-6132
ph: 703-368-6982 or 703-847-7530
fax: 703-848-9583
hltzhaus@erols.com
*Serious advanced collector and dealer
in child's ceramics; interested in
purchasing one piece or a complete
set; interest is limited to child's china,
salt & pepper shakers, cookie jars and
ceramic planters.*

Judy Posner
Judy Posner Collectibles
P.O. Box 2194
Englewood, FL 34295
ph: 941-475-1725
fax: 941-475-2645
judyandjef@yahoo.com
http://www.judyposner.com
*Wants Disney bisque figures, Disney
dinnerware, character cookie jars &
shakers; buying, selling collecting for
over 25 years.*

DIVING EQUIPMENT

(see NAUTICAL ANTIQUES, Diving;
SCUBA)

DIXIE CUP LIDS

Collectors

Leonard Schneir
184 Sixth Ave.
New York, NY 10013
ph: 212-966-4357
Wants one or an entire collection.

Leigh Giarde
P.O. Box 2243
Redlands, CA 92373-0741
ph: 909-792-8681
fax: 909-792-8681
onlyleigh@cpl.net
*President, circus, animal and movie
star lids and premiums wanted.*

DOCUMENTS

(see AUTOGRAPHS; BOOKS;
HISTORICAL AMERICANA; PAPER
COLLECTIBLES; MANUSCRIPTS)

DOILIES

(see TEXTILES, Needlework)

DOLL HOUSES & FURNISHINGS

(see also CHILDREN'S THINGS;
DOLLS; MINIATURES)

Appraisers

Judy Owen, ISA
Antique Appraisers - Grand Traverse
10332 Stoneybeach Pointe
Traverse City, MI 49686-8584
ph: 231-946-2534
fax: 231-946-2573
judy@antiqueappraisers.com
http://www.antiqueappraisers.com
*Specializing in doll houses and
miniatures.*

Clubs/Associations

Lorraine Punchard
Treasures of Little Children
Newsletter: Tiny Times, The
8201 Pleasant Ave. So.
Minneapolis, MN 55420
rainyp@earthlink.net
http://www.treasuresforlittlechildren.com
*A club for collectors of children's
dishes, toy glass, toy graniteware, tin
tea sets, miniature furniture, doll
houses, kitchen doll accessories, and
related toys.*

Russian Association of Dollhouses &
Miniatures Masters
Box 9
Moscow, 109004 Russia
fax: 095 706 98 77
info@miniature.ru
http://www.miniature.ru
*Icons, matryoshka, samovars, bast
shoes, eggs, lacquered boxes, caskets,
doll houses, etc.*

Collectors

Brian Cleary
P.O. Box 155
Poland, NY 13431-0155
ph: 315-826-3610
bgcsjc@ntcnet.com
*Wants to buy old cast iron doll
furniture in nice condition with
original paint.*

Sharon Wilkins
1105 Burnham St.
Cocoa, FL 32922-6836
ph: 321-631-0102
paulinescoll@bellsouth.net
*Wants to buy 1940s and 1950s doll
houses.*

Jerry A. Phelps
1500 Van Buren Rd.
Mount Eden, KY 40046-9552
ph: 502-859-4063
phelps-vbv@dcr.net
*Wants to buy old doll houses with
paper lithography on wood; also
wants early clockwork toys.*

F.J. Steffen
9705 Mill Creek Dr.
Eden Prairie, MN 55347
ph: 952-944-1041
*Wants to buy children's dishes, doll
houses, furniture, kitchen and shops,
etc.*

R.L. Rice
612 E. Front St.
Bloomington, IL 61701-5314
*Wants to buy metal doll house
furniture; one piece or an entire set;
please state brand and price.*

Dealers

Judith Armistead
Doll Works, The
P.O. Box 195
Lynnfield, MA 01940-0195
ph: 781-334-5577
judy@thedollworks.net
http://www.TheDollWorks.net
*Interested in buying and selling
antique dolls, doll houses and
miniatures; in business for 20 years
dealing in German, American and
French dolls and accessories.*

Ann Mechan
51 Pinehurst Rd.
Portsmouth, NH 03801
ph: 603-433-5650
fax: 603-431-7055
*Buy and sell pre-1900 antique doll
houses, furnishings and accessories.*

Shelley Smith
P.O. Box 159
Bethlehem, CT 06751-0159
ph: 203-266-7496
*Buys and sells toys, doll houses and
miniatures, Steiff, children's
collectibles, and country smalls.*

Robert Dankanics
Dollhouse Factory, The
P.O. Box 456
Lebanon, NJ 08833-0456
ph: 908-236-6404
fax: 908-236-7899
Wants old doll houses and miniatures.

Abbie Kelly
5196 Onodaga Rd.
Syracuse, NY 13215
ph: 315-487-7451
*Wants to buy German kitchens and
stores, doll dishes, doll accessories.*

Diane Sanchez
Diane's Dollhouse Collectibles
5934 Hillside Lane
Garland, TX 75043
ph: 972-686-8450
diane@dianesdollhouse.com
http://www.dianesdollhouse.com
*Specializes in vintage doll houses,
plastic and wood furniture including
Renwal, Petite Princess, Ideal-
Reliable, Plasco, Marx, Superior,
Thomas Toy, Acme, Best, Common-
wealth, Jaydon, Kilgore, Tootsietoy,
Schoenhut, etc.*

Shirley Christie
Slight Lights
4872 Pullman Ave. SE
Salem, OR 97302
ph: 503-581-5448 or 503-587-7335
fax: 503-587-7335
*Sells miniature and scale doll house
battery powered lamps and self-
decorating sticker tablecloths.*

Museums/Libraries

Peabody Essex Museum
Essex & Libert Sts.
Salem, MA 01970
ph: 978-745-9500 or 800-745-4054
pem@pem.org
http://www.pem.org

Strong Museum, The
1 Manhattan Square
Rochester, NY 14607
ph: 585-263-2700
fax: 585-263-2493
http://www.strongmuseum.org
*Collection contains more than
500,000 objects: toys, doll houses,
miniatures, household furnishings,
and the world's most comprehensive
collection of dolls.*

Washington Dolls' House & Toy
Museum
5236 44th St. NW
Washington, DC 20015-2101
ph: 202-244-0024
fax: 202-237-1659

Wrecker's Museum
322 Duval St.
Key West, FL 33040-6510
ph: 305-294-9502
*Houses nautical photos and
memorabilia from the Key West
wrecking era.*

Art Institute of Chicago, Thorne
Miniature Rooms
111 S. Michigan Ave.
Chicago, IL 60603
ph: 312-443-0849
webmaster@artic.edu
http://www.artic.edu

Periodicals

Castle Press Publications
Magazine: Doll Castle News
P.O. Box 247
Washington, NJ 07882-0247
ph: 908-689-7042 or 800-572-6607
fax: 908-689-6320
dcn@toast.net
*A bi-monthly magazine focusing on
dolls, miniatures, doll houses and
related items; ads, paper doll section,
needlework, patterns, etc.*

Scott Publications
Magazine: Miniature Collector
30595 Eight Mile
Livonia, MI 48152-1798
ph: 800-458-8237 or 248-477-6650
fax: 248-477-6795
concatus@scottpublications.com
http://www.scottpublications.com
A monthly international publication

*devoted to the serious collector,
craftsperson and artist of contemporary and antique scale miniatures;
amply illustrated with large color
photographs, historical information,
auctions, and much more.*

Plastic

Collectors

Bobbie Segal
1007 North Federal Hwy., #226
Fort Lauderdale, FL 33304
ph: 954-524-9339
fax: 954-524-2034
rpurple3r@aol.com
*Wants plastic doll house furniture
from the 1940s through the 1960s; by
Renwal, Ideal, etc.*

Dealers

Judy Mosholder
Dollhouse Furniture - Renwal
186 Pine Springs Camp Rd.
Boswell, PA 15531-2421
ph: 814-629-9277
jlytwins@floodcity.net
http://www.RenwalToys.com
*Buys and sells doll houses and plastic
doll house furniture, especially
Renwal, Ideal, and Marx; send LSASE
for list of items for sale.*

DOLLS

(see also NATIVE AMERICAN,
Skookum Dolls; NATIVE AMERICAN,
Kachina Dolls; BOOKS, Reference
[Dolls]; CHARACTER
COLLECTIBLES; CHILDREN'S
THINGS; COLLECTIBLES
[MODERN], Dolls; ELVES; DOLL
HOUSES & FURNISHINGS; STEIFF;
TEDDY BEARS; TOYS; TROLLS)

Appraisers

AsktheAppraiser.com
4 Brussels St.
Worcester, MA 01610
ph: 781-821-0199
ata@collectingchannel.com
http://www.AsktheAppraiser.com
*The premiere online appraisal service
offered by CollectingChannel.com; all
appraisals comply with the "Uniform
Standards of Professional Appraisal
Practice" and with the standards of
the Association of Online Appraisers.*

Judith Katz-Schwartz
Twin Brooks Antiques & Collectibles
E-zine: Antiques & Collectibles
Newsletter
P.O. Box 6572
New York, NY 10128-0006
ph: 212-876-3512
fax: 212-876-3512
twinb@msjudith.net
http://www.msjudith.net
*Buys, sells, appraises dolls, wind-ups,
character toys, board games, battery
operated, Chein, Marx, Disney,
robots, Japanese celluloid, space toys,
etc.; member Assoc. of Online*

Appraisers (AOA) and Inter. Soc. of
Appraisers (ISA).

Darlene Joy Gengelbach
Darlene's Joys
4785 St. Paul Blvd.
Rochester, NY 14617
ph: 716-544-6997
fax: 716-266-4623
*Doll appraisals, lectures, research,
consultant, restoration, conservation;
private or museums; presently working
for two museums.*

Stuart Holbrook
Theriault's Auction
P.O. Box 151
Annapolis, MD 21404-0151
ph: 410-224-3655 or 800-638-0422
fax: 410-224-2515
info@theriaults.com
http://www.theriaults.com
*Chief appraiser and buyer for one of
the nation's largest doll auction
houses; one doll or entire collection
can be appraised.*

Tim Luke, ISA
Treasure Quest Auction Galleries, Inc.
2581 Jupiter Park Dr., Ste. E5
Jupiter, FL 33458
ph: 561-741-0777 or 888-741-0777
fax: 561-741-0757
tim@tqag.com
http://www.tqag.com
*Specializes in the appraisal of toys,
dolls, and bears.*

Sharon Niles
Carousel, Inc.
14409 Manchester Rd.
Ballwin, MO 63011
ph: 636-391-4900
fax: 636-391-3993
carouselinc@hotmail.com
*Specializes in the appraisal,
conservation and restoration of
antique dolls.*

Kristy Neal
Treasured Collectibles Doll Hospital
1928 First St.
Slidell, LA 70458
ph: 985-646-6077 or 985-645-9974
info@treasured-collectibles.com
http://www.treasured-collectibles.com
*Repairs most dolls including broken
bisque or composition; restyles wigs;
sets sleep eyes; finds missing parts;
repaints; also appraises, buys and
sells vintage dolls.*

R. Rebecca Moncrief, ISA
2007 Sea Cove Ct.
Houston, TX 77058-4228
ph: 281-333-3672
fax: 281-333-0201
becky@ufdc.org
Specializes in antique dolls.

Barbara De Feo
Janara Antique Dolls
ph: 619-482-8575
fax: 619-482-8575
janara@pacbell.net
Since 1978, appraisals, identification

*and conservation of antique dolls, pre-
1960 only; buys and sells at shows
and by mail; identifications given only
if provided with photo and pertinent
info by email.*

Nancy Burke Bosch, ISA
Bosch Appraisal Service
1610 Northstar Dr.
Petaluma, CA 94954-6607
ph: 707-773-3970
fax: 707-773-3974
nbbosch@pacbell.net
http://www.appraiseyourantiques.com
*Specializes in appraising European &
American furniture, fine art,
decorative art & accessories, china,
dolls, toys, crystal, silver, American
wicker, quilts, linen, other textiles,
other appreciable residential contents.*

Norene Ott
Antique & Collectible Doll Appraisal of
Seattle
P.O. Box 46134
Seattle, WA 98146-0134
ph: 206-246-2290 or 206-244-8007
fax: 206-244-8007
seniorott@aol.com

Caren L. Carlson, ISA
Ask an Appraiser
31313 NW Paradise Park Rd.
Ridgefield, WA 98642-8754
ph: 360-887-8686
fax: 360-887-8909
carenscubbyhole@netscape.net
*Specializes in the appraisal of early
20th century dolls, toys and
accessories.*

Carol Sheehan, CPPA
SCA Appraisals
12 Burt Court
Stoney Creek, Ontario L8H 3H4 Canada
ph: 905-664-6712
fax: 905-664-6712
csheehan1@cogeco.ca
*Buys, sells, appraises dolls; well
known collector of vintage Barbie,
Liddle Kiddles, Chatty Cathys,
Thumbelina, Mrs. Beasley, G.I. Joe,
etc. for over 15 years.*

Auction Services

Dorothy McGonagle
Skinner, Inc.
63 Park Plaza
The Heritage on the Garden
Boston, MA 02116
ph: 617-350-5400
fax: 617-350-5429
info@skinnerinc.com
http://www.skinnerinc.com
*Established in 1971, Skinner Inc. is
the fourth largest auction house in the
US; has offices in Boston and Bolton,
MA.*

Richard W. Withington, Inc.
590 Center Rd.
Hillsboro, NH 03244
ph: 603-464-3232
fax: 603-464-4901
withington@conknet.com
http://www.withingtonauction.com

James D. Julia Auctioneers Inc.
Rt. 201, Skowhegan Rd.
P.O. Box 830
Fairfield, ME 04937
ph: 207-453-7125
fax: 207-453-2502
jjulia@juliaauctions.com
http://www.juliaauctions.com
*Conducts specialized auctions of toys
and doll items and are one of the
leaders in this field in North America.*

Stuart Holbrook
Theriault's Auction
P.O. Box 151
Annapolis, MD 21404-0151
ph: 410-224-3655 or 800-638-0422
fax: 410-224-2515
info@theriaults.com
http://www.theriaults.com
*One of the oldest and perhaps largest
doll auction houses in America; will
send "Doll Information Guide"
pamphlet upon request and LSASE;
doll auction color catalogs are $189
for 10 issues per year; holds over 50
doll auctions per year.*

Dorothy Hunt
Sweetbriar
P.O. Box 37
Earleville, MD 21919-0037
ph: 410-275-2094
fax: 410-275-2213
dorothy.hunt@dol.net
*Auctions dolls and doll costumes; also
offers doll seminars and appraisals.*

Ann Hays, ISA CAPP
Hays & Associates, Inc.
120 South Spring St.
Louisville, KY 40206-1953
ph: 502-584-4297
fax: 502-585-5896
annhays@haysauction.com
http://www.haysauction.com
*Conducts specialty toy and doll
auctions; Ann Hays is a Certified
Appraiser of Personal Property with
the International Society of Appraisers; director of auction house antique
and collectible toy and doll
department for over 25 years.*

David M. Cobb
Cobb's Doll Auctions
1909 Harrison Rd. N.
Johnstown, OH 43031-9539
ph: 740-964-0444
fax: 740-927-7701
auctions@cobbsdolls.com
http://www.cobbsdolls.com
*Conducts quarterly antique doll,
automata, bears, etc. auctions; send
$30 for catalog; send address for
advance notice flyer.*

Shari McMasters
McMasters Harris Doll Auctions
5855 John Glen Hwy.
P.O. Box 1755
Cambridge, OH 43725
ph: 800-842-3526 or 740-432-7400
fax: 740-432-3191
info@mcmastersharris.com
http://www.mcmastersharris.com
*Specializes in auctioning antique and
collectible dolls and doll related items
such as teddy bears, Barbie dolls and
accessories, children's dishes, toys,
children's books, etc.*

Kurt R. Krueger
Krueger Auctions
P.O. Box 275
Iola, WI 54945-0275
ph: 715-445-3845
fax: 715-445-4100
*Specializing in the mail-bid auction of
tokens, advertising, brewery items,
Western Americana, postcards,
World's Fair & Expo., autographs,
sports, coins & currency, pinbacks,
military memorabilia, automotive,
Disneyana, toys, dolls, etc.*

Barbara Frasher
Frasher's Doll Auction
2323 South Mecklin
Oak Grove, MO 64075
ph: 816-625-3786
fax: 816-625-6079
Conducts doll specialty auctions.

Jon Baddeley
Sotheby's
34-35 New Bond St.
London, W1A 2AA U.K.
ph: 44 171 293 5000
fax: 44 171 293 5989
http://www.sothebys.com
*Conducts specialty auctions of tinplate
toys, diecasts, trains, antique dolls,
teddy bears, automata.*

Clubs/Associations

JoAnn Mathias, Treas.
Doll Doctor's Association
Newsletter: Doll Rx
6204 Ocean Front Ave.
Virginia Beach, VA 23451
ph: 757-428-1609 or 757-427-9131
dolldoc@gmdollseminar.com
http://www.gmdollseminar.com
*An association for doll repair and
restoration specialists.*

Jean Ann Moale
Magnolia Fashion Doll Club of Atlanta
P.O. Box 156
Duluth, GA 30096
moalej@bellsouth.net
*Members are collectors of all types of
dolls, with a focus on fashion-type
dolls such as Barbie, Gene, Tyler, etc.*

Carol Pugh-Aksdal
Fashion Doll Collector's Club of S.E.
  Georgia
P.O. Box 115
Pembroke, GA 31321
ph: 912-65305447
CPoTig8021@aol.com

Ruth Leif
Modern Doll Collectors, Inc.
319 55th Place
Downers Grove, IL 60516
ph: 630-968-0172
fax: 707-847-3134
RuthsToys@aol.com
http://www.moderndollcollectors.com
  *A not for profit doll group focusing
  on modern dolls, education, research,
  preservation and enjoyment of dolls;
  hosts an annual convention; current
  focus is on the modern fashion dolls
  such as Gene, Tyler, Alex, Barbie,
  Vogue's Ginny, etc*

Bettyanne Twigg
United Federation of Doll Clubs
Newsletter: Doll News
10920 N. Ambassador Dr., Ste. 130
Kansas City, MO 64153
ph: 816-891-7040 or 816-891-8417
fax: 816-891-8360
twigg@ufdc.org
http://www.ufdc.org
  Contact to locate a club in your area.

Yonne L. Baird
National Antique Doll Dealers
  Association
8037 Jim Court SE
Olympia, WA 98503
ph: 360-438-0067
fax: 360-493-1488
Baird2@attbi.com
  *Intention of the association is to build
  a foundation of honesty and integrity
  so that collectors can buy with
  confidence from members who have
  committed to standards of ethics.*

Arlene Martinez
Dolls R Us of Washington
19616 NE 163rd Ave.
Battle Ground, WA 98604
ph: 360-687-4321
Arlenedoll@aol.com
  *Doll collectors, UFDC affiliated;
  active club that hosts the Region I
  Annual Picnic; does community related
  volunteering; warm and friendly group
  of ladies who wish to further the love
  and education of dolls, both antique
  and modern.*

Carol Sheehan
Golden Horseshoe Fashion Doll Club
12 Burt Court
Stoney Creek, Ontario L8H 3H4 Canada
ph: 905-664-6712
fax: 905-664-6712
csheehan1@cogeco.ca
  *Established club of Barbie and
  Fashion doll collectors sharing their
  interest in vintage as well as newer
  dolls.*

Doll Club of Great Britain
16E Chalwin Industrial Estate
St. Clements Rd.
Parkstone Poole, Dorset BH15 3PE U.K.

Collectors

Linda L. Vines
2911 4th St., #112
Santa Monica, CA 90405
ph: 310-314-0402
lleigh2000@hotmail.com
  *Wants to buy antique bisque head
  dolls in excellent condition; also doll
  clothes and accessories.*

Kate Emburg
P.O. Box 1437
North Highlands, CA 95660-1437
ph: 916-331-7435 or 916-331-7352
dolladopt@aol.com
  *Collector especially interested in
  Madame Alexander, hard plastic and
  composition dolls; will identify and
  appraise post-1900 dolls.*

Dealers

Judith Armistead
Doll Works, The
P.O. Box 195
Lynnfield, MA 01940-0195
ph: 781-334-5577
judy@thedollworks.net
http://www.TheDollWorks.net
  *Interested in buying and selling
  antique dolls, doll houses and
  miniatures; in business for 20 years
  dealing in German, American and
  French dolls and accessories.*

Eileen Mosteller
Dollworks
62-C Franklin St., PMB #107
Westerly, RI 02891
ph: 401-596-4674
eileen@dollworks.com
http://www.dollworks.com
  *Buys/sells mint & mint-in-box 1930-
  1970 dolls, especially rare cloth,
  composition & hard plastic Madame
  Alexanders plus fabulous Ginnys,
  Jills, Mary Hoyers, Arranbees,
  Effanbees, Style Shows, Shirley
  Temples, Revelons, etc.; $2 for list.*

Linda Dalenberg
Timeless Pieces
246 West Main St.
Hillsboro, NH 03244-5239
ph: 603-464-5621 or 603-464-6747
  *Wants to buy antique dolls, doll
  clothes, and doll accessories; also
  wants adult and children's vintage
  clothing, estate linens, and pre WWII
  toys.*

Liz Olimpio
Aladdin Antiques
59 Governor's Rd.
Sanbornville, NH 03872-4415
ph: 603-522-8503
fax: 603-522-8933
  *Buy, sells, repairs antique dolls and
  antique clothing.*

Joy Kelleher
Special Joys
41 N. River Rd.
Coventry, CT 06238-1634
ph: 860-742-6359
fax: 860-742-9343
specjoys@aol.com
  *Specializes in antique dolls, Steiff,
  doll clothing and pre-1960 accessories.*

Debra Gulea
Debra's Dolls
20 N. Main St.
P.O. Box 705
Mullica Hill, NJ 08062
ph: 609-478-9778 or 609-694-2007
  *Antique dolls bought and sold; doll
  furniture, clothing; doll houses, and
  accessories also available; member of
  UFDC and NADDA; send for photo
  doll list.*

Louise Sleeter
Louise's Little Ladies
21 Commissioners Pike
Woodstown, NJ 08098
ph: 856-769-5544
louisesladies@earthlink.net
  *Buys, sells and repairs antique to
  modern dolls; specializes in
  composition dolls.*

Roberta's Doll House
140 Caryl Ave.
Yonkers, NY 10705
ph: 800-569-9739 or 914-968-3033
fax: 914-968-4173
robertasdollhous@aol.com
http://www.robertasdollhouse.com
  *Web site has a nice selection of
  antique dolls for sale.*

Lauren Jaeger Mikalov
18 Milford Court
Nanuet, NY 10954
ph: 845-425-0322
  Buys, sells, appraises antique dolls.

Bonnie J. Cook
P.O. Box 134
East Greenbush, NY 12061
ph: 518-477-7272
antiques@bonniejcook.com
http://www.bonniejcook.com
  *Wants to buy American and European
  antique dolls.*

Eugene Owens
Gilded Age, Ltd., The
H.C. 1, Box 14A, Route 10
Stamford, NY 12167-9701
ph: 607-652-2896
  Buys and sells quality antique dolls.

Jacqueline Henry
Antique Treasures, Toys & Dolls
2240 Academy St.
P.O. Box 17
Walworth, NY 14568-0017
ph: 315-986-1424
jhenry1@rochester.rr.com
http://www.cyberattic.com/~toysndolls
  *Buys and sells antique German and
  French bisque dolls, and mint
  condition 1950s hard plastic dolls in*

*original clothes such as Toni,
  Arranbee, Madame Alexander, Ginnys,
  Gingers, and Nancy Ann Storybooks.*

Sherri & Jack Dempsey
Dempsey & Baster
1009 East 38th St.
Erie, PA 16504
ph: 814-825-7690 or 814-825-6381
info@dempseyandbaxter.com
http://www.dempseyandbaxter.com
  *Specializes in antique dolls and Marx
  toys; also doll restorations.*

Nikki Kvitka
Nikel Enterprises, Inc.
4536 Custer Dr.
Harrisburg, PA 17110
ph: 717-236-7148
fax: 717-236-6807

Sidney W. Jeffrey
My Dolly Dearest
229 Grofftown Rd.
Lancaster, PA 17602
ph: 717-295-9454 or 800-295-9457
fax: 717-295-9454
sidneyjeffrey@mydollydearest.com
http://www.mydollydearest.com
  *Doll dealer, collector, appraiser with
  a Web site dedicated to the sale of
  dolls, bears, and accessories from
  antique to contemporary.*

Dawn Herlocher
Dawn's Dolls
Maple Ave.
Mackeyville, PA 17750-0000
ph: 570-726-6458
  *Specializing in fine quality Japanese
  Satsuma and cloisonne.*

W. Richard Wright
Richard Wright Antiques
P.O. Box 227
Birchrunville, PA 19421
ph: 610-827-7442
fax: 610-827-7939
rwantiquez@aol.com
  *Specializes in fine antique dolls;
  member of NADA and NADDA.*

W. Richard Wright
Richard Wright Antiques
P.O. Box 227
Birchrunville, PA 19421
ph: 610-827-7442
fax: 610-827-7939
rwantiquez@aol.com
  *Specializes in the appraisal of antique
  dolls from the 18th through mid-20th
  century.*

Erlene Reed
Aquataurian Doll & Gift Gallery
1794 Verbena St., NW
Washington, DC 20012
ph: 202-829-7170
fax: 202-723-7274
dollyasm@erols.com
http://www.townsqr.com/dolly
  *Buys and sells many (retired) Daddy's
  Long Legs dolls, Barbie dolls,
  Madame Alexander dolls, Cabbage
  Patch Kid dolls, and other artist dolls
  and modern dolls.*

Dollmasters
P.O. Box 2319
Annapolis, MD 21404
ph: 800-966-3655
fax: 410-224-2515
info@theriaults.com
http://www.dollmasters.com
*"The Dollmasters" is published
quarterly and contains articles about
doll market news as well as recent
auction reports and doll related
products and accessories.*

Joyce McCandless
Krazy Cat Collectibles
P.O. Box 1192
Emmitsburg, MD 21727
ph: 301-271-9851
KrazyCatCo@aol.com
http://www.krazycatcollectibles.com
*Buys and sells dolls: '60s and '70s era
dolls including Liddle Kiddles, Dolly
Darlings, Upsey Downseys, etc; also
vintage and mod Barbie (pre-1972),
antique bisque & china heads,
composition, vinyl, modern artist
dolls, etc.*

Walter LaValley
Bachelor II Dolls & Bears
5130 Duke St., Ste. 6
Wheaton Plaza
Alexandria, VA 22304-2955
ph: 703-823-BEAR
fax: 703-823-1787
Specializes in dolls and bears.

Julia Melton
Melton's Antique Dolls
3513 Byrn Brae Dr.
Virginia Beach, VA 23464
ph: 757-420-0351
fax: 757-420-1462
*Buys and appraises antique dolls; in
business for over 30 years.*

Gayle L. Shaw, Pres.
Treasure & Dolls, Inc.
518 Indian Rocks Rd., N.
Belleair Bluffs, FL 33770
ph: 888-584-7277 or 727-584-7277
fax: 727-581-7846
mshawl@tampabay.rr.com
http://www.antiquedoll.com
*Buys and sells antique and collectible
dolls, teddy bears, Madame Alexander,
Annalee, stuffed animals, half dolls,
Barbie, plastic/vinyl dolls, porcelain
dolls.*

Dot Wise
Penny Wise Dolls
P.O. Box 701305
Saint Cloud, FL 34770-1305
dolls@pennywisedolls.com
http://www.pennywisedolls.com
*Specializing in collectibles dolls:
Ideal, Horsman, Alexander, Mattel,
Effanbee, Pin Cushions, etc.*

Wilder's Doll Center
3345 Dixie Highway
Waterford, MI 48328-1606
ph: 248-618-9506
fax: 248-618-9507
*Repairs and restores old dolls; also
buys and sells.*

Robert Zacher
Heirloom Doll Shoppe/Hospital/Museum
416 E. Broadway
Waukesha, WI 53186
ph: 414-544-4739

Gary Sowatzka
Sowatzka's Dolls
7273 Kelly Dr.
Lake Tomahawk, WI 54539
ph: 715-277-4591
sowatdol@newnorth.net
http://www.sowatzka.com
*Dolls for sale; doll appraisals, doll
repairs and doll restoration classes;
site has tips on collecting dolls and
has a unique area where you can
submit your own doll story; a doll is
given to everyone who has their story
put on the site.*

Valerie LaBreche
Enchanted World Doll Museum
615 North Main
Mitchell, SD 57301-1945
ph: 605-996-9896
fax: 605-996-0210
*Buys and sells antique and collectible
dolls and accessory items; specializes
in 1800 to early 1900s bisque and
china dolls.*

Barbara Earnshaw-Cain
Hers & Mine Antiques, Inc.
P.O. Box 14381
Shawnee Mission, KS 66285-4381
ph: 913-888-5297
fax: 913-888-5297
barbara@hersmine.com
http://www.hersmine.com
*Carries wide assortment of modern as
well as antique collectible dolls.*

Barbara's Dolls
P.O. Box 126095
Fort Worth, TX 76126
ph: 817-249-2069
info@barbarasdolls.com
http://www.barbarasdolls.com
*Buys and sells antique dolls and doll
accessories, composition dolls,
collectible dolls from the 1950s
through 1980s, old Barbie dolls and
vintage Barbie clothes, Madame
Alexander.*

David & Brenda Greener
7313 Wind Chime Dr.
Fort Worth, TX 76133
ph: 817-292-0909
*Buys, sells and appraises dolls;
former doll show promoter.*

Turn of the Century Antiques
1475 S. Broadway
Denver, CO 80210
ph: 303-722-8700 or 303-778-7077
toc@rare-dolls.com
http://www.rare-dolls.com
*Specializes in antique and collectible
dolls.*

Jeri Cotherman
Doll & Bear's Paradise, A
855 1/2 N. Cedar
Laramie, WY 82072-2469
ph: 307-742-3429
dolls2fix@fiberpipe.net
http://www.adollsandbearsparadise.com
*Restores dolls, stuffed animals; makes
artist specialty bears; sells dolls and
bears; buying dolls, patterns, old
material, fur and fake fur.*

Dolls & Lace
P.O. Box 1384
Orem, UT 84059
ph: 801-226-3737
Bubblefly3@aol.com
http://www.dollsandlace.com
*Specializes in antique dolls and bears,
antique doll clothes and accessories,
buttons, lace and linen.*

Gert Leonard
E & G Antiques
P.O. Box 296
San Dimas, CA 91773-0296
ph: 909-599-2723
fax: 909-559-4355
gert@eandgantiques.com
http://www.eandgantiques.com

Barbara De Feo
Janara Antique Dolls
ph: 619-482-8575
fax: 619-482-8575
janara@pacbell.net
*Since 1978, appraisals, identification
and conservation of antique dolls, pre-
1960 only; buys and sells at shows
and by mail; identifications provided
only if provided with with photo and
pertinent info by email.*

Rosalie Whyel Museum of Doll Art
1116 108th Ave. NE
Bellevue, WA 98004
ph: 425-455-1116
fax: 425-455-4793
dollart@dollart.com
http://www.dollart.com
*Here history unfolds through the
vision of master doll makers; dolls,
teddy bears, toys, and miniatures; also
features two stores which support this
privately funded museum; seeks good
dolls or collections to buy.*

Carol Sheehan
I Remember That!!
12 Burt Court
Stoney Creek, Ontario L8H 3H4 Canada
ph: 905-664-6712
fax: 905-664-6712
csheehan1@cogeco.ca
*Buys, sells, appraises dolls; well
known collector of vintage Barbie,
Liddle Kiddles, Chatty Cathys,
Thumbelina, Mrs. Beasley, G.I. Joe,
etc. for over 15 years.*

Kathryn Davies
Antique Dolls
7 Puma Dr.
Howick
Auckland, 1705 New Zealand
ph: 6490336-0862
info@antiquedolls.nz
http://www.antiquedolls.co.nz

Experts

Judith Izen
P.O. Box 623
Lexington, MA 02420
jizen@rcn.com
http://www.dollsofourchildhood.com
*A noted doll historian who has
written about several American doll
companies including Ideal, Vogue,
Eegee, Mattel, Deluxe Reading; also
American character dolls including
Tiny Tears, Betsy McCall, Tressy,
Toni, Toodles, Sweet Sue, etc.*

Patricia Snyder
My Dear Dolly
P.O. Box 303
Sparta, NJ 07871-0303
ph: 201-729-8087
dolly@sparta.csnet.net
http://www.mydeardolly.com
*Wants old dolls, bodies, parts, doll
clothing, accessories, doll dishes,
snowbabies; publishes monthly list of
dolls for sale; also appraises; on staff
of two appraisal services; offers
detailed lists of items for sale for $1
and LSASE.*

K. Darden
P.O. Box 210182
Nashville, TN 37221-0182
ph: 615-662-4243
barbieintn@yahoo.com
http://www.geocities.com/
FashionAvenue/6487/tips.html
*Expert in vintage Barbie dolls, Gene,
Alex, Tyler, Eve and all other fashion
dolls.*

Carol Sumpter
Cardan's Doll Shop
3808 Loughborough
Saint Louis, MO 63116
ph: 314-351-7955
*Buys, sells, collects, specializes in,
and appraises dolls.*

Patsy Moyer
P.O. Box 311
Deming, NM 88031
moddoll@yahoo.com
http://www.zianet.com/patsyandfriends
*Author of "Doll Values" (7th Ed.),
"Modern Collectible Dolls" (Vol.
VI)," "How to be a Doll Detective,"
and "Scouting Dolls Through the
Years."*

Ellen Charland, ANA, MCPA
1407 Foothill Blvd., #19
La Verne, CA 91750
ph: 909-592-0101 or 626-963-7695
fax: 626-335-6651
antiquetea@aol.com
http://members.tripod.com/~antiquetalk/
index-4.html
Specializes in dolls from the 1930s to modern dolls; offers online appraisals.

Don & Vella Painter
23483 Shephard Rd.
Clatskanie, OR 97016
ph: 888-763-5122 or 503-728-3503
webmaster@webdolls.com
http://www.webdolls.com
Buys, sells, appraises, collects and repairs dolls: antiques, compositions, pull string and battery operated talkers, mechanical, toys, vinyl; also reroots hair.

Internet Resources

About.com Hobbies
220 East 42nd St.
New York, NY 10017
pr@about-inc.com
http://home.about.com/hobbies
Online source for information about action figures, antiques, book collecting, coin collecting, collectibles, comic books, costume jewelry, dolls, mineral collecting, pin collecting, sports and trading cards, stamps, toy collecting.

Vicky Lewis
Vicky's Home on the Net
P.O. Box 951116
Lake Mary, FL 32795-1116
vicky@vicky-web.com
http://www.vicky-web.com
Comprehensive Web site for the modern doll collector: links to artists, doll clubs, doll links, Disney activities such as conventions and cruises, Barbie showcases and trivia, and much more.

Don Thompson
Vintage Toy Encyclopedia, The
P.O. Box 8701
Kansas City, MO 64114
http://www.toynfo.com
Great Web site with informative articles about scores and scores of action figures, dolls, toys and other collectibles.

Flossy Eddy
Flossy's Dolls & Collectibles
153 Sundance Dr.
Grand Junction, CO 81503
ph: 970-242-1358
flossysdolls@youfoundme.com
http://www.youfoundme.com/
dollarea.htm
Huge Web site with free doll classified ads, chat room, guestbook, email discussion group, free doll newsletter, collector books, dolls, toys and more.

Don & Vella Painter
WebDolls
23483 Shephard Rd.
Clatskanie, OR 97016
ph: 888-763-5122 or 503-728-3503
webmaster@webdolls.com
http://www.webdolls.com
WebDolls is the ultimate online resource to find anything related to dolls: museums, artist listings, clubs, shows, classifieds, doll businesses, etc.

Misc. Services

Dwaine E. Gipe
Dollologist
1406 Sycamore Rd.
Montoursville, PA 17754-9519
ph: 570-323-9604
Teaches four-day doll restoration seminar; brochure available; also sells step-by-step video covering use of modern restoration materials including air brush, sources provided, tools used, tricks.

JoAnn Mathias
G & M Doll Restoration Seminar
6204 Ocean Front Ave.
Virginia Beach, VA 23451
ph: 757-428-1609 or 757-427-9131
dolldoc@gmdollseminar.com
http://www.gmdollseminar.com
Teaching four-day seminars on restoration of bisque, composition, tin, china, papier mache, and felt dolls.

Museums/Libraries

Eleanor E. Thompson, Dir.
Wenham Museum
132 Main St.
Wenham, MA 01984-1520
ph: 978-468-2377
fax: 978-468-1763
http://www.nosh.net/wenhammuseum
Largest permanent display of toy soldiers in the US; collection includes pre-war Britains, large and small scale Heyde, composition figures and more; also model train room with operating layouts.

Yesteryears Doll & Toy Museum
Newsletter: Yesteryears Museum News
Main & River Sts.
P.O. Box 609
Sandwich, MA 02563
ph: 508-888-1711

Doll Museum, The
520 Thames St.
Newport, RI 02840-6711
ph: 401-849-0405
fax: 401-849-0405
DollMuseum@aol.com
http://www.dollmuseum.com
Featuring a fine collection of antique and modern dolls; museum toy shop carries antiques, collectibles, etc.; offers repairs and appraisals.

Curator
Fairfield Historical Society
636 Old Post Rd.
Fairfield, CT 06430-6647
ph: 203-259-1598
fax: 203-255-2716
info@fairfieldhs.org
http://www.fairfieldhistoricalsociety.org

Sheila Clark
Museum of the City of New York
1220 5th Ave. at 103rd St.
New York, NY 10029-5221
ph: 212-534-1672
fax: 212-534-5974
http://www.mcny.org
Access by appointment; research fee charged.

Aunt Len's Doll & Toy Museum
6 Hamilton Terrace
New York, NY 10031
ph: 212-281-4143

Linda Greenfield
Victorian Doll Museum
4332 Buffalo Rd.
North Chili, NY 14514-1206
ph: 585-247-0130
A wonderland exhibiting over 2,000 identified dolls from mid-1800s to present; puppet show, toy circus, doll houses, paper dolls, etc.

Strong Museum, The
1 Manhattan Square
Rochester, NY 14607
ph: 585-263-2700
fax: 585-263-2493
http://www.strongmuseum.org
Collection contains more than 500,000 objects: toys, doll houses, miniatures, household furnishings, and the world's most comprehensive collection of dolls.

Marjorie Darrah
Mary Merritt Doll Museum, The
843 Benjamin Hwy.
Douglassville, PA 19518
ph: 610-385-3809
fax: 610-689-4538
info@merritts.com
http://www.merritts.com/dollmuseum
Dolls on display range from a 17th century bone doll to French wax mini-manequins, bisque dolls, and Jumeaus.

Washington Dolls' House & Toy
Museum
5236 44th St. NW
Washington, DC 20015-2101
ph: 202-244-0024
fax: 202-237-1659

National Museum of American History
14th & Constitution Ave. NW
Washington, DC 20560
ph: 202-357-2700
webmaster@si.edu
http://www.si.edu/organiza/museums/
nmah/nmah.htm

Angela Peterson Doll & Miniatures
Museum
101 W. Green Dr.
High Point, NC 27260
ph: 336-885-3655
fax: 336-884-4352
hpcvb@highpoint.org
More than 1,600 dolls, 800 miniatures and 15 fully furnished doll houses on display including Shirley Temple and Bob Timberlake Collection and an extraordinary creche doll display.

Edwina Gill
Mary Miller Doll Museum
209-211 Gloucester St.
Brunswick, GA 31520
ph: 912-267-7569
fax: 912-267-7569
dollmuseum@thebest.net
3,000 dolls, doll houses, miniatures from 90 countries; dolls dating from 1850 to present; largest museum of this kind in the Southeast; gift shop on premises.

Milan Historical Museum, Inc.
Newsletter: New Milan Ledger
P.O. Box 308
Milan, OH 44846-0308
ph: 419-499-2968
fax: 419-499-9004
museum@milanhistory.org
http://www.milanhistory.org
A seven-building complex 500 yards from the birthplace of Thomas A. Edison; restored home, carriage shed, blacksmith shop, general store, collections from the 19th century.

Valerie LaBreche
Enchanted World Doll Museum
615 North Main
Mitchell, SD 57301-1945
ph: 605-996-9896
fax: 605-996-0210
4,000 antique & collectible dolls set in 400 unique displays; gift shop features dolls, doll books, paper dolls, doll accessories, and Dept. 56, Dickens and Snow Babies.

Marion Briton
House of a Thousand Dolls
106 First St.
Loma, MT 59460
ph: 406-739-4338
Collection of toys and dolls from 1830 to present.

Frances Kerber Walrond, Dir.
Eugene Field House & St. Louis Toy
Museum
Newsletter: Field Notes
634 So. Broadway St.
Saint Louis, MO 63102
ph: 314-421-4689
ExecDir@EugeneFieldHouse.org
http://www.eugenefieldhouse.org
Birthplace and childhood home of Eugene Field, the children's poet; large collection of antique toys always on display; home of Roswell M. Field, lawyer for Dred Scott and his family

when they sued for their freedom from slavery.

Sandi Russell
Toy & Miniature Museum of Kansas City
5235 Oak St.
Kansas City, MO 64112-2877
ph: 816-333-2055 or 816-333-9328
fax: 816-333-2055
bergr@umkc.edu
http://www.umkc.edu/tmm
Museum housed in an elegant mansion features collections of miniatures, antique dolls' houses and antique toys.

Eliza Cruce Hall Doll Museum
320 E. St., N.W.
Ardmore, OK 73401
ph: 405-223-8290
fax: 405-223-2033

Francis & Clara Franks
Franks Antique Doll Museum
211 West Grand Ave.
Marshall, TX 75670
ph: 903-935-3065 or 903-935-3070

Denver Museum of Miniatures, Dolls & Toys
1880 Gaylord St.
Denver, CO 80206-1211
ph: 303-322-1053
fax: 303-322-3704
dmmdt@juno.com
Displays miniatures, dolls and toys dating back to the 18th century.

Rosalie Whyel Museum of Doll Art
1116 108th Ave. NE
Bellevue, WA 98004
ph: 425-455-1116
fax: 425-455-4793
dollart@dollart.com
http://www.dollart.com
Here history unfolds through the vision of master doll makers; dolls, teddy bears, toys, and miniatures; also features two stores which support this privately funded museum; seeks good dolls or collections to buy.

Paul Gray
Bethnal Green Museum of Childhood
Cambridge Heath Rd.
London, E2 9PA U.K.
ph: 0181-980-2415
fax: 0181-983-5225
p.gray@vam.ac.uk
A division of the Victoria & ALbert Museum; national collection of dolls, toys, games, puppets, and children's costumes.

Periodicals

Ashton International Media, Inc.
Magazine: Doll Reader
44 Front St., Ste. 590
Worcester, MA 01608
ph: 800-437-5828
fax: 717-657-9552
DRMsubs@aol.com
http://www.dollreader.com
Gives both the beginning & advanced collector information on antique,

collectible and modern dolls; current collecting trends, popular manufacturers and artists, new product releases, events calendar, display ideas.

Castle Press Publications
Magazine: Doll Castle News
P.O. Box 247
Washington, NJ 07882-0247
ph: 908-689-7042 or 800-572-6607
fax: 908-689-6320
dcn@toast.net
A magazine focusing on dolls, miniatures, doll houses and related items; ads, paper doll section, needlework, patterns, etc.

Donna Kaonis, Ed.
Magazine: Antique Doll Collector
6 Woodside Ave., Ste 300
Northport, NY 11768
ph: 516-261-4100 or 888-800-2588
fax: 516-261-9684
adc@tias.com
http://www.antiqueDollCollector.com
Articles about antique dolls, vintage teddy bears, doll houses and miniatures; articles by leading doll experts, visits to major collections, coverage of shows and auctions; published bi-monthly.

Vicky Lewis
Vicky's NetResults, Inc.
Magazine: Dolls In Print
P.O. Box 951116
Lake Mary, FL 32795-1116
vicky@vicky-web.com
http://www.dollsinprint.com
A 90-page, four color glossy magazine focusing on contemporary dolls.

Martha Pullen Co.
Magazine: Sew Beautiful Magazine
149 Old Big Cover Rd.
Brownsboro, AL 35741
ph: 800-547-4176
info@marthapullen.com
http://www.marthapullen.com
The magazine about heirloom sewing, primarily children's clothing but also includes patterns for dolls.

Jones Publishing, Inc.
Magazine: Dolls Magazine
P.O. Box 5000
Iola, WI 54945
ph: 715-445-5000 or 800-331-0038
fax: 715-445-4053
jonespub@jonespublishing.com
http://www.dollsmagazine.com
Information and feature articles from the doll world's most renowned professionals: collecting values, new issues, limited edition pieces, restoration, costuming; hints & tricks, latest artist designs, contests.

Magazine: Antique & Collectible Dolls
218 W. Woodin Blvd.
Dallas, TX 75224
ph: 214-943-2107
A bi-monthly magazine with ads and articles about dolls, auctions, and shows.

Brian Savage
Fun Publications
Newspaper: Master Collector
225 Cattle Baron Parc Dr.
Fort Worth, TX 76108
ph: 800-772-6673 or 817-448-9863
fax: 817-448-9843
brian@mastercollector.com
http://www.mastercollector.com
Ads-only newspaper; dolls (antique and modern collectible), toys, banks, models, cars, Matchbox, monsters, puzzles, political, toy trains, etc.; subscribers receive free 30-word ad each month; published monthly; reaches 20,000.

Patsy Moyer
Newsletter: Patsy & Friends
P.O. Box 311
Deming, NM 88031
moddoll@yahoo.com
http://www.zianet.com/patsyandfriends
Newsletter focuses on composition & travel dolls, and more.

Sandra Hood, Pub.
Krause Regional Antique Publications
Newsmagazine: Antique Journal
P.O. Box 12589
500 Fesler St., Ste. 201
El Cajon, CA 92020
ph: 619-593-2925 or 619-593-2927
fax: 619-447-7187
AntiqueJournal@aol.com
The largest monthly newspaper in Northern California, Oregon and Washington covering the antiques and collectibles industry with focus on Nevada and southern California; 76+ pages; auctions, events and show selection, features, etc.

Sandra Hood, Pub.
Krause Regional Antique Publications
Newsmagazine: Antique & Collectables
P.O. Box 12589
500 Fesler St., Ste. 201
El Cajon, CA 92022
ph: 619-593-2925 or 619-593-2927
fax: 619-447-7187
antiquequill@aol.com
The largest monthly newspaper in southern California covering the antiques & collectibles industry with focus sections on Nevada and Arizona; 64+ pages; events and show section, auctions, feature articles; columns, ads.

Ashdown Publishing
Magazine: Doll Magazine
Avalon Court, Star Rd.
Partridge Green, West Sussex RH13 8RY U.K.
ph: +44 (0) 1403 711511 or 513-353-4052 (in US)
fax: +44 (0) 1403 711521
mark@ashdown.co.uk
http://www.dollmagazine.com
An English doll publication.

Repair Services

Leon Trefler
Trefler & Sons Antique Restoring Studio, Inc.
99 Cabot St.
Needham, MA 02494
ph: 781-444-2685
fax: 781-444-0659
trefler@trefler.com
http://www.trefler.com
Restoration of porcelain and ceramic dolls.

Doll'tor Jean's Doll Hospital
RR 2, Box 573
Chadbourne Ridge Rd.
West Buxton, ME 04093
ph: 207-727-5385
Complete modern and antique doll repair and restoration.

Pat Travisano
Doll Lady Doll Hospital, The
94 Pent Rd.
Branford, CT 06405-4013
ph: 203-488-6193
docpatricia@webtv.net
Repair all types of dolls; supplier of parts and reproduction service; costume work; send parts to be matched; wigs, dresses, shoes, doll jewelry, hats, pinafores, etc.; all work done by appointment only; over 25 years experience.

Doll Room, The
9 Stuart Rd. W.
Bridgewater, CT 06752
ph: 860-354-8442
fax: 860-355-0546
dollrm@aol.com
Doll repairs.

Louise Sleeter
Louise's Little Ladies
21 Commissioners Pike
Woodstown, NJ 08098
ph: 856-769-5544
louisesladies@earthlink.net
Buys, sells and repairs antique to modern dolls; specializes in composition dolls.

New York Doll Hospital
787 Lexington Ave.
New York, NY 10021-8164
ph: 212-838-7527
Buy, restore antique dolls, Teddy Bears, mechanical toys.

Linda Greenfield
Victorian Doll Museum & Chili Doll Hospital
4332 Buffalo Rd.
North Chili, NY 14514-1206
ph: 585-247-0130
Recognized expert in doll restoration; repairs all types of dolls; restringing, leather body repair, replacement of cloth bodies.

Dwaine E. Gipe
Dollologist
1406 Sycamore Rd.
Montoursville, PA 17754-9519
ph: 570-323-9604
Can solve most doll problems: papier-mâché, bisque, composition; conservation, restoration; reset eyes, wigs, missing parts, recoloring.

JoAnn Mathias
Beach Doll Hospital
6204 Ocean Front Ave.
Virginia Beach, VA 23451
ph: 757-428-1609 or 757-427-9131
dolldoc@gmdollseminar.com
http://www.gmdollseminar.com
Doll restoration of dolls made before 1950; specializing in bisque and composition repair.

Marcel Faulkner
Doll Repair Service
221 N. Lynnhaven Rd.
Virginia Beach, VA 23452
ph: 757-431-1911
Professional repair to all dolls and stuffed toys; a lifetime of craft experience and 20 years specializing in dolls; originality preserved whenever possible but basket cases welcomed; reasonable turnover time on average.

Ann Gough
1610 Smithville Rd.
Dayton, OH 45410
ph: 937-256-7280
asiabooby@aol.com
Restoring dolls for over 35 years.

Dolly Heaven
502 Broadway
New Haven, IN 46774
ph: 800-660-1912 or 260-493-6428
dolly.heaven@gte.net
Doll restoration & repair; specializing in broken bisque and composition dolls; modern, antique, collector dolls; all materials.

Wilder's Doll Center
3345 Dixie Highway
Waterford, MI 48328-1606
ph: 248-618-9506
fax: 248-618-9507
Repairs and restores old dolls; also buys and sells.

Gary Sowatzka
Sowatzka's Dolls
7273 Kelly Dr.
Lake Tomahawk, WI 54539
ph: 715-277-4591
sowatdol@newnorth.net
http://www.sowatzka.com
Dolls for sale; doll appraisals, doll repairs and doll restoration classes; site has tips on collecting dolls and has a unique area where you can submit your own doll story; a doll is given to everyone who has their story put on the site.

Clare Erickson
Auntie Clare's Doll Hospital Shop
2543 Seppela Blvd., N
North Saint Paul, MN 55109-3016
ph: 651-770-7522
clare@antieclares.com
http://www.antieclares.com
Offers professional restorations of dolls, bears, animals and plush, figurines and statues.

Stacy Spicer
Stacy's Vintage Specialties
2610 Olive St.
Grand Forks, ND 58201
ph: 701-775-9982
srspicer@corpcomm.net
http://www.corpcomm.net/~srspicer
Specializes in hair rerooting, facial retouches and repaints, green ear treatment, custom doll jewelry and custom designs; says all dolls can be saved; also buys, sells and trades; free estimates via email.

Mary Gates
Doll Doctor, The
1204 4h Park Rd.
Pontiac, IL 61764-9105
ph: 815-842-3442
Doll repairs; specializes in composition work; work shown in museums and sold in antique shops; also does custom dressing of old dolls using her own designs.

Sharon Niles
Carousel, Inc.
14409 Manchester Rd.
Ballwin, MO 63011
ph: 636-391-4900
fax: 636-391-3993
carouselinc@hotmail.com
Specializes in the appraisal, conservation and restoration of antique dolls.

Kristy Neal
Treasured Collectibles Doll Hospital
1928 First St.
Slidell, LA 70458
ph: 985-646-6077 or 985-645-9974
info@treasured-collectibles.com
http://www.treasured-collectibles.com
Repairs most dolls including broken bisque or composition; restyles wigs; sets sleep eyes; finds missing parts; repaints; also appraises, buys and sells vintage dolls.

Doll Hospital
419 Gentry St., #102
Spring, TX 77373
ph: 281-350-6722
fax: 281-446-3353
BHarden473@aol.com
http://www.aaadollhospital.com
Doll repair and restoration: antique and classic, modern, reproduction porcelain, original artist dolls, stuffed animals.

Jenny Moore
P.O. Box 360295
Lakewood, CO 80226
ph: 303-888-8255
Repair and restoration of dolls and stuffed animals; over 17 years experience; custom patterns/designs for vintage dolls.

Jeri Cotherman
Doll & Bear's Paradise, A
855 1/2 N. Cedar
Laramie, WY 82072-2469
ph: 307-742-3429
dolls2fix@fiberpipe.net
http://www.adollsandbearsparadise.com
Restores dolls, stuffed animals; makes artist specialty bears; sells dolls and bears; buying dolls, patterns, old material, fur and fake fur.

Darla Waters
Doll Restoration
1115 Bear Ave.
Idaho Falls, ID 83402-2050
ph: 208-522-4255
dlwaters@onewest.net
http://www.onewest.net/~dlwaters
Antique and bisque doll restoration; reconstruct broken parts, repaint, refurbish old wigs, reset eyes, redress; specializes in basket cases.

Don & Vella Painter
Homestead Doll Hospital
23483 Shephard Rd.
Clatskanie, OR 97016
ph: 888-763-5122 or 503-728-3503
webmaster@webdolls.com
http://www.webdolls.com
Buys, sells, appraises, collects and repairs dolls: antiques, compositions, pull string and battery operated talkers, mechanical, toys, vinyl; also reroots hair.

Rita Mauze
Life's Little Treasures
P.O. Box 585
Winston, OR 97496
ph: 541-697-3472 or 800-932-3472
Buys, sells, repairs, restores antique & modern dolls.

Arlene Martinez
Dolls by Arlene
19616 NE 163rd Ave.
Battle Ground, WA 98604
ph: 360-687-4321
Arlenedoll@aol.com
Dolls appraiser, collector, dealer, expert and restorer; complete porcelain art studio; specializes in the repair of modern as well as antique dolls; graduate of McDowell Museum restoration course; over 20 years experience.

Suppliers

Nick Hill
Twin Pines of Maine, Inc.
P.O Box 1178
Scarborough, ME 04070-1178
ph: 207-883-5541
fax: 207-883-1239
nick@twinpines.com
http://www.twinpines.com
Supplier of doll and doll clothes cleaning supplies; author of "The Definitive Book on the Care and Preservation of Vinyl Dolls and Action Figures."

Ron Lipstein
Dollspart Supply Co.
99 Gold Steet, 5th Floor
Brooklyn, NY 11201
ph: 718-243-0425 or 800-336-3655
fax: 718-243-0023
Sells full range of doll books and parts: eyes, wigs, bodies, clothing, tools, etc.

Banner Doll Supply Inc.
P.O. Box 32
Mechanicsburg, PA 17055
ph: 717-766-1503 or 800-637-8305
Metal doll stands manufacturer, also has bodies, hair, displays, eyes & eyelashes, footwear, hats, molds, paints, patterns, reference books, wigs.

Advertising

(see also ADVERTISING COLLECTIBLES, Figures)

Experts

Mary Jane Lamphier
Quilted Keepsakes & Unique Dolls Exhibit
577 Main St.
Arlington, IA 50606-9712
ph: 319-633-5885
Buys, sells and trades advertising dolls and characters such as Jolly Green Giant, the Ronald McDonald collection, Campbell Soup Kids, etc.; author of "Zany Characters of the Ad World" (Collector Books, 1995).

Annalee

Clubs/Associations

June Rogier, PR Mngr.
Annalee Doll Society
Magazine: Collector, The
P.O. Box 1137
Meredith, NH 03253
ph: 800-433-6557 or 603-279-3333
fax: 603-279-6659
jrogier@annalee.com
http://www.annalee.com
A collectors club sponsored by the Annalee Doll Co.; conducts annual Annalee doll auction.

Dealers

Sue Coffee
Laysville Hardware
10 Saunders Hollow Rd.
Old Lyme, CT 06371-1126
ph: 860-434-5641
fax: 860-434-3640
SueCoffee@aol.com
http://www.suecoffee.com
*A leading source for buying or selling
Annalee dolls; over 15,000 current
and retired Annalee dolls in stock;
secure online ordering; consulting
expert for "Annalee Mobilitee Dolls
Price Guide."*

Experts

Sue Coffee
10 Saunders Hollow Rd.
Old Lyme, CT 06371-1126
ph: 860-434-5641
fax: 860-434-3640
SueCoffee@aol.com
http://www.suecoffee.com
*A leading source for buying or selling
Annalee dolls; over 15,000 current
and retired Annalee dolls in stock;
secure online ordering; consulting
expert for "Annalee Mobilitee Dolls
Price Guide."*

Larry Koon
P.O. Box 808
Belpre, OH 45714-0808
Author of "Annalee Mobilitee Dolls."

Man./Prod./Dist.

June Rogier, PR Mngr.
Annalee Mobilitee Dolls, Inc.
P.O. Box 1137
Meredith, NH 03253
ph: 800-433-6557 or 603-279-3333
fax: 603-279-6659
jrogier@annalee.com
http://www.annalee.com
*Creates, produces and distributes
posable felt dolls of distinction which
contain wire armatures for flexibility
and repositioning.*

Museums/Libraries

June Rogier, PR Mngr.
Annalee Doll Museum
P.O. Box 1137
Meredith, NH 03253
ph: 800-433-6557 or 603-279-3333
fax: 603-279-6659
jrogier@annalee.com
http://www.annalee.com
*Over 1,000 Annalee Dolls on display
representing the work of founder and
creator Annalee Thorndike; open
Memorial Day to Labor Day or by
appointment.*

Artist

Appraisers

Michael Hinkle
Figurative, The
ph: 760-564-6060 or 760-564-0012
michael@thefigurative.com
http://www.thefigurative.com/appraisals
*Specializes in the appraisal of one-of-
a-kind sculpture and contemporary
doll art.*

Dealers

Nancie Mann
Mann Gallery - Art of the Doll
P.O. Box 1106
Boston, MA 02117
ph: 617-266-6266
fax: 617-696-6667
artmann@worldnet.att.net
http://www.manngallery.com
*Appraiser deals in one-of-a-kind and
very small editions of dolls created by
contemporary doll artists; mixed
media figurative sculptures by artists
from varied disciplines.*

Joyce McCandless
Krazy Cat Collectibles
P.O. Box 1192
Emmitsburg, MD 21727
ph: 301-271-9851
KrazyCatCo@aol.com
http://www.krazycatcollectibles.com
*Buys and sells dolls: '60s and '70s
ears dolls including Liddle Kiddles,
Dolly Darlings, Upsey Downseys, etc;
also vintage and mod Barbie (pre-
1972), antique bisque & china heads,
composition, vinyl, modern artist
dolls, etc.*

Dollcity USA
2080 S. Harbor blvd.
Anaheim, CA 92802
ph: 714-750-3585
fax: 714-750-3584
dale@dollcity.com
http://www.dollcity.com
*Large selection of collectible and play
dolls.*

Carol Salmon
Claymates Porcelain Dolls
827 Shanahan Blvd.
Newmarket, Ontario L3X 1P9 Canada
ph: 905-898-7926
claymates@rogers.com
*Carries unique one-of-a-kind
handmade porcelain dolls individually
created; also carries a line of
dollmaking supplies and accessories
for all dolls.*

Experts

Larry Koon
P.O. Box 808
Belpre, OH 45714-0808
*Author of "Contemporary Doll Artists
of the 1980s."*

Man./Prod./Dist.

Terressa Kaminski
Limited Original Dolls by Tre'
792 Caskey St.
Bay Point, CA 94565
ph: 925-709-9691 or 925-458-2148
fax: 925-458-2148
trelimitedoriginal@attbi.com
http://www.limitedoriginal.com/
*Internationally known doll artist; well
publicized in International publications; award winning and known as
"artist to the stars."*

Periodicals

Ashton International Media, Inc.
Magazine: Doll Reader
44 Front St., Ste. 590
Worcester, MA 01608
ph: 800-437-5828
fax: 717-657-9552
DRMsubs@aol.com
http://www.dollreader.com
*Gives both the beginning & advanced
collector information on antique,
collectible and modern dolls; current
collecting trends, popular manufacturers and artists, new product releases,
events calendar, display ideas.*

Suppliers

Carol Salmon
Claymates Porcelain Dolls
827 Shanahan Blvd.
Newmarket, Ontario L3X 1P9 Canada
ph: 905-898-7926
claymates@rogers.com
*Carries unique one-of-a-kind
handmade porcelain dolls individually
created; also carries a line of
dollmaking supplies and accessories
for all dolls.*

Automatons

Collectors

Frank DeMayo
1511 Holliston Trail
Fort Wayne, IN 46825
ph: 219-489-0053 or 800-258-8243
fax: 219-484-8605
seeburgh@aol.com
*Wants coin-operated slot, gum, card,
dice machines; also wants to buy
automatons and key wound figures.*

Dealers

Don Levison
Don Levison Antiques
P.O. Box 22262
San Francisco, CA 94122
ph: 415-753-0455
fax: 415-753-5206
dlevison@juno.com
http://www.antiquehorology.com
*Buys and sells antique and better
quality pocket and wrist watches,
clocks, music boxes, singing birds,
and other small automata; also
mercury barometers from the 17th
century to present.*

Barbie

Appraisers

Annette Givens
1958 Matador Way, #222
Northridge, CA 91330-2222
fax: 818-993-0228
AnnetteMG@aol.com
http://members.aol.com/annettemg/
aolla.html

Caren L. Carlson, ISA
Ask an Appraiser
31313 NW Paradise Park Rd.
Ridgefield, WA 98642-8754
ph: 360-887-8686
fax: 360-887-8909
carenscubbyhole@netscape.net
*Specializes in the appraisal of early
20th century dolls, toys and
accessories.*

Auction Services

Shari McMasters
McMasters Harris Doll Auctions
5855 John Glen Hwy.
P.O. Box 1755
Cambridge, OH 43725
ph: 800-842-3526 or 740-432-7400
fax: 740-432-3191
info@mcmastersharris.com
http://www.mcmastersharris.com
*Specializes in auctioning antique and
collectible dolls and doll related items
such as teddy bears, Barbie dolls and
accessories, children's dishes, toys,
children's books, etc.*

Clubs/Associations

Barbie Doll Club of Eastern Oklahoma
sarah@alphabetsoup.net
http://www.geocities.com/
FashionAvenue/1959

Dora Lerch
Barbie Doll Collectors Club International
Newsletter: Barbie Newsletter
P.O. Box 245
Garnerville, NY 10923
ph: 914-362-4657
fax: 914-362-3258
info.bdcci@juno.com
*Ads, upcoming shows, show reports,
identification tips, convention news,
etc.*

Kathryn E. Darden
Belle Meade Plantation Belles
P.O. Box 210182
Nashville, TN 37221-0182
barbieintn@yahoo.com
http://www.geocities.com/
FashionAvenue/6487/clubinfo.html
*A club for Barbie collectors in the
Belle Meade/Bellevue area of
Nashville.*

K. Darden
Tennessee Internet Pink Society
P.O. Box 210182
Nashville, TN 37221-0182
ph: 615-662-4243
barbieintn@yahoo.com
http://www.geocities.com/
FashionAvenue/6487/tips.html
*An Internet club for both vintage and
modern Barbie doll collectors.*

Jackie Burton
Memphis Barbie Doll Club
5706 Fieldcrest Cove
Memphis, TN 38134
ph: 901-386-6264

Julie Birenbaum
Windy City Collectors Barbie Doll Club
P.O. Box 417518
Chicago, IL 60641
ph: 847-357-1675
purpink@aol.com
A Chicago-based Barbie doll club; one of the largest in the country; monthly meetings; bimonthly newsletter and other club benefits.

Annette Givens
1958 Matador Way, #222
Northridge, CA 91330-2222
fax: 818-993-0228
AnnetteMG@aol.com
http://members.aol.com/annettemg/aolla.html
Club for Barbie collectors in the Los Angeles area.

Collectors

Keri Jones
420 Winthrop St.
Taunton, MA 02780-2157
Wants to buy vintage Barbie dolls and clothing from the 1960s to early 1970s; send description and price.

David & Becky Beane
Beane's Antiques & Photography
92 River Rd.
Benton, ME 04901
ph: 207-453-6790
fax: 207-453-6790
Collector of pre-1970 Barbie dolls, fashions and accessories; call or write with descriptions and prices.

Dan Stapleton
8237 Banyan Blvd.
Orlando, FL 32819
ph: 407-345-1132
Wants to buy mint condition (not removed from box), Holiday Barbies.

Laura Cordery
P.O. Box 0215
Elfers, FL 34680-0215
Enthusiast and collector of America's plastic princess, Barbie; over 50 in her collection; also an html programmer and Web page designer.

Tim Gordon, ISA
P.O. Box 5813
2717 Highland Dr.
Missoula, MT 59802
ph: 406-728-1812 or 888-720-1812
timbgordon@aol.com
http://www.xntrx.com
Wants singles, collections, accessories, clothing, related dolls; offers appraisal services.

Cheryl & Nick Shimp
Nick & Cheryl's Toy Collectors
749 Nottingham Lane
Crystal Lake, IL 60014
ph: 815-455-3308
ncshimp@dls.net
Buys, sells, trades, collects and appraises vintage Barbie dolls, fashions, accessories and structures; also collects Toni dolls and clothes;

appraises various vintage dolls from the 1940s through the 1970s.

Lois Burger
2323 Lincoln
Beatrice, NE 68310-3306
ph: 402-228-2797
BarbieLJB@yahoo.com
Wants pre-1966 Barbie clothes, accessories, Ken, Midge, Skipper & their clothes; also anything Barbie related such as comics, cars; also Terri Lee dolls.

Dealers

Patty & Fred Meyer
Meyer's Toy World New Barbie Center
ph: 800-963-1963
info@meyerstoyworld.com
http://www.meyerstoyworld.com

Marl B. Davidson
MARL & B Inc.
10301 Braden Run
Bradenton, FL 34202-1744
ph: 941-751-6275
fax: 941-751-5463
Marlbe@aol.com
http://www.marlbe.com
Buys vintage Barbies; carries full line of vintage and hard-to-find Barbies from 1959 to the present; also Tyler Wentworth, Alex, Willow/Daisy, Gene, Dawn, and other fashion dolls.

Paul David
Newsletter: Paul David Exclusively Barbie
610 Blackwater Rd.
Chillicothe, OH 45601-9004
ph: 740-642-2747
fax: 740-642-2755
Carries all the latest Barbies and old stock and accessories; newsletter is 40 pages, hundreds of Barbies listed for sale, articles, news, what's new, limited editions, special editions, values, updated prices, gossip, etc.

Denise Davidson
Deni's Vintage Barbies
7321 Seymour Rd.
Owosso, MI 48867
ph: 517-723-4611
fax: 517-725-5696
davidson@tir.com
http://www.dolls4play.com
Extensive list of vintage Barbie and friends for sale; Web site has comprehensive vintage Barbie and friends ID Guide for viewing; select clothing ID Guide for viewing at photo gallery; also has Modern Barbie sales list.

Deanna Overdorf
D's Dolls
4 Lakeridge Dr.
Adrian, MI 49221
ph: 517-264-1862 or 888-239-0176
fax: 517-264-1863
jrodjc@msn.com
http://www.dsdolls.com
Specializes in vintage Barbie, Dawn, Liddle Kiddles and other fashion dolls from the 1960s and 1970s including

cars, houses, clothes and other accessories.

Deanna Overdorf
D's Dolls
4 Lakeridge Dr.
Adrian, MI 49221
ph: 517-264-1862
fax: 517-264-1863
jrodjc@msn.com
http://www.dsdolls.com
An Internet store specializing in vintage Barbie, Dawn and Liddle Kiddles dolls, clothes and all other accessories.

Cheryl & Nick Shimp
Nick & Cheryl's Toy Collectors
749 Nottingham Lane
Crystal Lake, IL 60014
ph: 815-455-3308
ncshimp@dls.net
Buys, sells, trades, collects and appraises vintage Barbie dolls, fashions, accessories and structures; also collects Toni dolls and clothes; appraises various vintage dolls from the 1940s through the 1970s.

Judy Kuster
Bear Essentials Dolls, Bears & Collectible Toys
1502 Park St.
Paso Robles, CA 93446
ph: 805-237-8697
Offers vintage to present Barbie, GI Joe, action figures, Beanie Babies, Starting Lineup, Boyds Bears, Steiff, Muffy Vanderbear, Superman, Batman, Star Wars, Star Trek, and more.

Craig Dawson
Baddog Collectibles
115 Oakley Blvd.
Scarborough, Ontario M1P 3P8 Canada
baddog@thebulletin.net
http://www.thebulletin.net
Buys, sells, trades 1959-1974 Barbie dolls and friends (Ken, Skipper, Francie, Christie, Stacey, Casey, Twiggy, Scooter, Allan, Ricky, Tutti, Midge and others); also interested in celebrity items from the 1960s to 1970s.

Experts

Jane Sarasohn-Kahn
125 Shelbourne Lane
Phoenixville, PA 19460-5710
ph: 610-933-5710
fax: 610-933-5636
jskahn@aol.com
http://www.dollreport.com
Author of "Contemporary Barbie 1980 to Present," "Contemporary Barbie, 1998 Edition" (2nd edition), and Editor, Dollreport.com (www.dollreport.com).

Kathryn E. Darden
Newsletter: Tennessee Dolls
P. O. Box 218427
Nashville, TN 37221-0181
barbieintn@yahoo.com
Regular columnist for "Dolls in

Print" magazine; also known for her work in the doll collecting world as a free-lance writer, and doll show promoter; publishes bimonthly newsletter of interest to local Tennessee Barbie collectors.

Joe Blitman
Joe's: BARBIE & Other Fashion Dolls
5163 Franklin Ave.
Los Angeles, CA 90027-3601
ph: 323-953-6490
fax: 323-953-0888
joeblitman@aol.com
http://www.joeslist.com
Publisher of "Oh, You Beautiful Doll" Barbie videotape; author of "Barbie and her Mod, Mod, Mod, Mod World of Fashion," and "Francis and her Mod, Mod, Mod, Mod, World of Fashion" (Hobby House Books, 1996); partner is Kevin Mulligan.

Caroline Myers
2920 North Shingle Rd.
Shingle Springs, CA 95682
ph: 530-677-4060
fax: 530-677-4060
dollhabit4u@yahoo.com
http://www.dollhabit.com
Informative Web site for the Barbie enthusiast.

Internet Resources

Roseann Quaranto
Barbie Club Online
59 Selden Blvd.
Centereach, NY 11720
roeq@optonline.net
http://www.geocities.com/bcosite
Online Barbie Club and Web site with daily updated gossip, giveaways for members, message board, weekly chats and more.

Vivian Arzola
La Princesa Plastica
lpp1414@yahoo.com
http://home.earthlink.net/~vivian2
A bilingual (English/Spanish) Barbie Web site with Barbie news, gossip, photos, for sale, message board, classified ads.

Man./Prod./Dist.

Mattel Toys
8400 Fairway Place
P.O. Box 628218
Middleton, WI 53562-8218
ph: 800-491-7514
proxyadm@mattel.com
http://www.barbiecollectibles.com
Manufacturer of Barbie dolls; Web site includes Collecting Barbie Dolls, Product Showcase (the showcase edition, collector edition, limited edition and children's collection), and Barbie Shoppe.

Periodicals

Jacqueline Horning
Journal: Barbie Talks Some More
19 Jamestown Dr.
Cincinnati, OH 45241-1435
ph: 513-779-3708
A 65-page journal with 13 years of vital information for the Barbie collector; the author is a dealer/ collector herself; $12.95 ppd.

Barbie Bazaar, Inc.
Magazine: Barbie Bazaar
5711 8th Ave.
Kenosha, WI 53140
ph: 262-658-1004 or 262-658-1881
fax: 262-658-0433
mcpub@barbiebazaar.com
http://www.barbiebazaar.com
The Official Barbie Collectors magazine; news, classifieds, price guide, collector interviews.

Brian Savage
Fun Publications
Newspaper: Master Collector
225 Cattle Baron Parc Dr.
Fort Worth, TX 76108
ph: 800-772-6673 or 817-448-9863
fax: 817-448-9843
brian@mastercollector.com
http://www.mastercollector.com
Ads-only newspaper; dolls (antique and modern collectible), toys, banks, models, cars, Matchbox, monsters, puzzles, political, toy trains, etc.; subscribers receive free 30-word ad each month; published monthly; reaches 20,000.

Repair Services

Kristin Peterson
Must B Vintage
2908 Durbin Place
Virginia Beach, VA 23456
ph: 757-468-9841
KPeter24@aol.com
http://hometown.aol.com/kpeter24/index.html
Dealer who also specializes in the repair and restoration of vintage Barbie dolls: hair restyling, retouching face paint, reconstruction of nose nips, eyelash ridges, missing digits, limb reattachment and more.

Suppliers

Nick Hill
Twin Pines of Maine, Inc.
P.O Box 1178
Scarborough, ME 04070-1178
ph: 207-883-5541
fax: 207-883-1239
nick@twinpines.com
http://www.twinpines.com
Supplier of doll and doll clothes cleaning supplies; author of "The Definitive Book on the Care and Preservation of Vinyl Dolls and Action Figures."

Action Figure Display Case Co.
512 North Spruce St.
Valley, NE 68064-9670
ph: 402-359-5539
fax: 773-395-3495
sales@usadisplay.net
http://www.usadisplay.net
Manufactures high quality display cases for all 12" action figures; full color combat backgrounds or cityscapes for Barbie; perfect for gifts, home or office.

Linda Holt
Bits n' Pieces Lady
1141 Belfair Dr.
Pinole, CA 94564
ph: 510-724-1855
fax: 510-724-4143
pieceslady@aol.com
The place to get your Barbie accessories: vintage Barbie doll clothing, dresses, shoes, gloves, etc.

Betsy McCall

Experts

Marci Van Ausdall
4532 Fertile Valley Rd.
Newport, WA 99156
ph: 509-292-1311
betsymccallfanclub@hotmail.com
Buys, sells, appraises, specializes in Betsy McCall of all sizes as well as clothing and related merchandise (toys, paperdolls, etc.); one item or collection; Marci is author of "Betsy McCall - A Collector's Guide."

Periodicals

Marci Van Ausdall
Betsy McCall Fan Club
Newsletter: Betsy's Fan Club Newsletter
4532 Fertile Valley Rd.
Newport, WA 99156
ph: 509-292-1311
betsymccallfanclub@hotmail.com
Dedicated to providing collectors with information on both vintage and modern (Tonner Co.) Betsy McCall dolls; since 1994; over 200 members.

Black

(see also BLACK MEMORABILIA)

Dealers

Erlene Reed
Aquataurian Doll & Gift Gallery
1794 Verbena St., NW
Washington, DC 20012
ph: 202-829-7170
fax: 202-723-7274
dollyasm@erols.com
http://www.townsqr.com/dolly
Buys and sells many (retired) Daddy's Long Legs dolls, Barbie dolls, Madame Alexander dolls, Cabbage Patch Kid dolls, and other artist dolls and modern dolls.

Laverne Hall
Laverne's Place
P.O. Box 1212
Bellevue, WA 98009-1212
ph: 425-687-5815
fax: 425-687-5889
halllcmbh@aol.com
http://www.dollstreetdreamers.com/Laverne.htm
Specializes in contemporary African and African-American dolls and doll making; produces black doll shows.

Misc. Services

Laverne Hall
Laverne's Place
P.O. Box 1212
Bellevue, WA 98009-1212
ph: 425-687-5815
fax: 425-687-5889
halllcmbh@aol.com
http://www.dollstreetdreamers.com/Laverne.htm
Specializes in contemporary African and African-American dolls and doll making; produces black doll shows.

Bobbing Head

(see also SPORTS COLLECTIBLES, Baseball)

Clubs/Associations

Barry Larkins
Bobbin Head Collectors Club
P.O. Box 9297
Daytona Beach, FL 32120
ph: 940-253-7040
fax: 904-253-1115
bobbin1013@aol.com

Collectors

William Rose
Nostalgia Man
607 Meadowbrook Dr.
Georgetown, TX 78628
ph: 512-863-5080 or 512-682-6900 x8167
nostalgiaman@beer.com
http://whoathatscool.freeyellow.com/WantedList.html
Wants to buy or trade character bobbin' heads or sports nodders from the 1970s or earlier.

Dealers

Nelson Sports Collectibles
105 E. Broadway
Monmouth, IL 61462
support@bobhead.com
http://www.bobhead.com
Sells bobbing head dolls produced by Sports Accessories & Memorabilia, Inc. since 1992.

Experts

Tim Hunter
4301 W. Hidden Valley Dr.
Reno, NV 89502-9537
ph: 775-856-4357
fax: 775-856-4354
thunter885@aol.com
Buys, sells and specializes in sports and advertising bobbing head dolls;

author of "The Bobbing Head Price Guide."

Boudoir

Collectors

Rhiannon Mars
mars@boudoirdoll.com
http://www.boudoirdoll.com
1920s flapper boudoir bed doll collector; boudoir dolls are also known as pillow dolls; all types of dolls as well as photos depicting boudoir dolls wanted.

Cabbage Patch Kids

Clubs/Associations

Cabbage Connection, The
610 W. 17th
Fremont, NE 68025
ph: 402-721-0954

Man./Prod./Dist.

Original Appalachian Artworks, Inc.
Newsletter: Limited Edition
73 West Underwood St.
Cleveland, GA 30528
ph: 706-865-2171
fax: 706-865-5862
sales@cabbagepatchkids.com
http://www.cabbagepatchkids.com
Manufacturer of Cabbage Patch Kids dolls.

Periodicals

Marty Liston
Newsletter: Cabbage Line, The
553 Church St.
Oak Harbor, OH 43449
ph: 419-898-7106
cabline@winesburg.com
http://members.hmcltd.net/doug
Published bi-monthly; focuses mostly on mass-market dolls by Coleco, Hasbro and Mattel; covers the most current and past events happening in the Cabbage Patch.

Ann Wilhite
Newsletter: Cabbage Connection, The
610 W. 17th
Fremont, NE 68025
ph: 402-721-0954
acwilhite@teknetwork.com
Focuses mostly on mass-market dolls by Coleco, Hasbro and Mattel.

Celebrity

Collectors

Joedi Johnson
P.O. Box 565
Billings, MT 59103
ph: 406-248-4875
fax: 407-248-4875
Joedi@dawndollsplus.com
http://www.dawndollsplus.com
Wants to buy Mego 12" Cher doll and other girl dolls such as Diana Ross, Jaclyn Smith, Wonder Woman and others; also girl doll fashions and accessories.

Chatty Cathy

(see also TOYS, Talking [Pullstring])

Clubs/Associations

Melissa Gilkey Mince, Ed.
Chatty Cathy Collector's Club
Newsletter: Chatty News
P.O. Box 4426
Seminole, FL 33775-1426
ph: 727-319-6250
ChattyNme@aol.com
http://www.ttinet.com/chattycathy
For collectors of Chatty Cathy; share and learn all about Mattel's 1960s line of talking dolls; send SASE for information; bi-monthly 24-page newsletter; annual luncheon, Internet chats, club projects, collecting resources.

Repair Services

Kelly McIntyre
Chatty Cathy's Haven
19528 Ventura Blvd. #495
Tarzana, CA 91356-2917
ph: 818-881-3878
cchaven@aol.com
http://www.chattycathyshaven.com
Repairs, buys and sells pullstring talkers.

Cloth

Collectors

Chloe Ross
7553 Norton Ave. Apt. 4
Los Angeles, CA 90046-5500
ph: 213-874-3044
trstrap@aol.com
Wants Dollywood Defense Dolls: cloth dolls from the 1940s made by Dollywood Defense Studios, Hollywood, CA; these are well made, cloth dolls with sewn on uniforms: soldiers, sailors, WACS, nurse and bathing beauty, etc.

Periodicals

Judy Beswick
Magazine: Cloth Doll Magazine, The
P.O. Box 2167
Lake Oswego, OR 97035-0051
ph: 503-244-3539 or 800-695-7005
fax: 503-244-2370
theclothdoll@earthlink.com
http://www.theclothdoll.com
Quarterly magazine serving the interests of cloth dollmakers and collectors; each issue contains at least three patterns, articles on techniques, feature artists, collectibles, new products, events listings, and more.

Clothing

Clubs/Associations

Patricia Gosh
Doll Costumers Guild, Inc.
Journal: Doll Costumers Guild Journal
5042 Wilshire Blvd., PMB 573
Los Angeles, CA 90036
ph: 323-939-1482
fax: 323-939-3696
patgosh@aol.com
http://www.dollcostumersguild.com
Goal is to promote cooperation and interchange of ideas among those who are engaged or interested in doll costuming.

Misc. Services

William K. Jones
Carter & Jones, Inc.
4026 Melrose Ave.
Roanoke, VA 24017
ph: 800-476-5781 or 540-362-3751
fax: 540-362-1822
info@folkartnet.com
http://www.folkartnet.com
Specialist in cleaning and restoring antique doll clothes and accessories.

Repair Services

William K. Jones
Carter & Jones, Inc.
4026 Melrose Ave.
Roanoke, VA 24017
ph: 800-476-5781 or 540-362-3751
fax: 540-362-1822
info@folkartnet.com
http://www.folkartnet.com
Specialist in cleaning and restoring antique doll clothes and accessories.

Suppliers

Nick Hill
Twin Pines of Maine, Inc.
P.O Box 1178
Scarborough, ME 04070-1178
ph: 207-883-5541
fax: 207-883-1239
nick@twinpines.com
http://www.twinpines.com
Supplier of doll and doll clothes cleaning supplies; author of "The Definitive Book on the Care and Preservation of Vinyl Dolls and Action Figures."

Computer Programs For

Man./Prod./Dist.

Niche Software, Inc.
Software: Doll & Figurine Collector, The
7118 NW Terrace
Parkland, FL 33076
ph: 954-344-6561
marketing@collectiblessoftware.com
http://www.collectiblessoftware.com
Designed for the collector of dolls, figurines, and accessories.

Customized

Collectors

Sarah Worley
Sarah's Style
306 Blount St.
Clinton, NC 28328
sworli@hotmail.com
http://sarahstyle.terrashare.com
Collector of Barbie dolls, and doll makeover artist or fashion dolls; gallery of creations on Web site.

Loanne Ostlie
Tabloach Productions
719 North Ave. 51
Los Angeles, CA 90042
ph: 323-257-7645
Loanne@Tabloach.com
http://www.Tabloach.com
Specializes in one-of-a-kind customized fashion dolls including Kelly, Barbie, Tyler and Gene.

Dealers

Ella Trumpfeller
PurrFashion Designs - Custom Cat Dolls
2151 Harvey Mitchell Pkwy. South
College Station, TX 77840
ph: 979-764-3187
ekt@tca.net
http://www.purrfashiondesigns.com
Specializes in customizing fashion dolls into cats but also does fantasy dolls (Fairy Fashions), and novelty dolls (Pretty Boy Designs - Drag Queens/Cross Dressers, Texas Trailer Trash).

Man./Prod./Dist.

Angel Mitchell
Custom Doll Designs
941 CR 603
Green Forest, AR 72638
ph: 870-423-7147
angel@customdolldesigns.com
http://www.customdolldesigns.com
Specializing in one-of-a-kind designer fashion dolls including doll restoration.

Dawn

Collectors

Joedi Johnson
P.O. Box 565
Billings, MT 59103
ph: 406-248-4875
fax: 407-248-4875
Joedi@dawndollsplus.com
http://www.dawndollsplus.com
Buying all Dawn collections, dolls, fashions and accessories; looking for additional material for second printing of her Dawn price and guidebook; especially interested in international items, promotions, store displays.

Dealers

DeannaOverforf
D's Dolls
4 Lakeridge Dr.
Adrian, MI 49221
ph: 517-264-1862
fax: 517-264-1863
jrodjc@msn.com
http://www.dsdolls.com
An Internet store specializing in vintage Barbie, Dawn and Liddle Kiddles dolls, clothes and all other accessories.

Experts

Joedi Johnson
P.O. Box 565
Billings, MT 59103
ph: 406-248-4875
fax: 407-248-4875
Joedi@dawndollsplus.com
http://www.dawndollsplus.com
Author of "Dawn & Her World: A Collector's Identification & Price Guide."

Ginny

Clubs/Associations

Ginny Doll Club
Newsletter: Ginny Doll Journal
987 Wakefield Dr.
P.O. Box 756
Oakdale, CA 95361
ph: 877-848-0300 or 209-848-0300
fax: 209-848-4423
info@voguedolls.com
http://www.voguedolls.com
Club sponsored by the manufacturer, Vogue Doll Co.

Experts

Jeanne Niswonger
305 West Beacon Rd.
Lakeland, FL 33803-7248
ph: 863-682-8484
Author of "That Doll, Ginny," "The Ginny Doll Family," and "Ginny and Vogue Dolls."

Golliwoggs

Clubs/Associations

Juliet Savage
International Golliwogg Collectors Club
Newsletter: IGCC Newsletter
P.O. Box 612
Woodstock, NY 12498
ph: 914-679-5769
fax: 914-679-5769
ohgolli@aol.com
http://www.teddybears.com/golliwog

Collectors

Beth B. Savino
Westgate Village
3301 West Central Ave.
Toledo, OH 43606
ph: 419-531-2839 or 800-862-8697
fax: 419-531-2730
info@toystorenet.com
http://www.toystorenet.com
Golliwoggs are black characters dolls based on a series of British children's

books originating in 1895 and written by American authoress Florence Upton.

Half

Collectors

Sharon Wilkins
1105 Burnham St.
Cocoa, FL 32922-6836
ph: 321-631-0102
paulinescoll@bellsouth.net
Wants half dolls; porcelain half dolls decorated a lady's dresser in the '20s and '30s.

Iaulanda's

Experts

Jamie Saloff
P.O. Box 339
Edinboro, PA 16412
ph: 814-734-5189
fax: 814-734-7162
jlsaloff@erie.net
http://www.saloff.com/Iaulandas
Daughter of Iaulanda Turner Downey, creator of Iaulanda's Storyteller Dolls (high quality, handcrafted felt dolls made in the 1960s-'70s for the Christmas tree.)

Ideal Toy Co.

Collectors

Elizabeth Arnold
205 Penns Lane
Malvern, PA 19355
ph: 610-647-8468
Wants to buy Saucey Walker dolls by Ideal.

Experts

Judith Izen
Dolls of Our Childhood
P.O. Box 623
Lexington, MA 02420
jizen@rcn.com
http://www.dollsofourchildhood.com
Noted doll historian; has books on several American doll companies including Ideal and Vogue; her book on American character dolls includes Tiny Tears, Betsy McCall, Tressy, Toodles, Sweet Sue, Toni and the Whimseys.

Beth Gunther
BethEllenGA@aol.com
http://expage.com/page/69idealcrissy
Author of "Crissy Doll and Her Friends."

Kewpie

(see also ROSE O'NEILL COLLECTIBLES)

Clubs/Associations

Len Witkowski
International Rose O'Neill Club
P.O. Box 61
Golden, CO 80402-0061
ph: 303-273-5763 or 303-908-5295
agdc1@aol.com

Collectors

Kitty Watson
201 Dena Dr.
Guthrie, OK 73044-9043
ph: 405-282-2287
Wants to buy Kewpies, Scootles, and Rose O'Neill items, preferably "action" bisque, and metal pieces, signed.

Tadg Galleran
2911 4th St., #112
Santa Monica, CA 90405
ph: 310-314-0402
tadggalleran@hotmail.com
Wants to buy German bisque Kewpies - the "action" pieces such as Kewpie gardener, Kewpie with dog, Kewpie soldier; must be in excellent original condition; also wants Kewpies made of celluloids and Kewpie tea sets.

Dealers

Wilma Schiebel
No Place Like Home Collectibles
2200 S. Hwy 62-65
Harrison, AR 72601
ph: 870-741-9494
nplhc@alltel.net
Wants anything related to Kewpies: dolls, bells, plates, paper, puzzles, jewelry, figurines, old postcards, fabric, signs, advertisements, etc.

Liddle Kiddles

Clubs/Associations

Laura Miller
Liddle Kiddles Klub
Newsletter: Liddle Kiddles Klub Newsletter
3639 Fourth Ave.
La Crescenta, CA 91214-2441
A bi-monthly newsletter all about Liddle Kiddles (dolls by Mattel 1966-1971); classifieds; send SASE for more information or $3 for sample newsletter.

Collectors

Jill Salerno
245 Sunnyridge Ave., Unit #41
Fairfield, CT 06430-4646
ph: 203-332-1469
Wants to buy Liddle Kiddles by Mattel; old stock, mint on card, or childhood collections.

Linda Strumski
74 Pierpont RD E-7
Waterbury, CT 06705-3847
ph: 203-757-8103
JSmicro633@aol.com
Collector wants to buy Liddle Kiddles dolls, accessories, cases, and related paper items.

Joedi Johnson
P.O. Box 565
Billings, MT 59103
ph: 406-248-4875
fax: 407-248-4875
Joedi@dawndollsplus.com
http://www.dawndollsplus.com
Buying Kiddle collections, especially

coloring books, riddle books, puzzles, vinyl wallet, magic slate and paper dolls; also buying Mattel Upsy Downsy dolls, accessories and books.

Dealers

Deanna Overforf
D's Dolls
4 Lakeridge Dr.
Adrian, MI 49221
ph: 517-264-1862
fax: 517-264-1863
jrodjc@msn.com
http://www.dsdolls.com
An Internet store specializing in vintage Barbie, Dawn and Liddle Kiddles dolls, clothes and all other accessories.

Experts

Paris Langford
Kollecting Kiddles
415 Dodge Ave.
Jefferson, LA 70121-3311
ph: 504-733-0676 or 504-733-0676
bbean415@aol.com
Buy, sell, trade Liddle Kiddles by Mattel and other small dolls from '60s to '70s; send SASE for current list of offerings; author of "Liddle Kiddles Identification and Value Guide," (Collector Books, 1995).

Nisbet

Clubs/Associations

Howard & Sarah Wade
Peggy Nisbet International Collectors' Society
Newsletter: PNICS Newsletter
P.O. Box 325
Orrville, OH 44667-0325
ph: 330-682-8551
fax: 330-682-3655
RBCollectr@aol.com
Clearinghouse for information about Peggy Nisbet portrait and costume dolls and Nisbet bears from Britain, both primary and secondary markets.

Man./Prod./Dist.

Howard & Sarah Wade
Nisbet Dolls & Bears
P.O. Box 325
Orrville, OH 44667-0325
ph: 330-682-8551
fax: 330-682-3655
RBCollectr@aol.com
US distributor for Peggy Nisbet dolls and Nisbet bears from Britain.

Paper

(see also PAPER COLLECTIBLES)

Clubs/Associations

Jenny R. Taliadoros
Original Paper Doll Artists Guild, The
Magazine: OPDAG's Paper Doll Studio News
P.O. Box 14
Kingfield, ME 04947-0014
ph: 207-265-2500
fax: 207-265-2500
info@opdag.com
http://www.opdag.com
An organization of paper doll enthusiasts to promote the PD hobby; magazine has PD news, how-tos, paper dolls, artist features, etc.

Collectors

Loretta Willis
808 Lee Ave.
Tifton, GA 31794-4134
Deals with many paper doll and doll collectors who collect PD's as a hobby; wants PD movie stars, nostalgia, new & old for collection.

Lois Helen Brown
154 W. 500 S
Peru, IN 46970-7621
ph: 765-473-3983
Wants cut or uncut paper dolls dating from the 1930s through 1960s.

Virginia Crossley
685 Canyon Rd.
Rochester, MI 48306-2621
ph: 248-651-3203
Wants pre-1960 uncut paper dolls.

Jerry Brand
10612 W. 101st Terr.
Shawnee Mission, KS 66214-2528
ph: 913-888-4739
brandjjerryl@aol.com
Wants to buy pre-1970 paperdolls, cut or uncut; no magazines; also wants Little Golden Books with paperdolls and older Katy Keen comics with paperdolls in them.

Beverly Wethington
P.O. Box 871189
Wasilla, AK 99687-1189
ph: 907-745-4334

Dealers

Carolyn Thompson
P.O. Box 157
Orleans, MA 02653
ph: 508-896-6748

Jo Ann Reisler
360 Glyndon St., NE
Vienna, VA 22180-3537
ph: 703-938-2967
fax: 703-938-9057
email@joannreisler.com
http://www.joannreisler.com
Wants to buy paper dolls, fine and unusual children's, illustrated books, and illustrative art; issues about four color catalogs per year with almost all items in stock illustrated; sample catalog for $15.

R.H. Stevens
R.H. Stevens Antiques
17838 South East Hwy. 452
Umatilla, FL 32784
ph: 352-821-3276
http://www.opdag.com/Stevens.html
Paper dolls wanted: cut or uncut; send $1 for list.

Judy M. Johnson
Judy's Place
115 Kreiger Dr.
P.O. Box 216
Skandia, MI 49885-0176
ph: 906-942-7865
fax: 906-942-7865
Judysplc@aol.com
http://www.papergoodies.com
Author/artist artist buys, sells, collects & designs paper dolls & Magicloth dolls; wants paper dolls, especially original art and unique or comic paper dolls; also buys vintage paper dolls; send 2 first class stamps for catalog (NOT SASE).

Johana Gast Anderton
6408 North Flora
Kansas City, MO 64118-3609
ph: 816-468-0558
Specializes in original & antique paper dolls and other paper collectibles, antique dolls and teddy bears, original doll clothes, patterns; lecturer, author, paper doll artist; updated sales list available via email.

Kim Brecklein
Brecklein Paper Miniatures
7949 S. 161st W. Ave.
Sapulpa, OK 74066
ph: 918-224-7307 or 918-595-7522
kim@breckpaperdoll.com
http://www.breckpaperdoll.com
Collects and deals in paper doll ladies and children with lavish historically accurate costumes from Renaissance, Victorian, Edwardian eras plus from the 1920s through 1950s.

Experts

Marta Krebs
3116 Gracefield Rd., #412
Silver Spring, MD 20904
ph: 301-572-5004
rkrebs@erols.com
Buys and sells paper dolls; publisher of former "Paper Doll Update" newsletter - back issues available; author of "Royalty of Paper Dolls," "Advertising Paper Dolls," and several Dover books.

Mary Young
P.O. Box 9244
Dayton, OH 45409-9244
Buys, sells and specializes in paper dolls; welcomes questions; author of "Paper Dolls & Their Artists," "Magazine Paper Dolls" with price guide, and other books.

Emma Terry
P.O. Box 807
Vivian, LA 71082-0807
Publisher of the quarterly "Paper Doll News" newsletter.

Denis C. Jackson
P.O. Box 6433
Kingman, AZ 86401
ticn@olypen.com
http://www.olypen.com/ticn
Author of "The Price & Identification Guide to Old Magazine Paperdolls," 3rd Edition; with a strong focus on the golden age of paper, 'teens through the 1960s; send LSASE for information.

Periodicals

Marilyn Henry, Ed.
Magazine: Paper Doll Review
P.O. Box 14
Kingfield, ME 04947-0014
ph: 207-265-2500
fax: 207-265-2500
info@paperdollreview.com
http://www.paperdollreview.com
Published quarterly; a paper doll printed in color in each issue; lots of paper doll photos, and articles about paper dolls and related items; send LSASE for subscription information.

Arlene Del Fava
Newsletter: Now & Then
67-40 Yellowstone Blvd.
Forest Hills, NY 11375-2614
Newsletter published three times a year; covers some new but mostly nostalgic paper dolls and their times; about 30 pages; plus small auction.

Loretta Willis
Newsletter: Loretta's Place Paper Doll Newsletter
808 Lee Ave.
Tifton, GA 31794-4134
Focuses on original artists' paper dolls and features artists work and paper dolls in each issue; also old paper dolls; 4 issues ("in color" paper doll on front page) per year for $15.

Loretta Willis
Newsletter: Yesterday's Paper Dolls
808 Lee Ave.
Tifton, GA 31794-4134
Identification guide newsletter that illustrates, identifies, and prices old nostalgic paper dolls; 4 issues per year for $12.

Emma Terry
Newsletter: Paper Doll News
P.O. Box 807
Vivian, LA 71082-0807
A quarterly newsletter sharing news of the paper doll world; review paper dolls and share all known information regarding paper dolls; promote paper doll artists and share addresses in every issue of "Paper Doll News."

Nan Moorehead
Newsletter: Golden Opportunities: Paper Doll & Toy Quarterly
P.O. Box 252
Golden, CO 80402-0252
Concentrates on antique and collectible paper dolls.

Sharon Hill
Newsletter: Cornerstone Paper Doll Journal
2216 S. Autumn Ln.
Diamond Bar, CA 91789

Lorna Thomopoulos
Newsletter: Paperdoll Circle, The
28 Ferndown Gardens
Cobham, Surrey KT11 2BH U.K.
fax: 01932 866275
currie.thomopoulos@talk21.com
A 36-page newsletter published three times a year; has a cover and original paperdoll in full color; has a European slant but is for enthusiasts worldwide.

Lorna Currie Thomopoulos
Newsletter: Paperdoll Circle, The
28 Ferndown Gdns
Cobham, Surrey Kt11 2BH U.K.
ph: 01932 866274
fax: 01932 866274
currie.thomopoulos@talk21.com
The only British paperdoll newsletter; in print for 18 years; 36-page publication includes color in its format and covers all things paperdoll, particularly European; three times per year.

Pincushion
Dealers

Linda Gibbs
Heirloom Keepsakes
10380 Miranda Ave.
Buena Park, CA 90620-4447
ph: 714-827-6488
Will consider any vintage type pincushion 1/2 dolls.

Raggedy Ann & Andy
Collectors

Kathleen Ray
28 Kathy Ann Rd.
Bass River, MA 02664
ph: 508-394-9668
raggedy@capecod.net
Wants Raggedy Ann books and ephemera.

Katherine James
487 Oak Ridge Rd.
Dyersburg, TN 38024-6511
ph: 901-286-2025
Serious Raggedy Ann and Raggedy Andy collector.

Dealers

Dawn Herlocher
Dawn's Dolls
Maple Ave.
Mackeyville, PA 17750-0000
ph: 570-726-6458
Expert in Raggedy Ann & Andy dolls.

Gwen Daniel
18 Belleau Lake Ct.
O Fallon, MO 63366-3144
ph: 636-978-3190
SimGirl200@aol.com
Wants Raggedy Ann & Andy's, books and related items; also vintage teddy bears, Lulu & Tubby, Nancy & Sluggo, Howdy Doody and early Barbie.

Internet Resources

Charles & Cheryl Platt
Raggedy Ann & Andy Homepage
131 Northridge Dr.
Macon, GA 31220
ph: 478-757-0001
fax: 478-757-1200
charles@raggedyland.com
http://www.raggedyland.com
Contains everything Raggedy Ann & Andy on the Web: artwork, doll dealers, stamps, Raggedy Ann Festival, costumes, and catalog items.

Museums/Libraries

Johnny Gruelle Raggedy Ann & Andy Museum
Newsletter: Heart of the Matter, The
P.O. Box 183
110 East Main Sgt.
Arcola, IL 61910
ph: 217-268-4908
tom@raggedyann-museum.org
http://www.raggedyann-museum.org
Preserves the life and times of Johnny Gruelle, creator of Raggedy Ann and Andy; offers a positive educational experience for children as well as collectors.

Periodicals

Rankin Publishing Co.
Newsletter: Rags
118 E. Main
P.O. Box 0130
Arcola, IL 61910-0130
ph: 217-268-4959
fax: 217-268-4815
DRankin125@aol.com
http://www.raggedyland.com/rags.htm
A quarterly newsletter devoted to the creations of Johnny Gruelle; ads, articles, photos, etc. for Raggedy Ann and other cloth dolls.

Strawberry Shortcake
Clubs/Associations

Peggy Jimenez
Strawberry Shortcake Collectors' Club
Newsletter: Berry-Bits
1409 72nd St.
North Bergen, NJ 07047-3827
ph: 201-868-7334

Periodicals

Jennifer Bowles
Doll Patch, The
Newsletter: Strawberryland Gazette
138 E. Main Cross
Greenville, KY 42345
ph: 502-338-5213 or 502-338-4318
dollnutt@aol.com
http://strawberrybonkers.com
A bi-monthly newsletter for Strawberry Shortcake collectors; free ads; color photos.

Toni

Clubs/Associations

Newsletter: Toni Dolls Newsletter
7431-A LeMunyan Rd.
Addison, NY 14801

Collectors

Cheryl & Nick Shimp
Nick & Cheryl's Toy Collectors
749 Nottingham Lane
Crystal Lake, IL 60014
ph: 815-455-3308
ncshimp@dls.net
Buys, sells, trades, collects and appraises vintage Barbie dolls, fashions, accessories and structures; also collects Toni dolls and clothes; appraises various vintage dolls from the 1940s through the 1970s.

Dealers

Cheryl & Nick Shimp
Nick & Cheryl's Toy Collectors
749 Nottingham Lane
Crystal Lake, IL 60014
ph: 815-455-3308
ncshimp@dls.net
Buys, sells, trades, collects and appraises vintage Barbie dolls, fashions, accessories and structures; also collects Toni dolls and clothes; appraises various vintage dolls from the 1940s through the 1970s.

Vogue

Collectors

Victoria Broadhurst
P.O. Box 4078
Dana Point, CA 92629
mrscdrew@aol.com
Wants to buy Vogue dolls and accessories.

Experts

Judith Izen
P.O. Box 623
Lexington, MA 02420
jizen@rcn.com
http://www.dollsofourchildhood.com
Co-author with Carol Stover of "Vogue Dolls" (1998), values updated 2000; covers all Vogue dolls including Ginny, Jill, Ginnette, Li'l Imp, Baby Dear, Toddles, Jeff, Jan, etc. and their children; send SASE for more information.

Judith Izen
Dolls of Our Childhood
P.O. Box 623
Lexington, MA 02420
jizen@rcn.com
http://www.dollsofourchildhood.com
Co-author with Carol Stover of "Vogue Dolls" (1998); covers all Vogue dolls including Ginny, Jill, Ginnette, Li'l Imp, Baby Dear, Toddles, Jeff, Jan, etc. and their children; send SASE for more information.

DOLPHINS

(see WHALES)

DOORKNOBS

(see also HARDWARE; LOCKS)

Book Sellers

Maudie L. Eastwood
Antique Doorknob Publishing Company
17300 135th Ave. NW, #103
P.O. Box 2609
Woodinville, WA 98072
ph: 206-483-5848
Books about doorknobs and other builders' hardware.

Clubs/Associations

Rich Kennedy, Sec.
Antique Doorknob Collectors of America, The
Newsletter: Doorknob Collector, The
P.O. Box 31
Chatham, NJ 07928-0031
ph: 973-635-6338
fax: 973-635-6993
knobnews@aol.com
http://www.antiquedoorknobs.org
A club for doorknob and related hardware collectors and enthusiasts; conventions, seminars, banquets, trading sessions.

Collectors

Richard C. Hubbard
162 Poplar Ave.
Hackensack, NJ 07601
ph: 201-342-1274
DoorKnobID@aol.com
Wants to buy old doorknobs; historical, figural or emblematic knobs; please describe and price.

Charles W. Wardell
P.O. Box 195
Trinity, NC 27370-0195
ph: 336-434-1145
Wants ornate doorknobs, escutcheon plates, store door handles, push plates, door knockers, doorbells, mail slots, etc.; 1870-1920.

Loretta & Raymond Nemec
P.O. Box 126
Eola, IL 60519-0126
ph: 630-357-2381
fax: 630-357-2391
dornoblady@aol.com

Dealers

H. Weber & Jill Wilson
WebWilson.com
P.O. Box 506
Portsmouth, RI 02871
ph: 800-508-0022
fax: 401-683-1644
hww@webwilson.com
http://www.webwilson.com
Buys and sells vintage door hardware, especially doorknobs; also wants vintage plumbing items.

Marvin & Donna Stewart
Mardon Collectibles
P.O. Box 6385
Oceanside, CA 92052
mardon_collect@yahoo.com
Collects, buys and sells antique doorknobs.

Experts

Maudie L. Eastwood
Antique Doorknob Publishing Company
17300 135th Ave. NW, #103
P.O. Box 2609
Woodinville, WA 98072
ph: 206-483-5848
Researcher, expert, collector and consultant specializing in antique builders hardware and author of books on early American door and other builders hardware.

DOORKNOCKERS

Dealers

John & Nancy Smith
American Sampler
P.O. Box 371
Barnesville, MD 20838-0371
ph: 301-972-6250
Wants cast iron doorstops, figural bottle openers, doorknockers, paperweights, banks, bookends, etc.

DOORSTOPS

(see also CAST IRON ITEMS)

Auction Services

Bertoia Auctions
2141 DeMarco Dr.
Vineland, NJ 08360
ph: 856-692-1881
fax: 856-692-8697
bill@bertoiaauctions.com
http://www.bertoiaauctions.com
Specializing in the auctioning of antique toys, banks, trains, and doorstops; offers online auctions.

Collectors

Bill Price
Paperweight Potentate of Pittsburgh, The
P.O. Box 82501
Pittsburgh, PA 15218-0501
ph: 412-351-5297
fax: 724-271-4329
paperwghts@aol.com
Wants to buy glass paperweights advertising businesses or with people's portraits; also wants glass doorstops advertising businesses or with people's portraits.

Dealers

John & Nancy Smith
American Sampler
P.O. Box 371
Barnesville, MD 20838-0371
ph: 301-972-6250
Wants cast iron doorstops, figural bottle openers, doorknockers, paperweights, banks, bookends, etc.

Experts

Jeanne Bertoia
2141 DeMarco Dr.
Vineland, NJ 08360
ph: 856-692-1881
fax: 856-692-8697
bill@bertoiaauctions.com
Collector and dealer of cast iron figural doorstops; wants to buy painted cast iron doorstops; author of "Doorstop Identification & Values."

Craig Dinner
P.O. Box 4399
Long Island City, NY 11104-0399
ph: 718-729-3850
ferrouswheel123@aol.com
Advisor to "Warman's Antiques & Collectibles Price Guide."

DR. SEUSS COLLECTIBLES

Collectors

Michael Gessel
P.O. Box 748
Arlington, VA 22216-0748
ph: 703-524-0462
mgessel@cheerful.com
Wants Dr. Seuss books, pamphlets, posters, advertising, ephemera, original illustrations, anything related to Dr. Seuss.

Dealers

Helen & Marc Younger
Aleph-Bet Books, Inc.
85 Old Mill River Rd.
Pound Ridge, NY 10576
ph: 914-764-7410
fax: 914-764-1356
helen@alephbet.com
http://www.alephbet.com
Specializing in fine first editions of collectible and rare children's and illustrated books; always interested in buying books in fine condition; business established in 1978.

Daniel Hirsch
Daniel Hirsch - Fine & Rare Books
P.O. Box 5096
Chapel Hill, NC 27514
ph: 919-542-1816
fax: 919-542-1817
rhirsch@interserv.com
http://rarechildrensbooks.homestead.com/
  home.html
  *Wants Dr. Seuss: posters, books,
  dolls, etc.; also wants fairy tale
  books, pop-ups, movable books,
  panoramas and first editions; Hans
  Christian Andersen, Grimm, Perrault,
  Madame D'Aulnoy, Chris Van
  Allsburg, Maurice Sendak, and others.*

DRAMA

(see PERFORMING ARTS)

DRAWINGS

(see ART; PRINTS)

DRESSER ITEMS

(see also BUTTON HOOKS;
CLOTHING & ACCESSORIES,
Vintage; COMPACTS; COMBS &
HAIR ACCESSORIES)

Dealers

Judith Armistead
Doll Works, The
P.O. Box 195
Lynnfield, MA 01940-0195
ph: 781-334-5577
judy@thedollworks.net
http://www.TheDollWorks.net
  *Selling antique porcelain dresser
  boxes dating from 1860s to 1920s.*

Kathy Burch
Tri-State Antique Center
47 W. Pike
Canonsburg, PA 15317
ph: 724-745-9116
fax: 412-291-1367
kathy&ed@tri-stateantiques.com
http://tri-stateantiques.com
  *Specializes in lady's beaded and mesh
  purses, Lucite purses, chatelaines,
  compacts, and other ladies vanity
  items.*

Dawn Kinnaman
Vanity Treasures
303 W. Brown St.
Knightstown, IN 46148
ph: 765-345-7387
dawn@vanity-treasures.com
http://www.vanity-treasures.com
  *Buys and sells ladies' compacts, rouge
  powders & tins, talcum powders,
  lipsticks & holders, perfume bottles,
  hair net envelopes, hair pin cards,
  hosiery/stockings boxes, vanity bags,
  etc.*

Hatpins & Hatpin Holders

Clubs/Associations

Lillian Schoephoerster
International Club for Collectors of
  Hatpins & Hatpin Holders
Newsletter: Points
1013 Medhurst Rd.
Columbus, OH 43220
ph: 614-451-7368
  *For collectors of hatpins and hatpin
  holders; also publishes an annual 32-
  page Pictorial Journal.*

Virginia J. Woodbury
American Hatpin Society
Newsletter: American Hatpin Society
  Newsletter
20 Montecillo Dr.
Rolling Hills Estates, CA 90274-4249
ph: 310-326-2196
hatpnginia@aol.com
http://www.collectoronline.com/AHS
  *A society for hatpin & hatpin holder
  collectors and enthusiasts; meetings
  held quarterly; newsletter published
  quarterly.*

Hatpin Society of Great Britain, The
P.O. Box 110
Cheadle, Cheshire SK8 1GG U.K.
enquiries@hatpinsociety.org.uk
http://www.hatpinsociety.org.uk
  *For collectors of hatpins - the once
  fashionable piece of jewelry dating
  from the Victorian era through to the
  1950s.*

Collectors

Lillian Schoephoerster
1013 Medhurst Rd.
Columbus, OH 43220
ph: 614-451-7368

Dealers

Debbie Woolley
Favorite Past-Times Antiques
6 Main Hill
Bridgton, ME 04009
ph: 207-647-4486
info@maine-antiques.com
http://www.maine-antiques.com/fpt/Index
  *Dealing in authentic hatpins from
  simple to elaborate; send email to be
  put on email advance notice of new
  hatpin items.*

Gail & John Dunn
P.O. Box 234
Waterville, OH 43566
ph: 419-878-9515
  *Buys and sells vintage purses and
  hatpins.*

Diane Richardson
Gold Hatpin, The
125 N. Marion St.
Oak Park, IL 60301-1087
ph: 708-848-3247 or 708-445-0610
goldhatpin@comcast.net
  *Wants all types hatpins & holders:
  Satsuma, vanity, enameled, figural,
  fancy & the unusual; no repros.*

Internet Resources

Frankie
Hatpin Resource Page for Collectors
frankie854@aol.com
http://members.aol.com/frankie854
  *Great resource with lots of informa-
  tion and links for hatpin collectors.*

Linda Pullen
Thimbles, Needlework Tools & Hatpins
U.K.
linda.pullen@virgin.net
http://freespace.virgin.net/linda.pullen/
  homepage.htm
  *Web site is a pictorial tour of hatpins,
  hatpin holders, thimbles, needlework
  tools and ladies compacts; recommended reading and online book store;
  makers and their marks; clubs and
  links to other sites.*

DRUM & BUGLE CORPS

Collectors

Lawrence Hogan
36457 N. 83
Lake Villa, IL 60046
ph: 847-356-2875
  *Wants Drum & Bugle Corps records,
  tapes, videos and memorabilia.*

DUCK CALLS

(see SPORTING COLLECTIBLES,
Game Calls)

DUCK DECOYS

(see DECOYS, Waterfowl)

Here are some tips when contacting someone who is listed in this book:

When requesting information about a particular item, include a description (material, dimensions, maker's mark, model number, etc.) and a photo, sketch, digital image or photocopy of the item in question.

Always ask if there are charges for samples or for the services that you are requesting.

When corresponding by letter, please be sure to include a Large (#10 business size) Self-Addressed and Stamped Envelope (LSASE) if requesting a reply or the return of photographs.

Never call collect unless otherwise directed. When calling, be considerate of time zone differences and always ask if the party you are calling has time to talk. When leaving an answering machine message, always instruct the party to call you back collect.

EASTER COLLECTIBLES

(see HOLIDAY COLLECTIBLES;
RUSSIAN ITEMS, Faberge)

ECCLESIASTICAL ITEMS

(see RELIGIOUS COLLECTIBLES)

EDGED WEAPONS

(see also ARMS & ARMOR; NATIVE
AMERICAN; BAYONETS; SWORDS;
KNIVES; MILITARIA)

Appraisers

Richard Koster
Personal Property Consultant
P.O. Box 987
Parker, CO 80134
ph: 303-840-1565
fax: 303-841-6687
swordcoll@attbi.com
*Specializes in collecting edged
weapons: American swords, knives,
bayonets, European hunting and
forestry swords, Swiss swords; also
appraises all types and origins of
edged weapons.*

Auction Services

SoldUSA.com
1418 Industrial Dr., Box 11
Matthews, NC 28105
ph: 704-815-1500
fax: 704-844-6436
support@soldusa.com
http://www.soldusa.com
*Specializes in hunting and fishing
collectibles, especially firearms; does
online appraisals for
www.CollectingChannel.com's Ask the
Appraiser online appraisal service.*

Clubs/Associations

Minnesota Weapons Collectors
Association
P.O. Box 662
Hopkins, MN 55343
ph: 612-721-8976
fax: 612-721-8976
info@mwca.org
http://www.mwca.org
*For arms collectors: antique arms,
edged weapons, modern day arms,
ammunition, accessories, accouterments.*

Collectors

Hank McGonagle
26 Broad St.
Newburyport, MA 01950-2103
ph: 978-462-2354
saber12@mediaone.net
*Seeking edged weapons and Japanese
swords.*

Jim Manteris
1613 Barnard Way
Bowling Green, KY 42103
ph: 270-846-4931
manteris@insightbb.com
*Specializes in ethnographic weapons
from Indonesia, Philippines, India,
Africa, any type of club; wants police
clubs, saps, billy clubs, blackjacks,
brass knuckles, and old knives; also
wants African and Asian weapons.*

Richard Koster
P.O. Box 987
Parker, CO 80134
ph: 303-840-1565
fax: 303-841-6687
swordcoll@attbi.com
*Specializes in collecting edged
weapons: American swords, knives,
bayonets, European hunting and
forestry swords, Swiss swords; also
appraises all types and origins of
edged weapons.*

John S. Fischer
P.O. Box 47
Van Nuys, CA 91408
jsfischer1@aol.com
*Wants British and American edged
weapons from WWI and WWII; no
bayonets, please; state description,
price and phone number.*

Dealers

David L. Hartline
P.O. Box 775
Columbus, OH 43085-0775
fax: 614-760-5427
*Buys and sells edged weapons; has
large library and over 30 years
experience; specialty is pre-1920
Bowie knives; has had many articles
published on edge weapons; answers
every letter; does appraisals and will
authenticate.*

Robert B. Miller
LionGate Arms & Armour, Inc.
P.O. Box 14952
Scottsdale, AZ 85267
ph: 480-948-6348
hussar@antiquesswords.com
http://www.antiquesswords.com
*Buys and sells fine antique edged
weapons and armour; specializes in
European swords.*

Experts

Daniel Morrison
11 Maple Ave.
Demarest, NJ 07627
ph: 201-784-8486
fax: 201-768-4957
djmconsult@aol.com
Over 30 years of collecting, buying,

*selling military bayonets and knives;
specializing in US pieces; knowledgeable for identification and valuation;
also interested in buying one or more
pieces.*

Internet Resources

Kevin Carney
Military Collectors Consortium, The
154A Locust Ave.
Fairmont, WV 26554
ph: 304-367-9612
fax: 304-416-2811
CarneyK@labyrinth.net
http://www.lee-enfield.com
*Global resource for collectors of
military firearms, edged weapons, and
militaria from 1750-1970; appraisal,
brokerage, and consulting services
relating to arms and militaria;
publishes monthly "Military
Collectors Journal" online.*

German

Collectors

Greg Souchik
P.O. Box 161
Custer City, PA 16725-0161
ph: 814-362-2642
fax: 814-362-7356
Mg34@mg34.com
http://www.mg34.com
*Wants to buy all WWII German and
Japanese swords and daggers.*

Dealers

Thomas T. Wittmann
Wittmann Antique Militaria
P.O. Box 350
Moorestown, NJ 08057
ph: 856-866-8733 or 856-231-0323
fax: 856-235-4954
TWittm350@aol.com
http://www.wwiidaggers.com
*Buys and sells edged weapons:
daggers, swords and certain bayonets;
specializing in German 3rd Reich or
Imperial period weapons; author of
"Exploring the Dress Daggers of the
German Army," "German Luftwaffe,"
and other books.*

Experts

Thomas T. Wittmann
Wittmann Antique Militaria
P.O. Box 350
Moorestown, NJ 08057
ph: 856-866-8733 or 856-231-0323
fax: 856-235-4954
TWittm350@aol.com
http://www.wwiidaggers.com
*Buys and sells edged weapons:
daggers, swords and certain bayonets;
specializing in German 3rd Reich or
Imperial period weapons; author of
"Exploring the Dress Daggers of the
German Army," "German Luftwaffe,"
and other books.*

LTC(Ret) Thomas M. Johnson
Johnson Reference Books & Militaria
403 Chatham Square Office Park
Fredericksburg, VA 22405
ph: 540-373-9150 or 540-371-2665
fax: 540-373-0087
ww2daggers@aol.com
http://www.johnsonreferencebooks.com
*Wants to buy German War booty;
specific interest is in edged weapons
(dress swords, daggers, bayonets and
other quality items); author of
eighteen books about Imperial and
Third Reich German edged weapons
and militaria.*

EDUCATIONAL TOYS

(see TOYS, Construction Sets)

EGGCUPS

Clubs/Associations

Dr. Joan M. George
Eggcup Collectors Club
Newsletter: Eggcup Collectors' Corner
67 Stevens Ave.
Old Bridge, NJ 08857-2244
ph: 732-679-8924
fax: 732-679-6102
drjgeorge@nac.net
*A quarterly newsletter for eggcup
collectors; buy, sell, trade ads; share
information, review books, meetings of
collectors arranged.*

Sue Wright
Egg Cup Collectors' Club of Great
Britain
Newsletter: Egg Cup World
Bryn Hywel, Llangranog Rd.
Coed Y Bryn
Llandysul, Ceredigion, Wales SA44 5JL
U.K.
suewright@suecol.freeserve.co.uk
http://www.eggcupworld.co.uk
*About 500 members who are collectors
of eggcups.*

EIFFEL TOWER

(see SOUVENIR &
COMMEMORATIVE ITEMS, Buildings
[Eiffel Tower])

ELECTRICITY RELATED ITEMS

(see also AUDIO-VISUAL; CLOCKS,
Electric; COIN-OPERATED
MACHINES; FANS, Mechanical;
INSULATORS; KITCHEN
COLLECTIBLES; LAMPS &
LIGHTING; LIGHT BULBS;
MODERNISM; RADIOS;
TELEGRAPH ITEMS; TELEVISIONS;
TOASTERS, Electric; VACUUM
CLEANERS; WASHING MACHINES)

Clubs/Associations

Harry Goldman
Tesla Coil Builders' Association
Newsletter: TCBA News
3 Amy Lane
Queensbury, NY 2804-9432
ph: 518-792-1003
stcole@deltanet.com
http://www.eskimo.com/~billb/tesla/
tcba.html
*TCBA is a clearinghouse on the
history of electricity, wireless,
electrotherapy, etc.; acts as
consultants for high voltage historical
equipment.*

Collectors

Dean Thatcher
deanthatcher@yahoo.com
http://www.iavalley.cc.ia.us/~thatcher
*Collector of generators, motors,
meters, gauges, etc.*

Harvey Greenspan
15 Chatham Circle
Brookline, MA 02146
ph: 617-566-4191
*Wants early electric motors,
generators, dynamos and other pre-
1900 electrical/mechanical instruments
for science, industry, business.*

Steve Leffel
1790 Edison St.
Green Bay, WI 54302
fax: 414-465-6505
steve97979@yahoo.com
*Wants to buy tube testers and other
used test equipment.*

C. T. Little
183 Rainbow Dr., #8348
Livingston, TX 77399-1083
ladylight2000@yahoo.com
*Wants memorabilia relating to
electrical inventors such as Edison,
Westinghouse and Tesla.*

Mike's Electric Stuff
U.K.
mike@electricstuff.co.uk
http://www.electricstuff.co.uk
*Collector of electric items: valves, arc
rectifiers, photoelectric cells, Geisler
tubes, neon lamps, Tesla coils, etc.*

Dealers

Jim & Felicia Kreuzer
New Wireless Pioneers
1541 Bronson Rd.
Grand Island, NY 14072
ph: 716-773-4999
fax: 716-773-5757
wireless@pce.net
http://www.marconi-wireless.com
*Buys and sells 1850-1950 books,
catalogs, magazines, autographs, and
other literature dealing with early
radio, telegraph, wireless, pre-1940
television, medical, telegraphy, early
computers, television, X-ray and
electricity.*

Internet Resources

David Dahle
dave_d@watthourmeters.com
http://www.watthourmeters.com
*Meter collector with Web site designed
for those interested in electrical meters
or other antique electrical equipment.*

Museums/Libraries

Edison National Historic Site
Main St. at Lakeside Ave.
West Orange, NJ 07052
ph: 973-736-0550
fax: 973-736-8496
EDIS_Webmaster@nps.gov
http://www.nps.gov/edis/home.htm
*A museum with exhibits in all fields of
Edison's contributions.*

National Museum of American History
14th & Constitution Ave. NW
Washington, DC 20560
ph: 202-357-2700
webmaster@si.edu
http://www.si.edu/organiza/museums/
nmah/nmah.htm
*The most extensive research facility in
the US for electric relics; trade
catalogs, electric razors, refrigerators, TV's, radios, etc.*

Edison - Ford Winter Estates
2350 McGregor Blvd.
Fort Myers, FL 33901
ph: 941-334-7419
estateinfo@cityftmyers.com
http://www.edison-ford-estate.com
*Contains Edison-related displays:
appliances, early bulbs, and scientific
equipment.*

Laurence J. Russell, Curator
Thomas Edison Birthplace Museum
9 Edison Dr.
P.O. Box 451
Milan, OH 44846-0451
ph: 419-499-2135
fax: 419-499-3241
rwheeler@accnorwalk.com
http://www.tomedison.org
*An Edison exhibit featuring
phonographs, lamps, fans, photos,
and other items related to Thomas
Edison.*

Bakken Library & Museum, The
3537 Zenith Ave. South
Minneapolis, MN 55416
ph: 612-927-6508
fax: 612-927-7265
webmaster@thebakken.org
http://www.bakkenmuseum.org
*Collects medical electricity items (no
violet rays needed); over 2,000
artifacts relating to the historical role
of electricity in life; also a collection
of 11,000 rare books.*

Appliances

Clubs/Associations

Jack Santoro
Old Appliance Club, The
Magazine: Old Road Home, The
P.O. Box 65
Ventura, CA 93002
ph: 805-643-3532
fax: 805-643-3532
toac@sbcglobal.net
http://www.antiquestoves.com/toac/
about.htm
*The only vintage American appliance
information clearinghouse in the
world; parts, service, information,
sources, referrals, buy/sell classifieds,
historical articles on vintage stoves,
refrigerators and appliances.*

Collectors

Daniel Zilka
P.O. Box 885
Providence, RI 02901
ph: 401-331-8575 x102 or 401-461-7932
fax: 401-351-0127
dzilka@faithinphysics.com
http://www.dinermuseum.org
*Wants to buy older coffee pots,
percolators, waffle irons, mixers,
vaculator coffee makers; performs
restorations; seeking manufacturers'
promotional material and brochures.*

William Blakeslee
116 S. Bethlehem Pike
P.O. Box 56
Ambler, PA 19002
ph: 215-646-6593
fax: 215-646-5459
readferry@snip.net
*Wants unusual electric toasters as
well as any pre-1910 electric
appliance: GE, Simplex, American
Electric Heat, Heinrichs.*

Mary Faria
P.O. Box 32321
San Jose, CA 95152-2321
ph: 408-258-0413 or 408-258-0416
izmars@sbcglobal.net
*Collects excellent condition small
kitchen appliances, c. 1930s;
especially wants toasters, cake mixers
attachments such as Sunbeam and
Magic Maid, juicers.*

Experts

Jim Barker
Toaster Master
P.O. Box 746
Allentown, PA 18102
ph: 610-439-0751
fax: 610-439-1925
jbar@enter.net
*Dealer, collector, historian, authority
on early electric appliances.*

K. M. Scotty Mitchell
Millchell
2112 Lipscomb St.
Ft. Worth, TX 76110-2047
ph: 817-923-3274
fax: 817-926-1970
*Collector of small electrical kitchen
appliances (1893-1940): toaster,
waffle irons, coffee makers and
specialty items, etc.*

Gary L. Miller
Millchell
2112 Lipscomb St.
Ft. Worth, TX 76110-2047
ph: 817-923-3274
fax: 817-926-1970
*Collector of small electrical kitchen
appliances (1893-1940): toaster,
waffle irons, coffee makers and
specialty items, etc.*

Appliances (Coffee Pots)

Collectors

Carole Lundy
3 Long Lane Dr.
Hummelstown, PA 17036-9545
ph: 717-566-6016
boxerlines@comcast.net
*Wants to buy porcelain coffee pots
made by Hall, Westinghouse, Robeson
Rochester, and Porcelier.*

Appliances (Mixers)

Collectors

Dennis Thompson
P.O. Box 26067
Cleveland, OH 44126-0067
ph: 440-235-8548
dthomp@core.com
http://my.core.com/~dthomp
*Collects and researches early electric
mixers, concentrating on pre-1950
mixers; collection is online at Web
site.*

Appliances (Porcelier)

Clubs/Associations

Shirley Hall
Porcelier Collectors Club
Newsletter: Porcelier Paper, The
21 Tamarac Swamp Rd.
Wallingford, CT 06492-5529
ph: 203-265-5791
ThePPLady@aol.com
*For collectors of Porcelier dinner-
ware, service pieces and all-ceramic
small electrical kitchen appliances; bi-
monthly newsletter features
information and pictures of patterns,
new finds, and research; free ads for
members.*

Collectors

Carole Lundy
3 Long Lane Dr.
Hummelstown, PA 17036-9545
ph: 717-566-6016
boxerlines@comcast.net
*Wants to buy Porcelier brand electric
coffee pots, toasters, waffle irons,
sandwich grills, and related items.*

Batteries (9-Volt)

Clubs/Associations

Cliff Watts
World 9-Volt Battery Collectors Club
51 Glendale Rd.
Brantfors, Ontario N3T 1P5 Canada
ph: 519-753-9049
*Members collect 9-volt batteries like
those used in smoke detectors and
transistor radios; looking for as many
brands and graphic styles as possible;
new or old.*

Collectors

Cliff Watts
51 Glendale Rd.
Brantfors, Ontario N3T 1P5 Canada
ph: 519-753-9049
*Wants to buy 9-volt batteries like
those used in smoke detectors and
transistor radios; looking for as many
brands and graphic styles as possible;
new or old.*

Battery Jars

Collectors

W.M. Dickey
P.O. Box 7323
Macon, GA 31209-7223
ph: 912-471-0902
fax: 912-471-0902
*Wants to buy glass battery jars; used
as containers to hold lead plates and
acid; used in the home and industry
until the late 1930s where electricity
was not available.*

Motors

Collectors

Steve Cunningham
3200 Ashland Dr.
Bedford, TX 76021-6502
ph: 817-267-9851 or 800-991-0165
fax: 817-267-0387
*Collects antique electric motors; from
lemon-sized to medium-sized; these
motors all have open frames where all
the workings are exposed; brand
names include Weeded, Rex, Ajax,
K&D, Voltamp, Perrett, Crocker-
Wheeler.*

Repair Services

Mike Frost
Time Guard, Inc.
9655 Richmond St.
Manassas, VA 20110
ph: 800-390-5540
lincoln@mnsinc.com
*Specializes in the repair of obsolete
electric motors.*

Power Utilities Items

Collectors

Tommy Bolack
3901 Bloomfield Hwy.
Farmington, NM 87401-2831
ph: 505-325-7873 or 505-325-4275
fax: 505-323-1434
*Wants any early watthour meter: GE,
Thompson, Edison-Chemical, Duncan,*

*Fort Wayne, Sangamo, pre-pay meters
of any type; also any other early or
foreign types; also wants early
transformers and electrical distribution items.*

Museums/Libraries

Rocky Reach Dam, Gallery of Electricity
P.O. Box 1231
Wenatchee, WA 98801-1231
ph: 509-663-8121 or 888-663-8121
fax: 509-664-2870
publicinfo@chelanpud.org
http://www.chelanpud.org
*The museum features communications
and power relics.*

ELECTRONICS

(see AUDIO-VISUAL; ELECTRICITY
RELATED ITEMS; HI-FI
EQUIPMENT; RADIOS; TELEGRAPH
ITEMS; TELEVISIONS)

ELONGATED COINS

Clubs/Associations

Lurene Haines
Elongated Collectors, The
Newsletter: TEC News
P.O. Box 786
College Park, MD 20741-0786
tec@hainesworld.com
http://www.money.org/clubs/tec.html
*Focuses on elongated coins but
includes all denominations plus tokens
and foreign coins rolled under extreme
pressure through steel rollers forming
custom designed oblong souvenirs
commemorating people, places, things,
and events.*

Anne Robinson
Copper Memories Collectors Club
1364 London Bridge Rd., Ste. 101
Virginia Beach, VA 23456
ph: 800-517-3669 or 757-468-4090
fax: 757-468-6407
admin@coppermemories.com
http://www.coppermemories.com
*A club sponsored by a coin-press
manufacturing company; quarterly
newsletter, free elongated coins,
exclusive limited-edition elongated
coins, members only sales, latest news
about elongated coins.*

Collectors

Stuart Liss
Universal Studios Elongated Coins
  Checklists
liss@liss.olm.net
http://www.liss.olm.net/ec/universal
*Wants to buy elongated coins from
Universal Studios Florida and
Hollywood; Web site has many images
of elongated coins.*

Ronald Dupont, Jr.
3783-C Pompano Dr. SE
Saint Petersburg, FL 33705
ph: 727-550-2253
flaron@mindspring.com
http://www.ronald-dupont.com/
  pennies.htm
*Collects crushed pennies and quarters;
Web site contains images of many
from his collection.*

C. Meccarello
1572 Bowmans Trail
Lakeland, FL 33809-5006
ph: 941-859-7194 or 941-859-7194
*Buys, sells, collects OPA tokens, Bank
postcard, elongated coins.*

Dealers

Rich Hartzog
World Exonumia
P.O. Box 4143CNZ
Rockford, IL 61110-0643
ph: 815-226-0771
hartzog@exonumia.com
http://www.exonumia.com
*Wants any elongated coins, tokens,
medals, exonumia: badges, buttons,
World's Fair items, political items,
banners, etc.*

Internet Resources

Kathy Reddin
Penny Page, The
kredding@yahoo.com
http://www.pennypage.com
*The largest photo collection of
elongated coins (squashed, squished,
pressed, etc.); also message board,
links, news and penny FAQ.*

Maggie Nguyen
Elongated Coin Collection, The
elongatedcoincollection@hotmail.com
http://www.geocities.com/mainguy_1998
*Personal elongated coin collection,
including information about machine
location, elongated coin books and
articles, trade list, links, FAQs,
message boards and chat room.*

Man./Prod./Dist.

William C. Massey
Luck "E" Penny
P.O. Box 1511
Beltsville, MD 20704-1511
ph: 301-937-7732
willy@wcmassey.com
http://www.wcmassey.com/lep
*Produces elongated coins for any event
or special occasion; informative Web
site for the elongated coin collector.*

Copper Memories, Inc.
1364 London Bridge Rd., Ste. 101
Virginia Beach, VA 23456
ph: 800-517-3669 or 757-468-4090
fax: 757-468-6407
admin@coppermemories.com
http://www.coppermemories.com
*Manufacturer of coin-press machines
that make elongated coins for the
tourist industry.*

Museums/Libraries

Squished Penny Museum, The
416 T St. NW
Washington, DC 20001
ph: 202-9896-5644
spm@squished.com
http://www.squished.com

ELSIE THE BORDEN COW ITEMS

(see also ANIMAL COLLECTIBLES,
Cows; DAIRY COLLECTIBLES)

Collectors

Susan Schwartz
291 E. 4th St.
Brooklyn, NY 11218
Wants Elsie the Cow novelties.

Richard Reddock
914 Isle Ct.
Bellmore, NY 11710-1545
ph: 516-826-2032 or 800-223-PNUT
pnutfanclb@aol.com
*Wants to buy all Elsie Cow items:
clocks, signs, rubber Elsie doll, papier
mache Elsie head, letter opener,
drinking glasses.*

Lynny Borden
307 Stonebebridge Dr.
Longwood, FL 32779-3326
ph: 407-788-0780 or 407-788-0225
fax: 407-788-8161
*Wants to buy all types of Borden &
Elsie items: soda fountain containers,
clocks, neon or lighted signs, mugs,
glassware, cream top and unusual
bottles, bowls, watches, lighters,
Danbury Mint Borden vehicles,
paperweights, belt buckles.*

Ron Selcke
P.O. Box 237
Bloomingdale, IL 60108-0237
ph: 630-543-4848
*Wants Elsie games, cookbooks, comic
books, cups, glasses, Christmas cards,
books, pictures, blotters, postcards,
clocks, signs, neon signs, Borden Milk
bottles and creamers, Borden Milk
postcards, Borden Condensed Milk
trade cards.*

Dealers

Marty Blank
P.O. Box 405
Flushing, NY 11365-0405
ph: 516-485-8071
*Wants to buy Elsie, Campbell Kids,
Reddy Kilowatt, Coke, figural vinyl
advertising and Country Store items.*

ELVES

(see also GNOMES)

Collectors

Sally Kimmel
1471 Lark Lane
Concord, CA 94521-2942
ph: 925-689-4138
sallyraek@yahoo.com
Elf lover wants to buy elves and pixies: Christmas tree, wall, hanging, table decorations and ornaments and any other holiday (Easter, Valentines Day, St. Patrick's Day, etc.) elves, pixies, fairies and leprechauns - anything with elves!

EMBALMING ITEMS

(see FUNERAL ITEMS)

EMBROIDERY

(see MILITARIA, Silk Embroideries; TEXTILES, Embroidery)

ENAMELS

(see also BATTERSEA ENAMEL BOXES; BOXES; CLOISONNE; GLASS; METAL ITEMS; RUSSIAN ITEMS)

Clubs/Associations

Tom Ellis, Ed.
Enamelist Society, The
Magazine: Glass on Metal
P.O. Box 631704
Cincinnati, OH 45263-1704
ph: 859-291-3800
fax: 859-291-1849
thompson@rm1.net
http://www.craftweb.com/org/enamel/enamel.htm
Over 1,300 members worldwide with interests in all aspects of enameling - glass on metal; the magazine is published 5 times per year plus 2 bulletins; magazine tells of Guilds to join, conventions, workshops, exhibitions.

Dealers

Marvin Sokolow
425 West Fairy Chasm Rd.
Milwaukee, WI 53217
ph: 414-351-5750
msokolow@msn.com
Specializes in the buying, selling, appraising Asian antiques, silver, and European and Russian enamels.

Kathleen M. Bailey, AAA, ISA CAPP
Antique Appraisal & Estate Sale Service - the Original
160 NW Gilman Blvd., Ste. #1
Issaquah, WA 98027
ph: 425-746-2777
fax: 425-746-3793
antiquabailey@aol.com
Buys and sells Russian, French and Viennese enamels.

ENDANGERED SPECIES

(see also ANIMAL COLLECTIBLES; ANIMAL TROPHIES; IVORY; NAUTICAL ANTIQUES; SCRIMSHAW; SPORTING COLLECTIBLES)

Canadian

Misc. Services

Canadian Wildlife Service Headquarters, CITES Administrator
351 St. Joseph Blvd., 3rd Floor
Place Vincent Massey
Hull, Quebec J8Y 3Z5 Canada
ph: 819-953-1411
fax: 819-994-4065
cws-scf@ec.gc.ca
http://www.cws-scf.ec.gc.ca/cwshom_e.html
Canadian HQ contact for inquiries regarding CITES (the Convention on International Trade in Endangered Species of Wild Fauna & Flora); an international agreement that protects endangered and threatened species of animals & plants.

Canadian Wildlife Service, Pacific & Yukon Region
P.O. Box 340
5421 Robertson Rd.
Delta, British Columbia V4K 3Y3 Canada
ph: 604-946-8643
fax: 604-946-8359
Regional Canadian contact for inquiries regarding CITES (the Convention on International Trade in Endangered Species of Wild Fauna & Flora); an international agreement that protects endangered and threatened species of animals & plants

Canadian Wildlife Service, Western & Northern Region
115 Perimeter Rd.
Saskatoon, Saskatchewan S7N 0X4 Canada
ph: 306-975-4290 or 306-975-4919
fax: 306-975-6061
Regional Canadian contact for inquiries regarding CITES (the Convention on International Trade in Endangered Species of Wild Fauna & Flora); an international agreement that protects endangered and threatened species of animals & plants

Environment Canada, Canadian Wildlife Service, Ontario Region
70 Fountain St. E
Guelph, Ontario N1H 3N6 Canada
ph: 519-826-2100
fax: 519-826-2108
enviroinfo@ec.gc.ca
http://www.on.ec.gc.ca/wildlife/intro.html
Regional Canadian contact for inquiries regarding CITES (the Convention on International Trade in Endangered Species of Wild Fauna & Flora); an international agreement

that protects endangered and threatened species of animals & plants

Canadian Wildlife Service, Atlantic Region
P.O. Box 1590
Sackville, New Brunswick E0A 3C0 Canada
ph: 506-364-5044
fax: 506-364-5062
Regional Canadian contact for inquiries regarding CITES (the Convention on International Trade in Endangered Species of Wild Fauna & Flora); an international agreement that protects endangered and threatened species of animals & plants

Canadian Wildlife Service, Quebec Region
C.P. 10100
Ste-Foy, Quebec G1V 4H5 Canada
ph: 418-648-7028
fax: 418-648-4613
Regional Canadian contact for inquiries regarding CITES (the Convention on International Trade in Endangered Species of Wild Fauna & Flora); an international agreement that protects endangered and threatened species of animals & plants

National Marine Fisheries Ser.

Misc. Services

Special Agent in Charge
NOAA/NMFS Office of Enforcement, Northeast Region
1 Blackburn Dr., Room 206
Gloucester, MA 01930
ph: 978-281-9213
fax: 978-281-9317
http://www.nmfs.noaa.gov/ole/northeast.html
National Oceanic & Administration/ National Marine Fisheries Service enforcement office, Northeast Region; call to join the NOAA Fisheries Enforcement PARTNERS program to help find solutions to marine resource problems.

Chief
NOAA/NMFS Office of Enforcement, Headquarters
8484 Georgia Ave., Ste. 415
Silver Spring, MD 20910
ph: 301-417-2300
fax: 301-427-2055
http://www.nmfs.noaa.gov/ole
National Oceanic & Administration/ National Marine Fisheries Service Office of Enforcement, Headquarters; call to join the NOAA Fisheries Enforcement PARTNERS program to help find solutions to marine resource problems.

National Marine Fisheries Service, Office of Protected Resources
1335 East-West Hwy., 13th Fl.
Silver Spring, MD 20910-3226
ph: 301-713-2332
fax: 301-713-0376
pr.webmaster@noaa.gov
http://www.nmfs.noaa.gov/prot_res/prot_res.html
Contact for permits and inquiries regarding The Marine Mammal Protection Act for all whales, dolphins, seals, and sea lions (i.e., marine mammals other than polar bears, manatees, otters, walruses and dungongs.)

Special Agent in Charge
NOAA/NMFS Office of Enforcement, Southeast Region
9721 Executive Center Dr., Room 130
Saint Petersburg, FL 33702
ph: 727-570-5344
fax: 727-570-5343
http://www.nmfs.noaa.gov/ole/southeast.html
National Oceanic & Administration/ National Marine Fisheries Service enforcement office, Southeast Region; call to join the NOAA Fisheries Enforcement PARTNERS program to help find solutions to marine resource problems.

Special Agent in Charge
NOAA/NMFS Office of Enforcement, Southwest Region
501 W. Ocean Blvd., Ste. 4400-A
Long Beach, CA 90802
ph: 562-980-4050
fax: 562-980-4058
rick.deering@noaa.gov
http://swr.ucsd.edu/enf
National Oceanic & Administration/ National Marine Fisheries Service enforcement office, Southwest Region; call to join the NOAA Fisheries Enforcement PARTNERS program to help find solutions to marine resource problems.

Special Agent in Charge
NOAA/NMFS Office of Enforcement, Northwest Region
7600 Sand Point Way NE
Seattle, WA 98115
ph: 206-526-6133
fax: 206-526-6528
NW.Enforcement@noaa.gov
http://www.nmfs.noaa.gov/ole/northwest.html
National Oceanic & Administration/ National Marine Fisheries Service enforcement office, Northwest Region; call to join the NOAA Fisheries Enforcement PARTNERS program to help find solutions to marine resource problems.

Special Agent in Charge
NOAA/NMFS Office of Enforcement,
  Alaska Region
709 W. 9th St., Room M09C
P.O. Box 21767
Juneau, AK 99802
ph: 907-586-7225
fax: 907-586-7200
AED.webmaster@noaa.gov
http://www.nmfs.noaa.gov/ole/Alaska
*National Oceanic & Administration/
National Marine Fisheries Service
enforcement office, Alaska Region; call
to join the NOAA Fisheries
Enforcement PARTNERS program to
help find solutions to marine resource
problems.*

State Conservation Agencies

Misc. Services

Commissioner
Massachusetts Department of Fisheries,
  Wildlife & Environmental Law
  Enforcement
100 Cambridge St., Rm. 1901
Boston, MA 02202
ph: 617-727-1614
Mass.Wildlife@state.ma.us
http://www.magnet.state.ma.us/dfwele/
  dpt_toc.htm
*Each state has its own wildlife laws
which may differ from Federal laws.
Check with state and local authorities
for restrictions on ownership or
commercial transactions of protected
wildlife.*

Chief
Rhode Island Division of Fish &
  Wildlife
4808 Tower Hill Rd.
Wakefield, RI 02879
ph: 401-222-3075
fax: 401-783-4460
*Each state has its own wildlife laws
which may differ from Federal laws.
Check with state and local authorities
for restrictions on ownership or
commercial transactions of protected
wildlife.*

Director
New Hampshire Fish & Game
  Department
2 Hazen Dr.
Concord, NH 03301
ph: 603-271-3211
info@wildlife.state.nh.us
http://www.wildlife.state.nh.us/
  home.html
*Each state has its own wildlife laws
which may differ from Federal laws.
Check with state and local authorities
for restrictions on ownership or
commercial transactions of protected
wildlife.*

Commissioner
Maine Department of Inland Fisheries &
  Wildlife
284 State St.
41 State House Station
Augusta, ME 04333-0041
ph: 207-287-8000
fax: 207-287-6395
ifw.webmaster@maine.gov
http://www.state.me.us/ifw
*Each state has its own wildlife laws
which may differ from Federal laws.
Check with state and local authorities
for restrictions on ownership or
commercial transactions of protected
wildlife.*

Department of Fish & Wildlife, Vermont
  Agency of Natural Resources
103 South Main St.
Waterbury, VT 05671-0501
ph: 802-479-3242
fax: 802-241-3205c
jhall@fpr.anr.state.vt.us
http://www.anr.state.vt.us/fw/fwhome/
  index.htm
*Each state has its own wildlife laws
which may differ from Federal laws.
Check with state and local authorities
for restrictions on ownership or
commercial transactions of protected
wildlife.*

Commissioner
Connecticut Department of
  Environmental Protection
79 Elm St.
Hartford, CT 06106-5127
ph: 860-423-3000
fax: 860-424-4051
dep.webmaster@po.state.ct.us
http://dep.state.ct.us
*Each state has its own wildlife laws
which may differ from Federal laws.
Check with state and local authorities
for restrictions on ownership or
commercial transactions of protected
wildlife.*

Director
New Jersey Division of Fish & Wildlife
501 E. State St., 3rd Floor
P.O. Box 400
Trenton, NJ 08625-0400
ph: 609-292-2965
njwildlife@nac.net
http://www.state.nj.us/dep/fgw
*Each state has its own wildlife laws
which may differ from Federal laws.
Check with state and local authorities
for restrictions on ownership or
commercial transactions of protected
wildlife.*

Director
Outdoors & Natural Resources, New
  York Department of Environmental
  Conservation
50 Wolf Rd.
Albany, NY 12233-4750
ph: 518-457-5690
fax: 518-457-0341
fwinfo@gw.dec.state.ny.us
http://www.dec.state.ny.us/website/
  dfwmr
*Each state has its own wildlife laws
which may differ from Federal laws.
Check with state and local authorities
for restrictions on ownership or
commercial transactions of protected
wildlife.*

Executive Director
Pennsylvania Game Commission
2001 Elmerton Ave.
Harrisburg, PA 17110-9797
ph: 717-787-4250
pgccomments@state.pa.us
http://www.pgc.state.pa.us
*Each state has its own wildlife laws
which may differ from Federal laws.
Check with state and local authorities
for restrictions on ownership or
commercial transactions of protected
wildlife.*

Director
Delaware Division of Fish & Wildlife
89 Kings Highway
Dover, DE 19901
ph: 302-739-5295
http://www.dnrec.state.de.us/fw
*Each state has its own wildlife laws
which may differ from Federal laws.
Check with state and local authorities
for restrictions on ownership or
commercial transactions of protected
wildlife.*

Director
Maryland Department of Natural
  Resources
Tawes State Office Building
Annapolis, MD 21401
ph: 410-260-8200
customerservice@dnr.state.md.us
http://www.dnr.state.md.us
*Each state has its own wildlife laws
which may differ from Federal laws.
Check with state and local authorities
for restrictions on ownership or
commercial transactions of protected
wildlife.*

Executive Director
Virginia Department of Game & Inland
  Fisheries
4010 W. Broad St.
Richmond, VA 23230
ph: 804-367-1000
dgifweb@dgif.state.va.us
http://www.dgif.state.va.us
*Each state has its own wildlife laws
which may differ from Federal laws.
Check with state and local authorities
for restrictions on ownership or
commercial transactions of protected
wildlife.*

Director
West Virginia Department of Natural
  Resources
State Capitol Complex, Bldg. 3
1900 Kanawha Blvd.
Charleston, WV 25305-0060
ph: 304-558-2784
wildlife@dnr.state.wv.us
http://www.dnr.state.wv.us
*Each state has its own wildlife laws
which may differ from Federal laws.
Check with state and local authorities
for restrictions on ownership or
commercial transactions of protected
wildlife.*

John Pechmann, Ch.
North Carolina Wildlife Resources
  Commission
512 N. Salisbury St.
Raleigh, NC 27604-1188
ph: 919-661-4872
http://www.state.nc.us/wildlife
*Each state has its own wildlife laws
which may differ from Federal laws.
Check with state and local authorities
for restrictions on ownership or
commercial transactions of protected
wildlife.*

Dr. Paul Sandifer, Dir.
South Carolina Department of Natural
  Resources
1000 Assembly St.
Columbia, SC 29201
ph: 803-734-3888
http://www.dnr.state.sc.us
*Each state has its own wildlife laws
which may differ from Federal laws.
Check with state and local authorities
for restrictions on ownership or
commercial transactions of protected
wildlife.*

Director
Georgia Department of Natural Resources
116 Rum Creek Dr.
Forsyth, GA 31029
ph: 912-994-1438
fax: 912-933-3050
http://www.dnr.state.ga.us
*Each state has its own wildlife laws
which may differ from Federal laws.
Check with state and local authorities
for restrictions on ownership or
commercial transactions of protected
wildlife.*

Allan Egbert, Ex. Dir.
Florida Fish & Wildlife Conservation
  Commission
620 S. Meridian St.
Tallahassee, FL 32399-1600
ph: 850-488-2975
fax: 850-921-5786
http://www.state.fl.us/fwc
*Each state has its own wildlife laws
which may differ from Federal laws.
Check with state and local authorities
for restrictions on ownership or
commercial transactions of protected
wildlife.*

Director
Game & Fish Division, Alabama Dpt. of
   Conservation & Natural Resources
64 N. Union St.
Montgomery, AL 36130
ph: 334-242-3467 or 334-242-3465
ghouston@dcnr.state.al.us
http://www.dcnr.state.al.us/agfd
   *Each state has its own wildlife laws
   which may differ from Federal laws.
   Check with state and local authorities
   for restrictions on ownership or
   commercial transactions of protected
   wildlife.*

Gary Myers, Ex. Dir.
Tennessee Wildlife Resources Agency
Ellington Agricultural Center
P.O. Box 40747
Nashville, TN 37204
ph: 615-781-6500
stephanie.palm@state.tn.us
http://www.state.tn.us/twra
   *Each state has its own wildlife laws
   which may differ from Federal laws.
   Check with state and local authorities
   for restrictions on ownership or
   commercial transactions of protected
   wildlife.*

Mississippi Department of Wildlife,
   Fisheries & Parks
1505 Eastover Dr.
Jackson, MS 39211-6374
ph: 601-432-2400
http://www.mdwfp.com
   *Each state has its own wildlife laws
   which may differ from Federal laws.
   Check with state and local authorities
   for restrictions on ownership or
   commercial transactions of protected
   wildlife.*

Commissioner
Kentucky Department of Fish & Wildlife
   Resources
#1 Game Farm Rd.
Frankfort, KY 40601
ph: 502-564-3400 or 800-858-1549
info.center@mail.state.ky.us
http://www.kdfwr.state.ky.us/
   *Each state has its own wildlife laws
   which may differ from Federal laws.
   Check with state and local authorities
   for restrictions on ownership or
   commercial transactions of protected
   wildlife.*

Director
Ohio Division of Wildlife
1840 Belcher Dr.
Columbus, OH 43224-1329
ph: 614-265-6300 or 800-WILDLIFE
dnrmail@dnr.state.oh.us
http://www.dnr.state.oh.us/wildlife
   *Each state has its own wildlife laws
   which may differ from Federal laws.
   Check with state and local authorities
   for restrictions on ownership or
   commercial transactions of protected
   wildlife.*

Director
Division of Fish & Wildlife, Indiana
   Department of Natural Resources
402 W. Washington St., Rm W273
Indianapolis, IN 46204
ph: 317-232-4080
rmaharjan@dnr.state.in.us
http://www.state.in.us/dnr
   *Each state has its own wildlife laws
   which may differ from Federal laws.
   Check with state and local authorities
   for restrictions on ownership or
   commercial transactions of protected
   wildlife.*

Director
Michigan Department of Natural
   Resources
P.O. Box 30028
Lansing, MI 48909
ph: 517-373-2329
http://www.michigan.gov/dnr
   *Each state has its own wildlife laws
   which may differ from Federal laws.
   Check with state and local authorities
   for restrictions on ownership or
   commercial transactions of protected
   wildlife.*

Daryl Howell
Fish & Wildlife Division, Iowa
   Department of Natural Resources
Wallace State Office Building
502 E. 9th St.
Des Moines, IA 50319
ph: 515-281-4687
fax: 515-281-6794
daryl.howell@dnr.state.ia.us
http://www.state.ia.us/dnr/fwdiv.htm
   *Each state has its own wildlife laws
   which may differ from Federal laws.
   Check with state and local authorities
   for restrictions on ownership or
   commercial transactions of protected
   wildlife.*

Secretary
Wisconsin Department of Natural
   Resources
P.O. Box 7921
Madison, WI 53707
ph: 608-226-7012
http://www.dnr.state.wi.us
   *Each state has its own wildlife laws
   which may differ from Federal laws.
   Check with state and local authorities
   for restrictions on ownership or
   commercial transactions of protected
   wildlife.*

Director
Minnesota Department of Natural
   Resources
500 Lafayette Rd.
Saint Paul, MN 55146-4040
ph: 651-296-6157
info@dnr.state.mn.us
http://www.dnr.state.mn.us
   *Each state has its own wildlife laws
   which may differ from Federal laws.
   Check with state and local authorities
   for restrictions on ownership or
   commercial transactions of protected
   wildlife.*

Secretary
South Dakota Department of Game, Fish
   & Parks
523 East Capitol Ave.
Pierre, SD 57501-3182
ph: 605-773-3381
Wildinfo@gfp.state.sd.us
http://www.state.sd.us/gfp
   *Each state has its own wildlife laws
   which may differ from Federal laws.
   Check with state and local authorities
   for restrictions on ownership or
   commercial transactions of protected
   wildlife.*

Director
North Dakota Game & Fish Department
100 N. Bismark Expressway
Bismarck, ND 58501-5095
ph: 701-328-6300
fax: 701-328-6352
ndgf@state.nd.us
http://state.nd.us/gnf/index.html
   *Each state has its own wildlife laws
   which may differ from Federal laws.
   Check with state and local authorities
   for restrictions on ownership or
   commercial transactions of protected
   wildlife.*

Patrick Graham, Dir.
Montana Fish, Wildlife & Parks
1420 East Sixth
Helena, MT 59620
ph: 406-444-2950
http://www.fwp.state.mt.us
   *Each state has its own wildlife laws
   which may differ from Federal laws.
   Check with state and local authorities
   for restrictions on ownership or
   commercial transactions of protected
   wildlife.*

Director
Illinois Department of Natural Resources
524 South Second St.
Springfield, IL 62706
ph: 217-782-6302
endspec@dnrmail.state.il.us
http://dnr.state.il.us
   *Each state has its own wildlife laws
   which may differ from Federal laws.
   Check with state and local authorities
   for restrictions on ownership or
   commercial transactions of protected
   wildlife.*

Director
Missouri Department of Conservation
P.O. Box 180
Jefferson City, MO 65102-0180
ph: 573-751-4115
fax: 573-751-4467
http://www.conservation.state.mo.us
   *Each state has its own wildlife laws
   which may differ from Federal laws.
   Check with state and local authorities
   for restrictions on ownership or
   commercial transactions of protected
   wildlife.*

Kansas Department of Wildlife & Parks
512 SE 25th Ave.
Pratt, KS 67124-8174
ph: 316-672-5911
feedback@wp.state.ks.us
http://www.kdwp.state.ks.us
   *Each state has its own wildlife laws
   which may differ from Federal laws.
   Check with state and local authorities
   for restrictions on ownership or
   commercial transactions of protected
   wildlife.*

Director
Nebraska Game & Parks Commission
2200 N. 33rd St.
Lincoln, NE 68503
ph: 402-471-0641
webmaster@ngpc.state.ne.us
http://www.ngpc.state.ne.us/
   homepage.html
   *Each state has its own wildlife laws
   which may differ from Federal laws.
   Check with state and local authorities
   for restrictions on ownership or
   commercial transactions of protected
   wildlife.*

Keith LaCaze
Louisiana Department of Wildlife &
   Fisheries Law Enforcement Division
P.O. Box 98000
Baton Rouge, LA 70898-9000
ph: 225-765-2469
fax: 225-765-2832
lacaze_bk@wlf.state.la.us
http://www.wlf.state.la.us
   *Each state has its own wildlife laws
   which may differ from Federal laws.
   Check with state and local authorities
   for restrictions on ownership or
   commercial transactions of protected
   wildlife.*

Director
Arkansas Game & Fish Commission
#2 Natural Resources Dr.
Little Rock, AR 72205
ph: 501-223-6300 or 800-364-4263
fax: 501-223-6447
http://www.agfc.com
   *Each state has its own wildlife laws
   which may differ from Federal laws.
   Check with state and local authorities
   for restrictions on ownership or
   commercial transactions of protected
   wildlife.*

Director
Oklahoma Department of Wildlife
   Conservation
1801 N. Lincoln
Oklahoma City, OK 73105
ph: 405-521-3851
fax: 405-521-6535
pmoore@odwc.state.ok.us
http://www.wildlifedepartment.com
   *Each state has its own wildlife laws
   which may differ from Federal laws.
   Check with state and local authorities
   for restrictions on ownership or
   commercial transactions of protected
   wildlife.*

Executive Director
Texas Parks & Wildlife Department
4200 Smith School Rd.
Austin, TX 78744
ph: 512-389-4800 or 800-792-1112
http://www.tpwd.state.tx.us
*Each state has its own wildlife laws
which may differ from Federal laws.
Check with state and local authorities
for restrictions on ownership or
commercial transactions of protected
wildlife.*

Colorado Division of Wildlife
Magazine: Colorado Outdoors
6060 Broadway
Denver, CO 80216
ph: 303-297-1192
dnr.feedback@state.co.us
http://www.dnr.state.co.us/wildlife
*Each state has its own wildlife laws
which may differ from Federal laws.
Check with state and local authorities
for restrictions on ownership or
commercial transactions of protected
wildlife; source for hunting and
fishing info.*

Director
Wyoming Game & Fish Department
5400 Bishop Blvd.
Cheyenne, WY 82006
ph: 307-777-4600
fax: 307-777-4699
http://gf.state.wy.us
*Each state has its own wildlife laws
which may differ from Federal laws.
Check with state and local authorities
for restrictions on ownership or
commercial transactions of protected
wildlife.*

Commissioner
Idaho Department of Fish & Game
600 South Walnut St.
Boise, ID 83707
ph: 208-334-3736
idfginfo@idfg.state.id.us
http://www2.state.id.us/fishgame/
  fishgame.html
*Each state has its own wildlife laws
which may differ from Federal laws.
Check with state and local authorities
for restrictions on ownership or
commercial transactions of protected
wildlife.*

Director
Utah Department of Wildlife Resources
P.O. Box 146301
Salt Lake City, UT 84114-6301
ph: 801-538-7200
dwrcomment@utah.gov
http://www.nr.utah.gov
*Each state has its own wildlife laws
which may differ from Federal laws.
Check with state and local authorities
for restrictions on ownership or
commercial transactions of protected
wildlife.*

Duane Shroufe, Dir.
Arizona Game & Fish Department
2221 West Greenway Rd.
Phoenix, AZ 85023-4399
ph: 602-942-3000
http://www.gf.state.az.us
*Each state has its own wildlife laws
which may differ from Federal laws.
Check with state and local authorities
for restrictions on ownership or
commercial transactions of protected
wildlife.*

Director
New Mexico Department of Game &
  Fish
405 Galisteo
P.O. Box 25112
Santa Fe, NM 87504
ph: 505-827-7911 or 800-862-9310
fax: 505-827-7915
ispa@state.nm.us
http://www.gmfsh.state.nm.us
*Each state has its own wildlife laws
which may differ from Federal laws.
Check with state and local authorities
for restrictions on ownership or
commercial transactions of protected
wildlife.*

Director
Nevada Department of Wildlife
P.O. Box 10678
1100 Valley Rd.
Reno, NV 89520
ph: 702-688-1500
fax: 702-688-1595
ndowinfo@govmail.state.nv.us
http://www.state.nv.us/cnr/nvwildlife
*Each state has its own wildlife laws
which may differ from Federal laws.
Check with state and local authorities
for restrictions on ownership or
commercial transactions of protected
wildlife.*

Director
California Department of Fish & Game
1416 Ninth St.
Sacramento, CA 95814
ph: 916-653-7664
smorris@dfg.ca.gov
http://www.dfg.ca.gov/dfghome.html
*Each state has its own wildlife laws
which may differ from Federal laws.
Check with state and local authorities
for restrictions on ownership or
commercial transactions of protected
wildlife.*

Director
Hawaii Department of Land & Natural
  Resources
1151 Punchbowl St.
Honolulu, HI 96813
ph: 808-587-0400
fax: 808-587-0390
dlnr@pixi.com
http://www.hawaii.gov/dlnr/
  Welcome.html
*Each state has its own wildlife laws
which may differ from Federal laws.
Check with state and local authorities
for restrictions on ownership or*

*commercial transactions of protected
wildlife.*

Director
Oregon Department of Fish & Wildlife
2501 SW First Ave.
Portland, OR 97207
ph: 503-872-5268
Rodney.A.Lemeni@state.or.us
http://www.dfw.state.or.us
*Each state has its own wildlife laws
which may differ from Federal laws.
Check with state and local authorities
for restrictions on ownership or
commercial transactions of protected
wildlife.*

Director
Washington Department of Fish &
  Wildlife
600 Capitol Way North
Olympia, WA 98501-1091
ph: 360-902-2200
fax: 360-902-2230
webmaster@dfw.wa.gov
http://www.wa.gov/wdfw
*Each state has its own wildlife laws
which may differ from Federal laws.
Check with state and local authorities
for restrictions on ownership or
commercial transactions of protected
wildlife.*

Frank Rue, Comm
Alaska Department of Fish & Game
P.O. Box 25526
Juneau, AK 99802-5526
ph: 907-465-4100
fax: 907-465-2332
commrrue@fishgame.state.ak.us
http://www.state.ak.us/local/akpages/
  FISH.GAME
*Each state has its own wildlife laws
which may differ from Federal laws.
Check with state and local authorities
for restrictions on ownership or
commercial transactions of protected
wildlife.*

U.S. Fish & Wildlife Service

Experts

Special Agent John Brooks
U.S. Fish & Wildlife Service
185 West F St., Ste. 440
San Diego, CA 92101-6025
ph: 619-557-5063
fax: 619-557-2997
John_L_Brooks@fws.gov
*Specializes in regulations regarding
endangered species; will direct you in
the realm of Federal wildlife laws as
they relate to your business.*

Misc. Services

Regional Director
U.S. Fish & Wildlife Service, Region 5
300 Westgate Center Dr.
Hadley, MA 01035-9589
ph: 413-253-8200
fw5ea_web@fws.gov
http://northeast.fws.gov
*Regional US Fish & Wildlife Service
contact for inquiries regarding laws
pertaining to endangered and
threatened species of wild fauna and*

*wild flora; covers CT, DE, DC, ME,
MD, MA, NH, NJ, NY, PA, RI. VT,
VA, WV.*

U.S. Fish & Wildlife Service, Office of
  Endangered Species
4401 N. Fairfax Dr., Room 420
Arlington, VA 22203
ph: 703-358-2171
endangered@fws.gov
http://endangered.fws.gov
*Contact for current information on
endangered flora and fauna species,
other than marine (in which case
contact National Marine Fisheries
Service); point of contact for issues
relating to the Endangered Species Act
and the Lacey Act.*

U.S. Fish & Wildlife Service, Division
  of Law Enforcement
4401 North Fairfax Dr., Room 500
P.O. Box 3247
Arlington, VA 22203-3247
ph: 703-358-1949
fax: 703-358-2271
R9LE_WWW@fws.gov
http://www.le.fws.gov
*Check with the US Fish & Wildlife
Service about regulations for
importing and exporting wildlife or
wildlife products.*

Sam Hamilton, Reg. Dir.
U.S. Fish & Wildlife Service, Region 4
1875 Century Blvd.
Atlanta, GA 30345
ph: 404-679-7292
fax: 404-679-7286
fw4_web_manager@fws.gov
http://southeast.fws.gov
*Regional US Fish & Wildlife Service
contact for inquiries regarding laws
pertaining to endangered and
threatened species of wild fauna and
wild flora; covers AL, AR, FL, GA,
KY, LA, MS, NC, SC, TN, Puerto
Rico, US Virgin Islands.*

U.S. Fish & Wildlife Service, Region 3
One Federal Dr., 6th Floor
BHW Federal Building
Fort Snelling, MN 55111
ph: 612-713-5360
MidwestNews@fws.gov
http://midwest.fws.gov
*Regional US Fish & Wildlife Service
contact for inquiries regarding laws
pertaining to endangered and
threatened species of wild fauna and
wild flora; covers IL, IN, IA, MI, MN,
MO, OH, WI.*

Regional Director
U.S. Fish & Wildlife Service, Region 6
134 Union Blvd.
Lakewood, CO 80228
ph: 303-236-7917
MountainPrairie@fws.gov
http://www.r6.fws.gov
*Regional US Fish & Wildlife Service
contact for inquiries regarding laws
pertaining to endangered and
threatened species of wild fauna and
wild flora; covers CO, KS, MT, NE,
ND, SD, UT, WY.*

Nancy Kaufman, Reg. Dir.
U.S. Fish & Wildlife Service, Region 2
P.O. Box 1306
Albuquerque, NM 87103
ph: 505-248-6911
fax: 505-248-6915
Cathy_Carrillo@fws.gov
http://ifw2irm2.irm1.r2.fws.gov
Regional US Fish & Wildlife Service contact for inquiries regarding laws pertaining to endangered and threatened species of wild fauna and wild flora; covers AZ, NM, OK, TX.

Anne Bdgley, Reg. Dir.
U.S. Fish & Wildlife Service, Region 1
911 N.E. 11th Ave.
Portland, OR 97232-4181
ph: 503-231-6121
FW1Webmaster@r1.fws.gov
http://www.r1.fws.gov
Regional US Fish & Wildlife Service contact for inquiries regarding laws pertaining to endangered and threatened species of wild fauna and wild flora; covers CA, HI, ID, NV, OR, WA, American Samoa, Marinas Islands, Guam.

Susan Detwiler
U.S. Fish & Wildlife Service, Region 7
1011 E. Tudor Rd.
Anchorage, AK 99503
ph: 907-786-3520
fax: 907-786-3350
sue_detwiler@fws.gov
http://www.r7.fws.gov
Regional US Fish & Wildlife Service contact for inquiries pertaining to endangered and threatened species of wild fauna and wild flora; covers Alaska.

ENESCO

(see also COLLECTIBLES [MODERN]; COLLECTIBLES [MODERN], Ornaments [Enesco])

Experts

Steve Johnson
4003 Jefferson St.
Sioux City, IA 51108
ph: 712-239-5188
Consultant to "The Official Price Guide to Pottery and Porcelain."

ENGINES

(see also BOATS, Engines; FARM MACHINERY; GAUGES; LAWN MOWERS; MAYTAG; MODELS; STEAM-OPERATED, Models & Equipment; TRACTORS; WASHING MACHINES)

Collectors

Tom Copper
Tom's Small Engines
1416 Ralapen St.
Roxboro, NC 27573-4232
ph: 336-599-6908
tcopper@person.net
http://members.person.net/~tcopper/index.html
Collector of Maytag, Briggs & Stratton and other engines; repairs, rebuilds, and restores most small engines; locates parts and/or related supplies and services.

Ed & Karen Laginess
6896 N. Telegraph Rd.
Monroe, MI 48162
ph: 734-654-9269 or 734-241-9403
autosales@globalbiz.net
Wants to buy unusual flywheel engines and old spark plugs.

Experts

Charles Chiarchiaro
Owls Head Transportation Museum
Rte. 73 Box 277
Owls Head, ME 04854
ph: 207-594-4418
fax: 207-594-4410
info@ohtm.org
http://www.ohtm.org
Mr. Chiarchiaro is an expert in pre-1910 internal combustion and steam engines, and related technologies.

Internet Resources

Harry Matthews
Harry's Old Engine Page
P. O. Box 5612
Sarasota, FL 34277
oldengine@hotmail.com
http://www.old-engine.com
A pioneering Web site started in 1995 to present antique engines to the Web; collecting, restoring, showing antique stationary gas and steam engines; lots of resources for suppliers as well as a selection of books about engines.

Harry Matthews
Enginads
P.O. Box 5612
Sarasota, FL 34277
http://www.enginads.com
Great site for engine related ads, conversation, engine parts and tools, services and related materials for collectors of antique gas engines and steam engines.

Museums/Libraries

Rod Groenewold
Vista Antique Gas & Steam Engine Museum, Inc.
Newsletter: Ignitor
2040 Santa Fe Ave.
Vista, CA 92803
ph: 760-941-1791 or 800-587-2286
fax: 760-941-0690
rod_agsem@yahoo.com
http://www.agsem.com
40-acre living history museum focused on the period (1840-1950). Collec-

tions include historic agricultural and industrial equipment. Reference library on-site. Biennial Threshing Bee and Antique Engine Shows.

Periodicals

Erika Daileda
Wise Owl Worldwide Publications
Magazine: Model Engineers' Workshop
5150 Candlewood St., Ste. 1
Lakewood, CA 90712-1900
ph: 562-461-7574
fax: 562-461-7212
info@wiseowlmagazines.com
http://www.wiseowlmagazines.com
An English magazine published eight times per year; helps the amateur machinist get the most from his tools and equipment in the home engineering workshop.

Gasoline

Book Sellers

Alan C. King
King's Books
P.O. Box 86
Radnor, OH 43066-0086
ph: 614-595-3332
Carries tractor and gas engine manuals.

Clubs/Associations

David Rotigel
Fort Allen Antique Farm Equipment Association
RD #4 Box 143
Greensburg, PA 15601
ph: 724-668-7897
rotigel@westol.com
http://www.oldengine.org/members/rotigel
Buys, sells, trades stationary antique engines: farm, oil, steam.

Alvin Confer
Tri-State Gas Engine & Tractor Association, Inc.
9597 W. Division Rd.
Dunkirk, IN 47336
ph: 765-369-2656

Ona Cook, Sec.
North Texas Antique Tractor & Engine Club
9112 Leaside Dr.
Dallas, TX 75238
ph: 214-341-4539
http://www.north-texas-antique-tractor-and-engine-club.org
Meet regularly to share knowledge and interest in the tractors, engines and farm equipment that mechanized our early 20th century farms.

Ruth Warnock, Sec./Treas.
Early Day Gas Engine & Tractor Association, Inc.
Newsletter: National, The
1537 Weekend Villa Rd.
Ramona, CA 92065
ph: 760-789-3402
fax: 760-789-3769
rawarnock@sbcglobal.net
http://www.edgeta.org
A national organization with 90 regional "Branches" interested in early gas engines and tractors.

Collectors

Rob Skinner
Rusty Iron Gallery
rskinner@rustyiron.com
http://www.rustyiron.com/rustiron.html
Collects, restores and displays antique stationary engines and related farm equipment.

Dealers

David Rotigel
RD #4 Box 143
Greensburg, PA 15601
ph: 724-668-7897
rotigel@westol.com
http://www.oldengine.org/members/rotigel
Buys, sells, trades stationary antique engines: farm, oil, steam.

Larry Sikes
Rock Ridge Farm - The Florida Tractor Connection
1813 NW 97th Terr.
Pompano Beach, FL 33071
ph: 954-527-7360
larry@rockridgefarm.com
http://www.rockridgefarm.com
Collects, restores, buys and sells antique tractors, stationary engines and farm equipment.

Internet Resources

Craig Prucha
Antique Gas Engine Homepage
cprucha@antique-engine.com
http://www.antique-engine.com
Gas engine work shop, gatherings, collections, images.

Kate Smalley
Antique Tractor Resource Page
P.O. Box 896
Branford, CT 06405
anttrac@antiquetractors.com
http://www.antiquetractors.com
A complete reference site for collectors and restorers of antique tractors, stationary engines and farm equipment; also provides Web sites and advertising services for businesses and individuals.

Jim Dunmyer
OldEngine.org
4440 Samaria Rd.
Temperance, MI 48182
ph: 734-856-4190
jdunmyer@toltbbs.com
http://www.oldengine.org
An online site dedicated to lovers of old iron; many pictures taken at area shows.

Periodicals

Ogden Publications, Inc.
Magazine: Gas Engine Magazine
1503 SW 42nd St.
Topeka, KS 66609-1265
ph: 785-274-4383 or 785-274-4300
fax: 785-274-4305
rbackus@ogdenpubs.com
http://www.gasenginemagazine.com
G.E.M. is the leading magazine for antique tractor and gas engine collectors; articles, ads, auctions, models, Maytag gas engines, restoration tips, histories, auctions, suppliers, parts, etc.; published monthly.

Repair Services

David Rotigel
RD #4 Box 143
Greensburg, PA 15601
ph: 724-668-7897
rotigel@westol.com
http://www.oldengine.org/members/rotigel
Buys, sells, trades stationary antique engines: farm, oil, steam.

Suppliers

Bill Starkey
Starbolt Engine Supplies
3403 Buckeystown Pike
Adamstown, MD 21710
ph: 301-874-2821 or 301-694-6840
starbolt4u@aol.com
Sells parts for old gas engines; mail order only; open evenings until 9 p.m.

Simpson Motors
3708 S. Amherst Hwy.
Madison Heights, VA 24572
ph: 804-929-4468
New and used Maytag engine parts, restoration supplies, engines, etc.; rebuild, restore, supply parts for early gasoline engines that powered early washing machines; no appliance parts; makes parts not otherwise available.

Steam

(see also TOYS, Steam/Hot Air)

Clubs/Associations

John Cooper, Sec./Treas.
International Stationary Steam Engine Society
Newsletter: ISSES Bulletin
73 Coniston Way
Bewdley, Worcestershire DY12 2QA U.K.
ph: 01299-402946 or 718-636-3694
john.cooper@isses2.freeserve.co.uk
http://www.steamenginesociety.org
Members interested in the history, documentation and preservation of stationary steam engines throughout the world; publishes a quarterly "Bulletin" and an annual "Journal."

Collectors

R. Bruce Cynar
10023 St. Clair's Retreat
Fort Wayne, IN 46825
ph: 260-489-5004
oldtchnlgy@msn.com
Wants steam engines (small but not toys), steam whistles, and steam gauges.

Museums/Libraries

Dixie Gun Work's Old Car & Steam Engine Museum
1200 N. Highway 51 S
Union City, TN 38261
ph: 901-885-0700
http://www.dixiegun.com

EPHEMERA

(see ADVERTISING COLLECTIBLES; PAPER COLLECTIBLES)

EQUIPMENT

(see MACHINERY & EQUIPMENT; RAILROADS)

ERECTOR SETS

(see TOYS, Construction Sets [Erector])

EROTICA

(see also BATHING BEAUTIES, Nudies & Naughties; PIN-UP ART; PLAYBOY ITEMS; STRIPTEASE)

Auction Services

Robert Bessette
Green Dragon Arts
P.O. Box 588
Burlington, VT 05402-0588
ph: 802-862-1930
fax: 802-862-1930
Conducts auctions specializing in the sale of early erotica from 18th century to present; also underground adult comics and men's girlie magazines.

Gail Wolpin, ISA
Phoebus Auction Gallery
14-16 E. Mellen St.
Hampton, VA 23663
ph: 757-722-9210
fax: 757-723-2280
bwelch@phoebusauction.com
http://www.phoebusauction.com
Conducts auctions of antiques, collectibles, estates, furniture, decorative and fine arts, etc.

Dealers

Mojo Mustapha
World Art Erotica
yoni@wae.org
http://www.wae.org
Sellers of erotic art with an online museum of sensual art and literature from around the world; for a small fee members have access to virtual updates, royalty-free art, free catalog of items for sale, 20% discount off purchases.

Naomi Wilzig
Miss Naomi International Co. Inc.
4 Windermere Ct.
Livingston, NJ 07039
ph: 973-597-0717
fax: 973-992-0799
missnaomi@mindspring.com
http://www.missnaomi.com
Buying fine erotica and erotic art; sells erotic art books by Miss Naomi.

Edward Swain
Edward Swain Erotic Fine Art
P.O. Box 7420
Wayne, PA 19087-7420
ph: 610-688-2882
fax: 610-688-2882
Buys and sells all types of erotic fine art and artifacts: American paintings, drawings, prints, sculpture and photos; European and Asian artists of the 18th-20th C.; no catalogs at this time but photos of specific items upon request.

Naomi Wilzig
Miss Naomi Antiques & Erotica
Box 1421
Lutz, FL 33549-1421
ph: 813-949-3412
fax: 813-949-3148
missnaomi@mindspring.com
http://www.missnaomi.com
Wants erotic art, all mediums, for wall or display.

Experts

Terry Arellano
EroticArt.com
P.O. Box 6276
2191 S. El Camino Real, Ste. 6
San Mateo, CA 94403-0991
ph: 888-887-3444 or 650-906-8003
fax: 650-577-1485
Terry@eroticart.com
http://www.eroticart.com/main.html
Collector, dealer, expert, appraiser of fine erotic art.

Internet Resources

Terry Arellano
EroticArt.com
P.O. Box 6276
2191 S. El Camino Real, Ste. 6
San Mateo, CA 94403-0991
ph: 888-887-3444 or 650-906-8003
fax: 650-577-1485
Terry@eroticart.com
http://www.eroticart.com/main.html
The international marketplace for buyers and sellers of erotic art.

ESKIMO

(see INUIT & NORTHWEST COAST NATIVES; NATIVE AMERICAN)

ESTATE JEWELRY

(see GEMS & JEWELRY, Vintage & Estate)

EXIT GLOBES

Collectors

Michael Bruner
2615 Echo Lane
Ortonville, MI 48462
ph: 248-627-6351
Wants exit globes in all style, shapes and colors.

EXONUMIA

(see COINS; BADGES; BOOKS, Reference [Exonumia]; FRATERNAL ORGANIZATION ITEMS; MEDALS, ORDERS & DECORATIONS; POLITICAL COLLECTIBLES; TOKENS; VETERAN ITEMS; WOODEN MONEY)

EXPOSITIONS

(see WORLD'S FAIRS & EXPOSITIONS)

EYE RELATED ITEMS

(see also MEDICAL, DENTAL & PHARMACEUTICAL; OPTICAL ITEMS)

Clubs/Associations

V. Mellor
Opthalmic Antiques International Collectors' Club
3 Moor Park Rd.
Northwood, Middlesex HA6 2DL U.K.
michael.mellor1@btinternet.com
http://www.college-optometrists.org/college/museum/oaicc.htm
A club for those interested in the history vision aids, and in collecting optical items such as spectacles, instruments, magnifiers, eye baths, quizzers, books, etc.

Eyecups

Collectors

Ken Jermac
215 Westridge Ct.
Chapin, SC 29036-8725
ph: 803-345-9780
jjermac@aol.com
Buys and trades eyecups and eye related items.

Dealers

Doris K. Bagwell, R.N.
Bagwell Antiques
5607 Concord Dr.
Jackson, MS 39211-4239
ph: 601-956-3508
fax: 601-956-4190
DKay5607@aol.com
Wants to buy eye wash baths (eye cups).

Eyeglasses

Appraisers

J. William Rosenthal, MD, ISA
3434 Prytania St., Ste. 250
New Orleans, LA 70115-3551
ph: 504-891-1988 or 504-895-1673
fax: 504-845-1657
JWRosenHar@aol.com
Buys, sells, specializes in and appraises visual aids, spectacles, lorgnettes, opera glasses; author of "Spectacles and Other Visual Aids: A History and Guide to Collecting."

Collectors

Charles Letocha
444 Rathton Rd.
York, PA 17403
ph: 717-846-0428
fax: 717-854-9728
cm.letocha@gte.net
Wants to buy antique spectacles, opthalmoscopes, spectacle catalogs, trade cards, etc.

John Boggs
P.O. Box 66833
Seattle, WA 98166-0833
ph: 206-246-6777
Wants to buy eyeglasses from the 1960s or older including unused frames and especially round lens wire rim; minimum seven; also buying real ugly jewelry and cuff links.

Dealers

Ed Welch
Ed Welch Antiques
Rt. 201
RFD 3 Box 1290
Winslow, ME 04901
ph: 207-872-5849
edwelch@metiques.com
http://www.metiques.com/catalog/antiques.html
Specializes in eyeglasses, spectacles, related tools and optical equipment; Revolutionary and Civil War era spectacles, Pince-Nez and Lorgnettes, eyeglasses worn by famous people,

designer glasses from the 1950s to 1960s.

Gail Busche
Archangel Antiques
334 East Ninth St.
New York, NY 10003-7924
ph: 212-260-9313
richgail38@aol.com
Specializes in vintage and antique clothing buttons, cufflinks, eyewear, lighters, and home furnishings; also Art Deco and Art Nouveau, and classic 1950s and 1960s home furnishings and decorative items.

Man./Prod./Dist.

Alexander Vinyar
Gor. 3, Dom 23, Kv. 138
Ubilney, Moskovskaya 141090 Russia
ph: 095-515-8933 or 095-515-4481
fax: 095-515-8933
vinyar@mail.ru
http://www.geocities.com/vinyar_ru
Makes unique custom eyeglasses from ivory and precious woods; worn by celebrities.

Museums/Libraries

Optometry Museum, Ohio State
 University College of Optometry
338 W. Tenth Ave.
Columbus, OH 43210-1240
ph: 614-292-3246
fax: 614-292-7493
Optometry@osu.edu
Large collection of eyeglasses once owned by famous people; also spectacle styles on display as well as related items.

Here are some tips when contacting someone who is listed in this book:

When requesting information about a particular item, include a description (material, dimensions, maker's mark, model number, etc.) and a photo, sketch, digital image or photocopy of the item in question.

Always ask if there are charges for samples or for the services that you are requesting.

When corresponding by letter, please be sure to include a Large (#10 business size) Self-Addressed and Stamped Envelope (LSASE) if requesting a reply or the return of photographs.

Never call collect unless otherwise directed. When calling, be considerate of time zone differences and always ask if the party you are calling has time to talk. When leaving an answering machine message, always instruct the party to call you back collect.

FAIRIES

(see ELVES; GNOMES; TOOTH FAIRY)

FAIRINGS

Experts

Mel & Barbara Alpren
14 Carter Rd.
West Orange, NJ 07052-4612
ph: 973-731-9427
Advisor to "Warman's Antiques & Collectibles Price Guide."

Janice & Richard Vogel
8420 SW 92nd St., Unit B
Ocala, FL 34481-9317
ph: 352-854-0799
fax: 352-854-0799
vogels@contaandboehme.com
http://www.contaandboehme.com

Ray Begley
2 Lydiate Ash Rd.
Bromsgrove, Worcestershire B61 OHU U.K.
ph: (44) 121 457 9181
fax: (44) 121 457 9212
Collector and expert in Conta & Boehme fairings and match holders/strikers.

FAIRS

(see CARNIVAL ITEMS; WORLD'S FAIRS & EXPOSITIONS)

FAIRY LAMPS

(see also LAMPS & LIGHTING, Miniature; PERFUME LAMPS)

Clubs/Associations

Jim & Pat Sapp
Fairy Lamp Club
Newsletter: Fairy Lamp Newsletter
6422 Haystack Rd.
Alexandria, VA 22310-3308
ph: 703-971-3229
fax: 508-448-8917
sapp@erols.com
http://www.fairylampclub.com
A club for collectors of candle burning lamps (Fairy Lamps).

Collectors

George A. Coupe
1243 1st St. S.E.
Washington, DC 20003
ph: 202-554-1000 or 800-368-5466
fax: 202-863-0775
shootthemoonok@webtv.net
Wants to buy fairy lamps.

Jim & Pat Sapp
6422 Haystack Rd.
Alexandria, VA 22310-3308
ph: 703-971-3229
fax: 508-448-8917
sapp@erols.com
http://www.fairylampclub.com
Collector wants to buy Victorian era fairy lamps; editor of newsletter, member of Night Light Miniature Lamp Club.

Bob Ruf
4165 Fallingwater Dr.
Reno, NV 89509
ph: 775-747-2675
fax: 775-747-2675
bpr@powernet.net
Buys and sells fairy lamps and miniature oil lamps.

Experts

Bob Ruf
4165 Fallingwater Dr.
Reno, NV 89509
ph: 775-747-2675
fax: 775-747-2675
bpr@powernet.net
Author of "Fairy Lamps elegance in candle Lighting" (Schiffer).

FAN CLUBS

(see also AUTOGRAPHS, Celebrity; COMIC BOOKS; CHARACTER COLLECTIBLES; MOVIE MEMORABILIA; PERSONALITIES; PHOTOGRAPHS, Celebrity; SCIENCE FICTION; TELEVISION SHOWS & MEMORABILIA; SPORTS COLLECTIBLES)

Internet Resources

Brad Lang
Fan Clubs for Classic Movie Stars
classicfilm.guide@about.com
http://classicfilm.about.com
Online source of fan clubs, both online clubs as well as snail mail clubs.

Periodicals

Harry Hopkins, Pub.
FANDATA Publications
Directory: FANDOM Directory
7614 Cervantes Ct.
Springfield, VA 22152-1608
ph: 703-913-5575 or 888-FAN-DATA
fax: 703-913-5575
email@fandata.com
http://www.fandata.com
Fandom Directory (R) lists over 20,000 fans, collectors, dealers, stores, clubs, and conventions world-wide: science fiction, TV shows, Star Trek, etc.; now in its 19th annual edition; your listing published free of charge upon request.

FANS

Hand-Held

Clubs/Associations

Dorothy Fowler
Fan Association of North America
Journal: FANA Quarterly
P.O. Box 24118
St. Simons Island, GA 31522
dotfowler@earthlink.net
http://www.fanassociation.org
Promotes fans as art objects and historical artifacts; supports fan research; guides members and non-members in fan collecting; encourages fan exhibits; has active grants program; holds annual conferences with lectures and displays.

Mrs. J.D. Milligan
Fan Circle International
Magazine: Fans
Cronk-Y-Voddy, Rectory Rd.
Coltishall, Norwich NR12 7HF U.K.
ph: 01603 737270
jdm@coltishall.freeserve.co.uk
http://www.fancircleinternational.org
A worldwide society to promote the interest and knowledge in all aspects of fan collecting.

Collectors

Gretchen Walberg
P.O. Box 101
Sunbury, PA 17801-0101
ph: 570-286-6225
fax: 570-286-6229
Wants hand fans with depictions: American historical, ballooning, printed or painted, World's Fair, etc.

Mark Turner
216 Normandy Dr.
Silver Spring, MD 20901
ph: 301-589-2809 or 301-306-2826
MarkITurner@netscape.net
Wants to buy charade fans, i.d. folding fans with rhyming riddles printed on them; these are late 18th to early 19th century fans from U.K., France and Colonial America.

Dorothy Fowler
P.O. Box 24118
St. Simons Island, GA 31522
dotfowler@earthlink.net
http://www.fanassociation.org

Anita F. Palmer
678 Key Royal Dr.
Holmes Beach, FL 34217
ph: 941-778-6805
Serious collector interested in antique hand fans to buy for personal collection; send photocopy with condition and price.

Cynthia Fendel
5128 Spyglass Dr.
Dallas, TX 75287
ph: 972-931-1025
handfanpro@aol.com
http://www.handfanpro.com
Wants to buy fans: folding, advertising, commemorative, novelty, etc.; send photo or photocopy and price.

Cheryl Melnick
P.O. Box 790
Cupertino, CA 95015
ph: 408-559-7799 x222
webmistress@hand-fan.org
http://www.hand-fan.org
Serious collector wants to buy hand-held fans for personal collection and for reenacting to teach living history to others as a volunteer.

Dealers

Eureka, I Found It! Antiques & Collectibles
P.O. Box 2192
Petaluma, CA 94953-2192
eureka@eureka-i-found-it.com
http://www.eureka-i-found-it.com
An online dealer specializing in vintage textiles and clothing, toy and model steam engines, buttons, fans, Art Deco, costume jewelry, toy sewing machines.

Experts

Mary S. Frazier
Frazier at D.H.S./Wedgwood
P.O. Box 215
Dedham, MA 02027-0215
ph: 781-843-5091
msfrazier@hotmail.com
Wrote only book on American hand fans; lectures extensively; author of "Hunt and Allen Fans."

Gretchen Walberg
P.O. Box 101
Sunbury, PA 17801-0101
ph: 570-286-6225
fax: 570-286-6229
Collector of rare and unusual hand fans; author of "Fans Patented in the United States."

Wendy Blue
2118 Van Buren Dr.
Whitehall, PA 18052
ph: 610-799-2072
bluebrd@aol.com
Lectures, writes about fans; curates; wants to buy any type of good quality hand fan: fashion accessories (ivory, tortoise, folding, cockade, etc.); advertising, historical; good graphics & condition; send photo & description & SASE.

Cynthia Fendel
Hand Fan Productions
5128 Spyglass Dr.
Dallas, TX 75287
ph: 972-931-1025
handfanpro@aol.com
http://www.handfanpro.com
Has over 25 years collecting, publishing articles, speaking, and assessing collections; author of "Celluloid Hand Fans."

Grace R. Grayson
2133 Pine Knoll Dr. #16
Walnut Creek, CA 94595-2187
ph: 925-256-0949
A FAN-atic! Collects antique and contemporary fans; European, Oriental, ethnic, etc.; also fan related advertising and literature; lecturer, writer, curator.

Paul Van Saanen
Ch. de la Becque 50
La Tour De Peilz
Switzerland
ph: 0041219445022 or 0041219445320
fax: 0041219441243
Paul.vanSaanen@urbanet.ch

John Brooker
Fan Attic, The
The Square, East Rudham
King's Lynn, Norfolk PE31 8RB U.K.
johnbrooker@fanmaker.co.uk
Maker of fine hand-held fans; also restores fans.

Internet Resources

Cynthia Fendel
Hand Fan Productions
5128 Spyglass Dr.
Dallas, TX 75287
ph: 972-931-1025
handfanpro@aol.com
http://www.handfanpro.com
Informative Web site for hand fan enthusiasts: caring for fans, purchasing fans, glossary of terms, fan museums, types of fans, etc.

International Fan Collector's Guild, The
P.O. Box 790
Cupertino, CA 95015
ph: 408-559-7799 x222
fax: 408-558-2322
webmistress@hand-fan.org
http://www.hand-fan.org
The official online resource for fan collectors: fan museum, art, fan jewelry, Victorian fans, fans for sale, resources, conservation, history, books, vintage fans and more; list your fans or fan-related items on this Web site for free.

Misc. Services

Cynthia Fendel
Hand Fan Productions
5128 Spyglass Dr.
Dallas, TX 75287
ph: 972-931-1025
handfanpro@aol.com
http://www.handfanpro.com
A multi-faceted resource for those with

an interest in antique and collectible hand fans: speaking engagements, assessing collections, providing wedding fans are a few of the services offered.

Museums/Libraries

Colonial Williamsburg
P.O. Box 1776
Williamsburg, VA 23187-1776
ph: 757-229-1000 x8540 or 800-HISTORY
mmartin@cwf.org
http://www.history.org
Specializes in early American furniture and the decorative arts.

Alexandra Alexander
Fan Museum, The
Newsletter: Friends Newsletter
12 Crooms Hill
Greenwich, London SE10 8ER U.K.
ph: (0) 181 305-1441
fax: (0) 181 293-1889
admin@fan-museum.org
http://www.fan-museum.org
The only fan museum in the world entirely dedicated to the history of fans and to the art and craft of fan-making.

Repair Services

T. W. DeLeo
Cereus, Inc.
31 Brook Lane
Cortlandt Manor, NY 10567-6501
ph: 914-737-3769 or 914-739-0754
fax: 914-737-4333
Specializes in the conservation of hand fans: folding, pleated, brise, fixed; European or Oriental.

Mechanical

(see also ELECTRICITY RELATED ITEMS)

Clubs/Associations

Nancy J. Taussig
Antique Fan Collectors Association, Inc.
Newsletter: Fan Collector, The
P.O. Box 5473
Sarasota, FL 34277-5473
ph: 941-955-8232
fax: 941-952-1491
membership@fancollectors.org
http://www.fancollectors.org
Dedicated to the preservation and promotion of antique fans whether powered by water, air, alcohol, or electricity.

Collectors

Kevin Shail
30 Old Middle Rd.
Brookfield, CT 06804-1131
ph: 203-775-7015
fax: 203-775-2536
Interested in old mechanical fans, especially non-electric fans such as those driven by hot-air (kerosene), water power, or wind-ups; also wants early motors.

Rick Padron
1005 E. Idlewild Ave.
Tampa, FL 33604-6831
ph: 813-238-8535 or 813-624-5919
electricfan@aol.com
Serious collector wants to buy pre-1920 fans.

Howard Hazelcorn
6731 Ashley Ct.
Sarasota, FL 34241-9696
ph: 941-921-1815
mrpropane@aol.com
Specializes in early (1889-1905) battery type electric fans.

Jim Daggs
617 Main St.
Ackley, IA 50601
ph: 515-847-2623 or 515-847-2700
fax: 515-847-3588
Author of "A Scrapbook of Fans" (1997).

Michael Breedlove
1875 SE Hwy. 96
Leon, KS 67074
ph: 316-742-9995

Guinn Rigsby
4306 Idlewild Ave.
North Little Rock, AR 72116-8276
ph: 501-753-4073
Imafanman@aol.com
Wants to buy early antique fans with brass blades and brass cages, ornate castings, 6 blades, unusual oscillating mechanisms, Art Deco, unusual, or mint fans; also wants pre-1910 motors, and parts and advertising related to all.

Steve Cunningham
3200 Ashland Dr.
Bedford, TX 76021-6502
ph: 817-267-9851 or 800-991-0165
fax: 817-267-0387
Buying antique electric table fans with brass blades and brass cages; also very old ornate ceiling fans (paddle type); especially interested in very old antique electric motors; also wants books and catalogs on these items.

Alan Bies
357 N. Oak Post Rd.
Houston, TX 77008
ph: 713-869-3332
biesboehck@mindspring.com
Wants to buy early electric fans.

Dealers

Normand Mainville
Machine Age
354 Congress St.
Boston, MA 02210
ph: 617-482-0048

Phil Massie
Wind Wizards, The
1924 Hilton Ave.
Dover, PA 17315-3834
ph: 717-764-2359
Wants antique electric fans with brass blades, related advertising and

ephemera, especially metal signs, books and publications on electricity and pre-1900 electrical lighting.

Donald E. Taussig
Sanders' Antique Mall
527 S. Pineapple Ave.
Sarasota, FL 34236
ph: 941-366-0400
fax: 941-952-1491
sandersant@aol.com
http://www.sandersantiques.com
Buys, sells, restores ceiling and desk fans pre-1900 through 1940s: electric, hot-air, water-powered, etc.

Kurt House
Fan Man, The
218 Country Wood
San Antonio, TX 78216-1607
ph: 210-490-2433
fax: 210-490-3433
cowboyhous@aol.com
Author of "Antique Mechanical Fans" and "Guide to Mechanical Fan Collecting & Emerson Identification;" founder of the America Fan Collectors Association, paid lecturer to museums and clubs on mechanical fans; sells/buys antique fans.

Experts

Scott MacClymonds
Classic Fans & Lighting
10525 Airline Dr.
Houston, TX 77037
ph: 713-448-4739 or 713-697-0069
fax: 713-448-0189
Wants to buy unusual pre-1939 electric, water, kerosene power fans with ornate castings, brass blades and cages, fancy ornamentation, unusual mechanisms, ceiling or desk.

Kurt House
Fan Man, The
218 Country Wood
San Antonio, TX 78216-1607
ph: 210-490-2433
fax: 210-490-3433
cowboyhous@aol.com
Author of "Antique Mechanical Fans" and "Guide to Mechanical Fan Collecting & Emerson Identification;" founder of the America Fan Collectors Association, paid lecturer to museums and clubs on mechanical fans; sells/buys antique fans.

Museums/Libraries

Michael Coup
American Fan Collectors Museum
Vornado Air Circulation Systems
415 E. 13th St.
Andover, KS 67002
ph: 316-733-0035 or 800-297-0883
membership@fancollectors.org
http://www.fancollectors.org
Over 350 fans on display including many rare and one-of-a-kind items, the oldest dating back to the mid-1800s; the most comprehensive collection of air moving devices in the world.

Repair Services

Sidney Lamb
1501 Kesser Dr.
Plano, TX 75025
ph: 972-517-4526
*Motor rewinding; old motors and
choke coils rewound.*

FANTASY

(see HORROR; SCIENCE FICTION)

FARM COLLECTIBLES

(see also CORN COLLECTIBLES;
ENGINES; FARM MACHINERY;
ANIMAL COLLECTIBLES, Horses;
TOYS, Diecast; TOYS, Farm;
WATCH FOBS, Farm Related;
TRACTORS; WEANERS, Calf &
Cow; WINDMILL COLLECTIBLES)

Collectors

Gary Van Hoozer, Ed.
812 N. Third St.
Tarkio, MO 64491
ph: 660-736-4528
*Collects and specializes in farm toys,
antiques, collectibles and farm
equipment; contributor and former
editor of "Farm Collector."*

Dealers

Stephen G. DelSordo
Heritage Resource Group
305 Oakley St.
Cambridge, MD 21613
ph: 410-228-8934
fax: 410-221-8061
sdelsordo@comcast.net
http://www.heritageresource.com
*A cultural resource management/
historic preservation firm that has
contracts to locate, provide,
authenticate artifacts for museums and
collectors; areas of expertise include
architecture, industry, domestic,
agriculture, and maritime.*

Museums/Libraries

Esther Munroe Smith, Lib.
Billings Farm Museum
P.O. Box 489
Woodstock, VT 05091
ph: 802-457-2355
billings-farm@valley.net
*Museum of farm life & technology of
the late 19th century; dairying,
haying, general store, ice cutting,
apple orchard, etc.*

New York State Historical Association &
The Farmers' Museum, Inc., The
P.O. Box 800
Lake Rd., State Highway 80
Cooperstown, NY 13326
ph: 607-547-1400 or 888-547-1450
cliggio@nysha.org
http://www.nysha.org

Bruce Bomberger, Cur.
Landis Valley Museum
2451 Kissel Hill Rd.
Lancaster, PA 17601-4809
ph: 717-569-0401
fax: 717-560-1247
http://www.landisvalleymuseum.org
*Interprets Pennsylvania German rural
culture.*

Tory Fowler, Cur.
Carroll County Farm Museum
500 S. Center St.
Westminster, MD 21157-5615
ph: 410-848-7775 or 800-654-4645
fax: 410-876-8544
*Focuses on Victoriana in rural
America.*

Ron & Lois Smith
Neverrest Farm Family Museum
1911 Harper Rd.
Mason, MI 48854-9260
ph: 517-676-9391
*Located on a working farm and open
on a "by chance" or by appointment.*

Steve Davis
Living History Farms
2600 111th St.
Urbandale, IA 50322
ph: 515-278-2400 or 515-278-5286
fax: 515-278-9808
info@lhf.org
http://www.livinghistoryfarms.org
*A 600-acre, open-air museum
specializing in the past 300 years of
Midwest agriculture; interpreters in
period clothing work out of authentic
buildings with historically accurate
tools and machinery to recreate
routines of early farmers.*

State Agricultural Heritage Museum
925 11th St.
P.O. Box 2207
Brookings, SD 57007-0999
ph: 605-688-6226
fax: 605-688-6303
sdsu_agmuseum@sdstate.edu
http://www.agmuseum.com
*Dedicated to the preservation of South
Dakota's agricultural history and
rural heritage from 1860 to 1950.*

W. Vernon, Dir.
National Agricultural Center & Hall of
Fame
630 Hall of Fame Dr.
Bonner Springs, KS 66012
ph: 913-721-1075
fax: 913-721-1202
http://www.aghalloffame.com
*Collection of a wide range of farming
and farm family related items: plows,
tools, implements, art, dishes,
schoolhouse items, etc.*

Periodicals

Richard Van Vleck
Greybird Publishing
Journal: American Artifacts
P.O. Box 412
Taneytown, MD 21787
ph: 301-447-2680
smma@americanartifacts.com
http://americanartifacts.com/smma
*For collectors, dealers and research-
ers; recent articles include reaper knife
grinders, grain cradles, early cow
milkers, hand corn shellers and rope
machines; free ads for subscribers.*

Cast Iron Seats

Clubs/Associations

Cast Iron Seat Collectors Association
Newsletter: CISCA Newsletter
604 Washington St.
Woodstock, IL 60098-2251
ph: 815-338-6464
fax: 815-338-3556
bud@castironseatclub.org
http://www.castironseatclub.org
*Club for collectors of cast iron seats
from farm implements and machinery;
newsletter contains articles, notices of
meets and shows, auction sale results,
collector profiles.*

Haying Tools

Collectors

Robert Rauhauser
P.O. Box 324
Thomasville, PA 17364-0324
ph: 717-792-0278
*Buys haying tools (forks, carriers &
knives), corn items (shellers, planter
lids, etc.), hog oilers, wrenches, horse
mower tool box lids, etc.*

Hog Oilers

Collectors

Robert Rauhauser
P.O. Box 324
Thomasville, PA 17364-0324
ph: 717-792-0278
*Author of "Good-Bye Mr. Louse - Hog
Oiler Patents 1903 to 1995."*

Literature

Collectors

Clarence L. Goodburn
RR 2, Box 157
Madelia, MN 56062-9531
ph: 507-642-8481
fax: 507-642-8481
goodlit@madtelco.net
*Wants to buy sales literature,
calendars, magazines, hardback
books, etc. about farm tractors and
equipment, crawler tractors, heavy
construction, mining equipment,
logging equipment, and trucks.*

David Yates
321 West Church St.
Genoa, IL 60135
ph: 815-784-3369
deere@tbcnet.com
*Wants to buy farm sales literature, all
brands.*

FARM MACHINERY

(see also AUTOMOBILIA; ENGINES;
FARM COLLECTIBLES; HORSE-
DRAWN VEHICLES; MACHINERY &
EQUIPMENT; STEAM-OPERATED,
Models & Equipment; TOYS, Farm;
TRACTORS; WINDMILL
COLLECTIBLES)

Appraisers

Jay Proost
American Society of Agricultural
Appraisers, Inc.
834 Falls Ave., Ste. 1130
P.O. Box 186
Twin Falls, ID 83303-0186
ph: 208-733-2323 or 800-488-7570
fax: 208-733-2326
ag@amagappraisers.com
http://www.amagappraisers.com
*Members of this society's "American
Society of Farm Equipment Appraisers" division appraise farm
equipment.*

Auction Services

Iron Horse Auction Co.
413 South Hancock St.
P.O. Box 1267
Rockingham, NC 28380
ph: 910-997-2248 or 800-997-2248
fax: 910-895-1530
horse@infoave.net
http://www.auctionweb.com/ironhorse
*Conducts auctions specializing in the
sale of antique steam engines, tractors
and farm related items.*

Bill Dean
Waverly Sale Co.
P.O. Box 355
Waverly, IA 50677
ph: 319-352-2804
fax: 319-352-5642
waverlysalescompany@kca.net
http://www.waverlysales.com
*Specializes in the sale of old and new
farm machinery and equipment.*

Kurt Aumann
Aumann Auctions Inc.
20114 IL Rt. 16
Nokomis, IL 62075
ph: 217-563-2523
info@aumannauctions.com
http://www.aumannauctions.com
*Specializes in the auction sales of
estates, antiques and collectibles.*

Clubs/Associations

David Rotigel
Fort Allen Antique Farm Equipment
    Association
RD #4 Box 143
Greensburg, PA 15601
ph: 724-668-7897
rotigel@westol.com
http://www.oldengine.org/members/
    rotigel
*Buys, sells, trades stationary antique
engines: farm, oil, steam.*

Susan Knaub
Early American Steam Engine & Old
    Equipment Society
P.O. Box 652
Red Lion, PA 17356
ph: 717-244-2912
*Interested in old steam and gas
powered equipment, especially
engines, tractors and other farm
machinery.*

David Semmel
Antique Engine, Tractor & Toy Club,
    Inc.
Newsletter: AETTC Newsletter
5731 Paradise Rd.
Slatington, PA 18080-4028
ph: 610-767-4768
*Organized in 1986 with over 500
members; dedicated primarily to
collecting, preserving and enjoying old
time farm engines and tractors; a
lesser emphasis put on farm toys;
newsletter three times per year.*

David Schnakenberg
Farm Machinery Advertising Collectors
Newsletter: Farm Machinery Advertising
    Collectors Newsletter
10108 Tamarack Dr.
Vienna, VA 22182-1843
schnakenbergdd@erols.com
*A network of over 300 collectors of
farm machinery advertising literature
and memorabilia.*

David Schnakenberg
Farm Machinery Advertising Collectors
10108 Tamarack Dr.
Vienna, VA 22182-1843
ph: 703-938-8606
schnakenbergdd@erols.com
http://www.farmmachineryadvertise.com
*A network of collectors, dealers,
preservationists, historians of all
forms of farm machinery advertising
with interests spanning all manufacturers and time periods from 1830s to
1970s.*

Ona Cook, Sec.
North Texas Antique Tractor & Engine
    Club
9112 Leaside Dr.
Dallas, TX 75238
ph: 214-341-4539
http://www.north-texas-antique-tractor-
    and-engine-club.org
*Meet regularly to share knowledge and
interest in the tractors, engines and
farm equipment that mechanized our
early 20th century farms.*

Internet Resources

Antique Gas Engine Homepage
cprucha@antique-engine.com
http://www.antique-engine.com

Kate Smalley
Antique Tractor Resource Page
P.O. Box 896
Branford, CT 06405
anttrac@antiquetractors.com
http://www.antiquetractors.com
*A complete reference site for collectors
and restorers of antique tractors,
stationary engines and farm
equipment; also provides Web sites
and advertising services for businesses
and individuals.*

Spencer Yost
Antique Tractor Internet Services
3160 MacBrandon Ln.
Pfafftown, NC 27040
ph: 910-924-6109
yostsw@atis.net
http://www.atis.net
*The oldest and most complete Web site
on the Internet that specializes in
antique tractors and farm equipment;
thousands of people access the site
monthly to buy and sell and research
farm equipment.*

Misc. Services

Austin Farms Salvage
Rte. 4 Box 241
Butler, MO 64730
ph: 660-679-4080
fax: 660-679-6488
*Send $20 for a directory listing
names, addresses, phone numbers of
800 used agri-parts yards; for new
used and antique farm equipment.*

Museums/Libraries

Bucks County Historical Society
Newsletter: Penny Lots
84 S. Pine St.
Doylestown, PA 18901-4930
ph: 215-345-0210
fax: 215-230-0823
info@mercermuseum.org
http://www.mercermuseum.org/bchs
*Operates three Nat. Historical
Landmarks; Mercer Museum has over
40,000 tools of Early American
trades/crafts; Spruance Library has
research material on trades & crafts;
Fonthill Museum is a concrete castle
laden with tiles & treasures.*

State Agricultural Heritage Museum
925 11th St.
P.O. Box 2207
Brookings, SD 57007-0999
ph: 605-688-6226
fax: 605-688-6303
sdsu_agmuseum@sdstate.edu
http://www.agmuseum.com
*Dedicated to the preservation of South
Dakota's agricultural history and
rural heritage from 1860 to 1950.*

Darwin Quandt
Makoti Threshing Association Museum
P.O. Box 53
Makoti, ND 58756
ph: 701-726-5643
*Show each year first full weekend in
October; come see antique machines
run.*

W. Vernon, Dir.
National Agricultural Center & Hall of
    Fame
630 Hall of Fame Dr.
Bonner Springs, KS 66012
ph: 913-721-1075
fax: 913-721-1202
http://www.aghalloffame.com
*Collection of a wide range of farming
and farm family related items: plows,
tools, implements, art, dishes,
schoolhouse items, etc.*

Country Heritage Park
8560 Tremaine Rd.
P.O. Box 38
Milton, Ontario L9T 2Y3 Canada
ph: 905-878-8151 or 888-307-3276
fax: 905-876-4530
info@countryheritagepark.com
http://www.countryheritagepark.com
*An interactive heritage park depicting
agriculture and rural life over the last
150 years; 80 acre site, 30 exhibit
buildings, 20,000 artifacts.*

Periodicals

Christina Gargano
Heartland Communications Group, Inc.
Magazine: Farmers Hot Line &
    Manufacturer's Editions
1003 Central Ave.
P.O. Box 1052
Fort Dodge, IA 50501
ph: 800-247-2000 or 515-955-1600
fax: 515-574-2233
libbie@hlipublishing.com
http://www.hlipublishing.com
*Regional and state editions are edited
for buyers and sellers of farm
equipment.*

Christina Gargano
Heartland Communications Group, Inc.
Magazine: Farmers Hot Line Parts
    Edition
1003 Central Ave.
P.O. Box 1052
Fort Dodge, IA 50501
ph: 800-247-2000 or 515-955-1600
fax: 515-574-2233
libbie@hlipublishing.com
http://www.hlipublishing.com
*Directory for the largest selection and
the best prices of new, used, rebuilt
parts and attachments.*

Christina Gargano
Heartland Communications Group, Inc.
Magazine: Hot Line Farm Equipment
    Guide
1003 Central Ave.
P.O. Box 1052
Fort Dodge, IA 50501
ph: 800-247-2000 or 515-955-1600
fax: 515-574-2233
libbie@hlipublishing.com
http://www.hlipublishing.com
*The only monthly locating and pricing
guide for farm equipment.*

Chad & Katie Elmore
Magazine: Belt Pulley
P.O. Box 58
Jefferson, WI 53549
ph: 920-674-9732
elmore@jefnet.com
*Bi-monthly magazine featuring farm
machinery, all makes and models,
1900 to 1970: antique tractors, farm
machinery and related equipment.*

Magazine: Engineers & Engines
    Magazine
2240 Oak Leaf St.
P.O. Box 2757
Joliet, IL 60434-2757
ph: 815-741-2240
fax: 815-741-2243
barb@engineersandengines.com
http://www.engineersandengines.com
*Bi-monthly magazine for tractors, gas
engine, steam, farm machinery and
railroad enthusiasts.*

Shawn Rogers
Magazine: Rusty Iron Monthly
P.O. Box 342
Sandwich, IL 60548-0342
ph: 815-496-9267
rusty@indianvalley.com
*Focuses on the old iron marketplace:
early gas and steam engines, tractors
and related equipment; published
monthly: classified ads for antique
tractors and gasoline engines,
collectibles, literature, etc.*

Ogden Publications, Inc.
Magazine: Steam Traction Magazine
1503 SW 42nd St.
Topeka, KS 66609-1265
ph: 785-274-4383 or 800-678-4883
fax: 785-274-4305
rbackus@ogdenpubs.com
http://www.steamtraction.com
*Published six times per year; carries
articles, ads, auctions for steam
traction machinery: tractors,
threshers, steam engines, etc.*

Ogden Publications, Inc.
Directory: Farm Collector Show
    Directory
1503 SW 42nd St.
Topeka, KS 66609-1265
ph: 785-274-4379 or 800-678-4883
fax: 785-274-4305
kwinford@farmcollector.com
http://
    www.farmcollectorshowdirectory.com
*The annual show directory guides old-
time farming enthusiasts to over 900*

shows in the US and Canada; $8 postpaid.

Ogden Publications, Inc.
Magazine: Farm Collector
1503 SW 42nd St.
Topeka, KS 66609-1265
ph: 785-274-4380 or 800-678-4883
fax: 785-274-4305
jharmon@ogdenpubs.com
http://www.farmcollector.com
Monthly magazine focusing on the preservation of vintage farm equipment covering everything from antique tractors to engines, windmills, cream separators, horse-drawn implements, steam engines, farm toys and pedal tractors.

Elenore Wilson, Ed.
Magazine: Old Machinery Magazine, The
P.O. Box 1200
Port Macquarie, New South Wales 2444
   Australia
ph: (02) 65 850055
fax: (02) 65 850755
tomm_mag@turboweb.net.au
http://www.tomm.com.au
Australian bi-monthly magazine with 96 pages of color inserts, color covers, regular feature writers; published over 15 years; focuses on stationary engines, tractors, steam and various farm machinery; strong international readership.

Suzanne Wright
Kelsey Publishing Ltd.
Magazine: Stationary Engine
Cudham Tithe Barn
Berry's Hill
Cudham, Kent TN16 3AG U.K.
ph: 01959 541444
fax: 01959 541400
info@kelsey.co.uk
http://www.kelsey.co.uk
A 40-page British monthly magazine for the stationary engine enthusiast: news, restorations, history.

Kelsey Publishing Ltd.
Magazine: Farm & Horticultural
   Equipment Collector
Cudham Tithe Barn
Berry's Hill
Cudham, Kent TN16 3AG U.K.
ph: 01959 541444
fax: 01959 541400
info@kelsey.co.uk
http://www.kelsey.co.uk
A 16-page bi-monthly illustrated British magazine solely devoted to farm equipment and implement collecting; packed with information, pictures; plus articles covering barn machinery, sawing machinery, garden machinery, hand tools, etc.

International Harvester

Clubs/Associations

Allen Dummler, Mem. Sec.
International Harvester Collectors
Newsletter: Harvester Highlights
310 Busse Hwy.
PMB 250
Park Ridge, IL 60068-3251
ph: 847-823-8612
fax: 847-823-7069
ihcclub@aol.com
http://www.ihcollectors.org
An association of International Harvester equipment and memorabilia collectors and enthusiasts; sanctions regional chapters.

Collectors

Terry & Kay Klepey
P.O. Box 553
Forks, WA 98331-0553
ph: 360-327-3726 or 360-374-5717
slvrbllt@olypen.com
http://www.olypen.com/slvrbllt
Wants to buy International Harvester items: calendars, advertisements, tools, misc.

Periodicals

Daryl Miller
Newsletter: Red Power
P.O. Box 277
Battle Creek, IA 51006
ph: 712-365-4873
Bi-monthly periodical about International Harvester and their products.

FASHION

(see CLOTHING & ACCESSORIES)

FAST FOOD COLLECTIBLES

(see also FOOD COLLECTIBLES;
GLASSES, Drinking; HAMBURGERS;
PREMIUMS; RESTAURANT
COLLECTIBLES)

Dealers

Bob Gobeil
Bobby's Toys & Collectibles
P.O. Box 1416
Biddeford, ME 04005
bob@bobbystoys.com
http://www.bobbystoys.com
Offers character toys from the 1970s and 1980s from Alfs to Wuzzles; also TV and movie memorabilia, cereal premiums, fast food collectibles.

Bill & Pat Poe
220 Dominica Circle E.
Niceville, FL 32578-4085
ph: 850-897-4163
fax: 850-987-2606
bpoe@cox.net
Buys, sells, trades; specializes in McDonald's; buys old McDonald's collections and collections of PEZ and Smurfs.

Debi Chaltraw
Debi's Fast Food Toys
437 Leslie Dr.
Frankenmuth, MI 48734
gabrielc@cris.com
http://www.concentric.net/~Gabrielc
Buys, sells, trades fast food collectibles, mint-in-package or loose, sets or singles; Web site contains the McDonald's Collectors Club home page.

DeAnna Mansoor
Scribbles Toys & Collectibles
P.O. Box 93
Copperas Cove, TX 76522
ph: 254-542-8121
fax: 254-542-4427
deanna@sagelink.net
http://www.sagelink.net/deanna
Specializes in fast food collectibles from around the world; also action figures, Star Wars, Beanie Babies, Plushes, Smurfs, Care Bears, Disney, PEZ, Flintstones.

Richard Eymann
2619 E. Lynne Ln.
Phoenix, AZ 85040-4724
ph: 602-243-7064
richarde@mctoystore.com
http://www.mctoystore.com
Buy, sell, trade fast food toys from most restaurants and international toys; also action figures, non-sports cards, lunch boxes, advertising premiums.

Camille Boone
ph: 702-564-7380
fax: 702-564-7380
Booneclan@aol.com
http://members.aol.com/booneclan
Buys, sells and collects fast food collectibles from the past and present.

Sandy Hall
Che & Sandy's Fast Food Toys
5954 11th Ave.
Sacramento, CA 95820
burgertoys@comcast.net
http://www.burgertoys.com
Has extensive collection of fast food toys from most restaurants including many hard-to-find pieces.

Experts

Alex G. Malloy
Alex G. Malloy, Inc.
P.O. Box 38
South Salem, NY 10590-0038
ph: 203-438-0396 or 203-438-9652
fax: 203-438-6744
alexmalloy@aol.com
http://members.aol.com/AlexMalloy/
   agmalloy.htm
Specializes in fast food collectibles; co-author of "Kiddie Meal Collectibles" (Krause).

Internet Resources

Rick & Daphne's Webguide for Fast
   Food Toy Collectors
Netherlands
rick.van.der.geest@tip.nl
http://fastfoodtoys.50megs.com
Buys and sells PEZ and European fast food toys.

Burger King

Dealers

Randy Kemple
Randy's Fast Food Toys
rantoys@yahoo.com
http://members.tripod.com/kemple_r/
   index-2.html
Buys, sells, trades Burger King items.

Kentucky Fried Chicken

Museums/Libraries

Colonel Harland Sanders Museum, KFC
   Headquarters
1441 Gardiner Lane
Louisville, KY 40232-2070
ph: 502-456-8353
Col. Sanders was the creator of Kentucky Fried Chicken; the museum shows the history of KFC.

McDonald's

Clubs/Associations

Bill & Pat Poe
Sunshine Chapter, McDonald's
   Collectors Club
Newsletter: Sunshine Express
220 Dominica Circle E.
Niceville, FL 32578-4085
ph: 850-897-4163
fax: 850-987-2606
bpoe@cox.net
Membership is open to all; send SASE for membership form.

McDonald's Collectors Club
Newsletter: McDonald's Collectors Club
   News
PMB 200
1153 So. Lee St.
Des Plaines, IL 60016-6503
secretary@mcdclub.com
http://www.mcdclub.com
For collectors of McDonald's memorabilia: Happy Meal toys and boxes, advertising, ephemera, glassware, pins, garments, etc., quarterly newsletter; this club has regional chapters.

Bill & Betty McCormick
Metro St. Louis MacDonald's Collectors
   Club
725 "A" Woodside Trails
Ballwin, MO 63021-6192
ph: 636-230-3181
WMccorm418@aol.com
http://members.aol.com/wmccorm418/
   collect

Collectors

Charles Wichmann
255 New Lenox Rd.
Lenox, MA 01240-2242
ph: 413-637-3334
charmac@aol.com

Tenna Greenberg
5400 Waterbury Rd.
Des Moines, IA 50312
ph: 515-279-0741

Bill & Betty McCormick
725 "A" Woodside Trails
Ballwin, MO 63021-6192
ph: 636-230-3181
WMccorm418@aol.com
http://members.aol.com/wmccorm418/
collect
Collectors of MacDonald's Happy Meal toys and related items since 1987.

Meredith Williams
P.O. Box 633
Joplin, MO 64802-0633
ph: 417-624-2518 or 417-781-3855
willictn@joplin.com
Wants to buy McDonald's items: buttons, postcards, displays, old uniforms, kids clothes, Happy Meal boxes, toys, annual reports, old and rare comic books, signs, etc.

Dealers

Chris Rucho
7 Colonial Hill Dr.
West Boylston, MA 01583
ph: 508-835-4141
Buys and sells McDonald's collectibles.

Experts

Terry & Joyce Losonsky
SKI Publishing
7506 Summer Leave Lane
Columbia, MD 21046-2455
joyceusa@aol.com
http://members.aol.com/joyceusa/books/
joycebks.htm
Authors of "Collectors Guide to McDonald's Happy Meal Boxes and Premiums;" available from author for $7 plus $2 postage.

Barbara Hunt
1001 Sullins Ct.
Virginia Beach, VA 23455-6902
ph: 757-518-1426
fax: 757-518-1427
Collector, dealer, expert interested in purchasing older pre-1980 McDonald's collectibles, especially paper and slashed arches.

Matt Welch
P.O. Box 30444
Tucson, AZ 85751-0444
ph: 520-886-0505
matwelch@aol.com
Wants to buy any unusual items from McDonald's restaurants: uniforms, glasses, paper items, souvenirs, pins & buttons, regional items, reports, books, displays, signage, items not made available to the public.

Internet Resources

Werner Zemanek
McD-Collect
Lange Gasse 14/13a
Vienna, A-1080 Austria
ph: +43-1-403 32 68-0
fax: +43-1-403 32 68-88
webringmaster@bigfoot.com
http://www.mcd-collect.at
Site of The Official Austrian McDonald's Happy Meal Toys Museum; also McDonald gallery, news, rarities, trade and sell, club; English and Dutch versions.

Periodicals

Meredith Williams
Newsletter: Collecting Tips Newsletter
P.O. Box 633
Joplin, MO 64802-0633
ph: 417-624-2518 or 417-781-3855
willictn@joplin.com
A monthly newsletter filled with up-to-date information about old and new McDonald's restaurant collectibles; also buy, sell and trade ads; send two stamps plus SASE for sample copy.

McDonald's (Happy Meal Toys)

Experts

Meredith Williams
P.O. Box 633
Joplin, MO 64802-0633
ph: 417-624-2518 or 417-781-3855
willictn@joplin.com
Author of "Tomart's Price Guide to McDonald's Happy Meal Collectibles - List - Pictures - Prices - All Happy Meals 1977-1995," $30.95 ppd. from the author.

McDonald's (Japan)

Internet Resources

Happy Meal Toys Collectibles in Japan
Japan
chinq@yo.rim.or.jp
http://www.yo.rim.or.jp/%7Ehac/
world.html
Specializing in Japanese McDonald's toys; archives, links.

McDonald's (Pins)

Clubs/Associations

Michael Fountaine
McDonald's International Pin Club
Newsletter: MIPC Newsletter
P.O. Box 328
Coopersburg, PA 18036-0328
ph: 800-647-2746 or 610-282-8964
fax: 610-282-8963
mike@mipc.com
http://www.mipc.com/index2.html
For collectors of McDonald's lapel pins; newsletter published two times per year; catalog of over 500 McDonald's pins for sale; sponsors shows to meet other collectors.

FASTENERS

Collectors

Mel Kirsner
726 Deal Ct.
San Diego, CA 92109
ph: 619-488-9805
fax: 619-488-0919
pellmel@sd.znet.com
http://www.mellsfastenermuseum.org
Wants fasteners, bolts, nuts, washers or screw related items, pre-1950 only: advertising displays, promotional items, wooden boxes, metal tins, signs, catalogs, etc.

Museums/Libraries

Mel Kirsner
Mell's Fastener Museum
3128 Pera Alta
Julian, CA 92036
ph: 760-765-0569
fax: 619-488-0919
pellmel@sd.znet.com
http://www.mellsfastenermuseum.org
Not-for-profit museum of fasteners, bolts, nuts, washers or screw related items; advertising displays, promotional items, wooden boxes, metal tins, signs, catalogs, etc.; open by appointment only.

FATHER TIME

Collectors

Lee Davis
4150 Old Orchard Rd.
York, PA 17402-3319
ph: 717-757-7267
davisleeh66@aol.com
Collects pre-WWII Father Time items: advertising, postcards, etc.

FEEDSACKS

(see also TEXTILES; QUILTS)

Clubs/Associations

Jane Clark Stapel
Feedsack Club, The
Newsletter: Switches & Swatches
25 S. Starr Ave., Apt. 16
Pittsburgh, PA 15202-3424
ph: 412-766-3996
baglady@stargate.net
http://www.baglady3.com
Members buy, sell, trade and exhibit feedsacks which are used to make quilts, vests, baby quilts, doll quilts, miniatures, clothing and for decorating; lecture programs on request.

Collectors

Diane Holmes
Jasmine Quilt & Supplies
32 Crestview Dr.
Fleetwood, PA 19522
ph: 610-987-9622
fax: 619-987-0742
JasmineQlt@aol.com
Collects feedsacks to make quilts from patterns she designs and publishes; quilt lecturer, instructor, designer.

Karen Bush
Birdsong Collections
409 Morningside Dr.
Richmond, MO 64085
ph: 816-470-8976
Birdsong@worldnet.att.net
http://www.karenbushquilts.com

Dealers

Betsey Telford
Betsy Telford's Antique Quilts dba
Rocky Mountain Quilts
130 York St.
York Village, ME 03909
ph: 800-762-5940
fax: 207-351-3381
betsey@btantiquequilts.com
http://www.rockymountainquilts.com
Dealer, appraiser, expert specializes in quilts, feedsacks and textile restoration; buys, sells and restores antique quilts; has over 400 quilts dating from 1740 to 1940 in stock; restores quilts and hooked using period fabrics.

Jane Clark Stapel
25 S. Starr Ave., Apt. 16
Pittsburgh, PA 15202-3424
ph: 412-766-3996
baglady@stargate.net
http://www.baglady3.com
Specializes, buys, sells, lectures on feedsacks and their use in quilts, clothing and as decoration.

Experts

Jane Clark Stapel
25 S. Starr Ave., Apt. 16
Pittsburgh, PA 15202-3424
ph: 412-766-3996
baglady@stargate.net
http://www.baglady3.com
Specializes, buys, sells, lectures on feedsacks and their use in quilts, clothing and as decoration.

FENCE COLLECTIBLES

(see also BARBED WIRE)

Collectors

L. W. Love
1520 N. Buckner
Dallas, TX 75218
Wants advertising, salesman samples, and patent models related to barbed wire and fence tools.

Posts

Museums/Libraries

Post Rock Museum, The
202 West 1st St.
P.O. Box 473
La Crosse, KS 67548-0473
ph: 785-222-2719 or 785-222-3508
howell@kotn.org
http://skyways.lib.ks.us/towns/LaCrosse/
postrock.html
Documents the quarrying and use of

limestone for fence posts and buildings in the Midwest; displays stone quarry tools; open mid-May through mid-September.

FIESTA

(see CERAMICS [AMERICAN DINNERWARE], Homer Laughlin/ Fiesta)

FIGURINES

(see also ANIMAL COLLECTIBLES; BATHING BEAUTIES, Nudies & Naughties; BOSSONS; CERAMICS; COLLECTIBLES [MODERN]; REPAIR/RESTORATION/ CONSERVATION; TOYS, Action Figures; TOYS, Playsets)

Dealers

Mary Carter
Mary's Memories
P.O. Box 2342
Kansas City, MO 20122
mm@tias.com
http://www.tias.com/stores/mm
Carries a wide line of figurines including Beswick, Rosemeade, De Lee, Josef Originals, animals, Kay Finch, Sebastian, Lefton, Shawnee, Hummel and others.

Beatrix Potter

Dealers

Sarah Hamilton
Beatrix Potter Figurines
squigglywiggly@hotmail.com
http://www.geocities.com/Wellesley/ Atrium/4662

Box of Porcelain
51d Icen Way
Dorchester, Dorset DT1 1EW U.K.
ph: +44(0) 1305 267110
fax: +44(0) 1305 263201
rlunn@boxofporcelain.net
http://www.boxofporcelain.net
Specializes in Beswick, Royal Doulton, Beatrix Potter, Royal Worcester, and Spode.

Boehm

Clubs/Associations

Boehm Porcelain Society, The
Magazine: Boehm Guild Advisory, The
25 Princess Diana Lane
Trenton, NJ 08638
ph: 609-392-2207 or 800-257-9410
fax: 609-392-1437
boehmporcelain@att.net
http://www.boehmporcelain.com
A Boehm manufacturer-sponsored club.

Collectors

Leon Reimert
121 Highland Dr.
Coatesville, PA 19320-1709
ph: 610-383-6969
theboehmer@aol.com
Wants to buy Boehm porcelain dogs, horses, colts, and other animal figurines.

Dealers

Benjamin Gallery
1303 Pennsylvania Ave.
Hagerstown, MD 21742
ph: 301-797-4775
Carries large selection of Boehm porcelain figurines.

Gwendolyn R. Reasoner, Ph.D.
Re Vann Galleries
125 Arthur Lane
Hackberry, LA 70645-3001
ph: 337-762-4280 or 800-821-4278
revanngal@aol.com
Largest Boehm dealer in the US; specializes in the Boehm secondary market; also Cybis, Royal Worcester, Erte; also appraises.

Allan & Pat Clay
Clemons-Eicken Fine European Imports
6166 N. Scottsdale Rd., #204
Scottsdale, AZ 85253
ph: 602-998-9042 or 800-250-5423
fax: 602-998-3755
Carries Lladro, Armani, Boehm, Lalique, Cybis.

Man./Prod./Dist.

Boehm Porcelain, Inc.
25 Princess Diana Lane
Trenton, NJ 08638
ph: 609-392-2207 or 800-257-9410
fax: 609-392-1437
boehmporcelain@att.net
http://www.boehmporcelain.com
Boehm manufacturer, repair/ restoration; appraisals.

Repair Services

Boehm Porcelain, Inc.
25 Princess Diana Lane
Trenton, NJ 08638
ph: 609-392-2207 or 800-257-9410
fax: 609-392-1437
boehmporcelain@att.net
http://www.boehmporcelain.com
Boehm manufacturer, repair/ restoration; appraisals.

Borsato

Appraisers

Allan Koskela
Borsato Collectors Archives
1417 Third St.
Webster City, IA 50595
ph: 515-832-2437
repair@wmtel.net
http://borsato.20m.com
Appraisals and consulting; appraisals minimum $25; catalog available; request information sheet by letter;

also restorations with Borsato factory made parts.

Clubs/Associations

Allan Koskela
Borsato Collectors Club
1417 Third St.
Webster City, IA 50595
ph: 515-832-2437
repair@wmtel.net
http://borsato.20m.com
World's largest database on Italian porcelain and artist, Antonio Borsato; newsletter, appraisal, largest Borsato library in the world.

Cybis

Dealers

Gwendolyn R. Reasoner, Ph.D.
Re Vann Galleries
125 Arthur Lane
Hackberry, LA 70645-3001
ph: 337-762-4280 or 800-821-4278
revanngal@aol.com
Largest Boehm dealer in the US; specializes in the Boehm secondary market; also Cybis, Royal Worcester, Erte; also appraises.

Man./Prod./Dist.

Cybis Porcelains
65 Norman Ave.
Trenton, NJ 08618-3003
ph: 609-392-6074
info@cybisporcelain.com
http://www.cybisporcelain.com
Creates fine porcelain sculptures; contact for purchasing or appraising limited or open edition figurines; also offers authentic Cybis restorations.

Dahl Jensen

Collectors

Allan Nobel
Nobel Antik Webservice
Strommen 17
Randers, Jylland 8900 Denmark
ph: +45 86412220 or +45 86439166
fax: +45 86407952
on@it.dk
http://www.nobelantik.dk
Collects photos and numbers of Dahl Jensen porcelain figurines for posting on Web site to share with others.

Dealers

Peg Zurkowski
Becker Brooks Antiques
8027 Ellingson Dr.
Chevy Chase, MD 20815-3029
ph: 301-588-8558
fax: 301-608-2167
pegbeckz@aol.com
Buys and sells figurines designed by the Danish artist Dahl Jensen.

Erich Stauffer

Collectors

Joan Oates
685 S. Washington
Constantine, MI 49042-1407
ph: 269-435-8353
koates120@earthlink.net
Wants to buy Erich Stauffer child-like figurines; must say "Designed by Erich Stauffer" underneath and give style number; price, describe activity, give height.

Hagen-Renaker

Clubs/Associations

Debra Kerr
Hagen-Renaker Collector's Club, The
2055 Hammock Moss Dr.
Orlando, FL 32820
ph: 407-568-3551
fax: 407-650-2564
HRCC@lucky-seven.com
http://www.lucky-seven.com

Dealers

Arthur Brock
ARB Productions
155 Chestnut Dr.
Richboro, PA 18954-1530
ph: 215-953-9624
fax: 215-942-8761
arthurbrock@comcast.net
http://www.purplemountains.com
Sell, trade, buy retired Hagen Renakers; has large inventory of retired pieces as well as current pieces in stock.

Debra Kerr
Lucky Seven Enterprises
2055 Hammock Moss Dr.
Orlando, FL 32820
ph: 407-568-3551
fax: 407-650-2564
HRCC@lucky-seven.com
http://www.lucky-seven.com
Buys and sells Hagen-Renaker figurines.

Internet Resources

T. Phillips
Read-Me-First.com
feedback@read-me-first.com
http://www.read-me-first.com
Internet resource center for collectors of Hagen-Renaker figurines: glossary, forum, repair tips, identification.

Man./Prod./Dist.

Hagen-Renaker
P.O. Box 427
San Dimas, CA 91773
ph: 909-592-2341
fax: 909-592-8315
nikas.sue@gte.net
http://www.hagenrenaker.com
Manufacturer of collectible ceramic figurines for over 50 years.

Hartland

Collectors

Steve McPherson
RR 2 Box 139-A
La Belle, MO 63447-9569
ph: 660-213-3994
Wants to buy statues by Hartland Plastics: western, baseball, football, religious; also buying Marx playsets.

Dealers

Kevin Cloutier
Kevin Cloutier's Hartland Figurines
19 Vista Dr.
South Portland, ME 04106
ph: 207-767-5156
Kevin@hartlands.com
http://www.hartlands.com
Buys and sells figurines made by Hartland Plastics from 1950s to 1990s: baseball and football, Westerns, horses.

Pam Pramuka
Horsies.net - Model Horses Great & Small
122 Sunrise Hill Rd.
Norwalk, CT 06851
ph: 203-846-8246
pzp@horsies.net
http://www.horsies.net
Expert, dealer buys and sells Breyer model horses; also Hartland and Peter Stone horse and animal models; vintage, special-run, new-in-box, hard-to-find; search service available.

Hummel

(see also COLLECTIBLES [MODERN], Figurines [Goebel])

Appraisers

Larry L. Jensen
Hummels at Half Price
1524 S. Tucson St.
Aurora, CO 80012-5343
ph: 303-751-3782
fax: 303-752-0970
Experienced appraiser of Hummel collections for insurance coverage or claims, estate, and divorce settlements.

Auction Services

Cindy Isennock, CAI
Isennock Auctions & Appraisals, Inc.
4106B Norrisville Rd.
White Hall, MD 21161-9306
ph: 410-557-8052
fax: 410-692-6449
info@isennockauction.com
http://www.isennockauction.com
Appraises Hummel figurines and conducts sales of Hummels.

Clubs/Associations

M.I. Hummel Club
Newsletter: Insights
Goebel Plaza, Rte. 31
P.O. Box 11
Pennington, NJ 08534-0011
ph: 609-737-8777 or 800-666-2582
fax: 609-737-1545
memsrv@mihummel.com
http://www.mihummel.com/
  fs_m_club.html
Oldest collectors club of its kind; members receive information on Hummel figurines, plates & bells history & artistry; Web site with great resource information on Hummel identification and appraising.

Dorothy Dous, Pres.
Hummel Collector's Club, Inc.
Newsletter: Hummel Collector's Club
  Quarterly
1261 University Dr.
Yardley, PA 19067-2857
ph: 215-493-6705 or 888-5-HUMMEL
fax: 215-321-7367
customerservice@hummels.com
http://www.hummels.com
Specializing in M.I. Hummel items; fact-filled newsletter includes new releases, discontinued and older figurines, sale items and monthly figurine giveaway; also conducts monthly mail auctions of 2000-2500 items.

Tampa Area M.I. Hummel Club
114 W. Bloomingdale Ave.
Brandon, FL 33511
ph: 813-855-5680 or 813-654-1938
cjohns@aol.com

Larry L. Jensen
Mountaineers, The
1524 S. Tucson St.
Aurora, CO 80012-5343
ph: 303-751-3782
fax: 303-752-0970
The Mountaineers is one of the largest chapters of the M.I. Hummel Club.

Dealers

Don & Beth Woodworth
Dustables, Inc.
5866 W. Sweden Rd.
Bergen, NY 14416
ph: 800-560-6996
fax: 716-494-1617
service@dustables.com
Buys and sells M.I. Hummel figurines by mail order; checks, money orders, major credit cards accepted; free catalog available upon request.

Arnie Berger
Yesterdays South, Inc.
P.O. Box 565097
Miami, FL 33256
ph: 800-368-5866 or 305-251-1988
fax: 305-254-5977
arnieb@bellsouth.net
http://www.yesterdayssouth.com
Send SASE for list of almost 1,000 Doultons, Hummels, and Lladros for sale.

Larry L. Jensen
Hummels at Half Price
1524 S. Tucson St.
Aurora, CO 80012-5343
ph: 303-751-3782
fax: 303-752-0970
Buys, sells, trades Hummel figurines; selling new and old figurines at reduced prices.

Donald M. Hardisty
Don's Collectibles
3020 E. Majestic Ridge
Las Cruces, NM 88011
ph: 505-522-3721
fax: 505-522-7909
donshummels@zianet.com
http://www.zianet.com/donsbossons
Internationally recognized expert, collector, supplier, appraiser, and restoration artist recommended by Bossons; also specializes in Hummels and rare coins; member Inter. Bossons Collectors Society, MI Hummel Club, Amer. Numismatic Assoc.

Donald M. Hardisty
Don's Collectibles
3020 E. Majestic Ridge
Las Cruces, NM 88011
ph: 505-522-3721
fax: 505-522-7909
don@donsbossons.com
http://www.donsbossons.com
Internationally recognized expert, collector, supplier, appraiser, and restoration artist recommended by Bossons; also specializes in Hummels and rare coins; member Inter. Bossons Collectors Society, MI Hummel Club, Amer. Numismatic Assoc.

Paul Gillespie
HummelExchange
7737 Fair Oaks Blvd. #451
Carmichael, CA 95608
ph: 530-301-0717
webmaster@hummelexchange.com
http://www.hummelexchange.com
Buys and sells a large variety of M.I. Hummel figurines as well as other Hummels.

Experts

Dorothy Dous
1261 University Dr.
Yardley, PA 19067-2857
ph: 215-493-6705 or 888-5-HUMMEL
fax: 215-321-7367
customerservice@hummels.com
http://www.hummels.com
Buys, sells, collects, appraises, auctions and specializes in Hummels; runs the Hummel Collector's Club.

Dean A. Genth
Miller's Gift Gallery
500 Hallmark Dr.
Eaton, OH 45320
ph: 937-472-4072
fax: 937-472-4081
dean@millershallmark.com
http://www.millershallmark.com
Offers replacements and loss claim

analysis; author of the "Price Guide to M.I. Hummel."

Larry L. Jensen
1524 S. Tucson St.
Aurora, CO 80012-5343
ph: 303-751-3782
fax: 303-752-0970
Available for lectures across the country sharing his extensive knowledge with displays of Hummel figurines, original Hummel artwork and the world's largest collection of 800 Hummel art postcards; Hummel dealer, appraiser.

Fred Roberts
Bah Humbug Collectibles
P.O. Box 5733
Lake Montezuma, AZ 86342-5733
ph: 928-567-5941
fax: 815-425-9394
bahhumbug@juno.com
Hummel advisor to "Schroeder's Price Guide."

Internet Resources

Hans J. Schindhelm
M.I. Hummel & Precious Moments
Internet Sites Directory
8 John Walsh Blvd., Ste. 412
Peekskill, NY 10566
ph: 914-734-8410
fax: 914-762-1719
siegmar@aol.com
http://members.aol.com/hummel2001
Free online directory of Web pages and Internet sites relating to M.I. Hummel and Precious Moments collectibles.

Man./Prod./Dist.

M.I. Hummel
Goebel Plaza, Rte. 31
P.O. Box 11
Pennington, NJ 08534-0011
ph: 609-737-8777 or 800-666-2582
fax: 609-737-1545
memsrv@mihummel.com
http://www.mihummel.com
The official Web site for M.I. Hummel; price list for current Hummel figurines at http:// www.mihummel.com/collection/ pricelist_all.html.

Museums/Libraries

Doreen Schaeffer
New Braunfels Museum of Art
199 Main Plaza
P.O. Box 311100
New Braunfels, TX 78131-1100
ph: 830-625-5636
fax: 830-625-5966
nbma@nbtx.com
http://www.nbtx.com/nbma
Exhibits the world's largest collection of original drawings by M.I. Hummel; figurines and other Hummel items for sale in gift shop.

Repair Services

Hans J. Schindhelm
Ceramic Restorations of Westchester, Inc.
8 John Walsh Blvd., Ste. 412
Peekskill, NY 10566
ph: 914-734-8410
fax: 914-762-1719
siegmar@aol.com
http://www.swiftsite.com/hummel-preciousmoments/repair.html
Repair and restoration service for any brand of porcelain and ceramic collectibles, antiques and art objects; specializing in Precious Moments and Hummels; also Disney, Cybis, Boehm, Hutschenreuther, Rosenthal and others.

Fredi W. Boese
M.I. Hummel Restoration
P.O. Box 933
Harriman, NY 10926
ph: 845-783-4438
fax: 845-783-4438
fredi@frediboese.com
http://www.frediboese.com
One of the country's leading restorers of fine porcelain and art; 38 years experience as a master M.I. Hummel artist.

Dona Danziger
Clay Werks, Ltd.
4058 S. Main St.
P.O. Box 352
Exmore, VA 23350
ph: 757-414-0567
fax: 757-414-0571
info@claywerksltd.com
http://www.claywerksltd.com
Crazing corrections - trademarked in 1995; this is a kiln-fired process for the Hummels which eliminates crazing; call for free information sheet.

Hummel Look-Alikes

Collectors

Joan Oates
685 S. Washington
Constantine, MI 49042-1407
ph: 269-435-8353
koates120@earthlink.net
Interested in child-like, Hummel look-alikes marked "Designed by Erich Stauffer" and numbered, made in Japan and imported by Arnart Imports, NY; these 4 1/2" to 10" figurines resemble Hummels, but are not.

Josef Originals

Clubs/Associations

Karen Wagner
Josef Collectors Club
13566 "Z" St.
Omaha, NE 68136
SanToa@aol.com

Dealers

Jim Whitaker
Eclectic Antiques
P.O. Box 475
Lynnwood, WA 98046-0475
ph: 425-774-6910
eclectic@gte.net
http://www.eclecticantiques.com

Periodicals

Jim Whitaker
Newsletter: Josef Originals Newsletter
P.O. Box 475
Lynnwood, WA 98046-0475
ph: 425-774-6910
eclectic@gte.net
http://www.eclecticantiques.com
Newsletter is published bi-annually.

Kaiser

Man./Prod./Dist.

Kaiser - Porzellan, Alboth & Kaiser GmbH & Co. KG
Auwaldstr. 8
Staffelstein, Bavaria 96231 Germany
ph: 09573/336 - 0
fax: 09573/336 - 101
sales@kaiser-porzellan.com
http://www.kaiser-porzellan.com
Porcelain dinnerware and bone china; porcelain flowers, vases, figurines and wallplates, giftware and collectibles.

Lady

Collectors

Virginia Youngren
111 Temple St.
West Newton, MA 02465-2313
ph: 617-244-6144
fax: 617-244-5689
youngren@earthlink.net
Wants to buy witty Victoria bisque figurines, especially naughties and nudies.

Lipstick Ladies

Collectors

Bobbie & Alan Bryson
1 St. Eleanoras Ln.
Tuckahoe, NY 10707-1307
ph: 914-779-1405
napkindoll@aol.com
Collects lipstick ladies: figurines having holes or looks to hold tubes of lipstick.

Lladro

Clubs/Associations

Lladro Collectors Society
Magazine: Expressions
1 Lladro Dr.
Moonachie, NJ 07074
ph: 201-807-1177 or 800-634-9088
fax: 201-807-1168
http://www.lladro.com
Focuses on the collectible Lladro figurines. Sponsored by Lladro Co.

Dealers

Gregg Shienbaum
Lladro Connection, A
30 NE 1st St.
Miami, FL 33132
ph: 800-984-5586
illum1@aol.com
http://www.illumcollectibles.com
Specializing in current and retired Swarovski and Lladro; also carries a complete line of Lalique and Kosta Boda.

Arnie Berger
Yesterdays South, Inc.
P.O. Box 565097
Miami, FL 33256
ph: 800-368-5866 or 305-251-1988
fax: 305-254-5977
arnieb@bellsouth.net
http://www.yesterdayssouth.com
Send SASE for list of almost 1,000 Doultons, Hummels, and Lladros for sale.

Janet Gale Hammer
Lladro: A Retired Collection
550 Harbor Cove Circle
Longboat Key, FL 34228-3544
ph: 941-387-0102 or 800-332-8594
fax: 941-383-8865
janet@lladrolady.com
http://lladrolady.com
Secondary market dealer specializing in Lladro.

Clark Sanchez
Sanchez Collectibles
1555 East Glendale Ave.
Phoenix, AZ 85020
ph: 602-395-9974 or 602-277-1661
fax: 602-241-0702
Buys, sells, appraises Lladros; does not sell new pieces, only pre-owned pieces no longer being manufactured; list available for free; will assist in identifying pieces and estimating their value.

Allan & Pat Clay
Clemons-Eicken Fine European Imports
6166 N. Scottsdale Rd., #204
Scottsdale, AZ 85253
ph: 602-998-9042 or 800-250-5423
fax: 602-998-3755
Carries Lladro, Armani, Boehm, Lalique, Cybis.

Ben Swan
Golden Swan Collectibles
881 Lincoln Way
Auburn, CA 95603
ph: 530-823-7926 or 800-231-9055
fax: 530-823-1945
Offers a "search and find" and a listing service to collectors, buyers and sellers of Lladro figurines; also for Swarovski, Walt Disney Classics, and Disneyana Convention figurines.

Experts

Clark Sanchez
Sanchez Collectibles
1555 East Glendale Ave.
Phoenix, AZ 85020
ph: 602-395-9974 or 602-277-1661
fax: 602-241-0702
Buys, sells, appraises Lladros; does not sell new pieces, only pre-owned pieces no longer being manufactured; list available for free; will assist in identifying pieces and estimating their value.

Man./Prod./Dist.

Lladro USA, Inc.
1 Lladro Dr.
Moonachie, NJ 07074
ph: 201-807-1177 or 800-634-9088
fax: 201-807-1168
http://www.lladro.com
Manufactures and distributes quality handcrafted porcelains from Valencia, Spain.

Museums/Libraries

Lladro Museum
43 West 57th St.
New York, NY 10019
ph: 212-838-9356
A manufacturer-sponsored museum and retail outlet; includes the largest collection of retired Lladro porcelain figurines - over 1,000 pieces occupying five floors.

Periodicals

Lladro USA, Inc.
Newsletter: Lladro Antique News
1 Lladro Dr.
Moonachie, NJ 07074
ph: 201-807-1177 or 800-634-9088
fax: 201-807-1168
http://www.lladro.com
Focuses on the current secondary market values of Lladro's 3,000 hard-paste porcelain figurines produced since 1941; also covers history of hard-paste porcelain (1000 AD to present) such as Meissen, Sevres, Nymphenburg, etc.

Morten Studio

Dealers

Denise Hamilton
899 Latta Brook Rd.
Elmira, NY 14901-9226
ph: 607-732-2550
Buys dogs collectibles: figurines, old dog postcards, jewelry with dogs in it, etc.; Borzoi (Russian Wolfhound), greyhound, all Morten Studio and Erphila dogs and animals.

PenDelfin

Dealers

George Sparacio
Miscellania Antiques & Collectibles
P.O. Box 791
Malaga, NJ 08328
ph: 856-694-4167
fax: 856-694-4536
mrvesta1@aol.com
http://members.aol.com/mrvesta1
Dealer, expert wants to buy pre-1975 retired PenDelfin figurines; will buy one or entire collection; quality items only.

Royal Doulton

(see CERAMICS [ENGLISH], Doulton; CERAMICS [ENGLISH], Royal Doulton; COLLECTIBLES [MODERN], Royal Doulton)

Royal Dux

Dealers

Mary Ann Swietlik
Just Dux It, Inc.
4 Gillingham Court
Algonquin, IL 60102
ph: 773-593-0921 or 773-330-6567
fax: 847-669-1376
info@justduxit.com
http://www.justduxit.com
Specializes in collectible porcelain figurines by Royal Dux Bohemia; imported from Czechoslovakia; famous "Pink Triangle" mark guarantees authenticity; individually numbered and handcrafted.

Man./Prod./Dist.

Royal Bohemian Inc. (USA)
P.O. Box 1533
115 Industrial Dr., Ste. F
Saint Marys, GA 31558
ph: 912-673-7197 or 800-231-0208
fax: 800-222-0163
info@royalbohemia.com
http://www.royalbohemia.com
Manufacturer of Royal Dux figurines; online retail price guide for new pieces.

FILMS

(see also AUDIO-VISUAL; CAMERAS & CAMERA EQUIPMENT; MOVIE MEMORABILIA)

Appraisers

Larry Urbanski
Urbanski Film
P.O. Box 438
Orland Park, IL 60462-0438
ph: 708-460-9082
fax: 708-460-9099
info@urbanskifilm.com
http://www.urbanskifilm.com
Film collection appraisals (8mm, 16mm, 35mm) for legal purposes and/ or insurance claims; 35 years experience; member of AMIA

(Association of Moving Image Archivists).

Dr. Steve Johnson
Behavioral Images, Inc.
Newsletter: Ten Thousands Words
302 Leland St., Ste. 101
Bloomington, IL 61701-5646
ph: 309-829-3931 or 800-988-6427
fax: 309-829-9677
sjohnson@mediavalue.com
http://www.mediavalue.com
Film, video, recordings, photographs, negatives; author of "Appraising Audio-visual Media; A Guide for Attorneys, Trust Officers, Insurance Professionals, & Archivists" (1993); $34.95 & $3 S&H; publishes newsletter ten times per year.

Clubs/Associations

Association of Moving Image Archivists
1313 North Vine St.
Los Angeles, CA 90028
ph: 323-463-1500
fax: 323-463-1506
amia@amianet.org
http://www.amianet.org
Advancing the field of moving image archiving by fostering cooperation among individuals and organizations concerned with the collection, preservation, exhibition, and use of moving image materials.

Collectors

Gil O'Gara
P.O. Box 36172
Des Moines, IA 50315-0310
ph: 515-287-0404
Collects original silent (pre-1930) movies in these formats: 35mm nitrate, 16mm Kodascope, 28mm, 8mm, 9.5mm; no video, please.

Dealers

Larry Urbanski
Urbanski Film
P.O. Box 438
Orland Park, IL 60462-0438
ph: 708-460-9082
fax: 708-460-9099
info@urbanskifilm.com
http://www.urbanskifilm.com
Specializes in 16mm, 8mm, 35mm film and equipment; specializing in cartoons, educational, features, TV shows, and shorts; archival cans, reels, film cleaner; also buys same; send two stamps for list of wants.

Christopher Perry
Photoplay Orchestra
7470 Church St., Ste. A
Yucca Valley, CA 92284-3248
ph: 760-365-0475
fax: 760-365-0495
evildoctor3d@yahoo.com
http://www.photoplayorchestra.com
Wants motion picture films of all kinds, especially pre-1928 silent movies and also any 3-D movies; 8mm films are not desirable unless they are

complete movies and not shorter, condensed versions.

Videos

Man./Prod./Dist.

Larry Urbanski
Moviecraft Inc.
P.O. Box 438
Orland Park, IL 60462-0438
ph: 708-460-9082
fax: 708-460-9099
info@moviecraft.com
http://www.moviecraft.com
Offers a nostalgic/historical line of home videos including TV shows, World Fair, automotive, rare cartoons, classics, unique contemporary releases, war newsreels and propaganda, special interest subjects, and feature films.

FINANCIAL PAPER

(see BANKING; CIVIL WAR ARTIFACTS, Confederate Bonds; COINS & CURRENCY, Paper Money; PAPER COLLECTIBLES; SCRIP; STOCKS & BONDS)

FINE ART

(see ART; PAINTINGS & DRAWINGS; PRINTS; SCULPTURES)

FIRE FIGHTING MEMORABILIA

Auction Services

Chuck Deluca
Maritime Auctions
P.O. Box 322
York, ME 03909
ph: 207-363-4247
fax: 207-363-1416
info@maritiques.com
http://www.maritiques.com
Author of "Firehouse Memorabilia - A Collector's Reference;" two cataloged auctions per year in April and August.

Clubs/Associations

David Cerull
Fire Collectors Club
P.O. Box 992
Milwaukee, WI 53201-0992
Collectors of Fire Service medals.

Collectors

Joseph J. Kaminski
Firetiques
82 Stockburger Rd.
Moodus, CT 06469
ph: 860-873-2379
jjkaminski@snet.net
http://www.firetiques.com
Buy, sell, collect fine fire department and related antiques and memorabilia; will buy a single item or an entire collection: fire fighting folk art, paintings; parade hats, buckets, grenades, helmets, trumpets, etc.

Jim Piatti
P.O. Box 244
Oakland, NJ 07436
ph: 973-962-6470
jpiatti@ramapo.edu
Wants to buy fire fighting memorabilia: pre-1900, trumpets, steamers, hand pumpers, fire toys, presentation items, fire helmets, gold badges, engine lights, badges, etc.

Ralph Jennings
675 Forest Creek Dr.
Ambler, PA 19002-4934
ph: 215-646-7178
Interested in fire fighting and fire insurance related collectibles; prefers pre-1900 items.

Jeb S. Fuller
9 Durey Ct.
Cartersville, GA 30120
ph: 770-387-9758
Wants to buy firehouse items: postcards, ads or photographs featuring firemen or fire trucks, old fire trucks, extinguishers, trumpets, badges, alarms, helmets, etc.

David Cerull
P.O. Box 992
Milwaukee, WI 53201-0992
Wants Fire Service medals from any country; send detailed description, rubbing or photocopy along with price.

Larry Zeleznik
139 Badger Lane
Green Bay, WI 54303
wawrzekski@worldnet.att.net
Focuses on collecting fire fighting related memorabilia of the Chicago Fire Department.

Don Vessey
4425 Jonquil Ln.
Minneapolis, MN 55442
ph: 615-559-8047

Stan Zukowski
1867 Ellard Place
Concord, CA 94521-1545
ph: 925-687-6426
Wants fire department antiques: fire alarm boxes, wood cased fire station bells, desk bells, keys, books, catalogs, parts; anything fire alarm related in any condition; also wants helmets, lanterns, trumpets, glass grenades, etc.

Alan Miller
P.O. Box 128
Selma, OR 97538
ph: 541-597-4452
alan@webvenues.net
http://www.webvenues.net
Fire fighting memorabilia collector who operates Web hosting and development for firefighting collectibles; fire associations and clubs; Crown Fire Trucks, Face the Fire, Rusty Bucket, apparatus, badges, fire alarms, antique trucks, etc.

Dealers

Paul Klaver
5 Viking Court, #43
Arlington, MA 02474
ph: 781-648-3910
paul.klaver@verizon.net
*Buys all types of fire fighting items
including helmets, buckets, parade
hats, alarm equipment, toys, folk art,
apparatus, and related ephemera.*

Robert A. Fratkin
American Experience, The
1650 Tysons Blvd., 10th Floor
Mc Lean, VA 22102
ph: 703-556-8108 or 703-629-1941
fax: 703-356-6492
coxfdr@erols.com
*Buys and sells fire fighting memora-
bilia; willing to give telephone
assistance in identifying and valuing;
please have item in hand when calling.*

Stan Willis
Handcuffs & Badges
P.O. Box 36474
Cincinnati, OH 45236
handcuffs@isoc.net
http://www.handcuffsandbadges.com
*Buys, sells restraining devices
(handcuffs, leg irons, thumbcuffs,
etc.), police badges, fire badges and
other fire and police antiques;
specializes in items related to
Cincinnati and area.*

Robert H. Harper
Cary Station Antiques
22 Spring St.
Cary, IL 60013
ph: 847-639-7434
fax: 847-639-8982
rharper@carystationantiques.com
http://www.carystationantiques.com
*Wants helmets, trumpets, presentation
badges, painted leather buckets,
lamps, parade hats, alarm equipment,
etc.*

Dave Miller
Firecollector.com
P.O. Box 2393
Conroe, TX 77305-2393
ph: 936-756-9699
fax: 936-756-5256
info@firecollector.com
http://www.firecollector.com
*Offers fire department and fire
fighting memorabilia of fire
departments and fire fighting from
around the world.*

Marvin Karsten
Old Tyme Fire Classics
6217 Crystal Dr.
Alta Loma, CA 91701-3411
ph: 909-987-5084
firegoods@aol.com
http://members.aol.com/firegoods/
    firegoods/home.html
*Dealer, collector, expert wants to buy
firehouse memorabilia: American fire
helmets, wood cased fire alarm bells,
street boxes, speaking trumpets,*
*Gamewell equipment, fire insurance
advertising, fire toys, fire lanterns.*

Experts

Joseph J. Kaminski
Firetiques
82 Stockburger Rd.
Moodus, CT 06469
ph: 860-873-2379
jjkaminski@snet.net
http://www.firetiques.com
*Collects and specializes in firefighting
antiques and related items: grenades,
helmets, buckets, folk art that is fire
related including watercolors and oil
paintings, trumpets, and insurance
signs.*

Jim Piatti
P.O. Box 244
Oakland, NJ 07436
ph: 973-962-6470
jpiatti@ramapo.edu
*Author of "Confident Collector Series
- Firehouse Memorabilia," (Avon
Books).*

Tom & Patricia Laun
Little Century
215 Paul Ave.
Syracuse, NY 13206-3220
ph: 315-437-4156 or 315-654-3244
tlaun@twcny.rr.com
*Buys and sells fire related antiques
and collectibles, any number; supplies
and manufactures parts for firematic
items; also repairs; call 315-437-4156
in the winter, and 315-654-3244 in
summer.*

Germaine Broussard
1650 Tysons Blvd., 10th Floor
Mc Lean, VA 22102
ph: 703-556-8183 or 800-336-0156
fax: 703-356-6492
watrwitch@erols.com
*Buys, sells, appraises fire department
memorabilia; one piece or collection;
early ribbons are a specialty; will
answer questions for new collectors;
former firefighter and paramedic.*

Museums/Libraries

Eugene I. Morris, Dir.
New England Fire & History Museum
Newsletter: Siren Soundings
1439 Main St. (Rte. 6A)
Brewster, MA 02631
ph: 508-896-5711
http://www.nefiremuseum.org
*One of the world's most varied
collections of antique fire engines; 35
historic fire engines; Mr. Morris
appraises and has written many
articles relating to fire fighting,
apothecary and blacksmithing
material.*

Joseph Doyle, Jr.
Friendship Fire Company No. 1
29 Delaware St.
Woodbury, NJ 08096
ph: 856-845-0066 or 856-845-5174
dwayne@jersey.net
http://www.jersey.net/~dwayne/
    history1.htm
*Volunteer fire company in existence for
over 200 years; museum contains many
artifacts, apparatus, and other fire
fighting related items.*

Mina R. Weiner, Dir.
New York City Fire Museum, The
Newsletter: Burning Issues
278 Spring St.
New York, NY 10013-1405
ph: 212-691-1303
fax: 212-924-0403
http://www.nycfiremuseum.org
*Houses one of the nation's most
important collections of fire related
art and artifacts from the late 18th
century to present: painted leather
water buckets, helmets, parade hats
and belts, lanterns, tools, hand-
pumped fire engines, etc.*

R. Dennis Randall, Cur.
Firemen's Association of the State of
    New York Museum of Firefighting
117 Harry Howard Ave.
Hudson, NY 12534
ph: 518-828-1875 or 877-347-3687
fax: 518-822-8520
fasnyfiremus@mhcable.com
http://www.fasnyfiremuseum.org
*Focuses on the preservation of fire
fighting history; over 86 antique
engines dating from 1725 to 1974 are
displayed along with over thousands
of related fire fighting memorabilia;
admission is free.*

Fire Museum of Maryland
1301 York Rd.
Lutherville, MD 21093
ph: 410-321-7500
fax: 410-769-8433

Glenn Hartley, Sr.
Smokey's Fire Museum
1025 Roberts Dr.
Sugar Hill, GA 30518
ph: 678-714-3128
ghartleysr@aol.com
*Private museum displaying fire
department and fire insurance fire
marks, signs, badges, buckets,
helmets, postcards, stamps, toy, postal
covers, etc.*

Toledo Firefighters Museum
Newsletter: Hook & Letter, The
918 W. Sylvania Ave.
Toledo, OH 43612
ph: 419-478-3473
boconnor@wcnet.org
http://www.fishnews.com/museum.htm
*Comprehensive collection of fire
fighting antiques and 2000 volume
library.*

Oklahoma Firefighters Museum
2716 NE 50th St.
P.O. Box 11507
Oklahoma City, OK 73136
ph: 405-424-3440 or 800-308-5336
fax: 405-424-1032
osfa@brightok.net
http://www.osfa.info/muse.html
*Houses the large, colorful Ben Dancy
shoulder patch collection of over
4,500 pieces.*

Hall of Flame Museum of Firefighting
6101 East Van Buren St.
Phoenix, AZ 85008
ph: 602-275-3473
fax: 602-275-0896
webmaster@Halloflame.org
http://www.halloflame.org
*Over 35,000 square feet of exhibits,
with almost 90 fully restored pieces of
fire apparatus on display dating from
1725 to 1968; sponsored by the
National Historical Fire Foundation.*

San Francisco Fire Department Memorial
    Museum
655 Presidio Ave.
San Francisco, CA 94115
ph: 415-558-3546
ashen@crossnet.org
http://www.sffiremuseum.org
*Contains fire apparatus and fire
artifacts relating to the history of San
Francisco.*

Periodicals

Dave Miller
Firecollector.com
Magazine: Fire Patch Collector
P.O. Box 2393
Conroe, TX 77305-2393
ph: 936-756-9699
fax: 936-756-5256
info@firecollector.com
http://www.firecollector.com
*Loaded with articles about patch
collecting, how to obtain patches, lists
of traders, buy-sell-swap ads,
identification guides; covers all kinds
of fire patches, from regular fire dept.
patches to Company patches from NY,
Boston, etc.*

Dave Miller
Firecollector.com
Newsletter: Fire Collector News
P.O. Box 2393
Conroe, TX 77305-2393
ph: 936-756-9699
fax: 936-756-5256
info@firecollector.com
http://www.firecollector.com
*Published quarterly and contains
articles about fire department
memorabilia and collectibles offered
for sale: fire helmets, fire extinguishers, postcards, badges, lanterns,
Smokey Bear, insurance items, etc.*

FIRE FIGHTING MEMORABILIA

Repair Services

Tom & Patricia Laun
Little Century
215 Paul Ave.
Syracuse, NY 13206-3220
ph: 315-437-4156 or 315-654-3244
tlaun@twcny.rr.com
Repairs fire fighting antiques and collectibles; wood and metal parts fabricated including fire truck bells and associated brackets and parts.

Apparatus

(see also TRUCKS, Emergency)

Clubs/Associations

Anita Ford
Gibson Rd. Antique Fire Association
1545 Gibson Rd.
Bensalem, PA 19020
ph: 215-245-1545 or 215-638-0531
alf@grafa.org
http://www.grafa.org
A family-oriented group committed to the restoration and preservation of antique and classic fire apparatus; ownership of fire apparatus is not a requirement for membership; muster and picnic each Sept., annual Christmas part.

William A. Conn
Great Lakes International Antique Fire
    Apparatus Association
P.O. Box 2519
Detroit, MI 48231
ph: 248-684-1521

Barbara Connors, Mbrship.
Society for the Preservation &
    Appreciation of Motor Fire Apparatus
    in America
5420 S. Kedvale Ave.
Chicago, IL 60632-4232
ph: 773-585-1301
bconnors@spaamfaa.org
http://www.spaamfaa.org
Over 3,000 members in over 50 chapters; ownership of an antique piece of fire apparatus is not a requirement of membership.

Collectors

Bob Ward
2461 E. High St.
Pottstown, PA 19464-3189
ph: 610-970-6299
kunmingcbi@aol.com
Seeks information regarding fire trucks.

Periodicals

Magazine: Fire Apparatus Journal
P.O. Box 141295
Staten Island, NY 10314-1295
ph: 718-448-5009
fax: 718-981-2359
fireappjnl@aol.com
http://fireapparatusjournal.com
Focuses on all sorts of fire fighting apparatus: trucks, boats; also related modeling.

Fire Alarm Telegraphy

Collectors

Gary Carino
805 W. 3rd St.
Duluth, MN 55806-2201
ph: 218-722-6565
fax: 218-878-0488
gcarino@pawcom.com
Wants wood cased gongs by Gamewell or Moses G. Crane.

Grenades

Collectors

Jerry Pajak
4457 285th St.
Toledo, OH 43611-1912
ph: 419-726-4325
Wants turn-of-the-century fire fighting hand grenade fire extinguisher bottles (empty or full) which were originally sealed with a cork or with cement.

Larry Meyer
4001 Elmwood
Berwyn, IL 60402-4146
ph: 708-749-1564
lmeyer1212@aol.com

FIRE INSURANCE RELATED COLLECTIBLES

(see also INSURANCE COLLECTIBLES)

Collectors

Ralph Jennings
675 Forest Creek Dr.
Ambler, PA 19002-4934
ph: 215-646-7178
Interested in fire fighting and fire insurance related collectibles; prefers pre-1900 items.

Glenn Hartley, Sr.
1025 Roberts Dr.
Sugar Hill, GA 30518
ph: 678-714-3128
ghartleysr@aol.com
Buys and sells at area fire musters and apparatus shows: signs, plaques, policies, fire dept. memorabilia.

Museums/Libraries

Glenn Hartley, Sr.
Smokey's Fire Museum
1025 Roberts Dr.
Sugar Hill, GA 30518
ph: 678-714-3128
ghartleysr@aol.com
Private museum displaying fire department and fire insurance fire marks, signs, badges, buckets, helmets, postcards, stamps, toy, postal covers, etc.

Fire Marks

Clubs/Associations

Glenn Hartley, Sr.
Fire Mark Circle of the Americas, The
Newsletter: Signeverist, The
1025 Roberts Dr.
Buford, GA 30518
ph: 678-714-3128
ghartleysr@aol.com
http://www.firemarkcircle.org
Contains club news, auction prices, and articles about fire marks; also publishes the "FMCA Journal;" published addendum and booklets on fire marks and automobile insurance tags; also "Signs of Insurance," a book on insurance co. signs.

FIREARMS

(see also ADVERTISING COLLECTIBLES, Firearms Related; AIRGUNS; ARMS & ARMOR; BOOKS, Reference [Firearms]; CIVIL WAR ARTIFACTS; MILITARIA; AMMUNITION & EXPLOSIVE ORDNANCE; POWDER HORNS; SPORTING COLLECTIBLES; TARGET SHOOTING MEMORABILIA; TOY GUNS; TRAPSHOOTING)

Appraisers

Frank Pereny
Saisho International
P.O. Box 176
Spring Grove, PA 17362-0176
ph: 717-225-0176
fax: 717-225-9221
Collector for over 30 years; full-time dealer since 1980; Accredited Member of the International Society of Appraisers.

Robert A. Dewar, ISA
Robert A. Dewar & Assoc.
512 Canal St.
New Smyrna Beach, FL 32168
ph: 386-428-3331
coro1@ucnsb.net
Dealer and appraiser in both antique and modern firearms.

Terry L. Stull
4567 Alps Ct.
Columbus, OH 43230-1101
ph: 614-475-3535 or 614-571-8662
fax: 614-475-3535
antguns@aol.com
Specializes in buying, selling, restoring, and appraising antique guns from the period 1816 to 1946.

Richard Binger
Stott's Creek Armory, Inc.
2526 S. 475 W.
Morgantown, IN 46160-8405
ph: 317-878-5489
sccalendar@aol.com
Appraises and specialist in antique firearms; Life Member NRA, American Single Shot Rifle Assn., National Muzzle Loading Rifle Assn., Ohio Gun Collectors Assn.

Paul E. Jurgens
2330 DuClaire Rd.
Decatur, IL 62521
ph: 217-423-8303
jurgens@springnet1.com
Specializes in appraising firearms.

Jim Supica
Old Town Station, Ltd. Antique Arms
P.O. Box 14040
Lenexa, KS 66285
ph: 913-492-3000
fax: 913-492-3022
OldTownSta@aol.com
http://www.ArmchairGunShow.com
Buys and sells antique firearms; co-author of "Standard Catalog of S&W," contributing editor to "Blue Book of Gun Values" and "American Rifleman" magazine, pricing panel for "Std. Catalog of Firearms," and "Flayderman's Guide."

Brad Witherell
Witherell's
300 20th St.
Sacramento, CA 95814
ph: 916-683-3266
fax: 916-683-5625
brad@witherells.com
http://www.witherells.com
Specializes in the appraisal of investment-grade firearms and Western Americana.

Auction Services

William "Pete" Harvey
Pete Harvey Auctions
P.O. Box 280
Cataumet, MA 02534
ph: 508-548-0660
fax: 508-457-0660
http://www.firearmsauctions.com

James D. Julia Auctioneers Inc.
Rt. 201, Skowhegan Rd.
P.O. Box 830
Fairfield, ME 04937
ph: 207-453-7125
fax: 207-453-2502
jjulia@juliaauctions.com
http://www.juliaauctions.com
One of the leading firearms auctioneers in North America.

SoldUSA.com
1418 Industrial Dr., Box 11
Matthews, NC 28105
ph: 704-815-1500
fax: 704-844-6436
support@soldusa.com
http://www.soldusa.com
Specializes in hunting and fishing collectibles, especially firearms; does online appraisals for www.CollectingChannel.com's Ask the Appraiser online appraisal service.

Kim Richardson
GunBroker.com
P.O. Box 19137
Atlanta, GA 31126
ph: 770-234-4174
fax: 770-234-4174
admin@gunbroker.com
http://www.gunbroker.com
A premiere firearms auction on the Internet; allows the user to buy and sell guns, gun accessories, air guns, and archery equipment; extensive FFL Holder network assists with the legal transfer of firearms; free to buyers & sellers.

Larry Garner
Garner Realty & Auctioneers
332 S. Lison St.
P.O. Box 323
Carrollton, OH 44615
ph: 800-452-8452 or 330-627-5573
fax: 330-627-3788
larrygarner@bright.net
http://www.garner-acutioneers.com
Specializes in the auction sale of modern and antique firearms.

Rock Island Auction Company
4507 49th Ave.
Moline, IL 61265
ph: 309-797-1500 or 800-238-8022
fax: 309-797-1655
info@rockislandauction.com
http://www.rockislandauction.com

Jim Supica
Old Town Station, Ltd. Antique Arms
P.O. Box 14040
Lenexa, KS 66285
ph: 913-492-3000
fax: 913-492-3022
OldTownSta@aol.com
http://www.ArmchairGunShow.com
Conducts periodic collectible arms auction sales.

Greg Martin Auctions
298 San Bruno Ave.
San Francisco, CA 94103
ph: 800-509-1988 or 415-522-5700
fax: 415-522-5701
info@rabin.com
http://www.gmartinauctions.com
Specializes in the auction sale of sporting arms, historical Americana, arms & armor.

Clubs/Associations

Jack Ackerman
New York State Arms Collectors Association
24 South Mountain Terrace
Binghamton, NY 13902-3128
ph: 607-723-5668
fax: 607-722-7261

Edward R. Clark
Potomac Arms & Collectors Association
P.O. Box 6641
Silver Spring, MD 20916-6641
ph: 703-534-4250 or 301-949-5008

Attn: Membership
National Rifle Association
Magazine: American Rifleman
11250 Waples Mill Rd.
Fairfax, VA 22030
ph: 800-NRA-3888
membership@NRAhq.org
http://www.nrahq.org

Betty Hancock, Sec.
Dallas Arms Collectors Association, Inc.
P.O. Box 704
De Soto, TX 75123
ph: 972-223-3006
bettyhancock@netscape.net
http://www.dallasarms.com
Dedicated to the encouragement, education and protection of the collecting of arms of all types; strives to increase the number of collectors and provide a continuation of value of historical artifacts.

Cindy Hale, Sec.
Arizona Arms Association
P.O. Box 46464
Phoenix, AZ 85063-6464
ph: 623-435-3969
azarms@azarms.com
http://www.azarms.com
Oldest and largest gun collector's organization in Arizona; formed in 1958; goal is to inform the public regarding education as to the role of arms and armaments has had in our history, gun safety, and gun collecting.

Collectors

Dr. Anthony Sapienza
East 106 Ridgewood Ave.
Paramus, NJ 07652
ph: 201-262-6310
fax: 201-262-3990
siringo45@aol.com
Serious collector wants anything related to trick or exhibition shooting (Annie Oakley, Doc Carver, Gus Peret, etc.); wants posters, pin-backs, glass target balls, souvenir targets; plus shot items such as coins, playing or business cards.

Dealers

New England Arms Co.
6 Lawrence Land
P.O. Box 278
Kittery Point, ME 03905
ph: 207-439-0593
fax: 207-439-6726
info@newenglandarms.com
http://www.newenglandarms.com
Largest display of modern and antique sporting arms on the East Coast: Purdey, Boss, Woodward, Holland & Holland, Sauer, Merkel, Browning, Dumoulin, Ferlib, Fabbri, Piotti, Rizzini, Arrazabalaga, Arrieta, etc.

Greg Souchik
TMP Co.
P.O. Box 161
Custer City, PA 16725-0161
ph: 814-362-2642
fax: 814-362-7356
Mg34@mg34.com
http://www.mg34.com
Buys all broken and old firearms including parts.

William A. Kelley, Jr.
Gun Center, The
1713 Rosemont Ave.
Frederick, MD 21702
ph: 301-694-6887
fax: 301-694-6887
A full service gun store offering special order services, gunsmithing, and firearms appraisals; buy, sell, trade, consignment.

Dave Condon
David Condon, Inc.
P.O. Box 7
109 East Washington St.
Merrifield, VA 22118
ph: 540-687-5642
fax: 540-687-5649
dcondon@mediasoft.net
http://www.davidcondon.com
Antique firearms bought and sold.

Will Gorges
Battleground Antiques, Inc.
3910 US Highway 70 East
New Bern, NC 28560
ph: 252-636-3039 or 252-636-5445
fax: 252-637-1862
rebel@civilwarantiques.com
http://www.civilwarshop.com
Appraiser, dealer specializes in world militaria through Vietnam; licensed Federal Firearms dealer; rifles, pistols, swords, uniforms, flags, relics, photographs, accouterments.

Forrest Buckwald
Buck's Gun Rack
607 W. International Speedway Blvd.
Daytona Beach, FL 32114
ph: 904-252-8471 or 800-717-0727
fax: 904-255-0696
info@bucksgunrack.com
http://www.bucksgunrack.com
Dealer and appraiser of firearms since 1954.

Chuck Love
Love's Gun & Pawn
1411 S. Woodland Blvd.
Deland, FL 32724
ph: 386-736-1411
fax: 386-736-1410
lgp@bitstorm.net
Specializes in modern and antique weapons; also militaria.

Bill Williams
Guncraft Sports Inc.
10737 Dutchtown Rd.
Knoxville, TN 37932-3208
ph: 865-966-4545
fax: 865-966-4500
findit@guncraft.com
http://www.usit.net/hp/guncraft
Serving the shooting public since 1947; a multi-faceted supplier of guns, accessories, appraisal services, training, gunsmithing, gun related books.

Dixie Gun Work's Old Car & Steam Engine Museum
1200 N. Highway 51 S
Union City, TN 38261
ph: 901-885-0700
http://www.dixiegun.com
Specializes in the sale of black powder rifles.

Antique & Modern Firearms
2263 Niholasville Rd.
Lexington, KY 40503
ph: 859-276-1419
fax: 859-278-0838
amguns@am-firearms.com
http://www.am-firearms.com
Dealers in firearms since 1974: modern handguns, rifles & shotguns, Colts, collectibles handguns and long guns.

Ohio Gun Collectors Association
P.O. Box 406
Northfield, OH 44067-0406
ph: 330-467-5733
fax: 330-467-5793
ogca@ogca.com
http://www.ogca.com
A non-profit corporation that promotes friendships amongst those interested in the collection, possession, and use of arms by responsible persons.

Douglas R. Carlson
Antique American Firearms
P.O. Box 71035
Des Moines, IA 50325-0035
ph: 515-224-6552
Mail order catalogs of fine antique firearms for sale: American revolvers and Derringers, 1848 to 1898; Colt, Remington, Smith & Wesson, Merwin & Hulbert, and others; each item pictured in catalog which sells for $20 for 6 issues.

LeRoy Merz
LeRoy Merz Antique Guns
Rt. 1, Box 380
Fergus Falls, MN 56537
ph: 218-739-3255
fax: 218-739-4599
leroy@merzantique.com
http://www.merzantique.com

Randy Donley
Donley's Wild West Town & Museum
8512 S. Union Rd.
Union, IL 60180-9661
ph: 815-923-9000
fax: 815-923-2253
mdonley@dls.net
http://www.wildwesttown.com
*Buys, sells and collects antique
firearms of all sorts.*

Collectors Firearms
140 S. Seminary St.
Galesburg, IL 61401-4805
ph: 309-342-5800
fax: 309-342-5730
simpsonltd@gallatinriver.net
http://www.simpsonltd.com
*Wants antique firearms, Civil War
carbines and muskets, Colts,
European muskets, Derringers,
Winchester, etc.*

Michael Wamsher
17732 W. 67th St.
Shawnee Mission, KS 66217
ph: 913-631-0686
Specializes in military firearms.

Jim Supica
Old Town Station, Ltd. Antique Arms
Catalog: Old Town Station Dispatch
P.O. Box 14040
Lenexa, KS 66285
ph: 913-492-3000
fax: 913-492-3022
OldTownSta@aol.com
http://www.ArmchairGunShow.com
*Buys and sells antique firearms; co-
author of "Standard Catalog of
S&W," contributing editor to "Blue
Book of Gun Values" and "American
Rifleman" magazine, pricing panel for
"Std. Catalog of Firearms," and
"Flayderman's Guide."*

Terry Porter
Fine Antique Arms
P.O. Box 870337
Mesquite, TX 75150
ph: 214-679-7418
fax: 972-681-8992
Terry.Porter@FineAntiqueArms.com
http://www.fineantiquearms.com
*Dealing in fine antique arms, rapiers,
swords, pistols, guns, muskets.*

Marc Wade
Antique & Collectable Firearms &
Militaria Headquarters
P.O. Box 95021
South Jordan, UT 84095
ph: 801-947-9442
hq@oldguns.net
http://oldguns.net
*Buys, sells, appraises; interesting and
useful information for collectors of
antique and collectible firearms and
militaria; questions answered, gun
show listings, catalog, gun related
software.*

John Spangler
John Spangler Professional Services, LC
P.O. Box 711282
Salt Lake City, UT 84171
ph: 801-947-9442
hq@oldguns.net
http://www.oldguns.net
*Serving collectors and students of
firearms and military history; huge
inventory on Web site; single pieces,
entire collections, or deaccessioned
museum inventory wanted; appraisals
for estate, divorce.*

Walt Moreau
P.O. Box 14764
San Francisco, CA 94114
ph: 415-861-8319
fax: 415-255-2335
WMoreau130@aol.com
http://www.moreau.com
*Dealer and collector of classic antique
firearms; also Americana and Plains
Indian art.*

Antique Arms America, Inc.
P.O. Box 107
Depoe Bay, OR 97341-0107
ph: 541-764-4096
ejtedbell@hotmail.com
http://www.antiquearmsamericainc.com
*Dealer in fine antique arms only, Civil
War firearms, Indian Wars, Old
West, Bowie knives, badges, gun
leather.*

Experts

Robert W.D. Ball
26 Byron Dr.
Avon, CT 06001-4507
*Author of "Remington Firearms; the
Golden Age of Collecting,"
"Springfield Armory Shoulder
Weapons, 1795-1968," and "Mauser
Military Rifles of the World."*

Courtney Wilson
American Military Antiques
8398 Court Ave.
Ellicott City, MD 21043-4514
ph: 410-465-6827
fax: 410-461-6820
*Wants to buy collectible and antique
firearms; all periods.*

Bill Williams
Guncraft Sports Inc.
10737 Dutchtown Rd.
Knoxville, TN 37932-3208
ph: 865-966-4545
fax: 865-966-4500
findit@guncraft.com
http://www.usit.net/hp/guncraft
*Serving the shooting public since
1947; a multi-faceted supplier of guns,
accessories, appraisal services,
training, gunsmithing, gun related
books.*

Jim Supica
Old Town Station, Ltd. Antique Arms
P.O. Box 14040
Lenexa, KS 66285
ph: 913-492-3000
fax: 913-492-3022
OldTownSta@aol.com
http://www.ArmchairGunShow.com
*Buys and sells antique firearms; co-
author of "Standard Catalog of
S&W," contributing editor to "Blue
Book of Gun Values" and "American
Rifleman" magazine, pricing panel for
"Std. Catalog of Firearms," and
"Flayderman's Guide."*

Bruce Canfield
P.O. Box 6177
Shreveport, LA 71136-6117
fax: 419-818-3698
collect@brucecanfield.com
http://www.brucecanfield.com
*Gun collector, author, authority on
post-Civil War military firearms.*

Internet Resources

Springfield Armory Historic Site's Cyber
Museum
One Armory Square
Springfield, MA 01105
ph: 413-734-8551
fax: 413-747-8062
spar_interpretation@nps.gov
http://www.rediscov.com/spring.htm
*Search the Springfield Armory
National Historic Site's collection of
firearms using online searching
software.*

Rob Robles
antiqueguns.com
325 S. Maple Dr.
Salem, UT 84653
ph: 801-423-7831
fax: 801-423-7794
robles@antiqueguns.com
http://www.antiqueguns.com
*This site is devoted to antique
firearms manufactured prior to 1898;
dealers, gun shows, parts, ask the
experts, classifieds.*

Ben Loving
Gun Room, The
531 Main St., Ste. #518
El Segundo, CA 90245
ph: 310-546-6484
fax: 310-564-6484
ben@doublegun.com
http://www.doublegun.com
*A Web site with many dealers and
collectors offering firearms for sale
and listing firearms wanted to
purchase.*

Man./Prod./Dist.

Smith & Wesson
2100 Roosevelt Ave.
Springfield, MA 01104
ph: 413-781-8300 or 800-826-5481
qa@smith-wesson.com
http://www.smith-wesson.com

Greg Souchik
Allegheny Arsenal, Inc.
P.O. Box 161
Custer City, PA 16725-0161
ph: 814-362-2642
fax: 814-362-7356
Mg34@mg34.com
http://www.mg34.com
*Manufacturers of Guardian Gun Care
products: gun wipe, lubricant,
corrosive ammo neutralizer, and
Parkerizing kits; also surplus firearms
parts and parts kits.*

Museums/Libraries

Springfield Armory National Historic
Park
1 Armory Square
Springfield, MA 01105-1204
ph: 413-734-8551
fax: 413-747-8062
spar_superintendent@nps.gov
http://www.nps.gov/spar

American Precision Museum Association, Inc.
Newsletter: Tools & Technology
P.O. Box 679
196 Main St.
Windsor, VT 05089
ph: 802-674-5781
fax: 802-674-2524
curator@americanprecision.org
http://www.americanprecision.org
*Collections include examples of all of
the guns manufactured in the museum
building over its long history as an
armory; examples include Sharpes,
Jennings, Palmer, Ball, Robbins &
Lawrence, Enfield, and L.G.Y.*

Fort Ticonderoga Museum
Newsletter: Bulletin of the Fort
Ticonderoga Museum
P.O. Box 390
Ticonderoga, NY 12883
ph: 518-585-2821
fax: 518-585-2210
fort@fort-ticonderoga.org
http://www.fort-ticonderoga.org
*10,000 volume research library
specializing in 18th century military
history and the history of the
Champlain Valley; museum depicts
history of the area and the campaigns
during the 7 Year War and the
Revolutionary War.*

National Firearms Museum
11250 Waples Mill Rd.
Fairfax, VA 22030
ph: 800-NRA-3888
membership@NRAhq.org
http://www.nrahq.org

Museum of Weapons & Early American
History
81-C King St.
Saint Augustine, FL 32084
ph: 904-829-3727
*Rich collection of firearms including
flintlocks, percussion rifles, carbines;
also swords, bayonets, assorted tools,
and photographs; artifacts in the
collection date from 1500 to 1900.*

Randy Donley
Donley's Wild West Town & Museum
8512 S. Union Rd.
Union, IL 60180-9661
ph: 815-923-9000
fax: 815-923-2253
mdonley@dls.net
http://www.wildwesttown.com

J.M. Davis Arms & Historical Museum
333 Lynn Riggs Blvd.
Claremore, OK 74018
ph: 918-341-5707
http://www.jmdavis.state.ok.us
40,000 sq. ft. museum houses a diverse collection of firearms and related items, Western artifacts, Native American artifacts, Civil War era artifacts, music boxes and instruments, steins, swords, knives, John Rogers' statuary.

Periodicals

Stewart Mowbray
Andrew Mowbray Publishing
Magazine: Man at Arms
P.O. Box 460
Lincoln, RI 02865
ph: 800-999-4697 or 401-726-8011
fax: 401-726-8061
stuart@manatarmsbooks.com
http://www.manatarmsbooks.com
"Man at Arms" is the official arms collecting periodical of the NRA, a non-shooting magazine focusing on collectible firearms, arms and armor.

PRIMEDIA Enthusiast Group
Magazine: Guns & Ammo
745 Fifth Ave.
New York, NY 10151
ph: 212-745-0100
fax: 212-745-0121
gunsandammo@neodata.com
http://www.gunsandammomag.com
The world's leading firearms sporting journal for 40 years; edited for recreational hunting and shooting enthusiasts.

Magazine: Arms Collecting
P.O. Box 70
Alexandria Bay, NY 13607-0070
ph: 613-393-2980
mrsarms@kos.net
Reaches collectors, museums and librarians in 35 countries.

Second Amendment Foundation
Newspaper: Gun Week
P.O. Box 488
Buffalo, NY 14209-0488
ph: 716-885-6408
fax: 716-884-4471
safsub@broadviewnet.net
http://www.gunweek.com
Covers all aspects of the shooting sport: new products, hunting regulations, gun legislation, shows and collecting.

Peggy Tartaro, Ed.
Magazine: Women & Guns
P.O. Box 488
Buffalo, NY 14209-0488
ph: 716-885-6408
fax: 716-884-4471
safsub@broadviewnet.net
http://www.womenshooters.com
The only magazine of its kind; written and edited by women for women.

Magazine: Double Gun Journal, The
P.O. Box 550
East Jordan, MI 49727
ph: 231-536-7439
fax: 231-536-7450
info@gunshop.com
http://www.gunshop.com/doublegunjournal.htm
The world's only periodical dedicated to double barrel shotguns and rifles; outstanding photographs, articles written by experts in the field, packed with information about fine firearms.

Magazine: BIG Show Journal
P.O. Box 217
Iola, WI 54945
ph: 715-445-2708
paul@xlcom.com
http://www.showjournal.com
The guide to knife and gun shows nationwide.

Stacie Berger
Krause Publications
Newsmagazine: Gun List
700 E. State St.
Iola, WI 54990-0001
ph: 715-445-2214
fax: 715-445-4087
stacie.berger@fwpubs.com
http://www.krause.com
Ad newspaper for buying/selling collectible firearms, parts & accessories; gunsmithing services; reloading supplies; archery and knives; over 50,000 alphabetized guns in each issue.

Stacie Berger
Krause Publications
Magazine: Gun Show Calendar
700 E. State St.
Iola, WI 54990-0001
ph: 715-445-2214
fax: 715-445-4087
stacie.berger@fwpubs.com
http://www.krause.com
Largest listing of gun shows available; lists shows throughout the US and Canada; listings updated quarterly.

World-Wide Gun Report, Inc.
Magazine: Gun Report, The
P.O. Box 38
Aledo, IL 61231-0038
ph: 309-582-5311 or 309-582-5312
fax: 309-582-5555
gunrprt@winco.net
The monthly magazine serving the antique gun collector and dealer for over 40 years.

Citizens Committee for the Right to Keep & Bear Arms
Magazine: Gun News Digest
12500 N.E. Tenth Place
Bellevue, WA 98005
ph: 425-454-7012
info@ccrkba.org
http://www.ccrkba.org/publilc_gd1.html
Quarterly magazine; in-depth coverage of important issues that effect gun owners.

Repair Services

Doug Turnbull
Doug Turnbull Restoration
6680 Route 5 & 20
P.O. Box 471
Bloomfield, NY 14469
ph: 716-657-6338
fax: 716-657-6338
turnbullrest@mindspring.com
http://www.turnbullrestoration.com
Specializes in the accurate recreation of historical metal finishes on period firearms: from polishing to final finish: color case hardening, rust blue, charcoal blue, nitre blue.

John G. Zimmerman
1195 Washington St.
P.O. Box 1351
Harpers Ferry, WV 25425
ph: 304-535-2558
http://www.edsmart.com/jz
Over 35 years experience in the production, restoration, repair and modification of firearms; has worked on all types of firearms; specialty is to build, repair, and modify Civil War era firearms.

Browning Company

Clubs/Associations

Anthony Vanderlinden, Sec.
Browning Collectors Association
5603-B West Friendly Ave., Ste. 166
Greensboro, NC 27410
ph: 336-349-5427
belgianpistol@worldnet.att.net
http://www.castblast.com/brmember.htm

Colt

Clubs/Associations

Colt Collectors Association
P.O. Box 2241
Los Gatos, CA 95031-2241
fax: 408-353-3613
ccacolt@aol.com
http://www.coltcollectorsassoc.com
Founded in 1980 by a group of avid Colt collectors; promotes the collecting of all types of Colt firearms and memorabilia.

Collectors

Tim Schmoyer
91 South Fairview St.
Macungie, PA 18062
taschmoyer@earthlink.net
Collector of Colt memorabilia, ephemera, firearms; buys, sells, shares information on Colt.

John S. Fischer
Coltania
P.O. Box 47
Van Nuys, CA 91408
jsfischer1@aol.com
Buys and sells Colt factory items: original catalogs, pamphlets, advertising & promotional, books, posters: anything Colt, his factory or guns.

Experts

John T. Ogle
P.O. Box 252
Ocean Springs, MS 39566-0252
Collects memorabilia of the Colt Firearms Companies; author of Krause "Price Guide to Colt COmpany Collectibles" (1998).

Computer Programs For
Man./Prod./Dist.

Niche Software, Inc.
Software: Gun Collector, The
7118 NW Terrace
Parkland, FL 33076
ph: 954-344-6561
marketing@collectiblessoftware.com
http://www.collectiblessoftware.com
Designed for the gun collector including pistols, antique firearms, rifles, accessories.

Connecticut Arms & Mfg. Co.

Collectors

Edward R. Clark
P.O. Box 6641
Silver Spring, MD 20916-6641
ph: 703-534-4250 or 301-949-5008
Collecting and researching Hammond Bulldog single shot pistols manufactured by the Connecticut Arms & Mfg. Co. from 1863 to 1868.

Garand (M1)

Clubs/Associations

Frank Walter
Garand Collectors Association
P.O. Box 181
Richmond, KY 40476-0181
ph: 606-623-2795
fwalter@garandcollector.org
http://www.garandcollector.org
For collectors of M1 and M14 rifles made by John Garand originally in the 1950s.

Periodicals

Anthony Pucci, Jr.
Orion 7 Enterprises, Inc.
Magazine: Garand Times
P.O. Box 1592
Rocky Point, NY 11778
ph: 516-744-5842 or 800-653-4272
fax: 516-821-8446
orionrige1@yahoo.com
http://www.m1garandrifle.com
A quarterly magazine for the M1 collector, enthusiast, and shooter.

German

Clubs/Associations

German Gun Collectors Associations
Journal: Der Waffenschmied
438 Willow Brook Rd.
P.O. Box 385
Meriden, NH 03770-0385
ph: 603-469-3438
fax: 603-469-3800
jaeger@valley.net
http://www.germanguns.com
An organization to preserve the rich heritage of German hunting and sporting guns of the last 150 years.

Dealers

Tom Heller
Heller Arms, Ltd.
P.O. Box 398
Saint Charles, MO 63302-0398
ph: 636-447-3006
hellerarms@webtv.net
Autoloading pistols bought, sold, and appraised; Luger, Walther, Mauser; carries parts for most German pistols, plus original factory magazines and accessories for most pistols.

Repair Services

Tom Heller
Heller Arms, Ltd.
P.O. Box 398
Saint Charles, MO 63302-0398
ph: 636-447-3006
hellerarms@webtv.net
Autoloading pistols repaired, bought, sold, and appraised; also parts; Luger, Walther, Mauser; carries parts for most German pistols, plus original factory magazines and accessories for most pistols.

Gunsmithing

Dealers

Richard Binger
Stott's Creek Armory, Inc.
2526 S. 475 W.
Morgantown, IN 46160-8405
ph: 317-878-5489
sccalendar@aol.com
Antique only; buys, sells and collects flintlocks and cartridge rifles and muskets.

Repair Services

William Kennedy
Kennedy Firearms
10 North Market St.
Muncy, PA 17756
ph: 570-546-6695
Muzzleloading gunsmith specializing in the restoration and recreation of black powder rifles; manufactures replacement metal parts, stocks and forearms for muskets, Sharps, Maynard & Gallager.

William A. Kelley, Jr.
Gun Center, The
1713 Rosemont Ave.
Frederick, MD 21702
ph: 301-694-6887
fax: 301-694-6887
Offers a full line of gunsmithing services: repair, hot blueing, custom metal and stock work, etc.

Ron E. Dilliott
Dilliott Gunsmithing, Inc.
657 Scarlett Rd.
Dandridge, TN 37725
ph: 865-397-9204
gunsmithD@aol.com
http://www.dilliottgunsmithing.com
Appraisal, repair and restoration of antique firearms; make obsolete parts; metal and wood refinishing; 35 years experience.

Richard Binger
Stott's Creek Armory, Inc.
2526 S. 475 W.
Morgantown, IN 46160-8405
ph: 317-878-5489
sccalendar@aol.com
Appraises, buys and sells muzzle loaders and cartridge rifles and muskets; specializing in antique gunsmithing and restoration.

Dave Norin
Mike Schrank's Smoke & Gun
2010 Washington St.
Waukegan, IL 60085
ph: 847-662-4034
Color case hardening, factory quality hot blueing, rust blueing, nitre blueing, collector quality restorations, custom 45 auto work a specialty, complete custom rifles rebuilt, repairs on all firearms.

Japanese Matchlocks

Collectors

Raymond Macy
P.O. Box 11
West Alexandria, OH 45381-0011
ph: 937-839-5721 or 937-839-5203
yarycam@voyager.net
Wants Japanese swords, daggers, sword parts, matchlock guns, anything samurai.

Mannlicher

Clubs/Associations

Don Henry, Bd. Mem.
Mannlicher Collectors Association
Newsletter: Mannlicher Collector, The
P.O. Box 7144
Salem, OR 97303
ph: 503-472-7710
For collectors of the Continental firearms by Mannlicher.

Internet Resources

Mannlicher-Schoenauer
kanotex@discover-net.net
http://discover-net.net/~kanotex/mannlicher
Great informative Web site for the Mannlicher-Schoenauer rifle collector.

Miniature

Internet Resources

Derek F. Dredge
Miniature Firearm Collecting
La Repose
83 Feltham Hill Rd.
Ashford, Middlesex TWI5 2DQ U.K.
ph: 01784 24288
fax: 01784 24288
Dredge@madasafish.com
http://www.pinfire.homestead.com/miniaturePinfires.html
A reference site for collectors and dealers of miniature 2mm pinfire and rimfire firearms.

Mossberg

Clubs/Associations

National Mossberg Collectors Association
Newsletter: NMCA News
P.O. Box 487
Festus, MO 63028-0487
ph: 636-937-6401
O.F.Mossberg@worldnet.att.net
http://www.mossberg.com/collectors.htm
For the collector or sporting enthusiast interested in Mossberg firearms, optics, and history; special assistance given to members in locating obsolete parts and accessories; newsletter published bi-monthly.

Collectors

Art Snyder
6086 W. Boggstown Rd.
Boggstown, IN 46110
ph: 317-835-7121
emshaw@in.net
Buys, sells, trades all pre-1950 Mossberg firearms, especially hammerless pump action rifles and smooth bore Targo guns; also wants any related accessories or literature.

Victor Havlin
P.O. Box 487
Festus, MO 63028
ph: 636-937-6401
President, National Mossberg Collectors Association.

Man./Prod./Dist.

O.F. Mossberg & Sons, Inc.
7 Grasso Ave.
North Haven, CT 06473
ph: 203-230-5300
fax: 203-230-5420
O.F.Mossberg@worldnet.att.net
http://www.mossberg.com
World's largest manufacturer of pump-action shotguns.

Pistols

Clubs/Associations

Thompson Knox, Sr.
National Automatic Pistol Collectors Association
Newsletter: Auto Mag
P.O. Box 15738
Saint Louis, MO 63163
ph: 314-638-6505
info@napca.net
http://www.napca.net
For the automatic hand gun enthusiast.

Remington

Museums/Libraries

Remington Firearms Museum
P.O. Box 179
Ilion, NY 13357-0179
ph: 315-895-3200
fax: 315-895-3237
webmaster@remington.com
http://www.remington.com
Affiliated with the Remington Arms Company, Inc.

Rifles

Experts

Richard Binger
Stott's Creek Armory, Inc.
2526 S. 475 W.
Morgantown, IN 46160-8405
ph: 317-878-5489
sccalendar@aol.com
Appraises and specialist in antique firearms; Life Member NRA, American Single Shot Rifle Assn., National Muzzle Loading Rifle Assn., Ohio Gun Collectors Assn.

Rifles (Single Shot)

Clubs/Associations

Rudi Prusok, Archivist
American Single Shot Rifle Association
Journal: Single Shot Rifle Journal
625 Pine St.
Marquette, MI 49855-3723
ph: 906-225-1828
fax: 906-227-1819
rprusok@nmu.edu
http://www.assra.com
Organization dedicated to the shooting and collecting of single shot rifles from the turn of the century: German Schuetzen, buffalo, benchrest, and long range traditions; also interested in related memorabilia; free journal sample.

Periodicals

Magazine: Single Shot Exchange, The
P.O. Box 1055
York, SC 29745-1055
ph: 803-628-5326
fax: 803-628-5326
t_bird@mindspring.com
http://singleshotexchange.com
The magazine for black powder cartridge, silhouette, and Schuetzen shooters and antique gun collectors; monthly buy-sell-trade publication includes historical articles, collector's

information, product reviews, match schedules, and more.

Shooting Awards

Collectors

Richard Koster
Personal Property Consultant
P.O. Box 987
Parker, CO 80134
ph: 303-840-1565
fax: 303-841-6687
swordcoll@attbi.com
Collector of Swiss shooting festival (Schutzenfest) items including awards, medals, cups, watches, posters, photographs, and rifles.

Shotguns

Collectors

Pat McKune
P.O. Box 3168
Duluth, MN 55803
ph: 218-525-2596
sporting@sportingcollectibles.com
http://www.sportingcollectibles.com
Wants to buy shotguns and gun powder hunting related collectibles: prints, annual catalogs, calendars, cardboard advertising materials; anything the American shotgun makers and powder companies used to sell their wares.

Dealers

Ron B. Frodelius
Open Season, The
P.O. Box 125
Fayetteville, NY 13066-0125
Wants shotguns made in Syracuse, NY: LeFever, Baker, L.C. Smith, Syracuse Arms, Hollenbeck; prefers 20 gauges.

Thompson/Center Arms Co.

Clubs/Associations

Joe Wright, Pres.
Thompson/Center Association
Magazine: One Good Shot
P.O. Box 792
Northborough, MA 01532
TCA@aol.com
http://members.aol.com/TCA
Members dedicated to the collecting of Thompson/Center products and related memorabilia.

Winchester

Clubs/Associations

David P. Bichrest, Ex. Sec.
Winchester Arms Collectors Association, Inc., The
Magazine: Winchester Collector
P.O. Box 367
Silsbee, TX 77656-0367
ph: 903-852-4027
fax: 903-852-3029
davidwaca@msn.com
http://www.winchestercollector.org
Anything and everything for the collectors of Winchester firearms, ammunition, sporting goods,

hardware items, posters, and anything else made by Winchester.

Dealers

LeRoy Merz
Merz Antique Firearms
Rt. 1, Box 380
Fergus Falls, MN 56537
ph: 218-739-3255
fax: 218-739-4599
leroy@merzantique.com
http://www.merzantique.com
One of the most respected dealers of collectible firearms for over 30 years; specializes in antique and collectible Winchesters; also Colt, Marlin, Sharps, Spencer, Frank Wesson, Stevens, Savage, Henry.

Doug Clemence
Treasure Chest
436 North Chicago
Salina, KS 67401-2020
ph: 785-827-9371 or 785-825-4111
Buys, sells, trades Winchester related items.

Museums/Libraries

Shozo Kagoshima, Gen. Mngr.
Winchester Mystery House, Historic Firearms Museum
525 South Winchester Blvd.
San Jose, CA 95128
ph: 408-247-2000
fax: 408-247-2090
http://www.winchestermysteryhouse.com
Medium size display of firearms through the ages.

FIRECRACKERS

(see FIREWORKS MEMORABILIA)

FIREPLACE ITEMS

Firebacks

Repro. Sources

Charles Euston
Woodbury Blacksmith & Forge
P.O. Box 268
125 Main St. So.
Woodbury, CT 06798
ph: 203-263-5737
info@blacksmithandforge.com
http://www.blacksmithandforge.com
Makes and sells reproduction solid cast iron firebacks.

Wendy Stoughton
Country Iron Foundry
800 Laurel Oak Dr., Ste. 200
Dept. MAC99
Naples, FL 34108-2713
ph: 941-513-1400 or 800-233-9945
fax: 941-513-0969
Firebacks are decorative cast iron plates that protect the rear wall of the fireplace from heat damage; call for catalog of firebacks.

Fireboards

Repro. Sources

Hope R. Angier
P.O. Box 246
Alna, ME 04535
ph: 207-586-5692
hopera@tidewater.net
http://www.hopeangier.com
Handpainted fireboards, theorem paintings and wall hangings using early American decorative techniques.

Mantels

Dealers

Joseph Holahan
Urban Artifacts
4700 Wissahickon Ave.
Philadelphia, PA 19144
ph: 215-844-8330
fax: 215-844-8687
Over 15 years experience; currently has one of the largest mantle inventories in the country; Sotheby's associate.

Repro. Sources

Park Pigott
Mantels of Yesteryear
70 W. Tennessee Ave.
P.O. Box 908
Mc Caysville, GA 30555
ph: 706-492-5534
fax: 706-492-3758
mantels@mantelsofyesteryear.com
http://www.mantelsofyesteryear.com
Builds a line of reproduction mantel places that meet the National Building Codes.

Tools

Repro. Sources

Lemee's Fireplace Equipment
815 Bedford St.
Bridgewater, MA 02324-3007
ph: 508-697-2672
lemeesfirep@aol.com
http://www.lemeesfireplace.com

Charles R. Messner
Colonial Lighting & Tinware Reproductions
316 Franklin St.
Denver, PA 17517-1240
ph: 717-336-6295 or 717-336-0424
Makes Early American tinware: cookie cutters, coffee pots, wall sconces, chandeliers (electric and non-electric), post lights.

Virginia Metalcrafters
1010 East Main St.
Waynesboro, VA 22980-5855
ph: 540-949-9400 or 800-368-1002
fax: 540-949-9446
wcs@netlos.net
http://www.vametal.com
Makes and sells andirons, fireplace tools and fenders, chandeliers, candlesticks, sconces, garden sculpture.

Steve Kayne
Kayne & Son Custom Forged Hardware
100 Daniel Ridge Rd.
Candler, NC 28715-9434
ph: 828-667-8868 or 828-665-1988
fax: 828-665-8303
kaynehdwe@charter.net
http://www.customforgedhardware.com
Fireplace tools, cranes, oven doors, enclosures, andirons, kitchen utensils, etc.; also does repairs, restoration & conservation; $5 for two catalogs.

FIREWORKS MEMORABILIA

(see also TOYS, Cannons; TOY GUNS)

Collectors

Brian J. Zompanti
411 Shuttle Meadow Ave.
New Britain, CT 06052-1844
ph: 860-223-8872
Wants to buy old firecracker packs, boxes, catalogs, labels, etc.

Richard J. Scheurer
23 Cherry Ct.
Cresskill, NJ 07626-2409
ph: 201-568-2376
Wants fireworks, 1850-1967 4th of July memorabilia, firecracker labels, packs, posters and catalogs.

Stuart Schneider
P.O. Box 64
Teaneck, NJ 07666-0064
ph: 201-599-4250
fax: 201-599-4251
Stuart@wordcraft.net
http://www.wordcraft.net
Wants old firecracker pack labels from the turn of the century to the 1950s.

Barry Zecker
Collectors Exchange, Inc.
P.O. Box 217
Martinsville, NJ 08836-0217
ph: 908-253-3400
collexch@hotmail.com
Wants firecracker packs, fireworks catalogs; boxes for Sparklers, caps, salutes, torpedoes; also price lists, flyers, salesman's samples, photos of old fireworks plants & employees; happy to appraise items you have; 42 years experience.

Rick Fuith
5429 N. Linder
Chicago, IL 60630-1328
ph: 773-775-6792
abbott49@aol.com
Wants firecracker labels, packs, catalogs, anything on fireworks.

Bill Scales
130 Fordham Circle
Pueblo, CO 81005-1649
ph: 719-561-0603
Especially wants old firecracker packs, labels, catalogs, etc.

Dealers

Kevin Hurt
July 4th Antiques
P.O. Box 6185
Battlement Mesa, CO 81636
ph: 970-285-7041 or 970-285-9141
fax: 970-285-1302
j4antiques@aol.com
Collector, expert, appraiser buying old 4th of July memorabilia: old firecracker packs, labels, boxes, old fireworks, catalogs, posters, cap gun caps; free appraisals; also conducts periodic fireworks memorabilia auctions.

Experts

Barry Zecker
Collectors Exchange, Inc.
P.O. Box 217
Martinsville, NJ 08836-0217
ph: 908-253-3400
collexch@hotmail.com
Wants firecracker packs, fireworks catalogs; boxes for Sparklers, caps, salutes, torpedoes; also price lists, flyers, salesman's samples, photos of old fireworks plants & employees; happy to appraise items you have; 42 years experience.

George Moyer
403 Adams St.
Pottsville, PA 17901
ph: 570-622-3640
fax: 570-622-5787
venom1@infi.net
Specializes in firecrackers; co-author of "Firecrackers the Art & History."

Hal Kantrud
Prairie Pyrotechnics
Rt. 7 Box 52
Jamestown, ND 58401
ph: 701-252-5639
HalK995@daktel.com
Wants old Chinese firecracker packs and labels plus other fireworks related items.

FISHING COLLECTIBLES

(see also AQUARIUMS; BOOKS, Reference [Fishing]; DECOYS, Fish; SPORTING COLLECTIBLES)

Appraisers

Dr. Michael Echols
Fishing Collectibles
6300 Whiskey Creek Dr.
Fort Myers, FL 33919
ph: 239-489-0587
drechols@att.net
http://www.braceface.com/lures
Specializes in the appraisal of pre-1930 Heddon and Shakespeare lures and boxes; Web site has extensive information.

Auction Services

Richard W. Withington, Inc.
590 Center Rd.
Hillsboro, NH 03244
ph: 603-464-3232
fax: 603-464-4901
withington@conknet.com
http://www.withingtonauction.com

SoldUSA.com
1418 Industrial Dr., Box 11
Matthews, NC 28105
ph: 704-815-1500
fax: 704-844-6436
support@soldusa.com
http://www.soldusa.com
Specializes in hunting and fishing collectibles, especially firearms; does online appraisals for www.CollectingChannel.com's Ask the Appraiser online appraisal service.

Lindy Egan
Lures Etc.
4052 Sequoia Ave.
Grove City, OH 43123
ph: 614-871-3162

Clubs/Associations

Ron Gast
Florida Antique Tackle Collectors, Inc.
P.O. Box 420703
Kissimmee, FL 34742-0703
rkgast@magicnet.net
http://www.fatc.net

Joe Szabo
Michigan Lure Collectors Club
201 Doepker Rd.
Owosso, MI 48867-9377
ph: 517-723-5919
For those interested in old lures and other fishing tackle.

Drew Reese, Mem.
National Fishing Lure Collectors Club
Newsletter: NFLCC Gazette
197 Scottsdale Circle
Reeds Spring, MO 65737
ph: 417-338-4427
pennistn@wekz.net
http://www.nflcc.com
3,500 members; fosters awareness of fishing tackle collecting as a hobby; assists members in identification, location and valuing fishing tackle, etc.; 26 pg. newsletter published quarterly; also publishes NFLCC full color magazine.

Collectors

Mark R. Van Sciver
120 Elm St. AG-5
Beverly, NJ 08010
ph: 609-877-2271
Collector of antique tackle, specializing in saltwater.

Paul Webber
P.O. Box K
Stockton, NJ 08559-0350
ph: 609-397-8727

Sam G. Husselman
Sam's Fishing Page
474 Johnston Dr.
Bethlehem, PA 18017-1815
ph: 610-866-7984 or 877-305-3287
husselman@enter.net
http://www.enter.net/~husselman/
sam.html
Very familiar with the identification and pricing of most antique fishing lures and other fishing collectibles; his Web page has original research and information on the Heddon Crazy Crawler and 210 lures, two of his specialties.

Kevin Fiedler
RR 6, Box 6195
Moscow, PA 18444
ph: 570-842-4371
fax: 570-842-4247
Diablo12@aol.com
http://members.aol.com/Diablo12
Specializes in fishing tackle made by the Fred Arbogast Co., Heddon, and Creek Chub Bait Co.

Philip W. Hartman
1 South Eighth Alley
P.O. Box 263
New Market, MD 21774
ph: 301-865-5651
fax: 301-865-0518
Phil@newmarketmd.com
http://www.newmarketmd.com/
grange.htm
Buys lures, reels (including German silver reels), tackle, bobbers, etc.; wrote the first article, "Fishing Pike Floats & Bobbers" in "Antique Angler" (Aug. 1985); expert on bobbers.

David A. Gladwell
P.O. Box 238
Bedford, VA 24523-0238
ph: 540-586-1488 or 540-586-9575
dagladwell@aol.com
Wants old fishing tackle, especially lures or plugs, and advertisements.

Brian Shillito
5501 65th Ave. North
Pinellas Park, FL 33781
ph: 727-541-7540
Wants pre-1950 fishing lures and tackle.

Ron Gast
2306 Leeward Cove
Kissimmee, FL 34746
ph: 407-933-7435
rkgast@cfl.rr.com
http://home.cfl.rr.com/rkgast
Collector of antique fishing tackle for over 20 years; especially interested in lures made in Florida and reels made in Kentucky; always interested in talking with people about their tackle.

Bill Whitesell
306 Hale Ave.
Murfreesboro, TN 37130
wwhites@aol.com
http://members.aol.com/wwhites
Collects antique fishing lures.

Jim Fleming
518 Heather Place
Nashville, TN 37204
ph: 615-292-1463 or 615-595-5810
fax: 615-292-1465
mrprinting@comcast.net
Collects duck, turkey and goose calls; mostly antique calls but some contemporary as well; also collects old fishing lures with a special interest in the William Shakespear Company.

Lindy Egan
4052 Sequoia Ave.
Grove City, OH 43123
ph: 614-871-3162
Wants to buy most anything having to do with fishing.

David Twigg
Creek Chub Collectors Corner, The
9017 Dudley
Taylor, MI 48180
ph: 313-477-0166
twigg@peoplepc.com
http://www.geocities.com/Yosemite/
Rapids/9043
Creek Chub Bait Co. lures collector and expert; almost two decades of research; has experience and references to answer most general lure questions, but specializes as an expert in Creek Chub.

Raymond L. Carver
22325 B Dr. South
Marshall, MI 49068-9722
ph: 616-781-5668
fax: 616-781-9023
Author of "Bud Stewart - Michigan's Legendary Lure Maker."

Thomas Jacomet
1255 Crown Court
Mukwonago, WI 53149
ph: 262-363-9528
lurelore@wi.rr.com
http://www.lurelore.com
Collector and trader of old fishing tackle, specializing in Heddon River Runt Spooks; author of "Lure Lore," online bi-weekly articles on fishing tackle collectibles.

John A. Kolbeck
1610 Michigan Ave.
Stevens Point, WI 54481
ph: 715-341-5687
jkolbeck@g2a.net
http://www.bomberbaits.com
Buys and sells and trades all types of old fishing tackle; known as Capt. John on the Internet; sells tackle for others on eBay and other online auction sites.

Stephen Bassler, Jr.
Steve's Fishing Homepage
7 Rolling Ridge Rd.
Winnetka, IL 60093
ph: 847-446-2334
sjbassler2@aol.com
http://www.geocities.com/bassallure
Serious collector; interests range from baits, rods and reels, to miscellaneous equipment; interest in Heddon, Creek Chub, Shakespeare, Pflueger, and others.

John & JoAnn Monk
P.O. Box 261123
Plano, TX 75026
ph: 972-672-5114
jwmonk@airmail.net
Wants to buy pre-1950 fishing tackle: wooden lures, plastic lures, small fly rods, metal spoons and spinners, ice fishing decoys, wooden factory tackle boxes, two-piece cardboard boxes for lures, etc.

Frank Miller
49192 McKenzie Hwy.
Vida, OR 97488
ph: 714-870-5902
fax: 714-879-9049
fshnfrank@aol.com
Wants to buy fishing collectibles.

Dealers

Bill Crowley
Antique Fishing Tackle Connection
mrbill@antiquefishingstuff.com
http://www.antiquefishingstuff.com
Fishing art, fishing tackle, lures, rods, reels, bobbers, trout landing nets, hooks, creels, plugs, catalogs, minnow traps, etc.

Martin J. Keane
Classic Rods & Tackle, Inc.
P.O. Box 288
Ashley Falls, MA 01222
ph: 413-229-7988
Buys and sells antique rods, reels, and exotic accessories; high grade rods and reels bought and appraised.

Bob Greenbaum
Bob & Shirley's Antiques
6151 Beverly Hills Rd.
Coopersburg, PA 18036-1872
ph: 610-282-4881
bobshirleyantiq@aol.com
Wants all items related to the sport of fishing.

Hugh Fisher
Anglers Antiques
tydwater@msn.com
http://www.anglersantiques.com
Antique fishing tackle collector, dealer, expert, appraiser: all kinds including Heddon, Creek Chub Bait Co., Meisselbach, Bristol, C.A. Clark, fish decoys, etc.; specializes in Charles A Clark baits produced in Springfield, MO.

Jeff Savage
Drexel Grapevine Antiques
2784 US 70 East
Valdese, NC 28690
ph: 828-437-5938
jeff@drexelantiques.com
http://www.drexelantiques.com
Buy, sell antique fishing tackle as well as hunting and fishing licenses.

Neil Ghingold
Neil Ghingold Antiques
1230-32 Broad St.
Augusta, GA 30901-1116
ph: 706-722-3483
Wants to buy fishing collectibles.

Ed & Carolyn Corwin
P.O. Box 1133
Hastings, FL 32145-1133
ph: 904-692-2037
fax: 904-692-2037
reellures@aol.com
Buys, sells and appraises; general information no charge; send SASE with request; include photos or photocopies if possible (lures can be photocopied); specializes in pre-1960 fishing related items, the older the better.

Nancy & Glenn Darst
Boston Store, The
P.O. Box 190394
Mobile, AL 36619
ph: 334-666-9265 or 334-666-2079
gdarst@zebra.net
Buys and sells fishing and hunting collectibles from 1800s to 1950s: Girl Scout and Boy Scout knives, hatchets, axes; also landing & trout nets, backpacks, lures, bobbers, knives, creels, pack baskets, fishing catalogs, pre-1950 LL Bean.

Dean Sova
OldLures.com
10650 Birch
Taylor, MI 48180
ph: 313-299-9533
dean@sova.net
http://www.oldlures.org
Dealer, appraiser, collector of old fishing lures and antique tackle; wants Heddon, Creek Chub, Moonlight, CCBC, Shakespeare, and early lures or their boxes.

John E. Shoffner
624 Merritt St.
Fife Lake, MI 49633-9142
ph: 231-879-3912
Issues 6 lists a year with approx. 600 fish decoys and antique fishing tackle items for sale.

Arthur G. Politte
Antique Tackle Box
P.O. Box 106
Crystal City, MO 63019
ph: 314-937-1411
fax: 314-937-7116
apolitte@jcn1.com
http://www.antiquetacklebox.com
Wants to buy reels, rods, books, reel

boxes, lures, minnow traps, and other fishing related items.

Brian Cooper
Short Stop Collectible Tackle Site
5511 W. 99 Terr.
Shawnee Mission, KS 66207
ph: 816-225-3747 or 913-642-4316
Comprehensive auction and sales list for vintage tackle enthusiasts with detailed descriptions and photos of items; consignments accepted (subject to item by item approval.)

Phil White
14099 Lakeshore Dr.
Nampa, ID 83686
ph: 208-466-1746
editor@oldfishingstuff.com
http://www.oldfishingstuff.com
Collector of fishing tackle and sporting collectibles, specializing in fishing reels, catalogs, and related paper items; author of two books on fishing collectibles and editor of two fishing tackle newsletters.

Mike Berry
Mike's Tackle Box
P.O. Box 5827
Bellingham, WA 98227
ph: 360-734-7379
mike@mikestackle.com
http://www.mikestackle.com
Online catalog of collectible rods, reels, and lures which can be purchased over the Internet.

Experts

Gary Wood
Fishing Lure & Angling Collector
733 Myrtle Rd.
North Brunswick, NJ 08902-2549
ph: 732-821-7633
woodrasp@aol.com
Buying and appraising old fishing lures, reels, floats, and related advertising; feel free to call and chat; please enclose SASE with all US mail inquiries; "If it's got a hook, I'll take a look!"

Sam G. Husselman
Sam's Fishing Page
474 Johnston Dr.
Bethlehem, PA 18017-1815
ph: 610-866-7984 or 877-305-3287
husselman@enter.net
http://www.enter.net/~husselman/sam.html
Is an expert in all antique fishing tackle.

Ed & Carolyn Corwin
P.O. Box 1133
Hastings, FL 32145-1133
ph: 904-692-2037
fax: 904-692-2037
reellures@aol.com
Buys, sells and appraises; general information no charge; send SASE with request; include photos or photocopies if possible (lures can be photocopied); specializes in pre-1960

fishing related items, the older the better.

Byron Parker
Fishing Memories
117 Morgan Court
Clarksville, TN 37040-4369
ph: 931-648-1168
parkerb4@bellsouth.net
http://www.geocities.com/Yosemite/Gorge/3965
Collector, expert, appraiser of fishing lures made by the Fred Arbogast Bait Company; has published an identification guide on these lures; has a collection of over 4,000 lures.

David Twigg
Creek Chub Collectors Corner, The
9017 Dudley
Taylor, MI 48180
ph: 313-477-0166
twigg@peoplepc.com
http://www.geocities.com/Yosemite/Rapids/9043
Creek Chub Bait Co. lures collector and expert; almost two decades of research; has experience and references to answer most general lure questions, but specializes as an expert in Creek Chub.

Arlan Carter
Northland Fishing Museum & Wildlife Art Gallery
P.O. Box 107
Fall Creek, WI 54742
ph: 715-597-2551 or 715-877-3349
Author of "19th Century Fishing Lures."

Doug Jobe
Doug's Old Fishing Lures
217 S. College St.
Batavia, IL 60510
ph: 630-879-5104
luresdog@inil.com
http://www.inil.com/users/luresdog
Antique fishing lure collector; buy/sell/trade and appraise; buying old fishing and hunting magazines and catalogs; always happy to just talk old fishing tackle.

Russ Gulledge
Old Tackle Collections
1941 Heather Lane
Pacific, MO 63069
ph: 314-271-8078
fax: 314-271-8078
tackle99@aol.com
http://members.aol.com/tackle99/page1.htm
Expert, appraiser, collector buys single lures or entire collections of pre-WWII fishing lures.

Mark Copeland
Fishing Unlimited Antique Tackle
1710 Effie
Pasadena, TX 77502
ph: 281-487-8111
Collector, expert, appraiser, repairer of antique fishing tackle.

Phil White
14099 Lakeshore Dr.
Nampa, ID 83686
ph: 208-466-1746
editor@oldfishingstuff.com
http://www.oldfishingstuff.com
*Collector of fishing tackle and
sporting collectibles, specializing in
fishing reels, catalogs, and related
paper items; author of two books on
fishing collectibles and editor of two
fishing tackle newsletters.*

Robert Whitaker
2810 E. Desert Cove Ave.
Phoenix, AZ 85028-2620
ph: 602-992-7304
fax: 602-493-5598
whitakr@msn.com

Rick Edmisten
P.O. Box 686
North Hollywood, CA 91603-0686
ph: 818-763-9406
fax: 818-763-5974
info@flc.com
http://www.flc.com
*Wants to buy pre-1940 wooden lures,
quality reels, catalogs, some high
grade rods, tackle boxes, art prints,
etc.; collect calls O.K.; offers free
appraisal of any and all fishing tackle
from photos sent if SASE included.*

Gabby Talkington
4703 Upland Dr.
Richmond, CA 94803-3227
ph: 510-223-1142 or 800-233-4616
fax: 510-233-3388
oldlures@aol.com
http://www.antiquelures.com
*Longtime buyer/seller/appraiser of
vintage fishing tackle: wood fishing
lures, reels, rods, advertising and
catalogs; sale list available; free
appraisals; life member National
Fishing Lures Collectors Club.*

Richard Streater
P.O. Box 393
Mercer Island, WA 98040-0393
ph: 206-232-9060
fax: 206-232-9060
lureguru@aol.com
*Collector of antique fishing lures and
tackle; author of "The Fishing Lure
Collector's Bible," available from the
author; fishing gadgetry a specialty.*

Internet Resources

Dick Spurr
Classic Angler, The
256 Nashua Court
Grand Junction, CO 81503
ph: 970-243-8780
fax: 970-243-6503
spurr@classic-angler.com
http://www.classic-angler.com
*A comprehensive Internet site for
aficionados of classic tackle: bamboo
rods and old fishing tackle; for
collectors, builders and restorers of
bamboo rods.*

Gabby Talkington
AntiqueLures.com
4703 Upland Dr.
Richmond, CA 94803-3227
ph: 510-223-1142 or 800-233-4616
fax: 510-233-3388
oldlures@aol.com
http://www.antiquelures.com
*Information on pre-1940 fishing lures
with a heavy emphasis on Heddon,
Shakespeare, Flyrod lures, and early
miscellaneous lures; over 516 Web
pages of photos, articles, color charts,
catalogs, and advice on collecting
antique lures.*

Museums/Libraries

Gary Tanner, Ex. Dir.
American Museum of Fly Fishing
Magazine: American Fly Fisher, The
P.O. Box 42
Manchester, VT 05254
ph: 802-362-3300
fax: 802-362-3308
amffish@sover.net
http://www.amff.com
*Non-profit educational institution
dedicated to preserving the rich
history of fly fishing and American
angling; over 1,500 rods, 800 reels,
40,000 flies, 2,500 books, manuscripts, photos, etc.*

Ted Dzialo, Dir.
National Fresh Water Fishing Hall of
Fame
Newsletter: Splash, The
10360 Hall of Fame Dr.
P.O. Box 690
Hayward, WI 54843-0690
ph: 715-634-4440
fax: 715-634-4440
fishhall@cheqnet.net
http://www.freshwater-fishing.org
*Custodian of historical sport fishing
artifacts; world record qualifier;
clearinghouse for contemporary &
historical fishing facts.*

Periodicals

Abenaki Publishers, Inc.
Magazine: American Angler Magazine
160 Benmont Ave.
P.O. Box 4100
Bennington, VT 05201-4100
ph: 802-447-1518 or 800-877-5305
fax: 802-447-2471
americanangler@flyfishingmagazines.com
http://www.flyfishingmagazines.com
*Contains occasional articles about
vintage fishing collectibles.*

Stan Van Etten, Pub.
Magazine: Hunting & Fishing
Collectibles Magazine
P.O. Box 40
Lawsonville, NC 27022
ph: 336-593-9477
fax: 336-593-8085
HFcollectibles@aol.com
http://www.HFcollectibles.com
*Focuses on the artifacts that were
created as a part of America's hunting
& fishing traditions: decoys, fishing*

collectibles, game bird calls, old
sporting arms and related items,
wildlife & sporting art, historic
trapping items, licenses.

Creels

Clubs/Associations

Creel Collectors Association International
ph: 888-4-CREELS
polorule18@aol.com

Fly Fishing (Flies)

Experts

David Klausmeyer
New England Angler, The
P.O. Box 105
Steuben, ME 04680-0105
ph: 207-546-2018

Ice Fishing Spears

Experts

Marcel L. Salive, Ph.D.
1483 Dunster Lane
Potomac, MD 20854-6107
ph: 301-762-1909
msalive@erols.com
*Author of "Ice Fishing Spears"
(MarJac Publishing).*

Reels

Clubs/Associations

Roger Schulz, Sec./Treas.
Old Reel Collectors Association
Newsletter: Reel News, The
160 Shoreline Walk
Alpharetta, GA 30022
ph: 770-521-1877
sroger748@aol.com
http://www.orcaonline.org
*Purpose is the further the knowledge
about reels used in fishing from 1800
through 1970.*

Dealers

Tom Greene
Antique Reels
ph: 954-781-5600 or 800-940-4886
anreels@bellsouth.net
http://www.antiquereels.com
*Specializes in antique fishing reels,
small or big game; Web site has
discussion on grading reels, pricing
reels, evaluating reels, list of
markings, and more.*

Steve Vernon
Antique Fishing Reels
145 Ellis Rd.
Havertown, PA 19083
ph: 610-449-7227
reelsrus@icdc.com
http://www.antiquefishingreels.info
*Specializes in antique fishing reels;
will appraise; Web site has lots of
helpful information for the beginning
as well as advanced collector; links to
Web pages of manufacturers.*

Experts

Steve Vernon
Antique Fishing Reels
145 Ellis Rd.
Havertown, PA 19083
ph: 610-449-7227
reelsrus@icdc.com
http://www.antiquefishingreels.info
*Author of "Antique Fishing Reels"
(1985), "Fishing Reel Makers of
Kentucky" (1992), and articles on old
reels; Web site has information for
both the beginning as well as the
advanced collector.*

Phil White
14099 Lakeshore Dr.
Nampa, ID 83686
ph: 208-466-1746
editor@oldfishingstuff.com
http://www.oldfishingstuff.com/
meisselbach_assn.htm
Collector and expert in fishing reels.

Reels (Fly Fishing)

Experts

Jim Brown
97 Franklin St.
Stamford, CT 06901-1309
ph: 203-324-5441
fax: 203-324-5441
jbrown55@optonline.net
*Specializes in collecting American fly
reels and fly rod lures; author of
"Fishing Reel Patents of the US, 1838
- 1940" (1985) and "A Treasury of
Reels" (1990); consultant to American
Museum of Fly Fishing; Lifetime
Member of ORCA.*

Rods (Bamboo)

Collectors

Lee Pattison
P.O. Box 60
Cuba, NY 14727-0060
ph: 716-933-8112
*Wants old and new fishing tackle,
antique reels, old wood tackle boxes,
fishing books, tackle catalogs.*

Udwary
629 Spencer Circle
Spartanburg, SC 29307-2507
*Buys, sells, trades bamboo fly rods,
pre-1965, 7', 7-1/2', 8' sizes; Edwards,
Leonard, Thomas, High-Grade
Granger, Hardy, Heddon, Phillipson;
OK if in need of repair, but must be
priced accordingly.*

Experts

David Klausmeyer
P.O. Box 105
Steuben, ME 04680-0105
ph: 207-546-2018
*Buys and sells quality bamboo fly
rods; also manufacturers bamboo rods
and provides expert appraisal services
for quality bamboo fly rods.*

Internet Resources

Dick Spurr
Classic Angler, The
256 Nashua Court
Grand Junction, CO 81503
ph: 970-243-8780
fax: 970-243-6503
spurr@classic-angler.com
http://www.classic-angler.com
A comprehensive Internet site for aficionados of classic tackle: bamboo rods and old fishing tackle; for collectors, builders and restorers of bamboo rods.

Man./Prod./Dist.

Cal Harvey
Cal Harvey Custom Fly Rods
401 E. 12th
Littlefield, TX 79339
ph: 806-385-4298
bldarter@camalott.com
http://members.tripod.com/~BradBanner/
flyrod.html
Maker of custom fly rods since 1940.

FLAGS & FLAG RELATED COLLECTIBLES

(see also MILITARIA)

Clubs/Associations

David Martucci, Ed.
North American Vexillological
Association
Newsletter: NAVA News
PMB 225
1977 N. Olden Ave. Ext
Trenton, NJ 08618-2193
ph: 207-845-2857
pres@nava.org
http://www.nava.org
Dedicated to the promotion of vexillogy, the scientific & scholarly study of flag history and symbolism; publishes bi-monthly newsletter and annual "Raven" journal, annual meetings, publishes booklets, undertakes special projects.

Flag Institute, The
Magazine: Flagmaster
44 Middleton Rd.
Acomb
York, YO24 3AS U.K.
ph: +44 1904 339985
info@flaginstitute.org
http://www.flaginstitute.org
One of the world's main research and documentation centers for flags and vexillogy; collects and provides all kinds of flag information, from past and present, from all over the world.

Collectors

Jon Radel
6917 Ridgeway Dr.
Springfield, VA 22150-3027
jon@radel.com
http://www.radel.com
Collects flags, flag books, and other printed matted concerning flags, including postcards; older foreign and

local flags, foreign publications of special interest. No common or 20th c. US flags or flag items, please.

Mark Sutton
2035 St. Andrews Circle
Carmel, IN 46032-9547
ph: 317-844-5648
mdsutton2@comcast.net
Buys/trades old cloth American flags with 47 or less than 45 stars; wants original flags from 6" to HUGE; also unusual star patterns.

Dealers

Dallas & Ann Dutson
Flag Store, The
20089 Broadway
Sonoma, CA 95476
ph: 707-996-8140 or 888-GET-FLAG
fax: 707-996-8171
flags@vom.com
http://www.flagemporium.com
Dealer, expert, vendor, manufacturer; the most complete flag site on the Internet!

Man./Prod./Dist.

Carrot-Top Industries, Inc.
328 Elizabeth Brady Rd.
P.O. Box 820
Hillsborough, NC 27278-0820
ph: 800-628-3524 or 919-732-6200
fax: 919-732-5526
service@carrot-top.com
http://www.carrot-top.com
Sells new flags and related hardware: US, states and territories, international, flagpoles, mounting hardware, parade accessories, NASCAR, special interest flags, historical and military flags, globes, pennants, custom designed flags.

Military

Experts

Ben K. Weed
Colours, The
P.O. Box 4643
Stockton, CA 95204
B.K.Weed@worldnet.att.net
http://members.tripod.com/
~oldflagswanted/usa.html
Largest private collector of worldwide military flags; buys flags, parts and photos.

FLASHLIGHTS

Clubs/Associations

Bill Utley
Flashlight Collectors of America
Newsletter: Flashlight Collectors
Newsletter
P.O. Box 4095
Tustin, CA 92781
ph: 714-730-1252
fax: 714-505-4067
flashlight1@cox.net
The 8-page flashlight newsletter is printed quarterly: articles on flashlight history, great finds, questions & answers, classified ads,

old flashlight catalog reprints; annual meeting.

Collectors

Stuart Schneider
Flashlight Museum, The
P.O. Box 64
Teaneck, NJ 07666-0064
ph: 201-599-4250
fax: 201-599-4251
Stuart@wordcraft.net
http://www.wordcraft.net
Buys odd and unusual or early flashlights and flashlight advertising; author of "Collecting Flashlights."

Bill Utley
P.O. Box 4095
Tustin, CA 92781
ph: 714-730-1252
fax: 714-505-4067
flashlight1@cox.net
Collector/historian wants old flashlights, flashlight advertising, flashlight catalogs and other flashlight related items; interested in almost any portable object containing a dry cell battery and a light bulb.

Dealers

Shaw
P.O. Box 5096
Southfield, MI 48086
Wants to buy 1920s-1960s vintage flash lights: brass, chrome, enamel, etc.

Experts

Stuart Schneider
Flashlight Museum, The
P.O. Box 64
Teaneck, NJ 07666-0064
ph: 201-599-4250
fax: 201-599-4251
Stuart@wordcraft.net
http://www.wordcraft.net
Buys odd and unusual or early flashlights and flashlight advertising; author of "Collecting Flashlights."

Bill Utley
P.O. Box 4095
Tustin, CA 92781
ph: 714-730-1252
fax: 714-505-4067
flashlight1@cox.net
Author of the flashlight reference book, "Flashlights."

FLATWARE

(see also SILVER; SILVERPLATE; TABLEWARE)

Appraisers

Judith Livingston, ISA
ph: 360-379-3028
heirlooms@olympus.net
Collects and appraises unusual Victorian silver and silverplate flatware and hollowware.

Matching Services

J.P. Faddoul Company, Inc.
115 Boston Turnpike
Shrewsbury, MA 01545
ph: 508-755-5505
inquire@jpfaddoul.com
http://www.jpfaddoul.com
Carries discontinued and active china, crystal, and flatware; all merchandise is new, first quality and was purchased directly from the manufacturers.

Paul & Pearl Hoffman
China Brokers, Ltd.
11 Westgate Ct.
Colts Neck, NJ 07722-1650
ph: 732-780-5062
chinabrokers@worldnet.att.net

Tony Garfield
Yudin & Associates
P.O. Box 490
Columbus, NJ 08022
ph: 609-324-1205
fax: 609-324-7678
yudassoc@dandy.net
Community, Gorham, Holmes & Edwards, National, Oneida, 1847 Rogers, Wallace, silverplate.

Alice Korman
Alice's Past & Presents Replacements
P.O. Box 465
Merrick, NY 11566-0465
ph: 516-379-1352
fax: 516-379-7302
alicechina@aol.com
http://hometown.aol.com/alicechina/
myhomepage/business.html
Matching and locating service for stainless and silverplate flatware: Community, Oneida, Gorham, International, Reed & Barton, Towle, Wallace, National, Yamazaki, W.M. Frazer, Kirk, Mikasa, Sasaki, Lunt, others.

Michael Round Fine China & Crystal, Inc.
7845 Wisconsin Ave.
Bethesda, MD 20814
ph: 301-656-2626 or 800-467-6863
fax: 703-550-7881
feedback@Mround.com
http://www.michaelround.com
Impressive Web site for matching china, crystal or flatware.

Mary Ann Lowery
Crystal Corner, Inc., The
317 Billy Dyar Blvd.
P.O. Box 756
Boaz, AL 35957-0756
ph: 256-593-6169
fax: 256-593-6560
ccorner@hiwaay.net
http://www.crystalcorner.com
Specializes in stainless and silverplate flatware.

Chris & Tom Heichel
Sterling Buffet
P.O. Box 1665
Mansfield, OH 44901-1665
ph: 800-537-5783 or 419-529-0505
fax: 419-529-0506
info@sterlingbuffet.com
http://www.sterlingbuffet.com
Sterling, silverplate, stainless, dirilyte; all manufacturers; current and discontinued.

Dona Miller
Ann Arbor Dinnerware Exchange
P.O. Box 6054
Ann Arbor, MI 48106-6054
ph: 734-663-9883
fax: 734-663-5766
aadinex@aadinex.com
http://www.aadinex.com
Offers new patterns including some previously unavailable in the US: Magnum and Vantage (now called Aztec) stainless, flatware from Norway, Georg Jensen; also some previously discontinued Oneida patterns.

Barron's
P.O. Box 994
Novi, MI 48376
ph: 800-538-6340
fax: 800-523-4456
barronsdw@aol.com
http://www.barronsdinnerware.com
Matches stainless, silverplate, and sterling flatware.

China Replacements
P.O. Box 508
High Ridge, MO 63049
ph: 800-562-2655 or 636-677-5577
fax: 636-376-6319
chinarep@swbell.net
http://www.chinareplacements.com
Matches all major brands of sterling, silverplate, and stainless.

Joanne Cone
Joanne Cone Matching Service
34 Silverwood
Irvine, CA 92604
ph: 949-551-3173
jochina@aol.com
All manufacturers; stainless and silverplate; Oneida specialist, Fraser, Gense, Gorham, International, Lauffer, Mikasa, National, Noritake, Oxford Hall, Reed & Barton, Roberts, Towle, Wallace, etc.

Past & Present
14851 Ave. 360
Visalia, CA 93292
ph: 559-798-0029
fax: 559-798-1415
info@china-crystal-flatware.com
http://www.pastpresent.net
Silverplate, sterling, stainless, Dirilyte; by Alvin, Easterling, Frank Smith, Fraser, Gorham, International, Jensen, Kirk, Lunt, Manchester, Oneida, Reed & Barton, Steiff, Tiffany, Towle, Wallace, Westmoreland, etc.

Juanita Mallorie
Sterling Shop, The
P.O. Box 595
Silverton, OR 97381-0595
ph: 503-873-6315
fax: 503-873-3006
Marysc@mindspring.com
http://www.sterlingshop.com
Sterling and silverplate flatware matching service.

Grace Ann Kupferschmid
Matchmaker of Iowa
109 Discovery Bay St.
Sequim, WA 98382-9327
ph: 360-683-7517
gakup@olypen.com
Major brands of discontinued stainless, pewter, gold electroplated including Lunt, Wallace-International, Gorham, Oneida, Reed & Barton, Towle (including Lauffer, Supreme Cutlery), Fraser, Mikasa, Sasaki, Yamazaki,Dansk, Dalia, Kirk Stieff.

Periodicals

Susan Ranta
Ranta Enterprises
Directory: Set Your Table Discontinued
   Tableware Dealers
P.O. Box 22481
Lincoln, NE 68542-2481
ph: 800-600-2127 or 402-423-4865
fax: 402-423-4865
sranta@setyourtable.com
http://www.setyourtable.com
Looking for stainless, sterling, silverplate, pewter, "Set Your Table" has a growing list of dealers who can help you find your missing pieces; dealer listings are indexed by manufacturer; Web site is always up to date.

Silverplate

Matching Services

Michael Kucharski
Vintage Silver
33 LeMay Court
Williamsville, NY 14221-3628
ph: 716-631-0419
fax: 716-433-2850
mikekuch@localnet.com
Buys and sells; specializes in matching 1890-1950 silverplated flatware; 20,000 pieces in stock; 100s of patterns.

Carman's Collectables
P.O. Box 1484
Levittown, PA 19058
ph: 215-946-9315
fax: 215-946-9451
carmansc@aol.com
http://www.carmanscollectables.com
Buys and sells sterling silver and silverplate flatware.

Silver Girls
168 Riverview Rd. SW
Eatonton, GA 31024-6836
ph: 478-968-5225
fax: 478-968-5225
silvergirls@communicomm.com
http://www.silvergirls.com
Silverplated flatware; all major manufacturers of discontinued/ collectible patterns.

Phil & Angela Dreis
Antique Cupboard
1936 MacArthur Rd.
Waukesha, WI 53188
ph: 800-637-4583 or 262-548-0556
info@antiquecupboard.com
http://www.antiquecupboard.com
Over 900 sterling and 1,000 plated patterns in stock; buys and sells current and obsolete patterns and rare and unusual pieces; largest inventory in the Midwest.

Joyce Stewart
Joyce's Silver & Antiques
5207 Illini Court
Rockford, IL 61107
ph: 815-226-8255
fax: 815-226-8255
joycestew@aol.com

Helen Lawler
Helen Lawler's Silverplate Matching
   Service
5400 East County Rd. #2
Blytheville, AR 72315
ph: 573-720-8502
hlawler@missconet.com
Large inventory of only silverplated flatware (no stainless or sterling); call or write for your pattern listing with prices; antique and recently discontinued patterns.

Tom Maxwell
Maxwell Silver Matching service
5690 Feather River Place
Paradise, CA 95969
ph: 530-872-7330
tom@maxwellsilver.com
http://www.maxwellsilver.com
Specializes in obsolete, inactive and active patterns of sterling silver; professional polishing and repair services.

Sterling Silver

Internet Resources

Benjamin Randolph
Eden Sterling
7672 Montgomery Rd., #244
Cincinnati, OH 45236
ph: 800-385-3336 or 513-561-3700
info@edensterling.com
http://www.silvercollecting.com
Web site has online encyclopedia of the most often seen marks of American coin silversmiths and sterling silver manufacturers.

Matching Services

Silver Lady Antiques, The
P.O. Box 27
Newton, MA 02164
ph: 781-784-9184
silant@aol.com
Tiffany, Jensen, Gorham, Kirk flatware and hollowware.

Ross-Simons
#9 Ross-Simmons Dr.
Cranston, RI 02920-4476
ph: 800-521-7677 or 800-835-0919
fax: 800-896-9191
customerservice@ross-simons.com
http://www.ross-simons.com
Sells new, active patterns for Gorham, Reed & Barton, Wallace, Towle, Lunt, Kirk-Stieff, International; several outlets on East Coast.

Michael Negrotti
Tabletop Designs
P.O. Box 448
Cheshire, CT 06410
ph: 800-801-4084
lenox@ntplx.net
http://www.tabletopdesigns.com
A small, personal matching service with a constantly changing inventory; want lists are kept; send photocopy or photo when unsure of pattern name.

R. S. Goldberg
R. S. Goldberg
67 Beverly Rd.
Hawthorne, NJ 07506-3201
ph: 800-252-6655 or 201-427-6555
hello@rsgoldberg.com
http://www.rsgoldberg.com
Hundreds of patterns in stock; always buying and selling.

Joy Mercer
Silver Joy, Inc.
P.O. Box 1675
Morristown, NJ 07962-1675
ph: 877-745-88759
joy@silverjoy.com
http://www.silverjoy.com

Nathan Horowicz
Nathan Horowicz Antiques
1050 2nd Ave., Gallery 82
New York, NY 10022
ph: 800-214-6320 or 212-755-6320'
fax: 212-755-6438
horowicz82@aol.com
http://www.classicsilver.com
Large assortment of flatware, tea sets, hollowware; Tiffany, Georg Jensen; all American and European manufacturers.

Pattern Finders, A
P.O. Box 206
Port Jefferson Station, NY 11776-0206
ph: 631-928-5158 or 800-216-2446
fax: 631-928-5170
apattern@aol.com
http://www.patternfinders.com

Carman's Collectables
P.O. Box 1484
Levittown, PA 19058
ph: 215-946-9315
fax: 215-946-9451
carmansc@aol.com
http://www.carmanscollectables.com
*Buys and sells sterling silver and
silverplate flatware.*

Thurber's
2256C Dabeny Rd.
Richmond, VA 23230-3342
ph: 804-278-9080 or 800-848-7237
fax: 804-278-9480
*Carries only active patterns; will
locate old patterns.*

Joe Batista
Replacements Ltd.
P.O. Box 26029
1089 Knox Rd.
Greensboro, NC 27420
ph: 800-737-5223 or 336-697-3000
fax: 336-697-3100
inquire@replacements.com
http://www.replacements.com
*China, crystal and flatware (obsolete,
active and inactive.)*

Beverly H. Bremer
Beverly Bremer Silver Shop
3164 Peachtree Rd. NE
Atlanta, GA 30305
ph: 404-261-4009 or 800-270-4009
fax: 404-261-9708
sterlingsilver@worldnet.att.net
http://www.beverlybremer.com
*Buys, sells and matches sterling silver
flatware, new and antique sterling
silver holloware & giftware; send
for inventory of your sterling pattern
or send photocopy of your pattern; no
SASE required; answers all inquiries.*

Sterling Antique Silver
1201 N. Federal Hwy., #4C
Fort Lauderdale, FL 33304
ph: 954-561-9570 or 954-525-1920
fax: 954-561-9638
info@sterlingantiquesilver.com
http://www.sterlingantiquesilver.com
*Complete matching service for sterling
flatware and holloware, both
current and obsolete; also carries a
supply of silver chests, wraps, and
silver polish.*

Silver Queen
730 N. Indian Rocks Rd.
Belleair Bluffs, FL 33770
ph: 800-262-3134 or 727-581-6827
fax: 727-586-0822
sales@tampabay.rr.com
http://www.silverqueen.com
*High quality, estate and new flatware;
call or write for inventory list of your
pattern; also buys sterling silver
flatware; over 1,500 patterns in stock.*

Antique Silver House, The
8976 Seminole Blvd.
Seminole, FL 33772
ph: 813-392-7250 or 800-SIL-VER5

Sterling Matching Service
P.O. Box 46
Topsfield, MA 01983-1614
ph: 978-887-2610
dorothy@sterlingmatching.com
http://www.sterlingmatching.com/
*Carries elegant sterling silver
flatware including exotic antique
silver by Tiffany, Victorian sterling
serving pieces and many flatware
patterns, coin silver (handwrought)
and Medallion silver.*

Tim & Nancy Young
Alcove Antiques
9825 Concord Rd.
Brentwood, TN 37027
ph: 615-776-5152 or 800-525-8170
fax: 615-776-3039
mail@alcoveantiques.com
http://www.alcoveantiques.com

Carol Lewis
Sterling Buffet
P.O. Box 1665
Mansfield, OH 44901
ph: 800-537-5783 or 419-529-0505
fax: 419-529-0506
info@sterlingbuffet.com
http://www.sterlingbuffet.com
*A matching service for discontinued
and current sterling tableware, both
flatware and holloware; also carries
current and back years of sterling and
crystal Christmas ornaments.*

Benjamin Randolph
Eden Sterling
7672 Montgomery Rd., #244
Cincinnati, OH 45236
ph: 800-385-3336 or 513-561-3700
info@edensterling.com
http://www.edensterling.com
*Web site has online encyclopedia of
the most often seen marks of American
coin silversmiths and sterling silver
manufacturers.*

Phil & Angela Dreis
Antique Cupboard
1936 MacArthur Rd.
Waukesha, WI 53188
ph: 800-637-4583 or 262-548-0556
info@antiquecupboard.com
http://www.antiquecupboard.com
*Over 900 sterling and 1,000 plated
patterns in stock; buys and sells
current and obsolete patterns and rare
and unusual pieces; largest inventory
in the Midwest.*

Jane Rosenow
Jane's Silver
1210 NW 3rd Ave.
Galva, IL 61434
ph: 309-932-3953
fax: 309-932-3068
jarose@inw.net

Dining Elegance, Ltd.
P.O. Box 4203
Saint Louis, MO 63163
ph: 314-865-1408
de-3@earthlink.net
http://www.diningelegance.com

Silverwarehouse
4311 NE Vivion Rd.
Kansas City, MO 64119-2890
ph: 816-454-1990
fax: 816-454-1605
sales@silverwarehouse.com
http://www.silverwarehouse.com
*Largest sterling flatware inventory in
the country; buys/sells sterling; also
polishes, repairs, reblades knives; big
buyer of sterling silver flatware and
holloware; also stainless,
silverplate, pewter, Dirilyte.*

Madeleine Guice Nicoladis
Melange Sterling
5421 Magazine St.
New Orleans, LA 70115
ph: 800-513-3991 or 504-899-4796
fax: 504-899-6265
melangesterling@msn.com
http://www.melangesterling.com
*Specializes in active, inactive, and
obsolete American, British and
Continental sterling flatware: Alvin,
Amston, Baker, Birks, Buccellati,
Christofle, Concord, Dominick &
Haff, Duhme, Durgin, Easterling,
Georg Jensen, Tuttle, etc.*

Helen & Duncan Cox
As You Like It Silver Shop
3033 Magazine St.
New Orleans, LA 70115-2232
ph: 800-828-2311 or 504-897-6915
fax: 504-895-6933
ayliss@bellsouth.net
http://www.asyoulikeitsilvershop.com
*Large inventory of active and inactive
patterns; also tea services, goblets,
mint juleps, etc.*

William Pillsbury
Pillsbury-Michel Silver
2311 Westheimer Rd.
Houston, TX 77098
ph: 877-522-4797 or 713-522-4797
fax: 713-522-4797
info@pillsbury-michel.com
http://www.pillsbury-michel.com

Barry Rosenstein
Sunset Sterling
2219 E. Thousand Oaks Blvd., #459
Thousand Oaks, CA 91362
ph: 800-468-6966 or 805-374-9114
fax: 805-374-9113
sunsetag@aol.com
*Alvin, Amston, Dominick & Haff,
Durgin, Easterling, Fine Arts,
Gorham, International, Kirk-Stieff,
Lunt, Manchester, National, Oneida,
Reed & Barton, Royal Crest, State
House, Towle, Wallace,
Westmoreland, Frank Whiting,
Whiting Mfg. Co.*

Nancy's Silver Shop
21550 Oxnard St., 3rd Floor
Woodland Hills, CA 91367
ph: 800-352-8927 or 818-703-5000
fax: 818-703-5082
hello@nancysilver.com
http://www.nancysilver.com
Matching service, silverware sets,

*baby gifts, silver flatware pattern
finder.*

Betty Overton
Betty's Sterling Silver Matching Service
200 Avenida Santa Margarita
San Clemente, CA 92672
ph: 949-498-5330 or 949-498-4027
fax: 949-498-5330
edwhiffen@aol.com
*Active, inactive, and obsolete sterling
silver patterns; all manufacturers;
send want lists and photocopy; also
sterling silver holloware and
sterling silver ornaments from 1970 to
present.*

Silver Lane Antiques
P.O. Box 322
San Leandro, CA 94577-0032
ph: 510-483-0632
*American sterling flatware in complete
sets or by the piece; tea services, trays,
etc. also available; specializing in
unique pieces for advanced collectors.*

Florence Kinzie
Kinzie's Silver Matching
P.O. Box 522
Turlock, CA 95381
ph: 209-634-4880
fax: 209-634-1134
kinzies@mymailstation.com

Tom Maxwell
Maxwell Silver Matching service
5690 Feather River Place
Paradise, CA 95969
ph: 530-872-7330
tom@maxwellsilver.com
http://www.maxwellsilver.com
*Specializes in obsolete, inactive and
active patterns of sterling silver;
professional polishing and repair
services.*

FLEA MARKETS

(see also ANTIQUES SHOP
DIRECTORIES; TOURS/BUYING
TRIPS)

Directories

Periodicals

House of Collectibles
Directory: Official Directory to U.S. Flea
Markets
201 East 50th St.
New York, NY 10022-7703
ph: 212-751-2600 or 800-733-3000
fax: 212-572-8700
bfi@randomhouse.com
http://www.randomhouse.com/catalog
*Covers about 500 markets; provides
quality information about each.*

Dorothy Clark
Clark's Publications
Directory: Clark's Flea Market U.S.A.
5469 Inland Cove Ct.
Milton, FL 32583
ph: 850-623-0794
fax: 850-626-2088
fleaUSA@aol.com
A national flea market directory issued quarterly; over 1,800 flea markets and swap meets listed; subscription.

Jim Goodridge
Goodridge Guides
Directory: Flea Market Shoppers Companion
P.O. Box 16314
Saint Louis, MO 63125
ph: 314-416-0346
jim@goodridgeguides.com
http://www.goodridgeguides.com
Covers all 50 states; contains over 3,500 separate listings of flea markets across North America.

Directories (Foreign)

Periodicals

Peter Manston
Travel Keys
Directory: Manston's Flea Market Guides
P.O. Box 160691
Sacramento, CA 95816-0691
ph: 916-452-5200
Publishes a series of Flea Market Guides, for Britain, France and Germany; $9.95 plus $4.00 shipping; accepts credit card orders.

FLICKERS

Dealers

Joe Statkus
Eat at Joe's Collectibles
84 State Rd.
Eliot, ME 03903
ph: 207-439-7429
yozi2@aol.com
http://www.toyring.com
Carries a wide selection of flicker rings and specializes in hard-to-find flickers.

Gary Kraut
Alphaville
226 W. Houston St.
New York, NY 10014-4846
ph: 212-675-6850
fax: 212-741-2609
alphavil@mindspring.com
http://www.alphaville.com
Sells ring, button, pin, key chain flickers; flickers are those specially coated dimestore images mounted on cardboard backings that "moved" or shifted scenes as if animated when moved or viewed from a different angle.

FLOORCLOTHS

Man./Prod./Dist.

Angie Nelson
Free Rein Studio
1882 Kennedy Farm Rd. N
Thomasville, NC 27360-8335
ph: 336-472-6396
fax: 336-472-6396
angie@freereinart.com
http://www.freereinart.com
Offers handpainted canvas floorcloths and wall hangings; custom designed floorcloths, beautiful family tree design; also new hand built and hand painted furniture, house and pet portraits.

FLOWER "FROGS"

Collectors

William G. Sommer, MD
9 W. 10th St.
New York, NY 10011-8748
ph: 212-260-0999
wgs2@columbia.edu
Wants ceramic figural flower "frogs:" dancing ladies or nudes American (Cowan, Fulper, Rookwood) or European (Germany, England.)

Christie McCann
3019 Winter Pine Ct.
Fairfax, VA 22031
ph: 703-385-0551
olga@erols.com
http://users.erols.com/aaac
Collects, researches Depression glass flower frogs; wrote a small pamphlet to accompany a glass show display, copies available upon request.

Kescia Moore
2225 Casa Vista Dr.
Palm Harbor, FL 34683
ph: 727-784-9664
r2kmoore@gte.net

Marcia Bradley
FroggieB Treasures
P.O. Box 337
Chamberlain, SD 57325-0337
ph: 605-234-1180 or 605-734-9096
treasures@froggieb.com
http://www.froggieb.com
An avid flower frog collector interested in buying all types of flower frogs.

Lew & Joyce Hendrick
6526 Spring Brook Rd., #208
Rockford, IL 61114
ph: 815-636-4627
Wants to buy flower frogs.

Susan Cox
800 Murray Dr.
El Cajon, CA 92020
ph: 619-697-5922
antiqfever@aol.com
Wants American pottery flower frogs.

Internet Resources

Bonnie Bull
Flower Frog Gazette Online
P.O. Box 596
Wirtz, VA 24184
bbull@flowerfrog.com
http://www.flowerfrog.com
Great resource Web site for collectors where they can interact and learn about flower frogs.

FOBS

(see WATCH FOBS)

FOLK ART

(see also ART, Outsider; BOTTLES, Puzzle; CAROUSELS & CAROUSEL FIGURES; CIGAR STORE COLLECTIBLES; COVERLETS; DECOYS; EAGLES; FRAKTURS; PAINTINGS & DRAWINGS; POPULAR CULTURE; QUILTS; RUGS, Hooked; SAMPLERS; SCRIMSHAW; SILHOUETTES; TRAMP ART)

Appraisers

Patricia Anne Reed
144 Bristol Rd.
Damariscotta, ME 04543
ph: 207-563-5633 or 561-744-0373
patreedantiques@aol.com
Over 45 years as a folk art collector, appraiser and painter, and 35 years as an active dealer in folk art and antiques.

Helaine Fendelman
Helaine Fendelman & Assoc.
60 Gramercy Park North
New York, NY 10010
ph: 212-228-6440
fax: 212-228-8577
HFendelman@aol.com
http://www.appraisersassoc.org/biography/HF0002/page.html
Appraises and liquidates estates; author of the "Official Identification and Price Guide to American Folk Art," co-author with Joe Rosson of "Treasures in Your Attic" and of "Price it Yourself" (Harper Collins).

Susan D. Kleckner
Susan D. Kleckner, LLC
P.O. Box 877
Grand Central Station
New York, NY 10163
ph: 415-221-4869
info@susandkleckner.com
http://www.susandkleckner.com
Specializes in the appraisal of American folk art.

Ken Farmer
Ken Farmer Auctions & Appraisals, LLC
105 Harrison St.
Radford, VA 24141
ph: 540-639-0939
fax: 540-639-1759
ken@kfauctions.com
http://www.kfauctions.com
Specializes in real estate and personal property auctions; also offers appraisals of Southern material culture, American furniture, folk art, decorative arts, collectibles and fine art.

Auction Services

Willis Henry
Willis Henry Auctions, Inc.
22 Main St.
Marshfield, MA 02050
ph: 781-834-7774 or 800-244-8466
fax: 781-826-3520
wha@willishenry.com
http://www.willishenry.com
Specializes in the sale of American antiques of all kinds, particularly Shaker, American Indian and Early American.

John McClain
York Town Auction Inc.
1625 Haviland Rd.
York, PA 17404
ph: 717-751-0211
fax: 717-767-7729
info@yorktownauction.com
http://www.yorktownauction.com
Antique & specialty auctions, lecture & appraisal services; antiques also purchased; American & English furniture, related specialties & accessories, Americana, folk art, jewelry, art, clocks & watches, militaria, steins, Oriental rugs.

Steve Slotin
Slotin Folk Art Auction House
5967 Blackberry Lane
Buford, GA 30518
ph: 770-932-1000
fax: 770-932-0506
folkfest@bellsouth.net
http://www.slotinfolkart.com
Leading venue for self-taught, Outsider, Folk Art and Southern folk pottery.

Clubs/Associations

Richard Trump
Folk Art Association of the Southwest
3993 Old Santa Fe Trail
Santa Fe, NM 87501
ph: 505-984-8680
Founded in 1992 to promote, preserve, and encourage interest in folk art.

Collectors

Michael J. Hennigan
20816 E. Eleven Mile
Saint Clair Shores, MI 48081-1565
ph: 313-822-9730 or 810-779-9992
fax: 313-821-2766
Wants to buy figures made by tradesmen to advertise their

businesses, such as figures made from mufflers and parts, radiators, heating/cooling/furnace fixtures, plumbing parts, leaf or coil springs, etc.

Dealers

Gene & Linda Kangas
Creekside Art Gallery
Kangas@CreeksideArtGallery.com
http://www.creeksideartgallery.com
Dealers in folk art and hunting decoys.

Susan Stella
Susan Stella Antiques
9 Masconomo St.
Manchester, MA 01944
ph: 978-526-7371
sstella@banet.net
http://www.susanstella.com
Specializes in buying and selling 18th and 19th century American folk art; also formal and country furniture, paintings, samplers, hooked rugs, quilts, ship models, and weathervanes.

Russ & Karen Goldberger
RJG Antiques
P.O. Box 60
Rye, NH 03870
ph: 603-433-1770
fax: 603-433-3937
decoys@rjgantiques.com
http://www.rjgantiques.com
Specializes in quality working decoys, folk art, and American furniture and accessories in their original painted surfaces.

Gary Guyette
Gary Guyette Antiques
P.O. Box 522
West Farmington, ME 04992
ph: 207-778-6256
fax: 207-778-6501
decoys@guyetteandschmidt.com
http://www.guyetteandschmidt.com
Buys, sells, auctions antique decoys.

Marguerite Riordan
Marguerite Riordan Antiques
8 Pearl St.
Stonington, CT 06378
ph: 860-535-2511
fax: 860-535-0580
mr@kx3.com
Specializes in Folk Art, American furniture, paintings and decorative accessories; by appointment.

Jeffrey Tillou Antiques
33 & 39 West St.
Litchfield, CT 06759
ph: 860-567-9693
fax: 860-567-2781
jtillouantiques@earthlink.net
Specializes in 18th and early 19th century, folk art and accessories.

Frank Maresca
Ricco/Maresca Gallery
529 W. 20th St., 3rd Floor
New York, NY 10011
ph: 212-627-4819
fax: 212-627-5117
rmgal@aol.com
http://www.riccomaresca.com
Deals in American self-taught, folk and outsider art.

John Sholl
Sholl Antiques
P.O. Box 9
Norwood, NY 13668
ph: 315-353-2474
info@tramp-art.com
http://www.tramp-art.com
Specializes in folk crafts of the early 20th century: tramp art, penknife whimseys, marquetry, fretwork, pyrography.

Art Pietraszewski
60 Grant St.
Depew, NY 14043
ph: 716-681-2339
pie48@hotmail.com
Buys folk art: wooden decoys, bird carvings, folk art of any type of condition, including damaged or separate heads, bodies, parts; send close up images or photos.

Ronald Korman
Muleskinner Antiques
5548 Main St.
Williamsville, NY 14221
ph: 716-633-4077
rkorman@worldnet.att.net
http://www.muleskinnerantiques.com
Buys and sells redware, antique lighting, folk art, game boards, primitives, weathervanes, early glass, decoys, trade signs, etc.

Joe Adams
America, Oh Yes!
P.O. Box 3075
Hilton Head Island, SC 29938
ph: 843-785-2649
folkart@hargray.com
http://www.americaohyes.com
Wants Folk Art paintings, carvings, quilts, crafts by Southern artisans (contemporary and antique.)

Donald E. Taussig
Sanders' Antique Mall
527 S. Pineapple Ave.
Sarasota, FL 34236
ph: 941-366-0400
fax: 941-952-1491
sandersant@aol.com
http://www.sandersantiques.com
Buys and sells decoys, antique lighting, trade signs, decorative accessories.

Matt Lippa
Artisans
P.O. Box 256
Mentone, AL 35984-0256
ph: 256-634-4037
fax: 256-634-4037
artisans@folkartisans.com
http://www.folkartisans.com
Buy and sell folk art, outsider art, fine art; Internet WWW site offers links to additional dealers; also offers non-profit clubs and museums with an outlet to post notices, press releases, calendar items, etc. at no charge.

Marcia Weber
Marcia Weber - Art Objects
1050 Woodley Rd.
Montgomery, AL 36106
ph: 334-262-5349
fax: 334-567-0060
weberart@mindspring.com
http://www.marciaweberartobjects.com
Has specialized in collecting art created by self-taught artists for many years; has an inventory of over 400 works available through photographs sent to prospective purchasers; gallery opened by appointment only.

Ivan Gilbert, MD
Miran Art & Books
2824 Elm Ave.
Columbus, OH 43209
ph: 614-231-3707 or 614-818-3222
fax: 614-818-3223
IGilbert@ahhinc.com

J.E. Porcelli American Folk Art.
ph: 216-932-9087 or 216-932-3270
fax: 216-932-3270
jeporcelli@en.com
Carries quality 19th and early 20th century examples of American folk art: textiles, walking sticks, tramp art, trade signs, paintings, carvings, etc.

Louis Picek
Main St. Antiques & Art
110 West Main
P.O. Box 340
West Branch, IA 52358-0340
ph: 319-643-2065
msantiques@bigplanet.com
Buys and sells folk art; offers a monthly list of items for sale.

Frank & Barbara Pollack
1214 Green Bay Rd.
Highland Park, IL 60035-4011
ph: 847-433-2213 or 847-433-2295
fax: 312-372-8343
fpollack@compuserve.com
Have available and wish to purchase American primitive paintings, furniture, textiles, toleware, folk art and related accessories of the 18th and 19th centuries and furniture, jewelry and accessories of the 20th century.

Bonnie Grossman
Ames Gallery, The
Newsletter: Ames News
2661 Cedar St.
Berkeley, CA 94708-1933
ph: 510-845-4949
fax: 510-845-6219
info@amesgallery.com
http://www.amesgallery.com
Specializes in self-taught, visionary, and outsider art; carved canes, quilts, hooked rugs, tramp art, whirligigs, and whimseys; emphasis is on homemades and handmades; call for appointment.

Experts

Helaine Fendelman
Helaine Fendelman & Assoc.
60 Gramercy Park North
New York, NY 10010
ph: 212-228-6440
fax: 212-228-8577
HFendelman@aol.com
http://www.appraisersassoc.org/biography/HF0002/page.html
Appraises and liquidates estates; author of the "Official Identification and Price Guide to American Folk Art," co-author with Joe Rosson of "Treasures in Your Attic" and of "Price it Yourself" (Harper Collins).

Clifford Wallach
81 Washington St., #7J
Brooklyn, NY 11201
ph: 718-596-5325
fax: 718-596-5581
info@trampart.com
http://www.trampart.com
Author of "Tramp Art, One Notch at a Time" published by Wallace-Irons; buys, sells exceptional forms of tramp art and other folk art and outsider art.

George H. Meyer
100 West Long Lake Rd., Ste. 100
Bloomfield Hills, MI 48304
ph: 248-646-2907
fax: 248-647-5079
gmeyer@meyerkirk.com
Collector and expert wants to purchase early American face jugs, snake jugs, and other figural American pottery; author of "American Folk Art Canes - Personal Sculpture."

Internet Resources

Matt Lippa
Artisans
P.O. Box 256
Mentone, AL 35984-0256
ph: 256-634-4037
fax: 256-634-4037
artisans@folkartisans.com
http://www.folkartisans.com
Buy and sell folk art, outsider art, fine art; Internet WWW site offers links to additional dealers; also offers non-profit clubs and museums with an outlet to post notices, press releases, calendar items, etc. at no charge.

Museums/Libraries

Peggy Kempton, Deputy Dir.
Fruitlands Museums, Inc.
102 Prospect Hill Rd.
Harvard, MA 01451-1301
ph: 978-456-3924
fax: 978-456-8078
PKempton@fruitlands.org
http://www.fruitlands.org
A 19th century American art and history museum complex.

Museum of Fine Arts, Boston
465 Huntington Ave.
Boston, MA 02115-5523
ph: 617-267-9300
webmaster@mfa.org
http://www.mfa.org

Yale University Art Gallery, Garvan
Collection
P.O. Box 208271
New Haven, CT 06520-8271
ph: 203-432-0600 or 203-432-0601
http://www.yale.edu/artgallery
One of the most comprehensive collections of early American arts and crafts in the nation.

America Folk Art Museum
45 West 53rd St.
New York, NY 10019
ph: 212-265-1040
http://www.folkartmuseum.org
Dedicated to exploring the diversity of American culture as expressed through folk art.

New-York Historical Society, The
Two West 77th St.
New York, NY 10024
ph: 212-873-3400
fax: 212-874-8706
nyhs@interport.net
http://www.nyhistory.org
An unparalleled resource for the study and appreciation of American art, history, and culture.

Albany Institute of History & Art
125 Washington Ave.
Albany, NY 12210
ph: 518-463-4478
information@albanyinstitute.org
http://www.albanyinstitute.org
One of the oldest museums in the US; spans four centuries of regional history, art and culture; highlights include Hudson River School landscape paintings, silver, and other decorative arts, furniture, contemporary regional art and more.

New York State Historical Association &
The Farmers' Museum, Inc., The
P.O. Box 800
Lake Rd., State Highway 80
Cooperstown, NY 13326
ph: 607-547-1400 or 888-547-1450
cliggio@nysha.org
http://www.nysha.org

Bruce Bomberger, Cur.
Landis Valley Museum
2451 Kissel Hill Rd.
Lancaster, PA 17601-4809
ph: 717-569-0401
fax: 717-560-1247
http://www.landisvalleymuseum.org
Interprets Pennsylvania German rural culture.

Bucks County Historical Society
Newsletter: Penny Lots
84 S. Pine St.
Doylestown, PA 18901-4930
ph: 215-345-0210
fax: 215-230-0823
info@mercermuseum.org
http://www.mercermuseum.org/bchs
Operates three Nat. Historical Landmarks; Mercer Museum has over 40,000 tools of Early American trades/crafts; Spruance Library has research material on trades & crafts; Fonthill Museum is a concrete castle laden with tiles & treasures.

Pennsylvania Academy of Fine Arts
118 N. Broad St.
Philadelphia, PA 19102
ph: 215-972-7600
pafa@pafa.org
http://www.pafa.org/museum/exhibitions
Founded in 1805, the Academy is America's oldest art museum and school of fine arts; collects and exhibits the work of distinguished American artist; renowned for its reputation in training artists from the US and across the world.

Daughters of the American Revolution
Museum
1776 D St. NW
Washington, DC 20006-5392
ph: 202-879-3241 or 202-879-3208
fax: 202-628-0820
museum@dar.org
http://www.dar.org/museum
Washington DC's only American Decorative Arts collection; 33,000 objects made or used in America prior to 1840 are exhibited in 33 period rooms and two galleries.

Library of Congress American Folklife
Center
Newsletter: Folklife Center News
101 Independence Ave. SE
Washington, DC 20540-4610
ph: 202-707-5510
fax: 202-707-2076
folklife@loc.gov
http://lcweb.loc.gov/folklife
Created in 1976 to preserve and present American folk life: online digital collections, resources in ethnographic studies, folk life resources; primary strength is music and occupational-folklore interviews.

National Museum of American History
14th & Constitution Ave. NW
Washington, DC 20560
ph: 202-357-2700
webmaster@si.edu
http://www.si.edu/organiza/museums/
nmah/nmah.htm

Abby Aldrich Rockefeller Folk Art
Center
P.O. Box 1776
Williamsburg, VA 23187-1776
ph: 757-229-1000 x8540 or 800-
HISTORY
mmartin@cwf.org
http://www.history.org

Paula Chamblee
Museum of Early Southern Decorative
Arts
Journal: Journal of the Early Southern
Decorative Arts
P.O. Box 10310
Winston Salem, NC 27108-0310
ph: 336-721-7360 or 888-653-7253
fax: 336-721-7367
webmaster@oldsalem.org
http://www.mesda.org
Focuses on Southern decorative arts; has Research Center, Catalog of Early Southern Decorative Arts, and Index of Southern Artists.

David Warren
Bayou Bend Collection & Gardens, The
P.O. Box 6826
Houston, TX 77265-6826
ph: 281-639-7750
fax: 281-639-7770
hirsch@mfah.org
http://mfah.org/bayou.html
One of the nation's premier American decorative arts collections, housed in the former residence of Houston philanthropist Miss Ima Hogg; collection includes over 4,800 works of American art: furniture, textiles, paintings, etc.

Joyce Ice, Ph.D., Dir
Museum of International Folk Art
P.O. Box 2065
Santa Fe, NM 87505-2065
ph: 505-476-1200
fax: 505-982-0606
jice@moifa.org
http://www.moifa.org
Home of the world's largest folk art collection from around the globe; over 125,000 artifacts from over 100 nations; Museum is located at the Museum Hill Complex, 3 miles from the downtown plaza.

Periodicals

America Folk Art Museum
Magazine: Folk Art
45 West 53rd St.
New York, NY 10019
ph: 212-265-1040
http://www.folkartmuseum.org

Carvings

Repro. Sources

Vaughn Rawson
Whimsical Whittler, The
1745 W. Columbia Rd.
Mason, MI 48854-9259
ph: 517-676-4846
whimsicalwhit@aol.com
http://www.whimiscalwhittler.com
Specializes in reproduction of traditional and whimsical hand-carved Santas, Nativities, Angels, Americana, and other folk designs.

Contemporary

Clubs/Associations

Folk Art Society of America
Newsletter: Folk Art Messenger
P.O. Box 17041
Richmond, VA 23226-7041
ph: 804-285-4532 or 800-527-3655
fax: 804-285-4532
folkart@rmond.mindspring.com
http://www.folkart.org
Non-profit organization formed to discover, study, promote, preserve, exhibit, and document contemporary folk art, folk artists, and folk environments; newsletter published quarterly.

Museums/Libraries

Joan M. Bendetti, Lib.
Craft & Folk Art Museum
5800 Wilshire Blvd.
Los Angeles, CA 90036-4591
ph: 323-934-9684 or 323-937-5544
fax: 323-937-5576
Specializing in contemporary craft, design, folk art: clay, fiber, wood, glass, paper, costume, dolls, masks, etc.; artist's registry.

Periodicals

Florence Laffal, Ed.
Gallery Press
Newsletter: Folk Art Finder
1 River Rd.
Essex, CT 06426
ph: 860-767-0313
FAF is devoted to news and information on contemporary folk art; calendar, feature stories, readers exchange, new artists, ads, etc.; published quarterly.

Mexican

Experts

Donna McMenamin
5100 W. Rhyolite Loop
Tucson, AZ 85745
ph: 520-743-2940
fax: 520-743-2941
donnamcm@worldnet.att.net
http://www.donnamcmenamin.com
Author of "Popular Arts of Mexico 1850-1950," "Traditional Mexican Style Interiors," and "Traditional Mexican Style Exteriors;" buys and sells.

Stoneware

Dealers

Richard Hume
Liberty Forever Auctioneers
P.O. Box 281
Bay Head, NJ 08742
ph: 732-899-8707 or 732-244-7007
libertyforever76@hotmail.com

Theorems

Repro. Sources

Hope R. Angier
P.O. Box 246
Alna, ME 04535
ph: 207-586-5692
hopera@tidewater.net
http://www.hopeangier.com
Handpainted fireboards, theorem paintings and wall hangings using early American decorative techniques.

Tinware

Museums/Libraries

Cooper-Hewitt Museum National
Museum of Design, Smithsonian
Institution
2 East 91st St.
New York, NY 10128
ph: 212-860-6868 or 212-849-8300
publicinfo@ch.si.edu
http://www.si.edu/ndm

Weathervanes

Museums/Libraries

Heritage Plantation of Sandwich
P.O. Box 566
Sandwich, MA 02563
ph: 508-888-3300 or 508-888-1222
fax: 508-833-2916
heritage@heritageplantation.org
http://www.heritageplantation.org/
autos.htm

Repro. Sources

Lemee's Fireplace Equipment
815 Bedford St.
Bridgewater, MA 02324-3007
ph: 508-697-2672
lemeesfirep@aol.com
http://www.lemeesfireplace.com

Brian Chabot
Cape Cod Cupula
78 State Rd.
North Dartmouth, MA 02747-2922
ph: 508-994-2119
fax: 508-997-2511
http://www.capecodcupola.com
Sells reproduction weathervanes and custom-made copulas.

Copper House, The
1747 Dover Rd., RT 4
Epsom, NH 03234-4416
ph: 800-281-9798
fax: 603-736-4921
lights@thecopperhouse.com
http://www.thecopperhouse.com
Handmade copper reproduction lighting fixtures and weathervanes.

No imports. Catalog $4 deducted from purchase.

FOOD COLLECTIBLES

(see also BANANA COLLECTIBLES;
CEREAL BOXES; COFFEE;
COOKBOOKS; COOKIES & COOKIE
SHAPING; FAST FOOD
COLLECTIBLES; GROCERY STORE
ITEMS; HAMBURGERS; LABELS;
MENUS; NUT-RELATED
COLLECTIBLES; POPCORN ITEMS;
PREMIUMS, Cereal Box;
RESTAURANT COLLECTIBLES)

Dealers

Louise Pennisi
Around the Kitchen
P.O. Box 840
Georgetown, CT 06829
ph: 203-438-2338
Buying and selling collectible cookbooks (19th & 20th century), cookery booklets (Pillsbury, Baker's Chocolate, Jell-O, etc.), antique kitchen instruction & recipe pamphlets; issues catalogs of items for sale.

Internet Resources

Tom & Meredith Hughes
Food Museum, The
9908 La Paz, NW
Albuquerque, NM 87114
ph: 505-898-0909
fax: 505-898-3434
hughes@foodmuseum.com
http://www.foodmuseum.com
Web site provides a virtual tour of the world's foods based on artifacts in the museum's collections.

Fake Food

Man./Prod./Dist.

Fake-Foods.com
P.O. Box 231780
Encinitas, CA 92023
ph: 760-942-7235
fax: 760-942-7246
info@fake-foods.com
http://www.fake-foods.com
Manufacturer or replica food products.

Replica Food Limited
800 Highgate Studios
53-79 Higate Rd.
London, NW5 1TL U.K.
ph: +44 (20) 7485 3485
fax: +44 (20) 7485 3484
sales@replica.co.uk
http://www.replica.co.uk
Specializes in making plastic food models for use in restaurants, etc.

Ketchup

Collectors

Ralph Finch
34007 Hillside Ct.
Farmington, MI 48335-2513
ph: 248-476-4893 or 800-678-6400
x6023
Wants antique material relating to ketchup.

Mustard

Clubs/Associations

Mount Horeb Mustard Museum
109 E. Main St.
P.O. Box 468
Mount Horeb, WI 53572
ph: 608-437-3986 or 800-438-6878
curator@mustardmuseum.com
http://www.mustardmuseum.com
Over 3,000 mustard-related artifacts on display.

Collectors

Barry Levinson
c/o Mount Horeb Mustard Museum
109 E. Main St.
P.O. Box 468
Mount Horeb, WI 53572
ph: 608-437-3986 or 800-438-6878
curator@mustardmuseum.com
http://www.mustardmuseum.com
Collector of mustard-related items: mustard jars, advertising, knickknacks, etc.

FOSSILS

(see also ARCHAEOLOGY;
MINERAL SPECIMENS; NATURAL
HISTORY; PREHISTORIC
ARTIFACTS; SKELETONS)

Appraisers

Nathaniel Ludlum, ISA
Natural History Appraisals
7323 Tucker Rd.
Centerburg, OH 43011-9200
ph: 740-625-7956
fax: 614-436-0124
ludlum@ecr.net
Specializes in the appraisal of mineral and fossil collections for insurance, donation or estate purposes.

Auction Services

Jeremy Fuller
Mineral, Fossil & Gemstones Auctions
Co.
997 N. Chapel Dr., Ste. #4
Bountiful, UT 84010
ph: 801-296-2516
fax: 801-292-5439
info@minmarket.com
http://www.minmarket.com
The first mineral, fossil, and gemstone "mall" auction of its kind on the Web.

Collectors

Scott Young
P.O. Box 8452
Port Saint Lucie, FL 34985-8452
ph: 561-878-5634
fax: 561-878-2209
Buys, sells, trades vertebrate fossils from around the world.

Dealers

Ken LeBlanc
PaleoPlace
60 E. Fox Meadow Rd.
Leominster, MA 01453
ph: 978-537-3614
rand50@tiac.net
http://www.paleoplace.com
PaleoPlace is "The Old Earth Catalog" for genuine fossils from around the world; the beauty of life from the ancient preserved in stone.

Al Prandi
Two Guys Fossils
1 Lynne's Way
East Bridgewater, MA 02333-2131
ph: 800-FOS-SILS
fax: 508-378-7081
app@twoguysfossils.com
http://www.twoguysfossils.com
Insects in amber, dinosaurs.

Lang's Fossils
290 Brewer Rd.
Ilion, NY 13357
ph: 315-894-0513
fax: 315-894-0513
info@langsfossils.com
http://www.langsfossils.com
Sells fossils and meteorites; excavating, preparing, and supplying superior fossils since 1971; private quarry is world's finest source for eurypterids.

Gene Harris
Art By God
50 Upper Alabama, Store No. 248
Underground Atlanta
Atlanta, GA 30303
ph: 404-577-7311 or 800-940-4449
fax: 305-573-9343
artbygod@netside.net
Mineral specimens, fossils, gems, sea shells, animal mounts, animal pelts, insects/butterflies, snail shells, skulls.

Gene Harris
Art By God
3705 Biscayne
Miami, FL 33137
ph: 305-573-3011 or 305-573-3691
fax: 305-573-9343
artbygod@netside.net
Mineral specimens, fossils, gems, sea shells, animal mounts, animal pelts, insects/butterflies, snail shells, skulls.

Eric S. Kendrew
Fossil Store, The
4436 Tevallo Dr.
Valrico, FL 33594-7343
ph: 813-681-4350
fax: 813-685-0425
ktrex911@tampabay.rr.com
http://www.geocities.com/fossilstore
Buy, sell fossils worldwide; prepare fossils; gives lectures; supplies schools and museums with fossils; expert underwater and land excavations; written articles on fossils; featured in many magazines and newspaper articles.

Jim & Susan Pendergraft
J & S Fossils
17 Jeff Rd.
Largo, FL 33774-2038
ph: 813-595-2661
fax: 813-595-8544
Fossils@gte.net
http://home1.gte.net/fossils/jaws.htm
Supplies discerning collectors with fossil specimens from ancient sharks, whales, mastodons and mammoths; visit the Web site to see a reconstruction from the gigantic miocene shark megalodon.

Jerry & Sandy Sherman
Paleoworld Connection
2029 Iroquois Trail
Columbus, IN 47203
ph: 812-314-4731
fax: 812-314-2253
paleoworld@voyager.net
http://www.paleoworld.com
Deals in Native American, prehistoric artifacts and fossils worldwide.

John & Karen Mediz
Copper City Rock Shop
566 Ash St.
Globe, AZ 85501
ph: 520-425-7885 or 520-425-4506
fax: 520-425-4506
Buys and sells mining artifacts; also wants to buy minerals and fossils, especially old collections.

Richard B. Troyanowski
Rich Relics
P.O. Box 432
Sandia Park, NM 87047-0432
ph: 505-281-2611 or 505-281-2329
Buys/sells prehistoric/historic Indian artifacts, cowboy, militaria, old world antiquities & coins, fossils & ethnographic collectibles.

Jesse Wellman
High Grade Treasures
17865 Owl Court
Reno, NV 89506
info@highgradetreasures.com
http://www.highgradetreasures.com
Carries a wide selection of primarily minerals and some fossils; field collects in the western US and purchases from mine direct importers, as well as travels to Mexico to obtain quality common and rare specimen; advice given freely.

Internet Resources

Jeremy Fuller
Mineral Market
997 N. Chapel Dr., Ste. #4
Bountiful, UT 84010
ph: 801-296-2516
fax: 801-292-5439
info@minmarket.com
http://www.minmarket.com
Online mineral and fossil auctions, dealer lists, online mineral and fossil museum.

Museums/Libraries

American Museum of Natural History
Central Park West & 79th St.
New York, NY 10024
ph: 212-769-5100
http://www.amnh.org
Six halls of exhibits tell the story of vertebrate evolution through the single largest and most diverse array of vertebrae fossils in the world.

Fick Fossil & History Museum
700 W. 3rd St.
Oakley, KS 67748
ph: 758-672-4839
fickmuseum@ruraltel.net
http://www.oakley-kansas.com/fick
Museum features Cretaceous Period fossils from the personal collection of Earnest and Vi Fick; over 11,000 shark teeth, complete dinosaur specimens, mineral and rock specimens.

Periodicals

Adam Moskow, Ed.
PRIMEDIA Enthusiast Group
Magazine: Lapidary Journal
60 Chestnut Ave., Ste. 201
Devon, PA 19333-1312
ph: 610-293-1112 or 800-676-4336 (sub)
fax: 610-293-1717
LapidaryJournal@primediasi.com
http://www.lapidaryjournal.com
Covers gems, beads, jewelry, minerals, and fossils, for artisans and collectors, including profiles, step-by-step instructions, and a show calendar.

FOUNTAIN PENS

(see PENS)

FOURTH OF JULY ITEMS

(see FIREWORKS MEMORABILIA; HOLIDAY COLLECTIBLES)

FRAKTURS

(see also FOLK ART; STATE RELATED MEMORABILIA, Pennsylvania German Heritage)

Dealers

Corinne & Russell Earnest
P.O. Box 1007
East Berlin, PA 17316-0507
ph: 717-259-0299
rdearnest@aol.com
Buys and sells fraktur including printed fraktur, birth and baptism certificates, bookplates, fraktur-like watercolors, or other decorated manuscripts; send photo or clear photocopy; describe and state price.

Experts

Corinne & Russell Earnest
P.O. Box 1007
East Berlin, PA 17316-0507
ph: 717-259-0299
rdearnest@aol.com
Author of "Fraktur: Folk Art & Family."

Pstr. Frederick Weiser
55 Kohler School Rd.
New Oxford, PA 17350-9201
ph: 717-624-4106

Ron Lieberman
Family Album, The
4887 Newport Rd.
Kinzers, PA 17535
ph: 717-442-0220
fax: 717-442-7904
rarebooks@POBox.com
http://www.sellbooks.net
Buys, sells and appraises German Americana: fraktur, books, manuscripts, artwork, etc.

Museums/Libraries

Free Library of Philadelphia
1901 Vine St.
Philadelphia, PA 19103
ph: 215-686-5322 or 215-686-5416
http://www.library.phila.gov
The Henry S. Borneman collection of Pennsylvania German Fraktur.

FRAMES

(see also REPAIR/RESTORATION/ CONSERVATION, Gilding)

Appraisers

Luke Biggs
L. L. Biggs Conservator
P.O. Box 3091
Summerville, SC 29484-3091
ph: 843-851-9293
fax: 843-873-0165
biggsconservator@msn.com
Appraises and restores fine art and frames.

Jerome S. Feig, CPF, ISA
Field Art Studio
24242 Woodward Ave.
Pleasant Ridge, MI 48069-1144
ph: 248-399-1320
fax: 248-399-7018
jsfieldart@aol.com
http://www.custompictureframe.com
Frame specialist and appraiser:

restoration of art, frames, objects, gilding; period frame reproductions made; fine art and frame appraisals; conservation of picture frames.

Auction Services

Justin Wessels
Framefinders Inc.
454 East 84th St.
New York, NY 10028
ph: 212-396-3896
fax: 212-396-3899
framefinders@aol.com
http://www.framefinders.com
Antique frame dealers, restorers, experts, brokerage firm; specializes in the sale and acquisition of high quality antique frames; holds frame-only auctions bi-annually in New York City.

Clubs/Associations

William Adair
International Institute for Frame Study
1523 22nd St., NW, Rear
Washington, DC 20037
ph: 202-833-3200
fax: 202-347-4569
bill@goldleafstudios.com
http://www.goldleafstudios.com
Established in 1992 as the first public archive devoted exclusively to the history of picture frames; archive has hundreds of photographs, drawings, out-of-print books, auction and frame makers' catalogs, articles, videos, etc.

Dealers

John Baker
50 Granite St.
Foxboro, MA 02035
ph: 508-543-4626
Wants to buy ornate gilt frames.

Brad Shar
Lowy
223 East 80th St.
New York, NY 10021
ph: 212-861-8585
fax: 212-988-0443
bshar@lowyonline.com
http://www.lowyonline.com
Specializes in buying and selling antique frames; also offers fine art conservation and restoration services.

Eli Wilner
Eli Wilner & Co.
1525 York Ave.
New York, NY 10028
ph: 212-744-6521
fax: 212-628-0264
info@eliwilner.com
http://www.eliwilner.com/index2.htm
Sells, buys and restores fine 19th and 20th century frames; author of "Antique American Frames: Identification and Price Guide," editor of "The Gilded Edge - The Art of the Frame" (Chronicle Books).

Justin Wessels
Framefinders Inc.
454 East 84th St.
New York, NY 10028
ph: 212-396-3896
fax: 212-396-3899
framefinders@aol.com
http://www.framefinders.com
*Antique frame dealers, restorers,
experts, brokerage firm; specializes in
the sale and acquisition of high
quality antique frames; holds frame-
only auctions bi-annually in New York
City.*

Mary Webster
Mary Webster Antique Picture Frames
12 Edwards St.
Binghamton, NY 13905
ph: 607-722-1483
mwebster@lightlink.com
http://www.marywebster.com
*Carries large inventory of mainly
American period frames in many styles
including Federal, Victorian,
Renaissance Revival, Eastlake,
Aesthetic, Arts & Crafts, folk art;
also frames for photographs and
mirror frames; buys and sells.*

Historic Frames
1185 Mt. Aetna Rd.
Hagerstown, MD 21740
ph: 301-665-9000
fax: 301-665-9775
jc@historicframes.com
http://www.historicframes.com
*Specializes in period frames; also
works on paper, watercolors, and
prints.*

Carol Payne
Carol's Antique Gallery
14455 Big Basin Way
Saratoga, CA 95070-6008
ph: 408-867-7055
*Wants to buy pre-1940 stand-up
frames of wood, silver, brass, ivory,
enamel, etc.; send photocopy of front
and back of frame plus description for
a cash offer.*

Experts

Suzanne Smeaton, Gallery Assoc.
Eli Wilner & Co.
1525 York Ave.
New York, NY 10028
ph: 212-744-6521
fax: 212-628-0264
ssmeaton@eliwilner.com
http://www.eliwilner.com/index2.htm
*Gallery director for Eli Wilner & Co.
in NYC; over 20 years experience in
appraising frames.*

Jeffrey Hayman, Gallery Dir.
Eli Wilner & Co.
1525 York Ave.
New York, NY 10028
ph: 212-744-6521
fax: 212-628-0264
jhayman@eliwilner.com
http://www.eliwilner.com/index2.htm
*Eight years with with Eli Wilner &
Co. in NYC, currently as Gallery*

*Director; also an exhibiting artist and
photographer.*

William Adair
Gold Leaf Studios, Inc.
1523 22nd St., NW, Rear
Washington, DC 20037
ph: 202-833-3200
fax: 202-347-4569
bill@goldleafstudios.com
http://www.goldleafstudios.com

Internet Resources

Art & Framing Headquarters
webmaster@artframing.com
http://www.artframing.com
*Provides a centralized source for
people who have an interest in the art
and picture framing industry; vendors
can promote their products; customers
can purchase artwork or get items
framed.*

Scott Kublin
Art Directory
P.O. Box 1616
Rincon, GA 31326
ph: 912-826-6840
admin@artframing.com
http://www.artframing.com
*Centralized resource for businesses in
the art and framing industry.*

Periodicals

Tricia Bisoux, Sr. Ed.
Magazine: DECOR
330 N. Fourth St.
Saint Louis, MO 63102
ph: 314-421-5445 or 800-280-5445
fax: 314-421-1070
decor@pfpublish.com
http://www.decormagazine.com
*Aimed at art gallery and custom frame
shop owners with articles about
successful business management,
effective marketing and promotions,
gallery design, frame shop floor
plans, art media, technology, and new
trends; annual sources dir.*

Repair Services

Susan B. Jackson
Harvard Art
49 Littleton County Rd.
Harvard, MA 01451-1729
ph: 978-456-9050
fax: 978-456-9050
sbj@ma.ultranet.com
*Restoration and conservation of
period frames and other gilded
objects; stabilization, replacement of
missing pieces, gilding and toning to
match the existing surface.*

Alexandra Hadik
Gilder's Studio, The
34 Jarvis St.
Chester, NH 03036-4123
ph: 508-833-0782
chestergilder@msn.com
*Custom gold leaf framing and
conservation; also offers gilding of
weathervanes as well as instruction in
gold leaf.*

William Adair
Gold Leaf Studios, Inc.
1523 22nd St., NW, Rear
Washington, DC 20037
ph: 202-833-3200
fax: 202-347-4569
bill@goldleafstudios.com
http://www.goldleafstudios.com
*Frame repairs, gold leaf repair; also
makes copies of antique frames in
different sizes.*

R. Wayne Reynolds
R. Wayne Reynolds, Inc.
3618 Falls Rd.
Baltimore, MD 21211
ph: 410-467-1800 or 410-467-1890
*Specializes in the application of gold
leaf; complete restoration services for
gilded art objects, including furniture,
frames, and mirrors.*

Paul J. Buco
Fine Arts Services, Inc.
5725 Olkander Dr., Ste. 3
Wilmington, NC 28403
ph: 910-794-8859
*Restoration of frames including oil
and water gilding, recasting and
replacement of lost ornament.*

Luke Biggs
L. L. Biggs Conservator
P.O. Box 3091
Summerville, SC 29484-3091
ph: 843-851-9293
fax: 843-873-0165
biggsconservator@msn.com
*Appraises and restores fine art and
frames.*

Gordon Ponsford
Ponsford, Ltd.
2405 Highway 92
Acworth, GA 30102
ph: 770-924-4848
fax: 770-529-2278
ponsford@bellsouth.net
http://www.antiqueconservation.com
*Largest conservation group in the
Southwest; 14 of the finest experts
available in their respective fields
working in one studio; Ponsford has
worked with government pieces,
museum collections, private collectors,
family heirlooms.*

Jerome S. Feig, CPF, ISA
Field Art Studio
24242 Woodward Ave.
Pleasant Ridge, MI 48069-1144
ph: 248-399-1320
fax: 248-399-7018
jsfieldart@aol.com
http://www.customepictureframe.com
*Frame specialist and appraiser:
restoration of art, frames, objects,
gilding; period frame reproductions
made; fine art and frame appraisals;
conservation of picture frames.*

Dick Doeren
Lumber Mill Gallery & Framery
107 Smith Ave.
Oconto, WI 54153
ph: 920-834-4494 or 877-889-1085
fax: 920-834-4494
lumbermillgallery@msn.com
*Antique frame, photograph, and
document restoration and preservation; old world craftsmanship;
members of The Society of Guilders.*

Picture

Experts

Stuart Schneider
P.O. Box 64
Teaneck, NJ 07666-0064
ph: 201-599-4250
fax: 201-599-4251
Stuart@wordcraft.net
http://www.wordcraft.net
*Author of "Collecting Picture &
Photo Frames" with price guide,
photos of picture frames made from
1800 to 1870.*

FRANK LLOYD WRIGHT

(see also ARCHITECTURE &
RELATED ITEMS; ARTS & CRAFTS)

Clubs/Associations

Margo Stipe, Registrar
Frank Lloyd Wright Foundation,
Taliesin West
Magazine: FLLW Quarterly
P.O. Box 4430
Scottsdale, AZ 85261
ph: 480-860-2700
fax: 480-451-0254
archives@franklloydwright.org
http://www.franklloydwright.org
*Established by Frank Lloyd Wright in
1940 as a repository for his life's
work; committed to advancing the
ideas and principles of organic
architecture, organic education, and
conservation of the natural environment.*

Dealers

Michael FitzSimmons
Michael FitzSimmons Decorative Arts
311 West Superior St.
Chicago, IL 60610
ph: 312-787-0496
fax: 312-787-6343
contact@fitzdecarts.com
http://www.fitzdecarts.com
*Specializing in 20th century
architecture and decorative arts
especially Frank Lloyd Wright and the
Prairie School of design; also Gustav
Stickley and others.*

J.B. Muns
Fine Arts Books & Musical Autographs
1162 Shattuck Ave.
Berkeley, CA 94707-2635
ph: 510-525-2420
fax: 510-525-1126
jbmuns@aol.com
Specializes in Frank Lloyd Wright;

catalogs issued since 1964; by appointment only.

Internet Resources

Lists of Frank Lloyd Wright Links
usonia@hotmail.com
http://www.geocities.com/SoHo/1469/
flwlinks.html
Web site contains Frank Lloyd Wright links to organizations, items for sale, Frank Lloyd Wright discussion groups, etc.

FRANKART

(see also ART DECO)

Collectors

David Negley
David Negley's Gallery
438 W. 47th St., #1A
New York, NY 10036-2330
ph: 212-459-8954
negleyd@nyc.rr.com
http://www.davids-deco.com
Frankart dealer, collector, expert; buys and sells all Frankart items.

Adrienne Leff
1550 S. Dixie Hwy. #210
Coral Gables, FL 33146-3034
ph: 305-667-4214
fax: 305-668-2592
Buys, sells, trades and collects Frankart lamps, ashtrays, bookends and candlestick holders.

Jeff Leegood
DecoLectibles
P.O. Box 596553
Dallas, TX 75227-1429
ph: 214-275-4370
jleegood@yahoo.com
Buys all types of Frankart: nude figures, animals, etc.; Frankart made lamps, bookends, ashtrays, etc.; items were made in the '20s & '30s and are of cast metal; most pieces are marked; also buys other similar Art Deco figures.

Dealers

David Negley
David Negley's Gallery
438 W. 47th St., #1A
New York, NY 10036-2330
ph: 212-459-8954
negleyd@nyc.rr.com
http://www.davids-deco.com
Frankart dealer, collector, expert; buys and sells all Frankart items.

Experts

David Negley
David Negley's Gallery
438 W. 47th St., #1A
New York, NY 10036-2330
ph: 212-459-8954
negleyd@nyc.rr.com
http://www.davids-deco.com
Frankart dealer, collector, expert; buys and sells all Frankart items.

Walter Glenn
Geode, Ltd.
3393 Peachtree Rd.
Atlanta, GA 30326-1162
ph: 404-261-9346
Buys and sells Frankart, Inc. items; also advisor to collectors, dealers, auction houses, etc.

FRATERNAL ORGANIZATION ITEMS

(see also BADGES; VETERAN ITEMS; SOCIAL CAUSES)

Collectors

James Berkel
420 Arthur Ave.
Endicott, NY 13760
ph: 607-748-0393
Wants Union and lodge badges 7" long with fringe on bottom; also wants any Improved Order of the Red Man badges or pins.

American Legion

Collectors

Bob Bowen
13516 Kingsman Rd.
Woodbridge, VA 22193
ph: 703-590-3945
Buy American Legion convention badges or related Legion memorabilia.

Elks

Collectors

David Wendel
F.E.I. Collectibles
P.O. Box 1187
Poplar Bluff, MO 63902-1187
ph: 573-686-1926 or 573-785-2075
fax: 573-686-8450
dwendel@ldd.net
Wants Elks Lodge memorabilia; BPOE badges, tankards, steins, souvenir plates, programs, jewelry, etc.

Knights Of Columbus

Museums/Libraries

Mary Lou Cummings, Cur.
Knights of Columbus Museum
1 State St.
New Haven, CT 06511-0236
ph: 203-865-0400 x223
fax: 203-865-0351
info@kofc.org
http://www.kofc.org/knights/museum/
museum.htm
Museum and archives revealing the history, formation and activities of the K. of C. as an international, Catholic, service-oriented, fraternal organization with insurance benefits.

Lions

Collectors

Frank Johnson
73 West Johnston St.
Washington, NJ 07882-1332
Wants Lions Club pins and other memorabilia.

Thomas R. Owen
P.O. Box 435
Marshfield, MO 65706-0435
ph: 417-858-0000
tomrowen@msn.com
Wants to buy Lion's Club pins.

Masonic

Collectors

Dave
315 So. 4th St.
P.O. Box 522
Manhattan, KS 66505-0522
ph: 785-776-1433
Wants Masonic/Shriners jewelry, coins, tokens, books, paper items, memorabilia, anything Masonic needed for collection.

Dealers

Frank Everts
Frank Everts & Associates
11846 Donore
Dallas, TX 75218-1845
ph: 214-349-5577
fax: 214-553-0446
Collector of Masonic jewelry, fobs and pins (except Shrine); also manufactures Masonic jewelry.

Experts

Stanley W. Johnson
P.O. Box 462
Auburn, MA 01501-0462
ph: 508-799-6300
Specializes in the material culture of Freemasons including the obscure, cryptic, esoteric, enigmatic and genre; also Blue Lodge, Scottish Rite, York Rite, Royal Arch, Knights Templar, Shrine; Member, National Heritage Museum.

Museums/Libraries

National Heritage Museum, Van Gorden-Williams Library
33 Marrett Rd.
Lexington, MA 02421
ph: 781-861-6559
fax: 781-861-9846
library@monh.org
http://vgw.library.net
Research library specializing in the history of Freemasonry and related fraternal organizations in the US.

Iowa Masonic Library & Museum
813 First St. SE
P.O. Box 279
Cedar Rapids, IA 52406-0279
ph: 319-365-1438
fax: 319-365-1439
Librarian@gl-iowa.org
http://wwww.gl-iowa.org
Collection displays a great number of Masonic relics.

Masonic Grand Lodge Library &
Museum of Texas
715 Columbus Ave.
P.O. Box 446
Waco, TX 76703
ph: 254-753-7395
fax: 254-753-2944
texasmason@gltexas.org
http://www.library-museum.grandlodgeoftexas.org

Odd Fellows

Collectors

Greg Spiess
230 E. Washington St.
Joliet, IL 60433-1006
ph: 815-722-5639
fax: 815-722-0171
spiessantq@aol.com
Wants to buy Odd Fellows items: steins, badges, medals, pins, ritual prints, coffins, banners, ark of covenants, flags, pedestals, heart in hand items, carvings with symbolism, supply catalogs.

FREAKS

(see MORBID & ODD ITEMS)

FRENCH FOREIGN LEGION

Collectors

David Stevens
680 North Lake Shore Dr.
Chicago, IL 60611
ph: 773-751-8000
Wants to buy French Foreign Legion ephemera.

FRUIT JARS

(see also BOTTLES; JELLY CONTAINERS; INSULATORS)

Clubs/Associations

Norman & Junne Barnett
Midwest Antique Fruit Jar & Bottle
Club
Newsletter: Midwest Glass Chatter, The
P.O. Box 38
Flat Rock, IN 47234
ph: 812-587-5560
thebarnetts@lightbound.com
http://www.fruitjar.org
An organization for those interested in collecting and learning about fruit jars and bottles; sponsors two fruit and bottle shows each year in Indianapolis.

Mason Bright
Ball Collectors Club
Newsletter: Ball Collectors Club
  Newsletter
497 Fox Dr.
Monroe, MI 48161
ph: 734-241-0113 or 734-242-3430
fax: 734-242-3436
balljars@cheerful.com
*Focuses on collecting Ball fruit jars
and GO-WITHS; newsletter includes
information on Ball jars; lists jars for
sale by members.*

Wendy Smith, Mem.
Federation of Historical Bottle
  Collectors, Inc.
Magazine: Bottles & Extras
401 Johnston Court
Raymore, MO 64083
ph: 816-318-0160
osubuckeyes71@aol.com
http://www.fohbc.com
*"Bottles & Extras" contains articles,
pictures, letters, show dates, and
show and auction reports in the field
of antique bottles, insulators, fruit
jars and associated items; check Web
site for list of scores of clubs by
region.*

Collectors

Richard Dalton
30 Primrose Lane
Brick, NJ 08724
ph: 732-458-7650
jerseyjar@aol.com
*Collects, buys, sells, trades old fruit
jars or canning jars.*

Claude Bellar
1750 Keyes Rd.
Greenbrier, TN 37073
ph: 615-643-0290
fax: 615-643-0290
cbellar@aol.com

Art Snyder
6086 W. Boggstown Rd.
Boggstown, IN 46110
ph: 317-835-7121
emshaw@in.net
*Buys/sells/trades all types of fruit jars
especially Ball jars, odd closures, pint
sizes, midgets and highly whittled
quart size examples.*

Greg Spurgeon
10644 US 41 North
10644 US 41 North
Rosedale, IN 47874
ph: 812-466-6521
xx78@msn.com
http://www.hoosierjar.com
*Wants antique fruit jars; scarce and
colored jars.*

Harry Fisher
Rte. 1 Box 197
Owensville, MO 65066
ph: 573-437-4227
*Wants Globe, Lightning, Masons
amber, Millville Atmospherics and
Improveds, Princess, Perfections, The
Darling, Royal Amber, etc.; any*

*unusual jars, please describe and
price.*

Scott Grandstaff
63742 Applegate Dr.
P.O. Box 409
Happy Camp, CA 96039
ph: 530-493-2032
scottg@snowcrest.net
*Past-Publisher of "Bottles & Extras"
magazine; casual appraisals done
free; detailed appraisals and
professional consulting are available
for a fee.*

Dealers

John Hathaway
Hathaway's Antiques
3 Mills Rd.
Bryant Pond, ME 04219
ph: 207-665-2124
fax: 207-665-2124
meidea@megalink.net
http://www.megalink.net/~meidea
*Buys and sells fruit jars; hundreds of
rare jars to inexpensive jars in all
categories; midgets and half pints;
mail order a specialty.*

Experts

Bill & Jill Meier
Glass Insulators
103 Canterbury Ct.
Carlisle, MA 01741-1860
ph: 978-369-0208
bill@insulators.com
http://www.insulators.com
*Specialists in Hemingray, H.G. Co.
and DEC 19 1871 insulators and
other Hemingray items such as water
bottles and H.G. Co. fruit jars;
looking to expand collection;
interested in sharing knowledge with
others.*

John Hathaway
Hathaway's Antiques
3 Mills Rd.
Bryant Pond, ME 04219
ph: 207-665-2124
fax: 207-665-2124
meidea@megalink.net
http://www.megalink.net/~meidea
*Buys and sells fruit jars; hundreds of
rare jars to inexpensive jars in all
categories; midgets and half pints;
mail order a specialty.*

Mike Jordan
M & B Antiques
310 SW 35 St.
Ocala, FL 34474
ph: 352-291-1024
bjordan850@aol.com
http://members.aol.com/Potomacbtl/
  bottle2.htm
*Buy, sells, appraises and specializes
in rare, early American fruit jars;
specializing in odd closures and
colors.*

Mason Bright
497 Fox Dr.
Monroe, MI 48161
ph: 734-241-0113 or 734-242-3430
fax: 734-242-3436
balljars@cheerful.com
*Specialist and collector of BALL fruit
jars; wants jars, letterheads,
advertising items, GO-WITHS; has
largest collection in the US.*

Doug Leybourne
P.O. Box 5417
Muskegon, MI 49445-0417
ph: 231-744-2003
fax: 231-719-1672
leybourneredbook@bigplanes.com
*Author of "Red Book No. 9: The
Collector's Guide to Old Fruit Jars,"
a price guide describing over 10,000
known jars; available from the author
for $35 ppd.; also author of "The
Fruit Jar Works."*

Jerry McCann
Phoenix Press
5003 West Berwin
Chicago, IL 60630
ph: 773-777-0443
fjar@aol.com
http://www.antiquebotl.com/mccann.htm
*Wants to buy unusual fruit jars;
publishes "Fruit Jar Annual," a price
guide, for $30.*

Periodicals

Tom Caniff
Newsletter: Fruit Jar News, The
1223 Oak Grove Ave.
Steubenville, OH 43952
ph: 740-282-8918
tomcaniff@aol.com
*Covers new finds, glass factory
histories, jar news in general plus
want ads, for-sale page and show
dates.*

FUNERAL ITEMS

(see also MORBID & ODD ITEMS)

Collectors

Rich Hartzog
World Exonumia
P.O. Box 4143CNZ
Rockford, IL 61110-0643
ph: 815-226-0771
hartzog@exonumia.com
http://www.exonumia.com
*Wants advertising items showing or
issued by funeral parlors; tokens,
badges, medals, ribbons, and other
small collectibles.*

Museums/Libraries

National Museum of Funeral History
415 Barren Springs Dr.
Houston, TX 77090
ph: 281-876-3063 or 800-238-8861
fax: 281-876-2961
info@nmfh.org
http://www.nmfh.org
The nation's largest collection of

*funeral service memorabilia: historic
coffins, death wagons, embalming
instruments, etc.; a creation of Service
Corporation International, the
world's largest funeral provider.*

FURNITURE (ANTIQUE)

(see also ARTS & CRAFTS; ART
DECO; ART NOUVEAU; GARDEN
FURNITURE; MODERNISM;
ORIENTALIA; REPAIR/
RESTORATION/CONSERVATION,
Furniture [Antique Only]; SHAKER
ITEMS; WALLACE NUTTING;
WICKER)

Appraisers

David J. LeBeau
David J. LeBeau Appraisal Services
119 South Main St.
Sheffield, MA 01257
ph: 413-229-3445
djlebeau@rcn.com
http://www.appraisalbylebeau.com
*Specializes in the appraisal of
furniture, silver, ceramics and
decorative arts; former ASA (1974-99)
& Past Pres. NY Chapter ASA;
retired Asst. Prof. Appraisal Studies
NYU, founding faculty of Appraisal
Studies program Yeshiva U.*

Mary M. Kuhrtz, ISA
Cape Code Appraisal Service
P.O. Box 1082
East Dennis, MA 02641-1082
ph: 508-385-4978 or 781-341-4444
fax: 781-341-9315
mkuhrtz@aol.com
*Specializes in the appraisal of 18th
and 19th century American furniture
and decorative arts; complete estates,
insurance, donation appraisals for the
Cape, Islands, and Southeastern
Massachusetts.*

Nickolas Kotula, ASA
493 Simsbury Rd.
Bloomfield, CT 06002-1512
ph: 860-243-1646
fax: 860-243-8899
*Appraiser, expert witness, lecturer,
writer, author of articles in "Maine
Antique Digest," "The Faking of
Antique Furniture," and "Historical
Cabinetmaking Construction."*

William Oakley
Oakley Restoration & Finishing, LLC
30 South End Plaza
New Milford, CT 06776
ph: 860-350-6410
fax: 630-214-8237
oakleyrestoration@earthlink.net
http://www.oakleyrestoration.com
*Appraises, restores, conserves antique
furniture; appraisals for general and
legal purposes; offers digital video
archiving for accurate "visual"
documentation; specializes in 17th,
18th and 19th century American and
European furniture.*

Lynn Magnusson
Personal Property Consultants, Inc.
271 Parsippany Rd.
Parsippany, NJ 07054
ph: 973-884-2466
fax: 973-884-1781
info@ppcappraisals.com
http://www.ppcappraisals.com
Specializes in the appraisal of furniture, ceramics, silver and other residential contents for insurance, equitable distribution, donation, matrimonial; offers expert witness and litigation services; appraisals comply with USPAP.

Diane Patalano
Country Girls Appraisal & Liquidation Service
P.O. Box 376
Saddle River, NJ 07458
ph: 201-327-2499
fax: 20-327-2094
dp@microdsi.net
Specializes in 19th to 20th century furniture.

Eldred A. Stenzel, ISA
10 Blue Hills Dr.
Holmdel, NJ 07733-2218
ph: 732-946-8437
fax: 732-946-7980
antiques@iop.com
Specializes in the appraisal of Early American furniture; over 25 years experience.

M. Barden Prisant, FRICS
Telepraisal
32 Union Sq., #1016
New York, NY 10003
ph: 212-614-9090 or 800-645-6002
fax: 212-780-9539
info@telepraisal.com
http://www.telepraisal.com
For over 21 years, Telepraisal has been gathering pricing data on approximately 200,000 artists and sales of their works; printouts of the data can be purchased for $35 per search, or more formal appraisals can be generated.

Norman S. Young
P.O. Box 766
Nassau, NY 12123-0766
ph: 518-766-3445
fax: 518-766-9826
nsyoung@aol.com
http://www.antiekllc.com
Buys, sells, appraises 19th century country and formal furniture; author of "Fabulous But Fake" (H/C book), the professional's guide to fake antiques; available from the author for $44.95.

Catherine M. Sankey, ISA CAPP
Catherine's Antiques & Appraisals
7419 County Line Rd.
Auburn, NY 13021
ph: 315-685-5306
c.m.sankey@worldnet.att.net
Specializes in appraising 19th century furniture and Shaker.

Herbert & Joyce Windle
Windle's Antiques
5716 Kennett Pike
Centreville, DE 19807
ph: 302-651-9222
herbnjoyce@netzero.net
Specializes in the appraisal of antique American furniture; also carries a large inventory of decoys from the St. Lawrence areas - both from NY and Ontario sides, early lighting and fireplace cooking equipment.

James Callear
Barnesville Antiques & Appraising
P.O. Box 314
Barnesville, MD 20838
ph: 301-972-7490
clearviewmeadow@msn.com
Specializes in the appraisal of American and English furniture the 18th through 20th centuries; member of ISA.

Paula Hantman, ASA
Hantman's Auctioneers & Appraisers
P.O. Box 59366
Potomac, MD 20859-9366
ph: 301-770-3720
fax: 301-770-4135
hantman@hantmans.com
http://www.hantmans.com
American, European and Asian antiques (furniture, porcelain, silver, decorative arts, Americana), collectibles, residential contents; estates; insurance replacement and damage claims; estate planning; family division; also auctioneer.

C. Robert Harrison, ISA
Harrison Appraisals, LLC
3435 Uniontown Rd.
Westminster, MD 21158
ph: 410-775-1351
fax: 410-775-1351
bob@harrisonappraisals.com
http://www.harrisonappraisals.com
Offers appraisals of antiques & residential contents; specializes in 18th and 19th century American furniture and Pennsylvania German decorative arts, particularly American "backcountry" furniture from the Shenandoah Valley region.

J. Michael Flanigan
J. M. Flanigan American Antiques
1607 Park Ave.
Baltimore, MD 21217
ph: 410-225-3463
fax: 410-523-9637
jmf745i@aol.com
Specializes in buying, selling and appraising antique American furniture.

Mary Ellen Heibel, ISA, ASA
Personal Property Consultants, Inc.
1009 Old Bay Ridge Rd.
Annapolis, MD 21403-4228
ph: 410-267-7708 or 410-269-5909
fax: 410-269-5909
mehjlh@cs.com
Specializes in the appraisal of antique furniture, antique silver and

metalware, antiques and decorative arts.

Bruce M. Schuettinger, ISA
Antique Restorations Ltd.
17 N. Alley
P.O. Box 244
New Market, MD 21774-0244
ph: 301-865-3009
fax: 301-865-3009
bschuettinger@erols.com
Expert specializing in the appraisal of antique period furniture.

Todd Sigety
Washington Square Antiques
425 South Washington St.
Alexandria, VA 22314
ph: 703-836-1020
fax: 703-360-0803
info@washingtonsquareantiques.com
http://
　www.washingtonsquareantiques.com
Specializes in the appraisal of antique furniture, fine and decorative arts.

Jeffrey Evans
Green Valley Auctions, Inc.
2259 Green Valley Lane
Mount Crawford, VA 22841
ph: 540-434-4260
fax: 540-434-4532
gvai@shentel.net
http://www.greenvalleyauctions.com
Specializes in the appraisal of American glass and furniture.

Anna C. Sim
235 Richard Burbydge
Williamsburg, VA 23185
ph: 757-258-1113
fax: 757-229-5050
acsiminc@cox.net

Christine N. Corbin, ISA
Motley's Auctions, Inc.
4402 West Broad St.
Richmond, VA 23230
ph: 804-355-2100
fax: 804-359-6954
cncorbin@motleys.com
http://www.motleysgroup.com
Auctioneers and appraisers of furniture, silver, fine art, decorative arts, real estate, general goods and vehicles.

Mary Armistead
Armistead Appraisal Services
2608 Seaford Rd.
P.O. Box 495
Seaford, VA 23696
ph: 757-989-5901
fax: 757-989-1828
m.armistead@cox.net
http://members.cox.net/m.armistead/
An Accredited Member of the International Society of Appraisers; has studied at Winterthur, George Washington University, Asheford Institute, and attends the annual Williamsburg Antiques Forum.

Louise Phillips
Alexander Appraisal Service
3116 Weddington Rd. #900 PMB 190
Matthews, NC 28105
ph: 704-849-7352
flownlogic@aol.com
Specializes in appraising furniture, silver, ceramics as well as antiques & residential contents for insurance, liquidation, marital dissolution; also consulting services for clients wishing to sell their items in the highest, best market.

Caroline T. Gray, ISA CAPP
Thistle, The
P.O. Box 220064
Charlotte, NC 28222-0064
ph: 704-365-4539
fax: 704-365-4539
cgray@carolina.rr.com
Certified Appraiser of Personal Property with the International Society of Appraisers; specializes in the appraisal of furniture, ceramics and silver.

Jean Mallory, ISA
Mallory Appraisals
6431 Gardenia St.
Panama City, FL 32404
ph: 850-747-0025
fax: 850-747-0025
jmal88@aol.com
Specializes in the appraisal of antique furniture, residential contents, and collectibles.

Jane Washburn, ISA CAPP
Washburn Appraisals
13121 SW 30th Court
Fort Lauderdale, FL 33330
ph: 954-723-1997
fax: 954-723-0450
jwashburn@hotmail.com
Certified appraiser specializing in the appraisal of American and English furniture, decorative arts and accessories.

Bill Carner, ISA CAPP
Birmingham Appraisal Services
400 Lance Way
Birmingham, AL 35206-3035
ph: 205-836-8009
fax: 205-836-8009
billcarner@aol.com
http://www.billcarner.com
Specializes in appraising 18th to 20th century furniture, glass, ceramics, silver.

Jane Mabry, ISA CAPP
Antiques, Etc. Appraisals
P.O. Box 10045
Huntsville, AL 35801-3670
ph: 256-533-7647 or 256-533-7647
fax: 256-883-8839
jmabry@hiwaay.net
http://fly.highway.net/~jmabry
Specializes in the appraisal of antiques, collectibles, glass, pottery, and furniture.

Judy L. Campbell
Judy L. Campbell Appraisal & Estate
 Sales
5500 Summerset Dr.
Midland, MI 48640-2931
ph: 989-631-9263 or 989-631-4874
fax: 989-631-4874
go4nteks@aol.com
http://www.judycampbell.com
*Appraiser of antique furniture, fine &
decorative arts, American & European
paintings and sculpture, American and
European ceramics, antiques & 20th
century collectibles; also other
personal property.*

Martha C. Arney, ISA
Dunes Antiques Center, Inc.
12825 Red Arrow Highway
Sawyer, MI 49125-9173
ph: 616-426-4043
fax: 616-426-8283
dunesantiques@qtm.net
http://www.dunesantiques.com
*Appraiser of residential contents, art
glass, pottery, decorative arts.*

Frederick P. Dose, Jr.
Frederick Dose Appraisals Ltd.
778 Pleasant Ave.
Highland Park, IL 60035-4613
ph: 847-433-7870 or 847-433-1090
fdoseappraisals@comcast.net
*Appraises US, British, Continental
paintings and furniture, prints,
porcelain, silver, decorative arts,
coins, antiquities; for corporate,
private, and attorneys; references on
request; 6 year full-time as University
art historian.*

Matthew Peckham, ISA CAPP
Peckham & Associates Gallery
118 E. University Ave.
Champaign, IL 61820
ph: 217-351-7777
fax: 217-351-7777
peckham@soltec.net
*Specializes in the appraisal of 20th
century furniture and decorative arts;
Certified Appraiser with the
International Society of Appraisers.*

Brant Laird
Brant Laird Antiques & Appraisals
2901 N. Henderson Ave.
Dallas, TX 75206-6402
ph: 214-823-4100
fax: 214-823-4108
blaird2@earthlink.net
*Accredited Member of the ISA,
Graduate Gemologist; specializes in
the appraisal of jewelry, 18th and
19th century furniture, art objects and
accessories.*

Jerry W. Holley, ISA
Holley Appraisals
5600 W. Lovers Ln., Ste. 116
Dallas, TX 75209-4311
ph: 972-743-6071
fax: 214-350-4330
jwholley@ev1.net
Specializes in the appraisal of 18th

*and 19th century English and French
furniture; also clocks.*

Donald K. Cowan, ISA
New England Antiques & Interiors
P.O. Box 190966
Dallas, TX 75219-0966
ph: 214-522-2228 or 800-520-2228
fax: 214-522-2228
dkingc@earthlink.net
*Specializes in the appraisal of
Americana including furniture, folk
art, and decorative accessories.*

Rachel Pabst, ISA CAPP
Rachel Pabst Estate Sales & Appraisal
 Associates
ph: 713-626-0179
fax: 713-877-8087
r_pabst@yahoo.com
*Certified appraiser specializing in fine
art and Americana; over 16 years
experience; Attingham, Winterthur
Institute, Bayou Bend docent,
Sotheby's and Christie's courses.*

Jane C. Brennom
Zaisan Enterprises, Inc.
3240 Las Palmas
Houston, TX 77027-0184
ph: 713-527-0124
fax: 713-527-0124
brennom@sbcglobal.net
*Specializes in the appraisal of bronze
sculptures; also other decorative arts
and furniture.*

Dewey W. Smith, ASA
Dewey W. Smith, ASA Antique
 Appraisals
P.O. Box 2029
Littleton, CO 81061-2029
ph: 303-930-9899
fax: 303-930-9919
dwsmithasa@aol.com
*Provides appraisal and consultation
service for bankruptcy, collectors,
dealers, divorce, estates, individuals,
insurance companies and all other
manner of appraisal assignments.*

Michael Sassoon
Arte Gallery
9000 Wilshire Blvd.
Beverly Hills, CA 90211
ph: 310-858-7666
fax: 310-858-0525
artela@aol.com
*Specializes in the appraisal of 18th
through 20th century antique furniture
and Continental ceramics as well as
other antiques, collectibles, and
household contents.*

Bill Novotny, ISA, CGA
Novotny's Antiques & Appraisal
 Services
1138 Fairview Ave., #2
Arcadia, CA 91007
ph: 626-446-9663
fax: 626-446-2503
findvalu@aol.com
*Specializes in estate sales and in the
appraisal of general residential
contents, antiques, furniture,
Victoriana, glass, ceramics, lighting,*

*Native American, ethnographic and
Oriental items, and other residential
contents.*

Nancy Alison Martin, ASA
Nancy Martin Appraisals
ph: 626-304-0900
fax: 626-304-0928
namartin@pacbell.net
http://www.nancymartinappraisals.com
*Carefully researched and well
documented appraisals of antiques,
furniture, silver, ceramics, glass and
residential contents for litigation
support, compensation, insurance,
dissolution, estates, fraud and
charitable contribution.*

Carolyn Mani, ISA
18550 Hatteras St., #67
Tarzana, CA 91356
ph: 818-343-0118
fax: 818-343-0118
cme4ants@aol.com
*Specializes in the appraisal of
American furniture; also ceramics,
glassware, musical instruments, and
costume jewelry.*

Diana Sanders
Specialty Appraisals
P.O. Box 17461
Encino, CA 91416
ph: 877-255-5445
dlsanders@earthlink.net
http://www.specialtyappraisals.com
*Specializes in the appraisal of 19th
and 20th century furniture; member of
Appraisers National Association.*

K. C. Self, Jr., AIAA
The Gregg Rogers
616 Second Ave.
Chula Vista, CA 91910
ph: 619-425-4793
fax: 619-420-7788
Kcself@aaia.com
http://www.aaia.com/consultants.html
*Specializes in 18th and 19th century
American and European furniture.*

Kathryn Wolk, ISA
Antique Appraisal Services
P.O. Box 1834
Fallbrook, CA 92088
ph: 760-728-2346 or 760-505-7654
aprazit@earthlink.net
*Specializes in the appraisal of
ceramics, Orientalia, and furniture;
Accredited member of the International
Society of Appraisers and the
Appraisers National Association.*

Mike Aversa, ISA
Aversa Estate & Appraisal Service
P.O. Box 863
Yorba Linda, CA 92885
ph: 717-777-3848 or 714-749-3887
AversaAntiques@mindspring.com
http://www.aversaantiques.com
*Specializes in the appraisal of antique
furniture.*

Alice S. Karle, ANA
3463 State St., #178
Santa Barbara, CA 93105
ph: 805-682-2234
askappraiser@cox.net
*Certified member of the ANA; has
developed and taught courses in
American antique furniture and in
antiques in general, including silver.*

Nancy Burke Bosch, ISA
Bosch Appraisal Service
1610 Northstar Dr.
Petaluma, CA 94954-6607
ph: 707-773-3970
fax: 707-773-3974
nbbosch@pacbell.net
http://www.appraiseyourantiques.com
*Specializes in appraising European &
American furniture, fine art,
decorative art & accessories, china,
crystal, silver, American wicker,
quilts, linen, other textiles, other
appreciable residential contents;
consultations, estate sales.*

Christine Zachary
P.O. Box 82906
Portland, OR 97282-0906
ph: 503-234-8143 or 503-777-5813
christineZC@aol.com
*Over 25 years experience in dealing in
furniture and related items; gives
lectures and presentations on how to
identify furniture styles, woods, and
the distinctions between regions.*

Paul G. Bailey, ISA
Antique Appraisal & Estate Services
12819 SE 38th St., PMB 320
Bellevue, WA 98006-1395
ph: 425-746-2777
fax: 425-746-3793
antiquabailey@aol.com
*30 years experience in appraising
American, French and English
furniture.*

Kathleen M. Bailey, AAA, ISA CAPP
Antique Appraisal & Estate Sale Service
 - the Original
160 NW Gilman Blvd., Ste. #1
Issaquah, WA 98027
ph: 425-746-2777
fax: 425-746-3793
antiquabailey@aol.com
*Specialist in American, English,
German, Continental ceramics,
furniture, silver, glass, enamels,
Victoriana and decorative arts of the
18th to 20th centuries; full service
appraiser & estate sales since 1973.*

Robert G. Jason-Ickes
3600 14th Ave., SE #19-201
Olympia, WA 98501
ph: 360-455-9914
fax: 360-459-7154
r.jason-ickes@attbi.com
*Specializes in 19th and 20th century
furniture including "Depression" era
furniture of the 1920s through 1940s;
also lectures.*

Brent J. W. Cheung
Century Services Inc.
200, 105 - 10 Ave. S.E.
Calgary, Alberta T2G 0V8 Canada
ph: 403-303-2562 or 403-560-0918
fax: 403-294-9409
bcheung@centuryservices.com
http://www.centuryservices.com/
　FineFurnishings
*Specializes in the appraisal of
antiques, fine furniture, estate jewelry,
objects d'art.*

Auction Services

Michael B. Grogan
Grogan & Company Auctioneers
22 Harris St.
Dedham, MA 02026
ph: 781-461-9500
fax: 781-461-9625
grogans@groganco.com
http://www.groganco.com
*Specializes in the auction sale of 18th
and 19th century American, English
and Continental furniture and
decorations; also buys, auctions,
appraises 18th through 20th century
fine art, silver, oriental rugs, and
entire estates.*

Clubs/Associations

Mickey Callahan, Sec/Treas
Society of American Period Furniture
Makers
6 Irving Rd.
Wallingford, PA 19086
mcallahan@usainc.com
http://www.sapfm.org
*An organization intended for anyone
having a passionate interest in the
making, reproducing and conservation
of American period furniture.*

Dealers

Russ & Karen Goldberger
RJG Antiques
P.O. Box 60
Rye, NH 03870
ph: 603-433-1770
fax: 603-433-3937
decoys@rjgantiques.com
http://www.rjgantiques.com
*Specializes in quality working decoys,
folk art, and American furniture and
accessories in their original painted
surfaces.*

R. Jorgensen Antiques
502 Post Rd.
Wells, ME 04090
ph: 207-646-9444
fax: 207-646-4954
*Family business on historical property
selling 18th and 19th C. American,
British and Continental period
antique furniture and accessories; also
fireplace equipment and clocks.*

Wayne Pratt & Company
346 Main St. South
Woodbury, CT 06798
ph: 203-263-5676
fax: 203-266-4766
info@prattantiques.com
http://www.prattantiques.com
*Fine American 18th and 19th century
furniture with an emphasis on
original condition and patina; also a
selection of fine line-for-line
handmade copies of authentic
antiques.*

Arthur Pappas
Art Pappas Antiques
161 Main St. South
Woodbury, CT 06798-3405
ph: 203-266-0374
paptiques@aol.com
http://www.artpappas.com
*Specialist in 18th century American
furniture and architectural materials.*

Leigh Keno
Leigh Keno American Antiques
127 East 69th St.
New York, NY 10021
ph: 212-734-2381
fax: 212-734-0707
leigh@leighkeno.com
http://www.leighkeno.com
*Specializes in fine American antique
furniture, paintings, and decorative
arts from the late 17th through early
19th century.*

Lewis Baer
Newel Art Galleries, Inc.
425 East 53rd St.
New York, NY 10022
ph: 212-758-1970
fax: 212-371-0166
info@newel.com
http://www.newel.com
*One of the largest resources of quality
antique furniture from the 17th to
20th centuries: Biedermeier, Art
Nouveau, Art Deco, Neoclassic,
Bamboo, and period French, English
and Italian.*

Richard & Eileen Dubrow
Richard & Eileen Dubrow Antiques &
Books
P.O. Box 128
Flushing, NY 11361-0128
ph: 718-767-9758
fax: 718-767-8172
er4books@aol.com
*Specializing in 19th century American
cabinet maker furniture and decorative
arts; will identify pieces as to maker
by photo; also sells books (out-of-
print and current) about 19th C.
furniture, fine art and decorative arts.*

Joan Bogart
Joan Bogart Antiques
P.O. Box 21
Rockville Centre, NY 11571
ph: 516-764-5712
fax: 516-764-0529
joanbogart@yahoo.com
http://www.classical-america.com
American Classical or Empire

*furniture dating 1820 to 1840 with
emphasis on pieces by Phyfe,
Querville, Meeks; also classical
accessories such as gilt mirrors, Old
Paris porcelains, Parian ware, and
Argand, astral, and sinumbra lamps*

Terry Husk
Buttermilk Hill Antiques
1135 Liberty St.
Franklin, PA 16323
ph: 814-432-5691
buttermilkhill@webtv.net
http://www.buttermilkhillantiques.com

John J. McClain
York Town Auction Inc.
1625 Haviland Rd.
York, PA 17404
ph: 717-751-0211
fax: 717-767-7729
info@yorktownauction.com
http://www.yorktownauction.com

H.L. Chalfant Antiques
1352 Paoli Pike
West Chester, PA 19380-6263
ph: 610-696-1862
fax: 610-696-1863
*Specializes in American antique
furniture.*

Herbert & Joyce Windle
Windle's Antiques
5716 Kennett Pike
Centreville, DE 19807
ph: 302-651-9222
herbnjoyce@netzero.net
*Specializes in the appraisal of antique
American furniture; also carries a
large inventory of decoys from the St.
Lawrence areas - both from NY and
Ontario sides, early lighting and
fireplace cooking equipment.*

G.K.S. Bush, Inc.
2828 Pennsylvania Ave. NW
Washington, DC 20007
ph: 202-965-0653
fax: 202-342-6560
*Specializes in fine 18th and early 19th
century American antique furniture
and other decorative arts.*

J. Michael Flanigan
J. M. Flanigan American Antiques
1607 Park Ave.
Baltimore, MD 21217
ph: 410-225-3463
fax: 410-523-9637
jmf745i@aol.com
*Specializes in buying, selling and
appraising antique American
furniture.*

Bob O'Dell
Era of Elegance Antiques
Kennerly Rd.
Irmo, SC 29063
ph: 803-345-1689
*Buys and sells period antiques from
1830-1890; by appointment; East
Coast only.*

David E. Newman
Newman & Assoc.
2476 Bolsover, #504
Houston, TX 77005-2518
ph: 713-521-7044
newmanassoc@aol.com
*Specializes in buying, selling,
authenticating and appraising
American, English and Continental
19th century furniture and accessories.*

Paul G. Bailey, ISA
Antique Appraisal & Estate Services
12819 SE 38th St., PMB 320
Bellevue, WA 98006-1395
ph: 425-746-2777
fax: 425-746-3793
antiquabailey@aol.com
*30 years experience in buying and
appraising American, French and
English furniture.*

Kathleen M. Bailey, AAA, ISA CAPP
Antique Appraisal & Estate Sale Service
- the Original
160 NW Gilman Blvd., Ste. #1
Issaquah, WA 98027
ph: 425-746-2777
fax: 425-746-3793
antiquabailey@aol.com
*30 years experience buying and selling
antique furniture; specializes in
American, French and English
furniture from the 1770s to the 1890s.*

Experts

Nickolas Kotula, ASA
493 Simsbury Rd.
Bloomfield, CT 06002-1512
ph: 860-243-1646
fax: 860-243-8899
*Reaccredited Senior Member of the
American Society of Appraisers,
Personal Property, Furniture
designation; author of articles in
"Maine Antique Digest:" "The Faking
of Antique Furniture," and
"Historical Cabinetmaking
Construction."*

Suzy McLennan Anderson, ISA CAPP
Heritage Antiques & Appraisal Services
65 East Main St.
Holmdel, NJ 07733-2310
ph: 732-946-8801
fax: 732-946-1036
andersonauctions@aol.com
http://www.andersonauctions.net
*Authentication service offered for pre-
1840 American furniture; also buys
and sells.*

Robert F. Weinhagen, Jr.
221 Cameron St.
Alexandria, VA 22314-3203
ph: 703-549-2560
*Author of "Assume Nothing: A
Manual For Buyers of American and
English Antique Furniture."*

J. Robert Boykin, III
Boykin Appraisals, Inc.
P.O. Box 7440
Wilson, NC 27895
ph: 252-237-1700
fax: 252-237-2314
boykinappraisals@coastalnet.com
*Specializing in American & English
antique furniture, decorative arts, and
appreciable residential contents.*

Fred & Gail Taylor
P.O. Box 215
Crystal River, FL 34423
ph: 352-563-2916 or 800-387-6377
fax: 352-563-2916
fmtaylor@aol.com
*Produces a video for identifying
antique furniture based on construction techniques, materials, and style;
compilation of "Common Sense
Antiques" articles in book form is
available; offers a variety of classes
on antique furniture.*

Peter Blundell
P.O. Box 6
Vernon, British Columbia V1T 6M1
Canada
ph: 250-542-4540
petersblundell@shaw.ca
*Author of "The Marketplace Guides" -
Oak Furniture (1980), Victorian
Furniture (1981); specializes in North
American furniture from 1800 to
present.*

Misc. Services

Fred & Gail Taylor
P.O. Box 215
Crystal River, FL 34423
ph: 352-563-2916 or 800-387-6377
fax: 352-563-2916
fmtaylor@aol.com
*Produces a video for identifying
antique furniture based on construction techniques, materials, and style;
compilation of "Common Sense
Antiques" articles in book form is
available; offers a variety of classes
on antique furniture.*

Museums/Libraries

Society for the Preservation of New
England Antiquities, The
141 Cambridge St.
Boston, MA 02114
ph: 617-570-9105
http://www.spnea.org
*A museum of cultural history that
preserves, interprets, and collects
buildings, landscapes, and objects
reflecting New England life from the
17th century to present.*

Society for the Preservation of New
England Antiquities, The
Conservation Center
185 Lyman St.
North Waltham, MA 02154
ph: 781-891-4882
fax: 781-893-7832
info@spnea.org
http://www.spnea.org
Owns and operates 35 properties from

*the 17th to 20th centuries; SPENA's
library and archives contains more
than 1.5 million historical photos,
architectural drawings, and other
documents related to New England as
well as 110,000 artifacts.*

Rhode Island School of Design Museum
224 Benefit St.
Providence, RI 02903-2723
ph: 401-454-6500
fax: 401-454-6556
mshaw@risd.edu
http://www.risd.edu/museum.cfm
*Apparel, architecture, furniture,
graphic design, industrial design,
interior architecture, landscape
architecture.*

Bennington Museum, The
West Main St.
Bennington, VT 05201
ph: 802-447-1571
fax: 802-442-8305
bennmuse@sover.net
http://www.benningtonmuseum.com
*One of the finest regional art history
museums in the country; works by
Grandma Moses, American glass, VT
furniture, Bennington pottery, the
oldest Stars & Stripes in existence, the
1925 luxury touring car "The Wasp,"
and much more.*

Winterthur Museum
ph: 800-448-3883 or 302-888-4600
webmaster@winterthur.org
http://www.winterthur.org

Colonial Williamsburg
P.O. Box 1776
Williamsburg, VA 23187-1776
ph: 757-229-1000 x8540 or 800-
HISTORY
mmartin@cwf.org
http://www.history.org
*Specializes in early American furniture
and the decorative arts.*

Bernice Bienenstock Furniture Library
1009 North Main St.
High Point, NC 27262
ph: 336-883-4011
fax: 336-883-6579
info@furniturelibrary.com
http://www.furniturelibrary.com
*Comprehensive library covering
furniture design, styles, periods,
motifs, production, history, etc.*

Houston Museum of Decorative Arts,
The
201 High St.
Chattanooga, TN 37403
ph: 423-267-7176
houston@chattanooga.net
http://www.chattanooga.net/houston
*Contains one of the world's finest
collections of antique glass, furniture,
and ceramics.*

Henry Ford Museum & Greenfield
Village
20900 Oakwood Blvd.
P.O. Box 1970
Dearborn, MI 48121-1970
ph: 313-982-6001 or 313-271-1620
fax: 313-271-9621
info@hfmgv.org
http://www.hfmgv.org
*Museum houses a collection of over
one million three-dimensional
artifacts, defined by the following
general categories: agricultural and
industrial production, transportation,
communication, and domestic life.*

Repro. Sources

Thomas E. McGarry
Birnam Wood Joinery, The
302 N. Mildred St.
Charles Town, WV 25414-1834
ph: 304-728-0373 or 800-700-5959
fax: 304-728-0373
tom@benchmadefurniture.com
http://www.benchmadefurniture.com
*Maker of American country furniture
in William & Mary, Queen Anne,
Chippendale, Hepplewhite and classic
Shaker styles; beds, case pieces,
tables, Windsor chairs, etc. made to
order.*

American Antique Reproductions, Inc.
P.O. Box 72846
Chattanooga, TN 37407-5846
ph: 800-221-1988 or 423-867-1988
fax: 423-867-1788
service@americanantiques.com
http://www.americanantiques.com
*Wholesale only: handcrafted American
oak furniture and mahogany
reproduction furniture from Indonesia;
also reproduction leaded glass table
lamps, and reproduction American
made ice cream table and chair sets,
signs, prints, posters.*

Antler & Horn

Collectors

J.A. Higgins
5017 Walnut
Kansas City, MO 64112-2758
ph: 816-931-4095
fax: 816-363-5927
smojer@aol.com
Wants to buy old horn furniture.

Experts

Alan Rogers
1012 NE Shady Lane Dr.
Gladstone, MO 64188
ph: 816-436-9008
kcstockyards@aol.com
*Has studied and collected Texas cattle
horns, horn furniture, and related
items since 1972; wants to buy old
steer horns, but not horns wrapped in
tooled leather or vinyl and rope; also
buys horn furniture and related items.*

Beds

Dealers

Mendes Antiques
Rte. 44
52 Blanding Rd.
Rehoboth, MA 02769-1116
ph: 508-336-7381
*Specializing in antique four-poster
beds, all sizes.*

Loading Dock, The
P.O. Box 455
Murchison, TX 75778
ph: 866-469-3201 or 903-469-3200
loadingdockantiques@tyler.net
http://www.antiquelamps-ironbeds.com
*Specializes in the sale of cast iron
beds, as-is or in restored condition:
full beds, twin size, 3.4 size, baby
beds and cribs.*

Belter

Dealers

Richard & Eileen Dubrow
Richard & Eileen Dubrow Antiques &
Books
P.O. Box 128
Flushing, NY 11361-0128
ph: 718-767-9758
fax: 718-767-8172
er4books@aol.com
*Specializing in 19th century American
cabinet maker furniture and decorative
arts; will identify pieces as to maker
by photo; also sells books (out-of-
print and current) about 19th C.
furniture, fine art and decorative arts.*

British

Experts

David P. Lindquist
Whitehall at the Villa
1213 E. Franklin St.
Chapel Hill, NC 27514-3307
ph: 919-942-3179 or 919-933-3305
fax: 919-942-6600
whchnc@aol.com
*Author of "The Official Price Guide
to Antiques & Collectibles: English &
Continental Furniture - With Prices;"
co-author with Caroline Warren of
"English and Continental Furniture -
With Prices."*

Chinese

Dealers

Evelyn's Antique Chinese Furniture, Inc.
381 Hayes St.
San Francisco, CA 94102-2440
ph: 415-255-1815
fax: 415-255-0688
et@evelynantique.com
http://www.evelynantique.com
*Offers a large inventory of Classic
Chinese furniture and works of art
from the Ming & Qing Dynasties.*

Shen's Gallery
1368 Pacific Ave.
Santa Cruz, CA 95060-3932
ph: 831-457-4422
customerservice@shensgallery.com
http://www.shensgallery.com
Offers fine Oriental furniture and antiques; also ancient Chinese ceramics, carvings and statuary.

Colonial Revival
Experts

David P. Lindquist
Whitehall at the Villa
1213 E. Franklin St.
Chapel Hill, NC 27514-3307
ph: 919-942-3179 or 919-933-3305
fax: 919-942-6600
whchnc@aol.com
Co-author with Caroline Warren of "Colonial Revival Furniture - With Prices."

Museums/Libraries

Reynolda House Museum of American Art
P.O. Box 11765
Winston Salem, NC 27116
ph: 336-725-5325 or 888-663-1149
fax: 336-721-0991
reynolda@reynoldahouse.org
http://www.reynoldahouse.org
Magnificent former home of Richard J. Reynolds, founder of the R. J. Reynolds Tobacco Company; houses the finest fine art collection in the area; gardens and restored Historic Village adjacent to the museum.

Bernice Bienenstock Furniture Library
1009 North Main St.
High Point, NC 27262
ph: 336-883-4011
fax: 336-883-6579
info@furniturelibrary.com
http://www.furniturelibrary.com
Comprehensive library covering furniture design, styles, periods, motifs, production, history, etc.

Grand Rapids Public Library Furniture Design Collection
60 Library Plaza, Northeast
Grand Rapids, MI 49503-3903
rraz@grapids.lib.mi.us
http://www.grapids.lib.mi.us

Christian G. Carron
Grand Rapids Public Museum
272 Pearl St. NW
Grand Rapids, MI 49504-5371
ph: 616-456-3977
fax: 616-456-3873
staff@grmuseum.org
http://www.grmuseum.org
Focus is on furniture made in the Grand Rapids area; exhibits, publications and research information relating to all styles of 19th and 20th century furniture manufactured in Grand Rapids.

Continental
Experts

David P. Lindquist
Whitehall at the Villa
1213 E. Franklin St.
Chapel Hill, NC 27514-3307
ph: 919-942-3179 or 919-933-3305
fax: 919-942-6600
whchnc@aol.com
Author of "The Official Price Guide to Antiques & Collectibles: English & Continental Furniture - With Prices;" co-author with Caroline Warren of "English and Continental Furniture - With Prices."

French
Appraisers

Barbara Samuel
La Reine Abeille Antiques & Appraisals
11821 Brookhill Lane
Dallas, TX 75230
ph: 972-386-5066 or 972-239-8400
bslareine@aol.com
A long-time Dallas area antique dealer and ISA appraiser; specializes in French furniture.

Keith De Long
Keith C. De Long & Associates
Appraisal Service
32031 4th Ave. SW
Federal Way, WA 98023
ph: 253-874-6088
delong99@hotmail.com
Has 40 years experience in appraising 18th and 19th century French furniture.

Dealers

Cascade Antique Gallery
318 Grove St.
New Castle, PA 16101
ph: 724-657-6888
fax: 724-657-3391
Specializes in fine French antique furniture and French Quimper ceramics.

Nancy Kramer
Sparrows Inc.
4115 Howard Ave.
Kensington, MD 20895-2417
ph: 301-530-0175 or 888-800-1235
fax: 301-530-0189
sparrows@sparrows.com
http://www.sparrows.com
Specializes in 19th and early 20th century French antique furniture and decorative arts.

Cyril Tucci
Nicole Maleine Antiques, Inc.
121 North Goldthwaite St.
Montgomery, AL 36104
ph: 334-834-8530 or 877-855-8530
fax: 334-834-8530
nicmaleine@aol.com
http://www.nicolemaleineantiques.com
A direct importer of French antiques for over 12 years: 18th and 19th century furniture, mirrors, chande-

liers, sconces, decorative accessories, doors, windows, etc.

Renee Hunt
French Quarters Antiques
11 N. Block Ave.
Fayetteville, AR 72701
ph: 479-443-3355
fax: 479-443-3355
webmaster@french-quarters.com
http://www.french-quarters.com
Direct importers of fine French antiques including furniture, new custom chairs handcrafted in France, lighting, mirrors, Majolica, and other French accessories.

Barbara Samuel
La Reine Abeille Antiques & Appraisals
11821 Brookhill Lane
Dallas, TX 75230
ph: 972-386-5066 or 972-239-8400
bslareine@aol.com
A long-time Dallas area antique dealer and ISA appraiser; specializes in French furniture.

Horn

(see FURNITURE [ANTIQUE], Adirondack; FURNITURE [ANTIQUE], Antler & Horn; WESTERN AMERICANA)

Kitchen Cabinets
Dealers

Marcy A. Rau
Marcy A. Rau Antiques & Collectibles
R.D. #2, Box 431
Dalton, PA 18414
ph: 570-378-2198
marcyrau@hotmail.com
http://www.angelfire.com/biz/marcyrau
Specializes in Hoosiers and "Hoosier" type kitchen cabinets.

Experts

Phyllis & Phil Kennedy
Phyllis Kennedy Hardware, Inc.
10655 Andrade Dr.
Zionsville, IN 46077
ph: 317-873-1316
fax: 317-873-8662
philken@kennedyhardware.com
http://www.kennedyhardware.com
Author of "Hoosier Cabinets."

Suppliers

Clifford Rufkahr
Rufkahr's
P.O. Box 56112
Virginia Beach, VA 23456
ph: 757-721-9154 or 800-545-7947 (orders)
fax: 757-426-8484
rufkahrs@rufkahrs.com
http://www.rufkahrs.com
Reproduction hardware, lamp parts, mirror supports and brackets, knobs, pie safe tins, bed parts, Hoosier cabinet parts, brass handles, brass knobs, trunk hardware, caning supplies, rocker runners, Simichrome, Nev'r Dull, and more.

Phyllis & Phil Kennedy
Phyllis Kennedy Hardware, Inc.
10655 Andrade Dr.
Zionsville, IN 46077
ph: 317-873-1316
fax: 317-873-8662
philken@kennedyhardware.com
http://www.kennedyhardware.com
Author of "Hoosier Cabinets;" stocks parts for Hoosier cabinets including flour sifters, cardboard door charts, metal tags, sugar bins, etc.; send for catalog.

Phyllis & Phil Kennedy
Phyllis Kennedy Hardware
10655 Andrade Dr.
Zionsville, IN 46077
ph: 317-873-1316
fax: 317-873-8662
philken@kennedyhardware.com
http://www.kennedyhardware.com
Hardware for antique furniture, ice boxes, Hoosier cabinets and trunks; manufacturer of flour bins and sifters for Hoosier cabinets; pulls, bails, knobs, latches, chair seats and caning, hinges, locks and keys, coat hooks, etc.

Gary Hahn
Muff's Antiques
135 S. Glassell St.
Orange, CA 92866-1421
ph: 714-997-0243
fax: 714-997-1601
muffs@earthlink.net
http://home.earthlink.net/~muffs
Mail order source for kitchen cabinet hardware (Hoosiers) including hinges, labels, canisters, castors, and rolls; also 25 sizes of lids for jars, and salt & pepper canisters from Hoosier & Depression items; catalog $5.

Oak
Museums/Libraries

Christian G. Carron
Grand Rapids Public Museum
272 Pearl St. NW
Grand Rapids, MI 49504-5371
ph: 616-456-3977
fax: 616-456-3873
staff@grmuseum.org
http://www.grmuseum.org
Focus is on furniture made in the Grand Rapids area; exhibits, publications and research information relating to all styles of 19th and 20th century furniture manufactured in Grand Rapids.

Rustic
Dealers

Bert Savage
Rte. 126 Box 11
Center Strafford, NH 03815
ph: 603-269-7411
rustic@worldpath.net
Wants to buy rustic furniture: Adirondack, Indiana Hickory, twig, birch bark, root, burl.

Christine Guille
Country & Cabin Antiques
256 Osbrook Pt.
Stonington, CT 06378
ph: 860-535-0244
fax: 860-535-9104
cwguille@aol.com
*Wants quality Adirondack furniture
and accessories: Old Hickory,
Rittenhouse, birch bark, rustic lamps,
coat racks, mirrors, Black Forest
carved bears and clocks, miniature
canoes, pond boats, camp signs, art
and advertising.*

Ralph Kylloe
Kylloe Antiques
P.O. Box 669
Lake George, NY 12845-0669
ph: 518-696-4100
*Specializes in buying and selling
antiques for the cabin; old hickory,
Adirondack, root, twig, antler
furnishings, and rustic accessories;
also creels, snowshoes, skis,
sailboats, fishing nets, camp signs,
birch bark frames, canoes, etc.*

Bob Berman
441 S. Jackson St.
Media, PA 19063-3715
ph: 610-566-1516 or 888-784-2554
ber441@aol.com
http://www.bermangallery.com
*Especially wants wild and ornate
pieces of rustic furniture, Old Hickory.*

Museums/Libraries

Lori Sullivan
Adirondack Museum, The
Rte. 30
P.O. Box 99
Blue Mountain Lake, NY 12812-0099
ph: 518-352-7311
fax: 518-352-7653
lsullivan@adkmuseum.org
http://www.adirondackmuseum.org
*The "Smithsonian" of the
Adirondacks; 20 outdoor and indoor
exhibit buildings; live programming
tells the story of the Adirondacks from
mid-1800s to present; new Visitors
Center with Museum store, magnificent views, landscaped grounds.*

Soap Hollow
Museums/Libraries

Julie Robinson
Conemaugh Township Area Historical
Society
100-106 South Main St.
P.O. Box 307
Davidsville, PA 15928
ph: 814-479-2211 or 814-479-2067
*Historical information on the
furniture makers of Soap Hollow;
lecture frequently on furniture style,
hallmarks and stencils of the unique
Mennonite craftsmen.*

Stickley
Dealers

Dennis Lucier
1034 Mammoth Rd.
Dracut, MA 01826
ph: 978-957-0143
*Buys and sells Gustav, L & JG
Stickley mission oak furniture.*

Jerry Cohen
Aurora Studios
109 Main St.
Putnam, CT 06260
ph: 860-928-1965 or 800-448-7828
fax: 860-928-1966
jerry@mypinelake.com
http://www.artsncrafts.com
*Original antique Stickley and other
Mission style furniture makers; over
4,000 square feet furniture on display.*

Bob Berman
441 S. Jackson St.
Media, PA 19063-3715
ph: 610-566-1516 or 888-784-2554
ber441@aol.com
http://www.bermangallery.com
*Wants all Mission style furniture:
Gustav Stickley, L. & J.G. Stickley,
Roycroft, and good generic pieces.*

Caren Fine
11603 Gowrie Ct.
Potomac, MD 20854-3623
ph: 301-299-6886 or 301-854-6262
fine2beme@aol.com
*Buys, sells, trades Arts & Crafts
items such as furniture and copper by
Stickley, Dirk Van Erp, Roycroft,
Limbert, Harden, Rohlfs, Wright;
pottery, paintings, Nakashima
furniture.*

Robert Raynolds
California-art.com
7343 El Camino Real, PMB 311
Atascadero, CA 93422
ph: 805-462-2301 or 805-440-1579
fax: 805-462-1943
info@california-art.com
http://www.california-art.com
*Specializes in paintings and
watercolors from the California
Impressionism Movement (1880-1940);
also buys and sells original Stickley
furniture.*

Museums/Libraries

Craftsman Farms Foundation, Inc.
2352 Rt. 10-W, Box 5
Morris Plains, NJ 07950
ph: 973-540-1165
fax: 973-540-1167
setabit@njskylands.com
http://njskylands.com/hscrfarm.htm
*Runs Stickley's National Landmark
family home in Parsippany, NJ;
sponsors Stickley exhibits and related
catalogs.*

Repro. Sources

L. & J.G. Stickley, Inc.
One Stickley Dr.
P.O. Box 480
Manlius, NY 13104-0480
ph: 315-682-5500
fax: 315-682-6306
http://www.stickley.com

Twig

(see FURNITURE [ANTIQUE],
Adirondack)

Victorian
Auction Services

Rob Slawinski
Slawinski Auction Company
6192 Highway 9
P.O. Box 1513
Felton, CA 95018
ph: 831-335-9000
antiques@slawinski.com
http://www.slawinski.com
*One of the largest auctioneers in the
country specializing in Victorian
antiques including works by Herter,
Belter, Meeks, Roux, J.J. Horner and
others; monthly estate auctions also
feature fine art & accessories.*

Dealers

Joan Bogart
Joan Bogart Antiques
P.O. Box 21
Rockville Centre, NY 11571
ph: 516-764-5712
fax: 516-764-0529
joanbogart@yahoo.com
http://www.joanbogart.com
*Dealer, expert, appraiser specializing
in Victorian furniture by Belter,
Meeks, Horner, Herter, etc.; also
specializes in Victorian lighting, gas
chandeliers, astrals, kerosene lamps,
epergnes, silverplate, majolica, Parian
ware.*

Bill Norris
Sweet William Antiques
121 South LA Hwy. 1
Morganza, LA 70759
ph: 225-694-0777
bnorrisswa@aol.com
http://www.sweetwilliamantiques.com
*Specializes in quality Victorian
furniture, with a large selection of
Southern Plantation beds, banquet
tables, armoires and accent items.*

Museums/Libraries

Newark Museum, Ballantine House
49 Washington St.
Newark, NJ 07101
ph: 973-596-6550 or 800-7-MUSEUM
fax: 973-642-0459
webmaster@newarkmuseum.org
http://www.newarkmuseum.org
*Built in 1885, this 27-room brick and
limestone house is filled with things
found in people's homes from the
1650s to present including Victorian
furniture.*

Lyndhurst
635 S. Broadway
Tarrytown, NY 10591-6401
ph: 914-631-4481 or 914-631-0046
fax: 914-631-5634
lyndhurst@nthp.org
http://www.lyndhurst.org
*America's finest Gothic Revival
mansion; furniture, paintings,
decorative arts, library, archive;
Gothic Revival mansion on 67 acre
European-style park; tours, special
events, catering for parties, gallery.*

Wallace Nutting
Museums/Libraries

Wadsworth Atheneum Museum of Art
600 Main St.
Hartford, CT 06103
ph: 860-278-2670
fax: 860-527-0803
info@wadsworthatheneum.org
http://www.wadsworthatheneum.org
*The Wallace Nutting Collection of
17th century American furniture, the
largest of its kind, includes a wide
array of "Pilgrim-Century"
housewares and tools; also has two
fully-restored period rooms.*

Wooton Desks
Clubs/Associations

Richard & Eileen Dubrow
Wooton Desk Owners Society, Inc.
Newsletter: Wooton Desk Owners
Society Newsletter, The
P.O. Box 128
Flushing, NY 11361-0128
ph: 718-767-9758
fax: 718-767-8172
er4books@aol.com
*Archival records, authentication, and
sales of Wooton desks.*

FURS
Appraisers

Richard A. Newman, ISA
Newman Fur Appraisers & Consultants,
Inc.
11 Penn Plaza, 5th Floor
New York, NY 10001-2006
ph: 212-946-2680
fax: 201-864-4838
rangfn@att.net
*Fur appraiser, consultant, all phases
of the fur industry; damage claim
consultant.*

Farhad Radfar, ISA
MIR Appraisal Services, Inc.
307 N. Michigan Ave., Ste. 308
Chicago, IL 60601
ph: 312-814-8510
fax: 312-814-8511
appraisers@mirgallery.com
http://www.mirgallery.com
*Offers expert appraisals of personal
property including Continental
ceramics, Oriental rugs, furs, fine art,
antiques, jewelry, furniture, silver,*

*porcelain, marble, bronze, and other
fine items.*

Dealers

Farhad Radfar, ISA
MIR International Gallery, Inc.
307 N. Michigan Ave., Ste. 308
Chicago, IL 60601
ph: 312-814-8510
fax: 312-814-8511
mirgallery@aol.com
http://www.mirgallery.com

Museums/Libraries

Gail DeBuse Potter, Dir.
Museum of the Fur Trade
Magazine: MFT Quarterly
6321 Highway 20
Chadron, NE 69337-9501
ph: 308-432-3843
fax: 308-432-5963
museum@furtrade.org
http://www.furtrade.org
*Dedicated to the study of the American
fur trade from colonial times to the
present; furs, traps, trade guns, trade
goods, Indians; not involved with
present day trapping.*

**Here are some tips
when contacting
someone who is listed
in this book:**

When requesting
information about a
particular item, include
a description (material,
dimensions, maker's
mark, model number,
etc.) and a photo,
sketch, digital image or
photocopy of the item
in question.

Always ask if there are
charges for samples or
for the services that
you are requesting.

When corresponding
by letter, please be
sure to include a Large
(#10 business size)
Self-Addressed and
Stamped Envelope
(LSASE) if requesting a
reply or the return of
photographs.

Never call collect
unless otherwise
directed. When
calling, be considerate
of time zone differ-
ences and always ask
if the party you are
calling has time to talk.
When leaving an
answering machine
message, always
instruct the party to
call you back collect.

G-MAN

(see LAW ENFORCEMENT
MEMORABILIA, FBI)

G.A.R. MEMORABILIA

(see VETERAN ITEMS, Civil War)

G.I. JOE

(see TOYS, Action Figures [G.I. Joe])

GAMBLING COLLECTIBLES

(see also COIN-OPERATED
MACHINES, Slot Machines; DICE;
MATCHCOVERS, Casino; PLAYING
CARDS; SALOON & BAR
COLLECTIBLES; TOKENS)

Collectors

Robert Eisenstadt
140 Cadman Plaza West, #26-C
Brooklyn, NY 11202
ph: 718-625-3553
chipe@ix.netcom.com
http://www.antiquegamblingchips.com/
*Collects and buys all kinds of
gambling chips (casino, ivory, mother
of pearl, clay poker chips, etc. but no
light plastic chips); also wants
gambling-related items such as
equipment, books, catalogs, playing
cards, etc.*

John A. Greget
John A. Greget - Magic Lists
5575 E. Sheena Dr.
Scottsdale, AZ 85254-2961
ph: 602-404-3100
fax: 602-404-3200
*Buys and appraises gambling books or
equipment.*

Kitty & Russell Umbraco
P.O. Box 5331
Richmond, CA 94805-0331
ph: 510-235-1656
fax: 510-237-6019
russellu1@juno.com
*Wants to buy gambling collectibles
including Faro, playing cards, etc.*

Dealers

Steve Lerner
42 Barefoot Hill Rd.
Sharon, MA 02067
ph: 781-784-2286
slerner@attbi.com
http://www.gamblingcollectibles.com
*Buys and sells dice, punchcards, and
gaffed gambling items and equipment.*

Larry Lubliner
Avant Carde
3814 N. Fremont #3
Chicago, IL 60613-9998
ph: 773-883-0073
fax: 773-883-1199
joker1854@aol.com
http://www.avantcarde.com
*Buys and sells gambling items
including playing cards, poker chips,
Faro, poker, roulette, dice; also wants
coin-operated gambling machines,
related advertising items, sales
catalogs, and books.*

Beth Marshall
Marshall's Brocante
8505 Broadway
San Antonio, TX 78217
ph: 210-804-6320
fax: 210-804-6321
info@marshallsbrocante.com
http://www.marshallsbrocante.com
*Specializes in gambling collectibles:
antique ivory gambling chips, mother-
of-pearl counters, Bakelite chips, crest
and seal chips, chips from illegal
casinos in Texas and Louisiana,
gambling paraphernalia, card
shavers, etc.*

Periodicals

Magazine: Gaming Times
1350 E. Flamingo Rd., #494
Las Vegas, NV 89119
ph: 702-876-6020 or 800-784-4452
fax: 702-866-6020
chips@gamingtimes.com
http://www.gamingtimes.com
*Monthly publication containing news
and stories about chips, dice, casino
memorabilia, and more; new chip
releases, Atlantic City news, electronic
chipping, dice department, casino
news and histories.*

Tom Pleau
Magazine: Casino Collectible Magazine
P.O. Box 7438
Laguna Niguel, CA 92607-7438
ph: 714-362-9101

Gambling Chips & Gaming Tokens

Auction Services

Robert Buntin
SilverStrike Auctions
P.O. Box 20942
Reno, NV 89502
ph: 775-856-2286
fax: 775-856-2287
buntin@nvbell.net
http://www.silverstriker.com
*Buy or sell your collectible casino
chips, tokens, silver strikes, bullion,
coins and more.*

Clubs/Associations

Michael Knapp
Casino Chips & Gaming Tokens
Collectors Club
Magazine: Casino Chips & Token News
P.O. Box 340345
Columbus, OH 43234
ph: 614-451-0006 or 614-723-1092
fax: 614-723-1704
ChipProf@aol.com
http://www.ccgtcc.com
*Collectors of casino chips and gaming
tokens; ANA affiliation, yearly
convention in Las Vegas, 100+ page
quarterly newsletter; over 1,600
members.*

Collectors

Andrew R. Young III
5 Meadowbrook Rd.
East Longmeadow, MA 01028
ph: 413-525-8211
ayoung@map.com
http://pages.map.com/~ayoung
*A collector of Las Vegas, Atlantic
City, and Caribbean casino chips.*

Archie A. Black
P.O. Box 63
Brick, NJ 08723-0063
ph: 732-458-8827
fax: 732-458-8871
ablack2@optonline.net
http://www.callzia.com/dghome/acchips

George T. Davis
67 Franklin Ave.
Yonkers, NY 10705
ph: 914-963-6436
gtdyonkers@cs.com
*Wants to buy casino chips: Cuba,
Puerto Rico, Caribbean, Atlantic City,
Las Vegas, etc.; author of "The
Obsolete Casino Chips of Puerto
Rico."*

Robert Eisenstadt
140 Cadman Plaza West, #26-C
Brooklyn, NY 11202
ph: 718-625-3553
chipe@ix.netcom.com
http://www.antiquegamblingchips.com/
*Collects and buys all kinds of
gambling chips (casino, ivory, mother
of pearl, clay poker chips, etc. but no
light plastic chips); also wants
gambling-related items such as
equipment, books, catalogs, playing
cards, etc.*

Neal Silverman
585 Merrick Rd.
Lynbrook, NY 11563
fax: 732-576-8852
http://www.chequers.com
Wants to buy casino chips.

Nate Pincus
P.O. Box 693
Havertown, PA 19083-0693
ph: 610-668-4273
fax: 815-425-2792
nate@chipcollector.com
http://www.chipcollector.com
*Collector of casino chips from all
areas; buy, sell, trade.*

John "Top" Newby, USMC Ret.
10676 Sun Up Court
Milton, FL 32583
ph: 850-9891-0440
Top@TopUsmc.com
http://TopUsmc.com
*Buys and trades casino chips; wants
old chips that might be laying around
from your travels around the world:
Las Vegas, Atlantic City, foreign
chips; call or send fax with
descriptions.*

John Benedict
P.O. Drawer 1423
Loxahatchee, FL 33470-1423
ph: 561-798-2520 or 800-844-3397
fax: 561-798-2520
benedict@webtv.net
http://www.netmar.com/~creator/benedict
*Wants old casino chips and ivory
poker chips.*

Kevin Anthony Norris
6908 Sky Blue Ave.
Louisville, KY 40258
ph: 502-935-1283 or 502-499-7510
fax: 502-499-7514
kingofchip@aol.com
*Wants to buy old club poker chips
from all states; used at clubs from
1920s to 1950s; also wants casino
chips.*

Michael Knapp
P.O. Box 340345
Columbus, OH 43234
ph: 614-451-0006 or 614-723-1092
fax: 614-723-1704
ChipProf@aol.com
*Buys, collects and specializes in poker
chips; author of books and articles
about chips and chip collecting.*

Greg Johnson
3344 S. Raible Ave.
Anderson, IN 46011
g-johnson@excite.com
http://www.homepagez.com/gregjohnson
Buy, sell, trade casino chips.

George Conrad
3609 Dalecrest Dr.
Las Vegas, NV 89129
ph: 702-645-1955
http://members.aol.com/georgecon
*Collector, trader, buyer, seller of
Nevada casino chips.*

Mike & Dianne Draper
4970 Stagecoach Dr.
Silver Springs, NV 89429
ph: 702-629-9148
*Collector of Nevada casino items,
especially Harolds Club, Reno; also*

wants to buy native American Indian items.

Charles T. Rodgers
P.O. Box 4572
Lakewood, CA 90711-4572
ph: 562-408-2463
ctcoins@aol.com

Dealers

Don Anthony
505 Halsey Rd.
North Brunswick, NJ 08902-2616
ph: 732-297-2422
Collects, sells, trades casino gaming chips; specializing on denominations from 25 cents to $10; has chips from all over the world, including Nevada, Atlantic City, river boats, Colorado, Australia, Aruba and many other locations.

John Rudden
Starchip Enterprises
P.O. Box 140557
Jamaica, NY 11414
ph: 718-738-8125
starchip@nyc.rr.com
http://www.starchip.com
Collector and dealer buys, sells and trades casino chips, gaming tokens and slot cards; free downloadable catalog; monthly contests; Web site had scanned images of chips, slot cards; links, news and much more.

Jim Smith
Chip Chamber, The
4220 Judd Rd.
Milan, MI 48160
ph: 734-439-2510
Dealer in worldwide casino chips with emphasis on limited edition chips; member Casino Chip & Gaming Token Collector's Club.

Larry Lubliner
Avant Carde
3814 N. Fremont #3
Chicago, IL 60613-9998
ph: 773-883-0073
fax: 773-883-1199
joker1854@aol.com
http://www.avantcarde.com
Buys and sells gambling collectibles, poker chips, playing cards, coin-operated gambling machines.

Wilcox Enterprises
P.O. Box 395
Carthage, IL 62321-0395
ph: 217-357-3308
rwc@acm.org
Buys and sells chips, tokens, cards, matches and dice from river boats, Indian reservations, Deadwood, Colorado.

Greg Susong
P.O. Box 654
Wellington, KS 67152
ph: 316-326-2202
fax: 316-326-3893
greg@chipguide.com
http://www.chipguide.com
Buys, sells casino chips of all kinds;

specializes in chips from Riverboats and Indian casinos; Web site has an online guide, "Greg Susong's CyberGuide To Casino Chips," a state-by-state reference work for casino chip collectors.

Andy Jung
4800 Bissonet Dr.
Metairie, LA 70003-1136
ph: 504-454-7927
Buys and sells mainly New Orleans area chips and tokens; also some Lake Charles, LA, MS, and Gulf Coast.

Allen Banick
Colorado Casino Chip Exchange
Newsletter: Colorado Casino Chip Newsletter
P.O. Box 260575
Highlands Ranch, CO 80163-0575
fax: 303-683-0433
info@abanick.com
http://www.abanick.com
Collector and expert who buys, sells and trades collectible casino chips from all around the world; specializes in chips from Colorado, New Mexico, and South Dakota.

Scott Hartman
Chip Man, The
P.O. Box 387
Agoura Hills, CA 91376-0387
ph: 818-706-1197 or 800-LUCK-707
fax: 818-706-1986
scott@chipman.com
http://www.chipman.com
Largest shop on line casino chip catalog and reference guide, over 5,600 chips in color.

Gary Snover
P.O. Box 9696
San Bernardino, CA 92427-0696
ph: 909-883-5849
fax: 909-886-6874
garysnover@cs.com
http://www.coinmall.com/snover
Send $1 for price list.

Dean Richmond
Casino Collectibles
P.O. Box 666
Waldport, OR 97394
ph: 541-563-4529
fax: 541-563-4531
jodean@pioneer.net
http://www.ocvirtual.com/jodean
Full time dealer in casino collectibles since 1987; colored, monthly mail/fax bid auctions.

Experts

Archie A. Black
P.O. Box 63
Brick, NJ 08723-0063
ph: 732-458-8827
fax: 732-458-8871
ablack2@optonline.net
http://www.callzia.com/dghome/acchips
Author of "Black's Catalog of Atlantic City Casino Chips & Gaming Tokens," and "Black's Catalog of Puerto Rico Casino Chips."

Travis H. D. Lewin
Syracuse Univ. College of Law
Syracuse, NY 13244-1030
ph: 315-443-1222 or 315-446-8678
fax: 315-443-5394
thdlewin@law.syr.edu
http://web.syr.edu/~thlewin
Collects, buys and trades ivory, mother-of-pearl, and clay composition poker chips and casino checks and tokens.

Eugene M. Lonstein
4440 NE 20th Ave.
Fort Lauderdale, FL 33308
ph: 954-771-9600
fax: 954-943-9511
jebsam2000@attbi.com
Long time collector of casino chips worldwide; buys, sells, appraises.

Michael Knapp
P.O. Box 340345
Columbus, OH 43234
ph: 614-451-0006 or 614-723-1092
fax: 614-723-1704
ChipProf@aol.com
Buys, collects and specializes in poker chips; author of books and articles about chips and chip collecting.

Greg Susong
P.O. Box 654
Wellington, KS 67152
ph: 316-326-2202
fax: 316-326-3893
greg@chipguide.com
http://www.chipguide.com
Buys, sells casino chips of all kinds; specializes in chips from Riverboats and Indian casinos; Web site has an online guide, "Greg Susong's CyberGuide To Casino Chips," a state-by-state reference work for casino chip collectors.

Art Becker
2232 S. Nellis Blvd, #227
Las Vegas, NV 89104
artbecker@artbecker.com
http://www.artbecker.com
Specializes in slot club cards and Silver Strikes which are $10 souvenir tokens that were won from special casino slot machines; publishes print and CD-ROM catalogs; has Web site with message boards about collecting them.

Scott Hartman
Chip Man, The
P.O. Box 387
Agoura Hills, CA 91376-0387
ph: 818-706-1197 or 800-LUCK-707
fax: 818-706-1986
scott@chipman.com
http://www.chipman.com
Expert, collector and dealer of casino chips, specializing in mainly obsolete Nevada chips.

Dale Seymour
11170 Mora Dr.
Los Altos, CA 94024-6536
ph: 650-948-0948
fax: 650-941-3695
seymourdg@aol.com
Wants old poker chips; ivory, clay, or casino; no paper, plain or plastic chips wanted. Author of book on same.

Marv Weaver
P.O. Box 8595
Pittsburg, CA 94565-8595
Collector of Silver Strikes only; author of "Nevada Silver Premium Gaming Tokens Price Guide."

Internet Resources

Neal Silverman
Chequers
585 Merrick Rd.
Lynbrook, NY 11563
fax: 732-576-8852
http://www.chequers.com
An online directory for casino chip collectors; presently over 400 members with email addresses and homepages; site is full of information on the hobby submitted weekly by members; free to all collectors and dealers.

Periodicals

Magazine: Gaming Times
1350 E. Flamingo Rd., #494
Las Vegas, NV 89119
ph: 702-876-6020 or 800-784-4452
fax: 702-866-6020
chips@gamingtimes.com
http://www.gamingtimes.com
Monthly publication containing news and stories about chips, dice, casino memorabilia, and more; new chip releases, Atlantic City news, electronic chipping, dice department, casino news and histories.

Punchboards

(see also COIN-OPERATED MACHINES; GAMES; PAPER COLLECTIBLES)

Dealers

Steve Lerner
42 Barefoot Hill Rd.
Sharon, MA 02067
ph: 781-784-2286
slerner@attbi.com
http://www.gamblingcollectibles.com
Buys and sells dice, punchcards, and gaffed gambling items and equipment.

Ken Durham
GameRoomAntiques
909 26th St. NW
Washington, DC 20037-2029
durham@gameroomantiques.com
http://www.GameRoomAntiques.com
Buys and sells punchboards with gambling, sport, pin-up and other colorful decorations.

Clark Phelps
Amusement Sales Co.
7610 Main St.
Midvale, UT 84047-7106
ph: 801-255-4731
clarkp@aros.net
Buys and sells punchboards.

Internet Resources

Marcus Stafford
punchboard.com
2012 Oliver
Memphis, TN 38104
ph: 901-274-1472
marcus@punchboard.com
http://www.punchboard.com
All about punchboards; loaded with tips for the collector of gambling memorabilia; includes historical information and an extensive photo gallery of vintage punchboards.

GAME ROOM AMUSEMENTS

(see BILLIARD RELATED ITEMS; BOOKS, Reference [Coin-Op.]; COIN-OP. MACHINES; GAMBLING COLLECTIBLES, Punchboards; LAMPS & LIGHTING, Traffic Lights; REPAIR/RESTORATION/ CONSERVATION, Metal Items; SCALES; SOFT DRINK COLLECTIBLES, Soda Machines

GAMES

(see also BILLIARD RELATED ITEMS; BRIDGE; CHESS SETS; DICE; FRISBEES; GAMBLING COLLECTIBLES; MARBLES; PAPER COLLECTIBLES; PLAYING CARDS; PUZZLES; TOYS)

Auction Services

Richard W. Withington, Inc.
590 Center Rd.
Hillsboro, NH 03244
ph: 603-464-3232
fax: 603-464-4901
withington@conknet.com
http://www.withingtonauction.com

Clubs/Associations

Association of Game & Puzzle Collectors
Journal: Game & Puzzle Collectors
  Quarterly
PMB 321
197M Boston Post Rd. West
Marlborough, MA 01752
juckett@attglobal.net
http://www.agpc.org
Members are devoted to collecting, researching, preserving games, jigsaw puzzles, mechanical puzzles, and other pastimes.

Robert R. Grew
Antique Toy Collectors of America, Inc., The
Newsletter: Toy Chest
c/o Carter, Ledyard & Milburn
Two Wall St. - 13th Floor
New York, NY 10005
ph: 212-238-8803
fax: 212-732-3232
grew@clm.com
A non-profit organization focusing on antique toys and games; since membership is by invitation only for established collectors, there is a waiting list; bi-monthly newsletter available only to members & to libraries/museums on request.

H.M. Levy, Pres.
Gamers Alliance
Newsletter: Gamers Alliance Report
P.O. Box 197 -CIC
East Meadow, NY 11554-0197
gamers@gamersalliance.com
http://www.gamersalliance.com
Members receive quarterly reports with news, views and reviews on games plus FREE out-of-print catalogs, FREE research service, and more; send SASE for more information; also buys games - one or one thousand.

Dealers

Bruce Whitehill
Big Game Hunter, The
E-zine: All in the Game
11 South Angell St., #116
Providence, RI 02906
games@thebiggamehunter.com
http://www.thebiggamehunter.com
Buys, sells, collects; one of the world's foremost authorities on American games; author of "Games: American Games & Their Makers, 1822-1992, With Values" (Wallace-Homestead, 1992); on Advisory Board of Inter. Soc. for Board Game Studies.

Paul Fink
Fun & Games
P.O. Box 488
Kent, CT 06757-0488
ph: 860-927-4001
Buys and sells Victorian games, comic and cartoon games, TV & nostalgia games; dealer and mail order.

Chick Darrow
Darrow's Fun Antiques
1101 1st Ave.
New York, NY 10021-8737
ph: 212-838-0730 or 888-DARROWS
fax: 212-838-3617
george@fun-antiques.com
http://www.fun-antiques.com
Buys & sells antique games, toys, ad signs, animated art, jukeboxes, slot machines, comic watches, bicycles & memorabilia of all types; also prop rentals.

Marjorie Jeffreys
Going to Pieces
P.O. Box 390
Cibolo, TX 78108
ph: 210-659-2458
Buys and sells old games, toys, blocks and children's dishes and children's baking items.

Maurice & Laya Jakubowicz
Affiche Francaise
128 Avenue de la Chevre d'Or
Vallauris, 06220 France
ph: 33 (0)493 63 45 92
fax: 33 (0)493 63 45 92
ml@affiche-francaise.com
http://www.affiche-francaise.com
Large collection of "saussine" board games from 1880-1940.

Experts

Lee Dennis
447 Park Ave., Apt. 12
Keene, NH 03431-6506
ph: 603-358-0060
Author of "Warman's Antique American Games, 1840 - 1940;" former curator-owner of the country's largest collection of board games; continues to offer slide film presentation about games to clubs/ associations/Historical Societies.

Alex G. Malloy
Alex G. Malloy, Inc.
P.O. Box 38
South Salem, NY 10590-0038
ph: 203-438-0396 or 203-438-9652
fax: 203-438-6744
alexmalloy@aol.com
http://members.aol.com/AlexMalloy/ agmalloy.htm
Specialist in board and card games; author of "American Games" (Krause).

Bob Cereghino
6400 Baltimore National Pike, Ste. 170A-319
Baltimore, MD 21228-3914
ph: 410-766-7593
jwbc@juno.com

Museums/Libraries

Peabody Essex Museum
Essex & Libert Sts.
Salem, MA 01970
ph: 978-745-9500 or 800-745-4054
pem@pem.org
http://www.pem.org

Washington Dolls' House & Toy Museum
5236 44th St. NW
Washington, DC 20015-2101
ph: 202-244-0024
fax: 202-237-1659

University of Waterloo Museum & Archive of Games
Dept. of Recreation & Leisure Studies
Faculty of Applied Health Sci.
Waterloo, Ontario N2L 3G1 Canada
ph: 519-888-4424 or 519-885-4567
fax: 519-746-6776
eavedon@healthy.uwaterloo.ca
http://www.ahs.uwaterloo.ca/~museum/ index.html
2,000 references: books, journals, reports, patent information, scholarly studies, and other printed materials concerning games and playing behavior; also many games, photos, advertisements, catalogs, and rules about games.

Periodicals

Peter Sarrett
Magazine: Game Report, The
1920 N. 49th St.
Seattle, WA 98103
ph: 206-547-3449
editor@gamereport.com
http://www.gamereport.com
A quarterly publication dedicated to board, card, dice, party, family, and strategy games (but not war games or role playing games): game reviews, articles, interviews, classifieds; Web site has online game auctions.

Bagatelle

Dealers

Harold Balde
Fungus Amungus
21 Wellington St.
Orangeville, Ontario L9W 2L2 Canada
ph: 519-938-8808
boardwalk12345@yahoo.com
http://www.fungus-amungus.com
Collector and dealer in 1800s through 1940s bagatelles; will help new collectors with pricing and general information.

Baseball Related

Experts

Mark Cooper
Baseball Games & Memorabilia
816 Chauncey Rd.
Narberth, PA 19072
ph: 215-952-9153 or 610-667-7401
fax: 610-667-2341
A premier collector of 1860-1980 baseball games; has published the definitive text on the subject; will provide free information to all interested; always buying, selling, trading baseball games.

Board

Clubs/Associations

Association of Game & Puzzle Collectors
Journal: Game & Puzzle Collectors
Quarterly
PMB 321
197M Boston Post Rd. West
Marlborough, MA 01752
juckett@attglobal.net
http://www.agpc.org
Members are devoted to collecting, researching, preserving games, jigsaw puzzles, mechanical puzzles, and other pastimes.

Collectors

Bill Smith
56 Locust St.
East Douglas, MA 01516-2440
ph: 508-476-2015
Wants all board games; any age or theme.

Bernard Newman
2004 Delancy Place
Philadelphia, PA 19103-6510
ph: 800-523-3256
fax: 215-332-8586
bnewman@erols.com
Wants pre-1930 board games, especially by McLoughlin, Parker, Bliss, Bradley, Ives; must be in excellent condition with excellent graphics.

Dealers

Debra Krim
P.O. Box 764
Middleton, MA 01949
ph: 978-304-3140
fax: 978-304-3140
mrkrim@attbi.com
http://www.old-toys.com
Wants boxed & board games from 1843 to 1970: McLoughlin, Ives, Bliss and other companies; baseball and TV games; cartoon strip games.

Paul Fink
Fun & Games
P.O. Box 488
Kent, CT 06757-0488
ph: 860-927-4001
Buys and sells Victorian games, comic and cartoon games, TV & nostalgia games; dealer and mail order.

Bill & Joanne Bruegman
Toy Scouts, Inc.
137 Casterton Ave.
Akron, OH 44303-1543
ph: 330-836-0668
orders@toyscouts.com
http://www.toyscouts.com
Specializes in Baby-Boomer era toys and television memorabilia.

Jeff Lowe
Jeff Lowe's ExtravaGAMEza
2868 Redick Ave.
Omaha, NE 68112
ph: 402-592-8186
info@extravagameza.com
http://www.extravagameza.com
Collector and dealer with catalog of over 2,500 games available for nominal postage charge.

Experts

Bruce Whitehill
Big Game Hunter, The
E-zine: All in the Game
11 South Angell St., #116
Providence, RI 02906
games@thebiggamehunter.com
http://www.thebiggamehunter.com
Buys, sells, collects; one of the world's foremost authorities on American games; author of "Games: American Games & Their Makers, 1822-1992, With Values" (Wallace-Homestead, 1992); on Advisory Board of Inter. Soc. for Board Game Studies.

Lee Dennis
447 Park Ave., Apt. 12
Keene, NH 03431-6506
ph: 603-358-0060
Author of "Warman's Antique American Games, 1840 - 1940;" former curator-owner of the country's largest collection of board games; continues to offer slide film presentation about games to clubs/associations/Historical Societies.

David Galt
Games & Names
302 W. 78th St.
New York, NY 10024
ph: 212-769-2514
david@spacedominoes.com
http://www.spacedominoes.com
One of the premier playing card and board game collectors in America.

Pat McFarland
P.O. Box 400
Averill Park, NY 12018-0400
ph: 518-674-8390
greatgames@webtv.net
Buyer of American board games 1800s to 1940s; McLoughlin, Bliss, Ives, Doan, early Parker and Bradley; also wants game catalogs and ephemera; pre-1936 Monopoly; player related Baseball; The Landlord's Game; related information.

Ellen Charland, ANA, MCPA
1407 Foothill Blvd., #19
La Verne, CA 91750
ph: 909-592-0101 or 626-963-7695
fax: 626-335-6651
antiquetea@aol.com
http://members.tripod.com/~antiquetalk/index-4.html
Specializes in post WWII board games; offers online appraisals.

Internet Resources

Richard J. Rabe
Web Museum of Board Games, The
rjrabe@hotmail.com
http://www.geocities.com/rjrabe1989/
An online museum of board games dating from the 1880s to present.

Card

Experts

Bruce Whitehill
Big Game Hunter, The
E-zine: All in the Game
11 South Angell St., #116
Providence, RI 02906
games@thebiggamehunter.com
http://www.thebiggamehunter.com
Buys, sells, collects; one of the world's foremost authorities on American games; author of "Games: American Games & Their Makers, 1822-1992, With Values" (Wallace-Homestead, 1992); on Advisory Board of Inter. Soc. for Board Game Studies.

Lee Dennis
447 Park Ave., Apt. 12
Keene, NH 03431-6506
ph: 603-358-0060
Author of "Warman's Antique American Games, 1840 - 1940;" former curator-owner of the country's largest collection of board games; continues to offer slide film presentation about games to clubs/associations/Historical Societies.

Checkers

Clubs/Associations

Anthony Bishop, Treas.
American Checker Foundation
5304 Barton Bale Court
Nashville, TN 37221
lymanal@yahoo.com
http://www.acfcheckers.com

Collectors

Henry A. Justice
30 Thomas Ct.
Stockbridge, GA 30281-2900
ph: 770-389-8527
Wants checkers: plastic, wood, etc.; loose, boxed, sets, with or without board.

Experts

Don Deweber
John Caldwell-Irving Windt Library of Checkers
3520 Hillcrest, Apt. 4
Dubuque, IA 52002
Wants to buy old checker sets, checker books, and other checker memorabilia.

Museums/Libraries

International Checkers Hall of Fame
P.O. Box A
220 Lynn Ray Rd.
Petal, MS 39465
ph: 601-582-7090
Hosts international checkers competitions

Cribbage Boards

Clubs/Associations

Bette L. Bemis
Cribbage Board Collectors Society
Newsletter: Members of the Board
P.O. Box 170
Carolina, RI 02812-0170
ph: 401-364-7241
bbemis7@cox.net
For collectors of cribbage boards; newsletter published quarterly.

Experts

Bette L. Bemis
P.O. Box 170
Carolina, RI 02812-0170
ph: 401-364-7241
bbemis7@cox.net
Author of book "Cribbage Boards 1863-1998," as well as articles on cribbage board collecting published on the American Cribbage Congress Web site, http://www.cribbage.org.

Mah Jong

Clubs/Associations

Allan & Lila Weitz
Mah Jong Collectors Club
12 Van Every Circle
Kirkland, Quebec H9J 2P5 Canada
ph: 514-697-3276
allanweitz@yahoo.com
An informal international club; membership is open to anyone having an interest in the game of Mah Jong.

Collectors

Allan & Lila Weitz
12 Van Every Circle
Kirkland, Quebec H9J 2P5 Canada
ph: 514-697-3276
allanweitz@yahoo.com
Collector, expert wishing to share mah jong information; buys, sells, trades old Chinese sets; has large mah jong library, research network, travelling exhibition as well as first class collection; will travel.

Experts

Jim May
Mah Jong Cyber Museum
P.O. Box 4139
Hazelwood, MO 63042-0739
webmaster@mahjongmuseum.com
http://www.mahjongmuseum.com
Collector, dealer, expert in the ancient game of mah jong; Web site has lots of great information about the game at this site, even a Mah Jong Cyber Museum, and a personal collection and gift shop.

Beverly L. Walrath
5601 Tioga NW
Albuquerque, NM 87120
ph: 505-897-4615
nanabevs@spinn.net
Reference for early materials used for tiles (ivory, bone, celluloid, wood, Bakelite, Catalin, Pyralin, Ivoride, Lucite, etc.); wants to buy unusual

sets, especially tortoise shell; extensive collections of Mah Jong sets.

Allan & Lila Weitz
12 Van Every Circle
Kirkland, Quebec H9J 2P5 Canada
ph: 514-697-3276
allanweitz@yahoo.com
Collector, expert wishing to share mah jong information; buys, sells, trades old Chinese sets; has large mah jong library, research network, travelling exhibition as well as first class collection; will travel.

Internet Resources

Jim May
Mah Jong Cyber Museum
P.O. Box 4139
Hazelwood, MO 63042-0739
webmaster@mahjongmuseum.com
http://www.mahjongmuseum.com
Collector, dealer, expert in the ancient game of mah jong; Web site has lots of great information about the game at this site, even a Mah Jong Cyber Museum, and a personal collection and gift shop.

Skill & Action

Experts

Bruce Whitehill
Big Game Hunter, The
E-zine: All in the Game
11 South Angell St., #116
Providence, RI 02906
games@thebiggamehunter.com
http://www.thebiggamehunter.com
Buys, sells, collects skill & action games: Mouse Trap, Operation, spinner games, Pick-Up Sticks (Jack Straws), Tiddly Winks, marble games, ball games, table top billiards/ croquet/pinball (bagatelle), Twister, Hungry Hippo, etc.

Video Games

Clubs/Associations

Video Arcade Preservation Society
keeper@vaps.org
http://www.vaps.org
Web site has a Killer List of Video Games.

Dealers

Blast from the Past Amusements
543 West Betteravia Blvd., Ste. E
Santa Maria, CA 93455
ph: 805-347-1981 or 877-922-5278
fax: 208-247-3853
games@arcadeclassics.com
http://www.arcadeclassics.com
Restored classic arcade video games: Pac-Man, Asteroids, Defender, Ms. Pac, Galga, Robotron and new titles; for home, office, studio.

Waterfuls

Collectors

Garrett Perryman
56 Sunset Blvd.
Trenton, NJ 08690
ph: 609-587-4676
Wants to buy Waterfuls and Watergames; these are water-filled plastic toys designed as a game.

GANGSTER RELATED COLLECTIBLES

(see LAW ENFORCEMENT MEMORABILIA; PERSONALITIES [CRIMINAL]; PROHIBITION ITEMS)

GARDEN FURNITURE

Furniture & Ornaments

(see also ARCHITECTURAL ELEMENTS; CAST IRON ITEMS)

Dealers

New England Garden Ornaments
38 East Brookfield Rd.
P.O. Box 235
North Brookfield, MA 01535-0235
ph: 508-867-4474
fax: 508-867-8409
nego@bx.com
http://www.negardenornaments.com
Carries old and new garden architecture and ornamentation: sundials, statuary, planters, urns, wrought iron, pedestals, birdbaths, etc.

Barbara Israel
Barbara Israel Garden Antiques
296 Mount Holly Rd.
Katonah, NY 10536
ph: 212-744-6281
fax: 212-744-2188
eva@bi-gardenantiques.com
http://www.bi-gardenantiques.com
Specializes in American, English and Continental statues, fountains, urns, benches, sundials, and other period garden ornaments.

Experts

H. Weber & Jill Wilson
WebWilson.com
P.O. Box 506
Portsmouth, RI 02871
ph: 800-508-0022
fax: 401-683-1644
jill@LooLooDesign.com
http://www.LooLooDesign.com
Sells architectural antiques; garden ornaments, vintage plumbing, quality furniture, antique door hardware.

Elizabeth Schumacher
Garden Accents
4 Union Hill Rd.
West Conshohocken, PA 19428
ph: 610-825-5525
fax: 610-825-4817
eschuatga@aol.com
Buys and sells best assortment of

antique garden accessories: urns, planters, statuary, benches, fountains; bronze, iron, lead, etc.

Repro. Sources

John C. Allen, Jr.
Robinson Iron
P.O. Box 1119
Alexander City, AL 35011-1119
ph: 256-329-8486 or 800-824-2157
fax: 256-329-8960
sales@robinson-iron.com
http://www.robinson-iron.com
Makes reproduction furniture and fountains; catalog $5.

GARDEN HOSE NOZZLES

(see CAST IRON ITEMS)

GAS STATION COLLECTIBLES

(see also AUTOMOBILIA; GAUGES; HIGHWAY COLLECTIBLES; LICENSE PLATES; TOYS, Trucks & Equipment; TRAILERS & RVs)

Clubs/Associations

John Logsdon
Iowa Gas Swap Meet
2417 Linda Dr.
Des Moines, IA 50322-5200
ph: 515-251-8811
IowaGasJon@aol.com
http://www.iowagas.com
An organization dedicated to the collecting of all oil, gas, petroleum and auto advertising including signs, globes, pumps, cans, bottles, and related memorabilia. The annual convention held each August is the largest of its kind.

Collectors

Lee M. Fox
1715 S.H. 45
Mullica Hill, NJ 08062
ph: 856-478-6225
Wants to buy gas station collectibles including signs, pumps, pump globes.

Larry Spilkin
P.O. Box 5039
Southfield, MI 48086-5039
ph: 248-642-3722
Wants postcards and matchbook covers of drive-ins, diners, cafes, gas stations and 1930s-1950s motels, restaurant/bar, cabins and Art Deco streamline hotels.

Peter Capell
1838 West Grace St.
Chicago, IL 60613-2724
ph: 773-871-8735
pcapell@cometlink.com
Collects gasoline company/service station items: pump globes, giveaways such as banks, thermometers, salt & pepper shaker sets in the shape of gas pumps.

Ben Eckart
1121 Hylton Heights
Manhattan, KS 66502
ph: 785-539-7562
fax: 785-539-0822
enarco@flinthills.com
http://www.enarco.com
Collects anything from the National Refining Company, Cleveland, Ohio; produced White Rose gasoline and EN-AR-CO motor oil; signs, cans, maps, national news booklets, calendars, photographs, etc.

Jeffrey Herman
3333 N. Carson St.
Carson City, NV 89706
ph: 775-888-3333
fax: 775-883-4214
Wants to buy oil cans; also wants gas station collectibles such as signs, pumps, globes, etc.

Ace Feek
P.O. Box 1358
Chelan, WA 98816
ph: 509-682-5345 or 800-573-8847 x55
Wants to buy oil company and service station cap badges: Mobile, Union Oil, Mohawk Gasoline, Texaco, Shell, Union 76, etc.

Dealers

Ed Natale, Jr.
Retro Petro
P.O. Box 222
Wyckoff, NJ 07481-0222
ph: 201-493-7172
jednat@att.net
Wants to buy gas station and petroliana signs, uniform pins and badges, oil cans, pre-WWII road maps, map racks, credit card signs, rest room signs & key tags; photos of items would be helpful.

Experts

Wayne Henderson
338 Spartan Rd.
Wilmington, NC 28405
ph: 910-395-4279
fax: 910-793-0631
PCMPublishing@worldnet.att.net
http://www.pcmpublishing.com
World's largest collection of historical material concerning service stations and oil company collectibles; co-author of over 10 books on the subject of petroleum collectibles and oil company histories.

Scott Anderson
Time Passages, Ltd.
P.O. Box 65596
West Des Moines, IA 50265-0596
ph: 515-223-5105 or 515-223-5104
fax: 515-223-5149
timepass@netins.net
http://www.time-pass.com
Author of "Check the Oil" (Wallace-Homestead).

Jim Potts
9925 Reavis Rd.
Saint Louis, MO 63123
admin@oldgas.com
http://www.oldgas.com
Specializes in gas station collectibles.

Internet Resources

Jim Potts
Primarily Petroliana
9925 Reavis Rd.
Saint Louis, MO 63123
admin@oldgas.com
http://www.oldgas.com
An Internet service bringing gas station memorabilia collectors, dealers, publishers and service providers together for the benefit of all; Web site features event schedules and reports, articles and images, links and roster of collectors.

Periodicals

Jerry Keyser
International Petroliana Collectors
Association
Magazine: Check the Oil!
30 W. Olentangy St.
Powell, OH 43065-9764
ph: 614-848-5038 or 800-228-6224
fax: 614-436-4760
ctomagazine@aol.com
http://www.oldgas.com/info/cto.htm
Pumps, oil cans, signs, oil bottles, pens, pump globes; anything to do with the petroleum industry of days gone by.

Scott Benjamin, Co-Ed.
Petroleum Collectibles Monthly, Inc.
Newsletter: Petroleum Collectibles
Monthly
P.O. Box 556
Lagrange, OH 44050-0556
ph: 440-355-6608
fax: 440-355-4955
scott@pcmpublishing.com
http://www.pcmpublishing.com
Research on all phases of gasoline marketing; world's largest collection of historical material concerning service stations and oil company collectibles: cans, signs, paper, toys, gas pumps, globes, large ad section.

Suppliers

Walt & Terry Koz
Past Gas Company
308 Willard St.
Cocoa, FL 32922-7640
ph: 321-636-0449
fax: 321-636-1006
pastgas@telsurf.net
http://www.pastgas.com
Sells restoration parts for 1920s to 1950s gas pumps; no appraisal requests, please.

Weber's Nostalgia Supermarket
6611 Anglin Dr.
Fort Worth, TX 76119-7555 Canada
ph: 817-654-2002
fax: 817-534-3316
info@weberspump.com
http://www.weberspump.com
Restoration parts, supplies for vintage gas pumps, decals; castings, glass, I.D. tags, brass nozzles, hose, etc.

Conoco

Collectors

Paul A. Wilson
P.O. Box 290
Hondo, TX 78861
ph: 830-426-8663
fax: 830-426-8645
Wants any Conoco collectibles: toy trucks, maps, tour aides, pumps, dolls, signs, oil cans, filters, gas pump globes, etc.

Experts

Todd Helms
1023 East 5th Ave.
Lancaster, OH 43130-3276
ph: 740-681-6151 or 740-654-6179
fax: 740-681-6076
Collects Conoco (Continental Oil Company) and Maryland-related oil company items such as signs, cans, maps, pumps, giveaways; especially interested in "Minuteman" era of Conoco (1913-1929); author of "The Conoco Collector's Bible."

Frontier

Collectors

Jim Hollabaugh
3800 Congress Parkway
P.O. Box 460
Richfield, OH 44286-0460
ph: 330-659-3888 or 800-662-6344
fax: 330-659-9410
Wants to buy Shell & Frontier petroliana: containers, globes, signs, toys, promotional items, shell pocket watches with fobs; specializes in Shell and Frontier.

Hess

Collectors

Bob Ford
4804 Bensalem Blvd.
Bensalem, PA 19020
ph: 215-638-0531
toytrucks@comcast.net
http://www.webvenues.net/modelts/
Collects and sells Hess, Wilco, Servco, Texaco (Ertl) and other gasoline promotional toy trucks by Ertl and others; also collects Hess memorabilia.

Experts

Tom Nefos
779 E. Merritt Island Cswy #1282
Merritt Island, FL 32952
NationalToy@aol.com
http://members.aol.com/NationalToy/
HessTrucks.html
Publishes "Original Price Guide to Hess Toys," and "Hess Photo Album and Toys" on CD.

Oil Cans

Dealers

Jim Natale
Retro Petro
P.O. Box 222
Wyckoff, NJ 07481-0222
ph: 201-493-7172
jednat@att.net
Buying "handy oil" tins (like 3-in-1 type) with metal or plastic spout; full or empty; also household, gun, automotive, sewing machine oil cans, lighter fluid, gas station brands.

Pumps & Globes

Collectors

Gary Hildman
3240 Sevier Rd.
Marcellus, NY 13108-9624
ph: 315-673-2535
fax: 315-673-2412
pelican@baldcom.net
Wants gasoline pump globes and related items: inserts, glass and metal bodies; also wants porcelain, tin, and neon signs.

Kent Blaine
505 N. Mission Rd.
Winona, MS 38967-9534
ph: 662-624-2947 or 662-283-3524
sherriblaine2000@yahoo.com
Wants pre-1960 gas station items through 1950s; especially brass padlocks with oil company logos, e.g., Texaco, Pan Am, Crown, etc.; also wants 15" single globe lens; always has items for trade and for sale.

Scott Benjamin
Oil Company Collectibles, Inc.
P.O. Box 566
Lagrange, OH 44050-0556
ph: 440-355-6608
fax: 440-355-4955
scottpcm@aol.com
http://www.pcmpublishing.com
Wants gasoline globes, inserts, etched globes, aviation, Benzol and others.

Dealers

Ron Rogers
Gas Pumps & Parking Meters
ph: 418-673-1067
impala1@bright.net
http://www.bright.net/~impala1
Specializes in buying, selling and restoring old gas pumps and parking meters; also other gas station memorabilia such as oil cans,

porcelain and tin signs; pedal cars, too.

Don Creekmore
Nations Attic, The
ph: 316-371-1828
dcreekmore@cox.net
http://www.nationsattic.com
Wants to buy vintage gas pumps, especially wants visible gas pumps and clock face pumps; not interested in "computer" type pumps made after 1960.

Experts

Walt Feiger
Walt's Antiques
2513 Nelson Rd.
Traverse City, MI 49686-8557
ph: 231-223-7386 or 231-223-4123
feiger@pentel.net
http://www.pentel.net/antiques
Buys and sells gas pumps, globes, signs, auto memorabilia, and slot machines.

Repro. Sources

Benkin & Co.
16 E. Main
Tripp City, OH 45371
ph: 937-667-5975
Handmade antique-style gas pumps, wide selection of colors, 35 oil company globes to chose from; sold in kits or completely finished; write for flyer.

Suppliers

Walt & Terry Koz
Past Gas Company
308 Willard St.
Cocoa, FL 32922-7640
ph: 321-636-0449
fax: 321-636-1006
pastgas@telsurf.net
http://www.pastgas.com
Sells restoration parts for 1920s to 1950s gas pumps; no appraisal requests, please.

Scott Anderson
Time Passages, Ltd.
P.O. Box 65596
West Des Moines, IA 50265-0596
ph: 515-223-5105 or 515-223-5104
fax: 515-223-5149
timepass@netins.net
http://www.time-pass.com
Supplies restoration parts and supplies for vintage gasoline pumps.

Weber's Nostalgia Supermarket
6611 Anglin Dr.
Fort Worth, TX 76119-7555 Canada
ph: 817-654-2002
fax: 817-534-3316
info@weberspump.com
http://www.weberspump.com
Restoration parts, supplies for vintage gas pumps, decals; castings, glass, I.D. tags, brass nozzles, hose, etc.

Road Maps

Clubs/Associations

Richard Horwitz, Pres.
Road Map Collectors of America
Newsletter: RMCA Newsletter
P.O. Box 22624
Oklahoma City, OK 73123
rhorwitz@featurephoto.com
http://www.roadmaps.org
A club for researchers, collectors, dealers of North American road maps.

Collectors

Jeff Hubbard
2900 91st St.
Sturtevant, WI 53177-2013
ph: 262-886-0477
jeffh27@yahoo.com
Buys older Hot Wheel cars and pre-1960 oil company highway maps.

David Schul
2214 Princeton Blvd.
Lawrence, KS 66049
ph: 785-864-5143
dave@roadmaps.org
Looking for official Rd. maps, Rd. atlases, highway maps (all states and provinces) and pre-1940 road atlases (any publisher).

Peter Sidlow
5895 Duneville St.
Las Vegas, NV 89118
ph: 702-873-1818
fax: 702-248-6671
pedro666@earthlink.net
Wants early road maps; oil company or other issues; prefers colorful graphics.

Dealers

Noel Levy
20th Century Maps
1109 Silentglade Rd.
Owings Mills, MD 21117-2455
ph: 410-363-9040
megamapster@comcast.net
http://www.20thcenturymaps.com
Road map collector, expert, dealer; more than 12,000 different oil companies, official state and miscellaneous road maps from almost every year of 20th c.; for cartographers, history buffs, genealogists, collectors, etc.

James Willinger
Wide World of Maps
2626 W. Glenrosa
Phoenix, AZ 85017
ph: 602-455-0616
fax: 602-433-0695
azmapman@prodigy.net
http://www.maps4u.com
Buys, sells and trades old maps and travel related brochures with a focus on the Southwestern states.

Experts

Douglas Yorke
19 Oak Lane
Rumson, NJ 07760-1306
ph: 732-842-6283
Co-author with John Margolies of "Hitting the Road."

Noel Levy
20th Century Maps
1109 Silentglade Rd.
Owings Mills, MD 21117-2455
ph: 410-363-9040
megamapster@comcast.net
http://www.20thcenturymaps.com
Road map collector, expert, dealer; more than 12,000 different oil companies, official state and miscellaneous road maps from almost every year of 20th c.; for cartographers, history buffs, genealogists, collectors, etc.

David Schul
2214 Princeton Blvd.
Lawrence, KS 66049
ph: 785-864-5143
dave@roadmaps.org
Dealer and expert looking for official road maps, road atlases, highway maps (all states and provinces) and pre-1940 road atlases (any publisher).

Shell

Collectors

Jim Hollabaugh
3800 Congress Parkway
P.O. Box 460
Richfield, OH 44286-0460
ph: 330-659-3888 or 800-662-6344
fax: 330-659-9410
Wants to buy Shell & Frontier petroliana: containers, globes, signs, toys, promotional items, shell pocket watches with fobs; specializes in Shell and Frontier.

Texaco

Collectors

Richard Eaves
9838 Rustic Gate Rd.
La Porte, TX 77571-4100
ph: 281-470-2191
Wants Texaco toys, literature, memorabilia.

Ed Smith
Texaco Collector's Resource, The
P.O. Box 1086
Scappoose, OR 97056
ed@texacollector.com
http://www.texacollector.com
Major collector of Texaco memorabilia; Web site has interesting facts, images, reproductions, events for collectors, and more.

Dealers

Cecil Buchanan
1589 Curfman Rd.
Greensboro, NC 27455
ph: 336-288-3780
fax: 336-288-2745
Wants to buy pre-1950 Texaco advertising items.

GAUGES

(see also GAS STATION COLLECTIBLES; INSTRUMENTS & DEVICES; STEAM-OPERATED, Models & Equipment)

Collectors

R. Bruce Cynar
10023 St. Clair's Retreat
Fort Wayne, IN 46825
ph: 260-489-5004
oldtchnlgy@msn.com
Wants all steam whistles and large brass steam gauges.

Steam

Experts

Brian Lerohl
29048 486th Ave.
Fairview, SD 57027-6204
ph: 605-987-5378
fax: 605-987-5378
boilers@dtgnet.com
Appraiser, collector and historian of fluid pressure gauges, especially Bourdon tube and diaphragm type steam gauges; also does gauge repairs.

Repair Services

Brian Lerohl
29048 486th Ave.
Fairview, SD 57027-6204
ph: 605-987-5378
fax: 605-987-5378
boilers@dtgnet.com
Appraiser, collector and historian of fluid pressure gauges, especially Bourdon tube and diaphragm type steam gauges; also does gauge repairs.

GEMS & JEWELRY

(see also NATIVE AMERICAN, Jewelry; BEADS; BOOKS, Reference [Gems/Jewelry]; CHATELAINES; COMBS & HAIR ACCESSORIES; COMPACTS; CRAFTS, Jewelry; CUFF LINKS; GOLD; DRESSER ITEMS, Hatpins & Hatpin Holders; IVORY; JADE; LAPIDARY; MINERAL SPECIMENS; WATCHES)

Appraisers

Karin Ann Esposito, ISA, GG, NJA
KAE Gemological Services, Inc.
9124 East Hope
Christiansted, VI 00820
ph: 340-778-6634
fax: 340-778-6634
kae@viaccess.net

Martin D. Haske, GG, ISA
Adamas Gemological Laboratory
P.O. Box 470828
Brookline Village, MA 02147-0828
ph: 617-232-5508
fax: 617-232-5508
adamas@gis.net

Judith Fineblit Anderson, GG, ISA
  CAPP
Bijoux Extraordinaire, Ltd.
P.O. Box 1424
Manchester, NH 03105-1424
ph: 603-624-8672
fax: 603-624-8673
judi@jewelryexpert.com
http://www.jewelryexpert.com
Appraises diamonds, colored gems, antique & period jewelry, and contemporary designer jewelry for insurance, estate, divorce, charitable donation, damage reports, expert witness testimony.

Trina McCandless, ISA CAPP
McCandless Custom Jewelry &
  Appraisal
567 Vauxhaul St. Ext.
Groton, CT 06340
ph: 860-443-3039
trina@unidial.com
http://www.mccandlessjewelry.com
ISA CAPP, GIA GG, NAJA, SNAG; specializes in gemology & gemstones, antique & period jewelry, custom jewelry; laser welding repair and restoration; appraisals for estate, insurance, etc.

Paul D. Indorf, ISA CAPP, GG
Peter Indorf Jewelers
1022 Chapel St.
New Haven, CT 06510-2412
ph: 203-776-4833 or 860-526-3043
fax: 203-777-8423
paulindorf@snet.net
http://www.peterindorf.com

Richard Henion, ISA
Another Facet
150 W. Pleasant
Maywood, NJ 07607-1335
ph: 201-368-9433 or 800-992-4410
fax: 201-368-9337
rich@anotherfacet.com
http://www.anotherfacet.com
Appraisals of gems and jewelry for insurance, re-sale, estate liquidation, equitable distribution; appraisals done in conformance with The Uniform Standards of Professional Appraisal Practice.

Barbara R. Nevius, ISA, GG
106 Tower Hill Dr.
Red Bank, NJ 07701
ph: 732-345-0460 or 732-859-9194
fax: 732-345-0460
bjrn@att.net

David Wolf, ASA, GG
Just Appraisers
135 Columbia Turnpike, Ste. 202
Florham Park, NJ 07932
ph: 973-822-2222 or 212-812-7945 (NY)
fax: 973-236-9111
justappraisers@servenet.com
http://www.justappraisers.com
*Holds the designated title of Master
Gemologist Appraiser from the
American Society of Appraisers; a
Graduate Gemologist from the GIA;
USPAP certified in strict accordance
to The Appraisal Foundation;
consultant to Chubb & Sons.*

Karen J. Russo, G.G.
Karen Jocelyn, Inc.
792 Partridge Dr.
P.O. Box 6795
Bridgewater, NJ 08807
ph: 908-526-8440
fax: 908-526-8348
*Provides a full range of appraisal and
consultation services for studio/art
jewelry, antique/estate jewelry,
mineral specimens, and collector
gemstones; market research,
identification, photography,
provenance research, portable
services.*

Jerry Ehrenwald, GG, ISA
International Gemological Institute
579 5th Ave.
New York, NY 10017-1917
ph: 212-398-1700 or 212-398-1701
fax: 212-869-8047
igi@interport.net
http://www.igiworldwide.com
*Devoted to identification, authentica-
tion and valuation of gems and
jewelry from an unbiased point of
view; no buying or selling.*

Robert C. Aretz, ISA GG
Gem Appraisers & Consultants
608 5th Ave., Ste. 602
New York, NY 10020-2303
ph: 212-333-3122 or 800-318-5412
fax: 212-333-2281
robaretz@eclipse.net

Theodore Baer
Theodore M. Baer, Inc.
608 Fifth Ave., Ste. 706
New York, NY 10020-2303
ph: 212-245-6330
fax: 212-245-6331
baertm@aol.com
*Buys, sells, appraises estate and
previously owned contemporary and
antique jewelry.*

Barry Block, GG, NGJA, ASA
Jewelry Judge Ltd., The
Master Gemologist Appraiser
320 Old Country Rd., Ste. 204
Garden City, NY 11530
ph: 516-248-8130
fax: 516-248-5477
bblock@jewelryjudge.net
http://www.jewelryjudge.net
*Expert appraiser of all fields and
periods of fine jewelry; does not buy
or sell jewelry; work done on site*

*while you watch; offers a fully
computerized appraisal system for
gemologists.*

Paul Cassarino ISA CAPP, FGA
Gem Lab, The
4098 W. Henrietta Rd.
Rochester, NY 14623-5222
ph: 585-359-3900 or 888-356-4367
fax: 585-359-8932
paul@thegemlab.com
http://www.thegemlab.com
*Specializing in insurance and estate
appraisals of contemporary gold,
diamond and gemstone jewelry;
gemstone quality and price verification
consultation services; Certified
Gemological Laboratory.*

Paula Fox
P.O. Box 1697
Bensalem, PA 19020
ph: 215-639-8724
fax: 215-639-8124
paulafox@comcast.net
http://www.paulafoxappraisers.com

William Schuh, ISA, GIA GG
Independent Jewelry Appraisal Co.
124 Hunter Ct.
Wilmington, DE 19808-1978
ph: 302-239-2255
fax: 410-244-6169
appraisede@aol.com
*Specializes in the appraisal of
gemstones and jewelry.*

Pennye Jones-Napier, FGA, ISA
Jewellery Appraisal Sciences
236 Walnut St. NW
Washington, DC 20012-2157
ph: 202-291-5575 or 202-251-0494
fax: 202-318-0694
jas@triratna.com
http://www.threegemsinc.com/jas
*Appraiser specializing in vintage and
antique jewelry targeting the 19th and
20th centuries; contemporary Studio/
Design jewelers; also offers
consultation services for the brokerage
of jewelry and gemstones through
auction or private sales.*

Edwin W. Baker, Ex. VP
American Society of Appraisers
P.O. Box 17265
Washington, DC 20071
ph: 703-478-2228 or 800-272-8258
fax: 703-742-8471
asainfo@appraisers.org
http://www.appraisers.org
*The only appraisal organization in the
US representing all the disciplines of
appraisal specialists; call 800-ASA-
VALU for free referral or membership
directory, or visit Web site.*

Dan James, GG
Antique Jewelry Specialists
4212 Gallatin St.
Hyattsville, MD 20781-2049
ph: 301-779-3696
danjames34@hotmail.com
*Graduate gemologist, appraiser,
specialist in antique jewelry,
diamonds and colored gemstones;*

*Georgian to modern; gemological lab
on premises for appraisals and
evaluations; by appointment only.*

Thomas J. Terpilak, GG, ASA, AAA
Metro Gem Consultants
7315 Wisconsin Ave.
Bethesda, MD 20814-3202
ph: 301-654-0838 or 301-654-8678
*Gemological consultant and
professional jewelry appraiser.*

Barry Rogers, AAA, GAA
16650 Georgia Ave.
Olney, MD 20832
ph: 301-570-0779
frogers930@aol.com
*Appraising gems & jewelry for over
30 years; also appreciable and
depreciable residential contents.*

James Jolliff
National Association of Jewelry
  Appraisers, The
Newsletter: Jewelry Appraiser, The
P.O. Box 6558
Annapolis, MD 21401-0558
ph: 410-897-0889
*Members perform gem and jewelry,
silver flatware and holloware, and
watch valuations exclusively.*

James Jolliff
JEI Gemological Laboratory
P.O. Box 6558
Annapolis, MD 21401-0558
ph: 410-897-0889
*Appraises antique to contemporary
gems and jewelry, silver flatware and
holloware, and watches exclusively.*

Association of Online Appraisers, Inc.
P.O. Box 2049
Frederick, MD 21702-1049
ph: 301-228-2279
fax: 301-695-6491
info@AOAonline.org
http://www.AOAonline.org
*Not-for-profit association for online
as well as traditional appraisers;
establishes standards of appraisal
ethics & professional practice; offers
550+ page "Complete Online Course
in Personal Property Appraising" free
to members.*

Kim Decker Hammer
Heirlooms, Inc.
792 N. Stratford Rd.
Winston Salem, NC 27104
ph: 336-725-1036
dhammer@triad.rr.com
Graduate Gemologist (GIA).

Joette Humphrey
329 N. Main St.
Hendersonville, NC 28792
ph: 828-698-8485 or 828-692-3615
fax: 828-693-4305
joette@shelleysauction.com
http://www.shelleysauction.com
*Specializes in the appraisal of
diamonds, antique and estate jewelry,
pearls, gemstones.*

Joette Humphrey, GG
Shelley's Jewelry/Shelley's Auction
  Gallery
429 N. Main St.
Hendersonville, NC 28792-4903
ph: 828-698-8485 or 828-692-3615
fax: 828-693-4305
joette@shelleysauction.com
http://www.shelleysauction.com
*Buy, consign and auction antiques and
collectibles with a heavy emphasis on
antique jewelry and diamonds.*

Bill Lerner
Lerner Jewelry, Inc.
6065 Roswell Rd., Ste. 750
Atlanta, GA 30328
ph: 404-231-2277
fax: 404-233-1556
blerner@carsljco.com
http://www.carsljco.com
*Offers jewelry appraisals, sales,
repair, reproduction; third generation
jeweler; GIA graduate gemologist
since 1982; training with the
American Gem Society; Affiliate
member of the ISA.*

Karen Gross
Possessions
1830 Bay Dr.
Miami, FL 33141
ph: 305-861-3718
kgross1605@aol.com
*Dealer and appraiser of gems and
jewelry.*

Rose & Lornie Mueller, ISA, GG
Lithos Jewelry
344 Corey Ave.
Saint Petersburg, FL 33706
ph: 727-367-9010
fax: 727-367-9011
lithos@tampabay.rr.com
http://www.lithosjewelry.com
*High-end jewelry dealer; trained and
accredited appraisers.*

Jo Anne Whitteaker, ISA CAPP, GG
American Appraisal Diamond & Gem
  Lab
19727 Gulf Blvd., Ste. 204
Roselle Park, NJ 33785
ph: 727-596-6900 or 888-288-5432
fax: 757-596-1223
appraise@tampabay.rr.com
*Professional gemological examina-
tions, grading, appraisals, fraudulent
claims investigations, expert witness;
appraisals for casualty loss, insurance
replacement, liquidation, damage,
equitable distribution, donation,
estate, etc.*

Melissa Brookes, ISA, GG
D & M Diamonds & Appraisals
P.O. Box 8924
Port Saint Lucie, FL 34985-8924
ph: 561-879-0814
fax: 561-879-0814
dmdia@aol.com

362

Angelia D. Miller, ISA, GG
Raul Haas Jewelers
2709 Erie Ave.
Cincinnati, OH 45208-2103
ph: 513-321-7679 or 800-797-7285
fax: 513-321-3074
admgg@aol.com
*Specializing in appraisals of antique
and modern jewelry, diamond
grading, insurance reports, estate
appraisals.*

Pamela L. Hickman, ISA, GG
International Diamond & Gold Design
4026 E. 82nd St.
Indianapolis, IN 46250-4209
ph: 317-578-4653 or 800-626-5398
fax: 317-578-9335
info@idgd.com
http://www.idgd.com
*Specializes in gems, jewelry,
diamonds, colored stones, gold,
platinum, pearls, and estate and
custom jewelry.*

Charles M. Ellias, GG, ISA CAPP
Astrein's Fine Jewelry
120 W. Maple Rd.
Birmingham, MI 48009-3322
ph: 248-644-1651 or 586-704-7055
fax: 248-644-7477
cmeggisa@aol.com
http://www.ggappraiser.com
*Full appraisal services, consultations,
diamond, colored gemstone and pearl
grading reports, insurance claims
settlements, diamond and colored
gemstone recutting and salvage
services, custom design jewelry and
full manufacturing facility.*

Betty Trybuski
Suburban Appraisal Services
31300 Plymouth Rd.
Livonia, MI 48150
ph: 313-207-8227
fax: 313-937-1142
BTsJewelry@aol.com
*Accredited Member ISA, GIA
Gemologist providing jewelry
appraisal and repair services.*

Katherine Vandygriff, GG,ISA CAPP
Katherine's
501 Hogan Court
Muscatine, IA 52761
kkvgriff@attbi.com
*Professional, independent gems &
jewelry appraiser.*

Brant Laird
Brant Laird Antiques & Appraisals
2901 N. Henderson Ave.
Dallas, TX 75206-6402
ph: 214-823-4100
fax: 214-823-4108
blaird2@earthlink.net
*Accredited Member of the ISA,
Graduate Gemologist; specializes in
the appraisal of jewelry, 18th and
19th century furniture, art objects and
accessories.*

Alan Winston
Winston Studio & Imports
4448 West Lovers Lane
Dallas, TX 75209
ph: 214-357-0081 or 214-824-2842
fax: 214-821-8583
wsimports@aol.com
http://www.alanwinstonsmith.com
*Specializes in the appraisal of fine
gemstones and jewelry; BFA UT 1965
minor in jewelry, studied under
George Lacmman who was an
assistant of Georg Jensen; experienced
expert witness.*

Margaret C. Gronberg, ISA, GG
M. Gronberg Appraisal Services, Inc.
5924 Royal Lane, Ste. 170
Dallas, TX 75230
ph: 214-369-5361
fax: 214-369-5374
jgallery@dallas.net
*Specializes in the appraisal of gems &
Jewelry.*

Richard I. Pongratz, GG, ISA, ASA
Richard Pongratz Appraisal Services Inc.
3105 Ira E. Woods Ave., Ste. 130
PMB 170
Grapevine, TX 76051
ph: 817-545-6696 or 817-247-0821
fax: 817-545-6688
appraisal-services@att.net
*Provides contract appraisal services to
jewelers.*

Shelley Sandler, ISA, GG
S. Sandler, Appraiser of Fine Jewelry
21 Briar Hollow Ln., #306
Houston, TX 77027
ph: 713-355-3552
fax: 888-727-7269
shelley@wt.net
*Appraiser, consultant and experienced
expert witness specializing in
diamonds, gems and jewelry.*

Ben Gordon
1900 West Loop South, #960
Houston, TX 77027
ph: 713-961-1432 or 713-623-6111
fax: 713-961-5539
bgordon@jewelryjudge.net
http://www.jewleryjudge.net/gordon.htm

Steven Silver
Jewelry Appraisal Services
2425 West Loop South, Ste. 600
Houston, TX 77027
ph: 713-622-9070
fax: 713-622-9303
smsilver@swbell.net
http://www.jewelryappraisalservices.com
*A gemological lab staffed by GIA
gemologists providing appraisals for
insurance, estate, probate, liquidation
and dissolution of property; sells GIA
and EGL certified diamonds;
manufactures custom designed fine
jewelry; broker services.*

Amy J. Lawch, ISA, GG
A.A. Benjamin Ltd.
2200 Post Oak Blvd., #101
Houston, TX 77056
ph: 713-965-0555 or 713-965-0660
fax: 713-965-0222
aabenltd@netropolis.net
*Specializes in fine antique and estate
jewelry; offers repairs and appraisals
for all fine jewelry and watches
including work for estate and
insurance; also custom design and
antique wedding jewelry.*

Karen Jensen
3511 Shadowfern Dr.
Houston, TX 77082
ph: 281-558-1591 or 281-217-1636
fax: 281-589-1397
loupe@kjappraisals.com
http://www.kjappraisals.com
*Offers well-researched, accurate
jewelry appraisals; by appointment
only.*

Rudy M. Pena, ISA, GIA GG
Pena & Associates
7330 San Pedro Ave., Ste. 175
San Antonio, TX 78216-6257
ph: 210-349-4367
fax: 210-366-1802
pena544@world-net.net
http://www.appraisalsbypena.com
*Specializes in the appraisal of gems,
jewelry, diamonds, pearls, estate
jewelry.*

Anne Hawken, GG, ASA
Anne Hawken Gems
P.O. Box 160906
Austin, TX 78716-0906
ph: 512-328-9411
agx@earthlink.net
*Buys, sells, brokers, and appraises
fine and collectible gemstones; also
collection consultant, expert witness,
educator; Accredited Senior Appraiser
(ASA), AGA-Certified Gem Laboratory.*

Mary Weber, ISA, NAJA
Five Star Jewelry Appraisers
3636 Bee Cave Rd., Ste. 106
Austin, TX 78746
ph: 512-328-4367 or 512-329-8888
fax: 512-328-2164
mary@fivestarjewelers.com
http://www.fivestarjewelers.com
*Senior certified appraiser with the
National Association of Jewelry
Appraises and a gemologist from the
Gemological Institute of America;
specializes in estate and period
jewelry appraisals.*

Neil Bety
American Gem Registry, Inc.
451 E. 58th Ave., #2535-231
Denver, CO 80216
ph: 303-223-4944
fax: 720-528-8043
neil@gemlab1.com
http://www.gemlab1.com
*An independent AGA accredited
gemological laboratory; member of the
International Society of Appraisers;*
*diamond grading, diamond
certificates, stone identification,
Gemprint registration.*

Sharon Wakefield
Northwest Gemological Lab
P.O. Box 8243
Boise, ID 83707-2243
ph: 208-362-3938
fax: 208-362-2889
sharon@gem-science.com
http://www.gem-science.com
*Noted expert, appraiser, lecturer and
author specializing in the appraisal of
diamonds, gems and jewelry.*

LaVerne Larson, GG (GIA)
Gemological & Appraisal Services
1120 E. Mead Dr.
Chandler, AZ 85249
ph: 480-802-8092
l-m-larson-gg@worldnet.att.net
*Independent appraiser of gemstones
and jewelry; insurance, hypothetical,
estate, fair market value appraisals;
also special services such as stone
plots/diagrams, fully descriptive lists
for inheritance/gift designations,;
NAJA Certified.*

Larry Phillips, GG, ISA
Phillips & Associates
P.O. Box 51327
Albuquerque, NM 87181-1327
ph: 505-299-7999
fax: 505-299-7999
phillips@gemologist-appraiser.com
*Master Gemologist Appraiser;
specializes in Native American
jewelry.*

Joanna S. Stearns, ISA CAPP, GG
J. Stearns & Associates
7412 Silver Palm Ave.
Las Vegas, NV 89117-1442
ph: 702-360-8991
fax: 702-360-8938
joannastearns@earthlink.net
*Specializes in the appraisal of fine
art, residential contents, and gems &
jewelry.*

Robert F. Trapp, ISA CAPP, GG
Robert F. Trapp Gemological Services
P.O. Box 33397
Las Vegas, NV 89133-3397
ph: 702-363-0991
fax: 702-363-8725
bobtrapp@lvcm.com
http://www.trappgem.com

Gina D'Onofria, FGAA, ISA
GinaJewels
9615 Brighton Way
Beverly Hills, CA 90210
ph: 310-273-8471
ginala@earthlink.net
http://www.ginajewels.com
*Specializes in diamond grading,
gemstone and jewelry authentication,
and in the appraisal of watches and
jewelry; Accredited Member of the
Inter. Soc. of Appraisers.*

Danusia Niklewicz, ISA CAPP, GG
Paradise & Associates
23852 Pacific Coast Hwy. PMB 549
Malibu, CA 90265-4879
ph: 310-829-5286
fax: 310-829-5286
http://www.paradiseassociates.com

Stuart Locascio, ISA, GG
Appraisal Service, The
18645 Sherman Way, #111
Reseda, CA 91335
ph: 818-343-9016
fax: 818-343-5320
DiamondShoppe@ev1.net
http://www.DiamondShoppe.com

Norman K. Monteau
AIG Labs/Monteau Gemological Services
21250 Califa St., #203
Woodland Hills, CA 91367
ph: 818-712-9750
fax: 818-712-9755
aig-labs@pacbell.net
Offers appraisals and laboratory grading for diamonds and colored stones.

Cameron Pelle
Monteau Gemological Services
21250 Califa St., Ste. 203
Woodland Hills, CA 91367
ph: 818-712-9750
fax: 818-712-9755
Graduate gemologist appraiser, expert witness, gems & jewelry evaluations and appraisals.

Jennifer Thornton-Davis, ISACAPP
In Depth Appraisals
P.O. Box 56591
Van Nuys, CA 91411
ph: 818-988-5583
fax: 818-988-4341
indepth260@earthlink.net
http://www.indepthappraisals.com
Appraisals of fine jewelry; offers researched value conclusions; Graduate Gemologist (GIA); ISA Certified Appraiser of Personal Property; ASA Master Gemologist Appraiser.

Diana Sanders
Specialty Appraisals
P.O. Box 17461
Encino, CA 91416
ph: 877-255-5445
fax: 805-496-9843
dlsanders@earthlink.net
http://www.specialtyappraisals.com
Certified gemologist, appraiser and lecturer, specializing in 19th and 20th century fine and costume jewelry.

Diana Sanders
Specialty Appraisals
P.O. Box 17461
Encino, CA 91416
ph: 877-255-5445
dlsanders@earthlink.net
http://www.specialtyappraisals.com
Certified gemologist with an AA in gemology from Santiago Canyon College; certificate in pearl grading from GIA; graduated from College for

Appraisers; has taught "Antique & Collectible Jewelry" as well as "Antique Metals" courses.

Thom Underwood, ISA, GG
San Diego Gemological Labs
1851 San Diego Ave.
San Diego, CA 92110
ph: 619-286-6614
fax: 619-286-7541
thomu@cox.net
http://www.sdgemlab.com
Provides gemological and valuation services for the purpose of insurance, probate, post loss assessment and expert witness needs; Member of ISA, NGJA, and is a Master Gemologist Appraiser with the American Society of Appraisers.

Rene Johnson
Accredited Gemological Appraisals
24681 La Plaza, Ste. 220
Dana Point, CA 92629
ph: 949-903-8841 or 949-933-0144
rene.johnson@cox.net
http://www.AGemAppraisals.com
Graduate Gemologist through the Gemological Institute of America (GIA), Accredited Member of the International Society of Appraisers; jewelry and watch appraisals for insurance and estate.

Polina Vasilevskaya
5542 Geary Blvd.
San Francisco, CA 94121
ph: 415-752-5546 or 415-412-7843
fax: 415-752-5721
polina@torgsyn.com
Specializes in the appraisal of gems and jewelry as well as in Russian and European antique jewelry, silver and porcelain.

Nancy Stacy, ASA, GG
Jewels by Stacy Appraisals
712 Bancroft, #436
Walnut Creek, CA 94598-1531
ph: 925-939-4367
nancy@appraiser.net
http://www.jewelry-appraisal.com
Over 20 years; appraisals for insurance, claims, equitable distribution, liquidation, estates, trusts, conservatorships, etc.; forensic gemologist; litigation support, experienced in expert testimony; ASA Master Gemologist Appraiser.

Susan Bickford
Pacific Gemological Services
PMB 118, 38 Miller Ave.
Mill Valley, CA 94941
ph: 415-381-5642
fax: 415-380-1922
pacgems@yahoo.com
Specializes in on-site appraisals of gems & jewelry making use of a portable gemological lab; appraisals of contemporary or vintage jewelry for estate or insurance purposes.

Brenda Reichel, ISA, GG, NGJA
Carats & Karats Fine Jewelry
1254 S. King St.
Honolulu, HI 96814
ph: 808-593-8122 or 877-593-8122
fax: 808-591-9124
flawless@lava.net
http://www.caratsandkarats.com
Specializes in appraising, buying and selling diamonds, gold, ivory, jade, mineral specimens, pearls, silver, and Hawaiian shell jewelry (Niihau shells).

International Society of Appraisers
Newsletter: Professional Appraisers
Information Exchange
1131 SW 7th St., Ste. 105
Renton, WA 98055
ph: 206-241-0359 or 888-472-4732
fax: 206-241-0436
ISA@isa-appraisers.org
http://www.isa-appraisers.org
Largest assoc. of professional appraisers devoted solely to personal property; over 1,300 members specializing in all areas of antiques & residential contents, gems & jewelry, fine art, machinery & equipment; member directory on Web site.

Karen Lorene, ISA, NAJA
Facere Jewelry Art Gallery
1420 5th Ave., #108
Seattle, WA 98101-2333
ph: 206-624-6768
fax: 206-624-2852
facereart@aol.com
http://www.facerejewelryart.com
Over thirty years of experience in the world of antique jewelry and modern jewelry art; author of "Buying Antique Jewelry: Skipping the Mistakes."

Deborah Wieditz, G.G.
Sterling Gemological Services Inc.
P.O. Box 2600
Everett, WA 98203
ph: 425-347-4721 or 425-343-gems
fax: 425-347-4731
sterling.gemserv@verizon.net
http://www.sterlinggemological.com
Graduate Gemologist with over 23 years of experience in the jewelry industry; Associate Member of the International Society of Appraisers and a member of the GIA Alumni Association.

Vince C. Rundhaug, ISA, GG
Columbia Gem & Jewelry
8390 W. Gage Blvd., Ste. 105
Kennewick, WA 99336-8105
ph: 509-783-6363
fax: 509-783-0211
vrundhaug@aol.com
Specializing in natural fancy colored diamonds, forensic gemology, investigatory gemology, insurance valuation issues.

James Poag, GG, ISA CAPP
James O. Poag Jewellers, Ltd.
94 Frank St.
P.O. Box 39
Strathroy, Ontario N7G 3J1 Canada
ph: 519-245-1040 or 519-245-1580
fax: 519-245-6073
james@poags.com
http://www.poags.com
ISA appraiser certified in gems & jewelry, and in antique & period jewelry; also sells and restores new and estate jewelry; four goldsmiths on staff, as well as a GIA Graduate Gemologist.

Gary Coyle, MGGA
Coyle's Jewellery & Gifts, Ltd.
5876 Wyandotte St. East
Windsor, Ontario N8S 1MB Canada
ph: 519-945-1969
gcoyle@mnsi.net
Appraiser and retailer of contemporary jewelry.

Debra Sawatzky, ISA CAPP
21 Dundas Square
Toronto, Ontario M5BG 1B7 Canada
ph: 416-362-9011
sawatzky@attcanada.ca
Certified Appraiser of Personal property through the International Society of Appraisers with a specialty study in antique, period and estate jewelry; Accredited Appraiser through the Canadian Jewelers Institute.

Auction Services

Gloria Lieberman
Skinner, Inc.
63 Park Plaza
The Heritage on the Garden
Boston, MA 02116
ph: 617-350-5400
fax: 617-350-5429
info@skinnerinc.com
http://www.skinnerinc.com
Established in 1971, Skinner Inc. is the fourth largest auction house in the US; has offices in Boston and Bolton, MA.

Sotheby's
1334 York Ave.
New York, NY 10021
ph: 212-606-7000
fax: 212-606-7107
http://www.sothebys.com
Over 70 collecting areas are featured at Sotheby's auctions including toys, dolls, porcelain, furniture, silver, art, books; exhibitions are free and everyone is welcome; for a free copy of "Sotheby's Newsletter," call 212-606-7245.

John S. Weschler
Weschler's
909 E. St. NW
Washington, DC 20004-2006
ph: 202-628-1281 or 800-331-1430
fax: 202-628-2366
fineart@weschlers.com
http://www.weschlers.com
*Specializes in the auction sale of
jewelry, coins, and watches.*

Joette Humphrey, GG
Shelley's Jewelry/Shelley's Auction
  Gallery
429 N. Main St.
Hendersonville, NC 28792-4903
ph: 828-698-8485 or 828-692-3615
fax: 828-693-4305
joette@shelleysauction.com
http://www.shelleysauction.com
*Buy, consign and auction antiques and
collectibles with a heavy emphasis on
antique jewelry and diamonds.*

Joseph Mackley
Mackley & Company
9724 Kingston Pike, Ste. 1012
Knoxville, TN 37922
ph: 423-693-3097
joseph@mackley.com
http://www.mackley.com
*Online and live auction sales of gems
& jewelry, pocket watches, enameled
jewelry, estate jewelry, silver, chiming
watches, gold watch fobs, gold
charms, etc.; also buys.*

Joseph DuMouchelle, G.G.
Joseph DuMouchelle Fine & Estate
  Jewelry Auctions
5 Kercheval Ave.
Grosse Pointe Farms, MI 48236
ph: 313-884-4800 or 800-475-4367
fax: 313-884-7662
info@dumouchelleauction.com
http://www.dumouchelleauction.com
*Specializes in the sale of fine and
estate jewelry and small objects of art;
large diamonds and colored; also
Russian objects of art.*

Clubs/Associations

Manufacturing Jewelers & Silversmiths
  of America, Inc.
Magazine: American Jewelry Manufacturer
One State St., 6th Floor
Providence, RI 02908
ph: 401-274-3840 or 800-444-6572
fax: 401-274-02665
mjsa@mjsainc.com
http://mjsa.polygon.net
*A national trade association for the
jewelry manufacturing industry; for
jewelry manufacturers, goldsmiths and
silversmiths, casters, refiners,
electroplaters, gemstone dealers,
findings manufacturers, suppliers,
sales reps.*

Master Jewelers & Suppliers of America
Magazine: American Jewelry Manufacturer
One State St.
Providence, RI 02908-5035
ph: 401-274-3840
fax: 401-274-0265
mjsa@mjsainc.com
http://www.mjsainc.com
*A jewelry trade association; the
monthly glossy trade publication
contains industry articles, ads for
jewelry manufacturing goods and
services.*

International Colored Gemstone
  Association
3 East 48th St., 5th Floor
New York, NY 10017
ph: 212-688-8452
fax: 212-688-9006
ica@gemstone.org
http://www.gemstone.org
*Represents the international gemstone
industry (miners, cutters, wholesalers); working to increase the
understanding, appreciation of
colored gemstones worldwide; Web
site with great information for the
public; members are trade only.*

Jewelry Information Center
52 Vanderbilt Ave., 19th Floor
New York, NY 10017
ph: 800-459-0130 or 646-658-0240
fax: 646-658-0245
info@jic.org
http://www.jewelryinfo.org
*A trade association founded in 1946
to provide public relations for the
entire jewelry industry; provides
consumers with information about fine
jewelry, how to buy, how to care for
it, its history, and new product trends.*

Jewelers of America, Inc.
52 Vanderbilt Ave., 19th Floor
New York, NY 10017
ph: 800-223-0673 or 646-658-0246
info@jewelers.org
http://www.jewelers.org
*A national association of retail
jewelers; part of their mission is to
provide consumers with information
and education about fine jewelry; Web
site offers information on how to
select a jeweler, consumer news, test
your jewelry knowledge.*

American Society of Jewelry Historians
Newsletter: ASJH Newsletter
1333A North Ave., Box 103
New Rochelle, NY 10804
ph: 914-235-0983
fax: 914-235-0983
info@jewelryhistorians.com
http://www.jewelryhistorians.com
*Promotes education and appreciation
of antique jewelry, crossing all
periods from ancient to present;
quarterly newsletter informs members
of related lectures, exhibitions, and
book reviews; also publishes a
periodic journal.*

Lucille Tempesta
Vintage Fashion & Costume Jewelry
  Club
Newsletter: VFCJ Newsletter
P.O. Box 265
Glen Oaks, NY 11004-0265
ph: 718-939-3095
fax: 718-939-7988
VFCJ@aol.com
http://www.lizjewel.com/vf

Bob Mitchell
Society of North American Goldsmiths
Journal: Metalsmith
710 East Ogden Ave., Ste. 600
Naperville, IL 60563-8603
ph: 630-579-3272
fax: 630-369-2488
DSinger@SNAGmetalsmith.org
http://www.snagmetalsmith.org
*An association for jewelers and metal
artisans; quarterly magazine devoted
to the development and appreciation
for the craft of fine metalsmithing:
jewelry, decorative art, etc.*

Robert Bridel, Ex. Dir.
American Gem Society
8881 West Saraha Ave.
Las Vegas, NV 89117
ph: 702-255-6500
fax: 702-255-7420
http://www.ags.org
*Founded in 1934 to protect consumers
in their purchases of fine jewelry.*

Gemological Institute of America
5345 Armada Dr.
Carlsbad, CA 92008
ph: 760-603-4000 or 800-421-7250
fax: 760-603-4266
pr@gia.edu
http://www.gia.edu
*An independent nonprofit organization
recognized as the world's foremost
authority in the grading and
identification of diamonds, gemstones
and pearls; protects the interests of
the jewelry industry and consumer
alike.*

Accredited Gemologists Association
Journal: Cornerstone
888 Brannan St., Ste. 1175
San Francisco, CA 94103
president@AccreditedGemologists.org
http://www.accreditedgemologists.org
*Professional association of gemstone
experts, quality grading laboratories,
appraisers, and dealers; all
professional members are advanced,
degree-holding gemologists,
subscribing to a strong code of ethics
and professional practice.*

Myra McKeen
Canadian Jewellers Association
Newsletter: CJA News
27 Queen St. East, Ste. 600
Toronto, Ontario M5C 2M6 Canada
ph: 416-368-7616 or 800-580-0942
fax: 416-368-1986
cja@canadianjewellers.com
http://canadianjewellers.com
*A professional association with a
membership that is obligated to*

*maintain the highest level of personal
integrity, honesty and business ethics.*

W. Wight, Ed.
Canadian Gemmological Association
Magazine: Canadian Gemmologist, The
1767 Ave. Rd.
North York, Ontario M5M 3Y8 Canada
ph: 416-785-0962 or 877-244-3090
fax: 416-785-9043
info@canadiangemmological.com
http://www.canadiangemmological.com
*A non-profit educational institution
which teaches gemmology; founded in
1958; affiliated with the
Gemmological Association and Gem
Testing Laboratory of Great Britain;
magazine published quarterly.*

Canadian Institute of Gemmology
Newsletter: Gemmology Canada
P.O. Box 57010
Vancouver, British Columbia V5K 5G6
  Canada
ph: 604-530-8569
fax: 604-530-8569
wolf@cigem.ca
http://www.cigem.ca
*Offers members training courses,
information exchange, electronic
library of gems, and more.*

Gemmological Association & Gem
  Testing Laboratory of Great Britain
27 Greville St., 1st Floor
London, EC1N 8TN U.K.
ph: +44 (0)207 404 3334
fax: +44 (0)207 404 8843
gagtl@btinternet.com
http://www.gagtl.ac.uk/gagtl
*Offers correspondence and in-
residence classes in gemology.*

Dealers

Judith Fineblit Anderson, GG, ISA
  CAPP
Bijoux Extraordinaire, Ltd.
P.O. Box 1424
Manchester, NH 03105-1424
ph: 603-624-8672
fax: 603-624-8673
judi@jewelryexpert.com
http://www.jewelryexpert.com
*Buys, sells, brokers fine quality
antique and estate jewelry, contemporary designer jewelry, diamonds and
colored gemstones; also custom design
and restorations of antique jewelry;
appraisal services; lecturer on jewelry.*

Antoinette Matlins
Antoinette Leonard Matlins, PG
P.O. Box 237
Woodstock, VT 05091
ph: 802-457-5145
fax: 802-457-5191
AMatlins@aol.com
*Internationally respected gemologist
and jewelry expert, author and
lecturer; dedicated consumer advocate;
popular media guest and has been
seen on ABC, CBS, NBC, and CNN;
also seeks fine, rare or unusual gems
and jewels for clients.*

Elissa Cohen ISA CAPP, GG
Suburban Jewelers
126 East Front St.
Plainfield, NJ 07060-1202
ph: 908-756-1774 or 800-272-1315
fax: 908-756-6596
lisa@suburbanjewelers.com
http://www.suburbanjewelers.com
Dealer and appraiser of modern and period jewelry, GIA Graduate Gemologist, Certified Member of the ISA, appraiser of diamonds, gemstones, pearls, jewelry.

S.J. Moore
5 E. Genesee St.
Skaneateles, NY 13152-1317
ph: 315-685-8758
moore90w@adelphia.net
Buys and sells fine jewelry and diamonds, ruby, sapphire, emeralds.

Paul Cassarino ISA CAPP, GG
Gem Lab, The
4098 W. Henrietta Rd.
Rochester, NY 14623-5222
ph: 585-359-3900 or 888-356-4367
fax: 585-359-8932
paul@thegemlab.com
http://www.thegemlab.com
Diamonds, gemstones, cultured pearls, gold and platinum jewelry, estate jewelry; custom-made jewelry and jewelry restoration services.

Dan James, GG
Antique Jewelry Specialists
4212 Gallatin St.
Hyattsville, MD 20781-2049
ph: 301-779-3696
danjames34@hotmail.com
Buys and sells diamonds and colored stone jewelry, antique to 1940s; including platinum, enameled and costume jewelry.

Tony Laughter
Perry's at SouthPark
SouthPark Mall
4400 Sharon Rd.
Charlotte, NC 28211
ph: 704-364-1391
Deals in fine, antique and estate jewelry; Accredited Member of the International Society of Appraisers.

Chris & John Evans
Evans & Son Fine Jewelers
250 South Beach St.
Daytona Beach, FL 32114
ph: 904-255-5922
Dealer and appraiser of fine jewelry.

John Almasi
Salon Gems
2901 Vassar St.
P.O. Box 3345
Melbourne, FL 32901
ph: 407-725-8740
fax: 407-725-8740
Specializing in fine gemstones and gold products, including, but not limited to bullion, diamonds, alexandrite, and finished gold jewelry.

Rose & Lornie Mueller, ISA, GG
Lithos Jewelry
344 Corey Ave.
Saint Petersburg, FL 33706
ph: 727-367-9010
fax: 727-367-9011
lithos@tampabay.rr.com
http://www.lithosjewelry.com
High-end jewelry dealer; trained and accredited appraisers.

Jerry Forrest, GG, ISA CAPP
Jewelry Forrest, Inc.
9100 N. Central Expy., Ste. 185
Dallas, TX 75231-5901
ph: 214-368-5352 or 800-368-5376
fax: 214-750-1141
jerryforrest@compuserve.com
Custom jewelers and gemologists; an American Gem Society Accredited Gem Laboratory; Certified Member, ISA.

Robert Whiteside
Robert Whiteside Goldsmith
Rt. 1 Box 98
Mount Vernon, TX 75457
ph: 903-588-2402
mail@robertwhiteside.com
http://www.robertwhiteside.com
A master jeweler who specializes in recreating Faberge style jewelry and objects of art using original techniques including 19th century machinery to reproduce engine-turned enamel ware (guilloche); operates a school of jewelry.

Amy J. Lawch, ISA, GG
A.A. Benjamin Ltd.
2200 Post Oak Blvd., #101
Houston, TX 77056
ph: 713-965-0555 or 713-965-0660
fax: 713-965-0222
aabenltd@netropolis.net
Specializes in fine antique and estate jewelry; offers repairs and appraisals for all fine jewelry and watches including work for estate and insurance; also custom design and antique wedding jewelry.

Dottie A. Parliament
Timeless Treasurers, Inc.
4343 McCullough Ave.
San Antonio, TX 78212
ph: 210-829-7861
fax: 210-829-7862
Buys and sells diamonds and other quality gems; has an impressive collection of fine estate jewelry; gemologist and certified appraiser on the premises.

Robert E. Spomer
Buena Vista Gem Works
P.O. Box 476
Buena Vista, CO 81211
ph: 719-395-4327
respomer@buenavistagemworks.com
http://www.buenavistagemworks.com
A professional gem cutter by trade, specializing in custom collector's gemstones and fancy-cut jewelry grade stones; also collects and mines minerals and gems, especially in

Colorado; also collects Fairburn and other banded agates.

Anne Foster
1913 Hyde St.
San Francisco, CA 94109
ph: 415-776-8865
neilcalvin@aol.com
Wants Bakelite jewelry, bracelets, pins, necklaces, earrings, rings, etc.

Brenda Reichel, ISA, GG, NGJA
Carats & Karats Fine Jewelry
1254 S. King St.
Honolulu, HI 96814
ph: 808-593-8122 or 877-593-8122
fax: 808-591-9124
flawless@lava.net
http://www.caratsandkarats.com
Full service jewelry manufacturer; also appraises Niihau Shells and other items from the Pacific basin; Graduate Gemologist and Appraisers of jewelry, collectibles, knives; complete gemological laboratory on premises.

Ray L. Elsey
TradeShop Inc.
P.O. Box 40624
Portland, OR 97240-0624
ph: 800-224-8086 or 503-916-8688
fax: 503-226-6787
ray@tradeshop.com
http://www.tradeshop.com/master/lobby.html
A union professional fine jewelry trade shop, designing, building and servicing fine jewelry since 1974; refined working drawings, custom wax carving, special order manufacturing, platinum manufacturing, Celtic design bands.

James Poag, GG, ISA CAPP
James O. Poag Jewellers, Ltd.
94 Frank St.
P.O. Box 39
Strathroy, Ontario N7G 3J1 Canada
ph: 519-245-1040 or 519-245-1580
fax: 519-245-6073
james@poags.com
http://www.poags.com
Retail clock, jewellery, china and gift stores; staff includes 3 goldsmiths, 2 stone setters, watchmaker, clockmaker and ISA Certified Appraiser; largest selection of clocks in Ontario; in business since 1959.

Christopher Krokos
ThailandTradeNet.com
79/41 Moo 2 Highway
Chiang Mai, Doi Saket 50220 Thailand
ph: +66-53-867-497
fax: +66-53-867-497
webmaster@thailandtradenet.com
http://www.thailandtgradenet.com
Home of Thai gems & jewelry specializing in rare gems from Burma, Thailand and Africa: zircon, Burmese, Mongok and Mongshu rubies, Thai cabochon, star sapphires, African rubies, blue natural sapphire.

Experts

Judith Fineblit Anderson, GG, ISA CAPP
Bijoux Extraordinaire, Ltd.
P.O. Box 1424
Manchester, NH 03105-1424
ph: 603-624-8672
fax: 603-624-8673
judi@jewelryexpert.com
http://www.jewelryexpert.com
Buys, sells, brokers fine quality antique and estate jewelry, contemporary designer jewelry, diamonds and colored gemstones; also custom design and restorations; offers extensive consulting and appraisal services; lecturer on jewelry.

Antoinette Matlins
Antoinette Leonard Matlins, PG
P.O. Box 237
Woodstock, VT 05091
ph: 802-457-5145
fax: 802-457-5191
AMatlins@aol.com
Author of "Jewelry & Gems: The Buying Guide," and other books about pearls, diamonds, colored gemstones, and gem identification; a leading gem and jewelry expert, lecturer and educator; works as consultant to acquire rare gems & jewels.

William D. Hoefer, FGA, GG
Hoefers' Gemological Services
5016 Alan Ave., Ste. B4
San Jose, CA 95124-5741
ph: 408-264-0670
fax: 408-264-0725
editor@appraiserunderoath.com
http://www.appraiserunderoath.com
Specializes in the appraisal of gemstones, diamonds, and contemporary jewelry; also offers expert testimony for attorneys, court, etc.

Internet Resources

All About Jewels: Illustrated Dictionary of Jewelry
jewelrydictionary@allaboutjewels.com
http://www.allaboutjewels.com/jewel
Great descriptions and images of gems, jewelry and related terms.

John Kejr, Marketing Mngr.
Polygon, The Jewelry Industry WebCenter
First Bank Center, #201
P.O. Box 4806
Dillon, CO 80435
ph: 800-221-4425 or 970-468-1245
fax: 970-468-1247
sales@polygon.net
http://www.polygon.net
World's largest cluster of Web site-based online services for the jewelry industry; operated within a password-protected environment for trade-only communication; the public can find a local jeweler, and get tips for buying jewelry.

John Kejr, Marketing Mngr.
Tradelock.com
First Bank Center, #201
P.O. Box 4806
Dillon, CO 80435
ph: 800-221-4425 or 970-468-1245
fax: 970-468-1247
sales@polygon.net
http://www.polygon.net
*The jewelry industry's most complete
Web site search directory: equipment,
designer jewelry, clocks and watches,
materials, trade associations,
publications, trade shows, etc.*

Ray L. Elsey
TradeShop Inc.
P.O. Box 40624
Portland, OR 97240-0624
ph: 800-224-8086 or 503-916-8688
fax: 503-226-6787
ray@tradeshop.com
http://www.tradeshop.com/master/
 lobby.html
*Great Web site for consumer
information about gemstones; judging
cut, color, clarity, carat; how
gemstones are classified; gem
substitutes; grading; caring for your
gemstones; check out the jewelry Hall
of Shame.*

GemNet
P.O. Box 22
Victoria St.
Bourton-on-the-Water, The Cotswolds
 GL54 2ZA U.K.
ph: +44 1451 810595
fax: +44 1451 810594
info@gemnet.co.uk
http://www.gemnet.co.uk
*International gem links, online forum,
second hand jewelry, trade and press
associations, watch buying sources.*

Misc. Services

Cecilia Gardner, Ex. Dir.
Jewelers Vigilance Committee, Inc.
25 West 45th St., Ste. 400
New York, NY 10036
ph: 212-997-2002 or 800-JOIN-JVC
fax: 212-532-2217
clgjvc@aol.com
http://www.jvclegal.org
*The jewelry industry's guardian of
ethics and integrity; has published
"Recommended Minimum Guidelines
for Insurance Replacement Cost
Estimate Documentation for
Jewelers;" provides low cost dispute
mediation within the industry.*

Howard Rubin
GemDialogue Systems, Inc.
P.O. Box 7683
Rego Park, NY 11374-7683
ph: 718-997-0231
fax: 718-997-9057
gemdialog@aol.com
http://www.gemdialog.com
*GemDialogue is a gemstone
descriptive system for colored stones
and fancy colored diamonds; it gives
you visual comparison points for over*

*60,000 colors; a grading system is
also included.*

Holland Jewelry School
1034 Dawson Ave.
P.O. Box 882
Selma, AL 36702
ph: 800-469-8507 or 334-874-4245
fax: 334-872-3504
HollandSchool@Zebra.net
http://www.hollandjewelryschool.com
Offers training for jewelers.

Robert Whiteside
Robert Whiteside Goldsmith
Rt. 1 Box 98
Mount Vernon, TX 75457
ph: 903-588-2402
mail@robertwhiteside.com
http://www.robertwhiteside.com
*Operates a School of Jewelry
exploring the techniques of the
goldsmith/jeweler/designer, and a
School of Faberge for instruction in
the art of guilloche enamel.*

Gemological Institute of America
5345 Armada Dr.
Carlsbad, CA 92008
ph: 760-603-4000 or 800-421-7250
fax: 760-603-4266
pr@gia.edu
http://www.gia.edu
*Since 1931, GIA has been the most
respected source of gemological
education; courses in gemology &
jewelry manufacturing; Graduate
Gemologist (G.G.) diploma is
internationally recognized as the most
prestigious credential in the industry.*

GIA's Gem Trade Laboratory
5345 Armada Dr.
Carlsbad, CA 92008
ph: 760-603-4000 or 800-421-7250
fax: 760-603-4266
pr@gia.edu
http://www.gia.edu
*In 1953 the GIA created the
international diamond grading system,
now recognized by virtually every
professional jeweler in the world; GIA
offers gemstone grading and
identification services to the domestic
and international trade.*

Periodicals

James Pavia, Ed.
Magazine: National Jeweler
770 Broadway, 5th Floor
New York, NY 10003-9595
ph: 646-654-5080
info@nationaljeweler.com
http://www.nationaljeweler.com
*The most popular jewelry industry
resource; up-to-the-minute news twice
a month.*

Martin Rapaport, Pres.
Magazine: Rapaport Diamond Report
15 West 47th St.
New York, NY 10036
ph: 212-354-0575
fax: 212-840-0243
rap@diamonds.com
http://www.diamonds.com
*A weekly report of world wide activity
relating to diamonds, colored stones
and jewelry; price performances, cash
asking prices, precious metal prices,
actual transaction prices for diamonds
and diamond jewelry, etc.*

Cygnus Business Media, Inc.
Magazine: Modern Jeweler
45 Broad Hollow Rd.
Melville, NY 11747
ph: 631-845-2700
fax: 631-845-7109
tim.murphy@cygnuspub.com
http://www.modernjeweler.com
*Monthly trade magazine for the
jewelry industry.*

Morgan Beard, Ed.
PRIMEDIA Enthusiast Group
Magazine: Colored Stone
60 Chestnut Ave., Ste. 201
Devon, PA 19333-1312
ph: 610-294-6300 or 800-676-4336 (sub)
fax: 610-293-0977
cseditorial@primediasi.com
http://www.colored-stone.com
*The international reporter of the
gemstone trade; features also include
The Tucson Show Guide - a guide to
the largest US gemstone shows held
annually in Arizona; also The Fall
Show Guide, and the Vegas Show
Guide.*

Cahners Publishing
Magazine: JCK - Jewelers' Circular-
 Keystone
1018 West 19th St.
King Of Prussia, PA 19406
ph: 610-205-1122
fax: 610-205-1139
hschupak@cahners.com
http://www.jckgroup.com
*A monthly trade magazine focusing on
new and antique gems, jewelry, and
watches.*

Megan Watts
Gemworld International, Inc.
Magazine: Guide, The
630 Dundee Rd., Ste. 230
Northbrook, IL 60062
ph: 847-564-0555
fax: 847-564-0557
TheGuide@gemguide.com
http://www.gemguide.com
*"The Guide" is the industry standard
for wholesale diamond and colored
stone pricing; impartial and
extensively researched references are
easy to use; advisors are trusted
industry leaders.*

Gemological Institute of America
Magazine: Gems & Gemology
5345 Armada Dr.
Carlsbad, CA 92008
ph: 760-603-4000 or 800-421-7250
fax: 760-603-4266
pr@gia.edu
http://www.gia.edu
*Award-winning quarterly journal of
the GIA; publishes up-to-date technical
information about diamonds and
colored stones: where they are found,
their special characteristics, simulants
& synthetics, treatments, ID
techniques.*

Ornament, Inc.
Magazine: Ornament
P.O. Box 2349
San Marcos, CA 92079-2349
ph: 760-599-0222
fax: 760-599-0228
ornament@cts.com
http://www.ornamentmagazine.com
*A quarterly magazine focusing on
craft and art items of personal
adornment in any media or form:
fiber, glass, metal, ancient historic/
ethnic ornament; ethnographic and
tribal jewelry; also reviews of museum
exhibits and publications.*

Magazine: JQ Magazine
585 Fifth St. West
Sonoma, CA 95476
ph: 707-938-1082
fax: 707-935-6585
pfox@aip.com
http://www.jqmagazine.com
*The premier magazine for the
professional jeweler, jewelry designer
and jewelry manufacturer; for upscale
marketing of fine jewelry and luxury
Swiss watches.*

Carol Besler, Ed.
Magazine: Canadian Jeweller
555 Richmond St. W., Ste. 701
Toronto, Ontario M5V 3B1 Canada
ph: 416-203-6737
fax: 416-203-1057
carol@style.ca
http://www.canadianjeweller.com
*A bi-monthly glossy magazine focusing
on gems, jewelry and timepieces; trade
shows, business news, products and
services.*

Repair Services

Richard P. Hegeman
Hegeman & Co.
361 S. Main St.
Providence, RI 02903-2912
ph: 401-831-6812
*Cutters of all precious/semi-precious
stones; specializing in the repair &
restoration of all types of jewelry
(antique and contemporary); gemstone
replacements and repairs.*

Pat Morse
Edelstein & Morse Antique Jewelry
   Repair
62 Canaan Back Rd.
Barrington, NH 03825
ph: 603-664-2205
fax: 603-664-9699
pat@trunk.com
*Specializes in the fine repair and
restoration of antique jewelry,
hollowware and small objects of art
including gold, platinum, silver,
gemstones, diamonds.*

Mark S. Powell
A. Ludwig Klein & Son, Inc.
683 Sumneytown Pike
P.O. Box 145
Harleysville, PA 19438
ph: 215-256-9004 or 800-379-2929
fax: 215-256-9644
mark@aludwigklein.com
http://www.aludwigklein.com
*Specializing in the repair and
restoration of all types of glass, china
and porcelain as well as ivory, jade,
brass, pewter.*

Ray L. Elsey
TradeShop Inc.
P.O. Box 40624
Portland, OR 97240-0624
ph: 800-224-8086 or 503-916-8688
fax: 503-226-6787
ray@tradeshop.com
http://www.tradeshop.com/master/
lobby.html
*A union professional fine jewelry
trade shop, designing, building and
servicing fine jewelry since 1974; does
remanufacturings and restorations;
specializes in platinum.*

Suppliers

Stuart M. Matlins
GemStone Press
P.O. Box 237
Woodstock, VT 05091-0237
ph: 802-457-4000 or 800-962-4544
fax: 802-457-4004
everyone@longhillpartners.com
http://www.gemstonepress.com
*International source for books and
gem identification equipment and
other items designed to help people in
the gem trade and consumers learn
more about gems & jewelry.*

Amber

Dealers

Leslie Schwing
Amber Lady, The
P.O. Box 38109
Baltimore, MD 21231
ph: 410-342-1832
fax: 410-675-7565
amberlady@amberlady.com
http://amberlady.com/amberlady
*Features genuine 40-million-year-old
insects in polished honey colored
amber; also offers more traditional
amber jewelry such as neckware,
earrings, etc.*

Bakelite

Dealers

Karima Parry
Plastic Fantastic
info@plasticfantastic.com
http://www.plasticfantastic.com
*One of the largest sites of its kind on
the Internet, offering over 300 pieces
of vintage Bakelite, Lucite and
celluloid jewelry; also selected signed
designer costume jewelry; author of
"Collecting Bakelite Bangles Price &
ID Guide."*

Eve Lickver
P.O. Box 1778
San Marcos, CA 92079-1778
ph: 760-761-0868
*Dealer/collector buys and sells carved
and figural Bakelite jewelry, celluloid
and rhinestone bracelets; also wants
signed costume jewelry of 1920s
through 1950s including sterling and
enamel.*

Experts

Mary Hamburg
Tootsie's Antiques
20 Cedar Ave.
Danville, IL 61832-1525
ph: 217-446-2323 or 217-442-2725
tootsies@allarounddanville.com
*Specializes in antique costume jewelry,
especially Bakelite.*

Cameos

Dealers

Rita Perloff
Remember When Vintage
355 Summer St.
Bristol, NH 03222
ph: 603-744-2191
rewhen@tias.com
http://www.tias.com/stores/rewhen
*Features a wide range of vintage
carved shell cameos as well as cameos
of contemporary design.*

Jan Campbell
Cameo Heaven
3818 Atlanta Highway
Flowery Branch, GA 30542
ph: 770-965-9219
cameolady@mindspring.com
http://www.cameoheaven.com
*Specializes in hand carved shell
cameos dating back to 1840; many
rare scenes; also Victorian silver and
costume jewelry.*

Christmas

Dealers

Gerry Kempe
Carrie Richmond Antiques
P.O. Box 844
Barrington, IL 60011
ph: 847-428-1313
fax: 847-428-9824
antiques@carrie-richmond.com
http://www.carrie-richmond.com
*Inventory contains thousands of fine
pieces including a major collection of
Christmas jewelry.*

Billie & John McBride
South Texas Trading Company
P.O. Box 857
Port Aransas, TX 78373
ph: 361-749-6149 or 800-484-9293
   x3474
STFNandTRADING@centurytel.net
http://www.southtexastrading.com
*Specializing in the sale of vintage and
collectible costume jewelry,
specializing in Bakelite, Christmas
tree pins, and 20th century costume
jewelry; has 350-member online
jewelry group; nationwide pickers
available.*

Experts

Mary Morrison
ph: 503-648-7888
snowbaby@mail.com
Author of "Christmas Jewelry."

Kathy Flood
Jeweled Forest, The
P.O. Box 155
Kimmswick, MO 63053
ph: 636-461-0563
bizstyle@aol.com
http://www.christmastreepins.com
*Collector, dealer, researcher,
historian, expert specializing in
Christmas motif pins.*

Internet Resources

Kathy Flood
Jeweled Forest, The
P.O. Box 155
Kimmswick, MO 63053
ph: 636-461-0563
bizstyle@aol.com
http://www.christmastreepins.com
*The only all-Christmas-pins Web site
on the Internet; features antique,
vintage and contemporary jewelry with
holiday motifs, in addition to news
and information updates for
collectors.*

Computer Programs For

Appraisers

Megan Watts
Gemworld International, Inc.
Software: Guide Appraisal Software
630 Dundee Rd., Ste. 230
Northbrook, IL 60062
ph: 847-564-0555
fax: 847-564-0557
TheGuide@gemguide.com
http://www.gemguide.com
*A fast, accurate, effective appraisal
tool to assist you with your efficient
appraisal business; fully integrated
with diamond and colored gemstone
prices in "The Guide;" can build a
complete appraisal report with
minimal typing.*

Costume

Appraisers

Kathy Finch, ISA
5815 La Vista Court
Dallas, TX 75206
ph: 214-824-4684
klfelvis@aol.com
*Accredited member of the International
Society of Appraisers; appraises and
collects vintage and estate costume
jewelry.*

Linda H. Richard, ISA
Cajun Collection
3308 White Oak
Temple, TX 76502-3028
ph: 254-774-8608
cajun@vvm.com
http://www.vvm.com/~cajun
Buys, sells, appraises costume jewelry.

Diana Sanders
Specialty Appraisals
P.O. Box 17461
Encino, CA 91416
ph: 877-255-5445
fax: 805-496-9843
dlsanders@earthlink.net
http://www.specialtyappraisals.com
*Certified gemologist, appraiser and
lecturer, specializing in 19th and 20th
century fine and costume jewelry.*

Kathaleen Victor, ISA CAPP
Victor Appraisal Services
6356 138th Ave., N.E., #209
Redmond, WA 98052
ph: 425-882-9003
kathleenvictor@msn.com
http://groups.msn.com/
   VictorAppraisalServices
*Specializes in the appraisal of costume
jewelry including, but not limited to,
bone, ivory, jet, coral, amber,
celluloid, turquoise and Bakelite
jewelry.*

Collectors

Patti Vahary
Curious Cat, The
41 Crosby Dr.
Battle Creek, MI 49014
pattiv0204@aol.com
*Buys estate jewelry, especially costume
signed work and 1800s style jewelry;
also interested in Art Deco and
jewelry from the 1920s through 1940s.*

Dealers

Marilyn Ostrow
Terezi Vintage Costume Jewelry
ph: 508-335-6139
TereziB@aol.com
http://www.Terezi.com
*Vintage costume jewelry of the 1920s
to 1960s; specializing in glitz; also
vintage glass beads; member of
JewelCollect and Vintage Fashion &
Costume Jewelry Club.*

Andrea Maloney
Lochthyme Antiques
21 Anderson Ave., Apt. 7G
Middleboro, MA 02346
ph: 508-946-4654
lochthym@attbi.com
http://www.lochthyme.com
*Buys and sells vintage and designer
original costume jewelry including
one-of-a-kind designs: Andrea,
Bakelite, Lucite, sterling, copper,
rhinestones, etc.*

Elaine Kula
Antiquing On Line - Costume, Victorian
& Estate Jewelry
P.O. Box 7905
Nashua, NH 03060
ph: 603-888-7464
fax: 603-888-5648
webmistress@antiquingonline.com
http://www.antiquingonline.com
*Online catalog specializing in high
quality designer (Haskell, Eisenberg,
Trifari, Carnegie), Mexican,
Edwardian, Czech, Bakelite, antique,
and collectible vintage costume
jewelry, Victorian jewelry, estate
jewelry and accessories.*

Rita Perloff
Remember When Vintage
355 Summer St.
Bristol, NH 03222
ph: 603-744-2191
rewhen@tias.com
http://www.tias.com/stores/rewhen
*Specializes in costume jewelry ranging
from Victorian era pieces to
contemporary designs; features
cameos, Mexican & Scandinavian
sterling, unusual figural designs,
Bohemian glass beads, signed and
unsigned jewelry in all categories.*

Deborah J. Robinson
Vintage Jewelry & Collectibles
ph: 860-645-1525
vinjewels@aol.com
http://www.theplace2b.com/
    VintageJewels
*Appraiser, dealer, expert, collector,
repair person specializing in estate
and signed vintage jewelry from the
1850s to 1960s: pins, necklaces,
bracelets, rings, earrings by Trifari,
Vendome, Hobe, Hollycraft, Weiss,
Bakelite, etc.*

Belford
TwinklingJewels.com
2 Park Lane
New Milford, CT 06776
ph: 860-355-7707
DianeGem@aol.com
http://www.twinklingjewels.com
Costume jewelry appraiser and dealer.

Jan Gaughan
Eclectic Vintage Costume Jewelry &
    Collectibles
2588 Upper Mt. Rd.
Sanborn, NY 14132
ph: 716-731-3502
eclecticvintage@adelphia.net
http://www.electicvintage.com
*Carries quality vintage jewelry and
vanity items; specializes in Fabulous
Florenza; exclusive to RubyLane.com
since 1999; over 25 years experience;
buys and sells costume jewelry.*

Collectible Costume Designer Jewelry
P.O. Box 631
Green Lane, PA 18054
ph: 215-234-2818
char@collectiblejewels.com
http://www.collectiblejewels.com
*Buys and sells vintage and costume
jewelry; Web site displays large
collection of vintage necklaces,
earrings, bracelets, brooches,
compacts and other collectible items.*

Isabelle & Liz Bryman
Liz Collectible Jewelry
P.O. Box 1368
Bristol, PA 19007
ph: 215-781-1174
ibryman@lizjewel.com
http://www.lizjewel.com
*Online worldwide collectible costume
jewelry shopping; home of
JewelCollect Online Email Club.*

Deborah G. Kosnett
Rhinestone Rainbow
24 Solitaire Court
Gaithersburg, MD 20878
ph: 301-990-9473
dkos@radix.net
http://www.rhinestonerainbow.com
*Specializing in vintage costume
jewelry from the 1930s to the 1960s;
designer, Lea Stein, Lucite, bakelite,
rhinestones.*

Bonnie Plimack
Goodtimes Collectibles
P.O. Box 10477
Baltimore, MD 21202
ph: 410-653-2223 or 410-685-4426
fax: 410-602-2097
plimack@tias.com
http://www.tias.com/stores/goodtime
*Buying and selling costume jewelry for
many years; specializes in Czech and
pre-1950 jewelry; also has a large
collection of compacts.*

Claire Doyle
BC Jewels & Collectibles
3405 Sweetwater Rd., #836
Lawrenceville, GA 30044
ph: 770-381-7378
http://server2.hypermart.net/cad/
    bcjewels.html
*Buys and sells collectible costume and
vintage jewelry; member of
JewelCollect.*

Marcia Oliver
Marcia's Putting On The Glitz!
P.O. Box 211
Carnesville, GA 30521
ph: 706-245-9593
marcia@vintagecostumejewelry.com
http://www.vintagecostumejewelry.com
*Offers quality antique and collectible
costume jewelry: Victorian, Deco,
Bakelite, signed, unsigned; also
carries purses, perfumes, compacts.*

Jan Campbell
Cameo Heaven
3818 Atlanta Highway
Flowery Branch, GA 30542
ph: 770-965-9219
cameolady@mindspring.com
http://www.cameoheaven.com
*Specializes in hand carved shell
cameos dating back to 1840; many
rare scenes; also Victorian silver and
costume jewelry.*

Gloria Quincy
Q-Tiques Vintage Jewelry & Collectibles
6475 Ferber Rd.
Jacksonville, FL 32277
ph: 904-745-0618
fax: 904-743-9159
gloria@q-tiques.com
http://www.q-tiques.com
*Specializes in costume designer
jewelry, bakelite, and Mexican Silver.*

Wendy Hankins
Black Cat Collectibles
P.O. Box 864
Geneva, FL 32732
ph: 407-349-9150
wendy@blackcatcollectibles.com
http://www.blackcatcollectibles.com
*Specializing in collecting vintage and
costume jewelry; features both
designer pieces and unsigned pieces
from the 1920s through the 1970s:
rhinestones, sterling, copper, Bakelite,
Lucite, celluloid; also carries estate
jewelry.*

Suzie Bell
Bells Jewels
2200 Winter Springs Blvd., Ste. 106-
    225
Oviedo, FL 32765-9344
ph: 407-366-4747
fax: 407-366-4747
suzbell@cfl.rr.com
http://www.bellsjewels.com
*Specializing in high quality vintage
costume jewelry.*

Cathy Corday
Vintage Jewelry & More
ph: 954-632-0629
ccorday102@aol.com
http://members.aol.com/ccorday102/
    vintage.html
*Buys and sells vintage costume jewelry
and accessories; carries an assortment
of signed as well as unsigned pieces;
lots of rhinestones; also carries
vintage purses.*

Donna Barr
Victorian Elegance, A
P.O. Box 2091
Plant City, FL 33564-2091
ph: 813-719-8392
designs@gator.net
http://victorianelegance.com
*Specializing in vintage jewelry,
ranging from collectible costume to
Victorian mourning and hair jewelry.*

Joan M. Redden
Joan's Jewels & Collectibles
P.O. Box 462
Tallevast, FL 34270-0462
ph: 941-355-9171
fax: 941-355-9171
jmrrar@comcast.net
http://
    www.joansjewelsandcollectibles.com
*Buys and sells costume jewelry from
antique to contemporary; also vintage
clothing, purses, shoes, men's jewelry,
compacts; designs one-of-a-kind
jewelry predominantly made from
vintage jewelry components; will
design to order.*

Cindy Butler
607 Melody Lane
Bessemer, AL 35020
ph: 205-425-9340
cvbmomof3@aol.com
*Buys and sells costume and fine estate
jewelry; specializes in rhinestone and
signed pieces as well as vintage
diamond pieces.*

Lonny Rosen
Ooh Aah Antique Jewelry
492 S. Parkview Ave.
Columbus, OH 43209
ph: 614-237-6884
oohaah@iwaynet.net
http://www.iwaynet.net/~oohaah
*An online catalog of rare jewelry;
specializes in Victorian, Mexican,
Scandinavian, costume, fun and ethnic
jewelry; includes Georg Jensen,
William Spratling, Miriam Haskell,
WW2 Sweetheart to early Native
American.*

Brenda Sue Lansdowne
BSue Boutiques
1441 North Market St. Ext.
East Palestine, OH 44413
ph: 800-868-4393
fax: 330-426-6905
bsue1441@aol.com
http://www.tias.com/stores/bsue
*Actively dealing in vintage costume
Victorian to 1970s for over ten years;
dealer approvals are a specialty; any
qualified dealer may receive a package
- email or call for details.*

Ann Mills
Collections by Ann: Vintage Jewelry &
    Accessories
P.O. Box 102
Clawson, MI 48017
ph: 248-588-7232
amills@annscollection.com
http://www.annscollection.com
Specializing in quality vintage jewelry,

Bakelite, sterling sliver, and glittering evening bags.

Elizabeth Armstrong
Link to the Past, A
30W262 Bedford
Warrenville, IL 60555
elizabeth@alinkto.com
http://www.alinkto.com
Buys and sells Victorian jewelry through costume jewelry of the 1940s.

Peggy
Pegasus Antiques
162 West Hubbard
Chicago, IL 60610
ph: 847-338-0780
peggy@antiqueshop.com
http://www.antiqueshop.com
Carries vintage costume jewelry.

Kim & Larry Cummins
Just Jewelry
20 Burcham Dr.
East Saint Louis, IL 62208
ph: 618-398-2173
kimc@jstjewelry.com
http://www.jstjewelry.com
Specializes in quality vintage costume jewelry from the 1920s through the 1970s: Boucher, Haskell, KJL, Schiaparelli, Trifari, Weiss, and other designers.

George & Dotty Stringfield
Illusion Jewels
215 Plum Creek Rd.
Longview, TX 75605
ph: 903-663-3415
ijjewels@yahoo.com
http://www.illusionjewels.com
Buys and sells vintage and collectible costume jewelry; carries original designs by Dorothea; home of "Researching Costume Jewelry," recognized online resource for dates and historical information on jewelry designers and companies.

Billie & John McBride
South Texas Trading Company
P.O. Box 857
Port Aransas, TX 78373
ph: 361-749-6149 or 800-484-9293 x3474
STFNandTRADING@centurytel.net
http://www.southtexastrading.com
Specializing in the sale of vintage and collectible costume jewelry, specializing in Bakelite, Christmas tree pins, and 20th century costume jewelry; has 350-member online jewelry group; nationwide pickers available.

Christina Felps
Cat's Fancy, The
12221 Chisholm Valley Dr., #423
Round Rock, TX 78681
ph: 512-238-8037
catfancy@io.com
http://www.io.com/~catfancy
Buys and sells vintage and costume jewelry; Web site contains an online store front; maintains wish list for customers wanting to add to their

collection; also repairs and restores (replace pin shanks and clasps, match/replace stones).

JhaRee Miller
Effervescence!
P.O. Box 322
Osage, WY 82723
ph: 307-465-2484
eff@trib.com
http://www.rubylane.com/shops/effervescence
Offers costume jewelry and handcrafted lace.

Janet Lawwill
Azillion SPARKLZ
P.O. Box 36269
Tucson, AZ 85750
ph: 520-907-2839
fax: 413-683-7503
Jewel@Sparklz.com
http://www.sparklz.com
Buys and sells vintage costume jewelry: Victorian, Nouveau, Deco, rhinestones through the 1960s; cuff links, charms, buckles, shoe buckles, cameos, hair, sterling, gold; guides for cleaning, relating, storing, buying, and selling.

Patsy Comer
Patsy Comer's Antiques & Jewelry
7249 Reseda Blvd.
Reseda, CA 91335-3046
ph: 818-345-1631
fax: 818-345-1914
patsycomer@yahoo.com
Buys and sells costume and fine jewelry from all eras including designer; also costume jewelry, gold and sterling; 1960s memorabilia such as peace signs, designer costume and 1960s and '70s jewelry; sells to the trade, does mail order.

Eve Lickver
P.O. Box 1778
San Marcos, CA 92079-1778
ph: 760-761-0868
Dealer/collector buys and sells carved and figural Bakelite jewelry, celluloid and rhinestone bracelets; also wants signed costume jewelry of 1920s through 1950s including sterling and enamel.

Susan Murphy
29668 Orinda Rd.
San Juan Capistrano, CA 92675-1211
ph: 949-364-4333
Wants to buy pre-1950 costume jewelry; please enclose SASE.

Melinda Abbott
Vintage Jewelry Collect
P.O. Box 446
Benicia, CA 94510
ph: 707-751-1551
vintagejewelryco@aol.com
http://www.vintagejewelrycollect.com
Offers a large selection of collectible costume jewelry: collection spans over 130 years of costume jewelry adornment; signed pieces as well as unsigned beauties.

Sheila Pamfiloff
Glitter Box, The
P.O. Box 35
Walnut Creek, CA 94596
ph: 925-937-7554
pamfil@glitterbox.com
http://www.glitterbox.com
Specializing in vintage designer costume jewelry including Haskell, Schiaparelli, Hagler, Eisenberg, DeMario, Mazer, Boucher; also vintage Mexican sterling silver from the great designers of Taxco.

Eureka, I Found It! Antiques & Collectibles
P.O. Box 2192
Petaluma, CA 94953-2192
eureka@eureka-i-found-it.com
http://www.eureka-i-found-it.com
An online dealer specializing in vintage textiles and clothing, toy and model steam engines, buttons, fans, Art Deco, costume jewelry, toy sewing machines.

Pandora L. McKinnon
Pandora's Jewelry Box
4841 Martin Luther King Blvd.
Sacramento, CA 95820-4932
ph: 916-452-6728
fax: 916-452-6728
lfjantiquenews@angelfire.com
http://members.fortunecity.com/jewels4u2
Antique and collectible costume jewelry for sale.

Hillary Parsons
Hillary's Antiques
8441 SE 68th St. #313
Mercer Island, WA 98040
ph: 206-232-5309
fax: 206-236-0142
jewelry@hillarysantiques.com
http://www.hillarysantiques.com
Buys and sells antique and vintage jewelry including Victorian, Art Deco, Art Nouveau and costume jewelry.

Rosalie Sayyah
Rhinestone Rosie
606 West Crockett
Seattle, WA 98119
ph: 206-283-4605
rhinestonerosie@yahoo.com
Wants to buy big, colorful, "ugly" old costume jewelry.

Experts

Deborah J. Robinson
Vintage Jewelry & Collectibles
ph: 860-645-1525
vinjewels@aol.com
http://www.theplace2b.com/VintageJewels
Appraiser, dealer, expert, collector, repair person specializing in estate and signed vintage jewelry from the 1850s to 1960s: Trifari, Vendome, Hobe, Hollycraft, Weiss, Bakelite, sterling, vintage rings, compacts, cuff links.

Joan Vogel Elias
Absolutely Vintage Designer & Collectible Jewelry
51 Regents Park
Westport, CT 06880
ph: 203-255-6600
fax: 203-255-0898
JVEjewel@aol.com
http://www.absolutelyvintage.net
Dealer of quality vintage, designer, collectible and estate jewelry and accessories; over 1,175 pieces listed on the Web site which is updated weekly; interested in buying one piece or an entire jewelry collection.

Harrice Simons Miller
Harrice Miller Collection
40 West 25th St., Gallery #230
New York, NY 10010
ph: 212-242-0910
fax: 212-532-1394
Collectible costume jewelry appraiser, dealer and expert; author of "The Confident Collector: Costume Jewelry" and "Kenneth Jay Lane: Faking It;" consultant to Christie's, lecturer.

Judith Katz-Schwartz
Twin Brooks Antiques & Collectibles
E-zine: Antiques & Collectibles Newsletter
P.O. Box 6572
New York, NY 10128-0006
ph: 212-876-3512
fax: 212-876-3512
twinb@msjudith.net
http://www.msjudith.net
Buys, sells, appraisers signed and unsigned pieces of costume jewelry: brooches & pins, bracelets, earrings, rings, rhinestone jewelry, dress clips, Bakelite, sets, etc.; author of "Collectors Compass: Jewelry;" member of AOA and ISA.

Cherri Simonds
102 Tess Circle
Huntsville, AL 35811
ph: 256-851-0130
Author of "Collectible Costume Jewelry: Identification & Values;" appraises and offers costume jewelry seminars.

Mary Hamburg
Tootsie's Antiques
20 Cedar Ave.
Danville, IL 61832-1525
ph: 217-446-2323 or 217-442-2725
tootsies@allarounddanville.com
Specializes in antique costume jewelry, especially Bakelite.

Kathy Flood
Jeweled Forest, The
P.O. Box 155
Kimmswick, MO 63053
ph: 636-461-0563
bizstyle@aol.com
http://www.christmastreepins.com
Collector, dealer, researcher, historian, expert specializing in

370

vintage costume jewelry with a focus on Christmas pins.

Ann M. Pitman
8006 Hertfordshire Circle
Spring, TX 77379-4645
AnnMPitman@cs.com
Specializes in rhinestone vintage costume jewelry; writes the "Jewelry Box" column on vintage and antique jewelry, fine and costume jewelry; author of "Inside the Jewelry Box - A collector's Guide to Costume Jewelry."

Christie Romero
Center for Jewelry Studies
P.O. Box 424
Anaheim, CA 92815-0424
ph: 714-778-1828
fax: 714-778-3432
CR4jewelry@aol.com
http://www.center4jewelrystudies.org
One of America's leading scholars on antique, period & vintage jewelry; author of "Warman's Jewelry - A Fully Illustrated Identification & Price Guide to 18th, 19th & 20th Century Fine & Costume Jewelry;" lecturer, consultant.

Internet Resources

About.com Hobbies
220 East 42nd St.
New York, NY 10017
pr@about-inc.com
http://home.about.com/hobbies
Online source for information about action figures, antiques, book collecting, coin collecting, collectibles, comic books, costume jewelry, dolls, mineral collecting, pin collecting, sports and trading cards, stamps, toy collecting.

George & Dotty Stringfield
Researching Costume Jewelry
215 Plum Creek Rd.
Longview, TX 75605
ph: 903-663-3415
ijjewels@yahoo.com
http://www.illusionjewels.com
A recognized online resource for dates and historical information on jewelry designers and companies.

Misc. Services

Leigh Leshner
Venture Entertainment Group
P.O. Box 55113
Sherman Oaks, CA 91413-0113
ph: 818-981-7813
fax: 818-981-3466
venture818@aol.com
http://www.tias.com/stores/memories
Producers of the award winning video cassette series on vintage & costume jewelry from 1800s to 1960; a visual price guide for signed and unsigned costume jewelry by Trifari, Coro, Corocraft, Haskell, Hobe, Eisenberg, Chanel, etc.

Periodicals

Elyse Zorn Karlin, Ed.
1333A North Ave., Box 103
New Rochelle, NY 10804
ph: 914-235-0983
fax: 914-235-0983
info@jewelryhistorians.com
http://www.jewelryhistorians.com
Quarterly newsletter covering ancient, antique, contemporary studio, costume and vintage jewelry, historic costume, antique buttons and beads; contains articles, book reviews, terminology, extensive calendar, and more.

Davida Baron
Newsletter: Glittering Times
P.O. Box 656675
Flushing, NY 11365
ph: 718-969-2320
glittering_times@bigfoot.com
For collectors and dealers of vintage costume jewelry.

Repair Services

William Semmens
Costume Jewelry Repair House, The
55 East Washington St., Ste. 435
Chicago, IL 60602
ph: 312-782-7810 or 312-782-7815
fax: 312-782-7815
diamondgirl1003@aol.com
http://www.costumejewelryrepair.com
Offers hard-to-find costume jewelry repair service; never refuses a repair inquiry no matter of size or detail; also offers a jewelry finding inventory for objects dating back to 1900.

Rosalie Sayyah
Rhinestone Rosie
606 West Crockett
Seattle, WA 98119
ph: 206-283-4605
rhinestonerosie@yahoo.com
Offers repair and restoration of costume jewelry: professional lead soldering, stone replacement, restyling, etc.

Suppliers

Matthew Ribarich
Antique & Costume Jewelry Replacement Stones
P.O. Box 10104
Costa Mesa, CA 92627
ph: 949-645-9017 or 949-645-9020
fax: 949-645-9020
MRstones4U@aol.com
http://www.mrstones.com
Supplies a wide variety of antique and costume jewelry replacement stones including marcasites, rhinestones, imitation pearls, rose cut garnets and jadeite jade; over 6 million stones in inventory; stone matching services available.

Diamonds

Appraisers

Kathleen D. Paskman, GG
14236 Lake Price Dr.
Orlando, FL 32826
diamondgolden@prodigy.net
Specializes in the appraisal of diamonds.

Jeff Marcus
Marcus Jewelers
4047 Okeechobee Blvd.
West Palm Beach, FL 33409
ph: 561-689-2002 or 800-780-2357
fax: 561-689-2008
jnmar689@aol.com
http://marcusjewelers.com
Staff of gemologists with over 115 years of combined experience in buying, selling and appraising diamonds.

Dealers

Joseph W. Tenhagen
J.W. Tenhagen Gemstones, Inc.
36 NE 1st St., #419
Miami, FL 33132
ph: 305-374-2411
joeten@bellsouth.net
Specializes in the sale of diamonds and colored gemstones.

Rose Proler, GG, ISA
Rose Proler, Inc.
5433 Westheimer, Ste. 1105
Houston, TX 77056-5300
ph: 713-627-3098 or 800-627-3098
fax: 713-627-0504
texarose@msn.com
Specializes in rough and polished diamonds.

Misc. Services

Norman Monteau
American International Gemologists
Scientific Laboratory for Gem Identification
21250 Califa St., Ste. 203
Woodland Hills, CA 91367
ph: 818-712-9750
fax: 818-712-9755
aig-labs@pacbell.net
Diamond grading laboratory: full certificates, passports, consultation cards and appraisals; each diamond graded by three to five graduate gemologists; grades over 10,000 diamonds per years.

Periodicals

Martin Rapaport, Pres.
Price Guide: Rapaport Diamond Report
15 West 47th St.
New York, NY 10036
ph: 212-354-0575
fax: 212-840-0243
info@diamonds.com
http://www.diamonds.net
Can subscribe to a monthly or to a weekly price report; these reports are considered the primary source of diamond price information by the jewelry trade.

Hair

(see GEMS & JEWELRY, Mourning; HAIRWORK)

Hawaiian Shell

Appraisers

Brenda Reichel, ISA, GG, NGJA
Carats & Karats Fine Jewelry
1254 S. King St.
Honolulu, HI 96814
ph: 808-593-8122 or 877-593-8122
fax: 808-591-9124
flawless@lava.net
http://www.caratsandkarats.com
Specializes in appraising, buying and selling diamonds, gold, ivory, jade, mineral specimens, pearls, silver, and Hawaiian shell jewelry (Niihau shells).

Jade

Dealers

AntiqueJades.com
P.O. Box 600895
Springfield, MA 32260-0895
ph: 904-288-8190
sales@antiquejades.com
http://www.antiquejades.com
Carries authentic and certified Chinese jades from all time periods.

Don Kay
Mason-Kay Fine Jade Jewelry
P.O. Box 65015
Denver, CO 80206
ph: 800-722-7575 or 303-393-7575
fax: 303-393-0201
don@masonkay.com
http://www.masonkay.com
Specializes in the sale and appraisals of nephrite jade.

Mourning

(see also HAIRWORK)

Dealers

Darlene Tzavaras
Things Gone By
P.O. Box 325
Reedsville, WV 26547
ph: 304-864-5921
fax: 304-864-0519
darlene@thingsgoneby.com
http://www.thingsgoneby.com
Specializes in sentimental and mourning jewelry of high quality and variety; also offers extensive inventory of other antique jewelry from the Georgian, Victorian, Edwardian, and Art Nouveau periods.

Rachell Frazien
Poes Attic
2901 Beverly Blvd., #704
Los Angeles, CA 90057
webmaster@poesattic.com
http://www.poesattic.com
Specializes in mourning jewelry.

Opals

Experts

Paul B. Donning
Majestic Gems & Carvings
P.O. Box 1348
Estes Park, CO 80517
ph: 800-468-0324 or 970-586-2411
fax: 970-586-0996
Importer of rough opal; cutter and designer; author of three books on opals: "Opal Identification and Value," "Opal Adventures," and "Opal Cutting Made Easy."

Pearls

Dealers

Betty Sue King
King's Ransom
3030 Bridgeway, Ste. 209
Sausalito, CA 94965
ph: 415-331-2650 or 877-331-2650
fax: 415-331-9402
kransom@pacbell.net
Specializes in fine to gem quality pearls from the South Seas, Tahiti; also Akoya pearls from Japan; selects only the finer quality pearls from China; natural diamond crystals also available.

Periodicals

Richard Torrey, Editor
Pearl World LLC
Journal: Pearl World - The International Pearling Journal
5501 N. 7th Ave., PMB 331
Phoenix, AZ 85021-1755
ph: 602-678-5799
fax: 602-678-6799
prlwrld@aol.com
Covers whatever is happening in the pearling industry: statistics, market developments, auctions, interviews with cultivators and importers, coverage of major trade fairs, educational materials, history of pearling, etc.

Pearls (Majorican)

Man./Prod./Dist.

Carat & Under, A
33 Elm St.
Springfield, MA 01103
ph: 888-714-4441
LTJ@map.com
http://www.caratandunder.com/majorica.htm
Distributor of Majorican simulated pearls.

Pearls (Mikimoto)

Man./Prod./Dist.

Mikimoto (America) Co., Ltd.
40 West 57th St., 24th Fl.
New York, NY 10019-4001
ph: 212-457-4501
fax: 212-457-4635
contact@mikimotoamerica.com
http://www.mikimoto.com
Manufacturer of fine pearl jewelry, pearls, pearl strands; Web site has

tips on buying pearls, pearl care, becoming an expert.

Rhinestone

Appraisers

Rosalie Sayyah
Rhinestone Rosie
606 West Crockett
Seattle, WA 98119
ph: 206-283-4605
rhinestonerosie@yahoo.com
Specializes in the appraisal of rhinestone jewelry.

Experts

Ann M. Pitman
8006 Hertfordshire Circle
Spring, TX 77379-4645
AnnMPitman@cs.com
Specializes in rhinestone vintage costume jewelry; writes the "Jewelry Box" column on vintage and antique jewelry, fine and costume jewelry; author of "Inside the Jewelry Box - A collector's Guide to Costume Jewelry."

Marcia Brown
Sparkles
P.O. Box 2314
White City, OR 97503-0314
ph: 541-826-3039
fax: 541-836-5385
marciasparkles@aol.com
Author of books and videos about rhinestone jewelry including "Signed Beauties," "Unsigned Beauties," and "Hidden Treasure" video series.

Stick Pins

Collectors

Elynore "Pet" Kerins
82 Briarwood
Terre Haute, IN 47803-1770
ph: 812-877-1264
Serious stickpin collector with over 2,700 in many categories: cameos, pearls, enamel, mourning, carved, dogs, cats, other animals, advertising, political and patriotic, colored stones, diamonds, etc.

Experts

Elynore "Pet" Kerins
82 Briarwood
Terre Haute, IN 47803-1770
ph: 812-877-1264
Co-author with Jack Kerins of "Collecting Antique Stickpins - Identification & Value Guide."

Supplies For

(see also ANTIQUES DEALERS & COLLECTORS, Supplies For; BLACKLIGHTS [UV LAMPS])

Suppliers

Kassoy
16 Midland Ave.
Hicksville, NY 11801
ph: 800-452-7769 or 516-942-0560
fax: 516-942-0402
sales@kassoy.com
http://www.kassoy.com
Mail order source for tools, supplies and instruments for the jewelry trade: diamond testers, gold testers, loupes, gauges, diamond scales, gold scales, colorimeters, magnifiers, polishing equipment, watch repair tools, etc.

Robert Gitnick
R & D Jewelry Supply Co.
1310 Apple Ave.
Silver Spring, MD 20910
ph: 301-588-7296
fax: 301-495-7312
Phone or mail order for jewelry tools and supplies: loupes, diamond testers, tweezers, gold test equipment, black lights, diamond measuring gauges, etc.

Brenda Sue Lansdowne
BSue Boutiques
1441 North Market St. Ext.
East Palestine, OH 44413
ph: 800-868-4393
fax: 330-426-6905
bsue1441@aol.com
http://www.tias.com/stores/bsue
Carries basic supplies for jewelry dealers and collectors: sunshine cloths, simichrome, loupes, ziplocks, mailing supplies, hypo-tube cement, various pliers, tweezers, cutters, clamps, Jewelry Key; hatpin making supplies, beads, trays.

Indiana Jewelers Supply Inc.
31 E. Georgia, #202
Indianapolis, IN 46204-3621
ph: 317-632-6346 or 800-382-9973
Supplier of jewelers tools and equipment, and watch parts.

Swest Inc.
11090 North Stemmons Freeway
P.O. Box 59389
Dallas, TX 75229-1389
ph: 972-247-7744 or 800-527-5057
fax: 800-441-5162
email@swestinc.com
http://www.swestinc.com
Mail order source for tools, supplies and instruments for the jewelry trade; diamond testers, loupes, scales, gold testing kits, etc.

David D. Harleston
Lathrop's Jeweler Supplies & Findings
6704 Ferris St.
Bellaire, TX 77401
ph: 713-665-2699
fax: 713-665-0214
Jeweler supplies and findings; loupes, scales, test kits.

John & Jacqueline Foutz
550 Silver & Supply
4187 US Highway 64
Kirtland, NM 87417
ph: 505-598-5322
fax: 505-598-0974
sales@metalworks.com
http://www.metalworks.com
Supplies metal and bead crafters with the finest possible jewelry supplies, tools, materials and services: sterling silver, .999 fine silver, silver filled, 14k gold, gold filled, nickel, copper, red and yellow brass, bead supplies, etc.

Jack Slevkoff
Jack Slevkoff's Prized Possessions
4460 West Shaw Ave., Ste. 140
Fresno, CA 93722
ph: 559-275-6498
fax: 559-276-7485
jack@gemworld.com
http://www.gemworld.com
Gems, minerals, fossils, gemstone rough, equipment, supplies; provides opals, gemstones, collector stones, synthetics, cabbing and faceting rough, lapidary equipment and supplies, appraisals, etc.; extensive Web site.

Otto Frei & Jules Borel
P.O. Box 796
Oakland, CA 94604
ph: 510-832-0355 or 800-772-3456
fax: 800-900-3734
info@Ofrei.com
http://www.ofrei.com
Carries complete line of clock parts.

Vintage & Estate

Appraisers

Joyce Chapman
Joyce Chapman Enterprises
P.O. Box 2143
Port Washington, NY 11050
ph: 516-944-6313
fax: 516-944-6313
joychap@rcn.com
http://www.unusual1.com
Specializes only in vintage antique and period estate fine jewelry; no costume jewelry; Member of Appraisers Association of America.

Gail Brett Levine, GG
Timeless, Inc.
P.O. Box 7683
Rego Park, NY 11374-7683
ph: 718-897-7305
fax: 718-997-9057
76766.614@compuserve.com
http://www.auctionmarketresource.com
Graduate Gemologist, appraiser, lecturer, publisher of "Auction Market Resource For Gems & Jewelry," a semi-annual jewelry price, condition, quality report.

C. Jeanenne Bell, G.G., N.G.J.A.
Jewelry Box Antiques, Inc.
7325 Quivira Rd., Ste. 238
Shawnee Mission, KS 66216
ph: 913-962-8533
fax: 913-963-4418
cjbell@msn.com
http://www.jewelryboxantiques.com
*Vintage jewelry dealer and expert;
author of "Collectors Encyclopedia of
Hairwork Jewelry," "Answers to
Questions About Old Jewelry 1840-
1950" 6th Ed., "How to be a Jewelry
Detective," "Warman's Field Guide to
Antique Jewelry."*

Pamela Y. Wiggins
P.O. Box 745
Round Rock, TX 78680-0745
ph: 512-789-3803
fax: 512-388-9935
antiques.guide@about.com
http://antiques.about.com
*Specializes in the appraisal of vintage
costume jewelry and ladies'
accessories; also serves as the
Antiques Guide for www.about.com.*

Robin K. Hancock, ISA
RSK Independent Appraiser of Fine
Jewelry
ph: 512-694-9136
rskappraiser@msn.com
*Accredited member of the ISA;
graduate gemologist of the GIA;
studied history of jewelry at Sotheby's
in London; specializes in the
appraisal of estate and vintage
jewelry.*

Theresa Peregory, GG, ISA
Classic Facets Ltd.
942 Pearl St.
Boulder, CO 80302-5109
ph: 303-938-8851 or 720-940-8901
fax: 303-546-9811
gemnerd@earthlink.net
*Graduate Gemologist from the
Gemological Institute of America;
specializing in the appraisals of
antique, vintage and estate jewelry.*

Meriwether McGettigan
Meriwether
3701 Sacramento St., #362
San Francisco, CA 94118
ph: 415-921-6895
meriwether@earthlink.net
http://www.meriwether.net
*Specializes in the appraisal of
diamonds and estate jewelry.*

Neola Caveny, ISA, GIA GG
Neola Caveny Gem & Jewelry Appraisals
42 Pua Ole St.
Paia, HI 96779
ph: 808-579-9769
fax: 808-579-9769
neola@tiki.net
*Graduate Gemologist, GIA; Accredited
Member, ISA; 22 years in the jewelry
industry, 12 as an independent
appraiser for retailers, attorneys,
banks, and consumers; specializing in*

*the appraisal of antique & period
jewelry.*

James Poag, GG, ISA CAPP
James O. Poag Jewellers, Ltd.
94 Frank St.
P.O. Box 39
Strathroy, Ontario N7G 3J1 Canada
ph: 519-245-1040 or 519-245-1580
fax: 519-245-6073
james@poags.com
http://www.poags.com
*ISA appraiser certified in gems &
jewelry, and in antique & period
jewelry; also sells and restores new
and estate jewelry; four goldsmiths on
staff, as well as a GIA Graduate
Gemologist.*

Clubs/Associations

Lucille Tempesta
Vintage Fashion & Costume Jewelry
Club
Magazine: VF&CJ Magazine
P.O. Box 265
Glen Oaks, NY 11004-0265
ph: 718-939-3095
fax: 718-939-7988
VFCJ@aol.com
http://www.lizjewel.com/vf
*Over 1,000 members in 50 states and
overseas; quarterly magazine;
conventions; oldest club devoted to
vintage costume jewelry collecting.*

Pandora L. McKinnon, Ed.
Leaping Frog Antique Jewelry &
Collectible Club
Newsletter: LFAJCC Newsletter
4841 Martin Luther King Blvd.
Sacramento, CA 95820-4932
ph: 916-452-6728
fax: 916-452-6728
lfjantiquenews@angelfire.com
http://members.fortunecity.com/
jewels4u2
*Articles of interest regarding antique
and collectibles jewelry and other
collectible items such as hats, furs,
smoking items, compacts, purses and
more; annual convention.*

Collectors

Elyse Zorn Karlin
1333A North Ave., Box 103
New Rochelle, NY 10804
ph: 914-235-0983
fax: 914-235-0983
info@jewelryhistorians.com
http://www.jewelryhistorians.com

Dena Share
4349 LaVale Ct.
Clemmons, NC 27012-9009
ph: 336-766-6579
denarnc@aol.com
*Interested in buying fine jewelry by
Erte and Carrera Y Carrera.*

Jane Spies
ph: 330-534-8948
Lark5000@aol.com
Specializes in photographic jewelry.

Doris M. Diabo
19953 Great Oaks Circle S.
Clinton Township, MI 48036-2440
ph: 810-463-5651
*Wants to buy butterfly pins (brooches)
- designer names or not - especially
those flashy with colored rhinestones;
send photocopies, price, condition,
SASE.*

Patti Vahary
Curious Cat, The
41 Crosby Dr.
Battle Creek, MI 49014
pattiv0204@aol.com
*Buys estate jewelry, especially costume
signed work and 1800s style jewelry;
also interested in Art Deco and
jewelry from the 1920s through 1940s.*

Daniel Brown
P.O. Box 149
Davenport, CA 95017-0149
ph: 831-426-0134 or 800-492-6786
green-garnet@sbcglobal.net
*Wants to buy old jewelry from A to Z;
fine antique Victorian and Art
Nouveau gold to Edwardian and Art
Deco platinum; especially with fine
colored stones; Taxco silver, especially
Spratling, Aquilar, Davis, etc., pre-
1940 Navajo pieces.*

Dealers

Nancy Janeliunas
Janeliunas Jewelry
P.O. Box 417
Townsend, MA 01469
ph: 978-597-5939
nancyjan@prodigy.net
http://www.jansjewells.com
*Sells antique, vintage, collectible &
estate jewelry.*

Elaine Kula
Antiquing On Line - Costume, Victorian
& Estate Jewelry
P.O. Box 7905
Nashua, NH 03060
ph: 603-888-7464
fax: 603-888-5648
webmistress@antiquingonline.com
http://www.antiquingonline.com
*Online catalog specializing in high
quality designer (Haskell, Eisenberg,
Trifari, Carnegie), Mexican,
Edwardian, Czech, Bakelite, antique,
and collectible vintage costume
jewelry, Victorian jewelry, estate
jewelry and accessories.*

Judith Fineblit Anderson, GG, ISA
CAPP
Bijoux Extraordinaire, Ltd.
P.O. Box 1424
Manchester, NH 03105-1424
ph: 603-624-8672
fax: 603-624-8673
judi@jewelryexpert.com
http://www.jewelryexpert.com
*Buys, sells, brokers fine quality
antique and estate jewelry, contemporary designer jewelry, diamonds and
colored gemstones; also custom design*

*and restorations of antique jewelry;
appraisal services; lecturer on jewelry.*

Elisha Morgan
Elisha Morgan & Associates
Gemologists
P.O. Box 533
Hanover, NH 03755
ph: 603-643-3600
fax: 603-643-6556
rockman@aol.com
http://www.emgemologist.com
*Dealer and purchaser of fine estate
jewelry, gemstones, and vintage
watches; specialist in fine blue
sapphire and ruby; also in Victorian
and Edwardian jewelry.*

Debbie Woolley
Favorite Past-Times Antiques
6 Main Hill
Bridgton, ME 04009
ph: 207-647-4486
info@maine-antiques.com
http://www.maine-antiques.com/fpt/Index

Chris Peck
All That Glitters
3000 Fairfield Ave.
Bridgeport, CT 06605
ph: 203-333-5836
fax: 203-333-5840
atg1@snet.net
*Buys and sells fine estate jewelry,
including diamonds; also appraises.*

Koblenz & Co., Estate Jewelry
P.O. Box 9
South Kent, CT 06785
ph: 877-927-0179 or 860-927-0179
fax: 860-927-0179
merle@koblenzestatejewelry.com
http://www.koblenzestatejewelry.com
*Specializes in antique and estate
jewelry and appraisals.*

Suzanne W. Smith
Collectible Costume Jewelry
P.O. Box 431
Andover, NJ 07821
ph: 973-300-4101
swsmith@costumejewelry.com
http://www.costumejewelry.com
*Features signed and unsigned vintage
and collectible jewelry.*

Leigh Nacht
Bernard Nacht & Co., Inc.
589 Fifth Ave., Ste. 910
New York, NY 10017-1923
ph: 212-371-8100 or 800-348-3419
fax: 212-371-8284
*Buys and sells antique, estate and
period jewelry and objects as well as
diamonds and gemstones.*

Barry Weber
Edith Weber & Associates Antique
Jewelry
994 Madison Ave.
New York, NY 10021
ph: 212-570-9668
fax: 212-570-9668
info@antique-jewelry.com
http://www.antique-jewelry.com
One of America's premier antique

jewelry specialist dealers; featured at many of the country's charity auctions for over 30 years; retail store is located on Madison Ave. in Historic Upper East Side, Manhattan; great Web site.

A La Vieille Russie, Inc.
781 Fifth Ave.
New York, NY 10022
ph: 212-752-1727
alvr@alvr.com
http://www.alvr.com
Specializes in fine European and American antique jewelry, Faberge, gold snuff boxes and objects de vertu; also specializes in Russian decorative and fine arts.

Joyce Chapman
Joyce Chapman Enterprises
P.O. Box 2143
Port Washington, NY 11050
ph: 516-944-6313
fax: 516-944-6313
joychap@rcn.com
http://www.unusual1.com
Specializes only in vintage antique and period estate fine jewelry; no costume jewelry; Member of Appraisers Association of America.

Claudia Naragon
Claudia's Closet
7 East St.
Oneonta, NY 13820
ph: 607-432-7037
bcgems@digital-marketplace.net
http://www.101jewelrylane.com/claudiascloset
Specializes in estate, vintage, fine, and costume jewelry.

Collectible Costume Designer Jewelry
P.O. Box 631
Green Lane, PA 18054
ph: 215-234-2818
char@collectiblejewels.com
http://www.collectiblejewels.com
Buys and sells vintage and costume jewelry; Web site displays large collection of vintage necklaces, earrings, bracelets, brooches, compacts and other collectible items.

Ronald Talley
Talley Jewelry, Inc.
3035 Festival Way
P.O. Box 245
Waldorf, MD 20604-0245
ph: 301-645-5144 or 301-870-9593
fax: 301-870-9593
talleyjlry@earthlink.com
http://www.talleyjewelry.com
Buys, sells, appraises, repairs, and restores jewelry.

Linda Miller
Victorian Lady, The
P.O. Box 613
Jarrettsville, MD 21084
ph: 410-557-7071
victorianldy@earthlink.net
http://www.pacificws.com/victorianlady
Specializes in Victorian and vintage

jewelry along with ladies things including purses, dolls, vanity items.

Eugene Rooney, GG
Victorian Manor Jewelry
33 Main St.
P.O. Box 285
New Market, MD 21774-0285
ph: 301-865-3083 or 877-865-3083
fax: 301-865-0649
sales@victorianmanorjewelry.com
http://www.victorianmanorjewelry.com
Buys and sells antique and estate jewelry; repairs, restores, re-enameling, remounting, restring, and custom design jewelry.

Evie Myatt
Echoes of Time
700 Norfolk Ave.
Virginia Beach, VA 23451
ph: 757-428-2332
fax: 757-428-8099
eechoes@msn.com
http://www.echoes-of-time.com
Specializes in vintage clothing, costume, jewelry from the 1920s through 1970s.

Darlene Tzavaras
Things Gone By
P.O. Box 325
Reedsville, WV 26547
ph: 304-864-5921
fax: 304-864-0519
darlene@thingsgoneby.com
http://www.thingsgoneby.com
Specializes in sentimental and mourning jewelry of high quality and variety; also offers extensive inventory of other antique jewelry from the Georgian, Victorian, Edwardian, and Art Nouveau periods.

Susan M. Black
Susan's Vintage Boutique
120 Mopar Lane
West End, NC 27376
ph: 910-295-6575
fax: 910-295-9109
susans@tias.com
http://www.tias.com/stores/susans
In business since 1984.

Claire Doyle
BC Jewels & Collectibles
3405 Sweetwater Rd., #836
Lawrenceville, GA 30044
ph: 770-381-7378
http://server2.hypermart.net/cad/bcjewels.html
Buys and sells collectible costume and vintage jewelry; member of JewelCollect.

Marcia Oliver
Marcia's Putting On The Glitz!
P.O. Box 211
Carnesville, GA 30521
ph: 706-245-9593
marcia@vintagecostumejewelry.com
http://www.vintagecostumejewelry.com
Offers quality antique and collectible costume jewelry: Victorian, Deco, Bakelite, signed, unsigned; also carries purses, perfumes, compacts.

Jan Campbell
Cameo Heaven
3818 Atlanta Highway
Flowery Branch, GA 30542
ph: 770-965-9219
cameolady@mindspring.com
http://www.cameoheaven.com
Specializes in hand carved shell cameos dating back to 1840; many rare scenes; also Victorian silver and costume jewelry.

Peter Thurber
Ritzi & Thurber, Inc.
160 S. Beach St.
Daytona Beach, FL 32114
ph: 904-252-2552 or 904-226-8489
fax: 904-226-8490
ritzi1881@earthlink.net
http://www.ritzi-thurber.com
Founded in 1881, firm is one of the largest buyers of estate jewelry in Florida.

Wendy Hankins
Black Cat Collectibles
P.O. Box 864
Geneva, FL 32732
ph: 407-349-9150
wendy@blackcatcollectibles.com
http://www.blackcatcollectibles.com
Specializing in collecting vintage and costume jewelry; features both designer pieces and unsigned pieces from the 1920s through the 1970s: rhinestones, sterling, copper, Bakelite, Lucite, celluloid; also carries estate jewelry.

Donna Barr
Victorian Elegance, A
P.O. Box 2091
Plant City, FL 33564-2091
ph: 813-719-8392
designs@gator.net
http://victorianelegance.com
Specializing in vintage jewelry, ranging from collectible costume to Victorian mourning and hair jewelry.

Fred Hare
Headdress Jewelry & Accessories, Inc.
1135 9th Ave. N
Saint Petersburg, FL 33705
ph: 727-894-2280
fax: 727-894-2280
headress@tampabay.rr.com
http://www.headress.com
Online catalog of antique and estate jewelry and vintage designer accessories.

Denise Kowal
Denise Kowal & Sons Jewelry
530 S. Orange Ave.
P.O. Box 1676
Sarasota, FL 34236
ph: 941-364-3384 or 941-364-3385
fax: 941-364-3385
dkowalsons@aol.com
Purchasing and selling fine antique, estate, custom and modern jewelry; Graduate Master Appraiser of Jewelry.

Kim Paff
Vintage Jewelry Arts & Antiques
4137 Des Prez Court
Spring Hill, FL 34607
ph: 352-596-6119
kim@vintagejewelryartsandantiques.com
http://www.vintagejewelryartsandantiques.com
Buys and sells vintage costume jewelry: Bakelite, unsigned and designer-signed jewelry, fine jewelry, copper and handmade silver jewelry.

Cindy Butler
607 Melody Lane
Bessemer, AL 35020
ph: 205-425-9340
cvbmomof3@aol.com
Buys and sells costume and fine estate jewelry; specializes in rhinestone and signed pieces as well as vintage diamond pieces.

Elaine Luartes, GG
Athena Antiques
100 Beta Dr.
Franklin, TN 37064-3912
ph: 615-377-3442
Specializes in antique and estate jewelry; contributor to "Collector's Compass - Jewelry" (Martingale), Board of Advisors for "Warman's;" wants jewelry emphasizing craftsmanship and design.

Pam Huskey
P.O. Box 599
Sweetwater, TN 37874
ph: 423-337-2540
milesofhistory@charter.net
http://www.milesofhistory.com
Specializes in late Georgian to mid-Victorian estate jewelry.

Patricia A. Thompson, GG, ISA CAPP
Way-Fil Jewelry
1123 West Main St.
Tupelo, MS 38801
ph: 662-844-2427
fax: 662-840-4791
wayfil@juno.com
http://www.way-filjewelry.com
Manufacturer, appraisals, repairs, buy/sell, consignments, estate disposal.

Lonny Rosen
Ooh Aah Antique Jewelry
492 S. Parkview Ave.
Columbus, OH 43209
ph: 614-237-6884
oohaah@iwaynet.net
http://www.iwaynet.net/~oohaah
An online catalog of rare jewelry; specializes in Victorian, Mexican, Scandinavian, costume, fun and ethnic jewelry; includes Georg Jensen, William Spratling, Miriam Haskell, WW2 Sweetheart to early Native American.

Ed & Carolyn Sunday
Sunday & Sunday
P.O. Box 1240
Uniontown, OH 44685
ph: 330-966-6746
csunday@neo.rr.com
http://www.sundayandsunday.com
Specializes in pocket and wrist watches and in fine estate jewelry; has restored pocket watches for over 25 years.

Ann Mills
Collections by Ann: Vintage Jewelry & Accessories
P.O. Box 102
Clawson, MI 48017
ph: 248-588-7232
amills@annscollection.com
http://www.annscollection.com
Specializing in quality vintage jewelry, Bakelite, sterling sliver, and glittering evening bags.

Kathleen Kielkopf
AntiqueJewelry.com
2073 Ford Parkway
Saint Paul, MN 55116
ph: 800-328-1179 or 651-690-0842
fax: 651-698-0316
info@antiquejewelry.com
http://www.antiquejewelry.com
Source for buying and selling estate and antique jewelry.

Ron Geweniger
Old World Jewelers Ltd.
1301 West 22nd St., Ste. 308
Oak Brook, IL 60523
ph: 630-990-0100 or 800-322-3871
fax: 630-928-0880
sales@oldworldjewelers.com
http://www.oldworldjewelers.com
Dealers in fine antique and estate jewelry and timepieces for over 20 years; featuring toy Swiss made watches; also new watches.

Elizabeth Armstrong
Link to the Past, A
30W262 Bedford
Warrenville, IL 60555
elizabeth@alinkto.com
http://www.alinkto.com
Buys and sells Victorian jewelry through costume jewelry of the 1940s.

Dixie Markun Scott
Miss Dixie's Dazzlers
249 CR 5603
Berryville, AR 72616
ph: 870-545-3232
fax: 870-545-3232
dixie@missdixiesdazzlers.com
http://www.missdixiesdazzlers.com
Specializes in vintage jewelry: designer, sets, Victorian, Art Deco, Art Nouveau, Trifari, rhinestones, Haskell, Hobe, Alice Caviness.

Janice Costiloe
Jan's Jewels
3325 Eastman Dr.
Oklahoma City, OK 73112
ph: 405-840-2341
fax: 405-840-1057
jan@jansjewels.com
http://www.jansjewels.com
Buys and sells all kinds of vintage and antique jewelry: Lucite, Bakelite, celluloid, Victorian, rhinestone jewelry and much more.

Jan Thomas
J'antiques & Collectibles
9307 Mercer Dr.
Dallas, TX 75228
ph: 214-320-0489
fax: 214-320-1660
jthomas@jantiques.com
http://www.jantiques.com
Specializing in antique and vintage jewelry in all price ranges.

Jerry Forrest, GG, ISA CAPP
Jewelry Forrest, Inc.
9100 N. Central Expy., Ste. 185
Dallas, TX 75231-5901
ph: 214-368-5352 or 800-368-5376
fax: 214-750-1141
jerryforrest@compuserve.com
Custom jewelers and gemologists; an American Gem Society Accredited Gem Laboratory; Certified Member, ISA.

George & Dotty Stringfield
Illusion Jewels
215 Plum Creek Rd.
Longview, TX 75605
ph: 903-663-3415
ijjewels@yahoo.com
http://www.illusionjewels.com
Buys and sells vintage and collectible costume jewelry; carries original designs by Dorothea; home of "Researching Costume Jewelry," recognized online resource for dates and historical information on jewelry designers and companies.

Billie & John McBride
South Texas Trading Company
P.O. Box 857
Port Aransas, TX 78373
ph: 361-749-6149 or 800-484-9293 x3474
STFNandTRADING@centurytel.net
http://www.southtexastrading.com
Specializing in the sale of vintage and collectible costume jewelry, specializing in Bakelite, Christmas tree pins, and 20th century costume jewelry; has 350-member online jewelry group; nationwide pickers available.

Christina Felps
Cat's Fancy, The
12221 Chisholm Valley Dr., #423
Round Rock, TX 78681
ph: 512-238-8037
catfancy@io.com
http://www.io.com/~catfancy
Buys and sells vintage and costume jewelry; Web site contains an online store front; maintains wish list for

customers wanting to add to their collection; also repairs and restores (replace pin shanks and clasps, match/replace stones.)

Greg DeMark
DeMark Jewelry & Antiques
P.O. Box 6301
Longmont, CO 80501
ph: 303-678-0545
Specializes in antique and vintage jewelry, particularly in Victorian, Edwardian, Deco, Retro and modern jewelry in gold, silver, platinum; also costume jewelry.

Janet Lawwill
Azillion SPARKLZ
P.O. Box 36269
Tucson, AZ 85750
ph: 520-907-2839
fax: 413-683-7503
Jewel@Sparklz.com
http://www.sparklz.com
Buys and sells vintage costume jewelry: Victorian, Nouveau, Deco, rhinestones through the 1960s; cuff links, charms, buckles, shoe buckles, cameos, hair, sterling, gold; guides for cleaning, relating, storing, buying, and selling.

Jane H. Clarke
Morning Glory Antiques & Jewelry
12815 Central NE
Albuquerque, NM 87123
ph: 505-296-2300
jane@morninggloryantiques.com
http://www.morninggloryantiques.com
Buys and sells vintage jewelry.

Susan Hayes
Antique Jewelry Mall
P.O. Box 2648
Palos Verdes Peninsula, CA 90274
ph: 800-292-4900
info@antiquejewelrymall.com
http://www.antiquejewelrymall.com
Large online collection of estate and antique jewelry, including Victorian, Art Deco, filigree, antique rings, white gold, wedding & engagement rings, earrings, cufflinks, charms, bracelets, etc.

Patsy Comer
Patsy Comer's Antiques & Jewelry
7249 Reseda Blvd.
Reseda, CA 91335-3046
ph: 818-345-1631
fax: 818-345-1914
patsycomer@yahoo.com
Buys and sells costume and fine jewelry from all eras including designer; also costume jewelry, gold and sterling; 1960s memorabilia such as peace signs, designer costume and 1960s and '70s jewelry; sells to the trade, does mail order.

Leigh Leshner
Thanks for the Memories
P.O. Box 55113
Sherman Oaks, CA 91413-0113
ph: 818-981-7813
fax: 818-981-3466
venture818@aol.com
http://www.tias.com/stores/memories
Carries a large variety of antique and vintage jewelry covering all styles and periods.

Adrienne Shivers
Garden Party Collection
123 Marian Way
Pismo Beach, CA 93449
ph: 805-689-5574
fax: 805-473-2090
info@costumejewel.com
http://www.costumejewel.com
Specializing in antique, vintage and collectible costume and estate jewelry including designer, rhinestone, Bakelite, sterling and period jewelry pieces.

Janice Friedli
Gold Turtle & Co.
1315 W. Lockeford St.
Lodi, CA 95242
ph: 209-334-1909 or 209-334-5108
fax: 209-334-5108
gturtle@inreach.com
http://www.tace.com/vendors/gturtle.html
Buys and sells vintage jewelry: Victorian cameos and other authentic Victorian era jewelry set with jet, coral, garnets, and mosaics.

Candy Warmee
Heirloom Estate Jewelry
8698 Elk Grove Blvd., Ste. 3, PMB 225
Elk Grove, CA 95624-3300
ph: 916-684-0788
buyoldjewelry@aol.com
http://www.buyoldjewelry.com
Specializes in Art Deco and Victorian jewelry; has inventory of hundreds of gold and silver movable charms.

Pandora L. McKinnon
Pandora's Jewelry Box
4841 Martin Luther King Blvd.
Sacramento, CA 95820-4932
ph: 916-452-6728
fax: 916-452-6728
lfjantiquenews@angelfire.com
http://members.fortunecity.com/jewels4u2
Antique and collectible costume jewelry for sale.

Randeen Cummings, ISA CAPP
Cummings & Associates
P.O. Box 5484
Eugene, OR 97405-0484
ph: 541-345-5856
fax: 541-345-8192
avaluequest@uswest.net
http://www.avaluequest.com
Specializes in selling & appraising residential contents, fine art, estate jewelry, 18th & 19th century antiques, American Brilliant period cut glass; also specialized marketing for clients:

consultations, estate, and Internet sales.

Hillary Parsons
Hillary's Antiques
8441 SE 68th St. #313
Mercer Island, WA 98040
ph: 206-232-5309
fax: 206-236-0142
jewelry@hillarysantiques.com
http://www.hillarysantiques.com
Buys and sells antique and vintage jewelry including Victorian, Art Deco, Art Nouveau and costume jewelry.

Terri Krantz
Lovejoys Antique Jewelry & Silver
P.O. Box 28366
Bellingham, WA 98228
fax: 360-715-3757
tkrantz@nas.com
http://www.nas.com/lovejoy/love.html
Specializes in antique jewelry and silver with an emphasis on Victorian, Art Deco, and Art Nouveau.

Experts

Peter J. Shemonsky, GG, ISA
24 Horace St.
Boston, MA 02128-1534
ph: 617-569-1502
fax: 617-846-4767
pshemonsky@butterfields.com

Peter J. Theriault, FGA, GG
Northeast Gemlab, Inc.
58 Bayview St.
Camden, ME 04843-2242
ph: 207-236-3933
fax: 207-236-3933
gemlab@midcoast.com
http://www.antiquejewelrytimes.com
Independent gems and jewelry appraiser; publishes "The Art & Antique Service Directory," the "Redbook;" writes gemology column for "Maine Antique Digest" and "Antiques West."

Joan Vogel Elias
Absolutely Vintage Designer &
   Collectible Jewelry
51 Regents Park
Westport, CT 06880
ph: 203-255-6600
fax: 203-255-0898
JVEjewel@aol.com
http://www.absolutelyvintage.net
Dealer of quality vintage, designer, collectible and estate jewelry and accessories; over 1,175 pieces listed on the Web site which is updated weekly; interested in buying one piece or an entire jewelry collection.

Gail Brett Levine, GG
Timeless, Inc.
P.O. Box 7683
Rego Park, NY 11374-7683
ph: 718-897-7305
fax: 718-997-9057
76766.614@compuserve.com
http://www.auctionmarketresource.com
Graduate Gemologist, appraiser, lecturer, publisher of "Auction Market Resource For Gems & Jewelry," a

semi-annual jewelry price, condition, quality report.

Time Warp Custom & Vintage Attire
P.O. Box 9186
Schenectady, NY 12305-0186
ph: 518-347-1126
fax: 518-347-1126
timewarp@timewarp.com
http://www.timewarp.com
Buys/sells/appraises vintage clothing, jewelry, accessories; reproduces vintage and historical clothing for museums, reenactment, theater, ballroom dancing, etc.; also restores, repairs and alters clothing, textiles and costume jewelry.

Roseann Ettinger
Remember When
21-23 W. Broad St.
Hazleton, PA 18201
ph: 570-454-8465 or 570-450-5542
popgems2001@hotmail.com
Author of "Popular Jewelry 1840-1940," "Forties and Fifties Popular Jewelry," and "Popular Jewelry of the '60s, '70s, & '80s."

Arthur Guy Kaplan
P.O. Box 1942
Baltimore, MD 21203
ph: 410-752-2090 or 410-664-8350
fax: 410-783-2723
Author of "The Official Price Guide to Antique Jewelry."

C. Jeanenne Bell, G.G., N.G.J.A.
Jewelry Box Antiques, Inc.
7325 Quivira Rd., Ste. 238
Shawnee Mission, KS 66216
ph: 913-962-8533
fax: 913-963-4418
cjbell@msn.com
http://www.jewelryboxantiques.com
Vintage jewelry dealer and expert; author of "Collectors Encyclopedia of Hairwork Jewelry," "Answers to Questions About Old Jewelry 1840-1950" 6th Ed., "How to be a Jewelry Detective," "Warman's Field Guide to Antique Jewelry."

Ann M. Pitman
8006 Hertfordshire Circle
Spring, TX 77379-4645
AnnMPitman@cs.com
Specializes in rhinestone vintage costume jewelry; writes the "Jewelry Box" column on vintage and antique jewelry, fine and costume jewelry; author of "Inside the Jewelry Box - A collector's Guide to Costume Jewelry."

Christie Romero
Center for Jewelry Studies
P.O. Box 424
Anaheim, CA 92815-0424
ph: 714-778-1828
fax: 714-778-3432
CR4jewelry@aol.com
http://www.center4jewelrystudies.org
One of America's leading scholars on antique, period & vintage jewelry; author of "Warman's Jewelry - A

Fully Illustrated Identification & Price Guide to 18th, 19th & 20th Century Fine & Costume Jewelry;" lecturer, consultant.

Pandora L. McKinnon
Pandora's Jewelry Box
4841 Martin Luther King Blvd.
Sacramento, CA 95820-4932
ph: 916-452-6728
fax: 916-452-6728
lfjantiquenews@angelfire.com
http://members.fortunecity.com/
   jewels4u2
Writes articles about jewelry and other accessories.

Internet Resources

Peter J. Theriault, FGA, GG
Antique Jewelry Times On-Line
58 Bayview St.
Camden, ME 04843-2242
ph: 207-236-3933
fax: 207-236-3933
gemlab@midcoast.com
http://www.antiquejewelrytimes.com
An online magazine dedicated to antique jewelry and collectible watches; educational articles for dealers and collectors.

Robert S. Koppelman
JewelShow
1712 SE 13th St.
Fort Lauderdale, FL 33316
ph: 954-524-0770
fax: 954-524-1999
rokogrp@ix.netcom.com
http://www.jewelshow.com
The ultimate locator and showcase for fine antique and estate jewelry, rare gems, unusual timepieces.

Man./Prod./Dist.

Ron Edelstein
Ron's Rhinestones
P.O. Box 2028
New York, NY 10159-2028
ph: 212-253-6299 or 800-299-2185
fax: 212-253-6299
rhinestones@mindspring.com
http://www.ronsrhinestones.com
Specializes in contemporary rhinestone jewelry of Austrian crystal made in the USA: earrings, necklaces, bracelets, hair ornaments, chokers, pins.

Misc. Services

Leigh Leshner
Venture Entertainment Group
P.O. Box 55113
Sherman Oaks, CA 91413-0113
ph: 818-981-7813
fax: 818-981-3466
venture818@aol.com
http://www.tias.com/stores/memories
Producers of the award winning video cassette series on vintage & costume jewelry from 1800s to 1960; a visual price guide for signed and unsigned costume jewelry by Trifari, Coro, Corocraft, Haskell, Hobe, Eisenberg, Chanel, etc.

Periodicals

Elyse Zorn Karlin, Ed.
Newsletter: Adornment
1333A North Ave., Box 103
New Rochelle, NY 10804
ph: 914-235-0983
fax: 914-235-0983
info@jewelryhistorians.com
http://www.jewelryhistorians.com
Quarterly newsletter covering ancient, antique, contemporary studio, costume and vintage jewelry, historic costume, antique buttons and beads; contains articles, book reviews, terminology, extensive calendar, and more.

Gail Brett Levine, GG
Timeless, Inc.
Magazine: Auction Market Resource for
   Gems & Jewelry
P.O. Box 7683
Rego Park, NY 11374-7683
ph: 718-897-7305
fax: 718-997-9057
76766.614@compuserve.com
http://www.auctionmarketresource.com
A semi-annual publication providing data for a wide range of jewelry items including antique through contemporary, diamonds and colored stones; detailed text with photographs; offers research services to track fads, trends, etc.

Repair Services

Vogue & Vintage
106 Middle Neck Rd.
Great Neck, NY 11021
ph: 516-773-3338
fax: 516-773-3447
gifts@vogueandvintage.com
http://www.vogueandvintage.com
Specializes in the repair and restoration of antique and estate jewelry including Hobe, Whiting & Davis, Judith Jack, Haskell and others.

Eugene Rooney, GG
Victorian Manor Jewelry
33 Main St.
P.O. Box 285
New Market, MD 21774-0285
ph: 301-865-3083 or 877-865-3083
fax: 301-865-0649
sales@victorianmanorjewelry.com
http://www.victorianmanorjewelry.com
Buys and sells antique and estate jewelry; repairs, restores, re-enameling, remounting, restring, and custom design jewelry.

Suppliers

Matthew Ribarich
MrStones.com
P.O. Box 10104
Costa Mesa, CA 92627
ph: 949-645-9017 or 949-645-9020
fax: 949-645-9020
MRstones4U@aol.com
http://www.mrstones.com
Supplies a wide variety of antique and costume jewelry replacement stones including marcasites, rhinestones,

imitation pearls, rose cut garnets and jadeite jade; over 6 million stones in inventory; stone matching services available.

GENEALOGY

(see also HERALDRY; IMMIGRATION)

Internet Resources

Ancestry.com
360 W. 4800 N.
Provo, UT 84604
ph: 801-705-7000
fax: 801-705-7001
pr@myfamilyinc.com
http://www.ancestry.com
Premiere resource for family genealogy news, views and how-tos.

Misc. Services

Marie Varrelman Melchiori, CGRS
121 Tapawingo Rd. SW
Vienna, VA 22180-5964
ph: 703-938-8103
fax: 703-938-7279
mvmcgrs@aol.com
http://www.ancestordetective.com/
speakers/melchiori.htm
Certified Genealogical Record Specialist in Civil War research; will help identify owners of historical items; will assist members of the legal profession locate missing heirs.

Family History Library, Genealogical
Society of Utah
35 North West Temple St.
Salt Lake City, UT 84150-3400
ph: 800-453-3860 x22331
fax: 801-240-5551
fhl@ldschurch.org
http://www.familysearch.org

Museums/Libraries

Western Reserve Historical Society
10825 East Blvd.
Cleveland, OH 44106-1703
ph: 216-721-5722
fax: 216-721-0645
webmaster@wrhs.org
http://www.wrhs.org
Oldest cultural institution in Cleveland, with a research/ genealogical library, costume wing, auto & aviation museum and restored mansion under one roof; special interest area in genealogical research.

Periodicals

Magazine: Heritage Quest
P.O. Box 329
Bountiful, UT 84011
ph: 800-760-2455
sales@agll.com
http://www.heritagequest.com
America's leading magazine for genealogists and family historians; published bi-monthly.

Newsletter: Ancestry Newsletter
P.O. Box 476
Salt Lake City, UT 84110
Published bi-monthly.

GERMAN ITEMS

(see ANTIQUES & COLLECTIBLES, German; MILITARIA; NAZI ITEMS)

GHOSTS & HAUNTINGS

(see also HALLOWEEN COLLECTIBLES; HORROR; WITCHES)

Book Sellers

Chris Woodyard
Invisible Ink: Books on Ghosts & Hauntings
1811 Stonewood Dr.
Beavercreek, OH 45432-4002
ph: 937-426-5110
fax: 937-320-1832
invisiblei@aol.com
http://www.invink.com
Collector of nonfiction books on ghosts & hauntings; also dealer in new and paranormal books; founder of Invisible Ink Collection at BGSU Popular Collection Library.

GILBERT

(see TOYS, Construction Sets; TRAINS, Toy [American Flyer])

GIRL SCOUT MEMORABILIA

(see also BOY SCOUT MEMORABILIA)

Collectors

Phyllis Palm
P.O. Box 5272
Hamden, CT 06518-0272
ph: 203-288-9190
poohdingaling@worldnet.att.net
Wants to buy old Girl Scout uniforms (also uniform parts), insignia, dolls, etc.

D. Nordlinger Stern
385 Bayview Dr. NE
Saint Petersburg, FL 33704-2430
ph: 727-894-4000
fax: 727-894-1040
dnordstern@aol.com
Wants Girl Scout memorabilia; please send list of items you have with asking prices.

Jerry King
8429 Katy Freeway
Houston, TX 77024-1903
ph: 713-465-2500
fax: 713-465-0824
jerry@kinglok.com
Wants Girl Scout memorabilia: pre-1960 catalogs, postcards, magazines, handbooks, 1912-1920 uniforms,

equipment, etc.; do not send items without prior arrangements.

Dealers

Roland Sayers
Southeastern Antiques & Collectibles
P.O. Box 629
Brevard, NC 28712
ph: 828-883-9562
Wants to buy pre-1960 Boy Scout and Girl Scout collectibles.

Darrell Wessinger
dwessinger.com
1036 Two Notch Rd.
Lexington, SC 29073-8953
ph: 803-359-6752
darrell@dwessinger.com
http://www.dwessinger.com
Dealer, collector, expert with over 35 years specializing in Boy Scout and Girl Scout memorabilia; buys all kinds of scouting memorabilia; collections bought and sold.

Doug Bearce
P.O. Box 4742
Salem, OR 97302-8742
ph: 503-399-9872
fax: 503-399-0559
bearce@prodigy.net
http://www.scouting-collectables.com
Buys and sells Boy Scout & Girl Scout items: books, uniforms, patches, pins, Order of the Arrow items, Jamboree, etc.

Experts

Roy More
Scout Patch Auction
2484 Dundee
Ann Arbor, MI 48103
ph: 734-663-6203
fax: 734-663-7227
spa@msen.com
http://www.tspa.com
Collector, dealer, appraiser expert in Girl Scout memorabilia.

Museums/Libraries

Mrs. Ralph Zitelman
Zitelman Scout Museum
123 Beard St.
Danville, IL 61832-6009
ph: 217-442-6678
Worldwide Scouting: patches, books, uniforms & equipment including Boy and Girl Scouts, Brownies, Explorers, Scoutmasters, etc.

GLASS

(see also BOOKS, Reference [Glass]; CUP PLATES; CRAFTS, Glass; ENAMELS; GLASS KNIVES; GLASSES; KITCHEN COLLECTIBLES; POWDER JARS; REPAIR/RESTORATION/ CONSERVATION, Glass; SALOON & BAR COLLECTIBLES; TABLEWARE)

Appraisers

Vivian A. Highberg, ISA
Hilding & Larson Emporium
473 Carnegie Dr.
Pittsburgh, PA 15243
ph: 412-563-2898
vivianahighberg@aol.com
Appraiser of glass: blown, molded, mold-blown, pressed, etched, engraved, enameled, cut, cameo, etc.; Victorian, Pattern, Art, Depression, Elegant, Modern and Studio Glass; English, American, Continental, Swedish; 1800s to 2000s.

Barbara M. Lessig, ISA CAPP
Pleasant Valley Antiques
21000 Georgia Ave.
Brookeville, MD 20833-1138
ph: 301-924-2293
fax: 301-570-1625
bmlessig@aol.com
http://www.lessigs.com
Specializes in the appraisal of glass, ceramics, silver, furniture, and household contents.

Dianne Gregg
Glassnob Antiques
10413 Gary Rd.
Potomac, MD 20854
ph: 301-299-6456
fax: 301-299-6456
glassnob@aol.com
Appraiser specializing in European glass from the 18th-20th century, American art glass, and contemporary studio glass.

Jeffrey Evans
Green Valley Auctions, Inc.
2259 Green Valley Lane
Mount Crawford, VA 22841
ph: 540-434-4260
fax: 540-434-4532
gvai@shentel.net
http://www.greenvalleyauctions.com
Specializes in the appraisal of American glass and furniture.

Christine N. Corbin, ISA
Motley's Auctions, Inc.
4402 West Broad St.
Richmond, VA 23230
ph: 804-355-2100
fax: 804-359-6954
cncorbin@motleys.com
http://www.motleysgroup.com
Auctioneers and appraisers of furniture, silver, fine art, decorative arts, real estate, general goods and vehicles.

Karen Rook
3339 Balsam Dr.
Winter Park, FL 32792
ph: 407-677-5560 or 407-310-1120
karenspiegler@aol.com
Specializes in the appraisal of glass from the period 1830 to 1940 including Early American and Victorian glassware.

Sharon Niles
Carousel, Inc.
14409 Manchester Rd.
Ballwin, MO 63011
ph: 636-391-4900
fax: 636-391-3993
carouselinc@hotmail.com
*Specializes in the appraisal,
conservation and restoration of glass.*

Linda H. Richard, ISA
Cajun Collection
3308 White Oak
Temple, TX 76502-3028
ph: 254-774-8608
cajun@vvm.com
http://www.vvm.com/~cajun
*Specializing in glass with emphasis on
1950s Modern glass, particularly
American, Swedish, and Scandinavian;
also collects glass from WV, including
Morgantown, Pilgrim, Blenko,
Kanawha, Seneca, Rainbow, and
Bischoff.*

Sandra Millius
1530 NE 48th Ave.
Portland, OR 97213
ph: 503-282-3838 or 503-515-7309
smillius@mindspring.com
http://jmot.home.sprynet.com
*Specializes in the appraisal of 19th
and 20th century glassware: Early
American pattern glass, art glass,
Depression glass, Elegant and mid-
century glass.*

Kathleen M. Bailey, AAA, ISA CAPP
Antique Appraisal & Estate Sale Service
- the Original
160 NW Gilman Blvd., Ste. #1
Issaquah, WA 98027
ph: 425-746-2777
fax: 425-746-3793
antiquabailey@aol.com
*Specialist in American, English,
German, Continental ceramics,
furniture, silver, glass, enamels,
Victoriana and decorative arts of the
18th to 20th centuries; full service
appraiser & estate sales since 1973.*

Auction Services

Dudley Browne
James D. Julia Auctioneers Inc.
Rt. 201, Skowhegan Rd.
P.O. Box 830
Fairfield, ME 04937
ph: 207-453-7125
fax: 207-453-2502
jjulia@juliaauctions.com
http://www.juliaauctions.com
*Conducts specialized auctions of all
types of quality glassware including
Tiffany, Galle, Royal Flemish, fine
quality cut glass, Victorian glass and
early glassware; uses nationally
recognized experts to catalog sales.*

James Hagenbuch
Glass Works Auctions
P.O. Box 180
102 Jefferson St.
East Greenville, PA 18041
ph: 215-679-5849
fax: 215-679-3068
glswrk@enter.net
http://www.glswrk-auction.com
*Specializes in the auction of historical
flasks, fruit jars, food & milk bottles,
sodas, poisons, whiskeys, medicines,
inks, barber bottles, bitters bottles,
scent bottles, shaving mugs, target &
range balls, etc.*

Tom Harris Auction Center
203 South 18th Ave.
Marshalltown, IA 50158
ph: 641-754-4890
tomharris@tomharrisauctions.com
http://www.tomharrisauctions.com
*Specialized auctions of flint glass,
Sandwich, carnival, Pittsburgh; also
ceramics such as transferware, lustre,
historical Staffordshire, etc.*

Pacific Glass Auctions
1507 21st St., Ste. 203
Sacramento, CA 95814
ph: 916-443-3296 or 916-443-3210
fax: 916-443-3199
info@pacglass.com
http://www.pacglass.com
*The largest antique bottle auction
house currently on the Internet.*

Clubs/Associations

Glass Research Society of New Jersey
1501 Glasstown Rd.
Millville, NJ 08332-1566
ph: 856-825-6800 or 800-998-4552
fax: 856-825-2410
mail@wheatonvillage.org
http://www.wheatonvillage.org

Nancy Sheriff, Member. Chair
National American Glass Club, The,
Ltd.
Newsletter: Glass Club Bulletin
P.O. Box 8489
Silver Spring, MD 20907-8489
nagc@att.net
http://www.glassclub.org
*An international organization devoted
to the study and appreciation of glass
from antiquity to present; the semi-
annual newsletter of the NAGC covers
glass exhibits, chapter activities, etc.;
also publishes "Glass Shards."*

Bill Donalson
Tallahassee Glass & Antiques Club
Newsletter: TGAC Newsletter
3808 Forsythe Way
Tallahassee, FL 32308-2532
ph: 904-893-9794
*Collectors of glass, china, pottery,
silver and tools; meets 4th Tuesday
from September through June.*

Alvina Breckel
Greater Chicago Glass Collectors' Club
Newsletter: Glass Club Bulletin
185 Fuller Lane
Winnetka, IL 60093
ph: 847-441-8626
alvina@oakton.edu
*A chapter of the National American
Glass Club.*

Alvina Breckel
Greater Chicago Glass Collectors' Club
185 Fuller Lane
Winnetka, IL 60093
ph: 847-441-8626
alvina@oakton.edu
*A Chicago area chapter of the
National American Glass Club; meets
first Thursday of each month, Sept.
through June; members interested in
all types of glass.*

Lenette Heidman
Houston Glass Club
P.O. Box 1254
2728 First St.
Rosenberg, TX 77471-1254
ph: 281-342-4876 or 281-342-7722
*Club specializes in Depression and
Elegant glassware from the 1920s
through 1950s; sponsors annual
Depression glass show in August in
Rosenberg, TX; meets 2nd Tuesday of
each month in Houston, TX.*

Collectors

Tim Mason
Sweet Glass Antiques & Collectibles
719 Rawdon Rd.
Hillsvale, Nova Scotia B0N 1Z0 Canada
ph: 902-757-2780
fax: 902-757-2238
sweetglass@gosea.com
http://www.gosea.com/sweetglass
*Specializes in collecting glass from the
1930s to 1960s.*

Dealers

Bud Marchant
Lil-Bud Antiques
142 Main St.
Yarmouth Port, MA 02675
ph: 508-362-8984

Christopher Woods
Historic Glasshouse
157 Fairgrounds Rd.
Plymouth, NH 03264-3326
ph: 516-759-6744 or 603-536-3137
fax: 509-461-1572
john@antiquebottles-glass.com
http://www.antiquebottles-glass.net
*One of the largest dealers in 17th -
19th century antique bottles and glass;
Web site lists a wide variety of fine
quality items for sale; professionally
clean staining on glass items; will
search for specific items; also
appraises.*

William Banks
Classical Glass
P.O. Box 364
Wiscasset, ME 04578-0364
ph: 207-882-9393
inventor@gwi.net
http://www.gwi.net/~inventor
*Specializing in antique and collectible
glassware and art pottery; author of a
price guide on Victorian opalescent
glass.*

Rosemary Trietsch
Glass Cupboard, The
23 Lee Ave.
Albertson, NY 11507
ph: 516-248-5730
cupboard@optonline.net
http://www.theglasscupboard.com
*Specializing in Depression-era
glassware.*

George Kamm
George Kamm's 20th Century Glass,
Pottery, Etc.
23 Phillip Dr.
Kirkwood, PA 17536-9511
ph: 717-529-3741
fax: 717-529-2042
gkamm@earthlink.net
http://www.artglass-pottery.com
*Sells contemporary art glass,
paperweights, pottery, Raku, animal
and bird figurines, and more.*

Barbara M. Lessig, ISA CAPP
Pleasant Valley Antiques
21000 Georgia Ave.
Brookeville, MD 20833-1138
ph: 301-924-2293
fax: 301-570-1625
bmlessig@aol.com
http://www.lessigs.com
*Specialist in appraising and selling
all types of glassware.*

Stephen G. DelSordo
Heritage Resource Group
305 Oakley St.
Cambridge, MD 21613
ph: 410-228-8934
fax: 410-221-8061
sdelsordo@comcast.net
http://www.heritageresource.com
*A cultural resource management/
historic preservation firm that has
contracts to locate, provide,
authenticate artifacts for museums and
collectors; areas of expertise include
architecture, industry, domestic,
agriculture, and maritime.*

Michael Smeresky
Heritage Antiques
39 E. Patrick St.
Frederick, MD 21701
ph: 301-668-0299
hantq@aol.com
http://www.heritageantiques.com
*Specializes in 1920s through 1940s
dining room antiques and accessories:
dinnerware, glassware, furniture.*

Meryl Goldstein
All Antique Glass
P.O. Box 3515
Norfolk, VA 23514
ph: 757-625-1888
majn@visi.net
http://www.allantiqueglass.com
*Features Early American Pattern
Glass (EAPG), pressed, historical,
Victorian colored glass, Carnival,
Depression, Elegant, etc.*

Crystal Eye Antique Glass
5750 N. Powerline Rd.
Fort Lauderdale, FL 33309
brett@tvtaxi.com
*Buys and sells antique glassware:
Depression, art glass, pattern,
Fostoria, crackle, Imperial, Fenton,
L.G. Wright, Janet Glass Co., Tiffin,
Viking, Northwood, Jefferson, Dugan,
vaseline, Westmoreland, and others.*

Bargain Shack
P.O. Box 524
Wadsworth, OH 44282
ph: 330-925-9751
bargainhunters@bargainshack.com
http://www.bargainshack.com
*Buys and sells collectible glass: Boyd,
Mosser, L.G. Wright, Summit,
Guernsey, Pilgrim, and Gibson glass:
animal figurines, open & covered
salts, toothpicks, covered dishes, fairy
lights, vaseline glass a specialty.*

Reyne Haines
Just Glass
P.O. Box 20146
Cincinnati, OH 45220
ph: 513-961-5794
reyne@mindspring.com
http://www.justglass.com
*An Internet glass-only online mall
with dealers offering glass at fixed
prices: art glass, carnival and
Depression glass, modern and Elegant
glass, studio glass, opalescent and
pattern glass, etc.*

Jim & Barbara Payne
Liberty Ridge Antiques
9634 St. Rt. 12 West
Findlay, OH 45840
ph: 419-422-7920
Barbpain@aol.com
*Dealer, appraiser, expert specializes
in buying and selling antique
glassware, especially Findlay,
Fostoria, Tiffin.*

Carol Ann Clary
House of Glass, The
7102 Langdon
Houston, TX 77074
ph: 713-777-3347
carolclary@aol.com
*Glass dealer and appraiser; over 23
years specializing in American
glassware and pottery.*

Sue Morse
Emma's Antiques
P.O. Box 889
Redlands, CA 92373
ph: 909-864-3426
fax: 909-864-3426
emmastrunk@aol.com
http://www.emmasantiques.com
*Buys and sells unusual glass of the
Victorian era, 1837 to 1901.*

Randy & Debbie Coe
Coe's Mercantile
2459 SE TV Hwy PMB #321
Hillsboro, OR 97123-7919
ph: 503-640-9122
fax: 503-648-2261
elegantglass@aol.com
*Authors of a book on Elegant Glass;
specializes in Cambridge, Depression,
Elegant, Fenton, Fostoria,
Franciscan, Heisey, Hull, McKee,
Tiffin, and Westmoreland glass.*

Tony Hayter
1st.Glass
U.K.
1st@glassman.com
http://www.1st.glassman.com
*Glass dealer and expert; Web site
offers a unique online Victorian glass
registration lozenge translator to give
an easy method of dating and finding
the manufacturer of any English glass
registered between 1842 and 1883.*

Experts

Frank Chiarenza
39 West Main St.
Meriden, CT 06451-4110
ph: 203-639-9778
fax: 203-238-7025
chiarenzaglassmuseum@snet.net
*Director of the Frank Chiarenza
Museum of Glass, co-author with
James Slater of "The Milk Glass
Book," a frequent contributor to glass
publications, and former president of
the National Milk Glass Collectors
Society.*

Dianne Gregg
Glassnob Antiques
10413 Gary Rd.
Potomac, MD 20854
ph: 301-299-6456
fax: 301-299-6456
glassnob@aol.com
*Appraiser specializing in European
glass from the 18th-20th century,
American art glass, contemporary
studio glass.*

Mark Pickvet
5071 Watson Dr.
Flint, MI 48506
ph: 810-736-9320
MPickvet@aol.com
*Author of "Official Price Guide to
Glassware."*

Internet Resources

Dictionary of Glass Marks
2412 Sawyer Lane
Aransas Pass, TX 78336
ph: 800-484-6604 x789
bpepau@msn.com
http://www.heartland-discoveries.com/
dictionary.htm
*Thumbnail images of glass marks
indexed according to animals, birds,
crowns, shields, buildings, ovals,
stars, words, etc.*

Angela Bowey
Glass Museum On-Line
P.O. Box 113
Paihia Mall
Paihia, Bay of Islands 0252 New Zealand
ph: 649-402-8416
fax: 649-402-8538
abowey@clear.net.nz
http://www.glass.co.nz
*Extensive online articles about glass;
information message board; glass
encyclopedia.*

Man./Prod./Dist.

Joe Rice
House of Glass, Inc., The
7900 E. State Rd. 28
Elwood, IN 46036-8449
ph: 765-552-6841
fax: 765-552-6854
*Makes paperweights all signed by
owner, Joe Rice; also makes all sorts
of other solid glass: ashtrays, pears,
ringholders, etc.*

Misc. Services

R. Wayne Lowry
Jar Doctor
401 Johnston Ct.
Raymore, MO 64083
ph: 816-318-0161
fax: 816-318-0162
Jardoctor@aol.com
http://www.jardoctor.com
*Manufacturers a bottle and jar
cleaning system; also manufactures
glass cleaning equipment for
insulators, marbles as well - any
antique glass.*

Museums/Libraries

Bennington Museum, The
West Main St.
Bennington, VT 05201
ph: 802-447-1571
fax: 802-442-8305
bennmuse@sover.net
http://www.benningtonmuseum.com
*One of the finest regional art history
museums in the country; works by
Grandma Moses, American glass, VT
furniture, Bennington pottery, the
oldest Stars & Stripes in existence, the
1925 luxury touring car "The Wasp,"
and much more.*

Frank Chiarenza, Dir.
Frank Chiarenza Museum of Glass, The
39 West Main St.
Meriden, CT 06451-4110
ph: 203-639-9778
fax: 203-238-7025
chiarenzaglassmuseum@snet.net
*Museum displays an eclectic collection
of American and European glass,
mainly pressed, 1850 to present,
including many animal covered dishes,
historical and commemorative
tablewares, lamps, inkwells, Victorian
novelties, etc.*

Museum of American Glass at Wheaton
Village
1501 Glasstown Rd.
Millville, NJ 08332-1566
ph: 856-825-6800 or 800-998-4552
fax: 856-825-2410
mail@wheatonvillage.org
http://www.wheatonvillage.org
*Covers all types of American glass:
Stiegel, Amelung, flasks, pressed, art
glass, Art Nouveau, paperweights,
lamps & lighting, cut glass, 20th
century art glass, reproductions, pre-
studio movement, contemporary studio
glass, etc.*

Corning Museum of Glass, The
Journal: Journal of Glass Studies
One Museum Way
Corning, NY 14830-2253
ph: 607-937-5371
fax: 607-937-3352
pr@cmog.org
http://www.cmog.org
*Over 35,000 glass objects, innovative
exhibits, videos, models; glass history,
archaeology, and early manufacturing;
great Web site with lots of information about glass.*

Chrysler Museum of Art, The
245 West Olney Rd.
Norfolk, VA 23510-1587
ph: 757-664-6200
fax: 757-664-6201
museum@chrysler.org
http://www.chrysler.org
*Fine collection of early to 20th century
glass; also ancient to modern artifacts
from all over the world.*

West Virginia Museum of American
Glass
P.O. Box 574
Weston, WV 26452
ph: 304-269-5006
wvmuseumofglass@aol.com
http://members.aol.com/
wvmuseumofglass
*The museum shares the diverse and
rich heritage of glass as a product
and historical object as well as telling
of the lives of glass workers, their
families and communities, and of the
tools and machines they used in glass
houses.*

Houston Museum of Decorative Arts,
The
201 High St.
Chattanooga, TN 37403
ph: 423-267-7176
houston@chattanooga.net
http://www.chattanooga.net/houston
*Contains one of the world's finest
collections of antique glass, furniture,
and ceramics.*

Toledo Museum of Art, The
2445 Monroe St.
P.O. Box 1013
Toledo, OH 43697-1013
ph: 419-255-8000 or 800-644-6862
marketing@toledomuseum.org
http://www.toledomuseum.org
*Internationally recognized collections
of glass, paintings, and decorative
and graphic arts.*

Glass Museum at the Dunkirk Library
309 S. Franklin
Dunkirk, IN 47336-1209
ph: 765-768-6872
fax: 765-768-6872
*Collection contains 25 leaded-glass
windows, 25 hanging lamps and
hundreds of hand-blown and hand-
pressed glass creations.*

Jan Smith, Curator
Bergstrom-Mahler Museum
165 N. Park Ave.
Neenah, WI 54956
ph: 920-751-4670
*Extensive collection of glass
paperweights, Bohemian Glass and
Victorian Art Glass.*

Historical Glass Museum
Newsletter: Looking Glass
1157 Orange St.
P.O. Box 921
Redlands, CA 92373
ph: 909-798-0868
http://www.rth.org/lookingglass
*A breathtaking display of American
glassware.*

Periodicals

James Hagenbuch
Magazine: Antique Bottle & Glass
Collector
P.O. Box 180
102 Jefferson St.
East Greenville, PA 18041
ph: 215-679-5849
fax: 215-679-3068
glswrk@enter.net
http://www.glswrk-auction.com
*A monthly magazine for the glass and
bottle collector.*

West Virginia Museum of American
Glass
Magazine: All About Glass
P.O. Box 574
Weston, WV 26452
ph: 304-269-5006
wvmuseumofglass@aol.com
http://members.aol.com/
wvmuseumofglass
The voice of the glass collecting

*community; focuses on 20th century
American glass including fine art
glass, pattern glass, paperweights,
marbles and other glass-related
topics.*

Repair Services

Sharon Niles
Carousel, Inc.
14409 Manchester Rd.
Ballwin, MO 63011
ph: 636-391-4900
fax: 636-391-3993
carouselinc@hotmail.com
*Specializes in the appraisal,
conservation and restoration of glass.*

Akro Agate/Westite

Clubs/Associations

Roger Hardy
Akro Agate Collector's Club, Inc.
Newsletter: Clarksburg Crow
10 Bailey St.
Clarksburg, WV 26301
ph: 304-624-4523 or 304-624-7600
rhardy0424@citynet.net
http://www.mkl.com/akro/club
*Focuses on Akro marbles, children's
dishes and general line items.*

Collectors

Albert Morin
668 Robbins Ave. #23
Dracut, MA 01826
ph: 978-454-7907
akroal@attbi.com
*Wants either Akro Agate or Westite
items.*

Experts

Roger Hardy
West End Antiques
97 Milford St.
Clarksburg, WV 26301
ph: 304-624-4523 or 304-624-7600
rhardy0424@citynet.net
*Author of "The Complete Line of Akro
Agate, With Prices."*

Art

(see also GLASS, Studio
[Contemporary]; LAMPS &
LIGHTING, Tiffany/Handel/Pairpoint;
TIFFANY ITEMS)

Appraisers

Paul Royka
AppraisalDay.com
210 Park Avenue, #295
Worcester, MA 01609
ph: 978-582-8207
fax: 978-582-8207
appraisalday@aol.com
http://www.appraisalday.com
*Expert, author and appraiser of art
glass.*

Vivian Riegelman, ISA CAPP
AAA Appraisal Co., Inc.
10612-D Providence Rd., #225
Charlotte, NC 28277
ph: 704-843-4033
fax: 704-843-7562
vivri@carolina.rr.com
*Certified Member of the International
Society of Appraisers and the
American Society of Appraisers.*

Patricia Yocom, ISA
Private Stock
P.O. Box 81189
Cleveland, OH 44149
ph: 440-238-3522
fax: 440-238-3522
lctfavrile@aol.com

Martha C. Arney, ISA
Dunes Antiques Center, Inc.
12825 Red Arrow Highway
Sawyer, MI 49125-9173
ph: 616-426-4043
fax: 616-426-8283
dunesantiques@qtm.net
http://www.dunesantiques.com
*Appraiser of residential contents, art
glass, pottery, decorative arts.*

Brian Severn
Severn's Art Glass
150 Cleaveland Ave.
Pleasant Hill, CA 94523
http://home.earthlink.net/~bsevern/
artglass.htm
*Dealer, collector, appraiser of art
glass; offers antique, Art Nouveau,
contemporary: Steuben, Loetz, Quezal,
Durand, Tiffany, Orient & Flume,
Lundberg Studios, PHOENIX Studios,
Mashlach, Correia, perfumes and
more.*

Sylvia Fitzgerald, ISA
A.A.E.S.
P.O. Box 2509
Sacramento, CA 95812
ph: 800-471-9841 or 916-448-2428
sylfitz@compuserve.com
*Accredited ISA appraiser specializing
in Art Nouveau, Art Deco, Arts &
Crafts, art glass, art pottery, and fine
porcelains.*

Brill Lee
Brill Lee Appraisal Services
P.O. Box 244
Bellevue, WA 98009-0244
ph: 425-885-4518
fax: 425-895-1022
brilllee@hotmail.com
*Has appraised, collected, bought, sold
Tiffany, Steuben, Quezal, Fostoria,
and other art glass electric and
kerosene lamp shades for over 30
years; also will sell on consignment
for clients.*

Kathleen M. Bailey, AAA, ISA CAPP
Antique Appraisal & Estate Sale Service
- the Original
160 NW Gilman Blvd., Ste. #1
Issaquah, WA 98027
ph: 425-746-2777
fax: 425-746-3793
antiquabailey@aol.com
*Specialist in American, English,
German, Continental ceramics,
furniture, silver, glass, enamels,
Victoriana and decorative arts of the
18th to 20th centuries; full service
appraiser & estate sales since 1973.*

Auction Services

Jane Prentiss
Skinner, Inc.
63 Park Plaza
The Heritage on the Garden
Boston, MA 02116
ph: 617-350-5400
fax: 617-350-5429
info@skinnerinc.com
http://www.skinnerinc.com
*Established in 1971, Skinner Inc. is
the fourth largest auction house in the
US; has offices in Boston and Bolton,
MA.*

Jane Prentiss
Skinner, Inc.
63 Park Plaza
The Heritage on the Garden
Boston, MA 02116
ph: 617-350-5400
fax: 617-350-5429
info@skinnerinc.com
http://www.skinnerinc.com
*Established in 1971, Skinner Inc. is
the fourth largest auction house in the
US; has offices in Boston and Bolton,
MA.*

Early Auction Co.
123 Main St.
Milford, OH 45150
ph: 513-831-4833
fax: 513-831-1441
info@earlyauctionco.com
http://www.earlyauctionco.com
Specializes in art glass auctions.

James L. Jackson, ISA
Jackson's Auctioneers & Appraisers
2229 Lincoln St.
P.O. Box 50613
Cedar Falls, IA 50613
ph: 319-277-2256
fax: 319-277-1252
jacksons@jacksonsauction.com
http://www.jacksonsauction.com
*Conducts specialty auctions of
Victorian, Art Nouveau and Art Deco
glass, leaded and reverse painted
lamps, etc.*

Joy Luke
Joy Luke Auction Gallery
300 E. Grove St.
Bloomington, IL 61701-5232
ph: 309-828-5533
fax: 309-829-2266
robert@joyluke.com
http://www.joyluke.com
Conducts auctions specializing in fine art glass.

Clubs/Associations

Reyne Haines
Art Glass Discussion Group
405 Lafayette Ave.
Cincinnati, OH 45220
ph: 513-559-1405
fax: 513-651-0860
reyne@mindspring.com
http://www.tias.com/stores/RHA
Collectors talk about book reviews, auction information, reproduction information, buying and selling; no dues; email access essential.

Collectors

John O. Burgess
10738 Harley Rd.
Lorton, VA 22079-3908
ph: 703-339-5359
Wants to buy Burmese art glass from any source or time period.

Henry Tyler
13 Bellevue Dr.
Saint Petersburg, FL 33706-1201
Interested in Mount Washington, Crown Milano, Web art glass, English cameo.

Dealers

William Pitt
16 Sconticut Neck Rd., #312
Fairhaven, MA 02719
ph: 508-993-9434
wipitt@aol.com
http://www.wpitt.com
Specializes in art glass and paperweights; has appeared on PAX TV's "Treasures in Your Home."

William Banks
Classical Glass
P.O. Box 364
Wiscasset, ME 04578-0364
ph: 207-882-9393
inventor@gwi.net
http://www.gwi.net/~inventor
Specializing in antique and collectible glassware and art pottery; author of a price guide on Victorian opalescent glass.

Valerie Sevene
Route 7 Antiques & Treasures
388 Shelburne Rd.
Burlington, VT 05401
ph: 802-859-0917
sevene@together.net
Wants to buy Murano and other art glass and high quality cut glass and Waterford crystal.

Lenore Monleon
33 Fifth Ave.
New York, NY 10003-4338
ph: 212-475-7871 or 212-675-7771
Wants Galle, Lalique, silver overlay, Art Deco, Art Nouveau.

Stan & Arlene Weitman
P.O. Box 1186
N. Massapequa, NY 11758
ph: 516-799-2619
scrackle@earthlink.net
http://www.crackleglass.com
Buys and sells crackle glass and other Victoria Art Glass, e.g., Moser, Loetz, Rindskopf, Stevens & Williams, Webb, etc.

Allan Teal
P.O. Box 429
Chester Heights, PA 19017
ph: 610-459-5265
deldare@aol.com
Partner with Dottie Freeman; buys and sells Victorian era art glass.

Gerald Schultz
Antique Gallery, The
8523 Germantown Ave.
Philadelphia, PA 19118-3316
ph: 215-248-1700
fax: 215-247-8411
geraldluv@aol.com
Galle, Daum, Moser, Lalique, Legras, Durand, Tiffany, Venetian, Quezal, Bohemian, Steuben.

Alain Fournier
La Verrerie D'Art
P.O. Box 757
Bowie, MD 20718-0757
ph: 301-464-3251
Mail@decoesque.com
http://www.decoesque.com
Buys, sells and specializes in European art glass of the Art Nouveau and Art Deco eras (1880-1940); Schneider, Daum, Muller Fres., Loetz, D'Avesn.

Caren Fine
11603 Gowrie Ct.
Potomac, MD 20854-3623
ph: 301-299-6886 or 301-854-6262
fine2beme@aol.com
Buys, sells, trades glass and lamps by Renee Lalique, Tiffany, Galle, Handel, Quezal; also wants 1950s Italian glass.

L. Michael Boak
Initialed Duck Antiques & Collectibles
3812 Hamilton Ave.
Baltimore, MD 21206-3505
ph: 410-319-7529
Buys, sells and collects Steuben, Mt. Washington, Webb, Libbey, Venetian, Stevens & Williams, Hobbs & Brockunier; wants American, English and Continental art glass.

Angie Hudock
Angie's Antiques & Collectibles
11550 Wiles Rd., #3
Pompano Beach, FL 33076
ph: 954-341-8913
pupular@bellsouth.net
http://www.tias.com/stores/aca
Buys and sells antique art glass such as Mt. Washington, Crown Milano, Burmese, Wavecrest, Kelva, Nakara, Webb, Stevens & Williams, peachblow, peachbloom, mother of pearl satin glass.

Adele & Alan Grodsky
5722 South Flamingo Rd., #297
Fort Lauderdale, FL 33330
ph: 800-431-8256
adrianna53@aol.com
Buys, sells Pairpoint puffies and painted scenic lamps; also Tiffany and Handel painted lamps and accessories; also art glass: Tiffany, Durand, Quezal, Steuben.

Patricia Carta
Artpickers
P.O. Box 811689
Boca Raton, FL 33481-1689
ph: 561-239-1214
lct1890@aol.com
http://www.artpickers.com
Buys and sells vintage artwork and art glass: Tiffany, Daum, Schneider, A. Walter, Galle, etc.

Allan Dowling
Allan & Company Antiques Inc.
P.O. Box 254
Berea, OH 44017-0254
ph: 440-238-8474
Dealers and appraisers of art glass: Tiffany, Quezal, Loetz, Durand, Steuben, Moser and cameo; buy and sell both American and European examples of art glass.

Reyne Haines
Vintage Glass
17 East 8th St.
Cincinnati, OH 45202
ph: 513-559-1405
fax: 513-651-0860
reyne@mindspring.com
http://www.reyne.com
Buys and sells Tiffany glass, lamps, bronze, jewelry and windows; also buys art glass of the same period.

Mike Fabian
13367 Budd Rd.
Burt, MI 48417
ph: 989-770-9951
mjfabes@aol.com
Wants to buy art glass from American manufacturers: Steuben, Tiffany, Hobbs, Northwood, New England Glass Co., Pairpoint, Mt. Washington, Wave Crest, others; vases, perfumes, table forms, electric and oil lamps.

Mary L. Brinkman
Cedars Antiques, The
P.O. Box 215
Aurelia, IA 51005
ph: 712-434-2244
mbrinkman@aurelia.k12.ia.us
http://www.csmonline.com/cedars
Search or browse entire inventory and order online.

Fred Wishnie
Wishful Things Art Glass & Antiques
730 N. Plankinton Ave.
Milwaukee, WI 53203
ph: 414-765-1117 or 414-225-9905
luvglass@execpc.com
http://www.wishfulthings.com
Collector, dealer, expert, specializing in American and European art glass from Victorian to Contemporary; Web site features 300+ pieces with full color photos and descriptions: Tiffany, Steuben, Moser, Loetz, Bohemian, French, English, etc.

Dr. David Schwab
Dr. David Schwab Antiques
18 Silman Ave.
Hammond, LA 70401-1083
ph: 504-429-0143
gfrog@I-55.com
Art glass collector, dealer, expert, appraiser; has been the glass business for 30 years and has extensive library; deals in art glass of all kinds and better production items such as Elegant Depression-era glass.

William L. Geary
Nordic Art Glass, Inc.
P.O. Box 2247
Colorado Springs, CO 80901-2247
ph: 719-527-0810
fax: 719-527-0810
nordglass@aol.com
http://www.glass.co.nz/nordglass.htm
Dealer, appraiser of American and European art glass with a specialty in Scandinavian art glass; producer of video "Lyricism of Swedish Glass;" advisor to "Schroeder's Antiques Price Guide;" author of "Scandinavian Glass-Creative Energies".

Brian Severn
Severn's Art Glass
150 Cleaveland Ave.
Pleasant Hill, CA 94523
http://home.earthlink.net/~bsevern/artglass.htm
Dealer, collector, appraiser of art glass; offers antique, Art Nouveau, contemporary: Steuben, Loetz, Quezal, Durand, Tiffany, Orient & Flume, Lundberg Studios, PHOENIX Studios, Mashlach, Correia, perfumes and more.

Steve Hetherington
Glasstiques
P.O. Box 6177
Vacaville, CA 95696-6177
ph: 707-451-3688
glass@glasstiques.com
http://www.glasstiques.com
Wants to buy art glass: Rose Amber,

Peachblow, Napoli, Crown Milano, Colonial Ware, Royal Flemish, Burmese, Lava, M.O.P., Verona, Alexandrite, Silveria, Agata, Pink Slag, Holly Amber, Amberina, Plated Amberina; also fairy lamps.

Kathleen M. Bailey, AAA, ISA CAPP
Antique Appraisal & Estate Sale Service
- the Original
160 NW Gilman Blvd., Ste. #1
Issaquah, WA 98027
ph: 425-746-2777
fax: 425-746-3793
antiquabailey@aol.com
Specializing in fine Art Glass; Tiffany, Steuben, Lalique, Moser, Webb, Galle, Daum, etc.

Kathleen M. Bailey, AAA, ISA CAPP
Antique Appraisal & Estate Sale Service
- the Original
160 NW Gilman Blvd., Ste. #1
Issaquah, WA 98027
ph: 425-746-2777
fax: 425-746-3793
antiquabailey@aol.com
Buys and sells glass: American, Bohemian, French, German, Austrian and other European from the 18th to 20th centuries; Tiffany, Steuben, Moser, Bohemian, Cameo, Loetz, Lobemeyer, etc.

Experts

Louis O. St. Aubin, Jr.
Brookside Antiques "Art Glass Gallery"
44 North Water St.
New Bedford, MA 02740
ph: 508-993-4944
Museum consultant, expert, established in 1964, author of "Pairpoint Lamps: A Collectors Guide;" nationally known authority, lecturer, appraiser, auction house consultant; founder of the New Bedford Glass Museum.

Scott Roland
Glimmer Glass Antiques
P.O. Box 262
Schenevus, NY 12155-0262
ph: 607-638-9543
Buys, sells, specializes in and appraises Victorian glass, art glass, milk glass, water pitchers and tumblers, etc.

Clarence Maier
Burmese Cruet, The
P.O. Box 432
Montgomeryville, PA 18936-0432
ph: 215-855-5388
Specializes in Burmese, Crown Milano, and Royal Flemish art glass; advisor to "Warman's Antiques & Collectibles Price Guide" and to "Schroeder's Price Guide."

Mildred & Ralph Lechner
P.O. Box 554
Mechanicsville, VA 23111-0554
ph: 804-737-3347
Feature writers on antique glassware for "AntiqueWeek;" authors of "The World of Salt Shakers," Vols. 1, 2 & 3; Victorian art and pattern glass reproduction identification experts; collectors of art and pattern glass salt & pepper shakers.

Robin & June Greenwald
June Greenwald Antiques, Inc.
3096 Mayfield Rd.
Cleveland, OH 44118
ph: 216-932-5535
Nationally recognized art glass dealers.

Carl Heck
Carl Heck Decorative Arts
P.O. Box 8416
Aspen, CO 81612-8416
ph: 970-925-8011
fax: 970-925-8011
carlheck5@aol.com
http://www.carlheck.com
Collector/dealer/expert specializing in lamps by Tiffany, Pairpoint, Handel, Galle; also Tiffany windows, art glass, enamels for over 32 years; currently Tiffany advisor for "Schroeder's," "Antique Trader" price guides.

Museums/Libraries

Wadsworth Atheneum Museum of Art
600 Main St.
Hartford, CT 06103
ph: 860-278-2670
fax: 860-527-0803
info@wadsworthatheneum.org
http://www.wadsworthatheneum.org
Collection of decorative art glass includes examples ranging from Roman times to Victorian America.

Milan Historical Museum, Inc.
Newsletter: New Milan Ledger
P.O. Box 308
Milan, OH 44846-0308
ph: 419-499-2968
fax: 419-499-9004
museum@milanhistory.org
http://www.milanhistory.org
A seven-building complex 500 yards from the birthplace of Thomas A. Edison; restored home, carriage shed, blacksmith shop, general store, collections from the 19th century.

Art (1950s)
Collectors

Dennis Boyd
Dennis Boyd, Unlimited
P.O. Box 8925
Richmond, VA 23225
ph: 804-560-0753
dboydant@ix.netcom.com
Wants 1950s art glass by Venini, Sarpaneva, Tapio Wirkkala, Kosta, Orrefors, Kaj Franck, Nutajari-Notsjo, Flysfors, Leerdam, Toso, Barovier, Seguso; any Italian or Scandinavian art glass (signed or unsigned.)

Art (Austrian)
Dealers

Eric's Antiques
381 Elliot St.
Newton Upper Falls, MA 02164
ph: 617-332-3744
Specializes in fine Austrian art glass.

Baccarat

(see also PAPERWEIGHTS)

Matching Services

Past & Present
14851 Ave. 360
Visalia, CA 93292
ph: 559-798-0029
fax: 559-798-1415
info@china-crystal-flatware.com
http://www.pastpresent.net
Baccarat, Cambridge, Denby, Duncan & Miller, Fostoria, Franciscan, Gorham, Heisey, Imperial, Lalique, Lenox, Mikasa, Nancy Prentiss, Noritake, Orrefors, Sasaki, Tiffin, Towle, Val St. Lambert, Waterford, etc.

Black
Experts

Marlena Toohey
c/o Antique Publications
217 Union St.
P.O. Box 553
Marietta, OH 45750-0553
ph: 800-533-3433 or 740-373-6146
fax: 740-373-6917
info@glasscollectingbooks.com
http://www.glasscollectingbooks.com
Author of "A Collector's Guide to Black Glass."

Blenko
Museums/Libraries

Richard Blenko
Blenko Glass Visitor Center Museum & Wholesale Outlet
Newsletter: Antique Notes
P.O. Box 67
Milton, WV 25541-0067
ph: 304-743-9081
fax: 304-743-0547
blenko@usa.net
http://www.blenkoglass.com
Museum and outlet for nationally known blown glassware; also stained glass studio.

Bohemian
Collectors

Tom Price
11947 Marbon Meadows Dr.
Jacksonville, FL 32223
ph: 904-886-8955 or 904-629-5421
TPrice1227@aol.com
Wants to buy Bohemian glass; especially interested in glass made by Rossler.

Experts

Bob Truitt
13550 Ashbury Dr.
Carmel, IN 46032
ph: 301-929-2539
randdglass@sbcglobal.net
Author of "Collectible Bohemian Glass 1880-1940" (1995) and "Collectible Bohemian Glass Vol. II 1915-1945" (1998); research, consulting, and public speaking about Bohemian glass.

Boyd's Crystal Art
Dealers

Darrell Crim
Jody & Darrell's Glass Collectibles
P.O. Box 180833
Arlington, TX 76096-0833
ph: 817-467-5483
scribeink@aol.com

Man./Prod./Dist.

John Boyd
Boyd's Crystal Art Inc.
Newsletter: Boyd's Crystal Art Glass Newsletter
1203 Morton Ave.
P.O. Box 127
Cambridge, OH 43725
ph: 740-439-2077
fax: 740-432-1827
boydglass@hotmail.com
http://www.boydglass.com
Manufacturers many collectible glass items in a wide array of colors.

Periodicals

Jody Best
Newsletter: Jody & Darrell's Glass Collectibles Newsletter
P.O. Box 180833
Arlington, TX 76096-0833
ph: 817-467-5483
scribeink@aol.com
Published bi-monthly, focuses on Boyd's Crystal Art Glass and other contemporary glass collectibles; subscription includes an exclusive figurine produced by Boyd's Art Glass; articles, secondary market price information, classified ads.

Cambridge
Clubs/Associations

Charles A. Upton
National Cambridge Collectors, Inc.
Newsletter: Cambridge Crystal Ball
P.O. Box 416
Cambridge, OH 43725-0416
ph: 740-432-4245 or 740-432-6794
fax: 740-432-4245
webmaster@cambridgeglass.org
http://www.cambridgeglass.org
Preserves and studies the products of the Cambridge Glass Co., Cambridge, OH; please send a SASE when requesting information.

Collectors

Susan Leite
44 Glenwood Rd.
Brewster, MA 02631-2202
ph: 508-385-4905
Wants to buy Cambridge Etch #520 in pink.

Dealers

Penny Drucker
Mother Drucker's
P.O. Box 50261
Irvine, CA 92619-0261
ph: 888-637-8253 or 949-551-5529
fax: 949-551-2116
Penny@Motherdruckers.com
http://www.motherdruckers.com
Carries hard-to-find as well as common pieces of Cambridge glass.

Museums/Libraries

Charles A. Upton
Museum of the National Cambridge
 Collectors, Inc.
P.O. Box 416
Cambridge, OH 43725-0416
ph: 740-432-4245 or 740-432-6794
fax: 740-432-4245
webmaster@cambridgeglass.org
http://www.cambridgeglass.org
Preserves and studies the products of the Cambridge Glass Co., Cambridge, OH.

Judy Bennett
Cambridge Glass Museum, The
812 Jefferson Ave.
Cambridge, OH 43725-2846
ph: 740-432-3045
Over 5000 pieces of Cambridge glass on display dating from 1902 to 1958; also 100 pieces of Cambridge Art Pottery; private museum; gift shop; open June 2st to Nov. 1st; 1 - 4 daily except Sunday and holidays.

Cameo

Appraisers

Shawn Voils
430 Redding #1911
Breckinridge Court
Lexington, KY 40517
ph: 859-245-1089
shvoils@aol.com
Specializes in French Cameo glass by makers such as Galle, Daum Nancy, Muller Freres, and Schneider.

Candlewick

Clubs/Associations

Candlewick Collectors Club of Florida
cccfl@candlewickfl.com
http://www.candlwickfl.com

National Imperial Glass Collectors
 Society
Newsletter: Glasszette
P.O. Box 534
Bellaire, OH 43906
ph: 603-424-1146
fax: 603-424-1213
info@nigcs.org
http://www.imperialglass.org
Members interested in the history and glassware produced by the Imperial Glass Corp.; conducts an annual convention offering seminars, show and sale, and "members only" auction; establishing an Imperial museum.

Connie Doll, Mem.
National Candlewick Collector's Club,
 The
Newsletter: Candlewick Collector
 Newsletter, The
17609 Falling Water Rd.
Strongsville, OH 44136
ph: 440-846-9610
RonConDoll@aol.com
http://members.aol.com/_ht_a/vrs1cw/
 myhomepage/club.html
The newsletter is devoted to the Candlewick pattern, collectors, finds, prices, questions answered, look-alikes and repros. discussed.

Lucille R. Geisler
Michiana Association of Candlewick
 Collectors
Newsletter: Spyglass
17370 Battles Rd.
South Bend, IN 46614

Collectors

Lucille R. Geisler
17370 Battles Rd.
South Bend, IN 46614

Dealers

Kathy Burch
221 N. Maple
Ithaca, MI 48847-1025
ph: 517-875-3138
Buys and sells unusual pieces of Candlewick glass including colored pieces.

Penny Drucker
Mother Drucker's
P.O. Box 50261
Irvine, CA 92619-0261
ph: 888-637-8253 or 949-551-5529
fax: 949-551-2116
Penny@Motherdruckers.com
http://www.motherdruckers.com
Always changing inventory of color, cut, rare and common pieces; send LSASE for list.

Experts

Virginia R. Scott
275 Milledge Terrace
Athens, GA 30606-4937
ph: 706-548-5966
vrs1cw@aol.com
Researcher, author of "The Collector's Guide to Imperial Candlewick;" a very complete book illustrating almost every known Candlewick pattern piece, including colors, variations, cuttings; has look-alike and reproduction appendix.

Internet Resources

Laura Miller
CandlewickCollector
5134 Neptune Square
Oxnard, CA 93035
ph: 805-382-8729
glassmurf@aol.com
http://groups.yahoo.com/group/
 CandlewickCollector
A mailing list created especially for collectors of Imperial Glass Company's Candlewick; join fellow Candlewickers read the latest CW news, report your finds, ask questions, share information.

Museums/Libraries

National Imperial Glass Museum
P.O. Box 534
Bellaire, OH 43906
ph: 603-424-1146
fax: 603-424-1213
info@nigcs.org
http://www.imperialglass.org
Displays include cases filled with Imperial glass, including a large display of Candlewick.

Carnival

Auction Services

Tom Burns
Burns Auction Service
109 E. Steuben St.
Bath, NY 14810
ph: 607-776-7942
Sells Victorian and art glass, Nippon, Noritake, lamps, carnival glass.

Randy S. Burdette
Riverbend Auction
P.O. Box 800
103 South Monroe St.
Alderson, WV 24910
ph: 304-445-2897 or 800-726-2897
fax: 304-445-2900
rivauction@newwave.net
http://www.riverbendauction.com

Jim Wroda
Jim Wroda Auction Service
P.O. Box 111
Gettysburg, OH 45328
ph: 937-447-8909 or 937-447-8909
jwrodamidwest@earthlink.net
http://www.jimwrodaauction.com
Specializes in the auction sale of R.S. Prussia and Carnival Glass.

Tom Harris Auction Center
203 South 18th Ave.
Marshalltown, IA 50158
ph: 641-754-4890
tomharris@tomharrisauctions.com
http://www.tomharrisauctions.com
Specialized auctions of flint glass, Sandwich, carnival, Pittsburgh; also

ceramics such as transferware, lustre, historical Staffordshire, etc.

Jim & Jan Seeck
Seeck Auctions
P.O. Box 377
Mason City, IA 50402
ph: 641-424-1116
jimjan@seeckauction.com
http://www.seeckauction.com
Auctioning since 1982 with an emphasis on Carnival Glass.

Jason Woody
Woody Auction Company
P.O. Box 618
317 S. Forrest St.
Douglass, KS 67039-9800
ph: 316-747-2694
fax: 316-747-2145
woodyauction@earthlink.net
http://www.woodyauction.com

Clubs/Associations

Eva Backer
New England Carnival Glass Club
12 Sherwood Rd.
W Hartford, CT 06117-2738
ph: 860-233-3961

Dave Sharp
Keystone Carnival Glass Club
Newsletter: Keystoner
16 Green Acre Rd.
Lititz, PA 17543-8770
ph: 717-626-8231
dsharp@dejazzd.com
Members share common interest in old carnival glass; monthly meetings, newsletter, annual convention.

Jackie Poucher, Sec.
Sunshine State Carnival Glass
 Association
9087 Baywood Park Dr.
Seminole, FL 33777
ph: 727-398-1866
poucher@carnivalglass.net
http://www.carnivalglass.net/sscga

Barbara Hobbs
Tampa Bay Carnival Glass Club
Newsletter: Tampa Bay Carnival Glass
 Club Newsletter
5501 101st Ave. N
Pinellas Park, FL 33782-3311
ph: 813-541-6164
carnivalbarb@aol.com
Non-profit group, meetings, convention held 2nd weekend in February, auctions, shows, monthly newsletter.

National Imperial Glass Collectors
 Society
Newsletter: Glasszette
P.O. Box 534
Bellaire, OH 43906
ph: 603-424-1146
fax: 603-424-1213
info@nigcs.org
http://www.imperialglass.org
Members interested in the history and glassware produced by the Imperial Glass Corp.; conducts an annual convention offering seminars, show

and sale, and "members only" auction; establishing an Imperial museum.

Carole Richards
American Carnival Glass Association
Newsletter: American Carnival Glass News
44 Water St.
Poland, OH 44514
ph: 330-757-2001
http://www.woodsland.com/acga
Learn about highly collectible carnival glass; news, conventions; send SASE for full color brochure.

Lee Markley, Sec.
International Carnival Glass Association
Newsletter: Town Pump, The
P.O. Box 306
Mentone, IN 46539-0306
ph: 219-353-7678
rjc4470@dcccd.edu
http://www.internationalcarnivalglass.com
Promotes interest in collecting old Carnival Glass; holds annual convention featuring displays, seminars and banquet.

Ellen Hemm, Sec.
Lincoln Land Carnival Glass Club
N 951 Highway 27
Conrath, WI 54731
ph: 715-532-5816
LLCGC@aol.com
http://members.aol.com/LLCGC

Karen Skinner
Gateway Carnival Glass Club
108 Riverwoods Cove
East Alton, IL 62024
ph: 618-259-1373

Ann McMorris
Heart of America Carnival Glass Association
Newsletter: HOACGA Bulletin
P.O. Box 4361
Topeka, KS 66604-0361
ph: 785-478-9004
mcmorris@woodsland.com
Focuses on old carnival glass; members share information; monthly newsletter contains articles about OLD carnival glass, club meeting dates and secretary reports; members can advertise free of charge; annual convention in April.

Matzi Thrasher
Texas Carnival Glass Club
611 W. Main
Tomball, TX 77375
ph: 281-351-2202
cglady@sbcglobal.net
http://www.texascarnivalglass.org
Founded in 1979 to educate and enlighten its members about the historical and current significance of carnival glass.

Anne Swafford
Pacific Northwest Carnival Glass Club
17625 SW Frederick Lane
Sherwood, OR 97140
http://www.woodsland.com/pacific

Pauline Birkett, Treas.
Canadian Carnival Glass Association
Newsletter: CCAA Newsletter
34 Belholme Ave.
Brantford, Ontario N3T 1S1 Canada
birketts@sympatico.ca
Meetings are held every six weeks in the southwestern area of Ontario; holds annual convention; newsletter published every six weeks with articles, auction reports, sales, shows, etc.

Carnival Glass Society (UK), The
P.O. Box 14
Hayes, Middlesex UB3 5NU U.K.
PhylDon@btinternet.com
Objective of the society is to promote interest in the collecting of Carnival Glass, to encourage accurate research, and to circulate information.

Collectors

Eva Backer
12 Sherwood Rd.
W Hartford, CT 06117-2738
ph: 860-233-3961

Dick Hatscher
142 Walnut Hill Rd.
Bethel, CT 06801
ph: 203-743-1468
hatscher@worldnet.att.net
Wants to buy Carnival glass, Milk Glass, colored glass, Fenton Hob Nail, Fostoria American Glass.

John O. Burgess
10738 Harley Rd.
Lorton, VA 22079-3908
ph: 703-339-5359
Wants pre-1950 US carnival glass.

Larry Yung
9621 Springwater Ln.
Miamisburg, OH 45342

Cliff McCaslin
Rocliff Communications
8422 N. Park Ct.
Kansas City, MO 64155
ph: 816-436-7719
fax: 816-436-6955
vitrify@swbell.net
Wants to buy several manufacturers of carnival glass, stretch and art glassware patterns including Northwood, Dugan-Diamond, Millersburg.

Dealers

Duane Parkman
Bird Song Farm Carnival Glass
18 West Maple St.
Dover Foxcroft, ME 04426-3733
ph: 207-564-2006
birdsong@kynd.com
http://www.kynd.com/~birdsong
Buys and sells carnival glass including Northwood, Fenton, Imperial, Dugan, Millersburg, and others.

W. J. Warren
38 Mosher Dr.
Tonawanda, NY 14150-5218
ph: 716-692-2886
wwa38@aol.com
Buys and sells; wants all colors of carnival glass; one piece or a collection.

Peggy Guy
Happy Pastime
10114 Frederick Rd.
Ellicott City, MD 21042
ph: 410-480-8119 or 410-203-1101
sales@happypastime.com
http://www.happypastime.com
Buys and sells; specializes in carnival glass, Royal Doulton, M.I. Hummel, Royal Copenhagen, Bing & Grondahl, Lladro, Goebel, Beswick, Royal Worcester.

Barbara Hobbs
5501 101st Ave. N
Pinellas Park, FL 33782-3311
ph: 813-541-6164
carnivalbarb@aol.com
Buys, sells, collects only old carnival glass, carnival glass hatpins, carnival glass bottles, carnival glass beaded purses, novelties and oddities.

Mike Fabian
13367 Budd Rd.
Burt, MI 48417
ph: 989-770-9951
mjfabes@aol.com
Buying 1900-1930 carnival glass: Northwood, Millersburg, Fenton, Dugan, others.

Kevin Thorne
Eclectiques Carnival Glass
1470 Gamble Oaks Dr.
Elizabeth, CO 80107
Buys and sells carnival glass; over 400 pieces online for sale; detailed description, iridescence available.

Gary Lickver
P.O. Box 1778
San Marcos, CA 92079-1778
ph: 760-744-5686 or 760-803-0927
California's largest carnival glass dealer, collector; consistently at most quality indoor antique shows in California, Atlantic City, NJ and others; wants to buy one piece or entire collections; member of 9 Carnival glass clubs.

Experts

Glen & Steve Thistlewood
Thistlewoods
s.g.thistlewood@btinternet.com
http://www.carnival-glass.net

Helen Greguire
Helen's Antiques
216 Mountain View Rd.
Landrum, SC 29356
ph: 864-457-7340
Author of "Carnival Lighting," focusing on carnival glass used in lighting such as Gone With The Wind

lamps, electric and kerosene lamp shades, chandeliers, etc.; the book is out-of-print but copies are still available from the author.

Donald & Lynda Grizzle
Sanctified Cross-Eyed Bear, The
P.O. Box 1296
Huntsville, AL 35807-0296
ph: 256-534-9076 or 256-534-9049
sanctxbear@aol.com
Publishes the most extensive sales references available for carnival glass: reports on over 70,000 actual sales during the past five years; clarifies upward and downward price trends.

Tom & Sharon Mordini
36 North Mernitz Ave.
Freeport, IL 61032
ph: 815-235-4407
fax: 815-232-3911
TomMordini@aol.com
http://www.woodsland.com/mordini
Publishes "Carnival Glass Auction Prices," an annual list of 5,000 carnival glass auction prices.

Kitty & Russell Umbraco
P.O. Box 5331
Richmond, CA 94805-0331
ph: 510-235-1656
fax: 510-237-6019
russellu1@juno.com
Buys and sells; author of "Iridescent Stretch Glass."

Internet Resources

Fred Stone
Woodsland World Wide Carnival Glass Association
fstone@woodsland.com
http://www.woodsland.com
Online resource for carnival glass collectors.

Museums/Libraries

James Measell
Fenton Art Glass Company, The
700 Elizabeth St.
Williamstown, WV 26187-1028
ph: 304-375-6122 or 800-249-4527
fax: 304-375-7833
askfenton@fentonartglass.com
http://www.fentonartglass.com
Large attractive display of early Fenton and Upper Ohio Valley glass.

Carnival (Post-1960)

Clubs/Associations

Annetta M. Bosselman
Collectible Carnival Glass Association
Newsletter: CCGA Newsletter
3101 Brentwood Circle
Grand Island, NE 68801-7217
ph: 308-382-6384
For collectors of newer carnival glass made after 1960; quarterly newsletter has articles about carnival glass, and for sale and want ads; annual convention with sale and seminars.

Collectors

Annette M. Bosselman
3101 Brentwood Circle
Grand Island, NE 68801-7217
ph: 308-382-6384

Dealers

John Valentine
Contemporary Carnival Glass
19930 SW 92nd Ave.
Miami, FL 33157
ph: 305-235-8704
johnval@carnivalglass.net
http://www.carnivalglass.net
*Buys and sells; main focus in glass
made from 1950s through 1990s; Web
site lists glass companies and a brief
story of their history and samples of
carnival glass; also books and glass
clubs involved with contemporary
carnival glass.*

Wilma Thurston
2360 N. Old S.R. 9
Columbus, IN 47203-9430
ph: 812-546-5724

Coin

Experts

Tim Timmerman
11655 S.W. Allen Blvd. #31
Beaverton, OR 97005-4850
ph: 503-646-8300
timt@wa-net.com
*Author of "U.S. Coin Glass" (dated
1892); 70-page book includes pictures
and descriptions of 88 pieces and also
a section on reproductions; available
from author for $20.*

Computer Programs For

Man./Prod./Dist.

Niche Software, Inc.
Software: Antique Bottle & Glass
Collector, The
7118 NW Terrace
Parkland, FL 33076
ph: 954-344-6561
marketing@collectiblessoftware.com
http://www.collectiblessoftware.com
*Designed for the collector of antique
bottles, glass, insulators and any type
of glass collectible.*

Consolidated

Clubs/Associations

Tom Jiamachello, Sec.
PHOENIX & Consolidated Glass
Collectors' Club
Newsletter: PHOENIX & Consolidated
Collectors News & Views
41 River View Dr.
Essex Junction, VT 05452
ph: 802-878-2268 or 412-561-3379
TOPofVT@aol.com
http://www.collectoronline.com/club-
PCGCC-wp.html
*For collectors/dealers of art glass
produced by PHOENIX GLASS Co. of
Monaca, PA and Consolidated Lamp
& Shade Co. of Coraopolis, PA; bi-
monthly newsletter - market trends,*

*repro. alerts, buy/sell ads, price
reports, articles.*

Collectors

Barbara Norman Milin
ph: 561-995-7300
fax: 561-995-0096
bamilin@aol.com
*Wants to buy Ruba Rombic, red or
cased pieces of PHOENIX or
Consolidated Art Glass, Catalonian,
and Muncie Ruba Rombic.*

Experts

Jack D. Wilson
1514 Eagle Ridge Rd.
Prescott, AZ 86301-5418
ph: 520-445-5137
jdwilson1@earthlink.net
http://home.earthlink.net/~jdwilson1
*Author of "PHOENIX & Consoli-
dated Art Glass: 1926-1980;" features
in-depth research, 48 color pages
illustrating over 750 items (out-of-
print); wants original Consolidated
catalogs & company literature.*

Consolidated (Ruba Rombic)

Collectors

Paul Galli
ph: 408-730-4010
eichlerera1@comcast.net
*Wants to buy Consolidated's Ruba
Rombic pattern glass.*

Experts

Jack D. Wilson
1514 Eagle Ridge Rd.
Prescott, AZ 86301-5418
ph: 520-445-5137
jdwilson1@earthlink.net
http://home.earthlink.net/~jdwilson1
*Wants to buy examples of the Ruba
Rombic pattern of art glass made by
the Consolidated Lamp & Glass Co.
of Coraopolis, PA; author of
"PHOENIX & Consolidated Art
Glass: 1926-1980;" advisor to
Schroeder's.*

Crackle

Dealers

Stan & Arlene Weitman
P.O. Box 1186
N. Massapequa, NY 11758
ph: 516-799-2619
scrackle@earthlink.net
http://www.crackleglass.com
*Author of "Crackle Glass Identifica-
tion & Value Guide Book 1 & 2;"
buys and sells crackle glass and other
Victoria Art Glass, e.g., Moser, Loetz,
Rindskopf, Stevens & Williams,
Webb, etc.*

Experts

Stan & Arlene Weitman
P.O. Box 1186
N. Massapequa, NY 11758
ph: 516-799-2619
scrackle@earthlink.net
http://www.crackleglass.com
*Author of "Crackle Glass Identifica-
tion & Value Guide Book 1 & 2."*

Cranberry

Clubs/Associations

Pilgrim Cranberry Glass Collectors Club
Newsletter: PCGCC Newsletter
P.O. Box 395
Ceredo, WV 25507
ph: 304-453-3553
fax: 304-453-6849
http://www.pilgrimglass.com
*For those interested in Pilgrim
cranberry glass; club sponsored by the
world's largest cranberry glass and
"cameo" art glass manufacturer; free
catalogs, advance notice of new
offerings.*

Cranberry Opalescent

Collectors

Larry W. Nellans
9131 College Pkwy.
Fort Myers, FL 33919
ph: 941-481-6665
fax: 941-481-7391
larryn@strato.net
*Advanced collector of cranberry
opalescent Victorian glass; will pay
highest prices for rare cranberry
opalescent barber bottles, water
pitchers, table sets, oil lamps, etc.*

Crystal

(see also GLASS, Elegant; LAMPS &
LIGHTING, Chandeliers;
TABLEWARE)

Matching Services

J.P. Faddoul Company, Inc.
115 Boston Turnpike
Shrewsbury, MA 01545
ph: 508-755-5505
inquire@jpfaddoul.com
http://www.jpfaddoul.com
*Carries discontinued and active china,
crystal, and flatware; all merchandise
is new, first quality and was
purchased directly from the
manufacturers.*

Michael Negrotti
Tabletop Designs
P.O. Box 448
Cheshire, CT 06410
ph: 800-801-4084
lenox@ntplx.net
http://www.tabletopdesigns.com
*A small, personal matching service
with a constantly changing inventory;
want lists are kept; send photocopy or
photo when unsure of pattern name;
specializes in Lenox.*

Paul & Pearl Hoffman
China Brokers, Ltd.
11 Westgate Ct.
Colts Neck, NJ 07722-1650
ph: 732-780-5062
chinabrokers@worldnet.att.net

Alice Korman
Alice's Past & Presents Replacements
P.O. Box 465
Merrick, NY 11566-0465
ph: 516-379-1352
fax: 516-379-7302
alicechina@aol.com
http://hometown.aol.com/alicechina/
myhomepage/business.html
*Matching and locating service for
Lenox, Gorham, Mikasa, Orrefors,
Franciscan, Noritake, Wedgwood,
Royal Doulton, Tiffin, Towle,
Galway, Cambridge, Fostoria, Denby,
Royal Leerdam, Atlantis, Stuart, Val
St. Lambert, Sasaki, others.*

Pattern Finders, A
P.O. Box 206
Port Jefferson Station, NY 11776-0206
ph: 631-928-5158 or 800-216-2446
fax: 631-928-5170
apattern@aol.com
http://www.patternfinders.com
*All major brands of dinnerware and
crystal stocked in huge inventory;
locating service for hard-to-find
patterns; Rosenthal specialists.*

Sophia Papapanu
Sophia's China & Crystal
141 Sedgwick Rd.
Syracuse, NY 13203-1136
ph: 315-472-6834
sophia@sophiaschina-crystal.com
http://www.sophiaschina-crystal.com
*Discontinued china and crystal
patterns; over 22 years service;
American, English, and other
manufacturers; mail order or by
special appointment; email or please
send SASE with requests for
information*

Constance Stolz
China Match & Crystal Match
72 Longacre Rd.
Rochester, NY 14621-1019
ph: 585-338-3781
chinamat@frontiernet.net
*Replacements of discontinued glass
and crystal stemware; Fostoria,
Gorham, Lenox, Noritake, Mikasa,
Royal Doulton; buy and sell.*

Michael Round Fine China & Crystal,
Inc.
7845 Wisconsin Ave.
Bethesda, MD 20814
ph: 301-656-2626 or 800-467-6863
fax: 703-550-7881
feedback@Mround.com
http://www.michaelround.com
*Impressive Web site for matching
china, crystal or flatware.*

Thurber's
2256C Dabeny Rd.
Richmond, VA 23230-3342
ph: 804-278-9080 or 800-848-7237
fax: 804-278-9480
Carries only active patterns; will locate old patterns.

David Thompson
Replacements Ltd.
P.O. Box 26029
1089 Knox Rd.
Greensboro, NC 27420
ph: 800-737-5223 or 336-697-3000
fax: 336-697-3100
inquire@replacements.com
http://www.replacements.com
China, crystal and flatware (obsolete, active and inactive.)

D & J Locations
1601 E. Canal St.
Tarboro, NC 27886
ph: 252-823-5333 or 800-818-5565
Discontinued crystal: Fostoria, Franciscan, Gorham, Imperial, Lenox, Lotus, Mikasa, Noritake, Seneca, Tiffin, Wedgwood, and other major brands; buys, sells, locates.

China Cabinet, The
214 Hillside Dr.
P.O. Box 426
Clearwater, SC 29822-0426
ph: 803-593-9655 or 800-787-1605
fax: 803-593-9655
thechinacabinet@aol.com
Matches fine & casual crystal; Cambridge, Franciscan, Fostoria, Galway, Glastonbury, Gorham, Imperial, Lenox, Lotus, Mikasa, Noritake, Royal Doulton, Seneca, Tiffin, Towle, etc.

China & Crystal Matchers, Inc.
2379 John Glenn Dr., Ste. #108-M
Atlanta, GA 30341-1924
ph: 770-455-1162 or 800-286-1107
fax: 770-452-8616
chinacmi@bellsouth.net
http://www.chinaandcrystal.com
All manufacturers; buys, sells, locates; member of the International Association of Dinnerware Matchers.

Paul Church
Replacement Service, A
500 Oregon Ave.
Saint Cloud, FL 34769
ph: 407-957-1719 or 800-337-9075
fax: 649-915-2469
chinacrystal@juno.com
http://www.chinacrystalandmore.com
Buys, sells and locates Fostoria and Lenox crystal.

Mary Ann Lowery
Crystal Corner, Inc., The
317 Billy Dyar Blvd.
P.O. Box 756
Boaz, AL 35957-0756
ph: 256-593-6169
fax: 256-593-6560
ccorner@hiwaay.net
http://www.crystalcorner.com
Fostoria, Tiffin, Mikasa, Lenox, Imperial, Gorham, Franciscan, etc.

Barron's
P.O. Box 994
Novi, MI 48376
ph: 800-538-6340
fax: 800-523-4456
barronsdw@aol.com
http://www.barronsdinnerware.com

Colleen Becker
Heritage China of Iowa
P.O. Box 244
Palo, IA 52324
ph: 888-416-1595 or 319-227-3688
fax: 319-227-7781
dischina@aol.com
http://www.dish-china.com
Large inventory of china and crystal; crystal by Fostoria, Heisey, Imperial, Candlewick, Lenox, Noritake, Sasaki.

N. Skaja
Crystal Connection
8661 West Midland Dr.
Greendale, WI 53219-1038
ph: 414-425-1321
nskaja@execpc.com
A discontinued crystal matching service specializing in Lenox, Fostoria and Cambridge.

China & Crystal Replacements
P.O. Box 187
5613 Country Rd. 19
Excelsior, MN 55331
ph: 612-474-6418 or 800-432-4448
Discontinued and active china, dinnerware and crystal bought and sold.

China Replacements
P.O. Box 508
High Ridge, MO 63049
ph: 800-562-2655 or 636-677-5577
fax: 636-376-6319
chinarep@swbell.net
http://www.chinareplacements.com
Matches Lenox, Fostoria, Tiffin, Cambridge, Gorham, Lotus, Stuart, Noritake, Mikasa, and many others.

Dining Elegance, Ltd.
P.O. Box 4203
Saint Louis, MO 63163
ph: 314-865-1408
de-3@earthlink.net
http://www.diningelegance.com

Barbara Coleman
Finders Keepers China Lady
1537 Metairie Rd.
Metairie, LA 70005-3938
ph: 504-455-1530 or 504-831-4514
fax: 504-885-2512
Stock or locate Doulton, Lenox/

Oxford, Minton, Noritake, Pickard, Spode, Wedgwood; also other china and crystal.

edish, inc.
2311 Westheimer
Houston, TX 77098
ph: 713-942-7171
fax: 713-521-2546
questions@edish.com
http://www.edish.com
Browse the online inventory of discontinued and current china, crystal, dinnerware.

Larry & Anne McDonald
A & A Dinnerware Locators
P.O. Box 50222
Austin, TX 78763-0222
ph: 512-264-1054 or 888-898-4202
info@aadinnerware.com
http://www.aadinnerware.com
Locate/match discontinued crystal patterns; all major manufacturers: American, European, Japanese; primarily mail order.

edish, inc.
815 East 2100 South
Salt Lake City, UT 84106
ph: 801-486-8282 or 888-767-8282
fax: 801-485-7644
questions@edish.com
http://www.edish.com
Buy and sell most major brands: Fostoria, Lenox, Tiffin, Waterford, Stuart, Baccarat, etc.

Glass Urn, The
456 West Main St.
Mesa, AZ 85201-6523
ph: 480-833-2702 or 480-838-5936
Specializing in discontinued American made glass: Cambridge, Fostoria, Heisey, Tiffin, etc.; from 1890s to 1970s; open shop or mail order.

Past & Present
14851 Ave. 360
Visalia, CA 93292
ph: 559-798-0029
fax: 559-798-1415
info@china-crystal-flatware.com
http://www.pastpresent.net
Baccarat, Cambridge, Denby, Duncan & Miller, Fostoria, Franciscan, Gorham, Heisey, Imperial, Lalique, Lenox, Mikasa, Nancy Prentiss, Noritake, Orrefors, Sasaki, Tiffin, Towle, Val St. Lambert, Waterford, etc.

Silver Lane Antiques
P.O. Box 322
San Leandro, CA 94577-0032
ph: 510-483-0632
Discontinued crystal available by most major manufacturers.

Old China Patterns Ltd.
1560 Brimley Rd.
Scarborough, Ontario M1P 3G9 Canada
ph: 800-663-4533 or 416-299-8880
fax: 416-299-4721
ocp@chinapatterns.com
http://www.chinapatterns.com
Canada's largest matching service; buys and sells internationally; since 1966; specializing in English china and crystal; charter member International Association of Dinnerware Matchers.

Periodicals

Susan Ranta
Ranta Enterprises
Directory: Set Your Table Discontinued Tableware Dealers
P.O. Box 22481
Lincoln, NE 68542-2481
ph: 800-600-2127 or 402-423-4865
fax: 402-423-4865
sranta@setyourtable.com
http://www.setyourtable.com
From Anchor Hocking to Westmoreland crystal, "Set Your Table" has a growing list of dealers who can help you find your missing pieces; dealer listings are indexed by manufacturer; Web site is always up to date.

Repair Services

Allan B. Mittelmark
366 Clinton Ave.
Cedarhurst, NY 11516
ph: 516-569-2000
fax: 516-569-2001
Crystal repair including lead crystal and Swarovski crystal.

Curved

(see also REPAIR/RESTORATION/CONSERVATION, Glass)

Suppliers

Hudson Glass
219 North Division St.
Peekskill, NY 10566-2716
ph: 800-431-2964 or 914-737-2124
fax: 914-737-4447
Sells bent glass for china cabinets; convex picture frame glass; also carries restoration/old house glass in stock; sells stained glass tools and supplies (no stained glass repair); stained glass supply catalog available for $3.

B & L Antiqurie, Inc.
P.O. Box 453
6217 S. Lakeshore Rd.
Lexington, MI 48450-0453
ph: 800-840-1110 or 810-359-8623
fax: 810-359-7498
information@bentglasscentral.com
http://www.bentglasscentral.com
Bent glass, convex portrait glass, antique flat glass, beveled mirror shapes, domes, and other specialty glass products for over 30 years.

Central Glass Products
405 West Hamon Ave.
Pocola, OK 74902-3702
ph: 918-436-2401 or 888-236-8452
fax: 888-236-8452
info@bentglass.com
http://www.bentglass.com
*Custom bent glass for furniture,
solariums, architecture and
limousines; bent, laminated, insulated;
specialty is antique seeded glass for
cabinet manufacturers and replacement dealers.*

PECO Glass Bending
P.O. Box 777
Smithville, TX 78957
ph: 512-237-3600
glass@pecoglassbending.com
http://www.pecoglassbending.com
*Bends glass for antique china cabinets
and similar items; can do "J" bends,
"S" bends, "serpentines," "irregu-
lar" bends and convex glass for
picture frames; in business for over 26
years.*

Custard

Clubs/Associations

Michael Coulon
Custard Glass Collectors Society
Newsletter: Custard Connection, The
591 SW Duxbury Ave.
Port Saint Lucie, FL 34983
ph: 772-785-9946
fax: 772-785-9011
mike378880@aol.com
http://www.homestead.com/
custardsociety
*The only glass club in existence;
primary focus is on antique custard
glass; over 100 members; striving to
preserve and share knowledge about
custard glass.*

Experts

Michael Coulon
591 SW Duxbury Ave.
Port Saint Lucie, FL 34983
ph: 772-785-9946
fax: 772-785-9011
mike378880@aol.com
*Has done in-depth research and study
of antique custard glass for over 10
years; expert in all patterns and
makers; appraisals or questions are
welcomed.*

Cut

Appraisers

Joel Stuart Litzky, ISA
Walnut Leaf Antique Marketplace
95 Pt. Somerset Lane
Severna Park, MD 21146
ph: 410-544-7372 or 800-224-7355
fax: 410-544-7372
jlitzky@comcast.net
*Specializes in the appraisal of
American Brilliant Period cut glass,
European & Oriental porcelains,
nautical, Naval Academy collectibles,
antique furniture.*

Clubs/Associations

Kathy Emerson
American Cut Glass Association, Inc.
Newsletter: Hobstar, The
P.O. Box 482
Ramona, CA 92065-0482
ph: 768-789-2715
fax: 768-789-7112
acgakathy@aol.com
http://www.cutglass.org
*Focuses on the Brilliant Period (1880-
1915) of American glass.*

Collectors

Charles Blanton
118 Magothy Bridge Rd.
Severna Park, MD 21146-1221
ph: 410-647-2841
fax: 410-647-2841
Bblanbet@aol.com
*Advanced collector wants one piece or
entire collection.*

Dealers

Randeen Cummings, ISA CAPP
Cummings & Associates
P.O. Box 5484
Eugene, OR 97405-0484
ph: 541-345-5856
fax: 541-345-8192
avaluequest@uswest.net
http://www.avaluequest.com
*Specializes in selling & appraising
residential contents, fine art, estate
jewelry, 18th & 19th century antiques,
American Brilliant period cut glass;
also specialized marketing for clients:
consultations, estate, and Internet
sales.*

Experts

Joan & Dick Randles
From the Cutter's Wheel Antiques
P.O. Box 285
Webster, NY 14580-0285
ph: 716-671-3760
*Specializes, buys and sells American
Brilliant period cut glass and
engraved glass; members ACGA; eves
and weekends best time to call.*

Chet Cassel
910 Pheasant Run
Newark, DE 19711
ph: 302-737-3819
*Buys, sells (retail/wholesale) and
collects examples of fine cut glass.*

Bill & Louise Boggess
4016 Martin Dr.
San Mateo, CA 94403-3623
ph: 650-345-5230
*Authors of "Identifying American
Brilliant Cut Glass" "Collecting
American Brilliant Cut Glass," and
"Reflection on American Brilliant Cut
Glass."*

Martha Louise Swan
3930 SE 162nd Ave., Unit 61
Portland, OR 97236-7006
ph: 503-669-8697
*Author of "American Cut & Engraved
Glass: The Brilliant Period in*

*Historical Perspective (1876-1916),"
3rd revision (Krause), updated price
guide, available from author.*

Misc. Services

Dean & Sharon DeOgny
Sentimental Journey Antiques
121 S. Washington Ave.
Minneapolis, MN 55401
ph: 612-332-3270
fax: 612-630-9496
deogny@sentimentaljourney.net
http://www.sentimentaljourney.net
*Produces a series of videos about cut
glass: signatures, assembly line
cutting, details of cutting, pattern
names, why stoppers are not
interchangeable, figured blanks, what
to do with broken pieces, etc.*

Dean & Sharon DeOgny
Sentimental Journey Antiques
121 S. Washington Ave.
Minneapolis, MN 55401
ph: 612-332-3270
fax: 612-630-9496
deogny@sentimentaljourney.net
http://www.sentimentaljourney.net
Dealers in cut glass for over 29 years.

Museums/Libraries

Dorflinger Glass Museum
Long Ridge Rd.
P.O. Box 356
White Mills, PA 18473
ph: 570-253-1185
fax; 570-253-5196
dglassmus@aol.com
http://www.dorflinger.org
*A tribute to the life and accomplish-
ments of Christian Dorflinger, known
throughout the world as the creator of
fine crystal and exquisite cut glass.*

High Museum of Art, The
1280 Peachtree St.
Atlanta, GA 30309
ph: 404-733-4400
fax: 404-733-4502
http://www.high.org
*A leading art museum in the
Southeastern US; collections include
African art, decorative arts, European
art, folk art, modern and contemporary art, and photography.*

Lightner Museum
P.O. Box 334
75 King St.
Saint Augustine, FL 32085
ph: 904-824-2874
info@lightnermuseum.org
http://www.lightnermuseum.org
*Exhibits relics of America's Gilded
Age: cut glass, Victorian art glass,
stained glass of Tiffany, costumes,
furnishings, mechanical musical
instruments, and other artifacts that
give a glimpse into 19th century daily
life*

Czechoslovakian

Appraisers

Peggy Sebek, ISA, AAA
Century Antiques & Appraisals, Inc.
3255 Glencairn Rd.
Shaker Heights, OH 44122-3407
ph: 216-991-2356 or 216-533-5874
fax: 216-991-2935
peggys@hpyday.com
*Accredited Member of the Interna-
tional Society of Appraisers, Member
of the Appraisers Association of
America.*

Dealers

Czech Cottage
100 16th Ave. SW
Cedar Rapids, IA 52404-2955
ph: 319-366-4937
fax: 319-366-4937
czechcottage@uswest.net
http://www.czechcottage.com
*Carries a large selection of
traditional Bohemian glass and
porcelain from the Czech Republic.*

Experts

Charles & Barbara Plummer
11417 Sherrie Lane
Silver Spring, MD 20902

Joseph Mattis
Black Swan
P.O. Box 925
Spencer, WV 25276
ph: 304-927-5064

Andries van Dam
Andries van Dam Fine Art & Antiques
1318 Sunnyhill Dr.
Camden, SC 29020
ph: 803-425-1710
fax: 803-425-8818
*Dealer and expert in art glass, Czech
glass (especially that by Josef
Drahonovsky), and paintings.*

Polly Enloe, ISA
Century Antiques & Appraisals, Inc.
212 Miller St.
Lafayette, LA 70503
ph: 318-234-7146
*Specializes in and appraises
Czechoslovakian glass.*

Museums/Libraries

Bob Truitt
Friends of the Glass Museum at Novy
Bor
13550 Ashbury Dr.
Carmel, IN 46032
ph: 301-929-2539
randdglass@sbcglobal.net
*Organizes symposia and other
research and educational functions
focusing on the glassware produced or
decorated in the Novy Bor region of
Czechoslovakia; supports the Glass
Museum at Novy Bor, Czechoslovakia.*

Degenhart

Clubs/Associations

Friends of Degenhart
Newsletter: Heartbeat
65323 Highland Hills Rd.
P.O. Box 186
Cambridge, OH 43725-0186
ph: 740-432-2626
degmus@clover.net
Open to all Degenhart collectors and supporters; free museum admission, 5% discount on most purchases, newsletter, annual "Gathering."

Museums/Libraries

Degenhart Paperweight & Glass
Museum, Inc.
65323 Highland Hills Rd.
P.O. Box 186
Cambridge, OH 43725-0186
ph: 740-432-2626
degmus@clover.net
History of glass in the Ohio valley; video, exhibits, research library, gift shop.

Depression

Clubs/Associations

W. Walker
North Jersey Dee Geer's
P.O. Box 741
Oradell, NJ 07649
ph: 201-384-6703

Long Island Depression Glass Club
P.O. Box 148
West Sayville, NY 11796
ph: 516-421-5065
dgemma@webspan.net

Depression Glass Club of Greater
Rochester
Newsletter: Bits & Pieces
657 East Ave.
Rochester, NY 14609

Millie Downey
Land of Sunshine Depression Glass Club
Newsletter: LSDGC Newsletter
P.O. Box 560275
Orlando, FL 32856-0275
ph: 407-298-3355 or 407-855-5502
milliesglass@webtv.net
Purpose of the club is to preserve the history of Depression glass and to encourage new collectors and familiarize the public with glassware of the era.

Central Florida GLASSaholics
P.O. Box 2319
Lakeland, FL 33806
information@glassaholics.com
http://www.glassaholics.com
Purpose of the club is to broaden the knowledge of and to aid in the preservation of glassware, pottery, and other collectibles of the Depression era.

Ruth Gullis, Mem.
Western Reserve Depression Glass Club
8669 Courtland Dr.
Strongsville, OH 44136

Jeff Settell
Iowa Depression Glass Association
Newsletter: ISGA Newsletter
ph: 515-963-9210
jeff_wdms@earthlink.net

20-30-40's Society, Inc.
Newsletter: Society Page, The
P.O. Box 856
La Grange, IL 60525-0856
ph: 630-734-9912
glassclub@aol.com
http://www.20-30-40society.org
Formed in 1972; devoted to collecting and learning about Depression-era glassware.

Margaret Davis
Lincoln Land Depression Era Glass &
Pottery Club
21 Foresters Lane
Springfield, IL 62704
margaret_davis37@sbcglobal.net
Club meets first Monday of the month at the Lincoln Library in Springfield, IL from 7-9 p.m.; goal is to learn and educate members about the American-made glass and pottery of the Depression era through 1970; sponsors annual glass show.

Don C. Baker
Gateway Depressioners Glass Club of
Greater St. Louis
2040 Flight Dr.
Florissant, MO 63031-2216
ph: 314-839-2874
DonCBak@juno.com
Club meets monthly in Kirkwood, MO.

Sarah VanDalsem, Mem.
National Depression Glass Association,
The
Newsletter: News & Views
P.O. Box 8264
Wichita, KS 67208-0264
ph: 918-241-1205
info@ndga.net
http://www.ndga.net
A central organization for Depression glass collectors; sponsors an annual show and sale in July.

Greater Tulsa Depression Era Glass Club
P.O. Box 470763
Tulsa, OK 74147-0763
jrj74012@aol.com

A. Nicholson
Big "D" Pression Glass Club
10 Winding Creek Trail
Garland, TX 75043

Anita Wood
Permian Basin Depression Glass Club
1412 Alamosa St.
Odessa, TX 79763
ph: 915-337-1297
dganita@aol.com

Walter Lemiski
Canadian Depression Glass Association
Newsletter: CDGA Newsletter
119 Wexford Rd.
Brampton, Ontario L6Z 2T5 Canada
ph: 905-846-2835
walt@waltztime.com
http://www.waltztime.com
Formed in 1976, members receive the CDGA Newsletter with ads, articles, finds, a dealer directory, show reports, book reviews, repro alerts and more.

Collectors

Anita Wood
1412 Alamosa St.
Odessa, TX 79763
ph: 915-337-1297
dganita@aol.com

Mary Faria
P.O. Box 32321
San Jose, CA 95152-2321
ph: 408-258-0413 or 408-258-0416
izmars@sbcglobal.net
Wants to buy pink or apple green Depression glass in non-etched designs for kitchen, soda fountain, desk ware, barware, perfume, vanity and bath ware; especially wants pink straw holder, desk blotter sets.

Dealers

Susan Leite
44 Glenwood Rd.
Brewster, MA 02631-2202
ph: 508-385-4905
Wants to buy all pink, green and jadite (creamy green) Depression glass; must be undamaged.

Fred & Linda Suzman
Suzman's Antiques
P.O. Box 301
Rehoboth, MA 02769
ph: 508-252-5729
suzmanf@ride.ri.net
Buys and sells Depression glass and Fiestaware.

Jay Adams
71 Ackerman Ave., #289
Clifton, NJ 07011-1501
ph: 973-365-5907
fax: 973-471-5325
jadams7811@aol.com
Specializing in Depression-era glass and china: also wants to buy Elegant glass such as Cambridge, Tiffin, Fostoria and others; send SASE with wants; will search and keep want list on file; best to call 6-11 EST; mail order only.

Gerald Manitone
657 East Ave.
Rochester, NY 14609
Buys, sells, and collects Depression glass.

Seth Price
Antiques Nook, The
402 Benfield Rd.
Severna Park, MD 21146
ph: 410-544-5607
theprices@telocity.com
http://www.antiquesnook.com
Buys and sells Elegant Depression glass; Adam to Windsor; mail order or Internet sales; no shop.

Hatchett's Glass Treasures
3033 Allison Rd.
Pelham, NC 27311
ph: 336-694-6244
hgt@tias.com
http://www.tias.com/stores/hgt
Specializes in Depression Glass.

Millie Downey
Millie's Glass & China
P.O. Box 560275
Orlando, FL 32856-0275
ph: 407-298-3355 or 407-855-5502
milliesglass@webtv.net
Wants to buy Depression glass; collects many patterns.

Lorrie Kitchen
Lorrie Kitchen Antiques
ph: 419-475-1759
lorrie@kitchenantiques.com
http://www.kitchenantiques.com
Specializes in Depression-era glass and ceramics.

Jeanne Ceyler
Old Parsonage Antiques
P.O. Box 581
Anna, OH 45302
ph: 937-394-3805
jceyler@oldparsonage.com
http://www.oldparsonage.com
Buys and sells Depression glass; also Elegant glass, kitchen glass, children's glass, and Fire King.

Victor Elliott
Closet Classics
P.O. Box 909
Orangevale, CA 95662
ph: 916-988-6333
Buys, sells and specializes in Depression-era glassware.

Anne Shatrau
Auntie Q's Antiques & Collectibles
P.O. Box 3411-AQ
Albany, OR 97321-0716
ph: 541-928-6180
fax: 541-928-0202
dg@auntieqs.com
http://www.auntieqs.com
Specializes in Depression glass and post Depression-era glassware.

Experts

Gene Florence
P.O. Box 22186
Lexington, KY 40522-2186
ph: 606-266-4615
jafo@iglou.com
http://www.geneflorence.com
Author of several books about Depression glass.

Margaret & Kenn Whitmyer
K & M Antiques
P.O. Box 30806
Columbus, OH 43230
junquer9@columbus.rr.com
http://www.kandmantiques.com
*Specializing in Depression-era
bedroom and bathroom glassware.
Author of "Bedroom & Bathroom
Glassware of the Depression Years."*

Nadine Pankow
8825 W. 98th St.
Palos Hills, IL 60465
ph: 708-599-9107
nadineglas@aol.com
http://members.aol.com/nadineglas
*Specializes in mail order of
Depression, Elegant and some kitchen
glassware; in business for over 25
years.*

Internet Resources

Anne Shatrau
Depression Glass Shopper Online
P.O. Box 3411
Albany, OR 97321-0716
ph: 541-928-6180
fax: 541-928-0202
editor@dgshopper.com
http://www.dgshopper.com
*The Internet's first Depression-era
glassware magazine and marketplace;
daily chat, weekly sales, monthly
articles, online price guides; free one
week trial; Web site also includes
book sellers, periodicals and dealers;
subscription fee.*

Domes

Suppliers

Ben Bowen
Antique Clocks & Domes
Rt 3, Box 134C
Monticello, FL 32344
ph: 850-997-3979
fax: 850-997-3797
Ben@glassdomes.com
http://www.glassdomes.com
Sells round and oval domes.

B & L Antiqurie, Inc.
P.O. Box 453
6217 S. Lakeshore Rd.
Lexington, MI 48450-0453
ph: 800-840-1110 or 810-359-8623
fax: 810-359-7498
information@bentglasscentral.com
http://www.bentglasscentral.com
*Bent glass, convex portrait glass,
antique flat glass, beveled mirror
shapes, domes, and other specialty
glass products for over 30 years.*

Lew Oswald
Mile Hi Clock Supplies
625 Poppy Way
Broomfield, CO 80020
ph: 303-469-1220
fax: 303-439-0186
milehiclck@aol.com
http://members.aol.com/milehiclck/
domes.htm
*Carries clock supplies including glass
domes.*

Duncan & Miller

Clubs/Associations

National Duncan Glass Society
Journal: National Duncan Glass Journal
525 Jefferson Ave.
P.O. Box 965
Washington, PA 15301
ph: 724-225-9950
http://www.duncan-glass.com
*Focuses on the glassware produced by
the Duncan & Miller Glass Co.*

Collectors

Cliff McCaslin
Rocliff Communications
8422 N. Park Ct.
Kansas City, MO 64155
ph: 816-436-7719
fax: 816-436-6955
vitrify@swbell.net
*Wants to buy Duncan and Duncan-
Miller glass; all patterns.*

Museums/Libraries

Duncan Miller Glass Museum
525 Jefferson Ave.
P.O. Box 965
Washington, PA 15301
ph: 724-225-9950
http://www.duncan-glass.com
*Museum has over 1,400 pieces of
Duncan glass in five display rooms;
annual show and sale in July.*

Durand

Dealers

Edward J. Meschi
129 Pinyard Rd.
Monroeville, NJ 08343-1870
ph: 856-358-7293
fax: 856-358-7789
ed@meschiarts.com
http://www.meschiarts.com
*Buys and sells Durand art glass;
wants original sales catalogs for
Durand Art Glass which operated
under the name of Vineland Flint
Glass Co. in the 1920s; author of
"Durand - The Man and His Glass."*

Early American

Auction Services

Norman C. Heckler
Norman C. Heckler & Company
79 Bradford Corner Rd.
Woodstock Valley, CT 06282-2002
ph: 860-974-1634
fax: 860-974-2003
info@hecklerauction.com
http://www.hecklerauction.com
*Specializes in the sale of early glass
and bottles; Heckler & Co. sold a
single bottle for $66,000 at auction in
1993.*

Clubs/Associations

Walter B. Moore
Early American Glass Traders
RD 5 Box 638
Milford, DE 19963-9805
ph: 302-422-0932
*Association of collectors of early
American pressed glass who are
interested in improving their
collections by trading or selling their
duplicates amongst themselves.*

Collectors

Calvin L. Hackeman
8865 Olde Mill Run
Washington, DC 20010-6132
ph: 703-368-6982 or 703-847-7530
fax: 703-848-9583
hltzhaus@erols.com
*Serious advanced collector of
Hawaiian Ley by Higbee; wants hard-
to-find or unusual pieces; also
interested in purchasing colored Flint
Glass, especially Sandwich items.*

Experts

Jamie Houdeshell
16255 Normandy South
Perrysburg, OH 43551
ph: 419-872-1966
*Buys, sells, appraises and specializes
in antique bottles and early American
glass.*

Museums/Libraries

Sandwich Glass Museum
Newsletter: Cullet, The
109 Main St.
P.O. Box 103
Sandwich, MA 02453-0103
ph: 508-888-0251
glass@sandwichglassmuseum.org
http://www.sandwichglassmuseum.org
*The museum preserves and displays
the glass manufactured in Sandwich
1825-1907.*

Elegant

(see also GLASS, Cambridge;
GLASS, Crystal; GLASS, Duncan &
Miller; GLASS, Fostoria; GLASS,
Heisey; GLASS, Imperial; GLASS,
Tiffin)

Dealers

Jay Adams
71 Ackerman Ave., #289
Clifton, NJ 07011-1501
ph: 973-365-5907
fax: 973-471-5325
jadams7811@aol.com
*Specializing in Depression-era glass
and china; wants to buy Elegant glass
such as Cambridge, Tiffin, Fostoria
and others; send SASE with wants;
will search and keep want list on file;
best to call 6-11 EST.; mail order
only.*

Christie McCann
Always Available Antiques &
Collectibles
3019 Winter Pine Ct.
Fairfax, VA 22031
ph: 703-385-0551
olga@erols.com
http://users.erols.com/aaac
*Specializes in Elegant, Depression and
kitchen glassware.*

Kelly O'Kane
Elegant American Glass
P.O. Box 16303
Saint Paul, MN 55116-0303
kelly@kellyokane.com
http://www.kellyokane.com
*Author of "Tiffin Glassmasters: the
Modern Years," which identifies all
artware production at Tiffin from
1938 to 1984; dealer in Elegant
American glass (all major companies),
and collector of Tiffin Modern glass.*

Constance Crow
Crow's Nest Antiques - CyberGlass
Shop
1601 S. IH 35, Ste. 400
Round Rock, TX 78664
ph: 512-218-4290 or 512-918-1709
fax: 512-310-0680
cnest@antiquetexas.com
http://www.antiquetexas.com/crow
*Specializes in Elegant glassware from
the Depression era: Heisey,
Cambridge, Fostoria, Tiffin,
Morgantown, etc.; has large inventory
of rare and not-so-rare American
Elegant glassware.*

Darlene Simpson
Simpsons, The
4628 Morris Ave. S
Renton, WA 98055
ph: 524-277-0819 or 206-369-1869
fax: 425-277-0821
thesimpsons1@attbi.com
http://www.simpsonscollect.com
*Specializes in Elegant and Depression-
era glassware; also dolls, figurines,
crystal, and Steiff teddy bears.*

Experts

Randy & Debbie Coe
Coe's Mercantile
2459 SE TV Hwy PMB #321
Hillsboro, OR 97123-7919
ph: 503-640-9122
fax: 503-648-2261
elegantglass@aol.com
*Authors of a book on Elegant Glass;
specializes in Cambridge, Depression,
Elegant, Fenton, Fostoria,
Franciscan, Heisey, Hull, McKee,
Tiffin, and Westmoreland glass.*

Matching Services

Florence & Jay Solito
Solito
54 Old Stafford Rd.
Tolland, CT 06084
ph: 860-872-3294
solito@ix.netcom.com
*Tiffin, Morgantown, Imperial,
Fostoria, Depression glass,
Cambridge, and other Elegant
glassware.*

Fran Jay
Fran Jay's Glass
10 Church St.
Lambertville, NJ 08530-2102
ph: 609-397-1571
kelly@glassshow.com
http://www.GlassShow.com
*Cambridge, Depression glass, Fenton,
Fostoria, Heisey, and other Elegant
glass companies; daily hours, also
mail order.*

Harry Weitkemper
China Finders
2823 Central Ave.
St. Petersburg, FL 33781
ph: 888-244-6239 or 800-900-2557
fax: 727-321-3868
ChinaFinders@aol.com
http://www.chinafinders.com
*Candlewick, Fostoria, Cambridge,
Tiffin, Libby, etc.*

Wayne Carpenter
Country Store, The
2156 S. 7th St.
Lincoln, NE 68502-3301
ph: 402-476-2254
*Cambridge, Duncan Miller, Fenton,
Fostoria, Heisey, Imperial, Tiffin,
Westmoreland, Depression glass.*

Milbra Long
Milbra's Crystal
P.O. Box 784
Cleburne, TX 76033-0784
ph: 817-645-6066 or 817-294-9837
longseat@sbcglobal.net
http://www.fostoriacrystal.com
*Crystal matching: Fostoria, Tiffin,
Lenox & others; buy and sell; requests
kept on file; send SASE for reply.*

European

Auction Services

Ron Fox
Ron Fox Auctions
416 Throop St.
North Babylon, NY 11704
ph: 631-376-0916
fax: 631-376-0916
oz@webspan.net
*Conducts periodic auctions of
European glass: Bohemian and
Germanic, cut and enameled.*

Dealers

Ron Fox
416 Throop St.
North Babylon, NY 11704
ph: 631-376-0916
fax: 631-376-0916
oz@webspan.net
*Wants old European glass:
transparent or opaque enamel, wheel
cut, engraved, overlay, iridescent, etc.*

Fenton

Clubs/Associations

Kay Kenworthy, Ed.
Fenton Art Glass Collectors of America,
Inc.
Newsletter: Butterfly Net, The
P.O. Box 384
Williamstown, WV 26187
ph: 304-375-6196
fax: 304-375-4679
kkenworthy@foth.com
http://www.collectoronline.com/club-
FAGCA.html
*FAGCA is a non-profit educational
corporation dedicated to learning
about Fenton art glass.*

Bob Stein
National Fenton Glass Society
Newsletter: Fenton Flyer, The
P.O. Box 4008
Marietta, OH 45750-7008
ph: 614-374-3345
nfgs@ee.net
http://www.axces.com/nfgs

Jackie Shirley
Pacific Northwest Fenton Association
Newsletter: Fenton Nor'Wester
P.O. Box 881
Tillamook, OR 97141-0881
ph: 503-842-4815
*Annual convention each June in
Springfield, OR; check Web page for
membership details.*

Collectors

John O. Burgess
10738 Harley Rd.
Lorton, VA 22079-3908
ph: 703-339-5359
Wants pre-1970 Fenton art glass.

Dealers

Connie Frye
Attic Shoppee
ph: 330-745-7104 or 330-701-5335
fax: 330-745-9304
murmaid44@aol.com
http://members.aol.com/atticshoppee/
atticshoppee.html
*Buying and selling Fenton Art Glass
and Murano Art Glass.*

Gilbert Nadeau
Karats & Sterling Jewelers
202 S. George St.
Rome, NY 13440
ph: 315-336-0897
karatsandsterl@aol.com
http://www.fentonglassestore.com
*Sells new Fenton art glass: Burmese,
cranberry, Fenton lamps, milk glass.*

Darcie Smith
Puppets Glass
17 Lobue Lane
Cheektowaga, NY 14225
ph: 716-685-0060
puppet531@aol.com
http://www.puppetsglass.com
*Buys and sells Fenton art glass; also
Westmoreland.*

Jack R. Skaw
Glass Castle, The
48399 Kingwood Ave.
Mill City, OR 97360
jackr@wvi.com
http://www.glasscastle.com
*Buys and sells Fenton Art Glass both
old and new.*

Fenton Glass Man, The
2211 Simpson Ave.
Aberdeen, WA 98520
ph: 888-643-9134 (orders)
abart@techline.com
http://www.fentonglassman.com
*Carries hundreds of current Fenton
art glass collectibles: glass baskets,
glass, bells, limited editions, hand
painted glassware, vases, glass
animals, art glass lamps; an
authorized Fenton Showcase dealer.*

Experts

Margaret & Kenn Whitmyer
K & M Antiques
P.O. Box 30806
Columbus, OH 43230
junquer9@columbus.rr.com
http://www.kandmantiques.com
*Author of two books on Fenton
glassware.*

Ferill J. Rice
302 Pheasant Run
Kaukauna, WI 54130-1802
ph: 920-766-9176 or 920-991-9072
fax: 920-991-9078
*Advisor to "Warman's Antiques &
Collectibles Price Guide" and
"Warman's Flea Market."*

Randy & Debbie Coe
Coe's Mercantile
2459 SE TV Hwy PMB #321
Hillsboro, OR 97123-7919
ph: 503-640-9122
fax: 503-648-2261
elegantglass@aol.com
*Authors of a book on Elegant Glass;
specializes in Cambridge, Depression,
Elegant, Fenton, Fostoria,
Franciscan, Heisey, Hull, McKee,
Tiffin, and Westmoreland glass.*

Internet Resources

Frank Sereno
528 West Ave.
Morris, IL 60450
ph: 815-942-2595
fsereno@uti.com
http://groups.yahoo.com/group/fenton-
glass
*An email based group for the
discussion of and appreciation of
Fenton art glass; assistance in
identifying art glass, news,
information.*

John Gager
Fenton Fanatics Home Page
4403 W. Winston Court #19
Spokane, WA 99205
ph: 509-326-5821
fax: 503-961-7837
jgager@fentonfan.com
http://www.fentonfan.com
*A resource for Fenton art glass
collectors; contains articles, a monthly
"What's New?" column, QVC Fenton
database, links to a Fenton chat room,
Fenton classifieds, and more.*

Man./Prod./Dist.

James Measell
Fenton Art Glass Company, The
Newsletter: Glass Messenger
700 Elizabeth St.
Williamstown, WV 26187-1028
ph: 304-375-6122 or 800-249-4527
fax: 304-375-7833
askfenton@fentonartglass.com
http://www.fentonartglass.com
*Manufacturer of unique art glass such
as Burmese and Rosalene; currently
manufactures plates, figurines, bells,
ornaments and a "Connoisseur
Collection."*

Periodicals

Ferill J. Rice
Newsletter: Butterfly Net
302 Pheasant Run
Kaukauna, WI 54130-1802
ph: 920-766-9176 or 920-991-9072
fax: 920-991-9078
*Published six times per year; advisor
to "Warman's Antiques & Collectibles Price Guide" and
"Warman's Flea Market."*

Findlay

Clubs/Associations

Barbara Payne, Pres.
Collectors of Findlay Glass
Newsletter: Findlay Glass Press
P.O. Box 256
Findlay, OH 45839-0256
ph: 419-422-7920
Barbpain@aol.com
Club for members to share information about Findlay Glass and the current activity in the marketplace; quarterly newsletter.

Dealers

Jennifer Payne
Gifts In Time
540 S. Main St.
Findlay, OH 45840
ph: 419-422-7227
fax: 419-422-3824
Buys and sells Findlay pattern glass.

Fire-King

Dealers

John Pritchett
Prairie Collectibles 183
2700 Prairie College SW
Canton, OH 44706
ph: 330-484-2678
Buys and sells Fire-King, Hazel Atlas, Depression glass, Fenton, Anchor Hocking glass.

Experts

April M. Tvorak
P.O. Box 94
Warren Center, PA 18851
Author of "History and Price Guide to Fire-King," "Fire-King II," and "Fire-King '95," "Fire-King 5th Ed.- 97 Values," "Fire-King Fever, 95-96 Values" updated values; please include a SASE with all correspondence.

Fostoria

Clubs/Associations

Clifford Bucy
Fostoria Glass Society of America, The
Newsletter: Facets of Fostoria
P.O. Box 826
Moundsville, WV 26041-0826
ph: 304-845-9188 or 304-845-2170
mailme@fostoriaglass.org
http://www.fostoriaglass.org

Melvin Murray
Fostoria Glass Association
109 N. Main St.
Fostoria, OH 44830
mmurray419@aol.com

Tom Rosenburg, Ed.
Fostoria Glass Collectors, Inc.
Newsletter: Glass Works, The
P.O. Box 1625
Orange, CA 92856
ph: 949-770-4088
info@fostoriacollectors.org
http://www.fostoriacollectors.org
A nonprofit organization dedicated to

the study and preservation of Fostoria glass as well as all American handmade glassware.

Dealers

Penny Drucker
Mother Drucker's
P.O. Box 50261
Irvine, CA 92619-0261
ph: 888-637-8253 or 949-551-5529
fax: 949-551-2116
Penny@Motherdruckers.com
http://www.motherdruckers.com
Carries large selection of Fostoria glassware.

Experts

Milbra Long
Milbra's Crystal
P.O. Box 784
Cleburne, TX 76033-0784
ph: 817-645-6066 or 817-294-9837
longseat@sbcglobal.net
http://www.fostoriacrystal.com
Co-author with Emily Seate of "Fostoria Stemware," "Fostoria Tableware: 1924-1943," "Fostoria Tableware: 1944-1986," and "Fostoria, Useful and Ornamental" (Collector Books).

Juanita Williams
P.O. Box 1626
Medford, OR 97501
ph: 541-776-2442
juanita@fostorialady.com
http://www.fostorialady.com
Author on Fostoria glass and co-author on many study guides on Fostoria including "Fostoria's Master Etchings," "Fostoria Chintz," and "Fostoria By Ye Candlelight;" an avid collector and lecturer on Fostoria glass; online matching services.

Matching Services

Charlotte Krauch
Charlotte's Glass Reflections
5619 29th St. West
Bradenton, FL 34207
ph: 941-756-1940
grmc@tampabay.rr.com
http://www.facets.net/glassreflections
Specializes in Fostoria glassware; all discontinued patterns; locating service; send wants; SASE for reply.

Museums/Libraries

Clifford Bucy
Fostoria Glass Museum
P.O. Box 826
Moundsville, WV 26041-0826
ph: 304-845-9188 or 304-845-2170
mailme@fostoriaglass.org
http://www.fostoriaglass.org

Fry

Clubs/Associations

H.C. Fry Glass Society
Newsletter: Shards, The
P.O. Box 41
Beaver, PA 15009-0041
http://www.rochesterpa.com/fryglass/society.htm
Formed for the study, preservation of information and appreciation of the glass made at the H.C. Fry Glass Co. in Rochester, PA.

Gay Fad Studios

Experts

Donna McGrady
301 E. Walnut St.
P.O. Box 14
Waynetown, IN 47990-0014
ph: 765-234-2187
dmcg@tctc.com
Collects and specializes in glassware decorated from 1945-1964 by the Gay Fad Studios of Lancaster, Ohio; Gay Fad was known for applying hand decorations to many pieces of glass including Fire King.

Goofus

Collectors

John Martin Davis, Jr.
2705 Swiss Ave.
Dallas, TX 75204
ph: 214-824-2556
marty@texascpa.com

Experts

Steve Gillespie
400 NE Martin Blvd.
Kansas City, MO 64118
ph: 816-455-5558
stegil@sbcglobal.net
Publisher of the "Goofus Glass Gazette," dealer and collector of Goffus glass for over 30 years; developer of a Goofus Glass Museum; Goffus glass advisor to price guides, books; writing an illustrated book on Goffus glass & its history.

Internet Resources

David & Maureen Ballentine
Goofus Glass Museum & Information Center
639 E. Amelia St.
Orlando, FL 32803
gballens@bellsouth.net
http://www.goofus.org
The only known Internet Web site dedicated specifically to Goofus glass; subscribe online to an Goffus glass email newsletter.

Gorham

Man./Prod./Dist.

Gorham, Inc.
100 Lenox Dr.
Lawrenceville, NJ 08648
ph: 609-896-2800 or 800-635-3669
http://www.lenox.com
Sterling and stainless steel flatware,

sterling and silverplated hollowware; fine china, crystal stemware, giftware and dolls; a division of Lenox Brands.

Greentown

Clubs/Associations

National Greentown Glass Association
Newsletter: National Greentown Glass Association Newsletter
P.O. Box 107
Greentown, IN 46936-0107
ph: 765-628-6206
membership@greentownglass.org
http://www.greentownglass.org
Non-profit corporation dedicated to the promotion, preservation and collecting of Greentown Glass; active in disseminating information concerning Greentown Glass Co. which operated from 1894 to 1903.

Collectors

LeAnne Milliser
19596 Glendale Ave.
South Bend, IN 46637-1814
ph: 574-272-1184

Dealers

Jerry Garrett
Jerry's Antiques & Postcards
1807 West Madison St.
Kokomo, IN 46901-1829
ph: 765-457-5256
Buys and sells Greentown Glass as well as chocolate glass made by other National Company factories.

Experts

Jim & Mira Houdeshell
Houdeshell's Antiques Center
1610 South Main St.
Findlay, OH 45840
ph: 419-423-2895 or 419-434-4551
fax: 419-434-6974
houdeshell@findlay.edu

Museums/Libraries

Gary Buckley
Greentown Glass Museum
112 N. Meridian
P.O. Box 161
Greentown, IN 46936-0161
ph: 765-628-6206
http://www.eastern.k12.in.us/gpl/MUSEUM.HTM
An exhibit from the old Indiana Tumbler & Goblet Co. (1894-1903.)

Grand Rapids Public Museum
272 Pearl St. NW
Grand Rapids, MI 49504-5371
ph: 616-456-3977
fax: 616-456-3873
staff@grmuseum.org
http://www.grmuseum.org
Large collection of Greentown Glass; publisher of the book "Greentown Glass - the Indiana Tumbler & Goblet Company."

Hazel-Atlas

Collectors

Kenneth G. Sloan
5707 S. Kenwood
Chicago, IL 60637-1718
ph: 773-752-4247
kennethsloanHA@msn.com
General Hazel-Atlas collector, primarily marked items; also wants related literature.

Heisey

Clubs/Associations

Larry D. Burgess
Heisey '76ers
ldburg48@aol.com
Small but active study club located in Central OH (a.k.a. "Heisey Country"); dedicated to the preservation and promotion of Heisey glass, with an emphasis on education.

"Butch" Jones
National Capital Heisey Collectors
Newsletter: Heisey Herald
P.O. Box 23
Clinton, MD 20735
ph: 301-505-0041
Purpose is to study and preserve Heisey glassware; meetings held second Monday of each month except July and August; programs on Heisey patterns, pieces, colors, etc.

Heisey Collectors of America, Inc.
Newsletter: Heisey News, The
169 W. Church St.
Newark, OH 43055
ph: 740-345-2932
fax: 740-345-9638
curator@heiseymuseum.org
http://www.heiseymuseum.org
Every production color and pattern is on display in the King House, built in 1831.

Collectors

Cliff McCaslin
Rocliff Communications
8422 N. Park Ct.
Kansas City, MO 64155
ph: 816-436-7719
fax: 816-436-6955
vitrify@swbell.net
Wants to buy glassware by Heisey.

Dealers

Robert Henicksman
Classic Glass
916 Q St.
Sacramento, CA 95814
ph: 916-448-0840
Buys and sells all patterns of Heisey glass; also maintains want lists and will search for customer needs.

Museums/Libraries

National Heisey Glass Museum, The
169 W. Church St.
Newark, OH 43055
ph: 740-345-2932
fax: 740-345-9638
curator@heiseymuseum.org
http://www.heiseymuseum.org
Owned and operated by Heisey Collectors of America; hundreds of patterns of glass made by A.H. Heisey & Co. 1895-1957 on display.

Higgins

Man./Prod./Dist.

Higgins Glass Studio
33 E. Quincy Rd.
Riverside, IL 60546
ph: 708-447-2787
Manufacturer of the fused glass that was popular in the 1950s and 1960s.

Imperial

Clubs/Associations

National Imperial Glass Collectors
Society
Newsletter: Glasszette
P.O. Box 534
Bellaire, OH 43906
ph: 603-424-1146
fax: 603-424-1213
info@nigcs.org
http://www.imperialglass.org
Members interested in the history and glassware produced by the Imperial Glass Corp.; conducts an annual convention offering seminars, show and sale, and "members only" auction; establishing an Imperial museum.

Collectors

Kathy Doub
5359 Iron Pen Place
Columbia, MD 21044-1811
ph: 410-995-1254

Cliff McCaslin
Rocliff Communications
8422 N. Park Ct.
Kansas City, MO 64155
ph: 816-436-7719
fax: 816-436-6955
vitrify@swbell.net
Collects Depression and Elegant glassware; produces videos on Depression and Elegant glass.

Dealers

Cliff McCaslin
Rocliff Communications
8422 N. Park Ct.
Kansas City, MO 64155
ph: 816-436-7719
fax: 816-436-6955
vitrify@swbell.net
Wants to buy all patterns of Imperial glass.

Penny Drucker
Mother Drucker's
P.O. Box 50261
Irvine, CA 92619-0261
ph: 888-637-8253 or 949-551-5529
fax: 949-551-2116
Penny@Motherdruckers.com
http://www.motherdruckers.com
Always changing inventory of color, cut, rare and common pieces; send LSASE for list.

Experts

Myrna & Bob Garrison
Collector's Loot
3816 Hastings Dr.
Arlington, TX 76013-1900
ph: 817-275-6342
fax: 817-275-6342
Authors of "Imperial's Vintage Milk Glass," "Imperial's Boudoir, Etcetera," "Imperial Cape Cod Tradition to Treasure," and "Imperial Candlewick, Little Known Facts A look at the Rare & Unusual;" books available from author.

Internet Resources

Laura Miller
Imperial Glass
5134 Neptune Square
Oxnard, CA 93035
ph: 805-382-8729
glassmurf@aol.com
http://groups.yahoo.com/group/
CandlewickCollector
A mailing list created especially for collectors of Imperial Glass; join fellow collectors, read the latest Imperial news, report your finds, ask questions, share information.

Misc. Services

Cliff McCaslin
Rocliff Communications
8422 N. Park Ct.
Kansas City, MO 64155
ph: 816-436-7719
fax: 816-436-6955
vitrify@swbell.net
Offers videotapes on popular glassware patterns of the Depression era, Imperial Candlewick, Imperial Slag, Imperial Cape Cod.

Italian

(see also MODERNISM)

Clubs/Associations

William Scott Bata
Murano Glass Society
32040 Mt. Hermon Rd.
Salisbury, MD 21804
ph: 410-546-5881
fax: 410-546-5881

Dealers

Connie Frye
Attic Shoppee
ph: 330-745-7104 or 330-701-5335
fax: 330-745-9304
murmaid44@aol.com
http://members.aol.com/atticshoppee/
atticshoppee.html
Buying and selling Fenton Art Glass and Murano Art Glass.

William Scott Bata
Glassfinders
32040 Mt. Hermon Rd.
Salisbury, MD 21804
Collector, expert, dealer specializes in Venetian and Italian glass from the island of Murano; 19th century to present day; buying and selling.

David Huffman
P.O. Box 26151
Charlotte, NC 28221-6151
ph: 800-327-9654 or 704-598-7720
Wants to buy Italian glass.

Kenneth P. Lesko
Kenneth Paul Lesko 20th Century
Decorative Arts
P.O. Box 16099
Rocky River, OH 44116-0099
ph: 440-356-0275
fax: 440-331-1280
kplesko@aol.com
http://members.aol.com/kplesko/
kplesko.html
Specialist in Italian glass 1920-1970; wants to buy Venini, Matinuzzi, Scarpa, Seguso, Barovier, Cenedese, A. Toso/Dino Martens, MVM Cappelin, CVM, Avem, Salir, Nason, Fratelli Toso, Salviati, Vistosi, A. Barbini.

Ara Tavitian
Retro Gallery
524 1/2 N. La Brea Ave.
Los Angeles, CA 90036-2016
ph: 323-936-5261
fax: 323-936-5262
retrogalleryLA@aol.com
http://www.retroglass.com
Art glass from the 1940s through the 1960s; specializing in Italian and Scandinavian glass.

Experts

Howard Lockwood
P.O. Box 191
Fort Lee, NJ 07024
ph: 201-969-0373
fax: 201-969-0373
vetri@webspan.net
http://www.vetri-italianglassnews.com
Buys, sells and specializes in Venini and other Italian glass.

Dan Ripley
Dan Ripley Antiques
907 E. Michigan St., Ste. 102
Indianapolis, IN 46202
ph: 317-955-5900
fax: 317-630-9384
dnripley@iei.net
http://www.danripley.com
A most experienced dealer; specializes in Italian and Scandinavian glass and ceramics; thousands of pieces sold privately and at auction; guest speaker at International Society of Appraisers' convention.

Man./Prod./Dist.

Brenda Nishimoto
Venetian Glass Art.com
1404 Sarita Way
Cupertino, CA 95015
ph: 408-241-3408
fax: 408-985-5780
info@venetianglassart.com
http://www.venetianglassart.com
Direct importer of modern Venetian glass sculptures: vases, Murano glass chandeliers, Murano clowns, Murano paperweights.

Periodicals

Howard Lockwood
Vetri Italian Glass
Newsletter: VETRI: Italian Glass News
P.O. Box 191
Fort Lee, NJ 07024
ph: 201-969-0373
fax: 201-969-0373
vetri@webspan.net
http://www.vetri-italianglassnews.com
A quarterly newsletter focusing on 20th century Italian glass and its makers.

Jack-in-the-Pulpit

Clubs/Associations

David M. Issitt
Jack-in-the-Pulpit Appreciation Society
33B Holyoake Ct.
Kettering, Northamptonshire NN16 9DN
U.K.
ph: 10536 483520
glasswriter@hotmail.com
http://www.homestead.com/jipas/
JIPAS.html
A society for collectors of Jack-in-the-Pulpit glass vases.

Experts

David M. Issitt
Touch of Glass - England, A
33B Holyoake Ct.
Kettering, Northamptonshire NN16 9DN
U.K.
ph: 10536 483520
glasswriter@hotmail.com
http://www.homestead.com/jipas/
ATouchofGlass.html
Specializing in Jack-in-the-Pulpit vases; full research service.

Kosta Boda

Dealers

Gregg Shienbaum
Lladro Connection, A
30 NE 1st St.
Miami, FL 33132
ph: 800-984-5586
illum1@aol.com
http://www.illumcollectibles.com
Specializing in current and retired Swarovski and Lladro; also carries a complete line of Lalique and Kosta Boda.

Man./Prod./Dist.

Royal Scandinavian, Inc.
140 Bradford Dr.
West Berlin, NJ 08091
ph: 609-768-5400 or 800-431-1992
fax: 800-448-7553
http://www.royalscandinavia.com
Swedish full lead crystal glassware, giftware and accessories.

Lalique

Auction Services

Amory Spizzirri, Client Svc.
William Doyle Galleries
175 E. 87th St.
New York, NY 10128-2205
ph: 212-427-2730
fax: 212-369-0892
info@doylegalleries.com
http://www.doylegalleries.com
Holds over 50 auctions annually of furniture and decorations, paintings and sculpture, jewelry, books and prints, couture and textiles, 20th century art & design, majolica, Lalique, Asian works of art and other specialty categories.

Clubs/Associations

Lalique Collectors Society
Newsletter: Lalique
400 Veterans Blvd.
Carlstadt, NJ 07072-2704
ph: 800-993-2580
fax: 201-939-4492
info@lalique.com
http://www.lalique.com/lcs.htm
Focuses on the collectibles issued by Lalique North America.

Collectors

Jeff Myers
P.O. Box 26151
Charlotte, NC 28221-6151
ph: 800-327-9654 or 704-598-7720
Wants to buy R. LALIQUE glass; also wants Galle, Daum and Tiffany glass.

Dealers

Shai H. Bandmann
Paul Stamati Gallery
1050 2nd Ave.
New York, NY 10022
ph: 212-754-4533
fax: 718-271-6958
paul@stamati.com
http://www.stamati.com
A leading dealer and expert in works by Rene Lalique.

David Huffman
P.O. Box 26151
Charlotte, NC 28221-6151
ph: 800-327-9654 or 704-598-7720
Wants to buy R. LALIQUE glass; also wants Loetz, Daum, and Italian glass.

Gregg Shienbaum
Lladro Connection, A
30 NE 1st St.
Miami, FL 33132
ph: 800-984-5586
illum1@aol.com
http://www.illumcollectibles.com
Specializing in current and retired Swarovski and Lladro; also carries a complete line of Lalique and Kosta Boda.

Allan & Pat Clay
Clemons-Eicken Fine European Imports
6166 N. Scottsdale Rd., #204
Scottsdale, AZ 85253
ph: 602-998-9042 or 800-250-5423
fax: 602-998-3755
Carries Lladro, Armani, Boehm, Lalique, Cybis.

Experts

Nicholas Dawes
67 East 11th St.
New York, NY 10003-4613
ph: 212-473-5111
fax: 212-353-3845
nmdawes@aol.com
Buys, sells and specializes in pre-war works by Rene Lalique; author of "Lalique Glass" (Crown Publishers, 1986).

Randy Monsen
Monsen & Baer Inc.
P.O. Box 529
Vienna, VA 22183-0529
ph: 703-938-2129
fax: 703-242-1357
monsenbaer@erols.com
Wants perfume bottles by Lalique; prefers pre-1940 pieces by Rene Lalique but will consider later pieces; premium prices paid for early bottles with their original boxes.

John D. Shearer
55 Ave. R., 2nd Fl.
Office #2975
Toronto, Ontario M5R 3L2 Canada
ph: 416-922-9322
fax: 416-922-8487
deco1925@bellnet.ca
http://www.gemmologist.com
One of Canada's foremost Lalique

specialists; buys and sells unique and unusual pieces of Lalique.

Internet Resources

John D. Shearer
55 Ave. R., 2nd Fl.
Office #2975
Toronto, Ontario M5R 3L2 Canada
ph: 416-922-9322
fax: 416-922-8487
deco1925@bellnet.ca
http://www.gemmologist.com
A collector's Web site with great Lalique information: judging quality, signatures, history, Lalique glass and perfume bottles, Lalique mascots, and more.

Man./Prod./Dist.

Lalique North America, Inc.
400 Veterans Blvd.
Carlstadt, NJ 07072-2704
ph: 201-939-4199
fax: 201-939-4492
info@lalique.com
http://www.lalique.com
French porcelain, crystal, stemware, dinnerware and giftwares; distributor of Lalique porcelain, crystal, jewelry, leather goods, watches, silk scarves, and "parfum" in US (crystal patterns are never discontinued.)

Lenox

Man./Prod./Dist.

Lenox China & Crystal Consumer Service
100 Lenox Dr.
Lawrenceville, NJ 08648
ph: 609-896-2800 or 800-635-3669
http://www.lenox.com
Offers Matching Services List of dealers who offer replacements for current of discontinued Lenox items; also gives insurance estimates.

Matching Services

Cee Cee China
3904 Parsons Rd.
Chevy Chase, MD 20815
ph: 301-652-6226 or 800-619-6226
ceeceechina@aol.com
http://www.ceeceechina.com
Buys, sells and locates Lenox crystal.

Carol Ulrey
Unique Antiques
P.O. Box 15815
San Diego, CA 92175-5815
ph: 619-281-8650
fax: 619-282-8407
culrey@webcc.net
Specializing in china matching: Haviland, old French and American; also Lenox china and crystal; publishes booklet "Matching Services for Haviland China," updated yearly and lists matching services in 24 states & Canada, cost is $4 ppd.

Forget-Me-Not China
17255 SE Licorice Way
Renton, WA 98059
ph: 425-254-0200 or 800-553-6693
fax: 425-254-0239
info@forgetmenotchina.com
http://www.forgetmenotchina.com
Lenox only; specializing in discontinued patterns of Lenox Elegant stemware, casual crystal and barware; brochure available.

Loetz

Internet Resources

Eddy Scheepers
Loetz.com
eddy@loetz.com
http://www.loetz.com
Web site focuses on Bohemian art glass maker, Loetz: history, publications, museums, how to identify, articles, etc.

Lotton

Dealers

Lotton Glass Gallery
900 N. Michigan Ave.
Chicago, IL 60601
ph: 312-664-6203
fax: 312-664-6253

Man./Prod./Dist.

Jacqueline Reiner, Dir. of Sales
Lotton Glass
24760 Country Lane
Crete, IL 60417
ph: 800-661-0950 or 708-672-1400
charles.lotton@worldnet.att.net
http://www.lottonglass.com

Mary Gregory

Experts

Bob Truitt
13550 Ashbury Dr.
Carmel, IN 46032
ph: 301-929-2539
randdglass@sbcglobal.net
Author of "Mary Gregory Glassware; 1880-1990."

Milk

Clubs/Associations

Dee Sacherich, Treas.
National Milk Glass Collectors Society
Newsletter: Opaque News
500 Union Cemetery Rd.
Greensburg, PA 15601
Membership@nmgcs.org
http://www.nmgcs.org
Dedicated to the study, collection and preservation of milk glass items.

Collectors

Helen Storey
46 Almond Dr.
Hershey, PA 17033-1759
ph: 717-534-8585
fax: 717-520-0965
hdstorey@aol.com

John Vosevich
7418 Apple Cross
Plainfield, IN 46168
ph: 317-272-4959

June Sohl
Stan & June's Heirlooms Shop
P.O. Box 2291
Salina, KS 67402-2291
ph: 785-823-1320 or 785-823-6627
Milk glass collector and dealer; shop features early lighting, art glass, pottery, toys, milk glass, quilts, furniture.

Experts

Frank Chiarenza
39 West Main St.
Meriden, CT 06451-4110
ph: 203-639-9778
fax: 203-238-7025
chiarenzaglassmuseum@snet.net
Director of the Frank Chiarenza Museum of Glass, co-author with James Slater of "The Milk Glass Book," a frequent contributor to glass publications, and former president of the National Milk Glass Collectors Society.

Barbara Joyce Kaye
P.O. Box 20346
Cherokee Station
New York, NY 10021-0065
Author of "White Gold: A Primer for Previously Unlisted Milk Glass, Book 1" (out-of-print) and "White Gold: A Primer for Previously Unlisted Milk Glass, Book II."

April M. Tvorak
P.O. Box 94
Warren Center, PA 18851
Buys and sells pink milk glass including Jeanette, Cambridge, Fenton, Westmoreland, etc.

Myrna & Bob Garrison
Collector's Loot
3816 Hastings Dr.
Arlington, TX 76013-1900
ph: 817-275-6342
fax: 817-275-6342
Authors of "Imperial's Vintage Milk Glass," "Imperial's Boudoir, Etcetera," "Imperial Cape Cod Tradition to Treasure," and "Imperial Candlewick, Little Known Facts A look at the Rare & Unusual;" books available from author.

Phyllis Osjecki
Phyllis'
P.O. Box 792
Canyonville, OR 97417
ph: 541-839-4135 or 541-839-6151
Buys, sells, and appraises milk glass.

Museums/Libraries

Houston Museum of Decorative Arts, The
201 High St.
Chattanooga, TN 37403
ph: 423-267-7176
houston@chattanooga.net
http://www.chattanooga.net/houston
Contains one of the world's finest collections of antique glass and ceramics.

Moser

Experts

Gary Baldwin
Touch of Glass, A
P.O. Box 213
Simpsonville, MD 21150-0213
ph: 410-997-8425 or 410-765-2439
Buys, sells and collects European enameled glass; co-author with Lee Carno of "Moser - Artistry in Glass."

Man./Prod./Dist.

Bohemia-Moser
110 00 Praha 1, NA
Prikope, 12 Czechoslovakia
The Moser factory.

Mount Washington

Clubs/Associations

Kenneth C. Depew
Mount Washington Art Glass Society
Magazine: Mount Washington Art Glass Newsletter, The
P.O. Box 24094
Fort Worth, TX 76124-1094
ph: 817-457-3246 or 817-457-9315
fax: 817-451-9357
A national society dedicated to the appreciation, preservation and study of the art glass wares made by the Mount Washington Glass Co. from 1870 to 1900.

Collectors

Henry Tyler
13 Bellevue Dr.
Saint Petersburg, FL 33706-1201

Old Morgantown

Clubs/Associations

Jim Wiley, Pres.
Old Morgantown Glass Collectors' Guild
Newsletter: Topics
P.O. Box 894
Morgantown, WV 26507-0894
ph: 724-941-2546
jwiley1@adelphia.net
http://www.oldmorgantown.org
Dedicated to the education of members and the preservation of Old Morgantown glass through the establishment of a museum in Morgantown, WV.

Orrefors

Man./Prod./Dist.

Royal Scandinavian, Inc.
140 Bradford Dr.
West Berlin, NJ 08091
ph: 609-768-5400 or 800-431-1992
fax: 800-448-7553
http://www.royalscandinavia.com
Crystal stemware and giftware, bar accessories, Christmas ornaments, and art glass.

Paden City

Clubs/Associations

Paul Torsiello
Paden City Glass Collectors Guild
42 Aldine Rd.
Parsippany, NJ 07054
ph: 973-428-4885
pcguild1@yahoo.com

Experts

Paul & Debbie Torsiello
42 Aldine Rd.
Parsippany, NJ 07054
ph: 973-428-4885
debziesglass@earthlink.net
Paden City glass experts, collectors, dealers; co-authors of "Paden City Glassware" (Schiffer).

Michael Krumme
P.O. Box 35014
Los Angeles, CA 90035-0014
ph: 323-937-1470
mkrumme@pacbell.net
Author/researcher seeks any printed information regarding the Paden City Glass Mfg. Co. of Paden City, WV; 1916-1952 catalogs, trade journal ads, previously published articles; please price & describe; no Paden City Pottery Co., please.

Pairpoint

Man./Prod./Dist.

Valerie Kelly
Pairpoint Glass Co.
851 Sandwich Rd.
P.O. Box 515
Sagamore, MA 02561
ph: 508-888-2344 or 800-899-0953
fax: 508-888-3537
Blowing room open to visitors; catalog $2 (refundable); reproduces hand blown full led crystal liners for salts and other silver items.

Pattern

Clubs/Associations

Fred Phelps
Early American Pattern Glass Society
Newsletter: News Journal, The
P.O. Box 266
Colesburg, IA 52035
fredlmia@msn.com
http://www.eapgs.org
Focuses on the broad spectrum of pattern glassware manufactured primarily from 1850 to 1915; newsletter published quarterly.

Collectors

Fred Phelps
P.O. Box 217
Colesburg, IA 52035-0217
ph: 319-856-2025
Specializes in early American pattern glass.

Dealers

Phyllis Petcoff
Phyllis Petcoff Antique Glassware
876 Crews Rd.
Wickliffe, KY 42087
fax: 270-335-3328
petcoff@earthlink.net
http://www.petcoff.com
Buys and sells primarily American glassware dating from 1850 through 1920; also some out-of-print books on the subject.

Glenda Ridgway
P.O. Box 231
Anna, IL 62906
ph: 618-833-7971

Bill & Elaine Henderson
PatternGlass.com
1220 Monroe, NE
Albuquerque, NM 87110
ph: 505-268-0819
fax: 505-266-7204
Elaine@PatternGlass.com
http://www.patternglass.com
Pattern matching service exclusively for early American pattern glass tableware, 1850-1910; sellers may list their inventory in a computer database at no charge; free computer searches for collectors.

Experts

Dori Miles
Pattern Glass Historian
B20
Crown Point, NY 12928
ph: 518-597-3432
dori@Capital.Net
Buys, sells, appraises, collects, specializes in pattern glass; over 13,000 pieces in stock; lid and base matching service; want lists wanted; former pattern glass editor for Warman's; contributing editor for Glass Collectors Digest.

John & Alice Ahlfeld
2634 Royal Rd.
Lancaster, PA 17603
ph: 717-397-7313
fax: 717-397-7931
ahlfelds@aol.com
Advisor to "Warman's Antiques & Collectibles Price Guide."

Mildred & Ralph Lechner
P.O. Box 554
Mechanicsville, VA 23111-0554
ph: 804-737-3347
Feature writers on antique glassware for "AntiqueWeek;" authors of "The World of Salt Shakers," Vols. 1, 2 & 3; Victorian art and pattern glass reproduction identification experts;

collectors of art and pattern glass salt & pepper shakers.

Pattern (Moon & Star)

Clubs/Associations

Dick Balsley
Society of Moon & Star Pattern Glass
200 East Olson Rd.
Midland, MI 48640
ph: 517-631-2543
daneluv@aol.com

Collectors

Corina Jolley
106 Charlett
Sikeston, MO 63801
Collects Moon & Star; runs egroup Web site for collectors.

Internet Resources

Corina Jolley
Moon & Star Glass Group
106 Charlett
Sikeston, MO 63801
Egroup Web site for collectors.

PHOENIX

Clubs/Associations

Tom Jiamachello, Sec.
PHOENIX & Consolidated Glass Collectors' Club
Newsletter: PHOENIX & Consolidated Collectors News & Views
41 River View Dr.
Essex Junction, VT 05452
ph: 802-878-2268 or 412-561-3379
TOPofVT@aol.com
http://www.collectoronline.com/club-PCGCC-wp.html
For collectors/dealers of art glass produced by PHOENIX GLASS Co. of Monaca, PA and Consolidated Lamp & Shade Co. of Coraopolis, PA; bi-monthly newsletter - market trends, repro. alerts, buy/sell ads, price reports, articles.

Collectors

Kathy Hansen
1621 Princess Ave.
Pittsburgh, PA 15216-3738
ph: 412-561-3379
khansen1@pghboe.net
Wants to buy PHOENIX GLASS vases, bowls, boxes, oil lamps, light shades, catalogs, ads, photos, postcards, Reuben-Line, Vollenden Ware; compiling history of the PHOENIX GLASS Co., Monaca, PA, 1880 to present; seeks PG employees, collectors.

Barbara Norman Milin
ph: 561-995-7300
fax: 561-995-0096
bamilin@aol.com
Wants to buy Ruba Rombic, red or cased pieces of PHOENIX or Consolidated Art Glass, Catalonian, and Muncie Ruba Rombic.

Mark Lawyer
P.O. Box 3847
Edmond, OK 73083-3847
ph: 405-341-0020
mcdd@flash.net

Scott Montroy
P.O. Box 11166
Fort Worth, TX 7611001166
ph: 817-927-5119
connix@swbell.net
http://home.swbell.net/connix
Previous editor of the "PHOENIX & Consolidated Glass Collectors News & Views" newsletter; current owner and moderator of the Internet email discussion group, "PHOENIX & Consolidated Art Glass Discussion List."

Experts

Kathy Hansen
1621 Princess Ave.
Pittsburgh, PA 15216-3738
ph: 412-561-3379
khansen1@pghboe.net
Wants to buy PHOENIX GLASS vases, bowls, boxes, oil lamps, light shades, catalogs, ads, photos, postcards, Reuben-Line, Vollenden Ware; compiling history of the PHOENIX GLASS Co., Monaca, PA, 1880 to present; seeks PG employees, collectors.

Jack D. Wilson
1514 Eagle Ridge Rd.
Prescott, AZ 86301-5418
ph: 520-445-5137
jdwilson1@earthlink.net
http://home.earthlink.net/~jdwilson1
Author of "PHOENIX & Consoli-dated Art Glass: 1926-1980;" features in-depth research, 48 color pages illustrating over 750 items (out-of-print); wants original Consolidated catalogs & company literature.

Pilgrim

Clubs/Associations

Pilgrim Art Glass Club
Newsletter: PAGC Notebook
P.O. Box 395
Ceredo, WV 25507
ph: 304-453-3553
fax: 304-453-6849
http://www.pilgrimglass.com
Focuses on Pilgrim cameo/art glass.

Pilgrim Cranberry Glass Collectors Club
Newsletter: PCGCC Newsletter
P.O. Box 395
Ceredo, WV 25507
ph: 304-453-3553
fax: 304-453-6849
http://www.pilgrimglass.com
For those interested in Pilgrim cranberry glass; club sponsored by the world's largest cranberry glass and "cameo" art glass manufacturer; free catalogs, advance notice of new offerings.

Man./Prod./Dist.

Shelly Adkins
Pilgrim Glass Corp.
P.O. Box 395
Ceredo, WV 25507
ph: 304-453-3553
fax: 304-453-6849
http://www.pilgrimglass.com
The world's largest cranberry glass and "cameo" art glass manufacturer.

Post-WWII

Matching Services

April M. Tvorak
P.O. Box 94
Warren Center, PA 18851
Buys, sells, matches any glassware from 1940-1970; please include SASE with all correspondence.

Periodicals

April M. Tvorak
Newsletter: 50's Flea!!!, The
P.O. Box 94
Warren Center, PA 18851
Members interested in 1940s-1970s glass and other items; the yearly covers any kitchen glass subject from 1940-1970; free for members; please include SASE with all correspondence.

Pressed

Clubs/Associations

Pressed Glass Collectors Club
Newsletter: Marking Times
4 Bowshot Close Castle
Bromwich, W. Midlands B36 9UH U.K.
ph: 0121 681 4872
glassman@blueyonder.co.uk
http://www.pressedglasscollectorsclub.pwp.blueyonder.co.uk
Postal based club with an interna-tional membership; club journal issued 3 timer per year; member discounts, identification service; discount entry fares to glass shows.

Museums/Libraries

Schminck Memorial Museum
128 South E St.
Lakeview, OR 97630-1721
ph: 541-947-3134
Large collection of American pressed glass, 1830-1920.

Pyrex

Experts

Susan Tobier
Sue 21 Antiques
414 Spotswood Gravel Hill Rd.
Monroe Township, NJ 08831
ph: 732-521-1620
fax: 732-521-1673
SuZeQuZe@aol.com
Author of "Pyrex of Corning: A Collector's Guide" and "Pyrex by Corning: A Supplement and Price Guide."

Barbara Mauzy
Today's Pleasures Tomorrow's
Treasures
P.O. Box 207
Akron, PA 17501
tptt@aol.com
http://www.tptt.net
Buys, sells, collects Pyrex; author of
"PYREX - The Unauthorized
Collector's Guide" as well as many
other titles related to kitchen
collectibles from the 1920s to the
1950s; offers speaker programs and
articles.

Reed & Barton

Man./Prod./Dist.

Reed & Barton
144 W. Britannia St.
Taunton, MA 02780
ph: 508-824-6611 or 800-822-1824
fax: 508-822-7269
information@reedbarton.com
http://www.reedbarton.com
Produces china, crystal, silver,
silverplate, and stainless flatware,
collectible plates, bells, dolls,
ornaments and accessories.

Riverside

Collectors

Becky Lyle
EAPGlass.com
eapglass@hotmail.com
http://www.eapglass.com
Collects and studies all glass made by
the Riverside Glass Works of
Wellsburg, WV, c. 1879-1907.

Experts

Cliff Gorham
Heartlights
P.O. Box 2962
Springfield, MO 65801
ph: 800-833-2007 or 417-833-4725
fax: 417-473-6466
Author of "Riverside Glasswork of
Wellsburg, WV 1879-1907," available
from author for $35 ppd.; focuses on
Riverside bar accessories, vases,
bowls, decorative objects, presentation
awards.

Rose Bowls

Collectors

Johanna & Sean Billings
P.O. Box 244
Danielsville, PA 18038-0244
ph: 610-760-8134 or 610-760-1814
bankie@enter.net
Author of "Collectible Glass Rose
Bowls" as well as numerous articles
on rose bowls.

Sandwich

Museums/Libraries

Sandwich Glass Museum
Journal: Cullet, The
109 Main St.
P.O. Box 103
Sandwich, MA 02453-0103
ph: 508-888-0251
glass@sandwichglassmuseum.org
http://www.sandwichglassmuseum.org
The museum preserves and displays
the glass manufactured in Sandwich
1825-1907.

Scandinavian Art

Appraisers

William L. Geary
Nordic Art Glass, Inc.
P.O. Box 2247
Colorado Springs, CO 80901-2247
ph: 719-527-0810
fax: 719-527-0810
nordglass@aol.com
http://www.glass.co.nz/nordglass.htm
Dealer, appraiser of American and
European art glass with a specialty in
Scandinavian art glass; producer of
video "Lyricism of Swedish Glass;"
advisor to "Schroeder's Antiques
Price Guide;" author of "Scandina-
vian Glass-Creative Energies".

Dealers

Anita L. Grashof
Gallerie Ani'tiques
Stage House Village
366 Park Ave.
Scotch Plains, NJ 07076-1121
ph: 908-322-4600
Buys, sells, appraises Swedish
(Orrefors, Kosta, glass by Gate,
Hald, Lindstand) and Finish
(Karhula, Ittala, glass by Wirkkala,
Sarpaneva) art glass; also Finnish
(Ittala, Karhula, Wirkkala,
Sarpaneva).

Ara Tavitian
Retro Gallery
524 1/2 N. La Brea Ave.
Los Angeles, CA 90036-2016
ph: 323-936-5261
fax: 323-936-5262
retrogalleryLA@aol.com
http://www.retroglass.com
Art glass from the 1940s through the
1960s; specializing in Italian and
Scandinavian glass.

Shoes

Collectors

J.P. (Phil) Jamieson
2546 Sinclair Rd.
Victoria, British Columbia V8N 1B8
 Canada
ph: 250-477-3034
philjamieson@shaw.ca
Collector of glass shoes and glass
slippers, US or European; also
interested in glass hens-on-nests and
Carnival glass.

Silver Overlay

Dealers

John Marshall
For Love or Money
16693 NW Meadowgrass Ct.
Beaverton, OR 97006
john@europa.com
http://home.europa.com/~john
Buys and sells silver overlay and silver
deposit on glass.

Souvenir & Commemorative

(see SOUVENIR &
COMMEMORATIVE ITEMS)

St. Louis

(see PAPERWEIGHTS)

Steuben

Dealers

Jeffrey E. Purtell
P.O. Box 28
Amherst, NH 03031-0028
ph: 603-673-4331 or 800-973-4331
fax: 603-673-1525
jfpurtell@steubenpurtell.com
http://www.steubenpurtell.com
Buys and sells Steuben animals,
exhibition pieces, etc.

Steuben Glass Flagship Store
67 Madison Ave.
New York, NY 10022
ph: 212-752-1441 or 800-447-9876
fax: 212-753-1354
info@steuben.com
http://www.steuben.com
Source for new bar accessories, vases,
bowls, lead crystal, decorative objects,
presentation awards.

David Weiss, GG
Weiss Gallery
P.O. Box 2415
Birmingham, MI 48012
ph: 248-932-2600
fax: 248-932-2600
weissgallery@worldnet.att.net
Specializes in Steuben glass in
addition to 20th century paintings,
prints, art glass, and jewelry; has
appeared on PAX TV's "Treasures in
Your Home."

Man./Prod./Dist.

Daniel Collins, Corp. Comm.
Corning Inc.
One Riverfront Plaza
Corning, NY 14831
ph: 607-974-9000 or 800-424-4240
info@corning.com
http://www.corning.com
Manufacturer of Steuben glass.

Stretch

Clubs/Associations

Helen Jones, Pub.
Stretch Glass Society
Newsletter: SGS Newsletter
508 Turnberry Lane
St. Augustine, FL 32080
stretchgl@aol.com
http://members.aol.com/stretchgl
For collectors of iridescent stretch
glass made by such companies as
Fenton, Imperial and Northwood;
annual convention late April;
newsletter contains articles submitted
by membership; line drawings of
shapes by company.

Dealers

Calvin L. Hackeman
8865 Olde Mill Run
Washington, DC 20010-6132
ph: 703-368-6982 or 703-847-7530
fax: 703-848-9583
hltzhaus@erols.com
Collects, buys and sells stretch glass.

William Crowl
1500 Avery St.
Parkersburg, WV 26101-3914
ph: 304-422-5042
Buys and sells unusual shapes and
colors of stretch glass; one piece or
entire collection.

Experts

Kitty & Russell Umbraco
P.O. Box 5331
Richmond, CA 94805-0331
ph: 510-235-1656
fax: 510-237-6019
russellu1@juno.com
Buys and sells; author of "Iridescent
Stretch Glass."

Studio (Contemporary)

Clubs/Associations

Jerry Cloninger
American Scientific Glassblowers Society
Magazine: Fusion
302 Red Bud Lane
Thomasville, NC 27360
ph: 336-882-0174
fax: 336-882-0172
jerry.cloninger@chemistry.gatech.edu
http://www.science.wayne.edu/~asgs/
 asgshome.htm
A professional organization of
scientific glassblowers and vendors
associated with the glassblowing
industry.

Penny Berk, Ex. Dir.
Glass Art Society
Journal: GAS News
1305 4th Ave. Ste. 711
Seattle, WA 98101-2401
ph: 206-382-1305
fax: 206-382-2630
info@glassart.org
http://www.glassart.org
An international organization to
encourage excellence and to advance

the appreciation, understanding and development of the glass arts.

FUSION: Ontario Clay & Glass Association, The
Magazine: Fusion Magazine
225 Confederation Dr.
Toronto, Ontario M1G 1B2 Canada
ph: 416-438-8946
fax: 416-438-0192
2fusion@interlog.com
http://www.clayandglass.on.ca
An arts organization dedicated solely to makers and collectors of handmade clay and glass; focuses on contemporary potters, glassmakers and their products and techniques.

Dealers

Sally Hansen
Glass Gallery
4820 Hampden Lane, Ste. 150
Bethesda, MD 20814
ph: 301-657-3478
fax: 301-657-3478
salgall@worldnet.att.net
http://www.theglassgallery-usa.com
A pioneer in the contemporary glass movement since 1971; retails one-of-a-kind contemporary glass sculptures and wall pieces; emphasizes glass as an art form.

Betsy Lane
2002 Jimmy Durante Blvd.
Del Mar, CA 92014
ph: 619-581-1088

Misc. Services

Creative Glass Centre of America
1501 Glasstown Rd.
Millville, NJ 08332-1566
ph: 845-825-6800 x2733 or 800-998-4552
fax: 856-825-2410
cgca@wheatonvillage.org
http://www.wheatonvillage.org
Located in Wheaton Village, CGCA awards 12 fellowships per year to gifted students; provides glass artists with time and resources necessary to work without the restrictions imposed by the high cost of glass production.

Barbara Jones, Ex. Dir.
Pilchuck Glass School
430 Yale Ave. North
Seattle, WA 98109-5431
ph: 206-621-8422
fax: 206-621-0713
pilchuck-info@pilchuck.com
http://www.pilchuck.com
Largest and most comprehensive center for artists who create with glass.

Museums/Libraries

High Museum of Art, The
1280 Peachtree St.
Atlanta, GA 30309
ph: 404-733-4400
fax: 404-733-4502
http://www.high.org
A leading art museum in the Southeastern US; collections include

African art, decorative arts, European art, folk art, modern and contemporary art, and photography.

Sulphides-Cameos In Glass

Museums/Libraries

Alex Vance, ExDir
Bergstrom-Mahler Museum
165 N. Park Ave.
Neenah, WI 54956
ph: 920-751-4670

Tiffin

Clubs/Associations

Ruth Hemminger, Pres.
Tiffin Glass Collectors' Club
Newsletter: Tiffin Glassmasters
P.O. Box 554
25 South Washington St.
Tiffin, OH 44883-0554
ph: 419-447-5505 or 419-448-0200
overholt@bpsom.com
http://www.tiffinglass.org
Established in 1985 to study and preserve the fine glassware produced from 1889-1980 by the Tiffin Glass Company, Tiffin, OH; holds glass shows and fund raisers to benefit the Tiffin Glass Museum; monthly meetings in Tiffin.

Russ Gangloff
Tiffin Glass Collectors
950 Pierce St.
San Francisco, CA 94115
svcdude@yahoo.com
http://groups.yahoo.com/group/tiffin-glass-collectors
Internet online club for Tiffin glass collectors.

Collectors

Cliff McCaslin
Rocliff Communications
8422 N. Park Ct.
Kansas City, MO 64155
ph: 816-436-7719
fax: 816-436-6955
vitrify@swbell.net
Collects all patterns of Tiffin glassware (US Glass Company - Factory R).

Russ Gangloff
950 Pierce St.
San Francisco, CA 94115
svcdude@yahoo.com
http://groups.yahoo.com/group/tiffin-glass-collectors

Experts

Kelly O'Kane
Elegant American Glass
P.O. Box 16303
Saint Paul, MN 55116-0303
kelly@kellyokane.com
http://www.kellyokane.com
Author of "Tiffin Glassmasters: the Modern Years," which identifies all artware production at Tiffin from 1938 to 1984; dealer in Elegant American glass (all major companies), and collector of Tiffin Modern glass.

Museums/Libraries

Ruth Hemminger
Tiffin Glass Museum
P.O. Box 554
25 South Washington St.
Tiffin, OH 44883
ph: 419-448-0200
overholt@bpsom.com
http://www.tiffinglass.org/glassmuseum.html
Honors the heritage of the men and women of Tiffin's Glass House; displays popular lines of Tiffin stemware, lamps, optics, and colors.

Toy

(see CHILDREN'S THINGS)

Val St. Lambert

Experts

R. Rosenberg
P.O. Box 554
Hicksville, NY 11802-0554
ph: 516-669-5321
fax: 516-333-4149
rudyrr@worldnet.att.net
Wants to buy Verlys, also Val St. Lambert and Baccarat.

Matching Services

Past & Present
14851 Ave. 360
Visalia, CA 93292
ph: 559-798-0029
fax: 559-798-1415
info@china-crystal-flatware.com
http://www.pastpresent.net
Baccarat, Cambridge, Denby, Duncan & Miller, Fostoria, Franciscan, Gorham, Heisey, Imperial, Lalique, Lenox, Mikasa, Nancy Prentiss, Noritake, Orrefors, Sasaki, Tiffin, Towle, Val St. Lambert, Waterford, etc.

Vaseline

Clubs/Associations

Dave Peterson, Ed.
Vaseline Glass Collectors, Inc.
Newsletter: Glowing Report
14560 Schleisman Rd.
Corona, CA 92880
ph: 405-392-3924
vaselineglass@vaselineglass.org
http://www.vaselineglass.org
A non-profit organization dedicated to educating and unifying vaseline glass collectors everywhere.

Verlys

Experts

Rudy Rosenberg
P.O. Box 554
Hicksville, NY 11802-0554
ph: 516-669-5321
fax: 516-333-4149
rudyrr@worldnet.att.net
Wants to buy Verlys, also Val St. Lambert and Baccarat.

Carole & Wayne McPeek
McPeek Antiques & Books
1211 Pembroke Rd.
Newark, OH 43055-1627
ph: 740-344-7846
Authors of "Verlys of America Decorative Art, 1935-1951" (1992); advisor to "Warman's Antiques & Collectibles Price Guide;" author of "Verlys of France" (1993).

Waterford

Man./Prod./Dist.

Waterford/Wedgwood USA Inc.
P.O. Box 1276
Wall, NJ 07719
ph: 732-938-5800 or 800-444-1997
fax: 732-938-6915
feedback@wedgwood.com
http://www.wedgwood.com
Crystal stemware.

Wave Crest

Appraisers

Peggy Sebek, ISA, AAA
Century Antiques & Appraisals, Inc.
3255 Glencairn Rd.
Shaker Heights, OH 44122-3407
ph: 216-991-2356 or 216-533-5874
fax: 216-991-2935
peggys@hpyday.com
Accredited Member of the International Society of Appraisers, Member of the Appraisers Association of America.

Clubs/Associations

Wave Crest Collectors Club
P.O. Box 2013
Santa Barbara, CA 93120
nanm@flash.net

Dealers

Lyn Livingston, ISA CAPP
Remember When Antiques & Collectibles
3601 N. Classen Blvd., Ste. 103
Oklahoma City, OK 73118
ph: 405-524-9391
fax: 405-524-5550
LynL@keytech.com
http://www.WhatsItsWorth.com
Desires exchange of ideas, identification tips and impressions on C.F. Monroe glass with other collectors; also buys and sells.

Westmoreland

Clubs/Associations

Terry Porterfield, Pres.
National Westmoreland Glass Collectors Club
P.O. Box 100
Grapeville, PA 15634
vrflowers@aol.com
http://www.westmorelandglassclubs.org

Westmoreland Glass Society
Newsletter: Westmoreland Glass Society
Newsletter
P.O. Box 2883
Iowa City, IA 52244-2883
jlm2020@simcon.net
http://www.westmorelandglassclubs.org
*Sponsors annual Westmoreland Glass
convention, auction and souvenir
limited edition items.*

Dealers

Cynthia Pergantides
MediaSpecialists Westmoreland Gallery
On-Line
28 Revell Ave.
Northampton, MA 01060
ph: 413-586-7571 or 413-584-1034
fax: 413-584-1034
media@mediaspec.com
http://www.mediaspec.com/GNET/
wmoreland
*Buys, sells, specializes in
Westmoreland glass; checkout the
online catalog.*

Betty J. Viecelli
Viecelli Antiques & Collectibles
615 Gaskill Ave.
Jeannette, PA 15644
ph: 724-527-2222

Experts

John & Carol Wiese
Wiese's Elegant Glassware
P.O. Box 1311
Orange, CA 92856
inquiries@jcwiese.com
http://www.jcwiese.com
*Buy, sell, trade Westmoreland glass;
main collection consists of Paneled
Grape and decorated and etched
Specialty Co. pieces; also collects
original Westmoreland catalogs from
1889 to 1983.*

Museums/Libraries

Phillip Rosso
Rosso's Westmoreland Glass Museum
1725 Trimble Ave.
Port Vue, PA 15133
ph: 412-678-7352 or 412-678-7352
fax: 412-672-0593
RossoWhol1@aol.com
http://wholesale-glass-dealer.com
*Over 4,000 pieces on display; original
photos, tools, molds, etc.; also
wholesales glass.*

Wheaton

Clubs/Associations

Bob Purner
Classic Wheaton Club
Newsletter: Classic Wheaton Club
Newsletter
c/o Creative Wheaton Collectibles
P.O. Box 59
Downingtown, PA 19335
ph: 610-692-4474
cwc@cwcusa.com
http://www.cwcusa.com

Whimsies

20 Windermere Court
Downingtown, PA 19335-1113
ph: 610-269-9698 or 610-269-9698
hglazer@nni.com
*Wants to buy whimseys, glass canes,
end-of-day glass, glass pens.*

Clubs/Associations

Lon Knickerbocker
Glasshouse Whimsey Club, The
Newsletter: Whimsical Notions
#2 Hessler Ct.
Dansville, NY 14437
ph: 716-335-6506
mountainmonster@mountain.net
http://www.whimsey.org
*For collectors of hand blown glass
whimsies such as ink pens, smoke
bells, flip flops, witch balls, canes,
darners, horns, rolling pins, etc.*

Experts

Joyce Blake
1220 Stolle Rd.
Elma, NY 14059
ph: 716-652-7752
*Advisor to "Warman's Antiques &
Collectibles Price Guide;" author of
"Glasshouse Whimsies," available
from author.*

Whimsies (Pens)

(see also PENS)

Experts

Lon Knickerbocker
#2 Hessler Ct.
Dansville, NY 14437
ph: 716-335-6506
mountainmonster@mountain.net
http://www.whimsey.org
*Collects glass ink pens, darners,
horns, and all glass whimsies; advisor
to "Warman's Antiques & Collectibles Price Guide."*

Wilkerson Glass Company

Dealers

Juanita Williams
P.O. Box 1626
Medford, OR 97501
ph: 541-776-2442
juanita@fostorialady.com
http://www.fostorialady.com
*Avid collector/dealer of items made by
the Wilkerson Glass Company of
Moundsville, WV; specializes in
custom designed paperweights, unique
figurals and abstract rocks of glass.*

GLASS KNIVES

Collectors

Brenda Macomber
RD 3 Box 201-K
Delta, PA 17314-9588
ph: 717-456-6116
cruzegal@aol.com
*Wants Depression-era glass knives,
daggers, and butter spreaders.*

Wilbur Peterson
711 Kelly Dr.
Lebanon, TN 37087
ph: 615-444-4303

GLASSES

(see also BREWERIANA; EYE
RELATED ITEMS, Eyeglasses; FAST
FOOD COLLECTIBLES; SPORTS
COLLECTIBLES, Thoroughbred
Racing; STEINS; SWANKYSWIGS)

Drinking

Auction Services

Tom Hoder
Tom Hoder Collectables
444 S. Cherry
Itasca, IL 60143-2109
ph: 630-773-2635
*Conducts mail/phone-bid auctions of
cartoon, character, and horse racing
drinking glasses three times each year
(January, April, and October.)*

Clubs/Associations

Promotional Glass Collectors Association
Newsletter: Collector Glass News
61 S. Second St.
Central Point, OR 97502
ph: 541-664-1503
webmaster@pgcaglassclub.com
http://www.pgcaglassclub.com
*Association of promotional drinking
glass collectors - cartoon, character,
sports, soft drink, root beer,
advertising, Disney, etc.; regional and
national meetings; buy, sell, trade.*

Collectors

Paul Merolle
ph: 603-879-9104
pmerolle@erols.com
http://users.erols.com/pmerolle
*Buys small and large collections of
cartoon drinking glasses, especially
Looney Tunes and Merry Melodies
glasses from the 1930s; also interested
in early Disney glasses as well as
Pepsi character glasses from the
1970s.*

Matt Maloney
390 S. Broadway
Lindenhurst, NY 11757-4701
ph: 631-957-2521
borrrris@aol.com
*Specializes in older and lesser known
cartoon and comics characters on
promotional glasses.*

Mark E. Chase
P.O. Box 308
Slippery Rock, PA 16057
ph: 724-946-2838
fax: 724-946-9012
mark@glassnews.com
http://www.glassnews.com
*Buys and sells cartoon, sports, and
fast-food drinking glasses: Disney,
super heroes from '30s to present;
author of books on same.*

Steve Zehr
P.O. Box 74
Fogelsville, PA 18051

Carl Sehnert
1020 SW 149 Lane
Fort Lauderdale, FL 33326
ph: 954-475-7289
fax: 954-475-7290
glassnert@aol.com
*Collecting & dealing in character
promotional drinking glasses; on
board of directors of Promotional
Glass Collectors Association.*

Ed Dunwoody
3055 Landview Dr.
Rochester Hills, MI 48306
ph: 248-361-3280 or 810-659-9322
fax: 248-656-1910
*Specializes in collectible cartoon
drinking glasses and in measuring
glasses; editor of "New Issues"
column in Collector Glass News.*

Tom Hoder
444 S. Cherry
Itasca, IL 60143-2109
ph: 630-773-2635
*Specializing in cartoon, character and
horse racing drinking glasses.*

Bev Chapman
P.O. Box 638
Lindsay, CA 93247-0638
Major collector of drinking glasses.

Keith Cooper
2654 S.E. 23rd
Albany, OR 97321
ph: 541-967-7586
spacemouse@Prodigy.net
*Collector of drinking glasses
decorated with any type of picture or
advertisement.*

Dealers

Dale & Debbie Morrison
1810 Ferry St.
Easton, PA 18042
ph: 610-250-0242
poppy95@enter.net
*Wants to buy cartoon, super heroes,
sports drinking glasses.*

Jimmy Driver
Glasses Galore
934 Greenbriar Dr.
Harrisonburg, VA 22801
ph: 540-434-5193
glasgalore@aol.com
*Buy, sell, trade cartoon and
promotional drinking glasses: Pepsi,*

Coke, Sports, Disney, McDonald's, and other fast foods; also Kentucky Derby glasses.

Jay Honan
4349 Robertson Rd.
Stuart, FL 34997
ph: 561-286-8845
Buys, sells and trades cartoon and character drinking glasses.

Pat & Larry Aikins
P & L Collectibles
101 Trail Ridge Rd.
Athens, TX 75751
ph: 903-675-3765
fax: 903-677-3643
Buys and sells collectible drinking glasses.

Experts

Mark E. Chase
P.O. Box 308
Slippery Rock, PA 16057
ph: 724-946-2838
fax: 724-946-9012
mark@glassnews.com
http://www.glassnews.com
Buys and sells cartoon, sports, and fast-food drinking glasses: Disney, super heroes from '30s to present; author of books on same.

William Friedberg
462 Hillcreek Rd.
Shepherdsville, KY 40165-6927
ph: 502-957-4039
Author of Bill Friedberg's drinking glass collector's price guide "Racing into the 21st Century Special 'Millenium' Edition," 1999 - 2000; $13.50 ppd. from author; color photographs; Ky. Derby, Preakness, Belmont, Breeder's Cup and more.

Pete Kroll
P.O. Box 207
Sun Prairie, WI 53590-0207
ph: 608-837-4818
fax: 608-825-4205
pkroll@chorus.net
http://www.gmskroll.com
Buys and sells collectible advertising glasses, mugs, & steins.

Lynn Geyer
Lynn Geyer Advertising Auctions
300 Trail Ridge
Silver City, NM 88061-6071
ph: 505-538-2341
fax: 505-388-3493
Conducts semi-annual mail/phone bid specialized auctions on all aspects of breweriana and soda-pop; also contemporary steins, mugs & drinking glasses.

Shot

Auction Services

Lawrence Powers
Shot Glass Exchange
P.O. Box 219
Western Springs, IL 60558-0219
ph: 708-246-1559
fax: 708-246-1559
Created in 1989 to provide an open national market for buyers and sellers of whiskey tumblers and shot glasses via the semi-annual mail-bid auction; color photos and bid tab provided for each catalog; sells books on shot glasses.

Collectors

Carl F. Pflanzer
205 US Hwy. 22
Green Brook, NJ 08812
ph: 732-424-7811
fax: 732-424-7814
ewa@ewacars.com
http://www.ewacars.com
Wants to buy shot glasses, advertising spirits glasses, and foreign shot glasses.

Experts

Mark Pickvet
5071 Watson Dr.
Flint, MI 48506
ph: 810-736-9320
MPickvet@aol.com
Author of "Shot Glasses: An American Tradition" (Antique Publications.)

Spirit (Advertising)

Collectors

Carl F. Pflanzer
205 US Hwy. 22
Green Brook, NJ 08812
ph: 732-424-7811
fax: 732-424-7814
ewa@ewacars.com
http://www.ewacars.com
Wants to buy shot glasses, advertising spirits glasses, and foreign shot glasses.

GLIDERS

(see AIRPLANES, Sailplanes)

GLOBES

(see also ATLASES; EXIT GLOBES; GAS STATION COLLECTIBLES, Pumps & Globes; GAS STATION COLLECTIBLES, Road Maps; INSTRUMENTS & DEVICES; MAPS & CHARTS)

Dealers

George D. Glazer
28 East 72nd St., 3rd Flor
New York, NY 10021
ph: 212-535-5706
fax: 212-658-9512
worldglobe@georgeglazer.com
http://www.georgeglazer.com
Buys and sells terrestrial and celestial globes, armillary spheres, orreries, and maps; American, British, Continental; floor-standing, table, and miniature sizes; broad range of antique and vintage globes.

James E. Hess
Heritage Map Museum
49 N. Broad St.
P.O. Box 412
Lititz, PA 17543
ph: 717-626-5002
fax: 717-626-8858
heritage@carto.com
http://www.carto.com
One of the largest map and atlas, and globe dealers in the world; buys, sells, collects, appraises.

John Forster
Barometer Fair
P.O. Box 25502
Sarasota, FL 34277
ph: 941-923-6136
fax: 941-923-6136
john@barometerfair.com
Buys, sells, restores all antique barometers; also deals in antique maps, globes, compasses, telescopes and other scientific instruments.

Murray Hudson
Murray Hudson Antiquarian Books, Maps, Prints & Globes
109 S. Church St.
P.O. Box 163
Halls, TN 38040-0163
ph: 731-836-9057 or 800-748-9946
fax: 731-836-9017
mapman@ecsis.net
http://www.murrayhudson.com
Buys/sells pre-1900 antique maps (especially pocket, wall, Civil War and railroad maps) & books with maps (e.g. atlases, travel guides, geographies, land surveys, etc.); esp. of S.E. & S.W. US; also wants pre-1950 world globes.

Jonathan Blackman
Yellow Room, The
511 N. Robertson Blvd.
Los Angeles, CA 90048
ph: 310-274-3190
fax: 310-274-0129
Specializes in globes, maps and scientific instruments; great resource information on the Web site.

Scott Brake
Scott Brake Antiques
17420 Mt. Hermann St., Unit "D"
Fountain Valley, CA 92708
ph: 714-556-8333
fax: 714-556-8333
antiquechi@aol.com
Specializes in special acquisitions for entertainment and theme park clients; prop rentals.

GNOMES

(see also COLLECTIBLES [MODERN], Sculptures [Tom Clark]; ELVES)

Clubs/Associations

Liz Spera
International Gnome Club, The
Newsletter: Gnome News
6740 Duncan Lane
Carmichael, CA 95608-2817
ph: 916-944-2741
gnomegnet@aol.com
http://www.gnomereserve.co.uk/club
Mission is to unite Gnomes and their human-keepers throughout the world.

GOLD

(see also COINS & CURRENCY; GEMS & JEWELRY)

Dealers

Blanchard & Co.
P.O. Box 61740
New Orleans, LA 70161-1740
ph: 888-524-2646
fax: 504-837-4884
info@blanchardonline.com
http://www.blanchardonline.com
Dealers in rare coins and precious metals.

Beth Scott
Affordable Jewelry & Precious Metals
304 SW Washington St.
Portland, OR 97204
ph: 800-690-4995 or 503-224-7520
fax: 503-227-4204
sight@ajpm.com
http://www.ajpm.com
Gold, silver and platinum bullion dealers.

Misc. Services

Big Ten, Inc.
P.O. Box 321231
Cocoa Beach, FL 32932-1231
ph: 321-783-4595
http://www.goldmaps.com
Big Ten's gold maps are used by thousands of families for gold panning and outdoor recreation when vacationing, RVing, camping, hiking, biking, backpacking, etc.

Periodicals

Newsletter: Silver & Gold Report
P.O. Box 109665
West Palm Beach, FL 33410
ph: 800-289-9222 or 561-627-3300
fax: 561-625-6685
sgr@weissinc.com
Financial advice newsletter in precious medals, and gold & silver bullion and coins.

Scrap

Dealers

Jim Sciuto
GoldTek
P.O. Box 128
Methuen, MA 01844
ph: 978-374-2254 or 603-645-4717
fax: 978-373-1088
Buys scrap gold and silver: class rings, wedding bands, gold coins, gold watches, gold plated circuit boards, gold solder, gold wire, gold teeth; also scrap sterling silver flatware, coins, bars, silver flake, silver anodes, etc.

Greg Walsh
32 River View Lane
P.O. Box 747
Potsdam, NY 13676-0747
ph: 315-265-9111
fax: 315-265-9222
gwalsh@twcny.rr.com
http://www.walshauction.com
Wants to buy gold and silver rings, coins, estate jewelry, pocket watches, diamonds, sterling silver items, scrap gold, broken or damaged jewelry, dental gold, etc.; 24-hour turn around; ship on approval or call for quote; since 1979.

Michael A. Merrill
Michael A. Merrill, Inc.
Crestar Bank Building
2045 York Rd.
Timonium, MD 21093
ph: 410-453-9400
http://www.michaelmerrill.com
Buying precious metals from the public, dealers since 1974; buys scrap gold, diamonds, old gold, dental gold, school rings, gold & silver numismatic coins, sterling silver (Kirk & Steiff), Franklin Mint, platinum, palladium, exotics.

Jaime Raskansky
Gold & Silver Traders
5959 Westheimer, Ste. 30
Houston, TX 77057
ph: 713-520-5111 or 713-223-0777
fax: 713-223-0707
gstforex@msn.com
Buys and sells gold and silver scrap and bullion.

GOLD LEAF

(see REPAIR/RESTORATION/
CONSERVATION, Gilding)

GOLD RUSH MEMORABILIA

Collectors

Chester Jaffee
2321 Russel St.
Berkeley, CA 94705
ph: 510-845-0774
Wants items relating to the California Gold Rush 1848-1858.

Museums/Libraries

Georgia Fox, Cur.
Amador County Museum
500 Argonaut Lane
Jackson, CA 95642
ph: 209-223-6386
museum@volcano.net
http://www.amadorarchives.org/
museum.html
Mailing address is as listed above; the museum's physical address is 225 Church St., Jackson, CA.

Klondike Gold Rush National Historical
Park, Skagway Unit
P.O. Box 517
Skagway, AK 99840
ph: 907-983-2921
fax: 907-983-9249
KLGO_Ranger_Activities@nps.gov
http://www.nps.gov/klgo

Yukon Archives
Box 2703
Whitehorse, Yukon Territory Y1A 2C6
Canada
ph: 867-667-5321 or 800-661-0408
fax: 867-393-6253
Yukon.Archives@gov.yk.ca
http://www.yukoncollege.yk.ca/archives/
yuarch.html
Responsible for acquiring, preserving, displaying documentary sources related to the Yukon including the Klondike gold rush; 100,000 photos, 12,000 maps, newspapers, 1,600 hours of sound recordings, etc.

Dawson City Museum & Historical
Society
P.O. Box 303
Dawson City, Yukon Territory Y0B 1G0
Canada
ph: 867-993-5291
fax: 867-993-5839
dcmuseum@yknet.yk.ca
http://users.yknet.yk.ca/dcpages/
Museum.html
Maintains an extensive collection of records and photographs and provides research services; has over 7,000 photos.

GOOD LUCK ITEMS

Collectors

J.A. Higgins
5017 Walnut
Kansas City, MO 64112-2758
ph: 816-931-4095
fax: 816-363-5927
smojer@aol.com
Wants items with "Good Luck" on them.

GRANITEWARE

(see also KITCHEN COLLECTIBLES)

Clubs/Associations

National Graniteware Society
Newsletter: National Graniteware News
P.O. Box 9248
Cedar Rapids, IA 52409-9248
info@graniteware.org
http://www.graniteware.org
For collectors to share information about graniteware.

Collectors

Dan Allers
P.O. Box 10013
Cedar Rapids, IA 52410-0013
ph: 319-393-0252

Peggy Way
11334 Mesa Verde Lane
Parker, CO 80138
ph: 303-805-5884
purrrr@worldnet.att.net
http://home.att.net/~muffinway/granite
Buys and sells gray graniteware and cobalt blue and white swirl graniteware.

Dealers

Rita Mueller
Grange Hall Antiques
1 South Eighth Alley
P.O. Box 263
New Market, MD 21774
ph: 301-865-5651
fax: 301-865-0518
Rita@newmarketmd.com
http://www.grangehallantiques.com
Quality Steiff animals from 1950s through 1980s; always buying one piece or entire collection: teddy bears, Schuco, Hermann, Steiff; also available - fine country graniteware from Germany available; mail orders and layaways.

Bob Techav
Techav's Antiques
705 8th Ave.
De Witt, IA 52742
ph: 319-659-8365
Buys and sells graniteware; all types and all colors.

Experts

David T. Pikul
1 Fourth Ave.
Amsterdam, NY 12010-3803
ph: 518-843-3983
fax: 518-843-3983
dtpikul@telenet.net
http://www.enameledware.com
Co-author of "Collectible Enameled Ware - American & European," and "Enameled Kitchenware - American & European" (Schiffer).

Helen Greguire
Helen's Antiques
216 Mountain View Rd.
Landrum, SC 29356
ph: 864-457-7340
Author of "The Collector's Encyclopedia of Granite Ware."

Gregg Ellington
Upper Loft Antiques
47 Columbus St.
Wilmington, OH 45177
ph: 937-382-4311
Buys, sells, trades and collects graniteware and American ceramics including mochaware, yellowware, spatterware, spongeware, etc.; appraisals provided for a small fee; if writing, enclose SASE for reply.

Gary & Lorraine Boggio
North Wind Antiques
P.O. Box 198
Hennepin, IL 61327
ph: 815-925-7264
fax: 815-925-7264
nwind@ivnet.com
Buy, sell and specializes in graniteware.

French

Dealers

David T. Pikul
Chuctanunda Antique Company, The
1 Fourth Ave.
Amsterdam, NY 12010-3803
ph: 518-843-3983
fax: 518-843-3983
dtpikul@telenet.net
http://www.enameledware.com
Sells French and European enameled ware: coffee pots, canisters, utensil racks, etc.; colorful and highly decorative; free color brochure available.

GRAVESTONES

Clubs/Associations

Association for Gravestone Studies
Newsletter: AGS Quarterly
278 Main St., Ste. 207
Greenfield, MA 01301-3230
ph: 413-772-0836
info@gravestonestudies.org
http://www.gravestonestudies.org
Mission is to foster appreciation for gravestones and cemeteries through study and preservation; offers information and restoration referrals for gravestones; NOTE: Respect gravestones; they are sacred and not collectible!

GREETING CARDS

(see HOLIDAY COLLECTIBLES;
PAPER COLLECTIBLES;
POSTCARDS; VALENTINES)

GROCERY STORE ITEMS

(see CEREAL BOXES; FOOD COLLECTIBLES; PREMIUMS, Cereal Box)

GUIDES

(see ANTIQUE SHOP DIRECTORIES; FLEA MARKET GUIDES; TOURS/BUYING TRIPS)

GUINNESS WORLD RECORDS

Museums/Libraries

Guinness World of Records Museum
2780 Las Vegas Blvd., South
Las Vegas, NV 89109-1102
ph: 702-792-0640
fax: 702-792-0530
This unique museum brings the Guinness Book of World Records to three-dimensional life via life-sized replicas, computerized databanks and color videos.

GUITARS

(see MUSICAL INSTRUMENTS, String [Guitars]; TOYS, Guitar)

GUM

(see BUBBLE GUM CARDS; BUBBLE GUM & CANDY WRAPPERS; TRADING CARDS, Non-Sport)

GUMBALL MACHINES

(see COIN-OPERATED MACHINES, Vending Machines)

GUNFIGHTERS

(see WESTERN AMERICANA)

GUNS

(see ADVERTISING, Firearms Related; AIRGUNS; ARMS & ARMOR; CIVIL WAR ARTIFACTS; FIREARMS; MILITARIA; TOY GUNS; TRAPSHOOTING; WESTERN AMERICANA)

Here are some tips when contacting someone who is listed in this book:

When requesting information about a particular item, include a description (material, dimensions, maker's mark, model number, etc.) and a photo, sketch, digital image or photocopy of the item in question.

Always ask if there are charges for samples or for the services that you are requesting.

When corresponding by letter, please be sure to include a Large (#10 business size) Self-Addressed and Stamped Envelope (LSASE) if requesting a reply or the return of photographs.

Never call collect unless otherwise directed. When calling, be considerate of time zone differences and always ask if the party you are calling has time to talk. When leaving an answering machine message, always instruct the party to call you back collect.

HAIR ACCESSORIES

(see BARBERSHOP COLLECTIBLES; BEAUTY SHOP COLLECTIBLES; CLOTHING & ACCESSORIES, Vintage; COMBS & HAIR ACCESSORIES; DRESSER ITEMS, Hatpins & Hatpin Holders; GEMS & JEWELRY; SHAVING COLLECTIBLES)

HAIRWORK

(see also BARBERSHOP COLLECTIBLES; BEAUTY SHOP COLLECTIBLES; COMBS & HAIR ACCESSORIES; GEMS & JEWELRY, Mourning; SHAVING COLLECTIBLES)

Clubs/Associations

Ruth Gordon
H.A.I.R.
Newsletter: H.A.I.R. Line
1939 Elizabeth Blvd.
Newport, MI 48166
ph: 734-586-2027
ruthgordon@foxberry.net
http://www.hairworkvirtu.com
H.A.I.R. ("Hair Art International Restorers") is a society focused on the lost art of making intricate & beautiful flowers & jewelry using hair (even in miniature!); for collectors, hair workers, and persons interested in art.

Marlys Fladeland
Victorian Hairwork Society
P.O. Box 806
Pleasant Grove, UT 84062
ph: 801-785-7210
fax: 801-785-6235
marlys@hairwork.com
http://www.hairworksociety.org
A Web site and membership organization for networking anyone who is interested in the art of Victorian hairwork; includes articles on hairwork, instructions on braiding, items for sale, and much more; dealers, collectors, historians welcomed.

Collectors

Jerry Denzler
P.O. Box 127
Marengo, IA 52301-0127
ph: 319-642-3528 or 319-642-7777
Wants to buy human hair jewelry and other items made of hair or with hair such as framed mourning wreaths, postcards, buttons, purses; also wants

samples of tablework and equipment used in weaving hair.

Dealers

Vince Tartaglione
T-Graphix
P.O. Box 2116
Patterson, NJ 07509-2116
thairapy97@aol.com
Buys hair and hair related items: video, photographs, books, ads, labels, haircutting; long hair or no hair; Rapunzel, Sutherland Sisters; also buys braids, ponytails.

Nancy Robertson
Hair Art
1501 NE 49th St.
Kansas City, MO 64118
ph: 816-454-9601
hairart@swbell.net
Collector, expert, reproduction source for Victorian hairwork; makes both wreaths and jewelry items; does custom work for the public; especially interested in antique wreaths and cutwork; demonstrates at living history festivals.

Marlys Fladeland
P.O. Box 806
Pleasant Grove, UT 84062
ph: 801-785-7210
fax: 801-785-6235
marlys@hairwork.com
http://www.hairwork.com
Collects, buys and sells Victorian hairwork; also sells supplies, books and instructions for the art of hairwork.

Experts

Ruth Gordon
Cherished Memories
1939 Elizabeth Blvd.
Newport, MI 48166
ph: 734-586-2027
ruthgordon@foxberry.net
http://www.hairworkvirtu.com
Practices the lost art of Victorian "hairwork" creating flowers and jewelry out of hair; also does repairable repairs; hair artist, jeweler, lecturer, teacher, journalist, author, and founder of "H.A.I.R."

Wreaths

Museums/Libraries

Leila Cohoon
Leila's Hair Museum, College of Cosmetology
815 West 23rd St.
Independence, MO 64055
ph: 816-252-HAIR
Lcohoon@aol.com
http://www.hairwork.com/leila
An interesting display of various items made from human hair and dating back to 1610; over 200 wreaths and 2,000 pieces of jewelry.

HALLMARK

(see COLLECTIBLES [MODERN], Ornaments [Hallmark])

HALLOWEEN COLLECTIBLES

(see also ANIMAL COLLECTIBLES, Cats; GHOSTS & HAUNTINGS; HOLIDAY COLLECTIBLES; HORROR; WITCHES)

Collectors

Bob Merck
44 Newtown Turnpike
Weston, CT 06883-2118
fax: 203-761-8777
santa@optonline.net
Wants pre-1950 jack-o'-lanterns, other lanterns, candy containers; also photos of old Halloween parties and people in costume.

Tom Rutledge
3015 Bever Ave., SE
Cedar Rapids, IA 52403-3028
ph: 319-399-1427
Wants only pre-1950 Halloween collectibles including decorations, postcards, candy containers, lanterns, invitations, papier-mâché items, plaster of Paris items, etc.; also old mail order catalogs and flyers featuring Halloween.

Tom Pritchard
4905 Drew Ave. So.
Minneapolis, MN 55410-1743
ph: 800-473-3815 or 612-926-3815
fax: 612-926-3815
TomPumpkin@aol.com
http://www.halloweencollectibles.com
Wants to buy Halloween collectibles: jack-o'-lanterns, noisemakers, candy containers, nodders, hard plastic, German diecuts, pumpkin tea set pieces, Bogie books, etc.

Dawn Kroma
P.O. Box 143
Brookfield, IL 60513-0143
ph: 708-387-0334 or 708-387-0334
fax: 708-387-0334
BooNews@aol.com
http://www.boonews.com

David Welch
P.O. Box 714
Murphysboro, IL 62966-0714
ph: 618-687-2282
fax: 618-684-2243
PEZDude1@aol.com
http://www.pezheads.net/dwelch
Wants Don Post rubber monster masks (sold through Famous Monster magazines only); also '50s-'60s monster, TV, movie, comic, and cartoon costumes; must be in original boxes; $500 for Captain Action.

Gwen Daniel
18 Belleau Lake Ct.
O Fallon, MO 63366-3144
ph: 636-978-3190
SimGirl200@aol.com

Linda L. Vines
2911 4th St., #112
Santa Monica, CA 90405
ph: 310-314-0402
lleigh2000@hotmail.com
Wants to buy pre-1950 decorations including candy containers, jack-o'-lanterns, witches, black cats, skeletons.

Dealers

Leila Dunbar
Dunbar's Gallery
76 Haven St.
Milford, MA 01757-3821
ph: 508-634-8697
fax: 508-634-8698
dunbars@dunbarsgallery.com
http://www.dunbarsgallery.com
Mail order Americana - no reproductions; buys, sells and specializes in vintage character and comic toys, banks, advertising, automobilia, and Halloween related items.

Mark Bergin
Mark Bergin Toys Ltd.
P.O. Box 3073
Peterborough, NH 03458-3073
ph: 603-924-2079
fax: 603-924-2022
mbergin@bergintoys.com
http://www.bergintoys.com
Wants jack-o'-lanterns, candy containers, nodders, any figures, diecuts, crepe paper, noise makers, postcards, anything Halloween.

Hugh Alan Luch Collections, The
P.O. Box 111
Wenonah, NJ 08090
ph: 609-464-9751
Buys and sells illustrator and holiday collectibles with emphasis on Maxfield Parrish and Halloween.

Diane Richardson
Gold Hatpin, The
125 N. Marion St.
Oak Park, IL 60301-1087
ph: 708-848-3247 or 708-445-0610
goldhatpin@comcast.net
Wants old German Halloween items: veggie people, candy containers, diecuts, hard plastic toys, jewelry, lanterns, noisemakers, etc.

Jenny Tarrant
Holly Daze Antiques
4 Gardenview Dr.
Saint Peters, MO 63376-3507
ph: 314-397-1763
jennyjol@aol.com
http://www.holly-days.com
Wants Halloween items, papier-mâché candy containers, jack-o'-lanterns, Halloween party books, party decorations and favors, Halloween postcards, plastic toys.

Paul W. Schofield
Lion's Den Antiques
7988 Bethel Burley Rd. SE
Port Orchard, WA 98366
ph: 360-876-3364
fax: 360-876-5421
*Buys, sells, appraises, and specializes
in old Santas, candy containers,
Halloween, Easter, Christmas, Easter,
Dresden, figural lights.*

Experts

Pamela E. Apkarian-Russell
4 Lawrence St. & Rte. 10
P.O. Box 499
Winchester, NH 03470-0499
ph: 603-239-8875
fax: 603-239-8875
halloweenqueen@cheshire.net
http://userpages.cheshire.net/
~halloweenqueen
*Author of nine Halloween books
including "Tastes & Smells of
Halloween," and "Halloween
Decorations & Games."*

Stuart Schneider
Halloween Museum, The
P.O. Box 64
Teaneck, NJ 07666-0064
ph: 201-599-4250
fax: 201-599-4251
Stuart@wordcraft.net
http://www.wordcraft.net
*Full of Halloween collectibles, party
ideas, yard haunt pictures; author of
the illustrated book "Halloween in
America;" has appeared on ABC,
CollectingChannel.com, FOX, CNN,
and other TV and radio talk shows.*

Internet Resources

Halloween Collectibles
halween@aol.com
http://www.spookshows.com
*Discover the whimsical world of
antique Halloween decorations;
fantastic and creative designs of the
1900s come alive.*

Periodicals

Pamela E. Apkarian-Russell
Chris Russel & The Halloween Queen
Newsletter: Trick or Treat Trader, The
4 Lawrence St. & Rte. 10
P.O. Box 499
Winchester, NH 03470-0499
ph: 603-239-8875
fax: 603-239-8875
halloweenqueen@cheshire.net
http://userpages.cheshire.net/
~halloweenqueen
*For the collector of Halloween related
memorabilia including Salem Witch,
paranormal and metaphysical;
published quarterly; 20 years old.*

Dawn Kroma
Kromazone Media
Newsletter: BooNews
P.O. Box 143
Brookfield, IL 60513-0143
ph: 708-387-0334 or 708-387-0334
fax: 708-387-0334
BooNews@aol.com
http://www.boonews.com
*Quarterly, full color subscription
based newsletter for Halloween
enthusiasts; provides information and
networking regarding old and modern
Halloween collectibles, reproductions,
history, photos, interviews, events,
shows, etc.*

HAMBURGERS

(see also FAST FOOD
COLLECTIBLES; FOOD
COLLECTIBLES)

Collectors

Harry Sperl
Hamburger Harry
1000 North Beach St.
Daytona Beach, FL 32117
ph: 904-254-8753
fax: 904-255-2460
harry@burgerweb.com
http://www.burgerweb.com
*Owner of the Hamburger-Harley, the
Good Burger Mobile, and The
International Hamburger Hall of
Fame.*

Museums/Libraries

Harry Sperl
Hamburger Museum
1000 North Beach St.
Daytona Beach, FL 32117
ph: 904-254-8753
fax: 904-255-2460
harry@burgerweb.com
http://www.burgerweb.com
*Collection contains more than 500
different hamburgers and related
material: hamburger banks, badges,
biscuit jars, clocks, hats, trays,
erasers, salt & pepper shakers, music
boxes, pencil holders, pillows, signs,
posters, cups, etc.*

HANDBAGS

(see PURSES)

HARDWARE

(see also ARCHITECTURAL
ELEMENTS; ARCHITECTURE &
RELATED ITEMS; CATALOGS,
Trade; DIAMOND EDGE;
DOORKNOBS; FASTENERS; KEEN
KUTTER [SIMMONS HARDWARE];
PLUMBING; REPAIR/
RESTORATION/CONSERVATION,
Woodworking; TOOLS;
WINCHESTER COLLECTIBLES)

Appraisers

Rilla Simmons, CAGA
Simmons & Company Auctioneers
40706 E. 144th St.
Richmond, MO 64085
ph: 816-776-2936 or 800-646-2936
fax: 816-470-5016
bob@simmonsauction.com
http://www.simmonsauction.com
*Appraises Keen Kutter (Simmons
Hardware), Diamond Edge (Shapleigh
Hardware), Winchester tools.*

Auction Services

H. Weber & Jill Wilson
WebWilson.com
P.O. Box 506
Portsmouth, RI 02871
ph: 800-508-0022
fax: 401-683-1644
hww@webwilson.com
http://www.webwilson.com
*Conducts two phone/fax auctions per
year of quality builders' hardware
including door knobs, bells, shutter
pulls, plates, etc.*

Clubs/Associations

Barbara Huhn, Mem.
Hardware Companies Kollectors' Klub,
The
Newsletter: Winchester Keen Kutter
Diamond Edge Chronicles
432 S. Gore St.
Saint Louis, MO 63119
ph: 314-968-0304
dhuhn@earthlink.net
http://www.thckk.org
*A non-profit organization to serve as
an interactive information distribution
center for collectors of E.C. Simmons/
Keen Kutter, Winchester Store (non-
gun), A.F. Shapleigh/Diamond Edge,
Hibbard, and other hardware store
brands.*

Collectors

Larry Eastley
46460 Hwy. 10
Hardin, MO 64035
ph: 660-398-4617
eastley@iland.net
*Collector of Keen Kutter, Diamond
Edge, Winchester Store (non-gun),
Simmons & Shapleigh and other
hardware store brands.*

Dealers

John K. Spahr
Lilac Shed Antiques
P.O. Box 258
20 Spahr Rd.
Washington, ME 04574
ph: 207-845-2270
jspahr@pivot.net
http://www.victorianhardware.com
*Specializes in Victorian brass, bronze
and cast iron hardware, oil lamps,
gas lamps, electrical lighting, and
builder's hardware from the mid-
1700s to present; also stoves and
bells.*

Ed Donaldson
Hardware Restorations
1488 York Rd.
Carlisle, PA 17013-9237
ph: 717-249-3624
fax: 717-249-5647
ed@eddonaldson.com
http://eddonaldson.com
*Sells restored hardware and hardware
replacement parts.*

Steve Robinson
Robinson's Antiques
763 West Bippley Rd.
Lake Odessa, MI 48849
ph: 616-374-7750 or 616-374-7751
fax: 616-374-7752
antiquehardware@robinsonsantiques.com
http://www.robinsonsantiques.com
*Specializes in original 1650-1925
antique architectural hardware, door
knobs, furniture hardware hardware,
hinges, mirror restoration, latches,
locks, registers, tear drops, door
bells, escutcheons, ice box hardware
since 1967.*

Experts

H. Weber & Jill Wilson
WebWilson.com
P.O. Box 506
Portsmouth, RI 02871
ph: 800-508-0022
fax: 401-683-1644
hww@webwilson.com
http://www.webwilson.com
*Author of "Price Guide to Antique
Hardware," buying and selling
hardware daily; use Web site to
research articles and to list hardware
for sale for free; conducts online
hardware auctions ever 4-6 weeks.*

Repro. Sources

Period Furniture Hardware Co., Inc.
123 Charles St.
P.O. Box 314
Boston, MA 02114-0911
ph: 617-227-0758
fax: 617-227-2987
*Supplies fine quality reproduction
hardware for furniture and the home;
specializes in solid brass fittings and
accessories.*

Barbara Horton Rockwell
Horton Brasses Inc.
49 Nooks Hill Rd.
Cromwell, CT 06416
ph: 800-754-9127 or 860-635-4400
fax: 860-635-6473
orion@horton-brasses.com
http://www.horton-brasses.com
*Sells authentic period reproduction
hardware of the finest quality.
Manufactured of solid brass or
handforged black iron in CT factory;
catalog available upon request.*

William Simpson
18th Century Hardware Co., Inc.
131 East 3rd St.
Derry, PA 15627-1607
ph: 724-694-2708
fax: 724-694-9587
   *Clean, polish & repair brass, bronze,
   silver, pot metal items; makes, sells
   reproduction hardware; clean and
   electrify brass lamps, or reverse
   electrification; will duplicate any style
   or pattern.*

Londonderry Brasses, Ltd.
P.O. Box 415
Cochranville, PA 19330
ph: 610-593-6239
fax: 610-593-6246
info@londonderry-brasses.com
http://www.londonderry-brasses.com
   *Offers high quality period brass
   hardware; handmade using the direct
   lost wax process casing of the original
   period example.*

Bill Ball
Ball & Ball Antique Hardware
   Reproduction & Restorations
463 W. Lincoln Highway
Exton, PA 19341
ph: 800-257-3711 or 610-363-7330
fax: 610-363-7639
billball@ptd.net
http://www.ballandball-us.com
   *Sells reproduction hardware; 18th
   century reproduction brass and iron
   chandeliers, sconces, candle stands
   and candlesticks; also offers a
   recasting service.*

Paxton Hardware Ltd.
P.O. Box 256
Upper Falls, MD 21156-0256
ph: 410-592-8505 or 800-241-9741
fax: 410-592-2224
paxton@ix.netcom.com
http://www.paxtonhardware.com
   *Supplies authentic solid brass, hard-
   to-find reproduction hardware in
   period styles: pulls, knobs, hinges,
   locks, casters, table hardware, bed
   hardware.*

Robert Hershberger
Hershberger's Hardware
1411 Township Rd. 178
Baltic, OH 43804
ph: 330-893-2464 or 800-734-8044
fax: 330-698-3200
   *Catalog of specialty products for
   antiques and woodworking such as
   spool cabinet decals, high chair trays,
   antique telephone parts, Hoosier
   cabinet parts, lamp parts; $4 for 64-
   page catalog (refundable).*

Phyllis & Phil Kennedy
Phyllis Kennedy Hardware, Inc.
10655 Andrade Dr.
Zionsville, IN 46077
ph: 317-873-1316
fax: 317-873-8662
philken@kennedyhardware.com
http://www.kennedyhardware.com
   *Hardware for antique furniture, ice
   boxes, Hoosier cabinets and trunks;*

*manufacturer of flour bins and sifters
for Hoosier cabinets; pulls, bails,
knobs, latches, chair seats and caning,
hinges, locks and keys, coat hooks, etc.*

WSI Distributors - Antique Restoration
   Supplies
405 N. Main St.
Saint Charles, MO 63301-2034
ph: 800-447-9974 or 636-946-5811
fax: 636-946-5832
talk2us@wsidistributors.com
http://www.wsidistributors.com
   *Wholesale source for furniture &
   trunk hardware, cane & weaving
   materials, fiber chair seats, veneer,
   wood ornaments, Zap glues, and much
   more; over 1200 items for professional
   furniture restorers. Sorry, dealers
   only.*

Scott's-Becker's Hardware Inc.
1411 S. 3rd St.
Ozark, MO 65721-9188
ph: 888-991-0151 or 417-581-6525
fax: 417-581-4771
scotbeckhdw@aol.com
http://www.scotbeckhdw.com
   *Carries hardware for antique
   furniture: trunk hardware, bed parts,
   kitchen cabinets, Hoosier, pulls,
   latches, hinges, locks keys.*

Gary Hahn
Muff's Antiques
135 S. Glassell St.
Orange, CA 92866-1421
ph: 714-997-0243
fax: 714-997-1601
muffs@earthlink.net
http://home.earthlink.net/~muffs
   *Has thousands of pieces of hardware
   in stock both new and old for
   restoration of furniture and homes
   from antique to modern: door plates,
   locks/keys, knobs, light fixtures,
   electric and oil lamps; catalog $5.*

Mary Ann Aldrich
Thor's Hardware
1740 Myers St.
Oroville, CA 95966
ph: 530-533-9121 or 530-533-7614
fax: 530-533-9180
oldthings@cncnet.com
http://www.lumarmall.com/thors/
   thors.htm
   *Supplier of antique reproduction
   hardware, including locks, hinges, ice
   box hardware, trunk hardware,
   Victorian, Eastlake, Mission and
   Waterfall furniture hardware; also
   bar railing, door hardware and
   lighting.*

Roy Prange
House of Antique Hardware
3439 NE Sandy Blvd.
PMB 106
Portland, OR 97232
ph: 888-223-2545 or 503-231-4089
fax: 503-233-1312
sales@HouseofAntiqueHardware.com
http://
   www.HouseofAntiqueHardware.com
   Offers one of the largest selections of

*antique and reproduction house
hardware online.*

Fernando Viola
Viola S.L.
Aparisi y Guijarro, 4
Mislata, Valencia 46920 Spain
ph: +34 963 793 242
fax: +34 963 791 614
fernandoviola@viola.biz
http://www.viola.biz
   *Spanish manufacturer of solid brass
   decorative hardware for arts and
   crafts period cabinetry and furniture;
   clock parts, box hardware, furniture
   hardware, hooks, framing hardware.*

HAWAIIANA

   (see STATE RELATED
   MEMORABILIA, Hawaii)

HEALTH & BEAUTY

Devices To Restore

Collectors

Olg Lindan
1404 Dorsh Rd.
Cleveland, OH 44121-3840
ph: 216-382-7113
   *Wants old electrotherapeutic and
   controversial healing devices and
   related literature; also wants medical,
   scientific instruments.*

HEBRAICA

   (see JUDAICA)

HERALDRY

   (see also ARMS & ARMOR; BOOKS,
   Heraldry; GENEALOGY)

Clubs/Associations

David R. Wooten
American College of Heraldry, The
Newsletter: Armiger's News, The
P.O. Box 1899
Little Rock, AR 72203-1899
fax: 501-834-4038
davidwu10@sbcglobal.net
http://www.americancollegeofheraldry.org
   *A private body for the recording of
   arms in the US; lots of great links to
   other heraldry related sites.*

Heraldry Society, The
P.O. Box 32
Maidenhead, Berkshire SL6 3FD U.K.
ph: +44 (0) 118 932 0210
secretary@theheraldrysociety.com
http://www.theheraldrysociety.com
   *Exists to increase and extend interest
   in and knowledge of heraldry, armory,
   chivalry, genealogy and allied
   subjects.*

Experts

William Chandler
Chandler Art Consulting Services
3820 4th Ave.
San Diego, CA 92103
ph: 619-291-7765
   *Art expert with an extensive
   background in heraldry.*

Internet Resources

James P. Wolf
Heraldry on the Internet
jawolf@earthlink.net
http://www.digiserve.com/heraldry
   *Great online resource for heraldry
   information: heraldic glossary,
   castles, medieval resources,
   dictionaries, organizations,
   genealogical research tips and
   techniques.*

Brian R. Price
Knighthood, Chivalry & Tournament
   Glossary of Terms
4226 Cambridge Way
Union City, CA 94587
ph: 650-961-2187
brian@chronique.com
http://www.chronique.com
   *Web site with extensive glossary of
   terms relating to knighthood, chivalry
   and tournaments.*

Misc. Services

College of Arms, The
Queen Victoria St.
London, EC4V 4BT U.K.
ph: +44 171 248 2762
fax: +44 171 248 6448
http://www.college-of-arms.gov.uk
   *Charged with maintaining the system
   of heraldry; online Web site includes
   how it all began, heralds in modern
   times, granting of arms today, tracing
   your family.*

HERITAGE RESOURCES

   (see also NATIVE AMERICAN;
   ARCHAEOLOGY; PREHISTORIC
   ARTIFACTS)

Clubs/Associations

National Institute for the Conservation of
   Cultural Property
1730 K St. NW, Ste. 566
Washington, DC 0006-3836
ph: 888-767-7285 or 202-634-1422
fax: 202-634-1435
astone@heritagepreservation.org
http://www.heritagepreservation.org/
   PROGRAMS/SOS/sosmain.htm
   *Provides national leadership to
   promote & facilitate the conservation
   and preservation of the nation's
   heritage, including works of art,
   anthropological artifacts, documents,
   historic objects, architecture and
   natural science specimens.*

Misc. Services

Repatriation Coordin'tr
American Indian Ritual Object
  Repatriation Foundation
463 East 57th St.
New York, NY 10022-3003
ph: 212-980-9441
fax: 212-421-2746
circle@repatriationfoundation.org
http://www.repatriationfoundation.org
*A non-federally funded intercultural
partnership committed to assisting in
the return of ceremonial material to
American Indian Nations and to
educating the public about the
importance of repatriation.*

Licensing Officer
National Trust for Historic Preservation
Magazine: Preservation Magazine
1785 Massachusetts Ave., NW
Washington, DC 20036
ph: 202-588-6000
fax: 202-588-6292
members@nthp.org
http://nthp.org
*Licenses some of America's leading
home furnishings, decorative arts,
giftware and collectibles manufacturers to reproduce objects related to
Nat. Trust sites, and American history
& culture; educates public about
historic preservation.*

Naval Historical Center, Office of the
  Senior Historian
Washington Navy Yard
901 M St. SE
Washington, DC 20374-5060
ph: 202-433-7229 or 202-433-7230
fax: 202-433-3593
*Department of Navy ship and aircraft
wrecks remain government property;
questions and information concerning
historic US Navy aircraft and
shipwrecks should be addressed to the
Naval Historical Center.*

Museums/Libraries

National Museum of Natural History,
  Anthropology Department
Smithsonian Institution
Washington, DC 20560
dennis@smithson.si.edu
http://www.mnh.si.edu
*Contact about "Anthro Notes," a
bulletin for teachers.*

National Park Service

Misc. Services

National Park Service, Northeast
  Regional Office
200 Chestnut St., 5th Floor
Philadelphia, PA 19106
ph: 215-597-7013
fax: 215-597-0815
marie_rust@nps.gov
*Technical assistance, publications,
training, Secretary of the Interior's
Report on Federal Archeology,
National Archeological Database
(NADB), Listing of Education in
Archeology Projects (LEAP), Regional
Office Programs.*

National Register of Historic Places
National Park Service, DOI
1849 C St. NW, NC400
Washington, DC 20240
ph: 202-343-9500
fax: 202-343-1836
nr_info@nps.gov
http://www.cr.nps.gov/nr
*For information on the National
Register of Historic Places and
"Teaching With Historic Places."*

Richard Waldbauer
National Park Service, DOI, Archeology
  & Ethnography Program
1849 C St. NW
Washington, DC 20240
ph: 202-343-4113
fax: 202-523-1547
richard_waldbauer@nps.gov
http://www.cr.nps.gov/aad
*Can convey information concerning
the federal archaeological program
from a land management perspective.*

Tim McKeown
NAGPRA Team Leader, Archeology &
  Ethnography Program, National Park
  Service
1849 C St. NW
Washington, DC 20240
ph: 202-343-4101
fax: 202-523-1547
tim_mckeown@nps.gov
http://www.cast.uark.edu/products/
  NAGPRA
*Can convey information concerning
Native American human remains,
funerary objects, sacred objects, and
objects of cultural patrimony as
defined by the Native American Graves
Protection & Repatriation Act
(NAGPRA).*

National Park Service, DOI, Archeology
  & Ethnography Program
1849 C St. NW
Suite NC210 (2275)
Washington, DC 20240-0001
ph: 202-344-2100
fax: 202-371-5102
dca@nps.gov
http://www.cr.nps.gov/aad
*Can convey information concerning
both criminal and civil federal law
relating to heritage resources from
both a lawyer's and archeologist's
perspective.*

National Park Service, National Capital
  Region
1100 Ohio Srive, SW
Washington, DC 20242
ph: 202-619-7000
fax: 202-619-7220
tammy_stidham@nps.gov
http://www.nps.gov/ncro
*Technical assistance, publications,
training, Secretary of the Interior's
Report on Federal Archeology,
National Archeological Database
(NADB), Listing of Education in
Archeology Projects (LEAP), Regional
Office Programs.*

National Park Service, Southeast
  Regional Office
100 Alabama St. SW
NPS/Atlanta Federal Center
Atlanta, GA 30303
ph: 404-562-3100
fax: 404-562-3263
jerry_belson@nps.gov
*Technical assistance, publications,
training, Secretary of the Interior's
Report on Federal Archeology,
National Archeological Database
(NADB), Listing of Education in
Archeology Projects (LEAP), Regional
Office Programs.*

National Park Service, Midwest Region
B102 Steenbock
550 Babcock Dr.
Madison, WI 53706
ph: 608-265-3515
fax: 608-262-2500
peter_budde@nps.gov
*Technical assistance, publications,
training, Secretary of the Interior's
Report on Federal Archeology,
National Archeological Database
(NADB), Listing of Education in
Archeology Projects (LEAP), Regional
Office Programs.*

National Park Service, Intermountain
  Region
12795 West Alameda Parkway
P.O. Box 25287
Denver, CO 80225-0287
ph: 303-969-2653
fax: 303-696-2644
theresa_ely@nps.gov
*Technical assistance, publications,
training, Secretary of the Interior's
Report on Federal Archeology,
National Archeological Database
(NADB), Listing of Education in
Archeology Projects (LEAP), Regional
Office Programs.*

National Park Service, Pacific West
  Region
300 Ala Moana Blvd.
P.O. Box 50165, Room 6-226
Honolulu, HI 96850
ph: 808-541-2693
fax: 808-541-3696
melia_lane-kamahele@nps.gov
http://www.nps.gov/pwro
*Technical assistance, publications,
training, Secretary of the Interior's
Report on Federal Archeology,
National Archeological Database
(NADB), Listing of Education in
Archeology Projects (LEAP), Regional
Office Programs.*

National Park Service, Alaska Regional
  Office
2525 Gambell St., Rm. 107
Anchorage, AK 99503-2892
ph: 907-257-2489
fax: 907-264-5428
george_dickison@nps.gov
*Technical assistance, publications,
training, Secretary of the Interior's
Report on Federal Archeology,
National Archeological Database*

*(NADB), Listing of Education in
Archeology Projects (LEAP), Regional
Office Programs.*

State Archaeologists

Misc. Services

Elizabeth Righter
Senior Archaeologist, Dept. of Planning
  & Natural Resources, Div. of
  Archaeology
17 Kongens Gade
Charlotte Armalie, VI 00802
ph: 340-776-8605
fax: 340-776-7236
sankofa@viaccess.net
*Provides information on laws,
procedures, current research,
education programs, and other aspects
of archaeology for this state or
possession.*

Miguel Bonini
Puerto Rico State Historic Preservation
  Office
La Fortaleza
P.O. Box 82
San Juan, PR 00901
ph: 809-721-3737
fax: 809-723-0957
*Provides information on laws,
procedures, current research,
education programs, and other aspects
of archaeology for this state or
possession.*

Brona Simon
State Archaeologist, D-SHPO,
  Massachusetts Historical Commission
220 Morrissey Blvd.
Dorchester, MA 02125
ph: 617-727-8470
fax: 617-727-5128
bsimon@sec.state.ma.us
http://nasa.uconn.edu/massosa.html
*Provides information on laws,
procedures, current research,
education programs, and other aspects
of archaeology for this state or
possession.*

Principal/State Archaeologist, Rhode
  Island Historic Preservation
  Commission
Old State House
150 Benefit St.
Providence, RI 02903
ph: 401-277-2678
fax: 401-277-2968
*Provides information on laws,
procedures, current research,
education programs, and other aspects
of archaeology for this state or
possession.*

New Hampshire State Archaeologist,
Division of Historical Resources
19 Pillsbury St.
P.O. Box 2043
Concord, NH 03302-2043
ph: 603-271-3483 or 603-271-3558
fax: 603-271-3433
preservation@nhdhr.state.nh.us
http://webster.state.nh.us/nhdhr
*Provides information on laws,
procedures, current research,
education programs, and other aspects
of archaeology for this state or
possession.*

Archaeologist, Maine Historic
Preservation Commission
55 Capitol St.
State House Station 65
Augusta, ME 04333-0065
ph: 207-287-2132
fax: 207-287-2335
arthur.spiess@state.me.us
http://janus.state.me.us/mhpc
*Provides information on laws,
procedures, current research,
education programs, and other aspects
of archaeology for this state or
possession.*

Giovanna Peebles
State Archaeologist, Division for Historic
Preservation
National Life, Drawer 20
Montpelier, VT 05620-0501
ph: 802-828-3050
fax: 802-828-3206
giovanna.peebles@state.vt.us
http://nasa.uconn.edu/vtosa.html
*Provides information on laws,
procedures, current research,
education programs, and other aspects
of archaeology for this state or
possession.*

State Archaeologist, Connecticut State
Museum of Natural History
U-23 University of Connecticut
Storrs Mansfield, CT 06269-3023
ph: 860-486-5248
fax: 860-486-4460
nbell@uconnvm.uconn.edu
http://nasa.uconn.edu/connosa.html
*Provides information on laws,
procedures, current research,
education programs, and other aspects
of archaeology for this state or
possession.*

Lorraine Williams
New Jersey State Archaeologist, New
Jersey State Museum
205 W. State St., CN 530
Trenton, NJ 08625
ph: 609-292-8594
fax: 609-599-4098
*Provides information on laws,
procedures, current research,
education programs, and other aspects
of archaeology for this state or
possession.*

Robert Kuhn
Archaeologist, Office of Parks, Recreation
& Historic Preservation
Peebles Island
P.O. Box 189
Waterford, NY 12188
ph: 518-237-8643 x255
fax: 518-237-9049
rdkdelmar@aol.com
http://nasa.uconn.edu/nyosa.html
*Provides information on laws,
procedures, current research,
education programs, and other aspects
of archaeology for this state or
possession.*

Kurt Carr
Chief, Pennsylvania Division of
Archaeology & Protection
P.O. Box 1026
Harrisburg, PA 17120-1026
ph: 717-783-9926
fax: 717-783-1073
kcarr@state.pa.us
http://www.phmc.state.pa.us
*Provides information on laws,
procedures, current research,
education programs, and other aspects
of archaeology for this state or
possession.*

Faye Stocum
State of Delaware, Dept. of State,
Division of Historical & Cultural
Affairs
15 The Green
Dover, DE 19901-3611
ph: 302-739-5685
fax: 302-739-5660
http://www.state.de.us/sos/histcult.htm
*Provides information on laws,
procedures, current research,
education programs, and other aspects
of archaeology for this state or
possession.*

Richard Hughes
Maryland Office of Archaeology, Division
of Historical/Cultural Programs
100 Community Place
Crownsville, MD 21032-2032
ph: 410-514-7600
fax: 410-987-4071
http://www.marylandhistoricaltrust.net/
archeol.html
*Provides information on laws,
procedures, current research,
education programs, and other aspects
of archaeology for this state or
possession.*

Catherine Slusser
State Archaeologist, Virginia Department
of Historic Resources
2801 Kensington Ave.
Richmond, VA 23219
ph: 804-367-2323
fax: 804-367-2391
cslusser@dhr.state.va.us
http://www.dhr.state.va.us
*Provides information on laws,
procedures, current research,
education programs, and other aspects
of archaeology for this state or
possession.*

Senior Archaeologist, West Virginia
Division of Culture/History
The Cultural Center
1900 Kanawha Blvd. East
Charleston, WV 25305-0300
ph: 304-558-0220 x179
fax: 304-558-2779
joanna.wilson@wvculture.org
http://www.wvculture.org
*Provides information on laws,
procedures, current research,
education programs, and other aspects
of archaeology for this state or
possession.*

Stephen Claggett
North Carolina State Archaeologist
4619 Mail Service Center
Raleigh, NC 27699-4619
ph: 919-733-7342
fax: 919-715-2671
steve.claggett@ncmail.net
http://www.arch.dcr.state.nc.us/fosa.htm
*Provides information on laws,
procedures, current research,
education programs, and other aspects
of archaeology for this state or
possession.*

Bruce Rippeteau
Director/State Archaeologist, SC
Institute of Archaeology/Anthropology
University of South Carolina
1321 Pendleton St.
Columbia, SC 29201-0071
ph: 803-777-8170 or 803-734-0567
fax: 803-254-1338
rippeteau@sc.edu
http://www.cla.sc.edu/sciaa/sciaa.html
*Provides information on laws,
procedures, current research,
education programs, and other aspects
of archaeology in and for South
Carolina; maintains archaeological
collections, site files; accepts private
giving for research.*

Dave Crass
Georgia State Archaeologist, Historic
Preservation Division
156 Trinity Ave. SW, Ste 101
57 Forsyth St., NW
Atlanta, GA 30303-3600
ph: 404-656-9344
fax: 404-657-1040
david_crass@dnr.state.ga.us
http://www.dnr.state.ga.us/dnr/histpres
*Provides information on laws,
procedures, current research,
education programs, and other aspects
of archaeology for this state or
possession.*

James Miller
State Archaeologist, Florida Division of
Historical Resources
500 S. Bronough St.
Tallahassee, FL 32399-0250
ph: 850-245-6444
fax: 850-245-6436
bswann@dos.state.fl.us
http://dhr.dos.state.fl.us
*Provides information on laws,
procedures, current research,
education programs, and other aspects*

*of archaeology for this state or
possession.*

Thomas Maher
Chief, Archaeological Services Division,
Alabama Historical Commission
468 S. Perry St.
Montgomery, AL 36130-0900
ph: 334-230-2645
fax: 334-240-3477
TMaher@mail.preserveala.org
http://nasa.uconn.edu/alaosa.html
*Provides information on laws,
procedures, current research,
education programs, and other aspects
of archaeology for this state or
possession.*

Nick Fielder
TN State Archeologist, Dept. of
Environment & Conservation, Div. of
Archaeology
5103 Edmonson Pike
Nashville, TN 37211-5129
ph: 615-741-1588
fax: 615-741-7329
nick.fielder@state.tn.us
http://www.state.tn.us/environment/arch
*Provides information on laws,
procedures, current research,
education programs, and other aspects
of archaeology for this state or
possession.*

Samuel McGahey
Chief, Mississippi Department of
Archives & History
P.O. Box 571
Jackson, MS 39205
ph: 601-359-6940
fax: 601-359-6955
refdesk@mdah.state.ms.us
http://www.mdah.state.ms.us
*Provides information on laws,
procedures, current research,
education programs, and other aspects
of archaeology for this state or
possession.*

Kentucky State Archaeologist,
Department of Anthropology
University of Kentucky
1020-A Export St.
Lexington, KY 40506-0024
ph: 859-257-8208
fax: 859-323-1968
*Provides information on laws,
procedures, current research,
education programs, and other aspects
of archaeology for this state or
possession.*

Ohio Historic Preservation Office, Ohio
Historical Society
567 East Hudson St.
Columbus, OH 43211-1030
ph: 614-298-2000
fax: 614-298-2037
webmaster@ohiohistory.org
http://www.ohiohistory.com/resource/
histpres
*Provides information on laws,
procedures, current research,
education programs, and other aspects
of archaeology for this state or
possession.*

Jon Smith, Dir.
Indiana Dept. of Natural Resources, Div.
  of Historic Preservation/Archaeology
402 W. Washington, Rm. W274
Indianapolis, IN 46204
ph: 317-232-1646
fax: 317-232-8036
jsmith@dnr.state.in.us
http://www.state.in.us/dnr/historic
  *Provides information on laws,
  procedures, current research,
  education programs, and other aspects
  of archaeology for this state or
  possession.*

John R. Halsey
State Archaeologist, Michigan Historical
  Center
717 W. Allegan St.
Lansing, MI 48918-1847
ph: 517-373-6358
fax: 517-373-0851
webspinners@sosmail.state.mi.us
http://www.sos.state.mi.us/history/
  archeol
  *Provides information on laws,
  procedures, current research,
  education programs, and other aspects
  of archaeology for this state ör
  possession.*

William Green
Iowa State Archaeologist, University of
  Iowa
700 Clinton St. Bldg.
Iowa City, IA 52242-1030
ph: 319-384-0732
fax: 319-384-0768
OSA@uiowa.edu
http://www.uiowa.edu/~osa
  *Provides information on laws,
  procedures, current research,
  education programs, and other aspects
  of archaeology for this state or
  possession.*

John H. Broihahn
Archaeologist, Wisconsin State
  Historical Society of Wisconsin
816 State St.
Madison, WI 53706
ph: 608-264-6496
fax: 608-264-6504
jhbroihahn@whs.wisc.edu
http://www.wisconsinhistory.org/arch/
  osa
  *Provides information on laws,
  procedures, current research,
  education programs, and other aspects
  of archaeology for this state or
  possession.*

Mark Dudzik
Minnesota State Archaeologist
Fort Snelling History Center
Saint Paul, MN 55111
ph: 612-725-2411
fax: 612-725-2427
mark.dudzik@state.mn.us
http://nasa.uconn.edu/minnosa.html
  *Provides information on laws,
  procedures, current research,
  education programs, and other aspects
  of archaeology for this state or
  possession.*

James Haug
South Dakota State Archaeologist, State
  Archaeological Research Center
2425 E. St. Charles St.
P.O. Box 1257
Rapid City, SD 57709-1257
ph: 605-394-1936
fax: 605-394-1941
archaeology@state.sd.us
http://www.sdsmt.edu/wwwsarc
  *Provides information on laws,
  procedures, current research,
  education programs, and other aspects
  of archaeology for this state or
  possession.*

Fern Swenson
Chief Archaeologist, State Historical
  Society of ND, Arch. & Hist. Pres.
  Div.
North Dakota Heritage Center
612 E. Blvd. Ave.
Bismarck, ND 58505-0830
ph: 701-328-2672
fax: 701-328-3710
fswenson@state.nd.us
http://nasa.uconn.edu/ndosa.html
  *Provides information on laws,
  procedures, current research,
  education programs, and other aspects
  of archaeology for this state or
  possession.*

Stan Wilmoth
State Archaeologists, Montana Historical
  Society
P.O. Box 201201
Helena, MT 59620-1201
ph: 406-444-7719
fax: 406-444-6575
swilmoth@state.mt.us
http://www.his.state.mt.us
  *Provides information on laws,
  procedures, current research,
  education programs, and other aspects
  of archaeology for this state or
  possession.*

State Archaeologist, Preservation
  Services Div., IL Historic Preservation
  Agency
500 East Madison St.
Springfield, IL 62701
ph: 217-785-4999
fax: 217-782-8161
  *Provides information on laws,
  procedures, current research,
  education programs, and other aspects
  of archaeology for this state or
  possession.*

Senior Archaeologist, Missouri Historic
  Preservation Program
P.O. Box 176
Jefferson City, MO 65102
ph: 573-751-7958 or 800-361-4827
fax: 573-526-2852
moshpo@mail.dnr.state.mo.us
http://www.dnr.state.mo.us/shpo/
  Archaeology.htm
  *Provides information on laws,
  procedures, current research,
  education programs, and other aspects
  of archaeology for this state or
  possession.*

Kansas State Archaeologist, Kansas
  History Center
6425 SW 6th Ave.
Topeka, KS 66615-1099
ph: 785-272-8691
fax: 785-272-8682
rhoard@kshs.org
http://www.kshs.org/archeologisgts
  *Provides information on laws,
  procedures, current research,
  education programs, and other aspects
  of archaeology for this state or
  possession.*

Rob Bozwell
Director for Archaeology, Nebraska State
  Historical Society
1500 R St.
P.O. Box 82554
Lincoln, NE 68501
ph: 402-471-4790
fax: 402-471-3114
archnshs@nebraskahistory.org
http://www.nebraskahistory.org/archeo
  *Provides information on laws,
  procedures, current research,
  education programs, and other aspects
  of archaeology for this state or
  possession.*

Thomas Eubanks
Louisiana State Archaeologist, Division
  of Archaeology
1051 North Third St., Rm. 405
P.O. Box 44247
Baton Rouge, LA 70804-4247
ph: 225-342-8170
fax: 225-342-4480
teubanks@crt.state.la.us
http://nasa.uconn.edu/luosa.html
  *Provides information on laws,
  procedures, current research,
  education programs, and other aspects
  of archaeology for this state or
  possession.*

Ann Early
State Archaeologist, Arkansas
  Archeological Survey
2475 N. Hatch Ave.
Fayetteville, AR 72704
ph: 501-575-3556
fax: 501-575-5453
amearly@uark.edu
http://cavern.uark.edu/campus-resources/
  archinfo/statearch.html
  *Provides information on laws,
  procedures, current research,
  education programs, and other aspects
  of archaeology for this state or
  possession.*

Robert Brooks
Oklahoma Archeological Survey
111 East Chesapeake, Rm. 102
Norman, OK 73019
ph: 405-325-7211
fax: 405-325-7604
rbrooks@ou.edu
http://www.ou.edu/cas/archsur
  *Provides information on laws,
  procedures, current research,
  education programs, and other aspects
  of archaeology for this state or
  possession.*

Patricia Mercado-Allinger
State Archaeologist, Texan Historical
  Commission
Box 12276
Austin, TX 78711-2276
ph: 512-463-8882
fax: 512-463-2530
pat.mercado-allinger@thc.state.tx.us
http://www.thc.state.tx.us
  *Provides information on laws,
  procedures, current research,
  education programs, and other aspects
  of archaeology for this state or
  possession.*

State Archaeologist, Colorado Historical
  Society
1300 Broadway
Denver, CO 80203-2137
ph: 303-886-2736
fax: 303-866-2711
oahp@chs.state.co.us
http://coloradohistory-oahp.org
  *Provides information on laws,
  procedures, current research,
  education programs, and other aspects
  of archaeology for this state or
  possession.*

Mark Miller
Wyoming State Archaeologist's Office
Box 3413
University Station
Laramie, WY 82071
ph: 307-766-5301
fax: 307-766-4052
mmiller@uwyo.edu
http://wyoarchaeo.state.wy.us/default.htm
  *Provides information on laws,
  procedures, current research,
  education programs, and other aspects
  of archaeology for this state or
  possession.*

Ken Reid, Administrator
Idaho State Archaeologist
210 Main St.
Boise, ID 83702
ph: 208-334-3847
fax: 208-334-2775
Kreid@ishs.state.id.us
http://www2.state.id.us/ishs/SHPO.html
  *Provides information on laws,
  procedures, current research,
  education programs, and other aspects
  of archaeology for this state or
  possession.*

Kevin Jones
Utah State Archaeologist, Division of
  State History
Antiquities Section
310 Rio Grande
Salt Lake City, UT 84101
ph: 801-533-3524
fax: 801-533-3503
ktjones@utah.gov
http://history.utah.gov/archaeology
  *Provides information on laws,
  procedures, current research,
  education programs, and other aspects
  of archaeology for this state or
  possession.*

Paul Fish
Curator of Archaeology, Arizona State
  Museum
University of Arizona
Tucson, AZ 85721
ph: 520-621-2556
fax: 520-621-2976
pfish@u.arizona.edu
http://nasa.uconn.edu/arizosa.html
  Provides information on laws,
  procedures, current research,
  education programs, and other aspects
  of archaeology for this state or
  possession.

Glenna Dean
New Mexico State Archaeologist,
  Historic Preservation Division
Villa Rivera Bldg.
228 E. Palace Ave.
Santa Fe, NM 87501
ph: 505-827-3989
fax: 505-827-6338
gdean@lvr.state.nm.us
http://nasa.uconn.edu/nmosa.html
  Provides information on laws,
  procedures, current research,
  education programs, and other aspects
  of archaeology for this state or
  possession.

Barbara Prudic
Nevada State Historic Preservation Office
100 N. Stewart St.
Carson City, NV 89710
ph: 702-684-3448
fax: 702-687-3442
blprudic@clan.lib.nv.us
http://dmla.clan.lib.nv.us/docs/shpo/
  default.htm
  Provides information on laws,
  procedures, current research,
  education programs, and other aspects
  of archaeology for this state or
  possession.

California Office of Historic Preservation
P.O. Box 942896
Sacramento, CA 94296-0001
ph: 916-322-9623
fax: 916-653-9824
calshpo@ohp.parks.ca.gov
http://ohp.parks.ca.gov
  Provides information on laws,
  procedures, current research,
  education programs, and other aspects
  of archaeology for this state or
  possession.

Hawaii State Dept. of Land & Natural
  Resources Division, Historic Pres.
  Division
601 Kamokila Blvd., Ste. 555
Kapolei, HI 96707
ph: 808-692-8015
fax: 808-962-8020
Clifford.G.Inn@hawaii.gov
http://www.hawaii.gov/dlnr/hpd/
  hpgreeting.htm
  Provides information on laws,
  procedures, current research,
  education programs, and other aspects
  of archaeology for this state or
  possession.

Guam Department of Parks & Recreation
Building 13-8 Tiyan
P.O. Box 2950
Agana, GU 96910
ph: 671-475-6290
fax: 671-477-2822
http://ns.gov.gu/dpr/hrdhome.html
  Provides information on laws,
  procedures, current research,
  education programs, and other aspects
  of archaeology for this state or
  possession.

Archaeologist, Oregon State Historic
  Preservation Office
1115 Commercial St., NE, Ste. 2
Salem, OR 97310-1012
ph: 503-378-4168 x232
fax: 503-378-6447
park.info@state.or.us
http://www.prd.state.or.us/home.html
  Provides information on laws,
  procedures, current research,
  education programs, and other aspects
  of archaeology for this state or
  possession.

Robert Whitlam
State Archaeologist, Washington Dept.
  of Community, Trade & Economic
  Development
P.O. Box 48343
Olympia, WA 98504-8343
ph: 360-407-0771
fax: 360-407-6217
robw@cted.wa.gov
http://nasa.uconn.edu/waosa.html
  Provides information on laws,
  procedures, current research,
  education programs, and other aspects
  of archaeology for this state or
  possession.

Robert Shaw
Alaska Office of History & Archaeology
550 W. 7th Ave., Ste. 1310
Anchorage, AK 99501-3565
ph: 907-269-8721
fax: 907-269-8908
oha@alaska.net
http://www.dnr.state.ak.us/parks/
  oha_web
  Provides information on laws,
  procedures, current research,
  education programs, and other aspects
  of archaeology for this state or
  possession.

HI-FI EQUIPMENT

(see also AUDIO-VISUAL;
PHONOGRAPHS; RADIOS;
RADIOS, Vacuum Tubes for;
RECORDS)

Collectors

Jeffrey Viola
784 Eltone Rd.
Jackson, NJ 08527-4351
ph: 732-928-0666
  Wants to buy old tubes and tube-type
  Hi-fi & stereo equipment by such
  manufacturers as Marantz, Mcintosh,
  Fisher, Dynaco, Eico, Harman

Kardon, Heathkit, Acrosound,
Western Electric, Altec Lansing,
Fairchild, others; no Japanese
equipment.

Sonny Goldson
1413 Magnolia Lane
Midwest City, OK 73110
ph: 405-737-3312
fax: 405-737-3355
  Wants commercial tube hi-fi sound
  equipment: speakers, horns, and tubes;
  McIntosh, Altec, Jensen, Marantz,
  Heath, Dynaco, James Lansing,
  Western Electric, Fisher, Scott, Eico,
  Electrovoice, Tannoy, RCA, etc.

Dealers

John E. Kendall
Vintage Electronics
P.O. Box 436
Fallston, MD 21047-0436
maloney@vintage-electronics.com
http://www.vintage-electronics.com
  Wants radios from the 1920s through
  1960s; buys, sells tube and transistor
  radios, unusual TV's, early miniature
  or handheld TVs, tube audio and
  other early odd electronics; also
  related items such as books,
  schematics, tubes, ads, etc.

Experts

Jeffrey Viola
784 Eltone Rd.
Jackson, NJ 08527-4351
ph: 732-928-0666
  Hi-Fi equipment adviser to "The
  Official Guide to Flea Market Prices."

HIGHWAY COLLECTIBLES

(see also AUTOMOBILIA; GAS
STATION COLLECTIBLES; HOTEL
COLLECTIBLES; DINERS &
RELATED ITEMS; SOUVENIR &
COMMEMORATIVE ITEMS;
TRAILERS & RVs)

Experts

Laurel Kane
6036 Chip Shot Rd.
Grove, OK 74344
laurelrk66@aol.com
http://www.PostcardsFromTheRoad.net
  Expert and advanced collector of
  postcards and other US highway-
  related memorabilia such as maps,
  travel guides, and motel guides;
  especially wants those related to Route
  66; buys, sells, trades.

Periodicals

Mock Turtle Press
Magazine: American Road
P.O. Box 3168
Lynnwood, WA 98046
americanroad@mockturtlepress.com
http://www.mockturtlepress.com
  This magazine is aimed at the vast
  market of nostalgia lovers, family
  vacationers, retirees, and other road-
  bound tourists with a yearning to

learn about our nation's vintage
highways and auto trails.

Decals

Dealers

Richard Schneider
Lost Highway Art Co.
P.O. Box 164
Bedford Hills, NY 10507-1064
ph: 914-234-9029
losthwyart@aol.com
  Buys and sells souvenir water-dip
  decals: states, parks, cities,
  attractions, etc., wants singles or
  collections or inventories.

Repro. Sources

Richard Schneider
Lost Highway Art Co.
P.O. Box 164
Bedford Hills, NY 10507-1064
ph: 914-234-9029
losthwyart@aol.com
  Large variety of vintage travel images
  available for graphic artists or
  reproduced on mugs, magnets and t-
  shirts.

Lincoln Highway

Collectors

Lynn Christian
1114 Wilson Ave.
Ames, IA 50010-5570
ph: 515-232-2222
  Wants old "Lincoln Highway" related
  items.

Route 66 Items

Clubs/Associations

Route 66 Association of Illinois
2743 Veterans Parkway, #166
Springfield, IL 62704
ph: 847-392-0860 or 847-577-2501
teague66@eosinc.com
http://www.il66assoc.org/idx_1a.htm
  Organization focusing on protecting
  and promoting Rt. 66 (The Mother
  Road) and collecting items relating
  thereto.

International Route 66 Association
2700 Kiowa S.
Lake Havasu City, AZ 86403
http://www.route66.com

Experts

Laurel Kane
6036 Chip Shot Rd.
Grove, OK 74344
laurelrk66@aol.com
http://www.PostcardsFromTheRoad.net
  Expert and advanced collector of
  postcards and other US highway-
  related memorabilia such as maps,
  travel guides, and motel guides;
  especially wants those related to Route
  66; buys, sells, trades.

Museums/Libraries

Texas Old Route 66 Association
   Museum and Hall of Fame
100 Kingsley St.
P.O. Box 290
Mclean, TX 79057-0290
ph: 806-779-2225 or 806-779-3164
barbwiremuseum@centramedia.net
http://www.barbwiremuseum.com
   *1800 sq. ft. of 450 authentic Route 66
   artifacts; Route 66 gift shop.*

Bob Lundy
Route 66 Museum & Gift Shop
2400 San Dimas Cnayon Rd., #318
La Verne, CA 91750
ph: 909-592-2090 or 800-JOG-RT66
rte66@citivu.com
http://www.citivu.com/rc/rte66/
   rte66.html

Periodicals

Paul Taylor
Magazine: Route 66 Magazine
326 W. Route 66
Williams, AZ 86046
ph: 520-635-4322
fax: 520-635-4470
info@route66magazine.com
http://www.route66magazine.com
   *A glossy magazine loaded with news,
   photos and plenty of Route 66
   nostalgia.*

Signs & Traffic Devices

Collectors

Jeff Saltzman
Jeff's St.light Site
jeffsaltzman@iname.com
http://members.tripod.com/streetlights
   *Street light enthusiast; also interested
   in general highway and transit related
   things; Web site has photo gallery,
   roadside fixture links, transit links,
   and other road. and highway stuff.*

John Rietveld
SignalFan
signalfan@hotmail.com
http://www.signalfan.com
   *Interested in typical traffic signals
   from the 1960s: traffic signals, traffic
   controllers, historical signals, and
   more.*

Internet Resources

Signalfan's Club, The
signalfan@hotmail.com
http://www.signalfan.com
   *An online community for those
   interested in traffic signals or road
   signs.*

Periodicals

Jeff Francis
Newsletter: Signpost
P.O. Box 41381
Saint Petersburg, FL 33743-1381
ph: 727-345-6627
fax: 727-343-8977
gobucs13@aol.com
   An association focusing on the

*research and preservation of traffic
devices, markers and signs.*

Suppliers

Bill Andreas
Lights To Go!
P.O. Box 533
Derby, KS 67037
ph: 316-304-3051 or 316-788-4911
ltg@trafficlights.com
http://www.trafficlights.com
   *Sells traffic light control sequencer for
   antique or collectible traffic lights;
   compact unit installs in any traffic
   light to make it operational.*

HIPPIE ITEMS

(see SOCIAL CAUSES, Hippie Items)

HISTORICAL AMERICANA

(see also AUTOGRAPHS; GLASS,
Commemorative; IMMIGRATION;
MANUSCRIPTS; MILITARIA; PAPER
COLLECTIBLES; POLITICAL
COLLECTIBLES; SOCIAL CAUSES;
UNCLE SAM; VETERAN ITEMS)

Appraisers

Brian Kathenes
National Appraisal Consultants, LLC
P.O. Box 482
Hope, NJ 07844-0482
ph: 908-459-5996 or 800-323-5996
fax: 908-459-4899
Brian@nacvalue.com
http://www.nacvalue.com
   *Specialist Certified Appraiser of
   Personal Property in Autographs,
   Manuscripts and Historical
   Documents; expert appraisal,
   valuation and consulting services for
   Hollywood, sports and celebrity
   memorabilia and collectibles.*

Auction Services

East Coast Books
P.O. Box 849
Wells, ME 04090
ph: 207-646-3584
fax: 207-646-0416
   *Specializes in mail-bid auctions of
   historically significant autographs,
   manuscripts and letters, art works on
   paper.*

Donald Ackerman
Provenance Auction
P.O. Box 3487
Wallington, NJ 07057-1621
ph: 973-779-8785
assortedpast@comcast.net
   *Conducts periodic mail catalog
   auctions featuring historical
   Americana such as political items,
   early photography, autographs, Civil
   War, broadsides, etc.*

Robert Lifson
Robert Edward Auctions
P.O. Box 7256
Watchung, NJ 07069
ph: 908-226-9900 or 800-766-9324
fax: 908-226-9920
reaauct@aol.com
http://www.robertedwardauctions.com
   *Specializes in the auction sale of
   historical Americana, political
   material, autographs and manuscripts, and original illustration art.*

Caroline Birenbaum
Swann Galleries, Inc.
104 E. 25th St.
New York, NY 10010-2977
ph: 212-254-4710
fax: 212-979-1017
swann@swanngalleries.com
http://www.swanngalleries.com
   *Oldest/largest US auctioneer
   specializing in rare books, autographs
   & manuscripts, maps, atlases,
   photographs, and works of art on
   paper including vintage posters.*

Robert H. Snyder
Cohasco, Inc.
P.O. Drawer 821
Yonkers, NY 10702-0821
ph: 914-476-8500
fax: 914-476-8573
info@cohascodpc.com
http://www.cohascodpc.com
   *Mail bid auctions of paper and
   Americana: medallic art, Civil War,
   presidential ephemera and letters,
   music, old newspapers, prints, maps,
   political, financial, aviation, Judaica,
   legal, Lincolniana, personalities,
   royalty, sports, etc.*

Ted Hake
Hake's Americana & Collectibles
   Auction
P.O. Box 1444
York, PA 17405-1444
ph: 717-848-1333
Ted@hakes.com
http://www.hakes.com
   *Always purchasing, consigning items
   for 5 mail-bid & online auctions per
   year; hundreds of categories including
   toys, character collectibles, Disney,
   cowboy heroes, premiums, television,
   politicals, pin-back buttons,
   advertising and more.*

Robert Coup
Historicana
P.O. Box 348
Leola, PA 17540-0348
ph: 717-656-7855
fax: 717-656-8233
POLBANDWGN@aol.com
   *Specializes in mail-bid auctions of
   character collectibles, Disneyana,
   political items & historical
   Americana; sample catalog $2.*

Robert Raynor
Historical Collectible Auctions
24 NW Court Sq. #201
Graham, NC 27253
ph: 336-570-2803
fax: 336-570-2748
bids4hca@aol.com
http://www.hcaauctions.com
   *Specializes in historical Americana:
   Black Americana, Civil War artifacts
   and paper items, historic artifacts,
   Judaica, Indian War, Abraham
   Lincoln, militaria, photography,
   political, sports, Western, printed/
   manuscript Americana.*

C. Wesley Cowan
Cowan's Historic Americana
673 Wilmer Ave.
Cincinnati, OH 45226
ph: 513-871-1670
fax: 513-871-1670
info@historicamericana.com
http://www.historicamericana.com
   *Sells historical Americana: photo-
   graphic images, political items,
   manuscripts, autographs, etc.*

Al Anderson
Anderson Auction
P.O. Box 644
Troy, OH 45373-0644
ph: 937-339-0850
fax: 937-339-8620
aaauctn@erinet.com
http://www.erinet.com/aaauctn
   *Specializes in mail-bid auctions of
   political items and historical
   Americana.*

Tom Slater
Political Gallery, The
5335 North Takoma Ave.
Indianapolis, IN 46220
ph: 317-257-0863
fax: 317-254-9167
   *Specializing in mail-bid auctions of
   Disneyana, historical Americana, toys,
   political items, and other collectibles.*

U.I. "Chick" Harris
Harris Auctions
1010 Lemon St.
Highland, IL 62249-1678
ph: 618-651-1144
   *Collector/specialist in all types of
   political Americana; conducts
   specialized mail-auctions of political
   and historical Americana.*

Early American History Auction
P.O. Box 3341
La Jolla, CA 92038
ph: 858-459-4159
fax: 858-459-4373
auctions@earlyamerican.com
http://www.earlyAmerican.com
   *Autographs, currency, coins,
   Americana, Civil War, Lincoln,
   slavery, weapons, maps.*

Greg Martin Auctions
298 San Bruno Ave.
San Francisco, CA 94103
ph: 800-509-1988 or 415-522-5700
fax: 415-522-5701
info@rabin.com
http://www.gmartinauctions.com
Specializes in the auction sale of sporting arms, historical Americana, arms & armor.

Collectors

Sheldon Lerman
7505 Osler Dr.
Baltimore, MD 21204-7736
ph: 410-321-1514 or 410-828-1928
fax: 410-825-5710
Wants to buy historical documents, presidential and historical signatures.

Cary Demont
P.O. Box 16013
Minneapolis, MN 55416
ph: 763-522-0957
Serious collector looking for historical ephemera including political campaign items of all kinds, the woman's suffrage movement, prohibition and Carrie Nation items, Civil War period broadsides, and interesting Wild West material.

Ralf Mulhern
3710 Alabama St., Apt. 24
San Diego, CA 92104-3344
Wants to buy autographs, manuscripts, historical related items; send photocopy of items for sale and asking price; send lists and auction catalogs of items for sale.

Dealers

Rex Stark
Rex Stark Americana
P.O. Box 1029
Gardner, MA 01440-6029
ph: 978-630-3237
fax: 978-630-2388
rexstark@yahoo.com
Publishes fully illustrated fixed price catalog of historical Americana; averages 500 to 1,000 items per catalog with prices from $20 to $50,000: political, photography, Old West, advertising, early sports, graphic arts, glass, exonumia.

University Archives
49 Richmondville Ave.
Westport, CT 06880
ph: 800-237-5692 or 203-454-0111
fax: 203-454-3111
john@universityarchives.com
http://www.universityarchives.com
Buying and selling fine historical autographs, manuscripts, documents, autographed books and autographed photographs of notable people including US presidents, Revolutionary and Civil War, literary, aviation, science, art, and music.

Kenneth Rendell
Kenneth W. Rendell Gallery, The
989 Madison Ave.
New York, NY 10021
ph: 800-447-1007 or 212-717-1776
fax: 212-717-1492
gallery@kwrendell.com
http://www.kwrendell.com
Leading dealer in historical documents, autographs and manuscripts' author of "Autographs and Manuscripts: A Collector's Manual," "Faking Forgery: The Detection of Fake Letters and Documents," and other books.

Peter Hlinka
Peter Hlinka Historical Americana
P.O. Box 310
New York, NY 10028-0017
ph: 718-409-6407
Buys, sells, and appraises historical Americana; publishes a large catalog of militaria, military insignia, war relics, related books, and other historical Americana; also foreign.

Historical Collections
P.O. Box 42
Waynesboro, PA 17268-0042
ph: 717-762-3068

Tom Lingenfelter
Heritage Collectors' Society, Inc.
P.O. Box 2131
Doylestown, PA 18901
ph: 215-235-7955
fax: 215-230-7197
heritagecs@heritagecs.com
http://www.heritagecs.com
Dealers in investment quality historical documents and autographs; in business for over 25 years.

Donald Blincoe
Uncle Davey's Americana
6140 St. Augustine Rd.
Jacksonville, FL 32217
ph: 904-730-8932 or 904-777-6478
fax: 904-730-8932
uncledv@collectorsnet.com
http://www.collectorsnet.com/uncledv
Expert who buys, sells, appraises vintage historical US military related items from 1740 to 1885: weapons, documents, currency, coins, autographs, slavery, photos, books, newspapers, jewelry, clothing, maps, letters, etc.

Robert Richshafer
2929 First Ave. #L
San Diego, CA 92103
ph: 619-294-7950 or 619-975-4512
For 30 years a source of photographs, historic newspapers, broadsides, pamphlets, Americana, documents, ledgers, advertising, prints for collectors, dealers and museum.

Steve Schmale
Out West
2231 Creekside Rd.
Santa Rosa, CA 95405-8022
ph: 707-838-1859 or 707-575-5406
outweststv@aol.com
Buys and sells better vintage postcards since 1976; approval service; strong in Western states views; always buying better cards and real photos; also wants railroad paper, stereoviews, photos, brochures, trade cards; member IFPD.

Charles Zeder
Zeder's Antiques
1320 SW 10th St.
North Bend, WA 98045
ph: 425-888-6697
royalbritish@aol.com
Deals in 19th century ephemera, Civil War items, stock certificates, bonds, fruit box labels, 19th century advertising.

Ruth A. Miller Knott
Paperpreneur, The
1248 Ash St.
Lynden, WA 98264
ph: 360-318-8193
ruthie@nas.com
http://www.thepaperpreneur.com
Offers a unique selection of quality paper ephemera and historical documents: advertising, Americana, agriculture, Colonial, maritime, transportation, maritime, reward or merit, fraternal; does research, will answer questions.

Internet Resources

Library of Congress, American Memory
101 Independence Ave. SE
Washington, DC 20540
ph: 202-707-8000
ndlpcoll@loc.gov
http://memory.loc.gov/ammem
Historical collections from the National Digital Library: Washington's Papers, Lincoln's Papers, baseball cards, photos, prints, maps, motion pictures, sound recordings.

Making of America
University of Michigan
209 Graduate Library
Ann Arbor, MI 48103-1205
ph: 313-764-1148
fax: 313-764-0259
moa-feedback@umich.edu
http://moa.umdl.umich.edu
The MOA Collection is a digital library of primary sources in American social history from the antebellum period through reconstruction: 1,600 books, 50,000 journals with 19th century imprints; all scanned in their entirety.

HITCHING POSTS

Collectors

Bob Maclin
1436 Lakewood
Lexington, KY 40502
ph: 859269-4450
Interested in corresponding with others who are interested in hitching posts; also horse bridles, bridle bits, boot jacks.

HOBBY HORSES

(see RIDING TOYS, Rocking Horses)

HOBBY TOYS

(see TOYS, Construction Sets)

HOLIDAY COLLECTIBLES

(see also CHRISTMAS COLLECTIBLES; COLLECTIBLES [MODERN], Ornaments; ELVES; GEMS & JEWELRY, Christmas; HALLOWEEN COLLECTIBLES; VALENTINES; ST. PATRICK)

Collectors

Ann C. Bergin
P.O. Box 105
Amherst, NH 03031-0105
fax: 978-649-6807
acbergin@aol.com
Wants items relating to holidays, and ceremonies of life (Christenings, baptisms, weddings, confirmations, graduations, birthdays, etc.).

Linda L. Vines
2911 4th St., #112
Santa Monica, CA 90405
ph: 310-314-0402
lleigh2000@hotmail.com
Wants to buy pre-1950 holiday decoration including German Christmas, Halloween, Easter and patriotic candy containers, pumpkins, and Santas.

Dealers

Chris Savino
P.O. Box 419
Breesport, NY 14816-0419
ph: 607-739-3106
chrissavino@stny.rr.com
Wants holiday items including Christmas, Halloween, Easter; Santas, papier mache items such as ornaments, party favors, decorations, candy containers; tin toys, devils, skulls, witches; items made in Germany, Japan or USA.

Bettie Petzoldt
178 Woolen Mill Rd.
New Park, PA 17352
ph: 717-382-1416
bpetzoldt@supernet.com
http://www.mindyourbusiness.com/
ornaments
*Wants pre-1940 Christmas items:
unusual, collectible (figural)
Christmas ornaments, snow babies,
lights, Santas; other holiday items
too.*

Kit Carter Weilage
506 Briar Hill Rd.
Louisville, KY 40206
ph: 502-561-5030
kit1@bellsouth.net
*Buys and sells Christmas collectibles,
specializing in German-made Santa
candy containers.*

Jenny Tarrant
Holly Daze Antiques
4 Gardenview Dr.
Saint Peters, MO 63376-3507
ph: 314-397-1763
jennyjol@aol.com
http://www.holly-days.com
*Wants German Santas, Halloween
candy containers, jack-o'-lanterns,
German rabbits, and George
Washington composition candy
containers; also wants Easter
collectibles such as Easter toys and
candy containers from the 1950s.*

Repair Services

Jerry Arnold
3250 Dellwood Rd.
Cleveland, OH 44118
ph: 216-321-7418
*Repairs papier-mâché, fur Santa
beards, and other antique holiday
items.*

Easter

Dealers

Paul W. Schofield
Lion's Den Antiques
7988 Bethel Burley Rd. SE
Port Orchard, WA 98366
ph: 360-876-3364
fax: 360-876-5421
*Buys, sells, appraises, and specializes
in old Santas, candy containers,
Halloween, Easter, Christmas, Easter,
Dresden, figural lights.*

HOLLOWWARE

(see SILVER; SILVERPLATE)

HOLLYWOOD POSTERS

(see MOVIE MEMORABILIA, Movie
Posters; PHOTOGRAPHS, Celebrity)

HOLSTERS

(see TOY GUNS; WESTERN
AMERICANA)

HOLT HOWARD

(see also CERAMICS, Pixieware)

Collectors

Patrick Batzler
8118 Virginia Circle North
St. Louis Park, MN 55426
ph: 952-525-9590
fax: 952-545-7662
patrickbatzler@aol.com
*Seeks kitchen collectibles from the
1950s and 1960s: Holt Howard and
similar makers.*

HOMESPUN

(see TEXTILES)

HOOSIER CABINETS

(see FURNITURE [ANTIQUE],
Kitchen Cabinets)

HORNS & WHISTLES

(see also NAUTICAL ANTIQUES;
SPORTING COLLECTIBLES, Game
Calls; STEAM-OPERATED, Models &
Equipment)

Clubs/Associations

Harry D. Barry
Air Horn & Steam Whistle Enthusiasts
Newsletter: Horn & Whistle
275 Windswept Dr.
North East, PA 16428
ph: 814-725-8150
*Purpose is to preserve, increase, and
disseminate knowledge concerning
horns, whistles, sirens, and bells in
industrial, marine, transportation,
signaling, and warning applications.*

James C. Fitch
Call & Whistle Collectors Association
Newsletter: Whistle Notes
2839 E. 26th Place
Tulsa, OK 74114-4309
ph: 918-747-3202
jfitch@noria.com
*Club for collectors of game calls,
antique whistles, bo's'n pipes, flutes,
bird calls, advertising whistles, toy
whistles, and folk art whistles.*

Collectors

Harry D. Barry
275 Windswept Dr.
North East, PA 16428
ph: 814-725-8150
*Collects steam whistles and horns
which were and are used on
locomotives, ships, factories, boilers,
etc.*

Harry Warner
740 W. Clover Dr.
Memphis, TN 38120
ph: 800-850-9106
*Wants whistles; also dove, turkey and
dove calls; call after 5 p.m. EST.*

R. Bruce Cynar
10023 St. Clair's Retreat
Fort Wayne, IN 46825
ph: 260-489-5004
oldtchnlgy@msn.com
*Wants all steam whistles and large
brass steam gauges.*

Sirens

Collectors

Adam Smith
23 Carver Rd. East
Watertown, MA 02472
ph: 617-924-2260
adam@airraidsirens.com
http://www.airraidsirens.com
*Collects air raid sirens, both electric
and hand-cranked; especially wants
Carters, Secomak, Grifco, Klaxon
dual-tone electric siren.*

HORROR

(see also GHOSTS & HAUNTINGS;
MORBID & ODD ITEMS; MOVIE
MEMORABILIA; SCIENCE FICTION;
TRADING CARDS, Non-Sport;
WITCHES)

Collectors

Clayton Sayre
105 Francis St.
Portsmouth, VA 23702
ph: 757-487-8858
http://www.geocities.com/Hollywood/
Theater/1645
*Wants to buy classic movie monster
items: Frankenstein, Dracula,
Wolfman, Creature from the Black
Lagoon, etc.*

Dracula

Clubs/Associations

Dr. M. Jeanne Youngson
Count Dracula Fan Club
Journal: Dracula News
29 Washington Square West
New York, NY 10011-9180
ph: 212-982-6754
*Club keeps members of the CDFC up
on everything happening in the world
of the undead; also publishes other
newsletters.*

Museums/Libraries

Dr. M. Jeanne Youngson
Count Dracula Permanent Collection of
Vampire Memorabilia
29 Washington Square West
New York, NY 10011-9180
ph: 212-982-6754
*Figurines, posters, games, pulps,
autographed photos of Lugosi,
Hamilton Deane, Karloff, Langella,
Kinski, Price, Cushing, Lanchester,*

*etc., original art, early playbills; also
Frankenstein and Wolfman memorabilia.*

Frankenstein

Museums/Libraries

Dr. M. Jeanne Youngson
Count Dracula Permanent Collection of
Vampire Memorabilia
29 Washington Square West
New York, NY 10011-9180
ph: 212-982-6754
*Figurines, posters, games, pulps,
autographed photos of Lugosi,
Hamilton Deane, Karloff, Langella,
Kinski, Price, Cushing, Lanchester,
etc., original art, early playbills; also
Frankenstein and Wolfman memora-
bilia.*

Wolfman

Museums/Libraries

Dr. M. Jeanne Youngson
Count Dracula Permanent Collection of
Vampire Memorabilia
29 Washington Square West
New York, NY 10011-9180
ph: 212-982-6754
*Figurines, posters, games, pulps,
autographed photos of Lugosi,
Hamilton Deane, Karloff, Langella,
Kinski, Price, Cushing, Lanchester,
etc., original art, early playbills; also
Frankenstein and Wolfman memora-
bilia.*

HORSE RACING

(see SPORTS COLLECTIBLES,
Thoroughbred Racing)

HORSE-DRAWN VEHICLES

(see also FARM COLLECTIBLES;
FARM MACHINERY; ANIMAL
COLLECTIBLES, Horse-Related)

Auction Services

Paul Martin, Jr.
Martin Auctioneers, Inc.
12 North Railroad Ave.
P.O. Box 99
New Holland, PA 17557
ph: 717-354-6671
fax: 717-354-8248
martinauctioneer@frontiernet.net
http://www.martinauctioneers.com
*Specializes in the sale of horse drawn
carriages, buggies, hitch wagons, tack
and other horse-related items; buys
and sells through private transactions
and public auction; will buy complete
collections or single pieces.*

Larry Garner
Garner Realty & Auctioneers
332 S. Lison St.
P.O. Box 323
Carrollton, OH 44615
ph: 800-452-8452 or 330-627-5573
fax: 330-627-3788
larrygarner@bright.net
http://www.garner-acutioneers.com
*Conducts auctions of horse-drawn
carriages, buggies, hitch wagons, tack
and other horse-related items.*

Dealers

Horse-Drawn Carriages
P.O. Box 1392
Santa Rosa, CA 95402-1392
*Wants horse-drawn wagons, fifth
wheel wagons, light delivery wagons,
stagecoaches, etc.*

Periodicals

Thom Mezick
Magazine: Driving Digest Magazine
211 West Main St.
P.O. Box 110
New London, OH 44851-0110
ph: 419-929-6781
fax: 419-929-3800
thom@drivingdigest.com
http://www.drivingdigest.com
*A magazine for horsemen interested in
competitive driving of a single horse,
pairs and four-in-hands.*

Draft Horse Journal, Inc.
Magazine: Draft Horse Journal
P.O. Box 670
Waverly, IA 50677
ph: 319-352-4046
fax: 319-352-2232
horshoes@horseshoes.com
http://www.horseshoes.com
*A trade magazine of the Draft Horse
and Mule Industry; present day uses
along with historical material; horses,
mules, and equipment advertised.*

Repro. Sources

Cumberland General Store
657 Old Mountain Rd.
Marietta, GA 30064-1339
ph: 770-427-6434
fax: 770-422-8807
info@cumberlandgeneral.com
http://www.cumberlandgeneral.com

Carriages

Auction Services

Paul Martin, Jr.
Martin Auctioneers, Inc.
12 North Railroad Ave.
P.O. Box 99
New Holland, PA 17557
ph: 717-354-6671
fax: 717-354-8248
martinauctioneer@frontiernet.net
http://www.martinauctioneers.com
*Specializes in the sale of horse drawn
carriages, buggies, hitch wagons, tack
and other horse-related items; buys
and sells through private transactions*

*and public auction; will buy complete
collections or single pieces.*

Clubs/Associations

Jill Ryder, Ed. Dir.
Carriage Association of America, The
Journal: Carriage Journal, The
177 Pointers-Auburn Rd.
Salem, NJ 08079
ph: 856-935-1616 or 856-935-2547
fax: 865-935-9362
carrassc@mindspring.com
http://www.caaonline.com
*Founded in 1960; devoted to the
knowledge, collecting, restoring,
driving and research of horse-drawn
vehicles; more than 3,500 members in
25 countries.*

American Driving Society
Newsletter: Whip, The
P.O. Box 160
Metamora, MI 48455
ph: 810-664-8666
fax: 810-664-2405
info@americandrivingsociety.org
http://www.americandrivingsociety.org
*Promotes the sport of carriage driving
and horse training for sport and
pleasure; articles, ads, competitions,
carriage maintenance.*

Mrs. Jenny Dillon, Sec.
British Driving Society, The
Newsletter: British Driving Society
Newsletter
27 Dugard Place
Barford, Warwick CV35 8DX U.K.
ph: 01926 624420
fax: 01926 624633
*Focuses on carriage driving and horse
training.*

Collectors

Peter Morris
2 Lisa Court
Hammonds Plains, NS B4B 1K4 Canada
ph: 902-835-7692
*Wants to buy all Canadian horse-
drawn vehicle trade catalogs, very
early (c. 1860s) American horse-
drawn vehicle trade catalogs, and
other very early trade catalogs.*

Museums/Libraries

Long Island Museum of American Art,
History & Carriages
Newsletter: News & Events
1200 Route 25A
Stony Brook, NY 11790-1992
ph: 631-751-0066
fax: 631-751-0353
mail@longislandmuseum.org
http://www.longislandmuseum.org
*Large collection of American Art,
decoys, horse-drawn vehicles,
costumes, and miniature period
rooms; museum shop.*

Susan Green
Carriage Museum of America-Library
P.O. Box 417
Bird In Hand, PA 17505
ph: 717-656-7019
fax: 717-656-6251
susangreen@carriagemuseumlibrary.org
http://www.carriagemuseumlibrary.org
*A research library that serves as a
source for historically accurate
technical information on horse-drawn
vehicles and related subjects; books on
technical information for horse-drawn
vehicles: engineering drawings,
colored plates, etc.*

Rose Hill Manor
1611 N. Market St.
Frederick, MD 21701
ph: 301-694-1650
*Established in 1976 from the Robert
H. Renneberger collection, Rose Hill
Manor exhibits a variety of restored
carriages and sleighs.*

Henry Ford Museum & Greenfield
Village
20900 Oakwood Blvd.
P.O. Box 1970
Dearborn, MI 48121-1970
ph: 313-982-6001 or 313-271-1620
fax: 313-271-9621
info@hfmgv.org
http://www.hfmgv.org
Over 100 horse-drawn vehicles.

Periodicals

Magazine: Carriage Driving World
P.O. Box 36
Springtown, TX 76082
ph: 817-523-4111
fax: 817-523-4111
editor@carriagedrivingworld.com
http://www.carriagedrivingworld.com
*A bi-monthly magazine about carriage
driving for carriage driving
enthusiasts.*

Repair Services

Old World Wheel Works
12252 Highway 41 N.
Evansville, IN 47725
ph: 800-430-8747
http://www.gazebos.com/wheel.html
*Specializes in the repair and
restoration of horse drawn carriages
and buggies; reproductions, custom
made-to-order parts.*

HORSES

(see also ANIMAL COLLECTIBLES,
Horse Related; LIVESTOCK)

Appraisers

Stephanie S. Thiele
Path Valley Manor Stables
3624 Path Valley Rd.
Fort Loudon, PA 17224
ph: 717-369-0102
fax: 717-369-0026
EquineAppraisal@aol.com
*Appraises horses for insurance and
tax purposes, divorces, loans,
bankruptcies, establishing and/or
dissolving business partnerships,
donations, purchasing & selling, etc.;
familiar with a variety of breeds.*

Jay Proost
American Society of Agricultural
Appraisers, Inc.
834 Falls Ave., Ste. 1130
P.O. Box 186
Twin Falls, ID 83303-0186
ph: 208-733-2323 or 800-488-7570
fax: 208-733-2326
ag@amagappraisers.com
http://www.amagappraisers.com
*Members of this society's "Society of
Equine Appraisers" division appraise
horses.*

Auction Services

Professional Auction Services, Inc.
P.O. Box 1399
Leesburg, VA 20177
ph: 800-240-7900 or 703-777-6975
fax: 703-777-5580
pasinc@aol.com
http://professionalauction.com
*One of America's leading show horse
auction companies.*

Shipshewana Auction, Inc.
345 S. Van Buren St.
P.O. Box 185
Shipshewana, IN 46565
ph: 219-768-4129
tradingplace@shipshenet.com
http://www.tradingplaceamerica.com

HOTEL COLLECTIBLES

(see also HIGHWAY
COLLECTIBLES; SOUVENIR &
COMMEMORATIVE ITEMS;
TRAILERS & RVs)

Collectors

Larry Spilkin
P.O. Box 5039
Southfield, MI 48086-5039
ph: 248-642-3722
*Wants postcards and matchbook
covers of drive-ins, diners, cafes, gas
stations and 1930s-1950s motels,
restaurant/bar, cabins and Art Deco
streamline hotels.*

Hyatt Hotels

Collectors

Michael Hickey
1512 Chasewood Dr.
Austin, TX 78727
ph: 512-989-0188
fax: 512-989-0112
*Collects anything to do with Hyatt
Hotels & Resorts (has over 1,600
Hyatt items)!*

HOUSEWARES

(see ELECTRICITY RELATED
ITEMS, Appliances; KITCHEN
COLLECTIBLES)

HUMIDORS

(see SMOKING COLLECTIBLES)

HUMMELS

(see COLLECTIBLES [MODERN],
Figurines [Goebel]; FIGURINES,
Hummel)

HUNTING & FISHING

(see ANIMAL TROPHIES; ART,
Sporting; ART, Wildlife; CAMPING
EQUIPMENT; DECOYS;
ENDANGERED SPECIES;
FIREARMS; FISHING
COLLECTIBLES; LICENSES, Hunting
& Fishing; MAGAZINES, Sporting;
TARGET SHOOTING MEMORABILIA;
TICKETS; TRAP SHOOTING; TRAP

**Here are some tips
when contacting
someone who is listed
in this book:**

When requesting
information about a
particular item, include
a description (material,
dimensions, maker's
mark, model number,
etc.) and a photo,
sketch, digital image or
photocopy of the item
in question.

Always ask if there are
charges for samples or
for the services that
you are requesting.

When corresponding
by letter, please be
sure to include a Large
(#10 business size)
Self-Addressed and
Stamped Envelope
(LSASE) if requesting a
reply or the return of
photographs.

Never call collect
unless otherwise
directed. When
calling, be considerate
of time zone differ-
ences and always ask
if the party you are
calling has time to talk.
When leaving an
answering machine
message, always
instruct the party to
call you back collect.

ICE CREAM COLLECTIBLES

(see also ICE INDUSTRY; MOLDS, Ice Cream; SODA FOUNTAIN COLLECTIBLES)

Clubs/Associations

Donald D. Snyder
Ice Screamers, The
Newsletter: Ice Screamer, The
P.O. Box 465
Warrington, PA 18976-0465
ph: 215-343-2676
smoothsail@aol.com
http://www.icescreamers.com
For anyone who likes ice cream, who wants to learn more about the history of ice cream or who collects ice cream/soda fountain memorabilia.

Collectors

Ed Marks
521 West Second Ave., Ste. 1008
Lititz, PA 17543
ph: 717-625-6167
fax: 717-569-0220
paka2@ptd.net
http://www.icecreamhistorian.info
Ice cream collector and historian; wants ice cream ephemera, books, pamphlets, and any other printed material relating to ice cream.

Mary & Gus Brunner
2209 Township Rd.
Quakertown, PA 18951-3344
ph: 610-346-6650
Wants to buy ice cream scoops, tip trays, and pre-1930 ice cream memorabilia.

Donald D. Snyder
P.O. Box 465
Warrington, PA 18976-0465
ph: 215-343-2676
smoothsail@aol.com
Collector of ice cream related memorabilia.

Dealers

Bill & Anne Shaner
Shaner's Antiques & Collectibles
403 N. Charlotte St.
Pottstown, PA 19464-5311
ph: 610-326-0165
Wants ONLY Burdans Ice Cream items such as trays, signs, ads, and paper.

Experts

Ed Marks
521 West Second Ave., Ste. 1008
Lititz, PA 17543
ph: 717-625-6167
fax: 717-569-0220
paka2@ptd.net
http://www.icecreamhistorian.info
Author of "Ice Cream Collectibles;" 160 pages with 525 pictures and prices covering 26 categories of the most popular ice cream collectibles; order from author for $29.50.

Allan Mellis
Mr. Ice Cream
1115 West Montana
Chicago, IL 60614-2220
ph: 773-327-9123
fax: 773-327-9456
mellisfamily@rcn.com
Wants all graphically pleasing ice cream and soda fountain items: postcards, ice cream tip trays, and ice cream related watch fobs, magazines (pre-1925), valentines, pin-back buttons, trade cards, pre-1920 ephemera, supply catalogs, etc.

Dippers

Collectors

Billy Sprague
2009 Cedarmont Dr.
Franklin, TN 37067
billyscoop@aol.com
Wants to buy unusual ice cream dippers.

Chris Potts
8104 Fontana St.
Prairie Village, KS 66208
ph: 913-642-8269
cpotts8104@aol.com
Long time buyer of old ice cream scoops with a special interest in the rare and unusual scoops.

Danny Saleh
1520 Clubview Dr.
Tyler, TX 75701
ph: 903-595-6465
Wants to buy ice cream scoops (dippers).

Steve Elliott
1600 Tennessee St.
Vallejo, CA 94590-4629
ph: 707-552-8400 or 707-642-1949
fax: 707-552-0881
Wants to buy old ice cream scoops.

Dealers

Mike & Judi Powers
Memory Peddlers
6 Loubier Dr.
Essex Junction, VT 05452
ph: 802-878-8701
memorypdlr@aol.com
Collector, dealer, expert buys and sells rare and unusual ice cream scoops/dippers.

Experts

Mike & Judi Powers
Memory Peddlers
6 Loubier Dr.
Essex Junction, VT 05452
ph: 802-878-8701
memorypdlr@aol.com
Collector, dealer, expert buys and sells rare and unusual ice cream scoops/dippers.

Wayne Smith
P.O. Box 418
Walkersville, MD 21793-0418
ph: 301-845-6066
Author of "Ice Cream Dippers," an illustrated history and collectors guide to early ice cream dippers; $23.90 from author; send LSASE for free brochure entitled "An Introduction to Collecting Ice Cream Dippers."

ICE INDUSTRY

Collectors

Thom & Lucia Lucia
ICEBOX Memories
2145 Wilbraham Rd.
Springfield, MA 01129-1806
icebox@tiac.net
http://www.tiac.net/users/icebox
Wants to buy ice business memorabilia: ice cards, shavers, ice tongs, crushers, advertising, ice tools, ice picks with ice company names, photos, etc.; send asking price and description.

Joe Pedro
9 Whitcomb Ave.
Ayer, MA 01432-1627
ph: 978-772-2971
icetools2@ourweb.net
Wants ice memorabilia: signs, paper, tokens, photos, badges, watches, fobs, tools, delivery bags, picks, axes; anything to do with the ice business.

City Ice Co.
475 N. Main St.
Janesville, WI 53545
ph: 608-754-6619
Wants ice harvesting tools and ice items: plows, markers, fork bars, chisels, splitting bars, pictures, books, catalogs on ice harvesting.

John E. Somers
4524 Rialto Place
Stockton, CA 95207
ph: 209-477-1662
Wants ice tongs, picks, signs, bottles, scales, crushers, shavers; anything to do with the ice business.

Museums/Libraries

Ice House Museum
303 Franklin St.
Cedar Falls, IA 50613-2747
ph: 319-266-5149
fax: 319-268-1812
dschmitz@cfu.net
http://www.cedarfallshistorical.org/ics_house_museum.htm
Focuses on ice harvesting on the Cedar River.

ICONS

(see also RUSSIAN ITEMS)

Appraisers

Tad Sviderskis
Icon Painting, Restoration, Expertise & Appraisals
1298 Indian Mountain Lakes
Albrightsville, PA 18210-3119
ph: 800-510-9799 or 570-643-8732
fax: 570-643-8730
sviders@aol.com
Specializing in appraisals of 14th to 19th century Russian and Greek icon painting; provides documented reports in compliance with the Uniform Standards of Professional Appraisal Practice; serving collectors and museums.

Dealers

Don E. Springer
Slava Gallery
P.O. Box 2893
Fairfax, VA 22301
ph: 703-323-6185 or 800-210-0113
slavagal@fcc.net
http://www.slavagal.com
Collector, dealer, expert in icons: Russian, Orthodox Church, Eastern Church, Byzantine; also offers icon restoration service.

James L. Jackson, ISA
Jackson's Sacred Heart
2229 Lincoln St.
P.O. Box 50613
Cedar Falls, IA 50613
ph: 319-277-2256
fax: 319-277-1252
jacksons@jacksonsauction.com
http://www.jacksonsauction.com
Specializing in quality 17th, 18th and 19th century Russian icons and related items; quarterly full color catalog offering Russian icons and related items.

Experts

Tad Sviderskis
Icon Painting, Restoration, Expertise & Appraisals
1298 Indian Mountain Lakes
Albrightsville, PA 18210-3119
ph: 800-510-9799 or 570-643-8732
fax: 570-643-8730
sviders@aol.com
Specializing in professional conservation, restoration treatment of ancient icon painting; consolidation of

deteriorated paint layer, grounding, cleaning of grime & darkened varnish; services televised nationwide; video tape available.

James L. Jackson, ISA
Jackson's Sacred Heart
2229 Lincoln St.
P.O. Box 50613
Cedar Falls, IA 50613
ph: 319-277-2256
fax: 319-277-1252
jacksons@jacksonsauction.com
http://www.jacksonsauction.com
Has written and lectured widely on Russian icons, and has traveled extensively throughout Russia and the former Soviet Union studying Russian icons.

Museums/Libraries

Dr. Gary Vikan
Walters Art Museum
600 N. Charles St.
Baltimore, MD 21201
ph: 410-547-9000
klavin@thewalters.org
http://www.thewalters.org
One of only a few museums worldwide to present a comprehensive history of art from the third millennium B.C. to the early 20th century.

Repair Services

Tad Sviderskis
Icon Painting, Restoration, Expertise & Appraisals
1298 Indian Mountain Lakes
Albrightsville, PA 18210-3119
ph: 800-510-9799 or 570-643-8732
fax: 570-643-8730
sviders@aol.com
Specializing in professional conservation, restoration treatment of ancient icon painting; consolidation of deteriorated paint layer, grounding, cleaning of grime & darkened varnish; services televised nationwide; video tape available.

Don E. Springer
Slava Gallery
P.O. Box 2893
Fairfax, VA 22301
ph: 703-323-6185 or 800-210-0113
slavagal@fcc.net
http://www.slavagal.com
Collector, dealer, expert in icons: Russian, Orthodox Church, Eastern Church, Byzantine; also offers icon restoration service.

ILLUSTRATORS

(see also ART; BOOKS, Illustrated; MAGAZINES; PAINTINGS & DRAWINGS; PAPER COLLECTIBLES, Illustrated; PERSONALITIES [ARTISTS]; PIN-UP ART; PRINTS)

Auction Services

Robert Lifson
Robert Edward Auctions
P.O. Box 7256
Watchung, NJ 07069
ph: 908-226-9900 or 800-766-9324
fax: 908-226-9920
reaauct@aol.com
http://www.robertedwardauctions.com
Specializes in the auction sale of historical Americana, political material, autographs and manu-scripts, and original illustration art.

Walter A. Reed
Illustration House
96 Spring St., 7th Floor
New York, NY 10012-3923
ph: 212-966-9444
fax: 212-966-9425
info@illustrationhouse.com
http://www.illustrationhouse.com
Conducts specialized auctions for original illustrative paintings and drawings dating from the late 19th to mid-20th centuries.

James Halperin
Heritage Galleries & Auctioneers
Dallas, TX 75219
ph: 800-872-6467 or 214-528-3500
fax: 214-520-7108
auctions@HeritageGalleries.com
http://www.HeritageGalleries.com
Specializes in buying and selling illustrator art; auctioneers of The Famous American Illustrators collection.

Collectors

Charles Martignette
P.O. Box 293
Hallandale, FL 33008-0293
ph: 954-454-3474
American illustration art historian wants to buy original illustration artwork: original paintings and drawings, magazine front-cover art, magazine story illustrations, advertising art; please send photos, dimensions, price.

Timothy F. Isaacson
1002 Clinton
Oak Park, IL 60304
ph: 708-383-5646
moeknows1007@msn.com
Wants to buy original (cover) paintings; paintings that were used for the cover art for pulps, magazines, paperback and digest books, and movie posters: lurid, sleazy dames, hard boiled detective action, sexy gals, monsters, sci-fi, etc.

Wendy Hoffman
Wendy Hoffman Gallery
Mission Rd. Antique Mall
4101 W. 83rd St.
Shawnee Mission, KS 66208
ph: 702-839-9999
fax: 702-839-9494
wendysart@aol.com
http://www.wendysart.com
Wants to buy art by illustrators Fox,

Parrish, Gutmann, Humphrey; Esquire magazines with Vargas gatefolds; pin-up calendars/prints by Elvgren, Moran, Mozert and Armstrong; sporting calendars/prints by Goodwin, Stick, etc.

Wendy Hoffman
Wendy Hoffman Gallery
P.O. Box 35647
Las Vegas, NV 89133-5647
ph: 702-839-9999
fax: 702-839-9494
wendysart@aol.com
http://www.wendysart.com
Wants to buy art by illustrators Fox, Parrish, Gutmann, Humphrey; Esquire magazines with Vargas gatefolds; pin-up calendars/prints by Elvgren, Moran, Mozert and Armstrong; sporting calendars/prints by Goodwin, Stick, etc.

Danny Eskenazi
Jack Hammer Ltd.
ph: 206-679-5777
desk@nwlink.com
Wants to buy 1900s original American illustration paintings.

Dealers

Joan Jenkins
4 Henchman St., unit #8
Boston, MA 02113-1445
ph: 617-742-2345
JollyJoan@aol.com
Buys and sells illustrator art by Parrish, Fox, Thompson, Icart, Pressler, Goodwin, Gutmann, and Indian Maidens.

Kendra Krienke
140 Ashley Place
Park Ridge, NJ 07656
ph: 201-930-9709
fax: 201-930-9765
kendraart@mac.com
Specializes in original vintage illustrative art: watercolors, drawings, and oils; for children and fantasy 1880 through 1950 including Arthur Rackham, Edmund Dulac, Harrison Cady, etc.

Judy Goffman Cutler
American Illustrators Gallery
18 East 77th St.
New York, NY 10021
ph: 212-744-5190
fax: 212-744-0128
art@americanillustrators.com
http://www.americanillustrators.com
Specializing in paintings, watercolors and drawings from the "Golden Age" of American illustration 1880-1940.

Matt Iarocci
Matt's
P.O. Box 290H
Scarsdale, NY 10583-8790
ph: 914-472-6361
Buys and sells original illustrator art; done for magazine covers, stories, pulps, ads, calendars, posters, comics, etc.; subjects include Western,

adventure, fashion, pin-up, horror, sports, movies, travel.

Jordan Bermer
Illustrated Gallery, The
400 Commerce Dr., Ste. B
Fort Washington, PA 19034
ph: 215-2646-5466 or 214-740-0205
tig@illustratedgallery.com
http://www.illustratedgallery.com
Focuses on the golden age of original illustrated art 1900 to 1960: John Clyner, Steven Dohanos, Bernie Fuchs, Maud Humphrey, Mort Kunstler, J.C. Leyendecker, Tom Lovell, Norman Rockwell, Andrew Loomis, Dick Sargent, Ben Stahl and others.

Jo Ann Reisler
360 Glyndon St., NE
Vienna, VA 22180-3537
ph: 703-938-2967
fax: 703-938-9057
email@joannreisler.com
http://www.joannreisler.com
Wants to buy fine and unusual children's, illustrated books, and illustrative art; issues about four color catalogs per year with almost all items in stock illustrated; sample catalog for $15.

John Cosgriff
American Illustration
204 Wickham Dr.
Schaumburg, IL 60194
ph: 847-882-0839
fax: 847-882-1245
pulpmonger@aol.com
Buys and sells original artwork done for magazines, books, advertising, and comic strips; also buys and sells illustrated books, magazines, newspapers, comic strips and comic books; over 25 years experience selling ephemera.

Jeff Mark
JMARK
P.O. Box 5178
Santa Monica, CA 90409-5178
ph: 800-644-8537
fax: 310-396-2666
bigjoho@hotmail.com
Wants to buy original illustration art for comic books & other publications, especially cover art from 1880 to 1980: science fiction, pin-up, mystery, Americana, pulps, Disney, Wild West; special interest in R. Crumb, Underground Comix art.

Internet Resources

Denis C. Jackson, Ed.
E-zine: Illustrator Collector's News, The
P.O. Box 6433
Kingman, AZ 86401
ticn@olypen.com
http://www.olypen.com/ticn
An online publication for collectors of magazines and other paper illustra-tions; free classifieds and articles, no charge Web site information; new and old prints.

Museums/Libraries

Society of Illustrators Museum of
American Illustration
128 E. 63rd. St.
New York, NY 10021
ph: 212-838-2560
fax: 212-838-2561
society@societyillustrators.org
http://www.societyillustrators.org
*Permanent collection of the Society is
the home for hundreds of works of art
by many of the greatest names in
American painting and illustration.*

Arthur Szyk

Clubs/Associations

Irvin Ungar
Arthur Szyk Society, Inc.
Newsletter: Arthur Szyk Newsletter
1200 Edgehill Dr.
Burlingame, CA 90410
ph: 650-343-9588
fax: 650-579-6014
szyksociety@szyk.com
http://www.szyk.com
*Arthur Szyk (1894-1951, artist,
miniaturist, illuminator, illustrator) is
regarded as the greatest miniature
painter and illustrator of his times;
newsletter published six timer per
year.*

Bessie Pease Gutmann

Collectors

George & Janice Parola
43 Oakfield Ave.
Freeport, NY 11520-1935
ph: 516-868-8439
fax: 516-379-1534
georgejanp@aol.com
*Wants Bessie Pease Gutmann prints,
magazine covers, postcards,
calendars, etc.; also Meta Grimball
and Eda Doench.*

Dr. Victor J.W. Christie
Cheshire Cat, The
1050 West Main St.
Ephrata, PA 17522
ph: 717-738-4032
thecheshirecat@onemain.com
*Wants to buy prints, illustrated books,
postcards, calendars, etc. done by the
artists Bessie Pease Gutmann, Meta
M. Grimball, ad Eda S. Doench.*

Eleanor Popelka
124 Elizabeth Harrison Lane
Williamsburg, VA 23188
ph: 757-258-1713
popedel@msn.com
*Collector of prints, postcards,
magazine covers, books and calendars
illustrated by Bessie Pease Gutmann,
Meta Grimball, and Eda Doench; no
reproductions, please.*

Jim & Sharon Eckert
P.O. Box 62
Colfax, IL 61728-0062
ph: 309-723-4241
anchorsb@mtco.com
*Wants Wallace Nutting, Bessie Pease
Gutmann prints.*

Dealers

Edward J. Meschi
129 Pinyard Rd.
Monroeville, NJ 08343-1870
ph: 856-358-7293
fax: 856-358-7789
ed@meschiarts.com
http://www.meschiarts.com
*Buying paintings, calendars, original
works of art.*

Coles Phillips

Experts

Denis C. Jackson
P.O. Box 6433
Kingman, AZ 86401
ticn@olypen.com
http://www.olypen.com/ticn
*Covered magazines from 1900 to
1926; author of "The Price & ID
Guide to Coles Phillips," 2nd
Edition; send LSASE for information.*

Fern Bisel Peat

Collectors

Cathy Cook
10 E. 13th St., #2D
New York, NY 10003-4467
ph: 212-691-2406
fax: 212-691-2406
ccook710@aol.com
*Collector interested in buying, selling
and trading books, paper dolls,
puzzles, tin-lithographed toys, etc. by
children's illustrator Fern Bisel Peat.*

Experts

David W. Peat
1225 Carroll White
Indianapolis, IN 46219-3907
ph: 317-357-6895
typenut@comcast.net
http://www.davidpeat.com
*Wants books, tin toys, other metal or
paper children's items from 1927-1947
illustrated by my aunt, Fern Bisel
Peat.*

Periodicals

Peggy Welch Mershon
Newsletter: Fern Bisel Peat Newsletter
105 Main St., Apt. W
Bellville, OH 44813
marwelmer@aol.com
http://www.fernbiselpeat.com
*Fern Bisel Peat (1893-1971) is a
highly regarded illustrator of
children's books (Saalfield, Harter),
toys (Ohio Art), and magazines
(Children's Play Mate); newsletter
published quarterly and dedicated to
the legacy of Fern Bisel Peat.*

Grace Drayton

Experts

G.L. Wine
649 Bayview Dr.
Akron, OH 44319-1502
*Researcher who specializes in the life
and art of Campbell Kids' creator,
Grace G. Drayton.*

Harrison Fisher

(see also POSTCARDS)

Clubs/Associations

Deena M. Zachritz, Dir.
Harrison Fisher Society, The
Newsletter: Harrison Fisher Society
Newsletter
123 N. Glassell
Orange, CA 92666
ph: 714-633-5206
fax: 714-633-5726
*The Society gathers and researches
references and works by or about
Harrison Fisher.*

Experts

Naomi Welch
Images of the Past
309 Playa Blvd., Ste. 110
La Selva Beach, CA 95076-1737
ph: 831-689-0318
naomilaurawelch@sprintmail.com
*Collector, dealer, expert specializes in
Harrison Fisher; author of two books,
published in 1999, entitled "The
Complete Works of Harrison Fisher
Illustrator," and "American &
European Postcards of Harrison
Fisher Illustrator."*

Hy Hintermeister

Clubs/Associations

Carole Schwartz
Hy Hintermeister Collectors Group
Newsletter: Hy H Notes
5 Pasture Rd.
Whitehouse Station, NJ 08889-3357
ph: 908-236-9675
HYHNOTESed@worldnet.att.net
*Brings together collectors of
Hintermeister illustration art.*

Collectors

Hugh Hetzer
209 Homevale Rd.
Reisterstown, MD 21136
ph: 410-833-5170
hhetzer@prodigy.net

Dealers

Jo Havens-Wright
Wright Enterprises
610 N. Delaware Ave.
Roswell, NM 88201-2135
ph: 505-623-8053
johavens@dfn.com
http://www.dfn.com/~johavens
*Specializes in Hy Hintermeister and
William M. Thompson prints but also
carries others.*

J.C. & F.X. Leyendecker

Experts

Denis C. Jackson
P.O. Box 6433
Kingman, AZ 86401
ticn@olypen.com
http://www.olypen.com/ticn
*Specializes in illustrators from 1890s
through 1950s; author of "The Price
Guide to JC & FX Leyendecker" 3rd
edition; 350 Saturday Evening Post
covers listed and valued; send LSASE
for information.*

Joan Walsh Anglund

Experts

Ann C. Bergin
P.O. Box 105
Amherst, NH 03031-0105
fax: 978-649-6807
acbergin@aol.com
*Working on a book of Anglund
collectibles; seeks pictures of Joan
Walsh Anglund items.*

Periodicals

Ann C. Bergin
Newsletter: Joan Walsh Anglund
Collectors News
P.O. Box 105
Amherst, NH 03031-0105
fax: 978-649-6807
acbergin@aol.com
*An annual newsletter containing
information on children's book
illustrator Joan Walsh Anglund; free
buy, sell ad for subscribers.*

Kate Greenaway

Clubs/Associations

Dr. James Lewis Lowe, Dir.
Kate Greenaway Society
P.O. Box 8
Norwood, PA 19074
ph: 610-485-8572
PostcardClassics@juno.com
http://www.Deltiologists-America.com

Maxfield Parrish

Appraisers

Michelle Ferretta
Maxfield Parrish Collectibles
1314 Oak St.
Alameda, CA 94501-4506
ph: 510-522-1823
mpferretta@aol.com
*Dealer, expert buys and sells Maxfield
Parrish; in business over 28 years;
large collection in stock; vintage
prints, books, calendars, advertising,
estate items, original artwork; has
done Maxfield Parrish appraisals for
over 20 years.*

Collectors

John Buonaguidi
540 Reeside Ave.
Monterey, CA 93940-1828
ph: 831-375-7345
sportmsm@redshift.com
Wants to buy Maxfield Parrish

collectibles including calendars, posters, books, advertising items, paintings, prints, etc. - anything Parrish!

Dealers

John S. Zuk
106 Orchard St.
Belmont, MA 02478-2940
ph: 617-484-4800 or 617-588-5709
fax: 810-283-5371
Buys and sells Maxfield Parrish prints, books, and originals (pen & ink, watercolor, etc.); premium paid for Edison Mazda calendars, lamp testers, etc.

Hugh Alan Luch Collections, The
P.O. Box 111
Wenonah, NJ 08090
ph: 609-464-9751
Buys and sells illustrator and holiday collectibles with emphasis on Maxfield Parrish and Halloween.

Edward J. Meschi
129 Pinyard Rd.
Monroeville, NJ 08343-1870
ph: 856-358-7293
fax: 856-358-7789
ed@meschiarts.com
http://www.meschiarts.com
Buys and sells Maxfield Parrish prints and paintings.

John Walkowiak
3452 Humbolt Ave. S.
Minneapolis, MN 55408-3332
ph: 612-824-0785
Maxfield Parrish prints, books, calendars, advertising, reference items, posters, and other items bought and sold.

Michelle Ferretta
Maxfield Parrish Collectibles
1314 Oak St.
Alameda, CA 94501-4506
ph: 510-522-1823
mpferretta@aol.com
Dealer, expert buys and sells Maxfield Parrish; in business over 28 years; large collection in stock; vintage prints, books, calendars, advertising, estate items, original artwork; has done Maxfield Parrish appraisals for over 20 years.

Christine Daniels
Christine Daniels Antiques
135 E. Shiloh Rd.
Santa Rosa, CA 95403-1254
ph: 707-838-6083
fax: 707-838-6083
ctiques@aol.com
Buys and sells art: Maxfield Parrish, early California oil paintings.

Experts

Bill Holland
William Holland Fine Arts
1554 Paoli Pike
PMB #300
West Chester, PA 19380
ph: 610-344-9848
fax: 610-344-0651
bill@hollandarts.com
http://www.hollandarts.com
Buys and sells Parrish art prints, calendars, posters, advertising items, books, and magazine covers; author of "The Collectible Maxfield Parrish," $60 ppd.

John Goodspeed Stuart
Parrish House, The
1740 Marion St.
Denver, CO 80218-1121
ph: 303-831-0055
fax: 303-831-4901
jgstuart@aol.com
http://www.parrish-house.com
Buys, sells, appraises and specializes in Maxfield Parrish prints, books, etc.; send for free price list; author of "Young Maxfield Parrish" and "The Art of MAxfield Parrish."

Denis C. Jackson
P.O. Box 6433
Kingman, AZ 86401
ticn@olypen.com
http://www.olypen.com/ticn
Maxfield Parrish prints, calendars, books, magazines; author of "The Price and Identification Guide to Maxfield Parrish" 11th edition; send LSASE for information.

Norman Rockwell

(see also COLLECTIBLES [MODERN], Norman Rockwell)

Clubs/Associations

Michael J.P. Collins, Pres.
Rockwell Society of America
Newsletter: Rockwell Society of America Newsletter
P.O. Box 705
Ardsley, NY 10502-0705
Founded in 1974 and dedicated to the appreciation of America's most famous artist, Norman Rockwell; specializing in original paintings, drawings, collectibles, e.g., Saturday Evening Post covers/magazines, illustrated books, etc.

Dealers

Marshall Stoltz, Cur.
Rockwell Gallery Collection of Norman Rockwell Art
P.O. Box 126
Huntingdon Valley, PA 19006-0126
ph: 215-969-5619
fax: 215-969-6466
stoltzmarsh@snip.net
http://www.rockwellsite.com
Sells new prints and posters based on the works of Norman Rockwell.

Experts

Denis C. Jackson
P.O. Box 6433
Kingman, AZ 86401
ticn@olypen.com
http://www.olypen.com/ticn
Magazines and paper items from 1914 to present; author of "The Price Guide to Norman Rockwell," 4th edition; send LSASE for information.

Museums/Libraries

Norman Rockwell Museum at Stockbridge, The
Route 183
Stockbridge, MA 01262
ph: 413-298-4100 or 800-298-9450
postmaster@nrm.org
http://www.nrm.org
Exhibiting the world's largest collection of original Rockwell art, the museum preservers and studies the life, art and spirit of Rockwell's work; Museum offers limited edition prints signed by Normal Rockwell for sale.

Laurie Buckholt, Manager
Museum of Norman Rockwell Art
227 S. Park St.
Reedsburg, WI 53959-1945
ph: 608-524-2123
fax: 608-524-0611
Private museum with gift shop.

Palmer Cox

Experts

Wayne Morgan
69 Main St. East
Grimsby, Ontario L3M 1N5 Canada
ph: 905-945-5754
fax: 905-945-5768
morgan.modculture@sympatico.ca
Advice on Palmer Cox (1840-1924) author/illustrator famous for The Brownie's books and others; illustrator Dudley Ward (1879-1935) (developed The Dingbats for commercial use); illustrators of Mounties in popular culture, ephemera, prints.

Museums/Libraries

McGill University Libraries, Dept. of Rare Books & Special Collections
3459 McTavish St.
Montreal, QC H3A 2K6 Canada
ph: 514-398-4711
fax: 514-398-5143
webmaster.library@mcgill.ca
http://www.library.mcgill.ca/rarebook/cube.htm
Extensive collection of Canadian-born children's author and book illustrator Palmer Cox (1840-1924); Cox was the author of the famous Brownie books: drawings and other illustrative work, sketchbook from 1864-1865, and more.

Philip Boileau

Clubs/Associations

Karen Gamlin
Philip Boileau Collector's Society
Newsletter: PBCS Newsletter
1025 Redwood Blvd.
Redding, CA 96003
ph: 530-241-2166
Gamlin@aol.com
http://members.aol.com/PBoileauCC
Founded in 1995; publishes quarterly newsletter; members are collectors of illustrations, art, drawings, postcards by Philip Boileau (1863-1917).

Experts

Karen Gamlin
1025 Redwood Blvd.
Redding, CA 96003
ph: 530-241-2166
Gamlin@aol.com
http://members.aol.com/PBoileauCC
Buys, sells, collects and specializes in illustrations by Philip Boileau (1863-1917).

R. Atkinson Fox

Clubs/Associations

Ron & Cora Grassman
R. Atkinson Fox Society
Newsletter: Fox Tales
635 E. Palm
Altadena, CA 91001
ph: 626-791-8070
ronandcora@earthlink.net

Collectors

Sharon Gergen
8141 Main
Kansas City, MO 64114-2401
ph: 816-361-7530
LovellFam@prodigy.net
Paper and print dealer since 1983; past-President of the R.A. Fox Society; wants to buy illustrations by R. Atkinson Fox, Zula Kenyon, Heibel, Hintermeister, Desch, Coffin, Pressler, Gutmann, Grimball, and others.

Pat Gibson
38280 Guava Dr.
Newark, CA 94560
ph: 510-792-0586
Always looking for any R.A. Fox prints, calendars, oils, postcards, and anything with his work on it.

Experts

Rita Mortenson
727 North Spring
Independence, MO 64050
R. Atkinson Fox (1860-1927) was a Canadian artist. Rita Mortenson is author of "R. Atkinson Fox: His Life and Work" (Vol. I & II.); SASE required for reply.

Ruth E. Newton

Periodicals

Peggy Welch Mershon
Newsletter: Ruth E. Newton Newsletter
105 Main St., Apt. W
Bellville, OH 44813
marwelmer@aol.com
Dedicated to the life and work of artist Ruth E. Newton (1884-1972), who illustrated advertising, greeting cards, children's books; also designed dolls for Sun Rubber (Amosandra, So-Wee, Chunk, Rompy, etc.).

IMMIGRATION

Collectors

Kathy Sheeran
P.O. Box 520251
Miami, FL 33152-0251
Wants photos, documents and passports from pre-1950 immigrants to the US; also wants buttons and ribbons from immigrant groups (A.O.H., Sons of Italy, etc.); also Ellis Island and anti-immigrant items.

Canadian

Collectors

Richard Huntley
11 Hendon Place N.W.
Calgary, Alberta T2K 2A2 Canada
ph: 403-284-1660 or 403-292-5978
lhuntley@telusplanet.net
Wants to buy old Canadian Customs or Canadian Immigration items including documents, uniform items, pins, badges, and photographs; also French Police badges, French gendarme badges.

IMPLEMENT SEATS

(see FARM COLLECTIBLES, Cast Iron Seats)

INAUGURATION ITEMS

(see PERSONALITIES [HISTORICAL]; POLITICAL COLLECTIBLES; WHITE HOUSE MEMORABILIA)

INCOLAY

Collectors

Pat Marsh
915 Glenway Dr.
Saint Louis, MO 63122
ph: 314-965-2150
pattgatt@hotmail.com
Collector on Incolay Stone items; Incolay is a combination of minerals such as quartz, carnelian, onyx, agate combined with hand inlaid white artwork and a hand stratified variegated background; wants Incolay plates, boxes, etc.

INDIA

(see ART, Asian)

INDIAN ITEMS

(see ART, Western; NATIVE AMERICAN; NATIVE AMERICAN, Jewelry; WESTERN AMERICANA)

INDIAN WARS ITEMS

(see also NATIVE AMERICAN; MILITARIA; MILITARY HISTORY)

Clubs/Associations

Jerry L. Russell, Nat. Ch.
Order of the Indian Wars, The
Newsletter: Order of the Indian Wars Communique
P.O. Box 7388
Little Rock, AR 72217
ph: 501-225-3996
milhistory@aristotle.net
http://www.civilwarbuff.org
The only national organization devoted to the study & preservation of Indian Wars history.

Collectors

Thomas W. Pooler
P.O. Box 1861
Grass Valley, CA 95945-1861
ph: 530-268-1338
Wants to buy INDIAN WARS medals and insignia; also wants National and United Indian War Veterans medals, convention ribbons, pins, flags, photos, etc.

INDONESIA

(see also ART, Asian; ORIENTALIA; PHILIPPINES)

Dealers

B.C. Galleries Ancient & Tribal Art
1069 High St.
Armadale, Victoria 3143 Australia
ph: +61 3 9804 3353
fax: +61 3 9804 3353
b.c.galleries@bigpond.com.au
http://www.bcgalleries.com.au
Buys and sells ancient and tribal art: Oceanic, Melanesia, New Guinea, Pacific Islands, Australian Aboriginal, African tribal, tribal arts of Asia and of the Americas.

Antik Indonesia
Jl. Kemuning 4-B no. 8
RT.013 RW.06, Pejaten Timur
Jakarta, 12510 Indonesia
ph: +62-21-794-9435
fax: +62-21-723-4676
general@alabanza.com
http://www.alabanza.com/kamajaya/antik
Specializes in antiques from Indonesia: bead, stone, books, banknotes, clocks, furniture, mask, statue, stamps, textiles, costume,

ceramics, brass and metal work, weapons.

Experts

Dr. Daphne L. Rosenzweig, ISA CAPP
Rosenzweig Associates
P.O. Box 3976
Sarasota, FL 34230-3976
ph: 941-371-4643
fax: 941-342-6893
rosetwig@aol.com
Asian/Islamic art, Japanese prints, jades, Asian ceramics, sculpture, metalworks, cloisonne, scholar's studio objects, ivories, netsuke, paintings, screens, Himalayan, Indian, Southeast Asian Buddhist art, Indian & Persian miniatures.

Borneo

Experts

Michael G. Price
P.O. Box 468
Michigan Center, MI 49254
ph: 517-764-4517
mgprice@acd.net
Wants Philippine picture postcards, photos, magazines, books, maps; also wants items from nearby islands such as Borneo.

INDUSTRIAL DESIGN

(see MODERNISM)

INDUSTRY RELATED ITEMS

(see also BEEKEEPING MEMORABILIA; CONSTRUCTION EQUIPMENT; CRANBERRY INDUSTRY; FARM MACHINERY; FASTENERS; ICE INDUSTRY; LOGGING; MACHINERY & EQUIPMENT; MILLING; MINING; MODERNISM; SCRIP; SOCIAL CAUSES; TOOLS; WHISKEY INDUSTRY ITEMS)

Appraisers

Robert L. Johnson
Whistles in the Woods Museum Services
P.O. Box 309
Chickamauga, GA 30707-0309
ph: 706-375-4326
oldgoat@voy.net
Consultants & booksellers specializing in 1750-1930 historic machinery; power-generation, tools, wood- and metalworking machines, scientific & technical instruments, mining, milling, transportation, logging & lumbering, steam engines, etc.

Clubs/Associations

Elton W. Hall, Ex. Dir.
Early American Industries Association, The
Newsletter: Shavings, The
167 Bakersville Rd.
South Dartmouth, MA 02748-4198
ph: 508-993-4198
eaiainfo@worldnet.att.net
http://www.eaiainfo.org
Interested in old tools, implements, utensils, vehicles, "Whatsits;" and to discover, identify and preserve same; also publishes the magazine "Chronicle."

Museums/Libraries

Keith R. Gill
Museum of Science & Industry
5700 S Lake Shore Dr.
Chicago, IL 60637
ph: 773-684-1414
fax: 773-684-0026
msi@msichicago.org
http://www.msichicago.org
Archives contains documents & photos of the 1893 Columbian Exposition.

INFANT FEEDERS

(see also BOTTLES)

Clubs/Associations

John Giffird, Sec./Treas.
American Collectors of Infant Feeders
Newsletter: Keeping Abreast
1849 Ebony Dr.
York, PA 17402-4706
mrwoodyz@hotmail.com
http://www.acif.org
Founded in 1973 for those interested in feeding infants and the devices used therefore: nursers, baby bottles, infant/invalid feeders; book, "A Guide to American Nursing Bottles" is now available.

INK BLOTTERS

(see BLOTTERS; INKWELLS & INKSTANDS; PAPER COLLECTIBLES; PENS)

INKWELLS & INKSTANDS

(see also BOTTLES; BLOTTERS; PAPER COLLECTIBLES; PENCILS; PENS; SEALS, Wax)

Clubs/Associations

Charles L. Van Tine
Society of Inkwell Collectors, The
Newsletter: Stained Finger, The
P.O. Box 324
Mossville, IL 61552
ph: 309-579-3040
inkwellsociety@aol.com
http://www.soic.com
Features articles about inkwells, pens and writing accessories; has catalog offering books about inkwells, and

replacement inserts, quills, rocker blotters, etc; newsletter published quarterly; annual convention.

Bevy & Ray Jaegers
St. Louis Inkwell Collectors Society
P.O. Box 29396
Saint Louis, MO 63126-0396
USPsiSquad@aol.com

John Daniels, Mem. Sec.
Writing Equipment Society
Journal: Journal of the Writing
  Equipment Society
33 Glanville Rd.
Hadleigh
Ipswich, Suffolk IP7 5SQ U.K.
wes.sec@btinternet.com
http://www.wesonline.org.uk
  Devoted to the conservation and study of writing instruments and accessories: pens of all types and materials, pencils, nibs, inkwells, stamp boxes, quill cutters, scriveners' knives, seals, writing slopes, blotters, paper knives, etc.

Collectors

Robert Kwalwasser
168 Camp Fatima Rd.
Renfrew, PA 16053-9104
ph: 724-789-7766
fax: 724-789-9771
robertk@tcis.net
  Wants to buy traveling inkwells.

John E. Kochenburger
1304 Robertson St.
Fort Collins, CO 80524-4258
ph: 304-484-0274
koch@frii.com
  Collects a variety of inkstands, inkwells, ink bottles and "go-withs;" also buys and sells.

Gary Bahr
P.O. Box 2115
Salinas, CA 93902-2115
ph: 831-663-2671
fax: 831-663-1007
garyb5@earthlink.net

Dealers

Gene Bensen
AntiqueLine, Inc.
585-C Heritage Hills
Somers, NY 10589
ph: 914-276-0666
fax: 914-276-0666
antiqueline@rcn.com
http://www.antiqueline.com
  Specializes in inkwells, desk accessories, bookends, and fountain pens for the home or office.

Harold "Kap" Henson
Kapar Antiques
348 Cool Hollow Lane
Needmore, PA 17238-8707
ph: 717-573-2831
fax: 717-573-2831
kaplar@nb.net
http://www.kaplar.com
  Specializing in inkwells and inkstands.

Gerald Schultz
Antique Gallery, The
8523 Germantown Ave.
Philadelphia, PA 19118-3316
ph: 215-248-1700
fax: 215-247-8411
geraldluv@aol.com
  Buys and sells inkwells: ceramic, brass, glass, traveling, figural.

Sam Fiorella
Pendemonium
P.O. Box 447
Fort Madison, IA 52627-0447
ph: 888-372-2050 or 319-372-0881
fax: 319-372-0882
sam@pendemonium.com
http://www.pendemonium.com
  Buys and sells fountain pens, inkwells, ink bottles, pen stands, blotters, pen catalogs, magazine covers and advertisements.

Buck & Sandy Van Tine
Lora's Memory Lane
13133 N. Caroline St.
Chillicothe, IL 61523-9115
ph: 309-579-3040
fax: 309-579-2696
lorasink@aol.com
  Buys and sells inkwells, inkstands, and ink related items.

Carol Payne
Carol's Antique Gallery
14455 Big Basin Way
Saratoga, CA 95070-6008
ph: 408-867-7055
  Wants to buy inks of any material; sometimes considers broken ones for parts; also wants desk items like letter racks, wax seals, blotters, pens, pen stands, pen wipers, etc.

Experts

Veldon Badders
692 Martin Rd.
Hamlin, NY 14464-9744
ph: 716-964-3360
  Author of "Collector's Guide to Inkwells."

Beverly & Raymond Jaegers
P.O. Box 29396
Saint Louis, MO 63126-0396
USPsiSquad@aol.com
http://www.uspsisquad.com
  Experts and historians; authors of "The Write Stuff - A Collector's Guide to Inkwells, Fountain Pens & Desk Accessories."

INSECTS

Museums/Libraries

Frost Entomological Museum,
  Pennsylvania State University
501 ASI Building
University Park, PA 16802
ph: 814-863-2863
fax: 814-865-3048
kck@psu.edu

Butterflies

Internet Resources

Butterfly Website
butterfly@mgfx.com
http://mgfx.com/butterfly
  The most complete information on butterfly gardening, farming, ecology and education; lots of links to all sorts of butterfly resources including collections.

Cockroaches

Museums/Libraries

Michael Bohdan
Cockroach Hall of Fame Museum
2231-B West Fifteenth St.
Plano, TX 75075
ph: 972-519-0355
bugman@pestshop.com
http://www.pestshop.com
  Come see dressed up cockroaches like Roach Pero or Liberoachi!

Mosquitos

Experts

Richard Streater
P.O. Box 393
Mercer Island, WA 98040-0393
ph: 206-232-9060
fax: 206-232-9060
lureguru@aol.com
  Wants mosquito related items: tins, bottles, sprays, powders, ointments, etc.; working on a reference book for mosquito collectors.

Ticks

Museums/Libraries

Dr. James E. Keirans, Curator
U.S. National Tick Collection, Institute
  of Anthropodology & Parasitology
Georgia Southern University
Landrum, Box 8056
Statesboro, GA 30460
ph: 912-681-5564
fax: 912-681-0559
jkeirans@gasou.edu
http://www2.gasou.edu/iap/ustick.htm
  Collection of over one million ticks - the smallest fits on the head of a pin, the largest is the size of a quarter; history of each includes location collected and the "host" organism.

INSTRUMENTS & DEVICES

(see also ARCHITECTURE & RELATED ITEMS; ASTRONOMICAL ITEMS; BAROMETERS; GAUGES; GLOBES; MEDICAL, DENTAL & PHARMACEUTICAL; MICROSCOPES; NAUTICAL ANTIQUES; OFFICE EQUIPMENT; SCALES; SLIDE RULES; SPY EQUIPMENT; SURVEYING INSTRUMENTS; THERMOMETERS)

Compasses

Dealers

Michael Iannettoni
P.O. Box 1182
Syracuse, NY 13201
ph: 315-454-3231
MIannetton@aol.com
  Buys and sells all types of small, handheld compasses and instruments.

David S. Bennett
Bennett Antiques
15800 26th Ave. N.
Minneapolis, MN 55447-1940
  Wants to buy military compasses, pocket variety of WWI, WWII and earlier; pocket compasses in wooden boxes; old sport compasses; Boy Scout and Girl Scout pocket compasses; also pocket transits.

Kornelia Takacs
Pocket Compass Guide
9402 Grand Dr.
Huntington Beach, CA 92646
ph: 714-963-9939
kornelia@pocket-compass.com
http://www.pocket-compass.com
  Specializes in antique pocketwatch-style compasses from 1800s to 1920s; Web site contains information about many different pocket compasses; buys and sells.

Egg Related

Collectors

John Weber
50 Erobi Ln.
Iowa City, IA 52240
ph: 319-354-6920
  Wants to buy egg scales, egg washers, egg graders; single, multiple, dial, balance; for turkey, duck, chicken eggs, any kind; also wants figurines, etc. depicting children hatching from eggs.

Scientific

Appraisers

Prof. Thomas Perera
Telegraph & Scientific Instrument On-Line Cyber-Museum
P.O. Box 122
Hancock, VT 05748
ph: 802-767-3265
pererat@mail.montclair.edu
http://www.w1tp.com
  Online museum dedicated to the preservation of telegraph history, lore, and instrumentation; downloadable images; telegraph history, bibliography, and related links; email appraisals available.

Auction Services

George Glastris
Skinner, Inc.
63 Park Plaza
The Heritage on the Garden
Boston, MA 02116
ph: 617-350-5400
fax: 617-350-5429
info@skinnerinc.com
http://www.skinnerinc.com
Established in 1971, Skinner Inc. is the fourth largest auction house in the US; has offices in Boston and Bolton, MA.

Sotheby's
1334 York Ave.
New York, NY 10021
ph: 212-606-7000
fax: 212-606-7107
http://www.sothebys.com
Over 70 collecting areas are featured at Sotheby's auctions including toys, dolls, porcelain, furniture, silver, art, books; exhibitions are free and everyone is welcome; for a free copy of "Sotheby's Newsletter," call 212-606-7245.

Don V. Yeier
VERNONScope & Company
5 Ithaca Rd.
Candor, NY 13743
ph: 607-659-7000 or 888-333-3526
fax: 607-659-4000
sales@vernonscope.com
http://www.vernonscope.com
Two scientific antique instrument auctions each year: telescopes, microscopes, surveying, nautical, meteorologic equipment offered.

Jon Baddeley
Sotheby's
34-35 New Bond St.
London, W1A 2AA U.K.
ph: 44 171 293 5000
fax: 44 171 293 5989
http://www.sothebys.com
Conducts regular auctions of scientific instruments.

Book Sellers

John Ptak
J.F. Ptak Science Books
1531 33rd St., NW
Washington, DC 20007
ph: 202-337-0945
jfptak@thesciencebookstore.com
http://www.thesciencebookstore.com
Specializes in books about science and scientific instruments.

Clubs/Associations

Zeiss Historica Society
Journal: Zeiss Historica Society Journal
300 Waxwing Dr.
Cranbury, NJ 08512
ph: 540-981-1036
msmall@roanoke.infi.net
http://showcase.netins.net/web/crye/zi-hist.htm
Dedicated to the study & exchange of information on the history of Carl Zeiss Optical Co. and Zeiss-Ikon, its

people and products (cameras, accessories, and optical equipment of all types) from 1846 to present; semi-annual journal.

Dr. Sam Koslov
Maryland Microscopical & Scientific Instrument Society
8621 Polk St.
Mc Lean, VA 22102
ph: 703-893-9102
Focuses on instruments and devices: medical, surveying, photographic, microscopical, navigational, horological, astronomical, etc.

Scientific Instrument Society
Newsletter: Bulletin of the Scientific Instrument Society
31 High St.
Stanford in the Vale
Faringdon, Oxon SN7 8LH U.K.
ph: 01367 710223
sis@hidex.demon.co.uk
http://www.sis.org.uk
A British organization that travels extensively; quarterly journal with polished articles.

Collectors

Stephen Buczko
27 Surrey Rd.
Salem, MA 01970-4362
ph: 978-744-4683
nsbuczko@aol.com
Collector buying early American mathematical, surveying, nautical and engineering instruments.

Prof. Thomas Perera
P.O. Box 122
Hancock, VT 05748
ph: 802-767-3265
pererat@mail.montclair.edu
http://www.w1tp.com
Wants to buy early scientific instruments; has been collecting for over 40 years.

Dr. Allan Wissner
P.O. Box 102
Ardsley, NY 10502-0102
ph: 914-693-4628
wissner@bestweb.net
http://www.bestweb.net/~wissner
Wants microscopes, medical, scientific instruments: Zentmayer, Grunow, Bullock, McAllister, Gundlack, McIntosh, Tolles, Queen, Pike.

Paul Ferraglio
3332 W. Lake Rd.
Canandaigua, NY 14424-2441
ph: 585-394-7663
fax: 585-394-5424
p4alyo@aol.com
Buys old scientific instruments: microscopes, surveying instruments, mineralogical and other optical instruments in any condition; also books & catalogs; also wants parts.

Wayne Feely
1172 Lindsay La.
Jenkintown, PA 19046-1839
ph: 215-884-5640
wef@comcast.net
Wants unusual drafting and navigation equipment, coast artillery manuals and memorabilia.

Dr. Sam Koslov
8621 Polk St.
Mc Lean, VA 22102
ph: 703-893-9102
Wants to buy medical, surveying, photographic, microscopical, navigational, horological, astronomical, etc. instruments & devices.

Jon Lewin
622 Raleigh Ave., Apt. 3
Norfolk, VA 23507-2034
ph: 757-625-6732
Wants to buy floor-standing electro-medical machines, electro-static generators, leyden jars, oddly-shaped vacuum tubes or X-ray tubes, hand-operated vacuum pumps, glass-legged tables and stools, glass-handled rods, astronomical models.

John M. Shannon
7319 West Cedar Circle
Lakewood, CO 80226-2019
ph: 303-232-1534
rovers@aol.com
Wants to buy assay balances (wood and glass encased with small pans) - both laboratory and portable; also wants brass scientific instruments.

Stuart Johnson
710 Taylor Ave. #B
Alameda, CA 94501
ph: 510-523-1089
Wants to buy antique scientific, surveying, medical instruments, nautical antiques, Japanese swords.

Paul H. Hayashi, PE
18 Tarabrook Dr.
Orinda, CA 94563-3121
ph: 925-254-5074 or 925-253-1038
fax: 925-253-0592
Buys old scientific instruments: surveying, microscopes, barometers, calculators, drafting sets, chronometers, navigational devices, etc.

Robert De Cesaris
7429 Bree Ann Ct.
Citrus Heights, CA 95610-2455
ph: 916-356-5769
rdecesar@pcocd2.intel.com
Serious collector of slide rules, early mechanical adders and calculators; special interests include circular, cylindrical or other unusual slide rules and lever set calculators right up to the Curta calculator.

Dealers

David L. Isabelle
MediaSpecialies
28 Revell Ave.
Northampton, MA 01060
ph: 413-586-7571 or 413-584-1034
fax: 413-584-1034
http://www.mediaspec.com/GNET/mediaspecialties
Specializing in medical, scientific, optical, cameras, images, and cinema.

Parke Madden
Weather Store, The
146 Main St.
P.O. Box 729
Sandwich, MA 02563
ph: 800-646-1203
pmadden@wxstore.com
http://www.wxstore.com
Specializes in weather instruments ranging from marine related antiques to weathervanes.

David & Yola Coffeen
Tesseract
P.O. Box 151
Hastings On Hudson, NY 10706-0151
ph: 914-478-2594
fax: 914-478-5473
coffeen@aol.com
http://www.etesseract.com
Issues a series of well illustrated catalogs of early scientific instruments: astronomy, microscopy, sundials, surveying, calculation, demonstration, medical, surgical, navigation, etc.; interested in buying single items of collections.

Don V. Yeier
VERNONScope & Company
5 Ithaca Rd.
Candor, NY 13743
ph: 607-659-7000 or 888-333-3526
fax: 607-659-4000
sales@vernonscope.com
http://www.vernonscope.com
Buys and sells scientific instruments: telescopes, eyepieces, filters, astronomical accessories; binoculars, globes, etc.

James & Norvell Kennedy
James Kennedy Antiques, Ltd.
905 W. Main St.
Durham, NC 27701-2054
ph: 919-682-1040 or 800-236-1868
fax: 919-683-9633
kantiques@earthlink.net
http://www.jameskennedyantiques.com
Specialist in scientific, medical, and nautical antiques and prints.

John Forster
Barometer Fair
P.O. Box 25502
Sarasota, FL 34277
ph: 941-923-6136
fax: 941-923-6136
john@barometerfair.com
Buys, sells, restores all antique barometers; also deals in antique maps, globes, compasses, telescopes and other scientific instruments.

Alex Peck
Antique Scientifica
P.O. Box 710
Charleston, IL 61920-0710
ph: 217-348-1009
antiques@advant.net
http://antiquescientifica.com
  *Wants to buy early microscopes,
  telescopes, telegraphs, globes,
  electrical, patent models, surveying
  instruments, scales, nautical,
  demonstration items.*

Jonathan Blackman
Yellow Room, The
511 N. Robertson Blvd.
Los Angeles, CA 90048
ph: 310-274-3190
fax: 310-274-0129
  *Wants to buy brass telescopes, solar
  system models (orrery, tellurium,
  planetarium), and nautical items
  including passenger steam ship items,
  and compasses.*

Al & Bobbie Roberts
Rational Past, The
221 Oceano Dr.
Los Angeles, CA 90049-4123
ph: 310-476-6277
fax: 310-476-6278
malinfo@therationalpast.com
http://www.therationalpast.com
  *Organizer of West Coast Scientific &
  Technical Antique and Collectible
  Shows (Los Angeles and San
  Francisco.)*

R.C. & Faye Blankenhorn
Gemmary, The
P.O. Box 2560
Fallbrook, CA 92088
ph: 760-728-3321
fax: 760-728-3322
rcb@gemmary.com
http://www.gemmary.com/rcb
  *Antique scientific instruments: 18th &
  19th C. mathematical, philosophical,
  optical instruments, microscopes,
  telescopes, globes, orreries, sundials,
  compasses, surveying, navigating,
  drawing, medical, laboratory.*

Rod & Becky Cardoza
West Sea Company
2495 Congress St.
San Diego, CA 92110-2820
ph: 619-296-5356
fax: 619-216-1097
wsco@cox.net
http://www.westsea.com
  *Buys, sells all types of marine
  paintings, scrimshaw, ships' carvings,
  ship models, navigational and
  scientific instruments, sailor
  handcrafts, campaign furniture, hard
  hat diving, antique marine photography, nautical books, Naval ceramics.*

Scott Brake
Scott Brake Antiques
17420 Mt. Hermann St., Unit "D"
Fountain Valley, CA 92708
ph: 714-556-8333
fax: 714-556-8333
antiquechi@aol.com
  *Specializes in special acquisitions for
  entertainment and theme park clients;
  prop rentals.*

Lynn Harding
Antique Instruments of the Professions &
  Sciences
103 West Aliso St.
Ojai, CA 93023-2603
ph: 805-646-0204
fax: 805-646-0204
lynnhardingojai@aol.com
  *Specializes in buying and selling
  antique scientific and technological
  instruments: orreries, steam,
  calculating, optics, electrical, golfing,
  tennis, medical, microscopes, scales &
  weights, measuring, books, tools,
  drafting, surveying.*

Carole Meeker
Antiques of a Mechanical Nature
5702 Vacation Blvd.
Somerset, CA 95684-9324
ph: 530-620-7019 or 888-607-6090
fax: 530-620-7020
clm@antiqbuyer.com
http://www.antiqbuyer.com
  *Wants to buy early patented scientific
  instruments: calculation, surveying,
  telegraph, farm-related, tools, patent
  models, salesman samples, etc.*

Gloria Dekter
Ashton-Blakey Antiques & Collectibles
6021 Yonge St., Ste. 895
Toronto, Ontario M2M 3W2 Canada
ph: 905-886-5122
fax: 905-886-8566
ashtonb@netcom.ca
http://www.ashton-blakey-antiques.com
  *A complete Internet shop specializing
  in vintage wrist watches, antique
  pocket watches, watch fobs, chains;
  Web site contains images of all items;
  also specializes in scientific
  instruments.*

Marsh Graham
Marsh of Tockholes
Rockmount, Weasel Lane
Darwen, Lancs BB3 0NJ U.K.
ph: +(44)585 875848
fax: +(44)1254 760217
Graham@asiuk.net
http://www.asiuk.net
  *Buys, sells, researches and repairs
  antique scientific instruments such as
  microscopes, telescopes, theodolites,
  sextants, compasses, barographs,
  barometers, and electrical instruments.*

Experts

Prof. Thomas Perera
P.O. Box 122
Hancock, VT 05748
ph: 802-767-3265
pererat@mail.montclair.edu
http://www.w1tp.com
  *Maintains Internet telegraph and
  scientific instrument museum and
  collector's guide.*

Dale R. Beeks
Perceptions Scientifica
P.O. Box 117
Mount Vernon, IA 52314-0117
ph: 800-880-5178 or 319-895-0506
dbeeksci@aol.com
  *Buys fine microscopes; old scientific,
  surveying, technical, medical and
  precision instruments; pre-1900
  typewriters, calculating devices,
  medical items & quackery.*

Internet Resources

Prof. Thomas Perera
Telegraph & Scientific Instrument On-
  Line Cyber-Museum
P.O. Box 122
Hancock, VT 05748
ph: 802-767-3265
pererat@mail.montclair.edu
http://www.w1tp.com
  *Online museum dedicated to the
  preservation of telegraph history, lore,
  and instrumentation; downloadable
  images; telegraph history, bibliography, and related links; email
  appraisals available.*

Richard Van Vleck
Scientific Medical & Mechanical
  Antiques
P.O. Box 412
Taneytown, MD 21787
ph: 301-447-2680
smma@americanartifacts.com
http://americanartifacts.com/smma
  *Items for sale and wanted, US Patents
  search, SMMA articles and regular
  features, auction announcements,
  scientific instrument show schedules,
  books for the collector, links to related
  sites.*

R.C. & Faye Blankenhorn
Gemmary, The
P.O. Box 2560
Fallbrook, CA 92088
ph: 760-728-3321
fax: 760-728-3322
rcb@gemmary.com
http://www.gemmary.com/rcb
  *Online catalog of items for sale,
  conservation products, restoration
  materials, archival supplies,
  recommended scientific instrument
  reference books, other useful Web
  sites.*

Museums/Libraries

Adrianne Noe, Dir.
National Museum of Health & Medicine
6900 Georgia Ave. NW, Bldg. 54
Washington, DC 20307-5001
ph: 202-782-2200
fax: 202-782-3573
nmhminfo@afip.osd.mil
http://www.natmedmuse.afip.org
  *Collection contains medical
  technology since the early 17th century
  with objects ranging in size from a
  suture needle to a two-ton MRI
  magnet; X-Ray equipment, microscopes, surgical instruments,
  numismatics, and anatomical models.*

Periodicals

David & Yola Coffeen
Tesseract
Journal: Rittenhouse
P.O. Box 151
Hastings On Hudson, NY 10706-0151
ph: 914-478-2594
fax: 914-478-5473
coffeen@aol.com
http://www.etesseract.com
  *A bi-annual periodical to facilitate
  communication among collectors,
  curators & historians of scientific
  instruments; provides a forum for
  information about instruments made
  and/or sold in America.*

Richard Van Vleck
Greybird Publishing
Journal: American Artifacts
P.O. Box 412
Taneytown, MD 21787
ph: 301-447-2680
smma@americanartifacts.com
http://americanartifacts.com/smma
  *A bi-monthly newsletter about
  scientific, medical and mechanical
  devices; microscopy, surveying, scales,
  navigation, surgical, quackery, steam,
  electrical, agriculture, astronomy,
  calculators, etc.; ads, auction reports,
  article.*

Repair Services

Marsh Graham
Marsh of Tockholes
Rockmount, Weasel Lane
Darwen, Lancs BB3 0NJ U.K.
ph: +(44)585 875848
fax: +(44)1254 760217
Graham@asiuk.net
http://www.asiuk.net
  *Buys, sells, researches and repairs
  antique scientific instruments such as
  microscopes, telescopes, theodolites,
  sextants, compasses, barographs,
  barometers, and electrical instruments.*

INSULATORS

(see also BOTTLES; TELEPHONES)

Appraisers

John & Carol McDougald
Grampa Mac's Antique Insulator
Emporium
P.O. Box 1003
Saint Charles, IL 60174
ph: 630-513-1544
fax: 630-513-8278
emporium@crownjewelsofthewire.com
http://www.insulators.com/personal/
cmcdoug.htm
*Buys, sells, appraises glass
insulators.*

Auction Services

Dwayne Anthony
28390 Saffron Ave.
Highland, CA 92346
ph: 909-862-4312
insulators@open-wire.com
http://www.open-wire.com
Auctions, buys, sells insulators.

Clubs/Associations

Bill & Jill Meier
Yankee Polecat Insulator Club, The
Newsletter: YPIC Newsletter
103 Canterbury Ct.
Carlisle, MA 01741-1860
ph: 978-369-0208
bill@insulators.com
http://www.insulators.com
*Oldest continuing insulator club in the
country; members throughout New
England and surrounding areas;
annual show, swap meets.*

Kevin Lawless, VP
Capital Region Antique Bottle &
Insulator Club
Newsletter: Watercloset Gazette, The
3363 Guilderland Ave., Apt. 3
Schenectady, NY 12306-1820
ph: 518-357-2333
fax: 518-344-7485
kflbostons@aol.com
*Club for collectors of antique bottles
and electrical insulators; membership
based in Northeast US; annual show;
regular club swaps and meetings.*

John Hunsaker, Historian
Chesapeake Bay Insulator Club
7651 Wesley Rd.
Manassas, VA 20109-3321
ph: 703-361-5996
cbic@clubs.insulators.com
http://www.insulators.com/clubs/cbic
*Services most of the mid-Atlantic area
and meets quarterly in the Baltimore-
Washington DC area; holds shows/
sales in March and a swap meet in
September.*

Keith Roloson
Dixie Jewels Insulator Club
Newsletter: Dixie Jewels Newsletter
6220 Carriage Ct.
Cumming, GA 30040-9111
ph: 770-781-5021 or 770-750-6429
kroloson@mindspring.com
http://www.insulators.com/clubs/
djic.htm
*Newsletter published quarterly;
complimentary back issue available*

upon request; includes calendar of
upcoming shows, show reports,
insulator hunt plans, research
articles, and more.

Jacque Linscott
Central Florida Insulator Collectors Club
Newsletter: Newsnotes
3557 Nicklaus Dr.
Titusville, FL 32780-5356
ph: 321-267-9170
fax: 321-269-7767
bluebellwt@aol.com
http://www.insulators.com/clubs/cfic.htm

Joe J. Beres, Mem.
National Insulator Association
Newsletter: Drip Point
1315 Old Mill Path
Broadview Heights, OH 44147-3276
ph: 440-526-3478
jjjb@aol.com
http://www.nia.org
*An organization for those interested in
collecting electrical insulators and
other artifacts connected with related
industries.*

Alan Stastny
National Trails Insulator Club
6332 Clark Rd.
West Manchester, OH 45382
ph: 937-678-4745
ntic@clubs.insulators.com
http://www.insulators.com/clubs/
ntic.htm

Ed Peters
North Western Insulator Club
5424 Dufferin Dr.
Savage, MN 55378
ph: 612-447-2422
nic@clubs.insulators.com
http://www.insulators.com/clubs/nic.htm

Rick Soller
Greater Chicago Insulator Club
Newsletter: GCIC Newsletter
4086 Blackstone Ave.
Gurnee, IL 60031
ph: 847-782-8602 or 847-543-2958
fax: 847-548-3383
rick-soller@clc.cc.il.us
http://www.insulators.com/clubs/
gcic.htm
Hosts shows, swap meets and hunts.

Wendy Smith, Mem.
Federation of Historical Bottle
Collectors, Inc.
Magazine: Bottles & Extras
401 Johnston Court
Raymore, MO 64083
ph: 816-318-0160
osubuckeyes71@aol.com
http://www.fohbc.com
*"Bottles & Extras" contains articles,
pictures, letters, show dates, and
show and auction reports in the field
of antique bottles, insulators, fruit
jars and associated items; check Web
site for list of scores of clubs by
region.*

Dennis & Jeanne Weber
Missouri Valley Insulator Club
3609 Jackson
Saint Joseph, MO 64501-1940
ph: 816-364-1312
mvic@clubs.insulators.com
http://www.insulators.com/clubs/
mvic.htm

Elton Gish
Lone Star Insulator Club
Newsletter: Lone Star Lines
P.O. Box 1317
Buna, TX 77612-1317
ph: 409-994-5662 or 409-989-7161
fax: 409-989-7407
elton@r-infinity.com
http://www.insulators.com/clubs/
lsic.htm
*Meets monthly on the 3rd Friday in
Houston, TX; educational programs
offered at each meeting.*

Matt Poage
Triple Ridge Insulator Club
12510 Dahlia Way
Thornton, CO 80241
ph: 720-872-8298
tric@clubs.insulators.com
http://www.insulators.com/clubs/tric.htm

Steve Marks
Grand Canyon State Insulator Club
Newsletter: Arizona Telegraph Times
3655 W. Anthem Way, Ste. A-109
Phoenix, AZ 85086
ph: 623-551-1305
fax: 623-551-1306
gcsic@clubs.insulators.com
http://www.insulators.com/clubs/
gcsic.htm
*Open to anyone interested in
insulators; club meets four times per
year, publishes quarterly newsletter,
holds swap meets, and hosts shows.*

Tom Katonak
Enchantment Insulator Club
1024 Camino de Lucia
Corrales, NM 87048-8314
ph: 505-898-5592
eic@clubs.insulators.com
http://www.insulators.com/clubs/eic.htm
*Specialty area includes telegraph,
telephone, and power insulators; glass
and porcelain; experts in identification
and evaluation.*

Ron Norton
Central/Southern Counties Insulator
Club
P.O. Box 1423
Port Hueneme, CA 93044
ph: 805-488-7445
cscic@clubs.insulators.com
http://www.insulators.com/clubs/
cscic.htm

Larry Shumaker
Nor-Cal Insulator Club
P.O. Box 3434
Citrus Heights, CA 95611
ph: 916-725-8252
hemi19shu@attbi.com
http://www.insulators.com/clubs/
ncic.htm
*This club draws its members from
Northern California; four or five club
meetings held each year in conjunction
with Nor-Cal events; four to six
newsletters published each year; hosts
annual shows and annual awards.*

Collectors

Dario Dimare
1 Elda Rd.
Framingham, MA 01701-4335
ph: 508-877-4444 or 508-877-0958
fax: 508-877-4474
dario@dariodesigns.com
*Buys, sells, appraises glass
insulators; one piece or entire
collection; wants threadless and good
colored glass such as cobalt blue,
purple, yellow, citron, 7-Up green,
and amber; also wants pre-1900
telegraph maps, books and catalogs.*

Dick Bowman
1253 LaBaron Circle
Webster, NY 14580-9529
ph: 716-872-4015
dickevbow@aol.com
*Wants to buy quality insulators,
especially threadless insulators.*

John Hunsaker
7651 Wesley Rd.
Manassas, VA 22110-3321
ph: 703-361-5996

Keith Roloson
6220 Carriage Ct.
Cumming, GA 30040-9111
ph: 770-781-5021 or 770-750-6429
kroloson@mindspring.com
http://www.insulators.com/clubs/
djic.htm
*Interested in all glass and porcelain
insulators; seeks Southeastern
threadless-pinhole styles; specializes
in radio antenna "strain" insulators,
early (1860-1890) telegraph styles;
also offers free appraisals.*

Jim Meyer
3310 State Rd. 40
Ormond Beach, FL 32174-2537
ph: 386-677-0530
fax: 386-673-9883
hugo1074@aol.com
Wants to buy better insulators.

Mark Reutebuch
3125 Redwing Ln.
Rapid City, SD 57701
ph: 605-393-9707
marksanr@enetis.net
*Buys, sells, trades glass and wooden
insulators.*

Ross Baird
8617 Crosswind Dr.
Fort Worth, TX 76179
ph: 817-236-5580
*Wants to buy glass insulators
embossed Boston Bottle Works, Cal.
Elec. Works, Emminger, Seilers,
Harloe, Chester, E.C.M. & Co.
(color), Combination Safety.*

Matt Poage
12510 Dahlia Way
Thornton, CO 80241
ph: 720-872-8298
tric@clubs.insulators.com
http://www.insulators.com/clubs/tric.htm
*Always interested in glass and
porcelain insulators.*

Jim
Insulator Picture Gallery
cd102@aol.com
http://members.aol.com/Milstkr2/
EYECANSY/indexpic.html
*Web site has over 370 color images of
insulators and related items.*

Dealers

Doug MacGillvary
79 New Bolton Rd.
Manchester, CT 06040
ph: 860-649-0477
fax: 860-649-0477
*Glass & porcelain insulators,
collections or singles bought/sold/
traded; a reputation built on over
twenty-five years of honest dealing.*

Dwayne Anthony
28390 Saffron Ave.
Highland, CA 92346
ph: 909-862-4312
insulators@open-wire.com
http://www.open-wire.com
Auctions, buys, sells insulators.

Experts

Bill & Jill Meier
Glass Insulators
103 Canterbury Ct.
Carlisle, MA 01741-1860
ph: 978-369-0208
bill@insulators.com
http://www.insulators.com
*Specialists in Hemingray, H.G. Co.
and DEC 19 1871 insulators and
other Hemingray items such as water
bottles and H.G. Co. fruit jars;
looking to expand collection;
interested in sharing knowledge with
others.*

Kevin Lawless
3363 Guilderland Ave., Apt. 3
Schenectady, NY 12306-1820
ph: 518-357-2333
fax: 518-344-7485
kflbostons@aol.com
*Buys and sells all types of antique
insulators; glass, porcelain,
threadless, foreign, colored, rare,
common, singles or collections.*

Keith Roloson
6220 Carriage Ct.
Cumming, GA 30040-9111
ph: 770-781-5021 or 770-750-6429
kroloson@mindspring.com
http://www.insulators.com/clubs/
djic.htm
*Interested in all glass and porcelain
insulators; seeks Southeastern
threadless-pinhole styles; specializes
in radio antenna "strain" insulators,
early (1860-1890) telegraph styles;
also offers free appraisals.*

Jacqueline C. Linscott
3557 Nicklaus Dr.
Titusville, FL 32780-5356
ph: 321-267-9170 or 321-480-1800
fax: 321-269-7767
bluebellwt@aol.com
*Wants "eared" glass electrical
insulators; especially CD#250-
CD#270; also those with rare colors
of embossing errors; sells book solely
devoted to insulators; willing to assist
the novice collector with insulator
information & ID.*

Michael Bruner
2615 Echo Lane
Ortonville, MI 48462
ph: 248-627-6351
*Wants rare or unusual style
insulators; single or entire collections;
also wants related telephone/telegraph
items such as signs, catalogs.*

John & Carol McDougald
Grampa Mac's Antique Insulator
  Emporium
P.O. Box 1003
Saint Charles, IL 60174
ph: 630-513-1544
fax: 630-513-8278
emporium@crownjewelsofthewire.com
http://www.insulators.com/personal/
cmcdoug.htm
*Buys, sells, trades insulators &
telephone related items & lightning
rod balls and weathervanes; authors
of "Insulators-A History and Guide to
North Amer. Glass Pintype Insulators,
Vol. 1 & 2;" $68.50 both vols. &
current price guide.*

Elton Gish
P.O. Box 1317
Buna, TX 77612-1317
ph: 409-994-5662 or 409-989-7161
fax: 409-989-7407
http://www.insulators.com/icon/
collectors/egish.htm
*Wants 1890-1930 unipart or multipart
porcelain insulators; author of
"Multipart Porcelain Insulators,"
"Biography of Fred M. Locke - The
Father of Porcelain Insulators,"
"Value Guide for Porcelain
Insulator;" writes insulator column.*

Michael G. Guthrie
1209 West Menlo
Fresno, CA 93711-1477
ph: 559-435-6127
mgg17@cvip.fresno.com
http://www.insulators.com
*Author of "A Handbook for the
Recognition & Identification of Fake,
Altered and Repaired Insulators."*

Paul Keating
1705 S. 41st St.
Tacoma, WA 98405-1610
ph: 253-474-9659
*Author of an "Milholland Price
Guide," an insulator price guide;
published about every two years; does
appraisals; enclose SASE when
writing.*

Internet Resources

Bill & Jill Meier
Glass Insulators
103 Canterbury Ct.
Carlisle, MA 01741-1860
ph: 978-369-0208
bill@insulators.com
http://www.insulators.com
*Great Web site: general information,
photo albums, clubs, shows, reference
material.*

Patti Norton
P.O. Box 1423
Port Hueneme, CA 93044
ph: 805-488-7445
rrtp@ix.netcom.com
Ads, stories, interesting articles.

Periodicals

Carol McDougald
Magazine: Crown Jewels of the Wire
P.O. Box 1003
Saint Charles, IL 60174
ph: 630-513-1544
fax: 630-513-8278
editor@crownjewelsofthewire.com
http://www.crownjewelsofthewire.com
*76-page monthly magazine of
insulator and telephone history; glass,
porcelain; foreign columns; classified
ads, show dates, etc.*

Foreign

Experts

Marilyn Albers
14715 Oak Bend Dr.
Houston, TX 77079-6418
ph: 281-497-4146 or 281-497-3320
fax: 281-497-3957
marilynAFI@aol.com
*Co-author of "Glass Insulators From
Outside North America," "Worldwide
Porcelain Insulators," "Price Guide
for Glass Insulators from Outside
North America" (1996); specialist in
foreign insulators.*

INSURANCE MEMORABILIA

(see also FIRE INSURANCE
RELATED COLLECTIBLES)

Collectors

Byron Gregerson
P.O. Box 713
Modesto, CA 95353-0713
ph: 209-523-3300
fax: 209-523-3399
ByronGregerson@worldnet.att.net
*Collector wants pre-1930 auto and
fire (no life insurance items, please)
insurance memorabilia especially
advertising signs: reverse-painting-on-
glass, tin & lithography.*

State Farm

Collectors

Ken Jones
100 Manor Dr.
Columbia, MO 65203
ph: 573-445-7171
nanken@mchsi.com
http://www.msinter.net/tweety

INTERNET CLASSIFIEDS FOR COLLECTORS

Internet Resources

International Arts, Antiques &
  Collectibles Forum
1095 Washington St.
P.O. Box 69
Norwood, MA 02062
ph: 781-762-4209
fax: 781-762-8708
hschlesi@tiac.net
http://www.the-forum.com

Sam & Sally Pennington
Maine Antique Digest, Inc.
Newspaper: Maine Antique Digest
911 Main St.
P.O. Box 1429
Waldoboro, ME 04572-1429
ph: 207-832-7534
fax: 207-832-7341
mad@maine.com
http://www.maineantiquedigest.com
*The major monthly newspaper on
antiques, art and Americana; photos
with prices, dealers.*

Erik J. Wheeler
Collector Online
ph: 802-655-5400 or 800-546-2941
info@collectoronline.com
http://www.collectoronline.com
*Established in 1995, is one of the
oldest and largest dealer communities
online providing resources and
buying/selling opportunities; free
inventory management system for
collectors and dealers allows for
unlimited number of items.*

Brian Stanton
AntiqueArts.com
56 Valleywood Rd.
Cos Cob, CT 06807
ph: 888-262-7599
sales@antiquearts.com
http://www.antiquearts.com
*Online resources to find buyers and
sellers of antiques and collectibles;*

online search capability; multi-dealer antique mall featuring thousands of antiques pictured to browse and buy.

Susan Kopsch, Cust. Serv.
Internet Antique Shop, The
16 Heath Place
Garden City, NY 11530
ph: 248-288-9074 or 888-OLD-STUF
Phil@tias.com
http://www.tias.com
The Web's largest online antiques and collectibles mall, with over 480,000 items for sale online; serving collectors and dealers on the Web since 1995.

Arts & Antiques Network
National Press Bldge., Ste. 2003
Washington, DC 20045
ph: 703-553-0472
fax: 703-243-6012
webmaster@newsolutions.com
Internet source for information on the arts, antiques, collectibles, and cultural heritage.

Larry L. Krug
Collectors.Org
18222 Flower Hill Way, #299
Gaithersburg, MD 20879-5300
ph: 301-926-8663
fax: 301-926-7648
info@collectors.org
http://www.collectors.org
An information Web site for collector clubs and collectors, show calendar, theft reports, industry news, events calendar, auctioneer listings; official Web site for the National Association of Collectors.

Cindy Tipton
Collectibles.com
5388 Hickory Hollow Parkway
Antioch, TN 37013-8084
ph: 888-365-7467 or 615-263-8563
fax: 615-263-8084
collectibles@sath.com
http://www.collectibles.com
Web site for collectors; from sports figurines and jewelry to die casts, crystal, and plush toys; hard-to-find one-of-a-kind items; chat rooms and clubs for collectors, message boards, auctions; secure ordering.

Kathy Kamnikar
Antique Networking, Inc.
1350 West Fifth Ave., Ste. 300
Columbus, OH 43212
ph: 614-481-5750
fax: 614-481-5751
support@antiqnet.com
http://www.antiqnet.com
Internet online database that networks buyers and sellers of antiques locally, nationally, internationally.

Kathy Kamnikar
BuyCollectibles.Com
1350 West Fifth Ave., Ste. 300
Columbus, OH 43212
ph: 614-481-5750
fax: 614-481-5751
support@antiqnet.com
http://www.buycollectibles.com
Internet online database that networks buyers and sellers of collectibles locally, nationally, internationally.

Stacie Berger
Collectit.net Classifieds
Krause Publications
700 E. State St.
Iola, WI 54990-0001
ph: 715-445-2214
stacie.berger@fwpubs.com
http://www.collect.com/buysell/
  classifieds/default.asp
Brought to you by Krause Publications, one of the world's largest hobby publishers; includes the classified ads from more than 30 collectibles periodicals that Krause publishes.

Tom Johnson
Ruby Lane
1576 Waller St.
San Francisco, CA 94117
help@rubylane.com
http://www.rubylane.com
Search this Web site for antiques, collectibles, fine art being offered by many, many dealers.

icollector.com
United House
9 Penbridge Rd.
London, W11 3JY U.K.
ph: +44 (0)20 7313 2300 or +
fax: +44 (0)20 7221 7463
customer.services@icollector.com
http://www.icollector.com
An online site for buying and selling fine arts, antiques and collectibles.

INUIT & NORTHWEST COAST NATIVES

(see also NATIVE AMERICAN)

Appraisers

Donald Ellis
Donald Ellis Gallery
RR#3
Dundas, Ontario L9H 5E3 Canada
ph: 905-648-1837
ellisgal@interlynx.net
Dealer and appraiser specializing in North American Indian art in Canada: 18th and 19th century Northwest Coast and Eskimo art indigenous to Canada.

Auction Services

Seahawk Auctions
P.O. Box 231
Aldergrove, British Columbia V2X 7G1
Canada
ph: 604-657-1147 or 604-657-2072
fax: 604-462-7228
info@seahawkauctions.com
http://www.seahawkauctions.com
Specializes in the sale of Northwest Indian items.

Waddington's
111 Bathurst St.
Toronto, Ontario M5V 2R1 Canada
ph: 416-504-9100 or 877-504-5700
fax: 416-504-0033
info@waddingtonsauctions.com
http://www.waddingtonsauctions.com
Canada's oldest and largest auction house specializing in decorative arts, jewelry, antique furniture, Inuit and native Canadian arts, European and Canadian arts, books, militaria, Orientalia, toys, ceramics, etc.

Dealers

Norman Hurst, ISA CAPP
Hurst Gallery
53 Mount Auburn St.
Cambridge, MA 02138-5030
ph: 617-491-6888 or 212-744-6488
  (NYC)
fax: 617-661-0439
NHurst@compuserve.com
http://www.hurstgallery.com
Buys, sells, appraises Eskimo, Oceanic, Native American, Precolumbian and Asian art; has been appraising, dealing and publishing American Indian & Eskimo art for over 20 years: baskets, pottery, beadwork, masks, ivory.

Carol Halberstadt
Migrations
P.O. Box 543
Newton, MA 02456
carol@migrations.com
http://www.migrations.com
Specializes in older and contemporary Native American and Inuit/Eskimo art: weavings, pottery, baskets, jewelry, sculpture; online gallery with links to a wide variety of Native American resources.

Jack Bryan
Alaska on Madison - Gallery of Eskimo Art
937 Madison Ave.
New York, NY 10021
ph: 212-879-1782
fax: 212-327-4877
http://www.alaskaonmadison.com
Specializes in prints, wallhangings, Northwest Coast art, Inuit sculpture, Alaskan artifacts.

Jeffrey R. Myers
Jeffrey R. Myers, Primitive Arts
12 East 86th St.
New York, NY 10028-0506
ph: 212-472-0115
fax: 212-472-1665
jmyersprimitives@aol.com
Buys, sells, specializes and appraises pre-1915 NW masks, rattles, frontlets, bowls, textiles, boxes; pre-1915 Eskimo masks, carved boxes, bow drills, figural pieces, etc.

Arthur W. Erickson
Arthur E. Erickson, Inc.
1030 SW Taylor
Portland, OR 97205-2504
ph: 503-227-4710
fax: 503-279-9146
arthur@arthurwerickson.com
Buys and sells antique Native American and Eskimo arts with an emphasis on Columbian River items such as Wasco Saily bags, corn husk bags, Klicitat baskets and plateau figural and contour beadwork.

Lee
Northwest Tribal Art
1417 1st Ave.
Seattle, WA 98101
ph: 206-467-9330
fax: 206-624-6154
Carries a wide assortment of contemporary Native Eskimo and Pacific Northwest Coast Indian art, carvings, petrified walrus tusk, stone carvings, textiles, etc.

Jack Curtright
Curtright & Son Tribal Art
759 Saint Helens Ave.
Tacoma, WA 98402-3705
ph: 253-383-2969
Specialty is Northwest Coat materials, plains beadwork, and Eskimo art: Baskets, beadwork, carvings, jewelry, pottery, rugs.

Richard A. Wood
Alaskan Heritage Bookshop
P.O. Box 22165
Juneau, AK 99802-2165
ph: 907-789-8450
fax: 907-789-8450
dick@AlaskaWanted.com
http://www.ALaskaWanted.com
Buys and sells Northwest Coast antique Indian art objects including model boats, canoes, and kayaks, masks, baskets, handmade silver spoons, totem poles, Athabaskan beadwork, photographs.

Geoff Ryan
Uqqurmiut Centre for Arts & Crafts
P.O. Box 453
Pangnirtung, Northwest Territory X0A 0R0 Canada
ph: 867-473-8870 or 867-473-8669
fax: 867-473-8634
inuitart@nunanet.com
http://www.uqqurmiut.com
Producers of the Annual Pangnirtung limited edition Community Print Collection, Pangnirtung limited

edition Tapestries, and handmade
crafts.

Victor Topper
Topper Gallery
111 Finch Ave. W, Ste. 214
Markham, Ontario M3J 2E5 Canada
ph: 416-665-7554
fax: 416-665-8164
topperart@rogers.com
http://www.topperart.com
*Chinese art, Japanese art, Buddhistic
art, Precolumbian, Judaica, Inuit art,
Northwest Coast Indians.*

Experts

Patricia Feheley
Feheley Fine Arts
14 Hazelton Ave.
Toronto, Ontario M5R 2E2 Canada
ph: 416-323-1373
fax: 416-323-0121
gallery@feheleyfinearts.com
http://www.feheleyfinearts.com
*Dealers, experts, educators in Inuit
and Northwest Coast native art.*

Museums/Libraries

Samuel K. Fox Museum
Seward & D Sts.
P.O. Box 237
Dillingham, AK 99576
ph: 907-842-2322
fax: 907-842-2322
*Collection includes Southwestern
Yupik Eskimo arts and crafts, basket
weaving, and skin sewing (clothing).*

Sheldon Jackson Museum
104 College Dr.
Sitka, AK 99835-7657
ph: 907-747-8981
fax: 907-747-3004
bruce_kato@eed.state.ak.us
http://www.museums.state.ak.us
*Focuses on Aleut, Athabaskan, and
Northwest Coast Indians: Haida
argillite carvings, Eskimo implements,
ivory carvings, masks, skin clothing,
baskets, kayaks, umiaks, totem poles,
garments, ceremonial equipment, etc.*

Totem Heritage Center
601 Deermount St.
Ketchikan, AK 99901
ph: 907-225-5600
museumdir@city.ketchikan.ak.us
http://www.city.ketchikan.ak.us/ds/
tonghert
*Established in 1976 to house and
display a collection of 19th century
totem poles retrieved from uninhabited
Tlingit and Haida village sites near
Ketchikan; promotes the traditional
arts and crafts of the Tlingit, Haida,
Tsimshian.*

Inuit Art Centre
Indian & Northern Affairs Canada
10 Wellington St., Rm. 1415
Hull, Quebec K1A 0H4 Canada
ph: 819-997-0380
fax: 819-953-3017
infopubs@inac.gc.ca
http://www.inac.gc.ca/art
*A long-standing cultural center that
supports and promotes the visual arts
of the Inuit in Canada; artists'
biographies, stories and legends,
sources for materials, information on
art galleries.*

IRONS

Pressing

(see also KITCHEN COLLECTIBLES;
CLOTHES SPRINKLERS)

Clubs/Associations

Bruce Baumunk, Sec./Treas.
Mid-West Sad Iron Collectors Club
Newsletter: Pressing News
6903 Singingwood Lane
Saint Louis, MO 63129
ph: 314-846-9573
Bruce.Baumunk@gte.net
http://www.irons.com/msicc.htm
*Founded in 1984 to further the many
aspects of the collecting of pressing
irons; worldwide membership; annual
convention; lending reference library;
quarterly newsletter.*

Julia Morgan
British Iron Collectors Club
19 Churchill Rd.
Frome, Somerset BA11 4ED U.K.
ph: 01373-46-49-11
noridas@aol.com

Collectors

Kevin & Kate McCartney
Old Iron Inn B&B, The
155 High St.
Caribou, ME 04736
ph: 207-492-4766
oldiron@mfx.net
http://www.oldironinn.com
*Private museum has a great collection
of over 250 pressing irons: flat irons,
detachable-handle irons, tailor,
polishing, slug, coal, sleeve, hat, fuel,
electric, fluting, and goffering.*

William "Buck" Carson
936 Dove Island Rd.
Newton, NJ 07860-4512
ph: 973-383-4894
fax: 973-300-5946
bcarson@garden.net
*Editor of the "Pressing News," the
newsletter of the Midwest Sad Iron
Collectors Club.*

Jerry Jankowski
754 34th Place
West Des Moines, IA 50265-3126
ph: 515-223-8757
jmjan44@aol.com

Paul & Lynette Conrad
24 Nob Hill Dr.
Saint Louis, MO 63138-1458
ph: 314-741-4171

Jay Poirier
5964 S. Lee Way
Littleton, CO 80127
ph: 303-973-4255
fax: 303-288-1790
*Wants mint or near mint gasoline,
kerosene, or alcohol fueled pressing
irons; also wants parts.*

George Keech
U.K.
ph: 01204 591333
fax: 01204 602636
b.argekeech@btinternet.com
*Private collector of genuine antique
pressing irons; charcoal, gas, spirit,
naphtha, box & miniature irons, all
types of trivets (pieced brass) in
particular; exchanges info with other
pressophiles worldwide.*

Dealers

Leo & Nina Smith
Ironing Things
53 Dawn Dr.
Pleasant Hill, CA 94523
ph: 925-685-3236 or 209-258-8859
fax: 925-689-0535
leonina48@attbi.com
*Serious pressing iron collectors for 32
years; collection includes many types
of irons and accessories; ironing
boards, washing machines, trivets,
500 miniature irons, salesman
samples, advertisements, sprinkler
bottles.*

Carole & Larry Meeker
Antiques of a Mechanical Nature
5702 Vacation Blvd.
Somerset, CA 95684-9324
ph: 530-620-7019 or 888-607-6090
fax: 530-620-7020
clm@antiqbuyer.com
http://www.antiqbuyer.com
*Sells, buys and collects unusual
pressing irons with special interest in
fluters, fuel irons, and revolving/
combination irons; also interested in
many other early patented or
mechanical household devices.*

Experts

David & Sue Irons
Dave Irons Antiques
223 Covered Bridge Rd.
Northampton, PA 18067
ph: 610-262-9335
fax: 610-262-2853
dave@ironsantiques.com
http://www.ironsantiques.com
*Buys and sells; issues semi-annual
catalog of irons for sale; advisor to
"Warman's" and "Schroeder's;"
author of "Irons by Irons," "Pressing
Iron Patents," "More Irons by Irons,"
& "Even More Irons by Irons;"
available from author.*

Victor A. Papp
Tiber Island
490 M St., S.W., #W_705
Washington, DC 20024
ph: 202-484-8321 or 202-619-2296
vapapp@voa.gov
*Collecting antique pressing, sad, flat,
miniature irons.*

Internet Resources

Bill & Peggy Heyman
Shaker Brook Farm Antique Pressing
Iron Museum
P.O. Box 550
Marlborough, NH 03455
ph: 603-876-3636
fax: 603-876-4001
irons@irons.com
http://www.irons.com
*Internet resource for those interested
in pressing irons, iron auctions,
washing machines, wood stoves.*

Museums/Libraries

Nederlands Strijkijzer Museum
Noorderstraat 4
2635 TG Noorbroek, The Netherlands
ph: 0598 452075
fax: 0598 451181
strijkijzer@dolfijn.nl
http://www.expositiewijzer.nl/musea/
strijkijzermuseum.html
*A Dutch museum of ironing
instruments; lots of great images; in
Dutch.*

ISRAEL

(see JUDAICA)

IVER JOHNSON ARMS & CYCLE WORKS

Experts

William E. Goforth
13561 Castilian
Houston, TX 77015
ph: 713-451-5235
bgoforth@ev1.net
*Author of "Iver Johnson's Arms &
Cycle Works 1871-1978."*

Charles W. Best
11523 Pine Valley Dr.
Franktown, CO 80116-8708
ph: 303-660-2318
Budbest@aol.com
*Advanced collector and historian for
Iver Johnson Arms & Cycle Works of
Fitchburg, MA; interested in any Iver
Johnson product including guns,
tools, bicycles, motorcycles, signs,
advertising and memorabilia.*

IVOREX PLAQUES

Collectors

Ron & Sharon Edgar
4edgars@msn.com
http://www.ivorexplaques.com
Serious collectors of Ivorex Plaques.

IVORY

(see also ENDANGERED SPECIES;
GEMS & JEWELRY; NAUTICAL
ANTIQUES; NETSUKE;
ORIENTALIA; SCRIMSHAW)

Clubs/Associations

Robert E. Weisblut
International Ivory Society
Newsletter: International Ivory Society
   Newsletter
11109 Nicholas Dr.
Silver Spring, MD 20902-3532
ph: 301-649-4002
rweisblut@yahoo.com
*Provides a basis for people interested
in ivory to network worldwide and
learn to identify ivory and its history,
care, and current pricing.*

Collectors

Bill Simmons
181 NW 78th Ave.
Margate, FL 33063
ph: 954-984-9647
wsim1206@aol.com
*Wants all ivory: Chinese, Japanese,
African, Eskimo, netsukes, carvings,
tusks.*

David Warther II
David Warther Carving Museum
2561 Crestview Dr. NW
Dover, OH 44622-7405
ph: 330-343-1865 or 330-343-1868
ivorybuyer@adelphia.net
http://www.ivorybuyer.com
*Purchases estate elephant tusks for
ongoing ivory carving art project; only
wants tusks from African elephants
and they must be estate tusks within
the US.*

Dealers

Brian J. Kiracofe
Newport Scrimshander, The
14 Bowen's Wharf
Newport, RI 02840
ph: 401-849-5680 or 800-635-5234
fax: 401-849-9306
newportscrimshaw@juno.com
http://www.scrimshanders.com
*Carries an extensive collection of
European and Far Eastern carved
ivory antiques.*

T. Cronn
1399 S. Harbour City Blvd.
Melbourne, FL 32901
*Wants to buy ivory: whale, walrus,
elephant, any kind; raw and carved;
please state asking price.*

David Boone
Boone's Trading Company
P.O. Box 669
Brinnon, WA 98320
ph: 360-796-4330 or 800-423-1945
fax: 360-796-4551
sales@boonetrading.com
http://www.boonetrading.com
*Buys and sells legal ivory, scrimshaw,
furs and skulls: scrimshaw, netsuke,
Eskimo artifacts, carvings, walrus,
hippo, warthog, mammoth, jewelry,
pistol grips, ivory beads, old trade
beads, scrimshaw supplies and
reproductions.*

Experts

Ed Tripp
Collector's World
139 Main St.
Cooperstown, NY 13326
ph: 607-547-5509
fax: 607-547-5483
edtripp@collectors-world.com
http://www.collectors-world.com

Robert E. Weisblut
11109 Nicholas Dr.
Silver Spring, MD 20902-3532
ph: 301-649-4002
rweisblut@yahoo.com
*Wants to buy books about ivory: care,
identification, collections, the ivory
trade, etc.; also looking for ivory
carvings and tusks.*

Museums/Libraries

David Warther II
David Warther Carving Museum
2561 Crestview Dr. NW
Dover, OH 44622-7405
ph: 330-343-1865 or 330-343-1868
ivorybuyer@adelphia.net
http://www.ivorybuyer.com
*Purchases estate elephant tusks for
ongoing ivory carving art project; only
wants tusks from African elephants
and they must be estate tusks within
the US.*

Periodicals

Joan L. Cervi
Newsletter: Netsuke & Ivory Carving
   Newsletter-Video
3203 Adams Way
Ambler, PA 19002-3741
ph: 215-628-2026
fax: 215-628-2026
jcnetsuke@aol.com
*A wholesaler who offers VHS videos
and a monthly newsletter about
imported netsuke, ivory carvings and
other Orientalia.*

**Here are some tips
when contacting
someone who is listed
in this book:**

When requesting
information about a
particular item, include
a description (material,
dimensions, maker's
mark, model number,
etc.) and a photo,
sketch, digital image or
photocopy of the item
in question.

Always ask if there are
charges for samples or
for the services that
you are requesting.

When corresponding
by letter, please be
sure to include a Large
(#10 business size)
Self-Addressed and
Stamped Envelope
(LSASE) if requesting a
reply or the return of
photographs.

Never call collect
unless otherwise
directed. When
calling, be considerate
of time zone differ-
ences and always ask
if the party you are
calling has time to talk.
When leaving an
answering machine
message, always
instruct the party to
call you back collect.

JACOULET

(see PRINTS, Woodblock [Jacoulet])

JADE

(see GEMS & JEWELRY, Jade; ORIENTALIA)

JAMES BOND

(see CHARACTER COLLECTIBLES, Spy Memorabilia [James Bond])

JAPANESE ITEMS

(see ART, Oriental; ARMS & ARMOR, Japanese; BOOKS, Reference [Japanese Items]; FIREARMS, Japanese Matchlocks; OCCUPIED JAPAN; MILITARIA; ORIENTALIA, Japanese Items; PRINTS, Woodblock [Japanese])

JAPANESE WOODBLOCK PRINTS

(see ART, Oriental; ORIENTALIA; PRINTS, Woodblock [Japanese])

JARS

(see ADVERTISING COLLECTIBLES, Counter Jars; BOTTLES; CANDY CONTAINERS, Jars; FRUIT JARS; JELLY CONTAINERS; TOBACCO COLLECTIBLES, Jars)

JELL-O MEMORABILIA

Collectors

Ron Schieber
P.O. Box 72057
Akron, OH 44372
ph: 330-836-9442
dschiebe@neo.rr.com

JELLY CONTAINERS

(see also FRUIT JARS)

Clubs/Associations

Art Snyder, Treas.
Jelly Jammers
Newsletter: Jelly Jammers' Journal
6086 W. Boggstown Rd.
Boggstown, IN 46110
ph: 317-835-7121
emshaw@in.net
Jelly Jammers focuses on collecting jelly jars, glasses, molds, cups, mugs and samples or miniatures, and on the education of its members; newsletter published quarterly.

Collectors

Art Snyder
6086 W. Boggstown Rd.
Boggstown, IN 46110
ph: 317-835-7121
emshaw@in.net
Buys/sells/trades all types of jelly glasses, jars, molds and cups, especially patented examples; also wants all related material.

Margaret Shaw
6086 W. Boggstown Rd.
Boggstown, IN 46110-9731
ph: 317-835-7121
emshaw@in.net

JEWELRY

(see ART DECO; GEMS & JEWELRY)

JOHNSON SMITH CO.

Collectors

Stan & Mardi Timm
Uniquely Racine
6001 Leeward Lane
Racine, WI 53402-9783
ph: 414-639-2304 or 414-639-3312
rjbafact@borg.com
Wants to buy Johnson Smith Co. catalogs and items sold by the company; writing book about the company and would be interested in any anecdotes, stories or experiences with the company and its products.

JUDAICA

(see also ART, Jewish; AUTOGRAPHS, Jewish; STAMP COLLECTING, Holly Land; TEXTILES, Needlework [Judaic])

Appraisers

Y. Michael "Max" Rottenberg
Hebraica & Judaica Consultant
1524 56 St.
Brooklyn, NY 11219
ph: 718-435-7691

Auction Services

Kerry Shrives
63 Park Plaza
The Heritage on the Garden
Boston, MA 02116
ph: 617-350-5400
fax: 617-350-5429
info@skinnerinc.com
http://www.skinnerinc.com
Established in 1971, Skinner Inc. is the fourth largest auction house in the US; has offices in Boston and Bolton, MA.

Daniel E. Kestenbaum
Kestenbaum & Company
12 West 27th St.
New York, NY 10011
ph: 212-366-1197
fax: 212-366-1368
kestenbook@aol.com
http://www.kestenbaum.net
Specializes in the sale of Judaica and Hebraica.

Sotheby's
1334 York Ave.
New York, NY 10021
ph: 212-606-7000
fax: 212-606-7107
http://www.sothebys.com
Over 70 collecting areas are featured at Sotheby's auctions including toys, dolls, porcelain, furniture, silver, art, books; exhibitions are free and everyone is welcome; for a free copy of "Sotheby's Newsletter," call 212-606-7245.

Book Sellers

Gary Broder
Broder's Rare & Used Books
205 Columbia Blvd.
Waterbury, CT 06710
ph: 203-755-1114
fax: 203-575-9308
bookssss@aol.com
http://members.aol.com/bookssss
Rare and used books on the Web; great searchable Web pages with a wide selection of books with Judaica a specialty; books in English, Yiddish, and Hebrew.

Clubs/Associations

Israel I. Bick, Pres.
Judaica Collectors Society
Newsletter: Judaica Collectors Society Newsletter
P.O. Box 854
Van Nuys, CA 91408-0854
ph: 818-997-6496
fax: 818-988-4337
iibick@aol.com
http://www.bick.net
Dealing with and promoting the knowledge of all things related to Judaica and the state of Israel.

Collectors

Cheryl Weitzman
P.O. Box 790
Cupertino, CA 95015
ph: 408-559-7799 x222
cheryl@sessionware.com
Volunteer curator of historical displays, Congregation Kol Emeth, Palo Alto, CA; seeks Judaica for private collection and to create Jewish history displays at the synagogue; Webmaster for Southern Jewish Historical Soc.

Cheryl Melnick
P.O. Box 790
Cupertino, CA 95015
ph: 408-559-7799 x222
webmistress@hand-fan.org
http://www.hand-fan.org
Seeks the loan, donation or sale of items of Jewish interest (Judaica) to add to the display at the Congregation Kol Emeth Jewish Historic Displays.

Dealers

Ezra M. Holczer
Queen Esther Judaica Autographs
1417 East 28th St.
Brooklyn, NY 11210
ph: 718-253-2581
fax: 718-253-2581
qejudaica@aol.com
http://www.judaicaautographs.com
Deals exclusively in all areas of Judaica autographs; specializes in buying and selling vintage material autographed by American Jews and Zionists.

Alan Scop
Menorah Antiques, Ltd.
1303 Coney Island Ave.
Brooklyn, NY 11230-3520
ph: 718-692-3683
fax: 718-692-0084
menorahantiques@netscape.net
Buys and sells Judaica: postcards, posters, prints, photos, menorahs, spice boxes, kiddush cups, esrog boxes, Holocaust memorabilia; illustrated books, Haggadas, paintings.

Gary Niederkorn
Niederkorn Silver
Newspaper: Silver Edition
2005 Locust St.
Philadelphia, PA 19103-5606
ph: 215-567-2606
fax: 215-567-2606
niederkornsilver@aol.com
Specializes in 19th and 20th c. silver novelties, jewelry, napkin rings, Judaica, picture frames, etc.; also Tiffany, Jensen, Mexican.

Allan & Ita Fogel
Twin Tankard Antiques
P.O. Box 4847
Silver Spring, MD 20914-4847
ph: 301-236-9391
fax: 301-236-0427
twintankard@aol.com
http://www.twintankard.com
Specializes in European pewter; also buys and sells Russian and Judaica.

Joan Wurmbrand
Good Buy Girls
2691 East Main St., Ste. 102
Bexley, OH 43209
ph: 614-231-0437 or 866-886-0467
fax: 614-231-3140
goodbuygirls@tias.com
http://www.goodbuygirls.com
Seeks unique Jewish ritual and artistic items.

Israel I. Bick
Bick International
P.O. Box 854
Van Nuys, CA 91408-0854
ph: 818-997-6496
fax: 818-988-4337
iibick@aol.com
http://www.bick.net
Wants to buy Jewish postcards, Hollywood memorabilia, stamps, coins, documents, currency, photos, bonds, religious articles, everything from the 1933-1945 Holocaust era.

Historicana
1200 Edgehill Dr., Ste. D
Burlingame, CA 94010
ph: 650-343-9578
Wants to buy Jewish rare books, manuscripts, documents, works by Arthur Szyk.

Experts

Lael Bower
6751 School Rd.
Peck, MI 48466
ph: 810-378-5785
Wants to buy Christian and Judaic collectibles; co-author with Penny Forstner of "Guide to Collecting Christian and Judaic Artifacts."

Arthur M. Feldman
Arthur M. Feldman Galleries
1815 St. Johns Ave.
Highland Park, IL 60035-3215
ph: 847-432-8858
fax: 847-266-1199
arsdura@aol.com
http://www.judaicaconnection.com
Buys, sells and specializes in Judaica; former Director, Jewish Museum of Chicago; former Curator at Smithsonian; former Visiting Curator at the Victoria & Albert Museum.

Joshua Yacobovits
Rehov Katznelbogen 53
Har Nof, Jerusalem 93871 Israel
ph: 972 2 6541962
judaicaman@yahoo.com
http://y42.photos.yahoo.com/judaicaman
Evaluates Judaica and Hebraica; will

broker your items to private collectors and museums.

Museums/Libraries

Museum of Jewish Heritage
18 First Place
Battery Park City, NY 10004-1484
ph: 212-509-6130 or 212-968-1800
fax: 212-968-1368
http://www.mjhnyc.org
Three floors of artifacts and film history covering pre-Holocaust, Holocaust, post-Holocaust eras.

Yeshiva University Museum at the Center for Jewish History
15 West 16th St.
New York, NY 10011
ph: 212-294-8330
fax: 212-294-8335
info@yum.cjh.org
http://www.yu.edu/museum
Exhibits and programs relating to Jewish themes, featuring fine and decorative art, textiles and costumes, photography, manuscripts, contemporary crafts and sculpture.

Jewish Museum, The
1109 5th Ave.
New York, NY 10128
ph: 212-423-3200
fax: 212-423-3232
http://www.jewishmuseum.org
A major American art museum and largest Jewish museum in the Western hemisphere; collections, exhibitions, programs illustrating the diversity of Jewish culture for more than 4,000 years.

National Museum of American Jewish History
55 N. 5th St.
Independence Mall East
Philadelphia, PA 19106-2197
ph: 215-923-3811
fax: 215-923-0763
nmajh@nmajh.org
http://www.nmajh.org
Established in 1976; dedicated exclusively to collecting, preserving and interpreting artifacts pertaining to the American Jewish experience; over 10,000 artifacts from the history of more than 300 years of American Jewish life.

B'nai B'rith Klutznick Museum
Diana Altman
2020 K Street NW
Washington, DC 20006
ph: 202-857-6603
fax: 202-857-6604
http://www.bnaibrith.org/
http://bbi.koz.com/bbi/klutznik
The only museum in Washington, DC offering the sweep of Jewish culture and history; exhibits and programs on ethnography, history, and art which examines the contributions of Jewish culture to human civilization.

Jewish Museum of Maryland
15 Lloyd St.
Baltimore, MD 21202
ph: 410-732-6400
fax: 410-732-6451
info@jewishmuseummd.org
http://www.jhsm.org

Marcia Zerivitz, Ex. Dir.
Sanford L. Ziff Jewish Museum of Florida
301 Washington Ave.
Miami Beach, FL 33139-6965
ph: 305-672-5044
fax: 305-672-5933
mzerivitz@aol.com
http://www.jewishmuseum.com

Sylvia Plotkin Judaica Museum of Temple Beth Israel
10460 N. 56th St.
Scottsdale, AZ 85253
ph: 480-951-0323
fax: 480-951-7150
museum@templebethisrael.org
http://www.angelfire.com/az2/judaicamuseum
One of the most important collections of Judaic artifacts in the southwestern US.

Judah L. Magnes Museum
2911 Russell St.
Berkeley, CA 94705
ph: 510-549-6950
fax: 510-849-3673
info@magnesmuseum.org
http://www.magnesmuseum.org
Third largest Jewish museum in the US; permanent collections, changing exhibitions, library, archives, educational and outreach programs.

Holocaust

Museums/Libraries

Museum of Jewish Heritage
18 First Place
Battery Park City, NY 10004-1484
ph: 212-509-6130 or 212-968-1800
fax: 212-968-1368
http://www.mjhnyc.org
Dedicated to the Jewish history of the 20th century with a focus on the Holocaust.

United States Holocaust Memorial Museum
100 Raoul Wallenberg Place SW
Washington, DC 20024-2150
ph: 202-488-0400
web_administrator@ushmm.org
http://www.ushmm.org
America's national institution for the documentation, study, and interpretation of Holocaust history; serves as this country's memorial to the millions of people murdered during the Holocaust.

C.A.N.D.L.E.S. Holocaust Museum
1532 S. Third St.
Terre Haute, IN 47802
ph: 812-234-7881
fax: 812-235-2665
Candles@abcs.com
http://users.abcs.com/candles
Purpose of C.A.N.D.L.E.S. (Children of Auschwitz Nazi Deadly Lab Experiments Survivors) is to educate the public about the horrors of the Holocaust, and to tell the story of the children who survived.

JUGS

(see CERAMICS, Jugs; CERAMICS, Stoneware; SALOON & BAR COLLECTIBLES, Whiskey Pitchers;)

KALEIDOSCOPES

(see also OPTICAL TOYS)

Clubs/Associations

Cozy Baker
Brewster Society
Newsletter: Brewster Society New Scope
P.O. Box 1073
Bethesda, MD 20817
ph: 301-365-1855
fax: 301-365-2284
cozybaker1@aol.com
http://www.brewstersociety.com
A club for designers, collectors and lovers of kaleidoscopes; sponsors an annual kaleidoscope convention.

Collectors

Coleen Detzel
28 Lacresta Dr.
Florence, KY 41042-9663
ph: 606-647-6156
Wants to buy quality kaleidoscopes, especially unusual and older pieces.

Dealers

Lucille Malitz
Lucid Antiques
P.O. Box KH
Scarsdale, NY 10583
ph: 914-636-7825 or 914-636-5171
fax: 914-636-7825
lithopha@optonline.net
Invented by Sir David Brewster in the middle of the 19th century, early kaleidoscopes were beautifully crafted scientific instruments, made of ivory, brass and shagreen leather; some silver plated & contained ampules of colored liquid.

William P. Carroll
ACR Books
8500 La Entrada
Whittier, CA 90605
ph: 562-693-8421
fax: 562-945-6011
acrbooks@concentric.net
http://webtch.com/ACRbooks
Buys, sells and collects modern, top

quality kaleidoscopes and, at times, antique kaleidoscopes.

Eric Sinizer
Light Opera Retail Gallery
460 Post Rd.
San Francisco, CA 94102-1502
ph: 415-956-9866
fax: 415-956-5624
eric@lightoperagallery.com
http://www.lightoperagallery.com

Experts

Cozy Baker
P.O. Box 1073
Bethesda, MD 20817
ph: 301-365-1855
fax: 301-365-2284
cozybaker1@aol.com
http://www.brewstersociety.com

Internet Resources

Tim Beyer
Kaleidoscopes of America
15825 95th Ave. N
Maple Grove, MN 55369-4473
ph: 888-838-4067
fax: 612-416-9660
kaleido@kaleido.com
http://www.kaleido.com
Great Web site resource page for information about kaleidoscopes both new and old: artist info, special events, about kaleidoscopes in America, collector clubs, resources to make your own, and more.

Man./Prod./Dist.

Jan & Shel Haber
Hand of the Craftsman
Five South Broadway
Nyack, NY 10960
ph: 914-358-6622 or 914-358-3366
fax: 914-735-7669
k@habersite.com
http://www.kaleidoscopesUSA.com
Showing virtually every contemporary collectible American kaleidoscope by over 50 of the best American designers.

KEEN KUTTER (SIMMONS HARDWARE)

(see also DIAMOND EDGE; HARDWARE; KNIVES; TOOLS; WINCHESTER COLLECTIBLES)

Auction Services

Bob Simmons
Simmons & Company Auctioneers
40706 E. 144th St.
Richmond, MO 64085
ph: 816-776-2936 or 800-646-2936
fax: 816-470-5016
bob@simmonsauction.com
http://www.simmonsauction.com
Conducts annual specialty auctions of Winchester, Keen Kutter (E.C. Simmons Hardware) and Diamond Edge (Shapleigh Hardware) collectibles; has a well-established

reputation for expertise and high quality merchandise.

Clubs/Associations

Barbara Huhn, Mem.
Hardware Companies Kollectors' Klub, The
Newsletter: Winchester Keen Kutter Diamond Edge Chronicles
432 S. Gore St.
Saint Louis, MO 63119
ph: 314-968-0304
dhuhn@earthlink.net
http://www.thckk.org
A non-profit organization to serve as an interactive information distribution center for collectors of E.C. Simmons/ Keen Kutter, Winchester Store (non-gun), A.F. Shapleigh/Diamond Edge, Hibbard, and other hardware store brands.

Collectors

John M. Otte
800 N. Moulton St.
Perryville, MO 63775
ph: 573-547-6386
Interested in Keen Kutter advertising items that were given away by hardware stores; also interested in rare Keen Kutter tools and postcards with Keen Kutter logo or name on them.

Larry Eastley
46460 Hwy. 10
Hardin, MO 64035
ph: 660-398-4617
eastley@iland.net
Collector of Keen Kutter, Diamond Edge, Winchester Store (non-gun), Simmons & Shapleigh and other hardware store brands.

Experts

Jerry & Elaine Heuring
28450 US Highway 61
Scott City, MO 63780
ph: 573-264-3947
Authors of "Collectors Guide to Keen Kutter," 192 pages with over 750 color photos: advertising, tools, lawn & garden, showcases, farm items, electrical products, kitchen items, pocket knives, company history; available from author.

Jerry & Elaine Heuring
28450 US Highway 61
Scott City, MO 63780
ph: 573-264-3947
Buys and sells Keen Kutter related memorabilia.

Bob Simmons
40706 E. 144th St.
Richmond, MO 64085
ph: 816-776-2936 or 800-646-2936
fax: 816-470-5016
bob@simmonsauction.com
http://www.simmonsauction.com
Collects and specializes in Keen Kutter (E.C. Simmons Hardware) items especially advertising items and unusual items (household, sporting

goods, catalogs, signs) made for this St. Louis firm from the late 1800s to 1940.

KENTUCKY DERBY

(see SPORTS COLLECTIBLES, Thoroughbred Racing)

KEY CHAINS

Clubs/Associations

Dr. Edward H. Miles
License Plate Key Chain & Mini License Plate Collectors
Newsletter: DAV Keychain & Chauffeur Badge Collectors News
888 Eighth Ave.
New York, NY 10019-5704
ph: 212-765-2660
emiles33@aol.com
Focuses on miniature Disabled American Veterans key chains, chauffeurs' badges, gum cards featuring license plates, windshield stickers, mini license plates.

KEYS

(see also KEY CHAINS; LOCKS; RESTRAINT DEVICES; SAFES)

Clubs/Associations

Bob Heilemann
West Coast Lock Collectors
Newsletter: West Coast Lock Collectors Newsletter
1427 Lincoln Blvd.
Santa Monica, CA 90401-2732
ph: 310-454-7295 or 310-230-3004
locksmann@earthlink.net
http://www.wclca.org
Call evenings; no collect calls, please.

Collectors

Joseph Biunno
129 West 29th St.
New York, NY 10001
ph: 212-629-5630
fax: 212-268-4577
Wants furniture locks and keys; barrel, skeleton, door, drawer, old or new; also wants escutcheons in all styles and sizes.

Bruce Axler
Ansonia Station
P.O. Box 1288
New York, NY 10023-1288
ph: 212-579-0348
Wants pocket items, i.e., items/gadgets designed to fit in the pocket: tools, knives, lighters, compacts, folding cups, items which look like a pocket watch but are not, calculators, leather items, matchsafes, candle safes, travel items.

Mark Lyons
6020 Paseo Del Norte, Ste. B
Carlsbad, CA 92009
ph: 760-431-5397
fax: 760-607-3299
cuffsandstuff@sbcglobal.net
Wants unusual keys, original handcuff keys, keys to the city, padlock keys, jail/prison keys; also wants old locks and handcuffs.

KITCHEN COLLECTIBLES

(see also APPLE PARERS; CAST IRON ITEMS; CATALOGS; CERAMICS; COOKIES & COOKIE SHAPING; COOKIE JARS; DAIRY COLLECTIBLES; ELECTRICITY RELATED ITEMS, Appliances; GRANITEWARE; IRONS; MOLDS; PIE BIRDS; RANGES; RANSBURG; SPOONS; STOVES; STRING HOLDERS; TOASTERS)

Clubs/Associations

Janet Hoy
Kollectors of Old Kitchen Stuff
3038 E. Woodland Dr.
Port Huron, MI 48060
ph: 810-985-6230 or 810-841-0231
jndhoy@earthlink.net
For collectors, dealers interested in mechanical kitchen, laundry devices: egg beaters, apple parers, raisin seeders, washing and house cleaning items; primarily interested in items dating from 1850s to 1950s; convention every other year.

Collectors

Patrick Batzler
8118 Virginia Circle North
St. Louis Park, MN 55426
ph: 952-525-9590
fax: 952-545-7662
patrickbatzler@aol.com
Seeks kitchen collectibles from the 1950s and 1960s: Holt Howard and similar makers.

Reid Cooper
32942 Josheroo Ct.
Temecula, CA 92592
ph: 909-302-3348
res20rs2@verizon.net
Collector will purchase tin egg separators or tea strainers with embossed advertising in good or better condition; also buys any premium or item of any kind from the "Egg Baking Powder Co." of New York.

Dealers

Louise Pennisi
Around the Kitchen
P.O. Box 840
Georgetown, CT 06829
ph: 203-438-2338
Buys and sells food and kitchen advertising, including kitchen appliance, recipe pamphlets, cookery booklets (Pillsbury, Baker's Chocolate, Jell-O, etc.), and

collectible cookbooks (19th & 20th c.); catalogs, searches, co. histories.

Jerry Harmyk
Kitschen
380 Bleecker St.
New York, NY 10014
ph: 212-727-0430
Buys and sells kitchen collectibles from the 1920s through 1970s.

Stephen G. DelSordo
Heritage Resource Group
305 Oakley St.
Cambridge, MD 21613
ph: 410-228-8934
fax: 410-221-8061
sdelsordo@comcast.net
http://www.heritageresource.com
A cultural resource management/ historic preservation firm that has contracts to locate, provide, authenticate artifacts for museums and collectors; areas of expertise include architecture, industry, domestic, agriculture, and maritime.

Tom Lawson
Buckeye Appliance & Antiques
714 W. Fremont
Stockton, CA 95203-2702
ph: 209-464-9643
calbuck@aol.com
http://www.BuckeyeAppliance.com
Specializes in the sales, parts and restoration of antique gas stoves; also sells kitchen collectibles, Hoosiers, 1950s chrome dinettes, and porcelain-top tables, architectural, garden.

Jennifer & Co. Antiques & Fine Gifts
18744 Main St.
P.O. Box 884
Groveland, CA 95321-0884
ph: 209-962-7112
jennifer@jenniferandcompany.com
http://www.jenniferandcompany.com
Specializes in much-sought-after kitchen collectibles and cookie jars.

Carole & Larry Meeker
Antiques of a Mechanical Nature
5702 Vacation Blvd.
Somerset, CA 95684-9324
ph: 530-620-7019 or 888-607-6090
fax: 530-620-7020
clm@antiqbuyer.com
http://www.antiqbuyer.com
Wants to buy rare and unusual small patented mechanical antiques, early American technology and occupational-related photography, advertising and catalogs.

Experts

Jim Barker
Toaster Master
P.O. Box 746
Allentown, PA 18102
ph: 610-439-0751
fax: 610-439-1925
jbar@enter.net
Dealer, collector, historian, authority on early electric appliances.

Museums/Libraries

Johnson & Wales Culinary Archives & Museum
315 Harborside Blvd.
Providence, RI 02905-5202
ph: 401-598-2805
Housed at Johnson & Wales University, features more than 300,000 culinary and hospitality related items: cooking tools, antique kitchen appliances, 19th century stoves, graphic prints, cookbooks, menus, etc.

Periodicals

Alan R. Blakeman
B.B.R. Publishing
Magazine: British Bottle Review & Collectors Mart
Elsecar Heritage Centre
Nr Barnsley, South Yorks S74 8HJ U.K.
ph: 01226 745156
fax: 01226 361561
sales@onlinebbr.com
http://www.onlinebbr.com
Published for over 22 years; full color magazine; the world's longest continuous running publication covering the multitudinous areas of antique bottles; including world news; published quarterly.

Butter Churns

Dealers

Wendell W. Stream
Churn Castle Antiques
809 Maple Ave.
Woodward, IA 50276
ph: 515-438-4142
xisp142@netins.net
http://showcase.netins.net/web/churns
Appraiser, dealer and collector of butter churns; Web site has information on most kinds of butter churns.

Egg Separators

Collectors

Don Thornton
P.O. Box 57
Moss Beach, CA 94038
ph: 650-728-7978
fax: 650-728-7980
info@thorntonhouse.com
http://www.thorntonhouse.com
Wants old tin or aluminum egg separators, with advertising.

Egg Timers

Collectors

Lance V. Kuntzman
21 Perry
South Dartmouth, MA 02748-1803
ph: 508-994-5934
tomcaper@aol.com
Wants to buy unusual or figural egg timers with sand glass attached.

Phyllis Eisenach
3759 SW Whispering Sound Dr.
Palm City, FL 34990-7735
ph: 561-223-8275
eisenach@webtv.net
Specializes in figural egg timers; interested particularly in German Goebel and Japanese ceramic figures with glass timer attached.

Patrick Batzler
8118 Virginia Circle North
St. Louis Park, MN 55426
ph: 952-525-9590
fax: 952-545-7662
patrickbatzler@aol.com
Wants figural egg timers.

Eggbeaters

Collectors

Craig Dinner
P.O. Box 4399
Long Island City, NY 11104-0399
ph: 718-729-3850
ferrouswheel123@aol.com
Wants early or unusual egg beaters.

Dana & Darlene DeMore
4645 Laurel Ridge Dr.
Harrisburg, PA 17110-3446
ph: 717-545-7320
Wants to buy old eggbeaters; one or entire collection.

Terry Beams
219-B Stribling Ave.
Charlottesville, VA 22903
ph: 434-971-1983
beamspainting@beamspainting.com
Seeking unusual eggbeaters.

Clay Tontz
4043 Nora Ave.
Covina, CA 91722-3819
ph: 626-338-9976

Reid Cooper
Mixer Mania
32942 Josheroo Ct.
Temecula, CA 92592
ph: 909-302-3348
res20rs2@verizon.net
Advanced collector/researcher buying pre-1920 US-made eggbeaters, mayonnaise mixers, cream whips and stoneware beater bowls in top working order and/or condition; no electrics, plastic, or stainless; send price, photo or sketch.

Experts

Don Thornton
P.O. Box 57
Moss Beach, CA 94038
ph: 650-728-7978
fax: 650-728-7980
info@thorntonhouse.com
http://www.thorntonhouse.com
Wants old eggbeaters and related memorabilia and paper items, especially old catalogs; author of "Beat This, The Eggbeater Chronicles," (1994) and "The Eggbeater Book," (1983).

Flour Sifters

Collectors

Dana & Darlene DeMore
4645 Laurel Ridge Dr.
Harrisburg, PA 17110-3446
ph: 717-545-7320
Wants to buy mechanical flour sifters.

Frisbie Pie Pans

Collectors

Jerome Gundrum
200 Duncaster Rd.
Bloomfield, CT 06002
ph: 860-342-5714
DrRootbeer@aol.com
http://www.rootbeer.net
Buys, sells, trades pie tins having bakery names on them.

Mark Daniels
4786 Forest Grove Dr.
Brunswick, OH 44212
ph: 330-220-2722 or 440-669-8621
fax: 330-220-2715
Wants to buy any Frisbie Pie Co. collectible: pie pans, pie safes, advertising items, etc.

Victor Malafronte
909 Marina Village Pkwy., #321
Alameda, CA 94501
ph: 510-814-9639
Wants to buy Frisbie pie pans (made by the Frisbie Pie Co., Bridgeport, CT); will pay up to $5 each if in good condition.

Ice Shavers

Collectors

Don Thornton
P.O. Box 57
Moss Beach, CA 94038
ph: 650-728-7978
fax: 650-728-7980
info@thorntonhouse.com
http://www.thorntonhouse.com
Wants old ice shavers, cast iron planes and bowls.

Lemon Squeezers

Collectors

Stanley D. Watson
2959 Hundred Oaks Ave.
Baton Rouge, LA 70808-1536
ph: 225-383-1594
Wants to buy cast iron lemon squeezers with glass or porcelain bowls.

Mangles

Collectors

Nancy Alford
Mrs. Mangles
alford@pipeline.com.au
http://www.pipeline.com.au/users/alford
Collects antique mangles.

Mixers

Collectors

Norman Hagey
Mr. Sunbeam
19672 Steavens Creek #424
Cupertino, CA 95014-2465
ph: 408-973-8129
Wants to buy old Sunbeam mixers only: complete mixers, attachments, bowls, toasters, and information on model numbers and types; books, pamphlets about Sunbeam mixers.

Nutmeg Grinders

Collectors

Dana & Darlene DeMore
4645 Laurel Ridge Dr.
Harrisburg, PA 17110-3446
ph: 717-545-7320
Wants to buy mechanical nutmeg grinders.

Pie Crimpers/Jaggers

Collectors

Priscilla Hinners
2711 Jaynia Place
Lemon Grove, CA 91945-1319
ph: 619-265-1046
phinners@yahoo.com
Wants all types of pie crimpers (jaggers): ceramic, ivory, metal, unusual wooden, etc.

Pot Scrubbers

Collectors

Don Thornton
P.O. Box 57
Moss Beach, CA 94038
ph: 650-728-7978
fax: 650-728-7980
info@thorntonhouse.com
http://www.thorntonhouse.com
Wants old pot scrubbers - the ugly chain-mail variety.

Reamers

Clubs/Associations

Deborah Gillham
National Reamer Collectors Association
Newsletter: NRCA Quarterly Review
47 Midline Ct.
Gaithersburg, MD 20878-1996
ph: 301-977-5727
reamers@erols.com
http://www.reamers.org
A non-profit organization with over 350 members devoted to promoting citrus and juice reamer and squeezer collecting; interested in reamers of all materials - porcelain, glass, wood, metal, etc.

Gail Richards
Mid-American Reamer Collectors
Newsletter: Juicy Journal
8947 Briarclift Rd.
Indianapolis, IN 46256
ph: 317-845-1566
Club is an affiliate of the National Reamers Collectors Association;

membership in the NRCA is required for Regional Club membership.

John Brown, Pres.
Southwest Reamer Collectors Association
2824 Willing
Fort Worth, TX 76110
ph: 817-923-2026
sandyjohn@charter.net
http://www.reamers.org
Club is an affiliate of the National Reamers Collectors Association; membership in the NRCA is required for Regional Club membership.

Terry McDuffee
Western Regional Reamer Collectors Association
1478 W. Cypress Ave.
Redlands, CA 92373-5613
ph: 909-739-9534
fax: 909-335-8354
Club is an affiliate of the National Reamers Collectors Association; membership in the NRCA is required for Regional Club membership.

Collectors

Bobbie & Alan Bryson
1 St. Eleanoras Ln.
Tuckahoe, NY 10707-1307
ph: 914-779-1405
napkindoll@aol.com
Wants figural reamers; Bobbie is co-author of the pictorial reference guide "Collectibles For The Kitchen, Bath & Beyond" (Antique Trader Books).

Judy Smith
1702 Lamont St., NW
Washington, DC 20010
ph: 202-332-3020
fax: 202-234-6653
judy@quilt.net
http://www.quiltart.com/judy/glass.html
Interested in unusual glass, china and metal reamers and other Depression-era kitchen glassware; Webmaster for National Reamer Collector's Association (http://www.reamers.org/).

Deborah Gillham
47 Midline Ct.
Gaithersburg, MD 20878-1996
ph: 301-977-5727
reamers@erols.com
http://www.reamers.org
Membership chairman for the National Reamer Collectors Association.

Patrick Batzler
8118 Virginia Circle North
St. Louis Park, MN 55426
ph: 952-525-9590
fax: 952-545-7662
patrickbatzler@aol.com
Seeking kitchen collectibles including reamers or juicers.

Ray Maxwell
222 Cooper Ave.
Elgin, IL 60120-2128
ph: 847-695-6284
Collects all reamers; especially interested in glass reamers from the Depression era.

Jim Pulliam
1925 Ashley Dr.
Edmond, OK 73034
ph: 405-340-8710

Terry McDuffee
1478 W. Cypress Ave.
Redlands, CA 92373-5613
ph: 909-739-9534
fax: 909-335-8354
Buys and sells reamers, juicers and kitchen glassware; rare and unusual items wanted; please price and describe.

Rolling Pins

Collectors

Priscilla Hinners
2711 Jaynia Place
Lemon Grove, CA 91945-1319
ph: 619-265-1046
phinners@yahoo.com
Wants all types of rolling pins: Nailsea, Meissen, Harker, ceramic, glass, stoneware, advertising, metal, unusual wooden, springerle, and other types of rollers.

Sausage Stuffers

Collectors

Dale Schmidt
610 Howell Prairie Rd. SE
Salem, OR 97301-9097
ph: 503-364-0499
fax: 503-585-3071
jschm62655@aol.com
Wants all types; complete or parts.

Wire Ware

Repro. Sources

Mathews Wire, Inc.
654 West Morrison
Frankfort, IN 46041-1670
ph: 800-826-9650
fax: 765-659-1059
mwire@mathewswire.com
http://www.mathewswire.com
Wholesale supplier of wire reproductions; egg baskets, display racks, etc.; also reproduction toys and advertising signs.

KITES

Experts

Valerie Govig
KiteLines Bookstore, LLC
17A Hogarth Circle
Cockeysville Hunt Valley, MD 21030
ph: 410-683-8562
kitelines@compuserve.com
http://www.kitelinesbookstore.com
Former editor of "Kite Lines" magazine; offers kite books by mail

order; edits newsletter for the Maryland Kite Society.

Museums/Libraries

World Kite Museum & Hall of Fame
112 - 3rd St. NW
P.O. Box 964
Long Beach, WA 98631-0964
ph: 360-642-4020
jkite@willapabay.org
http://www.funbeach.com/Attrac9.html
Collection contains more than 600 kites from around the world; exhibits change annually.

KITS

(see also MODELS; SCIENCE FICTION)

Dealers

Fred Sterns
Fred's Model World
48 Standish Rd.
Buffalo, NY 14216
ph: 716-838-6797
fax: 716-836-6057
fsterns@aol.com
http://members.aol.com/jftully/fjs
Over 30 years of experience in model kits: building, buying, selling and appraisals; expert in kits made by AMT, MPC, Johan, Revell, Monogram, Aurora, and most foreign manufacturers.

Experts

Fred Sterns
Fred's Model World
48 Standish Rd.
Buffalo, NY 14216
ph: 716-838-6797
fax: 716-836-6057
fsterns@aol.com
http://members.aol.com/jftully/fjs
Over 30 years of experience in model kits: building, buying, selling and appraisals; expert in kits made by AMT, MPC, Johan, Revell, Monogram, Aurora, and most foreign manufacturers.

Periodicals

Fred DeRuvo, Ex. Pub.
Magazine: Modeler's Resource, The
4120 Douglas Blvd., #306-372
Granite Bay, CA 95746-5936
ph: 916-784-9517
fax: 916-784-8384
modres@surewest.net
http://www.modelersresource.com
Bi-monthly, promptly published magazine with up-to-date information including "how-tos" profiles, reviews, show coverage, etc. for the Sci-Fi, Fantasy, Vehicular, and Figure model builder.

Figures

Dealers

Gordy Dutt
Gordy's
P.O. Box 201
Sharon Center, OH 44274-0201
ph: 330-239-1657
fax: 330-239-2991
Gordysmag@aol.com
http://www.gordyskitbuilders.com
Buys and sells plastic, vinyl, and resin figure or Sci/Fi type model kits from the 1950s to present; also toys from the late '50s to the early '80s.

John F. Green
John F. Green, Inc.
P.O. Box 55787
Riverside, CA 92517
ph: 909-684-5300 or 800-807-4759
fax: 909-684-8819
ML@greenmodels.com
http://www.greenmodels.com
Sells, buys, trades plastic model kits from and of science fiction, TV, figures, space movies, etc.; old and new; send for free sales catalog.

Experts

Terry J. Webb
P.O. Box 30885
Columbus, OH 43230-0885
ph: 614-882-2125
fax: 614-882-6012
vlad2001@earthlink.net
http://www.amazingmodeler.com
Internationally renowned expert on the Garage Kit hobby; author of "Reverence of the Garage Kit That Ate My Wallet."

Gordy Dutt
Gordy's
P.O. Box 201
Sharon Center, OH 44274-0201
ph: 330-239-1657
fax: 330-239-2991
Gordysmag@aol.com
http://www.gordyskitbuilders.com
Dealing in figure related plastic, vinyl and resin model kits since 1986 (some boats, cars, planes); a mail order business.

Periodicals

Terry J. Webb
Amazing Publications & Communications Inc.
Magazine: Amazing Figure Modeler
P.O. Box 30885
Columbus, OH 43230-0885
ph: 614-882-2125
fax: 614-882-6012
vlad2001@earthlink.net
http://www.amazingmodeler.com
A quarterly magazine that focuses on the international garage and model figure kit market.

Plastic

Clubs/Associations

Jim Bates, Sec.
International Plastic Modelers Society
USA
Journal: IPMS/USA Modelers Journal
P.O. Box 2475
Canton, OH 44720-2475
ph: 330-478-3882
fax: 330-494-5456
jbates2@stratos.net
http://www.ipmsusa.org
Journal includes review of new kits and accessories, scratch-building, convention articles, IPMS news, etc.

John W. Burns
Society for the Preservation & Encouragement of Scale Model Kit Collecting
Magazine: Kit Collectors Clearinghouse
3213 Hardy Dr.
Edmond, OK 73013-5319
ph: 405-341-4640
cheersjb@swbell.net
A bi-monthly magazine for kit collectors; covers plastic model kits of aircraft, cars, tanks, ships, etc.; buy and sell ads, re-issue notices, information on new kits, vacuum-formed and resin kits, etc.

Collectors

Wally Krocsko
P.O. Box 307
Atlasburg, PA 15004-0307
ph: 724-947-5671
Sell plastic model kits; must enclose a LSASE to get a reply to buy/sell/trade inquiries; please call evenings.

John Krupienski
5200 Hilltop Dr.
P.O. Box AA6
Brookhaven, PA 19015-1200
ph: 610-874-3003

Jim Crane
15 Clemson Ct.
Newark, DE 19711-4301
ph: 302-738-6031
spcjpc@earthlink.net
Wants Aurora, Revell, Monogram plastic kits; built or unbuilt; any condition; wants figures, planes, boats and catalogs.

Experts

John W. Burns
3213 Hardy Dr.
Edmond, OK 73013-5319
ph: 405-341-4640
cheersjb@swbell.net
Author of "Plastic Aircraft Kits of the 20th Century And Beyond;" 425-page book with value guide and complete data on 32,000 plastic aircraft kits; wants to buy unbuilt plastic kits of all subjects.

Plastic (Aurora)

Experts

Bill & Joanne Bruegman
Toy Scouts, Inc.
137 Casterton Ave.
Akron, OH 44303-1543
ph: 330-836-0668
orders@toyscouts.com
http://www.toyscouts.com
Author of "Aurora History and Price Guide."

David Welch
P.O. Box 714
Murphysboro, IL 62966-0714
ph: 618-687-2282
fax: 618-684-2243
PEZDude1@aol.com
http://www.pezheads.net/dwelch
Specializing in Aurora figure kits; buying any pre-1977 TV, science fiction, comic, movie, monster related kits; must have original boxes unless factory promos; contributor to "O'Brien's Collecting Toys" and Tomart's "Garage Sale Gold."

KNIFE RESTS

Clubs/Associations

Dean Rockwell
Knife Rest Collectors Society
P.O. Box 970373
Ypsilanti, MI 48197
ph: 734-485-1442
fax: 734-487-2636

Doreen Hornsblow
Knife Rest Collectors Club
Braughingbury
Braughing
Hertfordshire, SG11 2RD U.K.
ph: 01920 822654
fax: 01920 822654
dorkrcc@hotmail.com

Collectors

Beverly Schell Ales
4046 Graham St.
Pleasanton, CA 94566-5619
ph: 925-846-5297
fax: 925-846-5297
kniferests@sbcglobal.net

KNIVES

(see also ARMS & ARMOR; BLACKSMITHING ITEMS; BOOKS, Reference [Knives]; DIAMOND EDGE; EDGED WEAPONS; KEEN KUTTER; KNIFE RESTS)

Auction Services

Blade Auction
6 University Dr., #249
Amherst, MA 01004-6000
fax: 603-710-8124
frontdesk@bladeauction.com
http://www.bladeauction.com
Online knife auction service: automatica, microtech, benchmade, Robbi Dalton, custom knives, long blades, production knives, antique knives, military knives, southpaw, multi tools, collections, supplies.

J. Bruce Voyles
J. Bruce Voyles, Auctioneers
P.O. Box 22007
Chattanooga, TN 37422
ph: 423-894-8319
fax: 423-892-7254
bruce@jbrucevoyles.com
http://www.jbrucevoyles.com
Primarily knife auctioneers specializing in Bowies, vintage pocket knives, fine handmade and custom knives; anything with an edge.

Clubs/Associations

Caroline Levine
Northeast Cutlery Collectors Association
P.O. Box 415
Dracut, MA 01826
ph: 978-454-5027
cklevine@att.net

Jay Tinker
Chesapeake Bay Knife Club, Inc.
Newsletter: CBKC Newsletter
939-I Beards Hill Rd., PMB #122
Aberdeen, MD 21001-1714
ph: 410-343-0380 or 410-686-5529
webmaster@knifeshows.com
http://www.knifeshows.com/clubs/cbkc
Club meets monthly on the second Monday at 7:30pm Rodesale Federal S&L on Rte. 1 in Perry Hall, MD; visits to local knifemakers' shops are scheduled; members' interests are varied, but all are cutlery related.

Palmetto Cutlery Club
P.O. Box 1356
Greer, SC 29652
ph: 864-877-0303
Members are collectors of knives and related objects.

Chattachoochee Cutlery Club
P.O. Box 568
Tucker, GA 30084-0568

Jimmy Green
Three Rivers Knife Club
783 NE Jones Mill Rd.
Rome, GA 30165-9075
ph: 706-235-0581 or 706-234-2540

Deep South Knife Collectors
P.O. Box 9001
Pensacola, FL 32513-9001
ph: 850-477-2202
fax: 850-477-2202

Mitch Weiss
Art Knife Collector's Association
Newsletter: Art Knife Trader
2211 Lee Rd., Ste. 104
Winter Park, FL 32789
ph: 407-740-8778
fax: 407-740-8283
mitch@artknife.com
http://www.artknife.com

Gary G. Nichols
Heart of Dixie Cutlery Club
4141 Camp Coleman
Trussville, AL 35173-2818
ph: 205-655-7789

Frank Centofante, Sec./Treas.
Knifemaker's Guild, The
P.O. Box 1019
Madisonville, TN 37354-1019
ph: 423-442-5767
fax: 423-442-5767
cento@compfxnet.com
http://www.kmg.org
*Recognized as the organization of the
finest custom handmade knifemakers in
the world, where more than 250
members display and offer for sale
handcrafted knives of the finest quality
at an annual show.*

National Knife Collectors Association
Newsletter: NKCA Gazette
5924-B Shallowford Rd.
P.O. Box 21070
Chattanooga, TN 37424-0070
ph: 423-892-5007
fax: 423-899-9456
nkca@aol.com
http://www.nationalknife.org
*A not-for-profit association dedicated
to promoting the hobby of knife
collecting; sponsors six knife shows
each year and sanctions many other
local knife shows.*

Western Reserve Cutlery Association
P.O. Box 355
Dover, OH 44622
rmacmac@aol.com

James Webb
Johnny Appleseed Knife Collectors
668 Lenox Ave.
Mansfield, OH 44906
ph: 419-747-7551

Ed Etchason
Indiana Knife Collectors
P.O. Box 101
Fountaintown, IN 46130-0101
ph: 317-835-7487

Patrick Donovan
Wolverine Knife Collectors Club
Newsletter: Wolverine Knife Collectors
    Newsletter
P.O. Box 52
Belleville, MI 48112-0052
ph: 586-786-5549
patrickjdonovan@comcast.net
http://expage.com/page/wkcc
*Michigan's largest knife collectors
club; members are expert in most knife
collecting categories; annual show is
one of the largest in the Midwest; new
annual mini-show in Sept.; affiliated
with the National Knife Collectors
Association.*

Bob Schrap
Badger Knife Club, Inc.
Newsletter: Badger Knife Club
    Newsletter
P.O. Box 511
Elm Grove, WI 53122-0511
ph: 414-479-9765 or 414-771-6472
fax: 262-784-2996
RSchrap@aol.com
*Club for all knife collectors; custom,
factory, military, antique knives; for
knife collectors, makers and dealers.*

Joe Kertzman
International Blade Collectors
Association
c/o Krause Publications
700 E. State Ste.
Iola, WI 54990
ph: 715-445-4612
fax: 715-445-4087
kertzmanj@krause.com

North Star Blade Collectors
P.O. Box 20523
Bloomington, MN 55420
http://www.knifecorner.com/nsbc
*Members interested in various forms
of cutlery.*

Willard C. Patrick, Pres.
Professional Knifemakers Association,
Inc.
2905 N. Montana Ave., Ste. 30027
Helena, MT 59601
ph: 770-449-7809
fax: 770-446-0644
president@proknifemakers.com
http://www.proknifemakers.com
*An association for professional
knifemakers, purveyors of custom
knives, suppliers to the trade.*

Louie Jamison, Pres.
American Edge Collectors Association
Newsletter: AECA Newsletter
24755 Hickory Ct.
Crete, IL 60417
ph: 708-868-7784 or 708-672-8838

Larry Hancock
Jefferson County Custom Knife Club
12193 E. Turner Dr.
Mount Vernon, IL 62864-2672
ph: 618-242-4514
fax: 618-244-5536
safety103@hotmail.com

Kansas Knife Collectors Association
P.O. Box 1125
Wichita, KS 67201
ph: 316-838-0540

Knife Collectors Club, Inc., The
1920 N. 2th St., US 540
Lowell, AR 72745-8989
ph: 479-631-0130 or 800-255-9034
fax: 479-631-8493
http://www.k-c-c.com

Texas Knifemakers & Collectors
Association
Newsletter: TKCA Newsletter
853 House St.
Fort Worth, TX 76103
ph: 817-451-8243
fax: 817-446-6982
tkca@tkca.org
http://www.tkca.org
*Promotes handmade knives and Texas
knifemakers; increases public
awareness of knifemakers as skilled
and versatile craft persons.*

Mike Moeskau
Gulf Coast Knife Club
P.O. Box 265
Pasadena, TX 77501-0265
ph: 281-554-6791 or 713-788-6016

Mike Moss. Pres.
Rocky Mountain Blade Collectors
P.O. Box 324
Westminster, CO 80230-0324
ph: 303-680-0408

Joseph G. Cordova
American Blacksmith Society
P.O. Box 977
Peralta, NM 87042-0977
ph: 505-869-3912
fax: 505-869-2509
abs@rt66.com
*An international society composed of
knifemakers who use the forging
method to make the blade and of
collectors who appreciate the forged
blade.*

Joseph G. Cordova
American Bladesmith Society
P.O. Box 977
Peralta, NM 87042-0977
ph: 505-869-3912
fax: 505-869-2509
abs@rt66.com
http://www.americanbladesmith.com
For knifemakers and knife enthusiasts.

Lowell Shelhart
Southern California Blades Knife
Collectors Club
P.O. Box 1140
Lomita, CA 90717-5140
ph: 310-530-8412
fax: 310-784-1330

Bay Area Knife Collectors Association
P.O. Box 2787
Dublin, CA 94568-1029
jeffrey.pelz@gte.net
http://www.bakca.org

Oregon Knife Collectors
P.O. Box 2091
Eugene, OR 97402
ph: 541-484-5564
okca@oregonknifeclub.org
http://www.oregonknifeclub.org

Paul Johnston, Sec./Treas.
Canadian Knifemakers Guild
8 Forest Dr. RR#4
Smiths Falls, Ontario K7A 4S5 Canada
ph: 613-472-5644
cdnguild@ckg.org
http://www.ckg.org
*Goal is to increase public awareness
of knifemakers, not as makers of
weapons, but as skilled and versatile
crafts people producing high quality
implements which happen to be knives.*

Collectors

Bruce Axler
Ansonia Station
P.O. Box 1288
New York, NY 10023-1288
ph: 212-579-0348
*Wants pocket items, i.e., items/gadgets
designed to fit in the pocket: tools,
knives, lighters, compacts, folding
cups, items which look like a pocket
watch but are not, calculators, leather
items, matchsafes, candle safes, travel
items.*

Kenneth D. Smith
55 Howard Ave.
Staten Island, NY 10301-4404
*Wants to buy Fairbairn-Sykes fighting
knives with personalized Wilkinson
blades.*

Bill Campesi
P.O. Box 140
Merrick, NY 11566-0140
ph: 516-546-9630
*Buy, sell, trade all cutlery and related
advertising: catalogs, postcards,
cutlery display items; pocket, sheath,
Bowie knives.*

Gerald A. Shaw
1928 Causton Bluff Rd.
Savannah, GA 31404-1310
ph: 912-232-0771
*Wants knives by Remington, Boker,
Winchester, CASE, Russell, Western,
Ka-Bar, etc.; also wants razors, knife
books, daggers, hunting knives, pocket
knives, etc.*

Gordon White
P.O. Box 181
Cuthbert, GA 31740
ph: 912-732-6982
*Wants to buy M.S.A., Marbles,
Scagel, and R.H. Ruana knives and
hatchets; also Loveless, Morseth,
Randall, and Remington sheath knives;
any Heiser, V.L. & A., or A&F Co.
marked knives or ax sheaths.*

Guy Manwaring
P.O. Box 361
Tecumseh, MI 49286-0361
ph: 517-423-4466
fax: 517-423-4466
*Collects knives: pocket, Bowie,
hunting, American switchblades, etc.;
also wants old magazine ads for
knives or Keen Kutter hardware,
cardboard pocket knife boxes,*

countertop displays, postcards, catalogs, any cutlery items.

A.L. Hunt
P.O. Box 711
Excelsior Springs, MO 64024
ph: 816-637-8464
Wants to buy military knives & bayonets from WWI, WWII, Korea, Vietnam: Special Forces stilettos & bolos, Seals dive knives, USMC recon knives & KA Bars, presentation knives, trench knives, M-4s, M-6s, bayonets, Randalls, EKS.

Dealers

Dennis Blaine
Cutlery Specialties
22 Morris Lane
Great Neck, NY 11024-1707
ph: 516-829-5899 or 800-229-5530 (orders)
fax: 516-773-8076
Dennis13@aol.com
http://www.restorationproduct.com
Buys, sells, trades, designs knives and other related cutlery items.

Glenn Smit
Wolf's Knives - Murphy's Way
627 Cindy Court
Aberdeen, MD 21001-1714
ph: 410-272-2959
fax: 410-278-2191
wolfsknife@aol.com
Buy, sell, trade knives produced throughout the history of the Murphy Knife Companies of Gresham, OR; also hand makes custom knives based on these past designs.

Tom Clark
Blue Ridge Knives
166 Adwolfe Rd.
Marion, VA 24354-9351
ph: 540-783-6143
fax: 540-783-9298
brk@netva.com
http://www.blueridgeknives.com
Will purchase entire knife collections or by the piece; interested in antique pocket, hunting and Bowie knives, commemorative knives, custom handmade knives, and business inventories of factory knives.

Rhett & Janie Stidham
Stidham's Knives
P.O. Box 570
Roseland, FL 32957
ph: 561-589-0618
fax: 561-589-3162
rstidham@gate.net
http://www.kmg.org/stidham
Over 29 years in business; specializes in older makers and in particular Loveless, Horn, Moran, Cronk, Hibben, Draper, Lile, Cooper, and Scagel; buys and sells at all major shows; buys collections large & small; specializes in Bowie knives.

Parkers' Knife Collector Service
6715 Heritage Business Court
P.O. Box 23522
Chattanooga, TN 37422
ph: 800-247-0599 or 423-892-0448
fax: 615-892-9165
Distributes all kinds of knives including Winchester, antique Case, Remington, Club knives, Marbles, Fightn' Rooster, New German knives, antique knives, Bulldog Brand Pit Bull collector knives, prototypes, etc.

J. Bruce Voyles
Heritage Antique Knives
P.O. Box 22007
Chattanooga, TN 37422
ph: 423-894-8319
fax: 423-892-7254
bruce@jbrucevoyles.com
http://www.jbrucevoyles.com
Buys, sells, collects, appraises and specializes in all kinds of knives including store closing inventories, Bowie knives, old pocket knives, antique, current, commemorative, advertising; also store displays, knife memorabilia, etc.

Steve Koontz
Riverside Cutlery Co.
P.O. Box 278
Kodak, TN 37764-0278
ph: 865-453-9558
fax: 865-453-2682
http://www.riversidecutlery.com
Specializes in new and old cutlery; over 1,000 rare and collectible knives.

Smokey Mountain Knife Words
2320 Winfield Dunn Pkwy.
Sevierville, TN 37862
ph: 800-251-9306
fax: 423-429-0182
Possibly the world's largest cutlery store: 40,000 square feet of sales and display floor space.

Charles D. Stapp
7037 Haynes Rd.
Georgetown, IN 47122-8610
ph: 812-923-3483
dennyjoyce@aol.com
Wants all kinds of old knives in any condition; will buy, appraise or sell on consignment; use color photos or send a trace drawing; please show blade and note all markings; SASE appreciated.

Byron Rogers
Cutler's Cove Knife Emporium
P.O. Box 3171
San Angelo, TX 76092-3171
ph: 325-655-4839
fax: 325-659-1404
info@cutlerscove.com
http://www.cutlerscove.com
Since 1991, dealing in quality vintage, used, old, antique, scarce and rare knives; specializes in vintage pocketknives, folders and fixed blades; Web site has over 2,000 links to other knife, sword, cutlery Web sites.

Lowell Shelhart
S&S and Sons Cutlery
P.O. Box 501
Lomita, CA 90717-0501
ph: 310-326-3869
snsandsons@earthlink.net
http://www.snsandsonscutlers.com
Dealer in collector grade knives.

Experts

J. Bruce Voyles
P.O. Box 22007
Chattanooga, TN 37422
ph: 423-894-8319
fax: 423-892-7254
bruce@jbrucevoyles.com
http://www.jbrucevoyles.com
Former publisher of "Blade Magazine" and "Edges, The Journal of American Knife Collecting;" author of 16 books on knives including price guides; edits the Knives entry of the "World Book Encyclopedia;" member Cutlery Hall of Fame.

Jim Weyer
Weyer International
2740 Nebraska Ave.
Toledo, OH 43607-3245
ph: 419-534-2020
law-weyerinternational@msn.com
Author of the "Knives: Points of Interest" book series which focuses on custom made knives.

Charles D. Stapp
7037 Haynes Rd.
Georgetown, IN 47122-8610
ph: 812-923-3483
dennyjoyce@aol.com
Wants all kinds of old knives in any condition; will buy, appraise or sell on consignment; use color photos or send a trace drawing; please show blade and note all markings; SASE appreciated.

Alex Peck
Antique Scientifica
P.O. Box 710
Charleston, IL 61920-0710
ph: 217-348-1009
antiques@advant.net
http://antiquescientifica.com
Collects early Bowie knives, American or English, especially with a motto and Civil War era; also California knives, knives by Rose, Goulding, Schively, Bell, Rees.

Charles H. Clements, III
Gryphon Studio
1741 Dallas St.
Aurora, CO 80010-2018
ph: 303-364-0403
fax: 303-739-9824
chas@pcisys.net
http://www.combase.com/~carregal/kuntao/chas.htm
Appraises and specializes in arms & armor, hunting, gaming, military and leisure material for men, frontier, fur-trade and Indian artifacts, etc.

Bernard Levine
P.O. Box 2404
Eugene, OR 97402-0124
ph: 541-484-0294
brlevine@ix.netcom.com
http://www.knife-expert.com
Identification and appraisal, museum consultation, expert witness, research, writing; author of "Levine's Guide to Knives and Their Values;" offers online evaluations of knives.

Internet Resources

Larry Burton
Knife Trader, The
burtonld@chattanooga.net
Great resource Web site for knife collectors.

Byron Rogers
Knife Web Guide
P.O. Box 3171
San Angelo, TX 76092-3171
ph: 325-655-4839
fax: 325-659-1404
info@cutlerscove.com
http://www.KinfeWebGuide.com
A gateway to knife, sword and cutlery information; Guide includes over 2,000 links in theme-based categories; regularly updated.

Russell L. Horn
International Knife Directory
1878 Galaxy Way
Redding, CA 96002
ph: 530-226-9488
info@knifecollector.com
http://www.horn-net.com/ikd
Internet site for knife enthusiasts: custom makers, manufacturers, retailers, suppliers, specialists, shows, classifieds, organizations, ads, and more.

Museums/Libraries

National Knife Museum, The
Magazine: National Knife Magazine
7201 Shallowford Rd.
P.O. Box 21070
Chattanooga, TN 37424-0070
ph: 423-892-5007
fax: 423-899-9456
nkca@aol.com
http://members.aol.com/nkca/nkm.htm
Collection includes over 15,000 knives from the Bronze Age to present; owned and operated by the National Knife Collectors Association.

Periodicals

Newspaper: Knife World
P.O. Box 3395
Knoxville, TN 37927-3395
ph: 865-397-1955 or 800-828-7751
fax: 865-397-1969
knifepub@knifeworld.com
http://www.knifeworld.com
A monthly newspaper with ads, shows, knife makers, knife artistry, knife making supplies, knife books, articles of interest to collectors and knife historians; has knife identification and value columns.

Magazine: BIG Show Journal
P.O. Box 217
Iola, WI 54945
ph: 715-445-2708
paul@xlcom.com
http://www.showjournal.com
The guide to knife and gun shows nationwide.

Stacie Berger
Krause Publications
Magazine: Blade
700 E. State St.
Iola, WI 54990-0001
ph: 715-445-2214
fax: 715-445-4087
stacie.berger@fwpubs.com
http://www.krause.com
A monthly magazine focusing on all aspects of knives, razors, pocket knives, knife making, care, sharpening, etc.

Stacie Berger
Krause Publications
Magazine: Blade Trade
700 E. State St.
Iola, WI 54990-0001
ph: 715-445-2214
fax: 715-445-4087
stacie.berger@fwpubs.com
http://www.krause.com
Directed at the retailer who sells cutlery; provides important tips and product knowledge on how to sell cutlery; full range of cutlery is covered.

Suppliers

Dennis Blaine
Cutlery Specialties
22 Morris Lane
Great Neck, NY 11024-1707
ph: 516-829-5899 or 800-229-5530 (orders)
fax: 516-773-8076
Dennis13@aol.com
http://www.restorationproduct.com
Preservation products for flatware: waxes, polishes, cleaners, glues, epoxies, adhesives, chamois, buffs, putty; Renaissance Wax/Polish to restore, refresh, protect antiques, cutlery, furniture, precious metals, armory and more.

Jim Lemcke
Texas Knifemakers Supply
10649 Haddington #180
Houston, TX 77043
ph: 713-461-8632 or 888-461-8632 (orders)
fax: 713-461-8221
jimlemcke@texasknife.com
http://www.texasknife.com
An extensive selection of micarta, steel, exotic woods, brass, stag horn, bone handle fasteners, rod tubing, ox horn, belt sanders, buffing wheels, rouge, epoxy, heat treating ovens, custom sheaths; large catalog, online shopping.

Bowie
Clubs/Associations

Paul L. Holmer
Antique Bowie Knife Association
Newsletter: Antique Bowie Journal
Buley Library, S. Court State U
501 Crescent St.
New Haven, CT 06515-1330
ph: 203-248-6318
fax: 203-392-5740
holmer@scsu.ctstateu.edu
The ABKA exists to serve collectors and students of antique Bowie-type knives; the Journal is published four times per year and an annual meeting features a board to authenticate members' knives.

Collectors

David Wallach
P.O. Box 150285
San Rafael, CA 94915-0285
ph: 415-777-0123 or 415-883-7121
fax: 415-284-5364
vcsrs@aol.com
Wants to buy find old Bowie knives.

Dealers

John Sexton
Stone Mountain Relics, Inc.
1551 Annapolis Way
Stone Mountain, GA 30017
ph: 770-329-4984
fax: 770-972-1953
john@civilwardealer.com
http://www.civilwardealer.com
Offers authentic Civil War memorabilia and collectibles; Confederate items a specialty.

Rhett & Janie Stidham
Stidham's Knives
P.O. Box 570
Roseland, FL 32957
ph: 561-589-0618
fax: 561-589-3162
rstidham@gate.net
http://www.kmg.org/stidham
Over 29 years in business; specializes in older makers and in particular Loveless, Horn, Moran, Cronk, Hibben, Draper, Lile, Cooper, and Scagel; buys and sells at all major shows; buys collections large & small; specializes in Bowie knives.

David L. Hartline
P.O. Box 775
Columbus, OH 43085-0775
fax: 614-760-5427
Buys and sells edged weapons; has large library and over 30 years experience; specialty is pre-1920 Bowie knives; has had many articles published on edge weapons; answers every letter; does appraisals and will authenticate.

Experts

Paul L. Holmer
P.O. Box 6091
Hamden, CT 06517-0091
ph: 203-392-5746
fax: 203-392-5740
holmer@scsu.ctstateu.edu
Always interested in talking with collectors or students and sharing information; has special interest in knives (e.g. Bowie, folding dirks, silver-mounted American daggers) made in the northeastern states during the 19th century.

Buck
Clubs/Associations

W. Murray Andrews
Buck Collectors Club, Inc.
P.O. Box 3
Enon, OH 45323-0003
ph: 937-767-7613
fax: 937-767-1773
For collectors of both fixed blade and folding pocket knives produced by Buck Knives, Inc. and their founders; Andrews is a former newsletter editor and has written for some periodicals pertaining to Buck knives.

Case
Collectors

Frank Miller
49192 McKenzie Hwy.
Vida, OR 97488
ph: 714-870-5902
fax: 714-879-9049
fshnfrank@aol.com
Wants CASE knives in mint condition: Doctors, Peanuts, Toothpicks, Melon Tasters, Flyfishermen and Appaloosa; also CASE memorabilia.

Computer Programs For
Man./Prod./Dist.

Niche Software, Inc.
Software: Knife Collector, The
7118 NW Terrace
Parkland, FL 33076
ph: 954-344-6561
marketing@collectiblessoftware.com
http://www.collectiblessoftware.com
Designed for the collector of knives, swords, daggers, accessories, etc.

Fight'n Rooster
Clubs/Associations

Frank Buster
Fight'n Rooster Cutlery Club
Newsletter: FRCC Newsletter
P.O. Box 936
Lebanon, TN 37087
ph: 615-444-8070
frank@fightnrooster.com
http://www.fightnrooster.com
A company-sponsored collector's club.

Man./Prod./Dist.

Frank Buster
Fight'n Rooster Cutlery Company
P.O. Box 936
Lebanon, TN 37087
ph: 615-444-8070
frank@fightnrooster.com
http://www.fightnrooster.com
Manufacturer of Fight'n Rooster knives.

Military
Collectors

Rickie Marquette
P.O. Box 343133
Homestead, FL 33034
ph: 305-246-5431 or 305-245-2323
fax: 305-245-9295
rangerson@aol.com
Wants to buy military fighting knives, especially John Ek, Scagel, Randall, and Gerber knives; also Special Forces, S.O.G. knives, presentation pieces, and edged weapons in general.

Miniature
Clubs/Associations

Kranning
Miniature Knifemakers' Society
1900 W. Quinn Rd.
Pocatello, ID 83202-2801
ph: 208-237-9047
terrykranning@juno.com
Promotes the collecting and making of miniature knives.

Pocket
Collectors

Dino Bakeris
417 Old Line Ave.
Laurel, MD 20724
ph: 301-604-6739
fax: 301-604-6746
dinob213@aol.com
Buys, sells, collects pocket knives.

Dealers

Rhett & Janie Stidham
Stidham's Knives
P.O. Box 570
Roseland, FL 32957
ph: 561-589-0618
fax: 561-589-3162
rstidham@gate.net
http://www.kmg.org/stidham
Over 29 years buying and selling antique pocket knives, hunting knives, Bowie knives and custom knives as a full-time business; does 25 knife shows per year; founders and owners of the Randall Knife Society; buy collections large & small.

Randall

Clubs/Associations

Rhett & Janie Stidham
Randall Knife Society of America
Newsletter: Randall Knife Society
 Newsletter
P.O. Box 539
Roseland, FL 32957
ph: 561-589-0618
fax: 561-589-3162
rstidham@gate.net
http://www.randallknifesociety.com
 Formed with the approval of the
 Randall Made Knives, Orlando, FL;
 over 2,000 members; newsletter on old
 and new knives, military Randall's,
 Randall history, latest shop news,
 ads, etc.

Man./Prod./Dist.

Randall Made Knives
4857 S. Orange Blossom Trail
Orlando, FL 32839
ph: 407-855-8075
fax: 407-855-9054
grandall@randallknives.com
http://www.randallknives.com

Sheaths

Suppliers

Bob Schrap
Custom Leather Knife Sheath Co.
7024 W. Wells St.
Milwaukee, WI 53213
ph: 414-771-6472 or 414-784-0863
fax: 262-784-2996
RSchrap@aol.com
http://www.customsheaths.com
 Maker of custom leather knife sheaths.

Switchblade/Automatic

Periodicals

Magazine: Automatic Knife Resource
 Guide & Newsletter
2269 Chestnut St., Ste. 212
San Francisco, CA 94123
ph: 415-664-2105
info@thenewsletter.com
http://www.thenewsletter.com
 Issued quarterly; photos, in-depth
 articles, maintenance and repair tips,
 latest trends, resources of ALL kinds
 of automatic knives, free classified ads
 and more.

Here are some tips when contacting someone who is listed in this book:

When requesting information about a particular item, include a description (material, dimensions, maker's mark, model number, etc.) and a photo, sketch, digital image or photocopy of the item in question.

Always ask if there are charges for samples or for the services that you are requesting.

When corresponding by letter, please be sure to include a Large (#10 business size) Self-Addressed and Stamped Envelope (LSASE) if requesting a reply or the return of photographs.

Never call collect unless otherwise directed. When calling, be considerate of time zone differences and always ask if the party you are calling has time to talk. When leaving an answering machine message, always instruct the party to call you back collect.

LABELS

(see also ADVERTISING
COLLECTIBLES; AIRLINE
MEMORABILIA; BANANA
COLLECTIBLES, Stickers;
BREWERIANA, Labels; CIGAR
BOXES, LABELS & BANDS;
MATCHBOXES; PAPER
COLLECTIBLES)

Appraisers

Barbara Pickett, GCA, MCA, GGAC
Pickett Fence Productions
P.O. Box 771
Lakewood, CA 90714-0771
ph: 562-425-4149
fax: 562-425-4149
pickettB2@aol.com
*Specializes in the appraisal of fruit
crate and cigar labels.*

Clubs/Associations

Joe Davidson
American Antique Graphics Society
5185 Windfall Rd.
Medina, OH 44256-8703
ph: 330-723-7172
*Members interested in graphic arts
prints: from medieval, natural history
to cigar labels, can labels, fruit
labels.*

Dealers

Steve Zeigfinger
Athens Antique Prints
RR 2, P.O. Box 169A
Athens, VT 05143
ph: 802-869-2722
oldlabel@sover.net
http://www.sover.net/~oldlabel
*Sells original antique labels that have
been scavenged from abandoned
packing houses: food, cigar, seed.*

Bill Weinberger
21 Luddington Rd.
West Orange, NJ 07052
weinberb@anchorcon.com
*Buys and sells hotel & baggage
labels, Cinderella stamps, Poster
Stamps, and all other labels with the
exception of Christmas seals and can/
fruit/vegetable labels.*

David & Barbara Freiberg
Cerebro
P.O. Box 327
East Prospect, PA 17317-0327
ph: 717-252-2400 or 800-69L-ABEL
fax: 717-252-3685
cerebro@cerebro.com
http://www.cerebro.com
Wants cigar labels, pictorial cigar

bands, fruit crate labels, firecracker
labels, can labels, and other
graphically pleasing labels.

Frank Gallucci
2335 Solari Dr.
Reno, NV 89509
ph: 775-825-6174
JRude18550@aol.com
*Quality selection of crate box labels
(citrus, apple, pear), can labels, cigar
labels, lug box labels, old seed
packets, salmon labels, cherry box
labels, asparagus labels, beer labels,
collectible advertising.*

Paul Jasmusz
2845 D St. NE
Salem, OR 97301
ph: 503-371-0868
*Wants labels: fruit crate, vegetable
crates, cans, seeds, etc.*

Paul Jarmusz
Vintage Original Fruit Crate Labels
2845 D St. N.E.
Salem, OR 97301-1600
ph: 503-371-0868
fax: 503-371-0868
mikajz@attbi.com
http://www.labelcollector.com
*Buys and sells original fruit crate or
vegetable crate labels, old can labels,
beer labels, soda labels, medical
labels, cosmetic labels, etc.; unused
stock found from old packing houses,
canneries, produce businesses.*

Paul Klym
Cubehouse Collectible Labels
202-1531 Beach Ave.
Vancouver, British Columbia V6G 1Y5
Canada
ph: 604-687-4249
*Online gallery of antique fruit crate
labels and salmon can labels;
specializing in authentic Canadian
labels.*

Bread Package Ends

Experts

Christopher Benjamin
P.O. Box 4020
Saint Augustine, FL 32085-4020
*Author of "Bread End Labels,
Illustrated Price Guide."*

Fruit Crate

Clubs/Associations

Jerry Chicone
Florida Citrus Label Collectors
  Association
P.O. Box 547636
rlando, FL 32854-7636
ph: 407-877-1044
fax: 407-877-1137

Citrus Label Society, The
Newsletter: Citrus Peal
131 Miramonte Dr.
Fullerton, CA 92635
ph: 714-871-2864
jeffdillon@yahoo.com
http://www.citruslabelsociety.com
*Members concentrate on the collection
of citrus fruit crate labels and on the
history of the citrus fruit industry.*

Dealers

Harol Haskins
Labelman I
P.O. Box 44
Gainesville, FL 32602-0044
ph: 352-372-3823
haskins@gru.net

Thomas P. "Pat" Jacobsen
California Fresh Fruit Label Exchange
P.O. Box 791
Weimar, CA 95736-0791
ph: 530-637-5923
fax: 530-637-5923
patj@fruitcratelabels.com
http://www.fruitcratelabels.com
Buys and sells fruit crate labels.

Lloyd "Hoke" Crim
Stage Stop Antiques, Inc.
513 Webster Ave.
Chelan, WA 98816-9773
ph: 509-682-5879
fax: 509-682-5879
*Specializes in buying and selling fruit
crate labels; also in historical paper
and pictures of NW Washington.*

Experts

Lloyd "Hoke" Crim
513 Webster Ave.
Chelan, WA 98816-9773
ph: 509-682-5879
fax: 509-682-5879
*Buys, sells, appraises, and specializes
in fruit crate labels and the history of
apple growing and processing.*

Internet Resources

Thomas P. "Pat" Jacobsen
California Fresh Fruit Label Exchange
P.O. Box 791
Weimar, CA 95736-0791
ph: 530-637-5923
fax: 530-637-5923
patj@fruitcratelabels.com
http://www.fruitcratelabels.com
*Site has images, trading, history of
fruit crate labels.*

Periodicals

Thomas P. "Pat" Jacobsen
Newsletter: Pacific Label News, The
P.O. Box 791
Weimar, CA 95736-0791
ph: 530-637-5923
fax: 530-637-5923
patj@fruitcratelabels.com
http://www.fruitcratelabels.com
A bimonthly newsletter.

Luggage

(see also AIRLINE MEMORABILIA,
Baggage I.D. Labels; PAPER
COLLECTIBLES)

Collectors

Daniel Kusrow
P.O. Box 158
Herndon, VA 20172
ph: 404-495-1593
dkusrow@us.net
*Avid collector/researcher of luggage
labels, particularly those issued by
airlines, hotels, railways, and ocean
liners.*

Leigh Giarde
P.O. Box 2243
Redlands, CA 92373-0741
ph: 909-792-8681
fax: 909-792-8681
onlyleigh@cpl.net
*Wants Scandinavian hotel labels and
USA travel decals.*

Dealers

Bill Weinberger
21 Luddington Rd.
West Orange, NJ 07052
weinberb@anchorcon.com
*Buys and sells hotel & baggage
labels, Cinderella stamps, Poster
Stamps, and all other labels with the
exception of Christmas seals and can/
fruit/vegetable labels.*

Charles Rabinovitz
Cinderella Co.
P.O. Box 265
Sykesville, MD 21784-0265
ph: 410-549-2412
fax: 410-795-8936
chuckrab@aol.com
*Wants to buy poster stamps,
matchcovers, matchbox labels,
baggage labels.*

Pat Sweeney
Pat Sweeney Ephemera
511 Woods End
Portage, MI 49002
ph: 269-381-9416
pse@tias.com
http://www.patsweeneyephemera.com
*Specializes in paper ephemera
including cigar labels, sheet music,
hotel luggage labels, vintage posters.*

Internet Resources

Ian Nicholson
Vintage Labels
ian@vintagelabels.org
http://www.vintagelabels.org
A Web site dedicated to the history and lost art of the luggage label as visualized by the world's hotels, airlines, railroads and oceanliner companies.

LABOR UNION ITEMS

(see BADGES; BUTTONS, Pin-Back; MINING RELATED ITEMS; PINS; POLITICAL COLLECTIBLES; SOCIAL CAUSES, Labor Unions)

LADY HEAD VASES

(see CERAMICS, Head Vase Planters)

LAMPS & LIGHTING

(see also ART DECO; CAMPING EQUIPMENT, Coleman; ELECTRICITY RELATED ITEMS; FAIRY LAMPS; FLASHLIGHTS; HIGHWAY COLLECTIBLES, Signs & Traffic Devices; LIGHT BULBS; MINING RELATED ITEMS, Lamps; PERFUME LAMPS; RAILROAD COLLECTIBLES, Signal Lamps)

Appraisers

Jerry & Marsha Ritch
J & M Antiques
6407 Transit Rd.
East Amherst, NY 14051
ph: 716-636-5874 or 716-636-5933
Jerry.Ritch@bms.com
http://www.eastamherstantiques.com
Antique lighting appraiser, collector, dealer, expert; specializes in antique lamps and lighting, with student lamps being a specialty; also Tiffany lamps, chandeliers, kerosene and oil lamps, gasoliers, sconces.

Randy Knox
714 E. Brown Ave.
Bellefontaine, OH 43311
ph: 937-599-3367
Specializes in lamps from the 1930s and 1940s.

Auction Services

Jane Prentiss
Skinner, Inc.
63 Park Plaza
The Heritage on the Garden
Boston, MA 02116
ph: 617-350-5400
fax: 617-350-5429
info@skinnerinc.com
http://www.skinnerinc.com
Established in 1971, Skinner Inc. is the fourth largest auction house in the US; has offices in Boston and Bolton, MA.

Dudley Browne
James D. Julia Auctioneers Inc.
Rt. 201, Skowhegan Rd.
P.O. Box 830
Fairfield, ME 04937
ph: 207-453-7125
fax: 207-453-2502
jjulia@juliaauctions.com
http://www.juliaauctions.com
Conducts specialized auctions of fine glass and lamps of all types including miniature lamps, early lighting devices, fluid lamps, art glass such as Tiffany, Handel, Pairpoint, etc.

Clubs/Associations

Dan Mattusch
Rushlight Club, Inc., The
<u>Journal: Rushlight, The</u>
260 Maryland Ave. NE
Washington, DC 20002
fax: 561-760-8018
info@rushlight.org
http://www.rushlight.org
One of the oldest organizations focusing on early lighting including lighting devices and fuels; journal published quarterly; also publishes the "Flickerings" newsletter; three meetings a year, heavily devoted to serious study.

Alan Goulding
Historical Lighting Society of Canada
<u>Newsletter: HLSC Font & Flame</u>
P.O. Box 561, Postal Station R
Toronto, Ontario M4G 4E1 Canada
ph: 416-724-0703 or 905-824-4117
goulding@idirect.com
http://www.historical-lighting.on.ca
Dedicated to the restoration and preservation of kerosene lamps and early lighting; general meetings held in April and October feature keynote speakers, theme tables, and a silent auction.

Historic Lighting Club
Causeway House
1 Dane St.
Bishops Stortford, Hertfordshire
CM233BT U.K.
ph: +44 (0) 1752 221980
fax: +44 (0) 1752 221908
caunteris@aol.com

Collectors

Bruce Axler
Ansonia Station
P.O. Box 1288
New York, NY 10023-1288
ph: 212-579-0348
Wants to buy pocket, portable, and travel lighting devices and fire appliances: cap lighters, pocket lamps, folding candlesticks, matchsafes, candle safes, lamps in cases.

Robert Kwalwasser
168 Camp Fatima Rd.
Renfrew, PA 16053-9104
ph: 724-789-7766
fax: 724-789-9771
robertk@tcis.net
Wants to buy fat, grease, candle and rush lights, tinder pistols, miners' lanterns.

Carole Lundy
3 Long Lane Dr.
Hummelstown, PA 17036-9545
ph: 717-566-6016
boxerlines@comcast.net
Wants to buy porcelain or ceramic light fixtures: ceiling lights or wall sconces.

Anthony Glab
6708 Duluth Ave.
Baltimore, MD 21222-1011
ph: 410-633-5354
z.zz@verizon.net
Wants CARBIDE miners and bicycle lamps; no railroad lanterns; any self-contained carbide lighting lamps, i.e., for household, industrial, mining.

David O. Benson
Lamps & Lanterns
1116 Villeroy Dr.
Sun City Center, FL 33573
ph: 813-634-2091
antiquelam@aol.com
http://www.antiquelamps.net
Specializes in angle lamps and Rayos.

Dealers

Chris Osborne
City Lights
2226 Massachusetts Ave.
Cambridge, MA 02140
ph: 617-547-1490
fax: 617-497-2074
lights@citylights.nu
http://www.citylights.nu
Antique lighting from 1850-1930 including ceiling fixtures, wall sconces and table and floor lamps; specialists in 1870 neo-Grecian white metal and brass fixtures and 1880 aesthetic fixtures with porcelain components.

Dan Johnson
Continuum: Quality Antique Lighting
#7 Rte. 28
Orleans, MA 02653
ph: 508-255-8513
fax: 508-255-8515
dan@oldlamp.com
http://www.oldlamp.com
Carries hundreds of restored antique lamps and lighting fixtures.

Judy Oppert
Victorian Lighting, Inc.
29 York St.
P.O. Box 1067
Kennebunk, ME 04043-1067
ph: 207-985-6868
Buys and sells antique lighting, 1840-1930; gas, kerosene and early electric, chandeliers, wall sconces, table lamps, floor lamps and outdoor lighting; fixtures and shades.

JoAnne Fuerst
Pine Bough Antiques
Main St.
P.O. Box 46
Northeast Harbor, ME 04662-0046
ph: 207-276-5079
Quarter century as scholar, dealer, author, with broad knowledge of pre-1860 lighting devices.

Ray Christensen
Metzger's Lamps & Lighting
15 South Main St.
W Hartford, CT 06107
ph: 860-232-1843
fax: 860-232-5267
rayp10@aol.com
Buys and sells 1880-1930 antique lamps and lighting.

Hugo A. Ramirez, Pres.
Hugo Ltd.
233 East 59th St.
New York, NY 10022-1425
ph: 212-750-6877
fax: 212-750-7346
A leading authority on 19th c. lighting; restorer and supplier to US Senate, Treasury Deptartment, Nantucket Historical Society, Gracie Mansion NYC, Metropolitan Museum NYC; restores and conserves to factory original finish all by hand.

Joan Bogart
Joan Bogart Antiques
P.O. Box 21
Rockville Centre, NY 11571
ph: 516-764-5712
fax: 516-764-0529
joanbogart@yahoo.com
http://www.antiqueslighting.com
Specializes in antique Victorian lighting: gas chandeliers, astral, Argands, sinumbra, kerosene and gas; 1820 to 1900.

Dan Edminster
Lampworks, The
435 Main St.
Hurleyville, NY 12747
ph: 845-434-6155
fax: 845-434-8677
lampworks@firebringer.com
http://www.firebringer.com/lampworks
Specializes in antique lamps & lighting; research, lamps, ephemera, lamp parts, books, accessories.

Peter B. Gregory
Gatehouse, The
125 Main St.
P.O. Box 195
Morris, NY 13808-0195
ph: 607-263-5855
fax: 607-263-5746
pgregory@dmcom.net
Lighting dealer and appraiser since 1966; wants to buy early lighting, kerosene lamps, pre-kerosene lamps.

Jerry & Marsha Ritch
J & M Antiques
6407 Transit Rd.
East Amherst, NY 14051
ph: 716-636-5874 or 716-636-5933
Jerry.Ritch@bms.com
http://www.eastamherstantiques.com
*Antique lighting appraiser, collector,
dealer, expert; specializes in antique
lamps and lighting, with student
lamps being a specialty; also Tiffany
lamps, chandeliers, kerosene and oil
lamps, gasoliers, sconces.*

Jeffery Venturella
Architectural Emporium
207 Adams Ave.
Canonsburg, PA 15317
ph: 724-746-4301
salesml@architectural-emporium.com
http://architectural-emporium.com
*Carries a full line of architectural
antiques; specializes in restoring
antique lighting, chandeliers, and
sconces.*

Fred Neece, Jr.
1307 Hadtner St.
Williamsport, PA 17701-3707
ph: 570-323-4679
fax: 570-323-5293
*Wants to buy candle, kerosene, and
gas lamps, lighting fixtures,
chandeliers, pieces, parts, shades, etc.*

Stephen G. DelSordo
Heritage Resource Group
305 Oakley St.
Cambridge, MD 21613
ph: 410-228-8934
fax: 410-221-8061
sdelsordo@comcast.net
http://www.heritageresource.com
*A cultural resource management/
historic preservation firm that has
contracts to locate, provide,
authenticate artifacts for museums and
collectors; areas of expertise include
architecture, industry, domestic,
agriculture, and maritime.*

Richard Dudley
A-Bit-of-Antiquity
1412 Forest Lane
Woodbridge, VA 22191-3024
ph: 703-491-2878
dudley@lampdoctor.com
http://www.lampdoctor.com
*Expert restoration, repair, replating
& polishing of oil, gas and electric
lamps; specializing in oil lighting
repair; also has huge inventory of all
manner of oil lighting to include
table, piano, student, hanging, bracket
lights.*

David & Phyllis Helphenstine
Phyllis' Antique Lamp Shop
2112 Old Main St.
Maysville, KY 41056-8929
ph: 606-759-7423
fax: 606-759-7423
phyllis@maysvilleky.net
http://www.phyllisantiques.com
*Buys, sells, repairs lamps of all sorts;
custom lamp repair, rewire, polish,*

lacquered, complete antique lamp
restoration, glass lampshades, hand
painted and artist signed shades,
custom shades.

Tom & Linda Millman
231 S. Main St.
Bethel, OH 45106-1327
ph: 513-734-6884 or 513-382-2978
*Dealer/collector buys, sells, trades
early lamps using heavy oil (lard, etc.)
or burning fluid as a fuel, e.g., solar,
sinumbra, Argand, camphene, etc.*

Treasured Friends Lamp Shoppe
P.O. Box 46
Waveland, IN 47989
ph: 765-435-3145
fax: 765-435-3845
mikec@wico.net
http://www.wico.net/~losttreasure/lamps
*Offers antique oil and electric lamps,
lamp parts, shades, chimneys, wicks
and other lamp related items.*

Treasured Friends Lamp Shoppe
226 N. Cross St.
P.O. Box 46
Waveland, IN 47989
ph: 765-435-3145
fax: 765-435-3845
mikec@wico.net
http://www.tflampshop.com
*Buys and sells old lamps including
antique oil and electric lamps; also
lamp parts, shades, chimneys, wicks
and other lamp related items.*

Robert Daly
Historic Lighting Restoration Sales &
Service
10341 Jewell Lake Ct.
Fenton, MI 48430-2418
ph: 810-629-4934
fax: 810-714-1009
Ldaly1@aol.com
http://www.dalys-historic-lighting.com
*Buying, selling and restoration of old
kerosene, gas and electric lighting
fixtures (chandeliers & sconces);
especially interested in 1800 to 1920
style lighting; iron, brass and tin.*

Karl Kester
Karlucci Studios
1255 Lincoln Ave.
Saint Paul, MN 55105
ph: 651-690-2975
karlucci@gte.net
http://home1.gte.net/karlucci/index.htm
*Buys, sells, restores antique lighting;
this homepage gives information about
the history of lighting and architectural styles in the US; regularly
updated listing with pictures of
fixtures and lamps for purchase
online.*

Scott MacClymonds
Classic Fans & Lighting
10525 Airline Dr.
Houston, TX 77037
ph: 713-448-4739 or 713-697-0069
fax: 713-448-0189
*Wants to buy art glass lighting,
especially by Quezal.*

Michael Dalio
Light Years Antiques & Restorations
8006 Grandview Ave.
Arvada, CO 80002-2404
ph: 303-422-4379
lightyrs48@aol.com
*Extensive inventory of antique,
reproduction lighting fixtures, parts,
shades, etc. consisting of floor, table,
and desk lamps also chandeliers, wall
sconces, exterior lighting & street
lights; also does custom plating and
appraisals.*

John D. McKenna
McKenna Bros. Wholesale
801 W. Cucharras St., #803
Colorado Springs, CO 80905-1619
ph: 719-630-8732 or 719-488-0818
*Buys, sells and trades gas, fluid and
electric lighting devices 1850-1930.*

Joyce Martinez
I Lite 4 U
1421 N. Freeman St.
Santa Ana, CA 92706
ph: 714-318-7022
joyce@ilite4u.com
http://www.ilite4u.com
*Repairs, restores antique electric
lamps; also manufactures one-of-a-
kind lamps making use of antique
lamp parts and shades.*

Charles Morgenstern
Woodchuck Antiques
3597 Sacramento St.
San Francisco, CA 94118-1846
ph: 415-922-6416
Buys and sells antique lamps.

Ross Levine
Levine Antique Lighting
ph: 415-455-8657
ron@levineantiquelighting.com
http://www.levineantiquelighting.com
*Collector, expert, and dealer in
original antique lighting; also offers
lighting repair and restoration
services.*

Greg Davidson
Greg Davidson Antiques
1020 1st Ave.
Seattle, WA 98104-1008
ph: 206-625-0406
greg@antiquelighting.biz
http://www.antiquelighting.biz
*Carries an outstanding selection of
original Victorian chandeliers, wall
sconces and other lighting devices;
gas, electric, kerosene, Tiffany,
Handel, Pairpoint, etc.*

Michael Peiffer
Assorted Treasures
1969 Oak Bay Ave.
Victoria, British Columbia V8R 1E3
Canada
ph: 250-370-1926
*Specializes in vintage ceiling fixtures,
wall sconces, table and floor lamps as
well as reproduction lighting.*

Experts

Phillip M. Sullivan
580 S. Orleans Rd.
P.O. Box 69
South Orleans, MA 02662-0069
ph: 508-255-8495
fax: 5080-240-1665
*Lighting expert, collector, appraiser;
specializes in early whale oil &
kerosene lighting, especially nautical
and marine related; currently
President of The Rushlight Club,
founded in 1932 & dedicated to the
study of historic lighting.*

Thomas Fritz
P.O. Box 1814
Bel Air, MD 21014
Fritter@prodigy.net
http://pages.prodigy.net/fritter/
gaslite.htm
*Collector and restorer of lamps,
including oil, gas and electric hanging
fixtures.*

Michael Dalio
Light Years Antiques & Restorations
8006 Grandview Ave.
Arvada, CO 80002-2404
ph: 303-422-4379
lightyrs48@aol.com
*Restores, designs, builds, fabricates
lighting fixtures: Denver Mint, Stanley
Hotel, Scottish Rites Temple, Love Oil
Company; provides lighting fixtures
for movies, commercials and plays;
consultant.*

Peter Blundell
P.O. Box 6
Vernon, British Columbia V1T 6M1
Canada
ph: 250-542-4540
petersblundell@shaw.ca
*Involved in research since 1969;
specializing in kerosene, gas, early
electric lighting.*

Internet Resources

Geoff Inglis
234 Parrish Rd.
Honeoye Falls, NY 14472
ph: 716-624-2638
inglis@envmed.rochester.edu
*Great Internet resource page for lamps
and lighting collectors: events,
organizations, museums, Web sites,
books; focus on antique lighting from
the 1850s to 1910.*

Man./Prod./Dist.

Imtiaz Sayed
Brighton Collection, The
230 Rt. 206 South
Building 4, Ste. 4
Flanders, NJ 07836
ph: 973-598-1580
fax: 973-598-1583
us@sayed.com
http://www.thebrightoncollection.com
*Manufacturers of traditional lighting
and accessories.*

Museums/Libraries

Tod Swormstedt
American Sign Museum
407 Gilbert Ave.
Cincinnati, OH 45202
ph: 800-925-1110 or 513-421-2050 x336
fax: 513-421-5144
tod@signmuseum.org
http://www.signmuseum.org
Preserves, archives, displays a historical collection of signs in their many types and forms; documents and surveys the products and equipment used in the design and manufacturing of signs; a 501(c)3 tax-exempt organization.

Periodicals

Tom Barnard
Newsletter: Light Revival
35 West Elm Ave.
Quincy, MA 02170-2423
ph: 617-773-3255
Quarterly newsletter for collectors and dealers of medium-priced lamps with a focus on late 19th and early 20th century lighting.

Repair Services

Richard Dermody
Brass n' Bounty
68 Front St.
Marblehead, MA 01945-3275
ph: 781-631-3864 or 781-631-6204
bnb@brassandbounty.com
http://www.brassandbounty.com
Restores brass chandeliers, sconces, floor and table lamps; also refinishes metal, rewires.

Tom Barnard
Light Revival
Newsletter: Light Revival Newsletter
35 West Elm Ave.
Quincy, MA 02170-2423
ph: 617-773-3255
Committed to the restoration of 1890-1930 period lighting; seeks out and restores quality fixtures and lamps, especially turn-of-the-century gas & electric lighting devices.

Leon Trefler
Trefler & Sons Antique Restoring
   Studio, Inc.
99 Cabot St.
Needham, MA 02494
ph: 781-444-2685
fax: 781-444-0659
trefler@trefler.com
http://www.trefler.com
Repairs, cleaning, rewire.

Stephen W. Conant
Conant Custom Brass
266-270 Pine St.
Burlington, VT 05401-4737
ph: 802-658-4482 or 800-832-4482
fax: 802-864-5914
store@conantcustombrass.com
http://www.conantcustombrass.com
Offers metal restoration and repair; specializes in repairing antique brass lighting fixtures.

Ray Christensen
Metzger's Lamps & Lighting
15 South Main St.
W Hartford, CT 06107
ph: 860-232-1843
fax: 860-232-5267
rayp10@aol.com
Repairs all types of lamps and lamp shades, new and antique; family-owned since 1925; no job too large or too small.

V. Diane Upton-Hagan
Upton Studios LLC
22 E. Mill Creek Rd.
Mount Holly, NJ 08060
ph: 609-261-2015
fax: 609-261-7326
felixxus@comcast.net
http://www.uptonstudios.com
A museum quality lamp and lighting conservation service specializing in the metal finishes of 19th century lighting devices; offers external parts for retail; also offers internal repairs, restorations and wiring.

Hugo A. Ramirez, Pres.
Hugo Ltd.
233 East 59th St.
New York, NY 10022-1425
ph: 212-750-6877
fax: 212-750-7346
A leading authority on 19th c. lighting; restorer and supplier to US Senate, Treasury Department, Nantucket Historical Society; restores and conserves to factory original finish (no plating or polishing, all hand restoration).

Gail Saucier
Aurora Lampworks Inc.
172 N. 11 St.
Brooklyn, NY 11211
ph: 718-384-6039
fax: 718-384-6198
ask@auroralampworks.com
http://www.auoralampworks.com
Offers conservation, restoration and replication of historic lighting fixtures; also a line of custom luminaries inspired by history.

John Batruch
Batruch Studio
P.O. Box 72
331 Main St.
Aurora, NY 13026
ph: 315-364-7815 or 315-246-6723
fax: 315-364-7815
jbatruch@rochester.rr.com
Over 30 years of quality lamp repairs; dedicated to safety and aesthetic originality through nearly invisible repairs to electricals, metals and original finishes.

Thomas Fritz
P.O. Box 1814
Bel Air, MD 21014
Fritter@prodigy.net
http://pages.prodigy.net/fritter/
   gaslite.htm
Collector and restorer of lamps,

including oil, gas and electric hanging fixtures.

David & Carol Baker
Baker's Metal & Wood Shop
11956 Augustine Herman Hwy.
P.O. Box 68
Kennedyville, MD 21645-0068
ph: 410-778-6681
fax: 410-348-5966
Polishing/lacquering/repairing gas/electric/oil lighting; new and old parts available, prisms, shades, etc.; rewiring, gilding, leafing, antiquing in bronze and brass; repair candlesticks; also architectural and fireplace items.

Don L. Reedy
Brass & Copper Polishing Shop, The
13 South Carroll St.
Frederick, MD 21701-5606
ph: 301-663-4240
fax: 301-694-9190
shineit4u@aol.com
http://www.frederickcouonty.com/
   antiques/brass.htm
Repair and restore antique lighting; 1,000s or antique and new lamp parts and supplies in stock; replacement glass shades and chimneys.

Kip Young
Copper Kettle Metal Polishing
158 1/2 South Potomac St.
Hagerstown, MD 21740
ph: 301-791-4555
Specialists in antique lamps and lighting sales, repairs and restorations; metal polishing, fabrication of missing metal parts; also specializes in crystal chandelier repair.

Richard Dudley
A-Bit-of-Antiquity
1412 Forest Lane
Woodbridge, VA 22191-3024
ph: 703-491-2878
dudley@lampdoctor.com
http://www.lampdoctor.com
Expert restoration, repair, replating & polishing of oil, gas and electric lamps; specializing in oil lighting repair; also has huge inventory of all manner of oil lighting to include table, piano, student, hanging, bracket lights.

Jim & Sheri Van Es
Wooden Shoe Antiques
222 W. Washington St.
Charles Town, WV 25414
ph: 304-725-1673 or 703-435-9045
wdnshu@aol.com
http://www.woodenshoeantiques.com
Buys, sells, and repairs all types of kerosene and electric lamps: Aladdin, Rayo, student, Gone With The Wind, and hanging lamps.

David & Phyllis Helphenstine
Phyllis' Antique Lamp Shop
2112 Old Main St.
Maysville, KY 41056-8929
ph: 606-759-7423
fax: 606-759-7423
phyllis@maysvilleky.net
http://www.phyllisantiques.com
Buys, sells, repairs lamps of all sorts; custom lamp repair, rewire, polish, lacquered, complete antique lamp restoration, glass lampshades, hand painted and artist signed shades, custom shades.

Mike Cook
Treasured Friends Lamp Shoppe
P.O. Box 46
Waveland, IN 47989
ph: 765-435-3145
fax: 765-435-3845
mikec@wico.net
http://www.wico.net/~losttreasure/lamps
Carries oil and electric lamps, glass and silk shades; repairs and reconditions all types of lamps, and has many lamp parts; also manufactures some parts that are no longer available.

Robert Daly
Historic Lighting Restoration Sales &
   Service
10341 Jewell Lake Ct.
Fenton, MI 48430-2418
ph: 810-629-4934
fax: 810-714-1009
Ldaly1@aol.com
http://www.dalys-historic-lighting.com
Buying, selling and restoration of old kerosene, gas and electric lighting fixtures (chandeliers & sconces); especially interested in 1800 to 1920 style lighting; iron, brass and tin.

Rick Charpie
Crystal Clear Chandelier Care
9602 W. 156th St.
Overland Park, KS 66221-9709
ph: 913-681-6700 or 800-373-7804
fax: 913-897-7608
Crystal & glass chandeliers a specialty: repair/cleaning/restoration, electrification of gas or candle devices, replacement of parts & prisms, buys whole or broken chandeliers and old trade catalogs, chandelier consultant, etc.

Antique Lighting Restoration & Sales
   Co.
316 E. 11th St.
Little Rock, AR 72202
ph: 501-375-8000
fax: 501-374-1700
antiquelighting@hotmail.com
Commercial, church, government, residential restoration, repair, sales of antique and old lighting fixtures; chandelier installation, maintenance, cleaning.

D & E Brass Buffing
101 Wagonsheel Lane
Rowlett, TX 75088
ph: 972-412-2260
fax: 972-527-5373
Professional polishing, lacquering and antique restoration of anything brass.

Joyce Martinez
I Lite 4 U
1421 N. Freeman St.
Santa Ana, CA 92706
ph: 714-318-7022
joyce@ilite4u.com
http://www.ilite4u.com
Repairs, restores antique electric lamps; also manufactures one-of-a-kind lamps making use of antique lamp parts and shades.

Alois Zajec
Bay Area Restoration
850 Airport St., #3
Moss Beach, CA 94038-9683
ph: 650-728-1662
fax: 650-728-1663
alzajec@pacbell.net
http://www.enterit.com/Bay1662
Offers total restoration of antiques and furniture; crystal chandelier parts and restoration; insurance casualty loss and moving industry claims adjusters.

Elegance
321 SE 6th St.
Grants Pass, OR 97526
ph: 541-476-0570
theraskins@yahoo.com
Repairs, restyles lamps: antique, vase, and items of interest electrified; offers fabric and glass replacement shades

Dorothy West
Glass Painting by Dorothy
251 Starlight Ave.
London, Ontario N5W 4X8 Canada
ph: 519-455-5742
fax: 519-455-2941
dwest@execulink.com
http://www.execulink.com/~dwest
Expert restores Victorian painted oil lamps; custom shade matched to your original base; glass paint is used and the shades are kiln fired so paint will not wash off; has blank ball shades and half shades available; some other parts.

Repro. Sources

Copper House, The
1747 Dover Rd., RT 4
Epsom, NH 03234-4416
ph: 800-281-9798
fax: 603-736-4921
lights@thecopperhouse.com
http://www.thecopperhouse.com
Handmade copper reproduction lighting fixtures and weathervanes. No imports. Catalog $4 deducted from purchase.

Renovator's Supply
P.O. Box 2515
Conway, NH 03818
ph: 800-659-2211 or 603-447-8500
fax: 603-447-1717
Offers catalog of Victorian reproduction accessories, lighting, hardware, bath fixtures, and door, window and cabinet hardware.

Ray Christensen
Metzger's Lamps & Lighting
15 South Main St.
W Hartford, CT 06107
ph: 860-232-1843
fax: 860-232-5267
rayp10@aol.com
Has huge stock of reproduction lighting and parts plus catalog orders.

Hugh C. Pribell
Early Lighting Specialties
24219 West Main St.
Columbus, NJ 08022-1917
ph: 609-298-9125
hugh1nj@aol.com
Reproduction early lighting burners and cut glass shades: camphene fluid burners, whale oil burners, Noyes 1855 patent lamp extinguishers for camphene fluid burners, brass fluid burner with coronets, betty lamps, other brass burners.

John Blowers
Olde Mill House Shoppes, Inc.
105 Strasburg Pike
Lancaster, PA 17602
ph: 717-299-0678
fax: 717-299-5822
oldemillhouse@comcast.net
http://www.oldmillhouse.com
Dealer in reproduction colonial and country indoor and outdoor lighting.

Jack Cunningham
American Period Lighting, Inc.
3004 Columbia Ave.
Lancaster, PA 17603-4001
ph: 717-392-5649
fax: 717-509-3127
conygham@yahoo.com
http://www.americanperiod.com
Sells complete line of reproduction period style lighting fixtures including lanterns, post lights, and chandeliers; also offers restoration of antiques lighting fixtures.

Mitchell K. Smith
Mitchell K. Smith - Blacksmith
P.O. Box 61
Morgantown, PA 19543
ph: 610-389-0213
fax: 610-363-8333
http://www.theblacksmith.com
Reproduction of 18th century iron chandeliers, sconces, candle stands and candlesticks; also rush lights and grease lamps.

Paxton Hardware Ltd.
P.O. Box 256
Upper Falls, MD 21156-0256
ph: 410-592-8505 or 800-241-9741
fax: 410-592-2224
paxton@ix.netcom.com
http://www.paxtonhardware.com
Authentic reproductions of oil lamps and lamp parts including glass, fabric, and parchment shades.

Cumberland General Store
657 Old Mountain Rd.
Marietta, GA 30064-1339
ph: 770-427-6434
fax: 770-422-8807
info@cumberlandgeneral.com
http://www.cumberlandgeneral.com
Aladdin, Dietz; send $4 for catalog.

Tracy Klosterman
Rejuvenation Lamp & Fixture
2550 NW Nicolai
Portland, OR 97210
ph: 888-401-1900 or 503-526-7329
fax: 800-526-7329
tklosterman@rejuvenation.com
http://www.rejuvenation.com
Manufactures reproduction lighting fixtures: Victorian, Arts & Crafts, etc.; send for free 88-page catalog; also repairs lighting fixtures.

Suppliers

Lamp Glass
2230 Massachusetts Ave.
Cambridge, MA 02140
ph: 617-497-0770
fax: 617-497-2074
lamps@lampglass.nu
http://www.lampglass.nu
A unique mail-order business specializing in replacement glass lamp shades; over one hundred in stock: Gone-With-The-Wind globes, student shades, chimneys, hurricanes, banker's shades, cased glass, prisms, glass shades, sconce glass, etc.

Ray Christensen
Metzger's Lamps & Lighting
15 South Main St.
W Hartford, CT 06107
ph: 860-232-1843
fax: 860-232-5267
rayp10@aol.com
Sells and manufactures parts for new and old lamps.

Kirks Lane Lamp Parts Co. Inc.
2541 Pearle Buck Rd.
Bristol, PA 19007
ph: 215-785-1251
fax: 215-785-1651
kirkslane@kirkslane.com
http://www.kirkslane.com
Source for lamp parts including sockets, bases, harps, finials, chimneys, shades, etc.

Mike Barnes
B & P Lamp Supply, Inc.
843 Old Morrison Highway
McMinnville, TN 37110
ph: 931-473-3016 or 800-822-3450
fax: 931-473-3014
bplamp@blomand.net
Wholesale distributor of early style lamp parts including oil burners, chimneys, shades, lamp cord, and wiring devices; mail order to the trade only.

Steve Kaye
Brass Light Gallery
131 South First St.
Milwaukee, WI 53204
ph: 414-271-8300 or 800-243-9595
fax: 800-505-9404
comments@brasslight.com
http://www.brasslight.com
Specializes in parts for gas wall sconces and chandeliers, and for early electric lamps; also does lamp repairs including metal work.

Aladdin

Clubs/Associations

J. W. "Bill" Courter
Aladdin Knights, The
Newsletter: Mystic Light, The
3935 Kelley Rd.
Kevil, KY 42053-9431
ph: 270-488-2116
fax: 270-488-2055
brtknight@aol.com
http://www.aladdinknights.org
Purpose is to preserve Aladdin kerosene and electric lamps and Aladdin advertising history and memorabilia; sponsors annual national lamp and lighting show.

Dealers

Jim & Sheri Van Es
Wooden Shoe Antiques
222 W. Washington St.
Charles Town, WV 25414
ph: 304-725-1673 or 703-435-9045
wdnshu@aol.com
http://www.woodenshoeantiques.com
Buys, sells, and repairs all types of kerosene and electric lamps: Aladdin, Rayo, student, Gone With The Wind, and hanging lamps.

Experts

J. W. "Bill" Courter
3935 Kelley Rd.
Kevil, KY 42053-9431
ph: 270-488-2116
fax: 270-488-2055
brtknight@aol.com
http://www.aladdinknights.org
Wants Aladdin and "angle" lamps; author of "Aladdin Collectors Manual & Price Guide Kerosene Mantle Lamps;" free 8-page "Brief History of Aladdin Lamps" if you send SASE with request.

Internet Resources

Darrell Kleckner
darrellkleckner@mchsi.com
http://www.aladdincollector.com
Web site includes an introduction to Aladdin lamps, collecting tips and tricks, identification tips, photo gallery.

Man./Prod./Dist.

Aladdin Mantle Lamp Company
P.O. Box 100255
Nashville, TN 37224
support@aladdinlamps.com
http://www.aladdinlamps.com

Repair Services

Richard Dudley
A-Bit-of-Antiquity
1412 Forest Lane
Woodbridge, VA 22191-3024
ph: 703-491-2878
dudley@lampdoctor.com
http://www.lampdoctor.com
Expert restoration, repair, replating & polishing of oil, gas and electric lamps; specializing in oil lighting repair; also has huge inventory of all manner of oil lighting to include table, piano, student, hanging, bracket lights.

Suppliers

John Lapp
Leacock Coleman Center, Inc.
89 Old Leacock Rd.
P.O. Box 307
Ronks, PA 17572-0307
ph: 717-768-7174
fax: 717-768-7673
leacock@prodigy.net
http://www.leacockcoleman.com
Replacement parts for Coleman table lamps and lanterns; also Aladdin lamps, parts and shades in stock.

Bruce B. Phillips
Phillips Lamp Shades Ltd.
172 Main St.
Toronto, Ontario M4E 2W1 Canada
ph: 416-691-7372
fax: 416-691-7360
aladdinorth@on.aibn.com
Parts & expert repairs for Aladdin lamps; wicks, chimneys, mantles, holders, decorated glass shades, electric adapters; dealing in lighting since 1925.

Angle

Collectors

David O. Benson
Lamps & Lanterns
1116 Villeroy Dr.
Sun City Center, FL 33573
ph: 813-634-2091
antiquelam@aol.com
http://www.antiquelamps.net
Specializes in angle lamps and Rayos.

Dealers

Tom & Linda Millman
231 S. Main St.
Bethel, OH 45106-1327
ph: 513-734-6884 or 513-382-2978
Dealer and collector; buys, sells, trades wall-mounted cast-metal angle lamps (glass desired, but not necessary); also old angle chimneys and elbows; send description and price.

Experts

J. W. "Bill" Courter
3935 Kelley Rd.
Kevil, KY 42053-9431
ph: 270-488-2116
fax: 270-488-2055
brtknight@aol.com
http://www.aladdinknights.org
Wants Aladdin and "angle" lamps; author of "Aladdin Collectors Manual & Price Guide Kerosene Mantle Lamps."

Bellova

Collectors

Bruce Bleier
73 Riverdale Rd.
Valley Stream, NY 11581
ph: 516-791-4353
fax: 516-792-0519
emeralite@aol.com
http://www.emeralite.com
Author of numerous articles on Bellova and Emeralite lamps; collects, buys, sells these lamps.

Experts

Bruce Bleier
73 Riverdale Rd.
Valley Stream, NY 11581
ph: 516-791-4353
fax: 516-792-0519
emeralite@aol.com
http://www.emeralite.com
Author of numerous articles on Bellova and Emeralite lamps; collects, buys, sells these lamps.

Candlesticks

Collectors

William G. Hodges
Ridgefield, Inc.
12509 Patterson Ave.
Richmond, VA 23233-6414
ph: 804-784-2760
ridgefield@mindspring.com
Wants to buy unusual candlesticks.

Carriage

Collectors

Larry Sluiter
4053 S. Springfield Rd.
Freeport, IL 61032-9510
ph: 815-362-6002
Wants coach, hearse, and carriage lamps in pairs; also wants horse-drawn carriages.

Chandeliers

Experts

Rick Charpie
Crystal Clear Chandelier Care
9602 W. 156th St.
Overland Park, KS 66221-9709
ph: 913-681-6700 or 800-373-7804
fax: 913-897-7608
Crystal & glass chandeliers a specialty: repair/cleaning/restoration, electrification of gas or candle devices, replacement of parts & prisms, buys whole or broken chandeliers and old trade catalogs, chandelier consultant, etc.

Repair Services

Kip Young
Copper Kettle Metal Polishing
158 1/2 South Potomac St.
Hagerstown, MD 21740
ph: 301-791-4555
Specialists in antique lamps and lighting sales, repairs and restorations; metal polishing, fabrication of missing metal parts; also specializes in crystal chandelier repair.

Suppliers

Maurice Electrical Supply
1500 Rockville Pike
Rockville, MD 20852
ph: 301-468-7300
mkogod@mauriceelectric.com
http://www.mauriceelectric.com
Carries large selection of crystal chandeliers.

Kurt Keifer
Kiefer Supply
417 Stanton Ave.
Fergus Falls, MN 56537
ph: 218-736-7000 or 888-543-3377
fax: 218-736-7474
kurtkiefer@aol.com
http://www.kiefers.com
Chandelier parts, wrapping pads, banners, blacklights, bubble wrap, cartons, cash boxes, dollies, easels, fasteners, forms holders, inventory items, jewelry tags, knobs & finials, labels, laminated signs, magnifiers, pennants, etc.

Coleman

Clubs/Associations

International Coleman Collectors Club
Newsletter: Coleman Collector, The
7472 Dumosa Ave.
Yucca Valley, CA 92284
webmaster@colemancollectorsclub.com
http://www.colemancollectorsclub.com
For collectors of any Coleman products such as lamps, lanterns, irons, camp stoves and other pressurized liquid fuel appliances; also literature, old repair manuals, sales samples.

Suppliers

John Lapp
Leacock Coleman Center, Inc.
89 Old Leacock Rd.
P.O. Box 307
Ronks, PA 17572-0307
ph: 717-768-7174
fax: 717-768-7673
leacock@prodigy.net
http://www.leacockcoleman.com
Replacement parts for Coleman table lamps and lanterns; also Aladdin lamps, parts and shades in stock.

Emeralite

Collectors

Jerry Propst
P.O. Box 45
Janesville, WI 53547-0045
ph: 608-752-2816
fax: 608-752-7691
Buys and sells Emeralite, Amrolite and Bellova shades and lamp bases; also literature on same; when writing, please include a LSASE if requesting a reply.

Dealers

Bruce Bleier
73 Riverdale Rd.
Valley Stream, NY 11581
ph: 516-791-4353
fax: 516-792-0519
emeralite@aol.com
http://www.emeralite.com
Author of numerous articles on Emeralite and Bellova lamps; collects, buys and sells these lamps.

Experts

Bruce Bleier
73 Riverdale Rd.
Valley Stream, NY 11581
ph: 516-791-4353
fax: 516-792-0519
emeralite@aol.com
http://www.emeralite.com
Author of numerous articles on Emeralite and Bellova lamps; collects, buys and sells these lamps.

Gas

Dealers

Federico Santi
Drawing Room of Newport, The
152 Spring St.
Newport, RI 02840-6806
ph: 401-841-5060
fax: 401-848-0953
zsolnay@drawrm.com
http://www.drawrm.com
Buys and sells high style 19th century gas lighting and gas shades.

Experts

Dan Mattausch
Cortelyou House
260 Maryland Ave., NE
Washington, DC 20002
ph: 202-544-4415
fax: 561-760-8018
Dan@Gaslights.org
http://www.gaslights.org
*Researching and collecting gaslight
burners, igniters, galleries, and
mantles; also any related new-old-
stock, packaging, catalogs, or
advertising; wants anything that
comes off a gaslight fixture when it is
electrified.*

Kerosene

Collectors

Geoff Inglis
234 Parrish Rd.
Honeoye Falls, NY 14472
ph: 716-624-2638
inglis@envmed.rochester.edu
*Interested in kerosene lamps from
1850s to 1910, especially in
mechanical lamps, i.e., a lamp that
has to be wound up.*

Dealers

Jerry & Marsha Ritch
J & M Antiques
6407 Transit Rd.
East Amherst, NY 14051
ph: 716-636-5874 or 716-636-5933
Jerry.Ritch@bms.com
http://www.eastamherstantiques.com
*Specializes in antique lamps and
lighting, with student lamps being a
specialty; also Tiffany lamps,
chandeliers, kerosene and oil lamps,
gasoliers, sconces.*

Carleton L. Cotting
1441 Crowell Rd.
Vienna, VA 22182-1512
ph: 703-759-5646
*Collects, buys and sells oil lamps -
miniature and full size.*

Tom & Linda Millman
231 S. Main St.
Bethel, OH 45106-1327
ph: 513-734-6884 or 513-382-2978
*Dealer/collector buys, sells, trades
early metal and colored glass kerosene
lamps; figural glass electric lamps;
parts for kerosene lamps; original
shades for both kerosene and electric;
send description and price.*

Experts

Dennis Hearn
Www.Oillamp.Com
Radio City Station
P.O. Box 1555
New York, NY 10101-1555
ph: 212-307-9397
dhearn@oillamp.com
http://www.oillamp.com
*Has appeared as an expert on the
subject of oil lamps in the pages of
national magazines and on television;
lecturer and feature article contributor*

*to trade publications; lamp designer
on Broadway stage; founded
Www.Oillamp.Com in 1996.*

Fil Graff
Lamp Shop at Lamplighters Farm, The
10111 Lincoln Way West
Saint Thomas, PA 17252-9513
ph: 717-369-3577
fax: 717-369-5546
fgraff@epix.net
http://www.dapllc.com/lampguild
*Expert, dealer, collector of Aladdin
kerosene lamps, other kerosene and
gasoline lamps, and early electric
lamps; old patent flat wick or round
wick burners and chimneys, gas
lighting fixtures, lamp glass; also
offers repair services.*

Internet Resources

Dennis Hearn
Www.Oillamp.Com
Radio City Station
P.O. Box 1555
New York, NY 10101-1555
ph: 212-307-9397
dhearn@oillamp.com
http://www.oillamp.com
*The information and market resource
for oil lamps.*

Fil Graff, Sec.
International Guild of Lamp Researchers
Newsletter: Light International
10111 Lincoln Way West
Saint Thomas, PA 17252-9513
ph: 717-369-3577
fax: 717-369-5546
fgraff@epix.net
http://www.dapllc.com/lampguild
*An excellent Web site to get your
questions about antique liquid fueled
lamps (kerosene and gasoline)
answered.*

Lanterns

Experts

Anthony Hobson
40 Palmer Terrace
Gansevoort, NY 12831
ph: 518-587-7827
fax: 518-587-7827
*Specializes in and appraises railroad,
marine, fire, carriage, farm, and other
lanterns; author of "Lanterns That
Lit Our World."*

Lava Lamps

Internet Resources

Lava World International, Inc.
430 Kimberly Dr.
Carol Stream, IL 60188
webmaster@Lavaworld.com
http://www.lavaworld.com
*Creators of the Lava Lite take you on
a journey through time; Lava Lite
FAQs, graphics and links to other
sites.*

Miniature

(see also FAIRY LAMPS; PERFUME
LAMPS)

Clubs/Associations

Bob Culver
Night Light Miniature Lamp Club
Newsletter: Night Light Newsletter
38619 Wakefield Ct.
Northville, MI 48167-9060
ph: 248-473-8575
rculver107@aol.com
*The goal of Night Light is to further
the hobby of collecting miniature oil
lamps; newsletter published quarterly.*

Motion

Collectors

Amy Kanis
5000 W. 96th St.
Indianapolis, IN 46268
ph: 317-873-2727
*Wants 1930s-60s revolving lamps,
i.e., plastic or glass w/light bulb-heat
propelled inner cylinder; all
applications desired.*

Jim Whitaker
P.O. Box 475
Lynnwood, WA 98046-0475
ph: 425-774-6910
eclectic@gte.net
http://www.eclecticantiques.com
*Collects, buys and sells motion
(revolving) lamps.*

Dealers

Jim Whitaker
Eclectic Antiques
P.O. Box 475
Lynnwood, WA 98046-0475
ph: 425-774-6910
eclectic@gte.net
http://www.eclecticantiques.com
*Collects, buys and sells motion
(revolving) lamps.*

Experts

Sam & Anna Samuelian
SMS Noveltiques
P.O. Box 504
Edgemont, PA 19028-0504
ph: 610-566-7248
fax: 610-566-7285
sms@bee.net
http://www.motionlamp.com
*Buys, sells, restores motion lamps:
Econolite, L.A. Goodman, Scene-In-
Action, Roto-Vue, etc.; leading buyers
and sellers with largest collection in
the world from 1920s-1980s; can
reproduce parts.*

Neon

(see also NEON)

Collectors

Len Davidson
2140 Mount Vernon St.
Philadelphia, PA 19130-3134
ph: 215-232-0478
fax: 215-232-0478
LnDavidson@aol.com
http://www.signmuseum.com
Wants to buy antique neon signs.

Stephen Seltzer
7912 Georgia Ave.
Silver Spring, MD 20910-4837
ph: 301-565-2444 or 301-565-3339
fax: 301-565-2228
eseltzer@aol.com
*Wants to buy neon signs - new and
antique - working or not.*

Dealers

Dennis Clark
Off the Wall Antiques, Inc.
7325 Melrose Ave.
Los Angeles, CA 90046
ph: 323-930-1185
fax: 323-930-1595
weirdstuff@earthlink.net
http://www.offthewallantiques.com
*Wants to buy figural neon signs; die
cut and animated preferred; porcelain
or painted; send photos.*

Experts

Len Davidson
Davidson Neon Design/Neon Museum of
  Philadelphia
2140 Mount Vernon St.
Philadelphia, PA 19130-3134
ph: 215-232-0478
fax: 215-232-0478
LnDavidson@aol.com
http://www.signmuseum.com
Author of "Vintage Neon" (Schiffer).

Museums/Libraries

Len Davidson
Davidson Neon Design/Neon Museum of
  Philadelphia
2140 Mount Vernon St.
Philadelphia, PA 19130-3134
ph: 215-232-0478
fax: 215-232-0478
LnDavidson@aol.com
http://www.signmuseum.com
*Museum restores & displays antique
neon signs.*

Museum of Neon Art
501 W. Olympic Blvd.
Los Angeles, CA 90015
ph: 213-489-9918
info@neonmona.org
http://www.neonmona.org
*A non-profit, cultural and educational
organization which exhibits,
documents and preserves contemporary
fine art in electric media; founded in
1981.*

Shades

Appraisers

Brill Lee
Brill Lee Appraisal Services
P.O. Box 244
Bellevue, WA 98009-0244
ph: 425-885-4518
fax: 425-895-1022
brilllee@hotmail.com
*Has appraised collected, bought, sold
Tiffany, Steuben, Quezal, Fostoria,
and other art glass electric and
kerosene lamp shades for over 30*

years; also will sell on consignment for clients.

Man./Prod./Dist.

Vintage Lampshades
5209 Williamsburg Rd., NW
Cincinnati, OH 45215
ph: 513-821-2079 or 800-605-3022
kelly@vintageshades.com
http://www.vintageshades.com
Sells custom fabric Victorian style lamp shades.

Faith Kovach
201 W. Alyea St.
P.O. Box 522
Hebron, IN 46341-0522
ph: 219-996-2924
kvchfaith@netscape.net
Makes Victorian lamp shades made with silk, satin lace and fringes.

Silk Shade, The
923 4th St.
P.O. Box 243
Santa Monica, CA 90406-0243
ph: 310-395-6360
Makes turn-of-the-century silk lamp shades using vintage fabrics.

Daniel Primo
Lampshades of Antique
P.O. Box 1507
Medford, OR 97501
ph: 541-826-9737
fax: 541-826-1086
shadesofantique@aol.com
http://www.lampshader.com
Designers, manufacturers, vendor for elegant lampshades for restaurants, hotels, movies, casinos, antiques, lighting stores; extensive selection of fabrics, laces & trim; also repairs and restores.

Repair Services

Daniel Primo
Lampshades of Antique
P.O. Box 1507
Medford, OR 97501
ph: 541-826-9737
fax: 541-826-1086
shadesofantique@aol.com
http://www.lampshader.com
Designers, manufacturers, vendor or elegant lampshades for restaurants, hotels, movies, casinos, antiques, lighting stores; extensive selection of fabrics, laces & trim; also repairs and restores.

Tiffany/Handel/Pairpoint

Appraisers

Paul Royka
AppraisalDay.com
210 Park Avenue, #295
Worcester, MA 01609
ph: 978-582-8207
fax: 978-582-8207
appraisalday@aol.com
http://www.appraisalday.com
Expert, author and appraiser of American art glass lamps.

Shawn Voils
430 Redding #1911
Breckinridge Court
Lexington, KY 40517
ph: 859-245-1089
shvoils@aol.com
Specializes in Tiffany Studios lamps & accessories, early 20th c. lamps by Handel, Pairpoint, Duffner & Kimberly, Chicago Mosaic, Jefferson, Bradley & Hubbard, etc.

Carl Heck
Carl Heck Decorative Arts
P.O. Box 8416
Aspen, CO 81612-8416
ph: 970-925-8011
fax: 970-925-8011
carlheck5@aol.com
http://www.carlheck.com
Collector, dealer, appraiser of lamps by Tiffany Studios, Duffner-Kimberly, Handel, Pairpoint, Steuben, Quezal, Galle and others; also collector of Tiffany Studios stained glass windows, art glass, enamels and pottery.

Collectors

Harvey Weinstein
22 Halifax Dr.
Morganville, NJ 07751
ph: 201-536-4467 or 800-321-0204
weinsteingal@earthlink.net
Wants lamps and glass by Tiffany, Galle, Daum Nancy, Handel, Lotz, Pairpoint, Lalique, etc.

Mark Kaplan
135 W. Penn St.
Long Beach, NY 11561-4040
ph: 800-626-1752
Wants Pairpoint puffies, painted scenes; also Handel painted lamps and accessories.

Robert Ogorek
6400 Davidson Rd.
Burton, MI 48509
ph: 810-743-5358
Serious collector of Tiffany lamps.

Dr. Neil Superfon
2121 W. Indian School Rd.
Phoenix, AZ 85015-4908
ph: 602-277-1449 or 800-258-0216
fax: 602-263-8523
Wants Handel, Galle, Pairpoint, Tiffany lamps and glass.

Dealers

Adele & Alan Grodsky
5722 South Flamingo Rd., #297
Fort Lauderdale, FL 33330
ph: 800-431-8256
adrianna53@aol.com
Buys, sells Pairpoint puffies and painted scenic lamps; also Tiffany and Handel painted lamps and accessories; also art glass: Tiffany, Durand, Quezal, Steuben.

Tom & Linda Millman
231 S. Main St.
Bethel, OH 45106-1327
ph: 513-734-6884 or 513-382-2978
Dealer/collector buys, sells complete reverse painted or stained glass lamps or shades: by Handel, Pairpoint, Pittsburgh, Jefferson, Tiffany, Wilkerson, Moe Bridges, Chicago Mosaic, etc.; items must be signed or otherwise identified.

Bob Ogorek
Plantation Galleries, Inc.
6400 Davison Rd.
Burton, MI 48509-1612
ph: 810-743-5258
fax: 810-743-5791
Specializes in the buying and selling of art glass lamp shades.

David E. Newman
Newman & Assoc.
2476 Bolsover, #504
Houston, TX 77005-2518
ph: 713-521-7044
newmanasoc@aol.com
Specializes in buying, selling, restoring, authenticating and appraising early 20th century electrified table and floor lamps including Tiffany, Handel, Pairpoint and French cameo.

Experts

Sheila & Edward Malakoff
276 Princeton Dr.
River Edge, NJ 07661-1031
ph: 201-487-1989
fax: 201-489-0179
pairpoint@worldnet.att.net
Authors of "Pairpoint Lamps."

Carole Hibel
Carole Hibel Art & Antiques
181 Broadview Rd.
Woodstock, NY 12498
ph: 845-679-2966 or 800-426-3357
fax: 845-679-9101
efshnc6@nyc.rr.com
Buys, sells, collects, appraises Tiffany, Pairpoint, Handel lamps; author of "Handel Lamps - Painted Shades & Glassware," and "The Handel Lamps Book."

Carl Heck
Carl Heck Decorative Arts
P.O. Box 8416
Aspen, CO 81612-8416
ph: 970-925-8011
fax: 970-925-8011
carlheck5@aol.com
http://www.carlheck.com
Collector/dealer/expert specializing in lamps by Tiffany, Pairpoint, Handel, Galle; also Tiffany windows, art glass, enamels for over 32 years; currently Tiffany advisor for "Schroeder's," "Antique Trader" price guides.

Museums/Libraries

Edward Malakoff
Pairpoint Lamp Museum
276 Princeton Dr.
River Edge, NJ 07661-1031
ph: 201-487-1989
fax: 201-489-0179
pairpoint@worldnet.att.net
Author of "Pairpoint Lamps."

Repair Services

Joan Meyer
104 Colwyn Lane
Bala Cynwyd, PA 19004
ph: 610-664-3174
Repairs Tiffany lamps; expert craftsmanship, only uses Tiffany glass, damaged shades purchased.

Paul Crist
Paul Crist Studios
8317 Secura Way
Santa Fe Springs, CA 90670
ph: 562-696-9992
fax: 562-696-9392
joe@mosaicshades.com
http://www.mosaicshades.com
Specializes in the restoration of Tiffany lamps and bronzeware; will do simple repatination jobs to complex reconstructions; also offers reproductions of original Tiffany hardware.

Repro. Sources

Asher Shahar
3146 J.P. Curcie Dr., Bldg. 3-A
Hallandale, FL 33009
ph: 954-981-7440
fax: 954-981-0472
stglass@bellsouth.net
Sells 2, 3, 12, and 18 light Lily Lamps and many other Tiffany reproductions.

TV Lamps

Clubs/Associations

Honey Jacobs
tvlamps.com
P.O. Box 324
Piermont, NY 10968
ph: 914-358-5311
Sadiehv@optonline.net
http://www.tvlamps.com
Focuses on 1950s TV lamps.

Experts

Honey Jacobs
P.O. Box 324
Piermont, NY 10968
ph: 914-358-5311
Sadiehv@optonline.net
http://www.tvlamps.com
Collector, dealer, expert specializing in 1950s TV lamps.

LANDMARK REPLICAS

(see SOUVENIR & COMMEMORATIVE ITEMS, Buildings)

LANTERNS

(see LAMPS & LIGHTING; MINING RELATED ITEMS, Lamps; RAILROAD COLLECTIBLES, Signal Lamps)

LAPIDARY

(see also GEMS & JEWELRY; MARBLE & STONE; MINERAL SPECIMENS)

Clubs/Associations

Jeff Ursillo
Gem & Mineral Society of Palm Beaches
Newsletter: Rockhound, The
1240 NW 22nd Ave.
Delray Beach, FL 33445
ph: 561-278-1120
fax: 561-272-3828
bnmjeff@aol.com
http://www.gemandmineral.cc
An educational organization teaching members various lapidary techniques.

Jonathan M. Moehring
Rollin' Rock Club
Magazine: Rollin' Rock Club Newsletter
6004 Cohoke Dr.
Arlington, TX 76018-2366
jmarkm@flash.net
http://home.flash.net/~jmarkm
Interest is in lapidary: cutting, shaping and polishing of stones.

Jay DePuy
Ute Mountain Gem & Mineral Society
P.O. Box 385
Cortez, CO 81321

Faceter's Guild of Northern California
1727 Arroyo Dr.
Auburn, CA 95603
ph: 916-885-3349

Dealers

R. A. "Art" Guyon
International Gem Mart
P.O. Box 7EE
San Antonio, TX 78201-1034
ph: 210-341-1789 or 800476-3992
fax: 210-822-6598
baumendow@stic.net
Offers a fine jewelry collection of wearable lapidary art pieces.

Kim Hansen
Dad's Rock Shop
P.O. Box 6124
Fort Mohave, AZ 86446
ph: 928-788-2513 or 800-844-3237
fax: 928-788-2514
sales@dadsrockshop.com
http://www.dadsrockshop.com
Dealers in lapidary equipment and supplies, rock carving material, rockhound books, and much more.

Susan McCune
GemFacets
20649 Keswick St.
Winnetka, CA 91306-2028
ph: 818-348-6701
fax: 818-348-6701
Active in the lapidary arts field; represents lapidary artists.

Misc. Services

Suzanne Wagner
William Holland School of Lapidary Arts
P.O. Box 980
Young Harris, GA 30582-0980
ph: 706-379-2126
lapidary@alltel.net
http://www.lapidaryschool.org
Offers classes in the lapidary arts: beading, cabochons, casting, chain making, faceting, channel, gem identification, glass bead making, glass fusing, intarsia, opals, silver, stained glass, and more.

Museums/Libraries

Lizzadro Museum of Lapidary Art
220 Cottage Hill Ave.
Elmhurst, IL 60126-3351
ph: 630-833-1616
webmaster@elmhurst.org
http://www.elmhurst.org/
LIZZMUS.HTML
Large collection of hard stone carvings (especially Chinese jade carvings), rocks, minerals, and a unique gift shop.

Periodicals

Adam Moskow, Ed.
PRIMEDIA Enthusiast Group
Magazine: Lapidary Journal
60 Chestnut Ave., Ste. 201
Devon, PA 19333-1312
ph: 610-293-1112 or 800-676-4336 (sub)
fax: 610-293-1717
LapidaryJournal@primediasi.com
http://www.lapidaryjournal.com
Covers gems, beads, jewelry, minerals, and fossils, for artisans and collectors, including profiles, step-by-step instructions, and a show calendar.

Repair Services

Richard P. Hegeman
Hegeman & Co.
361 S. Main St.
Providence, RI 02903-2912
ph: 401-831-6812
Cutters of all precious/semi-precious stones; specializing in the repair & restoration of all types of jewelry (antique and contemporary); gemstone replacements and repairs.

Gem Art

Appraisers

Charles M. Ellias, GG, ISA CAPP
North American Appraisal Services
P.O. Box 1394
Birmingham, MI 48012
ph: 810-397-7109 or 586-704-7055
gemartappraiser@aol.com
Full appraisal services, consultations, diamond, colored gemstone and pearl grading reports, insurance claims settlements, diamond and colored gemstone recutting and salvage services, custom design jewelry and full manufacturing facility.

Alan Winston
Winston Studio & Imports
4448 West Lovers Lane
Dallas, TX 75209
ph: 214-357-0081 or 214-824-2842
fax: 214-821-8583
wsimports@aol.com
http://www.alanwinstonsmith.com
Appraiser of lapidary art as well as custom faceted items, carvings, assemblages, fine art as lapidary art.

Clubs/Associations

Gem Artists of North America
P.O. Box 81504
Grand Junction, CO 81504
ganapage@aol.com
http://www.gemartists.org
Formed in 1995 to create a forum for artists and professionals of the gemstone art industry; supports the needs of gem artists and related professionals.

Misc. Services

Charles M. Ellias, GG, ISA CAPP
North American Lapidary Laboratory
P.O. Box 1394
Birmingham, MI 48012
ph: 810-397-7109 or 586-704-7055
gemartappraiser@aol.com
The first gem lab of its kind specializing in lapidary art; offering Grading Reports for colored stones, gem sculptures, diamonds, and pearls; also offers Gem Identification Reports.

LARKIN SOAP COMPANY

Collectors

Jerome P. Puma
55 Grant Rd.
Snyder, NY 14226-4536
ph: 716-839-3739
jpp@buffnet.net
http://groups.yahoo.com/group/
larkincompany
Would like any items pertaining to the Larkin Soap Co. of Buffalo, NY: catalogs, calendars, other paper items and Larkin items; also any item dealing with the Larkin administration building designed by Frank Lloyd Wright.

LAW ENFORCEMENT MEMORABILIA

(see also BADGES; OUTLAWS & LAWMEN; RESTRAINT DEVICES; WESTERN AMERICANA)

Collectors

Kenneth Nix
307 Rosewood Dr.
Dublin, GA 31021-4133
ph: 478-275-0281
fax: 478-272-1744
knix@nlamerica.com
Looking for any police badges from the state of Georgia; also wants sponsor pins for the 1996 Olympics and 1996 Atlanta Session badges.

James Manteris
1613 Barnard Way
Bowling Green, KY 42103
ph: 270-846-4931
manteris@insightbb.com
Specializes in ethnographic weapons from Indonesia, Philippines, India, Africa, any type of club; wants police clubs, saps, billy clubs, blackjacks, brass knuckles, and old knives; also wants African and Asian weapons.

Dealers

Stan Willis
Handcuffs & Badges
P.O. Box 36474
Cincinnati, OH 45236
handcuffs@isoc.net
http://www.handcuffsandbadges.com
Buys, sells restraining devices (handcuffs, leg irons, thumbcuffs, etc.), police badges, fire badges and other fire and police antiques; specializes in items related to Cincinnati and area.

Experts

Lt. Talbert Kanigher, Ret.
Tal's Nostalgia
P.O. Box 6294
Burbank, CA 91505-6294
ph: 818-848-6469
fax: 818-848-6469
Collecting for over 30 years; interested in anything pertaining to outlaws, lawmen, police, gangsters, murderers.

FBI

Collectors

Richard Guttler
P.O. Box 2114
Garden City, NY 11531-9998
ph: 516-931-2433
fax: 516-931-2433
Wants law enforcement FBI material related to G-Man, Melvin Purvis, Gangbusters; books, badges, toys, collectibles.

William R. Strieder
335 South Green Haven Rd.
Stormville, NY 12570
ph: 845-221-9371
toybill@aol.com
*Wants to buy F.B.I. Wanted posters;
all years.*

Barry O'Neill
6500 Ridge Rd.
Mount Airy, MD 21771
ph: 301-829-2050
*Wants G-Man, Melvin Purvis, FBI
collectibles.*

Police & Sheriff

Clubs/Associations

Sgt. James Post
International Police Historical Society
15677 Highway 62 West
Eureka Springs, AR 72632
ph: 501-253-4948
fax: 501-253-4949
jcasey@policeguide.com
http://www.policeguide.com/IPHS/
iphs.html
*Focus is to encourage the preservation
of appropriate police material relating
to the history of the police.*

Garry Neesam
Police Insignia Collectors Association of
Great Britain
Magazine: PICA Magazine
County Police Station
Baldock Rd.
Buntingford, Hertfordshire SG9 9DB
U.K.
garry@pica.co.uk
http://www.pica.co.uk
*Purpose is to keep alive the history of
the Police Service through the
collecting and preservation of related
insignia, photographs, and other
recorded information.*

Collectors

Hervey P. Cote
P.O. Box 2053
Westford, MA 01886-5053
ph: 978-692-2161
*Collector of police memorabilia
including badges, uniforms, hats,
Bobby helmets, etc.; especially
interested in older badges and
memorabilia from MA and New
England.*

Bob Fischer
P.O. Box 9763
Baldwin, MD 21013
Wants to buy old police badges.

Daryl Weseloh
P.O. Box 606
Minier, IL 61759-0741
ph: 309-497-9322
weseloh@mtco.com
*Wants to buy all sorts of police
uniform articles, equipment, police
toys, badges, shoulder patches, etc.*

Walt Gist
4190 Juniper Creek Rd.
Reno, NV 89509
ph: 775-747-2888
fax: 775-747-0926
*Wants to buy law enforcement
memorabilia including paper, photos,
badges, etc.; has over 39 years
experiencing collecting.*

Donald G. Robinson
United States Marshals Posse
P.O. Box 590487
San Francisco, CA 94159
ph: 415-386-1565
fax: 415-386-2316
*Wants to buy police and sheriff
memorabilia.*

Richard A. Perry
Perry's Cyber - P.I.G. page
3149 C St.
Sacramento, CA 95816-3328
ph: 916-448-6960
fax: 916-444-3011
*Collector and dealer in police
memorabilia; antique CA badges,
patches, US Marshal badges, patches
and highly detailed customized Road
Champs models.*

Patrick Cleary
Pamur
30 Tara Lawn
Glasheen Road, Cork City
Ireland
garda@hotmail.com
http://homepage.tinet.ie/~rcleary/pat/src/
letter.html
*An avid collector of police breast
badges, cap badges, and shoulder
patches; member of Police Insignia
Collectors Associations of Northern
Ireland/Great Britain/Australia/New
Zealand/Canada/Slovenia, International Police Association.*

Dealers

Baird Co.
P.O. Box 7240
Moreno Valley, CA 92303-7240
ph: 909-943-4180
fax: 909-943-8491
bedoya2@aol.com
http://www.bairdco.com
*Publishes lists of law enforcement
memorabilia available; also conducts
specialty mail auctions of same.*

Experts

Chip Greiner
P.O. Box 125
Bogota, NJ 07603
rrbadges@aol.com
*Specializes in Railroad Police;
produced a one hour cable TV special
on the topic the the History Channel.*

Gene Matzke
Gene's Badges & Emblems
439 Big Horn Ct.
Hancock, WI 54943
ph: 715-249-5695
fax: 414-645-8288
badgeone@uniontel.net
http://www.woodsters.com/emblems
*Wants police/fire/sheriffs & related
law enforcement badges; also old
cabinet police photos, handcuffs, leg
irons and related items.*

George E. Virgines
P.O. Box 13761
Albuquerque, NM 87192-3761
ph: 505-292-3853
*Consultant, historian and author of
"Badges of Law and Order" and
"Police Collectibles Pictorial Guide;"
collector of lawmen badges;
consultant to Franklin Mint for the
Great Western Lawman badges.*

Internet Resources

Darrell Haynes
Police Emblem Collectors Page
P.O. Box 9072
Wichita, KS 67277-0072
emblems@iname.com
http://members.cox.net/emblems
*Great resource Web site for those
interested in collecting police
emblems, especially US Federal Police
(US Government), also Capitol City,
Native American, Tribal police,
Foreign police.*

Museums/Libraries

New York City Police Museum
100 Old Slip
New York, NY 10005
ph: 212-480-3100
fax: 212-480-9757
http://www.nycpolicemuseum.org
*Devoted to exhibits of police
memorabilia and crime-related items
covering the 150 year history of the
NYPD.*

Suffolk County Police Department
  Museum
30 Yaphank Ave.
Yaphank, NY 11980
ph: 516-345-6011
*Contains various law enforcement
displays from the turn of the century
to present day.*

Jim Gordon
American Police Hall of Fame &
  Museum
Magazine: Chief of Police and Police
  Times
6350 Horizon Dr.
Titusville, FL 32780
ph: 321-264-0911
fax: 321-264-0033
policeinfo@aphf.org
http://www.aphf.org
*Over 11,000 items on display;
equipment, uniforms, firearms, etc.
from the 1700s; wants anything
related to law enforcement.*

Sgt. James Post
Last Precinct Police Museum, The
15677 Highway 62 West
Eureka Springs, AR 72632
ph: 501-253-4948
fax: 501-253-4949
jcasey@policeguide.com
http://www.policeguide.com/police-
museum.htm
*Over 150 years of law enforcement
history, movie memorabilia, police
toys, advertising, badges, weapons,
uniforms; also four decades of police
cars and motorcycles.*

Periodicals

Mike R. Bondarenko, Ed.
Newsletter: Police Collectors News
2392 US Highway 12
Baldwin, WI 54002
ph: 715-684-2216
fax: 715-684-3098
jcasey@policeguide.com
http://www.p-c-news.com
*The premier vehicle for the Police
Emblem collector.*

LAWMEN

(see LAW ENFORCEMENT
MEMORABILIA, Police & Sheriff;
OUTLAWS & LAWMEN; WESTERN
AMERICANA)

LAWN FURNITURE &
ORNAMENTS

(see GARDEN FURNITURE,
Furniture & Ornaments)

LAWNMOWERS

Clubs/Associations

Keith Wootton
Old Lawnmower Club
Newsletter: Grassbox
Milton Keynes Museum
Southern Way
Wolverton, Milton Keynes MK12 5EJ
U.K.
ph: +44 (0) 1327 830675
enquiry@oldlawnmowerclub.co.uk
http://www.oldlawnmowerclub.co.uk
*For collectors of vintage lawn
mowers.*

Museums/Libraries

Ian Britstone
British Lawnmower Museum
106-114 Shakespeare St.
Southport, Lancashire PR8 5AJ U.K.
ph: (0044) (0) 1704 501336
fax: (0044) (0) 1704 500564
help@lawnmowerworld.co.uk
http://www.lawnmowerworld.co.uk
*Over 100 machines on display
including those of the rich and
famous.*

LEAD SOLDIERS

(see SOLDIER, Toy)

LEADED WINDOWS

(see STAINED GLASS)

LEATHER

(see also ANIMAL COLLECTIBLES, Horses; ANIMAL COLLECTIBLES, Mules; KNIVES, Sheaths; LUGGAGE; OUTLAWS & LAWMEN; PURSES; SADDLES; SPORTS COLLECTIBLES, Equipment; TRUNKS)

Clubs/Associations

Dan Preston
Saddle, Harness & Allied Trades
　Association
Magazine: Shop Talk!
1101 Broad St.
Oriental, NC 28571
ph: 252-249-3409
fax: 252-249-3415
thsn@always-online.com
http://www.proleather.net
　Members are makers of saddles, chaps, harnesses, whips, holsters; carving & tooling, luggage making & repair, other leather goods, sewing machine maintenance.

Collectors

Bill Mackin
1137 Washington St.
Craig, CO 81625-1613
ph: 970-824-6717 or 970-824-6360
fax: 970-824-7175
　Wants pre-1940s cowboy and tack items: guns, cartridge belts, chaps, law badges, neckerchiefs, brands and brand books, spurs, knives, quirts, cowboy boots, hats, neckerchiefs, vests, cuffs, gauntlets, gun and saddle catalogs, etc.

Periodicals

Dan Preston
Proleptic, Inc.
Magazine: Shop Talk!
1101 Broad St.
Oriental, NC 28571
ph: 252-249-3409
fax: 252-249-3415
thsn@always-online.com
http://www.proleather.net
　For professional leather workers, saddle makers, shoe and saddle repairmen, holster manufacturers, harness makers, boot makers; ads, calendar of events.

Magazine: Leather Crafters & Saddlers
　Journal, The
331 Annette Court
Rhinelander, WI 54501-2902
ph: 715-362-5393
fax: 715-362-5391
journal@newnorth.net
　An instructional, how-to journal with leather projects using illustrations for the professional to the novice; news from the business world of leather, important ads to locate tools, leather, machinery, allied materials.

Repair Services

Bruce Hamilton
R. Bruce Hamilton, Furniture
　Restoration
P.O. Box 815
West Newbury, MA 01985
ph: 978-363-2638 or 800-439-8774
fax: 978-363-2638
rbruce.hamilton@verizon.net
http://www.patinarestoration.net
　Repairs and replaces leather and cloth table tops; brochure available; over 20 years in business.

Maria Pukownik
Fine Art & Paper Conservation
1045 Orrtanna Rd.
Orrtanna, PA 17353-9691
ph: 717-337-0668
conspuk@yahoo.com
　Surface cleaning, softening of cockled and distorted leather, stabilizing and flattening, calligraphy, conservation of wax seals and other materials.

Michael Weller
Metro Leather Furniture Restoration
202 Lane Court, Ste. E
Sterling, VA 20166
ph: 703-450-6850 or 800-553-3872
fax: 703-471-1776
metroleather@msn.com
http://www.metroleather.com
　Cleans, repairs, refinishes, reupholsters, colors leather furniture, auto leather, etc.

James Lane
James Lane & Son
8834 N. Virginia Ave.
Palm Beach Gardens, FL 33418
ph: 561-615-0622
fax: 561-694-8118
antiquef@bellsouth.net
　Standard and custom colors; leathers custom colored to match for desk tops and upholstery.

Charles H. Clements, III
Gryphon Studio
1741 Dallas St.
Aurora, CO 80010-2018
ph: 303-364-0403
fax: 303-739-9824
chas@pcisys.net
http://www.combase.com/~carregal/
　kuntao/chas.htm
　Conservation, repair, restoration of leather goods: luggage, cases, saddlery, frontier, cowboy, militaria, gun leather.

Suppliers

C.S. Osborne & Co.
125 Jersey St.
Harrison, NJ 07029
ph: 973-483-3232
fax: 973-484-3621
cso@csosborne.com
http://www.csosborne.com
　Supplier of fine leather working tools for over 160 years.

Wickett & Craig of America
120 Copper Rd.
Curwensville, PA 16833
ph: 800-TAN-NERY or 814-236-2220
fax: 814-236-3333
office@wickett-craig.com
http://www.wickett-craig.com
　Leather supplier for use in personal leather goods and equestrian products; tanning in North America for over 130 years.

Smucker's Harness Shop
2014 Main St.
Narvon, PA 17555
ph: 717-445-5956
fax: 717-445-7752
sales@smuckersharness.com
http://www.smuckersharness.com
　Carries complete line of leather working supplies including solid brass and plated brass bells for harnesses and decorative purposes.

Mast Harness Hardware
115E C.R. 500N
Arthur, IL 61911
ph: 217-543-3463
fax: 800-331-MAST
　Specializing in hardware, tools, leather oils, sleigh bells, and machines for the harness maker.

Bill Confer
Hereford Bi-Products, Inc.
P.O. Box 2257
Hereford, TX 79045
ph: 800-858-4384
fax: 806-364-6583
　American made rawhide for saddle & tree makers, braiders and craftsmen.

Charles H. Clements, III
Gryphon Studio
1741 Dallas St.
Aurora, CO 80010-2018
ph: 303-364-0403
fax: 303-739-9824
chas@pcisys.net
http://www.combase.com/~carregal/
　kuntao/chas.htm
　Makes cases, luggage, specialty items for Rodeo, Circus, Safari, Fashion/ Commercial, Advertising/Cinema, etc.

R. Stephen Dorsey
Pecard
P.O. Box 263
Eugene, OR 97440-0263
ph: 541-937-3348
mail@rsdmilitaria.com
http://www.rsdmilitaria.com
　Sells the very best antique leather preservative - moisturizes, preserves, colorless, softens, odorless, long lasting, safe; 6 oz. sample tub $9.50 ppd.; other, larger sizes available.

LETTERS (FAMILY)

(see MANUSCRIPTS; PAPER COLLECTIBLES)

LEVIS

(see CLOTHING & ACCESSORIES, Denim)

LICENSE PLATES

(see also AUTOMOBILIA; BICYCLES & RELATED MEMORABILIA; GAS STATION COLLECTIBLES)

Collectors

William Caswell
3 Buxton Place
Concord, NH 03302-2242
wscaswell@aol.com
http://members.aol.com/wscaswell/
　billhome.htm

Andy Bernstein
43-60 Douglaston Pkwy., Apt. #524
Flushing, NY 11363
ph: 718-279-1890 or 561-793-8422
andybnyork@aol.com
http://www.platehut.com
　Avid license plate collector wants all types of license plates; any year, type or place; will answer questions or help out those interested in the hobby; speaks Spanish and French.

Dan Segal
Great License Plate Trade Page, The
5 Pine Dr.
Woodbury, NY 11797
segaldan@aol.com
http://members.aol.com/segaldan
　Great Web site for finding license plates or for getting questions answered.

Trent Culp
P.O. Box 550
Misenheimer, NC 28109-0550
ph: 704-463-2857
　Collects license plates from all states: porcelain, early tin, motorcycle, Presidential Inauguration, early Alaskan & Hawaiian, etc.

Dealers

Ed English
PlatesUSA.com
4 Moors Circle
Scituate, MA 02066
fax: 801-340-3199
getplates@aol.com
http://www.PlatesUSA.com
　Internet license plate Web store; license plates stocked from all 50 states plus Canada; pictures on Web site of each plate style.

Greg Glaude
130 Coomer Hill Rd.
Dayville, CT 06241
Specializing in collecting, trading and selling US license plates; Web site has listing of Motor Vehicle Administration addresses to obtain sample plates (some of which are free!)

Drew Steitz
PL8S Magazine
P.O. Box 222
East Texas, PA 18046-0222
ph: 610-791-7979
fax: 610-791-7979
pl8seditor@aol.com
http://www.pl8s.com
Collects, buys, sells and trades all types of license plates: porcelain, leather, US or Canada, foreign, errors, blanks, tests, political, low number, motorcycle, movie props or prototypes, etc.

Billy Moore
3128 Kline Dr.
Virginia Beach, VA 23452-6226
moore@exis.net
http://wwwp.exis.net/~moore/us.htm
Collector and dealer of modern special issue US graphic license plates; also will trade for interesting foreign plates; specializes in VA graphic plates - for sale or trade.

Jeff Francis
P.O. Box 41381
Saint Petersburg, FL 33743-1381
ph: 727-345-6627
fax: 727-343-8977
gobucs13@aol.com

Chuck Batey
1115 Theresa St.
Stuart, FL 34996-3610
ph: 772-283-5335
fltagman@aol.com
Buys and sells license plates from 1910 to present.

Denny Williams
Denny's Trading Company
4038 Saltspring Dr.
Ferndale, WA 98248
ph: 360-380-1670
fax: 360-380-1477
denny4plat@aol.com
License plate dealer, appraiser, expert; very active member of numerous collector clubs; deals world wide in license plates; one or 1,000 at a time.

Leonard Heller
Automobile License Plates
2909 280 St. NW
Stanwood, WA 98292
ph: 360-629-4692
LPL8MAN@whidbey.net
http://www.whidbey.net/licenseplate
Dealer in automobile and motorcycle license plates from the US, Canada, Australia and over 100 other countries available to collectors; Web site contains hundreds of license plate

graphics; snail mail price lists available.

Dwayne Spark
Nostalgia Plus
8441 Sublaines
Anjou, Quebec H1K 2C1 Canada
ph: 514-352-6892
fax: 514-352-1856
dspark@videotron.ca
Wants to buy current passenger license plates and commemorative from US sates and Canadian provinces; prefers to buy in lots of 50 or more plates.

Experts

Tom Smith
License Plate Collectibles
3064 River Rd. West
P.O. Box 238
Goochland, VA 23063
ph: 804-556-3598
fax: 804-556-6224
tomvsmith@aol.com
http://users.erols.com/plates/lp/collect
Collector, dealer, expert in license plates worldwide; many plates available for sale or trade; technical consultant to the movie industry for the use of authentic license plates in productions.

Walt Feiger
Walt's Antiques
2513 Nelson Rd.
Traverse City, MI 49686-8557
ph: 231-223-7386 or 231-223-4123
feiger@pentel.net
http://www.pentel.net/antiques
Wants all kinds of older Michigan license plates.

Denny Williams
Denny's Trading Company
4038 Saltspring Dr.
Ferndale, WA 98248
ph: 360-380-1670
fax: 360-380-1477
denny4plat@aol.com
License plate dealer, appraiser, expert; very active member of numerous collector clubs; deals world wide in license plates; one or 1,000 at a time.

Repair Services

Dan & Judy Landino
D & J Restorations
37037 E. Almont
Sterling Heights, MI 48310
ph: 810-268-8692
djlrest@comcast.net
http://www.dnjauctions.com
Over 35 years experience in restoration of antiques: from carousel figures and antique furniture to soda machines and license plates.

Automobile

Clubs/Associations

Automobile License Plate Collectors
Association, Inc.
Newsletter: ALPCA Newsletter
7365 Main St., #214
Stratford, CT 06614-1300
pl8mail@alpca.org
http://www.alpca.org
A non-profit organization to promote interest in the collecting of motor vehicle license plates and to share information among members.

Collectors

Ken Stratton
Ken Stratton License Plates
strattonkm34@msn.com
http://www.geocities.com/
~ktrk_alpca3628
Specializes in collecting license plates from WA and WY as well as Wildlife, Environmental and Optional plates from all states; Web site has hundreds of images of plates in his collection.

Dealers

Conrad Hughson
Self Help Services
P.O. Box 941
Brattleboro, VT 05302-0399
ph: 802-387-4223
chughson@sover.net
Collector of US and Canadian license plates since 1952; will buy entire collections of early plates; many duplicates; appraisal service available; consignment sales of license plates and related collectibles; since 1952.

Experts

Chuck Crisler
P.O. Box 114
Ponchatoula, LA 70454-0114
p42@4rr.com
http://www.lp1.com
Author of "License Plates Values."

Periodicals

Drew Steitz
Magazine: PL8S - The License Plate
Collector's Hobby Paper
P.O. Box 222
East Texas, PA 18046-0222
ph: 610-791-7979
fax: 610-791-7979
pl8seditor@aol.com
http://www.pl8s.com
A bi-monthly hobby magazine dedicated to the license plate collecting hobby; license plate photos, puzzles, cartoons, giveaways, games, ads, and lots more.

Automobile (Delaware)

Collectors

Dave Lincoln
P.O. Box 331
Yorklyn, DE 19736-0331
ph: 610-444-4144
tagbarn@msn.com
Collector seeks Delaware plates of all types, variety, and vintage for comprehensive display and forthcoming book. Largest DELAWARE collection extant; finders fees paid; references available; information requests are welcome.

Automobile (Porcelain)

Collectors

Tom Mills
P.O. Box 424
Spencer, MA 01562
ph: 508-885-9550
Wants to buy porcelain license plates and signs; best to write and send photos first.

Stephen S. Uss
60 Homecrest Ave.
Yonkers, NY 10703
ph: 914-423-0442
Wants early porcelain, leather and tin auto or motorcycle license plates; also chauffeurs badges and dashboard registration discs.

Dave Lincoln
P.O. Box 331
Yorklyn, DE 19736-0331
ph: 610-444-4144
tagbarn@msn.com
Active hobbyist for over 30 years; will buy expired plates from anywhere; any type, any number, any vintage; will travel to purchase collections; has some for swap or sale; specializes in researching PORCELAIN-ENAMEL plates.

Jim Crilly
8261 141st St. N.
Seminole, FL 33776-2835
ph: 727-393-7295
jascrilly@aol.com
Collects state and city porcelain license plates; also wants 1940 B.F. Goodrich license plate key chain tags.

Government

Experts

Jake Eckenrode
310 Wallace Rd.
Bellefonte, PA 16823
ph: 814-355-8769
Wants old US Government license plates from any agency including old Civilian Conservation Corps (CCC) signs, and Pennsylvania licenses (vehicle, hunting, fishing, dog); author of "Collector's Guide to Pennsylvania Licenses."

Miniature

Clubs/Associations

Dr. Edward H. Miles
License Plate Key Chain & Mini License
Plate Collectors
Newsletter: DAV Keychain & Chauffeur
Badge Collectors News
888 Eighth Ave.
New York, NY 10019-5704
ph: 212-765-2660
emiles33@aol.com
*Focuses on miniature Disabled
American Veterans key chains,
chauffeurs' badges, gum cards
featuring license plates, windshield
stickers, mini license plates.*

Collectors

Virginia Young
15463 McNeill Rd.
Sterling, NY 13156-4212
ph: 315-947-5840 or 315-947-5782
fax: 315-947-6905
ginny@zlink.net
*Wants Idento Tag, DAV and BFG
miniature license keychain tags; also
gumball charms from 1950 depicting
license plates; all years, all state;
especially looking for older, Western
or Southern states, or a 1943 round
DAV tag.*

LICENSES

(see also AUTOMOBILIA; LICENSE
PLATES)

Collectors

Ken Mitzel
5225 N. George
Manchester, PA 17345-9400
ph: 717-266-2783
*Wants to buy hunting & fishing
licenses, dog licenses, bicycle licenses,
sidepath licenses, PA Dept. of
Forestry & Waters licenses and
badges.*

Animal

Clubs/Associations

William Bone
International Society of Animal License
Collectors
Newsletter: Paw Prints
928 SR 2206
Clinton, KY 42031
ph: 270-653-6060
*Animal license collectors united for
the exchange of hobby material;
annual convention in various areas of
the US; Sec./Treas. of the International Society of Animal License
Collectors; editor of "Paw Prints."*

Collectors

Henry Keyes
P.O. Box 1683
Cedar Rapids, IA 52406
ph: 319-355-2427 or 319-366-1323
fax: 319-366-2427
*Has a collection of over 7,000
licenses.*

Experts

William Bone
928 SR 2206
Clinton, KY 42031
ph: 270-653-6060
*Has published a book on pre-1900
animal license tags; Sec./Treas. of the
International Society of Animal
License Collectors; editor of "Paw
Prints."*

Dog

Collectors

James C. Case
10189 Crane Rd.
Lindley, NY 14858-9719
ph: 607-524-6606
hftlicense@aol.com
http://hometown.aol.com/hftlicense/
myhomepage/profile.html
*Wants dog licenses and dog tags
dated before 1920; especially
interested in pre-1917 tags from New
York state.*

Jerome Schaeper, Jr.
365 Meadowlark Dr.
Edgewood, KY 41018-2608
ph: 859-341-3769
*Collects and appraises early dog
(canine) license tags, especially pre-
1920, from any state or country.*

Hunting & Fishing

Clubs/Associations

Jim Nedla
Michigan Hunting & Fishing License
Collectors Club
P.O. Box 785
Mount Pleasant, MI 48858
ph: 989-773-7764
licenses@charter.net
http://www.mhflcc.citymax.com
*Club formed to enhance and promote
the collection, preservation and
knowledge of Michigan hunting and
fishing history, and to assist other
groups and organizations with a
similar purpose.*

Collectors

Eric T. Hado
145 Summit Ave., #106
Summit, NJ 07901
ph: 973-912-7735
fax: 973-376-5813
ericth@hotmail.com
*Wants hunting, fishing, and trapping
license buttons from New Jersey and
New York state (mainly pre-WWII);
also wants metal "no hunting/no-
trespassing" signs from NJ and NY.*

James C. Case
10189 Crane Rd.
Lindley, NY 14858-9719
ph: 607-524-6606
hftlicense@aol.com
http://hometown.aol.com/hftlicense/
myhomepage/profile.html
*Wants hunting, fishing, trapping
licenses and license buttons as well as
guide badges from all states (mainly
pre-1945.)*

Ron Brownawell
331 Old State Rd.
Shermans Dale, PA 17090-8431
ph: 717-582-2088
*Wants hunting and fishing licenses;
especially PA related; also pin-back
type licenses from all states and
Canada.*

Ken Mitzel
5225 N. George
Manchester, PA 17345-9400
ph: 717-266-2783
*Wants old hunting and fishing
licenses from all states and Canada;
game warden, fish warden, fire
warden; duck stamps, animal calls,
dog licenses; also conservation, guide,
forestry and other badges and related
items.*

Howard Share
4349 LaVale Ct.
Clemmons, NC 27012-9009
ph: 336-766-6579
fax: 336-766-5445
HowSha43@aol.com
*Wants to buy state hunting and
fishing licenses, especially from the
Southern states and Hawaii; will also
trade.*

Howard Share
4349 LaVale Ct.
Clemmons, NC 27012-9009
ph: 336-766-6579
denarnc@aol.com
*Wants Southern State license badges,
especially from AL, FL, GA, MS, NC,
SC, TN, VA; wants all nonresident
licenses and any trapping-only
licenses.*

Phil Taylor
Outdoors Michigan
519 Melita Rd.
Sterling, MI 48659-9649
ph: 517-654-2218
*Wants to buy old Michigan hunting
licenses and Michigan successful deer,
bear, turkey patches.*

Greg Woodland
480 Maiden Lane
Pleasant Lake, MI 49272-9713
ph: 517-769-6276
woodys@cablespeed.com

Joe Edson
316 Stanford St.
Brush, CO 80723
ph: 970-842-4841
fishback@webtv.net
Specializes in hunting and fishing

*licenses from CO, CA, OR, NE, and
OK; searching for licenses from all
these states, especially early examples.*

Dealers

Jeff Savage
Drexel Grapevine Antiques
2784 US 70 East
Valdese, NC 28690
ph: 828-437-5938
jeff@drexelantiques.com
http://www.drexelantiques.com
*Buy, sell antique fishing tackle as well
as hunting and fishing licenses.*

Walt Feiger
Walt's Antiques
2513 Nelson Rd.
Traverse City, MI 49686-8557
ph: 231-223-7386 or 231-223-4123
feiger@pentel.net
http://www.pentel.net/antiques
*Buys old Michigan hunting or fishing
licenses.*

Experts

Jake Eckenrode
310 Wallace Rd.
Bellefonte, PA 16823
ph: 814-355-8769
*Wants old US Government license
plates from any agency including old
Civilian Conservation Corps (CCC)
signs, and Pennsylvania licenses
(vehicle, hunting, fishing, dog);
author of "Collector's Guide to
Pennsylvania Licenses."*

Robert F. Miller
401 Old Rt 6
Ulysses, PA 16948
ph: 814-435-2140
*Collects and appraises; author of "A
Guide to Collecting Pennsylvania
Hunting and Fishing Licenses," 1992
edition; $6 plus $2 P&H; also collects
PA Game Commission items, patches
and posters.*

LIDS

(see also OINTMENT POTS & POT
LIDS)

Suppliers

Charles Bodiker
Lid Lady, The
7790 East Ross Rd.
New Carlisle, OH 45344-9624
ph: 937-845-1266
*Carries replacement lids for ceramic,
glass, metal, and plastic vessels and
containers.*

LIGHT BULBS

(see also CHRISTMAS
COLLECTIBLES; ELECTRICITY
RELATED ITEMS; LAMPS &
LIGHTING; PERSONALITIES
[INVENTORS], Thomas Alva Edison)

LIGHT BULBS

Collectors

Rob M. Simon
245 N. Stewart
Lombard, IL 60148-2026
ph: 630-620-4770
rsimon2424@aol.com
Wants to buy pre-1900 light bulbs and anything pertaining to light bulbs.

Dealers

Tim Tromp
Kilokat's Antique Light Bulb Site
P.O. Box G
Fruitport, MI 49415
kilokat7@bulbcollector.com
http://www.bulbcollector.com
A Web site for the bulb and vacuum tube collector.

Experts

C. T. Little
183 Rainbow Dr., #8348
Livingston, TX 77399-1083
ladylight2000@yahoo.com
Collects and specializes in light bulbs; wants light bulbs with tips or unusual light bulbs, Glow Lamps (neon) with figurals inside, meters, sockets, bulbs with figural or decorative filaments, Edison, Westinghouse, Reddy Kilowatt, etc.

Internet Resources

Tim Tromp
Kilokat's Antique Light Bulb Site
P.O. Box G
Fruitport, MI 49415
kilokat7@bulbcollector.com
http://www.bulbcollector.com
A Web site for the bulb and vacuum tube collector; research paper archives, time line, discussion boards, information, pictures; also covers tube advertising art.

Museums/Libraries

Carolyn T. Little
Light Bulb Museum
1655 Morena Blvd.
San Diego, CA 92110
ph: 619-276-1500

LIGHTERS

(see also CIGARETTE COLLECTIBLES; SMOKING COLLECTIBLES)

Clubs/Associations

Pocket Lighter Preservation Guild & Historical Society, Inc.
Newsletter: Flint & Flame
P.O. Box 327
Wentzville, MO 63385-0327
ph: 314-651-0693
fax: 636-639-8990
PLPG1@aol.com
An organization to help promote, maintain and preserve interest in the hobby of lighter collecting; newsletter published bi-monthly.

Judith Sanders, Editor
On the LIGHTER Side International Lighter Collectors
Newsletter: On The Lighter Side
P.O. Box 1733
Quitman, TX 75783-1733
ph: 903-763-2795
fax: 903-763-4953
info@otls.com
http://www.otls.com
Members collect cigar & cigarette lighters & research lighter history; bi-monthly newsletter; send SASE for information.

Christian Wenger
Spark International
P.O. Box 1656
Olten, 4600 Switzerland
ph: ++41622963381
fax: ++41622963381
intSpark@aol.com
http://members.aol.com/IntSpark/welcome.html
International lighter collector's club; world wide bilingual (English/German) operation; quarterly newsletter, Web services and annual conventions; members are from all around the world.

Richard Ball
Lighter Club of Great Britain
30 Heathfield Rd.
Croydon, Surrey CRO iEU U.K.
ph: 011-44-688-7673
Richard-Ball@msn.com
http://www.lighterclub.co.uk

Collectors

Barry D. Hoffman
7 Stonemeadow
Westwood, MA 02090
ph: 617-584-5555 or 781-326-3333
fax: 617-266-6666
pakistan@tiac.net
Wants to buy Ronson, Zippo and Dunhill cigarette lighters; also offers free appraisal service.

Wes & Elaine Hart
963 Westhaven St.
Columbus, OH 43228
ph: 614-870-7141
tiquestoys@webtv.net
Wants to buy "trench" lighters and other vintage or unique lighters; also pre-1960 Zippo pocket lighters with advertising, and Zippo table lighters.

John E. Shoffner
624 Merritt St.
Fife Lake, MI 49633-9142
ph: 231-879-3912

Terry & Karen Cairo
Cairo Lighters
P.O. Box 1054
Addison, IL 60101-8054
ph: 630-543-9120 or 630-220-1953 cell
fax: 630-834-4051
lightergod@aol.com
Wants to buy cigar and cigarette lighters made in US or in Europe; prefers pre-1970 items: pocket or table

models, figural, complicated mechanisms, case and lighter sets, solid gold lighters with watches, advertising displays, etc.

Leonard Shafer
3202 West Magnolia Blvd.
Burbank, CA 91505-2905
ph: 818-846-5655
Wants to buy Ronson, Zippo and Dunhill cigarette lighters.

Christian Wenger
Saelistgrasse 131
Olten, 4600 Switzerland
ph: +41622963381
fax: +41622963381
c.wenger@spectraweb.ch
Lighter collector and expert wants to buy high quality pre-WWII lighters: Dunhill, Cartier, Ronson, Evans, Carlton, Elgin, Douglas, Lincoln, etc.

Dealers

Ira Pilossof
Vintage Lighters, Inc.
P.O. Box 1325
Fair Lawn, NJ 07410-8325
ph: 201-797-6595 or 888-454-4483
fax: 201-797-8642
vintageltr@aol.com
http://www.vintagelightersinc.com
Experienced collector and dealer in vintage cigarette lighters since 1979; always interested in buying, especially entire collections; Zippo, Ronson, Dunhill; author of "Handbook of Vintage Cigarette Lighters."

Richard Weinstein
International Vintage Lighter Exchange
30 W. 57th St.
New York, NY 10019
ph: 212-586-0947
fax: 212-586-1296
vinlighter@aol.com
http://www.vintagelighters.com
Buying vintage Zippo, Dunhill, Tiffany, Ronson, Cartier, Evans, Thorens, and Marathon, lighters; especially interested in sterling, gold, enameled lighters and lighters with watches.

Shaw
P.O. Box 5096
Southfield, MI 48086
Wants to buy table model cigarette lighters: Dunhill, Ronson, Evans, Thorens, etc.

Michael A. Pratt, Sr.
Lighter Chest, The
512 North Spruce St.
Valley, NE 68064-9670
ph: 402-359-5539
fax: 402-359-5539
sales@usadisplay.net
http://www.usadisplay.net
Buys and sells unique cigarette lighters links of all kinds; also sells display cases for cuff links and collectibles of all types.

Bob Rogers
Wick'd Ways
P.O. Box 245
Lafayette, CA 94549
ph: 925-681-0451
wickdways@netvista.net
Buys and sells cigarette lighters.

Experts

Ira Pilossof
Vintage Lighters, Inc.
P.O. Box 1325
Fair Lawn, NJ 07410-8325
ph: 201-797-6595 or 888-454-4483
fax: 201-797-8642
vintageltr@aol.com
http://www.vintagelightersinc.com
Experienced collector and dealer in vintage cigarette lighters since 1979; always interested in buying, especially entire collections; Zippo, Ronson, Dunhill; author of "Handbook of Vintage Cigarette Lighters."

Internet Resources

Ted & Pat Ballard
National Lighter Museum
5714 So. Sooner Rd.
Guthrie, OK 73044
ph: 405-282-3025
nlm@natlitrmus.com
http://www.natlitrmus.com
An online museum with thousands of lighters on display: table model, pocket models, advertising, WWI, WWII, Zippos, Ronsons and more.

Man./Prod./Dist.

Zippo Manufacturing Company
33 Barbour St.
Bradford, PA 16701
ph: 814-368-2700
lmeabon@zippo.com
http://www.zippo.com
Offers a free "Zippo Collector's Guide" to vintage Zippo lighters; Web site has Zippo trivia and collector's and museum pages.

Repair Services

Richard Weinstein
International Vintage Lighter Exchange
30 W. 57th St.
New York, NY 10019
ph: 212-586-0947
fax: 212-586-1296
vinlighter@aol.com
http://www.vintagelighters.com
Specializes in the sales, repairing and purchasing of vintage lighters such as Zippo, Dunhill, Ronson, Evans, Thorens, Marathon, Cartier, Tiffany, Occupied Japan, and lighters of precious metals and with watches.

Zippo

Collectors

Frank Briola
P.O. Box 44022
Pittsburgh, PA 15205-0222
ph: 412-937-8787 or 800-372-6509
fax: 412-937-1959
americana@mail.com
Wants to buy Zippo lighters.

Dealers

Jerry Korn
Lighters Galore Plus
P.O. Box 534
San Marcos, CA 92079
ph: 800-853-3941 or 760-734-1414
fax: 760-744-6666
info@pipeshop.com
http://www.pipeshop.com
*Collector, dealer, appraiser, expert
specializes in collectible Zippo
lighters and handcarved Meerschaum
pipes; also carries many other hard-
to-find smoking accessories.*

Experts

Philip K. Taggart
1000 Edgefield Dr.
Plano, TX 75075
ph: 972-509-2214
*Expert on advertising Zippo cigarette
lighters; author of "Zippo & The
American Automobile."*

Jeff Mogilner
Racine & Laramie, Ltd.
2737 San Diego Ave.
San Diego, CA 92110-2731
ph: 619-291-7833
fax: 619-297-6653
axracine@znet.com
*Wants to buy old Zippo lighters: US
Navy ships and squadrons, US Marine
Corps and squadrons; also wants
antique or unusual lighters.*

LIGHTING

(see LAMPS & LIGHTING)

LIGHTNING BALLS & RODS

(see LIGHTNING PROTECTION
COLLECTIBLES)

LIGHTNING PROTECTION COLLECTIBLES

Collectors

John Gephart
1 Firestone Ct.
Fairfield, OH 45014
ph: 513-858-3368
fax: 513-595-2661
*Lightning rods, balls, arrows, vanes,
all related catalogs, paper and
advertising.*

Larry Bergman
N33015 Square Bluff Rd.
Whitehall, WI 54773-9148
ph: 715-985-3310
bergman@ecol.net
*Wants to buy lightning rod items:
balls, arrows, vanes, pendants.*

Dealers

Ted & Jeanne Storb
Storb Antiques
319B Rowayton Ave.
Rowayton, CT 06853
ph: 203-866-6244
fax: 203-866-6244
storbantiq@optonline.net
*Specializes in collectible lightning rod
weathervanes, balls and stands; also
repairs and restores those items for
sale and for past customers.*

Experts

Michael Bruner
2615 Echo Lane
Ortonville, MI 48462
ph: 248-627-6351
*Wants lightning rod balls, catalogs,
installation tags, rods, braces, etc.;
co-author of "The Complete Book of
Lightning Rod Balls."*

Rod Krupka
2615 Echo Lane
Ortonville, MI 48462
ph: 248-627-6351
*Collector, dealer, expert; buys, sells
lightning rod balls, weathervanes,
related catalogs and ads; co-author of
"The Complete Book of Lightning Rod
Balls."*

Russell Barnes
P.O. Box 141994
Austin, TX 78714-1994
csindian@flash.net
http://eula.home.texas.net/lrod1.htm
*Author of the "Lightning Rod
Collectibles Price Guide," available
from the author for $49.95 ppd.*

Periodicals

Newsletter: Crown Point, The
P.O. Box 23
Winfield, IL 60190
ph: 630-876-1316
crownpoint@ntsource.com
http://www.crownpointmagazine.com
*Devoted to the history of lightning
protection and the collecting of related
items: lightning rod balls, pendants,
weathervanes, points, etc.*

LIMITED EDITION COLLECTIBLES

(see COLLECTIBLES [MODERN])

LINCOLN

(see PERSONALITIES
[HISTORICAL], Abraham Lincoln)

LINENS

(see TEXTILES; TEXTILES, Lace &
Linens)

LITERATURE

(see AUTOGRAPHS; BOOKS;
MANUSCRIPTS; PERSONALITIES
[LITERARY])

LITHOPHANES

(see also COLLECTIBLES
[MODERN], Lithophanes)

Collectors

Donald Gorlick
P.O. Box 24541
Seattle, WA 98124-0541
ph: 206-824-0508
*Wants "Berlin transparencies:" looks
like bisque but when turned to light it
has a picture in it; in tea sets, lamp
shades, beer steins.*

Dealers

Lucille Malitz
Lucid Antiques
P.O. Box KH
Scarsdale, NY 10583
ph: 914-636-7825 or 914-636-5171
fax: 914-636-7825
lithopha@optonline.net
*These 19th century porcelain plaques,
made with the lost wax process; when
illuminated from the back they depict
famous paintings or portraits of
popular personalities of the times
because of the varying thickness of the
porcelain.*

LIVESTOCK

(see also ANIMAL COLLECTIBLES;
HORSES)

Appraisers

Jay Proost
American Society of Agricultural
  Appraisers, Inc.
834 Falls Ave., Ste. 1130
P.O. Box 186
Twin Falls, ID 83303-0186
ph: 208-733-2323 or 800-488-7570
fax: 208-733-2326
ag@amagappraisers.com
http://www.amagappraisers.com
*Members of this society's "Interna-
tional Society of Livestock Appraisers" division appraise livestock.*

LIVING HISTORY

(see also CLOTHING &
ACCESSORIES, Costumes;
MILITARY HISTORY)

Clubs/Associations

James Dassatti, Ex. Dir.
Living History Association
Newspaper: Living Historian
P.O. Box 1389
Wilmington, VT 05363
ph: 802-464-5569
info@livinghistoryassn.org
http://www.livinghistoryassn.org
*One of the largest group of reenactors
in the country; members dress up
according to the era, and act our
battles, home life, balls, etc.; catalog
of merchandise, lectures, school
programs, teaches workshops, etc.;
quarterly magazine.*

Internet Resources

Living History Online
P.O. Box 77
Fairfax, VA 22030
ph: 703-913-6319 or 703-758-5838
72774.2240@compuserve.com
http://www.LivingHistoryOnline.com
*Your best online source for living
history events and articles.*

Periodicals

Magazine: Artilleryman, The
234 Monarch Hill Rd.
Tunbridge, VT 05077
ph: 802-889-3500 or 800-777-1862
fax: 802-889-5627
mail@civilwarnews.com
*Published quarterly, the only
magazine exclusively for the 1750-
1898 artillery enthusiast: artillery
history, unit profiles, shell collecting,
etc.*

Newspaper: Civil War News, The
234 Monarch Hill Rd.
Tunbridge, VT 05077
ph: 802-889-3500 or 800-777-1862
fax: 802-889-5627
mail@civilwarnews.com
http://www.civilwarnews.com
*A current events newspaper published
eleven times per year for people with
an active interest in Civil War history:
coming events, book reviews, columns,
ads, news, features, photos.*

Magazine: Smoke & Fire News
P.O. Box 166
Grand Rapids, OH 43522-0166
ph: 419-832-0303
dmeyers@smoke-fire.com
http://www.smoke-fire.com
*Contains national listings of living
history events; emphasis on the 18th
century and Rendezvous period
primarily in the Midwest; good
coverage on War of 1812 era;
numerous ads, classifieds, reenacting
articles.*

Magazine: Backwoodsman Magazine
P.O. Box 627
Westcliffe, CO 81252
bwmmag@ris.net
http://purelight.com/bwmmag/home.htm
*The magazine for the twentieth century
frontiersman specializing in*

muzzleloading, woodslore, survival, homesteading, history, Indian lore and much more.

Suppliers

Collector's Armoury
P.O. Box 59
Alexandria, VA 22313-0059
ph: 877-276-6879 or 703-684-6111
fax: 703-683-5486
sales@collectorsarmoury.com
http://www.armoury.com
Offers museum quality reproductions: Civil War swords, knives, pistols and field gear; non-firing Western pistols, rifles and collectibles; medieval, Samurai and military swords; historic miniature Gatling guns and cannons.

Civil War Reenactors

Clubs/Associations

Arthur W. Henrick
American Civil War Association, Union Brigade
P.O. Box 61075
Sunnyvale, CA 94088-1075
ph: 510-843-2627
Union/CSA reenactors don authentically reproduced clothing and uniforms, shoulder period muskets, cook over open fires, sleep in canvas tents, participate in battle reenactments and some even speak in the dialect of the era.

American Civil War Association, Confederate Brigade
Newsletter: Courier, The
P.O. Box 83333
San Jose, CA 95155
marcusmulkins@yahoo.com
http://www.acwa.org
Confederate reenactors don authentically reproduced clothing and uniforms, shoulder period muskets, cook over open fires, sleep in canvas tents, participate in battle reenactments and some even speak in the dialect of the era.

Internet Resources

Robert Szabo
Civil War Reenactors, The
rjs@cwreenactors.com
http://www.cwreenactors.com
Web site devoted to reenacting and Civil War history.

Bill Cyders
P.O. Box 5614
Novato, CA 94948
ph: 415-474-2377
bcyders@marin.org
http://reenact.org
Great Internet site with lots of Civil War reenactor Web sites.

Periodicals

Dan Preston
Proleptic, Inc.
Magazine: Shop Talk!
1101 Broad St.
Oriental, NC 28571
ph: 252-249-3409
fax: 252-249-3415
thsn@always-online.com
http://www.proleather.net
Original McClellans, sources for military hardware, accouterments, and reproductions; professional leather workers, saddle makers, saddle & shoe repairmen, holster manufacturers, harness makers, boot makers; ads, calendar of events.

Jeff H. Grzelak
Department of the South
Newspaper: Hilton Head Dispatch
7214 Laurel Hill Rd.
Orlando, FL 32818-5233
ph: 407-295-7510
Carries the latest information on all Southeastern Civil War events: shows, reenactments, book fairs; for historians, reenactors, buffs in S.E.

William Holschuh, Pub.
Newspaper: Camp Chase Gazette
P.O. Box 707
Marietta, OH 45750
ph: 740-373-1865 or 800-449-1865
fax: 740-374-5710
CampChase@compuserve.com
http://www.campchase.com
For 28 years the voice of the Civil War reenactor: recruiting, events, equipment, etc.; Web site has links to many Civil War sites, including reenactors.

Suppliers

Regimental Quartermaster, The
P.O. Box 553
Hatboro, PA 19040
ph: 215-672-6891
fax: 215-672-9020
regtqm@aol.com
http://www.regtqm.com
Civil War reproduction Muskets, Revolvers, Swords, Uniforms, Leather Goods, Buckles, Buttons, Accouterments, Accessories, etc.; send $3 for list.

Southern Exposure
710 Caroline St.
Fredericksburg, VA 22401
ph: 540-899-6464
fax: 540-373-2469
sutler@erols.com
http://www.staleyssundries.com
Carries American Revolution and Civil War era gifts, flags, music, accessories, accouterments, etc.

Joy Melcher
P.O. Box 351
Clarinda, IA 51632
ph: 712-542-5239
fax: 712-542-5239
joy@civilwarlady.com
http://www.civilwarlady.com
Produces women's historical Civil War ball gowns, day dresses, corsets, bonnets and accessories; also original Victorian jewelry including broaches, earrings, bracelets; serves Civil War reenactors, theatrical and movie production.

WWII Reenactors

Internet Resources

WW2 German Army Reenacting Page
Soldaten@aol.com
http://members.aol.com/soldaten/main.htm
Specializing in WWII German army reenacting.

LOBBY CARDS

(see MOVIE MEMORABILIA; PAPER COLLECTIBLES)

LOCKS

(see also BANKS; DOORKNOBS; HARDWARE; KEYS; RESTRAINT DEVICES; SAFES)

Clubs/Associations

Robert Dix
American Lock Collectors Association
Newsletter: American Lock Collectors Association Newsletter
8576 Barbara Dr.
Mentor, OH 44060
ph: 440-257-2346
fax: 440-257-2373
dixlock@aol.com
Club newsletter reports on coming lock shows, also articles on locks, keys, handcuffs; prices, unusual items, historical information.

Bob Heilemann
West Coast Lock Collectors
Newsletter: West Coast Lock Collectors Newsletter
1427 Lincoln Blvd.
Santa Monica, CA 90401-2732
ph: 310-454-7295 or 310-230-3004
locksmann@earthlink.net
http://www.wclca.org
Call evenings; no collect calls, please.

Collectors

Alene Saap
400 Calaf St., Ste. 80
San Juan, PR 00918-1314
ph: 787-758-5606 or 787-782-0020
Wants antique or unusual padlocks with key.

Richard C. Hubbard
162 Poplar Ave.
Hackensack, NJ 07601
ph: 201-342-1274
DoorKnobID@aol.com
Interested in old US key or combination padlocks, embossed RR locks, figural shapes and unusual mechanisms or early patent dates.

Joseph Biunno
129 West 29th St.
New York, NY 10001
ph: 212-629-5630
fax: 212-268-4577
Wants furniture locks and keys; barrel, skeleton, door, drawer, old or new; also wants escutcheons in all styles and sizes.

Franklin Arnall
Collector, The
P.O. Box 253
Claremont, CA 91711-0253
ph: 909-621-2461
Wants to buy antique padlocks: brass railroad and express, odd miniatures, any unusual cast iron of brass; any quantity.

Mark Lyons
6020 Paseo Del Norte, Ste. B
Carlsbad, CA 92009
ph: 760-431-5397
fax: 760-607-3299
cuffsandstuff@sbcglobal.net
Wants antique pad locks or collectible and unusual locks and keys; also wants jail and prison locks.

Daniel C. Zolezzi
2211 Froude St.
San Diego, CA 92107-1721
ph: 619-223-7440
Wants to buy old padlocks, keys and locks; buys, sells and repairs.

Gregory King
7 Cone Way Pinelands
Cape Town, Western Cape 7405 South Africa
ph: 27 21 5320755
gregk@cashpower.co.za
Wants to buy any brass or steel padlocks.

Syd Wareman
Lock Collectors Review
U.K.
syd@lockcollectors.com
http://www.lockcollectors.com
Web site contains information about this collection; videos for purchase, discussion area, recent purchases; lots of quality images with history of each type of lock shows.

Dealers

Joseph & Pamela Tanner
Wheeler-Tanner ESCAPES
6442 Canyon Creek Way
Elk Grove, CA 95758
ph: 916-684-4006
fax: 916-684-4006
JnPwLrTnr@aol.com
Wants padlocks of all sizes and shapes; figural, combination, round pancake types, railroad, Winchester, Wells Fargo, Express companies, etc.

Experts

Charles Cameron
2818 Sherwood St.
Greensboro, NC 27403-1906
ph: 336-852-9211
ccameron@mail.com
Collector, dealer, repairer, expert in antique padlocks; also repairs.

Bob Heilemann
1427 Lincoln Blvd.
Santa Monica, CA 90401-2732
ph: 310-230-3004
locksmann@earthlink.net
Collector and historian of antique padlocks; also repairs and restores padlocks; call evenings; no collect calls, please.

Internet Resources

Syd Wareman
Lock Collectors Review
U.K.
syd@lockcollectors.com
http://www.lockcollectors.com
Web site contains information about this collection; videos for purchase, discussion area, recent purchases; lots of quality images with history of each type of lock shows.

Museums/Libraries

Thomas F. Hennessy, Curator
Lock Museum of America
Newsletter: Lock Museum of America Newsletter
230 Main St., Rte. 6
P.O. Box 104
Terryville, CT 06786-0104
ph: 860-589-6359
fax: 860-589-6359
thomasnsc@aol.com
http://www.lockmuseum.com
Collection contains over 1,000 locks and keys manufactured from 1854 to 1954.

Repair Services

Daniel C. Zolezzi
2211 Froude St.
San Diego, CA 92107-1721
ph: 619-223-7440
Wants to buy old padlocks, keys and locks; buys, sells and repairs.

Gary Hahn
Muff's Antiques
135 S. Glassell St.
Orange, CA 92866-1421
ph: 714-997-0243
fax: 714-997-1601
muffs@earthlink.net
http://home.earthlink.net/~muffs
Specializes in the repairing and rekeying of antique locks.

LODGE BADGES

(see FRATERNAL ORGANIZATION ITEMS)

LOGGING RELATED ITEMS

(see also SCRIP)

Museums/Libraries

Ashland Logging Museum, Inc.
P.O. Box 348
Ashland, ME 04732
ph: 207-435-6039

Lumberman's Museum
P.O. Box 300
Patten, ME 04765
ph: 207-528-2650
jimwalk@mainerec.com
http://www.mainerec.com/logger.html

Carol Riggs, Dir.
Texas Forestry Museum
P.O. Box 1488
Lufkin, TX 75902-1488
ph: 409-632-9535
cets@sfasu.edu
http://www.cets.sfasu.edu/TFM.html
One of the largest museums of its kind in the US: offers a historic look at early logging, lumberjacks, and sawmill towns.

LOOMS

(see COVERLETS; SPINNING WHEELS)

LORGNETTES

(see EYE RELATED ITEMS, Eyeglasses)

LOTTERY TICKETS
Instant (Used)
Clubs/Associations

Arthur Rein
Global Lottery Collectors Society
Newsletter: Lotologist, The
642 Locust St., Apt. 2J
Mount Vernon, NY 10552-2620
ph: 914-668-1668
lotteryfan@aol.com
http://www.LotteryCollectors.com
Unites lottery collectors and provides services such as newsletters, ticket catalog, and trading roster.

Collectors

Arthur Rein
642 Locust St., Apt. 2J
Mount Vernon, NY 10552-2620
ph: 914-668-1668
lotteryfan@aol.com
http://www.lotterycollectors.com
Collects all versions of instant scratch-off lottery tickets: scratched tickets (losers), tickets that have not been scratched (mint), and promotional versions (sample voids); also items with lottery logos: pens, keychains, magnets, etc.

Bill Pasquino
1824 Lyndon Ave.
Lancaster, PA 17602-4711
ph: 717-393-0843
Wants losing instant lottery tickets; instant rub off lottery tickets from the 1970s and early 1980s.

Scott Simon
301 Goodman Dr.
Paducah, KY 42003
ph: 270-441-7008
Always looking to buy scratch-offs and paper tickets from US and abroad.

LUGGAGE

VintageLuggage.com, a Division of Yank Azman Toronto
Toronto Antique Center
276 King St. West
Toronto, Ontario M5V 1J2 Canada
ph: 416-260-5662 or 877-260-5662
info@vintageluggage.com
http://www.vintageluggage.com
Specializes in the sale of vintage luggage: briefcases, attaches, campaign bags, carpet bags, club bags, coach bags, dresser cases for men or ladies, hat boxes, hat cases, instrument cases, trunks, suitcases, steamers, wardrobes.

(see also CLOTHING & ACCESSORIES, Vintage; LEATHER; LABELS, Luggage; TRUNKS)

Dealers

Lilit Eclectiques
483 Broome St.
New York, NY 10013
ph: 212-966-0650
Carries designer trunks, bags and steamers from 18th century to 1920s.

Louis Vuitton
Dealers

Ron Cook
R. Cook & Co.
1835 E. Hallandale Beaceh Blvd.
Hallandale, FL 33009
ph: 352-690-7395 or 800-232-0356
fax: 352-690-7379
info@rcookco.com
http://www.rcookco.com
One of the nation's largest dealers of vintage Louis Vuitton trunks,

wardrobes and suitcases; has a 400-page Web site dedicated to Louis Vuitton: vintage Louis Vuitton catalogs, posters, vintage luggage, handbags and more.

Duane S. Bietz
Les Meilleurs
6461 S.E. Thorburn
Portland, OR 97215-1378
ph: 503-238-6888
fax: 503-233-1602
dbietz@aol.com
Collects and sells Louis Vuitton hard luggage and trunks; specialty pieces, cosmetic, cigar, liquor, shoe, hat, collar, car trunks; any Louis Vuitton memorabilia and promotional items; email or write with photos for appraisals or to sell.

Man./Prod./Dist.

Louis Vuitton of North America
Customer Service
1 Front St., 6th Floor
San Francisco, CA 94111
ph: 866-VUITTON
http://www.vuitton.com

LUMBERING

(see LOGGING RELATED ITEMS)

LUNCH BOXES
Collectors

Bryan Los
Lunch Box Pad
22 School St.
Holyoke, MA 01040-3317
ph: 413-533-0157
http://www.lunchboxpad.com
Lunch box collector, expert with great lunch box Web site: chat, message board, history, resources, for sale, and more.

Dennis Visco
P.O. Box 20152
London Terrace Station
New York, NY 10011
ph: 212-802-7314
captaindennyUSA@aol.com
Wants to buy lunch boxes (metal or vinyl) from the 1950s to the 1960s.

Peter Reginato
60 Green St.
New York, NY 10012-5139
ph: 212-925-9787
Wants lunch boxes from 1950s through 1970s; also Howard Miller clocks from the 1950s.

David Reed
841 West Main St.
Madison, OH 44057-9763
ph: 440-428-6666
Wants Jetsons, Lost in Space, Westerns, TV Shows, Space: metal and vinyl.

Andy Galbus
Pak-Rat
900 8th St. NW
Kasson, MN 55944-1079
http://www.geocities.com/lhpakrat
Wants to buy lunch boxes.

Fred & Jan Carlson
P.O. Box 2
Hillsboro, OR 97123-0002
ph: 503-648-8477
fax: 503-642-2534
Wants to buy lunch pails and thermoses.

Dealers

Jim Cassidy
Lunch Box Bonanza
P.O. Box 157
West Boylston, MA 01583
lunchbox@cassidyframes.com
http://www.cassidyframes.com/box
Has been buying, collecting, selling, trading lunch boxes and thermoses since 1991.

Allen Woodall
2 Shalom Place
Columbus, GA 31904-2847
ph: 706-322-0516
fax: 706-322-0515
Co-author of "The Illustrated Encyclopedia of Metal Lunchboxes."

Terry Stueckrath
Terry's Collectibles
13901 "L" St.
Omaha, NE 68137-1598
ph: 402-332-5976
horseman@compuserve.com
http://ourworld.compuserve.com/
   homepages/horseman
Web site has lunch boxes for sale, classic lunch boxes, new and reproduction boxes, grading scale.

Terri Mardis-Ivers
Terri's Toys & Nostalgia
114 Whitworth Ave.
Ponca City, OK 74601-3438
ph: 580-762-8697
toylady@cableone.net
Buys and sells metal and vinyl lunch boxes, and metal or plastic thermoses from the late 1940s to the present; the most desirable are from the 1950s through 1984; also wants Western, space, and character related collectibles.

Experts

Sean Brickell
Reflections III, Ste. 121
Virginia Beach, VA 23452
ph: 757-463-4500
fax: 757-498-5948
sean@brickellpr.com
Co-author of "The Illustrated Encyclopedia of Metal Lunchboxes."

Allen Woodall
2 Shalom Place
Columbus, GA 31904-2847
ph: 706-322-0516
fax: 706-322-0515
Co-author of "The Illustrated Encyclopedia of Metal Lunchboxes."

Larry Aikins
P & L Collectibles
101 Trail Ridge Rd.
Athens, TX 75751
ph: 903-675-3765
fax: 903-677-3643
Author of "Pictorial Price Guide to Vinyl & Plastic Lunch Boxes" and "Pictorial Price Guide to Metal Lunch Boxes" (L-W Book Sales); wants to buy lunch boxes, thermos bottles: metals, soft vinyls, promotional, odd shaped plastics boxes.

Internet Resources

Bryan Los
Lunch Box Pad
22 School St.
Holyoke, MA 01040-3317
ph: 413-533-0157
http://www.lunchboxpad.com
Web site has price guide, chat room, discussion board, history and pictures, and more.

Museums/Libraries

Lunch Box Museum
River Market Antiques Mall
3226 Hamilton Rd.
Columbus, GA 31904
ph: 706-653-6240
fax: 706-221-4658
webmaster@rivermarketantiques.com
http://www.rivermarketantiques.com
Collection of over 2000 lunch boxes and 1400 thermoses accumulated by lunch box collector and expert, Allen Woodall.

LURAY

(see CERAMICS [AMERICAN DINNERWARE], Taylor, Smith & Taylor/LuRay)

LURES

(see FISHING COLLECTIBLES)

Here are some tips when contacting someone who is listed in this book:

When requesting information about a particular item, include a description (material, dimensions, maker's mark, model number, etc.) and a photo, sketch, digital image or photocopy of the item in question.

Always ask if there are charges for samples or for the services that you are requesting.

When corresponding by letter, please be sure to include a Large (#10 business size) Self-Addressed and Stamped Envelope (LSASE) if requesting a reply or the return of photographs.

Never call collect unless otherwise directed. When calling, be considerate of time zone differences and always ask if the party you are calling has time to talk. When leaving an answering machine message, always instruct the party to call you back collect.

M&M/MARS CANDY

Clubs/Associations

David Archer, Treas.
M & M Collector's Club
Newsletter: MMCC Newsletter
8814 Patricia Ct.
College Park, MD 20740
treasurer@mnmclub.com
http://www.mnmclub.com
*Collector's club not affiliated with
Mars/M&M; quarterly newsletter,
annual convention.*

Collectors

Frederick Kraut
120 Covington Dr.
Warwick, RI 02886-1936
ph: 401-738-2277
uki845@aol.com
*Big collector of M&M items,
memorabilia, toys and related
collectibles; also carries pre-1975
baseball cards and baseball
memorabilia.*

Dealers

Ken Clee
P.O. Box 11412
Philadelphia, PA 19111-0412
ph: 215-722-1979
waxntoys@aol.com
http://members.aol.com/waxntoys/main/
kidsmeal.htm
*Buys and sells anything related to
Mars M&M candy, including
NASCAR, dispensers, toppers,
advertising & displays.*

MACERATED CURRENCY ITEMS

Collectors

Bertram M. Cohen
169 Marlborough St.
Boston, MA 02116-1830
ph: 617-247-4754
fax: 617-247-9093
marblebert@aol.com
http://www.marblebert.com
*Wants items made from macerated US
money 1880-1940, original advertisements for macerated currency items,
and any magazine articles regarding
macerated money.*

Donald Gorlick
P.O. Box 24541
Seattle, WA 98124-0541
ph: 206-824-0508
*Wants macerated currency - items
made up of ground-up money pulp;*

*usually souvenir items, statues, plates,
animals; often with a tag.*

MACHINE AGE

(see MODERNISM)

MACHINERY & EQUIPMENT

(see also AIRPLANES;
CONSTRUCTION EQUIPMENT;
FARM MACHINERY; INDUSTRY
RELATED ITEMS; LAWN MOWERS;
RAILROADS; TOOLS; WASHING
MACHINES)

Appraisers

Michael Saperstein, ISA
Paul E. Saperstein Co., Inc.
148 State St., Ste. 520
Boston, MA 02109
ph: 617-227-6553
fax: 617-227-4538
msaperstein@pesco.com
http://www.pesco.com
*Machinery & equipment appraisers
and auctioneers.*

Equipment Appraisers Association of
North America
1309 Todd Ave.
Aliquippa, PA 15001
ph: 800-790-1053
fax: 724-378-0574
http://www.eaana.com
*A professional appraisal society
representing all aspects of the
industrial equipment industries; actual
market experience is a requirement for
all designated member appraisers.*

Edwin W. Baker, Ex. VP
American Society of Appraisers
P.O. Box 17265
Washington, DC 20071
ph: 703-478-2228 or 800-272-8258
fax: 703-742-8471
asainfo@appraisers.org
http://www.appraisers.org
*The only appraisal organization in the
US representing all the disciplines of
appraisal specialists; call 800-ASA-
VALU for free referral or membership
directory, or visit Web site.*

Association of Online Appraisers, Inc.
P.O. Box 2049
Frederick, MD 21702-1049
ph: 301-228-2279
fax: 301-695-6491
info@AOAonline.org
http://www.AOAonline.org
*Not-for-profit association for online
as well as traditional appraisers;
establishes standards of appraisal
ethics & professional practice; offers
550+ page "Complete Online Course
in Personal Property Appraising" free
to members.*

Association of Machinery & Equipment
Appraisers (AMEA)
315 S. Patrick St.
Alexandria, VA 22314-3501
ph: 800-537-8629 or 703-836-7900
fax: 703-836-9303
amea@amea.org
http://www.amea.org
*Association of machinery and
equipment appraisers; publishes
directory of appraisers who are used
machinery dealers and/or auctioneers
actively involved in the used machinery
marketplace.*

C.D. Gallimore, ISA CAPP, CAI
AMC Appraisal Co. Inc.
P.O. Box 2757
Duluth, GA 30096
ph: 770-497-8090 or 800-938-2121
fax: 770-497-1827
cdatamc@aol.com
http://www.amcvalu.com
*Certified appraiser, licensed and
bonded appraiser.*

Harry Stampler, ISA
Stampler Auctions
2801 Evans St.
Hollywood, FL 33020-1119
ph: 954-921-8888
fax: 954-927-2939
hps@stamplerauctions.com
http://www.stamplerauctions.com
*Specializes in machinery & equipment
appraisals and in business liquidations.*

Phillip D. Peck, ISA
Revpro Appraisal Service
8585 Antioch Rd.
Baton Rouge, LA 70817
ph: 225-755-7002
fax: 225-755-0302
revpro@cox.net
http://
www.appraisermachineryequipment.com

James Pharr, ISA
James Pharr Machinery Co.
P.O. Box 38385
Shreveport, LA 71133
ph: 318-636-6050
fax: 318-636-6608
jamespharr@worldnet.att.net
*Buys and sells earth moving
equipment.*

Noel L. Novak, MVS, ISA
American Appraisal Associates, Inc.
18881 Von Karman Ave., Ste. 700
Tustin, CA 92612
ph: 949-756-5030
fax: 949-440-0351
nnovak@american-appraisal.com
*Specializes in the appraisal of
fixtures, equipment and inventory.*

Noel L. Novak, MVS, ISA, ASA
American Appraisal Associates, Inc.
18881 Von Karman Ave., Ste. 700
Laguna Hills, CA 92612
ph: 949-756-5030
fax: 949-440-0351
nnovak@american-appraisal.com
Appraises all tangible business assets

*including fixtures, machinery,
equipment, tenant improvements, and
inventory; experienced as an expert
witness.*

Jeffrey A. Donahue, ASA
Equipment Valuation Consultants, Inc.
23010 Lake Forest Dr., Ste. D, PMB
404
Laguna Hills, CA 92653-1351
ph: 949-831-6166
fax: 949-831-1255
jdonahueevc@aol.com
*Appraises all tangible business assets
including fixtures, machinery,
equipment, tenant improvements, and
inventory; experienced as an expert
witness.*

Dennis West, ISA
D.B. West Auctioneers
P.O. Box 278
Woodland, CA 95776-0278
ph: 530-661-0490
fax: 530-661-2499
dennis@westauction.com
http://www.westauction.com

International Society of Appraisers
Newsletter: Professional Appraisers
Information Exchange
1131 SW 7th St., Ste. 105
Renton, WA 98055
ph: 206-241-0359 or 888-472-4732
fax: 206-241-0436
ISA@isa-appraisers.org
http://www.isa-appraisers.org
*Largest assoc. of professional
appraisers devoted solely to personal
property; over 1,300 members
specializing in all areas of antiques &
residential contents, gems & jewelry,
fine art, machinery & equipment;
member directory on Web site.*

John C. Craughan, ISA
Equipment Consulting
32009 162nd Ave. SE
Auburn, WA 98092-5905
ph: 253-350-0752
fax: 253-887-8120
jcraughan@attbi.com
*Specializes in the appraisal of
machinery & equipment, construction,
logging, mining & farm, trucks, cars,
tools.*

Cameron Carter, ISA
Normac Appraisals, Ltd.
G-105 - 2480 Spruce St.
Vancouver, British Columbia V6H 2P6
U.K.
ph: 604-221-8285
fax: 604-224-1445
normacappraisals@telus.net
*M&E appraiser specializes in welding
equipment, semi-trailers, office
furniture & equipment, water/sewage
treatment plants, pump stations,
landscaping improvements; also
specializes in replacement cost
appraisals for any building type.*

Auction Services

Larry Martin
Martin Auction Co.
Rt. 51 S.
Clinton, IL 61727
ph: 217-935-8211
fax: 217-935-3795
lmcs2000@yahoo.com
http://wwww.martinauctioncompany.com

Larry Mitchell
Superior Asset Management
P.O. Box 792427
San Antonio, TX 78279-2427
ph: 210-499-0777
fax: 210-495-1319
info@saami.com
http://www.saami.com
*Specializes in the auction sale
machinery and equipment, oil rigs,
classic cars.*

Emilio & Olga Lemeni
Abamex Auction Co.
10050 Via de la Amistad #2452
San Diego, CA 92154-7248
ph: 800-841-3364 or 858-279-2846
fax: 858-576-9577
auctions@abamex.com
http://www.abamex.com
*Conducts auctions in Southern CA;
real estate, business asset auctions
including FF&E, restaurant
equipment; also art and collectibles
auctions.*

Museums/Libraries

American Precision Museum Association, Inc.
Newsletter: Tools & Technology
P.O. Box 679
196 Main St.
Windsor, VT 05089
ph: 802-674-5781
fax: 802-674-2524
curator@americanprecision.org
http://www.americanprecision.org
*Housed in the original Robbins &
Lawrence Armory and Machine Shop,
the museum features the largest
collection of historic precision
machine tools in the nation.*

Periodicals

National Auto Research
Magazine: Black Book Official Auction
   Report
2620 Barrett Rd.
P.O. Box 758
Gainesville, GA 30503-0758
ph: 770-532-4111 or 800-367-3759
fax: 770-532-4792
http://www.blackbookguides.com
*Publishes weekly, monthly, bimonthly,
annual guides (Black Books)
containing new and used car and truck
values for the automotive and finance
industries including used and new car
dealers, bankers, wholesale buyers,
credit unions.*

Marcia Gruver, Ed.
Randall Publishing Co.
Magazine: Equipment World
3200 Rice Mine Rd., N.E.
Tuscaloosa, AL 35406
ph: 205-349-2990 or 800-633-5953
fax: 205-750-8070
tkillgore@randallpub.com
http://www.randallpub.com
*Monthly magazine with articles about
new equipment on the market.*

Randall Publishing Co.
Magazine: Top Bid
3200 Rice Mine Rd., N.E.
Tuscaloosa, AL 35406
ph: 205-349-2990 or 800-633-5953
fax: 205-750-8070
tkillgore@randallpub.com
http://www.randallpub.com
*Monthly auction report listing
machinery & equipment prices
realized as well as an upcoming
auction schedule.*

Christina Gargano
Heartland Communications Group, Inc.
Magazine: Contractors Hot Line
   Equipment Guide
1003 Central Ave.
P.O. Box 1052
Fort Dodge, IA 50501
ph: 800-247-2000 or 515-955-1600
fax: 515-574-2233
libbie@hlipublishing.com
http://www.hlipublishing.com
*Lists construction equipment
manufacturer's addresses, basic
equipment specs., original selling
prices, current market values;
published annually; information
source for buyers, sellers, dealers,
auctioneers, appraisers.*

Christina Gargano
Heartland Communications Group, Inc.
Magazine: Hot Line's Parts Connection
1003 Central Ave.
P.O. Box 1052
Fort Dodge, IA 50501
ph: 800-247-2000 or 515-955-1600
fax: 515-574-2233
libbie@hlipublishing.com
http://www.hlipublishing.com
*Directory for the largest selection and
best prices of new, used, rebuilt parts
and attachments for construction
equipment.*

Christina Gargano
Heartland Communications Group, Inc.
Magazine: Industrial Machine Trade
1003 Central Ave.
P.O. Box 1052
Fort Dodge, IA 50501
ph: 800-247-2000 or 515-955-1600
fax: 515-574-2233
libbie@hlipublishing.com
http://www.hlipublishing.com
*The only weekly nationwide
publication that links active buyers
and sellers of new and used industrial
machinery.*

Christina Gargano
Heartland Communications Group, Inc.
Magazine: Mine & Quarry Hot Line
1003 Central Ave.
P.O. Box 1052
Fort Dodge, IA 50501
ph: 800-247-2000 or 515-955-1600
fax: 515-574-2233
libbie@hlipublishing.com
http://www.hlipublishing.com
*Offers the buyers and sellers of
aggregate equipment a direct way to
reach thousands of highly qualified
customers in their specific industry.*

Dataquest Incorporated
Magazine: Green Guide
251 River Oaks Pkwy.
San Jose, CA 95134
ph: 408-468-8000 or 800-669-3282
fax: 408-954-1780
help@gartner.com
http://www.gartner.com
*Professionally researched market
values on construction equipment;
average resale values to 20 years old;
3,000 equipment models, all types;
original and current prices, serial
numbers for years of manufacture,
basic specs.*

Dataquest Incorporated
Magazine: Serial Number Guide
251 River Oaks Pkwy.
San Jose, CA 95134
ph: 408-468-8000 or 800-669-3282
fax: 408-954-1780
help@gartner.com
http://www.gartner.com
*Lists year of manufacture by maker
and model.*

Catalogs

(see also CATALOGS, Trade)

Collectors

Marvin McKinley
1652 State Rte. 511
Ashland, OH 44805-9214
ph: 419-289-1706
*Wants old sales catalogs and manuals
for machinery, steam engines, gas
engines, windmills, farm machinery,
buggies, sleighs, etc.*

Dealers

Eldon Bryant
Broken Kettle Books
702 East Madison St.
Fairfield, IA 52556-3649
ph: 641-472-8643
bkettle@kdsi.net
*Wants old sales catalogs and manuals
for machinery, steam engines, gas
engines, windmills, farm machinery,
buggies, sleighs, etc.*

Construction

Appraisers

Jerry Lyngby
1-Contractors Solution.com
6508 S. Frontage Rd.
Billings, MT 59101
ph: 406-294-1936 or 866-865-1936
fax: 406-204-1935
rjl@1contractorssolutions.com
http://www.1contractorssolutions.com
*A 30 year veteran of the construction
industry; specializes in construction
equipment appraisals.*

Clubs/Associations

Historical Construction Equipment
Association
16623 Liberty Hi Rd.
Bowling Green, OH 43402
ph: 419-352-5616
fax: 419-352-6086
info@hcea.net
http://www.hcea.net
*Dedicated to preserving the history of
all types of construction, surface
mining and dredging equipment.*

Restaurant Equipment

Periodicals

David Marketing Group
Price Guide: Official Used Restaurant
   Equipment Guide
P.O. Box 2757
Duluth, GA 30096
ph: 770-497-8090 or 800-938-2121
fax: 770-497-1827
cdatamc@aol.com
*Price guide for used restaurant
equipment: baking, refrigeration units,
stockpots, trash cans, utensils, brazier
pots, oven items, popcorn, etc.*

Road Making

Clubs/Associations

D.J. Crampton, Mem.
Road Roller Association
Newsletter: Rolling
6 Norwood Close
Mackworth, Derby DE3 4GA U.K.
ph: +44 1904 331926
derek@invicta1915.freeserve.co.uk
http://www.surf.to/rra
*Caters specifically to those interested
in the science of road making and
road repair and in the associated
equipment involved with these
operations, including steam and motor
rollers.*

Woodworking

Experts

Mr. Dana Martin Batory
402 E. Bucyrus St.
Crestline, OH 44827-1506
*Wants catalogs, photographs,
advertising, manuals, reminiscences,
etc. pertaining to woodworking
machinery and/or their manufacturers;
author of "Vintage Woodworking
Machinery - An Illustrated Guide to*

Four Manufacturers" (Astragal Press).

Suppliers

Mr. Dana Martin Batory
402 E. Bucyrus St.
Crestline, OH 44827-1506
Supplies photocopies of manuals for vintage woodworking machinery; 70+ page catalog, $7.50, updated quarterly.

MAGAZINES

(see also BOOKS; COLLEGE COLLECTIBLES, Humor Magazines; ILLUSTRATORS; MYSTERY/ DETECTIVE ITEMS; PAPER COLLECTIBLES; PERIODICALS; SPORTING COLLECTIBLES, Magazines; TELEVISION SHOWS & MEMORABILIA, TV Guide)

Collectors

Bob Havey
P.O. Box 183
North Sullivan, ME 04664-0183
ph: 207-422-3083
fax: 207-422-3430
Wants many magazines from the 1800s to 1950: "Movie Magazine," "Vogue," "Pictorial Review," "Esquire," "Good Housekeeping," "McCall's," etc.

Gary Olsen
505 S. Royal Ave.
Front Royal, VA 22630
ph: 540-635-7157 or 800-954-7374
fax: 540-635-1818
olsenhp@hpfri.com
http://www.hpfri.com
Wants pre-1970 "Life," "Look," "Colliers," "Post," etc. especially with WWI and/or WWII stories and articles.

Dealers

Richard West
Periodyssey
116 Pleasant St., 2nd Fl.
Easthampton, MA 01027
ph: 413-527-1900
fax: 413-527-1930
questions@periodyssey.com
http://www.oldmagazines.com
Specializes in significant and unusual pre-1950 American magazines.

Charles Zayic
Magazine Man, The
P.O. Box 57
Ellsworth, ME 04605-0057
ph: 207-667-7342
magman@acadia.net
Wants old magazines from the teens and 1920s; especially "Ladie's Home Journal," "Pictorial Review," "Woman's Home Companion," "McCall's," "Delineator," "Modern Priscilla," and "Needlecraft."

Jonie Williams
143-11, 105th Ave.
Jamaica, NY 11435
ph: 718-297-8130
renee20161196141@aol.com
http://www.expage.com/jonie
Buys and sells magazine back issues: "Rollingstone," "MAD," "Life," "Body Building," and more.

Clifford Aliperti
things-and-other-stuff
ph: 631-455-6381
things@things-and-other-stuff.com
http://www.things-and-other-stuff.com
Specializes in vintage magazines from the world of sports and entertainment, literary and historical, plus the classics such as "Time," "Life," "Look."

Sandra Odegard
OldMags.com
P.O. Box 67
Fairfield, MT 59436
ph: 406-467-2189
fax: 406-467-2189
sales@oldmags.com
http://www.oldmags.com
Buys and sells vintage magazines; buy your birthday "Life" online.

Stan Gold
As Time Goes By
7042 Dartbrook Dr.
Dallas, TX 75240
ph: 972-239-8621 or 214-352-2765
fax: 972-239-9622
record@astimegoesby.com
http://www.astimegoesby.com
Wants to buy "Life" 1936-1972, "Post," "Time," "Playboy" 1953-1965, "Sports Illustrated" 1954-1970s, "TV Guides" 1947-1970s, vintage movie magazines, aviation, men's adventure, automotive, sports, pin-up magazines 1920s to 1960s, world's fair pre-1940.

Jerry Rodnitzky
All America Paper Collectibles
1832 Westcrest Dr.
Arlington, TX 76013
ph: 817-861-8199
jrodprof@yahoo.com
http://www.aapapercollect.com.
Buys and sells vintage paperbacks, illustrated magazines, movie posters, sports collectibles, other paper items.

Mike Sandusky
Million Magazines
221 E. 6th St., #125 (rear)
Tucson, AZ 85705
ph: 800-877-9887 or 520-628-7872
fax: 520-623-5159
mike@millionmagazines.com
http://www.millionmagazines.com
Over one million magazines in stock dating from 1843 to present; over 750,000 pieces of magazine art available in most categories; in the trade since 1976; databases and indexes available for research.

Jim Kremer
Magazine Baron
1236 S. Magnolia Ave.
Anaheim, CA 92804
ph: 714-527-0358
fax: 714-527-5634
jim@magazinebaron.com
http://www.magazinebaron.com
Buys and sells back issue magazines: movies from 1914 to present, 1,000s of "Sports Illustrated," '50s to '90s "Playboy," fashion, pulps, teen magazines, aviation, art, historical, hobbies.

Ken Mitchell
710 Conacher Dr.
Willowdale, Ontario M2M 3N6 Canada
ph: 416-222-5808
Appraises, collects, buys and sells 1890 to 1970s comic books, newspapers, comic strips, "Big Little" books, popular music/jazz books/magazines/tapes; pulp magazines, original comic art, radio and cereal premiums.

Vintage Magazines & Paper Ephemera
Mare St. Studios
203-213 Mare St.
London, E8 3QE U.K.
ph: 020-8533-7588
fax: 020-8533-7283
thearchive@ndirect.co.uk
http://www.vinmag.com
Specializes in comics and magazines covering fashion, science fiction, movies, pulp fiction, glamour, social history and more; buys and sells.

Experts

Mike Sandusky
Million Magazines
221 E. 6th St., #125 (rear)
Tucson, AZ 85705
ph: 800-877-9887 or 520-628-7872
fax: 520-623-5159
mike@millionmagazines.com
http://www.millionmagazines.com
Over one million magazines in stock dating from 1843 to present; over 750,000 pieces of magazine art available in most categories; in the trade since 1976; databases and indexes available for research.

Denis C. Jackson
P.O. Box 6433
Kingman, AZ 86401
ticn@olypen.com
http://www.olypen.com/ticn
Buys, sells, collects and specializes in OLD magazines; author of "The Masters Price & Identification Guide to Old Magazines" 5th edition 2000/ 01; 1st through 5th editions cover 1,600 publishers from 1800 to present; LSASE for information.

Internet Resources

S. G. Honeck
Back Issue Finder
1303 S. 10th St.
Sheboygan, WI 53081
ph: 920-459-7901
fax: 505-204-7937
http://www.javahousebooks.com/ booklink/booklink/ephemera-txt.htm
A Web site marketplace for locating and selling hard-to-find, out-of-print and back issue periodicals including newspapers, magazines and comic books; also ephemera such as programs, postcards, posters, trading cards, etc.

Denis C. Jackson, Ed.
E-zine: Illustrator Collector's News, The
P.O. Box 6433
Kingman, AZ 86401
ticn@olypen.com
http://www.olypen.com/ticn
An online publication for collectors of magazines and other paper illustrations; free classifieds and articles, no charge Web site information; new and old prints.

Periodicals

Doug Watson
Magazine: Paper Collectors' Marketplace
470 Main St.
P.O. Box 128
Scandinavia, WI 54977-0128
ph: 715-467-2379
fax: 715-467-2243
pcmpaper@gglbbs.com
http://www.pcmpaper.com
Monthly magazine for collectors of autographs, paperbacks, postcards, advertising, photographica, magazines; all types of paper ephemera.

Automotive

Dealers

Dave Allen
Imperial Palace Auto Collection
3535 Las Vegas Blvd., So.
Las Vegas, NV 89109
ph: 702-794-3174
fax: 702-369-7430
info@autocollections.com
http://www.autocollections.com
Buys and sells out-of-print motorcycle and automotive magazines: "Hot Rod," "Motor Trend," "Speed Age," "Road Track," also all half-size magazines.

Computer Programs For
Man./Prod./Dist.

Niche Software, Inc.
Software: Book, Magazine & Paper Collector, The
7118 NW Terrace
Parkland, FL 33076
ph: 954-344-6561
marketing@collectiblessoftware.com
http://www.collectiblessoftware.com
Designed for the collector of books,

magazines, documents, fruit labels, etc.

Covers & Tear Sheets

Dealers

Mary Ann Hahn
Second Hand Mary Ann's
103 Ocean Point Rd.
Boothbay Harbor, ME 04538
ph: 207-633-2426
fax: 207-633-2586
maryann@gwi.net
Buys and sells magazine covers and tear sheets of any advertisement or illustration.

Charles Zayic
Magazine Man, The
P.O. Box 57
Ellsworth, ME 04605-0057
ph: 207-667-7342
magman@acadia.net
Buys and sells vintage magazines ads, 11" x 14", full page color originals, mixed subjects, 1920s, 1930s, 1940s and 1950s; send SASE for list.

Kim Anderson
Vintage Ads Online
RR #2
Mill Bay, British Columbia V0R 2P0 Canada
ph: 250-743-9113
anderson@vintageadsonline.com
http://www.vintageadsonline.com
Buys and sells vintage magazine ads; browse online; suitable for framing; categories include cars, Coca-Cola, fashion, movies, household products, and many others.

Life

Dealers

Charles Zayic
Magazine Man, The
P.O. Box 57
Ellsworth, ME 04605-0057
ph: 207-667-7342
magman@acadia.net
Buys and sells "Life" magazines 1936 through 1972; maintains active inventory of over 5,000 copies for sale, send SASE for list.

Dwayne Spark
Nostalgia Plus
8441 Sublaines
Anjou, Quebec H1K 2C1 Canada
ph: 514-352-6892
fax: 514-352-1856
dspark@videotron.ca
Wants to buy "Life" magazines from 1970 and earlier in small or large quantities.

Experts

Denis C. Jackson
P.O. Box 6433
Kingman, AZ 86401
ticn@olypen.com
http://www.olypen.com/ticn
Author of "Life Magazines," 3rd

edition (2000), every issue from 1898 to 1994 listed and valued.

MAD

Auction Services

Michael Lerner
32862 Springside Lane
Solon, OH 44139-2067
ph: 440-349-3776
Buys and sells "MAD" memorabilia.

Collectors

Ed Norris
91 Kelly Dr.
Lancaster, MA 01523
ph: 978-365-7628
Wants items from 1890 to present that have the likeness of Alfred E. Neuman from "MAD" magazine.

Roland Coover
1537 E. Strasburg Rd.
West Chester, PA 19380-6380
ph: 610-692-3112
rlcoover@aol.com
Wants anything related to "MAD" magazine or Alfred E. Neuman: jewelry, presidential campaign kits, Halloween costume, clothing, straight jacket, postcards, toys, etc.; no paperbacks or magazines, please.

Casey Nicholson
415 Vancleave Ave.
Ocean Springs, MS 39564-4733
ph: 228-872-8864 or 228-872-4280

Gary Kritzberg
P.O. Box 47
Yorkville, IL 60560
ph: 630-553-7653
yorkmaddoc@aol.com
Wants "MAD" magazine collectibles: magazines, comics, toys, shirts, records, hardback books, jewelry, pins, buttons, etc.

Experts

Michael Lerner
32862 Springside Lane
Solon, OH 44139-2067
ph: 440-349-3776
Buys and sells "MAD" memorabilia.

Internet Resources

Doug Gilford
MAD Cover Site
gilford@e-z.net
http://www.collectmad.com/madcoversite
A resource for collectors and fans of "MAD" magazine.

Men's

(see also PLAYBOY ITEMS)

Dealers

Kenneth E. Ritchie
P.O. Box 22604
Memphis, TN 38122
admin@kenritchie.com
http://www.kenritchie.com
Source for a huge selection of vintage adult erotica including Marilyn

Monroe and Bettie Page, pin-up art by Alberto Vargas and Gil Elvgren, and real-time auction of vintage men's magazines.

Experts

Denis C. Jackson
P.O. Box 6433
Kingman, AZ 86401
ticn@olypen.com
http://www.olypen.com/ticn
Author of "The Price & Identification Guide to Men's (Girlie) Magazines," 4th edition; covers all issues from 1920s forward.

Men's (Playboy)

Dealers

Passaic Books
267 Passaic St.
Passaic, NJ 07055
ph: 973-778-0416
fax: 973-778-6823
info@passaicbooks.com
http://www.passaicbooks.com
Sells a price guide devoted strictly to "Playboy" magazines; $10.95 postpaid.

Kenneth E. Ritchie
P.O. Box 22604
Memphis, TN 38122
admin@kenritchie.com
http://www.pbmags.com
Carries a wide selection of Playboy publications including rare back-issues, flats, calendars, collector cards, Playmate autographs and much more; nearly anything Playboy can be found here.

Douglas L. Tracy
Centerfold Shop, The
1220 23rd St., Ste. 2-M
San Diego, CA 92102-1960
ph: 619-235-6010
fax: 619-235-8005
Dealer, appraiser, expert, specializing in Playboy magazines from the 1950s since 1968; mail order only; 24-page catalog $10; stock of 50,000 issues; strict grading; internationally recommended by Playboy Enterprises, Inc.; buy pre-1964.

Experts

Denis C. Jackson
P.O. Box 6433
Kingman, AZ 86401
ticn@olypen.com
http://www.olypen.com/ticn
Author of "The Price & Identification Guide to Playboy Magazines," 2000, 5nd Edition; send LSASE for information.

Douglas L. Tracy
Centerfold Shop, The
1220 23rd St., Ste. 2-M
San Diego, CA 92102-1960
ph: 619-235-6010
fax: 619-235-8005
Dealer, appraiser, expert, specializing in Playboy magazines from the 1950s

since 1968; mail order only; 24-page catalog $10; stock of 50,000 issues; strict grading; internationally recommended by Playboy Enterprises, Inc.; buy pre-1964.

Monster

Collectors

Steve Dolnick
P.O. Box 69
East Meadow, NY 11554-0069
ph: 516-486-5085
fax: 516-458-5085
sdmonster@aol.com
Buys, sells and trades monster magazines: wants "Famous Monsters," "Vampirella," "Monsters Parade," "World Famous Creatures," "Little Shoppe of Horrors," and other monster magazines and fanzines.

Movie

(see also MOVIE MEMORABILIA)

Experts

Denis C. Jackson
P.O. Box 6433
Kingman, AZ 86401
ticn@olypen.com
http://www.olypen.com/ticn
Author of "The Old Movie, Television, Soap Opera, Radio Magazines Price & Identification Guide," 1st edition, 1994, 1914 through 1994.

Mystery

Collectors

Jack Deveny
6805 Cheyenne Trail
Edina, MN 55439-1158
ph: 612-941-2457
plane@itol.net
Wants Spider, Shadow, Doc Savage, Spicy, Detective, Mystery, Horror, Terror, etc.

National Geographic

Collectors

William Barr
6341 Werk Rd.
Cincinnati, OH 45248-2924
ph: 513-451-6174
fax: 513-922-1478
Buys and sells pre-1916 National Geographic Magazines, maps, publications: extensive collection for sale, 1888 to present; magazines, bound volumes, reprints, indexes, maps, atlases, videos, school bulletins, posters, ephemera, etc.

Norman Hagey
19672 Steavens Creek #424
Cupertino, CA 95014-2465
ph: 408-973-8129
Wants "National Geographic" magazines from the late 1800s and early 1900s including magazines bound in books; has over 3,000 magazines and many old "National Geographic" maps.

Dealers

Vernon Ford
18119 Sandy Pines Cir.
Fort Myers, FL 33917
ph: 239-567-0819
v8ford1@juno.com
Buys and sells 20th century "National Geographic" magazines.

Don Smith
Don Smith's National Geographic
  Magazines
3930 Rankin St.
Louisville, KY 40214-1748
ph: 502-366-7504
Wants magazines from 1888; buying and selling; author of "National Geographic Magazines (1888-2000) For Collectors" price guide booklet.

Randolph M. Moss
Eclectic Books
9 Clipper Way
Friday Harbor, WA 98250
ph: 360-378-5732
eclecticbk@aol.com
Buys and sells "National Geographic:" pre-1915 magazines, bound sets, reprint, books; all publications by The National Geographic Society.

Office Related

Collectors

Darryl Rehr
P.O. Box 641824
Los Angeles, CA 90064-6824
ph: 310-477-5229
fax: 310-268-8420
dcrehr@earthlink.net
http://home.earthlink.net/~dcrehr/
  collecting.html
Wants pre-1920 magazines & articles relating to old office equipment: "System," "Business Man's Monthly," "Phonographic World," etc.

Puck & Judge

Collectors

Bob Putnam
9129 Lake Braddock Dr.
Springfield, VA 22153
ph: 703-644-9711
putmanb@email.msn.com
Wants to buy "Puck" and "Judge" periodicals, especially political cartoons pages, dating from 1876 to 1910; whole issues preferred; also wants to buy cartoons by Thomas Nast (1840-1902.)

Dealers

Mary Ann Hahn
Second Hand Mary Ann's
103 Ocean Point Rd.
Boothbay Harbor, ME 04538
ph: 207-633-2426
fax: 207-633-2586
maryann@gwi.net
Buys "Puck & Judge" periodicals as well as "Brown Book," "The Truth," "Verdict & Vim" prior to 1910.

Pulp

(see also ART, Pulp; BOOKS, Paperback; SCIENCE FICTION/ FANTAST/HORROR)

Clubs/Associations

Ron Hanna
Secret Society of the Sanctum, The
Newsletter: Secret Sanctum
17803 Superior St., #204
Northridge, CA 91325
Newsletter features new pulp fiction, articles, and artwork; critically acclaimed with award-winning writers (Nick Carr, Will Murray); newsletter published bi-monthly.

Collectors

Jack Deveny
6805 Cheyenne Trail
Edina, MN 55439-1158
ph: 612-941-2457
plane@itol.net
Wants Spider, Shadow, Doc Savage, Spicy, Detective, Mystery, Horror, Terror, etc.

Doug Ellis
13 Spring Lane
Barrington, IL 60010
ph: 847-458-7097
pulpvault@msn.com
Wants to buy all pulp magazines, especially adventure genre pulps, pulps published by Clayton, and "spicy" pulps; also issues sale catalogs from time to time; also wants original pulp art.

Dealers

Jerry Peters
Chestnut Hollow, Ltd.
6060 Bordman Rd.
P.O. Box 6
Almont, MI 48003-0006
ph: 810-798-3158
jpeters@expression.org
Wants pulp magazines from the 1900s to 1950s: "The Shadow," "Doc Savage," weird tales, amazing stories, astounding, astonishing, planet stories, "The Spider," spicy detective, thrilling wonder stories, detective stories, "G-man," adventure.

David Smith
Rocket Comics
P.O. Box 30183
Seattle, WA 98103
ph: 206-784-7300
fax: 206-782-2844
rocket@jetcity.com
http://www.jetcity.com/~rocket
Dealer/expert buying and selling vintage comic books and pulp magazines since 1969; store has 2,500 sq. ft. of vintage comic books, pulp magazines, mass market magazines and paper books, and related paper collectibles.

Neil Mechem
Girasol Collectables
1409-3501 Glen Erin Dr.
Mississauga, Ontario L5L 2E9 Canada
ph: 905-820-7572
info@girasolcollectables.com
http://www.girasolcollectables.com
Wants all types of pulp magazines: The Shadow, G-8, Spider, Doc Savage; adventure, weird tales, horror, terror, spicy titles, mystery, detective, aviation, etc.

Experts

Ray Walsh
Curious Book Shop
307 E. Grand River
East Lansing, MI 48823-4324
ph: 517-332-0112
fax: 517-332-1915
mmabda@curiousbooks.com
http://www.curiousbooks.com
Dealer/expert; owner of three book shops in Michigan; hosts radio call-in show about books and paper collectibles; writes columns; send a SASE for reply when writing.

Internet Resources

William Lampkin
ThePulp.Net
mailbag@thepulp.net
http://www.thepulp.net
Great site for Pulp lovers: links, sources, files, history, memories, forum, gatherings, "The Shadow," "Doc Savage," "The Spider."

Museums/Libraries

San Francisco Academy of Comic Art
170 W. Cliff Dr., #15
Santa Cruz, CA 95060-5432
ph: 831-427-1737
fax: 831-427-1737
Millions of newspaper strips, bound files, major dailies from 1890-1960, pulps, all science fiction, crime fiction, film history, children's books, comic books; excellent copies made of all graphic material; dup material for trade.

Periodicals

Randy Cox
Journal: Dime Novel Round-Up
P.O. Box 226
Dundas, MN 55019-0226
ph: 507-645-5711
cox@stolaf.edu
http://www.readseries.com
A magazine devoted to the collecting, preservation and literature of the old-time dime and nickel novels and popular story papers, series books, and pulp magazine.

Doug Ellis
Tattered Pages Press
Magazine: Pulp Vault
13 Spring Lane
Barrington, IL 60010
ph: 847-458-7097
pulpvault@msn.com
Irregularly published magazine devoted to pulps; approx. 128 pgs, 8-1/2x11, perfect-binding; reprints fiction stories from pulps; articles about the pulps; recollections of the pulp era; priced per issue; no subscriptions.

Pulp (Doc Savage)

Periodicals

Howard Wright
Green Eagle Publications
Newsletter: Bronze Gazette, The
2900 Standiford Ave., #136
Modesto, CA 95350-6567
The only publication devoted exclusively to the invincible Man of Bronze, Doc Savage.

Scandal/Cult/R 'N' R

Experts

Wayne Betrock
Shake Books
P.O. Box 267
Cold Spring Harbor, NY 11724
ph: 516-978-1314
shakebooks@aol.com
Author of "Unseen America - The Greatest Cult Exploitation Magazines 1950-1966," "Illustrated Price Guide to Cult Magazines, 1945-1969," and "Hitsville: The Greatest Rock 'n Roll Magazines, 1954-1968."

Sporting

Dealers

Ron B. Frodelius
Open Season, The
P.O. Box 125
Fayetteville, NY 13066-0125
Wants any magazines related to trapping; pre-1955 only: ads, books, catalogs, magazines, hunt-trader-trapper, fur-fish-game magazines, and pre-1925 hunting magazines.

Toy

Collectors

Christmas Catalog Collector, The
175 East Delaware, #7403
Chicago, IL 60611-1731
ph: 800-879-6948 or 312-337-3123
fax: 312-266-7982
Collector eager to buy pre-1970 back copies of toy industry magazines such as "Playthings" and "Toys and Novelties;" also wants toy and Christmas catalogs.

TV Guide

Dealers

Rick Brown
Synergy
6031 Winterset
Lansing, MI 48911
ph: 517-887-1255
info@historybuff.com
http://www.historybuff.com
*Appraises, auctions, collects and
specializes in "TV Guide" magazines;
buying and selling Pre-National and
National editions 1948-1986.*

TV Guide Specialists
P.O. Box 20
Macomb, IL 61455-0020
ph: 309-833-1809
*Buys and sells "TV" Guide and
newspaper TV magazines, 1948-1997.*

MAGIC LANTERNS & SLIDES

(see also CAMERAS & CAMERA
EQUIPMENT; OPTICAL ITEMS;
TOYS, Optical)

Auction Services

Auction Team Breker
Bonner Str. 528-530
Koln, D-50968 Germany
ph: 49 221 387049 or 941-925-0385 (US
Rep)
fax: 49 221 374878
auction@breker.com
http://www.breker.com
*German auction company specializes
in the sale of old office equipment,
scientific instruments and devices,
photographica, and old technology
including toasters, typewriters, sewing
machines, tools, telecommunications,
etc.*

Clubs/Associations

Ralph Shape
Magic Lantern Society of the U. S. &
Canada
Newsletter: Magic Lantern Gazette
3757 South 194th St.
Seattle, WA 98188
ph: 206-592-8270
fax: 206-592-8269
RShape@compuserve.com
http://www.magiclanternsociety.org
*Collectors, restorers, preservers of the
history of magic lanterns - the
forerunner of cinema; members are
also interested in magic lantern glass
slides as well as other optical devices.*

Mike Smith, Hon. Sec.
Magic Lantern Society, The
South Park, Galphay Rd.
Kirkby Malzeard
Ripon, North Yorkshire HG4 3RX U.K.
lmh.smith@magiclanternsocy.demon.co.uk
http://www.magiclantern.org.uk
*Aim of the Society is to exchange,
coordinate research and disseminate
information about the history and
developments of the magic lantern and
lantern slides.*

Michael Pritchard, Editor
Photographic Collectors Club of Great
Britain
Magazine: Photographica World
5 Buntingford Rd.
Puckeridge
Ware, SG11 1RT U.K.
ph: (0044) (0)929 821611
info@pccgb.org
http://www.pccgb.org
*Club aims to promote the study and
collection of photographic equipment
and images by publications, meetings,
auctions and shows; covers cameras,
lenses, photographers, optical toys,
stereoscopes, magic lanterns, and
related areas.*

Collectors

Sherry L. Werdon
400 N. Washington
Lowell, MI 49331-1465
ph: 616-897-9580
*Wants unusual magic lanterns or
mechanical lantern slides; also round
and extra large slides and wooden
viewers, pantoscope, etc.*

Jack Judson, Jr.
1419 Austin Hwy.
San Antonio, TX 78209
ph: 210-805-0011
fax: 210-822-1226
castle@magiclanterns.org
http://www.magiclanterns.org
*Wants to buy magic lanterns and
slides.*

Alan Heim
8007 West 4th St.
Los Angeles, CA 90048-4414
ph: 213-935-0865
fax: 213-931-9549
*Collector and sometimes trader of all
forms of early film equipment with a
focus on editing equipment; movie
cameras, magic lanterns, pre-cinema.*

Dealers

Bryan W. Ginns
2109 Cty. Rte. 21
Valatie, NY 12184-6001
ph: 518-392-5805
fax: 518-392-7925
the3dman@aol.com
*Wants large collections of stereo
views, old cameras, daguerreotypes,
magic lanterns, optical toys; anything
relating to photographics.*

Ronald Krueger
R. W. Krueger's
P.O. Box 741
Oak Park, IL 60303-0741
ph: 708-788-8235
*Collects glass slides used to advertise
movies (coming attraction slides); also
wants song slides.*

Experts

Jack Judson, Jr.
1419 Austin Hwy.
San Antonio, TX 78209
ph: 210-805-0011
fax: 210-822-1226
castle@magiclanterns.org
http://www.magiclanterns.org
*Has extensive knowledge, collection/
museum, and research facilities
focusing on the magic lantern and
other optical devices.*

Internet Resources

Derek Greenacre
Thrill in The Dark, A
U.K.
magiclantern14@hotmail.com
http://
www.magiclantern14.btinternet.co.uk
*Offers an introduction to the lost
world of Victorian magic lanterns.*

Museums/Libraries

Jack Judson, Jr.
Magic Lantern Castle Museum
1419 Austin Hwy.
San Antonio, TX 78209
ph: 210-805-0011
fax: 210-822-1226
castle@magiclanterns.org
http://www.magiclanterns.org
*Open by appointment; one man's
collection of optical projection devices
and items relating to the science of
optics and optical projection.*

MAGICIANS PARAPHERNALIA

(see also MORBID & ODD ITEMS;
PERFORMING ARTS; POSTERS;
RESTRAINT DEVICES; WITCHES)

Appraisers

Ted J. Bogusta
Martinka & Co., Inc.
103 Godwin Ave., 262M
Midland Park, NJ 07432
ph: 201-847-9297 or 212-279-6079
fax: 201-848-9087
mrd@martinka.com
http://www.martinka.com
*Buying and accepting consignments
for quarterly auctions of vintage
magic; specializes in and appraises
magic posters, books, photos and
autographs of magicians; established
in 1877.*

Auction Services

Ted J. Bogusta
Martinka & Co., Inc.
103 Godwin Ave., 262M
Midland Park, NJ 07432
ph: 201-847-9297 or 212-279-6079
fax: 201-848-9087
mrd@martinka.com
http://www.martinka.com
*Buying and accepting consignments
for quarterly auctions of vintage
magic; specializes in and appraises
magic posters, books, photos and*

*autographs of magicians; established
in 1877.*

Clubs/Associations

Edward Hill
New England Magic Collectors
Association
3 Chandler St.
North Providence, RI 02911-2210
ph: 401-231-1215
ride0167@ride.ri.net
*Association of serious collectors of
magic who reside in the New England
area; three meetings/year; all
collectors welcome as guests.*

David Meyer
Magic Collector's Association
Magazine: Magicol
P.O. Box 511
Glenwood, IL 60425-0511
magic.collectors.assoc@att.net
*An association for collectors of all
kinds of memorabilia related to magic
as a performing art; magazine
published quarterly.*

Collectors

Joseph Gargano
P.O. Box 170
Lake Hiawatha, NJ 07034-0170
ph: 973-538-2501
*Wants to buy original old pre-1940
magic related ephemera, posters and
lithographs of magicians; also wants
to buy original Houdini material;
please state condition and price.*

Mark Whipple
102 Clarette Rd.
Pittsburgh, PA 15237-1058
ph: 412-366-9459
whip123@hotmail.com
*Collects anything to do with magic
and magicians: tricks, books,
magazines, posters, etc.*

Ken Trombly
1050 17th St., NW, Ste. 1250
Washington, DC 20036
ph: 800-673-8158 or 202-887-5000
fax: 202-457-0343
trombly@erols.com
http://www.magicposters.com
*Wants original stone litho magic
posters, Houdini items (photos,
letters, advertising, scrapbooks, etc.),
19th century broadsides and old
photos of magicians.*

Dan Stapleton
8237 Banyan Blvd.
Orlando, FL 32819
ph: 407-345-1132
*Collector only, not a dealer; wants to
buy old magic kits (pre-1965), magic
lithographs and posters (pre-1950).*

LaVerne Anderson
944 35th St.
Des Moines, IA 50312-3102
ph: 515-274-4443 or 515-274-9196
fax: 515-274-9196
*Wants old magic books and magic
tricks.*

Andy Gross
P.O. Box 6134
Beverly Hills, CA 90212-1134
ph: 310-362-4372 or 310-614-1944
fax: 310-680-6495
apedoll69@aol.com
http://www.lamagictoy.com
Wants old magic tricks, kits, books, posters.

Michael Jaffe
Brookman Stamp Company
P.O. Box 61484
Vancouver, WA 98666-1484
ph: 360-695-6161 or 800-782-6770
fax: 360-695-1616
mjaffe@brookmanstamps.com
http://www.brookmanstamps.com
Wants to buy magic, magicians, escape artists, ventriloquists, jugglers; also related photo cards, advertising cards.

Dealers

David Winkler
Winkler's Warehouse & Services
24 Doyle Rd.
Oakdale, CT 06370-1052
ph: 860-859-3474
fax: 860-859-3135
david.winkler@snet.net
http://www.winklerswarehouse.com
Buys, sells collectible and pre-owned magic items of all types, plus books, periodicals, anything magic related; Web site features large list of used magic items and books; always seeking to buy.

Ted J. Bogusta
Martinka & Co., Inc.
103 Godwin Ave., 262M
Midland Park, NJ 07432
ph: 201-847-9297 or 212-279-6079
fax: 201-848-9087
mrd@martinka.com
http://www.martinka.com
Wants to buy all magician and Houdini related items: old magic books, ads, letters, photos, prints, posters, cards, postcards, tricks, magic sets; especially wants items related to Houdini, Herrman, Kellar, Thurston, Blackstone, Soo.

Kenna Thompson
KT Magic, Inc.
P.O. Box 260
Hebron, KY 41048
ph: 859-689-7080
fax: 859-689-0227
kennat@earthlink.net
http://www.ktmagic.com
Buys, sells & appraises Magic, collectible, vintage, antique and rare: apparatus, books, lithograph posters (especially Strobridge), broadsides, sets, photos and autographs, memorabilia, collector item magic, Houdini, Kellar, Thurston.

Ed Verba
Magic Old & New
7655 Lexington Green
Cleveland, OH 44130-6864
ph: 440-243-2424 or 440-243-2350
everba@adelphia.net
Dealer in new and old magic (conjuring); used books, videos, illusions, antique magic, ephemera, and memorabilia; quarterly mailings of items for sale; no charge for mailing for first two years; many items on consignment.

Ron Allesi
P.O. Box 62029
Cincinnati, OH 45262
ph: 513-678-6146
ronallesi@fuse.net
http://www.ronallesimagic.com
Buying, selling and trading used and antique magic equipment, posters, books and anything else pertaining to magic.

Frank Herman
710 Anchor Way
Carlsbad, CA 92008
ph: 760-434-2254
Buys and sells magician related items: autographs, posters, programs, Mysto Magic sets, toys; also mentalists, escape artists, ventriloquists, fire eaters, spiritualists; plus all related books and apparatus; all offering lists answered.

Experts

Mario Carrandi
Mario Carrandi Inc. Antiquarian Magic
& Collectibles
122 Monroe Ave.
Belle Mead, NJ 08502-4608
ph: 908-874-0630
fax: 908-874-4892
mario@carrandimagic.com
http://www.carrandimagic.com
Buys, sells, appraises and specialize in all categories of magic; one of the oldest and largest dealer in the field.

Herb Jacobs
P.O. Box 5390
Pompano Beach, FL 33074-5390
ph: 954-943-4213
fax: 954-943-4213
Buys, sells, appraises and specializes in magic and conjuring memorabilia.

Kenna Thompson
KT Magic, Inc.
P.O. Box 260
Hebron, KY 41048
ph: 859-689-7080
fax: 859-689-0227
kennat@earthlink.net
http://www.ktmagic.com
Buys, sells & appraises Magic, collectible, vintage, antique and rare: apparatus, books, lithograph posters (especially Strobridge), broadsides, sets, photos and autographs, Taytelbaum; author of bi-weekly column for "The Magic Collector."

Dan Bradbury
Bradbury Books & Beyond
3318 Karnes Blvd.
Kansas City, MO 64111
ph: 816-531-2468
fax: 816-531-2468
dbjb@sky.net
http://www.bradburybooks.com
Buys and sells books (primarily out-of-print and used) and ephemera related to magic (conjuring) and its allied arts and entertainments: history and bibliography of magic, advertising, instructions, programs, books on performing.

John A. Greget
John A. Greget - Magic Lists
5575 E. Sheena Dr.
Scottsdale, AZ 85254-2961
ph: 602-404-3100
fax: 602-404-3200
Buys and appraises magic books, posters, magazines, ephemera, equipment, etc.; singles or collection.

Internet Resources

Gary Hunt, Ed.
Magical Past-Times
garyhunt@mindspring.com
http://www.uelectric.com/pastimes
The online journal of magic history; learn more about the fascinating history of magic; provides resources for everyone from the merely curious to the hard core collector.

Museums/Libraries

Elaine Lund
American Museum of Magic
107 E. Michigan
P.O. Box 5
Marshall, MI 49068
ph: 616-781-7666
http://www.marshallmi.org/tours/virtual/magic.html
Museum with holdings of approximately 250,000 items, all on magic; by appointment.

Periodicals

Magazine: Magic Magazine
7380 South Eastern, Ste. #124-179
Las Vegas, NV 89123
ph: 702-798-4893
fax: 702-798-0220
editor@magicmagazine.com
http://www.magicmagazine.com

Houdini

Collectors

Sidney Radner
1050 Northampton St.
Holyoke, MA 01040-1321
ph: 413-532-6009 or 561-588-5811
(winter)
hollisrendar@aol.com
Wants Houdini posters, playbills, books, ephemera, etc.; honorary curator of the Houdini Historical Center; owns one of the most extensive collections of Houdini memorabilia;

curator of Houdini Museum, Venetian Hotel, Las Vegas.

Joseph Gargano
P.O. Box 170
Lake Hiawatha, NJ 07034-0170
ph: 973-538-2501
Wants to buy original old pre-1940 magic related ephemera, posters and lithographs of magicians; also wants to buy original Houdini material; please state condition and price.

Kevin Connolly
257 E. Woodland Rd.
New Milford, NJ 07646-2321
ph: 201-262-9693
houdini26@aol.com
Wants anything Houdini or about magic: books, posters, autographs, tricks, tokens, sets, apparatus, etc.

Ken Trombly
1050 17th St., NW, Ste. 1250
Washington, DC 20036
ph: 800-673-8158 or 202-887-5000
fax: 202-457-0343
trombly@erols.com
http://www.magicposters.com
Wants magic posters, Mysto Magic sets, magic books and Houdini items; also wants broadsides and old photos of magicians; will pay top dollar or will trade from his collection.

Arthur Moses
4205 Hildring Dr. East
Fort Worth, TX 76109-4717
ph: 817-921-2840
aem102@aol.com
Wants to buy Houdini and related items: books, articles, posters, photos, autographs, personal effects, programs, pamphlets, playbills, scrapbooks, letters, lobby cards, films, etc.

Dealers

A. Peter Monticup
MagicTricks.Com
2768 Columbia Rd.
Gordonsville, VA 22942
ph: 540-832-0900
peter@magictricks.com
http://www.magictricks.com

Michael Griffin
International Handcuff Exchange
356 W. Powell Rd.
Powell, OH 43065-9650
ph: 614-846-0585 or 614-846-6790
escapeguy@aol.com
Buys/sells Houdini memorabilia and old collectible magic; also handcuffs, leg irons, etc.; list of items for sale available.

Joseph & Pamela Tanner
Wheeler-Tanner ESCAPES
6442 Canyon Creek Way
Elk Grove, CA 95758
ph: 916-684-4006
fax: 916-684-4006
JnPwLrTnr@aol.com
Wants Houdini & other escape artist items: autographs, posters, letters,

postcards, books, photos, playbills, equipment, etc.

Internet Resources

A. Peter Monticup
MagicTricks.Com
2768 Columbia Rd.
Gordonsville, VA 22942
ph: 540-832-0900
peter@magictricks.com
http://www.magictricks.com
Great Houdini Web site: research, read and learn about the most famous magician in history: biography, odditorium, seances, photo gallery, etc.

Museums/Libraries

Houdini Museum
1433 N. Main Ave.
Scranton, PA 18508
ph: 714-342-5555
magicusa@microserve.net
http://www.microserve.net/~magicusa/houdini.html
The only museum dedicated to Harry Houdini.

Kimberly Louagie, Curator
Houdini Historical Center
Magazine: Mystifier, The
330 East College Ave.
Appleton, WI 54911-5715
ph: 920-733-8445
ochs@foxvalleyhistory.org
http://www.foxvalleyhistory.org/houdini
Dedicated to the gathering, interpretation, and dissemination of information and artifacts related to the life and career of Harry Houdini; collection features the Sidney H. Radner collection of Houdini memorabilia.

Magic Sets

Collectors

Phil Temple
P.O. Box 561
Novato, CA 94948
ph: 415-897-5130
fax: 415-897-5130
magiccircus@earthlink.net
Collector and archivist for America's largest collection of magic sets and related items.

Periodicals

Phil Temple, Pub.
Newsletter: Magic Set Collector's NEWSLETTER
P.O. Box 561
Novato, CA 94948
ph: 415-897-5130
fax: 415-897-5130
magiccircus@earthlink.net
America's first and only publication dedicated to the history of magic sets in the United States and around the world; includes color pages and price guides.

MAGNETS (REFRIGERATOR)

Collectors

Louise J. Greenfarb
Magnet Lady, The
307 John Henry Dr.
Henderson, NV 89014-1610
ph: 702-433-4604
mgntldy@aol.com
http://hometown.aol.com/mgntldy
Has held Guiness record since 1995 for owning over 30,000 different refrigerator magnets; 7,000 are on display at the Guiness Museum in Las Vegas, NV; has a network of "magpal" traders world wide.

Man./Prod./Dist.

Chris Gwynn
Fridgedoor.com
21 Dixwell Ave.
Quincy, MA 02169
ph: 800-955-3741 or 617-770-7913
fax: 617-689-0601
chris@fridgedoor.com
http://www.fridgedoor.com
The Web's largest retailer of refrigerator magnets.

MAILBOXES

Collectors

Charles W. Wardell
P.O. Box 195
Trinity, NC 27370-0195
ph: 336-434-1145
Wants 1870-1940 cast iron mailboxes; these boxes were fancy in design and served on homes and shops; usually with many coats of paint.

MANUALS & INSTRUCTION BOOKLETS

(see PAPER COLLECTIBLES)

MANUSCRIPTS

(see also AUTOGRAPHS; BOOKS; HISTORICAL AMERICANA; PAPER COLLECTIBLES)

Appraisers

Brian Kathenes
National Appraisal Consultants, LLC
P.O. Box 482
Hope, NJ 07844-0482
ph: 908-459-5996 or 800-323-5996
fax: 908-459-4899
Brian@nacvalue.com
http://www.nacvalue.com
Specialist Certified Appraiser of Personal Property in Autographs, Manuscripts and Historical Documents; expert appraisal, valuation and consulting services for Hollywood, sports and celebrity memorabilia and collectibles.

Ray Nugent, ASA
Nugent Appraisal Services
P.O. Box 11984
Naples, FL 34101
ph: 888-353-7152 or 941-353-7122
fax: 941-353-8884
renugent@aol.com
http://www.appraisalreferrals.com
ASA senior accredited appraiser of rare books, documents, manuscripts, autographs and antique maps; member of ISA, AAA, AIC, SAA.

Auction Services

Robert Lifson
Robert Edward Auctions
P.O. Box 7256
Watchung, NJ 07069
ph: 908-226-9900 or 800-766-9324
fax: 908-226-9920
reaauct@aol.com
http://www.robertedwardauctions.com
Specializes in the auction sale of historical Americana, political material, autographs and manuscripts, and original illustration art.

Clubs/Associations

David R. Smith, Ex. Dir.
Manuscript Society, The
Magazine: Manuscripts
350 N. Niagara St.
Burbank, CA 91505-3648
manuscrip@aol.com
http://www.manuscript.org
An organization of collectors, dealers, librarians, archivists, scholars and others interested in autographs and manuscripts.

Dealers

George & Julie Perron
Old Paperphiles, The
P.O. Box 135
Tiverton, RI 02878-0135
ph: 401-624-9420
opac108@netzero.net
Buys and sells paper collectibles: autographs, sheet music, postcards, photos, stereoviews, documents, old letters; sells on eBay, seller name is "opac."

Peter Pehrson
Written by Hand
Yale Station
Box 206581
New Haven, CT 06520
ph: 203-380-9940
writtenbyhand@aol.com
http://www.writtenbyhand.com
Specializes in primary manuscript Americana source material for institutions, collectors, dealers, archivists, libraries and museums; please no autographs, postcards or celebrity items; always buying and selling.

University Archives
49 Richmondville Ave.
Westport, CT 06880
ph: 800-237-5692 or 203-454-0111
fax: 203-454-3111
john@universityarchives.com
http://www.universityarchives.com
Buying and selling fine historical autographs, manuscripts, documents, autographed books and autographed photographs of notable people including US presidents, Revolutionary and Civil War, literary, aviation, science, art, and music.

Kenneth Rendell
Kenneth W. Rendell Gallery, The
989 Madison Ave.
New York, NY 10021
ph: 800-447-1007 or 212-717-1776
fax: 212-717-1492
gallery@kwrendell.com
http://www.kwrendell.com
Leading dealer in historical documents, autographs and manuscripts' author of "Autographs and Manuscripts: A Collector's Manual," "Faking Forgery: The Detection of Fake Letters and Documents," and other books.

Gary J. Zimet
Moments in Time, Inc.
5 Cardinal Dr.
Washingtonville, NY 10992
ph: 914-497-7373
fax: 914-496-6367
vie1@aol.com
http://www.momentsintime.com
Wants to buy rare letters and manuscripts: Washington, Adams, Jefferson, Lincoln, M.L. King, Malcolm X, Churchill, Disney, Ruth, Lee, Grant, Custer, etc.

Carmen D. Valentino
Rare Books & Manuscripts
2956 Richmond St., Drawer 19
Philadelphia, PA 19134-5720
ph: 215-739-6056
fax: 215-739-6453
Antiquarian bookseller specializing in pre-WWI rare books, manuscripts, documents, early newspapers, handwritten diaries, account books, ledgers, ephemera, broadsides, trade catalogs, pamphlets; collections of old family/business letters.

Thomas J. Joyce
Joyce And Company
400 N. Racine Ave., #103A
Chicago, IL 60622
ph: 312-738-1933
fax: 312-243-6252
tjoyceco@comcast.net
Buys, sells, appraises rare books and manuscripts for over 25 years; members of the Antiquarian Booksellers Association of America & International League of Antiquarian Booksellers; Thomas Joyce appears on HGTV's "The Appraisal Fair."

John Wilson
Painswick Lawn
7 Painswick Rd.
Cheltenham, GL50 2EZ U.K.
ph: _44(0)1242 580344
fax: +44(0)1242 580355
web@manuscripts.co.uk
http://www.manuscripts.co.uk
*Long-established dealers in the UK
specializing in autograph letters,
historical documents and textual
manuscripts; also signed photographs
and other related material having a
close association with historical
figures in all fields.*

Pennsylvania

Experts

Ron Lieberman
Family Album, The
4887 Newport Rd.
Kinzers, PA 17535
ph: 717-442-0220
fax: 717-442-7904
rarebooks@POBox.com
http://www.sellbooks.net
*Buys, sells, appraises all Pennsylvania
related books, manuscripts, artwork,
etc.*

MAPS & CHARTS

(see also ATLASES; GAS STATION
COLLECTIBLES, Road Maps;
GLOBES; NAUTICAL ANTIQUES,
Maps & Charts; PAPER
COLLECTIBLES; PRINTS; STAMP
COLLECTING, Maps & Charts;
TRAILERS & RVs)

Appraisers

Jacqueline Grace
Grace Galleries, Inc.
20 West Cundys Point Rd.
Harpswell, ME 04079
ph: 207-729-1329
fax: 207-729-0385
jackie@gracegalleries.com
http://www.gracegalleries.com
*Buys and sells original maps & sea
charts; US and worldwide; from late
16th to late 19th centuries; specializes
in sea and sea related maps & charts;
member Appraisers Association of
America.*

Donald H. Cresswell
Philadelphia Print Shop, Ltd., The
8441 Germantown Ave.
Philadelphia, PA 19118
ph: 215-242-4750
fax: 215-242-6977
cresswell@PhilaPrintShop.com
http://www.philaprintshop.com
*Buys, sells, appraises prints, maps,
related rare books and atlases.*

Ray Nugent, ASA
Nugent Appraisal Services
P.O. Box 11984
Naples, FL 34101
ph: 888-353-7152 or 941-353-7122
fax: 941-353-8884
renugent@aol.com
http://www.appraisalreferrals.com
*ASA senior accredited appraiser of
rare books, documents, manuscripts,
autographs and antique maps; member
of ISA, AAA, AIC, SAA.*

Auction Services

James E. Hess
49 N. Broad St.
P.O. Box 412
Lititz, PA 17543
ph: 717-626-5002
fax: 717-626-8858
heritage@carto.com
http://www.carto.com

Joke Vrijenhoek
Paulus Swaen Internet Auction
P.O. Box 1238
Indian Rocks Beach, FL 33785
ph: 727-596-8734
fax: 727-596-8734
paulus@swaen.com
http://www.swaen.com
*Buys and sells old maps; conducts
interactive map auctions on the
Internet; offices in US and The
Netherlands.*

Curt & Marti Griggs
Old World Auctions
P.O. Box 2224
Sedona, AZ 86339
ph: 928-282-3944 or 800-664-7757
fax: 928-282-3945
marti@oldworldauctions.com
http://www.oldworldauctions.com
*Auction specialists in antique maps,
globes and prints; buys, sells, and
takes consignments.*

Clubs/Associations

David Cobb
Boston Map Society
Harvard College Library
Cambridge, MA 02138
ph: 617-495-2417
fax: 617-496-0440
cobb@husc.harvard.edu
http://icg.harvard.edu/~maps/hpbms.htm
*Brings together people with an
interest in collecting, studying, using
and preserving maps.*

Eric Riback
NorthEast Map Organization
Newsletter: NEMO Newsletter
2504 Kerry Lane
Charlottesville, VA 22901
ph: 804-975-6423
fax: 509-461-4285
eric@mapville.com
http://ublib.buffalo.edu/libraries/units/sel/
collections/maps/nemo.html

Maureen Farrell
Northern Ohio Map Society
c/o Map Department, Cleveland Public
Library
325 Superior Ave.
Cleveland, OH 44111
ph: 216-623-2880
fax: 216-902-4978
Maureen.Farrell@cpl.org
http://www.csuohio.edu/CUT/MapSoc/
NOMS.htm

Chicago Map Society, The
Newsletter: Mapline
The Newberry Library
60 West Walton St.
Chicago, IL 60610-7324
ph: 312-255-3659
fax: 312-255-2502
smithctr@newberry.org
http://www.newberry.org/nl/smith/
cms.html
Oldest map society in North America.

International Map Trade Association
P.O. Box 1789
Kankakee, IL 60901
ph: 815-939-4627
fax: 815-933-8320
imta@maptrade.org
http://www.maptrade.org
*Fostering and promoting the sales,
usage, awareness and understanding
of maps and map related products; for
map retailers, map publishers, globe
manufacturers, travel produce
manufacturers, bookstores, educators
and collectors.*

Texas Map Society
Newsletter: Neatline, The
c/o Department of History, Univ. of
Texas
P.O. Box 19497
Arlington, TX 76019-0497
ph: 817-272-5329
fax: 817-272-3360
goodwin@uta.edu
http://libraries.uta.edu/txmapsociety
*Organized in 1996 to foster the study,
understanding and collecting of
historical maps and cartography.*

William J. Warren
California Map Society
1109 Linda Glen Dr.
Pasadena, CA 91105
ph: 626-792-9152
fax: 626-568-4945
wjwarren@aol.com
http://www.raremaps.com/cms
*Anyone with an interest in maps may
join; members are mainly nonacademic
types, many are collectors, some are
dealers in maps and antiquarian
books; two meetings per year and a
quarterly newsletter.*

Jenny Harvey
International Map Collectors Society
(IMCoS)
Journal: IMCoS Journal
27 Landford Rd.
Putney, London SW15 1AQ U.K.
ph: +44 (0) 20 8789 7358
fax: +44 (0) 20 8788 7819
jeh@harvey27.demon.co.uk
http://www.imcos-mapcollecting.org
*Members from 22 countries worldwide
who are a mix of collectors,
academics, dealers and others who
love old maps; members have access to
important national and international
map collections not normally available
to the public.*

Collectors

Norman D. Leckert
P.O. Box 363
Bethel, VT 05032-0363
ph: 802-234-5657 or 800-717-2021
fax: 802-234-6104
Wants pre-1900 atlases and maps.

Dealers

Siegfried Feller
Cartomania Plus
8 Amherst Rd.
Pelham, MA 01002-9739
ph: 413-253-3115
*Sells maps and map related
memorabilia.*

Jon K. Rosenthal
Amherst Antiquarian Maps
P.O. Box 12
Amherst, MA 01004-0012
ph: 413-256-8900
fax: 413-256-6291
office@amherst-maps.com
http://www.amherst-maps.com
*General stock of antique maps and
charts; former publisher of "Antique
Map Price Record."*

Thomas E. Carroll
31 Main St.
Hatfield, MA 01038
ph: 413-247-9767
fax: 413-247-3080
tecmaps@rcn.com
*Specializing in maps and charts; has
appeared on PAX TV's "Treasures in
Your Home."*

Marshall Cook
Baldwin's Old Prints & Maps
P.O. Box 745
Vineyard Haven, MA 02568
ph: 508-693-5903
maps@baldwinsmaps.com
http://www.baldwinsmaps.com
*Specializes in prints, maps and charts;
US Coast Survey charts, historical
prints, biblical/religious maps, US
Civil War maps, etc.*

Lynn Vigeant
Maps of Antiquity
1022 Route 6A
West Barnstable, MA 02668
ph: 508-362-7169
http://www.mapsofantiquity.com
Buys and sells historical, decorative maps, 19th century and earlier.

Reg & Sally Lombard
Lombard Antiquarian Maps & Prints
P.O. Box 6565
Scarborough, ME 04070
ph: 207-885-9177
fax: 207-885-9575
rtl@lombardmaps.com
http://www.lombardmaps.com
Specializes in fine maps, charts, fore-edge-painted books and miniature books, rare botanical, natural history and architectural prints; also maps, prints, and books relating to Napoleon I.

Jacqueline Grace
Grace Galleries, Inc.
20 West Cundys Point Rd.
Harpswell, ME 04079
ph: 207-729-1329
fax: 207-729-0385
jackie@gracegalleries.com
http://www.gracegalleries.com
Buys and sells original maps & sea charts; US and worldwide; from late 16th to late 19th centuries; specializes in sea and sea related maps & charts; member Appraisers Association of America.

Antiquaries Manasek
P.O. Box 1204
Norwich, VT 05055
ph: 802-649-1722
fax: 802-649-2256
office@antiquaries.com
http://www.antiquaries.com
Buys maps and atlases from almost any region; also star maps, city plans and sea charts; folding (pocket), wall and roller maps of states, countries, continents and the world.

Christopher Watters
Cartographics of Vermont
P.O. Box 645
East Middlebury, VT 05740-0645
ph: 802-388-6229
watters@middlebury.edu
Buys and sells all forms of separately issued 19th c. American maps including: wall and pocket maps, school exercise maps, family and school atlases, government and commercial publications related to exploration, games & quiz maps, etc.

Patrick M. O'Brien
Laughing Moon, The
P.O. Box 254
West Simsbury, CT 06092
TheLaughingMoon@aol.com
http://members.aol.com/
thelaughingmoon/Index.html
Collector and dealer of primarily 19th century antique maps and prints.

Latitudes
P.O. Box 66
Essex, CT 06426-0066
ph: 860-767-3001 or 860-526-2100
Dealer/collector buys and sells unusual format maps (folding, strip, ribbon of rivers, canals), wall maps (CT & MA counties & entire US), harbor charts (USCS, Blunt, Eldridge, New England), coast pilot books, Nantucket, Block Island.

Neil St.
Street & O'Neill Galleries
152 Danbury Rd.
Wilton, CT 06897
ph: 203-762-3474
fax: 203-762-5545
mapmaker@vintagemaps.com
http://www.vintagemaps.com
Specializes in antique prints, maps and charts; custom framing available in gallery.

Bruce Morgan
Maps of Olde
11 Lenape Rd.
Cherry Hill, NJ 08002
ph: 856-488-1432
mapsofolde@comcast.net
http://www.mapsofolde.com
Buys and sells old maps.

George D. Glazer
28 East 72nd St., 3rd Flor
New York, NY 10021
ph: 212-535-5706
fax: 212-658-9512
worldglobe@georgeglazer.com
http://www.georgeglazer.com
Buys and sells 19th and early 20th century atlases and maps; emphasis is on United States, especially NY, FL, and New England, and on star and celestial charts; also wants novelty maps and world maps.

High Ridge Books, Inc.
P.O. Box 286
Rye, NY 10580
ph: 914-967-3332
fax: 914-967-6056
highridge@pipeline.com
http://www.highridgebooks.com
Wants to buy 19th century American cartography; atlases, wall maps, sea charts, pocket maps.

Michael Tokman
A-ha! Books, Inc.
17 Railroad St., Ste. #3
Freeville, NY 13068
ph: 607-844-5555
fax: 607-844-5555
info@ahabooks.com
http://www.ahabooks.com
Buys and sells rare, antiquarian and out-of-print books, autographs, and maps; online catalog, book search service.

James E. Hess
49 N. Broad St.
P.O. Box 412
Lititz, PA 17543
ph: 717-626-5002
fax: 717-626-8858
heritage@carto.com
http://www.carto.com
One of the largest map and atlas, and globe dealers in the world; buys, sells, collects, appraises.

Heritage Antique Maps
551 Christopher Ln.
Doylestown, PA 18901-3127
ph: 215-340-9662
fax: 215-340-9662
mapking7@hotmail.com
http://www.HeritageAntiqueMaps.com
Interested in purchasing maps.

Christopher W. Lane
Philadelphia Print Shop, Ltd., The
8441 Germantown Ave.
Philadelphia, PA 19118
ph: 215-242-4750
fax: 215-242-6977
PhilaPrint@PhilaPrintShop.com
http://www.philaprintshop.com
Buys, sells, appraises prints, maps, related rare books and atlases; also bookstore of reference books related to antique prints and maps; also paper conservation and restoration, museum quality framing.

Judith Blakely
Old Print Gallery, The
1220 31st St. NW
Washington, DC 20007-3422
ph: 202-965-1818
fax: 202-965-1869
info@oldprintgallery.com
http://www.oldprintgallery.com
Wants antique maps and prints: American or foreign, 16th to 19th centuries.

J. Baldwin
Baldwin's Attic
P.O. Box 3515
Norfolk, VA 23514
ph: 757-625-1888
baldwins@visi.net
http://www.shoporium.com/shops/
baldwinsattic
Specializes in antique prints, maps, books, and paper ephemera.

Luke & Patricia Vavra
Cartographic Arts
P.O. Box 2202
Petersburg, VA 23804-1502
ph: 804-861-6770
fax: 804-861-3021
carto@dogstar.com
http://www.CartographicsArts.com
Buys and sells only antique maps and charts; no reproductions.

Joel Kovarsky
Prime Meridian: Antique Maps & Books
385 Thistle Trail
Danville, VA 24540
ph: 434-724-1106
fax: 434-799-0218
tpm@theprimemeridian.com
http://www.theprimemeridian.com
Buys and sells antiquarian maps and related books; stocks a broad general inventory, with special interests in military cartographic material; browsing and secured ordering available at online Web site; member IAMA.

Bernard Rogers, Jr.
Appalachian Arts
P.O. Box 1274
2314 W. Dolphin Dr.
Blue Ridge, GA 30513
ph: 347-487-5781
bud@oldcharts.com
http://www.oldcharts.com
Specializes in 19th century antique state, city, and world maps, antique nautical charts, and antique decorative prints.

Charles Neuschafer
New World Maps, Inc.
1123 South Broadway
Lake Worth, FL 33462-4522
ph: 561-586-8723
newworldmaps@prodigy.net
Active dealer in antique and collectible maps; buys and sells antique and collectible maps and charts; author of a column on map collecting in "Paper Collectors' Marketplace," members of several professional map societies.

Michael Slicker
Lighthouse Books
1735 First Ave. North
Saint Petersburg, FL 33713
ph: 727-822-3278
lighthousebooks@sprintmail.com
Specializes in books and maps.

John Forster
Barometer Fair
P.O. Box 25502
Sarasota, FL 34277
ph: 941-923-6136
fax: 941-923-6136
john@barometerfair.com
Buys, sells, restores all antique barometers; also deals in antique maps, globes, compasses, telescopes and other scientific instruments.

Don McDonald
PastPresent Gallery
660 Celebration Ave., Ste. 150
Celebration, FL 34747
ph: 407-566-1899 or 877-4-PAST-MAPS
fax: 407-566-1030
curator@pastpresent.com
http://store.pastpresent.com
Deals in authentic 19th century antique maps, prints and engravings.

Murray Hudson
Murray Hudson Antiquarian Books,
  Maps, Prints & Globes
109 S. Church St.
P.O. Box 163
Halls, TN 38040-0163
ph: 731-836-9057 or 800-748-9946
fax: 731-836-9017
mapman@ecsis.net
http://www.murrayhudson.com
  *Buys/sells pre-1900 antique maps
  (especially pocket, wall, Civil War
  and railroad maps) & books with
  maps (e.g. atlases, travel guides,
  geographies, land surveys, etc.); esp.
  of S.E. & S.W. US; also wants pre-
  1950 world globes.*

J. Newcome-Beill
Abstract Eye Books
1517 Vivian Lane
Louisville, KY 40205
abstracteyebooks@cox.net
http://www.abstracteyebooks.com
  *Buys and sells used and rare
  photography books, maps, and prints.*

Charles Puckett
Charles Edwin Puckett
3867 West Market St., #253
Akron, OH 44333
ph: 330-668-0032
fax: 330-668-0037
charles@cepuckett.com
http://www.cepuckett.com
  *Specializes in maps, medieval and
  Renaissance illuminated manuscripts,
  prints.*

Mary & George Ritzlin
George Ritzlin Maps & Prints
473 Roger Williams Ave.
Highland Park, IL 60035-4704
ph: 847-433-2627
fax: 847-433-6389
maps@ritzlin.com
http://www.ritzlin.com
  *Buys and sells antique maps and
  atlases 1500-1900; cartographic
  references; books on early travel and
  exploration; pre-WWII Baedekers;
  illuminated medieval manuscripts;
  natural history prints; antique fashion
  plates; since 1976.*

Art Source International
1237 Pearl St.
Boulder, CO 80302-5204
ph: 303-444-4080
fax: 303-444-4298
info@mapsandprints.com
http://www.mapsandprints.com
  *Specializes in maps, globes, prints,
  and posters; in business for over 20
  years.*

Jonathan Blackman
Yellow Room, The
511 N. Robertson Blvd.
Los Angeles, CA 90048
ph: 310-274-3190
fax: 310-274-0129
  *Specializes in globes, maps and
  scientific instruments; great resource
  information on the Web site.*

Barry Lawrence Ruderman
Barry Lawrence Ruderman Antique Maps
6141 Soledad Mountain Rd.
La Jolla, CA 92037
ph: 858-551-8500
fax: 858-456-4095
blr@raremaps.com
http://www.raremaps.com
  *Large Internet gallery featuring 15th
  through 19th century antique maps
  from all parts of the world,
  specializing in Americana.*

Scott Brake
Scott Brake Antiques
17420 Mt. Hermann St., Unit "D"
Fountain Valley, CA 92708
ph: 714-556-8333
fax: 714-556-8333
antiquechi@aol.com
  *Specializes in special acquisitions for
  entertainment and theme park clients;
  prop rentals.*

Steve & Laurie Armistead
Deja View Antique Maps & Prints
P.O. Box 61722
Vancouver, WA 98666
ph: 360-696-3252
sarmis@dejaviewmaps.com
http://www.dejaviewmaps.com
  *Specializes in antique maps and
  atlases.*

Bruce Magnotti
Aesthetic Image
309 West Fifth Ave.
Ellensburg, WA 98926
ph: 509-962-5204
  *Buys and sells rare prints, maps and
  illustrated books.*

Alec Parley
Beach Antique Maps & Prints
390 Queens Quay West
Toronto, Ontario M5V 3A6 Canada
beachmap@sympatico.ca
http://www.beachmaps.com
  *Sells genuine engraved antique maps
  and prints dating from 1540 to 1895;
  every item in stock is over 100 years
  old.*

John Hulot
Print World
John Sebastian Bach Str. 11
Pullach, Bavaria 82049 Germany
ph: ++49-89-79367709
fax: ++49-89-79367708
info@artelino.com
http://www.artelino.com
  *Buys, sells old and modern prints and
  antique maps; also offers an online
  auction service.*

Yasha Beresiner
InterCol Gallery
43 Templars Crescent
London, N3 3QR U.K.
ph: (00 44) 208349 2207 or (00 44)
  207354 2599
fax: (00 44) 208346 9539
yasha@compuserve.com
http://www.intercol.co.uk
  *Buys and sells world banknotes, all

playing cards, old maps, related books
on Free Masonry.*

W.D.J. Bennett
Postaprint
Taidswood House
Iver Heath, Bucks SL0 0PQ U.K.
ph: +44 1 895 833 720
fax: +44 1 895 834 890
sales@postaprint.co.uk
http://www.postaprint.co.uk
  *Antiquarian books, maps, prints,
  historic engravings, and atlases; has
  an online database of over 200,000
  antique maps, steel, copper or wood
  engravings available for searching;
  items date from 1550 to 1899; library
  of scanned images.*

Richard Nicholson
Richard Nicholson of Chester
Stoneydale, Pepper St.
Christleton
Chester, Cheshire CH3 7AG U.K.
ph: (44)(1) 244 336004
fax: (44)(1) 244 336138
richard@earlymaps.com
http://www.antiquemaps.com
  *Large selection of antique maps of the
  British Isles and other parts of the
  world.*

Atlea Maps & Books
91 Regent St., 3rd Floor
London, W1B 4EL U.K.
ph: +44 20 7494 9060
fax: +44 20 7287 7938
info@alteamaps.com
http://www.alteamaps.com
  *Specialist in antique maps and atlases
  dating from the 15th to 19th century.*

Roger Baynton-Williams
Baynton-Williams Maps & Prints
37A High St.
Arundel, West Sussex BN18 9AG U.K.
ph: (01903) 883588
baynton@btinternet.com
http://www.baynton-williams.com
  *Dealers in antiques maps and prints
  since 1946.*

Experts

Charles Neuschafer
New World Maps, Inc.
1123 South Broadway
Lake Worth, FL 33462-4522
ph: 561-586-8723
newworldmaps@prodigy.net
  *Active dealer in antique and
  collectibles maps; belongs to several
  professional map associations; writes
  a regular column on maps for "Paper
  Collectors Marketplace."*

Joke Vrijenhoek
Paulus Swaen Old Maps & Prints
P.O. Box 1238
Indian Rocks Beach, FL 33785
ph: 727-596-8734
fax: 727-596-8734
paulus@swaen.com
http://www.swaen.com
  *Buys and sells old maps; conducts
  interactive map auctions on the

Internet; offices in US and The
Netherlands.*

Derek Nichloos, Dir.
Art-Emporium
Camford Square
Corner Douglas & Dorsey Sts.
Milton, Queensland 4064 Australia
ph: +61 7 3368 2637
fax: +61 7 3368 2847
printco@art-emporium.com
http://www.art-emporium.com/maps
  *Web site with great resource
  information on identifying and
  appraising Hummel figurines.*

Internet Resources

Ashley Baynton-Williams
MapForum.com
P.O. Box 28107
London, SE6 4ZZ U.K.
MapForum@btinternet.com
http://www.mapforum.com
  *Online magazine for the antique map
  collector with articles for all levels of
  interest.*

Museums/Libraries

David Cobb
Harvard Map Collection
Harvard College Library
Cambridge, MA 02138
ph: 617-495-2417
fax: 617-496-0440
cobb@husc.harvard.edu
http://icg.harvard.edu/~maps/hpbms.htm
  *One of the largest and oldest
  collections of cartographic materials
  in the US*

James E. Hess
Heritage Map Museum
49 N. Broad St.
P.O. Box 412
Lititz, PA 17543
ph: 717-626-5002
fax: 717-626-8858
heritage@carto.com
http://www.carto.com
  *The only museum in the world
  dedicated to the 15th through 19th
  century original maps; a commercial
  enterprise, map services include
  auctioning, buying, selling, consulting
  and educational services.*

British Library Map Collection
96 Euston Rd.
London, NW1 2DB U.K.
ph: +44 171 412 7702
fax: +44 171 412 7780
maps@bl.uk
http://www.bl.uk/collections/maps
  *The Map Library provides access to
  maps, atlases and globes from all
  parts of the world dating back to the
  15th century.*

Periodicals

International Map Collectors Society (IMCoS)
Journal: IMCoS Journal
27 Landford Rd.
Putney, London SW15 1AQ U.K.
ph: +44 (0) 20 8789 7358
fax: +44 (0) 20 8788 7819
jeh@harvey27.demon.co.uk
http://www.imcos-mapcollecting.org
Members are academics, dealers and others who love old maps; members have access to important national and international map collections not normally available to the public..

Folding

Dealers

Paul Mahoney
Old Map Gallery, The
1746 Blake St.
Denver, CO 80202
ph: 303-296-7725
fax: 303-296-7725
oldmapgallery@denver.net
http://www.oldmapgallery.com
Wants atlases and folding pocket maps.

Map Related Memorabilia

Clubs/Associations

Siegfried Feller
Association of Map Memorabilia Collectors
8 Amherst Rd.
Pelham, MA 01002-9739
ph: 413-253-3115
For collectors & lovers of maps: on postcards, stamps/envelopes, postmarks/cancels, labels, fabrics, trays/plates, etc.

MARBLE & STONE

(see also LAPIDARY; MINERAL SPECIMENS; NATURAL HISTORY; SCULPTURES)

Internet Resources

Walter S. Arnold
Families of Marble
ph: 847-568-1188
fax: 847-568-1187
walter@stonecarver.com
http://www.stonecarver.com/marble.html
An amazing Web site; everything you ever wanted to know about marble; hundreds of names of marbles within family groups and accompanying images; also marble history, tools, techniques and more.

Natural-Stone.com
8711 E. Pinnacle Peak Rd.
PMB 196
Scottsdale, AZ 85255
ph: 480-502-5354
fax: 781-394-0599
info@natural-stone.com
http://www.natural-stone.com
Internet marketplace for stone products, including materials, stone giftware, semi-precious stone knobs and accent tiles, fireplaces, etc.; information about the stone industry and stone companies; restoration products, sources, etc.

Periodicals

Alex Bachrach, Pub.
Magazine: Stone World
299 Market St., 3rd Floor
Saddle Brook, NJ 07663
ph: 201-291-9001
fax: 201-291-9002
alex@stoneworld.com
http://www.stoneworld.com
The premier magazine for stone and tile related products and services; Web sites has lots of links for stone and machinery suppliers.

Alex Bachrach, Pub.
Magazine: Contemporary Stone Design
299 Market St., 3rd Floor
Saddle Brook, NJ 07663
ph: 201-291-9001
fax: 201-291-9002
alex@stoneworld.com
http://www.stoneworld.com

Repair Services

David Modine
Irwin Stone
601 East Gude Dr.
Rockville, MD 20852
ph: 301-762-5800
fax: 301-294-9726
irwinstone@aol.com
http://www.irwinstone.com
Cuts and repairs marble tops.

Ron Leatherman
Leatherman Services
509 Mairo
Austin, TX 78748
ph: 512-282-1556 or 512-799-7871
fax: 512-282-1562
ron@kdi.com
Restores marble, granite, miscellaneous stone, plaster and wood art objects, ornate picture frames, obsolete ceramic or porcelain tile; 25 years experience.

Absolute Granite & Restoration Co.
67 Hoff, Ste. B
San Francisco, CA 94110
ph: 415-437-1966
fax: 650-637-1228
http://www.datamania.com/absolutegranite
Marble fabrication and repair; specializing in the restoration of antique stone and terracotta.

MARBLES

Auction Services

Robert Block
Chip Off the Old Block, A
P.O. Box 233
Trumbull, CT 06611-0051
ph: 203-926-8448
fax: 203-261-7033
blockschip@aol.com
http://www.marblecollecting.com/chip
Largest marble auctioneer; conducts live online marble CyberAuctions several nights a week; several mail marble auctions a year; two live marble auctions a year; sells approx. 15k-20K lots of marbles each year.

Lloyd & Chris Huffer
Gold Medal Videos
Star Route C
Damascus, PA 18415
ph: 570-224-4012
fax: 570-224-6796
olmarblz@ptd.net
http://www.oldmarbles.com
Conducts twice-yearly auctions by video.

Danny & Gretchen Turner
Running Rabbit Video Auctions
P.O. Box 701
Waverly, TN 37185-0701
ph: 931-296-3600
fax: 931-296-1732
marbles@waverly.net
http://www.runningrabbit.com
Conducts marble mail auctions using VHS video tape/catalog or full color catalog. Quality marbles are shown on well-detailed 2 hr. tape. Excellent educational tool!

Clubs/Associations

Beverly Brule
Marble Collectors Unlimited
Newsletter: Marble Mart/Newsletter
P.O. Box 206
Northborough, MA 01532-0206
ph: 508-393-2923
marblesbev@aol.com
The newsletter is published for and by members of MCU; contains items of interest such as meets, auctions, member buy/sell/trade ads, etc.

Stanley Block
Marble Collectors Society of America
Newsletter: Marble Mania
P.O. Box 222
Trumbull, CT 06611-0222
ph: 203-261-3223
Stan@marblemania.com
http://www.marblemania.com
Established to gather and disseminate information and to perform services to further the hobby of marbles and marble collecting.

Jim Ridpath
National Marble Club of America
Newsletter: National Marble Club of America Newsletter
440 Eaton Rd.
Drexel Hill, PA 19026-1205
ph: 610-622-4444
To keep marble collectors informed, to encourage children to once again play the game, to advise members on all aspects of marbles including about books and publications about marbles and buying/selling marbles; offers appraisals.

Roger Dowdy
Blue Ridge Marble Club
Newsletter: Marble Circle News
2401 Brookmont Ct.
Richmond, VA 23233
ph: 804-754-8371
fax: 804-754-8379
rdowdy-cp@mindspring.com
For collectors, dealers, and shooters.

Brenda Longbrake, Sec.
Buckeye Marble Collectors Club
Newsletter: BMC Newsletter
P.O. Box 6
Franklin, OH 45005
brendal@wcoil.com
http://www.buckeyemarble.com
Active club sponsoring annual convention in Columbus, OH; newsletter contains articles, buy/sell ads, calendar of events, etc.

Larry Van Dyke
Sea-Tac Marble Collectors Club
Newsletter: Marble Monitor
P.O. Box 33611
North Las Vegas, NV 89030
ph: 702-656-1513
stmccone@mindspring.com
http://www.marbleclub.com
Holds meetings, picnics, shows in five Western states.

Sherry Ellis
California Marble Collectors Society
Newsletter: Mainly Marbles
P.O. Box 6913
San Pedro, CA 90734-6913
ph: 310-548-4906
fax: 310-833-3892
sellis9439@aol.com
Marble shows; buy, sell, trade antique and machine made marbles.

Canadian Marble Collectors Association
59 Mill St.
Milton, Ontario L9T JR8 Canada

Collectors

Beverly Brule
P.O. Box 206
Northborough, MA 01532-0206
ph: 508-393-2923
marblesbev@aol.com
Buy/sell/trade marbles and marble related items.

David & Becky Beane
Beane's Antiques & Photography
92 River Rd.
Benton, ME 04901
ph: 207-453-6790
fax: 207-453-6790
Buys, sells and trades marbles; will travel for collections.

Peter Caparelli
3528 204th St.
Bayside, NY 11361-1232
ph: 718-352-9010
fax: 707-202-1769
prc@landofmarbles.com
http://www.landofmarbles.com
Dealer, collector, expert in antique and contemporary marbles.

Jack Whistance
288 Rte. 28
Kingston, NY 12401
ph: 914-338-4397
Wants old handmade marbles: swirls, onion skins, Lutz, slags, opaques, micas, sulphides, etc.; also wants pre-1940's machine made marbles.

Yvonne Marie Holmberg
7229 Pine Island Dr., NE
Comstock Park, MI 49321-9534
ph: 616-784-1715
vonniesvault@aol.com
Serious collector of all pre-1940 glass marbles except sulphides; will buy single marble or boxful; does not buy for resale, but to add to private collection, so will pay "current book" prices.

Gary Huxford
503 West Pine St.
Marengo, IA 52301
ph: 319-642-3891

Bill Tinkcom
2406 West Madison
Sioux Falls, SD 57104
ph: 605-331-5740
Wants to buy all kinds of marbles and marble type items such as marble games and old time marble boxes or bags.

Dealers

Bertram M. Cohen
Great American Marble Co.
169 Marlborough St.
Boston, MA 02116-1830
ph: 617-247-4754
fax: 617-247-9093
marblebert@aol.com
http://www.marblebert.com
Marbles bought and sold, especially "art glass" marbles; also wants postcards showing children playing with marbles; organizes the Northeast Marble Meet in October of each year.

Bill Sweet
14 Diana Dr.
P.O. Box 4736
Rumford, RI 02916-0736
ph: 401-434-4548
Marble dealer, collector and appraiser.

Jerry Biern
Rare Marbles, etc.
65 Crest Dr.
Cranston, RI 02921-3313
ph: 401-826-3933
fax: 401-826-4460
raremarble@aol.com
Buys and sells rare, antique marbles; free appraisals backed with data from previous sales.

Ardyth & John Stimson
AJS Marbles & Records
P.O. Box 8052
Glen Ridge, NJ 07028
Buys, sells, collects machine-made or antique marbles; will trade, buy or sell; also deals in old records, especially jazz, R&B, 33/45/78 rpm.

Charles Eson
Hawkeye Collectibles
128 Western Ave.
Altamont, NY 12009-6230
ph: 518-861-6256
hawkphil2@aol.com
Buys and sells antique and machine made collectible marbles; also sells selected contemporary handmade marbles.

Bill Blair
Blair Collectibles
P.O. Box 655
Pine Hill, NY 12465
ph: 845-254-4717
blaircol@aol.com
http://www.collectoronline.com/booths/booth-50
Buys, sells, appraises marbles of all types, especially machine-made marbles from the 1930s to present and handmade marbles from 1870 to 1915.

Gloria Munsell
Allenwood Americana Antiques
P.O. Box 116
Allenwood, PA 17810-0116
ph: 570-538-1440 or 570-538-1932
fax: 570-538-1932
kwkipp@ptd.net
Buying and selling marbles and marble games, etc.

Elliot Pincus
Elliot's Marbles
P.O. Box C
Jenkintown, PA 19046
ph: 215-886-7421

Alan Zimmerman
Marvelous Marbles
20940-C Frederick Rd.
Germantown, MD 20876
alan_zimmerman@hotmail.com
http://www.marblecollector.com
Handmade marbles, fakes, Peltier, Akro Agate, grading marbles, marble

identification, Marble King, machine made marbles, Christensen, contemporary marbles, etc.

B. Alan Basinet
Alan's Marble Connection
ph: 904-389-2713
Marblealan@aol.com
http://www.marblealan.com
Web site offers 1,000 antique, collectible, and contemporary marbles for sale, along with marble collecting supplies; comprehensive identification guide, message board, consignment services, and more.

Wayne E. Sanders
2202 Livingston St.
Jefferson City, MO 65109-0850
ph: 573-636-7515
Buys, sells and collect antique handmade marbles and collectible machine-made marbles; no contemporary marbles; looking for single ribbon cores, clouds and unusual or colored figure sulphides.

Michael A. Pratt, Sr.
Marble Emporium, The
512 North Spruce St.
Valley, NE 68064-9670
ph: 402-359-5539
fax: 402-359-5539
sales@usadisplay.net
http://www.usadisplay.net
Buys and sells marbles of all kinds; also sells display cases for cuff links and collectibles of all types.

Steve Gorin
Collectmarbles.com
2592 Caballo Ranchero
P.O. Box 773
Diablo, CA 94528
ph: 925-837-8445
marblemania@aol.com
http://www.collectmarbles.com
Appraises, buys and sells antique collectible marbles.

Experts

Robert Block
Chip Off the Old Block, A
P.O. Box 233
Trumbull, CT 06611-0051
ph: 203-926-8448
fax: 203-261-7033
blockschip@aol.com
http://www.marblecollecting.com
Buys, sells, and specializes in marbles; experts on identification and valuation of marbles; Web site has tons of information about marbles.

Cathy C. Runyan
Marble Lady, The
7812 N.W. Hampton Rd.
Kansas City, MO 64152-4940
ph: 816-587-8687 or 816-587-1203
fax: 816-587-8687
marbleldy@aol.com
Author of "Knuckles Down - A Fun Guide to Marble Play;" helps people identify & value their marbles; also teaches, demonstrates & lectures about marbles and marble playing;

interested in handmades, machine made, and marble memorabilia.

Larry Castle
Castle Fair
3387 Polk Ave.
Ogden, UT 84403
ph: 801-393-8131
antiquemarbles@msn.com
Advanced collector and nationally recognized expert with over 10 years experience with marbles; buys, appraises and repairs marbles.

Larry Van Dyke
P.O. Box 33611
North Las Vegas, NV 89030
ph: 702-656-1513
stmccone@mindspring.com
http://www.marbleclub.com
Marble collector, dealer, appraiser and expert.

Internet Resources

Robert Block
MarbleCollecting.com
P.O. Box 233
Trumbull, CT 06611-0051
ph: 203-926-8448
fax: 203-261-7033
blockschip@aol.com
http://www.marblecollecting.com
Largest Web site for anyone who is interested in marble collecting, marble making or marble playing; tons of information.

Peter Caparelli
LandofMarbles.com
E-zine: Marbleous News
3528 204th St.
Bayside, NY 11361-1232
ph: 718-352-9010
fax: 707-202-1769
prc@landofmarbles.com
http://www.landofmarbles.com
Web site is a hub of information for marble collectors: tips, clubs, marble sales, community bulletin board (learn, chat, free ID help).

Marble Museum
491 Chicago Dr.
Holland, MI 49423
ph: 616-396-1249
http://www.macatawa.org/~rlo
Photo museum, links, and more.

Museums/Libraries

Chris Cooper
Marble Museum, Inc., The
P.O. Box 1093
Yreka, CA 96097
marblemuseum@marblemuseum.org
http://www.marblemuseum.org
Dedicated to the collection, education and preservation of art glass marbles, historical marbles and related articles and documentation for the public benefit; promotes the art, history and game.

Repair Services

Larry Castle
Castle Fair
3387 Polk Ave.
Ogden, UT 84403
ph: 801-393-8131
antiquemarbles@msn.com
Restores and regrinds glass marbles; over ten years experience and more that 6,000 marbles restored.

Suppliers

Michael Cosentino
Marble Show-Case
6936 N. Overhill Ave.
Chicago, IL 60631
fax: 773-594-9479
mikecoz@mc.net
http://www.marbleshowcase.com
Sells display cases for marbles and other small collectibles; also sells and appraises marbles.

Michael A. Pratt, Sr.
Marble Emporium, The
512 North Spruce St.
Valley, NE 68064-9670
ph: 402-359-5539
fax: 402-359-5539
sales@usadisplay.net
http://www.usadisplay.net
Manufactures unique inexpensive cases to display, organize, and protect small collectibles of all types including marbles; send SASE for more information.

MARDI GRAS ITEMS

Collectors

Derek Franklin
2737 Canal St.
New Orleans, LA 70119
ph: 504-482-9869 or 504-522-9959
fax: 504-524-9027
Wants Mardi Gras memorabilia: Rex, Comus, Momus, Proteus Ball invitations, photos, admit cards, dance cards, envelopes, stereoviews, postcards, medals, pins, favors, carnival bulletins, newspaper foldouts, float designs; 1870s to 1940s.

Michael Reese II
P.O. Box 5704
South San Francisco, CA 94083-5704
ph: 415-641-5920
creole@shutmymouth.com
http://www.shutmymouth.com
Wants anything relating to New Orleans and Mardi Gras: invitations, medals, call out gifts, etc.

New Orleans

Collectors

Marilyn & Celeste Bordelon
1750 St. Charles Ave., Ste. 303
New Orleans, LA 70130
ph: 504-596-6550 or 504-897-2603
marilyn@enochsframing.com
http://www.enochsframing.com
Wants to buy pre-1950 New Orleans

Mardi Gras items: ball invitations, dance cards, admit, newspaper print of floats, carnival bulletins, programs, pendants, pins, buttons, favors, postcards, medal or rhinestone badges.

Experts

Arthur Hardy
Arthur Hardy Enterprises, Inc.
602 Metairie Rd., Ste. C
Metairie, LA 70005-4009
ph: 504-838-6111
fax: 504-838-0100
mardihardy@aol.com
http://mardigrasneworleans.com/arthur
Buys, collects and specializes in Mardi Gras memorabilia such as ball invitations, postcards, carnival bulletins (parade papers), photos, illustrated feature articles, brochures, etc.; author of the annual "Mardi Gras Guide."

Museums/Libraries

Mardi Gras World
23 Newton St.
New Orleans, LA 70114
ph: 504-361-7821 or 800-362-8213
briankern@mardigrasworld.com
http://www.mardigrasworld.com

Periodicals

Arthur Hardy
Arthur Hardy Enterprises, Inc.
Magazine: Arthur Hardy's Mardi Gras Guide
602 Metairie Rd., Ste. C
Metairie, LA 70005-4009
ph: 504-838-6111
fax: 504-838-0100
mardihardy@aol.com
http://mardigrasneworleans.com/arthur
Published annually on December 31st: Mardi Gras history, stories about collectibles, interviews, parade routes, etc.

Arthur Hardy
Arthur Hardy Enterprises, Inc.
Newsletter: Arthur Hardy's Carnival Times Newsletter
602 Metairie Rd., Ste. C
Metairie, LA 70005-4009
ph: 504-838-6111
fax: 504-838-0100
mardihardy@aol.com
http://mardigrasneworleans.com/arthur

MARINE ARTIFACTS

(see NAUTICAL ANTIQUES)

MARINE CORPS ITEMS

Collectors

Dick Weisler
53-07 213th St.
Flushing, NY 11364-1823
ph: 718-428-9829 or 718-626-7110
fax: 718-726-2011
Wants Marine Corps related recruiting posters, sheet music, belt

buckles, cigarette lighters, steins, trucks, toy soldiers, documents, trench art, etc.

Stan Clark
Stan Clark Military Books
915 Fairview Ave.
Gettysburg, PA 17325-2905
ph: 717-337-1728
fax: 717-337-0581
Wants Marine Corps items: books (unit histories, memoirs, campaigns, etc.), postcards, tapestries, recruiting, letters, documents, embroideries, prints, photographs, scrap books, toy soldiers, etc.

Bruce Updegrove
52 Woodside Lane
Boyertown, PA 19512-8479
ph: 610-369-1798
Interested in pre-1946 Marine Corps items; also wants any women's uniforms of WWII.

LtCol J.K. Williams, USMC (Ret'd.)
6025 Makely Dr.
Fairfax Station, VA 22039-1324
ph: 703-250-8421 or 202-371-8880
fax: 202-371-8258
mudmarine5@aol.com
Wants US Marine Corps WWI-era recruiting posters, photos, bus/trolley cards, tin signs, brochures, advertisements, etc.

Harold Dylhoff
23511 Paulson's Rd.
Gobles, MI 49055-8651
ph: 269-628-4051
hdylxrds@aol.com
Wants to buy letters and postal history from US Marine Corp (WWI through WWII), including postmarks from bases, camps and other locations; send photocopies and LSASE for reply.

Frank Anguiano, III
214 Medicine Bow Trail
Del Rio, TX 78840
ph: 830-778-1825
Wants any WWI 4th Marine Brigade items: uniforms with Indian-head patches, helmets, EGA devices, 2nd Division citations, French Croix de Guerre citations, medals/medal groups, Occupation pillow cases, photographs, Marine documents, etc.

MARIONETTES

(see PUPPETS)

MARITIME ANTIQUES

(see NAUTICAL ANTIQUES)

MASCOTS

(see AUTOMOBILIA, Hood Ornaments)

MATCH SAFES

(see also CIGARETTE COLLECTIBLES; CIGAR STORE COLLECTIBLES; LIGHTERS; MATCHBOXES & LABELS; MATCHCOVERS; TOBACCO COLLECTIBLES)

Appraisers

George Sparacio
P.O. Box 791
Malaga, NJ 08328-0791
ph: 856-694-4167
fax: 856-694-4536
mrvesta1@aol.com
http://members.aol.com/mrvesta2
Appraises, buys, sells and trades pocket match safes; especially interested in fancy, figural and unusual match safes; also interested in pre-1915 match safe related catalogs, advertisements and ephemera; will answer all correspondence.

Clubs/Associations

George Sparacio
International Match Safe Association
Newsletter: IMSA Newsletter
P.O. Box 791
Malaga, NJ 08328-0791
ph: 856-694-4167
fax: 856-694-4536
IMSAoc@aol.com
http://www.matchsafe.org
Focuses on pocket match safes; newsletter published quarterly; annual meetings featuring buying/selling session, information and networking opportunities.

Dealers

George Sparacio
P.O. Box 791
Malaga, NJ 08328-0791
ph: 856-694-4167
fax: 856-694-4536
mrvesta1@aol.com
http://members.aol.com/mrvesta2
Appraises, buys, sells and trades pocket match safes; especially interested in fancy, figural and unusual match safes; also interested in pre-1915 match safe related catalogs, advertisements and ephemera; will answer all correspondence.

Lenore Monleon
33 Fifth Ave.
New York, NY 10003-4338
ph: 212-475-7871 or 212-675-7771
Wants enamel and sterling match safes and cigarette boxes.

MATCHBOOKS

(see MATCHCOVERS)

MATCHBOXES

(see also MATCHCOVERS; MATCH SAFES; TOYS, Diecast [Matchbox])

Clubs/Associations

Linda Clavette
New Moon Matchbox & Label Club
Newsletter: New Moon News
13 Creekstone Dr.
Mont Alto, PA 17237
Newsletter is published 5 times per year.

Collectors

Stanislav Dmitriev
11-42 Segezhskaya St.
Petrozavodsk, Karelia 185033 Russia
ph: +7(8142) 52357
fax: +1(443) 9470697
stasdm@onego.ru
http://phillumeny.onego.ru
Collects matchbox labels, matchboxes and matchcovers.

Internet Resources

Mogens Rasmussen
Privat
Aebleparken 66-2
Odense, Fyn 5270 Denmark
mlrdk@hotmail.com
http://www.phillumenie.dk
An Internet site for and about the collecting of matchboxes; no buying or selling.

MATCHCOVERS

(see also MATCHBOXES; MATCH
SAFES; PAPER COLLECTIBLES)

Clubs/Associations

Janet Penny
Liberty Bell Matchcover Club
Newsletter: Liberty Bell Crier
2501 Maryland Ave., #7
Willow Grove, PA 19090-1835
http://groups.yahoo.com/group/
libertybellmatchcoverclub
Members are interested in the collecting of matchcovers & matchboxes; hosts annual national convention; holds shows, auctions, bi-monthly meetings with displays and trading.

Bill Retskin
American Matchcover Collecting Club
E-zine: Front Striker Bulletin, The
P.O. Box 18481
Asheville, NC 28814-0481
ph: 828-254-4487
bill@matchcovers.com
http://www.matchcovers.com
Devoted to the study and collecting of older matchcovers; the publication includes a matchcover mail auction and covers history and current status of the matchbook industry as well as the matchcover collecting hobby.

Mark J. Quilling
Great Lakes Match Club
Newsletter: Phillumenator, The
1000 Edgerton St., #1313
Saint Paul, MN 55101-3958
ph: 651-772-9398
markmatch@isd.net
One of over 30 regional match collecting clubs that promotes the hobby of collecting matchbooks, matchboxes, matchcovers and other match-related items; based in the Twin Cities area; meets on a monthly basis; bi-monthly bulletin.

Nancy Bailey
Angelus Matchcover Club
1231 Edmund Ave.
Saint Paul, MN 55104
sjbnab@aol.com
Publishes bi-monthly newsletter.

Annie Johnson
Windy City Matchcover Club
Newsletter: Windy City Matchcover
News
1307 College Ave., Apt. 12
Wheaton, IL 60187
Ltlb1t@aol.com
Editor of the Badger State Matchcover Club (Wisconsin) newsletter.

Emily Hiller, Treas.
Long Beach Matchcover Club
Newsletter: Matchcover Beachcomber
2501 West Sunflower, H-5
Santa Ana, CA 92704-7503
ph: 714-540-8220
fax: 714-751-2750

Mike Prero
Sierra-Diablo Matchcover Club
12659 Echard Way
Auburn, CA 95603
fax: 978-389-0396
Rmseditor@ev1.net
http://www.matchcover.org/sierra
Second largest regional matchcover club in the country; monthly color newsletter.

Mike Prero, Ed.
Rathkamp Matchcover Society
Newsletter: RMS Bulletin
12659 Eckard Way
Auburn, CA 95603
rmseditor@ev1.net
http://www.matchcover.org
Membership is open to all matchcover and matchbox collectors; annual convention, six bulletins per year, tips, list of local clubs, Web page ads.

Pacific Northwest Matchcover Collector's
Club
6225 SW Mad Hatter Lane
Beaverton, WA 97008-8547
rescorpion@aol.com
http://home1.gte.net/res0c4r5/
pnmcc.html
Membership is open to all collectors of matchcovers, matchboxes, and matchbooks.

Bill Ryan
Sydney Phillumenist Club
14 Weston Ave.
Narwee, New South Wales 2209
Australia
ph: 612 915 36672
fax: 612 915 36672
bryan@tpgi.com
Members collects anything related to matches.

Arthur Alderton, Mem.
British Matchbox Label & Booklet
Society
122 High St.
Melbourn, Cambridgeshire SG8 6AL
U.K.
http://enterprise.hb.se/~match/bml&bs/
new

Collectors

Joe DeGennaro
309 East 87th St., Apt. 6E
New York, NY 10128
ph: 212-975-4108
fax: 212-975-8424
jtdegennaro@cbs.com
Matchcover and matchbox collector for over thirty years; collection consists of over 100,000 covers and boxes in many categories; past president of the Rathkamp Matchcover Society.

Marc Edelman
8822 Hargrave St.
Philadelphia, PA 19152-1511
ph: 215-969-6258

Mike Landis
P.O. Box 814
Adamstown, PA 19501
ph: 888-248-2291
landis2@ptd.net
Buys and sells matchcovers; full books and especially feature matches; call toll free.

John C. Williams
1359 Surrey Rd., Dept. CH
Vandalia, OH 45377-1646
ph: 937-890-8684
Matchcover collector and expert; member of the Rathkamp Matchcover Society.

Mark J. Quilling
1000 Edgerton St., #1313
Saint Paul, MN 55101-3958
ph: 651-772-9398
markmatch@isd.net
http://home.thirdage.com/collections/
matchsite/index.html
Collecting matchcovers for over 25 years; very knowledgeable on the subject and has excellent reference resources available if needed.

Charles Specht
2306 Belmore Dr.
Champaign, IL 61821-6263
ph: 217-356-3176
charlesspecht@hotmail.com
Collects, trades, sells matchcovers, matchboxes and related material.

Charles E. Eberhart
Lead Cannon, The
3616 Seward
Topeka, KS 66616-1652
ph: 785-235-1016
Wants to buy match book covers relating to military and those showing Kansas towns.

Dean Hodgdon
2920 E. 77th St.
Tulsa, OK 74136-8723
ph: 918-494-0225 or 918-582-9918
d.hodgdon@worldnet.att.net

Susan Cox
800 Murray Dr.
El Cajon, CA 92020
ph: 619-697-5922
antiqfever@aol.com
Wants to buy matches, book type, old only; matches inside, unused and boxes a plus; good condition.

Mike Prero
Vault, The
12659 Eckard Way
Auburn, CA 95603-3516
rmseditor@ev1.net
http://users.ev1.net/~rmseditor
Editor for three hobby publications; collects matchcovers from around the world; Web site is a resource for matchcover collectors.

Richard W. Lauck
6225 SW Mad Hatter Lane
Beaverton, WA 97008-8547
res0c4r5@verizon.net
Wants to buy 1930s to 1950s matchcovers and matchbooks.

Bill Ryan
14 Weston Ave.
Narwee, New South Wales 2209
Australia
ph: 612 915 36672
fax: 612 915 36672
bryan@tpgi.com
Collects anything related to matches; specialty includes the topics Sweden, China, India, Australia, trees, sea, air, land, travel.

Stanislav Dmitriev
11-42 Segezhskaya St.
Petrozavodsk, Karelia 185033 Russia
ph: +7(8142) 52357
fax: +1(443) 9470697
stasdm@onego.ru
http://phillumeny.onego.ru
Collects matchbox labels, matchboxes and matchcovers.

Dealers

Charles Rabinovitz
Cinderella Co.
P.O. Box 265
Sykesville, MD 21784-0265
ph: 410-549-2412
fax: 410-795-8936
chuckrab@aol.com
Wants to buy poster stamps, matchcovers, matchbox labels, baggage labels.

Experts

Bill Retskin
P.O. Box 18481
Asheville, NC 28814-0481
ph: 828-254-4487
bill@matchcovers.com
http://www.matchcovers.com
*Author of "The Matchcover Resource
Book and Price Guide," and "The
Matchcover Collectors Price Guide,"
1st and 2d editions.*

Wray Martin
221 Upper Paradise
Hamilton, Ontario L9C 5C1 Canada
ph: 905-383-0454
lwmartin@mountaincable.net
*Buys, trades matchbooks in the
categories of transportation, military,
sports, covers advertising a product
rather than a service; prefers older
unused covers, but will consider all.*

Internet Resources

Mike Prero
Vault, The
12659 Eckard Way
Auburn, CA 95603-3516
rmseditor@ev1.net
http://users.ev1.net/~rmseditor
*Editor for three hobby publications;
collects matchcovers from around the
world; Web site is a resource for
matchcover collectors.*

Stanislav Dmitriev
Virtual Matchbox Labels Collectors Club
11-42 Segezhskaya St.
Petrozavodsk, Karelia 185033 Russia
ph: +7(8142) 52357
fax: +1(443) 9470697
stasdm@onego.ru
http://phillumeny.onego.ru/collect.html
*A site for sharing information
amongst those interested in phillumeny
(the collecting of matchcovers,
lighters, matchboxes, matchbox
labels).*

Casino

Clubs/Associations

Richard D. Hagerman
Casino Matchcover Collectors Club
Newsletter: Gambling Gazette
824 Peachy Canyon Cir., #101
Mount Laurel, NJ 89144-0907
ph: 702-243-9340
*Members are dedicated to the
collection of all casino and gaming
establishment matchbooks and
matchboxes which are displayed and
traded at regular meetings throughout
the US and Canada; bi-monthly
newsletter.*

Collectors

Richard D. Hagerman
824 Peachy Canyon Cir., #101
Mount Laurel, NJ 89144-0907
ph: 702-243-9340
*Collects casino matchcovers,
matchboxes; also wants those from
older Atlantic City hotels, restaurants*

*and businesses; also general
matchcovers and matchboxes.*

MATCHING SERVICES

(see DINNERWARE; FLATWARE;
GLASS, Elegant; GLASS, Crystal)

MAYTAG

(see also WASHING MACHINES)

Clubs/Associations

Mark A. Shulaw
Maytag Collectors Club Eastern Division
452 County Rd. 33
Bluffton, OH 45817-9601
ph: 419-358-5206
frappi@wcoil.com
http://www.maytagclub.com
*A chapter of the national Maytag
Collectors Club; dedicated to the
preservation and restoration of all
types of Maytag items, anything built
by Maytag.*

Nate & Charlene Stoller
Maytag Collectors Club
Newsletter: Maytag Collectors Club
Newsletter
960 Reynolds Dr.
Ripon, CA 95366
ph: 530-676-1000
nate@maytagclub.com
http://www.maytagclub.com
*Over 250 members nationwide
collecting all types of Maytag items;
lots of ads for Maytag engines, meat
grinders, washers, new and used
parts, gaskets, replacement decals, etc.*

Collectors

Tom Copper
Tom's Small Engines
1416 Ralapen St.
Roxboro, NC 27573-4232
ph: 336-599-6908
tcopper@person.net
http://members.person.net/~tcopper/
index.html
*Collector of Maytag, Briggs &
Stratton and other engines; repairs,
rebuilds, and restores most small
engines; locates parts and/or related
supplies and services.*

Dealers

Mark A. Shulaw
452 County Rd. 33
Bluffton, OH 45817-9601
ph: 419-358-5206
frappi@wcoil.com
*Buying anything Maytag: cans,
engines, washer accessories,
literature, tools, new old stock and
used engine parts, promotional items,
almost anything that is Maytag; will
answer questions; please send SASE
with inquiries.*

Man./Prod./Dist.

Orville Butler, Hist.
Maytag Company Archives
403 West Fourth St. N.
Newton, IA 50208
ph: 641-792-7000
fax: 641-791-8376
*Private company archives include
paper artifacts, production records,
old catalogs; will help identify or date
your Maytag machine.*

Museums/Libraries

Hans J. Brosig, Dir.
Maytag Exhibit, Jasper County
Historical Museum
1700 South 15th Ave. West
P.O. Box 834
Newton, IA 50208-0834
ph: 641-792-9118
jascomus@netins.net
http://www.jaspercountymuseum.org
*A museum about Jasper County, Iowa;
contains a large artifact collection of
the Maytag Company: washing
machines, seed cleaners, ironers,
dryers, advertising & promotional
items.*

Suppliers

Simpson Motors
3708 S. Amherst Hwy.
Madison Heights, VA 24572
ph: 804-929-4468
*New and used Maytag engine parts,
restoration supplies, engines, etc.;
rebuild, restore, supply parts for early
gasoline engines that powered early
washing machines; no appliance
parts; makes parts not otherwise
available.*

MEDALLIC SCULPTURES

(see also MEDALS, ORDERS &
DECORATIONS; SCULPTURES)

Clubs/Associations

American Medallic Sculpture Association
Newsletter: Members Exchange
56 North Plant Rd., Ste. 1-685
Newburgh, NY 12550
info@amsamedals.org
http://www.amsamedals.org
*A group of sculptors, collectors,
suppliers, producers and scholars
interested in high relief medallic
sculptures; annual exhibitions;
newsletter published bi-monthly,
"Medallic Sculpture" magazine
published annually.*

MEDALS

(see BADGES; COINS &
CURRENCY; MEDALS, ORDERS &
DECORATIONS; MILITARIA,
Insignia; RELIGIOUS
COLLECTIBLES; TOKENS;
VETERAN ITEMS)

MEDALS, ORDERS & DECORATIONS

(see also HISTORICAL AMERICANA;
MEDALLIC SCULPTURES;
VETERAN ITEMS; MILITARIA;
MILITARIA, Russian; TOKENS)

Auction Services

Lawrence Stack
Stack's Coin Galleries
123 West 57th St.
New York, NY 10019-2280
ph: 212-582-2580
fax: 212-245-5018
info@stacks.com
http://www.stacks.com
*Specializes in the auctions of coins,
medals, tokens, silver, paper currency.*

David M. Gale
C & D Gale
2404 Berwyn Rd.
Wilmington, DE 19810-3525
ph: 302-478-0872
fax: 302-478-6866
cdgale@dol.net
http://www.cdgale.com/catalog/
exonumia.htm
*Conducts mail bid auctions of medals,
tokens, religious items, trade checks,
miscellaneous items, Civil War tokens
and other exonumia; issues fixed-price
exonumia catalogs.*

Jeffrey B. Floyd
Floyd, Johnson & Paine, Inc.
P.O. Box 9791
Alexandria, VA 22304-0469
ph: 703-461-9582
fax: 703-461-3059
fjp4floyd@aol.com
http://www.FJPauction.com
*Conducts four sales per year of
orders, medals and decorations.*

H. Joseph Levine
Presidential Coin & Antique Co. Inc.
6550-I Little River Turnpike
Alexandria, VA 22312
ph: 703-354-5454
fax: 703-914-0547
JLevine968@aol.com
*Conducts periodic auctions of
Presidential and other medals,
badges, decorations, tokens, World's
Fair and other exonumia,*

Floyd, Johnson & Paine, Inc.
P.O. Box 34679
Chicago, IL 60634
ph: 703-461-9582
fax: 703-461-3059
mail@fjpauction.com
http://www.fjpauction.com
*Conducts four sales per year of
orders, medals and decorations.*

Rich Hartzog
World Exonumia
P.O. Box 4143CNZ
Rockford, IL 61110-0643
ph: 815-226-0771
hartzog@exonumia.com
http://www.exonumia.com
Pre-1940 items preferred; collections and quantities wanted.

Roy Butler
Wallis & Wallis
West St. Auction Galleries
Lewes, East Sussex BN7 2NJ U.K.
ph: 01273-480208
fax: 01273-476562
wallisandwallis@mcmail.com
http://www.wallisandwallis.co.uk
Britain's specialist auctioneers of arms, armor, militaria and military orders.

Julia Walker
Spink & Son, Ltd.
69 Southampton Row
Bloomsbury
London, WC1B 4ET U.K.
ph: +44 (0) 20 7563 4000
fax: +44 (0) 20 7563 4066
info@spinkandson.com
http://www.spink-online.com
Auctioneers and dealers of coins (ancient to present), banknotes, medals, orders, tokens, decorations and other numismatic items; also stamps and postal history as well as fine European, Indian and Islamic art.

Clubs/Associations

Dr. Ute Wartenberg, Ex. Dir.
American Numismatic Society, The
Magazine: American Numismatic Society Magazine, The
Broadway at 155th St.
New York, NY 10032
ph: 212-234-3130
fax: 212-234-3381
info@amnumsoc.org
http://www.amnumsoc.org
Has a major collection of American coins in addition to major and important collections of ancient, Latin American, Islamic, European, and other material; also publishes "American Journal of Numismatics" and "Numismatic Literature."

Token & Medal Society
Journal: Token & Medal Society Journal
5224 West SR 46, #408
Sanford, FL 32771-9230
mlighter@bellsouth.net
http://www.angelfire.com/id/TAMS/index.html
Promotes and stimulates "exonumia," the study of non-government issue tokens and medals; an organization of collectors and researchers of tokens, medals and related items.

Christopher Cipoletti, Ex. Dir.
American Numismatic Association
Magazine: Numismatist, The
818 N. Cascade Ave.
Colorado Springs, CO 80903-3279
ph: 719-632-2646 or 800-367-9723
fax: 719-634-4085
ana@money.org
http://www.money.org
Worldwide nonprofit assoc. chartered by US Congress to promote the study and collection of money including coins, tokens, paper currency, for research, interpretation, preservation of history and culture from ancient time to present.

Cameron Ward
Canadian Society of Military Medals & Insignia
Journal: Journal, The
64 Edgemont St. South
Hamilton, Ontario L8K 2H5 Canada
ph: 905-547-1815 or 905-547-8293

Peter Helmore, Gen. Sec.
Orders & Medals Research Society
P.O. Box 1904
Southam, CV47 2ZX U.K.
phil@ihug.co.nz
http://homepages.ihug.co.nz/~phil/omrs.htm
Promotes and fosters a general interest in the study of orders, decorations and medals and all matter related thereto; assists members in their researches.

Collectors

Stanley Steinberg
P.O. Box 2219
Salem, NH 03079-1154
Wants tokens and all engraved awards and medals: military, political, merchant advertising, agriculture, schools & colleges, historical, city and town, associations, expositions, lifesaving awards, etc.

Dr. Paul Rohe
P.O. Box 122
Martinville, NJ 08336-0122

Howard Averbach
1919 Delaware Ave.
Pittsburgh, PA 15218-1801
ph: 412-441-6904
Wants to buy quality US Military campaign medals and decorations; no reproductions; send photos and asking price.

David Schwind
ForValor.com Military Historical Research
9 Sonneborn Lane
Severna Park, MD 21146
ph: 410-757-1131
dave@forvalor.com
http://www.forvalor.com
Collecting and researching Soviet medals and orders since 1991; can assist new collectors with starting their collection, as well as add new items to advanced collections; can also

assist with researching Soviet awards and preservation.

Mark Piersall
mark@marksmedals.com
http://www.marksmedals.com
Collector of military medals specializing in all periods of Romanian and US medals.

Rickie Marquette
P.O. Box 343133
Homestead, FL 33034
ph: 305-246-5431 or 305-245-2323
fax: 305-245-9295
rangerson@aol.com
Wants to buy American medals and orders, especially named and/or numbered pieces, valor awards, and Southern Crosses of Honor.

Jerome Schaeper, Jr.
365 Meadowlark Dr.
Edgewood, KY 41018-2608
ph: 859-341-3769
Collects, appraises United Confederate reunion badges, WWI homecoming medals and Civil War dog tags.

Alan Harrow
2292 Chelan Dr.
Los Angeles, CA 90068-2621
ph: 323-874-3474
genoff@webtv.net
Primarily interested in military campaign and gallantry medals of most countries, especially US and Great Britain, as well as related documents; also wants civilian medals for heroism.

Dealers

Peter Hlinka
Peter Hlinka Historical Americana
P.O. Box 310
New York, NY 10028-0017
ph: 718-409-6407
Buys, sells, and appraises historical Americana; publishes a large catalog of militaria, war medals, military insignia, war relics, related books, and other historical Americana; also foreign.

Medals of America
1929 Fairview Rd.
Fountain Inn, SC 29644
ph: 800-308-0849
medals@usmedals.com
http://www.usmedals.com
One of America's largest insignia dealers: all US military badges, medals, patches, and books; publishes an annual catalog of items for sale.

Steve Johnson
Steve Johnson Medals & Militaria
P.O. Box 4706
Aurora, IL 60507
ph: 630-851-0744
fax: 630-851-0866
Large dealer; issues 3 to 4 catalogs per year.

Dan Farek
P.O. Box 1212
Bellaire, TX 77402-1212
ph: 713-666-2629
fax: 713-666-2629
Dealer in military medals of the world; issues list of items for sale for $8/yr.; sample list $1.

Sydney Vernon
P.O. Box 890280
Temecula, CA 92589-0280
ph: 909-698-1646
fax: 909-698-7091
svernon@inland.net
http://home.earthlink.net/~svernon
Dealer in orders, medals & decorations since 1967; offers hundreds of items, including books, in mail order sales catalogs 3 to 4 times each year.

Michael Rice
Michael Rice Collectibles
P.O. Box 286
Saanichton, British Columbia V8M 2C5 Canada
ph: 250-652-9412
fax: 250-652-7866
mrice@pacificcoast.net
Wants pre-1946 medals and badges from all English speaking countries; military (except US), fraternal, sports, academic, memberships, etc.; approvals or photocopies welcome; will make offer; send 2 stamps to ensure reply; call after 6 PST.

Eugene G. Ursual
Eugene G. Ursual, Military Antiquarian, Inc.
P.O. Box 788
Kemptville, Ontario K0G 1J0 Canada
ph: 613-258-5999
fax: 613-258-9118
egu@magma.ca
http://www.medalsofwar.com
British & Canadian groups, medals for gallantry and distinguished service, single British campaign medals, British Orders, LSGC medals, Coronations and Jubilees. medals of the US and of the world.

John F. Williams
Southern Medals
P.O. Box 50
Knebworth, Herts. SG3 6UE U.K.
ph: 01438 811657
fax: 01438 813320
smedalsJ@aol.com
http://www.southernmedals.co.uk
Buys and sells medals, orders and decorations: campaign, gallantry, casualty, long service, miniatures, WWI, WWII, foreign.

Jamie Cross
Jamie Cross Militaria
P.O. Box 73
Newmarket, Suffolk CB8 8RY U.K.
ph: (0) 1638 750132
fax: (0) 1638 750132
Jamiecross@aol.com
http://www.thirdreichmedals.com
Appraiser, expert, dealer buys and

sells original Third Reich orders, medals and badges; also Imperial German, British WWI and WWII medals, and foreign awards and decorations; writes for magazines on the subject of Third Reich awards.

Experts

Jeffrey B. Floyd
P.O. Box 9791
Alexandria, VA 22304-0469
ph: 703-461-9582
fax: 703-461-3059
fjp4floyd@aol.com
http://www.FJPauction.com
Buys, sells, trades, specializes in all military medals & decorations; specializing in Imperial German, British and American awards; all periods.

Edward J. Emering
Emering Companies, LLC, The
414 North Orleans, Ste. 205
Chicago, IL 60610
ejemering@aol.com
http://www.emering.com/medals
Medal collector, appraiser, book author and columnist; specializes in Communist Vietnam, Royal Cambodia, Royal Laos, French Colonial, former French Colonies, Spain, Persian Gulf War, Peace keeping in former Yugoslavia, current Afghanistan.

Sydney Vernon
P.O. Box 890280
Temecula, CA 92589-0280
ph: 909-698-1646
fax: 909-698-7091
svernon@inland.net
http://home.earthlink.net/~svernon
Author of "Vernon's Collectors' Guide to Orders, Medals & Decorations (with valuations," and "The Medal Collector's Companion."

Jamie Cross
Jamie Cross Militaria
P.O. Box 73
Newmarket, Suffolk CB8 8RY U.K.
ph: (0) 1638 750132
fax: (0) 1638 750132
Jamiecross@aol.com
http://www.thirdreichmedals.com
Appraiser, expert, dealer buys and sells original Third Reich orders, medals and badges; also Imperial German, British WWI and WWII medals, and foreign awards and decorations; writes for magazines on the subject of Third Reich awards.

Museums/Libraries

Museum of the American Numismatic Association
Magazine: Numismatist, The
818 N. Cascade Ave.
Colorado Springs, CO 80903-3279
ph: 719-632-2646 or 800-367-9723
fax: 719-634-4085
ana@money.org
http://www.money.org
A museum collection including

400,000 items; collection includes medals, orders and decorations from all countries and time periods.

John Langton, Jr.
Military Medal Museum & Research Center
448 N. San Pedro St.
San Jose, CA 95110-2232
ph: 408-298-1100
Send for free "History of the U.S.S. Washington" of WWII fame.

Periodicals

Token Publishing, Ltd.
Magazine: Medal News
Orchard House
Duchy Rd., Heathpark
Honiton, Devon EX14 1YD U.K.
ph: +44 1404 46972
fax: +44 1404 44788
info@medal-news.com
http://www.medal-news.com
A monthly English publication focusing on military history, medals, and badge collecting.

Medal of Honor

Clubs/Associations

Congressional Medal of Honor Society, The
40 Patriots Point Rd.
Mount Pleasant, SC 29464
ph: 843-884-8662
fax: 843-884-1471
medalhq@earthlink.net
http://www.cmohs.org
It is illegal to buy or sell the Congressional Medal of Honor. The Mission of the Society is to protect the name of the Medal and the individual recipients from exploitation, and to preserve the dignity and honor of the Medal at all times.

Museums/Libraries

National Medal of Honor Museum of Military History
400 Georgia Ave.
Chattanooga, TN 37403
ph: 423-267-1737
fax: 423-266-7771
dsmith0344@worldnet.att.net
http://www.smoky.com/medalofhonor

Purple Heart

Collectors

Ed Maier
Purple Hears of World War II
elmiii@aol.com
http://hometown.aol.com/medalcol/
purple_hearts_of_world_war_ii.htm
Collector of Purple Hearts that were awarded to US sailors and airmen who gave their lives in battle during WWII; preserves the memory of these Servicemen with dignity and honor.

MEDICAL, DENTAL & PHARMACEUTICAL

(see also BOOKS, Medical & Dental; CIVIL WAR ARTIFACTS, Medical; EYE RELATED ITEMS; HEALTH & BEAUTY; INSTRUMENTS & DEVICES, Scientific; OPTICAL ITEMS; STAMP COLLECTING, Medical; VETERINARY MEDICINE ITEMS)

Appraisers

Peggy Landt
LHL Services
9065 La Serena Dr.
Fair Oaks, CA 95628
ph: 916-962-0592
Complete soda fountain and pharmacy appraisal services.

Clubs/Associations

Dr. M. Donald Blaufox, MD, PhD
Medical Collectors Association
Newsletter: Medical Collectors Newsletter
Montefiore Medical Park
1695 A Eastchester Rd., #1695A
Bronx, NY 10461-2374
ph: 718-405-8454
fax: 718-824-0625
blaufox@aecom.yu.edu
The association meets once a year and issues its newsletter semi-annually.

Dr. Sam Koslov
Maryland Microscopical & Scientific Instrument Society
8621 Polk St.
Mc Lean, VA 22102
ph: 703-893-9102
Focuses on instruments and devices: medical, surveying, photographic, microscopical, navigational, horological, astronomical, etc.

Collectors

Dr. Allan Wissner
P.O. Box 102
Ardsley, NY 10502-0102
ph: 914-693-4628
wissner@bestweb.net
http://www.bestweb.net/~wissner
Wants microscopes, medical, scientific instruments: Zentmayer, Grunow, Bullock, McAllister, Gundlack, McIntosh, Tolles, Queen, Pike.

Douglas Arbittier, MD
MedicalAntiques
P.O. Box 478
Watertown, NY 13601
ph: 315-788-2063
darbitt@imcnet.net
http://www.medicalantiques.com
Seeks pre-1890 medical antiques: surgical, dental and bloodletting, especially rare bleeding devices and cased surgical sets; Web site has information about medical and surgical related antiques.

Dr. F. Terry Hambrecht
14015 Manorvale Rd.
Rockville, MD 20853
fh2@cu.nih.gov

Richard Van Vleck
Greybird Publishing
P.O. Box 412
Taneytown, MD 21787
ph: 301-447-2680
smma@americanartifacts.com
http://americanartifacts.com/smma
Wants medical and scientific antiques of all sorts; especially microscopes, eye-related instruments, laboratory and demo devices.

Dr. Robert Greenspan, MD
7922 Washington Ave.
Alexandria, VA 22308
ph: 703-550-4517
fax: 703-765-5152
BobGreenspan2000@aol.com
http://www.collectmedicalantiques.com
Extensive collector of medical, dental, apothecary, and quack medical antiques; Web site contains important information on all aspects of collecting for those in the hobby.

Jon Lewin
622 Raleigh Ave., Apt. 3
Norfolk, VA 23507-2034
ph: 757-625-6732
Buying medical & scientific items: bleeding instruments, wood/bone-handled surgical tools, phrenology heads, electric or violet ray quack boxes, electric belts, microscopes, 19th C. medical books, eye-massagers, ear trumpets, etc.

Howard G. Johnson
8570 Wood Mills Dr. West
Cordova, TN 38018
ph: 901-737-3787
Wants to buy any medical or sick room device having a black, hard rubber nozzle/tip that penetrates any body orifice such as rubber douche syringes (bag or bulb); also pre-1950 enema equipment.

Jerry A. Phelps
1500 Van Buren Rd.
Mount Eden, KY 40046-9552
ph: 502-859-4063
phelps-vbv@dcr.net
Wants pre-1900 medical and apothecary antiques, especially colored pontiled medicine bottles, bleeding items, leeching jars; also pre-1900 country store items and advertising items.

Colin R. Voorneveld, MD
27 Roncesvalles Ave., #408
Toronto, Ontario M6R 3B2 Canada
ph: 416-516-4751
fax: 416-516-4751
Avid collector specializing in pre-1900 medical and pharmaceutical antiques; actively seeks medical instruments, spectacles, historic medicine, etc.

Dealers

C. Keith Wilbur, M.D.
Doctor's Bag, The
397 Prospect St.
Northampton, MA 01060-2089
ph: 413-584-1440
doctorsbag@juno.com
Buys, sells, appraises apothecary, medical, dental, surgical, optical & quack instruments, equipment, advertising, books, etc.; catalogs available 3 to 4 times a year; author of "Antique Medical Instruments" and other books.

Ed Welch
Ed Welch Antiques
Rt. 201
RFD 3 Box 1290
Winslow, ME 04901
ph: 207-872-5849
edwelch@metiques.com
http://www.metiques.com/catalog/
    antiques.html
Specializes in medical and dental antiques 1600 to 1930; including tools, books, charts, photographs, old teaching props, instruments; also forensic science, undertaking and mortuary, death and dying.

Mike Gordon
M & R Gordon
57 Bundy Lane
Storrs, CT 06268
ph: 860-429-3834
fax: 860-429-3834
Wants to buy pre-WWII medical and dental items: diagnostic, surgical, bloodletting instruments, tooth extractors, opthalmic devices, obstetric forceps, hearing aids, phrenological heads and quack items.

Lucille Malitz
Lucid Antiques
P.O. Box KH
Scarsdale, NY 10583
ph: 914-636-7825 or 914-636-5171
fax: 914-636-7825
lithopha@optonline.net
Interested in the most collectible medical and dental antiques dating from the 19th century before the period of sterilization.

David & Yola Coffeen
Tesseract
P.O. Box 151
Hastings On Hudson, NY 10706-0151
ph: 914-478-2594
fax: 914-478-5473
coffeen@aol.com
http://www.etesseract.com
Issues a series of well illustrated catalogs of early scientific instruments: astronomy, microscopy, sundials, surveying, calculation, demonstration, medical, surgical, navigation, etc.; interested in buying single items of collections.

Eric P. Kane
285 Sills Rd., Bldg #7
Patchogue, NY 11772
ph: 516-475-2144
fax: 516-475-1588
epk@aol.com
Wants to buy medical antiques from the Civil War and earlier: medical instruments, cased sets, especially marked "USA Hospital/Medical Dept.," medical texts, and associated materials such as medicine bottles, tins, etc.

Rod Harmic
Harmic's Antique Gallery
550 Rose Dale Lane
Dover, DE 19904
ph: 302-736-1174 or 302-736-1266
rodney.harmic@dol.net
http://www.harmic.com
Wants to buy medical antiques.

J. Glen & Violet Moore
Main St. Antiques
47 W. Main St.
P.O. Box 627
New Market, MD 21774-0627
ph: 301-865-3710
Buys and sells early medical devices, quack devices, signs and curiosities; eye, vet, dentist and other fields; patent medicines; appointments preferred.

Willisia Holbrook
Armbrook Antiques
531 Doub Rd.
Lewisville, NC 27023
ph: 888-393-8025 or 336-945-9477
fax: 336-945-9914
Buys and sells early medical and pharmaceutical antiques; specializes in pre-1930s items; Web site has full online catalog including descriptions and photos.

James & Norvell Kennedy
James Kennedy Antiques, Ltd.
905 W. Main St.
Durham, NC 27701-2054
ph: 919-682-1040 or 800-236-1868
fax: 919-683-9633
kantiques@earthlink.net
http://www.jameskennedyantiques.com
Specialist in scientific, medical, and nautical antiques and prints.

Dr. John S. Gimesh, M.D.
Stein's Antiques
202 Stedman St.
P.O. Box 53788
Fayetteville, NC 28305-3788
ph: 910-484-2219
steinmed@foto.infi.net
Buys and sells medical, dental, apothecary items, spectacles, books, etc.

Doris K. Bagwell, R.N.
Bagwell Antiques
5607 Concord Dr.
Jackson, MS 39211-4239
ph: 601-956-3508
fax: 601-956-4190
DKay5607@aol.com
Buys and sells any medical related items: surgical, instruments, supplies, books, etc.

Dr. Craig A. Maxwell
Roosa & Ratliff Drug Co., The
3553 Springdale Rd.
Cincinnati, OH 45251
ph: 800-431-7626 or 513-741-8653
fax: 513-741-7994
themaxwellhouse@earthlink.net
25 years experience collecting, dealing, appraising pharmacy and medical antiques; buys old medicine bottles, tins, pharmacy & medical books/catalogs, showglobes, pill rollers, advertising, quack items, displays, medical kits, etc.

Dale B. Peterson
Past Times Treasures
22762 Woodridge Dr.
Claremore, OK 74017
ph: 918-341-5475
cpeters2@mail.com
http://www.geocities.com/cdpet1
Actively seeking drug store and country store show globes, pedestal candy jars, old shelf stock, all forms of advertising, counter top containers; NOS products; anything old drug store or country store related; restorations & appraisals.

Al & Bobbie Roberts
Rational Past, The
221 Oceano Dr.
Los Angeles, CA 90049-4123
ph: 310-476-6277
fax: 310-476-6278
malinfo@therationalpast.com
http://www.therationalpast.com
Organizer of West Coast Scientific & Technical Antique and Collectible Shows (Los Angeles and San Francisco.)

Chris Jennings
Absolutely Wonderful Antiques
P.O. Box 70532
Shasta Lake, CA 96079
ph: 877-275-0637
Wants to buy medical, pharmaceutical, dental and veterinary items, including medical instruments.

Experts

L.C. & C.G. Richardson
Mortar & Pestle Antiques
1176 South Dogwood Dr.
Harrisonburg, VA 22801-1535
ph: 540-434-1506
dcknlill@gte.net
Buys, sells and specializes in medical and pharmaceutical antiques; authors of "A Book on Apothecary Antiques and Collectibles" (Old Fort Press.)

Paul Wherry
Pharmatiques
20 West North St.
Columbus, OH 43085-4133
ph: 614-885-1322
Collects and appraises pharmacy antiques.

Dr. Craig A. Maxwell
Roosa & Ratliff Drug Co., The
3553 Springdale Rd.
Cincinnati, OH 45251
ph: 800-431-7626 or 513-741-8653
fax: 513-741-7994
themaxwellhouse@earthlink.net
25 years experience collecting, dealing, appraising pharmacy and medical antiques; buys old medicine bottles, tins, pharmacy & medical books/catalogs, showglobes, pill rollers, advertising, quack items, displays, medical kits, etc.

Dale R. Beeks
Perceptions Scientifica
P.O. Box 117
Mount Vernon, IA 52314-0117
ph: 800-880-5178 or 319-895-0506
dbeeksci@aol.com
Buys fine microscopes; old scientific, surveying, technical, medical and precision instruments; pre-1900 typewriters, calculating devices, medical items & quackery.

Dr. Robert E. Kravetz, M.D.
Medical Museum
c/o Administration, Phoenix Baptist Hospital
2000 W. Bethany Home Rd.
Phoenix, AZ 85015-2467
ph: 602-246-5319
fax: 602-433-6646
Medical museum curator, collector and historian; deals mainly with 18th and 19th century medical & pharmaceutical antiques.

Richard M. Wiedhopf, Cur.
University of Arizona College of Pharmacy, History of Pharmacy Museum
1703 E.. Mabel
P.O. Box 210207
Tucson, AZ 85721
ph: 520-626-4429
fax: 520-626-4063
wiedhopf@pharmacy.arizona.edu
http://www.pharmacy.arizona.edu/
    museum/history.shtml
Collector and expert specializing in pharmaceutical collectibles.

Internet Resources

Douglas Arbittier, MD
Medical Antiques
P.O. Box 478
Watertown, NY 13601
ph: 315-788-2063
darbitt@imcnet.net
http://www.medicalantiques.com
Information about medical and surgical related antiques.

U.S. National Library of Medicine
(NLM)
8600 Rockville Pike
Bethesda, MD 20894
ph: 888-346-3656 or 301-594-5983
publicinfo@nlm.nih.gov
http://www.nlm.nih.gov
*Image library of nearly 60,000 images
in prints and photograph collection;
search by keyword or browse.*

Richard Van Vleck
Scientific Medical & Mechanical
Antiques
P.O. Box 412
Taneytown, MD 21787
ph: 301-447-2680
smma@americanartifacts.com
http://americanartifacts.com/smma
*Items for sale and wanted, US Patents
search, SMMA articles and regular
features, auction announcements,
scientific instrument show schedules,
books for the collector, links to related
sites.*

Dr. Robert Greenspan, MD
7922 Washington Ave.
Alexandria, VA 22308
ph: 703-550-4517
fax: 703-765-5152
BobGreenspan2000@aol.com
http://www.collectmedicalantiques.com
*Extensive collector of medical, dental,
apothecary, and quack medical
antiques; Web site contains important
information on all aspects of
collecting for those in the hobby.*

Dr. Michael Echols
Medical Antiques
6300 Whiskey Creek Dr.
Fort Myers, FL 33919
ph: 239-489-0587
fax: 941-481-0100
drechols@att.net
http://www.braceface.com/medical
*An extensive Web site which
specializes in pre-1900 medical,
surgical, and dental instruments;
extensive information and photographs
on evaluating, pricing and collecting
pre-1870 American surgical sets.*

Museums/Libraries

Gretchen Worden, Dir.
Mutter Museum, College of Physicians
of Philadelphia
19 South 22nd St.
Philadelphia, PA 19103-3097
ph: 215-563-3737 x242
fax: 215-561-6477
muttref@collphyphil.org
http://www.collphyphil.org/
muttpg1.shtml
*Collection consists of antique medical
instruments and equipment primarily
from the 19th and 20th centuries, and
rare anatomical specimens and
medical curiosities such as 2,000
swallowed objects removed from food
and air passages.*

James Connor
National Museum of Health & Medicine
of the Armed Forces Institute of
Pathology
Bldg. 54
Walter Reed Medical Center
Washington, DC 20306
ph: 202-782-2200
fax: 202-782-3573
connorj@afip.osd.mil
http://nmhm.washingtondc.museum
*Historical collections containing over
1100 artifacts documenting the history
of medicine; actively seeking medical
instruments.*

Hugh Mercer Apothecary Shop
1020 Caroline St.
Fredericksburg, VA 22401-3814
ph: 540-373-3362

Country Doctor Museum, The
P.O. Box 34
Bailey, NC 27807
ph: 252-235-4165
fax: 252-291-2756
*Founded in 1968, this is the only
museum in the country dedicated to the
rural physicians who practiced
medicine in North Carolina and the
South during the 19th and early 20th
centuries.*

McDowell House & Apothecary Shop
125 S. Second St.
Danville, KY 40422-1801
ph: 859-236-2804
tourbc@bellsouth.net
http://www.danville-ky.com/
BoyleCounty/mcdowell.htm
*Has an outstanding apothecary shop
museum.*

James M. Edmonson, PhD
Dittrick Museum of Medical History
11000 Euclid Ave.
Cleveland, OH 44106-1714
ph: 216-368-3648
fax: 216-368-6421
jme3@po.cwru.edu
http://www.cwru.edu/chsl/hist_div.htm
*Collection of 75,000 artifacts: medical
history, diagnostic instruments,
microscopes, surgical and obstetric
instruments, etc.*

Hook's American Drugstore Museum,
Inc.
201 North Meridian St.
Indianapolis, IN 46225
ph: 317-951-2222
fax: 317-951-2224
pharmuseum@aol.com
*A museum dedicated to the American
drugstore; collecting anything related
to drugstore, apothecary, pharmacy,
soda fountain; any period from
Colonial to present.*

Bakken Library & Museum, The
3537 Zenith Ave. South
Minneapolis, MN 55416
ph: 612-927-6508
fax: 612-927-7265
webmaster@thebakken.org
http://www.bakkenmuseum.org
*Collects medical electricity items (no
violet rays needed); have 2,000
artifacts; 10,000 books.*

International Museum of Surgical Science
1524 North Lake Shore Dr.
Chicago, IL 60610
ph: 312-642-6502
info@imss.org
http://www.imss.org

Dr. Robert E. Kravetz, M.D.
Medical Museum
c/o Administration, Phoenix Baptist
Hospital
2000 W. Bethany Home Rd.
Phoenix, AZ 85015-2467
ph: 602-246-5319
fax: 602-433-6646
*Mailing address is as above; physical
location is at 6025 N. 20th Ave.,
Phoenix, AZ.*

Richard M. Wiedhopf, Cur.
University of Arizona College of
Pharmacy, History of Pharmacy
Museum
1703 E.. Mabel
P.O. Box 210207
Tucson, AZ 85721
ph: 520-626-4429
fax: 520-626-4063
wiedhopf@pharmacy.arizona.edu
http://www.pharmacy.arizona.edu/
museum/history.shtml
*Spanning all four floors of the
Pharmacy building, the museum
contains a collection of over 60,000
bottles, original drug containers,
books, display cases, and artifacts
from 1880 to 1930.*

David Pearson
Wellcome Library for the History &
Understanding of Medicine
183 Euston Rd.
London, NW1 2BE U.K.
ph: +44 020 7611 8582
fax: +44 020 7611 8369
library@wellcome.ac.uk
http://library.wellcome.ac.uk
*The Wellcome Library provides
insight and information to anyone
seeking to understand medicine and its
role in society, past and present.*

Periodicals

Richard Van Vleck
Greybird Publishing
Journal: American Artifacts
P.O. Box 412
Taneytown, MD 21787
ph: 301-447-2680
smma@americanartifacts.com
http://americanartifacts.com/smma
*For collectors, dealers, researchers;
recent articles include formaldehyde
disinfectors, galvanic spectacles and*

*electric dumbbells; free ads for
subscribers.*

Civil War

Dealers

Alex Peck
Antique Scientifica
P.O. Box 710
Charleston, IL 61920-0710
ph: 217-348-1009
antiques@advant.net
http://antiquescientifica.com
*Wants surgical and bloodletting
instruments, any Civil War (and pre-
1890) medical gear, USA Hosp. Dept.,
etc.; anything Civil War.*

Dental

Collectors

William Winburn, Jr.
1502 Showalter Rd.
Grafton, VA 23692
ph: 757-898-8246
fax: 757-898-6689
*Dental instruments especially
extracting; also contents of old dental
offices.*

Ralph Nix
P.O. Box 655
Red Bay, AL 35582-0655
ph: 256-356-2997
*Wants dental antiques such as fancy
wooden dental cabinets, four-leg
dental chairs, wood or ivory handled
instruments, foot engines, etc.*

Dr. Barry Janov
2454 Dempster St., Ste. 416
Des Plaines, IL 60016-5320
marconifon@aol.com
*Collector of early dental tools and
related memorabilia.*

Museums/Libraries

Dr. Scott D. Swank
Dr. Samuel D. Harris National Museum
of Dentistry
31 South Greene St.
Baltimore, MD 21201-1504
ph: 410-706-0600
fax: 410-706-8313
sswank@dentalmuseum.umaryland.edu
http://www.dentalmuseum.org
*Opened in 1996 with 7,000 sq. ft. of
exhibit spaces, archives, reference
library; collections consist of dental
advertising art, pre-1950 dentist's
directories (e.g. Polk's, Beecher's),
trade catalogs, etc.*

Dr. John Harris Dental Museum
P.O. Box 344
Bainbridge, OH 45612
ph: 740-634-2228
*Mailing address is as above, but
located in Bainbridge, OH.*

Drug Store

Appraisers

Jim McMahon
James L. McMahon & Sons
635 Gilbert Hwy.
Fairfield, CT 06430-1646
ph: 203-226-3430
fax: 203-226-3430
Buys, sells, collects, and appraises antique apothecary (pharmacy) and medical items.

Clubs/Associations

American Institute of the History of
  Pharmacy
777 Highland Ave.
Madison, WI 53705-2222
ph: 608-262-5378
aihp@aihp.org
http://www.aihp.org
A non-profit national organization devoted to advancing knowledge and understanding of the place of pharmacy in history; supports both public and private collections of manuscript material and artifacts related to the profession.

Collectors

Christopher D. Riley, R.Ph.
175 Wood Duck Run
Lexington, NC 27295
crileyrph@yahoo.com
Registered pharmacist wants to buy antique apothecary and pharmacy related antiques: LUG bottles, crude drug jars, M&Ps; almost anything.

Mart James
487 Oak Ridge Rd.
Dyersburg, TN 38024-6511
ph: 901-286-2025
Wants to buy label-under-glass apothecary bottles, show globes, porcelain and show jars, medicine advertising, drug store window display pieces, etc.

Andrew E. Thomas
4681 North 84th Way
Scottsdale, AZ 85251-1864
ph: 888-255-0664 or 480-947-5693
fax: 480-994-4382
andrew-thomas@qwest.net
Buying apothecary antiques and drug store collectibles; show globes, drug jars, drug mills, mortars and pestles, balances and scales, displays, pill tiles, labels and label cabinets; specialty is show globes.

Dealers

Jim McMahon
James L. McMahon & Sons
635 Gilbert Hwy.
Fairfield, CT 06430-1646
ph: 203-226-3430
fax: 203-226-3430
Buys, sells, collects, and appraises antique apothecary (pharmacy) and medical items.

Museums/Libraries

Eugene I. Morris, Dir.
New England Fire & History Museum
Newsletter: Siren Soundings
1439 Main St. (Rte. 6A)
Brewster, MA 02631
ph: 508-896-5711
http://www.nefiremuseum.org
"The Schmidt Apothecary Shop" contains the largest collection of pharmaceutical bottles, original medicines and prescriptions; library contains many volumes dealing with pharmaceutical history.

Eli Lilly & Co.

Collectors

Charles T. Davaney
8888 Classic View Dr.
Indianapolis, IN 46217-6017
ph: 317-888-8401
cdavaney@lilly.com
Buys, sells, trades Eli Lilly & Company bottles, books, periodicals, etc.

John Many
8307 Hi-Vu Dr.
Indianapolis, IN 46227
ph: 317-882-2279
jmany@iquest.net
Wants to buy pre-1940 Eli Lilly & Co. cork bottles, books, advertisements, periodicals, ephemera, etc.

Hearing Aids

Collectors

Jon Kolger
6906 Meade Dr.
Colleyville, TX 76034-6416
ph: 817-329-5262
jkolger@gte.net
Wants to buy all sorts of primitive hearing-aid devices such as conversation tubes, ear trumpets, early battery-powered hearing-aids, etc.

Military Related

Museums/Libraries

U.S. Army Medical Department Museum
P.O. Box 340244
Ft. Sam Houston, TX 78234
ph: 210-221-6358
fax: 210-221-6781
Mission is to preserve exhibit and interpret artifacts related to the history of the US Army Medical Department from 1775 to present including significant events in history of the AMEDD, scientific advances, medical field services.

Patent Medicines

Collectors

Mark S. McNee
Nostrums & Quackery
1009 Vassar Dr.
Kalamazoo, MI 49001-4483
ph: 269-343-8393
nostrums@chartermi.net
Collector for 25 years wants pre-1910 patent medicine bottles, tins,

packages, and pills; also wants to buy advertising items and contents of old drug stores.

Harold Dylhoff
23511 Paulson's Rd.
Gobles, MI 49055-8651
ph: 269-628-4051
hdylxrds@aol.com
Wants to buy Hadacol patent medicine memorabilia, almanacs, flyers, Captain Hadacol comics, Col. LeBlanc items; send photocopies and LSASE for reply.

Dan Cowman
22911 Kuykendahl Rd.
Spring, TX 77389-4326
ph: 281-376-1799
kcowman@aol.com
Wants to buy any items relating to patent medicines: almanacs, trade cards, billheads, labeled bottles, boxes, packages, tins, plasters, advertising, druggist trade catalogs, tin and paper patent medicine advertising signs, etc.

Dealers

Gary Hofe
Gypsy's Treasures
Rt 4, Box 665
Berkeley Springs, WV 25411
ph: 304-258-1617
Wants to buy medicine bottles; patent medicines from 1800s to mid 1900s; S&D, Merck, J&J, Lilly and others; also spice, talc, other tins and general advertising; mail order and shows.

Dr. Craig A. Maxwell
Roosa & Ratliff Drug Co., The
3553 Springdale Rd.
Cincinnati, OH 45251
ph: 800-431-7626 or 513-741-8653
fax: 513-741-7994
themaxwellhouse@earthlink.net
25 years experience collecting, dealing, appraising pharmacy and medical antiques; buys patent medicines, tins, pharmacy & medical books/catalogs, showglobes, pill rollers, advertising, quack items, displays, medical kits, etc.

Phrenology Busts

Collectors

Jon Lewin
622 Raleigh Ave., Apt. 3
Norfolk, VA 23507-2034
ph: 757-625-6732
Wants to buy phrenology heads, instruments or machines for measuring the head, fortune telling hands marked with zones, and related books, signs, etc.

Quackery

(see also HEALTH & BEAUTY, Devices to Restore)

Collectors

David Rickert
301 E. Rayamond Ave.
Alexandria, VA 22301
ph: 703-535-6502
Rickertd@gdls.com
http://www.radiantslab.com/quackmed
Wants to buy antique quack medical, electrotherapy, diathermy, X-Ray equipment by Wappler, McIntosh, Victor, etc.

Jeff Behary
16797 60th Lane N.
Loxahatchee, FL 33470
jeff_behary@hotmail.com
http://www.lvstrings.com/quack.htm
Collects turn of the century electrotherapy devices: magneto-electric machines, Faradic medical batteries, violet rays, ultra violet ozone lamps, carbon arc lamps, Tesla coils, induction coils, high frequency apparatus.

O. Lindan
1404 Dorsh Rd.
Cleveland, OH 44121-3840
ph: 216-382-7113
Wants old electrotherapeutic and controversial healing devices and related literature; also wants medical, scientific instruments.

Ed Keller
1205 Imperial Dr.
Pittsburg, KS 66762-6123
Wants quack medical devices, cure-all devices, and old electrotherapeutic gadgets which shock, spark, buzz, light up or remain silent; no violet-rays, please; please send name, brief description and price.

Dealers

Dr. Craig A. Maxwell
Roosa & Ratliff Drug Co., The
3553 Springdale Rd.
Cincinnati, OH 45251
ph: 800-431-7626 or 513-741-8653
fax: 513-741-7994
themaxwellhouse@earthlink.net
25 years experience collecting, dealing, appraising pharmacy and medical antiques; buys old medicine bottles, tins, pharmacy & medical books/catalogs, showglobes, pill rollers, advertising, quack items, displays, medical kits, etc.

Experts

Robert W. McCoy, Dir.
Museum of Questionable Medical
  Devices
201 Main St., SE
Minneapolis, MN 55414
ph: 763-545-1113 or 612-379-4046
fax: 763-540-9999
quack@mtn.org
http://www.mtn.org/quack
Author of "Quack - Tales of Medical Fraud from the Museum of Questionable Medical Devices" (Santa Monica Press).

Internet Resources

Jeff Behary
Electrotherapy Museum, The
16797 60th Lane N.
Loxahatchee, FL 33470
jeff_behary@hotmail.com
http://www.lvstrings.com/quack.htm
Great source of information on violet rays, portable Tesla home quackery, diathermy machines, surgical Tesla coils, high frequency apparatus, Faradic coils, induction coils, magneto-electric machines, carbon arc lamps and more.

Museums/Libraries

O. Lindan
Lindan Hist. Coll. of Electrotherapeutic
& Controversial Medical Devices, The
1404 Dorsh Rd.
Cleveland, OH 44121-3840
ph: 216-382-7113
Focuses on old electrotherapeutic and controversial healing devices and related literature.

Robert W. McCoy, Dir.
Museum of Questionable Medical
Devices
201 Main St., SE
Minneapolis, MN 55414
ph: 763-545-1113 or 612-379-4046
fax: 763-540-9999
quack@mtn.org
http://www.mtn.org/quack
Nation's largest display of quack devices, from the AMA, FDA, St. Louis Science Center, Bakken Library and the National Council Against Health Fraud; publishes copies of old posters & advertising brochures dealing with medical quackery.

Bakken Library & Museum, The
3537 Zenith Ave. South
Minneapolis, MN 55416
ph: 612-927-6508
fax: 612-927-7265
webmaster@thebakken.org
http://www.bakkenmuseum.org
Collects medical electricity items (no violet rays needed); have 2,000 artifacts; 10,000 books; maintains a special collection of quack devices.

Audrey Kamprath, Curator
Diablo Valley College Museum
321 Golf Club Rd.
Pleasant Hill, CA 94523-1529
ph: 925-685-1230 x303
fax: 925-685-1551

Stethoscopes

Experts

Erik Soiferman, D.O.
Medical Antiques Online
114 Myrtle Ave.
Havertown, PA 19083
ph: 610-789-4588
fax: 610-668-9949
erik@antiquemed.com
http://www.antiquemed.com
Expert on the history of the stethoscope; collector of binaural stethoscopes; extensive online collection.

MEDICINE RELATED ITEMS

(see MEDICAL, DENTAL &
PHARMACEUTICAL)

MENUS

(see also COOKBOOKS; PAPER
COLLECTIBLES; RESTAURANT
COLLECTIBLES)

Collectors

Barbara & Richard DePalma
Deer Park Books
609 Kent Rd., Route 7
Gaylordsville, CT 06755
ph: 860-350-4140
deerparkbooks@earthlink.net
http://www.deerparkbooks.com
Collector of 19th century menus, preferably American; will purchase single menu or entire collection.

Internet Resources

Menu Database, Los Angeles Public
Library
ph: 213-228-7272
ppersic@lapl.org
http://www.lapl.org/elec_neigh
This online collection of menus allows you to browse the dishes of thousands of restaurants; searchable by keyword, cuisine, or date, it covers American to Vietnamese.

Museums/Libraries

Strong Museum, The
1 Manhattan Square
Rochester, NY 14607
ph: 585-263-2700
fax: 585-263-2493
http://www.strongmuseum.org
Has a small collection of 100 menus dating back to the 1840s; fully cataloged on a computer database.

Cornell University Hotel School Library,
Nestle Collection
G80 Statler Hall
Cornell University
Ithaca, NY 14853-6902
ph: 607-255-3673
fax: 607-255-0021
djb4@cornell.edu
http://www.nestlelib.cornell.edu
Over 10,000 menus from the 1850s through the 1940s.

MERMAIDS

Collectors

Jennifer Sykes
9018 Balboa Blvd. #595
Northridge, CA 91325-2610
ph: 818-993-1916
fax: 818-993-7612
Veeda10@aol.com
Wants to buy mermaid items: wall plaques, figurines.

Wayne Babcock
4846 Carpenteria Ave.
Carpinteria, CA 93013-1935
ph: 805-684-8148
oldsurfin@cs.com
Collects mermaid figurines, clocks, artwork; any mermaid items.

Dealers

Stephanie M. Schnatz
17 Tallow Ct.
Baltimore, MD 21244-2516
ph: 410-944-0819
chelsealady@hotmail.com
http://www.geocities.com/Paris/Palais/
7498
Buys and sells any printed materials with mermaids, mermen, merbabies on them; also wants antique merpeople in porcelain, silver, metal, china, wood, ivory, linens, lace, jewelry, etc.; items must be pre-1930.

METAL DETECTING

(see TREASURE HUNTING)

METAL ITEMS

(see also ALUMINUM, Hammered;
BRASS ITEMS; BRONZES; CAST
IRON ITEMS; CHROME; COPPER
ITEMS; GOLD, Scrap; PLATINUM,
Scrap; SILVER, Scrap; REPAIR/
RESTORATION/CONSERVATION,
Metal Items)

Dealers

Eve Stone
Eve Stone Antiques, Ltd.
22 Selden St.
Woodbridge, CT 06525
ph: 203-389-6665 or 800-833-1665
fax: 203-389-6103
info@evestoneantiques.com
http://www.evestoneantiques.com
Specializes in period brass and copper French and English antiques; a nationally known expert in copper and brass.

Michael J. Whitman Antiques
427 Bethlehem Pike
Fort Washington, PA 19034-2315
ph: 215-646-8639
fax: 215-641-5831
margaux@voicenet.com
Specializes in early metalware: brass, copper, iron, pewter, tin, paktong bronze.

Bette & Melvyn Wolf, Inc.
1196 Shady Hill Court
Flint, MI 48532
ph: 810-732-6595
fax: 810-732-1467
b.m.wolf@worldnet.att.net
Specializes in antique pewter: American, English, Continental; also in other metal antiques in copper, iron and brass.

Museums/Libraries

James Wallace, Dir.
National Ornamental Metal Museum
Newsletter: Museum News
374 Metal Museum Dr.
Memphis, TN 38106
ph: 901-774-6380
fax: 901-774-6382
metal@wspice.com
http://www.metalmuseum.org
Conservation and restoration services available to the public and private sector; changing exhibits of historic and contemporary metalwork, classes, metalsmithing demonstrations.

Repro. Sources

Steve Kayne
Kayne & Son Custom Forged Hardware
100 Daniel Ridge Rd.
Candler, NC 28715-9434
ph: 828-667-8868 or 828-665-1988
fax: 828-665-8303
kaynehdwe@charter.net
http://www.customforgedhardware.com
Steel, brass, bronze reproductions of locks, pulls, hinges, thumb latches, furniture & interior/exterior hardware, fireplace tools & accessories, military accouterments, etc.; also does repairs, restoration; $5 for two catalogs.

Suppliers

Glenn Hayes
Right Stuff Company, The
6246 Mission Rd.
Shawnee Mission, KS 66205-3253
ph: 913-722-4002 or 877-4-POLISH
fax: 913-722-6819
info@rtstuf.com
http://www.rtstuf.com
Sells Cape Cod Metal Polishing Cloths: moist cotton cloths that remove tarnish on silver, gold, brass, copper, pewter, aluminum - all metals' pleasant vanilla scent; anti-tarnish formula so shine lasts longer.

Heintz Art Metal

Collectors

David Surgan
328 Flatbush Ave., Ste. 123
Brooklyn, NY 11238-4302
ph: 718-638-3768
fax: 718-638-3768
surgheintz@aol.com
Dealer, author, exhibit curator, avid collector of Heintz Art Metal Shop items including vases, bowls, lighting, boxes, bookends, picture frames, etc.

METALSMITHS

(see CRAFTS; METAL ITEMS;
REPAIR/RESTORATION/
CONSERVATION, Metal Items)

METTLACH

(see STEINS)

MICROSCOPES

(see also INSTRUMENTS & DEVICES, Scientific; OPTICAL ITEMS)

Clubs/Associations

Manuel del Cerro, MD
Microscope Historical Society
Journal: Journal of the MHS
14 Tall Acres Dr.
Pittsford, NY 14534
m.delcerro@worldnet.att.net
Members are interested in the antique microscopes, parts, and history.

Dr. Sam Koslov
Maryland Microscopical & Scientific Instrument Society
8621 Polk St.
Mc Lean, VA 22102
ph: 703-893-9102
Focuses on instruments and devices: medical, surveying, photographic, microscopical, navigational, horological, astronomical, etc.

Lafrry Albright
Microscopical Society of Southern California
11815 Indianapolis St.
Los Angeles, CA 90066-2046
ph: 310-397-8357
albrite@Plasma-Art.com
http://www.plasma-art.com/MSSC.html
One of the largest and most active societies in the U.S; membership is worldwide.

Fritz Schulze
Historical Microscopical Society of Canada
Newsletter: HMSC Bulletin
RR #2
Priceville, Ontario NOC 1K0 Canada
ph: 519-369-2855
fax: 519-369-2855
glenelly@wightman.ca
http://www.geocities.com/
CapeCanaveral/Hangar/5485
Members are hobby microscopists and collectors of optical instruments and related books, etc.; some do repairs and restorations, some buy and sell.

Collectors

Dr. Allan Wissner
P.O. Box 102
Ardsley, NY 10502-0102
ph: 914-693-4628
wissner@bestweb.net
http://www.bestweb.net/~wissner
Wants to buy antique brass microscopes and all kinds of microscope accessories including lenses, parts, microscope oil lamps, prepared slides, slide preparation equipment, slide cabinets; also related books and trade catalogs.

Paul Ferraglio
3332 W. Lake Rd.
Canandaigua, NY 14424-2441
ph: 585-394-7663
fax: 585-394-5424
p4alyo@aol.com
Wants to buy antique brass microscopes, scientific and surveying instruments in any condition; also wants related books and catalogs; also wants parts.

Richard Van Vleck
Greybird Publishing
P.O. Box 412
Taneytown, MD 21787
ph: 301-447-2680
smma@americanartifacts.com
http://americanartifacts.com/smma
Seeking pre-1900 American microscopes by Zentmayer, Tolles, Gundlach, McIntosh, McAllister, Bulloch, Grunow, Spencer, Baush & Lomb and others.

Paul H. Hayashi, PE
18 Tarabrook Dr.
Orinda, CA 94563-3121
ph: 925-254-5074 or 925-253-1038
fax: 925-253-0592
Wants to buy pre-1900 microscopes.

Dealers

C. Keith Wilbur, M.D.
Doctor's Bag, The
397 Prospect St.
Northampton, MA 01060-2089
ph: 413-584-1440
doctorsbag@juno.com
Buys, sells, appraises apothecary, medical, dental, surgical, optical & quack instruments, equipment, advertising, books, etc.; catalogs available 3 to 4 times a year; author of "Antique Medical Instruments" and other books.

Experts

Dale R. Beeks
Perceptions Scientifica
P.O. Box 117
Mount Vernon, IA 52314-0117
ph: 800-880-5178 or 319-895-0506
dbeeksci@aol.com

Randy D. Watson, M.D.
545 SE Oak, Ste. D
Hillsboro, OR 97123-4147
ph: 503-297-7424 or 503-640-1614
fax: 503-681-0925
gate@teleport.com
Advanced collector wants all microscopes; antique and toy; also wants related books; says "I never met a microscope I didn't like!;" has private museum of over 2500 microscopes and 200 meteorites.

Internet Resources

Moody Medical Library
Univ. of Texas Medical Branch
Galveston, TX 77555-1035
ref@utmb.edu
http://www.utmb.edu/mml/scopes/welcome.htm
Museum with a collection of 40 microscopes on display; Web site has resources for makers, anatomy of a microscope, toy microscopes, replicas, and more.

Museums/Libraries

Adrianne Noe, Dir.
National Museum of Health & Medicine
6900 Georgia Ave. NW, Bldg. 54
Washington, DC 20307-5001
ph: 202-782-2200
fax: 202-782-3573
nmhminfo@afip.osd.mil
http://www.natmedmuse.afip.org
Approx. 1,000 microscopes and 700 accessories; documents histological techniques by the inclusion of microtomes, accessories & microslides.

MILITARIA

(see also ARMS & ARMOR; AVIATION; BADGES; CANNONS; CIVIL WAR; FIREARMS; FLAGS; FRENCH FOREIGN LEGION; INDIAN WARS; KNIVES; MEDALS, ORDERS & DECORATIONS; MILITARY HISTORY; AMMUNITION; POSTERS; SWORDS; TRENCH ART; VETERAN ITEMS; VIETNAM ITEMS)

Appraisers

Frank Pereny
Saisho International
P.O. Box 176
Spring Grove, PA 17362-0176
ph: 717-225-0176
fax: 717-225-9221
Collector for over 30 years; full-time dealer since 1980; Accredited Member of the International Society of Appraisers.

Robert A. Dewar, ISA
Robert A. Dewar & Assoc.
512 Canal St.
New Smyrna Beach, FL 32168
ph: 386-428-3331
coro1@ucnsb.net
Dealer and appraiser in both antique and modern firearms.

Bruce B. Herman
P.O. Box 195
Pasadena, CA 91102-0195
ph: 626-357-3485
bbh1122@aol.com
Specializes in the appraisal of Western European and American militaria.

Richard J. Richter, ISA
R. Richter Appraisals
P.O. Box 16201
Portland, OR 97292-001
ph: 503-253-9195
r-richter@att.net
Buys, sells, appraises military relics from the Civil War through WWII.

Auction Services

Raymond J. Zyla
Mohawk Arms Inc.
P.O. Box 157
Bouckville, NY 13310
ph: 315-893-7888
fax: 315-893-7707
mohawk@militaryrelics.com
http://www.militaryrelics.com
Three auctions per year: original historical militaria, personality items, daggers, swords, medals, award documents, uniforms, headgear, art items, presentation pieces, etc.

Stephen Flood, Pres.
AAG, International Militaria Mail Auction
1226-B Sans Souci Parkway
Wilkes Barre, PA 18702-1230
ph: 570-822-5300
fax: 570-822-9992
aagintl1@aol.com
http://www.aag-militaria.com
Specializing in mail-bid auctions of militaria from Revolutionary War to Vietnam with emphasis on WWII, guns, Nazi, Japanese swords; all countries; 3 catalogs with over 7,000 items for $35; a large, fine auction house.

Roger S. Steffen
Steffen's Historical Militaria
14 Murnan Rd.
Cold Spring, KY 41076-9723
ph: 859-431-4499
fax: 859-431-3113
http://www.steffensmilitaria.com
Conducts periodic mail bid militaria auctions: firearms, military art, rare books, medals, uniforms, photos, etc.

Manion's Auction House
P.O. Box 12214
Kansas City, KS 66112-0214
ph: 913-299-6692
fax: 913-299-6792
collecting@manions.com
http://www.manions.com
The largest auction service in the US handling military related antiques and items from U.S, Germany, Japan & all other countries.

Roy Butler
Wallis & Wallis
West St. Auction Galleries
Lewes, East Sussex BN7 2NJ U.K.
ph: 01273-480208
fax: 01273-476562
wallisandwallis@mcmail.com
http://www.wallisandwallis.co.uk
Britain's specialist auctioneers of arms, armor, militaria and military orders.

Bosley's Military Auctioneers
The White House
Marlow, Buckinghamshire SL7 1AH
U.K.
ph: 01628 488188
fax: 01628 488111
sales@bosleys.co.uk
http://www.bosleys.co.uk
Military auctioneers and appraisers.

Clubs/Associations

Jon Jacobus
Militaria Collectors Society of Florida
Newsletter: Frontal Dispatch, The
140 N.E. 55th St.
Fort Lauderdale, FL 33334
ph: 954-772-6226
rangerson@aol.com
http://
www.militariacollectorssociety.com
*Purpose is to promote the knowledge,
study and preservation of military
relics from ancient to modern and to
support militaria collectors in the
pursuit of their hobby; club meets
monthly; sponsors military relics
shows.*

Rob Morgan
Civil War Collectors Society & the
American Militaria Exchange
5970 Toylor Ridge Dr.
West Chester, OH 45069
ph: 513-874-0483
RWMorgan@jackrouse.com
http://www.civilwar-collectors.com
*Established to promote the preserva-
tion and collecting of material
relating to our nation's rich military
heritage, from pre-Revolutionary times
to present day.*

American Society of Military History
Los Angeles Patriotic Hall
1816 S. Figueroa
Los Angeles, CA 90015
ph: 213-746-1776
tankland@aol.com
*Society of men and women dedicated
to developing programs to perpetuate
and maintain the great American
military heritage; library has over
25,000 titles and 10 periodical
subscriptions.*

Mike Hanlon, Mem.
Great War Society, The
Magazine: Relevance
P.O. Box 4585
Stanford, CA 94309
medwardh@hotmail.com
http://www.mcs.com/~mikei/tgws
*Encourages discussion, learning,
scholarship and independent research
on the events surrounding the First
World War.*

Robert Yaxley
Victorian Military Society
P.O. Box 58377
Newbury, RG14 7FJ U.K.
ry003e5671@blueyonder.co.uk
http://www.vms.org.uk
*Aim is to encourage and foster the
study of military aspects of the
Victorian era - from 1837 to 1914.*

Collectors

Warren K. Tice
W. Tice & Company
8 Orchard Terrace
Essex Junction, VT 05452-3501
ph: 802-878-3835
*Wants to purchase US Military,
Confederate, and high quality
decorative buttons; also wants to buy
military antiques.*

Kenneth D. Smith
55 Howard Ave.
Staten Island, NY 10301-4404
*Wants to buy WWII OSS memorabilia,
relics and documents; also buys
espionage items, cryptographic and
code/cipher machines, devices, books
and manuals; any era, any nation.*

Gene Christian
3849 Bailey Ave.
Bronx, NY 10463-2503
ph: 718-548-0243
*Wants Foreign Legion, Free French-
Vichy, Devils Island, China (Marines,
15th Inf., gunboats, French
Concession, White Russians,
Warlords), Imperial Chinese
headdress with finials, dogs (mascots,
war, rescue, heroism); please enclose
SASE.*

Charles Dubsky
686 N. Dupont Blvd. #328
Milford, DE 19963-1002
ph: 302-422-7766
fax: 302-424-4428
buying@yahoo.com
*Buys and appraises military and
airline items of all kinds: US,
German, Japanese: US Army patches,
medals, pins, wings, hats, flags,
paper documents, etc.; any amount
from one to one thousand items.*

Richard Fleming
P.O. Box 8394
Virginia Beach, VA 23450-8394
ph: 757-622-1343 or 757-463-2800 x205
fax: 757-463-3052
rfleming@milcom-systems.com
*Specializes in Japanese swords
brought back by our veterans and
servicemen; also interested in WWII
Army Air Force, Troop Carrier
Command, and Airborne items; free
translation of signed swords; book
about 1868-1945 swords available.*

Pat Olson
4533 Rutledge Ave.
Minneapolis, MN 55436-1418
ph: 952-927-0560
ptbasil@aol.com
*Wants military war souvenirs from all
countries and all periods: daggers,
swords, uniforms, helmets, flags,
papers, badges, wings, patches,
medals, squadron insignia.*

Charles G. Kratz, Jr.
17821 Golfview
Homewood, IL 60430-1210
ph: 708-799-8478 or 312-951-0336
*Wants old military cannons (only full-
size, authentic type) in any condition;
also want US artillery clothing and
equipment such wooden artillery
carriages and ammunition chests.*

Ron L. Willis
2110 Fox Ave.
Moore, OK 73160-4217
ph: 405-793-9604
*Wants US Navy - any period - patches,
wings, uniforms, books, documents,
edged weapons, photos, plaques,
flags, etc.*

Ed Royse
112 N. Broadway St.
Walters, OK 73572
ph: 580-357-8000
fax: 580-875-2063
edroyse@juno.com
*Wants to buy US military collectibles,
US Army firearms, swords, knives and
accouterments from Civil War to
present; also wants US WWI and
WWII posters, patriotic, recruiting,
Red Cross, propaganda.*

Dealers

Blue Cape Antiques
620 Great Rd., Rte. 119
Littleton, MA 01460
ph: 978-486-4709
*Wants to buy military collectibles; US,
German, Japanese.*

George P. van Duinwyk
Articles of War
358 Blvd.
Middletown, RI 02842-5467
ph: 401-846-8503
fax: 508-672-9699
dutch5@ids.net
*Buys, sells, appraises, collects and
specializes in antique militaria
including weapons and accouterments
dating from 1680 to 1945.*

Tom & Dave's Militaria
P.O. Box 725
Wyoming, RI 02898-0725
pir3@msn.com
http://www.TDWW2militaria.com
*WWII militaria dealers specializing in
American, German and Japanese
military collectibles and the stories
behind them; want to buy helmets,
uniforms, edged weapons, and
anything that a soldier would have
carried or used.*

Military Specialties, Inc.
2543 Berlin Tnpk.
Newington, CT 06111-4109
ph: 860-666-4275
fax: 860-666-1939
morforles@aol.com
http://www.militaryspecialtiesinc.com
*Buys and sells WWI and WWII
German, US, Japanese, British
military souvenirs: helmets, hats,
uniforms, swords, daggers, knives,
medals, patches, insignia, firearms,
etc.; carries a wide variety of new and
used clothing, insignia, surplus.*

William H. Guthman
Guthman Americana
P.O. Box 392
Westport, CT 06881
ph: 203-259-9763
fax: 203-319-0882
ejstilling@yahoo.com
*Specializes in Colonial and Federal
period military and historical
materials, such as weapons, powder
horns, and documents; also American
Indian objects.*

Jacques Noel Jacobsen, Jr.
Collector's Antiquities
60 Manor Rd.
Staten Island, NY 10310-2698
ph: 718-981-0973
jnjacobsen@mail.volusiacable.com
http://home.fiam.net/milantique
*American military antiques 1840-
1940; large annual illustrated
catalog, $12 ($15 overseas).*

Eric P. Kane
285 Sills Rd., Bldg #7
Patchogue, NY 11772
ph: 516-475-2144
fax: 516-475-1588
epk@aol.com
*Wants to buy Civil War and earlier
antique guns and militaria, uniforms,
photographs; also wants books on
guns.*

Raymond J. Zyla
Mohawk Arms Inc.
P.O. Box 157
Bouckville, NY 13310
ph: 315-893-7888
fax: 315-893-7707
mohawk@militaryrelics.com
http://www.militaryrelics.com

Dale C. Anderson Co.
P.O. Box 3516
Gettysburg, PA 17325
http://www.andersonmilitaria.com
*Sells antique firearms, swords,
uniforms, headgear, accouterments,
and more from the period 1775 to
1945; US and foreign; emphasis on
1860 to 1900 era; 40-page bimonthly
catalog $12/yr and by Web site; since
1961.*

Ken Kipp
Allenwood Americana Antiques
P.O. Box 116
Allenwood, PA 17810-0116
ph: 570-538-1440 or 570-538-1932
fax: 570-538-1932
kwkipp@ptd.net
*Established militaria dealer and
Veteran with over 20 years experience;
especially interested in WWI and
WWII memorabilia; buys and sells.*

J. T. Gallaghan
Faded Glories
Ardmart Antiques Mall
Drexel Hill, PA 19026
ph: 215-370-6138 or 215-937-1546
hero1954@aol.com
*Appraises, buy, sells all militaria
from the Revolutionary War to the
Spanish American War; specializing
in the period from 1860 to 1870:
muskets, sabers, rifles, carbines,
uniforms, accouterments, insignia,
swords.*

Terry Hannon, Pres.
Phoenix Militaria, Inc.
P.O. Box 245
Lyon Station, PA 19536-9986
ph: 610-682-1010 or 800-446-0909
fax: 610-682-1066
TerryHannon@msn.com
http://www.phoenixmilitaria.com
*Buys/sells general militaria; also sells
militaria collecting books &
periodicals.*

Randy Gravenor
E.R.G. Militaria
P.O. Box 299
Delmar, DE 19940
ph: 410-835-2280
info@gisurplus.com
http://www.gisurplus.com
*Over 12 years old and has rare,
unusual military collectibles; always
buying items of interest.*

Erik Padison
15127 Frederick Rd.
Rockville, MD 20850-1109
ph: 301-424-0053
elnor57@comcast.net
*Buys, sells, collects, appraises,
specializes in Japanese swords and
militaria.*

LTC(Ret) Thomas M. Johnson
Johnson Reference Books & Militaria
403 Chatham Square Office Park
Fredericksburg, VA 22405
ph: 540-373-9150 or 540-371-2665
fax: 540-373-0087
ww2daggers@aol.com
http://www.johnsonreferencebooks.com
*Wants to buy German War booty;
specific interest is in edged weapons
(dress swords, daggers, bayonets and
other quality items); author of
eighteen books about Imperial and
Third Reich German edged weapons
and militaria.*

Newton Carter
King's Own, The
P.O. Box 46
Wallace, NC 28466
ph: 910-285-5506
fax: 910-285-8042
kingsown@duplinnet.com
http://www.thekingsown.com
*Produces a catalog with over 1,000
British and American military
antiques; Queen Victorian period
through WWII; send $3.*

Will Gorges
Battleground Antiques, Inc.
3910 US Highway 70 East
New Bern, NC 28560
ph: 252-636-3039 or 252-636-5445
fax: 252-637-1862
rebel@civilwarantiques.com
http://www.civilwarshop.com
*Appraiser, dealer specializes in world
militaria through Vietnam; licensed
Federal Firearms dealer; rifles,
pistols, swords, uniforms, flags,
relics, photographs, accouterments.*

Andrew Lipps
Wartime Collectables Military Antiques
P.O. Box 165
532 Dekalb St.
Camden, SC 29020
ph: 803-424-5273
fax: 803-424-5278
wartime@wartimecollectables.com
http://www.wartimecollectables.com
*Buys and sells authentic military items
from the Civil War to the Vietnam
War with an emphasis on US material
from Spanish American War to WWII;
authentic material only.*

Scott Vezeau
Scottiques
446 Dixie Bee Rd.
Clarksville, TN 37043
ph: 931-358-3097
scottiques1@msn.com
*Dealer, collector of Civil War through
WWII militaria with emphasis on
Civil War photographs; also wants
antique photographs from early
daguerreotypes to snapshot albums of
the 1950s.*

Big Sky Enterprises
P.O. Box 493
Piedmont, SC 29673
ph: 864-299-1375
fax: 864-299-1391
sales@bigskyenterprises.com
http://www.bigskyenterprises.com
*Specializes in prehistoric as well as
historic Indian artifacts of all types;
also militaria of all countries from
1865 to 1945: swords, bayonets,
medals, badges, insignia, fieldgear,
uniforms, documents.*

Paul Kosek
P & K Military Collectables
1323 Washington Ave.
Savannah, GA 31401
ph: 912-355-6806
paulk@sysconn.com
http://www.pandkmilitaryantiques.com
*Specializes in high-quality military
collectibles from 1800s through
Vietnam: edged weapons, headgear,
home front items, sweetheart jewelry,
trench art, photos, booklets and
pamphlets, etc.*

Ron Gordon
San Juan Precious Metals Corp.
4818 San Juan Ave.
Jacksonville, FL 32210-3232
ph: 904-387-3466
fax: 904-387-5166
sjpm@bigfoot.com
http://www.ejewelry.com/sjpm
*Wants German, US, Japanese,
Vietnam military items: helmets, flags,
uniforms, badges, swords, coins,
daggers, etc.*

Donald Blincoe
Uncle Davey's Americana
6140 St. Augustine Rd.
Jacksonville, FL 32217
ph: 904-730-8932 or 904-777-6478
fax: 904-730-8932
uncledv@collectorsnet.com
http://www.collectorsnet.com/uncledv
*Expert who buys, sells, appraises
vintage historical US military related
items from 1740 to 1885: weapons,
documents, currency, coins,
autographs, slavery, photos, books,
newspapers, jewelry, clothing, maps,
letters, etc.*

Chuck Love
Love's Gun & Pawn
1411 S. Woodland Blvd.
Deland, FL 32724
ph: 386-736-1411
fax: 386-736-1410
lgp@bitstorm.net
*Specializes in modern and antique
weapons; also militaria.*

Frank & Bill Muir
Grande Armee Military Antiques
256 Worth Ave.
Palm Beach, FL 33480
ph: 800-278-8212 or 561-835-1958
fax: 561-835-0020
info@grandearmee.com
http://www.grandearmee.com
*Buys and sells armor, medals and
orders, regimental tankards, edged
weapons, aviation models, helmets
and headgear, toy soldiers, GI Joe and
Action Man, firearms, military
miniatures, etc.*

Donald E. Taussig
Sanders' Antique Mall
527 S. Pineapple Ave.
Sarasota, FL 34236
ph: 941-366-0400
fax: 941-952-1491
sandersant@aol.com
http://www.sandersantiques.com
*Buys and sells military related
swords, medals.*

William Skelton
Highland's Vault
P.O. Box 55448
Birmingham, AL 35255-5548
ph: 205-939-1178 or 205-939-3166
fax: 205-939-3166
*Wants to buy all military collectibles
from Civil War through WWII.*

Roger S. Steffen
Steffen's Historical Militaria
14 Murnan Rd.
Cold Spring, KY 41076-9723
ph: 859-431-4499
fax: 859-431-3113
http://www.steffensmilitaria.com
*Antique firearms, accouterments,
swords, helmets, orders, medals;
Revolutionary War, Civil War, WWI,
WWII, Korean War, Vietnam War;
American, Imperial German and Third
Reich, British, French, Russian.*

Ted & Sallie Caldwell
Caldwell & Co. Civil War Antiques
816 Pleasant St.
Lebanon, IN 46052
ph: 765-482-0292 or 765-482-6280
civilwr@in-motion.net
http://www.caldwellandcompany.net
*Actively buy, sell, trade all military
items from Revolutionary War through
Indian War era; also rewraps leather
grips on swords and sabers.*

John W. Poling
Military & Political Collectibles
P.O. Box 333
Pendleton, IN 46064-0333
ph: 765-778-2714
polingjw@aol.com
*Mail order dealer in military
collectibles (helmets, uniforms,
medals, war souvenirs); issues
periodic catalog of items for sale;
send $2 for latest catalog; most prices
in catalog well below current retail.*

Last Square, The
5944 Odana Rd.
Madison, WI 53719
ph: 800-750-4401 or 608-278-4401
fax: 608-278-4402
orders@lastsquare.com
http://www.lastsquare.com
*A military/militaria art & books/
historical miniatures dealer catering
to all aspects of the military history
hobby; from collectible art to large-
scale hand-painted figures to
wargaming miniatures.*

Bob Johnson
Battlefield Bookstore
3915 Highway 7
Minneapolis, MN 55416
ph: 952-920-3820
fax: 952-929-3714
military@globalcrossing.net
http://www.battlefieldstore.com
Buys and sells militaria.

Hayes Otoupalik
14000 Highway 93 N.
Missoula, MT 59802
ph: 406-549-4817
*Wants to buy all American military
items from 1845 to 1945: Civil War,
Indian and Spanish American Wars,
blue wool uniforms and caps, WWI
doughboy uniforms and helmets,
WWII flyers jackets, paratrooper
uniforms, patch collections, etc.*

Randy Donley
Donley's Wild West Town & Museum
8512 S. Union Rd.
Union, IL 60180-9661
ph: 815-923-9000
fax: 815-923-2253
mdonley@dls.net
http://www.wildwesttown.com
*Buys and sells souvenirs and relics
from all wars: uniforms, helmets,
medals, weapons, guns, swords, etc.*

Marc Wade
Antique & Collectable Firearms &
  Militaria Headquarters
P.O. Box 95021
South Jordan, UT 84095
ph: 801-947-9442
hq@oldguns.net
http://oldguns.net
*Buys, sells, appraises; interesting and
useful information for collectors of
antique and collectible firearms and
militaria; questions answered, gun
show listings, catalog, gun related
software.*

John Spangler
Antique & Collectible Firearms &
  Militaria Headquarters
P.O. Box 711282
Salt Lake City, UT 84171
ph: 801-947-9442
hq@oldguns.net
http://www.oldguns.net
*Appraises, buys, sells, specializes in
firearms & militaria; Web site has
interesting and useful information for
collectors of antique and collectible
firearms and militaria; questions
answered, gun show listings, catalog.*

Warren Anderson
America West Archives
P.O. Box 100
Cedar City, UT 84721-0100
ph: 435-586-9497 or 435-586-7323
awa@netutah.com
http://www.americawestarchives.com
*Buys and sells pre-1900 US military
documents, letters, autographs,
photos, especially interested in Civil
War, Indian Wars, and military
documents from the Western US;
author of "Owning Western History."*

Stewart's Military Antiques
108 W. Main St.
Mesa, AZ 85201
ph: 602-834-4004
fax: 602-834-3380
*Buys and sells helmets, medals,
insignia, uniforms, photos, swords,
and other military collectibles from
1860 to 1945.*

Barrett Behnke
Barrett's Toys & Collectibles
7063 E. Blue Lake Dr.
Tucson, AZ 85715-3218
ph: 520-290-2864
barrettnan@aol.com
*Buys and sells US militaria from the
Civil War to present; also general
military items of all countries.*

Robert C. Thomas, Jr.
P.O. Box 28191
Santa Ana, CA 92799-8191
ph: 714-572-1985 or 714-345-8092
fax: 714-546-0110
robert@thomashouse.org
*Buys and sells military collectibles,
primarily WWII items; also collects
WWII US Airborne related items.*

AntiquesWest.com
P.O. Box 6218
Moraga, CA 94570
ph: 925-934-4137
jd@antiqueswest.com
http://www.antiqueswest.com
*Specializes in antique guns, swords,
militaria, and American Civil War.*

Military Antiques & Museum
300 Petaluma Blvd. North
Petaluma, CA 94952
ph: 707-763-2220
fax: 707-763-5964
warstuff@sonic.net
http://
www.militaryantiquesmuseum.com
*Military antiques from the Civil War
to WWII; US, Japanese, German,
Italian, French; books, video and
audio tapes, uniforms, badges,
medals, edged weapons, headgear,
antique firearms, posters.*

Geoff Pollard
Geoff Pollard Militaria
P.O. Box 89
Lytham St. Annes, Lancashire FY8 3UQ
U.K.
ph: 01253 721070
*Specializes in German and WWII
memorabilia.*

Experts

Stephen Flood, Pres.
AAG, International Militaria Mail
  Auction
1226-B Sans Souci Parkway
Wilkes Barre, PA 18702-1230
ph: 570-822-5300
fax: 570-822-9992
aagintl1@aol.com
http://www.aag-militaria.com
*Buys and sells militaria from
Revolutionary War to Vietnam with
emphasis on WWII; all countries;
issues a catalog approximately every
six months; a large, fine auction
house.*

Courtney Wilson
American Military Antiques
8398 Court Ave.
Ellicott City, MD 21043-4514
ph: 410-465-6827
fax: 410-461-6820
*Military antiques 1700-1900:
appraiser, consultant, broker, dealer;
arms, uniforms, equipment,
memorabilia - especially Civil War.*

Kevin Carney
Military Collectors Consortium, The
154A Locust Ave.
Fairmont, WV 26554
ph: 304-367-9612
fax: 304-416-2811
CarneyK@labyrinth.net
http://www.lee-enfield.com
*Dealer, collector and expert in
military firearms, edged weapons, and
militaria from 1750 to 1970;
appraises, brokers, consults.*

Sheperd Paine
P.O. Box 34679
Chicago, IL 60634
ph: 703-461-9582
fax: 703-461-3059
mail@fjpauction.com
http://www.fjpauction.com
*Wants British, French and German
pre-1914 uniforms, helmets, swords;
familiar with military items from most
countries & periods.*

David C. Williams
Lost Cause Relics
2237 Brookhollow Dr.
Abilene, TX 79605-5507
ph: 915-692-1858
dcjew@swbell.net
*Collector and dealer in US medals
and medal groupings of all periods;
also military photography, documents,
uniforms, aviation items, etc.; Special
Forces (Green Berets) a specialty.*

R. Stephen Dorsey
R. Stephen Dorsey Antique Militaria
P.O. Box 263
Eugene, OR 97440-0263
ph: 541-937-3348
mail@rsdmilitaria.com
http://www.rsdmilitaria.com
*Has authored or co-authored nine
books relating to militaria; staff
editor for "The Gun Report"
magazine; antique guns, edged
weapons, accouterments, cavalry
items.*

Internet Resources

Jonathan Gawne
Militaria.com
P.O. Box 2925
Framingham, MA 01703
jgawne@militaria.com
http://www.militaria.com/gij.html
*A place for military collectors and
military historians; home of the "G.I.
Journal," with information on some
of the best military magazines, books,
collectibles, and militaria sites.*

Kevin Carney
Military Collectors Consortium, The
154A Locust Ave.
Fairmont, WV 26554
ph: 304-367-9612
fax: 304-416-2811
CarneyK@labyrinth.net
http://www.lee-enfield.com
*Global resource for collectors of
military firearms, edged weapons, and
militaria from 1750-1970; appraisal,*

*brokerage, and consulting services
relating to arms and militaria;
publishes monthly "Military
Collectors Journal" online.*

Steve Baker
Antique Militaria & Collectibles
  Network
106 Osprey Ct.
Morehead City, NC 28557
ph: 252-393-7821
ddesign@ddesigns.com
http://www.collectorsnet.com/
  militariaindex.html
*A network dedicated to militaria
dealers of all eras; put your list online
for as little as $21.50 per month and
advertise to over 12,000 visitors per
day.*

Chris Armold
Militaria Collector's Exchange, The
124 Mary Lane
Jacksonville, AR 72076
ph: 501-988-2565
tmcx@infinet.com
http://www.tmcx.com
*An internationally recognized Web site
devoted to the preservation and
collecting of military relics; great Web
site with just about everything related
to militaria.*

John Spangler
Antique & Collectible Firearms &
  Militaria Headquarters
P.O. Box 711282
Salt Lake City, UT 84171
ph: 801-947-9442
hq@oldguns.net
http://www.oldguns.net
*Impressive site with loads of helpful
information for the beginning or
advanced collector as well as highly
detailed catalog listings (many with
photos) of militaria: guns, swords,
bayonets, modern firearms; also
consignments & repairs.*

Olive Drab
chuck@olive-drab.com
http://www.olive-drab.com
*Web site where you will find original
materials on many military subjects
and links: military vehicles, military
movies and books, vehicle/parts
dealers, organizations, surplus
dealers, military photos and clip art,
etc.*

Museums/Libraries

Greg Souchik
Allegheny Arms & Armor Museum, Inc.
P.O. Box 161
Custer City, PA 16725-0161
ph: 814-362-2642
fax: 814-362-7356
Director@armormuseum.com
http://www.armormuseum.com
*Firearms, cannons, all types of
historical military material.*

George W. Marinos
Battlefield Military Museum
900 Baltimore Pike
P.O. Box 3192
Gettysburg, PA 17325-0192
ph: 717-334-6568
Wants war relics - US, German, any country and any war; guns, swords, medals, helmets, belts, buckles, flags, etc.

U.S. Marine Corps Historical Center & Museum
Washington Navy Yard, Bldg. 58
1254 Charles Morris St., SE
Washington, DC 20374-0540
ph: 202-433-3483
fax: 202-433-4691
http://www.usmc.mil/historical.nsf/Nav3
Marine Corps art, personal papers, military music.

Naval Historical Center
Washington Navy Yard
805 Kidder Breese SE
Washington, DC 20374-5060
ph: 202-433-4882
fax: 202-433-8200
archives@navy.mil
http://www.history.navy.mil
Mission is to enhance the Navy's effectiveness by preserving, analyzing and interpreting its history: museum, art gallery, research library, archives.

Director
U.S. Army Transportation Museum
Bldg. 300, Besson Hall
Ft. Eustis, VA 23604-5259
ph: 757-878-1115
fax: 757-878-5656
atzfptm@eustis.army.mil
http://www.eustis.army.mil/dptmsec/
  museum.htm
Collects, exhibits and interprets the history of US Army transportation activities from the Revolutionary War to present.

Parris Island Museum, The
Commanding General, Attn: MCRD
  ERR
Box 19001
Beaufort, SC 29905-9001
ph: 843-228-2951
fax: 843-228-3065
http://www.parrisisland.com/
  museum.htm
Museum features large exhibit halls of the history of recruit training, 20th century Marine Corps history, and the history of Parris Island.

National Infantry Museum of the National
  Infantry Association
U.S. Army Infantry School
ATSH-OTN Building 396
Fort Benning, GA 31905-5593
ph: 706-545-2958 or 706-545-6762
fax: 706-545-5158
infantryassn@earthlink.net
http://www.infantryassn.com
Over 30,000 sq. ft. of exhibits honoring the infantry soldier and over two centuries of service.

Richard L. Uppstrom, Dir.
U.S. Air Force Museum
1100 Spaatz St.
Dayton, OH 45433-7102
ph: 937-255-3286
fax: 937-255-0523
usaf.museum@wpafb.af.mil
http://www.wpafb.af.mil/museum
World's largest aviation museum with 10 1/2 acres of aircraft and other exhibits under roof.

Randy Donley
Donley's Wild West Town & Museum
8512 S. Union Rd.
Union, IL 60180-9661
ph: 815-923-9000
fax: 815-923-2253
mdonley@dls.net
http://www.wildwesttown.com
Large display of souvenirs and relics from all wars: uniforms, helmets, medals, weapons, guns, swords, etc.

Military Antiques & Museum
300 Petaluma Blvd. North
Petaluma, CA 94952
ph: 707-763-2220
fax: 707-763-5964
warstuff@sonic.net
http://
  www.militaryantiquesmuseum.com
Military antiques from the Civil War to WWII; US, Japanese, German, Italian, French; books, video and audio tapes, uniforms, badges, medals, edged weapons, headgear, antique firearms, posters.

Periodicals

Terry Hannon, Ed.
Phoenix Militaria, Inc.
Directory: American Militaria
  Sourcebook & Directory
P.O. Box 245
Lyon Station, PA 19536-9986
ph: 610-682-1010 or 800-446-0909
fax: 610-682-1066
TerryHannon@msn.com
http://www.phoenixmilitaria.com
A complete listing of militaria dealers, service companies and organizations.

PRIMEDIA Enthusiast Group
Magazine: Military History
741 Miller Dr., SE, Ste. D-2
Leesburg, VA 20175
ph: 703-779-8318
fax: 703-779-8310
david.masini@primedia.com
http://www.thehistorynet.com/
  MilitaryHistory
A guide through history focusing on armed conflicts; incisive accounts of land, naval and air warfare in world history from ancient to modern times; published bi-monthly.

PRIMEDIA Enthusiast Group
Magazine: World War II
741 Miller Dr., SE, Ste. D-2
Leesburg, VA 20175
ph: 703-779-8318
fax: 703-779-8310
david.masini@primedia.com
http://www.thehistorynet.com/
  WorldWarII
A bi-monthly magazine; the ultimate authority on WWII: weapons, personalities, tactics.

Chris George
War of 1812 Consortium, The Star
  Spangled Banner Flag House & 1812
  Museum
Magazine: Journal of the War of 1812 &
  the Era 1800 to 1840
844 E. Pratt St.
Baltimore, MD 21202
ph: 410-223-1638 or 410-243-5635
chrisdonna@erols.com
http://www.cronab.demon.co.uk/
  jour.htm
For those interested in the early years of our history.

Stacie Berger
Antique Trader Publications, Inc.
Magazine: Military Trader
P.O. Box 1050
Dubuque, IA 52004-1050
ph: 800-334-7165 or 800-482-4155
fax: 800-531-0880
stacie.berger@fwpubs.com
http://www.militarytrader.com
Monthly publication focusing on military collectibles: articles, collecting, interviews with dealers, military toy column, book reviews, collectibles for sale, espionage.

Thomas O. Berndt, Pub.
Magazine: Militaria International
P.O. Box 43400
Minneapolis, MN 55443-0400
ph: 888-428-1942 or 612-428-4345
fax: 612-428-7575
militintl@aol.com
http://members.aol.com/militintl
A monthly worldwide magazine with articles, features and photos; for all types of collectible militaria: uniforms and field gear, weapons, vehicles and parts, travel and museums, clubs and organizations, sale and show information.

Newsmagazine: Military
2122 28th St.
P.O. Box 189490
Sacramento, CA 95818
ph: 800-366-9192 or 916-457-8990
fax: 916-457-7339
editor@milmag.com
http://www.milmag.com
Monthly newsmagazine with articles, ads, etc.; many articles on military aviation.

Service Publications
Newsletter: Military Artifact
55 Abingdon Dr.
Nepean, Ontario K2H 7M5 Canada
ph: 613-820-7350
fax: 613-820-1288
sales@servicepub.com
http://www.servicepub.com
A quarterly newsletter dedicated to collectible artifacts of the British Empire, Commonwealth and specifically Canada; covers the period of the Crimea to Korea, 1854 to 1953.

Phillipe Charbonnier, Ed.
Histoire et Collections
Magazine: Militaria Magazine
5, Ave de la Republique
75541 Paris Cedex, 11 France
ph: 01 40 21 18 20
fax: 01 47 00 51 11
militaria@histecoll.com
http://www.militariamag.com
A French monthly magazine written in French featuring pristine examples of existing memorabilia, supported with historical photos.

Imperial War Museum
Magazine: Imperial War Museum
  Review
Mail Order Department
Duxford, Cambridge CB2 4QR U.K.
mail@iwm.org.uk
http://www.iwm.org.uk
A richly illustrated journal from the UK's museum of 20th century conflict; covering war history and art; primary source material covering documents, films, posters, photographs; invaluable for the historian, student or teacher.

Beaumont Publishing
Magazine: Armourer Magazine, The
Adelphi Mill, 1st Floor
Bollington, Cheshire SK10 5JB U.K.
ph: +44 (0) 1625 575700
fax: +44 (0) 1625 575700
editor@armourer.u-net.com
http://www.armourer.u-net.com
Bi-monthly English magazine; has everything for the militaria, arms, armor and weapon enthusiast and collector and those with an interest in WWI, WWII, and military history; ads, articles on ordnance, bayonets, medals, insignia, etc.

Repro. Sources

Collector's Armoury
P.O. Box 59
Alexandria, VA 22313-0059
ph: 877-276-6879 or 703-684-6111
fax: 703-683-5486
sales@collectorsarmoury.com
http://www.armoury.com
Offers museum quality reproductions: Civil War swords, knives, pistols and field gear; non-firing Western pistols, rifles and collectibles; medieval, Samurai and military swords; historic miniature Gatling guns and cannons.

Anti-Axis

Collectors

Kenneth E. Fleck
Fleck Auctioneering
496 2nd St.
Highspire, PA 17034-1505
ph: 717-939-8441
fax: 717-939-0064
*Wants to buy WWII Anti-Axis items
depicting anti-Hitler, anti-Mussolini,
anti-Tojo, etc. sentiments: toys,
games, coin-ops, banks, ashtrays,
paper, textiles, etc.*

Martin Jacobs
World War II Homefront Collectibles
P.O. Box 22026
San Francisco, CA 94122-0026
ph: 415-661-7552
fax: 415-731-4668
MJacobs784@aol.com
*Collector seeks WWII memorabilia
from the Homefront 1941-1945; will
purchase any size collection; wants
victory pins, Cinderella stickers and
stamps, envelope art, war propaganda, Anti-Axis art, matchcovers,
postcards, etc.*

British

Clubs/Associations

Hubert H. Long
Military Heraldry Society
Magazine: Formation Sign, The
77 Chiltern Gardens
Dawley
Telford, Shropshire TF4 2QH U.K.
ph: 01952 408830
*Formed in 1951 for collectors of cloth
formation signs: shoulder sleeve
insignia, shoulder titles, regimental
and unit flashes, etc.; all countries.*

A.N. McClenaghan
Indian Military Historical Society
Magazine: Durbar
33 High St.
Tilbrook
Hungingdon, Cambridgeshire PE28 0JP
U.K.
imhs@zetnet.co.uk
*Formed in 1983 to bring together
those interested in the military history
of the Indian Subcontinent; a forum
for the dissemination of knowledge of
uniforms, medals, badges, buttons,
and other militaria & history of
Service units.*

Experts

Brian Whitely
British Regalia Imports
P.O. Box 1416
Palm Harbor, FL 34682-1416
ph: 727-736-6750
fax: 727-736-6585
execucom@gte.net
*British and Scottish regimental
insignia and accessories: cap badges,
rank badges, uniform buttons,
patches, wings, garrison belts, berets,
blazer crests, ties, officers' swagger*

canes, swords, flags, medals, maps,
etc.

Decals

Collectors

Steve Billings
6429 Cheekwood Ave.
Memphis, TN 38134
sbillin9@bellsouth.net
*Collects military unit and equipment
manufacturer's stickers and decals
(a.k.a. "zappers"); American or
foreign, Air Force, Navy, Army.*

German

Clubs/Associations

J.J. Daub
Imperial German Military Collectors
Association
Journal: Kaiserzeit
82 Atlantic St.
Keyport, NJ 07735-1857
ph: 908-739-1799 or 816-455-3214
*Military collectors and historians with
a wide range of interests in all aspects
of the Imperial German military (pre-
1919).*

Collectors

John Telesmanich
P.O. Box 62
White Plains, NY 10604-0062
ph: 914-949-5519
militarybuyer@aol.com
*Wants WWII or earlier German
daggers, swords, medals, uniforms,
helmets, flags, books, documents,
patches, belt buckles, postcards, etc.*

J. Burnet
P.O. Box 1472
Massapequa, NY 11758-0908
*Wants to buy WWII Nazi relics: flags,
helmets, badges, etc.; also wants
Adolf Hitler memorabilia: postcards,
cigarette cards and albums,
silverware, etc.; anything pertaining
to Hitler.*

Daniel E. Lee
P.O. Box 1142
Brentwood, TN 37024-1142
ph: 615-370-3220 or 615-429-5336
6lees@msn.com
*Private collector seeking 3rd Reich
(Nazi) war relics for personal
collection; references available;
discreet.*

Tommy Foster
501 E. Main St.
Arlington, TX 76010
ph: 800-342-2409
fax: 817-275-3225
tfoster@attglobal.net
Collector of Third Reich arm bands.

Dealers

Diane Schreiber
Brandenburg Historica
63 Emerald St., PMB 500
Keene, NH 03431-3626
ph: 603-352-1961
fax: 603-357-5364
info@brandenburghistorica.com
http://www.brandenburghistorica.com
*Buys and sells German militaria:
decorations and badges of the German
Armed Forces, police civil and
paramilitary organizations from 1871-
1945 and 1957 to present; historical
German military music and soldiers'
songs on CD.*

Brent's Military Antiques
P.O. Box 9255
Greensboro, NC 27429-0255
ph: 336-288-5061
bsmith1181@aol.com
*Wants WWII Nazi military items:
swords, daggers, helmets, medals,
hats, uniforms, autographs, etc.*

Marc J. Cohen
P.O. Box 100637
Fort Lauderdale, FL 33310-0637
ph: 954-565-9754
*Wants to buy German war souvenirs
(especially WWII German Navy, the
Kriegsmarine, items): helmets,
uniforms, medals, gas masks, buttons,
canteens, badges, hats, belts, buttons,
bayonets, patches, daggers, flags,
knives, etc.*

Dr. Robert A. Hiett
Maple City Coin
P.O. Drawer 47
Monmouth, IL 61462-0047
ph: 309-734-3212
fax: 309-734-8083
hiett@gallatinriver.net
Wants any Nazi or SS related items.

Ronald J. Weinand
Weinand Militaria
P.O. Box 323
Quincy, IL 62306-0323
ph: 217-223-2322
fax: 217-223-2552
relic@warrelic.com
http://www.warrelic.com
*Appraiser, collector, dealer
specializing in German militaria;
author of "German Helmets 1933-
1945" (Vol. 1 and 2), "NPEA
Daggers and Associated Knives," and
"German Clamshells & Other
Bayonets."*

World Militaria
ph: 503-296-2080 or 888-481-3727
worldmilitaria@mindspring.com
http://www.worldmilitaria.com
*Specializing in WWII German
militaria, especially in items relating
to Adolf Hitler.*

Mark Sansom
German Militaria & Collectables
12 Broughton Ave.
Redhill, Ensbury Park
U.K.
ph: 01202 466672 or 07968 066764
info@german-militaria.co.uk
http://www.german-militaria.co.uk
*Established dealer wants to buy
German war booty and souvenirs:
helmets, uniforms, medals, gas masks,
buttons, canteens, badges, hats, belts,
buttons, bayonets, patches, daggers,
flags, knives, etc.*

Experts

Richard J. Kimmel
P.O. Box 19
Bayville, NJ 08721-1412
ph: 732-557-4485
KoreaVeteran@aol.com
*Author of "The Phenomenon of Third
Reich Badge Collecting: From the
Hocus Bogus to True Genuine;" wants
WWII combat cameras: military
versions with subdued olive drab and
black finish only.*

Ronald J. Weinand
Weinand Militaria
P.O. Box 323
Quincy, IL 62306-0323
ph: 217-223-2322
fax: 217-223-2552
relic@warrelic.com
http://www.warrelic.com
*Appraiser, collector, dealer
specializing in German militaria;
author of "German Helmets 1933-
1945" (Vol. 1 and 2), "NPEA
Daggers and Associated Knives," and
"German Clamshells & Other
Bayonets."*

German (East)

Clubs/Associations

Lee Stewart
Society of East German Militaria
Collectors
Magazine: SEGMC Magazine
P.O. Box 2153
Reston, VA 20195-0153
ph: 703-715-0683
*Source for information on history,
uniforms, and insignia of former East
German forces; quarterly newsletter.*

Helmets

Dealers

Casey Hubbke
Papa Hoth Militaria
5945 West Parker Rd., Ste. 3027
Plano, TX 75093
ph: 972-473-6736
fax: 972-473-7278
*Collectors and dealers in military
helmets; also restores helmets, but not
original period pieces; buys all types
of helmets and helmet parts.*

Insignia

(see also BADGES; MEDALS,
ORDERS & DECORATIONS;
PATCHES; VETERAN ITEMS)

Clubs/Associations

Scott G. hughes
American Society of Military Insignia
  Collectors
Journal: Trading Post
3415 Tilley Morris Rd.
Matthews, NC 28105-7121
ph: 704-846-0541
fax: 704-846-0540
adjutant@asmic.org
http://www.asmic.org
  *Dedicated to the collection and
  preservation of US military cloth and
  metal insignia; newsletter available
  only to members and contains
  members' buy/sell ads; approximately
  2500 members; send for application
  and dues information.*

Chute & Dagger
P.O. Box 7201
Arlington, VA 22207-7201
fax: 703-276-3033
hfp@ix.netcom.com
http://www.chuteanddagger.com
  *Parachute and Special Force insignia
  collectors.*

Collectors

Hank McGonagle
26 Broad St.
Newburyport, MA 01950-2103
ph: 978-462-2354
saber12@mediaone.net
  *Wants to buy medals and cloth
  shoulder insignia; all nations and
  eras.*

Don Sexton
400 Flamingo Circle
Greeneville, TN 37743-6126
ph: 423-639-4725
fax: 423-639-3960
  *President of the American Society of
  Military Insignia Collectors.*

Rex M. "Wess" Wessling
15706 North East 56th Way
Redmond, WA 98052
ph: 425-497-1480
wwesslin@ix.netcom.com
http://www.rexmwess.com
  *Collects, buys, sells, trades,
  documents US Coast Guard patches;
  Web site has 200-400 patches
  available for sale; also illustrations of
  several hundred C.G. patches and
  books for sale regarding C.G. patches
  and history.*

Dealers

H.J. Saunders
H.J. Saunders U.S. Military Insignia,
  Inc.
5025 Tamiami Trail East
Naples, FL 34113-4126
ph: 941-775-2100 or 800-442-3133
fax: 941-774-3323
Insignia@naples.net
http://www.SaundersInsignia.com
  *America's largest retail insignia
  company; offering over 14,000
  different US military insignia items
  from WWII; insignia; shoulder
  patches, aviation wings, National*

Guard, Special Forces, squadron
patches; also 150 books on insignia.

J. Polder
Aeroemblem
P.O. Box 6206
Wichita Falls, TX 76311-6202
ph: 940-855-0988 or 940-855-8606
fax: 940-855-0072
AEROEMBLEM@aol.com
http://www.aeroemblem.com
  *Has been in the business of trading,
  buying and selling Air Force patches
  since the 1950s.*

McGrogan's Military Patches
P.O. Box 2254
Hayden, ID 83835
ph: 208-762-4481
fax: 208-762-3931
macpatch@mcgrogans.com
http://www.mcgrogans.com
  *1,000s of submarine, ship, Navy,
  Marine, Air Force, Army and Air
  Borne patches in stock.*

Experts

Mario De Marco
152 Maple St.
West Boylston, MA 01583-1825
ph: 508-835-4085
  *Has books on Naval ships and
  aircraft, insignias and history; also
  Naval and Marine; price $9 each ppd.*

David C. Williams
Lost Cause Relics
2237 Brookhollow Dr.
Abilene, TX 79605-5507
ph: 915-692-1858
dcjew@swbell.net
  *Collector and dealer in US medals
  and medal groupings of all periods;
  also military photography, documents,
  uniforms, aviation items, etc.; Special
  Forces (Green Berets) a specialty.*

Internet Resources

Richard Operhall
U.S. Air Force Patch Collectors
  Homepage
usafpatches@yahoo.com
http://www.usafpatches.com
  *A Web site dedicated to the US Air
  Force patch/insignia collector; patches
  for sale, where to buy patches, etc.*

Insignia (British)

Dealers

Ian Kelly
Major Ian G. Kelly Militaria
P.O. Box 66
Ellesmere, Shropshire SY12 0YS U.K.
fax: 44 1691 624964
Ian@KellyBadge.co.uk
http://www.KellyBadge.co.uk
  *Buys and sells original post-1881
  British military and police badges;
  send 3 international postal response
  coupons for free substantial catalog:
  caps and collar insignia, buttons,
  trade & proficiency badges, shoulder
  titles, etc.*

Japanese

(see ARMS & ARMOR; FIREARMS,
Japanese Matchlocks; ORIENTALIA,
Japanese Items)

Manuals

Dealers

George Kastner
Daddy Warbooks
P.O. Box 6397
Los Osos, CA 93412-6397
ph: 805-528-1614
  *Wants to buy military books and
  manuals from 1900-1965.*

Medals

(see also MEDALS, ORDERS &
DECORATIONS)

Clubs/Associations

John E. Lelle, Sec.
Orders & Medals Society of America
Newsletter: Medal Collector, The
P.O. Box 484
Glassboro, NJ 08028-0484
dlriley@hopkinsville.net
http://www.omsa.org
  *Interested in collecting and studying
  military and civil orders, decorations
  and medals of all countries.*

Nuclear

Museums/Libraries

National Atomic Museum
1905 Mountain Rd. NW
Albuquerque, NM 87104
ph: 505-245-2137
fax: 505-242-4537
rekenny@sandia.gov
http://www.sandia.gov/museum
  *Exhibits cover the complete history of
  US nuclear development.*

Polish

Experts

John Scott Mathews
SLM Consulting
1051 E. Kent Place
Chandler, AZ 85225
ph: 480-786-4215
JScottMathews@netscape.net
  *Thirty years collecting experience in
  Polish militaria: headgear, uniforms,
  badges, medals, flags, bayonets and
  swords; professional historian
  employed as a professor at a major
  institution of higher learning.*

Russian

(see also RUSSIAN ITEMS)

Dealers

Igor Moiseyev
Atlantic Crossroads, Inc.
P.O. Box 144
Tenafly, NJ 07670
ph: 201-567-8717
fax: 201-567-6855
Nat@CollectRussia.com
http://www.collectrussia.com
  *Sells 1918-1980s Russian military and
  civilian decorations, documented
  award groups, WWII and 1950s
  uniforms and field gear, historical
  documents, reference books, military
  badges and insignia; offers
  appraisals, research, translations.*

Robert Natanzon
Original Soviet Militaria
2536 Hubbard St.
Brooklyn, NY 11235-6223
ph: 718-769-1446
fax: 718-769-5617
rob1329@aol.com
http://www.fine-russian-antiques.com
  *Specializes in Russian militaria,
  icons, crosses, silver, etc.*

Silk Embroideries

Collectors

Howard Averbach
1919 Delaware Ave.
Pittsburgh, PA 15218-1801
ph: 412-441-6904
  *Wants to buy patriotic/military silk
  embroideries purchased as souvenirs
  by US soldiers and sailors in the
  Orient; embroidered ships, flags,
  eagles, mottoes; wallhangings only;
  no pillowcases or clothing; send
  photos & asking price.*

Spanish-American War

Collectors

Morris Pickerell, Jr.
100 A. Lyon Ave.
Glasgow, KY 42141
ph: 270-678-5848 or 270-783-3124
fax: 270-678-7888
  *Wants to buy anything relating to
  Admiral George Dewey, the Spanish-
  American War, including battleship
  Maine.*

Stickers

Collectors

Jim
Military Program Sticker & Patch
  Collector
cd102@aol.com
http://members.aol.com/Milstkr1/
  indexsp1.htm
  *Buys and traders military program
  stickers such as Patriot Missile,
  Harpoon Missile, Star Wars, DOD,
  etc.*

U-Boats

Clubs/Associations

Harry Cooper
Sharkhunters International Inc.
Magazine: KTB Magazine (Kriegs Tag Buch)
P.O. Box 1539
Hernando, FL 34442
ph: 352-637-2917
fax: 352-637-6289
sharkhunters@sharkhunters.com
http://www.sharkhunters.com
Locates and preserves the history of the German and Italian U-Boat forces; recognized leading authority on the subject; Sharkhunters is the largest research center in the Western hemisphere on German U-Boat history.

Museums/Libraries

Keith R. Gill
Museum of Science & Industry
5700 S. Lake Shore Dr.
Chicago, IL 60637
ph: 773-684-1414
fax: 773-684-0026
msi@msichicago.org
http://www.msichicago.org

Uniforms

Clubs/Associations

Gil Sanow, II, Editor
Association of American Military Uniform Collectors
Newsletter: Footlocker
P.O. Box 1876
Elyria, OH 44036
ph: 440-365-5321
aamucfl@aol.com
http://www.naples.net/clubs/aamuc/index.html
Members are interested in improving their personal collections and in sharing information, ideas and knowledge about US military uniforms.

Collectors

Joe Weber
604 Centre St.
Ashland, PA 17921-1332
ph: 570-875-4787 or 570-875-4401
Wants to buy Victorian, WWI (especially aviation), and WWII (especially CBI theater-made uniforms); all countries (US, Britain, German, France, Russia.)

Dealers

Dan Kelley
Experienced Denim
P.O. Box 239
Fayetteville, AR 72702-0239
ph: 501-444-7541 or 800-336-4694
fax: 501-521-8331
exd@edenim.com
http://www.edenim.com
Wants to buy vintage fatigue wear, denim wear, khaki pants, nylon flight jackets, tanker boots, etc.

Repair Services

Lynn Gorges
Historic Textiles Studio
3910 US Highway 70 East
New Bern, NC 28560
ph: 252-636-3039 or 252-636-5445
fax: 252-637-1862
palampore@aol.com
http://www.textilepreservation.com
Specializes in the restoration, conservation, appraisal, evaluation of military uniforms, including Civil War uniforms and Civil War flags.

Vehicles

Clubs/Associations

S. Sebring
Red Ball Military Transport
400 Ave. C
Stroudsburg, PA 18360
ph: 717-421-2950

Joe McClain
Indiana Chapter of the Military Vehicle Preservation Association
2330 Crystal St.
Anderson, IN 46012-1726
ph: 765-649-8265
fax: 765-642-0262

Kay Hinga
Military Vehicle Preservation Association
Newsletter: Army Motors & Supply Line
P.O. Box 520378
Independence, MO 64052-0378
ph: 816-737-MVPA or 800-365-5798
fax: 816-833-5115
mvpa-hq@mvpa.org
http://www.mvpa.org
Since 1976, an international organization dedicated to the preservation of military transport from trucks to tanks.

Gary Roberts, Pres.
California Inland Empire Military Vehicle Preservation Association
455 N. Dahlia
Ontario, CA 91762
ph: 909-983-8755
A world-wide organization dedicated to the preservation and restoration of military vehicles.

Frank Von Rosenstiel
Ontario Military Vehicle Association
1248 Dartmoor St.
Oshawa, Ontario L1K 2K2 Canada
ph: 905-721-0840
http://www.eagle.ca/~harry/vehicles/omva

Nigel Godfrey, Mem. Sec.
Military Vehicle Trust, The
Magazine: Windscreen
P.O. Box 6
Fleet, Hants. GU13 9PE U.K.
fax: +44 (0) 1264 392951
nigelgodfrey@mvt.org.uk
http://www.mvt.org.uk

Dealers

David W. Uhrig
David W. Uhrig Military Vehicles Sales & Appraisals
P.O. Box 726
Chillicothe, OH 45601
ph: 740-772-1540
fax: 740-772-1540
daveuhrig@armyjeeps.net
http://www.armyjeeps.net
Buys, sells, brokers, appraises military vehicles.

Jack Tomlin
Tomlin Ordnance Depot
P.O. Box 778
Tooele, UT 84074
ph: 801-882-0420
fax: 801-882-5042
Buys and sells all sorts of military vehicles from trailers to tanks.

Museums/Libraries

Joe McClain
Historical Military Armor Museum
2330 Crystal St.
Anderson, IN 46012-1726
ph: 765-649-8265
fax: 765-642-0262
One of the most complete collections of Light US Tanks; plus a dozen prototypes of various vehicles; 30,000 sq. ft. of displays; collection has armored vehicles from WWI through Desert Storm.

Periodicals

Stacie Berger
Krause Publications
Magazine: Military Vehicles
700 E. State St.
Iola, WI 54990-0001
ph: 715-445-2214
fax: 715-445-4087
stacie.berger@fwpubs.com
http://www.krause.com
A bi-monthly magazine for military vehicle (wheeled & tracked) enthusiasts.

Nick Bullock, Ed.
Magazine: MV Magazine
North House
Northside
Patrington, East Yorkshire HU12 0PB U.K.
ph: 01964 631244
fax: 01964 631576
mv@tradingnorthwest.demon.co.uk
http://www.tradingnorthwest.demon.co.uk/military.vehicles
A bi-monthly British publication for military vehicle collectors and enthusiasts: restoration tips, tales, news, contacts, photos, illustrations.

Repair Services

John A. Headley, Jr.
Doncar Equipment Co.
P.O. Box 133
Flanders, NJ 07836
ph: 201-927-0940
fax: 201-584-8118
Restores, appraises military vehicles.

Suppliers

Daniel Janquitto
Beachwood Canvas Works
P.O. Box 137
Island Heights, NJ 08732
ph: 732-929-3168
fax: 732-929-3479
beachwoodcanvas@comcast.net
http://www.beachwoodcanvas.com
Provides parts for WWII military vehicles such as Jeeps.

Vehicles (Armored)

Internet Resources

Olive Drab
chuck@olive-drab.com
http://www.olive-drab.com
Web site where you will find original materials on many military subjects; links to military vehicles, military movies and books, vehicle/parts dealers, organizations, surplus dealers, military photos and clip art, etc.

Museums/Libraries

Bill Gasser
American Armoured Foundation, Tank & Ordnance War Memorial Museum
2383 5th Ave.
Ronkonkoma, NY 11779
ph: 516-588-0033
fax: 516-981-4992
aaf.tank.museum@erols.com
http://www.aaftankmuseum.com
Museum of armored vehicles, weapons and militaria dedicated in the honor of all veterans.

Patton Museum of Cavalry & Armor
P.O. Box 208
Fort Knox, KY 40121-0208
ph: 502-624-3812
fax: 502-624-6968
pattonweb@aol.com
http://www.generalpatton.org
Established to preserve historical materials relating to Cavalry and Armor and to make these properties available for public use.

American Society of Military History Military Museum
Whittier Narrows Rec. Area
1918 North Rosemead Blvd.
El Monte, CA 91732
ph: 626-442-1776
fax: 626-443-1776
tankland@aol.com
http://hometown.aol.com/tankland/museum.htm
Maintained by the American Society of Military History; contains the largest

collection of tanks and military
vehicles in the US.

Vietnam Items

Dealers

Michael Tucker
Authentic Militaria
2119 SE Wild Meadow Circle
Port Saint Lucie, FL 34952
ph: 561-398-4878
webmaster@authenticmilitaria.com
http://www.authenticmilitaria.com
*Specializes in militaria from WWII
and Vietnam era: badges, patches,
medals, uniforms, hats, daggers,
helmets, field gear, bayonets, swords,
flags, documents, personal items.*

WWI Items

Collectors

Peter M. Bennethum
P.O. Box 6523
Reading, PA 19610
ph: 610-678-1730
*Wants to buy WWI and WWII war
souvenirs: swords, daggers, photos,
medals, paratrooper items, helmets,
flight jackets, uniforms, patches.*

Randy Trawnik
1228 Lausanne
Dallas, TX 75208
ph: 214-941-2445
fax: 214-739-8361
dallaseye@airmail.net
*Wants WWI German spiked helmets,
uniforms, etc.; wants in any condition;
also identification and restoration.*

Dealers

Dale C. Anderson Co.
P.O. Box 3516
Gettysburg, PA 17325
http://www.andersonmilitaria.com
*Sells antique firearms, swords,
uniforms, headgear, accouterments,
and more from the period 1775 to
1945; US and foreign; emphasis on
1860 to 1900 era; 40-page bimonthly
catalog $12/yr and by Web site; since
1961.*

Ken Greenfield
Der Rittmeister Militaria
P.O. Box 841
New Port Richey, FL 34656-0841
ph: 727-857-0912
fax: 727-857-0912
rittmeister@earthlink.net
http://www.derrittmeister.com
*Specializes in German Imperial WWI
collectibles with an emphasis on
aviation-related items.*

Museums/Libraries

Liberty Memorial Museum of World
War One, The
Newsletter: Signals
100 West 26th St.
Kansas City, MO 64108
ph: 816-931-0749
fax: 816-221-8981
staff@libertymemorialmuseum.org
http://www.libertymemorialmuseum.org
*The only public museum in the US
dedicated solely to the history of
World War One.*

WWI Items (Photographs)

Collectors

Scott A. Swanson
50 Gloucester St.
Boston, MA 02115-3141
ph: 617-536-8013
speer707@aol.com
*Wants photos of American, European
soldiers, sailors; all fronts, all
branches; albums, single snapshots,
photos taken by soldiers, official or
press photos; no printed cards or
reproductions; also German and
P.O.W.*

WWI Items (Posters)

(see also POSTERS)

Collectors

Ken Khuans
155 Harbor Dr. #4812
Chicago, IL 60601-7378
ph: 312-642-0554
kenkhu@aol.com
*Collector wants American WWI
posters; also books relating to WWI
posters.*

Dealers

Maurice & Laya Jakubowicz
Affiche Francaise
128 Avenue de la Chevre d'Or
Vallauris, 06220 France
ph: 33 (0)493 63 45 92
fax: 33 (0)493 63 45 92
ml@affiche-francaise.com
http://www.affiche-francaise.com
*Buys and sells posters, mainly French,
some foreign; catalog sent on request.*

Experts

George Theofiles
Miscellaneous Man
P.O. Box 1776
New Freedom, PA 17349-0076
ph: 717-235-4766
fax: 717-235-2853
miscman@adelphia.net
*Collects, buys and sells; since 1970
offering catalogs of rare posters and
early advertising and ephemera on
hundreds of subjects; descriptive flyer
available; author of "American
Posters of World War I."*

WWII Items

Collectors

Richard Harrow
8523 210 St.
Jamaica, NY 11427
ph: 718-740-1088
fax: 718-740-1088
*Wants any item relating to WWII:
allied forces, anti-fascist propaganda,
Jewish Holocaust, soldier benevolent
aid, etc.*

Peter M. Bennethum
P.O. Box 6523
Reading, PA 19610
ph: 610-678-1730
*Wants to buy WWI and WWII war
souvenirs: swords, daggers, photos,
medals, paratrooper items, helmets,
flight jackets, uniforms, patches.*

Roger Reece
2241 Danver Circle
Jonesboro, GA 30236-2619
reichrelic@aol.com
*Wants to buy WWII items, memora-
bilia, paper items; specializes in items
belonging to Eva Braun.*

Daniel E. Lee
P.O. Box 1142
Brentwood, TN 37024-1142
ph: 615-370-3220 or 615-429-5336
6lees@msn.com
*Federally licensed firearms collector
seeking Third Reich era (WWII) items,
especially Mauser, Luger, Walther
manufactured and related accessories.*

Harry Fisher
Rte. 1 Box 197
Owensville, MO 65066
ph: 573-437-4227
*Wants WWII items: books, magazines,
unit records (especially 8th Air Force
memorabilia), etc.; please describe
and price.*

Dealers

Gerald Rubackin
Jerry's Cards & Collectibles
P.O. Box 1271
Framingham, MA 01701-0207
ph: 508-788-0946
fax: 508-788-5197
jermyrauto@att.net
http://www.uacc.org/dealers/
   rubackin.html
*Buys and sells WWII fighter aces
autographs and other WWII military
signatures; also want autographed
material by the crew of the Enola Gay
which dropped the first atomic bomb
on Hiroshima.*

Dale C. Anderson Co.
P.O. Box 3516
Gettysburg, PA 17325
http://www.andersonmilitaria.com
*Sells antique firearms, swords,
uniforms, headgear, accouterments,
and more from the period 1775 to
1945; US and foreign; emphasis on
1860 to 1900 era; 40-page bimonthly*

catalog $12/yr and by Web site; since
1961.

Ron Wolin
437 Bartell Dr.
Chesapeake, VA 23322-5707
ph: 757-547-2764
ronwolin@cox.net
*Specializes in WWII military
souvenirs, curios of all kinds; German
and US.*

Michael Tucker
Authentic Militaria
2119 SE Wild Meadow Circle
Port Saint Lucie, FL 34952
ph: 561-398-4878
webmaster@authenticmilitaria.com
http://www.authenticmilitaria.com
*Specializes in militaria from WWII
and Vietnam era: badges, patches,
medals, uniforms, hats, daggers,
helmets, field gear, bayonets, swords,
flags, documents, personal items.*

Anthony Jessen
Jessen's Relics, Inc.
P.O. Box 9523
Birmingham, AL 35220
ph: 205-681-6382
fax: 205-680-9171
*Specializing in German WWII relics,
some US and other nations, 400 to
500 German insignia each catalog:
medals, badges, pins, buckles, flags,
cloth insignia, visor hats, helmets and
uniforms, field gear, edged weapons;
catalog $10.*

Don Creekmore
Nations Attic, The
ph: 316-371-1828
dcreekmore@cox.net
http://www.nationsattic.com
*Wants to buy WWII leather bomber
jackets; any condition; with or without
patches, art work, etc.*

WWII Items (Homefront)

Collectors

Martin Jacobs
World War II Homefront Collectibles
P.O. Box 22026
San Francisco, CA 94122-0026
ph: 415-661-7552
fax: 415-731-4668
MJacobs784@aol.com
*Collector seeks WWII memorabilia
from the Homefront 1941-1945; will
purchase any size collection; wants
victory pins, Cinderella stickers and
stamps, envelope art, war propaganda, Anti-Axis art, matchcovers,
postcards, etc.*

WWII Items (Paratroop)

Collectors

Ed Hicks
P.O. Box 42324
Fayetteville, NC 28309
ph: 910-425-7000
edhicks82@aol.com
http://www.warpathmilitaria.com
Airborne collector/historian wants to

buy WWII Paratroop and Elite militaria: jump jackets, pants, boots, M1C helmets, A-2 leather jackets, fighting and jump knives, T-5 parachutes, unit histories, all related equipment.

WWII Items (Photographs)

Collectors

Scott A. Swanson
50 Gloucester St.
Boston, MA 02115-3141
ph: 617-536-8013
speer707@aol.com
Wants photos of American, European soldiers, sailors; all fronts, all branches; albums, single snapshots, photos taken by soldiers, official or press photos; no printed cards or reproductions; also German and P.O.W.

WWII Items (Posters)

(see also POSTERS)

Collectors

John Stachmus
RR 1 Box 110
Homer, IL 61849
ph: 217-896-2859
Collector wants WWII posters.

Dealers

Jim Meehan
Meehan Military Collectibles
P.O. Box 477
New York, NY 10028-0018
ph: 212-734-5683
fax: 212-535-4249
meehan@interport.net
http://www.posterfair.com/mm/ storefront.htm

Maurice & Laya Jakubowicz
Affiche Francaise
128 Avenue de la Chevre d'Or
Vallauris, 06220 France
ph: 33 (0)493 63 45 92
fax: 33 (0)493 63 45 92
ml@affiche-francaise.com
http://www.affiche-francaise.com
Buys and sells posters, mainly French, some foreign; catalog sent on request.

Experts

George Theofiles
Miscellaneous Man
P.O. Box 1776
New Freedom, PA 17349-0076
ph: 717-235-4766
fax: 717-235-2853
miscman@adelphia.net
Catalogs issued.

MILITARY HISTORY

(see also AVIATION, Military; AVIATION MEMORABILIA; BOOKS, Collector [Militaria]; CIVIL WAR HISTORY; INDIAN WARS; LIVING HISTORY; MARINE CORPS ITEMS; MILITARIA; SOLDIERS, Toy; VIETNAM ITEMS)

Book Sellers

Richard S. Gardner
Battery Press, Inc., The
P.O. Box 198885
Nashville, TN 37219-8885
ph: 615-298-1401
fax: 615-298-1401
batterybks@aol.com
http://www.sonic.net/~bstone/battery
Carries books about WWI and WWII; specializes in aviation, military and naval titles.

Internet Resources

State of New York Division of Military & Naval Affairs; Military History Links
aikeym@dmna.state.ny.us
http://www.dmna.state.ny.us/historic/ histlink.html
Links to major military history Web sites.

Jonathan Gawne
Militaria.com
P.O. Box 2925
Framingham, MA 01703
jgawne@militaria.com
http://www.militaria.com/gij.html
A place for military collectors and military historians; home of the "G.I. Journal," with information on some of the best military magazines, books, collectibles, and militaria sites.

Air War College Gateway to Military History & Related Information
AU Public Affairs
55 South LeMay Plaza
Maxwell AFB, AL 361112
ph: 334-953-2014
maxwell.webmaster@maxwell.af.mil
http://www.au.af.mil/au/awc/awcgate/ awc-hist.htm
Many links to Web sites containing military history information: heraldry, history sources, aces, US operations, Gulf War, Kosovo, WWII, WWI, medieval period, ancient war, etc.

Misc. Services

Meredith Vezina
Traditions Military History
102 West 6th Ave.
Escondido, CA 92025
ph: 800-277-1977 or 760-735-9313
fax: 760-432-9043
cservice@militaryvideo.com
http://www.militaryvideo.com
Sells hard-to-find government-produced films originally recorded in the 1930s through 1980s on 16 and 35 mm film by combat camera teams; films have been transferred to video.

Museums/Libraries

Massachusetts National Guard Military Museum & Archives
Worcester Armory
44 Salisbury St.
Worcester, MA 01609
ph: 508-797-0334 or 508-757-2410
PAO@ma.ngb.army.mil
http://www.state.ma.us/guard/Museum/ museum.htm
Military history museum and archive related to the history of the Massachusetts National Guard from 1638 to present.

Fort Ticonderoga Museum
Newsletter: Bulletin of the Fort Ticonderoga Museum
P.O. Box 390
Ticonderoga, NY 12883
ph: 518-585-2821
fax: 518-585-2210
fort@fort-ticonderoga.org
http://www.fort-ticonderoga.org
10,000 volume research library specializing in 18th century military history and the history of the Champlain Valley; museum depicts history of the area and the campaigns during the 7 Year War and the Revolutionary War.

Virginia War Museum
9285 Warwick Blvd.
Newport News, VA 23607-1537
ph: 757-247-8523 or 757-247-8522
fax: 757-247-8627
info@warmuseum.org
http://www.warmuseum.org
Museum interprets US military history from 1775 to present; featuring over 60,000 artifacts.

Periodicals

Magazine: Artilleryman, The
234 Monarch Hill Rd.
Tunbridge, VT 05077
ph: 802-889-3500 or 800-777-1862
fax: 802-889-5627
mail@civilwarnews.com
Published quarterly, the only magazine exclusively for the 1750-1898 artillery enthusiast: artillery history, unit profiles, shell collecting, etc.

PRIMEDIA Enthusiast Group
Magazine: MHQ: The Quarterly Journal of Military History
741 Miller Dr., SE, Ste. D-2
Leesburg, VA 20175
ph: 703-779-8318
fax: 703-779-8310
david.masini@primedia.com
http://www.thehistorynet.com/MHQ
A quarterly magazine containing a wide variety of articles on military history.

Erika Daileda
Wise Owl Worldwide Publications
Magazine: Regiment
5150 Candlewood St., Ste. 1
Lakewood, CA 90712-1900
ph: 562-461-7574
fax: 562-461-7212
info@wiseowlmagazines.com
http://www.wiseowlmagazines.com
An English magazine published 9 timer per year; regimental and unit histories presented through pictorial records; weapons, vehicles, accouterments, uniforms, medals and decorations, equipment, model soldiers, etc.

Erika Daileda
Wise Owl Worldwide Publications
Magazine: Military Illustrated
5150 Candlewood St., Ste. 1
Lakewood, CA 90712-1900
ph: 562-461-7574
fax: 562-461-7212
info@wiseowlmagazines.com
http://www.wiseowlmagazines.com
A monthly English publication; all periods of military history from ancient to WWII; in-depth research, rare photos, specially commissioned artwork make this magazine one of the finest reference sources for collectors and enthusiasts.

Cavalry

Clubs/Associations

Patricia S. Bright, Ex. Dir.
U.S. Cavalry Association & US Cavalry Memorial Research Library
Journal: Cavalry Journal
Bldg. 247, Cameron St.
P.O. Box 2325
Fort Riley, KS 66442-0325
ph: 785-784-5759
fax: 785-784-5797
cavalry@flinthills.com
http://www.uscavalry.org
Mission is to preserve for posterity the history, equipment, and traditions of the US Cavalry from its inception as a horse mounted force during the Revolutionary War into the 21st century; sponsors the US Cavalry Museum.

Collectors

Mitchell Fenton
334 Mountain Rd.
Lebanon, NJ 08833
ph: 908-534-1438
m3fenton@aol.com
Collector/historian of the four regiments of horse cavalry and remount/veterinarian corp that served in France during WWI; wants related uniforms, photos, equipment, etc.

Museums/Libraries

Terry Van Meter
U.S. Cavalry Museum
P.O. Box 2325
Fort Riley, KS 66442-0325
ph: 785-239-2737
cavalry@flinthills.com
http://www.wtvi.com/cavalry/
  museum.html
*Preserves and displays the uniforms,
weapons and equipment used by
cavalry soldiers from the Revolutionary War through WWII.*

Unit Histories

Collectors

Bill Baumann
P.O. Box 319
Esperance, NY 12066-0319
ph: 518-875-6753
*Collects military unit history books
from all American wars (i.e., Civil
War, Spanish American War, WWI,
WWII, Korea, Vietnam); also wants
unit photos, holiday menus, albums,
posthumous decorations; specializes in
black militaria.*

Museums/Libraries

U.S. Military History Institute
22 Ashburn Dr.
Carlisle Barracks
Carlisle, PA 17013-5008
ph: 717-245-3611
http://carlisle-www.army.mil/usamhi
*Specialized library to research
military history including unit
histories; department of the US Army
War College; the Army's central
repository for historical materials;
collects, preserves, and makes
available military history.*

U.S. Army Center of Military History
103 Third Ave.
Ft. McNair, DC 20319-5058
ph: 202-272-0310
cmhonline@hqda.army.mil
http://www.army.mil/cmh-pg/default.htm
*Specialized library to research
military unit histories.*

U.S. Marine Corps Historical Center &
  Museum
Washington Navy Yard, Bldg. 58
1254 Charles Morris St., SE
Washington, DC 20374-0540
ph: 202-433-3483
fax: 202-433-4691
http://www.usmc.mil/historical.nsf/Nav3
*Specialized library to research
military unit histories.*

Library of Congress
101 Independence Ave. SE
Washington, DC 20540
ph: 202-707-5000 or 202-707-8000
http://www.loc.gov
*Specialized library to research
military unit histories.*

U.S. Army Women's Museum
Newsletter: WAC Newsletter
2100 Adams Ave.
Building P-5219
Fort Lee, VA 23801-2100
ph: 804-734-4326
awmweb@lee.army.mil
http://www.awm.lee.army.mil
*Does purchase some items; cannot sell
or appraise items; can provide
information to collectors and
researchers.*

U.S. Army Military Police Corps
  Regimental Museum
495 South Dakota Ave, Bldg. 1607
Fort Leonard Wood, MO 65473-8851
USAMHI@carlisle.army.mil
http://www.wood.army.mil/usamps/
  Museum/Museum.htm
*Displays the role of the Military
Police (MP) during major US
conflicts, including the Civil War;
collection includes firearms, uniforms,
military vehicles, and Civil War
photographs and artifacts.*

MILLENNIUM COLLECTIBLES

Clubs/Associations

Millenium Collectors, The
18222 Flower Hill Way, #299
Gaithersburg, MD 20879-5300
ph: 301-926-8663
fax: 301-926-7648
info@millenniumcollectors.com
http://www.millenniumcollectors.com
*For collectors of memorabilia
associated with the Millennium.*

MILLING

Appraisers

Robert L. Johnson
Whistles in the Woods Museum
  Services
P.O. Box 309
Chickamauga, GA 30707-0309
ph: 706-375-4326
oldgoat@voy.net
*Consultants & booksellers specializ-
ing in 1750-1930 historic machinery;
power-generation, tools, wood- and
metalworking machines, scientific &
technical instruments, mining, milling,
transportation, logging & lumbering,
steam engines, etc.*

Book Sellers

Sidney Halma
Mill Book Store
P.O. Box 1055
Newton, NC 28658
ph: 828-465-0383 or 828-465-0928
fax: 828-465-9813
eamedit@aol.com
http://www.spoom.org
*Sells books relating to milling; many
reprints.*

Clubs/Associations

Sidney Hamla
Society for the Preservation of Old Mills
  (SPOOM)
Magazine: Old Mill News
P.O. Box 1055
Newton, NC 28658
ph: 828-465-0383 or 828-465-0928
fax: 828-465-9813
eamedit@aol.com
http://www.spoom.org
*Organization focuses on the milling
industry: mills, millwrights,
equipment, techniques; ads, mills for
sale, millwrights, stones, etc.; in
existence for over 20 years; over 2,000
members.*

Collectors

Fred Foley
1333 Randolph Ave.
Saint Paul, MN 55105-2957
ph: 612-690-0993 or 612-699-0859
fax: 612-699-0859
FredFromMN@webtv.net
*Collector seeks pre-1940 flour milling
memorabilia: calendars, signs,
thermometers, flour bags with
graphics, trade cards, store
advertising displays; anything related
to the milling industry.*

Museums/Libraries

Hanford Mills Museum
P.O. Box 99
East Meredith, NY 13757
ph: 607-278-5744 or 800-295-4992
fax: 607-278-5840
hanford4@hanfordmills.org
http://www.catskillguide.com/
  hanford.htm

Bobbins & Spools

Dealers

David W. Harris
Joel S. Perkins & Son, Inc.
P.O. Box 299
South Strafford, VT 05070-0209
ph: 802-889-3260
fax: 802-889-3316
jsperk@sover.net
http://www.joelsperkins.com
*Textile mill supplies, bobbins, spools,
shuttle, mill memorabilia.*

Man./Prod./Dist.

Dirk & Ann Poole
Ma's Bobbin Works, Inc.
P.O. Box 667
Newcastle, ME 04553-0667
ph: 207-563-1210 or 800-782-8581
fax: 207-633-2313
http://www.woodenbobbins.com
*Manufactures a wide assortment of
items (candle holders, lamps, etc.)
from old textile mill bobbins.*

MINERAL SPECIMENS

*(see also FOSSILS; GEMS &
JEWELRY; GOLD; LAPIDARY;
MARBLE & STONE; MINING
RELATED ITEMS; NATURAL
HISTORY; SAND)*

Appraisers

Nathaniel Ludlum, ISA
Natural History Appraisals
7323 Tucker Rd.
Centerburg, OH 43011-9200
ph: 740-625-7956
fax: 614-436-0124
ludlum@ecr.net
*Specializes in the appraisal of mineral
and fossil collections for insurance,
donation or estate purposes.*

Auction Services

Jeremy Fuller
Mineral, Fossil & Gemstones Auctions
  Co.
997 N. Chapel Dr., Ste. #4
Bountiful, UT 84010
ph: 801-296-2516
fax: 801-292-5439
info@minmarket.com
http://www.minmarket.com
*The first mineral, fossil, and gemstone
"mall" auction of its kind on the
Web.*

Clubs/Associations

Mineralogical Society of America
Magazine: American Mineralogist
1015 Eighteenth St. NW, Ste. 601
Washington, DC 20036-5274
ph: 202-775-4344
fax: 202-775-0018
j_a_speer@minsocam.org
http://www.minsocam.org
*Members are interested in mineralogy,
crystallography, and petrology;
promotes, through education and
research, the understanding and
application of mineralogy by industry,
universities, government and the
public.*

Gem & Mineral Society of the Virginia
  Peninsula
Newsletter: Virginia Pen, The
P.O. Box 6424
Hidenwood Station
Newport News, VA 23606
vapen@widowmaker.com
http://www.widowmaker.com/~finn/
  vapen/index.html
*Purpose is to facilitate the exchange of
information and general cooperation
between its members by promoting the
study of lapidary arts, mineralogy,
paleontology and allied fields of earth
sciences.*

Duncan Heron
Carolina Geological Society
P.O. Box 90234
Durham, NC 27708-0234
ph: 919-684-5321
fax: 919=684-5833
duncan.heron@duke.edu
http://www.carolinageologicalsociety.org

Steve Henegar
Middle Tennessee Gem & Mineral
Society
Newsletter: Mid_Tenn Gem'ers
P.O. Box 1256
Murfreesboro, TN 37133-1256
ph: 615-896-1472
steve.henegar@nashville.com
http://www.mtgms.org
*Dedicated to the study and enjoyment
of the earth sciences; monthly meetings
3rd Thursday, Farm Bureau Bldg.,
818 South Church St.; annual gems &
mineral show.*

John Watkins
Southeast Federation of Mineralogical
Societies
299 Edwards School Rd.
Loudon, TN 37774
sfms@amfed.org
http://www.amfed.org/sfms
*Brings together those clubs and
societies devoted to the study of earth
sciences and the practice of lapidary
arts and crafts in the Southeast part
of the US.*

John Teague, Webmaster
Knoxville Gem & Mineral Society
P.O. Box 51554
Knoxville, TN 37950-0291
volgems@icx.net
http://www.korrnet.org/kgms
*A family-oriented organization for
those interested in studying,
collecting, sharing rocks, minerals
and fossils.*

Evansville Lapidary Society
1304 North Willow Rd.
Evansville, IN 47711
ph: 812-425-GEMS
mylines@evansville.net
http://www.evansville.net/~mylines/
els.html

Hellgate Mineral Society
P.O. Box 3015
Missoula, MT 59807
Macsgems@aol.com
http://macsgems.freeyellow.com

American Federation of Mineralogical
Societies
P.O. Box 26523
Oklahoma City, OK 73126-0523
afms@amfed.org
http://www.amfed.org
*A non-profit educational federation of
seven similar regional organizations
of gem, mineral and lapidary
societies.*

Al Pennington
Clear Lake Gem & Mineral Society
Newsletter: Stoney Statements
P.O. Box 891533
Houston, TX 77289
ph: 281-481-1591
fax: 281-481-2002
gpenning@ghg.net
http://www.ghg.net/gpenning/clgms.htm
*The club Web site gives those
individuals interested in rocks,
minerals, faceting and lapidary a*

*source for information on the earth
sciences and supporting organizations.*

Clark County Gem Collectors, The
P.O. Box 89125
Las Vegas, NV 89125
admin@ccgc.org
http://www.ccgc.org
*An educational and social club for
those who enjoy collecting and
learning about rocks, gems, minerals,
fossils, and the lapidary arts.*

Dr. Rodney Burroughs
Fluorescent Mineral Society
Newsletter: UV Waves
P.O. Box 572694
Tarzana, CA 91357-2694
71543.3343@compuserve.com
*Over 500 members worldwide
specialize in the collection and study
of fluorescent minerals.*

Fluorescent Mineral Society, Inc.
Newsletter: UV Waves
P.O. Box 572694
Tarzana, CA 91357-2694
questions@uvminerals.org
http://www.uvminerals.org
*A society for professional mineralo-
gists, gemologists, amateur collectors,
and anyone else sharing an interest in
minerals that glow under invisible
ultraviolet light.*

Garth Bricker
Fallbrook Gem & Mineral Society
Newsletter: Lithoshpere
P.O. 62
Fallbrook, CA 92088-0062
ph: 760-728-1333
gbricker@sd.znet.com
http://fgms.home.att.net
*Amateur gem and mineral society, free
gem and mineral museum.*

Everett Rock & Gem Club
P.O. Box 1615
Langley, WA 98260
sheeeeesh@msn.com
http://www.geocities.com/Yosemite/
Trails/3085

Collectors

Stephen Seltzer
7912 Georgia Ave.
Silver Spring, MD 20910-4837
ph: 301-565-2444 or 301-565-3339
fax: 301-565-2228
eseltzer@aol.com
*Wants to buy specimen size minerals
and fossils for display.*

Gary E. Fleck
P.O. Box 2886
Hot Springs National Park, AR 71914-
2886
ph: 501-623-4098
fax: 501-623-4098
*Wants to buy mineral collections,
natural rock crystals, cutting rough
rock.*

Robert E. Spomer
Buena Vista Gem Works
P.O. Box 476
Buena Vista, CO 81211
ph: 719-395-4327
respomer@buenavistagemworks.com
http://www.buenavistagemworks.com
*A professional gem cutter by trade,
specializing in custom collector's
gemstones and fancy-cut jewelry grade
stones; also collects and mines
minerals and gems, especially in
Colorado; also collects Fairburn and
other banded agates.*

Dealers

John Betts
John Betts Fine Minerals
215 West 98 St., No. 2F
New York, NY 10025
ph: 212-678-1942
fax: 212-242-7020
jhbnyc@aol.com
http://www.johnbetts-fineminerals.com
*Wide range of natural history
collectibles: fossils, crystals, minerals,
books on earth sciences; specializes in
large, aesthetic mineral crystal
specimens from around the world;
have sold to museums, collectors and
decorators.*

Les Tolonen
Keweenaw Agate Shop
P.O. Box 41
Copper Harbor, MI 49918
ph: 906-289-4491
http://www.copperharbor.org/
keweenaw_agate_shop.htm
*Polished agates, mineral specimens,
coppersmith, rock tours, native
copper.*

Deb & Dave McClain
Mac's Gems
2204 South 8th St.
Missoula, MT 59801
ph: 406-549-7003
Macsgems@aol.com
*Offers Montana gems and crystals:
sapphire, garnets, agate, quartz
crystals, and very large smoky quartz
points; also Canadian ammolite,
ammetrine, Brazilian amethyst, and
much more.*

David M. Crawford
David M. Crawford Mining Antiques &
Mineral Specimens
3421 Fremont St.
Rockford, IL 61103
ph: 815-637-6720
dmcxls4u@aeroinc.net
*Mining dealer, appraiser, collector
expert; wants to buy all mining items:
oil, safety, and carbide lamps;
blasting cap tins, photos, postcards;
ore cars, powder boxes, Miner Union
ribbons, pins, patches; also seeking
mineral collections.*

Jayne Horak
Crystal Springs Mining & Jewelry
P.O. Box 40
Royal, AR 71968
ph: 501-991-3557
fax: 501-991-3281

John & Karen Mediz
Copper City Rock Shop
566 Ash St.
Globe, AZ 85501
ph: 520-425-7885 or 520-425-4506
fax: 520-425-4506
*Buys and sells mining artifacts; also
wants to buy minerals and fossils,
especially old collections.*

Jesse Wellman
High Grade Treasures
17865 Owl Court
Reno, NV 89506
info@highgradetreasures.com
http://www.highgradetreasures.com
*Carries a wide selection of primarily
minerals and some fossils; field
collects in the western US and
purchases from mine direct importers,
as well as travels to Mexico to obtain
quality common and rare specimen;
advice given freely.*

Gem & Mineral Exploration Company,
The
4141 Ball Rd. #373
Cypress, CA 90630
ph: 714-826-2132
hwmroch@attbi.com
http://www.gemandmineral.com
*Dealers in exquisite mineral
specimens.*

George Campbell
OsoSoft Mineral Collection
2122 9th St., Ste. 202
Los Osos, CA 93402
ph: 805-528-1759
fax: 805-528-3074
ososoftminerals@yahoo.com
http://www.osomin.com
*Buys and sells high quality mineral
specimens.*

Sharon Cisneros
Mineralogical Research Company
15840 East Alta Vista Way
San Jose, CA 95127-1737
ph: 408-923-6800 or 408-926-6015
fax: 408-926-6015
xtls@minresco.com
http://www.mineresco.com
*Over 35 years in the mail order and
gem show business: minerals for
collection & research, meteorites &
tektites; also books, loupes, ultraviolet
lamps, specimen boxes, fulgurites,
trinitite, mineral & gemstone gifts,
gift certificates.*

MINERAL SPECIMENS

Doug Miller
Northern Lights Minerals
8B - 186, 3110 8th St. E.
Saskatoon, SK S7H 0W2 Canada
ph: 306-373-5013
fax: 306-477-1727
minerals@minerals.sk.ca
http://www.minerals.sk.ca
Specializes in fine quality Canadian mineral specimens.

Experts

Dr. Abraham Rosenzweig
Rosenzweig Associates
P.O. Box 3976
Sarasota, FL 34230-3976
ph: 941-371-4643
fax: 941-342-6893
rosetwig@aol.com
Consultant specializing in mineralogy and gemology.

Lanny R. Ream
P.O. Box 2043
Coeur d'Alene, ID 83816-2043
ph: 208-664-2448
lanny@mineralnews.com
http://www.mineralnews.com
Editor of "Mineral News," the mineral collectors newsletter.

Internet Resources

Scott Shrader
Gems, Minerals & Fossils Webring
sshrader@mindspring.com
http://www.geocities.com/Yosemite/2352/gmf.html
Webring has scores of links to rockhound Web sites.

About.com Hobbies
220 East 42nd St.
New York, NY 10017
pr@about-inc.com
http://home.about.com/hobbies
Online source for information about action figures, antiques, book collecting, coin collecting, collectibles, comic books, costume jewelry, dolls, mineral collecting, pin collecting, sports and trading cards, stamps, toy collecting.

Smithsonian Gem & Mineral Collection, National Museum of Natural History
10th St. & Constitution Ave.
Washington, DC 20560-0119
ph: 202-357-2060
fax: 202-357-2476
minsciweb@volcano.si.edu
http://www.nmnh.si.edu/minsci
A Smithsonian Web site with a great selection of mineral specimen images with descriptions.

Jeremy Fuller
Mineral Market
997 N. Chapel Dr., Ste. #4
Bountiful, UT 84010
ph: 801-296-2516
fax: 801-292-5439
info@minmarket.com
http://www.minmarket.com
Online mineral and fossil auctions,

dealer lists, online mineral and fossil museum.

Bob Keller
Bob's Rock Shop
227 West Rillito St.
Tucson, AZ 85705
ph: 520-624-1899
fax: 520-624-1891
bkeller@rockhounds.com
http://www.rockhounds.com
The Internet's first 'zine for mineral collectors, lapidary hobbyists, and rockhounds.

Museums/Libraries

Earth & Mineral Sciences Museum & Art Gallery, Pennsylvania State University
122 Steidle Bldg.
Pollock Rd.
University Park, PA 16802
ph: 814-865-6427
fax: 814-863-7708
sicree@geosc.psu.edu
http://www.ems.psu.edu/Museum
Displays of minerals, materials, gemstones, and art work related to mining; displays of old lamps and other mining artifacts.

Daniel Lazar, Ex. Dir.
Colburn Gem & Mineral Museum
Newsletter: Touchstone
P.O. Box 1617
Asheville, NC 28802-1617
ph: 828-254-7162
fax: 828-251-5652
http://www.main.nc.us/colburn
Features gems and minerals from North Carolina and around the world.

Susan Celestian, Cur.
Arizona Mining & Mineral Museum
1502 W. Washington
Phoenix, AZ 85007
ph: 602-255-3795
fax: 602-255-3777
SusanCelestian@hotmail.com
http://www.admmr.state.az.us
Over 3,000 specimens on display, prominently featuring Arizona minerals, lapidary materials and fossils; outstanding outside exhibits include a huge mining shovel bucket, a 13' diameter truck tire, stamp mill; also rock shop.

Periodicals

Heldref Publications
Magazine: Rocks & Minerals
1319 18th St., NW
Washington, DC 20036-1802
ph: 800-365-9753 or 202-296-6267
fax: 202-296-5149
rm@heldref.org
http://www.heldref.org
America's oldest popular magazine about minerals; bi-monthly; mineralogy, geology, and paleontology.

Lanny R. Ream
Newsletter: Mineral News
P.O. Box 2043
Coeur d'Alene, ID 83816-2043
ph: 208-664-2448
lanny@mineralnews.com
http://www.mineralnews.com
A monthly newsletter for mineral collectors; contains news and information on minerals and mineral localities; show reports, new discoveries, new collecting opportunities; abstracts of new minerals; show information.

Magazine: Mineralogical Record, The
P.O. Box 35565
Tucson, AZ 85750
ph: 520-297-6709
fax: 520-544-0815
minrec@aol.com
http://www.minrec.org
Each bimonthly issue packed with in-depth articles about minerals and mineral localities; lavishly illustrated with beautiful color photos of some of the world's finest mineral specimens; prominent collectors, mineral museums, etc.

Miller Magazines, Inc.
Magazine: Rock & Gem
4880 Market St.
Ventura, CA 93003-7783
ph: 805-644-3824
editor@rockngem.com
http://www.rockngem.com
Since 1971, R&G has been the leading magazine for the lapidary and mineral hobbyist; captures the fun and excitement of rockhounding, gathering mineral specimens at their source; step-by-step processes for jewelry making, and more.

Suppliers

Carl W. Haywood
Rockman's Trading Co.
P.O. Box 7174
Loveland, CO 80537-0174
ph: 970-622-0869
fax: 970-622-0869
rockman@rocksandminerals.com
http://www.rocksandminerals.com
Sells earth science supplies for classroom and collector: starter rock, mineral, fossil, and ore collections; handbooks, display cases, magnifiers, etc.

Jack Slevkoff
Prized Possessions
4460 West Shaw Ave., Ste. 140
Fresno, CA 93722
ph: 559-275-6498
fax: 559-276-7485
jack@gemworld.com
http://www.gemworld.com
Gems, minerals, fossils, gemstone rough, equipment, supplies; provides opals, gemstones, collector stones, synthetics, cabbing and faceting rough, lapidary equipment and supplies, appraisals, etc.; extensive Web site.

Fluorescent

Clubs/Associations

Fluorescent Mineral Society, Inc.
Newsletter: UV Waves
P.O. Box 572694
Tarzana, CA 91357-2694
questions@uvminerals.org
http://www.uvminerals.org
Founded in 1971, an international organization of professional mineralogists, gemologists, amateur collectors, and others who study and collect fluorescent minerals.

Meteorites

Clubs/Associations

International Meteorite Collectors Association
3201 Leith Lane, Apt. 516
Louisville, KY 40218
questions@meteoritecollectors.org
http://www.meteoritecollectors.org
International association for collectors of meteorites.

Collectors

Blaine Reed
P.O. Box 1141
Delta, CO 81416-1141
ph: 970-874-1487
fax: 970-874-1487
Buy, sell, trade all types of meteorites; free list; free identification on suspected meteorites for people who believe they may have found one.

Robert Haag
P.O. Box 27527
Tucson, AZ 85726-7527
ph: 520-882-8804
fax: 520-743-7225
bobhaag@meteoriteman.com
http://www.meteoriteman.com
One of the world's largest meteorite dealers.

Dealers

Geoffrey Cintron
Island Meteorite
ph: 516-731-8218
geoffcin@aol.com
http://www.islandmeteorite.com

Darryl Pitt
Macovich Collection of Meteorites
1501 Braodway, Ste. 1304
New York, NY 10036
ph: 212-3-2-9200
fax: 212-382-1639
curator@macovich.com
http://www.macovich.com
Dealer, collector and expert in meteorites; involved in the natural history auctions at Phillips and Butterfields auction houses; collection is one of the finest in the world.

RA Langheinrich Meteorites & Fossils
290 Brewer Rd.
Ilion, NY 13357
ph: 732-764-0879
fax: 732-764-0879
meteorite@compuserve.com
http://www.nyrockman.com
Numerous links to Web sites focusing on archaeology, ancient history, ancient medicine, ancient Greek, Roman and Egyptian cultures, ancient coins, etc.

Lang's Fossils
290 Brewer Rd.
Ilion, NY 13357
ph: 315-894-0513
fax: 315-894-0513
info@nyrockman.com
http://www.nyrockman.com
Sells fossils and meteorites; excavating, preparing, and supplying superior fossils since 1971; private quarry is world's finest source for eurypterids.

Michael Casper
Michael I. Casper Meteorites, Inc.
P.O. Drawer J
Ithaca, NY 14851
ph: 607-257-5349
fax: 607-266-7904
info@meteorites.com
http://www.meteorites.com
Meteorite dealer, collector, expert and appraiser; buys, sells, trades meteorites; has an extensive inventory; guarantees authenticity; world's largest volume meteorite dealer.

Marvin Killgore
Killgore Southwest
P.O. Box 95
Payson, AZ 85547
ph: 928-474-9515
fax: 928-474-2474
email@meteoritelab.com
http://www.meteoritelab.com

Norm Lehrman
Tektite Source!, The
3535 Comstock Dr.
Reno, NV 89512
nlehrman@nvbell.net
http://www.tektitesource.com
The world's only exclusive tektite dealer; has a quarter million meteorite impacted glass specimens in stock; will answer your meteorite questions.

Mike Martinez
MARE Meteorites
P.O. Box 19041
Oakland, CA 94619
ph: 925-743-8146
fax: 925-743-8146
meteors@flash.net
http://www.flash.net/~meteors
Collector, dealer in meteorites and tektites; small collectors welcome; also sell related books.

Sharon Cisneros
Mineralogical Research Company
15840 East Alta Vista Way
San Jose, CA 95127-1737
ph: 408-923-6800 or 408-926-6015
fax: 408-926-6015
xtls@mineresco.com
http://www.mineresco.com
Over 35 years in the mail order and gem show business: minerals for collection & research, meteorites & tektites; also books, loupes, ultraviolet lamps, specimen boxes, fulgurites, trinitite, mineral & gemstone gifts, gift certificates.

Eric Twelker
Meteorite Market, The
P.O. Box 33873
Juneau, AK 99803
ph: 907-789-6800
fax: 907-789-3742
twelker@alaska.net
http://www.alaska.net/~meteor
A place to buy or learn about meteorites; a full-color online catalog of hundreds of affordable meteorite specimens.

Experts

Darryl Pitt
Macovich Collection of Meteorites
1501 Braodway, Ste. 1304
New York, NY 10036
ph: 212-3-2-9200
fax: 212-382-1639
curator@macovich.com
http://www.macovich.com
Dealer, collector and expert in meteorites; involved in the natural history auctions at Phillips and Butterfields auction houses; collection is one of the finest in the world.

Michael Casper
Michael I. Casper Meteorites, Inc.
P.O. Drawer J
Ithaca, NY 14851
ph: 607-257-5349
fax: 607-266-7904
info@meteorites.com
http://www.meteorites.com
Meteorite dealer, collector, expert and appraiser; buys, sells, trades meteorites; has an extensive inventory; guarantees authenticity; world's largest volume meteorite dealer.

Randy D. Watson, M.D.
545 SE Oak, Ste. D
Hillsboro, OR 97123-4147
ph: 503-297-7424 or 503-640-1614
fax: 503-681-0925
gate@teleport.com
Advanced collector pays top dollar; will buy any and all meteorites; also wants to buy meteorite books and pictures; says "I never met a meteorite I didn't like!;" has private museum of over 2500 microscopes and 200 meteorites.

Periodicals

Joel Schiff, Ed.
Pallasite Press
Magazine: METEORITE
P.O. Box 33-1218
Takapuna, Auckland
New Zealand
ph: +69-9-486-6750
fax: +64-9-489-6750
j.schiff@auckland.ac.nz
http://crash.ihug.co.nz/~afs
Meteorite collecting and collections, scientific research, new falls and finds, craters, asteroids, Tektites, historical events, new discoveries, and more.

MINIATURES

(see also ART, Portraits [Miniature]; BOOKS, Miniature; BOTTLES, Miniature; BOTTLES, Puzzle; CHILDREN'S THINGS; DOLL HOUSES & FURNISHINGS; IRONS, Pressing [Miniature]; MODELS, Cars; PIANOS, Miniature; TRUCKS, Miniature)

Appraisers

Judy Owen, ISA
Antique Appraisers - Grand Traverse
10332 Stoneybeach Pointe
Traverse City, MI 49686-8584
ph: 231-946-2534
fax: 231-946-2573
judy@antiqueappraisers.com
http://www.antiqueappraisers.com
Specializing in doll houses and miniatures.

Clubs/Associations

Miniatures Industry Association of America
P.O. Box 3388
Zanesville, OH 43702-3388
ph: 740-452-4541
fax: 740-452-2552
miaa.info@offinger.com
http://www.miaa.com
A trade organization; purpose is to promote the common interests of the miniatures industry; approximately 400 company members; Web site has some good information about miniatures with links to related sites.

John Purcell
National Association of Miniature Enthusiasts
Magazine: Miniature Gazette
P.O. Box 69
Carmel, IN 46032
ph: 317-571-8094
fax: 317-571-8105
name@miniatures.org
http://www.miniatures.org
N.A.M.E. serves the miniature collector and builder; the monthly magazine contains articles, ads, dealer listings, etc.

Tony Liguori, Mem.
Cottage Industry Miniaturists Trade Association, Inc.
Newsletter: CIMTA Ink
P.O. Box 42849
Chicago Ridge, IL 60805-0849
ph: 732-651-2162
taylorjademini@aol.com
http://www.cimta.org
Non-profit organization whose membership is limited to professional handcrafters of doll house miniatures.

International Guild of Miniature Artisans
Newsletter: Cube
P.O. Box 629
Freedom, CA 95019-0629
ph: 800-711-IGMA or 831-724-7974
fax: 831-724-8605
info@igma.org
http://www.igma.org
Dedicated to the recognition of excellence in the field of miniatures.

Miniature Enthusiasts Across Canada
1133 Sixth Line
Oakville, Ontario L6H 1W6 Canada
ph: 905-294-0902
meac@miniature.net
http://www.miniature.net/meac
An association for people interested in doll house miniatures.

Dealers

Judith Armistead
Doll Works, The
P.O. Box 195
Lynnfield, MA 01940-0195
ph: 781-334-5577
judy@thedollworks.net
http://www.TheDollWorks.net
Interested in buying and selling antique dolls, doll houses and miniatures; in business for 20 years dealing in German, American and French dolls and accessories.

Natalie Bell
Open House Miniatures
402 Railroad Ave. W.
Allendale, SC 29810
Carries highest quality Russian miniatures available; also painted eggs, matreshkas (nesting dolls), icons, and Palekh boxes made by the Russian Association of Dollhouse & Miniature Masters (see examples at http://www.aha.ru/~vladin/).

Internet Resources

About.com Hobbies
220 East 42nd St.
New York, NY 10017
pr@about-inc.com
http://home.about.com/hobbies
Online source for information about action figures, antiques, book collecting, coin collecting, collectibles, comic books, costume jewelry, dolls, mineral collecting, pin collecting, sports and trading cards, stamps, toy collecting.

Museums/Libraries

Long Island Museum of American Art,
    History & Carriages
Newsletter: News & Events
1200 Route 25A
Stony Brook, NY 11790-1992
ph: 631-751-0066
fax: 631-751-0353
mail@longislandmuseum.org
http://www.longislandmuseum.org
    *Large collection of American Art,
    decoys, horse-drawn vehicles,
    costumes, and miniature period
    rooms; museum shop.*

Toy & Miniature Museum of Delaware
P.O. Box 4053
Route 141
Wilmington, DE 19807
ph: 302-427-8697
fax: 302-427-8654
toys@thomes.net
http://www.thomes.net/toys
    *Collections include doll houses,
    miniatures, dolls, toys, trains, boats,
    and planes; both European and
    American; 18th to 20th centuries.*

Delaware Toy & Miniature Museum
P.O. Box 4053
Wilmington, DE 19807
ph: 302-427-8697
fax: 302-427-8654
toys@thomes.net
http://www.thomes.net/toys
    *A historical reference of antique and
    contemporary doll houses, miniatures
    and sample furniture as well as dolls,
    toys, trains, boats and planes, both
    European and American from the 18th
    to 20th centuries.*

Washington Dolls' House & Toy
    Museum
5236 44th St. NW
Washington, DC 20015-2101
ph: 202-244-0024
fax: 202-237-1659

Art Institute of Chicago, Thorne
    Miniature Rooms
111 S. Michigan Ave.
Chicago, IL 60603
ph: 312-443-0849
webmaster@artic.edu
http://www.artic.edu
    *These 68 rooms were designed and in
    large part created by Carcissa Niblack
    Thorne; many are exact replicas of
    existing houses in the US and Europe;
    made at a scale of 1:12; other rooms
    in Phoenix Art Museum, Knoxville
    Museum of Art.*

Sandi Russell
Toy & Miniature Museum of Kansas
    City
5235 Oak St.
Kansas City, MO 64112-2877
ph: 816-333-2055 or 816-333-9328
fax: 816-333-2055
bergr@umkc.edu
http://www.umkc.edu/tmm
    *Museum housed in an elegant mansion
    features collections of miniatures,*

*antique dolls' houses and antique
toys.*

Laura Douglas, Ex. Dir.
Denver Museum of Miniatures, Dolls &
    Toys
1880 Gaylord St.
Denver, CO 80206-1211
ph: 303-322-1053
fax: 303-322-3704
dmmdt@juno.com
    *Displays miniatures, dolls and toys
    dating back to the 18th century.*

Carole & Barry Kaye
Carole & Barry Kaye Museum of
    Miniatures
5900 Wilshire Blvd.
Los Angeles, CA 90036
ph: 323-937-6464 or 323-937-7766
fax: 323-937-2126
carolekaye@aol.com
http://www.museumofminiatures.com
    *14,000 square feet containing
    hundreds of exhibits, most done in
    remarkable 1/12 scale.*

Periodicals

Castle Press Publications
Magazine: Doll Castle News
P.O. Box 247
Washington, NJ 07882-0247
ph: 908-689-7042 or 800-572-6607
fax: 908-689-6320
dcn@toast.net
    *A magazine focusing on dolls,
    miniatures, doll houses and related
    items; ads; paper doll section,
    needlework, patterns, etc.*

Scott Publications
Magazine: Miniature Collector
30595 Eight Mile
Livonia, MI 48152-1798
ph: 800-458-8237 or 248-477-6650
fax: 248-477-6795
concatus@scottpublications.com
http://www.scottpublications.com
    *A monthly international publication
    devoted to the serious collector,
    craftsperson and artist of contempo-
    rary and antique scale miniatures;
    amply illustrated with large color
    photographs, historical information,
    auctions, and much more.*

Candice St. Jacques, Ed.
Kalmbach Publishing Co.
Magazine: Dollhouse Miniatures
P.O. Box 1612
21027 Crossroads Circle
Waukesha, WI 53187
ph: 262-796-8776 or 800-533-6644
fax: 262-796-1615
web@dhminiatures.com
http://www2.dhminiatures.com/dhm
    *Monthly magazine with techniques,
    how-tos, projects, plans, collections,
    artists profiles, reviews of miniature
    shows, extensive calendar of events,
    etc.*

Magazine: Dolls & Miniatures
1040 Bentoak Lane
San Jose, CA 95129
dollsmini@aol.com
http://members.aol.com/dollsinmin
    *Quarterly magazine featuring the work
    of talented miniature doll and bear
    artisans and collectors; also covers
    accessories for the well-dressed doll
    and many other doll house items.*

Ashdown Publishing
Magazine: Dolls House World
Avalon Court, Star Rd.
Partridge Green, West Sussex RH13
    8RY U.K.
ph: +44 (0) 1403 711511 or 513-353-
    4052 (in US)
fax: +44 (0) 1403 711521
mark@ashdown.co.uk
http://www.dollshouseworld.com
    *Britain's top selling miniatures
    magazine.*

Repro. Sources

Duane Sylor
49 Horner Rd.
Angelica, NY 14709-8780
ph: 716-466-7700
    *Makes & sells authentically crafted
    1:2 scale traditionally painted
    furniture accurately copying Early
    American examples; great for dolls,
    teddies, tots.*

Dishes

Clubs/Associations

Lorraine Punchard
Treasures of Little Children
Newsletter: Tiny Times, The
8201 Pleasant Ave. So.
Minneapolis, MN 55420
rainyp@earthlink.net
http://www.treasuresforlittlechildren.com
    *A club for collectors of children's
    dishes, toy glass, toy graniteware, tin
    tea sets, miniature furniture, doll
    houses, kitchen doll accessories, and
    related toys.*

Military

(see also SOLDIERS, Toy; TOYS,
Playsets)

Appraisers

Barry Carter
Knightstown Antiques Mall
136 W. Carey St.
Knightstown, IN 46148-1111
ph: 765-345-5665
bcarter@spitfire.net
    *Buys, sells, appraises and specializes
    in toy soldiers and military
    miniatures; consultant for
    AntiqueWeek; promoter of the Indiana
    Toy Soldier Show (last Sunday in
    March.)*

Auction Services

Glenn Butler
Wallis & Wallis
West St. Auction Galleries
Lewes, East Sussex BN7 2NJ U.K.
ph: 01273-480208
fax: 01273-476562
wallisandwallis@mcmail.com
http://www.wallisandwallis.co.uk
    *Britain's specialist auctioneers of
    diecast & tin plate toys & models
    including model soldiers.*

Clubs/Associations

Terry Martin, Sec.
Atlanta Military Figure Society
ph: 770-972-8226
tmartin@tacticaldimensions.com
http://www.atlantaminiatures.com

Miniature Figure Collectors of America
Newsletter: Guidon, The
102 St. Paul's Rd.
Ardmore, PA 19003-2811
ph: 610-649-4144
Pkelly@synnlech.com
    *Non-profit corporation; members
    interested in military history,
    miniature figures of military personnel
    in uniform, dioramic scenes, painting,
    casting, conversion of miniature
    figures; annual exhibition, competition
    and show each May.*

Andy Hansen
Military Miniature Society of Illinois
Newsletter: Scabbard, The
529 S. Burno Dr.
Palatine, IL 60067-6711
andyhansen@ailch.com
http://www.mmsichicago.com
    *Sponsors an annual exhibition on the
    3rd Saturday in October; features the
    best work from the US, Canada and
    Europe.*

Len Johnson
Rendezvous! - Historical Miniature
    Figure Society of Colorado
17601 E. Eastman Place
Aurora, CO 80013

Jim Hill
Southern California Area Historical
    Miniature Society
3057 Lakeview Circle
Fullerton, CA 92835
ph: 714-526-9339
fax: 714-520-4740
j1776h@aol.com
http://home1.gte.net/sulla1

Recruitment Officer
British Model Soldier Society
75 Mill Rd.
Woodford
Kettering, Nortants NN14 4HL U.K.
Model.Soldiers@btinternet.com
http://www.btinternet.com/
    ~MODEL.SOLDIERS
    *The largest and longest established
    association of model soldier
    enthusiasts.*

Dealers

Arquebus Military Miniatures
101 Fire Tower Rd.
Pomfret Center, CT 06259
webshop@arquebus.com
http://www.arquebus.com
Collectible toy soldiers and military miniatures.

Jim Hillestad
Toy Soldier, The
RR 1, Box 379
Cresco, PA 18326
ph: 570-629-7227
fax: 570-629-9205
jimhill@ptd.net
http://www.The-Toy-Soldier.com
Deals in all major toy soldier makers, furniture-quality display cases, Michael Sutty bone china military sculptures, regimental drums, bugles and more; also has a 3,000 sq. ft. museum of figures and dioramas.

Bob Hornung
Hornung Art
32 Charlotte Ave.
Cincinnati, OH 45215
ph: 513-761-8518
fax: 513-761-0950
bob@hornungart.com
http://www.hornungart.com
Buys and sells toy and miniature soldiers.

Barry Carter
Knightstown Antiques Mall
136 W. Carey St.
Knightstown, IN 46148-1111
ph: 765-345-5665
bcarter@spitfire.net
Buys, sells, appraises and specializes in toy soldiers and military miniatures; consultant for AntiqueWeek; promoter of the Indiana Toy Soldier Show (last Sunday in March.)

Mark Avery
Toy Soldier
Avalon Court, Star Rd.
Partridge Green, West Sussex RH13 8RY U.K.
ph: +44 (0) 1403 711511 or 513-353-4052 (in US)
fax: +44 (0) 1403 711521
mark@ashdown.co.uk
http://www.toy-soldier.com
Toy soldier dealer and expert; specializes in antique and modern toy soldiers and 54mm collectors figures; also sells books and special edition figurines for the discerning collector.

Man./Prod./Dist.

Dr. Paul Rohe
Museum Quality Miniatures
P.O. Box 122
Martinville, NJ 08336-0122
Produces the world's finest quality, detailed and accurate miniatures (54mm) painted to absolute perfection; most popular are Knights and Civil War themes; wholesale and resale.

Periodicals

Hank Olsen
Newsletter: Mini Soldier Gazette
P.O. Box 15
Eatontown, NJ 07724
minisoldier@minisoldier.com
http://www.minisoldier.com
A 64-page quarterly newsletter for collectors of toy soldiers, miniature figures and associated items.

Erika Daileda
Wise Owl Worldwide Publications
Magazine: Military Modelling
5150 Candlewood St., Ste. 1
Lakewood, CA 90712-1900
ph: 562-461-7574
fax: 562-461-7212
info@wiseowlmagazines.com
http://www.wiseowlmagazines.com
A monthly English publication; for modelers, enthusiasts and historians.

MINING RELATED ITEMS

(see also INDUSTRY RELATED ITEMS; MINERAL SPECIMENS; SCRIP; SOCIAL CAUSES; STOCKS & BONDS, Mining Related)

Appraisers

Robert L. Johnson
Whistles in the Woods Museum Services
P.O. Box 309
Chickamauga, GA 30707-0309
ph: 706-375-4326
oldgoat@voy.net
Consultants & booksellers specializing in 1750-1930 historic machinery; power-generation, tools, wood- and metalworking machines, scientific & technical instruments, mining, milling, transportation, logging & lumbering, steam engines, etc.

Clubs/Associations

National Mining Memorabilia Association
Northcliffe Cottage
Newton Rd.
Newton Solney, Burton-on-Trent DE15 0TG U.K.
mark.smith30@virgin.net
http://freespace.virgin.net/mark.smith30
British association of collectors of mining related collectibles such as tokens, medals and awards, passes, stock certificates, ephemera, lamps.

Collectors

Len Gaska
gaska@nilenet.com
http://ra.nilenet.com/~gaska/mining
Always in the market for mining antiques, especially miners' lamps.

John M. Shannon
7319 West Cedar Circle
Lakewood, CO 80226-2019
ph: 303-232-1534
rovers@aol.com
Wants to buy mining memorabilia

including assay balances (wood and glass encased with small pans) - both laboratory and portable; also wants brass scientific instruments.

Cap Tin Bob
P.O. Box 687
Twin Peaks, CA 92391
ph: 909-337-7833
bschroth@aol.com
Wants mining related artifacts: blasting cap tins, carbide cap lamps, miners candle holders, miners oil wicks.

Robert Murray
2530 Camden Ct.
Fairfield, CA 94533-1321
ph: 707-425-7366
rlmurra@pacbell.net
http://home.pacbell.net/rlmurra
Collects mining collectibles: blasting cap tins, wooden boxes used to carry dynamite, explosives and powder.

Manfred Stutzer
Madenburgstr. 6
Ludwigshafen, 67065 Germany
ph: 0621-5792432
fax: 0621-5792433
mkstu@t-online.de
http://home.t-online.de/home/mkstu/hptmp.htm
Wants to buy miner's flame safety lamps, mining artifacts, and mining medals.

Dealers

David M. Crawford
David M. Crawford Mining Antiques & Mineral Specimens
3421 Fremont St.
Rockford, IL 61103
ph: 815-637-6720
dmcxls4u@aeroinc.net
Mining dealer, appraiser, collector expert; wants to buy all mining items: oil, safety, and carbide lamps; blasting cap tins, photos, postcards; ore cars, powder boxes, Miner Union ribbons, pins, patches; also seeking mineral collections.

Leo Stambaugh
Powder Cache Antiques
P.O. Box 984
612 6th St. Unit C - 2nd Floor
Georgetown, CO 80444-0779
ph: 303-569-2109
leomining@aol.com
http://www.powderchacheantiques.com
Wants to buy mining books, catalogs, photos, equipment, maps; anything mining related and pre-1930; also maintains the Mining Museum, the largest collection of miners' personal items, tools, lamps on permanent display in CO.

Warren Anderson
America West Archives
P.O. Box 100
Cedar City, UT 84721-0100
ph: 435-586-9497 or 435-586-7323
awa@netutah.com
http://www.americawestarchives.com
Buys and sells pre-1920 mining related documents including letters, maps, photos, checks, stock certificates, prospectuses, etc.; author of "Owning Western History."

John & Karen Mediz
Copper City Rock Shop
566 Ash St.
Globe, AZ 85501
ph: 520-425-7885 or 520-425-4506
fax: 520-425-4506
Buys and sells mining artifacts; also wants to buy minerals and fossils, especially old collections.

Experts

David Johnson
ph: 502-327-7559 or 502-540-6988
jana@iglou.com
http://www.miningartifacts.org
Active collector of all types of mine lighting, carbide flasks, oil cadgers, tools and equipment, caps and helmets, blasting items, photos, UMWA items, Coal & Iron Police badges, tokens, statues, mine signs, etc.; free appraisals.

Andy Martin
3030 N. Sarsparilla Place
Tucson, AZ 85749
ph: 520-760-0337
fax: 520-806-3227
oldadit@iname.com
http://www.nmt.edu/~tromero/caps/tins.html
Mining collectibles collector, dealer, expert; author of the "Blasting Cap Tin Catalog" (available from author); has considerable expertise with cap tins, candle boxes, dynamite boxes, and other relics found in abandoned mines.

Mike Serino
Carbide Cap Lamps
26074 Ave. Hall, Ste. 5
Valencia, CA 91355
ph: 661-510-4160 or 661-295-8717
fax: 661-295-1199
mserino@mindspring.com
http://www.carbidelamps.com
Collector of mining gear from the 1880s to the early 1930s including carbide lamps, safety lamps, detonators, cap tins, and miners' candle sticks; buy, sell, trade.

Internet Resources

Dave Thorpe
Eureka! The Online Journal of Mining Collectibles
dhthorpe@earthlink.net
http://eurekamagazine.net
A site for collectors and historians of antique mining artifacts.

David Johnson
ph: 502-327-7559 or 502-540-6988
jana@iglou.com
http://www.miningartifacts.org
A wealth of mining information; all types of mine lighting, carbide flasks, oil cadgers, tools and equipment, caps and helmets, blasting items, photos, UMWA items, Coal & Iron Police badges, tokens, statues, mine signs; free appraisals.

Museums/Libraries

Earth & Mineral Sciences Museum & Art Gallery, Pennsylvania State University
122 Steidle Bldg.
Pollock Rd.
University Park, PA 16802
ph: 814-865-6427
fax: 814-863-7708
sicree@geosc.psu.edu
http://www.ems.psu.edu/Museum
Displays of minerals, materials, gemstones, and art work related to mining; displays of old lamps and other mining artifacts.

National Mining Hall of Fame & Museum
P.O. Box 981
120 W. 9th
Leadville, CO 80461
ph: 719-486-1229
fax: 719-486-3927
nationalminingmuseum@bemail.com
http://www.leadville.com/
    miningmuseum/index.htm
Seeks to inform and educate the public regarding development of mineral resources and to honor the people responsible for creating the mining industry; memorials, museum displays, library.

Bisbee Mining & Historical Museum
P.O. Box 14
5 Copper Queen Plaza
Bisbee, AZ 85603
ph: 520-432-7071
fax: 520-432-7800
info@bisbeemuseum.org
http://www.bisbeemuseum.org

Periodicals

Ted Bobrink
Newsletter: Mining Artifact Collector, The
34612 Ave. B
Yucaipa, CA 92399-4185
mineantiques@earthlink.net

Cap Tins

Experts

Andy Martin
3030 N. Sarsparilla Place
Tucson, AZ 85749
ph: 520-760-0337
fax: 520-806-3227
oldadit@iname.com
http://www.nmt.edu/~tromero/caps/
    tins.html
Mining collectibles collector, dealer, expert; author of the "Blasting Cap

Tin Catalog" (available from author); has considerable expertise with cap tins, candle boxes, dynamite boxes, and other relics found in abandoned mines.

Coal Mining

Collectors

William Blake
506 Driftwood Dr. Lot A
Charleston, WV 25306-6306
ph: 304-925-3780
Coal mine items wanted; all categories: carbide lights, safety lamps, oil wicks, etc.

Museums/Libraries

Museum of Anthracite Mining
Pine & 17th St.
Ashland, PA 17921
ph: 570-875-4708
Tools, machinery, models, photographs and graphic displays explain the mining and processing of anthracite.

National Coal Museum, The
3197 Route 37 North
P.O. Box 369
West Frankfort, IL 62896
ph: 618-YES-COAL
fax: 618-932-2347
coalmuseum@aol.com
http://www.coalmuseum.com
Tour an actual coal mine 600 feet underground.

Colorado

Collectors

George Foott
120 W. Park Ave.
Salida, CO 81201-1548
ph: 719-530-0344
sfgfco@chaffee.net
Wants to buy early Western mining memorabilia (especially Colorado): photographs, maps, promotional pamphlets, books, mining directories, miners' candleholders; also wants Old West cattle brand books, saddle catalogs, cowboy items.

Lamps

(see also LAMPS & LIGHTING)

Collectors

Anthony Glab
6708 Duluth Ave.
Baltimore, MD 21222-1011
ph: 410-633-5354
z.zz@verizon.net
Wants CARBIDE miners and bicycle lamps; no railroad lanterns; any self-contained carbide lighting lamps, i.e., for household, industrial, mining.

Brian Williamson
4690 Springgate Dr.
Powder Springs, GA 30073
ph: 770-439-7003
brianrwi@bellsouth.net
Buys, sells, restores and specializes in older carbide mining lamps, especially

those made by Justrite, Baldwin, Autolite, etc.; also interested in lamp parts and in British mining lamps.

John W. Coons
9757 S. Isabel Ct.
Littleton, CO 80126-4717
ph: 303-791-6496
coons-jw@msn.com
Wants to buy mining lamps, candlestick holders, carbide lamps.

Manfred Stutzer
Madenburgstr. 6
Ludwigshafen, 67065 Germany
ph: 0621-5792432
fax: 0621-5792433
mkstu@t-online.de
http://home.t-online.de/home/mkstu/
    hptmp.htm
Wants to buy miner's flame safety lamps, mining artifacts, and mining medals.

Dealers

David M. Crawford
David M. Crawford Mining Antiques & Mineral Specimens
3421 Fremont St.
Rockford, IL 61103
ph: 815-637-6720
dmcxls4u@aeroinc.net
Mining dealer, appraiser, collector expert; wants to buy all mining items: oil, safety, and carbide lamps; blasting cap tins, photos, postcards; ore cars, powder boxes, Miner Union ribbons, pins, patches; also seeking mineral collections.

Experts

Mike Serino
Carbide Cap Lamps
26074 Ave. Hall, Ste. 5
Valencia, CA 91355
ph: 661-510-4160 or 661-295-8717
fax: 661-295-1199
mserino@mindspring.com
http://www.carbidelamps.com
Collector of mining gear from the 1880s to the early 1930s including carbide lamps, safety lamps, detonators, cap tins, and miners' candle sticks; buy, sell, trade.

MIRRORS

(see POCKET MIRRORS; REPAIR/RESTORATION/CONSERVATION, Mirrors)

MISSILES

(see ROCKETS; SPACE COLLECTIBLES)

MISSION STYLE

(see ARTS & CRAFTS; COPPER ITEMS, Stickley; FURNITURE [ANTIQUE], Stickley)

MIXERS

(see KITCHEN COLLECTIBLES, Eggbeaters; KITCHEN COLLECTIBLES, Mixers)

MOBILE HOMES

(see also TRAILERS & RVs)

Auction Services

Florida's Manufactured Home Auctions & Wholesale
P.O. Box 61
Candler, FL 32111
ph: 352-288-2328
fax: 352-288-9108
florida@mobilehome.com
http://florida.mobilehome.com
Buys and sells manufactured homes online.

MODEL KITS

(see KITS)

MODELS

(see also AIRLINE MEMORABILIA, Models [Desk]; AIRPLANES, Model; BOATS, Model; KITS; MILITARY HISTORY; NAUTICAL ANTIQUES, Models [Ships]; SOLDIERS, Toy; STEAM-OPERATED; TOYS, Diecast; TOYS, Transportation; TRAINS, Model)

Collectors

Joel Balsam
#4 Pickwick Hills Dr.
Huntington Station, NY 11746-1241
ph: 631-271-3267
satch.3428@earthlink.net
Wants to buy pre-1955 model airplane, car, and boat engines; also wants model race cars and other related items.

Dealers

Toys for Collectors
P.O. Box 1406
North Attleboro, MA 02763
ph: 508-695-0588 or 888-445-3322
fax: 508-699-8649
tfcusa@northweb.com
http://www.tfcusa.com
If you collect models of cars, trucks, fire trucks, construction equipment, cranes, buses, race cars, NASCARS, etc. this is the source for better quality 1:43 scale models as well as 1:50, 1:18 and 1:14 scale models.

Colleen Lewis
Buffalo Rd. Hobby
10120 Main St.
Clarence, NY 14031-2049
ph: 716-741-8399
fax: 716-759-7462
bripvc@toyline.com
http://www.toyline.com/clubs/pcc
Dealer, collector, appraiser, distributor of construction scale

models; also diecast scale model military vehicles, aircraft, ships, soldiers; also replacement parts for old models.

James Banko
Creative Three Hobbies
122 Independence Court
Bethlehem, PA 18020
ph: 610-837-4507
fax: 610-837-4507
CTH1@prodigy.net
http://www.swiftsite.com/creativethreehobbies
Buys and sells collectible plastic model kits; specializing in 1950s kits with an emphasis on early Aurora and Revell "S" kits; from aircraft to Sci-fi.

Lelan Kuhlmann
M & L Records & Models
6504 Ravenna Ave.
Seattle, WA 98115
ph: 206-522-8189
mlrecmod@halcyon.com
http://www.halcyon.com/mlrecmod
Seattle storefront with an online catalog having over 22,000 LPs and 2,000 models, rare and used.

Internet Resources

L.T. Wang
ScaleModel.NET
Taiwan
ltwang@mail.ntust.edu.tw
http://www.scalemodel.net
A Web site for all things related to scale modeling: manufacturers, hobby shops, model clubs, modeling techniques, slot cars, roller coaster/ park rides, live steam, engineering, airplanes, static models, railroading, supplies, resources.

Periodicals

Kalmbach Publishing Co.
Magazine: FineScale Modeler
P.O. Box 1612
21027 Crossroads Circle
Waukesha, WI 53187
ph: 262-796-8776 or 800-533-6644
fax: 262-796-1383
tthompson@finescale.com
http://www2.finescale.com/fsn
For those interested in the scaled-down universe including aircraft, military vehicles, ships, cars or dioramas; how-to tips and techniques, new project ideas and step-by-step instructions that make modeling more fun.

Suppliers

Ernie Weinberg
Superior Aircraft Materials
12020 Centralia Ave. #G
Hawaiian Gardens, CA 90716-1064
ph: 562-865-3220
fax: 562-860-0327
balsa@ix.netcom.com
Specializes in supplying wood materials (balsa, spruce, plywood) for the model builder.

Aircraft

(see also AVIATION MEMORABILIA; KITS; TOYS, Airplane Related; TOYS, Diecast)

Collectors

Charles Martignette
P.O. Box 293
Hallandale, FL 33008-0293
ph: 954-454-3474
Wants to buy travel agency and airport counter displays of model airplanes; please send length, width, height and asking price along with photographs.

Periodicals

Erika Daileda
Wise Owl Worldwide Publications
Magazine: Aeromodeller
5150 Candlewood St., Ste. 1
Lakewood, CA 90712-1900
ph: 562-461-7574
fax: 562-461-7212
info@wiseowlmagazines.com
http://www.wiseowlmagazines.com
Great Britain's favorite model aircraft magazine; a monthly featuring reviews, plans and news from the world of aircraft modeling and flight.

Erika Daileda
Wise Owl Worldwide Publications
Magazine: Plastic Kit Constructor
5150 Candlewood St., Ste. 1
Lakewood, CA 90712-1900
ph: 562-461-7574
fax: 562-461-7212
info@wiseowlmagazines.com
http://www.wiseowlmagazines.com
A U.K. quarterly magazine for plastic model aircraft modelers.

Aircraft (Flying)

Internet Resources

Bill Kelsey
Kit Collector Illustrated
2322 Hemlock Ave.
Portage, MI 49024
ph: 616-327-5974
skylane42@aol.com
http://members.aol.com/skylane42a/collector.html
Site contains pictures and prices for out-of-production radio control plains and ready-to-fly control line planes like Cox, Wen Mac, Aurora, Comet.

Periodicals

Harold H. Carstens
Carstens Publications
Magazine: Flying Models
108 Phil Hardin Rd.
P.O. Box 700
Newton, NJ 07860-0700
ph: 973-383-3355 or 800-474-6995
fax: 973-383-4064
carstens@carstens-publications.com
http://www.carstens-publications.com

Richard Gaynor, Ed.
Magazine: FlightSmith Radio Control Magazine
P.O. Box 59905
Chicago, IL 60659-0905
RGaynor@flightsmith.com
http://www.flightsmith.com/rcmaster.htm
Bi-monthly publication for radio control flying; includes construction articles, beginner sections, product reviews.

Magazine: R/C Modeler Magazine
144 West Sierra Madre Blvd.
Sierra Madre, CA 91024
ph: 626-355-1476
info@rcmmagazine.com
http://www.rcmmagazine.com
Complete R/C publication for the remote control enthusiast; construction, how-tos; equipment, contests, etc.

Cars

(see also AUTOMOBILIA; KITS; NASCAR; TOYS, Cars; TOYS, Diecast; TOYS, Transportation)

Clubs/Associations

Ray Denney
Model Car Collectors Association
Journal: Model Car Collectors Association Journal
5113 Sugar Loaf Dr. SW
Roanoke, VA 24018
editor@vintagekarts.com
http://www.vintagekarts.com/MCCA/MCCA.htm
Dedicated to the promotion & enjoyment of the model car hobby; a bi-monthly journal features kit reviews, how-tos, free member ads.

Peter H. Foss
Michigan Model Car Collectors
Newsletter: Model car Breeze
4301 Orchard Lake, 163
West Bloomfield, MI 48323
ph: 248-682-0272
fax: 248-682-5782
FossOhl@aol.com
Friends of The Toy Car Collectors Association, meets with the United Detroit Car Modelers; monthly meetings, 10-15 people, mostly modelers.

Michael Knab
Diecast Car Collectors Club
Newsletter: Diecast Collectors' Journal
1415 Dayton St.
Chicago, IL 60622
ph: 312-337-2010
mknab@priva.com
http://www.diecast.org
For collectors of Danbury Mint and Franklin Mint models and all other precision die cast models; published bi-monthly newsletter with photos and reviews of new models, classifieds, etc.; Web site is "Diecast Car Collectors' Zone."

1/87th Scale Vehicle & Equipment Club, The
102 Plymouth Park S/C #168
Irving, TX 75061
info@1-87vehicles.org
http://www.1-87vehicles.org
Covers intermodal, modern truck, vintage vehicles and equipment, military, logging, carnival, emergency, construction, bus and coach, maintenance and automobiles, all in 1/87th scale.

Tucson Miniature Auto Club
Newsletter: Tucson Miniature Auto Club Newsletter
1111 E. Limberlost Dr., #164
Tucson, AZ 85719-1062
ph: 520-293-3178 or 800-484-1097 pin 2984

Collectors

Ken Katz
354 Townline Rd.
Commack, NY 11725-1423
ph: 631-462-5808
fax: 631-499-0366
kennyskars@aol.com
Wants models of automotive vehicles: plastic, friction, built or unbuilt kits, promotional models.

Bill Whelan
P.O. Box 617
Daly City, CA 94017-0617
ph: 650-756-1189
fax: 650-756-4772
slotdynasty@earthlink.net
Wants to buy 1/25 scale dealer promotional Corvette and Camaro models; also 1/43 Corvette race cars (by Vitesse, Eagle, etc.); buys, sells and trades other makes or model cars; no list available.

Dealers

Dean Klein
Distinctive Die-Cast Inc.
P.O. Box 656
Tallman, NY 10982
ph: 914-357-3382
Specializing in Dinky and Corgi diecast toys.

Michael Knab
Legacy Motors
c/o Gennera Knab
1415 Dayton St.
Chicago, IL 60622
ph: 877-534-2733 or 312-337-3010
fax: 312-337-2433
customercare@legacydiecast.com
http://www.legacydiecast.com
The official online store for Diecast Zone, offering precision model cars in all scales and from around the world; Web site has images and independent reviews.

Rod Ward
MODELAUTO
P.O. Box SM2
Leeds, LS25 5XA U.K.
ph: 0113-2686685
fax: 01977-681991
modelauto@zeteo.com
http://www.zeteo.com/mar
Worldwide mail order specializing in 1:43 and 1:50 scales, but other models stocked as well; see advertisement in "Model Auto Review."

Man./Prod./Dist.

ExotiCar Model Company
2-8 New York Ave.
Framingham, MA 01701
ph: 508-620-6784 or 800-348-9159
fax: 508-620-6786
pitcrew@exoticar.com
http://www.exoticarmodel.com
The complete one-stop source for the automobile enthusiast; the largest US distributor for 1/18 scale; also carries 1/24th, 1/43rd and 1/12th scale models; also sells automobile clothing and accessories.

EWA Miniature Cars USA, Inc.
205 US Hwy. 22
Dunellen, NJ 08812
ph: 732-424-0200 or 732-424-7811
fax: 732-424-7814
ewa@ewacars.com
http://www.ewacars.com
Carries North America's largest inventory of scale model automobiles - over 90,000 in stock from 350 manufacturers including many rare and hard-to-find pieces.

Liberty Classics, Inc.
235 Peterson Rd.
Libertyville, IL 60048
ph: 847-367-1288
fax: 847-367-1295
A leader in manufacturing of diecast vehicles and collectibles for the premium and collector markets since 1991; over 100 unique castings; specializes in 1/64th scale trucks, airplanes and engines.

Periodicals

Magazine: Diecast Digest Magazine
P.O. Box 12510
Knoxville, TN 37912-0510
ph: 865-922-1091
fax: 865-922-1614
dccarcollector@yahoo.com
http://www.diecastdigest.com
A monthly magazine focusing on diecast model cars including NASCAR and Formula 1; articles, advertising, models.

Terry Thompson, Ed.
Kalmbach Publishing Co.
Magazine: Scale Auto Enthusiast
P.O. Box 1612
21027 Crossroads Circle
Waukesha, WI 53187
ph: 262-796-8776 or 800-446-5489
fax: 262-796-1383
tthompson@kalmbach.com
http://www2.scaleautomag.com
Covers the complete automotive modeling hobby including the newest and most successful kit building techniques, collector's market insight, new kit and product releases, and today's greatest modelers.

Stacie Berger
Krause Publications
Magazine: Toy Cars & Vehicles
700 E. State St.
Iola, WI 54990-0001
ph: 715-445-2214
fax: 715-445-4087
stacie.berger@fwpubs.com
http://www.krause.com
One-stop marketplace and information for collectors of scale vehicles: toy cars, trucks, military vehicles, and construction vehicles; model kits, diecasts, motor sports, promotional models.

Jeff Atkinson
Newsletter: Traders Horn
1903 Schoettler Valley Rd.
Chesterfield, MO 63017-5203
ph: 636-532-3871
thorn@gloryroad.net
The oldest, largest bi-monthly periodical dedicated to the sales, trading of diecast toy vehicles, promotional models, model kits; obsolete, rare, current automotive & other transportation miniatures and related memorabilia; all scales.

Rod Ward
Magazine: Model Auto Review
P.O. Box SM2
Leeds, LS25 5XA U.K.
ph: 0113-2686685
fax: 01977-681991
modelauto@zeteo.com
http://www.zeteo.com/mar
MAR is a bi-monthly glossy magazine with many color and b/w photos; covering model cars, trucks, buses, military vehicles.

Cars (Dinky)

Clubs/Associations

Jerry Fralick
Dinky Toy Club of America
Newsletter: DTCA Newsletter
P.O. Box 11
Highland, MD 20777
ph: 301-854-2217
fax: 301-854-2217
MrDinky@erols.com
http://users.erols.com/dinkytoy
For Dinky collectors.

Engines

Collectors

Joel Balsam
#4 Pickwick Hills Dr.
Huntington Station, NY 11746-1241
ph: 631-271-3267
satch.3428@earthlink.net
Wants to buy pre-1955 model airplane, car, and boat engines; also wants model race cars and other related items.

Bill Bickel
3121 W. Cavedale Dr.
Phoenix, AZ 85085-7637
ph: 623-582-0211
wbickel@msn.net
Wants to buy or trade for old model plane engines and gas powered race cars; also wants gas powered planes and cars that were originally sold as ready-to-run toys; incomplete or damaged items and parts also wanted.

Clark Smith
27653 Taryn Dr.
Santa Clarita, CA 91350
ph: 661-263-9049
Wants old model airplane and model race car engines.

Periodicals

Robert A. Washburn, Ed.
Magazine: Strictly I.C.
24920 43th Ave. S.
Kent, WA 98032-4160
fax: 253-946-5253
strictlyic@earthlink.net
http://www.scrictlyic.com
A bi-monthly periodical of information promoting the design and construction of internal combustion miniature model engines in the home shop.

Trucks & Equipment (Winross)

Collectors

Jim Brandt
TruckHobby.com
280 Meadow Lane
Lebanon, PA 17042
ph: 717-273-5776
jim@truckhobby.com
http://www.truckhobby.com
Avid collector of Winross trucks since 1987.

Man./Prod./Dist.

David & Patty Lowe
Winross
Newsletter: Collector Series
P.O. Box 390
East Rochester, NY 14445
ph: 716-381-5638
fax: 716-381-5884
http://www.winross.com
Produces scale model promotional trucks.

MODERNISM

(see also ART, Outsider; ART DECO; CERAMICS [AMERICAN], Russel Wright Designs; ELECTRICITY RELATED ITEMS, Appliances; GLASS, Italian; POPULAR CULTURE; SOCIAL CAUSES)

Appraisers

Christoper A. Kennedy
e-modern
P.O. Bbox 751
Northampton, MA 01061
ph: 800-366-3376 or 413-584-6804
fax: 413-586-2249
chris@e-modern.net
http://www.e-modern.net
Appraiser specializing in 20th century modern.

John Bruno
Appraisal Associates
P.O. Box 57
Northport, NY 11768
ph: 631-261-4590
fax: 631-262-1912
johnwbruno@aol.com
http://www.flamingoshows.com
Avid collector, dealer for over 38 years specializing in Modernism; Show Promoter for over 15 years offering general, formal, country, antiquarian book, and ephemera shows.

Auction Services

David Rago
David Rago Auctions Inc.
333 North Main St.
Lambertville, NJ 08530
ph: 609-397-9374
fax: 609-397-9377
info@ragoarts.com
http://www.ragoarts.com
Specializing in the sale of 20th century decorative and applied arts from 1920 to present.

Phillips de Pury & Luxembourg
450 West 15th St.
New York, NY 10011
ph: 212-940-1200
fax: 212-688-1647
inquiry.desk@phillips-dpl.com
http://www.phillips-dpl.com
Specializes in the auction sale of American art, Contemporary art, Impressionist and Modern art, jewelry, photographs, and 20th and 21st century Modern design.

Don Treadway
Treadway Gallery, Inc.
2029 Madison Rd.
Cincinnati, OH 45208
ph: 513-321-6742
fax: 513-871-7722
treadway2029@earthlink.net
http://www.treadwaygallery.com
Special auction sales of 1950s/Modern design.

Peter Loughrey
L.A. Modern Auctions
P.O. Box 462006
Los Angeles, CA 90046
ph: 323-904-1950
fax: 323-904-1954
info@lamodern.com
http://www.lamodern.com
Auctions twice a year specializing in 20th century decorative arts with an emphasis on works by Designers; publishes full-color catalogs for each auction.

Collectors

John M. England, Jr.
103 Old River Rd.
Lincoln, RI 02865
Buys, collects, and sells machine age design, Art Deco and Moderne furnishings, radios.

Dealers

Jim Medeiros
Twentieth Century Designs
P.O. Box 3386
Fayville, MA 01745-0386
ph: 508-370-7330
jim@fiestajim.com
http://www.fiestajim.com
Jim Medeiros and his partner Ken Paruti Specialize in modern American dinnerware and pottery, kitchen and barware, Jadite, Deco, Fifties, etc.

Dennis Bradbury
Deco Reflections
44 Market St.
Amesbury, MA 01913-2424
ph: 978-388-6250
fax: 978-388-6250
Specializing in items from the 20th century: Chase chrome, Manhattan glass, kitchen appliances, toasters, blenders, lamps & lighting, clocks, dinnerware, furniture, and costume jewelry.

Normand Mainville
Machine Age
354 Congress St.
Boston, MA 02210
ph: 617-482-0048
Buys and sells vintage modern furniture and decorative arts from the '30s to the '50s: desks, chairs, lamps, vases, ceramics, radios, telephones, ashtrays, sofas, clocks, fans, irons, mirrors, toys, globes, toasters, blenders, etc.

Ed Welch
Ed Welch Antiques
Rt. 201
RFD 3 Box 1290
Winslow, ME 04901
ph: 207-872-5849
edwelch@metiques.com
http://www.metiques.com/catalog/antiques.html
Carries Modern furniture and decorative items by Charles Eames, Russell Wright, Eero Saarinen, and other 20th century designers; also

Herman Miller and Knoll International.

Steven Caitai
New Era Antiques
7304 5th Ave., Ste. 112
Brooklyn, NY 11209
ph: 718-232-0889
fax: 718-232-0889
http://www.neweraantiques.com
Specializing in 1920 to 1950 industrial design, Art Deco, electrical antiques, vintage radios, televisions, World's Fair, lighting, Chase chrome, and American Moderne style.

John Bruno
Appraisal Associates
P.O. Box 57
Northport, NY 11768
ph: 631-261-4590
fax: 631-262-1912
johnwbruno@aol.com
http://www.flamingoshows.com
Avid collector, dealer for over 38 years specializing in Modernism; Show Promoter for over 15 years offering general, formal, country, antiquarian book, and ephemera shows.

Carole Hibel
Carole Hibel Art & Antiques
181 Broadview Rd.
Woodstock, NY 12498
ph: 845-679-2966 or 800-426-3357
fax: 845-679-9101
efshnc6@nyc.rr.com
Buying 1950s Heywood-Wakefield furniture, period lighting, ceramics, pottery, etc.

Wes & Mary Ann Waters
ERA, The
1419 E. Daby Rd.
Havertown, PA 19083-3701
ph: 610-449-0781
m6guy@aol.com
A 20th century decorative arts business dedicated to Art Deco, Industrial design, Machine Age, Cubist and Moderne collectibles.

Michael Wilson
Mode Moderne
159 N. 3rd St.
Philadelphia, PA 19106
ph: 215-627-0299
fax: 215-627-0299

Michael Smeresky
Heritage Antiques
39 E. Patrick St.
Frederick, MD 21701
ph: 301-668-0299
hantq@aol.com
http://www.heritageantiques.com
Specializes in 1920s through 1940s dining room antiques and accessories: dinnerware, glassware, furniture.

Ken Forster
5501 Seminary Rd., Ste. 1311 South
Falls Church, VA 22041-3907
ph: 703-379-1142
kencforster@aol.com
Dealer in American art pottery and tiles, specializing in American tiles from 1860 to 1940; also Art Nouveau, Art Deco, Georg Jensen silver, and American Modernism.

Daniel Donnelly
Daniel Donnelly Modern Design Studio
520 N. Fayette St.
Alexandria, VA 22314
ph: 703-549-4672
fax: 703-549-4733
info@danieldonnelly.com
http://www.danieldonnelly.com

Boomerang Modern
3301 South Dixie Highway
West Palm Beach, FL 33405
ph: 561-835-1865
boomerangmodern@earthlink.net
http://www.boomerangmodern.com
Buys and sells 20th century modern design items; top quality Knoll, Herman-Miller, Heywood-Wakefield; American and European.

Suite Lorain
7105 Lorain Ave.
Cleveland, OH 44102
ph: 216-281-1959
Specializes in Deco to 1950s: vintage fabric, kitchen kitsch, ceramics and glass, lighting, Herman Miller, Heywood-Wakefield, Eames, Saarinen, Herman Miller, clocks, televisions, radios.

Steve Hachen
Just 50's
2109 Luray Ave.
Cincinnati, OH 45206-2630
ph: 513-221-1959
Wants 1950s accessories and designer furniture by Herman Miller, Charles Eames, George Nelson, Knoll, Harry Bertoia, Russell Wright, Eero Saarinen, Isamu Noguchi.

Don Treadway
Treadway Gallery, Inc.
2029 Madison Rd.
Cincinnati, OH 45208
ph: 513-321-6742
fax: 513-871-7722
treadway2029@earthlink.net
http://www.treadwaygallery.com
Wants to buy mid-20th century "modern design" furniture and decorative arts by designers Charles and Ray Eames, Kem Weber, Gio Ponti, George Nakashima, Isamu Noguchi, George Nelson, Herman Miller, Lloyd Manufacture, Troy, etc.

Lee Hay
Weird & Wonderful
P.O. Box 14898
Cincinnati, OH 45250-0898
ph: 513-621-6034
fax: 513-621-6448
heywood@sprintmail.com
Wants to buy Peter Max, 1960's protest items, books on 1930-1970 designers; strange one-of-a-kind items from the 1930s through the 1970s.

Connie Zeigler
Durwyn Smedley Antiques
431 Massachusetts Ave.
Indianapolis, IN 46204
ph: 317-822-0102
Buys and sells 20th century design: Arts & Crafts era, Art Deco, Mid-Century Modern, upscale '50s; art pottery from all eras and designer dinnerware; the first Indiana antique shop in the World Wide Web.

Kathryn Wiese Gibson
Retrospective Modern Designs
P.O. Box 305
Manning, IA 51455
ph: 712-653-3678 or 888-301-6829
fax: 712-653-3027
inquire@retrospective.net
http://www.retrospective.net
Mid-century modern dinnerware & home designs sold exclusively on the Internet and by phone; featuring Russel Wright, Ben Seibel, Eva Zeisel, Metlox Poppytrail, Franciscan, Chase, Sascha Brastoff, Vernon and more; storefront sales by appt.

Steve Savitt
Josie's
545 Ridge Rd.
Wilmette, IL 60091-2439
ph: 847-256-7646
fax: 847-256-7604
josies545@attbi.com
Specializes in Art Deco, 20th century Modern, art pottery, art glass and jewelry; no reproductions.

Don Colclough
Mr. Modern
807 Madison, #104
Oak Park, IL 60302
ph: 800-775-5078 or 708-848-7496
mrmodern@aol.com
Specialist in Art Deco lighting (commercial and residential), Heywood-Wakefield furniture, period hardware; also interested in vintage clothing.

Zig Zag
3419 North Lincoln Ave.
Chicago, IL 60657
ph: 773-525-1060
xaviers20thcenturyfurniture@msn.com
http://www.antiqnet.com/m&m/2000/modernism/booth/zig-zag.htm
Buys, sells, and rents Art Deco and Moderne furnishings, Bakelite jewelry, industrial design, radios, purses, etc.

Urban Artifacts
2928 N. Lincoln
Chicago, IL 60657-4109
ph: 773-404-1008
  *Buys and sells vintage modern
  furniture and decorative arts from the
  '40s to the '70s.*

20th Century Classics
3017-B Routh St.
Dallas, TX 75201
ph: 214-880-0020
fax: 214-351-6208
  *Wants 20th century collectibles:
  Knoll, H. Miller, Juhl, Artlo,
  Noguchi, Venini, etc.*

Scott Crow
Century Modern
2928 Main St.
Dallas, TX 75226
ph: 214-651-9200
cmodern@airmail.net
http://www.centurymodern.com
  *Buys, sells, appraises mid-20th
  century tables, seating and accessories; writes quarterly column for
  "Modernism" magazine.*

Aqua 20th Century Modern
1415 S. Congress
Austin, TX 78704-2434
ph: 512-916-8800
fax: 512-916-8800
  *Herman Miller, ethnic, 20th century
  modern, architectural.*

Jet Age
250 Oak St.
San Francisco, CA 94102
ph: 415-864-1950
  *Buys and sells classic modern
  furnishings from the 1930s to 1960s;
  Art Deco, '30s and '40s modern,
  Eames, Nelson, Noguchi, Saarinen,
  Bertoia, Aalto, Herman-Miller, Knoll,
  etc.*

Peter & Deborah Keresztury
Deco to '50s
149 Gough St.
San Francisco, CA 94102-5919
ph: 415-553-4500
  *Wants to buy furniture, accessories,
  rugs, art, fabric, jewelry, and
  decorative objects of the 20th century.*

Kevin Vanderkolk
Fifty-Sixty
P.O. Box 8353
Medford, OR 97504
ph: 541-944-7378
kvander2@uswest.net
http://www.50-60.com
  *Specializes in 1950s and 1960s
  modern: Higgins Glass, California
  Ceramics, Italian glass, Gay Fad,
  Glidden, Howard Holt, etc.*

Mike Fahlgren
ModNorthWest.com
432 SW 6th St.
Redmond, OR 97756
ph: 541-923-0164
sales@modnorthwest.com
http://www.modnorthwest.com
  *Specializes in Mid 20th century
  modernism: furniture and decor.*

Wrinkled Bohemia
1125 Pike St.
Seattle, WA 98101
ph: 206-464-0850
  *Buys and sells mid-20th century
  furniture, dishware, and decorative
  arts by Russell Wright, Eva Zeisel,
  Charles and Ray Eames, Ken Weber,
  Noguchi, George Nelson, Herman
  Miller, Knoll Associates, Paul
  McCobb, Heywood-Wakefield, etc.*

Experts

Scott Crow
Century Modern
2928 Main St.
Dallas, TX 75226
ph: 214-651-9200
cmodern@airmail.net
http://www.centurymodern.com
  *Buys, sells, appraises mid-20th
  century tables, seating and accessories; writes quarterly column for
  "Modernism" magazine.*

Jan Lindenberger
P.O. Box 7224
Colorado Springs, CO 80933
ph: 719-591-9558
fax: 719-591-9558
  *Buys and sells '50s and '60s
  memorabilia; author of "'50s-'60s
  Memorabilia - Information & Price
  Guide" (Schiffer Pub., 1993).*

Steve Cabella
Modern "i," The
500 Red Hill Ave.
San Anselmo, CA 94960-2409
ph: 415-456-3960
  *Collecting modern furniture, products
  and design facts for over 20 years;
  specialize in the work of Ray and
  Charles Eames; also always buying
  '50s modernist craft jewelry and
  ceramics; settle estates of artists,
  architects, designers.*

Museums/Libraries

Annabel Hanson
Walter Gropius House, Society for the
  Preservation of New England
  Antiquities
68 Baker Bridge Rd.
Lincoln, MA 01773
ph: 781-259-8098 or 781-227-3957
fax: 781-227-9204
http://www.spnea.org/visit/tout/
  house.asp
  *Designed and lived in by architect
  Walter Gropius (founder of the
  German design school known as
  Bauhaus), SPNEA's Gropius House is*

*open to the public; house tours run
regularly; admission charged.*

Periodicals

Deco Echoes Publications
Magazine: Echoes Magazine
P.O. Box 155
Cummaquid, MA 02637
ph: 508-362-3822 or 800-695-5768
fax: 508-362-6670
publisher@deco-echoes.com
http://www.deco-echoes.com/echoes
  *Glossy, elegantly designed quarterly
  dedicated to the styles & designs of
  the mid-20th C.; emphasis on 1920s-
  1960s eras including Art Deco,
  Streamline Moderne, Biomorphic '50s,
  Abstract '60s styles and movements
  from kitsch to high-end.*

David Rago
Magazine: Modernism Magazine, The
333 North Main St.
Lambertville, NJ 08530
ph: 609-397-9374
fax: 609-397-9377
info@ragoarts.com
http://www.ragoarts.com
  *A quarterly publication focusing on
  modernism and the Machine Age.*

Heywood-Wakefield

Dealers

Kathy Burch
Tri-State Antique Center
47 W. Pike
Canonsburg, PA 15317
ph: 724-745-9116
fax: 412-291-1367
kathy&ed@tri-stateantiques.com
http://tri-stateantiques.com
  *Extensive Internet gallery featuring
  Heywood-Wakefield and other mid-
  20th century modern designer
  furniture; also mid-century modern
  and Art Deco, beaded & mesh purses,
  compacts, ladies vanity items.*

Boomerang Modern
3301 South Dixie Highway
West Palm Beach, FL 33405
ph: 561-835-1865
boomerangmodern@earthlink.net
http://www.boomerangmodern.com
  *Buys and sells 20th century modern
  design items; top quality Knoll,
  Herman-Miller, Heywood-Wakefield;
  American and European.*

Lee Hay
Weird & Wonderful
P.O. Box 14898
Cincinnati, OH 45250-0898
ph: 513-621-6034
fax: 513-621-6448
heywood@sprintmail.com
  *Wants to buy Heywood-Wakefield
  advertising pieces, catalogs, and
  furniture.*

Don Colclough
Mr. Modern
807 Madison, #104
Oak Park, IL 60302
ph: 800-775-5078 or 708-848-7496
mrmodern@aol.com
  *Specialist in Art Deco lighting
  (commercial and residential),
  Heywood-Wakefield furniture, period
  hardware; also interested in vintage
  clothing.*

Bill Lewis
Spotlight on Modern
The Antique Center on Broadway
1235 S. Broadway
Denver, CO 80210-1503
ph: 303-744-1857
Spotmodern@aol.com
http://members.aol.com/spotmodern
  *Specialists in vintage Heywood-
  Wakefield furniture and other 1950s
  mid-century modern.*

Penny Lane
2820 Gilroy St.
Los Angeles, CA 90039
ph: 800-775-5078
  *Featuring the largest selection of
  Heywood-Wakefield furniture in the
  country; total restoration available;
  buy, sell, trade.*

Experts

Lee Stanley
Antique Store, An
3858 N. Lincoln Ave.
Chicago, IL 60613-3543
ph: 773-935-6060
fax: 773-871-6660
  *Buys, sells, appraises Heywood-
  Wakefield furniture and original
  catalogs, signs, advertising, etc.; also
  wants Dunbar and Widdicomb
  furniture catalogs, brochures, etc.*

Peter Max

Appraisers

Timmy W. Miller
Flat Signed Rare Books
3415 West End Ave., #1101
Nashville, TN 37203
ph: 615-292-3528
fax: 615-298-2757
timmiller@flatsigned.com
http://www.flatsigned.com
  *Appraiser, collector, dealer; one of the
  world's largest sellers of rare books,
  political memorabilia, and works by
  Peter Max.*

Collectors

Bill Triola
1114 E. Mt. Hope Ave.
Lansing, MI 48910
ph: 517-332-1203 or 517-484-5414
fax: 517-484-3480
triolas@aol.com

Dealers

Lee Hay
Weird & Wonderful
P.O. Box 14898
Cincinnati, OH 45250-0898
ph: 513-621-6034
fax: 513-621-6448
heywood@sprintmail.com
Wants to buy Peter Max memorabilia.

MOLDS

(see also ICE CREAM
COLLECTIBLES; KITCHEN
COLLECTIBLES)

Butter

Collectors

Priscilla Hinners
2711 Jaynia Place
Lemon Grove, CA 91945-1319
ph: 619-265-1046
phinners@yahoo.com
Wants butter molds, stamps, multiple prints, rollers.

Dealers

Carleton L. Cotting
1441 Crowell Rd.
Vienna, VA 22182-1512
ph: 703-759-5646
Collects, buys and sells butter molds and stamps.

Candy

Collectors

Priscilla Hinners
2711 Jaynia Place
Lemon Grove, CA 91945-1319
ph: 619-265-1046
phinners@yahoo.com
Wants candy molds, chocolate, maple sugar, rollers, etc.

Museums/Libraries

Wilbur Chocolate's Candy Americana
  Museum
48 N. Broad St.
Lititz, PA 17543-1026
ph: 717-626-3249 or 888-294-5287
http://www.wilburbuds.com
Collection contains over 1,000 varieties of candy molds, tins, and candy boxes.

Chocolate

Dealers

Wendy Mullen
P.O. Box 846
San Juan Bautista, CA 95045
ph: 831-623-1681
fax: 831-623-4134
wendy@victorianchocolatemolds.com
http://www.victorianchocolatemolds.com
Author of "Collectors Guide to Antique Chocolate Molds with Values."

Experts

Lorry & Bruce Hanes
Dad's Follies
40 Kingston Ct.
Gibsonville, NC 27249-3353
ph: 336-449-0494
fax: 336-449-9670
dadsfollie@aol.com
http://www.dadsfollies.com
Buys, sells, and specializes in ice cream molds; carries large inventory of tin and pewter chocolate and ice cream molds.

Wendy Mullen
P.O. Box 846
San Juan Bautista, CA 95045
ph: 831-623-1681
fax: 831-623-4134
wendy@victorianchocolatemolds.com
http://www.victorianchocolatemolds.com
Author of "Collectors Guide to Antique Chocolate Molds with Values."

Ice Cream

Dealers

Mike & Judi Powers
Memory Peddlers
6 Loubier Dr.
Essex Junction, VT 05452
ph: 802-878-8701
memorypdlr@aol.com
Collector, dealer and expert buys and sells pewter American and European ice cream molds (moulds); interested in both individual and banquet size molds.

Experts

Mike & Judi Powers
Memory Peddlers
6 Loubier Dr.
Essex Junction, VT 05452
ph: 802-878-8701
memorypdlr@aol.com
Collector, dealer and expert buys and sells pewter American and European ice cream molds (moulds); interested in both individual and banquet size molds.

Lorry & Bruce Hanes
Dad's Follies
40 Kingston Ct.
Gibsonville, NC 27249-3353
ph: 336-449-0494
fax: 336-449-9670
dadsfollie@aol.com
http://www.dadsfollies.com
Buys, sells, and specializes in ice cream molds; carries large inventory of tin and pewter chocolate and ice cream molds.

Allan Mellis
Mr. Ice Cream
1115 West Montana
Chicago, IL 60614-2220
ph: 773-327-9123
fax: 773-327-9456
mellisfamily@rcn.com
Wants postcards, pewter molds, ice cream trays, and ice cream-related watch fobs, magazines, valentines, buttons, ice cream and soda fountain real photo postcards, trade cards, pre-1920 ephemera, and supply catalogs.

MONEY

(see BANKING; CIVIL WAR ARTIFACTS, Currency; COINS & CURRENCY; CREDIT CARDS & CHARGE ITEMS; MONEYCARDS; TELEPHONE CARDS; WOODEN MONEY)

MONEY CLIPS

(see CUFF LINKS)

MONEYCARDS

(see also BANKING; CIVIL WAR ARTIFACTS, Currency; COINS & CURRENCY; CREDIT CARDS & CHARGE ITEMS; TELEPHONE CARDS; WOODEN MONEY)

MONSTER COLLECTIBLES

(see CHARACTER COLLECTIBLES; COMIC BOOKS; HORROR; SCIENCE FICTION; TELEVISION SHOWS & MEMORABILIA; MOVIE MEMORABILIA; TOYS, Monsters; TRADING CARDS, Non-Sport; UFOs & UNEXPLAINED PHENOMENA)

MONUMENT REPLICAS

(see SOUVENIR & COMMEMORATIVE ITEMS, Buildings)

MORBID & ODD ITEMS

(see also CIRCUS COLLECTIBLES;
FUNERAL ITEMS; GHOSTS &
HAUNTINGS; RIPLEY'S BELIEVE IT
OR NOT!; SKELETONS; SCIENCE
FICTION; SHRUNKEN HEADS;
TATTOO RELATED ITEMS; UFOs &
UNEXPLAINED PHENOMENA;
WITCHES)

Collectors

Great American Sideshow Museum
P.O. Box 15243
Philadelphia, PA 19125-0243
profcouch@aol.com
http://www.profouch.com
*Wants freaks, oddities, banners,
museum shows, dime museum, tattoo,
motodrome, girlshow, daredevils:
books, postcards, cabinet cards,
broadsides, cartes de visites,
handbills, business papers, props,
stage outfits, etc.*

Dealers

A. Peter Monticup
MagicTricks.Com
2768 Columbia Rd.
Gordonsville, VA 22942
ph: 540-832-0900
peter@magictricks.com
http://www.magictricks.com
*Buys and sells sideshow, freak show
and carnival items and curiosities;
souvenir photos, autographs,
sideshow banners, giant's rings,
posters, memorabilia, sideshow
illusions and actual exhibits.*

Harvey Lee Boswell
Palace of Wonders Museum
P.O. Box 446
Elm City, NC 27822-0446
*Wants to buy anything strange, odd
and unusual: Tibetan items, 2-headed
calf, shrunken head, mummy, skeleton,
tombstones, antique funeral items,
mounted reptiles/fish/animals, circus
& carnival sideshow items, jungle
weapons, etc.*

Museums/Libraries

Gretchen Worden, Dir.
Mutter Museum, College of Physicians
of Philadelphia
19 South 22nd St.
Philadelphia, PA 19103-3097
ph: 215-563-3737 x242
fax: 215-561-6477
muttref@collphyphil.org
http://www.collphyphil.org/
muttpg1.shtml
*Collection consists of antique medical
instruments and equipment primarily
from the 19th and 20th centuries, and
rare anatomical specimens and
medical curiosities such as 2,000
swallowed objects removed from food
and air passages.*

MORMON ITEMS

Dealers

Rick Grunder
Rick Grunder Books
2922 Eager Rd.
La Fayette, NY 13084
ph: 315-677-0035
fax: 315-677-0035
RickBook@aol.com
http://members.aol.com/rickbook
*Wants Mormon related items; pro and
con, in every form; early books,
manuscripts, artifacts, newspaper
articles, and ephemera of all kinds.*

Joe & Jeff Buhler
Copperton Trading Post
501 E. State Highway
Copperton, UT 84006
ph: 801-569-2722
books@utahldsbooks.com
http://www.utahldsbooks.com
*Buys and sells used, out-of-print
Mormon books; also books on county,
city, and family histories, Western
Americana.*

Warren Anderson
America West Archives
P.O. Box 100
Cedar City, UT 84721-0100
ph: 435-586-9497 or 435-586-7323
awa@netutah.com
http://www.americawestarchives.com
*Buying and selling documents, letters,
autographs and other types of printed
ephemera related to Mormonism;
author of "Owning Western History."*

MOTOR SCOOTERS

(see also MOTORCYCLES)

Collectors

Chris Savino
P.O. Box 419
Breesport, NY 14816-0419
ph: 607-739-3106
chrissavino@stny.rr.com
*Wants to purchase any motor scooters
made in America or Europe:
Cushman, Sears Allstate, Salsbury,
Doodlebug, Motoscoot, etc.; also need
Whizzers or Mustangs; parts and
scooters in any condition wanted; also
motorcycle literature and memorabilia.*

Howard Murrill
826 DeWitt Dr.
Lenoir City, TN 37772-5514
ph: 865-986-3042
hmurrill@ix.netcom.com
*Wants unrestored motor scooters and
parts, especially Cushman, Silver
Pigeon, Vespa, Powell, Autoglide,
Salsbury, Fuji Rabbit, Zun Dap,
Doodlebug; must be 30 years old or
older; also need cycle license plates,
Cushman signs.*

Cushman

Clubs/Associations

Tom O'Hara, Sec.
Cushman Club of America
Magazine: Cushman Club of America
  Member Magazine
P.O. Box 661
Union Springs, AL 36089-0661
ph: 334-738-3874
fax: 334-738-5145
ccoa@ustconline.net
http://www.cushmancluboamerica.com
*Dedicated to the preservation and
restoration of Cushman Motor
Scooters.*

MOTORCYCLES

(see also AUTOMOBILIA;
MAGAZINES, Motorcycle; MOTOR
SCOOTERS)

Auction Services

Jerry Wood
J. Wood Co. Auctioneers
RR1, Box 316
Stockton Springs, ME 04981
ph: 207-567-4250 or 901-795-8895
fax: 207-567-4252
jwoodandco@mindspring.com
http://www.jwoodandcompany.com

Clubs/Associations

Gary Sweet
American Motorcyclist Association
Magazine: American Motorcyclist
13515 Yarmouth Dr.
Pickerington, OH 43147
ph: 614-856-2222
fax: 614-856-2221
gsweet@ama-cycle.org
http://www.ama-cycle.org
*Has over 200,000 members; monthly
magazine often contains articles about
vintage motorcycles.*

Dick Winger, Mem.
Antique Motorcycle Club of America
Magazine: Antique Motorcycle, The
P.O. Box 310
Sweetser, IN 46987
ph: 765-384-5421 or 800-782-2622
fax: 765-384-5700
amc@comteck.com
http://www.antiquemotorcycle.org
*A club of 9,000 members worldwide
dedicated to the preservation,
restoration and enjoyment of antique
motorcycles; have approximately 8-10
shows and swap meets, and road rides
around the country each year.*

Women On Wheels (WOW)
Magazine: WOW Magazine
P.O. Box 26
Fall River, WI 53932-0026
ph: 800-322-1969 or 608-337-4676
fax: 608-337-4419
PR1@womenonwheels.org
http://www.womenonwheels.org
*Has over 65 chapters in the US and
Canada; over 2,000 members.*

Oregon Vintage Motorcyclists
P.O. Box 14645
Portland, OR 97293-0645
ovm@efn.org
http://www.oregonvintage.org
*Dedicated to the preservation,
maintenance, and enjoyment of antique
motorcycles.*

Collectors

Wayne R. Batten
303 Landing St.
Lumberton, NJ 08048
ph: 609-267-5953 or 609-714-9495
fax: 609-267-2477
*Serious collector interested in buying
antique motorcycles, motor attachments and related memorabilia
pertaining to old motorcycles:
advertisements, parts, clothing,
licenses.*

Herb Glass
531 Burlingham Rd.
Pine Bush, NY 12566-6820
ph: 845-361-3657
*Wants to buy antique American pre-
1920 motorcycles, motorcycle
literature and motorcycle advertising
items: factory sales catalogs, manuals,
magazines, pins, fobs, trophies,
medals, etc.*

Bob "Sprocket" Eckardt
P.O. Box 172
Saratoga Springs, NY 12866
ph: 518-584-2405
sprocketbe@aol.com
*Buys motorcycle memorabilia:
literature, posters, toys, trophies,
medals, fobs, pennants, programs,
photos, jerseys, F.A.M., AMA, Gypsy
tour items, advertising items, clocks,
signs, showroom items; anything to do
with motorcycles.*

Chris Savino
P.O. Box 419
Breesport, NY 14816-0419
ph: 607-739-3106
chrissavino@stny.rr.com
*Wants to buy motorcycle literature,
pins, awards, motorcycles, clothing
toys, shop signs, old parts inventory,
motorcycle license plates, dealer
plates, anything related to motor
scooters and motorcycles!*

Jack C. Bishop
209 Tebbs Rd.
Montgomery, PA 17752-9733
ph: 570-547-2578
fax: 570-547-2578
jackcbishop@yahoo.com
*A collector of pre-1970 European and
antique American motorcycles,
clothing, pins, literature, and
advertising; wants motorcycle related
pins, hats, signs, literature, oil cans -
anything related to motorcycles.*

Richard L. Weiss
1885 Klines Mill Rd.
Breinigsville, PA 18031
ph: 610-285-4122
mrsdlw@prodigy.net
*Specialized wants: Smith, Briggs &
Stratton, Merkel, Steffy motor wheels;
Whizzer & pre-1940 American
motorcycles; whole or parts.*

Dealers

Ed Natale, Jr.
Retro Petro
P.O. Box 222
Wyckoff, NJ 07481-0222
ph: 201-493-7172
jednat@att.net
*Wants motorcycle related item: club/
gang items such as photos, pins,
patches, jackets, vests; also oil cans,
advertising, pre-war license plates,
etc.; photos helpful.*

Chris Savino
P.O. Box 419
Breesport, NY 14816-0419
ph: 607-739-3106
chrissavino@stny.rr.com
*Buy & sells motorcycle literature,
pins, awards, motorcycles, clothing
toys, shop signs, old parts inventory,
motorcycle license plates, dealer
plates, anything related to motor
scooters and motorcycles!*

David Gaylin
Motor Cycle Days
P.O. Box 9686
Baltimore, MD 21237
ph: 410-665-6295
*Author of "Triumph Motorcycles in
America," (1993) and "Triumph
Motorcycle Restoration Guide,"
(1997); always seeking original
motorcycle literature, art, especially
from British and Japanese makers;
also wants motorcycle movie posters.*

Al Bogg
Al Bogg Motorscooters & Motorcycles
P.O. Box 839
Poplar Bluff, MO 63902
ph: 573-785-0172 or 573-785-0385
fax: 573-785-0015
al@albogg.com
http://www.albogg.com
*Specializes in classic, vintage and
antique motorcycles, motor scooters
and bicycles.*

Mick Stamm
Antique & Vintage Motorcycles
3401 S. 1st
Abilene, TX 79605-1708
ph: 915-676-8788
*American motorcycles, parts,
advertising items, Harley/Indian
dealer items, signs, clocks, mirrors,
original boxed parts, oil/paint cans,
clothing, toys, jewelry, ash trays,
literature, pins, awards, ribbons,
fobs, license plates.*

Museums/Libraries

Mark Mederski
Motorcycle Hall of Fame Museum
13515 Yarmouth Dr.
Pickerington, OH 43147
ph: 614-856-2222
fax: 614-856-2221
mmederski@motorcyclemuseum.org
http://www.motorcyclemuseum.org
*Over 150 motorcycles on display
tracing the history of motorcycling in
America; also 298 famous motorcyclists honored in the Hall of Fame
with many of the motorcycles they rode
on display.*

Rocky Mountain Motorcycle Museum &
Hall of Fame
308 E. Arvada
Colorado Springs, CO 80906-1439
ph: 719-633-6392
*A non-profit Colorado corporation
dedicated to the preservation of early
American motorcycling and the
pioneers of the sport.*

Periodicals

American Motorcyclist Association
<u>Magazine: AMA Official Motorcycle
Value Guide</u>
P.O. Box 3190
Laurel, MD 20709
ph: 800-972-5312
CPI4Values@aol.com
http://www.cpivalueguide.com/main/
AMAGuide.htm
*A quarterly periodical covering
motorcycles, ATVs, personal
watercraft, and snowmobiles going
back to 1980.*

<u>Magazine: Walneck's Classic Cycle
Trader</u>
P.O. Box 9059
Clearwater, FL 34618-9059
ph: 727-712-0035 or 800-548-8889
fax: 727-712-0034
idowu@traderonline.com
http://www.traderonline.com
*Buy, sell, trade; color photos, road
tests, bikes and parts; published
monthly.*

Kelley Blue Book
<u>Price Guide: Kelley Blue Book</u>
5 Oldfield
Irvine, CA 92618
ph: 949-770-7704
fax: 949-837-1904
kelley@kbb.com
http://www.kbb.com/indexv.html
*Web site offers current trade-in values
for all makes and model cars for the
past 21 years; also publishes printed
value guides for cars, RVs, motorcycles, snowmobiles, motor homes,
travel trailers, personal watercraft,
etc.*

Steve Ferguson, Ed.
National Automobile Dealers Association
<u>Price Guide: N.A.D.A. Official Used Car
Guide</u>
P.O. Box 7800
Costa Mesa, CA 92628
ph: 800-544-6232 or 714-556-8511
fax: 714-556-8715
info@nadaguides.com
http://www.nada.org
*A series of value guides for domestic
and foreign cars, trucks, vans, RVs,
mobile homes, motorcycles,
snowmobiles, and boats, small and
large; also Heavy Duty Trucks and
Aircraft Book, car clubs & organizations, museums.*

<u>Magazine: Canadian Biker Magazine</u>
P.O. Box 4122
Victoria, British Columbia V8X 2X4
Canada
ph: 604-384-0333 or 800-667-5667
canbike@islandnet.com
http://www.canadianbiker.com
*Six-time winner of the prestigious
MAX Award for publishing excellence;
honored with the Media of the Year
Award for "improving the image of
motorcycling;" Internet edition,
Canadian Biker Online.*

Repair Services

Antique Motorcycle Restoration
14611 N. Nebraska Ave.
Tampa, FL 33613-1430
ph: 813-972-9297
fax: 813-979-9475
*Complete ground-up restoration;
painting, sheet metal repair, sand
blasting, engine repair, transmission
repair, welding.*

Don Doody
North West Classic Motorcycles
P.O. Box 7783
Riverside, CA 92513
sadams02@earthlink.net
*Sells and repairs antique Harley and
Indian motorcycles.*

Randy Hilberg
Collector's Nectar
Box 431
Morro Bay, CA 93443
ph: 805-772-2968
fax: 805-772-2968
gd57@hotmail.com
*Always buying antique motorcycles,
scooters; offers complete restoration
services; appraisals; master
technician; all makes and models; no
collection too big or too small to
purchase or restore; the only lifetime
guarantee in the business.*

BMW

Clubs/Associations

Yankee Beemers Motorcycle Club
<u>Newsletter: Boxer Shorts</u>
101 South Ave., Box 22
Attleboro, MA 02703
webmaster@yankeebeemers.org
http://www.yankeebeemers.org

Roland Slabon, Ed
Vintage BMW Motorcycle Owners, Ltd.
<u>Newsletter: Vintage BMW Bulletin</u>
P.O. Box 67
Exeter, NH 03833
ph: 603-772-9799
vintagebmw@attbi.com
http://www.vintagebmw.org
*Dedicated to the preservation,
enjoyment and use of antique (1923-
1945), vintage (1948-1969) and
classic (1970 on if more than 25 years
old) BMW motorcycles; over 6,500
members in 27 countries.*

Experts

Craig Vechorik
Bench Mark Works
3400 Earles Fork Rd.
Sturgis, MS 39769
ph: 662-465-6444
fax: 662-465-6444
vechbmw@aol.com
http://members.aol.com/vechbmw
*Buy, sell, collect, repair, expert; for
over 25 years dedicated to the
preservation, enjoyment and use of
BMW motorcycles: classic (1969-
1975), vintage (1948-1969), WWII
production (1940-1945), and antique
(1923-1945).*

British

Clubs/Associations

British Iron Association of Connecticut
<u>Newsletter: British Iron Association of
Connecticut Newsletter</u>
P.O. Box 280893
Lattimore, NC 280893
ph: 860-585-5102
dksierra@concentric.net
http://www.britironct.org
*A club for British motorcycle
enthusiasts; dedicated to the
restoration and enjoyment of British
motorcycles.*

Dealers

James Bernier
Bernier Vintage Motorcycles
Old Concord Rd.
P.O. Box 967
Henniker, NH 03242
ph: 603-428-7493
jbernier@attbi.com
http://www.berniervintage.com
*Supplier of new and used parts for
British motorcycles.*

British (Triumph)

Clubs/Associations

John W. Healy
Triumph International Owners Club/
British Motorcycle Association
<u>Newsletter: TIOC/BMA Newsletter</u>
P.O. Box 6676
Holliston, MA 01746-6676
ph: 508-429-4221
fax: 508-429-6213
JohnTIOC@aol.com
http://members.aol.com/JohnTIOC/
tioc.htm
Dedicated to the riding, restoration

and racing of Triumph motorcycles; 3,000 members; annual rally in various parts of the US; newsletter includes rallies, ads, classifieds, and varying social and technical articles.

Triumph International Owners Club
Magazine: Vintage Bike
P.O. Box 6676
Holliston, MA 01746-6676
ph: 508-429-4221
fax: 508-429-6213
JohnTIOC@aol.com
http://tioc.com

Harley-Davidson
Clubs/Associations

National Harley Owners Group
P.O. Box 453
Milwaukee, WI 53201
ph: 800-258-2464
fax: 414-343-4515
http://www.hog.com

Man./Prod./Dist.

Harley-Davidson Motor Company
3700 W. Juneau Ave.
Milwaukee, WI 53208
ph: 414-343-4056
http://www.harley-davidson.com

Periodicals

Ehlert Publishing Group, Inc.
Magazine: American Rider
601 Carlson Parkway, Ste. 600
Hopkins, MN 55305
mallmaster@atving.com
http://www.powersportsmall.com/ehlert
A quarterly magazine for the Harley-Davidson enthusiast; historical profiles, technical information, racing coverage, club news, road tests, product evaluations, etc.

Indian
Clubs/Associations

Steve Adams
Indian Motorcycle Club International
Magazine: Vintage Indian Magazine
P.O. Box 7783
Riverside, CA 92513
sadams02@earthlink.net
A club dedicated to the enjoyment of Indian motorcycles.

Dealers

Starklite Cycle
21230 Gold Valley Rd.
Perris, CA 92570
ph: 909-780-0421
fax: 909-780-0857
sales@starklite.com
http://www.starklite.com
World's largest supplier of quality antique Indian (made from 1901-1953) motorcycle parts, accessories and complete restorations.

Museums/Libraries

Esta Manthos, Dir.
Indian Motorcycle Museum & Hall of Fame
33 Hendee St.
P.O. Box 90003 Mason Sq. Sta.
Springfield, MA 01139-3003
ph: 413-737-2624

Japanese
Clubs/Associations

Ben Gundy, Mem.
Classic Japanese Motorcycle Club
Newsletter: Classic Japanese Motorcycle Club Newsletter
667 Cuesta Dr.
Los Altos, CA 94024-4135
ph: 650-948-2229
membership@cjmc.org
http://www.cjmc.org
Dedicated to having fun with pre-1984 Japanese motorcycles; newsletter has information, technical help, and the largest Japanese motorcycle want ad section; free want ads!

Vintage Japanese Motorcycle Club
Magazine: TANSHA
P.O. Box 14
Corwen, Ll21 9WF U.K.
ph: +44 (0) 870 013 8562
fax: +44 (0) 870 013 8562
vjmc@vjmc.com
http://www.vjmc.com
Welcomes collectors, riders, restorers, and racers of vintage Japanese motorcycles; 21 year old club; 6,500+ members; make contact with others involved in all aspects of vintage and classic Japanese motorcycles.

Moto Guzzi
Clubs/Associations

Frank Wedge
Moto Guzzi National Owners Club
P.O. Box 3
Larned, KS 67550-0003
ph: 316-285-7432
fax: 316-285-7344
mgnochq@cox.net
http://www.mgnoc.com
Focuses on the collection and restoration of Moto Guzzi motorcycles and related items.

Motor Scooter
Clubs/Associations

Joyce Lee
Vintage Motor Bike Club, Inc.
537 W. Huntington St.
Montpelier, IN 47359
ph: 765-728-5318
http://www.cantrellbarnes.com/vmbc.html
Founded in 1972; focuses on out-of-production motor scooters (generally defined as vehicles that go under 50 mph).

Sidecars
Clubs/Associations

United Sidecar Association
130 South Michigan Ave. South
Villa Park, IL 60181
ph: 630-833-6732
jcain2@csc.com
http://www.sidecar.com
The world's premier sidecar Web site.

Periodicals

Magazine: Hack'd
P.O. Box 250
Chandler, IN 47610
ph: 812-925-3931
hackdmag1@sbcglobal.net
http://www.sidecar.com/hacked.htm
The magazine for and about sidecarists.

Suzuki
Clubs/Associations

Suzuki Owners Club
30 Lavender Place
Carterton
Oxford, Oxfordshire OX18 3XR U.K.
webmaster@suzuki-club.co.uk
http://www.suzuki-club.co.uk
For owners of Suzuki motorcycles.

Whizzer
Collectors

Robert J. Lee
P.O. Box 465
Franklin, TN 37065
rjustinlee@yahoo.com
http://userweb.nashville.com/~robert.lee
Buys and sells Whizzer and Triumph motorcycles.

Ron Klaus
35769 Simon Dr.
Clinton Township, MI 48035
ph: 810-791-5594

MOTTOES (PICTURE POEMS)
Clubs/Associations

Howard & Sarah Wade
Mad About Mottoes
Newsletter: Mad About Mottoes Newsletter
P.O. Box 325
Orrville, OH 44667-0325
ph: 330-682-8551
fax: 330-682-3655
RBCollectr@aol.com

Collectors

Howard & Sarah Wade
P.O. Box 325
Orrville, OH 44667-0325
ph: 330-682-8551
fax: 330-682-3655
RBCollectr@aol.com
Has extensive collection of mottoes and picture poems by Buzza, P.F. Volland, Cincinnati Art Publishers, Mottograph, Buckbee-Grehn, and Gibson.

MOUNTS

(see ANIMAL TROPHIES)

MOVIE MEMORABILIA

(see also AUDIO-VISUAL; AUTOGRAPHS; BROADCASTING; COWBOY HEROES; DISNEY COLLECTIBLES; FAN CLUBS; FILMS; HORROR; MAGAZINES, Movie; PERSONALITIES [MOVIE STARS]; PHOTOGRAPHS, Celebrity; SCIENCE FICTION; TELEVISION SHOWS & MEMORABILIA)

Auction Services

Bonhams & Butterfields
220 San Bruno Ave.
San Francisco, CA 94103
ph: 415-861-7500 or 800-223-2854
fax: 415-861-8951
info.US@butterfields.com
http://www.butterfields.com
Auctioneers and appraisers of antiques, fine art and collectibles in all categories; specialty sales include posters, toys, decorative arts, furniture, photography, etc.; the largest full service auction in the West.

Miles Barton
Sotheby's
34-35 New Bond St.
London, W1A 2AA U.K.
ph: 44 171 293 5000
fax: 44 171 293 5989
http://www.sothebys.com
Conducts regular auctions of movie memorabilia.

Clubs/Associations

British Film Institute
21 Stephen St.
London, W1P 1LN U.K.
ph: 020 7255 1444
library@bfi.org.uk
http://www.bfi.org.uk
Provides information and maintains collections pertaining to the history of film and television; making movies, collections & archives, facts on film, museum of the moving image, and more.

Collectors

Bob Havey
P.O. Box 183
North Sullivan, ME 04664-0183
ph: 207-422-3083
fax: 207-422-3430
Wants to buy 1930s-1940s posters, lobby cards, advertising, magazines; anything movie related.

Bill Simmons
181 NW 78th Ave.
Margate, FL 33063
ph: 954-984-9647
wsim1206@aol.com
Wants all movie memorabilia, autographs, posters, photos; especial wants anything on Chuck Connors

including baseball and basketball items.

James Carlson, #73536
Arizona State Prison - Florence
P.O. Box 8400 - South Unit
Florence, AZ 85232-8400
Inmate collects autographs, scripts, documents in the entertainment field; accepts donations of autographs only (no money); writes to stars and celebrities to obtain autographs; member of UACC; seeks penpals with similar interests.

Scott Weiss
1158 26th St., #489
Santa Monica, CA 90403
ph: 310-264-7202
fax: 310-264-7203
sweiss5905@aol.com
Wants to buy movie and TV imprinted promotional advertising objects; metal, wood, plastic, glass, ceramic: pin-back buttons, pins, paperweights, tokens, snowdomes, watches, radios, rings, matchbooks, flashlights, letter openers, etc.

Talbert Kanigher
Tal's Nostalgia
P.O. Box 6294
Burbank, CA 91505-6294
ph: 818-848-6469
fax: 818-848-6469
Wants movie autographs, photographs, etc.; collecting movie memorabilia for over 40 years.

Dealers

Jon Allan
Elmer's Nostalgia, Inc.
3 Putnam St.
Sanford, ME 04073-2024
ph: 207-324-2166
elmers@gwi.net
http://www.elmers.net

Vaughn K. Mann
Cinema Recall
P.O. Box 1021
New London, CT 06320
ph: 840-447-2286
Buys and sells nearly any and all movie collectibles and memorabilia.

Van Polla
16-64 155 St.
Flushing, NY 11357-3233
ph: 718-746-0911
fax: 718-746-0911
info@hollywoodcollector.com
http://www.hollywoodcollector.com
Buying, selling, trading and auctioning movie posters, lobby cards, photos, stills, vintage sheet music, animation art, toys, magazines, comics, records, 8mm films, books, movie star postcards and some sports and TV paper collectibles.

Dennis & Mary Luby
Casey's Collectible Corner
HCR 31 Box 30
No. Blenheim, NY 12131
ph: 607-588-6464
caseyscc@aol.com
Buys and sells collectible toys: comic characters, TV shows and personalities; also space and monster toys, sports collectibles, etc.

Sandra Hollman
Global Music Enterprises
488 Archer Lane
Kissimmee, FL 34746
ph: 407-396-4176
fax: 407-396-4176
globaltreasures@webtv.net
Buys and sells vintage sheet music and movie/movie star memorabilia, Marilyn Monroe, pin-ups; send want lists or email requests.

Bruce Hubbard IV
Williams Collection, The
260 Ridgeview Dr.
Wayzata, MN 55391
ph: 612-473-9591
bedlum@aol.com
http://www.bedlum.net
Large movie prop dealer; drama, horror, Sci-fi, action; deals only in authentic movie props and wardrobe; no common posters, concert tickets, common movie items, or T-shirts; head of MPA.

Silver Screen Film Collectibles & Gifts
6336 Clayton Ave.
Saint Louis, MO 63139
ph: 314-781-0077 or 800-317-6947
fax: 314-781-2208
pmcedwards@aol.com
http://www.vintagefilm.com
Inventory constantly changing; check Web site for stock; call 800-317-6957 for orders ONLY.

Book City Collectables
6631 Hollywood Blvd.
Hollywood, CA 90028
ph: 323-466-0120
fax: 323-962-6742
hwdbookcity@earthlink.net
http://www.hollywoodbookcity.com
Sells movie memorabilia, books and TV and movie scripts.

Hollywood Book City Collectables
6627 Hollywood Blvd.
Los Angeles, CA 90028
ph: 323-466-2525 or 800-4CINEMA
fax: 323-962-6742
hwdbookcity@earthlink.net
Buys and sells books, autographed celebrity pictures, movie and television scripts, and other movie memorabilia.

Larry Edmunds
Larry Edmunds Bookshop, Inc.
6644 Hollywood Blvd.
Los Angeles, CA 90028-6208
ph: 323-463-3273
fax: 323-463-4245
edmunds@artnet.net
http://www.larryedmunds.com
Sells movie memorabilia, stills, posters, books and TV and movie scripts.

Myron Ross
Heroes & Legends
P.O. Box 9088
Calabasas, CA 91372
ph: 818-346-9220
heroesross@aol.com
http://www.heroesandlegends.net
Wants character memorabilia, books, comic books, Fanzines, movie memorabilia, etc.; science fiction or fantasy, rock 'n' roll, autographs.

Israel I. Bick
Bick International
P.O. Box 854
Van Nuys, CA 91408-0854
ph: 818-997-6496
fax: 818-988-4337
iibick@aol.com
http://www.bick.net
Buy, sell, trade and appraises Princess Diana, Hollywood, Beatles, Churchill, Lincoln, James Dean, Disney, Elvis, Marilyn Monroe, Bruce Lee, movies, Sherlock Holmes, Judaica, space, Star Trek, Streisand, etc.

Heather Holmberg
Heather Holmberg Auctions
3727 W. Magnolia Blvd., #247
Burbank, CA 91505
ph: 818-765-7341
fax: 818-765-7342
heather@collectible.com
http://www.collectible.com
Buys, sells, auctions movie posters, props and costumes, autographs, letters and documents, photographs, original art; also rock 'n' roll, animation, postcards, ephemera.

Eddie Brandt's Saturday Matinee
5006 Vineland Ave.
North Hollywood, CA 91601
ph: 818-506-4242 or 818-506-7722
fax: 818-506-5649
A great source for stills, posters, and lobby cards.

Reel Clothes & Props
5525 Cahuenga Blvd.
North Hollywood, CA 91601
ph: 818-508-7762
sales@reelclothes.com
http://www.reelclothes.com
Sells off clothing and props from movies and TV.

Christopher Perry
Photoplay Orchestra
7470 Church St., Ste. A
Yucca Valley, CA 92284-3248
ph: 760-365-0475
fax: 760-365-0495
evildoctor3d@yahoo.com
http://www.photoplayorchestra.com
Buys glass slides that were used in movie theaters; prefers pre-1940 slides but buys slides from all eras; these slides measure 4" x 3-1/4"; also buys all 3-D movie memorabilia (says "3D" or "3-Dimension" on it).

Trudy Prescott
Star Struck International
2791 F. North Texas St., Ste. 112
Fairfield, CA 94533
ph: 707-426-0811
fax: 707-426-0811
sales@starcollectibles.com
http://www.starcollectibles.com
Buys and sells memorabilia from TV, film and music: costumes, autographs, memorabilia.

Ann Daman
Big Picture Movie Posters & Collectibles
bigpix@dnai.com
http://www.big-pix.com
Movie posters, press kits, banners, standees, buttons and other miscellaneous movie memorabilia from the 1960s to present.

William Rumpf
Memorabilia Mine
P.O. Box 21026
San Jose, CA 95151
ph: 408-270-1072
fax: 408-270-1072
sirwgr@memomine.com
http://www.memomine.com
Movie memorabilia collector, dealer, expert and appraiser.

Thomas Bauer
Nonstop Collectibles
6152 Terrebonne
Montreal, Quebec H4B 1A3 Canada
ph: 514-489-5499
thomasbauer@sympatico.ca
http://www.thomasbauer.ca
Internet sales consultant and broker since 1993; active in online sales and marketing of movie memorabilia, other collectibles; will do qualified evaluations of your collection; list items for sale for 20% commission; good comic info.

STARticles
58 Stewart St., Studio 301
Totonto, Ontario M5V 1H6 Canada
ph: 416-504-8286
info@starticles.com
http://www.starticles.com
Hollywood props, wardrobe used in films, gold records, signed guitars, stage worn items, autographs, sports items, movie "star articles."

Eric G. Lilley
Charles Clore Court, Flat 59
139 Appleford Rd.
Reading, Berkshire RG30 3NT U.K.
ph: 0118 9599540
*Buys and sells memorabilia from the
"Golden Era" of Hollywood (1930s
to 1950s): American Westerns, swash
bucklers, dancers, dramatic stars,
British stars: posters, photographs,
autographs, films, rare books, etc.*

Experts

Richard C. De Thuin
875 West End Ave., Apt. 11F
New York, NY 10025-4954
Rdethuin@aol.com
*Welcomes written inquiries; please
keep inquiries to a max of two items
and include both condition and a
photograph; SASE required for reply
which will be dictated by volume of
mail received; please be patient.*

Richard Alan Davis
Bijou Dream
9500 Old Georgetown Rd.
Bethesda, MD 20814-1724
ph: 301-530-5904
fax: 301-530-8532
rdavis9500@aol.com
*Wants vintage movie memorabilia;
sorry, no photographs of movie stars.*

Richard L. Wilson
Norma's Jeans
3511 Turner Lane
Chevy Chase, MD 20815-3213
ph: 301-652-4644
fax: 301-652-9888
normasjeans@msn.com
*Buys, sells, collects and appraises
entertainment costumes, props, promo
items; also belongings of famous
people, historical relics and artifacts;
issues periodic catalog of celebrity
items for sale.*

Morris Everett, Jr.
Last Moving Picture Company, The
10535 Chillicothe Rd.
Willoughby, OH 44094
lastmo@aol.com
*Expert, appraiser of movie memora-
bilia.*

Internet Resources

Internet Movie Database, Inc.
feedback@imdb.com
http://www.imdb.com
*Search a database of filmography by
movie title, cast or crew name,
character name, taglines, biographies,
business, credits, goofs, locations,
plots, quotes, soundtracks, trivia,
versions, years, etc.*

Mark Crawley
MovieProp.com
mrmovieprop@movieprop.com
http://www.movieprop.com
*For movie prop and costume
collectors; information about the
hobby of collecting production used
Hollywood memorabilia such as*

*celebrity wardrobe, Sci-Fi weapons,
spaceships, replicas, and more.*

Baseline.Hollywood.com
30 Irving Place, 5th Floor
New York, NY 10003
ph: 212-254-8235 or 800-242-7546
fax: 212-529-3330
info@baseline.hollywood.com
http://www.pkbaseline.com
*Facts for the entertainment industries;
databases for accurate, timely
information about feature films,
television series & movies, video
distribution, cable TV, film &
television projects in production,
analysis of the media industries.*

Sue D'Agostino, PR
All Movie Guide
301 East Liberty, Ste. 400
Ann Arbor, MI 48104
ph: 734-887-5600
fax: 734-827-2492
suedag@aent.com
http://allmovie.com
*Movie Guide glossary of movie and
film-related terms; search databases
by keywords for actor filmographies,
factoids, and lots more.*

Heather Holmberg
Collectible.com, Inc.
3727 W. Magnolia Blvd., #247
Burbank, CA 91505
ph: 818-765-7341
fax: 818-765-7342
heather@collectible.com
http://www.collectible.com
*A movie memorabilia information hub:
dealer and show listings, resources
for collectors, discounts on products
and services.*

National Film Preservation Foundation
870 Market St., Ste. 1113
San Francisco, CA 94102
ph: 415-392-7291
fax: 415-392-7293
info@filmpreservation.org
http://www.filmpreservation.org
*Dedicated to the preservation of
America's film heritage.*

Museums/Libraries

Library & Museum of the Performing
Arts
40 Lincoln Center Plaza
New York, NY 10023-7498
ph: 212-870-1630
performingarts@nypl.org
http://www.nypl.org/research/lpa/
lpa.html
*Houses one of the world's most
extensive combination of circulating,
reference, and rare archival
collections in the field: historic
recordings, autograph manuscripts,
sheet music, stage designs, press
clippings, programs, posters, etc.*

American Museum of the Moving Image
35 Ave. at 36 St.
Astoria, NY 11106
ph: 718-784-4520 or 718-784-0077
fax: 718-784-4681
info@ammi.org
http://www.ammi.org
*The only museum in the US devoted to
the art, history, technology of film,
television, video, interactive media;
collection includes costumes, dolls,
movie posters, magazines, TV sets,
movie cameras, and other items of film
& TV history.*

American Film Institute, The
2021 N. Western Ave.
Los Angeles, CA 90027
ph: 323-856-7600 or 800-774-4AFI
fax: 323-467-4578
information@afi.com
http://www.afi.com
*Promotes the art and appreciation of
American film.*

Periodicals

Kevin Celment, Ed.
Magazine: Chiller Theatre
P.O. Box 23
Rutherford, NJ 07070
*A magazine for fans of the early
Horror movies; four issues per year.*

Magazine: Cineaste
P.O. Box 2242
New York, NY 10009
ph: 212-982-1241
fax: 212-982-1241
cineaste@cineaste.com
http://www.cineaste.com
*A quarterly magazine on the art and
politics of the cinema; interviews,
articles, and reviews of films, videos
and books; funded by the New York
State Council on the Arts.*

Magazine: American Movie Classics
P.O. Box 469082
Marion, OH 469082
ph: 888-262-4700
info@amctv.com
http://www.amctv.com/
amcmagazine.html

Brian A. Bukantis
Arena Publishing, Inc.
Newspaper: Movie Collector's World
P.O. Box 309
Fraser, MI 48026
ph: 810-774-4311
fax: 810-774-5450
mcw@mcwonline.com
http://www.mcwonline.com
*Largest leading biweekly movie poster
& memorabilia collecting publication
existing; posters, stills, videos, etc.
offered in each issue; over 625
consecutive biweekly issues published.*

Stacie Berger
Antique Trader Publications, Inc.
Magazine: Big Reel
P.O. Box 1050
Dubuque, IA 52004-1050
ph: 800-334-7165 or 800-482-4155
fax: 800-531-0880
stacie.berger@fwpubs.com
http://www.bigreel.com
*A monthly tabloid for movie and
television memorabilia collectors and
fans: ads, news, current & nostalgic
feature articles, obits, etc.*

Bob King
Newspaper: Classic Images
301 East 3rd St.
Muscatine, IA 52761
ph: 319-263-2331
fax: 319-262-8042
classicimages@classicimages.com
http://www.classicimages.com
*Monthly tabloid featuring articles and
advertisements directed at film buffs;
classic screen biographies,
filmographies, interviews, and
historical articles on the film industry.*

Bob King
Classic Images
Magazine: Films of the Golden Age
301 East 3rd St.
Muscatine, IA 52761
ph: 319-263-2331
fax: 319-262-8042
classicimages@classicimages.com
http://www.classicimages.com
*For classic movie buffs; beautifully
produced stories and art will take you
back to Hollywood's Golden Age; 100
pages in each issue; published
quarterly.*

Doug Watson
Magazine: Paper Collectors' Marketplace
470 Main St.
P.O. Box 128
Scandinavia, WI 54977-0128
ph: 715-467-2379
fax: 715-467-2243
pcmpaper@gglbbs.com
http://www.pcmpaper.com
*Monthly magazine for collectors of
autographs, paperbacks, postcards,
advertising, photographica,
magazines; all types of paper
ephemera.*

Randy Skretvedt
Past Times Nostalgia Network
Newsletter: Past Times
7308-H Filmore Dr.
Buena Park, CA 90620
ph: 714-527-5845
fax: 714-527-5845
skretved@ix.netcom.com
http://www.ptnostalgia.com
*A quarterly newsletter covering music,
movies, and radio programs from the
1920s, '30s, and '40s.*

Jordan Young
Past Times Nostalgia Network
Directory: Nostalgia Entertainment
Sourcebook
7308-H Filmore Dr.
Buena Park, CA 90620
ph: 714-527-5845
fax: 714-527-5845
skretved@ix.netcom.com
http://www.ptnostalgia.com
*Complete resource guide to classic
movies, vintage radio, old time music,
and theater: programs, sheet music,
equipment, where to replace and
repair, where to rent or buy old
movies, theater posters.*

Darrell Talbert
Odyssey Publications, a Division of
Collectors Universe
Magazine: Pop Culture Collecting
510-A S. Corona Mall
Corona, CA 91720-1420
ph: 909-371-7137 or 800-99-ODYSSEY
fax: 909-371-7139
DBTOGI@aol.com
http://www.autographs.com/collect.htm
*A monthly magazine focusing on
collecting autographs, movie
memorabilia, movie posters,
television, rock & roll, props,
costumes, sports, space collectibles,
animation art and more.*

Gone With The Wind

(see also PERSONALITIES
[LITERARY], Margaret Mitchell)

Collectors

Robert Buchanan
277 W. 22nd St.
New York, NY 10011-2755
ph: 212-989-3917
*Wants any GWTW items; also any
Vivien Leigh and Clark Gable.*

John Wiley, Ed.
1347 Greenmoss Dr.
Richmond, VA 23225-4112
ph: 804-330-5484
fax: 804-771-3054
tsl_gwtw@hotmail.com
http://www.thescarlettletter.com
*Wants to buy early copies of the novel
in dust jackets and limited editions
(US and foreign); Margaret Mitchell
items (personal effects, business
cards, etc.), movie & stage version
items (programs, scarves, novelties,
scripts, etc.).*

Herb Bridges
P.O. Box 192
Sharpsburg, GA 30277-0192
ph: 404-253-4934
herb-gwtw@mindspring.com
*Seeks the many GWTW movie tie-in
items which were produced in the
1940s: figurines, dolls, games,
jewelry, perfume bottles, powder
boxes, book ends, candy boxes,
handkerchiefs, stationary boxes; also
GWTW posters, programs, banners.*

Kenneth Nix
307 Rosewood Dr.
Dublin, GA 31021-4133
ph: 478-275-0281
fax: 478-272-1744
knix@nlamerica.com
*Especially wants merchandising tie-ins
associated with both the book and film
versions of GWTW. "Scarlett's
Chocolates" candy box, neckties,
scarves, handkerchiefs, puzzles,
games, etc.; publisher of "Gone With
The Wind Marketplace."*

Dealers

June Crawford
JG Enterprises
P.O. Box 2589
Goose Creek, SC 29445
ph: 843-569-3260
jkscarlett@aol.com
*Buys and sells any and all "Gone
With The Wind" items; has a catalog
of over 100 GWTW items, both old
and new.*

J. Faye Bell
Gone With the Wind Memories
1701 S. Alexander St., Ste. 109
Plant City, FL 33566
ph: 813-752-7700
fax: 813-754-8211
GWTWfaye@aol.com
http://www.gwtwmemories.com
*Buying and selling GWTW; has
thousands of items from which to
choose, from 1936 to present.*

Museums/Libraries

Clayton County Convention & Visitors
Bureau
104 North Main St.
Jonesboro, GA 30236
ph: 770-478-4800 or 800-662-7829
*Learn about Gone With The Wind
related attractions.*

Susan Vaccaro, Off. Mngr.
Margaret Mitchell House & Museum
990 Peachtree St.
Atlanta, GA 30309
ph: 404-249-7012
fax: 404-249-7015
susan@gwtw.org
http://www.gwtw.org
*Memorabilia from around the world
has been collected and offered in over
6,000 square feet of displays, artwork
and artifacts that are of interest to the
serious historian as well as the
curious traveler.*

Periodicals

John Wiley, Ed.
Newsletter: Scarlett Letter, The
1347 Greenmoss Dr.
Richmond, VA 23225-4112
ph: 804-330-5484
fax: 804-771-3054
tsl_gwtw@hotmail.com
http://www.thescarlettletter.com
*Published quarterly; honors both book
and film; keeps collectors up-to-date*

*on all aspects of GWTW; articles,
auction results, ads, etc.*

Horror Films & Literature

(see HORROR; SCIENCE FICTION)

Movie Posters

Auction Services

James Halperin
Heritage Galleries & Auctioneers
Dallas, TX 75219
ph: 800-872-6467 or 214-528-3500
fax: 214-520-7108
auctions@HeritageMoviePosters.com
http://www.HeritageMoviePosters.com
*Specializes in buying and selling
movie posters; over $1.5M sold at
auction in 2002; free online
community, auction prices archive,
weekly newsletter.*

Collectors

Ed Royse
112 N. Broadway St.
Walters, OK 73572
ph: 580-357-8000
fax: 580-875-2063
edroyse@juno.com
*Wants to buy movie posters, B
Westerns, any Audie Murphy or John
Wayne movie posters.*

Gene Arnold
2234 South Blvd.
Houston, TX 77098-5225
ph: 713-528-1880
*Wants any old movie posters or
11" x 14" lobby cards.*

Dealers

Rudy Franchi
Nostalgia Factory, The
50 Terminal St., Bldg 2
Charlestown, MA 02129
ph: 617-241-8300 or 800-479-8754
fax: 617-241-0710
posters@nostalgia.com
http://www.nostalgia.com
*Always buying all forms of movie
advertising from 1900 to present;
posters, lobby cards, stills, press
books, press kits, inserts, etc.*

Bowers & Merena, Inc.
P.O. Box 1224
Wolfeboro, NH 03894-1224
ph: 800-458-4646 or 603-569-5095
fax: 603-569-5319
directsales@Bowersandmerena.com
http://www.bowersandmerena.com
*Wants American film posters from
1895-1915.*

Marty Davis
Vintage Film Posters
12 Thronebrook Rd.
West Granby, CT 06090
ph: 860-653-4228
fax: 860-653-4425
onesheet@aol.com
http://www.vintagefilmposters.com
*Buys and sells movie posters, all sizes
and periods; also related movie*

*memorabilia; specialist in silent era,
especially Chaplin, Keaton and Lloyd.*

Alan Levine
P.O. Box 1577
Bloomfield, NJ 07003
ph: 973-743-5288
posterking@aol.com
*Buys and sells movie posters and
lobby cards.*

Marc Zydiak
Star Archives
P.O. Box 285
Westfield, NJ 07091-0285
ph: 908-654-6505
mzunderstood@hotmail.com

Poster World
9 Bolton Place
Fair Lawn, NJ 07410
ph: 201-791-1073
*Specializing in movie posters from
1940 through 1970.*

Jerry Ohlinger
Jerry Ohlinger's Movie Material Store,
Inc.
242 W. 14th St.
New York, NY 10011-7206
ph: 212-989-0869
fax: 212-989-1660
jomms@aol.com
http://www.moviematerials.com
*Buys and sells motion picture photos
and posters from 1920 to present; also
TV photos; research services
available; free lists available;
complete lists of 100,000 black &
white photos or of 100,000 color
photos are $4 each.*

Sam Sarowitz
Posteritati Movie Posters
239 Centre St.
New York, NY 10013
ph: 212-226-2207
fax: 212-226-2102
mail@posteritati.com
http://www.posteritati.com
*Wants movie posters, lobby cards;
1900-1970s; small or large collections
bought; immediate cash available;
call, fax or write.*

Joe Burtis
Motion Picture Arts Gallery
133 E. 58th St., 10th Floor
New York, NY 10022
ph: 212-223-1009
fax: 212-371-0809
info@mpagallery.com
http://www.mpagallery.com
*Buys and sells posters, lobby cards,
etc.*

Todd Richard Feiertag
Poster City
P.O. Box 94
Orangeburg, NY 10962-0094
ph: 800-272-3323 or 201-869-1692
toddfeiertag@msn.com
*Buys and sells movie posters; entire
collections purchased; free appraisals;
will travel anywhere.*

Ken Farrell
Just Kids Nostalgia
310 New York Ave.
Huntington, NY 11743
ph: 631-423-8449
info@justkidsnostalgia.com
http://www.justkidsnostalgia.com
*Buys and sells vintage movie posters:
Humphrey Bogart, Judy Garland,
Audrey Hepburn, monsters, science
fiction, serials, comedy, Abbot &
Costello, Godfather, Batman, etc.*

John Kisch
Separate Cinema Archive(TM)
P.O. Box 114
Hyde Park, NY 12538-0114
ph: 845-452-1998
fax: 845-454-7131
http://www.separatecinema.com

George Theofiles
Miscellaneous Man
P.O. Box 1776
New Freedom, PA 17349-0076
ph: 717-235-4766
fax: 717-235-2853
miscman@adelphia.net
*Collects, buys and sells vintage film
posters; since 1970 offering catalogs
of rare posters and early advertising
and ephemera on hundreds of subjects.
Descriptive flyer available.*

Bill Fisher
How Sweet It Was
16104 Delaire Landing Rd.
Philadelphia, PA 19114
ph: 888-3-POSTER
fax: 215-551-4068
*Sells linen-backed and restored posters
from the past.*

Rick's Movie Graphics & Posters
P.O. Box 23709
Gainesville, FL 32602
ph: 352-373-7202 or 800-252-0425
fax: 352-373-2589
ricks@ricksmovie.com
http://www.ricksmovie.com

John Green
Movie Poster Page
2729 Cranbrook Rd.
Ann Arbor, MI 48104
ph: 734-973-7303
fax: 734-973-7304
john@musicman.com
http://www.musicman.com/mp/mp.html
*Buys and sells vintage as well as new
movie posters; also repairs and
restores.*

Celebrity Graphics
P.O. Box 385
Flushing, MI 48433-0385
ph: 810-659-8751
fax: 810-659-1215
birdsrus4@comcast.net
*Wants movie posters, lobby cards, any
vintage, any quantity.*

Galactic Highway Movie Posters
113 Colonial Parkway, Ste. B
Yorkville, IL 60560
ph: 630-553-2994
support@galactic-hwy.com
http://www.movieposters.net

Dwight M. Cleveland
P.O. Box 10922
Chicago, IL 60610-0922
ph: 773-525-9152
fax: 773-525-2969
posterboss@aol.com
http://www.movieposterbiz.com
*Buys, sells and collects movie posters,
lobby cards, 1-sheets, 3-sheets,
window cards, glass slides, studio
annuals, motion picture heralds, etc.;
highest prices paid.*

Bruce Hershenson
Hershenson-Allen Archive
P.O. Box 874
West Plains, MO 65775-0874
ph: 417-256-9616
fax: 417-257-6948
mail@brucehershenson.com
http://www.brucehershenson.com
*Wants high quality original posters
from major pre-1970 Hollywood films;
publisher of 18 books of full-color
reproductions of movie posters; sells
posters through sales lists and annual
auctions.*

Don Creekmore
Nations Attic, The
ph: 316-371-1828
dcreekmore@cox.net
http://www.nationsattic.com
*Want to buy pre-1970 vintage movie
posters.*

Gene Arnold
Movieposters.com
2315 SW Frwy., Ste. 120
Houston, TX 77098
ph: 713-524-9000
info@movieposters.com
http://www.movieposters.com
*Buys and sells old movie posters; in
business since 1965; carries a wide
variety of original posters covering the
obscure to the well-known; also has
access to newer movie posters.*

Cyber-cinema
P.O. Box 1944
Tempe, AZ 85280-1944
info@cyber-cinema.com
http://www.cyber-cinema.com
*Specializes in new releases and classic
movie reprints.*

Harry Lemay
LeMay Movie Posters
P.O. Box 480879
Los Angeles, CA 90048
ph: 323-935-4053 or 800-565-3629
fax: 323-933-4465
LeMayCo@aol.com

CINEMAGIC
852 Fifth Ave., Ste. #317
San Diego, CA 92101
ph: 619-291-2500
fax: 619-295-7626
cinemagic@classicmovieposters.com
http://www.classicmovieposters.com
*Buys and sells original movie posters
and lobby cards from the 1930s
through the early 1980s.*

James Dietz
J.S. Dietz Vintage Movie Posters
2726 Shelter Island Dr.
San Diego, CA 92106
ph: 619-223-1563
fax: 619-223-8944
jsdietz@earthlink.net
http://www.jimdietz.com/poster.html
*Collector, dealer, expert, appraiser
has one of the oldest and largest
Internet sites for pre-1970 vintage US
and foreign movie posters.*

David Kneubuhl
Movie Memories Poster Shop
502 Waverly St.
Palo Alto, CA 94301
ph: 650-328-6265
fax: 650-328-6265
kneubuhl1@excite.com
http://www.businessquest.com/
movie.htm
*Carries posters and other movie
memorabilia.*

Ann Daman
Big Picture Movie Posters & Collectibles
bigpix@dnai.com
http://www.big-pix.com
*Movie posters, press kits, banners,
standees, buttons and other
miscellaneous movie memorabilia from
the 1960s to present.*

Mark Welch
P.O. Box 11355
Pleasanton, CA 94588-1355
ph: 925-462-8483
markwelch@markwelch.com
http://www.markwelch.com
*Buys movie posters, movie memora-
bilia, movie lobby cards, still photos.*

Robert Candel
Movie Poster Shop
1314 S. Grand Blvd., #2-156
Spokane, WA 99202
ph: 403-250-7588
fax: 403-250-7589
mail@moviepostershop.com
http://www.moviepostershop.com
*15,000 original movie posters from
1925 to present; 20,000 photos,
posters and reproductions.*

Hollywood Canteen, The
1516 Danforth Ave.
Toronto, Ontario M4J 1N4 Canada
ph: 416-461-1704
fax: 416-461-7089
hcanteen@interlog.com
http://www.hcanteen.com
*Buys and sells movie posters and
movie books, new and out-of-print.*

CinePosters
4705 Doherty
Montreal, Quebec H4B 2B2 Canada
ph: 877-736-1023
info@cineposters.com
http://www.cineposters.com
*Specializes in movie posters from the
classics to present.*

Experts

Cinemonde
138 2nd Ave. North, Ste. #104
Nashville, TN 37201
ph: 615-742-3048
fax: 615-742-9945
cinemonde@earthlink.net
http://home.earthlink.net/~cinemonde
*Buys, sells, specializes in movie
posters; also sells country music
memorabilia; has a consulting office
in San Francisco.*

Jon Warren
Iguide Media Inc.
2401 Broad St.
Chattanooga, TN 37408
ph: 423-265-5515
fax: 423-265-5515
jon@iguide.net
http://www.iguide.net
*Author of "Movie Poster Price
Guide;" wants to buy movie posters as
well as comic books, cartoon art,
Disney, Big Little Books, pulp
magazines, baseball and non-sport
cards.*

Periodicals

John Kisch
Price Guide: Movie Poster Price
Almanac
P.O. Box 114
Hyde Park, NY 12538-0114
ph: 845-452-1998
fax: 845-454-7131
posterprice@moviegoods.com
http://www.posterprice.com
An annual movie poster price guide.

Movie Posters (Black)

Dealers

John Kisch
Separate Cinema Archive(TM)
P.O. Box 114
Hyde Park, NY 12538-0114
ph: 845-452-1998
fax: 845-454-7131
http://www.separatecinema.com
*Buys, sells and exhibits historic all
black cast movie posters and
ephemera.*

Movie Posters (Silent Movies)

Dealers

Ronald Krueger
R.W. Krueger's
P.O. Box 741
Oak Park, IL 60303-0741
ph: 708-788-8235
*Buys, sells, and trades silent movie
related posters, stills, portraits,
magazines, glass slides, etc.;
especially wants Mary Miles Minter
and Valentino.*

Oscars

Internet Resources

Academy of Motion Picture Arts &
Sciences
8949 Wilshire Blvd.
Beverly Hills, CA 90211-1972
ph: 310-247-3000
fax: 310-859-9351
ampas@oscars.org
http://www.oscars.org
*Everything you wanted to know about
the Oscars: nominees, history, fun &
games, store; behind the scene on
Oscar night, Governors Ball, the
Academy Awards show team, etc.*

Scripts

Collectors

Grayson D. Cook
Grayson D. Cook, Bookseller
367 W. Ave. 42
Los Angeles, CA 90065-3905
ph: 213-227-8899
*Wants to buy screenplays and movie
scripts; prefers original studio
production copies; will consider
agency copies or photocopies; please
send description (title, writer, and
draft).*

Dealers

Mad Morgan Enterprises
P.O. Box 6698
Burbank, CA 91510
ph: 818-848-1445
fax: 818-840-1252
morgancooke@earthlink.net
http://www.madmorgan.com
*Specializes in scripts from movies,
mini series, pilots, TV shows, movies
of the week, unproduced titles,
storyboards.*

Serials

Periodicals

Linda S. Downey
World of Yesterday, The
Journal: Cliffhanger
104 Chestnut Wood Dr.
Waynesville, NC 28786-6514
ph: 828-646-6864
Periodic journal focusing on serials.

Silent Films

Experts

Richard Alan Davis
Bijou Dream
9500 Old Georgetown Rd.
Bethesda, MD 20814-1724
ph: 301-530-5904
fax: 301-530-8532
rdavis9500@aol.com
*Wants silent movie items: posters,
lobby cards, programs, stills, Star
Garment Co. hangers with head/
shoulder of movie stars.*

Star Wars

Collectors

Martin Thurn
Star Wars Collector's Bible, The
mthurn@megapipe.net
http://www.sandcrawler.com/SWB
*An extensive list of Star Wars
collectibles and resources.*

David Welch
P.O. Box 714
Murphysboro, IL 62966-0714
ph: 618-687-2282
fax: 618-684-2243
PEZDude1@aol.com
http://www.pezheads.net/dwelch
*Wants 1977-1984 complete items with
original packaging only; especially
interested in Kenner Action Figure
related items; paying over $2000 for
rarer items; no books, records or
comics, please.*

Dealers

411 Toys
16054 Sherman Way
Van Nuys, CA 91406
ph: 818-786-9760 or 888-411-TOYS
fax: 818-786-4655
http://www.411toys.com

Brian Rachfal
P.O. Box 7772
San Jose, CA 95150-3766
ph: 408-298-9070 or 408-629-3980
*Wants to buy Star Wars action figures
and related items.*

David Roberts
D & S Sci-fi Toy World
4701 NE 72nd Ave. #J222
Vancouver, WA 98661
ph: 360-666-4774
fax: 360-666-4868
dave@dnstoys.com
http://www.dnstoys.com
*Specializes in Star Wars, Star Trek,
Aliens and other sci-fi movie related
toys and collectibles.*

Experts

Nick J. Lehrling
P.O. Box 18536
Tucson, AZ 85731
ph: 520-749-3897 or 520-749-2621
fax: 520-749-3897
Star Wars collector and expert.

Internet Resources

Gus Lopez
Star Wars Collectors Archives
lopez@halcyon.com
http://www.toysrgus.com
*A virtual tour of some of the finest
Star Wars collections in the world; an
exhaustive archive of Star Wars
information and photographs.*

NewsDroid Star Wars Headline News
editor@newsdroid.com
http://www.newsdroid.com
*Headline news for Star Wars fans
featuring every aspect of the Star
Wars universe: prequels, games,
books, and other news topics.*

Martin Thurn
Star Wars Collector's Bible, The
mthurn@megapipe.net
http://www.sandcrawler.com/SWB
*An extensive list of Star Wars
collectibles and resources.*

Guillermo Rivera
Star Wars Fan's Web Page
Cesba@aol.com
http://hometown.aol.com/Cesba/
index.html
*Star Wars collecting information;
buying and selling.*

Force.net, The
P.O. Box 690681
Houston, TX 77269-0681
fax: 305-675-8103
contact@theforce.net
http://www.theforce.net
*All the latest Star Wars news,
collectibles, trivia, new episodes, etc.;
encyclopedia, time lines, humor, fan
art museum, events, and more.*

Sameer Ketkar
Star Wars Database
fax: 208-330-4751
ketkar@usc.edu
http://www.swdatabase.com
*Hundreds of pages of Star Wars
information and multimedia including
prequels, chat, animated .gifs, games,
movie mistakes, and more.*

ForceCollectors.com
force@forcecollectors.com
http://www.forcecollectors.com
*An online community dedicated to the
buying, selling, trading of Star Wars
collectibles: action figures, toys,
trading cards, comics, games, and all
related memorabilia.*

Star Wars (Art)

Experts

William Plumb
2503 Floradale Way
Lincoln, CA 95748
ph: 916-434-1772
disneyp@starstream.net
*Collects all Star Wars original art:
drawings, sketches, paintings; plans
on opening a museum of original Star
Wars art.*

Trade Publications

Collectors

George Reed
7216 Kindred St.
Philadelphia, PA 19149-1124
ph: 215-725-3003
Wants illustrated movie advertising trade books, coming attraction folios, pamphlets, etc., in color or black and white; also exhibitors/trade magazines and publications, pressbooks and souvenir programs, and related material.

Westerns

(see also COWBOY HEROES)

Clubs/Associations

Milo Holt
Old Time Western Film Club
Newsletter: Old Time Western Film
Newsletter
P.O. Box 142
Siler City, NC 27344-0142
Interested in promoting the showing of old Westerns and in the collecting of memorabilia relating thereto; meets every other month for Western film festival; 500 on mailing list; over 30 years.

Nikki Ellerbe
Western Film Preservation Society, Inc., Raleigh Chapter
Newsletter: Western Film Preservation Society Newsletter
2404 Rock Ridge Court
Raleigh, NC 27612
Began in 1981 for the purpose of keeping "B" Western movies of the 1920 through 1950s alive for future generations to enjoy; over 200 members; regular meetings.

Norman Kietzer
Westerns & Serials Fan Club
Magazine: Westerns & Serials
527 S. Front St.
Mankato, MN 56001-3718
ph: 507-344-8913
fax: 507-344-0255
kietzer@mctcnet.net
http://www.angelfire.com/biz2/normankietzerpubs
A club for collectors as well as non-collectors interested in westerns and serials of the silver screen; also interested in related memorabilia.

Alan Dobrey
Western Film Appreciation Club of Alberta
Newsletter: Western Film Appreciation Society Bulletin
9826 171A Ave.
Edmonton, Alberta T5X 3Y4 Canada
ph: 403-456-3769
Dedicated to keeping the Western films of yesteryear (1930s to 1950s) alive through the screening and promoting of these films; holds monthly meetings; open to the public.

Eric G. Lilley, Pres.
Boys Hollywood
Charles Clore Court, Flat 59
139 Appleford Rd.
Reading, Berkshire RG30 3NT U.K.
ph: 0118 9599540
Focuses on the great Hollywood Western film stars of the 1930s to 1950s: Roy Rogers, Gene Autry, William Boyd.

Dealers

Jerry Ohlinger
Jerry Ohlinger's Movie Material Store, Inc.
242 W. 14th St.
New York, NY 10011-7206
ph: 212-989-0869
fax: 212-989-1660
jomms@aol.com
http://www.moviematerials.com
Buys and sells motion picture photos and posters from 1920 to present; also TV photos; research services available; free lists available; complete lists of 100,000 black & white photos or of 100,000 color photos are $4 each.

Periodicals

Linda S. Downey
World of Yesterday, The
Journal: Under Western Skies
104 Chestnut Wood Dr.
Waynesville, NC 28786-6514
ph: 828-646-6864
Focuses on the old west of the Silver Screen & TV.

Colin Momber
Magazine: Wrangler's Roost
23 Sabrina Way
Bristol, BS9 1ST U.K.
ph: 0117-9684776
fax: 0117-9684776
colin.momber@cliffhanger.me.uk
A 32-page periodical published three times per year; longest running fanzine in the Western field; printed on gloss paper and is directed at enthusiasts of the old "B" Western movies.

Westerns (Italian)

Periodicals

Tom Betts
Newsletter: Westerns...All' Italiana!
P.O. Box 25042
Anaheim, CA 92825-5042
fax: 714-836-9040
Quarterly newsletter focusing on Italian Westerns.

MOVIE PROJECTORS

(see CAMERAS & CAMERA EQUIPMENT, Movie; FILMS; MAGIC LANTERNS)

MOVING & STORAGE ASSOCIATIONS

(see also REPAIR/RESTORATION/CONSERVATION)

Clubs/Associations

Household Goods Forwarders Association of America
2320 Mill Rd., Ste. 102
Alexandria, VA 22314
ph: 703-684-3780
fax: 703-684-3784
hhgfaa@aol.com
http://www.hhgfaa.org
World's largest union of moving and shipping companies in the world; business links, Congressional addresses, industry terms, industry abbreviations, etc.

American Moving & Storage Association
Magazine: Moving World, The
1611 Duke St.
Alexandria, VA 22314-3482
ph: 703-683-7411
fax: 703-683-7525
amconf@amconf.org
http://www.moving.org
Provides educational and certification programs for the moving & storage industry; approx. 3,500 members worldwide who provide goods & services to those who are relocating; actively involved in government and military affairs.

Chuck Naylor, Ex. Dir.
Claims Prevention & Procedure Council
Newsletter: CPPC Newsletter
P.O. Box 1367
Englewood, FL 34295-1367
ph: 941-473-2772
fax: 941-473-2775
cppc@comcast.net
http://www.claimsnet.org
A moving industry related organization of repairmen, van lines, appraisers, insurance companies, lawyers and claims adjusters.

MOXIE

(see SOFT DRINK COLLECTIBLES, Moxie)

MR. PEANUT

(see PLANTERS PEANUTS ITEMS)

MUGS

(see BARBERSHOP COLLECTIBLES, Shaving Mugs; COLLECTIBLES [MODERN], Steins; GLASSES, Drinking; RESTAURANT COLLECTIBLES; STEINS)

MUSIC

(see also AUTOGRAPHS, Music Related; BOOKS, Reference [Music]; DRUM & BUGLE CORPS; MUSIC BOXES; MUSICAL INSTRUMENTS; PERFORMING ARTS; PERSONALITIES [MUSICIANS]; PHONOGRAPHS; PIANO ROLLS; ROCK 'N' ROLL COLLECTIBLES; RECORDS; SHEET MUSIC; TICKETS)

Clubs/Associations

Music Library Association, Inc.
Magazine: Notes
8551 Research Way, Ste. 180
Middleton, WI 53562
ph: 608-836-5825
fax: 608-831-8200
mla@areditions.com
http://www.musiclibraryassoc.org
For music scholars, teachers, performers, librarians: scholarly articles, reviews, CR reviews, music publishers' information; also ads for records, scores, books, journals and other services.

Dealers

Campagna Christian
Rounder Records
Newsletter: Roundup
1 Camp St.
Cambridge, MA 02140-1194
ph: 617-661-6308 or 800-768-6337
fax: 617-868-8769
info@rounder.com
http://www.rounder.com
Mail order CDs, LPs, cassettes; specializing in hard-to-find blues, country, R&B, Rock 'N' Roll, jazz, bluegrass, etc.; "Roundup" is a bimonthly catalog/newsletter.

Bob Iuliucci
MusicandVideo.com
One Surrey Lane
Allendale, NJ 07401
ph: 201-236-9107
fax: 201-236-2916
riuliu6832@aol.com
http://www.musicandvideo.com
Web site updated weekly; items for sale include rare records, CDs, sheet music, music laser discs, designed guitars, concert tickets, rock books, DVDs, memorabilia and industry record awards; memorabilia featuring thousands of artists.

Gary Hein
Hein's Rare Collectibles
P.O. Box 179
Little Silver, NJ 07739-0179
ph: 732-219-1988
fax: 732-219-5940
ibuybeatles@comcast.net
http://www.Beatles4me.com
Buys, sells original 1960s Beatles: records, autographs, motion displays, bongos, guitars, record players, full and used concert tickets, kaboodle kits, costumes, color forms, kits, dolls,

school supplies, Yellow Submarine
items.

Jim Weaver
PMB 345, 322 Mall Blvd.
Monroeville, PA 15146-2229
*Wants to buy Rock & Roll/Rhythm &
Blues paper collectibles from the
1950s through the early 1970s: sheet
music, autographs, concert posters
and placards (especially for small
venues, clubs, bars, etc.); also movie/
TV autographs.*

Trudy Prescott
Star Struck International
2791 F. North Texas St., Ste. 112
Fairfield, CA 94533
ph: 707-426-0811
fax: 707-426-0811
sales@starcollectibles.com
http://www.starcollectibles.com
*Buys and sells memorabilia from TV,
film and music: costumes, autographs,
memorabilia.*

Internet Resources

Sue D'Agostino, PR
All Music Guide
301 East Liberty, Ste. 400
Ann Arbor, MI 48104
ph: 734-887-5600
fax: 734-827-2492
suedag@aent.com
http://allmovie.com
*History, description of music styles
dating back to 1920's; history of
artists; key albums, essays.*

Periodicals

Stacie Berger
Krause Publications
Magazine: Goldmine
700 E. State St.
Iola, WI 54990-0001
ph: 715-445-2214
fax: 715-445-4087
stacie.berger@fwpubs.com
http://www.krause.com
*A biweekly magazine containing
articles, ads about records &
recording artists from 1940s to
present; the record & CD marketplace.*

1960s & 1970s

Dealers

Charles F. Rosenay
Liverpool Productions
315 Derby Ave.
Orange, CT 06477
ph: 203-891-8131
rosenay@aol.com
http://www.toursandevents.com
*Buys and sells '60s music and
memorabilia relating to the Beatles,
British Invasion, Rolling Stones,
Monkees and Beach Boys.*

Big Band

3116 Teesdale St.
Philadelphia, PA 19152-4514
joeruttar@aol.com
*Wants to buy big band era music on
compact discs.*

Collectors

John L. Mickolas
172 Liberty St.
Trenton, NJ 08611-2631
ph: 609-599-9672
jmickolas@aol.com
*Wants Glenn Miller, Bunny Berigan,
autographs, recordings, photos, sheet
music, magazines, films, anything
related.*

Mark Rosenblum
10776 Blackley St.
Temple City, CA 91780-3501
ph: 626-453-8890
*Wants big band memorabilia: concert
posters, programs, advertising,
magazines, ballroom tickets pertaining
to Miller, Goodman, Dorsey, James,
Ellington, etc.*

Country

Museums/Libraries

Country Music Hall of Fame & Museum
222 Fifth Ave. South
Nashville, TN 37203
ph: 615-416-2096
http://www.countrymusichalloffame.com
*The largest museum devoted to a
single form of popular music: movies,
videos, computer interactives,
instruments, costumes, personal items
of the stars; NEW museum to open in
downtown Nashville in 2001.*

Periodicals

Disc Collector Publications
Newsletter: Disc Collector
P.O. Box 315
Cheswold, DE 19936-0315
ph: 302-674-3632
*Focuses on bluegrass and old time
country music.*

Dixieland & Ragtime

Collectors

Don Hoffman
P.O. Box 4231
Salinas, CA 93912-4231
ph: 831-449-7311
*Wants to buy blues, jazz, ragtime,
minstrel, Dixieland related items:
posters, tickets, programs, autographs, videos, broadsides, antique
photos, souvenirs, ephemera,
memorabilia, books, booklets,
souvenirs; describe and price, please.*

Periodicals

Richard Zimmerman, Ed.
Maple Leaf Club
Newsletter: Rag Times, The
15522 Ricky Ct.
Grass Valley, CA 95949-6672
*A bi-monthly newsletter with
everything about ragtime - past and
present; since 1967; also sheet music
ads and articles.*

Jazz & Blues

Auction Services

George Wilson
AllJazz
1079 Stuart Rd.
Princeton, NJ 08540
ph: 800-303-6557
gwilson@alljazz.com
http://www.alljazz.com
*Conducts auction sales of jazz,
personality, blues, C&W records
including 78s, LPs, CDs, etc.; over
20,000 items per year.*

Clubs/Associations

Bill Steinberg
New Jersey Jazz Society
1 Beechtree Rd.
Roseland, NJ 07068
ph: 800-303-6557
fax: 908-850-8258
anord@mindspring.com
http://www.njjs.org
*Mission is to promote and preserve
interest in jazz; many members are
collectors of jazz related music and
records.*

Charles E. Swan, Ex. Dir.
American Federation of Jazz Societies,
Inc.
Newsletter: Federation Jazz
P.O. Box 84063
Phoenix, AZ 85071-4063
ph: 602-942-8348
fax: 480-946-5598
info@jazzfederation.com
http://www.jazzfederation.com
*Serving jazz societies, individuals,
musicians, and the music industry.*

Collectors

Stanley King
260 Fifth Ave.
New York, NY 10001-6408
ph: 212-447-1880
fax: 212-447-0728
*Wants to nuy jazz band and jazz
musician memorabilia: photos,
posters, advertisements, postcards,
contracts, letters, etc.*

Don Hoffman
P.O. Box 4231
Salinas, CA 93912-4231
ph: 831-449-7311
*Wants to buy blues, jazz, ragtime,
minstrel, Dixieland related items:
posters, tickets, programs, autographs, videos, broadsides, antique
photos, souvenirs, ephemera,*

memorabilia, books, booklets,
souvenirs; describe and price, please.

Chuck Moore
P.O. Box 280
Gladstone, OR 97027
ph: 503-654-9994
fax: 503-656-7603
*Wants Jazz LP's, singles, 78's; also
older books, magazines, sheet music
on jazz.*

Dealers

Gary Alderman
G's Jazz
P.O. Box 259164
Madison, WI 53725-9164
ph: 608-274-3527
fax: 608-277-1999
gjazz@tds.net
http://www.gjazz.com
*Wants to buy jazz LP's, jazz
literature, jazz photos, autographs,
etc.; carries rare and out-of-print jazz
recordings and memorabilia for
collectors.*

Rock 'N' Roll

(see also AMERICAN BANDSTAND)

Auction Services

Stephen Maycock
Sotheby's
34-35 New Bond St.
London, W1A 2AA U.K.
ph: 44 171 293 5000
fax: 44 171 293 5989
http://www.sothebys.com
*Conducts regular auctions of Rock 'N
Roll memorabilia.*

Clubs/Associations

Dave Frees
American Bandstand 1950's Fan Club
Magazine: Bandstand Boogie
P.O. Box 131
Adamstown, PA 19501-0131
ph: 717-738-2513
popfrosty@webtv.net
http://www.fiftiesweb.com/davey-
frees.htm
*Focuses on "American Bandstand"
from the 1950s and 1980s; magazine
published twice a year; sells "Dave's
Collectables Catalog" ('50s through
'80s photos, magazines, etc.) for $1 -
free to members.*

Museums/Libraries

Rock & Roll Hall of Fame & Museum
One Key Plaza
751 Erieside Ave.
Cleveland, OH 44114
ph: 216-781-ROCK or 888-764-ROCK
director@rockhall.org
http://www.rockhall.com

MUSIC BOXES

(see also DOLLS, Automatons;
MUSICAL INSTRUMENTS,
Mechanical)

Appraisers

William Bunch
William Bunch Auctions & Appraisals
One Hillman Dr.
Chadds Ford, PA 19317
ph: 610-558-1800
fax: 610-558-0885
whb@williambunchauctions.com
http://www.williambunchauctions.com
Specializes in the appraisal of antique clocks, music boxes, silver, paintings and other decorative objects.

Clubs/Associations

Ralph Schack, VP
Musical Box Society International
Magazine: Journal of Mechanical Music
P.O. Box 551083
Indianapolis, IN 46205-5583
fax: 317-251-6443
mbsi@estreet.com
http://www.mbsi.org
Members collect, study, preserve all types of instruments that mechanically produce music: musical boxes, orchestrions, band organs, player pianos, musical clocks, automata, etc.; "News Bulletin" contains Mart for buying & selling.

Alan Wyatt, Sec.
Musical Box Society of Great Britain
Journal: Music Box, The
P.O. Box 299
Waterbeach, Cambridge CB4 8DT U.K.
mbsbg@reedman.org.uk
http://www.mbsgb.org.uk
For collectors, dealers and enthusiasts of all types of mechanical music boxes, large and small; journal published quarterly.

Collectors

Sherlock S. Holmes, D.D.
P.O. Box 3
Worcester, MA 01613-0003
ph: 888-651-0421
fax: 888-651-0421
mail@SherlockHolmes.com
http://www.Sherlock.Holmes.Name
Wants to buy pre-1950 WORKING music boxes; cylinder type, disk type, etc.; please send complete details including asking price.

John W. Hess
244 Bernaski Rd.
Amsterdam, NY 12010-7827
ph: 518-843-6117
Wants to buy Vogue picture disc records, horn phonographs, music boxes, roller organs; also wants parts, empty cabinets, horns; any condition, any material.

Dave Ogden
P.O. Box 223
Northbrook, IL 60062-5951
ph: 847-564-2893
fax: 847-564-2893
musical@flash.net
http://www.flash.net/~musical
Wants disc and cylinder music boxes;

Regina; also monkey organs and any self playing musical instruments.

Dealers

Porter Music Box Co., Inc.
Rte. 66, Box 424
Randolph, VT 05060
ph: 800-728-9694 or 800-635-1938
fax: 802-728-9699
info@portermusicbox.com
http://www.portermusicbox.com
Repairs and sells antique music boxes; also manufactures copperplated discs for Regina, Polyphone, and Porter music boxes in 11", 12 1/4", and 15 1/2" sizes.

Bill Wineburgh
P.O. Box 47
Flanders, NJ 07836
wwineburgh@aol.com
http://members.aol.com/WWineburgh
Out-of-print books about mechanical music and automata, piano rolls, music box discs and an occasional music box for sale; also maintains an online virtual music box museum.

Al Meekins
Meekins Music Box Co.
P.O. Box 161
Collingswood, NJ 08108
ph: 856-858-6421
fax: 856-858-1642
ameek37754@aol.com
http://www.finest1.com/antiques
Buys, sells, restores antique music boxes.

Rita Ford Music Boxes
19 E. 65th St.
New York, NY 10021
ph: 973-379-6636
fax: 973-564-9497
http://www.ritaford.com
Buys, sells, repairs antique music boxes; since 1947.

John T. Johnston
John T. Johnston's Jukebox Classics & Vintage Slot Machines, Inc.
6742 Fifth Ave.
Brooklyn, NY 11220-5418
ph: 718-833-8455
fax: 718-833-0560
Buys, sells, rents, trades and repairs slot and jukeboxes; wants to buy old jukeboxes, slot machines, vending, arcade, old gambling items, neons, cash registers, music boxes, phonographs, syrup dispensers.

Rick Cooley
Cooley's Old Tyme Piano Shoppe, Inc.
700 Walnut Hill Rd.
Hockessin, DE 19707
ph: 302-239-5658
fax: 302-234-1684
cotps@aol.com
http://www.members.aol.com/cotps
Collects, studies, restores, sells all types of vintage automated music instruments including antique musical boxes, automata, orchestrions, band organs, player pianos, musical clocks;

over 200 items for sale; in business for over 30 yrs.

Jim Brady
Brady Sales & Restorations of Pianos & Music Boxes
2725 E. 56th St.
Indianapolis, IN 46220
ph: 317-259-4307
fax: 317-259-4340
jlbrady@mindspring.com
http://www.mindspring.com/~jlbrady
Music boxes wanted; any type or condition; also jukeboxes.

Jim Brady
Brady Sales & Restorations
2725 East 56th St.
Indianapolis, IN 46220
ph: 317-259-4307 or 317-849-1469
jlbrady@mindspring.com
http://www.bradymusicboxes.com
Buys, sells and restores automatic musical instruments: music boxes; tooth replacement, comb dampening, governor work, cylinder repining, new gears, sound board restoration, case refinishing, tuning, inlay repair, etc.

Doug Negus
Phonograph Phanatic
215 Mason St.
Sutherland, IA 51058-7606
ph: 712-446-2270
Music boxes, phonographs, cylinder records, pianos, NO piano rolls, older mechanical musical instruments, pre-1930; any parts or repairables wanted.

Martin Roenigk
Mechantiques
The Crescent Hotel
75 Prospect St.
Eureka Springs, AR 72632
ph: 800-671-6333 or 501-253-0405
mroenigk@aol.com
http://www.mechantiques.com
Wants all types of mechanical music instruments: music boxes, player organs, coin pianos, singing birds, Wurlitzer 78 rpm jukeboxes, etc.

Rick Wilkins
Olden Year Musical Museum
P.O. Box 381951
Duncanville, TX 75138
ph: 972-298-5587 or 214-213-4056
museum1@airmail.net
Buys, sells, repairs and appraises all types of windup automated musical machines including Victrolas, Gramophones, music boxes, grind organs, etc.

Margaret Marcus
Music Box Shop, The
7236 E. 1st Ave.
Scottsdale, AZ 85251
ph: 480-945-0428 or 800-932-2745
fax: 480-200-9365
musicboxshop@cox.net
http://www.themusicboxshop.com
Buys, sells, appraises, repairs music boxes; over 3000 music boxes: Reuge, Sankyo, Porter, Hummel.

Experts

William H. Edgerton
P.O. Box 88
Darien, CT 06820-0588
ph: 203-655-0566
fax: 203-655-8066
wedgerton@aol.com
Buys, sells, repairs pianos and rolls, musical boxes, player organs, nickelodeons, and automata.

Nancy Fratti
Panchronia Antiquities
P.O. Box 400
Canastota, NY 13032-0400
ph: 315-684-9977
fax: 315-684-9976
musicbox@dreamscape.com
Specializes in, buys, sells and restores antique cylinder and disc musical boxes, restoration supplies; restoration school, books, discs, recordings of automatic musical instruments; catalog available for $6.

Ken Danckaert
231 Kennedy Ct.
Severna Park, MD 21146-3039
ph: 410-544-0260
kend@lemur.org
Collects, buys, sells, appraises, and restores music boxes and hand-crank phonographs; in business since 1972; an expert who gives lectures, presentations and videos.

David & Carol Beck
DB Musical Restorations
75 Waters Edge Lane
Newnan, GA 30263-3579
ph: 770-253-1903
fax: 770-253-7601
cbeck93435@aol.com
http://www.dbmusicalrestorations.com
Specializes in cylinder and disc music boxes; offers quality repair of cylinder and disc music boxes.

Susan & Al Choffnes
Collector's World, Inc.
P.O. Box 1512
Northbrook, IL 60065-1512
ph: 847-948-1472
fax: 847-948-1486
cworldinc@aol.com
http://www.collectorsworldinc.com
Buys, sells and specializes in disc and cylinder music boxes: Regina, large German glass front upright music boxes, table models, console models, Stella, Mira; also cylinder music boxes, mechanical organs and pianos.

Marty Persky
6514 N. Trumbull Ave.
Lincolnwood, IL 60712-3835
ph: 847-675-6144
fax: 847-675-6160
persky@worldnet.att.net
Specializes in automatic musical instruments.

Christian Eric
Antique Music Box Restoration
1825 Placentia Ave.
Costa Mesa, CA 92627-3565
ph: 949-548-1542
fax: 949-631-9996
musicbox@email.com
http://www.antique-music-box.com
*Specialists in antique musical boxes,
emphasis on early cylinder, miniature
and sur plateau mechanisms; author
on subject; buys, sells and repairs.*

Museums/Libraries

Lockwood-Mathews Mansion Museum
295 West Ave.
Norwalk, CT 06850
ph: 203-838-9799
fax: 203-838-1434
lockmathew@aol.com
http://www.lockwoodmathews.org
*The Music Box Society International
has a permanent exhibit of beautifully
crafted, antique music boxes kept on
the second floor of the Mansion; they
can be seen and heard during guided
tours only.*

Museum of Musical Instruments, The
Schubert Club
302 Landmark Center
75 W. 5th St.
Saint Paul, MN 55102
ph: 651-292-3267
fax: 651-292-4317
schubert@schubert.org
http://www.schubert.org
*More than 100 pianofortes,
harpsichords, clavichords and organs
spanning more than 425 years; also
various musical instruments from
around the world, automatic musical
instruments and phonographs; early
composer & musician letters.*

Repair Services

David Adamitis
Antique Musical Machines
RR #5, Box 5295
Moscow, PA 18444
ph: 570-689-7263
fax: 570-689-3703
davediane@ezaccess.net
http://www.antiqnet.com/
antiquemusicalmachines
*Sells, services, restores music boxes,
phonographs, band organs,
nickelodeons, violanos, barrel pianos,
orchestrions, jukeboxes; anything that
plays music automatically.*

Chet Ramsay
Chet Ramsay Antiques
2460 Strasburg Rd.
Coatesville, PA 19320-4339
ph: 610-384-0514
*Wants all types of pre-1912 music
boxes; buy, sell and repair; also wants
parts.*

David & Carol Beck
DB Musical Restorations
75 Waters Edge Lane
Newnan, GA 30263-3579
ph: 770-253-1903
fax: 770-253-7601
cbeck93435@aol.com
http://www.dbmusicalrestorations.com
*Specializes in cylinder and disc music
boxes; offers quality repair of cylinder
and disc music boxes.*

Emerson E. Whitacre
Mechanical Music Man
7550 President Court
Dayton, OH 45414-3671
ph: 937-898-6044 or 937-898-0865
*Repairs, adjusts and cleans disc music
boxes, cylinder music boxes, antique
phonographs, etc.*

Jim Brady
Brady Sales & Restorations
2725 East 56th St.
Indianapolis, IN 46220
ph: 317-259-4307 or 317-849-1469
jlbrady@mindspring.com
http://www.bradymusicboxes.com
*Buys, sells and restores automatic
musical instruments: music boxes;
tooth replacement, comb dampening,
governor work, cylinder repining, new
gears, sound board restoration, case
refinishing, tuning, inlay repair, etc.*

Ralph J. Schultz
Mechanical Musicologist
420 W. State St.
Belle Plaine, MN 56011
ph: 612-873-6704
fax: 612-873-6704
Repairs all types of music boxes.

K.R. Powers
K.R. Powers Antique Music Boxes
28 Alton Circle
Rogers, AR 72756-9252
ph: 501-636-2643
*Disc and cylinder music box
restoration, sales and repairs.*

Bill Gesswein
Clock Doctor, Inc., The
10610 N. 71st Place
Scottsdale, AZ 85254
ph: 888-256-2537
clockdr@clockdr.com
http://www.clockdr.com
*Sells and repairs wall, mantel,
grandfather, cuckoo clocks; also music
boxes.*

Christian Eric
Antique Music Box Restoration
1825 Placentia Ave.
Costa Mesa, CA 92627-3565
ph: 949-548-1542
fax: 949-631-9996
musicbox@email.com
http://www.antique-music-box.com
*Specialists in antique musical boxes,
emphasis on early cylinder, miniature
and sur plateau mechanisms; fine
precision restoration; all facets of*

*restoration personally undertaken in
house; also buys and sells.*

Birds & Bird Boxes (Singing)

Dealers

Don Levison
Don Levison Antiques
P.O. Box 22262
San Francisco, CA 94122
ph: 415-753-0455
fax: 415-753-5206
dlevison@juno.com
http://www.antiquehorology.com
*Buys and sells antique and better
quality pocket and wrist watches,
clocks, music boxes, singing birds,
and other small automata; also
mercury barometers from the 17th
century to present.*

Steve Bogoff
Bogoff Antique Timepieces
P.O. Box 408
Mill Valley, CA 94942
ph: 415-383-8100
fax: 415-383-8112
info@bogoff.com
http://www.bogoff.com
*Buys, sells, appraises and has online
catalog of complicated, rare, early,
unusual, beautiful pocket watches,
vintage wrist watches, small clocks,
singing bird boxes and more.*

Cylinder

Experts

Susan & Al Choffnes
Collector's World, Inc.
P.O. Box 1512
Northbrook, IL 60065-1512
ph: 847-948-1472
fax: 847-948-1486
cworldinc@aol.com
http://www.collectorsworldinc.com
*Buys, sells and specializes in disc and
cylinder music boxes: Regina, large
German glass front upright music
boxes, table models, console models,
Stella, Mira; also cylinder music
boxes, mechanical organs and pianos.*

Steve Boehck
357 N. Oak Post Rd.
Houston, TX 77008
ph: 713-869-3332
biesboehck@mindspring.com
Specializes in cylinder music boxes.

David Wells
P.O. Box 280368
Lakewood, CO 80228-0368
ph: 303-985-4481
fax: 303-985-4481
*Specializes in the restoration of pre-
20th century cylinder music boxes
since 1978.*

Repair Services

David Wells
P.O. Box 280368
Lakewood, CO 80228-0368
ph: 303-985-4481
fax: 303-985-4481
Specializes in the restoration of pre-

*20th century cylinder music boxes
since 1978.*

Disc

Experts

Coulson Conn
432 Old Forge Rd.
Media, PA 19063-5511
ph: 610-459-0367
fax: 610-358-9424
*Collects rare and particularly melodic
disc and other musical boxes, and is a
clearinghouse of information about
disc music boxes.*

Susan & Al Choffnes
Collector's World, Inc.
P.O. Box 1512
Northbrook, IL 60065-1512
ph: 847-948-1472
fax: 847-948-1486
cworldinc@aol.com
http://www.collectorsworldinc.com
*Buys, sells and specializes in disc and
cylinder music boxes: Regina, large
German glass front upright music
boxes, table models, console models,
Stella, Mira; also cylinder music
boxes, mechanical organs and pianos.*

Alan Bies
357 N. Oak Post Rd.
Houston, TX 77008
ph: 713-869-3332
biesboehck@mindspring.com
Specializes in disc music boxes.

Barry Johnson
1305 Hoover St.
Menlo Park, CA 94025-4218
ph: 650-964-0685
*Specializes in disc music boxes; also
makes new discs for music boxes.*

Toy

Clubs/Associations

Jan Norwood
Modern Musical Boxes & Toys
P.O. Box 1396
Brookings, OR 97415
seniorlink@nwtec.com
*For collectors of small, tabletop or
handheld modern as well as vintage
(pre-1970) music boxes and musical
toys, i.e., those containing chips,
batteries, or key-wound mechanisms;
not for collectors of automatons or
large musical antiques.*

MUSICAL INSTRUMENTS

(see also CAROUSELS &
CAROUSEL FIGURES; DRUM &
BUGLE CORPS; MUSIC; MUSIC
BOXES)

Appraisers

Billy Birthrong
Brass & Reed Music Center, Inc.
675 Mason Ave.
Daytona Beach, FL 32117
ph: 386-252-5544
fax: 386-253-4171
brassnreed@earthlink.net
Specializes in the appraisal of brass wind band instruments, violins and guitars and other fretted instruments; also offers repairs and restorations.

Charles Rudig
5815 Crabtree Lane
Cincinnati, OH 45243
ph: 513-561-8093
fax: 513-561-8094
charlesrudig@fuse.net
Specialist appraiser of musical instruments.

Albert R. Rice
495 St. Augustine Ave.
Claremont, CA 91711
ph: 909-625-7649
fax: 909-625-7649
arrice@rocketmail.com
http://www.musical-instrument-appraisals.com
Dr. Rice has worked as an appraiser of musical instruments since 1989 for institutional and private collections throughout the US.

Auction Services

David Bonsey
Skinner, Inc.
63 Park Plaza
The Heritage on the Garden
Boston, MA 02116
ph: 617-350-5400
fax: 617-350-5429
info@skinnerinc.com
http://www.skinnerinc.com
Established in 1971, Skinner Inc. is the fourth largest auction house in the US; has offices in Boston and Bolton, MA.

Christie's
20 Rockefeller Plaza
New York, NY 10020
ph: 212-636-2000
info@christies.com
http://www.christies.com

Graham Wells
Sotheby's
34-35 New Bond St.
London, W1A 2AA U.K.
ph: 44 171 293 5000
fax: 44 171 293 5989
http://www.sothebys.com
Conducts regular auctions of vintage musical instruments.

Clubs/Associations

Albert R. Rice
American Musical Instrument Society
Newsletter: Newsletter & Journal of the AMIS
495 St. Augustine Ave.
Claremont, CA 91711
ph: 909-625-7649
fax: 909-625-7649
arrice@rocketmail.com
http://www.amis.org
Inter. organization founded to promote the study of the history, design and use of musical instruments; all periods and cultures; also publishes the "Journal of the AMIS."

Dealers

William D. Voiers
William D. Voiers Fine Musical Instruments
P.O. Box 23
North Egremont, MA 01252-0023
ph: 413-528-3321 or 800-788-3521
fax: 413-528-5801
Dealer, collector, appraiser of the violin family of instruments: violins, violas, cellos, bows, banjos, ukuleles, guitars and mandolins; electric or acoustic; also saxes, brasses, drums, percussion; also buys, sells, collects and trades.

Dominic S. Cucinotti
Dominic's Music
27 Lexington Ave.
Magnolia, MA 01930
ph: 978-525-2323
fax: 978-525-2916
dominic@world.std.com
http://dominicsmusic.com
Buys, sells, and repairs musical instruments.

Steve Sassano
Black Rock Music Center LLC
3004 Fairfield Ave.
Bridgeport, CT 06605
ph: 203-331-0040 or 203-384-2207
fax: 203-366-6416
SSassano@erols.com
http://www.blackrockmusiccenter.com
Buys and sells all types of musical instruments, new or old: guitars and amps, violins, mandolins, banjos, ukes, cellos; also wants related memorabilia, catalogs, and anything to do with instrument manufacturers.

Sid Glickman
Sid Glickman, Musical Instruments
5901 Spencer Ave.
Bronx, NY 10471
ph: 718-548-6008
fax: 718-548-6008
sidglick@earthlink.net
http://www.AllMusicalInstruments.net
Major collector and dealer in antique and vintage musical instruments.

John G. McAuliffe
Ardagh Vintage Musical Instruments
P.O. Box 810
Carmel, NY 10512
ph: 914-225-1746 or 800-217-1746
Buys, sells, collects, appraises buy fine violins, violas, cellos, bows, guitars, banjos, mandolins, ukes, harps, concertinas, wood flutes, ivory flutes, glass flutes, silver flutes by Powell, Haynes, Badger, etc.

Louis J. Porsi, Jr.
King Louie Music
115 Marbeth Ave.
Carlisle, PA 17013-1626
ph: 717-258-1177
luigibosco@webtv.net
http://members.aol.com/kingloumus/index.htm
Vintage musical instruments including drums, guitars and basses, microphones, amplifiers, etc.; also instrument catalogs, banners, advertising pieces, salesman promos and dealer items.

Frederick W. Oster
Vintage Instruments
1529 Pine St.
Philadelphia, PA 19102-4623
ph: 215-545-1100
fax: 215-735-3634
vintageFO@aol.com
http://www.vintage-instruments.com
Since 1975; dealer, appraiser, consultant; rare & antique musical instruments; specializing in violins, violas, cellos, bows; American fretted instruments - guitars, mandolins, banjos; antique wind instruments, etc.; SASE for reply.

Mickie Zekley
Lark in the Morning
P.O. Box 799
Fort Bragg, CA 95437
ph: 707-964-5569
fax: 707-964-1979
larkinam@larkinam.com
http://www.larkinam.com
Mail order musician's service specializing in hard-to-find musical instruments, music and instructional materials.

Eva Flynn
Eva Flynn Collectibles & Antiques
P.O. Box 1011
Carlsborg, WA 98324-1011
ph: 360-683-7725
evaflynn@tenforward.com
http://www.isnbiz.com/evaflynn
Wants to buy musical instruments: bowed string instruments, guitars/parts/books.

Experts

Sid Glickman
Sid Glickman, Musical Instruments
5901 Spencer Ave.
Bronx, NY 10471
ph: 718-548-6008
fax: 718-548-6008
sidglick@earthlink.net
http://www.AllMusicalInstruments.net
Buys and sells all types of musical instruments, especially antique and ethnic; availability lists to collectors; send SASE for copy; free estimates to dealers and collectors; also answers questions about musical instruments.

Frederick W. Oster
Vintage Instruments
1529 Pine St.
Philadelphia, PA 19102-4623
ph: 215-545-1100
fax: 215-735-3634
vintageFO@aol.com
http://www.vintage-instruments.com
Since 1975; dealer, appraiser, consultant; rare & antique musical instruments; specializing in violins, violas, cellos, bows; American fretted instruments - guitars, mandolins, banjos; antique wind instruments, etc.; SASE for reply.

Museums/Libraries

Yale University Collection of Musical Instruments
15 Hillhouse Ave.
P.O. Box 208278
New Haven, CT 06520
ph: 203-432-0822
fax: 203-432-8342
http://www.yale.edu/musicalinstruments
Collection contains over 1,000 instruments.

Prof. Joseph Lam, Dir.
University of Michigan, Stearns Collection of Musical Instruments
Newsletter: Stearns Newsletter, The
Earl V. More School Of Music Building
1100 Baits Dr.
Ann Arbor, MI 48109-2085
ph: 734-763-4389
http://www.music.umich.edu/resources/stearns
A collection of over 2,000 musical instruments from around the world.

America's Shrine to Music Museum
University of South Dakota
414 East Clark St.
Vermillion, SD 57069-2390
ph: 605-677-5309
fax: 605-677-5073
smm@usd.edu
http://www.usd.edu/smm
One of the great institutions of its kind in the world: collection includes more than 10,000 American, European, and non-Western instruments from virtually all cultures and historical periods.

Albert R. Rice
Kenneth G. Fiske Museum of the
  Claremont Colleges
495 St. Augustine Ave.
Claremont, CA 91711
ph: 909-625-7649
fax: 909-625-7649
arrice@rocketmail.com
http://www.cuc.claremont.edu/fiske/
  welcome.htm
  *One of the most diverse collections of
  musical instruments in the US;
  contains over 1,400 American,
  European and ethnic instruments
  dating from the 17th century to
  present.*

Periodicals

Christina Gargano
Heartland Communications Group, Inc.
Magazine: Midwest Musicians Hot Line
1003 Central Ave.
P.O. Box 1052
Fort Dodge, IA 50501
ph: 800-247-2000 or 515-955-1600
fax: 515-574-2233
libbie@hlipublishing.com
http://www.hlipublishing.com
  *The monthly buy, sell and trade
  magazine by performing musicians for
  performing musicians in the Midwest.*

String Letter Publishing, Inc.
Price Guide: Musical Instrument Auction
  Price Guide
P.O. Box 7767
San Anselmo, CA 94979
ph: 415-485-6946 or 800-827-6837
fax: 415-485-0831
editors.st@stringletter.com
http://www.stringsmagazine.com
  *Lists values for musical instruments
  that are sold at auction; string
  instruments, wind instruments,
  pianos, etc.*

Repair Services

Frederick W. Oster
Vintage Instruments
1529 Pine St.
Philadelphia, PA 19102-4623
ph: 215-545-1100
fax: 215-735-3634
vintageFO@aol.com
http://www.vintage-instruments.com
  *Since 1975; dealer, appraiser,
  consultant; rare & antique musical
  instruments; specializing in violins,
  violas, cellos, bows; American fretted
  instruments - guitars, mandolins,
  banjos; antique wind instruments,
  etc.; SASE for reply.*

Martin O'Brien
Martin O'Brien Cabinetmaker
606 N. Trade St.
Winston Salem, NC 27101
ph: 3336-773-1334
martin@martinobriencabinetmaker.com
http://
  www.martinobriencabinetmaker.com
  *Offers design, construction and
  conservation of furniture, musical
  instruments and other wooden objects;*
  *carving, turning, gilding, French
  polishing, surface cleaning of painted
  and varnished surfaces, color
  matching, museum quality reproductions.*

Billy Birthrong
Brass & Reed Music Center, Inc.
675 Mason Ave.
Daytona Beach, FL 32117
ph: 386-252-5544
fax: 386-253-4171
brassnreed@earthlink.net
  *Specializes in the repair and
  restoration of brass wind band
  instruments, violins and guitars and
  other fretted instruments.*

Accordions

Collectors

Jared Snyder
524 B Glen Echo Rd.
Philadelphia, PA 19119-2916
ph: 215-247-8996
  *Wants anything accordion related:
  photographs, illustrations, postcards,
  etc. with emphasis on button
  accordions and exotic locales.*

Drums

Dealers

Ned Ingberman
Vintage Drum Center
2243 Ivory Dr.
Libertyville, IA 52567-8533
ph: 800-729-3111 or 641-693-3611
fax: 641-693-3101
vintagedrum@lisco.com
http://www.vintagedrum.com
  *Wants to buy pre-1980 drums, and
  cymbals; also wants drum catalogs.*

Experts

Dan Paul
Paul-Mueller Percussion Studio
3049 W. 71st St.
Indianapolis, IN 46268-2241
ph: 317-293-5057 or 317-842-6165
fax: 317-842-6165
  *Percussion instrument specialist,
  collector and appraiser; drums and
  related memorabilia including
  catalogs and magazines.*

Repair Services

Dan Paul
Paul-Mueller Percussion Studio
3049 W. 71st St.
Indianapolis, IN 46268-2241
ph: 317-293-5057 or 317-842-6165
fax: 317-842-6165
  *Restorations of all percussion
  instruments including drums,
  xylophones, marimbas, timpani, traps,
  etc.*

Harmonicas

Appraisers

Rick Nielsen, ISA
Fleur-De-Lis Appraisals
1132 Westmoor Place
Saint Louis, MO 63131
ph: 314-997-7963
fax: 801-858-2907
rn1132@earthlink.net
http://home.earthlink.net/~rn1132a/
  harmonicas
  *Serious harmonica collector and
  expert with one of the largest
  harmonica collections in the world.*

Clubs/Associations

Doug Tate
Society for the Preservation &
  Advancement of the Harmonica
P.O. Box 865
Troy, MI 48099-0865
fax: 248-542-5793
HarpSPAH@spah.org
http://www.spah.org
  *Maintains a database of over 3,000
  harmonicas from all over the world;
  does not buy or sell antique
  harmonicas.*

Harland Crain
Harmonica Collectors International
Newsletter: Trumpet Call, The
741 Cedar Field Ct.
Chesterfield, MO 63017
ph: 314-434-8875
fax: 314-576-6154
hcrain@harleysharps.com
http://www.harleysharps.com
  *Serves harmonica collectors' interests
  around the world.*

Collectors

Harland Crain
741 Cedar Field Ct.
Chesterfield, MO 63017
ph: 314-434-8875
fax: 314-576-6154
hcrain@harleysharps.com
http://www.harleysharps.com
  *Harmonica collector, dealer, expert,
  repair service; collects harmonicas
  and any related items such as
  displays, posters, catalogs, books and
  booklets, price lists, signs, ads, etc.*

Rick Nielsen, ISA
Fleur-De-Lis Appraisals
1132 Westmoor Place
Saint Louis, MO 63131
ph: 314-997-7963
fax: 801-858-2907
rn1132@earthlink.net
http://home.earthlink.net/~rn1132a/
  harmonicas
  *Serious harmonica collector and
  expert with one of the largest
  harmonica collections in the world.*

Horns

Dealers

Charles Fail Music, Inc.
4710-G Ecton Dr.
Marietta, GA 30066-1095
ph: 770-591-0645 or 800-965-2263
fax: 770-591-9893
cfail@mindspring.com
http://www.charlesfail.com
  *Wants to buy saxophones, any age or
  condition; also wants to buy old brass
  and woodwind band instruments.*

Paul Ayick
Paul Ayick Vintage Brass
4800 SW 70th Terrace
Fort Lauderdale, FL 33314
ph: 954-321-9368
bulos@earthlink.net
http://www.paulayickvintagebrass.com
  *Buys, sells, trades vintage trumpets,
  cornets, and other brass and wind
  instruments; satisfied customers
  include Chicago Symphony and Boston
  Pops orchestras; strives for accuracy
  in descriptions; enjoys sharing
  knowledge with others.*

Repair Services

Billy Birthrong
Brass & Reed Music Center, Inc.
675 Mason Ave.
Daytona Beach, FL 32117
ph: 386-252-5544
fax: 386-253-4171
brassnreed@earthlink.net
  *Specializes in the repair and
  restoration of brass wind band
  instruments, violins and guitars and
  other fretted instruments.*

Horns (Brass)

Clubs/Associations

Historic Brass Society
Journal: Historic Brass Society Journal
148 West 23rd St., #2A
New York, NY 10011
ph: 212-627-3820
fax: 212-627-3820
President@historicbrass.org
http://www.historicbrass.org
  *An international music organization
  concerned with the entire range of
  early brass music, from antiquity and
  Biblical period to 20th century;
  interested in the history, music,
  literature and performance practice of
  early brass instruments.*

Collectors

Chuck Hollocker
2501 Honeysuckle Dr.
Richardson, TX 75082
ph: 972-333-7769 or 972-669-2596
fax: 972-690-3490
  *Interested in vintage saxophones of all
  major manufacturers, in any
  condition; specializes in CONN
  saxophones; also interested in related
  items such as catalogs, books and
  booklets, price lists, signs, ads, etc.*

Dealers

David Reed
841 West Main St.
Madison, OH 44057-9763
ph: 440-428-6666
Buys, sells and collects woodwinds, saxophones and band instruments: silver plated or brass; any condition; also wants parts, early sax sales brochures, etc.

Robb Stewart
Robb Stewart Brass Instruments
140 E. Santa Clara St., #18
Arcadia, CA 91006-3204
ph: 626-447-1904
fax: 626-447-1904
oldbrass@worldnet.att.net
Will buy all brass instruments, especially pre-1880 and high quality later instruments; also wants interesting woodwinds; offers restoration, repair and conservation of brass instruments; send for free price guide and sale list.

Museums/Libraries

Ralph Dudgeon
Instrumentenmuseum, Schloss Kremsegg
Schloss Kremsegg
Kremseggerstrasse 59
Kremsmunster, 4550 Upper Austria
ph: 0 75 83/247
dudgeonr@cortland.edu
A major collection over 1,170 brass instruments; also prints, recordings, books, figurines, sheet music, etc.

Mechanical

Clubs/Associations

Musical Box Society International
Magazine: Journal of Mechanical Music
P.O. Box 551083
Indianapolis, IN 46205-5583
fax: 317-251-6443
mbsi@estreet.com
http://www.mbsi.org
Members collect, study, preserve all types of instruments that mechanically produce music: musical boxes, orchestrions, band organs, player pianos, musical clocks, automata, etc.; "News Bulletin" contains Mart for buying & selling.

I. Savins
Australian Collectors of Mechanical
  Musical Instruments
Newsletter: Bulletin
19 Waipori St.
St. Ives
Sydney, NSW 2075 Australia
ph: 61 2 9449 5296
acmmi@optushome.com.au
http://www.zip.com.au/~job

Jurgen Hocker
Society of Self-Playing Musical
  Instruments
Journal: Das Mechanische
  Musikinstrument
Heiligenstock 46
Bergisch Gladbach, D-51465 Germany
ph: 49-2202-932524
fax: 49-2202-932526
Juergen.Hocker@t-online.de
http://www.geocities.com/Vienna/2831/
  Gsmev_e.htm
Has the aim of investigating, maintaining and encouraging the cultural tradition of self-playing musical instruments.

Dealers

John S. Zuk
106 Orchard St.
Belmont, MA 02478-2940
ph: 617-484-4800 or 617-588-5709
fax: 810-283-5371
Buys, sells and repairs musical boxes, phonographs, and related mechanical music machines.

Danilo Konvalinka
Musical Wonder House Museum, The
18 High St.
P.O. Box 604
Wiscasset, ME 04578-0604
ph: 207-882-7163 or 800-336-3725
musicbox@musicalwonderhouse.com
http://www.musicalwonderhouse.com
Buys & sells music boxes, wind-up phonographs, player pianos & rolls, cylinder records, complete or parts; full repair services: combwork, gearwork, spring repairs.

Out-Back Mechanical Music
6 Front St.
Bainbridge, NY 13733
ph: 607-967-8909
outback@mkl.com
http://home.mkl.com/~outback
Collects and restores all types of antique musical machines including: player pianos, nickelodeons, reproducing pianos, player organs, reed organs, organettes, harmoniums, and plain pianos, too.

Rick Cooley
Cooley's Old Tyme Piano Shoppe, Inc.
700 Walnut Hill Rd.
Hockessin, DE 19707
ph: 302-239-5658
fax: 302-234-1684
cotps@aol.com
http://www.members.aol.com/cotps
Collects, studies, restores, sells all types of vintage automated music instruments including antique musical boxes, automata, orchestrions, band organs, player pianos, musical clocks; over 200 items for sale; in business for over 30 yrs.

Doug Negus
Phonograph Phanatic
215 Mason St.
Sutherland, IA 51058-7606
ph: 712-446-2270
Music boxes, phonographs, cylinder records, pianos, NO piano rolls, older mechanical musical instruments, pre-1930; any parts or repairables wanted.

Jerry Biasella
286 W. 14th Place
Chicago Heights, IL 60411
ph: 708-756-3307
Specializes in band organs, coin-operated pianos, nickelodeons, music boxes, antique phonographs; buys, sells, restores.

Martin Roenigk
Mechantiques
The Crescent Hotel
75 Prospect St.
Eureka Springs, AR 72632
ph: 800-671-6333 or 501-253-0405
mroenigk@aol.com
http://www.mechantiques.com
Largest business in the US specializing in mechanical musical instruments; buys disc & cylinder music boxes, horn phonographs, player organs, carousel organs, musical clocks & watches, monkey organs, coin pianos, mechanical birds, etc.

Richard W. Oliver, Jr.
Clock Guy Antique Brokerage, The
ph: 760-604-0262
fax: 760-598-0327
theclockguy@clockguy.com
http://www.clockguy.com
Largest broker of antique clocks in North America; represents collectors, estates and those down-sizing; also brokers mechanical music devices; their extensive search database helps in locating specific items for their clients.

Ragtime Automated Music
4218 Jesup Rd.
Ceres, CA 95307
ph: 209-667-5525
fax: 209-668-8922
ragtimewest@earthlink.net
http://www.ragtimewest.com
Carousel organs, nickelodeons, musical counters, custom parade vehicles, automated player pianos.

Experts

William H. Edgerton
P.O. Box 88
Darien, CT 06820-0588
ph: 203-655-0566
fax: 203-655-8066
wedgerton@aol.com
Buys, sells, repairs pianos and rolls, musical boxes, player organs, nickelodeons, and automata.

Marty Persky
6514 N. Trumbull Ave.
Lincolnwood, IL 60712-3835
ph: 847-675-6144
fax: 847-675-6160
persky@worldnet.att.net
Specializes in automatic musical instruments.

Museums/Libraries

Danilo Konvalinka
Musical Wonder House Museum, The
18 High St.
P.O. Box 604
Wiscasset, ME 04578-0604
ph: 207-882-7163 or 800-336-3725
musicbox@musicalwonderhouse.com
http://www.musicalwonderhouse.com
America's unique Music Museum in an 1852 sea captain's mansion; antique music boxes, player pianos, wind-up phonographs; restored pieces in rooms furnished with antiques of the period; founded 1963; instruments bought, sold, repaired.

Neil Ratliff
Music Library, University of Maryland
Hornbrake 3210
College Park, MD 20742
ph: 301-405-9217
fax: 301-314-7170
webmaster@itd.umd.edu
http://www.lib.umd.edu/UMCP/
  MUSIC/music.html

Marvin Yagoda
Marvin's Marvelous Mechanical
  Museum
31005 Orchard Rd.
Farmington, MI 48334
ph: 248-626-5020
fax: 248-626-7945
adamant726@aol.com
http://www.marvin3m.com

Music House Museum, The
7377 US 31 North
P.O. Box 297
Acme, MI 49610
ph: 231-938-9300
MusicMachines@juno.com
http://www.musichouse.org
Opened in 1983, this museum is dedicated to the historical restoration and preservation of mechanical musical instruments.

Repair Services

Danilo Konvalinka
Musical Wonder House Museum, The
18 High St.
P.O. Box 604
Wiscasset, ME 04578-0604
ph: 207-882-7163 or 800-336-3725
musicbox@musicalwonderhouse.com
http://www.musicalwonderhouse.com
Buys & sells music boxes, wind-up phonographs, player pianos & rolls, cylinder records, complete or parts; full repair services: combwork, gearwork, spring repairs.

Andy Witkowski
Old Crank, An
oldcrank@adelphia.net
http://users.adelphia.net/~oldcrank
*Specialty is in collecting and repairing
and restoring old phonographs, reed
organs, and other mechanical musical
machines.*

David Adamitis
Antique Musical Machines
RR #5, Box 5295
Moscow, PA 18444
ph: 570-689-7263
fax: 570-689-3703
davediane@ezaccess.net
http://www.antiqnet.com/
antiquemusicalmachines
*Sells, services, restores music boxes,
phonographs, band organs,
nickelodeons, violanos, barrel pianos,
orchestrions, jukeboxes; anything that
plays music automatically.*

Jerry Biasella
286 W. 14th Place
Chicago Heights, IL 60411
ph: 708-756-3307
*Specializes in band organs, coin-
operated pianos, nickelodeons, music
boxes, antique phonographs; buys,
sells, restores.*

John H. Pohlpeter
Another Time Restorations
502 4th Ave.
Oregon City, OR 97045-3100
ph: 503-656-9757 or 503-656-9757
*Buys, sells, restores clocks, player
pianos, band organs and orchestrions,
pump and reed organs.*

Carl Kehret
P.O. Box 303
Wilkeson, WA 98396
ph: 360-829-3161
pegkehre@tx3.net
*Thirty years experience in the
restoration of both large and small
vintage mechanical musical
instruments; member of AMICA and
MBSI; specializes in restoring player
pianos, crank organs, and other
mechanical musical instruments.*

Mechanical (Band Organs)

(see also CAROUSELS &
CAROUSEL FIGURES; MUSICAL
INSTRUMENTS, Organs)

Clubs/Associations

Terry Haughawout
American Band Organ Association
3766 Mann Rd.
Blacklick, OH 43004
ph: 419-454-3671
*Members interested building, re-
building, and playing band,
fairground, and monkey organs.*

Dealers

Rick Cooley
Cooley's Old Tyme Piano Shoppe, Inc.
700 Walnut Hill Rd.
Hockessin, DE 19707
ph: 302-239-5658
fax: 302-234-1684
cotps@aol.com
http://www.members.aol.com/cotps
*Collects, studies, restores, sells all
types of vintage automated music
instruments including antique musical
boxes, automata, orchestrions, band
organs, player pianos, musical clocks;
over 200 items for sale; in business
for over 30 yrs.*

Bill Hall
Hall International
5525 Nova Rd.
Saint Cloud, FL 34771
ph: 407-892-1144 or 407-420-5636
fax: 407-420-5761
gavioli@nivets.com
http://www.bandorgans.com
*Appraiser, collector, dealer, expert in
band organs; also antique carnival
equipment and antique trucks.*

Danie Horenberger
Brass Ring Entertainment
11001 Peoria St.
Sun Valley, CA 91352
ph: 818-394-0028
fax: 818-394-0062
sales@carousell.com
http://www.carousell.com
*20 years experience, sales, restoration,
parts, service.*

Alan S. Erb, P.E. (M.E.)
Erb Engineering
P.O. Box 124
Mt. Eden, CA 94557-0124
ph: 510-783-5068
fax: 510-783-5068
erbmusic@earthlink.net
http://www.mechanicalmusicbox.com
*Expert buys, sells, restores, music
boxes, coin-op pianos, organs and
parts; offers the finest pipework
including reed pipes; also makes
custom made organs and calliopes to
any customer specification (commercial use, home use, etc.).*

Experts

Jerry Biasella
286 W. 14th Place
Chicago Heights, IL 60411
ph: 708-756-3307
*Specializes in band organs, coin-
operated pianos, nickelodeons, music
boxes, antique phonographs; buys,
sells, restores.*

Art Reblitz
Reblitz Restorations Inc.
P.O. Box 7392
Colorado Springs, CO 80933-7392
orchestrion@juno.com
*Specializes in the restoration of
orchestrions and band organs; also
music arranging for these instruments.*

Repair Services

David Adamitis
Antique Musical Machines
RR #5, Box 5295
Moscow, PA 18444
ph: 570-689-7263
fax: 570-689-3703
davediane@ezaccess.net
http://www.antiqnet.com/
antiquemusicalmachines
*Sells, services, restores music boxes,
phonographs, band organs,
nickelodeons, violanos, barrel pianos,
orchestrions, jukeboxes; anything that
plays music automatically.*

Art Reblitz
Reblitz Restorations Inc.
P.O. Box 7392
Colorado Springs, CO 80933-7392
orchestrion@juno.com
*Specializes in the restoration of
orchestrions and band organs; also
music arranging for these instruments.*

Alan S. Erb, P.E. (M.E.)
Erb Engineering
P.O. Box 124
Mt. Eden, CA 94557-0124
ph: 510-783-5068
fax: 510-783-5068
erbmusic@earthlink.net
http://www.mechanicalmusicbox.com
*Expert buys, sells, restores, repairs
organs and parts; offers the finest
pipework including reed pipes; also
makes custom made organs and
calliopes to any customer specification
(commercial use, home use, etc.).*

Repro. Sources

Stinson Organ Co.
4691 Co. Rd. 91
Bellefontaine, OH 43311
ph: 937-593-5709 or 888-470-4442
fax: 937-593-5553
sales@stinsonorganco.com
http://www.stinsonorganco.com
*Since 1965 has been manufacturing
quality, custom-built concert and band
organs.*

Organs

(see also MUSIC BOXES; MUSICAL
INSTRUMENTS, Mechanical [Band
Organs])

Clubs/Associations

James Quashnock, Mem.
Reed Organ Society, Inc.
Magazine: Reed Organ Society Quarterly
3575 State Highway 258 E.
Wichita Falls, TX 76310-7037
ph: 940-691-7809
Quashnock@aol.com
http://sponsor.globalknowledge.nl/ros
*A non-profit organization devoted to
the appreciation, study, collection,
restoration, and preservation of reed
organs; includes harmonicas,
accordions, concertinas, lap organs,
melodeons, harmoniums, mechanical
and player organs.*

Dr. Hans van Oost, Gen. Sec.
Dutch Mechanical Organ Society - Kring
van Draaiorgelvriended (KDV)
Naaldwijkseweg 262-264
PW's-Gravenzande, 2691 The
Netherlands
ph: (31) 174 41 54 38
fax: (31) 174 41 54 38
havo@kabelfoon.nl
http://home.kabelfoon.nl/~havo/
en_idx2.htm
*For those interested in self-playing
organs: street organs, fairground
organs, dance hall organs,
orchestrions.*

John Page, Mem. Sec.
Fair Organ Preservation Society
Magazine: Key Frame, The
43 Woolmans
Fullers Slade
Milton Keynes, Bucks MK11 2BA U.K.
ph: +44 1908 263717
fax: +44 1908 263717
memsec@fops.org
http://www.fops.org/
*For the enthusiast of fair organs and
mechanical music instruments.*

Andrew Paterson, Mem. Sec.
Cinema Organ Society
Journal: Cinema Organ
80 Merrylee Rd.
Newlands, Glasgow G43 2QZ U.K.
john@leemingj.demon.co.uk
http://www.cinema-organs.org.uk
*For those interested in organ music as
entertainment; the society is building
an extensive archive of printed
material and recordings.*

Dealers

John F. Morningstar
Beehive Reed Organ Service, The
11 Oak St.
P.O. Box 41
Alfred, ME 04002-0041
ph: 207-324-0990
info@alfred-beehive.org
http://www.alfred-beehive.org
*Reed organs, harmoniums, antique
pump organs bought, sold, repaired,
rebuilt including case work and tuning
reeds.*

Gary Besteman
Pump & Pipe Shop, The
7945 Kraft Ave.
Caledonia, MI 49316-8387
ph: 616-891-8743
*Specializes in the restoration, buying
and selling of reed organs; also buys
parts.*

Don Bryant
Bryant Antique Players
4819 Stallcup
Mesquite, TX 75150-1143
ph: 972-270-0135
fax: 972-613-1627
aplayr@airmail.net
http://www.bryanantiques.net
*Sales, service and rebuilding of player
pianos, pump organs, reproducing &*

coin-operated instruments, pin balls, & game room equipment; since 1975

Internet Resources

Jerrell Kautz
Theatre Organ Home Page
2250 Holly Trail
Houston, TX 77054
ph: 713-797-6173
jkautz@theatreorgans.com
http://theatreorgans.com
An organization for those interested in theatre pipe organs and Hammond and other electronic organs.

Repair Services

John F. Morningstar
Beehive Reed Organ Service, The
11 Oak St.
P.O. Box 41
Alfred, ME 04002-0041
ph: 207-324-0990
info@alfred-beehive.org
http://www.alfred-beehive.org
Reed organs, harmoniums, antique pump organs bought, sold, repaired, rebuilt including case work and tuning reeds.

Johnson Music
117 Colonel's Trail
P.O. Box 615
Mount Airy, NC 27030
ph: 336-320-2212 or 336-320-3286
jmusic@surry.net
Repairs and restores pump organs.

Gary Besteman
Pump & Pipe Shop, The
7945 Kraft Ave.
Caledonia, MI 49316-8387
ph: 616-891-8743
Specializes in the restoration, buying and selling of reed organs; also buys parts.

Organs (Roller)

Experts

Todd Augsburger
Todd Augsburger's Roller Organs
30 N. Main St.
Kenton, OH 43326
todd@rollerorgans.com
http://www.rollerorgans.com
Cob-type roller organ collector, expert, dealer; Web site with roller organ information, list of rollers, reference books/materials, parts/accessories, free buy/sell/trade listings for all types of mechanical music.

Organs (Theatre)

Clubs/Associations

Michael Fellenzer, Ex. Sec.
American Theatre Organ Society
Magazine: Theatre Organ Journal
P.O. Box 551081
Indianapolis, IN 46205-5581
ph: 317-251-6441
fax: 317-251-6443
fellenzer@atos.org
http://www.atos.org
Dedicated to the restoration,

preservation and presentation of the theatre pipe organ and its music; originally developed as a replacement for the orchestra accompanying silent films, these majestic instruments are now used in concerts.

Scottish Theatre Organ Preservation Society
New Palace Centre
Greenlaw, Berwickshire TD10 6XD
Scottland
unusual.museum@stops.org
http://www.stops.org/STOPS/
Founded in 1972 and dedicated to the preservation of the theatre pipe organ.

Pianos

(see also PIANOS, Miniature)

Dealers

Legay Piano Resales
ph: 925-735-8625
pianos@webcom.com
http://www.legacypiano.com
Specializes in the sales of pre-owned Steinway pianos.

Roger's Piano
879 Washington St.
Hanover, MA 02339
ph: 781-826-0453
fax: 781-826-1212
roger@usedsteinways.com
http://usedsteinways.com
Buys, sells and restores fine quality vintage Steinway pianos; also other makers of similar handcrafted quality pianos.

Pyrianos Collection, Inc., The
P.O. Box 1655
Greenwich, CT 06836
ph: 203-661-2566
fax: 203-661-2566
mmw@pyrianos.com
http://www.pyrianos.com
Specializes in the acquisition, restoration, and sales of vintage Steinway & Sons pianos.

Leopold Holder
New York Piano Center, Inc.
121 W. 19th St., 7th Floor
New York, NY 10011-4114
ph: 212-229-2600
fax: 212-229-2668
info@newyorkpianocenter.com
http://www.newyorkpianocenter.com
A thoroughly complete piano rebuilding, restoration and refinishing workshop; also offers other services such as sales, rentals and appraisals of vintage pianos.

Ted Snyder
Olde Towne Piano Shop
427 East Patrick St.
Frederick, MD 21701
ph: 301-695-6150
fax: 301-698-2740
info@townpiano.com
http://www.townpiano.com
Sells used piano (like-new, refurbished, rebuilt, restored) and piano

accessories; also does piano restorations.

Mike Evola
Evola Music
48800 Van Dyke
Utica, MI 48317
ph: 810-726-6570
fax: 810-726-0416
pianoman@evola.com
http://www.evola.com
Buys, sells, restores, appraises pianos: Baldwin, Bosendorfer, Wurlitzer, PianoDisc, Schimmel, Estonia, Yamaha Claviona, Chickering, Knabe, Mason & Hamlin.

Melvin Besbrode
Besbrode Piano
Galways Mill
Leeds, West Yorkshire LS11 9XE U.K.
ph: 00 44 1132 448344 or 00 44 1132 663225
fax: 00 44 1132 456960
melvin@legend.co.uk
http://www.piano-uk.com
Piano dealer and appraiser specializing in Steinway, Bechstein, Erard, Pleyel artcased grand pianos; suppliers of all types of new and used pianos.

Experts

Mike Aversa, ISA
Aversa Estate & Appraisal Service
P.O. Box 863
Yorba Linda, CA 92885
ph: 717-777-3848 or 714-749-3887
AversaAntiques@mindspring.com
http://www.aversaantiques.com
Expert in 20th century guitars including Fender, Gibson, Martin, Guild; also 19th and 20th century pianos.

Internet Resources

Bluebook of Pianos
bluebookofpiano@aol.com
http://www.bluebookofpianos.com
Web site provides list of manufacturers with serial numbers to assist in determining the age of your piano.

Piano World
38 Parky Dr.
Enfield, CT 06082
ph: 860-745-5826
fax: 860-741-2625
ideas@pianoworld.com
http://www.pianoworld.com
Great Web site for piano related information: how old is your piano?, tuners, CD's, books, dealers, for sale, restoring, care, moving, supplies, organs.

Piano Technicians Guild
3930 Washington
Kansas City, MO 64111-2963
ph: 816-753-7747
fax: 816-531-0070
ptg@ptg.org
http://www.ptg.org
Web site offers an incredible collection of piano resources: dealers,

industry, literature, merchandise, piano museum, organs, research, software, teachers, technicians.

Man./Prod./Dist.

Steinway & Sons
1 Steinway Place
Long Island City, NY 11105
ph: 800-366-1853
info@steinway.com
http://www.steinway.com
Great Web site with music links, links to Steinway artists, caring for your Steinway, Steinway Restoration Center, find out the weight and age of a Steinway, sizes of "modern" grand pianos, Steinway patents, and more.

Museums/Libraries

Museum of the American Piano
291 Broadway
New York, NY 10007-1814
ph: 212-246-4646 or 212-406-6060
fax: 212-406-5245
http://www.museumforpianos.org

Museum of Musical Instruments, The
Schubert Club
302 Landmark Center
75 W. 5th St.
Saint Paul, MN 55102
ph: 651-292-3267
fax: 651-292-4317
schubert@schubert.org
http://www.schubert.org
More than 100 pianofortes, harpsichords, clavichords and organs spanning more than 425 years; also various musical instruments from around the world, automatic musical instruments and phonographs; early composer & musician letters.

Repair Services

Roger's Piano
879 Washington St.
Hanover, MA 02339
ph: 781-826-0453
fax: 781-826-1212
roger@usedsteinways.com
http://usedsteinways.com
Buys, sells and restores fine quality vintage Steinway pianos; also other makers of similar handcrafted quality pianos.

Pyrianos Collection, Inc., The
P.O. Box 1655
Greenwich, CT 06836
ph: 203-661-2566
fax: 203-661-2566
mmw@pyrianos.com
http://www.pyrianos.com
Specializes in the acquisition, restoration, and sales of vintage Steinway & Sons pianos.

Leopold Holder
New York Piano Center, Inc.
121 W. 19th St., 7th Floor
New York, NY 10011-4114
ph: 212-229-2600
fax: 212-229-2668
info@newyorkpianocenter.com
http://www.newyorkpianocenter.com
A thoroughly complete piano rebuilding, restoration and refinishing workshop; also offers other services such as sales, rentals and appraisals of vintage pianos.

Ted Snyder
Olde Towne Piano Shop
427 East Patrick St.
Frederick, MD 21701
ph: 301-695-6150
fax: 301-698-2740
info@townpiano.com
http://www.townpiano.com
Sells used piano (like-new, refurbished, rebuilt, restored) and piano accessories; also does piano restorations.

Piano World, The
2732 Cherokee St.
Saint Louis, MO 63118
ph: 314-772-6676 or 800-589-5824
fax: 314-664-1358
dlbullock@att.net
http://www.thepianoworld.com
One of the largest musical instrument restoration facilities in the Midwest; restores and sells both vintage used and new keyboard musical instruments including post-1900 pianos, vintage antique pianos, players, etc.

Steve Kinchen
Hall Piano Co., Inc.
901 David Dr.
Metairie, LA 70003
ph: 504-733-8863 or 800-527-9480
fax: 504-736-0109
skinchen@earthlink.net
http://www.hallpiano.com

Daniel S. Reed
Piano Arts
1909 Lilac Court
Richardson, TX 75080
ph: 972-699-7463
fax: 972-644-1304
pianoarts@attbi.com
Provides restoration, regulating and tuning ervices for turn-of-the-century keyboard instruments; Dan Reed is a Registered Piano Technician, pianist and composer.

Pianos (Player)

(see also PIANO ROLLS)

Clubs/Associations

Bill Chapman, Mem.
Automatic Musical Instrument Collectors
  Association (AMICA)
Magazine: AMICA News Bulletin
2150 Hastings Court
Santa Rosa, CA 95405-8377
ph: 707-570-2258
amica_webmaster@cometlink.com
http://www.amica.org
Purpose is to foster preservation and appreciation of instruments and recordings of roll-actuated instruments, especially player pianos and organs.

J.J.I.M. ten Horn, Sec.
Nederlandse Pianola Vereniging (Dutch
  Pianola Association)
Newsletter: Pianola Bulletin
Eikendreef 24
HR OSS, NL-5342 The Netherlands
ph: (0412) 623369
fax: (0412) 623369

Everson Whittle, Sec.
North West Player Piano Association,
  The
Journal: NWPPA Journal
11 Smiths Rd.
Darcy Lever
Bolton, Greater Manchester BL3 2PP
U.K.
ph: 01204 529939
nwppa@hotmail.com
Association dealing in all aspects of Mechanical Music, repair of instruments, and interest in the hobby.

Dealers

David M. Hall, Sr.
Cabin Fever Pianos
P.O. Box 161
Uxbridge, MA 01569
ph: 508-278-2874
Player piano sales and service since 1959; pickup and deliver on the East Coast with own trucks.

Rick Cooley
Cooley's Old Tyme Piano Shoppe, Inc.
700 Walnut Hill Rd.
Hockessin, DE 19707
ph: 302-239-5658
fax: 302-234-1684
cotps@aol.com
http://www.members.aol.com/cotps
Collects, studies, restores, sells all types of vintage automated music instruments including antique musical boxes, automata, orchestrions, band organs, player pianos, musical clocks; over 200 items for sale; in business for over 30 yrs.

Pauls & Gale Bullock
P & G Investments
P.O. Box 30139
Columbia, MO 65205
ph: 573-445-8918
fax: 573-445-0871
olebear@pgtigercat.com
http://www.pgtigercat.com
Buys, sells, brokers old antique player pianos.

Don Bryant
Bryant Antique Players
4819 Stallcup
Mesquite, TX 75150-1143
ph: 972-270-0135
fax: 972-613-1627
aplayr@airmail.net
http://www.bryanantiques.net
Sales, service and rebuilding of player pianos, pump organs, reproducing & coin-operated instruments, pin balls, & game room equipment; since 1975.

Mr. Kim Bunker
Orange Coast Piano
2658 S. Grand Ave.
Santa Ana, CA 92705
ph: 714-432-7426
fax: 714-543-0835
webmaster@playerpianos.com
http://www.playerpianos.com
Buys, sells and restores player pianos; also rare and exotic mechanical musical instruments.

Internet Resources

John Tuttle
John Tuttle "Self-Playing Pianos"
407 19th Ave.
Brick, NJ 08724
ph: 732-840-8787
john@player-care.com
http://www.player-care.com
Dedicated to player and reproducing pianos: service, repair, rebuilding; also sells new QRS and Tempola music rolls online; lots of technical information and information about used rolls and roll auctions on Web site; lists technicians.

Jody Kravitz
Player Piano & Mechanical Music
  Exchange
P.O. Box 502230
San Diego, CA 92150-2230
ph: 619-559-8055
kravitz@foxtail.com
http://mmd.foxtail.com
Buy, sell, trade player pianos; also piano roll suppliers (new & used), music and MIDI files, mechanical music suppliers, museums, sources for restoration and repair of player pianos, societies and organizations.

Michael Waters
Player Piano
P.O. Box CP 15
Mildura, Victoria 3502 Australia
ph: 03 50212249
fax: 03 50211572
mwaters@ruralnet.net.au
http://www.pianoworld.com
Great resource Web site for player pianos: restoration, societies, links, roll manufacturers.

Museums/Libraries

International Piano Archives at
  Maryland, Neil Ratliff Music Library
Hornbrake 3210
College Park, MD 20742
ph: 301-405-9217
fax: 301-314-7170
webmaster@itd.umd.edu
http://www.lib.umd.edu/UMCP/
  MUSIC/music.html

Repair Services

John Tuttle
John Tuttle "Self-Playing Pianos"
407 19th Ave.
Brick, NJ 08724
ph: 732-840-8787
john@player-care.com
http://www.player-care.com
Dedicated to player and reproducing pianos: service, repair, rebuilding; also sells new QRS and Tempola music rolls online; lots of technical information and information about used rolls and roll auctions on Web site; lists technicians.

Sam Harris
Player Piano Restorations
640 Allegheny Rd.
Greenville, NC 27834
ph: 252-758-6944 or 252-752-4179
fax: 252-752-2943
http://www.geocities.com/Heartland/
  Ranch/9374
Specializes in the complete restoration of standard 88 note player pianos in the Southeast US.

Hazel Inzer
Inzer Pianos, Inc.
2473 Canton Rd.
Marietta, GA 30066-5376
ph: 770-422-2664
inzerpianos@hotmail.com
Repairs pump organs, antique pianos, and player pianos; also has small catalog of parts, tools, and books for the repair of pianos, player pianos and pump organs.

Brian Thornton
Short Mountain Music Works
207 South McCrary St.
Woodbury, TN 37190
ph: 615-563-5814
smmw@mindspring.com
http://www.shortmountainmusic.com
Restoration of player pianos and all types of pneumatically operated musical devices.

Steve Grattan
Lost Chord Clinic
1602 Griswold St.
Port Huron, MI 48060
ph: 810-984-2757
lostchordclinic@ameritech.net
All phases of restoration available; some custom parts duplication; restores pianos, players, reproducing pianos, orchestrions, reed organs; all work guaranteed.

Daniel M. Armstrong
2053 24th St. SW
Pine River, MN 56474
ph: 218-587-3292
pianodan@uslink.net
http://www.uslink.net/~pianodan
Rebuilding of player units of all types, piano actions rebuilt/reconditioned, keyboards recovered, tuning and miscellaneous repairs.

Mel Septon
Player Pianos Plus
9045 N. Karlov Ave.
Skokie, IL 60076
ph: 847-679-3455
notpes@aol.com
Specializes in the repair of reproducing pianos.

Craig Brougher
Brougher Restorations
3500 Claremont Ave.
Independence, MO 64052
ph: 816-254-1693
fax: 816-254-2710
craigbr@worldnet.att.net
http://www.player-care.com/cb
Complete restoration facilities for reproducers, orchestrions and fine grand pianos; also case and veneer repairs.

Laura Hielman
Vintage Piano Restorations
1702 Doubletree Dr.
Mesquite, TX 75149
ph: 214-773-8958
kdivad@aol.com
Offers restoration of pianos, antique player pianos, and other automatic musical instruments.

Alan S. Erb, P.E. (M.E.)
Erb Engineering
P.O. Box 124
Mt. Eden, CA 94557-0124
ph: 510-783-5068
fax: 510-783-5068
erbmusic@earthlink.net
http://www.mechanicalmusicbox.com
Expert buys, sells, restores, repairs nickelodeon/coin-op pianos, parts; offers the finest pipework.

John H. Pohlpeter
Another Time Restorations
502 4th Ave.
Oregon City, OR 97045-3100
ph: 503-656-9757 or 503-656-9757
Buys, sells, restores clocks, player pianos, band organs and orchestrions, pump and reed organs.

Suppliers

Durrell Armstrong
Player Piano Co., Inc.
704 East Douglas
Wichita, KS 67202-3506
ph: 316-263-1714 or 316-263-3241
fax: 316-263-5480
http://www.playerpianocompany.com
Complete line of player piano restoration supplies, service manuals,

music rolls; catalog if mailed free upon request.

Picks

Collectors

Carl Oates
2003 Ave. L
Galveston, TX 77550
ph: 409-762-9995
fax: 409-762-9996
lynchrox@aol.com
http://members.aol.com/lynchrox/coates.html
Trades guitar picks with other collectors and makes purchases for his own collection; looking for imprinted guitar picks from bands and individual musicians: actual stage used, mint, promotional, fan club picks.

Dennis Chase
Picknet
7637 S. Goosseberry Way
Tucson, AZ 85747
Avid collector of picks; always willing to talk with others having a similar interest.

Experts

Will Hoover
92-1553-B Aliinui Dr.
Kapolei, HI 96707
ph: 808-679-0114
Author of "Picks! The Colorful Saga of Vintage Celluloid Guitar Plectrums."

Internet Resources

Hand Pick'd
bdaleiden@hotmail.com
http://members.tripod.com/~bdaleiden

Jeff White
Universal Guitar Pick Trader, The
28 K Corniche Dr.
Dana Point, CA 92629
ph: 949-487-7050
Has many celebrity, promo and vintage picks to trade.

String

Appraisers

Luke Biggs
L. L. Biggs Conservator
P.O. Box 3091
Summerville, SC 29484-3091
ph: 843-851-9293
fax: 843-873-0165
biggsconservator@msn.com
Specializes in the appraisal of 19th and 20th century American stringed instruments including guitars, banjos and mandolins.

Jeffrey Holmes
Shar Fine Instruments
2465 South Industrial Highway
Ann Arbor, MI 48106
ph: 800-438-4538 or 734-665-4626
fax: 734-665-0829
fineinst@sharmusic.com
http://www.sharmusic.com
Specializes in the appraisal of stringed instruments and bows.

Fritz Reuter
Fritz Reuter & Sons, Inc.
3917 W. Touhy Ave.
Chicago, IL 60712-1027
ph: 847-677-7255 or 847-677-7257
fax: 847-677-7256
freuter@fritz-reuter.com
http://www.fritz-reuter.com
Master violin makers and dealers; international consultants and expert appraisers; specializes in string instruments (violins, violas, cellos, bows); also repairs and restores string instruments.

Collectors

Richard Schwartz
24550 Hawthorne Dr.
Cleveland, OH 44122-2314
ph: 216-464-0183
richs48969@aol.com
Wants to buy older violins, violas, cellos, basses, bows, etc.; also wants books and catalogs about string instruments.

Dealers

Jim Bollman
Music Emporium, Inc., The
165 Massachusetts Ave.
Lexington, MA 02420
ph: 781-860-0049
fax: 781-860-0051
sales@themusicemporium.com
http://www.themusicemporium.com
Wants old guitars, ukuleles, banjos, mandolins, concertinas, wooden flutes or other stringed instruments in any condition; specializes in fretted instruments, especially the banjo.

Toys from the Attic
203 Mamaroneck Ave.
White Plains, NY 10601
ph: 914-421-0069
fax: 914-328-3852
guitars@tfta.com
http://www.tfta.com
Wants to buy guitars, basses, amplifiers, effects, other stringed instruments.

Fritz Reuter
Fritz Reuter & Sons, Inc.
3917 W. Touhy Ave.
Chicago, IL 60712-1027
ph: 847-677-7255 or 847-677-7257
fax: 847-677-7256
freuter@fritz-reuter.com
http://www.fritz-reuter.com
Master violin makers and dealers; international consultants and expert appraisers; specializes in string instruments (violins, violas, cellos,

bows); also repairs and restores string instruments.

Periodicals

String Letter Publishing, Inc.
Magazine: Strings
P.O. Box 7767
San Anselmo, CA 94979
ph: 415-485-6946 or 800-827-6837
fax: 415-485-0831
editors.st@stringletter.com
http://www.stringsmagazine.com
The bi-monthly magazine for players and makers of bowed instruments; articles, profiles, instrument making and repair, music schools, ads; also publishes annual auction Price Guide and annual Resource Guide.

String (Fretted)

Appraisers

Stanley M. Jay
Mandolin Brothers, Ltd.
Newsletter: Vintage News, The
629 Forest Ave.
Staten Island, NY 10310-2515
ph: 718-981-3226 or 718-981-8585
fax: 718-816-4416
mandolin@ix.netcom.com
http://www.mandoweb.com
Buy guitars, banjos & mandolins by fine American brands: Gibson, C.F. Martin, National, Dobro, D'Angelico, Fender, Gretsch, Rickenbacker, Paramount, Vega, B&D, Epiphone, Stromberg, S.S. Stewart; free telephone appraisals; repairs.

George Gruhn
Gruhn Guitars, Inc.
400 Broadway
Nashville, TN 37203-3931
ph: 615-256-2033
fax: 615-255-2021
gruhn@gruhn.com
http://www.gruhn.com
Buys, sells, appraises, and specializes in American vintage or custom-made fretted instruments; Web site featuring over 1,500 vintage guitars, mandolins and banjos is updated five times per week; offers online appraisal service.

Stan Werbin
Elderly Instruments
1100 N. Washington
Lansing, MI 48906
ph: 517-372-7890 or 517-372-7880
fax: 517-372-5155
swerbin@elderly.com
http://www.elderly.com
Collector, dealer, expert, appraiser specializes in American made fretted stringed instruments including guitars, banjos, mandolins: by Martin, Gibson, Vega, B&D, D'Angelico, Stromberg, Maurer, Fender, etc.

Collectors

K. Wiley
719 Baldwin SE
Grand Rapids, MI 49503-4470
ph: 616-451-8410
*Wants older (pre-1970) guitars,
banjos, ukuleles, mandolins; pieces,
junkers, basket cases; also buying tube
amplifiers.*

Dealers

Steve Sassano
Black Rock Music Center LLC
3004 Fairfield Ave.
Bridgeport, CT 06605
ph: 203-331-0040 or 203-384-2207
fax: 203-366-6416
SSassano@erols.com
http://www.blackrockmusiccenter.com
*Buys and sells all types of musical
instruments, new or old: guitars and
amps, violins, mandolins, banjos,
ukes, cellos; also wants related
memorabilia, catalogs, and anything
to do with instrument manufacturers.*

Stanley M. Jay
Mandolin Brothers, Ltd.
Newsletter: Vintage News, The
629 Forest Ave.
Staten Island, NY 10310-2515
ph: 718-981-3226 or 718-981-8585
fax: 718-816-4416
mandolin@ix.netcom.com
http://www.mandoweb.com
*Buy guitars, banjos & mandolins by
fine American brands: Gibson, C.F.
Martin, National, Dobro, D'Angelico,
Fender, Gretsch, Rickenbacker,
Paramount, Vega, B&D, Epiphone,
Stromberg, S.S. Stewart; free
telephone appraisals; repairs.*

Stan Werbin
Elderly Instruments
1100 N. Washington
Lansing, MI 48906
ph: 517-372-7890 or 517-372-7880
fax: 517-372-5155
swerbin@elderly.com
http://www.elderly.com
*Collector, dealer, expert, appraiser
specializes in American made fretted
stringed instruments including
guitars, banjos, mandolins: by
Martin, Gibson, Vega, B&D,
D'Angelico, Stromberg, Maurer,
Fender, etc.*

Experts

Jim Bollman
Music Emporium, Inc., The
165 Massachusetts Ave.
Lexington, MA 02420
ph: 781-860-0049
fax: 781-860-0051
sales@themusicemporium.com
http://www.themusicemporium.com
*Wants old guitars, ukuleles, banjos,
mandolins, concertinas, wooden flutes
or other stringed instruments in any
condition; specializes in fretted
instruments, especially the banjo.*

David E. Schenkman
Turtle Hill Banjo Co.
P.O. Box 265
Bryantown, MD 20617-0265
ph: 301-274-3441
turtlehill@olg.com
http://www.turtlehillbanjo.com
*Buying vintage stringed instruments:
banjos, guitars, mandolins, and
ukuleles; especially wants instruments
made by Gibson, Martin, Fairbanks,
B & D, Bacon, Vega, Paramount,
Weymann, etc.*

George Gruhn
Gruhn Guitars, Inc.
400 Broadway
Nashville, TN 37203-3931
ph: 615-256-2033
fax: 615-255-2021
gruhn@gruhn.com
http://www.gruhn.com
*Buys, sells, appraises, and specializes
in American vintage or custom-made
fretted instruments; Web site featuring
over 1,500 vintage guitars, mandolins
and banjos is updated five times per
week; offers online appraisal service.*

Repair Services

Stanley M. Jay
Mandolin Brothers, Ltd.
Newsletter: Vintage News, The
629 Forest Ave.
Staten Island, NY 10310-2515
ph: 718-981-3226 or 718-981-8585
fax: 718-816-4416
mandolin@ix.netcom.com
http://www.mandoweb.com
*Buy guitars, banjos & mandolins by
fine American brands: Gibson, C.F.
Martin, National, Dobro, D'Angelico,
Fender, Gretsch, Rickenbacker,
Paramount, Vega, B&D, Epiphone,
Stromberg, S.S. Stewart; free
telephone appraisals; repairs.*

Billy Birthrong
Brass & Reed Music Center, Inc.
675 Mason Ave.
Daytona Beach, FL 32117
ph: 386-252-5544
fax: 386-253-4171
brassnreed@earthlink.net
*Specializes in the repair and
restoration of brass wind band
instruments, violins and guitars and
other fretted instruments.*

Repro. Sources

John & Ann Rawdon
Dulcimers by JR
10068 Stonecreek Rd.
Newcomerstown, OH 43832-9118
ph: 614-498-7753
*Builders of fine quality lap and
hammered dulcimers; price lists upon
request; some wholesale, ask for
details.*

String (Guitars)

Auction Services

GuitarAuction.com
37 South Park St.
Dahlonega, GA 30533
vintage@guitarauction.com
http://www.guitarauction.com
*A Web-based guitar auction for used,
new, and vintage guitars by Martin,
Gibson, Fender, Takoma and others.*

Collectors

Sonny Goldson
1413 Magnolia Lane
Midwest City, OK 73110
ph: 405-737-3312
fax: 405-737-3355
*Wants to buy old guitars, amplifiers
and effects: Gibson, Fender, VOX,
Gretsch, Ricken Backer, Mosrite,
Silvertone, Guico, Harmony, Martin,
Epiphone, National, Valco.*

Dealers

Southworth Guitars
7854 Old Georgetown Rd.
Bethesda, MD 20814
ph: 301-718-1667
fax: 301-718-0391
southworthguitar@aol.com
http://www.southworthguitars.com
*Sells vintage and used guitars;
electrics, arch tops, flat tops,
acoustics, lap and table guitars, bass
guitars, lefty instruments, amplifiers,
mandolins, ukuleles, banjos, etc.*

Guitar Emporium
1610 Bardstown Rd.
Louisville, KY 40205
ph: 502-459-4153
fax: 502-454-3661

Gordy's Music
3341 Hilton Rd.
Ferndale, MI 48200
ph: 248-546-7447
fax: 248-546-5249

Nate Westgor
Willie's American Guitars
254 Cleveland Ave., S
Saint Paul, MN 55105
ph: 651-699-1913
fax: 651-690-1766
willies@ix.netcom.com
http://www.williesguitars.com
*Specializes in vintage, used, new
electric and acoustic guitars as well
as tube amplifiers.*

Steve Evans
Jacksonville Guitar Center
1105 Burman Dr.
Jacksonville, AR 72076-4386
ph: 501-982-4933
jvilguitar@aol.com
http://members.aol.com/jvilguitar
*Buys, collects, and specialized in
stencil-painted cowboy guitars, toy
guitars, and vintage guitars.*

Terri Mardis-Ivers
Terri's Toys & Nostalgia
114 Whitworth Ave.
Ponca City, OK 74601-3438
ph: 580-762-8697
toylady@cableone.net
*Buys and sells many brands of guitars
and amps with special interest in
American made items and especially
interested in vintage items: Gibson,
Martin, Rickenbacker, Danelectro,
Fender, Gretsch, VOX, National,
Hofner, etc.*

Guitar Heaven
1892 Contra Costa Blvd.
Pleasant Hill, CA 94523
ph: 800-797-5750 or 925-687-5750
guitarheaven@juno.com
http://www.guitarheaven.com
*Wants to buy pre-1970 old guitars:
Fender, Gibson, Gretsch, Guild and
Martins only.*

Guitarville
19258 15th NE
Seattle, WA 98155
ph: 206-363-8188
fax: 206-363-0478

Experts

Mike Aversa, ISA
Aversa Estate & Appraisal Service
P.O. Box 863
Yorba Linda, CA 92885
ph: 717-777-3848 or 714-749-3887
AversaAntiques@mindspring.com
http://www.aversaantiques.com
*Expert in 20th century guitars
including Fender, Gibson, Martin,
Guild; also 19th and 20th century
pianos.*

Internet Resources

GuitarBase GuitarMall
3107 Douglas Rd.
Flushing, NY 11363-1043
ph: 718-229-4289
fax: 718-229-3061
info@gbase.com
http://www.gbase.com
*Great Web site for guitar enthusiasts:
search dealer database for guitars for
sale, guitar links.*

Man./Prod./Dist.

Gibson Musical Instruments
ph: 800-4-GIBSON
relations@gibson.com
http://www.gibson.com
*Search for date of a Gibson guitar,
mandolin or banjo using serial
number online.*

C.F. Martin Guitar & Co., Inc.
510 Sycamore St.
P.O. Box 329
Nazareth, PA 18064-0329
ph: 610-759-2937
fax: 610-759-5757
info@martinguitar.com
http://www.mguitar.com
*Offers Woodworker's Guitar Makers
Connection for Woodworkers &*

Luthiers; tools, materials, parts for the fretted instrument maker; factory tours M-F; Guitar Makers Connection catalog $2 ppd.

Museums/Libraries

Steve Evans
Jacksonville Guitar Center
1105 Burman Dr.
Jacksonville, AR 72076-4386
ph: 501-982-4933
jvilguitar@aol.com
http://members.aol.com/jvilguitar
Large collection of vintage guitars on permanent display; includes over 100 cowboy guitars, c. 1930s-1950s, made with painted cowboy scenes showing Gene Autry, Roy Rogers, Buck Jones and others.

Periodicals

Larry Acunto
Magazine: 20th Century Guitar
135 Oser Ave.
Hauppauge, NY 11788
ph: 631-273-1674 or 800-291-9687
fax: 631-434-9057
tcguitar@tcguitar.com
http://www.tcguitar.com
A monthly magazine covering the vintage guitar market; up-to-date reports on technical information, guitar prices, shows, photo classifieds, as well as interesting, off-beat interviews with celebrity musicians who collect.

Magazine: Bluegrass Unlimited
P.O. Box 111
Broad Run, VA 20137-0111
ph: 540-349-8181 or 800-258-4727
fax: 540-341-0011
info@bluegrassmusic.com
http://www.bluegrassmusic.com
Bluegrass Festival calendar, artist interviews, personal appearance calendar, some articles about vintage guitars; classified ads with many instruments.

Magazine: Guitar Digest
P.O. Box 66
Athens, OH 45701
ph: 740-592-4614
alexmack@frognet.net
http://www.guitardigest.com
The magazine for guitar players and collectors.

Vintage Guitar Inc.
Magazine: Vintage Guitar Magazine
P.O. Box 7301
Bismarck, ND 58507
ph: 701-255-1197 or 800-844-1197
fax: 701-255-0250
vguitar@vguitar.com
http://www.vintageguitar.com
Guitar related articles, ads, parts, supplies, books, music, used and new guitars for sale, amps, price guides, guitar factories, repairs, interviews, guitar cases.

Vintage Guitar Inc.
Magazine: VG Classics
P.O. Box 7301
Bismarck, ND 58507
ph: 701-255-1197 or 800-844-1197
fax: 701-255-0250
vguitar@vguitar.com
http://www.vintageguitar.com
A quarterly glossy magazine dedicated to vintage guitars and other stringed instruments; also publishes "The Official Vintage Guitar Magazine Instrument Price Guide."

Miller Freeman, Inc.
Magazine: Guitar Player
600 Harrison St.
San Francisco, CA 94107
ph: 650-655-4308 or 800-289-9839
guitarplayer@neodata.com
http://www.guitarplayer.com
Monthly glossy magazine serving the guitar playing community; some articles about collectible vintage guitars.

String Letter Publishing, Inc.
Magazine: Acoustic Guitar
P.O. Box 767
San Anselmo, CA 94979-0767
ph: 415-485-6946 or 800-827-6837
fax: 415-485-0831
editors.ag@stringletter.com
http://www.acousticguitar.com
The magazine for those interested in acoustic guitars.

String (Violin Family)

Appraisers

Robert Portukalian
Providence Violin Shop
1279 North Main St.
Providence, RI 02904
ph: 401-521-5145
Professional expert and appraiser specializing in antique violins, bows, violas, and cellos.

Andrew Dipper
Givens Violins
1004 Marquette Ave., Ste. 205
Minneapolis, MN 55403
ph: 612-375-0708
fax: 612-375-0096
adipper@citilink.com
http://www.givensviolins.com
Specializes in the restoration and appraisal of historic string instruments.

Collectors

Richard Schwartz
24550 Hawthorne Dr.
Cleveland, OH 44122-2314
ph: 216-464-0183
richs48969@aol.com
Wants to buy older violins, violas, cellos, basses, bows, etc.; also wants books and catalogs about string instruments.

Dealers

Ron Midgett
Easthampton Violin Company
15 Lovefield St.
Easthampton, MA 01027-1167
ph: 413-527-8033 or 800-207-2400
info@easthamptonviolin.com
http://www.easthamptonviolin.com
Wants violins, violas, cellos and bows; American or European; especially wants violins made by Massachusetts makers and any related photographs, books, advertising, etc.; buys and sells; also restorer of violin-family instruments & bows.

William D. Voiers
William D. Voiers Fine Musical Instruments
P.O. Box 23
North Egremont, MA 01252-0023
ph: 413-528-3321 or 800-788-3521
fax: 413-528-5801
Dealer, collector, appraiser of the violin family of instruments: violins, violas, cellos, bows, banjos, ukuleles, guitars and mandolins; electric or acoustic; also saxes, brasses, drums, percussion; also buys, sells, collects and trades.

Robert Portukalian
Providence Violin Shop
1279 North Main St.
Providence, RI 02904
ph: 401-521-5145
Professional expert and appraiser specializing in antique violins, bows, violas, and cellos.

Frederick W. Oster
Frederick W. Oster Fine Violins
1529 Pine St.
Philadelphia, PA 19102-4623
ph: 215-545-1100
fax: 215-735-3634
vintageFO@aol.com
http://www.fredoster.com
Since 1975; dealer, appraiser, consultant; rare & antique musical instruments; specializing in violins, violas, cellos, bows; American fretted instruments - guitars, mandolins, banjos; antique wind instruments, etc.; SASE for reply.

Lillian Zaret
Angelico Violins, Inc.
861 W. 46th St.
Norfolk, VA 23508-2009
ph: 800-222-2998 or 757-423-3336
fax: 757-423-4768
info@angelicoviolins.com
http://www.angelicoviolins.com
Sells all sizes of new and old violins including violins made in China and Eastern Europe; also deals in violas, cellos and their bows; instruments & bows by contemporary luthier also available; expert repairs & bow rehairing.

John Montgomery
John Montgomery, Inc.
509 Hillsborough St.
Raleigh, NC 27603-1729
ph: 919-821-4459
fax: 919-821-1072
john@montgomeryviolins.com
http://www.montgomeryviolins.com
Dealer in the violin family of instruments; violin maker and restorer.

Al Stancel
Casa Del Sol Violins, Ltd.
4302 East 62nd St.
Indianapolis, IN 46220-4568
ph: 800-423-0236 or 317-257-9923
cdsviolins@iquest.net
http://www.violincasa.com
Buys, sells, and restores old violins; also makes and sells new violins; especially wants French bows and Italian violins.

Experts

William L. Monical
William Monical & Son, Inc. - Dealers & Restorers of Fine Violins
288 Richmond Terrace
Staten Island, NY 10301-1512
ph: 718-816-7878 or 800-816-4424
fax: 718-816-7711
wmonical@con2.com
Specializes in bowed string instruments of modern & Baroque violin and viola da gamba families: sales, restoration, appraisals, cases.

Internet Resources

Violink
Italy
info@violink.com
http://www.violink.com
Lots of information about violins, fiddles, etc.: conferences, violin and bow makers, violin making schools, organizations, dealers, shops, museums, books, journals.

Periodicals

Orpheus Publications Ltd.
Magazine: Strad, The
P.O. Box 648
Harrow, Middlesex HA1 2EE U.K.
ph: +44 (0)20 8863 4040 or +44 (0)20 8863 2020
fax: +44 (0)20 8863 2444
thestrad@orpheuspublications.com
http://www.thestrad.com
A monthly magazine covering all aspects of violin-family stringed instruments: playing, making, teaching; includes great performers, teachers and luthiers, news, reviews; US subscriptions call 1-800-688-6247.

Repair Services

Ron Midgett
Easthampton Violin Company
15 Lovefield St.
Easthampton, MA 01027-1167
ph: 413-527-8033 or 800-207-2400
info@easthamptonviolin.com
http://www.easthamptonviolin.com
*Wants violins, violas, cellos and
bows; American or European;
especially wants violins made by
Massachusetts makers and any related
photographs, books, advertising, etc.;
buys and sells; also restorer of violin-
family instruments & bows.*

Andrew Dipper
Givens Violins
1004 Marquette Ave., Ste. 205
Minneapolis, MN 55403
ph: 612-375-0708
fax: 612-375-0096
adipper@citilink.com
http://www.givensviolins.com
*Specializes in the restoration and
appraisal of historic string
instruments.*

MYSTERY/DETECTIVE ITEMS

(see also BOOKS, Mystery;
CAMERAS & CAMERA EQUIPMENT,
Subminiature; CHARACTER
COLLECTIBLES, Sherlock Holmes;
CHARACTER COLLECTIBLES, Spy
Memorabilia; MAGAZINES, Mystery;
SPY EQUIPMENT)

Collectors

Beverley Furlow-Cleary
2620 Stewart Rd.
Signal Mountain, TN 37377
ph: 423-517-0703
beverleyf@aol.com
http://www.BeverleyFurlowClearly.net
*Buys, sells, and appraises collectible
mystery/detective items: books, vintage
clothing and hats.*

MYSTICAL ARTS

(see UFOs & UNEXPLAINED
PHENOMENA)

**Here are some tips
when contacting
someone who is listed
in this book:**

When requesting
information about a
particular item, include
a description (material,
dimensions, maker's
mark, model number,
etc.) and a photo,
sketch, digital image or
photocopy of the item
in question.

Always ask if there are
charges for samples or
for the services that
you are requesting.

When corresponding
by letter, please be
sure to include a Large
(#10 business size)
Self-Addressed and
Stamped Envelope
(LSASE) if requesting a
reply or the return of
photographs.

Never call collect
unless otherwise
directed. When
calling, be considerate
of time zone differ-
ences and always ask
if the party you are
calling has time to talk.
When leaving an
answering machine
message, always
instruct the party to
call you back collect.

N-O

NAPKIN DOLLS

Collectors

Bobbie & Alan Bryson
1 St. Eleanoras Ln.
Tuckahoe, NY 10707-1307
ph: 914-779-1405
napkindoll@aol.com
A napkin doll is a ceramic figurine of a girl with slits in her skirt for holding a folded napkin; Bobbie is co-author of the pictorial reference guide "Collectibles For The Kitchen, Bath & Beyond;" 150 photos of napkin dolls plus ads.

Dealers

Bobbie & Alan Bryson
1 St. Eleanoras Ln.
Tuckahoe, NY 10707-1307
ph: 914-779-1405
napkindoll@aol.com
A napkin doll is a ceramic figurine of a girl with slits in her skirt for holding a folded napkin; Bobbie is co-author of the pictorial reference guide "Collectibles For The Kitchen, Bath & Beyond;" 150 photos of napkin dolls plus ads.

NAPKIN RINGS

Figural

Collectors

Maria E. Raymond
Plow & Pen, Inc.
P.O. Box 758
Knights Landing, CA 95645-0758
ph: 530-735-6596
mariaraymond@afes.com
Interested in buying Meriden Company napkin rings only.

Dealers

Sandra Whitson
Van Anda's Antiques
P.O. Box 272
Lititz, PA 17543-0272
ph: 717-626-4978
fax: 717-626-7625
npknring@desupernet.net
Buys and sells fine quality Victorian figural napkin rings; co-author of "Figural Napkin Rings" (1996), a collector's identification and value guide.

Barbara & Steve Aaronson
Victorian Lady, The
P.O. Box 7522
Northridge, CA 91327
ph: 818-368-6052
bjaaronson@aol.com
http://www.thevictorianlady.com
Specializes in buying and selling American Victorian figural napkin rings.

NASA

(see SPACE COLLECTIBLES)

NATIVE AMERICAN

(see also ARCHAEOLOGY; ART, Western; BASKETS; BEADS, Trade; BOOKS, Reference [Native American]; CIGAR STORE COLLECTIBLES; EDGED WEAPONS; HERITAGE RESOURCES; INDIAN WARS; PREHISTORIC ARTIFACTS; TEXTILES, Blankets; WESTERN AMERICANA)

Appraisers

Glenn A. Long
Long & Manzi Fine Art Services, Inc.
ph: 518-854-3388
fax: 518-854-3999
topappraisers@hotmail.com
Private dealers and appraisers serving collectors and museums for over 25 years; specializes in art, drawings, paintings, photography & photographs, 19th and 20th century sculpture, African, Native American, Precolumbian.

David Summers
Native American Artifacts
45 West Parkway
Victor, NY 14564-1243
ph: 585-924-5167
fax: 585-924-5167
naasummers@aol.com
Dealer, appraiser, collector; one of the world's largest dealers in American Indian art and antiquities; buys and sells; specializing in Northeastern Indian specimens.

Gary L. Fogelman
245 Fairview Rd.
Turbotville, PA 17772-9063
ph: 570-437-3698
fax: 570-437-3411
iam@uplink.net
http://www.indian-artifacts.net
Author of "A Projectile Point Typology for PA and the Northeast" and "An Identification and Price Guide for Indian Artifacts of the Northeast."

Roy Harrell
P.O. Box 95
Ocean View, DE 19970
ph: 302-537-6287
roywow@aol.com
Specializes in the appraisal of Native American Indian items.

Maryann L'Heureux
Native American Arts Appraisals
6172 Devon Dr.
Columbia, MD 21044-3821
ph: 410-730-8084
Maryann@happyones.com
http://www.happyones.com/maryann
Senior member of the American Society of Appraisers, tested in North American Indian art and artifacts.

Linda Dyer
P.O. Box 1104
Franklin, TN 37065-1104
ph: 615-791-9242
Ledyer256@aol.com
Specializes in the appraisal of American Indian art and ethnographica.

Gwen Yeaman, ISA
Native Appraisal, LLC
gwen@nativeappraisal.com
http://www.nativeappraisal.com
Appraiser of Native American art; graduated top of class "Case Law & the Legal Appraisal Environment" Amer. Soc. of Appraisers; Accredited Appraiser Inter. Soc. of App.; consultant, author, professional speaker on native culture & art.

Cynthia Hale
7930 S. Hudson
Tulsa, OK 74136
ph: 918-524-9338
cj-hale@swbell.net
Specializes in the appraisal of Native American art; also other fine art, paintings, sculpture.

Bruce M. Shackelford
Western Services
P.O. Box 15707
San Antonio, TX 78212
ph: 210-698-3217
fax: 210-698-0073
bruce@bshack.com
http://www.bshack.com
Specializes in appraising Western Americana and North American Indian art.

Corinne Cain, ISA, ASA
Corinne Cain Ltd.
326 West Harmont Dr.
Phoenix, AZ 85021
ph: 602-906-1633
fax: 602-906-0677
corinne@savvycollector.com
http://www.savvycollector.com
Appraises fine arts and Native American arts.

John C. Hill
Gallery of American Indian Art
6962 East First Ave., Ste. 104
Scottsdale, AZ 85251-4302
ph: 480-946-2910
fax: 480-946-7410
antqindart@aol.com
Expert dealer and appraiser of old Southwestern Indian, and Indian beadwork.

Sarah Ann Bowler-Hill
Peter Eller Gallery & Appraisers
12432 Prospect Ave. NE
Albuquerque, NM 87112
ph: 505-249-3925 or 505-268-7437
fax: 505-268-6442
bowlerhill@yahoo.com
http://www.peterellergallery.com
Appraising Southwestern and contemporary Native American arts, antiques and general residential contents; video and photographic inventory services available.

Joan Caballero, ISA
Joan Caballero Appraisals
P.O. Box 822
Santa Fe, NM 87504
ph: 505-982-8148
fax: 505-982-7048
joancaballero@msn.com
Specializes in the appraisal of Native American arts (antique & contemporary), New Mexican Hispanic arts, and Southwest Regional fine arts (Taos and Santa Fe schools and living artists).

Gene Quintana
P.O. Box 533
Carmichael, CA 95609
ph: 916-485-8232
vipbasketman@aol.com
Collector and appraiser of American Indian basketry and blankets.

Phil Moerschell
Western Collectables
P.O. Box 21
Bend, OR 97709
ph: 541-923-2140
fax: 541-923-9894
phm3@westerncollectables.com
http://www.westerncollectables.com
Collector, appraiser of Western Americana: cowboy spurs, bits and chaps, Indian baskets, beadwork, etc.

Brill Lee
Brill Lee Appraisal Services
P.O. Box 244
Bellevue, WA 98009-0244
ph: 425-885-4518
fax: 425-895-1022
brilllee@hotmail.com
Buys, sells, and appraises pre-1960 Native American Indian artifacts, beadwork, baskets, clothing, parfleche, weapons and related items; Eastern Oregon University: Master's Thesis on the Umatilla Indian Reservation, 1855-1926.

Scott Zema, ISA CAPP
ph: 425-486-6310
scottzema@msn.com
http://www.arklimited.com

Auction Services

Willis Henry
Willis Henry Auctions, Inc.
22 Main St.
Marshfield, MA 02050
ph: 781-834-7774 or 800-244-8466
fax: 781-826-3520
wha@willishenry.com
http://www.willishenry.com
Specializes in the sale of American antiques of all kinds, particularly Shaker, American Indian and Early American.

Douglas Deihl
Skinner, Inc.
63 Park Plaza
The Heritage on the Garden
Boston, MA 02116
ph: 617-350-5400
fax: 617-350-5429
info@skinnerinc.com
http://www.skinnerinc.com
Established in 1971, Skinner Inc. is the fourth largest auction house in the US; has offices in Boston and Bolton, MA.

Sotheby's
1334 York Ave.
New York, NY 10021
ph: 212-606-7000
fax: 212-606-7107
http://www.sothebys.com
Over 70 collecting areas are featured at Sotheby's auctions including toys, dolls, porcelain, furniture, silver, art, books; exhibitions are free and everyone is welcome; for a free copy of "Sotheby's Newsletter," call 212-606-7245.

Garth's Auction, Inc.
2690 Stratford Rd.
P.O. Box 369
Delaware, OH 43015
ph: 740-362-4771
fax: 740-363-0164
info@garths.com
http://www.garths.com
Specializing in Early American, English, Continental, Oriental antiques and accessories; paintings, fine art, folk art, American Indian, military, jewelry, toys, dolls, advertising, collectibles.

Jan Sorgenfrei
Old Barn Auction
10040 S.R. 224 West
Findlay, OH 45840
ph: 419-422-8531
fax: 419-522-5321
Manningdg@aol.com
http://www.oldbarn.com
Conducts specialized auctions of American Indian items.

Steve Allard
Allard Auctions, Inc.
419 Flathead St.
Saint Ignatius, MT 59865
ph: 406-745-0500 or 800-314-0343
fax: 406-745-0502
steve@allardauctions.com
http://www.allardauctions.com
Conducts live and live Internet auctions specializing in American Indian items.

Preston E. Miller
Four Winds Indian Auction
P.O. Box 580
Saint Ignatius, MT 59865-0580
ph: 406-745-4336
fax: 406-745-3595
Conducts mail/phone bid auctions of contemporary Indian artifacts and collectibles: beadwork, old photos, stone relics, parfleches, weapons, pottery, trade beads, baskets, replicas, Navajo rugs, etc.; photo illustrated catalog $20.

Joy Luke
Joy Luke Auction Gallery
300 E. Grove St.
Bloomington, IL 61701-5232
ph: 309-828-5533
fax: 309-829-2266
robert@joyluke.com
http://www.joyluke.com
Conducts periodic auctions specializing in Indian items.

Bonhams & Butterfields
220 San Bruno Ave.
San Francisco, CA 94103
ph: 415-861-7500 or 800-223-2854
fax: 415-861-8951
info.US@butterfields.com
http://www.butterfields.com
Auctioneers and appraisers of antiques, fine art and collectibles in all categories; specialty sales include posters, toys, decorative arts, furniture, photography, etc.; the largest full service auction in the West.

Clubs/Associations

Genuine Indian Relic Society
Magazine: Prehistoric American
937 Eventide, Ste. 2
San Antonio, TX 78209-5546
amartin2@earthlink.net
http://www.artifactsetc.com/girs.htm

Alice Kaufman, Ex. Dir.
Antique Tribal Art Dealers Association, The
Newsletter: ATADA Newsletter
215 Sierra SE
Albuquerque, NM 87108
ph: 415-863-3173
fax: 415-431-1939
acek33@aol.com
http://www.atada.org
Offers buyers a guarantee that objects members sell are as represented regarding age, authenticity and extent of restoration (if any); members also

guarantee refunds if objects prove to be other than represented.

Collectors

Dr. Fred Cesana
49 E. Main St.
Plainville, CT 06062
ph: 860-747-2759 or 860-379-0054
fax: 860-793-6019
Wants pre-1880 Plains Indian weapons: tomahawks, knives, lances, clubs, rifles; also wants important beadwork.

Joe Liberkowski
P.O. Box 2161
Medford, NJ 08055-7161
Wants American Indian items; also pre-1940 Mexican and South American Santos, Retablos, Ex Votos, crucifixes, religious, historical autographs/documents.

Jan Sorgenfrei
10040 S.R. 224 West
Findlay, OH 45840
ph: 419-422-8531
fax: 419-522-5321
Manningdg@aol.com
http://www.oldbarn.com

Larry Jarvinen
313 Condon Rd.
Manistee, MI 49660-1008
ph: 231-723-5063
Wants to buy American Indian trade beads, silver, axes, beadwork, brass kettles, muskets, etc.

Charles Arnold
1200 Madison St.
P.O. Box 554
Denver, CO 80206
ph: 303-394-2941 or 800-747-1062
Collector of 19th to mid 20th century Native American Indian artifacts: art, Navajo blankets and rugs, beadwork, baskets, Pueblo pottery, Kachinas, weapons, pre-1930 Navajo jewelry; special interest in Pueblo Indian material.

Bob Temarantz
2824 N. Bentley Ave.
Tucson, AZ 85716-5513
ph: 520-326-6704 or 520-741-9751
fax: 520-294-6052
azsnipe@hotmail.com
Wants old Southwestern Indian baskets, pottery, jewelry, textiles, etc.; also wants old trading post tokens from Arizona.

Mike Kramer
P.O. Box 3257
Vallejo, CA 94590-0676
ph: 800-568-8883 or 800-446-6581
fax: 707-642-2456
Wants early American Indian items: model totems, trade totems, quality baskets.

Daniel Brown
P.O. Box 149
Davenport, CA 95017-0149
ph: 831-426-0134 or 800-492-6786
green-garnet@sbcglobal.net
Wants to buy museum quality Indian relics: pre-1900 Plains Indian material including shirts, shields, weapons, beadwork, quillwork; large Pueblo pots, early Navajo blankets, saltillos, old Navajo jewelry, fine baskets, NW Coast, etc.

Dealers

Barry Walsh
Buffalo Barry's Indian Art
76 Laurelwood Rd.
Holden, MA 01520
ph: 508-829-6297
fax: 508-393-1279
bbia@gis.net
Native American art dealer and appraiser specializing in Hopi Kachina dolls, Pueblo pottery, Southwest baskets, beadwork, Northeast baskets, Penobscot root clubs, Northwest Coast masks, Inuit carvings, Navajo rugs, etc.

Norman Hurst, ISA CAPP
Hurst Gallery
53 Mount Auburn St.
Cambridge, MA 02138-5030
ph: 617-491-6888 or 212-744-6488 (NYC)
fax: 617-661-0439
NHurst@compuserve.com
http://www.hurstgallery.com
Buys, sells, appraises African, Oceanic, Native American, Precolumbian and Asian art; has been appraising, dealing and publishing American Indian & Eskimo art for over 20 years: baskets, pottery, beadwork, masks, ivory.

Carol Halberstadt
Migrations
P.O. Box 543
Newton, MA 02456
carol@migrations.com
http://www.migrations.com
Specializes in older and contemporary Native American and Inuit/Eskimo art: weavings, pottery, baskets, jewelry, sculpture; online gallery with links to a wide variety of Native American resources.

Trotta-Bono American Indian Art
P.O. Box 34
Shrub Oak, NY 10588
ph: 914-528-6604
fax: 914-526-2714
tb788183@aol.com
Specializes in North American Indian art; early native objects from all tribal areas: bowls, ladles, weapons, pottery, basketry, weavings, paintings.

David Summers
Native American Artifacts
45 West Parkway
Victor, NY 14564-1243
ph: 585-924-5167
fax: 585-924-5167
naasummers@aol.com
Dealer, appraiser, collector; one of the world's largest dealers in American Indian art and antiquities; buys and sells; specializing in Northeastern Indian specimens.

Crown & Eagle Antiques
P.O. Box 181
New Hope, PA 18938
ph: 215-794-7972
fax: 215-794-7392
artifact@voicenet.com
http://www.corwneagle.com
Dealer, expert, appraiser in fine quality American Indian art: old pawn, rugs, basketry, beadwork, pottery.

Stephen Barnett
American Indian Art
524 Elm Ave.
Upper Darby, PA 19082
ph: 610-352-3976
Specializes in antique Native American Indian art: dolls from Plains, Northeastern, Seminole, Mojave, Cherokee; also Indian beadwork of all kinds.

Ramona Morris
Ramona Morris Fine Art
P.O. Box 135
Delaplane, VA 20144
ph: 540-592-3873
fax: 540-592-3342
rmfineart@earthlink.net
Specializes in antique Native American art and Shamanic art; offers appraisals, curatorial services, collection building and brokerage.

Big Sky Enterprises
P.O. Box 493
Piedmont, SC 29673
ph: 864-299-1375
fax: 864-299-1391
sales@bigskyenterprises.com
http://www.bigskyenterprises.com
Specializes in prehistoric as well as historic Indian artifacts of all types; also militaria of all countries from 1865 to 1945: swords, bayonets, medals, badges, insignia, fieldgear, uniforms, documents.

Von Hilliard
Indian Shop, The
P.O. Box 246
Independence, KY 41051-0246
ph: 859-428-0449
For $2 you receive the current relic catalog consisting of 50 to 80 pages filled with arrowheads, spearheads, axes, Precolumbian, Plains Indian and Eskimo items, and more - all photographed.

Bradley S. Vite
Bradley Vite Fine Arts
1600 West Beardsley Ave.
Elkhart, IN 46514-1800
ph: 219-293-1616
fax: 219-293-1616
bradley@finearts.com
Interested in Native American weavings and basketry.

Gerald E. Czulewicz
Antiques Americana
25699 Highway 65 NE
Isanti, MN 55040
ph: 763-444-9216
fax: 763-444-9218
charliezebra@msn.com
Buys and sells important pieces of Native American art and artifacts.

World City, Inc.
6935 James Ave. South
Minneapolis, MN 55423-2147
Buys and sells Indian items such as beaded items, pottery, Navajo rugs, quilled items, Kachinas, Northwest Coast items; both pre-historic and historic; send price wanted (unless unsure), description, photos, and SASE.

Donald Baughman
Donald James Baughman Fine Arts
P.O. Box 2348
Bigfork, MT 59911
ph: 406-982-3837
ybh@digisys.net
Second generation antiquarian; has been collecting since the age of five; associate of the Antiquities Show; full member of the Antiques Tribal Arts Association; buys, sells and offers an independent appraisal service.

John Buxton
Shango Galleries
6717 Spring Valley
Dallas, TX 75254
ph: 972-239-4620 or 972-239-9943
fax: 972-239-9766
jbuxton@arttrak.com
http://www.arttrak.com
Buys, sells, and appraises African, Precolumbian, Oceanic, and American Indian art.

William W. Wynn
2117 Hillcrest St.
Fort Worth, TX 76107-4329
ph: 817-763-8424
Wants to buy Skookum Indian dolls, beaded Zuni dolls, pre-1950 Plains Indian and Navajo rag dolls; pre-1950 Kachina dolls, Navajo rugs, Pima & Apache baskets, and San Ildefonso, Hopi, Cochiti, Santo Domingo pottery.

Pat Dunnegan
Pat's Authentic Indian Artifacts
201 Harrison Ave.
Gustine, TX 76455
ph: 888-841-9386 or 915-667-7210
teddun@itexas.net
http://www2.itexas.net/~teddun
Online close-up photos of quality authentic American Indian artifacts offered for sale; also a selected list of related books; over 40 years in business.

David Cook
David Cook Fine American Art
1637 Wazee St.
Denver, CO 80202
ph: 303-623-8181
fax: 303-623-4817
info@davidcookgalleries.com
http://
www.davidcookfineamericanart.com
Buys, sells, collects and appraises antique Native American art; also interested in American paintings (specializing in Colorado and New Mexico artists), sculpture, and arts & crafts.

Squash Blossom & Cogswell Gallery
2531 W. Colorado Ave.
Colorado Springs, CO 80904
ph: 719-632-1899
fax: 719-635-4304
staff@squashblossom.com
http://www.squashblossom.com
Dealer/appraiser specializing in Southwestern Native American jewelry and art including pottery, weaving, Kachinas (both prehistoric and historic.)

John Hartman
Globalarts
17897 Hwy. 160
Durango, CO 81301
ph: 970-247-5589
fax: 970-259-6020
Buys and sells antique Frontier memorabilia, Native American Indian items, Cowboy items; also Ethnic Rarities from around the world.

Corinne Cain, ISA, ASA
Corinne Cain Ltd.
326 West Harmont Dr.
Phoenix, AZ 85021
ph: 602-906-1633
fax: 602-906-0677
corinne@savvycollector.com
http://www.savvycollector.com
A veteran art appraiser for over 25 years selling fine art and Native American arts online; guaranteed condition, authenticity verified, value is assured; Accredited Senior Appraiser, Certified Appraiser of Personal Property.

Deborah Begner
Turkey Mountain Traders
7008 East Main St.
Scottsdale, AZ 85251
ph: 480-423-8777 or 480-951-8678
fax: 480-423-8778
info@turkey-mountain.com
http://www.turkey-mountain.com
Specializes in only antique American Indian artifacts; also Mission furniture and American folk art.

John C. Hill
Hill Antique Indian Art Gallery
6962 East First Ave.
Scottsdale, AZ 85251
ph: 480-946-2910
fax: 480-946-7410
Antqindart@aol.com
http://www.maineantiquedigest.com/
adimg/johnhill.htm
Dealer, expert, appraiser of early Native American Indian art; specialist in Hopi material culture (Hopi Kachinas), historic pottery of the Southwest, Native American jewelry (old pawn), Navajo & Pueblo textiles, baskets, beadwork, etc.

John C. Hill
Gallery of American Indian Art
6962 East First Ave., Ste. 104
Scottsdale, AZ 85251-4302
ph: 480-946-2910
fax: 480-946-7410
antqindart@aol.com
Wants to buy early Southwest Indian items including classic Navajo & Pueblo silver & turquoise, Indian blankets and other textiles, Kachina dolls, early pottery; also wants Plains and Northeast Indian beadwork, and fine Indian basketry.

Michael D. Higgins
Michael D. Higgins & Son Antique Indian Art
4429 N. Campbell Ave.
Tucson, AZ 85718
ph: 520-577-8330
mdhiggins@earthlink.net
http://www.mhiggins.com
Appraises, buys and sells antique American Indian, PreColumbian, Mexican and Spanish Colonial antiques; since 1972; also wants paintings of the American West; museum references available.

Donna McMenamin
5100 W. Rhyolite Loop
Tucson, AZ 85745
ph: 520-743-2940
fax: 520-743-2941
donnamcm@worldnet.att.net
http://www.donnamcmenamin.com
Buys and sells historical Native American baskets, pre-1900 beadwork, and Navajo rugs.

Richard B. Troyanowski
Rich Relics
P.O. Box 432
Sandia Park, NM 87047-0432
ph: 505-281-2611 or 505-281-2329
Buys/sells prehistoric/historic Indian artifacts, cowboy, militaria, old world antiquities & coins, fossils & ethnographic collectibles.

Thomas Baker
Tanner Chaney Gallery
410 Romero NW
Albuquerque, NM 87104
ph: 505-247-2242
fax: 505-298-3434
tbaker@tannerchaneygallery.com
http://www.tannerchaneygallery.com
Sells and appraises contemporary and antique Native American jewelry, weavings and pottery.

Robert V. Gallegos
Robert Gallegos Fine Art
215 Sierra SE
Albuquerque, NM 87108
ph: 505-262-0620
fax: 505-260-0383
gallegos@nmia.com
Specializes in American Indian and Mexican Colonial antiques.

Terry Schurmeier
Cowboys & Indians Antiques
4000 Central SE
Albuquerque, NM 87108
ph: 505-255-4054 or 505-255-5775
fax: 505-255-1730
cowgirls@rt66.com
http://www.cowboysandindiansnm.com
Carries large inventory of pre-1940s Native American pottery, baskets, beadwork, jewelry, textiles; antique devotional art, art of the Old West; also Old West, Spanish colonial, old pawn & Mexican jewelry; buy, sell, trade, appraise.

Jed Foutz
Shiprock Trading Co.
P.O. Box 3379
Highway 64
Shiprock, NM 87420
ph: 505-368-4585 or 800-210-7847
fax: 505-368-5583
jed@shiprocktrading.com
http://www.shiprocktrading.com
Fifth generation dealer in American Indian items.

Joe Rivera
Morning Star Gallery, Ltd.
513 Canyon Rd.
Santa Fe, NM 87501
ph: 505-982-8187
fax: 505-984-2368
indian@morningstargallery.com
http://www.morningstargallery.com
Pottery, baskets, bags, textiles, rugs, parfleche, moccasins, clothing, jewelry, weapons, musical instruments, dolls.

Matthew Maxwell
Matthew Chase Ltd.
503 Canyon Rd.
Santa Fe, NM 87501
ph: 505-986-1095
art@matthewchaseltd.com
http://www.mathewchaseltd.com
Gallery of fine antique American Indian art and paintings of the American West.

Michael Kokin
Sherwoods Spirit of America
130 Lincoln Ave.
Santa Fe, NM 87501
ph: 505-988-1776
fax: 505-992-1812
americanwest1776@aol.com
http://www.sherwoodspirit.com
Collector, dealer, expert, specializes in exceptional and important American history antiquities and collectibles: antique guns, Native American, Civil War, cowboy and Western memorabilia.

Christopher Selser
American Indian & Tribal Art
830 Canyon Rd.
Santa Fe, NM 87501
ph: 505-984-1481
fax: 505-984-1481
tribalart@newmexico.com
Dealer in American antiquities for over 30 years; author of "Navajo Weaving Tradition;" current president of Antique Tribal Art Dealers Association.

Pierre G. Bovis
Bovis Primitive Arts
P.O. Box 5529
Santa Fe, NM 87502
ph: 505-474-6598 or 505-577-4723
fax: 505-474-6598
louberlugan@earthlink.net
http://www.bovisprimitivearts.com
Specializes in Oceanic, African, and North American artifacts.

Don Bennett
Don Bennett & Associates
P.O. Box 283
Agoura Hills, CA 91376-0283
ph: 818-991-5596
fax: 818-991-6866
artofwest@aol.com
Collects, buys, sells and appraises high quality antique Native American items: Navajo, baskets, etc.; also paintings by deceased Western artists; since 1968.

Jimmy Vitanza
Peregrine Galleries
508 Brinkerhoff Ave.
Santa Barbara, CA 93101-3441
ph: 805-963-3134
fax: 805-963-3134

John W. Barry
Indian Rock Arts
P.O. Box 583
Davis, CA 95617-0583
ph: 530-758-2561
Dealer wants California Indian baskets, Pueblo Indian pottery, beadwork, Navajo rugs, old Navajo jewelry; also wants pre-1970 photographs and postcards of American Indian potters for research purposes.

Syd Bottomley, ISA
Sagebrush Gallery
P.O. Box 1842
Nevada City, CA 95959-1842
ph: 530-272-6367
fax: 530-272-2820
findsyd@oro.net
http://www.sagebrushgallery.com
Buys, collects, appraises and specializes in American Indian art: baskets, rugs, pottery, early California paintings.

Arthur W. Erickson
Arthur E. Erickson, Inc.
1030 SW Taylor
Portland, OR 97205-2504
ph: 503-227-4710
fax: 503-279-9146
arthur@arthurwerickson.com
Buys and sells antique Native American and Eskimo arts with an emphasis on Columbian River items such as Wasco Sally bags, corn husk bags, Klicitat baskets and plateau figural and contour beadwork.

Randeen Cummings, ISA CAPP
Cummings & Associates
P.O. Box 5484
Eugene, OR 97405-0484
ph: 541-345-5856
fax: 541-345-8192
avaluequest@uswest.net
http://www.avaluequest.com
Specializes in selling & appraising residential contents, fine art, estate jewelry, 18th & 19th century antiques, American Brilliant period cut glass; also specialized marketing for clients: consultations, estate, and Internet sales.

Kevin C. McIntosh
Kevin's Fine American Indian Art
270 Southridge Way
Grants Pass, OR 97527
ph: 541-476-1028
mkjudy@qwest.net
Collector and dealer of southern OR and northern CA native American Indian basketry and related ethnographic material; specializes in Hupa, Yurok, and Karuk areas; seeking sinew-backed painted bows, wood stemmed pipes, elk horn items.

Brill Lee
P.O. Box 244
Bellevue, WA 98009-0244
ph: 425-885-4518
fax: 425-895-1022
brilllee@hotmail.com
Buys, sells, and appraises pre-1960 Native American Indian artifacts, beadwork, baskets, clothing, parfleche, weapons and related items.

Experts

Gary L. Fogelman
245 Fairview Rd.
Turbotville, PA 17772-9063
ph: 570-437-3698
fax: 570-437-3411
iam@uplink.net
http://www.indian-artifacts.net
Specializes in and buys Indian artifacts: single pieces or entire collections; appraisals; author of "A Projectile Point Typology for PA and the Northeast" and "An Identification and Price Guide for Indian Artifacts of the Northeast, etc."

Roy Harrell
P.O. Box 95
Ocean View, DE 19970
ph: 302-537-6287
roywow@aol.com
Expert in Native American Indian items.

Terry L. Schafer
American Indian Art & Antiques
Rt #9 Box 295
Marietta, OH 45750
ph: 740-374-2807
wj_tschafer@seovec.org
Wants old Indian items: baskets, blankets, beadwork, Navajo rugs and old pawn jewelry.

Peter Eller, ISA
Peter Eller Gallery & Appraisers
206 Dartmouth
Albuquerque, NM 87106
ph: 505-268-7437
fax: 505-268-6442
pelgal@nmia.com
http://www.peterellergallery.com
Specializes in and appraises American, Southwest, and "Western" art; also Pueblo pottery, Navajo rugs and other weavings, Spanish colonial artifacts of the Southwest.

Mary Elizabeth McDonald
620 Sierra Dr. SE
Albuquerque, NM 87108-3377
ph: 505-265-2842

Don Bennett
Don Bennett & Associates
P.O. Box 283
Agoura Hills, CA 91376-0283
ph: 818-991-5596
fax: 818-991-6866
artofwest@aol.com
Collects, buys, sells and appraises high quality antique Native American items: Navajo, baskets, etc.; also paintings by deceased Western artists; since 1968.

Internet Resources

Longhouse Marketplace
1425 NE Irving, Ste. 225
Portland, OR 97232
longhouse@indianbaskets.com
http://www.indianbaskets.com
A Web site bringing together buyers and sellers of authentic American Indian baskets and clothing.

Museums/Libraries

Donald Cumberland, Mus. Ser.
U.S. Department of the Interior Museum, The
1849 C. St. NW
Mail Stop 1024
Washington, DC 20240
ph: 202-208-4743
Donald_R_Cumberland@nbc.gov
http://museums.doi.gov/museum
Educates the public and DOI employees about the missions and programs of the Dept. of Interior; acquires objects appropriate for promoting understanding of the Department's activities.

National Museum of Natural History
10th St. & Constitution Ave.
Washington, DC 20560
ph: 202-357-2700
dennis@smithson.si.edu
http://www.mnh.si.edu

National Museum of the American Indian
470 L'Enfant Plaza, SW, Ste. 7102
Washington, DC 20560
ph: 301-238-6624
NIN@ic.si.edu
http://www.si.edu/nmai
The museum will open on the Mall in Washington, DC, in the year 2002, on a site between the National Air & Space Museum and the US Capitol; will be a center for exhibitions, ceremonies, performances, and educational activities

Museum of the Cherokee Indian
P.O. Box 1599
Cherokee, NC 28719-1599
ph: 828-497-3481
fax: 828-497-4985
littlejohn@cherokeemuseum.org
http://www.cherokeemuseum.org
Located on the Cherokee Indian Reservation, the museum tells the story of the Cherokee Indians through dramatic exhibits.

Erik Alexander
Grand Rapids Public Museum
272 Pearl St. NW
Grand Rapids, MI 49504-5371
ph: 616-456-3977
fax: 616-456-3873
staff@grmuseum.org
http://www.grmuseum.org
Exhibits, publications and research information relating to West Michigan's Ottawa, Potawatomi, and Chippewa people; also Great Lakes Indian beadwork.

Field Museum of Natural History
1400 S. Lake Shore Dr.
Chicago, IL 60605-2496
ph: 312-922-9410
webmaster@fmnh.org
http://www.fieldmuseum.org

Jerry P. Martin, Dir.
Mid-America All-Indian Center
650 North Seneca
Wichita, KS 67203
ph: 316-262-5221
fax: 316-262-4216
info@theindiancenter.com
http://www.theindiancenter.com
Dedicated to the preservation of Native American Heritage; features a wide range of exhibitions displaying contemporary art as well as traditional artifacts.

Diana Pardue
Heard Museum, The
2301 N. Central Ave.
Phoenix, AZ 85004
ph: 602-252-8848 or 602-252-8840
fax: 602-252-9757
webmaster@heard.org
http://www.heard.org
Has over 32,000 works of art and ethnographic objects including more than 4,000 objects from the Fred Harvey Company Fine Art Collection.

Betty L. Cornelius
Colorado River Indian Tribes Museum
Rte. 1 Box 23-B
Parker, AZ 85344-9704
ph: 520-669-9211
fax: 520-669-8262
Displays Mohave, Chemehuevi, Navajo, and Hopi artifacts and prehistoric Mogollon, Anasazi, Hohokam, and Patayan collections.

Amerind Foundation, Inc.
P.O. Box 400
Dragoon, AZ 85609
ph: 520-586-3666
fax: 520-586-4679
amerind@amerind.org
http://www.amerind.org
Archaeology and ethnology museum, art gallery, and research library; archaeological collections from the Americas; ethnological material from the SW, Mexico, Great Plains, Eastern Woodlands, CA, Arctic.

Institute of American Indian Arts Museum
108 Cathedral Place
Santa Fe, NM 87501
ph: 505-983-1777 or 505-983-8900
canoka@iaiancad.org
http://www.iaiancad.org
Home to a unique collection of contemporary American Indian and Alaska Native art and some historical material; over 6,500 paintings, sculpture, ceramics, jewelry, graphics, costumes, beadwork, textiles.

Museum of New Mexico
107 West Palace Ave.
P.O. Box 2087
Santa Fe, NM 87501
ph: 505-827-6463
fax: 505-476-5076
jmarshall@mnm.state.nm.us
http://www.museumofnewmexico.org
Made up of four museums which house the country's most intriguing collection of New Mexico art, history and culture: Museum of Indian Arts & Culture, Museum of International Folk Art, Museum of Fine Arts, Palace of the Governors.

Jonathan Batkin, Dir.
Wheelwright Museum of the American Indian, The
Newsletter: Messenger, The
704 Camino Lejo
Santa Fe, NM 87505
ph: 505-982-4636 or 800-607-4636
fax: 505-988-7386
info@wheelwright.org
http://www.wheelwright.org
Hosts changing exhibitions of contemporary and history Native American art with an emphasis on the Southwest.

Southwest Museum
234 Museum Dr.
Los Angeles, CA 90065
ph: 323-221-2164
info@southwestmuseum.org
http://www.southwestmuseum.org
Holds one of the nation's most important collections related to the American Indian; also extensive holdings of prehistoric, Spanish Colonial, Latino, and Western American art and artifacts.

Bev Cornwall
Favell Museum of Western Art & Indian Artifacts
125 W. Main St.
Klamath Falls, OR 97601
ph: 541-882-9996
fax: 541-850-0125
favmusem@internetcds.com
http://www.favellmuseum.com
Collection contains works by over 300 Western artists as well as over 100,000 Indian artifacts; has art sales gallery and gift shop at the museum.

Maryhill Museum of Art
35 Maryhill Museum Dr.
Goldendale, WA 98620-4601
ph: 509-773-3733
fax: 509-773-6138
MaryHill@gorge.net
http://www.maryhillmuseum.org
The extensive 5,000 piece Native American collection comprises rare prehistoric rock carvings, baskets, beadwork, and other objects which are seen as both art and artifact.

Periodicals

Gary L. Fogelman
Magazine: Indian Artifact Magazine
245 Fairview Rd.
Turbotville, PA 17772-9063
ph: 570-437-3698
fax: 570-437-3411
iam@uplink.net
http://www.indian-artifacts.net
An easy reading quarterly focusing on American Indian prehistory: artifacts, tools, lifestyles, customs, archaeology, book reviews; everything about collecting, buying, finding and enjoying Indian artifacts.

Jack Heriard
Written Heritage, Inc.
Magazine: Whispering Wind Magazine
P.O. Box 1390
Folsom, LA 70437
ph: 985-796-5433 or 800-301-8009
fax: 985-796-9236
whiswind@i-55.com
http://www.whisperingwind.com
Crafts, pow-wows, books, history, tradition; subscribers are crafts people, book buyers and Indian art and antique collectors.

American Indian Art, Inc.
Magazine: American Indian Art Magazine
7314 E. Osborn Dr.
Scottsdale, AZ 85251-6418
ph: 480-994-5445
fax: 480-945-9533
Quarterly art journal devoted to native American art from prehistoric to modern; gorgeous photographs, auction reports, reports on ethnographic and fine arts items, "Legal Briefs" column.

Martin Link, Pub.
Newspaper: Indian Trader, The
P.O. Box 1421
Gallup, NM 87305-1421
ph: 505-722-6694 or 800-748-1624
fax: 505-722-6696
trader@cia-g.com
http://www.cia-g.com/~trader/index.htm
Focuses on old and new Indian art and artifacts.

John M. Gogol
Magazine: American Indian Basketry
P.O. Box 66124
Portland, OR 97260-6124
ph: 503-233-8131
A magazine dedicated to Native American Indian arts: basketry, beadwork, pottery, baskets and weaving, textiles, masks, jewelry, etc.

Baskets

Collectors

John R. Joiner
130 Peninsula Circle
Newnan, GA 30265
ph: 770-502-9565
propjj@numail.org
Buying Cherokee Indian rivercane baskets; prefers older baskets in good condition, but will consider buying any rivercane basket.

Dealers

Syd Bottomley, ISA
Sagebrush Gallery
P.O. Box 1842
Nevada City, CA 95959-1842
ph: 530-272-6367
fax: 530-272-2820
findsyd@oro.net
http://www.sagebrushgallery.com
Buys, collects, appraises and specializes in American Indian art:

baskets, rugs, pottery, early
California paintings.

Experts

Barry Friedman
P.O. Box 55492
Valencia, CA 91385-0492
ph: 661-255-2365
BarryF@thevine.net
http://www.blanketboy.com
*Wants to buy pre-1940 undamaged
Indian baskets; please send good
photo, dimensions and price; all
letters answered!*

Brenda Butler Focht
Riverside Municipal Museum
3580 Mission Inn Ave.
Riverside, CA 92501
ph: 909-826-5273
fax: 909-369-4970
bfocht@ci.riverside.ca.us
http://www.ci.riverside.ca.us/museum
*Can identify Native American
basketry; Riverside Museum Press
published 3 catalogs written by Chris
Moser: 1986 "Basketry of Central
California," 1989 "Basketry of
Northern California," 1993 "Basketry
of Southern California."*

Museums/Libraries

Diana Pardue
Heard Museum, The
2301 N. Central Ave.
Phoenix, AZ 85004
ph: 602-252-8848 or 602-252-8840
fax: 602-252-9757
webmaster@heard.org
http://www.heard.org
*Has over 32,000 works of art and
ethnographic objects including more
than 4,000 objects from the Fred
Harvey Company Fine Art Collection;
has an extensive collection of Native
American baskets.*

Grenfell Labrador Industries

Experts

Barry Friedman
P.O. Box 55492
Valencia, CA 91385-0492
ph: 661-255-2365
BarryF@thevine.net
http://www.blanketboy.com
*Wants to buy any textile or purses
labeled "Grenfell Labrador
Industries." These always picture
Northern scenes (polar bears,
Eskimos, etc.); undamaged pieces only;
send photo, dimensions, and price; all
letters answered!*

Repro. Sources

Norma Larkin
Grenfell Handicrafts
P.O. Box 280
St. Anthony, Newfoundland AOK 4S0
Canada
ph: 709-454-3576
fax: 709-454-4047
info@grenfell-properties.com
http://www.grenfell-properties.com
*Send for free catalog of new Grenfell
mats currently for sale.*

Jewelry

Appraisers

Larry Phillips, GG, ISA
Phillips & Associates
P.O. Box 51327
Albuquerque, NM 87181-1327
ph: 505-299-7999
fax: 505-299-7999
phillips@gemologist-appraiser.com
*Master Gemologist Appraiser;
specializes in Native American
jewelry.*

Dealers

Navajo Silversmith, The
ph: 928-339-1948
sales@navajosilversmith.com
http://www.navajosilversmith.com
*Specializes in traditional Navajo
jewelry designs; all jewelry is custom
made from start to finish; Web
contains FAQs about silversmithing
and turquoise.*

Dianne Kennedy
Tribal Offerings
394 Commercial St.
Provincetown, MA 02657
ph: 508-587-4857
info@tribalofferings.com
http://www.tribalofferings.com
*Specializes in American Indian
jewelry.*

Lani Randall, GG
Rocking Horse Southwest Jewelry
2415 W. Glenrosa Ave.
Phoenix, AZ 85015
ph: 602-265-1061
fax: 602-285-3067
info@indianjewelry.com
http://www.indianjewelry.com
*Dedicated to the fine art of Native
American Indian jewelry; since 1945;
consumer information, appraisals.*

Skystone Creations
833 E. Broadway
Mesa, AZ 85204
ph: 480-964-1922
fax: 480-964-2859
skystonecreations@worldnet.att.net
http://www.skystonecreations.com
*Carries high quality Navajo Indian
jewelry.*

Yellowhorse Museum & Gallery
9100 North Morning Glort Rd.
Paradise Valley, AZ 85253
ph: 480-948-9273
fax: 480-948-1999
info@yellowhorse.com
http://www.yellowhorse.com
*Great source for high quality Native
American and Western jewelry and
art.*

Lisa Barret
Kokopelli Traders
P.O. Box 5462
Tucson, AZ 85703-0462
ph: 520-743-4356
fax: 520-743-4356
info@kokopellitraders.com
http://www.kokopellitraders.com
*Authentic handcrafted jewelry created
by skilled Navajo craftsmen.*

Terry Schurmeier
Cowboys & Indians Antiques
4000 Central SE
Albuquerque, NM 87108
ph: 505-255-4054 or 505-255-5775
fax: 505-255-1730
cowgirls@rt66.com
http://www.cowboysandindiansnm.com
*Carries large inventory of pre-1940s
Native American pottery, baskets,
beadwork, jewelry, textiles; antique
devotional art, art of the Old West;
also Old West, Spanish Colonial, old
pawn & Mexican jewelry; buy, sell,
trade, appraise.*

Thunderbird Jewelry Company
1923 West Historic Route 66
Gallup, NM 87301
ph: 800-545-7998
fax: 505-722-9250
webmaster@thunderbird-jewelry.com
http://www.thunderbird-jewelry.com

Dave Elkins
Navajo Shopping Center
P.O. Box 77
Gamerco, NM 87317
ph: 800-825-5777 or 505-863-6897
fax: 505-722-9120
info@navajoshop.com
http://www.navajoshop.com
Specializes in quality Navajo jewelry.

Julia & Harry Theobald
Skystone Trading Co.
7 Avenida Vista Grande #159
Santa Fe, NM 87505-9199
ph: 505-466-4588
fax: 505-466-4587
theo@skystonetrading.com
http://www.skystonetrading.com
*Offers only the highest quality
Southwest American Indian turquoise
and silver jewelry.*

Kachina Dolls

Dealers

World City, Inc.
6935 James Ave. South
Minneapolis, MN 55423-2147
*Buys and sells Indian items such as
beaded items, pottery, Navajo rugs,*

quilled items, Kachinas, Northwest
Coast items; both pre-historic and
historic; send price wanted (unless
unsure), description, photos, and
SASE.

Squash Blossom, The
2531 W. Colorado Ave.
Colorado Springs, CO 80904
ph: 719-632-1899
fax: 719-635-4304
staff@squashblossom.com
http://www.squashblossom.com
*Dealer/appraiser specializing in
Southwestern Native American jewelry
and art including pottery, weaving,
Kachinas (both prehistoric and
historic.)*

John C. Hill
Gallery of American Indian Art
6962 East First Ave., Ste. 104
Scottsdale, AZ 85251-4302
ph: 480-946-2910
fax: 480-946-7410
antqindart@aol.com
*Wants to buy early Southwest Indian
items including classic Navajo &
Pueblo silver & turquoise, Indian
blankets and other textiles, Kachina
dolls, early pottery; also wants Plains
and Northeast Indian beadwork, and
fine Indian basketry.*

Alexander Anthony, Jr.
Adobe Gallery
413 Romero NW
Albuquerque, NM 87104-1421
ph: 505-243-8485 or 800-821-5221
fax: 505-243-8403
info@adobegallery.com
http://www.adobegallery.com
*Specializing in art of the Southwest
Indian: historic Pueblo pottery,
Navajo blankets and rugs, Hopi
Kachina dolls and Navajo and Pueblo
pawn jewelry.*

Experts

John C. Hill
Hill Antique Indian Art Gallery
6962 East First Ave.
Scottsdale, AZ 85251
ph: 480-946-2910
fax: 480-946-7410
Antqindart@aol.com
http://www.maineantiquedigest.com/
adimg/johnhill.htm
*Dealer, expert, appraiser of early
Native American Indian art; specialist
in Hopi material culture (Hopi
Kachinas), historic pottery of the
Southwest, Native American jewelry
(old pawn), Navajo & Pueblo textiles,
baskets, beadwork, etc.*

Museums/Libraries

Diana Pardue
Heard Museum, The
2301 N. Central Ave.
Phoenix, AZ 85004
ph: 602-252-8848 or 602-252-8840
fax: 602-252-9757
webmaster@heard.org
http://www.heard.org
Has over 32,000 works of art and ethnographic objects and one of the largest collections of Hopi Kachina dolls including 437 historic Kachina dolls from the Barry Goldwater Collection.

Navajo

Dealers

Tyrone Campbell
Tyrone D. Campbell Gallery
8900 E. Pinnacle Peak Rd., B-2
Scottsdale, AZ 85255
ph: 480-502-8899 or 602-741-4505
fax: 480-502-4795
tyronecampbell@qwest.net
Buys and sells antique American Indian weavings: Navajo, Pueblo and Hispanic weavings and folk art; specializes in appraising collections, consultations, and research of 19th & 20th C. Navajo weavings.

Experts

Gregg Leighton
Notah Dineh
345 West Main
Cortez, CO 81321
ph: 800-444-2024 or 970-565-9607
notah@fone.net
http://subee.com/nd/home.html
Buys and sells wide range of Navajo rugs, antique and contemporary; also carries large assortment of contemporary American Indian crafts and jewelry.

Steve Getzwiller
Classic & Contemporary Amerind Art
P.O. Box 36
Spear G Ranch
Benson, AZ 85602
ph: 520-586-2579
fax: 520-586-2960
getzwiller@theriver.com
Recognized authority, dealer and collector of American Indian art; specializing in Navajo weavings, historic and contemporary; author of "The Fine Art of Navajo Weaving;" buys and sells Indian art collections.

Barry Friedman
P.O. Box 55492
Valencia, CA 91385-0492
ph: 661-255-2365
BarryF@thevine.net
http://www.blanketboy.com
Wants to purchase pre-1940 Navajo rugs; send photo, condition, and price; undamaged items only; all letters answered!

Museums/Libraries

Navajo National Monument Museum
HC 71 Box 3
Tonalea, AZ 86044-9704
ph: 520-672-2700
fax: 520-672-2703
http://www.nps.gov/nava
A national monument featuring the best preserved cliff dwellings in the SW; small museum and library (no checkout) for research (copier not available); prehistoric Pueblo and Navajo exhibits.

Pottery

Appraisers

Casey Reed
Material Culture
1727 Dietz Plaza, NW
Albuquerque, NM 87107
ph: 505-344-8492
fax: 505-344-8492
Casey@material-insight.com
http://www.material-insight.com/PuebloPotteryRestoration.htm
Conservation and restoration of Pueblo pottery; application of traditional and unique methodologies to preserve the past; also collects and appraises Pueblo pottery.

Collectors

Terry Ahlberg
1000 Irvine Blvd.
Tustin, CA 92780-3527
ph: 714-730-1000 or 949-856-9395
fax: 714-730-1752
emailit@earthlink.net
Wants American Indian pottery primarily from the tribes of Hopi, Santa Clara, San Ildefonso, Acoma, Laguna, Santo Domingo, and Zuni; also interested in Navajo rugs and other Native American items.

Experts

John W. Barry
Indian Rock Arts
P.O. Box 583
Davis, CA 95617-0583
ph: 530-758-2561
Appraises Pueblo Indian pottery; author of "American Indian Pottery" (Books Americana), 1981; contributor to "Encyclopedia Native American in the 20th Century" (Garland Publishing) and "North American Artifacts" by Lar Hothem.

Internet Resources

James A. Ringold
Pueblo Pottery Classroom
jringold@umich.edu
http://www.ipl.org/div/pottery/classroom.htm
An introduction to Pueblo pottery: peoples of the Southwest, manufacturer of pottery, prehistoric pottery, historic Pueblo pottery, images, artifacts.

Museums/Libraries

Cherokee National Museum
P.O. Box 515
Tahlequah, OK 74465-0515
ph: 918-456-6007
fax: 918-456-6165
http://www.powersource.com/heritage/museum.html
The only facility devoted to the preservation of the heritage of the Cherokee Nation, the second largest American tribe.

Diana Pardue
Heard Museum, The
2301 N. Central Ave.
Phoenix, AZ 85004
ph: 602-252-8848 or 602-252-8840
fax: 602-252-9757
webmaster@heard.org
http://www.heard.org
Has over 32,000 works of art and ethnographic objects including an extensive collection of pottery, especially pieces made by Native American cultures in the Southwestern United States.

Repair Services

Andy Goldschmidt
Ceramicare
P.O. Box 1812
Corrales, NM 87048
ph: 505-898-2728
agoldschmidt@earthlink.net
http://home.earthlink.net/~agoldschmidt/wizzg.html
Repairs and restores ceramic art; specializing in Native American Indian pottery - prehistoric, historic and contemporary.

Casey Reed
Material Culture
1727 Dietz Plaza, NW
Albuquerque, NM 87107
ph: 505-344-8492
fax: 505-344-8492
Casey@material-insight.com
http://www.material-insight.com/PuebloPotteryRestoration.htm
Conservation and restoration of Pueblo pottery; application of traditional and unique methodologies to preserve the past; also collects and appraises Pueblo pottery.

Skookum Dolls

Dealers

William W. Wynn
2117 Hillcrest St.
Fort Worth, TX 76107-4329
ph: 817-763-8424
Wants to buy Skookum Indian dolls, beaded Zuni dolls, pre-1950 Plains Indian and Navajo rag dolls; pre-1950 Kachina dolls, Navajo rugs, Pima & Apache baskets, and San Ildefonso, Hopi, Cochiti, Santo Domingo pottery.

Experts

Linda Larouche
Linda Larouche Antiques & Collectibles
P.O. Box 702
New York, NY 10018
ph: 718-230-3830
skookumgal@aol.com
http://www.skookumgal.com
Wants to buy Skookum Indian dolls in good condition.

Lesley Mitchell Polinko
Skookumkid
P.O. Box 91233
Pittsburgh, PA 15217
ph: 42-901-3953
http://www.skookumdoll.com
Author of "Skookum: The Great Indian Character Doll; A History and Guide;" always looking for new Skookum information; wants Skookum dolls and catalogs showing the dolls from the Arrow Novelty Co. of NY and H.H. Tammen Co. of Colorado.

Barry Friedman
P.O. Box 55492
Valencia, CA 91385-0492
ph: 661-255-2365
BarryF@thevine.net
http://www.blanketboy.com
Wants to buy undamaged Skookum Indian dolls over 20"; these dolls wear colorful Indian design blankets; send photo, size, and price; all letters answered!

Internet Resources

Linda Larouche
Linda Larouche Antiques & Collectibles
P.O. Box 702
New York, NY 10018
ph: 718-230-3830
skookumgal@aol.com
http://www.skookumgal.com
Web site has the first online history of Skookum Indian dolls.

Totems

Dealers

John Cavanagh
Linda Larouche Antiques & Collectibles
606 Carlton Ave.
Brooklyn, NY 11238-3407
ph: 718-230-3830 or 212-431-5225
jcav@stray-light.com
http://www.skookumgal.com
Buys and sells well-carved pre-1945 Pacific NW and Eskimo model totems in wood, bone or ivory; also wants ivory carved animals, fish, salt & peppers; Native American made dolls.

NATIVE AMERICAN (MODERN)

Clubs/Associations

Indian Arts & Crafts Association
Newsletter: IACA Newsletter
4010 Carlisle NE, Ste. C
Albuquerque, NM 87107
ph: 505-265-9149
fax: 505-265-8251
info@iaca.com
http://www.iaca.com
Purpose is to collect, promote, preserve, protect and enhance the understanding of authentic American Indian crafts and arts.

Dealers

Bonnie Pulver
Wild Wind Creations
279 East Central St., Ste. 105
Franklin, MA 02038
bpulver@norfolk-county.com
http://www.wildwind.com
Sells items made by Native Americans and provides support for their efforts to preserve their culture.

Carol Halberstadt
Migrations
P.O. Box 543
Newton, MA 02456
carol@migrations.com
http://www.migrations.com
Specializes in older and contemporary Native American and Inuit/Eskimo art: weavings, pottery, baskets, jewelry, sculpture; online gallery with links to a wide variety of Native American resources.

Carol Halberstadt
Black Mesa Weavers for Life and Land
P.O. Box 543
Newton, MA 02456
carol@migrations.com
http://www.migrations.com/blackmesa/
blackmesa.html
A nonprofit enterprise selling weavings and wool of the Diné (Navajo) of Black Mesa, AZ; proceeds help sustain their lives, land and culture.

Richard Sutton
Kiva Trading Company
117 Main St.
Cold Spring Harbor, NY 11724
ph: 631-367-2875 or 800-947-8461
fax: 631-367-2834
http://www.kivatrading.com
NY metro's most complete selection of authentic American Indian handcrafted arts: jewelry, pottery, Kachina dolls, fetish carvings, weavings, fine hanging arts, sculpture; no imports or knock-offs; Web site has lots of images.

Peyton M. Alexander
Native American Traders
151 Dekalb Industrial Way
Decatur, GA 30030-2201
ph: 404-787-1787
fax: 770-496-9797
pma@nativeamericantraders.com
http://www.nativeamericantraders.com
Carries Native arts including Kachina dolls, Navajo weavings, prehistoric pots, paintings, "Arizona Highway" and "American Indian Art" magazines along with a large selection of "Indian Event" posters.

White Buffalo Collectibles
3113 S. Ridgewood Ave.
Edgewater, FL 32141
ph: 386-427-8522 or 877-9BUFFALO
fax: 386-427-3915
sales@whitebuffalo1.com
http://www.whitebuffalo1.com
Carries Native American artifacts, Kachinas, Shalakos, pottery, fetishes, weapons, quivers, bow & arrows, war clubs, shields, masks, knives, spears, turquoise, and other authentic Native American crafts; Ute, Navajo, Acoma; Santa Clara.

Adobe East
328 East Atlantic Ave.
Delray Beach, FL 33483
ph: 561-330-8484 or 800-242-3623
fax: 908-277-1483
Hopi, Kachina dolls, Native American Pueblo pottery and jewelry, sculpture, paintings, Zuni fetishes.

Red Crow Snapp
Native American Connection
3215 Brainerd Rd
Chattanooga, TN 37411
ph: 423-624-5061
Specializes in antique repair and replating, and design and creation of custom jewelry; carries a variety of Native American crafts.

WhiteBark Design
P.O. Box 6739
Kokomo, IN 46904-6739
ph: 765-459-8741
barri@iquest.net
http://www.nativecreations.com
Native American made and related art, artifacts, books, apparel, supplies and more.

Harry Bradshaw
Reflections of Culture
P.O. Box 764
1413 Montclair Place
Fort Atkinson, WI 53538
ph: 800-655-0553 or 608-423-3223
fax: 608-423-9744
culture@charter.net
http://www.reflectionsofculture.com
Specializing in the sale of Native art from all North America; member of the Indian Arts & Crafts Association; galleries located in Cambridge, WI and Monona, WI.

Colleen Miller
Prairie Edge, Inc.
P.O. Box 8303
Rapid City, SD 57709
ph: 605-342-3086
fax: 605-341-6415
prairie@rapidnet.com
http://www.prairieedge.com
Deals in contemporary reproductions of Plains Indians arts, crafts and jewelry.

Merritt L. Smith
Indian Sun Gallery
1805 Fairview St.
Houston, TX 77006
ph: 866-494-5939
info@indiansun.net
http://www.indiansun.net
Offers Native American and Latin American pottery, jewelry, fine art and folk art; specializes in Navajo, Zuni, and Hopi jewelry and pottery.

Jill Giller
Native American Collections, Inc.
338 Eudora St.
Denver, CO 80220
ph: 303-321-1071
fax: 303-321-1156
Jillspots@aol.com
http://www.nativepots.com
A unique contemporary gallery showcasing the finest in handmade Pueblo pottery, Zuni Fetishes, Navajo folk art, sculpture, and Indian jewelry; welcomes special orders.

Anne Goldstein
Elk Ridge Art Company
25918 Genessee Trail Rd., #150
Golden, CO 80401
ph: 303-526-1561 or 800-713-0763
fax: 303-526-5271
GoldAnne@aol.com
http://www.elkridgeart.com
Carries fine Native American art, paintings, pottery, Navajo rugs and jewelry.

Georgiana Kennedy Simpson
Kennedy Indian Arts
P.O. Box 39
Bluff, UT 84512
ph: 435-672-2405
fax: 435-672-2406
kennedyi@frontiernet.net
Since 1908 specializing in pottery, jewelry, fetishes, rugs, baskets, Kachinas, novelties, folk art.

John & Sharon Bryant
Dancing Horses
P.O. Box 30357
Mesa, AZ 85275-0357
ph: 602-924-3226
fax: 602-981-6281
jsbryant@amug.org
Authentic Native American collectibles handcrafted by artists: dream catchers, to tomahawks.

Stephen Osborne
Desert Son American Indian Art
4759 E. Sunrise Dr.
Tucson, AZ 85718
ph: 520-299-0818
info@desertson.com
http://www.desertson.com
Dealing in quality Indian goods for over 30 years; handmade traditional Southwestern moccasins, gold and silver jewelry, Kachinas, rugs, pottery, buckles, belts; excellent buckle collection including Ranger sets; Hopi Kachina repair.

Jay Tallant
Canyon Country Originals
6030 E. Fangio Place
Tucson, AZ 85750
ph: 520-529-5545
fax: 520-529-1456
cainfo@canyonart.com
http://canyonart.com
Web site has large collection of Southwestern Indian arts & crafts; specializing in pottery from Hopi, Acoma, Zuni, Jemez, Cochiti, San Ildefonso, Santa Clara, San Juan pueblos; authentic Navajo rugs, jewelry.

Ron McGee
McGee's Indian Art Gallery
P.O. Box 607, Hwy. 264
Keams Canyon, AZ 86034
ph: 928-738-2295
fax: 928-738-5250
sales@hopiart.com
http://www.hopiart.com
Located on the Hopi Reservation for over 50 years; specializing in Hopi jewelry, Kachinas and pottery.

Ancient Nations: Indigenous Arts
P.O. Box 1346
Keams Canyon, AZ 86034
ph: 800-854-1359
sales@ancientnations.com
http://www.ancientnations.com

Lucky Mokhesi
Van's Trading Company
P.O. Box 7
Tuba City, AZ 86045
ph: 520-283-5343
fax: 520-283-4333
lm1@citlink.net
Navajo owned and operated trading post on the Navajo Reservation; dating back to 1940s; authentic Navajo arts & crafts, rugs, Hopi Kachina carvings; pawn jewelry; monthly auctions.

Pueblo Pottery Gallery
P.O. Box 366
San Fidel, NM 87049
ph: 505-552-6748 or 800-933-5771
fax: 505-552-6748
pueblopottery@mindspring.com
http://www.pueblopotterygallery.com
Featuring quality pottery, Kachinas, jewelry, fetishes, rugs, Acoma photographs and prints; numerous artists represented.

Thomas Baker
Tanner Chaney Gallery
410 Romero NW
Albuquerque, NM 87104
ph: 505-247-2242
fax: 505-298-3434
tbaker@tannerchaneygallery.com
http://www.tannerchaneygallery.com
Sells and appraises contemporary and antique Native American jewelry, weavings and pottery.

Alexander Anthony, Jr.
Adobe Gallery
413 Romero NW
Albuquerque, NM 87104-1421
ph: 505-243-8485 or 800-821-5221
fax: 505-243-8403
info@adobegallery.com
http://www.adobegallery.com
Specializing in art of the Southwest Indian: historic Pueblo pottery, Navajo blankets and rugs, Hopi Kachina dolls and Navajo and Pueblo pawn jewelry.

Georgiana Kennedy Simpson
Kennedy Gallery
P.O. Box 6526
Albuquerque, NM 87197
ph: 505-344-7538
fax: 505-343-1382
kennedyi@frontiernet.net
Showcases top examples of contemporary Native American art: weavings, basketry, Navajo folk art, contemporary Indian jewelry, pottery.

Ron Fernandez
Bien Mur Indian Market Center
I-25 N & Tramway Rd.
P.O. Box 91148
Albuquerque, NM 87199
ph: 505-821-5400 or 800-365-5400
info@bienmur.com
http://www.bienmur.com
Sells original Native American Indian art & crafts: fetishes, turquoise, Kachinas, Navajo rugs, sand paintings, jewelry, pottery, etc.

Bill Foutz
Foutz Trading Co.
P.O. Box 1094
Shiprock, NM 87420-1904
ph: 505-368-5790 or 800-383-0615
fax: 505-368-4441
info@foutzrug.com
http://www.foutzrug.com
Specializing in Navajo rugs, sand paintings, Kachinas, sculptures, Navajo pottery, beadwork.

Arch Thiessen
Sunshine Studio
3180 Vista Sandia
Santa Fe, NM 87501
ph: 800-348-9273 or 505-985-3216
fax: 505-986-0765
sunshine@sunshinestudio.com
http://www.sunshinestudio.com
Specializes in Southwest American Indian art, including antique and contemporary: Zuni fetishes, American Indian silver and turquoise jewelry, Pueblo pottery, Navajo rugs, Hopi

Kachinas, Native American paintings, baskets, etc.

Peter Kahn
Keshi the Zuni Connection
227 Don Gaspar
Santa Fe, NM 87501
ph: 509-989-8728
zuniart@keshi.com
http://www.keshi.com
Your connection to authentic arts & crafts from the Zuni Pueblo: traditional Zuni jewelry, fetish carvings and medicine bags.

Buzz Trevathan
Cristof's
420 Old Santa Fe Trail
Santa Fe, NM 87501
ph: 505-988-9881 or 877-389-6393
fax: 505-986-8652
buzzart@cristofs.com
http://www.cristofs.com
An internationally recognized primary source for contemporary museum quality Navajo weavings such as rugs, tapestries, wall hangings; also carries Hopi Kachinas, Navajo sand paintings, Navajo Yeibichai carvings, and other works of art.

Matthew Maxwell
Pueblo Pottery New Mexico
503 Canyon Rd.
Santa Fe, NM 87501
ph: 505-986-1095
fax: 505-986-0051
pottery@pueblopottery.com
http://www.pueblopottery.com
Online gallery of contemporary Pueblo Indian pottery including Hopi, Santa Clara, San Ildefonso, Acoma, Santa Domingo and others.

Lisa Trujillo
Centinela Traditional Arts
CHR 64, Box 4
Chimayo, NM 87522
ph: 877-351-2180 or 505-351-2180
fax: 505-351-4008
centinela@newmexico.com
http://www.chimayoweavers.com
A tapestry gallery in New Mexico specializing in handwoven wool products using natural dyes, custom-dyed yarns, handspun yarns, and the traditional New Mexico Hispanic Rio Grande styles.

Rainmaker-Art
P.O. Box 3801
Hollywood Station
Los Angeles, CA 90078-3801
ph: 818-951-3663
fax: 818-951-3663
Rainmaker@Rainmaker-art.com
http://www.Rainmaker-Art.com
Dealer, expert, appraiser of modern Native American arts & crafts for over 20 years: Hopi Kachina dolls, Navajo rugs, Zuni fetishes, old pawn jewelry, beadwork, weapons, clothing, basketry, pottery.

Gallery of the American West
121 K St.
Sacramento, CA 95814
ph: 916-446-6662
fax: 916-446-1432
gallerywest@gallerywest.com
http://www.gallerywest.com
Buys and sells highest quality Native American handmade pieces.

Misc. Services

Indian Arts & Crafts Board
U.S. Dept. of the Interior
Room 4004 - MIB
Washington, DC 20240-0001
ph: 202-208-3773
fax: 202-208-5196
iacb@ios.doi.gov
http://www.iacb.doi.gov
Promotes American Indian and Alaska Native economic development; contact for information on how to order a "Source Directory" which lists Indian-owned and operated arts & crafts businesses throughout the country.

Periodicals

Magazine: Native Peoples
5333 N. 7th St., Ste. 224
Phoenix, AZ 85012
ph: 888-262-8483 or 602-265-4855
fax: 602-265-3113
sphillips@nativepeoples.com
http://www.nativepeoples.com
Focuses on contemporary Native American arts and crafts.

American Indian Art, Inc.
Magazine: American Indian Art Magazine
7314 E. Osborn Dr.
Scottsdale, AZ 85251-6418
ph: 480-994-5445
fax: 480-945-9533
Quarterly art journal devoted to native American art from prehistoric to modern; gorgeous photographs, auction reports, reports on ethnographic and fine arts items, "Legal Briefs" column.

Martin Link, Pub.
Newspaper: Indian Trader, The
P.O. Box 1421
Gallup, NM 87305-1421
ph: 505-722-6694 or 800-748-1624
fax: 505-722-6696
trader@cia-g.com
http://www.cia-g.com/~trader/index.htm
Focuses on old and new Indian art and artifacts.

John M. Gogol
Magazine: American Indian Basketry
P.O. Box 66124
Portland, OR 97260-6124
ph: 503-233-8131
A magazine dedicated to Native American Indian arts: basketry, beadwork, pottery, baskets and weaving, textiles, masks, jewelry, etc.

NATURAL HISTORY

(see also ANIMAL COLLECTIBLES; ASTRONOMICAL ITEMS; BOOKS, Reference [Natural History]; CAVE RELATED ITEMS; FOSSILS; HERITAGE RESOURCES; LAPIDARY; MARBLE & STONE; MINERAL SPECIMENS; SEASHELLS)

Book Sellers

Frank J. Mikesh
1356 Walden Rd.
Walnut Creek, CA 94596-3158
ph: 925-934-9243
fax: 925-947-6113
natscibooks@netvista.net
http://www.netvista.net/~natscibooks
Interested in out-of-print natural history, hunting, fishing, sporting, and wildlife books, and related art.

Museums/Libraries

Amy Chionchio, Marketing
Milwaukee Public Museum
800 W. Wells St.
Milwaukee, WI 53233-1478
ph: 414-278-2702
amy@mpm.edu
http://www.mpm.edu
A museum of human and natural history: permanent butterfly wing with hundreds of live butterflies in a tropical garden; an American POW-WOW; authentic rain forest; IMAX Theater.

NAUTICAL ANTIQUES

(see also ART, Marine; BOATS; COAST GUARD; DIVING EQUIPMENT; INSTRUMENTS & DEVICES; MAPS & CHARTS; IVORY; OCEAN LINER MEMORABILIA; SCRIMSHAW; SEASHELLS; SHIPPING; SHIP RELATED; STEAMBOAT COLLECTIBLES; TITANIC MEMORABILIA; WHALING)

Appraisers

Peter C. Sorlien, ASA
Accredited Appraisers
17-1/2 State St.
Marblehead, MA 01945-3536
ph: 781-631-5956
fax: 781-631-6550
appraisr@shore.net
Professional nautical antiques and marine art appraisals; experience with divorce, donation, estate, insurance, litigation, and tax matters; does not buy or sell.

Sara Conklin, ISA
Nautical Appraisals
P.O. Box 30203
Blairsden, CA 96103
ph: 415-467-6249 or 800-464-4208
fax: 415-467-6249
sconklin2@pngusa.net
http://home.earthlink.net/~sconklin2
Appraises maritime items and collections: ship models, scrimshaw,

navigational instruments, figurehead carvings, marine art, paper & ephemera archival collections, telescopes, shipwrecks, diving equip., ocean liner memorabilia, whaling.

Auction Services

Chuck Deluca
Maritime Auctions
P.O. Box 322
York, ME 03909
ph: 207-363-4247
fax: 207-363-1416
info@maritiques.com
http://www.maritiques.com
Three catalog auctions per year in March, July and October.

Clubs/Associations

National Maritime Historical Society
Magazine: Sea History
5 John Walsh Blvd.
Peekskill, NY 10566
ph: 914-737-7378 or 800-221-6647
nmhs@seahistory.org
http://www.seahistory.org
Preservation (full-rigger ship, brigantine, schooner, tug boat), education to heighten the maritime awareness of young Americans across the country, and publication of the magazines "Sea History" and the monthly newsletter "Gazette."

Harry D. Barry
Air Horn & Steam Whistle Enthusiasts
Newsletter: Horn & Whistle
275 Windswept Dr.
North East, PA 16428
ph: 814-725-8150
Purpose is to preserve, increase, and disseminate knowledge concerning horns, whistles, sirens, and bells in industrial, marine, transportation, signaling, and warning applications.

Collectors

Stephen Buczko
27 Surrey Rd.
Salem, MA 01970-4362
ph: 978-744-4683
nsbuczko@aol.com
Collector wants to purchase nautical antiques such as navigation instruments, marine clocks, whaling artifacts, scrimshaw, early books, ships' log books & documents, pond model sailboats, etc.

Dick Hawkins
Columbia Trading Company
One Barnstable Rd.
Hyannis, MA 02601
ph: 508-778-2929
fax: 508-778-2922
info@columbiatrading.com
http://www.columbiatrading.com
Wants to buy all marine items; items relating to lighthouses, Coast Guard, naval, yachting, marine architecture, marine engineering, boating, sailing, marine engines, outboard motors, boat building, ship building, etc.

Stephen Seltzer
7912 Georgia Ave.
Silver Spring, MD 20910-4837
ph: 301-565-2444 or 301-565-3339
fax: 301-565-2228
eseltzer@aol.com
Wants to buy authentic brass items salvaged form ships.

Sam McDowell
P.O. Box 3546
Carmel, CA 93921
ph: 831-624-6787
fax: 831-624-6787
Wants to buy 19th century scrimshaw and other nautical collectibles.

Dealers

James W. Claflin
Kenrick A. Claflin & Son Nautical Antiques
30 Hudson St.
Northborough, MA 01532
ph: 508-869-6955
jclaflin@ma.ultranet.com
http://www.ultranet.com/~jclaflin
Collectors and dealers in fine nautical antiques; specializing in US Lighthouse Service, US Lifesaving Service, US Revenue Cutter Service, US Coast Guard.

Andrew Jacobson
Andrew Jacobson Marine Antiques
P.O. Box 437
Ipswich, MA 01938
ph: 978-356-5583
fax: 978-356-8705
andrew@marineantiques.com
http://www.marineantiques.com
Fine marine artifacts, paintings, models, half-hulls, antique scrimshaw, navigational instruments, photography, out-of-print books, manuscript material; regularly updated online catalog; storefront open by appointment.

Richard Dermody
Brass n' Bounty
68 Front St.
Marblehead, MA 01945-3275
ph: 781-631-3864 or 781-631-6204
bnb@brassandbounty.com
http://www.brassandbounty.com
Buys and sells navigation instruments, telescopes, binnacles, compasses, sextants, clocks, barometers; also yachting items.

Ed Lefkowicz
Edward J. Lefkowicz, Inc.
500 Angell St.
Providence, RI 02906
ph: 800-201-7901
fax: 401-277-1459
seabooks@saltbooks.com
http://www.saltbooks.com
Appraiser and dealer specializes in rare books and manuscripts relating to the sea, the islands, and nautical science: voyages, naval, navigation, polar, the Pacific, sea charts.

Stevens Bunker
China Sea Marine Trading Company
229 Portland Rd.
Gray, ME 04039
ph: 207-657-2117
chinasea@chinaseatrading.com
http://www.chinaseatrading.com
Carries a unique jumble of maritime artifacts, antiques and curios gathered from around the world.

John Rinaldi
John Rinaldi Nautical Antiques
P.O. Box 765
Kennebunkport, ME 04046-0765
ph: 207-967-3218
fax: 207-967-2918
jfrinaldi@adelphia.net
Buys and sells marine antiques, antique scrimshaw, paintings, naval items; fully illustrated catalog for $5.

Michael Leslie
Port 'N Starboard Gallery
53 Falmouth St.
Falmouth, ME 04105
ph: 207-781-4214
fax: 207-781-4208
mleslie@maine.rr.com
Specializes in marine antiques, art, paintings and folk art: ship portraits, yachting, Nantucket, Hudson River, ship models, half hulls, dioramas, whirligigs, weathervanes, carved eagles, trade signs, lighthouses.

Bernhard W. Sund
Jonesport Nautical Antiques
Cogswell & Main St., Box 401
Jonesport, ME 04649
ph: 207-497-5655
bsund@NauticalAntiques.com
http://www.NauticalAntiques.com
Specializes in nautical art, nautical antiques, and nautical reproductions: carries compasses, sextants, engine order telegraphs, diving helmets, binnacles, charts, items for restaurant decoration, and other items of interest.

James P. Marenakos
Quester Gallery
77 Main St.
P.O. Box 32
Stonington, CT 06378
ph: 860-535-3860
fax: 860-535-3533
info@questergallery.com
http://www.questergallery.com
Internationally recognized as a leading source for exceptional 18th, 19th and 20th century marine and sporting paintings; buys and takes on consignment fine marine and sporting paintings and antiques.

J. Tobin
Antique & Classic Boats
12 Carstead Dr.
Slingerlands, NY 12159
ph: 518-439-0477
fax: 518-439-0477

Robert Shourot
Coastal Diving Operations
10297 Rainbow Rd.
Carrollton, VA 23314-4109
ph: 757-826-3945
fax: 757-826-7879
Specialty is nautical artifacts and diving antiques including pumps, helmets, bells, steam gauges, engine telegraphs, portholes, lights, etc.

Daniel Alex Haase
Haase's Nautical Antiques & Furnishings
6150 Virginia Beach Blvd.
Norfolk, VA 23502-2702
ph: 757-461-2465 or 757-461-6150
Makers of resin-covered hatch cover tables; buys and sells nautical antiques: brass lights, ship's wheels, sextants, etc.; also specializes in restoring nautical antiques.

James & Norvell Kennedy
James Kennedy Antiques, Ltd.
905 W. Main St.
Durham, NC 27701-2054
ph: 919-682-1040 or 800-236-1868
fax: 919-683-9633
kantiques@earthlink.net
http://www.jameskennedyantiques.com
Specialist in scientific, medical, and nautical antiques and prints.

Raymond & Lyn Newman
Martifacts, Inc.
P.O. Box 350190
Jacksonville, FL 32235-0190
ph: 904-645-0150
fax: 904-645-0150
martifacts@aol.com
http://www.martifacts.com
Dealer in authentic nautical items from scrapped ships: lights, blocks, clocks, barometers, sextants, clinometers, grates, US Navy items including china and silver; US Lines items, etc.; buys and sells.

Marc J. Cohen
P.O. Box 100637
Fort Lauderdale, FL 33310-0637
ph: 954-565-9754
Buys, sells and collects antique "hard hat" diving gear: helmets, hoses, shoes, knives, weights, belts, dresses, pumps, tools, catalogs, books, pictures, and other related "hard hat" diving equipment items.

Bob Elsner
Heights Antiques
29 Clubhouse Ln.
Boynton Beach, FL 33436-6056
ph: 561-736-1362
fax: 561-736-1914
rjelsner@aol.com
Barometer expert who buys, sells, appraises and repairs all types of barometers: gimbaled, mercury, aneroid, altimeters, barographs; antique and reproduction.

Bruce Littler
Olde Nautical Shoppe
25 Causeway Blvd.
Clearwater, FL 33727
ph: 727-441-3036
fax: 727-443-5032
oldnaut@aol.com
http://www.oldenauticalshoppe.com
Carries a large selection nautical antiques, ship artifacts, scientific instruments, navigation instruments, vintage fishing tackle, antique marine art, ship and boat models, weather instruments, ship clocks, etc.

Donald E. Taussig
Sanders' Antique
527 S. Pineapple Ave.
Sarasota, FL 34236
ph: 941-366-0400
fax: 941-952-1491
sandersant@aol.com
http://www.sandersantiques.com
Buys and sells ship models, helmets, instruments, maps, clocks, bells, etc.

Nauticals Ltd.
4101 Windsor Pkwy.
Dallas, TX 75205
ph: 214-522-2366
fax: 214-522-2218
nauticalA@aol.com
Specializes in nautical antiques: telescopes, sextants, compasses, running lights, brass port holes, etc.

Gordon Stanley
Maritime Gallery
P.O. Box 40
Fulton, TX 78358
ph: 361-729-4026
fax: 361-729-7967
pamelamstanley@aol.com
Specializes in 1800s to 1900s maritime artifacts; shows at high quality antique shows.

Al & Bobbie Roberts
Rational Past, The
221 Oceano Dr.
Los Angeles, CA 90049-4123
ph: 310-476-6277
fax: 310-476-6278
malinfo@therationalpast.com
http://www.therationalpast.com
Organizer of West Coast Scientific & Technical Antique and Collectible Shows (Los Angeles and San Francisco.)

Maidhof Bros. International
1891 San Diego Ave.
San Diego, CA 92110
ph: 800-SEA-JUNK
fax: 619-574-1894
nautical@seajunk.com
http://www.seajunk.com
Carries Old ship relics from dead and dying ships of the world: real ship furniture, nautical lamps & lanterns, brass hardware, seagoing clocks and barometers, portholes, ships' wheels, etc.

Rod & Becky Cardoza
West Sea Company
2495 Congress St.
San Diego, CA 92110-2820
ph: 619-296-5356
fax: 619-216-1097
wsco@cox.net
http://www.westsea.com
Buys, sells all types of marine paintings, scrimshaw, ships' carvings, ship models, navigational and scientific instruments, sailor handcrafts, campaign furniture, hard hat diving, antique marine photography, nautical books, Naval ceramics.

Scott Brake
Scott Brake Antiques
17420 Mt. Hermann St., Unit "D"
Fountain Valley, CA 92708
ph: 714-556-8333
fax: 714-556-8333
antiquechi@aol.com
Specializes in special acquisitions for entertainment and theme park clients; prop rentals.

Kathryn Retzer
Kathryn's Collectibles
2650 Emma Dr.
Pinole, CA 94564
ph: 800-424-3339 or 510-741-9976
fax: 510-741-1689
shipnsea@aol.com
Collectors and dealers in all types of nautical antiques with a special interest in deep sea diving equipment and naval items.

Fred Von Wiegen
Ship Store Galleries
P.O. Box 1058
Kapaa, HI 96746-1058
ph: 808-822-4999 or 800-877-1948
fax: 808-822-2506
von@ssgalleries.com
http://www.ssgalleries.com
Buys and sells 18th and 19th century shipboard items: old maps and charts, models, scrimshaw; particularly Pacific vessels and South Sea items.

James W. Coulson
Cuttysark of Bellevue
10235 Main St.
Bellevue, WA 98004-6121
ph: 425-453-1265 or 888-453-1265
fax: 425-451-8779
jlcutty@aol.com
http://www.cuttysark.net
Buys and sells a general line of marine items: flags, marine antiques, models, clocks, etc.

A. Rex Bennett
Anchor Antiques Co.
5129 No. Pearl St.
Tacoma, WA 98407
ph: 253-752-1134
Specializes in diver's helmets and old oil lamps.

Experts

Sara Conklin, ISA
Nautical Appraisals
P.O. Box 30203
Blairsden, CA 96103
ph: 415-467-6249 or 800-464-4208
fax: 415-467-6249
sconklin2@pngusa.net
http://home.earthlink.net/~sconklin2
Appraises maritime items and collections: ship models, scrimshaw, navigational instruments, figurehead carvings, marine art, paper & ephemera archival collections, telescopes, shipwrecks, diving equip., ocean liner memorabilia, whaling.

Internet Resources

John Kohnen
Mother of All Maritime Links, The
jkohnen@boat-links.com
http://www.boat-links.com
Web site contains an incredible number of links to other nautical sights; boat builders and dealers, canoes, Coast Guard, diving, events, navies, hardware, lighthouses, modeling, nautical history, sailing, steamboats, etc.

Bill Momsen
Nautical Brass Online
P.O. Box 3966
Fort Myers, FL 33918-3966
nbrass1@earthlink.net
http://home.earthlink.net/~nbrass1/ezine.htm
Provides free online information about nautical antiques.

Museums/Libraries

Peabody Essex Museum
Magazine: American Neptune
Essex & Libert Sts.
Salem, MA 01970
ph: 978-745-9500 or 800-745-4054
pem@pem.org
http://www.pem.org

Mystic Seaport Museum
Magazine: Log of Mystic Seaport, The
75 Greenmanville Ave.
P.O. Box 6000
Mystic, CT 06355-0990
ph: 860-572-0711 or 888-9SEAPORT
info@mysticseaport.org
http://www.mysticseaport.org
General focus is 19th century seafaring America: scrimshaw, figureheads, instruments, maritime art, carvings, etc.

U.S. Naval Academy Museum
118 Maryland Ave.
Annapolis, MD 21402-5034
ph: 410-293-2180
fax: 410-293-5220
jsharmon@nadn.navy.mil
http://www.nadn.navy.mil/Museum
Focuses on the heritage of the US Navy; ship models, paintings, prints, flags, uniforms, swords, medals, sculptures, rare books, photographs,

instruments and gear, personal memorabilia.

Pete Lesher, Cur.
Chesapeake Bay Maritime Museum
Magazine: CBMM Quarterly
P.O. Box 636
St. Michaels, MD 21663-0636
ph: 410-745-2916
fax: 410-745-6088
library@cbmm.org
http://www.cbmm.org
A major regional maritime museum with a 10,000 volume research library; collections include 9,000 objects, 32,000 photos, 1,200 ships' plans, 120 linear feet of manuscripts; decoys, oystering, lighthouses, charts, nautical, tools.

Mariners' Museum, The
100 Museum Dr.
Newport News, VA 23606
ph: 757-596-2222 or 800-581-7245
fax: 757-591-7310
info@mariner.org
http://www.mariner.org

Keith R. Gill
Museum of Science & Industry
5700 S. Lake Shore Dr.
Chicago, IL 60637
ph: 773-684-1414
fax: 773-684-0026
msi@msichicago.org
http://www.msichicago.org

Maritime Museum of Monterey
5 Custom House Plaza
Monterey, CA 93940-2430
ph: 831-375-9259
fax: 831-665-3054
mhaamm@mbay.net
http://www.mhaamm.org

San Francisco Maritime National
    Historical Park, Museum & Library
Bldg. E, Fort Mason Center
San Francisco, CA 94123
ph: 415-556-9870 or 415-556-9871
fax: 415-556-3540
safr_maritime_library@nps.gov
http://www.nps.gov/safr/local/lib/libtop.html

Periodicals

Robert R. McKenna, Ed.
Magazine: Nautical Collector
One Whale Oil Row
New London, CT 06320
ph: 860-444-0127
fax: 860-444-0129
nautworld@aol.com
An authoritative bi-monthly magazine on the antiques, collectibles, art, artifacts, literature and memorabilia associated with the seas, lakes and waterways.

Repair Services

Richard Dermody
Brass n' Bounty
68 Front St.
Marblehead, MA 01945-3275
ph: 781-631-3864 or 781-631-6204
bnb@brassandbounty.com
http://www.brassandbounty.com
Repairs nautical instruments such as compasses, sextants, telescopes; polishes and lacquers marine hardware and lights.

James P. Connor
J.P. Connor & Co.
P.O. Box 305
Devon, PA 19333-0305
ph: 610-644-1474
fax: 610-993-0760
Specialist in antique and modern marine chronometers, deck watches, ship's clocks, barometers, and sextants; buys and sells, appraisals, evaluating, dating; catalog available; repair and restoration services also available.

Repro. Sources

Cyrus Doomasia
Avesta Collectibles
2911 Bayview Ave.
Toronto, Ontario M2K 1E8 Canada
ph: 416-250-1333
fax: 416-250-7999
cdavesta@hotmail.com
http://www.avesta-collectibles.com
Dealer and manufacturer of fine navigational and nautical instruments.

Diving

(see also SCUBA)

Clubs/Associations

Historical Diving Society USA
Magazine: Historical Diver Magazine
2022 Cliff Dr., #405
Santa Barbara, CA 93109
ph: 805-692-0072
fax: 805-692-0042
hds@hds.org
http://www.hds.org
Dedicated to the preservation, study and promotion of our diving heritage; enables individuals, organizations and divers interested in the historical aspect of diving to make academic, social and practical contacts on a national level.

Mike Fardell, Mem. Sec.
Historical Diving Society, The
Magazine: Historical Diving Times
Little Gatton Lodge
25 Gatton Rd.
Reigate, Surrey RH2 0HB U.K.
ph: +44 (0) 1737 249961
info@thehds.com
http://www.thehds.com
Dedicated to the preservation, study and promotion of our diving heritage; enables individuals, organizations and divers interested in the historical aspect of diving to make academic,

social and practical contacts on a national level.

Collectors

Stephen Buczko
27 Surrey Rd.
Salem, MA 01970-4362
ph: 978-744-4683
nsbuczko@aol.com
Wants to purchase antique diving apparatus: diving helmets, pumps, trade catalogs; anything related to early diving.

Dealers

Leon Lyons
Helmets of the Deep
P.O. Box 190
Saint Augustine, FL 32085-0190
ph: 904-825-0184
amoebus103@aol.com
Collects all types and material of deep sea diving equipment; wrote and published the book "Helmets of the Deep," available from author.

Experts

Leslie Leaney
Silent World Antiques
2022 Cliff Dr. #119
Santa Barbara, CA 93109
ph: 805-899-3200
fax: 805-962-3810
LLeaney@aol.com
Specializes in antique and collectible diving equipment; amassed collection over 20 years with assistance of a network of contacts; authored various articles on early manufacturers; consultant to Discovery Channel, History Channel.

Diving Helmets

Collectors

Dan Cramer
P.O. Box 447
Swartz Creek, MI 48473-0447
ph: 810-635-4957
Wants deep sea diving helmets and related items.

Dealers

Larry Pitman
Pioneer Peddler Antiques
5424 Bryan Station Rd.
Paris, KY 40361-9062
ph: 859-299-5022
fax: 859-299-4522
Wants diving helmets.

Repair Services

DESCO Corp.
240 N. Milwaukee St.
Milwaukee, WI 53202
ph: 414-272-2371
fax: 414-272-2373
diveq@execpc.com
http://www.divedesco.com
Old helmets repaired and reconditioned; in business since 1937.

Figureheads & Ships Carvings

Appraisers

Sara Conklin, ISA
Nautical Appraisals
P.O. Box 30203
Blairsden, CA 96103
ph: 415-467-6249 or 800-464-4208
fax: 415-467-6249
sconklin2@pngusa.net
http://home.earthlink.net/~sconklin2
Managed the collections of the National Maritime Museum in San Francisco for ten years and is an expert in appraising figureheads and other ship carvings such as trailboards, sternboards, beakboards, and billetheads.

Experts

Sara Conklin, ISA
Nautical Appraisals
P.O. Box 30203
Blairsden, CA 96103
ph: 415-467-6249 or 800-464-4208
fax: 415-467-6249
sconklin2@pngusa.net
http://home.earthlink.net/~sconklin2
Managed the collections of the National Maritime Museum in San Francisco for ten years and is an expert in appraising figureheads and other ship carvings such as trailboards, sternboards, beakboards, and billetheads.

Fishing Floats

Collectors

Gerald Wightman
floats@glass-floats.com
http://www.glass-floats.com
Buys colored European and Japanese glass fishing floats.

John Honl
P.O. Box 1201
Kailua Kona, HI 96745-1201
ph: 808-325-9905
jhh@kona.net
Buys and trades glass fishing floats; looking to buy floats with embossing; also wants odd shapes and colors.

Connie Woodward
1177 S. Main St.
Colville, WA 99114
ph: 509-684-4186
glassfloats@hotmail.com
http://www.homestead.com/floats
Collector of glass fishing floats; offers appraisals.

Experts

Stu Farnsworth
P.O. Box 847
Wilsonville, OR 97070-0847
ph: 503-393-9115
Wants to buy glass fishing floats; unusual colors such as pink, lavender, purple, black, cobalt blue, red, orange, etc.; also wants rolling pin floats with writing on side, European

floats with embossed markings or characters; no repros.

Lighthouses

Clubs/Associations

Lighthouse Preservation Society, The
4 Middle St.
Newburyport, MA 01950
ph: 508-499-0011 or 800-727-BEAM
fax: 508-499-0026
http://www.mayday.com/lps
Catalyst for the preservation of lighthouses up and down the nation's coasts.

Timothy Harrison
New England Lighthouse Foundation
P.O. Box 1690
Wells, ME 04090
ph: 800-758-1444 or 207-646-0515
fax: 207-646-0516
timh@lhdigest.com
http://www.lhdigest.com
Mission is to act as an agency to encourage Historic Preservation, to foster and support local lighthouse initiatives, and to improve public awareness and appreciation of and access to all of New England's lighthouses.

United States Lighthouse Society
Magazine: Keeper's Log
244 Kearney St., 5th Floor
San Francisco, CA 94108
ph: 415-362-7255 or 415-362-7464
http://www.maine.com/lights/uslhs.htm
Nonprofit historical/educational society; maintains comprehensive library and archives on lighthouse matters, conducts regional and foreign lighthouse tours, conducts research, hosts photography contests, has state chapters.

Collectors

Dick Hawkins
Columbia Trading Company
One Barnstable Rd.
Hyannis, MA 02601
ph: 508-778-2929
fax: 508-778-2922
info@columbiatrading.com
http://www.columbiatrading.com
Wants to buy items relating to lighthouses.

Timothy Harrison
P.O. Box 1690
Wells, ME 04090
ph: 800-758-1444 or 207-646-0515
fax: 207-646-0516
timh@lhdigest.com
http://www.lhdigest.com
Wants to buy memorabilia from US Lighthouse Service (USLHS) or US Lighthouse Establishment (USLHE): badges, flags, dinnerware, buttons, uniforms, old photographs of keepers and their families, postcards, newspaper stories.

J. Carol Duncan
Keeper's Lighthouse Establishment
1027 Garden St.
Santa Barbara, CA 93101-1416
ph: 805-963-9129 or 805-965-1174
fax: 805-962-5054
jcduncan@aol.com
Wants to buy lighthouse artifacts and antiques: lamps, lanterns, oil cans, maps, photographs, lighthouse keeper items, lighthouse ephemera, Fresnel lens (whole or in parts); also wants to buy Coast Guard items.

Man./Prod./Dist.

Lighthouse Depot
P.O. Box 427
Wells, ME 04090-0427
ph: 800-758-1444
fax: 207-646-0516
lhdigest@lhdigest.com
http://www.biddeford.com/~lhdigest/catalog/home.html
Issues catalog containing new items having the lighthouse motif: clocks, lamps, figurines, clothing, lighthouse replicas, prints, steins, jewelry boxes, glassware, watches, candles, key fobs, snow globes, etc.

Museums/Libraries

Pete Lesher, Cur.
Chesapeake Bay Maritime Museum
Magazine: CBMM Quarterly
P.O. Box 636
St. Michaels, MD 21663-0636
ph: 410-745-2916
fax: 410-745-6088
library@cbmm.org
http://www.cbmm.org
A major regional maritime museum with a 10,000 volume research library; collections include 9,000 objects, 32,000 photos, 1,200 ships' plans, 120 linear feet of manuscripts; decoys, oystering, lighthouses, charts, nautical, tools.

Periodicals

Timothy Harrison
Newspaper: Lighthouse Digest
P.O. Box 1690
Wells, ME 04090
ph: 800-758-1444 or 207-646-0515
fax: 207-646-0516
timh@lhdigest.com
http://www.lhdigest.com
America's only monthly Lighthouse newspaper; issues catalog of a large selection of contemporary lighthouse collectibles.

Marine Chronometers

Collectors

Paul H. Hayashi, PE
18 Tarabrook Dr.
Orinda, CA 94563-3121
ph: 925-254-5074 or 925-253-1038
fax: 925-253-0592
Wants to buy precision wall regulators with different escapements.

Dealers

Marine Antiques & Timepieces
8028 - 238th SW
Edmonds, WA 98020
ph: 425-774-8159
Specializes in Elgin and Hamilton marine chronometers, military timepieces and parts; also other antique and modern marine instruments.

Experts

James P. Connor
J.P. Connor & Co.
P.O. Box 305
Devon, PA 19333-0305
ph: 610-644-1474
fax: 610-993-0760
Specialist in antique and modern marine chronometers, deck watches, ship's clocks, barometers, and sextants; buys and sells, appraisals, evaluating, dating; catalog available; repair and restoration services also available.

Repair Services

Philip M. Poniz
European Watch & Casemakers, Ltd.
P.O. Box 1314
Highland Park, NJ 08904-1314
ph: 732-777-0111
fax: 732-777-0118
horology@webspan.net
Restoration of watches, clocks, and music boxes; museum experience; can make any part and restore any watch; clients include Sotheby's, Cartier, collectors in USA, Asia and Europe; appraises, researches, restores chronometers.

Merchant Marine

Museums/Libraries

Harvey Lee Boswell
Palace of Wonders Museum
P.O. Box 446
Elm City, NC 27822-0446
Wants Merchant Marine and US Maritime Service items: flags, uniforms, photos, medals, etc.

Models (Sailboats)

Clubs/Associations

Bruce Bollenbach
Rocky Mountain Shipwrights
Newsletter: Scuttlebutt, The
8046 Lee Court
Arvada, CO 80005
ph: 303-424-7578
BDBoll@aol.com
A club for those interested in ship models, especially wooden sailing models; for beginners or advanced; newsletter posted on the Internet at http://www.naut-res-guild.org/newsletr/nl-rms.html.

Models (Ship)

Appraisers

Sara Conklin, ISA
Nautical Appraisals
P.O. Box 30203
Blairsden, CA 96103
ph: 415-467-6249 or 800-464-4208
fax: 415-467-6249
sconklin2@pngusa.net
http://home.earthlink.net/~sconklin2
Managed the collections of the National Maritime Museum in San Francisco for ten years & is an expert in appraising ship models, ships-in-bottles, marine art, scrimshaw, figureheads, paper ephemera, instruments, whaling, diving equipment.

Clubs/Associations

Lloyd V. Warner
Nautical Research Guild, Inc.
Journal: Nautical Research Journal
31 Water St., Ste. 7
Cuba, NY 14727
ph: 585-968-8111
nrg@a-znet.com
http://www.naut-Res-Guild.org
Has been linking researchers, collectors, builders of the highest quality ship models for nearly 50 years; focuses on the story of the ship, the technologies of marine transportation, the shipwrights and sailors.

Dealers

Arrangements Inc., Marine Div.
P.O. Box 126
Mount Kisco, NY 10549-0126
ph: 914-238-1300
fax: 914-238-9776
gablouise@aol.com
Buys, sells, custom builds, appraises, and restores ship models.

Experts

R. Michael Wall
American Marine Model Gallery, Inc.
12 Derby Square
Salem, MA 01970-3704
ph: 978-745-5777
fax: 978-745-5778
wall@shipmodel.com
http://www.shipmodel.com
Buys, sells, appraises and specializes in model ships; representing the finest work of internationally acclaimed model makers; all models fully documented; 92 pg. illustrated catalog $10.

Sara Conklin, ISA
Nautical Appraisals
P.O. Box 30203
Blairsden, CA 96103
ph: 415-467-6249 or 800-464-4208
fax: 415-467-6249
sconklin2@pngusa.net
http://home.earthlink.net/~sconklin2
Managed the collections of the National Maritime Museum in San Francisco for ten years & is an expert in appraising ship models, ships-in-bottles, marine art, scrimshaw, figureheads, paper ephemera, instruments, whaling, diving equipment.

Internet Resources

Lloyd V. Warner
Nautical Research Guild, Inc.
Journal: Nautical Research Journal
31 Water St., Ste. 7
Cuba, NY 14727
ph: 585-968-8111
nrg@a-znet.com
http://www.naut-Res-Guild.org
Has been linking researchers, collectors, builders of the highest quality ship models for nearly 50 years; focuses on the story of the ship, the technologies of marine transportation, the shipwrights and sailors.

Repair Services

R. Michael Wall
American Marine Model Gallery, Inc.
12 Derby Square
Salem, MA 01970-3704
ph: 978-745-5777
fax: 978-745-5778
wall@shipmodel.com
http://www.shipmodel.com
Offers complete professional restoration services, custom models, cases, appraisals.

Rick Fortenberry
Cape Cod Scale Watercraft
1335 Rt. 134
Box 1459
East Dennis, MA 02641-1459
ph: 508-385-4019 or 508-385-5010
fax: 508-385-4019
whaler@aol.com
Construction, restoration, acquisition and display of fine watercraft models.

Al August
44 Cambridge Dr.
Mashpee, MA 02649-2219
ph: 508-477-4169
Ship model repair; also buys and sells wood ship models old or new in any condition; will buy total or partial wrecks, hulls, kits; will give repair or restoration quotes from good photos; also will buy and sell through photos.

Models (Ships-In-Bottles)

Appraisers

Sara Conklin, ISA
Nautical Appraisals
P.O. Box 30203
Blairsden, CA 96103
ph: 415-467-6249 or 800-464-4208
fax: 415-467-6249
sconklin2@pngusa.net
http://home.earthlink.net/~sconklin2
Managed the collections of the National Maritime Museum in San Francisco for ten years & is an expert in appraising ship models, ships-in-bottles, marine art, scrimshaw, figureheads, paper ephemera, instruments, whaling, diving equipment.

NAUTICAL ANTIQUES

NEWSBOY ITEMS

533

Clubs/Associations

Don Hubbard
Ships In Bottles Association of America
Newsletter: Bottle Shipwright, The
P.O. Box 180550
Coronado, CA 92178
hubbarddon@aol.com

Experts

Sara Conklin, ISA
Nautical Appraisals
P.O. Box 30203
Blairsden, CA 96103
ph: 415-467-6249 or 800-464-4208
fax: 415-467-6249
sconklin2@pngusa.net
http://home.earthlink.net/~sconklin2
*Managed the collections of the
National Maritime Museum in San
Francisco for ten years & is an expert
in appraising ship models, ships-in-
bottles, marine art, scrimshaw,
figureheads, paper ephemera,
instruments, whaling, diving
equipment.*

Internet Resources

Artem Popov
Ships-in-Bottles
Russia
popov@galaktika.ru
http://www.shipbottle.ru
*Russian Web site focusing on ships-in-
bottles, links to associations world
wide, how-to tips and instructions.*

Shipwrecks

Appraisers

Sara Conklin, ISA
Nautical Appraisals
P.O. Box 30203
Blairsden, CA 96103
ph: 415-467-6249 or 800-464-4208
fax: 415-467-6249
sconklin2@pngusa.net
http://home.earthlink.net/~sconklin2
*Managed the collections of the
National Maritime Museum in San
Francisco for ten years and is an
expert in appraising shipwreck
material such as vessel fragments and
related objects.*

Experts

Sara Conklin, ISA
Nautical Appraisals
P.O. Box 30203
Blairsden, CA 96103
ph: 415-467-6249 or 800-464-4208
fax: 415-467-6249
sconklin2@pngusa.net
http://home.earthlink.net/~sconklin2
*Managed the collections of the
National Maritime Museum in San
Francisco for ten years and is an
expert in appraising shipwreck
material such as vessel fragments and
related objects.*

Telescopes

Dealers

Daniel J. Vaughn
Spyglass, The
618 Main St.
Chatham, MA 02633
ph: 508-945-9686
*Buys, sells, repairs and restores
telescopes (especially mounted scopes);
world's largest dealer.*

NEEDLEWORK

(see TEXTILES, Needlework)

NEON

(see also BREWERIANA; COIN-
OPERATED MACHINES; LAMPS &
LIGHTING, Neon)

Collectors

Roark Vane
6839 Havenside Dr.
Sacramento, CA 95831-2168
ph: 916-392-3864
neonclock@aol.com
*Wants to buy vintage neon clocks,
small advertising neon signs, neon
light bulbs, or other unusual
illuminated advertising signs; also
signs with "bubble tubes" - glass
tubes or letters are filled with a liquid
that "bubbles."*

Periodicals

Tim Ferrante
Magazine: Gameroom Magazine
P.O. Box 41
Keyport, NJ 07735-0041
ph: 732-739-1955
fax: 732-739-2834
coinop@gameroommagazine.com
http://www.gameroommagazine.com
*A great source of information for the
collector and dealer of jukeboxes,
pinballs, slot machines, Coke and
other soda machines, arcade games,
classic arcade video, and other
gameroom collectibles.*

Repair Services

Stephen Kuhn
Neon Radio, The
503 E. Market St.
Lockhart, TX 78644
ph: 512-398-7777
stephen@neonradio.com
http://www.neonradio.com
*Repairs vintage neon signs electri-
cally; also refinished tube radios.*

Clocks

Collectors

Van Stueart
2240 Hwy 27 N
Nashville, AR 71852
ph: 870-845-4864 or 800-577-1810
sodaman@iosa.com
Buys and trades all types of

*advertising neon clocks; also wants
Cleveland type neon thermometers.*

Dealers

David A. Dyer
Neon Clock
246 Third Ave.
New Lenox, IL 60451
ph: 815-485-5573
fax: 815-485-0483
Old neon clocks bought and sold.

Robert Newman
17220 Silver Lane
Encino, CA 91316
ph: 310-559-0539
*Wants to buy pre-1960 neon and
lighted clocks, with or without
advertising; wants any clock with neon
numbers or hands.*

Repair Services

Tom Arrington
Neon Specialties
P.O. Box 2292
Chapel Hill, NC 27515-2292
ph: 919-932-5747
fax: 919-932-1782
*Reproduction and restoration of
vintage neon clocks.*

Bob Olds
364 Vinewood Ave.
Tallmadge, OH 44278
ph: 330-633-5938
Repairs neon electric clocks.

NETSUKE

(see also ORIENTALIA)

Clubs/Associations

International Netsuke Society
Journal: International Netsuke Society
Journal
P.O. Box 833272
Richardson, TX 75083-3272
ph: 972-596-8250
fax: 972-866-9946
info@netsuke.org
http://www.netsuke.org
*Over 600 members in 25 countries;
celebrates 20th anniversary in 1995.*

Dealers

James Sisk
Netsuke Store, The
105A Beacon Rd.
Baltimore, MD 21220
ph: 410-686-4216
fax: 410-574-8160
info@fareastgallery.com
http://www.netsukestore.com
*Online store offering a large selection
of netsuke carved from ivory, horn and
wood.*

Bill Egleston
509 Brentwood Rd.
Marshalltown, IA 50158-3727
ph: 800-798-4579
fax: 515-752-4570
Specializing in mail order sale of

*Oriental art, jade, cloisonne, netsuke,
etc.; send for catalog.*

Sagemonoya
Yanane K.K.
Yotsuya 4-chrome 28-20-703
Tokyo, 160 Japan
ph: 813 33.52.62.86
fax: 813 33.56.65.81
sagemonoya@gol.com
http://www.netsuke.com
*Sells only netsuke and other fine
Sagemono.*

Experts

Richard R. Silverman
838 N. Doheny Dr. #1102
West Hollywood, CA 90069-4851
ph: 310-271-1896 or 310-273-3838
fax: 310-273-3843
*Specializes in Japanese prints and
ceramics; netsuke and inro; also Thai,
Burmese, Indian and Nepalese items;
call 12:00 noon to 12:00 midnight
PST; BOD of Inter. Netsuke Kenkyukai
(1991-present), Certified Member of
ISA.*

Periodicals

Joan L. Cervi
Newsletter: Netsuke & Ivory Carving
Newsletter-Video
3203 Adams Way
Ambler, PA 19002-3741
ph: 215-628-2026
fax: 215-628-2026
jcnetsuke@aol.com
*A wholesaler who offers VHS videos
and a monthly newsletter about
imported netsuke, ivory carvings and
other Orientalia.*

NEWSBOY ITEMS

(see also NEWSPAPERS)

Clubs/Associations

B. J. Hughes
Newspaper Memorabilia Collectors
Network
P.O. Box 797
Watertown, NY 13601-0797
*Newsletter published quarterly;
members interested in old newspapers
as well as newsboy related memora-
bilia.*

Collectors

Mark Peters
504 Boynton Ave.
Berkeley, CA 94707-1704
ph: 510-525-7972
fax: 510-525-7972
*Wants to buy newsboy memorabilia
including badges, buttons, ephemera,
figurines, photos, books, etc.;
anything related to newsboys.*

Experts

Tony Lee
P.O. Box 134
Monmouth Junction, NJ 08852-0134
ph: 201-429-1531
*Collector and dealer of badges and
other credentials issued to newsboys,
as well as the buttons, ribbons,
aprons and hats they wore to advertise
the newspapers they sold.*

NEWSPAPERS

(see also COMIC STRIPS, Sunday
Newspaper; PAPER COLLECTIBLES;
PERIODICALS; NEWSBOY ITEMS)

Appraisers

Mark E. Mitchell
Original Historic Newspapers, Letters &
  Documents
3002 Winter Pine Ct.
Fairfax, VA 22031-1125
ph: 703-591-3150
fax: 703-385-3152
info@mitchellarchives.com
http://www.mitchellarchives.com
*Specializing in the appraisal of old
and historic newspapers; appraised
$4M collection of rare newspapers at
the Newseum in Washington, DC.*

Auction Services

Robert Raynor
Historical Collectible Auctions
24 NW Court Sq. #201
Graham, NC 27253
ph: 336-570-2803
fax: 336-570-2748
bids4hca@aol.com
http://www.hcaauctions.com
*Buys, sells historic newspapers from
1760 through 1945; also conducts
periodic mail/phone bid auctions of
old collectible newspapers.*

Rick Brown
History Buff's Auction
6031 Winterset
Lansing, MI 48911
ph: 517-887-1255
help@historybuffauction.com
http://www.historybuffauction.com
*Online auction specializing in paper
collectibles from 1600s to 1990s:
newspapers, magazines, pulps,
documents, Civil War, old catalogs,
photography, tobacco cards,
stereoviews, postcards, souvenir
folders, booklets, advertising, etc.*

Clubs/Associations

B. J. Hughes
Newspaper Memorabilia Collectors
  Network
P.O. Box 797
Watertown, NY 13601-0797
*Newsletter published quarterly;
members interested in old newspapers
as well as newsboy related memora-
bilia.*

Collectors

E. Alexander Peters
'Tiques
P.O. Box 3267
Farmingdale, NY 11735-0679
ph: 631-842-9549
*Wants 18th and 19th C. newspapers
and articles documenting the African-
American experience, including
Caribbean, South America and Africa.*

B. J. Hughes
P.O. Box 797
Watertown, NY 13601-0797

Joe Weber
604 Centre St.
Ashland, PA 17921-1332
ph: 570-875-4787 or 570-875-4401
*Wants to buy pre-1890 newspapers,
especially those discussing important
events; also papers from Pennsylvania;
will advise others.*

Dealers

Phil Barber
Historic Newspapers & Early Imprints
P.O. Box 8694
Boston, MA 02114-0036
ph: 617-492-4653
fax: 617-868-1534
philb@historicpages.com
http://www.historicpages.com
*Buying and selling fine paper
collectibles since 1979; specializes in
historic newspapers from the period
1775 to 1865; also early Bible leaves,
and ephemera dating 1440 to 1940.*

Eric Caren
Caren Archives, The
P.O. Box 185
Lincolndale, NY 10540-0185
ph: 914-248-8038
fax: 914-248-6439
eccaren@prodigy.net
http://www.historicalnews.com
*Buys and sells Americana, Western,
rare newspapers.*

Kyle Rothgeb
Yesterday's News
67 Chapel St.
Kingston, NY 12401
ph: 914-339-8930
*Collector and dealer of old and rare
newspapers dating from the late 1700s
to present; has written a manual,
"Yesterday's News," for other
collectors to explain the proper way of
storing and displaying newspapers.*

Timothy Hughes
Timothy Hughes Rare & Early
  Newspapers
P.O. Box 3636
Williamsport, PA 17701-8636
ph: 570-326-1045
fax: 570-326-7606
tim@rarenewspapers.com
http://www.rarenewspapers.com
*Buys and sells old newspapers; 1600s
through 1970; catalog of offerings for
$2.*

Steve Goldman
Stephen Goldman Historical Newspapers
P.O. Box 359
Parkton, MD 21120-0359
ph: 410-357-8204
fax: 410-343-3507
info@historicalnews.com
http://www.historicalnews.com
*Buys and sells historical newspapers,
large or small quantities, bound
volumes, single issues; from 18th,
19th, or 20th centuries.*

Mark E. Mitchell
Original Historic Newspapers, Letters &
  Documents
3002 Winter Pine Ct.
Fairfax, VA 22031-1125
ph: 703-591-3150
fax: 703-385-3152
info@mitchellarchives.com
http://www.mitchellarchives.com
*Buys and sells 1620-1945 original
high quality newspapers and
periodicals; including Amer. Rev.,
Civil War, Harper's Weekly.*

Robert Raynor
Vintage Cover Story
24 NW Court Sq. #201
Graham, NC 27253
ph: 336-570-2803
fax: 336-570-2748
bids4hca@aol.com
http://www.hcaauctions.com
*Buys, sells historic newspapers from
1760 through 1945; also conducts
periodic mail/phone bid auctions of
old collectible newspapers.*

Experts

Rick Brown
6031 Winterset
Lansing, MI 48911
ph: 517-887-1255
info@historybuff.com
http://www.historybuff.com
*Collects, appraises and specializes in
old newspapers.*

Internet Resources

Rick Brown
Newspaper Collectors Society of America
6031 Winterset
Lansing, MI 48911
ph: 517-887-1255
info@historybuff.com
http://www.historybuff.com
*Online magazine with over 600 files of
information about old and historic
newspapers; files include price guide,
collector primer, reprint guide and
much more.*

Museums/Libraries

Newseum
1101 Wilson Blvd.
Arlington, VA 22209
ph: 703-284-3725 or 888-NEWSEUM
newseum@freedomforum.org
http://www.newseum.org
*World's only interactive museum of
news, news gathering, news reporting,
journalism; showcases hundreds of*

*objects associated with news events
and news people, historic broadcasts,
newspapers and magazines.*

Repro. Sources

AnyDate.com
1504 East North Ave.
Milwaukee, WI 53202
ph: 414-908-0404
info@anydate.com
http://www.Anydate.com
*A source for original historic
newspapers and historic newspaper
reproductions; great place to find
items for birthdays, holidays, or other
special events.*

Harpers Weekly

Dealers

Dale W. Rose
104 Tern Court
Wilmington, DE 19808
ph: 302-239-3150
*"Harpers Weekly" specialist offers
original engravings: Civil War
through 1897; all sports, city views,
firemen, Indians, Santas, Presidents
and other political.*

NICKELODEONS

(see CAROUSELS & CAROUSEL
FIGURES; MUSICAL
INSTRUMENTS, Mechanical [Band
Organs])

NIGHT LIGHTS

(see FAIRY LAMPS; LAMPS &
LIGHTING, Miniature; PERFUME
LAMPS)

NIPPER

(see PHONOGRAPHS, Nipper)

NORMAN ROCKWELL

(see ILLUSTRATORS, Norman
Rockwell; COLLECTIBLES
[MODERN], Norman Rockwell)

NORTHWEST COAST

(see ART, Canadian; INUIT &
NORTHWEST COAST NATIVES;
NATIVE AMERICANS)

NUMISMATICS

(see COINS & CURRENCY;
MEDALS, ORDERS &
DECORATIONS; SOUVENIR
CARDS; TOKENS)

NURSES

(see also RED CROSS)

Collectors

M. Brunswick
P.O. Box 9729
Baltimore, MD 21286-9729
Wants books illustrating baby and child care, home nursing, basic nursing treatments and procedures, sick care, home health, nursing school manuals and films, etc.; prefer 1900-1970, especially photo-illustrated; also foreign.

Dealers

UHR Books
P.O. Box 306
Hollis Center, ME 04042
ph: 207-929-5100
uhrbooks@uhrbooks.com
http://www.uhrbooks.com
Wants nurse and nursing related items: old books, postcards, magazines, sheet music, prints, posters, photos, dolls, diplomas, letters, diaries, pins and caps.

NUT-RELATED COLLECTIBLES

Museums/Libraries

Elizabeth Tashjian
Nut Museum, The
303 Ferry Rd.
Old Lyme, CT 06371-1615
ph: 860-434-7616
http://www.roadsideamerica.com/nut/
CTOLDmus.html
Focuses on the hard-shell fruit.

Nutcrackers

Clubs/Associations

Steinbach/KSA Collectible Nutcracker
Club
1107 Broadway
New York, NY 10010
ph: 212-924-0900 or 800-243-9627
fax: 212-807-0575
info@kurtadler.com
http://www.kurtadler.com
Collectors of contemporary German hand-carved wooden figurals.

Susan Otto, Editor
Nutcracker Collectors' Club
Newsletter: Nutcracker Collectors' Club
Newsletter
12204 Fox Run Dr.
Chesterland, OH 44026-2044
ph: 440-729-2686
nutsue@core.com
Members focus on collecting brass, cast iron, carved wood, figural or mechanical nutcrackers; but not toy soldier nutcrackers such as those made by Steinbach.

Collectors

Nutcrackers, Etc.
P.O. Box 6337
Tyler, TX 75711-6337
ph: 903-561-7005 or 903-597-8090
Wants to buy ornamental and figural nutcrackers, plus carved wooden heads and figurals.

Claudia J. Davis
2350 Finch
Hayden Lake, ID 83835
ph: 208-772-6801
fax: 208-772-5311
World's largest nutcracker collection; bronze, iron, ivory, brass, porcelain, wood.

Experts

Judith Rittenhouse
1860 Winding Brook Way
Scotch Plains, NJ 07090
Author of "Ornamental & Figural Nutcrackers: An Identification and Value Guide."

James E. Anthony
6300 Indian Creek Dr.
Fort Worth, TX 76116
ph: 817-732-4724 or 817-279-7056
fax: 817-279-7057
anthony6@swbell.net
Nutcracker collector and expert.

NUTS & BOLTS

(see FASTENERS)

OCCUPIED GERMANY

Collectors

Larry L. Krug
Americana Resources, Inc.
18222 Flower Hill Way, #299
Gaithersburg, MD 20879-5300
ph: 301-926-8663
fax: 301-926-7648
info@amres.com
http://www.amres.com

OCCUPIED JAPAN

Clubs/Associations

Florence Archambault
Occupied Japan Club, The
Newsletter: Upside Down World of an
O.J. Collector, The
29 Freeborn St.
Newport, RI 02840-1821
ph: 401-846-9024
florence@aiconnect.com
Focuses on Japanese-made items marked "Occupied Japan;" newsletter includes free buy/sell ads, up-to-date price information, lots of photos, and more; newsletter published bi-monthly; send SASE for more information.

Collectors

Margaret Bolbat
8714 Alicia St.
Philadelphia, PA 19115-4103
ph: 215-671-1766
Advanced collector looking for quality bisque and porcelain, large bisque birds, American children, objects with Mioj Hokutosha mark, books pamphlets, maps or paper marked "Printed in Occupied Japan."

Linda Trew Ahlfield-Bruhn
Divine Inc.
4441-C Mohala Place
Wahiawa, HI 96786
kagneys@aol.com
Wants figurines only: Pixies, any figurines over 6" high, ethnic figurines, mermaids and dancers; no cups, plates, fans or metal items.

Experts

Florence Archambault
29 Freeborn St.
Newport, RI 02840-1821
ph: 401-846-9024
florence@aiconnect.com
Author of "Occupied Japan Collectibles," and "Occupied Japan for the Home."

OCEAN LINER COLLECTIBLES

(see also DINNERWARE, Advertising; NAUTICAL ANTIQUES; SHIPPING; SHIP RELATED; STEAMBOAT COLLECTIBLES; TITANIC MEMORABILIA; TRANSPORTATION COLLECTIBLES)

Appraisers

Sara Conklin, ISA
Nautical Appraisals
P.O. Box 30203
Blairsden, CA 96103
ph: 415-467-6249 or 800-464-4208
fax: 415-467-6249
sconklin2@pngusa.net
http://home.earthlink.net/~sconklin2
Managed the collections of the National Maritime Museum in San Francisco for ten years and is an expert in appraising Titanic and other ocean liner objects and related paper ephemera and archival collections.

Clubs/Associations

Sue Ewen
Steamship Historical Society of America,
Inc.
Magazine: Steamboat Bill
300 Ray Dr., Ste. #4
Providence, RI 02906
ph: 401-274-0805
http://www.sshsa.net
For those interested in maritime history; publishes high quality quarterly magazine; has photo bank of thousands of negatives of powered vessels, national and regional meetings.

Charles Ira Sachs
Oceanic Navigation Research Society,
Inc.
Journal: Ship To Shore
P.O. Box 8797
Universal City, CA 91618-8797
ph: 818-985-1345
fax: 818-985-1345
onrs@earthlink.net
Studies the history of ocean liner travel with a focus on the transatlantic service from 1840 to present;

quarterly journal focuses on a topic or ship using rare illustrations and memorabilia to highlight this romantic era of travel.

Collectors

Ken Schultz
P.O. Box M753
Hoboken, NJ 07030
ph: 201-656-0966
fax: 201-418-8640
kschultz@midplains.net
http://userpages.chorus.net/kschultz
Wants all items relating to ocean liners: brochures, deck plans, souvenirs, postcards, models, menus, etc.

Frederick Lingenfelser
814 Byram St.
Reading, PA 19606-1446
lingy@afo.net
Wants to buy pre-1945 ocean liner collectibles: postcards, letters, ship blue prints, deck plans, books, tickets, brochures, dinnerware, souvenirs, models, menus, etc.; especially wants Titanic items.

Dave Cooper
2900 Faulkland Rd.
Wilmington, DE 19808-2514
ph: 302-999-9940
dcooper@synerfac.com
Collects White Star Line china, silver, souvenirs (no paper, please).

Randy Ridgely
447 Oglethorpe Ave.
Athens, GA 30606-2236
ph: 706-549-6264
erie@negia.net
Wants railroad, steamship and airline items.

Robert L. Loewenthal
10161 SW 1st Court
Fort Lauderdale, FL 33324-2226
ph: 954-474-4246
fax: 954-888-1199
bobship@bellsouth.net
Wants to buy ocean liner memorabilia: postcards, china, silver, deck plans, models, posters, books, paper, etc.

Derek Horn
3320 West Belmont Ave.
Phoenix, AZ 85051
ph: 602-589-0184
fax: 602-589-0184
olympicCBO@aol.com
Wants to buy ocean liner memorabilia, especially that pertaining to transatlantic routes from 1850 to 1970; also collects items relating to ocean liners during duty as troopships.

New Steamship Consultants
P.O. Box 30088
Mesa, AZ 85275-0088
ships@oceanliner.com
http://www.oceanliner.com
Wants ocean liner deck plans, brochures, menus, etc.; world's

largest buyers of all ships and lines; quote or send on approval.

Bill Gardner
P.O. Box 1031
Desert Hot Springs, CA 92240-0914
ph: 760-288-3167
Wants old liner cabin plans, view booklets, posters, pictures, reference books, etc. that promote ship travel.

Kathleen Lathom
P.O. Box 5053
Bellingham, WA 98227-5053
ph: 360-676-0715
chinacoll@earthlink.net
Wants to buy US and Canadian steamship china and memorabilia, especially Pacific Coast, Northwest, and Great Lakes and river boat operations.

E.S. Radcliffe
3732 Colonial Lane SE
Port Orchard, WA 98366-1846
ph: 206-876-8615
Wants pre-1940 ocean liner related items: brochures, labels, cards, tableware, books, souvenirs and all paper items.

Dealers

Don Leavitt
Nautiques.net
P.O. Box 930
Canaan, NH 03741
ph: 800-558-7134
info@nautiques.net
http://www.nautiques.net
Carries over 2,500 ocean liner and cruise ship antiques for sale: deck plans, furniture, paper, china, more.

Richard C. Faber, Jr.
230 E. 15th St.
New York, NY 10003
ph: 212-228-7353
fax: 212-477-9392
rfaber@accesshub.net
http://www.accesshub.net/rfaber
Wants booklets, china, deck plans, models, souvenirs, posters, etc. from Lusitania, Titanic, Normandie, Queen Mary, Andrea Doria, etc.

George Theofiles
Miscellaneous Man
P.O. Box 1776
New Freedom, PA 17349-0076
ph: 717-235-4766
fax: 717-235-2853
miscman@adelphia.net
Buys and sells posters and ocean liner ephemera.

David Rhinehart
ShipShape
1041 Tuscany Place
Winter Park, FL 32789-1017
ph: 407-644-2892
fax: 407-644-1833
DWP1041@aol.com
Buy, sell ocean liner (passenger ships) china, silver, models, deck plans, souvenirs, ephemera.

Robert L. Loewenthal
10161 SW 1st Court
Fort Lauderdale, FL 33324-2226
ph: 954-474-4246
fax: 954-888-1199
bobship@bellsouth.net
Wants ocean line memorabilia: postcards, china, books, pictures, silverplate, posters, deck plans, models, etc.

Ered Matthew
Cabin Class Collectibles
P.O. Box 740474
Dallas, TX 75374-0474
ph: 972-235-8639
fax: 972-235-8614
mailroom@cabinclass.com
http://www.cabinclass.com
Buys and sells fine ocean liner, airline, and other transportation memorabilia on the Internet.

New Steamship Consultants
P.O. Box 30088
Mesa, AZ 85275-0088
ships@oceanliner.com
http://www.oceanliner.com
World's largest dealer of original ocean liner memorabilia.

Drake Jasso
Catalyst
1191 Huntington Dr., Ste. 1
Duarte, CA 91010
ph: 626-674-2885 or 562-499-1768
fax: 626-357-8147
drakejasso@earthlink.net
Collector, dealer, expert in oceanliner memorabilia, vintage magazines, vintage newspapers; owner of Past Times Collectibles, a shop aboard the Queen Mary in Long Beach, CA.

Experts

Charles Ira Sachs
TransAtlantic Research
P.O. Box 8797
Universal City, CA 91618-8797
ph: 818-985-1345
fax: 818-985-1345
onrs@earthlink.net
Buys/sells/specializes/lectures on ocean liner and zeppelin history & memorabilia from the high seas (i.e., none from coastal or river steamers) dating from 1840 to 1960s; posters, postcards and related material for collectors/museums.

Sara Conklin, ISA
Nautical Appraisals
P.O. Box 30203
Blairsden, CA 96103
ph: 415-467-6249 or 800-464-4208
fax: 415-467-6249
sconklin2@pngusa.net
http://home.earthlink.net/~sconklin2
Managed the collections of the National Maritime Museum in San Francisco for ten years and is an expert in appraising Titanic and other ocean liner objects and related paper ephemera and archival collections.

Museums/Libraries

South St. Seaport Museum
207 Front St.
New York, NY 10038
ph: 212-748-8600
fax: 212-748-8610
emunoz@southstseaport.org
http://www.southstseaport.org
Devoted to tracing the history of the port of New York; collections comprise artworks, artifacts and documents.

ODDITIES

(see MORBID & ODD ITEMS; GUINNESS WORLD RECORDS; RIPLEY'S BELIEVE IT OR NOT)

OFFICE EQUIPMENT

(see also ADDING MACHINES; CALCULATORS; CLOCKS, Time; INSTRUMENTS & DEVICES; PAPER CLIPS; PENCIL SHARPENERS; PENS; PENCILS; STAPLERS; TYPEWRITERS)

Clubs/Associations

Chuck Dilts, Ed.
Early Typewriter Collectors Association
Magazine: ETCetera
P.O. Box 286
Southborough, MA 01772
ph: 508-229-2064
etcetera@writeme.com
http://typewriter.rydia.net/etcetera.htm
An international club for collectors of old office equipment including typewriters, adding machines, pencil sharpeners, staplers, ribbon tins, etc.; provides contact with worldwide network of members; free ads.

Internationales Forum Historische Burowelt e.V.
Magazine: Historische Burowelt
Gemarkenstr. 61
Essen, D-45147 Germany
ph: 02 01/77 87 99
fax: 941-925-0487
ifhbev@t-online.de
http://www.ifhb.de
Publishes quarterly magazine in German for members of the I.F.H.B. only; in non-German speaking countries with English summaries only.

Collectors

William Feigin
Dualoy, Inc.
45 W. 34th St., Ste. 811
New York, NY 10001-3008
ph: 212-736-3360
fax: 212-594-8327
Wants to buy very old check writers, check perforators, staplers in working condition.

Uwe H. Breker
Bonner Str. 528-530
Koln, D-50968 Germany
ph: 49 221 387049 or 941-925-0385 (US Rep)
fax: 49 221 374878
auction@breker.com
http://www.breker.com
Wants to buy office equipment, typewriters, calculators, pre-1900 printing presses and equipment, adding machines, pencil sharpeners, office literature and magazines.

Dealers

William Feigin
c/o Dualoy, Inc.
45 W. 34th St., Ste. 811
New York, NY 10001-3008
ph: 212-736-3360
fax: 212-594-8327
Buys and sells very old check writers, check perforators, staplers in working condition.

Thor Konwin
Olde Office, This
36564 Camino Del Mar
Cathedral City, CA 92234
ph: 760-328-5690 or 760-409-0970
fax: 760-328-5690
thorkonwin@aol.com
Complete online catalog of vintage office equipment including typewriters, adding machines, check protectors and other office items.

Carole & Larry Meeker
Antiques of a Mechanical Nature
5702 Vacation Blvd.
Somerset, CA 95684-9324
ph: 530-620-7019 or 888-607-6090
fax: 530-620-7020
clm@antiqbuyer.com
http://www.antiqbuyer.com
Buys early office devices as well as other early patented technological items from the home, shop or office: typewriters, pencil sharpeners, calculators, slide rules, early electric or water-powered fans, etc.

Experts

Trent Condellone, Esq.
P.O. Box 2741
Springfield, MO 65801-2741
ph: 417-868-8274
fax: 417-831-7688
Buys, collects and specializes in adding machines, calculating devices, teletypes, clipless stand machines, and any advertising pieces, manuals, parts, tools, etc. relating to the above.

OIL COMPANY MEMORABILIA

(see GAS STATION COLLECTIBLES)

OIL DRILLING COLLECTIBLES

Museums/Libraries

Graham County Historical Oil Museum
P.O. Box 155
Hill City, KS 67642-0155
ph: 785-421-5621
fax: 785-421-6247
ghcoeco@ruraltel.net
http://www.ruraltel.net/gced/oil.htm
Museum is located at 821 West Main St. in Hill City; tours are self-guided; call in advance for a group tour to arrange for a guide.

OINTMENT POTS & POT LIDS

Auction Services

Alan R. Blakeman
B.B.R. Auctions
Elsecar Heritage Centre
Nr Barnsley, South Yorks S74 8HJ U.K.
ph: 01226 745156
fax: 01226 361561
sales@onlinebbr.com
http://www.onlinebbr.com
England's leading specialists and auction house for antique bottles, pot lids and related advertising material.

Collectors

James Hagenbuch
P.O. Box 180
102 Jefferson St.
East Greenville, PA 18041
ph: 215-679-5849
fax: 215-679-3068
glswrk@enter.net
http://www.glswrk-auction.com
Wants to buy American pot lids for private collection. (Pot lids are decorated lids from small ceramic containers from 1840s to 1880s; pot lids first appeared in England.)

Experts

Mark Priestley
Ointment Pot, The
Romer House
Grendon Underwood, Bucks HP18 OSU U.K.
Buys, sells, collects, appraises Victorian ointment pots; also offers advice, expert comment on the subject; these are small, ceramic pots from the turn of the century and earlier claiming to cure all wounds and diseases.

Mark Priestley
Ointment Pot, The
Romer House
Grendon Underwood, Bucks HP18 OSU U.K.
Buys, sells, collects, appraises Victorian ointment pots and pot lids.

Alan R. Blakeman
Elsecar Heritage Centre
Nr Barnsley, South Yorks S74 8HJ U.K.
ph: 01226 745156
fax: 01226 361561
sales@onlinebbr.com
http://www.onlinebbr.com
Author or "Collector's Guide to Ointment Pots."

Internet Resources

Mike Sheridan
World of Bottles & Bygones
30 Brabant Rd.
Cheadle Hulme
Cheadle, Cheshire SK8 7AU U.K.
ph: 011 44 7931 812156
fax: 011 44 7931 812156
bygonz@yahoo.com
http://members.tripod.co.uk/~MikeSheridan
Britain's biggest and busiest Internet site relating to old bottles, pot lids and old advertising.

OLD SLEEPY EYE

Clubs/Associations

Gary Schroeder
Old Sleepy Eye Collectors Club of America
Newsletter: Sleepy Eye Newsletter
P.O. Box 5445
Rockford, IL 61125
ph: 507-282-7899
fax: 507-282-4693
ose@oldsleepyeyecollectors.org
http://www.oldsleepyeyecollectors.org
Based in Monmouth, IL, home of Western Stoneware Co., the plant where Sleepy Eye pottery was produced; club dedicated to the collecting and preservation of items related to the Sleepy Eye Milling Co. of Sleepy Eye, MN.

OLYMPIC GAMES COLLECTIBLES

(see also PINS; SPORTS COLLECTIBLES; STAMP COLLECTING, Sports Related)

Auction Services

Coubertin.com Olympic Collectors Auction
admin@coubertin.com
http://www.coubertin.com
Conducts online Olympic memorabilia and collectibles auctions: medals, tickets, torches, programs, posters, postcards, mascots, philately, badges, buttons and pins.

Clubs/Associations

Paula Burger
Society of Olympic Collectors
Journal: Society of Olympic Collectors Journal
19 Hanbury Path
Sheerwater
Working, Surrey GU21 5RB U.K.

Collectors

Kevin Cummings
Kevin's Olympic Memorabilia
3301 Pinetree Lane
Greenville, NC 27858
ph: 919-412-0583

Kenneth Nix
307 Rosewood Dr.
Dublin, GA 31021-4133
ph: 478-275-0281
fax: 478-272-1744
knix@nlamerica.com
Wants Olympic memorabilia from the Atlanta, 1996 Games; especially wants media pins and badges, and Atlanta Session badges.

Jim Greensfelder
5825 Squire Hill Ct.
Cincinnati, OH 45241-6021
ph: 513-489-6750 or 513-703-5319
fax: 513-489-6757
medal_man@fuse.net
http://www.olympicmedals.info
Wants to buy, sell or trade Olympic pins, medals, torches, automobile items, clothing, banners, uniforms, badges, mugs, steins, anything; author of "Olympic Medals, A Reference Guide."

Jim Clark
6100 Walnut St.
Kansas City, MO 64113-2236
ph: 816-361-4311
fax: 816-333-2635
paradedres@aol.com
Wants anything related to the Olympics: pins, dolls, coins, toys, mascots, displays, and anything marked with the Olympic rings.

Alan Polsky
11845 West Olympic Blvd., #1245
Los Angeles, CA 90064
OLYARP@aol.com
Wants any original Olympic Games' winners' medals, torches, participation medallions, badges worn by athletes or officials, Official Reports, etc. from all Olympics, 1896 to present.

John & Virginia Torney
P.O. Box 2387
Huntington Beach, CA 92647-0387
ph: 714-840-7778
vjtorney@earthlink.net
Olympic Games memorabilia wanted; all years; winter and summer games; wants medals, badges, torches, pins, flags, diplomas, documents, programs, uniforms, etc.

Sy & Ronnie Margolis
17853 Santiago Blvd., #107-210
Villa Park, CA 92861-4113
ph: 714-974-5938
fax: 714-921-0731
smargol@adelphia.net
Wants to buy automobile related items connected with the 1932 Olympics: license plate toppers, radiator badges, hood ornaments, etc.

Dealers

Ray Smith
P.O. Box 254
Elizabeth, NJ 07207-0254
ph: 908-354-5224
fax: 908-352-1576
cgs918@aol.com
Buys and sells Olympic memorabilia: posters, pins, medals, ephemera, wire photos, programs, cigarette cards, uniforms, autographs, tickets, etc.

Steve Milwich
Sign of the Times
105 Gilmore Blvd.
Floral Park, NY 11001
fax: 413-473-2063
steve@signofthetimes.com
http://www.signofthetimes.com
Olympic collector and dealer for over 17 years; carries Olympic torches and medals.

Craig R. Perlow
Olympian Artifacts
P.O. Box 923311
Norcross, GA 30010-3311
craigatl@mindspring.com
http://www.olympianartifacts.com
Largest and most comprehensive Web site devoted exclusively to Olympic memorabilia; site featured on CNN; currently has listings for over 5,500 Artifacts, 1,200 Bid Pins, and 1,400 NOC Pins spanning the years 1912 to 2012.

Ingrid O'Neil
Ingrid O'Neil Sports & Olympic Memorabilia
P.O. Box 872048
Vancouver, WA 98687
ph: 360-834-5202
fax: 360-834-2853
info@ioneil.com
http://www.ioneil.com
Buys and sells all Olympic memorabilia: winner's medals, participation medals, torches, badges, pins, official reports, programs, tickets, posters, diplomas, and souvenirs.

Experts

Craig R. Perlow
Olympian Artifacts
P.O. Box 923311
Norcross, GA 30010-3311
craigatl@mindspring.com
http://www.olympianartifacts.com
Listed by the International Olympic Memorabilia Federation as one of the top experts in the area of Olympic memorabilia.

Jim Greensfelder
5825 Squire Hill Ct.
Cincinnati, OH 45241-6021
ph: 513-489-6750 or 513-703-5319
fax: 513-489-6757
medal_man@fuse.net
http://www.olympicmedals.info
Wants to buy, sell or trade Olympic pins, medals, torches, automobile items, clothing, banners, uniforms, badges, mugs, steins, anything; author

of "Olympic Medals, A Reference Guide."

Internet Resources

U.S. Olympic Committee Online
One Olympic Plaza
Colorado Springs, CO 80909-5760
ph: 719-578-4948
fax: 719-632-02504
usoc.online@usoc.org
http://www.usolympicteam.com
The US Olympic Committee offers officially-licensed merchandise, authentics and collectibles.

Pins & Buttons

Clubs/Associations

Don Bigsby
Olympic Pin Collector's Club
1386 5th St.
Schenectady, NY 12303
ph: 518-355-9445 or 518-356-6525
fax: 518-356-1559
dbigsby1@nycap.rr.com
The largest and oldest pin trading club in North America.

Rowan Fay
International Pin Collectors Club
Newsletter: IPCC Newsletter
602 Chenango St.
Binghamton, NY 13901-2029
ph: 607-724-4583 or 607-723-7421
fax: 607-723-3687
rhfay@juno.com
Interested in all sorts of pins: Olympic, Coca Cola, sports, Desert Storm, media, etc.

Collectors

Don Bigsby
1386 5th St.
Schenectady, NY 12303
ph: 518-355-9445 or 518-356-6525
fax: 518-356-1559
dbigsby1@nycap.rr.com
Interested in Olympic pins as well as other Olympic related memorabilia.

Dealers

Rick Amari
Wreckme's Olympic Pin Trader
111 Misty Oak Place
Gahanna, OH 43230
ph: 614-471-1112
fax: 614-471-3606
sales@wreckme.com
http://www.wreckme.com/index2.htm
Great Web site for Olympic pin traders and enthusiasts; site includes over 400 pins (with photos) from all Olympics from 1980 through 2004; new pins added every week; links to pin discussion groups, pin auctions, pin information.

Bill Nelson
Newsletter: Bill Nelson Newsletter, The
P.O. Box 41630
Tucson, AZ 85717-1630
ph: 520-629-0868 or 800-368-8434
fax: 520-629-0387
sales@pinsbymail.com
http://www.pinsbymail.com
Monthly newsletter with news, tips, and sources for collectors of Olympic, Sport, Disney, Coca Cola pins; over a million pins in inventory; established in 1985.

OPENERS

(see BOTTLE OPENERS; CAN OPENERS; CORKSCREWS)

OPTICAL ITEMS

(see also BINOCULARS; CAMERAS & CAMERA EQUIPMENT; EYE RELATED ITEMS; INSTRUMENTS & DEVICES; KALEIDOSCOPES; MEDICAL, DENTAL & PHARMACEUTICAL; MAGIC LANTERNS & SLIDES; MICROSCOPES; STANHOPES; STEREO VIEWERS & STEREOVIEWS; 3-D PHOTOGRAPHICA; TOYS, Optical)

Appraisers

J. William Rosenthal, MD, ISA
3434 Prytania St., Ste. 250
New Orleans, LA 70115-3551
ph: 504-891-1988 or 504-895-1673
fax: 504-845-1657
JWRosenHar@aol.com
Buys, sells, specializes in and appraises visual aids, spectacles, lorgnettes, opera glasses; author of "Spectacles and Other Visual Aids: A History and Guide to Collecting."

Auction Services

Bryan W. Ginns
2109 Cty. Rte. 21
Valatie, NY 12184-6001
ph: 518-392-5805
fax: 518-392-7925
the3dman@aol.com
Conducts mail sales specializing in optical items such as cameras, magic lantern slide projectors, stereographica, polyorama pantoptiques, praxinoscopes, zeotropes, kinoras, coin-operated mutoscopes, etc.

Clubs/Associations

J. William Rosenthal, MD, ISA
Ocular Heritage Society
3434 Prytania St., Ste. 250
New Orleans, LA 70115-3551
ph: 504-891-1988 or 504-895-1673
fax: 504-845-1657
JWRosenHar@aol.com
Annual meetings, sale, lectures.

Ralph Shape
Magic Lantern Society of the U. S. & Canada
Newsletter: Magic Lantern Gazette
3757 South 194th St.
Seattle, WA 98188
ph: 206-592-8270
fax: 206-592-8269
RShape@compuserve.com
http://www.magiclanternsociety.org
Collectors, restorers, preservers of the history of magic lanterns - the forerunner of cinema; members are also interested in magic lantern glass slides as well as other optical devices.

Frank Barraclough
Opthalmic Antiques International Collectors' Club
3 Moor Park Rd.
Northwood, Middlesex HA6 2DL U.K.
michael.mellor1@btinternet.com
http://www.college-optometrists.org/college/museum/oaicc.htm
A club for those interested in the history of spectacles and in collecting optical instruments, magnifiers, quizzers, spectacles, books, eye baths, etc.

Collectors

Maret Webb
5101 E. Monterey Way
Phoenix, AZ 85018-6623
ph: 602-957-0653
fax: 602-957-1631
maret@vehrwebbstudio.com
Wants to buy antique spyglasses, telescopes, microscopes.

Dealers

C. Keith Wilbur, M.D.
Doctor's Bag, The
397 Prospect St.
Northampton, MA 01060-2089
ph: 413-584-1440
doctorsbag@juno.com
Buys, sells, appraises apothecary, medical, dental, surgical, optical & quack instruments, equipment, advertising, books, etc.; catalogs available 3 to 4 times a year; author of "Antique Medical Instruments" and other books.

Al & Bobbie Roberts
Rational Past, The
221 Oceano Dr.
Los Angeles, CA 90049-4123
ph: 310-476-6277
fax: 310-476-6278
malinfo@therationalpast.com
http://www.therationalpast.com
Organizer of West Coast Scientific & Technical Antique and Collectible Shows (Los Angeles and San Francisco.)

ORDNANCE

(see AMMUNITION & EXPLOSIVE ORDNANCE)

ORIENTALIA

(see also ARMS & ARMOR; ART, Asian; ART, Oriental; BRONZES; CERAMICS [ORIENTAL]; CLOISONNE; FURNITURE [ANTIQUE], Chinese; GEMS & JEWELRY, Jade; INDONESIA; IVORY; JADE; PHILIPPINES; NETSUKE; PRINTS, Woodblock [Japanese]; SILVER, Chinese; SNUFF BOTTLES)

Appraisers

AsktheAppraiser.com
4 Brussels St.
Worcester, MA 01610
ph: 781-821-0199
ata@collectingchannel.com
http://www.AsktheAppraiser.com
The premiere online appraisal service offered by CollectingChannel.com; all appraisals comply with the "Uniform Standards of Professional Appraisal Practice" and with the standards of the Association of Online Appraisers.

Sandra Andacht
P.O. Box 94
Little Neck, NY 11363-0094
ph: 718-229-6593
Orientalia@aol.com
http://hometown.aol.com/orientalia/index.html
Author of "Collector's Value Guide to Japanese Woodblock Prints," "Collector's Value Guide to Oriental Decorative Arts," and "Oriental Antiques Art - An Identification & Value Guide" (Krause).

Marvin Sokolow
425 West Fairy Chasm Rd.
Milwaukee, WI 53217
ph: 414-351-5750
msokolow@msn.com
Specializes in the buying, selling, appraising Asian antiques, silver, and European and Russian enamels.

Patricia Graham
Asian Art Research & Appraisals
1641 Rhode Island St.
Lawrence, KS 66044
ph: 785-841-1477
fax: 785-841-1477
pgraham@ku.edu
Serves as a consultant on Asian fine arts to private collections, businesses, and museums; does IRS, estate and insurance appraisals; specializes in Japanese paintings, prints and ceramics; also Chinese, and Korean.

Rhonda C. Tollstrup, ISA
R.C. Tollstrup Appraisals
2221 Valley Mill
Carrollton, TX 75006
ph: 972-416-5613
randd.art@verizon.net
http://www.randdorientalart.com
Specializes in the appraisal of Asian antiques.

Dana Franklin
Antiquity
3916 W. Runge Ct.
Irving, TX 75038
ph: 972-570-4740
danafranklin1@yahoo.com
Buys, sells, appraises Orientalia:
Chinese, Japanese, Thai, Korean, and
other Asian antiques and collectibles;
Accredited Member of the Interna-
tional Society of Appraisers; since
1985.

Elisabeth Douglas, ASA, ISA
China Coast, The
P.O. Box 610
Austin, TX 78767
ph: 512-330-9524 or 512-789-7507
fax: 512-330-9348
wien@texas.net
http://www.asianartappraisals.com
Active in the field of Asian art and
antiques for over twenty years;
specializing in damage, insurance and
IRS appraisals; also offers brokerage
of Chinese, Japanese, and Southeast
Asian Art.

Fuji Murakami, ASA
Asian Art Appraisal Service
P.O. Box 24999
Denver, CO 80224-0999
ph: 303-758-8379
fax: 303-758-0816
fmarkm@qwest.net
Bronze, Asian ivory, netsuke,
ceramics, costumes/robes/embroider-
ies, jade and other mineral carvings,
snuff bottles, paintings, calligraphy,
prints, screens and scrolls, textiles of
China, Korea, Japan, Southeast Asia,
some India/Tibet.

Kathryn Wolk, ISA
Antique Appraisal Services
P.O. Box 1834
Fallbrook, CA 92088
ph: 760-728-2346 or 760-505-7654
aprazit@earthlink.net
Specializes in the appraisal of
ceramics, Orientalia, and furniture;
Accredited member of the International
Society of Appraisers and the
Appraisers National Association.

Scott Zema, ISA CAPP
Ark Limited Appraisals, Inc.
ph: 425-486-6310
scottzema@msn.com
http://www.arklimited.com

Scott Singer, ISA
Singer Antique Galleries, Inc.
411 W. Galer St.
Seattle, WA 98119
ph: 206-285-0394
fax: 206-283-5264
singer@tias.com
http://www.tias.com/stores/singer
Specializes in Asian art, furniture,
porcelain, pottery, ceramics.

Auction Services

James Callahan
Skinner, Inc.
63 Park Plaza
The Heritage on the Garden
Boston, MA 02116
ph: 617-350-5400
fax: 617-350-5429
info@skinnerinc.com
http://www.skinnerinc.com
Established in 1971, Skinner Inc. is
the fourth largest auction house in the
US; has offices in Boston and Bolton,
MA.

John H. Schofield
Eldred's
P.O. Box 796
East Dennis, MA 02641-0796
ph: 508-385-3116
fax: 508-385-7201
eldreds@capecod.net
http://www.eldreds.com
Specialists with annual week-long
series of auction dedicated to
Orientalia for over 25 years.

Christie's
20 Rockefeller Plaza
New York, NY 10020
ph: 212-636-2000
info@christies.com
http://www.christies.com

Sotheby's
1334 York Ave.
New York, NY 10021
ph: 212-606-7000
fax: 212-606-7107
http://www.sothebys.com
Over 70 collecting areas are featured
at Sotheby's auctions including toys,
dolls, porcelain, furniture, silver, art,
books; exhibitions are free and
everyone is welcome; for a free copy of
"Sotheby's Newsletter," call 212-606-
7245.

Freeman's Auction Gallery
1808 Chestnut St.
Philadelphia, PA 19103
ph: 215-563-9275
fax: 215-563-8236
proberts@freemansauction.com
http://www.freemansauction.com
America's oldest auction house:
Continental, English and American
furniture, paintings, silver and
decorative arts; Oriental rugs, rare
books, fine jewelry, Orientalia.

Isadore M. Chait
I.M. Chait Gallery
9330 Civic Center Dr.
Beverly Hills, CA 90210
ph: 310-285-0182
fax: 310-285-9740
IMChait@chait.com
http://www.chait.com
Appraiser, auctioneer, expert in
Oriental antiques and art; monthly
auctions of approximately 450 mostly
period lots; also has a retail store;
specializes in Han, T'ang, Sung,
Ming, Ching, and other dynasties.

Bonhams & Butterfields
220 San Bruno Ave.
San Francisco, CA 94103
ph: 415-861-7500 or 800-223-2854
fax: 415-861-8951
info.US@butterfields.com
http://www.butterfields.com
Auctioneers and appraisers of
antiques, fine art and collectibles in
all categories; specialty sales include
posters, toys, decorative arts,
furniture, photography, etc.; the
largest full service auction in the
West.

McClain Auctions
825 Halekauwila St.
Honolulu, HI 96813-5315
ph: 808-538-7227 or 808-596-3900
fax: 808-545-7007

Clubs/Associations

Chase Gilmore
Oriental Art Society of Chicago
Intern. Antique Center
6122 N. Clark St.
Chicago, IL 60660
ph: 773-761-4901
Brings together and enriches members
through viewing and sharing of
knowledge and information about
Orientalia; programs and field trips.

Dealers

Robert & Vinka Berg
Ichiban Japanese & Oriental Antiques
P.O. Box 395
Marion, CT 06444-0395
ph: 203-272-7392
TheBergs@snet.net
http://www.ichibanantiques.com
Carries a fine collection of Asian art
including ceramics, bronzes, Ukiyo-E,
cloisonne, tea articles, paintings,
Buddhist art, scholars items, Mingei
art.

Anthony Blower
Anthony's Asian Art
1 Devonshire Dr.
Hazlet, NJ 07730-1671
ph: 732-335-1515
fax: 732-335-1977
ablo2000@aol.com
http://www.trocadero.com/anthonys
Specializing in Imari, Satsuma,
cloisonne, rootwood, metalwork, arms
& armor, bronzes.

Richard Spence
Circle of the Moon Antiques
219P Berlin Rd., Ste. 160
Cherry Hill, NJ 08034
ph: 856-428-3546
fax: 856-428-9282
info@circleofthemoon.com
http://www.circleofthemoon.com
Specializing in Orientalia including
netsuke, woodblock prints, porcelain
and pottery, snuff bottles, textiles, and
lacquerware.

Jeffrey L. Andacht
Oriental Antiques Shop Miracle Ventures
 Inc.
P.O. Box 75
Little Neck, NY 11363
ph: 718-225-1461
fax: 718-822-1461
Samuari66@aol.com
http://members.aol.com/Samuari66/
 orientalantiques.html
An online shop specializing in
Chinese, Japanese and Korean
antiques including Imari, Kutani,
Satsuma, woodblock prints,
metalwares, etc.; always interested in
purchasing items.

Sandra Andacht
P.O. Box 94
Little Neck, NY 11363-0094
ph: 718-229-6593
Orientalia@aol.com
http://hometown.aol.com/orientalia/
 index.html
Buys and sells Oriental antiques,
collectibles, fine art: Asian, Japanese,
Chinese, Korean, Southeast Asia.

Susan Akins
Oriental Antiques by Susan Akins
3740 Howard Ave.
Kensington, MD 20895-3347
ph: 301-946-4609
http://www.kensingtonantiquerow.com/
 orientalantiquesbysusan
All Asian countries: China, Japan,
Indonesia, S.E. Asia, India, etc.;
specializing in fine porcelains,
furniture, ivories, carvings, hangings,
ancient artifacts.

James Sisk
Far East Gallery, The
105A Beacon Rd.
Baltimore, MD 21220
ph: 410-686-4216
fax: 410-574-8160
info@fareastgallery.com
http://www.netsukestore.com
Offers a large selection of Asian arts
and crafts, and collectibles; extensive
history and culture section.

Joe Arnold
East & Beyond, Ltd.
6727 Curran St.
Mc Lean, VA 22101
ph: 703-448-8200
fax: 703-821-1272
EandBeyond@aol.com
http://www.eandbeyond.com
A three-story gallery specializing in
antiques from China, Japan and
Korea: furniture, boxes, benches,
chairs, porcelain, and textiles.

Sharon & Arno Ziesnitz
7835 Painted Daisy Dr.
Springfield, VA 22152
ph: 703-451-1033
fax: 703-569-4221
ziesnitz@aol.com
Lecturers, authors, consultants want
fine works of art: netsuke, inro, ojime,
sword accessories, cloisonne,
Satsuma, ivory and wood carvings,

Chinese snuff bottles, Japanese traveling shrines, and Japanese metalworks.

Chong Leong
Kay's Antiques & Gifts
Beach St. Antiques Mall
116 S. Beach St.
Daytona Beach, FL 32114
ph: 386-252-1656
kaysantiques@cs.com
Buys and sells fine oriental objects and works of art.

AntiqueJades.com
P.O. Box 600895
Springfield, MA 32260-0895
ph: 904-288-8190
sales@antiquejades.com
http://www.antiquejades.com
Carries authentic and certified Chinese jades from all time periods.

Susie Lorin
Asianantiques, Inc.
130 North Park Ave.
Winter Park, FL 32789
ph: 407-629-9118
fax: 407-629-0818
questions@asiantiques.com
http://www.asiantiques.com
Specializes in high quality and rare Korean, Japanese and Chinese antiques: Chinese snuff bottles, Japanese netsuke, Chinese jade; especially archaic pieces.

Cynthia "Sachi" Wagner
Midori Gallery
3170 Commodore Plaza
Miami, FL 33133
ph: 305-443-3399
fax: 305-569-0911
Specializes in Chinese and Japanese antique furniture and works of art: Japanese tansu chests and Chinese hardwood furniture, paintings, screens, archaic ceramic sculpture, Buddhist icons, netsuke and sagemono, tapestries, bronze, etc.

Mary Morrison
Tiananmen Trading
2512 North Greenway Dr.
Miami, FL 33134
ph: 786-552-1311
fax: 786-552-1311
tiananmentrading@aol.com
http://www.tiananmentrading.com
Largest collection of original 1910-1940 Chinese advertising lithographs (also known as the 1920s "Shanghai Posters"); beware of the cheap reproductions being sold by others.

Bill Egleston
509 Brentwood Rd.
Marshalltown, IA 50158-3727
ph: 800-798-4579
fax: 515-752-4570
Specializing in mail order sale of Oriental art, jade, cloisonne, netsuke, etc.; send for catalog.

Marvin Sokolow
425 West Fairy Chasm Rd.
Milwaukee, WI 53217
ph: 414-351-5750
msokolow@msn.com
Specializes in the buying, selling, appraising Asian antiques, silver, and European and Russian enamels.

Dana Franklin
Antiquity
3916 W. Runge Ct.
Irving, TX 75038
ph: 972-570-4740
danafranklin1@yahoo.com
Buys, sells, appraises Orientalia: Chinese, Japanese, Thai, Korean, and other Asian antiques and collectibles; Accredited Member of the International Society of Appraisers; since 1985.

Byla Simon Kunis, ISA
Oriental Treasures Antiques
1851 June Lake Dr.
Henderson, NV 89052
ph: 702-492-1174
fax: 702-432-1456
Orientbyla@aol.com
Specializes in Chinese and Japanese antiques and objets d'art: textiles, ivory, jade, lacquer, metal; also appraises.

Isadore M. Chait
I.M. Chait Gallery
9330 Civic Center Dr.
Beverly Hills, CA 90210
ph: 310-285-0182
fax: 310-285-9740
IMChait@chait.com
http://www.chait.com
Appraiser, auctioneer, expert in Oriental antiques and art; specializes in Han, T'ang, Sung, Ming, Ching, and other dynasties; also sells Japanese woodblock prints, netsuke, jades, ivory, snuff bottle, furniture, Tibetan, SE Asia.

Larry Nelson
Orientalia.com
31653 Outer Hwy. 10
Redlands, CA 92373
ph: 909-794-3594
info@orientalia.com
http://www.orientalia.com
Specializing in Asian antiques and art since 1976.

Marsha L. Vargas, ASA
Xanadu/Folk Art International
871 Santa Cruz Ave.
Menlo Park, CA 94022
ph: 650-329-9999
fax: 650-328-3918
info@folkartintl.com
http://www.folkartintl.com
Interested in Asian, African and Oceanic antiques and works of art; has one of the largest collections on the West Coast of fine antique Tibetan//Nepalese bronzes and works of art as well as exceptional Khmer sculpture.

Robyn Buntin
Robyn Buntin of Honolulu
848 So. Beretania St.
Honolulu, HI 96813
ph: 808-523-5913
fax: 808-536-6305
rbuntin@lava.net
http://www.robynbuntin.com
Buys and sells extraordinary Chinese and Japanese items such as netsuke, scholar's table items, paintings, prints, screens, jade and lacquer ware.

Bernie
755 Isenberg St., 305
Honolulu, HI 96826-4504
ph: 808-941-8639
fax: 808-845-9638
Appraiser, dealer specializes in pre-1920 artifacts from Hawaii, China, Korea, Japan and other Asia countries.

Scott Singer, ISA
Singer Antique Galleries, Inc.
411 W. Galer St.
Seattle, WA 98119
ph: 206-285-0394
fax: 206-283-5264
singer@tias.com
http://www.tias.com/stores/singer
Specializes in buying, selling, appraising Asian art, furniture, porcelain, pottery, ceramics.

Victor Topper
Topper Gallery
111 Finch Ave. W, Ste. 214
Markham, Ontario M3J 2E5 Canada
ph: 416-665-7554
fax: 416-665-8164
topperart@rogers.com
http://www.topperart.com
Chinese art, Japanese art, Buddhistic art, Precolumbian, Judaica, Inuit art, Northwest Coast Indians; early Chinese bronze vessels, snuff bottles, early Jade carvings.

Ed Pramuk
Art Source Asia
7A Merry Court 10 Castle Rd.
Hong Kong
ph: 852-2803-7430 or 852-9520-7022
fax: 852-2546-1660
artsourceasia@aol.com
http://www.artsourceasia.com
Direct source for Asian antiques, art and collectibles.

Peter
Oriental Art Collection
Blk 3, New Bugis St., #01-21
Singapore, 188867 Singapore
ph: 3369208
boyseen@cyberway.com.sg
Specializes in Oriental fine arts from: wood carvings, jade, paintings, netsuke, ivory, bronzes.

Christopher Krokos
ThailandTradeNet.com
79/41 Moo 2 Highway
Chiang Mai, Doi Saket 50220 Thailand
ph: +66-53-867-497
fax: +66-53-867-497
webmaster@thailandtradenet.com
http://www.thailandtgradenet.com
Specializes in Asian art: jade sculptures, Thai benjarong, sterling silver, fine porcelain, woodcarvings, tapestry, lacquerware, furniture, marble and bronze sculptures, etc.

Anita Gray
Fine Antique Porcelain
58 Davies St.
London, W1Y 2LP U.K.
ph: +44 (0) 171 408 1638
fax: +44 (0) 171 495-0707
info@chinese-porcelain.com
http://www.chinese-porcelain.com
For over 30 years specializing in antique Chinese and Japanese porcelain and works of art.

Experts

Patricia M. Grove
PMG Antique Appraisal Research
3 Ober St.
Beverly, MA 01915-4639
ph: 978-927-2979
fax: 978-927-8625
Collects, researches and appraises decorative and fine arts of the China, Japan, India and Russia export trades, 17th through mid-19th centuries: paintings, silver, ivory, tortoise carvings, furniture, fans, lacquer.

Sandra Andacht
P.O. Box 94
Little Neck, NY 11363-0094
ph: 718-229-6593
Orientalia@aol.com
http://hometown.aol.com/orientalia/index.html
Author of "Collector's Value Guide to Japanese Woodblock Prints," "Collector's Value Guide to Oriental Decorative Arts," and "Oriental Antiques Art - An Identification & Value Guide."

Dr. Daphne L. Rosenzweig, ISA CAPP
Rosenzweig Associates
P.O. Box 3976
Sarasota, FL 34230-3976
ph: 941-371-4643
fax: 941-342-6893
rosetwig@aol.com
Consultant and appraiser dealing with Oriental Art; author of "Selected Works from the Fine Arts Group of Later Chinese Painting;" specializes in Chinese art, and Japanese prints and ceramics.

Richard R. Silverman
838 N. Doheny Dr. #1102
West Hollywood, CA 90069-4851
ph: 310-271-1896 or 310-273-3838
fax: 310-273-3843
Specializes in Japanese prints and ceramics; netsuke and inro; also Thai,

Burmese, Indian and Nepalese items; call 12:00 noon to 12:00 midnight PST; International Society of Appraiser, Certified Appraiser in netsuke.

Museums/Libraries

Charles Jones
University of Chicago's Oriental Institute Museum
ph: 773-702-9537
cejo@midway.uchicago.edu
http://www-oi.uchicago.edu/OI/MUS/OI_Museum.html

George Walter Vincent Smith Art Museum
220 State St.
Springfield, MA 01103-1703
ph: 413-263-6800
fax: 413-263-6889
info@spfldlibmus.org
http://www.quadrangle.org/GWVS.htm
Recognized collections of American paintings; Orientalia including Japanese arms & armor, screens, lacquers, textiles and ceramics; Islamic rugs; and the largest collection of Chinese cloisonne in the Western world.

Arthur M. Sackler Gallery
Smithsonian Institution
1050 Independence Ave. SW
Washington, DC 20560
ph: 202-357-3200
edsonmi@asia.si.edu
http://www.asia.si.edu
The Chinese Dept. will authenticate your Chinese works of art; call to make an appointment; limit 5 items per visit, 10 items per year; may be able to work from good photographs.

Art Institute of Chicago
111 S. Michigan Ave.
Chicago, IL 60603
ph: 312-443-3600
webmaster@artic.edu
http://www.artic.edu
Galleries of Chinese, Japanese, and Korean art contain 20,000 works covering nearly 5,000 years representing a variety of media from China, Japan, Korea, Southeast Asia, India, and the Near and Middle East.

Pacific Asia Museum
Newsletter: Pacific Asia Museum Member Newsletter
46 N. Los Robles Ave.
Pasadena, CA 91101
ph: 818-449-2742
fax: 818-449-2754
PacAsiaMus@aol.com
http://www.pacasiamuseum.org
Preserves, presents, and interprets to the public the arts and culture of the Pacific Islands and Asia.

Asian Art Museum of San Francisco
Magazine: Treasures
200 Larkin St.
San Francisco, CA 94102
ph: 415-581-3500
pr@asianart.org
http://www.asianart.org
One the largest museums in the Western world devoted exclusively to Asian art with nearly 15,000 treasures spanning 6,000 years of history; over 2,500 works on display; constitutes a comprehensive introduction to all major Asian cultures.

Repair Services

Isadore M. Chait
I.M. Chait Gallery
9330 Civic Center Dr.
Beverly Hills, CA 90210
ph: 310-285-0182
fax: 310-285-9740
IMChait@chait.com
http://www.chait.com
Restorers of all types of Asian antiques: ceramics, paper, wood, metal, etc.

Repro. Sources

Joan L. Cervi
Arts of Asia
3203 Adams Way
Ambler, PA 19002-3741
ph: 215-628-2026
fax: 215-628-2026
jcnetsuke@aol.com
Importer of statues, netsuke, snuff bottles, etc.; wholesale prices; annual catalog with updates $5; annual video $5.

Manny Shaool
Manny's Oriental Rugs
72 W. Washington St.
Hagerstown, MD 21740
ph: 301-797-7434
Importer of Oriental ivory, porcelain, reverse paintings, rugs; also Remington recast bronzes, clocks, lacquered furniture.

Chinese Items

Appraisers

Elisabeth Douglas, ASA, ISA
China Coast, The
P.O. Box 610
Austin, TX 78767
ph: 512-330-9524 or 512-789-7507
fax: 512-330-9348
wien@texas.net
http://www.asianartappraisals.com
Active in the field of Asian art and antiques for over twenty years; specializing in damage, insurance and IRS appraisals; also offers brokerage of Chinese, Japanese, and Southeast Asian Art.

Dealers

Joe Arnold
East & Beyond, Ltd.
6727 Curran St.
Mc Lean, VA 22101
ph: 703-448-8200
fax: 703-821-1272
EandBeyond@aol.com
http://www.eandbeyond.com
A three-story gallery specializing in antiques from China, Japan and Korea: furniture, boxes, benches, chairs, porcelain, and textiles.

Deb Youtie
Chinese Antiquities
3038L N. Federal Highway
Fort Lauderdale, FL 33308
ph: 954-563-2622 or 954-772-4164
fax: 954-772-3722
debyoutie@aol.com
http://www.chineseantiques.com
Buys and sells Chinese antiques including furniture; most furniture is from the Ming and Qing dynasties.

Michael Yip
Han Palace Fine Arts
11665 Powell St.
San Francisco, CA 94108
ph: 415-788-5338
fax: 415-788-5233
yip@hanpalace.com
http://www.hanpalace.com
A private antique gallery in San Francisco specializing in high quality authentic Chinese antiques.

Jadestone Gallery
10922 N.E. St. Johns Rd.
Vancouver, WA 98686
ph: 360-573-2580 or 800-854-JADE
fax: 360-573-4834
artinfo@jadestonegallery.com
http://www.jadestonegallery.com
Specializes in Chinese art and antiquities: Neolithic, tomb sculptures, pottery and porcelain, fine jade and other carvings.

Misc. Services

Arthur M. Sackler Gallery
Smithsonian Institution
1050 Independence Ave. SW
Washington, DC 20560
ph: 202-357-3200
edsonmi@asia.si.edu
http://www.asia.si.edu
The Chinese Dept. will authenticate your Chinese works of art; call to make an appointment; limit 5 items per visit, 10 items per year; may be able to work from good photographs.

Japanese Items

(see also ARMS & ARMOR, Japanese; BOOKS, Reference [Japanese Items]; FIREARMS, Japanese Matchlocks; OCCUPIED JAPAN; PRINTS, Woodblock [Japanese])

Appraisers

Mr. Masatoshi Fukumaru
Heian Art
8700 Commerce Park St., Ste. 212
Houston, TX 77036
ph: 888-333-6254 or 713-541-0203
fax: 713-541-0318
art@japaneseantiqueart.com
http://www.japaneseantiqueart.com
Dealer, collector, appraiser buys and sells high quality Japanese art and antiques.

Elisabeth Douglas, ASA, ISA
China Coast, The
P.O. Box 610
Austin, TX 78767
ph: 512-330-9524 or 512-789-7507
fax: 512-330-9348
wien@texas.net
http://www.asianartappraisals.com
Active in the field of Asian art and antiques for over twenty years; specializing in damage, insurance and IRS appraisals; also offers brokerage of Chinese, Japanese, and Southeast Asian Art.

Auction Services

John H. Schofield
Eldred's
P.O. Box 796
East Dennis, MA 02641-0796
ph: 508-385-3116
fax: 508-385-7201
eldreds@capecod.net
http://www.eldreds.com
Specialists with annual week-long series of auction dedicated to Orientalia for over 25 years.

Collectors

Alistair C.G. Seton
Daruma Magazine
Mukonoso Higashi 1-12-5
Amagasaki, 661-0032 Japan
ph: 81-78-851-6654 or 81-6-6436-5874
fax: 81-6-6438-1882
momoko@gao.ne.jp
http://www.darumamagazine.com
Collector of Japanese art and antiques.

Dealers

Richard Murphy
Asahi Japan Collectibles
19 Timberwood Rd.
Kensington, CT 06037
ph: 888-282-4452 or 860-828-3106
fax: 860-828-3106
info@asahi-jc.com
http://www.asahi-jc.com
Provides customers world wide with high quality Japanese culture related goods: kimono, Ukiyo-E art, Japanese dolls, Buddha, etc.

Robert & Vinka Berg
Ichiban Japanese & Oriental Antiques
P.O. Box 395
Marion, CT 06444-0395
ph: 203-272-7392
TheBergs@snet.net
http://www.ichibanantiques.com
Carries a fine collection of Asian art including ceramics, bronzes, Ukiyo-E, cloisonne, tea articles, paintings, Buddhist art, scholars items, Mingei art.

Michael R. Bernstein
Fine Japanese Art
16 West 16th St., Apr. 7JN
New York, NY 10011
ph: 646-230-7993
fax: 646-230-7992
netsukeninro@worldnet.att.net
http://www.netsuke-inro.com
Deals exclusively in Japanese art, specializing in netsuke, inro, pipe cases, ojime, tsuba and lacquer; has sold works which now appear in the collections of major museums and the most prominent private collectors.

Denis Szeszler
Antique Oriental Art
P.O. Box 714
New York, NY 10028-0044
ph: 212-427-4682
fax: 212-860-4426
Specializes in antique netsuke and related works of art: inro and other sagemono, pipe cases, yatate, okimono, etc.; buys and sells; researches and appraises.

Jeffrey L. Andacht
Oriental Antiques Shop Miracle Ventures Inc.
P.O. Box 75
Little Neck, NY 11363
ph: 718-225-1461
fax: 718-822-1461
Samuari66@aol.com
http://members.aol.com/Samuari66/
orientalantiques.html
An online shop specializing in Chinese, Japanese and Korean antiques including Imari, Kutani, Satsuma, woodblock prints, metalwares, etc.; always interested in purchasing items.

Yoneyama
Ginza, "Things Japanese"
1721 Connecticut Ave., NW
Washington, DC 20009-1108
ph: 202-331-7991
fax: 202-265-1319
ginzashop@msn.com
http://www.ginzaonline.com
Specialty gift store 80% Japanese imports/collectibles/decorative accessories: fine china, sake sets, tea sets, kimono & happi coats, futons, bonsai/ikebana, origami, toys, dolls/cases, shoji screens & lamps, prints, lanterns, etc.

Joe Arnold
East & Beyond, Ltd.
6727 Curran St.
Mc Lean, VA 22101
ph: 703-448-8200
fax: 703-821-1272
EandBeyond@aol.com
http://www.eandbeyond.com
A three-story gallery specializing in antiques from China, Japan and Korea: furniture, boxes, benches, chairs, porcelain, and textiles.

Mr. Masatoshi Fukumaru
Heian Art
8700 Commerce Park St., Ste. 212
Houston, TX 77036
ph: 888-333-6254 or 713-541-0203
fax: 713-541-0318
art@japaneseantiqueart.com
http://www.japaneseantiqueart.com
Dealer, collector, appraiser buys and sells high quality Japanese art and antiques.

Gary Myers
Yoshino Japanese Antiques
1240 E. Colorado Blvd.
Pasadena, CA 91106
ph: 626-356-0588
yoshinoja@earthlink.net
http://www.yoshinoantiques.com
Offers the finest in Japanese antiques, art, and folk craft.

Geri Servi
McMullen's Japanese Antiques
260A Lambert St.
Oxnard, CA 93030
ph: 877-407-4491
hosoge@mcmullens.com
http://www.mcmullens.com
One of the largest dealers of Japanese antiques in the US; offers hundreds of unique items ranging from tansu to handpainted folding screens, fine art, scrolls, rare dolls, armor, porcelain, textiles and kimono.

Imari, Inc.
40 Filbert Ave.
Sausalito, CA 94965-1842
ph: 415-332-0245
fax: 415-332-3621
Specializes in Japanese antiques and screens.

Lars Nordin
Meiji Art
Tallidsvagen 8c
Nacka, 131 37 Sweden
ph: +46 8 7478529
fax: +46 8 7478529
oni@meijiart.se
http://www.meijiart.se
Specializes in Japanese art such as netsuke, inro, cloisonne and metalwork.

Tansu Ltd.
Skopos Mills
Bradford Rd.
Batley, West Yorkshire WF17 6LZ U.K.
ph: 44-1924-422391
fax: 44-1924-443856
Specializes in Tansu.

Experts

Dr. Daphne L. Rosenzweig, ISA CAPP
Rosenzweig Associates
P.O. Box 3976
Sarasota, FL 34230-3976
ph: 941-371-4643
fax: 941-342-6893
rosetwig@aol.com
Consultant and appraiser dealing with Oriental Art; author of "Selected Works from the Fine Arts Group of Later Chinese Painting;" specializes in Chinese art, and Japanese prints and ceramics.

Misc. Services

Barbara Brooks
Arthur M. Sackler Gallery
Smithsonian Institution
1050 Independence Ave. SW
Washington, DC 20560
ph: 202-357-3200
edsonmi@asia.si.edu
http://www.asia.si.edu
The Japanese Dept. will authenticate your Japanese works of art; call to make an appointment; limit 5 items per visit, 10 items per year; may be able to work from good photographs.

Museums/Libraries

Morikami Museum & Japanese Gardens
4000 Morikami Park Rd.
Delray Beach, FL 33446-2305
ph: 561-495-0233
fax: 561-499-2557
morikami@co.palm-beach.fl.us
http://www.morikami.org
Focuses on Japanese utilitarian objects of everyday use; also contains a comprehensive collection of Japanese textiles, folk crafts, tea ceremony utensils, and folding screens; 5,000 artifacts on permanent display; 4,500 books in library.

Periodicals

Magazine: Daruma Magazine
Mukonoso Higashi 1-12-5
Amagasaki, 661-0032 Japan
ph: 81-78-851-6654 or 81-6-6436-5874
fax: 81-6-6438-1882
momoko@gao.ne.jp
http://www.darumamagazine.com
The only English language full-color quarterly magazine devoted to the arts and antiques of Japan; founded in 1993.

Japanese Items (Tsuba)

Internet Resources

Jim Gilbert
Tsuba
jggilbert@earthlink.net
http://home.earthlink.net/~jggilbert/
tsuba.htm
THE place for tsubas (handguards mounted on Japanese swords) and related information.

Korean Items

Dealers

Sandra Andacht
P.O. Box 94
Little Neck, NY 11363-0094
ph: 718-229-6593
Orientalia@aol.com
http://hometown.aol.com/orientalia/
index.html
Buys and sells Oriental antiques, collectibles, fine art: Asian, Japanese, Chinese, Korean, Southeast Asia.

Joe Arnold
East & Beyond, Ltd.
6727 Curran St.
Mc Lean, VA 22101
ph: 703-448-8200
fax: 703-821-1272
EandBeyond@aol.com
http://www.eandbeyond.com
A three-story gallery specializing in antiques from China, Japan and Korea: furniture, boxes, benches, chairs, porcelain, and textiles.

Lacquer

Experts

Janet Francine Cobert
Fine Art of Asia
P.O. Box 2976
Beverly Hills, CA 90213
ph: 310-470-2176
fax: 818-986-5584
asianart1@earthlink.net
Specializes in and appraises Oriental lacquer.

Repair Services

Janet Francine Cobert
Fine Art of Asia
P.O. Box 2976
Beverly Hills, CA 90213
ph: 310-470-2176
fax: 818-986-5584
asianart1@earthlink.net
Restores Oriental lacquer and ceramic wares.

Near East Items

Misc. Services

Arthur M. Sackler Gallery
Smithsonian Institution
1050 Independence Ave. SW
Washington, DC 20560
ph: 202-357-3200
edsonmi@asia.si.edu
http://www.asia.si.edu
The Near East Dept. will authenticate your Near East works of art; call to make an appointment; limit 5 items

per visit, 10 items per year; may be able to work from good photographs.

South & Southeast Asia

Appraisers

Elisabeth Douglas, ASA, ISA
China Coast, The
P.O. Box 610
Austin, TX 78767
ph: 512-330-9524 or 512-789-7507
fax: 512-330-9348
wien@texas.net
http://www.asianartappraisals.com
Active in the field of Asian art and antiques for over twenty years; specializing in damage, insurance and IRS appraisals; also offers brokerage of Chinese, Japanese, and Southeast Asian Art.

Christine Zachary
P.O. Box 82906
Portland, OR 97282-0906
ph: 503-234-8143 or 503-777-5813
christineZC@aol.com
Specializes in collecting, selling, appraising SE Asian art and antiques of the Himalayan regions as well as China; main expertise is in painted Buddhist thangkas and bronzes; also Chinese ceramics, textiles, statuary.

Collectors

John Rudak
32 Princess Lane
North Stonington, CT 06359-1117
ph: 860-599-8489
Wants Asian Buddhist & Hindu art; all representations desired; interested in all Asian artistic mediums including metalwork, wood carvings, porcelain, pottery, works on paper, etc.; special interest in Buddhist art & artifacts.

Dealers

Art of the Past
1242 Madison Ave.
New York, NY 10128-0515
ph: 212-860-7070
fax: 212-876-5373
ArtofPast@aol.com
http://www.artofpast.com
Specializing in paintings, sculptures, textiles, Islamic and other works of art from India, Tibet, Nepal, and Southeast Asia.

Marsha L. Vargas, ASA
Xanadu/Folk Art International
871 Santa Cruz Ave.
Menlo Park, CA 94022
ph: 650-329-9999
fax: 650-328-3918
info@folkartintl.com
http://www.folkartintl.com
Interested in Asian, African and Oceanic antiques and works of art; has one of the largest collections on the West Coast of fine antique Tibetan//Nepalese bronzes and works of art as well as exceptional Khmer sculpture.

Carlo Raineri
Loft Antiques, The
36 Talang Rd.
Phuket, Phuket 83000 Thailand
ph: 6676 258160 or 6619 699845
fax: 6676 258159
theloft@phuket.ksc.co.th
http://www.theloft-antiques.com
Specializes in Southeastern Asian art spanning all periods from the Mon civilization up to and including the Colonial era; emphasis is on rare and unusual examples from Burma and Thailand.

Misc. Services

Arthur M. Sackler Gallery
Smithsonian Institution
1050 Independence Ave. SW
Washington, DC 20560
ph: 202-357-3200
edsonmi@asia.si.edu
http://www.asia.si.edu
The South & Southeast Dept. will authenticate your South & Southeast Asian works of art; call to make an appointment; limit 5 items/visit, 10 items/year; may be able to work from good photographs.

OSBORNE IVOREX

Collectors

Andy Jackson
501 Falcon Lane
West Chester, PA 19382-5716
ph: 610-692-0269 or 610-272-7900
mrivorex@aol.com
Wants wall plaques, figurines, calendars and advertising brochures; will buy, sell or trade.

Experts

John Smith
28 Garfield Rd.
Bitterne
Southampton, Hampshire S019 4BU
U.K.
ph: 023 80 331582
Ivorex@btinternet.com
http://www.ivorex.btinternet.co.uk
Collector and dealer of Osborne Ivorex plaques; all subjects covered; Web site packed with history and information on the subject.

OUTBOARD MOTORS

(see BOATS, Engines; NAUTICAL ANTIQUES; TOYS, Boats & Outboards)

OUTDOOR COLLECTIBLES

(see ANIMAL TROPHIES; ART, Sporting; CAMPING EQUIPMENT; DECOYS; FISHING COLLECTIBLES; LICENSES, Hunting & Fishing; SPORTING COLLECTIBLES; TARGET SHOOTING MEMORABILIA; TRAP SHOOTING; TRAPS)

OUTHOUSES

Collectors

J. W. "Bill" Courter
3935 Kelley Rd.
Kevil, KY 42053-9431
ph: 270-488-2116
fax: 270-488-2055
brtknight@aol.com
http://www.aladdinknights.org
Wants items relating to outhouses: postcards, books, old photographs, plans, catalogs, models, etc.

OUTLAWS & LAWMEN

(see also LAW ENFORCEMENT MEMORABILIA, Police & Sheriff; WESTERN AMERICANA)

Clubs/Associations

Hank Clark
National Association for Outlaw & Lawman History
Newsletter: NOLA Newsletter & Quarterly
P.O. Box 812
Waterford, CA 95386-0812
ph: 209-874-2640
fax: 209-874-5750
conchosmith@hotmail.com
Members interested in Western outlaw and lawmen history and artifacts; sponsors annual Rendezvous.

Collectors

Dr. Anthony Sapienza
East 106 Ridgewood Ave.
Paramus, NJ 07652
ph: 201-262-6310
fax: 201-262-3990
siringo45@aol.com
Serious collector wants photographs, autographs, documents, Wanted posters and postcards, original Western Law officers' badges, invitations to hangings, telegrams, etc.

Bill Mackin
1137 Washington St.
Craig, CO 81625-1613
ph: 970-824-6717 or 970-824-6360
fax: 970-824-7175
Author of "Cowboy and Gunfighter Collectibles" price guide; sells books for Old West collectors by mail and at shows; over 45 years collecting; wants nice gun leather and cowboy gear; appraises, consults, lectures.

OVENS

(see RANGES)

OYSTER RELATED COLLECTIBLES

Clubs/Associations

Andrea H. Sullivan, Sec.
Oyster Plate & Collectibles Society International
Newsletter: OPCS Newsletter
P.O. Box 632
Brigantine, NJ 08203
ph: 215-342-6450
fax: 410-378-9431
http://www.geocities.com/Heartland/Bluffs/1570

Collectors

Donald C. Bell
89 Canoe Brook Rd.
Trumbull, CT 06611
ph: 203-268-7380
Wants old oyster cans, bottles, boxes, barrels, advertising and related items; no oyster plates, please.

Sheldon Katz
18 Cliffside Dr.
Port Jefferson, NY 11777-1118
ph: 631-928-1800

Carlton G. Riggin
Rt. 617
Marionville, VA 23408
ph: 757-442-5321 or 757-442-2179
fax: 757-442-5321
Wants to buy old oyster cans and containers, oyster advertising, envelopes and letterheads, postcards, trade cards, and other oyster related items.

Jan & Dick Wilson
Seasonal Seafoods
P.O. Box 356
Bay Center, WA 98527
ph: 360-875-5519
fax: 360-875-5937
jan_dick@willapabay.org
http://www.willapabay.org/~jan_dick
Collectors of oyster plates.

Dealers

France
Majolica@noos.fr
http://www.oysterplates.com
Buys and sells oyster plate; Web site has photos of hundreds of patterns and styles.

Experts

Vivian & James Karsnitz
1428 Jerry Lane
Manheim, PA 17545-9353
ph: 717-665-4202
Buys and sells oyster cans, advertising and related items; authors of "Oyster Plates" and "Oyster Cans" (Schiffer, 1993.)

OZ

(see WIZARD OF OZ)

PADLOCKS

(see LOCKS)

PAINT

Collectors

Irene Davis
27036 Withams Rd.
Oak Hall, VA 23416-2606
ph: 757-824-5524
fax: 757-824-3350
paintcan@ccisp.net
http://www.creekhouseantiques.com
Wants to buy old paint cans, paint advertising displays, or retail items; send photos for offer.

Experts

Randy Smith
1977 Fairway Circle
Atlanta, GA 30319
ph: 404-633-1679
paintmaker@mailcity.com
Maintains company history, collects historical items such as paint color charts, paint cans, etc. relating to F. W. Devoe & Co. and C. T. Raynolds, Co. (1754 to present), also known as Devoe Paint Co.

PAINTINGS & DRAWINGS

(see also ART; FOLK ART; ILLUSTRATORS; REPAIR/ RESTORATION/CONSERVATION, Art; REPAIR/RESTORATION/ CONSERVATION, Paper Items)

Appraisers

Paul Royka
AppraisalDay.com
210 Park Avenue, #295
Worcester, MA 01609
ph: 978-582-8207
fax: 978-582-8207
appraisalday@aol.com
http://www.appraisalday.com
Expert, author and appraiser of 20th century art including works by Arthur Wesley Dow and the Boston Society of Arts & Crafts members.

Peter Kostoulakos
Peter Kostoulakos Fine Art
15 Sayles St.
Lowell, MA 01851-1625
ph: 978-453-8888
peter@pkart.com
http://www.pkart.com
Appraiser, expert offers valuations, oil

painting condition reports, conservation estimates.

Peter C. Sorlien, ASA
Accredited Appraisers
17-1/2 State St.
Marblehead, MA 01945-3536
ph: 781-631-5956
fax: 781-631-6550
appraisr@shore.net
Professional art appraisals; experience with divorce, donation, estate, insurance, litigation, and tax matters; does not buy or sell.

M. Barden Prisant, FRICS
Telepraisal
32 Union Sq., #1016
New York, NY 10003
ph: 212-614-9090 or 800-645-6002
fax: 212-780-9539
info@telepraisal.com
http://www.telepraisal.com
For over 21 years, Telepraisal has been gathering pricing data on approximately 200,000 artists and sales of their works; printouts of the data can be purchased for $35 per search, or more formal appraisals can be generated.

Nancy Harrison
Nancy Harrison Fine Art Consultant LLC
10 Mitchell Place, Ste. 12GH
New York, NY 10017
ph: 212-371-1935
fax: 212-371-0312
Nharrisonart@aol.com
Specializes in appraisal of European paintings, drawings, sculpture (Old Masters, 19th century, Modern), Amer. paintings & drawings; Member Appraisers Assoc. of America; former Dir., 19th Cent. European Paintings & Drawings at Sotheby's.

Debra J. Force
Debra Force Fine Art, Inc.
14 E. 73rd St., #4B
New York, NY 10021
ph: 212-734-3636
fax: 212-734-1042
debra@debraforce.com
http://www.debraforce.com
Specializes in the appraisal of American paintings, drawings, prints and sculpture of the 19th through 20th centuries.

Denise J. Levy
Art Find Associates, Inc.
135 Central Park West, Ste. 2 South
New York, NY 10023
ph: 212-595-5267
fax: 212-595-7666
djjl@nyc.rr.com
Fine art appraiser specializing in Modern and Contemporary art of all media: site-specific, prints, paintings, sculpture, unique works on paper; appraisals for insurance, charitable gift, estate planning, division of property.

Dr. Charles J. Semowich
Charles Semowich Fine Arts
242 Broadway
Rensselaer, NY 12144-2705
ph: 518-449-4756
semowich@att.net
Appraiser of art, antiques and decorative arts.

Pamela E. Mayo, ISA
710 Washington St.
Sewickley, PA 15143-1845
ph: 412-749-0760 or 412-390-3707
fax: 412-390-3708
pandjr@usaor.net
Fine art appraiser (paintings, drawings, prints, sculpture), specializing in 19th and early 20th century American art with a general background in 18th-20th century American and European art; specializes in sporting art and Southern art.

Cecilia Gillespie, ISA CAPP
Perry Arts, The
212 Pine Court
Pittsburgh, PA 15237
ph: 412-364-8500 or 412-364-3063
fax: 412-364-3063
perryart@aol.com
Certified Member of the International Society of Appraisers; Certified, Professional Picture Framers Association; specializing in appraising fine art; restoration services, conservation services.

Kathleen Harwood
Harwood Fine Arts, Inc.
P.O. Box 380
Montrose, PA 18801
ph: 570-278-9393
harwoodart@aol.com
Appraises 19th and 20th century American and European paintings and drawings.

Cindy Charleston, ISA
Appraisal Firm, The
P.O. Box 8904
Cheltenham, PA 19012
ph: 215-469-0010
ccpgallery@msn.com
http://www.theappraisalfirm.net
Has been in the fine art field for over 10 years; specializes in the appraisal of 19th and 20th century American and European oil paintings.

Rochelle Eisenberg, ASA
Art Directives, Inc.
455 Pennsylvania Ave., Ste 130
Fort Washington, PA 19034
ph: 215-646-0233
fax: 215-646-1894
info@artdirectives.com
http://www.artdirectives.com
Appraiser, consultant, writer, lecturer, author, advisor for Montgomery County newspapers, appeared on "Chubb Antiques Roadshow," instructor at Temple University.

William Bunch
William Bunch Auctions & Appraisals
One Hillman Dr.
Chadds Ford, PA 19317
ph: 610-558-1800
fax: 610-558-0885
whb@williambunchauctions.com
http://www.williambunchauctions.com
Specializes in the appraisal of antique clocks, music boxes, silver, paintings and other decorative objects.

Randall C. Hunt
Fine Arts Appraisals
3503 Fulton St., NW
Washington, DC 20007-1438
ph: 202-333-4035
randallhunt@starpower.net
Specializes in the appraisal of fine art including American and European 18th through 20th century paintings, prints and sculpture; Certified Appraiser, Appraisers Association of America.

Edwin W. Baker, Ex. VP
American Society of Appraisers
P.O. Box 17265
Washington, DC 20071
ph: 703-478-2228 or 800-272-8258
fax: 703-742-8471
asainfo@appraisers.org
http://www.appraisers.org
The only appraisal organization in the US representing all the disciplines of appraisal specialists; call 800-ASA-VALU for free referral or membership directory, or visit Web site.

Charles B. Goldstein, ISA CAPP
Charles Barry International
8 Hardwicke Place
Rockville, MD 20850-3010
ph: 301-340-6775
fax: 301-340-1726
chadeg@erols.com
Buys, sells, and appraises 19th and 20th century, modern and contemporary American and European paintings; Certified Member, International Society of Appraisers; expert witness and trial consultant.

Association of Online Appraisers, Inc.
P.O. Box 2049
Frederick, MD 21702-1049
ph: 301-228-2279
fax: 301-695-6491
info@AOAonline.org
http://www.AOAonline.org
Not-for-profit association for online as well as traditional appraisers; establishes standards of appraisal ethics & professional practice; offers 550+ page "Complete Online Course in Personal Property Appraising" free to members.

Michele R. Marceau, ISA
Principle Gallery
208 King St.
Alexandria, VA 22314
ph: 703-739-9326
fax: 703-739-0528
princgal@erols.com
http://www.principlegallery.com
Specializes in the appraisal of paintings.

Melanie Smith, ISA
Seaside Art Gallery
2716 Virginia Dare Trail South
P.O. Box 1
Nags Head, NC 27959-0001
ph: 252-441-5418 or 800-828-2444
fax: 252-441-8563
info@seasideart.com
http://www.seasideart.com
Accredited member of the International Society of Appraisers; specializes in fine art (paintings, graphics, sculpture) and animation art.

William Gordon
Gordon's Fine Art
5665 Highway 9, Ste. 103
Alpharetta, GA 30004
ph: 678-777-9034
fax: 770-569-1255
bill@gordonsfineart.com
http://www.gordonsfineart.com
Specializes in the sale and appraisal of fine art paintings and prints by listed 20th century artists; Associate Member of the International Society of Appraisers specializing in the appraisal of fine art, paintings, and prints.

Mark Alexander, ISA
Art Services 2000 Ltd., Co.
P.O. Box 1205
New Smyrna Beach, FL 32170
ph: 386-428-2980 or 386-748-3531
fax: 386-428-2981
artserv2000@yahoo.com
http://www.artservices2000.com
Fine art consulting, documentation, research, appraisals, curatorial services; also offers fine art packing and transportation services; appraisals for insurance, charitable donation, liquidation, equitable distribution, estate planning.

Albert Post, ISA
Albert Post Galleries
2291 Newbury Dr.
West Palm Beach, FL 33414
ph: 561-707-3024
albertpost@aol.com
Specializes in the appraisal of American paintings and drawings.

Richard Carta, Administrator
International Association of Fine Art Appraisers
6401 East Rogers Circle, Ste. 9
Boca Raton, FL 33487
ph: 561-997-8007 x203
fax: 561-997-6653
artpikr@artpickers.com

Bryan Roberts
Bryan H. Roberts Gallery, The
539 South Drexel Ave.
Columbus, OH 43209
ph: 614-236-1245
fax: 614-236-1252
brobert3@ix.netcom.com
http://www.robertsgallery.com
Fine art gallery dealing in paintings of the 18th, 19th, and 20th centuries; framing, restoration, and appraisal services also offered.

James Corcoran, ISA
Corcoran Fine Arts Limited, Inc.
2915 Fairfax Rd.
Cleveland, OH 44118-4015
ph: 216-431-0025 or 216-397-0777
fax: 216-397-0222
corcoranfa@aol.com
http://www.corcoranfinearts.com
Appraises European, American, Canadian, Latin American paintings and drawings; Renaissance to contemporary.

Caroline Ashleigh
Caroline Ashleigh Associates, Inc.
800 E. Lincoln
Birmingham, MI 48009
ph: 248-613-4056
fax: 248-792-2545
carolineashleigh@appraiseyourart.com
http://www.appraiseyourart.com
Specializes in professional appraisals of fine art, antiques, textiles, residential contents; participating appraiser in the "Antiques Roadshow;" Certified Senior Member and Regional Representative of the Appraisers Association of America.

Judy L. Campbell
Judy L. Campbell Appraisal & Estate Sales
5500 Summerset Dr.
Midland, MI 48640-2931
ph: 989-631-9263 or 989-631-4874
fax: 989-631-4874
go4nteks@aol.com
http://www.judycampbell.com
Appraiser of antique furniture, fine & decorative arts, American & European paintings and sculpture, American and European ceramics, antiques & 20th century collectibles; also other personal property.

Patricia M. Knight
Finetooth Comb Antiques Research & Appraisal Service
P.O. Box 1177
Ames, IA 50014-1177
ph: 515-292-9028
ftcres@aol.com
Consultant and qualified appraiser of 19th century and early 20th century oil paintings; also Oriental images on paper; please send SASE for reply; does not purchase; send SASE if requesting return of photos.

Frederick P. Dose, Jr.
Frederick Dose Appraisals Ltd.
778 Pleasant Ave.
Highland Park, IL 60035-4613
ph: 847-433-7870 or 847-433-1090
fdoseappraisals@comcast.net
Appraises US, British, Continental paintings and furniture, prints, porcelain, silver, decorative arts, coins, antiquities; for corporate, private, and attorneys; references on request; 6 year full-time as University art historian.

Victoria L. Scogland
Victoria L. Scogland Fine Art, Inc.
414 West Deerpath Rd.
Lake Forest, IL 60045
ph: 847-6151-1098
fax: 847-615-1132
vscogland@aol.com
Fine art appraiser, consultant, dealer.

Sybil Tillman, ISA
Artco Inc.
3013 Harrow Gate Dr.
Woodstock, IL 60098-7410
ph: 815-338-3600
SybilTillman@msn.com
http://www.e-Artco.com
Specializing in fine art appraisals and research; also buying and selling 19th and 20th century, important and contemporary American artists and American Indian Art.

Farhad Radfar, ISA
MIR Appraisal Services, Inc.
307 N. Michigan Ave., Ste. 308
Chicago, IL 60601
ph: 312-814-8510
fax: 312-814-8511
appraisers@mirgallery.com
http://www.mirgallery.com
Offers expert appraisals of personal property including fine art, antiques, jewelry, furniture, silver, porcelain, rugs, marble, bronze, and other fine items.

William Lavendusky, M.S., ISA
William Lavendusky, Fine Art
3345 So. Harvard, Bldg. 100
Tulsa, OK 74135
ph: 918-747-5336
fax: 918-742-3425
Dealer and appraiser of paintings and sculpture; specialist in 19th century French animal bronzes.

Brenda Mohle, ISA CAPP
Signet Art
2211 High Point Dr.
Carrollton, TX 75007-1705
ph: 972-306-1963 or 972-849-3053
fax: 972-306-1963
signetart@attbi.com
http://www.signetart.com
Appraiser of prints, paintings, drawings, sculptures and other fine art.

Robert Banks, AAA, ISA
Banks Fine Art, LLC
1231 Dragon St.
Dallas, TX 75207
ph: 214-352-1811
fax: 214-352-6360
bob@banksfineart.com
http://www.banksfineart.com
Has been dealing in 19th and 20th century fine art for over 20 years; to the trade; certified member of Appraisers Association of America; clientele includes established galleries and collectors.

Genae Fields, ISA
Image One International
16126 Rainbow Lake Rd.
Houston, TX 77095-4053
ph: 281-856-8866
fax: 281-550-8618
gfields@imageoneinternational.com
http://www.imageoneinternational.com
Specializes in the appraisal of Impressionist, modern and contemporary paintings.

Richard Casagrande, ISA CAPP
Casagrande Appraisals
8546 Broadway, Ste. 203
San Antonio, TX 78217
ph: 210-820-3097
fax: 210-820-3097
rlcasagrande@sbcglobal.net
Appraiser specializing in 19th century American art; also the art of Texas and the San Antonio region.

Corinne Cain, ISA, ASA
Corinne Cain Ltd.
326 West Harmont Dr.
Phoenix, AZ 85021
ph: 602-906-1633
fax: 602-906-0677
corinne@savvycollector.com
http://www.savvycollector.com
A veteran art appraiser for over 25 years selling fine art and Native American arts online; guaranteed condition, authenticity verified, value is assured; Accredited Senior Appraiser, Certified Appraiser of Personal Property.

Jnanideva Shanmuga
Appraisal & Connoisseur Associates
620 Sierra Dr. SE
Albuquerque, NM 87108-3377
ph: 505-265-2842
jshan@nmia.com
Appraisers, artists and brokers serving the Southwest in painting, prints and sculpture; also appraise residential contents nationwide.

James Haddad, ISA
Poulsen Galleries, Inc.
910 San Pasqual St.
Pasadena, CA 91106
ph: 626-792-7410
fax: 626-792-7247
poulsengalleries@compuserve.com
http://www.poulsengalleries.com
Fine art appraiser; buys and sells 19th and 20th century American and

European paintings; also California paintings.

Kathleen DeBolt, ISA
Debolt Fine Art
18353 Sycamore Creek Rd.
Escondido, CA 92025-2302
ph: 858-676-5913 or 619-857-5913
fineart@adnc.com
http://www.onlineartline.com
Specializes in the appraisal of 19th and 20th century American Art, California Impressionism, American scene, New Mexico modernists, Western art.

Marcia Osterkamp, ISA
Poulsen Galleries, Inc.
327 Terrace Dr.
Brawley, CA 92227-3040
ph: 760-344-4810
fax: 760-344-4778
poulsengalleries@compuserve.com
http://www.poulsengalleries.com
Fine art appraiser; buys and sells 19th and 20th century American and European paintings; also California paintings.

Michael Hinkle
Figurative, The
ph: 760-564-6060 or 760-564-0012
michael@thefigurative.com
http://www.thefigurative.com/appraisals
Specializes in the appraisal of 20th century paintings, contemporary art, sculpture, collectibles, paintings and drawings; Associate member of the International Society of Appraisers and of the Appraisers Association of America.

Nancy Burke Bosch, ISA
Bosch Appraisal Service
1610 Northstar Dr.
Petaluma, CA 94954-6607
ph: 707-773-3970
fax: 707-773-3974
nbbosch@pacbell.net
http://www.appraiseyourantiques.com
Specializes in appraising European & American furniture, fine art, decorative art & accessories, china, crystal, silver, American wicker, quilts, linen, other textiles, other appreciable residential contents; consultations, estate sales.

Richard C. Frey, ISA CAPP
R.T.L.H. Enterprises
1275 East Ave.
Chico, CA 95926-1020
ph: 530-343-4528 or 800-567-7854
fax: 530-343-9380
RFREYRTLH@aol.com
http://www.richardcfreyfineart.com
Certified appraiser of American and European art, paintings, watercolors, drawings, prints, sculpture, bronzes, etc.; appraises for estates, arbitration, and has testified as expert witness.

Susanne L. Gavigan, ISA, CPF
Artiques Appraisal Service
16425 Trail Dr.
Redding, CA 96001
ph: 530-244-2100 or 530-244-6147
fax: 530-244-0166
gartiques@aol.com
http://www.appraisalsbyrequest.com
Art dealer, expert, collector, conservator and appraiser since 1970: paintings, water colors, drawings, etchings, original prints, sculpture, etc.; Accredited Member of the International Society of Appraisers;

Candy Moffett, ISA
Alder Gallery & Antiques
P.O. Box 8517
Coburg, OR 97408
ph: 541-342-6411
fax: 541-683-9797
candy@alderart.com
http://www.alderart.com
Buys, sells, repairs and restores art; specializes in the appraisal of fine art and antiques; Accredited Member of the International Society of Appraisers (ISA).

Keith De Long
Keith C. De Long & Associates
Appraisal Service
32031 4th Ave. SW
Federal Way, WA 98023
ph: 253-874-6088
delong99@hotmail.com
Has 40 years experience in appraising paintings and drawings; Master of Arts degree in Art History and accreditation by the International Society of Appraisers.

International Society of Appraisers
Newsletter: Professional Appraisers
Information Exchange
1131 SW 7th St., Ste. 105
Renton, WA 98055
ph: 206-241-0359 or 888-472-4732
fax: 206-241-0436
ISA@isa-appraisers.org
http://www.isa-appraisers.org
Largest assoc. of professional appraisers devoted solely to personal property; over 1,300 members specializing in all areas of antiques & residential contents, gems & jewelry, fine art, machinery & equipment; member directory on Web site.

Haydee Allred
807 "W" Ave.
Anacortes, WA 98221
ph: 360-588-8995
m.allred@juno.com
Specializes in the appraisal of paintings, drawings and prints.

Lorraine Pierce-Hull
Pierce-Hull Art Appraisers & Advisors
23 Seaforth Rd.
Kingston, Ontario K7M 1E1 Canada
ph: 613-542-2228 or 877-205-5866
fax: 613-542-1474
piercehull@sympatico.ca
Appraiser of Canadian and European

paintings, textiles, sculpture, photographs and prints.

Edith Yeomans, ASA
Appraisal Associates
80 Richmond St. West, Ste. 1101
Toronto, Ontario M5H 2A4 Canada
ph: 416-368-4334
fax: 416-368-6679
emy@appraisalassociates.ca
http://www.appraise.org
Specialist in the valuation of fine art, antiques, decorative art, including Canadian, American and European art.

Stephen P. Sweeting
Appraisal Associates
80 Richmond St. West, Ste. 1101
Toronto, Ontario M5H 2A4 Canada
ph: 416-368-4334
fax: 416-368-6679
sps@appraisalassociates.ca
http://www.appraise.org
Specialist in the valuation of fine art, antiques, decorative art, including Canadian, American and European art.

Kathryn Minard, ISA
Contemporary Fine Art Services Inc.
184 Pearl St., Ste. 201A
Toronto, Ontario M5A 1L5 Canada
ph: 416-366-9770
fax: 416-366-8541
art.advisory.biz@on.aibn.com
Art expert and appraiser specializing in Canadian contemporary and historical art; also Canadian Indian and Inuit.

David Peckman
U.K.
dpeckman@btinternet.com
Specializes in the appraisal of European and American art, primarily works on paper including prints, photography, drawings, and watercolors from the 20th and 21st centuries.

Auction Services

Michael B. Grogan
Grogan & Company Auctioneers
22 Harris St.
Dedham, MA 02026
ph: 781-461-9500
fax: 781-461-9625
grogans@groganco.com
http://www.groganco.com
Auctioneer and appraiser specializing in 18th through 20th century American & European paintings, sculpture, oriental rugs, and fine silver; accepts consignments year round for two semi-annual sales.

Willis Henry
Willis Henry Auctions, Inc.
22 Main St.
Marshfield, MA 02050
ph: 781-834-7774 or 800-244-8466
fax: 781-826-3520
wha@willishenry.com
http://www.willishenry.com
Specializes in the sale of American

antiques of all kinds, particularly Shaker, American Indian and Early American.

Colleene Fesko
Skinner, Inc.
63 Park Plaza
The Heritage on the Garden
Boston, MA 02116
ph: 617-350-5400
fax: 617-350-5429
info@skinnerinc.com
http://www.skinnerinc.com
Established in 1971, Skinner Inc. is the fourth largest auction house in the US; has offices in Boston and Bolton, MA.

Christie's
20 Rockefeller Plaza
New York, NY 10020
ph: 212-636-2000
info@christies.com
http://www.christies.com

Sotheby's
1334 York Ave.
New York, NY 10021
ph: 212-606-7000
fax: 212-606-7107
http://www.sothebys.com

Amory Spizzirri, Client Svc.
William Doyle Galleries
175 E. 87th St.
New York, NY 10128-2205
ph: 212-427-2730
fax: 212-369-0892
info@doylegalleries.com
http://www.doylegalleries.com
Holds over 50 auctions annually of furniture and decorations, paintings and sculpture, jewelry, books and prints, couture and textiles, 20th century art & design, majolica, Lalique, Asian works of art and other specialty categories.

Margot Chuatal
Weschler's
909 E St. NW
Washington, DC 20004-2006
ph: 202-628-1281 or 800-331-1430
fax: 202-628-2366
fineart@weschlers.com
http://www.weschlers.com
Conducts specialized auction sales of art, paintings, prints and graphics.

Frank Boos
Frank H. Boos Gallery, Inc.
420 Enterprise Court
Bloomfield Hills, MI 48302
ph: 248-332-1500
fax: 248-332-6370
artandauction@boosgallery.com
http://www.boosgallery.com
Specializes in the auction and appraisal of fine art, antiques and decorative arts.

James Halperin
Heritage Galleries & Auctioneers
Dallas, TX 75219
ph: 800-872-6467
auctions@HeritageGalleries.com
http://www.HeritageGalleries.com
Specializes in buying and selling illustrator art.

Waddington's
111 Bathurst St.
Toronto, Ontario M5V 2R1 Canada
ph: 416-504-9100 or 877-504-5700
fax: 416-504-0033
info@waddingtonsauctions.com
http://www.waddingtonsauctions.com
Canada's oldest and largest auction house specializing in decorative arts, jewelry, antique furniture, Inuit and native Canadian arts, European and Canadian arts, books, militaria, Orientalia, toys, ceramics, etc.

Clubs/Associations

Association of Online Appraisers, Inc.
P.O. Box 2049
Frederick, MD 21702-1049
ph: 301-228-2279
fax: 301-695-6491
info@AOAonline.org
http://www.AOAonline.org
Not-for-profit association for online as well as traditional appraisers;
establishes standards of appraisal ethics & professional practice; offers 550+ page "Complete Online Course in Personal Property Appraising" free to members.

Collectors

John Clement
36 Oakwood Ave.
Fitchburg, MA 01420-7421
ph: 978-345-5863
Collector and expert, special interests include worldwide master works of art, particularly works on paper, including Japanese woodblock prints; also fine paintings.

Elias London
Parke Lloyds International, Inc.
9408 NW 70 St.
Fort Lauderdale, FL 33321-3002
ph: 954-726-4107 or 954-724-4274
Wants to buy paintings, watercolors, drawings; send description, photo, condition, size, artist's name if signed, asking price.

Dealers

Henry B. Holt
125 Golden Hill
P.O. Box 699
Lee, MA 01238-0699
ph: 413-243-3184
fax: 413-243-9918
hbholt@vgernet.net
Buys and sells American art, oils or watercolors; conservation, framing and appraisals available; wants to buy marines, still life, impressionist, Hudson River, and folk art; member Appraisers Association of America, Inc.

John Clement
36 Oakwood Ave.
Fitchburg, MA 01420-7421
ph: 978-345-5863
Specializes in American, European Old Master, and modern paintings and works on paper.

Tony Fusco
Fusco & Four, Associates
One Murdock Terrace
Brighton, MA 02135-2817
ph: 617-787-2637
fax: 617-782-4430
fuscofour@aol.com
Specializes in European and American paintings from 1900-1950, with an emphasis on Art Deco, WPA, Modernist, Regionalists and American Scene; will assist individuals and organizations buying and selling paintings and fine art.

Jim Martin
Martin Antiques
75 Meadowbrook Rd.
East Greenwich, RI 02818
trader@traderantiques.com
http://www.traderantiques.com
Specializes paintings: Rhode Island art, New England art, American art primarily from the period 1860 to 1940.

Annette & Rob Elowitch
Barridoff Galleries
P.O. Box 9715
Portland, ME 04104
ph: 207-772-5011
fax: 207-772-5049
fineart@barridoff.com
http://www.barridoff.com
Buys, sells and auctions fine American and European art.

Jane Allinson
Allinson Gallery, Inc.
ph: 860-429-2322
fax: 860-429-2825
allinson@neca.com
http://www.allinsongallery.com
Buys and sells American & European fine prints, drawings, paintings, watercolors; also offers fine art appraisals; member of Appraisers Association of America, International Fine Print Dealers Association.

James P. Marenakos
Quester Gallery
77 Main St.
P.O. Box 32
Stonington, CT 06378
ph: 860-535-3860
fax: 860-535-3533
info@questergallery.com
http://www.questergallery.com
Internationally recognized as a leading source for exceptional 18th, 19th and 20th century marine and sporting paintings; features works by artists such as James Butterworth, Montague Dawson, Jack Gray, Antonio Jacobsen, and John Stobart.

Peter Hastings Falk
Falk Art Management, LLC
P.O. Box 833
Madison, CT 06443
ph: 203-245-4761
pfalk@cshore.com
http://www.soundviewpressbooks.com
Researches, writes and publishes books about artists listed in "Who's Who in American Art;" also publishes/sells art reference dictionaries; promotes and manages artist estate collections.

Don Barese
Don Barese Fine Art & Antiques
3651 Whitney Ave.
Hamden, CT 06518
ph: 203-248-2700 or 800-733-4254
fax: 203-281-7438
D.Barese.artantiques@snet.net
http://www.donbaresefineart.com
Buys and sells American & European fine art, 19th and 20th century paintings and prints.

Ellen Sragow
Sragow Gallery
73 Spring St.
New York, NY 10012-5800
ph: 212-219-1793
fax: 212-219-1793
Specializes in American art from the 1920s to the 1950s: paintings, prints, sculpture; WPA era, abstract expressionist prints, Mexican prints, works by African American artists.

Alex Acevedo
Alexander Gallery
942 Madison Ave.
New York, NY 10021
ph: 212-472-1636
fax: 212-734-6937
hudson3@worldnet.att.net
Specializes in 18th, 19th, and 20th century art.

Hirschl & Adler Galleries, Inc.
21 East 70th St.
New York, NY 10021
ph: 212-535-8810
fax: 212-772-7237
gallery@hirschlandadler.com
http://www.hirschlandadler.com
American and European paintings, watercolors, drawings, and sculptures, 18th century to present;

also American prints and decorative arts 1810 to 1910.

James Graham & Sons Gallery
1014 Madison Ave. at 78th
New York, NY 10021-0103
ph: 212-535-5767
fax: 212-794-2454
info@jamesgrahamandsons.com
http://www.jamesgrahamandsons.com
Specializes in 19th and early 20th century American paintings, American and European sculpture, contemporary art and British ceramics.

Margaret McAuliffe
Ardagh Fair
P.O. Box 810
Carmel, NY 10512
ph: 914-225-1746 or 800-217-1746
Buys and sells fine art: oils, watercolors, prints, sculpture, photographs.

Sydney L. Germansky
Europa Master Gallery
16 A Lafayette Ave.
Suffern, NY 10901-5406
ph: 914-368-2707

P. Bruce Marine
Marine-Hardy Collection
2918 M. St. NW
Washington, DC 20007-3713
ph: 202-337-2224
fax: 202-337-2224
Specializes in 19th century through 1940s African-American art; buys, sells, collects; oils, drawings, watercolors; by Bannister, Lawrence, Lewis, Douglas, Lee-Smith, etc.

Ted Cooper
Adams Davidson Galleries
2727 29th St. NW, Ste. 504
Washington, DC 20008
ph: 202-965-3800
fax: 202-265-3395
cooper@adgal.com
http://www.adgal.com
Wants to buy exceptional European paintings from the 16th through 19th centuries.

Robert B. Mayo
Gallery Mayo, Inc.
11758 River Crest Dr.
Gloucester, VA 23061-2516
ph: 804-693-2516
hightide@visi.net
Buys and sells 19th through early 20th century American art, with a specialty in Southern and sporting art.

Kathy Hughes
Tudor House Galleries
4126 Park Rd., Ste. E.
Charlotte, NC 28209
ph: 704-676-4871 or 704-676-4872
fax: 704-676-5197
tudorhouse@aol.com
http://www.tudorhouse.com
Buys, sells and appraises 19th century oil paintings and watercolors; Accredited Member, International Society of Appraisers.

Peter Thurber
Ritzi & Thurber, Inc.
160 S. Beach St.
Daytona Beach, FL 32114
ph: 904-252-2552 or 904-226-8489
fax: 904-226-8490
ritzi1881@earthlink.net
http://www.ritzi-thurber.com
Founded in 1881, gallery buys and sells 18th to early 20th century works of art; up-to-date, comprehensive art reference library is maintained; all subjects sought, especially still lifes, animals, and marine subjects.

Robert Thames
Robert Thames Art & Antiques
P.O. Box 4175
Ormond Beach, FL 32175
ph: 904-677-8835
rthamesa@bellsouth.net
Specializes in fine art: paintings, drawings and prints.

Elaine Kwan
8022 SE Osprey St.
Hobe Sound, FL 33455
ph: 772-545-9939
fax: 772-545-9939
elaine@artcollect.com
http://www.artcollect.com
Buys and sells modern and contemporary art; resale; fine art appraiser; collections cataloging; member, Appraisers Association of America (AAA).

Ivan Gilbert, MD
Miran Art & Books
2824 Elm Ave.
Columbus, OH 43209
ph: 614-231-3707 or 614-818-3222
fax: 614-818-3223
IGilbert@ahhinc.com
Interested especially in prints and paintings by 20th century artists, but only if of quality and with adequate provenance.

Bryan Roberts
Bryan H. Roberts Gallery, The
539 South Drexel Ave.
Columbus, OH 43209
ph: 614-236-1245
fax: 614-236-1252
brobert3@ix.netcom.com
http://www.robertsgallery.com
Fine art gallery dealing in paintings of the 18th, 19th, and 20th centuries; framing, restoration, and appraisal services also offered.

Randy Sandler
Cincinnati Art Galleries
225 East 6th St.
Cincinnati, OH 45202
ph: 513-381-2128
fax: 513-381-7527
info@cincinnatiartgalleries.com
http://www.cincinnatiartgalleries.com
Buying paintings.

Don Treadway
Treadway Gallery, Inc.
2029 Madison Rd.
Cincinnati, OH 45208
ph: 513-321-6742
fax: 513-871-7722
treadway2029@earthlink.net
http://www.treadwaygallery.com

Timothy Haines
405 Lafayette Ave.
Cincinnati, OH 45220
ph: 513-559-1405
fax: 513-651-0860
relostrat1@aol.com
http://members.aol.com/ReyneH
Wants to buy 19th-20th century American and European paintings, Cincinnati artists, watercolors and drawings by listed artists.

Bradley S. Vite
Bradley Vite Fine Arts
1600 West Beardsley Ave.
Elkhart, IN 46514-1800
ph: 219-293-1616
fax: 219-293-1616
bradley@finearts.com
Buys, sells and appraises 19th and 20th century American and European prints, paintings, watercolors, and sculpture; especially interested in Audubon prints and McKenney & Hall prints.

Sybil Tillman, ISA
Artco Inc.
3013 Harrow Gate Dr.
Woodstock, IL 60098-7410
ph: 815-338-3600
SybilTillman@msn.com
http://www.e-Artco.com
Specializing in fine art appraisals and research; also buying and selling 19th and 20th century, Old Masters, important and contemporary American artists and American Indian Art; Accredited member of the ISA, Member of AAA.

Susan Larson
Susan Larson Fine Art
1150 Old Mill Dr.
Palatine, IL 60067
ph: 847-359-7799
fax: 847-359-6796
Specialist in buying, selling and appraising fine art including paintings and prints; also consults and advises on the development of private and corporate fine art collections.

Farhad Radfar, ISA
MIR International Gallery, Inc.
307 N. Michigan Ave., Ste. 308
Chicago, IL 60601
ph: 312-814-8510
fax: 312-814-8511
mirgallery@aol.com
http://www.mirgallery.com

Robert Henry Adams
Adams Fine Art
715 N. Franklin St.
Chicago, IL 60610-3511
ph: 312-642-8700
fax: 312-642-8785
info@adamsfineart.com
http://www.adamsfineart.com
Specializes in 19th and 20th century American and European paintings and works on paper; Impressionism, Regionalism, Modernism.

George T. Clark
Taylor Clark Gallery
2623 Government St.
Baton Rouge, LA 70806-5408
ph: 225-383-4929 or 888-725-5251
fax: 225-383-4920
taylorclark@taylorclark.com
http://www.taylorclark.com
Specializes in 18th, 19th, and 20th century oil paintings, watercolors, and prints, especially all editions of Audubon prints.

Robert Banks, AAA, ISA
Banks Fine Art, LLC
1231 Dragon St.
Dallas, TX 75207
ph: 214-352-1811
fax: 214-352-6360
bob@banksfineart.com
http://www.banksfineart.com
Has been dealing in 19th and 20th century fine art for over 20 years; to the trade; certified member of Appraisers Association of America; clientele includes established galleries and collectors.

David Cook
David Cook Fine American Art
1637 Wazee St.
Denver, CO 80202
ph: 303-623-8181
fax: 303-623-4817
info@davidcookgalleries.com
http://www.davidcookfineamericanart.com
Buys, sells, collects and appraises antique Native American art; also interested in American paintings (specializing in Colorado and New Mexico artists), sculpture, and arts & crafts.

Jan Wilson
Jan Wilson Gallery
P.O. Box 6649
Ketchum, ID 83340
ph: 208-622-7799
fax: 208-726-5975
Buys and sells print, fine art, sculpture.

Art Brokerage, Inc.
P.O. Box 3730
544 East Fork Rd.
Ketchum, ID 83340
ph: 208-788-1484 or 208-788-1491
fax: 208-788-1492
drose@earthlink.net
http://www.artbrokerage.com
Online service for buying and selling art; specializes in selling limited

edition prints and sculpture; accepts consignments; list your artwork for sale in classifieds.

Goldfield Galleries
8380 Melrose Ave.
West Hollywood, CA 90069-5422
ph: 323-651-1122
fax: 323-651-1168
Specializes in 19th and 20th century American Impressionist art, and California and Western art.

James Haddad, ISA
Poulsen Galleries, Inc.
910 San Pasqual St.
Pasadena, CA 91106
ph: 626-792-7410
fax: 626-792-7247
poulsengalleries@compuserve.com
http://www.poulsengalleries.com
Fine art appraiser; buys and sells 19th and 20th century American and European paintings; also California paintings.

Don Bennett
Don Bennett & Associates
P.O. Box 283
Agoura Hills, CA 91376-0283
ph: 818-991-5596
fax: 818-991-6866
artofwest@aol.com
Collects, buys, sells and appraises high quality antique Native American items: Navajo, baskets, etc.; also paintings by deceased Western artists; since 1968.

Marcia Osterkamp, ISA
Poulsen Galleries, Inc.
327 Terrace Dr.
Brawley, CA 92227-3040
ph: 760-344-4810
fax: 760-344-4778
poulsengalleries@compuserve.com
http://www.poulsengalleries.com
Fine art appraiser; buys and sells 19th and 20th century American and European paintings; also California paintings.

Jimmy Vitanza
Peregrine Galleries
508 Brinkerhoff Ave.
Santa Barbara, CA 93101-3441
ph: 805-963-3134
fax: 805-963-3134

Christine Daniels
Christine Daniels Antiques
135 E. Shiloh Rd.
Santa Rosa, CA 95403-1254
ph: 707-838-6083
fax: 707-838-6083
ctiques@aol.com
Buys and sells art: Maxfield Parrish, early California oil paintings.

Randeen Cummings, ISA CAPP
Cummings & Associates
P.O. Box 5484
Eugene, OR 97405-0484
ph: 541-345-5856
fax: 541-345-8192
avaluequest@uswest.net
http://www.avaluequest.com
Specializes in selling & appraising residential contents, fine art, estate jewelry, 18th & 19th century antiques, American Brilliant period cut glass; also specialized marketing for clients: consultations, estate, and Internet sales.

Candy Moffett, ISA
Alder Gallery & Antiques
P.O. Box 8517
Coburg, OR 97408
ph: 541-342-6411
fax: 541-683-9797
candy@alderart.com
http://www.alderart.com
Buys, sells, repairs and restores art; specializes in the appraisal of fine art and antiques; Accredited Member of the International Society of Appraisers (ISA).

Experts

Mike Stakis
3 Brookside Ave., Room #3
Newburgh, NY 12550-3018
ph: 845-565-7378
Appraiser, expert, collector of oil paintings, miniature paintings on ivory, reverse paintings on glass; any paintings of American paintings.

A. Everette James, Jr.
St. James Place
205 New Castle Place
Chapel Hill, NC 27514
ph: 919-933-6853
fax: 919-942-0437
everette@nc.rr.com
Art collector, writer, historian; serves on the Art Committee of the Cosmos Club; affiliated with numerous boards and has been a guest curator and lecturer both nationally and internationally; his collections have been widely exhibited.

Terry L. Schafer
American Indian Art & Antiques
Rt #9 Box 295
Marietta, OH 45750
ph: 740-374-2807
wj_tschafer@seovec.org
Expert in old oil paintings and period frames.

Robert Banks, AAA, ISA
Banks Fine Art, LLC
1231 Dragon St.
Dallas, TX 75207
ph: 214-352-1811
fax: 214-352-6360
bob@banksfineart.com
http://www.banksfineart.com
Has been dealing in 19th and 20th century fine art for over 20 years; to the trade; certified member of

Appraisers Association of America; clientele includes established galleries and collectors.

Museums/Libraries

Andrea Henderson Fahnestock
Museum of the City of New York
1220 5th Ave. at 103rd St.
New York, NY 10029-5221
ph: 212-534-1672
fax: 212-534-5974
http://www.mcny.org
Special paintings and sculpture collections; access by appointment; research fee charged.

National Museum of American Art
Catalog: Inventory of Amer. Paintings
  Executed Before 1914
8th & G Sts. N.W.
Washington, DC 20560
ph: 202-357-2504
nmaainfo@nmaa.si.edu
http://www.nmaa.si.edu
A computerized index of over 230,000 records of pre-1914 paintings in public and private collections; artist, location, subject, photo.

Repro. Sources

Wang Zhachui
Beijing Dream Works
P.O. Box 23
Shuang Yu Shu
Beijing, 100086 China
ph: (86) 13901185127
fax: (86) 1062151536
gordon@cnindex.net
http://www.oilpaintingshop.com
Specializes in hand-painted oil on canvas reproductions of old masterpieces.

Isabel Art Gallery
241, Route de Longwy
Luxembourg, L-1941 Luxembourg
info@isabel.com
http://www.isabel.com
Reproduces thousands of works by Old Masters; high quality oil reproductions, entirely hand crafted by specialized and talented artists: Carraaci, Cezenne, David, Degas, Goya, Klimt, Renoir, Van Gogh, Vermeer, Manet, and others.

Vincent Art Gallery
Hoge Slagen 343
SM's - Hertogenbosch, 5233 The Netherlands
ph: +31 73 6417807
fax: +31 73 6400576
theo@vincent.nl
http://www.vincent.nl
Oil painting on canvas reproductions: Van Gogh, Aersten, Botticelli, Boudin, Cabanel, Constable, Degas, Fragonard, Goya, Klimt, Lastman, Leyden, Mauve, Orley, Patinir, Parmigianino, and others.

Ray Lukassen
ING Inc.
P.O. Box 1800
1000 BV Amsterdam, The Netherlands
fax: +31 (0)20 87664021
euro-art-gallery@planet.nl
http://www.euro-art-gallery.net
Sells high quality reproductions of masterpieces of the world: Renaissance, Baroque, Neo Classicism, Romanticism, 20th century, Realism, Impressionism, Post Impressionism; will paint from photos you provide - family, pets, etc.

California

Appraisers

Kathleen DeBolt, ISA
Debolt Fine Art
18353 Sycamore Creek Rd.
Escondido, CA 92025-2302
ph: 858-676-5913 or 619-857-5913
fineart@adnc.com
http://www.onlineartline.com
Specializes in the appraisal of 19th and 20th century American Art, California Impressionism, American scene, New Mexico modernists, Western art.

Richard C. Frey, ISA CAPP
R.T.L.H. Enterprises
1275 East Ave.
Chico, CA 95926-1020
ph: 530-343-4528 or 800-567-7854
fax: 530-343-9380
RFREYRTLH@aol.com
http://www.richardcfreyfineart.com
Certified appraiser of American and European art, paintings, watercolors, drawings, prints, sculpture, bronzes, etc.; appraises for estates, arbitration, and has testified as expert witness.

Auction Services

Bonhams & Butterfields
7601 Sunset Blvd.
Los Angeles, CA 90046-2714
ph: 323-850-7500
fax: 323-850-5843
info@butterfields.com
http://www.butterfields.com

John Moran
John Moran Auctioneers, Inc.
735 W. Woodbury Rd.
Altadena, CA 91001-5310
johnmoran@pop.net
http://www.johnmoran.com

Dealers

Goldfield Galleries
8380 Melrose Ave.
West Hollywood, CA 90069-5422
ph: 323-651-1122
fax: 323-651-1168
Specializes in 19th and 20th century American Impressionist art, and California and Western art.

Marcia Osterkamp, ISA
Poulsen Galleries, Inc.
327 Terrace Dr.
Brawley, CA 92227-3040
ph: 760-344-4810
fax: 760-344-4778
poulsengalleries@compuserve.com
http://www.poulsengalleries.com
*Fine art appraiser; buys and sells
19th and 20th century American and
European paintings; also California
paintings.*

Ray Redfern
Redfern Galleries
1540 South Coast Hwy.
Laguna Beach, CA 92651
ph: 949-497-3356
fax: 949-497-1324
mail@redferngallery.com
http://www.redferngallery.com
*One of California's finest galleries
specializing in American Impressionism with an emphasis on paintings by
the early California Plein Air Artists
(1890-1940): William Wendt, Franz
Bischoff, Donna Schuster, Alson
Clark, etc.*

Jimmy Vitanza
Peregrine Galleries
508 Brinkerhoff Ave.
Santa Barbara, CA 93101-3441
ph: 805-963-3134
fax: 805-963-3134

Robert Raynolds
California-art.com
7343 El Camino Real, PMB 311
Atascadero, CA 93422
ph: 805-462-2301 or 805-440-1579
fax: 805-462-1943
info@california-art.com
http://www.california-art.com
*Specializes in paintings and
watercolors from the California
Impressionism Movement (1880-1940);
also buys and sells original Stickley
furniture.*

William A. Karges Fine Art
P.O. Box D-1
Carmel, CA 93921
ph: 800-833-9185
fax: 831-625-8850
karges@ix.netcom.com
http://www.kargesfineart.com
*Buys and sells California, American,
and Hoosier school paintings.*

Paul Galli
ph: 408-730-4010
eichlerera1@comcast.net
*Buys and sells San Francisco and New
York abstract expressionist art by such
artists as John Saccard, James Budd
Dixon, Edward Corbett, and other
artists.*

Alfred C. Harrison, Jr.
Northpoint Gallery, The
407 Jackson St.
San Francisco, CA 94111
ph: 415-781-7550
fax: 415-781-7553
northpoint@macol.net

John Garzoli
Garzoli Gallery
930 B. St.
San Rafael, CA 94901
ph: 415-459-4321
fax: 415-459-4368
*Specializes in pre-1945 paintings by
California artists with an emphasis
on Northern California artists.*

Christine Daniels
Christine Daniels Antiques
135 E. Shiloh Rd.
Santa Rosa, CA 95403-1254
ph: 707-838-6083
fax: 707-838-6083
ctiques@aol.com
*Buys and sells art: Maxfield Parrish,
early California oil paintings.*

Syd Bottomley, ISA
Sagebrush Gallery
P.O. Box 1842
Nevada City, CA 95959-1842
ph: 530-272-6367
fax: 530-272-2820
findsyd@oro.net
http://www.sagebrushgallery.com
*Buys, collects, appraises and
specializes in American Indian art:
baskets, rugs, pottery, early
California paintings.*

Experts

Don Bennett
Don Bennett & Associates
P.O. Box 283
Agoura Hills, CA 91376-0283
ph: 818-991-5596
fax: 818-991-6866
artofwest@aol.com
*Specializes in works of art by deceased
California and Western artists.*

Museums/Libraries

Irvine Museum, The
18881 Von Karman Ave., Ste. 100
Irvine, CA 92612
ph: 949-476-0294 or 949-476-2565
fax: 949-476-2437
http://www.irvinemuseum.org
*Dedicated to the preservation and
display of California art of the
Impressionist Period (1890-1930).*

Portraits
Misc. Services

Robert Stewart, Cur. Emeritus
4104 46th St. NW
Washington, DC 20016-5608
ph: 202-244-0252
*Will authenticate paintings and
sculpture brought in for inspection;
make an appointment first; may be
able to work from good photographs.*

Museums/Libraries

Linda Thrift, Keeper
National Portrait Gallery
Catalog: Catalog of American Portraits
750 Ninth St., Ste. 8300
Washington, DC 20560-0973
ph: 202-275-1738
fax: 202-275-1887
npgweb@npg.si.edu
http://www.npg.si.edu
*Research database documenting more
than 100,000 American portraits in
public and private collections; offers
online catalog on the Internet.*

Portraits (Miniature)
Collectors

Sheldon Lerman
7505 Osler Dr.
Baltimore, MD 21204-7736
ph: 410-321-1514 or 410-828-1928
fax: 410-825-5710
*Wants to buy American portrait
miniatures on ivory.*

Dealers

Elle Shushan
Augustus Decorative Arts, Ltd.
P.O. Box 7000
New York, NY 10101
ph: 212-333-7888
fax: 212-489-9380
elle@portrait-miniatures.com
http://www.portrait-miniatures.com
*Specializes in portrait miniatures and
portrait waxes from America, Britain
and Europe of the 16th through 19th
centuries.*

Experts

Mike Stakis
3 Brookside Ave., Room #3
Newburgh, NY 12550-3018
ph: 845-565-7378
*Appraiser, expert, collector of oil
paintings, miniature paintings on
ivory, reverse paintings on glass; any
paintings of American paintings.*

Museums/Libraries

Gibbes Museum of Art
135 Meeting St.
Charleston, SC 29401
ph: 843-722-2706
fax: 843-720-1682
http://www.gibbes.com
*Has one of the oldest and finest
collections of miniature portraits in
the US; the collection of more than
500 works ranges from the earliest
produced in Charleston in 1740 to
20th century artists such as Leila
Waring.*

Reverse Painting On Glass
Experts

Mike Stakis
3 Brookside Ave., Room #3
Newburgh, NY 12550-3018
ph: 845-565-7378
*Appraiser, expert, collector of oil
paintings, miniature paintings on
ivory, reverse paintings on glass; any
paintings of American paintings.*

Shirley R. Mace
Shadow Enterprises
P.O. Box 1602
Mesilla Park, NM 88047-1602
ph: 505-524-6717
fax: 505-523-0940
shadow-ent@zianet.com
http://www.geocities.com/
MadisonAvenue/Boardroom/1631
*Author of "Vintage Silhouettes on
Glass & Reverse Paintings" (2000);
painted black on reverse of glass; sold
in dimestores from the 1920s to
1950s; often with advertising and
attached thermometers or calendars.*

Repair Services

Ingrid Sanborn
Ingrid Sanborn & Daughters
85 Church St.
West Newbury, MA 01985-1018
ph: 978-363-2253
fax: 978-363-2049
sanbornanddaughters@attbi.com
http://www.isd.pair.com
*Specializes in the restoration of
reverse paintings on glass and antique
painted finishes; philosophy is to
preserve as much of the original finish
as possible and restore only those
areas that have been lost or damaged.*

Wyeth
Appraisers

Frank E. Fowler
120 Watauga Lane
P.O. Box 247
Lookout Mountain, TN 37350-0247
ph: 423-821-3081
fax: 423-821-5779
ffowl@aol.com
http://www.awyeth.com
*Has specialized in appraising Wyeth
for over 30 years with an emphasis on
Andrew Wyeth; by appointment only.*

PAMPHLETS

(see PAPER COLLECTIBLES)

PAPER CLIPS
Collectors

John T. Ogle
P.O. Box 252
Ocean Springs, MS 39566-0252
*Wants to buy paper clips and notched
bookmarks: antique, foreign, plastic,
novelty, advertising; also wants early
paper clip advertising.*

PAPER COLLECTIBLES

(see also ADVERTISING
COLLECTIBLES; AUTOGRAPHS;
BLOTTERS; BOOKS; BUSINESS
CARDS; CALENDARS; CARDS;
CATALOGS; HISTORICAL
AMERICANA; MAPS & CHARTS;
MAGAZINES; NEWSPAPERS;
POSTCARDS; POSTERS; REPAIR/
RESTORATION/CONSERVATION,
Paper Items; SHEET MUSIC)

Appraisers

Ken Sowman
Vista Group, The
229 Foster Dr.
Barrie, Ontaria LN4 3X9 Canada
ph: 705-739-0482
fax: 705-739-7544
*Appraises, deals in all kinds of paper
collectibles; any subject, any age.*

Auction Services

Russell Mascieri
Victorian Images
P.O. Box 284
Marlton, NJ 08053
ph: 609-985-7711
fax: 609-985-8513
RMascieri@aol.com
http://www.tradecards.com/vi

Robert H. Snyder
Cohasco, Inc.
P.O. Drawer 821
Yonkers, NY 10702-0821
ph: 914-476-8500
fax: 914-476-8573
info@cohascodpc.com
http://www.cohascodpc.com
*In business over 55 years, specializing
in paper collectibles, autographs,
documents, Americana, ephemera, etc.;
mail auction catalogs issued.*

Dale Sorenson
Waverly Auctions, Inc.
4931 Cordell Ave.
Bethesda, MD 20814-2508
ph: 301-951-8883
fax: 301-718-8375
waverly1660@earthlink.net
http://www.waverlyauctions.com
*Specializes in the auction of graphic
art, books, paper, atlases, prints,
postcards, autographs, and other
paper ephemera.*

Ron Meininger
Antebellum Covers
P.O. Box 3494
Gaithersburg, MD 20885
ph: 888-268-3235 or 240-498-3535
fax: 301-869-2623
antebell@antebellumcovers.com
http://www.antebellumcovers.com
*Offers Civil War and 19th century
American paper for sale through
monthly auctions, net price lists and
private treaty: soldier's letters,
autographs, images, engravings,
patriotic envelopes, images, general
orders, slavery items.*

Rick Brown
History Buff's Auction
6031 Winterset
Lansing, MI 48911
ph: 517-887-1255
help@historybuffauction.com
http://www.historybuffauction.com
*Online auction specializing in paper
collectibles from 1600s to 1990s:
newspapers, magazines, pulps,
documents, Civil War, old catalogs,
photography, tobacco cards,
stereoviews, postcards, souvenir
folders, booklets, advertising, etc.*

Joseph Millard
Grandma's Trunk
102 N. Mill St.
Northport, MI 49670
ph: 616-386-5351
*Trade cards, rewards of merit,
valentines, etc.*

Kurt R. Krueger
Krueger Auctions
P.O. Box 275
Iola, WI 54945-0275
ph: 715-445-3845
fax: 715-445-4100
*Specializing in the mail-bid auction of
paper collectibles: stocks & bonds,
advertising, books, letters, manuscripts, children's books, prints,
photographs, historical Americana,
posters, etc.*

Michael Hickey
Accumulations & Collections
1512 Chasewood Dr.
Austin, TX 78727
ph: 512-989-0188
fax: 512-989-0112
*Conducts six auctions per year; directs
auctions to a database of collectors
who are interested in paper
collectibles.*

Clubs/Associations

Ephemera Society of America Inc., The
Newsletter: Ephemera News
P.O. Box 95
Cazenovia, NY 13035-0095
ph: 315-655-9139
fax: 315-655-9139
info@ephemerasociety.org
http://www.ephemerasociety.org
*The major organization for collectors
and dealers of paper collectibles;
focuses on the preservation and study
of ephemera (short-lived printed
matter); "Ephemera News" published
quarterly; also publishes "The
Ephemera Journal."*

Friedl Wolaskowitz
Ephemera Society of Austria, The
Journal: Ephemera Journal
Baumlegarten 5
Hoehst, A-6973 Austria
ph: 0043 5578 76903
*Members collect mostly coffee cream
lids (peel offs) and lids from honey,
lemon, jam, marmalade containers;
also collect packaging items and
advertising collectibles and promotion*

*items from food and drink; want
contact with US collectors.*

Ephemera Society of Canada, The
Newsletter: Ephemera Canada
36 Macauley Dr.
Thornhill, Ontario L3T 5S5 Canada
ph: 416-492-5958
fax: 416-492-5958
ephemera@tht.net
*Dedicated to the preservation, study
and display of Canada's printed
heritage.*

Ephemera Society of England, The
Journal: Ephemerist, The
P.O. Box 112
Northwood, HA6 2WT U.K.

Collectors

Paul R. Lafavore
2131 6th St., NW
Hickory, NC 28601-1703
ph: 828-323-8221
lafavore@twave.net
*Collecting 19th century or earlier
broadsides or handbills relating to
photography, medicine, or the state of
Maine.*

Tom Rutledge
3015 Bever Ave., SE
Cedar Rapids, IA 52403-3028
ph: 319-399-1427
*Wants rare and antiquarian books,
paper, manuscripts, documents,
calendars, postcards, valentines, trade
cards, maps, atlases, autographs,
railroadiana, cook books, posters,
rewards of merit, and children's
books.*

James E. Kattner
P.O. Box 11132
Spring, TX 77391-1132
ph: 281-376-4826
victorio1sw@yahoo.com
*Wants to buy Texas saloon letter-
heads, envelopes, advertising cards,
photographs, and other saloon paper
collectibles; also wants same from
pre-1919 Texas liquor dealers.*

Dealers

Gerald Rubackin
Jerry's Cards & Collectibles
P.O. Box 1271
Framingham, MA 01701-0207
ph: 508-788-0946
fax: 508-788-5197
jermyrauto@att.net
http://www.uacc.org/dealers/
rubackin.html
*Buys and sells WWII fighter aces
autographs and other WWII military
signatures; also want autographed
material by the crew of the Enola Gay
which dropped the first atomic bomb
on Hiroshima.*

George & Julie Perron
Old Paperphiles, The
P.O. Box 135
Tiverton, RI 02878-0135
ph: 401-624-9420
opac108@netzero.net
*Buys and sells paper collectibles:
autographs, sheet music, postcards,
photos, stereoviews, documents, old
letters; sells on eBay, seller name is
"opac."*

Deborah Lavoie
Deborah Lavoie Fine Books & Paper
Treasures
P.O. Box 117
New Boston, NH 03070-0117
ph: 603-487-2369
fax: 603-487-2333
rare@worldnet.att.net
http://abebooks.com/home/RARE
*Buys/sells rare and antiquarian books,
paper, letters, documents, catalogs,
newspapers, postcards, trade cards,
diaries, ledgers, atlases, maps, etc.*

Kit Barry
Kit Barry Ephemera
136 High St., Box 3
Brattleboro, VT 05301
ph: 802-254-3634
kbarry@surfglobal.net
http://www.tradecards.com/kb
*Specializes in fine ephemera, scarce
and rare, including trade cards,
billheads, labels, and posters; also
sells a complete line of ephemera
supplies: plastic pages, matchbook
pages, rigid print holders, soft plastic
sleeves, et.*

Ron & Carol Haglund
Yesterday's Paper
2 Terrill Dr.
Califon, NJ 07830
ph: 908-832-6729
ydayspaper@aol.com
http://www.yesterdayspaper.com
*Buys and sells anything made of old
paper: books, maps, prints, comics,
catalogs, stock certificates, sheet
music, posters, newspapers,
documents, Disneyana, magazines, etc.*

Mark Forder
1800s ephemera
23 Dell Rd.
Stanhope, NJ 07874
mforder@worldnet.att.net
http://home.att.net/~mforder
*Specializes in 19th century paper
ephemera: railroad, baseball, theatre,
advertising, banking, photographs,
and more.*

Old Paper Archive, The
122 West 25th St.
New York, NY 10001-7401
ph: 212-645-3983
*Specializing in antique prints, ads,
books, movie posters, sports,
postcards, photographica, magazines.*

Judith Katz-Schwartz
Twin Brooks Antiques & Collectibles
E-zine: Antiques & Collectibles
  Newsletter
P.O. Box 6572
New York, NY 10128-0006
ph: 212-876-3512
fax: 212-876-3512
twinb@msjudith.net
http://www.msjudith.net
  *Buys, sells, appraises postcards,
  photos, old magazines, valentines,
  advertising fans, cookbooks and
  pamphlets, 39 World's Fair,
  advertising trade cards, blotters, die
  cuts, calendars, etc.; member Assoc. of
  Online Appraisers (AOA).*

Stephen & Carol Resnick
4783 West Lake Rd.
Cazenovia, NY 13035-9671
ph: 315-655-2810
  *Specializes in 18th and 19th century
  ephemera, manuscripts, pamphlets,
  documents, broadsides, postal history,
  invitations, autographs, photographs,
  trade cards.*

Bill "Wolf" Berry
Paper Wolf, The
6950 Lain Rd.
Hornell, NY 14843-9419
ph: 607-324-1086
fax: 607-324-2001
thepaperwolf@dctmail.com
  *Buys and sells paper Americana and
  ephemera; also interested in stamps,
  art, books and records.*

Jack L. Dempsey
Dempsey & Baster
1009 East 38th St.
Erie, PA 16504
ph: 814-825-7690 or 814-825-6381
info@dempseyandbaxter.com
http://www.dempseyandbaxter.com
  *Owns the only one-of-a-kind American
  coin in existence - the 11-cent coin;
  buys coins and currency; also tin toys,
  paper ephemera, fine estate jewelry.*

Tom & Cindy Stone
Stone Enterprises
P.O. Box 414
Mechanicsburg, PA 17055
ph: 717-697-4524
fax: 717-697-1370
tcstone@papercollectibles.com
http://www.papercollectibles.com
  *Buying and selling paper collectibles
  since 1979; Web site has illustrated
  electronic price list in several
  categories.*

George Theofiles
Miscellaneous Man
P.O. Box 1776
New Freedom, PA 17349-0076
ph: 717-235-4766
fax: 717-235-2853
miscman@adelphia.net
  *Issues periodic catalog of paper items
  for sale including labels, poster
  stamps, etc.*

John Cuddy
2768 Willits Rd.
Philadelphia, PA 19136-1026
ph: 215-552-9855
cuddymailpouch@aol.com
  *Buys and sells illustrated advertising
  mailing envelopes dating from 1870s
  to 1940s from US manufacturers;
  please no stamps or 1st day covers.*

Fred Hollman
Global Music Enterprises
488 Archer Lane
Kissimmee, FL 34746
globaltreasures@webtv.net
  *Wants to buy vintage magazines,
  postcards, sheet music, newspapers,
  and other paper collectibles.*

Barbara Sweat
Ayers Collectibles
108 Coffman Circle
Athens, AL 35611
ph: 256-233-1954
jsweat51@aol.com
http://www.webspawner.com/users/
  ayerscollectibles
  *Specializes in all types of paper
  ephemera: letterheads, billheads,
  vintage checks, bank drafts,
  promissory notes, legal documents,
  books, vintage magazines, personal
  letters, vintage magazine ads,
  postcards, Elvis memorabilia.*

Pat Sweeney
Pat Sweeney Ephemera
511 Woods End
Portage, MI 49002
ph: 269-381-9416
pse@tias.com
http://www.patsweeneyephemera.com
  *Specializes in paper ephemera
  including cigar labels, sheet music,
  hotel luggage labels, vintage posters.*

Hugh Passow
306 Main St.
Eau Claire, WI 54701
ph: 715-832-2494
fax: 715-832-1863
mgallery@execpc.com
  *Wants large folio pre-1920 books,
  scrap albums, quantities of pre-1940
  magazines, old prints, miscellaneous
  paper items.*

Bindy Bitterman
Eureka! Antiques, Nostalgia &
  Collectibles
705 W. Washington
Evanston, IL 60202-2214
ph: 847-869-9090
rbitt356@aol.com
  *Specializes in buying and selling early
  paper advertising, catalogs,
  calendars, etc. especially relating to
  the Chicago area; a small but full
  shop - they send no lists but will reply
  by phone, email or letter; SASEs get
  first attention.*

Susan Nicholson
Greater Chicago Productions
P.O. Box 595
Lisle, IL 60532
ph: 630-964-5240
deltiology@aol.com
http://www.susanbrownnicholson.com
  *Buys and sells rare and unusual
  postcards, Victorian valentines,
  periodicals, advertising trade cards,
  etc.*

Jerry Rodnitzky
All America Paper Collectibles
1832 Westcrest Dr.
Arlington, TX 76013
ph: 817-861-8199
jrodprof@yahoo.com
http://www.aapapercollect.com.
  *Buys and sells vintage paperbacks,
  illustrated magazines, movie posters,
  sports collectibles, other paper items.*

John Butler
Vintage Paper Memories
P.O. Box 36010
Las Vegas, NV 89133
ph: 702-245-5320
vintagepm@aol.com
http://www.vintagepapermemories.com
  *Partner with Debbie Conner; wants to
  buy 1860s to 1930s quality paper
  images including paper money, cigar
  labels and postcards.*

Susan Mac Gregor
Whimzy Treasures
27372 Rock Rose Lane, #103
Canyon Country, CA 91387
ph: 661-251-4165
whimzy103@aol.com
http://www.whimzytreasures.com
  *Specializes in paper collectibles from
  1800s through 1900s: die-cut scraps
  from old Victorian albums, trade
  cards, postcards, Victorian paper
  collectibles, seed packages, decals, old
  photos, cabinet cards, CDVs,
  ephemera.*

Joyce Hewitt
Vintage Paper
28353 Paragon Dr.
Santa Clarita, CA 91390
ph: 661-263-6050
jhsunburst@aol.com
http://www.rubylane.com/shops/
  vintagepaper
  *Specializes in vintage paper from
  1800s to 1900s: postcards, photos,
  advertising, cabinet cards, CDVs,
  holiday items, Santa, valentines,
  Easter, Japanese woodblock prints,
  prints catalogs, flower seed catalogs,
  chromolithographs, etc.*

Vivian Briggs
Briggs Antiques
4443 Linwood Place
Riverside, CA 92506
ph: 909-781-3121
fax: 909-781-3121
  *Buys and sells paper collectibles:
  checks, stocks, autographs, receipts,*

*invoices, etc. from 1850s through
early 1900s.*

David Yager
Old Paper
P.O. Box 271
La Honda, CA 94020
ph: 650-372-0780
dyager@alderwood.com
http://www.old-paper.com
  *Web site has over 6,000 collectible
  paper items for sale; sorted by date,
  city, category, company name; items
  priced.*

Ada Fitzsimmons
Paper Pile
P.O. Box 337
San Anselmo, CA 94979-0337
ph: 415-454-5552
fax: 415-454-2947
apaperpile@aol.com
http://www.paperpilecollectibles.com
  *Shop and mail order dealer of all
  kinds of paper items and ephemera;
  specialties are postcards, magazines,
  advertising trade cards, valentines,
  poster stamps and stickers, sheet
  music, advertising, handmade/
  primitive paper items, etc.*

Tom Osjecki
Phyllis' Philatelics
P.O. Box 792
Canyonville, OR 97417
ph: 541-839-4135 or 541-839-6151
  *Buys, sells and specializes in
  postcards, paper Americana, stamps
  and covers; over 25,000 covers and
  postcards listed by state or topic.*

Mac Johnson
Tanstaafl!
P.O. Box 292
Elmira, OR 97437
ph: 541-935-8603
mackie279@continet.com
http://www.prints-n-ephemera.com
  *Specializes in paper ephemera,
  postcards, books, photographs,
  original paintings and drawings,
  matted illustrator prints, old letters,
  old mailed envelopes, magazines,
  posters, calendars, etc.*

Ruth A. Miller Knott
Paperpreneur, The
1248 Ash St.
Lynden, WA 98264
ph: 360-318-8193
ruthie@nas.com
http://www.thepaperpreneur.com
  *Offers a unique selection of quality
  paper ephemera and historical
  documents: advertising, Americana,
  agriculture, Colonial, maritime,
  transportation, maritime, reward or
  merit, fraternal; does research, will
  answer questions.*

Ken Sowman
Vista Group, The
229 Foster Dr.
Barrie, Ontario LN4 3X9 Canada
ph: 705-739-0482
fax: 705-739-7544
Appraises, deals in all kinds of paper collectibles; any subject, any age.

Hava Getz
HGIMAGES
P.O. Box 6
Markfield, Leicstershir LE67 9TX U.K.
ph: 44 1530 244354
fax: 44 1530 244354
hgimages@dircon.co.uk
http://www.hgimages.dircon.co.uk
Has a large selection of playing cards and card games for sale on the Web; also carries large selection of ephemera including cigar box labels and old cigarette packets.

Eugenie Gelman
Victorian & Edwardian Scraps
U.K.
genie@websitegenie.co.uk
http://www.victorianscraps.co.uk
Buys, sells, collects original Victorian scraps, i.e., stamped embossed paper die-cut chromolithograph reliefs; no reproductions; only genuine period scraps.

Experts

A. David Rutstein
As Time Goes By Ephemera & Nostalgia Shop
P.O. Box 73
Great Barrington, MA 01230-0073
ph: 413-528-3002
davidr@bcn.net
Buys and sells paper collectibles and ephemera, especially WWI posters, Victorian scrapbooks, sheet music, Judaica, baseball, ethnic, non-sports trading cards, etc.; has spoken extensively on WWI propaganda and on sheet music.

Norman E. Martinus
Nostalgia Gallery, Inc.
3501 N. Croatan Hwy., Unit #4
Kill Devil Hills, NC 27948-8350
ph: 252-441-1881 or 252-261-2002
Co-author with Harry Rinker of "Warman's Paper" (Wallace-Homestead, 1994); wants to buy pre-1940 surfing paper, Wright Bros., paper related to spiders, US Coast Guard Stations in N.C.

Ray Walsh
Curious Book Shop
307 E. Grand River
East Lansing, MI 48823-4324
ph: 517-332-0112
fax: 517-332-1915
mmabda@curiousbooks.com
http://www.curiousbooks.com
Dealer/expert; owner of three book shops in Michigan; hosts radio call-in show about books and paper collectibles; writes columns; send a SASE for reply when writing.

Ken Prag
Ken Prag Paper Americana
P.O. Box 14817
San Francisco, CA 94114-0817
ph: 415-586-9386
kprag@planeteria.net
Eager to buy old stocks and bonds, quality picture postcards, western stereoviews, old timetables and brochures, etc.

Internet Resources

Printed Ephemera Collection, Library of Congress
101 Independence Ave. SE
Washington, DC 20540
ph: 202-707-8000
ndlpcoll@loc.gov
http://memory.loc.gov/ammem/rbpehtml/pehome.html
The Printed Ephemera Collection is a rich repository of Americana; 28,000 primary source items dating from the 17th century; Web site preview has 50 digitized images: posters, notices, advertisements, proclamations, leaflets, etc.

John Lobota
Antique Paper & Ephemera X-change
3089 Lillian Rd.
West Palm Beach, FL 33406
ph: 561-697-0055
fax: 561-433-3138
papertique@apex-ephemera.com
http://www.apex-ephemera.com
Buy, sell, trade your paper collectibles; APEX offers over 80 categories of paper collectibles; free classifieds for collectors; bulletin boards, search and more.

Back Issue Finder
1303 S. 10th St.
Sheboygan, WI 53081
ph: 920-459-7901
fax: 505-204-7937
http://www.javahousebooks.com/booklink/booklink/ephemera-txt.htm
A Web site marketplace for locating and selling hard-to-find, out-of-print and back issue periodicals including newspapers, magazines and comic books; also ephemera such as programs, postcards, posters, trading cards, etc.

Museums/Libraries

Crane Museum of Papermaking
30 South St.
Dalton, MA 01226
ph: 413-648-2600
info@crane.com
http://www.crane.com/about/ac_sets/set_ac_museum.html
Operated by the Crane Paper Company.

American Antiquarian Society
185 Salisbury St.
Worcester, MA 01609
ph: 508-755-5221
fax: 508-753-3311
library@mwa.org
A learned society founded in 1812;

maintains a research library of American history and culture in order to collect, preserve, and make available for study the printed record of the US; 3 million books, maps, pamphlets, etc.

Periodicals

Denise M. Sater, Ed.
Newspaper: Paper & Advertising Collector (P.A.C.)
P.O. Box 500
Mount Joy, PA 17552-0500
ph: 717-492-2540 or 800-800-1833
fax: 717-653-6165
dsater7650@aol.com
http://www.paperandadvertisingcollector.com
Specialty publication for collectors of paper, advertising, ephemera, country store, etc.

Doug Watson
Magazine: Paper Collectors' Marketplace
470 Main St.
P.O. Box 128
Scandinavia, WI 54977-0128
ph: 715-467-2379
fax: 715-467-2243
pcmpaper@gglbbs.com
http://www.pcmpaper.com
Monthly magazine for collectors of autographs, paperbacks, postcards, advertising, photographica, magazines; all types of paper ephemera.

Ada Fitzsimmons, Ed.
Paper Pile Press
Magazine: Paper Pile Quarterly
P.O. Box 337
San Anselmo, CA 94979-0337
ph: 415-454-5552
fax: 415-454-2947
apaperpile@aol.com
http://www.paperpilecollectibles.com
A 22 year old quarterly magazine for buyers and sellers of paper items: postcards, menus, ads, magazines, trade cards, etc.; also contains feature articles about collectibles, book reviews, auction reviews, show schedule.

Billheads

Collectors

Joseph F. Loccisano
Historic Photographs & Paper Americana
2264 Nicholson Square Dr.
Lancaster, PA 17601-3966
ph: 717-560-5182
always_buying@yahoo.com
http://www.always-buying.com
Wants to buy billheads and business letterheads (1850s - 1920s) that graphically show products, buildings, logos, etc.; send photo with asking price.

Canadian

Dealers

Michael Rice
Michael Rice Collectibles
P.O. Box 286
Saanichton, British Columbia V8M 2C5 Canada
ph: 250-652-9412
fax: 250-652-7866
mrice@pacificcoast.net
Wants pre-1940 Canadian and English picture postcards, and other pre-1940 Canadian interesting paper memorabilia; stock certificates, photographs, steamship souvenirs, posters, autographs; all queries answered; call after 6 PST.

Certificates

Repro. Sources

Mark Sutton
Victorian Certificates
2035 St. Andrews Circle
Carmel, IN 46032-9547
ph: 317-844-5648
mdsutton2@comcast.net
Reproduces Victorian-era certificates; add your own photos & calligraphy; commemorate weddings, anniversaries, births or baptisms.

Coloring Books

Collectors

Lois Helen Brown
154 W. 500 S
Peru, IN 46970-7621
ph: 765-473-3983
Wants coloring books from the 1930s through the 1960s, especially ones from the WWII era.

Computer Programs For

Man./Prod./Dist.

Niche Software, Inc.
Software: Book, Magazine & Paper Collector, The
7118 NW Terrace
Parkland, FL 33076
ph: 954-344-6561
marketing@collectiblessoftware.com
http://www.collectiblessoftware.com
Designed for the collector of books, magazines, documents, fruit labels, etc.

Dance Cards

Dealers

Federico Santi
Drawing Room of Newport, The
152 Spring St.
Newport, RI 02840-6806
ph: 401-841-5060
fax: 401-848-0953
zsolnay@drawrm.com
http://www.drawrm.com
Buys, sells, and collects late 19th century and early 20th century dance cards; prefers fancy examples; can buy from photo or photocopy.

Historical

Collectors

Gary Ronk
6247 Cove Rd.
Roanoke, VA 24019-1715
ph: 540-562-2368
papermemo@aol.com
*Wants to buy early deeds, indentures,
land grants, etc., especially those that
have revenue stamps or seals.*

Illustrated

Internet Resources

Denis C. Jackson, Ed.
E-zine: Illustrator Collector's News, The
P.O. Box 6433
Kingman, AZ 86401
ticn@olypen.com
http://www.olypen.com/ticn
*An online publication for collectors of
magazines and other paper illustrations; free classifieds and articles, no
charge Web site information; new and
old prints.*

Napkins

Experts

Moira Jaffe
255 W. 88 St.
New York, NY 10024
jaffer@earthlink.net
*Interested in pre-1950 decorative and
commemorative napkins.*

Radio Related

(see also RADIOS)

Dealers

Jim & Felicia Kreuzer
New Wireless Pioneers
1541 Bronson Rd.
Grand Island, NY 14072
ph: 716-773-4999
fax: 716-773-5757
wireless@pce.net
http://www.marconi-wireless.com
*Buys and sells 1850-1950 books,
catalogs, magazines and other
literature dealing with early radio,
telegraph, wireless, X-ray and
electricity.*

Southern

Dealers

Henry Barnet
Your Town, Inc.
516 Maverick Circle
Spartanburg, SC 29307-3707
ph: 864-579-2112
hbbarnet@cs.com
*Buys, sells, appraises paper, photos,
documents, maps, rare & collectible
books, autographs, and prints
associated with The Old South or New
South.*

Western

(see also WESTERN AMERICANA)

Auction Services

Warren Anderson
America West Archives
P.O. Box 100
Cedar City, UT 84721-0100
ph: 435-586-9497 or 435-586-7323
awa@netutah.com
http://www.americawestarchives.com
*Buys and sells paper Americana
associated with the Western US: old
documents, letters, photos, stocks,
maps, autographs, prints, etc.; author
of "Owning Western History."*

PAPERDOLLS

(see DOLLS, Paper)

PAPERWEIGHTS

(see also GLASS)

Appraisers

Debbie Tarsitano
Tarsitano Studio
dtglassart@aol.com
http://www.debbietarsitano.com
*Paperweight artist and designer; also
appraises antique as well as
contemporary paperweights; 25 years
experience in the field with major
glass museum affiliations; experienced
as paperweight consultant to
Sotheby's and Skinners.*

Auction Services

Robert Block
Block's Box
P.O. Box 51
Trumbull, CT 06611-0051
ph: 203-926-8448
fax: 203-261-7033
blockschip@aol.com
http://www.blocksite.com
*Conducts mail-bid auctions of
paperweights received from collectors,
dealers, estates, museums and others.*

Lawrence H. Selman
L.H. Selman, Ltd.
123 Locust St.
Santa Cruz, CA 95060
ph: 800-538-0766 or 831-427-1177
fax: 831-427-0111
lselman@got.net
http://www.paperweight.com
*Conducts periodic auctions of fine
paperweights.*

Clubs/Associations

Ben Drabeck
New England Paperweight Collectors
   Association
P.O. Box 188
Shutesbury, MA 01072
ph: 413-259-1575
*NEPCA holds meetings to provide
members the opportunity to learn more
about paperweights by offering
educational programs and to purchase
paperweights from dealers.*

Andrew Dohan
Delaware Valley Chapter, Paperweight
   Collectors Association
Newsletter: DVC-PCA Newsletter
20 Chester County Commons
Malvern, PA 19355-1942
ph: 610-722-5800
fax: 610-647-5476
Dohan@juno.com
*Full program meetings four times a
year; color photography quarterly
newsletter.*

Paperweight Collectors' Association,
   Inc.
Newsletter: Paperweight Collectors'
   Bulletin
274 Eastchester Dr., #117
High Point, NC 27262
ph: 336-869-2769
fax: 336-869-8974
info@paperweight.org
http://www.paperweight.org
*1,600 member association of
paperweight collectors; antique and
modern; dealers, artists, makers of
contemporary weights.*

Leo C. McNamee III
Paperweight Collectors Association of
   Chicago
Newsletter: PCAC Newsletter
535 Delkir Court
Naperville, IL 60565-4165
ph: 630-369-2242
*An association for collectors of
antique and contemporary glass
paperweights.*

Bob White
Paperweight Collectors Association of
   Texas
Newsletter: Paperweight, The
2900 Sussex Gardens Lane
Austin, TX 78748-2020
ph: 512-282-0061
white-rr@juno.com
http://www.main.org/pcatx
*Three or four meetings and five or six
newsletters per year.*

Lawrence H. Selman
International Paperweight Society
Newsletter: Paperweight News
123 Locust St.
Santa Cruz, CA 95060
ph: 800-538-0766 or 831-427-1177
fax: 831-427-0111
lselman@got.net
http://www.paperweight.com
*The purpose of the society is to
uncover knowledge about the history
and making of glass paperweights
(antique and contemporary), to bring
together collectors from around the
world, and to organize displays of
glass paperweights.*

Cambridge Paperweight Circle
Newsletter: CPC Newsletter
P.O. Box 941
Comberton, Cambridge PDO CB3 7GQ
   U.K.
kevh@clara.co.uk
http://www.kevh.clara.net
UK-based paperweight club with

*worldwide membership; centralized
and regional meetings, full color
newsletter.*

Collectors

James Lefever
P.O. Box 1263
Beltsville, MD 20704
ph: 410-828-0776
MrGlass@redrose.net

Barry Schultheiss
P.O. Box 6259
High Point, NC 27262
ph: 336-841-6966
fax: 336-841-6987
barrysppwt@aol.com

Alvin R. Bates
P.O. Box 40
Barker, TX 77413-0040
ph: 281-579-7413
fax: 281-579-7413
albates@worldnet.att.net
*Paperweight collector; also editor of
the Paperweight Collectors
Association of Texas newsletter.*

Aleen Burfening
21405 North 142nd Dr.
Sun City West, AZ 85375
ph: 623-546-4405
jwburf@aol.com

Margaret Gunn
10110 Longview
Atwater, CA 95301
ph: 209-394-7724

Dealers

William Pitt
16 Sconticut Neck Rd., #312
Fairhaven, MA 02719
ph: 508-993-9434
wipitt@aol.com
http://www.wpitt.com
*Specializes in art glass and
paperweights; has appeared on PAX
TV's "Treasures in Your Home."*

Robert Block
Block's Box
P.O. Box 51
Trumbull, CT 06611-0051
ph: 203-926-8448
fax: 203-261-7033
blockschip@aol.com
http://www.blocksite.com
*Buys and sells antique French and
modern Kaziun paperweights.*

Leo Kaplan
Leo Kaplan, Ltd.
114 East 57th St.
New York, NY 10022
ph: 212-355-7212
fax: 212-355-7209
leokaplan@mindspring.com
http://www.leokaplan.com
*Specializes in early English pottery
and porcelain; also antique and
contemporary glass paperweights.*

George Kamm
George Kamm's 20th Century Glass,
   Pottery, Etc.
23 Phillip Dr.
Kirkwood, PA 17536-9511
ph: 717-529-3741
fax: 717-529-2042
gkamm@earthlink.net
http://www.artglass-pottery.com
   *Sells contemporary art glass,
   paperweights, pottery, Raku, animal
   and bird figurines, and more.*

Andrew Dohan
20 Chester County Commons
Malvern, PA 19355-1942
ph: 610-722-5800
fax: 610-647-5476
Dohan@juno.com
   *Collector, dealer buys antique pre-
   1900s glass paperweights: French,
   American, English, Bohemian,
   Russian; buying one or entire
   collection; surface wear & minor
   chips to base not a problem; write or
   call first with description.*

Tad McKeon
2115 West Houston Way
Germantown, TN 38139
ph: 901-854-5683
mtad2@midsouth.rr.com
   *Wants to buy antique and modern
   paperweights (Baccarat, Perthshire,
   Whitefriars, St. Louis, etc.); singles
   or collections; will return all calls.*

Nancy Alfano
Portia Paperweights
1702 N. Damen Ave.
Chicago, IL 50547
ph: 773-862-1700
fax: 773-862-0142
nancy@portiapaperweights.com
http://www.portiapaperweights.com
   *Buys and sells contemporary as well
   as antique paperweights: Scottish,
   European, American, sulphides, etc.*

Betty & Larry Schwab
Paperweight Shoppe, The
2507 Newport Dr.
Bloomington, IL 61704-4525
ph: 309-662-1956 or 877-517-6518
mail@thepaperweightshoppe.com
http://www.thepaperweightshoppe.com
   *Purveyor of fine glass paperweights,
   both contemporary and antique; also
   sculptural art glass, vases and
   paperweight reference books; over
   2500 paperweights in inventory; also
   buys high quality glass paperweights
   and offers appraisals.*

Lawrence H. Selman
L.H. Selman, Ltd.
Newsletter: Paperweight News
123 Locust St.
Santa Cruz, CA 95060
ph: 800-538-0766 or 831-427-1177
fax: 831-427-0111
lselman@got.net
http://www.paperweight.com
   *World's largest dealer in fine
   paperweights, both antique and
   contemporary; mail order company*

*selling directly or through paper-
weight auctions offered twice yearly;
call for free brochure.*

Experts

Dan McNamara
P.O. Box 130 - 163
Boston, MA 02113
ph: 617-846-9465
theresemcnamara@msn.com
   *Buys and sells antique glass
   paperweights; has identified and
   cataloged paperweights for numerous
   museums; will identify paperweights
   for others who send photo and SASE.*

Louis O. St. Aubin, Jr.
Brookside Antiques "Art Glass Gallery"
44 North Water St.
New Bedford, MA 02740
ph: 508-993-4944
   *Museum consultant, expert,
   established in 1964, author of
   "Pairpoint Lamps. A Collectors
   Guide;" nationally known authority,
   lecturer, appraiser, auction house
   consultant; founder of the New
   Bedford Glass Museum.*

Paul H. Dunlop
Dunlop Collection, The
P.O. Box 6269
Statesville, NC 28687-6269
ph: 800-227-1996 or 704-871-2626
fax: 704-871-2329
   *Leading paperweight dealers; buys
   and sells all top quality antique and
   contemporary glass paperweights,
   paperweight books and related items;
   author of "The Jokelson Collection of
   Antique Cameo Incrustation."*

George N. Kulles
13441 Little Creek Dr.
Lockport, IL 60441-8686
ph: 708-301-0996
   *Buys, appraises and repairs antique
   paperweights.*

Steve Cole
Steve Cole Antiques
23897 Corte Emerado
Murrieta, CA 92562
ph: 909-600-0335
fax: 909-600-0445
   *Buy, sell, collect, trade glass
   paperweights from around the world;
   collections can be consigned for sale
   or appraised; member of the National
   Paperweight Collector's Association
   and numerous local collector groups;
   will answer questions.*

Lawrence H. Selman
L.H. Selman, Ltd.
123 Locust St.
Santa Cruz, CA 95060
ph: 800-538-0766 or 831-427-1177
fax: 831-427-0111
lselman@got.net
http://www.paperweight.com
   *Buys and sells antique paperweights;
   also repairs and polishes paperweights. Author of "Art of the
   Paperweight."*

Man./Prod./Dist.

Joe Rice
House of Glass, Inc., The
7900 E. State Rd. 28
Elwood, IN 46036-8449
ph: 765-552-6841
fax: 765-552-6854
   *Makes paperweights all signed by
   owner, Joe Rice; also makes all sorts
   of other solid glass: ashtrays, pears,
   ringholders, etc.*

Museums/Libraries

Museum of American Glass at Wheaton
   Village
1501 Glasstown Rd.
Millville, NJ 08332-1566
ph: 856-825-6800 or 800-998-4552
fax: 856-825-2410
mail@wheatonvillage.org
http://www.wheatonvillage.org
   *Covers all types of American glass:
   Stiegel, Amelung, flasks, pressed, art
   glass, Art Nouveau, paperweights,
   lamps & lighting, cut glass, 20th
   century art glass, reproductions, pre-
   studio movement, contemporary studio
   glass, etc.*

Corning Museum of Glass, The
Journal: Journal of Glass Studies
One Museum Way
Corning, NY 14830-2253
ph: 607-937-5371
fax: 607-937-3352
pr@cmog.org
http://www.cmog.org
   *Over 35,000 glass objects, innovative
   exhibits, videos, models; glass history,
   archaeology, and early manufacturing;
   great Web site with lots of information about glass.*

Degenhart Paperweight & Glass
   Museum, Inc.
65323 Highland Hills Rd.
P.O. Box 186
Cambridge, OH 43725-0186
ph: 740-432-2626
degmus@clover.net
   *Over 1,000 paperweights on exhibit;
   video, research library, gift shop.*

Alex Vance, Ex. Dir.
Bergstrom-Mahler Museum
165 N. Park Ave.
Neenah, WI 54956
ph: 920-751-4670
   *The museum houses one of the world's
   finest collections of glass paperweights.*

Repair Services

Edward Poore
Crystal Work Shop
794 Sandwich Rd.
P.O. Box 475
Sagamore, MA 02561-0475
ph: 508-888-9298 or 888-869-0867
fax: 508-888-9298
crystal.workshop@verizon.net
http://www.thecrystalworkshop.com
   *Repairs and recutting of damaged
   glass paperweights; impact fractures
   removed; recutting of faceted weights*

*and star bottom done when needed; 30
years experience; contact for free
detailed brochure.*

Art Cut Glass Studio
RD 1 -10 Fawn Dr.
Matawan, NJ 07747
ph: 732-583-7648
   *Restores fine antique glass such as
   Lalique, Steuben, Baccarat, Galle;
   also resurfaces paperweights.*

George N. Kulles
13441 Little Creek Dr.
Lockport, IL 60441-8686
ph: 708-301-0996
   *Restores and polishes damaged
   paperweight surfaces; author of
   "Identifying Antique Paperweights -
   Millifiore and Lampwork."*

Larry Castle
Castle Fair
3387 Polk Ave.
Ogden, UT 84403
ph: 801-393-8131
antiquemarbles@msn.com
   *Over ten years experience; all work is
   hand held using water-cooled diamond
   equipment to heal fractures.*

Advertising

Collectors

Bill Price
Paperweight Potentate of Pittsburgh, The
P.O. Box 82501
Pittsburgh, PA 15218-0501
ph: 412-351-5297
fax: 724-271-4329
paperwghts@aol.com
   *Wants to buy glass paperweights
   advertising businesses or with
   people's portraits; also wants glass
   doorstops advertising businesses or
   with people's portraits.*

John Andreae
P.O. Box 156
Granger, IN 46530-0156
ph: 219-675-9960
fax: 219-675-9961
jkandreae@aol.com
   *Wants glass paperweights with
   advertising on them.*

Glenn Fletcher
Wood Room, The
1070 State Highway 46 East
New Braunfels, TX 78130-2850
ph: 830-625-5384
   *Advanced collector wants standing
   promotional metal paperweights
   displaying cars, trucks, buildings, RR,
   ships, tools; also figural animals,
   human, medical or representing
   product advertising; must have
   company logo, name, or trademark.*

Experts

Stuart Kammerman
3262 West Chateau Ave.
Roseburg, OR 97470-2411
ph: 541-440-6754
slkamm@rosenet.net
   Collector, expert wants to buy glass

■ **PATENTS, TRADEMARKS & COPYRIGHTS**

advertising paperweights with the white milk glass appearance on the reverse side; especially wants those made by the Barnes & Abrams Co., Abram Paper Weight Co., and J.N. Abrams.

Cast Iron

Dealers

Richard Tucker
Argyle Antiques
P.O. Box 262
Argyle, TX 76226-0262
ph: 940-464-3752
fax: 940-464-7293
lead1234@gte.net
Buys and sells cast iron advertising paperweights; no reproductions or repaired items.

PAPERWEIGHTS (MODERN)

Clubs/Associations

Paperweight Collectors' Association, Inc.
Newsletter: Paperweight Collectors' Bulletin
274 Eastchester Dr., #117
High Point, NC 27262
ph: 336-869-2769
fax: 336-869-8974
info@paperweight.org
http://www.paperweight.org
1,600 member association of paperweight collectors; antique and modern; dealers, artists, makers of contemporary weights.

Dealers

Tad McKeon
2115 West Houston Way
Germantown, TN 38139
ph: 901-854-5683
mtad2@midsouth.rr.com
Wants to buy antique and modern paperweights (Baccarat, Perthshire, Whitefriars, St. Louis, etc.); singles or collections; will return all calls.

Joan Wurmbrand
Good Buy Girls
2691 East Main St., Ste. 102
Bexley, OH 43209
ph: 614-231-0437 or 866-886-0467
fax: 614-231-3140
goodbuygirls@tias.com
http://www.goodbuygirls.com
Carries Gibson (West Virginia) glass paperweights as well as one-of-a-kind paperweights by Midwest artists.

Eric Sinizer
Light Opera Retail Corp.
460 Post Rd.
San Francisco, CA 94102-1502
ph: 415-956-9866
fax: 415-956-5624
eric@lightoperagallery.com
http://www.lightoperagallery.com
Specializes in contemporary glass paperweights and other studio glass.

Experts

Paul H. Dunlop
Dunlop Collection, The
P.O. Box 6269
Statesville, NC 28687-6269
ph: 800-227-1996 or 704-871-2626
fax: 704-871-2329
Leading paperweight dealers; buys and sells all top quality antique and contemporary glass paperweights, paperweight books and related items; author of "The Jokelson Collection of Antique Cameo Incrustation."

Man./Prod./Dist.

Bob Banford
Banford Paperweights
2010 Skip Morgan Dr.
Hammonton, NJ 08037
ph: 609-561-7575
fax: 609-704-0197
rbpwt@erols.com
http://www.banfordpaperweights.com
Making fine glass paperweights since 1973.

Ron & Sherry Blankenship
Baron Creek Glassworks
Rt. 2, Box 176
Westville, OK 74965
ph: 918-778-3243
baroncreek@aol.com
http://hometown.aol.com/baroncreek/shells.html
Creates elegant studio art glass with an emphasis on intricacy and beauty; also creates mouth blown, hand shaped vases and other vessels, perfumes, pendants, decorative platters, lamps.

Caithness

Clubs/Associations

Caithness Glass Paperweight Society
Newsletter: Caithness Report, The
141 Lanza Ave., Bldg. 12
Garfield, NJ 07026-3530
ph: 973-340-3330 or 800-452-7987
fax: 973-340-9415
caithglas@aol.com
http://www.caithnessglass.co.uk/caithness.htp
Company sponsored society for collectors of Caithness glass paperweights; also publishes the magazine "Reflections" twice a year.

Man./Prod./Dist.

Caithness Glass Inc.
141 Lanza Ave., Bldg. 12
Garfield, NJ 07026-3530
ph: 973-340-3330 or 800-452-7987
fax: 973-340-9415
caithglas@aol.com
http://www.caithnessglass.co.uk/caithness.htp
The largest producer of museum-quality glass paperweights in the world in both traditional and modern styles; email in Scotland at collector@caithnessglass.co.uk.

PASSPORTS

Collectors

Dan M. Jacobson
P.O. Box 277101
Sacramento, CA 95827-7101
United States and overseas.

PATCHES

(see BADGES; BOY SCOUT MEMORABILIA; FIRE FIGHTING MEMORABILIA; LAW ENFORCEMENT MEMORABILIA; MILITARIA, Insignia; GIRL SCOUT MEMORABILIA)

PATENT MODELS

Collectors

Alan W. Rothschild
4796 West Lake Rd.
Cazenovia, NY 13035
ph: 315-655-9367
Maxertaxer@aol.com
http://www.patentmodel.org
Wants to buy patent models and Patent Office documents.

Skip Gladwin
11900 SE Shell Ave.
Hobe Sound, FL 33455
ph: 561-546-1500
fax: 561-746-8336
rfg101842@aol.com
Collects US Patent Models; requests information on models or literature pertaining to models; will assist in answering questions about patent models and can recommend others who might be able to help.

Internet Resources

Alan W. Rothschild
Rothschild Petersen Patent Model Museum
4796 West Lake Rd.
Cazenovia, NY 13035
ph: 315-655-9367
Maxertaxer@aol.com
http://www.patentmodel.org
The museum was established in 1998; contains nearly 4,000 patent models and related documents; very informative Web site containing images of interesting inventions and contraptions as well as patent model history.

Museums/Libraries

Alan W. Rothschild
Rothschild Petersen Patent Model Museum
4796 West Lake Rd.
Cazenovia, NY 13035
ph: 315-655-9367
Maxertaxer@aol.com
http://www.patentmodel.org
The museum was established in 1998; contains nearly 4,000 patent models and related documents; very informative Web site containing images of interesting inventions and

contraptions as well as patent model history.

U.S. Patent & Trademark Museum
2121 Crystal Dr.
Arlington, VA 22202
ph: 703-305-8341
http://www.uspto.gov/web/offices/ac/ahrpa/opa/museum
Strives to educate the public about the patent and trademark systems, and the important role intellectual property protection plays in our nation's social and economic health.

Patent Model Museum
400 North 8th St.
Fort Smith, AR 72901
ph: 501-782-9014 or 501-782-1555
fax: 501-782-1555
Collection contains over 80 miniature models and pictures of 19th century inventions.

PATENTS, TRADEMARKS & COPYRIGHTS

Internet Resources

United States Copyright Office, The
Library of Congress
101 Independence Ave. SE
Washington, DC 20559-6000
copyinfo@loc.gov
http://lcweb.loc.gov/copyright
Copyright basics, registration procedures, copyright records, application forms, form letters, copyright law, Federal regulations, international copyright, related resources.

Misc. Services

U.S. Government Printing Office, Superintendent of Document
P.O. Box 371954
Pittsburgh, PA 15250-7954
ph: 202-512-1800
fax: 202-512-2250
gpoaccess@gpo.gov
http://www.access.gpo.gov
Send $4 for "General Information Concerning Patents."

United States Patent & Trademark Office, Copy Sales
Box 9
Washington, DC 20231
ph: 703-305-4350 or 800-786-9199
fax: 703-305-8759
ptcs@uspto.gov
http://www.uspto.gov
Send $3 for copy of a patent; database of patent numbers and issue dates.

Richard Van Vleck
Greybird Publishing
P.O. Box 412
Taneytown, MD 21787
ph: 301-447-2680
smma@americanartifacts.com
http://americanartifacts.com/smma
Patent search and copy service for items in your collection; a copy of any patent from 1790 to present will be provided, including full text and

illustrations; cost is $15 for the first search and $9 for each additional search.

U.S. Patent & Trademark Office,
Scientific Library, Foreign Patents
Division
2021 Jefferson Davis Highway
Arlington, VA 22202
ph: 703-308-1076 or 800-786-9199
fax: 703-308-1000
ptcs@uspto.gov
http://www.uspto.gov/web/offices/pac/
dapp/sir/stic/newstic.html
*Can obtain copies of foreign patents
for $10.*

PAWNBROKERS

Clubs/Associations

National Pawnbrokers Association
2050 Stemmons, Ste. 107
P.O. Box 420028
Dallas, TX 75342-0028
ph: 214-745-4746 or 888-808-7296
fax: 214-745-1459
info@nationalpawnbrokers.org
http://www.nationalpawnbrokers.org
*Contributes to the professional and
personal development of member
pawnbrokers through enhancement of
the images/perceptions of the industry,
by advocating pawnbrokers rights,
responsibilities and issues, and by
representing the industry.*

Periodicals

Brian K. Burkart, Pub.
BKB Publications Inc.
Magazine: Today's Pawnbroker
98 Greenwich Ave., #1FL
New York, NY 10011-7743
ph: 212-807-6558
fax: 212-807-1821
bkbpub1@ix.netcom.com
*Trade news and articles, ads, refining
companies, buyers of jewelry and
coins, trade shows, etc.*

PEACE MOVEMENT ITEMS

(see CLOTHING & ACCESSORIES,
1960s & 1970s; MODERNISM;
MUSIC, 1960s & 1970s; POPULAR
CULTURE; SOCIAL CAUSES, Hippie
Items; VIETNAM ITEMS)

PEANUT MACHINES

(see COIN-OPERATED MACHINES,
Vending Machines)

PEANUTS

(see CHARACTER COLLECTIBLES,
Peanuts Characters; PLANTERS
PEANUTS ITEMS; TOM'S PEANUTS)

PEARL HARBOR

(see also MILITARIA)

Collectors

Martin Jacobs
World War II Homefront Collectibles
P.O. Box 22026
San Francisco, CA 94122-0026
ph: 415-661-7552
fax: 415-731-4668
MJacobs784@aol.com
*Collector seeks WWII memorabilia
from the Homefront 1941-1945; will
purchase any size collection; wants
victory pins, Cinderella stickers and
stamps, envelope art, war propaganda, Anti-Axis art, matchcovers,
postcards, etc.*

Experts

Harvey & Sandy Dolin
Harvey Dolin & Co.
111 Fulton St., Mezzanine Level
New York, NY 100386
ph: 212-267-0216
*Wants any item pertaining to Pearl
Harbor, WWI and WWII.*

PEDAL CARS

(see RIDING TOYS)

PEEP SHOWS

(see STANHOPES)

PENCIL SHARPENERS

Collectors

Craig Dinner
P.O. Box 4399
Long Island City, NY 11104-0399
ph: 718-729-3850
ferrouswheel123@aol.com
*Wants pre-1920 mechanical pencil
sharpeners.*

Robert Kwalwasser
168 Camp Fatima Rd.
Renfrew, PA 16053-9104
ph: 724-789-7766
fax: 724-789-9771
robertk@tcis.net
*Wants old pencil sharpeners, pocket
and desk types.*

Martha Crouse
4516 Brandon Lane
Beltsville, MD 20705-2601
ph: 301-937-2343
*Wants to buy old pencil sharpeners;
figural, celluloid, hand held; wants
one or entire collections.*

Bernice Kraker
9800 McMillan Ave.
Silver Spring, MD 20910-1149
ph: 301-589-2544
*Wants only hand-held, figural
sharpeners made from metal,
celluloid, or Bakelite from German,
USA and Japan from 1920s to 1940s;
wants no plastic or common bronzed
metal types; description important;
answers all mail and glad to share.*

Jay Bolante
3058 North Honore St.
Chicago, IL 60657-2050
ph: 773-327-5091
jaybee47@msn.com
*Collects and wants to buy mechani-
cally operated pencil sharpeners.*

Clay Tontz
4043 Nora Ave.
Covina, CA 91722-3819
ph: 626-338-9976
*Please send SASE if requesting a
reply.*

Experts

Bernice Kraker
9800 McMillan Ave.
Silver Spring, MD 20910-1149
ph: 301-589-2544
*Wants only hand-held, figural
sharpeners made from metal,
celluloid, or Bakelite from German,
USA and Japan from 1920s to 1940s;
wants no plastic or common bronzed
metal types; description important;
answers all mail and glad to share.*

PENCILS

(see also OFFICE EQUIPMENT;
PENCIL SHARPENERS; PENS)

Clubs/Associations

Sam Fiorella
Pen Collectors of America
Newsletter: PENnant
P.O. Box 447
Fort Madison, IA 52627-0447
ph: 319-372-0881
fax: 319-372-0882
info@pencollectors.com
http://www.pencollectors.com
*Association of fountain pen collectors;
maintains library of materials for pen
collectors; disseminates information,
holds regular meetings; promotes
collecting as a hobby and using pens;
newsletter published three times a
year.*

Louise Hiltz, Mem.
American Pencil Collectors Society
Newsletter: Pencil Collector, The
P.O. Box 547
Mountain View, WY 82939
webmaster@pencilcollector.org
http://www.pencilcollector.org
*Members focus on the collecting of
pens & pencils: unsharpened lead
pencils with advertisements or
addresses, old mechanical pencils.*

John Daniels, Mem. Sec.
Writing Equipment Society
Journal: Journal of the Writing
Equipment Society
33 Glanville Rd.
Hadleigh
Ipswich, Suffolk IP7 5SQ U.K.
wes.sec@btinternet.com
http://www.wesonline.org.uk
*Devoted to the conservation and study
of writing instruments and accesso-*

*ries: pens of all types and materials,
pencils, nibs, inkwells, stamp boxes,
quill cutters, scriveners' knives, seals,
writing slopes, blotters, paper knives,
etc.*

Collectors

Bruce Axler
Ansonia Station
P.O. Box 1288
New York, NY 10023-1288
ph: 212-579-0348
*Wants pocket items, i.e., items/gadgets
designed to fit in the pocket: tools,
knives, lighters, compacts, folding
cups, items which look like a pocket
watch but are not, calculators, leather
items, match safes, candle safes, travel
items.*

Bill Bean
3351 Jeffrey Lane
Eau Claire, WI 54703
ph: 715-832-4301
*Collects wooden pencils with
advertising.*

Andrew Westberg
Pencil Pushing
916 Wall St.
Mankato, MN 56003
ph: 507-344-0643
westberg@mctcnet.net
http://www.gotocrystal.net/~westberg/
pencil.htm
*Collects advertising pencils,
mechanical, bullet, golf and carpenter
pencils.*

Susan Cox
800 Murray Dr.
El Cajon, CA 92020
ph: 619-697-5922
antiqfever@aol.com
*Wants old, unsharpened pencils with
advertising on them.*

Dealers

David Nishimura
Vintage Pens & Writing Equipment
P.O. Box 41452
Providence, RI 02940-1452
ph: 401-351-7607
fax: 401-351-1168
info@vintagepens.com
http://www.vintagepens.com
*Buys and sells all sorts of vintage
fountain pens, pencils, and writing
equipment; maintains Web site catalog
with extensive reference resources.*

Experts

Judith & Cliff Lawrence
Pen Fanciers Club
1169 Overcash Dr.
Dunedin, FL 34698-5537
ph: 727-734-4742
fax: 727-738-0476
PenFanC@aol.com
*Buys, sells and specializes in old
fountain pens, dip pens and
mechanical pencils.*

Internet Resources

Doug Martin
Pencil Pages, The
17797 W. Toussaint N.
Graytown, OH 43432
ph: 419-862-2380
doug@pencilpages.com
http://www.pencilpages.com
Web site contains general information of use to pencil collectors, and can aid collectors in contacting one another.

PENS

(see also BLOTTERS; GLASS, Whimsies [Pens]; INKWELLS & INKSTANDS; OFFICE EQUIPMENT; PENCILS)

Appraisers

Jim Gaston
Jim Gaston Vintage Fountain Pens & Dip Pens
1777 River Rd.
Lakeview, AR 72642
ph: 870-431-5206 or 870-431-5204
fax: 870-431-5216
jim@jimgaston.com
http://www.jimgaston.com
Wants to buy vintage fountain pens, dip pens; will purchase entire collections, or appraiser single pen(s) or collections; also repairs.

Victor Topper
Topper Gallery
111 Finch Ave. W, Ste. 214
Markham, Ontario M3J 2E5 Canada
ph: 416-665-7554
fax: 416-665-8164
topperart@rogers.com
http://www.topperart.com
Pen appraiser, dealer collector specializing in pens of various materials made from 1890 to 1990: Waterman, Mont Blanc, etc.

Auction Services

PenBid.com, Inc.
P.O. Box 1187
Malvern, PA 19355
ph: 610-647-1771
support@penbid.com
http://www.penbid.com
Online auctions of vintage pens.

Clubs/Associations

Sam Fiorella
Pen Collectors of America
Newsletter: PENnant
P.O. Box 447
Fort Madison, IA 52627-0447
ph: 319-372-0881
fax: 319-372-0882
info@pencollectors.com
http://www.pencollectors.com
Association of fountain pen collectors; maintains library of materials for pen collectors; disseminates information, holds regular meetings; promotes collecting as a hobby and using pens; newsletter published three times a year.

Jim Griffiths, Sec.
Pan Pacific Pen Club, The
20197 Brittany Court
Castro Valley, CA 94546-4601
ph: 510-885-0965
fax: 510-588-4543
pan-pacific@attbi.com
http://pan-pacific.home.attbi.com
A Northern California club for collectors of vintage and modern fountain pens.

Canadian Association of Writing
  Instrument Collectors
1057 Steeles Ave. West, Ste. 642
North York, Ontario M2R 2S9 Canada
A not-for-profit club for writing instrument collectors and enthusiasts.

Dov Randel
Israel Pen Club
P.O. Box 16331
Tel Aviv, 81152 Israel
ph: 011 972 52 425784
dov@israelpenclub.org
http://www.israel.penclub.org
An international pen club devoted to collectors and users of all writing instruments and related ephemera; meets about every 6 weeks in Kibbutz Gaash: pen lectures, show and tell, swap and shop.

John Daniels, Sec.
Writing Equipment Society
Journal: Journal of the Writing
  Equipment Society
33 Glanville Rd.
Hadleigh
Ipswich, Suffolk IP7 5SQ U.K.
wes.sec@btinternet.com
http://www.wesonline.org.uk
Devoted to the conservation and study of writing instruments and accessories: pens of all types and materials, pencils, nibs, inkwells, stamp boxes, quill cutters, scriveners' knives, seals, writing slopes, blotters, paper knives, etc.

Collectors

Dan McNamara
P.O. Box 130 - 163
Boston, MA 02113
ph: 617-846-9465
theresemcnamara@msn.com
Buying fancy metal or overlay pens; will help identify fountain pens for others who send photo and SASE.

David & Becky Beane
Beane's Antiques & Photography
92 River Rd.
Benton, ME 04901
ph: 207-453-6790
fax: 207-453-6790
Collector of quality fountain pens, showcases, advertisements, and other pen related items: LeBouef, Waterman, Parker, Chilton and any quality pen wanted.

Gary Lehrer
16 Mulberry Rd.
Woodbridge, CT 06525-1717
ph: 203-389-5295
fax: 203-389-4515
garylehrer@aol.com
http://www.gopens.com
Wants pens of any age and condition; single items or large collections; call collect; write or send pens and pencils (insured); also offers fountain pen repair service.

Richard Carvell
249 Sportsmans Ave.
Freeport, NY 11520-5635
ph: 516-623-1325 or 800-767-7367
Wants old fountain pens; any large size pen; any ornate pens; also gold filled & silver filigree; pre-1910 pearl overlay and solid gold; also wants to buy pen ephemera.

Howard Share
4349 LaVale Ct.
Clemmons, NC 27012-9009
ph: 336-766-6579
fax: 336-766-5445
HowSha43@aol.com
Wants to buy high quality fountain pens, especially the oversized men's pens or the fancy pens with overlays or filigrees of gold silver, or mother-of-pearl.

Stephen Berger
7759 Seminary Ridge
Columbus, OH 43235
ph: 614-885-6083
fax: 614-436-8695
Wants to buy pens by Parker, Waterman, Conklin, Wahl-Eversharp, Chilton, Schnell.

Jim Beattie
3730 Augusta Lane
Elkhart, IN 46517
ph: 219-522-3467
fax: 219-875-6617
indianapens@msn.com
Wants quality old fountain pens or parts, 1870-1970; also does repairs.

Bob Arnell
P.O. Box 313
Grandview, MO 64030-0313
ph: 816-966-0544 or 816-213-4999
bobstuff11@excite.com
Wants to buy fountain pens.

Dale Beebe
11441 Montclair
Garden Grove, CA 92841
ph: 714-530-9270
Wants to buy old pens, American ink bottles with clean, intact labels; also wants metal/Bakelite desk sets with cast artwork, especially Art Deco.

Dealers

David Nishimura
Vintage Pens & Writing Equipment
P.O. Box 41452
Providence, RI 02940-1452
ph: 401-351-7607
fax: 401-351-1168
info@vintagepens.com
http://www.vintagepens.com
Buys collections, parts, and all pen-related material; maintains an extensive informational Web site and online catalog.

Albert B. Jerard
Odds 'N Ends
1000 Western Ave.
Brattleboro, VT 05301
ph: 802-254-5815
Buys and sells vintage fountain pens.

Gary Lehrer
GoPens
16 Mulberry Rd.
Woodbridge, CT 06525-1717
ph: 203-389-5295
fax: 203-389-4515
garylehrer@aol.com
http://www.gopens.com
Publishes quarterly catalog of pens for sale.

Geoffrey Berliner
Berliner Pen
Catalog: Pen Finder Quarterly
928 Broadway, Ste. 604
New York, NY 10010
ph: 800-444-PENS or 212-614-3020
fax: 212-614-3025
BerlinerPn@aol.com
http://www.berlinerpen.com
Buys and sells vintage and contemporary pens; restorations; newsletter is a monthly glossy color catalog designed to help dealers and collectors buy and sell vintage pens.

Charles M. Yassky
424 Madison Ave., 8th Floor
New York, NY 10017-1106
ph: 800-969-2345
fax: 212-826-6214
Active buyer of fountain pens and related advertising material; wants fountain pens by Wahl, Waterman, Parker, Conklin, etc.

Richard Weinstein
Authorized Repair Service
30 W. 57th St.
New York, NY 10019
ph: 212-586-0947
fax: 212-586-1296
vinlighter@aol.com
http://www.vintagelighters.com
Wants to buy unusual old fountain pens in precious metal or plastic by Parker, Waterman, Wahl, Eversharp, Conklin, Chilton, Esterbrook, etc.

Jonathan Steinberg
Fountain Pens
200 East 90th St.
New York, NY 10128
ph: 800-PEN-WRITER
fax: 212-722-2425
info@vintagepen.com
http://www.vintagepen.com
*Buys and sells better vintage fountain
pens.*

Gene Bensen
AntiqueLine, Inc.
585-C Heritage Hills
Somers, NY 10589
ph: 914-276-0666
fax: 914-276-0666
antiqueline@rcn.com
http://www.antiqueline.com
*Specializes in inkwells, desk
accessories, bookends, and fountain
pens for the home or office.*

Frank Briola
P.O. Box 44022
Pittsburgh, PA 15205-0222
ph: 412-937-8787 or 800-372-6509
fax: 412-937-1959
americana@mail.com
Wants to buy fountain pens.

Jim Monroe
Monroe's Pen Shop
P.O. Box 508
Edgemont, PA 19028
ph: 888-666-7637
fax: 877-666-7637
penshop@netaxs.com
http://www.penshop.com
*Avid pen collector; Web site serves pen
collectors world wide featuring
consignments, repairs, pen locator,
magazine subscriptions, vintage
fountain pens; also offers a large
selection of new and limited edition
pens.*

Fahrney's Pens
8329 Old Marlboro Pike, B-13
Upper Marlboro, MD 20772
ph: 800-624-7367 or 301-568-6550
fax: 301-736-2926
*Carries contemporary pen catalog;
also does repairs.*

Judith & Cliff Lawrence
Pen Fanciers Club
1169 Overcash Dr.
Dunedin, FL 34698-5537
ph: 727-734-4742
fax: 727-738-0476
PenFanC@aol.com
*Issues catalog with articles on
fountain pens and mechanical pencils;
vintage fountain pens, mechanical
pencils & pen parts for sale; quarterly
catalog; send $5 for sample copy.*

Terry Mawhorter
Gentle Ben's Antiques
P.O. Box 3324
Zanesville, OH 43702
ph: 740-454-2314
linklady@cyberzane.net
*Has been buying and selling pens
since 1983.*

Thomas Zoss
Zoss Communications, Inc.
3431 Willow Rd.
Bloomington, IN 47403
ph: 812-332-2334
tzoss@zoss.com
http://www.zoss.com/pens.htm
*Broker of pen-related items, moderator
of Internet mailing list of pen
collectors and experts; Web site offers
a free mailing list where people from
all over the world ask questions, buy
and sell, and explore fountain pen
collecting.*

Michael Clague
Clague's Antiques & Collectibles
515 North 7th St.
Estherville, IA 51334
ph: 712-362-2343
mpcac@ncn.net
http://www.ncn.net/~mpcac
*Buys and sells fountain pens and
mechanical pencils; will furnish
references; offers a five day return
privilege.*

Sam Fiorella
Pendemonium
P.O. Box 447
Fort Madison, IA 52627-0447
ph: 888-372-2050 or 319-372-0881
fax: 319-372-0882
sam@pendemonium.com
http://www.pendemonium.com
*Buys and sells fountain pens, inkwells,
ink bottles, pen stands, blotters, pen
catalogs, magazine covers and
advertisements.*

Michael A. Pratt, Sr.
Pen Palace, The
512 North Spruce St.
Valley, NE 68064-9670
ph: 402-359-5539
fax: 402-359-5539
sales@usadisplay.net
http://www.usadisplay.net
*Buys and sells unique pens of all
kinds; also sells display cases for cuff
links and collectibles of all types; also
can make old pens modern so they can
use cartridge ink without altering the
pen's appearance in any way.*

John Marshall
For Love or Money
16693 NW Meadowgrass Ct.
Beaverton, OR 97006
john@europa.com
http://home.europa.com/~john
*Buys and sells antique and collectible
fountain pens mostly Sheaffer and*

*Parker, occasionally more unusual
pens.*

Simon Gray
Battersea Pen Home
Catalog: Battersea Pen Home Quarterly
P.O. Box 6128
Epping, CM16 4GG U.K.
ph: +44 870-900 1888
fax: +44 870-909 1888
info@penhome.com
http://www.penhome.com
*Specialists in buying, selling and
restoring vintage fountain pens
including Montblanc, Waterman,
Conklin, Sheaffer, Parker, Pelikan and
all major brands. Organizer of the
annual London Pen Show.*

Hans Seiringer
Han's Vintage Fountain Pens
1, Hassocks Close
Eastbourn, BN23 8LT U.K.
ph: 44(0) 1323 765398
HSeiringer@aol.com
http://www.hanspens.com
*Buys, sells, repairs vintage fountain
pens: Parker, Watermans, Sheaffer,
Montblanc, Pelikan, Swan and others.*

Experts

Stuart Schneider
P.O. Box 64
Teaneck, NJ 07666-0064
ph: 201-599-4250
fax: 201-599-4251
Stuart@wordcraft.net
http://www.wordcraft.net
*Author of four leading books on
fountain pen collecting; has appeared
on television and has written for
dozens of magazines on the subject;
has a column in "Pen World"
magazine titled "Ask Miss Inky."*

Jonathan Steinberg
Fountain Pens
200 East 90th St.
New York, NY 10128
ph: 800-PEN-WRITER
fax: 212-722-2425
info@vintagepen.com
http://www.vintagepen.com
*Author of "Fountain Pens," the best
selling book and generally accepted
standard authoritative work on the
subject of vintage pens.*

Judith & Cliff Lawrence
Pen Fanciers Club
1169 Overcash Dr.
Dunedin, FL 34698-5537
ph: 727-734-4742
fax: 727-738-0476
PenFanC@aol.com
*Buys, sells and specializes in old
fountain pens, dip pens and
mechanical pencils.*

Jack Price
Vintage Fountain Pens
3481 North High St.
Columbus, OH 43214
ph: 614-267-8468 or 614-267-7978
fax: 614-267-8468
jproto1@aol.com
*Buys, sells, restores new as well as
antique pens.*

Beverly & Raymond Jaegers
P.O. Box 29396
Saint Louis, MO 63126-0396
USPsiSquad@aol.com
http://www.uspsisquad.com
*Experts and historians; authors of
"The Write Stuff - A Collector's
Guide to Inkwells, Fountain Pens &
Desk Accessories."*

Glen Benton Bowen
Fountain Pen Hospital - Texas
P.O. Box 6007
Kingwood, TX 77325-6007
ph: 281-359-4363
fax: 281-359-4468
info@penworld.com
http://www.penworld.com
*Repairs, buys and sells; offers a
consignment catalog, PENFINDER,
containing the world's most valuable
and rare pens; author of book about
pens.*

Simon Gray
Battersea Pen Home
P.O. Box 6128
Epping, CM16 4GG U.K.
ph: +44 870-900 1888
fax: +44 870-909 1888
info@penhome.com
http://www.penhome.com
*Specialists in buying, selling and
restoring vintage fountain pens
including Montblanc, Waterman,
Conklin, Sheaffer, Parker, Pelikan and
all major brands. Organizer of the
annual London Pen Show.*

Internet Resources

Dean Tweeddale
Pen Lovers - The Internet Fountain Pen
Homepage
deant@seanet.com
http://www.penlovers.com
*Pen bulletin boards, magazine,
glossary, history, pen shows, and
more.*

Pen Central
webmaster@pencentral.com
http://www.pencentral.com
*Fountain pens, collecting, modern and
vintage pens, pen repairs, fountain
pen history, links, pen clubs, pen
shows, pen books and magazines.*

Pentrace
info@pentrace.com
http://www.pentrace.com
*A online cooperative effort for
fountain pen enthusiasts: message
board, articles about pen finds,
heirloom pens, pen search stories;
also how-to articles, repair tips.*

Jonathan Steinberg
Fountain Pens
200 East 90th St.
New York, NY 10128
ph: 800-PEN-WRITER
fax: 212-722-2425
info@vintagepen.com
http://www.vintagepen.com
*Web site assists collectors to focus
their collecting efforts: what to look
for when collecting pens, what to buy,
how to negotiate.*

Thomas Zoss
Zoss Communications, Inc.
3431 Willow Rd.
Bloomington, IN 47403
ph: 812-332-2334
tzoss@zoss.com
http://www.zoss.com/pens.htm
*Broker of pen-related items, moderator
of Internet mailing list of pen
collectors and experts; Web site offers
a free mailing list where people from
all over the world ask questions, buy
and sell, and explore fountain pen
collecting.*

Bill Acker
Bill Acker's Fountain Pen Page
P.O. Box 338
Henderson, TX 75653
ph: 903-657-0558
Bill@billspens.com
http://www.billspens.com
*Web site includes information on
brands, repair information, literature,
shows, pen links.*

Fountain Pen Paradise, LLC
678 Wells Rd.
Boulder City, NV 89055
ph: 702-294-6582
fax: 702-294-6538
feedback@fountainpens.com
http://www.fountainpens.com
*Newsletter, many brands of pens for
sale, online collections, pen
information, etc.*

Glenn Marcus
Glenn's Pen Page
#6, 216 9th St.
New Westminster, British Columbia
V3M 3V3 Canada
ph: 604-522-3134
glenn@marcuslink.com
http://www.marcuslink.com/pens
*Web site has directory and reviews of
pen stores from around the world.*

Periodicals

Terry Monzo
World Publications
Magazine: Pen World International
P.O. Box 6007
Kingwood, TX 77325-6007
ph: 281-359-4363
fax: 281-359-4468
info@penworld.com
http://www.penworld.com
*Premier magazine for fountain pens
and fine writing instruments; bi-
monthly glossy color magazine to
provide histories of pen companies*

*and their products; full color
reproductions of worlds most valuable
pens; some articles on old pens.*

Repair Services

Gary Lehrer
GoPens
16 Mulberry Rd.
Woodbridge, CT 06525-1717
ph: 203-389-5295
fax: 203-389-4515
garylehrer@aol.com
http://www.gopens.com
*Vintage fountain pens bought, sold
and repaired.*

Fountain Pen Hospital
10 Warren St.
New York, NY 10007-2211
ph: 212-964-0580 or 800-253-7367
fax: 212-227-5916
info@fountainpenhospital.com
http://www.fountainpenhospital.com
*Repairs fountain pens; also sells
books, new and vintage pens, and
accessories.*

Thom D'Amico
Fine Italian Hand, A
P.O. Box 624
Putnam Valley, NY 10579
ph: 914-528-4350
afineitalianhand@pcrealm.net
*Antique and classic writing
instruments restored, repaired,
replated, and recreated; special
attention to nibs.*

George Daly
Mirans Pen Shop
2537 6th Ave.
East Meadow, NY 11554
ph: 516-826-6084
penrepair1@aol.com
http://www.fountainpenrepairs.com
*Repairs pens from 1900s to 1960s for
collectors, retailers, pen dealers; in
business for over 50 years worldwide.*

Simon Gray
Battersea Pen Home
P.O. Box 6128
Epping, CM16 4GG U.K.
ph: +44 870-900 1888
fax: +44 870-909 1888
info@penhome.com
http://www.penhome.com
*Specialists in buying, selling and
restoring vintage fountain pens
including Montblanc, Waterman,
Conklin, Sheaffer, Parker, Pelikan and
all major brands. Organizer of the
annual London Pen Show.*

Roy Zeff
Penfriend, Ltd.
10-13 Newbury St.
London, EC1A 7NW U.K.
ph: 0044 20 7606 6542 or 0044 20 7836
9809
fax: 0044 20 7606 6542
pen.london@btinternet.com
http://www.penfriend.co.uk
*World's largest restorer of writing
instruments: most makes and models*

*of fountain pens, pencils, ball point
pens.*

Suppliers

Michael A. Pratt, Sr.
Pen Palace, The
512 North Spruce St.
Valley, NE 68064-9670
ph: 402-359-5539
fax: 402-359-5539
sales@usadisplay.net
http://www.usadisplay.net
*Buys and sells unique pens of all
kinds; also sells display cases for cuff
links and collectibles of all types; also
can make old pens modern so they can
use cartridge ink without altering the
pen's appearance in any way.*

Pen Sac Company, The
P.O. Box 4470
Carlsbad, CA 92018
ph: 760-735-2501 or 888-PENSACS
fax: 760-735-2502
PenSacs@aol.com
*Manufactures ink sacs for vintage
fountain pens; has almost 50 different
sizes; can supply ink sacs for
practically every vintage pen.*

Floaty

Collectors

Beverly Broadstone
Go With The Flo-at!
P.O. Box 655
Lomita, CA 90717-0655
floatypenguin@earthlink.net
http://floatypens.tripod.com
*Trades and collects float pens; Web
site has a list of pens for trade as well
as collector information and
resources.*

Karen Rolstad
1 Via Honrado
Rancho Santa Margarita, CA 92688
Collector and trader of float pens.

Dealers

Diana Andra
Float About
1676 Millsboro Rd.
Mansfield, OH 44906-3374
ph: 419-529-8876
fax: 419-529-3354
DiAndra@FloatAbout.com
http://www.FloatAbout.com
*Floaty pens contain an image or other
object that floats in a small chamber
of liquid; offers over 500 floaty pen
designs for sale; also free online
floaty pen newsletter.*

Internet Resources

Diana Andra
Float About
1676 Millsboro Rd.
Mansfield, OH 44906-3374
ph: 419-529-8876
fax: 419-529-3354
DiAndra@FloatAbout.com
http://www.FloatAbout.com
*Floaty pens contain an image or other
object that floats in a small chamber*

*of liquid; offers over 500 floaty pen
designs for sale; also free online
floaty pen newsletter.*

Man./Prod./Dist.

Micale Maddox
Worldwide Marketing Services, Inc.,
a.k.a. Ideal Motion
1219 Connecticut Ave., NW 3rd Floor
Washington, DC 20036
ph: 202-775-4310
fax: 202-775-4309
micale@floatpens.com
http://www.floatpens.com
*Importers of Eskesen floating action
products such as floaty pens, a.k.a.
floating action pens, photoramic pens,
floating view pens, view pens, motion
pens, magic motion pens.*

Sharon Jones
Global Shakeup
235 East Colorado Blvd., #178
Pasadena, CA 91101
ph: 818-752-2542
fax: 818-752-2667
feedback@snowdomes.com
http://www.snowdomes.com
*Hundreds of unusual snowdomes,
snowglobes and float pens from
around the world; US and non-US
location theme snowdomes,
advertising, cartoon characters, and
more; also produces custom snow
dome and float pen designs.*

Sandy Medorf
Floaty Industries
2219 West Olive Ave., Dept. 260
Burbank, CA 91506
ph: 800-883-3627
fax: 818-566-4420
floaty@floaty.com
http://www.floaty.com
*Web site has a store of exclusive floaty
products and you can email or call to
request a free mail order catalog.*

Nibs

Collectors

John Gwin
1845 Anderson Dr.
Las Cruces, NM 88001
ph: 505-522-2171
*Since 1995 has collected antique steel
pen nibs, the boxes/tins in which they
came, and relate advertising,
equipment and ephemera.*

Repair Services

John Mottishaw
Classic Fountain Pens
P.O. Box 46723
Los Angeles, CA 90046
ph: 323-655-2641
fax: 323-651-0265
john@nibs.com
http://www.nibs.com
*Offers a complete fountain pen point
(or nib) repair service including
custom tipping, crack repair, and
straightening; most other pen repairs
provided as well (mail order business*

only offering return insured UPS shipping.)

PERAMBULATORS

(see also CHILDREN'S THINGS)

Museums/Libraries

Janet L. Pallo
Victorian Perambulator Museum
26 East Cedar St.
Jefferson, OH 44047
ph: 440-576-9588
Only Victorian perambulator museum in the US; over 100 examples of early wicker baby and doll carriages along with related items such as sleighs, velocipedes, farm wagons, games, dolls, etc.

PERFORMING ARTS

(see also MAGICIANS PARAPHERNALIA; MUSIC; POPULAR CULTURE; PUPPETS; SHEET MUSIC; STRIPTEASE; VENTRILOQUIST ITEMS)

Collectors

Don Hoffman
P.O. Box 4231
Salinas, CA 93912-4231
ph: 831-449-7311
Wants to buy minstrel, vaudeville, ragtime items: posters, broadsides, cabinet cards, CDVs, tintypes, daguerreotypes, ambrotypes, programs, tickets, antique photos, autographs, books, booklets, memorabilia; please describe and price.

Dealers

Jonathan & Lisa Reynolds
Dramatis Personae - Booksellers
P.O. Box 1070
Sheffield, MA 01257-1070
ph: 413-229-7735
fax: 413-229-7735
books@dramatispersonae.com
http://www.bibliocity.com/home/DP
Sale of antiquarian books, prints, ephemera, autographs, and manuscripts relating to theater, drama, circus, conjuring, puppetry, and popular entertainers; also select theatrical antiques; issues 4-5 catalogs per year.

Museums/Libraries

Consortium of Popular Culture Collections
Popular Culture Library
Bowling Green State University
Bowling Green, OH 43403-0001
ph: 419-372-2450
fax: 419-372-7996
atracy@bgnet.bgsu.edu
http://www.bgsu.edu/colleges/library/pcl/cpccm.html
Consortium composed of Bowling Green State U., Kent State U., Michigan State U., and Ohio State U.;

the largest academic library collections of primary research material in comic art, popular fiction, popular music, performing arts.

Dance

Collectors

William G. Sommer, MD
9 W. 10th St.
New York, NY 10011-8748
ph: 212-260-0999
wgs2@columbia.edu
Wants depictions of people dancing in social situations, e.g., Jitterbug, Tango, Disco; in any media or format; also wants dance related sheet music and postcards.

Gilbert & Sullivan

Collectors

David Trutt
3711 North Round Rock Dr.
Tucson, AZ 85750-2082
ph: 520-751-4215
davettt@aol.com
Wants Gilbert & Sullivan items: books, posters, antiques, collectibles; any item relating to W.S. Gilbert, Arthur Sullivan, or their operas.

Opera Mementos

Dealers

Roger Gross
Roger Gross, Ltd.
225 East 57th St.
New York, NY 10022-2822
ph: 212-759-2892
fax: 212-838-5425
rogergross@earthlink.net
http://www.rgrossmusicautograph.com
Buys and sells signed photos of singers, instrumentalists, conductors and composers; letters, musical quotes; classical music and operatic books, memorabilia, ephemera, unsigned photos, etc.

Museums/Libraries

Nordica Homestead Museum
Holly Rd.
Farmington, ME 04938
ph: 207-778-2042
Home of Maine's homegrown international opera diva, Lillian Norton, born in 1857.

Lester Dequaine, Dir.
Rosa Ponselle Museum, The
39 West Main St.
Meriden, CT 06451-4110
ph: 203-639-9778
fax: 203-639-9778
rosaponsellemuseum@snet.net
Museum displays artifacts of Rosa Ponselle's life and the opera world she knew; museum store sells Ponselle books and CDs; also buys related artifacts.

Marcella Sembrich Opera Museum
4800 Lakeshore Dr.
Bolton Landing, NY 12814-0417
ph: 518-644-9839
sembrich@webtv.net
http://www.operamuseum.com
Historical museum of opera diva Marcella Sembrich's gowns, period furnishings, and mementos.

Theatrical Memorabilia

Collectors

D. Eliot
400 W. 43rd St. #25T
New York, NY 10036-6312
Wants theater souvenirs; pre-1920 only; especially commemorative items, e.g., 50th performance, 100th, etc.; also wants anything related to the career of great Italian international actress, Elenora Duse (1858-1924).

Dealers

Lacy E. Long
199 Tarrytown Rd.
Manchester, NH 03103
ph: 603-622-5449
Buys, sells and trades theatrical memorabilia, holds periodic telephone auctions, sends out monthly price lists.

Museums/Libraries

Marty Jacobs
Museum of the City of New York
1220 5th Ave. at 103rd St.
New York, NY 10029-5221
ph: 212-534-1672
fax: 212-534-5974
http://www.mcny.org
Access by appointment; research fee charged.

Lennis Moore
Theatre Museum of Repertoire Americana
405 E. Threshers Rd.
Mount Pleasant, IA 52641
ph: 319-385-9432 or 888-826-6622
info@oldthreshers.org
http://www.oldthreshers.org
Largest American collection of 1850s-1950s middle plains Tent, Opera House, Repertoire Theatre and Chautauqua memorabilia, with Research Library and data base.

PERFUME LAMPS

(see also BOTTLES, Perfume & Scent; FAIRY LAMPS; LAMPS & LIGHTING, Miniature)

Collectors

Sandy Katz-Leegood
P.O. Box 596553
Dallas, TX 75227-1429
ph: 214-275-4370
jleegood@yahoo.com
Interested in all types of perfume lamps (similar to night lights, but has well/container to add/hold perfume; also small holes on top preventing

exploding and allows perfume to escape); porcelain, glass, ceramic, French, Robj, etc.

Dealers

Tom & Linda Millman
231 S. Main St.
Bethel, OH 45106-1327
ph: 513-734-6884 or 513-382-2978
Dealer and expert buys, sells, trades perfume lamps: Goebel, DeVilbiss, Fulper, Robj, Aladin, Aerozon, Aroma, and other foreign and domestic manufacturers.

PERIODICALS

(see also Various specialty-related Periodicals listed under specific categories throughout this Directory; also see Periodicals contained within listings for Clubs/Associations.)

Periodicals

Brimfield Antique Show Website
Newspaper: Brimfield Antique Guide, The
P.O. Box 442
Brimfield, MA 01010
ph: 413-245-9329
brimfieldp@aol.com
http://www.brimfieldshow.com/brimfield-publications.htm
Published 3 times per year; highlights any changes, news releases or other noteworthy information, etc. pertaining to the Brimfield Antique and Collectible shows.

Turley Publications
Newspaper: New England Antiques Journal, The
24 Water St.
Palmer, MA 01069
ph: 413-283-8393 or 800-824-6548
fax: 413-283-7071
visit@antiquesjournal.com
http://www.antiquesjournal.com
Monthly newspaper providing the best coverage of New England: Living with Antiques supplement; shops listed geographically; shows, auctions and a wide range of feature material.

Jody Young
Newspaper: Journal of Antiques & Collectibles, The
4 Charlton St.
P.O. Box 950
Sturbridge, MA 01566
ph: 508-347-1960 or 888-698-0734
fax: 508-347-1977
tothejournal@aol.com
http://www.journalofantiques.com
Monthly newspaper is a major source of information on antique shows and the Brimfield Flea Markets.

William Margolin
Newsletter: Collectors' Classified
P.O. Box 347
Holbrook, MA 02343-0347
ph: 781-961-1463
ccmay1975@aol.com
Published monthly; all collectibles -

especially cards, coins, stamps, books, memorabilia; published since 1975; free subscriber ads.

Treasure Chest Publishing
Newspaper: Treasure Chest
564 Eddy St., Ste. 326
Providence, RI 02903
ph: 401-272-9444 or 800-557-9662
fax: 401-647-0051
treasurechest@thesunchronicle.com
http://www.cjeans.com/JAN1.HTM
    A monthly information source & marketplace for collectors & dealers of antiques and collectibles; emphasis is on antique shop, show, auction and classified ads; distributed in the NY, NJ, PA, CT, MA, and RI area.

Kathy Greer, Ed.
Newspaper: Unravel the Gavel
14 Hurricane Rd. #1
Belmont, NH 03220-5603
ph: 603-524-4281
fax: 603-528-3565
Gavel96@worldpath.net
http://www.thegavel.net
    Focusing on the northern New England area: covers auctions, shows, flea markets, new shops, and antiques and collectibles in NH, VT, ME, MA, plus upstate NY.

Yankee Publishing Inc.
Magazine: Yankee Magazine
P.O. Box 520
Dublin, NH 03444
ph: 603-563-8111
dearyank@yankeepub.com
http://www.newengland.com

Charles Wibel, Pub.
Newspaper: New Hampshire Antiques Monthly
P.O. 546
Farmington, NH 03835-0546
ph: 603-755-4568
fax: 603-755-3990
tumeroll@s-way.com
    A monthly publication covering the antiques marketplace in the six New England states.

Sam & Sally Pennington
Maine Antique Digest, Inc.
Newspaper: Maine Antique Digest
911 Main St.
P.O. Box 1429
Waldoboro, ME 04572-1429
ph: 207-832-7534
fax: 207-832-7341
mad@maine.com
http://www.maineantiquedigest.com
    The major monthly newspaper on antiques, art and Americana; photos with prices, dealers.

Bee Publishing Co.
Newspaper: Antiques & The Arts Weekly
P.O. Box 5503
Newtown, CT 06470-5503
ph: 203-426-3141 or 203-426-8036
fax: 203-426-1394
liza@thebee.com
http://www.antiquesandthearts.com
    Leading weekly newspaper for auction advertising, show coverage, and other events in the world of antiques.

Larry Canale, Ed.
Magazine: Antiques Roadshow Insider
P.O. Box 2626
Greenwich, CT 06836
ph: 800-241-7519
    A monthly, 16-page full-color newsletter following the news, trends and analysis from the world of antiques.

Journal: Journal America
P.O. Box 459
Hewitt, NJ 07421
ph: 973-728-8355
fax: 973-728-7128
journal@warwick.net
http://www.ajournal.com
    Articles on all types of antiques and collectibles; also questions and answers.

Dorothy J. Graf, Ed.
Newspaper: Collector's Marketplace, The
P.O. Box 25
Stewartsville, NJ 08886-0025
ph: 908-479-4614
fax: 908-479-6158
cm@4-collectors.com
http://www.4-collectors.com
    A bi-monthly publication for collectors and dealers; an international advertising publication; classifieds and display ads for buying and selling collectibles.

Barbara Jacksier, Ed.
Harris Publications
Magazine: Country Collectibles
1115 Broadway
New York, NY 10010-2803
ph: 212-807-7100
fax: 212-627-4678
countryletters@harris-pub.com
http://www.countrycollector.com
    Full-color glossy magazine; features collectibles, antiques, bread & breakfast getaways, people who collect, favorite recipes, and decorating with collectibles.

Brant Art Publications
Magazine: Magazine Antiques, The
575 Broadway
New York, NY 10012
ph: 212-941-2800 or 800-925-8059
fax: 212-941-2897
brantpubs@aol.com
    A full-color monthly magazine featuring detailed articles about art and antiques.

Goodman Media Group, Inc.
Magazine: Country Accents
419 Park Ave. South
New York, NY 10016
ph: 212-541-7100 or 800-955-3870
fax: 212-245-1241
http://www.goodmanmediagroup.com
    Published six times per year; focuses on decorating, crafts, collectibles, and antiques.

Goodman Media Group, Inc.
Magazine: Victorian Decorating & Lifestyle
419 Park Ave. South
New York, NY 10016
ph: 212-541-7100 or 800-955-3870
fax: 212-245-1241
http://www.goodmanmediagroup.com
    A glossy bi-monthly magazine that focuses on decorating, crafts, collectibles, antiques, Victorian people and costumes.

Goodman Media Group, Inc.
Magazine: American Country Collectibles
419 Park Ave. South
New York, NY 10016
ph: 212-541-7100 or 800-955-3870
fax: 212-245-1241
http://www.goodmanmediagroup.com
    Published four times a year; focuses on collecting and decorating with collectibles.

Goodman Media Group, Inc.
Magazine: Collectibles/Flea Market Finds
419 Park Ave. South
New York, NY 10016
ph: 212-541-7100 or 800-955-3870
fax: 212-245-1241
http://www.goodmanmediagroup.com
    Published four times a year; focuses on fleamarket collectibles and 20th-century collectibles that are fun, affordable, and not the standard fare of other magazines: kitchenware, toys, vintage clothing; display ideas.

Hearst Corporation
Magazine: Country Living
224 West 57th St.
New York, NY 10019
ph: 212-649-3500 or 800-888-2665
countryliving@hearst.com
http://www.countryliving.com
    A monthly magazine that focuses on decorating, crafts, collectibles, and antiques.

Hearst Corporation
Magazine: Victoria
224 West 57th St.
New York, NY 10019
ph: 212-649-3720 or 800-888-2665
victoriamag@hearst.com
http://www.victoriamag.com
    Glossy monthly magazine; home decorating, recipes, gardening, architecture, country living; some articles about antiques & collectibles.

Newspaper: New York Antique Almanac
P.O. Box 2400
New York, NY 10021
ph: 212-988-2700
fax: 212-988-5255
    Antiques and collectibles trade newspaper with ads, articles, auction and show reports; nationwide coverage.

Maura Feeney, Ed.
Newspaper: Antiques News, The
P.O. Box 2054
New York, NY 10159-2054
ph: 212-675-8006
fax: 212-675-8007
info@nycan.com
http://www.nycan.com
    Serves the antiques and collectible markets in the NY, CT, NJ, and PA areas with original articles, full color photography, and information about local shops, auctions and shows.

Harold M. Hanson, Pub.
Newspaper: Northeast Journal of Antiques & Art
P.O. Box 37
Hudson, NY 12534
ph: 518-828-9327
fax: 518-828-3870
nejournl@mhcable.com
http://www.northeastjournal.com
    Focuses on eastern US; articles, ads, show and auction calendar.

Antique Collectors' Club, Ltd.
Magazine: Antique Collecting
91 Market St. Industrial Park
Wappingers Falls, NY 12590
ph: 800-252-5231 or 914-297-0003
fax: 914-297-0068
info@antiquecc.com
http://www.artbookservices.com/articles/antcol.html
    A sophisticated English magazine of the Antique Collectors' Club, the parent organization for dozens of regional antiques clubs within the U.K.

Messenger Post Newspapers
Newspaper: New York-Pennsylvania Collector, The
73 Buffalo St.
Canandaigua, NY 14424
ph: 585-394-1712 or 800-836-1868
fax: 585-394-7725
collector@MPNewspapers.com
http://www.NY-PACollector.com
    Informative articles on art, antiques & Americana; show and auction reviews; annual subject index in Jan.; monthly calendar of events.

Celtic Moon Publishing, Inc.
Magazine: Early American Homes Magazine
4707 N. Clearview Dr.
Camp Hill, PA 17011
ph: 717-730-6263
    All aspects of American life before 1850 and material culture, i.e., pottery, iron, textiles, furnishings, architecture, ornament, utilitarian

objects in depth (formerly "Early American Life").

Denise M. Sater, Ed.
Newspaper: Antiques & Auction News
P.O. Box 500
Mount Joy, PA 17552-0500
ph: 717-492-2540 or 800-800-1833
fax: 717-653-6165
dsater7650@aol.com
http://www.antiquesandauctionnews.net
A weekly newspaper featuring antiques, collectibles, auctions, sales, shows and exhibits.

Victorian Society in America, The
Magazine: 19th Century Magazine
205 South Camac St.
Philadelphia, PA 19107
ph: 215-545-8340
fax: 215-545-8379
info@victoriansociety.org
http://www.victoriansociety.org
Membership benefits include quarterly newsletter, semi-annual magazine, symposia on wide array of 19th century subjects, annual meeting; fostering appreciation in Victorian life through preservation and educational efforts; non-profit.

Editor
Newspaper: Renninger's Antique Guide
P.O. Box 495
Lafayette Hill, PA 19444-0495
ph: 610-828-4614 or 610-825-6392
fax: 610-834-1599
webmaster@renningers.com
http://www.renningers.com/news/
  renguide.html
Newspaper covering antique shows, shops, flea markets and auctions catering primarily to the mid-Atlantic region.

Penelope Callender, Ed.
PCCS Publishing
Magazine: Antique Traveller
P.O. Box 5216
Herndon, VA 20172-1974
ph: 703-437-4971
fax: 703-707-0458
pscpub@aol.com
http://www.antiquetraveller.com
Bi-monthly newsprint magazine covering the MD, DC, VA area; articles of area interest including historic sites, antiques shows, dealer ads, etc.

Brent Diamond
PRIMEDIA Enthusiast Group
Magazine: American History
741 Miller Dr., SE, Ste. D-2
Leesburg, VA 20175
ph: 703-779-8318
fax: 703-779-8310
david.masini@primedia.com
http://www.thehistorynet.com/
  AmericanHistory
Feature articles on all aspects of American history; coverage of military, social, and political events and the forces that have shaped American history; published bi-monthly.

Smithsonian Institution
Magazine: Smithsonian Magazine
900 Jefferson Dr. SW
Washington, DC 20560
ph: 202-786-2900
webmaster@si.edu
http://www.si.edu

David J. Maloney, ISA CAPP
Sales Online Direct, Inc.
Directory: Maloney's Antiques &
  Collectibles Resource Dir.
P.O. Box 2049
Frederick, MD 21702-1049
ph: 301-228-2279
fax: 301-695-6491
dave@maloney.com
http://www.davidmaloney.com/
  aboutbook.htm
Publishes major resource information source for collectors, sellers, claims adjusters, etc.: includes experts, buyers, clubs, periodicals, repairers, museums/libraries, appraisers, auctioneers, matching services, dealers, etc.

Oxford University Press, Inc., c/o
Journals Marketing Dept.
Journal: Journal of the History of
  Collections
2001 Evans Rd.
Cary, NC 27513
ph: 919-677-0977 or 800-852-7323
fax: 919-677-1714
www-admin@oup.co.uk
http://www3.oup.co.uk/jnls/list/hiscol
An international journal devoted to the study of collections from palaces and household accumulations to systematic museum collections.

Newspaper: Mid-Atlantic Antique News
P.O. Box 241114
Charlotte, NC 28224
ph: 888-212-1280
fax: 800-681-4963
editor@maano.com
http://www.maano.com
Regional antique and auction trade publication serving the Mid-Atlantic region.

Newspaper: Southern Antiques
P.O. Drawer 1107
Decatur, GA 30031-1107
ph: 404-289-0054 or 888-800-4997
fax: 404-286-9727
southernantiques@msn.com
The South's leading monthly antiques and collectibles newspaper.

Jim McElreath, Pub.
McElreath Printing & Publishing, Inc.
Magazine: Southeastern Antiquing &
  Collecting Magazine
P.O. Box 510
Acworth, GA 30101
ph: 770-974-6495 or 888-388-7827
fax: 770-975-7286
antiquing@go-star.com
http://www.go-star.com/antiquing
A monthly magazine featuring antique and collecting related articles, show

schedule, auction calendar, classifieds, shop and mall directory.

Billian Publishing Inc.
Magazine: Art & Antiques
2100 Powers Ferry Rd.
Atlanta, GA 30339
ph: 770-955-5656
fax: 770-952-0669
editor@artantiquesmag.com
http://www.ArtandAntiques.net
Glossy magazine focusing on the fine and decorative arts and in antiques: colorful ads, articles, auction reports, detailed listings, etc.

Bruce Causey
Newspaper: Antique Shoppe, The
P.O. Box 2175
Keystone Heights, FL 32656-2175
ph: 352-475-1679 or 800-847-1740
fax: 352-475-5326
antshoppe@aol.com
http://www.antiqueshoppefl.com
Florida's monthly antiques newspaper; interesting and entertaining articles about antiques and collectibles, historical landmarks and places of interest, including maps to Florida's best antique shops; serves FL and parts of GA.

Ralph & Terry Kovel
Newsletter: Kovels on Antiques &
  Collectibles
P.O. Box 22200
Beachwood, OH 44122-0200
ph: 800-829-9158 or 800-829-9158
fax: 216-752-3115
kovels@palmcoastd.com
http://www.kovels.com
Focuses on antiques, decorative arts and collectibles; identification and buying tips, prices, reproduction alerts, etc.

Susan Hogan, Ed.
Farm & Dairy Publishers
Newspaper: Antique Collector & Auction
  Guide, The
185 E. State St.
Salem, OH 44460-2842
ph: 330-337-3419 or 330-337-3164
fax: 330-337-9550
A weekly insert to "Farm and Dairy" newspaper; serving the antiques and collectibles trade; ads, auctions, articles, etc.

Art Wilson
Magazine: American Antiquities Journal
126 E. High St.
Springfield, OH 45502
ph: 937-322-6281 or 800-557-6281
fax: 937-322-0294
mail@americanantiquities.com
http://www.americanantiquities.com/
  journal.html
A tri-annual publication featuring "Map of America," a guide to shopping, eating and sleeping for the antiques enthusiast, interesting and informative articles, events and show calendar.

Connie Swaim, Ed.
DMG World Media
Newspaper: AntiqueWeek - Eastern
  Edition
P.O. Box 90
Knightstown, IN 46148
ph: 765-345-5133 or 800-876-5133
fax: 800-695-8153
connie@antiqueweek.com
http://www.antiqueweek.com
A leading antiques, auctions and collectors' newspaper published weekly every Monday in three regional editions - Eastern, Central and Western.

Connie Swaim, Ed.
DMG World Media
Newspaper: AntiqueWeek - Central
  Edition
P.O. Box 90
Knightstown, IN 46148
ph: 765-345-5133 or 800-876-5133
fax: 800-695-8153
connie@antiqueweek.com
http://www.antiqueweek.com
A leading antiques, auctions and collectors' newspaper published weekly every Monday in three regional editions - Eastern, Central and Western.

Connie Swaim, Ed.
DMG World Media
Newspaper: AntiqueWest
P.O. Box 90
Knightstown, IN 46148
ph: 765-345-5133 or 800-876-5133
fax: 800-695-8153
connie@antiqueweek.com
http://www.antiqueweek.com
A leading antiques, auctions and collectors' newspaper; published monthly.

Greg Wilcox, Pub.
Newspaper: Great Lakes Trader
P.O. Box 9
Williamston, MI 48895
ph: 517-655-5621 or 800-785-3637
fax: 517-655-5380
gltrader@aol.com
Michigan's prime antiques trade paper; monthly show listings, original articles on antiques and related items, monthly auction and show reviews, ads.

Lars Svendsen, Pub.
Newspaper: Auction Exchange &
  Collectors News, The
929 Indusgtrial Parkway
P.O. Box 57
Plainwell, MI 49080-0057
ph: 269-685-1343 or 888-339-3795
fax: 269-685-8840
info@eauctionexchange.com
http://www.eauctionexchange.com
The weekly auction and collectors guide for Michigan, N. Indiana, and NW Ohio.

Meredith Corporation
Magazine: Country Home Magazine
1716 Locust St.
Des Moines, IA 50309-3023
ph: 800-374-9431 or 515-284-2015
fax: 515-285-2552
countryh@mdp.com
http://www.countryhomemagazine.com
*A monthly magazine with lots of ads
and in-depth articles about antiques,
collectibles, decorative accessories,
reproductions, interior decorating and
architecture.*

Meredith Corporation
Magazine: Traditional Home
1716 Locust St.
Des Moines, IA 50309-3023
ph: 515-284-3762 or 800-374-8791
fax: 515-284-1083
traditionalhome@mdp.com
http://www.designerfinder.com
*Focuses on a classic, refined and
gracious way of living, interpreting
tradition as a style choice and a way
of life: interiors, architecture,
renovation, gardening, collecting,
cuisine, table settings, travel, new
products featured.*

Linda Kruger, Ed.
Pioneer Communications, Inc.
Magazine: Collectors News
506 Second St.
P.O. Box 306
Grundy Center, IA 50638
ph: 319-824-6981 or 800-352-8039
fax: 319-824-3414
collectors@collectors-news.com
http://www.collectors-news.com
*The monthly newsprint magazine for
antiquers & collectors nationwide;
complete show & sale calendar,
articles, limited edition collectibles,
expert advice, values, etc.; price guide
in every issue.*

Linda Kunkel, Ed.
Antique Trader Publications, Inc.
Newspaper: Cotton & Quail Antique
Trail
2728 Asbury Rd.
Cove Bldg., Ste 600
Dubuque, IA 52001
ph: 800-482-4150 or 563-588-2073
fax: 800-531-0880
kunkell@krause.com
*A monthly newspaper on antiques and
collectibles; wide variety of general
interest articles; covers the Southeast;
65,000 readers; distributed in over
2,200 antique malls, shops and
shows.*

Stacie Berger
Regional Antique Publications
Newspaper: Antique Gazette
P.O. Box 1050
Dubuque, IA 52004
ph: 319-588-2073 x130
stacie.berger@fwpubs.com
*Complete monthly antiques guide;
shop/mall locator, show calendar,
classifieds, articles; nationwide
distribution; featuring the exclusive*

*"Antiques Locator" - hundreds of
quality antiques listed for sale with
prices.*

Stacie Berger
Antique Trader Publications, Inc.
Magazine: Collector Magazine & Price
Guide
P.O. Box 1050
Dubuque, IA 52004-1050
ph: 800-334-7165 or 800-482-4155
fax: 800-531-0880
stacie.berger@fwpubs.com
http://www.collect.com/interest/
periodical.asp?Pub=CO
*A monthly magazine featuring stories
on hot collectibles, travelogue of great
antiquing towns, an in-depth look at
antique collecting with advice from
experts, exclusive 25-page price guide
in each issue.*

Connie Gewecke, Ed.
CarPac Publishing Co.
Newspaper: Collectors Journal
1800 W. D St.
P.O. Box 601
Vinton, IA 52349-0601
ph: 319-472-4763 or 319-472-4764
fax: 319-472-3117
connie@collectorsjournal.com
http://www.collectorsjournal.com
*Weekly auction paper for collectors
and antique lovers; weekly auction and
flea market calendar, auction results,
and articles.*

Bob & Jeni Olsze
Newspaper: Auction Action Antique
News. Inc.
1404 1/2 East Greenbay St.
Shawano, WI 54166-2258
ph: 715-524-3076
fax: 800-580-4568
auction@auctionactionnews.com
http://www.auctionactionnews.com
*A weekly newspaper in both printed
and online edition, by subscription;
ads and articles for auctions, shows,
and antique malls and shops; 100s of
items available for sale in each issue;
covers the Midwest; subscriptions
worldwide.*

Michael Jacobi
Newspaper: Yesteryear
P.O. Box 2
Princeton, WI 54968-0002
ph: 920-787-4808
fax: 920-787-7381
yesteryear@vbe.com
*A monthly newspaper featuring
articles and ads about antiques &
collectibles; shop directory, extensive
calendar of events covering flea
markets, antique shows, etc.; covering
the North Central states.*

Stacie Berger
Krause Publications
Newspaper: Antique Review
700 E. State St.
Iola, WI 54990
stacie.berger@fwpubs.com
http://www.collect.com
A monthly newspaper serving the

*dealers and collectors of Mid-America:
articles, shows, auctions, ads, etc.*

Stacie Berger
Krause Publications
Newspaper: Antique Trader Weekly, The
700 E. State St.
Iola, WI 54990-0001
ph: 715-445-2214
fax: 715-445-4087
stacie.berger@fwpubs.com
http://www.antiquetrader.com
*A weekly newspaper with ads, articles
and news on the antiques and
collectibles hobby; buy, sell, trade
smarter; over 2,000 ads in every issue;
comprehensive national show and
auction calendars; special feature
stories.*

Stacie Berger
Krause Publications
Magazine: Warman's Today's Collector
700 E. State St.
Iola, WI 54990-0001
ph: 715-445-2214
fax: 715-445-4087
stacie.berger@fwpubs.com
http://www.krause.com
*Monthly magazine with the latest news
and market reports for dozens of areas
of collector interest; classified ads,
nationwide auction results, updated
auction & collectibles show calendar
in every issue.*

Stacie Berger
Krause Publications
Magazine: eBay Magazine
700 E. State St.
Iola, WI 54990-0001
ph: 715-445-2214
fax: 715-445-4087
stacie.berger@fwpubs.com
http://www.krause.com
*Contains the latest news in
collectibles, e-commerce and person-
to-person trading, tips on how to buy,
sell, invest and collect online, advice
from experts in all types of fields.*

Stacie Berger
Krause Publications
Magazine: Guide to Collecting on the
Web
700 E. State St.
Iola, WI 54990-0001
ph: 715-445-2214
fax: 715-445-4087
stacie.berger@fwpubs.com
http://www.krause.com
*Produced twice yearly; easy-to-access
compact guide providing a road map
to navigate collectibles information
and value on the Internet.*

Tom Ratzloff
Newspaper: Old Times, The
P.O. Box 340
Maple Lake, MN 55350-0340
ph: 320-963-6010
fax: 320-963-6499
oldtimes@theoldtimes.com
http://www.theoldtimes.com
*Monthly newspaper serving antiques
collectors in MN, WI, IL, and IA.*

Dale K. Graham, Pub.
Lightner Publishing Corp.
Magazine: Antiques & Collecting
Magazine
1006 S. Michigan Ave.
Chicago, IL 60605-9840
ph: 312-939-4767
fax: 312-939-0053
lightnerpb@aol.com
*Informative articles on antiques &
collectibles; up-to-the-minute news
from the field, auction results,
exhibitions of interest, classified ads,
book reviews, antique show calendar;
published monthly since 1931
(formerly "Hobbies").*

Lois Bowman, Ed.
Newspaper: Collector, The
P.O. Box 148
Heyworth, IL 61745-0158
ph: 309-473-2466 or 309-473-2940
fax: 309-473-3610
collinc@mchsi.com
*Monthly newspaper for those
interested in antiques and collectibles;
flea markets, shows, articles, event
reviews, etc.; many ads for antiques
businesses in the Illinois region; free
"I Collect" and "For Sale" ads for
collectors.*

Jerry Reppert
Reppert Publications
Newspaper: Antique & Collectible News
& The Antique Times
P.O. Box 529
Anna, IL 62906-0529
ph: 618-833-2158 or 800-833-2699
fax: 618-833-5813
reppert@midwest.net
*A regional monthly with articles about
antiques, collectors, quilts, history,
crafts, craftsmen, special events,
collector clubs and other topics of
interest to collectors in IL, MO, KY
IN MS and TN.*

Bill Alexander, Ed.
Newspaper: Antiques Gazette, The
41429 W. I-55 Service Rd.
P.O. Box 305
Hammond, LA 70403
ph: 985-429-0575 or 800-386-0575
fax: 985-429-0576
gazette@i-55.com
http://www.theantiquesgazette.com
*A monthly newspaper focusing on the
heritage, antiques, collectibles and
attractions of the South; antiques
auctions and shows, stories on
collections, shops and museums,
historic attractions, etc.*

Newspaper: Arkansas Antiques
P.O. Box 575
Dardanelle, AR 72834-0575
ph: 501-229-2493
fax: 501-229-2493
Periodical includes ads, articles, calendar of events for the antique enthusiast in Arkansas; maps to antique stores in Arkansas.

Paul Averitt, Pub.
Antique Prime Publications LLC
Newspaper: Antique Prime
P.O. Box C
Waxahachie, TX 75168
ph: 972-935-0938
fax: 972-937-7326
info@antiqueprime.com
http://www.antiqueprime.com
Ad newspaper of antiques events and shows in central Texas.

Zorah Publications, Inc.
Magazine: Antique Traveler, The
P.O. Box 656
Mineola, TX 75773
ph: 800-446-3588 or 903-569-2487
antq@dctexas.net
Serving the American Southwest antiques trade; ads, dealer directory, articles, show and auction schedules nation wide.

Brian Savage
Fun Publications
Newspaper: Master Collector
225 Cattle Baron Parc Dr.
Fort Worth, TX 76108
ph: 800-772-6673 or 817-448-9863
fax: 817-448-9843
brian@mastercollector.com
http://www.mastercollector.com
Ads-only newspaper; dolls (antique and modern collectible), toys, banks, models, cars, Matchbox, monsters, puzzles, political, toy trains, etc.; subscribers receive free 30-word ad each month; published monthly; reaches 20,000.

Newspaper: Antiquing Texas
P.O. Box 7754
The Woodlands, TX 77378
ph: 281-364-9540
fax: 281-364-9701
A monthly ad-newspaper containing shop, mall ads throughout the state of Texas; handy as an antiquer's traveling companion; no articles, just ads; freely given out at antique malls in Texas.

Spree Enterprises, Inc.
Newspaper: Mountain States Collector
P.O. Box 2525
Evergreen, CO 80437-2525
ph: 303-674-1253
fax: 303-674-6281
spreepub@aol.com
http://www.mountainstatescollector.com
Primarily distributed through advertisers, but subscriptions are also available; focuses on the mountain states; show schedules, articles, columns, etc.

Elizabeth Lilien
Newspaper: Vintage Collector, The
P.O. Box 764
Hotchkiss, CO 81419-0764
ph: 970-872-2226
Western Colorado's information source for people who are passionate about collecting.

Rosalie Dannenbaum, Pub.
West Coast Peddler, Inc.
Newspaper: West Coast Peddler
P.O. Box 5134
Whittier, CA 90607
ph: 562-698-1718
fax: 562-698-1500
westcoastpeddler@earthlink.net
http://www.westcoastpeddler.com
Oldest monthly newspaper about antiques, the arts, and collectibles; serving California, Oregon, Washington, Nevada, Arizona and some areas of Idaho and Colorado.

Darrell Talbert
Odyssey Publications, a Division of Collectors Universe
Magazine: Pop Culture Collecting
510-A S. Corona Mall
Corona, CA 91720-1420
ph: 909-371-7137 or 800-99-ODYSSEY
fax: 909-371-7139
DBTOGI@aol.com
http://www.autographs.com/collect.htm
A monthly magazine focusing on collecting autographs, movie memorabilia, movie posters, television, rock & roll, props, costumes, sports, space collectibles, animation art and more.

Frank Donadee
Magazine: Collector Magazine
436 W. Fourth St. #222
Pomona, CA 91766-1620
ph: 909-620-9014
icollect@aol.com
http://www.collectorsconference.com
A monthly periodical; Southern California's most popular collecting newspaper; ads, calendar of events, auctions, service directory, etc.

Sandra Hood, Pub.
Krause Regional Antique Publications
Newsmagazine: Antique Journal
P.O. Box 12589
500 Fesler St., Ste. 201
El Cajon, CA 92020
ph: 619-593-2925 or 619-593-2927
fax: 619-447-7187
AntiqueJournal@aol.com
The largest monthly newspaper in Northern California, Oregon and Washington covering the antiques and collectibles industry with focus on Nevada and southern California; 76+ pages; auctions, events and show selection, features, etc.

Sandra Hood, Pub.
Krause Regional Antique Publications
Newsmagazine: Antique & Collectables
P.O. Box 12589
500 Fesler St., Ste. 201
El Cajon, CA 92022
ph: 619-593-2925 or 619-593-2927
fax: 619-447-7187
antiquequill@aol.com
The largest monthly newspaper in southern California covering the antiques & collectibles industry with focus sections on Nevada and Arizona; 64+ pages; events and show section, auctions, feature articles; columns, ads.

Victorian Homes, Inc.
Magazine: Victorian Homes
265 South Anita Dr., Ste. 120
Orange, CA 92868-3343
ph: 800-999-9718 or 714-939-9991 x332
fax: 714-939-9909
editorial@victorianhomesmag.com
http://www.victorianhomesmag.com
Glossy magazine with information sources for locating special items for restoring and decorating Victorian homes.

Newspaper: Hawaii Antiques, Art & Collectibles Quarterly
P.O. Box 853
Honolulu, HI 96808
ph: 808-591-0049
hibevgde@aloha.net
http://www.ukulele.com/haq.html

Ron & Donna Miller
Newspaper: Old Stuff
P.O. Box 1084
McMinnville, OR 97128-1084
ph: 503-434-5386
fax: 503-435-0990
oldstuff@oldstuffnews.com
http://www.oldstuffnews.com
Published 6 times/year; a newspaper about the antiques, collectibles, history, and nostalgia of the Northwest US; lots of ads, articles, show and auction calendar.

Andre Jaku, Pub.
Magazine: World of Antiques & Art, The
10 Spring St., Ste. 1b
P.O. Box 324
Bondi Junction, New South Wales 2022 Australia
ph: 612 9389 2919
fax: 612 9387 7487
editor@antiquesandart.com.au
http://www.worldaa.com

Paul Fiocca
Trajan Publishing Corp.
Magazine: Antique Showcase
103 Lakeshore Rd., Ste. 202
St. Catharines, Ontario L2N 2T6 Canada
ph: 905-646-7744
fax: 905-646-0995
fiocca@trajan.com
http://www.antiquesshowcase.net
National magazine with diverse articles, show and auction reports, museum exhibits, book reviews, upcoming trends, etc.; also contains lots of display and classified ads for buyers of Canadian, US and European antiques; 9 times per year.

Bill Dobson
Newspaper: Upper Canadian, The
30 D Chambers St.
P.O. Box 653
Smiths Falls, Ontario K7A 5B8 Canada
ph: 613-283-1168
fax: 613-283-1345
uppercanadian@recorder.ca
http://www.uppercanadian.com
A bi-monthly Canadian newspaper with auction and show coverage, educational content, photo-ads, show and auction calendar, restoration section, and price guides; presents current trends in the Canadian antiques and collectibles business.

Trajan Publishing Corporation
Newspaper: Collectibles Canada
103 Lakeshore Rd., Ste. 202
St. Catharines, Ontario L2N 2T6 Canada
ph: 905-646-7744
fax: 905-646-0995
rscott@trajan.com
http://www.tarjan.com

Jay Telfer
Good Writtens Publishing
Newspaper: Wayback Times, The
RR #1, 541 Rednersville Rd.
Belleville, Ontario K8N 4Z1 Canada
ph: 613-966-8749
fax: 613-966-8747
waybackt@magma.ca
http://www.waybacktimes.com
Ontario's largest antiques newspaper.

Connie Wills
Soaring Eagle Publications
Magazine: Georgian Antique Digest
22 Louisa St. East
Thornbury, Ontario N0H 2P0 Canada
ph: 519-599-5017
fax: 519-599-5017
gad@georgian.net
A quarterly magazine with informational articles on antiques to whet the

appetite of the collecting public; helps them become familiar with the shops and shows around South Central Ontario, close to the Eastern Great Lakes states.

Editoriale Tricolore srl
Magazine: Collezionare
via Panfilo Castaldo No. 1
Reggio Emilia, 42100 Italy
ph: 0522557893
fax: 0522557825
collezio@tin.it
http://www.collezionare.com
Monthly periodical written in Italian; covers antique fairs, markets, conventions, art exhibitions, auctions and auction results in Italy and abroad; also contacts in Italy and abroad to exchange, buy and sell antiques & collectibles.

Philip Bartlam, Pub.
Magazine: Antique Dealer & Collectors Guide, The
P.O. Box 805
Greenwich
London, SE10 8TD U.K.
ph: 0181-6914820
fax: 0181-6912489
antiquedealercollectorsguide@ukbusiness.com
http://www.ukbusiness.com/
   antiquedealercollectorsguide
An English glossy international monthly magazine for dealers and collectors: articles, ads, book reviews, auction reports, etc.

Mark Bridge
Metropress Ltd.
Newspaper: Antiques Trade Gazette
115 Shaftesbury Ave.
London, London WC2H 8AD U.K.
ph: 020 7420 6600
fax: 020 7420 6605
info@antiquestradegazette.com
http://www.antiquestradegazette.com
A substantial weekly newspaper with articles, calendar of shows and sales, ads, etc. focusing on the English market; founded in 1971; provides comprehensive international coverage of auctions, shows and dealers.

Magazine: Apollo Magazine
1 Castle Lane
London, SW1E 6DR U.K.
ph: 020 7233 6640
fax: 020 7233 7159
editorial@apollomag.com
http://www.apollomagazine.com
The international magazine of art and antiques; an English monthly publication with detailed articles and glossy color photos; for US postal subscriptions write P.O. Box 47, North Hollywood, CA 91603-0047.

H.P. Publishing
Magazine: Antiques Magazine
2 Hampton Court Rd.
Harborne, Birmingham B17 9AE U.K.
ph: (01210) 681 8003 or (01210) 681 8000
fax: (01210) 681 8005
editorial@antiquesmagazine.com
http://www.antiquesmagazine.com
A weekly English publication for dealers and collectors.

Philip Bartlam
Statuscourt Ltd.
Magazine: Antique Dealer & Collectors' Guide
P.O. Box 805
Greenwich, London SE10 8TD U.K.
ph: (0) 181 691 4820
fax: (0) 181 691 2489
antiquedealercollectorsguide@ukbusiness.com
http://www.collectiques.net/guide
Monthly English publication; the very latest on auctions, antiques fairs, exhibitions, and other events; informative articles on furniture, ceramics, silver, pictures, and collectibles; over 1,200 fair and auction dates each issue.

Tony Keniston
Newspaper: Antiques & Art Independent
1 Brambledean Rd.
Comely Bank, Edinburgh BN41 1LP U.K.
ph: +44 1273 705 827
fax: +44 1273 705 827
antiquesnews@hotmail.com
http://www.antiquesnews.co.uk
A newspaper for the British antique and art trade; widest circulating publication covering the antiques trade in Britain.

Antiques Information Services Ltd.
Magazine: Antiques Info Magazine
P.O. Box 93
Broadstairs, Kent CT10 3YR U.K.
ph: 01843 862069
fax: 01843 862014
john.ainsley@antiques-info.co.uk
http://www.antiques-info.co.uk
Search for fairs and auctions, market surveys and forecasts, fair and auction news and prices, informational and advisory pages.

Magazine: Antiques Diary
P.O. Box 30
Twyford
Reading, Berkshire RG10 8DQ U.K.
ph: +44 118 940 2165
fax: +44 118 940 4550
English publications: comprehensive listing of events, feature articles, fairs, auctions, markets.

Essential Publishing Ltd.
Magazine: Collect it!
The Tower
Phoenix Square
Colchester, Essex CO4 9PE U.K.
ph: +44 1206 851117
info@essentialpublishing.co.uk
http://www.collectit.co.uk
A full-color glossy monthly magazine

keeping you up-to-date with collecting news and in-depth features.

PERSONALITIES

(see AUTOGRAPHS; AUTOGRAPHS, Celebrity; FAN CLUBS; MOVIE MEMORABILIA; PHOTOGRAPHS, Celebrity; POLITICAL COLLECTIBLES; SPORTS COLLECTIBLES)

PERSONALITIES (ARTISTS)

(see also ART; CARTOON ART, Walt Kelly; ILLUSTRATORS)

Daniel Chester French

Museums/Libraries

Chesterwood Estate & Museum
4 Williamsville Rd.
P.O. Box 827
Stockbridge, MA 01262
ph: 413-298-3579
chesterwood@nthp.org
http://www.chesterwood.org
The 1920s summer home, studio and garden of sculptor Daniel Chester French (1850-1931); collection includes the working models of the seated Lincoln for the Lincoln Memorial in Washington, DC; also models for the Minute Man.

Edna Hibel

Clubs/Associations

Ralph Burg, Pres.
Edna Hibel Society
Magazine: Hibelletter
P.O. Box 9721
Coral Springs, FL 33075-9721
ph: 561-848-9633
fax: 561-858-9640
HibelSoc@aol.com
A fellowship to honor the art and achievements of internationally famous artist Edna Hibel; magazine published quarterly.

Man./Prod./Dist.

Andy Plotkin, Ph.D.
Edna Hibel Studio
Newsletter: Hibelletter
P.O. Box 10907
Riviera Beach, FL 33419-4967
ph: 561-848-9633 or 800-771-3362
fax: 561-848-9640
aplotkin@hibel.com
http://www.hibel.com
Publishes and distributes fine arts, collectibles, reproductions, gift items, and fashion and accessories designed by Edna Hibel, America's best loved artist.

Museums/Libraries

Andy Plotkin, Ph.D.
Hibel Museum of Art
Newsletter: Hibelleter
P.O. Box 10907
Riviera Beach, FL 33419-4967
ph: 561-848-9633 or 800-771-3362
fax: 561-848-9640
aplotkin@hibel.com
http://www.hibel.com
Oversees the world's oldest artist fellowship, and the world's only non-profit public museum dedicated to the art of a living American woman.

Grant Wood

Collectors

Jerry A. McCoy
800 Thayer Ave.
Silver Spring, MD 20910-4504
ph: 301-565-2519
sshistory@yahoo.com
Wants anything relating to Grant Wood: autographs, lithographs, etc.

Saint-Gaudens

Museums/Libraries

Saint-Gaudens National Historic Site
RR 3, Box 73
Cornish, NH 03745
ph: 603-675-2175
fax: 603-675-2701
saga@valley.net
http://www.sgnhs.org
Home of one of America's greatest sculptures.

PERSONALITIES (ENTERTAINERS)

(see also RADIO SHOWS, Old Time)

Abbott & Costello

Clubs/Associations

Bill Honor
Abbott & Costello Fan Club
Newsletter: Abbott & Costello Quarterly, The
P.O. Box 5566
Fort Wayne, IN 46895-5566
acqtrly@aol.com
http://members.aol.com/ACQtrly/
   club.html
Promotes the legacy of Abbott & Costello along with selling A&C Fan Club products and merchandise; sells A&C products on their Web site.

Collectors

Mark Stewart
PSC 816
Box 299
FPO, AE 09612
markmax_88@yahoo.com
Collects Abbot & Costello insert movie posters.

Eugene Kirschenbaum
723 E. 84th St., #2
Brooklyn, NY 11236-3501
ph: 718-531-1873
*Wants Abbott & Costello title cards;
anything related to Abbott & Costello
that is rare and unusual.*

Al Jolson

Clubs/Associations

International Al Jolson Society, Inc.
Magazine: Jolson Journal, The
P.O. Box 473
Stevenson, MD 21153-0473
ph: 888-4JOLSON
webmaster@jolson.org
http://www.jolson.org
*Dedicated to perpetuating the memory
"THE WORLD'S GREATEST
ENTERTAINER!" - AL JOLSON; also
publishes The Jolson News newsletter.*

Billie Holiday

Collectors

Thom
1389 Alexandria Dr., Ste. #7
Lexington, KY 40504-1777
ph: 859-255-2727 or 859-873-8787
fax: 859-255-2727
*Wants to buy memorabilia relating to
jazz singer Billie Holiday: sheet
music, phonographs, magazine
articles, contracts, etc.*

British

Periodicals

Bill King
Goody Press, The
Newsletter: Anglofile
P.O. Box 33515
Decatur, GA 30033-0515
ph: 404-633-5587
fax: 404-321-3109
mm@rarebeatles.com
*Anglofile keeps tabs on British
entertainment and entertainers and
when and where they're appearing in
the US.*

Dean Martin

Clubs/Associations

Dean Martin Fan Center
Magazine: Dean Martin Fan Center
Magazine
P.O. Box 660212
Arcadia, CA 91066-0212
admin@deanmartinfancenter.com
http://deanmartinfancenter.com
*Official organization; magazine
published quarterly: articles, news,
question and answer, auction section,
editorials, lots of photos, interviews,
contests, etc.*

Collectors

Neil T. Daniels
P.O. Box 660203
Arcadia, CA 91066-0203
webdir@deanmartinfancenter.com
http://deanmartinfancenter.com
*Wants to buy anything Dino: records,
photos, programs, videos, reel-to-reel
tapes, acetates, toys, novelties, comics,
posters, oddball items, etc.*

Eddie Cantor

Clubs/Associations

Michelle Malik
Eddie Cantor Appreciation Society
Newsletter: ECAS Newsletter
14611 Valley Vista Blvd.
Sherman Oaks, CA 91403
ecantor@aol.com
http://members.aol.com/ecantor
*Members receive a newsletter,
biographical information, and a
black-and-white photograph of the
1930s-1940s singer/entertainer.*

Frank Sinatra

Clubs/Associations

Sinatra Society of America
Newsletter: Sinatra Society of America
Newsletter
P.O. Box 2705
North Hollywood, CA 91610-0705
fssociety@aol.com
http://members.aol.com/BrianC101/
SSA.htm
*Interested in anything and everything
that has to do with Frank Sinatra.*

Collectors

Bill Brooks
31 Thorns Lane
Highland, NY 12528-1213
ph: 845-691-7370
poppopp4@aol.com

Scott Sayers
1800 Nueces St.
Austin, TX 78701
ph: 512-478-3483
fax: 512-473-2447
sayers@bencrenshaw.com
*Wants any Frank Sinatra-related
collectibles including records, toys,
books, etc.; issues an auction list
quarterly.*

Dealers

Footlight Records
113 East 12th St.
New York, NY 10003
ph: 212-533-1572
fax: 212-673-1496
footlight1@aol.com
http://www.footlight.com
*Offers large selection of Sinatra
records, tapes and CDs.*

Experts

Peter Barbato
917 South Bishop St.
Chicago, IL 60607-4019
ph: 312-733-7943 or 312-746-5369
Buys, collects, appraises Frank

*Sinatra memorabilia; author of
"Sinatra: 50th Anniversary
Collector's Guide, 1935-1985;"
serious Sinatra collectors; collecting
for over 35 years; no calls after 9 p.m.
CST; large collection now for sale.*

Fred Astaire

Collectors

M. Russell
1425 4th St. SW, A206
Washington, DC 20024-2240
RussellMA@webtv.net
*Wants to buy Fred Astaire costumes,
signed letters, contracts, and other
memorabilia.*

Jack Benny

Clubs/Associations

Laura Leff, Pres.
International Jack Benny Fan Club
Newsletter: Jack Benny Times, The
P.O. Box 11288
Piedmont, CA 94611
jackbenny@aol.com
http://www.jackbenny.org
*Forum for acquisition and trading of
memorabilia relating to Jack Benny &
his associates; also JB audio tape
lending library.*

Lily Langtry

Collectors

Cummings
P.O. Box 622
Saint Helena, CA 94574-0622
*Wants any Lily Langtry-related
memorabilia; stage posters, sheet
music, newspaper and magazine
articles, etc.*

Marx Brothers

Collectors

Ira Dolnick
241 Golf Mill center #718
Niles, IL 60714
ijdds@aol.com
*Wants anything relating to the Marx
Brothers: magazines, lobby cards,
sheet music, etc.*

Internet Resources

Frank Bland
Marx Brotherhood
feedback@whyaduck.com
http://www.whyaduck.com
*Web site offers Marx Brothers career
info, pictures, sounds, games, and
more.*

Sonja Henie

Collectors

Ann J. Bates
Trout Point
5660 Keefe Rd.
Land O' Lakes, WI 54540
ph: 715-547-3638
ajb@newnorth.net
*Long time, active collector of all
Sonja Henie memorabilia.*

PERSONALITIES (FAMOUS)

Charles A. Lindbergh

(see also AVIATION)

Clubs/Associations

Janet & Dick Hoerle, ExSec
C.A.L./N-X-211 Collectors Society
Newsletter: Spirit of St. Louis
727 Youn Kin Parkway, South
Columbus, OH 43207-4788
ph: 614-497-9517
*Organized to perpetuate the memory of
the man and the machine; interested in
items concerning Charles A.
Lindbergh (1902-1974) and the
aeroplane, The Spirit of St. Louis (N-
X-211).*

Collectors

Stanley King
260 Fifth Ave.
New York, NY 10001-6408
ph: 212-447-1880
fax: 212-447-0728
*A lifelong interest in collecting
Lindbergh-related material.*

Lou Lufker
Lufker Airport Flight Museum
115 Montauk Highway
East Moriches, NY 11940
ph: 631-878-6302
*Wants Lindbergh memorabilia;
anything about Lindy or the Spirit of
St. Louis.*

Robert A. Fratkin
1650 Tysons Blvd., 10th Floor
Mc Lean, VA 22102
ph: 703-556-8108 or 703-629-1941
fax: 703-356-6492
coxfdr@erols.com
*Buys, sells and collects all Lindbergh
memorabilia except books; will
appraise by phone, email or with
SASE.*

Doug Studer
16 Orchard Terrace
Cold Spring, KY 41076
ph: 606-441-2754
*Wants Lindbergh and Spirit of St.
Louis items.*

Janet & Dick Hoerle
727 Youn Kin Parkway, South
Columbus, OH 43207-4788
ph: 614-497-9517
*Collects items related to Charles A.
Lindbergh and the aeroplane, The
Spirit of St. Louis (N-X-211).*

Lyndon Sheldon
2019 Essex
Colorado Springs, CO 80909-1423
ph: 719-597-7066
*Buys, sells and trades Charles A.
Lindbergh/Spirit of St. Louis
memorabilia.*

Museums/Libraries

Missouri Historical Society
P.O. Box 11940
Saint Louis, MO 63112-0040
ph: 314-746-3150
fax: 314-746-4548
library@mohistory.org
http://www.mohistory.org

Dionne Quintuplets

Clubs/Associations

Fay & Jimmy Rodolfos
Dionne Quint Collectors
Newsletter: Quint News
P.O. Box 2527
Woburn, MA 01888-1027
ph: 781-933-2219
effanjay@webtv.net
*A 24-page quarterly newsletter
containing articles, columns and
classified ads; also reproduction
alerts of newly produced items such as
signs, pocket mirrors, and paper and
composition dolls.*

Collectors

Fay & Jimmy Rodolfos
P.O. Box 2527
Woburn, MA 01888-1027
ph: 781-933-2219
effanjay@webtv.net
Wants Dionne quintuplet items.

Ethelyn Hulit
236 Cape Rd.
Standish, ME 04084-6232
ph: 207-642-3091
*Wants to buy Dionne quintuplet items
including games, china, paper,
advertising, cloth, wooden, plaster
items, real photos, sketches, paintings,
unusual items; will reply.*

Marceil Drake
698 Posey Hill, Apt. 21
Roanoke, IN 46783
ph: 219-672-2475
*Wants Dionne quintuplet items:
games, china, toys, paper advertising,
etc.; anything related to Dionne
quintuplets or Quintland.*

Lois Helen Brown
154 W. 500 S
Peru, IN 46970-7621
ph: 765-473-3983
*Wants Dionne quintuplet and related
items such as postcards, games, china,
paper, advertising, etc.*

Museums/Libraries

Sharon Clark-Berard
Dionne Quints Home & Museum, North
　Bay Chamber of Commerce
P.O. Box 747
North Bay, Ontario P1B 8J8 Canada
ph: 705-472-8480 or 800-387-0516
fax: 705-472-8027
nbcc@efni.com
http://www.northbaychamber.com/
　dionnequ.htm

William Randolph Hearst

Collectors

Robert A. LeGresley
727 St. John's Mine Rd.
Vallejo, CA 94951
ph: 707-648-9377
rlegres@aol.com
*Wants to buy original autographs,
manuscripts, books and printed
material on Hearst and his family.*

PERSONALITIES (HISTORICAL)

(see also POLITICAL
COLLECTIBLES; WHITE HOUSE
COLLECTIBLES)

Abraham Lincoln

Clubs/Associations

Jonathan H. Mann
Rail Splitter
Magazine: Rail Splitter, The
P.O. Box 275
New York, NY 10044-0205
ph: 212-980-7031 or 212-691-1224
fax: 212-741-8756
splitter@interport.net
http://www.railsplitter.com
*Dedicated to the study and preserva-
tion of materials relating to Abraham
Lincoln; assists in appraising
Lincoln/Civil War and related
collectibles; publishes quarterly
journal on new finds and market
activity.*

Collectors

Donald Ackerman
P.O. Box 3487
Wallington, NJ 07057-1621
ph: 973-779-8785
assortedpast@comcast.net
*Devoted collector eager to buy Lincoln
memorabilia: campaign flags,
ribbons, banners, posters, photographic badges, glass, china.*

Cary Demont
P.O. Box 16013
Minneapolis, MN 55416
ph: 763-522-0957
*Wants Lincoln related items:
campaign badges, photographic
badges, ribbons, banners, political
flags, posters and the unusual; also
wants the same for any of Lincoln's
contemporaries.*

Dealers

Steve H. Nowlin
History Makers, Inc.
942 Ft. Wayne Ave.
Indianapolis, IN 46202
ph: 800-424-9259 or 317-842-4159
fax: 317-842-4198
Snowlin@indy.rr.com
http://www.rareautograph.com
*Wants autographs of heroes, legends,
superstars; any famous autographs
from 1600 to present.*

Chuck Hand
310 Monterey St.
Paris, IL 61944
ph: 217-463-4555
fax: 217-463-4555
butch@tigerpaw.com
*Extensive catalog of Lincoln
ephemera, books, and related material
issued every year.*

Experts

Stuart Schneider
Abraham Lincoln
P.O. Box 64
Teaneck, NJ 07666-0064
ph: 201-599-4250
fax: 201-599-4251
Stuart@wordcraft.net
http://www.wordcraft.net
*Collects and authenticates Lincoln
photographs taken and printed while
Lincoln was still living (first
generation photographs); author of
"Collecting Lincoln."*

Museums/Libraries

Abraham Lincoln Birthplace National
　Historical Site
2995 Lincoln Farm Rd.
Hodgenville, KY 42748
ph: 270-358-3137 or 270-358-3138
fax: 270-358-3874
abli_administration@nps.gov
http://www.nps.gov/abli

Elizabeth Kehoe, Dir. Mktng.
Lincoln Museum, The
200 E. Berry St.
Fort Wayne, IN 46802
ph: 219-455-3864
fax: 219-455-6922
TheLincolnMuseum@LNC.com
http://www.thelincolnmuseum.org
*Experience firsthand the legacy of
America's most famous president
through the award winning permanent
exhibit, programs, research
collections, and special events.*

Lincoln Boyhood National Memorial
P.O. Box 1816
Lincoln City, IN 47552
ph: 812-937-4541
libo_superintendent@nps.gov
http://www.nps.gov/libo

Lincoln's New Salem Historic Site
Rte. 1 Box 244A
Petersburg, IL 62675-9729
ph: 217-632-4000
fax: 217-632-4010
newsalem@lincolnsnewsalem.com
http://www.lincolnsnewsalem.com
*Reconstructed village where Lincoln
lived from 1831 to 1837.*

Abraham Lincoln Presidential
　Presidential Library & Museum
c/o Illinois Historic Preservation Agency
1 Old State Capitol Plaza
Springfield, IL 62701
ph: 217-785-7958
info@ALincoln-Library.com
http://www.alincoln-library.com
*Brings together the world's largest
collection of documentary material
related to the life of the 16th President
of the US.*

Lincoln Home National Historical Site
413 South Eighth St.
Springfield, IL 62701-1905
ph: 217-492-4241
Timothy_Good@nps.gov
http://www.nps.gov/liho
*At the park's center stands the two-
story home of Abraham Lincoln, the
only home he over owned.*

Lincoln Tomb State Historic Site
Oak Ridge Cemetery
Springfield, IL 62702
ph: 217-782-2717
http://www.state.il.us/HPA/hs/
Tomb.htm

George Washington

Museums/Libraries

Stacey Swigart, M&C Cur.
Valley Forge Historical Society
　Museum, The
Newsletter: VFHS Perspective
P.O. Box 122
Valley Forge, PA 19481-0122
ph: 610-783-0535 or 610-783-0448
fax: 610-783-0957
info@em-c.com
http://www.valleyforgemuseum.com
*Focuses on artifacts from the period
of the American War for Indepen-
dence; features a large collection of
Washingtonia.*

Mount Vernon Ladies' Association
P.O. Box 110
Mount Vernon, VA 22121
ph: 703-780-2000
mvinfo@mountvernon.org
http://www.mountvernon.org
*Mount Vernon is the estate, gardens,
farm, and burial site of George &
Martha Washington; owned and
maintained in trust for the people of
the United States by the Mount Vernon
Ladies' Association.*

Lafayette

Collectors

Andrew B. Golbert
RR 1 Box 1820
North Ferrisburg, VT 05473
ph: 802-453-2525
*Wants any Lafayette ephemera,
particularly relating to his visit to the
US in 1824-25: ribbons, medals,
tokens, prints, books, etc.*

Napoleon

Appraisers

Pierre G. Bovis
Bovis Primitive Arts
P.O. Box 5529
Santa Fe, NM 87502
ph: 505-989-1339 or 505-577-7992
fax: 505-989-1339
louberlugan@earthlink.net
http://www.bovisprimitivearts.com
*Buy, sells, appraises cowboy
memorabilia, primitive arts, American
Indian arts, Napoleonic artifacts; also
Polynesian, Hawaiian, New Guinea,
Pacific Islands and African art
including Shaman items, weapons,
fine carvings.*

Clubs/Associations

Douglas Allan, Ex. VP
Napoleonic Society of America
Newsletter: Member's Bulletin
1115 Ponce De Leon Blvd.
Clearwater, FL 33756
ph: 610-581-0400
fax: 610-581-0400
napoleonic1@juno.com
http://www.napoleonsociety.org
*Founded in 1983 to provide a means
of communicating and sharing views
on Napoleon as a man and as a
military genius; also memorabilia.*

Collectors

W.R. Morat
3942 Park Ave.
Memphis, TN 38111-6666
ph: 901-458-2633
fax: 901-458-6202
*Wants Napoleon or his family &
marshals; books, pictures, statues,
paintings, plates, tables, miniatures,
letters, manuscripts, newspapers,
swords, ink wells, etc.; especially in
America after exile.*

James & Evelyn Hilty
Balcony Row
216 S. Broad St.
Holly, MI 48442-1670
ph: 248-634-1400
*Wants items of Napoleonic history;
manuscripts, letters, diaries, maps,
documents, books, etc.*

Sir Winston S. Churchill

Clubs/Associations

Lorraine C. Horn, Bus. Mngr.
Churchill Societies, International
Magazine: Finest Hour
135 S. LaSalle St.
Chicago, IL 60603
ph: 800-621-1917
fax: 312-726-9474
dcraighorn@msn.com
http://www.winstonchurchill.org/
society.htm
*Educational/charitable assoc. devoted
to preserving the memory, thought,
writings, of Sir Winston S. Churchill
(1874-1965.)*

Churchill Center, The
Magazine: Finest Hour
1847 Stonewood Dr.
Baton Rouge, LA 70816
ph: 888-972-1874
Malakand@conknet.com
http://www.winstonchurchill.org/
center.htm
*Devoted to the promotion of all
aspects of Churchill studies, including
a broad academic program of
seminars, lectures and symposia;
publishes specialty handbooks on
Churchill-related stamps, books and
memorabilia.*

PERSONALITIES (INVENTORS)

Thomas Alva Edison

Collectors

John W. Hess
244 Bernaski Rd.
Amsterdam, NY 12010-7827
ph: 518-843-6117
*Wants to buy or trade any Edison
related merchandise: inventions,
antique phonographs, cylinders,
advertising, prototypes; also original
documents, photographs, etc.*

Steven Ramm
420 Fitzwater St.
Philadelphia, PA 19147-3109
ph: 610-922-7050 or 610-545-3290
steveramm@aol.com
*Wants items related to Thomas Alva
Edison, such as books, articles, stock
certificates, products from various
Edison companies; no magazine ads
please.*

David Giovannoni
ph: 301-869-1501
fax: 301-987-2511
dgio-inquiries@ara.net
http://www.aranet.com/phono/main.htm
*Advanced collector of primary
documents and materials related to
Thomas Alva Edison: photographs,
letters and autographs, patent models,
or other original items.*

C. T. Little
183 Rainbow Dr., #8348
Livingston, TX 77399-1083
ladylight2000@yahoo.com
*Wants miniature busts, Edison
commemoratives, Edison memorabilia,
etc.; also seeks memorabilia relating
to other electrical inventors such as
Westinghouse and Tesla.*

Experts

David C. Heitz
Edison Connection, The
P.O. Box 518
New Hope, PA 18938
ph: 215-862-5717
*Wants to buy Thomas A. Edison
memorabilia: autographs, stock
certificates, company letters,
advertising, anything Edison; no
magazine ads please.*

Museums/Libraries

Edison National Historic Site
Main St. at Lakeside Ave.
West Orange, NJ 07052
ph: 973-736-0550
fax: 973-736-8496
EDIS_Webmaster@nps.gov
http://www.nps.gov/edis/home.htm
Edison's home and laboratory.

David C. Heitz
Edison Connection, The
P.O. Box 518
New Hope, PA 18938
ph: 215-862-5717
*Edison Museum open by appointment
only - school groups, clubs, Seniors
Groups are all welcome; lectures and
demonstrations about Edison; no
charge.*

Laurence J. Russell, Curator
Thomas Edison Birthplace Museum
9 Edison Dr.
P.O. Box 451
Milan, OH 44846-0451
ph: 419-499-2135
fax: 419-499-3241
rwheeler@accnorwalk.com
http://www.tomedison.org
*An Edison exhibit featuring
phonographs, lamps, fans, photos,
and other items related to Thomas
Edison.*

PERSONALITIES (LITERARY)

(see also LITERATURE)

Charles Dickens

Collectors

Gerald DiMinico
105 Park St.
Montclair, NJ 07042-2905
ph: 973-744-2092
JDiMinico@comcast.net
*Wants Charles Dickens material;
seeking primarily prints, lithographs
or original art work pertaining to
Dickens' books.*

Edgar Allan Poe

Museums/Libraries

Edgar Allan Poe House & Museum
203 N. Amity St.
Baltimore, MD 21202
ph: 410-396-7932

Edgar Rice Burroughs

(see also CHARACTER
COLLECTIBLES, Tarzan)

Clubs/Associations

George McWhorter
Burroughs Bibliophiles
Magazine: Burroughs Bulletin
Burroughs Memorial Collection
University of Louisville
Louisville, KY 40292-0001
ph: 502-852-8729 or 502-852-6752
fax: 502-852-8734
tyner@taliesan.com
*International club interested in Edgar
Rice Burroughs; the "Gridley Wave"
newsletter is published monthly; the
"Burroughs Bulletin" is a quarterly
magazine; annual convention since
1960 with buying, selling, speakers.*

Horatio Alger, Jr.

(see also BOOKS, Horatio Alger, Jr.)

Clubs/Associations

Horatio Alger Society
Newsletter: Newsboy, The
P.O. Box 70361
Richmond, VA 23255
has@ihot.com
http://www3.ihot.com/~has
*To further the philosophy of Horatio
Alger, Jr. and to encourage the spirit
of Strive & Succeed.*

Internet Resources

Bill Roach
Horatio Alger, Jr. Resources Web Site &
Listserv
School of Business
Washburn University
Topeka, KS 66621
ph: 785-231-1010 x1748 or 785-231-
1010 x1306
fax: 785-231-1063
zzroac@acc.wuacc.edu
http://www.wuacc.edu/sobu/broach/
algerres.html
*Provides a forum for discussing the
work and world of Horatio Alger;
submissions on the novels, short
stories, and/or poetry are welcome;
works that deal with Alger or the
philosophical or historical significance of his writing.*

Jack London

Museums/Libraries

Jack London State Historic Park
2400 London Ranch Rd.
Glen Ellen, CA 95442
ph: 707-938-5216
jacklondonshp@aol.com
http://parks.sonoma.net/JLPark.html
*House of Happy Walls museum wants
Jack London books, magazines, letters
and other memorabilia.*

Lewis Carroll

Clubs/Associations

Ellie Luchinsky, Sec.
Lewis Carroll Society of North America
Newsletter: Knights Letter, The
P.O. Box 204
Napa, CA 94559
webcontact@lewiscarroll.org
http://www.lewiscarroll.org
*Many members also collect books and
other Lewis Carroll related materials.*

Margaret Mitchell

(see also MOVIE MEMORABILIA,
Gone With The Wind)

Collectors

John Wiley, Ed.
1347 Greenmoss Dr.
Richmond, VA 23225-4112
ph: 804-330-5484
fax: 804-771-3054
tsl_gwtw@hotmail.com
http://www.thescarlettletter.com
*Wants to buy early copies of Gone
With The Wind in dust jackets &
limited editions (U.S. & foreign);
original Macmillan promotional
material (catalogs, counter displays,
etc.); Margaret Mitchell items
(personal effects, business cards.)*

Mark Twain

Dealers

Chuck Haley
Sherlock's
13926 Double Girth Ct.
Matthews, NC 28105-4068
ph: 704-847-5480
mirepoix2@aol.com

Experts

Kevin MacDonnell
MacDonnell Rare Books
9307 Glenlake Dr.
Austin, TX 78730
ph: 512-345-4139
macbooks@jump.net
http://www.macdonnellrarebooks.com
*Wants to buy Mark Twain memora-
bilia: photos, autographs, advertising
statues, relics, books, postcards,
dinner menus, recordings, lecture
tickets, etc.; published author of
articles about Mark Twain.*

Museums/Libraries

Mark Twain House
Newsletter: Mark Twain News
351 Farmington Ave.
Hartford, CT 06105
ph: 860-247-0998 or 860-493-6411
fax: 860-246-1557
http://www.MarkTwainHouse.org
*Now a historic house museum, this
19-room Picturesque Gothic home was
built for Samuel Clemens (aka Mark
Twain) in 1874 and was the Clemens
family residence until 1891; extensive
photo archive and collections relating
to Mark Twain.*

Henry Sweets, Dir.
Mark Twain Home & Museum
Newsletter: Fence Painter, The
208 Hill St.
Hannibal, MO 63401
ph: 573-221-9010
*Museum operates Mark Twain's
boyhood home, J.M. Clemens Law
Office, Grant's Drug Store, and three
museum buildings; the newsletter
contains historical notes on mark
Twain and Hannibal, MO as well as
museum news.*

Sir Arthur Conan Doyle

Collectors

Robert C. Hess
559 Potter Blvd.
Brightwaters, NY 11718-1615
ph: 516-665-8365
hessmudlark@aol.com
*Wants Sherlock Holmes/Sir Arthur
Conan Doyle items: figurines,
sculpture, statuary, dolls, original
artwork, illustrations, etc.*

Zane Grey

Clubs/Associations

Zane Grey's West Society
Newsletter: Zane Grey Review
708 Warwick Ave.
Fort Wayne, IN 46825-5653
ph: 219-484-2904
tbolin3194@aol.com
http://www.zanegreysws.org
*Members are collectors of Zane Grey
books and memorabilia.*

PERSONALITIES (MILITARY)

Audie Murphy

Clubs/Associations

Terry M. Murphy
Audie Murphy Research Foundation
P.O. Box 1804
Orinda, CA 94563
ph: 888-314-AMRF
fax: 925-253-0504
Audiemurphy@juno.com
http://www.audiemurphy.com/amrf.htm
*A non-profit, public benefit
organization established for the
purpose of collecting, preserving, and
making available to the public
historical information concerning the
life and times of Audie Murphy.*

Gen. George S. Patton

Clubs/Associations

Charles M. Province, Pres.
George S. Patton, Jr. Historical Society
Newsletter: Patton Blade, The
3116 Thorn St.
San Diego, CA 92104-4618
ph: 619-282-4404
fax: 619-282-1920
http://www.pattonhq.com/homeghq.html
*Founded in 1970 for the purpose of
perpetuating the history of the
achievements of General Patton and
the men who served with him.*

Museums/Libraries

Katie Talbot
Patton Museum of Cavalry & Armor
P.O. Box 208
Fort Knox, KY 40121-0208
ph: 502-624-3812
fax: 502-624-6968
museum@knox.army.mil
http://knox-www.army.mil/museum
*The "Patton Gallery" and the Emert
L. "Red" Davis Library contains Gen.
George S. Patton, Jr. artifacts and
reference materials.*

PERSONALITIES (MOVIE STARS)

(see also AUTOGRAPHS, Celebrity;
MOVIE MEMORABILIA)

Ava Gardner

Museums/Libraries

Melody Godwin
Ava Gardner Museum
Newsletter: Ava Advocate
205 S. 3rd St.
P.O. Box 1182
Smithfield, NC 27577
ph: 919-934-5830 or 919-934-0887
fax: 919-934-5830
jmivey@ipass.net
http://www.avagardner.org
*Collection of posters, costumes,
photographs and personal items
relating to the famous Hollywood
movie star, Ava Gardner.*

Bette Davis

Collectors

James L. Harmon
P.O. Box 25
Banks, OR 97106
ph: 503-324-9099
*Wants to buy Bette Davis movie
posters, lobby cards, magazines,
unusual paper items; original and
vintage material only.*

Clint Eastwood

Collectors

Fred & Jan Carlson
P.O. Box 2
Hillsboro, OR 97123-0002
ph: 503-648-8477
fax: 503-642-2534
*Wants to buy Rawhide and Clint
Eastwood items including comics,
books, records, tapes, posters, etc.*

Errol Flynn

Clubs/Associations

Eric G. Lilley, Pres.
International Errol Flynn Society
Magazine: Sword Magazine
Charles Clore Court, Flat 59
139 Appleford Rd.
Reading, Berkshire RG30 3NT U.K.
ph: 0118 9599540
*Founded 1977, over 6,000 members in
23 countries; an international club
devoted to Errol Flynn.*

Frances Farmer

Collectors

Henry Heiman, III
P.O. Box 316
South Salem, NY 10590-0316
*Wants anything relating to actress
Frances Farmer (1913-1970).*

Greta Garbo

Collectors

Rick Rann
P.O. Box 877
Oak Park, IL 60303-0877
ph: 708-442-7907
ukczech@aol.com
*Wants to buy Greta Garbo movie
posters, lobby cards, glass slides,
magazines, coming attraction flyers,
books, and pressbooks from 1920s to
1940s.*

James Dean

Museums/Libraries

David Loehr
James Dean Memorial Gallery
425 North Main St.
P.O. Box 55
Fairmount, IN 46928-0055
ph: 765-948-3326
fax: 765-948-3389
dl@jamesdeangallery.com
http://www.jamesdeangallery.com
*Houses the world's largest collection
of memorabilia dealing with James
Dean; wants James Dean plates,
posters, records, novelties, photos,
autographs, etc.*

Jimmy Stewart

Museums/Libraries

Jimmy Stewart Museum
P.O. Box 1
Indiana, PA 15701
ph: 724-349-6112 or 800-83-JIMMY
fax: 724-349-6140
curator@jimmy.org
http://www.jimmy.org

John Wayne

Periodicals

Mario De Marco
Newsletter: John Wayne, The All-
American Hero
152 Maple St.
West Boylston, MA 01583-1825
ph: 508-835-4085
Has a number of books on other western and serial stars; send large SASE for book list.

Tim Lilley
Journal: Trail Beyond, The
540 Stanton Ave.
Akron, OH 44301-1554
ph: 330-724-9225
BigTrailak@aol.com
Published annually on the films of John Wayne: John Wayne movie reviews, items for sale, feature articles.

Laurel & Hardy

Collectors

Gino Dercola
10134 Cape Ann Dr.
Columbia, MD 21046
ph: 301-596-6547
gvd57@yahoo.com
Wants Laurel & Hardy toys, games, novelties, dolls, comics, etc.

Marilyn Monroe

Collectors

Ann Bartoli
1230 Woodridge Ct.
Princeton, IL 61356-2842
ph: 815-875-8925
Wants to buy magazines with Marilyn on the cover (American and foreign), sheet music, press books; especially wants older magazines including pre-national TV Guides; also Sunday sections newspapers like NY Daily News.

Dealers

Clark Kidder
3219 E. County Rd. "N"
Milton, WI 53563
ph: 608-868-4185
fax: 608-868-6808
ckidder@jvlnet.com
http://www.jvlnet.com/marilyn
Collects, buys, sells, appraises and specialize in Marilyn Monroe memorabilia.

Experts

Clark Kidder
3219 E. County Rd. "N"
Milton, WI 53563
ph: 608-868-4185
fax: 608-868-6808
ckidder@jvlnet.com
http://www.jvlnet.com/marilyn
Collects, buys, sells, appraises and specialize in Marilyn Monroe memorabilia.

Denis C. Jackson
P.O. Box 6433
Kingman, AZ 86401
ticn@olypen.com
http://www.olypen.com/ticn
Author of "The Price & Identification Guide to Marilyn Monroe" 3rd edition, 1996; lists mens' magazines, movie magazines, paper, books, etc.; send LSASE for information.

Internet Resources

Peggy Wilkins
Marilyn Monroe
mozart@uchicago.edu
http://glamournet.com/legends/Marilyn
Web site listing many resources relating to Marilyn Monroe: fan clubs, videos, recent publications, films, etc.

Mary Miles Minter

Experts

Ronald Krueger
P.O. Box 741
Oak Park, IL 60303-0741
ph: 708-788-8235
Always buying photos, posters, lobby cards, postcards, glass slides, theater handbills or anything related to this silent film actress; also interested in making contact with other Minter collectors.

Shirley Temple

Clubs/Associations

Shirley Temple Collectors by the Sea
Newsletter: Lollipop News
P.O. Box 6203
Oxnard, CA 93031
http://www.shirleytemplefans.com/
html_files/clubs/stclub.htm

Collectors

Gen Jones
294 Park St.
Medford, MA 02155-2668
ph: 781-395-8598
genjones@world.std.com
Serious collector wants anything related to Shirley Temple.

Internet Resources

ShirleyTempleFans.Com
fax: 781-344-7782
questions@shirleytemplefans.com
http://www.shirleytemplefans.com

W.C. Fields

Clubs/Associations

Ted Wioncek, Jr.
W.C. Fields Fan Club
Newsletter: Lompoc Picayune-
Intelligencer
P.O. Box 506
Stratford, NJ 08084-0506
fieldsfanc@aol.com
http://www.webtrec.com/wcfields
Official W.C. Fields fan club; members receive an 8" x 10" photo of Fields, membership card, W.C. Fields films list, discounts on related

memorabilia, newsletter four times per year, free classifieds to buy/sell W.C. Fields collectibles.

PERSONALITIES (MUSICIANS)

(see also ROCK 'N' ROLL COLLECTIBLES)

Beatles

Clubs/Associations

B. Whatmough
Working Class Hero Beatles Club
Newsletter: Working Class Hero, The
3311 Niagara St.
Pittsburgh, PA 15213-4223
Non-profit organization for and by true Beatles fans; three newsletters per year cover news, pictures and articles about the Beatles; please send SASE for information.

Beatles Connection
Newsletter: Beatles Connection
Newsletter
P.O. Box 1066
Miami, FL 33780-1066

Collectors

Marc Zydiak
P.O. Box 285
Westfield, NJ 07091-0285
ph: 908-654-6505
mzunderstood@hotmail.com
Wants to buy rare Beatles items: Butcher Album covers, important autograph material, original photographs, etc.

Herb Van Vliet
35 Roberta Dr.
Howell, NJ 07731-2720
ph: 732-458-3950
herbvan@earthlink.net
Wants to buy Beatles memorabilia: toys, records, memorabilia and rock concert ticket stubs 1955-1975.

Gretchen Dziadosz
333 Grentree Lane NE
Ada, MI 49301-9796
gretchen@aol.com
Wants original 1960s items only: games, dolls, other memorabilia; please write (include SASE if you want reply) or email; please include asking price.

Dennis Toll
127 Blackfair Lane
Brantford, Ontario N3R 7X6 Canada
ph: 519-753-8655 or 519-752-0689
fax: 519-753-1195
dtoll@bfree.on.ca
Collector of high-end Beatles items: autographs, personal items, etc.

Dealers

Gary Hein
Hein's Rare Collectibles
P.O. Box 179
Little Silver, NJ 07739-0179
ph: 732-219-1988
fax: 732-219-5940
ibuybeatles@comcast.net
http://www.Beatles4me.com
Buys, sells original 1960s Beatles: records, autographs, motion displays, bongos, guitars, record players, full and used concert tickets, kaboodle kits, costumes, color forms, kits, dolls, school supplies, Yellow Submarine items.

Gary Mayes
PopCultureToday.Com
P.O. Box 630521
Irving, TX 75063
revolver@popculturetoday.com
http://www.popculturetoday.com/
revolver
A source for Beatles and other pop culture related collectibles.

Mitch McGeary
Ticket to Ryde, Ltd.
P.O. Box 3393
Lacey, WA 98509
fax: 360-491-7343
sps@rarebeatles.com
http://www.rarebeatles.com
Specializing in buying, selling, trading Beatles records and memorabilia; in business for over 25 years; especially wants original Beatles concert tickets from North America 1964-1966.

Experts

Joseph Hilton
6 Wheelwright Dr.
Durham, NH 03824-6607
ph: 603-659-3987
JHilton@aol.com
Collecting original 1960s items only: Beatles lunch boxes, games, toys, Yellow Submarine items, promo displays, anything Beatles.

Charles F. Rosenay
Liverpool Productions
315 Derby Ave.
Orange, CT 06477
ph: 203-891-8131
rosenay@aol.com
http://www.toursandevents.com
Editor of Beatles Fan Club magazine; produces Beatles conventions; trades and sells memorabilia by mail; recognized expert.

Bob Gottuso
BOJO
P.O. Box 1403
Mars, PA 16066-0403
ph: 724-776-0621
fax: 724-776-0621
bojo@zbzoom.net
http://www.bojoonline.com
Beatles collector and expert buys, sells, trades, and collects 1960's Beatles items; send $3 for 32-page

sales catalog filled with Beatles and Yellow Sub items.

Marty Eck
P.O. Box 764
Elburn, IL 60119
ph: 630-365-5468
Toys, dolls, guitars, record player, hair spray, records, concert tickets, movie items, magazines; co-author of book on same.

Rick Rann
P.O. Box 877
Oak Park, IL 60303-0877
ph: 708-442-7907
ukczech@aol.com
Wants to buy toys, dolls, guitars, record player, hair spray, records, concert tickets, movie items, magazines; co-author of book on The Beatles.

Jeff Augsburger
507 Normal Ave.
Normal, IL 61761-2412
ph: 309-452-9376
fax: 309-664-1771
beatles.normal@verizon.net
Buys, collects, sells Beatles memorabilia: toys, dolls, guitars, record player, hair spray, records, concert tickets, movie items, magazines; co-author of book on same.

Matt Hurwitz
P.O. Box 661008
Los Angeles, CA 90066-9608
ph: 310-391-0778
fax: 301-390-7475
gds1964@aol.com
Noted Beatles expert; publisher of the former "Good Day Sunshine," which was a leading Beatles magazine in the U.S

Mitch McGeary
Ticket to Ryde, Ltd.
P.O. Box 3393
Lacey, WA 98509
fax: 360-491-7343
sps@rarebeatles.com
http://www.rarebeatles.com
Specializing in buying, selling, trading Beatles records and memorabilia; in business for over 25 years; especially wants original Beatles concert tickets from North America 1964-1966.

Internet Resources

Michelle King
Beatles Worldsite Museum, The
michelle@beatlespost.zzn.com
http://beatlesmuseum.netfirms.com
An online museum showcasing one of the world's largest online collections of Beatles collectibles and memorabilia.

Mitch McGeary
Mitch McGeary's Songs, Pictures & Stories of the Beatles Website
P.O. Box 3393
Lacey, WA 98509
fax: 360-491-7343
sps@rarebeatles.com
http://www.rarebeatles.com
Web site had hundreds of the rarest and unique Beatles collectibles available; several contributors combined their experience to present images, descriptions, values of many items of Beatles memorabilia.

Museums/Libraries

Jeff Augsburger
Beatles Mobile Museum, The
507 Normal Ave.
Normal, IL 61761-2412
ph: 309-452-9376
fax: 309-664-1771
beatles.normal@verizon.net
Has the largest collection of Beatles memorabilia in the US; actively buying for the collection; will buy one item or 1,000.

Periodicals

Magazine: Beatlefan
P.O. Box 33515
Decatur, GA 30033-0515
ph: 404-633-5587
fax: 404-321-3109
mm@rarebeatles.com
A bi-monthly magazine for Beatles fans; a news-oriented, professional publication; articles, books for sale, ads, etc.

Andrew Croft, Pub.
Magazine: Beatology Magazine
P.O. Box 90
260 Adelaide St. East
Toronto, Ontario M5A 1N1 Canada
ph: 416-360-8902 or 888-844-0826
fax: 416-360-0588
publisher@beatlology.com
http://www.beatlology.com
The magazine for Beatles fans and collectors around the world.

Def Leppard

Collectors

Tammy Clack
101 Queensbury Circle
Goose Creek, SC 29445-5524
ph: 843-863-0857
tammy5145@aol.com
http://www.angelfire.com/sc/strangebehaviourdisc
Wants to buy rare, important and promo records and memorabilia relating to the rock band Def Leppard; also Phil, Collen & Girl.

Duran Duran

Dealers

Tammy Clack
Strange Behavior Discs & Collectibles
101 Queensbury Circle
Goose Creek, SC 29445-5524
ph: 843-863-0857
tammy5145@aol.com
http://www.angelfire.com/sc/strangebehaviourdisc
Wants to buy Duran Duran items, single items or collections.

Elvis

Auction Services

Jerry Osborne
Elvis Auctions
P.O. Box 255
Port Townsend, WA 98368
ph: 360-385-1200
fax: 360-385-6572
jpo@olympus.net
http://www.jerryosborne.com
Conducts periodic auctions of Elvis memorabilia.

Clubs/Associations

Susan Still
Elvis Forever TCB Fan Club
Newsletter: Elvis Forever TCB Fan Club Newsletter
P.O. Box 1066
Miami, FL 33780-1066

Collectors

Burt Atwood
894 Greenway Rd.
Woodbridge, CT 06525-2413
ph: 203-799-9825
Buyer of rare Elvis memorabilia.

Eddie Hammer
735 Roosevelt Ave.
Carteret, NJ 07008-2318
fax: 908-353-8091
Authority on current releases of Elvis recordings; writes "Elvis News" column for "DISCoveries;" largest Elvis collection in the world; buy, sell, trade anything Elvis.

Dealers

Ed Wall
Big Boys Toys
242 Main St.
Gloucester, MA 01930
ph: 978-283-8384
Buys, sells and trades Elvis memorabilia.

Peter Weldon
Pete's Music
815 2nd Ave.
Troy, NY 12182-2131
ph: 518-235-1318 or 518-235-6795
petesmusic@aol.com
http://www.petes.gemm.com
Issues catalog containing Elvis albums, 45s, LPs, picture sleeves, colored vinyl, picture discs, magazines, books, memorabilia, etc.

Tod Hutchinson
P.O. Box 915
Griffith, IN 46319-0915
ph: 219-923-8334
fax: 219-923-8334
Toddtcb@aol.com
Specializes in Elvis collectibles, records, movie posters, etc.

Dwayne Spark
Nostalgia Plus
8441 Sublaines
Anjou, Quebec H1K 2C1 Canada
ph: 514-352-6892
fax: 514-352-1856
dspark@videotron.ca
Buys and sells Elvis memorabilia.

Sid Shaw
Elvisly Yours
233 Baker St.
London, NW1 6XE U.K.
ph: 44-20-7486-2005
fax: 44-20-7486-0550
sid@elvisly-yours.com
http://www.elvisly-yours.com
The world's leading supplier of Elvis Presley memorabilia with over 400 different Elvis souvenirs - inexpensive, good quality and excellent designs; now in their 25th year; totally independent of Elvis Presley Enterprises.

Experts

Eddie Hammer
735 Roosevelt Ave.
Carteret, NJ 07008-2318
fax: 908-353-8091
Authority on current releases of Elvis recordings; writes "Elvis News" column for "DISCoveries;" largest Elvis collection in the world; buy, sell, trade anything Elvis.

Sean O'Neal
6218 Braden Run
Bradenton, FL 34202
ph: 941-727-8316
fax: 941-756-9437
Buys, sells, trades vintage Elvis Presley memorabilia; looking for personal items, unpublished photographs, film footage, unreleased sound recordings, 1956 novelty items, Las Vegas memorabilia; also holds quarterly Elvis auction.

Jerry Osborne
P.O. Box 255
Port Townsend, WA 98368
ph: 360-385-1200
fax: 360-385-6572
jpo@olympus.net
http://www.jerryosborne.com
Author of "The Official Price Guide to Elvis Presley Records and Memorabilia" (House of Collectibles).

Misc. Services

Niche Software, Inc.
Software: Elvis Collector!, The
7118 NW Terrace
Parkland, FL 33076
ph: 954-344-6561
marketing@collectiblessoftware.com
http://www.collectiblessoftware.com
Software to catalog, inventory, sort, group anything in an Elvis collection.

Museums/Libraries

Graceland
3734 Elvis Presley Blvd.
P.O. Box 16508
Memphis, TN 38186-0508
ph: 800-238-2000 or 901-332-3322
fax: 901-344-3119
http://www.elvis.com

Billy Beeny
Elvis Is Alive Museum
P.O. Box 377
Wright City, MO 63390
ph: 636-745-3154
Cafe/arcade/museum filled with Elvis photos, memorabilia and printed material related to the controversy.

KISS

Collectors

Bob Gottuso
BOJO
P.O. Box 1403
Mars, PA 16066-0403
ph: 724-776-0621
fax: 724-776-0621
bojo@zbzoom.net
http://www.bojoonline.com
Buys and sells memorabilia related to KISS, the 1970s rock band: original KISS toys, dolls, household items, etc.; send SASE for sales list.

Liberace

Museums/Libraries

Liberace Foundation for the Performing
 & Creative Arts/Liberace Museum
Newsletter: Liberace Museum Newsletter
1775 E. Tropicana Ave.
Las Vegas, NV 89119-6529
ph: 702-798-5595
fax: 702-798-7386
info@liberace.org
http://www.liberace.org
A non-profit Foundation, Museum, Archives, and gift shop with proceeds funding scholarships in the Arts; collection includes Liberace pianos, furnishings, costumes, cars, jewelry, film, photographs, and recordings.

Monkees

Clubs/Associations

Charles F. Rosenay
Liverpool Productions' Monkees
 Buttonmania Club
315 Derby Ave.
Orange, CT 06477
ph: 203-891-8131
rosenay@aol.com
http://www.toursandevents.com
Produces Monkees conventions.

Collectors

Bob Gottuso
BOJO
P.O. Box 1403
Mars, PA 16066-0403
ph: 724-776-0621
fax: 724-776-0621
bojo@zbzoom.net
http://www.bojoonline.com
Buys and sells original '60s memorabilia related to the Monkees: toys, dolls, and other licensed '60s items.

Rick Rann
P.O. Box 877
Oak Park, IL 60303-0877
ph: 708-442-7907
ukczech@aol.com
Wants to buy 1960s Monkees memorabilia: toys, dolls, concert tickets, magazines, books, fan club items, etc.

Tex Ritter

Clubs/Associations

Sharon L. Sweeting
Tex Ritter Fan Club
Newsletter: Gringo, The
828 Wandering Creek Dr.
Bothell, WA 98021
sharons55@juno.com
12-page newsletter packed with news, reports, clippings, a trading post, discography, and more relating to Tex Ritter.

PETROLIANA

(see GAS STATION COLLECTIBLES)

PEWTER

(see also REPAIR/RESTORATION/
CONSERVATION, Metal Items)

Clubs/Associations

Louise Graver, Mem.
Pewter Collectors Club of America, Inc.
504 W. Lafayette St.
West Chester, PA 19380-2210
ph: 860-673-6637
gpewter@bellatlantic.net
http://members.aol.com/pewterpcca
Association of private collectors and interested parties; annual national as well as regional meetings; semi-annual newsletter.

Peter Hayward
Pewter Society, The
Journal: Journal of the Pewter Society
Llananant Farm
Penallt
Monmouth, NP25 4AP U.K.
fax: +44 870 167 4633
secretary@pewtersociety.org
http://www.pewtersociety.org
Stimulates interest in and appreciation of pewter by encouraging research into its history, manufacture and social context, disseminating information through meetings, advising on its care and preservation.

Dealers

Abbott's Arcade of Antiques
DwAbbott@aol.com
http://members.aol.com/dwabbott/
antiques.htm
Buys and sells old pewter.

Allan & Ita Fogel
Twin Tankard Antiques
P.O. Box 4847
Silver Spring, MD 20914-4847
ph: 301-236-9391
fax: 301-236-0427
twintankard@aol.com
http://www.twintankard.com
Specializes in European pewter; also buys and sells Russian and Judaica.

Bette & Melvyn Wolf, Inc.
1196 Shady Hill Court
Flint, MI 48532
ph: 810-732-6595
fax: 810-732-1467
b.m.wolf@worldnet.att.net
Specializes in antique pewter: American, English, Continental; also in other metal antiques in copper, iron and brass.

Repro. Sources

Pewter Crafter of Cape Cod
791 Rt. 28
Harwich Port, MA 02646
ph: 508-432-5858
fax: 508-432-5858
http://www.pewtercrafterofcapecod.com
Handcrafted American pewter hollowware in traditional and contemporary designs.

PEZ

(see also CANDY CONTAINERS)

Collectors

pezananda@yahoo.com
http://www.geocities.com/pezananda
Collector interested in footed, non-footed, mint, and other PEZ.

Maureen Winer
5900 Brackenridge Ave.
Baltimore, MD 21212-3526
ph: 410-435-5226
fax: 410-464-9213
mwiner@jhu.edu
Interested in buying all PEZ containers.

Richard Belyski
P.O. Box 14956
Surfside, SC 29587
info@pezcollectorsnews.com
http://www.pezcollectorsnews.com
Buys, sells, trades and collects PEZ candy containers.

Jill Cohen
PEZMANIA
13900 Shaker Blvd., #714
Cleveland, OH 44120
ph: 216-283-5993
pezamania@msn.com
http://www.pezmania.com
The world's largest gathering of PEZ collectors; held annually every summer in Cleveland, OH.

Marcia Marshall
Pezheads
ph: 330-929-9588
gotfriends@aol.com
PEZ collector seeks to build private collection.

Sally Kimmel
1471 Lark Lane
Concord, CA 94521-2942
ph: 925-689-4138
sallyraek@yahoo.com
Wants to buy pre 1960s PEZ dispensers (the ones without feet); also other PEZ items.

Dealers

Mark McMahon
Cookie Jars, Etc.
806 Sixth Ave.
Asbury Park, NJ 07712
ph: 732-776-9216
peter@peterandmark.com
http://www.peterandmark.com
Buy, sell, trade cookie jars, banks, salt & peppers and PEZ; in partnership with Peter Linski.

Graham Trievel
P.O. Box 1625
West Chester, PA 19380
ph: 610-701-9193

Diane Davison
Indispensable PEZ
1517 Reisterstown Rd., Ste. 101
Baltimore, MD 21208
ph: 410-486-0900
fax: 410-486-0901
diane@lawgal.net
Buys, sells, collects and specializes in PEZ dispensers.

David A. Hull
Small Town Coins & Collectibles
7498 E. Davison Rd.
Davison, MI 48423-2014
ph: 810-658-1992
fax: 810-658-2977
towncoin@small-town.cnchost.com
http://small-town.cnchost.com
Has 100s of old PEZ for sale; wants to buy singles or entire collections.

Troy Huffer
Pez Sanctum, The
7723 N. 18th Ave.
Phoenix, AZ 85021-7021
ph: 602-994-8383
pezsanctum@rocketmail.com
PEZ expert/collector/dealer with a Web site to buy, trade, sell PEZ dispensers over the Internet; also contains the latest PEZ News.

Gary Doss
Burlingame Museum of Pez Memorabilia
214 California Dr.
Burlingame, CA 94010
ph: 650-347-2301
fax: 650-347-3840
gary@spectrumnet.com
http://www.burlingamepezmuseum.com
Buys and sells current and collectible PEZ candy dispensers; the museum, located 20 minutes south of San Francisco, features the largest public display of PEZ candy dispensers in the world.

Bob Tipton
1526 S. Ray St.
Spokane, WA 99223
ph: 509-534-8557
tipton@pezworld.com
http://www.pezworld.com

Experts

Chris MacTaggart
ph: 724-225-6441
chris@mactaggart.com
Send email to be added to an Internet email mailing list for PEZ collectors.

Steven J. Glew
5611 Lehman Rd.
Dewitt, MI 48820
ph: 517-669-5931
fax: 517-669-3581
josh@sjglew.com
http://www.sjglew.com
Buys, sells and specializes in PEZ.

David Welch
P.O. Box 714
Murphysboro, IL 62966-0714
ph: 618-687-2282
fax: 618-684-2243
PEZDude1@aol.com
http://www.pezheads.net/dwelch
Wants anything relating to PEZ before 1985 for collection and book research; paying over $5,000 for certain items; author of "A Pictorial Guide to Plastic Candy Dispensers" and "Collecting PEZ;" in Guiness for selling PEZ for record amount.

John Devlin
"The Cool PEZ Man"
5441 Oakville Center, Ste. 119
Saint Louis, MO 63129-3554
ph: 314-416-0333
coolpezman@aol.com
http://www.pezconvention.com
Buys, sells, collects, and trades PEZ candy containers; runs the annual National PEZ Collectors Convention (not affiliated with the PEZ Company.)

Robert Yarak
46 Santa Cruz
Palos Verdes Peninsula, CA 90274
ph: 310-377-2364
fax: 310-377-2629
Spectres@aol.com
http://members.aol.com/spectres/index.html
PEZ collector since 1976 always willing to help with any questions regarding PEZ candy dispensers; also buys and appraises.

Bob Tipton
Wonderful World of PEZ Collector's Association
1526 S. Ray St.
Spokane, WA 99223
ph: 509-534-8557
tipton@pezworld.com
http://www.pezworld.com
One stop source for all your PEZ Dispenser questions.

Internet Resources

Kurt Seefeld
Ultimate PEZ Resource, The
kurt@popapez.com
http://www.popapez.com
Lots of great PEZ information, free PEZ email newsletters, PEZ links.

Jamie Gerdes
Flip Me Some Pez!
P.O. Box 256
Boys Town, NE 68010
ph: 402-493-7737
fax: 402-493-7737
http://www.pezheads.org
On line PEZ price guide, PEZ for sale, forum and chat room, current PEZ news, info and history and facts, searchable price database.

Benjamin Scanlon
PEZ Central
pezcentral@hotmail.com
http://www.pezcentral.com
The PEZ collecting site with up-to-date information for everyone from the experienced collector to those who are just beginning: news, PEZ sightings, PEZ garage, PEZ poll, free PEZ graphics and more.

Man./Prod./Dist.

PEZ Candy, Inc.
ph: 888-777-2205
http://www.pez.com
Official PEZ Web site; site has list of all PEZ containers ever made.

Museums/Libraries

Gary Doss
Burlingame Museum of Pez Memorabilia
214 California Dr.
Burlingame, CA 94010
ph: 650-347-2301
fax: 650-347-3840
gary@spectrumnet.com
http://www.burlingamepezmuseum.com
Buys and sells current and collectible PEZ candy dispensers; the museum, located 20 minutes south of San Francisco, features the largest public display of PEZ candy dispensers in the world.

Periodicals

Richard Belyski
Newsletter: PEZ Collector's News
P.O. Box 14956
Surfside, SC 29587
info@pezcollectorsnews.com
http://www.pezcollectorsnews.com
Newsletter for collectors of PEZ candy dispensers; great Web site of PEZ resources, history, factory tour, and more.

PHARMACY

(see MEDICAL, DENTAL & PHARMACEUTICAL)

PHILATELICS

(see STAMP COLLECTING)

PHILIPPINES

(see also ART, Asian; ORIENTALIA; INDONESIA)

Experts

Michael G. Price
P.O. Box 468
Michigan Center, MI 49254
ph: 517-764-4517
mgprice@acd.net
Wants Philippine picture postcards, photos, magazines, books, maps; also wants items from nearby islands such as Borneo.

PHILLUMENY

(see MATCHBOXES; MATCHCOVERS; MATCH SAFES; LIGHTERS)

PHONOGRAPHS

(see also BOOKS, Reference [Phonographs]; HI-FI EQUIPMENT; MUSICAL INSTRUMENTS, Mechanical; PERSONALITIES [INVENTORS], Thomas Alva Edison; RECORDS)

Appraisers

Bruce & Charlotte Mager
Waves
251 W. 30th St.
New York, NY 10001
ph: 212-273-9616
c1wave@aol.com
http://www.wavesradio.com
Established in 1976, buys, sells, repairs, appraises and rents radios, phonographs, TVs, microphones, telephones, fans, neon clocks and signs, and related advertising and literature.

Book Sellers

Yesterday Once Again
P.O. Box 6773
Huntington Beach, CA 92615-6773
ph: 714-963-2474
fax: 714-963-1558
yesterdayonceagain@yahoo.com
http://www.yesterdayonceagain.net
Carries a large selection of books dealing with early phonographs and related ephemera.

Clubs/Associations

Allen Koenigsberg
Antique Phonograph Collectors Club
Newsletter: Antique Phonograph Monthly
502 E. 17th St.
Brooklyn, NY 11226-6606
ph: 718-941-6835
AllenAmet@aol.com
http://www.PhonoBooks.com
Books and information on the history, repair and identification of antique phonographs.

Steve Dando
Buckeye Radio & Phonograph Club
Newsletter: Soundings
4572 Mark Trail
Akron, OH 44321-1462
ph: 330-666-7222
Members exchange expertise in restoration of vintage radios and phonographs; club holds annual mall show (displaying radios and phonographs) and picnic.

Phil Stewart, Ed.
Michigan Antique Phonograph Society, Inc.
Newsletter: In The Groove
60 Central St.
Battle Creek, MI 49027
ph: 616-968-1299
fax: 616-968-1299
pgstewart@aol.com
http://www.lrbcg.com/pogo/MAPS.html
A highly recommended newsletter contains articles, member ads about

antique phonographs, records and music boxes.

Vintage Radio & Phonograph Society, Inc.
Newsletter: Reproducer, The
P.O. Box 165345
Irving, TX 75016-5345
ph: 214-337-2823 or 972-353-4862
http://www.radioremembered.org
Purpose is to preserve early radios, phonographs, and related material and to conduct historical research of same; also publishes "Soundwaves" newsletter.

Karyn Sitter
California Antique Phonograph Society
18242 Timberlane Dr.
Yorba Linda, CA 92686-5345
ph: 714-777-2486 or 714-368-6360
fax: 714-828-0166
nipperlover@yahoo.com

Jim M. Whitty, Historian
Wolverine Antique Music Society
252 Mill St.
Silverton, OR 97381
whitty@hevanet.com
http://www.teleport.com/~rfrederi

Bill Pratt
Canadian Antique Phonograph Society
Journal: Antique Phonograph News
122 Major St.
Toronto, Ontario M5S 2L2 Canada
ph: 416-924-8207
info@capsnews.org
http://www.capsnews.org
Members interested in sound recording and its history: phonographs, gramophones; also related ephemera and memorabilia; journal has original articles, repair tips and how-tos, auction results, ads.

Suzanne Coleman
City of London Phonograph & Gramophone Society
51 Brockhurst Rd.
Chesham
U.K.
clpgs@aol.com
http://www.musicweb.force9.co.uk/music/frms/clpgs.htm

Federation of Recorded Music Societies
67 Galleys Bank Kidsgrove
Staffordshire, ST7 4DE U.K.
frms.sec@virgin.net
http://www.musicweb.force9.co.uk/music/frms

Collectors

John W. Hess
244 Bernaski Rd.
Amsterdam, NY 12010-7827
ph: 518-843-6117
Wants to buy Vogue picture disc records, horn phonographs, music boxes, roller organs; also wants parts, empty cabinets, horns; any condition, any material.

Alvin Heckard
165 Orchard Grove Ave.
Lewistown, PA 17044-7511
ph: 717-248-7071 or 717-248-2816
aheckard@localnet.com
Wants wind-up type phonographs (outside horn type only, please), parts, literature and advertising.

Bernie Seinberg
1548 Bristol Pk.
c/o AFY
Bensalem, PA 19020
ph: 215-886-6124
fax: 215-638-2265
phonoman-bernie@worldnet.att.net
Wants Edison, RCA, Victor, and Columbia tabletop phonographs; also phonograph related advertising, trade cards, displays, needle tins, record dusters, puzzles, fans, pins, buttons, badges, mirrors, etc.

Steven Ramm
420 Fitzwater St.
Philadelphia, PA 19147-3109
ph: 610-922-7050 or 610-545-3290
steveramm@aol.com
Specializes in phonographs and pre-1930 records; wants to buy sheet music, postcards, and advertising with illustrations of phonographs, records, or Thomas A. Edison; also wants cylinder rolls in playable condition.

David Giovannoni
ph: 301-869-1501
fax: 301-987-2511
dgio-inquiries@ara.net
http://www.aranet.com/phono/main.htm
Advanced collector of certain phonographs and records from 1890s through 1920s; also looking for old photographs with phonographs in them, especially of people listening to phonographs that have horns.

John Greenstreet
1409 Cherry St.
Baltimore, MD 21226-1230
ph: 410-355-4437
fax: 410-354-2039
jgreenst@bcpl.net

Stuart Stein
P.O. Box 303
Frederick, MD 21705-0303
ph: 301-663-8369
fax: 301-663-8202
steincpa@ix.netcom.com
Wants disc type wind up phonographs with horns.

Leon Snyder
507 Liberty Ln.
New Prague, MN 56071
ph: 612-758-4622

Mike Ellingson
1412 2nd Ave. S.
Fargo, ND 58103-1612
ph: 701-280-1413
mikellingson@webtv.net
http://members.ebay.com/aboutme/phonomike
Has most phonographs he needs for

his personal collection, but is willing to help you determine what your phonograph is worth; will try to answer any antique phonograph question 10:00 a.m. to 10:00 p.m. CST M-F.

Loran T. Hughes
2883 Ross Lane
Central Point, OR 97502
ph: 541-732-0126
loran@www.oldcrank.com
http://www.oldcrank.com
Collector of pre-1930 wind-up phonographs; also want to buy early phonograph literature, especially instruction manuals.

Dealers

Rob Lomas
Edison Shop, The
rob@edisonshop.com
http://www.edisonshop.com

Howard Embleton
Vintage Talking Machines
P.O. Box 77262
Sussex, NJ 07461
ph: 973-786-7955 or 973-875-9227
vsphonos@nac.net
http://www.vintagetalkingmachines.com
Buys, sells, repairs windup phonographs: Edison, Victor, Columbia and others wanted for sale; parts available for most phonographs; also buys and sells cylinders, 78 records, and related memorabilia; work guaranteed; free estimates.

Bruce & Charlotte Mager
Waves
251 W. 30th St.
New York, NY 10001
ph: 212-273-9616
c1wave@aol.com
http://www.wavesradio.com
Over 20 years experience specializing in vintage radios, phonographs, telegraphy, televisions, assorted electrical and mechanical apparatus, and related advertising memorabilia, books and pamphlets.

John T. Johnston
John T. Johnston's Jukebox Classics & Vintage Slot Machines, Inc.
6742 Fifth Ave.
Brooklyn, NY 11220-5418
ph: 718-833-8455
fax: 718-833-0560
Buys, sells, rents, trades and repairs slot and jukeboxes; wants to buy old jukeboxes, slot machines, vending, arcade, old gambling items, neons, cash registers, music boxes, phonographs, syrup dispensers.

Allen Koenigsberg
502 E. 17th St.
Brooklyn, NY 11226-6606
ph: 718-941-6835
AllenAmet@aol.com
http://www.PhonoBooks.com
Author of the "Patent History of the Phonograph."

Dennis Valente
Antique Phonograph Supply Co.
P.O. Box 123
Rt. 23
Davenport Center, NY 13751
ph: 607-278-6218
fax: 607-278-5136
apsco@antiquephono.com
http://www.antiquephono.com
Buys, collects, sells, specializes and appraises phonographs; carries a comprehensive line of restoration parts, services, and books for the restoration of turn-of-the-century mechanical, wind up talking machines and phonographs.

Tim Fabrizio
Terra Firma Antiques
P.O. Box 10307
Rochester, NY 14610-0307
ph: 585-244-5546
fax: 585-244-7601
phonophan@aol.com
http://www.phonophan.com
Buys and sells talking machines, mechanical music, records and related books and ephemera; also sells phonograph parts and supplies.

Greg & Jane Rush
Rush's Talking Machines
591 Getz Rd.
Pen Argyl, PA 18072
ph: 610-759-5919 or 610-759-6000
fax: 610-759-9790
rush12griz@fast.net
Buys, sells, repairs antique phonographs.

Peter S. Liebert
Nipperhead Antique Phonographs
peter@nipperhead.com
http://www.nipperhead.com
Buying and selling phonographs; Web site serves the phonograph community by offering information pertaining to antique phonographs, gramophones, Victor, Edison, Columbia, Nipper.

Joel Straley
Rose & Gracey's Antiques
5806 South First St.
Arlington, VA 22204
ph: 703-998-6208
info@TalkingMachines.com
http://www.TalkingMachines.com
Specializes in restored pre-1929 spring-driven phonographs and talking machines; in business since 1986.

Doug Negus
Phonograph Phanatic
215 Mason St.
Sutherland, IA 51058-7606
ph: 712-446-2270
Music boxes, phonographs, cylinder records, pianos, NO piano rolls, older mechanical musical instruments, pre-1930; any parts or repairables wanted.

Robin & Joan Rolfs
Audio Antique LLC
W6273 Cedar Cliff Dr.
Hortonville, WI 54944
nipper@dataex.com
http://www.audioantique.com
Specializes in the repair, restoration, sale of vintage phonographs & gramophones including Edison, Columbia, Victor talking machines; features Edison, Victor, Nipper and talking doll collectibles; also expert papier-mâché restorations.

Shawn Borri
North American Phonograph Company
26594, 2600N Ave.
La Moille, IL 61330-9801
ph: 815-638-2243
fax: 815-638-2243
northamericanphonograph@yahoo.com
http://www.waxcylinders.com
Expert knowledge on early hand-cranked phonographs, Victrolas, and other talking machines; author of "The Antique Phonograph Corner;" also offers repair and restoration services as well as appraisals; also makes wax cylinders.

Rick Wilkins
Olden Year Musical Museum
P.O. Box 381951
Duncanville, TX 75138
ph: 972-298-5587 or 214-213-4056
museum1@airmail.net
Buys, sells, repairs and appraises all types of windup automated musical machines including Victrolas, Gramophones, music boxes, grind organs, etc.

Yesterday Once Again
P.O. Box 6773
Huntington Beach, CA 92615-6773
ph: 714-963-2474
fax: 714-963-1558
yesterdayonceagain@yahoo.com
http://www.yesterdayonceagain.net
Equipped to supply almost any part necessary to restore the old handcranked phonographs; also sells accessories such as steel phonograph needles, paper record sleeves, books, instruction manual reprints, and related items.

Experts

Aaron Cramer
2056 E. 28th St.
Brooklyn, NY 11229
ph: 718-332-3330
aaronalva@aol.com
Has written columns about phonographs, or talking machines; discovered and owns "The World's Oldest Playable Recording" which is presently on long term loan to the National Watch & Clock Collectors Museum; will offer advice.

John P. Andolina, Jr.
Early Sound Man, The
28 Glen Oaks Dr.
Rochester, NY 14624-1405
ph: 716-247-3056
Over 24 years experience in the collecting, repair, and research of crank type phonographs and related items; buys, sells, collects, repairs; also supplies original and reproduction parts and related items; Edison reproducers in stock.

Ken Danckaert
231 Kennedy Ct.
Severna Park, MD 21146-3039
ph: 410-544-0260
kend@lemur.org
Collects, buys, sells, appraises, and restores music boxes and hand-crank phonographs; in business since 1972; an expert who gives lectures, presentations and videos.

Howard Hazelcorn
6731 Ashley Ct.
Sarasota, FL 34241-9696
ph: 941-921-1815
mrpropane@aol.com
Collector and author of "Collectors Guide to Columbia Spring-Wound Cylinder Phonographs," and "Hazelcorn's Guide to the Columbia Cylinder Graphophone" (1999).

Robin & Joan Rolfs
Audio Antique LLC
W6273 Cedar Cliff Dr.
Hortonville, WI 54944
nipper@dataex.com
http://www.audioantique.com
Specializes in the repair, restoration, sale of vintage phonographs & gramophones including Edison, Columbia, Victor talking machines; authors of phonograph articles, as well as "Phonograph Dolls That Talk and Sing."

Randy & Larry Donley
Donley's Wild West Town & Museum
8512 S. Union Rd.
Union, IL 60180-9661
ph: 815-923-9000
fax: 815-923-2253
mdonley@dls.net
http://www.wildwesttown.com
Experts in antique phonographs; buys, sells, collects and repairs.

Shawn Borri
North American Phonograph Company
26594, 2600N Ave.
La Moille, IL 61330-9801
ph: 815-638-2243
fax: 815-638-2243
northamericanphonograph@yahoo.com
http://www.waxcylinders.com
Expert knowledge on early hand-cranked phonographs, Victrolas, and other talking machines; author of "The Antique Phonograph Corner;" also offers repair and restoration services as well as appraisals; also makes wax cylinders.

Steve Oliphant
5255 Allott Ave.
Van Nuys, CA 91401-5902
ph: 818-789-2339 or 818-865-1400
fax: 818-865-1450
jlo55@aol.com
Adviser and dealer of old phonographs; buys entire collections or individual pieces.

Internet Resources

Peter S. Liebert
Nipperhead Antique Phonographs
peter@nipperhead.com
http://www.nipperhead.com
Serving the phonograph community for over 50 years; a premiere Web site for information pertaining to antique phonographs, gramophones, Victor, Edison, Columbia, Nipper; repair instructions, resource listings, online catalogs, more.

Steve Adams
RadioGallery.com
P.O. Box 90
Moody, AL 35004
ph: 205-640-2701
fax: 205-640-2701
radios@RadioGallery.com
http://www.radiogallery.com
RadioGallery.com features classified ads with color photos of antique and collectible radios, phonographs, and other radio-related items for sale; free wanted and "help" ads; free notices of radio club events.

Rick Salsman
Antique Phonograph Gallery Online
2645 San Pablo Ave.
Berkeley, CA 94702
inky@emf.net
http://www.inkyfingers.com/Record.html
Web site has several personal collections of antique phonographs and related items; also an index of machines by category.

Tim Gracyk
9180 Joy Lane
Granite Bay, CA 95746-9682
tgracyk@garlic.com
http://www.garlic.com/~tgracyk
Great resource Web site phonographs and phonograph records/cylinders.

Loran T. Hughes
2883 Ross Lane
Central Point, OR 97502
ph: 541-732-0126
loran@www.oldcrank.com
http://www.oldcrank.com
Great list of phonograph links: organizations and museums, publications and history, newsgroups and mailing lists, dealers in phonograph ephemera, parts, sales & service, recordings, turntables, and other phonograph related sites.

Museums/Libraries

Edison National Historic Site
Main St. at Lakeside Ave.
West Orange, NJ 07052
ph: 973-736-0550
fax: 973-736-8496
EDIS_Webmaster@nps.gov
http://www.nps.gov/edis/home.htm
A museum with exhibits in all fields of Edison's contributions.

Madeline Dunn
Johnson Victrola Museum
c/o Delaware State Visitor's Center
406 Federal St., Box 1401
Dover, DE 19903
ph: 302-739-4266
fax: 302-739-3943
jistewart@state.de.us
http://www.destatemuseums.org/jvm
Museum is a tribute to Eldridge Reeves Johnson, inventor and businessman who founded the Victor Talking Machine Company; extensive collection of talking machines, Victrolas, "Nipper," early recordings, equipment, Johnson memorabilia.

Randy & Larry Donley
Donley's Wild West Town & Museum
8512 S. Union Rd.
Union, IL 60180-9661
ph: 815-923-9000
fax: 815-923-2253
mdonley@dls.net
http://www.wildwesttown.com
Large exhibit of Edison phonographs, cylinder and disc music machines, and other music memorabilia.

Periodicals

Newsletter: Jerry's Musical Newsletter
4624 West Woodland Rd.
Minneapolis, MN 55424-1553
ph: 612-926-7775
fax: 612-926-7775
jerryclare@aol.com
Focuses on phonograph toys, memorabilia, needle tins, books, etc.

Repair Services

Randle Pomeroy
54 12th St.
Providence, RI 02906-2925
ph: 401-272-5560
Specializes in repairing, cleaning and restoring old phonographs.

Victrola
206 Cliff St.
Saint Johnsbury, VT 05819
ph: 800-239-4188
victrola@together.net
http://www.angelfire.com/vt/victrola
Victrola sales and repair.

Rod Lauman
Victrola Repair Service
206 Cliff St.
Saint Johnsbury, VT 05819-1002
ph: 802-748-4893 or 800-239-4188
victrola@together.net
http://homepages.together.net/~victrola
Repairs Victrolas and wind-up phonographs; repairs done via U.P.S.;

mainsprings, parts, needles also available; call between 10 a.m. and 10 p.m. EST.

Howard Embleton
Vintage Sounds & Antiques
P.O. Box 77262
Sussex, NJ 07461
ph: 973-786-7955 or 973-875-9227
vsphonos@nac.net
http://www.vintagetalkingmachines.com
Buys, sells, repairs windup phonographs: Edison, Victor, Columbia and others wanted for sale; parts available for most phonographs; also buys and sells cylinders, 78 records, and related memorabilia; work guaranteed; free estimates.

Floyd Silver
Antique Phonograph Center
P.O. Box 2574
Vincentown, NJ 08088-2574
ph: 609-859-8617
fsi5491160@aol.com
Antique phonograph sales and service; complete restorations of Edison, Victor and Columbia phonographs.

Dennis Valente
Antique Phonograph Supply Co.
P.O. Box 123
Rt. 23
Davenport Center, NY 13751
ph: 607-278-6218
fax: 607-278-5136
apsco@antiquephono.com
http://www.antiquephono.com
Buys, collects, sells, specializes and appraises phonographs; carries a comprehensive line of restoration parts, services, and books for the restoration of turn-of-the-century mechanical, wind up talking machines and phonographs.

John P. Andolina, Jr.
Early Sound Man, The
28 Glen Oaks Dr.
Rochester, NY 14624-1405
ph: 716-247-3056
Wants to buy outside horn phonographs, Edison, Victor, Columbia, others; records, brown wax cylinders, Berliner, Vogue picture discs, concert cylinders, need tins, record dusters, "Nipper;" also does repairs and adjustments.

Andy Witkowski
Old Crank, An
oldcrank@adelphia.net
http://users.adelphia.net/~oldcrank
Specialty is in collecting and repairing and restoring old phonographs, reed organs, and other mechanical musical machines.

David Adamitis
Antique Musical Machines
RR #5, Box 5295
Moscow, PA 18444
ph: 570-689-7263
fax: 570-689-3703
davediane@ezaccess.net
http://www.antiqnet.com/
 antiquemusicalmachines
Sells, services, restores music boxes, phonographs, band organs, nickelodeons, violanos, barrel pianos, orchestrions, jukeboxes; anything that plays music automatically.

Bill Hodges
Nipper & His Masters Voice Forever
2507 Mike Padgett Hwy.
Augusta, GA 30906
ph: 803-279-9309 or 706-793-6363
fax: 706-793-5253
bhhodges@aol.com
Buys, sells, repairs, supplies parts for old phonographs; collects Nipper related items.

Emerson E. Whitacre
Mechanical Music Man
7550 President Court
Dayton, OH 45414-3671
ph: 937-898-6044 or 937-898-0865
Repairs, adjusts and cleans disc music boxes, cylinder music boxes, antique phonographs, etc.

George Vollema
Great Lakes Antique Phonograph
5092 Muskego Dr.
Newaygo, MI 49337
ph: 231-652-5753
fax: 231-652-5753
victrola@triton.net
http://www.victroladoctor.com
Offers parts and repairs for most wind-up phonographs and Victrolas; all makes and models; over 20 years experience; also sells needles, cranks, reproducers, springs, tonearms, motors, etc.; wants to buy parts and nonworking machines.

Dan Reed
P.O. Box 169
Victorville, CA 92393
ph: 760-242-5748
Repairs hand-wound phonographs, Gramophones, and Victrolas.

Dwayne Wyatt
Wyatt's Musical Americana
P.O. Box 601
Lakeport, CA 95453-0601
ph: 707-263-5013
fax: 707-263-8823
http://www.wyattsmusical.com
Carries large supply of antique phonographs parts & accessories; also specializes in the repair and restoration of all types of windup phonographs; send $4 for 64-page catalog listing over 1,500 parts.

Repro. Sources

Shawn Borri
North American Phonograph Company
26594, 2600N Ave.
La Moille, IL 61330-9801
ph: 815-638-2243
fax: 815-638-2243
northamericanphonograph@yahoo.com
http://www.waxcylinders.com
Manufacturers "new" two-minute brown wax cylinder records and recording blanks for the old Edison Phonograph or Columbia Graphophone; all records are made of authentic metallic soap compound like all original "wax" cylinders.

Suppliers

Jerry Papovich
53 Magnolia Ave.
Pitman, NJ 08071
ph: 609-582-8279
Supplies needles and other parts for old phonographs.

Dennis Valente
Antique Phonograph Supply Co.
P.O. Box 123
Rt. 23
Davenport Center, NY 13751
ph: 607-278-6218
fax: 607-278-5136
apsco@antiquephono.com
http://www.antiquephono.com
Buys, collects, sells, specializes and appraises phonographs; carries a comprehensive line of restoration parts, services, and books for the restoration of turn-of-the-century mechanical, wind up talking machines and phonographs.

Shawn Borri
North American Phonograph Company
26594, 2600N Ave.
La Moille, IL 61330-9801
ph: 815-638-2243
fax: 815-638-2243
northamericanphonograph@yahoo.com
http://www.waxcylinders.com
Only maker of wax cylinders in the US - a slow process so be patient when ordering; each must be made by hand and cannot be rushed; also offers seminars on Talking Machine collecting, Thomas A. Edison and the history of sound recording.

Needle Tins
Dealers

Ruth Lambert
Needle Tins
U.K.
ruthlambert@needletins.co.uk
http://www.needletins.co.uk
Buys, sells, collects gramophone tins worldwide including from Britain, Canada, America, Germany, France, Switzerland, Japan and the Czech Republic.

Nipper
Collectors

Bernie Seinberg
1548 Bristol Pk.
c/o AFY
Bensalem, PA 19020
ph: 215-886-6124
fax: 215-638-2265
phonoman-bernie@worldnet.att.net
Wants any pre-1950s items picturing the RCA dog, Nipper.

Bill Hodges
Nipper & His Masters Voice Forever
2507 Mike Padgett Hwy.
Augusta, GA 30906
ph: 803-279-9309 or 706-793-6363
fax: 706-793-5253
bhhodges@aol.com
Buys, sells, repairs, supplies parts for old phonographs; collects Nipper related items.

Dealers

Yesterday Once Again
P.O. Box 6773
Huntington Beach, CA 92615-6773
ph: 714-963-2474
fax: 714-963-1558
yesterdayonceagain@yahoo.com
http://www.yesterdayonceagain.net
Largest selection of "Nipper" available: dogs, accessories, books, and more.

Internet Resources

Allen Koenigsberg
502 E. 17th St.
Brooklyn, NY 11226-6606
ph: 718-941-6835
AllenAmet@aol.com
http://www.PhonoBooks.com
Online information about Nipper and the story of "His Master's Voice."

PHOTOGRAPHICA

(see 3-D PHOTOGRAPHICA; CAMERAS & CAMERA EQUIPMENT; OPTICAL ITEMS; PHOTOGRAPHS; PHOTOGRAPHY; STANHOPES; STEREO VIEWERS & STEREOVIEWS)

PHOTOGRAPHS

(see also 3-D PHOTOGRAPHICA; AUDIO-VISUAL; CAMERAS & CAMERA EQUIPMENT; MILITARIA; MOVIE MEMORABILIA; PHOTOGRAPHY; REPAIR/ RESTORATION/CONSERVATION, Archival Supplies For; REPAIR/ RESTORATION/CONSERVATION, Paper Items; STEREO VIEWERS & STEREOVIEWS)

Appraisers

Larry Gottheim
BE-HOLD, Inc.
78 Rockland Ave.
Yonkers, NY 10705
ph: 914-423-5806
fax: 914-423-5802
behold@be-hold.com
http://www.be-hold.com
*Specializes in appraising vintage
photographs, daguerreotypes, tintypes,
stereo views; entire collections as well
as important single items, especially
rare and unique items with little
published record of sales.*

Pamela Leeds
Pamela Leeds Fine Art
P.O. Box 1339
Topanga, CA 90290
ph: 310-455-4227
fax: 310-455-4227
ArtProPL@earthlink.net
*27 years experience in art advising/
consulting, forming and curating
collections for private and corporate
collectors, and planning and executing
customized art tours for groups and
individuals.*

Julia Nelson-Gal
826 Alvarado
San Francisco, CA 94114-3116
ph: 415-641-8004
fax: 415-641-8053
*Specialist in appraisals of 19th and
20th century photographs and
photographic literature; will
authenticate and broker sales.*

Karen Kemball, ISA
Kemball Appraisals, Art Consultant &
Researcher
5735 DuDemainie, Apr. 302
Montreal, Quebec H4J 1P3 Canada
ph: 514-332-3840 or 305-613-7329
kemball.appraisals@aya.yale.edu
*Specializes in the appraisal of
photographs and fine art.*

David Peckman
U.K.
dpeckman@btinternet.com
*Specializes in the appraisal of
European and American art, primarily
works on paper including prints,
photography, drawings, and
watercolors from the 20th and 21st
centuries.*

Auction Services

Caroline Birenbaum
Swann Galleries, Inc.
104 E. 25th St.
New York, NY 10010-2977
ph: 212-254-4710
fax: 212-979-1017
swann@swanngalleries.com
http://www.swanngalleries.com
*Oldest/largest US auctioneer
specializing in rare books, autographs
& manuscripts, maps, atlases,
photographs, and works of art on
paper including vintage posters.*

Christie's
20 Rockefeller Plaza
New York, NY 10020
ph: 212-636-2000
info@christies.com
http://www.christies.com

Denise Bethel
Sotheby's
1334 York Ave.
New York, NY 10021
ph: 212-606-7000
fax: 212-606-7107
http://www.sothebys.com

Larry Gottheim
BE-HOLD, Inc.
78 Rockland Ave.
Yonkers, NY 10705
ph: 914-423-5806
fax: 914-423-5802
behold@be-hold.com
http://www.be-hold.com
*Conducts mail-bid auctions of vintage
photographs, daguerreotypes, tintypes,
stereo views, especially of historic and
aesthetic importance; well illustrated
informative catalogs $50 for 3 issues
plus auction results.*

Bonhams & Butterfields
220 San Bruno Ave.
San Francisco, CA 94103
ph: 415-861-7500 or 800-223-2854
fax: 415-861-8951
info.US@butterfields.com
http://www.butterfields.com
*Auctioneers and appraisers of
antiques, fine art and collectibles in
all categories; specialty sales include
posters, toys, decorative arts,
furniture, photography, etc.; the
largest full service auction in the
West.*

John Saddy
Jefferson Stereoptics
50 Foxborough Grove
London, Ontario N6K 4A8 Canada
ph: 519-641-4431
fax: 519-641-2899
john.saddy.3d@sympatico.ca
http://www3.sympatico.ca/
john.saddy.3d/home.htm
*Wants photography from early
daguerreotypes to View-Master
including antique stereo cards, cartes
des visites, cabinet cards, cased
images; specializes in consignments,
but will also buy outright.*

Clubs/Associations

Prof. Andrew Davidhazy, Webmaster
Photographic Historical Society, Inc.,
The
Newsletter: PHS Newsletter
P.O. Box 39563
Rochester, NY 14604
ph: 585-475-2592
fax: 585-475-7750
tphs@rochester.rr.com
http://www.tphs.org
*For those with an interest in the
history of photography; conducts
monthly meetings and a tri-annual
symposium.*

Association of International Photography
Art Dealers
1609 Connecticut Ave. NW #200
Washington, DC 20009-1034
ph: 202-986-0105
fax: 202-986-0448
ewingal@aol.com
http://www.photoshow.com
*Dedicated to creating and maintaining
high standards in the business of
exhibiting, buying, selling photographs as art.*

Michigan Photographic Historical
Society
Newsletter: Photogram, The
P.O. Box 2278
Birmingham, MI 48012-2278
ph: 313-882-1113 or 245-549-6026
pmotz@worldnet.att.net

Marv B. Chait, Pres.
Chicago Photographic Collectors Society
Newsletter: CPCS Bulletin
P.O. Box 1979
Evanston, IL 60204-1979
ph: 847-223-4348
info@chicagophotographic.org
http://www.chicagophotographic.org
*A non-profit organization since 1971;
over 200 US and foreign members;
sponsors two trade shows a year in
the Chicago area; "CPCS Bulletin" is
published monthly; also publishes the
journal "By Daylight" periodically.*

Tom Kowach
Historic Camera Collectors Club
ph: 310-645-3767
tomko@earthlink.net
http://www.historiccamera.com/
club.html
*An international club bringing
together camera collectors, photograph collectors, and photography
historians via the Internet; club
provides various information and Web
site resources; share collections,
information, answer questions.*

Michael Pritchard, Editor
Photographic Collectors Club of Great
Britain
Magazine: Photographica World
5 Buntingford Rd.
Puckeridge
Ware, SG11 1RT U.K.
ph: (0044) (0)929 821611
info@pccgb.org
http://www.pccgb.org
*Club aims to promote the study and
collection of photographic equipment
and images by publications, meetings,
auctions and shows; covers cameras,
lenses, photographers, optical toys,
stereoscopes, magic lanterns, and
related areas.*

Collectors

Norman D. Leckert
P.O. Box 363
Bethel, VT 05032-0363
ph: 802-234-5657 or 800-717-2021
fax: 802-234-6104
*Wants to buy old photographs and
daguerreotypes; especially wants
photos by E.S. Curtis (Curtis).*

Andy Rudoff
P.O. Box 111
Oceanport, NJ 07757-0111
ph: 732-542-3712
fax: 732-542-3712
shoreguy@comcast.net
*Wants pre-1940 photographs of
commercial interiors such as cigar
and drug stores, billiard parlors,
gambling establishments, soda
fountains, etc.*

Thomas Harris
223 E. Fourth St., Apt. #14
New York, NY 10009
ph: 212-420-9121
Saltprint@mindspring.com
http://www.EarlyPhotographs.com
*Serious buyer of and dealer in early
early photographs: Daguerreotypes,
salt prints, CDVs, tintypes, photo
albums, etc.; Abraham Lincoln, Civil
War, Black history, Indians and The
West, historic and unusual images of
all kinds.*

George Sullivan
330 East 33rd St.
New York, NY 10016-9466
ph: 212-689-9745
gjsbooks@aol.com
*Wants to buy cased images by Mathew
Brady.*

Karl L. Jannen
106 Bishops Rd.
Smithtown, NY 11787-1427
ph: 516-265-3654
*Wants to buy early photographs
showing humor or suggesting an
amusing caption; nothing sensational
expected—any smile-provoker
qualifies; will pay up to $25 per; send
photocopy first, please; will reply
promptly.*

Nicholas M. Graver
276 Brooklawn Dr.
Rochester, NY 14618-2923
ph: 585-244-4818
ngraver@rochester.rr.com
*Buys early and unusual daguerreo-
types, stereo views, cartes de visites,
early Kodak (round) photos, Civil
War photos, family albums,
photographers at work, ambrotypes,
tintypes; speech & hearing (19th c.
deaf & dumb) related.*

Ron Coddington
2233 N. Quantico St.
Arlington, VA 22205
ph: 703-532-3358
Collector of early historic photo-

graphs, 1840 to 1920; specializes in Civil War CDVs.

Gary Ronk
6247 Cove Rd.
Roanoke, VA 24019-1715
ph: 540-562-2368
papermemo@aol.com
Wants to buy CDVs of soldiers, animals, buildings, outdoor; tax stamped or any unusual is preferred.

Randy Beach
313 Julia St.
New Smyrna Beach, FL 32168
ph: 904-427-7444
Wants to buy daguerreotypes, ambrotypes, tintypes, postmortems, animals.

David L. Hartline
P.O. Box 775
Columbus, OH 43085-0775
fax: 614-760-5427
Wants Western photographs, Annie Oakley, Buffalo Bill, Indian, etc.; also images of Black soldiers, military forts and regiments; will answer all letters.

Betty Davis
5291 Ravenna Rd.
Newton Falls, OH 44444
ph: 330-872-0318 or 330-719-2735
noahsattic44444@yahoo.com
Collector of early photographic images including dags, tintypes and photo albums.

Betty Davis
5291 Ravenna Rd.
Newton Falls, OH 44444-9440
ph: 330-872-0318 or 330-872-0386
Collector wants interesting, unusual images (cased, tin, paper, etc.); also buys old (pre-1930) scrapbooks and albums.

Bill Becker
P.O. Box 7076
Huntington Woods, MI 48070
Seeking attractive photographs of all types that have interesting historical content; daguerreotypes, early glass stereo views, French tissue (hold-to-light) stereos with hidden balloons, ships, trains; Indians, Shakers, etc.

Dave Gorski
21045 N. 124th Ave.
Sun City West, AZ 85375
ph: 623-975-4061
fax: 623-975-4061
davegorski@yahoo.com
http://www.davegorski.com
Wants old photographic images and the cameras that took them; any image either large or very small on tintypes, ambrotypes, daguerreotypes, and old stereo cards; Indians, street scenes, animals, nudes, vehicles.

Jeff Mark
JMARK
P.O. Box 5178
Santa Monica, CA 90409-5178
ph: 800-644-8537
classicfilms@htmail.com
Wants old photographs from 1850-1900; prefers from Old America: cowboys, Indians, miners, slaves, occupationals (fireman, police, etc.), baseball, sports; especially wants larger, autographed, old photos.

Mike Aversa, ISA
Aversa Estate & Appraisal Service
P.O. Box 863
Yorba Linda, CA 92885
ph: 717-777-3848 or 714-749-3887
AversaAntiques@mindspring.com
http://www.aversaantiques.com
Buys, sells all types of photographs including daguerreotypes, ambrotypes, tintypes, stereo views, cabinet photos, CDVs, and all antique and vintage photographs.

Don Hoffman
P.O. Box 4231
Salinas, CA 93912-4231
ph: 831-449-7311
Wants old photographs, images, prints, stereoviews, CDVs, cabinet cards, calotypes, daguerreotypes, ambrotypes, negatives about sports, boxing, jazz, blues, minstrel, vaudeville, general Americana subjects; please describe and price.

David Wallach
P.O. Box 150285
San Rafael, CA 94915-0285
ph: 415-777-0123 or 415-883-7121
fax: 415-284-5364
vcsrs@aol.com
Wants to buy photographs, images, antique daguerreotypes, ambrotypes, tintypes; interested in military, Indian, armed civilians, nudes.

Dealers

Mack Lee
Lee Gallery
9 Mount Vernon St.
Winchester, MA 01890-2703
ph: 781-729-7445
fax: 781-729-4592
info@leegallery.com
http://www.leegallery.com
Buys, sells, and appraises fine 19th and 20th century photographs and daguerreotypes.

Sharon Lacasse
Sharon Lacasse Antiques
1424 Osterville - W. Barnstable Rd.
West Barnstable, MA 02668
ph: 508-428-0562
slacasse@capecod.net
http://www.capecod.net/wnutting
Buying and selling pictures, books, furniture and all memorabilia relating to Wallace Nutting; also interested in all other hand-colored photographs by any photographer.

David L. Spahr
Maine Antique Photographica Gallery
51 High Holborn St.
Gardiner, ME 04345
ph: 207-582-0402
dspahr3d@stereoviews.com
http://www.stereoviews.com
19th and 20th century photograph specialist focusing on stereoviews.

David & Becky Beane
Beane's Antiques & Photography
92 River Rd.
Benton, ME 04901
ph: 207-453-6790
fax: 207-453-6790
Actively buying early photography including but not limited to daguerreotypes, ambrotypes, tintypes, and all related forms of photographica.

Thomas Harris
EarlyPhotographs.com
223 E. Fourth St., Apt. #14
New York, NY 10009
ph: 212-420-9121
Saltprint@mindspring.com
http://www.EarlyPhotographs.com
Serious buyer of and dealer in early early photographs: Daguerreotypes, salt prints, CDVs, tintypes, photo albums, etc.; Abraham Lincoln, Civil War, Black history, Indians and The West, historic and unusual images of all kinds.

George D. Glazer
28 East 72nd St., 3rd Flor
New York, NY 10021
ph: 212-535-5706
fax: 212-658-9512
worldglobe@georgeglazer.com
http://www.georgeglazer.com
Buys and sells vintage photographs, mostly photojournalist, of popular subjects such as skiing, golf, landscapes and views, fashion, Grand Tour views of Italy.

Larry Gottheim
BE-HOLD, Inc.
78 Rockland Ave.
Yonkers, NY 10705
ph: 914-423-5806
fax: 914-423-5802
behold@be-hold.com
http://www.be-hold.com
Buys and sells by appointment and mail; specializes in vintage photographs, daguerreotypes, tintypes, stereo views, especially of historic and aesthetic importance; publishes well illustrated informative catalog, $50 for 3 issues.

Larry Berke
28 Marksman Ln.
Levittown, NY 11756-5110
ph: 516-796-7280
lhbke@optonline.net
Buys and sells photographs (daguerreotypes, stereoviews, tintypes, CDVs, cards) and 19th or 20th photos and unusual century cameras.

Joseph F. Loccisano
Historic Photographs & Paper Americana
2264 Nicholson Square Dr.
Lancaster, PA 17601-3966
ph: 717-560-5182
always_buying@yahoo.com
http://www.always-buying.com
Wants to buy good pre-1910 American photographs; original photographs of American storefronts, occupationals, mercantile views especially those showing trade signs, commercial interiors, factory close-ups; also images of cast iron toys.

Bruce Lancaster
P.O. Box 151541
Chevy Chase, MD 20825
fax: 301-718-1875

Kevin M. Lynn
Americana & Collectibles
3097 Crown Circle
Manchester, MD 21102
ph: 410-239-4491
klynn3097@aol.com
http://www.historicregister.com
A specialist in 19th century photography including daguerreotypes, tintypes, cabinet cards, etc.

Ronald & Kathy Fritz
Fritz Antiques
P.O. Box 575
Zephyrhills, FL 33539
ph: 813-788-2312
fritzantiques@earthlink.net
http://www.fritzantiques.com
Buys and sells vintage photographs: daguerreotypes, ambrotypes, ferrotypes, tintypes, Carte-de-Visites, CDVs, cabinet cards, stereoviews, real photograph postcards.

Ivan Gilbert, MD
Miran Art & Books
2824 Elm Ave.
Columbus, OH 43209
ph: 614-231-3707 or 614-818-3222
fax: 614-818-3223
IGilbert@ahhinc.com

Tom Molocea
Historic Images
P.O. Box 100
North Lima, OH 44452-0100
ph: 330-549-3245 or 330-629-1864
Buys photos of all categories and all formats; single images to entire collections.

Don Leone
Remains to be Seen
608 W. Main
Collinsville, IL 62234
ph: 618-344-6927
info@remainstobeseen.com
http://www.remainstobeseen.com
Purveyor of photographs and photograph cases.

Jennifer Moss
Photografique
11901 Santa Monica Blvd., #644
Los Angeles, CA 90025
ph: 310-442-0976
photo@jennifermoss.com
http://www.photografique.com
Antique and collectible photographs for sale and reprint; specializes in images from the 1840s through 1940s.

Norman Kulkin
Pixidiom
727 N. Fuller Ave.
Los Angeles, CA 90046-7504
ph: 323-653-6929
fax: 323-651-0640
pixidiom@aol.com
http://www.pixidiom.com
Buy, sell, trade vintage photographs: ambrotypes, tintypes, stereoviews, specialty is daguerreotypes; also early 19th century paper photos, early 20th century photos; also photographica including cameras.

Anthony Davis
Rainbow Creations
P.O. Box 8935
Universal City, CA 91618-8935
ph: 818-762-3540
fax: 818-762-2503
antiqphoto@earthlink.net
http://www.19cphoto.com
Collector/dealer wants images of all subjects particularly early flat mounts, stereo daguerreotypes, autochromes (early color photography), ambrotypes, albumen, CDVs, platinum prints; all subjects; will buy entire collections.

Jeffrey Fraenkel
Fraenkel Gallery
49 Geary St.
San Francisco, CA 94108
ph: 415-981-2661
fax: 415-981-4014
mail@fraenkelgallery.com
http://www.fraenkelgallery.com
With co-owner Frish Brandt specializes in 19th and 20th century photography.

Richard C. Frey, ISA
R.T.L.H. Enterprises
1275 East Ave.
Chico, CA 95926-1020
ph: 530-343-4528 or 800-567-7854
fax: 530-343-9380
RFREYRTLH@aol.com
http://www.richardcfreyfineart.com
Wants to buy 19th and 20th century photographs; prefers American Indian, art subjects, Oriental, and albums.

Tim McIntyre
Tim McIntyre's Antique Photographs
525 Nicola St., #908
Kamloops, British Columbia V2C 6J5
   Canada
ph: 250-374-6610
timoni@orc.ca
http://www.timoni.net
Buys and sells 19th and early 20th century photographs, especially

stereoviews, CDVs, cabinet cards, ambrotypes, tintypes, daguerreotypes and larger formats.

John Saddy
Jefferson Stereoptics
50 Foxborough Grove
London, Ontario N6K 4A8 Canada
ph: 519-641-4431
fax: 519-641-2899
john.saddy.3d@sympatico.ca
http://www3.sympatico.ca/
   john.saddy.3d/home.htm
Wants photography from early daguerreotypes to View-Master including antique stereo cards, cartes des visites, cabinet cards, cased images; specializes in consignments, but will also buy outright.

Experts

Marv B. Chait
P.O. Box 1979
Evanston, IL 60204-1979
ph: 847-853-8521
Marv5555@aol.com

Anthony Davis
Rainbow Creations
P.O. Box 8935
Universal City, CA 91618-8935
ph: 818-762-3540
fax: 818-762-2503
antiqphoto@earthlink.net
http://www.19cphoto.com
Collector/dealer wants images of all subjects particularly early flat mounts, stereo daguerreotypes, autochromes (early color photography), ambrotypes, albumen, CDVs, platinum prints; all subjects; will buy entire collections.

Julia Nelson-Gal
826 Alvarado
San Francisco, CA 94114-3116
ph: 415-641-8004
fax: 415-641-8053
Specialist in appraisals of 19th and 20th century photographs and photographic literature; will authenticate and broker sales.

David Rudd
Cycleback: Publishers & Collectors
   Services
P.O. Box 16311
Seattle, WA 98116
ph: 206-923-0367
drudd@cycleback.com
http://www.cycleback.com
One of the leading authorities on baseball memorabilia, early prints & photographs; author of numerous books on these subjects; is a forensic art examiner; teaches online courses in print & photograph authentication and forgery detection.

Internet Resources

Claudio Vanin
Fotobibliografica
24 Bye Side Rd. R.R. 2
Goulais River, Ontario P0S 1E0 Canada
ph: 705-649-0087
books@fotobibliografica.com
http://www.fotobibliografica.com
An Internet resource for collectors of fine photography monographs: works on and by Ansel Adams, Richard Avedon, Man Ray, Ray Metzker, Alfred Stieglitz, etc.; buys and sells similar works; links to related artist Web sites.

Misc. Services

Library of Congress, Prints &
   Photographs Reading Room
Library of Congress
James Madison Bldg., Rm LM-339
Washington, DC 20540-4730
ph: 202-707-6394 or 202-707-8000
http://www.lcweb.loc.gov/rr/print
Has a collection of over 13,000,000 images: prints, photographs, drawings, posters, and architectural and engineering drawings.

National Portrait Gallery, Catalog of
   American Portraits
Photo Dept.
750 9th St. NW
Washington, DC 20560
ph: 202-275-1738
fax: 202-275-1887
npgweb@npg.si.edu
http://www.npg.si.edu/inf/cap.htm
Will examine photographs brought in for inspection; make an appointment first; may be able to work from good photos of the items; no monetary values given.

Gordon's Art Reference, Inc.
Price Guide: Gordon's Photography
   Price Annual
306 West Coronado Rd.
Phoenix, AZ 85003-1147
ph: 602-253-6948 or 800-892-4622
   (orders)
fax: 602-253-2104
office@gordonsart.com
http://www.gordonsart.com
Comprehensive listing of over 14,000 worldwide auction results from 2002 organized by photographer and title: covers condition, negative and print dates, notes if signed, dated or annotated; also on CD-ROM or online with 150,000 entries.

Periodicals

Charles Stuart Lane, Ed.
Newspaper: Journal of the Print World
P.O. Box 978
Meredith, NH 03253-0978
ph: 603-279-6479
fax: 603-279-1337
sophia@cyberportal.net
http://www.journaloftheprintworld.com
A quarterly newspaper with articles, advertising and classifieds focusing on antique and contemporary works of

art on paper, photographs, prints and artists; features articles, ads, auction results, show reviews, calendar of events.

Journal: Art On Paper
39 E. 78th St., #501
New York, NY 10021-0213
ph: 212-988-5959
fax: 212-988-6107
info@artonpaper.com
http://www.artonpaper.com
Published bi-monthly, this journal reports on the entire print and photograph market and is considered a must by print collectors and dealers; also contains scholarly articles and reviews, and auction results.

Stephen Perloff, Ed.
Newsletter: Photograph Collector, The
140 East Richardson Ave., Ste. 301
Langhorne, PA 19047-2829
ph: 215-891-0214
fax: 215-891-9358
info@photoreview.org
http://www.photoreview.org
For photograph collectors, dealers and curators; also publishes "The Photographic Art Market," an annual compilation of auction prices.

Repair Services

Northeast Document Conservation Center
100 Brickstone Square
Andover, MA 01810-1494
ph: 978-470-1010
fax: 978-475-6021
nedcc@nedcc.org
http://www.nedcc.org
Paper conservation, preservation microfilming, photographic duplication, photograph conservation, book conservation, disaster assistance.

David Mishkin
Just Black & White
P.O. Box 4628
54 York Ave.
Portland, ME 04112
ph: 800-827-5881
photos@maine.com
http://www.maine.com/photos
Specializes in photographic copies, enhancements from faded originals and restorations; can lighten dark tintypes or provide sepia toning; can provide archival (lasts 100 years+) negatives or prints; in business for over 15 years.

Maria Pukownik
Fine Art & Paper Conservation
1045 Orrtanna Rd.
Orrtanna, PA 17353-9691
ph: 717-337-0668
conspuk@yahoo.com
Surface cleaning, mending tears and creases, removal/replacing of decayed backing board, B/W photographic copies of restored original.

Dick Doeren
Lumber Mill Gallery Framery
107 Smith Ave.
Oconto, WI 54153
ph: 920-834-4494 or 877-889-1085
fax: 920-834-4494
lumbermillgallery@msn.com
Antique frame, photograph, and document restoration and preservation; old world craftsmanship; members of The Society of Guilders.

Thomas E. Seal
DigiMatrix
1234 Court St.
Medford, OR 97501
ph: 541-734-2225
fax: 541-734-2476
Specializing in photo restoration, large format printing, art reproduction, scanning.

Suppliers

John A. Dunphy
University Products, Inc.
517 Main St.
P.O. Box 101
Holyoke, MA 01041-0101
ph: 413-532-3372 or 800-336-4847
fax: 800-532-9281
jadunphy@universityproducts.com
http://www.universityproducts.com
Carries safe products for the long term storage of postcards, posters, stamps, documents, photographs, textiles, costumes; acid-free archival supplies, and materials for conservation and preservation; send for free catalog.

Ansel Adams

Dealers

Edward Carter Galleries Ltd.
560 Broadway, 4th Floor
New York, NY 10012
ph: 212-966-1933
fax: 212-966-2145
contact@edwardcartergalleries.com
http://www.edwardcartergalleries.com
Offers the world's largest available inventory of Ansel Adams' work.

Michael Spencer
Ansel Adams Gallery, The
685 Cannery Row, #113
Monterey, CA 93940
ph: 831-375-7215
monterey@anseladams.com
http://www.anseladams.com
Buys and sells Ansel Adams photographs; studios in Yosemite and in Monterey, CA.

Glenn Crosby
Ansel Adams Gallery, The
Village Mall
Yosemite National Park, CA 95389
ph: 800-568-7398 or 209-372-4413
glenn@anseladams.com
http://www.anseladams.com
Buys and sells Ansel Adams photographs; studios in Yosemite and in Monterey, CA.

Cases

Dealers

Gene Groves
P.O. Box 2471
Baton Rouge, LA 70821-2471
ph: 225-387-3221 or 225-927-2795
fax: 225-346-8049
gene@tpbp.com
Buys, sells and collects early photo cases 1840-1865; big size, mother-of-pearl, tortoise, patriotic, signed, wall frames, Union, Mascher, etc.

Celebrity

(see also AUTOGRAPHS, Celebrity; MOVIE MEMORABILIA; TELEVISION SHOWS & MEMORABILIA)

Collectors

James Carlson, #73536
Arizona State Prison - Florence
P.O. Box 8400 - South Unit
Florence, AZ 85232-8400
Inmate collects autographed photographs; accepts donations of autographed photos only (no money); writes to stars and celebrities to obtain autographs; member of UACC; seeks penpals with similar interests.

Dealers

Scott Johnson
Celebrity Locators
P.O. Box 12
North Whitefield, ME 04353
ph: 207-832-6687
fax: 207-832-0546
Scott@CelebrityLocators.com
http://www.CelebrityLocators.com
Specialist in putting fans in contact with celebrities; carries a variety of celebrity-related products; publisher of "The Big Book of Celebrity Addresses," and "The Autograph Collecting News" (a free email newsletter).

Doug Wirth
Hummerdude's
P.O. Box 4348
Dunellen, NJ 08812-4348
ph: 732-424-9367
fax: 732-424-1619
sales@hummerdudes.com
http://www.hummerdudes.com
Celebrity photos, autographs and collectibles.

Movie Star News
134 West 18th St.
New York, NY 10011
ph: 212-620-8160
fax: 212-727-0634
info@moviestarnews.com
http://www.moviestarnews.com
Carries large variety of movie photos: rarest movie or the latest star.

Arbe Bareis
Safka & Bareis Autographs
P.O. Box 886
Forest Hills, NY 11375
ph: 718-263-2276
fax: 718-263-2276
safkabareis@yahoo.com
http://www.safka-bareis.com
Buys and sells signed and unsigned photographs in all categories, specializing in performing arts (film, opera, composers, musicians); free catalogs issued.

Robert M. Ready
Movie & TV Star Photos & Books
1410 Oak Tree Dr.
Houston, TX 77055-4316
Sells over 2,000 b&w and color 8" x 10" celebrity photographs from 1930s to present including Westerns, movie, TV stars; celebrity books are also available; catalog $5 (refundable); wholesale available to dealers.

Mike Gould
Hollywood Legends Gallery
6621A Hollywood Blvd.
Los Angeles, CA 90028
ph: 323-962-7411
fax: 323-962-6742
hwdbookcity@earthlink.net
http://www.hollywoodbookcity.com
Specializes in signed photographs of contemporary movie stars; also autographs of television stars.

Book City Collectables
6631 Hollywood Blvd.
Hollywood, CA 90028
ph: 323-466-0120
fax: 323-962-6742
hwdbookcity@earthlink.net
http://www.hollywoodbookcity.com
Sells autographed celebrity photos, movie and TV scripts, and other Hollywood memorabilia.

Hollywood Book City Collectables
6627 Hollywood Blvd.
Los Angeles, CA 90028
ph: 323-466-2525 or 800-4CINEMA
fax: 323-962-6742
hwdbookcity@earthlink.net
Buys and sells books, autographed celebrity pictures, movie and television scripts, and other movie memorabilia.

S. & P. Parker's Movie Market
P.O. Box 3900
Dana Point, CA 92629-8900
ph: 949-488-8444
fax: 949-488-8445
webmaster@moviemarket.com
http://www.moviemarket.com
Over 50,000 celebrity photographs to choose from.

Michelle Brown
Timeless Autographs
U.K.
fax: 01765 658040
autographs@timeless-collectables.com
http://www.timeless-collectables.com
Online catalog of autographed photographs from the world of

movies, music, animation and more; member of UACC.

Civil War

Collectors

Ron Coddington
2233 N. Quantico St.
Arlington, VA 22205
ph: 703-532-3358
Collector of early historic photographs, 1840 to 1920; specializes in Civil War CDVs.

Dealers

Scott Vezeau
Scottiques
446 Dixie Bee Rd.
Clarksville, TN 37043
ph: 931-358-3097
scottiques1@msn.com

Internet Resources

Civil War Photographs, Library of Congress
101 Independence Ave. SE
Washington, DC 20540
ph: 202-707-8000
ndlpcoll@loc.gov
http://memory.loc.gov/ammem/cwphome.html
Contains 1,118 photographs, most by Mathew Brady, including scenes of military personnel, preparations for battle, battle aftereffects; also includes portraits of both Confederate and Union officers, and a selection of enlisted men.

Daguerreotypes

Clubs/Associations

Mark Johnson, Pres.
Daguerreian Society, The
Newsletter: Daguerreian Society Newsletter
3045 W. Liberty Ave., Rear
Pittsburgh, PA 15216-2460
ph: 412-343-5525
fax: 412-563-5972
DagSocPgh@aol.com
http://www.daguerre.org
An organization dedicated to the history, art and science of the world's first form of photography - the daguerreotype; over 1,300 members worldwide; also publishes an annual journal in addition to the bi-monthly newsletter.

Collectors

Harold E. Boyer
2200 Clayton Rd.
Beaver Falls, PA 15010-1306
ph: 724-843-4774
Wants to buy Daguerreotype photos of very well-dressed ladies and men; experienced in identification research; also desires 1840-70 jewelry with portrait photos, especially of women and men who are important looking.

Paul R. Lafavore
2131 6th St., NW
Hickory, NC 28601-1703
ph: 828-323-8221
lafavore@twave.net
Collecting quality daguerreotype images of any subject, especially maker-marked Maine images; also collecting Daguerreian ephemera and broadsides.

John McWilliams
P.O. Box 3655
Los Altos, CA 94024
ph: 650-949-2615
jmcwilliam@aol.com
Long time collector of daguerreotypes and early photographs of the American West; wants images of armed civilians, Texans, California Gold Rush; especially wants images showing large brimmed hats, buckskins, pistols, and knives.

Dealers

Mack Lee
Lee Gallery
9 Mount Vernon St.
Winchester, MA 01890-2703
ph: 781-729-7445
fax: 781-729-4592
info@leegallery.com
http://www.leegallery.com
Buys, sells, and appraises fine 19th and 20th century photographs and daguerreotypes.

Dennis Waters
Dennis A. Waters, Fine Daguerreotypes
P.O. Box 1073
Exeter, NH 03833-1073
ph: 603-772-9065
finedags@attbi.com
http://www.finedags.com
Buys and sells daguerreotypes, thermoplastic cases, and related material.

Mark Koenigsberg
Daguerreotypes: 19th Century
  Photography
ph: 201-863-0868
dagmark@alum.mit.edu
http://www.geocities.com/~daguerreotype
Always interested in purchasing large or small collections of daguerreotypes.

Bryan W. Ginns
2109 Cty. Rte. 21
Valatie, NY 12184-6001
ph: 518-392-5805
fax: 518-392-7925
the3dman@aol.com
Wants large collections of stereo views, old cameras, daguerreotypes, magic lanterns, optical toys; anything relating to photographics.

Gene Groves
P.O. Box 2471
Baton Rouge, LA 70821-2471
ph: 225-387-3221 or 225-927-2795
fax: 225-346-8049
gene@tpbp.com
Buys, sells, repairs and collects

quality daguerreotypes: outdoors, occupationals, military, blacks, Louisiana, animals, signed, toys, large groups, etc.

Janos Novomeszky
8744 Castle View Ave.
Las Vegas, NV 89128-7680
ph: 702-228-3454
Wants to buy fine daguerreotypes and pre-1880 photographic equipment; single pieces or entire collections.

Norman Kulkin
Pixidiom
727 N. Fuller Ave.
Los Angeles, CA 90046-7504
ph: 323-653-6929
fax: 323-651-0640
pixidiom@aol.com
http://www.pixidiom.com
Buy, sell, trade vintage photographs: ambrotypes, tintypes, stereoviews, specialty is daguerreotypes; also early 19th century paper photos, early 20th century photos; also photographica including cameras.

Anthony Davis
Rainbow Creations
P.O. Box 8935
Universal City, CA 91618-8935
ph: 818-762-3540
fax: 818-762-2503
antiqphoto@earthlink.net
http://www.19cphoto.com
Collector/dealer specializing in daguerreotypes of outdoor scenes, military, occupationals; also hand-tinted portraits, stereo daguerreotypes all categories; wants single items or entire collections.

Experts

Anthony Davis
Rainbow Creations
P.O. Box 8935
Universal City, CA 91618-8935
ph: 818-762-3540
fax: 818-762-2503
antiqphoto@earthlink.net
http://www.19cphoto.com
Collector/dealer specializing in daguerreotypes of outdoor scenes, military, occupationals; also hand-tinted portraits, stereo daguerreotypes all categories; wants single items or entire collections.

Internet Resources

Mark Koenigsberg
Daguerreotypes: 19th Century
  Photography
ph: 201-863-0868
dagmark@alum.mit.edu
http://www.geocities.com/~daguerreotype
Learn about daguerreotypes at this site; email or call for information or an offer on any daguerreotypes you have.

Daguerreotype Collection, Library of
  Congress
101 Independence Ave. SE
Washington, DC 20540
ph: 202-707-8000
ndlpcoll@loc.gov
http://memory.loc.gov/ammem/daghtml/
  daghome.html
The collection consists of more than 650 photographs dating from 1839 to 1864 including portrait daguerreotypes and early architectural views.

Repair Services

Gene Groves
P.O. Box 2471
Baton Rouge, LA 70821-2471
ph: 225-387-3221 or 225-927-2795
fax: 225-346-8049
gene@tpbp.com
Professionally repairs daguerreotypes; replaces old and damaging glass which deteriorates with new safe glass.

Mathew Brady

Internet Resources

Mathew Brady's Portraits, National
  Portrait Gallery, Smithsonian
  Institution
750 Ninth St., Ste. 8300
Washington, DC 20560-0973
ph: 202-2785-1738
fax: 202-275-1887
npgweb@npg.si.edu
http://www.npg.si.edu/exh/brady
Web site contains Mathew Brady's National Portrait Gallery, carte de visite album, making a photograph, Brady's biography, a technical glossary, index of Brady's sitters, links to publications and programs.

Military

Dealers

Will Gorges
Battleground Antiques, Inc.
3910 US Highway 70 East
New Bern, NC 28560
ph: 252-636-3039 or 252-636-5445
fax: 252-637-1862
rebel@civilwarantiques.com
http://www.civilwarshop.com
Full time dealer buys, sells, collects and appraises authentic Civil War artifacts: firearms, accouterments, edged weapons, dug items, documents, uniforms, coins, etc.; catalog available.

Misc. Services

National Archives & Records Administration, Still Picture Branch
8601 Adelphi Rd.
College Park, MD 20740-6001
ph: 301-713-6660 or 866-272-6272
fax: 301-837-0483
http://www.archives.gov
Photos of movie stars in uniform while serving their country can be purchased.

Real War Photos
P.O. Box 728
Hammond, IN 46325-0728
ph: 219-931-3359
fax: 219-931-3359
realwarphotos@yahoo.com
Combat photographs taken by combat photographers can be obtained; catalogs available of Army, Navy, Marines, USAF, Civil War, Korea, WWII, WWI, Korea, ship histories, 1,000s of photos available; send $3 for catalog.

Periodicals

Phil Katcher
Magazine: Military Images
P.O. Box 2391
Southeastern, PA 19399
ph: 610-644-6337
milimage@yahoo.com
http://www.civilwar-photos.com
Focuses on military images from 1839 to 1900; six issues per year; since 1979.

Travel

Collectors

Scott A. Swanson
50 Gloucester St.
Boston, MA 02115-3141
ph: 617-536-8013
speer707@aol.com
Wants to buy travel photographs from all countries, especially Italy, Hawaii, West Indies, Middle East, Egypt, India, Asia; photos showing people, cities, landscapes.

PHOTOGRAPHY

(see also 3-D PHOTOGRAPHICA;
CAMERAS & CAMERA EQUIPMENT;
PHOTOGRAPHS; STEREO
VIEWERS & STEREOVIEWS)

Book Sellers

Joe Newcome-Beill
Abstract Eye Books
1517 Vivian Lane
Louisville, KY 40205
abstracteyebooks@cox.net
http://www.abstracteyebooks.com
Buys and sells used and rare photography books, maps, and prints.

Clubs/Associations

Adrian LeVesque
Photographic Historical Society of New
  England, Inc.
Journal: New England Journal of
  Photographic History
P.O. Box 65189
Newton, MA 02165-0189
ph: 617-731-6603 or 617-277-0207
fax: 617-277-7878
copley@ultranet.com
http://www.ultranet.com/~copley/
  PHSNE
800 member non-profit society; 60-page journal.

Gerald Fine
American Photographic Historical
   Society, Inc.
Magazine: Photographica
1150 Avenue of the Americas
New York, NY 10036
ph: 212-575-0483 or 732-617-3142
fax: 732-617-1360
   *International organization with
   educational meetings six times each
   year in NYC; conducts two fairs for
   the selling of antique cameras,
   equipment & photos; publishes
   "Photographica" quarterly and a
   monthly newsletter, "In Focus."*

Prof. Andrew Davidhazy, Webmaster
Photographic Historical Society, Inc.,
   The
Newsletter: TPHS Newsletter
P.O. Box 39563
Rochester, NY 14604
ph: 585-475-2592
fax: 585-475-7750
tphs@rochester.rr.com
http://www.tphs.org
   *For those with an interest in the
   history of photography; conducts
   monthly meetings and a tri-annual
   symposium.*

Photographic Society of America
3000 United Founders Blvd., Ste. 103
Oklahoma City, OK 73112-3940
ph: 405-843-1437
fax: 405-843-1438
hq@psa-photo.org
http://psa-photo.org/index.html

William P. Carroll
Western Photographic Collectors
   Association, Inc.
Magazine: Photographist, The
8500 La Entrada
Whittier, CA 90605
ph: 562-693-8421
fax: 562-945-6011
acrbooks@concentric.net
http://webtch/com/ACRbooks
   *Non-profit organization dedicated to
   the dissemination of information on,
   and to stimulate interest in, all
   aspects of photographica.*

Photographic Historical Society of
   Canada
Magazine: Photographic Canadiana
P.O. Box 54620
Toronto, Ontario M5M 4N5 Canada
ph: 416-736-2100
fax: 416-736-5838
phsc@phsc.ca
http://www.phsc.ca
   *Collectors and historians interested in
   the apparatus, processes, images, and
   history of photography; photographica
   fairs held in March and October;
   auction in April/March.*

Dealers

Jeremy Rowe
Jeremy Rowe Vintage Photography
P.O. Box 40577
Mesa, AZ 85275-0577
ph: 480-965-8622 or 480-820-5493
fax: 480-965-8698
jrowe@vintagephoto.com
http://www.vintagephoto.com
   *Appraiser, dealer in better 19th and
   early 20th century photographs and
   ephemera; serious researcher and
   collector of pre-1920 Arizona and
   Southwestern photographs and related
   material; photos, cased images,
   cabinet cards, albums, etc.*

Experts

Jeremy Rowe
Jeremy Rowe Vintage Photography
P.O. Box 40577
Mesa, AZ 85275-0577
ph: 480-965-8622 or 480-820-5493
fax: 480-965-8698
jrowe@vintagephoto.com
http://www.vintagephoto.com
   *Appraiser, dealer in better 19th and
   early 20th century photographs and
   ephemera; serious researcher and
   collector of pre-1920 Arizona and
   Southwestern photographs and related
   material; photos, cased images,
   cabinet cards, albums, etc.*

Internet Resources

Prof. Andrew Davidhazy, Webmaster
PhotoForum
RIT School of Photographic Arts &
   Sciences
Lomb Memorial Dr.
Rochester, NY 14623
ph: 716-475-2592
fax: 716-475-7750
andpph@rit.edu
http://www.rit.edu/~andpph/
   photoforum.html
   *Online educational network
   established to serve the photographic
   and imaging communities in general
   with a medium for exchange of ideas;
   has an accessible databank of
   informational files about a wide
   variety of photo/imaging subjects.*

Misc. Services

David Silver
International Photographic Historical
   Association
Newsletter: INPHO News
P.O. Box 16074
San Francisco, CA 94116-0074
ph: 415-681-4356
silver@well.com
http://www.well.com/user/silver
   *Corresponding research & resource
   center for those interested in studying/
   collecting cameras, photographs, or
   other objects pertaining to the history
   of photography; free appraisals and
   information services; speakers/
   presentation bureau.*

Museums/Libraries

International Center of Photography
1114 Avenue of the Americas at 43rd St.
New York, NY 10036
ph: 212-860-1776
fax: 212-722-3674
education@icp.org
http://www.icp.org

George Eastman House International
   Museum of Photography & Film
900 East Ave.
Rochester, NY 14607
ph: 716-271-3361
fax: 716-271-3970
tbannon@geh.org
http://www.eastman.org
   *The museum includes the restored
   house and garden of George Eastman
   (1854-1932), founder of Eastman
   Kodak Co., and displays the art,
   technology, and impact of photography and motion pictures over 150
   years.*

Bill Becker
American Museum of Photography
P.O. Box 7076
Huntington Woods, MI 48070
images@photographymuseum.com
http://www.photographymuseum.com
   *A very well done virtual museum based
   on a 75,000 piece collection of images
   from the first 75 years of photography: photos, museum bookstore, early
   photographic processes, links to
   related sites, protecting & preserving
   photos.*

National Museum of Photography, Film
   & Television
U.K.
ph: 01274 203305
talk.nmpft@nmsi.ac.uk
http://www.nmsi.ac.uk/nmpft
   *A popular British museum; collections
   contain exciting galleries outlining the
   past, present and future imaging
   technology.*

Periodicals

Taylor & Francis Ltd.
Magazine: History of Photography
Rankine Rd.
Basingstoke, Hants RG24 8PR U.K.
ph: +44(0) 1256 813000
fax: +44(0) 1256 479438
beverley.acreman@tandf.co.uk
http://www.tandf.co.uk/joournals/tf/
   03087298.html
   *An international publication devoted
   exclusively to the history and criticism
   of the photograph; covers photography
   from the earliest times to the present
   day; published quarterly.*

Suppliers

Dick Haviland
Film for Classics
P.O. Box 486
Honeoye Falls, NY 14472
ph: 716-624-4945
fax: 716-624-5651
joan@filmforclassics.com
http://www.filmforclassics.com
   *Provides film for collectors/users of
   classic and antique cameras all over
   the world.*

PIANO ROLLS

(see also MUSICAL INSTRUMENTS,
Pianos [Player])

Auction Services

Paul & Cindy Johnson
Piano Roll Shop, The
28 Prospect Hill
Burlington, VT 05401
ph: 802-660-8041
pianorol@globalnetisp.net
   *Holds periodic auctions of player
   piano rolls and nickelodeon rolls; also
   produces new rolls of the best in
   ragtime and jazz as well as rolls for
   reproducing pianos.*

QRS Music Rolls, Inc.
1026 Niagara St.
Buffalo, NY 14213-2099
ph: 716-885-4600
fax: 716-885-7510
bobb@qrsinc.com
http://www.qrsmusic.com
   *Offers bi-monthly auctions by mail of
   original antique 88-note and
   reproducing player piano rolls; buys
   collections of old rolls, but does not
   accept consignments.*

Collectors

Deno Buralli
P.O. Box 6
Spring Grove, IL 60081
ph: 815-675-2305
tgc@threadgageco.com
   *Reproducing rolls and standard 88-
   note rolls.*

Dealers

John Tuttle
John Tuttle "Self-Playing Pianos"
407 19th Ave.
Brick, NJ 08724
ph: 732-840-8787
john@player-care.com
http://www.player-care.com
   *Dedicated to player and reproducing
   pianos: service, repair, rebuilding;
   also sells new QRS and Tempola
   music rolls online; lots of technical
   information and information about
   used rolls and roll auctions on Web
   site; lists technicians.*

Sheet Music Center
Box 10
Old Bethpage, NY 11804
ph: 800-527-7626
smctr@sheetmusiccenter.com
http://www.sheetmusiccenter.com
*Buys and sells sheet music and piano
rolls; FREE catalog to readers of
"Maloney's Antiques & Collectibles
Resource Directory."*

Man./Prod./Dist.

L. Douglas Henderson
ARTCRAFT Music Rolls
16 Lee St., Red Brick House
P.O. Box 295
Wiscasset, ME 04578
ph: 207-882-7420
artcraft@wiscasset.net
http://www.wiscasset.net/artcraft
*New music rolls for standard 88 note
player pianos (pianolas), and Duo-Art
and Ampico reproducing pianos.*

QRS Music Rolls, Inc.
1026 Niagara St.
Buffalo, NY 14213-2099
ph: 716-885-4600
fax: 716-885-7510
bobb@qrsinc.com
http://www.qrsmusic.com
*World's oldest manufacturer of player
piano rolls; thousands of songs, old
and new, by famous pianists of past
and present.*

Rob DeLand
BluesTones Music Rolls
485 Gatewood Lane
Grayslake, IL 60030
ph: 847-548-6416
fax: 847-548-8615
rdeland@bluesrolls.com
http://www.bluesrolls.com
*88 note blues, ragtime, jazz plus
Ampico, Duo-Art, Welte, QRS XP and
Nickelodeon A rolls.*

Play-Rite Music Rolls
401 S. Broadway
P.O. Box 1024
Turlock, CA 95380
ph: 209-667-1996 or 800-826-5539
fax: 209-667-8241
*Sells new 10 to 16 tune "O" rolls for
player pianos.*

Paul & Cindy Johnson
Piano Roll Center, The
26390 Big Valley Rd. NE
Poulsbo, WA 98370
ph: 360-697-2422
fax: 360-697-2522
76651.1710@compuserve.com
*Ampico, Duo-Art, Welte and 88 note
ragtime, jazz and blues.*

PIANOS
Miniature
(see also MINIATURES; MUSICAL
INSTRUMENTS, Pianos)

Clubs/Associations

Janice E. Kelsh
Miniature Piano Enthusiast Club
Newsletter: Musically Yours!
633 Pennsylvania Ave.
Hagerstown, MD 21740-3769
ph: 301-797-7675
fax: 301-827-7039
mpec2000@hotmail.com
http://www.angelfire.com/music2/
miniaturepianoclub
*Established in 1990 to promote the
hobby of miniature piano collecting;
annual convention.*

Collectors

Janice E. Kelsh
633 Pennsylvania Ave.
Hagerstown, MD 21740-3769
ph: 301-797-7675
fax: 301-827-7039
mpec2000@hotmail.com
http://www.angelfire.com/music2/
miniaturepianoclub
*Interested in obtaining miniature
pianos of all kinds; also wants old
postcards depicting pianos.*

PICKLE CASTORS
Collectors

Gerald A. Young
15463 McNeill Rd.
Sterling, NY 13156-4212
ph: 315-947-5840 or 315-947-5782
fax: 315-947-6905
ginny@zlink.net
*Wants to buy pickle castors; frames
must have a mark; especially interested
in colored decorated jars or unusual
castors; must be in very good
condition; also seeking Victorian jewel
caskets.*

Dealers

Barbara & Steve Aaronson
Victorian Lady, The
P.O. Box 7522
Northridge, CA 91327
ph: 818-368-6052
bjaaronson@aol.com
http://www.thevictorianlady.com
*Specializes in buying and selling
unusual American Victorian pickle
castors.*

PIE BIRDS
(see also KITCHEN COLLECTIBLES)

Collectors

Jeannie Kolger
6906 Meade Dr.
Colleyville, TX 76034-6416
ph: 817-329-5262
jkolger@gte.net
*Wants to buy unusual old pie birds
and pie vents, particularly Disney
examples, Black Mammys and/or black
chefs.*

Dealers

Deborah Vanden Heuvel
Global Galleria, The
209 Riverwalk Circle
Cary, NC 27511
ph: 888-832-5616 or 919-859-5818
fax: 919-859-6396
*Has a large selection of whimsical
English pie birds; always wants to
buy more to add to inventory; straight
from the English countryside.*

Alan Pedel
Captivating Collectibles
Guineaford
Barnstaple, Devonshire EX31 4EA U.K.
fax: 011-44-1271-322514
sales@piebirds.net
http://www.piebirds.net
*Offers original and authentic British
piebirds direct from the heart of the
English countryside.*

Experts

Lillian Cole
14 Harmony School Rd.
Flemington, NJ 08822-2606
ph: 908-782-3198
*Interested in the older foreign and US
pie birds either in singles or in
collections; avid collector and
historian/researcher.*

Linda & Bobby Fields
158 Bagsby Hill Lane
Dover, TN 37058-6248
ph: 931-232-5099
fpiebird@compu.net
http://www.festivalusa.com/my-piebird
*Buy single birds or entire collections;
have a large selection of traders;
author of "Four & Twenty
Blackbirds," 184 pages, 623 color
photos, identification and value guide,
$33.95 ppd.; available from author.*

Man./Prod./Dist.

Donna Peterson
Donnaware
286 Louth Rd.
Scartho
Grimsby, DN33 2LB U.K.
ph: 01472 591817
enquiries@piebirds.co.uk
http://www.piebirds.co.uk
*Pie bird artist, expert; handmade
ceramic pie birds made in England.*

Periodicals

Patricia Donaldson
Newsletter: Piebirds Unlimited
P.O. Box 192
Acworth, GA 30101-0192
pldonaldson@mindspring.com
http://hometown.aol.com/acworthd/
PiebirdsUnlimited.html
*A quarterly publication printed in
color; a must for any pie bird
collector; send SASE for information.*

PIN-BACK BUTTONS
(see BUTTONS, Pin-Back)

PIN-UP ART
(see also AVIATION MEMORABILIA,
Military [Nose Art]; EROTICA;
PLAYBOY ITEMS)

Collectors

Louis & Susan Meisel
Meisel Gallery
141 Prince St.
New York, NY 10012-5315
ph: 212-677-1340
fax: 212-533-7340
lou@meisels.com
http://www.MeiselGallery.com
*Wants to buy pin-ups: oil paintings,
pastels, watercolors, drawings.*

David Kveragas
1943 Timberlane
Clarks Summit, PA 18411-9539
hiwind2000@aol.com
*Wants Vargas and Olivia illustra-
tions; Vargas prior to his Playboy
work, especially Shadowland mags,
Ziegfeld Follies sheet music. Olivia
items: catalogs, posters, greeting
cards, etc.; offers made; also Rolf
Armstrong items.*

Charles Martignette
P.O. Box 293
Hallandale, FL 33008-0293
ph: 954-454-3474
*Wants pin-up and glamour art;
original paintings.*

Jerry Peters
Chestnut Hollow, Ltd.
6060 Bordman Rd.
P.O. Box 6
Almont, MI 48003-0006
ph: 810-798-3158
jpeters@expression.org
*Collecting pin-up photos, art and
magazines; especially wants Vargas,
Petty, Elvghrenn, Moran, Olivia; also
wants old Playboy magazines and
Bettie Page photos.*

Ed Royse
112 N. Broadway St.
Walters, OK 73572
ph: 580-357-8000
fax: 580-875-2063
edroyse@juno.com
*Wants to buy Varga/Vargas pin-up
art, Esquire calendars, playing cards,
Esky cards, etc.*

Wendy Hoffman
Wendy Hoffman Gallery
P.O. Box 35647
Las Vegas, NV 89133-5647
ph: 702-839-9999
fax: 702-839-9494
wendysart@aol.com
http://www.wendysart.com
*Wants to buy art by illustrators Fox,
Parrish, Gutmann, Humphrey; Esquire
magazines with Vargas gatefolds; pin-
up calendars/prints by Elvgren,
Moran, Mozert and Armstrong;
sporting calendars/prints by Goodwin,
Stick, etc.*

Richard J. Perry
Collectors Press, Inc.
P.O. Box 230986
Portland, OR 97281-0986
ph: 503-684-3030 or 800-423-1848
fax: 503-684-3777
rperry@collectorspress.com
http://www.collectorspress.com
Buyer of illustrated pin-up art and glamour art originals, calendars, prints, and anything with a pin-up or glamour image on it; by artists such as Rolf Armstrong, Earl Moran, Gene Pressler, Gil Elvgren, Maxfield Parrish and others.

Dealers

Robert Bessette
Green Dragon Arts
P.O. Box 588
Burlington, VT 05402-0588
ph: 802-862-1930
fax: 802-862-1930
Buys and sells pin-up art works, calendars, fantasy and pin-up postcards, men's magazines, erotic books and paper books.

Clifford P. Catania
Joshua's Attic
518 Kimberton Rd.
Phoenixville, PA 19460-4737
ph: 610-917-1167
clifford@joshuasattic.com
http://www.davidchasegallery.com
Interested in French and American vintage "cheesecake" and pin-up photography of the 1960s and 1970s.

Experts

Denis C. Jackson, Ed.
P.O. Box 6433
Kingman, AZ 86401
ticn@olypen.com
http://www.olypen.com/ticn
Author of "The Price and Identification Guide to Pin-Ups & Glamour Art," 1996, 2nd edition; send LSASE for information; wants old prints, calendars, mutescope cards.

Internet Resources

Glamourcon
ph: 425-821-1760
glamourcon@aol.com
http://www.glamourcon.com
A marketplace of Pin-Up Art and Glamour from the past, present and future.

Denis C. Jackson, Ed.
E-zine: Illustrator Collector's News, The
P.O. Box 6433
Kingman, AZ 86401
ticn@olypen.com
http://www.olypen.com/ticn
An online publication for collectors of magazines and other paper illustrations; free classifieds and articles, no charge Web site information; new and old prints.

Periodicals

Steve Sullivan
Magazine: Glamour Girls: Then and Now
P.O. Box 34501
Washington, DC 20043-4501
ph: 202-232-2144
steve@ggtan.com
http://www.ggtan.com
Published approximately three times per year; focuses on pin-up art: interviews and features on glamour girls from the 1950s to present in movies, TV, burlesque, and men's magazines.

PINS

(see also BADGES; BUTTONS, Pin-Back; FAST FOOD COLLECTIBLES, McDonald's [Pins]; OLYMPIC GAMES COLLECTIBLES, Pins & Buttons; POLITICAL COLLECTIBLES; SOCIAL CAUSES; TIE BARS, CLIPS & TACKS)

Collectors

Gil & Marjorie Joanis
1329 14 St. East
Saskatoon, Saskatchewan S7H 0A6
Canada
ph: 306-665-9902
Buys, sells, trades metal pins, especially relating to curling (Brier, Scotch Cup, Silver Broom), media (CBC, SRC), figure skating (Worlds and other major events), Olympic Games; send photocopies.

Dealers

Robert M. Levine
#2 Troll Court
Ballwin, MO 63011-4036
ph: 636-394-4370 or 314-518-4872
fax: 636-394-8557
boblevine@hotmail.com
Wants any political item such as presidential campaign items, lapel pins; new or old; single or in quantity.

Bill Nelson
Newsletter: Bill Nelson Newsletter, The
P.O. Box 41630
Tucson, AZ 85717-1630
ph: 520-629-0868 or 800-368-8434
fax: 520-629-0387
sales@pinsbymail.com
http://www.pinsbymail.com
Monthly newsletter with news, tips, and sources for collectors of Olympic, Sport, Disney, Coca Cola pins; over a million pins in inventory; established in 1985.

Internet Resources

MyPins.com
mjm@mypins.com
http://www.mypins.com
The online reference for pin collecting: Olympic, Hard Rock Cafe, Disney, pin manufacturers, lapel pin accessories,
pin clubs, newsgroups, information and history, and much more.

About.com Hobbies
220 East 42nd St.
New York, NY 10017
pr@about-inc.com
http://home.about.com/hobbies
Online source for information about action figures, antiques, book collecting, coin collecting, collectibles, comic books, costume jewelry, dolls, mineral collecting, pin collecting, sports and trading cards, stamps, toy collecting.

Award

Collectors

Bob Lucian
33 Merritts Rd.
Farmingdale, NY 11735-1820
ph: 516-293-3927
bbluc@optonline.net
Wants to buy corporate service pins; pins given to employees reaching 5-10-15-20+ years of service; also other corporate awards: watches, tie pins, cuff links, medals, etc.; prefers national or international companies.

Hard Rock Cafe

Clubs/Associations

Hard Rock Cafe Pin Collectors CLub
vlaferney@attbi.com

Collectors

David Rodriguez
DavidRod.com
P.O. Box 813754
Hollywood, FL 33081-3754
ph: 954-483-5304
david@davidrod.com
http://www.davidrod.com
Hard Rock Cafe pin expert and appraiser also buys, sells, trades, collects Hard Rock Cafe pins.

Dealers

Michael Comer
2986 Kings Highway, Ste. E
Colonial Beach, VA 22443
ph: 804-224-9711
fax: 804-224-9712
http://www.3n.net/midatl/pins
Buys and sells Hard Rock Cafe pins worldwide.

PIONEERS

(see WESTERN AMERICANA)

PIPES

(see also CANES & WALKING STICKS; CHARACTER COLLECTIBLES, Sherlock Holmes; MATCH SAFES; SMOKING COLLECTIBLES; TOBACCO COLLECTIBLES)

Appraisers

Bob Spore
400 Riverside Dr.
Pasadena, MD 21122
ph: 410-437-2715
bobspore@erols.com
Collector seeking pre-smoked briar pipes; sells and appraises pipe collections; member T.U.C.O.P.S., P.C.C.A.

Bill Braddock
Bill's Pipe Repair
2909 SW 52nd Place
Oklahoma City, OK 73119
ph: 405-682-1558
fax: 405-682-1558
Restoration and repair of tobacco pipes; also buys, sells and appraises pipes; handmade pipes made from the highest quality plateau briar.

Clubs/Associations

Sailorman Jack
New York Pipe Club
Newsletter: New York Pipe Club Newsletter
440 East 81, Apt. 1C
New York, NY 10028
ph: 212-288-3832
Club meets on the first Tuesday of each month at 6 pm at Mary's of Madison Restaurant, 24 East 41 St., between 5th Ave. and Madison Ave.

Robert C. Hamlin
Pipe Collectors Club of America
Magazine: Pipe Smokers Pipeline
P.O. Box 5179
Woodbridge, VA 22194-5179
ph: 703-878-7655
fax: 703-878-7657
rch@pipeguy.com
http://www.pipesmoke.com

Bill Unger, Sec/Treas
North American Society of Pipe Collectors
Newsletter: Pipe Collector, The
P.O. Box 9642
Columbus, OH 43209-9642
ph: 614-252-2904
bill@naspc.org
http://www.naspc.org
A club of over 500 members dedicated to all aspects of pipe collecting and smoking; publishes a professional newsletter and produces a Fall swap/sell show in Columbus,s OH.

Dan Spaniola, Treas.
International Association of Pipe Smokers' Clubs
647 S. Saginaw St.
Flint, MI 48502
treasurer@iapsc.net
http://www.iapsc.net
Founded in 1949; holds annual pipe smoking contest and convention.

Michael Reschke
Chicagoland Pipe Collectors Club
540 South Westmore
Lombard, IL 60148-3028
ph: 630-889-0453
info@chicagopipeshow.com
http://www.chicagopipeshow.com
A local group of pipe collectors and smokers who gather once a month for an informal meeting and evening of fellowship; members have a common interest in pipes, cigars, and tobacciana.

P.C. Wiseman, Sec./Treas.
Pipe Club of London, The
Journal: Journal of the Pipe Club of
    London, The
40 Crescent Dr.
Petts Wood
Orpington, Kent BR5 1BD U.K.
ph: 0168 983 7761
webmaster@pcol.co.uk
http://www.pcol.co.uk
Premier pipe club in Great Britain; international in scope with over 500 members in 33 countries; promotes and protects the interests of pipe smokers; 12 meetings a year; free 26-page bi-annual Journal to all members; founded in 1970.

Collectors

Charles H. Strom
100 Bleecker St.
New York, NY 10012-2205
ph: 212-998-8480
charlie.strom@nyu.edu
Wants to buy ornately carved, top quality antique meerschaum pipes and cheroot holders.

Lee Pattison
P.O. Box 60
Cuba, NY 14727-0060
ph: 716-933-8112
Wants antique meerschaum pipes carved and plain, briar pipes of more recent manufacture brand names: Charatan, Barling, Dunhill, Sasieni, Stanwell, Larson, Savinelli and others; also wants to buy tobacco jars and cigar store items.

Gary L. Donachy
801 W. Sunset
Steeleville, IL 62288-1015
ph: 618-965-3189
Wants to buy antique meerschaum and high grade briar pipes; also wants tobacco-related books, trade cards, and advertising.

E.S. Radcliffe
3732 Colonial Lane SE
Port Orchard, WA 98366-1846
ph: 206-876-8615
Wants to buy cigar holders, cigarette holders, carved and ornamental pipes, meerschaum clay pipes.

Dealers

Bob Spore
400 Riverside Dr.
Pasadena, MD 21122
ph: 410-437-2715
bobspore@erols.com
Collector seeking pre-smoked briar pipes; sells and appraises pipe collections; member T.U.C.O.P.S., P.C.C.A.

Chuck Haley
Sherlock's
13926 Double Girth Ct.
Matthews, NC 28105-4068
ph: 704-847-5480
mirepoix2@aol.com
Specializing in estate pipes and related smoking accessories.

Don Duco
Pijpenkabinet & Smokiana
Prinsengracht 488
1017 KH Amsterdam
The Netherlands
ph: +(31) 020 42 11 779
info@pijpenkabinet.nl
http://www.pipeshop.nl
Best assorted pipe shop in Western Europe with over 2,000 modern briar, hundreds of meerschaums and clay; antique pipes and tobacco collectibles; also modern and antique books on pipes and tobacco.

Terry Josh
Antique Pipe Company
19 Challacombe
Southend on Sea, SS1 3TY U.K.
ph: +44 (0) 01702 585018
antiquepipeco@yahoo.com
http://www.antiquepipes.co.uk
Specialist dealer in antique smoking pipes including Meerschaum and oriental items.

Experts

Benjamin Rapaport
Antiquarian Tobacciana
Newsletter: Antiquarian Tobacciana
    Newsletter
11505 Turnbridge Ln.
Reston, VA 20194-1220
ph: 703-435-8133
fax: 703-435-3852
benrapaport@earthlink.net
Wants antique meerschaum, opium, porcelain, Meissen, chinoiserie, Wedgwood, metal, cloisonne, champleve, early wood, etc. pipes.

James Kesterson
3881 Fulton Grove Rd.
Cincinnati, OH 45245-2504
ph: 513-752-0949
Wants smoked or new briar pipes: brands like Barling, Caminetto, Charatan, Comoy, Dunhill, GBD, Larsen, Sasieni, Savinelli, etc.

Don Duco
Pijpenkabinet
Prinsengracht 488
1017 KH Amsterdam, The Netherlands
ph: +(31) 020 42 11 779
info@pijpenkabinet.nl
http://www.pijpenkabinet.nl
World renowned expert on the history of smoking and pipes; author of specialist books, giving expertise on pipes from archaeological sources, advising publishers and film makers on historical smoking equipment.

Museums/Libraries

Don Duco
Pijpenkabinet
Prinsengracht 488
1017 KH Amsterdam, The Netherlands
ph: +(31) 020 42 11 779
info@pijpenkabinet.nl
http://www.pijpenkabinet.nl
Exclusive museum covering tobacco smoking from preColumbian times to present day with over 20,000 items; special attention to clay and porcelain, including European, ethnographic and folk art.

Periodicals

SpecComm International, Inc.
Magazine: Pipes & Tobaccos
3000 Highwoods Blvd., Ste. 300
Raleigh, NC 27604-1029
ph: 919-872-5040
fax: 919-876-6531
mprice@pt-magazine.com
http://www.pt-magazine.com
Articles about pipes, tobaccos, famous smokers, collectible pipes.

Repair Services

Bill Braddock
Bill's Pipe Repair
2909 SW 52nd Place
Oklahoma City, OK 73119
ph: 405-682-1558
fax: 405-682-1558
Restoration and repair of tobacco pipes; also buys, sells and appraises pipes; handmade pipes made from the highest quality plateau briar.

Clay

Clubs/Associations

Susanne Atkin, Ed.
Society for Clay Pipe Research
30 Ongrils Close
Pershore, Worcestshire WR10 1QE U.K.
susatkin@aol.com
http://www.scpr.fsnet.co.uk
Formed in the U.K. in 1984 with the aim to further enhance the study of clay tobacco pipes and their makers.

Collectors

Paul Jung
P.O. Box 817
Bel Air, MD 21014-0817
ph: 410-638-1475
sjung93156@aol.com
Buys and collects clay pipes; researches the clay tobacco pipe

industry in the US, Canada, and Europe; especially wants clay pipes marked France or Paris, or with name of an American or Canadian city; has published books on smoking pipes.

Meerschaum

Collectors

Bernard Berlly
24 School House Ln.
Great Neck, NY 11020-1323
ph: 516-829-2777
fax: 516-829-2779
Wants antique carved meerschaum pipes.

Dealers

Jerry Korn
Lighters Galore Plus
P.O. Box 534
San Marcos, CA 92079
ph: 800-853-3941 or 760-734-1414
fax: 760-744-6666
info@pipeshop.com
http://www.pipeshop.com
Collector, dealer, appraiser, expert specializes in collectible Zippo lighters and handcarved Meerschaum pipes; also carries many other hard-to-find smoking accessories.

Pipe Cleaners

Collectors

Paul Scheuer
6753 Humbolt Ave.
Minneapolis, MN 55430-1533
ph: 763-561-7321
Collects old pipe cleaner containers; also Roll-Your-Own cigarette paper packets and related memorabilia.

PIRATES

(see NAUTICAL ANTIQUES)

PISTOLS

(see FIREARMS; TOY GUNS)

PIXIES

(see CERAMICS, Pixieware; GNOMES; ELVES)

PLANNING ITEMS

(see also ARCHITECTURE & RELATED ITEMS; STATE RELATED MEMORABILIA; MAPS & CHARTS)

Dealers

Gloria Munsell
Allenwood Americana Antiques
P.O. Box 116
Allenwood, PA 17810-0116
ph: 570-538-1440 or 570-538-1932
fax: 570-538-1932
kwkipp@ptd.net
Buys and sells city/town/regional planning items; early to current:

plans, maps, books, memorabilia of US community planners.

PLANTERS PEANUTS ITEMS

Clubs/Associations

John Paglialunga
Peanut Pals
Newsletter: Peanut Papers
P.O. Box 652
Saint Clairsville, OH 43950-0652
ph: 740-695-4286
sas-photo@juno.com
http://www.peanutpals.org
Focuses on Planters Peanuts and Mr. Peanut history and memorabilia; national and regional conventions, newsletter, classified ads for members only.

Collectors

Richard Reddock
914 Isle Ct.
Bellmore, NY 11710-1545
ph: 516-826-2032 or 800-223-PNUT
pnutfanclb@aol.com
Wants to buy all types of Mr. Peanut tin displays, signs, paper items, ceramic oil and vinegar, metal letter openers.

Joyce Spontak
804 Hickory Grade Rd.
Bridgeville, PA 15017
ph: 412-221-7599
Has over 2,000 Planters items in her collection.

Mike & Fran Nolan
1228 Oakdale Dr.
Sanatoga, PA 19464
ph: 610-718-9774
HyTyde3@aol.com
http://members.aol.com/fran247
Avid collectors of Planters Mr. Peanut items from the early 1900s to present; lots of rare and unusual items; club info available; Web site has a For Sale/Trade page.

Dealers

Joe Iozzia
Chameleon Collectibles
P.O. Box 1005
Pomona, NJ 08240-1005
ph: 609-652-8504
pinflyers@aol.com
http://members.aol.com/Pinflyers
Selling vintage Planters Mr. Peanut advertising items.

Judy Posner
Judy Posner Collectibles
P.O. Box 2194
Englewood, FL 34295
ph: 941-475-1725
fax: 941-475-2645
judyandjef@yahoo.com
http://www.judyposner.com
Buying, selling collecting for over 25 years.

Experts

Arleane Pawlowicz
5 Edgewood Rd.
Goshen, NY 10924-2303
ph: 845-294-3475
fax: 845-294-3475
epphoto@frontiernet.net
Long time and avid collector of anything relating to Planters Peanuts.

Marty Blank
P.O. Box 405
Flushing, NY 11365-0405
ph: 516-485-8071
Wants to buy unusual Mr. Peanut items, especially plastic toys, counter displays and older items; listed in "Planter's Peanut Collectibles" (Schiffer).

Judith & Bob Walthall
P.O. Box 4465
Huntsville, AL 35815-4465
ph: 256-881-9198
Serious collectors specializing in Planter Peanut items; founded Peanut Pals in 1978; has done extensive research over the years; has had many articles published.

PLASTIC COLLECTIBLES

(see also BOXES; CELLULOID ITEMS; CHARMS; DINNERWARE, Melmac; DOLLS HOUSES & FURNISHINGS; GEMS & JEWELRY, Bakelite; KITS; LUNCH BOXES; MODELS, Cars; SOLDIERS, Toy; TOYS; TOYS, Playsets; TRAINS, Toy [Plasticville])

Collectors

G. Marshall Naul
209 Glen St.
Chestertown, MD 21620-1417
ph: 410-810-1758
fenolix@dmv.com
Specializes in early 20th century plastics; also in daguerreotype Union Cases.

Dealers

Abby Nash
Malabar Enterprises
172 Bush Lane
Ithaca, NY 14850
ph: 607-255-2905 or 607-266-0690
fax: 607-255-4179
asn6@cornell.edu
Buying and selling 1920-1960 Bakelite and other plastic items.

Alicia & Jorge Valino
P.O. Box 1442
Montevideo, 11000 Uruguay
valino@valino.com
http://www.valino.com
Wants to buy items made of Bakelite.

Experts

Jan Lindenberger
P.O. Box 7224
Colorado Springs, CO 80933
ph: 719-591-9558
fax: 719-591-9558
Buys and sells plastic collectibles; author of "Plastic Collectibles - Information & Price Guide" (Schiffer Pub., Ltd., 1992).

Museums/Libraries

National Plastics Center & Museum
210 Lancaster St.
Leominster, MA 01453
ph: 978-537-9529
fax: 978-537-3220
npcm@plasticsmuseum.org
http://www.plasticsmuseum.org
Follow the history of plastic from Egypt into the Millennium; see exhibits of celluloid toys and turn of the century combs.

PLASTICVILLE

(see TRAINS, Toy [Plasticville])

PLATES

(see COLLECTIBLES [MODERN], Plates)

Dealers

Pat Klein
Nostalgia Unlimited
P.O. Box 262
East Berlin, CT 06023
ph: 860-828-3973
fax: 860-828-1544
pklein262@yahoo.com
Carries college, university, academy and preparatory school plates by such makers as Wedgwood, Spode, Lamberton, Balfour and Staffordshire; send email with wants.

PLATING

(see REPAIR/RESTORATION/ CONSERVATION, Metal Items)

PLATINUM

Dealers

Beth Scott
Affordable Jewelry & Precious Metals
304 SW Washington St.
Portland, OR 97204
ph: 800-690-4995 or 503-224-7520
fax: 503-227-4204
sight@ajpm.com
http://www.ajpm.com
Gold, silver and platinum bullion dealers.

Scrap

Dealers

Michael A. Merrill
Michael A. Merrill, Inc.
Crestar Bank Building
2045 York Rd.
Timonium, MD 21093
ph: 410-453-9400
http://www.michaelmerrill.com
Buying precious metals from the public, dealers since 1974; buys scrap gold, diamonds, old gold, dental gold, school rings, gold & silver numismatic coins, sterling silver (Kirk & Steiff), Franklin Mint, platinum, palladium, exotics.

PLAYBOY ITEMS

(see also EROTICA; MAGAZINES, Men's [Playboy]; PIN-UP ART)

Clubs/Associations

Tom Bonner
Playboy Collectors Association
P.O. Box 653
Phillipsburg, MO 65722-0653

Collectors

Ronnie Keshishian
P.O. Box 2654
Glendale, AZ 85311
ph: 623-435-2665
fax: 707-281-1444
ronniek1@cox.net
http://www.magazinesthatmenlike.com
Wants Playboy memorabilia: early calendars, special editions, puzzles, hand puppets, liquor caddies, feminine statues, rabbit dolls, club items, dinner plates, candles, menus, promo items, anything Playboy except magazines.

Dealers

Kenneth E. Ritchie
P.O. Box 22604
Memphis, TN 38122
admin@kenritchie.com
http://www.playboycollectibles.com
Vintage collectibles from Playboy clubs and casinos including glassware, table tokens, membership keys and fun money, plus other hard-to-find Playboy memorabilia such as puzzles and music.

Autographs

Collectors

David Kveragas
1943 Timberlane
Clarks Summit, PA 18411-9539
hiwind2000@aol.com
Wants Playboy playmate autographs; also autographs of other women who have appeared in the magazine. Items must be on Playboy related pages, covers, etc.; photocopies appreciated; offers made.

PLAYER PIANOS

(see MUSICAL INSTRUMENTS, Mechanical; MUSICAL INSTRUMENTS, Pianos [Player])

PLAYING CARDS

(see also AIRLINE MEMORABILIA, Playing Cards; BRIDGE; CARDS; GAMBLING COLLECTIBLES; PAPER COLLECTIBLES; GAMES, Cards; RAILROAD COLLECTIBLES, Playing Cards)

Clubs/Associations

Association of Game & Puzzle Collectors
Journal: Game & Puzzle Collectors Quarterly
PMB 321
197M Boston Post Rd. West
Marlborough, MA 01752
juckett@attglobal.net
http://www.agpc.org
Members are devoted to collecting, researching, preserving games, jigsaw puzzles, mechanical puzzles, and other pastimes.

Barbara Lunaburg, Trustee
Chicago Playing Card Collectors, Inc.
Newsletter: C.P.P.C. Bulletin
1826 Mallard Lake Dr.
Marietta, GA 30068-1644
ph: 770-992-7478
cpccink@aol.com
http://www.cpccinc.org
Purpose of the club is to encourage and promote the hobby of playing card collecting and to explore the history of playing cards; newsletter offers buy/sell/trade ads, articles, etc.

Barbara Clark
International Playing Card Society
Journal: IPCS Journal
3570 Delaware Common
Indianapolis, IN 46220
ph: 317-251-5980
brew@iquest.net
http://www.pagat.com/ipcs
U.S. area representative; members receive a journal six times per year, plus membership lists.

Larry Lubliner, Sec.
52 Plus Joker
Magazine: Clear the Decks
3814 N. Fremont #3
Chicago, IL 60613-9998
ph: 773-883-0073
fax: 773-883-1199
joker1854@aol.com
http://www.52PlusJoker.org
For those interested in collecting playing cards, antique and unusual decks; magazine is published quarterly.

Simon Wintle
English Playing Card Society & The World of Playing Cards
Newsletter: English Playing Card Society Newsletter, The
123 Washington Rd.
Portsmouth, Hants PO2 7DF U.K.
ph: +44 (0)23 92352404
swintle@wopc.co.uk
http://www.wopc.co.uk
For collectors, researchers, museums, archivists, manufacturers, etc. who are interested in English and other playing cards and card games; collections and old packs bought and sold; online sale list.

Collectors

Rhonda Hawes
204 Gorham Ave.
Hamden, CT 06514-3904
ph: 203-288-6584
rhawes@snet.net
http://members.aol.com/robertcard
Buys antique and unusual playing cards and playing card related ephemera.

Barbara Lunaburg
1826 Mallard Lake Dr.
Marietta, GA 30068-1644
ph: 770-992-7478
cpccink@aol.com
Trustee, Board of Directors of the Chicago Playing Card Collectors Club.

Bill Sachen
Sachen Associates
1075 Victory Dr., Apt. 227
Lindenhurst, IL 60046
ph: 847-265-3573
futilewill@aol.com
http://members.aol.com/FutileWill

Larry Lubliner, Sec.
3814 N. Fremont #3
Chicago, IL 60613-9998
ph: 773-883-0073
fax: 773-883-1199
joker1854@aol.com
http://www.52PlusJoker.org
Avid collector of playing cards.

Bernice De Somer
1559 West Pratt Blvd.
Chicago, IL 60626-4228
ph: 773-274-0250
Interested in playing cards, decks or single cards.

Cary Basse
6927 Forbes Ave.
Van Nuys, CA 91406-4504
ph: 818-781-4856

Ben Bornstein
6 Arlstan Dr.
Toronto, Ontario M3H 4V8 Canada
ph: 416-398-6249
5flush@sympatico.ca
http://www.erols.com/sbostin.cards

Dealers

Glenn Currie
P.O. Box 1342
Concord, NH 03302-1342
ph: 603-228-3328
glennkc@aol.com
Wants to buy antique or unusual decks of playing cards.

Larry Lubliner
Avant Carde
3814 N. Fremont #3
Chicago, IL 60613-9998
ph: 773-883-0073
fax: 773-883-1199
joker1854@aol.com
http://www.avantcarde.com
Wants to buy pre-1930 playing cards and related advertising.

Yasha Beresiner
InterCol Gallery
43 Templars Crescent
London, N3 3QR U.K.
ph: (00 44) 208349 2207 or (00 44) 207354 2599
fax: (00 44) 208346 9539
yasha@compuserve.com
http://www.intercol.co.uk
Buys and sells world banknotes, all playing cards, old maps, related books on Free Masonry.

Hava Getz
HGIMAGES
P.O. Box 6
Markfield, Leicstershir LE67 9TX U.K.
ph: 44 1530 244354
fax: 44 1530 244354
hgimages@dircon.co.uk
http://www.hgimages.dircon.co.uk
Has a large selection of playing cards and card games for sale on the Web; also carries large selection of ephemera including cigar box labels and old cigarette packets.

Experts

David Galt
Games & Names
302 W. 78th St.
New York, NY 10024
ph: 212-769-2514
david@spacedominoes.com
http://www.spacedominoes.com
One of the premier playing card and board game collectors in America.

Phil Bollhagen
7940 West Leroy Ave.
Greenfield, WI 53220
ph: 414-327-6220
bollhagp@rocketmail.com
Has one of the largest collections of antique railroad playing card decks in the US; wants to buy quality pre-1915 decks from all railroads; author of "The Great Book of Railroad Playing Cards;" railroad decks and singles.

Shami & Kathryn Maxwell
Parnell Publishing
P.O. Box 16432
Phoenix, AZ 85011-6432
ph: 602-279-2358
fax: 602-279-5754
Author of "Price Guide of Old & Unusual Playing Cards" and "Playing Cards - The Intentional Price Guide;" also recreates historical playing card decks.

Museums/Libraries

Cincinnati Art Museum
Eden Park
Cincinnati, OH 45202
ph: 513-639-2995
information@cincyart.org
http://www.cincinnatiartmuseum.com

Margery B. Griffith, Dir.
United States Playing Card Company Playing Card Museum
4590 Beech St.
Cincinnati, OH 45212
ph: 513-396-5700
fax: 513-396-6321
consumerrelations@usplayingcard.com
http://www.usplayingcard.com
Resource for research materials dealing with playing cards; largest playing card collection in the world.

Repro. Sources

Shami & Kathryn Maxwell
Parnell Publishing
P.O. Box 16432
Phoenix, AZ 85011-6432
ph: 602-279-2358
fax: 602-279-5754
Recreates playing cards, faro and Civil War; also makes faro equipment: casekeepers, layouts, dealing boxes.

PLUMBING

(see also ARCHITECTURAL ELEMENTS; CATALOGS; HARDWARE; OUTHOUSES)

Dealers

H. Weber & Jill Wilson
WebWilson.com
P.O. Box 506
Portsmouth, RI 02871
ph: 800-508-0022
fax: 401-683-1644
jill@LooLooDesign.com
http://www.LooLooDesign.com
Sells architectural antiques; garden ornaments, vintage plumbing, quality furniture, antique door hardware.

United House Wrecking
535 Hope St.
Stamford, CT 06906-1316
ph: 203-348-5371
fax: 203-961-9472
unitedhouse.wrecking@snet.net
http://www.unitedhousewrecking.com
Sells architectural elements; stained and beveled glass, fireplace mantels and accessories, antique furniture,

chandeliers and other lighting fixtures, etc.

Donald Hooper
Vintage Plumbing & Bathroom Antiques
9645 Sylvia Ave.
Northridge, CA 91324
ph: 818-772-1721 or 818-420-1233
vintageplumbing@juno.com
http://www.vintageplumbing.com
Buys, sells, rents and repairs c. 1900 American bath fixtures such as unusual claw foot bathtubs, ornamental toilets, fancy pedestal sinks, rib-cage showers and more; over 20 years in business.

Don Hooper
Vintage Plumbing Bathroom Antiques
9645 Sylvia Ave.
Northridge, CA 91324-1756
ph: 818-772-1721
fax: 818-772-4647
vintageplumbing@juno.com
http://www.vintageplumbing.com
Wants to buy high quality Victorian period antique bath tubs, toilets, sinks, showers, and nickel plated accessories.

Museums/Libraries

American Sanitary Plumbing Museum, The
39 Piedmont St.
Worcester, MA 01610
ph: 508-754-9453
Collection includes bathtubs, sinks, toilets, plumbing books and tools.

Periodicals

Hanley-Wood, Inc.
Directory: Old-House Journal Restoration Directory
Two Main St.
Gloucester, MA 01930
ph: 800-234-3797
jbutterf@hanley-wood.com
http://www.oldhousejournal.com
Sourcebook listing companies large and small which manufacture and sell traditional hard-to-find items for the old house owner: sinks, siding, lumber, plumbing, stoves, etc.; also call 800-931-2931.

Bathroom Antiques
Dealers

Donald Hooper
Vintage Plumbing & Bathroom Antiques
9645 Sylvia Ave.
Northridge, CA 91324
ph: 818-772-1721 or 818-420-1233
vintageplumbing@juno.com
http://www.vintageplumbing.com
Buys, sells, rents and repairs c. 1900 American bath fixtures such as unusual claw foot bathtubs, ornamental toilets, fancy pedestal sinks, rib-cage showers and more; over 20 years in business.

Repair Services

Premium Refinishing
300 Atlantic Ave.
Brooklyn, NY 11201
ph: 888-404-8827
premium123@aol.com
Restores antique bathtubs and sinks to customer specifications; also sells reproductions of antique fixtures.

PLUSH

(see STEIFF; TEDDY BEARS; TOYS, Plush; TOYS, Senna Bears)

POCKET KNIVES

(see KNIVES, Pocket)

POCKET MIRRORS

(see also ADVERTISING COLLECTIBLES)

Collectors

Howard Share
4349 LaVale Ct.
Clemmons, NC 27012-9009
ph: 336-766-6579
fax: 336-766-5445
HowSha43@aol.com
Wants high quality advertising pocket mirrors, especially those picturing Blacks, nudes, or unusual products.

Jerome Schaeper, Jr.
365 Meadowlark Dr.
Edgewood, KY 41018-2608
ph: 859-341-3769
Collects and appraises colorful, graphic celluloid advertising pocket mirrors.

James E. Kattner
P.O. Box 11132
Spring, TX 77391-1132
ph: 281-376-4826
victorio1sw@yahoo.com
Wants to buy pocket mirrors with celluloid backs that picture pretty ladies and young girls which advertise saloons and bars, or that specify a redemption value such as "12-1/2" cents or "One Drink" at a merchant's establishment.

Dealers

Dave Beck
P.O. Box 435
Mediapolis, IA 52637-0435
ph: 319-394-3943
fax: 319-394-3943
adman@mepotelco.net
Buys and sells advertising watch fobs, mirrors and pin-backs; send stamp for illustrated mail auction catalog.

POCKET-SIZE COLLECTIBLES
Collectors

Bruce Axler
Ansonia Station
P.O. Box 1288
New York, NY 10023-1288
ph: 212-579-0348
Wants pocket items, i.e., items/gadgets designed to fit in the pocket: tools, knives, lighters, items which look like a pocket watch but are not, calculators, leather items, match safes, candle safes, travel items.

POINTS

(see NATIVE AMERICAN; PREHISTORIC ARTIFACTS, Arrowheads & Points)

POKER CHIPS

(see GAMBLING COLLECTIBLES, Gambling Chips & Gaming Tokens)

POLICE & SHERIFF

(see LAW ENFORCEMENT MEMORABILIA, Police & Sheriff)

POLITICAL COLLECTIBLES

(see also AUTOGRAPHS; BADGES; BUTTONS, Pin-Back; CANES & WALKING STICKS; CARTOON ART; CERAMICS, Political Related; HISTORICAL AMERICANA; PERSONALITIES [HISTORICAL]; PINS; PROHIBITION ITEMS; SOCIAL CAUSES; UNCLE SAM; WHITE HOUSE COLLECTIBL

Appraisers

Mike Stakis
3 Brookside Ave., Room #3
Newburgh, NY 12550-3018
ph: 845-565-7378
Appraiser, expert, collector of political memorabilia; willing to help identify and value political items over the phone; buttons, china, ceramics, banners, textile items, etc.; also buys political items, single item or entire collections.

Timmy W. Miller
Flat Signed Rare Books
3415 West End Ave., #1101
Nashville, TN 37203
ph: 615-292-3528
fax: 615-298-2757
timmiller@flatsigned.com
http://www.flatsigned.com
Appraiser, collector, dealer; one of the world's largest sellers of rare books, political memorabilia, and works by Peter Max.

U.I. "Chick" Harris
1010 Lemon St.
Highland, IL 62249-1678
ph: 618-651-1144
Collects, specializes in, and appraises all types of political Americana; conducts specialized mail-auctions of political and historical Americana.

Auction Services

Robert Lifson
Robert Edward Auctions
P.O. Box 7256
Watchung, NJ 07069
ph: 908-226-9900 or 800-766-9324
fax: 908-226-9920
reaauct@aol.com
http://www.robertedwardauctions.com
Specializes in the auction sale of historical Americana, political material, autographs and manuscripts, and original illustration art.

Ted Hake
Hake's Americana & Collectibles Auction
P.O. Box 1444
York, PA 17405-1444
ph: 717-848-1333
Ted@hakes.com
http://www.hakes.com
Always purchasing, consigning items for 5 mail-bid & online auctions per year; hundreds of categories including toys, character collectibles, Disney, cowboy heroes, premiums, television, politicals, pin-back buttons, advertising and more.

Robert Coup
Historicana
P.O. Box 348
Leola, PA 17540-0348
ph: 717-656-7855
fax: 717-656-8233
POLBANDWGN@aol.com
Specializes in mail-bid auctions of character collectibles, Disneyana, political items & historical Americana; sample catalog $2.

Al Anderson
Anderson Auction
P.O. Box 644
Troy, OH 45373-0644
ph: 937-339-0850
fax: 937-339-8620
aaauctn@erinet.com
http://www.erinet.com/aaauctn
Specializes in mail-bid auctions of political items and historical Americana.

Tom Slater
Political Gallery, The
5335 North Takoma Ave.
Indianapolis, IN 46220
ph: 317-257-0863
fax: 317-254-9167
Specializing in mail-bid auctions of Disneyana, historical Americana, toys, political items, and other collectibles.

Slater's Americana, Inc.
5335 North Tacoma Ave., Ste. 24
Indianapolis, IN 46220
ph: 317-257-0863
fax: 317-254-9167
slater@indy.net
Specializes in political and presidential memorabilia as well as other historical Americana.

Kurt R. Krueger
Krueger Auctions
P.O. Box 275
Iola, WI 54945-0275
ph: 715-445-3845
fax: 715-445-4100

Clubs/Associations

Michael McQuillen
Indiana Political Collectors Club
Newsletter: IN A.P.I.C.
P.O. Box 50022
Indianapolis, IN 46250-0022
ph: 317-845-1721
mmcquillen@politicalparade.com
http://www.politicalparade.com
Club meets two times per year with annual show; send SASE to be placed on show mailing list.

Joseph Hayes, Sec./Treas.
American Political Items Collectors (APIC)
Newsletter: Political Bandwagon, The
P.O. Box 1149
Cibolo, TX 78108
ph: 210-945-2811
fax: 210-945-8232
apic@texas.net
http://www.apic.ws
Dedicated to the collection, study, preservation of items relating to the political campaigns of the US; also publishes the "Keynoter" magazine three times a year; ask about specialty and local chapters.

Collectors

Frank Consilvio
P.O. Box 552
Boston, MA 02128

Norwood H. Keeney, III
P.O. Box 1026
Georges Mills, NH 03751-1026
ph: 603-763-9157
acer@webryders.com
Wants items relating to Statesman John Hay (1838-1905), US Secretary of State.

Donald Ackerman
P.O. Box 3487
Wallington, NJ 07057-1621
ph: 973-779-8785
assortedpast@comcast.net
Wants to buy presidential campaign items; wants one item or collection; over 35 years in the hobby; will make an offer if requested, or will make an honest attempt to tell you what you've got.

Robert Kwalwasser
168 Camp Fatima Rd.
Renfrew, PA 16053-9104
ph: 724-789-7766
fax: 724-789-9771
robertk@tcis.net
Wants political parade torches, tinder pistols.

Christopher B. Hearn
125 Morven Park Rd., NW
Leesburg, VA 20176-2025
ph: 703-777-7181
Wants to buy political campaign items; political buttons, banners, flags, china, posters, ribbons; especially interested in Roosevelt and Women's Suffrage; also wants Presidential White House gift items and china.

Bob Cereghino
6400 Baltimore National Pike, Ste. 170A-319
Baltimore, MD 21228-3914
ph: 410-766-7593
jwbc@juno.com
Wants advertising, entertainment and political pin-back buttons.

Bob Putnam
9129 Lake Braddock Dr.
Springfield, VA 22153
ph: 703-644-9711
putmanb@email.msn.com
Wants to buy all presidential campaign items: buttons, banners, posters and political cartoons.

Lon Ellis
P.O. Box 99123
Raleigh, NC 27624
ph: 919-844-9962
fax: 919-844-9962
lellis@rocksolid.com
Active collector of pre-1960 political campaign pin-back buttons and other political campaign memorabilia including ribbons, badges, posters, postcards, banners, etc.

John Gingerich
P.O. Box 358
Lexington, GA 30648-0358
ph: 706-743-3420
lazydog2@earthlink.net
Wants political campaign items: buttons, ribbons, badges, posters, postcards, flags, 3-D items, etc.; also wants C.C.C., Bonus Army, United Confederate Veterans, Socialist Party, etc.; want lists sent on request; SASE please.

Peggy Dillard
P.O. Box 210904
Nashville, TN 37221-0904
ph: 615-646-1605
pdill43795@aol.com
Send SASE and photocopy of political campaign items and receive free appraisal and offer in the mail.

Don Beck
P.O. Box 15305
Fort Wayne, IN 46885-5305
ph: 2609-486-3010
Wants to buy Lincoln to Kennedy political pins, medals, flags, banners, autographs.

Ken Hosner
5692 Comstock
Kalamazoo, MI 49001
ph: 616-345-5983
mrbutton@cyberrealm.net
http://cyberrealm.net/~mrbutton
Wants to buy presidential campaign items; over 30 years in the business.

Joe Doerring
P.O. Box 35351
Des Moines, IA 50315
ph: 515-285-7702
JDoerring@aol.com
Wants poster stamps and labels dealing with presidential campaigns, women's suffrage, labor, and prohibition.

Paul Bengston
1225 N. 7th St.
Minneapolis, MN 55411-4060
ph: 612-975-3955 or 612-287-0223
fax: 612-522-0025
Wants pre-1964 political buttons, badges, ribbons, banners, tokens, flags, autographs, and related collectibles; send photocopy.

Cary Demont
P.O. Box 16013
Minneapolis, MN 55416
ph: 763-522-0957
Serious collector for over 35 years wants scarce and unusual campaign and presidential related items; pre-1964 campaign pins, badges, ribbons, posters, banners, political flags, postcards and 3-dimensional items.

David Yates
321 West Church St.
Genoa, IL 60135
ph: 815-784-3369
deere@tbcnet.com
Wants to buy political campaign pin-backs.

James Carlson, #73536
Arizona State Prison - Florence
P.O. Box 8400 - South Unit
Florence, AZ 85232-8400
Inmate collects political autographs, letters, documents; accepts donations of same only (no money); writes to stars and celebrities to obtain autographs; member of UACC; seeks penpals with similar interests.

John Gearhart
3267 S.E. Hawthorne
Portland, OR 97214
ph: 503-255-8108 or 503-234-0991
gearhart@teleport.com
http://www.teleport.com/~gearhart
Buttons, posters, ribbons, banners, etc.

Dealers

Rex Stark
Rex Stark Americana
P.O. Box 1029
Gardner, MA 01440-6029
ph: 978-630-3237
fax: 978-630-2388
rexstark@yahoo.com
Publishes fully illustrated fixed price catalog of historical Americana; averages 500 to 1,000 items per catalog with prices from $20 to $50,000: political, photography, Old West, advertising, early sports, graphic arts, glass, exonumia.

Paul Longo
Paul Longo Americana
P.O. Box 5510
Gloucester, MA 01930-0007
ph: 978-525-2290
Wants political pins, buttons, ribbons, banners, autographs, badges, etc.

Jon Allan
Elmer's Nostalgia, Inc.
3 Putnam St.
Sanford, ME 04073-2024
ph: 207-324-2166
elmers@gwi.net
http://www.elmers.net

James M. Russell
7 Meadow Lane
Gettysburg, PA 17325-8025
ph: 717-337-9018
bjmrussell@supernet.com
Buys, sells and collects any political collectibles including buttons, bandannas, textiles, pins, posters, etc.; especially interested in items relating to James G. Blaine and the election of 1884.

Larry L. Krug
Americana Resources, Inc.
18222 Flower Hill Way, #299
Gaithersburg, MD 20879-5300
ph: 301-926-8663
fax: 301-926-7648
info@amres.com
http://www.amres.com
Wants to buy political buttons/pins, ribbons, glassware and china, posters, autographs, and other memorabilia relating to US presidents, the White House, and Camp David; has over 30 years of experience.

Stephen Cresswell
Cresswell's List
Rte. 1, Box 185-A
Buckhannon, WV 26201
cress@msys.net
http://www.msys.net/cress/list.htm
A Web-based political collectibles business offering a monthly list as well as a permanent catalog of more that 1,000 political buttons; also offers quarterly Webzine as well as a large selection of back-issue articles.

Tom Peeling
P.O. Box 6661
West Palm Beach, FL 33405-0661
ph: 561-585-1351
trbuttons@aol.com
http://members.aol.com/TRbuttons
Collector and dealer of presidential/ political campaign buttons, 3-D items, etc.; Theodore Roosevelt a special want.

John W. Poling
John W. Poling: Military & Political Collectibles
P.O. Box 333
Pendleton, IN 46064-0333
ph: 765-778-2714
polingjw@aol.com
Mail order dealer in political collectibles; specializing in items from Alaska and Indiana; issues periodic catalog of items for sale; send $2 for latest catalog; most prices in catalog well below current retail.

Al & Rhonda Hunter
Hunter's Vault
P.O. Box 906
Westfield, IN 46074-0906
ph: 317-815-1975
fax: 317-815-1933
HuntVault@aol.com
Specializes in political memorabilia, sports memorabilia, and autographs.

Michael McQuillen
Political Parade
P.O. Box 50022
Indianapolis, IN 46250-0022
ph: 317-845-1721
mmcquillen@politicalparade.com
http://www.politicalparade.com
Buys, sells, collects, appraises political collectibles; wants political items of any age: presidentials and local candidates from any state or election; writes the "Political Parade" column for "AntiqueWeek;" send SASE for replies.

Robert M. Levine
#2 Troll Court
Ballwin, MO 63011-4036
ph: 636-394-4370 or 314-518-4872
fax: 636-394-8557
boblevine@hotmail.com
Wants any political item such as presidential campaign items, lapel pins; new or old; single or in quantity.

Ronald E. Wade
2100 Lafayette Dr.
Longview, TX 75601-3417
ph: 903-236-9615
fax: 903-236-9499
RonWadeGOP@aol.com
http://www.ronwadebuttons.com
Political buttons/pins JFK and older, posters, 3-dimensional political items, e.g., clocks, glassware, bandannas, etc.; free appraisals, send photocopy with SASE.

Drew Julian
Drew Julian's Political Collectibles
P.O. Box 150363
Austin, TX 78715-0363
ph: 512-447-8785 or 512-441-2020
drewjulian@sbcglobal.net
http://www.djpolitical.com
Member of APIC, an organization whose members work to improve and protect the collecting hobby; members are informed about known fake and fantasy items, current values and trends in the hobby.

Earl F. Dodge
P.O. Box 2635
Denver, CO 80201
ph: 303-237-4947
fax: 303-233-2099
earldodge@dodgeoffice.net
http://www.buttonsbydodge.com
20 years of buying and selling all political Americana: older items such as buttons, ferros, ribbons, etc.; specializes in Prohibition and Calvin Coolidge buy buy all types of political items; free appraisals; 50 fixed-price lists a year.

Gary L. Cohen
Political Memorabilia Marketplace
10780 Elk Lake Dr.
Las Vegas, NV 89144
ph: 702-233-0123 or 702-228-6624
fax: 702-233-0010
gary@politicalbuttons.com
http://www.politicalbuttons.com/ index.shtml
Online resource with market information, auctions, sales, related links, and more; every aspect of buying, selling, trading political related collectibles; FREE appraisals given on any item of value; can come to you if necessary.

Vivian Briggs
Briggs Antiques
4443 Linwood Place
Riverside, CA 92506
ph: 909-781-3121
fax: 909-781-3121
Buys and sells political collectibles: badges, paper items, ribbons, various souvenirs.

Experts

Mark Suozzi
P.O. Box 102
Ashfield, MA 01330
ph: 413-628-3241
fax: 413-628-3241
marklyn@valinet.com
http://www.marklynantiques.com
Buying all campaign badges, buttons, china, political flags from 1840 to 1912: Henry Clay, Harrison, Van Buren, Grant, Lincoln, Douglas through to Teddy Roosevelt's Bull Moose campaign.

Tony Lee
Le Politicals
P.O. Box 134
Monmouth Junction, NJ 08852-0134
ph: 201-429-1531
Collector and dealer in all types of political campaign memorabilia, from buttons and ribbons to badges and 3-D items; also president of the big Apple Chapter of the American Political Items Collectors group.

Mike Stakis
3 Brookside Ave., Room #3
Newburgh, NY 12550-3018
ph: 845-565-7378
Appraiser, expert, collector of political memorabilia; willing to help identify and value political items over the phone; buttons, china, ceramics, banners, textile items, etc.; also buys political items, single item or entire collections.

Robert A. Fratkin
1650 Tysons Blvd., 10th Floor
Mc Lean, VA 22102
ph: 703-556-8108 or 703-629-1941
fax: 703-356-6492
coxfdr@erols.com
Buys, sells, specializes in political collectibles; nationally recognized expert & lecturer on political collectibles; willing to give help on telephone in identifying & valuing items; send photo & SASE or have in front of you when calling.

Ed Krohn
P.O. Box 357309
Miami, FL 32635
ph: 305-237-2382
fax: 305-237-2635
ekx@inaugurals.com
http://www.inaugurals.com
Expert, appraiser, collector; author of "National Political Convention Tickets & Other Ephemera" catalog; illustrated catalog of tickets, programs and other ephemera for all National political conventions from 1856 to present.

Howard Hazelcorn
6731 Ashley Ct.
Sarasota, FL 34241-9696
ph: 941-921-1815
mrpropane@aol.com
Collects and specializes in political textiles and posters; especially wants buttons and 3-D items.

Michael McQuillen
P.O. Box 50022
Indianapolis, IN 46250-0022
ph: 317-845-1721
mmcquillen@politicalparade.com
http://www.politicalparade.com
Buys, sells, collects, appraises political collectibles; wants political items of any age: presidentials and local candidates from any state or election; writes the "Political Parade" column for "AntiqueWeek;" send SASE for replies.

Museums/Libraries

Museum of American Political Life,
  University of Hartford
200 Bloomfield Ave.
West Hartford, CT 06117
ph: 860-768-4090
fax: 860-768-5159
http://www.hartford.edu/polmus/ polmus1.html
The extraordinary collection of Mr. J. Doyle Dewitt donated to the University of Hartford forms the nucleus of the museum; 60,000 artifacts: posters, banners, textiles, prints, medals, pottery, glassware, ribbons, etc.

National Museum of American History
14th & Constitution Ave. NW
Washington, DC 20560
ph: 202-357-2700
webmaster@si.edu
http://www.si.edu/organiza/museums/ nmah/nmah.htm

Periodicals

Newspaper: Political Collector, The
P.O. Box 5171
York, PA 17405-5171
ph: 717-846-0418
A monthly newspaper focusing on political collectibles.

M. Jeannine Coup
Newspaper: Political Bandwagon, The
P.O. Box 348
Leola, PA 17540-0348
ph: 717-656-7855
fax: 717-656-8233
POLBANDWGN@aol.com
A monthly publication focusing on collecting historical and political memorabilia with articles, information on political memorabilia shows and items offered for sale; free sample.

Bill Clinton

Clubs/Associations

Philip J. Ross
Bill Clinton Political Items Collectors
Magazine: Arkansas Traveler, The
8226 McNeil St.
Vienna, VA 22180-6924
ph: 703-698-5883
politiphil@aol.com
http://www.apic.ws/chapters/sp- wjclinton.asp
Serves political collectors specializing in memorabilia relating to Bill Clinton campaigns, Presidential and other stages of his career; editor of "The Arkansas Traveler," writes articles about political memorabilia for other magazines.

Calvin Coolidge

Collectors

Larry L. Krug
Americana Resources, Inc.
18222 Flower Hill Way, #299
Gaithersburg, MD 20879-5300
ph: 301-926-8663
fax: 301-926-7648
info@amres.com
http://www.amres.com
Major collector for over 25 years of Calvin Coolidge campaign memorabilia and of items relating to the Coolidge administration.

Dealers

Earl F. Dodge
P.O. Box 2635
Denver, CO 80201
ph: 303-237-4947
fax: 303-233-2099
earldodge@dodgeoffice.net
http://www.buttonsbydodge.com
20 years of buying and selling all political Americana: older items such as buttons, ferros, ribbons, etc.; specializes in Prohibition and Calvin Coolidge buy buy all types of political items; free appraisals; 50 fixed-price lists a year.

Canadian

Dealers

Michael Rice
Michael Rice Collectibles
P.O. Box 286
Saanichton, British Columbia V8M 2C5
Canada
ph: 250-652-9412
fax: 250-652-7866
mrice@pacificcoast.net
Particularly interested in Canadian pin-back buttons and paper election memorabilia; call after 6 PST.

Dan Quayle

Museums/Libraries

Dan Quayle Center & Museum
815 Warren St.
P.O. Box 856
Huntington, IN 46750
ph: 219-356-6356
fax: 219-356-1455
info@quaylemuseum.org
http://www.quaylemuseum.org

Dwight D. Eisenhower

Museums/Libraries

Dwight D. Eisenhower Library
200 SE 4th St.
Abilene, KS 67410-2900
ph: 785-263-4751
fax: 785-263-4218
Eisenhower.Library@nara.gov
http://www.eisenhower.utexas.edu

Franklin D. Roosevelt

Clubs/Associations

Mike Craun
Franklin D. Roosevelt - Democratic
  Political Items Collectors
Newsletter: New Deal Spirit, The
2708 Pemberton Dr.
Toledo, OH 43606
ph: 419-531-0170
http://www.apic.ws/chapters/sp-fdr.asp
Provides a communications network among FDR collectors.

Collectors

Christopher Carroll
810 Verin Lane
Chula Vista, CA 91910-7830
ccarroll@cvesd.k12.ca.us
Wants FDR items, especially 3-D items.

Museums/Libraries

Franklin Delano Roosevelt Library
511 Albany Rd.
Hyde Park, NY 12538-1999
ph: 914-229-8114
fax: 914-229-0872
roosevelt.library@nara.gov
http://www.fdrlibrary.marist.edu

George Bush

Clubs/Associations

Michael McQuillen
Bush Political Items Collectors
Newsletter: Bush Bandwagon
P.O. Box 50022
Indianapolis, IN 46250-0022
ph: 317-845-1721
mmcquillen@politicalparade.com
http://www.apic.ws/chapters/sp-gwbush.asp

Museums/Libraries

George Bush Library
1000 George Bush Dr. West
College Station, TX 77843
ph: 979-260-9554
fax: 979-260-9557
library@bush.nara.gov
http://bushlibrary.tamu.edu

George Wallace

Experts

Ronald Krueger
P.O. Box 741
Oak Park, IL 60303-0741
ph: 708-788-8235
Always buying photos, posters, lobby cards, postcards, glass slides, theater handbills or anything related to this silent film actress; also interested in making contact with other Minter collectors.

Gerald R. Ford

Clubs/Associations

Roger Van Sickle
Gerald R. Ford Chapter oF APIC
614 PollyAnna Dr.
Delaware, OH 43015
ph: 740-362-1632
rmv610@aol.com
http://www.apic.ws/chapters/sp-grford.asp
Dedicated to the preservation of political memorabilia of President Gerald R. Ford, the 38th President of the United States.

Museums/Libraries

William H. McNitt, Archivist
Gerald R. Ford Library
1000 Beal Ave.
Ann Arbor, MI 48109-2114
ph: 734-741-2218
fax: 734-741-2341
ford.library@nara.gov
http://www.ford.utexas.edu
An archival institution with only manuscript and audio-visual holdings for the researcher; no collections of Gerald R. Ford related memorabilia.

Gerald R. Ford Museum
303 Pearl St., NW
Grand Rapids, MI 49504-5343
ph: 616-451-9263
fax: 616-451-9570
ford.museum@nara.gov
http://www.ford.utexas.edu/museum
Presents exhibits and programs as they relate to Gerald R. Ford and his presidency.

Harry S. Truman

Clubs/Associations

Lois Pile
Harry S. Truman Chapter of APIC
Newsletter: Buckstopper, The
ph: 915-697-2545
batfile@aol.com
http://www.apic.ws/chapters/sp-hstruman.asp
For those interested in the Truman Presidency, Truman's life, and related memorabilia.

Collectors

Mario Donald Thomas
860 18th Ave.
Salt Lake City, UT 84103-3719
ph: 801-532-5340
fax: 801-532-5340
Collects any items connected to President Harry S. Truman.

Museums/Libraries

Clay R. Bauske, Curator
Harry S. Truman Library & Museum
500 West US Highway 24
Independence, MO 64050-1798
ph: 816-833-1400 or 816-833-1225
fax: 816-833-4368
library@truman.nara.gov
http://www.trumanlibrary.org

Herbert Hoover

Collectors

Joe Doerring
P.O. Box 35351
Des Moines, IA 50315
ph: 515-285-7702
JDoerring@aol.com
Wants items from both campaigns of Herbert Hoover: pin-back buttons, ribbons, paper items, novelties, etc.

Museums/Libraries

Herbert Hoover Library
211 Parkside Dr.
P.O. Box 488
West Branch, IA 52358-0488
ph: 319-643-5301
fax: 319-643-5825
library@hoover.nara.gov
http://hoover.nara.gov

Jimmy Carter

Clubs/Associations

Roger Van Sickle
Carter Political Items Group
Newsletter: Carter Journal, The
614 PollyAnna Dr.
Delaware, OH 43015
ph: 740-362-1632
rmv610@aol.com
http://www.apic.ws/chapters/sp-jcarter.asp
Purpose is to preserve the memorabilia associated with the life, political administrations and family members of our nation's 39th president, Jimmy Carter; quarterly newsletter.

Museums/Libraries

Jimmy Carter Library
441 Freedom Parkway
One Copenhill Ave.
Atlanta, GA 30307-1498
ph: 401-331-3942
fax: 401-730-2215
carter.library@nara.gov
http://www.jimmycarterlibrary.org

John F. Kennedy

Clubs/Associations

Harvey Goldberg, Ed.
Kennedy Political Items Collectors
Newsletter: Hyannisporter
P.O. Box 922
Clark, NJ 07066-0922
ph: 732-382-4652
fax: 732-382-1325
heg@worldnet.att.net
http://www.apic.ws/chapters/sp-kpic.asp
KPIC is a world-wide organization for collectors of Kennedy political campaign items; members throughout the US and Canada and as far away as Australia and Europe.

Experts

Harvey Goldberg, Ed.
P.O. Box 922
Clark, NJ 07066-0922
ph: 732-382-4652
fax: 732-382-1325
heg@worldnet.att.net
http://www.apic.ws/chapters/sp-kpic.asp
Author of several books about Kennedy-related memorabilia and a noted expert on Kennedy materials; offers evaluations and liquidations of political collections.

Museums/Libraries

John Fitzgerald Kennedy Library & Museum
Columbia Point
Boston, MA 02125-3398
ph: 617-929-4500 or 877-616-4599
fax: 617-929-4538
kennedy.library@nara.gov
http://www.jfklibrary.org

Locals

Clubs/Associations

Ira Forman, Ed.
American Locals Political Items Collectors (ALPIC)
Newsletter: ALPIC Newsletter
1717 Webster St. NW
Washington, DC 20011
ira@njdc.org
http://www.apic.ws/chapters/sp-alpic.asp
Serves political collectors of state and local offices including governors, US senators and Congressmen, mayors, sheriffs, etc.

Lyndon Baines Johnson

Museums/Libraries

Carol Kay Johnson, Mngr.
Lyndon Baines Johnson Library & Museum
2313 Red River Rd.
Austin, TX 78705-5702
ph: 512-476-0029 or 512-936-5137 x249
fax: 512-478-9104
carol.johnson@nara.gov
http://www.lbjlib.utexas.edu
Established to preserve and make available for research the papers and memorabilia of President Lyndon Baines Johnson; the Library actively collects papers of Johnson's contemporaries.

Republican

Clubs/Associations

Jonathan A. Binkley
Republican Political Items Collectors
Newsletter: RPIC Trumpeter
1786 Bucklew Dr.
Toledo, OH 43613
ph: 419-472-1912
bjbinkley@webtv.net
http://www.apic.ws/chapters/sp-rpic.asp
Members specialize in Republican political leaders and their legacies.

Richard Nixon

Clubs/Associations

Eldon Almquist
Nixon Collector's Organization
Newsletter: NIXCO News
975 Maunawili Circle
Kailua, HI 96734-4620
ph: 808-262-9837
fax: 808-834-1046
nixco1@aol.com
http://www.homestead.com/nixco
For those interested in collecting Richard Nixon memorabilia and in studying the political career of our 37th president.

Collectors

Eldon Almquist
975 Maunawili Circle
Kailua, HI 96734-4620
ph: 808-262-9837
fax: 808-834-1046
nixco1@aol.com
http://www.homestead.com/nixco
Wants to buy Nixon related pin-backs, jewelry and novelties; send SASE and photocopy of your items for response and free appraisal or offer.

Museums/Libraries

Nixon Presidential Materials Staff, National Archives at College Park
8601 Adelphi Rd.
College Park, MD 20740-6001
ph: 301-713-6950
fax: 301-713-9616
nixon@arch2.nara.gov
http://www.nara.gov/nixon

Melissa Foley
Richard Nixon Library & Birthplace
18001 Yorba Linda Blvd.
Yorba Linda, CA 92886
ph: 714-993-3393 or 714-993-5075
fax: 714-528-0544
melissa@nixonlibrary.org
http://www.nixonlibrary.org
Museum store, Web site, and annual gifts catalog offers wide selection of Presidential and campaign memorabilia from contemporary administrations including Pres. Nixon; political memorabilia can be donated; will buy select items.

Ronald Reagan

Clubs/Associations

Thomas Lorincz
ph: 909-949-8402
tomcat@tstonramp.com
http://www.apic.ws/chapterse/sp-rreagan.asp

Museums/Libraries

Mark Burson, Ex. Dir.
Ronald Reagan Presidential Library & Museum
40 Presidential Dr.
Simi Valley, CA 93065-0666
ph: 805-522-8444 or 800-410-8354
fax: 805-522-9621
library@reagan.nara.gov
http://www.reaganlibrary.net
The museum store sells political items; store phone number is 805-522-9953.

Theodore Roosevelt

Clubs/Associations

Tom Peeling
Theodore Roosevelt Chapter of the American Political Items Collectors (APIC)
Newsletter: Bully Pulpit
P.O. Box 6661
West Palm Beach, FL 33405-0661
ph: 561-585-1351
trbuttons@aol.com
http://www.apic.ws/chapters/sp-troosevelt.asp
For collectors and scholars of the Theodore Roosevelt years and the political memorabilia associated with it.

Dealers

Tom Peeling
P.O. Box 6661
West Palm Beach, FL 33405-0661
ph: 561-585-1351
trbuttons@aol.com
http://members.aol.com/TRbuttons
Collector and dealer of presidential/political campaign buttons, 3-D items, etc.; Theodore Roosevelt a special want.

Third Party & Hopefuls

Clubs/Associations

Jon Curtis, Ed.
Third Party & Hopefuls Chapter of APIC
Newsletter: Bullmoose, The
1901 Ridgeway, Apt. #8
De Pere, WI 54115
ph: 920-339-6219
joncurtis99@hotmail.com
http://www.apic.ws/chapterse/sp-3rdparty.asp
Collectors interested in the memorabilia associated with third party political candidates and political hopefuls.

Collectors

Joe Doerring
P.O. Box 35351
Des Moines, IA 50315
ph: 515-285-7702
JDoerring@aol.com
Collects items associated with the Socialist, Communist, Union, and Prohibition parties.

Wendell L. Willkie

Clubs/Associations

Michael McQuillen
Wendell L. Willkie Political Items Collectors
Newsletter: Willkie World
P.O. Box 50022
Indianapolis, IN 46250-0022
ph: 317-845-1721
mmcquillen@politicalparade.com
http://www.apic.ws/chapters/sp-wlwillkie.asp
A group of collectors interested in buttons, ribbons, paper and all items related to Wendell Willkie's 1940 campaign; send SASE for replies.

POLYNESIAN COLLECTIBLES

Dealers

Mark Blackburn
Mauna Kea Galleries
65-1298 Kawaihae Rd.
Waimea, HI 96743
ph: 808-887-2244
fax: 808-887-2226
mkg@interpac.net
http://www.maunakeagalleries.com
Wants cultural art and artifacts from all the Polynesian islands; war clubs, items of personal adornment; also pre-1925 Hawaiian items.

POND BOATS

(see BOATS, Model)

POOL TABLES

(see BILLIARD RELATED ITEMS)

POP ART

(see MODERNISM)

POP CULTURE

(see AUTOGRAPHS; MAGAZINES, Scandal/Cult/R 'N' R; MODERNISM; MUSIC, Rock 'N' Roll; MOVIE MEMORABILIA; PERSONALITIES [MUSICIANS]; POSTERS, Music; RECORDS; SHEET MUSIC; TELEVISION SHOWS & MEMORABILIA)

POPCORN ITEMS

Collectors

Glenn Smith
3706 Westgate Rd.
Omaha, NE 68124
ph: 402-391-8876
Wants popcorn boxes and cans: 10 and 12 oz. size cans.

Jack Cory
7733 Spanish Bar Dr.
Las Vegas, NV 89113
ph: 702-364-1645 or 702-375-5339
fax: 702-365-5731
kernelcory@lvcm.com
*Wants to buy popcorn memorabilia,
popcorn boxes, bags, cans, crates,
brochures, catalogs, old machines and
their parts, Cretor's steam engines
and anything related to popcorn.*

Museums/Libraries

Wyandot Popcorn Museum
Heritage Hall
169 E. Church St.
Marion, OH 43302
ph: 740-383-4255 or 740-389-2948
fax: 740-389-2066
georgek@wyandotpopcornmus.com
http://www.wyandotpopcornmus.com
*Museum contains the world's largest
collection of popcorn poppers and
peanut roasters including all the
classics: Cretors, Dunbar, Kingery,
Holcomb and Hoke, Cracker Jack,
Long-Eakin, Manley, Burch, Star,
Royal, and Advance.*

POPULAR CULTURE

(see also ANTIQUES &
COLLECTIBLES; CARTOON ART;
MODERNISM; SOCIAL CAUSES;
TELEVISION SHOWS &
MEMORABILIA; TOYS, Action
Figures)

Auction Services

Ted Hake
Hake's Americana & Collectibles
Auction
P.O. Box 1444
York, PA 17405-1444
ph: 717-848-1333
Ted@hakes.com
http://www.hakes.com
*Always purchasing, consigning items
for 5 mail-bid & online auctions per
year; hundreds of categories including
toys, character collectibles, Disney,
cowboy heroes, premiums, television,
politics, pin-back buttons,
advertising and more.*

Clubs/Associations

Ephemera Society of America Inc., The
Newsletter: Ephemera News
P.O. Box 95
Cazenovia, NY 13035-0095
ph: 315-655-9139
fax: 315-655-9139
info@ephemerasociety.org
http://www.ephemerasociety.org
*The major organization for collectors
and dealers of paper collectibles;
focuses on the preservation and study
of ephemera (short-lived printed
matter); "Ephemera News" published
quarterly; also publishes "The
Ephemera Journal."*

Dealers

Gary Sohmers
Wex Rex Collectibles
P.O. Box 702
Hudson, MA 01749
ph: 508-788-5474
wexrex@aol.com
http://www.allcollectors.com
*Appraiser on PBX TV "Antiques
Roadshow;" specializes in Rock 'n
Roll, movies, TV memorabilia,
records, posters, magazines,
autographs, toys, and other pop
culture memorabilia from the 20th
century.*

Michael Torres
Howdy Do
72 E. 7th St.
New York, NY 10003
ph: 212-979-1618
howdy72@aol.com
http://members.aol.com/howdy72
*A New York City shop that specializes
in celebrity TV-related toys and other
popular culture memorabilia.*

Experts

Gary Sohmers
Wex Rex Collectibles
P.O. Box 702
Hudson, MA 01749
ph: 508-788-5474
wexrex@aol.com
http://www.allcollectors.com
*Appraiser on PBX TV "Antiques
Roadshow;" specializes in Rock 'n
Roll, movies, TV memorabilia,
records, posters, magazines,
autographs, toys, and other pop
culture memorabilia from the 20th
century.*

Museums/Libraries

Consortium of Popular Culture
Collections
Popular Culture Library
Bowling Green State University
Bowling Green, OH 43403-0001
ph: 419-372-2450
fax: 419-372-7996
atracy@bgnet.bgsu.edu
http://www.bgsu.edu/colleges/library/pcl/
cpccm.html
*Consortium composed of Bowling
Green State U., Kent State U.,
Michigan State U., and Ohio State U.;
the largest academic library
collections of primary research
material in comic art, popular fiction,
popular music, performing arts.*

Randall W. Scott
Russel B. Nye Popular Culture
Collection, Michigan State University
Libraries
Michigan State Univ. Libraries
Special Collections
East Lansing, MI 48824-1048
ph: 517-355-3770
fax: 517-353-5069
scottr@pilot.msu.edu
http://www.lib.msu.edu/coll/main/
spec_col/nye
*Includes a popular culture vertical file
of related ephemera; also has the
world's largest comic book collection
(150,000 items) plus large collections
of science fiction, mysteries, romances,
girls' and boys' series books,
Westerns.*

Periodicals

Ray B. Browne, Ed.
Popular Culture Association
Journal: Journal of American Culture
Popular Culture Center
Bowling Green State University
Bowling Green, OH 43403
ph: 419-372-7861 or 419-372-7867
fax: 419-372-8095
rbrowne@bgnet.bgsu.edu
http://www2.h-net.msu.edu/~pcaaca/
popindex.html
*The major center and source for the
study of popular culture (media,
music, folklore, ethnic popular
culture, cartoons, performing arts,
books, and more); maintains 200,000
volume reference library of clippings,
leaflets, pamphlets, etc.*

Baby Boomer

Auction Services

Gary Kraut
Alphaville
226 W. Houston St.
New York, NY 10014-4846
ph: 212-675-6850
fax: 212-741-2609
alphavil@mindspring.com
http://www.alphaville.com
*Along with partner Steve Karchin
conducts phone auctions of '50s and
'60s toys, games, and other
memorabilia.*

Dealers

Gary Kraut
Alphaville
226 W. Houston St.
New York, NY 10014-4846
ph: 212-675-6850
fax: 212-741-2609
alphavil@mindspring.com
http://www.alphaville.com
*Along with partner Steve Karchin buys
and sells vintage 1940s, '50s, and '60s
toys, games, and other memorabilia.*

David Hendrickson
Retroville
133 E. First St.
Port Angeles, WA 98362
ph: 360-452-1429 or 877-399-1429
fax: 360-457-3991
*Specializes in various items from
primitive to post modern - the things
we grew up with: 1950s Formica
dinette set, Bakelite flatware and
dinnerware from Bauer to Zeisel;
clothing, wall art, knickknacks,
barware, kitchenware, and more.*

Man./Prod./Dist.

Gene Rees
Gino's Malt Shop Collection
25 N. Jefferson
Canonsburg, PA 15317
ph: 724-743-1950
fax: 724-743-3275
*Sells '50s and '60s malt shop
furniture, decor and accessories:
booths, tables, chairs, stools,
moldings, metal trim, lighting
fixtures, quilted stainless sheets,
counter accessories, etc.*

PORCELAIN

(see CERAMICS; DINNERWARE;
FIGURINES; OCCUPIED JAPAN;
ORIENTALIA; REPAIR/
RESTORATION/CONSERVATION;
TABLEWARE)

POSTAGE STAMPS

(see POSTAL SERVICE ITEMS;
STAMP COLLECTING)

POSTAL SERVICE ITEMS

(see also POSTCARDS, Post Office
Related; STAMP COLLECTING)

Auction Services

Jim Mehrer
Jim Mehrer's Postal History
2405 - 30th St.
Rock Island, IL 61201
ph: 309-786-6539
fax: 309-786-4840
mehrer@postal-history.com
http://www.postal-history.com
*Dealer, auctioneer conducts six postal
history mail bid sales per year, each
containing 3,000+ lots; also
postcards, reference literature,
collectors' supplies and more; Web
site has dealers and show calendar
sections.*

Collectors

Tom Mills
P.O. Box 424
Spencer, MA 01562
ph: 508-885-9550
*Wants fire alarm and police boxes
especially ones with dates cast into
them; seeks cast iron signs and street*

letter pickup boxes marked "U.S. MAIL;" best to write and send photos.

Dr. Frank R. Scheer, Curator
Railway Mail Service Library
12 E. Rosemont Ave.
Alexandria, VA 22301-2325
ph: 703-549-4095
fax: 703-836-1955
fscheer@erols.com
http://members.ebay.com/aboutme/
  fscheer@erols.com
  Wants to buy obsolete official postal artifacts from any country: postmarking handstamps, badges, mail locks, street letterboxes, mail route schedules, postal hand guns, etc.; no stamps, postmarked envelopes or modern collectibles.

Harold Dylhoff
23511 Paulson's Rd.
Gobles, MI 49055-8651
ph: 269-628-4051
hdylxrds@aol.com
  Wants to buy postal history items: ship cancels, covers from 1946 atomic bomb tests Bikini Atoll "Operation Crossroads," any material Air Force 509th connected with XRDs tests; send photocopies and LSASE for reply.

Dealers

Paul & Becky Huber
Fairwinds
26450 Moore Farm Lane
Onancock, VA 23417
ph: 757-787-1569
  Dealers in naval and maritime postal history, postcards, historical documents and antiques; maintains an extensive stock and provides approval service; want lists appreciated.

Jim Mehrer
Jim Mehrer's Postal History
2405 - 30th St.
Rock Island, IL 61201
ph: 309-786-6539
fax: 309-786-4840
mehrer@postal-history.com
http://www.postal-history.com
  Dealer, auctioneer conducts six postal history mail bid sales per year, each containing 3,000+ lots; also postcards, reference literature, collectors' supplies and more; Web site has dealers and show calendar sections.

Internet Resources

Dr. Frank R. Scheer, Curator
Railway Mail Service Library
12 E. Rosemont Ave.
Alexandria, VA 22301-2325
ph: 703-549-4095
fax: 703-836-1955
fscheer@erols.com
http://members.ebay.com/aboutme/
  fscheer@erols.com
  A FREE computer Web page for postal history researchers interested in post items of the USA and other countries; replies to requests will be downloaded; upload articles to check

technical information; send email for current URL.

Museums/Libraries

Postal History Foundation, The
Newsletter: Heliograph
P.O. Box 40725
920 North First Ave.
Tucson, AZ 85719-0725
ph: 520-623-6652
phf3@mindspring.com
http://azstarnet.com/~phf/phf.html
  Houses artifacts, postmarks and covers dedicated to postal history.

Military

Clubs/Associations

Robert Kinsley
Military Postal History Society
Newsletter: MPHS Bulletin
5410 Fern Loop
West Richmond, WA 99353
kinsley@owt.com
http://www.militaryPHS.org
  Formed for the purpose of collecting and studying military mail of all periods: "Field Post" markings, censorship, occupation, internment, prisoner of war camp covers, and propaganda labels and leaflets; publishes books on the subject.

Collectors

Harold Dylhoff
23511 Paulson's Rd.
Gobles, MI 49055-8651
ph: 269-628-4051
hdylxrds@aol.com
  Collecting A.P.O.s (Army Post Office) especially from 1940s to 1950s; Alaska Highway construction, WWII Alaska Forts; also Canadian NWT postmarks and A.P.O.s; send photocopies and LSASE for reply.

Virginia

Collectors

Lewis Leigh, Jr.
38785 Leighfield Ln.
Leesburg, VA 20175-6810
ph: 703-771-1015
fax: 703-771-1432
  Wants to buy postal history items especially pertaining to early Virginia: equipment & forms, old letters, documents, etc.

POSTCARDS

(see also BOOKS, Reference [Postcards]; ILLUSTRATORS; PAPER COLLECTIBLES)

Auction Services

Virginia Postcard Mail Auction
P.O. Box 1765
Manassas, VA 20108

John H. McClintock
Virginia Postcard Mail Auction
P.O. Box 1765
Manassas, VA 20108-1765
ph: 703-368-2757
  Conducts 5 to 6 illustrated postcard mail auctions per year; also promotes 6 postcard shows per year.

Martin J. Shapiro
VintagePostcards.com
312 Feather Tree Dr.
Clearwater, CT 33765
ph: 727-467-0555
fax: 727-467-0333
quality@vintagepostcards.com
http://www.VintagePostcards.com
  Offers vintage picture postcards for collectors; offers online catalog at Web site; also a mail service for want lists.

Ron Playle
Playle's Online Auctions
P.O. Box 65918
West Des Moines, IA 50265
ph: 515-279-0884
fax: 515-279-0884
ron@playle.com
http://www.playle.com/main.html
  Buy and sell postcards, stamps, coins, antiques, collectibles online.

Roger Harvey
Card Source
170 Selwyn Lane
Buffalo Grove, IL 60089-4333
ph: 847-520-8145
fax: 847-520-8145
RHarvey@thepostcard.com
http://www.thepostcard.com
  Deals in antique, collectible and modern postcards; established the first postcard shop on the Internet/World Wide Web; also appraises and auctions postcards.

Bob Coalbran
Card Mine, The
P.O. Box 56
Telford, Shropshire TF1 3WQ U.K.
http://www.cardmine.co.uk
  Specializes in European thematic and Victorian advertising collectible trade cards (sport and non-sport); regular auctions on Web site.

Trevor Vennett-Smith
T. Vennett-Smith Auctioneers & Valuers
11 Nottingham Rd.
Gotham, Nottingham NG11 OHE U.K.
ph: +44 (0)115 983 0541
fax: +44 (0)115 983 0114
info@vennett-smith.com
http://www.vennett-smith.com
  Great Britain's leading professional autograph auction house, specializing in bi-monthly auctions of fine and varied autographs; also postcards, trade cards, ephemera, sporting memorabilia.

Clubs/Associations

Judi Kearney, Pres.
South Jersey Postcard Club
Newsletter: Postcard Courier
303 Forrest Ave.
Ambler, PA 19002
ph: 215-646-6247
pntjudith1@aol.com
  Club membership is open to all; meets 2nd Sunday of each month at Prince of Peace Lutheran Church, Marlton, NJ.

Dr. James Lewis Lowe, Dir.
Deltiologists of America
E-zine: Postcard Classics
P.O. Box 8
Norwood, PA 19074
ph: 610-485-8572
PostcardClassics@juno.com
http://www.Deltiologists-America.com
  International postcard society for collectors, dealers, librarians, and archivist; free e-zine, "Postcard Classics," published online.

John H. McClintock
International Federation of Postcard Dealers, Inc.
Directory: Annual IFPD Directory
P.O. Box 1765
Manassas, VA 20108
ph: 703-368-2757
thewishbone@erols.com
http://www.playle.com/IFPD
  The Annual IFPD Directory of nearly 300 postcard dealers is free for $1 postage.

John H. McClintock, Dir
Postcard Society, Inc.
P.O. Box 1765
Manassas, VA 20108-1765
ph: 703-368-2757

Jane Pepper
Gateway Postcard Club
Newsletter: GPPC News
P.O. Box 28941
St Louis, MO 63132
jrpepper@inlink.com

Hal Ottaway
Wichita Postcard Club
Newsletter: Wichita Postcard NEWS
P.O. Box 780282
Wichita, KS 67278-0282
kskon@networksplus.net
http://members.fortunecity.com/
  wichitapcclub
  Club supports members with educational and informative meetings, newsletters and shows; monthly newsletter with free ads, annual events such as swap meet, auction, show, and Christmas dinner; members worldwide.

Joan Gentry, Pres.
Tucson Postcard Exchange Club
820 Via Lucitas
Tucson, AZ 85718-1046
ph: 520-297-0980
fax: 520-575-7010
joangentry@email.msn.com
http://iwhome.com/tpcec
*Club for postcard collectors in the
southern Arizona region.*

Lewis Baer
San Francisco Bay Area Postcard Club
Newsletter: SFBAPCC Newsletter
P.O. Box 621
Penngrove, CA 94951
ph: 707-795-2650
fax: 419-791-7549
ursusmjr@sonic.net
http://www.postcard.org
*Dedicated to encouraging the
collecting and study of postcards,
particularly within the San Francisco
Bay area; monthly newsletter,
programs, meetings.*

Hawai'i Postcard Club
P.O. Box 15273
Honolulu, HI 96830
fax: 808-922-2343
enelani@hawaii.rr.com
http://www.stampshows.com/hpc.html

Peter James, Sec.
Postcard Traders Association
Glanrhyd Station House
Manordeilo
Llandeilo, Dyfed SA19 7BP U.K.
ph: +44 (0) 1550 777064
info@postcard.co.uk
http://www.postcard.co.uk
*Represents foremost dealers and
auctioneers, fair organizers and
publishers in U.K & many worldwide;
organizes annual "Picture Postcard
Show" in London; Web site provides
information on all aspects of
postcards: fairs, clubs, dealers, etc.*

Collectors

John H. McClintock
P.O. Box 1765
Manassas, VA 20108-1765
ph: 703-368-2757
Promotes 6 postcard shows.

Ben Egerton
13009 Dover Rd.
Reisterstown, MD 21136-5512
ph: 410-561-5062
bgesr@attglobal.net
*Has been collecting postcards for over
20 years.*

Gary Olsen
505 S. Royal Ave.
Front Royal, VA 22630
ph: 540-635-7157 or 800-954-7374
fax: 540-635-1818
olsenhp@hpfri.com
http://www.hpfri.com
*Wants postcards with maps, music
themes, real estate subjects and/or
famous "persons" autographs.*

Marguerite Cantine
Cantine Kilpatrick
223 Southeast 37th Ave.
Ocala, FL 34471-3045
ph: 352-694-4514
fax: 352-694-4514
designbycantine@aol.com
*Wants advertising trade cards and
postcards from 1800s to 1915; none
later than 1915; prefers children,
chromolithographs, and product ads;
no photographs; no city or state
cards; send photocopy and price by
mail, fax, email.*

Jerry Abert
631 Broadway
East Alton, IL 62024
ph: 618-259-0901

Lee Aronsohn
16430 Westfall Place
Encino, CA 91436
ph: 818-905-0225
fax: 818-905-6334
overpaid@metawire.com
*Collects material relating to
cartoonist Gary Trudeau and the
"Doonesbury" comic strip; also wants
humorous 3-D postcards marked
"Eden Plastics," "Postplax," or
"Cardell."*

Lewis Baer
P.O. Box 621
Penngrove, CA 94951
ph: 707-795-2650
fax: 419-791-7549
ursusmjr@sonic.net
*Writes postcard column for "Postcard
Collector" and "Barr's News"
magazines; world's leading collector
of goats on postcards.*

Dealers

Siegfried Feller
Cartomania Plus
8 Amherst Rd.
Pelham, MA 01002-9739
ph: 413-253-3115
Specializes in European locales.

Jim & Kayce Dimond
P.O. Box 362
Pittsford, VT 05763
ph: 802-483-6610 or 802-775-6722
Jimandkc@aol.com
*Collecting, buying, selling better
views and topicals; appraisals, open
shop, shows; 30 years experience.*

Barbara & Richard DePalma
Deer Park Books
609 Kent Rd., Route 7
Gaylordsville, CT 06755
ph: 860-350-4140
deerparkbooks@earthlink.net
http://www.deerparkbooks.com
*Collector/dealer wants View cards of
small towns in CT, MA, and NY.*

Don Pocher
Old Cape May Cards
11 S. Lafayette St.
Cape May, NJ 08204-5301
ph: 609-884-3115
mermaid1@dandy.net
*Advanced collectors of lightship and
Cape May postcards; authors of
"Cape May in Vintage Postcards;"
specializes in postcards from South
Jersey.*

Bob & Kay Schies
452 East Bissell Ave.
Oil City, PA 16301-2063
ph: 814-677-3182
*Buying pre-1930 postcards, any
amount.*

Harry R. McKeon, Jr.
18 Rose Lane
Flourtown, PA 19031-1910
ph: 215-233-4094
toyspost@aol.com
*Send your postcards want list for
large unpicked selection also Victorian
trade cards.*

Jay Miller
725 S. Schell St.
Philadelphia, PA 19147
ph: 215-925-3839
artpostjm@aol.com
*Specializing in photographs: linen,
chrome, advertising, Roadside,
photos, PA, NJ, NYC, MidAtlantic,
FL views and roadside attractions,
poster type advertising.*

Sheldon Dobres
S. Dobres Postcards
P.O. Box 1855
Baltimore, MD 21203-1855
ph: 410-486-6569 or 800-342-5983
fax: 410-486-6587
sdpost@aol.com
http://www.deltiology.com/dobres.html
*Postcards bought and sold; top prices
paid for all US and foreign postcards.*

Mary L. Martin, Ltd.
4899 Pulaski Highway
P.O. Box 787
Perryville, MD 21903
ph: 410-575-7768 or 800-899-9887
fax: 410-642-2053
marymartinpostcards@prodigy.net
http://www.maryLmartin.com
*Specializing in state views, signed
artists, sports, transportation,
political, Halloween, Santas, etc.*

Alan Ronk
Paper Memories, LLC
P.O. Box 164
Roanoke, VA 24002
ph: 540-774-1881
alanero@aol.com
*Dealer, collector, expert wants to
purchase estate accumulations of old
picture postcards from the period
1900-1960s.*

Joseph L. Mashburn
Colonial House
P.O. Box 609 - M
Enka, NC 28728-0609
ph: 828-667-1427
fax: 828-667-1111
jmashb0135@aol.com
http://www.postcard-books.com
*Buys and sells antique postcards;
interested mainly in artist-signed
beautiful ladies, children, fantasy,
animals, blacks, nudes, real photos,
sports; specializing in Harrison
Fisher and Philip Boileau.*

Martin J. Shapiro
VintagePostcards.com
312 Feather Tree Dr.
Clearwater, CT 33765
ph: 727-467-0555
fax: 727-467-0333
quality@vintagepostcards.com
http://www.VintagePostcards.com
*Offers vintage picture postcards for
collectors; offers online catalog at
Web site; also a mail service for want
lists.*

Betty Powell
P.O. Box 571
Columbus, OH 43085-0571
ph: 614-885-1962
fax: 614-885-1962
*Buys and sells US postcards: artist
signed, holidays, topicals, views.*

Jerry Garrett
Jerry's Antiques & Postcards
1807 West Madison St.
Kokomo, IN 46901-1829
ph: 765-457-5256
Wants to buy old postcards.

Roger Harvey
Card Source
170 Selwyn Lane
Buffalo Grove, IL 60089-4333
ph: 847-520-8145
fax: 847-520-8145
RHarvey@thepostcard.com
http://www.thepostcard.com
*Deals in antique, collectible and
modern postcards; established the first
postcard shop on the Internet/World
Wide Web; also buys, sells, appraises
and auctions postcards.*

Robert M. Weisz
4562 N. Austin Ave.
Chicago, IL 60630-3116
ph: 773-545-2929 or 773-297-1337
*Buys, sells, appraises stamps,
envelopes and postcards.*

Jim Mehrer
Jim Mehrer's Postal History
2405 - 30th St.
Rock Island, IL 61201
ph: 309-786-6539
fax: 309-786-4840
mehrer@postal-history.com
http://www.postal-history.com
*Dealer, auctioneer conducts six postal
history mail bid sales per year, each
containing 3,000+ lots; also
postcards, reference literature,*

collectors' supplies and more; Web site has dealers and show calendar sections.

Jim Taylor
P.O. Box 399
Neosho, MO 64850
ph: 417-451-3463
jmtaylor@ipa.net
http://www.courthousesquare.net

Trenton Boyd
P.O. Box 517
Columbia, MO 65205-0517
ph: 573-882-2461 or 573-442-5235
fax: 573-882-2950
vetlib@missouri.edu
Interested in veterinary postcards including schools and military veterinary; also wants teratology cards that show animals with birth defects (e.g. five-legged calves); Red Cross dogs, Humane Association.

Terri McDaniels
Kansas Konnection, The
6613 East 47th St. S
Derby, KS 67037
kskon@networksplus.net
http://www.networksplus.net/kskon/tkk.htm
Specializes in postcards depicting state views and roadside attractions.

Tom & Barbara Tripp
3839 Bonneymoore Dr.
Fort Collins, CO 80524
ph: 970-482-4448
coloradoattic@aol.com
Specializes in antique and collectible postcards.

Ed Anderson
Kraze Ed
P.O. Box 1915
Temple City, CA 91780
ph: 626-309-7545
krazeed@flash.net
http://www.web-pac.com/mall/kraze-ed
Buys, sells, trades, collects postcards; also supplier of postcard protection sleeves and pages.

Steve Schmale
Out West
2231 Creekside Rd.
Santa Rosa, CA 95405-8022
ph: 707-838-1859 or 707-575-5406
outweststv@aol.com
Buys and sells better vintage postcards since 1976; approval service; strong in Western states views; always buying better cards and real photos; also wants railroad paper, stereoviews, photos, brochures, trade cards; member IFPD.

Tom Osjecki
Phyllis' Philatelics
P.O. Box 792
Canyonville, OR 97417
ph: 541-839-4135 or 541-839-6151
Buys, sells and specializes in postcards, paper Americana, stamps and covers; over 25,000 covers and postcards listed by state or topic.

Alicia & Jorge Valino
P.O. Box 1442
Montevideo, 11000 Uruguay
valino@valino.com
http://www.valino.com

Experts

Dr. James Lewis Lowe, Dir.
P.O. Box 8
Norwood, PA 19074
ph: 610-485-8572
PostcardClassics@juno.com
http://www.Deltiologists-America.com

Roy Cox
P.O. Box 3610
Hamilton, MD 21214
Author of "How to Price and Sell Old Picture Postcards," available from the author for $9.95 ppd.

V. Lee Cox
Memory Lane Postcards, Inc.
P.O. Box 66
Keymar, MD 21757-0066
ph: 410-775-0188 or 410-775-0190
memorylane@erols.com
http://www.memorylanepostcards.org

Joseph L. Mashburn
Colonial House
P.O. Box 609 - M
Enka, NC 28728-0609
ph: 828-667-1427
fax: 828-667-1111
jmashb0135@aol.com
http://www.postcard-books.com
Buys and specializes in high quality postcards; author and publisher of postcard price guides "The Postcard Price Guide," "The Artist-Signed Postcard Price Guide," and "Super Rare Postcards of Harrison Fisher;" write for prices.

Martin J. Shapiro
VintagePostcards.com
312 Feather Tree Dr.
Clearwater, CT 33765
ph: 727-467-0555
fax: 727-467-0333
quality@vintagepostcards.com
http://www.VintagePostcards.com
Offers vintage picture postcards for collectors; offers online catalog at Web site; also a mail service for want lists.

Susan Nicholson
Greater Chicago Productions
P.O. Box 595
Lisle, IL 60532
ph: 630-964-5240
deltiology@aol.com
http://www.susanbrownnicholson.com
Buys and sells rare and unusual postcards, Victorian valentines, periodicals, advertising trade cards, etc.

Allan Mellis
Mr. Ice Cream
1115 West Montana
Chicago, IL 60614-2220
ph: 773-327-9123
fax: 773-327-9456
mellisfamily@rcn.com
Wants better ice cream and soda fountain postcards, especially real photo, advertising, interiors, artist signed and comic; the image must be primarily ice cream related, i.e., no postcards that have only a small ice cream sign, please.

Laurel Kane
6036 Chip Shot Rd.
Grove, OK 74344
laurelrk66@aol.com
http://www.PostcardsFromTheRoad.net
Expert and advanced collector of postcards and other US highway-related memorabilia such as maps, travel guides, and motel guides; especially wants those related to Route 66; buys, sells, trades.

Ada Fitzsimmons
P.O. Box 337
San Anselmo, CA 94979-0337
ph: 415-454-5552
fax: 415-454-2947
apaperpile@aol.com
http://www.paperpilecollectibles.com
Buys, sells, appraises, lectures and write about postcards.

Naomi Welch
Images of the Past
309 Playa Blvd., Ste. 110
La Selva Beach, CA 95076-1737
ph: 831-689-0318
naomilaurawelch@sprintmail.com
Collector, dealer, expert specializes in Harrison Fisher; author of two books, published in 1999, entitled "The Complete Works of Harrison Fisher Illustrator," and "American & European Postcards of Harrison Fisher Illustrator."

Internet Resources

Jack D. Mount
Postcard Resources
jdmount@cox.net
http://members.cox.net/jdmount/postcard.html
Huge Internet list of postcard resources: clubs, auctions, catalogs, directories, chatting, personal pages, dealers, FAQs, listserves and newsgroups, museums, publications, shows, events, exhibitions, Webrings, trading lists, giveaways.

Terry Stewart
Collector Link
71 John St. East
Waterloo, Ontario N2J 1G2 Canada
ph: 519-745-1745
stewart@collector-link.com
http://www.collector-link.com
Catalogs over 2,000 trading card related Web sites for: baseball, hockey, basketball, football, other

sports, non-sports, phone cards, credit-debit cards, business cards, postcards.

Museums/Libraries

Katherine Hamilton-Smith
Curt Teich Postcard Archives, Lake County Discovery Museum
Journal: Image File
27277 Forest Preserve Dr.
Wauconda, IL 60084-2016
ph: 847-968-3381 or 847-968-3400
fax: 847-526-1545
TeichArchives@co.lake.il.us
http://www.teicharchives.org
The Teich Archives contain over 370,000 postcard and photographic images of 20th century history and culture, dating from 1893 to present; photocopying and photographic reproduction services are available.

Periodicals

Stacie Berger
Antique Trader Publications, Inc.
Magazine: Postcard Collector
P.O. Box 1050
Dubuque, IA 52004-1050
ph: 800-334-7165 or 800-482-4155
fax: 800-531-0880
stacie.berger@fwpubs.com
http://www.postcardcollector.com
The hobby's leading publication; best source to buy, sell, and learn about postcards and other paper collectibles; calendar of upcoming shows, postcard profiles, a collecting guide for moderns through the mail, and more.

CarPac Publishing
Newspaper: Barr's Post Card News
1800 W. D St.
Vinton, IA 52349
ph: 319-472-4713
fax: 319-472-3117
barrspcn@aol.com
http://www.barrspcn.com
A weekly deltiology newspaper containing postcard events, shows, news, articles, club directory, current prices, ads, etc.

Gloria Jackson
Newsletter: Gloria's Corner
P.O. Box 507
Denison, TX 75021-0507
ph: 903-463-4878
fax: 903-463-4878
gmj@texoma.net
A bi-monthly newsletter about postcards and the people who collect them; publishing since 1988.

Brian & Mary Lund
Reflections of a Bygone Age
Magazine: Picture Postcard Monthly
15 Debdale Lane
Keyworth, Nottinghamshire NG12 5HT
U.K.
ph: 0115-9374079
fax: 0115-9376197
reflections@argonet.co.uk
http://www.argonet.co.uk/users/
reflections/index.htm
Magazine designed for collectors of old picture postcards whatever your interest, theme or area; events, clubs, checklists, values, etc.; also includes a supplement of modern picture postcards from 1950; new issues, event, shops, values.

Suppliers

Monmouth Stamp & Coin
39 Monmouth St.
Red Bank, NJ 07701-1613
ph: 732-741-0626
fax: 732-741-0479
Postcard albums with 4 and 6 pocket crystal clear vinyl pages; send SASE for price list.

Aviation Related

(see also AVIATION MEMORABILIA)

Dealers

Larry Myers
Postcard Post, The
2539 Millers Woods Rd.
Boonville, NY 13309-5020
postcard@borg.com
http://www.postcardpost.com
Expert, dealer, collector; buys and sells postcards, specializing in rare airline postcard; Web site has many illustrated postcard articles; also airline postcard sales and auctions.

Bank Related

Collectors

John & Nancy Wilson
Wilson's Syngraphics
9353 SW 92nd Place Rd.
Ocala, FL 34481-6502
ph: 352-291-0775
fax: 352-291-0776
johnancyw@aol.com
http://www.johnnancywilson.com
Wants any pre-1929 paper money issued in the US; also wants any pre-1930 postcards depicting banks.

Foreign

Dealers

Gerald Rubackin
Jerry's Cards & Collectibles
P.O. Box 1271
Framingham, MA 01701-0207
ph: 508-788-0946
fax: 508-788-5197
jermyrauto@att.net
http://www.uacc.org/dealers/
rubackin.html
Buys early foreign postcards from Philippines and Hawaii: people, street scenes, advertising, costumes, real photo; no general views; need early atlases and Harpers Book of the Philippines.

Mexican

Collectors

Susan Frost
806 Rosedale Terrace
Austin, TX 78704-3159
ph: 512-447-2575 or 512-447-0407
fax: 512-447-2575
sfrost@austin.rr.com
http://www.io.com/~reuter
Collector of Mexican and Guatemalan postcards and specialist in photographs and postcards by Hugo Brehme (Germany 1882 - 1954 Mexico).

Photo (Real)

Auction Services

Bob Ward
Antique Paper Guild
P.O. Box 5742
Bellevue, WA 98006-0242
ph: 425-643-5701
fax: 425-641-4363
rwardapg@interserv.com
http://www.web-pac.com
Conducts periodic auctions specializing in pre-1935 real photo postcards; six mail/phone auction catalogs per year for $30, 8 1/2" x 11", profusely illustrated.

Experts

Bob Ward
Antique Paper Guild
P.O. Box 5742
Bellevue, WA 98006-0242
ph: 425-643-5701
fax: 425-641-4363
rwardapg@interserv.com
http://www.web-pac.com
Specializes in pre-1935 real photo postcards, stereographs and photographica; also conducts specialized auctions of same; author of "Investment Guide to North American Real Photo Postcards," "Real Photo Postcards: The 'Life-Size' Edition."

Photo (Real) Canadian

Dealers

Michael Rice
Michael Rice Collectibles
P.O. Box 286
Saanichton, British Columbia V8M 2C5
Canada
ph: 250-652-9412
fax: 250-652-7866
mrice@pacificcoast.net
Active buyer of Canadian, US, English, foreign pre-1930 picture postcards; wants used or unused; especially wants "real photo" views of Western Canadian provinces and the Yukon Territory; cards may be sent on approval; will pay postage.

Piano Related

Collectors

Janice E. Kelsh
633 Pennsylvania Ave.
Hagerstown, MD 21740-3769
ph: 301-797-7675
fax: 301-827-7039
mpec2000@hotmail.com
http://www.angelfire.com/music2/
miniaturepianoclub
Interested in obtaining miniature pianos of all kinds; also want postcards depicting pianos.

Post Office Related

Collectors

Dr. Frank R. Scheer, Curator
Railway Mail Service Library
12 E. Rosemont Ave.
Alexandria, VA 22301-2325
ph: 703-549-4095
fax: 703-836-1955
fscheer@erols.com
http://members.ebay.com/aboutme/
fscheer@erols.com
Buys post office related postcards - any condition, era, location or country. Will send free list with buying prices. Also wants postcards with views of street letterboxes, postal vehicles, post office interiors, etc.

States

(see also STATE RELATED MEMORABILIA)

Collectors

Richard Pace
12556 Timber Hollow Place
Germantown, MD 20874-1561
ph: 301-916-4357 or 202-708-3944 x2621
richardpace@starpower.net
A photographer who collects and wants to buy modern postcards depicting or related to the 50 States, the US Territories, and the District of Columbia.

States (Florida)

Collectors

Steve Hess
P.O. Box 1747
Deland, FL 32720-1747
ph: 386-736-1067
Buying Florida postcards: small town, depots, blacks; anything pre-1915 Florida.

States (Maryland)

Collectors

Jerry A. McCoy
800 Thayer Ave.
Silver Spring, MD 20910-4504
ph: 301-565-2519
sshistory@yahoo.com
Wants any postcards or memorabilia of Silver Spring, Maryland.

States (North Carolina)

Collectors

J. Robert Boykin, III
P.O. Box 7440
Wilson, NC 27895
ph: 252-237-1700
fax: 252-237-2314
boykinappraisals@coastalnet.com
Buying pre-1930s North Carolina postcards; no mountains; prefers early or real photo.

States (Pennsylvania)

Collectors

Richard A. Wood
P.O. Box 22165
Juneau, AK 99802-2165
ph: 907-789-8450
fax: 907-789-8450
dick@AlaskaWanted.com
http://www.ALaskaWanted.com
Wants postcards of Penna. Pike County towns: Milford, Twin Lakes, Shohola, Parker's Glen, Walker Lake, Woodtown; also ALASKA postcards.

States (West Virginia)

Collectors

Jerry A. McCoy
800 Thayer Ave.
Silver Spring, MD 20910-4504
ph: 301-565-2519
sshistory@yahoo.com
Wants any postcard of Gassaway, WV.

Randy Bryant
P.O. Box 62
Cannelton, WV 25036-0062
ph: 304-442-4480
Wants pre-1930 real photos and postcards of West Virginia: small towns, coal mining, lumbering, interiors, exteriors, lynchings, sports teams of WV coal towns; no scenic views (mountains, rivers, statues, etc.).

POSTER STAMPS

(see also STAMP COLLECTING)

Clubs/Associations

Walter Schmidt
Poster Stamp Society
Newsletter: Poster Stamp Society Bulletin
3654 Applegate Rd.
Jacksonville, OR 97530
ph: 541-899-1642
fax: 541-899-8933
pssoc@cdsnet.net
Poster stamps are non-postal stamps that function like miniature posters; generally designed to advertise a product or announce a public event such as a fair, carnival, exhibition, or convention; often used as propaganda to promote ideas.

Collectors

Charles Johnson
24 Woodbridge St.
Cambridge, MA 02140

Ray Petersen
P.O. Box 270511
W Hartford, CT 06127

Art Groten
Printer's Stone, Ltd., The
P.O. Box 30
Fishkill, NY 12524
ph: 845-471-4179
fax: 845-471-3829
info@printerstone.com
http://www.printerstone.com
*Buys and sells poster stamps and
other small format graphics; prompt
reply to all inquiries.*

Robert Du Bois
838 Temple Rd.
Pottstown, PA 19465

Roger Riga
P.O. Box 326
Eaton, OH 45320

Don Reuter
P.O. Box 190
South Lyon, MI 48178

Frank Backeneimer
P.O. Box 230
Glenview, IL 60025

Walter Schmidt
3654 Applegate Rd.
Jacksonville, OR 97530
ph: 541-899-1642
fax: 541-899-8933
pssoc@cdsnet.net
*Collects stamps depicting posters from
all over the world.*

Dealers

C. Stetson Thomas
Cindstamp
P.O. Box 599
Middleboro, MA 02346-0599
stetthomas@attbi.com
http://www.cindstamp.com
*Dealer in "Cinderella" material, i.e.,
philatelic "odd and unusual" that is
not listed in the Scotts Catalog of
postage stamps such as labels, poster
stamps, locals, fantasies, forgeries,
phantoms, etc.*

Bill Weinberger
21 Luddington Rd.
West Orange, NJ 07052
weinberb@anchorcon.com
*Buys and sells hotel & baggage
labels, Cinderella stamps, Poster
Stamps, and all other labels with the
exception of Christmas seals and can/
fruit/vegetable labels.*

Charles Rabinovitz
Cinderella Co.
P.O. Box 265
Sykesville, MD 21784-0265
ph: 410-549-2412
fax: 410-795-8936
chuckrab@aol.com
*Wants to buy poster stamps,
matchcovers, matchbox labels,
baggage labels.*

Ada Fitzsimmons
Paper Pile
P.O. Box 337
San Anselmo, CA 94979-0337
ph: 415-454-5552
fax: 415-454-2947
apaperpile@aol.com
http://www.paperpilecollectibles.com
*Dealer in poster stamps and
advertising stickers (1900 through
1960s); sells primarily US stamps and
stickers: expositions, sports, travel,
geographic.*

POSTERS

(see also ADVERTISING
COLLECTIBLES, Posters; CARTOON
ART; MAGICIANS
PARAPHERNALIA; MARINE CORPS
ITEMS; MILITARIA, WWI [Posters];
MILITARIA, WWII [Posters]; MOVIE
MEMORABILIA, Movie Posters;
PAPER COLLECTIBLES; PRINTS;
PRINTS [MODERN])

Auction Services

Terry Shargel
Poster Auctions International Inc
601 West 26th St., 13th Floor
New York, NY 1001
ph: 212-787-4000
fax: 212-604-9175
jrennert@angel.net
http://www.posterauction.com
*Conducts two poster-only auctions per
year emphasizing original French
advertising posters of the Belle
Epoque; prices range from $1,000 to
$65,000; resource for books on all
aspects of poster art; catalogue
available.*

Caroline Birenbaum
Swann Galleries, Inc.
104 E. 25th St.
New York, NY 10010-2977
ph: 212-254-4710
fax: 212-979-1017
swann@swanngalleries.com
http://www.swanngalleries.com
*Oldest/largest US auctioneer
specializing in rare books, autographs
& manuscripts, maps, atlases,
photographs, and works of art on
paper including vintage posters.*

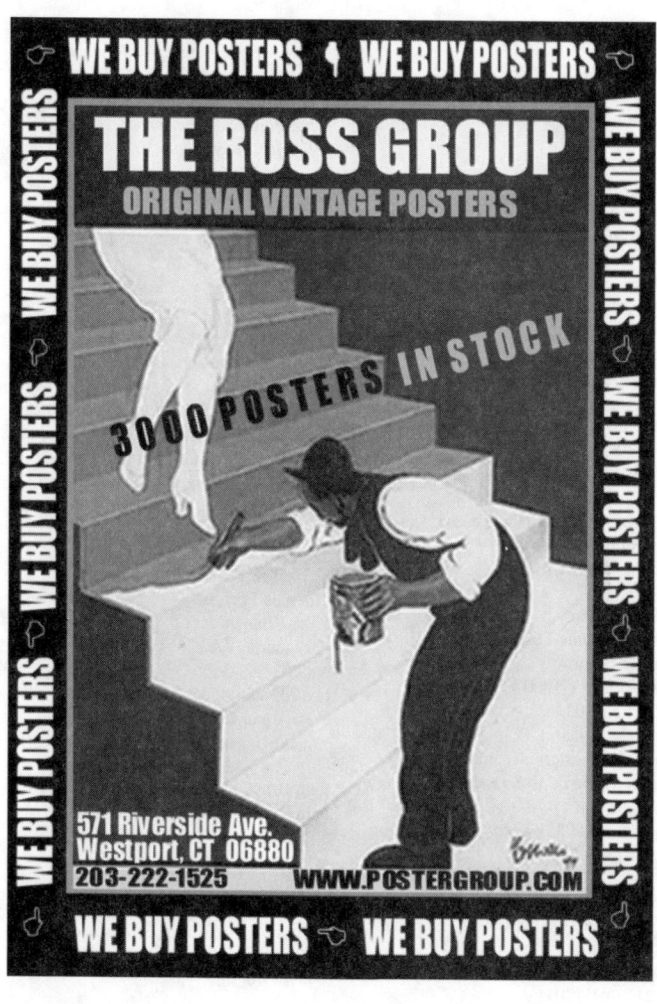

Clubs/Associations

International Vintage Poster Dealers
  Association
P.O. Box 501
New York, NY 10113-0501
ph: 212-355-8391
fax: 212-355-8391
info@ivpda.com
http://www.ivpda.com
*A trade association with strict
standards and guidelines for all its
members to insure the authenticity of
the posters which they sell and to
promote ethical and fair business
practices.*

Collectors

Dan Calandriello
10 Weston Place
Eatontown, NJ 07724
ph: 732-542-4770
danster-nj@comcast.net
*Wants Disney posters, tobacco
posters.*

Ken Trombly
1050 17th St., NW, Ste. 1250
Washington, DC 20036
ph: 800-673-8158 or 202-887-5000
fax: 202-457-0343
trombly@erols.com
http://www.magicposters.com
Wants original stone litho magic

*posters, Houdini items (photos,
letters, advertising, scrapbooks, etc.),
19th century broadsides and old
photos of magicians.*

Dealers

Nancy Steinbock
Nancy Steinbock Posters & Prints
12 Garrison St.
Chestnut Hill, MA 02467
ph: 800-438-1577
nancy@nancysteinbockposters.com
http://www.nancysteinbockposters.com
*Buys and sells posters 1880-present;
subjects: war, travel, circus, literary,
political, product advertising, etc.;
American or foreign.*

Mickey Ross
Ross Group Inc., The
571 Riverside Ave.
Westport, CT 06880
ph: 203-222-1525
fax: 203-222-1580
sales@postergroup.com
http://www.postergroup.com
*Buys and sells original vintage
advertising posters; a full service
gallery with over 3,000 posters on
display covering a wide variety of
topics.*

George Dembo
Poster Master
P.O. Box 657
Chatham, NJ 07928-0657
ph: 973-701-0713
fax: 973-701-0713
poster1776@aol.com
Wants to buy vintage posters (1860-1960) in good condition, especially War Posters; phone or write and send photos; wants one poster or a large collection.

Susan & Mario Carrandi
Carrandi Vintage Posters
122 Monroe Ave.
Belle Mead, NJ 08502-4608
ph: 908-874-0630
fax: 908-874-4892
mario@carrandimagic.com
http://www.carrandimagic.com
Buys and sells posters: French, circus, magic, Wild West, decorative.

Philip Williams
Philip Williams Posters
85 West Broadway
New York, NY 10007
ph: 212-513-0313
posters@mail.com
http://www.postermuseum.com
Specializing in posters since 1973; one of the largest poster galleries in the world; 50,000 original posters dating from 1870 to present.

Robert Chisholm
Chisholm Larsson Gallery
145 8th Ave.
New York, NY 10011
ph: 212-741-1703
fax: 212-645-6691
info@chisholm-poster.com
http://www.chisholm-poster.com
Deals in 100 years of original vintage posters: political, movie, circus, French advertisement, foreign posters; online catalog; also the only searchable database on the Internet with thousands of titles with prices and images.

Laura Gold
Park South Gallery at Carnegie Hall, The
154 West 57th St., Studio 11-114
New York, NY 10019
ph: 212-246-5900
fax: 212-541-5716
lauramgold@aol.com
http://www.parksouthgallery.com
Offering the finest examples of rare vintage original lithograph posters; specialty in classic French decorative posters from the 1880s through 1939; premier dealers in posters by Toulouse-Lautrec, Mucha, Steinlen, Cheret, Pal Grasset, et

Peggy Bronstein
646 Scranton Ave.
Lynbrook, NY 11563
ph: 516-599-5629
fax: 516-593-7527
posterpeg@aol.com
http://www.posterpeggy.com
In business since 1989; ardent

collectors; specializes in the sale of rare, original vintage advertising posters, c. 1890 to 1920: once advertised plays, concerts, liquor, bicycles, and other products; mainly France, Italy, Spain, US.

Debra Clifford
Vintage Poster Works
P.O. Box 88
Pittsford, NY 14534
ph: 716-218-9483
fax: 716-218-9035
debra@vintageposterworks.com
http://www.vintageposterworks.com
Buys and sells vintage posters including travel, military, advertising, French, European, magic, circus, and movie; online poster gallery, poster show, condition, grading and linen backing info; also sells books about vintage posters.

R. Neil Reynolds
Fine Old Posters
1015 King St.
Alexandria, VA 22314-2922
ph: 703-684-3656
fax: 703-684-4535
Buys and sells hundreds of original vintage posters.

Pam Brin
Pam Brin Gallery
8 Park Lane
Minneapolis, MN 55416-4340
ph: 612-920-3030
fax: 612-920-3031
Buys and sells posters; has over 150 WWI posters; issues periodic list of items for sale.

Spencer Weisz
Spencer Weisz Galleries
214 W. Ohio St.
Chicago, IL 60610
ph: 312-527-9420
grndvl@aol.com
http://www.spencerweisz.com
A full service gallery offering a huge selection of European vintage posters; specializes primarily in turn-of-the-century stone lithography featuring works by Toulouse Lautrec & Cappiello through post WWII artists such as Villemot.

Henry W. Taylor, Jr.
500 South Main St.
P.O. Box 2247
Ketchum, ID 83340-2247
ph: 208-726-5757
Wants to buy travel posters from the Western USA (especially Sun Valley, ID or Yellowstone Park), travel posters from Bavaria (Germany) or the Austrian Tyrol, old movie posters (especially Idaho and Montana).

Marty Rosenberg
MR Posters & Graphics
300 Vistoso Place
Santa Fe, NM 87501
ph: 505-986-8418
fax: 505-989-4396
rosenbergassociates@earthlink.net
http://www.mrposter.com
Carries an internationally recognized collection of award-winning posters spanning over 100 years.

Louis Bixenman
International Vintage Poster Fair
36 Vereda Serena
Santa Fe, NM 87505-5918
ph: 800-856-8069 or 505-438-0650
fax: 505-438-0060
pfair@dti.net
http://www.posterfair.com
A leading gallery of original vintage advertising posters from Europe, Asia, and the Americas; charter member of the International Vintage Poster Dealers Assoc.; inventory dates from 1890-1980; art Nouveau, Belle Epoque, etc.

Ken Taylor
La Belle Epoque
11661 San Vicente, #3304
Los Angeles, CA 90049-5110
ph: 310-442-0054 or 310-207-4345
fax: 310-826-6934
ktscicon@ix.netcom.com
Buys and sells vintage posters: travel, war, aviation, shipping, railway, advertising, Art Deco, Art Nouveau, sport, movie, etc.

Garrison Dover
Pacific Posters International
P.O. Box 3896
Santa Barbara, CA 93130
ph: 805-968-2384
webmaster@pacificposters.com
http://www.pacificposters.com
Buys and sells posters: alcohol & liquor, tobacco, food & beverages, clothing & products, theatre & stage, opera & musicals, music & dance, movies & cinema, travel & transportation, ski & sports.

Maurice & Laya Jakubowicz
Affiche Francaise
128 Avenue de la Chevre d'Or
Vallauris, 06220 France
ph: 33 (0)493 63 45 92
fax: 33 (0)493 63 45 92
ml@affiche-francaise.com
http://www.affiche-francaise.com
Buy and sell 1880-present vintage posters, mainly European, all subjects: advertising, travel, theater, sport, World War, cycles, political, etc.

Experts

Tony Fusco
Fusco & Four, Associates
One Murdock Terrace
Brighton, MA 02135-2817
ph: 617-787-2637
fax: 617-782-4430
fuscofour@aol.com
Vintage posters 1800s to WWII plus selected modern art posters; author of "The Confident Collector Identification & Price Guide to Posters;" offers appraisal and brokerage services for vintage 1870-1940 poster collectors.

George Theofiles
Miscellaneous Man
P.O. Box 1776
New Freedom, PA 17349-0076
ph: 717-235-4766
fax: 717-235-2853
miscman@adelphia.net
Collects, buys and sells; since 1970 offering catalogs of rare posters and early advertising and ephemera on hundreds of subjects. Descriptive flyer available.

Misc. Services

Phil Temple
Phil Temple Poster Mounting Service
P.O. Box 561
Novato, CA 94948
ph: 415-897-5130
fax: 415-897-5130
magiccircus@earthlink.net
Poster mounting service since 1980; linen mounting for posters of all sizes: 1/4 sheet to 20 sheets in size; highly competitive prices, excellent references.

Repair Services

Funny Face Productions
147 Main St.
Haydenville, MA 01039-0282
ph: 413-268-9215
artandfilm@cs.com
http://www.funnyfaceproductions.com
Fixes stains, missing pieces, faded areas and tears, remounts posters on Japanese paper and linen backs.

Eastern European

Dealers

Judy Sullivan
Eastern European Art Company
0208 Caballo
Carbondale, CO 81623
ph: 970-963-8789
fax: 970-963-9565
aspartmkt@aol.com
Sells rare, original posters from Eastern Europe, mainly from Poland, dating from 1945 of American and foreign films, sports, music, political, circus, travel, theater, and exhibits; posters have very unusual graphics and colors.

Music

Collectors

Jim Abicht
131 Main St.
P.O. Box 157
Smithfield, VA 23431
ph: 757-365-0223
bobani@visi.net
Collector of 1960s Rock music posters; any poster artist, musician, venue.

Dealers

J. Kastor
Psychedelic Solution
33 W. 8th St., 2nd Floor
New York, NY 10011
ph: 212-529-2462 or 800-558-7950
fax: 212-475-4395
info@psychedelicsolution.com
http://www.psychedelicsolution.com
Carries reference books on '60s and '70s rock art and psychedelic posters; publishes price lists; also offers appraisals and consultations.

Experts

Professor Poster
ph: 650-355-2311 or 650-993-6686
pfrpstr@best.net
http://www.best.com/~pfrpstr
Historian, archivist, collector, appraiser, restoration expert; specializes in Rockart, Rock posters for concerts and events; psychedelic posters and art from the 1960s to present day.

POSTMARKS

(see STAMP COLLECTING, Postmarks)

POT LIDS

(see OINTMENT POTS & POT LIDS)

POTTERY

(see CERAMICS; COOKIE JARS; DINNERWARE; FIGURINES; FLOWER "FROGS"; REPAIR/RESTORATION/CONSERVATION; SALT & PEPPER SHAKERS; STEINS; TILES)

POWDER HORNS

(see also ARMS & ARMOR; FIREARMS)

Collectors

David A. Galliher
2500 W. Berwyn Rd.
Muncie, IN 47304-5113
ph: 317-289-2233 or 317-284-6668
fax: 317-289-2376
Wants very early powder horns (late 1700s to 1812), engraved and with historical significance.

Dealers

William H. Guthman
Guthman Americana
P.O. Box 392
Westport, CT 06881
ph: 203-259-9763
fax: 203-319-0882
ejstilling@yahoo.com
Specializes in Colonial and Federal period military and historical materials, such as weapons, powder horns, and documents; also American Indian objects.

Experts

William H. Guthman
Guthman Americana
P.O. Box 392
Westport, CT 06881
ph: 203-259-9763
fax: 203-319-0882
ejstilling@yahoo.com
Author of "Drums A'beating, Trumpets Sounding: Artistically Carved Powder Horns in the Provincial Manner, 1746-1781."

Jim Dresslar
c/o Dresslar Publishing
P.O. Box 635
Bargersville, IN 46106
ph: 317-422-5147
Author of "Folk Art of Early America - The Engraved Powder Horn" (Dresslar Publishing), available from the author.

PRECOLUMBIAN

(see also PREHISTORIC ARTIFACTS)

Appraisers

Glenn A. Long
Long & Manzi Fine Art Services, Inc.
ph: 518-854-3388
fax: 518-854-3999
topappraisers@hotmail.com
Private dealers and appraisers serving collectors and museums for over 25 years; specializes in art, drawings, paintings, photography & photographs, 19th and 20th century sculpture, African, Native American, Precolumbian.

Anna C. Sim
235 Richard Burbydge
Williamsburg, VA 23185
ph: 757-258-1113
fax: 757-229-5050
acsiminc@cox.net

Tara Ana Finley
Anubis Appraisers & Estate Services, Inc.
1042 Sorolla Ave.
Miami, FL 33134-3560
ph: 305-446-1820 or 786-486-8042
fax: 305-648-1939
tara.finley@worldnet.att.net
Thirty years experience appraising
Precolumbian art for insurance, donation or probate purposes.

Auction Services

Greg Manning
Greg Manning Auctions, Inc.
775 Passaic Ave.
West Caldwell, NJ 07006
ph: 973-882-0004 or 800-221-0243
fax: 973-882-3499
gmauction@aol.com
http://www.gregmanning.com
Since 1905, a leading auctioneer of Americana, glass, stoneware, and antiquities.

Howard Rose
Arte Primitivo Gallery
3 East 65th St., Ste. 2
New York, NY 10021
ph: 212-570-6999 or 212-570-0393
fax: 212-570-1899
info@arteprimitivo.com
http://www.arteprimitivo.com
Specializes in Classical and Egyptian antiquities, Precolumbian art, ethnographic art, Asian antiquities, and books; conducts absentee/callback auctions biennially and publishes lavish color catalog with each auction.

Dealers

Norman Hurst, ISA CAPP
Hurst Gallery
53 Mount Auburn St.
Cambridge, MA 02138-5030
ph: 617-491-6888 or 212-744-6488 (NYC)
fax: 617-661-0439
NHurst@compuserve.com
http://www.hurstgallery.com
Buys, sells, appraises African, Oceanic, Native American, Precolumbian and Asian art; has been appraising, authenticating, and dealing in Precolumbian art of North and South America for over 25 years.

Jonathan T. Carofino
Jonathan T. Carofino Pre-Columbian Art
402 Essex Court
Torrington, CT 06790
ph: 860-965-5704
ancient@pre-columbian-art.com
http://www.pre-columbian-art.com
Buys, sells, appraises, specializes in Pre-Columbian art and other ancient art.

David Bernstein
David Bernstein Pre-Columbian Art
737 Park Ave., Ste. 11B
at 71st St.
New York, NY 10021
ph: 212-794-0389
fax: 212-861-8728
dbfinearts@att.net
http://www.precolumbianart4sale.com
Private dealer specializing in Andean and South American Pre-Columbian art including Taino Art from the Caribbean, metalwork and Peruvian textiles and weavings; established in
1979; deals with both the new and advanced collector.

John Buxton
Shango Galleries
6717 Spring Valley
Dallas, TX 75254
ph: 972-239-4620 or 972-239-9943
fax: 972-239-9766
jbuxton@arttrak.com
http://www.arttrak.com
Buys, sells, and appraises African, Precolumbian, Oceanic, and American Indian art.

Michael D. Higgins
Michael D. Higgins & Son Antique Indian Art
4429 N. Campbell Ave.
Tucson, AZ 85718
ph: 520-577-8330
mdhiggins@earthlink.net
http://www.mhiggins.com
Appraises, buys and sells antique American Indian, PreColumbian, Mexican and Spanish Colonial antiques; since 1972; also wants paintings of the American West; museum references available.

Joel & Michael Malter
Malter Galleries, Inc.
17003 Ventura Blvd., Ste. 205
Encino, CA 91316
ph: 818-784-7772 or 888-784-2131
fax: 818-784-4726
mike@maltergalleries.com
http://www.maltergalleries.com

David Markarian
Markarian Ancient Artifacts
P.O. Box 2476
Rancho Mirage, CA 92270-1087
ph: 760-202-5000
orion@inland.net
http://www.ancientart.org
Buys and sells Precolumbian artifacts.

Museums/Libraries

Dumbarton Oaks Research Library & Collection
1703 32nd St. NW
Washington, DC 20007
ph: 202-339-6400
DumbartonOaks@doaks.org
http://www.doaks.org

Dr. Ramiro Matos
National Museum of Natural History
10th St. & Constitution Ave.
Washington, DC 20560
ph: 202-357-2700
dennis@smithson.si.edu
http://www.mnh.si.edu
Distinguished Peruvian archaeologist.

PREHISTORIC ARTIFACTS

(see also NATIVE AMERICAN; ARCHAEOLOGY; FOSSILS; HERITAGE RESOURCES; MINERAL SPECIMENS; PRECOLUMBIAN)

Auction Services

Lolli Brothers
704 Main St., Ste. A
Macon, MO 63552
ph: 660-385-2516
lollibros@lollibros.com
http://www.lollibros.com

Book Sellers

Pat Dunnegan
Dunnegan Enterprises
P.O. Box 156
Gustine, TX 76455
ph: 888-841-9386
teddun@itexas.net
http://www.arrowheads-relics.com

Collectors

Bill Balinger
P.O. Box 296
North Lewisburg, OH 43060
ph: 937-747-2225
fax: 937-747-2784
Collector of prehistoric and native American Indian artifacts.

Lar Hothem
Hothem House
P.O. Box 458
Lancaster, OH 43130-0458
ph: 740-653-9030
shothem@greenapple.com
http://www.HothemHouse.com
Wants prehistoric American Indian artifacts, mainly from Ohio.

Dealers

Alton Martin
Artifacts, Inc.
P.O. Box 484
Cave Spring, GA 30124
ph: 770-487-3248
amartin2@earthlink.net
http://www.artifactsetc.com
Offers quality, investment grade, genuine American Indian prehistoric and historic artifacts: stone, flint, pottery; all legally obtained.

Kevin Dowdy
Flint River Trading Post
P.O. Box 234
Fowlstown, GA 31752
ph: 912-221-1999 or 912-243-7064
bolenbevel@aol.com
http://www.artifactsguide.com
Specializing in prehistoric Native American artifacts from Georgia, Alabama, and Florida; buys, sells, trades, takes on consignment, appraises only guaranteed genuine pieces; price and identification guide available.

Scott Young
Scott Young Stone Age Artifacts & Fossils
P.O. Box 8452
Port Saint Lucie, FL 34985-8452
ph: 561-878-5634
fax: 561-878-2209
Appraiser, dealer buys, sells, trades American Indian relics, pre-historic pottery, points, tools, stone, shell,

bone, etc.; also stone age artifacts world wide; Precolumbian artifacts; one item or whole collection.

Mark Clark
624 Providence Blvd.
Clarksville, TN 37042
ph: 931-645-9218 or 931-237-3646
markclarksville@aol.com

Tom & David Davis
Davis Artifacts, Inc.
P.O. Box 676
449 Oak Ridge Dr.
Stanton, KY 40380
ph: 606-663-2741
fax: 606-663-4370
support@tomdavisartifacts.com
http://www.tomdavisartifacts.com
Dealer, authenticator, appraiser of prehistoric native American artifacts including arrowheads, tools, pottery, etc.

Jerry & Sandy Sherman
Paleoworld Connection
2029 Iroquois Trail
Columbus, IN 47203
ph: 812-314-4731
fax: 812-314-2253
paleoworld@voyager.net
http://www.paleoworld.com
Deals in Native American, prehistoric artifacts and fossils worldwide.

Pat Dunnegan
Dunnegan Enterprises
P.O. Box 156
Gustine, TX 76455
ph: 888-841-9386
teddun@itexas.net
http://www.arrowheads-relics.com

Roger Dillard
Dillards Artifacts
135 Creekside Dr.
Boerne, TX 78006
ph: 830-249-5643
rdillard@hcadventures.com
http://www.texasmidwestartifacts.com
Buys, sells, trades, appraises Indian artifacts anywhere in the US; legally obtained artifacts only.

Richard B. Troyanowski
Rich Relics
P.O. Box 432
Sandia Park, NM 87047-0432
ph: 505-281-2611 or 505-281-2329
Buys/sells prehistoric/historic Indian artifacts, cowboy, militaria, old world antiquities & coins, fossils & ethnographic collectibles.

Jackson Galleries
3844 W. Channel Islands Blvd.
Oxnard, CA 93035
ph: 800-466-3836
fax: 805-985-3279
psychohill@hotmail.com
http://www.jacksongalleries.com
Specializes in arrow points and other prehistoric artifacts; uses latest technologies for appraising.

Experts

Kevin Dowdy
Flint River Trading Post
P.O. Box 234
Fowlstown, GA 31752
ph: 912-221-1999 or 912-243-7064
bolenbevel@aol.com
http://www.artifactsguide.com
Specializing in prehistoric Native American artifacts from Georgia, Alabama, and Florida; buys, sells, trades, takes on consignment, appraises only guaranteed genuine pieces; price and identification guide available.

Len Weidner
Indian River Industries
13706 Robins Rd.
Westerville, OH 43082
ph: 614-965-2868 or 800-444-1280
fax: 614-965-5913
janiew48@aol.com
http://members.aol.com/JanieW48
Collector, dealer, and expert paying cash for Indian relics, both historic and prehistoric; author of many books on Indian relics.

Museums/Libraries

Anne Kaupp
National Museum of Natural History, Anthropology Public Information Office
Smithsonian
NHBMRC112
Washington, DC 20560
ph: 202-357-1592
dennis@smithson.si.edu
http://www.mnh.si.edu
With questions about found artifacts first try calling your State Archaeology department or the anthropology department of a local natural history museum.

Bob McWilliam
Museum of the Texas Amateur Archaeological Association
102 Hwy 27E #108
Ingram, TX 78025
ph: 803-367-7012
fax: 803-367-7012
txcache@aol.com
http://arrowheads.com/taaa
A museum featuring ancient Indian artifacts from all over Texas; members of the TAAA put their collections on display on a rotating basis.

Periodicals

Gary L. Fogelman
Magazine: Indian Artifact Magazine
245 Fairview Rd.
Turbotville, PA 17772-9063
ph: 570-437-3698
fax: 570-437-3411
iam@uplink.net
http://www.indian-artifacts.net
An easy reading quarterly focusing on American Indian prehistory: artifacts, tools, lifestyles, customs, archaeology, book reviews; everything about

collecting, buying, finding and enjoying Indian artifacts.

Bill Balinger
Magazine: Prehistoric Antiquities & Archaeological News
P.O. Box 296
North Lewisburg, OH 43060
ph: 937-747-2225
fax: 937-747-2784
Quarterly magazine about archaeology and antiquities; articles, ads, etc.

Arrowheads & Points

Clubs/Associations

Kolomoki Society
Newsletter: Kolomoki Newsletter
P.O. Box 185
Jakin, GA 31761-0185
amartin2@earthlink.net
http://www.artifactsetc.com/kolomoki.htm

Bob McWilliam
Texas Amateur Archeological Association
Magazine: Texas Cache
102 Hwy 27E #108
Ingram, TX 78025
ph: 803-367-7012
fax: 803-367-7012
txcache@aol.com
http://arrowheads.com/taaa
A learning experience and adventure in archaeology, arrowhead hunting and collecting; photos and stories of Texas and Southwest points; national artifact show; archaeological digs.

Collectors

Mark Clark
624 Providence Blvd.
Clarksville, TN 37042
ph: 931-645-9218 or 931-237-3646
markclarksville@aol.com

David Crain
Texas Arrowheads & Indian Artifacts
Rt. 3 Box 107
Sweeny, TX 77480
davidcrain@mail.com
http://www.texasarrowheads.com
Artifact collector's Web site with lithic tool typology, updated archaeological information, descriptions and photos of Texas arrowheads and Indian artifacts.

Dealers

Bob's Flint Shop
ph: 877-244-8998 or 970-241-7295
fax: 970-241-7516
knowlton@gj.net
http://www.bobsarrowheads.com
Buys, sells, trades, arrowheads and other prehistoric artifacts; also accepts consignment sales.

David Summers
Native American Artifacts
45 West Parkway
Victor, NY 14564-1243
ph: 585-924-5167
fax: 585-924-5167
naasummers@aol.com
Dealer, appraiser, collector; one of the world's largest dealers in American Indian art and antiquities; buys and sells; specializing in Northeastern Indian specimens.

Alton Martin
Artifacts, Inc.
P.O. Box 484
Cave Spring, GA 30124
ph: 770-487-3248
amartin2@earthlink.net
http://www.artifactsetc.com
Offers quality, investment grade, genuine American Indian prehistoric and historic artifacts: stone, flint, pottery; all legally obtained.

Roy Mitchell
3104 Glenmere Place, S.W.
Decatur, AL 35603
ph: 256-350-3103
Wants to buy Indian relics.

Arkansas Ozarks Arrowheads
P.O. Box 68
Saint Joe, AR 72675
ph: 870-439-2542
Dealing in only 100% authentic Indian artifacts; offers warranty; over 200 artifacts online.

Pat Dunnegan
Pat's Authentic Indian Artifacts
201 Harrison Ave.
Gustine, TX 76455
ph: 888-841-9386 or 915-667-7210
teddun@itexas.net
http://www2.itexas.net/~teddun
Online close-up photos of quality authentic American Indian artifacts offered for sale; also a selected list of related books; over 40 years in business.

Roger Dillard
Dillards Artifacts
135 Creekside Dr.
Boerne, TX 78006
ph: 830-249-5643
rdillard@hcadventures.com
http://www.texasmidwestartifacts.com
Buys, sells, trades, appraises Indian artifacts anywhere in the US; legally obtained artifacts only.

Experts

Robert Overstreet
Gemstone Publishing, Inc.
1966 Greenspring Dr.
Lutherville Timonium, MD 21093
ph: 888-375-9800 or 410-560-5806
fax: 410-560-6107
obob@gemstonepub.com
http://www.gemstonepub.com
Author of "The Overstreet Indian Arrowheads Identification & Price Guide."

Sam Williams
Arrowheads Dot Com
1610 West Main
Eastland, TX 76448
ph: 254-629-2549 or 800-538-3490
fax: 254-629-2550
sam@arrowheads.com
http://www.arrowheads.com
Collector, dealer and expert specializing in arrowheads and other authentic American Indian artifacts.

Richard B. Troyanowski
Rich Relics
P.O. Box 432
Sandia Park, NM 87047-0432
ph: 505-281-2611 or 505-281-2329
Specializes in prehistoric lithics (stone items, e.g., arrowheads, points, clubs, bowls, etc.).

Internet Resources

Hugh Jarvis
Lithics Site, The
hjarvis@acsu.buffalo.edu
http://wings.buffalo.edu/anthropology/lithics.html
Great page with lots of links to all kinds of archaeological resources: lithics research projects, literary resources, related institutional sites, archaeological courses on lithics, artifact information, commercial concerns.

Sam Williams
Arrowheads Dot Com
1610 West Main
Eastland, TX 76448
ph: 254-629-2549 or 800-538-3490
fax: 254-629-2550
sam@arrowheads.com
http://www.arrowheads.com
Informational resource and an online chat room for artifact enthusiasts; legal issues, arrowheads for sale, trader's corner, calendar of events, arrowhead typology, products, arrowhead links.

PREMIUMS

(see also CEREAL BOXES; CRACKER JACK COLLECTIBLES; GROCERY STORE ITEMS; FAST FOOD COLLECTIBLES; PAPER COLLECTIBLES; TELEVISION SHOWS & MEMORABILIA)

Collectors

Chris Swain
P.O. Box 513
Williamsburg, MA 01096
ph: 413-628-3213
Bluejettoy@aol.com
Wants radio show and cereal premiums from the 1930s through the 1950s.

Bob Havey
P.O. Box 183
North Sullivan, ME 04664-0183
ph: 207-422-3083
fax: 207-422-3430
Wants radio and cereal box premiums: rings, badges, decoders, etc. from Superman, Tom Mix, Buck Rogers, cowboys, etc.

Ed Pragler
P.O. Box 284
Wharton, NJ 07885-0284
ph: 973-875-8293
radiopremium@aol.com
Wants to buy radio premiums, box top & cereal giveaways, comic character collectibles: rings, decoders, badges, manuals, maps, pin-back buttons, cereal boxes, figurines, etc. from Buck Rogers, Capt. Marvel, Capt. America, Flash Gordon, etc.

Dealers

Ken Mitchell
710 Conacher Dr.
Willowdale, Ontario M2M 3N6 Canada
ph: 416-222-5808
Appraises, collects, buys and sells 1890 to 1970s comic books, newspapers, comic strips, "Big Little" books, popular music/jazz books/magazines/tapes; pulp magazines, original comic art, radio and cereal premiums.

Experts

Ted Hake
Hake's Americana & Collectibles
Auction
P.O. Box 1444
York, PA 17405-1444
ph: 717-848-1333
Ted@hakes.com
http://www.hakes.com
Author of "Hake's Guide to TV Collectibles" and several other books on collectibles; always purchasing items for mail-bid auctions of Disneyana, historical Americana, toys, premiums, political items, character and other collectibles.

Cereal Box

(see also CEREAL BOXES)

Collectors

Roland Coover
1537 E. Strasburg Rd.
West Chester, PA 19380-6380
ph: 610-692-3112
rlcoover@aol.com
Wants cereal items: cereal boxes, premiums, and store displays from the 1950s to 1980s; Cap'n Crunch, Quisp, Quake, Freakies, Frankenberry, King Vitamin; also wants items from kids products such as Bosco, Fizzies, candy, cookies, etc.

Kevin Meisner
5400 Cheshire Meadows Way
Fairfax, VA 22032-3216
ph: 703-527-3485
Meisner65@aol.com
http://members.tripod.com/~Meisner65
Wants to buy Freakies stuff: cereal boxes, prizes from Freakies cereal, Freakies figures, Freakies boats, Freakies rings, Goody Goody Fruit Hat figure, and the Hamhose Good Friends Medal, magnets, flip-n-flys, fun dots, etc.

Aaron Sultan
3201 Arrowood Dr.
Raleigh, NC 27604
ph: 919-954-7111
Wants to buy cereal premiums and toys: Quisp, Cap'n Crunch, Freakies, Frankenberry, etc.

David Welch
P.O. Box 714
Murphysboro, IL 62966-0714
ph: 618-687-2282
fax: 618-684-2243
PEZDude1@aol.com
http://www.pezheads.net/dwelch
Wants giveaway or send-away items offered through cereal boxes and relating to TV, sports, comic, cartoon or movie characters, especially super heroes.

Dan Goodsell
Tick Tock Toys
P.O. Box 48021
Los Angeles, CA 90048
grickily@aol.com
http://www.theimaginaryworld.com/page4.html
Interested in all 1940s to 1970s kid's food packaging and premiums such as cereal boxes and cereal box prizes.

Dealers

Bob Gobeil
Bobby's Toys & Collectibles
P.O. Box 1416
Biddeford, ME 04005
bob@bobbystoys.com
http://www.bobbystoys.com
Offers character toys from the 1970s and 1980s from Alfs to Wuzzles; also TV and movie memorabilia, cereal premiums, fast food collectibles.

Experts

Tom Tumbusch
Tomart Publications
3300 Encrete Lane
Dayton, OH 45439-1944
ph: 937-294-2250
fax: 937-294-1024
office@tomart.com
http://www.tomart.com
Buys radio, cereal, comic book, etc. premiums, i.e., rings, badges, etc.; author of "Illustrated Radio Premium Catalog & Price Guide."

Comics

Collectors

John S. Fawcett
P.O. Box 1156
Waldoboro, ME 04572-1156
ph: 207-832-7398
fawcetoy@gwi.net
http://home.gwi.net/~fawcetoy
Wants to buy comic book subscription giveaway premiums; radio show rings, decoders, etc.

Dealers

Ken Mitchell
710 Conacher Dr.
Willowdale, Ontario M2M 3N6 Canada
ph: 416-222-5808
Appraises, collects, buys and sells 1890 to 1970s comic books, newspapers, comic strips, "Big Little" books, popular music/jazz books/magazines/tapes; pulp magazines, original comic art, radio and cereal premiums.

Radio Show

(see also CHARACTER COLLECTIBLES; COWBOY HEROES; RADIO SHOWS, Old Time [Straight Arrow], SPACE COLLECTIBLES)

Collectors

Bruce Thalberg
23 Mountain View Dr.
Weston, CT 06883-1317
ph: 203-227-8175
gortoh@yahoo.com
Wants Lone Ranger, Sky King, Space Patrol, Tom Mix, Roy Rogers, The Shadow, Capt. Midnight, Terry & the Pirates, etc., especially pre-1965 rings; all novelty rings considered; photocopy helpful; please price items & send SASE.

David Welch
P.O. Box 714
Murphysboro, IL 62966-0714
ph: 618-687-2282
fax: 618-684-2243
PEZDude1@aol.com
http://www.pezheads.net/dwelch
Wants giveaway or send-away items offered through radio programs and comic books relating to TV, sports, comic, cartoon or movie characters, especially super heroes.

Dealers

Leon Rue
18132 James Rd.
Cathedral City, CA 92861
ph: 714-998-6393
Buys and sells radio show premiums such as from Capt. Midnight, Little Orphan Annie, Tom Mix, Amos & Andy, etc.; has over 400 to sell; digital pictures available for all.

Ken Mitchell
710 Conacher Dr.
Willowdale, Ontario M2M 3N6 Canada
ph: 416-222-5808
Appraises, collects, buys and sells 1890 to 1970s comic books, newspapers, comic strips, "Big Little" books, popular music/jazz books/magazines/tapes; pulp magazines, original comic art, radio and cereal premiums.

Experts

Tom Tumbusch
Tomart Publications
3300 Encrete Lane
Dayton, OH 45439-1944
ph: 937-294-2250
fax: 937-294-1024
office@tomart.com
http://www.tomart.com
Buys radio, cereal, comic book, etc. premiums, i.e., rings, badges, etc.; author of "Illustrated Radio Premium Catalog & Price Guide."

Radio Show (Jimmie Allen)

Collectors

Jack Deveny
6805 Cheyenne Trail
Edina, MN 55439-1158
ph: 612-941-2457
plane@itol.net
Wants Jimmie Allen Flying Club wings, I.D. bracelets, knife, whistles, maps, blotters, membership cards, aircraft models, etc.

Rings

Collectors

Steve A. Geppi
Diamond Comic Distributors, Inc.
1966 Greenspring Dr., Ste. 300
Lutherville Timonium, MD 21093-4161
ph: 410-560-7100
webmaster@diamondcomics.com
http://www.diamondcomics.com
Wants to buy old and rare comic rings: Spider, Howdy Doody Jack-in-the-Box, Cisco Kid Secret Compartment, Tom Mix Spinner, Radio Orphan Annie Altascope, Superman, Lone Ranger Meteorite, Valric the Viking, Joe Louis, etc.

Dealers

Joe Statkus
Eat at Joe's Collectibles
84 State Rd.
Eliot, ME 03903
ph: 207-439-7429
yozi2@aol.com
http://www.toyring.com
Offers the world's largest inventory of post-1950s toy rings along with a huge emphasis on flicker rings; also carries some pre-1950s toy rings; Web site has over 700 different flicker rings; will evaluate rings for free.

Robert Overstreet
Gemstone Publishing, Inc.
1966 Greenspring Dr.
Lutherville Timonium, MD 21093
ph: 888-375-9800 or 410-560-5806
fax: 410-560-6107
obob@gemstonepub.com
http://www.gemstonepub.com
Author of "The Overstreet Toy Ring Price Guide."

Mark Farace
All American Collectibles
6510 Chippewa St.
Saint Louis, MO 63109-4107
ph: 314-353-9500 or 314-352-7700
mf@aac-mo.com
http://www.aac-mo.com

Experts

Danny Fuchs
209-80 18th Ave., #4K
Bayside, NY 11360-1424
ph: 718-225-9030
fax: 718-225-3688
superdf62@aol.com
"America's foremost Superman Collector;" co-author of "The Adventures of Superman Collecting."

Tom Tumbusch
Tomart Publications
3300 Encrete Lane
Dayton, OH 45439-1944
ph: 937-294-2250
fax: 937-294-1024
office@tomart.com
http://www.tomart.com
Buys radio, cereal, and comic book, premiums, i.e., rings, badges, etc.; author of "Illustrated Radio Premium Catalog & Price Guide."

PRESIDENTIAL MEMORABILIA

(see PERSONALITIES [HISTORICAL]; POLITICAL COLLECTIBLES; WHITE HOUSE MEMORABILIA)

PRINTING EQUIPMENT

(see also BOOK ARTS; NEWSPAPERS; TYPEWRITERS)

Clubs/Associations

Paul Romaine
American Printing History Association
Newsletter: APHA Newsletter
P.O. Box 4519
Grand Central Station
New York, NY 10163
membership@printinghistory.org
http://www.printinghistory.org
Encourages the preservation of printing artifacts and source materials for printing history, as well as the development of museums and libraries to house them; in addition to newsletter, publishes "Printing History" journal.

Mike O'Connor
Amalgamated Printers' Association
Magazine: APA Journal, The
P.O. Box 18117
Fountain Hills, AZ 85269
mikeatfh@earthlink.net
http://www.apa-letterpress.org
An organization composed of letterpress printing enthusiasts: printers, typecasters, collectors; Web site contains links to printing museums, private and professional letterpress shops, printing groups, type lore, and more.

Collectors

Briar Press, The
P.O. Box 490
Briarcliff Manor, NY 10510
bpress@aol.com
http://www.briarpress.org
Interested in purchasing small tabletop and card printing presses, wood type, type specimen catalogs, and anything printing related.

David W. Peat
1225 Carroll White
Indianapolis, IN 46219-3907
ph: 317-357-6895
typenut@comcast.net
http://www.davidpeat.com
Wants antique printers type, catalogs of printers type (typefounders specimen books), small presses, periodicals, stock certificates, medals, and other 19th c. printing items.

James L. Weygand
P.O. Box 215
Nappanee, IN 46550-0215
ph: 219-773-4832
Wants tabletop printing presses, catalogs, instruction booklets, literature, equipment, accessories, etc.

Paul Aken
39221 N. Lewis
Zion, IL 60099-3344
ph: 847-746-8170 or 847-731-1945
platenpress@iconnect.net
Wants printing items: presses, type, tools, books, manuals, catalogs, toy printing presses, multigraphs, litho stones, etc.

Uwe H. Breker
Bonner Str. 528-530
Koln, D-50968 Germany
ph: 49 221 387049 or 941-925-0385 (US Rep)
fax: 49 221 374878
auction@breker.com
http://www.breker.com
Wants to buy early printing presses, lithographic presses, typesetting hand presses, pre-1900 books on printing technology.

Dealers

Nancy Neale Silverman
Nancy Neale Typecraft
Steamboat Wharf Rd.
Bernard, ME 04612
ph: 207-244-5192 or 800-927-7469
fax: 207-244-5090
typenancy@aol.com
http://www.acadia.net/typecraft
*Collector, dealer, expert, appraiser;
specializes in antique printer's wood
type and other printing artifacts.*

David Schwartz
Schwartz's Antique Printing
9214 New Albion Rd.
Little Valley, NY 14755-9771
ph: 716-938-9807
okdk@eznet.net
*Wants to buy old printers type and
cuts, type specimen books, old printing
equipment & supply catalogs, books
about printing, certificates and badges
from printers unions; anything related
to letter press printing.*

Internet Resources

Elizabeth Nevin
Briar Press, The
P.O. Box 490
Briarcliff Manor, NY 10510
bpress@aol.com
http://www.briarpress.org
*A private press with a collection of
type, presses, printing equipment and
ephemera; has a comprehensive Web
site: an online Letterpress Museum,
resources, bookarts links for
letterpress printers and enthusiasts.*

Museums/Libraries

Paul Aken
Platen Press Museum
39221 N. Lewis
Zion, IL 60099-3344
ph: 847-746-8170 or 847-731-1945
platenpress@iconnect.net
*Large collection of presses, type,
typecasting machines, and bindery
equipment.*

International Printing Museum
315 East Torrance Blvd.
Carson, CA 90745
ph: 714-529-1832
printmuseum@earthlink.net
http://www.printmuseum.org
*Experience the development of the
printing press, rare antique printing
machines; offers printing equipment
for sale on occasion.*

Periodicals

Mike Phillips
Magazine: Printer, The
337 Wilson St.
Findlay, OH 45840
ph: 419-422-4958
fax: 419-422-2777
theprinter4918@aol.com
*Monthly publication; contains lots of
current items of interest to letterpress
printers: classified ads for presses and*

equipment for sale in US, Canada,
UK.

Type Founding Items

Collectors

David W. Peat
1225 Carroll White
Indianapolis, IN 46219-3907
ph: 317-357-6895
typenut@comcast.net
http://www.davidpeat.com
*Wants old type casting (founding)
equipment: hand molds, mats
(matrices) for casting antique type,
Bruce type caster, catalogs.*

PRINTS

(see also ART; BOOKPLATES;
ILLUSTRATORS; MAPS & CHARTS;
MOTTOES [PICTURE POEMS];
PAPER COLLECTIBLES;
PERSONALITIES [ARTISTS];
POSTERS; PRINTS [MODERN];
REPAIR/RESTORATION/
CONSERVATION, Paper Items;
WALLACE NUTTING)

Appraisers

AsktheAppraiser.com
4 Brussels St.
Worcester, MA 01610
ph: 781-821-0199
ata@collectingchannel.com
http://www.AsktheAppraiser.com
*The premiere online appraisal service
offered by CollectingChannel.com; all
appraisals comply with the "Uniform
Standards of Professional Appraisal
Practice" and with the standards of
the Association of Online Appraisers.*

Derek D. Cocovinis
DDC Fine Arts
P.O. Bbox 718
Montville, NJ 07045
ph: 973-316-0023
Art sales and appraisals.

M. Barden Prisant, FRICS
Telepraisal
32 Union Sq., #1016
New York, NY 10003
ph: 212-614-9090 or 800-645-6002
fax: 212-780-9539
info@telepraisal.com
http://www.telepraisal.com
*For over 21 years, Telepraisal has
been gathering pricing data on
approximately 200,000 artists and
sales of their works; printouts of the
data can be purchased for $35 per
search, or more formal appraisals can
be generated.*

Christopher W. Lane
Philadelphia Print Shop, Ltd., The
8441 Germantown Ave.
Philadelphia, PA 19118
ph: 215-242-4750
fax: 215-242-6977
PhilaPrint@PhilaPrintShop.com
http://www.philaprintshop.com
Gallery of antique prints and maps

with related rare books and atlases;
also bookstore of reference books
related to antique prints and maps;
appraisals, paper conservation and
restoration.

Donald H. Cresswell
Philadelphia Print Shop, Ltd., The
8441 Germantown Ave.
Philadelphia, PA 19118
ph: 215-242-4750
fax: 215-242-6977
cresswell@PhilaPrintShop.com
http://www.philaprintshop.com
*Buys, sells, appraises prints, maps,
related rare books and atlases.*

Randall C. Hunt
3503 Fulton St., NW
Washington, DC 20007-1438
ph: 202-333-4035
randallhunt@starpower.net
*Specializes in the appraisal of fine art
including American and European
18th through 20th century paintings,
prints and sculpture; Certified
Appraiser, Appraisers Association of
America.*

Charles B. Goldstein, ISA CAPP
Charles Barry International
8 Hardwicke Place
Rockville, MD 20850-3010
ph: 301-340-6775
fax: 301-340-1726
chadeg@erols.com
*Buys, sells, and appraises fine Old
Master, 19th and 20th century,
modern and contemporary, American
and European prints; Certified
Member, International Society of
Appraisers; expert witness and trial
consultant.*

Melanie Smith, ISA
Seaside Art Gallery
2716 Virginia Dare Trail South
P.O. Box 1
Nags Head, NC 27959-0001
ph: 252-441-5418 or 800-828-2444
fax: 252-441-8563
info@seasideart.com
http://www.seasideart.com
*Accredited member of the International
Society of Appraisers; specializes in
fine art (paintings, graphics,
sculpture) and animation art.*

Jerry Bengis, ISA
Bengis Fine Art
1440 Coral Ridge Dr., #166
Pompano Beach, FL 33071
ph: 954-757-2444
fax: 954-757-6222
yascha7@netrox.net
http://www.bengisfineart.com
*Fine art appraiser specializing in
prints (especially Salvador Dali),
graphics (Miro, Chagall, Picasso,
Warhol), etchings, engravings, prints,
bronzes.*

James Corcoran, ISA
Corcoran Fine Arts Limited, Inc.
2915 Fairfax Rd.
Cleveland, OH 44118-4015
ph: 216-431-0025 or 216-397-0777
fax: 216-397-0222
corcoranfa@aol.com
http://www.corcoranfinearts.com
*Appraises European, American,
Canadian and Latin American prints;
Renaissance to contemporary; Active
Associates of Sothebys.com offering
client property for sale online.*

Susan S. Pohle
Pigeon Creek Antiques
621 N. Main St.
Thiensville, WI 53092-1215
ph: 262-242-2072
*Sells and appraises fine art prints,
period furniture, lamps, toys, dolls.*

Corinne Cain, ISA, ASA
Corinne Cain Ltd.
326 West Harmont Dr.
Phoenix, AZ 85021
ph: 602-906-1633
fax: 602-906-0677
corinne@savvycollector.com
http://www.savvycollector.com
*A veteran art appraiser for over 25
years selling fine art and Native
American arts online; guaranteed
condition, authenticity verified, value
is assured; Accredited Senior
Appraiser, Certified Appraiser of
Personal Property.*

Linda Dunn
Dunn & Associates
8724 McCarty Ranch Dr.
San Jose, CA 95135
ph: 408-223-1095
fax: 408-223-1095
tpart@aol.com
http://www.art-appraiser.com
*Specializes in 19th and 20th century
European and American paintings,
contemporary limited edition prints,
and frescos and murals.*

David Peckman
U.K.
dpeckman@btinternet.com
*Specializes in the appraisal of
European and American art, primarily
works on paper including prints,
photography, drawings, and
watercolors from the 20th and 21st
centuries.*

Auction Services

Amory Spizzirri, Client Svc.
William Doyle Galleries
175 E. 87th St.
New York, NY 10128-2205
ph: 212-427-2730
fax: 212-369-0892
info@doylegalleries.com
http://www.doylegalleries.com
*Holds over 50 auctions annually of
furniture and decorations, paintings
and sculpture, jewelry, books and
prints, couture and textiles, 20th
century art & design, majolica,*

Lalique, Asian works of art and other specialty categories.

Clubs/Associations

American Historical Print Collectors
  Society
Magazine: Imprint
P.O. Box 201
Fairfield, CT 06430-0201
ph: 203-255-1627
rbraun@optonline.com
http://www.ahpcs.org
  *Objectives are to the foster preserva-
  tion, study and exhibition of historical
  American prints from the 17th through
  the 19th century; publishes "Imprint"
  magazine twice and "Newsletter" four
  times per year; scholarly meetings.*

International Fine Print Dealers
  Association
485 Madison Ave., 15th Floor
New York, NY 10022
ph: 212-759-4469
fax: 212-319-7752
ifpda@printdealers.com
http://www.printdealers.com
  *Membership of prestigious print
  dealers by election only; publishes
  membership directory.*

Dr. Charles J. Semowich
Print Club of Albany
Newsletter: Print Club of Albany
  Newsletter
P.O. Box 6578
Albany, NY 12206-0578
ph: 518-449-4756
semowich@att.net
http://www.pcaprint.com
  *Founded in 1933 for the purpose of
  promoting an appreciation of fine art
  prints among its members and
  community; each active member
  receives an original print; conducts
  lectures and workshops; holds artists
  papers in its archives.*

Joe Davidson
American Antique Graphics Society
5185 Windfall Rd.
Medina, OH 44256-8703
ph: 330-723-7172
  *Members interested in graphic arts
  prints: from medieval, natural history
  to etchings, engravings.*

Collectors

Joel Goleman
607 Chelten Hills Dr.
Elkins Park, PA 19027-1319
ph: 215-542-7700
fax: 215-542-7700
viol@webtv.net
  *Special interest in old master prints
  and Japanese woodblock prints;
  experienced as expert witness; teaches
  courses in print connoisseurship and
  curates print exhibitions.*

Terry Ahlberg
1000 Irvine Blvd.
Tustin, CA 92780-3527
ph: 714-730-1000 or 949-856-9395
fax: 714-730-1752
emailit@earthlink.net
  *Wants any prints or posters by artists
  Jo Mora (J.J. Mora), Till Goodan,
  Maynard Dixon, Frank Mechau, Ila
  McAfee, A.M. Cassandra.*

Dealers

John Clement
36 Oakwood Ave.
Fitchburg, MA 01420-7421
ph: 978-345-5863
  *Specializes in American, European
  Old Master, and modern prints; also
  Japanese woodblock prints.*

Jim Messineo
JMW Gallery
144 Lincoln St.
Boston, MA 02111-2523
ph: 617-338-9097
fax: 617-338-7636
mail@jmwgallery.com
http://www.jmwgallery.com
  *Buys, sells and specializes along with
  co-owner Mike Witt in the Arts &
  Crafts movement. Mission furniture:
  Lifetime, Limbert, Stickley; American
  Art Pottery 1875 to 1950s: Grueby,
  Newcomb, Marblehead, etc.;
  metalwork, Roycroft.*

Tony Fusco
Fusco & Four, Associates
One Murdock Terrace
Brighton, MA 02135-2817
ph: 617-787-2637
fax: 617-782-4430
fuscofour@aol.com
  *Specializing in 20th century European
  and American works on paper, 1900-
  1950, especially WPA, regionalists,
  and urban social realists; free
  quarterly illustrated lists.*

Ernest S. Kramer
Ernest S. Kramer Fine Arts & Prints
P.O. Box 81037
Wellesley, MA 02481-0001
ph: 781-237-3635
fax: 781-235-0112
eskramer@attbi.com
http://www.kramerfineart.com
  *Focuses on 19th and 20th century
  prints with an emphasis on the '20s
  through '40s, e.g., Arms, Benson,
  Benton, Cadmus, Lewis, Marsh;
  interested in purchasing single works
  or collections of prints, drawings,
  watercolors or oil paintings.*

Marshall Cook
Baldwin's Old Prints & Maps
P.O. Box 745
Vineyard Haven, MA 02568
ph: 508-693-5903
maps@baldwinsmaps.com
http://www.baldwinsmaps.com
  *Specializes in prints, maps and charts;
  US Coast Survey charts, historical*

*prints, biblical/religious maps, US
Civil War maps, etc.*

Jim Martin
Martin Antiques
75 Meadowbrook Rd.
East Greenwich, RI 02818
trader@traderantiques.com
http://www.traderantiques.com
  *Offers vintage lithographs and prints
  by Mucha, Lefevre, Vernuil, Parrish,
  Stillwell, Phillips, Pognay, Cheret,
  Grasset and others.*

Reg & Sally Lombard
Lombard Antiquarian Maps & Prints
P.O. Box 6565
Scarborough, ME 04070
ph: 207-885-9177
fax: 207-885-9575
rtl@lombardmaps.com
http://www.lombardmaps.com
  *Specializes in fine maps, charts, rare
  botanical, natural history and
  architectural prints.*

Robert Bessette
Green Dragon Arts
P.O. Box 588
Burlington, VT 05402-0588
ph: 802-862-1930
fax: 802-862-1930
  *Has over 20,000 old prints to choose
  from; buys and sells 18th to early 20th
  century lithographs, etchings,
  woodcuts, chromolithographs, hand
  colored book plates, etc.*

Jane Allinson
Allinson Gallery, Inc.
ph: 860-429-2322
fax: 860-429-2825
allinson@neca.com
http://www.allinsongallery.com
  *Buys and sells American & European
  fine prints, 1880-1960; also offers fine
  art appraisals; member of Appraisers
  Association of America, International
  Fine Print Dealers Association.*

Don Barese
Don Barese Fine Art & Antiques
3651 Whitney Ave.
Hamden, CT 06518
ph: 203-248-2700 or 800-733-4254
fax: 203-281-7438
D.Barese.artantiques@snet.net
http://www.donbaresefineart.com
  *Buys and sells American & European
  fine art, 19th and 20th century
  paintings and prints.*

Neil St.
Street & O'Neill Galleries
152 Danbury Rd.
Wilton, CT 06897
ph: 203-762-3474
fax: 203-762-5545
mapmaker@vintagemaps.com
http://www.vintagemaps.com
  *Specializes in antique prints, maps
  and charts; custom framing available
  in gallery.*

Marcy & Mindi Brahin
Antique Topical Prints
100 Sargent Rd.
Freehold, NJ 07728
ph: 732-462-7923
mbrahin@optonline.net
  *Specializes in antique topical prints,
  especially 19th century matter Harpers
  & Leslie's weeklies, Civil War,
  baseball, Nast Santas and others.*

Ellen Sragow
Sragow Gallery
73 Spring St.
New York, NY 10012-5800
ph: 212-219-1793
fax: 212-219-1793
  *American prints, paintings and works
  on paper 1920s through 1940s.*

Kenneth Newman
Old Print Shop, The
150 Lexington Ave. at 30th St.
New York, NY 10016
ph: 212-683-3950
fax: 212-779-8040
info@oldprintshop.com
http://www.oldprintshop.com
  *Wants 18th-20th century American
  prints; Currier & Ives, Endicott Hill,
  large folio American town views,
  marines, maps, historicals.*

W. Graham Arader III
Arader Galleries
29 East 72nd St.
New York, NY 10021
ph: 212-628-3668
fax: 212-879-8714
AraderGalleries@msn.com
http://www.aradergalleries.com
  *Buys & sells Audubon and other fine
  prints: Indians, natural history,
  sporting,, Currier & Ives, etc.; also
  maps, paintings and books; offices in
  Philadelphia, New York, San
  Francisco, and Houston.*

George D. Glazer
28 East 72nd St., 3rd Floor
New York, NY 10021
ph: 212-535-5706
fax: 212-658-9512
worldglobe@georgeglazer.com
http://www.georgeglazer.com
  *Buys and sells antique prints: birds,
  botanicals, sporting (golf, tennis,
  skiing), maritime, aviation,
  architectural, Americana, fashion;
  works with interior designers and
  corporate art consultants.*

Margaret McAuliffe
ARDAGH
P.O. Box 810
Carmel, NY 10512
ph: 914-225-1746 or 800-217-1746
  *Buys and sells fine art: oils,
  watercolors, prints, sculpture,
  photographs.*

Donald J. Bruckner
Bardon Antiques
37 August Lane
Hicksville, NY 11801-4419
ph: 516-931-5164
dbruck7@cs.com
Wants to buy historical 19th century American lithographs; normally has 500-600 for sale.

Dr. Charles J. Semowich
Charles Semowich Fine Arts
242 Broadway
Rensselaer, NY 12144-2705
ph: 518-449-4756
semowich@att.net
Buys and sells prints, especially American 20th century; also buys and sells paintings and drawings.

Ursula Hobson
Ursula Hobson Fine Art
1600 Spruce St.
Philadelphia, PA 19103
ph: 215-546-780
fax: 215-546-2424
Specializes in antique prints and fine art framing; appeared on PAX TV's "Treasures in Your Home."

Christopher W. Lane
Philadelphia Print Shop, Ltd., The
8441 Germantown Ave.
Philadelphia, PA 19118
ph: 215-242-4750
fax: 215-242-6977
PhilaPrint@PhilaPrintShop.com
http://www.philaprintshop.com
Gallery of antique prints and maps with related rare books and atlases; also bookstore of reference books related to antique prints and maps; appraisals, paper conservation and restoration.

John Dupree
Creighton-Davis Gallery
3222 M St. NW
Washington, DC 20007
ph: 202-333-3050
fax: 202-338-4470
info@rareart.com.
http://www.rareart.com
Specializes in contemporary, old and modern print artists with national and international reputations; also sells sculptures and paintings by newly emerging as well as established artists.

Judith Blakely
Old Print Gallery, The
1220 31st St. NW
Washington, DC 20007-3422
ph: 202-965-1818
fax: 202-965-1869
info@oldprintgallery.com
http://www.oldprintgallery.com
Wants antique prints: city views, historical scenes, Currier & Ives, Western, natural history, sporting, military and nautical scenes.

Monica Burdeshaw
Print Portfolio
4701 Sangamore Rd.
Bethesda, MD 20816
ph: 301-229-5800
Buys and sells fine prints.

Ray Moore
Heritage Historical Prints, Inc.
3772 Angelton Court
Burtonsville, MD 20866
ph: 301-890-4566 or 800-890-4566
fax: 301-890-5481
hhpi@pop.erols.com
http://www.heritageprints.com
Buys and sells 17th through 19th century prints; specializes in 17th through 19th century hand watercolored natural history lithographs; also offers restoration, conservation, framing, and documentation services.

Richard Kornemann
Museum Shop, Ltd.
20 N. Market St.
Frederick, MD 21701
ph: 301-695-0424
fax: 301-698-5242
fineartmuseum@erols.com
http://www.museumsholptd.com
Specializes in Japanese Ukiyo-E woodblock prints from the Edo period by masters such as Hiroshige, Kunisata, Utamaro, Yoshida, Hasui, and others; also specializes in 1930s era by Grant Wood, Whistler, T.H. Benton, WPA artists, etc.

David Allen
David Allen Fine Art
5839 20th St. N
Arlington, VA 22205-3306
ph: 703-536-4142
silveradotwo@yahoo.com
Dealer and expert specializing in 19th & 20th century American prints.

Billie Sue Bruce
Aquarian Gallery
P.O. Box 732
Jonesville, VA 24263
ph: 540-346-4257
AquarianGallery@pre1900prints.com
http://pre1900prints.com
Specializes in authentic antique prints and maps published during the 1800s and early 1900s.

John Sandberg
Yellowhouse Gallery
P.O. Box 554
2902 South Virginia Dare Trail
Nags Head, NC 27959
ph: 252-441-6928
yelnag@pinn.net
http://www.yellowhousegallery.com
Established in 1969, offers a comprehensive collection of antique prints and maps; specialties are Civil War maps and prints; wood engravings by Winslow Homer, Thomas Nast and Frederic Remington; old orchids, birds, shells, fish prints.

Shirley & Al Bowers
Pablo Prints
206 Pablo Rd.
Ponte Vedra Beach, FL 32082
ph: 904-285-2962
sbowers@aol.com
Specializes in McKenney & Hall prints, primarily Seminoles.

Robert Thames
Robert Thames Art & Antiques
P.O. Box 4175
Ormond Beach, FL 32175
ph: 904-677-8835
rthamesa@bellsouth.net
Specializes in fine art: paintings, drawings and prints.

Elaine Kwan
8022 SE Osprey St.
Hobe Sound, FL 33455
ph: 772-545-9939
fax: 772-545-9939
elaine@artcollect.com
http://www.artcollect.com
Buys and sells modern and contemporary art; resale; fine art appraiser; collections cataloging; member, Appraisers Association of America (AAA).

David Boshart
National Wildlife Galleries
8504 Charter Club Blvd., Ste. 10
Fort Myers, FL 33919
ph: 239-275-0500 or 800-382-5278
fax: 239-936-2788
stamps@nationalwildlife.com
http://www.nationalwildlife.com
Designs, produces and distributes duck and other wildlife conservation stamps, prints, and medallions; since 1976; also buys, sells, trades most other prints and sculpture of all subjects.

Don McDonald
PastPresent Gallery
660 Celebration Ave., Ste. 150
Celebration, FL 34747
ph: 407-566-1899 or 877-4-PAST-MAPS
fax: 407-566-1030
curator@pastpresent.com
http://store.pastpresent.com
Deals in authentic 19th century antique maps, prints and engravings.

J. Newcome-Beill
Abstract Eye Books
1517 Vivian Lane
Louisville, KY 40205
abstracteyebooks@cox.net
http://www.abstracteyebooks.com
Buys and sells used and rare photography books, maps, and prints.

Susan S. Pohle
Pigeon Creek Antiques
621 N. Main St.
Thiensville, WI 53092-1215
ph: 262-242-2072
Sells and appraises fine art prints, period furniture, lamps, toys, dolls.

Robert L. Butler, ISA
Robert L. Butler Galleries
390 A No. Euclid
Saint Louis, MO 631080
ph: 314-361-7013
fax: 314-768-7566
Private dealer and appraiser in antique and contemporary prints: lithographs, etchings and screen prints.

Sharon M. Gergen
Nostalgia Antiques
8141 Main
Kansas City, MO 64114-2401
ph: 816-361-7530
LovellFam@prodigy.net
Paper and print dealer since 1983; past-President of the R.A. Fox Society; wants to illustrations buy R. Atkinson Fox, Zula Kenyon, Heibel, Hintermeister, Desch, Coffin, Pressler, Gutmann, Grimball, and others.

Cynthia Alden
Michael Alden Assoc., Inc.
P.O. Box 26097
New Orleans, LA 70186
ph: 504-835-8081 or 936-273-9662
fax: 504-828-8669
cynthia@traditionalart.com
http://www.traditionalart.com
Specializes in traditional engravings and original antique prints from the 17th through 19th centuries.

Jeffery Measamer
Art Connections
8315 E. Copper Village Dr.
Houston, TX 77095
ph: 281-861-0244
fax: 281-861-0266
artconnections@sbcglobal.net
http://www.houstonarts.com
Specialists in fine prints and drawings from 1750-1950; deals primarily in British prints and drawings; always has a wide selection of American and European works in stock.

Robert & Jenny Kipp
Art & Old Print Restorations
4340 E. Kentucky Ave., Ste. 337
Denver, CO 80246
ph: 720-933-7649
JennyKipp@qwest.net
http://www.oldprints.com
Paper and print sales, conservation and restorations; specializing in 18th century to present prints; over 22 years in business.

Jan Wilson
Jan Wilson Gallery
P.O. Box 6649
Ketchum, ID 83340
ph: 208-622-7799
fax: 208-726-5975
Buys and sells print, fine art, sculpture.

Keith Bartelheim
Fallen Leaf Gallery
3675 Baker Lane
Reno, NV 89509
ph: 775-826-7477
fax: 775-826-7477
fallenleafgallery@yahoo.com
*Specializes in buying, selling,
appraising fine art including 19th and
20th century prints and graphics.*

Leila Lyons
Lyons Ltd. Antique Prints
Ten Town & Country Village
Palo Alto, CA 94301
ph: 650-325-9010 or 800-LYONS-LTD
fax: 650-325-8332
lyonsltd@gte.net
http://www.lyonsltd.com
*Specializes in fine original etchings,
engravings and lithographs dating
from 1490 to 1920: botanicals, maps,
city views, natural history, architecture, performing arts, fashion, and
children's illustrations; also custom
framing.*

Priscilla Anne Lowry
Lowry-James Fine Antique Prints
101 Athens
Langley, WA 98260
ph: 360-221-0477
fax: 360-221-0477
fineprints@lowryjames.com
http://www.lowryjames.com
*Specializes in fine and rare natural
history prints from the 17th through
the 19th centuries.*

Bruce Magnotti
Anchor in Time Antiques & Rare Books
309 West Fifth Ave.
Ellensburg, WA 98926
ph: 509-962-5204
*Buys and sells rare prints, maps and
illustrated books.*

Elisabeth Legge
Elisabeth Legge Fine Antique Prints
37 Hazelton Ave.
Toronto, Canada M5R 2E3 Canada
ph: 416-972-1378
elegge@sympatico.ca
http://www.LeggePrints.com
*Specializes in and appraises original
15th through 19th century prints and
manuscripts, specializing, but not
restricted to, natural history; also
offers traditional English framing and
restoration.*

John Hulot
Artelino
Johnn Sebastian Bach Str. 11
Pullach, Bavaria 82049 Germany
ph: ++49-89-79367709
fax: ++49-89-79367708
info@artelino.com
http://www.artelino.com
*Buys, sells old and modern prints and
antique maps; also offers an online
auction service.*

Peter McConnell
Fine Rare Prints
550 Scenic Dr.
Auckland, 1008 New Zealand
ph: +64 21 299 -824
enquiries@finerareprints.com
http://www.finerareprints.com
*Specializes in the sale of antique
prints: animals, birds, botanicals,
flowers, classical Rome, marine life,
people, topography; by makers such as
Brodtman, Edwards Van Houtte.*

W.D.J. Bennett
Postaprint
Taidswood House
Iver Heath, Bucks SL0 0PQ U.K.
ph: +44 1 895 833 720
fax: +44 1 895 834 890
sales@postaprint.co.uk
http://www.postaprint.co.uk
*Antique maps, prints, historic
engravings, antiquarian atlases and
books; has an online database of over
200,000 antique maps, steel, copper
or wood engravings available for
searching; items date from 1550 to
1899.*

Experts

Joel Goleman
607 Chelten Hills Dr.
Elkins Park, PA 19027-1319
ph: 215-542-7700
fax: 215-542-7700
viol@webtv.net
*Special interest in old master prints
and Japanese woodblock prints;
experienced as expert witness; teaches
courses in print connoisseurship and
curates print exhibitions.*

William G. Hodges
Ridgefield, Inc.
12509 Patterson Ave.
Richmond, VA 23233-6414
ph: 804-784-2760
ridgefield@mindspring.com
*Specializes in buying and selling
antique prints; 300,000 prints in
stock.*

David Rudd
Cycleback: Publishers & Collectors
Services
P.O. Box 16311
Seattle, WA 98116
ph: 206-923-0367
drudd@cycleback.com
http://www.cycleback.com
*One of the leading authorities on
baseball memorabilia, early prints &
photographs; author of numerous
books on these subjects; is a forensic
art examiner; teaches online courses in
print & photograph authentication
and forgery detection.*

Internet Resources

Denis C. Jackson, Ed.
E-zine: Illustrator Collector's News, The
P.O. Box 6433
Kingman, AZ 86401
ticn@olypen.com
http://www.olypen.com/ticn
*An online publication for collectors of
magazines and other paper illustrations; free classifieds and articles, no
charge Web site information; new and
old prints.*

Misc. Services

Library of Congress, Prints &
Photographs Reading Room
Library of Congress
James Madison Bldg., Rm LM-339
Washington, DC 20540-4730
ph: 202-707-6394 or 202-707-8000
http://www.lcweb.loc.gov/rr/print
*Has a collection of over 13,000,000
images: prints, photographs,
drawings, posters, and architectural
and engineering drawings.*

Wendy Reaves, Cur.
National Portrait Gallery
Prints & Drawings
750 Ninth St., Ste. 8300
Washington, DC 20560-0973
ph: 202-275-1738
fax: 202-275-1887
npgweb@npg.si.edu
http://www.npg.si.edu
*Will authenticate prints & drawings
brought in for inspection; make an
appointment first; may be able to work
from good photographs.*

Jodie Benson
Gordon's Art Reference, Inc.
Price Guide: Gordon's Print Price
Annual
306 West Coronado Rd.
Phoenix, AZ 85003-1147
ph: 602-253-6948 or 800-892-4622
(orders)
fax: 602-253-2104
office@gordonsart.com
http://www.gordonsart.com
*Over 50,000 worldwide print auction
results from 2002 organized by artist
and title; includes information about
conditions, print dates, notes if item is
signed, dated, or annotated; also on
CD-ROM and online with 675,000
entries.*

Jodie Benson
Gordon's Art Reference, Inc.
Price Guide: Lawrence's Dealer Print
Prices
306 West Coronado Rd.
Phoenix, AZ 85003-1147
ph: 602-253-6948 or 800-892-4622
(orders)
fax: 602-253-2104
office@gordonsart.com
http://www.gordonsart.com
*The only print price guide devoted
exclusively to prices in dealer catalogs
and inventory; features over 30,000
one-time entries organized by artist
and title; includes information about
condition, print dates, notes if signed
or dated.*

Museums/Libraries

Museum of Prints & Printmaking
P.O. Box 6578
Albany, NY 12206-0578
ph: 518-449-4756
semowich@att.net
http://www.pcaprint.com
*Shares space with the Print Club of
Albany; open by appointment.*

Periodicals

Charles Stuart Lane, Ed.
Newspaper: Journal of the Print World,
Inc.
P.O. Box 978
Meredith, NH 03253-0978
ph: 603-279-6479
fax: 603-279-1337
sophia@cyberportal.net
http://www.journaloftheprintworld.com
*A quarterly newspaper with articles,
advertising and classifieds focusing on
antique and contemporary works of
art on paper, photographs, prints and
artists; features articles, ads, auction
results, show reviews, calendar of
events.*

Journal: Art On Paper
39 E. 78th St., #501
New York, NY 10021-0213
ph: 212-988-5959
fax: 212-988-6107
info@artonpaper.com
http://www.artonpaper.com
*Published bi-monthly; only interna-
tional art magazine dedicated to
works on paper; renowned for its
coverage of prints, drawings, and
photography.*

Suppliers

Cronite Co., The
120 East Halsey Rd.
P.O. Box 6330
Parsippany, NJ 07054
ph: 973-887-7900
fax: 973-887-0015
info@cronite.com
http://www.cronite.com
*Suppliers to engravers, etchers, and
print makers for 100 years; plate
printing inks and oils, steel/copper/
zinc/brass plates, pantograph
machines and supplies, etching acids/
acid resists, photoengraving supplies,
engraving tools.*

Audubon

Dealers

Peter D. Cowen
225 Riverview Ave.
Waltham, MA 02466-1358
ph: 617-965-1985
fax: 617-965-1211
*Wants to buy museum-quality Havell
edition Audubon prints.*

Ed Kenney
Audubon Prints & Books
9720 Spring Ridge Ln.
Vienna, VA 22182-1449
ph: 703-759-5567
Audubonprints@aol.com
http://www.audubonprints-books.com
*Buys & sells natural history prints
and books by John James Audubon;
also prints by Wilson, Gould,
Catesby, Bodmer, Catlin and others.*

Leslie Kostrich
minniesland.com, LLC
P.O Box 16380
Alexandria, VA 22302
ph: 703-823-7436
leslie@minniesland.com
http://www.minniesland.com
*Specializes in original color-plate
books by Audubon & other natural
history artists; offers good selection of
reference books reference books; Web
site has detailed information on all
major Audubon editions including
authentication tips.*

George T. Clark
Taylor Clark Gallery
2623 Government St.
Baton Rouge, LA 70806-5408
ph: 225-383-4929 or 888-725-5251
fax: 225-383-4920
taylorclark@taylorclark.com
http://www.taylorclark.com
*Specializes in 18th, 19th, and 20th
century oil paintings, watercolors,
and prints, especially all editions of
Audubon prints.*

Internet Resources

Leslie Kostrich
minniesland.com, LLC
P.O Box 16380
Alexandria, VA 22302
ph: 703-823-7436
leslie@minniesland.com
http://www.minniesland.com
*Web site has extensive information on
all major Audubon editions including
how-to guides to authentication.*

Museums/Libraries

John James Audubon State Park &
Museum
P.O. Box 576
3100 US Highway 41 North
Henderson, KY 42420
ph: 270-826-2247 or 270-827-1893
fax: 270-826-2286
marydee.miller@mail.state.ky.us
http://www.state.ky.us/agencies/parks/
audubon2.htm
*The world's largest gathering of John
James Audubon memorabilia and one
of the most extensive collections of his
work in the world; four galleries
present his life, work and legacy.*

Repro. Sources

Edward Ziegele
Princeton Audubon Limited
P.O. Box 3179
Princeton, NJ 08543-3179
fax: 908-813-2397
audubonart@aol.com
http://www.princetonaudubon.com
*Producers of the world's only direct-
camera Audubon reproductions; these
are double-elephant, full size, limited
edition prints that are printed using
up to nine colors giving striking
detail.*

Cupid

Clubs/Associations

Juanita Ingles
Cupid Collectors Club
Newsletter: Cupid Capers
920 Newton St.
Waterloo, IA 50703
ph: 319-226-3718
ingles12@mchsi.com
http://www.cupidcollectors.com
*Purpose of this club is to promote the
appreciation of Cupid prints of all
types including the M.B. Parkinson
"Cupid Awake and Cupid Asleep"
print.*

Collectors

Cindy & Jerry Youngquist
P.O. Box 91
Gowrie, IA 50543
ph: 515-352-3798

Juanita Ingles
920 Newton St.
Waterloo, IA 50703
ph: 319-226-3718
ingles12@mchsi.com
http://www.cupidcollectors.com

Glen Tull
402 W. Montgomery
Creston, IA 50801-2206
ph: 515-782-2335

Currier & Ives

Dealers

Donald J. Bruckner
Bardon Antiques
37 August Lane
Hicksville, NY 11801-4419
ph: 516-931-5164
dbruck7@cs.com
*Wants to buy historical 19th century
American lithographs; normally has
500-600 for sale; especially interested
in Currier & Ives.*

George J. Cohenour
4301 Beaumont Rd.
Dover, PA 17315-2405
ph: 717-292-5345
cohenour@currierprints.com
http://www.currierprints.com
*Buys and sells original Currier & Ives
lithographs; carries large selection
and offers a free list; also offers
cleaning and restoration service.*

Experts

George J. Cohenour
4301 Beaumont Rd.
Dover, PA 17315-2405
ph: 717-292-5345
cohenour@currierprints.com
http://www.currierprints.com
*Author of "Currier & Ives Litho-
graphs Value Guide."*

John & Barbara Rudisill
Rudisill's Alt Print Haus
P.O. Box 199
Worton, MD 21678-0199
ph: 410-778-9290
fax: 410-778-9310
rudi@dmv.com
http://www.chesapeake-bay.com/
altprinthaus
*Buys and sells original Currier & Ives
prints; have written articles on the
history of Currier & Ives and on
identifying reproductions; send SASE
for free list.*

Internet Resources

John & Barbara Rudisill
Rudisill's Alt Print Haus
P.O. Box 199
Worton, MD 21678-0199
ph: 410-778-9290
fax: 410-778-9310
rudi@dmv.com
http://freepages.rootsweb.com/~vstern
*Online resource containing a gallery
of prints by Nathaniel Currier,
Currier & Ives, and Charles Currier;
goal is to eventually include all known
examples.*

Museums/Libraries

Bob Shamis
Museum of the City of New York
1220 5th Ave. at 103rd St.
New York, NY 10029-5221
ph: 212-534-1672
fax: 212-534-5974
http://www.mcny.org
*Access by appointment; research fee
charged.*

Repair Services

Robert & Jenny Kipp
Art & Old Print Restorations
4340 E. Kentucky Ave., Ste. 337
Denver, CO 80246
ph: 720-933-7649
JennyKipp@qwest.net
http://www.oldprints.com
*A noted expert and authority on
Currier & Ives prints; cleans, restores
and conserves prints for clients
throughout the US; send for brochure;
author of "Currier's Price Guide to
Currier & Ives Prints."*

Dali

Appraisers

Jerry Bengis, ISA
Bengis Fine Art
1440 Coral Ridge Dr., #166
Pompano Beach, FL 33071
ph: 954-757-2444
fax: 954-757-6222
yascha7@netrox.net
http://www.bengisfineart.com
*Fine art appraiser specializing in
prints (especially Salvador Dali),
graphics (Miro, Chagall, Picasso,
Warhol), etchings, engravings, prints,
bronzes.*

Joan Kropf
16111 Redington Dr.
Saint Petersburg, FL 33708
ph: 727-399-1915
rljk@ij.net
*Specializes in the appraisal of
Salvador Dali art, 19th and 20th
century.*

Bernard Ewell, ASA
Bernard Ewell Art Appraisals
1223-D South St. Francis Dr.
Santa Fe, NM 87505
ph: 505-954-4113 or 800-884-3254
fax: 505-954-4107
artpro@juno.com
http://www.colomar.com/artpro
*International expert on all Salvador
Dali artworks.*

Dealers

Bruce Hochman
Salvador Dali Gallery
15332 Antioch St., Ste. 108
Pacific Palisades, CA 90272
ph: 310-459-8883 or 800-275-3254
fax: 310-454-2090
Dalimaven@aol.com
http://www.daligallery.com
*A leading gallery dealing exclusively
in authentic works of Salvador Dali;
buys, sells, appraises Salvador Dali
works.*

Experts

Albert Field
Salvador Dali Archives, The
2020 29th St.
Astoria, NY 11105
ph: 718-274-0407
fax: 718-726-2469
daliarch@pipeline.com
http://www.daliarchives.com
*A private repository of information
about Salvador Dali; established with
the approval of the artist; provides an
authentication service; publisher of
several books on Dali.*

Museums/Libraries

Kathleen A. White
Salvador Dali Museum
Newsletter: Dali Newsletter
1000 Third St. South
Saint Petersburg, FL 33701
ph: 727-823-3767 or 800-442-DALI
fax: 727-894-6068
curatorial@salvadordalimuseum.org
http://www.salvadordalimuseum.org
*Permanent home of the world's most
comprehensive collection of Dali's
works; oil and watercolor paintings,
drawings, graphics, etc.; also a
library with over 5,000 books on Dali
and Surrealism.*

Salvador Dali Museum, The
Newsletter: Salvador Dali Museum
Newsletter
1000 Third St. South
Saint Petersburg, FL 33701
ph: 727-823-3767 or 800-442-DALI
fax: 727-894-6068
curatorial@salvadordalimuseum.org
http://www.salvadordalimuseum.org
*Permanent home to the world's most
comprehensive collection of works
exclusively by the late Spanish
surrealist, Salvador Dali; 94 original
oils, over 100 watercolors and
drawings, holograms, objects of art
and photographs.*

Periodicals

Bruce Hochman
Salvador Dali Gallery
Magazine: Dali Collectors Quarterly
15332 Antioch St., Ste. 108
Pacific Palisades, CA 90272
ph: 310-459-8883 or 800-275-3254
fax: 310-454-2090
Dalimaven@aol.com
http://www.daligallery.com
*Stay current on all the latest Dali
news; quarterly 8-page newsletter now
it its 11th year.*

French Boudoir

Dealers

Clifford P. Catania
Joshua's Attic
518 Kimberton Rd.
Phoenixville, PA 19460-4737
ph: 610-917-1167
clifford@joshuasattic.com
http://www.davidchasegallery.com
*Wants Icart-like etchings by Ablett,
Grellet, Felix, Helleu, Milliere, Robbe,
Hardy, Meunier, etc.*

Hirshfeld

Dealers

George J. Goodstadt
Antique Poster Collection Gallery, The
17 Danbury Rd.
Ridgefield, CT 06877
ph: 203-438-1836
fax: 203-431-8712
george@georgejgoodstadt.com
http://www.georgejgoodstadt.com
*Publishers of fine art, offers a variety
of original lithograph posters and*

*limited edition graphics: Al Hirschfeld
pencil signed etchings and lithographs, Apollo XIII and XIV lithos;
appeared on PAX TV's "Treasures in
Your Home."*

Icart

Collectors

Adrienne Leff
1550 S. Dixie Hwy. #210
Coral Gables, FL 33146-3034
ph: 305-667-4214
fax: 305-668-2592
*Buys, sell and collects original Louis
Icart etchings, oils and complete
books.*

Dr. Neil Superfon
2121 W. Indian School Rd.
Phoenix, AZ 85015-4908
ph: 602-277-1449 or 800-258-0216
fax: 602-263-8523
Wants to buy Icart etchings.

Paul Kelly
26576 Estanciero Dr.
Mission Viejo, CA 92691
ph: 949-770-1483
pkellyfineart@worldnet.att.net
*Buys, sells and collects Louis Icart
etchings, oils, and illustrated books.*

Dealers

Edward J. Meschi
129 Pinyard Rd.
Monroeville, NJ 08343-1870
ph: 856-358-7293
fax: 856-358-7789
ed@meschiarts.com
http://www.meschiarts.com
*Buys and sells Louis Icart etchings,
illustrated books, and oil paintings.*

Clifford P. Catania
Joshua's Attic
518 Kimberton Rd.
Phoenixville, PA 19460-4737
ph: 610-917-1167
clifford@joshuasattic.com
http://www.davidchasegallery.com
*Buys and sells original Icart etchings;
assisting major collectors. Author of
"Complete Etchings of Louis Icart"
(1990-Schiffer Pub.)*

Debra Freer
Freer & Associates, Fine Art & Antiques
P.O. Box 98327
Atlanta, GA 30359-2027
ph: 404-321-6369
fax: 404-636-8531
DFreer@attbi.com
http://www.artnet.com/freer.html
*Buys and sells original Icart etchings,
artwork and illustrated books;
publishes quarterly newsletter "The
Louis Icart Collector" which is
available for $10/yr.*

Experts

Carole Hibel
Carole Hibel Art & Antiques
181 Broadview Rd.
Woodstock, NY 12498
ph: 845-679-2966 or 800-426-3357
fax: 845-679-9101
efshnc6@nyc.rr.com
*Wants to buy Louis Icart etchings and
paintings.*

Bill Holland
William Holland Fine Arts
1554 Paoli Pike
PMB #300
West Chester, PA 19380
ph: 610-344-9848
fax: 610-344-0651
bill@hollandarts.com
http://www.hollandarts.com
*Buys and sells Louis Icart etchings,
oils and illustrated books; co-author
of "Louis Icart - The Complete
Etchings;" call for details or to order.*

P. Bruce Marine
Cherub Antiques Gallery
2918 M. St. NW
Washington, DC 20007-3713
ph: 202-337-2224
fax: 202-337-2224
*Nationally known author of articles,
and leading expert in original Louis
Icart etchings; also wants etchings
and pastels by Paul Cesar Helleu.*

Leroy Neiman

Dealers

Ralph Olsen
Hammer Graphics Gallery
33 W. 57th St.
New York, NY 10019
ph: 212-644-4405

Vanity Fair (Spy)

Collectors

Paul Davis
308 Landsende Rd.
Devon, PA 19333
ph: 610-644-1216
pwbsdavis@msn.com
*Wants Vanity Fair "Spy" caricature
prints.*

Ken Taylor
11661 San Vicente, #3304
Los Angeles, CA 90049-5110
ph: 310-442-0054 or 310-207-4345
fax: 310-826-6934
ktscicon@ix.netcom.com
*Wants to buy original Vanity Fair
lithographs ("Spy" prints) published
in England from 1869 to 1913.*

Wallace Nutting

Collectors

Bob & Pam Franscella
23 Newstar Ridge Rd.
Sparta, NJ 07871
ph: 973-726-9736
franscella@earthlink.net

Jim & Sharon Eckert
P.O. Box 62
Colfax, IL 61728-0062
ph: 309-723-4241
anchorsb@mtco.com
*Wants Wallace Nutting, Bessie Pease
Gutmann prints.*

Woodblock

Dealers

Steven Thomas
Steven Thomas, Inc.
P.O. Box 41
Woodstock, VT 05091-0041
ph: 802-457-1764 or 800-781-8028
fax: 802-457-1764
stinc@sover.net
http://www.woodblock-prints.com
*Dealer/expert wants to buy American,
European and Canadian woodblock
prints from 1895-1950; color or black
and white; interested in strong images
by major and minor artists alike;
write for free 4-page illustrated want
list.*

Woodblock (American)

Collectors

Peter Hastings Falk
P.O. Box 833
Madison, CT 06443
ph: 203-245-4761
pfalk@cshore.com
http://www.soundviewpressbooks.com
*Buys and sells color woodblock prints
by American artists; 1890s to 1920s.*

Woodblock (Jacoulet)

Auction Services

John H. Schofield
Eldred's
P.O. Box 796
East Dennis, MA 02641-0796
ph: 508-385-3116
fax: 508-385-7201
eldreds@capecod.net
http://www.eldreds.com
*Specializes in the sale of 20th century
Japanese-style woodblock prints by
artist Paul Jacoulet.*

Woodblock (Japanese)

(see also ART, Oriental;
ORIENTALIA)

Appraisers

Dr. Daphne L. Rosenzweig, ISA CAPP
Rosenzweig Associates
P.O. Box 3976
Sarasota, FL 34230-3976
ph: 941-371-4643
fax: 941-342-6893
rosetwig@aol.com
*Consultant and appraiser dealing
with Oriental Art; author of "Selected
Works from the Fine Arts Group of
Later Chinese Painting;" specializes
in Chinese art, and Japanese prints
and ceramics.*

Fuji Murakami, ASA
Asian Art Appraisal Service
P.O. Box 24999
Denver, CO 80224-0999
ph: 303-758-8379
fax: 303-758-0816
fmarkm@qwest.net
Bronze, Asian ivory, netsuke, ceramics, costumes/robes/embroideries, jade and other mineral carvings, snuff bottles, paintings, calligraphy, prints, screens and scrolls, textiles of China, Korea, Japan, Southeast Asia, some India/Tibet.

Frank Castle
Castle Fine Arts, Inc.
P.O. Box 557
San Ramon, CA 94583
ph: 925-735-3149
info@castlefinearts.com
http://www.castlefinearts.com
Specializes in 18th through 20th century Japanese prints and other Oriental art.

Auction Services

Paul Knuston
Asian Collection
4397 John's Point Rd.
Gloucester, VA 23061
ph: 800-693-2154 or 804-693-2154
fax: 804-693-2154
asiancol@inna.net
http://www.woodblockprint.com
Offers over 100 18th and 19th century woodblock prints for sale on a bimonthly auction; full color catalog.

Ukiyo-E World GmbH
Johann Sebastian Bach Str. 11
Pullach, Bavaria 82049 Germany
ph: ++49-(0)89-79367709
fax: ++49-(0)89-79367708
webmaster@ukiyo-e-world.com
http://www.ukiyo-e-world.com
An Internet site for collectors of high quality Japanese woodblock prints; monthly online auction, gallery, forum, reference articles, links, Japanese calendar, newsletter by email.

Clubs/Associations

Ukiyo-E Society of America, Inc.
Newsletter: President's Newsletter
P.O. Box 23062
Washington, DC 20026-3062
ukiyoe@earthlink.net
http://www.ukiyo-e.org
Promotes the study/appreciation of Japanese woodblock prints through monthly meetings, seminars & exhibitions; also publishes Journal.

Collectors

John Clement
36 Oakwood Ave.
Fitchburg, MA 01420-7421
ph: 978-345-5863
Collector and expert; special interests include worldwide master works of art, particularly works on paper,

including Japanese woodblock prints; also fine paintings.

Bob Vargas
P.O. Box 1284
Los Altos, CA 94023
ph: 650-949-3959
Wants 20th century and older Japanese woodblock prints.

Dealers

Jane Allinson
Allinson Gallery, Inc.
ph: 860-429-2322
fax: 860-429-2825
allinson@neca.com
http://www.allinsongallery.com
Buys and sells 19th and 20th century Japanese woodblock prints.

Roni Neuer
Ronin Gallery
605 Madison Ave.
New York, NY 10022
ph: 212-688-0188
fax: 212-593-9808
ronin@japancollection.com
http://www.japancollection.com
Specializes in Japanese woodblock prints and publishes catalogs on specialty artists.

John Bradley
John Bradley Gallery
1020 Burlingham Rd.
Pine Bush, NY 12566
ph: 845-744-3642
bradley4@hvc.rr.com
http://www.japaneseblockprints.com
Buys and sells Japanese woodblock prints.

Merlin C. Dailey
Merlin C. Dailey Associates, Inc.
29 East Main St.
Victor, NY 14564
ph: 585-924-5830
fax: 585-924-5838
daileysan@aol.com
http://www.merlindailey.com
Specializes in fine Japanese woodblock prints.

Shirley Luber
Gilbert Luber Collection
1420 Locust St.
Philadelphia, PA 19102
ph: 215-545-4975
fax: 215-546-2210
luber@lubergallery.com
http://www.lubergallery.com
Specializes in antique and contemporary Japanese prints: woodblocks, silk-screens, etchings, and mezzotints.

Shogun Gallery, Inc.
P.O. Box 5300
Gaithersburg, MD 20882
ph: 301-948-0899 or 800-926-4255
fax: 301-208-0725
shogungallery@shogungallery.com
http://www.shoguninc.com
One of the largest dealers of original, museum-quality Japanese woodblock prints in the US; selection spans three centuries; Web site contains

discussions about Japanese prints, exhibition schedule, price lists.

Richard Kornemann
Museum Shop, Ltd.
20 N. Market St.
Frederick, MD 21701
ph: 301-695-0424
fax: 301-698-5242
fineartmuseum@erols.com
http://www.museumsholptd.com
Specializes in Japanese Ukiyo-E woodblock prints from the Edo period by masters such as Hiroshige, Kunisata, Utamaro, Yoshida, Hasui, and others; also specializes in 1930s era by Grant Wood, Whistler, T.H. Benton, WPA artists, etc.

William Stein
Floating World Gallery
P.O. Box 148200
Chicago, IL 60614
ph: 312-587-7800
fax: 312-587-7888
artwork@floatingworld.com
http://www.floatingworld.com
Seeking Japanese paintings and prints; antique to the present.

Richard Waldman
Art of Japan, The
P.O. Box 507
Mountain View, CA 94042-0507
ph: 650-964-4464 or 888-570-4464
fax: 650-964-9310
rwaldman@theartofjapan.com
http://www.theartofjapan.com
Japanese print dealer specializing in 18th, 19th, and 20th century prints; Ukiyo-E, Shin Hanga and Sosaku Hanga; with emphasis on Shin Hanga and 19th century Ukiyo-E.

Elizabeth Danechild
Ukiyo-E Gallery
4736 Seventeenth St.
San Francisco, CA 94117-4329
ph: 415-731-5971
fax: 415-753-3415
danechild@inreach.com
Buys and sells Japanese color woodblock prints from the 18th to early 20th centuries; by appointment.

Peter Gilder
Arts & Designs of Japan
P.O. Box 22075
San Francisco, CA 94122
ph: 415-759-6233
fax: 415-759-9017
gilder@artsanddesignsjapan.com
http://www.artsanddesignsjapan.com
Specialist in fine 17th through 20th century Japanese woodblock prints since 1973; buys, sells and appraises.

Carolyn Staley
Carolyn Staley Fine Japanese Prints
314 Occidental Ave. S
Seattle, WA 98104-2840
ph: 206-621-1888
fax: 206-621-6493
info@carolynstaleyprints.com
http://www.carolynstaleyprints.com
Buys, sells, consigns fine Japanese

woodblock prints, including Ukiyo-E, shin nanga and sosaku hanga; Web site contains an extensive collection of more than 400 prints.

G. C. Uhlenbeck
Hotei Japanese Prints
Breestraat 113a
CL Leiden, 23211 The Netherlands
ph: (071) 514 35 52
fax: (071) 514 14 88
ukiyoe@xs4all.nl
http://www.nvva.nl/ukiyoe
Fine Japanese prints, paintings and illustrated books by appointment.

Experts

Sandra Andacht
P.O. Box 94
Little Neck, NY 11363-0094
ph: 718-229-6593
Orientalia@aol.com
http://hometown.aol.com/orientalia/index.html
Author of "Collector's Value Guide to Japanese Woodblock Prints," "Collector's Value Guide to Oriental Decorative Arts," and "Oriental Antiques Art - An Identification & Value Guide" (Krause).

Internet Resources

Ukiyo-E World GmbH
Johann Sebastian Bach Str. 11
Pullach, Bavaria 82049 Germany
ph: ++49-(0)89-79367709
fax: ++49-(0)89-79367708
webmaster@ukiyo-e-world.com
http://www.ukiyo-e-world.com
An Internet site for collectors of high quality Japanese woodblock prints; monthly online auction, gallery, forum, reference articles, links, Japanese calendar, newsletter by email.

John Laroche
artelino - The Magic of Art
Joh.-Seb.-Bach-Str. 11
Pullach, Bavaria 82049 Germany
webmaster@artelino.com
http://www.artelino.com
Art auctions, galleries and forum for art prints, old maps, Japanese art, Ukiyo-E, Orthodox icons; also contemporary artists, art resource listings and classifieds; extensive articles on art, prints, icons, etc.

Hans Olof Johansson
Ukiyo-E: The Pictures of the Floating World
Sweden
secutor@bahnhof.se
http://www.bahnhof.se/~secutor/ukiyo-e
Web site has lots of links to other Ukiyo-E (Japanese woodblock print) sites, and other sites relating to Japan and its culture and art.

Museums/Libraries

Honolulu Academy of Arts
900 S. Beretania St.
Honolulu, HI 96814-1495
ph: 808-532-8701 or 808-532-8700
webmaster@honoluluacademy.org
http://www.honoluluacademy.org
An encyclopedic museum of world art.

Yard-Long

Collectors

Al Little
151 Highway 173
Antioch, IL 60002
ph: 847-395-7752
fax: 847-395-7703
Buys and sells yard-long prints.

Sherry & Mike Miller
303 Holiday Dr. #130
Tuscola, IL 61953-2118
ph: 217-253-4991
miller1@net66.com
*Wants to buy yard-long lithograph
prints; only of lovely ladies dressed in
1900-1920s fashions; some have been
trimmed to fit smaller frames; some
have artist's name on front; most have
advertising and small calendar on
back.*

Dealers

Kathy Wilkins
K.W.'s Antiques
1181 Stelzer Rd.
Howell, MI 48843
ph: 517-552-0012 or 517-548-9346
*Calendar advertising distributed to
consumers from the early 1900s to the
1920s are known as Yard-Long prints;
these beautiful lithography prints are
in a multitude of subjects ranging
from polar bears to Victorian ladies.*

Linda Gibbs
Heirloom Keepsakes
10380 Miranda Ave.
Buena Park, CA 90620-4447
ph: 714-827-6488
*Wants yard-long prints from the
1800s to 1930s.*

Experts

Bill & June Keagy
Those Wonderful Yard-Long Prints &
More
P.O. Box 106
Bloomfield, IN 47424-0106
ph: 812-384-3471
fax: 812-384-8824
billjune@custom.net
*Co-authors of the yard-long books,
"Those Wonderful Yard-Long Prints
and More" (1989), "More Wonderful
Yard-Long Prints" (1992), and
"Yard-Long Prints" Book III (1995);
available from the author.*

Charles & Joan Rhoden
Rhoden Books & Publishing, Inc.
8693 N. 1950 East Rd.
Georgetown, IL 61846-6264
ph: 217-662-8046
rhoden@soltec.net
*Buys and collects yard-long prints; co-
author of "Those Wonderful Yard-
Long Prints," Books I, II and III
which are available from the author.*

PRINTS (MODERN)

(see also ART; COLLECTIBLES
[MODERN]; PRINTS; REPAIR/
RESTORATION/CONSERVATION,
Paper Items)

Dealers

Allen's Creations, Inc. - Frame & Art
Gallery
P.O. Box 452
Clemson, SC 29633-0452
ph: 864-654-3594 or 800-669-2731
aci@innova.net
http://www.allenscreations.com

David Boshart
National Wildlife Galleries
8504 Charter Club Blvd., Ste. 10
Fort Myers, FL 33919
ph: 239-275-0500 or 800-382-5278
fax: 239-936-2788
stamps@nationalwildlife.com
http://www.nationalwildlife.com
*Designs, produces and distributes
duck and other wildlife conservation
stamps, prints, and medallions; since
1976; also buys, sells, trades most
other prints and sculpture of all
subjects.*

BIGgallery.com
7130 Grammar Dr.
Fairview, TN 37062
ph: 615-799-8437 or 800-760-6491
(orders)
fax: 615-799-8459
staff@biggallery.com
http://www.big-gallery.com
*Great resource for searching tens of
thousands of modern prints by
thousands of artists.*

Jonathan Farrow
Media Group, The
7510 W. Sunset Blvd., #553
Los Angeles, CA 90024
ph: 323-661-3382
jfarrow@fineartsite.com
http://www.FineArtSite.com
*Limited edition prints, original
paintings, sculpture: Erte, Dali,
Haring, Hockney, Indiana,
Liechtenstein, Miro, Motherwell,
Picasso, Rosenquist, Vasarely,
Warhol, Hart, Kostabi, Max, Neiman,
Rockwell, Yamagata.*

Nielsen's Art
1356 Jadwin Ave.
Richland, WA 99352
ph: 509-946-8878 or 800-974-4278
fax: 509-783-4518
nielsenj@nielsensart.com
http://www.nielsensart.com
*Advertises that they can get any
limited edition print ever done.*

Internet Resources

Art Brokerage, Inc.
P.O. Box 3730
544 East Fork Rd.
Ketchum, ID 83340
ph: 208-788-1484 or 208-788-1491
fax: 208-788-1492
drose@earthlink.net
http://www.artbrokerage.com
*Online service for buying and selling
art; specializes in selling limited
edition prints and sculpture; accepts
consignments; list your artwork for
sale in classifieds.*

Man./Prod./Dist.

Greenwich Workshop, Inc.
1 Greenwich Place
Shelton, CT 06484-4618
ph: 203-925-0131
fax: 203-925-0262
http://www.greenwichworkshop.com
*Publishes aviation, Western, and
fantasy art in limited edition print
form.*

Periodicals

Westtown Publishing
Magazine: InformArt
P.O. Box 220
Bethel, CT 06801
ph: 203-205-0000 or 800-906-9600
fax: 203-205-0003
kathi@informartmag.com
http://www.informartmag.com
*A quarterly magazine focusing on
modern limited edition prints (signed
& numbered); ads, articles, new
releases, secondary market values.*

Julie MacDonald, Ed.
Advanstar Communications, Inc.
Magazine: Art Business News
270 Madison Ave.
New York, NY 10016-0601
ph: 888-527-7008
fax: 218-723-9437
jmacdonald@advanstar.com
http://www.artbusinessnews.com
*Focuses on the contemporary
photoreproduction print market and
the business aspect of art and
framing, but includes timely
information on tax changes and laws,
as well as analysis of markets.*

Tricia Bisoux, Sr. Ed.
Magazine: DECOR
330 N. Fourth St.
Saint Louis, MO 63102
ph: 314-421-5445 or 800-280-5445
fax: 314-421-1070
decor@pfpublish.com
http://www.decormagazine.com
*Aimed at art gallery and custom frame
shop owners with articles about
successful business management,
effective marketing and promotions,
gallery design, frame shop floor
plans, art media, technology, and new
trends; annual sources dir.*

Adolf Sehring

Man./Prod./Dist.

D. Gary Gibson, VP
American Artist Portfolio, Inc.
496 Clarks Tract
Keswick, VA 22947
ph: 434-295-4883
dggib@earthlink.net
http://www.adolfsehring.com
*Founded in 1988 to publish and
market the works of realist artist
Adolf Sehring.*

Barbara Hails

Man./Prod./Dist.

Barbara Hails Fine Art
18319 Georgia Ave.
Olney, MD 20832-1435
ph: 301-774-6249 or 800-451-6411
fax: 301-774-1128
http://www.barbarahails.com
*Produces limited edition fine prints
based on the pastels and oils of artist
Barbara Hails; recently introduced
canvas lithographs of her distinctive
art.*

Diane Graebner

Clubs/Associations

Diane Graebner Collector's Club
Newsletter: Diane Graebner Collector's
Club Newsletter
P.O. Box 530253
Millersburg, OH 89053-0253
ph: 800-626-4306
fax: 702-263-2954
dgraebner@aol.com
*Limited edition, paper prints depicting
the Amish lifestyle.*

Man./Prod./Dist.

Diane & Ted Graebner
Lynn's Prints
P.O. Box 530253
Millersburg, OH 89053-0253
ph: 800-626-4306
fax: 702-263-2954
dgraebner@aol.com
*Producer of limited edition prints,
cross stitch packets, other products
designed by Diane Graebner and
which depict Amish living.*

Fred Stone

Man./Prod./Dist.

American Artists
P.O. Box 536
Cold Spring Harbor, NY 11724
ph: 800-828-0086
AmericanArt1@aol.com

Jody Bergsma

Man./Prod./Dist.

Jody Bergsma Galleries
1344 King St.
Bellingham, WA 98226-6224
ph: 360-733-1101 or 800-237-4762
bergsma@bergsma.com
http://www.bergsma.com
*Publishes and markets the works of
artist Jody Bergsma.*

Marty Bell

Clubs/Associations

Marty Bell Collector's Society
Newsletter: Sounds of Bells, The
9550 Owensmouth Ave.
Chatsworth, CA 91311-4801
ph: 818-700-0754 or 800-637-4537
fax: 818-709-7668
info@martybell.com
http://www.martybell.com
*Focuses on the collectible prints of
English thatched, tiled and slate roof
cottages by Marty Bell.*

Man./Prod./Dist.

Marty Bell Fine Art, Inc.
9550 Owensmouth Ave.
Chatsworth, CA 91311-4801
ph: 818-700-0754 or 800-637-4537
fax: 818-709-7668
info@martybell.com
http://www.martybell.com
*Publishes limited edition lithographs
from the original paintings of Marty
Bell.*

Thomas Kinkade

Clubs/Associations

Thomas Kinkade Collectors' Society,
c/o Lightpost Publishing
Newsletter: Thomas Kinkade Collectors'
Society Newsletter
521 Charcot Ave.
San Jose, CA 95131
ph: 408-324-2020 or 800-366-3733
fax: 408-232-4822
customer_service@mediaarts.com
http://www.thomaskinkade.com
*Canvas lithographs and luminous
archival paper prints.*

Man./Prod./Dist.

Lightpost Publishing, Inc.
521 Charcot Ave.
San Jose, CA 95131
ph: 408-324-2020 or 800-366-3733
fax: 408-232-4822
customer_service@mediaarts.com
http://www.thomaskinkade.com
*Widely known in the limited edition
print field for its publishing of fine
art prints by artist Thomas Kinkade.*

PRISON RELATED ITEMS

(see LAW ENFORCEMENT
MEMORABILIA)

PRISONER-OF-WAR ART
Straw

Dealers

Lucille Malitz
Lucid Antiques
P.O. Box KH
Scarsdale, NY 10583
ph: 914-636-7825 or 914-636-5171
fax: 914-636-7825
lithopha@optonline.net
*Imprisoned by the British, French
prisoners of war escaped boredom by
fashioning ingenious items made of
straw or ivory.*

PROGRAMS

(see MOVIE MEMORABILIA; PAPER
COLLECTIBLES; SPORTS
COLLECTIBLES)

PROHIBITION ITEMS

(see also BREWERIANA;
PERSONALITIES [CRIMINAL];
POLITICAL COLLECTIBLES;
SALOON & BAR COLLECTIBLES;
WHISKEY INDUSTRY ITEMS)

Clubs/Associations

Earl F. Dodge
Partisan Prohibition Historical Society
Newsletter: National Statesman, The
P.O. Box 2635
Denver, CO 80201
ph: 303-237-4947
fax: 303-233-2099
earldodge@dodgeoffice.net
http://www.buttonsbydodge.com
*Wants to buy all Prohibition related
items*

Collectors

Cary Demont
P.O. Box 16013
Minneapolis, MN 55416
ph: 763-522-0957
*Wants early Prohibition, Temperance,
and Carrie Nation related items; early
badges, pins, postcards, posters,
broadsides, banners, etc.*

Dealers

Bob Lucian
33 Merritts Rd.
Farmingdale, NY 11735-1820
ph: 516-293-3927
bbluc@optonline.net
*Buys and sells old pre-prohibition
American beer items: mugs, steins,
advertising signs, bottle openers,
match safes, glasses, "giveaways,"
etc.; prefers items from the NYC and
L.I. area; also wants prohibition
items; call collect.*

PROMOTERS

(see ANTIQUES SHOW
PROMOTERS)

PROPHYLACTICS
Tins

Collectors

Dennis Elliot
323 Sandpiper Lane
Delray Beach, FL 33483-7135
ph: 410-889-3964
*Wants condom tins, especially Rough
Rider, 3 Pirates, Akron Tourist Tubes.*

Michael Dusek
1058 Lupin Dr. #5
Salinas, CA 93906
ph: 831-757-2526
*Wants prophylactic/condom tins:
Sphinx, Chariots, Napoleons,
Carmen, etc.; also wants related
advertising.*

Experts

George Goehring
Dennis & George Collectibles
323 Sandpiper Lane
Delray Beach, FL 33483
ph: 561-243-3072
dandgtins@aol.com
*Co-author with Dennis O'Brien of
"Remember Your Rubbers."*

Vending Machines

Collectors

Mr. Condom
1635 Acorn Ano Rd.
Somerset, KY 42501
ph: 606-274-4848
*Buys/sells collectible prophylactic and
feminine hygiene vending equipment
and related items.*

PSYCHEDELIC ITEMS

(see SOCIAL CAUSES, Hippie Items)

PUB JUGS

(see SALOON & BAR
COLLECTIBLES, Whiskey Pitchers)

PUPPETS

(see also PERFORMING ARTS;
VENTRILOQUIST ITEMS)

Clubs/Associations

Joyce & Chuck Berty, Mbrship.
Puppeteers of America, Inc.
Magazine: Puppetry Journal
P.O. Box 29417
Cleveland, OH 44129-0417
ph: 888-568-6235
pofajoin@aol.com
http://www.puppeteers.org
*A national nonprofit organization
founded in 1937, provides information, encourages performances, and
builds a community of people who love
puppet theatre; for professional
puppeteers, puppet makers, teachers,
hobbyists, etc.*

Puppetry Arts Institute
Newsletter: Puppetry Arts Institute
Newsletter
11025 E. Winner Rd.
Independence, MO 64052
ph: 816-833-9777
pai@att.net
http://www.hazelle.org
*Send SASE for price list of Hazelle
parts available and information of
Hazelle Rollins life and puppet
factory.*

Ontario Puppetry Association
Newsletter: Ontario Puppetry Association
Newsletter
171 Sherman St.
Mississaugua, Ontario K7M 5G9 Canada
ph: 800-379-0446 or 613-389-2966
webmaster@onpuppet.org
http://www.onpuppet.org
*Members include professional puppet
performers and makers, collectors,
and puppet enthusiasts.*

Collectors

Andy Gross
P.O. Box 6134
Beverly Hills, CA 90212-1134
ph: 310-362-4372 or 310-614-1944
fax: 310-680-6495
apedoll69@aol.com
http://www.lamagictoy.com
*Wants ventriloquist dummies and or
any related items such as puppets,
toys, games, photos, books,
marionettes, and old pro & toy
dummies, i.e., Jerry Mahoney,
Knucklehead Smiff, Charlie McCarthy,
Mortimer Snerd, Danny O'Day,
Farfel, etc.*

Experts

Bob Isaacson
1002 Clinton
Oak Park, IL 60304
ph: 708-383-5646
moeknows1007@msn.com
*Wants to buy professional ventrilo-
quist figures and wooden dummies
used by professional stage performers,
or amateur ventriloquists; please send
photos.*

Internet Resources

Rose Sage
Puppetry Homepage
rosesage@sagecraft.com
http://www.sagecraft.com/puppetry
A free resource for the puppetry community; dedicated to helping people connect with the world of puppetry: organizations, puppet news, festivals, theaters, definitions, using puppets, puppet traditions, schools, exhibits & museums, etc.

Museums/Libraries

Bread & Puppet Museum
743 Heights Rd.
Glover, VT 05839
ph: 802-525-3031
A large collection of gigantic puppets, masks and related graphics and paintings.

Library & Museum of the Performing Arts, Shelby Cullom Davis Museum
40 Lincoln Center Plaza
New York, NY 10023-7498
ph: 212-870-1630
performingarts@nypl.org
http://www.nypl.org/research/lpa/lpa.html

Center for Puppetry Arts Museum
1404 Spring St.
Atlanta, GA 30309
ph: 404-873-3089
fax: 404-873-9907
puppet@mindspring.com
http://www.puppet.org/museum_permanent.html
Library, videos, educational programs, exhibits, publications.

PURSES

(see also BEADS; CLOTHING & ACCESSORIES, Vintage; COMPACTS; DRESSER ITEMS)

Clubs/Associations

Molly Klumpfell
California Purse Collector's Club
Newsletter: California Purse Collectors' Club Newsletter
P.O. Box 572
Campbell, CA 95009
Members from across the US learn how to collect antique purses, store them, identify styles/type/quality; historical info on pre-1940 purses; holds meetings to swap and sell in the San Francisco area.

Collectors

Kathy Glaeser
142 Cimarand Dr.
Williamsville, NY 14221
ph: 716-639-7934
ibuypurses@aol.com
Wants to buy Victorian era beaded purses with scenes, people, animals, Egyptian motifs, fine florals, jeweled frames, etc.; also wants White & Davis and Mandalian colored mesh

purses, as well as fine petitpoint bags and unusual frames.

Lydia M. Jackson-Fryer
608 Winans Way
Baltimore, MD 21229-1430
ph: 410-233-6231
fax: 410-233-6231
ljackson@umbc.edu
Wants to buy antique purses: mesh, beaded, Bakelite, cloth, leather.

Barbara Hobbs
5501 101st Ave. N
Pinellas Park, FL 33782-3311
ph: 813-541-6164
carnivalbarb@aol.com
Wants to buy beaded purses.

Jennifer Sykes
Jennifer Sykes Antiques
9018 Balboa Blvd. #595
Northridge, CA 91325-2610
ph: 818-993-1916
fax: 818-993-7612
Veeda10@aol.com
Wants purses and vanity bags: mesh, enamel, bead, Bakelite, or celluloid; also wants girlie items such as mugs, ashtrays, figurines, novelties, etc.

Molly Klumpfell
Purse Snatchers
P.O. Box 572
Campbell, CA 95009
Wants to buy pre-1930 antique purses in good to excellent condition; wants unusual purses such as scenic beaded, carpet bags; also buys collections; send clear photo, or zerox copies with complete description; will respond in 5 days.

Leslie Holms
P.O. Box 596
Los Gatos, CA 95031-0596
ph: 408-354-1626
fax: 408-395-0803
Wants to buy pre-1930s beaded purses with scenes of people and places, abstracts, Persian carpet motifs; also wants enameled mesh, bright colors, bold designs; damaged purses are OK.

Dealers

Debbie Woolley
Favorite Past-Times Antiques
6 Main Hill
Bridgton, ME 04009
ph: 207-647-4486
info@maine-antiques.com
http://www.maine-antiques.com/fpt/Index
Specializing in enameled mesh purses.

Kathy Burch
Tri-State Antique Center
47 W. Pike
Canonsburg, PA 15317
ph: 724-745-9116
fax: 412-291-1367
kathy&ed@tri-stateantiques.com
http://tri-stateantiques.com
Specializes in lady's beaded and mesh purses, Lucite purses, chatelaines,

compacts, and other ladies vanity items.

Cindy Butler
607 Melody Lane
Bessemer, AL 35020
ph: 205-425-9340
cvbmomof3@aol.com
Buys and sells vintage beaded scenic/figural purses; selling beaded, mesh, petite point, decoupage, Lucite, and tapestry purses.

Gail & John Dunn
P.O. Box 234
Waterville, OH 43566
ph: 419-878-9515
Buys and sells vintage purses and hatpins.

Veronica Trainer
Bayhouse
P.O. Box 40442
Bay Village, OH 44140-0442
ph: 440-871-8584
Buys and sells purses by mail order; advisor to "Schroeder's Antiques Price Guide;" specializes in beaded and enameled mesh purses; paying top dollar for scenics and purses with jeweled and ornate frames; also wants damaged purses.

Marion Spitzley
Spitzley Data & Graphics
1118 Nottingham
Grosse Pointe, MI 48230
ph: 313-824-9435
esmee@io.com
http://www.io.com/~esmee/bag_lady/bag_lady.htm
Specializes in Lucite and Bakelite handbags and jewelry, but has a general knowledge of all types of purses: beaded, mesh, leather as well as 20th century jewelry and compacts.

Beth Pulsipher
Prairie Home Antiques
240 North Grand
P.O. Box 373
Schoolcraft, MI 49087-0373
ph: 616-679-2062
Buys and sells vintage beaded or mesh purses and hand bags, c. 1880 to 1940; sells by mail; available for lectures and seminars.

Diane Richardson
Gold Hatpin, The
125 N. Marion St.
Oak Park, IL 60301-1087
ph: 708-848-3247 or 708-445-0610
goldhatpin@comcast.net
Wants all types of beaded and mesh purses made before 1940, especially those with small beads, scenes, elaborate frames, etc.; also buys purse frames.

Andra Behrendt
Lady A Antiques
P.O. Box 217
Western Springs, IL 60558
ph: 708-246-2676
andra@lady-a.com
http://www.lady-a.com
Dealer specializing in ladies' accessory items including a large variety of compacts and mesh/beaded purses.

David E. Newman
Newman & Assoc.
2476 Bolsover, #504
Houston, TX 77005-2518
ph: 713-521-7044
newmanasoc@aol.com
Specializes in buying, selling, restoring and appraising vintage beaded, mesh and enameled purses: relining, refringe and reframe.

Experts

Jeannette Schoolsky
P.O. Box 95
Nashua, NH 03061
ph: 603-883-7931
fax: 603-882-3781
Purses@ArtDeco.com
Purse expert/collector wants to buy cut steel, mesh and glass beaded purses; especially seeking any "micro" glass beaded purse depicting oriental rug pattern, scenery, birds, people, animals; also does purse repairs and fee appraisals.

Roselyn Gerson
P.O. Box 100
Malverne, NY 11565
ph: 516-593-8746
fax: 516-593-0611
Author of "Vintage Vanity Bags & Purses" focusing on purses, bags and related items that have compacts.

Kathy Burch
Tri-State Antique Center
47 W. Pike
Canonsburg, PA 15317
ph: 724-745-9116
fax: 412-291-1367
kathy&ed@tri-stateantiques.com
http://tri-stateantiques.com
Specializes in lady's beaded and mesh purses, Lucite purses, chatelaines, compacts, and other ladies vanity items.

Roseann Ettinger
Remember When
21-23 W. Broad St.
Hazleton, PA 18201
ph: 570-454-8465 or 570-450-5542
popgems2001@hotmail.com
Author of "Handbags."

Sherry & Mike Miller
303 Holiday Dr. #130
Tuscola, IL 61953-2118
ph: 217-253-4991
miller1@net66.com
Wants unusual glass bead, ring mesh & flat mesh purses made in the 1920s

& 1930s with designs painted on the mesh; especially wants compact/mesh bag combinations; must be mint or near-mint condition; also wants vintage ads for mesh purses.

Museums/Libraries

Museum of Fine Arts, Boston
465 Huntington Ave.
Boston, MA 02115-5523
ph: 617-267-9300
webmaster@mfa.org
http://www.mfa.org
An outstanding collection of purses.

Repair Services

Jeannette Schoolsky
P.O. Box 95
Nashua, NH 03061
ph: 603-883-7931
fax: 603-882-3781
Purses@ArtDeco.com
Purse expert/collector wants to buy cut steel, mesh and glass beaded purses; especially seeking any "micro" glass beaded purse depicting oriental rug pattern, scenery, birds, people, animals; also does purse repairs and fee appraisals.

Naomi Godel
Nomago
532 Boyer Rd.
Cheltenham, PA 19012
ph: 215-663-1721
bagrestore@aol.com
Specializes in the repair and restoration of vintage beaded bags: beaded bodies, fringes, tassels, linings.

Plastic

Collectors

Melba Becker
2408 Las Verdes St.
Las Vegas, NV 89102
Wants to buy plastic handbags from the 1940s and 1950s.

PUZZLES

(see also BOTTLES, Puzzle; GAMES; PAPER COLLECTIBLES)

Clubs/Associations

Association of Game & Puzzle Collectors
Journal: Game & Puzzle Collectors
  Quarterly
PMB 321
197M Boston Post Rd. West
Marlborough, MA 01752
juckett@attglobal.net
http://www.agpc.org
Members are devoted to collecting, researching, preserving games, jigsaw puzzles, mechanical puzzles, and other pastimes.

Crosswords

Collectors

Will Shortz
55 Great Oak Lane
Pleasantville, NY 10570-2010
ph: 914-769-9128
wshortz@aol.com
http://www.crosswordtournament.com
Wants to buy crossword puzzles: books and magazines.

Jigsaw

Collectors

Mark G. Cappitella
MGC's Custom Hand Cut Wooden
  Jigsaw Puzzles & Fine Art
31 Bogue Lane
East Haddam, CT 06423
ph: 888-604-7654 or 860-873-3093
mark@mgcpuzzles.com
http://www.mgcpuzzles.com
Makes & collects custom hand crafted "wooden" jigsaw puzzles; great online puzzle Web site.

Jim Rohacs
9721 Lomond Dr.
Manassas, VA 22110-3104
ph: 703-369-5578
Wants pre-1950s puzzles.

Liz & Dick Wilmes
38W567 Brindlewood Ave.
Elgin, IL 60123-7976
ph: 847-697-9679
fax: 847-742-1054
Bblocks@bblocksonline.com
Especially interested in Depression-era advertising jigsaw puzzles; please send SASE for reply.

Dave Cooper
Clarendon, Parsonage Rd.
Herne Bay, Kent CT6 5TA U.K.
ji6sawman@aol.com
http://members.aol.com/ji6sawman/
  index.html
Collector of wooden and old card jigsaw puzzles and maker of new wooden puzzles to order from customers' own prints; buy, sell, swap puzzles; researching information regarding U.K. jigsaws and wants to expand knowledge of US puzzles.

Dealers

Robert J. Bergeron
CIA Group, The
2054 E. Balboa Dr.
Tempe, AZ 85282-4005
ph: 480-838-6266
fax: 480-839-5266
zagzaw@worldnet.att.net
Collects, buys, sells jigsaw puzzles, specializing in Zag-Zaw wooden puzzles by Raphael Tuck, particularly the Dickens 1812-1912 series and all of Tuck's catalogs; Centenary a.k.a. Carriage Series in 2 sizes and 16 prints.

Experts

Bob Armstrong
15 Monadnock Rd.
Worcester, MA 01609
ph: 508-799-0644
raahna@oldpuzzles.com
http://www.oldpuzzles.com
Old wood jigsaw puzzles, adult cut, pre-1950; collects, restores, displays, sells, answers information via Web site; author of "Jigsaw Puzzle Cutting Styles," "Game Researchers" Notes Issue No. 25, AGCA, and other articles.

Anne D. Williams
Economics Dept.
Bates College
Lewiston, ME 04240
ph: 207-783-8732
puzzles@bates.edu
Wants jigsaw puzzles and information about them (company catalogs, ephemera, etc.); special interest in history of small-scale puzzle makers; author of "Jigsaw Puzzles" (1990), "Cutting A Fine Figure" (1996), many articles about puzzles.

Chris McCann
658 MacElroy Rd.
Ballston Lake, NY 12019-2202
ph: 518-877-7303
Researcher of cardboard jigsaw puzzles from 1932 to 1960; has computer database of more than 13,500 titles; 10,200 titles have been identified with artist name; would like to hear from other collectors; author of "Master Pieces."

Harry L. Rinker
Puzzle Pit, The
5093 Vera Cruz Rd.
Emmaus, PA 18049-9554
ph: 610-965-1122
fax: 610-965-1124
rinkeron@fast.net
http://www.harryrinker.com
Wants wooden or cardboard jigsaw puzzles with advertising, mystery, personality, cartoon character, depression era, or WWII theme.

Jigsaw (Wood)

Collectors

Gordon Hayter
6232 Riviera Circle
Long Beach, CA 90815-4780
ph: 562-799-3797
Collector of wooden adult (not children's) interlocking jigsaw puzzles; long-time member of the Association of Game & Puzzle Collectors.

Mechanical

Collectors

Cary Basse
6927 Forbes Ave.
Van Nuys, CA 91406-4504
ph: 818-781-4856

Experts

Jerry Slocum
Slocum Puzzle Foundation
257 South Palm Dr.
Beverly Hills, CA 90212
ph: 310-273-2270
fax: 310-274-3644
jslocum@earthlink.net
http://anduin.eldar.org/~problemi/
  slocum/referenc.html
Wants mechanical & dexterity puzzles, trick locks, trick match safes, folding puzzles, advertising string puzzles, puzzle trade cards, checkerboard puzzles, catalogs with puzzles, puzzle books.

Mechanical (Rubik's Cubes)

Collectors

Peter M. Beck
Just Puzzles
P.O. Box 267
Wharton, NJ 07885
ph: 973-625-4191
just_puzzles@yahoo.com
http://justpuzzles.freeyellow.com
Wants to buy any type of Rubik's cube memorabilia; buys and sells all forms of mechanical puzzles; send SASE for brochure.

Paper

Collectors

Will Shortz
55 Great Oak Lane
Pleasantville, NY 10570-2010
ph: 914-769-9128
wshortz@aol.com
http://www.crosswordtournament.com
Wants to buy paper puzzles, also puzzle books and magazines.

PYROBILIA

(see FIREWORKS MEMORABILIA)

PYROGRAPHY ITEMS

Collectors

John Lewis
2906 Alamosa Ct.
Loveland, CO 80538
ph: 970-667-2960
john4real@aol.com
Wants quality "burnt wood" items such as plaques, boxes and furniture; also wants catalogs, wood burning kits, and books on pyrography.

Dealers

John Sholl
Sholl Antiques
P.O. Box 9
Norwood, NY 13668
ph: 315-353-2474
info@tramp-art.com
http://www.tramp-art.com
Specializes in folk crafts of the early 20th century: tramp art, penknife whimseys, marquetry, fretwork, pyrography.

Linda Gibbs
Heirloom Keepsakes
10380 Miranda Ave.
Buena Park, CA 90620-4447
ph: 714-827-6488
*Wants wooden boxes with flower
designs, beautiful ladies, etc., 1800s-
1900s; please send SASE and photos.*

Experts

Carole & Richard Smyth
Carole Smyth Antiques
P.O. Box 2068
Huntington, NY 11743-0861
ph: 631-673-8666
carolesmyth@yahoo.com
*Authors of "The Burning Passion - A
Study & Price Guide," now available
from the authors for $25 ppd.*

**Here are some tips
when contacting
someone who is listed
in this book:**

When requesting
information about a
particular item, include
a description (material,
dimensions, maker's
mark, model number,
etc.) and a photo,
sketch, digital image or
photocopy of the item
in question.

Always ask if there are
charges for samples or
for the services that
you are requesting.

When corresponding
by letter, please be
sure to include a Large
(#10 business size)
Self-Addressed and
Stamped Envelope
(LSASE) if requesting a
reply or the return of
photographs.

Never call collect
unless otherwise
directed. When
calling, be considerate
of time zone differ-
ences and always ask
if the party you are
calling has time to talk.
When leaving an
answering machine
message, always
instruct the party to
call you back collect.

QUILTS

(see also FEED & GRAIN BAGS;
FOLK ART; REPAIR/RESTORATION/
CONSERVATION, Textiles;
TEXTILES)

Appraisers

Phyllis Twigg
2775 Gingerview Lane
Annapolis, MD 21401
ph: 410-571-8847
ptwigg@radix.net
http://www.quilt-appraiser.com
*Qualified to appraise both antique
and new quilts, tops, blocks, and
quilted wearable art in all traditional,
contemporary, and innovative styles;
offers hands-on fabric dating
workshops, lectures, appraisal
sessions at quilt shows.*

Lynn Gorges
Historic Textiles Studio
3910 U.S. Highway 70 East
New Bern, NC 28560
ph: 252-636-3039 or 252-636-5445
fax: 252-637-1862
palampore@aol.com
http://www.textilepreservation.com
*Specializes in the restoration,
conservation, appraisal, evaluation of
quilts.*

American Quilter's Society
Magazine: American Quilter
P.O. Box 3290
Paducah, KY 42002-3290
ph: 800-626-5420 or 270-898-7903
fax: 270-898-8890
info@aqsquilt.com
http://www.aqsquilt.com
*Publishes list of certified quilt
appraisers.*

Laura Hobby Syler
Texas Quilt Co.
2401 Blue Cypress
Richardson, TX 75082
ph: 972-473-0884
texas_quilt.co@airmail.net
*Certified quilt appraiser, quilt
historian, quilt restoration, quilt
lecturer, and author; president &
founder of Texas Quilt Co. and the
Vintage Quilt & Textile Society.*

Terri Ellis, ISA
Mistletoe Estate Sales & Appraisals
1205 Mistletoe Dr.
Fort Worth, TX 76110-1018
ph: 817-926-9424
fax: 817-926-0386
tquilts@airmail.net
http://www.mistletoesales.net
*Certified quilt appraiser by the
American Quilter's Society; Accredited
Member of the ISA; also buys and sells
vintage textiles.*

Cindy Brick
3700 N. Collins
Castle Rock, CO 80104
ph: 303-688-0774
fax: 303-688-0774
brickworks@bigfoot.com
http://www.cindybrick.com
*Certified appraiser, American
Quilter's Society (textiles and quilts);
teacher, author, lecturer; managing
editor of Crazy Quilt Society; selling
vintage ephemera, quilt-related items,
and vintage-style fabric transfers.*

Deborah Roberts
P.O. Box 2176
Costa Mesa, CA 92626
ph: 714-557-5258
quiltevals@aol.com
http://www.quiltappraiser.com
*Historian, appraiser, specializing in
buying and selling antique hooked
rugs, quilts and quilt-related textiles;
certified by the American Quilter's
Society; wish list available; also
lectures on quilts.*

Deborah Roberts
Professional Association of Appraisers -
Quilted Textiles
1071 San Pablo
Costa Mesa, CA 92626
ph: 714-557-5258
quiltevals@aol.com
http://members.aol.com/NBolliger/
paaqt.html
*All members are certified by the
American Quilter's Society; search for
a quilt appraiser in your area on their
Web site.*

Nance Searle, ISA
Searle Appraisal Practice
1355 Paige Ave.
Eugene, OR 97405
ph: 541-684-4038
fax: 541-683-6084
nms@jps.net
*Appraises all quilt and household
related textiles including linens, lace,
soft furnishings, antique/vintage
sewing notions and toy sewing
machines.*

Ann Rogers Pfrender
2917 Timberline Dr.
Eugene, OR 97405-1233
ph: 541-484-9979
fax: 541-684-8076
Apfrender@aol.com
*Appraises antique and contemporary
quilts and quilted textiles; Member,
Professional Association of
Appraisers of Quilted Textiles;
Certified Member, American Quilters
Society.*

Bette G. Bell, ISA CAPP
Guildmark Appraisal & Estate Sale
Services, LLC
P.O. Box 952
Edmonds, WA 98020
ph: 425-775-5650
fax: 425-670-6957
stashn33@gte.net
http://www.guildmarkappraisal.com
*Appraises quilts and other textiles
such as samplers, ethnographic
textiles, linens; handles estate sales
throughout the NW; Certified Member
of the International Society of
Appraisers; appraising for over 16
years.*

Sally A. Ambrose, ISA CAPP
Ambrose Appraisal Service
P.O. Box 536
11156 North Rd.
Leavenworth, WA 98826-9512
ph: 509-548-7472
fax: 509-548-0240
sally@televar.com
*Specializes in the appraising of
antique and contemporary American
quilted textiles, contemporary
wearable art, and residential contents;
ASA accredited Senior Appraiser,
American Quilt Society Certified
Appraiser of Quilted Textiles.*

Diane Shink
Dimac Quilt
68 Strathearn North
Montreal West, Quebec H4X 1X7
Canada
ph: 514-486-2768
Dimacquilt@sympatico.ca
http://www3.sympatico.ca/dimacquilt
*American Quilt Society Certified quilt
appraiser; also gives lectures on quilt
care and repair.*

Clubs/Associations

National Quilting Association, Inc., The
Magazine: Quilting Quarterly
P.O. Box 393
Ellicott City, MD 21043-0393
ph: 410-461-5733
fax: 410-461-3693
nqa@erols.com
http://www.nqaquilts.org
*Purpose is to stimulate, maintain and
record interest in all matters
pertaining to the making, collecting
and preserving of quilts.*

American Quilter's Society
Magazine: American Quilter
P.O. Box 3290
Paducah, KY 42002-3290
ph: 800-626-5420 or 270-898-7903
fax: 270-898-8890
info@aqsquilt.com
http://www.aqsquilt.com
*Members receive bi-monthly
newsletter, discount admission to
Annual National AQS Quilt Show,
discounts on quilting books, American*
*Quilter Magazine; also publishes list
of certified quilt appraisers.*

Crazy Quilt Society
Newsletter: Crazy Quilt Newsletter
P.O. Box 19452
Omaha, NE 68119
ph: 800-599-0094
fax: 800-811-6101
QuiltHF@aol.com
http://www.crazyquilt.com
*Over 500 members who enjoy
collecting, making or studying crazy
quilts; newsletter published quarterly;
annual conference.*

Judy J. Brott Buss
American Quilt Study Group
Newsletter: Blanket Statements
P.O. Box 4737
Lincoln, NE 68504-0737
ph: 402-472-5361
fax: 402-472-5428
AQSG2@unl.edu
http://www2.h-net.msu.edu/~aqsq
*Goal is to develop a responsible and
accurate body of information about
quilts and their makers; membership
open to any person having an interest
in the history of quilt making; also
publishes the annual journal,
"Uncoverings."*

Collectors

A. Everette James, Jr.
St. James Place
205 New Castle Place
Chapel Hill, NC 27514
ph: 919-933-6853
fax: 919-942-0437
everette@nc.rr.com
*Focuses on African American folk art
quilts from North Carolina from the
period 1860 to 1950.*

Dealers

Betsey Telford
Betsy Telford's Antique Quilts dba
Rocky Mountain Quilts
130 York St.
York Village, ME 03909
ph: 800-762-5940
fax: 207-351-3381
betsey@btantiquequilts.com
http://www.rockymountainquilts.com
*Buys, sells and restores antique quilts;
has over 400 quilts dating from 1740
to 1940 in stock; restorations of quilts
and hooked rugs using period fabrics;
professional washing available;
custom quilting available.*

Lawrence Miller
Marie Miller Antique Quilts
1489 Route 30
Dorset, VT 05251
ph: 802-867-5969
fax: 802-867-0324
larry@antiquequilts.com
http://www.antiquequilts.com
*Buys, sells, appraises quilts; has over
300 from 1820 to 1930s: applique,
pieced, crazy quilts, crib, doll, Amish
and Mennonite, and quilt tops; see the*

online catalog; also sells quilt hangers and Ensure, a quilt wash.

Pattyann Wilson
Patty's Prettys
P.O. Box 282
Roosevelt, NJ 08555-0282
ph: 609-443-6081
msnearmint@juno.com
Specializes in antique and vintage lace, quilts, linen and other findings; buys, sells, trades.

Kris Driessen
Hickory Hill Antique Quilts
P.O. Box 273
Esperance, NY 12066
ph: 518-875-6133 or 888-817-6577
fax: 518-875-9141
krisdriessen@yahoo.com
http://www.HickoryHillQuilts.com
Offers antique quilt tops, blocks by catalog; also offers vintage and reproduction fabrics, as well as restoration supplies and Quilt Heritage reference books.

Tom Vonah
Tom's Quilts
15 East High St.
Lebanon, PA 17042
ph: 717-279-6262
tomsquilts@aol.com
http://www.starfaceinc.com/tom.quilt/tom.html
Sells antique quilts, tops, blocks, and sewing notions; stocks over 200 quilts from the 1870s to 1940s; Web site has about 100 photos.

Antique Quilt Source, The
3064 Bricker Rd.
Manheim, PA 17545
ph: 717-492-9876
fax: 717-492-0285
strongg@paonline.com
http://www.antiquequiltsource.com
Over 20 years in business buying and selling antique quilts.

Stella Rubin
12300 Glen Rd.
Potomac, MD 20854-1023
ph: 301-948-4187
fax: 301-948-0460
stella.rubin@att.net
http://www.stellarubinantiques.com
Buys and sells quality quilts; also Mexican silver jewelry.

Quilts Unlimited
444 A Duke of Gloucester St.
Williamsburg, VA 23185
ph: 757-253-8700
quilts@rlc.net
http://www.quiltsunlimited.com
Images, dates, descriptions, prices of quilts in inventory are available on the Web site.

Deborah Vanden Heuvel
Global Galleria, The
209 Riverwalk Circle
Cary, NC 27511
ph: 888-832-5616 or 919-859-5818
fax: 919-859-6396
Carries a large selection of Antique and Experienced American Quilts; many pieces of museum quality.

Matt Lippa
Artisans
P.O. Box 256
Mentone, AL 35984-0256
ph: 256-634-4037
fax: 256-634-4037
artisans@folkartisans.com
http://www.folkartisans.com
Buy and sell folk art, outsider art, fine art; Internet WWW site offers links to additional dealers; also offers non-profit clubs and museums with an outlet to post notices, press releases, calendar items, etc. at no charge.

Shelly Zegart
Shelly Zegart Quilts
300 Penruth Ave.
Louisville, KY 40207
ph: 502-897-7566
fax: 502-897-3819
info@shellyquilts.com
http://www.shellyquilts.com
Quilt appraiser, dealer, collector; author of "American Quilt Collections: Antique Quilt Masterpieces;" founding director of the Kentucky Quilt Project; has curated exhibitions, lectured on all aspects of quilt history and aesthetics.

Lisa Bennett
Fiber Art
N2212 10th Ave.
Montello, WI 53949
ph: 608-297-7909
Sells art quilts, specializing in the 1920s through 1960s quilts with an emphasis on unusual fabrics: silks, brocades, velvet, etc.; wants one-of-a-kind quilts or related fringe, tassels, fabric, drapes, etc.

Barbara Woodford
Historic American Quilts
4775 S. River Rd.
Hanover, IL 61041-9523
ph: 815-777-2009
fax: 815-777-4130
haq@galenalink.net
http://www.historic-american.com
Dealer and collector of high-quality antique quilts, principally from the 19th century.

Diane J. Reese
Antique Quilts & Vintage Textiles
6212 S. 177th St.
Omaha, NE 68135
Buys and sells antique quilts, quilt tops, quilt squares from 1880 to 1945; also antique fabric, feedsacks, lace and hand crochet trims, needlework magazines, etc.

Mary Ann Walters
Log Cabin Antiques
4200 Peggy Lane
Plano, TX 75074
ph: 972-881-2818
logcabin@flash.net
http://www.quiltsquilts.com
Buys and sells quilts, specializing in 19th and early 20th century quilts in excellent condition; online catalog features scores of quilts currently for sale with pictures, descriptions, and prices.

Frank Geeslin
American Quilts!
P.O. Box 370891
Upton, KY 89137-0831
ph: 702-247-4200 or 877-531-1619
amquilts@aol.com
http://www.AmericanQuilts.com
Over 1,200 American-made quilts: new and antique, custom-made, baby and doll, quilt tops, applique, cutter quilts, quilt clothing, contemporary and traditional quilts; also repairs; buying extraordinary quilts or tops.

Linda Gibbs
Heirloom Keepsakes
10380 Miranda Ave.
Buena Park, CA 90620-4447
ph: 714-827-6488
Wants to buy crazy quilts with fancy embroidery stitches.

Deborah Roberts
P.O. Box 2176
Costa Mesa, CA 92626
ph: 714-557-5258
quiltevals@aol.com
http://www.quiltappraiser.com
Historian, appraiser, specializing in buying and selling antique hooked rugs, quilts and quilt-related textiles; certified by the American Quilter's Society; wish list available; also lectures on quilts.

Sally Hale
Covered Wagon Quiltworks
710 S.E. Dora
Troutdale, OR 97060
ph: 503-665-6178
Specializes in American-made 19th and early-20th century quilts from all areas of the country.

Experts

Suzy McLennan Anderson, ISA CAPP
Heritage Antiques & Appraisal Services
65 East Main St.
Holmdel, NJ 07733-2310
ph: 732-946-8801
fax: 732-946-1036
andersonauctions@aol.com
http://www.andersonauctions.net
Authenticates, buys, sells, appraises, lectures; author of "The Collectors Guide to Quilts."

Merry May
Schoolhouse Enterprises
P.O. Box 305
Tuckahoe, NJ 08250-0305
ph: 609-628-2256
fax: 609-628-3048
Inspectr@delanet.com
http://www.cluesew.com
Has taught quilt making since 1988; quilt historian since 1989; offers lectures and workshops; writes articles for publications; interested in feedsacks; produces quilt patterns; designs and makes custom-made quilts; does not appraise.

Ardis & Robert James
Ardis & Robert James Quilt Collection, The
80 Ludlow Dr.
Chappaqua, NY 10514
ph: 914-666-3774
fax: 212-824-1102
bobjames@eassets.com
Exhibits, lends, lectures and writes about quilts; collection has been featured in several publications and is currently in the International Quilt Study Center at the University of Nebraska in Lincoln, Nebraska.

Yvonne Khin
9423 Longs Mill Rd.
Rocky Ridge, MD 21778
ph: 301-898-0091
Author of "Collector's Dictionary of Quilt Names and Patterns" (1980.)

Shelly Zegart
Shelly Zegart Quilts
300 Penruth Ave.
Louisville, KY 40207
ph: 502-897-7566
fax: 502-897-3819
info@shellyquilts.com
http://www.shellyquilts.com
Quilt appraiser, dealer, collector; author of "American Quilt Collections: Antique Quilt Masterpieces;" founding director of the Kentucky Quilt Project; has curated exhibitions, lectured on all aspects of quilt history and aesthetics.

Internet Resources

World Wide Quilting Page
QHomePage@quilt.com
http://quilt.com/MainQuiltingPage.html
All sorts of links to contemporary quilt resources; also to some resources for antique quilts.

Misc. Services

Quilter's Design Studio QuiltSoft
5441 Brockbank Place
San Diego, CA 92115
ph: 619-583-2970
fax: 619-583-2692
tech@quiltsoft.com
http://www.quiltsoft.com//fabriccd.html
Quilt design computer program for Windows or for Macintosh; copy, rotate, and flip blocks; print

templates, calculate yardage, unlimited colors.

Museums/Libraries

New England Quilt Museum
18 Shattuck St.
Lowell, MA 01852
ph: 978-452-4207
fax: 978-452-5405
mps@tiac.net
http://www.nequiltmuseum.org/default.htm

Shelburne Museum, Inc.
P.O. Box 10
Shelburne, VT 05482-0010
ph: 802-985-3346 or 802-985-3348
fax: 802-985-2331
info@shelburnemuseum.org
http://www.shelburnemuseum.org
37 historic structures and exhibit buildings; diverse collection of American folk, fine, decorative and utilitarian art.

National Museum of American History, Division of Textiles
14th & Constitution Ave. NW
Washington, DC 20560
ph: 202-357-2700
webmaster@si.edu
http://www.si.edu/organiza/museums/nmah/nmah.htm

Yvonne Khin
Doll & Quilts Barn
9423 Longs Mill Rd.
Rocky Ridge, MD 21778
ph: 301-898-0091
Quilt museum offering quilt repairs, enlarging, duplicating, quilting classes, storage, and research.

Virginia Quilt Museum
301 South Main St.
Harrisonburg, VA 22801
ph: 540-433-3818
fax: 540-433-3818
ceknight@postoffice.worldnet.att.net
http://www.folkart.com/~latitude/museums/m_vqm.htm
A resource center for the study of the role of quilts and quilting in the cultural life of society; collections include works by both early and contemporary quilt artisans.

Museum of the American Quilter's Society
Newsletter: Friends of MAQS Newsletter
215 Jefferson St.
P.O. Box 1540
Paducah, KY 42002-1540
ph: 270-442-8856
fax: 270-442-5448
info@quiltmuseum.org
http://www.quiltmuseum.org
World's largest quilt museum; changing displays of new and antique quilts; gift and book shop carries over 400 titles related to quilts and textiles.

Quilters Hall of Fame
P.O. Box 681
Marion, IN 46952-0681
ph: 765-664-9333
fax: 765-664-9333
quilters@comteck.com
http://www.quiltershalloffame.org
A non-profit organization dedicated to honoring those who have made outstanding contributions to the world of quilting.

James J. Prochaska, P.E. - Dir.
Rocky Mountain Quilt Museum
1111 Washington Ave.
Golden, CO 80401
ph: 303-277-0377 or 303-215-9001
fax: 303-215-1636
rmqm@att.net
http://www.rmqm.org
A non-profit conservator of historic and contemporary quilts; collection includes over 150 quilts; six special exhibitions each year.

San Jose Museum of Quilts & Textiles
Newsletter: Connections
110 Paseo de San Antonio
San Jose, CA 95112-3639
ph: 408-971-0323
fax: 408-971-7226
http://www.sjquiltmuseum.org
Non-profit, public benefit museum with regularly changing exhibits of traditional, contemporary and historical quilts and textiles; museum store.

Periodicals

PRIMEDIA Enthusiast Group
Magazine: Quilter's Newsletter Magazine
741 Corporate Circle, Ste. A
Golden, CO 80401
ph: 303-278-1010 or 800-477-6089
fax: 303-277-0370
questions@qnm.com
http://www.quiltersnewsletter.com/qnm
The magazine for quilt lovers; a glossy magazine published ten times per year; articles, appraisals, patterns, frames, old and new quilts, quilt history, fabric clubs, ads, calendar, techniques, supplies, shows, etc.

Leman Publications
Magazine: Quiltmaker
741 Corporate Circle, Ste. A
Golden, CO 80401
ph: 303-278-1010 or 800-477-6089
fax: 303-277-0370
questions@qnm.com
http://www.quiltersnewsletter.com/qnm
A bi-monthly magazine for today's quilters; a pattern magazine featuring original quilt art in addition to full color photographs of quilts; step-by-step instructions, yardage, and more.

Repair Services

Lynn Gorges
Historic Textiles Studio
3910 U.S. Highway 70 East
New Bern, NC 28560
ph: 252-636-3039 or 252-636-5445
fax: 252-637-1862
palampore@aol.com
http://www.textilepreservation.com
Specializes in the restoration, conservation, appraisal, evaluation of quilts.

Laura Hobby Syler
Texas Quilt Co.
2401 Blue Cypress
Richardson, TX 75082
ph: 972-473-0884
texas_quilt.co@airmail.net
Certified quilt appraiser, quilt historian, quilt restoration, quilt lecturer, and author; president & founder of Texas Quilt Co. and the Vintage Quilt & Textile Society.

Suppliers

Kris Driessen
Hickory Hill Antique Quilts
P.O. Box 273
Esperance, NY 12066
ph: 518-875-6133 or 888-817-6577
fax: 518-875-9141
krisdriessen@yahoo.com
http://www.HickoryHillQuilts.com
Offers antique quilt tops, blocks by catalog; also offers vintage and reproduction fabrics, as well as restoration supplies and Quilt Heritage reference books.

Miniature

Man./Prod./Dist.

Kate Adams
Kate Adams Designs
140 Beechwood Ave.
P.O. Box 3025
Kennebunkport, ME 04046
ph: 800-553-3766 or 207-967-5077
fax: 207-967-0972
Makes miniature quilts framed as wall decorations; unique folk art collectibles created with early pieces in mind and then adapted to 1:12 scale.

RACING

(see AIRPLANES, Racing; AUTO RACING MEMORABILIA; AUTOMOBILES, Racing; SPORTS COLLECTIBLES, Thoroughbred Racing; TOYS, Cars [Racing])

RADIO SHOWS

Old Time

(see also AUDIO-VISUAL; BROADCASTING; PERSONALITIES [ENTERTAINERS]; PREMIUMS, Radio Show; RADIOS)

Clubs/Associations

Robert D. Gariepy
Nostalgia Theater Club
P.O. Box 1585
Haverhill, MA 01831-2285
ph: 978-372-9942
Golden age of radio, TV, and movies: records, videos, books, tapes, CDs.

Gerald Eskin, Rec. Sec.
Radio Collectors of America
Newsletter: RCA Newsletter
28 Wolfe St., Unit #1
West Roxbury, MA 02132-3234
ph: 617-323-0938
Purpose is to collect, preserve and enjoy old radio shows. Does not collect old radios, the emphasis is strictly on radio shows.

Richard Olday
Old Time Radio Club
Newsletter: OTRC Newsletter
171 Parwood Trail
Depew, NY 14043-1071
ph: 716-684-1604
raolday@yahoo.com
http://www2.pcom.net/robmcd
A nationally oriented local chapter.

Owens Pomeroy, Co-founder
Golden Radio Buffs of Maryland, Inc.
Newsletter: On the Air
301 Jeanwood Ct.
Baltimore, MD 21222-2857
ph: 410-477-2550 or 410-477-3051
opomeroy@msn.com
http://members.aol.com/grbmd
International club interested in old time radio also has an Old Time radio exhibit in the Baltimore Museum of Industry, Baltimore, MD; lots of radios, artifacts, pictures, etc.; OTR tape lending library for members.

Jack French
Metro Washington Old Time Radio Club
Newsletter: Radio Recall
5137 Richardson Dr.
Fairfax, VA 22032-2810
ph: 703-978-1236
OTRpiano@erols.com
http://www.mwotrc.com
Club preserves, records, shares the Golden Age of Radio: audio copies of shows, books, scripts, magazines, and related materials; monthly meetings held in Arlington, VA; rent tapes, books, CDs and other items from lending libraries.

Robert W. Newman
Radio Listener's Lyceum
Journal: RLL on the Air
11509 Islandale Dr.
Forest Park, OH 45240-2319
ph: 513-825-3662
rto5@juno.com
http://www.starshines-place.com/otrmain.htm
Cassette library contains thousands of the classic old-time radio programs; publishers of "RLL on the Air," a quarterly informative journal about

old-time radio and those who participated in it; please send SASE with requests.

Barry Hill
Old Time Radio Collectors Association (O.R.C.A.)
Newsletter: Tune Into Yesterday
Rte. 1 Box 197
Belpre, OH 45714
ph: 740-423-4010 or 740-423-4104
fax: 740-423-4010
orca@eurekanet.com
http://www.eurekanet.com/~orca
Preserve English-spoken radio shows broadcasts around the world and makes them available for the enjoyment of the members.

Gordon Spiering
Milwaukee Area Radio Enthusiasts
16670 Harmony Ct.
New Berlin, WI 53151-6524
ph: 414-784-4642
Local group interested in old time radio programs; meets every other month; guest speakers and discussions about OTR; book and tape library; newsletter.

Richard R. King
Radio Historical Association of Colorado
Newsletter: Return With Us Now
P.O. Box 1908
Englewood, CO 80150-1908
ph: 303-761-4139
dickking@earthlink.net
http://www.rhac.org
Club rents over 13,000 old time radio shows to members for a nominal charge.

Don Aston, Sec./Treas.
North American Radio Archives
Newsletter: NARA News
P.O. Box 1392
Lake Elsinore, CA 92531
ph: 909-244-5242
aston@linkline.com
International club dedicated to the enjoyment of classic radio shows from the 1930s to present; has a printed materials as well as over 3,000 cassettes to loan out.

Collectors

David L. Easter
1900 Angleside Rd.
Fallston, MD 21047-1739
ph: 410-877-2949
fax: 410-877-0419
davideaster@comcast.net
Interested in all old time radio shows, especially in science fiction program; American, BBC or South African.

Fred B. Korb, Jr.
725 Cardigan Ct.
Naperville, IL 60565-1202
ph: 630-416-8968
skorb@ameritech.net
Looking for any new programs in circulation; member of O.R.C.A.T.S; personal library contains approxi-

mately 50,000 programs; trades shows on a limited basis.

Jack Mann
3883 Madrona Dr. SE, #204
Port Orchard, WA 98366
ph: 360-769-6275
rnovak@pe.net
http://www.pe.net/~rnovak/jack.htm
A great online resource for Old Time Radio fans and show collectors; over 250 links for everything related to OTR.

Dealers

Erstwhile Radio
P.O. Box 2284
Peabody, MA 01960-7284
Send $3 for catalog listing nearly 5,700 old time radio shows: The Whistler, Suspense, Jack Benny, Sherlock Holmes, The Lone Ranger, Fibber McGee & Molly, Lux Radio Theater, etc.; mail order only.

Heritage Radio Classics
P.O. Box 16
Chestnut Hill, MA 02467
fax: 617-965-9984
info@heritageradio.com
http://www.heritageradio.com
Super quality old-time radio shows from the 1930s to 1950s on TDK cassettes: Jack Benny, The Shadow, The Lone Ranger, Our Miss Brooks, The Great Gildersleeve, Lux Radio Theatre, Suspense and 100s more; catalog $1.50 refundable.

Al Bruton, III
Can Corner, The
P.O. Box 1173 - MA
Marcus Hook, PA 19061-7173
Jack Benny, Amos & Andy, Green Hornet, Lone Ranger, WWII broadcasts, comedy, drama, kid shows, comedy, Big Band specials, drama, old commercials for Chevrolet, Studebaker, etc.; send for list; over 1,000 one-hour audio cassettes; mail order.

Lawrence Rao
1009 Autumn Woods Ln. #106
Virginia Beach, VA 23454
Sells vintage radio broadcasts on audio-only VHS Hi-fi cassettes; broadcasts are also available on standard analog-Dolby cassettes; Vintage Radio catalog $6 ppd. refundable on first order.

Charlie Garant
P.O. Box 331
Greeneville, TN 37744-0331

Bob Burchett
Hello Again, Radio
10280 Gunpowder Rd.
Florence, KY 41042-8253
ph: 859-282-0333
fax: 859-282-1999
Free catalog of Old Time radio shows on cassette; catalog supplements approx. every five weeks.

Don Aston
AVPRO
P.O. Box 1392
Lake Elsinore, CA 92531
ph: 888-332-8776
fax: 909-244-0022
avpro@linkline.com
http://avpro.otr.com
Has been involved in Old Time Radio for over 35 years.

Experts

Jack French
5137 Richardson Dr.
Fairfax, VA 22032-2810
ph: 703-978-1236
OTRpiano@erols.com
Collecting, researching, and writing about the Golden Age of radio for over 20 years; former editor of "NARA News," current editor of "Radio Recall;" lecturer on old time radio, juvenile westerns, female detectives, soap operas, etc.

Internet Resources

Louis V. Genco
Old-Time Radio
webmaster@old-time.com
http://www.old-time.com
A wealth of information relating to Old Time Radio; fans can communicate with each other, and with experts in the area by accessing the several bulletin boards at the site; one of the largest and best known OTR sites on the Web.

Jack Mann
Jack's List of Old Time Radio Pages
3883 Madrona Dr. SE, #204
Port Orchard, WA 98366
ph: 360-769-6275
rnovak@pe.net
http://www.pe.net/~rnovak/jack.htm
A great online resource for Old Time Radio fans and show collectors; over 250 links for everything related to OTR.

Museums/Libraries

National Broadcasters Hall of Fame
2201 Marconi Rd.
Wall, NJ 07719
ph: 732-681-6018
fred-carl@infoage.org
http://www.infoage.org/NBHF.htm
Honors the men and women who made broadcasting a communications marvel in the 1930s, 1940s and 1950s.

Library of Congress, Recorded Sound Reference Center
101 Independence Ave. SE
Washington, DC 20540-4698
ph: 202-707-7833
fax: 202-707-8464
rsrc@loc.gov
http://www.loc.gov
Recorded sound collection includes old time radio broadcasts; copies can be made if you get permission from the rights holders.

American Radio Archive, Thousand Oaks Library
1401 East Janss Rd.
Thousand Oaks, CA 91362
ph: 805-449-2660
fax: 805-449-2675
library@toaks.org
http://www.tol.lib.ca.us/_tol/tol_ar.htm
Research collection of scripts, sound recordings, books, pamphlets, and correspondence relating to old-time radio; available for research use at facility only.

Periodicals

Jay A. Hickerson
Friends of Old-Time Radio
Newsletter: Hello Again
P.O. Box 4321
Hamden, CT 06514-0321
ph: 203-248-2887
fax: 203-281-1322
jayhick@aol.com
For collectors of old-time radio shows; sponsors an annual convention; send SASE for sample copy of newsletter.

Bob Burchett, Ed.
Audio Classic Press
Magazine: Old Time Radio Digest
10280 Gunpowder Rd.
Florence, KY 41042-8253
ph: 859-282-0333
fax: 859-282-1999
Published four times per year.

Jordan Young
Past Times Nostalgia Network
Directory: Nostalgia Entertainment Sourcebook
7308-H Filmore Dr.
Buena Park, CA 90620
ph: 714-527-5845
fax: 714-527-5845
skretved@ix.netcom.com
http://www.ptnostalgia.com
Complete resource guide to classic movies, vintage radio, old time music, and theater: programs, equipment, where to replace and repair, where to rent or buy old movies, theater posters.

Old Time (Lum 'n' Abner)

Clubs/Associations

Tim Hollis, ExSec
National Lum 'n' Abner Society
Newsletter: Jot 'Em Down Journal, The
#81 Sharon Blvd.
Dora, AL 35062
ph: 205-648-6110
fax: 205-674-0190
jtemple@inu.net
http://www.inu.net/stemple

Museums/Libraries

Lon & Kathy Stucker
Lum and Abner Museum
4562 Highway 88 W
General Delivery
Pine Ridge, AR 71966
ph: 870-326-4442
fax: 870-326-4442
nstucker@alltel.net
http://www.lum-abner.com
On National Register of Historic Places.

Old Time (Straight Arrow)

Clubs/Associations

Bill Harper
POW-WOW
Newsletter: POW-WOW Newsletter
P.O. Box 24751
Minneapolis, MN 55424-0751
WaltGrogan@aol.com
http://shazam.imginc.com/fca
POW-WOW is the definitive source for information on the Nabisco Straight Arrow Promotion 1948-1954; dedicated to the memory of the real Straight Arrow - Howard Culver (1919-1984) and announcer/narrator Frank Bingham (1914-1988.)

RADIOS

(see also ART DECO; AUDIO-VISUAL; BROADCASTING; ELECTRICITY RELATED ITEMS; PAPER COLLECTIBLES, Radio Related; PREMIUMS, Radio Shows; RADIO SHOWS, Old Time; TELEGRAPH ITEMS; TELEVISIONS)

Appraisers

Bruce & Charlotte Mager
Waves
251 W. 30th St.
New York, NY 10001
ph: 212-273-9616
c1wave@aol.com
http://www.wavesradio.com
Established in 1976, buys, sells, repairs, appraises and rents radios, phonographs, TVs, microphones, telephones, fans, neon clocks and signs, and related advertising and literature.

Mark Stein, Appraiser
Radiomania(R)
3100 Falls Cliff Rd., Ste. 6
Baltimore, MD 21211
ph: 410-366-3993
fax: 800-891-4484
rpbook@bellatlantic.net
http://www.radiomania.com
Appraiser of vintage radios, 20th century Art Deco clocks, 20th century industrial design collectibles; member Association of Online Appraisers (AOA).

Auction Services

Ronald Baker
Antique Radio Auction House
1600 Whitman, Ste. 100
Wheaton, IL 60187
ph: 630-665-5279
fax: 630-665-5279
service@virtualauctions.com
http://www.virtualauctions.com/ArtDecoAuctionHouse
Sells radios at auction; also buys direct.

Clubs/Associations

John Reinicke, Pres.
Michigan Antique Radio Club
Newsletter: Chronicle
ph: 248-626-4895
john.reinicke@fanucrobotics.com
http://www.antiqueradios.com/marc
Preserves the history and enhance the knowledge of radio, TV and related disciplines with special emphasis on contributions made from the state of Michigan.

George Kaczowka
New England Antique Radio Club
Newsletter: Escutcheon
P.O. Box 201
Spofford, NH 03462
gsk@oldradios.com
http://www.nearc.net
A group of radio collectors who share a love of preserving old radios; club meets four times a year in Nashua, NH with swap meet and sale; public invited; details and directions on Web site.

John Ellsworth
Connecticut Vintage Radio Collectors Club
Newsletter: Connecticut Wireless Gazette
563 West Avon Rd.
Avon, CT 06001
ph: 860-673-0518
fax: 860-675-9916
radioclctr@aol.com
http://members.aol.com/radioclctr
Museum, library, swap meets spring and fall.

John Dilks
New Jersey Antique Radio Club
Newsletter: NJARC Newsletter
125 Warf Rd.
Egg Harbor Twp., NJ 08234-8501
ph: 609-927-3873
oldradio@worldnet.att.net
http://www.eht.com/oldradio

Richard G. Brill
International Antique Radio Club, Div. of RGB Enterprises
P.O. Box 5367
Old Bridge, NJ 08857
ph: 732-607-0299
fax: 732-679-8024
rgbent@aol.com
http://www.rgbent.com

Chris Bacon
Greater New York Vintage Wireless Association
52 Uranus Rd.
Rocky Point, NY 11778-8842
ph: 516-821-7618

Allen W. Tomisman
Antique Radio Club of Schenectady
33 Bailey Ave.
Latham, NY 12110-2441
ph: 518-785-3117

Gary Parzy
Niagara Frontier Wireless Association
Newsletter: NFWA Newsletter
135 Autumnwood
Cheektowaga, NY 14227

Ed Gable
Antique Wireless Association, Inc.
Newsletter: Old Timer's Bulletin
Box E
Breesport, NY 14816
ph: 607-739-5443
fax: 607-796-6230
k2mp@eznet.net
http://www.antiquewireless.org
One of the world's largest and oldest historical radio collector organizations; purpose is to document and preserve the history of radio, telegraph and television artifacts.

Richard J. Harris, Sec.
Pittsburgh Antique Radio Society
407 Woodside Rd.
Pittsburgh, PA 15221
schaefer@nb.net
http://www.nb.net/~schaefer/pars.html

Bill Overbeck
Delaware Valley Historic Radio Club
Newsletter: Oscillator, The
P.O. Box 847
Havertown, PA 19803
ph: 610-853-3199
Billoradio@aol.com
http://pw2.netcom.com/~firstake/dvhrc.htm
Open to anyone with an interest in vintage radios.

Ken Mellgren, VP
Radio History Society, Inc.
13 Bitterroot Ct.
Rockville, MD 20853
kmellgren3@comcast.net
http://www.radiohistory.org
An IRS-recognized tax-exempt nonprofit organization set up primarily to establish a national vintage radio and television museum and library in Bowie, MD.

Paul R. Farmer, Mem.
Mid-Atlantic Antique Radio Club
Magazine: Radio Age
P.O. Box 352
Washington, VA 22747-0352
oldradiotime@hotmail.com
http://www.maarc.org
Published monthly since 1975 for collectors interested in the history of radio and television; restoration,

articles by early experts; free buy and sell ads; free sample.

Ron Lawrence
Carolina Chapter/AWA
P.O. Box 3015
Matthews, NC 28106-3015
ph: 704-289-1166
kc4yoy@trellis.net
http://www.cc-awa.org
Main focus in hosting collector events such as swap/mini meets in and around NC and SC; also holds annual 3-day conference in March in Charlotte NC with seminars of interest to the beginning as well as advanced collector.

Dennis G. Williams
Florida Antique Wireless Group
Newsletter: FAWGhorn News
4822 S. Orange Ave., #7
Orlando, FL 32806
ph: 407-895-9075
oldradio@cfl.rr.com
http://www.radiorelics.com
A group devoted to collecting old radios.

Alabama Historical Radio Society
Newsletter: Superflex, The
P.O. Box 26452
Birmingham, AL 35226
ph: 205-822-6759 or 205-631-6680
mbbarnes@mindspring.com
http://www.ahrs.org
The Society was founded in 1989 by Don Kresge, a retired GE engineer, to provide an opportunity for men and women of all ages to join together to pursue their interest in vintage radio; interested in listening to and restoring old radios.

Bill Moore
Southern Vintage Wireless Association
Newsletter: SVWA Newsletter
1901 Spanish Oaks
Huntsville, AL 35803-1379
ph: 256-885-0068
bmoore2nd@aol.com
Interested in antique radios; looking for Pilot and related advertising.

Mike Keller
Central Ohio Antique Radio Association
5861 Riverton Rd.
Columbus, OH 43232
ph: 614-866-7725
mkeller@wideopenwest.com
http://members.tripod.com/~COARA

Steve Dando
Buckeye Radio & Phonograph Club
Newsletter: Soundings
4572 Mark Trail
Akron, OH 44321-1462
ph: 330-666-7222
Members exchange expertise in restoration of vintage radios and phonographs; club holds annual mall show (displaying radios and phonographs) and picnic.

Karl Koogle
Antique Radio Collectors of Ohio
Newsletter: ARCO Newsletter
2929 Hazelwood Ave.
Dayton, OH 45419
ph: 937-294-8960
karlkradio@gemair.com
Newsletter published quarterly; holds several meetings and swap meets each year.

Dr. Edmund E. Taylor
Indiana Historical Radio Society
Newsletter: IHRS Bulletin
245 N. Oakland Ave.
Indianapolis, IN 46201-3360
ph: 317-638-1641
IndianaHistoricalRadio@worldnet.att.net
http://home.att.net/
%7indianahistoricalradio/ihrp2soc.htm
Society of antique radio collectors who meet quarterly in Indiana; sponsors swap-meets, auctions, museum projects, contests.

Dave Wiggert
Western Wisconsin Antique Radio
  Collectors Club
Newsletter: Radio Recollections
1611 Redfield St.
La Crosse, WI 54601

Greg Farmer, Sec.
Northland Antique Radio Club
Newsletter: Northland Antique Radio
  Club Newsletter
P.O. Box 18362
Minneapolis, MN 55418
gif@usfamily.net
http://www.geocities.com/
  TelevisionCity/4544
A non-profit organization with members across the country; purpose is to preserve the history of radios and related items through activities and meetings.

Antique Radio Club of Illinois
Newsletter: ARCI Newsletter
P.O. Box 1139
La Grange, IL 60526
clubinfo@antique-radios.org
http://www.antique-radios.org

Derek Cohn
Antique Radio Collectors & Historians
8141 Stratford Dr.
Saint Louis, MO 63105-3707
ph: 314-725-2333
vibroplex@mindspring.com
http://www.archradio.com
A club for collectors of old radios and related items; from crystal sets to modern communication receivers.

Robert Lane, Pres.
Mid-American Antique Radio Club
Newsletter: Broadcaster, The
10332 Mowhawk Lane
Shawnee Mission, KS 66206-2525
ph: 913-648-5296
fax: 913-341-1610
Historical preservation and collecting ratios with two auctions a year, April and October.

Steve Morton
Nebraska Antique Radio Collectors Club
Newsletter: NARCC Newsletter
905 West First
North Platte, NE 69101

Frank Karner
Oklahoma Vintage Radio Collectors
Newsletter: OKVRC Broadcast News
P.O. Box 50625
Midwest City, OK 73140-5625
ph: 405-769-4656
fkarner@cox.net
http://members.cox.net/okvrc

Vintage Radio & Phonograph Society,
Inc.
Newsletter: Reproducer, The
P.O. Box 165345
Irving, TX 75016-5345
ph: 214-337-2823 or 972-353-4862
http://www.radioremembered.org
Purpose is to preserve early radios, phonographs, and related material and to conduct historical research of same; also publishes "Soundwaves" newsletter.

Houston Vintage Radio Association
Newsletter: Grid Leak, The
P.O. Box 31276
Houston, TX 77231-1276
ritterhouse@prodigy.net
http://www.clarc.org/HVRA
Monthly meetings and electronic seminars, annual convention, swap meets, Christmas celebration, and two MEGA auctions.

Larry Weide, Ed.
Colorado Radio Collectors
Newsletter: Flash!, The
5270 East Nassau Circle
Englewood, CO 80110
ph: 303-758-8382
lweide@attglobal.net
Holds bi-monthly meetings and swap meets; annual auction, public displays, presentations, get-togethers/picnic.

Jeffrey Shields
Arizona Antique Radio Club, Inc.
Newsletter: AARC News
1820 W. Raven Dr.
Chandler, AZ 85248
jeffandkt@msn.com
http://www.azarc.org
Has swap meets in Phoenix and Tucson, regular meetings and exhibits, quarterly journal.

Charles Burch, Treas.
New Mexico Radio Collectors Club
Newsletter: New Mexico Radio
  Collectors Club Newsletter
39 Chaco Loop
Sandia Park, NM 87047
teneagles@juno.com
http://members.aol.com/NMRCC

Schoenbeck
Southern California Antique Radio
  Society
Magazine: California Antique Radio
  Gazette
24803 Pitcaris Way
Torrance, CA 90505-6614
ph: 818-993-4560

California Historical Radio Society,
  North Valley Chapter
Newsletter: NVC-CHRS Newsletter
P.O. Box 31659
San Francisco, CA 94131
ph: 415-821-9800
mhadams@got.net
http://www.antiqueradios.com/chrs/
  index.html

Hal Layer
California Historical Radio Society
Journal: Journal, The
P.O. Box 31659
San Francisco, CA 94131-0659
ph: 415-978-9100
mhadams@got.net
http://www.antiqueradios.com/chrs
Members focus on vintage radios and other old electronics.

Waldo T. Boyd, Exec. Sec.
Society of Wireless Pioneers Inc.
P.O. Box 86
Geyserville, CA 95441-0086
k6dzy@direcway.com
http://www.sowp.org
Dedicated to collecting, researching, recording, preserving the history of communications, particularly wireless and radio telegraphy related to ex-professional Morse wireless (especially spark) operators.

Sacramento Historical Radio Society
P.O. Box 162612
Sacramento, CA 95816-9998

Northwest Vintage Radio Society
Newsletter: NVRS Call Letter
P.O. Box 82379
Portland, OR 97282-0379
ph: 503-654-7387 or 503-281-6585
nwvrs@ironradio.com
http://nwvrs.org
Membership is open to all who are interested in vintage radio and wireless equipment.

Harold Hagen
Puget Sound Antique Radio Association
Newsletter: Horn of Plenty
P.O. Box 2095
Snohomish, WA 98291-2095
ph: 425-747-1323
hhagen@eskimo.com
http://www.eskimo.com/~hhagen/
  psara.html
Dedicated to the preservation, restoration of antique radio & wireless equipment; maintains a museum that is open to the public; activities include swap meets, auction, and monthly meetings featuring lectures, demonstrations.

Canadian Vintage Radio Society
Newsletter: Radio Waves
4895 Mahood Dr.
Richmond, British Columbia V4N 3V8
  Canada
ph: 604-275-2033
fax: 604-275-4282
Membership across Canada, USA, Europe, New Zealand, Australia, and Japan; dedicated to the preservation, restoration, enjoyment of antique radios and related items.

David Cantelon
London Vintage Radio Club
42 Clamatis Rd.
London, Ontario M2J 4X2 Canada
justradios@yahoo.com
http://www.geocities.com/Athens/Troy/
  9935

Mike Barker
British Vintage Wireless Society
Magazine: BVWS Bulletin
23 Rosendale Rd.
West Dulwich
London, SE21 8DS U.K.
ph: 020 8670 3667
murphymad@aol.com
http://www.bvws.org.uk

Collectors

George Kaczowka
P.O. Box 103
Boylston, MA 01505
ph: 508-869-6376
gsk@oldradios.com
http://www.oldradios.com/
Collector of antique radios from the 1930s, and early transistor radios from the 1950s and 1960s; over 20 years experience.

Steve Fullmer
110 Delmage Rd.
Swansea, MA 02777
sfullmer@ici.net
http://home.ici.net/~sfullmer/
  sfullmer.html
Specializes in collecting wood radios.

Harry Poster
Vintage TVs
P.O. Box 1883
South Hackensack, NJ 07606-0483
ph: 201-794-9606
fax: 201-794-9553
hposter@att.net
http://www.harryposter.com
Buying early and unusual radios including battery and crystal sets, kits, cathedrals, etc.; also wants pre-1950 4-pin tubes, speakers, horns, manufacturers' literature, books and signs.

Richard E. Lauber
P.O. Box 51
Alplaus, NY 12008-0051
ph: 518-399-0080
RichardLauber@earthlink.net
Wants to buy old radios made by Zenith, FADA, Emerson, Crosley, Bendix, Detrola, Grebe, Atwater Kent, and most others; early battery sets,

crystal sets, cathedrals, and colorful plastics; single pieces or entire collections.

Bill Wood
8 Oregon Place
Buffalo, NY 14207-1522
ph: 716-875-9874345
fax: 716-874-6724
merlin206@adelphia.net
Collects portable radios and microphones (both wired and wireless) from US and Europe.

John Rohrer
John's Antique Radios
567 Railroad St.
Windber, PA 15963
Collector of old radios; Web site has pictures of old radios, links to antique radio pages, parts for sale.

Alvin Heckard
165 Orchard Grove Ave.
Lewistown, PA 17044-7511
ph: 717-248-7071 or 717-248-2816
aheckard@localnet.com
Wants wood table model radios, colored Bakelite and plastic radios; also any parts, tubes, literature, service manuals, advertising, etc.

Gerald Schneider
3101 Blueford Rd.
Kensington, MD 20895-2726
ph: 301-929-8593
Wants to buy vintage radios, radio equipment, parts, and related literature; specialization in radios with Oriental-style cabinets, and radio/furniture combinations (radio lamps, bed headboards with radios, tables with radios, etc.).

Richard O. Gates
P.O. Box 187
Chesterfield, VA 23832-0187
ph: 804-748-0382 or 804-794-5146
fax: 804-748-6349
rogates@mindspring.com
Wants to buy 1930s and 1940s Catalin radios with names such as FADA, Emerson, Garod, etc.; also wants Charlie McCarthy, Hopalong Cassidy, and Sparton mirrored radios.

Edward K. Bell
5311 Woodsdale Rd.
Raleigh, NC 27606-3341
ph: 919-851-1517
fax: 919-851-1517
ebell@nc.rr.com
Wants to buy old radios: pre-1926 battery sets, crystal sets, interesting plastics, cathedrals, advertising, horn speakers, old tubes, etc. Will buy entire collections.

Robert P. Morrison
10238 117th Lane
Live Oak, FL 32060-6716
ph: 904-362-1521
fax: 903-848-0596
rmorison@suwanneevalley.net
http://home1.gte.net/cranshaw/ths2.htm
Former editor of "The Electronic Collector;" collects antique radios, electronics, test equipment, etc.

Gary B. Schneider
9511 Sunrise Blvd. #J-23
North Royalton, OH 44133-3410
ph: 440-582-3094 or 216-251-3714
fax: 216-251-3714
gbsptop@aol.com
http://www.oldradioparts.com
Wants pre-1940 radio items: radios, tubes, parts, speakers; also technical radio magazines, catalogs, books, advertising, etc.

Steve Dando
4572 Mark Trail
Akron, OH 44321-1462
ph: 330-666-7222

Jerry Rose
Jerry's Old Radio
4738 Branstetter Rd.
Nashville, IN 47448
ph: 812-988-4353
fax: 812-988-4347
Collects old radios and related items.

Larry Spilkin
P.O. Box 5039
Southfield, MI 48086-5039
ph: 248-642-3722
Wants Catalin & Bakelite radios especially colored, marbleized or Art Deco styles.

Dr. Barry Janov
2454 Dempster St., Ste. 416
Des Plaines, IL 60016-5320
marconifon@aol.com
Wants to buy early radios, micro-phones, speakers and related items.

William Ross
875 Gordon Terrace
Winnetka, IL 60093
ph: 847-441-6462 or 312-364-8722
Interested in old radios and TVs; also related premiums; organizes Radiofest, a major antique radio meet.

Pete & Shirley Petersen
5214 120th Ave. SE
Bellevue, WA 98006-2826
ph: 425-747-1323
wy7z@juno.com
Collectors of pre-1941 radios and related memorabilia.

John Jenkins
15736 NE 143 Place
Woodinville, WA 98072
ph: 425-936-8856
fax: 425-489-9566
johnj@halcyon.com
http://www.halcyon.com/johnj/radios
Long time collector of pre-1930 radios and wireless items; Web site is a

virtual Museum with hundreds of images of items in his collection.

Dealers

Adam Schoolsky
P.O. Box 95
Nashua, NH 03061
ph: 603-883-7931
fax: 603-882-3781
adam@ArtDeco.com
Buying one item of entire collections or estates; specializing in radios from 1910-1950 with Art Deco wood, plastic, mirrored cabinets; also buying any radio related advertising signs, banners, clocks, etc.; expert restorations.

John Sakas
P.O. Box 4124
South Hackensack, NJ 07606-4124
ph: 201-794-0437
fax: 201-794-8359
Specializing in Catalin, Deco, mirror radios; also in Art Deco clocks.

Richard G. Brill
RGB Enterprises
P.O. Box 5367
Old Bridge, NJ 08857
ph: 732-607-0299
fax: 732-679-8024
rgbent@aol.com
http://www.rgbent.com
Welcomes information & schematics on all antique foreign radios; radios from the 1930s to 1960s; specializes in foreign radios; needs info on former Eastern European country radios like Tesla, Goplana, etc.; appraises international radios.

Bruce & Charlotte Mager
Waves
251 W. 30th St.
New York, NY 10001
ph: 212-273-9616
c1wave@aol.com
http://www.wavesradio.com
Over 20 years experience specializing in vintage radios, phonographs, telegraphy, televisions, assorted electrical and mechanical apparatus, and related advertising memorabilia, books and pamphlets.

Allen W. Tomisman
33 Bailey Ave.
Latham, NY 12110-2441
ph: 518-785-3117

Gary Formica
Radio Research
823 91st St.
Niagara Falls, NY 14304
ph: 716-283-2274 or 716-283-2651
radioguy@adelphia.net
http://www2.pcom.net/radio
Buys and sells radios and related items; also telephones.

John Slusser
Radio Daze
7620 Omnitech
Victor, NY 14564
ph: 585-742-2020
fax: 585-742-2099
info@radiodaze.com
http://www.radiodaze.com
Specialists in antique and novelty tube and transistor radios; offers professional repair and restoration services; buys and sells radios, vacuum tubes, parts, literature, magazines, and advertising; major E.H. Scott radio collector.

Chris Savino
P.O. Box 419
Breesport, NY 14816-0419
ph: 607-739-3106
chrissavino@stny.rr.com
Buying plastic color radios from the 1930s to 1950s; by makers such as Air King, Addison, Arvin, Crosley, De Wald, Emerson, Espey, Fada, Garod, GE, RCA, Sentinel, Sonora, Sparton, and Stewart Warner; AM tabletop radios only.

Donald M. Maurer
Maurer Vintage Radios
29 South 4th St.
Lebanon, PA 17042
ph: 717-272-2481
dmradios@aol.com
http://hometown.aol.com/dmradios/
index.html
Supplier of hard-to-find vintage tube and transistor radios, phonos, vintage hi-fi, televisions, reel-to-reel tape decks, and other vintage radio related items; also new old stock radio/tv parts, tubes, manuals and pre-1960 TV Guides.

John Okolowicz
624 Cedar Hill Rd., Ste. 100
Ambler, PA 19002-1504
ph: 215-542-1597
john@grillecloth.com
http://www.grillecloth.com
Buys, sells, trades pre-1950 radios and TVs in unusual or ornate plastic or wooden cabinets; especially those made by Emerson, Stromberg Carlson, or Detrola; also sells 40 types of antique radio reproduction grille cloth.

Frank Johnson
530 Elford Rd.
Fairless Hills, PA 19030-3624
ph: 215-943-8295
fadacat@aol.com
Buys, sells, collects, and repairs/ restores antique radios.

John E. Kendall
Vintage Electronics
P.O. Box 436
Fallston, MD 21047-0436
maloney@vintage-electronics.com
http://www.vintage-electronics.com
Wants radios from the 1920s through 1960s; buys, sells tube and transistor radios, unusual TVs, early miniature

or handheld TVs, tube audio and
other early odd electronics; also
related items such as books,
schematics, tubes, ads, etc.

Tommy Meers
GARMCo
fax: 404-297-8161
*Buys and sells vintage electronics
including antique tube, crystal and
transistor radios, phonographs
(record players), microphones,
televisions and related collectibles; on
Internet since 1996; worldwide
insured shipping.*

David Snow
Antique Radios, Inc.
P.O. Box 6352
Jackson, MI 49204-6352
ph: 517-787-2985
arbeiii@yahoo.com
http://www.arbeiii.com
*Manufacturer of power supplies for
pre-1930s battery radios; complete
electrical restoration of early '20s
through '40s radios (no cabinet
work); no list of radios available;
appraisals on a fee-basis.*

Merrill Mabbs
Classic Radio Gallery
709 Pluma Dr.
Rapid City, SD 57702
ph: 605-342-4090
fax: 605-390-1456
boz@rushmore.com
http://www.classicradiogallery.com
*Specializes in early 1930s to 1940s
radios; schematics available for most
US-made radios made from the 1920s
to the 1950s; has an online virtual
radio museum at the Web site; also
schematic services; antique radios for
sale.*

Art Bilski
Art's Antique Radios
208 Green Mountain Dr.
Bolingbrook, IL 60440
ph: 630-739-1060
fax: 630-739-1060
art@myantiqueradio.com
http://www.myantiqueradio.com
*Consultation, repair, sales and
purchases of old tube style radios;
will buy your old radios or will refer
you to another resource who will buy.*

Dick Morgan
Radio Man, The
3630 Cavalier Dr.
Garland, TX 75042-7503
ph: 972-272-3581
fax: 972-272-1831
theradioman@att.net
*Buys, sells, trades antique radios;
also sells tubes for antique radios.*

Radio Era Archives
2043 Empire Central
Dallas, TX 75235
ph: 214-358-5195
fax: 214-357-4693
tsm@radioera.com
http://www.radioera.com
*Mail order and Internet business
servicing the antique radio collector,
restorer or repair person; sells
primarily old radio information,
catalogs, manuals, schematics and
technical data for most radios; also
restores and sells old radios.*

Henry Harmoney
508 Highland
Arlington, TX 76010
ph: 817-226-1140
*Buys, sells, repairs all types of radios;
Zenith and Art Deco a favorite.*

Stephen Kuhn
Neon Radio, The
503 E. Market St.
Lockhart, TX 78644
ph: 512-398-7777
stephen@neonradio.com
http://www.neonradio.com
*Buys, sells, trades, repairs vintage
radios.*

John D. McKenna
Radio King, The
801 W. Cucharras St., #803
Colorado Springs, CO 80905-1619
ph: 719-630-8732 or 719-488-0818
*Buys, sells, restores 1930-1950
vacuum tube radios, especially Zenith
wood radios.*

Henry Rogers
Virginia City Radio Museum
P.O. Box 511
109 "F" St.
Virginia City, NV 89440
ph: 775-847-9047
curator@radioblvd.com
http://www.radioblvd.com
*Buys, sells, and restores 1915 to
1950s antique radios.*

Steve Oliphant
5255 Allott Ave.
Van Nuys, CA 91401-5902
ph: 818-789-2339 or 818-865-1400
fax: 818-865-1450
jlo55@aol.com
*Dealer in old phonographs and
radios; buys entire collections or
individual pieces.*

Mike Harrod
Trailside Treasures
365 Victor St. "S"
Salinas, CA 93907
*Buy, sells and trades coin-operated
machines; many coin-ops, plastic
radios and other gameroom
collectibles in stock.*

C.E. "Sonny" Clutter
Radiola Guy, The
3634 NW 29th Circle
Camas, WA 98607
ph: 360-834-5741
Sonny@radiolaguy.com
http://www.radiolaguy.com
*Buys, sells, services old radios 1930
to 1950 and wireless 1900 to 1950s;
great Web page packed with helpful
radio-related information.*

Scott Primeau
916 Oxford St. West
London, Ontario N6H 1V3 Canada
ph: 519-657-4433
fax: 519-471-4095
info@primeaumusic.com
http://www.primeaumusic.com
*Specializes in rare and collectible
Bakelite radios in the full range of
colors.*

Malcom Bennett
Vintage Radios
Shirley, Munns Lane
Hartlip.
Sittingbourne, Kent ME9 7SY U.K.
ph: 01795 842616
mfb@valve.demon.co.uk
http://www.valve.demon.co.uk
*Purveyor and collector of vintage/
antique radios and valves (tubes); also
service data and components; plus full
repair restoration services offered.*

Experts

John M. England, Jr.
103 Old River Rd.
Lincoln, RI 02865
*Buys, collects, sells, appraises radios
and equipment made by Stromberg-
Carlson of Rochester, NY; also wants
to buy Stromberg-Carlson Co. radios,
Scott radios, mirrored radios, plus
related literature, magazines,
ephemera.*

Bob Eslinger
Antique Radio Restoration & Repair
20 Gary School Rd.
Pomfret Center, CT 06259-1212
ph: 860-928-2628
fax: 860-928-2628
bob@oldradiodoc.com
http://www.oldradiodoc.com
*Professional restorations for all tube
type antique table and console radios,
communication receivers and music
amplifiers; complete overhauls;
lacquer sprayed hand rubbed and
polished cabinet refinishing; also
appraises, buys & sells.*

Gerald Schneider
3101 Blueford Rd.
Kensington, MD 20895-2726
ph: 301-929-8593

Mark Stein
Radiomania(R)
3100 Falls Cliff Rd., Ste. 6
Baltimore, MD 21211
ph: 410-366-3993
fax: 800-891-4484
rpbook@bellatlantic.net
http://www.radiomania.com
*Publisher of radio price guides:
"Complete Price Guide to Antique
Radios," "Tabletop Radios"
(Machine Age to Jet Age series in 3
vols.), "Complete Price Guide to
Antique Radios: Pre-War Consoles."*

Gary B. Schneider
9511 Sunrise Blvd. #J-23
North Royalton, OH 44133-3410
ph: 440-582-3094 or 216-251-3714
fax: 216-251-3714
gbsptop@aol.com
http://www.oldradioparts.com
*Founding publisher of "Antique Radio
Classified;" author of "1988 Official
Price Guide to Antiques - Radio
Classification."*

David Lane
2515 W. 88th St.
Leawood, KS 66206
ph: 913-341-1610
*Co-author of "Transistor Radios - a
Collector's Encyclopedia and Price
Guide."*

Robert Lane
10332 Mowhawk Lane
Shawnee Mission, KS 66206-2525
ph: 913-648-5296
fax: 913-341-1610
*Co-author of "Transistor Radios - a
Collector's Encyclopedia and Price
Guide."*

Mike Adams
112 Crescent Ct.
Scotts Valley, CA 95066-2815
ph: 408-924-4545
fax: 408-924-4543
adams@email.sjsu.edu
http://www.mikeadams.org
*Specialty area is radio and broadcast
history; produced "Radio Collector"
series for PBS TV; writes for
"Antique Radio Classified."*

Jonathan F. Winter
American Museum of Radio
1312 Bay St.
Bellingham, WA 98225
ph: 360-738-3886
jwinter@americanradiomuseum.org
http://www.americanradiomuseum.org

Internet Resources

Don Adamson
Antique Radio Page
djadamson@aol.com
http://members.aol.com/djadamson/
arp.html
*Web site has a gallery of radios from
1920s to 1960s; also reference books,
articles, Web sites, and a directory of
information about 1,500 antique*

RADIOS   RADIOS

625

radios from Web sites around the world.

Tom Sundstrom
Radio Netherlands' Antique & Old Time
  Radio Page
P.O. Box 2275
Vincentown, NJ 08088-2275
ph: 609-859-2447
fax: 609-859-3226
antique_radio@trsc.com
http://www.rnw.nl/realradio/html/
  antiqueradio.html
A world-wide comprehensive compilation of several hundred Web sites about antique and old-time radio; with descriptions, grouped by categories; a free service.

Richard Lancaster
Nostalgia Air
P.O. Box 2328
Melbourne, FL 32902-2328
info-mo@nostalgiaair.org
http://www.nostalgiaair.org
Dedicated to the preservation, conservation and free dissemination of antique and vintage radio and electronics technical information, schematics, technical information, tube references, manuals, articles, vintage publications.

Steve Adams
RadioGallery.com
P.O. Box 90
Moody, AL 35004
ph: 205-640-2701
fax: 205-640-2701
radios@RadioGallery.com
http://www.radiogallery.com
RadioGallery.com features classified ads with color photos of antique and collectible radios, phonographs, and other radio-related items for sale; free wanted and "help" ads; free notices of radio club events.

Timothy Sullivan
All Things Radio
P.O. Box 371798
El Paso, TX 79937
ph: 915-838-8177
info@allthingsradio.com
http://www.allthingsradio.com
A comprehensive resource for the vintage radio enthusiast.

Warren Parks
Warren's Antique Radio Restoration
  Homepage
crash@ezlink.com
http://www.ezlink.com/~crash/parks/
  radio.html
Web site provides tips, hints, how-to and links on restoring and repairing antique radios: case histories, explanations of the restoration process and lots of pictures.

Phil Nelson
Phil's Old Radios
16104 167th Ave. NE
Woodinville, WA 98072
philnelson@antiqueradio.org
http://www.antiqueradio.org
Comprehensive Web site for antique radios; large online gallery with color photos, free ads for collectors, extensive information about restoration of old radios, special section for beginning collectors, links, and more.

Museums/Libraries

New England Wireless & Steam
  Museum, Inc.
1300 Frenchtown Rd.
East Greenwich, RI 02818
ph: 401-884-1710 or 401-885-0545
fax: 401-884-0683
newsm@ids.net
http://users.ids.net/~newsm
Composed of five buildings, the museum is a public, non-profit corporation run by volunteers; the wireless building shows the span of electrical communication from telegraph to TV: keys, sounders, crystal sets, tubes, ocean cable, etc.

John Ellsworth, Dir.
Vintage Radio & Communications
  Museum of Connecticut
33 Mechanics St.
Windsor, CT 06095
ph: 860-673-0518
radioclctr@aol.com
http://
  www.nationalcommunicationsmuseum.org
Displays include radio, television, motion picture and telephone equipment, as well as advertising and other communications related memorabilia.

Museum of Television & Radio
25 West 52nd St.
New York, NY 10019
ph: 212-621-6800 or 212-621-6600
publicrelations@mtr.org
http://www.mtr.org
Museum has two locations, one in New York City and one in Los Angeles.

Ed Gable
Antique Wireless Association's
  Electronic Communication Museum
Box E
Breesport, NY 14816
ph: 607-739-5443
fax: 607-796-6230
k2mp@eznet.net
http://www.antiquewireless.org
Open limited hours May through October; call or write before visiting; please enclose SASE if requesting a reply.

Richard Post
Museum of Radio & Technology, Inc.
1640 Florence Ave.
Huntington, WV 25701
ph: 304-525-8890
postr@ohiou.edu
http://oak.cats.ohiou.edu/~postr/MRT
Great displays of old radios from the 1930s to 1950s.

Indiana Historic Radio Museum
800 Lincolnway South
Ligonier, IN 46767-0353
ph: 888-417-3562 or 219-894-9000
olradio@ligtel.com
http://home.att.net/
  ~indianahistoricalradio/ihrp6mus.htm
Features radios from the 1920s through the 1960s, specialty radios, novelty radios, WWII radios including one from Nazi Germany, telegraph keys.

Steve Raymer
Pavek Museum of Broadcasting
3515 Raleigh Ave.
Minneapolis, MN 55416
ph: 952-926-8198
fax: 952-929-6105
sraymer@pavekmuseum.org
http://www.MuseumofBroadcasting.com
Houses one of the world's finest collections of antique radio, television, and broadcast equipment.

Keith R. Gill
Museum of Science & Industry
5700 S. Lake Shore Dr.
Chicago, IL 60637
ph: 773-684-1414
fax: 773-684-0026
msi@msichicago.org
http://www.msichicago.org

Henry Rogers
Western Historic Radio Museum
P.O. Box 511
109 "F" St.
Virginia City, NV 89440
ph: 775-847-9047
curator@radioblvd.com
http://www.radioblvd.com
Museum of antique radios from 1915 through 1950s; also radio accessories, photographs, vacuum tubes and history; antique radio restoration service also available.

Museum of Television & Radio
465 N. Beverly Dr.
Beverly Hills, CA 90210
ph: 310-786-1000
publicrelations@mtr.org
http://www.mtr.org
Museum has two locations, one in New York City and one in Los Angeles.

Jonathan F. Winter, Pres.
American Museum of Radio
1312 Bay St.
Bellingham, WA 98225
ph: 360-738-3886
jwinter@americanradiomuseum.org
http://www.americanradiomuseum.org
Collection includes seldom seen items

from the dawn of the electrical age (1650) through to the discovery of radio and on to the beginning of the transistor (1950); public, non-profit museum open to the public Wed. through Sat, 11-4.

Periodicals

John V. Terrey
Magazine: Antique Radio Classified
P.O. Box 2
Carlisle, MA 01741
ph: 978-371-0512
fax: 978-371-7129
arc@antiqueradio.com
http://www.antiqueradio.com
Antique radio's largest monthly about old radios, Art Deco, TVs, ham equip. - '40s, '50s, books, telegraph, etc.; lots of ads.

Tim Ferrante
Magazine: Gameroom Magazine
P.O. Box 41
Keyport, NJ 07735-0041
ph: 732-739-1955
fax: 732-739-2834
coinop@gameroommagazine.com
http://www.gameroommagazine.com
A great source of information for the collector and dealer of jukeboxes, pinballs, slot machines, Coke and other soda machines, arcade games, classic arcade video, and other gameroom collectibles.

Repair Services

Bob Eslinger
Antique Radio Restoration & Repair
20 Gary School Rd.
Pomfret Center, CT 06259-1212
ph: 860-928-2628
fax: 860-928-2628
bob@oldradiodoc.com
http://www.oldradiodoc.com
Professional restorations for all tube type antique table and console radios, communication receivers and music amplifiers; complete overhauls; lacquer sprayed hand rubbed and polished cabinet refinishing; also appraises, buys & sells.

Frank Johnson
530 Elford Rd.
Fairless Hills, PA 19030-3624
ph: 215-943-8295
fadacat@aol.com
Buys, sells, collects, and repairs/ restores antique radios.

Stan Watkins
5326 Doncaster Dr.
Charlotte, NC 28211
ph: 704-362-2147
stwradio@concentric.net
http://www.cris.com/~stwradio

Ed Romney
Romney Publishing
P.O. Box 487
Drayton, SC 29333
ph: 864-597-1882
ed@edromney.com
http://www.edromney.com
Fix your own cameras! Romney offers

camera repair manuals, courses, tools
and restoration supplies for most
cameras, old or new: Leica Graflex,
Rolleiflex, Nikon, Canon and many
more; also books on repairing old
radios.

Dennis G. Williams
Radio Relics
4822 S. Orange Ave., #7
Orlando, FL 32806
ph: 407-895-9075
oldradio@cfl.rr.com
http://www.radiorelics.com
*Repairs vacuum tube equipment,
primarily antique radios and vintage
tube radio amplifiers.*

Al Welch
Antique Radios
2248 S. 33 St.
Milwaukee, WI 53215-2414
ph: 414-383-9908
alwelch@ticon.net
http://www.ticon.net/~alwech
*Interested in pre-WWII radios, radios
parts, test equipment, history; owner
of the online community of radio
enthusiasts at antique-
radio@yahoogroups.com.*

David B. Johnson
2336 S. Kenilworth Ave.
Berwyn, IL 60402
ph: 708-484-2743
*Vintage TV and radio repair and
restorations; both electronics and
cosmetics.*

Art Bilski
Art's Antique Radios
208 Green Mountain Dr.
Bolingbrook, IL 60440
ph: 630-739-1060
fax: 630-739-1060
art@myantiqueradio.com
http://www.myantiqueradio.com
*Consultation, repair, sales and
purchases of old tube style radios;
will buy your old radios or will refer
you to another resource who will buy.*

Clinton Blais
Antique Radio Restorations
109 S. Oak St.
O Fallon, IL 62269-2000
ph: 618-632-7423
*Collects and restores old radios;
electronic consultant; also manufactures reproductions radio dials.*

Radio Era Archives
2043 Empire Central
Dallas, TX 75235
ph: 214-358-5195
fax: 214-357-4693
tsm@radioera.com
http://www.radioera.com
*Mail order and Internet business
servicing the antique radio collector,
restorer or repair person; sells
primarily old radio information,
catalogs, manuals, schematics and
technical data for most radios; also
restores and sells old radios.*

Henry Harmoney
508 Highland
Arlington, TX 76010
ph: 817-226-1140
*Buys, sells, repairs all types of radios;
Zenith and Art Deco are favorites.*

Stephen Kuhn
Neon Radio, The
503 E. Market St.
Lockhart, TX 78644
ph: 512-398-7777
stephen@neonradio.com
http://www.neonradio.com
*Buys, sells, trades, repairs vintage
radios.*

Mac's Old Time Radios & Radio
  Museum
4335 W. 147th St.
Lawndale, CA 90260
ph: 310-675-6017
Restores old radios and cabinets.

Malcom Bennett
Vintage Radios
Shirley, Munns Lane
Hartlip.
Sittingbourne, Kent ME9 7SY U.K.
ph: 01795 842616
mfb@valve.demon.co.uk
http://www.valve.demon.co.uk
*Purveyor and collector of vintage/
antique radios and valves (tubes); also
service data and components; plus full
repair restoration services offered.*

Suppliers

Electron Tube Enterprises
P.O. Box 8311
Essex, VT 05451
ph: 802-879-0611
fax: 802-879-7764
etetubes@adelphia.net
http://members.aol.com/etetubes
*Dealers in surplus electron tubes; free
catalog available; over 2000 different
types in stock; both new and used
tubes available.*

Michael Tannenbaum
A.G. Tannenbaum
P.O. Box 386
Ambler, PA 19002
ph: 215-540-8055
fax: 215-540-8327
k2bn@agtannenbaum.com
http://www.agtannenbaum.com
*Provides electronic service data for
new and antique electronic equipment
of all types from pre-1930s radios to
latest electronic equipment; sells
copies of manufacturer's documentation; collector books, hard-to-find
parts.*

John Okolowicz
Grillecloth Headquarters
624 Cedar Hill Rd., Ste. 100
Ambler, PA 19002-1504
ph: 215-542-1597
john@grillecloth.com
http://www.grillecloth.com
*Source for over 50 reproduction grille
cloth patterns for antique radios from*

*1920-1950; Web site also offers
helpful links to other radio parts
sources and club listings.*

Howard W. Granoff
Old Tyme Radio Co.
2445 Lyttonsville Rd., Ste. 317
Silver Spring, MD 20910-1931
ph: 301-587-5280
fax: 301-587-5280
*Carries hard-to-find radio parts:
vintage tubes, five types of fan wire,
hook up wire, audio transformers,
vintage headphones, etc.; also vintage
radio repair service and vintage radio
data packages; send LSASE for flyer.*

Merrill Mabbs
Classic Radio Gallery
709 Pluma Dr.
Rapid City, SD 57702
ph: 605-342-4090
fax: 605-390-1456
boz@rushmore.com
http://www.classicradiogallery.com
*Specializes in early 1930s to 1940s
radios; schematics available for most
US-made radios made from the 1920s
to the 1950s; has an online virtual
radio museum at the Web site; also
schematic services; antique radios for
sale.*

Radio Era Archives
2043 Empire Central
Dallas, TX 75235
ph: 214-358-5195
fax: 214-357-4693
tsm@radioera.com
http://www.radioera.com
*Mail order and Internet business
servicing the antique radio collector,
restorer or repair person; sells
primarily old radio information,
catalogs, manuals, schematics and
technical data for most radios; also
restores and sells old radios.*

Antique Electronic Supply
6221 S. Maple Ave.
Tempe, AZ 85283-2856
ph: 480-820-5411
fax: 800-706-6789
info@tubesandmore.com
http://www.tubesandmore.com
*Large catalog carrying tubes,
supplies, capacitors, transformers,
chemicals, test equipment, wire, parts,
tools, books, old fabric lamp cords,
etc.*

Larry Bordonaro
Old Time Replications
5744 Tobias
Van Nuys, CA 91411-3349
ph: 818-786-2500
fax: 818-909-0241
oldtimerep@aol.com
http://www.antiqueradioknobs.com
*Supplies replacement knobs, push-
buttons, escutcheons, plastic grills,
handles, etc.*

Mike Tobin
Rock-Sea Enterprises
323 E. Matilija St., #110-241
Ojai, CA 93023
ph: 805-646-7362
dials@juno.com
http://members.aol.com/RockSeaEnt
*Manufacturer of dial scales for
antique radios; specializing in plastic
and card/foil dial scales as
replacements for any radio including
glass and metal dials.*

Art Deco

Collectors

John M. England, Jr.
103 Old River Rd.
Lincoln, RI 02865
*Buys and sells Art Deco radios,
clocks, machine age design.*

Dealers

Carl Ratner
94 Mechanic St.
Reinholds, PA 17569-9701
ph: 717-484-1021
artdeco@epix.net
*Buys, collects, sells, trades, and
restores Art Deco radios from the
1930s and 1940s.*

Atwater Kent

Internet Resources

Vane Warner
1513 Meadow Way Ct.
Mansfield, TX 76063
ph: 817-473-0455
vanew@airmail.net
http://web2.airmail.net/vanew
*This Web site is devoted to providing
information about Atwater Kent
radios and the man who created them;
pictures, schematics, advertising, and
Web links dealing with Atwater Kent
radios.*

Hallicrafters

Clubs/Associations

Fred Mooney
Hallicrafters Collectors International
webmaster@w9wze.org
http://www.w9wze.org
*Dedicated to fans of vintage
Hallicrafters radios; Web site features
information about amateur radio and
shortwave listening; also extensive
archive of over a thousand photos of
Hallicrafters equipment from 1930s
through 1970s.*

Speakers

Repair Services

Lakes Loudspeaker Service
4400 W. Hillsboro Blvd.
Coconut Creek, FL 33073
ph: 800-367-7757 or 954-426-6369
lakeselec@aol.com
http://www.lakeselectronics.com
Loudspeaker rebuilding service.

Transistor

Collectors

Bob Davidson
19 Davis Court
Concord, MA 01742-2319
ph: 978-369-2007
bob@abetterpage.com
http://www.galaxym31.com/trans/
1trans.html
*Wants to buy Japanese pocket
transistor radios.*

Richard Lambert
166 East 34th St.
New York, NY 10016
ph: 212-684-6564
*Wants to buy 1950s and 1960s
transistor radios; Emerson, Regency,
Zenith, Sony, etc.*

Eric Wrobbel
20802 Exhibit Ct.
Woodland Hills, CA 91367-5205
ph: 818-884-2282
ewrobbel@aol.com
http://members.aol.com/ewrobbel/
pubpage.htm
*Wants shirt-pocket or coat-pocket size
transistor radios, working or not;
made in the US or in Japan; call or
write with radio brand name and
model number, or send photocopy of
front of radio; also wants toy crystal
radios.*

Mike Kramer
P.O. Box 3257
Vallejo, CA 94590-0676
ph: 800-568-8883 or 800-446-6581
fax: 707-642-2456
*Wants to buy shirt pocket size
Japanese transistor radios; also wants
Catalin table model radios.*

Mike Brooks
7335 Skyline
Oakland, CA 94611-1121
ph: 510-339-1751
deborahwb@aol.com
*Wants to buy early American and
Japanese transistor radios including
boys' models, earphone only, and
other miniature sets; also wants toy
pocket crystal radios from the 1920s
to 1960s.*

Dealers

Bob Roberts
P.O. Box 152
Guilderland, NY 12084-0152
*Wants to buy novelty transistor
radios, e.g., Atlas Battery, Brut
cologne, Budweiser, Pepsi, Coke,
McDonald's, etc.; also wants
telephones in unusual shapes, e.g.,
gas pumps, food items, cartoon
characters, cars, movie related, TV,
etc.*

Gary Arnold
Arnold's Novelty Radios
615 Oak St.
Marion, NC 28752
ph: 828-652-6893
gary@noveltyradio.com
http://www.noveltyradio.com
*Buys and sells novelty transistor
radios.*

Vacuum Tubes For

Clubs/Associations

Ludwell Sibley, Ed.
Tube Collectors Association
Newsletter: Tube Collector
P.O. Box 1181
Medford, OR 97501
ph: 541-855-5207
tubelore@internetcds.com
http://www.tubecollectors.org
*Collectors group focused on the
history and collecting of radio tubes.*

Collectors

Leo Gibbs
Radio Tubes
701 Brookfield Rd.
Dayton, OH 45429-3323
ph: 937-299-3965
Wants pre-1925 antique radio tubes.

Dealers

Richard Bergeron
Electron Tube Enterprise
P.O. Box 8311
Essex, VT 05451
ph: 802-879-1844
fax: 802-879-7764
etetubes@adelphia.net
http://members.aol.com/etetubes
*Specializes in old vacuum tubes for
radios, TVs, amplifiers, radio HAM
gear, etc.; both new and older,
pretested, used tubes are available; in
business for over 10 years.*

James P. Cross
Vacuum Tubes, Inc.
3246 Floridale Lane
Cincinnati, OH 45239-6203
ph: 513-385-3855
fax: 513-385-3855
vactubes@cinternet.net
http://www.cinternet.net/~vactubes
*Carries a full line of vacuum tubes for
audiophiles, radio enthusiasts,
industry, and collectors.*

Brent Jessee
Brent Jessee Recording Vacuum Tubes
1655 W. Algonquin Rd., #111
Hoffman Estates, IL 60195
ph: 847-496-4546
brentjes@audiotubes.com
http://www.audiotubes.com
*Supplies vacuum tubes (valves,
electronic tubes) for radios, Hi-Fi,
television, Ham radio, and industrial
uses; has antique tubes for antique
radios and audiophile tubes for tube
amplifiers.*

Dick Morgan
Electronic Communications
3630 Cavalier Dr.
Garland, TX 75042-7503
ph: 972-272-3581
fax: 972-272-1831
ec.inc@att.net
*Collector and dealer wants all types
of radio tubes; prefer new in box, old
stock tubes and new and used antique
tubes.*

Antique Electronic Supply
6221 S. Maple Ave.
Tempe, AZ 85283-2856
ph: 480-820-5411
fax: 800-706-6789
info@tubesandmore.com
http://www.tubesandmore.com
*Large catalog carrying tubes,
supplies, capacitors, transformers,
chemicals, test equipment, wire, parts,
tools, books, old fabric lamp cords,
etc.*

C.E. "Sonny" Clutter
Radiola Guy, The
3634 NW 29th Circle
Camas, WA 98607
ph: 360-834-5741
Sonny@radiolaguy.com
http://www.radiolaguy.com
*Collector and dealer of vintage
vacuum tubes for 1910 to 1960 radios
and TVs.*

Internet Resources

Tim Tromp
Kilokat's Antique Light Bulb Site
P.O. Box G
Fruitport, MI 49415
kilokat7@bulbcollector.com
http://www.bulbcollector.com
*A Web site for the bulb and vacuum
tube collector; research paper
archives, time line, discussion boards.*

RAILROAD COLLECTIBLES

(see also BOOKS, Railroad;
DINNERWARE, Advertising;
RAILROADS; STREETCAR LINE
COLLECTIBLES; TRAINS, Model;
TRAINS, Toy; TRANSPORTATION
COLLECTIBLES)

Appraisers

Bob Chase
Bob Chase, Railroad Collectibles
550 Veronica Place
Escondido, CA 92027
ph: 760-746-9392 or 760-443-4931
fax: 763-746-9392
chaser@cox.net
*Railroad memorabilia appraiser,
dealer and collector for over 17 years;
specialized in railroad china, silver,
paper and other assorted railroadiana
collectibles.*

Brad S. Lomazzi
Western Railroad Collectibles
1300 Liberty Ct.
Roseville, CA 95747-7440
ph: 916-782-6587
bslomazzi@att.net
*Appraiser, dealer and expert in
railroad and other transportation
collectibles; author of "Railroad
Timetables, Travel Brochures &
Posters," and "Railroad Collectibles
- A History and Price Guide."*

Brill Lee
Brill Lee Appraisal Services
P.O. Box 244
Bellevue, WA 98009-0244
ph: 425-885-4518
fax: 425-895-1022
brilllee@hotmail.com
*Collects handheld kerosene railroad
lanterns, padlocks, keys, telegraph
equipment, stock certificates, signs,
etc.; also model railroad items ("O"
and "027" gauge Marx and Lionel
trains and accessories.*

Clubs/Associations

Greg Gneier
American Southwestern Railway
Association
P.O. Box 39846
Los Angeles, CA 90039
ph: 213-668-0104
greg@traveltown.org
http://mcscom.com/asra
*Non-profit educational organization
formed in 1982 for the purpose of
preserving the history of American
railroading; collects and preserves
railroad artifacts.*

Bob Chase
Railroadiana Collectors Association, Inc.
Newsletter: Express
550 Veronica Place
Escondido, CA 92027
ph: 760-746-9392
fax: 763-746-9392
rcaisec@cox.net
http://www.railroadcollectors.org
*Members receive a quarterly
publication containing articles on
different aspects of railroad history;
shares knowledge on a wide range of
collectibles associated with railroads.*

Canadian Railroad Historical Association
- Toronto & York Division
Magazine: Turnout, The
527B Mount Pleasant Rd.
Toronto, Ontario M4S 2M4 Canada
mail@torontoyork.com
http://www.torontoyork.com
*Has library of books, magazines,
artifacts, photos and plans of
locomotives and stations; assists local
media with information on railway
history; holds ten meetings each year.*

Collectors

Jay Skidmore
P.O. Box 332
Princeton Junction, NJ 08550
ph: 609-799-5375
jjs2440@aol.com
Wants to buy railroad police badges, patches, police and railroad lanterns, locks, keys, restraining devices; specializes in items from the Pennsylvania Railroad; also wants US Postal Inspection Service memorabilia.

Harold Schreibman
P.O. Box 4323
Bayside, NY 11360
ph: 718-225-9480
harlod414@aol.com
Buying railroad collectibles: timetables, passes, calendars, lanterns, locks, keys, Poor's manuals, official guides, conductor badges, etc.

Harold Schreibman
P.O. Box 121
Mountain Dale, NY 12763-0121
ph: 914-434-6662 or 718-225-9480
Railroad timetables, annual passes, badges, depot items, calendars.

Randy Ridgely
447 Oglethorpe Ave.
Athens, GA 30606-2236
ph: 706-549-6264
erie@negia.net
Wants railroad china, silver, paper, etc.; also steamship and airline items.

Seth Bramson
330 N.E. 96th St.
Miami, FL 33138-2718
ph: 305-757-1016
fax: 305-895-8178
sbramson@bellsouth.net
Buys railroad and trolleyana; postage paid on approvals.

Richard Hebel
233 Dietrich Crescent Dr.
Lawrenceburg, IN 47025-1576
ph: 812-537-0150
bhebel@seidata.com
Collector buying railroad items: lanterns, globes, china, silver, brass locks, etc.

Howard Page
Old Depot Railroad Museum, The
651 West Hwy., #12
P.O. Box 99
Dassel, MN 55325-0099
ph: 320-275-3629 or 320-275-3876
fax: 320-275-3933
Seeks railroad artifacts: bells & whistles, uniforms, signs, signals, advertising toys & models, pictures, calendars, etc.

Michael Sullivan
Route 1, Box 45
Jonesburg, MO 63351
ph: 636-488-5677
mandgee@socket.net
http://www.sully-has-it.com
Buys, sells, trades railroad items;
especially wants MKT, Wabash, and TRRA items.

Greg Gneier
American Southwestern Railway
  Association
P.O. Box 39846
Los Angeles, CA 90039
ph: 213-668-0104
greg@traveltown.org
http://mcscom.com/asra
Collector and museum preservation of railroad artifacts; especially interested in dining car and passenger train related items: china, silverware, menus, promotional items; specializing in Union Pacific, Santa Fe, & Southern Pacific.

Richard Wright
P.O. Box 4894
Pomona, CA 91766-0894
ph: 909-681-4647 or 909-364-6620
wrights.rrstation@verizon.net
Wants railroad items such as china, silverware, lanterns, etc.; all inquiries answered.

Dealers

Fred N. Arone
Depot Attic, The
377 Ashford Ave.
Dobbs Ferry, NY 10522
ph: 914-693-5858
fax: 914-674-6030
rrauctco@aol.com
Buys and sells pre-1960 railroadiana: paper ephemera, books, hardware, silverware and chinaware, timetables, lanterns, brass locks, posters and display advertising, calendars, passes, porcelain signs, hat badges, playing cards, etc.

L. Michael Boak
Initialed Duck Antiques & Collectibles
3812 Hamilton Ave.
Baltimore, MD 21206-3505
ph: 410-319-7529
Buys, sells and collects primarily B&O railroad memorabilia.

Don Anderson
Railroad Collectibles Sales Agent
1831 N. Cambridge Ave., #1206
Milwaukee, WI 53202
ph: 414-291-5216
fax: 414-291-5216
wistrains@yahoo.com
http://www.apex-ephemera.com/
  RailroadSalesAgent
Buys and sells historic, antique and railroad maps; seeking pre-1910 atlases in any condition and by any publisher; list your items in the free "For Sale" and "Search" sections of the Web site.

Bob Chase
Bob Chase, Railroad Collectibles
550 Veronica Place
Escondido, CA 92027
ph: 760-746-9392 or 760-443-4931
fax: 763-746-9392
chaser@cox.net
Railroad memorabilia appraiser,
dealer and collector for over 17 years; specialized in railroad china, silver, paper and other assorted railroadiana collectibles.

Steve Schmale
Out West
2231 Creekside Rd.
Santa Rosa, CA 95405-8022
ph: 707-838-1859 or 707-575-5406
outweststv@aol.com
Buys and sells better vintage postcards since 1976; approval service; strong in Western states views; always buying better cards and real photos; also wants railroad paper, stereoviews, photos, brochures, trade cards; member IFPD.

Brad S. Lomazzi
Western Railroad Collectibles
1300 Liberty Ct.
Roseville, CA 95747-7440
ph: 916-782-6587
bslomazzi@att.net
Appraiser, dealer and expert in railroad and other transportation collectibles; author of "Railroad Timetables, Travel Brochures & Posters," and "Railroad Collectibles - A History and Price Guide."

Scott Arden
Antiques & Artifacts
20457 Highway 126
Noti, OR 97461-9706
ph: 541-935-1619
Leading RR mail order dealer for 31 years; catalog $1; buys and sells fine old transportation items, mostly non-paper; consignment.

Raul Roy
P.D.R.'s Train Shop
3874 Winlake Cres.
Burnaby, British Columbia V5A 2G5
  Canada
ph: 604-420-1292
fax: 604-420-1292
proy@direct.ca
http://www.direct.ca/adz/pdr/pdr.html
Trades, buys, sells railroad memorabilia, collectibles: cloth crests, RR pins, etc.

Experts

Richard C. Barrett
Railroad Research Publications
3400 Ridge Rd. West, Ste. 5-266
Rochester, NY 14626-3458
ph: 716-227-6903
rrpubl@frontiernet.net
Publisher of books on railroad collectibles and railroad history.

Charles Miller
Golden Spike Enterprises Inc.
3106 N. Rochester St.
Arlington, VA 22213
ph: 703-536-2954
fax: 703-241-7027
Sue & Bill Knous
Railroad Memories
1903 S. Niagara St.
Denver, CO 80224
ph: 303-759-1290
rrm@uswest.net
http://www.railroadmemories.com
Authors of "The Railroad Detective, a Guide to Replica & Counterfeit Railroad Collectibles."

Museums/Libraries

Ralph Justen
National Railroad Museum
Newsletter: Railines
2285 S. Broadway
Green Bay, WI 54304-7245
ph: 414-435-7623 or 414-435-7245
staff@nationalrrmuseum.org
http://www.nationalrrmuseum.org
One of the oldest railroad museums in the country; 75+ pieces of rolling stock; world's largest steam locomotive; seasonal train rides; well stocked gift shop.

Howard Page
Old Depot Railroad Museum, The
651 West Hwy., #12
P.O. Box 99
Dassel, MN 55325-0099
ph: 320-275-3629 or 320-275-3876
fax: 320-275-3933
An old Great Northern depot filled with railroad artifacts: bells & whistles, uniforms, signs, signals, advertising toys & models, two cabooses, freight car, section car, track bicycle, pictures, calendars, etc.

Denny Hainley
Santa Fe Depot Railroad & Heritage
  Museum
315 West Ave. B.
Temple, TX 76503
ph: 254-298-5172
fax: 254-298-5171
dhainley@ci.temple.tx.us
http://www.rrdepot.org

Periodicals

Birmingham Railway Publications
Magazine: Railway Collectors' Journal
P.O. Box 7001
Bingham, Nottingham NG13 9XA U.K.
ph: +44 1271 814315 or +44 781 517-6431
fax: +44 1271 814315
rcj@prorail.co.uk
http://www.prorail.co.uk
Covers all aspects of railway memorabilia collecting: auction listings, previews and results, historical research and informative articles on engines, carriages, wagons, plus objects used in railway stations, hotels, office, restaurants.

B & O Items

Collectors

Charles Boice
7003 Charles Ridge Rd.
Baltimore, MD 21204-3608
ph: 410-321-7149 or 301-897-8850
Wants to buy Baltimore & Ohio R.R. memorabilia and china.

Repro. Sources

B & O Railroad Museum
901 Pratt St.
Baltimore, MD 21223
ph: 410-752-2490
fax: 410-752-2499
sfay@borail.org
http://www.borail.org
Sells B & O railroad china and other B & O related items.

China

Collectors

Robert D'Achille
3972 NY Rt. 26
Whitney Point, NY 13862-2708
ph: 607-862-3914
rdachill@stny.rr.com
Wants any railroad china especially Railroad-marked; must be in good condition (no hairlines, cracks or chips, etc.).

Dealers

Charles Miller
Golden Spike Enterprises Inc.
3106 N. Rochester St.
Arlington, VA 22213
ph: 703-536-2954
fax: 703-241-7027
Wants to buy railroad china, especially by Buffalo or Syracuse China.

Experts

Douglas W. McIntyre
20 Cleveland Place
Lockport, NY 14094-3104
ph: 716-433-2235
Author of "The Official Guide to Railroad Dining Car China."

Museums/Libraries

B & O Railroad Museum, Chessie Shop
901 Pratt St.
Baltimore, MD 21223
ph: 410-752-2490
fax: 410-752-2499
sfay@borail.org
http://www.borail.org
Shop sells B&O railroad china.

Hat Badges

Experts

Jim Younger
4628 Old Dragon Path
Ellicott City, MD 21042-5970
ph: 410-964-1949
boomer-op@ragingbull.com
Wants railroad hat badges (from all railroads and in all occupations),

hats, uniforms, and brotherhood (RR Unions) lapel pins.

Paper Items

Collectors

Carl Loucks
P.O. Box 484
North Haven, CT 06473-0484
ph: 203-288-3765
fax: 203-234-2729
ct.direct.mail@snet.net
Wants railroad timetables, brochures, guides, maps, menus; also trolley, air and bus.

Passes

Collectors

George Johnson
P.O. Box 1449
Lexington, VA 24450-1449
ph: 540-464-4326
fax: 540-464-4326
gnjo@rockbridge.net
Wants to buy pre-1940 timetables for railroad, trolley, airline, and bus; also wants passes, catalogs, and postcards of small town depots.

Ed Lewis
P.O. Box 505
Aberdeen, NC 28315
ph: 919-367-0426
Collector wants to buy railroad timetables and passes from small railroads.

Playing Cards

Experts

Phil Bollhagen
7940 West Leroy Ave.
Greenfield, WI 53220
ph: 414-327-6220
bollhagp@rocketmail.com
Has one of the largest collections of antique railroad playing card decks in the US; wants to buy quality pre-1915 decks from all railroads; author of "The Great Book of Railroad Playing Cards;" railroad decks and singles.

Posters

Collectors

Charles G. Kratz, Jr.
17821 Golfview
Homewood, IL 60430-1210
ph: 708-799-8478 or 312-951-0336
Wants original railroad posters produced for American and Canadian companies; also original railroad paintings and any material relating to Chicago & Eastern Illinois Railroad.

Signal Lamps

Internet Resources

Paul Koren
Railroad Lantern Collecting Website
klnl@attbi.com
http://www.klnl.org/pgLanterns.htm
This Web site focuses on railroad lamps, lanterns and signal lamps.

Timetables

Collectors

Ed Lewis
P.O. Box 505
Aberdeen, NC 28315
ph: 919-367-0426
Collector wants to buy railroad timetables and passes from small railroads.

Uniforms

(see BUTTONS, Railroad/Transit Uniforms)

RAILROADS

(see also BOOKS, Railroad; RAILROAD COLLECTIBLES; STEAM-OPERATED, Models & Equipment; TRAINS, Model; TRAINS, Toy)

Appraisers

David J. Thebodo
Rail Merchants International
P.O. Box 2019
Fairfield, IA 52556-8019
ph: 641-472-2020
fax: 641-472-7927
caboose@kdsi.net
http://www.railmerchants.net
Buys and sells railroad rolling stock: cabooses, Fairmont motorcars, luxury passenger cars, box cars, bunk cars, flatcars, baggage cars, coaches, and other railroad equipment and railroadiana; escorts and appraises private rail cars.

Clubs/Associations

National Railway Historical Society
P.O. Box 58547
Philadelphia, PA 19102-8547
ph: 610-557-6606
fax: 610-557-6740
info@nrhs.com
http://www.nrhs.com
An organization for those who enjoy riding the railways, operating trains, taking photographs, restoring vintage equipment, preserving and revitalizing railroad structures, writing books, rail history, watching trains, etc.

Diane Elliott, Ex. Dir.
American Association of Private Railroad Car Owners
Magazine: Private Varnish
630-B Constitution Ave., NE
Washington, DC 20002
ph: 202-547-5696
fax: 202-547-5623
delliott155@earthlink.net
http://www.aaprco.com
For enthusiasts and owners of private railroad cars.

Chesapeake & Ohio Historical Society, Inc.
Magazine: Chesapeake & Ohio Historical Magazine
P.O. Box 79
Clifton Forge, VA 24422
ph: 540-862-2210
cohs@cfw.com
http://www.cohs.org
Monthly articles on history of the C&O RR and predecessors (PM RR in Mich., HV RR in Ohio, etc.), as well as successor CSX Transportation.

New York Central System Historical Society, Inc.
Magazine: Central Headlight
P.O. Box 81184
Philadelphia, PA 81184
jhands@nycshs.org
http://www.nycshs.org
Publishes quarterly magazine; information, drawings, photos available; research sources; inquiries welcome.

Tourist Railway Association, Inc.
Magazine: TrainLine
P.O. Box 1245
Chama, NM 87520-1245
ph: 800-67-TRAIN or 505-756-1240
fax: 505-756-1238
markg@gtownloop.com
http://www.traininc.org
Formed in 1972 to encourage creative railroading; membership open to railway museums, clubs, tourist railroads, product suppliers, railroad publishers, private car owners, excursion operators, etc.

William Lugg, Mem.
Railway & Locomotive Historical Society
Newsletter: R&LHS Newsletter
P.O. Box 292927
Sacramento, CA 95829-2927
aettlinger@worldnet.att.net
http://www.rlhs.org
A national organization devoted to railroad history; several chapters across the US.

Pacific Coast Chapter of the Railway & Locomotive Historical Society
Newsletter: Western Railroader
198 Wool St.
San Francisco, CA 96530-2596
ph: 916-985-4777 or 800-336-7547 (orders)
fax: 916-985-3763
A chapter of a national organization devoted to railroad history.

Collectors

Robert Gormley
334 Brownsburg Rd.
Newtown, PA 18940-9626
ph: 215-598-3520
bgormley@erols.com
Wants collectibles and souvenirs related to the Switchback Gravity railroad of Mauch Chunk, PA.

Dealers

D.F. Barnhardt
D.F. Barnhardt & Associates
Magazine: Railroad & Tourist Rail
   Magazine
8344 W. Franklin St.
P.O. Box 1089
Mount Pleasant, NC 28124-1089
ph: 704-436-9393
fax: 704-436-9399
dfba@mindspring.com
http://www.trains-trams-trolleys.com/
   home
*Sells rolling stock; magazine
advertises equipment for sale and
contains stories that focus on the use
of old time trains in tourist locations
such as parks and amusement centers.*

David J. Thebodo
Rail Merchants International
P.O. Box 2019
Fairfield, IA 52556-8019
ph: 641-472-2020
fax: 641-472-7927
caboose@kdsi.net
http://www.railmerchants.net
*Buys and sells railroad rolling stock:
cabooses, Fairmont motorcars, luxury
passenger cars, box cars, bunk cars,
flatcars, baggage cars, coaches, and
other railroad equipment and
railroadiana; escorts and appraises
private rail cars.*

Experts

Robert L. Johnson
Whistles in the Woods Museum
   Services
P.O. Box 309
Chickamauga, GA 30707-0309
ph: 706-375-4326
oldgoat@voy.net
*Consultants specializing in narrow-
gauge, steam, industrial, logging and
mining railroads; American, foreign
(European, Australian); also inclines,
aerial tramways, garden and large
scale model railroads.*

Internet Resources

Central Pacific Railroad Photographic
   History Museum
museum@cprr.org
http://www.cprr.org
*Site chronicles the history of the
transcontinental railroad through the
display of over 2,300 vintage photos;
images carefully researched; 2,380
pages of transcontinental railroad
history.*

Daniel Dawdy
Ribbon Rail Productions
319 N. Weber Rd.
PMB 348
Bolingbrook, IL 60490
ph: 815-584-1577
fax: 800-783-0127
webmaster@rrhistorical.com
http://www.rrhistorical.com
*Great first stop for railroad historical
information: links to railroad history,
clubs, historical and technical*

societies, museums, clip art, model
railroad manufacturers, etc.

Museums/Libraries

Larz Anderson Auto Museum
15 Newton St.
Brookline, MA 02146
ph: 617-522-6547
fax: 617-524-0170
director@mot.org
http://www.mot.org
*The museum collection includes many
unique and remarkable vehicles as
well as many other significant historic
artifacts.*

New York Museum of Transportation
P.O. Box 136
6393 East River Rd.
West Henrietta, NY 14586
ph: 585-533-1113
info@nymtmuseum.org
http://www.nymtmuseum.org
*Open all year on Sundays only;
exhibits collection of vehicles
including trolleys, rail, autos, buses,
trucks, and horse-drawn, as well as
related smaller artifacts and photos,
documents, stock certificates,
timetables, tickets.*

California State Railroad Museum
111 "I" St.
Sacramento, CA 95814-2265
ph: 916-445-7387
fax: 916-327-5655
http://www.csrmf.org

Periodicals

Harold H. Carstens
Carstens Publications
Magazine: Railfan & Railroad
108 Phil Hardin Rd.
P.O. Box 700
Newton, NJ 07860-0700
ph: 973-383-3355 or 800-474-6995
fax: 973-383-4064
carstens@carstens-publications.com
http://www.carstens-publications.com

Harold H. Carstens
Carstens Publications
Magazine: Railroad Model Craftsman
108 Phil Hardin Rd.
P.O. Box 700
Newton, NJ 07860-0700
ph: 973-383-3355 or 800-474-6995
fax: 973-383-4064
carstens@carstens-publications.com
http://www.carstens-publications.com

D.F. Barnhardt
D.F. Barnhardt & Associates
Magazine: Railroad & Tourist Rail
   Magazine
8344 W. Franklin St.
P.O. Box 1089
Mount Pleasant, NC 28124-1089
ph: 704-436-9393
fax: 704-436-9399
dfba@mindspring.com
http://www.trains-trams-trolleys.com/
   home
*Magazine advertises equipment for
sale and contains stories that focus on*

the use of old time trains in tourist
locations such as parks and
amusement centers.

Mark W. Hemphill, Ed.
Kalmbach Publishing Co.
Magazine: Trains
P.O. Box 1612
21027 Crossroads Circle
Waukesha, WI 53187
ph: 262-796-8776 or 800-446-5489
fax: 262-798-6468
editor@trains.com
http://www2.trains.com/trains
*For the railroad buff: capture the
power, history and drama of
railroading; learn about railroad
empires, see the newest high-tech
locomotives, enjoy award-winning
photography.*

Flying Scotsman

Collectors

Paul R. Dowie
P.O. Box 472
Chester Springs, PA 19425-0472
ph: 610-827-7561
lner4472fs@aol.com
*Collects anything related to LNER
4472 "Flying Scotsman" (both the
locomotive and the train of the same
name): photos (especially with second/
water tender), recordings, china and
flatware from the F.S. train; books,
posters, models.*

RANGES

(see also CAST IRON ITEMS;
KITCHEN COLLECTIBLES; STOVES)

Clubs/Associations

Antique Stove Association
Newsletter: Stove Parts Needed
   Newsletter
2617 Riverside
Houston, TX 77004-7610
ph: 713-528-2990
sales@antiquestoves.com
http://www.antiquestoves.com
*For those interested in antique stoves
and related items; you must join to
receive the benefits which are for
members only.*

Jack Santoro
Old Appliance Club, The
Newsletter: Old Road Home, The
P.O. Box 65
Ventura, CA 93002
ph: 805-643-3532
fax: 805-643-3532
toac@sbcglobal.net
http://www.antiquestoves.com/toac/
   about.htm
*The only vintage American appliance
information clearinghouse in the
world; parts, service, information,
sources, referrals, buy/sell classifieds,
historical articles on vintage stoves,
refrigerators and appliances.*

Dealers

Erickson's Antique Stoves, Inc.
P.O. Box 2275
At the Depot
Littleton, MA 01460
ph: 978-486-3589
fax: 978-486-3695
*Antique gas coal and wood stoves and
ranges; bought, sold, restored.*

Paul Schoenharl
Rectanus Stove Co.
1328 Aster Place
Cincinnati, OH 45224-3208
ph: 513-541-0450
*Buys, sells and restores antique stoves
and ranges (pre 1930) with emphasis
on antique gas ranges 1882-1930;
also lectures and writes magazine
articles about early kitchen stoves.*

Macy's Classic Stove Works
5515 Almeda Rd.
Houston, TX 77004-7443
ph: 713-521-0934 or 713-528-1297
fax: 713-521-0889
http://
   www.MacysClassicStoveWorks.com
*Buys, sells, brokers, repairs, and
restores old ranges; also sells parts
and publishes "Classic Ranges"
newspaper.*

Jack Santoro
J.E.S. Enterprises
P.O. Box 65
Ventura, CA 93002
ph: 805-643-3532
fax: 805-643-3532
toac@sbcglobal.net
http://www.antiquestoves.com/toac/
   about.htm
*Antique stove and appliance parts,
service, information: thermostats,
carbon rod regulators rebuilt, safety
systems fabricated, mechanical systems
rebuilt, How-To manuals, factory
service books, clocks & timers rebuilt,
etc.*

Museums/Libraries

Paul Schoenharl
Cincinnati Stove Museum
1328 Aster Place
Cincinnati, OH 45224-3208
ph: 513-541-0450
*Small museum of stoves and ranges;
no admission.*

Periodicals

Newsletter: Antique Stove Exchange,
   The
P.O. Box 2101
Waukesha, WI 53187
ph: 262-542-9190
fax: 262-542-9190
mail@theantiquestovexchng.com
http://www.theantiquestovexchng.com
*Since 1992, America's antique stove
publication: source for those using,
collecting, repairing and restoring
antique stoves; informative articles,
ads, locate a stove dealer, buy/sell/*

trade cookstoves, heating stoves, parts.

Repair Services

Antique Gas Stoves
P.O. Box 3175
Montclair, CA 91763
ph: 909-445-0300
cookin@antiquegasstoves.com
http://www.antiquegasstoves.com
Sales, parts, repair and restoration of antique gas stoves, specializing in 1940s and 1950 O'Keefe & Merritt, Wedgewood, Roper and Western Holly; fully restored stoves are available.

Jack Santoro
J.E.S. Enterprises
P.O. Box 65
Ventura, CA 93002
ph: 805-643-3532
fax: 805-643-3532
toac@sbcglobal.net
http://www.antiquestoves.com/toac/about.htm
Superior range restoration: mechanical systems rebuilt, genuine porcelain finishes, safety valves, Bakelite refinished, clocks & timers rebuilt, brilliant electroplating, oven controls, movie prop rentals; how-to-restore books.

RANSBURG

Internet Resources

Dave Ransburg
Ransburg Collection, The
P.O. Box 9555
Peoria, IL 61612-9555
ph: 888-726-7287
fax: 309-692-7057
webmaster@ransburgcollection.com
http://www.ransburgcollection.com
Web site for those interested in Ransburg collectibles; for over half of the 20th century, the Ransburg Company of Indianapolis, IN produced handpainted stoneware and metalware household products for the kitchen and bath.

RATIONING RELATED ITEMS

(see also MILITARIA, WWII Items)

Clubs/Associations

Thomas B. Smith
Society of Ration Token Collectors
Newsletter: Ration Board, The
618 Jay Dr.
Gallipolis, OH 45631-1314
Tomsue@ZOOMNET.net
Society collects, trades, sells paper & token home front ration items (for food, clothing, gasoline, tires, etc.); send SASE for info.

Collectors

Lee Poleske
P.O. Box 871
Seward, AK 99664-0871
Wants OPA tokens and other WWII ration items.

RAY GUNS

(see TOYS, Space & Robot [Ray Guns])

RAZORS

(see BARBERSHOP COLLECTIBLES; SHAVING COLLECTIBLES)

RECORD JACKETS

(see PAPER COLLECTIBLES; RECORDS)

RECORDED SOUND

(see also COMPACT DISCS; RADIO SHOWS, Old Time; RECORDS)

Appraisers

Dr. Steve Johnson
Behavioral Images, Inc.
Newsletter: Ten Thousands Words
302 Leland St., Ste. 101
Bloomington, IL 61701-5646
ph: 309-829-3931 or 800-988-6427
fax: 309-829-9677
sjohnson@mediavalue.com
http://www.mediavalue.com
Film, video, recordings, photographs, negatives; author of "Appraising Audio-Visual Media; A Guide for Attorneys, Trust Officers, Insurance Professionals, & Archivists" (1993); $34.95 & $3 S&H; publishes newsletter ten times per year.

Clubs/Associations

Peter Shambarger, ExDir
Association for Recorded Sound Collections, Inc.
Journal: ARSC Journal
P.O. Box 543
Annapolis, MD 21404-0543
ph: 410-757-0488 or 410-956-5600
fax: 410-349-0175
koprowski@stanford.edu
http://www.arsc-audio.org
Dedicated to the preservation and study of recordings in the fields of music and speech: Edison cylinders, rare discs, oral history, etc.; publishes the ARSC Journal twice a year and the ARSC Newsletter four times per year.

Collectors

David Giovannoni
ph: 301-869-1501
fax: 301-987-2511
dgio-inquiries@ara.net
http://www.aranet.com/phono/main.htm
Advanced collector of home and commercial recordings on wax cylinders, 78 rpm discs, or wire; also looking for old photographs with phonographs in them, especially of people listening to phonographs that have horns.

Soundtracks

Dealers

Don Kyle
Soundtracks!
P.O. Box 531156
Henderson, NV 89053
sndtrx@earthlink.net
http://www.lasvegasrecordcompany.com
Buys and sells soundtracks; original cast, children's, Disney and personality LPs; sells via mail order and at conventions; also trades and buys collections.

RECORDS

(see also BOOKS, Reference [Records]; AUDIO-VISUAL; COMPACT DISCS; DRUM & BUGLE CORPS; HI-FI EQUIPMENT; MUSIC; PHONOGRAPHS; RECORDED SOUND; ROCK 'N' ROLL COLLECTIBLES)

Appraisers

Scott Neuman
Forever Vinyl
P.O. Box 526
Lakehurst, NJ 08733
ph: 732-505-3646
fax: 732-505-5337
sneuman@forevervinyl.com
http://www.forevervinyl.com
Buys, sells, trades rare and hard-to-find vinyl records and albums, 45s picture sleeves; most anything to do with music; over 500,000 items in stock; over 20 years in business; appraise for estate, insurance, etc.

John Vogel
Phonograph Record Appraisals & Search Service
123B East Deer Park Dr.
Gaithersburg, MD 20877
ph: 301-208-8175 or 301-379-8178
fax: 301-379-8179
jdvee@aol.com
Appraises single records or entire collections; also offers a finders service to locate rare items for collectors; will help locate buyers for your collections.

Steven Smolian
Smolian Sound Preservation Studios
1 Worman's Mill Court #4
Frederick, MD 21701
ph: 301-694-5134
fax: 301-694-5179
smolians@erols.com
http://www.soundsaver.com
Record collections appraised for tax donation, estate & insurance loss purposes; all formats - 78s, 45s, LPs, cylinders, radio disks, etc.; rock, classical, country, old news broadcasts; over 20 years appraising major archives.

Jon S. Englund
American Estate Services
P.O. Box 600305
Saint Paul, MN 55106-0006
ph: 651-776-6105
fax: 651-771-5033
jenglund@americanestate.com
Specializes in the appraisal of records, albums, musical items and related items; also antiques, collectibles, Barbie.

Edward Odel
Hot Platters
P.O. Box 4213
Thousand Oaks, CA 91359-1213
ph: 805-493-0861
fax: 805-492-3682
HotPlatter@aol.com
http://www.HotPlatters.com
Appraiser of LPs, 45s, 78s, soundtracks, tapes and related books, magazines, CDs, reel-to-reel, posters, videos, sheet music, paper goods, rock and movie memorabilia.

Auction Services

Floyd Silver
Antique Phonograph Center
P.O. Box 2574
Vincentown, NJ 08088-2574
ph: 609-859-8617
fsi5491160@aol.com
Conducts special mail auctions of rare and unusual 78 rpm Edison diamond discs and cylinder records; $2 for catalog.

Clubs/Associations

Richard Phillips
Association of Independent Record Collectors
Newsletter: AIRC Newsletter
P.O. Box 222
Northford, CT 06472-0222
ph: 203-484-2023
dipdadip@aol.com

Record Collectors Guild
the_rcguild@hotmail.com
http://thercguild.tripod.com
For and about the collecting of vinyl records; tips and information on collecting and care of vinyl records; message boards; a rapidly growing club.

Bill Pratt
Canadian Antique Phonograph Society
Journal: Antique Phonograph News
122 Major St.
Toronto, Ontario M5S 2L2 Canada
ph: 416-924-8207
info@capsnews.org
http://www.capsnews.org
Members interested in sound recording and its history: phonographs, gramophones; also related ephemera and memorabilia; journal has original articles, repair tips and how-tos, auction results, ads.

Collectors

Dave A. Reiss
141 Cabot Rd.
Massapequa, NY 11758-8119
ph: 516-798-3381
Collects 78 rpm's, 1900 to 1930s: popular, classical, jazz, personalities, dance records, gospel, country & western, ethnic.

Gerard Ortman
Jerry's Record Room
1577 Hannington Ave.
Wantagh, NY 11793-2807
ph: 516-781-7380
jerrysrock1@yahoo.com
Record expert and collector wants to buy 1948-1965 records: jazz, blues, R&B, rock, blues, soundtracks.

Dealers

Jay Norman
Fast Hits Music
P.O. Box 1459
Meredith, NH 03253
ph: 603-279-0450
fax: 603-279-0008
info@fasthits.com
http://www.fasthits.com
Specializes in newly manufactured 45s, oldies and newies.

AB-CD Planetwide
21 N. Main St.
Norwalk, CT 06854
ph: 203-831-83-1
fax: 203-831-8238
shoptalk@ab-cd.com
http://www.ab-cd.com
Specializes in hard-to-find/independent labels, rarities and import titles; offers a complete selection of music.

Gerald Wilson
Select Circle Records
P.O. Box 302
Riverside, CT 06878
ph: 203-661-8421
Specializes in Frank Sinatra.

Stephen Mack
RPM Records
132 West 3rd St.
Bayonne, NJ 07002
ph: 732-565-8194
http://www.home.earthlink.net/~jlsmack/recordlist.html
Buys and sells vinyl records from 1930s to 1950s.

Bernard F. Lopez
DiscoMusic.com
267 Kentlands Blvd., #1036
Gaithersburg, MD 20878
bflop@earthlink.net
http://www.discomusic.com
Comprehensive site for collectors of Disco, Soul and dance music; 12" & LP vinyl records from the 1970s and 1980s; RealAudio samples, cover art pictures, articles and release data as well as info on compact disc reissues of classic tracks.

Ardyth & John Stimson
AJS Marbles & Records
P.O. Box 8052
Glen Ridge, NJ 07028
Buys, sells, collects machine-made or antique marbles; will trade, buy or sell; also deals in old records, especially jazz, R&B, 33/45/78 rpm.

Rod Baum
Rare Records
15 Mt. Vernon St.
Ridgefield Park, NJ 07660
ph: 201-994-0065
rarerecords2000@earthlink.net
http://www.rarerecords2000.com

Don Mennie
P.O. Box 75
Mendham, NJ 07945-0075
ph: 973-543-9520
fax: 973-543-6033
dgmennie@netscape.net
Sells records primarily at shows and on eBay: primarily from 1950 to 1968; 45's, LP's, some 78's; Rock 'N' Roll, R & B, vocal groups, pop music of the era.

Allen Radwill
23 Hunters Lane
Vincentown, NJ 08088-2837
ph: 609-953-5473
radwill1@aol.com
250,000 items related to rock & roll, rhythm & blues, soul, gospel, television, movies: records, sheet music, magazines; no CDs or videos.

Princeton Record Exchange
20 S. Tulane St.
Princeton, NJ 08542
ph: 609-921-0881
info@prex.com
http://www.prex.com
Buys and sells new and used CDs, LPs, and tapes: rock, jazz, alternative, imports, oldies, shows, new releases, soundtracks, classical, opera, etc.

Scott Neuman
Forever Vinyl
P.O. Box 526
Lakehurst, NJ 08733
ph: 732-505-3646
fax: 732-505-5337
sneuman@forevervinyl.com
http://www.forevervinyl.com
Buys, sells, trades rare and hard-to-find vinyl records and albums, 45s picture sleeves; most anything to do with music; over 500,000 items in stock; over 20 years in business; appraise for estate, insurance, etc.

Robert Hess
AAA Music Memorabilia
155 West 72nd St., Ste. 404
New York, NY 10023
ph: 212-579-0689
info@musiccollecting.com
http://www.musiccollecting.com
Buys, sells LP records (33-1/3 rpm), 45 rpm, 78 rpm, jazz, R&B-soul, classical, opera, country, folk, ethnic, spoken word, comedy, big bands,

doo wop, TV-radio, gospel-spirituals, etc.; also related sheet music, books, photos, posters.

Larry Augistover
Augie's 45 RPM Records
P.O. Box 932
Bellmore, NY 11710
vinyl@augiesrecords.com
http://www.augiesrecords.com
Collector and dealer with huge collection of 45 RPM records; Web site is organized by artist name.

Ken Farrell
Just Kids Nostalgia
310 New York Ave.
Huntington, NY 11743
ph: 631-423-8449
info@justkidsnostalgia.com
http://www.justkidsnostalgia.com
Buys and sells vintage records: personality, TV soundtracks, Rock 'n Roll, cartoon, Golden Records, 45s, promotional, EPs, LPs, children's records.

Peter Weldon
Pete's Music
815 2nd Ave.
Troy, NY 12182-2131
ph: 518-235-1318 or 518-235-6795
petesmusic@aol.com
http://www.petes.gemm.com
Sells 45 rpm records and some LPs; also books, vintage paperbacks, VHS, CD, DVD, older collectibles.

Revival Records
2132 Niskayuna Dr.
Niskayuna, NY 12309-4126
revivalrec@aol.com
Mail order record and music business; carries mostly vinyl LPs and 45s.

James Cancilla
D & J Records
212 E. Main St.
Carnegie, PA 15106
ph: 412-279-8888
fax: 412-279-5538
dj-beans@comcast.net
Record collector, dealer, expert; has over 1 million 45s in stock; buys and sells records and CDs from 1940s to present; specializes in doo wop, Northern Soul and Sweet Soul music.

Fred Bohn
Attic Record Store, Inc.
513 Grant Ave.
Pittsburgh, PA 15209-2657
ph: 412-821-8484
fax: 412-821-5179
atticrecords@cs.com
Over 4 million phonograph records in stock; buys collections of 45s, 78s, and LPs; no amount too large.

Jay Notartomaso
Musical Energi
59 N. Main St.
Wilkes Barre, PA 18701
ph: 570-829-2929
fax: 570-829-2929
orders@musicalenergi.com
http://www.musicalenergi.com
Buys and sells CDs, records, tapes, videos, DVDs, and computer games; also large selection of gifts.

Collectables Records
P.O. Box 35
Narberth, PA 19072
ph: 800-336-4627 or 610-649-7650
fax: 610-649-0315
webmaster@oldies.com
http://www.oldies.com
Over 3 million records in stock; 12" and current hits available; mail order with music from 1950s through 1990s.

Ken Clee
P.O. Box 11412
Philadelphia, PA 19111-0412
ph: 215-722-1979
waxntoys@aol.com
http://members.aol.com/waxntoys/main/kidsmeal.htm
Wants to buy 45s in bulk, old store stock, DJ collections or radio station stock; also has 45s for sale.

Mike Landis
P.O. Box 814
Adamstown, PA 19501
ph: 888-248-2291
landis2@ptd.net
Buys and sells 1950s-1960s black vocal groups; call toll free!

Tom Engle
P.O. Box 744
Riverdale, MD 20738-0744
ph: 410-533-1057 or 410-750-3730
deepgroove@comcast.net
Wants to buy jazz, classical LPs, rock 'n' roll, R&B "45s" and LP albums, posters, and related memorabilia.

Steven Smolian
Smolian Sound Preservation Studios
1 Worman's Mill Court #4
Frederick, MD 21701
ph: 301-694-5134
fax: 301-694-5179
smolians@erols.com
http://www.soundsaver.com
Wants large LP and 78rpm collections; classical and jazz music a specialty; also appraises records for donation purposes.

Walter Smith
Memory Lane Records
Newspaper: Record Finder
8508 Sanford Dr.
Richmond, VA 23228
ph: 804-266-1154 or 804-264-0300
fax: 804-264-9660
sales1@recordfinders.com
http://www.recordfinders.com
A monthly newspaper for the record collector: articles, ads, mail-bid

record auctions; also sells record collections on consignment.

Douglas Allen
Bananas Records, Tapes & CDs
2226 16th Ave. N.
Saint Petersburg, FL 33713-5624
ph: 813-327-4616 or 800-823-4113
fax: 813-343-0775
bananagram@aol.com
http://www.musicfinder.com
Over two million out-of-print records, CDs, LPs, 45s, 78s; books on music, sheet music; posters, memorabilia; 7,000 sq. ft. warehouse of records in all categories.

NVI Classical Records
2195 Woods Edge Dr., #4
Memphis, TN 38134
ph: 901-388-4168
fax: 901-377-6875
orders@nviclassical.com
http://www.nviclassical.com
International dealers in rare, out-of-print classical LPs and 78s; mail order and via e-commerce only; also buys collections of classical LPs only.

Jim Petrat
Old & Gold Music Store
jimpetrat@comcast.net
http://www.oldandgold.com
Specializes in vinyl records, picture sleeves, EPs, guitar tabs, song books, posters, electronics, big band, soundtracks, classical, country, jazz, Wop, Pop, R&B.

Dick Rosemont
Flat, Black & Circular
541 E. Grand River
East Lansing, MI 48823
ph: 517-351-0838
Has over 25 years experience buying and selling records.

Shelly G. Callies
4072 Scenic Rd.
Campbellsport, WI 53010
ph: 920-533-5593
Buying records, LPs, 45s, 78s, CDs; also magazines, books, and memorabilia relating to music and musicians; herself a musician collecting many kinds of recorded music, especially jazz.

Dusty Groove America
1180 N. Milwaukee Ave.
Chicago, IL 60622-4019
ph: 888-387-8947 (orders) or 773-342-5800
fax: 773-342-2180
jp@dustygroove.com
http://www.dustygroove.com
Specialist in Jazz, Soul, Funk, Latin, easy listening, Hip Hop, and Brazilian music; online retailer with an extensive array of hard-to-find titles; has a retail outlet in Chicago.

Arlene Levine
Record Ron's Good & Plenty
1129 Decatur St.
New Orleans, LA 70116
ph: 504-524-9444
Pop, jazz, R&B, soul, blues, gospel, oldies, zydeco, comedy, doo wop, Dixieland, big bands, spoken word, Broadway shows, country & western; LPs, 45s, CDs, tapes, sheet music, music memorabilia.

Stan Gold
As Time Goes By
7042 Dartbrook Dr.
Dallas, TX 75240
ph: 972-239-8621 or 214-352-2765
fax: 972-239-9622
record@astimegoesby.com
http://www.astimegoesby.com
Wants all formats from 78s to LPs; 1940s to 1960s jazz, rock and R&B 1950s to 1960s; also exotic/lounge, personalities, picture discs, classical, blues, folk, and related advertisements.

L.R. (Les) Docks
Shellac Shack
P.O. Box 691035
San Antonio, TX 78269-1035
ph: 210-492-6021
fax: 210-492-6489
docks@texas.net
http://docks.home.texas.net
Buying vintage popular records, especially 78's: jazz, blues, hillbilly, pop, rockabilly, etc.; wants list (a 72-page profusely illustrated booklet, including thousands of actual prices paid) for $2 (refundable).

Paula Major
Paula's House of Music
8205 Geneva Ave.
Lubbock, TX 79423-2823
ph: 806-793-0111
fax: 806-793-0111
paula@houseofmusic.com
http://www.houseofmusic.com
Thousands of vinyl albums, 45s and 12" singles from the 1950s to 1980s; specializing in 1950s and 1960s music; worldwide shipping; secure online ordering; in business since 1991; strict Goldmine grading, full money back guarantee.

Randy's Record Shop
157 East 900 S.
Salt Lake City, UT 84111
ph: 801-532-4413
Thousands of LPs, CDs, 45s, cassettes and collectibles.

Paul Bergquist
Vinyl Vendors
1800 S. Robertson Blvd., #279
Los Angeles, CA 90035
ph: 310-275-1444
paul@vinylvendors.com
http://www.vinylvendors.com
Huge selection of vinyl records.

Jerry Bouquard
California Albums
P.O. Box 3426
Los Angeles, CA 90078
ph: 323-461-9806
fax: 914-612-2302
calalbums@earthlink.net
http://www.californiaalbums.com
Well-stocked LP record dealer; 60 categories to browse.

Philip Smith
House of Records
3328 Pico Blvd.
Santa Monica, CA 90405
ph: 310-450-1222
fax: 310-450-5425
info@houseofrecords.com
http://www.houseofrecords.com
Buys, sells, trades new, used and collectible records and CDs.

Edward Odel
Hot Platters
P.O. Box 4213
Thousand Oaks, CA 91359-1213
ph: 805-493-0861
fax: 805-492-3682
HotPlatter@aol.com
http://www.HotPlatters.com
50 searchable categories; LPs, 45s, 78s, CDs, books, 'Zines, reel-to-reel, Elvis, video, sheet music, photos, press kits, posters, cassettes, memorabilia, movie & TV items; new set sale lists monthly, music links.

American Pie
P.O. Box 57347
Sherman Oaks, CA 91413
ph: 818-786-5788 or 888-876-8742 (orders)
fax: 818-786-5790
questions@ampie.com
http://www.ampie.com
Specializing in 1960s and 1960s vinyl; thousands of hard-to-find titles on CD and 45 RPM; every title guaranteed the original recording by the original artist.

Record Man, The
1322 El Camino Real
Redwood City, CA 94063
ph: 650-368-9065
fax: 650-368-2968
recordman@recordman.com
http://www.recordman.com
LPs, 45s, EPs, picture discs, 78s, CDs, cassettes, reel-to-reels, videos, memorabilia, posters, books, magazines, sheet music.

Ed Leimbacher
MisterE Books & Records
1501 Pike Place Market #432
Seattle, WA 98101
ph: 206-622-5182 or 206-463-3986
fax: 206-622-2697
mistere@mistere.com
http://www.wolfenet.com/~mistere
Collector, dealer and expert specializes in vinyl records from all eras; especially looking for great jazz,

blues, R&B, reggae and early Rock to purchase.

Lelan Kuhlmann
M & L Records & Models
6504 Ravenna Ave.
Seattle, WA 98115
ph: 206-522-8189
mlrecmod@halcyon.com
http://www.halcyon.com/mlrecmod
Seattle storefront with an online catalog having over 22,000 LPs and 2,000 models, rare and used.

Experts

James Cancilla
D & J Records
212 E. Main St.
Carnegie, PA 15106
ph: 412-279-8888
fax: 412-279-5538
dj-beans@comcast.net
Record collector, dealer, expert; has over 1 million 45s in stock; buys and sells records and CDs from 1940s to present; specializes in doo wop, Northern Soul and Sweet Soul music.

Paul C. Mawhinney
Record-Rama Sound Archives
1130 Perry Highway
Pines Plaza
Pittsburgh, PA 15237-2132
ph: 412-367-7330
fax: 412-367-7388
recrama@recordrama.com
http://www.recordrama.com
Expert in recorded sound, albums, compact discs, 45 rpm records; search services; DJ supplies, record and disc cleaning supplies, reference material on history of recorded sound; author of "MusicMaster: The 45 RPM Record Directory."

Douglas Allen
Bananas Records, Tapes & CDs
2226 16th Ave. N.
Saint Petersburg, FL 33713-5624
ph: 813-327-4616 or 800-823-4113
fax: 813-343-0775
bananagram@aol.com
http://www.musicfinder.com
Over two million out-of-print records, CDs, LPs, 45s, 78s; books on music, sheet music; posters, memorabilia; 7,000 sq. ft. warehouse of records in all categories.

L.R. (Les) Docks
Shellac Shack
P.O. Box 691035
San Antonio, TX 78269-1035
ph: 210-492-6021
fax: 210-492-6489
docks@texas.net
http://docks.home.texas.net
Author of "American Premium Record Guide" (Books Americana).

John Tefteller
World's Rarest Records, The
P.O. Box 1727
Grants Pass, OR 97528-0200
ph: 800-955-1326 or 541-476-1326
fax: 541-476-3523
teftellr@cdsnet.net
http://www.tefteller.com
Writes "On the Record" column about collectibles records.

Jerry Osborne
Osborne Enterprises
P.O. Box 255
Port Townsend, WA 98368
ph: 360-385-1200
fax: 360-385-6572
jpo@olympus.net
http://www.jerryosborne.com
Author of "The Official Price Guide to Records" (House of Collectibles).

Internet Resources

Brent Gutekunst
Records Universe
P.O. Box 6289
Newport Beach, CA 92658
ph: 949-567-1234
fax: 949-833-7955
http://www.collectors.com
Online collector news, buy and sell, information, auctions, grading & authentication services.

Periodicals

Joel Slotnikoff
Newsletter: 78 Quarterly
P.O. Box 283
Key West, FL 33041
joelslot@bluesworld.com
http://www.bluesworld.com/78QSubs
An English publication; focus is 78 rpm records, particularly blues and jazz.

Stacie Berger
Antique Trader Publications, Inc.
Magazine: DISCoveries
P.O. Box 1050
Dubuque, IA 52004-1050
ph: 800-334-7165 or 800-482-4155
fax: 800-531-0880
stacie.berger@fwpubs.com
http://www.collect.com/discoveries
The record collector's magazine; articles on artists, ads for 10s of thousands of CD's & related music memorabilia from 1930s to present; in-depth coverage of a variety of music, stars, and eras; music memorabilia wanted and for sale.

Stacie Berger
Krause Publications
Magazine: Goldmine
700 E. State St.
Iola, WI 54990-0001
ph: 715-445-2214
fax: 715-445-4087
stacie.berger@fwpubs.com
http://www.krause.com
A biweekly magazine containing articles, ads about records & recording artists from 1940s to present; the record & CD marketplace.

Suppliers

Andy's Record Supplies
48 Colonial Rd.
Providence, RI 02906
ph: 401-421-9453
fax: 401-421-0841
Japanese resealable mylar sleeves, poly sleeves, CD replacement cases, cardboard jackets, mailers, blister packs, storage boxes, cassette replacement cases, white plastic divider cards, quality paper sleeves.

Bags Unlimited
7 Canal St.
Rochester, NY 14608-1910
ph: 800-767-2247 or 716-436-9006
fax: 716-328-8526
info@bagsunlimited.com
http://www.bagsunlimited.com
Sells record collector supplies: poly and paper sleeves, mailers, filler pads, album jackets, storage boxes, divider cards, etc.

Jack Price
Cabco Products
3481 North High St.
Columbus, OH 43214
ph: 614-267-8468 or 614-267-7978
fax: 614-267-8468
jproto1@aol.com
Record collector supplies: replacement sleeves, jackets, covers, boxes, CD supplies, video supplies, storage boxes, frame displays, record holders, etc.

Big Band

Experts

L.R. (Les) Docks
Shellac Shack
P.O. Box 691035
San Antonio, TX 78269-1035
ph: 210-492-6021
fax: 210-492-6489
docks@texas.net
http://docks.home.texas.net
Expert, dealer and avid collector of 1920s-1930s jazz and big band 78s.

Children's

Experts

Peter Muldavin
Kiddie Rekord King
173 W. 78th St., Apt. 5-F
New York, NY 10024-6711
ph: 212-362-9606
fax: 586-314-4091
kiddie78s@aol.com
http://www.kiddierekordking.com
Expert, researcher, seller, collector of vintage Kiddie Records (78s and occasionally 45s); wants to buy any label, any year; should be in original covers; will make cassette recordings of hard-to-find kiddie records; compiling discography.

Computer Programs For
Man./Prod./Dist.

FNProgramvare
Software: CATraxx
Pb 721 Krapfoss
Moss, N-1536 Norway
info@fnprg.com
http://www.fnprg.com/catraxx/catraxx.html
Catalog information about the artist, album title, format, release date, company, label, catalog number, condition, playing time, purchase price, current value, song titles, songwriters, producers, studios, musicians, and instruments.

Cylinder Records

Collectors

Steven Ramm
420 Fitzwater St.
Philadelphia, PA 19147-3109
ph: 610-922-7050 or 610-545-3290
steveramm@aol.com
Specializes in phonographs and pre-1930 records; wants to buy sheet music, postcards, and advertising with illustrations of phonographs, records, or Thomas A. Edison; also wants cylinder rolls in playable condition.

David Giovannoni
ph: 301-869-1501
fax: 301-987-2511
dgio-inquiries@ara.net
http://www.aranet.com/phono/main.htm
Advanced collector of records from 1890s through 1920s: 78s, cylinder records, antique phonograph records.

Gospel

Collectors

Arthur Crowley
207 Hamilton Rd.
Teaneck, NJ 07666-6367
ph: 201-833-0152
arcrow@worldnet.att.net
Wants to buy gospel 78rpm records from the mid 1940s and 1950s on Chess, Downbeat, Gotham, Nashboro, VJ, and other labels.

Jazz & Blues

Clubs/Associations

Dick Peters, Mem.
International Association of Jazz Record Collectors
Journal: IAJRC Journal
12366 Quinlan Ave.
Port Charlotte, FL 33981
admiral@ewol.com
http://www.geocities.com/IAJRC
Promotes exchange of information and research on jazz, its musicians and recordings.

George Buck
George H. Buck Jazz Foundation, The
Newsletter: JazzBeat Magazine
61 French Market Place
New Orleans, LA 70116
ph: 504-525-5000
fax: 504-525-1776
info@jazzology.com
http://www.jazzology.com
Catalog is dedicated to the documentation and preservation of traditional jazz; excellent source for rare recordings from the 1920s and up.

Dealers

Robert Hess
AAA Music Memorabilia
155 West 72nd St., Ste. 404
New York, NY 10023
ph: 212-579-0689
info@musiccollecting.com
http://www.musiccollecting.com
Buys, sells LP records (33-1/3 rpm), 45 rpm, 78 rpm, jazz, R&B-soul, classical, opera, country, folk, ethnic, spoken word, comedy, big bands, doo wop, TV-radio, gospel-spirituals, etc.; also related sheet music, books, photos, posters.

Larry Raye
Cadence Building
Redwood, NY 13679
ph: 315-287-2852
fax: 315-287-2860
cadence@cadencebuilding.com
http://www.cadencebuilding.com
Buys and sells old and new jazz and blues LPs and CDs, books, etc.; handles/distributes over 900 different labels.

Experts

L.R. (Les) Docks
Shellac Shack
P.O. Box 691035
San Antonio, TX 78269-1035
ph: 210-492-6021
fax: 210-492-6489
docks@texas.net
http://docks.home.texas.net
Expert, dealer and avid collector of 1920s-1930s jazz and big band 78s.

Periodicals

Larry Raye
Magazine: Cadence
Cadence Building
Redwood, NY 13679
ph: 315-287-2852
fax: 315-287-2860
cadence@cadencebuilding.com
http://www.cadencebuilding.com
A monthly Jazz & Blues journal featuring interviews, oral histories, news and complete coverage of the entire record scene; the most complete coverage of jazz & blues, improvising music in the world.

Rock 'N' Roll

Collectors

Richard Phillips
Radio Disc-Jockey
Flyer: Rockin' Richard 50's - 60's
  Entertainment Guide
P.O. Box 222
Northford, CT 06472-0222
ph: 203-484-2023
dipdadip@aol.com
*Collectors show (3) hours long (2)
cassettes available for $20 ppd.;
features extremely rare recordings;
guest collectors chat and discuss rare
recordings; make check or money order
to Richard Phillips; list of shows with
first order.*

Dealers

Marc J. Cohen
P.O. Box 100637
Fort Lauderdale, FL 33310-0637
ph: 954-565-9754
*Buys and sells 1950s and early 1960s
rock and roll records: Bill Haley and
His Comets, Chuck Berry, Ricky
Nelson, Coasters, Bobby Darin,
Buddy Holly, Fats Domino, Platters,
Everly Brothers, Drifters, Elvis,
Connie Francis, etc.*

Soundtracks

Dealers

Footlight Records
113 East 12th St.
New York, NY 10003
ph: 212-533-1572
fax: 212-673-1496
footlight1@aol.com
http://www.footlight.com
*Specialty areas are cast recordings,
soundtracks and vocalists.*

Soundtrack Album Retailers
1176 Brownstone Ridge
P.O. Box 487
Soudersburg, PA 17577-0487
ph: 717-351-0847
fax: 717-251-0847
info@soundtrak.com
http://www.soundtrak.com
*Specializes in original cast and film
soundtracks; foreign film scores, film
scores, shows, compilations, original
casts and theatre works.*

Periodicals

Lukas Kendall
Newsletter: Film Score Monthly
8503 Washington Blvd.
Culver City, CA 90232
ph: 310-253-9595
fax: 310-253-9588
lukas@filmscoremonthly.com
http://www.filmscoremonthly.com
*Focuses on original movie
soundtracks.*

Vogue Picture

Collectors

John W. Hess
244 Bernaski Rd.
Amsterdam, NY 12010-7827
ph: 518-843-6117
*Wants to buy Vogue picture disc
records, horn phonographs, music
boxes, roller organs; also wants
parts, empty cabinets, horns; any
condition, any material.*

Bernie Seinberg
1548 Bristol Pk.
c/o AFY
Bensalem, PA 19020
ph: 215-886-6124
fax: 215-638-2265
phonoman-bernie@worldnet.att.net
*Wants to buy picture records, 78 rpm,
from Vogue and Victor; also any
picture records from the 1930s
through 1950s.*

John Widmar
5800 3rd Ave.
Kenosha, WI 53140-4237
ph: 262-654-6802
*Wants to buy Vogue picture records,
45s from the 1950s (Rock 'N Roll,
Rhythm & Blues) and 78s from 1925
to 1935 (jazz, dance); send list of
what you have for site; list label
number, artist, and record speed; all
types of picture records.*

John Coates
324 Woodland Dr.
Stevens Point, WI 54481-9285
ph: 715-341-6113
*Advanced Vogue picture record
collector.*

Experts

John Curry
5702 Parkview Lane
Everett, WA 98203
ph: 425-355-8886
*Author of "Vogue: The Picture
Record."*

Internet Resources

Judi Smith
Association of Vogue Picture Record
  Collectors
P.O. Box 1356
Springfield, MO 65801
info@voguepicturerecords.org
http://www.voguepicturerecords.org
*Online source of information about
Vogue picture records.*

RED CROSS

(see also NURSES)

Collectors

Dick Lavin
2908 Cleave Dr.
Falls Church, VA 22042
ph: 703-533-8402
lavinre@cs.com
*Wants to buy Red Cross medals,
patches, pins, posters, tabs, and sheet
music; please send photo or call.*

Shirley Powers
7964 Sartan Way N.E.
Albuquerque, NM 87109-3128
ph: 505-821-2735
fax: 505-821-0245
powerss@crossnet.org
http://www.collectarc.com
*Expert and collector who documents
American Red Cross pins, posters,
and uniforms; publisher of "The
Collector's Guide to Red Cross Pins"
and "A Guide to American Red Cross
"Uniforms;" collects all types of
American Red Cross memorabilia.*

Experts

Shirley Powers
7964 Sartan Way N.E.
Albuquerque, NM 87109-3128
ph: 505-821-2735
fax: 505-821-0245
powerss@crossnet.org
http://www.collectarc.com
*Expert and collector who documents
American Red Cross pins, posters,
and uniforms; publisher of "The
Collector's Guide to Red Cross Pins"
and "A Guide to American Red Cross
"Uniforms;" collects all types of
American Red Cross memorabilia.*

RED WING POTTERY

(see CERAMICS [AMERICAN],
Stoneware [Red Wing Pottery];
CERAMICS [AMERICAN ART
POTTERY], Red Wing; CERAMICS
[AMERICAN DINNERWARE], Red
Wing)

REDDY KILOWATT

(see ADVERTISING COLLECTIBLES,
Figures [Reddy Kilowatt])

RELICS

(see AMMUNITION & EXPLOSIVE
ORDNANCE; ARCHAEOLOGY;
CIVIL WAR ARTIFACTS; COINS &
CURRENCY; MILITARIA;
RELIGIOUS COLLECTIBLES;
TREASURE HUNTING)

RELIGIOUS COLLECTIBLES

(see also ART, Asian; BIBLES;
JUDAICA; HYMNS; MEDALS,
ORDERS & DECORATIONS;
MORMON ITEMS; STAMP
COLLECTING, Religion Related)

Appraisers

Leon Castner, ISA CAPP
National Appraisal Consultants
P.O. Box 482
Hope, NJ 07844
ph: 800-323-5996 or 908-459-5996
fax: 908-459-4899
castner@garden.net
http://www.nacvalue.com
*Extensive appraisal experience in
valuing stained glass, religious
interiors (churches, seminaries), and
related religious articles for
insurance, charitable contribution, or
claims purposes.*

Alan Winston
Winston Studio & Imports
4448 West Lovers Lane
Dallas, TX 75209
ph: 214-357-0081 or 214-824-2842
fax: 214-821-8583
wsimports@aol.com
http://www.alanwinstonsmith.com
*Specializes in the appraisal of
religious and ecclesiastical arts:
chalices, crosses, wood carving,
sculpture, stained glass, silver and
gold Christian religious objects,
icons, Santos, altar carvings,
rosaries, medals, paintings.*

Clubs/Associations

Emilio C. Botticelli
Foundation International for Restorers of
  Religious Medals
Newsletter: M.A.R.C., The
P.O. Box 2652
Worcester, MA 01603-2652
ph: 508-752-0612
*All types of old religious medals; club
focuses on medal history, values,
varieties, makers, rarity, countries of
origin, etc.*

Collectors

Emilio C. Botticelli
P.O. Box 2652
Worcester, MA 01603-2652
ph: 508-752-0612
*Wants to buy any and all types of old
religious medals in any metal; also
old Vatican medals.*

Jim Osella
216 Cumer Rd.
Canonsburg, PA 15057
ph: 866-873-3735 or 724-746-2451
fax: 724-746-2451
osella@usaor.net
http://www.usedchurchitems.com
*Major collector/dealer of old
traditional religious items: buys and
sells stained glass windows, altars,
statuary, vestments, sacred vessels,
reliquaries, pews, complete interiors
of churches.*

James D. Stambaugh, Dir.
Graham Center Museum
500 East College Ave.
Wheaton, IL 60187-1909
ph: 630-752-5909
fax: 630-752-5916
BGCMus@wheaton.edu
http://www.wheaton.edu/BGC/museum
Evangelism, revival, missions, 19th & 20th century prints & ephemera, postcards, artifacts, anything to do with the advancement of Evangelical Christianity in America.

Greg Spiess
230 E. Washington St.
Joliet, IL 60433-1006
ph: 815-722-5639
fax: 815-722-0171
spiessantq@aol.com
Wants to buy church furnishings, religious stained glass, altars, pews, railings, confessionals, pulpits, baptismals, lighting, architectural renderings and blueprints, stained glass cartoons, furnishings catalogs.

J.A. Higgins
5017 Walnut
Kansas City, MO 64112-2758
ph: 816-931-4095
fax: 816-363-5927
smojer@aol.com
Wants to buy Buddha and Hindu statues.

Ernie Reda
Crosses of Christianity
3997 Latimer Ave.
San Jose, CA 95130-1568
ph: 408-378-7786 or 408-378-4046
http://www.cyberstars.com/crosses
Accepting donation for the future Museum of All Religions; has collection of over 10,000 crosses and thousands of religious items from all over the world; Guiness Book of World Records.

Dealers

Lawrence Skilling
Antique Church Furnishings
Rivernook Farm
Sunnyside
Walton on Thames, Surrey KT12 2ET
  U.K.
ph: 00 44 1932 252736
antchurch@aol.com
http://www.freeride.co.uk/antique-church
A church antiques and architectural salvage business dealing in anything that can be found in a pre-WWII church: fonts, crosses, pews, furniture, etc.

Experts

Lael Bower
6751 School Rd.
Peck, MI 48466
ph: 810-378-5785
Wants to buy Christian and Judaic collectibles; co-author with Penny Forstner of "Guide to Collecting Christian and Judaic Artifacts."

Ann Ball
4726 Creekbend
Houston, TX 77035
ph: 713-526-7171 or 713-721-2981
fax: 713-721-2788
AnnAlert@aol.com
http://www.annball.com
Catholic writer and author; will provide help in identifying Catholic saints and miscellaneous sacramentals in various collectibles and in art; sorry, does not do valuations or appraisals.

Internet Resources

Ecclesiological Society
3 Sycamore Close
Court Rd.
U.K.
fax: +44 (0)20 7213 3181
ecclsoc@aol.com
http://www.ecclsoc.org
For those who love churches; founded in 1839.

Repair Services

Mueller Kaiser Plating Co.
5815 Hampton Ave.
Saint Louis, MO 63109
ph: 314-832-3553
fax: 314-832-3553
tmsk9111@yahoo.com
http://www.Mueller-KaiserPlating.com
Since 1911, fine metal finishing in silver, gold, bronze, copper and brass; flatware, tea services, antiques and church ware including chalices, ciboria, crosses, candelabra, sanctuary lamps, vases, alms basins, flagons, book stands, etc.

Church Pews

Repair Services

Don Mullen
Oak Grove Restorations, Inc.
299B Broad St.
Manchester, CT 06040
ph: 860-646-1951
fax: 860-646-0770
DohnM@aol.com
http://www.nvionline.com/donmullen
Furniture restoration service specializing in church pew restorations; since 1972.

Crosses

Collectors

Ernie Reda
Crosses of Christianity
3997 Latimer Ave.
San Jose, CA 95130-1568
ph: 408-378-7786 or 408-378-4046
http://www.cyberstars.com/crosses
Accepting donation for the future Museum of All Religions; has collection of over 10,000 crosses and thousands of religious items from all over the world; Guiness Book of World Records.

Holy Cards

Clubs/Associations

Chuck Thompson
Psalm Card Collectors & Traders
Newsletter: Psalm Card Collectors,
  Readers & Traders
10802 Greencreek Dr., Ste. 203
Houston, TX 77070-5365
ph: 281-970-0479
chilichuck@chilitech.com
Members focus on collecting the 23rd and others found on greeting cards, pocket cards, postcards, and bookmarks; publishes a directory of collectors twice a year.

Collectors

Fr. Eugene J. Carrella
St. Adalbert Roman Catholic Church
337 Morningstar Rd.
Staten Island, NY 10707
ph: 718-442-8476
fax: 718-727-1241
Eujoe@aol.com
Holy card collector and expert.

Rita Adams
3301 Stratford Hills Lane
Austin, TX 78746
ph: 512-328-6728
fax: 512-328-7274
ritadams@austin.rr.com
Buys and trades old small religious/ holy cards, Catholic or Protestant; serious inquiries only, please.

Experts

Brent Devitt
Saints Unlimited
35 Hawthorn Glen Trail
Dayton, OH 45440-3547
ph: 937-426-5394
Collector, expert, providing online information about collecting both antique and contemporary; Holy cards, Bible Lessons and small paper icons; online images, tips, and links.

Internet Resources

Brent Devitt
Saints Unlimited
35 Hawthorn Glen Trail
Dayton, OH 45440-3547
ph: 937-426-5394
Great Web site for information about devotional cards.

Yvonne Cariveau
Bible Cards
yvonne@cariveau.com
http://www.antiques-oronoco.com
Web site with great information on Holy Cards.

Jehovah's Witnesses

Collectors

Jeffrey Neumann
Bethal-Tower Books
9960 Mt. Eaton
Wadsworth, OH 44281-9028
ph: 330-334-1784
jneuman@neo.rr.com
Wants pre-1930 literature, books,

booklets, magazines, memorabilia relating to Pastor Russell, pre-1940 Watchtower, Tower Publishing, Golden Age, Herald of the Morning, International Bible Students Association, and Jehovah's Witnesses.

Rosaries

Museums/Libraries

Sharon Tiffany, Ex. Dir.
Don Brown Rosary Collection,
  Skamania Interpretive Center
P.O. Box 396
Stevenson, WA 98648
ph: 800-991-2338 or 509-427-5141
fax: 509-427-7429
beadsong@hotmail.com
http://www.rosaryworkshop.com/
  4000Rosaries.htm
The Historical Society interprets the human history surrounding and the natural events that created Columbia Gorge.

REMOTE CONTROL

(see BOATS, Model [Remote Control]; MODELS, Aircraft [Flying]; MODELS, Cars [Remote Control])

REPAIR/RESTORATION/ CONSERVATION

(see also Specialized Repair Services listed within specific categories throughout this Directory.)

Clubs/Associations

Andrea Daley
Association of Restorers & Council of
  Certified Artists
8 Medford Place
New Hartford, NY 13413
ph: 315-733-1952
fax: 315-724-7231
aorcca@adelphia.net
http://www.assoc-restorers.com
An association for repairers and restorers of furniture, ceramics, glass, textiles, etc.; offers one-on-one apprenticeship training programs, seminars, workshops.

John Swahn
International Restorers Guild
515 Lancaster Ave.
Haverford, PA 19041
ph: 610-525-5001
Non-profit organization designed around the needs of the restorer.

British Antique Furniture Restorers'
  Association
The Old Rectory
Warmwell
Dorchester, Dorset DT2 8HQ U.K.
ph: 01 305 854822
fax: 01 305 854822
headoffice@bafra.org.uk
http://www.bafra.org.uk
Foremost national organization of craftspeople concerned with maintaining the highest standards in

the field of antique furniture restoration and conservation.

Internet Resources

Walter Henry
Conservation Online, Stanford University
Libraries
Preservation Dept. University Libraries
Stanford, CA 94305-6004
cool-webmaster@sulmail.stanford.edu
http://palimpsest.stanford.edu
Resources for professionals involved with the conservation of museum, library, and archive materials: documentation, ethics, health & safety, mold, preservation organizations, pest management, suppliers, dictionaries, etc.

Misc. Services

Bruce Hamilton
Wood Finish School, The
P.O. Box 815
West Newbury, MA 01985
ph: 978-363-2638 or 800-439-8774
fax: 978-363-2638
rbruce.hamilton@verizon.net
http://www.thewoodfinishschool.com
A school for wood finishing and restoration.

Andrea Daley
Association of Restorers & Council of
Certified Artists
8 Medford Place
New Hartford, NY 13413
ph: 315-733-1952
fax: 315-724-7231
aorcca@adelphia.net
http://www.assoc-restorers.com
Offers restoration schooling in West Palm Beach, FL: furniture repair and refinishing, antique wood restoration, porcelain/pottery, glass, gilding, caning, claims handling, architectural building repair, oil painting repair, etc.

Janie Curtis
17550 S.E. 85th Place
Ocklawaha, FL 32179
ph: 352-288-3007
Offers classes in repair and restoration of ceramics.

DiAnna Tindell
Tindell's Restoration Schools & Studios
825 Sandburg Place
Nashville, TN 37214
ph: 615-885-1029 or 615-297-7412
fax: 615-391-0712
dianna@tindellsrestorationschools.com
http://
   www.tindellsrestorationschools.com
Offers restorations; also training for the repair of porcelain, crystal, glass, marble, and more.

Allan Koskela
Allan Koskela Restorations
1417 Third St.
Webster City, IA 50595
ph: 515-832-2437
repair@wmtel.net
http://
   restorationmaterials.safeshopper.com
Learn repair for invisible, ultra violet protected restorations on china, pottery, porcelain, bisque, composition, cold casts and ceramics; suitable for majolica, flow blue, Hummel, Lladro, Roseville, Weller, Hull, Royal Doulton, etc.

Allan Koskela
Nationwide Restoration Classes on
Video
1417 Third St.
Webster City, IA 50595
ph: 515-832-2437
repair@wmtel.net
http://
   restorationmaterials.safeshopper.com
Instructional videos available: "Repairing China, Pottery & Porcelain," "Airbrush Basics," "Color-Matching for the Restorer of Pottery & Porcelain," "Paintings: Cleaning & Repair," "Glass Cleaning & Repairing (Audio Tape)."

Gerlinde M. Kornmesser
China Mending & Restoration Course
1705 Glenview Rd.
Glenview, IL 60025
ph: 847-724-3059
fax: 847-724-3060
gkrestoration@yahoo.com
http://www.gkrestoration.com
China mending and restoration course; instructor on the campus of Lawrence University, Appleton, WI; practicing restorer and AIC member Gerlinde M. Kornmesser is successor to Morla Tsossen, founder and developer of the course.

Valorie Hays
School of Conservation Restoration
P.O. Box 55
Marietta, OK 73448
ph: 580-275-5834
t.hays@worldnet.att.net
Specializes in conservation restoration (invisible without overcoating) of ceramics including china, pottery and porcelain; offers classes in conservation restoration.

Shirley Vickers
Shirley Vickers School of China
Restoration
P.O. Box 688
Pine, AZ 85544-0688
ph: 928-476-3703
fax: 928-476-3703
shirley@shirleyvickers.com
http://www.shirleyvickers.com
Course lasts 7 to 8 days for those wishing to go into the repair business; also suited for collectors and dealers; restore chips, cracks, missing parts,

using airbrush art, learn to match colors and glazes.

Periodicals

Bob Flexner, Ed.
McCloskey Communications, Inc.
Magazine: Professional Refinishing
P.O. Box 306
Woodland Hills, CA 91365
ph: 818-715-9776
fax: 818-715-9059
main@ProRefinishing.com
http://www.ProRefinishing.com
Glossy, full color magazine for the wood restoration industry; how-to, ads, supplies, tools, etc.

Repair Services

Leon Trefler
Trefler & Sons Antique Restoring
Studio, Inc.
99 Cabot St.
Needham, MA 02494
ph: 781-444-2685
fax: 781-444-0659
trefler@trefler.com
http://www.trefler.com
Specializes in the repair and conservation of art objects: ceramics, paintings, furniture, frames, crystal, porcelain, marble, ivory, cloisonne, metals, jade, etc.

Georgiana Nedelcu
Universal Fine Art Conservation
267 Derby Ave.
Orange, CT 06477-1319
ph: 203-795-8849
fax: 203-795-8278
georgiana.nedelcu@snet.net
http://www.sculptdirect.com
Restoration of art, antiques, porcelain, gold leaf frames, marble statuary, oil paintings, wooden objects and carvings; insurance claims; sculptor on staff.

Patricia Little
Restorations by Patricia
420 Centre St.
Nutley, NJ 07110
ph: 973-235-0234 or 973-235-0732
patriciaA44@aol.com
Specialty in restoring religious statuary; also proficient in ceramics, china, pottery, porcelain, sculptures; recommended by Hummel/Goebel, G. Armani, Archdiocese of Newark, NJ, Dept. 56, Austin Galleries.

Ronald L. Aiello
Antique Restorations
1313 Mt. Holly Rd.
Burlington, NJ 08016-3773
ph: 609-387-2587
fax: 609-747-9340
ronaiello@comcast.net
Repairs and restores china, porcelain, pottery, dolls, objets d'art; specializes in professional repairs to figurines: Character and Toby Jugs, Lambeth, Burslem, Kingsware, stoneware, Flambe, etc.; 24 years full-time experience.

Lada Sultanova
Hess Restorations
200 Park Ave. South, #1514
New York, NY 10003-1503
ph: 212-260-2255
fax: 212-979-1143
hessrestorations@hotmail.com
Expert restorers of antiques since 1945; highly recommended by museums and leading galleries; proficient in the repair of porcelain, crystal, silver, ivory, wood, ceramics, paintings, sculptures, jewelry, lamps.

Walter C. Kahn, PE
1017 Constable Dr., S.
Mamaroneck, NY 10543-4702
ph: 914-381-3200
fax: 914-381-3200
Professional restoration of porcelain, china, glass, and pottery; also jade and ivory carvings and object d'art since 1972; life member of ASM, TMA, ASME, and SNDT.

Jim & Sylvia Sheehan
J & S Invisible Repairs
35 Leonard St.
Glens Falls, NY 12801
ph: 518-796-0132
fax: 518-745-5934
jsir@jandsinvisiblerepairs.com
http://www.jandsinvisiblerepairs.com
Furniture repair and restoration experts; specializes in the fields of transit, fire, and water damage repairs; on-site inspections/repairs conducted in upstate New York, Vermont, and Western Massachusetts.

Len Paradise, CR
Loss Recovery Systems, Inc.
10 Dwight Park Dr.
Syracuse, NY 13209-1029
ph: 315-451-9111 or 315-451-9299
fax: 315-451-9222
mparadi1@twcny.rr.com
http://www.ascr.org/ny/lrs.htm
Certified Restorer #94; repairs, cleans and restores following fire and flood loss, tree loss, smoke damage, structural collapse, etc.

Richard Michael Gramly, PhD
Great Lakes Artifact Repository
79 Perry St.
Buffalo, NY 14203-3037
ph: 716-849-0149
fax: 716-852-0093
Stores, sells, and conserves artifacts from all parts of the world in a secure, fireproof, climate-controlled working room and vault; examining room with drafting and photographic facilities; cataloguing of incoming collections, etc.

Philip Redman
Redman Restoration
2242 Cedar Rd.
York, PA 17404-4150
ph: 717-767-4003
Specializes in restoring collectibles.

Mark S. Powell
A. Ludwig Klein & Son, Inc.
683 Sumneytown Pike
P.O. Box 145
Harleysville, PA 19438
ph: 215-256-9004 or 800-379-2929
fax: 215-256-9644
mark@aludwigklein.com
http://www.aludwigklein.com
*Specializing in the repair and
restoration of all types of glass, china
and porcelain as well as ivory, jade,
brass, pewter.*

David Sim
Nonomura Studios
3432 Connecticut Ave. NW
Washington, DC 20008-1308
ph: 202-363-4025
fax: 202-244-1541
*Specializes in Korean, Japanese,
Chinese antiques; restores china,
glassware, screens, scrolls, ivory,
paintings, jade, lamps, etc.*

Sidney Williston
Mario's Conservation Services
1738 14th St. NW
Washington, DC 20009-4309
ph: 202-234-5795
*Restorers/conservators of decorative
arts objects: china, glass, plaster,
lacquer, metal, ivory, icons, frames,
gold leaf, glass grinding and drilling.*

Richard Kornemann
Museum Shop, Ltd.
20 N. Market St.
Frederick, MD 21701
ph: 301-695-0424
fax: 301-698-5242
fineartmuseum@erols.com
http://www.museumsholptd.com
*Highly-recommended conservator of
oils, paper (etchings, lithographs,
engravings, maps), icons, Oriental
art, photos, 23k gold leaf, etc.*

Joseph Howell
Pleasant Valley Restoration
1725 Reed Rd.
Knoxville, MD 21758-1118
ph: 301-432-6022
fax: 301-432-2721
jhowell371@aol.com
*Restoration, cleaning, and consulta-
tion services for china, glass,
porcelain, marble, ivory, and other
objets d'art; fine art and antique
repair; custom color matching and air
brushing.*

Mildred R. Shepherd
Shepherd Studio
5527 Third St., South
Arlington, VA 22204-1115
ph: 703-671-1789
JohnMilShep@aol.com
*Since 1970, conservation/restoration
of art objects; specializing in
porcelain, glass, pottery, plaster,
stoneware, ivory, jade; for private
clients and museums.*

Gordon Ponsford
Ponsford, Ltd.
2405 Highway 92
Acworth, GA 30102
ph: 770-924-4848
fax: 770-529-2278
ponsford@bellsouth.net
http://www.antiqueconservation.com
*Largest conservation group in the
Southwest; 14 of the finest experts
available in their respective fields
working in one studio; Ponsford has
worked with government pieces,
museum collections, private collectors,
family heirlooms.*

DiAnna Tindell
DiAnna Tindell's Restoration School
825 Sandburg Place
Nashville, TN 37214
ph: 615-885-1029 or 615-297-7412
fax: 615-391-0712
dianna@tindellsrestorationschools.com
http://
   www.tindellsrestorationschools.com
*Offers restorations; also training for
the repair of porcelain, crystal, glass,
marble, and more.*

Adrienne Kreinberg
Dunhill Restorations
2309 Lee Rd.
Cleveland, OH 44118-3413
ph: 216-291-1771
Restores porcelain figurines, etc.

Douglas A. Eisele
Old World Restorations, Inc.
5729 Dragon Way
Cincinnati, OH 45227
ph: 513-271-5459
fax: 513-271-5418
info@oldworldrestorations.com
http://www.oldworldrestorations.com
*Fine restoration and conservation of
paintings, porcelain, glass, china, art
pottery, metals, crystal, frames, ivory,
gold leaf, photographs, etc.;
nationwide service; free estimates; call
or write for more information and
brochures.*

Dan & Judy Landino
D & J Restorations
37037 E. Almont
Sterling Heights, MI 48310
ph: 810-268-8692
djlrest@comcast.net
http://www.dnjauctions.com
*Over 35 years experience in
restoration of antiques: from carousel
figures and antique furniture to soda
machines and license plates.*

Michael Fisher
Fisher's Furniture
9791 East Crain Hill Rd.
Traverse City, MI 49684
ph: 231-932-8676
fax: 231-932-8676
mfisher@traverse.net
*Offers complete claim handling, repair
service, including property damage,
in-home repairs, complete furniture
restoration, and a wide range of third*

*party services; serves Michigan's
northern half of the Lower Peninsula.*

Allan Koskela
Allan Koskela Restorations
1417 Third St.
Webster City, IA 50595
ph: 515-832-2437
repair@wmtel.net
http://
   restorationmaterials.safeshopper.com
*Repairs most natural materials: ivory,
jade, quartz, onyx, malachite, marble,
lapis, gemstones; also carvings,
figures, art objects, sculpture, clock
cases; scientific color matching
system; also conducts classes.*

Susan Johnson
Furniture Doctor, The
4465 Harbor Lane
Minneapolis, MN 55446
ph: 612-557-6519
fax: 612-557-6573
*Repairs all periods of furniture,
antiques and household items.*

Melinda Lockwood
Lockwood Refinishing & Restoration
7700 North Highway V v
Columbia, MO 65202
ph: 573-442-7109
fax: 573-449-9400
yankeeclipper@socket.net
http://www.lockwoodrefinishing.com
*Offers restoration and refinishing of
antique as well as contemporary
furniture; seat caning and rushing;
faux finishing service available;
handles moving claims.*

John Edward Cunningham
Fine Art Restoration
1525 E. Berkley
Springfield, MO 65804-3203
ph: 417-889-7702
*Restoration artist; porcelains, ivory,
jade, gold leaf, oil paintings, and
frames; registered Boehm and Royal
Worcester restorer.*

Suzy Lytle
Broken Arts Restoration
2739 Gladstone
Dallas, TX 75211-5206
ph: 214-331-6706 or 877-643-1121 pin
   #0869
brokenarts@sbcglobal.net
http://www.brokenarts.com
*Restores and repairs antique,
collectible, and heirloom objects:
Roseville, Lladro, Meissen, crystal,
glass, marble, cloisonne, gold leaf,
pottery, ceramics, gilded frames,
mother of pearl, lamp repair, etc.*

Ron Leatherman
Leatherman Services
509 Mairo
Austin, TX 78748
ph: 512-282-1556 or 512-799-7871
fax: 512-282-1562
ron@kdi.com
*Restores marble, granite, miscella-
neous stone, plaster and wood art
objects, ornate picture frames,*

*obsolete ceramic or porcelain tile; 25
years experience.*

Andrew A. Alden
LEGACY Art Restorations & Design
   International, Inc.
4221 North 16th St.
Phoenix, AZ 85016
ph: 602-263-5178
fax: 602-263-6009
restoration@legacyintlinc.com
http://www.legacyintlinc.com/main.html
*Specializes in the restoration and
conservation of paintings, porcelain,
ivory, marble, glass and jade.*

Billie Coleman
China & Crystal Clinic
1808 N. Scottsdale Rd.
Tempe, AZ 85281-1515
ph: 480-945-5510 or 602-478-7857
fax: 480-945-1079
billiecoleman@earthlink.net
http://www.chinaandcrystalclinic.com
*Repairs porcelain, crystal, jade,
pottery, dolls, clocks, Hummels,
Lladros, etc.*

Mary B. Steffen
Wilderness Sculptures
1421 West Basin Ave.
Pahrump, NV 89041-4500
ph: 775-751-8582
finearts@air-internet.com
*Restores porcelain, oil paintings,
lamps, furniture, frames, glass, metal
objects, wood sculptures, and jewelry.*

Mary Brooks-Steffen
Fine Art Restoration
1421 W. Basin Ave.
Pahrump, NV 89060-4500
ph: 775-751-8582
finearts@air-internet.com
*Repairs, restores, conserves porcelain,
ceramics, wood, enamels, and metals.*

Dr. Lawrence Vescera
Pick Up the Pieces
711 West 17th St., Unit C-12
Costa Mesa, CA 92627-4334
ph: 714-645-9953 or 800-934-9278
fax: 714-645-8381
putp@occc.com
*Repairs many types of materials
including porcelain, glass, crystal
collectibles, figurines, ceramics,
marble, enamels, ivory, alabaster,
antiques and paintings.*

Bonhams & Butterfields Restoration
   Department
220 San Bruno Ave.
San Francisco, CA 94103
ph: 415-861-7500 or 800-223-2854
fax: 415-861-8951
info.US@butterfields.com
http://www.butterfields.com
*Services include repair, restoration
and refinishing of furniture and
decorative arts: marquetry &
parquetry, veneer, carved wood
furniture, bronzes, ceramics,
porcelain.*

Janet Connolly
Venerable Classics
645 Fourth St., Ste. 208
Santa Rosa, CA 95404-4435
ph: 707-575-3626 or 800-531-2891
fax: 707-575-4913
venerable@prodigy.net
http://www.venerableclassics.com
Restoration of porcelain, ceramics, ivory, jade, marble, Dresden lace figurines, and other fragile objects.

Dolores Schwalb
Bluebird Gallery & Art Restoration
1263 N. Riverside, Ste. 4
Medford, OR 97501
ph: 541-773-7698
Specializes in the restoration, cleaning and repair of oil paintings; cleans, repair, conserves works on paper; also restores frames and ceramics.

Juergen Berndt
Auction Team Breker
Bonner Str. 528-530
Koln, D-50968 Germany
ph: 49 221 387049 or 941-925-0385 (US Rep)
fax: 49 221 374878
auction@breker.com
http://www.breker.com
Specializes in the repair and restoration of antique mechanical devices such as typewriters, calculators, telephones, telegraphs, sewing machines, etc.; a specialty is the repair of cast iron cracks.

Sarah Peek
Conservation of Ceramics, Glass & Enamels
The Battery House
Petworth House
Petworth, West Sussex GU28 0AN U.K.
ph: +44(0) 1798 342 763
conservation@sarahpeek.co.uk
http://www.sarahpeek.co.uk
Dedicated to the quality conservation and restoration of objects in terms of their future preservation; pottery, stoneware, enamels, bone china, porcelain, terracotta, earthenware, glass.

Raymond Konyn
Antique Restorations
Brasted Forge
Brasted
Brasted, Kent U.K. TN16 1JL
ph: +44 (0) 1959 563863
fax: +44 (0) 1959 561262
antique@antique-restorations.org.uk
http://www.antique-restorations.sorg.uk
Offers a complete range of antique and fine art services; from furniture restoration and conservation to solutions for preserving your art collections and other valuables.

Steve Christy
Christy Restorations
The Oast Hurst Farm
Mountain St.
Chilham, Kent CT4 8DH U.K.
ph: 01227-730924 or 01304-613585
fax: 01304-613585
steve@christyantiques.co.uk
http://www.christyantiques.co.uk
Offers restoration of antiques by skilled craftsmen; from minor repairs to full restorations.

Suppliers

Charles Lockwood
Finish it Right
7700 North Highway V v
Columbia, MO 65202
ph: 573-442-7109
fax: 573-449-9400
yankeeclipper@socket.net
http://www.finishitright.com
Sells finishing supplies for the professional or the do-it-yourselfer: stain, finish, hardware, caning supplies, advice for completing projects; also sells business start-up "kits" for those wanting to refinish professionally.

Archival Supplies For

(see also ANTIQUES DEALERS & COLLECTORS, Supplies For)

Suppliers

John Dunphy, Mkrtng.
University Products, Inc.
517 Main St.
P.O. Box 101
Holyoke, MA 01041-0101
ph: 413-532-3372 or 800-336-4847
fax: 800-532-9281
jadunphy@universityproducts.com
http://www.universityproducts.com
Carries safe products for the long term storage of postcards, posters, stamps, documents, photographs, textiles, costumes; acid-free archival supplies, and materials for conservation and preservation; send for free catalog.

John Coutu
Rising Paper Co., Division of Fox River
295 Park St.
P.O. Box 565
Housatonic, MA 01236-0565
ph: 413-274-3345
fax: 413-274-6684
General line of archival supplies including mat boards, framing and photographic supplies, mounting boards.

Bill Cole Enterprises, Inc.
P.O. Box 60
Randolph, MA 02368-0060
ph: 781-986-2653
fax: 781-986-2656
bcemylar@cwbusiness.com
http://www.bcemylar.com
Preservation supplies for comics, movie posters/stills, paperback books, sports cards, magazines, maps,

currency, newspapers, legal documents, animation cels, phonograph records; archival repair and cleaning supplies.

Nielsen & Bainbridge
17 S. Middlesex Ave.
Cranbury, NJ 08512
ph: 609-395-5550 or 800-927-8227
info@nielsen-bainbridge.com
http://www.nielsen-bainbridge.com
General line of archival supplies including mat boards, document storage boxes, framing and photographic supplies.

TALAS
568 Broadway
New York, NY 10012-3225
ph: 212-219-0770
fax: 212-219-0735
info@talasonline.com
http://www.talasonline.com
Archival supplies for artists, restorers, collectors, bookbinders, conservators, calligraphers, museums, vintage clothing restorers, archives, libraries, etc.

Robert H. Snyder
Cohasco, Inc. - Document Preservation Center
P.O. Drawer 821
Yonkers, NY 10702-0821
ph: 914-476-8500
fax: 914-476-8573
info@cohascodpc.com
http://www.cohascodpc.com
Sells acid-free products: protectors, boxes, tissues, tapes, wrapping paper, paste, board, and various types of binders.

Light Impressions
P.O. Box 22708
Rochester, NY 14692-2708
ph: 800-828-6216
fax: 800-828-5539
LiWebsite@limpressions.com
http://www.lightimpressionsdirect.com
General line of archival supplies including mat boards, document storage boxes, framing, ephemera storage and photographic supplies.

Brodart Company - Library Supplies
P.O. Box 3037
Williamsport, PA 17705
ph: 800-820-4377 or 570-769-3265
fax: 800-283-6087
SusanWinterle@brodart.com
http://www.brodart.com
Offers a comprehensive catalog of library and archival products, from acid-free folders to open shelving systems.

Kathy Hollinger
Conservation Resources International
8000 H Forbes Place
Springfield, VA 22151
ph: 703-321-7730 or 800-634-6932
fax: 703-321-0629
criusa@conservationresources.com
http://www.conservationresources.com
Archival supplies for works of art on

paper; document and photographic storage materials; chemicals; conservation tools; environmental monitoring supplies.

Hollinger Corporation
P.O. Box 8360
Fredericksburg, VA 22404
ph: 800-634-0491 or 540-898-7300
fax: 800-947-8814
hollingercorp@erols.com
http://www.hollingercorp.com
Archival supplies for storing works of art on paper, textiles, quilts and stamps; document and photographic storage materials; a variety of boxes, envelopes, folders, tubes, wrappers, labels, tapes, insert plastic sleeves, etc.; since 1945.

Metal Edge, Inc.
6340 Bandini Blvd.
Los Angeles, CA 90040
ph: 800-862-2228 or 213-721-7800
fax: 888-822-6938
mtledge@ix.netcom.com
http://www.metaledgeinc.com
Archival boxes, storage supplies, document cases, acid-free tissue, print folders, acid-free tissue, UV light filters, deacidification sprays, hygrometers, etc.

Art

Clubs/Associations

American Institute for Conservation of Historic & Artistic Works
Directory: AIC Directory
1717 K St. NW, Ste. 200
Washington, DC 20006
ph: 202-452-9545
fax: 202-452-9328
info@aic-faic.org
http://aic.stanford.edu
Purpose is to advance the knowledge, practice of the conservation of cultural property; the "Guide" lists conservators who are Fellows and Professional Associates of the AIC in paper, textiles, photographs, paintings, furniture, etc.

Misc. Services

Canadian Conservation Institute
Newsletter: CCI Newsletter
1030 Innes Rd.
Ottawa, Ontario K1A OM5 Canada
ph: 613-998-3721
fax: 613-998-4721
cci-icc_services@pch.gc.ca
http://www.cci-icc.gc.ca
Created in 1972 to promote the proper care and preservation of Canada's cultural heritage; works with Canadian museums and other cultural institutions to conserve and restore works of art & artifacts; scientific analysis, testing available.

Repair Services

Northeast Document Conservation Center
100 Brickstone Square
Andover, MA 01810-1494
ph: 978-470-1010
fax: 978-475-6021
nedcc@nedcc.org
http://www.nedcc.org
Paper and art on paper conservation, preservation microfilming, photo-graphic duplication, photograph conservation, book conservation, disaster assistance.

Peter Kostoulakos
Peter Kostoulakos Fine Art
15 Sayles St.
Lowell, MA 01851-1625
ph: 978-453-8888
peter@pkart.com
http://www.pkart.com
Conservation of oil paintings on canvas or solid supports; oil paintings cleaned and restored; by appointment.

Henry Lie
Center for Conservation & Technical Studies, The
Harvard University
32 Quincy St.
Cambridge, MA 02138
ph: 617-495-2392
Provides conservation and restoration services for fine arts, including works of art on paper, paintings, objects and sculpture.

Leon Trefler
Trefler & Sons Antique Restoring Studio, Inc.
99 Cabot St.
Needham, MA 02494
ph: 781-444-2685
fax: 781-444-0659
trefler@trefler.com
http://www.trefler.com
Cleaning and restoration of tears, punctures; also restores frames.

BD Mattozzi, Inc., Fine Art Restoration & Conservation
142 High St., Ste. 513
Portland, ME 04101
ph: 207-871-1678
fax: 207-871-1678
BDMattozzi@aol.com
Offers painting restoration and conservation.

John Squadra
Fine Art Restoration
93 Knowlton Rd.
Brooks, ME 04921
ph: 207-722-3464
fax: 207-722-3475
Specializes in the restoration of oil paintings; will send a written estimate from a photo of your damaged painting; upon approval, will UPS a wooden crate to you for shipment; work guaranteed.

Georgiana Nedelcu
Universal Fine Art Conservation
267 Derby Ave.
Orange, CT 06477-1319
ph: 203-795-8849
fax: 203-795-8278
georgiana.nedelcu@snet.net
http://www.sculptdirect.com
Restoration of art, antiques, porcelain, gold leaf frames, marble statuary, oil paintings, wooden objects and carvings; insurance claims; sculptor on staff.

Oscar & Debra Perez
Vigues Art Studio
54 Flanders Rd.
Woodbury, CT 06798-2103
ph: 203-263-4088
fax: 203-266-9118
viguesart@aol.com
Conservation, restoration of oil paintings (cleaning, lining, touch up and repair), frames (gold leaf repairs, casting of missing parts) and paper (cleaning, repairs of prints, documents); also porcelain & china repair.

Jill Pratzon
122 W. 26th St., Rm. 1006
New York, NY 10001-6804
ph: 212-807-7066
jpratzon@earthlink.net
Specializes in the restoration, cleaning, relining, repair of 19th and 20th century paintings; extensive knowledge in the field of original illustration art.

Brad Shar
Lowy
223 East 80th St.
New York, NY 10021
ph: 212-861-8585
fax: 212-988-0443
bshar@lowyonline.com
http://www.lowyonline.com
Specializes in buying and selling antique frames; also offers fine art conservation and restoration services.

Appelbaum & Himmelstein
444 Central Park West
New York, NY 10025
ph: 212-666-4630
fax: 212-316-1039
aandh@mindspring.com
Treats silk textiles, paintings and objects.

Leonard E. Sasso
21 Salem Lane
South Salem, NY 10590
ph: 914-248-8289
Master restorer of oil paintings & water colors; all periods; American, European, Old Masters; over 25 years experience; references available.

Sydney L. Germansky
Europa Master Gallery
16 A Lafayette Ave.
Suffern, NY 10901-5406
ph: 914-368-2707
Restorers of art, fine antiques, antique jewelry, old photographs.

Alexander Katlan
Alexander Katlan Conservation Inc.
56 - 38 Main St.
Flushing, NY 11355-5046
ph: 718-445-7458
fax: 718-445-7458
Conservation of paintings and panels, both European and American; author of "American Artists' Materials, Vol I: Suppliers Directory, 19th C." (Noyes Press 1987), and "Vol. II: A Guide to Stretchers, Panels, Millboards & Stencil Marks."

James Martin
Marmargar
32 Maple St.
Broadalbin, NY 12025
ph: 518-883-3354 or 518-866-9181
mmartin5@nycap.rr.com
Appraises, repairs, restores, conserves all fine art: canvas, paper and mixed medium; all work is museum quality and fully insured; member of the ISA and the American Institute for Conservation of Historic & Artistic Works (AIC).

Romayne Shay McMahon, ISA
Veronique's Antiques
124 S. Market St.
Mechanicsburg, PA 17055-6329
ph: 717-697-4924

Maria Pukownik
Fine Art & Paper Conservation
1045 Orrtanna Rd.
Orrtanna, PA 17353-9691
ph: 717-337-0668
conspuk@yahoo.com
Cleaning, old varnish removal, consolidation of flaking paint, relining, structural reinforcement of wooden panels, retouching, revarnishing.

Bob Porter
A. Ludwig Klein & Son, Inc.
683 Sumneytown Pike
P.O. Box 145
Harleysville, PA 19438
ph: 215-256-9004 or 800-379-2929
fax: 215-256-9644
bob@aludwigklein.com
http://www.aludwigklein.com
Specializing in the repair and restoration of all types of glass, china and porcelain as well as ivory, jade, brass, pewter.

Roy & Lois Blankenship
Blankenship Fine Art
P.O. Box 7221
Wilmington, DE 19803
ph: 302-529-1184
RoyBlankenship@aol.com
http://www.royblankenship.com
Offers professional restoration of fine paintings.

Justine S. Wimsatt
Wimsatt & Associates Art Conservation Studio, Inc.
4230 Howard Ave.
Kensington, MD 20895-2418
ph: 301-493-4250
fax: 301-493-9563
justine@artconservation.com
http://www.artconservation.com
For 20 years has provided profes-sional restoration of paintings, murals, icons, frames and related objects.

H.I. Gates
118 E. Church St.
Frederick, MD 21701-5404
ph: 301-663-3717
fax: 301-663-5961
samurai_gates@yahoo.com
Conservator of paintings.

Margaret Bardwell
Bardwell Conservation, Ltd.
11373 Park Dr.
Fairfax, VA 22030
ph: 703-385-8451
Conservation and restoration of paintings executed on canvas, metal or wood (including icons); also frames and small painted furniture.

Mark Wittl
Virginia Art Conservation & Restoration
7181 Bent Mountain Rd.
Roanoke, VA 24018
ph: 540-776-1740
mark@va-art.com
http://www.va-art.com
Provides specialized services in the conservation and restoration of easel paintings (principally oil paintings on canvas) for individuals, galleries, small museums or insurance companies.

Bryan Guarnieri
Animation & Fine Art Galleries
University Mall
201 S. Estes Dr.
Chapel Hill, NC 27514
ph: 919-968-8008
fax: 919-968-8064
bryan@animationandfineart.com
http://www.animationandfineart.com
Fine art, paintings, drawings, sculptures, and prints experts, dealers and appraisers; also offers repair services.

Luke Biggs
L. L. Biggs Conservator
P.O. Box 3091
Summerville, SC 29484-3091
ph: 843-851-9293
fax: 843-873-0165
biggsconservator@msn.com
Appraises and restores fine art and frames.

William Gordon
Gordon's Fine Art
5665 Highway 9, Ste. 103
Alpharetta, GA 30004
ph: 678-777-9034
fax: 770-569-1255
bill@gordonsfineart.com
http://www.gordonsfineart.com
Cleans and restores oil and acrylic paintings.

Chris Carpenter
Renaissance Group Inc., The
P.O. Box 9283
Tampa, FL 33674
ph: 813-238-0617
fax: 813-238-0617
RensGrpInc@aol.com
Specializes in the cleaning, stabilizing, and restoration of oil paintings; also specializes in the sale of old master paintings.

Bondstreet Gallery
870 Sixth Ave. S.
Naples, FL 34102
ph: 941-430-0039
fax: 941-430-4368
Certified Member of the International Society of Appraisers; Certified, Professional Picture Framers Association; specializing in appraising fine art; restoration services, conservation services.

Antique & Art Restoration By Wiebold
413 Terrace Place
Terrace Park, OH 45174-1164
ph: 513-831-2541 or 800-321-2541
fax: 513-831-2815
wiebold@eos.net
http://www.wiebold.com
Expert restoration of oil paintings, frames, mirrors, wooden artifacts, ivory, antiquities, etc.

Cornelia & Marcel Iclozan
Fine Arts Conservation
821 Ridge Rd.
Wilmette, IL 60091
ph: 847-256-8595
finearts@attbi.com
http://www.restorationlab.com
Restoration and conservation of oil paintings on canvas and panel, watercolor, pastel, polychrome sculptures, icons, art objects.

Heather Becker, VP
Chicago Conservation Center
730 N. Franklin
Chicago, IL 60610
ph: 312-944-5401
fax: 312-944-5479
chicagoconservation@yahoo.com
http://www.chicagoconservation.com
Restoration and conservation of paintings.

John Edward Cunningham
Fine Art Restoration
1525 E. Berkley
Springfield, MO 65804-3203
ph: 417-889-7702
Restoration artist; porcelains, ivory, jade, gold leaf, oil paintings, and frames; registered Boehm and Royal Worcester restorer.

Art Restorations, Inc.
7803 Inwood Rd.
Dallas, TX 75209
ph: 214-350-0811
epoxylady@aol.com
Professional restoration of porcelains, ceramics, crystal, paintings (cleaning, lining, mending), frames (reconstruction, gold leaf, custom finishes), metal objects, plating, marble, lacquer ware, cloisonne, ivory, tortoise, etc.

Anne W. Zanikos
Anne W. Zanikos Art Conservation
1023 Shook ave.
San Antonio, TX 78212
ph: 210-828-1925
fax: 210-828-1925
Offers conservation services for works of art.

Cheryl Carrabba
Carrabba Conservation, Inc.
2700 W. Anderson Ln., Ste. 512
Austin, TX 78757-1132
ph: 512-452-5880
fax: 512-452-6112
cherylc@io.com
Offers restoration and conservation services for fine artworks.

Scott M. Haskins
Fine Art Conservation Laboratories
P.O. Box 23557
Santa Barbara, CA 93121
ph: 805-564-3438
fax: 805-568-1178
Specializes in the preservation of paintings, murals, works of art on paper and period frames.

Carol Carney
Gainsborough Products Company
281 Lafayette Cir.
Lafayette, CA 94549-4316
ph: 925-283-4187 or 800-227-2186
fax: 925-283-3343
Service@gainsboroughproducts.com
http://www.gainsboroughproducts.com
Complete line of oil painting restoration supplies since 1974, including manual cleaning solvents, varnish removers, lining compound, putty, canvas, ultraviolet lights as

well as professional restoration services & classes.

Dolores Schwalb
Bluebird Gallery & Art Restoration
1263 N. Riverside, Ste. 4
Medford, OR 97501
ph: 541-773-7698
Specializes in the restoration, cleaning and repair of oil paintings; cleans, repair, conserves works on paper; also restores frames and ceramics.

Alan Pedel
Oil Paintings Restored
Guineaford
Barnstaple, Devonshire EX31 4EA U.K.
fax: 011-44-1271-322514
webmaster@paintingsrestored.com
http://www.paintingsrestored.com
London-trained professional oil painting restorer; based in Devonshire but commissions accepted from all over the United Kingdom as well as from overseas.

Suppliers

Carol Carney
Gainsborough Products Company
281 Lafayette Cir.
Lafayette, CA 94549-4316
ph: 925-283-4187 or 800-227-2186
fax: 925-283-3343
Service@gainsboroughproducts.com
http://www.gainsboroughproducts.com
Complete line of oil painting restoration supplies since 1974, including manual cleaning solvents, varnish removers, lining compound, putty, canvas, ultraviolet lights as well as professional restoration services & classes.

Cane & Basketry

Internet Resources

WeaveNet
P.O. Box 67
Warner, NH 03278-0067
ph: 603-938-2137
peter@83j.com
http://www.weavenet.com
This Web site provides a complete source of basketry, weaving and caning information; restoration supplies, ash strips, chair cane, dyes, patterns, raffia, seagrass, weaving guilds and associations, etc.

Repair Services

Bruce & Katherine Kreymborg
Bruce H. Kreymborg Furniture Repair
1659 North Sea Rd.
Southampton, NY 11968
ph: 631-283-5330
fax: 631-283-5845
BruceHKreymborg@aol.com
http://
www.brucehkreymborg.freeservers.com
Does all varieties of chair seat caning & weaving.

Susan Dilworth
Iron Bridge Farm Antiques
2953 Appleton Rd.
Elkton, MD 21921-2176
ph: 410-398-0954

Morris Wubbels
2812 170th St.
New Sharon, IA 50207-8067
ph: 641-632-8238
ewubbels@kdsi.net
Experienced cane seat weaving with 14 patterns.

Mickey Johnson
Mickey's Chair Caning
233 Byrnes Dr.
Waterloo, IA 50701
ph: 319-232-5934
mlj091554@aol.com
Specializes in antique/modern caning and rush seating; over 20 years in business; also sells caning supplies.

Louise Herriott
Dallas Caning
3816 Elfland
Dallas, TX 75229
ph: 214-850-1491
fax: 214-850-7529
herriott@airmail.net
Specializes in hand and prewoven caning repairs.

Suppliers

K.C. Parkinson
Connecticut Cane & Reed Co.
P.O. Box 762
Manchester, CT 06045
ph: 860-646-6586 or 800-227-8498
fax: 860-649-2221
canereed@ntplx.net
http://www.caneandreed.com
Largest selection of materials and books; source for cane, wicker and basket supplies; all types of materials to reseat a chair.

H.H. Perkins Co.
22 Universal Dr.
North Haven, CT 06473
ph: 800-462-6660 or 203-787-1123
fax: 203-787-1161
HPerkinsco@hhperkins.com
http://www.hhperkins.com
Oldest and largest importer and distributor of fine rattan products: basketry supplies and accessories, seat weaving supplies and accessories, furniture repair and restoration products.

Lilian Cummings
Canecraft
RD 1 Box 126-A (Rte 443)
Andreas, PA 18211-9784
ph: 570-386-2441
Sells cane, reed and rushing material for seating chairs, making baskets, and repairing wicker furniture; also instruction books.

Paige W. Beasley
Carolina Caning Supply
111 Fairfax Lane
Cary, NC 27513
ph: 800-346-0142 or 919-467-7773
Chair caning and repair supplies.

Peerless Rattan
5605 West National Rd.
Springfield, OH 45504-3220
ph: 937-882-9389
fax: 937-882-9389
hcribbs@woh.rr.com
http://www.peerlessrattan.com
*Source for cane, wicker, splints, fiber
rush, seagrass, and basket supplies.*

WSI Distributors - Antique Restoration
Supplies
405 N. Main St.
Saint Charles, MO 63301-2034
ph: 800-447-9974 or 636-946-5811
fax: 636-946-5832
talk2us@wsidistributors.com
http://www.wsidistributors.com
*Wholesale source for furniture &
trunk hardware, cane & weaving
materials, fiber chair seats, veneer,
wood ornaments, Zap glues, and much
more; over 1200 items for professional
furniture restorers. Sorry, dealers
only.*

Cane & Basket Supply Co.
1283 S. Cochran Ave.
Los Angeles, CA 90019
ph: 323-939-9644 or 800-468-3966
fax: 323-939-7237
cabasu@2cowherd.net
http://www.2cowherd.net/cabasu
*Source for cane, wicker and basket
supplies.*

Michael Frank
Frank's Cane & Rush Supply
7252 Heil Ave.
Huntington Beach, CA 92647
ph: 714-847-0707
fax: 717-843-5645
mfrank@franksupply.com
http://www.franksupply.com
*Carries high quality natural seat
weaving supplies.*

Ceramics

Appraisers

Sharon Niles
Carousel, Inc.
14409 Manchester Rd.
Ballwin, MO 63011
ph: 636-391-4900
fax: 636-391-3993
carouselinc@hotmail.com
*Specializes in the appraisal,
conservation and restoration of fine
porcelains.*

Repair Services

Sharon Smith Abbott
Fine Wares Restoration
P.O. Box 753
Bridgton, ME 04009-0753
ph: 207-647-2093
sharonsmithabbott@yahoo.net
*Restores ceramic & glass art objects
for private collectors and museums;
references of museum clients on
request.*

Christine Peltier
CP Restoration
6 South 3rd Ave.
Taftville, CT 06380-1428
ph: 860-886-1870 or 800-882-1870
fax: 860-887-9097
cprest@snet.net
http://www.cprestoration.com
*Restores damaged china or porcelain
based on severity of damage and
method of repair - not on the value of
the article.*

Oscar & Debra Perez
Vigues Art Studio
54 Flanders Rd.
Woodbury, CT 06798-2103
ph: 203-263-4088
fax: 203-266-9118
viguesart@aol.com
*Conservation, restoration of oil
paintings (cleaning, lining, touch up
and repair), frames (gold leaf repairs,
casting of missing parts) and paper
(cleaning, repairs of prints,
documents); also porcelain & china
repair.*

Patricia Little
Restorations by Patricia
420 Centre St.
Nutley, NJ 07110
ph: 973-235-0234 or 973-235-0732
patriciaA44@aol.com
*Specialty in restoring religious
statuary; also proficient in ceramics,
china, pottery, porcelain, sculptures;
recommended by Hummel/Goebel, G.
Armani, Archdiocese of Newark, NJ,
Dept. 56, Austin Galleries.*

Ronald L. Aiello
Antique Restorations
1313 Mt. Holly Rd.
Burlington, NJ 08016-3773
ph: 609-387-2587
fax: 609-747-9340
ronaiello@comcast.net
*Repairs and restores china, porcelain,
pottery, dolls, objets d'art; specializes
in professional repairs to figurines:
Character and Toby Jugs, Lambeth,
Burslem, Kingsware, stoneware,
Flambe, etc.; 24 years full-time
experience.*

Jonathan Mark Gershen
Jonathan Mark Gershen Porcelain,
Pottery & Glass Restoration
1463 Pennington Rd.
Ewing, NJ 08618-2656
ph: 609-882-9417
fax: 609-530-0660
*Second generation restorer and long
time member of the AIC; clients
include museums, collectors and
dealers worldwide; free brochure
available upon request.*

Jareth Holub
Ceramic Restorations, Inc.
224 W. 29th St., 12th Floor
New York, NY 10001
ph: 212-564-8669
fax: 212-843-3742
DMarekJHolub@netzero.net
*Specializes in the restoration &
conservation of ceramics (porcelain,
terracotta, bisque, etc.); over 20 yrs.
experience; everything from
Precolumbian to Art Pottery; also
marble, jade, ivory, cloisonne, tortoise
shell; free estimates.*

Hans J. Schindhelm
Ceramic Restorations of Westchester,
Inc.
8 John Walsh Blvd., Ste. 412
Peekskill, NY 10566
ph: 914-734-8410
fax: 914-762-1719
siegmar@aol.com
http://www.swiftsite.com/hummel-
preciousmoments/repair.html
*Repair and restoration service for any
brand of porcelain and ceramic
collectibles, antiques and art objects;
specializing in Precious Moments and
Hummels; also Disney, Cybis, Boehm,
Hutschenreuther, Rosenthal and
others.*

Fredi W. Boese
M.I. Hummel Restoration
P.O. Box 933
Harriman, NY 10926
ph: 845-783-4438
fax: 845-783-4438
fredi@frediboese.com
http://www.frediboese.com
*One of the country's leading restorers
of fine porcelain and art; 38 years
experience as a master M.I. Hummel
artist.*

Roger J. Krokey
Terra Nouva Restorations
38 Cedar Heights Rd.
Rhinebeck, NY 12572
ph: 914-876-3753
*Located 100 miles north of New York
City; complete restoration of ceramic
items.*

Christine Reynolds
P.O. Box 3440
Glens Falls, NY 12801
ph: 518-743-9416
*Restoration of all objects made of a
ceramic material such as china,*

*porcelain, pottery; in business for over
25 years.*

Mark Ninemire
Collector's Clinic
1209 Milton Ave.
Syracuse, NY 13204
ph: 315-488-1225
fax: 315-488-1225
mnpn@prodigy.net
*Specializes in the restoration and
repair of bisque, porcelain, cold cast
figurines, plaster/gypsum, Hummels,
Roseville, Royal Doulton, Lladro,
Moorcroft, etc.*

Romayne Shay McMahon, ISA
Veronique's Antiques
124 S. Market St.
Mechanicsburg, PA 17055-6329
ph: 717-697-4924

Grady Stewart
Grady Stewart Expert Porcelain
Restorations
2019 Sansom St.
Philadelphia, PA 19103-4416
ph: 215-567-2888
*Offering repairs for museums, dealers,
collectors; highest quality repairs of
fine porcelain, pottery, and stoneware.*

Bill Eberhardt
Harry A. Eberhardt & Son
2010 Walnut St.
Philadelphia, PA 19103-5608
ph: 215-568-4144
artfix@magpage.com
http://www.eberhardts.com
*America's oldest repair firm:
porcelain, glass, Orientalia, etc.*

Mark S. Powell
A. Ludwig Klein & Son, Inc.
683 Sumneytown Pike
P.O. Box 145
Harleysville, PA 19438
ph: 215-256-9004 or 800-379-2929
fax: 215-256-9644
mark@aludwigklein.com
http://www.aludwigklein.com
*Specializing in the repair and
restoration of all types of glass, china
and porcelain as well as ivory, jade,
brass, pewter.*

Sidney Williston
Mario's Conservation Services
1738 14th St. NW
Washington, DC 20009-4309
ph: 202-234-5795
*Restorers/conservators of decorative
arts objects: china, glass, plaster,
lacquer, metal, ivory, icons, frames,
gold leaf, glass grinding and drilling.*

R. Foster Holcombe
Art of Fire at Chaerie Farm
7901 Hawkins Creamery Rd.
Gaithersburg, MD 20882-3507
ph: 301-253-6642 or 800-639-6979
comments@artoffire.com
http://www.artoffire.com
*Offers glass blowing services; makes
replacement glass liners for silver*

*pieces; also porcelain and pottery
restorations.*

Mary Landess
Mary Landess Restorations
3102 Beverly Rd.
Baltimore, MD 21214
ph: 410-319-8684 or 410-267-7708
fax: 410-269-5909
marylandess@msn.com
*Repairs porcelain, pottery, chins and
some glass; will mend broken parts
together, make missing parts, and
match colors using quality materials
from England.*

Joseph Howell
Pleasant Valley Restoration
1725 Reed Rd.
Knoxville, MD 21758-1118
ph: 301-432-6022
fax: 301-432-2721
jhowell371@aol.com
*Restoration, cleaning, and consulta-
tion services for china, glass,
porcelain, marble, ivory, and other
objets d'art; fine art and antique
repair; custom color matching and air
brushing.*

Mildred R. Shepherd
Shepherd Studio
5527 Third St., South
Arlington, VA 22204-1115
ph: 703-671-1789
JohnMilShep@aol.com
*Since 1970, conservation/restoration
of art objects; specializing in
porcelain, glass, pottery, plaster,
stoneware, ivory, jade; for private
clients and museums.*

McHugh's Restoration Inc.
3461 W. Cary St.
Richmond, VA 232221
ph: 804-353-9596 or 804-353-9412
mchughs@aol.com
*China mending and restoration
service; repairs chips, cracks, and
fabricates missing pieces; Boehm
restorer; official Lladro and Hummel
restorer; also official restorers of
Swarovski Crystal & Thomas
Blackshear pieces produced by Willits.*

Dona Danziger
Clay Werks, Ltd.
4058 S. Main St.
P.O. Box 352
Exmore, VA 23350
ph: 757-414-0567
fax: 757-414-0571
info@claywerksltd.com
http://www.claywerksltd.com
*Acquired skills working for Boehm,
Goebel and the Franklin Mint;
restorations of all types of fine
porcelain and art pottery; specializes
in Hummels; missing parts made; fully
insured.*

Richard Beggs
Pottery Restoration
9553 White Trail Trail
Kernersville, NC 27284-8741
ph: 336-595-2753 or 336-993-6971
rtbeg@webtv.net
*Specializing in invisible restoration of
all types of ceramics, especially
American art pottery, e.g., Rookwood,
Weller, Roseville, Hull; also cookie
jars and Fiestaware.*

Gordon Ponsford
Ponsford, Ltd.
2405 Highway 92
Acworth, GA 30102
ph: 770-924-4848
fax: 770-529-2278
ponsford@bellsouth.net
http://www.antiqueconservation.com
*Largest conservation group in the
Southwest; 14 of the finest experts
available in their respective fields
working in one studio; Ponsford has
worked with government pieces,
museum collections, private collectors,
family heirlooms.*

Sharon Richford
147 Michigan Ave.
Daytona Beach, FL 32114-3297
ph: 386-239-0939
fax: 386-252-1700
srich4d@bellsouth.net
*Repair of porcelain, pottery, crockery,
chalkware, cement lawn ornaments,
statuary, etc.*

Jody Leak
Leak Enterprises
12500 SE Highway 301
Belleview, FL 34420-4410
ph: 352-245-8862
fax: 352-245-8862
jleak@leakenterprises.com
http://www.leakenterprises.com
*Specializing in the restoration of
objets d'art, either antique or
contemporary including Lladro,
Boehm, Cybis, Hummel, Meissen,
Orientalia, and all quality porcelain
and ceramics.*

Donna Riddick
Little River Restorations
3816 Wildwood Rd.
Maryville, TN 37804
ph: 865-977-9058
*Specializes in the repair of ceramics,
pottery, china, and figurines.*

Tice Goodson
985 Williams St.
Batesville, MS 38606
ph: 662-563-3051

Sharon Schlesinger
Sharlan Restorations
23111 Fairmont Blvd.
Cleveland, OH 44122
ph: 216-464-3434
shar2trvl@hotmail.com
http://www.rtantiques.com/sharlan.htm
Specializes in the restoration and

*repair of china, porcelain and pottery
collectibles.*

Antique & Art Restoration By Wiebold
413 Terrace Place
Terrace Park, OH 45174-1164
ph: 513-831-2541 or 800-321-2541
fax: 513-831-2815
wiebold@eos.net
http://www.wiebold.com
*Restoration of all types of art pottery,
fine porcelain, ceramics, glass,
crystal, sculpture, antiquities, etc.*

Anne R. Hackmann
Hackmann Restoration Services
2550 Kodiak Dr.
East Lansing, MI 48823-7208
ph: 517-351-2011
fax: 517-337-7234
stanhack1@juno.com
*Offers museum quality repair and
restoration of antiques and ceramic
art objects; specializing in Boehm and
Stangl birds; please call or write
before shipping.*

Clare Erickson
Auntie Clare's Doll Hospital Shop
2543 Seppela Blvd., N
North Saint Paul, MN 55109-3016
ph: 651-770-7522
clare@antieclares.com
http://www.antieclares.com
*Offers professional restorations of
dolls, bears, animals and plush,
figurines and statues.*

Corey & Jo Ann Keller
Keller China Restoration
4825 Windsor Dr.
Rapid City, SD 57702-0125
ph: 605-342-6756
kellerchina@rapidnet.com
http://kellerchina.rapidnet.com
*Professional repair of cracks, chips
and missing parts on antique china,
porcelain, dolls, Hummels, and
porcelain lace; authorized restorers
for the Lladro Society.*

Larry Crawford
North Plains Restoration
313 12 Ave. SW
Minot, ND 58701
ph: 701-838-5876
digitim@minot.ndak.net
*Pottery and porcelain restoration in
American Art Pottery; dedicated to
maintaining the integrity of antique
pottery and porcelain.*

William & Michelle Marhoefer
Broken Art Restoration
1841 West Chicago Ave.
Chicago, IL 60622-5513
ph: 312-226-8200 or 815-472-3900
fax: 815-472-3930
*Museum quality invisible repair
specializing in the professional
restoration of porcelain, pottery,
ceramics, wood, ivory, stone, art
objects; Chicago Institute Masters
Degree, qualified restorers since 1980;
call for shipping instructions.*

Mary Dillon
Mary's Porcelain & Pottery Restorations
Albany Park
Chicago, IL 60625
ph: 773-478-0994
marysrepairs@webtv.net
http://www.marysrepairs.com
*Expert, experienced work in
restoration of porcelain, pottery,
ceramics, lamps, chandeliers, object
d'art, antiques, collectibles; ship by
U.P.S.*

Sisel Langenstein
Bric-A-Brac, Inc.
ph: 504-284-1130
langenst@bellsouth.net
*Repairs porcelain figurines, vases,
objets d'art; broken pieces are fitted
together with epoxy; new pieces are
fabricated where needed; artists match
original color and patterns; crystal
objects can also be repaired including
grinding rims.*

Valorie Hays
School of Conservation Restoration
P.O. Box 55
Marietta, OK 73448
ph: 580-275-5834
t.hays@worldnet.att.net
*Specializes in conservation restoration
(invisible without overcoating) of
ceramics including china, pottery and
porcelain; offers classes in conservation restoration.*

Dale B. Peterson
Claremore Restoration Service
22762 Woodridge Dr.
Claremore, OK 74017
ph: 918-341-5475
cpeters2@mail.com
http://www.geocities.com/cdpet1
*Restoration service for pottery,
porcelain, ceramics and some glass;
uses invisible repair techniques; also
Lladro, Kay Finch, Brayton, Sequoia
and other collectibles and art glass.*

Linda Norris
Antique Restoration
1304 W. Virginia St.
Mc Kinney, TX 75069
ph: 972-529-2614
*Specializes in the repair and
restoration of fine pottery, porcelain,
and figurines.*

Nadia Wassef
303 Detering
Houston, TX 77007
ph: 713-880-0108
fax: 713-880-3544
nfwassef@msn.com
*Does stained glass, crystal and
porcelain repair; email or snail mail
photos to find out about restoration
possibilities; repair and return ship.*

Michael Blair
Restorations by Michael, Inc.
P.O. Box 387
Golden, CO 80403-0387
ph: 303-384-9121
mblair5028@aol.com
*Repairs glass and ceramics art such
as figurines.*

Sue Thiessen
25115 Cemetery Rd.
Middleton, ID 83644-5103
ph: 208-585-3243
*Specializing in restoring model
horses, Roseville, and other pottery;
also collector of Hagen Renaker horse
and animal figurines.*

Billie Coleman
China & Crystal Clinic
1808 N. Scottsdale Rd.
Tempe, AZ 85281-1515
ph: 480-945-5510 or 602-478-7857
fax: 480-945-1079
billiecoleman@earthlink.net
http://www.chinaandcrystalclinic.com
*Repairs porcelain, crystal, jade,
pottery, dolls, clocks, Hummels,
Lladros, etc.*

Andy Goldschmidt
Ceramicare
P.O. Box 1812
Corrales, NM 87048
ph: 505-898-2728
agoldschmidt@earthlink.net
http://home.earthlink.net/~agoldschmidt/
wizzg.html
*Repairs and restores ceramic art;
specializing in Native American Indian
pottery - prehistoric, historic and
contemporary.*

Casey Reed
Material Culture
1727 Dietz Plaza, NW
Albuquerque, NM 87107
ph: 505-344-8492
fax: 505-344-8492
Casey@material-insight.com
http://www.material-insight.com/
PuebloPotteryRestoration.htm
*Conservation and restoration of
Pueblo pottery; application of
traditional and unique methodologies
to preserve the past; also collects and
appraises Pueblo pottery.*

Cheleen Morgan
Antiques, Etc.
1270 Autumn Wind Way
Henderson, NV 89012
ph: 702-270-9910
*Specializing in museum-quality
restorations of pottery, porcelain,
china, ceramics and hand painted
items.*

Mark J. Dorian
Mark's China-Pottery
756 W. Pico Ave.
Fresno, CA 93705-1009
ph: 559-225-2261

Janet Connolly
Venerable Classics
645 Fourth St., Ste. 208
Santa Rosa, CA 95404-4435
ph: 707-575-3626 or 800-531-2891
fax: 707-575-4913
venerable@prodigy.net
http://www.venerableclassics.com
*Restoration of porcelain, ceramics,
ivory, jade, marble, Dresden lace
figurines, and other fragile objects.*

Dolores Schwalb
Bluebird Gallery & Art Restoration
1263 N. Riverside, Ste. 4
Medford, OR 97501
ph: 541-773-7698
*Specializes in the restoration, cleaning
and repair of oil paintings; cleans,
repair, conserves works on paper; also
restores frames and ceramics.*

Suppliers

Restorite Systems
P.O. Box 7096
West Trenton, NJ 08628-0096
ph: 609-530-1526
*Products for restoration and
conservation of porcelain, pottery, and
glass; sells a complete kit for
repairing breaks and chips; also
"How-to" videos available; send for
free catalog.*

Allan Koskela
Allan Koskela Restorations
1417 Third St.
Webster City, IA 50595
ph: 515-832-2437
repair@wmtel.net
http://
restorationmaterials.safeshopper.com
*Sells repair supplies including fillers,
glazes, lacquers, resins and cleaners;
no heat needed; how-to video,
"Repairing Pottery & Porcelain"
recommended by Harry L. Rinker;
restoration classes 6 times a year,
with glueless repairing.*

Figurines

(see REPAIR/RESTORATION/
CONSERVATION; REPAIR/
RESTORATION/CONSERVATION,
Ceramics)

Furniture

(see also HARDWARE; REPAIR/
RESTORATION/CONSERVATION,
Woodworking; WOOD; Repair
Services listed under REPAIR/
RESTORATION/CONSERVATION
and within other specific categories
throughout this Directory)

Experts

Lew Larason
2 E. Butler Ave.
Chalfont, PA 18914-3014
*Writes syndicated antique furniture
repair column.*

Man./Prod./Dist.

Minuteman Furniture Restoration
  Systems & Supplies
115 North Monroe St.
Waterloo, WI 53594-1124
ph: 800-733-1776
fax: 920-478-3966
*Free catalog features complete line of
wholesale furniture restoration
supplies, systems and equipment.*

Repair Services

Leon Trefler
Trefler & Sons Antique Restoring
  Studio, Inc.
99 Cabot St.
Needham, MA 02494
ph: 781-444-2685
fax: 781-444-0659
trefler@trefler.com
http://www.trefler.com
*Repair, restoration, conservation of
all furniture; specializing in all hand
finish work, custom color matching
and preserving original finishes.*

Robert Wiley
Restorations by Lord Robert
43 Prospect St.
Contoocook, NH 03229
ph: 603-746-6490
fax: 603-746-4920
Bwlordrobert@aol.com
*Complete furniture repair and
restoration for wooden and
upholstered furniture; also specializing in leather and vinyl repair.*

Don Mullen
Oak Grove Restorations, Inc.
299B Broad St.
Manchester, CT 06040
ph: 860-646-1951
fax: 860-646-0770
DohnM@aol.com
http://www.nvionline.com/donmullen
*Furniture restoration service
specializing in church pew restorations; since 1972.*

Dan Manning
Manning Claim Services
P.O. Box 212
Allendale, NJ 07401
ph: 201-825-8450 or 201-805-0577
fax: 201-825-8301
*Specializing in cargo claims handling,
and furniture and antiques repair
services.*

Wayne R. Batten
Cats Meow, The
303 Landing St.
Lumberton, NJ 08048
ph: 609-267-5953 or 609-714-9495
fax: 609-267-2477
*High quality furniture restorations
and custom lacquering on period to
modern fine furniture.*

Eric Saperstein
Artisans of the Valley
103 Corrine Dr.
Pennington, NJ 08534
ph: 609-737-9364 or 609-637-0450
fax: 609-637-0452
woodworkers@artisansofthevalley.com
http://www.artisansofthevalley.com
*Maker of quality period reproduction
furniture; also offers antique
restoration services including finish
and carving restoration.*

Brian Stair
Oxford Restoration, LLC
1916 Park Ave., Ste. 611
New York, NY 10037
ph: 212-860-0410
fax: 212-860-0140
briandstair@yahoo.com
*Formerly of Sotheby's Restoration,
offers quality furniture restoration
services.*

Bruce & Katherine Kreymborg
Bruce H. Kreymborg Furniture Repair
1659 North Sea Rd.
Southampton, NY 11968
ph: 631-283-5330
fax: 631-283-5845
BruceHKreymborg@aol.com
http://
  www.brucehkreymborg.freeservers.com
*Five professionals restoring furniture
and all items made of wood.*

Gus Hoogers
Furniture Care of Rochester NY
45 Southcross Trail
Fairport, NY 14450
ph: 585-482-4480 or 585-729-5734
fax: 585-425-7125
ghoogers@aol.com
*Old World craftsman specializing in
the repair and restoration of fine
furniture; full service shop with access
to many specialized services.*

Tom Barr
Community Woodworks
225 Julian Woods Lane
Julian, PA 16844
ph: 814-355-4592
fax: 814-355-4592
tcb1000@hotmail.com
*A full service furniture repair and
restoration company in business for
over 22 years; inspections and repairs
for the moving industry, insurance,
retail furniture industry; also custom
restorations and spot repairs for the
public.*

Andrew Gelinas
Burlesque Repair Service
18 W. 3rd. St.
Bethlehem, PA 18015-1222
ph: 610-867-3313 or 610-867-1665
fax: 610-867-4999
BurlesqueRep@enter.net
*Specializing in cargo claims handling
and repair services for moving,
insurance, retail companies; full shop
facilities; over 30 years experience.*

John Swahn
Niki Francis Furniture Restoration
515 Lancaster Ave.
Haverford, PA 19041
ph: 610-525-5001
fax: 610-581-7377
Specializing in furniture restoration.

David A. Glassberg
At the Shop Furniture Service
52 St. Rd.
Newtown Square, PA 19073
ph: 610-240-4822 or 877-SHOPGY2
fax: 610-240-3822
attheshop@msn.com
http://www.thefurnitureguy.com
A specialist in antique restoration and repair; furniture, breakables, frames.

Joseph Miller
Joseph Miller Furniture Restoration
4811 Catharpin Rd.
Gainesville, VA 20155
ph: 703-754-7598
fax: 703-754-3955
furnfoto@aol.com
Refinishing, repairing, caning.

Gene Shontere
Shontere Restoration, Inc.
P.O. Box 1805
Bowie, MD 20717-1805
ph: 301-753-6051
fax: 301-743-2128
shontere@erols.com
Specializing in furniture restoration of all types; complete insurance and transit claims service.

Bob Neiderlander
Yesteryear Antique Farms Inc.
7420 Hawkins Creamery Rd.
Gaithersburg, MD 20882-3206
ph: 301-948-3979
Repairs and restores new and antique furniture.

John Pyle
Glade Valley Furniture Repair
10464 Glade Rd.
Walkersville, MD 21793-9715
ph: 301-898-3795
fax: 301-898-3795
gvfr@xecu.net
Moving claims service.

Steve Rogowsky
Frederick Refinishing Center
P.O. Box 111
Woodsboro, MD 21798-0111
Commercial and residential furniture and antiques; repairs, refinishing, restorations, touch-up; water/fire/ moving damage claim work.

Peter C. Grygotis
BearTrace Furniture Works
30 Butler Rd.
Fredericksburg, VA 22405-2332
ph: 540-899-3166
fax: 540-899-9080
beartrace@aol.com
Furniture restoration, stripping, refinishing, repairs, resilvering, veneering, caning.

Bill Kala
Transportation Related Services of
  Virginia
154 Mountain Laurel Court
Fredericksburg, VA 22406
ph: 540-752-7546 or 540-752-7599
fax: 540-752-7599
Kala7546@msn.com
Offers claims services for household goods and residence damage to include inspections and repairs; also millwork, touch-up and refurbishing for churches and commercial establishments.

Bill Ivey
William Ivey Fine Furniture Ltd.
2710 W. Cary St.
Richmond, VA 23220
ph: 804-358-7545
Conservation, restoration and design of furniture.

Walter Hanger
Transit Claims Services
1128 Pechin Ave.
Roanoke, VA 24013
ph: 540-342-9392
fax: 540-342-9392
TransitClaims@aol.com
Over 20 years serving the moving industry and homeowners in repairing, refinishing and restoration.

Dwight E. Foster
Foster Bros.
1757 West Beverley St.
P.O. Box 1834
Staunton, VA 24402
ph: 540-885-1794
fax: 540-885-1795
Over 20 years experience in wood working, refinishing, and restoration of existing finishes.

Thomas E. McGarry
Birnam Wood Joinery, The
302 N. Mildred St.
Charles Town, WV 25414-1834
ph: 304-728-0373 or 800-700-5959
fax: 304-728-0373
tom@benchmadefurniture.com
http://www.benchmadefurniture.com
Specializes in the restoration of antiques including woven chairs of all kinds; restorations done by hand and restored to period appearance; custom reproductions of country styles from 1740-1840 made to standards of the originals.

Martin O'Brien
Martin O'Brien Cabinetmaker
606 N. Trade St.
Winston Salem, NC 27101
ph: 3336-773-1334
martin@martinobriencabinetmaker.com
http://
  www.martinobriencabinetmaker.com
Offers design, construction and conservation of furniture, musical instruments and other wooden objects; carving, turning, gilding, French polishing, surface cleaning of painted and varnished surfaces, color

matching, museum quality reproductions.

Larry Hinshaw
Custom Restorations, Inc.
3230-L Piper Lane
P.O. Box 19881
Charlotte, NC 28208
ph: 704-357-9929
fax: 704-357-0560
CustomerService@custom-restorations.com
http://www.custom-restorations.com
Quality furniture repair, restoration and refinishing; online catalog of restoration supplies.

Restoration Center
P.O. Box 988
Danielsville, GA 30633
ph: 800-332-2747
fax: 800-332-2017
Use their Hot Line to contact an authorized Restoration Center specialist for moving damage claims, insurance casualty damages, furniture manufacturers and distributors, adjusters, relocation departments, retailers, corporations.

James Braun
Braun Restoration Specialties
216 W. 42nd St.
Savannah, GA 31401
ph: 912-232-6482
Braun.Restoration@sysconn.com
Specializes in crystal glass grinding and polishing and in wood restoration.

Robert K. Kelly
Restoration, Ltd.
420 Bonaventure Rd.
Savannah, GA 31404
ph: 912-236-6910
fax: 912-897-2585
redowood@aol.com
Damage claims inspections, touch-ups, Member of the Claims Prevention & Procedure Council, Hot Line member.

Dick Adams, ISA CAPP
Specialists of the South, Inc.
544 East Sixth St.
Panama City, FL 32401-3066
ph: 850-785-2577
fax: 850-872-8662
dickadams@knology.net
Specializing in furniture restorations & repairs, upholstery, refinishing; designated restoration center for northwest Florida; repairs for individuals, and the moving and insurance industries; also repairs rugs, porcelain, glass, silver.

Richard Raines
Furniture Medic of Broward/Palm Beach
FL
3725 Hollywood Blvd.
Hollywood, FL 33021
ph: 954-981-9663
fax: 954-981-9663
Furnituremedic@hotmail.com
Furniture restoration and repair: burn-ins, scratches, dents, broken

chairs, broken legs, nail polish damage, fire and water damage, pet damage; moving claims, insurance, estimates, Furniture Medic.

Jack Craig
Craig's Limited Inc.
3595 N. Dixie Hwy #6
Boca Raton, FL 33431-5936
ph: 531-367-0096
Antique & fine furniture restoration, stripping, refinishing, repair; over 20 years experience; licensed and insured; free phone estimates.

James Cole
Elberta,, AL 26530
jac111@gulftel.com
ph: 251-986-3972
Offers furniture restoration including leather, gilding, French polishing; also custom reproductions.

Blake Soule'
Soule' Furniture Restorations, Inc.
5145 Raleigh LaGrange Rd., Ste. 102
Memphis, TN 38134
ph: 901-377-3646
fax: 901-377-3615
FurnitureRestoration@soule.com
http://www.FurnitureRestoration.net
Specializes in furniture repair: on site spot repair, fire and water damage, moving damage, office furniture refinishing and touch up, antique restorations, retail stores.

Jim & Helen Roose
Mt. Pleasant Restoration Shop
Township Rd. 100, House #222
P.O. Box 245
Mount Pleasant, OH 43939
ph: 740-769-7565
Furniture repair, hand stripping, refinishing, caning, custom millwork, furniture made to order; over 28 years experience.

Bob Kovach
201 W. Alyea St.
P.O. Box 522
Hebron, IN 46341-0522
ph: 219-996-2924
kvchfaith@netscape.net
Antique restorations, veneer work, wicker repair.

Michelle Schultz, ISA
Guaranteed Furniture Services Inc.
3380 West Eleven Mile Rd.
Berkley, MI 48072
ph: 248-545-1130 or 248-393-1705
fax: 248-545-1163
michelle@guaranteedfurniture.net
Furniture and contents appraisals, repairs, restorations; appraisals for estate, donations, liquidation, trust, divorce; extensive background in loss of value determination as a result of fire, water, transit damage; ISA Accredited Member.

Bill Witkowski
Michigan Antique Preservation Co., Inc.
2034 Eureka Rd.
Wyandotte, MI 48192
ph: 734-283-5700
fax: 734-283-4312
mapco@wyan.org
Furniture conservators; repair and restoration of everyday furniture as well as fine antiques; member of American Institute for Conservation.

Robert Thomas
Furniture Medic #1791
2177 Avon Industrial Dr.
Rochester, MI 48309
ph: 248-853-9886
fax: 248-853-2959
The Thomas family has been in the furniture industry since 1989; experienced in the repair, restoration, and conservation of all wooden furniture.

David Colglazier
Original Woodworks
4631 Lake Ave.
Saint Paul, MN 55110
ph: 651-429-2222
orgwood@iaxs.net
http://www.originalwoodworks.com
A full service shop specializing in wooden antique restorations including furniture and architectural elements requiring extensive restoration and repairs, especially veneers; by appointment only.

Kevin Southwick
Southwick Furniture Conservation Co.
3640 33rd Ave. S.
Minneapolis, MN 55406
ph: 612-250-1756
Specializes in high end antique furniture finish touch ups and finish repairs including French polish, gilding, faux finishes.

William W. Ingram
Refinishing Touch, Ltd., The
950 N. Rand Rd., Unit #103
Wauconda, IL 60084-1155
ph: 847-526-3113
A full service shop specializing in furniture repair, hand stripping, refinishing and antique restoration; also caning, veneers, and custom wood finishes.

Duane Mitch
Mercury Furniture Service
1017 W. Highland Ave.
Elgin, IL 60123
ph: 847-608-9553
fax: 847-608-9553
DuaneEMitch@aol.com
Refinishing, repairs, restoration.

James Bandy
Furniture Medic
2528 W. 183rd St.
Homewood, IL 60430
ph: 708-957-7910
fax: 708-957-8530
On-site repair, scratches and dents, gouges, scuffs and scrapes, broken

joints, chair regluing, refinish and restorations.

Dave Kummerow
Image Restoration Services Inc.
127 West Locust St.
Belvidere, IL 61008
ph: 815-547-5919 or 815-378-2845
fax: 815-547-6413
kummerowdl@aol.com
35 years in restoration field, moving claims; complete restoration services for furniture and all objects of art, wood, metal, glass and canvas.

Don Kistner
Kistner's Full Claims Service, Inc.
520 20th St.
Rock Island, IL 61201
ph: 309-786-5868
fax: 309-794-0559
kistners1@mchsi.com
http://www.kistners.com
Full claims service serving the eastern Iowa and northwestern Illinois area; furniture repair and touch up, manufacturing of new parts, furniture stripping, refinishing, marble repair, porcelains, etc.

Norm Shoults, Jr.
Workbench Furniture Restoration
8361 Gravois Rd.
Saint Louis, MO 63123
ph: 314-351-4224 or 800-810-4224
fax: 314-353-4664
workbenchfurniture@prodigy.net
Specializes in the furniture repair and restoration; also cane, rush, splint and tape work; in-home touch-ups and repairs.

Wood Works Inc., The
7710 West 63rd St.
Shawnee Mission, KS 66202
ph: 913-362-2432
fax: 913-362-0588
mgmt@thewws.com
http://www.thewoodworksinc.com
Furniture repair and refinishing, moving claims, woodworking, kitchen refacing, shutters, etc.

Dennis Furlow
Shaker Woodworks
1026 S. Broadway
Carrollton, TX 75006
ph: 972-436-7975
fax: 972-353-9446
dennis@shakerwoodworks.com
http://www.shakerwoodworks.com

Gary Wallace
Guardsman FurniturePro
221 Baker Rd., Bldg. D4/D5
Houston, TX 77094
ph: 281-345-6818 or 281-828-2920
fax: 281-345-6828
garymaryw@juno.com
http://
   guradsmanwoodpro.reliabilitymall.com
Furniture repair: structural, finish, complete refinishing, small leather repair.

Andrew Trapp
A & B United
1056 Co. Rd. 332
Bertram, TX 78605
ph: 512-355-2893 or 888-890-2893
fax: 512-355-9031
andrew_t_78605@yahoo.com
Second generation wood refinisher: antiques, office, restaurant, hotel furniture; also cane and rush weaving.

Ray Spencer
Ray Spencer Enterprises
25415 SE 219th St.
Maple Valley, WA 98038
ph: 425-413-1660 or 206-930-4364
fax: 425-413-1659
rayspencer@comcast.net
Specializing in cargo claims handling and in complete repair services.

Ron Lawrence
Town & Country Claim Service, Inc.
18421 Driftwood Dr. East
Sumner, WA 98390
ph: 253-826-0322
fax: 253-826-0324
TwnCntryInc@msn.com
Transit damage specialist; specializes in the repair and restoration of fine furniture and antiques.

Furniture & Upholstery
Repair Services

Christopher Tantillo
Furniture Medic
120 Magnolia Ave.
Westbury, NY 11590
ph: 516-333-9090
fax: 516-333-0805
ctantillo@spec.net
Full service repair, refinishing and restoration company; wood, upholstery, mica, marble, metal, and architectural elements; lead refinisher received apprenticeship in England; all technicians thoroughly trained.

Tom Kuhns
West Interior Services, Inc.
P.O. Box 540
Natrona Heights, PA 15065-0740
ph: 724-224-2215
fax: 724-226-3233
tomjr@westinteriorservices.com
http://www.westinteriorservices.com
Specializes in moving or insurance claims; furniture repair, refinishing & restoration, architectural refinishing; fire, smoke, water damage.

Timothy P. Hughes
MSS Furniture Service
211 Commerce Dr.
Montgomeryville, PA 18936-9641
ph: 800-433-1159 or 215-393-1900
fax: 800-835-0338
timh@mss1.com
http://www.mss1.com
Specializing in cargo claims handling, fire and water damage repairs, and furniture and antiques repair services; wood repairs and refinishing, woodworking and cabinetry, custom

upholstery, antique restoration, china, metal repairs.

L. Philip Oliver
Oliver's
24610 Frederick Rd.
Clarksburg, MD 20871-9732
ph: 301-428-3336
fax: 301-428-9282
Specializes in moving or insurance claims; complete line of furniture upholstery, repair, refinishing and restoration.

Peter Simonetti
Artisian Restoration, Inc.
P.O. Box 1265
Sykesville, MD 21784
ph: 410-489-9001 or 410-206-5100
fax: 410-489-9004
pete@simonetti.com
A complete furniture claims service specializing in cargo claims and fire water damage for insurance industry; repairs, refinishing, antique restoration, upholstery, touch-up, third party services; MD's largest furniture service.

Bill Crawford
Bill's Furniture Service
331 East Sullivan
Kingsport, TN 37660
ph: 423-245-8511
Repair and restoration of fine furniture; also complete upholstery services available.

Richard M. Montalbano
Montalbano Majestic International
3000 St. Charles Rd.
Bellwood, IL 60104-1544
ph: 708-547-1010
fax: 708-547-1032
info@montalbanofurniture.com
http://www.montalbanofurniture.com
Manufacturers, importers of period furniture; also offers complete refinishing, reupholstery, restoring of furniture.

Alois Zajec
Bay Area Restoration
850 Airport St., #3
Moss Beach, CA 94038-9683
ph: 650-728-1662
fax: 650-728-1663
alzajec@pacbell.net
http://www.enterit.com/Bay1662
Offers total restoration of antiques and furniture; crystal chandelier parts and restoration; insurance casualty loss and moving industry claims adjusters.

Suppliers

John K. Burch Co.
1818 Underwood Blvd.
Delran, NJ 08075
ph: 800-257-9112
fax: 609-461-7093
burchfab@burchfabrics.com
http://www.burchfabrics.com
Company's East coast mail order

source for upholstering supplies; also fabric books.

Minute-Man Upholstery Supply
 Company of North Carolina
1905 South Elm St.
High Point, NC 27260
ph: 800-457-0029 or 336-882-4100
fax: 336-885-6890
 Mail order source for upholstering supplies.

Bill Crawford
Bill's Furniture Service
331 East Sullivan
Kingsport, TN 37660
ph: 423-245-8511
 Upholstery fabric, foam, and other supplies.

Susan Bloomquist
Stitch Niche, The
208 Wild Tiger Rd.
Boulder, CO 80302
ph: 303-442-6556
fax: 303-546-6133
info@stitch1.com
http://www.stitch1.com
 Offers custom needlepoint textiles for fine wood furniture; authentic needlepoint reproduction of Berlin wool work.

Furniture (Antique Only)

Repair Services

Wade Holtzman
104 Bolton Rd.
Harvard, MA 01451
ph: 978-456-6850
 Professionally trained in England; over 22 years experience.

Bruce Hamilton
R. Bruce Hamilton, Furniture
 Restoration
P.O. Box 815
West Newbury, MA 01985
ph: 978-363-2638 or 800-439-8774
fax: 978-363-2638
rbruce.hamilton@verizon.net
http://www.patinarestoration.net
 Antique & fine furniture restoration; French polish, cleaning and restoration of existing finishes, false graining, removal of water stains & marks, leather work, veneering, carving, etc.; 20th century lacquer finishes repaired.

Nickolas Kotula, ASA
493 Simsbury Rd.
Bloomfield, CT 06002-1512
ph: 860-243-1646
fax: 860-243-8899
 Furniture conservator for museums and serious collectors; also does moving and insurance claims for fine furniture.

William Oakley
Oakley Restoration & Finishing, LLC
30 South End Plaza
New Milford, CT 06776
ph: 860-350-6410
fax: 630-214-8237
oakleyrestoration@earthlink.net
http://www.oakleyrestoration.com
 Appraises, restores, conserves antique furniture; appraisals for general and legal purposes; offers digital video archiving for accurate "visual" documentation; specializes in 17th, 18th and 19th century American and European furniture.

Peter Salamonski
A.R.S. Antiqua Co.
118 Eight St.
Brooklyn, NY 11215
ph: 718-788-3601
fax: 718-788-1316
peteratars@earthlink.net
http://www.ars-antiqua.com
 Restoration and conservation of fine antiques and objects of art including gilding, and veneer and marquetry repair.

John Sutton
John Sutton Antique Restorations
14 North Henry St.
Brooklyn, NY 11222
ph: 718-389-6101
yellowhouse39@earthlink.net
 Specializes in the restoration of 17th and 18th century English, French and American furniture.

Tom Matthews
Furniture Restoration Services
204 Smith Rd.
Eaton, NY 13334
ph: 315-684-7716
fax: 315-684-7716
Wefinish@dreamscape.com
http://wefinish.com
 A small shop allowing for consistent and high quality work; also does more contemporary furniture as well.

Eugene E. Landon
144 Quaker State Rd.
Montoursville, PA 17754
ph: 570-433-3476
fax: 570-433-3476
 Specializing in the restoration, conservation and replication of antique wooden furniture and artifacts.

Lawrence Bodine
Bodine Conservations
299 W. Mr. Pleasent Ave.
Ambler, PA 19002
ph: 215-646-1030
LDBodine4@aol.com
 Conservation, restoration and reproduction of antique American and European furniture including carving, marquetry, veneering, boulle, gold leaf conservation and historic finish conservation and restoration.

Stephen Rice
Heritage Restorations
4233 Howard Ave., Ste. #F
Kensington, MD 20895-8416
ph: 301-493-4458
 European trained craftsmen specializing in wooden objets d'art & antique furniture restoration; duplicating finishes, inlays, etc.

Walter Raynes
4900 Wetheredsville
Baltimore, MD 21207-6625
ph: 410-448-3515
fax: 410-448-0855
 Specializes in the restoration and conservation of antique furniture only; also builds reproduction of antique furniture.

Arnold Begleiter
Begleiter Antique Restorations
6801 Reisterstown Rd.
Baltimore, MD 21215
ph: 410-764-7467
fax: 410-486-2473

Bruce M. Schuettinger, ISA
Antique Restorations Ltd.
17 N. Alley
P.O. Box 244
New Market, MD 21774-0244
ph: 301-865-3009
fax: 301-865-3009
bschuettinger@erols.com
 Conservators and consultants of wooden artifacts, specializing in the preservation of original finishes, painted or gilt decoration, and structural elements; also inlay, marquetry, veneering, carving, and turned elements.

Howard Pletcher
Upshur Restoration
40 Mario St.
Buckhannon, WV 26201
ph: 304-473-0500 or 304-472-4353
fax: 304-473-1903
 Over 15 years restoring antique furniture; also offers complete claim service to the moving and insurance industry; wide variety of third party services available; also offers architectural restoration and salvage.

Martin O'Brien
Martin O'Brien Cabinetmaker
606 N. Trade St.
Winston Salem, NC 27101
ph: 3336-773-1334
martin@martinobriencabinetmaker.com
http://
www.martinobriencabinetmaker.com
*Offers design, construction and
conservation of furniture, musical
instruments and other wooden objects;
carving, turning, gilding, French
polishing, surface cleaning of painted
and varnished surfaces, color
matching, museum quality reproductions.*

Charles Smith
Antique Restorations
40779 Hearne Rd.
New London, NC 28127
ph: 704-463-5286
fax: 704-463-4730
*Specializes in the restoration and
refinishing of antique furniture; no
urethanes used, only oils; replacement
parts made from solid wood.*

Nemie Merkley
Merkley's Fine Wood Finishing Co.
111 Hausfeldt Lane
New Albany, IN 47150
ph: 812-944-7946 or 502-722-7727
fax: 812-944-7946
merkleys1@aol.com
*Family-owned and operated antique
restoration and refinishing business;
specializes in reproduction of missing
parts; a full service restoration/
refinishing business.*

Ran Sheller
Finishing Touch, The
319 Nebraska Ave., Ste. C
Columbia, MO 65201
ph: 573-874-9150
fax: 573-874-9149
ran@socket.net
*Master craftsman in business for 21
years; specializes in upper level
refinishing and repair of antique
furniture; references available.*

Gene & Deb Ruelle
Ruelle's
526 S. Broadway
Tyler, TX 75702
ph: 903-595-2176
fax: 903-595-1234
finishersformula@hotmail.com
http://www.ruelle.com
*Offers antique furniture restorations,
repairs, refinishing and appraising;
also chair caning, seat weaving,
rushing and wicker repair; member of
Appraisers National Association.*

Hal Resnikoff
Village Woodsmith, The
13043 N. Cave Creek Rd.
Phoenix, AZ 85022
ph: 602-867-2681
furniturefixer@cox.net
http://www.thevillagewoodsmith.com
Complete repair and restoration

*service for fine antiques and
collectibles.*

Suppliers

WSI Distributors - Antique Restoration
Supplies
405 N. Main St.
Saint Charles, MO 63301-2034
ph: 800-447-9974 or 636-946-5811
fax: 636-946-5832
talk2us@wsidistributors.com
http://www.wsidistributors.com
*Wholesale source for furniture &
trunk hardware, cane & weaving
materials, fiber chair seats, veneer,
wood ornaments, Zap glues, and much
more; over 1,200 items for professional furniture restorers. Sorry,
dealers only.*

Gilding

(see also FRAMES)

Repair Services

Susan B. Jackson
Harvard Art
49 Littleton County Rd.
Harvard, MA 01451-1729
ph: 978-456-9050
fax: 978-456-9050
sbj@ma.ultranet.com
*Restoration and conservation of
period frames and other gilded
objects; stabilization, replacement of
missing pieces, gilding and toning to
match the existing surface.*

Romayne Shay McMahon, ISA
Veronique's Antiques
124 S. Market St.
Mechanicsburg, PA 17055-6329
ph: 717-697-4924

William Adair
Gold Leaf Studios, Inc.
1523 22nd St., NW, Rear
Washington, DC 20037
ph: 202-833-3200
fax: 202-347-4569
bill@goldleafstudios.com
http://www.goldleafstudios.com
*Gilding of anything gold leafed:
frames, sculpture, sconces, etc.*

Bryan & Karen Parker
Parker's Gilding Studio, Inc.
8600 Foundry St., #1010, Ste. 118
Savage, MD 20763
ph: 301-490-8410
planetparker@msn.com
*Specializes in gilded antique
restorations: frames, furniture, etc.*

R. Wayne Reynolds
R. Wayne Reynolds, Inc.
3618 Falls Rd.
Baltimore, MD 21211
ph: 410-467-1800 or 410-467-1890
*Specializes in the application of gold
leaf; complete restoration services for
gilded art objects, including furniture,
frames, and mirrors.*

Richard Kornemann
Museum Shop, Ltd.
20 N. Market St.
Frederick, MD 21701
ph: 301-695-0424
fax: 301-698-5242
fineartmuseum@erols.com
http://www.museumsholptd.com
*23k gold leafing of antiques, picture
frames, signs, etc.; also complete art
and frame restoration.*

Society of Gilders
Newsletter: Tip, The
P.O. Box 478
Snellville, GA 30078-0478
ph: 770-979-7994
fax: 770-979-7994
information@societyofgilders.org
http://www.societyofgilders.org
*Promotes traditional gilding skills,
techniques and knowledge; gives
workshops and lectures on the art of
gilding.*

Jerome S. Feig, CPF, ISA
Field Art Studio
24242 Woodward Ave.
Pleasant Ridge, MI 48069-1144
ph: 248-399-1320
fax: 248-399-7018
jsfieldart@aol.com
http://www.customepictureframe.com
*Frame specialist and appraiser:
restoration of art, frames, objects,
gilding; period frame reproductions
made; fine art and frame appraisals;
conservation of picture frames.*

Glass

(see also GLASS, Curved)

Misc. Services

R. Wayne Lowry
Jar Doctor
401 Johnston Ct.
Raymore, MO 64083
ph: 816-318-0161
fax: 816-318-0162
Jardoctor@aol.com
http://www.jardoctor.com
*Manufacturers a bottle and jar
cleaning system; also manufactures
glass cleaning equipment for
insulators, marbles as well - any
antique glass.*

Repair Services

Leon Trefler
Trefler & Sons Antique Restoring
Studio, Inc.
99 Cabot St.
Needham, MA 02494
ph: 781-444-2685
fax: 781-444-0659
trefler@trefler.com
http://www.trefler.com
*Repair of all glass items; removal of
chips on glass.*

Edward Poore
Crystal Workshop
794 Sandwich Rd.
P.O. Box 475
Sagamore, MA 02561-0475
ph: 508-888-9298 or 888-869-0867
fax: 508-888-9298
crystal.workshop@verizon.net
http://www.thecrystalworkshop.com
*Repairs stemware, cut glass, and art
glass; chips removed; misc. repairs,
recutting, stoppers fitted; contact for
free detailed brochure; also engraved
glass panels from old houses
reproduced; new designs cut to order;
30 years experience.*

Sharon Smith Abbott
Fine Wares Restoration
P.O. Box 753
Bridgton, ME 04009-0753
ph: 207-647-2093
sharonsmithabbott@yahoo.net
*Restores ceramic & glass art objects
for private collectors and museums;
references of museum clients on
request.*

Sylvio Bettio
Sylvio's
44 Longhill Dr.
Clifton, NJ 07013
ph: 973-777-0288
fax: 973-779-7659
Sylvio11@aol.com
Repairs chipped glass and crystal.

Art Cut Glass Studio
RD 1 -10 Fawn Dr.
Matawan, NJ 07747
ph: 732-583-7648
*Restores fine antique glass such as
Lalique, Steuben, Baccarat, Galle;
also resurfaces paperweights.*

Jonathan Mark Gershen
Jonathan Mark Gershen Porcelain,
Pottery & Glass Restoration
1463 Pennington Rd.
Ewing, NJ 08618-2656
ph: 609-882-9417
fax: 609-530-0660
*Second generation restorer and long
time member of the AIC; clients
include museums, collectors and
dealers worldwide; free brochure
available upon request.*

Glass Restorations
1597 York Ave.
New York, NY 10028-6236
ph: 212-517-3287
fax: 212-517-3287
gusjochec@earthlink.net

Anton Laub Glass Corp.
1873 Second Ave.
New York, NY 10029-7453
ph: 212-734-4270 or 718-430-1901
*Installation, beveling and resilvering
of glass and mirrors; also fabrication
of reproduction antique mirrors,
repair and restoration of stained-glass
panels.*

Ernest Kionke
Dropped Shop, The
34 Elm St.
East Aurora, NY 14052
ph: 716-652-7053
ernie102@juno.com

Michael Andras
244 East Lake Rd.
Bear Rocks, PA 15610
ph: 724-547-6419
andras@cvzoom.net
   *Custom hand engraving using vintage
   equipment, stone or diamond wheel.*

Mark S. Powell
A. Ludwig Klein & Son, Inc.
683 Sumneytown Pike
P.O. Box 145
Harleysville, PA 19438
ph: 215-256-9004 or 800-379-2929
fax: 215-256-9644
mark@aludwigklein.com
http://www.aludwigklein.com
   *Specializing in the repair and
   restoration of all types of glass, china
   and porcelain as well as ivory, jade,
   brass, pewter.*

Henry Chaudron
Chaudron Glass & Mirror Co., Inc.
1801 Lovegrove St.
Baltimore, MD 21202-2815
ph: 410-685-1568
fax: 410-685-1591
   *Resilvers mirrors; also specializes in
   cutting, hand-beveling plate glass, and
   stone wheel engraving.*

Mildred R. Shepherd
Shepherd Studio
5527 Third St., South
Arlington, VA 22204-1115
ph: 703-671-1789
JohnMilShep@aol.com
   *Since 1970, conservation/restoration
   of art objects; specializing in
   porcelain, glass, pottery, plaster,
   stoneware, ivory, jade; for private
   clients and museums.*

Jim & Sheri Van Es
Wooden Shoe Antiques
222 W. Washington St.
Charles Town, WV 25414
ph: 304-725-1673 or 703-435-9045
wdnshu@aol.com
http://www.woodenshoeantiques.com
   Grinds and repairs chips on glass.

Ray Errett
Ray Errett - Glass Restoration
101 Mohican Trail
Wilmington, NC 28409-3418
ph: 910-792-1807
errettjr@aol.com
   *Restores glass figurines, sculpture
   crystal, cut glass, grinding, polishing;
   semi retired, Corning Museum of
   Glass.*

Gordon Ponsford
Ponsford, Ltd.
2405 Highway 92
Acworth, GA 30102
ph: 770-924-4848
fax: 770-529-2278
ponsford@bellsouth.net
http://www.antiqueconservation.com
   *Largest conservation group in the
   Southwest; 14 of the finest experts
   available in their respective fields
   working in one studio; Ponsford has
   worked with government pieces,
   museum collections, private collectors,
   family heirlooms.*

James Braun
Braun Restoration Specialties
216 W. 42nd St.
Savannah, GA 31401
ph: 912-232-6482
Braun.Restoration@sysconn.com
   *Specializes in crystal glass grinding
   and polishing and in wood restoration.*

Don & Joyce McCurley
McCurley Glass Repair
5011 Memorial Dr.
Sebring, FL 33870-1087
ph: 813-471-9814
fax: 941-471-3359
   *Repairs glass and crystal; chip
   removal, polishing, sawing, bells
   made from goblets; stopper specialist -
   carries large stock of replacement
   stoppers for bottles; also prism
   replacement.*

Antique & Collectible Restoration
   Services
P.O. Box 186
608 Des Moines St.
Webster City, IA 50595
ph: 515-832-6623
fax: 515-832-6623
   *Restoration of glass, supplies for
   glass repairs.*

Josef Puehringer
Crystal Cave, The
1141 Central Ave.
Wilmette, IL 60091
ph: 847-251-1160
fax: 847-251-1172
   *European trained craftsmen will
   restore your treasures with expert
   care; call or write for free estimates.*

Suzy Lytle
Broken Arts Restoration
2739 Gladstone
Dallas, TX 75211-5206
ph: 214-331-6706 or 877-643-1121 pin
   #0869
brokenarts@sbcglobal.net
http://www.brokenarts.com
   *Can repair glass including the
   fabrication of missing glass pieces
   such as the missing saw teeth on
   American Brilliant period cut glass;
   can also secure stress cracks.*

Michael Blair
Restorations by Michael, Inc.
P.O. Box 387
Golden, CO 80403-0387
ph: 303-384-9121
mblair5028@aol.com
   *Repairs glass and ceramics art such
   as figurines.*

Victor Coleman
Dr. Chips
1808 N. Scottsdale Rd.
Tempe, AZ 85281
ph: 800-658-9197
   *Restoration of glass and fine crystal;
   also porcelain, pottery restoration;
   gluing, making new parts when
   necessary, refinishing to match
   original; ships nationwide.*

Wayne Montano
Montano's Antique Glass Repair
P.O. Box 720783
Pinon Hills, CA 92372
ph: 760-868-6598
fax: 760-868-6598
info@montanosglassrepair.com
http://www.montanosglassrepair.com
   *In business since 1981; repairs about
   10,000 pieces per year; repairs on site
   at antique shows throughout
   California; also teaches professional
   glass repair at their shop.*

Attic Unlimited
22435 E. LaPalma
Yorba Linda, CA 92887
ph: 714-692-2940
fax: 714-692-2947
   Glass polishing, grinding, repair.

Kenny & Judy Lang
Miracle Glass Repair
125 Mill St.
Grass Valley, CA 95945
ph: 530-274-1917 or 530-274-0911
kjl71@juno.com
http://www.ourhouseantiques.com/
   miracle.htm
   *Professional glass repairs including
   rim chips.*

Suppliers

Valerie Kelly
Pairpoint Glass Co.
851 Sandwich Rd.
P.O. Box 515
Sagamore, MA 02561
ph: 508-888-2344 or 800-899-0953
fax: 508-888-3537
   *Blowing room open to visitors;
   catalog $2 (refundable); reproduces
   hand blown full led crystal liners for
   salts and other silver items.*

Restorite Systems
P.O. Box 7096
West Trenton, NJ 08628-0096
ph: 609-530-1526
   *Products for restoration and
   conservation of porcelain, pottery, and
   glass; sells a complete kit for
   repairing breaks and chips; also
   "How-to" videos available; send for
   free catalog.*

R. Foster Holcombe
Art of Fire at Chaerie Farm
7901 Hawkins Creamery Rd.
Gaithersburg, MD 20882-3507
ph: 301-253-6642 or 800-639-6979
comments@artoffire.com
http://www.artoffire.com
   *Offers glass blowing services; makes
   replacement glass liners for silver
   pieces; also porcelain and pottery
   restorations.*

Allan Koskela
Allan Koskela Restorations
1417 Third St.
Webster City, IA 50595
ph: 515-832-2437
repair@wmtel.net
http://
   restorationmaterials.safeshopper.com
   *Sells glass repair materials including
   Diamond Hand Pads, fillers, glues
   and cleaners; instructional videos on
   Lampworking, to make glass beads,
   jewelry, figurines, etc.; highly
   recommended by many publications
   including Glass Art.*

Ivory

Repair Services

Frank Funes
57 Maplewood Ave.
Hempstead, NY 11550
ph: 516-483-6712
   Restores ivory and other artifacts.

Mark S. Powell
A. Ludwig Klein & Son, Inc.
683 Sumneytown Pike
P.O. Box 145
Harleysville, PA 19438
ph: 215-256-9004 or 800-379-2929
fax: 215-256-9644
mark@aludwigklein.com
http://www.aludwigklein.com
   *Specializing in the repair and
   restoration of all types of glass, china
   and porcelain as well as ivory, jade,
   brass, pewter.*

Mildred R. Shepherd
Shepherd Studio
5527 Third St., South
Arlington, VA 22204-1115
ph: 703-671-1789
JohnMilShep@aol.com
   *Since 1970, conservation/restoration
   of art objects; specializing in
   porcelain, glass, pottery, plaster,
   stoneware, ivory, jade; for private
   clients and museums.*

Ron Fromkin
Japanese Repository, The
7705 NW 18th Court
Margate, FL 33063
ph: 954-972-0287
ivoryrepair@yahoo.com
http://www.ivoryrepair.com
   *Repair and restoration of ivory, bone,
   antler, horn; repairs carved in real
   ivory or other natural materials; inlay
   work, nautical, canes, chess sets, all
   styles.*

William & Michelle Marhoefer
Broken Art Restoration
1841 West Chicago Ave.
Chicago, IL 60622-5513
ph: 312-226-8200 or 815-472-3900
fax: 815-472-3930
Museum quality invisible repair specializing in the professional restoration of porcelain, pottery, ceramics, wood, ivory, stone, art objects; Chicago Institute Masters Degree, qualified restorers since 1980; call for shipping instructions.

John Edward Cunningham
Fine Art Restoration
1525 E. Berkley
Springfield, MO 65804-3203
ph: 417-889-7702
Ivory, highly detailed and handcarved; genuine ivory replacement parts for Art Deco and Japanese figurines; also ivory and mother-of-pearl inlays; will travel for large restorations.

Andrew A. Owen
LEGACY Art Restorations & Design
International, Inc.
4221 North 16th St.
Phoenix, AZ 85016
ph: 602-263-5178
fax: 602-263-6009
restoration@legacyintlinc.com
http://www.legacyintlinc.com/main.html
Specializes in the restoration and conservation of paintings, porcelain, ivory, marble, glass and jade.

Mattresses

Man./Prod./Dist.

Tucker Mattress Company
3926 Lawrenceville Hwy.
P.O. Box 2
Tucker, GA 30085-0002
ph: 770-938-1176
Manufacturer of customized mattresses for antique beds, adjustable beds, brass beds; also for boats, RV's and campers.

Clinton Bedding Company
255 Hiway Dr.
Clinton, TN 37716
ph: 800-822-2337 or 865-463-8330
fax: 865-457-0051
save@clintonbedding.com
http://www.clintonbedding.com
Specializes in custom made mattresses and box springs for hard-to-fit antique beds, such as "three-quarter" beds.

Metal Items

(see also SILVER)

Repair Services

Walter Allen
Specialty Castings
19 Mill Rd.
Boxford, MA 01921
ph: 978-887-9783
specialty@gis.net
http://www.gis.net/~specialty
Reproduces items for collectors by casting in cast iron, bronze, brass or aluminum; all items created through the lost wax process; also mold making, parts modification, and shrinkage compensation.

Leon Trefler
Trefler & Sons Antique Restoring
Studio, Inc.
99 Cabot St.
Needham, MA 02494
ph: 781-444-2685
fax: 781-444-0659
trefler@trefler.com
http://www.trefler.com
Repairs and polishes brass.

Howard & Mary Newman
Newmans Ltd.
55 Farewell St.
Newport, RI 02840
ph: 401-846-4784 or 401-847-8557
fax: 401-849-0611
newmansltd@cox.net
http://www.newmansltd.com
Fine metal restoration and conservation; master silversmith, specialist in bronze finishing and patination; trained at RI School of Design & in Italy; conservation & restoration of personal items & museum works; can ship anywhere.

Joseph J. Pistilli
Orum Silver Co., Inc.
51 S. Vine St.
P.O. Box 805
Meriden, CT 06450-0805
ph: 203-237-3037
fax: 203-237-3037
Orum@ct1.nai.net
http://www.orumsilver.com
Repairing, restoring, replating of antique and old silver, gold, nickel; brass & copper plating; cleaning, buffing, polishing.

Bill Berkowitz
Hartel Plating, Inc.
6205 Hudson Ave.
West New York, NJ 07093
ph: 201-861-2636
Specializes in metal restoration and plating.

Romayne Shay McMahon, ISA
Veronique's Antiques
124 S. Market St.
Mechanicsburg, PA 17055-6329
ph: 717-697-4924
Fine metals refinishing: replating, cleaning, polishing, lacquering, repairing; silver, brass, copper, pewter, bronze; chandeliers, lamps, etc. rewired and restored; brass beds a specialty.

Londonderry Brasses, Ltd.
P.O. Box 415
Cochranville, PA 19330
ph: 610-593-6239
fax: 610-593-6246
info@londonderry-brasses.com
http://www.londonderry-brasses.com
Offers high quality period brass hardware; handmade using the direct lost wax process casing of the original period example.

Alexander Bigler
Equestrian Forge
222 S. King St.
Leesburg, VA 20175-2110
ph: 703-777-2110
fax: 703-777-3949
Recasts replacement parts in various metals; also casts portrait sculptures.

Boris Paskvan
Awesome Metal Restorations, Inc.
4233-G Howard Ave.
Kensington, MD 20895-2449
ph: 301-897-3266
fax: 301-530-8428
European expert restores gold, gilt, bronze, silver, silver plating, icons, metal accessories, sculptures, etc. for museums, homes, insurance; repairs, solders, fabricates, duplicates parts, replates, rewires, retins, polishes, lacquers.

Abercombie & Company Silverplaters,
Inc.
9159A Brookeville Rd.
Silver Spring, MD 20910
ph: 301-585-2385 or 800-585-2387
fax: 301-587-5708
abernco@erols.com
http://www.silverplaters.com
Replates silverplate; repairs all sorts of metal; silver, brass, copper; also welding.

Robert Eagan
American Alloy Foundry
112 S. Eden St., #118
P.O. Box 13145
Baltimore, MD 21203-3145
ph: 410-276-1930
fax: 410-276-1947
Custom castings to replace broken or missing parts; has made castings for the Smithsonian, Washington DC, National Park Service, US Coast Guard, and many antique dealers in the mid-Atlantic area; small family business since 1935.

Don L. Reedy
Brass & Copper Polishing Shop, The
13 South Carroll St.
Frederick, MD 21701-5606
ph: 301-663-4240
fax: 301-694-9190
shineit4u@aol.com
http://www.frederickcouonty.com/
antiques/brass.htm
Repair and restore antique lighting; 1,000s or antique and new lamp parts and supplies in stock; professional metal polishing and repair; replacement glass shades and chimneys.

Pete Markey
Creative Metal Design
7935 Edgewood Church Rd.
Frederick, MD 21702-2713
ph: 301-473-5995
fax: 301-473-5995
Specializes in ornamental ironwork,
hand forged originals; metal repairs; made the Statue of Liberty gates.*

David Nelson
Jarnel Iron & Forge
221 Rowland Ave.
Hagerstown, MD 21740
ph: 301-733-0441
fax: 301-733-0919
Recasts replacement parts in various metals; also iron work.

Kip Young
Copper Kettle Metal Polishing
158 1/2 South Potomac St.
Hagerstown, MD 21740
ph: 301-791-4555
Specialists in antique lamps and lighting sales, repairs and restorations; metal polishing, fabrication of missing metal parts; also specializes in crystal chandelier repair.

Toombs, Ltd.
5730 Patterson Ave.
Richmond, VA 23226
ph: 804-282-6554
fax: 804-282-1371
toombsltd@aol.com
Brass, copper, pewter and silver polishing, repairing and plating.

Beth Walker
Oexning Silversmiths
320 Highway 197 South
Bakersville, NC 28705
ph: 828-688-9998 or 800-332-6857
fax: 828-688-9976
oexning@aol.com
http://www.oxningsilversmiths.com
Specializes in the refinishing, repair and replating of silver, copper, pewter, gold, and brass; two locations - in Minneapolis, MN and in Bakersville, NC.

Steve Kayne
Kayne & Son Custom Forged Hardware
100 Daniel Ridge Rd.
Candler, NC 28715-9434
ph: 828-667-8868 or 828-665-1988
fax: 828-665-8303
kaynehdwe@charter.net
http://www.customforgedhardware.com
Steel, brass, bronze reproductions of locks, pulls, hinges, thumb latches, furniture & interior/exterior hardware, fireplace tools & accessories, military accouterments, etc.; also does repairs, restoration; $5 for two catalogs.

Alfred L. Crabtree
Brass & Silver Workshop, The
758 St. Andrew Blvd.
Charleston, SC 29407
ph: 843-571-4342
fax: 843-571-7417
info@silvervaultcharleston.com
http://www.silvervaultcharleston.com
Museum quality restoration and conservation of most fine metal decorative arts; emphasis on 17th, 18th and 19th century brass and silver; also purchases Southern coin silver and unusual sterling items.

Gordon Ponsford
Ponsford, Ltd.
2405 Highway 92
Acworth, GA 30102
ph: 770-924-4848
fax: 770-529-2278
ponsford@bellsouth.net
http://www.antiqueconservation.com
*Largest conservation group in the
Southwest; 14 of the finest experts
available in their respective fields
working in one studio; Ponsford has
worked with government pieces,
museum collections, private collectors,
family heirlooms.*

Estes-Simmons Silverplating, Ltd.
1050 Northside Dr., NW
Atlanta, GA 30318
ph: 404-875-9581 or 800-645-4193
fax: 404-873-4826
info@estes-simmons.com
http://www.estes-simmons.com
*Repairs silver, silverplate, gold,
pewter, brass and copper; also
replates silver, gold, brass, nickel,
copper.*

Memphis Plating Works
682 Madison Ave.
Memphis, TN 38103
ph: 901-526-3051
*Gold, silver, copper, brass, nickel and
chrome plating; restoration of
chandeliers, floor lamps, brass beds,
fern tables, tea sets, trays, vanity sets,
etc.; repairs teapot feet, spouts,
missing parts, flatware, etc.*

Antique & Art Restoration By Wiebold
413 Terrace Place
Terrace Park, OH 45174-1164
ph: 513-831-2541 or 800-321-2541
fax: 513-831-2815
wiebold@eos.net
http://www.wiebold.com
*Silver repair and replating;
restoration of bronzes, brass, copper,
pewter, lead, combs, brushes, knife
blades, mirrors, chandeliers, glass,
etc.*

Steve Solomon
Solomon Metal Antique Restorations
13760 Sherwood
Oak Park, MI 48237
ph: 248-543-9411
fax: 248-543-9411
solomos1@hotmail.com
*Offers repairs on metal antiques:
brazing, soldering, fabricating,
casting, bronze, brass, silver, steel,
iron, pewter, pot metal.*

Electro-Coatings, Inc.
911 Shaver Rd., NE
Cedar Rapids, IA 52402
ph: 800-806-6059 or 319-363-9602
fax: 319-363-1187
sales@electro-coatings.com
http://www.platingforindustry.com/
electrocoatings
Specializes in chrome plating.

Roger A. Sundblom
Specialized Repair Service
1125 E. Wisconsin Ave.
Appleton, WI 54911-3905
ph: 920-993-9993
metlmstr@execpc.com
http://www.execpc.com/~metlmstr
*Repairs all metal items; also designs
and fabricates replacement metal
parts; machining, welding (tig,
heliarc, oxyacetylene, silver brazing,
casting in yellow and red brass, etc.;
if it can't be repaired, will remake
from scratch!*

Glenn Taylor
Courtesy Metal Polishing
735 N. Addison Rd.
Villa Park, IL 60181
ph: 630-832-1862
*All metals polished and buffed:
motorcycle, automobile, marine parts,
antique juke boxes and slot machines.*

Max Kaiser
Mueller Kaiser Plating Co.
5815 Hampton Ave.
Saint Louis, MO 63109
ph: 314-832-3553
fax: 314-832-3553
tmsk9111@yahoo.com
http://www.Mueller-KaiserPlating.com
*Since 1911, fine metal finishing in
silver, gold, bronze, copper and brass;
flatware, tea services, church ware,
antiques, and other items.*

Danny O'Brien, ISA
Star Forge & Anvil
1816 E. 135th St.
Grandview, MO 64030
ph: 816-763-4741
fatdog_autos@hotmail.com
*Custom forgings and ornamental iron
repair.*

D & E Brass Buffing
101 Wagonsheel Lane
Rowlett, TX 75088
ph: 972-412-2260
fax: 972-527-5373
*Professional polishing, lacquering
and antique restoration of anything
brass.*

Mike Taylor
5545 Celestial Rd.
Dallas, TX 75240
ph: 972-788-1411
fax: 972-385-0779
Mike@rememwhen.com
http://www.rememwhen.com
*Specializes in the restoration of metal
collectibles, toys, pedal vehicles, etc.:
cast iron, steel, aluminum, galvanized,
brass, copper, tin, stainless steel and
corrugated, stamped, rolled, pressed
and pot metal.*

Craig Bierman
Speed & Sport Chrome Plating
404 Broadway
Houston, TX 77012
ph: 281-921-0235
Specializing in chrome plating of

*antique jukeboxes, Coke machines, slot
machines, pedal cars, etc.*

Carmelo Tringali
Colonial Silver
1219 Forest Ave.
Pacific Grove, CA 93950
ph: 831-375-0355
*Recommended for silverplating and
replating.*

Tim Maple
Omega Silversmithing Inc.
11232 120th Ave. NE #118
Kirkland, WA 98033-4522
ph: 425-822-3727
*Expert repair and restoration of fine
silver, bronze, silverplate, spelter,
brass, pewter and copper; from tea
sets to brass beds, chandeliers, new
knife blades, mirrors and combs; full
service restoration.*

Suppliers

Jax Chemical Company, Inc.
78-11 267th St.
Floral Park, NY 11004
ph: 718-347-0057
fax: 914-668-8490
*Sells metal finishing solutions: green
patina, pewter black, black darkener,
gold finish, silver and copper plating
solutions; also brass, copper, gold
and marble cleaners.*

Delphi Stained Glass
3380 E. Jolly Rd.
Lansing, MI 48910
ph: 800-248-2048 or 517-394-4631
fax: 517-394-5364
webmaster@delphiglass.com
http://www.delphiglass.com
*Sells stained glass supplies; gives
lessons; large mail order business;
also sells chemical solutions to repair
damaged patina on brass and other
metals.*

Mirrors

Repair Services

Modern Glass Co., Inc.
384 Broadway
Pawtucket, RI 02860-1305
ph: 401-722-9644 or 877-722-9644
*Specializes in Native Americana and
Western collectibles and memorabilia.*

Anton Laub Glass Corp.
1873 Second Ave.
New York, NY 10029-7453
ph: 212-734-4270 or 718-430-1901
*Installation, beveling and resilvering
of glass and mirrors; also fabrication
of reproduction antique mirrors,
repair and restoration of stained-glass
panels.*

Sundial & Schwartz
159 E. 118th St.
New York, NY 10035
ph: 212-289-4969 or 800-876-4776
fax: 212-996-3236
*Custom resilvering and antiquing of
mirror and glass.*

Romayne Shay McMahon, ISA
Veronique's Antiques
124 S. Market St.
Mechanicsburg, PA 17055-6329
ph: 717-697-4924
Offers glass grinding and resilvering.

Henry Chaudron
Chaudron Glass & Mirror Co., Inc.
1801 Lovegrove St.
Baltimore, MD 21202-2815
ph: 410-685-1568
fax: 410-685-1591
*Resilvers mirrors; also hand-bevels
plate glass.*

Steve Robinson
Robinson's Antiques
763 West Bippley Rd.
Lake Odessa, MI 48849
ph: 616-374-7750 or 616-374-7751
fax: 616-374-7752
antiquehardware@robinsonsantiques.com
http://www.robinsonsantiques.com
*Specializes in original 1650-1925
antique architectural hardware, door
knobs, furniture hardware hardware,
hinges, mirror restoration, latches,
locks, registers, tear drops, door
bells, escutcheons, ice box hardware;
since 1967.*

Robert Easthope
Reflections Again
156 Goble Lane
San Jose, CA 95111
ph: 408-629-3942
mirrors@321.net
http://www.mirrorresilvering.com
*Specializes in mirror resilvering,
furniture stripping, furniture
refinishing.*

Painted Finishes

Repair Services

Ruby Newman
Roundabout Restoration Studio
P.O. Box 823
Forest Knolls, CA 94933-0823
ph: 415-488-9213
fax: 415-488-9213
*Restoration and recreating of classic
finishes; all painted surfaces including
furniture, mirror frames, carousel
carvings, etc.: trompe l'oeil,
contemporary murals, classical faux
marbles, wood grain, gold leaf, wall
treatments.*

Paper Items

(see also PRINTS; REPAIR/
RESTORATION/CONSERVATION,
Archival Supplies For)

Clubs/Associations

American Institute for Conservation of
Historic & Artistic Works
Directory: AIC Directory
1717 K St. NW, Ste. 200
Washington, DC 20006
ph: 202-452-9545
fax: 202-452-9328
info@aic-faic.org
http://aic.stanford.edu
*Purpose is to advance the knowledge,
practice of the conservation of cultural
property; the "Guide" lists
conservators who are Fellows and
Professional Associates of the AIC in
paper, textiles, photographs,
paintings, furniture, etc.*

Repair Services

Northeast Document Conservation Center
100 Brickstone Square
Andover, MA 01810-1494
ph: 978-470-1010
fax: 978-475-6021
nedcc@nedcc.org
http://www.nedcc.org
*Paper and art on paper conservation,
preservation microfilming, photographic duplication, photograph
conservation, book conservation,
disaster assistance.*

Center for Conservation & Technical
Studies, The
Harvard University
32 Quincy St.
Cambridge, MA 02138
ph: 617-495-2392
*Provides conservation and restoration
services for fine arts, including works
of art on paper, paintings, objects and
sculpture.*

Bridgitte Boyadjian
43 Fern St.
Lexington, MA 02173-6024
ph: 781-862-9395
fax: 781-862-9395
*Paper restoration and conservation;
fine prints, drawings, watercolors and
manuscripts.*

David E. Kenney
Conservation Gallery
32 Center St.
Yarmouth, ME 04096
ph: 207-846-9246 or 207-846-5176
*Conservation and restoration of art
on paper: watercolors, etchings,
lithographs, historical documents.*

Oscar & Debra Perez
Vigues Art Studio
54 Flanders Rd.
Woodbury, CT 06798-2103
ph: 203-263-4088
fax: 203-266-9118
viguesart@aol.com
*Conservation, restoration of oil
paintings (cleaning, lining, touch up
and repair), frames (gold leaf repairs,
casting of missing parts) and paper
(cleaning, repairs of prints,
documents); also porcelain & china
repair.*

Kenneth Newman
Old Print Shop, The
150 Lexington Ave. at 30th St.
New York, NY 10016
ph: 212-683-3950
fax: 212-779-8040
info@oldprintshop.com
http://www.oldprintshop.com
*Paper conservator: preservation,
restoration, cleaning, deacidification,
encapsulation.*

George J. Cohenour
4301 Beaumont Rd.
Dover, PA 17315-2405
ph: 717-292-5345
cohenour@currierprints.com
http://www.currierprints.com
*Cleans, deacidifies, repairs and
restores prints: American historical,
antique and decorative, handcolored
lithographs, chromolithographs,
etchings, engravings, watercolors, etc.*

Maria Pukownik
Fine Art & Paper Conservation
1045 Orrtanna Rd.
Orrtanna, PA 17353-9691
ph: 717-337-0668
conspuk@yahoo.com
*Watercolors, charcoal and pastel,
drawings, colored engravings,
autographs, maps; cleaning, leaf
casting, tears and cracks mending,
flattening, retouching, dry mounting
removal.*

Christopher W. Lane
Philadelphia Print Shop, Ltd., The
8441 Germantown Ave.
Philadelphia, PA 19118
ph: 215-242-4750
fax: 215-242-6977
PhilaPrint@PhilaPrintShop.com
http://www.philaprintshop.com
*Gallery of antique prints and maps
with related rare books and atlases;
also bookstore of reference books
related to antique prints and maps;
appraisals, paper conservation and
restoration, museum quality framing.*

Franklin Shores
Conservation of Works on Paper
612 S. 9th St.
Philadelphia, PA 19147
ph: 215-923-4929
*Conservation of works on paper,
prints, drawings, pastels; specializing
in the treatment of Penna. German
fraktur; conservation matting &
encapsulation under ultraviolet acrylic
sheeting also done; by appointment;
sorry, no books or photos.*

James Von Ruster
Old Print Gallery, The
1220 31st St. NW
Washington, DC 20007-3422
ph: 202-965-1818
fax: 202-965-1869
info@oldprintgallery.com
http://www.oldprintgallery.com
*Paper conservator: preservation,
restoration, cleaning, deacidification,
encapsulation.*

Dennis Dobson
Dobson Studios
810 N. Daniel St.
Arlington, VA 22201-1944
ph: 703-243-7363
fax: 703-243-2382
ddobson@erols.com
*Conservator of Oriental screens,
scrolls and wood block prints; repairs
and conservation to other paper items
as well.*

Christine Smith, Pres.
Conservation of Art on Paper, Inc.
2805 Mt. Vernon Ave., Ste. B
Alexandria, VA 22301-1125
ph: 703-836-7757
*Conservation of fine art and historic
artifacts on paper including Japanese
woodblock prints; conservation
treatments, collection surveys,
lectures, workshops, vault storage.*

Gordon Ponsford
Ponsford, Ltd.
2405 Highway 92
Acworth, GA 30102
ph: 770-924-4848
fax: 770-529-2278
ponsford@bellsouth.net
http://www.antiqueconservation.com
*Largest conservation group in the
Southwest; 14 of the finest experts
available in their respective fields
working in one studio; Ponsford has
worked with government pieces,
museum collections, private collectors,
family heirlooms.*

Ray Nugent, ASA
Nugent Appraisal Services
P.O. Box 11984
Naples, FL 34101
ph: 888-353-7152 or 941-353-7122
fax: 941-353-8884
renugent@aol.com
http://www.appraisalreferrals.com
*Professionally accredited Conservator,
with experience in paper, bindings,
and chemical treatment of all types of
paper and leather products.*

David L. Swift
6436 Brownlee Dr.
Nashville, TN 37205
ph: 615-352-0308
*Paper conservator: preservation,
restoration, cleaning, deacidification,
encapsulation.*

Okey J. Hatcher
Archival Conservation Center, Inc.
8225 Daly Rd.
Cincinnati, OH 45231-5701
ph: 513-521-9858
fax: 513-521-9859
*Repair and restoration of works of art
on paper: engravings, lithographs,
posters, prints, historical documents,
maps, family bible restorations, etc.*

Dick Doeren
Lumber Mill Gallery Framery
107 Smith Ave.
Oconto, WI 54153
ph: 920-834-4494 or 877-889-1085
fax: 920-834-4494
lumbermillgallery@msn.com
*Antique frame, photograph, and
document restoration and preservation; old world craftsmanship;
members of The Society of Guilders.*

Graphic Conservation Co.
329 W. 18th St., Ste. 701
Chicago, IL 60616
ph: 312-738-2657
fax: 312-738-3125
info@graphicconservation.com
http://www.graphicconservation.com
*Specializing in the conservation of
works of art on paper: cleaning, stain
reduction, deacidification, inpainting,
tear repairs, flattening.*

Robert & Jenny Kipp
Art & Old Print Restorations
4340 E. Kentucky Ave., Ste. 337
Denver, CO 80246
ph: 720-933-7649
JennyKipp@qwest.net
http://www.oldprints.com
*Paper and print sales, conservation
and restorations; specializing in 18th
century to present prints; over 22
years in business.*

Shawn Leubner, Conservator
Sierra Restoration Services
P.O. Box 1884
Nevada City, CA 95959-1884
ph: 530-478-0499
*Professional paper restoration and
conservation service; over 18 years of
archival experience; specializes in
comic book and original art
restoration; call or email to have free
information package sent to you.*

Suppliers

Light Impressions
P.O. Box 22708
Rochester, NY 14692-2708
ph: 800-828-6216
fax: 800-828-5539
LiWebsite@limpressions.com
http://www.lightimpressionsdirect.com
*General line of archival supplies
including mat boards, document
storage boxes, framing, ephemera
storage and photographic supplies.*

Porcelain

(see REPAIR/RESTORATION/
CONSERVATION, Ceramics)

Supplies For

Suppliers

Ronald L. Aiello
Antique Restorations
1313 Mt. Holly Rd.
Burlington, NJ 08016-3773
ph: 609-387-2587
fax: 609-747-9340
ronaiello@comcast.net
Repair and restoration supplies available.

Restorite Systems
P.O. Box 7096
West Trenton, NJ 08628-0096
ph: 609-530-1526
Products for restoration and conservation of porcelain, pottery, and glass; sells a complete kit for repairing breaks and chips; also "How-to" videos available; send for free catalog.

Dennis Blaine
Cutlery Specialties
22 Morris Lane
Great Neck, NY 11024-1707
ph: 516-829-5899 or 800-229-5530 (orders)
fax: 516-773-8076
Dennis13@aol.com
http://www.restorationproduct.com
Preservation products for flatware: waxes, polishes, cleaners, glues, epoxies, adhesives, chamois, buffs, putty: Renaissance Wax/Polish to restore, refresh, protect antiques, cutlery, furniture, precious metals, armory and more.

Doug Denruyter
Doug's Supplies
144 Sheldon
Climax, MI 49034
ph: 269-746-4104
fax: 269-746-5865
doug2@voyager.net
http://www.dougs-supplies.com
Reproduction hardware, gloves, wooden casters, wood carvings, oxalic acid, glue cleaner, degreaser, Finish Feeder, Restore-A-Finish refinishing supplies; paint strippers, brushes, gloves, steel wool, lacquers, sandpaper, outdoor canopies,

Van Dykes Restorer's
39771 S.D. Hwy. 34
P.O. Box 278
Woonsocket, SD 57385-0278
ph: 800-787-3355 or 605-796-4425
fax: 605-796-4085
http://www.vandykes.com
Supplies for woodworkers and antique restorers: isinglass, curved & bubble glass, roll top accessories, Hoosier accessories, carvings & moldings, furniture components, over 1,000 brass/glass/wooden hardware items; free catalog.

Michael Blair
Restorer Supplies, Inc.
P.O. Box 387
Golden, CO 80403-0387
ph: 303-384-9121
sales@restorersupplies.com
http://www.RestorerSupplies.com
One-stop supplier of a wide range of restoration products and supplies: airbrushes and accessories, adhesives, fill-in and impression materials, glazes, paints, fillers, powders, lighting.

Textiles

Clubs/Associations

American Institute for Conservation of Historic & Artistic Works
Directory: AIC Directory
1717 K St. NW, Ste. 200
Washington, DC 20006
ph: 202-452-9545
fax: 202-452-9328
info@aic-faic.org
http://aic.stanford.edu
Purpose is to advance the knowledge, practice of the conservation of cultural property; the "Guide" lists conservators who are Fellows and Professional Associates of the AIC in paper, textiles, photographs, paintings, furniture, etc.

Repair Services

Textile Conservation Center, Museum of American Textile History
491 Dutton St.
Lowell, MA 01854-4221
ph: 978-441-0400
fax: 978-441-1412
espear@athm.org
http://www.athm.org
TCC provides evaluation, treatment and educational services that pertain to the conservation and preservation of historic textiles.

Evelyn Kennedy
Sewtique, Inc.
391 Long Hill Rd.
P.O. Box 1293
Groton, CT 06340-1293
ph: 860-445-7320 or 800-332-9122
fax: 860-445-1448
sewtique@aol.com
http://www.sewtiqueonline.com
Specialist in restoration, preservation & conservation of apparel and textiles; full service by mail/phone or appt.; appraises textiles, laces, tapestries, etc.; removes spots & stains; teaches textile appraisal & restoration workshops.

Stephen & Carol Huber
40 Ferry Rd.
Old Saybrook, CT 06475
ph: 860-388-6809
fax: 860-434-9709
hubers@antiquesamplers.com
http://www.antiquesamplers.com
Specializes in the repair and conservation of antique needlework.

Appelbaum & Himmelstein
444 Central Park West
New York, NY 10025
ph: 212-666-4630
fax: 212-316-1039
aandh@mindspring.com
Treats silk textiles, paintings and objects.

Patsy Orlofsky
Textile Conservation Workshop
3 Main St.
South Salem, NY 10590
ph: 914-763-5805
textile@bestweb.net
http://www.rap-arcc.org/tcw.htm
Textile conservation lecturer and consultant; also does conservation and repairs of all types of textiles such as archaeological and ethnographic textiles, needlework, laces, quilts, coverlets, samplers, tapestries, costumes.

Linda Tomlin
Details in Design, A Needle Art Studio
4901 C. Helen Potts Place
Williamsburg, VA 23188
ph: 757-253-2483
fax: 757-253-2483
Linens and lace restoration, conservation; embroidered textiles; also reproduction embroidery for linens: arts & crafts, and 18th and 19th century period designs; sells marked linen kits on Irish linen for embroiderers.

Lynn Gorges
Historic Textiles Studio
3910 US Highway 70 East
New Bern, NC 28560
ph: 252-636-3039 or 252-636-5445
fax: 252-637-1862
palampore@aol.com
http://www.textilepreservation.com
Professional conservation and restoration services of vintage textiles including Civil War uniforms, flags, quilts and ladies wear; on-site deionized water stainless steel wash tank 8' x 10' for cleaning age, smoke and water damaged fabric.

Mini Magic, Inc.
3910 Patricia Dr.
Columbus, OH 43220
ph: 614-457-3687
fax: 614-459-2306
Cleaning and repairing; conservation supplies.

Frances K. Faile
Frances K. Faile Textile Conservation
512 S. Washington, #189
Royal Oak, MI 48067
ph: 248-288-2297
fkfaile@earthlink.net
Specializing in the care of antique samplers and needlework, Oriental embroideries, quilts, woven coverlets, hooked rugs, costume accessories, and all types of flat textiles; cleaning, repair & structural stabilization, framing.

Elizabeth L. Barbatelli
Linens Limited, Inc.
240 North Milwaukee St.
Milwaukee, WI 53202
ph: 414-223-1123 or 800-637-6334
fax: 414-223-1126
Expert specializing in the repair, restoration and cleaning of linens; restores both new and antique linens using old world European laundry techniques that are superior to simple laundering.

Emily Sanford
Sanford Restoration Works
2102 Speyer Ln.
Redondo Beach, CA 90278-4918
ph: 310-374-7412
fax: 310-798-2792
Restoration of antique textiles including oriental rugs, American Indian weavings, quilts, needlepoint, embroideries, and tapestries.

Margaret Geiss-Mooney
Textile/Costume Conservation
1124 Clelia Court
Petaluma, CA 94954-5617
ph: 707-763-8694
mgmooney@moonware.net
Has offered conservation services since 1979 for all types of textiles/costumes, antique to modern; assessment, stabilizing, cleaning, preparation for display, storage & transit; disaster recovery; workshops & lectures.

Suppliers

Mary Beth Temple
Mary Beth Temple.com
P.O. Box 4
Tenafly, NJ 07670
ph: 201-569-5571
fax: 201-569-9170
VintageLin@aol.com
http://www.marybethtemple.com
Sells Restoration (for old food stains), sodium perborate (stain removal), Orvus quilt soap.

Rita Marx
Cherish
205 W. 86th St.
New York, NY 10024-3327
ph: 212-724-1748
smarx@i2000.com
Carries Orvus soap and other conservation supplies including padded hangers, acid-free boxes and tissues, etc. for the storage, cleaning and displaying of vintage textiles and clothing.

Betsy Johnson
Nancy's Notions
333 Beichl Ave.
P.O. Box 683
Beaver Dam, WI 53916-0683
ph: 920-887-0391 or 800-833-0690
fax: 920-887-0391
johnson@nancysnotions.com
http://www.nancysnotions.com
Carries Orvus brand quilt soap.

June Roth-Splain
Lily-White Linens
1496 Rolling Acres
Argyle, TX 76226-6330
ph: 940-240-8800 or 940-565-9611
fax: 940-383-8809
*Lily-White Linens is a product that
can be safely used on antique linens
and quilts for stain and spot removal;
safe for the environment.*

Woodworking

(see also HARDWARE; REPAIR/
RESTORATION/CONSERVATION,
Furniture; WOOD; Repair Services
listed under REPAIR/RESTORATION/
CONSERVATION and within other
specific categories throughout this
Directory)

Misc. Services

Bess Naylor
Olde Mill Cabinet Shoppe
1660 Camp Betty Washington Rd.
York, PA 17402
ph: 717-755-8884
fax: 717-755-5688
http://www.oldemill.com
*Offers one and two day courses on
wood finishing, antique restoration,
carving, furniture construction and
several other topics; specialty wood
finishing supplies including dyes,
shellacs, pigments, milk paints, etc.*

Mitchell Kohanek, Instr.
Dakota County Technical College
1300 145th St. E.
Rosemount, MN 55068-2999
ph: 651-423-8362
fax: 651-423-8775
mitchell.kohanek@dctc.mnscu.edu
http://www.woodfinishing.org
*Offers a diploma program in Wood
finishing technology and a Certificate
in Furniture Service Technician.*

Suppliers

Woodworkers Warehouse
126 Oxford St.
Lynn, MA 01901-1132
ph: 800-877-7899 or 781-598-2000
fax: 781-485-2150
customerservice@woodworkerswarehouse.com
http://www.woodworkerswarehouse.com
*Mail order source for a good mix of
woodworking tools.*

Tremont Nail Company
P.O. Box 111
Wareham, MA 02571
ph: 617-295-0038 or 800-842-0560
tremont@mazenails.com
http://www.mazenails.com/tremont.htm
*Carries twenty different styles of
historic cut nails.*

Barbara Horton Rockwell
Horton Brasses Inc.
49 Nooks Hill Rd.
Cromwell, CT 06416
ph: 800-754-9127 or 860-635-4400
fax: 860-635-6473
orion@horton-brasses.com
http://www.horton-brasses.com
*Sells authentic period reproduction
hardware of the finest quality.
Manufactured of solid brass or
handforged black iron in CT factory;
catalog available upon request.*

Micro Mark
340 Snyder Ave.
Berkeley Heights, NJ 07922-1505
ph: 908-464-2984
fax: 908-665-9383
info@micromark.com
http://www.micromark.com
*Mail order source for small tools
only, e.g., X-Acto, knives, Dremel,
airbrushes, micro-sanders, etc.; 80-pg.
catalog $1.*

Garrett Wade Company, Inc.
161 Ave. Of The Americas
New York, NY 10013-1299
ph: 800-221-2942 or 212-807-1155
fax: 800-566-9525
mail@garrettwade.com
http://www.garrettwade.com
*Reproduction English solid brass
hardware; also 220-page catalog of
the world's finest specialty woodworking tools: planes, chisels, etc.*

Glenn Docherty
Constantine
2050 Eastchester Rd.
Bronx, NY 10461
ph: 800-223-8087
fax: 718-792-2110
glendoc@constantines.com
http://www.constantines.com
*A complete line of tools, hardware,
finishing supplies, marquetry kits,
books, moldings, parts, veneers,
hardwoods, etc.*

Mohawk Finishing Products
4715 State Highway 30
Amsterdam, NY 12010
ph: 800-545-0047 or 518-843-1380
fax: 518-842-3551
mohawkinfo@mohawk-finishing.com
http://www.mohawk-finishing.com
*Major supplier of finishing tools,
supplies and materials.*

Woodcrafter's Supply, Inc.
7703 Perry Highway
Pittsburgh, PA 15237
ph: 800-645-9292 or 412-367-4330
fax: 800-853-9663
http://www.woodcrafterssupply.com
*Mail order source for hand tools,
machinery, hardware, and finishes;
also stores located in Erie, PA and
Altoona, PA.*

William Simpson
18th Century Hardware Co., Inc.
131 East 3rd St.
Derry, PA 15627-1607
ph: 724-694-2708
fax: 724-694-9587
*Clean, polish & repair brass, bronze,
silver, pot metal items; makes, sells
reproduction hardware; clean and
electrify brass lamps, or reverse
electrification; will duplicate any style
or pattern.*

Bess Naylor
Olde Mill Cabinet Shoppe
1660 Camp Betty Washington Rd.
York, PA 17402
ph: 717-755-8884
fax: 717-755-5688
http://www.oldemill.com
*Offers one and two day courses on
wood finishing, antique restoration,
carving, furniture construction and
several other topics; specialty wood
finishing supplies including dyes,
shellacs, pigments, milk paints, etc.*

Bill Ball
Ball & Ball Antique Hardware
  Reproduction & Restorations
463 W. Lincoln Highway
Exton, PA 19341
ph: 800-257-3711 or 610-363-7330
fax: 610-363-7639
billball@ptd.net
http://www.ballandball-us.com
*Sells reproduction hardware; 18th
century reproduction brass and iron
chandeliers, sconces, candle stands
and candlesticks; also offers a
recasting service.*

Industrial Abrasives Co.
P.O. Box 14955
Reading, PA 19612-4955
ph: 800-451-1861
fax: 610-378-4868
indabrasives@msn.com
http://www.industrialabrasives.com/
  index.html
*Carries a large line of sandpaper and
other abrasives.*

Paxton Hardware Ltd.
P.O. Box 256
Upper Falls, MD 21156-0256
ph: 410-592-8505 or 800-241-9741
fax: 410-592-2224
paxton@ix.netcom.com
http://www.paxtonhardware.com
*Supplies authentic solid brass, hard-
to-find reproduction hardware in
period styles: pulls, knobs, hinges,
locks, casters, table hardware, bed
hardware.*

Clifford Rufkahr
Rufkahr's
P.O. Box 56112
Virginia Beach, VA 23456
ph: 757-721-9154 or 800-545-7947
  (orders)
fax: 757-426-8484
rufkahrs@rufkahrs.com
http://www.rufkahrs.com
Reproduction hardware, lamp parts,

*mirror supports and brackets, knobs,
pie safe tins, bed parts, Hoosier
cabinet parts, brass handles, brass
knobs, trunk hardware, caning
supplies, rocker runners, Simichrome,
Nev'r Dull, and more.*

Woodcraft
1177 Rosemar Rd.
Parkersburg, WV 26102
ph: 304-428-4866 or 800-225-1153
fax: 304-428-8271
custserv@woodcraft.com
http://www.woodcraft.com
*Mail order, retail and Internet source
for the Craftsman's most complete
offering of woodworking tools,
supplies and books.*

Highland Hardware
1045 N. Highland Ave., NE
Atlanta, GA 30306
ph: 800-241-6748 or 404-872-4466
fax: 404-876-1941
customerservice@highland-hardware.com
http://www.highland-hardware.com
*Mail order source for hand tools,
machinery, workbenches, books,
videos, and supplies; call 888-500-
4466 for free catalog.*

Power Kleen Corp.
101 Bayview Blvd.
Oldsmar, FL 34677
ph: 813-854-2648 or 800-844-2648
fax: 813-854-3133
*Wholesale chemicals and supplies for
refinishers; paint and varnish
removers, lacquer thinner, mineral
spirits.*

A & H Brass & Supply
126 W. Main St.
Johnson City, TN 37601-6210
ph: 423-928-8220 or 800-638-4252
fax: 423-928-8360
thelampdr@aol.com
*Carries a wide selection of lamp parts
and shades, furniture hardware,
veneers, caning supplies, trunk parts,
fiberboard seats, etc.*

Bob Morgan Woodworking Supplies
1121 Bardstown Rd.
Louisville, KY 40204-1301
ph: 502-225-5855
fax: 502-225-5844
info@morganwood.com
http://www.morganwood.com
*Mail order source for hundreds of
veneers, faces, flexibles, inlays, burls,
tiger oak, etc. for restoring antique
furniture; send for free catalog.*

Cherry Tree Toys, Inc.
408 S. Jefferson St.
P.O. Box 369
Belmont, OH 43718
ph: 614-484-4363 or 800-848-4363
fax: 888-848-4388
http://www.cherrytree-online.com
*Mail order source for children's toys,
doll houses, whirligig kits, parts,
books and supplies.*

Robert Hershberger
Hershberger's Hardware
1411 Township Rd. 178
Baltic, OH 43804
ph: 330-893-2464 or 800-734-8044
fax: 330-698-3200
Catalog of specialty products for antiques and woodworking such as spool cabinet decals, high chair trays, antique telephone parts, Hoosier cabinet parts, lamp parts; $4 for 64-page catalog (refundable).

Leichtung Workshops
4944 Commerce Parkway
Cleveland, OH 44128
ph: 800-321-6840
fax: 216-464-6764
Mail order source for hand tools, supplies and small kits.

Refinishing Store, The
1943 N. Cleveland-Massillon Rd.
P.O. Box 498
Bath, OH 44210-0498
ph: 330-668-2631
fax: 330-666-0586
http://www.refinish.com
A source of finishing products waxes, cleaners easily used by professionals and first time restorers alike; all tested for ease of use and results; also carries hard-to-find products such as Butchers Wax and Goddards Polishes.

Shopsmith Tool Guide
6530 Poe Ave.
Dayton, OH 45414
ph: 800-543-7586 or 800-762-7555
fax: 800-722-3965
shpsmith@aol.com
http://www.shopsmith.com
Mail order source for hand tools and supplies. Visit local Shopsmith Store or order by phone.

Phyllis & Phil Kennedy
Phyllis Kennedy Hardware, Inc.
10655 Andrade Dr.
Zionsville, IN 46077
ph: 317-873-1316
fax: 317-873-8662
philken@kennedyhardware.com
http://www.kennedyhardware.com
Hardware for antique furniture, ice boxes, Hoosier cabinets and trunks; manufacturer of flour bins and sifters for Hoosier cabinets; pulls, bails, knobs, latches, chair seats and caning, hinges, locks and keys, coat hooks, etc.

Doug Poe
Doug Poe Antiques
4213W 500N
Huntington, IN 46750-8941
ph: 800-348-5004
fax: 219-356-4358
Carries antique restoration hardware: stamped-brass pulls, diecast brass knobs, casters, teardrop pulls, brass keys, cupboard latches, etc.

Doug Denruyter
Doug's Supplies
144 Sheldon
Climax, MI 49034
ph: 269-746-4104
fax: 269-746-5865
doug2@voyager.net
http://www.dougs-supplies.com
Reproduction hardware, gloves, wooden casters, wood carvings, oxalic acid, glue cleaner, degreaser, Finish Feeder, Restore-A-Finish refinishing supplies; paint strippers, brushes, gloves, steel wool, lacquers, sandpaper, outdoor canopies,

Woodsmith Store
2625 Beaver Ave.
Des Moines, IA 50310
ph: 800-929-8854 or 515-255-8979
fax: 515-282-6741
woodstor@augusthome.com
http://www.woodsmithstore.com
Mail order source for woodworking tools, hardware, and project plans and supplies.

Van Dykes Restorer's
39771 S.D. Hwy. 34
P.O. Box 278
Woonsocket, SD 57385-0278
ph: 800-787-3355 or 605-796-4425
fax: 605-796-4085
http://www.vandykes.com
Mail order source for refinishing supplies; free catalog of reproduction simulated and solid wood carvings, hardware, pulls, knobs, leather seats, old fashioned nails, isinglass, etc.; also issues catalog of taxidermy supplies.

WSI Distributors - Antique Restoration Supplies
405 N. Main St.
Saint Charles, MO 63301-2034
ph: 800-447-9974 or 636-946-5811
fax: 636-946-5832
talk2us@wsidistributors.com
http://www.wsidistributors.com
Wholesale source for furniture & trunk hardware, cane & weaving materials, fiber chair seats, veneer, wood ornaments, Zap glues, and much more; over 1,200 items for professional furniture restorers. Sorry, dealers only.

Gay Barton
Briwax Midwest, Inc.
4400 E. Woodson Harris Rd.
Columbia, MO 65201
ph: 800-562-5855
Briwax is a restorative compound used mainly for restoring antique furniture and floors.

Scott's-Becker's Hardware Inc.
1411 S. 3rd St.
Ozark, MO 65721-9188
ph: 888-991-0151 or 417-581-6525
fax: 417-581-4771
scotbeckhdw@aol.com
http://www.scotbeckhdw.com
Carries hardware for antique furniture: trunk hardware, bed parts,

kitchen cabinets, Hoosier, pulls, latches, hinges, locks keys.

Woodworker's Supply, Inc.
5604 Alameda Place NE
Albuquerque, NM 87113
ph: 505-821-1511 or 800-645-9292
fax: 505-821-7331
robinm@woodworker.com
http://www.woodworker.com
Mail order source for wood finishing tools, supplies and brass hardware.

Gary Hahn
Muff's Antiques
135 S. Glassell St.
Orange, CA 92866-1421
ph: 714-997-0243
fax: 714-997-1601
muffs@earthlink.net
http://home.earthlink.net/~muffs
Mail order source for kitchen cabinet hardware (Hoosiers) including hinges, labels, canisters, castors, and rolls; also ice box parts, locks, keys (specializes in rekeying antique locks), window hardware, and much, much more; catalog $5.

Harbor Freight Tools
3491 Mission Oaks Blvd.
Camarillo, CA 93011-6010
ph: 800-423-2567 or 805-388-3000
fax: 805-388-0760
webmaster@harborfreight.com
http://www.harborfreight.com
Absolutely the lowest prices on quality name brand tools, equipment, machinery for both the home and professional workshop; free catalog.

Woodline, The Japan Woodworker
1731 Clement Ave.
Alameda, CA 94501-1204
ph: 510-521-1810 or 800-537-7820
fax: 510-521-1864
support@thejapanwoodworker.com
http://www.thejapanwoodworker.com
Mail order source for highest quality woodworking tools from Japan.

American Home Supply
191 Lost Lake Lane
P.O. Box 697
Campbell, CA 95009-0697
ph: 408-246-1962
fax: 408-296-2450
Carries the largest selection of antique reproduction hardware on the West Coast; has a 99.9% stock rate.

Vintage Hardware
P.O. Box 9486
San Jose, CA 95157-0486
ph: 408-246-9918
fax: 408-296-2450
vhprs@earthlink.net
Publishes a hardware catalog; brass hardware, household hinges, glass knobs, brass casters, nickel plate ice box hardware, wooden casters.

Ritter & Son Hardware
38001 Old Stage Rd.
P.O. Box 578
Gualala, CA 95445-9984
ph: 800-445-5044 or 707-884-3363
fax: 800-445-5043
flora@mcn.org
Supplier of furniture restoration hardware: carved oak gingerbread, Hoosier hardware, cast & stamped brass pulls, handles, etc.; dealers only.

Bridge City Tool Works, Inc.
1104 N.E. 28th Ave.
Portland, OR 97232
ph: 503-282-6997 or 800-253-3332
fax: 503-287-1085
bridgecitytools@uswest.net
http://www.bridgecitytools.com
Mail order source for fine woodworking hand tools.

RESTAURANT COLLECTIBLES

(see also CERAMICS; DINERS & RELATED ITEMS; FAST FOOD COLLECTIBLES; FOOD COLLECTIBLES; MENUS)

Collectors

Kathleen Lathom
P.O. Box 5053
Bellingham, WA 98227-5053
ph: 360-676-0715
chinacoll@earthlink.net
Wants top-marked restaurant china from ice cream parlors, lunch rooms, hamburger stands, grills, diners, sandwich stands, cafes, coffee shops, greasy spoon restaurants.

Dealers

Annaliese Whipple
Bee's Knees, The
3220 Storrington Dr.
Miccosukee Cpo, FL 32309
ph: 850-894-6571 or 850-894-6572
thebeesknees@comcast.net
http://www.thebeesknees.biz
Buys and sells restaurant ware china manufactured for use in cafe and railroad diners, shipping lines, transportation, and other companies; especially seeking unusual topmarks and rare patterns.

Ered Matthew
Dinner in the Diner.com
P.O. Box 740474
Dallas, TX 75374-0474
ph: 972-235-8639
fax: 972-235-8614
dinerchine@cabinclass.com
http://www.cabinclass.com/dinerinthediner
Offers replacement pieces for collectible, vintage restaurant ware; hundreds of vintage restaurant ware and commercial china patterns in stock.

Experts

Barbara J. Conroy
P.O. Box 2343
Santa Clara, CA 95055
restaurant-china@comcast.com
http://restaurant-china.home.comcast.net
*Author of "Restaurant China, Vol. 1
and 2;" specializes in restaurant,
hotel, steam ship, railroad, airline,
and other commercial dinnerware.*

Internet Resources

Chris Trent
Little Spoon's Virtual Museum of
Restaurant Ware
ph: 310-827-6510
spoon@littlespoon.com
http://www.littlespoon.com
*An online resource and virtual
museum of collectible vitrified
restaurant chinas.*

Barbara J. Conroy
P.O. Box 2369
Santa Clara, CA 95055
restaurantchina@attbi.com
http://home.attbi.com/~restaurantchina
*Site contains helpful information on
restaurant china: references, china
manufacturer marks, date codes,
restaurant china names and materials,
pattern names, topmark identification,
related links.*

Big Boy

Collectors

Steve Soelberg
29126 Laro Dr.
Agoura Hills, CA 91301-1635
ph: 818-889-9909
*Wants Big Boy collectibles such as
lamps, lunch boxes, cookie jars,
counter displays, buttons, nodders,
menus, ash trays, salt/peppers, etc.;
items must have the Big Boy logo on
them; no vinyl/rubber banks, please;
the older the better.*

Howard Johnson's

Collectors

Jeffrey C. McCurty
P.O. Box 882
Pleasant Valley, NY 12569-0882
ph: 845-635-3566
Jeffrey.McCurty@omr.state.ny.us
*Wants 1930-1980 Howard Johnson's
dishes, tins, candy boxes, toys, soda
cans, employee patches/service
awards; will seriously consider any
items.*

RESTRAINT DEVICES

(see also KEYS; LOCKS;
MAGICIANS PARAPHERNALIA;
LAW ENFORCEMENT
MEMORABILIA)

Collectors

Mark Lyons
6020 Paseo Del Norte, Ste. B
Carlsbad, CA 92009
ph: 760-431-5397
fax: 760-607-3299
cuffsandstuff@sbcglobal.net
*Wants to buy law enforcement and
magicians keys, handcuffs, leg irons,
thumbcuffs, slave irons, ball and
chains, and toy cuffs; American and
foreign; old or new; also Wells Fargo
strong boxes & locks.*

Dealers

Stan Willis
Handcuffs & Badges
P.O. Box 36474
Cincinnati, OH 45236
handcuffs@isoc.net
http://www.handcuffsandbadges.com
*Buys, sells restraining devices
(handcuffs, leg irons, thumbcuffs,
etc.), police badges, fire badges and
other fire and police antiques;
specializes in items related to
Cincinnati and area.*

Experts

Yossie Silverman
Yossie's Handcuff Collection
49 Hartford St.
San Francisco, CA 94114
yossie@blacksteel.com
http://www.blacksteel.com/hcs.html
*Collects and specializes in handcuffs
and other restraint devices.*

Internet Resources

Joseph W. Lauher
Handcuffs.Org
38 Segatogue Lane
Centereach, NY 11720
lauher@handcuffs.org
http://www.handcuffs.org
*This Web site presents a guide to
collecting handcuffs and related
restraint devices; the emphasis is on
vintage American handcuffs from the
American Civil War through the
1970s.*

Yossie Silverman
Yossie's Handcuff Collection
49 Hartford St.
San Francisco, CA 94114
yossie@blacksteel.com
http://www.blacksteel.com/hcs.html
*Displays handcuffs according to type,
manufacturer, and name.*

Handcuffs & Leg Shackles

Dealers

Joseph & Pamela Tanner
Wheeler-Tanner ESCAPES
6442 Canyon Creek Way
Elk Grove, CA 95758
ph: 916-684-4006
fax: 916-684-4006
JnPwLrTnr@aol.com
*Specialize in handcuffs, leg shackles,
balls & chains, restraints, padlocks,
locks & locking devices of all kinds
(including railroad).*

Peter D. McCahon
Handcuff Collection, The
96 Butely Rd.
Luton, Bedfordshire LU4 9EX U.K.
ph: +44 (0) 1582 564850
fax: +44 (0) 7973 135263
Peter@mccahon.co.uk
http://www.handcuffcollection.co.uk
*Collector and dealer in all forms of
handcuffs, leg irons, and manacles;
interest limited solely to antique,
police and magical related items.*

Experts

Michael Griffin
International Handcuff Exchange
356 W. Powell Rd.
Powell, OH 43065-9650
ph: 614-846-0585 or 614-846-6790
escapeguy@aol.com
*Buys/sells all types of handcuffs, leg
irons, locks, magicians escape items,
old or new; offers large quarterly list
of items for sale.*

REVERE GIFTWARE

Experts

Douglas M. Singleton
P.O. Box 416
Westmoreland, NY 13490-0416
ph: 315-336-7792
archaic123@aol.com
*Appraises and specializes in Revere
Giftware made of chrome, copper and
brass prior to 1942: cocktail shakers,
condiment sets, goblets, magazine
holders, pitchers, trays, etc.; no pots
and/or pans, please.*

REVOLUTIONARY WAR ITEMS

Collectors

Larry Jarvinen
313 Condon Rd.
Manistee, MI 49660-1008
ph: 231-723-5063
*Wants muskets, lamps, pipes, chests,
swords, polearms, tools, silverware,
compasses, bayonets, canteens,
cannons, etc.*

Alex Peck
Antique Scientifica
P.O. Box 710
Charleston, IL 61920-0710
ph: 217-348-1009
antiques@advant.net
http://antiquescientifica.com
*Wants uniforms, insignia, guns,
swords, diaries, medical instruments,
hats, medals, belt plates.*

REVOLVING LAMPS

(see LAMPS & LIGHTING, Motion)

REWARDS OF MERIT

(see PAPER COLLECTIBLES;
SCHOOL RELATED MEMORABILIA)

RIDING TOYS

(see also AUTOMOBILIA; BICYCLES
& RELATED MEMORABILIA)

Experts

Edmund Weinberg
Atlantic Highlands Animal Hospital
44 Thoreau Dr.
Freehold, NJ 07728
ph: 732-845-5117
fax: 732-845-5117
*Collects and specializes in riding toys,
velocipedes, wagons, wheel toys, and
rocking horses.*

Internet Resources

Bob Yuhas
CollectingShows.com
P.O. Box 1289
Mc Afee, NJ 07428-1289
ph: 973-697-4982 or 866-349-8697
pedalcar@netrom.com
http://www.collectingshows.com
*Web site showing images of ongoing
toy shows as well dates and times for
upcoming shows; purchase items while
online or direct from the dealer.*

Repair Services

Carl Kriewall
C & N Reproductions, Inc.
1341 Ashover Ct.
Bloomfield Hills, MI 48304
ph: 248-852-1998
fax: 248-852-1999
info@pedalcar.com
http://www.pedalcar.com
*Manufacturers parts and kits for pedal
cars and pedal planes, especially the
Pursuit plane.*

Repro. Sources

Carl Kriewall
C & N Reproductions, Inc.
1341 Ashover Ct.
Bloomfield Hills, MI 48304
ph: 248-852-1998
fax: 248-852-1999
info@pedalcar.com
http://www.pedalcar.com
*Sells reproduction pedal cars and
pedal planes; wholesale & retail.*

Trace Boley
Un4Gettable Toys
1907 Birchwood St.
Aurora, NE 68818
ph: 402-694-0214
fax: 402-694-6905
info@un4gettabletoys.com
http://www.un4gettabletoys.com
*Specializes in reproductions of classic
riding toys including Radio Flyer
cars, wagons and horses, pedal cars,
Krazy Cars, American-Retro and
Airflow.*

Pedal Vehicles

Clubs/Associations

Bruce Beimers
National Pedal Vehicle Association
1720 Rupert, N.E.
Grand Rapids, MI 49505
ph: 616-361-9887
Focuses on pedal cars.

Collectors

Frank Martin
7669 Winterberry Dr.
Youngstown, OH 44512-4723
ph: 330-758-4470 or 330-518-1160
*Wants any literature related to pedal
vehicles: catalogs, old photos,
advertisements, etc.; wants to buy
postwar pedal cars in original
excellent condition; also prewar pedal
cars in any condition; also wants old
tricycles.*

Nate Stoller
960 Reynolds Dr.
Ripon, CA 95366
ph: 530-676-1000
nate@maytagclub.com
http://www.maytagclub.com
*Wants to buy or trade pre-1960 pedal
cars.*

Dealers

Matthew Vaznaian
Juvenile Automobiles
291 High St.
Woonsocket, RI 02895
ph: 401-762-9661
vaz185@aol.com
Buys and sells antique pedal cars.

Bob Yuhas
Pedal Car Specialties, Inc.
P.O. Box 1289
Mc Afee, NJ 07428-1289
ph: 973-697-4982 or 866-349-8697
pedalcar@netrom.com
http://www.pressedsteeltoysmonthly.com
*Pedal car sales, restorations, parts &
accessories.*

Bob & Betty Lampman
20 Black Ave. West
Vernon, NY 13476
ph: 315-829-2345

Tom Vitunic
4684 Roland Rd.
Allison Park, PA 15101
ph: 412-487-1405
Buys, sells, trades pedal cars.

Stan Phillips
438 8th St.
Oakmont, PA 15139
ph: 412-828-7351

David Osborn
D & J Collectibles
101 Ridgecrest Dr.
Lawrenceville, GA 30045
ph: 770-962-7556 or 770-586-0338
fax: 770-962-5881
sr281@aol.com
http://members.aol.com/sr281
*Buys, sells, appraises pedal vehicles
from the 1920s to 1960s era.*

Pedal Car Bob
6690 Sterling Rd.
Hollywood, FL 33024
ph: 954-690-5630
Buys, sells, repairs pedal cars.

Harold Neal
7841 Owl Hollow Trail
Mc Donald, TN 37353
ph: 615-238-5421

David A. Hull
Small Town Coins & Collectibles
7498 E. Davison Rd.
Davison, MI 48423-2014
ph: 810-658-1992
fax: 810-658-2977
towncoin@small-town.cnchost.com
http://small-town.cnchost.com
*Has over 100 antique (1920-1970)
pedal cars for sale; also buys pedal
cars.*

Bill Guggemos
Lil Car Peddler, The
1104 N. Creyts Rd.
Lansing, MI 48917
ph: 517-323-2758
*Wants unrestored pedal cars from the
1920s to 1940s.*

Dan & Linda Portell
Portell Restorations
1574 Saddle Dr.
Festus, MO 63028
ph: 636-937-8192 or 636-931-8192
toypeddler@aol.com
http://www.pedalcarsandparts.com
*Collector, restorer and manufacturer
of pedal cars and parts; buys, sells,
trades pedal cars.*

Joe Moncado
15745 Beckett Lane
Olathe, KS 66062
ph: 913-764-0026
jmoncado@aol.com

Bill Hampton
17916 B Interstate 30
Benton, AR 72015
ph: 501-778-1327
*Specializing in pedal cars, pedal
airplanes, pedal boats, pedal tractors;
all antique toys with wheels.*

Tony Duran
Nostalgia Warehouse LLC
7801 US Hwy 287
Arlington, TX 76001
ph: 817-572-5012
fax: 817-563-0572
tonyduran@nostalgiawarehouse.com
http://www.nostalgiawarehouse.com
Buy/sell/restore jukeboxes, coke

*machines, radios, gas pumps, pedal
cars, neon signs, and more; an
authorized distributor for Wurlitzer
and Crosley Radio products; sells new
pedal car reproductions.*

Leroy Dyas
Leroy's Sidewalk Cruisers
P.O. Box 1864
Ramona, CA 92065
ph: 619-789-2962
*Buys, sells, restores all types of pedal
toys; tires, wheels, hub caps, decals,
reproduction parts, accessories.*

Roger Rocha
1114 Harvard Dr.
Davis, CA 95161
ph: 916-759-0345

Experts

Sanford Weltman
2 Roxbury Lane
Pittsford, NY 14534
ph: 585-249-9417 or 585-249-9499
*20 year veteran collector/buyer of
pedal vehicles and large riding toys;
buys pre-WWII pedal cars, pedal
planes, or pedal trucks; also will buy
post-WWII up to 1950s; any
condition; has parts; does not resell;
please send photos.*

Frank Martin
7669 Winterberry Dr.
Youngstown, OH 44512-4723
ph: 330-758-4470 or 330-518-1160
*Wants any literature related to pedal
vehicles: catalogs, old photos,
advertisements, etc.; wants to buy
postwar pedal cars in original
excellent condition; also prewar pedal
cars in any condition; also wants old
tricycles.*

Dennis Krupnow
PedalCarPlus.com
15150 Hannan Rd.
Romulus, MI 48174
ph: 734-941-5868
fax: 734-941-9212
pedalcarplus@aol.com
http://www.pedalcarplus.com
*Retail and wholesale distributor of
reproduction and customized pedal
cars for children and collectors;
manufacturer of pedal car accessories.*

Tom Christmann
Blue Diamond Classics
P.O. Box 81906
Lincoln, NE 68501
ph: 402-323-3220
fax: 402-323-3211
bdc@inebraska.com
http://www.bluediamondclassics.com
*Pedal vehicle collector and dealer; one
of the largest collections of pedal cars
in the world; buys and sells pre- and
post-war pedal vehicle parts,
accessories, graphics, and reproduction cars.*

George Medinilla
Pedal Cars by George Medinilla
14714 1/2 Chadron Ave.
Gardena, CA 90249-3505
ph: 310-679-8688
http://www.pedalcar.net
*Pedal car collector, dealer, expert,
repair and restoration service; also
makes reproduction pedal cars, planes
and boats; information books
available.*

Internet Resources

George Medinilla
Pedal Cars by George Medinilla
14714 1/2 Chadron Ave.
Gardena, CA 90249-3505
ph: 310-679-8688
http://www.pedalcar.net
*Appraisal, pedal car news, restoration
tips, classified ads, etc.*

Periodicals

Bob Yuhas
Magazine: Pressed Steel Toys
P.O. Box 1289
Mc Afee, NJ 07428-1289
ph: 973-697-4982 or 866-349-8697
pedalcar@netrom.com
http://www.pressedsteeltoysmonthly.com
*A monthly magazine dedicated to all
pressed steel toys from pedal cars to
toy trucks.*

John Rastall
Newsletter: Wheel Goods Trader, The
P.O. Box 435
Fraser, MI 48026-0435
ph: 586-949-6282
fax: 586-949-6282
wheelgoodstrader@ameritech.net
http://www.wgtpub.com
*Magazine for collectors pedal cars,
pedal airplanes; classifieds, calendar,
etc.*

Repair Services

John Bogan
Bogan Restoration Services
ph: 972-445-4800
fax: 972-445-8207
jbogan@mindspring.com
http://www.mindspring.com/~dagmara/
deere.html
*Buys, sells, restores vintage bicycles,
pedal cars, toys and metalware.*

Bob Yuhas
Pedal Car Specialties, Inc.
P.O. Box 1289
Mc Afee, NJ 07428-1289
ph: 973-697-4982 or 866-349-8697
pedalcar@netrom.com
http://www.pressedsteeltoysmonthly.com
*Pedal car sales, restorations, parts &
accessories.*

Ron Hanley
Mini-Motors
130 Main
Hobart, NY 13788
ph: 607-538-9926
Handcrafted "one-of-a-kind" pedal

cars manufactured; can hand craft
body parts and fenders for pedal cars.

Gerald Hochstetler
Gerald & Sons Restorations
72930 C.R. 100
Nappanee, IN 46550
ph: 219-773-7189

Darwin "Doc" Hunkler
2248 S. City Rd. 350 W.
Russiaville, IN 46979
ph: 765-453-1210
*Restores pedal cars and pressed steel
toys.*

Samuelson Pedal Tractor Part
234 1st Ave. East
P.O. Box 346
Dyersville, IA 52040
ph: 319-875-6222
fax: 319-875-6126
pedalparts@aol.com
http://www.pedaltractorparts.com
*Sells, repairs pedal tractors; also
supplies parts.*

Dan & Linda Portell
Portell Restorations
1574 Saddle Dr.
Festus, MO 63028
ph: 636-937-8192 or 636-931-8192
toypeddler@aol.com
http://www.pedalcarsandparts.com
*Collector, restorer and manufacturer
of pedal cars and parts; buys, sells,
trades pedal cars.*

Tom Christmann
Blue Diamond Classics
P.O. Box 81906
Lincoln, NE 68501
ph: 402-323-3220
fax: 402-323-3211
bdc@inebraska.com
http://www.bluediamondclassics.com
*Carries an extensive selection of
repair parts for a wide range of pedal
toys.*

Juan DeLeon
DeLeon's Restoration
202 Wickhamford Way
Houston, TX 77015
ph: 713-330-9073
juan@bikevato.com
http://www.bikevato.com
*Restores vintage bicycles as well as
pedal vehicles.*

Mike Harfield
Elantec
16 Blackbrook Rd.
Fareham, Hampshire PO15 5DJ U.K.
ph: +44 (0) 1329 285198
fax: +44 (0) 20 7681 3763
cars@elantec.co.uk
http://www.elantec.co.uk
*Reproduction and restoration of
Eureka pedal cars and spares; special
commissions also undertaken.*

Repro. Sources

Pedalcars.com - The Pedal Car Authority
1460 Betsy Lane
Randleman, NC 27317
ph: 336-672-3818
sales@pedalcars.com
http://www.pedalcars.com
Offers reproduction pedal vehicles.

Dennis Krupnow
PedalCarPlus.com
15150 Hannan Rd.
Romulus, MI 48174
ph: 734-941-5868
fax: 734-941-9212
pedalcarplus@aol.com
http://www.pedalcarplus.com
*Retail and wholesale distributor of
reproduction and customized pedal
cars for children and collectors;
manufacturer of pedal car accessories.*

Tony Duran
Nostalgia Warehouse LLC
7801 US Hwy 287
Arlington, TX 76001
ph: 817-572-5012
fax: 817-563-0572
tonyduran@nostalgiawarehouse.com
http://www.nostalgiawarehouse.com
*Buy/sell/restore jukeboxes, coke
machines, radios, gas pumps, pedal
cars, neon signs, and more; an
authorized distributor for Wurlitzer
and Crosley Radio products; sells new
reproductions of pedal cars.*

Bob Lowry
Foss Company, The
1224 Washington Ave.
Golden, CO 80401
ph: 303-279-3373
fax: 303-278-9556
BLowry@fossco.com
http://www.fossco.com
Sells reproduction pedal cars.

Mike Harfield
Elantec
16 Blackbrook Rd.
Fareham, Hampshire PO15 5DJ U.K.
ph: +44 (0) 1329 285198
fax: +44 (0) 20 7681 3763
cars@elantec.co.uk
http://www.elantec.co.uk
*Reproduction and restoration of
Eureka pedal cars and spares; special
commissions also undertaken.*

Suppliers

Matthew Vaznaian
Juvenile Automobiles
291 High St.
Woonsocket, RI 02895
ph: 401-762-9661
vaz185@aol.com
*Smallest pedal car parts supplier in
the world: tires, wheels, hubcaps,
hood ornaments, bells, bumpers,
steering wheels, headlights, pods,
windshields, etc.; send $6 for catalog.*

Jim & Sandy Kay
J&S Pedalin'
2536 Willow Dr.
Arnold, MO 63010-2829
ph: 314-296-5908
*Supplies parts for pedal cars: front
ends, rear ends, pedal rods, cranks,
ladder racks, wheels, tires, hubcaps,
steering wheels, windshields, hood
ornaments, etc.*

Tom Christmann
Blue Diamond Classics
P.O. Box 81906
Lincoln, NE 68501
ph: 402-323-3220
fax: 402-323-3211
bdc@inebraska.com
http://www.bluediamondclassics.com
*Pedal cars, car graphics, parts and
repairs; extensive catalog of parts and
decals available.*

J.D. Dorsey
Texas Pedal Car Peddler Inc.
213 Stone Dr.
Fort Worth, TX 76108
ph: 817-238-8363
fax: 817-238-7227
texped@aol.com
http://www.pedalcarparts.com
*320-page catalog/reference book for
$8.*

Rocking Horses
Experts

Edmund Weinberg
Atlantic Highlands Animal Hospital
44 Thoreau Dr.
Freehold, NJ 07728
ph: 732-845-5117
fax: 732-845-5117
*Collects and specializes in riding toys,
wheel toys, and rocking horses.*

Man./Prod./Dist.

Christopher Woolcock
Renaissance Rocking Horses
251C Windsor Rd.
Vineyard, New South Wales 2765
  Australia
ph: 61 2 4577-8697 or 61 2 4577-5061
info@rockinghorses.com.au
http://www.rockinghorses.com.au
*World renowned rocking horse maker/
restorer/appraiser; 25 yrs. experience;
sells new moving horses toys such as
hobby horses, tricycle horses, shoo-
flies, walker trainers, cabriolets,
small bow rockers, horse-drawns.*

Repair Services

Marsha A. Schloesser
Carousel Workshop, The
29915 Fullerville Rd.
Deland, FL 32720-5704
ph: 352-669-6449
fax: 352-669-5573
carouselworkshop@yahoo.com
http://www.carouselworkshop.com
*Dealer and lecturer; buys, sells,
restores carousel figures; also gliding*

*& rocking horses; antique and
reproduction carousel figures.*

Sleds
Collectors

Art Bransky
1840 Siegfriedale Rd.
Breinigsville, PA 18031-2246
ph: 610-285-6180
artbransky@enter.net
*Dealer, collector, expert, restorer of
children's sleds, bobsleds, and any
unusual sledding related items from
the past 100 years; a frequent museum
exhibitor and serious collector.*

Dealers

Lyle Palmiter
Canacadea Sled Shop
676 Tinkertown Rd.
Alfred Station, NY 14803
ph: 607-587-9450
sledman@infoblvd.net
http://www.infoblvd.net/sledman/home/
  home.htm
*Sled collector, dealer, expert, restorer;
buys old sleds regardless of condition;
parts accepted; also does sled
restorations.*

Art Bransky
1840 Siegfriedale Rd.
Breinigsville, PA 18031-2246
ph: 610-285-6180
artbransky@enter.net
*Dealer, collector, expert, restorer of
children's sleds, bobsleds, and any
unusual sledding related items from
the past 100 years; a frequent museum
exhibitor and serious collector.*

Experts

Joan Palicia
15 Canton Rd.
Wayne, NJ 07470
ph: 201-831-0527
*Flexible Flyer memorabilia,
membership cards, models, pins,
advertising, sleds; anything Flexible
Flyer; author of "Flexible Flyer and
other Great Sleds for Collectors."*

Museums/Libraries

Old Sled Works Sled Museum
722 North Market St.
Duncannon, PA 17020
ph: 717-834-9333
sledworks@aol.com
http://www.sledworks.com
*Now an antiques and crafts center, the
Old Sled Works made sleds from 1904
to 1990; museum evokes happy
childhood memories when sleds were
made of wood and metal.*

Repair Services

Lyle Palmiter
Canacadea Sled Shop
676 Tinkertown Rd.
Alfred Station, NY 14803
ph: 607-587-9450
sledman@infoblvd.net
http://www.infoblvd.net/sledman/home/
home.htm
*Sled collector, dealer, expert, restorer;
buys old sleds regardless of condition;
parts accepted; also does sled
restorations.*

Art Bransky
1840 Siegfriedale Rd.
Breinigsville, PA 18031-2246
ph: 610-285-6180
artbransky@enter.net
*Dealer, collector, expert, restorer of
children's sleds, bobsleds, and any
unusual sledding related items from
the past 100 years; a frequent museum
exhibitor and serious collector.*

RINGS

Character/Comic

(see PREMIUMS, Rings)

RIPLEY'S BELIEVE IT OR NOT!

(see also MORBID & ODD ITEMS)

Collectors

Dan Paulun
215 South Maple
West Lafayette, OH 43845-1138
ph: 740-545-9743
*Wants anything Ripley: blotters,
calendars, posters, museum &
odditorium postcards and booklets,
newspaper & magazine ads, etc.*

Glenn Carlisle
2163 Goshen Hill Rd. SE
New Philadelphia, OH 44663-6789
ph: 330-339-3859
*Wants "Ripley's Believe It or Not"
hardback books; also memorabilia
from museum, Odditorium programs,
postcards, giant rings, etc.*

Museums/Libraries

Ripley's Believe It Or Not! Museum
175 Jefferson St.
San Francisco, CA 94113
ph: 415-771-6188
fax: 415-771-1246
sanfran@ripleys.com
http://www.ripleysf.com/ripley/odd/
odd.html
*There are 17 Ripley's Believe It Or
Not! museums across the US and
Canada.*

RIVERBOAT COLLECTIBLES

(see STEAMBOAT COLLECTIBLES)

ROADSIDE MEMORABILIA

(see HIGHWAY COLLECTIBLES;
HOTEL COLLECTIBLES; SOUVENIR
& COMMEMORATIVE ITEMS)

ROBJ

Collectors

Charles Sorkin
63 Ward Dr.
New Rochelle, NY 10804-1918
ph: 914-235-4718
*Wants Robj porcelains: figural
bottles, inkwells, powder jars,
statuettes; any piece marked "Robj;"
call collect.*

Jeff Leegood
DecoLectibles
P.O. Box 596553
Dallas, TX 75227-1429
ph: 214-275-4370
jleegood@yahoo.com
*Seeks Robj perfume lamps, incense
burners, statues, powder boxes, and
liquor bottles; made in porcelain,
ceramic, glass during the 1920s; most
marked ROBJ, Paris France; also
wants other similar Art Deco perfume
lamps.*

Experts

Randy Monsen
Monsen & Baer Inc.
P.O. Box 529
Vienna, VA 22183-0529
ph: 703-938-2129
fax: 703-242-1357
monsenbaer@erols.com

ROBOTS

(see TOYS, Space & Robot)

ROCK 'N' ROLL COLLECTIBLES

(see also AUTOGRAPHS;
MAGAZINES, Scandal/Cult/R 'N' R;
MUSIC, Rock 'N' Roll;
PERSONALITIES [MUSICIANS];
POSTERS, Music; RECORDS;
SHEET MUSIC)

Collectors

Rick Rann
P.O. Box 877
Oak Park, IL 60303-0877
ph: 708-442-7907
ukczech@aol.com
*Wants to buy 1950s through 1970s
rock concert items such as tickets,
handbills, programs, posters, etc.*

Dealers

Ken Farrell
Just Kids Nostalgia
310 New York Ave.
Huntington, NY 11743
ph: 631-423-8449
info@justkidsnostalgia.com
http://www.justkidsnostalgia.com
*Buys and sells vintage Rock 'n Roll:
Beatles, Rolling Stones, Monkees, Led
Zeppelin, Jimi Hendrix, KISS,
Woodstock, concert posters and
tickets, photos.*

Terri Mardis-Ivers
Terri's Toys & Nostalgia
114 Whitworth Ave.
Ponca City, OK 74601-3438
ph: 580-762-8697
toylady@cableone.net
*Buys and sells Beatles, Kiss, Monkees,
Elvis & other original memorabilia
such as toys, novelties, guitars,
drums, vehicles (Yellow Submarine,
Monkeemobile, etc.), Sun Records, etc.*

Myron Ross
Heroes & Legends
P.O. Box 9088
Calabasas, CA 91372
ph: 818-346-9220
heroesross@aol.com
http://www.hereosandlegends.net
*Wants character memorabilia, books,
comic books, Fanzines, movie
memorabilia, etc.; science fiction or
fantasy, rock 'n' roll, autographs.*

Computer Programs For
Man./Prod./Dist.

Niche Software, Inc.
Software: Rock & Roll Collector, The
7118 NW Terrace
Parkland, FL 33076
ph: 954-344-6561
marketing@collectiblessoftware.com
http://www.collectiblessoftware.com
*Designed for the collector of Rock &
Roll memorabilia, from CDs to T-
shirts.*

ROCKETS

(see KITS; MODELS, Rockets;
SCIENCE FICTION; SPACE
COLLECTIBLES)

ROCKHOUNDS

(see LAPIDARY; MINERAL
SPECIMENS)

ROGERS GROUPS

Clubs/Associations

George Humphrey
Rogers Group, The
Newsletter: Minutes, News & Bits
4932 Prince George Ave.
Beltsville, MD 20705-1907
ph: 301-937-7899
*Focuses on the life and works of John
Rogers (1829-1904), American
sculptor.*

Dealers

George P. Lentros
179A Main St.
Ashland, MA 01721-1153
ph: 508-881-1160 or 508-881-1635
fax: 508-881-6475
pglentros@aol.com
*Collector and dealer; buys and sells
John Rogers groups: appraises and
consults on any collection; contact
with wants and any Groups to sell.*

Bruce Bleier
73 Riverdale Rd.
Valley Stream, NY 11581
ph: 516-791-4353
fax: 516-792-0519
emeralite@aol.com
*Author of "John Rogers Statuary;"
buys, collects, sells Rogers groups;
also offers restoration service; will
buy whole collections; questions
answered.*

Experts

Bruce Bleier
73 Riverdale Rd.
Valley Stream, NY 11581
ph: 516-791-4353
fax: 516-792-0519
emeralite@aol.com
*Author of "John Rogers Statuary;"
buys, collects, sells Rogers groups;
also offers restoration service; will
buy whole collections; questions
answered.*

Michael Semendinger
497 South Wellwood Ave.
Lindenhurst, NY 11757-4908
ph: 631-957-8953
mdsdaisy1@netscape.net
*Rogers Groups collector, dealer,
expert; active collector with 75 John
Rogers groups.*

George Humphrey
4932 Prince George Ave.
Beltsville, MD 20705-1907
ph: 301-937-7899
*Interested in the life and works of
John Rogers (1829-1904), American
sculptor; wants to purchase Rogers
groups for his collection.*

Museums/Libraries

John Rogers Studio & Museum of the
New Canaan Historical Society
13 Oenoke Ridge
New Canaan, CT 06840-4104
ph: 203-966-1776
fax: 203-972-5917
newcanaan.historical@snet.net
http://www.nchistory.org

Lightner Museum
P.O. Box 334
75 King St.
Saint Augustine, FL 32085
ph: 904-824-2874
info@lightnermuseum.org
http://www.lightnermuseum.org
*Exhibits relics of America's Gilded
Age: cut glass, Victorian art glass,
stained glass of Tiffany, costumes,
furnishings, mechanical musical
instruments, and other artifacts that
give a glimpse into 19th century daily
life*

ROLLER COASTERS

(see also AMUSEMENT PARK
ITEMS)

Clubs/Associations

American Coaster Enthusiasts, Inc.
Magazine: Rollercoaster!
P.O. Box 2412
Shawnee Mission, KS 66201
bpeters@aceonline.org
http://www.aceonline.org
*Promotes the preservation, apprecia-
tion and enjoyment of the roller
coaster; 4,700 members in 48 states
and 17 countries.*

Collectors

Peter Dusza
305 Mathew St.
Santa Clara, CA 95050
ph: 408-988-8161 or 408-723-0722
fax: 408-988-2206
pdusza@ix.netcom.com
*Wants to buy roller coaster souvenirs
and memorabilia: coffee cups,
drinking and shot glasses, pins,
patches, postcards, posters, and
buttons.*

ROSE O'NEILL COLLECTIBLES

(see also DOLLS, Kewpie)

Clubs/Associations

Len Witkowski
International Rose O'Neill Club
P.O. Box 61
Golden, CO 80402-0061
ph: 303-273-5763 or 303-908-5295
agdc1@aol.com

Jerrie Jorgensen, Pres.
California Rose O'Neill Association
972 E. Marjan St.
Anaheim, CA 92806
ph: 888-637-5747
rwarjorg@aol.com

Experts

Denis C. Jackson
P.O. Box 6433
Kingman, AZ 86401
ticn@olypen.com
http://www.olypen.com/ticn
*Author of "The Price & Identification
Guide to Rose O'Neill," 3rd edition;*

*covering magazine covers, advertising,
paper items from Puck, etc.; send
LSASE for information.*

ROYALTY COLLECTIBLES

(see also POSTCARDS, Royalty
Related; RUSSIAN ITEMS;
SOUVENIR & COMMEMORATIVE
ITEMS)

Clubs/Associations

Commemorative Collector's Society
Newsletter: Members Journal
Lumless House, Gainsborough Rd.
Winthrope
Near Newark, Nottinghamshire NG24
2NR U.K.
ph: 01636-671377
chris@royalcoll.fsnet.co.uk
http://www.royalcoll.fsnet.co.uk
*Members interested in commemorative
items including commemorative pieces
for Royal events and personages (both
US and worldwide): ceramics, glass,
printed tins, textiles, and ephemera.*

Collectors

Frank J. Buono
P.O. Box 1535
Binghamton, NY 13902-1535
ph: 607-724-4444 or 800-527-8893
fax: 607-723-1656
fbuono@stny.rr.com
http://www.fjbstamps.com
*Wants to buy royalty items: Victoria
1887, 1897 Jubilees, Edward &
Alexandra 1901.*

Dealers

Pat Klein
Nostalgia Unlimited
P.O. Box 262
East Berlin, CT 06023
ph: 860-828-3973
fax: 860-828-1544
pklein262@yahoo.com
*Carries stock of royalty collectibles
primarily from England, Germany,
Russia, Denmark, Norway, Monaco
and Belgium.*

Ian Ingham
Royal Pavilion, The
4741 East Palm canyon (PMB167)
Palm Springs, CA 92264
ph: 730-321-7305
info@theroyalpavilion.com
http://www.theroyalpavilion.com
*Buys and sells British Royalty
commemoraives; from King George III
to the present day.*

British

Collectors

Edward J. Sperling
Britannia Past
215 Beach Ave.
Kennebunk, ME 04043
ph: 207-967-5989
*Buys and sells by mail order British
Royalty commemoratives: china, glass,
silver, paper, textile, etc.*

Dealers

Anita L. Grashof
Gallerie Ani'tiques
Stage House Village
366 Park Ave.
Scotch Plains, NJ 07076-1121
ph: 908-322-4600
*Buys, sells and appraises British
Royal commemoratives from Queen
Victoria through Prince William.*

Douglas H. Flynn
126 East Main St.
P.O. Box 294
Lititz, PA 17543-0294
ph: 717-627-4567
fax: 717-627-7727
doug@dougflynn.com
http://www.dougflynn.com
*Buys and sells British Royalty items;
also publishes five or six catalogs per
year; co-author of "British Royalty
Commemoratives," $23.95 ppd.*

Audrey B. Zeder
British Royalty Commemoratives
1320 SW 10th St.
North Bend, WA 98045
ph: 425-888-6697
royalbritish@aol.com
*Buys, sells, British Royal commemora-
tive items for all royalty events; deals
in royalty ceramics, tins, textiles,
ephemera and souvenirs; for sale list
available for $3.*

Botany Bay Antiques
8 Grape Pane
Whitby
North Yorkshire, YO22 4BA U.K.
ph: 01947 602007
botanybay@madasafish.com
http://www.botanybayantiques.com
*Specializes in Royal memorabilia,
commemorative collectibles,
coronation mugs.*

Experts

Douglas H. Flynn
126 East Main St.
P.O. Box 294
Lititz, PA 17543-0294
ph: 717-627-4567
fax: 717-627-7727
doug@dougflynn.com
http://www.dougflynn.com
*Co-author with Alan H. Bolton of
"British Royalty Commemoratives,
19th and 20th Century Royal Events in
Britain Illustrated by
Commemoratives" (Schiffer).*

Audrey B. Zeder
British Royalty Commemoratives
1320 SW 10th St.
North Bend, WA 98045
ph: 425-888-6697
royalbritish@aol.com
*Author of "British Royal
Commemoratives."*

Internet Resources

British Monarch Official Web Site, The
U.K.
http://www.royal.gov.uk
*The British Monarchy Official Web
Site.*

Italian

Collectors

Mario Donald Thomas
860 18th Ave.
Salt Lake City, UT 84103-3719
ph: 801-532-5340
fax: 801-532-5340
*Buys any items connected to the Italian
royal families.*

Princess Diana

Experts

Charles Nobles
4708 Cobblestone Dr., Apt.. I-8
Myrtle Beach, SC 29577
ph: 843-467-2128
*Collecting Princess Diana memora-
bilia since 1981; author of "Diana,
Collecting on a Princess" (Hobby
House Press).*

Russian

Experts

Timothy A. Miller
ARTCo
P.O. Box 4011
Frederick, MD 21705-4011
ph: 301-668-6271
artco@mindspring.com
http://www.artcoantiques.com
*Buys, sells, brokers, appraises quality
Russian antiques: civil, military,
religious items from Russia 1700s to
1917; periodic auction catalogs.*

ROYCROFT

(see ARTS & CRAFTS, Roycroft)

RUBA ROMBIC

(see GLASS, Consolidated)

RUBBER ITEMS

Collectors

Mike Woshner
2306 Spokane Ave.
Pittsburgh, PA 15210-4414
ph: 412-884-9299
mwoshner@bellatlantic.net
*Collector, researcher, historian,
lecturer; author of "India-Rubber and
Gutta-Percha in the Civil War Era"
(1999).*

M. Brunswick
P.O. Box 9729
Baltimore, MD 21286-9729
*Wants rubber goods, manuals, films;
hot water bottle outfits, rubber
syringes, bulbs, enamel cans, etc.: pre-
1965 or foreign; also books,*

accessories, boxes, ads, catalogs, photos on use, etc.; also nursing, child care, sick care.

Howard G. Johnson
8570 Wood Mills Dr. West
Cordova, TN 38018
ph: 901-737-3787
Wants to buy any medical or sick room device having a black, hard rubber nozzle/tip that penetrates any body orifice such as rubber douche syringes (bag or bulb); also pre-1950 enema equipment.

Museums/Libraries

Goodyear World of Rubber
1201 East Market St.
Akron, OH 44316
ph: 330-796-2044 or 800-321-2136
pa@goodyear.com
http://www.goodyear.com

Clothing

Collectors

Standish H. Smith
P.O. Box 292
Villanova, PA 19085
Wants rubber raincoats, hats, rain suits, capes; any color; or photographs of firemen, policemen, fishermen, etc. wearing same.

M. Brunswick
P.O. Box 9729
Baltimore, MD 21286-9729
Wants to buy ladies rubber undergarments, solid or perforated girdles, corsets, Playtex, Kleinetts, etc.; also wants women's rubber boots and shoes (no black unless unusual).

RUBIK'S CUBES

(see PUZZLES, Mechanical [Rubik's Cubes])

RUGS

(see also NATIVE AMERICAN, Navajo)

Appraisers

James A. Ffrench
Beauvais Carpets
12 East 86th St., Apt. 736
New York, NY 10028
ph: 212-688-2265
Jaffrench@aol.com
http://www.beauvaiscarpets.com
Specializes in the appraisal of period carpets, tapestries and textiles of historical significance, both European and Eastern dating from 15th century to present.

Clubs/Associations

Stephanie Kline Morehouse
Textile Group of Los Angeles, Inc.
894 South Bronson Ave.
Los Angeles, CA 90005-3605
ph: 323-939-2240
fax: 323-939-2240
tglaincorp@aol.com
Non-profit society formed in 1979 to further the interest in all and any type of carpets, textiles or related arts; regular meetings, lectures, viewing private collections; textile design, conservation, history.

Dealers

Allan Arthur
Cyber Rug Center
25 Bennett St.
Atlanta, GA 30309
ph: 800-686-7030 or 404-350-9560
aarthur@cyberrug.com
http://www.cyberrug.com
Buys and sells antique Oriental rugs, Persian rugs, Art Deco rugs, Chinese rugs, Kelim & flat woven rugs, Coptic and Asian textiles, European rugs and tapestries, Kashmir shawls, and American hooked and folk art rugs.

Experts

J. Barry O'Connell
RugNotes
12700 Ardennes Ave.
Rockville, MD 20851
ph: 301-468-2131
jboc@spongobongo.com
http://www.spongobongo.com
A virtual magazine dealing with Oriental rugs, Persian carpets, Tribal rugs, etc.; covers rugs and the people who buy, sell, and collect them.

Repro. Sources

David C. Kline
Family Heir-Loom Weavers
775 Meadowview Dr.
Red Lion, PA 17356-8608
ph: 717-246-2431 or 717-246-2431
fax: 717-246-7439
PatKline@familyheirloomweavers.com
http://www.familyheirloomweavers.com
Makers of fancy jacquard coverlets, ingrain carpets & other historic textiles; carpets in the Abe Lincoln home & various other sites.

Hooked

(see also FOLK ART; REPAIR/ RESTORATION/CONSERVATION, Textiles; TEXTILES)

Dealers

Deborah Roberts
P.O. Box 2176
Costa Mesa, CA 92626
ph: 714-557-5258
quiltevals@aol.com
http://www.quiltappraiser.com
Specializing in buying and selling antique hooked rugs, quilts and quilt-related textiles; certified by the

American Quilter's Society; wish list available; also lectures on quilts.

Experts

Jessie A. Thurbayne
P.O. Box 2540
Westwood, MA 02090
ph: 781-769-4798
Author of "Hooked Rugs: History and the Continuing Tradition" and two other books on hooked rugs; all available from the author.

Internet Resources

Rug Hooker's Network, The
101 Cliff Nelson Rd.
Kingston, GA 30145
ph: 770-607-9713
fax: 770-607-9713
mailbox@rughookersnetwork.com
http://www.rughookersnetwork.com
Web site for rug hookers: suppliers, designers, locate a local teacher, workshops & events, exhibits and competitions.

Periodicals

Stackpole, Inc.
Magazine: Rug Hooking
1300 Market St., Ste. 202
Lemoyne, PA 17043-1420
ph: 717-234-5091 or 800-233-9055
fax: 717-234-1359
editor@rughookingonline.com
http://www.rughookingonline.com
Published five times yearly; provides how-to information as well as features on outstanding or historically significant hand-hooked rugs; also publishes special annual, "Celebrations."

Repair Services

Pamela Laubscher
Nutting House Antique Center
22 Center St.
P.O. Box 158
Brandon, VT 05733
ph: 802-247-3302 or 800-870-9866
nutnghse@sover.net
http://www.brandon.org/nutting.htm
Offers hooked rug repair and cleaning.

Linda Eliasom
513 Sykes Hollow Rd.
Pawlet, VT 05761
ph: 802-325-3026
Repairs hooked rugs.

Suppliers

Jean L. Edmonds
Sea Holly Hooked Rug Shop
114 Trenor Lane
Powells Point, NC 27966
ph: 252-491-5015
fax: 252-491-5015
rughooker@beachlink.com
http://www.seahollyhooked.com
Traditional rug hooking; sells finished pieces, patterns, wool and other supplies and equipment; also teaches classes and workshops.

Oriental

Appraisers

Peter B. Pap
Peter Pap Oriental Rugs
Rt. 101, Box 286
Dublin, NH 03444
ph: 603-563-8717
fax: 603-563-7158
ppordub@monad.net
http://www.peterpaporientalrugs.com
Specializes in the appraisal of Oriental rugs.

Alan F. Butler, ISA
P.O. Box 2818
Durham, NC 27715-2818
ph: 919-489-9342
fax: 919-489-9342

Sharon Kerwick, ISA
Kerwick Appraisals
1633 NE 24th St.
Fort Lauderdale, FL 33305-1402
ph: 954-565-9031
fax: 954-564-0648
sharon@kerwick.com
http://www.kerwick.com
Certified Member of the International Society of Appraisers specializing in the appraisal of Oriental rugs.

Jacqueline McMillan
McMillan Appraisal Group, Inc.
3340 Brownlow Ave.
Minneapolis, MN 55426
ph: 952-926-1000 or 612-423-1323
fax: 612-339-8691
jmcmillan@mcmillanappraisals.com
Extensive expertise in the appraisal of Oriental rugs.

Farhad Radfar, ISA
MIR Appraisal Services, Inc.
307 N. Michigan Ave., Ste. 308
Chicago, IL 60601
ph: 312-814-8510
fax: 312-814-8511
appraisers@mirgallery.com
http://www.mirgallery.com
Offers expert appraisals of personal property including Continental ceramics, Oriental rugs, furs, fine art, antiques, jewelry, furniture, silver, porcelain, marble, bronze, and other fine items.

Ellen Amirkhan, ISA CAPP
Oriental Rug Cleaning Co., Inc.
3907 Ross Ave.
Dallas, TX 75204-5248
ph: 214-821-9135
fax: 214-821-9136
eamirkhan@comcast.net
Oriental and specialty rugs custom cleaned; rug repairing (Oriental and specialty); Oriental rug appraising.

Samuel Abraham
Abrahams Oriental Rugs
5120 Woodway, Ste. 6010
Houston, TX 77056
ph: 713-622-4444
fax: 713-622-8928
abrahams.rugs@worldnet.att.net
http://www.abrahamsrugs.com
*Specializes in appraising Oriental
rugs, Persian rugs, European
tapestries, and contemporary rugs.*

Guido Muzzarelli
Appraisals & Valuations
4244 Laurelgrove Ave.
Studio City, CA 91604-1623
ph: 818-766-0605
fax: 818-766-3025
guidom@earthlink.net
*Accredited Senior Member of the
American Society of Appraisers and
Appraisers Association of America;
offers appraisals of Persian, Oriental
and European carpets, rugs and
tapestries for estates, insurance,
donations.*

Pamela Bensoussan, AAIA
616 Second Ave.
Chula Vista, CA 91910
ph: 619-420-7782
fax: 619-420-7788
http://www.aaia.com/appraisals.html
*Specializes in the appraisal of
Oriental rugs, tapestries, and
furniture.*

Val Arbab, ISA CAPP
P.O. Box 684
La Jolla, CA 92038-0684
ph: 858-453-4686
fax: 858-457-3647
valarbab@att.net
*Appraises all oriental rugs, shawls,
and other textiles; also buys, sells and
brokers collectible and old decorative
rugs; over 30 years experience;
member of the ASA, certified member
of the ISA.*

Jan Jocoy, ISA CAPP
Jan J. Jocoy & Associates
910 La Tierra Dr.
San Marcos, CA 92069
ph: 760-510-9220 or 760-402-2173
jjjocoy@att.net
*Specializes in the appraisal of
Oriental rugs and carpets.*

Auction Services

Michael B. Grogan
Grogan & Company Auctioneers
22 Harris St.
Dedham, MA 02026
ph: 781-461-9500
fax: 781-461-9625
grogans@groganco.com
http://www.groganco.com
*Auctioneer and appraiser specializing
in 18th through 20th century American
& European paintings, sculpture,
oriental rugs, and fine silver; accepts
consignments year round for two semi-
annual sales.*

Jo Kris
Skinner, Inc.
63 Park Plaza
The Heritage on the Garden
Boston, MA 02116
ph: 617-350-5400
fax: 617-350-5429
info@skinnerinc.com
http://www.skinnerinc.com
*Established in 1971, Skinner Inc. is
the fourth largest auction house in the
US; has offices in Boston and Bolton,
MA.*

Elisabeth C. Poole
Christie's
20 Rockefeller Plaza
New York, NY 10020
ph: 212-636-2000
info@christies.com
http://www.christies.com
*Specializes in the auction sale and
appraisal of carpets and Oriental
rugs.*

Sotheby's
1334 York Ave.
New York, NY 10021
ph: 212-606-7000
fax: 212-606-7107
http://www.sothebys.com
*Over 70 collecting areas are featured
at Sotheby's auctions including toys,
dolls, porcelain, furniture, silver, art,
books; exhibitions are free and
everyone is welcome; for a free copy of
"Sotheby's Newsletter," call 212-606-
7245.*

Freeman's Auction Gallery
1808 Chestnut St.
Philadelphia, PA 19103
ph: 215-563-9275
fax: 215-563-8236
proberts@freemansauction.com
http://www.freemansauction.com
*America's oldest auction house:
Continental, English and American
furniture, paintings, silver and
decorative arts; Oriental rugs, rare
books, fine jewelry, Orientalia.*

Book Sellers

Dennis Marquand
Dennis B. Marquand Books
P.O. Box 1187
Culver City, CA 90232-1187
ph: 310-313-0177
fax: 310-915-9922
dennis@rugbooks.com
http://www.rugbooks.com
*Specialize in books on ethnographic
textiles from around the world with a
focus on Oriental rugs, embroideries,
textiles from Central Asian, Navajo,
Tibet, Guatemala, Africa.*

Clubs/Associations

Sharon Fenlon, Pres.
American Conference on Oriental Rugs
scullent@aasd.k12.wi.us
http://www.acor-rugs.org
*Established to develop an understand-
ing of oriental rugs and textiles;
sponsors three-day conferences every*

two years: tribal and village rugs, rug
restoration, textile esthetics, effects of
light, design origins, rug books.

Jesie Fisher
Oriental Rug Society of Kansas City
ph: 818-221-0422
fax: 816-221-0422
jfisher@kc.rr.com

Joan Long
Cleveland Rug Society
ph: 330-666-4876
fax: 330-972-5574
jcl.ebl@att.net

Leslie Atiyeh
Portland Area Rug Society
ph: 503-538-7560
fax: 503-538-8239
pars@atiyeh.com

George Trotman
Philadelphia Oriental Rug Society
ph: 215-985-0889
fax: 215-985-0886
georgetrot@aol.com

Jim Morgan
Houston Oriental Rug Society
ph: 713-461-3080
jgmorgan@ix.netcom.com

Richard Stweart
Colorado Textile Group
ph: 303-444-3720
fax: 303-443-7712
Richard_Stewart@webTV.net

Basil Scaljon
Oriental Rug Club of Houston
ph: 713-526-2621
BasilScal@aol.com

Jessie Fisher
Oriental Rug Club of Kansas City
jfisher@kc.rr.com

Wendel Swan
International Hajji Baba Society, Inc.
6500 Pinecrest
Annandale, VA 22003
ph: 703-960-0343
fax: 703-683-7545
wdswan@erols.com
*A non-profit association of rug &
textile collectors & enthusiasts;
sponsors several lectures each year
featuring experts on Oriental rugs; the
events are held in the Washington DC
area and are academic, not social or
commercial.*

Wendel Swan
International Conference on Oriental
Carpets
ph: 703-960-0343
fax: 703-683-7545
wdswan@erols.com
http://www.icoc-international.org/
icoc.htm
*Sponsors conferences every three years
in which oriental rug collectors and
textile enthusiasts gather to see special
exhibits, hear academic sessions and*

view offerings of dealers from around
the world.

Wendel Swam
International Hajji Baba Society, The
ph: 703-960-0343
fax: 703-683-7545
wdswan@erols.com
*A Washington, DC based non-profit
society of oriental rug collectors and
textile enthusiasts; 6-8 meetings per
year featuring lectures by internationally recognized authorities on rugs
and textiles.*

Lucille Kimble
Triangle Rug Society
3100 Cornwall Rd.
Durham, NC 27707
ph: 919-489-2702
kimble@psych.duke.edu

Sharon Kerwick, ISA
South Florida Oriental Rug Club
1633 NE 24th St.
Fort Lauderdale, FL 33305-1402
ph: 954-565-9031
fax: 954-564-0648
sharon@kerwick.com
http://www.kerwick.com

Michael F. Wiley
Rug & Textile Society of Indiana
8940 Sassafras Ct.
Indianapolis, IN 46260
ph: 317-873-3494
*Dedicated to studying, collecting and
discussing rugs and textiles of central
Asia and Asia Minor; programs
presented 8 times each year at the
Indianapolis Museum of Art; open to
novice and expert alike.*

Suzanne Kaufman
Chicago Rug Society
240 Market St.
Rockford, IL 61107
ph: 815-963-6543
suzannekaufman@msn.com
*Meets five times each year in the
Chicago area; summer outing/
symposium.*

Sally Komerska
Arizona Oriental Rug/Textile Association
3804 E. Calle DeSoto
Tucson, AZ 85716
ph: 520-323-0320
fax: 520-299-7802
aorta@cox.net
*Group of collectors seeking to learn
more about oriental rugs by sharing
with one another and hearing talks
from collectors and dealers alike;
focus is on tribal rugs made for
everyday uses by the weavers
themselves.*

Dealers

Stephanie Kline Morehouse
Textile Group of Los Angeles, Inc.
894 South Bronson Ave.
Los Angeles, CA 90005-3605
ph: 323-939-2240
fax: 323-939-2240
tglaincorp@aol.com
Non-profit society formed in 1979 to further the interest in all and any type of carpets, textiles or related arts; regular meetings, lectures, viewing private collections; textile design, conservation, history.

Cheri Hunter
Textile Museum Associates of Southern California
P.O. Box 49160
Los Angeles, CA 90049
ph: 310-454-8221
fax: 310-454-8604
cherihunter@earthlink.net
Oriental rug and ethnic textile study club; 250 members, offers monthly lectures, programs, visits to museum exhibitions and private collections.

Ray Rosenberg
Rug Society of San Diego
1010 University Ave.
PMB 241
San Diego, CA 92103
ph: 619-291-4275
fax: 619-297-8240
rugbuff@aol.com
A group of San Diego area residents who have a common interest in collecting and studying the art of the Oriental rug; meetings are held four times each year.

Fred Ingham
Seattle Textile & Rug Society
Newsletter: Star News
2016 26th Ave. East
Seattle, WA 98112
ph: 206-325-8907
fax: 206-325-8907
fingham@yahoo.com
"STARS" is dedicated to encouraging the understanding and appreciation of collectible ethnographic rugs and textiles; meets several times a year for speaker programs; member of the American Conference of Oriental Rugs.

Jean Landa
New Calgary Rug & Textile Club
#201, 618 2nd Ave., NW
Calgary, Alberta T2N 0E1 Canada
ph: 403-270-2880
landa@acs.ucalgary.ca

Janice Summers
Quebec Oriental Rug & Textile Society
Canada
ph: 514-288-1218
fax: 514-288-1210
74643.335@compuserve.com

Robert Davidson
Davidson Oriental Rugs
P.O. Box 650114
West Newton, MA 02165-0114
ph: 617-630-9996 or 800-746-4320
davidsoncompany@cs.com
Buys all used, old and antique Oriental rugs; all sizes and condition.

A.E. Runge, Jr.
Runge Oriental Rugs
108 Main St.
Yarmouth, ME 04096
ph: 207-846-9000
runge@nlis.net
http://www.rungerugs.com
Specializes in pre-WWII decorative Persian and Caucasian village rugs: Heriz, Hamadans, Bijars, South Caucasians; also does repairs, restorations and appraisals.

Hard Cider Farm
45 Middle Rd., Rt. 9
Falmouth, ME 04105
ph: 800-346-6617 or 207-775-1600
rtirrel1@maine.rr.com
http://www.hardciderfarm.com
Buys, sells, repairs Oriental rugs.

Solomon Bassalely
Eliko Oriental Rugs
102 Madison Ave., Fl. 4
New York, NY 10016-7417
ph: 212-725-1600 or 800-733-5456
fax: 212-725-1885
ElikoRugs@aol.com
http://www.eliko-carpets.com
Appraises, buys, sells, and repairs Oriental rugs.

Jacobsen Oriental Rugs
401 N. Salina St.
Syracuse, NY 13203
ph: 315-422-7832
fax: 315-422-6909
rugpeople@jacobsenrugs.com
http://jacobsenrugs.com
In business since 1924; more than 6,000 handwoven Oriental rugs in stock; also repairs.

Peter Shihadeh
Worldwide Rug Market, The
116 Cricket Ave.
Ardmore, PA 19003
ph: 610-649-2000
fax: 610-649-6463
peter@orientalrugs.com
http://www.orientalrugs.com

David Zahirpour
David Zahirpour Oriental Rugs, Inc.
4922 Wisconsin Ave. NW
Washington, DC 20016
ph: 202-338-4141 or 202-244-1800
zahirpour@aol.com
Specialist in Oriental rugs; cleans and repairs; handwashing, stain removal, carpet reweaving and restoration, appraisals, etc.

Gerald W. Thompson
Gerald W. Thompson Oriental Rugs
P.O. Box 193
Shepherdstown, WV 25443-0193
ph: 304-876-2218
fax: 304-876-3640
kayethom@aol.com
Specialist in antique and semi-antique oriental rugs with 25 years experience; also does repairs, appraisals, padding, and lecturing; also buying and selling of Oriental rugs.

John Lucas
Oglukian Oriental Rugs
4600 Oglukian Rd.
Charlotte, NC 28226-5124
ph: 704-366-1972
Appraisals, cleaning, repair of handmade rugs.

Marla Mallett
Marla Mallett Textiles
1690 Johnson Rd. NE
Atlanta, GA 30306
ph: 404-872-3356 or 877-542-0841
marlam@mindspring.com
http://www.marlamallett.com
Specializes in antique flat woven tribal Oriental rugs, bags, kilims (kelims); also features handwoven tapestries, embroideries and other textile art from around the world; 2,800 photos illustrate a variety of textile topics.

Bob Anderson
Aaron's Oriental Rug Gallery
1217 Broadway
Fort Wayne, IN 46802-3303
ph: 260-422-5184
Buys, sells, trades and appraises Oriental rugs; the Midwest's finest selection.

Larry Bergman
Coulee Oriental Rugs
N33015 Square Bluff Rd.
Whitehall, WI 54773-9148
ph: 715-985-3310
bergman@ecol.net
Wants to buy older hand-knotted rugs, both throw rugs and room size rugs; especially wants rugs made before 1940.

Farhad Radfar, ISA
MIR International Gallery, Inc.
307 N. Michigan Ave., Ste. 308
Chicago, IL 60601
ph: 312-814-8510
fax: 312-814-8511
mirgallery@aol.com
http://www.mirgallery.com

Samuel Abraham
Abrahams Oriental Rugs
5120 Woodway, Ste. 6010
Houston, TX 77056
ph: 713-622-4444
fax: 713-622-8928
abrahams.rugs@worldnet.att.net
http://www.abrahamsrugs.com
Buying and selling Oriental rugs since 1974; Orientals, needlepoint rugs, new Kilims, new Pakistani and Persian rugs, Kashmir silk rugs.

Afshin Nejad
Oldcarpet.com
P.O. Box 1031
Brea, CA 92822
ph: 310-766-1820
fax: 419-781-4735
info@oldcarpet.com
http://www.oldcarpet.com
Specializes in Persian rugs including cleaning and repairs.

Jimmy Vitanza
Peregrine Galleries
508 Brinkerhoff Ave.
Santa Barbara, CA 93101-3441
ph: 805-963-3134
fax: 805-963-3134

Harold & Janice Bedoukian
Ararat Rug Company
3457 Park Ave.
Montreal, Quebec H2X 2H6 Canada
ph: 514-288-1218
fax: 514-288-1210
araratrug@compuserve.com
Specializes in antique and used Oriental carpets; has a large selection of oversized rugs in stock; also expert cleaning and restoration facilities.

Experts

Val Arbab, ISA CAPP
P.O. Box 684
La Jolla, CA 92038-0684
ph: 858-453-4686
fax: 858-457-3647
valarbab@att.net
Appraises all oriental rugs, shawls, and other textiles; also buys, sells and brokers collectible and old decorative rugs; over 30 years experience; member of the ASA, certified member of the ISA.

Internet Resources

Ron O'Callaghan
Oriental Rug Review
Sinclair Hill Rd.
New Hampton, NH 03256
ph: 603-744-9191
ronocal@lr.net
http://www.rugreview.com/orr.htm
Formerly a glossy magazine published bi-monthly and focusing primarily on old rugs; book reviews, auctions, ads, detailed articles, etc.; now an online reference source.

J. Barry O'Connell
RugNotes
12700 Ardennes Ave.
Rockville, MD 20851
ph: 301-468-2131
jboc@spongobongo.com
http://www.spongobongo.com
A virtual magazine dealing with Oriental rugs, Persian carpets, Tribal rugs, etc.; covers rugs and the people who buy, sell, and collect them.

Steve Price
TurkoTek
1862 Fox Downs Lane
Oilville, VA 23129
ph: 804-828-4485
sprice@hsc.vcu.edu
http://www.turkotek.com
A noncommercial Web site devoted to collectible weavings, Oriental rugs; has rugs and books about rugs for sale; also an online magazine, a discussion forum, and educational content.

David Miller
World Wide Weave, The
85 South Park Blvd.
Glen Ellyn, IL 60137
wwweave@aol.com
http://hometown.aol.com/wwweave/index.htm
World wide rug societies, rug conferences, shows and events, rug education and information.

Art Arena's Persian Carpets - A Brief History
4 Bennett Hill Close
Wootton Bassett
Wiltshire SN4 8LR U.K.
ph: (+44) 1793 848 742
katy@art-arena.com
http://www.art-arena.com/pcarpet.htm
Loads of information and images about Persian carpets; place to go for identification of types, dates, and other rug particulars.

Man./Prod./Dist.

Peerless Imported Rugs
3033 North Lincoln Ave.
Chicago, IL 60657
ph: 800-621-6573
fax: 773-525-4055
customerservice@peerlessrugs.com
http://www.peerlessrugs.com
Sells new oriental rugs and oriental style rugs.

Museums/Libraries

Jack Cassin
Weaving Art Museum & Research Institute
webmaster@weavingartmuseum.org
http://www.weavingartmuseum.org
Focuses on the masterpiece weavings produced in the eastern Mediterranean region.

Periodicals

Ron O'Callaghan
Asian Trade
Magazine: Oriental Rug Review
Sinclair Rd.
New Hampton, NH 03256
ph: 603-744-9191
ronocal@lr.net
http://www.rugreview.com/orr.htm
A bi-monthly journal of Oriental rugs and other textiles.

Museum Books, Inc.
Magazine: Rug News
90 John St., 5th Floor
New York, NY 10038
ph: 212-587-1340
fax: 212-587-1344
rugnews@rugnews.com
http://www.rugnews.com
Contains articles about the construction and quality of new Oriental rugs, primarily; also auction reports, shows, buy & sell ads.

HALI Publications, Ltd.
Magazine: HALI
St. Giles House
50 Poland St.
London, W1F 4AX U.K.
ph: 020 7970 4600
fax: 020 7578 7222
hali@centaur.co.uk
http://www.hali.com
"HALI" is the leading bi-monthly international publication in the field of carpet and textile art; an invaluable encyclopedic source of information with original research articles, reviews of museum collections, etc.; high color.

Repair Services

Solomon Bassalely
Eliko Oriental Rugs
102 Madison Ave., Fl. 4
New York, NY 10016-7417
ph: 212-725-1600 or 800-733-5456
fax: 212-725-1885
ElikoRugs@aol.com
http://www.eliko-carpets.com
Appraises, buys, sells, and repairs Oriental rugs.

Hayko Restoration & Conservation
857 Lexington Ave., 2nd Floor
New York, NY 10021
ph: 212-717-5400
fax: 212-717-5400
info@hayko.com
http://www.hayko.com
Restoration and conservation of antique rugs; 20 years experience with carpets and tapestries; at your home or in the studio; references on request.

Hayk Oltaci
Hayko Restoration Antique Rugs & Tapestry
857 Lexington Ave., 2nd Floor
New York, NY 10021
ph: 212-717-5400
fax: 212-717-2783
info@hayko.com
http://www.hayko.com
Has over 26 years of expertise gained in the carpet and tapestry ateliers of Istanbul, Strasbourg, Paris and New York.

Jacobsen Oriental Rugs
401 N. Salina St.
Syracuse, NY 13203
ph: 315-422-7832
fax: 315-422-6909
rugpeople@jacobsenrugs.com
http://jacobsenrugs.com
In business since 1924; more than 6,000 handwoven Oriental rugs in stock; also repairs.

David Zahirpour
David Zahirpour Oriental Rugs, Inc.
4922 Wisconsin Ave. NW
Washington, DC 20016
ph: 202-338-4141 or 202-244-1800
zahirpour@aol.com
Specialist in Oriental rugs; cleans and repairs; handwashing, stain removal, carpet reweaving and restoration, appraisals, etc.

Frank Shaia
Shaia Oriental Rugs
1325 Jamestown Rd.
Williamsburg, VA 23185
ph: 757-220-0400
fax: 757-229-3406
rugs@shaia.com
http://www.shaia.com
Expert Oriental rug repairs and restorations; reweave, reknot, overcast, selvedge; also cleaning and appraisals.

Ellen Amirkhan, ISA CAPP
Oriental Rug Cleaning Co., Inc.
3907 Ross Ave.
Dallas, TX 75204-5248
ph: 214-821-9135
fax: 214-821-9136
eamirkhan@comcast.net
Oriental and specialty rugs custom cleaned; rug repairing (Oriental and specialty); Oriental rug appraising.

Emily Sanford
Sanford Restoration Works
2102 Speyer Ln.
Redondo Beach, CA 90278-4918
ph: 310-374-7412
fax: 310-798-2792
Specializing in antique village and nomadic weavings.

Pamela Hiller
Pamela Hiller Oriental Rug Restorations'
1016 Aspen Way
Petaluma, CA 94954
ph: 707-789-0784
fax: 603-754-0724
pamhiller@aol.com
Offers hand done repairs to Oriental rugs allowing beauty and functionality to be returned to the damaged weaving.

Harold & Janice Bedoukian
Ararat Rug Company
3457 Park Ave.
Montreal, Quebec H2X 2H6 Canada
ph: 514-288-1218
fax: 514-288-1210
araratrug@compuserve.com
Specializes in antique and used Oriental carpets; has a large selection of oversized rugs in stock; also expert cleaning and restoration facilities.

Oriental (Moroccan)

Dealers

Brooke Pickering
Brooke Pickering Moroccan Rugs
1209 Route 213, 2nd Floor
P.O. Box 37
High Falls, NY 12440
ph: 914-687-8737
fax: 914-687-8889
BPrugs@aol.com
http://www.moraoccanrugs.com
One of the foremost authorities on Moroccan rugs and the only rug dealer in the Northeastern US specializing exclusively in the Moroccan material; author and lecturer about Moroccan rugs.

RUSSEL WRIGHT

(see also CERAMICS [AMERICAN], Russel Wright Designs)

Collectors

Dennis Boyd
P.O. Box 8925
Richmond, VA 23225
ph: 804-560-0753
dboydant@ix.netcom.com
Wants Russel Wright dinnerware (American Modern, Highlight, Iroquois, and other patterns); also wants Russel Wright stainless flatware, glassware, aluminum, Bauer, etc.

Dealers

Edward E. Stump
Raccoon's Tale
6 High St.
Mullica Hill, NJ 08062-9540
ph: 609-478-4488
ractale@fast.net
Wants Russel Wright items: china dinnerware, modern, Iroquois, sterling & highlights; also anything unusual.

Lee Hay
Weird & Wonderful
P.O. Box 14898
Cincinnati, OH 45250-0898
ph: 513-621-6034
fax: 513-621-6448
heywood@sprintmail.com
Wants to by Russel Wright dishes, silverware, furniture; also Bauer pottery.

Connie Zeigler
Durwyn Smedley Antiques
431 Massachusetts Ave.
Indianapolis, IN 46204
ph: 317-822-0102
Buys, sells, appraises all works by Russel Wright or Mary Wright including dinnerware, furniture, pottery, lighting, metalwork, textiles, glassware, books, and other related items.

RUSSIAN ITEMS

(see also CAMERAS & CAMERA
EQUIPMENT, Russian;
COLLECTIBLES [MODERN],
Russian; MILITARIA, Russian;
ROYALTY COLLECTIBLES, Russian;
STAMP COLLECTING, Russian;
TOYS, Russian)

Appraisers

Polina Vasilevskaya
5542 Geary Blvd.
San Francisco, CA 94121
ph: 415-752-5546 or 415-412-7843
fax: 415-752-5721
polina@torgsyn.com
*Specializes in the appraisal of gems
and jewelry as well as in Russian and
European antique jewelry, silver and
porcelain.*

Auction Services

Sotheby's
1334 York Ave.
New York, NY 10021
ph: 212-606-7000
fax: 212-606-7107
http://www.sothebys.com

Timothy A. Miller
ARTCo
P.O. Box 4011
Frederick, MD 21705-4011
ph: 301-668-6271
artco@mindspring.com
http://www.artcoantiques.com
*Buys, sells, brokers quality Russian
antiques: civil, military, religious
items from Russia 1700s to 1917;
periodic auction catalogs.*

Joseph DuMouchelle
Joseph DuMouchelle Fine & Estate
   Jewelry Auctions
5 Kercheval Ave.
Grosse Pointe Farms, MI 48236
ph: 313-884-4800 or 800-475-4367
fax: 313-884-7662
info@dumouchelleauction.com
http://www.dumouchelleauction.com
*Specializes in the sale of fine and
estate jewelry and small objects of art;
large diamonds and colored stones,
paintings, Oriental rugs, silver,
antique furniture and sculpture,
Russian objects of art.*

GELOS Antique Auctioneers & Dealers
2/6, 1st Botkinsky Dr.
P.O. Box 12
Russia
ph: (007*095) 946 1171
fax: (007*095) 946 0932
info@gelos.ru
http://www.gelos.ru
*The largest antique auctioneer and
dealer in Russia and CIS; founded in
1988.*

Dealers

Lacey Greer
Treasures of Imperial Russia
1771 Post Rd., East
PMB 185
Westport, CT 06880
ph: 203-319-1450
fax: 203-259-8045
laceygreer@art-of-imperial-russia.com
http://www.art-of-imperial-russia.com
*Specializes in unique and fine art from
pre-Revolutionary Russia, specializing
in rare icons from the 16th century
through the turn of the century:
paintings, prints, porcelain, brass,
silver, enamels, lacquer, papier-mâché
boxes, etc.*

Anita L. Grashof
Gallerie Ani'tiques
Stage House Village
366 Park Ave.
Scotch Plains, NJ 07076-1121
ph: 908-322-4600
*Buys, sells and appraises antique
Russian commemoratives in brass,
copper, silver and porcelain of the
Romanoff period*

Russian House
253 Fifth Ave.
New York, NY 10016
ph: 212-685-1010
fax: 212-685-1046
*Carries large selection of the best
selection of fine Russian books and
gifts: lacquered miniatures, icons,
amber jewelry, nesting dolls,
porcelain, hand-painted shawls,
Faberge-style eggs.*

A La Vieille Russie, Inc.
781 Fifth Ave.
New York, NY 10022
ph: 212-752-1727
alvr@alvr.com
http://www.alvr.com
*Specializes in fine European and
American antique jewelry, Faberge,
gold snuff boxes and objects de vertu;
also specializes in Russian decorative
and fine arts.*

Robert Natanzon
Fine Russian Antiques
2536 Hubbard St.
Brooklyn, NY 11235-6223
ph: 718-769-1446
fax: 718-769-5617
rob1329@aol.com
http://www.fine-russian-antiques.com
*Specializes in Russian icons, crosses,
silver, militaria, etc.*

Allan & Ita Fogel
Twin Tankard Antiques
P.O. Box 4847
Silver Spring, MD 20914-4847
ph: 301-236-9391
fax: 301-236-0427
twintankard@aol.com
http://www.twintankard.com
*Specializes in European pewter; also
buys and sells Russian and Judaica.*

Timothy A. Miller
ARTCo Russian Antiques
P.O. Box 4011
Frederick, MD 21705-4011
ph: 301-668-6271
artco@mindspring.com
http://www.artcoantiques.com
*Buys and sells Imperial Russian items:
enamels, metal, art; civil, military,
religious, etc.; send photo or
photocopy and price, please.*

Mimi Levine
Mimi & Steve Levine Antiques, Inc.
6205 Marilyn Dr.
Alexandria, VA 22310
ph: 703-971-3941
mimilev@erols.com
*Dealers, experts in Russian porcelain,
both Imperial and private factories.*

Mitch Siegler
Sovietski Collection
3450 Kurtz St.
San Diego, CA 92110
ph: 800-442-0002 or 619-294-2000
fax: 619-294-2500
info@sovietski.com
http://www.sovietski.com
*Antiques, gifts, and collectibles from
Russia, Eastern Europe, and the
former Soviet Union: militaria, optics,
timepieces, spy gear, lacquer boxes,
survival gear, coins, folk art, jewelry,
and other rare items.*

Andre Ruzhnikov
Andre Ruzhnikov Russian Art &
   Antiques
P.O. Box 1261
Palo Alto, CA 94302-1261
ph: 650-858-0469
fax: 650-858-1008
ruzhnikov@russianarts.com
http://www.russianarts.com
*Large inventory of Russian icons,
silver, enamels, paintings, watercolors, decorative arts and Faberge;
always interested in buying collections
of fine Russian antiques; appraisals,
consultation, and restoration services
available.*

Experts

Patricia M. Grove
PMG Antique Appraisal Research
3 Ober St.
Beverly, MA 01915-4639
ph: 978-927-2979
fax: 978-927-8625
*Collects, researches and appraises
decorative and fine arts of the China,
Japan, India and Russia export trades,
17th through mid-19th centuries:
paintings, silver, ivory, tortoise
carvings, furniture, fans, lacquer.*

Benedict J. Hastings
2006 Columbia Rd. N.W.
Washington, DC 20009
ph: 202-483-8575
bhastingsdc@aol.com
*Specializes in fine silver, Russian
decorative arts, Russian icons, 18th*

*and 19th century porcelain, military
medals, decorations and orders.*

Mimi Levine
Mimi & Steve Levine Antiques, Inc.
6205 Marilyn Dr.
Alexandria, VA 22310
ph: 703-971-3941
mimilev@erols.com
*Dealers, experts in Russian porcelain,
both Imperial and private factories.*

James L. Jackson, ISA
Jackson's Auctioneers & Appraisers
2229 Lincoln St.
P.O. Box 50613
Cedar Falls, IA 50613
ph: 319-277-2256
fax: 319-277-1252
jacksons@jacksonsauction.com
http://www.jacksonsauction.com
*Has written and lectured widely on
Russian icons, and has traveled
extensively throughout Russia and the
former Soviet Union studying Russian
icons.*

Museums/Libraries

Hillwood Museum & Gardens
Journal: Hillwood Studies
4155 Linnean Ave. NW
Washington, DC 20008
ph: 202-686-8500
fax: 202-966-7846
info@hillwoodmuseum.org
http://www.hillwoodmuseum.org
*Most comprehensive collection of
Russian art outside the former USSR;
plus gift shop and 25 acres of
gardens, greenhouses, and auxiliary
buildings.*

Repro. Sources

Robert Whiteside
Robert Whiteside Goldsmith
Rt. 1 Box 98
Mount Vernon, TX 75457
ph: 903-588-2402
mail@robertwhiteside.com
http://www.robertwhiteside.com
*A master jeweler who specializes in
recreating Faberge style jewelry and
objects of art using original
techniques including 19th century
machinery to reproduce engine-turned
enamel ware (guilloche); operates a
school of jewelry.*

Enamels

Experts

Mel & Barbara Alpren
14 Carter Rd.
West Orange, NJ 07052-4612
ph: 973-731-9427
*Advisor to "Warman's Antiques &
Collectibles Price Guide."*

Faberge

Auction Services

Joseph DuMouchelle
Joseph DuMouchelle Fine & Estate
  Jewelry Auctions
5 Kercheval Ave.
Grosse Pointe Farms, MI 48236
ph: 313-884-4800 or 800-475-4367
fax: 313-884-7662
info@dumouchelleauction.com
http://www.dumouchelleauction.com
  *Specializes in the sale of fine and
  estate jewelry and small objects of art;
  large diamonds and colored stones,
  paintings, Oriental rugs, silver,
  antique furniture and sculpture,
  Russian objects of art.*

Dealers

Philip M. Poniz
European Watch & Casemakers, Ltd.
P.O. Box 1314
Highland Park, NJ 08904-1314
ph: 732-777-0111
fax: 732-777-0118
horology@webspan.net
  *Restoration of watches, clocks, and
  music boxes; museum experience; can
  make any part and restore any watch;
  clients include Sotheby's, Cartier,
  collectors in USA, Asia and Europe;
  appraises, researches, restores
  Faberge.*

Lawrence Brewer, GM
St. Petersburg Collection
Eskdale Rd.
Uxbridge, Middlesex UB8 2RT U.K.
ph: +44 1895 238674
fax: +44 1895 810566
Creations@StPetersburgCollection.com
http://www.stpetersburgcollection.com
  *Offers creations by Theo Faberge and
  Sara Faberge in the style of Carl
  Faberge.*

Museums/Libraries

Forbes Magazine Galleries
62 Fifth Ave.
New York, NY 10011-8882
ph: 212-620-5548
  *Permanent exhibits include over 500
  toy boats, 12,000 miniature soldiers,
  twelve fabled Russian Imperial Easter
  Eggs made by the House of Faberge
  for the last two Russian czars, and
  over 300 jeweled items and objets
  d'art.*

Kirsten Lavin, PR Coord.
Walters Art Museum
600 N. Charles St.
Baltimore, MD 21201
ph: 410-547-9000
klavin@thewalters.org
http://www.thewalters.org
  *One of only a few museums worldwide
  to present a comprehensive history of
  art from the third millennium B.C. to
  the early 20th century.*

Frederick R. Brandt
Virginia Museum of Fine Arts, Lillian
  Thomas Pratt Collection
2800 Grove Ave.
Richmond, VA 23221-2466
ph: 804-340-1400
fax: 804-340-1548
webmaster@vmfa.state.va.us
http://www.vmfa.state.va.us
  *Fine arts museum covering the entire
  range of history of art.*

Lacquer Boxes

Dealers

Vika's Russia Direct
P.O. Box 79
Jackson, NH 03846
ph: 603-383-4110
info@russiancollect.com
http://www.russiancollect.com
  *One of the largest selections of
  lacquer boxes outside Russia.*

Tradestone International
803 Light St.
Baltimore, MD 21230
ph: 410-752-8085
ajstone@erols.com
http://www.lacquerbox.com
  *Specializes in new and antique
  Russian lacquer boxes.*

Art at the Power House
2000 Sycamore St.
Cleveland, OH 44113
ph: 216-696-1942
fax: 216-623-3884
artpower@yahoo.com

Experts

Vitaly Shukin
Russian Shop, The
1720 Ogden Ave.
Lisle, IL 60532-1230
ph: 630-963-5160 or 800-778-9404
fax: 630-963-5170
mail@TheRussianShop.com
http://www.TheRussianShop.com
  *Imports unusual Russian gifts and
  collectibles; experts in identifying
  authentic Russian lacquer boxes and
  nesting dolls; dealer in contemporary
  Russian porcelain; free catalog; family
  business for over 25 years.*

Eric Sinizer
Light Opera Retail Corp.
460 Post Rd.
San Francisco, CA 94102-1502
ph: 415-956-9866
fax: 415-956-5624
eric@lightoperagallery.com
http://www.lightoperagallery.com
  Appraises, buys, sells, rights catalogs.

Samovars

Collectors

Jerome M. Marks
Jerome M. Marks Agency
120 Corporate Woods, Ste. 260
Rochester, NY 14623-1464
ph: 585-475-0220
fax: 585-475-0208
  *Wants to buy older Russian samovars;
  also wants any samovar related
  literature; if selling, please send
  photo, description, condition,
  measurements, and asking price.*

Dealers

Mehmet Nabi Israfil
Fil Caravan Inc.
240 East 56th St., Ste. 2E
New York, NY 10022
ph: 212-421-5972
fax: 212-421-5976
filcaravan@att.net
http://www.filcaravan.com
  *Established in 1976, has large
  selection of authentic Russian
  samovars; has provided samovars to
  collectors worldwide; provides
  samovar restoration service as well as
  a limited supply of spare parts.*

RVs

(see TRAILERS & RVs)

**Here are some tips
when contacting
someone who is listed
in this book:**

When requesting
information about a
particular item, include
a description (material,
dimensions, maker's
mark, model number,
etc.) and a photo,
sketch, digital image or
photocopy of the item
in question.

———————————

Always ask if there are
charges for samples or
for the services that
you are requesting.

———————————

When corresponding
by letter, please be
sure to include a Large
(#10 business size)
Self-Addressed and
Stamped Envelope
(LSASE) if requesting a
reply or the return of
photographs.

———————————

Never call collect
unless otherwise
directed. When
calling, be considerate
of time zone differ-
ences and always ask
if the party you are
calling has time to talk.
When leaving an
answering machine
message, always
instruct the party to
call you back collect.

S

SABERS

(see SWORDS)

SACKS

(see CORN COLLECTIBLES; FEED SACKS; MILLING)

SAD IRONS

(see IRONS, Pressing)

SADDLES

(see also ANIMAL COLLECTIBLES, Horses; LEATHER; WESTERN AMERICANA)

Clubs/Associations

Dan Preston
Saddle, Harness & Allied Trades Association
Magazine: Shop Talk!
1101 Broad St.
Oriental, NC 28571
ph: 252-249-3409
fax: 252-249-3415
thsn@always-online.com
http://www.proleather.net
Members are makers of saddles, chaps, harnesses, whips, holsters; carving & tooling, luggage making & repair, other leather goods, sewing machine maintenance.

Collectors

Bill Mackin
1137 Washington St.
Craig, CO 81625-1613
ph: 970-824-6717 or 970-824-6360
fax: 970-824-7175
Author of "Cowboy and Gunfighter Collectibles" price guide; sells books for Old West collectors by mail and at shows; over 45 years collecting; wants nice gun leather and cowboy gear; appraises, consults, lectures.

Dealers

Sharon Myers
J & S Oldwestern Store, Saddle Shop & Museum
RR 1, Box 315-C-NT
Warsaw, MO 65355
ph: 660-438-2631
fax: 660-438-6517
oldwest@iland.net
http://www.jsoldwest.com
Over 200 antique saddles, hibacks, side-saddles, military, charro, etc.;

Admission to museum if free; also 1,300 Western collectibles for sale; 55-page catalog for $5; will advise customers as to age, value and history of saddles.

Museums/Libraries

Sharon Myers
J & S Oldwestern Store, Saddle Shop & Museum
RR 1, Box 315-C-NT
Warsaw, MO 65355
ph: 660-438-2631
fax: 660-438-6517
oldwest@iland.net
http://www.jsoldwest.com
Over 200 antique saddles, hibacks, side-saddles, military, charro, etc.; admission to museum is free.

Periodicals

Dan Preston
Proleptic, Inc.
Magazine: Shop Talk!
1101 Broad St.
Oriental, NC 28571
ph: 252-249-3409
fax: 252-249-3415
thsn@always-online.com
http://www.proleather.net
Professional leather workers, saddle makers, shoe and saddle repairmen, holster manufacturers, harness makers, boot makers, equipment manufacturers; ads, calendar of events.

Side

Clubs/Associations

Linda A. Bowlby, Pres.
World Sidesaddle Federation, Inc., The
Magazine: Aside World
P.O. Box 1104
Bucyrus, OH 44820-1104
ph: 419-284-3176
fax: 419-284-3176
WorldSFI@aol.com
http://www.sidesaddle.org
A non-profit organization for promoting the use of the sidesaddle; provides sources of equipment and information on the use of the sidesaddle.

SAFES

(see also ANTIQUES DEALERS & COLLECTORS, Supplies For; BANKS, Safe Shaped; LOCKS)

Clubs/Associations

Bob Heilemann
West Coast Lock Collectors
Newsletter: West Coast Lock Collectors Newsletter
1427 Lincoln Blvd.
Santa Monica, CA 90401-2732
ph: 310-454-7295 or 310-230-3004
locksmann@earthlink.net
http://www.wclca.org
Call evenings; no collect calls, please.

Collectors

Larry Egelhoff
4175 Millersville Rd.
Indianapolis, IN 46205-2966
ph: 317-846-7228
egelhoffl@juno.com
Collector and appraiser interested in key or combination safes.

SALOON & BAR COLLECTIBLES

(see also ADVERTISING COLLECTIBLES; ALCOHOLICS ANONYMOUS ITEMS; BOTTLES; BREWERIANA; GAMBLING COLLECTIBLES; GLASSES; PROHIBITION ITEMS; WHISKEY INDUSTRY ITEMS)

Collectors

James E. Kattner
P.O. Box 11132
Spring, TX 77391-1132
ph: 281-376-4826
victorio1sw@yahoo.com
Wants to buy Texas saloon, bar and liquor advertisement items such as shot glasses, match safes, miniature and larger jugs, pocket mirrors with celluloid backs illustrating pretty ladies, corkscrews, old dice, tokens, coin purses.

John Goetz
P.O. Box 1570
Cedar Ridge, CA 95924
ph: 530-272-4644
Wants saloon bottles: label under glass, bottles, flasks, mugs, bottles and flasks with silver overlay, bottles with multicolored enamel pictures; also wants beer trays or signs.

Dealers

Deborah & Paul Inglis
Bootleggers Nostalgia
P.O. Box 165
South Hadley, MA 01075-0165
ph: 413-533-0419
fax: 413-533-0419
bootleggers.nostalgia@worldnet.att.net
Buys pitchers, ashtrays, back bar statues, change receivers, and drip plates advertising Scotch whisky or other types of liquor.

Greg Spiess
Spiess Architectural Antiques
230 E. Washington St.
Joliet, IL 60433-1006
ph: 815-722-5639
fax: 815-722-0171
spiessantq@aol.com
Buys saloon fixtures, back and front bars, liquor cabinets, saloon doors, dividers, etc.; also wants saloon catalogs and related saloon fixture advertising such as Brunswick, Passow & Sons, American, Rothschilds, Merle & Heany, etc.

Experts

Steve Visakay
Stephen Visakay Cocktail Shakers
P.O. Box 1517
West Caldwell, NJ 07007-1517
svisakay@aol.com
Author of "Vintage Bar Ware," (Collector Books), an identification and value guide dedicated to cocktail shakers, stemware, ice buckets, serving trays, recipe books, paper collectibles, cocktail picks, swizzle sticks, etc.

Roger V. Baker
Baker's Lady Luck Emporium
P.O. Box 620417
Redwood City, CA 94062-0417
ph: 650-851-7188
fax: 650-851-7188
Specializing in saloon collectibles: gambling, bar bottles, shaving mugs, razors, Bowie knives, daggers, barber items, match safes.

Cocktail Shakers

Collectors

Andrew E. Thomas
4681 North 84th Way
Scottsdale, AZ 85251-1864
ph: 888-255-0664 or 480-947-5693
fax: 480-994-4382
andrew-thomas@qwest.net

Manuel Solano
P.O. Box 192
El Arenal
El Arenal Baleares Islands, Mallorca 07600 Spain
ph: 607 296 221
manuel.solano@teleline.es
Wants to buy cocktail shakers from around the world.

Experts

Steve Visakay
Stephen Visakay Cocktail Shakers
P.O. Box 1517
West Caldwell, NJ 07007-1517
svisakay@aol.com
Offers free appraisals, identification and history of the maker of your cocktail shaker; please enclose SASE for reply.

Corkstoppers

Collectors

Philly Rains
1401 Brentwood Dr.
Harrison, AR 72601
ph: 870-743-2040
fax: 419-735-0610
phillyr@anricarvings.com
http://www.anricarvings.com
Expert in antique ANRI Italian wood carvings, 1912 through 1960s; bottle stoppers, corkscrews, nutcrackers, bar sets, figurines, napkin rings, smoking accessories, and more; appraisals upon request.

Dealers

Joe Iozzia
Chameleon Collectibles
P.O. Box 1005
Pomona, NJ 08240-1005
ph: 609-652-8504
pinflyers@aol.com
http://members.aol.com/Pinflyers/
WOODEN.html
*Wants to buy figural handcarved
wood people, animals, elves, pirates,
monks, etc.; nutcrackers, cigarette
boxes, book sends, ashtrays, pipe
holders, figurines, bottle stoppers,
humidors, and unusual figural
handcarved items.*

Soda Syphons

Internet Resources

Mark Kerr
U.K.
mark@sable.co.uk
http://www.sodasyphons.co.uk
*Leading Web site for information on
soda syphons (seltzer bottles) with
image gallery, price guide, cleaning
tips, history, and related links.*

Swizzle Sticks

Clubs/Associations

Ray P. Hoare
International Swizzle Stick Collectors
  Association
Newsletter: Swizzle Stick News
P.O. Box 1117
Bellingham, WA 98227-1117
ph: 604-936-7636
fax: 604-654-1224
veray.issca@shaw.ca
http://www.swizzlesticks-issca.com
*Ray Hoare is co-founder of the
International Swizzle Stick Collectors
Association; sponsors convention every
other year.*

Collectors

Robert Akin
7351 Picardie Lane
Las Vegas, NV 89123-1251
ph: 702-361-0844
bandjakin@aol.com

Ray P. Hoare
P.O. Box 1117
Bellingham, WA 98227-1117
ph: 604-936-7636
fax: 604-654-1224
veray.issca@shaw.ca
*Ray Hoare is co-founder of the
International Swizzle Stick Collectors
Association; sponsors convention every
other year.*

Whiskey Pitchers

Clubs/Associations

Deborah & Paul Inglis
Pub Jug/Whiskey Pitcher Collectors
P.O. Box 165
South Hadley, MA 01075-0165
ph: 413-533-0419
fax: 413-533-0419
bootleggers.nostalgia@worldnet.att.net
*Members interested in buying, selling
and trading of whiskey pitchers/pub
jugs and related items.*

Whisky Pitcher Collectors Association of
  America
Newsletter: Black & White
8044 Tiger Lily Dr.
Mundelein, IL 34113-2636
ph: 941-732-7972
fax: 941-732-7972
dcdowdall@msn.com
http://www.pubjug.com
*An international collector's club;
annual convention/show; members
buy, sell and trade pub jugs, liquor
advertising, water jugs, whisky
pitchers.*

Collectors

Tom Duhn
8044 Tiger Lily Dr.
Mundelein, IL 34113-2636
ph: 941-732-7972
fax: 941-732-7972
dcdowdall@msn.com
http://www.pubjug.com
*Buys, sells and trades pub jugs, liquor
advertising, water jugs, whisky
pitchers.*

Alan R. Blakeman
Elsecar Heritage Centre
Nr Barnsley, South Yorks S74 8HJ U.K.
ph: 01226 745156
fax: 01226 361561
sales@onlinebbr.com
http://www.onlinebbr.com
*Wants pottery whiskey pitchers,
especially with colored tops or colored
transfer decorations; will trade.*

Dealers

Deborah & Paul Inglis
Bootleggers Nostalgia
P.O. Box 165
South Hadley, MA 01075-0165
ph: 413-533-0419
fax: 413-533-0419
bootleggers.nostalgia@worldnet.att.net
*Buys pitchers, ashtrays, back bar
statues, change receivers, and drip
plates advertising Scotch whisky or
other types of liquor.*

Experts

Pete Kroll
P.O. Box 207
Sun Prairie, WI 53590-0207
ph: 608-837-4818
fax: 608-825-4205
pkroll@chorus.net
http://www.gmskroll.com
*Buys and sells collectible advertising
glasses, mugs, & steins.*

SALT & PEPPER SHAKERS

Collectors

Coleen Detzel
28 Lacresta Dr.
Florence, KY 41042-9663
ph: 606-647-6156
*Wants to buy novel, unique salt and
pepper shakers, especially Holt
Howard of any kind.*

Tracy Nader
2322 Ninth St., N.W.
Canton, OH 44708
ph: 330-454-3060
mnader@aol.com
http://members.aol.com/mnader/private/
tracy.html
*Salt & pepper shaker collector for
over 5 years; member of the Ohio
chapter of Novelty Shaker Collectors
Club; Web site is dedicated to
"collector helping collectors."*

Dealers

Helene Guarnaccia
52 Coach Lane
Fairfield, CT 06430
ph: 203-374-6034
greatstufftwo@aol.com
Send requests.

Carol Silagyi
C.S. Antiques & Jewelry
P.O. Box 151
Wyckoff, NJ 07430
ph: 201-934-6528
csantiques@aol.com
*Wants to buy collections of salt and
pepper shakers.*

Mark McMahon
PeterAndMark.com, Inc./Cookie Jars,
  Etc.
806 Sixth Ave.
Asbury Park, NJ 07712
ph: 732-776-9216
peter@peterandmark.com
http://www.peterandmark.com
*Buy, sell, trade cookie jars, banks,
salt & peppers and PEZ; in
partnership with Peter Linski.*

Joyce McCandless
Krazy Cat Collectibles
P.O. Box 1192
Emmitsburg, MD 21727
ph: 301-271-9851
KrazyCatCo@aol.com
http://www.krazycatcollectibles.com
*Wants to buy salt and pepper shakers
of all kinds: animals, characters,*

*couples, nodders; especially wants cat
and dog s&p's; buys collections.*

Judy Posner
Judy Posner Collectibles
P.O. Box 2194
Englewood, FL 34295
ph: 941-475-1725
fax: 941-475-2645
judyandjef@yahoo.com
http://www.judyposner.com
*Collector and dealer wants figural
salt & pepper shakers: Black
Americana, Disneyana, Ceramic Art
Studio, Regal China, advertising
figurals, etc.; buying, selling
collecting for over 25 years.*

Charlene Green
P.O. Box 250421
West Bloomfield, MI 48325-0421
spcollect@aol.com
http://members.aol.com/spcollect
*Buys and sells novelty and figural salt
and pepper shakers; Parkcraft and
other states sets, Goebels, Ceramic
Arts Studio, Van Telligan Huggies,
Shawnee, Nodders, advertising sets;
Web site is always under construction
and changing.*

Lois & Ralph Behm
Lois' Collectibles of Antique Market III
413 W. Main St.
Saint Charles, IL 60174-1815
ph: 630-377-5599 or 847-831-5997
fax: 847-831-5998
*Buys and sells salt and pepper
shakers; will buy entire collections.*

Wilma Schiebel
No Place Like Home Collectibles
2200 S. Hwy 62-65
Harrison, AR 72601
ph: 870-741-9494
nplhc@alltel.net
*Wants salt and pepper shaker pairs or
singles as follows: advertising, black
Americana, figural, characters, novel,
unique, anthropomorphic (fruit and
vegetables with faces), etc.*

Experts

Larry Carey
Salt & Pepper Man, The
P.O. Box 329
Mechanicsburg, PA 17055-0329
ph: 717-766-0868
snpman@comcast.net
*Buys novelty salt and pepper shaker
collections; co-author of six books on
s&p's, "1001, 1002, 1003, 1004,
1005, and 1006 Salt & Pepper
Shakers."*

Mildred & Ralph Lechner
World of Salt Shakers
P.O. Box 554
Mechanicsville, VA 23111-0554
ph: 804-737-3347
*Feature writers on antique glassware
for "AntiqueWeek;" authors of "The
World of Salt Shakers," Vols. 1, 2 &
3; Victorian art and pattern glass
reproduction identification experts;*

collectors of art and pattern glass salt & pepper shakers.

Art Glass
Clubs/Associations

Antique & Art Glass Salt Shaker
Collector's Society
Newsletter: Pioneer, The
1775 Lakeview Dr.
Zeeland, MI 49464
ph: 616-772-7251
shakers@cbantiques.com
http://www.cbantiques.com/ssc
Promotes and encourages the collection and study of salt shakers of the Antique Victorian and Art Glass type; quarterly newsletter.

Dealers

Janice C. Eldridge
64 Burt Rd.
Springfield, MA 01118-1848
ph: 413-783-4629
Wants to buy art glass, colored Victorian glass salt and pepper shakers.

Novelty
Clubs/Associations

Novelty Salt & Pepper Shakers Club
Newsletter: Novelty Salt & Pepper
Shakers Club Newsletter
P.O. Box 416
Gladstone, OR 97027-0416
dmac925@yahoo.com
http://members.aol.com/spclub1234
Focuses on novelty salt and pepper shakers; also anything picturing shakers; offers "singles matching service" for members; newsletter published quarterly.

Ray Dodd, Sec.
British Novelty Salt & Pepper Collectors
Club
Newsletter: S & P Gazette
Coleshill, Clayton Rd.
Mold, Flintshire CH7 1SX U.K.
ph: 01352 759715

Collectors

Irene Thornburg
581 Joy Rd.
Battle Creek, MI 49014-0118
ph: 616-963-7954 or 616-964-9024
fax: 616-963-0118
itburg@attbi.com
Wants to buy unusual novelty shakers to add to collection.

SALTS
Open
Clubs/Associations

New England Society of Open Salts
Collectors
Newsletter: Salt Talk
4 Clear Pond Dr.
Walpole, MA 02681
lgsolkoske@snet.net
http://www.opensalts.info
Meets semi-annually usually in Marlborough, MA.

Rod Elser
Open Salt Collectors of the Atlantic
Region
Newsletter: OSCAR
1470 Morewood Dr.
Powhatan, VA 23139
rcelser@aol.com
http://www.opensalts.info

Carolyn Bugel
Open Salt Collectors South East
Newsletter: OSalt-CSE
P.O. Box 98267
Atlanta, GA 30359-1967
bugelc@peoplepc.com
http://www.opensalts.info
An Atlanta-based club for collectors of open salts.

Harry E. Bowman, Treas.
Midwest Open Salt Society
211 West 500 North
Hartford City, IN 47348
ph: 765-348-4542
edbowman@netusa1.net
http://www.opensalts.info

Sarah Kawakami
Open Salt Seekers of the West - Northern
California
2005 Putman St.
Antioch, CA 94509
ph: 925-757-9603
hgsalts@earthlink.net

Dealers

Elizabeth Jane Koble
Koble's Intaglios, Etc.
7 Camelot Arms
York, PA 17402
ph: 717-757-6484
intaglioetc@blazenet.net
Dealer, collector of open salts; offers a master sale listing; eBay name is intaglioetc.

Debi Raitz
Newsletter: Salt Trader Quarterly
3820 Meadowbrook
Troy, MI 48084-1767
ph: 248-528-9371
DRaitz@aol.com
http://www.opensalts.info
Buys and sells open salts.

Experts

Daniel Snyder
6957 Big Tree Rd.
Pavilion, NY 14525
ph: 585-584-8555
dasnyder@hfent.com
Specializes in master open salts.

Ed & Kay Berg
Delaware Salt Box
401 Nottingham Rd.
Newark, DE 19711-7404
ph: 302-731-5749
desaltbox@cs.com
Buys, sells, and specializes in open salts; writes columns on open salts for club newsletters; can provide information about open salt clubs.

Internet Resources

Debi Raitz
3820 Meadowbrook
Troy, MI 48084-1767
ph: 248-528-9371
DRaitz@aol.com
http://www.opensalts.info
Clubs, links, resources.

Periodicals

Ed & Kay Berg
Delaware Salt Box
Newsletter: Salty Comments
401 Nottingham Rd.
Newark, DE 19711-7404
ph: 302-731-5749
desaltbox@cs.com
The newsletter covers research on open salt dishes.

SALVATION ARMY ITEMS
Experts

David Miller
Salvation Army Collectables
U.K.
webmaster@sacollectables.co.uk
http://www.sacollectables.co.uk
Dealer, collector, expert in Salvation Army collectibles.

Internet Resources

David Miller
Salvation Army Collectables
U.K.
webmaster@sacollectables.co.uk
http://www.sacollectables.co.uk
Only site on the Internet devoted to collectors of Salvation Army memorabilia and artifacts including stamps, postcards, records, books and much more.

Museums/Libraries

George Scott Railton Heritage Center
2130 Bayview Ave.
North York, Ontario M4N 3K6 Canada
ph: 416-481-4441
fax: 416-481-6096
heritage_centre@can.salvationarmy.org
http://heritage.salvationarmy.ca/gsr.html
Museum contains artwork, artifacts,

photographs and texts that tell The Salvation Army's story.

SAMPLERS

(see also FOLK ART; REPAIR/
RESTORATION/CONSERVATION,
Textiles; TEXTILES)

Appraisers

Bette G. Bell, ISA CAPP
Guildmark Appraisal & Estate Sale
Services, LLC
P.O. Box 952
Edmonds, WA 98020
ph: 425-775-5650
fax: 425-670-6957
stashn33@gte.net
http://www.guildmarkappraisal.com
Appraises quilts and other textiles such as samplers, ethnographic textiles, linens; handles estate sales throughout the NW; Certified Member of the International Society of Appraisers; appraising for over 16 years.

Collectors

Donna Litwin
P.O. Box 494
Princeton Junction, NJ 08550-5225
ph: 609-275-1427 or 609-275-0996
fax: 609-275-1427
jsl58@comcast.net
Buys, sells, appraises American and English sampler; please send photo and price of items for sale.

Denise Hamilton
899 Latta Brook Rd.
Elmira, NY 14901-9226
ph: 607-732-2550
Buying pre-1900 samplers and other old needlework.

Dealers

Carol Huber
40 Ferry Rd.
Old Saybrook, CT 06475
ph: 860-388-6809
fax: 860-434-9709
hubers@antiquesamplers.com
http://www.antiquesamplers.com
Specializes in American and English samplers, silk embroideries, needlework pictures, and textile accessories from the 17th, 18th and 19th centuries.

Donna Litwin
P.O. Box 494
Princeton Junction, NJ 08550-5225
ph: 609-275-1427 or 609-275-0996
fax: 609-275-1427
jsl58@comcast.net
Buys, sells, appraises American and English sampler; please send photo and price of items for sale.

Carl McCann
Troy & Black, Inc.
P.O. Box 228
Red Creek, NY 13143-0228
ph: 315-754-8115
*Buys and sells high quality flow blue,
Staffordshire figurines, American
painted furniture, stoneware, redware,
coverlets, samplers, and other
American textiles, folk art, etc.*

Fassnachts, The
P.O. Box 795
Canandaigua, NY 14424
ph: 585-229-4199
fax: 585-229-4810
sampler@frontiernet.net
*Specialists in American samplers and
silk embroideries.*

M. Finkel & Daughter
936 Pine St.
Philadelphia, PA 19107
ph: 215-627-7797
fax: 215-627-8199
mailbox@finkelantiques.com
http://www.finkelantiques.com
*Specializes in schoolgirl samplers and
needlework from the 18th and 19th
centuries; publishes a catalog,
"Samplings," twice a year; available
by subscription.*

Ruth J. Van Tassel
Van Tassel Baumann
690 Sugartown Rd.
Malvern, PA 19355
ph: 610-647-3330
http://www.antiquesandfineart.com/
tasselbaumann
*With Donald O. Baumann, specializes
in samplers and other schoolgirl
needlework; also offers needlework
conservation.*

Peter Cifelli
P.O. Box 2160
Los Gatos, CA 95031
ph: 408-348-3444
samplerhi@aol.com
http://www.labellecollectibles.com
*Specializes in early American
schoolgirl samplers as well as
examples from the British Isles and
Europe.*

Experts

Suzy McLennan Anderson, ISA CAPP
Heritage Antiques & Appraisal Services
65 East Main St.
Holmdel, NJ 07733-2310
ph: 732-946-8801
fax: 732-946-1036
andersonauctions@aol.com
http://www.andersonauctions.net
*Authenticates, buys, sells, appraises,
lectures; author of "The Collectors
Guide to Quilts."*

Museums/Libraries

Cooper-Hewitt Museum National
Museum of Design, Smithsonian
Institution
2 East 91st St.
New York, NY 10128
ph: 212-860-6868 or 212-849-8300
publicinfo@ch.si.edu
http://www.si.edu/ndm

SAMURAI ITEMS

(see ARMS & ARMOR, Japanese
[Swords]; ORIENTALIA, Japanese
Items)

SAND

(see also DIRT)

Clubs/Associations

Nicholas D'Errico
International Sand Collectors Society
Newsletter: Sand Paper, The
P.O. Box 117
North Haven, CT 06473-0117
ph: 203-239-5488
fax: 203-239-5488
iscs@juno.com
http://www.sandcollectors.org
*Founded in 1969; serious and
whimsical collections for purposes of
keepsake, analysis, bon hommarie;
collector of sand, ore, or minerals;
divisions include Beach Sands,
Microscopy, etc.; all ages and sand
related interests welcome.*

Collectors

Jean-Pierre Seys
Sand Collection
1073, rue du Bourg Vieux
Voreppe, 38340 France
james38@multimania.com
http://www.multimania.com/james38/
sandcollection.shtm
*Has a collection of 2,000 samples of
sand from over 150 different
countries.*

SANTA CLAUS

(see CHRISTMAS COLLECTIBLES;
COLLECTIBLES [MODERN],
Christmas)

SCALES

(see also COIN-OPERATED
MACHINES; INSTRUMENTS &
DEVICES, Scientific)

Clubs/Associations

Steve Beare, Mem.
International Society of Antique Scale
Collectors (USA)
Magazine: Equilibrium
3616 Noakes St.
Los Angeles, CA 90023
ph: 323-263-6878
fax: 323-263-3147
stevebooks@aol.com
http://www.isasc.org
*Club focuses on antique scales;
several hundred members worldwide;
the "Equilibrium" magazine is
published quarterly and contains
articles on scales & scale manufacturers.*

Diana Crawforth-Hitchins
International Society of Antique Scale
Collectors (Europe)
Magazine: Equilibrium
P.O. Box 179
Haedington
Oxford, Oxon OX3 9JQ U.K.
fax: 01865 751797
LeHitchins@aol.com
*Club focuses on antique scales;
several hundred members worldwide;
the "Equilibrium" magazine is
published quarterly and contains
articles on scales & scale manufactur-
ers.*

Collectors

Jerry Neufeld
50 Saratoga Dr.
West Windsor, NJ 08550
ph: 609-936-8688
fax: 609-936-8688
jneufeld2@comcast.net
*Wants to buy unusual scales; send
description and picture.*

Steve Beare
7 E. Brookland Ave.
Wilmington, DE 19805
Stevebooks@aol.com

Bob Stein
300 West Adams, Ste. 821
Chicago, IL 60606
ph: 312-263-7500
fax: 312-263-7748
*Past-president of the International
Society of Antique Scale Collectors.*

John M. Shannon
7319 West Cedar Circle
Lakewood, CO 80226-2019
ph: 303-232-1534
rovers@aol.com
*Wants to buy assay balances (wood
and glass encased with small pans) -
both laboratory and portable; also
wants brass scientific instruments;
author of 260-page book on the
development of the assay balance and
history their manufacturers.*

Donald Gorlick
P.O. Box 24541
Seattle, WA 98124-0541
ph: 206-824-0508
*Wants dentist or dental scales, alloy
scales, any small dental scales; also
wants Dr. Fitch's Prescription Scales,
small self-contained scales, medical,
doctors small scales.*

Dealers

Jerome Katz
Katz Collectibles
1108 Pipestem Place
Rockville, MD 20854
ph: 301-279-9320
katzscales@aol.com
http://members.aol.com/katzscales/
antiques.htm
*Scale expert, collector, dealer; VP of
the International Society of Antique
Scale Collectors directing the Society's
research and reply service for public
inquiries.*

Repro. Sources

Sturbridge Yankee Workshop
90 Blueberry Rd.
Portland, ME 04102-1989
ph: 800-343-1144
fax: 207-774-2561
info@sturbridgeyankee.com
http://www.sturbridgeyankee.com

Toy

Collectors

Donald Gorlick
P.O. Box 24541
Seattle, WA 98124-0541
ph: 206-824-0508
*Wants old toy scales; small tin scales
like the old penny toys; any small toy
scale but not the pencil sharpener type
scales.*

SCHOOL RELATED
MEMORABILIA

Collectors

Lee Dennis
447 Park Ave., Apt. 12
Keene, NH 03431-6506
ph: 603-358-0060
*Wants early schoolhouse memorabilia
from 1840-1880: unusual slates,
pencil boxes, lunch boxes, sheet music
depicting schoolhouses, book holders,
etc,*

Tedd Levy
P.O. Box 20
Old Saybrook, CT 06475
teddlevy@aol.com
*Wants pre-1920 items related to
public schools, teaching, students,
playgrounds, school buses, etc.
including postcards, photos, journals,
documents, correspondence,
certificates and some 19th c. books
(none after 1860); prompt replies.*

Diplomas

Collectors

Bob Hut
P.O. Box 1495
Grand Central Station
New York, NY 10163-1495
ph: 800-321-7687
Wants only pre-1865 diplomas from institutions of higher learning.

SCIENCE FICTION

(see also ANIMATION ART; CARTOON ART; CHARACTER COLLECTIBLES; COMIC BOOKS; FAN CLUBS; HORROR; KITS; MOVIE MEMORABILIA; POPULAR CULTURE; SPACE COLLECTIBLES; SUPER HEROES; TELEVISION SHOWS & MEMORABILIA; TOYS, Science Fiction; UFOs & UNEXPLAINED PHENOMENA)

Clubs/Associations

Dale L. Ames
Galaxy Patrol
Newsletter: Galaxy Patrol Newsletter
144 Russell St.
Worcester, MA 01610
ph: 508-755-3830
Focuses on memorabilia relating to radio and TV show space heroes.

Dennis L. Davis
National Fantasy Fan Federation
Newsletter: National Fantasy Fan
25549 Byron St.
San Bernardino, CA 92404-6403
n3f_info@yahoo.com
http://www.simegen.com/fandom/n3f
An organization for Science Fiction and Fantasy fans to work and talk together for the enhancement and enjoyment of these interesting genres: from film to comic books, from role playing to conventions.

Collectors

Dale L. Ames
144 Russell St.
Worcester, MA 01610
ph: 508-755-3830
Interested in collectibles associated with science fiction TV & radio shows & recordings of the programs themselves; also sci-fi comics.

Dealers

Jon Warren
Iguide Media Inc.
2401 Broad St.
Chattanooga, TN 37408
ph: 423-265-5515
fax: 423-265-5515
jon@iguide.net
http://www.iguide.net
Specializes in science fiction and fantasy items; also wants to buy movie posters as well as comic books, cartoon art, Disney, Big Little Books, pulp magazines, baseball and non-sport cards.

Experts

Allen Shevy
P.O. Box 9421
Tampa, FL 33674-9421
ph: 813-933-7424
wofshevy@tampabay.rr.com
http://www.zipmall.com/wofmag
Collects, appraises and specializes in science fiction collectibles: movies, comic books, TV, music, toys, games, etc.

Internet Resources

Stephen Walker
Starland
P.O. Box 24955
Denver, CO 80224-0955
ph: 303-757-0955
fax: 303-757-4958
starland@starland.com
http://starland.com
Science fiction movie and television news, information, and collectibles.

Museums/Libraries

Los Angeles Science Fantasy Society Library
11513 Burbank Blvd.
North Hollywood, CA 91601-2309
ph: 818-760-9234
library@lasfs.org
http://www.lasfs.org
A club collection primarily for members' use, with 12,500 volumes and over 125 magazine titles; public use by appointment.

University of California, J. Lloyd Eaton Collection of Science Fiction
Special Collections Library Dep.
P.O. Box 5900
Riverside, CA 92519
ph: 909-787-3233 or 909-787-6385
fax: 909-787-4673
George.Slusser@ucr.edu
http://lib-www.ucr.edu/spec_coll/eaton.html
A comprehensive research resource for science fiction, fantasy and horror; over 75,000 volumes of hardbacks and paperbacks, related boy's books, pulp magazines, comic books, video and audio library, manuscripts, etc.

Periodicals

Roxanne Toser
Roxanne Toser Non-Sport Enterprises, Inc.
Magazine: Non-Sport Update
4019 Green St.
P.O. Box 5858
Harrisburg, PA 17110-0858
ph: 717-238-1936
fax: 717-238-3220
feedback@nonsportupdate.com
http://www.nonsportupdate.com
The foremost bi-monthly publication for non-sport card collectors; original artwork covers, glossy paper, lots of articles by the experts, great variety of ads, includes a 32-page "pop-out" price guide and free cards.

Harry Hopkins, Pub.
FANDATA Publications
Directory: FANDOM Directory
7614 Cervantes Ct.
Springfield, VA 22152-1608
ph: 703-913-5575 or 888-FAN-DATA
fax: 703-913-5575
email@fandata.com
http://www.fandata.com
Fandom Directory (R) lists over 20,000 fans, collectors, dealers, stores, clubs, and conventions worldwide: science fiction, TV shows, Star Trek, etc.; now in its 19th annual edition; your listing published free of charge upon request.

Warren Lapine, Pub.
Magazine: Science Fiction Chronicle
P.O. Box 2988
Radford, VA 24143-2988
ph: 540-763-2925
fax: 540-763-2924
publications@dnapublications.com
http://www.dnapublications.com
Monthly Science Fiction, fantasy and horror newsmagazine; news stories, interviews, columns, book buyers' forthcoming guide, market reports (updated every 4 months), 500+ book and small press reviews, author sales, etc.

Allen Shevy
World of Fandom
Magazine: World of Fandom Magazine
P.O. Box 9421
Tampa, FL 33674-9421
ph: 813-933-7424
wofshevy@tampabay.rr.com
http://www.zipmall.com/wofmag
Covers movies, comic books, TV, music, toys, games; many exclusive interviews and stories; 108 pages, 4-color glossy covers.

Costuming

Clubs/Associations

International Costumer's Guild
Newsletter: Costumer's Quarterly
P.O. Box 94538
Pasadena, CA 91109
icg@costume.org
http://www.costume.org
International club interested in science fiction, fantasy, comic and historical costuming.

Jana Keeler, Co-Founder
Greater Bay Area Costumer's Guild, The
Newsletter: Costumer's Scribe, The
PMB #320 5214-F Diamond Heights Blvd.
San Francisco, CA 94131
ph: 415-974-9333
jkeeler415@aol.com
http://www.gbacg.org
Local chapter of the International Costumer's Guild; lots of information and networking for costume lovers in the area; costume related workshops, extensive Web site and monthly newsletter included in membership.

SCIENTIFIC INSTRUMENTS

(see INSTRUMENTS & DEVICES)

SCIENTIFIC TOYS

(see TOYS, Construction Sets)

SCOOPS

(see ICE CREAM COLLECTIBLES, Dippers)

SCOOTERS

(see RIDING TOYS)

SCOTTISH COLLECTIBLES

(see also ART, Scottish; BOOKS, Scottish)

Clubs/Associations

Tom Moles, Sec.
Scottish Military Historical Society
Journal: Dispatch
4 Hillside Cottages
Glenboig
Lanarkshire, Scotland ML5 2QY U.K.
scottish.military@btinternet.com
http://www.btinternet.com/~james.mckay/dispatch.htm
Members share a common interest in the history of Scotland and its regiments; the Society is based in Scotland.

Dealers

Sir Alasdair T. Munro, BT.
Alba Antiques
384 RiverRidge Rd.
P.O. Box 940
Waitsfield, VT 05673-0940
ph: 802-496-2213
atmunroalba@madriver.com
Buys and sells antiques of Scottish origin or association: Mauchline ware, Tartanware, Scottish dress, dirks, powder horns, pistols, swords, Victorian Scottish silver jewelry, oil paintings, watercolors, prints, etc.

Experts

Sir Alasdair T. Munro, BT.
Alba Antiques
384 RiverRidge Rd.
P.O. Box 940
Waitsfield, VT 05673-0940
ph: 802-496-2213
atmunroalba@madriver.com
Author of "Scottish Antiques...Fine Victorian & Collectible" (Schiffer Publishing).

Museums/Libraries

Scottish Tartans Museum
86 East Main St.
Franklin, NC 28734
ph: 828-524-7472
fax: 828-524-1092
tartans@scottishtartans.org
http://www.scottishtartans.org
Displays Scottish Tartans and covers various aspects of the Scottish experience, culture, history, dress, and military.

Mauchline Ware

Clubs/Associations

Mauchline Ware Collectors' Club (UK)
Journal: Journal of the Mauchline Ware
  Collectors Club
P.O. Box 3780
New York, NY 10185
tknyc@earthlink.net
http://www.mauchlineclub.org
US club contact for collectors of Mauchline Ware; will provide membership application for mailing to the parent club in England.

William Hodges
Mauchline Ware Collectors' Club (UK)
Journal: Journal of the Mauchline Ware
  Collectors Club
Unit 37, Romsey Industrial Estate
Greatbridge Rd.
Romsey, Hants SO51 0HR U.K.
ph: +44 (0) 1903 775120
For collectors of Mauchline Ware, a wooden ware, souvenirs and furniture from Scotland decorated with transfer prints and photographs; also tartan and fern ware.

Dealers

Sir Alasdair T. Munro, BT.
Alba Antiques
384 RiverRidge Rd.
P.O. Box 940
Waitsfield, VT 05673-0940
ph: 802-496-2213
atmunroalba@madriver.com
Buys and sells antiques of Scottish origin or association: Mauchline ware, Tartanware, Scottish dress, dirks, powder horns, pistols, swords, Victorian Scottish silver jewelry, oil paintings, watercolors, prints, etc.

Experts

David Trachtenberg
c/o Thomas Keith
237 Eldridge St., #24
New York, NY 10002
ph: 212-643-1797
djustint@aol.com
Co-author of "The Collector's Guide to Mauchline Ware."

Thomas Keith
237 Eldridge St., #24
New York, NY 10002
ph: 212-533-8842
Co-author of "The Collector's Guide to Mauchline Ware."

SCOUTING MEMORABILIA

(see BOY SCOUT MEMORABILIA; CAMPING EQUIPMENT; GIRL SCOUT MEMORABILIA; LONE SCOUT MEMORABILIA; STAMP COLLECTING, Scouting)

SCRAP

(see GOLD, Scrap; PLATINUM, Scrap; SILVER, Scrap; GEMS & JEWELRY)

SCRAPBOOKS

(see ALBUMS; PAPER COLLECTIBLES)

SCRIMSHAW

(see also ENDANGERED SPECIES; FOLK ART; IVORY; NAUTICAL ANTIQUES; WHALING)

Appraisers

Sara Conklin, ISA
Nautical Appraisals
P.O. Box 30203
Blairsden, CA 96103
ph: 415-467-6249 or 800-464-4208
fax: 415-467-6249
sconklin2@pngusa.net
http://home.earthlink.net/~sconklin2
Appraises maritime items and collections: ship models, scrimshaw, navigational instruments, figurehead carvings, marine art, paper & ephemera archival collections, telescopes, shipwrecks, diving equip., ocean liner memorabilia, whaling.

Dealers

Albert L. Doucette
Whale's Tale Scrimshanders
42 North Water St.
New Bedford, MA 02740-6335
ph: 508-997-4233 or 508-758-3065
fax: 508-997-0752
http://www.whalestale.com
Specializes in contemporary ivory carvings and scrimshaw; appraisals, manufacturing, reproductions, repair and restoration.

Brian J. Kiracofe
Newport Scrimshander, The
14 Bowen's Wharf
Newport, RI 02840
ph: 401-849-5680 or 800-635-5234
fax: 401-849-9306
newportscrimshaw@juno.com
http://www.scrimshanders.com
Carries an extensive collection of scrimshaw items, whaler folk art c. 1870.

Experts

Albert L. Doucette
Whale's Tale Scrimshanders
42 North Water St.
New Bedford, MA 02740-6335
ph: 508-997-4233 or 508-758-3065
fax: 508-997-0752
http://www.whalestale.com
Specializes in contemporary ivory carvings and scrimshaw; appraisals, manufacturing, reproductions, repair and restoration.

Sara Conklin, ISA
Nautical Appraisals
P.O. Box 30203
Blairsden, CA 96103
ph: 415-467-6249 or 800-464-4208
fax: 415-467-6249
sconklin2@pngusa.net
http://home.earthlink.net/~sconklin2
Appraises maritime items and collections: ship models, scrimshaw, navigational instruments, figurehead carvings, marine art, paper & ephemera archival collections, telescopes, shipwrecks, diving equip., ocean liner memorabilia, whaling.

Museums/Libraries

New Bedford Whaling Museum
18 Johnny Cake Hill
New Bedford, MA 02740-6317
ph: 508-997-0046
fax: 508-994-4350
abrengle@whalingmuseum.org
http://www.whalingmuseum.org
A whaling and local historical museum.

Cold Spring Harbor Whaling Museum
279 Main St.
P.O. Box 25
Cold Spring Harbor, NY 11724
ph: 631-367-3418
fax: 631-692-7037
info@cshwhalingmuseum.org
http://www.cshwhalingmuseum.org
A museum of local whaling history which is accredited by The American Association of Museums; extensive collections of scrimshaw and whalecraft, and archival materials relating to the maritime history of Cold Spring Harbor & LI North Shore.

San Francisco Maritime National
  Historical Park, Museum & Library
Bldg. E, Fort Mason Center
San Francisco, CA 94123
ph: 415-556-9870 or 415-556-9871
fax: 415-556-3540
safr_maritime_library@nps.gov
http://www.nps.gov/safr/local/lib/
  libtop.html

Repro. Sources

Michelle Ochonicky
Stone Hollow Scrimshaw Studio
31 High Trail
Eureka, MO 63025-3563
ph: 314-938-9570
information@BestOfMissouriHands.com
http://www.bestofmissourihands.com/
  stonehollow.htm

SCRIP

(see also LOGGING RELATED ITEMS; MINING RELATED ITEMS; STOCKS & BONDS; TOKENS)

Clubs/Associations

W.C. Stump
National Scrip Collectors Association
Newsletter: Scrip Talk
P.O. Box 444
Loyall, KY 40854-0444
Promotes collecting of coal, lumber & all mining scrip (metal & paper scrip used as a medium of wages in industries such as coal mining), merchant tokens, & mining artifacts including mining lamps.

Periodicals

Walter Caldwell
Newsletter: Token Talk
P.O. Box 29
Fayetteville, WV 25840
ph: 304-574-0105
Periodical about coal, lumber & all mining scrip (metal & paper scrip used as a medium of wages in industries such as coal mining), merchant tokens, & mining artifacts including mining lamps.

Stacie Berger
Krause Publications
Newspaper: Bank Note Reporter
700 E. State St.
Iola, WI 54990-0001
ph: 715-445-2214
fax: 715-445-4087
stacie.berger@fwpubs.com
http://www.krause.com
Monthly news source and marketplace for collectors of US and world paper money, notes, checks and related fiscal paper.

Depression

Experts

Neil Shafer
P.O. Box 170138
Milwaukee, WI 53217
ph: 414-352-5962
fax: 414-352-5974
nelsshaf@aol.com
Co-author of "Standard Catalog of Depression Scrip of the United States;" the 1930s including Canada and Mexico.

SCUBA

(see also NAUTICAL ANTIQUES,
Diom.)

Collectors

Mark Howell
25151 Windwood Ln.
Lake Forest, CA 92630
ph: 949-770-4920
fax: 949-837-6209
lafireboat@aol.com
*Wants scuba diving equipment from
the 1950s: regulators, tanks, fins,
masks, old photos, repair manuals,
spare parts, sales catalogs, old diving
books.*

SCULPTURES

(see also ART; BRONZES;
COLLECTIBLES [MODERN],
Sculptures; FOLK ART; GARDEN
FURNITURE; MARBLE & STONE;
MEDALLIC SCULPTURES;
MINIATURES, Sculptures; ROGERS
GROUPS; WOOD, Carvings)

Appraisers

M. Barden Prisant, FRICS
Telepraisal
32 Union Sq., #1016
New York, NY 10003
ph: 212-614-9090 or 800-645-6002
fax: 212-780-9539
info@telepraisal.com
http://www.telepraisal.com
*For over 21 years, Telepraisal has
been gathering pricing data on
approximately 200,000 artists and
sales of their works; printouts of the
data can be purchased for $35 per
search, or more formal appraisals can
be generated.*

Nancy Harrison
Nancy Harrison Fine Art Consultant
LLC
10 Mitchell Place, Ste. 12GH
New York, NY 10017
ph: 212-371-1935
fax: 212-371-0312
Nharrisonart@aol.com
*Specializes in appraisal of European
paintings, drawings, sculpture (Old
Masters, 19th century, Modern), Amer.
paintings & drawings; Member
Appraisers Assoc. of America; former
Dir., 19th Cent. European Paintings
& Drawings at Sotheby's.*

Debra J. Force
Debra Force Fine Art, Inc.
14 E. 73rd St., #4B
New York, NY 10021
ph: 212-734-3636
fax: 212-734-1042
debra@debraforce.com
http://www.debraforce.com
*Specializes in the appraisal of
American paintings, drawings, prints
and sculpture of the 19th through 20th
centuries.*

Denise J. Levy
Art Find Associates, Inc.
135 Central Park West, Ste. 2 South
New York, NY 10023
ph: 212-595-5267
fax: 212-595-7666
djjl@nyc.rr.com
*Fine art appraiser specializing in
Modern and Contemporary art of all
media: site-specific, prints, paintings,
sculpture, unique works on paper;
appraisals for insurance, charitable
gift, estate planning, division of
property.*

Randall C. Hunt
Fine Arts Appraisals
3503 Fulton St., NW
Washington, DC 20007-1438
ph: 202-333-4035
randallhunt@starpower.net
*Specializes in the appraisal of fine art
including American and European
18th through 20th century paintings,
prints and sculpture; Certified
Appraiser, Appraisers Association of
America.*

Charles B. Goldstein, ISA CAPP
Charles Barry International
8 Hardwicke Place
Rockville, MD 20850-3010
ph: 301-340-6775
fax: 301-340-1726
chadeg@erols.com
*Buys, sells, and appraises 20th
century, modern and contemporary
sculpture; Certified Member,
International Society of Appraisers;
expert witness and trial consultant.*

Melanie Smith, ISA
Seaside Art Gallery
2716 Virginia Dare Trail South
P.O. Box 1
Nags Head, NC 27959-0001
ph: 252-441-5418 or 800-828-2444
fax: 252-441-8563
info@seasideart.com
http://www.seasideart.com
*Accredited member of the International
Society of Appraisers; specializes in
fine art (paintings, graphics,
sculpture) and animation art.*

William Lavendusky, M.S., ISA
William Lavendusky, Fine Art
3345 So. Harvard, Bldg. 100
Tulsa, OK 74135
ph: 918-747-5336
fax: 918-742-3425
*Dealer and appraiser of paintings and
sculpture; specialist in 19th century
French animal bronzes.*

Jnanideva Shanmuga
Appraisal & Connoisseur Associates
620 Sierra Dr. SE
Albuquerque, NM 87108-3377
ph: 505-265-2842
jshan@nmia.com
*Appraisers, artists and brokers
serving the Southwest in painting,
prints and sculpture; also appraise
residential contents nationwide.*

Richard C. Frey, ISA CAPP
R.T.L.H. Enterprises
1275 East Ave.
Chico, CA 95926-1020
ph: 530-343-4528 or 800-567-7854
fax: 530-343-9380
RFREYRTLH@aol.com
http://www.richardcfreyfineart.com
*Certified appraiser of American and
European art, paintings, watercolors,
drawings, prints, sculpture, bronzes,
etc.; appraises for estates, arbitration,
and has testified as expert witness.*

Susanne L. Gavigan, ISA, CPF
Artiques Appraisal Service
16425 Trail Dr.
Redding, CA 96001
ph: 530-244-2100 or 530-244-6147
fax: 530-244-0166
gartiques@aol.com
http://www.appraisalsbyrequest.com
*Art dealer, expert, collector,
conservator and appraiser since 1970:
paintings, water colors, drawings,
etchings, original prints, sculpture,
etc.; Accredited Member of the
International Society of Appraisers;*

Clubs/Associations

International Sculpture Center
Magazine: Sculpture
14 Fairgrounds Rd., Ste. B
Trenton, NJ 08619-3447
ph: 609-689-1051
fax: 609-689-1061
isc@sculpture.org
http://www.sculpture.org
*Not-for-profit organization founded in
1960 for sculptors, collectors,
architects, developers, journalists,
curators, historians, critics,
educators, foundries, galleries,
museums - anyone with an interest in
the field of sculpture.*

National Sculpture Society
Magazine: Sculpture Review
1177 Avenue of the Americas
New York, NY 10036
ph: 212-764-5645
fax: 212-764-5651
NSS1893@aol.com
http://www.sculptor.org/NSS
*Oldest organization of professional
sculptors in the US; purpose is to
promote excellence in figurative and
realist sculpture throughout the US.*

Texas Society of Sculptors
Newsletter: Third Dimension, The
P.O. Box 49291
Austin, TX 78765-9291
ph: 512-371-7606
webmaster@tsos.org
http://www.tsos.org
*This site features the works of member
sculptors in any medium including
terracotta, stone and bronze; lists
information about shows and
festivals, and provides links to lots of
sculpture-related sites.*

Dealers

Ellen Sragow
Sragow Gallery
73 Spring St.
New York, NY 10012-5800
ph: 212-219-1793
fax: 212-219-1793
*Specializes in American art from the
1920s to the 1950s: paintings, prints,
sculpture; WPA era, abstract
expressionist prints, Mexican prints,
works by African American artists.*

James Graham & Sons Gallery
1014 Madison Ave. at 78th
New York, NY 10021-0103
ph: 212-535-5767
fax: 212-794-2454
info@jamesgrahamandsons.com
http://www.jamesgrahamandsons.com
*Specializes in late 19th and early 20th
century European and American
sculpture as well as contemporary
bronzes: French Animalier school,
American Western and wildlife,
figurative, Neoclassical marbles,
historical subjects, etc.*

Robin & June Greenwald
June Greenwald Antiques, Inc.
3096 Mayfield Rd.
Cleveland, OH 44118
ph: 216-932-5535
*Buys and sells 19th and early 20th
century bronze and marble sculptures.*

Jan Wilson
Jan Wilson Gallery
P.O. Box 6649
Ketchum, ID 83340
ph: 208-622-7799
fax: 208-726-5975
*Buys and sells print, fine art,
sculpture.*

Man./Prod./Dist.

Robin Trudel
Pine Tree Studios
271 Bouchard Ave.
Dracut, MA 01826-2229
rtrudel@yahoo.com
*Provides wooden sculptures of all
sizes, specializing in small statuary
including all the popular saints;
member of NWCA and NEWC.*

Museums/Libraries

Andrea Henderson Fahnestock
Museum of the City of New York
1220 5th Ave. at 103rd St.
New York, NY 10029-5221
ph: 212-534-1672
fax: 212-534-5974
http://www.mcny.org
*Special paintings and sculpture
collections; access by appointment;
research fee charged.*

Repair Services

Boris Paskvan
Awesome Metal Restorations, Inc.
4233-G Howard Ave.
Kensington, MD 20895-2449
ph: 301-897-3266
fax: 301-530-8428
*European expert restores gold, gilt,
bronze, silver, silver plating, icons,
metal accessories, sculptures, etc. for
museums, homes, insurance; repairs,
solders, fabricates, duplicates parts,
replates, rewires, retins, polishes,
lacquers.*

Repro. Sources

Gothic Arts
2706 Devine St.
Columbia, SC 29205
ph: 803-765-1188 or 800-284-5435
fax: 803-779-9779
J.Musselman@mindspring.com
http://www.GothicArts.com
*Offers the finest quality reproductions
of art objects ranging from traditional
classic statuary to European
gargoyles.*

Erte

Dealers

Charles Huller
Benedetti Gallery
52 Prince St.
New York, NY 10012
ph: 212-226-2238
fax: 212-431-8106
fineart@benedetti.com
http://www.benedetti.com
*Specializing in sculpture by Erte with
over 60 sculptures on display; also
sculptures by Felix deWeldon (creator
of Iwo Jima War Memorial and over
2000 other monuments), Robazza,
Falai, Brescianine, Li Causi; art by
Anthony Quinn.*

Gwendolyn R. Reasoner, Ph.D.
Re Vann Galleries
125 Arthur Lane
Hackberry, LA 70645-3001
ph: 337-762-4280 or 800-821-4278
revanngal@aol.com
*Largest Boehm dealer in the US;
specializes in the Boehm secondary
market; also Cybis, Royal Worcester,
Erte; also appraises.*

Outdoor

Clubs/Associations

Save Outdoor Sculpture, Heritage
Preservation
1730 K St. NW, Ste. 566
Washington, DC 0006-3836
ph: 888-767-7285 or 202-634-1422
fax: 202-634-1435
astone@heritagepreservation.org
http://www.heritagepreservation.org/
PROGRAMS/SOS/sosmain.htm
*Non-profit organization that works to
preserve and increase awareness about
outdoor sculpture, works of art,
anthropological artifacts, documents,*
*historic objects, architecture and
natural science specimens.*

SEALS

(see also BOY SCOUT
MEMORABILIA, Seals; POSTER
STAMPS; SEALS & STAMPS; STAMP
COLLECTING)

Christmas & Charity

Clubs/Associations

Florence H. Wright, Sec.
Christmas Seal & Charity Stamp
Society, The
Newsletter: Seal News
P.O. Box 18615
Rochester, NY 14618-8615
ph: 585-461-9792
FHW-33@worldnet.att.net
http://homes.aol.com/betsychuck/
cscss.htm
*Focuses on stamp and metered seals
such as tuberculosis, veterans,
fraternal and civic, Jewish, ethnic,
pets, wildlife, medical, Easter, etc.
seals.*

SEALS & STAMPS

Wax

Collectors

Sherlock S. Holmes, D.D.
P.O. Box 3
Worcester, MA 01613-0003
ph: 888-651-0421
fax: 888-651-0421
mail@SherlockHolmes.com
http://www.Sherlock.Holmes.Name
*Wants to buy wax seals; seals are
used to impress a design in melted
wax on the back of an envelope or at
the bottom of a signed contract; made
of metal, porcelain, glass, etc.; all
types wanted.*

Irwin & Eileen Prince
142 Fairway Dr.
Indianapolis, IN 46260-4218
ph: 317-255-1913 or 317-334-9200
fax: 317-228-3355
noitall@netdirect.net
*Wants wood, sterling, bronze, agate,
glass, crystal, ivory, bone, mother-of-
pearl, etc. desk-type (non-fob type)
sealing wax seals; send photos and
price or call for an evaluation.*

SEASHELLS

(see also GEMS & JEWELRY,
Hawaiian Shell; NAUTICAL
ANTIQUES; NATURAL HISTORY)

Clubs/Associations

Mark Scott, Corr. Sec.
San Diego Shell Club
cmhertz@pacbell.net
http://www.molluscs.net/
SanDiegoShellClub
Hazel Andress, Editor
Palmetto Shell Club
Newsletter: Laddergram, The
4 Holly Tree Lane
Columbia, SC 29204
http://www.molluscs.net/
Palmetto_Shell_Club.htm
*A club for those interested in the study
of molluscs, shell collecting, shell arts
and crafts, and other activities related
to beachcombing, snorkeling and
diving.*

Georgia Shell Club, Inc.
Newsletter: Whelk Wavelength, The
3886 Rains Court
Atlanta, GA 30319
flowman@arches.uga.edu
http://www.arches.uga.edu/~amylyne/
GSC/gashell.htm
*Dedicated to all aspects of the science
and beauty of seashells.*

Astronaut Trail Shell Club
4812 Union Cypress Place
Melbourne, FL 32904
ph: 407-724-4585
fax: 407-724-4585
ejpower@ix.netcom.com
http://pw1.netcom.com/~ejpower/
atsc.html

Mark & Peta Bethke
Greater Miami Shell Club
Newsletter: Mollusk, The
3001 South Ocean Dr.
Hollywood, FL 33019
ph: 954-929-5967
*Members interested in collecting land
and marine shells from all over the
world; some shells are very rare and
command thousands of dollars;
regular meetings and shows held to
display member collections.*

St. Pete Shell Club, Inc.
P.O. Box 66873
Saint Petersburg, FL 33736
rlipe1@tampabay.rr.com
http://home.tampabay.rr.com/shellclub

Glen Deuel, Ed.
North Alabama Shell Club
Newsletter: Nautiloid, The
8011 Camille Dr. SE
Huntsville, AL 35802
ph: 256-881-4067
gmdeuel@hiwaay.net
http://fly.hiwaay.net/~dwills/nasc.html

Lynn Scheu, Editor
Conchologists of America
Journal: American Conchologist
1222 Holsworth Ln.
Louisville, KY 40222-6616
ph: 502-423-0469 or 502-458-5719
fax: 502-426-4336
AmConch@mindspring.com
http://coa.acnatsci.org/conchnet
*Amateurs, professionals interested in
the study, collection, conservation of
seashells; grants to deserving
malacology students & qualified
workers; annual convention with*
*lectures, field trips, exhibits, dealers'
bourse, auction.*

Judy Lewis Caldeira
North Texas Conchological Society
Newsletter: Conch Courier
2117 Via Estrada
Carrollton, TX 75006
ph: 972-416-4712
jcaldeira@earthlink.net
http://home.earthlink.net/~jcaldeira/
ntcs.html
*Society promotes and stimulates an
interest in shells and malacology, as
well as in the preservation of natural
habitats; members have diverse
interests in specimen shell collecting,
seashell art, etc.*

Lindsey T. Groves, Treas.
Conchological Club of Southern
California
c/o Malacology
900 Exposition Blvd.
Los Angeles, CA 90007
ph: 213-763-3376 or 213-744-3485
fax: 213-746-2999
lgroves@nhm.org
http://www.lam.mus.ca.us/~ccsc
Oldest shell club in the country.

Guam Shell Club, The
P.O. Box 4482
Agana, GU 96910
http://www.geocities.com/pittoale/
GSCI.html

Mike Cortie
Conchological Society of Southern Africa
7 Jan Booysen Str.
Annlin, Pretoria 0182 South Africa
ph: 11-709-4485
achatina@iafrica.com
http://www.molluscs.net/
ConchSocSoAfrica.html

Collectors

Mique & C.E. Pinkerton
Mique's Molluscs
7078 Westmoremand Dr.
Warrenton, VA 20817-4451
ph: 540-347-3839
fax: 540-347-9740
miques.molluscs.shells@erols.com
http://www.miquesmolluscs.com
*Collector and dealer in specimen
seashells (also includes land and
freshwater mollusks); appraisals on
collections for estate settlements; sells
collections on consignment; member
Conchologists of America and NC
Shell Club.*

Mark & Peta Bethke
3001 South Ocean Dr.
Hollywood, FL 33019
ph: 954-929-5967
*Collector specializing in "cone
shells;" when alive this animal is the
deadliest animal in the world — fast-
acting poison kills its victim within
minutes.*

Tony Lothian
12 Bluebeard Point
Hattiesburg, MS 39402
ph: 601-264-8598
fax: 601-264-0325
tlothian@netdoor.com
http://www2.netdoor.com/~tlothian
*A collector of sea shells for over 35
years; has over 500 species and 1,200
shells.*

Bret Raines
P.O. Box 3209
Victorville, CA 92393
ph: 760-949-1938
mtp@netvigator.com
http://www.molluscs.net
*Shell appraiser, collector, dealer,
expert and auctioneer.*

Dealers

Richard L. Goldberg
Worldwide Specimen Shells
P.O. Box 6088
Columbia, MD 21046
ph: 410-379-6583
fax: 410-379-6583
worldwide@erols.com
http://users.erols.com/worldwide
*Collector, expert, and retail mail
order specimen shell dealer since
1977.*

Shell World
4600 Cecile Dr.
Kissimmee, FL 34746
ph: 407-787-3362 or 888-9-SHELLS
fax: 407-787-3364
customerservice@cyberislandshops.com
http://www.seashellworld.com
*One of the largest selections of sea
shells, corals, and nautical and
tropical decorative items on the
Internet; over 22 years in business;
ships worldwide.*

John Bernard
Shelloak
32 Old Homestead Hwy.
Crossville, TN 38555
ph: 931-484-7167
shelloak@frontiernet.net
http://www.geocities.com/shelloak/
index2.html
*Appraises and sells specimen seashells
for the collector.*

Bob Foster
Abbey, The
P.O. Box 2119
Mammoth Lakes, CA 93546
ph: 760-924-2033
fax: 760-924-0014
Abbeyshell@aol.com
http://www.molluscs.net/The_Abbey/
index.html
*Offers specimen seashells for the
collector.*

Experts

Mique & C.E. Pinkerton
Mique's Molluscs
7078 Westmoremand Dr.
Warrenton, VA 20817-4451
ph: 540-347-3839
fax: 540-347-9740
miques.molluscs.shells@erols.com
http://www.miquesmolluscs.com
*Collector and dealer in specimen
seashells (also includes land and
freshwater mollusks); appraisals on
collections for estate settlements; sells
collections on consignment; member
Conchologists of America and NC
Shell Club.*

Bret Raines
P.O. Box 3209
Victorville, CA 92393
ph: 760-949-1938
mtp@netvigator.com
http://www.molluscs.net
*Shell appraiser, collector, dealer,
expert and auctioneer.*

Internet Resources

Richard L. Goldberg
Worldwide Specimen Shells
P.O. Box 6088
Columbia, MD 21046
ph: 410-379-6583
fax: 410-379-6583
worldwide@erols.com
http://users.erols.com/worldwide
*Collector, expert, and retail mail
order specimen shell dealer since
1977; highly illustrated site for
learning about and purchasing shells.*

Richard L. Goldberg
Conchology - The Art & Science of
Nature
P.O. Box 6088
Columbia, MD 21046
ph: 410-379-6583
fax: 410-379-6583
worldwide@worldwideconchology.com
http://www.worldwideconchology.com
*A non-commercial Web site designed
for shell collectors with a variety of
interests in the hobby and science of
Conchology; illustrates a wide variety
of shells from around the world; for
all those with an interest in shell
collecting.*

Bret Raines
Molluscs Net
P.O. Box 3209
Victorville, CA 92393
ph: 760-949-1938
mtp@netvigator.com
http://www.molluscs.net
*Network of shell dealers and
collectors; free classifieds, dealer's
lists, shell auctions, list of collectors
and clubs, chat rooms, online forum,
and links to related shell sites; free
Web pages for any shell club in the
world!*

Wesley M. Thorsson, Ed.
E-zine: Hawaiian Shell News
122 Waialeale Ste.
Honolulu, HI 96825-2020
ph: 808-395-3581
wthorsson@hits.net
http://home.att.net/~w.thorsson

Tom Rice
Sea & Shore, Inc., Of
Magazine: Of Sea & Shore
P.O. Box 219
Port Gamble, WA 98364
ofseashr@sinclair.net
http://www.ofseaandshore.com
*Dedicated to the study of mollusks; a
one-stop resource for biologists, shell
collectors, students, etc; quarterly
publication covers collecting trips,
descriptions of new species, ads; on-
site museum is free.*

Guido T. Poppe
Conchology
Stanislas Leclefstraat 8
Berchem, 2600 Belgium
ph: 32(2)217-01-10
fax: 32(2)217-36-28
guido@conchology.be
http://www.conchology.be
*A comprehensive Web site for
seashells: seashell gallery, shell links,
collecting shells, and much more all
about seashells.*

Museums/Libraries

Discovery Seashell Museum
P.O. Box 121
2717 Asbury Ave.
Ocean City, NJ 08226
ph: 609-398-2316
http://www.fieldtrip.com/nj/
93982316.htm
*Collection contains some of the rarest
and finest seashell specimens in the
world; over 10,000 varieties of
seashells can be seen as well as types
of coral, carved shells, and more.*

Kevin J. Roe, PhD., Curator
Delaware Museum of Natural History
Journal: Nemouria
4840 Kennett Pike
P.O. Box 3937
Wilmington, DE 19807-0937
ph: 302-658-9111
fax: 302-658-2610
http://www.delmnh.org
*Has seashell research collection;
accepts donations of shells having
locality data; loans material to bona
fide researchers at research institutes.*

Debbie Frederick, Office Mngr.
Bailey-Matthews Shell Museum
3075 Sanibel-Captiva Rd.
P.O. Box 1580
Sanibel, FL 33957
ph: 239-395-2233 or 888-679-6450
fax: 239-395-6706
shell@shellmuseum.org
http://www.shellmuseum.org

Shellorama Shell Museum (The Mikado
Collection)
Mauritius
mikado@intnet.mu
http://www.mikado.com/shellM.html

Periodicals

Maria Antonietta Fontana Angioy
Evolver srl
Magazine: La Conchiglia (The Shell)
Via Cesare Federici 1
Rome, 00147 Italy
ph: 0039 06 5132536
fax: 0039 06 5132796
conchiglia@pronet.it
http://www.evolver.it
*Published four times each year in both
English and Italian; plus a yearbook.*

Seashell Art

Experts

Carole & Richard Smyth
Carole Smyth Antiques
P.O. Box 2068
Huntington, NY 11743-0861
ph: 631-673-8666
carolesmyth@yahoo.com
*Authors of "Neptune's Treasures - A
Study and Price Guide" available
from the authors for $28.50 ppd.*

SEEDS

Collectors

Jean Riley
R 2, Box 2067
Equinunk, PA 18417
ph: 570-224-6330
fiddlinaround@ezaccess.net
*Wants to buy late 1800s to early
1900s seed catalogs, particularly
Peter Henderson's, Childs, Mandeville
& King; also wants seed packets.*

SERVICE STATION
COLLECTIBLES

(see GAS STATION COLLECTIBLES)

SEWING ITEMS & GO-WITHS

(see also BUTTONS; CLOTHING &
ACCESSORIES, Vintage; TEXTILES)

Appraisers

Julie Dearman, ISA
Boulevard Appraisals
2907 North Monroe St.
Spokane, WA 99205
ph: 509-324-2018 or 509-323-9200
fax: 509-323-9082
jubuttons@aol.com
*Button expert, collector, dealer,
specializes in the appraisal of clothing
buttons and sewing go-withs;
Accredited Member of the International Society of Appraisers.*

Collectors

Linda Malenich
207 Roosevelt Ave.
Mc Donald, PA 15057-2468
*Wants Victorian sewing tools and
gold thimbles; also chatelaines and
tools which hang on them; please
include SASE for reply.*

Sherry L. Werdon
400 N. Washington
Lowell, MI 49331-1465
ph: 616-897-9580
*Wants to buy figural tape measures;
also wants unusual sewing items such
as figural pin cushions, thimble
holders, etc.*

Wynneth Mullins
P.O. Box 381807
Duncanville, TX 75138-1807
ph: 972-780-8278
thimble_guild@msn.com
*Wants sewing thimbles and other
sewing related tools.*

Beth Szescila, ISA CAPP
Szescila Appraisal Services
224 Birdsall
Houston, TX 77007
ph: 713-869-4088
fax: 713-869-3728
BethSzescila@ev1.net
http://www.houstonappraiser.net
*Collects sewing items; looking for sets
of sewing tools, preferably in their
original containers; also interested in
18th and 19th century sewing boxes in
good condition, particularly those
with sewing tools.*

Dealers

Denise Hamilton
899 Latta Brook Rd.
Elmira, NY 14901-9226
ph: 607-732-2550
*Wants to buy needlework tools,
especially old needle cases and thimble
containers.*

Barbara Cooney
Cooney's Collectibles
729 Indian Beach Circle
Sarasota, FL 34234-5740
ph: 941-355-1843
bcooney9@aol.com
*Specializes in figural tape measures,
all types of needlework tools,
especially the unusual, chatelaines and
toy sewing machines; buy, sell and do
mail order.*

Beth Pulsipher
Prairie Home Antiques
240 North Grand
P.O. Box 373
Schoolcraft, MI 49087-0373
ph: 616-679-2062
*Buys, sells and specializes in unusual
and rare needlework tools, thimbles,
needle cases, lace bobbins, pincushions, silk winders, sewing clamps,
tape measures, etc.; sells by mail;
available for lectures and seminars.*

Diane Richardson
Gold Hatpin, The
125 N. Marion St.
Oak Park, IL 60301-1087
ph: 708-848-3247 or 708-445-0610
goldhatpin@comcast.net
*Wants needle cases, sterling thimbles,
scissors, unusual darning eggs,
sewing birds, thread winders, figural
tape measures, tatting shuttles, tool
sets, the unusual.*

Darners

Collectors

Linda A. Swierczewski
461 Brown Briar Circle
Horsham, PA 19044
ph: 215-441-0872
linda@fssnet.com
*Collects sock darners; prefers unusual
ones; also collects glove darners.*

Wayne Muller
P.O. Box 903
Pacific Palisades, CA 90272-0903
*Wants to buy darners; author of
"Darn It!: The History and Romance
of Darners: A Price Guide."*

Experts

Wayne Muller
Darn It!
P.O. Box 903
Pacific Palisades, CA 90272-0903
*Lecturer, author of "Darn It!: The
History and Romance of Darners: A
Price Guide;" comprehensive history
of darners and darning; 370 full color
photos, descriptions, background,
prices.*

Machines

Appraisers

Jan Sabin
Dog-N-Pony Show
1359 Crest View Dr.
Camano Island, WA 98282-8484
ph: 360-387-9348
stefnjan@camano.net
*Specializes in the appraisal of vintage
sewing machines, household as well
as children's toy sewing machines.*

Clubs/Associations

Canadian Sewing Machine Collectors
Society
Newsletter: Can-Sew
78 East St.
St. Thomas, Ontario N5P 2R5 Canada
al.lynn@sympatico.ca
http://www.sew2go.com/
cansewhome.htm
*World organization of sewing
machine collectors, restorers, authors,
and historians; nominal annual dues,
online digest/forum and exclusive
listing of machines offered by
members.*

Graham Forsdyke
International Sewing Machine Collectors
Society
Magazine: ISMACS News
158 Hampton Rd.
Chingford, London E1 9UB U.K.
ph: 181 529 0394
fax: 181 926 4492
graham@ismacs.net
http://www.ismacs.net
*An English-based collectors club; the
world's only society for collectors of
antique sewing machines.*

Collectors

Peter Frei
P.O. Box 500
Brimfield, MA 01010-0500
ph: 413-245-4660
peterfrei@prodigy.net
*Wants to buy handpowered vacuum
cleaners, pre-1875 sewing machines,
typewriters, calculators, and adding
machines.*

Frank Smith
804 West Abram
Arlington, TX 76013
ph: 817-275-0971

Alan Quinn
Alan Quinn's Treadles.com
U.K.
alan@treadles.com
http://www.treadles.com
*Collector of pre-1968 sewing
machines, specializing in those made
by Singer and the Jones Sewing
Machine Company.*

Dealers

Jim W. Slaten
Antique Sewing Machine Museum
3400 Park Blvd.
Oakland, CA 94610-2834
ph: 510-261-0413 or 800-474-8433
jws100@pacbell.net
*Buys and sells antique sewing
machines; also publishes the book
"Antique American Sewing Machines -
A Value Guide;" sells books relating
to all phases of sewing machine
interest.*

Sew2go.com
P.O. Box 58249
Renton, WA 98058 Canada
sew2go@sew2go.com
http://www.sew2go.com
*Canadian collector, restoration
expert, appraiser, author and dealer
in fine antique & vintage sewing
machines; mail order vintage sewing
machine needles, operating and service
manuals, hard-to-find and rare parts.*

Maggie Snell
158 Hampton Rd.
Chingford, London E1 9UB U.K.
ph: 181 529 0394
fax: 181 926 4492
maggie@ismacs.u-net.com
http://www.sew-sales.com
*Collects, buys and sells antique
sewing machines as part of a*

*mechanical-antique business; great
Web site with a virtual Maggie Snell
collection, fact files about makers,
collection of featherweights and toy
machines, and much more.*

Experts

Elizabeth S. Brown
45 Whippoorwill Way
Belle Mead, NJ 08502-5827
ph: 908-359-3395
fax: 908-874-7590
ebrown@nerc.com
*Specializes in pre-1920 American
sewing machines or early electric
machines, early sewing tools and
paper patterns for men or women, and
garment drafting tools and/or systems
for tailors or dressmakers..*

Carter Bays
143 Spring Lake Rd.
Columbia, SC 29206-2106
ph: 800-332-2297 or 888-PRE-1875
bays@cs.sc.edu
http://kbs.net/tt/zone/carter/carter.html
*One of the nation's leading sewing
machine collectors; wants only pre-
1875 machines; no oak machines; no
Wheeler & Wilson; no Wilcox &
Gibbs; author of "The Encyclopedia
of Early American Sewing Machines."*

Charles Law
900 Fort St. Mall #1405
Honolulu, HI 96813
fax: 808-545-4285
claw@geocities.com
http://www.geocities.com/Heartland/
Plains/3081
*Author of "The Encyclopedia of
Antique Sewing Machines," the
premiere source for information on
antique and vintage sewing machines.*

Maggie Snell
158 Hampton Rd.
Chingford, London E1 9UB U.K.
ph: 181 529 0394
fax: 181 926 4492
maggie@ismacs.u-net.com
http://www.sew-sales.com
*Appraiser, auctioneer, buyer, seller,
and specialist in antique sewing
machines.*

Internet Resources

Campbell's Guide to Toy Sewing
Machines
quilts@erols.com
http://users.erols.com/quilts/index.htm
*Provides electronic service data for
new and antique electronic equipment
of all types from pre-1930s radios to
latest electronic equipment; sells
copies of manufacturer's documentation; collector books, hard-to-find
parts.*

Melissa Bishop
Tangled Threads
475 Mill Rd.
Coram, NY 11727-4137
ph: 516-736-0320
mbishop@notes.cc.sunysb.edu
http://kbs.net/tt/faq
*Great information about antique
sewing machines.*

Charles Law
Online Antique Sewing Machine
  Resource
900 Fort St. Mall #1405
Honolulu, HI 96813
fax: 808-545-4285
claw@geocities.com
http://www.geocities.com/Heartland/
  Plains/3081

Alan Quinn
Alan Quinn's Treadles.com
U.K.
alan@treadles.com
http://www.treadles.com
*Care and restoration of machines,
recommended sites, sewing machine
mailing lists, images of various
makers, identifying shuttle types,
articles, history.*

Donald Quinn
NeedleBar, the; Vintage Sewing Machine
  Collectors' Group
U.K.
alan@meiboku.demon.co.uk
http://www.needlebar.com
*Members collect, use and research the
history of fine old examples of vintage
sewing machines from America and
Europe.*

Museums/Libraries

Frank Smith
Antique Sewing Machine Museum
804 West Abram
Arlington, TX 76013
ph: 817-275-0971
*America's first sewing machine
museum; over 100 antique sewing
machines, sewing memorabilia, and
old patterns on display.*

Jim W. Slaten
Antique Sewing Machine Museum
3400 Park Blvd.
Oakland, CA 94610-2834
ph: 510-261-0413 or 800-474-8433
jws100@pacbell.net
*Buys and sells antique sewing
machines; also publishes the book
"Antique American Sewing Machines -
A Value Guide;" sells books relating
to all phases of sewing machine
interest.*

Repair Services

Cathy & Stephen Racine
Simple Machine, The
18 Masonic Home Rd. - Rt. 31
P.O. Box 234
Charlton, MA 01507-0234
ph: 508-248-6632
*Buys, sells, repairs and restores old
treadle sewing machines and antique*

hand crank sewing machines; also
carries parts, belts, needles, bobbins
and manuals.

Machines (Miniature & Toy)
Appraisers

Jan Sabin
Dog-N-Pony Show
1359 Crest View Dr.
Camano Island, WA 98282-8484
ph: 360-387-9348
stefnjan@camano.net
*Specializes in the appraisal of vintage
sewing machines, household as well
as children's toy sewing machines.*

Collectors

Lanelle Hodnett
2965 Ave. Z
Brooklyn, NY 11235-1658
ph: 718-891-3489
*Collects all types of miniature and toy
sewing machines, as well as any
sewing machine motifs (especially
Singer); also wants related items.*

Dana & Darlene DeMore
4645 Laurel Ridge Dr.
Harrisburg, PA 17110-3446
ph: 717-545-7320
*Wants to buy miniature and toy
sewing machines.*

Jay Bolante
3058 North Honore St.
Chicago, IL 60657-2050
ph: 773-327-5091
jaybee47@msn.com
*Collects and wants to buy antique toy
and adult sewing machines.*

Dealers

Jude Seyk
Vintage Collection
356 Main St.
Half Moon Bay, CA 94019-1724
ph: 650-712-0366
fax: 650-726-545
vintgecol@aol.com
http://www.vintagecollection.net
*Appraises, buys and sells linen and
lace; also old yardage, buttons, quilts,
sewing implements, sewing machines
and miniature sewing machines.*

Eureka, I Found It! Antiques &
  Collectibles
P.O. Box 2192
Petaluma, CA 94953-2192
eureka@eureka-i-found-it.com
http://www.eureka-i-found-it.com
*An online dealer specializing in
vintage textiles and clothing, toy and
model steam engines, buttons, fans,
Art Deco, costume jewelry, toy sewing
machines.*

Carole & Larry Meeker
Antiques of a Mechanical Nature
5702 Vacation Blvd.
Somerset, CA 95684-9324
ph: 530-620-7019 or 888-607-6090
fax: 530-620-7020
clm@antiqbuyer.com
http://www.antiqbuyer.com
*Interested in purchasing early/unusual
sewing machines; focuses primarily on
small cast iron models with integral
clamps, many dating from the Civil
War era; also other early machines,
both large and small.*

Sew2go.com
P.O. Box 58249
Renton, WA 98058 Canada
sew2go@sew2go.com
http://www.sew2go.com
*Canadian collector, restoration
expert, appraiser, author and dealer
in fine antique & vintage sewing
machines; mail order vintage sewing
machine needles, operating and service
manuals, hard-to-find and rare parts.*

Internet Resources

Geoff & Norma Dickens
Sewing Machine Collector
U.K.
smc@dincum.com
http://www.dincum.com
*Online resource for enthusiasts of
antique and collectible toy sewing
machines.*

Needle Books
Internet Resources

Connie McGinnis
Rosie's Needle Book Museum
111 E. 7th St.
Metropolis, IL 62960
ph: 618-524-2418
rosierider@yahoo.com
http://www.geocities.com/rosierider
*Visit Rosie's Web site to view the
needle book exhibit, to learn about
needle books, or to obtain price
information; nothing for sale; just
sharing the collection.*

Thimbles
Clubs/Associations

Jina Samulka
Empire State Thimble Collectors
316 Parkwood Rd.
Vestal, NY 13850
ph: 607-785-1738
thimblyjina@stny.rr.com

Jina Samulka, Mem.
Thimble Collectors International
Newsletter: TCI Bulletin
316 Parkwood Rd.
Vestal, NY 13850-1262
thimblyjina@stny.rr.com
http://www.thimblecollectors.com
*TCI introduces members to various
aspects of thimble collecting; promotes
research & scholarship; quarterly
newsletter and booklets on thimbles
and related needlework; regional*

chapters; biennial convention; send
LSASE for information.

Wynneth Mullins
Thimble Guild, The
Newsletter: Thimble Guild
P.O. Box 381807
Duncanville, TX 75138-1807
ph: 972-780-8278
thimble_guild@msn.com

Thimble Society, The
P.O. Box 25362
London, NW5 4ZW U.K.
ph: +44 (0)207 419 9562
antiques@thimblesociety.co.uk
http://www.thimblesociety.com
*Members interested in thimbles and
other sewing tools including tape
measures, lace bobbins, pincushions,
chatelaines, sewing boxes, etc.*

Tony Forbes
Birchcroft Thimble Collectors Club
Sutherland Works
Longton
Stoke-on-Trent, ST3 1RH U.K.
ph: 01782-329535 or 01782-333883
fax: 01782-599041
tony@thimble.net
http://www.thimble.net
A company-sponsored collector's club.

Collectors

Barbara Acchino
2011 Tamarack Dr.
Rome, NY 13440-2245
ph: 315-336-4072
bacchino@twcny.rr.com
http://www.smartgroups.com/groups/
  cyberthimble
*Over 20 years collecting antique
sewing tools, especially thimbles;
always looking for sewing items with
Scottie dogs; creator of the first
electronic round robin for fellow
thimble collectors.*

Jina Samulka
316 Parkwood Rd.
Vestal, NY 13850
ph: 607-785-1738
thimblyjina@stny.rr.com
*Thimble collector as well as Editor of
the newsletter for the Empire State
Thimble Collectors club.*

Mary Innes Wagner
564 Linden St.
Rochester, NY 14620
ph: 716-271-8816
fax: 716-244-2673
saperry@aol.com
*Wants to buy all types of thimbles,
especially antique, needle holders.*

Robbie Crawford
Antique Treasures
346 Deer Run Dr.
Maryville, TN 37803
ph: 865-980-9212
fax: 865-980-9463
mc-rc@worldnet.att.net
http://www.antiquetreasures.com
*Collects thimbles, sewing tools,
thimble holders a specialty.*

Sarah Locker
9706 North 111th East Ave.
Owasso, OK 74055-4335
ph: 918-272-7285
admin@alphabetsoup.net
http://www.alphabetsoup.net/
lockerfamily/thimbles.htm
*A favorite among young and old,
thimbles are a wonderful, inexpensive,
and history-laden collectible; join the
growing number of thimble collectors
on the Web and start your collection
today.*

Kay Connors
2594 E. Upper Hayden Lake Rd.
Hayden, ID 83835
ph: 208-762-9520

Dealers

Vicky Fletcher
Thimbles Galore
53 Ancaster Court
Scunthorpe, North Lincolnshire DN17
2DD U.K.
ph: +44 (0) 1724 337011
fax: +44 (0) 1724 337011
thimblesgalore@aol.com
http://www.thimblesgalore.co.uk
*Sells collectible thimbles; Web site has
extensive information on collectible
thimbles; links to other thimble related
sites, message board, competitions
and more.*

Experts

Lorraine M. Crosby
93 Walnut Hill Rd.
Newton Highlands, MA 02461-1836
ph: 617-969-9358
jmcrosby@attbi.com
*Former editor of the "Thimbletter"
newsletter.*

Internet Resources

Barbara Acchino
CyberThimble
2011 Tamarack Dr.
Rome, NY 13440-2245
ph: 315-336-4072
bacchino@twcny.rr.com
http://www.smartgroups.com/groups/
cyberthimble
*An online round robin for collectors
of thimbles and other antique sewing
tools; over 200 collectors participate;
available databases include books on
the subject, recent thimble selling
prices and more.*

Robbie Crawford
Antique Treasures
346 Deer Run Dr.
Maryville, TN 37803
ph: 865-980-9212
fax: 865-980-9463
mc-rc@worldnet.att.net
http://www.antiquetreasures.com
*A online museum of antique sewing
items: thimbles, sewing tools, thimble
holders a specialty; over 500 images
of antique thimbles.*

Sarah Locker
Thimbles!
9706 North 111th East Ave.
Owasso, OK 74055-4335
ph: 918-272-7285
admin@alphabetsoup.net
http://www.alphabetsoup.net/
lockerfamily/thimbles.htm
Offers free thimbles newsletter.

Man./Prod./Dist.

Tony Forbes
Birchcroft Thimbles
Sutherland Works
Longton
Stoke-on-Trent, ST3 1RH U.K.
ph: 01782-329535 or 01782-333883
fax: 01782-599041
tony@thimble.net
http://www.thimble.net
*Manufacturer of porcelain souvenir
thimbles.*

SEX

(see BATHING BEAUTIES, Nudies &
Naughties; EROTICA; PIN-UP ART;
PLAYBOY ITEMS; STRIPTEASE)

SHAKER ITEMS

(see also FURNITURE [ANTIQUE])

Auction Services

David D. Newell
David D. Newell - Shaker Literature
39 Steady Lane
Ashfield, MA 01330
ph: 413-628-3240
fax: 413-628-3833
*Buys, sells, appraises, auctions
printed and manuscript items by/about
Shakers and other like sects; also
wants related photographica and
ephemera; consignments available;
catalog and mailing list placement $5.*

Willis Henry
Willis Henry Auctions, Inc.
22 Main St.
Marshfield, MA 02050
ph: 781-834-7774 or 800-244-8466
fax: 781-826-3520
wha@willishenry.com
http://www.willishenry.com
*Specializes in the sale of American
antiques of all kinds, particularly
Shaker, American Indian and Early
American.*

Clubs/Associations

Henry G. Williams, Ex. Dir.
Shaker Heritage Society, Shaker Meeting
House
Journal: Watervliet Shaker Journal, The
875 Watervliet-Shaker Rd., Ste. 2
Albany, NY 12211-1051
ph: 518-456-7890
fax: 518-452-7348
shakerwv@crisny.org
http://www.crisny.org/not-for-profit/
shakerwv

Karen Campbell
Western Shaker Study Group
1700 Penbrooke Trail
Dayton, OH 45459
http://www.shakerwssg.org
*Many members have expertise in
various areas of Shaker collecting.*

Collectors

Steve Miller
Six Park Place
New Britain, CT 06052
ph: 860-561-3342
fax: 860-223-6316
*Wants Shaker bottles, booklets, paper,
etc.*

Dealers

David D. Newell
David D. Newell - Shaker Literature
39 Steady Lane
Ashfield, MA 01330
ph: 413-628-3240
fax: 413-628-3833
*Buys, sells, appraises printed and
manuscript items by/about Shakers
and other like sects; also wants
related photographica and ephemera;
consignments available; catalog and
mailing list placement $5.*

Doug Hamel
Douglas H. Hamel Antiques
56 Staniels Rd.
Chichester, NH 03234
ph: 603-798-5912
fax: 603-798-5447
Doug@ShakerAntiques.com
http://www.ShakerAntiques.com
*Buys and sells quality Shaker items;
helping to build major private and
public collections for over 35 years.*

Richard Vandall
American Decorative Arts/Crows Run
Gallery
29 War Bonnet Rd.
RFD #1, Box 29
Canaan, NH 03741-9746
ph: 603-523-4276
fax: 603-523-4888
stevengraphs@yahoo.com
*Buying and selling Shaker, Americana
and English Staffordshire; prompt
complete service, confidential to the
seller; family business, second
generation; shipping service available.*

Experts

K.C. & Alana Parkinson
331 Broad St.
Manchester, CT 06040-7014
ph: 860-646-6586
fax: 860-649-2221
kc@caneandreed.com
http://www.caneandreed.com
*Former publisher of "Shakers World"
magazine.*

Gary D. Gardner
200 College St.
Hodgenville, KY 42748-1404
ph: 270-358-3222
*Collector, researcher of furniture,
tools, textiles, books, and crafts
produced by Shaker communities
during the 19th century, especially
Pleasant Hill and South Union in
Kentucky.*

Museums/Libraries

Hancock Shaker Village
P.O. Box 927
Pittsfield, MA 01202-0927
ph: 413-443-0188
fax: 413-447-9357
info@hancockshakervillage.org
http://www.hancockshakervillage.org
*A 200-year-old Shaker site encompass-
ing 20 restored buildings housing the
largest and finest collection of Shaker
furnishings & artifacts in an original
Shaker site.*

Karen Redd, Office Mngr.
Canterbury Shaker Village
288 Shaker Rd.
Canterbury, NH 03224
ph: 603-783-9511 or 866-783-9511
fax: 603-783-9152
info@shakers.org
http://www.shakers.org
*Archives open by appointment;
collectors' seminars, craft workshops,
demonstrations, museum book store
and gift shop, exhibitions, 25 antique
Shaker buildings on 694 acres.*

Erin Budis
Shaker Museum & Library, The
88 Shaker Museum Rd.
Old Chatham, NY 12136
ph: 518-794-9100
fax: 518-794-8621
shakeroldchat@taconic.net
http://www.shakermuseumoldchat.org
*The premier Shaker collection housing
24 galleries of furniture masterpieces,
oval boxes, baskets, ingenious tools
and machinery reflecting the "order,
harmony, and utility" of Shaker
design.*

Shaker Village of Pleasant Hill
3501 Lexington Rd.
Harrodsburg, KY 40330-9218
ph: 859-734-5411 or 800-734-5611
info@shakervillageky.org
http://www.shakervillageky.org
*America's finest, largest and most
completely restored Shaker village; 33
original buildings, 2,800 acres;
dining, lodging in original 19th*

century buildings; featured in books and magazines.

Shaker Museum at South Union
P.O. Box 30
South Union, KY 42283
ph: 502-542-4167 or 800-811-8279
fax: 502-542-7558
shakmus@logantele.com
http://www.logantele.com/~shakmus

Cathie Winans, Dir.
Shaker Historical Museum, The
Journal: Journal, The
16740 S. Park Blvd.
Cleveland, OH 44120-1641
ph: 216-921-1201
webmaster@ohiohistory.org
http://www.ohiohistory.org/places/shaker
Collection and display of artifacts and furniture designed and used by the North Union Shaker Settlement (now known as Shaker Heights); materials about local history including early developers of Shaker Heights.

Furniture

Repro. Sources

Brian Braskie
North Woods Chair Shop
237 Old Tilton Rd.
Canterbury, NH 03224-2224
ph: 603-783-4595
fax: 603-783-3328
brian@northwoodschairshop.com
http://www.northwoodschairshop.com
Manufactures chairs, tables and case pieces in the Shaker style.

SHAPLEIGH HARDWARE

(see DIAMOND EDGE [SHAPLEIGH HARDWARE])

SHARPENERS

(see PENCIL SHARPENERS; PENCILS)

SHAVING COLLECTIBLES

(see also BARBERSHOP COLLECTIBLES)

Experts

Phillip Krumholz
P.O. Box 4050
Peoria, IL 61607-0050
ph: 309-697-1120
Acknowledged expert on razors; author of "The Complete Gillette Collectors Handbook" as well as two other books on shaving collectibles and Barberiana.

Museums/Libraries

Lester Dequaine, Dir.
National Shaving & Barbershop Museum
39 West Main St.
Meriden, CT 06451-4110
ph: 203-639-9778
fax: 203-235-7025
shaving-bshopmuseum@snet.net
Displays barbershop and shaving furnishings and artifacts with on-site theater, sidewalk cafe, and museum store which buys and sells related collectibles and books including razor blade bank price guide.

Razor Sharpeners

Collectors

Jay Bolante
3058 North Honore St.
Chicago, IL 60657-2050
ph: 773-327-5091
jaybee47@msn.com
Collects and wants to buy mechanical gadgets use to sharpen razor blades; also wants wind-up or battery operated shavers and unusual safety razors.

Cary Basse
6927 Forbes Ave.
Van Nuys, CA 91406-4504
ph: 818-781-4856
Wants to buy safety razors, blade sharpeners, blades.

Razors

Collectors

D. Perkins
6335 W. 62nd St.
Indianapolis, IN 46278-1906
ph: 317-293-9962
Wants early fancy or odd safety razors in tins or sets; also fancy handled straight razors.

Dealers

Sigmund Wohl
Razor's Edge, The
P.O. Box 429
Bronxville, NY 10708-0429
ph: 914-476-5939
fax: 914-376-4160
sigwohl@optonline.net
Buys and sells barber and shaving collectibles, fancy and unusual razors, and related advertising.

Experts

Roy Ritchie
RBR Cutlery
P.O. Box 41822
Hindman, KY 41822
Co-author with Ron Stewart of "Standard Guide to Razors."

Charles D. Stapp
7037 Haynes Rd.
Georgetown, IN 47122-8610
ph: 812-923-3483
dennyjoyce@aol.com
Buys all straight razors but especially wants fancy handles, safety razors in original containers, strops, hones,

blade banks, and related items; free appraisal with SASE enclosed.

Hank Belasco
7939 Chastain Place
Reseda, CA 91335-2106
ph: 818-344-8790
Wants fancy or unusual straight razors; also wants safety razors, sharpeners, and blank blades; sent list and prices.

Razors (Safety)

Clubs/Associations

Safety Razor Collectors Guild
P.O. Box 885
Crescent City, CA 95531-0885
Promotes interest in collecting and preserving safety-razors, safety-razor blades and related items; provides information at no charge, but please include SASE with inquiries.

Collectors

Lester Dequaine
155 Brewster St.
Bridgeport, CT 06605-3149
ph: 203-335-6833
shaving-bshopmuseum@snet.net
Wants to buy early safety razors; also wants related advertisements, catalogs, instruction sheets, mechanical blade sharpeners, razor blade banks, figural shaving mugs, figural handle shaving brushes, counter & window displays.

Howard Hazelcorn
6731 Ashley Ct.
Sarasota, FL 34241-9696
ph: 941-921-1815
mrpropane@aol.com
Wants to buy turn-of-the-20th-century safety razors.

Clay Tontz
4043 Nora Ave.
Covina, CA 91722-3819
ph: 626-338-9976

Experts

Howard Hazelcorn
6731 Ashley Ct.
Sarasota, FL 34241-9696
ph: 941-921-1815
mrpropane@aol.com
Author of "Hazelcorn's Guide to Kampfe's Star Safety Razors."

Robert Waits
Safety Razors & Shaving Collectibles
594 Endicott Dr.
Sunnyvale, CA 94087-4426
rwaits@juno.com
http://www.geocities.com/safetyrazors
Author of "Safety Razor Reference Guide" and "Safety Razor Reference Guide - First Supplement;" these are not price guides.

SHAWLS

Kashmir (Paisley)

(see also TEXTILES)

Collectors

Stephanie M. Schnatz
17 Tallow Ct.
Baltimore, MD 21244-2516
ph: 410-944-0819
chelsealady@hotmail.com
http://www.geocities.com/Paris/Palais/7498
Wants to buy paisley shawls and scraps; please, no dry rot.

Dealers

Allan Arthur
Cyber Rug Center
25 Bennett St.
Atlanta, GA 30309
ph: 800-686-7030 or 404-350-9560
aarthur@cyberrug.com
http://www.cyberrug.com
Buys and sells antique Oriental rugs, Persian rugs, Art Deco rugs, Chinese rugs, Kelim & flat woven rugs, Coptic and Asian textiles, European rugs and tapestries, Kashmir shawls, and American hooked and folk art rugs.

Lavesh Jagasia
Shawl Gallery, The
Shop #1, Sunbeam Apartments
Perry Cross Rd., Bandra-West
Bombay, Maharashtra 400 050 India
ph: 91-22-6510505
shawlgallery@hotmail.com
http://www.shawlgallery.com
Deals in find antique shawls; also offers a shawl repair and restoration services.

Experts

Val Arbab, ISA CAPP
P.O. Box 684
La Jolla, CA 92038-0684
ph: 858-453-4686
fax: 858-457-3647
valarbab@att.net
Appraises all oriental rugs, shawls, and other textiles; also buys, sells and brokers collectible and old decorative rugs; over 30 years experience; member of the ASA, certified member of the ISA.

SHEET MUSIC

(see also MOVIE MEMORABILIA; MUSIC; PAPER COLLECTIBLES; PERFORMING ARTS; ROCK 'N' ROLL COLLECTIBLES)

Appraisers

Wayland Bunnell
Clean Sheets
199 Tarrytown Rd.
Manchester, NH 03103-2723
ph: 603-668-5466
wtarrytown@aol.com
Full service out-of-print sheet music

mail order business; 18 years in business; set-priced and auction lists available; nationally recognized expert on E.T. Paull sheet music; seeks "unpicked" sheet music lots or collections.

Auction Services

Beverly A. Hamer
Hamer Sheet Music Sales
P.O. Box 75
East Derry, NH 03041
ph: 603-432-3528
fax: 207-934-1481
hamersheetmusic@aol.com
Wants old collectible sheet music; publishes a set price list and conducts auctions of collectible sheet music; free search service.

Paul A. Riseman
2205 South Park Ave.
Springfield, IL 62704-4335
ph: 217-787-2634
fax: 217-787-0062
riseman@riseman.com
http://www.riseman.com
Send for free sheet music auction catalogs in the following categories: movie, broadway, rags, jazz, blues, rock, Berlin, Gershwin, transportation, sports, political, etc.

Lois Cordey
5623 N. 64th Ave.
Glendale, AZ 85301
ph: 623-931-2835
Conducts periodic sheet music auctions.

Clubs/Associations

Sam Teicher
New York Sheet Music Society
P.O. Box 354
Hewlett, NY 11557
ph: 516-295-0719
fax: 516-569-1493
samuelt313@aol.com
For collectors of all kinds of sheet music with an emphasis on popular music from 1890 to 1950.

Wanda W. Bond
1712 Winingridge Dr.
Richmond, VA 23233
ph: 804-303-1165 or 804-741-4985
bondww@erols.com
Identifier and appraiser of vintage and collectible sheet music; specializing in historical/military, E.T. Paull, ragtime, early 20th century and tin pan alley sheet music.

Lois Cordey, Ed.
Remember That Song
Newsletter: Remember That Song Newsletter
5623 N. 64th Ave.
Glendale, AZ 85301
ph: 623-931-2835
Sheet music collectors contribute informative articles and illustrations; illustrated newsletter covering every aspect of old-time popular music collecting; focuses on sheet music from

1840 to 1940; auctions; members get free ads.

Marilyn Brees, Sec.
National Sheet Music Society, Inc.
Newsletter: Song Sheet
1597 Fair Park Ave.
Los Angeles, CA 90041-2255
ph: 805-497-2212 or 818-761-0567
res0fek5@verison.net
http://www.nsmsmusic.org
Membership includes bi-monthly newsletter and yearly directory; members get free 40 word listings in each.

Marge Day
City of Roses Sheet Music Collectors Club
17401 SE 39th St.
Portland, OR 98683
ph: 360-253-8233
fax: 360-892-8969
An association of collectors of sheet music; hosts an annual sale of sheet music in September.

Collectors

Stanley King
260 Fifth Ave.
New York, NY 10001-6408
ph: 212-447-1880
fax: 212-447-0728
Wants to buy sheet music: jazz, KKK music, political music, and songsters.

Gary Olsen
505 S. Royal Ave.
Front Royal, VA 22630
ph: 540-635-7157 or 800-954-7374
fax: 540-635-1818
olsenhp@hpfri.com
http://www.hpfri.com
Wants sheet music with covers depicting sports, WWI, or first names in the titles.

Roger Burgoon
425 Zetterower Rd.
Statesboro, GA 30458
ph: 912-764-3195
rogerburgoon@hotmail.com

Jim Wiemers
5312 Seiler Rd.
Dorsey, IL 62021-1700
ph: 618-377-6379
wiemershmusic@juno.com
Hosts the annual Sheet Music Show in late June in Collinsville, IL; collector for over 25 years; will provide appraisal; please provide photocopies of covers.

Margaret Horning
13447 SE Brush St.
Portland, OR 97236-3323
ph: 503-761-3817

Marge Day
17401 SE 39th St.
Portland, OR 98683
ph: 360-253-8233
fax: 360-892-8969

Dealers

Beverly A. Hamer
Beverly A. Hamer Sheet Music Sales
P.O. Box 75
East Derry, NH 03041
ph: 603-432-3528
fax: 207-934-1481
hamersheetmusic@aol.com
Expert, collector, dealer wants old collectible sheet music; publishes a set price list and conducts auctions of collectible sheet music; free search service.

Wayland Bunnell
Clean Sheets
199 Tarrytown Rd.
Manchester, NH 03103-2723
ph: 603-668-5466
wtarrytown@aol.com
Full service out-of-print sheet music mail order business; 18 years in business; set-priced and auction lists available; nationally recognized expert on E.T. Paull sheet music; seeks "unpicked" sheet music lots or collections.

Allen Radwill
23 Hunters Lane
Vincentown, NJ 08088-2837
ph: 609-953-5473
radwill1@aol.com
250,000 items related to rock & roll, rhythm & blues, soul, gospel, television, movies: records, sheet music, magazines; no CDs or videos.

Robert Hess
155 West 72nd St., Ste. 404
New York, NY 10023
ph: 212-579-0689
info@musiccollecting.com
http://www.musiccollecting.com
Buys, sells LP records (33-1/3 rpm), 45 rpm, 78 rpm, jazz, R&B-soul, classical, opera, country, folk, ethnic, spoken word, comedy, big bands, doo wop, TV-radio, gospel-spirituals, etc.; also related sheet music, books, photos, posters.

Sheet Music Center
Box 10
Old Bethpage, NY 11804
ph: 800-527-7626
smctr@sheetmusiccenter.com
http://www.sheetmusiccenter.com
Buys and sells sheet music and piano rolls; FREE catalog to readers of "Maloney's Antiques & Collectibles Resource Directory."

Sandra Hollman
Global Music Enterprises
488 Archer Lane
Kissimmee, FL 34746
ph: 407-396-4176
fax: 407-396-4176
globaltreasures@webtv.net
Buys and sells vintage sheet music and movie/movie star memorabilia, Marilyn Monroe, pin-ups; send want lists or email requests.

Jeannie Peters
Mt. Washington Antiques
3742 Kellogg Ave.
Cincinnati, OH 45226-1514
ph: 513-231-6584 or 513-321-0919
Buys, sells and specializes in sheet music; over 200,000 available for sale; send want list, please.

Barbara Hospel
2836 Pleasant View Heights
Cottage Grove, WI 53527
ph: 608-209-0900
bhospel@mailbag.com
http://www.sheetmusiccollectibles.com
Specializes in collecting vintage sheet music.

Joe Schulte
Gift Music Book & Collectibles
420 Wallace St.
Chicago Heights, IL 60411
ph: 708-877-7099 or 708-755-7622
fax: 208-275-5014
jntschulte@rocketmail.com
http://www.tias.com/stores/gift
In stock or free search for individual and folios from mid-1800s to present; out-of-print, piano, organ, vocal, guitar, tablature, child and adult keyboard and instrumental methods, choral, ethnic, frameable, and/or playable.

Tom Morgan
913 Elysian Fields Ave.
New Orleans, LA 70117
ph: 504-944-7040
tom@jass.com
http://www.jass.com/tom
Author of "From Cakewalk to Concert Halls;" always looking for sheet music with photos of African Americans or sheet music published in New Orleans.

Heidi Wilson
P.O. Box 5231
Hercules, CA 94547
theotherheidi@aol.com
Buys and sells sheet music 1880-1975; send name and address along your list of wants; or ask for current list of sheet music for sale.

Jeanne Koch
Kookie Kollectorium
4312 SE Flavel St.
Portland, OR 97206-8426
ph: 503-771-2024
jkoch@aol.com
Send want lists.

SHEET MUSIC

Experts

Wayland Bunnell
Clean Sheets
199 Tarrytown Rd.
Manchester, NH 03103-2723
ph: 603-668-5466
wtarrytown@aol.com
Full service out-of-print sheet music mail order business; 18 years in business; set-priced and auction lists available; nationally recognized expert on E.T. Paull sheet music; seeks "unpicked" sheet music lots or collections.

Sandy Marrone
113 Oakwood Dr.
Cinnaminson, NJ 08077
ph: 856-829-6104
Smusandy@aol.com
Sheet music collector for over 25 years; appraises and lectures; has contacts throughout the hobby; willing to answer questions and give advice about sheet music; would prefer discussing by phone but will answer mail if SASE enclosed.

Lois Cordey
5623 N. 64th Ave.
Glendale, AZ 85301
ph: 623-931-2835
Collects, appraises and specializes in sheet music.

Lynn Wenzel
15134 Airport Rd.
Nevada City, CA 95959-9405
ph: 530-470-0360
fax: 530-478-5695
lwinparadise@sbcglobal.net
Co-author with Carol Binkowski of "I Hear American Singing;" features writer for antique and collectible publications nationwide under the syndicated name "Handed Down."

Internet Resources

American Sheet Music Collection,
Library of Congress
101 Independence Ave. SE
Washington, DC 20540
ph: 202-707-8000
ndlpcoll@loc.gov
http://memory.loc.gov/ammem/smhtml/smhome.html
The American Sheet Music Collection contains tens of thousands of pieces of sheet music registered for copyright during the post-Civil War era, 1870 to 1885: popular songs, piano music, sacred music, secular choral music, etc.

Museums/Libraries

American Antiquarian Society
185 Salisbury St.
Worcester, MA 01609
ph: 508-755-5221
fax: 508-753-3311
library@mwa.org
A learned society founded in 1812; maintains a research library of American history and culture in order to collect, preserve, and make available for study the printed record of the US; 3 million books, maps, pamphlets, etc.

Broadcast Music, Inc. (BMI)
320 West 57th St.
New York, NY 10019
ph: 212-586-2000
pr@bmi.com
http://www.bmi.com
A nationwide music performance rights organization, licenses for more than 120,000 songwriters and composers and more than 60,000 music publishers; significant sheet music collection.

Periodicals

Kirk Miller, Ed.
Good Music Group, The
Magazine: Sheet Music Magazine
333 Adams St.
Bedford Hills, NY 10507
ph: 800-759-3036 or 914-244-8500
fax: 914-244-8560
editor@sheetmusicmagazine.com
http://www.sheetmusicmagazine.com
Focuses on playable sheet music; some dealer ads for vintage sheet music.

Richard Zimmerman, Ed.
Maple Leaf Club
Newsletter: Rag Times, The
15522 Ricky Ct.
Grass Valley, CA 95949-6672
A bi-monthly newsletter with everything about ragtime - past and present; since 1967; also sheet music ads and articles.

Rock 'N' Roll

Collectors

Jim Weaver
PMB 345, 322 Mall Blvd.
Monroeville, PA 15146-2229
Wants 1950s-1960s rock 'n' roll photo cover sheet music; send lists and offers.

SHEFFIELD

(see also SILVER; SILVERPLATE)

SHELLS

(see AMMUNITION & EXPLOSIVE ORDNANCE, Shell Casings; SEASHELLS; TRENCH ART)

SHIP RELATED

(see also NAUTICAL ANTIQUES; SHIPPING; STEAMBOAT COLLECTIBLES; TITANIC MEMORABILIA)

Appraisers

Sara Conklin, ISA
Nautical Appraisals
P.O. Box 30203
Blairsden, CA 96103
ph: 415-467-6249 or 800-464-4208
fax: 415-467-6249
sconklin2@pngusa.net
http://home.earthlink.net/~sconklin2
Managed the collections of the National Maritime Museum in San Francisco for ten years & is an expert in appraising ship models, ships-in-bottles, marine art, scrimshaw, figureheads, paper ephemera, instruments, whaling, diving equipment.

Experts

Sara Conklin, ISA
Nautical Appraisals
P.O. Box 30203
Blairsden, CA 96103
ph: 415-467-6249 or 800-464-4208
fax: 415-467-6249
sconklin2@pngusa.net
http://home.earthlink.net/~sconklin2
Managed the collections of the National Maritime Museum in San Francisco for ten years & is an expert in appraising ship models, ships-in-bottles, marine art, scrimshaw, figureheads, paper ephemera, instruments, whaling, diving equipment.

U.S.S. Constitution

Collectors

Tim O'Callaghan
305 St. Lawrence Blvd.
P.O. Box 512
Northville, MI 48167
ph: 248-449-2652
timothyo@ameritech.net
http://www.hfha.org/fordtrimotor.htm
Wants USS Constitution "Old Ironsides" items made from the ship in the 1920s and sold to raise money for her restoration; also wants 1931 postal covers from her 1931-1934 cruise around the US; other related items considered.

Museums/Libraries

U.S.S. Constitution Museum
P.O. Box 1812
Boston, MA 02129
ph: 617-426-1812
info@ussconstitutionmuseum.org
http://www.ussconstitutionmuseum.org
Museum brings to life the stories of the individuals who authorized, built, served on and preserved the USS Constitution.

Warships

Clubs/Associations

Allan Harris
International Naval Research Organization
Magazine: Warship International
5905 Reinwood Dr.
Toledo, OH 43613
ph: 419-472-1331
editor@warship.org
http://www.warship.org
Dedicated to the study of post-1860 naval vessels: histories, elements of ballistics, design, careers, etc.; magazine issued quarterly.

Collectors

Stan Dickinson
307-1/2 E. Lake St., Apt. B
Petoskey, MI 49770-2417
ph: 231-347-1022
Collects prints or pictures of Spanish American War era, US Navy war ships, Great White Fleet.

SHIPPING

(see also NAUTICAL ANTIQUES; SHIP RELATED; STEAMBOAT COLLECTIBLES)

Canadian

Dealers

Michael Rice
Michael Rice Collectibles
P.O. Box 286
Saanichton, British Columbia V8M 2C5
Canada
ph: 250-652-9412
fax: 250-652-7866
mrice@pacificcoast.net
Looking for paper items from Canadian steamships and paddle wheelers, particularly menus, passenger lists, deck plans & similar items; also wants any envelopes used on board with appropriate postal markings such as "Posted on Board," etc.

Chesapeake Bay Steamship

Collectors

James Tigner, Jr.
P.O. Box 700
Fairfield, PA 17320-0770
oldbayline@hotmail.com
Collector wants to buy memorabilia relating to the Chesapeake Bay area steamship lines: time tables, brochures, tickets, menus, photographs, etc.

Great Lakes Related

Dealers

Kenneth Benjamin
Island Shipyard, The
P.O. Box 599
Put In Bay, OH 43456-0599
ph: 419-285-2585
fax: 419-285-2585
ksb@kenben.com
*Specializes in genuine Great Lakes
nautical antiques and ship models.*

Michael Kujat
Anchor In Antiques
2122 W. US 2
Saint Ignace, MI 49781-9647
ph: 906-643-9917
*Specializes in Great Lakes nautical
items.*

Experts

James A. Baumhofer
P.O. Box 4302
Saint Paul, MN 55104-0302
ph: 651-698-7151
fax: 651-690-5641
*Great Lakes ships, books, pictures,
photos; Green's or other directories.*

Museums/Libraries

Dossin Great Lakes Museum
100 Strand Dr.
Detroit, MI 48207
ph: 313-852-4051
amy@detroithistorical.org
http://www.detroithistorical.org/html/
information/dossin.html
*History of Great Lakes transport,
focusing on Detroit: ship model
gallery, pilot house, yachts of the Auto
Barons.*

SHIPS-IN-BOTTLES

(see NAUTICAL ANTIQUES, Models
[Ships-In-Bottles])

SHIRT STUDS

(see CLOTHING & ACCESSORIES,
Vintage; CUFF LINKS)

SHOESHINE STANDS

(see BARBERSHOP
COLLECTIBLES)

SHOULDER PATCHES

(see BADGES; MILITARIA;
PATCHES)

SHRUNKEN HEADS

(see MORBID & ODD ITEMS;
SKELETONS)

SIGNS

(see ADVERTISING COLLECTIBLES;
BREWERIANA; GAS STATION
COLLECTIBLES; HIGHWAY
COLLECTIBLES; LAMPS &
LIGHTING, Neon; MARINE CORPS
ITEMS)

SILHOUETTES

(see also FOLK ART)

Dealers

Janene Fawcett
Vintage Clothing
190 Parker Ave.
Rodeo, CA 94572
ph: 510-245-2443 or 800-636-1410
stone@vintagesilhouettes.com
http://www.vintagesilhouettes.com

Experts

Alda Horner
3700 Dean Dr., Unit #3301
Ventura, CA 93003
ph: 805-642-7953
Author, consultant, and dealer.

Museums/Libraries

Peabody Essex Museum
Essex & Libert Sts.
Salem, MA 01970
ph: 978-745-9500 or 800-745-4054
pem@pem.org
http://www.pem.org

National Portrait Gallery
750 Ninth St., Ste. 8300
Washington, DC 20560-0973
ph: 202-275-1738
fax: 202-275-1887
npgweb@npg.si.edu
http://www.npg.si.edu

Repro. Sources

Ellen Mischo
Profiles
P.O. Box 412
Leesburg, VA 22075-0412
ph: 703-771-7342
*Makes and sells authentic 18th and
19th century reproduction silhouettes.*

Glass

Experts

Shirley R. Mace
Shadow Enterprises
P.O. Box 1602
Mesilla Park, NM 88047-1602
ph: 505-524-6717
fax: 505-523-0940
shadow-ent@zianet.com
http://www.geocities.com/
MadisonAvenue/Boardroom/1631
*Author of "Vintage Silhouettes on
Glass & Reverse Paintings" (2000);
painted black on reverse of glass; sold
in dimestores from the 1920s to
1950s; often with advertising and
attached thermometers or calendars.*

SILK EMBROIDERIES

(see MILITARIA, Silk Embroideries;
STEVENGRAPHS; TEXTILES)

SILVER

(see also BOOKS, Reference
[Silver]; FLATWARE; GLASS, Silver
Overlay; GEMS & JEWELRY;
REPAIR/RESTORATION/
CONSERVATION, Metal Items;
SHEFFIELD; SILVERPLATE;
SPOONS; TABLEWARE)

Appraisers

David J. LeBeau
David J. LeBeau Appraisal Services
119 South Main St.
Sheffield, MA 01257
ph: 413-229-3445
djlebeau@rcn.com
http://www.appraisalbylebeau.com
*Specializes in the appraisal of
furniture, silver, ceramics and
decorative arts; former ASA (1974-99)
& Past Pres. NY Chapter ASA;
retired Asst. Prof. Appraisal Studies
NYU, founding faculty of Appraisal
Studies program Yeshiva U.*

Sarah Shinn Pratt
358 Main St. South
Woodbury, CT 06798
ph: 203-263-5636
fax: 203-263-6702
shinnpratt@aol.com
http://hometown.aol.com/shinnpratt/
index.html
*Specialist in decorative arts and
silver.*

Lynn Magnusson, AM
Personal Property Consultants, Inc.
271 Parsippany Rd.
Parsippany, NJ 07054
ph: 973-884-2466
fax: 973-884-1781
info@ppcappraisals.com
http://www.ppcappraisals.com
*Specializes in the appraisal of
furniture, ceramics, silver and other
residential contents for insurance,
equitable distribution, donation,
matrimonial; offers expert witness and
litigation services; appraisals comply
with USPAP.*

Linda Dawson
Dawson's
128 American Rd.
Morris Plains, NJ 07950
ph: 973-984-6900
fax: 973-984-6956
info@dawsons.org
http://www.dawsons.org
*Accredited Senior Appraiser in the
American Society of Appraisers and
silver specialist on the "Antiques
Roadshow."*

William Bunch
William Bunch Auctions & Appraisals
One Hillman Dr.
Chadds Ford, PA 19317
ph: 610-558-1800
fax: 610-558-0885
whb@williambunchauctions.com
http://www.williambunchauctions.com
*Specializes in the appraisal of antique
clocks, music boxes, silver, paintings
and other decorative objects.*

Rita Lang
Silver 2000
P.O. Box 845
Middleburg, VA 20118-0845
ph: 540-253-9966
silver2000@erols.com
*Specializing in the appraisal of fine
heirloom silver.*

James Callear
Barnesville Antiques & Appraising
P.O. Box 314
Barnesville, MD 20838
ph: 301-972-7490
clearviewmeadow@msn.com
*Specializes in the appraisal of
American, English, Continental silver
from the 18th through 20th centuries;
member of ISA.*

Paula Hantman, ASA
Hantman's Auctioneers & Appraisers
P.O. Box 59366
Potomac, MD 20859-9366
ph: 301-770-3720
fax: 301-770-4135
hantman@hantmans.com
http://www.hantmans.com
*American, European and Asian
antiques (furniture, porcelain, silver,
decorative arts, Americana),
collectibles, residential contents;
estates; insurance replacement and
damage claims; estate planning;
family division; also auctioneer.*

Mary Ellen Heibel, ISA, ASA
Personal Property Consultants, Inc.
1009 Old Bay Ridge Rd.
Annapolis, MD 21403-4228
ph: 410-267-7708 or 410-269-5909
fax: 410-269-5909
mehjlh@cs.com
*Accredited Senior Member of the
American Society of Appraisers;
specializes in the appraisal of antique
furniture, antique silver and
metalware, antiques and decorative
arts.*

Anna C. Sim
235 Richard Burbydge
Williamsburg, VA 23185
ph: 757-258-1113
fax: 757-229-5050
acsiminc@cox.net

Paula Barlowe
Paul L. Barlowe Appraisal Services
2933 W. Cary St., Ste. 201
Richmond, VA 23221
ph: 804-355-6566
sectime@erols.com
http://www.appraisers.org/pages/
   memberpage.cfm?id-46600
   Specializes in the appraisal of
   English, Scottish and American silver
   as well as in American Victorian-era
   silverplate.

Christine N. Corbin, ISA
Motley's Auctions, Inc.
4402 West Broad St.
Richmond, VA 23230
ph: 804-355-2100
fax: 804-359-6954
cncorbin@motleys.com
http://www.motleysgroup.com
   Auctioneers and appraisers of antique
   and modern silver, flatware,
   hollowware, jewelry, and other
   decorative items.

Carla S. Butler
Butler & Associates
P.O. Box 4510
Greensboro, NC 27404
ph: 336-299-6509
csbutler@vnet.net
http://users.vnet.net/csbutler
   Specializes in the appraisal of silver,
   antiques, decorative arts; also
   household contents; for the purposes
   of insurance, donation, division of
   property, estate.

Louise Phillips
Alexander Appraisal Service
3116 Weddington Rd. #900 PMB 190
Matthews, NC 28105
ph: 704-849-7352
flownlogic@aol.com
   Specializes in appraising furniture,
   silver, ceramics as well as antiques &
   residential contents for insurance,
   liquidation, marital dissolution; also
   consulting services for clients wishing
   to sell their items in the highest, best
   market.

Caroline T. Gray, ISA CAPP
Thistle, The
P.O. Box 220064
Charlotte, NC 28222-0064
ph: 704-365-4539
fax: 704-365-4539
cgray@carolina.rr.com
   Certified Appraiser of Personal
   Property with the International Society
   of Appraisers; specializes in the
   appraisal of furniture, ceramics and
   silver.

Sharon Kerwick, ISA
Kerwick Appraisals
1633 NE 24th St.
Fort Lauderdale, FL 33305-1402
ph: 954-565-9031
fax: 954-564-0648
sharon@kerwick.com
http://www.kerwick.com
   Very knowledgeable appraiser and

teacher/lecturer in 19th and 20th
century world wide silver.

James S. Harriss
James S. Harris Antiques & Appraisals
P.O. Box 672
Richmond, KY 40475
ph: 859-623-9100
jimant@ipro.net
   Specializes in the appraisal of coin
   and English hallmarked silver,
   American art pottery, stevengraphs,
   and English watercolors.

Patricia M. Knight
Finetooth Comb Antiques Research &
   Appraisal Service
P.O. Box 1177
Ames, IA 50014-1177
ph: 515-292-9028
ftcres@aol.com
   Does not purchase; send SASE if
   requesting return of photos.

Gloria Moroni, ISA CAPP
873 Havenshire Rd.
Naperville, IL 60565-6188
ph: 630-717-1380
fax: 630-717-1480
gloriamoroni@aol.com
   Specializes in the appraisal of silver
   and porcelain.

Matthew McNeil, ISA CAPP
McNeil & Hickman
3128 NW 26
Oklahoma City, OK 73107
ph: 405-524-9391 or 405-949-9935
fax: 405-524-5550
oklappraiser@aol.com
   Specializes in 18th and 19th century
   sterling silver flatware and
   hollowware with a concentration in
   British work; also some American
   post-1860; has interest in Continental
   and American art glass 1935-1965
   and Amer. Art pottery 1880-1960.

Barbara Samuel
La Reine Abeille Antiques & Appraisals
11821 Brookhill Lane
Dallas, TX 75230
ph: 972-386-5066 or 972-239-8400
bslareine@aol.com
   A long-time Dallas area antique
   dealer and ISA appraiser; specializes
   in French furniture.

Fred M. Nevill, ISA
Nevill Antiques
2723 Sackett St.
Houston, TX 77098-1131
ph: 713-529-8473
fax: 713-522-5195
fmnevill@houston.rr.com
   Specializes in the appraisal of silver
   and antique furniture.

Dewey W. Smith, ASA
Dewey W. Smith, ASA Antique
   Appraisals
P.O. Box 2029
Littleton, CO 81061-2029
ph: 303-930-9899
fax: 303-930-9919
dwsmithasa@aol.com
   Provides appraisal and consultation
   service for bankruptcy, collectors,
   dealers, divorce, estates, individuals,
   insurance companies and all other
   manner of appraisal assignments.

Nancy Alison Martin, ASA
Nancy Martin Appraisals
ph: 626-304-0900
fax: 626-304-0928
namartin@pacbell.net
http://www.nancymartinappraisals.com
   Carefully researched and well
   documented appraisals of antiques,
   furniture, silver, ceramics, glass and
   residential contents for litigation
   support, compensation, insurance,
   dissolution, estates, fraud and
   charitable contribution.

Diana Sanders
Specialty Appraisals
P.O. Box 17461
Encino, CA 91416
ph: 877-255-5445
dlsanders@earthlink.net
http://www.specialtyappraisals.com
   Certified gemologist with an AA in
   gemology from Santiago Canyon
   College; certificate in pearl grading
   from GIA; graduated from College for
   Appraisers; has taught "Antique &
   Collectible Jewelry" as well as
   "Antique Metals" courses.

Pearl Shiffman, ISA CAPP
Chatham Appraisal Service
P.O. Box 962
Tustin, CA 92781-0962
ph: 714-832-5101
fax: 714-544-6955
chathamappraisal@comcast.net
   ISA Certified Appraiser specializing in
   silver and antiques.

Alice S. Karle, ANA
3463 State St., #178
Santa Barbara, CA 93105
ph: 805-682-2234
askappraiser@cox.net
   Certified member of the ANA; has
   developed and taught courses in
   American antique furniture and in
   antiques in general, including silver.

Christine Zachary
P.O. Box 82906
Portland, OR 97282-0906
ph: 503-234-8143 or 503-777-5813
christineZC@aol.com
   Over 25 years experience buying,
   selling, appraising silver; has broad
   knowledge of silver hallmarks,
   manufacturing techniques and styles of
   fine antique silver, Old Sheffield
   silver, bronzes, snuff boxes, enamels,
   and precious objects.

Kathleen M. Bailey, AAA, ISA CAPP
Antique Appraisal & Estate Sale Service
   - the Original
160 NW Gilman Blvd., Ste. #1
Issaquah, WA 98027
ph: 425-746-2777
fax: 425-746-3793
antiquabailey@aol.com
   Antiques specialist since 1973;
   Certified ISA CAPP and AAA; estate
   sales specialist; specialist in
   American, English and Continental
   furniture of the 18th and 19th
   centuries, silver, glass, china,
   enamels, decorative arts, Victoriana.

Judith Livingston, ISA
ph: 360-379-3028
heirlooms@olympus.net
   Collects and appraises unusual
   Victorian silver and silverplate
   flatware and hollowware.

Auction Services

Michael B. Grogan
Grogan & Company Auctioneers
22 Harris St.
Dedham, MA 02026
ph: 781-461-9500
fax: 781-461-9625
grogans@groganco.com
http://www.groganco.com
   Auctioneer and appraiser specializing
   in 18th through 20th century American
   & European paintings, sculpture,
   oriental rugs, and fine silver; accepts
   consignments year round for two semi-
   annual sales.

Stuart Slavid
Skinner, Inc.
63 Park Plaza
The Heritage on the Garden
Boston, MA 02116
ph: 617-350-5400
fax: 617-350-5429
info@skinnerinc.com
http://www.skinnerinc.com
   Established in 1971, Skinner Inc. is
   the fourth largest auction house in the
   US; has offices in Boston and Bolton,
   MA.

Christie's
20 Rockefeller Plaza
New York, NY 10020
ph: 212-636-2000
info@christies.com
http://www.christies.com

John McClain
York Town Auction Inc.
1625 Haviland Rd.
York, PA 17404
ph: 717-751-0211
fax: 717-767-7729
info@yorktownauction.com
http://www.yorktownauction.com
   Antique & specialty auctions, lecture
   & appraisal services; antiques also
   purchased; American & English
   furniture, related specialties &
   accessories, Americana, folk art,
   jewelry, art, clocks & watches,
   militaria, steins, Oriental rugs.

Mary Kraus
Kraus Antiques, Ltd.
P.O. Box 12537
Fort Pierce, FL 34979
ph: 561-465-0770
fax: 561-468-9020
kraus@metrolink.net
http://www.antiqnet.com/kraus
Specializes in sterling silver flatware; conducts periodic auctions of obsolete and discontinued patterns; also conducts the largest souvenir spoon auction in the country.

Clubs/Associations

Jeffrey Herman, Ex. Dir.
Society of American Silversmiths
P.O. Box 72839
Providence, RI 02907
ph: 401-461-6840
fax: 401-461-6841
sas@silversmithing.com
http://www.silversmithing.com
Answers questions on silversmithing techniques, conservation and restoration, maker's mark identification and all other silver-related inquiries.

Nancy Yee, Sec./Treas.
International Association of Silver Art Collectors
Newsletter: Silver Bugle, The
P.O. Box 28415
Seattle, WA 98118-8415
iasacnancy@cs.com
Dedicated to the silver round and art bar collector and hobbyist; newsletter published six times per year.

Collectors

Bruce Johnson
25 Upper Brush Creek Rd.
Fletcher, NC 28732
ph: 828-628-1915
fax: 828-628-4070
bj1912@aol.com
http://www.arts-craftsconference.com
Wants to buy silver marked DODGE or ASHEVILLE SILVERCRAFT.

Bill Simmons
181 NW 78th Ave.
Margate, FL 33063
ph: 954-984-9647
wsim1206@aol.com
Wants most sterling flatware and hollowware, especially Tiffany, Georg Jensen, and early Gorham.

Dealers

Spencer Gordon
Spencer Marks
P.O. Box 303
East Walpole, MA 02032
ph: 508-668-6990
info@spencermarks.com
http://www.spencermarks.com
Fine American and English antiques and silver; also sells books about antiques.

Steve Duffy
Sea Eagles Sterling
20 Bridle Dr.
Winsted, CT 06098-3422
ph: 860-379-5749
fax: 860-379-5749
Specializes in active, inactive, and obsolete sterling silver flatware.

Betty & Bruce Comstock
Luxe, LLC
P.O. Box 604
Essex, CT 06426
ph: 860-767-0286
fax: 860-767-7018
bcomstock@snet.net
Buys and sells antique furniture, paintings, and sterling silver.

John C. Foy
P.O. Box 476
Fanwood, NJ 07023-0476
ph: 908-654-3867
Buys and sells antique American coin silver, American sterling silver and souvenir spoons, and English sterling silver; also sells books on silver.

Nathan Horowicz
Nathan Horowicz Antiques
1050 2nd Ave., Gallery 82
New York, NY 10022
ph: 800-214-6320 or 212-755-6320
fax: 212-755-6438
horowicz82@aol.com
http://www.classicsilver.com
Large assortment of flatware, tea sets, hollowware; Tiffany, Georg Jensen; all American and European manufacturers.

Fortunoff
681 5th Ave. at 54th St.
New York, NY 10022
ph: 212-758-6660
fax: 212-715-5906
service@fortunoff.com
http://www.dir-dd.com/fortunoff.html
Focuses on 19th and 20th century American, English, coin and Chinese silver; has over 1,000 pieces in stock including tea sets, tureens, centerpieces, candlesticks, vases, pitchers, flatware and more.

Lauren Stanley Gallery
300 E. 51st St.
New York, NY 10022
ph: 212-888-6732
fax: 212-486-2503
info@laurenstanley.com
http://www.laurenstanley.com
Specializing in American silver from 1840 to 1900: Shiebler, Tiffany, Gale, Wood & Hughes, Whiting, Gorham, Krider, Dominick & Haff, Duhme, Wendt, Kidney & Johnston, Kirk, Coles, and others; Medallion pattern flatware a specialty.

Gary Niederkorn
Niederkorn Silver
Newspaper: Silver Edition
2005 Locust St.
Philadelphia, PA 19103-5606
ph: 215-567-2606
fax: 215-567-2606
niederkornsilver@aol.com
Specializes in 19th and 20th c. silver novelties, Christmas ornaments, napkin rings, Judaica, picture frames, etc.; also Tiffany, Jensen, Mexican.

Gerald Schultz
Antique Gallery, The
8523 Germantown Ave.
Philadelphia, PA 19118-3316
ph: 215-248-1700
fax: 215-247-8411
geraldluv@aol.com
Interested in sterling silver and Victorian silverplate (no flatware): Jensen, Tiffany, Stone, Kirk, etc.

Rita Lang
Silver 2000
P.O. Box 845
Middleburg, VA 20118-0845
ph: 540-253-9966
silver2000@erols.com
Expert and dealer in early American silver.

Caren Fine
11603 Gowrie Ct.
Potomac, MD 20854-3623
ph: 301-299-6886 or 301-854-6262
fine2beme@aol.com
Buys, sells, trades silver objects by Liberty, Tiffany, Georg Jensen, Spratling, Shreve & Co., Jarvie, Kalo, Lebolt; jewelry by F.G. Nale, Edward Oakes; Judaica.

Pikesville Jewelry & Coin Exchange
1350 Reisterstown Rd.
Baltimore, MD 21208-3803
ph: 410-653-3430
fax: 410-653-8463

Beverly H. Bremer
Beverly Bremer Silver Shop
3164 Peachtree Rd. NE
Atlanta, GA 30305
ph: 404-261-4009 or 800-270-4009
fax: 404-261-9708
sterlingsilver@worldnet.att.net
http://www.beverlybremer.com
Buys, sells and matches sterling silver flatware, and new and antique sterling silver hollowware & giftware; large shop; sterling silver only; want lists kept; mail order; totally computerized.

Peter Thurber
Ritzi & Thurber, Inc.
160 S. Beach St.
Daytona Beach, FL 32114
ph: 904-252-2552 or 904-226-8489
fax: 904-226-8490
ritzi1881@earthlink.net
http://www.ritzi-thurber.com
Founded in 1881, firm purchases all types of silver and Sheffield, from scrap sterling to fine English, French

and Russian presentation pieces; very interested in purchasing American coin silver and any type of Art Nouveau sterling.

Sterling Matching Service
P.O. Box 46
Topsfield, MA 01983-1614
ph: 978-887-2610
dorothy@sterlingmatching.com
http://www.sterlingmatching.com/
Carries elegant sterling silver flatware including exotic antique silver by Tiffany, Victorian sterling serving pieces and many flatware patterns, coin silver (handwrought) and Medallion silver.

Robin & June Greenwald
June Greenwald Antiques, Inc.
3096 Mayfield Rd.
Cleveland, OH 44118
ph: 216-932-5535
Buys and sells 19th and 20th century silver; offers a matching service.

Marvin Sokolow
425 West Fairy Chasm Rd.
Milwaukee, WI 53217
ph: 414-351-5750
msokolow@msn.com
Specializes in the buying, selling, appraising Asian antiques, silver, and European and Russian enamels.

Mark
Silverwarehouse
4311 NE Vivion Rd.
Kansas City, MO 64119-2890
ph: 816-454-1990
fax: 816-454-1605
sales@silverwarehouse.com
http://www.silverwarehouse.com
Buys, sells, repairs silverware and hollowware of all types; also silver books, silverware chests, silver care products, online resources, appraisals, repairs.

Louise Richardson
Silver Thistle, The
3767 Forest Lane, Ste. 124-1264
Dallas, TX 75244
ph: 214-850-1491
thesilverthistle@hotmail.com
Silver appraiser, dealer, collector, expert specializes in Art Nouveau and Georgian sterling silver as well as some silverplate.

Connie & Bill McNally
McNally Co. Antiques, The
P.O. Box 1048
6033-L&M Paseo Delicias
Rancho Santa Fe, CA 92067
ph: 858-756-1922
fax: 858-756-9928
info@mcnallycompanyantiques.com
http://
www.mcnallycompanyantiques.com
Buys, sells, collects and specializes in 18th and 19th century furnishings, silver and objets d'art.

Sue Morse
Emma's Antiques
P.O. Box 889
Redlands, CA 92373
ph: 909-864-3426
fax: 909-864-3426
emmastrunk@aol.com
http://www.emmasantiques.com
*Buys and sells sterling silver,
silverplate serving pieces dating from
1870s to 1940s.*

Argentum - The Leopard's Head
414 Jackson St., Ste. 101
San Francisco, CA 94111
ph: 415-296-7757
fax: 415-296-7233
info@argentum-theleopard.com
http://www.argentum-theleopard.com
*Antique silver from all periods bought
and sold; large shop; full catalog with
prices available online; specializing in
18th c. English silver, early American
and Victorian silver; no pattern
matching except Shreve & Co., San
Francisco.*

Beth Scott
Affordable Jewelry & Precious Metals
304 SW Washington St.
Portland, OR 97204
ph: 800-690-4995 or 503-224-7520
fax: 503-227-4204
sight@ajpm.com
http://www.ajpm.com
*Gold, silver and platinum bullion
dealers.*

Sterling Shop, The
P.O. Box 595
Silverton, OR 97381-0595
ph: 503-873-6315
fax: 503-873-3006
Marysc@mindspring.com
http://www.sterlingshop.com
*Sterling and silverplate flatware
matching service.*

Kathleen M. Bailey, AAA, ISA CAPP
Antique Appraisal & Estate Sale Service
- the Original
160 NW Gilman Blvd., Ste. #1
Issaquah, WA 98027
ph: 425-746-2777
fax: 425-746-3793
antiquabailey@aol.com
*Specialist in American, English,
German, Continental ceramics,
furniture, silver, glass, enamels,
Victoriana and decorative arts of the
18th to 20th centuries; full service
appraiser & estate sales since 1973.*

Kathleen M. Bailey, AAA, ISA CAPP
Antique Appraisal & Estate Sale Service
- the Original
160 NW Gilman Blvd., Ste. #1
Issaquah, WA 98027
ph: 425-746-2777
fax: 425-746-3793
antiquabailey@aol.com
*30 years experience handling sterling
silver; American, French, English,
Continental; American, Tiffany,
Gorham, Durgin, Whiting.*

Experts

V. Stephen Vaughan
E.B. Horn Co.
429 Washington St.
Boston, MA 02108
ph: 617-542-3902
*Specializes in 19th century American
silver; vast library of period research
materials.*

Benedict J. Hastings
2006 Columbia Rd. N.W.
Washington, DC 20009
ph: 202-483-8575
bhastingsdc@aol.com
*Specializes in fine silver, Russian
decorative arts, Russian icons, 18th
and 19th century porcelain, military
medals, decorations and orders.*

Gwendolyn L. Kelso
Rampant Lion, The
P.O. Box 5887
Washington, DC 20016-1487
ph: 202-364-2431
fax: 202-364-2431
*Silver expert, appraiser, dealer; also
silver reference service with extensive
library; sells books about silver for
appraisers, collectors, museums.*

Jennifer F. Goldsborough
1688 Coventry Place
Annapolis, MD 21401
ph: 401-841-2634
*American silver expert, lecturer,
curator.*

Gary D. Gardner
200 College St.
Hodgenville, KY 42748-1404
ph: 270-358-3222
*Expert/collector specializing in
American pre-1870 coin grade silver
crafted by Southern silversmiths; seeks
examples of holloware & early
flatware, especially from KY, TN, VA;
also ledgers, receipts, inventories
mentioning silver.*

Rod Tinkler
Silver Vault, The
P.O. Box 911
Woodstock, IL 60098
ph: 815-337-3990
fax: 815-337-3738
SilverVlt@aol.com
*Buy, sell, trade, and appraises
American, English and Continental
silver.*

Internet Resources

SM Publications
353 West 56th St., MS7A
New York, NY 10019
ph: 212-246-5060 or 212-246-5216
info@SMPub.com
http://www.smpub.com
*An Internet resource center for silver
collectors, dealers and appraisers:
books on silver marks, evaluating
silver, identification; for flatware
holloware, silversmiths, silver
jewelry, silver antiques; also covers
gold.*

Illustrated Silver Collection
Italy
giobuse1@tin.it
http://www.silvercollection.it
*An illustrated review of a small
collection of antique silver and objects
of vertu from 18th to 20th century;
detailed images also showing
hallmarks.*

David R. Clarke
SilverMine
4 Mortimer Buildings
Bridge St., Nailsworth GL6 0AA U.K.
ph: (44)(0) 1453 836735
a.data@virgin.net
http://freespace.virgin.net/a.data
*SilverMine is a stand-alone hypertext
program to aid in the identification
and study of marks struck on British
silver; also contains brief details of
some 250 American silver makers.*

Man./Prod./Dist.

P.G. Gill Co.
9 Fowle St.
Woburn, MA 01801
ph: 781-933-3275
fax: 781-933-3751
gifts@patrickgillco.com
http://www.patrickgillco.com
*Silversmiths, metal finishers and
platers; a family tradition of
excellence since 1911; offers an
extensive selection of church goods
and religious gifts for all occasions;
also repairs, refinishes, replates
holloware, flatware.*

Museums/Libraries

Museum of Fine Arts, Boston
465 Huntington Ave.
Boston, MA 02115-5523
ph: 617-267-9300
webmaster@mfa.org
http://www.mfa.org

Wadsworth Atheneum Museum of Art
600 Main St.
Hartford, CT 06103
ph: 860-278-2670
fax: 860-527-0803
info@wadsworthatheneum.org
http://www.wadsworthatheneum.org
*Collections include the Elizabeth B.
Miles Silver Collection and the Philip
H. Hammerslough Collection of
American Silver.*

Yale University Art Gallery
P.O. Box 208271
New Haven, CT 06520-8271
ph: 203-432-0600 or 203-432-0601
http://www.yale.edu/artgallery

Dallas Museum of Art
1717 North Harwood
Dallas, TX 75201
ph: 214-992-1200
membership@dm-art.org
http://www.dm-art.org
*Holdings include an internationally
recognized collection of fine Victorian
silver.*

David Warren
Bayou Bend Collection & Gardens, The
P.O. Box 6826
Houston, TX 77265-6826
ph: 281-639-7750
fax: 281-639-7770
hirsch@mfah.org
http://mfah.org/bayou.html

Periodicals

Nanette Monmonier-Schweitzer
Price Guide: Silver Update, The
P.O. Box 2157
Ellicott City, MD 21041-2157
ph: 410-750-3282
fax: 410-418-5128
*Provides prices for current American
and popular foreign sterling silver
flatware manufacturers; published
three times each year.*

Nanette Monmonier-Schweitzer
Price Guide: Sterling Silver Hollowware
Update, The
P.O. Box 2157
Ellicott City, MD 21041-2157
ph: 410-750-3282
fax: 410-418-5128
*Provides illustrations and prices for
current American sterling silver
holloware.*

Newsletter: Silver & Gold Report
P.O. Box 109665
West Palm Beach, FL 33410
ph: 800-289-9222 or 561-627-3300
fax: 561-625-6685
sgr@weissinc.com
*Financial advice newsletter in
precious medals, and gold & silver
bullion and coins.*

Connie McNally
Silver Magazine Inc.
Magazine: Silver Magazine
P.O. Box 9690
Rancho Santa Fe, CA 92067-4690
ph: 800-756-1054 or 858-756-1054
fax: 858-756-9928
silver@silvermag.com
http://www.silvermag.com
*Top quality bi-monthly magazine for
silver collectors, dealers, researchers;
articles on antique American, English,
Continental, Colonial and contemporary silver; previews/reviews of
auctions, book reviews, opinion,
classified/display ads.*

Repair Services

Stephen Smithers
Smithers Restorations
1057 Hawley Rd.
Ashfield, MA 01330-9626
ph: 413-625-2994
stevesmithers@stevesmithers.com
http://www.stevesmithers.com
*Restoration of fine early silver and
brass; design and making of hand
hammered silver holloware and
brass lighting (chandeliers, lanterns,
sconces, candlesticks); also demonstrations, silversmithing talks for
museums and civic groups.*

P.G. Gill Co.
9 Fowle St.
Woburn, MA 01801
ph: 781-933-3275
fax: 781-933-3751
gifts@patrickgillco.com
http://www.patrickgillco.com
Silversmiths, metal finishers and platers; a family tradition of excellence since 1911; offers an extensive selection of church goods and religious gifts for all occasions; also repairs, refinishes, replates hollowware, flatware.

Beth A. Perry
Beth A. Perry, Hand Engraving
115 Newbury St., #502
Boston, MA 02116
ph: 617-859-8805
fax: 617-247-4940
Hand engraving, inscriptions, coats-of-arms, monogramming, logos, custom designs, engraver of fine jewelry and tableware for 16 years; call or send sample for estimate to copy old engraving of any style or to create new design.

Howard & Mary Newman
Newmans Ltd.
55 Farewell St.
Newport, RI 02840
ph: 401-846-4784 or 401-847-8557
fax: 401-849-0611
newmansltd@cox.net
http://www.newmansltd.com
Fine metal restoration and conservation; master silversmith, specialist in bronze finishing and patination; trained at RI School of Design & in Italy; conservation & restoration of personal items & museum works; can ship anywhere.

Jeffrey Herman
Jeffrey Herman Silver Restoration & Conservation
P.O. Box 72839
Providence, RI 02907
ph: 401-461-6840 or 800-584-2352
fax: 401-461-6841
jeff@silversmithing.com
http://www.silversmithing.com/silver
Museum quality silver restoration and conservation; 14 years in business; founder Society of American Silversmiths; listed with Jewelers Board of Trade; Web site has complete list of services, pricing, and special silver care guide.

Joseph J. Pistilli
Orum Silver Co., Inc.
51 S. Vine St.
P.O. Box 805
Meriden, CT 06450-0805
ph: 203-237-3037
fax: 203-237-3037
Orum@ct1.nai.net
http://www.orumsilver.com
Repairing, restoring, replating of antique and old silver, gold, nickel; brass & copper plating; cleaning, buffing, polishing.

Abercombie & Company Silverplaters, Inc.
9159A Brookeville Rd.
Silver Spring, MD 20910
ph: 301-585-2385 or 800-585-2387
fax: 301-587-5708
abernco@erols.com
http://www.silverplaters.com
Replates silverplate; repairs all sorts of metal; silver, brass, copper; also welding.

Harry Stock
Coventry Silversmiths
228 S. Washington St.
Alexandria, VA 22314
ph: 703-684-6821
fax: 703-684-6821
Silver plating and restoration: combs, brushes, mirrors, knife blades replaced.

Beth Walker
Oexning Silversmiths
320 Highway 197 South
Bakersville, NC 28705
ph: 828-688-9998 or 800-332-6857
fax: 828-688-9976
oexning@aol.com
http://www.oxningsilversmiths.com
Since 1947; specializes in the refinishing, repair and replating of silver, copper, pewter, gold, and brass; two locations - in Minneapolis, MN and in Bakersville, NC.

Estes-Simmons Silverplating, Ltd.
1050 Northside Dr., NW
Atlanta, GA 30318
ph: 404-875-9581 or 800-645-4193
fax: 404-873-4826
info@estes-simmons.com
http://www.estes-simmons.com
Repairs silver, silverplate, gold, pewter, brass and copper; also replates silver, gold, brass, nickel, copper.

Robert Kaynes
Senti-Metal Silver Restoration Company, The
1919 Memory Lane, Dept. 39CA97
Columbus, OH 43209
ph: 614-252-0967
fax: 614-252-4602
bronzeinfo@bronshoe.com
http://www.resilver.com
Will restore your silver at factory-direct prices; brings back life to old, worn silver heirlooms; quadruple silverplating is covered by 25 year warranty; write for FREE catalog.

Paul Trageser
Paul Trageser Metalsmith
10330 Howard Rd.
Harrison, OH 45030
ph: 513-367-6226
Finest quality silver repairs.

Silverwarehouse
4311 NE Vivion Rd.
Kansas City, MO 64119-2890
ph: 816-454-1990
fax: 816-454-1605
sales@silverwarehouse.com
http://www.silverwarehouse.com
Expert knife reblading, silverware repair, polishing, full-time silversmiths on staff; also sells loose knife blades; also stainless, silverplate, pewter, Dirilyte.

Carmelo Tringali
Colonial Silver
1219 Forest Ave.
Pacific Grove, CA 93950
ph: 831-375-0355
Recommended for silverplating and replating.

Tim Maple
Omega Silversmithing Inc.
11232 120th Ave. NE #118
Kirkland, WA 98033-4522
ph: 425-822-3727
Expert repair and restoration of fine silver, bronze, silverplate, spelter, brass, pewter and copper; from tea sets to brass beds, chandeliers, new knife blades, mirrors and combs; full service restoration.

Repro. Sources

Stephen Smithers
1057 Hawley Rd.
Ashfield, MA 01330-9626
ph: 413-625-2994
stevesmithers@stevesmithers.com
http://www.stevesmithers.com
Design and making of hand hammered silver hollowware & brass lighting (chandeliers, lanterns, sconces, candlesticks); also restoration of fine early silver and brass; demonstrations, silversmithing talks for museums and civic groups.

Suppliers

Jeffrey Herman
Herman's Best Silver Care Products
P.O. Box 72839
Providence, RI 02907
ph: 401-461-6840 or 800-584-2352
fax: 401-461-6841
jeff@silversmithing.com
http://www.silversmithing.com/silver
Supplies and instructions for caring for silver.

Baltimore

Dealers

Patrick Duggan
Imperial Half Bushel
831 N. Howard St.
Baltimore, MD 21201
ph: 410-462-1192
ihb@imperialhalfbushel.com
http://www.imperialhalfbushel.com
Specializes in Baltimore, Maryland silver dating from the 19th and 20th centuries.

Chinese

Experts

Stuart Slavid
9 Gryzboska Circle
Framingham, MA 01702-5519
ph: 508-620-2531
wedghead@rcn.com
Interested in Chinese silver.

Christofle

Man./Prod./Dist.

Christofle
contact@christofle.com
http://www.christofle.com
Manufacturer of fine silver flatware and hollowware, porcelain, table linens and crystal; Web site lists retail outlets worldwide.

Georg Jensen

Dealers

Soren Jensen
The Showplace
40 W. 25th St., Shop #204
New York, NY 10010
ph: 212-645-3671
fax: 212-924-5375
soren@jensensilver.com
http://www.jensensilver.com
Specializes in vintage Georg Jensen silver; also other Scandinavian designers, silversmiths and jewelers.

Michael James
Silver Fund, Ltd., The
1001 Madison Ave.
New York, NY 10021
ph: 212-794-4994
dealers@thesilverfund.com
http://www.thesilverfund.com
A leading dealer in Georg Jensen estate silver, including hollowware, flatware and jewelry.

Gary Niederkorn
Niederkorn Silver
Newspaper: Silver Edition
2005 Locust St.
Philadelphia, PA 19103-5606
ph: 215-567-2606
fax: 215-567-2606
niederkornsilver@aol.com
Specializes in hollowware and flatware matching for Georg Jensen silver and other Danish makers.

Ken Forster
5501 Seminary Rd., Ste. 1311 South
Falls Church, VA 22041-3907
ph: 703-379-1142
kencforster@aol.com
Dealer in American art pottery and tiles, specializing in American tiles from 1860 to 1940; also Art Nouveau, Art Deco, Georg Jensen silver, and American Modernism.

Man./Prod./Dist.

Royal Scandinavian, Inc.
140 Bradford Dr.
West Berlin, NJ 08091
ph: 609-768-5400 or 800-431-1992
fax: 800-448-7553
http://www.royalscandinavia.com
*Royal Copenhagen, Bing & Grondahl,
Holmegaard, and Georg Jensen are
the best of Scandinavian collectibles;
manufactures dinnerware, cobalt blue
underglaze collector plates, figurines,
bells, dolls, ornaments and gift
accessories.*

Matching Services

Caryl Rose Unger
Imagination Unlimited
4302 Alton Rd., Ste. 820
Miami, FL 33140-2893
ph: 305-534-2214 or 305-992-0176
fax: 305-538-0914
info@imaginationunlimited.com
http://www.imaginationunlimited.com
*Specializes in Georg Jensen silver;
offers a Jensen silver matching service;
buys and sells Jensen silver: single
pieces or sets, jewelry, serving pieces,
hollowware, and other Danish silver;
reprints of their Jensen articles
available.*

Gorham

Man./Prod./Dist.

Gorham, Inc.
100 Lenox Dr.
Lawrenceville, NJ 08648
ph: 609-896-2800 or 800-635-3669
http://www.lenox.com
*Sterling and stainless steel flatware,
sterling and silverplated hollowware;
fine china, crystal stemware, giftware
and dolls; a division of Lenox Brands.*

International

Man./Prod./Dist.

Brenda Ryzzek, PR
International Silver Co., a Division of
Syratech
175 McClellan Hwy.
Boston, MA 02128-9114
ph: 617-561-2200
fax: 617-568-1528
consumerservicest@syratech.com
http://www.syratech.com
*Syratech manufacturers items for
dining and decorating; divisions
include Wallace Silversmiths, Towle
Silversmiths, International Silver
Company.*

Kirk Stieff

Dealers

Michael A. Merrill
Michael A. Merrill, Inc.
Newsletter: Silver Letter, The
Crestar Bank Building
2045 York Rd.
Timonium, MD 21093
ph: 410-453-9400
http://www.michaelmerrill.com
Kirk & Stieff specialists; pattern

*matching, bridal registry, silver
replating, appraisals; newsletter lists
and pictures items for sale including
sterling silver and books about silver.*

Lunt

Man./Prod./Dist.

Lunt Silversmiths
298 Federal St.
Greenfield, MA 01301
ph: 413-774-2774 or 800-242-2774
fax: 413-774-5349
info@lunt-silversmiths.com
http://www.lunt-silversmiths.com
*Sterling and plated flatware and
hollowware.*

Mexican

Collectors

Jill A. Crawford
Crawford Design
7377 Birdview Ave.
Malibu, CA 90265
ph: 310-457-8076
fax: 310-457-3453
*Interested in buying Spratling and
other Mexican silver.*

Dealers

Gary Niederkorn
Niederkorn Silver
Newspaper: Silver Edition
2005 Locust St.
Philadelphia, PA 19103-5606
ph: 215-567-2606
fax: 215-567-2606
niederkornsilver@aol.com
*Specializes in 19th and 20th c. silver
novelties, Christmas ornaments,
napkin rings, Judaica, picture frames,
etc.; also Tiffany, Jensen, Mexican.*

Gloria Quincy
Q-Tiques Vintage Jewelry & Collectibles
6475 Ferber Rd.
Jacksonville, FL 32277
ph: 904-745-0618
fax: 904-743-9159
gloria@q-tiques.com
http://www.q-tiques.com
*Specializes in costume designer
jewelry, bakelite, and Mexican Silver.*

Joe Breidel
3113 10th Ave., S.
Minneapolis, MN 55407
ph: 612-721-2837
*Buys and sells Mexican silver; also
American Indian, Modernist and
Scandinavian silver.*

Susan Morton
Mexican Silver Shop
2542 S. IH-35, Ste. 200-238
Round Rock, TX 78664
ph: 512-930-0124
disorderlygirl@noisyboy.com
http://www.noisyboy.com
*Specializes in silver items and other
metalware from Mexico, pre-1960.*

Jimmy Vitanza
Peregrine Galleries
508 Brinkerhoff Ave.
Santa Barbara, CA 93101-3441
ph: 805-963-3134
fax: 805-963-3134

Sheila Pamfiloff
Glitter Box, The
P.O. Box 35
Walnut Creek, CA 94596
ph: 925-937-7554
pamfil@glitterbox.com
http://www.glitterbox.com
*Specializing in vintage designer
costume jewelry including Haskell,
Schiaparelli, Hagler, Eisenberg,
DeMario, Mazer, Boucher; also
vintage Mexican sterling silver from
the great designers of Taxco.*

Experts

Carole A. Berk
Carole A. Berk, Ltd.
4913 Hampden Lane
Bethesda, MD 20814
ph: 301-365-3400
fax: 301-365-8837
cab@caroleberk.com
http://www.caroleberk.com
*Specializes in 20th century decorative
art: Clarice Cliff, Keith Murray,
Charlotte Rhead, Mexican silver,
Bakelite, and costume jewelry; co-
author of "Mexican Silver;" an expert
in Keith Murray.*

Mexican (Spratling)

Experts

Phyllis Goddard
SpratlingSilver.com
11 Mary's Lane
Deer Isle, ME 04627
ph: 207-348-2713
fax: 207-248-2236
pmgoddard@earthlink.net
http://www.spratlingsilver.com
*Author of "Spratling Silver: A Field
Guide, Recognizing a William
Spratling Treasure;" 500 full color
photos, latest in hallmark research.*

Internet Resources

Phyllis Goddard
SpratlingSilver.com
11 Mary's Lane
Deer Isle, ME 04627
ph: 207-348-2713
fax: 207-248-2236
pmgoddard@earthlink.net
http://www.spratlingsilver.com
*Great Web site source for information
on Spratling silver: hallmark
identification, reference material, tips
on collecting, William Spratling
biography, Forum and more.*

Nielloware

Internet Resources

Charles Dittell
Siam Sterling Nielloware Site, The
cdittel@gate.net
http://www.gate.net/~cdittel
*Nielloware is silver and black Thai
sterling silver pieces popular in the
1950s through 1970s.*

Old Newbury Crafters

Man./Prod./Dist.

Jeanne Pritchard
Old Newbury Crafters
36 Main St.
Amesbury, MA 01913-2807
ph: 978-388-0983 or 800-343-1388
fax: 978-388-8430
info@silvercrafters.com
http://www.silvercrafters.com
*Sterling silver flatware and
hollowware, pewter giftware.*

Oneida

Man./Prod./Dist.

Oneida Silversmiths
Kenwood Station
Oneida, NY 13421-2829
ph: 315-361-3000
sales@oneida.com
http://www.oneida.com
*Sterling silver, silverplate, gold
electroplate, stainless steel, flatware;
stainless and silverplate hollowware,
crystal stemware and hollowware.*

Reed & Barton

Man./Prod./Dist.

Reed & Barton
144 W. Britannia St.
Taunton, MA 02780
ph: 508-824-6611 or 800-822-1824
fax: 508-822-7269
information@reedbarton.com
http://www.reedbarton.com
*Produces china, crystal, silver,
silverplate, and stainless flatware,
collectible plates, bells, dolls,
ornaments and accessories.*

Scrap

Dealers

Jim Sciuto
GoldTek
P.O. Box 128
Methuen, MA 01844
ph: 978-374-2254 or 603-645-4717
fax: 978-373-1088
*Buys scrap gold and silver: class
rings, wedding bands, gold coins,
gold watches, gold plated circuit
boards, gold solder, gold wire, gold
teeth; also scrap sterling silver
flatware, coins, bars, silver flake,
silver anodes, etc.*

Greg Walsh
32 River View Lane
P.O. Box 747
Potsdam, NY 13676-0747
ph: 315-265-9111
fax: 315-265-9222
gwalsh@twcny.rr.com
http://www.walshauction.com
*Wants to buy gold and silver rings,
coins, estate jewelry, pocket watches,
diamonds, sterling silver items, scrap
gold, broken or damaged jewelry,
dental gold, etc.; 24-hour turn
around; ship on approval or call for
quote; since 1979.*

Michael A. Merrill
Michael A. Merrill, Inc.
Crestar Bank Building
2045 York Rd.
Timonium, MD 21093
ph: 410-453-9400
http://www.michaelmerrill.com
*Buying precious metals from the
public, dealers since 1974; buys scrap
gold, diamonds, old gold, dental gold,
school rings, gold & silver
numismatic coins, sterling silver (Kirk
& Steiff), Franklin Mint, platinum,
palladium, exotics.*

Jaime Raskansky
Gold & Silver Traders
5959 Westheimer, Ste. 30
Houston, TX 77057
ph: 713-520-5111 or 713-223-0777
fax: 713-223-0707
gstforex@msn.com
*Buys and sells gold and silver scrap
and bullion.*

Towle

Man./Prod./Dist.

Brenda Ryzzek, PR
Towle Silversmiths, a Division of
  Syratech
175 McClellan Hwy.
Boston, MA 02128-9114
ph: 617-561-2200
fax: 617-568-1528
consumerservicest@syratech.com
http://www.syratech.com
*Syratech manufacturers items for
dining and decorating; divisions
include Wallace Silversmiths, Towle
Silversmiths, International Silver
Company.*

Wallace

Man./Prod./Dist.

Brenda Ryzzek, PR
Wallace Silversmiths, a Division of
  Syratech
175 McClellan Hwy.
Boston, MA 02128-9114
ph: 617-561-2200
fax: 617-568-1528
consumerservicest@syratech.com
http://www.syratech.com
*Syratech manufacturers items for
dining and decorating; divisions
include Wallace Silversmiths, Towle*

*Silversmiths, International Silver
Company.*

SILVERPLATE

(see also FLATWARE; SHEFFIELD;
SILVER; REPAIR/RESTORATION/
CONSERVATION, Metal Items;
TABLEWARE)

Appraisers

Paula Barlowe
Paul L. Barlowe Appraisal Services
2933 W. Cary St., Ste. 201
Richmond, VA 23221
ph: 804-355-6566
sectime@erols.com
http://www.appraisers.org/pages/
  memberpage.cfm?id-46600
*Specializes in the appraisal of
English, Scottish and American silver
as well as in American Victorian-era
silverplate.*

Judith Livingston, ISA
ph: 360-379-3028
heirlooms@olympus.net
*Collects and appraises unusual
Victorian silver and silverplate
flatware and holloware.*

Dealers

Paul Severino
Silver & Such
ph: 703-573-0509
severinop@aol.com
*Specializes in Victorian and Art
Nouveau silverplate, holloware and
flatware.*

Barbara & Steve Aaronson
Victorian Lady, The
P.O. Box 7522
Northridge, CA 91327
ph: 818-368-6052
bjaaronson@aol.com
http://www.thevictorianlady.com
*Specializes in buying and selling
unusual American Victorian
silverplate.*

Periodicals

Nanette Monmonier-Schweitzer
Price Guide: Silverplated Holloware
  Update, The
P.O. Box 2157
Ellicott City, MD 21041-2157
ph: 410-750-3282
fax: 410-418-5128
*Provides illustrations and prices for
current American silverplated
holloware manufacturers.*

Connie McNally
Silver Magazine Inc.
Magazine: Silver Magazine
P.O. Box 9690
Rancho Santa Fe, CA 92067-4690
ph: 800-756-1054 or 858-756-1054
fax: 858-756-9928
silver@silvermag.com
http://www.silvermag.com
*Top quality bi-monthly magazine for
silver collectors, dealers, researchers;*

*articles on antique American, English,
Continental, Colonial and contemporary silver; previews/reviews of
auctions, book reviews, opinion,
classified/display ads.*

SILVERPLATED FLATWARE

(see FLATWARE)

SILVERWARE

(see FLATWARE)

SIMMONS HARDWARE

(see KEEN KUTTER [SIMMONS
HARDWARE])

SINGING BIRDS

(see MUSIC BOXES, Birds & Bird
Boxes [Singing])

SKATING

(see SPORTS COLLECTIBLES, Ice
Skating; SPORTS COLLECTIBLES,
Roller Skating; SPORTS
COLLECTIBLES, Skateboards)

SKELETONS

(see also ANIMAL TROPHIES;
FOSSILS; HAIRWORK; MORBID &
ODD ITEMS)

Dealers

Bone Room, The
1569 Solano Ave.
Berkeley, CA 94707-2116
ph: 510-526-5252
evolve@boneroom.com
http://www.boneroom.com
*Premiere store for natural history
buffs and collectors: fossils, casts,
wonders from the animal and insect
kingdoms; wants to buy ivory,
skeletons, tusks, skulls, fossils, insect
collections, shrunken heads, etc.*

SLAVERY ITEMS

(see also ART, African-American;
BLACK MEMORABILIA)

Collectors

E. Alexander Peters
'Tiques
P.O. Box 3267
Farmingdale, NY 11735-0679
ph: 631-842-9549
*Wants documents, pictures, and
artifacts relating to the African-
American slavery experience, both
Continental and diasporic.*

James C. Allen
1178 Wildcreek Trail NE
Atlanta, GA 30324
ph: 404-321-5784
jim@southernpicker.com
*Wants memorabilia and objects from
the slave era through the Civil War
Movement; also lynching postcards
and photos; also wants items from
post-Civil War Reconstruction to the
Civil Rights era.*

Slave Tags

Collectors

Rich Hartzog
World Exonumia
P.O. Box 4143CNZ
Rockford, IL 61110-0643
ph: 815-226-0771
hartzog@exonumia.com
http://www.exonumia.com
*Wants slave tags, and other Black
tokens and medals.*

SLIDE RULES

(see also CALCULATORS;
COMPUTERS; INSTRUMENTS &
DEVICES, Scientific)

Clubs/Associations

Kate Matthews
Oughtred Society
Journal: Journal of the Oughtred Society
3425 Paiute St.
Winnemucca, NV 89445
ph: 9775-625-2235 or 775-427-5597
oughtred@winnemucca.net
http://www.oughtred.org
*Named for the inventor of the slide
rule, the Oughtred Society is for
collectors of slide rules and other
mechanical calculating tools such as
addiometers; biannual journal.*

Collectors

Wayne Feely
1172 Lindsay La.
Jenkintown, PA 19046-1839
ph: 215-884-5640
wef@comcast.net
*Wants slide rules: linear, circular or
cylindrical; also books on slide rules,
pre-1945 Army Field Manuals, and
K&E, Gurley, Buff, Dietzgen, or
Burger catalogs.*

Jay Francis
1409 Sandlewood Dr.
Plano, TX 75023
jay@slideruleguy.com
http://www.slideruleguy.com
*Collects slide rules and mechanical
calculators; collection includes over
900 slide rules.*

Robert Otnes
2160 Middlefield Rd.
Palo Alto, CA 94301-4022
ph: 650-324-1821
botnes@pacbell.net
*A leading collector of calculating
machines and slide rules.*

689

Paul H. Hayashi, PE
18 Tarabrook Dr.
Orinda, CA 94563-3121
ph: 925-254-5074 or 925-253-1038
fax: 925-253-0592
*Wants to buy old engineering
instruments, slide rules, drafting sets,
graphical integrators, planimeters.*

Rodger Shepherd, MD
10592 Englewood Dr.
Oakland, CA 94605-5014
ph: 510-632-1680
*Treasurer of The Oughtred Society, a
club for slide rule collectors.*

Wayne Lehnert
P.O. Box 99077
Emeryville, CA 94662
ph: 925-754-9337
e-mail@oughtred.org
http://www.oughtred.org
*Secretary of The Oughtred Society, a
club for slide rule collectors.*

Robert De Cesaris
7429 Bree Ann Ct.
Citrus Heights, CA 95610-2455
ph: 916-356-5769
rdecesar@pcocd2.intel.com
*Actively seeking slide rules and other
mechanical calculating devices:
especially interested in circular slide
rules, special purpose and special
function rules, 20" rules, pocket watch
type like Boucher, Sperry, Fowler, and
others.*

Experts

George Duckworth
12602 North 20 Ave.
Phoenix, AZ 85029-2610
ph: 602-944-4538
*Author of "Slide Rule Collector's
Guide," available from author.*

Internet Resources

Ronald Manley
78 Huntingdon Rd.
Cambridge, Cambs CB3 0HH U.K.
sliderules@clara.co.uk
http://www.sliderules.clara.net
*Web site has instructions for using
slide rules, an analysis of slide rule
prices on eBay and links to other slide
rule sites.*

SLOT CARS

(see TOYS, Cars [Racing])

SMOKEY BEAR ITEMS

Collectors

Pete Nowicki
1531 39th Ave.
San Francisco, CA 94122-3015
ph: 415-566-7506
portfire86@aol.com
*Collector seeks all licensed Smokey
Bear items for collection: toys, dolls,
posters, etc.*

SB Collector
P.O. Box 9007
Bend, OR 97708-9007
*Serious collector buying Smokey Bear
items.*

SMOKING COLLECTIBLES

(see also ADVERTISING
COLLECTIBLES, Trade Cards
[Tobacco]; CIGAR BOXES, LABELS
& BANDS; CIGARETTE
COLLECTIBLES; CIGAR STORE
COLLECTIBLES; LIGHTERS;
MATCHBOXES & LABELS;
MATCHCOVERS; MATCH SAFES;
PIPES; TOBACCO COLLECTIBLES)

Collectors

Lee Pattison
P.O. Box 60
Cuba, NY 14727-0060
ph: 716-933-8112
*Wants antique meerschaum pipes
carved and plain, briar pipes of more
recent manufacture brand names:
Charatan, Barling, Stanwell, Larson,
Dunhill, Savinelli and others; also
wants to buy tobacco jars and cigar
store items.*

Les Franics
129 South Van Buren St.
Rockville, MD 20850-2802
ph: 301-762-3003
*Buys and sells tobacco cards and
cigar related collectibles: silks, felts,
cutters, tobacco jars, tobacco tags,
books and ephemera.*

D. Nordlinger Stern
385 Bayview Dr. NE
Saint Petersburg, FL 33704-2430
ph: 727-894-4000
fax: 727-894-1040
dnordstern@aol.com
*Wants tobacco memorabilia,
particularly W. Duke and Duke's
Mixture.*

Cindy Porman
22044 Roosevelt Rd.
South Bend, IN 46614
ph: 219-291-6414
imaporman@yahoo.com
*Wants Copenhagen Snuff, Weyman &
Sons, Weyman Bros., Skoal Snuff, and
Key Snuff tobacco items including
crocks, pocket tins, store displays,
metal and paper signs, and related
advertising items.*

Dealers

Charles S. Levi
19 South Wabash
Chicago, IL 60603-3171
ph: 312-372-1306
fax: 312-372-1416
*Buy and sells all things related to
smoking: books, pipes, gadgets,
literature, etc.*

Experts

Benjamin Rapaport
Antiquarian Tobacciana
Newsletter: Antiquarian Tobacciana
Newsletter
11505 Turnbridge Ln.
Reston, VA 20194-1220
ph: 703-435-8133
fax: 703-435-3852
benrapaport@earthlink.net
*Wants antiquarian tobacciana:
domestic & foreign literature, pipes
& pipe smoking, snuff & its
accouterments, cigars & accessories,
smoking technology, ephemera &
lithography, pipe tampers, and
tobacco jars and boxes.*

Museums/Libraries

Duke Tobacco History Corporation
2828 Duke Homestead Rd.
Durham, NC 27705-2726
ph: 919-477-5498 or 919-479-7093
fax: 919-479-7092
maggot@sunsite.unc.edu
http://metalab.unc.edu/maggot/
dukehome2
*A non-profit support group for the
Duke Homestead State Historic Site;
collects materials relevant to the
preservation of tobacco history: pipe,
smoking, cigarette, advertising, etc.*

Holders

Collectors

Jay Opperman
78 Clinton Ave.
Montclair, NJ 07042-2116
ph: 973-509-0195
fax: 973-509-0881
*Wants to buy superb examples of
exquisite antique meerschaum pipes
and cigar holders.*

Smoking Stands (Figural)

Collectors

Claire Savitt
4141 Battersea Rd.
Coconut Grove, FL 33133
*Collector of figural smoking stands,
i.e., the butlers and bellboys of the
1920s and 1930s.*

Snuff Boxes

Collectors

Eli Hecht
Mineli Assoc.
19 Evelyn Lane
Syosset, NY 11791-5806
ph: 516-921-1837
*Wants to buy snuff boxes, nautical
items, and inkwells.*

SNOW BABIES

(see also COLLECTIBLES
[MODERN], Dept. 56)

Experts

Linda L. Vines
2911 4th St., #112
Santa Monica, CA 90405
ph: 310-314-0402
lleigh2000@hotmail.com
*Buys, sells and trades German bisque
snow babies; authored "Snow
Babies" in "Collectors Showcase"
magazine; Snow Babies advisor to
"Schroeder's;" lecturer and
appraiser.*

SNOWDOMES

Clubs/Associations

Nancy McMichael
Snowdome Collectors Club
Newsletter: Snow Biz Newsletter
P.O. Box 53262
Washington, DC 20009-9262
*"Snow Biz" aims to enhance the
knowledge, enjoyment and collections
of snowdome/waterglobe enthusiasts;
quarterly newsletter.*

Collectors

Miriam Bein
113 Cedar Rd.
Watchung, NJ 07060
ph: 908-561-0808 or 908-233-0115
fax: 908-232-7311
*Serious collector of snowdomes;
especially seeking plastic souvenir and
location domes with place names; also
wants advertising, Disney,
commemoratives, and figurals; has
snowdomes to sell and trade with
other collectors.*

Michael Muntner
6817 Capri Place
Bethesda, MD 20817
ph: 301-365-4784
fax: 301-365-4525
trylon@erols.com
http://www.muntner.com/snowdome.htm
*Wants snow domes (water globes),
glass or plastic; souvenir (e.g. cities),
tourist traps, events (e.g. Olympics),
product advertising, and figural; will
buy individual pieces or entire
collections; also have domes for sale
and trade.*

Diane Davison
1517 Reisterstown Rd., Ste. 101
Baltimore, MD 21208
ph: 410-486-0900
fax: 410-486-0901
diane@lawgal.net

Ian Luria
2620 N. 2nd Rd.
Arlington, VA 22201

Fiona Neary
12003 North Valley Pike
Broadway, VA 22815
ph: 540-896-2174
gallery@heritagestudio.com
http://www.heritagestudio.com
*Buys and sells old snowdomes of
various themes: religions, military,*

*snowbaby, animal, people, destina-
tion, and others; Web site has lots of
examples from the collection as well
as for sale.*

Linda Muether
7895 Watson Rd.
Saint Louis, MO 63129
ph: 314-961-1119
fax: 314-845-9942
lmuether@aol.com
http://hometown.aol.com/lmuether/
collect/index.htm

Dealers

Judy Posner
Judy Posner Collectibles
P.O. Box 2194
Englewood, FL 34295
ph: 941-475-1725
fax: 941-475-2645
judyandjef@yahoo.com
http://www.judyposner.com
*Buying, selling collecting for over 25
years.*

Experts

Helene Guarnaccia
52 Coach Lane
Fairfield, CT 06430
ph: 203-374-6034
greatstufftwo@aol.com
*Author of "Snowdomes, A Price
Guide."*

Nancy McMichael
P.O. Box 53262
Washington, DC 20009-9262
*"Snow Biz" aims to enhance the
knowledge, enjoyment and collections
of snowdome/waterglobe enthusiasts;
quarterly newsletter.*

Andy Zito
135 S. La Brea Ave.
Los Angeles, CA 90036-2980
ph: 323-931-1182
fax: 323-931-3091
andyzito@hotmail.com
http://www.andyzito.com/snowdomes
*Serious snowdome collector and
expert; especially seeking plastic,
souvenir, location or advertising
snowdomes with inside name plaques;
also plastic figurals; buys, sells,
trades; has extensive list of domes for
sale or trade.*

Man./Prod./Dist.

Herb Rabbin
P.O. Box 421205
Los Angeles, CA 90042
ph: 213-258-1776
fax: 213-258-1776
globerepair@earthlink.net
http://home.earthlink.net/~hrabbin
*This site is a resource for collectors
(and friends and relatives) who have
broken domes by accident and need to
have them repaired or refurbished;
also does custom domes fabricated
from 1 to 1,500 in glass or plastic.*

Sharon Jones
Global Shakeup
235 East Colorado Blvd., #178
Pasadena, CA 91101
ph: 818-752-2542
fax: 818-752-2667
feedback@snowdomes.com
http://www.snowdomes.com
*Hundreds of unusual snowdomes,
snowglobes and float pens from
around the world; US and non-US
location theme snowdomes,
advertising, cartoon characters, and
more; also produces custom snow
dome and float pen designs.*

Repair Services

Herb Rabbin
P.O. Box 421205
Los Angeles, CA 90042
ph: 213-258-1776
fax: 213-258-1776
globerepair@earthlink.net
http://home.earthlink.net/~hrabbin
*This site is a resource for collectors
(and friends and relatives) who have
broken domes by accident and need to
have them repaired or refurbished;
also does custom domes fabricated
from 1 to 1,500 in glass or plastic.*

Suppliers

National Artcraft Company
7966 Darrow Rd.
Twinsburg, OH 44087
ph: 800-793-0152
*Sells replacement glass globes, bases,
gaskets, snow, music boxes and more;
everything you need to make or repair
glass snowglobes.*

Location

Experts

Chloe Ross
7553 Norton Ave. Apt. 4
Los Angeles, CA 90046-5500
ph: 213-874-3044
trstrap@aol.com
*Seeking all plastic (NO GLASS)
souvenir location or advertising
snowshakers/snowdomes; any size or
condition; need not have water or
snow; prefer uncracked but small leaks
OK; must have inside plaque; no
holidays; wants LA; all answered.*

SNOWGLOBES

(see SNOWDOMES)

SNOWMOBILES

Clubs/Associations

Vintage Snowmobile Club of America
Magazine: Vintage Snowmobile
Magazine
P.O. Box 392
Fultonville, NY 12072
ph: 518-922-9053
admin@vsca.com
http://www.vsca.com
Caters to collectors and restorers of

*vintage and antique snowmobiles and
memorabilia from the early days to
1980; over 2400 subscribers/members
across the US and Canada.*

Dave Guenther, Pres.
Antique Snowmobile Club of America
Newsletter: Iron Dog Tracks
32832 Co. Rd. 39
Pequot Lakes, MN 56472
ph: 218-543-4146
http://www.ascoa.org

Museums/Libraries

New Hampshire Snowmobile Museum
Association
P.O. Box 10112
Concord, NH 03301-0112
ph: 603-648-2304
fax: 603-648-6683
info@nhsnowmobilemuseum.com
http://www.nhsnowmobilemuseum.com

Periodicals

American Motorcyclist Association
Magazine: AMA Official Motorcycle
Value Guide
P.O. Box 3190
Laurel, MD 20709
ph: 800-972-5312
CPI4Values@aol.com
http://www.cpivalueguide.com/main/
AMAGuide.htm
*A quarterly periodical covering
motorcycles, ATVs, personal
watercraft, and snowmobiles going
back to 1980.*

Kelley Blue Book
Price Guide: Kelley Blue Book
5 Oldfield
Irvine, CA 92618
ph: 949-770-7704
fax: 949-837-1904
kelley@kbb.com
http://www.kbb.com/indexv.html
*Web site offers current trade-in values
for all makes and model cars for the
past 21 years; also publishes printed
value guides for cars, RVs, motorcycles, snowmobiles, motor homes,
travel trailers, personal watercraft,
etc.*

Steve Ferguson, Ed.
National Automobile Dealers Association
Price Guide: N.A.D.A. Official Used Car
Guide
P.O. Box 7800
Costa Mesa, CA 92628
ph: 800-544-6232 or 714-556-8511
fax: 714-556-8715
info@nadaguides.com
http://www.nada.org
*A series of value guides for domestic
and foreign cars, trucks, vans, RVs,
mobile homes, motorcycles,
snowmobiles, and boats, small and
large; also Heavy Duty Trucks and
Aircraft Book, car clubs & organizations, museums.*

SNUFF BOTTLES

(see also ORIENTALIA; SMOKING
COLLECTIBLES)

Clubs/Associations

John Ford, Pres.
International Chinese Snuff Bottle
Society
Journal: Chinese Snuff Bottle Journal
2601 North Charles St.
Baltimore, MD 21218-4514
ph: 410-467-9400
fax: 410-243-3451
ICSBS.snuffbottle@verizon.net
http://www.snuffbottle.org
*Members interested in "Chinese"
snuff bottles.*

Dealers

James Sisk
Snuff Bottle Store, The
105A Beacon Rd.
Baltimore, MD 21220
ph: 410-686-4216
fax: 410-574-8160
info@snuffbottlestore.com
http://www.snuffbottlestore.com
*Offers about 500 Chinese snuff bottles
for sale; Web site has as an extensive
reference section for researching your
collection.*

Robert Hall
Robert Hall Chinese Snuff Bottles
15C Clifford St.
London, W1S 4JZ U.K.
ph: 020 7734 4008
fax: 020 7734 4408
roberthall@snuffbottle.com
http://www.snuffbottle.com
*Buys, sells, specializes in snuff
bottles; has produced eight publications and numerous articles about
snuff bottles.*

Experts

Robert Hall
Robert Hall Chinese Snuff Bottles
15C Clifford St.
London, W1S 4JZ U.K.
ph: 020 7734 4008
fax: 020 7734 4408
roberthall@snuffbottle.com
http://www.snuffbottle.com
*Buys, sells, specializes in snuff
bottles; has produced eight publications and numerous articles about
snuff bottles.*

Internet Resources

James Sisk
Snuff Bottle Store, The
105A Beacon Rd.
Baltimore, MD 21220
ph: 410-686-4216
fax: 410-574-8160
info@snuffbottlestore.com
http://www.snuffbottlestore.com
*Offers about 500 Chinese snuff bottles
for sale; Web site has as an extensive
reference section for researching your
collection.*

SOCIAL CAUSES

(see also BLACK MEMORABILIA;
BUTTONS, Pin-Back; HISTORICAL
AMERICANA; IMMIGRATION;
INDUSTRY RELATED ITEMS;
MINING RELATED ITEMS;
POLITICAL COLLECTIBLES;
POPULAR CULTURE; PROHIBITION
ITEMS; SLAVERY ITEMS; VIETNAM)

Auction Services

Dick Oestreicher
P.O. Box 407
Dallas, NC 28034
*Conducts mail/phone auctions of
American social history and social
movements: Blacks, Women, Ethnics,
Labor, Left, Anti-War, 1960s, Social
Movements.*

Collectors

Dick Oestreicher
P.O. Box 407
Dallas, NC 28034
*Wants items relating to history and
social movements: Blacks, Women,
Ethnics, Labor, Left, Anti-War,
1960s, Social Movements.*

Sylvia Marcotte-Cloutier
Sylvia Charles of Blythe
218 W. Hobson Way
Blythe, CA 92225-1619
ph: 760-922-3456
fax: 760-922-5651
ru4flowerpower@aol.com
*Wants 1960 to 1970 material relating
to Vietnam, counterculture organizations, Civil Rights: diaries, letters,
signed books, letters from military
men sent home; documents, photos of
sit-ins, marches, riots, demonstrations, etc.*

Dealers

Dr. Pamela Oestreicher
American Social History & Social
  Movements
P.O. Box 55066
Pittsburgh, PA 15207
ph: 412-421-5230
fax: 412-421-0903
*Produces a catalog of about 1,000
cause items for sale, many from 19th
century as well as 1960s through
1970s; African American, Civil War,
political, West, women, labor; social
movements: suffrage, KKK, anti-war,
prohibition, etc.*

Beatnik

Collectors

Rick Synchef
208 Summit Dr.
Corte Madera, CA 94925-1342
ph: 415-927-8844
*Wants 1960s "counterculture"
memorabilia: beatnik, hippie, Black
Panthers, Haight Ashbury, Tim Leary,
Abbie Hoffman, Vietnam war, LBJ,
Nixon, psychedelic, drugs, political,
music, handbills, leaflets, books.*

Dealers

James Musser
Skyline Books
P.O. Box T
Forest Knolls, CA 94933-0720
ph: 415-488-9491
skylinbk@ix.netcom.com
http://www.abebooks.com/home/
  SKYLINEBOOKS
*Wants hippie, the Beat generation,
'60s counterculture, drugs, student
activism, psychedelia; books,
pamphlets, posters, handbills,
ephemera, etc.*

Hippie Items

(see also WOODSTOCK)

Collectors

Ronald Krueger
R.W. Krueger's
P.O. Box 741
Oak Park, IL 60303-0741
ph: 708-788-8235
*Wants 1960s psychedelic hippie art:
underground newspapers, rock, pro-
drug, anti-war posters, handbills,
pamphlets, books, Peter Max.*

Rick Synchef
208 Summit Dr.
Corte Madera, CA 94925-1342
ph: 415-927-8844
*Wants 1960s "counterculture"
memorabilia: beatnik, hippie, Black
Panthers, Haight Ashbury, Tim Leary,
Abbie Hoffman, Vietnam war, LBJ,
Nixon, psychedelic, drugs, political,
music, handbills, leaflets, books.*

Dealers

James Musser
Skyline Books
P.O. Box T
Forest Knolls, CA 94933-0720
ph: 415-488-9491
skylinbk@ix.netcom.com
http://www.abebooks.com/home/
  SKYLINEBOOKS
*Wants hippie, the Beat generation,
'60s counterculture, drugs, student
activism, psychedelia; books,
pamphlets, posters, handbills,
ephemera, etc.*

Internet Resources

Psychedelic '60s, The
Univ. of Virginia, Special Collections
  Dept.
Charlottesville, VA 22903
lib-web@virginia.edu
http://www.lib.virginia.edu/exhibits/
  sixties/index.html
*Displays some of the great images of
the sixties; focuses on the literary
tradition, social change: Civil Rights,
Timothy Leary, Ken Kesey, Mountain
Poets, Rock music, social protest,
hippies, radical groups, Woodstock,
rock handbills.*

Labor Unions

Clubs/Associations

Michael Black
American Political Items Collectors
  (APIC) Labor History Chapter
Newsletter: Solidarity Forever!
P.O. Box 407
Dallas, NC 28034
*Purpose is to publicize and preserve
American labor history and to provide
communication among collectors of
labor movement memorabilia and
ephemera; send SASE for more
information.*

Collectors

Scott Molloy
550 Usquepaugh Rd.
West Kingston, RI 02892-1924
ph: 401-782-3614
fax: 401-874-2954
*Wants labor and left-wing items:
badges, ribbons, pins, photos, flyers,
books, pamphlets, posters, knickknacks; wants Knights of Labor,
Railroad unions, I.W.W., AFL-CIO,
etc.*

Daniel Neuspiel
8 Anthony Rd.
White Plains, NY 10605
ph: 914-946-3523
dneuspiel@compuserve.com
*Collects pin-back labor union buttons,
especially pre-1950.*

Joe Doerring
P.O. Box 35351
Des Moines, IA 50315
ph: 515-285-7702
JDoerring@aol.com
*Wants pre-1940 Industrial Workers of
the World (IWW) items: pin-back
buttons, ribbons, paper items, etc.*

Patrick J. Kehoe
3455 S. 83rd St.
Milwaukee, WI 53219-3840
ph: 414-541-2538
kehoe@voyager.net
*Wants labor union buttons, ribbon
badges, shop signs, especially 1960s
and older; topics covering: 8-hour
day, labor day, strikes, membership,
etc.; famous labor union leaders
memorabilia of Jimmy Hoffa, Eugene
Debs, John L. Lewis.*

Suffrage Items

Clubs/Associations

Ronnie Lapinsky Sax, Pres.
Woman Suffrage & Political Issues
  Chapter, APIC
Newsletter: Clarion, The
9820 Glenolden Dr.
Potomac, MD 20854
ph: 800-455-6622
fax: 301-299-2015
r.lapinskysax@rssmb.com
http://www.apic.ws/chapters/sp-
  womans.asp
*Collectors of items relating to woman
suffrage and other women's historical
material.*

Collectors

Andy Avery
P.O. Box 471
Jamaica, VT 05343-0471
ph: 802-874-4207
*Wants women's suffrage items: pins,
ribbons, postcards, ceramics, papers,
pennants, fans, stamps, cards, etc.;
interested in most any souvenir
memorabilia with a special interest in
women's suffrage.*

Ronnie Lapinsky Sax
9820 Glenolden Dr.
Potomac, MD 20854
ph: 800-455-6622 x6368
fax: 301-299-2015
r.lapinskysax@rssmb.com
*Over 25 years collecting and
preserving American women's
historical memorabilia of all kinds:
suffrage for women, ERA, women's
involvement in the '20s through '50s;
has collection of over 5,000 items
pertaining to women's issues.*

Cary Demont
P.O. Box 16013
Minneapolis, MN 55416
ph: 763-522-0957
*Wants early women's suffrage items
and Votes for Women material: pin-
back buttons, badges, posters,
banners, pennants, costumes,
postcards, and unusual 3-dimensional
items; also wants Carrie Nation
material of all kinds.*

Steve Sobel
5132 Topeka Dr.
Tarzana, CA 91356-3921
ph: 818-705-4063
fax: 818-705-1123
*Wants woman suffrage/votes for
women materials: buttons, ribbons,
posters, etc.*

John Gearhart
3267 S.E. Hawthorne
Portland, OR 97214
ph: 503-255-8108 or 503-234-0991
gearhart@teleport.com
http://www.teleport.com/~gearhart

Internet Resources

Woman Suffrage Association Collection,
  Library of Congress
101 Independence Ave. SE
Washington, DC 20540
ph: 202-707-8000
ndlpcoll@loc.gov
http://memory.loc.gov/ammem/naw/
  nawshome.html
*Collection consists of books,
pamphlets, and other artifacts
documenting the suffrage campaign,
1848 to 1921.*

SODA FOUNTAIN COLLECTIBLES

(see also ICE CREAM COLLECTIBLES; MOLDS, Ice Cream; SOFT DRINK COLLECTIBLES)

Appraisers

Peggy Landt
LHL Services
9065 La Serena Dr.
Fair Oaks, CA 95628
ph: 916-962-0592
Complete soda fountain and pharmacy appraisal services.

Clubs/Associations

Betty Davis, Pres.
National Association of Soda Jerks & Soda Fountain Preservation Association
Newsletter: Fiz Biz
P.O. Box 115
Omaha, NE 68101-0115
ph: 402-341-6965 or 712-322-8685
fax: 402-453-9448
Dedicated to the preservation of nostalgia and of the history related to the soda fountain and soda jerks; recipes, soda fountain visits, nostalgic remembrances, etc.

Collectors

Duvall & Barbara Sollers
P.O. Box 132
Monkton, MD 21111
iseditor@bellatlantic.net
Interested in buying antique soda fountain and ice cream collectibles.

Harold & Joyce Screen
2804 Munster Rd.
Baltimore, MD 21234-1131
ph: 410-661-6765
hscreen@comcast.net
Collector of soda fountain material for 30+ years; buying pre-1920 trade catalogs, trade magazines, pre-1910 original photos of soda fountains; will answer questions and do appraisals for a modest fee.

Coleen Detzel
28 Lacresta Dr.
Florence, KY 41042-9663
ph: 606-647-6156
Wants c. 1940s soda fountain and ice cream items: dispensers, fountains, malt mixers, signs, neons, bars, stools, tables, booths, etc.; also wants diner items c. 1940s and 1950s including furniture.

Dealers

Mike & Judi Powers
Memory Peddlers
6 Loubier Dr.
Essex Junction, VT 05452
ph: 802-878-8701
memorypdlr@aol.com
Collector, dealer interested in all soda fountain related collectibles with focus on ice cream scoops (dippers), ice cream molds (moulds), pennylicks, tip trays, pre-1900s iced cream freezers; also related items, e.g., pharmacy collectibles.

Experts

Harold & Joyce Screen
2804 Munster Rd.
Baltimore, MD 21234-1131
ph: 410-661-6765
hscreen@comcast.net
Historian wants: "Soda Fountain" pre-1925 trade magazines magazines, fountain equipment & pre-1930 supply catalogs, interior view photos of pre-1910 soda fountains; will reply to queries if accompanied by a SASE; appraisals for fee.

Man./Prod./Dist.

Gene Rees
Gino's Malt Shop Collection
25 N. Jefferson
Canonsburg, PA 15317
ph: 724-743-1950
fax: 724-743-3275
Sells '50s and '60s malt shop furniture, decor and accessories: booths, tables, chairs, stools, moldings, metal trim, lighting fixtures, quilted stainless sheets, counter accessories, etc.

Museums/Libraries

Hook's American Drugstore Museum, Inc.
201 North Meridian St.
Indianapolis, IN 46225
ph: 317-951-2222
fax: 317-951-2224
pharmuseum@aol.com
A museum dedicated to the American drugstore; collecting anything related to drugstore, apothecary, pharmacy, soda fountain; any period from Colonial to present.

SODA POP

(see SOFT DRINK COLLECTIBLES)

SOFT DRINK COLLECTIBLES

(see also BOTTLES; COIN-OPERATED MACHINES, Vending Machines; SODA FOUNTAIN COLLECTIBLES)

Collectors

Carolyn Hammond
P.O. Box 343
Black Mountain, NC 28711-0343
ph: 828-669-6262
Wants to buy soft drink collectibles: Pepsi, Coca-Cola, Dr. Pepper, Moxie, and Nu-Grape; signs, posters, calendars, trays, etc.

Wallace A. Newkirk
229 Tangelo Ave.
Fern Park, FL 32730-2811
ph: 407-834-2101
fax: 407-834-3101
Wants to buy old bottles, defunct brands of bottles from the US only.

Jim Carr
H.C. 30, Box 49-D
Brownwood, TX 76801
ph: 915-752-6818
Wants to buy older Coca-Cola, Pepsi, and 7-Up items; all types and any condition.

Dealers

Wayne Merritt
5 Hanson Ct.
Greenville, SC 29615-4331
ph: 864-297-3999
fax: 804-297-3999
Wants to buy soft drink collectibles: Coca-Cola, Pepsi-Cola; bottles, signs, calendars, paper items, colored soda bottles, displays, posters, etc.; please state price and condition in first letter.

Lois & Ralph Behm
Lois' Collectibles of Antique Market III
413 W. Main St.
Saint Charles, IL 60174-1815
ph: 630-377-5599 or 847-831-5997
fax: 847-831-5998
Buys and sells Coca-Cola and Pepsi collectibles.

Matt Holmes
Soda Pop Shop, The
P.O. Box 13382
Shawnee Mission, KS 66212
ph: 877-SODASHOP
fax: 877-SODASHOP
webmaster@sodashop.com
http://www.sodashop.com
Carries a wide variety of contemporary soda collectibles; all licensed by their respective companies.

Robert Newman
17220 Silver Lane
Encino, CA 91316
ph: 310-559-0539
Serious collector, dealer of Coca-Cola memorabilia and other pre-1965 soft drink collectibles: Pepsi, Dr. Pepper, Crush, Hires, etc.; cardboard, tin, porcelain and light-up signs, trays, clocks, thermometers, calendars, etc.

Tim Smokoff
Pop Shoppe, The
9208 128th St. Court NW
Gig Harbor, WA 98329
Buys, sells, trades, conducts auctions, and shares information about Soda Pop Collecting; specializing in Coke, Hires, Moxie and Orange Crush; also tracks 7-Up, Squeeze, Dads Rootbeer and Pepsi.

Harold Balde
Fungus Amungus
21 Wellington St.
Orangeville, Ontario L9W 2L2 Canada
ph: 519-938-8808
boardwalk12345@yahoo.com
http://www.fungus-amungus.com
Dealer of soda collectibles; specialty is Coca-Cola and Orange Crush items such as trays, bottles, clans, and paper material.

Experts

Craig Stifter
218 South Adams St.
Hinsdale, IL 60521
ph: 630-789-5780
mcstifte@gsb.uchicago.edu
Wants to buy older Coca-Cola, Pepsi-Cola, Dr. Pepper, Orange-Crush, Hires Root Beer and other brand soda memorabilia; writes columns for several antiques periodicals; also interested in items pertaining to country (general) stores.

Tim Smokoff
Pop Shoppe, The
9208 128th St. Court NW
Gig Harbor, WA 98329
Buys, sells, trades, conducts auctions, and shares information about Soda Pop Collecting; specializing in Coke, Hires, Moxie and Orange Crush; also tracks 7-Up, Squeeze, Dads Rootbeer and Pepsi.

Internet Resources

TheSodaFoundain.com
http://www.thesodafountain.com
An online resource created to assist people in their quest for information regarding soda pop collectibles and collecting.

Periodicals

Dan Kwate
Magazine: Club Soda
P.O. Box 489
Troy, ID 83871-0489
ph: 208-835-2306
fax: 208-835-2307
Articles about all types of soda collectibles: vending machines, signs, bottles, etc.; features include company histories, restoration tips, show and auction reviews, and free classified ads.

Blair Matthews
Playing With Words
Magazine: Soda Pop Dreams
P.O. Box 23037
Krug Postal Outlet, Ontario N2B 3V1 Canada
ph: 519-650-3969
fax: 519-650-2547
editor@sodapopdreams.org
http://www.sodapopdreams.org
A publication dedicated to soda pop collectors and enthusiasts from across North America and beyond; articles about all types of soda collectibles and brands including signs, bottles,

cans, machines, etc.; free classifieds for subscribers.

7-Up

Collectors

Gwen Daniel
18 Belleau Lake Ct.
O Fallon, MO 63366-3144
ph: 636-978-3190
SimGirl200@aol.com

Brian Adamson
6732 Arlington St.
Vancouver, British Columbia V5S 3N9
Canada
Wants 7-Up related collectibles: thermometers, calendars, signs, etc.; also wants Pepsi and Orange Crush items.

Applied Color Label Bottles

Clubs/Associations

Rick Sweeney
Painted Soda Bottle Collectors
Association
Newsletter: Soda Net
9418 Hilmer Dr.
La Mesa, CA 91942
ph: 619-461-4354
aclsrus@cox.net
http://www.collectoronline.com/PSBCA/
PSBCA.html
The only national organization for "painted" (silkscreened) soda bottle collectors.

Collectors

Ed Kassay
P.O. Box 4
Calimesa, CA 92320
ph: 909-795-5551
Wants to buy and trade painted label soda bottles from the 1940s through 1960s; also wants soda crown caps, especially if unused.

Experts

Thomas Marsh
914 Franklin Ave.
Youngstown, OH 44502
ph: 800-845-7930
Author of "Official Guide to Collecting Applied Color Label Soda Bottles." Applied color label (ACL) bottles (heyday was 1930s-1970s) had silkscreened labels, as opposed to a glued-on paper label or an embossed label.

Periodicals

Soda Mart - Can World
Newsletter: Painted-Label Soda Bottles
1055 Ridgecrest Dr.
Goodlettsville, TN 37072
ph: 615-859-5236 or 800-826-4929
fax: 615-859-5238
mbca@gono.com
http://www.gono.com/vir-mus/
museum.htm
An annual periodical that focuses on soda bottles having painted, silk-screened or enameled labels.

Coca-Cola

(see also ADVERTISING COLLECTIBLES, Tin Vienna Art Plates)

Auction Services

Allan Petretti
Nostalgia Publications
21 S. Lake Dr.
Hackensack, NJ 07601
ph: 201-488-4536
Conducts semi-annual mail-bid auctions of Coca-Cola related advertising items; catalogs are $10 for subscription.

Tom Fiese
Fiese's Auction Service
202 12th Ave.
Baraboo, WI 53913
ph: 608-356-2073
fax: 608-356-2073
auctions4you@baraboo.com
Conducts specialty Coca-Cola auctions.

Clubs/Associations

Tim Watkins, Pres.
Old Dominion Chapter of the Coca-Cola Collectors Club International
1401 Addison Rd.
Hampton, VA 23663
ph: 757-850-2822

Coca-Cola Collectors Club, The
Newsletter: Coca-Cola Collectors News
PMB 609
4780 Ashford-Dunwoody Rd, St A
Atlanta, GA 30338
webmaster@cocacolaclub.org
http://www.cocacolaclub.org
International communications with over 7,000 collectors, markets for buying/selling/trading, special monthly merchandise offerings for members, monthly newsletter with free classified.

Chris Wenzel
Florida West Coast Chapter of the Coca-Cola Collectors Club International
1007 Emerald Dr.
Brandon, FL 33511-6521
ph: 813-685-7242
fax: 813-645-0305
heintz54@earthlink.com
Contact with questions about the club or about Coca-Cola memorabilia.

John W. Heintz
Florida West Coast Chapter of the Coca-Cola Collectors Club
11735 Kay Court
Seminole, FL 33778
ph: 727-393-2203 or 727-302-4515
fax: 727-302-4550
heintz54@earthlink.net
An active club with about 75 members who have a special interest in Coca-Cola and other soda related items.

Collectors

Steve Sands
Steve's Coca-Cola Collection & Mini-Museum
1315 Washington St.
Weymouth, MA 02189-2333
ph: 781-335-6352
steve@cckid.net
http://www.cckid.net
Collects anything having to do with Coca-Cola.

Drew Steitz
Coke Bottles of the World Website, The
P.O. Box 222
East Texas, PA 18046-0222
ph: 610-791-7979
fax: 610-791-7979
pl8seditor@aol.com
http://www.pl8s.com/coke.htm
Wants to buy Coca-Cola bottles and cans from around the world; also looking for other international soft drink and bottled waters.

Scott Rosenman
1 E. Lexington St., Ste. 509
Baltimore, MD 21202
ph: 410-837-5897
visionsm@charm.net
Wants Coca-Cola and Pepsi-Cola items; pre-1960 and in excellent condition.

Jeffrey Smith
5940 McGinnis Circle
Norfolk, VA 23502
Wants to buy Coca-Cola memorabilia: signs, machines, and paper ephemera; has appeared on PAX TV's "Treasures in Your Home."

Thom Thompson
1389 Alexandria Dr., Ste. #7
Lexington, KY 40504-1777
ph: 859-255-2727 or 859-873-8787
fax: 859-255-2727
Serious collector and researcher of Coca-Cola collectibles since 1970; interested in buying older collectibles including posters, trays, coupons, calendars, knives, openers, fobs, etc.; especially chewing gum items; free appraisals.

Keith Johnson
236 N. Catherine
Ithaca, MI 48847
keithjo@edcen.ehhs.cmich.edu
Wants to buy Coca-Cola Christmas collectibles.

J. D. Moore
1111 Cartwright
Jonesboro, AR 72401
ph: 870-931-3772
bottle40@yahoo.com
Specializes in collecting Coca-Cola bottles.

Dealers

Larry & Debby Lawrence
Coca-Cola Collectibles
660 Kipps Lane
Blacksburg, VA 24060
cocacola@usit.net
http://www.public.usit.net/cocacola
Buying, selling, trading Coca-Cola memorabilia and advertising for over 20 years.

John Forrest
Cola Shop, The
137 Cherry St.
Black Mountain, NC 28711
ph: 828-669-4019
Buys and sells Coca-Cola memorabilia; fountain on site.

Richard Mix
Mix International
P.O. Box 425
Marietta, GA 30112
ph: 770-834-1655
fax: 770-634-5975
mixintl@aol.com
http://www.bottleworld.com
Coca-Cola collector, dealer, expert; noted world-wide expert on Coca-Cola memorabilia; has authored numerous books and articles on the subject; owns the world's largest collection of Coca-Cola bottles.

DaClassic 1's Coca-Cola Collector's
Corner
44123 Kendyl Dr.
Sterling Heights, MI 48314
ph: 248-265-3075
DaClassic1@aol.com
http://www.daclassic1.com
Buys, sells, collects Coca-Cola related items.

Dick & Kay Thompson
320 E. Washington St.
Pontiac, IL 61764
ph: 815-842-2586

Robert Newman
17220 Silver Lane
Encino, CA 91316
ph: 310-559-0539
Serious collector, dealer of Coca-Cola memorabilia and other pre-1965 soft drink collectibles: Pepsi, Dr. Pepper, Crush, Hires, etc.; cardboard, tin, porcelain and light-up signs, trays, clocks, thermometers, calendars, etc.

Dwayne Spark
Nostalgia Plus
8441 Sublaines
Anjou, Quebec H1K 2C1 Canada
ph: 514-352-6892
fax: 514-352-1856
dspark@videotron.ca
Buys and sells Coca-Cola memorabilia (old and new): cans, bottles, signs, "Life" ads, phone cards.

Experts

Allan Petretti
Nostalgia Publications
21 S. Lake Dr.
Hackensack, NJ 07601
ph: 201-488-4536
*Author of "Petretti's Coca-Cola
Collectibles Price Guide" - 10th
edition, and "Petretti's Soda-Pop
Collectibles Price Guide."*

Randy S. Schaeffer
C.C. Tray-ders
611 N. 5th St.
Reading, PA 19601-2201
ph: 610-373-3333 or 610-683-4401
schaeffe@kutztown.edu
*Advanced collector seeking the old,
rare and unusual in Coca-Cola
collectibles; also provides expert
appraisals and evaluations; author of
"Coca-Cola: A Collector's Guide to
New & Vintage Coca-Cola
Memorabilia."*

William E. Bateman
611 N. 5th St.
Reading, PA 19601-2201
ph: 610-373-3333 or 610-683-4412
bateman@kutztown.edu
*Advanced collector seeking the old,
rare and unusual in Coca-Cola
collectibles; also provides expert
appraisals and evaluations.*

Bill Ricketts
Nostalgia Store, The
P.O. Box 9605
Asheville, NC 28805-0605
ph: 828-669-2205 or 828-669-2668
fax: 828-669-2205
*Buys, sells and trades Coca-Cola
memorabilia: trays, signs, posters,
calendars, bottles, novelty items, etc.*

Richard Mix
P.O. Box 425
Marietta, GA 30112
ph: 770-834-1655
fax: 770-634-5975
mixintl@aol.com
http://www.bottleworld.com
*Noted world-wide expert on Coca-
Cola memorabilia; has authored
numerous books and articles on the
subject; owns the world's largest
collection of Coca-Cola bottles.*

Chris Wenzel
1007 Emerald Dr.
Brandon, FL 33511-6521
ph: 813-685-7242
fax: 813-645-0305
heintz54@earthlink.com
*Does Coca-Cola research for movie
companies.*

Thom Thompson
1389 Alexandria Dr., Ste. #7
Lexington, KY 40504-1777
ph: 859-255-2727 or 859-873-8787
fax: 859-255-2727
*Serious collector and researcher of
Coca-Cola collectibles since 1970;
interested in buying older collectibles
including posters, trays, coupons,*
calendars, knives, openers, fobs, etc.;
especially chewing gum items; free
appraisals.

Craig Stifter
218 South Adams St.
Hinsdale, IL 60521
ph: 630-789-5780
mcstifte@gsb.uchicago.edu
*Wants to buy older Coca-Cola, Pepsi-
Cola, Dr. Pepper, Orange-Crush,
Hires Root Beer and other brand soda
memorabilia; writes columns for
several antiques periodicals; also
interested in items pertaining to
country (general) stores.*

Internet Resources

DaClassic 1's Coca-Cola Collector's
Corner
44123 Kendyl Dr.
Sterling Heights, MI 48314
ph: 248-265-3075
DaClassic1@aol.com
http://www.daclassic1.com
*Internet Web Site homepage dedicated
to providing facts, information and
fun for Coke fans and collectors of
Coca-Cola memorabilia.*

Man./Prod./Dist.

Coca-Cola Store
6655 Sugarloaf Parkway
Duluth, GA 30097
ph: 800-746-7265
customerservice@coca-colastore.com
http://www.coca-colastore.com
*Carries a wide assortment of current
Coca-Cola material.*

Museums/Libraries

Phillip Mooney, Manager
Coca-Cola Company Archives
Department
P.O. Drawer 1734
Atlanta, GA 30301
ph: 800-GET-COKE or 404-676-3491
fax: 404-676-7701
*Request information about your Coca-
Cola collectibles directly from the
Company; will answer questions
about ingredients, recycling, products,
packaging, promotions, advertising,
history, and much, much more.*

Philip F. Mooney, Cur.
World of Coca-Cola Pavilion, The
55 Martin Luther King Dr., SW
Atlanta, GA 30303-3505
ph: 770-578-4325
http://www.woccatlanta.com
*A 45,000 square foot attraction
containing high-tech, interactive
exhibits and archival materials from
the company's 110+ year history.*

Biedenharn Candy Company & Museum
of Coca-Cola Memorabilia
1107 Washington St.
Vicksburg, MS 39180
ph: 601-638-6514
fax: 601-636-5010
*Collection contains reproduction
bottling works, Coca-Cola memora-*
bilia, 1900 soda fountain, restored
1890 candy store.

Channing Hardy
Schmidt's Coca-Cola Museum
1201 North Dixie
P.O. Box 848
Elizabethtown, KY 42701-0848
ph: 502-769-3320 x237
fax: 502-769-3323
*Contains the world's largest private
collection of Coca-Cola memorabilia;
will buy Coke items from 1890 to
1970, especially unusual paper items,
toys, cut-outs, etc.*

Periodicals

Tim Ferrante
Magazine: Gameroom Magazine
P.O. Box 41
Keyport, NJ 07735-0041
ph: 732-739-1955
fax: 732-739-2834
coinop@gameroommagazine.com
http://www.gameroommagazine.com
*A great source of information for the
collector and dealer of jukeboxes,
pinballs, slot machines, Coke and
other soda machines, arcade games,
classic arcade video, and other
gameroom collectibles.*

Coca-Cola Machines

(see COIN-OPERATED MACHINES,
Vending Machines; SOFT DRINK
COLLECTIBLES, Soda Machines)

Dr. Pepper

Clubs/Associations

Dr. Pepper 10-2-4 Collector's Club
Newsletter: Lions Roar
823 Hannock Glen Lane
Spring, TX 77373-8213
desiloo@earthlink.net
http://www.drpep.com/club.htm
*The 10-2-4 club is a national
organization of people dedicated to
the study of the history and collecting
of Dr. Pepper Co. memorabilia.*

Collectors

Gwen Daniel
18 Belleau Lake Ct.
O Fallon, MO 63366-3144
ph: 636-978-3190
SimGirl200@aol.com

Ed Royse
112 N. Broadway St.
Walters, OK 73572
ph: 580-357-8000
fax: 580-875-2063
edroyse@juno.com
*Wants to buy pre-1951 (script logo)
Dr. Pepper signs, cardboards, clocks,
trays, calendars, promotional
material, etc.*

Bob Thiele
620 Tinker
Pawhuska, OK 74056-4039
ph: 918-287-3845
rthiele@mmind.net
Wants early and unusual Dr. Pepper
items: celluloid, early paper, tokens,
jewelry, pins, pencils, clothing,
fountain pens, etc.; also items from
founding co. - "Artesian Mfg. &
Bottling Co." (AM&B Co.), Waco,
TX or other cities.

Wilton A. Lanning, Jr.
6433 Summit Ridge St.
Waco, TX 76710-1143
ph: 254-776-3130 or 254-772-2434
fax: 254-776-3153
*Collector of Dr. Pepper, Circle A and
Artesian Mfg. & Bottling memorabilia: bottles, signs, thermometers,
advertising, etc.*

Experts

Bill Ricketts
Pepper's Deli
P.O. Box 9605
Asheville, NC 28805-0605
ph: 828-669-2205 or 828-669-2668
fax: 828-669-2205
*Buy/sell/trade, collects and specializes
in pre-1960 Dr. Pepper advertising
items; especially interested in old
trays, signs, calendars; anything Dr.
Pepper; will buy single items,
duplicates, collections, or accumulations.*

Craig Stifter
218 South Adams St.
Hinsdale, IL 60521
ph: 630-789-5780
mcstifte@gsb.uchicago.edu
*Wants to buy older Coca-Cola, Pepsi-
Cola, Dr. Pepper, Orange-Crush,
Hires Root Beer and other brand soda
memorabilia; writes columns for
several antiques periodicals; also
interested in items pertaining to
country (general) stores.*

Museums/Libraries

Dr. Pepper Museum & Free Enterprise
Institute
Newsletter: Bottlecaps
300 S. 5th St.
Waco, TX 76701-2115
ph: 254-757-1025 or 800-527-7096
fax: 254-757-2221
dp-info@drpeppermuseum.com
http://www.drpeppermuseum.com
*The museum focuses on the soft drink
industry; gift shop.*

Grapette

Clubs/Associations

Van Stueart
Grapette Collectors Club
Newsletter: Grapette Collectors Club
Newsletter
2240 Hwy 27 N
Nashville, AR 71852
ph: 870-845-4864 or 800-577-1810
sodaman@iosa.com
*For collectors of Grapette soda
collectibles.*

Collectors

Van Stueart
2240 Hwy 27 N
Nashville, AR 71852
ph: 870-845-4864 or 800-577-1810
sodaman@iosa.com
Wants Grapette items: soda fountain glasses, cardboard signs, light-up clocks, tin signs, neon clocks, calendars, flange signs, porcelain signs.

Mountain Dew

Internet Resources

Wayne C. Burgess
Mountain Dew Bottle Collectors Home Page
mtdew@mountaindewbottles.com
http://www.mountaindewbottles.com
Web site authored by Wayne Burgess and Dick Bridgforth; there are over 724 unique Mountain Dew bottles and this Web site has images of all of them; also has some bottles listed for trade.

Tim Tromp
DewCollector.com
1729 Lee Ave.
Muskegon, MI 49444
ph: 231-788-1694
dewtimes@dewcollector.com
http://www.dewcollector.com
Dedicated to soda pop collecting and specifically vintage Mountain Dew; Web site has a discussion board to meet other collectors, sell and trade, and share information; search the master list of over 700 known bottles.

Moxie

Clubs/Associations

Kirt Kabelac
New England Moxie Congress
Newsletter: Nerve Food News
2783 N. Triphammer Rd.
Ithaca, NY 14850
http://www.xensei.com/users/iraseski/Congress.html
Provides a clearinghouse for all information and memorabilia relating to Moxie, supports Maine Moxie weekends, promotes the consumption of Moxie; annual meeting of NEMC 2nd weekend in July in Kennebunkport, ME at Trolley Museum.

Collectors

Jan Bacci
82 Wyman Rd.
Braintree, MA 02184-4721
ph: 781-848-1095
Advanced collector interested in rare and early Moxie items for personal collection.

Ira Seskin
657 Boylston St.
Newton Centre, MA 02459
ph: 617-965-9891
moxieman@rcn.com
http://www.xensei.com/users/iraseski
Dealer, collector, appraiser; has lectured and/or displayed on Moxie at the Museum of Our National Heritage, Lexington, MA as well as the Lowell National Historic Park, Lowell, MA; was the Moxie "historian" on History Channel series.

Experts

Ira Seskin
657 Boylston St.
Newton Centre, MA 02459
ph: 617-965-9891
moxieman@rcn.com
http://www.xensei.com/users/iraseski
Dealer, collector, appraiser; has lectured and/or displayed on Moxie at the Museum of Our National Heritage, Lexington, MA as well as the Lowell National Historic Park, Lowell, MA; was the Moxie "historian" on History Channel series.

Misc. Services

Frank Anicetti
Kennebec Fruit Company - The Moxie Festival
2 Main St.
Lisbon Falls, ME 04252
ph: 207-353-8173
Each year sponsors a Moxie Festival in Lisbon Falls, ME; offers contemporary Moxie collectibles.

Orange Crush

Experts

Craig Stifter
218 South Adams St.
Hinsdale, IL 60521
ph: 630-789-5780
mcstifte@gsb.uchicago.edu
Wants to buy older Coca-Cola, Pepsi-Cola, Dr. Pepper, Orange-Crush, Hires Root Beer and other brand soda memorabilia; writes columns for several antiques periodicals; also interested in items pertaining to country (general) stores.

Painted-Label Soda Bottles

(see SOFT DRINK COLLECTIBLES, Applied Color Label Bottles)

Pepsi-Cola

Clubs/Associations

Phyllis Dragovich
Ozark Mountain Pepsi Collectors Club
9101 Columbus Ave. S.
Bloomington, MN 55420
mnpepsidrago@bigfoot.com
Local club for collectors of Pepsi memorabilia.

Bob Stoddard
Pepsi-Cola Collectors Club
Newsletter: Pepsi Express
P.O. Box 817
Claremont, CA 91711
ph: 909-946-6026
fax: 909-946-4786
doubledot@earthlink.net
http://www.pepsigifts.com/pcccinfo.html

Collectors

Scott Rosenman
1 E. Lexington St., Ste. 509
Baltimore, MD 21202
ph: 410-837-5897
visionsm@charm.net
Wants Coca-Cola and Pepsi-Cola items; pre-1960 and in excellent condition.

Dolores Robinson
11309 Ten Oaks Dr.
Port Richey, FL 34669
Robinson@mciworldcom.net

Gwen Daniel
18 Belleau Lake Ct.
O Fallon, MO 63366-3144
ph: 636-978-3190
SimGirl200@aol.com

Dealers

Bill Ricketts
Nostalgia Store, The
P.O. Box 9605
Asheville, NC 28805-0605
ph: 828-669-2205 or 828-669-2668
fax: 828-669-2205
Wants to buy Pepsi-Cola items: advertising, trays, signs, posters, calendars, novelty items, bottles, etc.; please describe and price.

Experts

Scott Kinzie
ph: 804-748-5769
gandy60@prodigy.net
Collector, dealer, expert specializing in pre-1960 Pepsi advertising memorabilia with a strong interest in historically significant items.

Larry Woestman
14750 Karlov Ave.
Midlothian, IL 60445
pepcconn2@aol.com
Coauthor with Phil Dillman of "Pepsi Memorabilia - Then and Now."

Bob Stoddard
P.O. Box 817
Claremont, CA 91711
ph: 909-946-6026
fax: 909-946-4786
doubledot@earthlink.net
http://www.pepsigifts.com
Author of "Introduction to Pepsi Collecting."

Root Beer

Collectors

Jerome Gundrum
200 Duncaster Rd.
Bloomfield, CT 06002
ph: 860-342-5714
DrRootbeer@aol.com
http://www.rootbeer.net
Wants to buy root beer advertising items.

Bob Averill
1942 W. Market St.
Pottsville, PA 17901-2043
ph: 570-628-3084
Wants root beer advertising items: tin, porcelain or cardboard signs, dispensers, mugs, bottles, trade cards, postcards, or anything root beer.

Root Beer (Hires)

Collectors

Steve Sourapas
1212 9th Ave. West #2
Seattle, WA 98119-3445
ph: 206-282-9922
fax: 206-782-1039
stevesourapas@email.msn.com
Advanced collector seeks pre-1930 good to mint condition items.

Experts

Craig Stifter
218 South Adams St.
Hinsdale, IL 60521
ph: 630-789-5780
mcstifte@gsb.uchicago.edu
Wants to buy older Coca-Cola, Pepsi-Cola, Dr. Pepper, Orange-Crush, Hires Root Beer and other brand soda memorabilia; writes columns for several antiques periodicals; also interested in items pertaining to country (general) stores.

Soda Machines

(see also COIN-OPERATED MACHINES, Vending Machines)

Collectors

Richard O. Gates
P.O. Box 187
Chesterfield, VA 23832-0187
ph: 804-748-0382 or 804-794-5146
fax: 804-748-6349
rogates@mindspring.com
Wants coin-operated machines including Coca-Cola, Pepsi, Dr. Pepper, R.C., etc. machines, light-ups, advertising items and literature related to any of the above.

Dealers

Bill Mock
2640 SW 29th Way
Fort Lauderdale, FL 33312
ph: 954-584-8958
Buys, sells, restores Coca-Cola vending machines.

Hobbs Country Store
P.O. Box 158
Galveston, IN 46932
ph: 219-699-7505
Sells vintage soda machines.

Home Arcade Corp.
4611 Main St.
Lisle, IL 60532
ph: 630-964-2555
fax: 630-964-9367
arcadehom@aol.com
http://www.homearcadecorp.com
Sells restored vintage Coke machines; also juke boxes, phone booths, beer signs, tavern items, barber poles and other '50s memorabilia; send $5 for Coke Restoration Parts Catalog.

Tony Duran
Nostalgia Warehouse LLC
7801 US Hwy 287
Arlington, TX 76001
ph: 817-572-5012
fax: 817-563-0572
tonyduran@nostalgiawarehouse.com
http://www.nostalgiawarehouse.com
Buy/sell/restore jukeboxes, coke machines, radios, gas pumps, pedal cars, neon signs, and more; an authorized distributor for Wurlitzer and Crosley Radio products; sells vintage Coke machines, original as well as restored.

Periodicals

Dan Kwate
Magazine: Club Soda
P.O. Box 489
Troy, ID 83871-0489
ph: 208-835-2306
fax: 208-835-2307
Articles about all types of soda collectibles: vending machines, signs, bottles, etc.; features include company histories, restoration tips, show and auction reviews, and free classified ads.

Suppliers

Steve Ebner
Fun-Tronics
P.O. Box 448
Middletown, MD 21769
ph: 301-371-5246
Specializing in restoration supplies for vintage Coke machines; the source for in-stock inventory of quality reproduction parts, decals, and manuals.

Soft Drink Cans

Clubs/Associations

Rich Simmons, Dir.
National Pop Can Collectors
Newsletter: Can-O-Gram
19201 Sherwood Green Way
Gaithersburg, MD 20879
ph: 301-869-4899
fax: 301-601-9322
cokecans@aol.com
http://www.pinnaclecommunications.com/coke
Worldwide network of collectors focusing on soda cans & bottles as well as other soda memorabilia; articles, free ads and roster; regional trade sessions so members can meet and trade in person; club roster provided to each member.

Collectors

Rich Simmons
19201 Sherwood Green Way
Gaithersburg, MD 20879
ph: 301-869-4899
fax: 301-601-9322
cokecans@aol.com
http://www.pinnaclecommunications.com/coke

Jerry Glader
1017 Villa Gran Way
Fenton, MO 63026
ph: 636-343-9433
Collects Coca-Cola, Pepsi, and 7-Up cans and specializes in one can from every country in the world and cans from Africa.

Museums/Libraries

Museum of Beverage Containers & Advertising, The
1055 Ridgecrest Dr.
Goodlettsville, TN 37072
ph: 615-859-5236 or 800-826-4929
fax: 615-859-5238
mbca@gono.com
http://www.gono.com/vir-mus/museum.htm
The largest collection of soda and beer cans in the world (over, 50,000); buy, sell, trade beer & soda advertising items.

Squirt

Collectors

Jan Vonburg
3749 E. Gill Dr.
Denver, CO 80209-3510
ph: 303-777-9388
Wants Squirt picnic coolers, soda machines, clocks, decals, 6 pack holders, etc.

Vernors Ginger Ale

Experts

Keith Wunderlich
P.O. Box 300572
Waterford, MI 48330
ph: 248-682-6134
Wants to buy Vernors Ginger Ale advertising and memorabilia.

Michael Novak
10445 Fike Rd.
Blissfield, MI 49228
mnovak@scnc.blissfield.k12.mi.us
Avid collector of Vernors Ginger Ale advertising and memorabilia; also Vernors historian and will help identify and date Vernors items.

Whistle Soda

Collectors

Andy Fulks
P.O. Box 92
Whitestown, IN 46075
ph: 765-482-1861 or 317-769-1861
fax: 765-482-1848
ajf5577@aol.com
http://fcsutler.com/fcwanted.html
Serious collector of Whistle Soda and Cleo Cola advertising items: signs, calendars, die cuts, etc.

SOLDIERS

Toy

(see also MINIATURES, Military; TOYS; TOYS, Playsets)

Appraisers

Tara Ana Finley
Anubis Appraisers & Estate Services, Inc.
1042 Sorolla Ave.
Miami, FL 33134-3560
ph: 305-446-1820 or 786-486-8042
fax: 305-648-1939
tara.finley@worldnet.att.net
Expert in appraising toy soldiers; also appraises dolls and toys.

Barry Carter
Knightstown Antiques Mall
136 W. Carey St.
Knightstown, IN 46148-1111
ph: 765-345-5665
bcarter@spitfire.net
Buys, sells, appraises and specializes in toy soldiers and military miniatures; consultant for AntiqueWeek; promoter of the Indiana Toy Soldier Show (last Sunday in March.)

Auction Services

Henry Kurtz
Henry Kurtz Ltd.
163 Amsterdam Ave., Ste. 136
New York, NY 10023
ph: 212-642-5904
fax: 212-874-6018
Specializes in the sale of jewelry, paintings, prints, silver, coins,

stamps, toys (especially lead soldiers), and movie memorabilia.

Glenn Butler
Wallis & Wallis
West St. Auction Galleries
Lewes, East Sussex BN7 2NJ U.K.
ph: 01273-480208
fax: 01273-476562
wallisandwallis@mcmail.com
http://www.wallisandwallis.co.uk
Britain's specialist auctioneers of diecast & tin plate toys & models including model soldiers.

Bryan Goodall
Vectis Auctions Ltd.
Fleck Way
Thornaby
Stockton on Tees, TS17 9JZ U.K.
enquiries@vectis.co.uk
http://www.vectis.co.uk
A U.K. firm with offices in the US specializing in the auction sale of vintage toys and toy soldiers.

Clubs/Associations

Arley Pett, Past-Pres.
North East Toy Soldier Society
Newsletter: North East Toy Soldier Society Newsletter
12 Beach Rd.
Gloucester, MA 09130-3214
ph: 978-283-2612
fax: 978-283-2612
apett92117@aol.com
Monthly meetings usually in the Boston area; sponsors two toy soldier sales/shows in Boston area each year.

Charlie Duval
Toy Soldier Collectors of America
Newsletter: Communique
P.O. Box 179
New Ellenton, SC 29809
ph: 803-652-7932
toysoldiercollectorsamerica@yahoo.com
http://www.toysoldiercollectors.homestead.com/tsca.html
An information center for all toy soldier collectors worldwide.

Frank Burns
South Florida Toy Soldiers Club, Inc.
715 S.W. 15 St.
Boynton Beach, FL 33426
ph: 561-732-7295
Majortoyman@webtv.net
http://community.gopbi.com/ToySoldiers
Club host annual show first Sunday in February in West Palm Beach, FL.

William Britain Collectors Club
Magazine: Standard, The
P.O. Box 32
Workingham, RG40 4XZ U.K.
ph: 01189 737080
fax: 01189 733947
admin@wbritaincollectorsclub.com
http://www.wbritaincollectorsclub.com
A manufacturer-sponsored club for people interested in the hand painted,

white metal toy soldiers made by William Britain.

Collectors

Bill Lango
P.O. Box 4809
North Bergen, NJ 07047-4809
ph: 973-831-8900
fax: 973-831-8912
bill@vintagecastings.com
http://www.vintagecastings.com
Interested in Barclay vehicles, animals and soldiers from original and new molds.

Peter & Kathy Paul
1673A Town Point Rd.
Cambridge, MD 21613-3579
ph: 410-476-4627
Wants old toy soldiers; lead, iron, composition, rubber; any quantity.

David W. Francis
148 King St.
Wadsworth, OH 44281
ph: 330-335-3717
fax: 330-335-3617
fphadv@bright.net
Wants to buy toy soldiers of all types.

Dealers

John A. Rollins
Toy Soldiers
633 Route 6 Mm 98
South Wellfleet, MA 02663
ph: 508-349-1715

Helene Guarnaccia
52 Coach Lane
Fairfield, CT 06430
ph: 203-374-6034
greatstufftwo@aol.com
Specializes in Britains toy lead soldiers; sells related books.

Arley Pett
Arley L. Pett Antiques
12 Beach Rd.
Gloucester, MA 09130-3214
ph: 978-283-2612
fax: 978-283-2612
apett92117@aol.com
Collects, buys, sells and appraises toy soldiers and civilians, lead farm, zoo, circus, hunt, railroad figures, military vehicles and related items such as miniature gardens; manages two toy shows per year for NETSS.

Jamie & Jenny Delson
Toy Soldier Company, The
100 Riverside Dr.
New York, NY 10024
ph: 201-792-6665
fax: 201-792-2626
info@toysoldierco.com
http://www.toysoldierco.com
Large mail order resource for toy soldiers; stocks unpainted and painted plastic figures in 54mm, 60mm, and 70mm scales, unpainted plastic figures in HO scale, and painted metal figures in 54mm scale; send $6 for catalog of stock.

Chris Keller
Keller Enterprises
219 Ridge Rd.
Carlisle, PA 17013-9275
ph: 717-258-3573 or 717-245-1781
doktorkec@aol.com
Toy soldier collector, dealer and expert; buying and selling antique W. Britains, German composition, and Dimestore collections; free appraisals; 18 years experience.

Ron Ruddell
London Bridge Collector's Toys, Ltd.
401 Chestnut St.
Emmaus, PA 18049-2401
ph: 610-967-6887
fax: 610-967-6887
lbt@londonbridgetoys.com
http://www.londonbridgetoys.com

Jim Hillestad
Toy Soldier, The
RR 1, Box 379
Cresco, PA 18326
ph: 570-629-7227
fax: 570-629-9205
jimhill@ptd.net
http://www.The-Toy-Soldier.com
Deals in all major toy soldier makers, furniture-quality display cases, Michael Sutty bone china military sculptures, regimental drums, bugles and more; also has a 3,000 sq. ft. museum of figures and dioramas.

Michael & Norene Rosso
Stockade Miniatures, Inc.
4 North 6th St.
Stroudsburg, PA 18360
ph: 570-424-8507
fax: 570-424-8503
mrosso@ptd.net
http://www.stockade-miniatures.com
Deals in quality new and old toy soldiers from around the world; want lists accepted for old items.

Allen W. Smith
102 N. Cherry St.
Falls Church, VA 22046-3518
ph: 703-237-2164
Wants dimestore toy soldiers: lead, rubber, composition, paper; Auburn, Marx, Manoil, Barclay, Built-Rite, etc.; any number.

Stone Castle Imports
804 N. Third St.
P.O. Box 141
Bardstown, KY 40004
ph: 502-897-0207
fax: 502-897-6415
castle@toysoldiers.cc
http://www.toysoldiers.cc
Carries a wide variety of toy soldiers and playsets.

Joseph Saine
Joseph Saine Toy Soldiers
P.O. Box 50506
Toledo, OH 43624
ph: 419-691-0008
josaine@att.net
http://home.att.net/~nostalgiarama
Buys and sells antique and modern toy

soldiers, miniature figures, playsets: lead, composition, and plastic toy soldiers; any soldier or figure; issues periodic listings.

Barry Carter
Knightstown Antiques Mall
136 W. Carey St.
Knightstown, IN 46148-1111
ph: 765-345-5665
bcarter@spitfire.net
Buys, sells, appraises and specializes in toy soldiers and military miniatures; consultant for AntiqueWeek; promoter of the Indiana Toy Soldier Show (last Sunday in March.)

Rick Berry
Michigan Toy Soldier & Figure Co.
1406 E. 11 Mile Rd.
Royal Oak, MI 48067
ph: 248-586-1022
fax: 248-398-4436
michigantoysoldier@bigfoot.com
http://www.michtoy.com
Buys and sells new and old toy soldiers of all types; Web site contains one of the most comprehensive listings of information on the hobby available.

David S. Bennett
Bennett Antiques
15800 26th Ave. N.
Minneapolis, MN 55447-1940
Wants American dimestore toy soldiers made by Barclay, Manoil, Gray Ives, Jones, etc.

James Finn
James Finn Miniatures
4950 Lindell Blvd.
Saint Louis, MO 63108
ph: 314-454-0826
fax: 314-647-9388
fineas@prodigy.net
http://www.jamesfinnminiatures.theshoppe.com
Sells new and old German style toy soldiers, zinnfiguren (tin flats), semirounds and Heyde figures; professional painting service available.

Pam & Bill Brunton
Brunton's Barracks
1019 Country Club Dr.
Prescott, AZ 86303-3401
ph: 928-717-1698
fax: 928-717-1698
BruntonsBrcks@cableone.net
Dealer, appraiser of composition and plastic toy soldiers.

Paul Kemkemian
Ani Toy Soldiers
1125 S. Central Ave.
Glendale, CA 91204
ph: 818-242-6700
fax: 818-244-0097
info@anitoysoldiers.com
http://www.anitoysoldiers.com
Sells handmade and handpainted lead military soldiers.

Craig Mclain
Old Toy Soldier Home, The
977 S. Santa Fe, Ste. #11
Vista, CA 92083
ph: 760-758-5481
fax: 760-758-5481
info@oldtoysoldierhome.com
http://www.oldtoysoldierhome.com
A retail store dedicated to the toy soldier hobby; has over 15,000 figures on view covering all areas of history from ancient to modern times: Britain's and Mignot both new and old, Ducal, Imperial King & Country.

Bob Fisher
Old Toy Soldier Home, The
977 S. Santa Fe #11
Vista, CA 92083-6911
ph: 760-758-5481
fax: 760-758-5481
info@oldtoysoldierhome.com
http://oldtoysoldierhome.com
Buys and sells toy soldiers: Britains, Mignot (old and new), dime store, composition, new makers, King & Country, Ducal, AQM, Trophy, Imperial; has over 20,000 figures on display.

Mark Avery
Toy Soldier
Avalon Court, Star Rd.
Partridge Green, West Sussex RH13 8RY U.K.
ph: +44 (0) 1403 711511 or 513-353-4052 (in US)
fax: +44 (0) 1403 711521
mark@ashdown.co.uk
http://www.toy-soldier.com
Toy soldier dealer and expert; specializes in antique and modern toy soldiers and 54mm collectors figures; also sells books and special edition figurines for the discerning collector.

Experts

Chris Keller
Keller Enterprises
219 Ridge Rd.
Carlisle, PA 17013-9275
ph: 717-258-3573 or 717-245-1781
doktorkec@aol.com
Toy soldier collector, dealer and expert; buying and selling antique W. Britains, German composition, and Dimestore collections; free appraisals; 18 years experience.

K. Warren Mitchell
1008 Forward Pass
Pataskala, OH 43062-7505
ph: 740-927-1661
fax: 740-927-3183
Buys, sells, appraises and specializes in all kinds of old toy soldiers especially Britains, "dimestore," Mignot, Heyde (no plastic toys, please.) Author of articles on toy soldiers.

Internet Resources

Bill Hocker
Toy Soldier Resources
1605 Arch St.
Berkeley, CA 94709
ph: 510-841-4458
fax: 510-644-3433
bill@wmhocker.org
http://www.wmhocker.com
Manufacturer of collectible metal toy soldiers; Web site has many resources for the toy soldier collector.

Man./Prod./Dist.

Joseph DiVincenzo
Nickolson Miniatures
17877 St. Clair Ave.
Cleveland, OH 44110
ph: 216-531-7334
nickolson@worldnet.att.net
http://www.nickolson-toy-soldiers.com
Manufactures traditional high gloss toy soldiers depicting the British Empire, the Indian Army under British rule, WWII American and German paratroopers.

Bill Hocker
Wm Hocker Toy Soldiers
1605 Arch St.
Berkeley, CA 94709
ph: 510-841-4458
fax: 510-644-3433
bill@wmhocker.org
http://www.wmhocker.com
Manufacturer of collectible metal toy soldiers; Web site has many resources for the toy soldier collector.

Judiann & Bob O'Connell
Northcoast Miniatures
311 Biyle Dr.
Eureka, CA 95503
ph: 707-443-8915
oconnell@humboldt1.com
http://www.54mmtoysoldier.com/info
Manufactures metal 54mm scale cannons, wagons, and figures: Napoleonic era, Civil War era, Victorian Village, Early Americana, Nativity; fine line of wagons available.

Periodicals

Bill Lango
Magazine: Toy Soldier Review
P.O. Box 4809
North Bergen, NJ 07047-4809
ph: 973-831-8900
fax: 973-831-8912
bill@vintagecastings.com
http://www.vintagecastings.com
A worldwide quarterly magazine for the toy soldier enthusiast.

Magazine: Toy Soldiers & Collectibles
P.O. Box 301
Libertytown, MD 21762-0301
ph: 301-898-7686
ilewis4566@aol.com
http://www.angelfire.com/biz/
ToySoldierMag
Quarterly magazine covers Marx, Imex, Accurate, A Call to Arms, CTS,

Timpo, Hat Industries, and other brands of plastic toy soldiers.

Stacie Berger
Antique Trader Publications, Inc.
Magazine: Military Trader
P.O. Box 1050
Dubuque, IA 52004-1050
ph: 800-334-7165 or 800-482-4155
fax: 800-531-0880
stacie.berger@fwpubs.com
http://www.militarytrader.com
Monthly publication focusing on military collectibles: articles, collecting, interviews with dealers, military toy column, book reviews, collectibles for sale, espionage.

Jo & Steve Sommers
OTSN, Inc.
Magazine: Old Toy Soldier
209 North Lombard
Oak Park, IL 60302
ph: 708-383-6525
fax: 708-383-2182
dimestores@aol.com
http://www.oldtoysoldier.com
A quarterly publication published since 1976; articles cover the full range of toy soldier topics and makers; packed with articles on Britains, American Dimestore, Lineol, Elastolin; book reviews, shows, ads; some civilian lines, too.

Paul Stadinger
STAD's
Magazine: Plastic Warrior
65 Walton Court
Woking, Surrey GU21 5EE U.K.
ph: (0) 1483 722778
fax: (0) 1483 772723
editor@plasticwarrior.freeserve.co.uk
http://www.plasticwarrior.com
A British bi-monthly focusing on leading European plastic figures, firms (Britains, Timpo, etc.), reviews, Q&A, letters, news, ads, etc.

Mark Avery
Ashdown Publishing
Magazine: Toy Soldier & Model Figure
    Magazine
Avalon Court, Star Rd.
Partridge Green, West Sussex RH13
8RY U.K.
ph: +44 (0) 1403 711511 or 513-353-
    4052 (in US)
fax: +44 (0) 1403 711521
mark@ashdown.co.uk
http://www.toy-soldier.com
An English full color magazine and Web site devoted to collectors of antique and modern toy soldiers and 54mm collectors figures; also sells books and special edition figurines for the discerning collector.

SOUTH PACIFIC

(see ART, Oceanic; POLYNESIAN COLLECTIBLES)

SOUVENIR & COMMEMORATIVE ITEMS

(see also CERAMICS, Souvenir & Commemorative; DISNEY COLLECTIBLES, Disneyland Souvenirs; GLASS, Souvenir & Commemorative; HISTORICAL AMERICANA; MILITARIA, Silk Embroideries; ROYALTY COLLECTIBLES; SPOONS, Souvenir; STATE RELATED MEMORABILIA)

Collectors

Chloe Ross
7553 Norton Ave. Apt. 4
Los Angeles, CA 90046-5500
ph: 213-874-3044
trstrap@aol.com
Wants tablecloths with maps, graphics or states, amusement parks, locations; may be worn and some stains OK; no AK or CA; especially wants East Coast, Midwest, New England or FL; buy or trade.

David Ringering
Ray King Antiques
1395 59th Ave. SE
Salem, OR 97301
ph: 503-364-0464
ar1480@aol.com
Wants to buy Rowland & Marsellus rolled edge, 10" souvenir/historical plates; also any other c. 1890-1935 pictorial souvenirs with scenes of cities, towns, etc.; also wants German metal tumblers with American/ Canadian scenes.

Dealers

Gary Leveille
Antique Souvenir China
5 Brook Lane
Great Barrington, MA 01230
ph: 413-528-5490
garyleve@aol.com
http://www.berkshirecreative.com
Wants to purchase antique souvenirs: souvenir china, postcards.

Buildings

Clubs/Associations

Dixie Trainer
Souvenir Building Collectors Society
Newsletter: Souvenir Building Collector
P.O. Box 70
Nellysford, VA 22958-0070
ph: 804-361-1739
fax: 804-361-9151
souvenirbu@aol.com
http://www.SBCollectors.org
Aims to educate and entertain collectors of three-dimensional souvenir buildings and monuments worldwide; annual convention; newsletter published three times a year; free newsletter sample on request.

Collectors

Barry D. Hoffman
7 Stonemeadow
Westwood, MA 02090
ph: 617-584-5555 or 781-326-3333
fax: 617-266-6666
pakistan@tiac.net
Wants to buy metal souvenir buildings, all types: paperweight, bank, inkwells, etc.; wants anything that looks like a recognizable building model; free appraisals.

Bill Trainer
P.O. Box 70
Nellysford, VA 22958-0070
ph: 804-361-1739
billdix@aol.com
Buys, sells, trades metal souvenir buildings and banks from around the world; free telephone appraisals.

Dave Forman
215 - 10th Ave. North
Saint Petersburg, FL 33701
forvid@aol.com
Wants to buy potmetal souvenir building replicas of banks, S&Ps, etc. of famous buildings, landmarks, monuments, etc.

Mark Dittenbir
641 S. Shore Dr.
Kalamazoo, MI 49002
ph: 616-327-4227
Wants to buy metal replicas of landmark skyscrapers, cathedrals, bank buildings, etc. such as Chrysler Building, Capitol Records Building.

Fred Schwartz
135 RR 1
Hull, IL 62343
ph: 217-432-5796 or 217-432-5502
Wants to buy small metal buildings, can be banks or paperweights or anything else.

Margarete Majua
Ace Architects
332 2nd St.
Oakland, CA 94607
ph: 510-286-2290 or 925-283-3218
fax: 510-452-1175
ace@aceland.com
Wants to buy souvenir buildings; found in the form of banks, souvenirs, paperweights, inkwells, salt & pepper shakers, World's Fair memorabilia, pencil sharpeners, etc.

Dealers

Barbara Strand
Dullsville
143 E. 13th St.
New York, NY 10003
ph: 212-505-2505
Specializes in souvenir buildings.

Bob Kneisel
1278 Mare Vista Ave.
Pasadena, CA 91104-2951
ph: 626-797-2707
Buys and sells miniature buildings;

souvenir buildings, banks, monuments, statues; metal and other materials.

Man./Prod./Dist.

Dixie Trainer
Souvenir Building Network
P.O. Box 70
Nellysford, VA 22958-0070
ph: 804-361-1739 or 888-650-7999
fax: 804-361-9151
littlemonuments@aol.com
http://www.souvenirbuildings.com
Sells US and foreign souvenir buildings by mail and Web site; free catalog on request; produces custom replicas of buildings of buildings for real estate developers, banks and museums.

Anthony Tremblay
Microcosms
809 N. Rose St.
Burbank, CA 91505
ph: 818-558-7952
This company casts high-quality and affordable mini replicas of a number of buildings, including modern, classical and ancient structures.

Pillows

Collectors

J.J. Murphy
310 Vista Rd.
Madison, WI 53726
ph: 608-238-3378
jjmurphy@wisc.edu
Wants lithograph pillow tops: turn-of-the-century color lithographs on cloth; approximately 22 inches square; all subjects; condition important.

Dealers

Susan & Michelle Horowitz
Quilted Corner, The
124 Fourth Ave.
New York, NY 10003-4903
ph: 212-505-6568
michelle@quiltedcorner.com
http://www.quiltedcorner.com
Carries a wide assortment of vintage linens, tablecloths, napkins, tea towels, souvenir pillows, drapes and textiles.

Summer Resort Items

Collectors

David W. Francis
148 King St.
Wadsworth, OH 44281
ph: 330-335-3717
fax: 330-335-3617
fphadv@bright.net
Wants 1880-1930 summer resort souvenirs: Atlantic City, Coney Island, Cedar Point, etc. - postcards, booklets, pennants, tickets, etc.

Universal Theatres

Collectors

Edwin Snyder
P.O. Box 156
Lancaster, KY 40444-0156
ph: 606-792-4816
Wants to buy penny toys, pocket mirrors, dexterity games, compasses, small portrait plaques, mini books, etc. given away to children attending movies in the 1920s and 1930s; all toys marked "Souvenir of Universal Theatres - Chicago."

Yosemite

Collectors

Neal Austinson
P.O. Box 1691
Windsor, CA 95492-1691
ph: 707-838-9015
Wants old Yosemite items: photographs, souvenirs, etc.

SOVIET

(see RUSSIAN ITEMS)

SPACE COLLECTIBLES

(see also ASTRONOMICAL ITEMS; AUTOGRAPHS, Astronaut; BOOKS, Reference [Space Collectibles]; CHARACTER COLLECTIBLES; PREMIUMS; ROCKETS; SCIENCE FICTION; TELEVISION SHOWS & MEMORABILIA; TOYS, Space & Robot)

Auction Services

Superior Galleries
9478 West Olympic Blvd.
Beverly Hills, CA 90212-4246
ph: 310-203-9855 or 800-421-0754
fax: 310-203-0496
superior@superiorgalleries.com
http://www.superiorgalleries.com
Has been a retail and auction source for dealers and collectors for over 70 years; specializes in stamps, coins, sports memorabilia and other collectibles.

Clubs/Associations

David Brandt
National Space Society
Magazine: Ad Astra
600 Pennsylvania Ave. SE, Ste. 201
Washington, DC 20003-4316
ph: 202-543-1900 or 800-376-ORBIT
fax: 202-546-4189
nsshq@nss.org
http://www.nss.org
International organization promoting space development; 80 local and international chapters; holds annual Space Development Conference and regional conferences.

Jack Moore, Mktng.
International Space Hall of Fame
The Space Center
P.O. Box 533
Alamogordo, NM 88310
ph: 505-437-2840
fax: 505-434-2245
spacepr@zianet.com
http://www.spacefame.org

Collectors

Michael Mitchell
RR 1, Box 4440
Kents Hill, ME 04349
ph: 207-897-6855
Collects space related memorabilia: newspapers headlining space missions, photographs, books; non-flown items.

Harvey & Sandy Dolin
Harvey Dolin & Co.
111 Fulton St., Mezzanine Level
New York, NY 100386
ph: 212-267-0216
Wants to buy items relating to the space programs.

Larry McLaughlin
17 Seventh Ave.
Smithtown, NY 11787-4508
ph: 631-265-9224
larrymak@erols.com
Wants space items from Apollo, Mercury, or Gemini; also wants NASA logos.

Dealers

Gregg Linebaugh
SpaceSource, The
P.O. Box 604
Glenn Dale, MD 20769
ph: 301-871-6367
space@thespacesource.com
http://www.thespacesource.com
Buys and sells artifacts that have flown in space and to the moon; actual space craft hardware, space suits, videos, books, patches, medallions, flags, and other unusual items; large selection of astronaut autographed photos available.

Ron Kramer
Astro-Postal History
3105 Chamber Dr.
Raleigh, NC 28190-0439
ph: 704-291-9774 or 866-RJI-STAMP
fax: 704-296-9097
info@astropostal.com
http://www.astropostal.com
Deals in the history of space on covers, stamps, autographs, lithos, photos, letters, documents, postcards, memorabilia, trading cards, aerospace balloons, NASA issues medallions containing metal from vehicles flown to the moon, etc.

Russsell Herron
Galactic Voyager
12335 Kingsride #124
Houston, TX 77024-4116
ph: 713-467-0264
fax: 713-973-0456
contact@galacticvoyager.com
http://www.galacticvoyager.com
Historic & collectible items from the history of air & space including official NASA mission patches & pins, rare and hard-to-find scale models of historic spacecraft and aircraft, high quality diecast models, photos, commemorative, books.

Premiere Space Editions
P.O. Box 580056
Houston, TX 77258
ph: 281-486-4534
fax: 281-280-0774
info@premierespace.com
http://www.premierespace.com
Specializes in authenticated high-quality Apollo astronaut-autographed photographs and related Apollo-era memorabilia.

Jeff Mark
JMARK
P.O. Box 5178
Santa Monica, CA 90409-5178
ph: 800-644-8537 or 310-396-9767
fax: 310-396-2666
AirForce1944@hotmail.com
Wants any astronaut, NASA, Apollo, Shuttle, space program items: uniforms, gear, moon rocks, memorabilia, autographs, rocket, shuttle, capsule pieces, paperwork, insignia, photographs; Apollo, Mercury, Gemini, Sputnik; American or Russian.

Experts

Stuart Schneider
P.O. Box 64
Teaneck, NJ 07666-0064
ph: 201-599-4250
fax: 201-599-4251
Stuart@wordcraft.net
http://www.wordcraft.net
Items flown in space, toys, toy ray guns, Russian items, Sputnik, Welcome Back astronaut buttons, coin banks, artwork, etc.; author of "Collecting the Space Race" (1993).

Russ Still
P.O. Box 832
Roswell, GA 30077
write-stuff@earthlink.net
http://www.russellstill.com
Author of "Relics of the Space Race," which includes information on space related memorabilia: autographs (including autopen guide for every pre-Shuttle astronaut), philatelics, patches, badges and passes, flown currency, medallions, etc.

Tom Tumbusch
Tomart Publications
3300 Encrete Lane
Dayton, OH 45439-1944
ph: 937-294-2250
fax: 937-294-1024
office@tomart.com
http://www.tomart.com
Aliens, Flash Gordon, Empire Strikes Back, Star Wars, Star Trek, Captain Video; action figures, comic books, and all related memorabilia; author of "Space Adventure Collectibles;" only inquiries accompanied by a SASE will be answered.

Leslie Singer
7 Shackleford Plaza, Ste. C
Little Rock, AR 72211
ph: 501-221-2885
zenmotel@aol.com
Specializes in NASA artifacts and autographs: authentic items such as mission and contractor equipment, flown items, documents, early autographs.

Internet Resources

Astronaut Connection, The
info@nauts.com
http://www.nauts.com
Web site covering the history of space exploration, vehicles, astronaut chats, men and women astronauts, merchandise and memorabilia, astronaut appearances.

Robert Pearlman
collectSPACE.com
4350 N. Fairfax dr.
Arlington, VA 22203
robert@collectspace.com
http://www.collectspace.com
Web site dedicated to collecting space memorabilia; provides resources for beginner and advanced collectors including: guides, an astronaut appearance calendar, message boards, an international collector's directory, links to other sites.

Museums/Libraries

Jim Johnson
U.S. Space & Rocket Center
One Tranquility Base
Huntsville, AL 35805-3371
ph: 256-837-3400
http://www.spacecamp.com/museum
The public Visitor Center of the Marshall Space Flight Center.

International Space Hall of Fame, The
  Space Center
Magazine: SpaceLog
P.O. Box 533
Alamogordo, NM 88310-0533
ph: 505-437-2840 or 800-545-4021
fax: 505-437-7722
space@zianet.com
http://www.zianet.com/space
The ISHF is a four-story museum which chronicles the history of man's exploration of space; from earliest rockets to space shuttle.

SPAM

(see ADVERTISING COLLECTIBLES, Hormel)

SPECTACLES

(see EYE RELATED ITEMS, Eyeglasses; OPTICAL ITEMS)

SPIES

(see CHARACTER COLLECTIBLES, Spy Memorabilia; SPY EQUIPMENT; TELEVISION SHOWS & MEMORABILIA, Private Eye)

SPINNING WHEELS

Dealers

Holloway
Apple Hollow Fiber Arts
P.O. Box 242
Evansville, WI 53536
ph: 608-882-0668
fax: 608-882-0669
contact@applehollow.com
http://www.applehollow.com.
Always buying and selling used and antique spinning wheels and looms.

Museums/Libraries

American Textile History Museum
491 Dutton St.
Lowell, MA 01854-4221
ph: 978-441-0400
fax: 978-441-1412
espear@athm.org
http://www.athm.org
Outstanding collection of textiles and textile making machinery and equipment; tools, machines, prints, photographs, business records, industry periodicals, textiles, swatches, sample books, trade catalogs, etc.

Periodicals

Florence Feldman-Wood
Newsletter: Spinning Wheel Sleuth, The
P.O. Box 422
Andover, MA 01810-0008
ph: 978-475-8790
ffw@netway.com
http://www.spwhsl.com
A quarterly newsletter exploring all aspects of spinning wheels; feature articles include types of wheels, American and European, histories of wheels, biographies of wheel makers, and much more; for hand spinners, collectors, and museums.

Suppliers

Barbara Muret
Fleece & Unicorn
Seventh Avenue Center
123 West 7th Ave.
Stillwater, OK 74074-4665
ph: 405-377-7105
Designer of yarn and fibers;

international services, exceptional selections of doll hair and craft yarns.

Miniature

Collectors

Lanelle Hodnett
2965 Ave. Z
Brooklyn, NY 11235-1658
ph: 718-891-3489
Wants to buy miniature spinning wheels and motifs.

SPIRITUALISM

(see UFOs & UNEXPLAINED PHENOMENA)

SPOON WARMERS

Dealers

Vivian & James Karsnitz
1428 Jerry Lane
Manheim, PA 17545-9353
ph: 717-665-4202
Buying and selling spoon warmers.

SPOONS

(see also KITCHEN COLLECTIBLES; SILVER; SOUVENIR & COMMEMORATIVE ITEMS; SPOON WARMERS)

Clubs/Associations

Terry & Mary Haines
Silver Spoon Club of Great Britain, The
Journal: Finial, The
Glenleigh Park
Sticker
St. Austell, Cornwall PL26 7JD U.K.
ph: 01726-65269
fax: 01726-65269
enquiries@silver-spoon.com
http://www.silver-spoon.com
International postal club for experienced or beginner collectors of antique and other fine silver spoons and associated silver cutlery; worldwide membership; "The Finial" contains specialist articles and member's news and views; auctions.

Souvenir

(see also SOUVENIR & COMMEMORATIVE ITEMS)

Auction Services

Walter Kraus, Jr.
Kraus Antiques, Ltd.
P.O. Box 12538
Fort Pierce, FL 34979
ph: 561-465-0770
fax: 561-468-9020
kraus@metrolink.net
http://www.antiqnet.com/kraus
Specializes in sterling silver flatware; conducts periodic auctions of obsolete and discontinued patterns; also conducts the largest souvenir spoon auction in the country.

Chris McGlothlin
780 Rock Springs Rd.
Kingsport, TN 37664
ph: 423-239-6776
McSpoons@aol.com
http://hometown.aol.com/mcspoons/ home.html

Clubs/Associations

Norma Bowen
Northeastern Spoon Collectors Guild
Newsletter: Cauldron, The
P.O. Box 12072
Albany, NY 12212
bownor@aol.com
http://www.souvenirspoons.com/nscg
NSCG is dedicated to the perpetuation of the spoon collecting hobby.

Robert M. Wilhelm, Editor
American Spoon Collectors
Newsletter: Spooners Forum
P.O. Box 243
Rhinecliff, NY 12574
ph: 845-876-0303
fax: 845-876-2037
campania@one.net
http://www.campanian.org/ americanspoon.html

Trudy Geer
Spoon Club of Southern California
6032 Triangle Dr.
City of Commerce, CA 90040
tgantiques@aol.com
http://www.souvenirspoons.com/scsc/ index.html

Bob Corson
Washington State Spoon Collectors
1992 S. Elger Bay Rd., Box 151
Stanwood, WA 98292

Collectors

Erwin & Dorothy Goldman
8200 Blvd. East
North Bergen, NJ 07047-6039
ph: 201-662-1342
fax: 201-662-1342
erthy@aol.com

Chris McGlothlin
780 Rock Springs Rd.
Kingsport, TN 37664
ph: 423-239-6776
McSpoons@aol.com
http://hometown.aol.com/mcspoons/ home.html

John W. Coons
9757 S. Isabel Ct.
Littleton, CO 80126-4717
ph: 303-791-6496
coons-jw@msn.com
Wants souvenir spoons: enamel bowls, blacks, mining, hotels, libraries, skylines, etc.

Dealers

Spoon Search
spoons@spoonsearch.com

Gene L. Bagwell
Bagwell Antiques
5607 Concord Dr.
Jackson, MS 39211-4239
ph: 601-956-3508
fax: 601-956-4190
Gbagw28947@aol.com
*Collects, buys and sells quality
sterling silver souvenir spoons,
especially enamel bowls, blacks,
embossed, and engraved.*

T.K. Treadwell
4201 Nagle Rd.
Bryan, TX 77801-3938
ph: 409-846-0209
71222.1571@compuserve.com

Gary Lickver
P.O. Box 1778
San Marcos, CA 92079-1778
ph: 760-744-5686 or 760-803-0927
*Collector/dealer wants to buy sterling
silver souvenir spoons 1890-1930;
especially full bowl enamels, American
and European.*

Beth Jacobson
SpoonTown!
P.O. Box 23158
Seattle, WA 98102
inquiry@spoontown.com
http://www.spoontown.com
*Collector, dealer specializes in
buying, selling, collecting sterling
silver antique American souvenir
spoons.*

Experts

Jon Caron
jon@souvenirspoons.com
http://www.souvenirspoons.com
*Collector, dealer, expert, author of
"American Souvenir Teaspoon
Handbook."*

Bill Boyd
7408 Englewood Lane
Raytown, MO 64133-6913
ph: 816-356-7423
fax: 816-356-7423
*Wants souvenir spoons with
embossed, enameled or engraved
handles and bowls; also World's Fair
subjects, full-figured people, etc.*

Chuck Wasserman
11723 W. 101st
Shawnee Mission, KS 66214
ph: 913-492-5005
*Appraiser and serious collector of
1904 St. Louis World's Fair
memorabilia; specializes in spoons,
ceramics, and glass; especially foreign
exhibit material such as jasperware,
Haviland Limoges, Nippon, and
moriage.*

Wayne Bednersh
Souvenir Spoons Museum
ph: 818-225-7711
fax: 419-735-8201
souvenirspoons@yahoo.com
http://www.geocities.com/
souvenirspoons
*Author of two books about silver
souvenir spoons; also author of many
magazine articles about souvenir
spoons; buys, sells, trades, appraises
souvenir spoons.*

Internet Resources

Jon Caron
American Souvenir Spoons
jon@souvenirspoons.com
http://www.souvenirspoons.com
*Focus is on antique sterling silver
souvenir spoons only; stories, guides,
for sale, makers' marks, state seals
and links, glossary of terms, selling
your spoon collection, collecting tips,
and more.*

Wayne Bednersh
Souvenir Spoons Museum
ph: 818-225-7711
fax: 419-735-8201
souvenirspoons@yahoo.com
http://www.geocities.com/
souvenirspoons
*An eclectic mix of hundreds of unusual
silver spoons; also a forum for
collectors, a calendar of upcoming
events, FAQ, myths and misunder-
standings about spoons, links to
spoon clubs, history of souvenir
spoons, etc.*

SPORTING COLLECTIBLES

(see also ANIMAL TROPHIES; ART,
Sporting; ART, Wildlife; CAMPING
EQUIPMENT; DECOYS;
ENDANGERED SPECIES;
FIREARMS; FISHING
COLLECTIBLES; LICENSES, Hunting
& Fishing; MAGAZINES, Sporting;
TARGET SHOOTING MEMORABILIA;
TICKETS; TRAP SHOOTING;
TRAPS)

Appraisers

Kenny Lindsay
TCM Sports Memorabilia
18569 Southampton
Livonia, MI 48152
ph: 248-473-1547
productionline@msn.com
http://www.thecatchersmitt.com
*Specializes in vintage sports
memorabilia, autograph authentications and appraisals; the largest
vintage hockey memorabilia company
in the US; auctioneer, appraiser,
author of "Autograph Discoveries"
investigative newsletter.*

Auction Services

Gerard Giguere
Giguere Auction Co.
P.O. Box 1272
Windham, ME 04062-1272
ph: 207-892-3800 or 207-675-3207
fax: 207-675-3441
info@giguereauction.com
http://www.giguereauction.com
*Conducts sporting auctions: fishing,
hunting, decoys, sporting art,
taxidermy.*

Frank & Frank Sporting Collectibles
422 Lakewood-Farmingdale Rd.
Howell, NJ 07731
ph: 732-938-2988
fax: 732-938-2988
afrank1807rh@cs.com
http://www.frankandfrankdecoys.com
*Auctions, buys and sells decoys,
sporting collectibles, wildlife/sporting
art.*

SoldUSA.com
1418 Industrial Dr., Box 11
Matthews, NC 28105
ph: 704-815-1500
fax: 704-844-6436
support@soldusa.com
http://www.soldusa.com
*Specializes in hunting and fishing
collectibles, especially firearms; does
online appraisals for
www.CollectingChannel.com's Ask the
Appraiser online appraisal service.*

Kurt R. Krueger
Krueger Auctions
P.O. Box 275
Iola, WI 54945-0275
ph: 715-445-3845
fax: 715-445-4100
*Specializing in the mail-bid auction of
hunting, fishing, shooting, and
trapping memorabilia.*

Greg Martin Auctions
298 San Bruno Ave.
San Francisco, CA 94103
ph: 800-509-1988 or 415-522-5700
fax: 415-522-5701
info@rabin.com
http://www.gmartinauctions.com
*Specializes in the auction sale of
sporting arms, historical Americana,
arms & armor.*

Book Sellers

David E. Foley
David E. Foley - Sporting Books
76 Bonny View Rd.
West Hartford, CT 06107
ph: 860-561-0783
*Buys and sells fine sporting books:
angling, hunting, firearms, shooting,
archery, natural history.*

Judith & Jim Bowman
Judith Bowman Books
98 Pound Ridge Rd.
Bedford, NY 10506
ph: 914-234-7543
fax: 914-234-0122
Buys and sells rare and out-of-print

*books and ephemera on angling,
hunting, related natural history, guns,
dogs, old tackle and gun catalogs, etc.*

Dean Dashner
Hunting Rig Books
349 S. Green Bay Rd.
Neenah, WI 54956
ph: 920-725-4350 or 920-725-4421
dashners@athenet.net
http://www.huntingrigbooks.com
*Buys and sells decoys, duck calls,
Ducks Unlimited pin-backs, sporting
books, old sporting magazines.*

Wilderness Adventures
P.O. Box 627
Gallatin Gateway, MT 59730
ph: 800-925-3339 or 406-763-4900
books@wildadv.com
http://www.wildadv.com
*World's largest selection of hunting
and fishing books for the collector and
enthusiast.*

Collectors

Ron Willoughby
2281 Lime Kiln Rd.
North Haverhill, NH 03774
ph: 603-787-2060
fax: 603-787-2060
swillo@together.net
*Wants to buy shotshell boxes, gun
company posters and calendars, glass
target balls and traps, gunpowder
cans, pin-back buttons, and related
items; a very serious buyer; free
appraisals; estate purchases.*

Orville Hamman, Jr.
P.O. Box 421
10 Sprague St.
Naples, NY 14512
ph: 585-374-2431
naplesbigbucks@aol.com
*Wants any New York fish & game law
book, pamphlet, syllabus, guide,
annual reports, etc. issued by the NYS
Conservation Commission, NYS
Conservation Dept., NYS Dept. of
Environmental Conservation with NYS
fish & game laws.*

Bill Bramlett
P.O. Box 12600
Florence, SC 29504-1965
ph: 843-629-1965 or 843-662-0702 x102
BillBramlett@webtv.net
*Wants 1890-1931 firearms-related
advertising items such as calendars,
signs and posters that advertise
firearms, shotgun shells, gunpowders;
also wants Edmund Osthaus and G.
Muss-Arnolt bird dog and duck
hunting art, prints, pictures.*

Tommie Lee Horsley
P.O. Box 728
Jackson, AL 36545-0728
ph: 334-246-5000
leehorsley@mindspring.com
http://www.benleecalls.com
*Wants duck and turkey calls, hunting
magazines and photographs, hunting
books, old hunting and gun company*

advertising, Winchester items, all gun company catalogs.

Lynn "Dr. Duck" Troute
Lynn Troute Decoys
3808 Kingsley Dr.
Springfield, IL 62707-7250
ph: 217-787-3595
fax: 217-726-1801
kstroute@yahoo.com
Wants to buy duck stamps, duck decoys, duck calls, licenses, Illinois deer and turkey harvest pins, Ducks Unlimited buttons, and all hunting and fishing artifacts.

Bob Simmons
40706 E. 144th St.
Richmond, MO 64085
ph: 816-776-2936 or 800-646-2936
fax: 816-470-5016
bob@simmonsauction.com
http://www.simmonsauction.com
Collects all types of sporting goods, fishing tackle and related advertising from Simmons Hardware Co., St. Louis, MO; also items from Winchester-Simmons Hardware Co., Diamond Edge (Shapleigh), and Keen Kutter.

Bill Smith, Sr.
6326 Lakewood Park
San Antonio, TX 78239
ph: 800-982-9507
Wants to buy fishing and hunting items.

Dealers

Mary Ann Hahn
Second Hand Mary Ann's
103 Ocean Point Rd.
Boothbay Harbor, ME 04538
ph: 207-633-2426
fax: 207-633-2586
maryann@gwi.net
Buys and sells old fishing and hunting magazines prior to 1939.

Henry Fleckenstein
P.O. Box 577
Cambridge, MD 21613
ph: 410-221-0076
Appraiser, consultant, agent; buys and sells, sporting collectibles: decoys, rare books, shell boxes, powder tins, ammo advertising, sporting magazines and books, reels, lures, bobbers, game calls, old licenses, knives, fish decoys.

Len Codella
Heritage Sporting Collectibles
2201 S. Carnegie Dr.
Inverness, FL 34450
ph: 352-637-5454
fax: 352-637-5420
len@codella.com
http://www.codella.com
Wants to buy bamboo fly rods, reels, tackle, etc.; since 1969.

Tony Laws
Woods & Water, Inc.
1019 McFarland Blvd.
Northport, AL 35476
ph: 205-333-1214 or 800-383-9020
fax: 205-339-9573
info@woods-n-water.com
http://www.woods-n-water.com
Buys and sells sporting art: paintings, prints, drawings, classic firearms, rods & reels, sporting bronzes, wood carvings, advertising art, catalogs, brochures, books.

Robert Krause
Ravenwood Gallery
38745 Butternut Ridge Rd.
Elyria, OH 44035-8372
ph: 440-458-4929
Wants to buy paintings, prints, etchings, calendars, and posters relating to hunting and fishing, birds, dogs, guns, ammunition and power companies; also duck and crow calls, decoys, sporting books, bamboo fly rods, rods, reels, etc.

Dean Dashner
Hunting Rig Books
349 S. Green Bay Rd.
Neenah, WI 54956
ph: 920-725-4350 or 920-725-4421
dashners@athenet.net
http://www.huntingrigbooks.com
Buys and sells decoys, duck calls, Ducks Unlimited pin-backs, sporting books, old sporting magazines.

Joseph & Donna M. Tonelli
Fish-N-Fowl Antiques
29046 377th Ave.
P.O. Box 459
Lake Andes, SD 57356
ph: 605-337-2301 or 815-664-4580
tonelli47@hotmail.com
http://www.edecoy.com
Collector, dealer of quality hunting and fishing collectibles: duck decoys, fish decoys, vintage tackle and reels, gun advertising, sporting advertising, shotshell boxes, powder tins; author of "Top of the Line Hunting Collectibles."

Experts

Ralf Coykendall
P.O. Box 29
East Dorset, VT 05253-0029
ph: 802-362-5707
Writes a sporting collectibles column for "AntiqueWeek;" will answer questions if accompanied by a SASE; author of "Coykendall's Sporting Collectibles Price Guide" Vol. I, II and III.

Vivian & James Karsnitz
Vivian Karsnitz Antiques
1428 Jerry Lane
Manheim, PA 17545-9353
ph: 717-665-4202
Buys, sells sporting collectibles: decoys, shotshells, 2-pc. shotshell boxes, prints (especially Lynn Bogue Hunt), early sporting magazines, glass

target balls, etc.; authors of "Sporting Collectibles" (Schiffer, 1992.)

Kenny Lindsay
TCM Sports Memorabilia
18569 Southampton
Livonia, MI 48152
ph: 248-473-1547
productionline@msn.com
http://www.thecatchersmitt.com
Specializes in vintage sports memorabilia, autograph authentications and appraisals; the largest vintage hockey memorabilia company in the US; auctioneer, appraiser, author of "Autograph Discoveries" investigative newsletter.

Joseph & Donna M. Tonelli
Fish-N-Fowl Antiques
29046 377th Ave.
P.O. Box 459
Lake Andes, SD 57356
ph: 605-337-2301 or 815-664-4580
tonelli47@hotmail.com
http://www.edecoy.com
Collector, dealer of quality hunting and fishing collectibles: duck decoys, fish decoys, vintage tackle and reels, gun advertising, sporting advertising, shotshell boxes, powder tins; author of "Top of the Line Hunting Collectibles."

Red Johnson
130 4th St.
Santa Rosa, CA 95401
ph: 707-545-6357
warrenjo@pacbell.net
Appraiser of antique telephones, fishing tackle, knives, duck decoys; promoter of Santa Rosa, CA sporting collectibles show.

Periodicals

Ralf Coykendall
Newsletter: Coykendall's Sporting Collectibles Newsletter
P.O. Box 29
East Dorset, VT 05253-0029
ph: 802-362-5707

Stan Van Etten, Pub.
Magazine: Hunting & Fishing Collectibles Magazine
P.O. Box 40
Lawsonville, NC 27022
ph: 336-593-9477
fax: 336-593-8085
HFcollectibles@aol.com
http://www.HFcollectibles.com
Focuses on the artifacts that were created as a part of America's hunting & fishing traditions: decoys, fishing collectibles, game bird calls, old sporting arms and related items, wildlife & sporting art, historic trapping items, licenses.

Stacie Berger
Krause Publications
Magazine: Trapper & Predator Caller, The
700 E. State St.
Iola, WI 54990-0001
ph: 715-445-2214
fax: 715-445-4087
stacie.berger@fwpubs.com
http://www.krause.com
A monthly magazine about hunting, trapping and predator calling, and animal damage control.

Stacie Berger
Krause Publications
Magazine: Turkey & Turkey Hunting
700 E. State St.
Iola, WI 54990-0001
ph: 715-445-2214
fax: 715-445-4087
stacie.berger@fwpubs.com
http://www.krause.com
For serious, technical, year-round, gun and bow turkey hunters; features emphasize success and enjoyment of the sport; some articles on related collectibles.

Archery

Auction Services

Kim Richardson
GunBroker.com
P.O. Box 19137
Atlanta, GA 31126
ph: 770-234-4174
fax: 770-234-4174
admin@gunbroker.com
http://www.gunbroker.com
A premiere firearms auction on the Internet; allows the user to buy and sell guns, gun accessories, air guns, and archery equipment; extensive FFL Holder network assists with the legal transfer of firearms; free to buyers & sellers.

Clubs/Associations

Professional Bowhunters Society
P.O. Box 246
Terrell, NC 28682
ph: 704-664-2534
fax: 704-664-7471
Bowhunters@worldnet.att.net
http://www.bowsite.com/pbs

Collectors

Lowell Hobbs
P.O. Box 226
Lynnville, IN 47619-0226
Wants pre-1970s bows and archery equipment; wood or modern recurves and longbows, all metal bows, books magazines, catalogs, old photos, quivers, arrows, accessories.

Leslie Bolyard
787 Westbrooke Dr.
South Lyon, MI 48178-1665
ph: 248-486-3494
Wants to buy archery hunting memorabilia including wood long bows, wood arrows, leather back quivers, folk art with animal/hunting

theme, rustic furniture, and accessories.

Experts

Joe St. Charles
19807 1st Ave. S
Seattle, WA 98148
ph: 206-878-7391
Bow and arrow expert; curator of P & Y Archery Museum.

Curling

Museums/Libraries

John J. Roche, Curator
American Curling History Museum
555 Dundee Rd.
Northbrook, IL 60062
ph: 847-564-9877
jrochesr@aol.com
Housed in the Chicago Curling Club.

Game Calls

Book Sellers

Dean Dashner
Hunting Rig Books
349 S. Green Bay Rd.
Neenah, WI 54956
ph: 920-725-4350 or 920-725-4421
dashners@athenet.net
http://www.huntingrigbooks.com
Buys and sells decoys, duck calls, Ducks Unlimited pin-backs, sporting books, old sporting magazines.

Clubs/Associations

Jim Fleming
Callmakers & Collectors Association of America
Newsletter: CCAA Newsletter
518 Heather Place
Nashville, TN 37204
ph: 615-292-1463 or 615-595-5810
fax: 615-292-1465
mrprinting@comcast.net
http://www.quackin.com/ccaa
Purpose is to promote interest in and knowledge of the history of callmaking in America; annual meeting, quarterly swap meets, trade, buy, sell.

James C. Fitch
Call & Whistle Collectors Association
Newsletter: Whistle Notes
2839 E. 26th Place
Tulsa, OK 74114-4309
ph: 918-747-3202
jfitch@noria.com
Club for collectors of game calls, antique whistles, bo's'n pipes, flutes, bird calls, advertising whistles, toy whistles, and folk art whistles.

Collectors

Robert Christensen
Duck Call Collectors Homepage
outdoors@mc.net
http://user.mc.net/~outdoors/duckcalls

Jim Fleming
518 Heather Place
Nashville, TN 37204
ph: 615-292-1463 or 615-595-5810
fax: 615-292-1465
mrprinting@comcast.net
Collects duck, turkey and goose calls; mostly antique calls but some contemporary as well; also collects old fishing lures with a special interest in the William Shakespear Company.

Richard Tull
Rick's Antique Duck Calls
6310 Sea Haven Dr.
Hixson, TN 37343

Dealers

Doug Lodermeier
L & M Design
4600 Washburn Ave. South
Minneapolis, MN 55410
ph: 612-922-9674
fax: 612-922-9672
doug@dougandpaul.com
http://www.dougandpaul.com
Duck call collector, dealer, expert; buys, sells, trades game calls; resource for replacement parts.

Experts

Howard Harlan
Heavy Duty Duck Call Company
4920 Franklin Rd.
Nashville, TN 37210-2834
ph: 800-388-2556 or 615-832-0564
fax: 615-244-1553
http://www.quackin.com/HVY-DUTY
Expert and collector wants to collect all types of game calls as well as related historical information; author of "Duck Calls, An Enduring American Folk Art," and "Turkey Calls, An Enduring American Folk Art."

Doug Lodermeier
L & M Design
4600 Washburn Ave. South
Minneapolis, MN 55410
ph: 612-922-9674
fax: 612-922-9672
doug@dougandpaul.com
http://www.dougandpaul.com
Duck call collector, dealer, expert; buys, sells, trades game calls; resource for replacement parts; author and source for "Minnesota Duck Calls - yesterday's and today's folk artists."

Golf Balls

Experts

Kevin McGimpsey
P.O. Box 120
Deeside, CH5 3HE U.K.
ph: 01244 539414
fax: 01244 539414
kevin@golfballcollector.co.uk
http://www.golfballcollector.co.uk
Author of the definitive collector's book on antique and old golf balls.

SPORTS COLLECTIBLES

(see also ART, Sports; AUTO RACING MEMORABILIA; AUTOGRAPHS; CAPS; COLLECTIBLES [MODERN], Sports Related; DOLLS, Bobbing Head; FAN CLUBS; POSTCARDS; SPORTS HISTORY; TICKETS; TRADING CARDS, Non-Sport; TRAPSHOOTING)

Appraisers

Joel Szlosek
Rotman Auction
4 Brussels St.
Worcester, MA 01610
ph: 508-791-6710
fax: 508-797-5398
jszlosek@rotmanauction.com
http://www.rotmanauction.com
Sports collectibles expert and appraiser: sports cards, autographs, memorabilia.

Les Wolff, ISA
P.O. Box 917
Plainview, NY 11803
ph: 516-933-7787
fax: 516-933-7747
lwolff1823@aol.com
http://members.aol.com/lwolff1823
Buys, sells, trades, appraises sports memorabilia; specializes in all types of sports auctions fund raisers; specializing in autographs; appeared on PAX TV's "Treasures in Your Home."

Robert J. Connelly, ASA
Bob & Sallie Connelly Auctions
666 Chenango St.
Binghamton, NY 13901-2015
ph: 607-722-9593 or 607-722-3555
fax: 607-722-1266
connelly@clarityconnect.com
Gives litigation support; appeared on the TV show "Personal FX, The Collectibles Show" for four years; had own radio show for 14 years.

SoldUSA.com
1418 Industrial Dr., Box 11
Matthews, NC 28105
ph: 704-815-1500
fax: 704-844-6436
support@soldusa.com
http://www.soldusa.com
Specializes in hunting and fishing collectibles, especially firearms; also sports collectibles; does online appraisals for www.CollectingChannel.com's Ask the Appraiser online appraisal service.

Mark Jordan
4709 Colleyville Blvd., Ste. 580-245
Colleyville, TX 76034
ph: 817-281-8455
fax: 817-281-3050
markjspts@aol.com
A nationally recognized sports collectibles authentication authority: over 27 years as autograph collector/ dealer; principal authenticator for the National Sports Gallery in Washington, DC; auction house consultant.

Margaret A. Olsen, ASA
Westminster Coin, Jewelry & Sports
P.O. Box 276
Westminster, CO 80036-0276
ph: 303-428-9175
fax: 303-428-1842
marg@mysportsappraiser.com
http://www.4preciousmetals.com
Specializes in the appraisal of sports memorabilia and coins.

Auction Services

Richard Rotman
Rotman Auction
4 Brussels St.
Worcester, MA 01610-2904
ph: 508-791-6710
fax: 508-797-5398
rrotman@rotmanauction.com
http://www.rotmanauction.com
Specializes in the auction sales of sports memorabilia; also comic books, movie posters, trading cards.

Leland's
36 East 22nd St., 7th Floor
New York, NY 10010
ph: 212-254-2555
fax: 212-254-2389
info@lelands.com
http://www.lelands.com
Conducts specialty sports auctions.

B & E Collectibles
950 Broadway
Thornwood, NY 10594
ph: 914-769-1304

Ron Oser
Ron Oser Enterprises
P.O. Box 101
Huntingdon Valley, PA 19006-0101
ph: 215-947-6575
fax: 215-938-7348
Auctioneers of distinctive sports cards and memorabilia: 1880s-1960s baseball cards, early tobacco and gum cards, display advertising pieces, autographed baseballs, written letters, game-used uniforms, balls, gloves, etc.

David Hunt
Hunt Auctions, Inc.
75 E. Uwchlan Ave., Ste. 130
Exton, PA 19341
ph: 610-524-0822
fax: 610-524-0826
info@huntauctions.com
http://www.huntauctions.com
Specializes in auctioning fine vintage sports memorabilia.

Jay's Sports Connection
49 W. Aylesbury Rd.
Timonium, MD 21093
ph: 410-252-7700 or 800-628-2352
jaysport@erols.com
http://www.jaysports.com
Offering sports collectibles since 1976.

Just Encase
49 W. Aylesbury Rd.
Timonium, MD 21093
ph: 410-252-7700 or 800-628-2352
jaysport@erols.com
http://www.jaysports.com

John D. Compton
J.D. Compton Auctioneering
13833 Rockdale Rd.
Clear Spring, MD 21722
ph: 301-582-0727
fax: 301-582-6114
Specializes in the sale of sports collectibles; call toll-free in MD 1-800-499-3344.

Tom Slater
Political Gallery, The
5335 North Takoma Ave.
Indianapolis, IN 46220
ph: 317-257-0863
fax: 317-254-9167

William Mastro
MastroNet, Inc.
1515 W. 22nd, Ste. 125
Oak Brook, IL 60523-8412
ph: 630-472-1200
fax: 630-472-1201
info@mastronet.com
http://www.mastronet.com
Offers Internet, phone and mail auctions of fine sports memorabilia.

Superior Galleries
9478 West Olympic Blvd.
Beverly Hills, CA 90212-4246
ph: 310-203-9855 or 800-421-0754
fax: 310-203-0496
superior@superiorgalleries.com
http://www.superiorgalleries.com
Has been a retail and auction source for dealers and collectors for over 70 years; specializes in stamps, coins, sports memorabilia and other collectibles.

Sports Warehouse Inc.
P.O. Box 388
Wilsonville, OR 97070
ph: 503-263-8801
fax: 503-263-8804
sportswhse@aol.com
http://www.sportswarehouseinc.com
Deals exclusively with game-used uniforms and equipment; main focus is baseball, but also carries basketballs, football, and some paper items.

Trevor Vennett-Smith
T. Vennett-Smith Auctioneers & Valuers
11 Nottingham Rd.
Gotham, Nottingham NG11 OHE U.K.
ph: +44 (0)115 983 0541
fax: +44 (0)115 983 0114
info@vennett-smith.com
http://www.vennett-smith.com
Great Britain's leading professional autograph auction house, specializing in bi-monthly auctions of fine and varied autographs; also postcards, trade cards, ephemera, sporting memorabilia.

Collectors

Donald Wilson
P.O. Box 282
Roosevelt, NJ 08555
ph: 609-443-6081
Collector of sports cards and memorabilia; will buy, sell, trade.

Goodwin Goldfaden
P.O. Box 48677
Bicentennial Station
Los Angeles, CA 90048-0677
ph: 818-986-4914
Buy, sell, trade all sports related items: baseball, football, basketball, boxing, wrestling, billiards, track & field, body building, other sports; books magazines, programs other sports collectibles from 1860 to present.

John Buonaguidi
540 Reeside Ave.
Monterey, CA 93940-1828
ph: 831-375-7345
sportmsm@redshift.com
Wants any sports related item: baseball cards, World Series programs; autographed baseballs and photos, boxing posters, advertising, etc.; especially interested in museum-quality items for soon-to-open sports museum.

Dealers

Paul Longo
Paul Longo Americana
P.O. Box 5510
Gloucester, MA 01930-0007
ph: 978-525-2290
Wants baseball and other sports memorabilia: sports cards, balls, autographs, uniforms, pennants, yearbooks, statues, silks, etc.

Sportsworld
429 Broadway
Everett, MA 02149
ph: 617-387-7220
fax: 617-387-6177
comments@sportsworld-usa.com
http://www.sportsworld-usa.com
New England's largest sports memorabilia shop: baseball, basketball, football, hockey, wrestling.

Ken Thimmel
All American Collectibles
22-08 Route 208
Fair Lawn, NJ 07410
ph: 201-797-2555 or 800-872-8850
fax: 201-797-3357
score@aacteam.com
http://www.allamericancollectibles.com
Dealer, expert specializes in signed sports memorabilia; conducts online auctions of sports memorabilia.

Alan Rosen
Mr. Mint
70 Chestnut Ridge Rd.
Montvale, NJ 07645
ph: 201-307-0700
mrmint@mindspring.com
http://www.mrmint.net
Buys and sells baseball cards and sportscards.

Julie A. Baron
Fameabilia Corporation
42 Monmouth St.
Red Bank, NJ 07701
ph: 732-450-8411
fax: 732-450-8413
julie@fameabilia.com
http://www.fameabilia.com
Specializes in autographs, sports memorabilia, historical documents and letters.

Bob Rothschild
Bob R's
5 Fillmore Dr.
Clarksburg, NJ 08510
ph: 609-259-9338
bobrs@mindspring.com

Steve Milwich
Sign of the Times
105 Gilmore Blvd.
Floral Park, NY 11001
fax: 413-473-2063
steve@signofthetimes.com
http://www.signofthetimes.com
Buys and sells autographs, autographed photos, sports memorabilia, and more.

Brian Drucker
Cardboard Memories
3012 Jericho Trpke.
East Northport, NY 11731
ph: 631-462-1919 or 888-443-1919
fax: 631-462-4220
webmaster@cardboardmemories.com
http://www.cardboardmemories.com
Offers authentic autographed sports memorabilia and display cases; carries UDA, Steiner Sports, Green Diamond, and more.

Les Wolff, ISA
P.O. Box 917
Plainview, NY 11803
ph: 516-933-7787
fax: 516-933-7747
lwolff1823@aol.com
http://members.aol.com/lwolff1823
Buys, sells, trades, appraises sports memorabilia; specializes in all types of sports auctions fund raisers; specializing in autographs; appeared on PAX TV's "Treasures in Your Home."

James Spence III
James Spence Autographs
1604 Village Rd.
Orwigsburg, PA 17961
ph: 570-366-3138 or 888-947-7788
fax: 570-366-3139
autographs@jspence.com
http://www.jspence.com
Specializes in sports autographs;

fourth generation graphophiles; expertise used by law enforcement agencies against forgeries.

Mark F. Emerson
4040 Poste Lane Rd.
Columbus, OH 43221
ph: 614-771-7272 or 614-431-5800
fax: 614-431-4100
mark@max-ermas.com
Appraiser, dealer, collector, wants to buy old golf programs, tickets, badges, pairing sheets, passes, photos, autographs of deceased players.

Stephen Hansrote
Griffin Trading Company
159 Howell St.
Dallas, TX 75207
ph: 214-747-9234
fax: 214-747-0660
griffintc2@aol.com
http://www.griffintradingantiques.com
Buying and selling 19th and 20th century American and European sports equipment, clothing and trophies.

Ken & Mike Adelson
Adelson Sports
13610 N. Scottsdale Rd. #10
Scottsdale, AZ 85254-4037
ph: 480-596-1913
fax: 480-596-1914
adelson@adelsonsports.com
http://www.adelsonsports.com
Wants to buy sports memorabilia: yearbooks, ticket stubs, pennants, baseball, football, hockey, basketball, boxing; all items from all sports.

Jim Galusha
Sports World Collectibles
897 Oak Park Blvd., Ste 272
Pismo Beach, CA 93449
ph: 805-474-7999
sprtswrld@sprtswrld.com
http://www.sprtswrld.com

Gary Spoerle
Milestone Collectibles
P.O. Box 607
Troutdale, OR 97060-0607
ph: 503-695-3413
fax: 503-695-5406
Wants to buy baseball, golf, fishing and other sports memorabilia.

Experts

Rich Davis
Rich Davis Autograph Authentication & Collectible Investments
P.O. Box 563
Kingston, OH 45644
ph: 740-642-2024
prdavis@horizonview.net
http://authenticator.freeservers.com
Specializes in the authentication and appraisal of all types of autographs; expert on sports collectibles, coins & currency, comic books, and stamps; also provides services as a research/grading/appraisal expert.

David N. Berkowitz
Golf's Golden Years
P.O. Box 842
Palatine, IL 60078-0842
ph: 847-934-4108
fax: 847-934-4107
dave@golfsgoldenyears.com
http://www.golfsgoldenyears.com
*Buys, sells, collects, specializes in golf
collectibles; has appraised for over 20
years for collectors, estates, museums.*

Internet Resources

About.com Hobbies
220 East 42nd St.
New York, NY 10017
pr@about-inc.com
http://home.about.com/hobbies
*Online source for information about
action figures, antiques, book
collecting, coin collecting, collectibles,
comic books, costume jewelry, dolls,
mineral collecting, pin collecting,
sports and trading cards, stamps, toy
collecting.*

Brent Gutekunst
Sports Universe
P.O. Box 6289
Newport Beach, CA 92658
ph: 949-567-1234
fax: 949-833-7955
http://www.collectors.com
*Online collector news, buy and sell,
information, auctions, grading &
authentication services.*

Misc. Services

Steve Bass
Sports Collector's Radio Show
527 Third Ave. #294
New York, NY 10016
ph: 212-573-8100
fax: 212-573-8100
sportradio@aol.com
*Talk show on New York's WGBB
(1240 AM); heard Sunday 12-1 PM
and 9-10 PM; explores all aspects of
sports collecting; advice and insights
from well-known collectors & dealers;
cards, autographs - all types of sports
memorabilia.*

James Spence III
PSA/DNA Authentication Service
130 Brookshire Lane
Orwigsburg, PA 17961
ph: 570-943-7788 or 888-947-7788
fax: 570-943-7790
autographs@jspence.com
http://psadna.com
*Authentication service for sports
autographs.*

Museums/Libraries

Sports Museum of New England
Fleet Center
150 Causeway St.
Boston, MA 02114
ph: 617-624-1235
sportsmuseum@fleetcenter.com
http://www.sportsmuseum.org
*Not open to the public but archives
may be researched by appointment.*

Periodicals

Stacie Berger
Krause Publications
Newsmagazine: Sports Collectors Digest
700 E. State St.
Iola, WI 54990-0001
ph: 715-445-2214
fax: 715-445-4087
stacie.berger@fwpubs.com
http://www.krause.com
*A weekly newsmagazine for collectors
of sports memorabilia; everything
from baseball cards to game-worn
uniforms.*

Stacie Berger
Krause Publications
Magazine: Tuff Stuff
700 E. State St.
Iola, WI 54990-0001
ph: 715-445-2214
fax: 715-445-4087
stacie.berger@fwpubs.com
http://www.tuffstuffonline.com
*The complete monthly sports price
guide publication including baseball,
football, basketball, auto racing and
hockey: 95% sports cards, Kenner's
Starting Lineup sports figures, sports
autographs.*

Stacie Berger
Krause Publications
Newsletter: Trade Fax
700 E. State St.
Iola, WI 54990-0001
ph: 715-445-2214
fax: 715-445-4087
stacie.berger@fwpubs.com
http://www.krause.com
*Published each Monday and Thursday
morning; contains breaking hobby
news from shows, manufacturers, and
other sources; $500 per year.*

Hugh Murphy, PR
Beckett Publications, Inc.
Magazine: Beckett Sports Collectibles
Vintage
15850 Dallas Parkway
Dallas, TX 75248
ph: 972-448-9018 or 800-840-3137
hmurphy@beckett.com
http://www.beckett.com
*Focuses on sports autographs and
memorabilia; includes autograph,
memorabilia and Minor League and
draft pick sports card price guides.*

Chuck Kaufman
Kaufman Communications
Magazine: Sweet Spot
816 Congress Ave., Ste. 1280
Austin, TX 78701
ph: 512-708-1999
fax: 512-708-0333
ckaufman1@compuserve.com
http://www.sweetspotnews.com
*Bimonthly publication focusing on
vintage and autographed sports
memorabilia: reports on golf, boxing,
track & field, Olympics, baseball,
football, basketball, and hockey.*

Ed Kobak
Global Sports Productions, Ltd.
Directory: Sports Address Bible &
Almanac, The
1223 Broadway, Ste. 102
Santa Monica, CA 90404-2770
ph: 310-454-9480
fax: 310-454-6590
globalnw@earthlink.net
http://www.sportsbooksempire.com
*Worldwide reference guide (506
pages) with over 10K listings of
sports addresses, phone and fax
numbers, and contact person for
Leagues, teams, organizations, and
publications; major, minor, semi-pro,
amateur, international, college.*

Ed Kobak
Global Sports Productions, Ltd.
Directory: International Sports Directory
1223 Broadway, Ste. 102
Santa Monica, CA 90404-2770
ph: 310-454-9480
fax: 310-454-6590
globalnw@earthlink.net
http://www.sportsbooksempire.com
*464-page directory: listings for
Olympic organizations and committees, national sports governing bodies,
Olympic and multi-sport games
committees, teams/clubs sports for
foreign leagues & teams, collecting
periodicals and societies.*

Ed Kobak
Global Sports Productions, Ltd.
Directory: Athlete & Sport Personality
Address Book, The
1223 Broadway, Ste. 102
Santa Monica, CA 90404-2770
ph: 310-454-9480
fax: 310-454-6590
globalnw@earthlink.net
http://www.sportsbooksempire.com
*Over 17K sports athlete/personality
names and addresses from all sports;
includes current athletes, Hall of
Famers and former athletes, Negro
League Baseball players, broadcast-
ers/announcers, coaches, managers,
etc.*

Baseball

Appraisers

James Murphy
Philadelphia Bat Company
P.O. Box 456
266 W. Greenwood Ave.
Lansdowne, PA 19050-0456
ph: 610-623-8077
*Specializes in the professional
appraisals of baseball memorabilia:
balls, bats, gloves, displays, pictures,
equipment, ads, pennants, etc.*

Auction Services

Robert Lifson
Robert Edward Auctions
P.O. Box 7256
Watchung, NJ 07069
ph: 908-226-9900 or 800-766-9324
fax: 908-226-9920
reaauct@aol.com
http://www.robertedwardauctions.com
*Conducts specialty baseball
memorabilia auctions: baseball cards,
Babe Ruth & Lou Gehrig items,
tobacco cards, uncut sheets, buttons,
autographs, display pieces, postcards,
gum cards, world series items,
original artwork, documents, etc.*

Clubs/Associations

Robert E. Schmierer
Eastern Pennsylvania Sports Collectors
Club
P.O. Box 3037
Maple Glen, PA 19002-8037
ph: 215-643-0910
fax: 215-643-2697
http://www.phillyshow.org
*Focus is to promote baseball and
other sports memorabilia; formed in
1975.*

Society for American Baseball Research
Journal: Baseball Research Journal
812 Huron Rd. E., #719
Cleveland, OH 44115
ph: 216-575-0500
fax: 216-575-0502
info@sabr.org
http://www.sabr.org
*SABR's objectives are to facilitate and
disseminate baseball research
information and to establish an
accurate historical account of
baseball; membership is open to all
who have an interest in baseball
history.*

Collectors

Stan Block
128 Cynthia Rd.
Newton, MA 02159
*Wants to buy baseball items: leathers,
silks, postcards, pennants, cards,
banks, bats, clothing, autographs on
balls, etc.*

Ken Felden
2 Hemlock Lane
Marlboro, NJ 07746
ph: 732-536-5974
fax: 732-972-4646
linken1@aol.com
*Collector wants to buy baseball
related antiques: cards (1880s-1930s),
advertising, fans, pins, tins,
scorecards and programs, photos,
tickets (1860-1920), games, sheet
music, early trophies and statuary,
posters, etc.*

Bill Simmons
181 NW 78th Ave.
Margate, FL 33063
ph: 954-984-9647
wsim1206@aol.com
Wants to buy baseball memorabilia:

anything autographed including balls, bats, and gloves; old photos, postcards, cards, programs, statues, movie stuff, pens, lighters, etc.; especially wants anything relating to Chuck Connors.

Dealers

David Hall
Hall's Nostalgia
P.O. Box 408
Arlington, MA 02476
ph: 800-367-4255 or 781-595-7757
fax: 781-599-6737
hallsnost@aol.com
Buys and sells all major sport collectibles (sport cards, publications, autographs, etc.); oldest sports store on the East Coast; opened in 1976; appraises sports memorabilia.

Tom & Jill Kaczor
1550 Franklin Rd.
Langhorne, PA 19047
ph: 215-968-5776 or 215-946-6044
fax: 215-946-6056
Serious collectors who want all sorts of baseball memorabilia: early bats, gloves, photos, board games, fans, sheet music, advertising pieces with players in them, stadium artifacts, score cards, programs, signed balls, trophies, etc.

Bob McCann
P.O. Box 18
Gilbertsville, PA 19525
ph: 610-367-1827
bobmccann1@aol.com
Wants to buy quality Baseball memorabilia.

Scott Cowan
Vintage Cardboard
23632 Highway 99 #F173
Edmonds, WA 98026
vintage@vintagecardboard.com
http://www.vintagecardboard.com
Specializes in vintage baseball collectibles, especially pre-WWII cards and collectibles.

Experts

Mark Cooper
Baseball Games & Memorabilia
816 Chauncey Rd.
Narberth, PA 19072
ph: 215-952-9153 or 610-667-7401
fax: 610-667-2341
A premier collector of 1860-1980 baseball games; has published the definitive text on the subject; will provide free information to all interested; always buying, selling, trading baseball games.

Phil Wood
P.O. Box 204
Reisterstown, MD 21136-0204
ph: 410-833-9663
Editor of "Diamond Duds," a bi-monthly newsletter on game-used major league baseball uniforms; monthly memorabilia columnist in "Tuff Stuff" magazine.

Dennis Goldstein
1531 Beechcliff Dr. NE
Atlanta, GA 30329-3825
ph: 404-982-1075
Baseball historian looking for early photographs, books, programs, memorabilia.

David Rudd
Cycleback: Publishers & Collectors
  Services
P.O. Box 16311
Seattle, WA 98116
ph: 206-923-0367
drudd@cycleback.com
http://www.cycleback.com
One of the leading authorities on baseball memorabilia, early prints & photographs; author of numerous books on these subjects; is a forensic art examiner; teaches online courses in print & photograph authentication and forgery detection.

Internet Resources

Seth Nagdeman
19th Century Only, Inc.
P.O. Box 382
Bogota, NJ 07603
ph: 973-324-1444 or 888-340-9903
fax: 208-247-2390
info@19thcenturyonly.org
http://www.19thcenturyonly.org
An online collecting community focusing on vintage 19th century baseball memorabilia including Old Judge tobacco cards, cabinet cards, early baseball photographs, tintypes, Hall of Fame players, bats, balls, etc.

Museums/Libraries

National Baseball Hall of Fame &
  Museum, Inc.
P.O. Box 590
25 Main St.
Cooperstown, NY 13326
ph: 607-547-7200
fax: 607-547-2044
info@baseballhalloffame.org
http://baseballhalloffame.org

Periodicals

Stacie Berger
Krause Publications
Magazine: Fantasy Baseball
700 E. State St.
Iola, WI 54990-0001
ph: 715-445-2214
fax: 715-445-4087
stacie.berger@fwpubs.com
http://www.krause.com
Complete guide to fantasy baseball league; every major league player ranked from scrub to star; hottest hobby with more than 1M players.

Magazine: Diamond Angle, The
706 South Alu
Wailuku, HI 96793
ph: 808-244-7704
tdaflow@aloha.net
http://www.aloha.net/~tdaflow
A journal feature articles, book reviews, trivia, lore, monthly card

columns; sells cards plus has nationwide dealer ads.

Baseball (Books)

Collectors

R. Plapinger
P.O. Box 1062
Ashland, OR 97520-0063
ph: 541-488-1220
baseballbooks@opendoor.com
Wants any book about baseball: non-fiction, fiction, adult, juvenile, especially turn-of-the-century; send SASE for list of most wanted.

Dealers

Andy Moursund
Georgetown Book Shop
7770 Woodmont Ave.
Bethesda, MD 20814
ph: 301-907-6923
Specializes in baseball team history books.

R. Plapinger
R. Plapinger Baseball Books
P.O. Box 1062
Ashland, OR 97520-0063
ph: 541-488-1220
baseballbooks@opendoor.com
Specializes in catalog sales of baseball team history books.

Baseball (Washington Senators)

Clubs/Associations

Richard Bruce
Washington Senators Baseball
  Association
Newsletter: Save the Senators
11417 St. Rd. 535
Orlando, FL 32836
ph: 407-239-4482
Specializes in preservation of Washington Senators baseball club memorabilia, research and preservation to include specialty in autographs.

Collectors

Richard Bruce
11417 St. Rd. 535
Orlando, FL 32836
ph: 407-239-4482
Buys, sells, collects and specializes in memorabilia relating to the Washington Senators baseball team.

Baseball Cards

Collectors

Chuck Moore
P.O. Box 280
Gladstone, OR 97027
ph: 503-654-9994
fax: 503-656-7603
Wants baseball cards, publications, memorabilia; also older football and basketball memorabilia.

Dealers

Peggy Wolffrum
Peggy's Baseball Cards
6201 Gabriel St.
Bowie, MD 20720
ph: 301-390-6243
bbcards@speakeasy.org
http://www.baseballcardz.com
Buys, sells, trades baseball cards ranging from 1988 to present; star players as well as common cards available for sale; good selection at prices below Beckett.

Larry Fritsch
Larry Fritsch Cards, Inc.
735 Old Wassau Rd.
P.O. Box 863
Stevens Point, WI 54481
ph: 715-344-8687
fax: 715-344-1778
Larry@fritschcards.com
http://www.fritschcards.com
Over 55 million cards in stock; buys and sells.

Pat Yeary
Pat & Larry's Baseball Cards
3708 W. Pioneer Parkway
Arlington, TX 76013-2901
ph: 817-265-0006
Buy, sell, trade baseball, football, basketball cards; specializing in sports trading cards since 1960s.

David Levin
Dave's Vintage Baseball Cards
P.O. Box 49723
Los Angeles, CA 90049
ph: 310-471-1959
baseball@gfg.com
http://www.gfg.com/baseball
Comprehensive listings of vintage baseball cards for sale on the Internet; also football, basketball, hockey and boxing cards; all pre-1975; Topps, Fleer, Bowman, Leaf, Philly, Parkhurst, Wheaties, Post, Hostess, Kelloggs, etc.

Internet Resources

Baseball Cards 1887-1914, Library of
  Congress
101 Independence Ave. SE
Washington, DC 20540
ph: 202-707-8000
ndlpcoll@loc.gov
http://memory.loc.gov/ammem/bbhtml/
  bbhome.html
The collection presents a Library of Congress treasure - 2,100 early baseball cards dating from 1887 to 1914.

Man./Prod./Dist.

Fleer Corp.
1120 Route 73, Ste. 300
Mount Laurel, NJ 08054-5113
info@flrsbx.com
http://www.fleerskybox.com
A baseball card company.

Donruss/Leaf
P.O. Box 2038
Memphis, TN 38101
info@donruss.com
http://www.donruss.com
Web site has store locator.

Upper Deck Co. LLC, The
5909 Sea Otter Place
Carlsbad, CA 92008-6621
ph: 760-929-6500 or 800-873-7332
fax: 760-929-6500
customer_service@upperdeck.com
http://www.upperdeck.com
A baseball card company; Web site has trading cards, collectors clubs, card checklists.

Museums/Libraries

Metropolitan Museum of Art, The
Jefferson Burdick Collection
1000 Fifth Ave.
New York, NY 10028-0198
ph: 212-535-7710
fax: 212-794-9316
http://www.metmuseum.org

National Baseball Hall of Fame & Museum, Inc.
P.O. Box 590
25 Main St.
Cooperstown, NY 13326
ph: 607-547-7200
fax: 607-547-2044
info@baseballhalloffame.org
http://baseballhalloffame.org

Larry Fritsch
Larry Fritsch Collection, The
735 Old Wassau Rd.
P.O. Box 863
Stevens Point, WI 54481
ph: 715-344-8687
fax: 715-344-1778
Larry@fritschcards.com
http://www.fritschcards.com

Periodicals

Stacie Berger
Krause Publications
Newsmagazine: Sports Collectors Digest
700 E. State St.
Iola, WI 54990-0001
ph: 715-445-2214
fax: 715-445-4087
stacie.berger@fwpubs.com
http://www.krause.com
A weekly newsmagazine for collectors of sports memorabilia; everything from baseball cards to game-worn uniforms.

Stacie Berger
Krause Publications
Magazine: Sports Cards Magazine & Price Guide
700 E. State St.
Iola, WI 54990-0001
ph: 715-445-2214
fax: 715-445-4087
stacie.berger@fwpubs.com
http://www.krause.com
Full color monthly magazine featuring baseball, basketball, hockey and football cards from all eras; news,

columns, feature stories, price guides; ads for cards and related items.

Stacie Berger
Krause Publications
Magazine: Card Trade
700 E. State St.
Iola, WI 54990-0001
ph: 715-445-2214
fax: 715-445-4087
stacie.berger@fwpubs.com
http://www.krause.com
Card industry's official trade journal, touching on topics pertinent the sports hobby professional.

Hugh Murphy, PR
Beckett Publications, Inc.
Magazine: Beckett Baseball Collector
15850 Dallas Parkway
Dallas, TX 75248
ph: 972-448-9018 or 800-840-3137
hmurphy@beckett.com
http://www.beckett.com
A monthly baseball card price guide, articles, ads, show calendar.

Baseball Gloves

Clubs/Associations

Joe Phillips
Glove Collector Club, The
Newsletter: Glove Collector, The
14057 Rolling Hills Lane
Dallas, TX 75240-3807
ph: 972-699-1808
fax: 972-699-9851
jp@glovecollector.com
http://www.glovecollector.com
A bi-monthly newsletter containing buy/sell/trade ads and articles about old baseball gloves; also the club is a source for glove price guides and glove reference books.

Experts

David Bushing
217 Homewood Ave.
Libertyville, IL 60048-2123
ph: 847-816-6847
Author of "Vintage Baseball Glove Price Guide."

Repro. Sources

Joe Phillips
14057 Rolling Hills Lane
Dallas, TX 75240-3807
ph: 972-699-1808
fax: 972-699-9851
jp@glovecollector.com
http://www.glovecollector.com
Deals in re-issue USA made baseball gloves.

Baseball Uniforms

Collectors

Gary Hong, Pub.
603 Concerto Lane
Silver Spring, MD 20901
ph: 301-593-6763
fax: 301-681-1476
ghong@erols.com
Interested in game-worn major league baseball uniforms.

Basketball

Dealers

Basketball Bonanza
27 Currey Lane
West Orange, NJ 07052
ph: 973-731-2813 or 973-736-6321
Specializes in basketball memorabilia and cards.

Museums/Libraries

Naismith Memorial Basketball Hall of Fame
1150 W. Columbus Ave.
P.O. Box 179
Springfield, MA 01101-0179
ph: 413-781-6500
fax: 413-781-1939
robin@hoophall.com
http://www.hoophall.com

Basketball Cards

Dealers

Robert Cosner
Bob's Baseball Cards
20978 E. Berry Place
Aurora, CO 80015
ph: 303-693-3852
Bobplus@aol.com
http://www.Bobsbaseballcards.com
Buys and sells baseball cards; vintage and newer baseball stars and commons; Web site has monthly specials and free stuff.

Periodicals

Stacie Berger
Krause Publications
Magazine: Sports Cards Magazine & Price Guide
700 E. State St.
Iola, WI 54990-0001
ph: 715-445-2214
fax: 715-445-4087
stacie.berger@fwpubs.com
http://www.krause.com
Full color monthly magazine featuring baseball, basketball, hockey and football cards from all eras; news, columns, feature stories, price guides; ads for cards and related items.

Hugh Murphy, PR
Beckett Publications, Inc.
Magazine: Beckett Basketball Collector
15850 Dallas Parkway
Dallas, TX 75248
ph: 972-448-9018 or 800-840-3137
hmurphy@beckett.com
http://www.beckett.com
Articles, ads, basketball card price guide.

Bowling

Collectors

Walt Sill
557 Forest Retreat Rd.
Hendersonville, TN 37075
ph: 615-824-4646
fax: 615-822-6852
Wants to buy pre-1940 bowling items: wooden balls and pins, photos, equipment, posters, trophies, clocks,

mugs, plaques, ribbons, bags, china, advertising, medals, etc.

Museums/Libraries

International Bowling Hall of Fame & Museum
111 Stadium Plaza
Saint Louis, MO 63102
ph: 314-231-6340 or 800-966-BOWL
hofm@bowlingmuseum.com
http://www.bowlingmuseum.com
Collection includes artifacts covering the history of bowling.

Boxing

Clubs/Associations

Frederick Ryan
Boxiana & Pugilistica Collectors International
Newsletter: BPCI Newsletter
P.O. Box 83135
Portland, OR 97283-0135
ph: 503-286-3597 or 503-235-9559

Collectors

Lou Manfra
27 Rochelle St.
Staten Island, NY 10304
ph: 718-979-9556
Wants to buy boxing memorabilia: autographs, photos, documents, tickets, posters, programs, books, figurines.

Bob Bryla
1912 Sunset Ave.
Utica, NY 13502-5636
ph: 315-733-1846
fax: 315-733-7518
bryfour@dreamscape.com
Wants items relating to boxing and wrestling: strength books, magazines, programs, dolls, games, medals, pennants, bottles, etc. from 1860 to present.

Shawn Murphy
P.O. Box 103
Fithian, IL 61844-0103
Wants boxing memorabilia including programs, posters, tickets, books, souvenirs.

Don Hoffman
P.O. Box 4231
Salinas, CA 93912-4231
ph: 831-449-7311
Wants to buy boxing (all fighters) autographs, posters, tickets, programs, 8mm & 16mm films, old photos, silks, broadsides, cabinet cards, books, photo buttons, lithographs, banners, equipment, Golden Gloves, pins, etc.; describe & price.

Frederick Ryan
Arena Archives
P.O. Box 83135
Portland, OR 97283-0135
ph: 503-286-3597 or 503-235-9559
Boxing archivist, lifelong collector; owner of the "Grand Ave. Gym," organizer of the Annual Boxing

memorabilia show held annually in
Portland; wants tickets, programs,
fight films, posters, literature,
awards, mementos.

Lyle Whiteman
1526 Alki Ave. SW
Seattle, WA 98116
ph: 206-938-5746
fax: 206-938-0155
Wants to buy old boxing memorabilia.

Dealers

Richard R. Regan
293 Winter St. #5
Hanover, MA 02339-2528
ph: 781-826-3537
foregolf@tiac.net
*Wants to buy boxing posters &
broadsides, books, prints, cigarette
cards, programs, autographed photos,
early equipment; anything related to
boxing.*

Jerome Shochet
6144 Oakland Mills Rd., CIC
Sykesville, MD 21784-6916
ph: 410-795-5879
*Buys and sells boxing memorabilia of
all kinds.*

Bill Pollock
4267 Fox Hollow Circle
Casselberry, FL 32707-5240
ph: 407-695-9140
pollockwk@mindspring.com
*Wants boxing programs, tickets,
autographs, pins, pre-1980 posters,
buttons, trophies, estates of
professional boxers, boxing pennants,
and any items from restaurants owned
by pro boxers (Jack Dempsey's, Lew
Tendler's, etc.).*

Museums/Libraries

International Boxing Hall of Fame
1 Hall of Fame Dr.
Canastota, NY 13032
ph: 315-697-7095
publisher@ibhof.com
http://www.ibhof.com

Periodicals

Don Scott
Magazine: Boxing Collectors News
7541 Raleigh Lane
Jonesboro, GA 30236
ph: 770-472-7575
donscott@boxingcollectors.com
http://www.boxingcollectors.com
*Articles, addresses and ads for boxing
memorabilia; 12 years of monthly
publishing, 16-32 pages, editor/
publisher is columnist for "Ring"
magazine; also offers appraisals.*

Cards

(see also ADVERTISING
COLLECTIBLES, Trading Cards;
CARDS; SPORTS COLLECTIBLES,
Baseball Cards; SPORTS
COLLECTIBLES, Basketball Cards;
SPORTS COLLECTIBLES, Football
Cards; SPORTS COLLECTIBLES,
Hockey Cards)

Auction Services

Greg Manning
Greg Manning Auctions, Inc.
775 Passaic Ave.
West Caldwell, NJ 07006
ph: 973-882-0004 or 800-221-0243
fax: 973-882-3499
gmauction@aol.com
http://www.gregmanning.com
*Conducts four to six mail/phone bid
auctions per year containing primarily
sports and non-sports cards; also
autographs and varied memorabilia.*

Teletrade Sports Card Auctions
27 Main St.
Kingston, NY 12401-3853
ph: 800-232-1132 or 845-339-2900
fax: 845-339-3288
cust@teletrade.com
http://www.teletrade.com
*Conducts online auctions of sports
cards.*

Collectors

Peter Dean
2295 Benson Ave.
Santa Cruz, CA 95065-1670
ph: 831-457-4332
*Wants to buy 1960s and early 1970s
cards, all sports: baseball, football,
basketball, hockey.*

Dealers

Baystate Vintage Sportscards
ph: 508-764-2237
seanmurf@bellatlantic.net
http://www.bvscards.com
*Specializes in high-end, PSA graded
vintage sports cards including
baseball, hockey, football and
basketball; PSA 8, 9 and 10 cards
available from 1900 to 1994.*

Cavalcade of Sports
P.O. Box 150
Littlestown, PA 17340
ph: 717-359-1345
jaycos@qualitycards.com
http://www.qualitycards.com
*Buys and sells PSA graded cards:
football, baseball, basketball, hockey;
1910 to present.*

707 Sportscards Ltd.
P.O. Box 707
Plumsteadville, PA 18949
ph: 215-766-9700
jim@707sportscards.com
http://www.707sportscards.com
*Buys and sells pre-1980 baseball
cards and PSA graded sports cards.*

Burton's Coins & Cards
5831 Buckeystown Pike
Frederick, MD 21701
ph: 301-663-3223
fax: 3910663-3262
burtons@erols.com
http://www.collectingexchange.com/
  dealers/burtons
*Carries sports cards (baseball,
football, basketball, hockey),
memorabilia (bobbing heads, mini-*

helmets, jerseys), and coins (silver
dollars, Peace dollars, proof sets).

Shelley & Lanny Jennings
Batters Box, The
8416 Old Keene Mill Rd.
Springfield, VA 22152
ph: 703-455-6018 or 877-385-9600
lanny@erols.com
http://www.battersbox.com
*Specializes in wax (sports and non-
sports boxes), sports collectibles, diecast racing cars, and card/comic
supplies.*

Joe McPhee
Mr. M.V.P.
1219 Windwaerd Ct.
Largo, FL 33770
ph: 727-559-9513
fax: 727-584-1311
*Specializes in buying and selling
vintage sports cards and memorabilia:
baseball, football, basketball, hockey;
new releases as well as vintage cards
and rookie cards of all brands.*

Joe Stahura
Cheap Seats Sports Cards
1504 - 119th St.
Whiting, IN 46394
ph: 219-473-0022
fax: 219-473-0352
joe@cheapseatscards.com
http://www.cheapseatscards.com
*Full service sports cards and
collectibles store.*

Scott Geithman
Scotty G's Sports Cards
cardwiz118@attbi.com
http://www.egradedcards.com
*Specializes in Beckett and PSA graded,
game used, autographed insert, and
rookie cards from baseball, football,
basketball, NASCAR, golf, Hockey.*

All-Star Sports Cards
875 Comstock Ave., Ste. 18E
Los Angeles, CA 90024
ph: 310-274-2180
allstars@allstarsportscards.com
http://www.allstarsportscards.com

David Levin
Dave's Vintage Baseball Cards
P.O. Box 49723
Los Angeles, CA 90049
ph: 310-471-1959
baseball@gfg.com
http://www.gfg.com/baseball
*Comprehensive listings of vintage
baseball cards for sale on the Internet;
also football, basketball, hockey and
boxing cards; all pre-1975; Topps,
Fleer, Bowman, Leaf, Philly,
Parkhurst, Wheaties, Post, Hostess,
Kelloggs, etc.*

Chris Thorne
Thorne Collectibles
10206 Canmarillo Place
North Hollywood, CA 91602
ph: 818-415-6835
ct98@icnt.net
Family-owned sports card business,

specializing in hockey; also basketball,
football, baseball.

Derrick Jones
Derrick's Sports Cards
2177 Pine St.
Quincy, CA 95971
ph: 916-625-0625
dwjones@hotmail.com
http://www.angelfire.com/ca/
  derricksportscards
*Great Web site to buy, trade and sell
sports cards and sports-related
memorabilia: baseball cards,
basketball cards, football cards,
Wheaties cereal boxes, Corinthian
headliners, SLU's, coins, magazines,
and other sports-related items.*

Internet Resources

About.com Hobbies
220 East 42nd St.
New York, NY 10017
pr@about-inc.com
http://home.about.com/hobbies
*Online source for information about
action figures, antiques, book
collecting, coin collecting, collectibles,
comic books, costume jewelry, dolls,
mineral collecting, pin collecting,
sports and trading cards, stamps, toy
collecting.*

Terry Stewart
Collector Link
71 John St. East
Waterloo, Ontario N2J 1G2 Canada
ph: 519-745-1745
stewart@collector-link.com
http://www.collector-link.com
*Catalogs over 2,000 trading card
related Web sites for: baseball,
hockey, basketball, football, other
sports, non-sports, phone cards,
credit-debit cards, business cards,
postcards.*

Misc. Services

Sean Skeffington, Oper.
Sportscard Guaranty LLC
P.O. Box 6919
Parsippany, NJ 07054-6919
ph: 800-742-9212 or 973-984-0018
fax: 973-984-8447
service@sgccard.com
http://www.sgccard.com
*Offers accurate, consistent grading
and authentication for sports cards.*

WinCards
Software: WinCards
110 Brent Dr.
Wallingford, PA 19086
ph: 610-876-1202
sales@wincards.net
http://www.wincards.net
*A comprehensive sports card tracking
program; over 10,000 card sets
(850,000 cards) ships with WinCards
CD.*

Pick-N-Click Software
Software: Ultimate Card Collector
525 South Third St.
Smithfield, NC 27577
Sports card collection management system with over 260,000 (and growing) pre-loaded cards.

Hugh Murphy, PR
Beckett.com/Beckett Grading Services
15850 Dallas Parkway
Dallas, TX 75248
ph: 972-448-9018 or 800-840-3137
hmurphy@beckett.com
http://www.beckett.com
Offers grading services for sports cards.

Professional Sports Authenticator
P.O. Box 6180
Newport Beach, CA 92658
ph: 800-325-1121 or 949-833-8824
fax: 949-833-7955
info@psacard.com
http://www.PSAcard.com
Offers third party authentication and grading services for sports cards.

PrimaSoft PC, Inc.
Software: Sports Card Organizer
P.O. Box 456
Surrey, British Columbia V3T 5B7
Canada
ph: 800-371-7520 or 604-951-1085
fax: 604-951-7797
support@primasoft.com
http://www.primasoft.com
Designed for managing collections of sports cards.

Periodicals

Stacie Berger
Krause Publications
Magazine: Card Trade
700 E. State St.
Iola, WI 54990-0001
ph: 715-445-2214
fax: 715-445-4087
stacie.berger@fwpubs.com
http://www.krause.com
Card industry's official trade journal, touching on topics pertinent the sports hobby professional.

Richard Scott
Trajan Publishing Corporation
Newspaper: Canadian Sports Collector
103 Lakeshore Rd., Ste. 202
St. Catharines, Ontario L2N 2T6 Canada
ph: 905-646-7744
fax: 905-646-0995
rscott@trajan.com
http://www.tarjan.com
Canada's foremost source for sports cards and sports memorabilia collectors.

Computer Programs For

Man./Prod./Dist.

Niche Software, Inc.
Software: Sports Memorabilia Collector, The
7118 NW Terrace
Parkland, FL 33076
ph: 954-344-6561
marketing@collectiblessoftware.com
http://www.collectiblessoftware.com
Designed for the collector of sports memorabilia.

Crew Rowing

Collectors

Peter Hastings Falk
P.O. Box 833
Madison, CT 06443
ph: 203-245-4761
pfalk@cshore.com
http://www.soundviewpressbooks.com
Wants 19th century cigarette & trade cards, posters, broadsides, stereoviews, prints, sheet music, & books on rowing.

Cricket

Clubs/Associations

Steve Cashmore
Cricket Memorabilia Society
4 Stoke Park Court, Stoke Rd.
Bishops Cleeve
Cheltenham, Gloucestershire GL52 8US
U.K.
cms@cricinfo.com
http://www.uk.cricket.org/
link_to_database/SOCIETIES/ENG/
CMS
Aims to promote interest in and the preservation of cricket memorabilia.

Curling

Museums/Libraries

Turner's Curling Museum
530 Fifth St. N.E.
Weyburn, Saskatchewan S4H 2K6
Canada
ph: 306-842-3604 or 306-848-3283
Museum features many rare, historical curling pieces, including one of the largest collections of curling pins in the country.

Equipment

Experts

David Bushing
Vintage Sports Equipment
217 Homewood Ave.
Libertyville, IL 60048-2123
ph: 847-816-6847
Wants to buy old sports equipment: bats, gloves, catchers gear, old leather football helmets, old pennants, etc.; writes a sports collectibles column for "AntiqueWeek."

Football

Dealers

Athleticards
5638 Lake Murray Blvd., Ste. 110
La Mesa, CA 91942-1929
ph: 619-461-3451
fax: 619-461-2938
Wants to buy items relating to pro football: advertising displays, postcards, equipment, posters, records, team-issued photos, bread labels, bottle caps, books, toys, games, glassware, bottles, cans, programs/magazines, pennants, etc.

Museums/Libraries

Pro Football Hall of Fame
2121 George Halas Dr. NW
Canton, OH 44708
ph: 330-456-8207
http://www.profootballhof.com

Football Cards

Dealers

V & J Cards
P.O. Box 168
Furlong, PA 18925
ph: 215-348-8027
gradedfootball@aol.com
http://www.psafootball.com
Buys and sells vintage pre-1970 football cards; dealing in PSA graded as well as ungraded cards.

Periodicals

Stacie Berger
Krause Publications
Magazine: Sports Cards Magazine & Price Guide
700 E. State St.
Iola, WI 54990-0001
ph: 715-445-2214
fax: 715-445-4087
stacie.berger@fwpubs.com
http://www.krause.com
Full color monthly magazine featuring baseball, basketball, hockey and football cards from all eras; news, columns, feature stories, price guides; ads for cards and related items.

Hugh Murphy, PR
Beckett Publications, Inc.
Magazine: Beckett Football Collector
15850 Dallas Parkway
Dallas, TX 75248
ph: 972-448-9018 or 800-840-3137
hmurphy@beckett.com
http://www.beckett.com
Includes ads, show calendar, articles and football card price guide.

Golf

Appraisers

George Lewis
George Lewis/Golfiana
P.O. Box 291
Mamaroneck, NY 10543
ph: 914-835-5100
fax: 914-835-1715
george@golfiana.com
http://www.golfiana.com
Golf appraiser, dealer buying/selling golf collectibles; in business full-time since 1988; old golf books, antique clubs, equipment, art, prints, decorative items.

Auction Services

Kevin C. McGrath
Sporting Antiquities
44 Oakland St.
Melrose, MA 02176
ph: 781-662-6588
fax: 781-662-6588
Sells antique golf collectibles through auction and private sales; buys high quality golf paintings, prints, clubs, books, balls, etc.; also appraises golf collectibles for a fee.

Leo M. Kelly, Jr.
IGolf Auction
4977 Arquilla Dr.
Richton Park, IL 60471-1643
ph: 708-747-1045
fax: 708-747-1055
oldgolf@oldgolf.com
http://www.igolfauction.com
An online auction site dedicated exclusively to antique golf collectibles; consignments welcome.

Jon Baddeley
Sotheby's
34-35 New Bond St.
London, W1A 2AA U.K.
ph: 44 171 293 5000
fax: 44 171 293 5989
http://www.sothebys.com
Conducts regular auctions of golfing memorabilia.

Book Sellers

Rhod McEwan
Rhod McEwan Golf Books
Glengarden
Ballater, Aberdeenshire AB35 5UB
Scotland
ph: 013397-55429
fax: 013397-55995
rhodmcewan@easynet.co.uk
Specialist full-time dealer in rare, used, and out-of-print golf books; also golf ephemera and original paintings; always looking to purchase; member Antiquarian Bookseller's Association (UK) and Golf Collector's Society.

Clubs/Associations

Karen Bednarski, Ex. Dir.
Golf Collectors Society
Journal: Bulletin, The
P.O. Box 3103
Ponte Vedra Beach, FL 32004-3102
ph: 904-825-2191
fax: 904-810-5305
kbednarski@thegolfsource.net
http://www.golfcollectors.com
An international society for the preservation of the treasures and traditions of the Royal and Ancient game; largest in the world.

Collectors

Art DiProspero
Highlands Golf
P.O. Box 300
Watertown, CT 06795-0300
ph: 860-274-4203
seasidelinks@aol.com
Wants wooden shaft golf clubs, early trophies, pre-1920 golf books, golf bronzes, modern "classic" clubs, golf paintings & prints, balls, golf memorabilia, early golf magazines and programs, etc.

Norman Boughton
P.O. Box 1
Macedon, NY 14502
ph: 315-986-3851
nbought1@rochester.rr.com
http://www.woodenmoney.com
Wants to buy golf memorabilia including golf markers (used to mark a spot on the green), any material; especially those identifiable to a particular course or golfer.

Bob Greco
2817 Camelot Dr.
New Kensington, PA 15068
Wants golf related collectibles including postcards (no courses or clubhouses), postcards of famous golfers, trade cards, old advertising pieces, tins, old golf balls, Bobby Jones items.

Mark F. Emerson
4040 Poste Lane Rd.
Columbus, OH 43221
ph: 614-771-7272 or 614-431-5800
fax: 614-431-4100
mark@max-ermas.com
Appraiser, dealer, collector, wants to buy old golf programs, tickets, badges, pairing sheets, passes, photos, autographs of deceased players.

D. Perkins
6335 W. 62nd St.
Indianapolis, IN 46278-1906
ph: 317-293-9962
Wants wooden shaft golf clubs, early trophies or any antique sports related item.

Frank R. Zadra
N5830 Cty. Hwy. H.
Spooner, WI 54801-7242
ph: 715-635-2791
Wants old golf related items: unusual golf clubs, old balls, books, bronzes, quality china and ceramics, and miscellaneous related items; has been collecting for over 35 years.

Scott Sayers
1800 Nueces St.
Austin, TX 78701
ph: 512-478-3483
fax: 512-473-2447
sayers@bencrenshaw.com
Wants to buy golf related autographs and memorabilia.

Dealers

Richard R. Regan
293 Winter St. #5
Hanover, MA 02339-2528
ph: 781-826-3537
foregolf@tiac.net
Wants to buy wood shaft clubs, golf books, statues, china, paintings, prints, balls, scorecards, programs, autographs, sales catalogs, trophies, miniature golf clubs & games, pinball machines, cigarette & postcards; any golf related item.

George Lewis
George Lewis/Golfiana
P.O. Box 291
Mamaroneck, NY 10543
ph: 914-835-5100
fax: 914-835-1715
george@golfiana.com
http://www.golfiana.com
Golf appraiser, dealer buying/selling golf collectibles; in business full-time since 1988; old golf books, antique clubs, equipment, art, prints, decorative items.

Arthur H. Vanderbeek
15 Pearl St.
Rouses Point, NY 12979-1409
ph: 518-297-6146
Collector and dealer of golf collectibles including wood-shafted clubs, paper items, books, golf balls; from April to Nov. call 386-304-6382.

Allen Wallach
Heritage Hickory Golf Collectibles
300 Edge Hill Rd.
Glenside, PA 19038
ph: 215-886-8875
fax: 215-886-3463
info@heritagehickory.com
http://www.heritagehickory.com
Collector, expert, dealer buying and selling all types of antique golf collectibles; specializes in golf balls, wood shafted golf clubs, books on golf, tees, art, trophies, pottery, and all other aspects of golf collectibles.

George P. "Pat" Gillis
American Golf Classics, Inc.
114 Blackheath
Williamsburg, VA 23188
ph: 757-565-7237 or 757-565-7200
fax: 757-565-7249
pat@americangolfclassics.com
http://www.americangolfclassics.com
Appraiser, dealer, repair expert in antique, classic and modern golf clubs; in the golf business for over 25 years in pro shop management and retail along with repair which lead into the antique and classic trade in 1980.

Neil Ghingold
Neil Ghingold Antiques
1230-32 Broad St.
Augusta, GA 30901-1116
ph: 706-722-3483
Wants to buy golfing collectibles.

Gordon Page
Hickory Sticks
34643 Sunward Loop
Zephyrhills, FL 33541
ph: 813-780-8841
gpage@innet.com
http://www.webcom.com/oldgolf/mu/gpage.html
A well known dealer of antique golf collectibles specializing in antique wood shaft golf clubs; participates in many of the Golf Collectors Society shows throughout the US; has a Web site that lists early golf collectibles.

David N. Berkowitz
Golf's Golden Years
P.O. Box 842
Palatine, IL 60078-0842
ph: 847-934-4108
fax: 847-934-4107
dave@golfsgoldenyears.com
http://www.golfsgoldenyears.com
Buys and sells old golf items: balls, books, ceramics, tees, memorabilia, vintage golf autographs, wood shafted clubs, silver, trophies, etc.

Bob Lucas
P.O. Box 364
Geneva, IL 60134-0364
ph: 630-232-2665
fax: 630-262-1935
antqgolf@aol.com
Old golf items, wood-shafted clubs, books, prints, china, etc.

Leo M. Kelly, Jr.
Old Chicago Golf Shop
4977 Arquilla Dr.
Richton Park, IL 60471-1643
ph: 708-747-1045
fax: 708-747-1055
Ochicago@ix.netcom.com
http://www.oldgolf.com
Dealer, appraiser and collector of pre-1930s golf antiques, memorabilia, and collectibles.

Al Moore
Moore's of Omaha
9230 Burt St., #214
Omaha, NE 68114
ph: 402-392-2964
almor@cox.net
http://members.cox.net/almor/mainpage.htm
Wants old golf related items: caddy badges, wood shaft clubs, books, signature golf balls, etc.; also wants WWII Navy PT boat memorabilia.

Barry Smith
Barry O'Brien's Golf Clubs & Collectibles
P.O. Box 22145
Lincoln, NE 68542
ph: 402-488-7684
barry@solu.net
http://www.golfopia.com
Buys, sells, trades practically anything related to golf; specializes in Wooden Shaft Golf Clubs and classic golf clubs from the 1940s through the 1960s.

Chuck Furjanic
Golf Collectibles
P.O. Box 165892
Irving, TX 75016
ph: 972-594-7802 or 800-882-4825
fax: 972-257-1875
furjanic@directlink.net
http://www.golfforallages.com
Buys and sells golf collectibles, balls, books, autographs, wood shaft clubs and other golf memorabilia; issues monthly comprehensive Golf Collectibles Catalogue; will buy large collections.

Douglas MacKenzie
Antique Golf Clubs of Scotland - DMC Ltd.
2 La Belle Place
Glasgow, G3 7LH Scotland
ph: +44 141 333 9400
fax: +44 141 333 9490
douglas@dmcsoft.com
http://www.dmcsoft.com/antiquegolf
Buy an antique golf club: great gift for the golf nut, club prize or corporate gift.

Douglas MacKenzie
Antique Golf Clubs from Scotland
8 Easy Argyle St.
Helensburgh, Dunbartonshire G84 7RR Scotland
info@antiquegolfscotland.com
http://www.antiquegolfscotland.com
The leading online resource for antique golf clubs and golf memorabilia from Scotland, the birthplace of golf.

Iain Walker
Antique Golf
10 Glasgow Rd.
Paisley, PA1 3QG U.K.
ph: 0141-889-1860
fax: 0141-889-1880
info@antiquegolf.com
http://www.antiquegolf.com
Premier golf dealer with online catalog.

Experts

Bobby Farino
American Golf Classics, Inc.
114 Blackheath
Williamsburg, VA 23188
ph: 757-565-7200
fax: 757-565-7249
americangolf@cox.net
http://www.americangolfclassics.com
Author of "Golf Club Collectors Handbook;" appeared on PAX TV's "Treasures in Your Home."

John & Morton Olman
Old Golf Shop, Ltd.
P.O. Box 220
Pleasant Plain, OH 45162-0220
ph: 513-877-2676
fax: 513-241-7855
Authors of the "Golf Antiques & Other Treasures of the Game" (1997).

Leo M. Kelly, Jr.
Old Chicago Golf Shop
4977 Arquilla Dr.
Richton Park, IL 60471-1643
ph: 708-747-1045
fax: 708-747-1055
Ochicago@ix.netcom.com
http://www.oldgolf.com
Buys and sells golf related collectibles; issues a periodic catalog, "The Hickory Club Mart," packed with golf items for sale and having 40 to 70 B/W photos of antique golf collectibles; $35 for four issues; author of golf ball book.

Museums/Libraries

Andy Hunold, Curator
World Golf Hall of Fame
One World Golf Place
Saint Augustine, FL 32092
ph: 904-940-4000
http://www.wgv.com/hof/hof.html

Golf Ball Markers

Collectors

Norman Boughton
P.O. Box 1
Macedon, NY 14502
ph: 315-986-3851
nbought1@rochester.rr.com
http://www.woodenmoney.com
Wants golf markers (used to mark a spot on the green), any material; especially those identifiable to a particular course or golfer; also buys other golf memorabilia.

Golf Balls

Collectors

Bruce Broeffle
Golflogos Home Page
golflogos@yahoo.com
http://www.geocities.com/Augusta/4360
Logo golf balls for sale.

Roger Kleinschmidt
Golf Ball Art & Custom Displays
5303 Park Place Circle
Boca Raton, FL 33486
ph: 888-296-4133 or 561-417-5010
fax: 561-417-5010
golfart@gate.net
http://golfballart.com
Buys, trades, collects, sells logo golf balls; also builds and sells a more functional rack for storing or displaying a golf ball collection.

Kirk Harney
Logo Ball Web Site, The
712 Lucy Goff Dr.
Rantoul, IL 61866
ph: 217-893-8406
klharney@advancenet.net
http://www.advancenet.net/~klharney
A Web site for those who collect Logo Golf Balls; filled with information and pictures of logos and collections.

Misc. Services

Roger Kleinschmidt
Golf Ball Art & Custom Displays
5303 Park Place Circle
Boca Raton, FL 33486
ph: 888-296-4133 or 561-417-5010
fax: 561-417-5010
golfart@gate.net
http://golfballart.com
Builds golf ball display cases for collectors or to be given as awards or gifts; unique because of a new concept of attaching balls to a surface; made of oak or acrylic and of any size; takes up less wall or desk space.

Golf Clubs

Collectors

Samuel G. Scroggs
1073 Stonybridge Dr.
Chambersburg, PA 17201-9093
ph: 717-263-5422
Wants to buy older wooden shaft golf putters.

Dealers

George P. "Pat" Gillis
American Golf Classics, Inc.
114 Blackheath
Williamsburg, VA 23188
ph: 757-565-7237 or 757-565-7200
fax: 757-565-7249
pat@americangolfclassics.com
http://www.americangolfclassics.com
Appraiser, dealer, repair expert in antique, classic and modern golf clubs; in the golf business for over 25 years in pro shop management and retail along with repair which lead into the antique and classic trade in 1980.

Robin W. Berg
Golfingly Yours
5407 Pennock Point Rd.
Jupiter, FL 33458-3496
ph: 561-744-2553
fax: 561-744-2374
rokit8@aol.com
Dealer in fine collectible golfiana; buys, sells and appraises.

Barry Smith
Barry O'Brien's Golf Clubs & Collectibles
P.O. Box 22145
Lincoln, NE 68542
ph: 402-488-7684
barry@solu.net
http://www.golfopia.com
Buys, sells, trades practically anything related to golf; specializes in Wooden Shaft Golf Clubs and classic golf clubs from the 1940s through the 1960s.

John Hawes
Antique Golf
40 Allendale Rd.
Brampton, Ontario L6W 2YB Canada
ph: 905-796-3031 or 905-601-2631
deepgroove@sympatico.ca
http://www.geocities.com/Augusta/4053/pg1.html
Has been collecting wood shaft golf clubs for over 10 years; buys, sells and trades.

Experts

Bobby Farino
American Golf Classics, Inc.
114 Blackheath
Williamsburg, VA 23188
ph: 757-565-7200
fax: 757-565-7249
americangolf@cox.net
http://www.americangolfclassics.com
Author of "Golf Club Collectors Handbook;" appeared on PAX TV's "Treasures in Your Home."

Periodicals

Robin W. Berg, Pub.
Golfingly Yours
Newsletter: US Golf Classics
5407 Pennock Point Rd.
Jupiter, FL 33458-3496
ph: 561-744-2553
fax: 561-744-2374
rokit8@aol.com
A 24-30 page "buy-sell-trade" newsletter for classic and antique golf buffs; woods, irons, putters, wedges, sets and singles, books, memorabilia.

Harness Racing

Collectors

Cathy Ploumen
659 Milwaukee Court
Shakopee, MN 55379-2553
cploumen@aol.com
Interested in harness racing items, especially relating to Dan Patch and Rambling Willie.

Dealers

Lynne Matarrese
3163 Brixton Lane
Levittown, NY 11756
ph: 516-520-4090
Buys and sells harness racing memorabilia: photographs, programs, passes, tickets, menus, original correspondence, etc. from 1940s to 1980s.

Museums/Libraries

Trotting Horse Museum
Newsletter: Hall of Fame Trotters News
P.O. Box 590
240 Main St.
Goshen, NY 10924
ph: 914-294-6330
fax: 914-294-3463
Preserves the tradition of harness racing.

Hockey

Collectors

Scott Petterson
14560 White Lane SE
Jefferson, OR 97352
ph: 541-327-3841
hockeylegend@hotmail.com
http://www.hockeylegend.com
Collector of vintage (pre-1940) hockey memorabilia: original autographed photos and documents, programs and all other related NHL, PCHA, WCHL and minor league memorabilia and ephemera.

Internet Resources

GameWorn.net
jon@gameworn.net
http://www.gameworn.net
Online resource and community for collectors of game-used hockey jerseys and equipment: collecting tips, dealers, auctions, resources, forum, collector sites.

Museums/Libraries

U.S. Hockey Hall of Fame
801 Hat Trick Ave.
P.O. Box 657
Eveleth, MN 55734
ph: 218-744-5167 or 800-443-7825
fax: 218-744-2590
sersha@ushockeyhall.com
http://www.ushockeyhall.com

Hockey Hall of Fame
BCE Place
30 Yonge St.
Toronto, Ontario M5E 1X8 Canada
ph: 416-350-7765
fax: 416-360-1316
rellis@hhof.com
http://www.hhof.com/index.htm

Periodicals

Hugh Murphy, PR
Beckett Publications, Inc.
Magazine: Beckett Hockey Collector
15850 Dallas Parkway
Dallas, TX 75248
ph: 972-448-9018 or 800-840-3137
hmurphy@beckett.com
http://www.beckett.com
*Articles, ads, show calendar and
hockey card price guide.*

Hockey Cards

Dealers

Dan Donaldson
Slap Shot Hockey Cards
2922 Maple St.
Michigan City, IN 46360
webmaster@slapshothockey.com
http://www.slapshothockey.com

Experts

Andrew Koffman
Action Coin & Card
230 Sheppard Ave. West, Ste. 200
Toronto, Ontario M2N 1N1 Canada
ph: 416-222-6227
fax: 416-590-9991
andrew@actioncoin.com
http://www.actioncoin.com
*Canada's #1 source for hockey sports
cards.*

Periodicals

Stacie Berger
Krause Publications
Magazine: Sports Cards Magazine &
Price Guide
700 E. State St.
Iola, WI 54990-0001
ph: 715-445-2214
fax: 715-445-4087
stacie.berger@fwpubs.com
http://www.krause.com
*Full color monthly magazine featuring
baseball, basketball, hockey and
football cards from all eras; news,
columns, feature stories, price guides;
ads for cards and related items.*

Ice Skating

Clubs/Associations

Professional Skaters Association,
International
Magazine: Professional Skater
1821 2nd St. SW
Rochester, MN 55902
ph: 507-281-5122
fax: 507-281-5491
office@skatepsa.com
http://www.skatepsa.com

United States Figure Skating Association
Magazine: Skating
20 First St.
Colorado Springs, CO 80906
ph: 719-635-5200
fax: 719-635-9548
usfsa@usfsa.org
http://www.usfsa.org

Collectors

Lovena Harwood
P.O. Box 6139
Haverhill, MA 01831-6139
lovena@netway.com
http://www.netway.com/~lovena/
lovena.htm
*Ice skating memorabilia collector;
Web site has a bulletin board for
posting for sale, buy or trade ads.*

Karen Cameron
70-104 Scott St.
Meriden, CT 06450
ph: 203-238-3603
Cameron11@cox.net
*Collector of 18th and 19th century
antique ice skates, especially those
with a curly prow; also interested in
books about the history of skating.*

Dealers

Greg Walsh
32 River View Lane
P.O. Box 747
Potsdam, NY 13676-0747
ph: 315-265-9111
fax: 315-265-9222
gwalsh@twcny.rr.com
http://www.walshauction.com
*Wants to buy antique ice skates of
exceptional quality; appraises ice
skates and relate material; corresponding with others.*

Ice Skating (Ice Skates)

Clubs/Associations

Karen Cameron
Antique Ice Skate Club
Newsletter: Antique Skates, Inc.
70-104 Scott St.
Meriden, CT 06450
ph: 203-238-3603
Cameron11@cox.net
*Club formed by Karen Cameron and
Ann J. Bates; quarterly newsletter.*

Collectors

Ann J. Bates
Trout Point
5660 Keefe Rd.
Land O' Lakes, WI 54540
ph: 715-547-3638
ajb@newnorth.net
*Collector of unusual and rare antique
ice skates and Sonja Henie memorabilia; co-founder with Karen Cameron
of the Antique Ice Skate Club.*

Jerseys (Game Worn)

Dealers

Barry Meisel
MeiGray Group
185 Industrial Parkway, Ste. C
Branchburg, NJ 08876
ph: 908-541-0114 or 888-463-4472
fax: 908-541-1123
sales@meigray.com
http://www.meigray.com
Specializes in game worn jerseys.

Grey Flannel Collectibles, Inc.
731 Middle Neck Rd.
Great Neck, NY 11024
ph: 800-242-7647 or 516-466-5533
fax: 516-466-5592
gfcsports@aol.com
http://www.greyflannel.com
Leading dealers in game-used jerseys.

Jim Yackel
Jim's Jerseys - Game Worn Jerseys &
Helmets
P.O. Box 35885
Syracuse, NY 13235
ph: 315-449-4764
jimyackel@yahoo.com
http://www.jimyackel.com
*Buys and sells genuine game worn/
player used jerseys, helmets, bats, and
more for sports memorabilia and
uniform collectors: Major and Minor
League baseball, NFL, CFL, USFL,
WLAF, NCAA, Arena football.*

GameWornJerseys.com
2 Lake Crescent Dr.
East Rochester, NY 14445
ph: 716-820-GAME
http://www.gamewornjerseys.com
*Sells game worn jerseys and game
used equipment; items for sale, want
ads, auctions, collecting tips, sports
guide, price guide, photo gallery,
links.*

Jewelry

Collectors

M. B. Spragins
501 Adams St.
Huntsville, AL 35801
ph: 800-987-7464 x8424
mbs501@aol.com
*Wants to buy sports rings: football,
baseball, basketball, hockey, college,
minor league; also Super Bowl rings,
professional Cotton Bowl Rolexes.*

Experts

Mike Safran
Collectors' Collector, The
204 South Edisto Ave.
Columbia, SC 29205
ph: 803-771-6995
collect1@logicsouth.com
*Championship sports rings bought,
sold, traded; from the Sugar Bowl to
the Super Bowl, championship jewelry
from all aspects of sports.*

Lacrosse

Museums/Libraries

U.S. Lacrosse Museum & National Hall
of Fame
Magazine: Lacrosse Magazine
113 West University Parkway
Baltimore, MD 21210-3301
ph: 410-235-6882
fax: 410-366-6735
info@lacrosse.org
http://www.lacrosse.org
*US Lacrosse is the national governing
body of men's and women's lacrosse;*

*the Lacrosse Museum contains
national lacrosse archives.*

Little League

Museums/Libraries

Alan Robison
Peter J. McGovern Little League
Museum
P.O. Box 3485
South Williamsport, PA 17701
ph: 570-326-3607
publicrelations@littleleague.org
http://www.littleleague.org/museum
*Focuses on Little League Baseball/
softball memorabilia; vintage baseball
equipment; vintage magazine covers
featuring youths and baseball.*

Nike Sportswear

Dealers

Larry McKaugham
Heller's Far West Clothing
1000 Lenora, Ste. 116
Seattle, WA 98121
ph: 206-233-9014 or 800-328-5384
hellers@halcyon.com
http://www.hellerscafe.com
Wants old Nike sportswear.

Husky Boy Vintage
4441 S. Meridian, Ste. 471
Puyallup, WA 98373-5959
ph: 800-HUSKY-BO or 253-472-6341
steve@huskyboy.com
*Wants to buy Nike Air Jordan 1985-
1991 and 1970s-1980s Nike shoes and
sportswear; also buying vintage denim
workwear, i.e., Levi's, Lee, etc. and
vintage military flight jackets.*

Polo

Collectors

Dennis Amato
5 The Crow's Nest
Port Washington, NY 11050
ph: 212-503-7934
damato@iopener.net
*Wants anything related to the sport of
polo: books, magazines, programs,
autographs, ephemera.*

Rodeo

Clubs/Associations

Pro Bull Rider Fan Club
Magazine: Pro Bull Rider Magazine
6 South Tejon, Ste. 700
Colorado Springs, CO 80903
ph: 714-471-3008
fax: 719-471-4712
admin@pbrnow.com
http://www.pbrnow.com
*Merchandise, fashion, articles, behind
the chutes, chutin' the bull, etc.*

Professional Rodeo Cowboys Association
Magazine: ProRodeo Sports News
101 Pro Rodeo Dr.
Colorado Springs, CO 80919
ph: 719-593-8840
prca@prorodeo.com
http://www.prorodeo.com

Museums/Libraries

Pro Rodeo Hall of Fame & Museum of
the American Cowboy
101 Pro Rodeo Dr.
Colorado Springs, CO 80919
ph: 719-528-4764 or 719-593-8840
prca@prorodeo.com
http://www.prorodeo.com/html/
1.8.halloffame.html

Roller Skating

Clubs/Associations

Bill Wolf
USA Roller Skating
Magazine: US Roller Sports
4730 South St.
P.O. Box 6579
Lincoln, NE 68506-0579
ph: 402-483-7551 x20
fax: 402-483-1465
lmarciani@usarollersports.org
http://usarollersports.novia.net
*Governing body for amateur roller
skating: speed skating, roller hockey,
artistic skating.*

Collectors

Royal Duncan
7600 N. Galena Rd.
Peoria, IL 61615
ph: 309-691-2772
*Wants to buy Roller Derby autographs
and memorabilia.*

Museums/Libraries

National Museum of Roller Skating
Newsletter: Historical Roller Skating
Overview
4730 South St., Ste. 2
P.O. Box 6579
Lincoln, NE 68506-0579
ph: 402-483-7551 x16
fax: 402-483-1465
directorcurator@rollerskatingmuseum.com
http://www.rollerskatingmuseum.com
*Largest collection of historical roller
skates dating to 1819; roller skating
history as technology, sport,
recreation and personalities; sells
"The Evolution of the Roller Skate:
1820 - Present" by Scott Addison
Wilhite; also other books.*

Rugby

Clubs/Associations

David Fox, Sec.
Rugby Memorabilia Society
P.O. Box 1093
Thornbury
Bristol, BS35 1DA U.K.
rugby-memorabilia@blueyonder.co.uk
http://www.rugby-memorabilia.co.uk
*For those interested in collecting
rugby memorabilia.*

Skateboards

Collectors

Jack Koffron
8600 N. 53rd St.
Brown Deer, WI 53223
ph: 414-354-4850
fax: 414-765-1207
*Wants to buy wooden skateboards
with good graphics from the 1950s to
1970s; also wants hot rod car club
jackets and license plaques from the
1940s to 1960s.*

Wayne Babcock
4846 Carpenteria Ave.
Carpinteria, CA 93013-1935
ph: 805-684-8148
oldsurfin@cs.com
*Collects pre-1985 skateboards,
skateboard magazines, trophies, and
patches.*

Snow Skiing

Collectors

Mark Miller
Mark Miller Collection, The
P.O. Box 3836
Park City, UT 84060
ph: 888-753-7807 or 435-649-1858
fax: 435-649-1858
info@antiqueskis.com
http://www.antiqueskis.com
*Has compiled the largest collection of
antique wooden skis and snowshoes in
the country.*

Gary Schwartz
1099 D St., Penthouse A
San Rafael, CA 94901
ph: 415-256-9300
fax: 415-256-9400
gary@PicturesNow.com
http://www.picturesnow.com
*Wants pre-1940 books, company
catalogs, magazines, postcards, sheet
music, posters, photographs, etc.
relating to skiing.*

Museums/Libraries

Jeff Leich
New England Ski Museum
Journal: New England Ski Museum
Journal
P.O. Box 267
Parkway Exit 34B
Franconia, NH 03580-0267
ph: 603-823-7177
fax: 603-823-9505
staff@skimuseum.org
http://www.skimuseum.org
*Museum contains library research
materials and photo collections open
by appointment.*

U.S. National Ski Hall of Fame &
Museum
610 Palms Ave.
P.O. Box 191
Ishpeming, MI 49849
ph: 906-485-6323
fax: 906-486-4570
skihall@uplogon.com
http://www.skihall.com
*Walk through ski history with an
array of panels and cases displaying
items, old and new, telling the story of
skiing.*

Colorado Ski Museum - Ski Hall of
Fame
Newsletter: Making Tracks
231 S. Frontage Rd.
P.O. Box 1976
Vail, CO 81657
ph: 970-476-1876
fax: 970-476-1879
skimuse@vail.net
http://www.vailsoft.com/museum
*Traces 100 years of Colorado's ski
heritage through displays containing
equipment, artifacts and photographs.*

Bill Clark, Dir.
Western America Skisport Museum
P.O. Box 729
Soda Springs, CA 95728
ph: 916-426-3313
*Ski history, memorabilia, manuscript
collection.*

Soccer

Dealers

Frank Barr
Frank Barr, Inc.
10 Wren Court
Edison, NJ 08820
FrankBarrInc@juno.com
http://www.swiftsite.com/frankbarrinc
*Specializes in soccer cards and
memorabilia.*

Museums/Libraries

National Soccer Hall of Fame, The
Newsletter: 90 Minutes
18 Stadium Circle
Oneonta, NY 13820
ph: 607-432-3351
fax: 607-432-8429
info@soccerhall.org
http://www.soccerhall.org
*Information on soccer history,
especially American; wants all forms
of memorabilia relating to soccer
including photographs.*

International Football Hall of Fame
U.K.
info@ifhof.com
http://www.ifhof.com

Softball

Museums/Libraries

Ron Babb
Amateur Softball Association of America
Newsletter: Amateur Softball Hall of
Fame Newsletter
2801 N.E. 50th St.
Oklahoma City, OK 73111
ph: 405-424-5266
fax: 405-424-3855
info@softball.org
http://www.softball.org

National Softball Hall of Fame &
Museum
2801 NW 50th St.
Oklahoma City, OK 73111-7200
ph: 405-424-5266
info@softball.org
http://www.softball.org

Squash

Experts

Bert Armstrong
Bert Armstrong Squash Museum
8 McLeod Place
Mt. Waverley, Vic. 3149 Australia
ph: 613 9807-3102
fax: 613 9807-7378
bertarm@bigpond.net.au
*One of the largest collections (over
600) of squash rackets and memorabilia including balls, badges, flags,
stamps, pins, etc.; also collects lawn
and royal tennis items.*

Supplies For

Suppliers

BCW Supplies
P.O. Box 970
Anderson, IN 46015
ph: 800-433-4229 or 765-644-2033
info@bcwsupplies.com
http://www.bcwsupplies.com
*Sells protective supplies for sports
collectibles: albums, protective pages,
ball and bat holders, storage boxes,
snap and screw card holders, top
loads and card sleeves, card cases,
comic supplies, and more.*

Sports Collectibles Supplies
1933 E. Pomona St.
Santa Ana, CA 92705
ph: 714-259-0550 or 800-366-1425
fax: 714-259-0550
sales@cardboardgold.com
http://www.cardboardgoldstore.com
*A leading supplier of trading card
supplies and sports memorabilia
displays: semi rigid holders, pocket
pages, cube displays for balls, and
more.*

Surfing

Collectors

John Casper
2605 S. Peninsula Dr.
Daytona Beach, FL 32118-5603
ph: 904-767-2075
sandab66@hotmail.com
*Wants to buy 1960's and earlier
surfing memorabilia including surfing
magazines, books, advertising
literature/items, decals, patches, films,
original surf movie posters, clocks,
board games, comics, trophies, 8' or
longer boards, etc.*

Wayne Babcock
4846 Carpenteria Ave.
Carpinteria, CA 93013-1935
ph: 805-684-8148
oldsurfin@cs.com
*Collects old long surfboards, surfing
trophies, magazines, photos, books,*

*records, posters, and any pre-1968
surfing items; also wants any pre-
1980 Hawaiian items; especially
wants wooden surfboards and very old
items.*

Jim Winniman
399 E. Kawaili St.
Hilo, HI 96720
ph: 808-935-2341
scoops@hawaii.rr.com
*Major collector of all surfing or
surfboard related items: surfboards,
art, posters, old trophies, books,
magazines, figurines, decals, patches;
anything related to surfing; send
photos with detailed descriptions
including condition.*

Dealers

Surf N Hula
P.. Box 812
Haiku, HI 96708-0812
ph: 800-410-7648 or 808-935-2341
info@surfNhula.com
http://www.surfNhula.com
*Buys and sells everything that is
vintage Hawaiian and surfing related;
over 1,000 pieces in stock: paintings,
posters, postcards, Hula figurines and
nodders, artifacts, books, magazines,
Duke Kahanamoku, surfboards,
skateboards, etc.*

Mark Blackburn
Mauna Kea Galleries
65-1298 Kawaihae Rd.
Waimea, HI 96743
ph: 808-887-2244
fax: 808-887-2226
mkg@interpac.net
http://www.maunakeagalleries.com
*Wants only pre-1969 surfboards, price
lists, posters, programs, photos,
books, trophies, souvenirs, etc.*

Museums/Libraries

Tara Torburn, Sec.
California Surf Museum
223 North Coast Highway
Oceanside, CA 92054
ph: 760-721-6876
csm@surfmuseum.org
http://www.surfmuseum.org
*Surfboard collection, men's bathing
suits, record covers, surf advertising
art.*

International Surfing Museum
411 Olive
P.O. Box 782
Huntington Beach, CA 92648
ph: 714-960-3483
fax: 714-960-1434
intsurfing@earthlink.net
http://www.surfingmuseum.org
Surfboards from 1900 to present.

Swimming

Museums/Libraries

Bob Duenkel
International Swimming Hall of Fame
1 Hall of Fame Dr.
Fort Lauderdale, FL 33316-1611
ph: 954-462-6536
fax: 954-525-4031
bduenkel@ishof.org
http://ishof.org/museum.htm
*Seeks photos, memorabilia, etc.
regarding the great athletes and
history of the aquatic sports;
swimming, diving, water polo,
synchronized swimming, water safety,
pools, etc.*

Table Tennis

Clubs/Associations

Graham Trimming
Table Tennis Collectors Society, The
Magazine: Table Tennis Collector, The
17 Gwendale
Pinkneys Green
Maidenhead, Berkshire Sl6 6SH U.K.
ph: +44(0) 1628 636978
graham.trimming@virgin.net
http://freespace.virgin.net/
graham.trimming/TTCS/
TTCSHome.htm
*Purpose is to encourage research into
the history of racket sports; to share
information on collectible items; to
publicize news of auctions; to put
subscribers in touch with one another;
informal with occasional meetings.*

Tennis

Clubs/Associations

Gerald Gurney
Tennis Collectors Society, The
Magazine: Tennis Collector, The
The Guildhall Orchard
Mary Lane North, Great Bromley
Colchester, Essex CO7 7TU U.K.
ph: 1206 230330
fax: 1206 230330
*Purpose is to encourage research into
the history of racket sports; to share
information on collectible items; to
publicize news of auctions; to put
subscribers in touch with one another;
informal with occasional meetings.*

Collectors

Sheldon Katz
18 Cliffside Dr.
Port Jefferson, NY 11777-1118
ph: 631-928-1800

Paul Dowling
2312 Riverbend Rd.
Allentown, PA 18103
ph: 610-220-6263
fax: 610-391-1556
PAULD58103@aol.com
*Wants to buy tennis ball cans (key-
wind with metal lids); also wants
tennis ball boxes, porcelain tennis
figurines, and silver tennis items with
a tennis motif.*

Ken Benner
217 Hewett Rd.
Wyncote, PA 19095-1203
ph: 215-885-5876
fax: 215-885-4635
kenbenten@aol.com
*Wants to buy pre-1900 unusual
racquets, photos, trophies, programs,
tennis ball cans (metal lids), books,
prints, etc.*

Donald N. Jones
107 Rivers Edge Dr.
Savannah, GA 31406-8419
ph: 912-354-2133
*Wants to buy tennis items: rackets,
ball cans, and tennis ephemera.*

Larry Whitaker
1337 Joplin Dr., #2
San Jose, CA 95118
ph: 408-723-4665
LWhita@aol.com
Wants to buy old tennis ball cans.

Dealers

Richard R. Regan
293 Winter St. #5
Hanover, MA 02339-2528
ph: 781-826-3537
foregolf@tiac.net
*Wants to buy tennis posters &
broadsides, books, prints, cigarette
cards, programs, autographed photos,
early equipment such as balls, ball
containers and rackets; anything
related to tennis.*

Don Brenner
2292 Fair Oaks Rd.
Atlanta, GA 30333-1200
ph: 404-315-7782
dnadon@mediaone.net
*Dealer and collector of tennis
trophies, autographs, magazines,
guides, books, programs, tickets,
cards, photographs, and other tennis
memorabilia.*

Experts

Jeanne Cherry
Amaryllis Press
1402 San Vicente Blvd.
Santa Monica, CA 90402
ph: 310-395-3915
fax: 310-260-9425
info@tennisantiques.com
http://www.tennisantiques.com
*Collects, buys, appraises and
specializes in tennis collectibles;
author of "Tennis Antiques &
Collectibles," covering rackets, ball
cans, books, ephemera, silver and
ceramics.*

Internet Resources

Rick Roth
Racquet Collector, The
4710 Hilltop Dr.
Pasco, WA 99301
ph: 509-543-9239
reroth@theracquetcollector.com
http://www.theracquetcollector.com
Online service for buyers and sellers

*of tennis related memorabilia:
racquets, tennis balls and cans, art,
books, prints, trophies, etc.*

Museums/Libraries

Mark S. Young, II, Archivist
International Tennis Hall of Fame &
Tennis Museum
194 Bellevue Ave.
Newport, RI 02840-3515
ph: 401-849-3990
fax: 401-849-8780
newport@tennisfame.com
http://www.tennisfame.com
*Provides a chronology of the sport's
rich history, from its origins up to
today's superstars.*

Tennis Rackets

Collectors

Ralph Nix
P.O. Box 655
Red Bay, AL 35582-0655
ph: 256-356-2997
*Wants early lawn tennis rackets and
other tennis memorabilia.*

Norman Hagey
19672 Steavens Creek #424
Cupertino, CA 95014-2465
ph: 408-973-8129
*Wants old autographed tennis rackets
and related equipment; has over 250
autographed tennis rackets.*

Thoroughbred Racing

Appraisers

Joe Boone
Triple Crown Collectibles & Cigars
309 West Woodlawn Ave.
Louisville, KY 40214
ph: 502-361-1973 or 800-585-7237
joe@derbyglass.com
http://www.derbyglass.com
*Buys, sells, trades, appraises and
specializes in Kentucky Derby,
Preakness, Belmont, and Breeders'
Cup memorabilia: glasses, programs,
pins, artwork, admission items, etc.*

Auction Services

Dick Hering
311 Knollwood Dr.
Hampstead, NC 28443
ph: 910-270-7738
fax: 910-270-7739
drfager132@aol.com
http://members.aol.com/drfager132/
auction.htm
*Mail bid auctions of horse racing
(thoroughbred) memorabilia, glasses,
programs, pins, advertising signs,
games, books, stocks, etc.; Kentucky
Derby, Preakness, Belmont, etc.*

Collectors

Ken Grayson
P.O. Box 24586
Lexington, KY 40524-4586
ph: 859-278-7419
fax: 859-278-4268
Wants to buy Kentucky Derby,

Belmont, Preakness, and Breeder's Cup glasses, programs, etc.

Coleen Detzel
28 Lacresta Dr.
Florence, KY 41042-9663
ph: 606-647-6156
Wants thoroughbred racing items pertaining to Kentucky Derby and Jim Beam Stakes; also Latonia Race Track items: glasses, programs, photos, tickets, etc.

Gary Gatanis
3283-B Cardiff
Toledo, OH 43606-1867
ph: 419-475-3192
janis@buckeyeinet.com
Wants Kentucky Derby memorabilia including programs, advertising and glasses; also Dan Patch memorabilia.

Gary Medeiros
1319 Sayre St.
San Leandro, CA 94579
ph: 510-351-6193
fax: 510-351-6193
pharlap2@aol.com
Thoroughbred racing and Kentucky Derby memorabilia: programs, books, games, glasses, photos, passes, pins, postcards; any thoroughbred related items considered; has written articles on collecting racing programs.

Dealers

Paul Gundy
Horse Racing Memorabilia
5610 Pebble Brook Lane
Boynton Beach, FL 33437
ph: 561-364-8403
paulgundy@adelphia.net
http://www.derbystuff.com
Buys and sells drinking glasses, programs, books, magazines, decanters, posters, pins, trophies, track giveaways; anything to do with famous horses, races, tracks, jockeys, trainers, Kentucky Derby, Preakness, Belmont, Breeders' Cup.

Jim Settembre
Thoroughbred Racing Collectibles, Inc.
5115 Woodstone Circle E.
Lake Worth, FL 33463-5819
ph: 561-964-5434 or 561-964-8230
fax: 561-964-1143
bigred51@t-r-c.com
http://www.t-r-c.com
Wants Kentucky Derby, Breeder's Cup, Preakness, and Belmont Stakes glasses and programs; also wants to buy any related horse racing items; auction service also available.

Joe Boone
Triple Crown Collectibles & Cigars
309 West Woodlawn Ave.
Louisville, KY 40214
ph: 502-361-1973 or 800-585-7237
joe@derbyglass.com
http://www.derbyglass.com
Buys, sells, trades, appraises and specializes in Kentucky Derby, Preakness, Belmont, and Breeders'

Cup memorabilia: glasses, programs, pins, artwork, admission items, etc.

Douglas Joseph Burkhardt
533 East 4th St.
Newport, KY 41071
ph: 606-581-5490 or 606-341-8752
slugdb@hotmail.com
Buys and sells all Kentucky Derby, Jim Beam Stakes, and all other horse racing items.

Experts

Tom Sporney
1005 Sharon Dr.
Glen Burnie, MD 21061
ph: 410-863-5854
fax: 347-823-4895
equillector@horse-races.net
http://www.abouthorseraces.com/equillector

William Friedberg
462 Hillcreek Rd.
Shepherdsville, KY 40165-6927
ph: 502-957-4039
Author of Bill Friedberg's glass collector's price guide "Racing into the 21st Century Special "Millenium" Edition," 1999 - 2000; $13.50 ppd. from author; color photographs; Ky. Derby, Preakness, Belmont, Breeder's Cup and more.

Betty Hornback
Betty's Antiques
707 Sunrise Lane
Elizabethtown, KY 42701
ph: 502-765-2441 or 502-369-7279
Author of "Kentucky Derby Glass Price Guide;" specializes in Kentucky Derby glasses; sells nationwide; wants to buy pre-1974 glasses; send $2 for list of glasses for sale.

Cindy Dulay
Horse-Races.Net
11753 Sheppard Ave. E. #1207
Scarborough, Ontario M1B 5M3 Canada
editor@horse-races.net
http://www.horse-races.net
Collector/expert has large online museum of horse racing memorabilia and collectibles from glasses to advertising to programs; photos, info, online price guide.

Internet Resources

Tom Sporney
Equillector, The
1005 Sharon Dr.
Glen Burnie, MD 21061
ph: 410-863-5854
fax: 347-823-4895
equillector@horse-races.net
http://www.abouthorseraces.com/equillector
A guide for collectors of horse racing memorabilia; goal is to present realistic prices for items based on actual sales prices rather than arbitrary dealer prices, to aid in identifying items by giving descriptions and photos.

Museums/Libraries

National Museum of Racing & Hall of Fame
191 Union Ave.
Saratoga Springs, NY 12866
ph: 518-584-0400
fax: 518-584-4574
webmaster@racingmuseum.org
http://www.racingmuseum.org

Chris Goodlett
Kentucky Derby Museum, The
<u>Newsletter: Inside Track</u>
P.O. Box 3513
Louisville, KY 40201-3513
ph: 502-637-1111 or 800-273-3729
fax: 502-636-5855
info@derbymuseum.org
http://www.derbymuseum.org
Cannot provide appraisals, but can help identify and research; located at 704 Central Ave., Louisville, KY 40208.

Track & Field

Collectors

Ed Kozloff
10144 Lincoln
Huntington Woods, MI 48070-1539
ph: 248-544-9099
fax: 248-544-4601
racebreak@aol.com
http://www.motorcitystriders.com
Collector, expert on Olympic, running and track & field memorabilia; track & field, road races, Olympic material: medals, ribbons, trophies, annuals, books, magazines, etc.

Museums/Libraries

National Track & Field Hall of Fame
216 Fort Washington Ave.
New York, NY 10032
ph: 212-923-1803
fax: 212-923-1645
keats@armorytrack.com
http://www.armorynyc.org/trackhall
Three floors of exhibits in the sport of track and field.

Weightlifting

Experts

David Chapman
656 32nd Ave. East
Seattle, WA 98112
ph: 206-329-7573
fax: 206-329-7573
Says there is more to weight training than fat Russian guys or Arnold Schwarzenegger; is interested in the early days of "physical culture" (1895-1950): wants photos, books, magazines, posters, etc.; has written extensively.

Museums/Libraries

Barb Andrelczyk
York Barbell Hall of Fame
3300 Board Rd.
York, PA 17402
ph: 717-767-6481 or 800-358-9675
fax: 717-764-0044
info@yorkbarbell.com
http://www.yorkbarbell.com/
Weightlifting, body building, power lifting history and memorabilia.

Wrestling

Collectors

John Pantozzi
1000 Polk Ave.
Franklin Square, NY 11010-2018
ph: 516-488-7728
fax: 516-327-8984
mr4wrestle@aol.com
Wants to buy wrestling related toys, dolls, pennants, patches, trading cards, pins, postcards, books, posters, movie posters, board games, ring gear, autographs, photos, scrapbooks, etc.

Bob Bryla
"Dr. Wrestling"
1912 Sunset Ave.
Utica, NY 13502-5636
ph: 315-733-1846
fax: 315-733-7518
bryfour@dreamscape.com
Wants items relating to boxing and wrestling: strength books, magazines, programs, dolls, games, medals, pennants, bottles, etc. from 1860 to present.

Dealers

Tom Burke
31 Groveland St.
Springfield, MA 01108-2920
ph: 413-733-6015
tbgblmat@javanet.com
Buys and sells Professional Wrestling postcards, programs, magazines, and related items from any era.

Clifford Aliperti
things-and-other-stuff
ph: 631-455-6381
things@things-and-other-stuff.com
http://www.things-and-other-stuff.com
Specializes in Professional Wrestling memorabilia with an emphasis on wrestling magazines.

Main Event Wrestling Collectibles
P.O. Box 2351
Monroe, NC 28111
ph: 704-226-9966 or 800-613-9966
fax: 704-226-9955
gregprice@maineventwrestling.com
http://www.maineventwrestling.com
Source for Pro Wrestling collectibles and autographed memorabilia.

Bill Pollock
4267 Fox Hollow Circle
Casselberry, FL 32707-5240
ph: 407-695-9140
pollockwk@mindspring.com
*Wants pre-1980 wrestling related
items: posters, programs, tickets,
autographs, pennants.*

Museums/Libraries

Myron Roderick
National Wrestling Hall of Fame
405 W. Hall Of Fame Ave.
Stillwater, OK 74075
ph: 405-377-5243
fax: 405-377-5244
info@wrestlinghalloffame.org
http://www.wrestlinghalloffame.org
*America's shrine to the sport of
amateur wrestling.*

SPORTS HISTORY

Clubs/Associations

Chuck Hershberger, GM
Sports Hall of Oblivion
P.O. Box 69025
Pleasant Ridge, MI 48069-0025
ph: 248-543-9412
wheresports@hotmail.com
*The Sports Hall of Oblivion is an
organization dedicated to preserving
the memory of defunct sports teams
(HS, College, semi-pro, pro.); also
covering new and weird sports.*

SPRINKLERS

(see CAST IRON; CLOTHES
SPRINKLERS)

SPY EQUIPMENT

(see also CAMERAS & CAMERA
EQUIPMENT, Subminiature;
CHARACTER COLLECTIBLES, Spy
Memorabilia; MYSTERY/DETECTIVE
ITEMS; TELEVISION SHOWS &
MEMORABILIA, Private Eye)

Collectors

Kenneth D. Smith
55 Howard Ave.
Staten Island, NY 10301-4404
*Wants to buy cryptographic and code
machines, devices, books and manuals;
any era, any nation.*

Keith Melton
P.O. Box 2880
Jupiter, FL 33468-2880
ph: 561-743-1143
fax: 561-743-7504
*Pays top dollar for all types of old
Code machines: ENIGMA's, M-209's,
M-94's, M-138's, cipher disks and
wheels; also devices used by OSS,
SOE, KGB, MOSSAD, British
intelligence, etc.*

Mike & Gladys Kessler
25749 Anchor Circle
San Juan Capistrano, CA 92675-4002
ph: 949-661-3320
*Buys and specializes in unusual 1880-
1890s disguised or detective cameras;
also Simon Wing cameras.*

Uwe H. Breker
Bonner Str. 528-530
Koln, D-50968 Germany
ph: 49 221 387049 or 941-925-0385 (US
Rep)
fax: 49 221 374878
auction@breker.com
http://www.breker.com
*Wants secret service communication
machines and devices.*

Museums/Libraries

Jack E. Ingram, Cur.
National Cryptologic Museum
DIRNSA
Attn: S542/Museum
Fort George G Meade, MD 20755
ph: 301-688-5849 or 301-688-5848
fax: 301-688-5847
http://www.nsa.gov/museum
*Gov't. collection open free to the
public; thousands of artifacts which
collectively serve to sustain the history
of the cryptologic profession: books,
computers, cipher devices, Enigma,
cryptanalysis, research library by
appointment.*

ST. PATRICK

(see ELVES)

Periodicals

Chuck Thompson
Newsletter: St. Patrick Notes
10802 Greencreek Dr., Ste. 203
Houston, TX 77070-5365
ph: 281-970-0479
chilichuck@chilitech.com
*Legends, facts, quotes, stories, and
other notes about St. Patrick; for fans
of the Patron Saint of Ireland and
collectors of St. Patrick memorabilia.*

STAGECOACH ITEMS

(see WESTERN AMERICANA)

STAINED GLASS

(see also ARCHITECTURAL
ELEMENTS; CRAFTS, Glass)

Clubs/Associations

Katei Gross, Ex. Admin.
Stained Glass Association of America
Magazine: Stained Glass Quarterly, The
10009 East 62nd St.
Raytown, MO 64129
ph: 800-438-9581 or 816-737-2090
fax: 816-737-2801
sgaa@stainedglass.org
http://www.stainedglass.org
*A non-profit association founded in
1903 to promote the development and
advancement of the stained and
decorative art glass craft; members
receive "Stand Glass Quarterly" four
times each year.*

Collectors

Bob Ward
2461 E. High St.
Pottstown, PA 19464-3189
ph: 610-970-6299
kunmingcbi@aol.com
Wants stained glass windows.

Dealers

Jim Osella
Church Connection
216 Cumer Rd.
Canonsburg, PA 15057
ph: 866-873-3735 or 724-746-2451
fax: 724-746-2451
osella@usaor.net
http://www.usedchurchitems.com
*Wants to buy stained and beveled
glass windows, one or a hundred.*

David E. Newman
Newman & Assoc.
2476 Bolsover, #504
Houston, TX 77005-2518
ph: 713-521-7044
newmanasoc@aol.com
*Specializes in buying, selling,
authenticating and appraising vintage
stained and beveled leaded window
and door glass panels.*

Experts

H. Weber & Jill Wilson
WebWilson.com
P.O. Box 506
Portsmouth, RI 02871
ph: 800-508-0022
fax: 401-683-1644
hww@webwilson.com
http://www.webwilson.com
*Author of books on stained glass; also
sells architectural antiques.*

Carl Heck
Carl Heck Decorative Arts
P.O. Box 8416
Aspen, CO 81612-8416
ph: 970-925-8011
fax: 970-925-8011
carlheck5@aol.com
http://www.carlheck.com
*Collector/dealer/expert specializing in
lamps by Tiffany, Pairpoint, Handel,
Galle and Tiffany windows for over
32 years; currently Tiffany advisor for
"Schroeder's," "Antique Trader"
price guides.*

Internet Resources

Robert Daniels
Art Glass World
4403 Cleveland St.
Tampa, FL 33609
ph: 813-806-2923 x16
webmaster@artglassworld.com
http://www.artglassworld.com
*The largest Internet stained glass
resource in the world; great database
of stained glass professionals listed by
state.*

Man./Prod./Dist.

Stained Glass Resources, Inc.
15 Commercial Dr.
Hampden, MA 01036
ph: 800-883-5052
fax: 413-566-2935
sgr@map.com
http://www.stainedglassresources.com
*Specializes in the manufacture and
restoration of stained glass windows.*

Rohlf's Studio, Inc.
783 South Third Ave.
Mount Vernon, NY 10550
ph: 800-969-4106 or 914-699-4848
fax: 914-699-7091
Rohlf1@aol.com
http://www.RohlfStudio.com

Victor Rothman
Victor Rothman for Stained Glass
1468 Midland Ave., #5A
Bronxville, NY 10708
ph: 914-969-0919 or 212-255-2551
fax: 914-237-2032
vrothman@iwon.com
*Specializes in museum quality
restoration and conservation of all
styles of stained glass windows and
lamps; qualified to act as a consultant
and to write specifications for new
fabrication of windows.*

Durham Studios, Inc.
330 Eagle Ave.
West Hempstead, NY 11552
ph: 516-481-5656
fax: 516-481-7905
*Has been designing and installing
stained glass windows since 1902:
installations in churches, synagogues,
commercial and residential architectural settings.*

Hunt Stained Glass Studios, Inc.
1756 West Carson St.
Pittsburgh, PA 15219-1036
ph: 412-391-1796
fax: 412-391-1560
huntsg@msn.com
http://www.huntstainedglass.com
*Leaded glass, faceted glass,
residential, sculptures, etched glass,
restorations.*

E. Crosby Willet, ASA
Willet Stained Glass Studios
10 East Moreland Ave.
Philadelphia, PA 19118-3539
ph: 877-709-4106 or 215-247-5721
fax: 215-247-2951
crosbyw@earthlink.net
http://www.willetglass.com

Art-N-Glass Studio
693 Adams Hotel Rd.
Shoemakersville, PA 19555
ph: 610-562-4052
studio@art-n-glass.com
http://www.art-n-glass.com

Art in Glass, Inc.
414 Pine Ave.
Frederick, MD 21701-5764
ph: 301-663-1151 or 888-340-7888
fax: 301-620-7417
carvedglass@artinglass.com
http://www.artinglass.com
*Specializing in custom stained glass
designs for doors, sidelights,
skylights, cabinets; also sandblast
carving, etching, and repairs.*

Ray Gregory
Art Glass, Inc.
2708 Wyoming Ave.
Norfolk, VA 23513
ph: 757-855-4312
fax: 757-855-4312
*Design and create stained glass for
churches, synagogues, public
buildings, restaurants and private
homes; also repairs old stained glass
windows.*

Michael J. Marsh
Stained Glass Associates
P.O. Box 1531
Raleigh, NC 27602-1531
ph: 919-266-2493
fax: 919-266-2493
*Fabricates, repairs, restores and
installs stained glass windows; also
builds beveled window and door
inserts; established in 1958; member
of SGAA.*

Laws Stained Glass Studios, Inc.
145 Ebenezer Lane
Statesville, NC 28625
ph: 800-820-1292 or 704-876-3463
fax: 704-876-4238
http://www.lawsstainedglass.com
*Serving churches for over 50 years;
features work in 22 states as well as
Puerto Rico and Korea.*

Statesville Stained Glass, Inc.
136 Christopher Lane
Statesville, NC 28625
ph: 704-872-5147
fax: 704-872-7813
ssglass@vnet.net

Advent Glass Works, Inc.
P.O. Box 174
Fort White, FL 32038
ph: 800-207-4875 or 904-497-2050
fax: 904-497-2941

Bob Primm
Emmanuel Stained Glass Studios, Inc.
410 Maple Ave.
Nashville, TN 37210
ph: 800-326-2228 or 615-255-5446
fax: 615-255-5447
info@emmanuelstainedglass.com
http://www.emmanuelstainedglass.com

Franklin Art Glass Studios, Inc.
222 East Sycamore St.
Columbus, OH 43206-2144
ph: 614-221-2972 or 800-848-7683
fax: 614-221-5223
info@franklinartglass.com
http://www.franklinartglass.com
*Serving the stained glass industry
since 1924; a full service art glass
supplier; also fabricates stained
leaded glass products for residential,
commercial and churches.*

Whitney Stained Glass Studio, Inc.
2530 Superior Ave.
Cleveland, OH 44114
ph: 216-348-1616
fax: 216-348-1116
wsglass@aol.com
*Founded in 1985, offers outstanding
craftsmanship in the design,
fabrication and installation of
stained, leaded, faceted glass
windows; religions, commercial,
residential; also restores historic
stained glass windows.*

Shadetree Stained Glass Studio
417 Howard
Petoskey, MI 49770
ph: 616-347-1011
fax: 616-347-4826
shadetre@freeway.net
http://www.shadetreestudios.com

Ed Gilbertson
Gilbertson's Stained Glass Studio
705 Madison St.
Lake Geneva, WI 53147
ph: 262-248-8022
fax: 262-248-3044
gsgs@genevaonline.com
http://www.stainedartglass.com

Conrad Schmitt Studios, Inc.
2405 S. 162nd St.
New Berlin, WI 53151
ph: 800-969-3033 or 262-786-3030
fax: 262-786-9036
studio@conradschmitt.com
http://www.conradschmitt.com
*Since 1889; stained & art glass,
statuary, sculpture, mosaics, murals,
liturgical consulting.*

Reinart's Stained Glass Studios, Inc.
73 Washington St.
P.O. Box 872
Winona, MN 55987
ph: 800-533-4444 or 507-452-4465
fax: 507-452-4649
reinarts@hbci.com
http://www.reinarts.com
*Since 1950 specializing in traditional
stained glass, restoration of stained
glass windows on location, protective*

*storm coverings, new stained glass
windows, custom work.*

Kebrle Stained Glass Studio, Inc.
2829 Bachman Dr.
Dallas, TX 75220
ph: 214-357-5922
fax: 214-357-5922
*Commissions have ranged from
sculptural pieces at Texas A&M
University to glass at Jarvis Christian
College at Hawkins, Texas.*

Jenkyn Powell
Powell Brothers & Sons
4050 S. Howick St., Ste. 10E
Salt Lake City, UT 84107
ph: 888-484-5184 or 801-262-4002
fax: 801-262-4002
jenkyn@aros.net
http://www.powellbrosglassart.com

Judson Studios
200 South Ave. 66
Los Angeles, CA 90042
ph: 800-445-8376 or 323-255-0131
fax: 323-255-8529
djudson@judsonstudios.com
http://www.judsonstudios.com

Jean Myers
Jean Myers Architectural Glass
11 Willotta Dr.
Suisun City, CA 94585
ph: 707-864-3906
fax: 707-864-3467
jmyers@jmaglass.com
http://www.jmaglass.com
*Designs stained glass elements for
homes, places of worship, places
where people work and study, and
places where people recover physically
and spiritually.*

Museums/Libraries

Corning Museum of Glass, The
Journal: Journal of Glass Studies
One Museum Way
Corning, NY 14830-2253
ph: 607-937-5371
fax: 607-937-3352
pr@cmog.org
http://www.cmog.org
*Over 35,000 glass objects, innovative
exhibits, videos, models; glass history,
archaeology, and early manufacturing;
Robert Sowers (stained glass artist,
critic, author) collection of archival
materials pertaining to stained glass.*

Periodicals

Magazine: Glass Patterns Quarterly
8300 Hidden Valley Rd.
P.O. Box 69
Westport, KY 40077
ph: 502-222-5631 or 800-719-0769
fax: 502-222-4527
Gpqmag@aol.com
http://www.glasspatterns.com
*Glossy quarterly magazine for the
stained glass hobbyist: stained glass
patterns, techniques, ads, etc.; also
articles about sandblasting and
etching glass, glass kiln firing, glass*

*painting, lamps, windows, display
cases, etc.*

Richard Gross, Ed.
Magazine: Stained Glass Quarterly, The
10009 East 62nd St.
Raytown, MO 64129
ph: 800-438-9581 or 816-737-2090
fax: 816-737-2801
thequarterly@stainedglass.org
http://www.stainedglass.org/
*A quarterly publication that focuses
on architectural stained glass;
primarily a trade magazine, but also
contains articles and resources of
interest to owners of old stained
glass.*

Magazine: Glass Art Magazine
P.O. Box 260377
Highlands Ranch, CO 80126-0377
ph: 303-791-8998
fax: 303-791-7739
glassartm@aol.com
http://www.artglassworld.com/mag/
   glassart
*A bi-monthly magazine which includes
glass industry news including
upcoming museum and gallery
exhibitions.*

Repair Services

Stained Glass Resources, Inc.
15 Commercial Dr.
Hampden, MA 01036
ph: 800-883-5052
fax: 413-566-2935
sgr@map.com
http://www.stainedglassresources.com
*Specializes in the manufacture and
restoration of stained glass windows.*

John Owen
Stained Glass Lamp Repair
29 Murray St.
Augusta, ME 04330
ph: 207-622-3277
lamprepair@msn.com
http://www.stained-glass-lamp-
   restorations.com
*Specializes in the repair of stained
glass lamp shades with bent slag
glass panels; also repairs small piece
(Tiffany style) stained glass lamp
shades.*

Victor Rothman
Victor Rothman for Stained Glass
1468 Midland Ave., #5A
Bronxville, NY 10708
ph: 914-969-0919 or 212-255-2551
fax: 914-237-2032
vrothman@iwon.com
*Specializes in museum quality
restoration and conservation of all
styles of stained glass windows and
lamps; qualified to act as a consultant
and to write specifications for new
fabrication of windows.*

Art Glass Studio, Inc.
543 Union St., 3A
Brooklyn, NY 11215
ph: 718-596-4353
fax: 718-596-4353
Restores leaded and stained glass

windows; will duplicate stained glass windows and skylights.

Barbara Malinoski
Stained Glass Artworks
8634 Bertha Court
Manassas, VA 20110
ph: 703-330-5119
fax: 520-222-4036
barbara@stainedglassartworks.com
Restorer of bent panel lamps, stained glass panels, unusual stained glass objects, windows, copper foil, lead, churches, Victorian, original designs; does bending, slumping, etching, sand blasting, original designs; 30 years experience.

Drehobl Brothers Art Glass Company
2847 N. Lincoln Ave.
Chicago, IL 60657-4201
ph: 773-281-2022
fax: 773-281-2023
Repairs leaded glass and Tiffany lampshades; bent glass, custom designs.

Nadia Wassef
303 Detering
Houston, TX 77007
ph: 713-880-0108
fax: 713-880-3544
nfwassef@msn.com
Does stained glass, crystal and porcelain repair; email or snail mail photos to find out about restoration possibilities; repair and return ship.

Suppliers

Hudson Glass
219 North Division St.
Peekskill, NY 10566-2716
ph: 800-431-2964 or 914-737-2124
fax: 914-737-4447
Sells bent glass for china cabinets; convex picture frame glass; also carries restoration/old house glass in stock; sells stained glass tools and supplies (no stained glass repair); stained glass supply catalog available for $3.

Richard Blenko
Blenko Glass Company, Inc.
P.O. Box 67
Milton, WV 25541-0067
ph: 304-743-9081
fax: 304-743-0547
blenko@usa.net
http://www.blenkoglass.com
Supplies hand-blown "antique" glass for stained glass windows; colored handmade glassware, blown tableware, tumblers and stemware, vases, pitchers; custom mold work, awards and barware; stained glass studio.

Robert Danielss
Delphi Stained Glass
3380 E. Jolly Rd.
Lansing, MI 48910
ph: 800-248-2048 or 517-394-4631
fax: 517-394-5364
webmaster@delphiglass.com
http://www.delphiglass.com
Sells stained glass supplies; gives lessons; large mail order business; also sells chemical solutions to repair damaged patina on brass and other metals.

Steve
Stained Glass Web-Mart
2808 Broadway
Eureka, CA 95501
ph: 717-443-8157
antiques@glassmart.com
http://www.glassmart.com
Stained glass tools and supplies online.

STAINLESS STEEL FLATWARE

(see FLATWARE)

STAMP COLLECTING

(see also ADVERTISING COLLECTIBLES, Trading Cards; POSTER STAMPS; POSTAL SERVICE ITEMS; SEALS, Christmas & Charity; SEALS & STAMPS; TRADING CARDS, Non-Sport)

Appraisers

John Zak, III
437 North Clyde Morris Blvd.
Daytona Beach, FL 32114
ph: 386-255-4425
fax: 386-255-4511
kdough3925@aol.com
Stamp collector for over 40 years; member of APA, APRL, RPS; offers stamp appraisals.

Dave Cunningham
5 Waterberry Circle
Ormond Beach, FL 32174
cunn5393@bellsouth.net

Ray L. Coughlin
Coughlin's
71 Arnold St.
Mountain Home, AR 72653
ph: 870-491-5085
coughlin@raylcoughlin.com
http://www.raylcoughlin.com
Stamp expert, appraiser; buys and sells the stamps, postal stationary, postal history of the US Possessions, Canal Zone, pre-Castro Cuba, Guam, HI, Philippines (all eras), PR, The Ryukyus Islands, other places with US Postal facilities.

Auction Services

Stanley J. Richmond
Daniel F. Kelleher Company, Inc.
24 Farnsworth St., Ste. 605
Boston, MA 02210-1264
ph: 617-443-0033
fax: 617-443-0789
US and BNA stamps at auction; also autographs and documents.

Greg Manning
Greg Manning Auctions, Inc.
775 Passaic Ave.
West Caldwell, NJ 07006
ph: 973-882-0004 or 800-221-0243
fax: 973-882-3499
gmauction@aol.com
http://www.gregmanning.com
Dealer and auctioneer in all philatelic properties.

Jacques C. Schiff, Jr.
Jacques C. Schiff, Jr. Inc.
195 Main St.
Ridgefield Park, NJ 07660-1620
ph: 201-641-5566 or 212-662-2777
fax: 201-641-5705
Auctioneers of worldwide stamps and postal history; specialties include US stamps, world stamps, US and world postal history, errors and varieties; also purchase outright and sell consignments.

Robson Lowe
Christie's
20 Rockefeller Plaza
New York, NY 10020
ph: 212-636-2000
info@christies.com
http://www.christies.com

Elizabeth C. Pope
Robert A. Siegel Auction Galleries, Inc.
65 East 55th St.
New York, NY 10022-3219
ph: 212-753-6421
fax: 212-753-6429
siegelstp@aol.com
http://www.siegelauctions.com/home.htm

Thomas Droege
Stamp Auction Central
20 West Colony, Ste. 120
Durham, NC 27705
ph: 919-403-9459
fax: 919-403-8199
tldroege@mindspring.com
http://www.StampAuctionCentral.com/auctions.htm
The most comprehensive resource for online stamp auction catalogs; over 70 stamp auction firms have provided complete online catalogs for over 350 sales and 600,000 lost since inception in Jan 1996.

Charles G. Firby Auctions
6695 Highland Rd., Ste. 107
Waterford, MI 48327-1967
ph: 248-666-5333
fax: 248-666-5020
Firbystamps@prodigy.net

Ron Playle
Playle's Online Auctions
P.O. Box 65918
West Des Moines, IA 50265
ph: 515-279-0884
fax: 515-279-0884
ron@playle.com
http://www.playle.com/main.html
Buy and sell postcards, stamps, coins, antiques, collectibles online.

Dennis R. Abel
Stamps for Collectors
ph: 651-639-3957
Dennis@drabel.com
http://www.drabel.com
An online philatelic auction site offering stamps, covers, collections, and more; listings change daily; no fee for the buyer; over 25 years philatelic experience; member of APS and NSDA.

Bel-Aire Stamp Auctions
2589 Hamline Ave. North, Ste. D
Saint Paul, MN 55113
ph: 612-633-8553
fax: 612-633-8354
info@belairestamp.com
http://www.belairestamp.com

Rasdale Stamp Company
36 South St., Ste. 1102
Chicago, IL 60603
ph: 312-263-7334
fax: 312-263-1819
rasdales@aol.com
http://www.rasdalestamps.com
Frequent public and mail auctions of US and world stamps.

Superior Galleries
9478 West Olympic Blvd.
Beverly Hills, CA 90212-4246
ph: 310-203-9855 or 800-421-0754
fax: 310-203-0496
superior@superiorgalleries.com
http://www.superiorgalleries.com
Has been a retail and auction source for dealers and collectors for over 70 years; specializes in stamps, coins, sports memorabilia and other collectibles.

Northwestern Philatelic Auctions, Inc.
304 Martin St., Ste. 200
Penticton, British Columbia V2A 5K4
Canada
ph: 250-493-0145
fax: 250-493-4076
northwestern@img.net
http://vvv.com/~northwest

Harmers of London
91 New Bond St.
London, W1A 4EH U.K.
ph: 0171-629 0218
fax: 0171-495 0260
auctions@harmers.demon.co.uk
http://www.harmers.com
Harmers specializes in the sale of stamps, but also sells paper items such as autographs, manuscripts, maps, etc.

Book Sellers

David G. Phillips Company, Inc.
P.O. Box 611388
Miami, FL 33161-1388
ph: 305-895-0470
fax: 305-893-0234
dgp3@bellsouth.net
http://www.davidgphillips.com
*Deals in US covers and philatelic
literature; sells the basic important
references for the US stamp specialist.*

Clubs/Associations

George Young
Rainbow Study Unit of the American
Topical Association
Newsletter: Rainbow's Bend, The
P.O. Box 632
Tewksbury, MA 01876-0632
ph: 978-851-8283
george-young@msn.com
*Collectors of philatelic material
concerning the spectrum: radar to
gamma rays and all subtopics which
are the different parts of the spectrum
- astronomy, mineralogy, health,
police, the sciences; also the aurorae
on stamps.*

David Lee, Ex. Sec.
United States Stamp Society
Journal: United States Specialist, The
P.O. Box 722
Westfield, NJ 07091-0722
webmaster@usstamps.org
http://www.usstamps.org
*Focuses on all US and US-related
philatelic material; for the collector of
stamp and revenue paper produced for
use in the U.S and US-administered
areas.*

Collectors Club, The
Journal: Collectors Club Philatelist, The
22 East 35th St.
New York, NY 10016-3806
ph: 212-683-0559
fax: 212-481-1269
collectorsclub@nac.net
http://www.collectorsclub.org
*Membership open to those interested
in philately.*

American Stamp Dealers Association
3 School St., Ste. 205
Glen Cove, NY 11542-2548
ph: 516-759-7000
fax: 516-759-7014
asda@erols.com
http://www.asdaonline.com
*Trade association representing stamp
dealers; issues free list of dealers in
your area and by your special area of
interest; sponsors national and
regional stamp shows; offers free
brochures about stamp collecting,
dealing, etc.*

Charles Eson
Fort Orange Stamp Club
128 Western Ave.
Altamont, NY 12009-6230
ph: 518-861-6256
hawkphil2@aol.com
*Oldest continuously meeting stamp
club in the US; meets 2nd and 4th
Tuesday of the month from September
through May in Albany, NY.*

Robert Lamb, Ex. Dir.
American Philatelic Society
Magazine: American Philatelist
P.O. Box 8000
State College, PA 16803-8000
ph: 814-237-3803
fax: 814-237-6128
relamb@stamps.org
http://www.stamps.org
*The largest stamp collector
organization in the US; provides
services to 50,000 collectors in more
than 110 countries; 600 local allied
stamp clubs, 200 national "specialty
groups;" code of ethics, estate advice,
expertizing.*

American Philatelic Society Stamp Store
P.O. Box 8000
State College, PA 16803-8000
ph: 814-237-3803
fax: 814-237-6128
stampstore@stamps.org
http://www.stampstore.org
*A service for American Philatelic
Society members to make it convenient
to buy and sell stamps, covers and
other philatelic material on the
Internet.*

John Hotchner, Ed.
American Association of Philatelic
Exhibitors
Journal: Philatelic Exhibitor, The
P.O. Box 1125
Falls Church, VA 22041-0125
JMHstamp@ix.netcom.com
*Formed to provide a forum for stamp
exhibitors to share and discuss ideas
and techniques geared towards
improving standards to exhibit
preparation, judging, and show
management; members are beginners
through experienced stamp collectors.*

Peter J. Roberts
Atlanta Stamp Collectors Club
Newsletter: Postmark Club
2442 King Point Dr.
Atlanta, GA 30338-5927
ph: 770-986-4214 or 404-894-0281
peterebay@yahoo.com
http://www.gsu.edu/~libpjr/
atlstamps.htm

Wanda Miller
American Philatelic Congress
P.O. Box 8171
Cincinnati, OH 45208
wandy001@aol.com
http://members.aol.com/TongaJan/
APC.html
*Provides a service to philately by
editing, printing, and distributing to
members a quality hardbound book of
original research papers annually.*

Carriers & Locals Society
P.O. Box 1574
Dayton, OH 45401-1574
*Members interested in collecting and
study of US carriers and locals: US
official and semi-official carrier
services, 19th century local posts,
independent mails, package expresses
of the 19th century, fakes & forgeries.*

Indiana Stamp Club
Newsletter: Mule, The
P.O. Box 40792
indianapolis, IN 46240
indypex@aol.com
http://members.aol.com/indypex/isc
*Largest stamp club in Indiana and
home to INDYPEX, an APS World
Series of Philately show.*

Southwest Stamp Circuit Club
213 Redbud St.
Yukon, OK 73099
wadscom@aol.com
*Started in 1990, this club has
members worldwide.*

American Philatelic Foundation
7219 Hampton Ave.
Los Angeles, CA 90046
ph: 310-375-3256
fax: 213-874-9687
mdubasso@americanphilatelic.com
http://www.americanphilatelic.com
*Non profit organization answering
questions about stamp collecting;
specific emphasis is on young children
as potential collectors; offers free
appraisal services.*

Israel I. Bick, Ex. Dir.
International Coin & Stamp Collectors
Society
Newsletter: Interstamps
P.O. Box 854
Van Nuys, CA 91408-0854
ph: 818-997-6496
fax: 818-988-4337
iibick@aol.com
http://www.bick.net
*Promoting understanding in the world
through coin & stamp collecting.*

National Stamp Dealers Association
P.O. Box 7176
Redwood City, CA 94063
ph: 800-875-6633 or 650-364-6667
fax: 650-364-6972
stamps@fortunesofwar.com

Jennifer Arnold, Ex. Sec.
Junior Philatelists of America
Journal: Philatelic Observer
P.O. Box 2625
Albany, OR 97231
ph: 541-967-7043
fax: 541-967-9515
exec.sec@jpastamps.org
http://www.jpastamps.org
Organization for pre-adult collectors.

Rob Lund, Mem. Ch.
U.S. Philatelic Classics Society
Journal: Chronicle, The
293 Fulton St.
Everett, WA 98201-3733
MembershipChairman@uspcs.org
http://www.uspcs.org
*Focuses on stamps issued over one
hundred years ago; old, rare and
valuable stamps.*

Pete Jacobi, Sec.
British North American Philatelic
Society, Ltd.
Journal: BNA Topics
5295 Moncton St.
Richmond, British Columbia V7E 3B2
Canada
ph: 604-272-5090
beaver@telus.net
http://www.bnaps.org
*BNAPS is devoted to the study of
stamps and postal history of Canada
and the former colonies; also
publishes the "BNA Portraits," a
newsletter; annual convention.*

Dr. P. H. Dangerfield, Hon. Sec.
Liverpool Philatelic Society
Dept. of Human Anatomy, Univ. of
Liverpool
P.O. Box 147
Liverpool, L69 3BX U.K.
ph: _44 151 794 5502
fax: _44 151 794 5517
spine92@liv.ac.uk
http://lps.merseyworld.com
*One of the oldest philatelic societies in
the U.K.; founded in 1888.*

Collectors

Scott Kitchen
1301 Sunny Slope Rd.
Bridgewater, NJ 08807
*Stamp collector; worldwide; tanks and
chess.*

Carl Albrecht, Mem.
U.S. Philatelic Classics Society, Inc.
Journal: Chronicle of the U.S. Classic
Postal Issues
P.O. Box 82252
Columbus, OH 43202
calbrech@infinet.com
http://www.scruz.net/~eho/uspcs
*Members focus on US stamps from the
period 1851 to 1857.*

Tony Zollo, Pres.
International Society of Worldwide
Stamp Collectors
Newsletter: Circuit, The
P.O. Box 150407
Lufkin, TX 75915-0407
zolloam@lcc.net
*Serves the interests of all worldwide
stamp collectors.*

Richard Simon
1846 27th Ave.
San Francisco, CA 94122
ph: 415-566-3920 or 415-664-3381
RSimon4545@aol.com
*Stamp collector (not a dealer) wants
to buy US and foreign stamp
collections; fifth generation San
Franciscan and member of the
American Philatelic Society since
1986.*

James Yeaw
P.O. Box 1077
Rocklin, CA 95677
ph: 916-624-7281
fax: 916-624-9309
jyeaw@interests.com
http://www.philately.com

Dealers

C. Stetson Thomas
Cindstamp
P.O. Box 599
Middleboro, MA 02346-0599
stetthomas@attbi.com
http://www.cindstamp.com
Dealer in "Cinderella" material, i.e., philatelic "odd and unusual" that is not listed in the Scotts Catalog of postage stamps such as labels, poster stamps, locals, fantasies, forgeries, phantoms, etc.

Richard A. Champagne
P.O. Box 600372
Newtonville, MA 02460-0004
ph: 617-969-5719
Stocks US classics; does important stamp shows; an entertaining speaker at show seminars.

Brookman Barrett & Worthen
10 Chestnut Dr.
Bedford, NH 03110
ph: 800-332-3383 or 603-472-5575
fax: 603-472-8795
sales@coverspecialist.com
http://www.coverspecialist.com
Dealers in stamps and covers.

Bob Gobeil
Bobby's U.S. & Worldwide Stamp
Packets
P.O. Box 1416
Biddeford, ME 04005
bob@bobbystoys.com
http://www.bobbystoys.com
Source for older US and Worldwide stamp packets.

Andrew Levitt
Oldtime Stamp Shop
P.O. Box 342
Danbury, CT 06813
ph: 203-743-5291
fax: 203-730-8283
levstamp@mags.net
http://www.andrewlevitt.com
Former VP of Robert A. Siegel Auction Galleries and former president of Sotheby Parke Bernet Philatelic Auctions.

Anthony's
P.O. Box 1523
Englewood Cliffs, NJ 07632
ph: 800-451-9645 or 201-871-3705
manth@astampcoin.com
http://www.astampcoin.com
Buying and selling collections of coins, stamps, paper money since 1958.

Jacques C. Schiff, Jr.
Jacques C. Schiff, Jr. Inc.
195 Main St.
Ridgefield Park, NJ 07660-1620
ph: 201-641-5566 or 212-662-2777
fax: 201-641-5705
Buys, sells, auctions, and appraises US and World stamps, errors and varieties.

Sam Malamud
Ideal Stamp Company
460 West 34th St.
New York, NY 10001
ph: 212-629-7979
fax: 212-629-3350
Buying and selling stamps of the world, especially US, British, Israel, and United Nations.

John A. Rerecic
J.R. Stamps
30 West 26th St.
New York, NY 10001
ph: 212-663-4134 or 212-807-6477
Operates a store open only on Saturdays and Sundays from 10 a.m. to 6 p.m. at 110 W. 25th St., Store #609, New York, NY 10001.

Harvey & Sandy Dolin
Harvey Dolin & Co.
111 Fulton St., Mezzanine Level
New York, NY 100386
ph: 212-267-0216
Has been in the stamp and coin business for over 66 years.

Harry Hagendorf
Columbian Stamp Company, Inc.
700 White Plains Rd.
Scarsdale, NY 10583
ph: 914-725-2290
fax: 914-572-2576
Dealer in rare stamps, including the famous 1918 inverted Jenny biplane.

Don Black
405 Tarrytown Rd., Ste. 402
White Plains, NY 10607
ph: 914-347-3971
fax: 914-347-3971
don@donblack.com
http://www.donblack.com
Sells collectible world wide postage stamps and postcards.

Henry Gitner
Henry Gitner Philatelists, Inc.
2-20 Low Ave., Ste. 311
P.O. Box 3077
Middletown, NY 10940
ph: 800-947-8267 or 845-343-5151
fax: 845-343-0068
hgitner@hgitner.com
http://www.hgitner.com
One of America's most diverse stamp dealers with 15 rooms of stock; also offers valid postage for under face value.

Jack & Myrna Golden
Golden Philatelics
P.O. Box 484
Cedarhurst, NY 11516
ph: 516-791-1804
fax: 516-791-7846
mgolden922@aol.com
Good stock of US revenues, including cheaper but elusive varieties, bought and sold.

Doris Bode
Stamp Vault
P.O. Box 637
Lynbrook, NY 11563
ph: 516-295-3643
fax: 516-295-2194
questions@stampvault.com
http://www.stampvault.com
A leading supplier for worldwide new issues as well as older hard-to-find stamps from all over the world.

American Coin & Stamp Brokerage, Inc.
30 Merrick Ave.
Merrick, NY 11566
ph: 516-546-2300 or 800-682-2272
fax: 516-546-2315
acsb@acsb.com
http://www.wid.com/coin

Ron Alfin
Alfin's Philatelic Connection
Newsletter: Newsletter, The
3 Williamsburgh Lane
Nesconset, NY 11767
ph: 516-737-1694
ralfin@alfin.computerworks.net
http://www.apcstamps.com/ss
Stamp trading and sales for the beginner to pro; Web site has valuable terminology for the beginner; some special introductory stamps available; trade with others in the club.

Michael Teitelbaum
Advantage Associates, Inc.
P.O. Box 469
Plainview, NY 11803
ph: 516-692-0557 or 888-771-4322
fax: 516-692-0557
Specializes in high quality stamps and coins; buys and sells.

Alan Anderson
stampview.com
ph: 516-756-0167 or 718-248-7825
fax: 718-361-6550
alan@stampview.com
http://www.stampview.com
Sells stamps of the world, specializing in less common items, mostly via the Internet; appraisals also available; Web site includes high resolution scans of many stamps offered for sale; accepts consignments to be placed on Web site.

Charles Eson
Hawkeye Philatelics
128 Western Ave.
Altamont, NY 12009-6230
ph: 518-861-6256
hawkphil2@aol.com
Specializing in US coins, Revenues,

used, Canada, Mexico, and Mediterranean countries.

B. Congdon
Internet Stamp Store.com
115 Stafford Lane
Niskayuna, NY 12309
dislady@InternetStampStore.com
http://www.InternetStampStore.com
Specializes in topical philately; collectible stamps and souvenir sheets from all over the world, including Disney movies, entertainers, royalty, etc.

Mystic Stamp Company
9700 Mill St.
Camden, NY 13316
ph: 315-245-2690 or 800-433-7811
fax: 315-245-0036
info@mysticstamp.com
http://www.mysticstamp.com
Buys entire dealer stock, US stamp collections, worldwide and topical stamp collections, rare individual stamps both US and worldwide, mixed accumulations, US and worldwide covers.

Claude Held
Claude Held Collectibles
P.O. Box 515
Cheektowaga, NY 14225-0515
ph: 716-634-4842
Buys and sells stamp collections.

Bill "Wolf" Berry
Paper Wolf, The
6950 Lain Rd.
Hornell, NY 14843-9419
ph: 607-324-1086
fax: 607-324-2001
thepaperwolf@dctmail.com
Specializes in US stamps, covers and postal history items; old envelopes and letters with or without postal markings and stamps.

James J. Reeves
James J. Reeves, Inc.
P.O. Box 219
Huntingdon, PA 16652-0219
ph: 800-364-2948 or 814-643-5497
fax: 814-641-2600
comments@jamesjreeves.com
http://www.jamesjreeves.com
Buys and sells stamps, coins, currency, railroad, sportscards, comics, paper and nostalgic memorabilia; in business for over 25 years.

Dale Enterprises, Inc.
P.O. Box 539
Emmaus, PA 18049
ph: 610-433-3303
fax: 610-965-6089
daleent@fast.net
http://www.dalestamps.com

Earl P.L. Apfelbaum, Inc.
2006 Walnut St.
Philadelphia, PA 19103-5608
ph: 215-567-5200 or 800-523-4648
fax: 215-567-5445
mail@apfelbauminc.com
http://apfelbauminc.com
One of the oldest and largest stamp firms in the world.

Maryland Stamps & Coins
7720 Wisconsin Ave.
Bethesda, MD 20815
ph: 301-654-8828 or 800-426-5723
fax: 301-654-1923

Martin L. Barron, Jr.
AmeriCom Philatelic
P.O. Box 587
New Market, MD 21774-0587
ph: 301-631-5362
americom@fred.net
http://www.fred.net/americom
Specializing in mint US stamps from the Classic Period of 1890 to 1940.

William Sandrik
Ballston Philatelics
P.O. Box 3277
Arlington, VA 22203
ph: 703-524-9352
fax: 703-524-0350
sandrik@ballstonphilatelics.com
http://www.ballstonphilatelics.com
An online store offering a selection of stamps and covers.

Allen Jossim
Covington Stamps, Inc.
80 Lake Dr.
Covington, GA 30014
covington@stamps-philately.com
http://www.stamps-philately.com
Buys and sells classic worldwide stamps from the first century of philately, 1840 to 1940.

John Zak, III
437 North Clyde Morris Blvd.
Daytona Beach, FL 32114
ph: 386-255-4425
fax: 386-255-4511
kdough3925@aol.com
Stamp collector for over 40 years; member of APA, APRL, RPS; offers stamp appraisals.

Jim White
Winter Park Stamp Shop
325 South Orlando Ave.
Winter Park, FL 32789-3608
ph: 407-628-1120 or 800-845-1819
fax: 407-628-0091
stamps@winterparkstampshop.com
http://www.winterparkstampshop.com
Member of over 30 professional and collector societies.

Michael Rogers
Michael Rogers, Inc.
199 E. Welbourne Ave., Ste. 3
Winter Park, FL 32789-4324
ph: 407-644-2290 or 800-843-3751
fax: 407-645-4434
mrogersinc@aol.com
http://www.michaelrogersinc.com
Carries full line of US and foreign stamps; good selection of stamp collecting supplies.

Stampfinder
6175 NW 153rd St., Ste. 201
Hialeah, FL 33014
ph: 305-557-1832
USID@StampFinder.com
http://www.stampfinder.com
A multi-dealer buy site offering comparative side-by-side pricing of like items; search for stamps by topic, country or item; search for covers with full color images; download free inventory software; use the Internet to buy/sell stamps.

Len Ettinger
3865 Lancewood Dr.
Pompano Beach, FL 33065-6003
ph: 954-344-8106
fax: 954-344-8105
mintstamp@aol.com

Joachim Steltzer
Rudolf Steltzer International
5030 Champion Blvd., Ste. G-6 #116
Boca Raton, FL 33496-2496
ph: 561-852-1435
fax: 561-451-8774
Steltinter@aol.com
http://members.aol.com/Steltinter/Index.htm
Dealer and expert in stamps.

Jerry & Barbara Koepp
Stamps "n' Stuff
8190 Hickman Rd.
Des Moines, IA 50325-4405
ph: 800-999-5964 or 515-331-4307
fax: 515-331-4957
jbkoepp@msn.com
http://www.stampsnstuff.com

Bardo Stamps
P.O. Box 7437
Buffalo Grove, IL 60089
ph: 847-634-2676
jfb7437@aol.com
http://www.bardostamps.com
Specializes in modern stamps from 1847 to present; errors, scarce varieties, precancels, missing colors.

Robert M. Weisz
4562 N. Austin Ave.
Chicago, IL 60630-3116
ph: 773-545-2929 or 773-297-1337
Buys, sells, appraises stamps, envelopes and postcards.

Carlton King
L & C Stamps
P.O. Box 421
Sedalia, MO 65302-0421
ph: 660-826-0897
lncking@iland.net
http://www.landcstamps.com
US and foreign stamps, US covers, other philatelic accessories; member of American Philatelic Society, American Stamp Dealers Association, Midwest Stamp Dealers Association, and others.

Raymond Weill
Raymond H. Weill Company
407 Royal St.
New Orleans, LA 70130
ph: 504-581-7373
Carries a good stock of US stamps.

Ray L. Coughlin
Coughlin's
71 Arnold St.
Mountain Home, AR 72653
ph: 870-491-5085
coughlin@raylcoughlin.com
http://www.raylcoughlin.com
Stamp expert, appraiser; buys and sells the stamps, postal stationary, postal history of the US Possessions, Canal Zone, pre-Castro Cuba, Guam, HI, Philippines (all eras), PR, The Ryukyus Islands, other places with US Postal facilities.

Robert P. Hoover, ISA
Rice Coin & Stamp Co., Inc.
9440 Old Katy Rd., Ste., 121
Houston, TX 77055-6363
ph: 713-973-0030
Buying, selling, appraising coins, stamps, paper money, tokens; US and worldwide 1600 to present; member of ANA, APS, GHCC, TSDA, and NGC.

Paradise Valley Stamp Company
P.O. Box 8948
Scottsdale, AZ 85252-8948
ph: 602-970-1733
fax: 602-970-0332
tor@stamp-one.com
http://www.stamp-one.com/pvsc

Richard C. Frajola
P.O. Box 2679
Ranchos De Taos, NM 87557
ph: 501-751-7607
covers@rfrajola.com
http://www.rfrajola.com
Specializes in buying, selling, appraising, expertizing, collecting stamps, postmarks and covers.

George C. Baxley
P.O. Box 807
Alamogordo, NM 88311
ph: 505-437-8707
fax: 505-434-1571
gbaxley@netmdc.com
http://www.baxleystamps.com
Buying and selling worldwide stamps and covers; specializing in Asia.

Warren Sankey
United States Stamp Company
368 Bush St.
San Francisco, CA 94104
ph: 415-421-7398
fax: 415-421-3167
usstamp@pacbell.net
Buys and sells worldwide and US mint and used stamps; also carries supplies.

Ian Kimmerly Stamps
112 Sparks St.
Ottawa, Ontario K1P 5B6 Canada
kimmerly@cyberus.ca
http://www.cyberus.ca/~kimmerly
Buys, sells, auctions rare stamps.

Dave Ramsay
Stamp Dad, The
5900 Explorer Dr.
Mississauga, Ontario L4W 5L2 Canada
ph: 905-361-4189
fax: 905-361-4189
thestampdad@rogers.com
http://members.rogers.com/thestampdad
Dealer in Canadian mint, FDC's, blocks, sheets, booklets, etc.; all new issues from Canada; also British Royalty and Omnibus issues available.

Walter Christ
Philasearch.com
Gutwerkstr. 30
Aschaffenburg, 63743 Germany
ph: 0049 6021 98407 or 0049 6021 98408
fax: 0049 6021 94612
Walter.Christ@Philasearch.com
http://www.philasearch.com
One of the largest places on the Internet to search for stamps; thousands of offers from auction companies; well-known stamp dealers can search with a very advanced search engine; be notified of new arrivals; online stamp auctions.

Dauwalders of Salisbury
92/96 Fisherton St.
Salisbury, SP2 7QY U.K.
ph: 01722 412100 or 01793 530826
fax: 01722 410074
talk2us@worldstamps.co.uk
http://www.worldstamps.co.uk
UK based stamp dealers since 1958; mail order worldwide.

Black Swan Postal Sales
15 Burcrott Rd.
Purley, Surrey CR8 4AD U.K.
ph: (+44) 181 660 3335
fax: (+44) 181 660 3335
brian@bsps.freeserve.co.uk
http://www.bsps.freeserve.co.uk
Has online catalog of stamps; place bids via email; focuses only on pre-1970 stamps and covers of Great Britain and the British Empire - not rest of the world.

Experts

William T. Crowe
Philatelic Foundation
70 West 40th St.
New York, NY 10018
ph: 212-221-6555
fax: 212-221-6208

Rich Davis
Rich Davis Autograph Authentication &
  Collectible Investments
P.O. Box 563
Kingston, OH 45644
ph: 740-642-2024
prdavis@horizonview.net
http://authenticator.freeservers.com
  *Specializes in the authentication and
  appraisal of all types of autographs;
  expert on sports collectibles, coins &
  currency, comic books, and stamps;
  also provides services as a research/
  grading/appraisal expert.*

Internet Resources

StampUniverse.com
suggestions@collectors.com
http://www.stampworld.com
  *Provides a home base for stamp
  collectors, dealers, and stamp
  enthusiasts; site brings together a
  complete set of resources for
  collectors.*

Philatelic.com
webmaster@philatelic.com
http://www.philatelic.com

James T. McCusker
James T. McCusker, Inc.
804 Broadway
Raynham, MA 02767-1797
ph: 800-852-0076 or 508-822-7787
fax: 508-822-1230
mail@jamesmccusker.com
http://www.jamesmccusker.com
  *Offers monthly philatelic auction with
  1,500 lots offered weekly; indexes set
  up to search by topic and cachet
  maker.*

About.com Hobbies
220 East 42nd St.
New York, NY 10017
pr@about-inc.com
http://home.about.com/hobbies
  *Online source for information about
  action figures, antiques, book
  collecting, coin collecting, collectibles,
  comic books, costume jewelry, dolls,
  mineral collecting, pin collecting,
  sports and trading cards, stamps, toy
  collecting.*

Alex Barinov
Find Your Stamps Value Online
alexdoc@findyourstampsvalue.com
http://www.findyourstampsvalue.com
  *A fee service to find the value of
  stamps online.*

StampsNet
6175 NW 153rd St., Ste. 201
Hialeah, FL 33014
ph: 305-557-1832
usid@stampfinder.com
http://www.stamps.net
  *Online magazine for stamp enthusi-
  asts: stories, resources, loads of free
  information.*

Michael Laurence, Ed.
Amos Press, Inc.
Newspaper: Linn's Stamp News
P.O. Box 29
Sidney, OH 45365-0029
ph: 937-498-0801 or 800-448-7293
fax: 800-340-9501
linns@linns.com
http://www.linns.com
  *Great online resources for the stamp
  collector: local stamp clubs, postal
  history societies, currency guide,
  stamp issuing entities, glossary of
  terms, grading, collecting basics, and
  more.*

Joseph R. Luft
Joseph Luft's Philatelic Resource Page
7621 West Willowbrook Dr.
Mequon, WI 53097
ph: 414-242-5120
fax: 414-358-8066
joeluft@execpc.com
http://www.execpc.com/~joeluft/
  resource.html
  *Great links to stamp sites on the
  Internet; stamp price lists, discount
  postage, philatelic resources of all
  kinds.*

Arthur J. Ward
A.J.'s Encyclopedia of Stamp &
  Philatelic Links
P.O. Box 251334
Glendale, CA 91225
ph: 818-240-0928
ajward@mailcity.com
http://members.tripod.com/~ajward/
  stamps/links.htm
  *An index to stamp collecting resources
  on the Internet: basic collecting, care,
  perforations, value, glossary,
  identifiers, dealers and supplies,
  specialized collecting, cancellations,
  first day covers, topicals, stamp
  issuing entities.*

Roger Pearce
Stamp Ink
545 N. Mountain Ave., Ste. 109
Upland, CA 91786
ph: 909-861-9547
fax: 909-860-7557
roger@stamplink.com
http://www.stamplink.com
  *Jump-off platform to hottest Internet
  stamp sites around the world.*

Brent Gutekunst
Stamp Universe
P.O. Box 6289
Newport Beach, CA 92658
ph: 949-567-1234
fax: 949-833-7955
http://www.collectors.com
  Online collector news, buy and sell,

*information, auctions, grading &
authentication services.*

James Yeaw
Ideal Solutions
P.O. Box 1077
Rocklin, CA 95677
ph: 916-624-7281
fax: 916-624-9309
jyeaw@interests.com
http://www.philately.com
  *Large Internet site about stamps and
  stamp collecting.*

Misc. Services

Harold Effner
Stamps for Children
27 Pine St.
Lincroft, NJ 07738-1827
ph: 732-741-5537 or 212-969-1042
haroldeffn@aol.com
  *Not-for-profit organization that
  solicits donations of used stamps and
  then distributes them free of charge to
  any need children's group (schools,
  Scout groups, etc.); used to interest
  children in stamps, as educational
  aids, and for crafts.*

William T. Crowe
Philatelic Foundation
70 West 40th St.
New York, NY 10018
ph: 212-221-6555
fax: 212-221-6208
  *An expertizing organization which
  will verify the genuineness of a rare
  stamp; write for list of fees; enclose a
  SASE.*

A. Mercer Bristow
American Philatelic Society Expertizing
  Service
P.O. Box 8000
State College, PA 16803-8000
ph: 814-237-3803
fax: 814-237-6128
ambristo@stamps.org
http://www.stamps.org
  *Run jointly by the American Philatelic
  Society and the American Stamp
  Dealers Association; offers substantial
  discounts on fees to members of either
  organization for expertizing services;
  will evaluate stamps for a fee; send
  for info.*

Kim J. Kowalxzyk, Dir. of Ed.
American Philatelic Society
P.O. Box 8000
State College, PA 16803-8000
ph: 814-237-3803
fax: 814-237-6128
kim@stamps.org
http://www.stamps.org
  *Offers online and correspondence
  education courses, seminars, support,
  and resources to help collectors get
  more enjoyment from stamp collecting.*

Professional Stamp Experts
P.O. Box 6170
Newport Beach, CA 92658
ph: 877-782-6788
fax: 949-833-7955
infopse@collectors.com
  *Provides third party authentication,
  grading and encapsulation for stamps.*

Museums/Libraries

Cardinal Spellman Philatelic Museum,
  Inc. at Regis College
235 Wellesley St.
Weston, MA 02193
ph: 781-894-6735
fax: 781-894-8056
  *This museum houses the personal
  collections of Cardinal Spellman,
  President Eisenhower, and Jascha
  Heifetz.*

Collectors Club Research Library, The
22 East 35th St.
New York, NY 10016-3806
ph: 212-683-0559
fax: 212-481-1269
collectorsclub@nac.net
http://www.collectorsclub.org
  *Library has over 140,000 items and is
  one of the largest specialized
  philatelic library in the world.*

Robert Lamb, Ex. Dir.
American Philatelic Research Library
P.O. Box 8000
State College, PA 16803-8000
ph: 814-237-3803
fax: 814-237-6128
relamb@stamps.org
http://www.stamps.org
  *The largest general philatelic library
  in the US that's open to the public.*

National Museum of American History,
  National Philatelic Collection
14th & Constitution Ave. NW
Washington, DC 20560
ph: 202-357-2700
webmaster@si.edu
http://www.si.edu/organiza/museums/
  nmah/nmah.htm

David Umansky
National Postal Museum
2 Massachusetts Ave., NE
Washington, DC 20560-0001
ph: 202-633-9360
umanskyd@npm.si.edu
http://www.si.edu/postal
  *23,000 square feet of exhibition space,
  6,000 square foot research library, a
  stamp store and a museum shop.*

Larry D. Sall
Wineburgh Philatelic Research Library,
  Univ. of TX at Dallas
P.O. Box 830643
Richardson, TX 75083-0643
ph: 972-883-2570
sall@utdallas.edu
http://www.utdallas.edu/library/special/
  wprl.html
  *Contains over 5,000 stamp books,
  many journals, and auction catalogs.*

Postal History Foundation, The
Journal: Heliograph
P.O. Box 40725
920 North First Ave.
Tucson, AZ 85719-0725
ph: 520-623-6652
phf3@mindspring.com
http://azstarnet.com/~phf/phf.html
Houses artifacts, postmarks and covers dedicated to postal history; a hub of postal research and education.

Periodicals

Philatelic Communications Corp.
Magazine: Mekeel's & Stamps Magazine
175R Proctor Hill Rd.
Hollis, NH 03049
ph: 800-635-3351 or 603-465-9377
fax: 603-465-9377
stampnews@aol.com
http://www.stampnews.com
The world's oldest stamp weekly (founded in 1891) and the only stamp weekly in magazine format; "Mekeel's" now incorporates the former "Stamp Auction News."

Philatelic Communications Corp.
Magazine: U.S. Stamp News
175R Proctor Hill Rd.
Hollis, NH 03049
ph: 800-635-3351 or 603-465-9377
fax: 603-465-9377
stampnews@aol.com
http://www.stampnews.com
The only magazine for all US stamp & cover collectors.

Philatelic Foundation, The
Newsletter: Philatelic Focus
70 West 40th St.
New York, NY 10018
ph: 212-221-6555
fax: 212-221-6208
Discusses the Philatelic Foundation and expertization.

Michael Laurence, Ed.
Amos Press, Inc.
Newspaper: Linn's Stamp News
P.O. Box 29
Sidney, OH 45365-0029
ph: 937-498-0801 or 800-448-7293
fax: 800-340-9501
linns@linns.com
http://www.linns.com
World's largest stamp marketplace with up-to-the-minute hobby news, reports on topics from trends in values, special interest collections to under-collected stamps; well-respected in the hobby; indispensable for the stamp collector.

Amos Press, Inc.
Magazine: Scott's Stamp Monthly
P.O. Box 828
Sidney, OH 45365-0828
ph: 937-498-0802 or 800-5SC-OTT5
fax: 937-498-0807
cuserv@amospress.com
http://www.scottonline.com
Magazine features notices of new stamp issues (using copyrighted Scott

Numbering system) and other articles for the collector.

Stacie Berger
Krause Publications
Newspaper: Stamp Collector
700 E. State St.
Iola, WI 54990-0001
ph: 715-445-2214
fax: 715-445-4087
stacie.berger@fwpubs.com
http://www.krause.com
Covers a wide variety of US as well as foreign stamp news from the world over; articles, special features, and theme issues; every other issue contains Stamp Wholesaler, with extensive dealer information.

Bret Evans
Trajan Publishing Corp.
Newspaper: Canadian Stamp News
103 Lakeshore Rd., Ste. 202
St. Catharines, Ontario L2N 2T6 Canada
ph: 905-646-7744
fax: 905-646-0995
bret@trajan.com
http://www.tarjan.com
Insightful, up-to-date philatelic articles, world-wide new releases, reports on finds, errors and auctions.

Steve Fairclough, Ed.
Link House Magazines
Magazine: Stamp Magazine
Link House, Dingwall Ave.
Croydon, Surrey CR9 2TA U.K.
ph: +44 (0) 181 686 2599
fax: +44 (0) 181 781 6044
steve_fairclough@ipcmedia.com
http://www.ipcmedia.com
Britain's leading stamp publication; articles, G.B. covers, stamps, cancellations, postcards, auction news, stamp shows, etc.

Repair Services

Hans A. Sitt
FCI Stamp Restoration Service
306 Guelph St.
Kitchener, Ontario N2H 5X3 Canada
ph: 519-579-7208 or 519-579-7461
fax: 519-579-0288
hanssitt@golden.net
http://home.golden.net/~hanssitt/SRShtml/SRShome.html
Repair and restore postage stamps; regumming stamps, repairing thins and missing corners and reperforating; also cleans soiled stamps and can remove or improve most stains.

Air Mail Related

(see also AIRLINE MEMORABILIA)

Clubs/Associations

Jim Graue
American Air Mail Society
Journal: Airpost Journal, The
P.O. Box 110
Mineola, NY 11501-0110
ph: 509-924-4484 or 509-466-4602
fax: 509-466-4698
sr1501@aol.com
http://ourworld.compuserve.com/homepages/aams
Focuses on any stamps or covers relating to air mail; areas of specialty include Crash Mail, Lindberghiana, US and foreign first flights, Rocket Mail, Balloon Mail, Glider Mail, Zeppelin Mail, Amelia Earhart, Concord, etc.

Dealers

Airmail Collector
P.O. Box 99
Cardiff, CF23 6XP U.K.
ph: +44 (0)1222-754748
fax: +44 (0)1222-761076
airmails@fut.net
http://www.airmails.co.uk
Buys and sells airmail related philatelic material; concerned exclusively with the sale and purchase of flown items and first flight covers from the pioneer period of aviation to present.

Albrecht Durer

Clubs/Associations

Jack Denys
Albrecht Durer Study Unit of the American Topical Association
Newsletter: Durer Journal
3 East Cadillac Dr.
Somerville, NJ 08876
Life and works of Albrecht Durer.

Americana

Clubs/Associations

Dennis Dengel, Sec. Treas.
Americana Unit of the American Topical Association
Newsletter: Americana Philatelic News
17 Peckham Rd.
Poughkeepsie, NY 12603-2018
fax: 781-459-0392
membership@americanaunit.org
http://www.americanaunit.org
Group of stamp collectors interested in all phases of Americana on stamps of the world: American history, culture, and industry.

Archaeology

Clubs/Associations

Merle Farrington
Old World Archaeological Study Unit of the American Topical Association
Newsletter: Old World Archaeologist
10 Clark St.
Medway, MA 22053-2204
Focuses on stamps featuring archaeology of the World, excluding North and South America.

Art

Clubs/Associations

Bernard Seckler, Pres.
Fine & Performing Arts Society, a Unit of the American Topical Association
Journal: Journal of Fine & Performing Arts Philately
10393 Derby Dr.
Laurel, MD 20723
bersec@aol.com
http://www.philately.com/philately/fap.htm
For collectors and those interested in fine art and the performing arts on stamps.

Astronomy

Clubs/Associations

George Young
Astronomy Unit of the American Topical Association
Newsletter: Astrofax
P.O. Box 632
Tewksbury, MA 01876-0632
ph: 978-851-8283
george-young@msn.com
Astronomy, astrology, zodiac.

Australia

Clubs/Associations

Stuart Leven, Member.
Society of Australasia/Oceania Specialists
Newsletter: Informer, The
P.O. Box 24764
San Jose, CA 95154-4764
stulev@ix.netcom.com
http://members.aol.com/stampsho/saso.html
Founded in 1936 for collectors interested in Australasian philately.

Biblical

Clubs/Associations

Rev. Frank Pieper
Biblical Topics Study Unit of the American Topical Association
Newsletter: Biblical Philately
P.O. Box 169
Emden, IL 62635
Old and New Testaments.

Bicycle

Clubs/Associations

Bill Hofmann, Treas.
Bicycle Stamp Club of the American Topical Association
Newsletter: Bicycle Stamps
610 North Pin Oak Lane
Muncie, IN 47304
ph: 765-288-0648
NormBatho@worldnet.att.net
http://members.tripod.com/~bicyclestamps
In addition to stamps, items of interest to members include other postal material and Cinderella items; subjects are bicycles used in racing, touring, play; venues, riders, use of bicycles in military, law enforcement, etc.

Biology

Clubs/Associations

Christopher Dahle
Biology Unit of the American Topical
Association
Newsletter: Biophilately
1401 Linmare Dr. NE
Cedar Rapids, IA 52402-3724
*Animal and plant life, present and
prehistoric.*

Black Related

Clubs/Associations

Ebony Society of Philatelic Events &
Reflections
Newsletter: Reflections
P.O. Box 145
Montclair, NJ 07042-0145
fax: 361-980-8675
esperstamps@esperstamps.org
http://www.esperstamps.org
*Interested in collecting material
related to all philatelic services that
contribute to the long-term improve-
ment and enhancement of black stamp
collecting and black history makers,
past and present.*

Booklets

Dealers

Nome St.
P.O. Box 2693
Ellicott City, MD 21042
ph: 410-381-6840
NomeSt@aol.com
http://www.nomestreet.com
*Sells stamp booklets of the world; by
country or theme.*

British

Clubs/Associations

Royal Philatelic Society, London
Journal: London Philatelist
41 Devonshire Place
London, W1G 6JY U.K.
ph: +44 (0)20 7486 1044
fax: +44 (0)20 7486 0803
secretary@rpsl.org.uk
http://www.rpsl.org.uk
*Established in 1968, this is the oldest
philatelic society in the world; regular
meetings are held; the Society library
contains a magnificent collection of
several thousand philatelic works,
handbooks, monographs, journals,
etc.*

Dealers

British Commonwealth Stamp Company
P.O. Box 10218
Wilmington, NC 28404-0218
ph: 910-256-0971
bcstamp@stamp-mall.com
http://www.stamp-mall.com
*Fully interactive Web site focusing on
British Commonwealth stamps mint
and used prior to 1952.*

Bill Martin
William Lawrence Philatelics
P.O. Box 991756
Redding, CA 96099-1756
ph: 530-223-5448
fax: 530-223-5448
baldeagl2@earthlink.net
http://home.earthlink.net/~baldeagl2
*Buys and sells collectible postage
stamps of the British Empire.*

Butterfly & Moth

Clubs/Associations

Charles V. Covell, Jr.
Butterfly & Moth Stamp Society of the
American Topical Association
Newsletter: Swallowtail, The
2333 Brighton Dr.
Louisville, KY 40205

Canadian

Clubs/Associations

National Office
Royal Philatelic Society of Canada, The
Journal: Canadian Philatelist, The
P.O. Box 929, Station "Q"
Toronto, Ontario M4T 2P1 Canada
ph: 416-979-8874 or 888-285-4143
fax: 416-979-1144
info@rpsc.org
http://www.rpsc.org
*The RPSC holds an annual convention
in a different locale each year;
publishes the 60-page journal bi-
monthly.*

John Peebles
Canadiana Study Unit of the American
Topical Association
Newsletter: Canadian Connection, The
P.O. Box 3262
Station "A"
London, Ontario N6A 4K3 Canada
john.peebles@sympatico.ca
*History, culture, and industry of
Canada as seen on stamps of the
world.*

Museums/Libraries

Canadian Postal Archives
395 Wellington St.
Ottawa, Ontario K1A 0N3 Canada
ph: 613-995-5138 or 866-578-7777
fax: 613-995-6274
media@archives.com
http://www.archives.ca/08/
  080608__e.html
*Part of the National Archives of
Canada; houses a library of 10,000
philatelic volumes, as well as a large
collection of Canadian and
international stamps.*

Cancels

Clubs/Associations

Gary Carlson, Sec.
Machine Cancel Society
Journal: Machine Cancel Forum
3097 Frobisher Ave.
Dublin, OH 43017-1652
gcarlson@columbus.rr.com
http://www.machinecancel.org
*Dedicated to the study of Machine
Postal Markings, the machine
inventors, patents, and other related
history.*

Captain Cook

Clubs/Associations

Brian Sandford
Captain Cook Society
Newsletter: Cook's Log
173 Minuteman Dr.
Concord, MA 01742
ph: 978-369-7741
USagent@CaptainCookSociety.com
http://www.CaptainCookSociety.com
*Interested in all aspects of the life and
voyages of Captain James Cook, with
philately as a significant but not
dominant interest; main office in U.K.*

Caribbean

Clubs/Associations

Peter Kaulback
British Caribbean Philatelic Study Group
Journal: British Caribbean Philatelic
Journal
108 Byron Ave.
Ottawa, Ontario K1Y 3J2 Canada
kaulbackpe@rogers.com
http://www.bcpsg.com/

Cats

Clubs/Associations

Mary Ann Brown
Cats on Stamps Unit of the American
Topical Association
Newsletter: Cat Mews
3006 Wade Rd.
Durham, NC 27705-5627
Domestic and wild felines.

Chemistry & Physics

Clubs/Associations

Dr. Roland Hirsch
Chemistry & Physics Study Unit of the
American Topical Association
Journal: Philatelia Chimica et Physica
20458 Water Point Lane
Germantown, MD 20874
michael@cpossu.org
http://www.cpossu.org
*For anyone with an interest in how
there sciences are represented on
postage stamps around the world;
journal includes more than 250 pages
a year of articles on the topic,
including checklists of new stamp
issues, bios of scientists.*

Chess

Clubs/Associations

Ray Alexis
Chess on Stamps Study Unit of the
American Topical Association
Newsletter: Chesstamp Review
608 Emery St.
Longmont, CO 80501
ph: 303-776-8892
chessstuff911459@aol.com
*Members interested in chess-themed
stamps.*

China

Dealers

Simon Andrews
Simon Andrews Stamps
U.K.
simon@simonandrews.com
http://www.simonandrews.com
*London's oldest stamp shop
specializing in stamps from Asia,
China, Hong Kong, Thailand; stamps,
postal history, auctions and retail
sales.*

Chinese

Clubs/Associations

Paul H. Gault, Sec.
China Stamp Society, Inc., The
Magazine: China Clipper
P.O. Box 20711
Columbus, OH 43220
ph: 614-451-8034
pgault@columbus.rr.com
http://www.chinastampsociety.org
*Society provides various services for
members to obtain stamps of China
from all periods; holds auction twice
a year and sales on the Internet;
expertization of stamps from China is
provided by experts.*

Dealers

Stamps of China
335 Court St.
PMB #64
Brooklyn, NY 11231
info1@stampsofchina.com
http://www.stampsofchina.com
*Source for quality postage stamps
from China (1878-1949).*

Experts

John W. Humphries
P.O. Box 965
Los Molinos, CA 96055-0965
jhantiques@hotmail.com
*Author of "Catalog of Chinese
Revenue Stamps."*

Christmas

Clubs/Associations

Linda Lawrence, Sec.
Christmas Philatelic Club of the
    American Topical Association
Journal: Yule Log
312 Northwood Dr.
Lexington, KY 40505-2104
ph: 859-293-0151
stamplinda@aol.com
http://www.hwcn.org/link/cpc
For those interested in collecting
Christmas stamps from around the
world: seals, covers, postcards and
any related Christmas material.

Christmas & Charity

Clubs/Associations

Florence H. Wright, Sec.
Christmas Seal & Charity Stamp
    Society, The
Newsletter: Seal News
P.O. Box 18615
Rochester, NY 14618-8615
ph: 585-461-9792
FHW-33@worldnet.att.net
http://homes.aol.com/betsychuck/
    cscss.htm
Focuses on stamp and metered seals
such as tuberculosis, veterans,
fraternal and civic, Jewish, ethnic,
pets, wildlife, medical, Easter, etc.
seals.

Christopher Columbus

Clubs/Associations

David Nye
Christopher Columbus Philatelic Society
    of the American Topical Association
Newsletter: Discovery
P.O. Box 1492
Frankenmuth, MI 48734-9539
columbus@accn.org
http://home.prcn.org/~pauld/ata/units/
    columbus.htm
Life and voyage of Christopher
Columbus.

Commemorative

Collectors

Kim Malcom
6410 Sierra Dr. SE
Lacey, WA 98503
ph: 360-456-8424
Interested in US commemorative
stamps.

Computer Programs For

Man./Prod./Dist.

Roger S. Edelman
Software: Stamp Collector's Data Base
8505 River Rock Terrace, Ste. B
Bethesda, MD 20817-4321
ph: 800-321-SCDB or 301-320-2451
fax: 301-581-4591
staff@scdbsoft.com
http://www.scdbsoft.com

MMR Software
Software: StampPro
P.O. Box 34916
Bethesda, MD 20827
ph: 530-686-9470
fax: 413-723-9797
webmaster@mmrsoft.com
http://www.mmrsoft.com
Stamp inventory and tracking
program; wide range of features for
expert and novice alike.

Niche Software, Inc.
Software: Stamp Collector, The
7118 NW Terrace
Parkland, FL 33076
ph: 954-344-6561
marketing@collectiblessoftware.com
http://www.collectiblessoftware.com
Designed specifically for the collector
of stamps from any nation.

Changing Seasons Software, Inc.
Software: StampBase for Windows
5881 Roanoke Dr.
Madison, WI 53719
ph: 800-260-2739 or 608-273-2739
fax: 608-273-1965
technicalsupport@stampbase.com
http://www.stampbase.com
Scott Catalog Number System, yearly
catalog updates with market values,
print your want lists, design
customized inventory reports, store
and display pictures of your stamps,
and more.

PrimaSoft PC, Inc.
Software: Stamp Organizer
P.O. Box 456
Surrey, British Columbia V3T 5B7
    Canada
ph: 800-371-7520 or 604-951-1085
fax: 604-951-7797
support@primasoft.com
http://www.primasoft.com
Designed for managing stamp
collections.

Confederate

Clubs/Associations

Ronald Teffs
Confederate Stamp Alliance
Magazine: Confederate Philatelist
19540 Yuma St.
Castro Valley, CA 94546
fastoffshore@aol.com
http://www.csalliance.org
Focuses on the mail and postal
systems used during the Civil War
period. The bi-monthly booklet
contains extensively researched
articles; an association (nonpolitical)
of collectors of Confederate postage
stamps and covers.

Dealers

Patricia A. Kaufmann
10194 N. Old State Rd.
Lincoln, DE 19960
ph: 302-422-2656
fax: 302-424-1990
trish@webuystamps.com
http://www.webuystamps.com
Philatelic consultant specializing in
Confederate States stamps and postal
history.

Brian & Maria Green
Brian & Maria Green, Inc.
P.O. Box 1816
Kernersville, NC 27285-1816
ph: 336-993-5100
fax: 336-993-1801
bmgcivilwar@triad.rr.com
http://www.bmgcivilwar.com
Buy & sell Confederate States stamps,
postally used envelopes & related
material, military correspondences &
Generals' letters, etc.

Covers

Collectors

Lewis Leigh, Jr.
38785 Leighfield Ln.
Leesburg, VA 20175-6810
ph: 703-771-3081
fax: 703-771-1432
Wants to buy items pertaining to early
Virginia postal history: old letters
with interesting content, stampless
covers, etc.

Dealers

John Cuddy
2768 Willits Rd.
Philadelphia, PA 19136-1026
ph: 215-552-9855
cuddymailpouch@aol.com
Buys and sells illustrated advertising
mailing envelopes dating from 1870s
to 1940s from US manufacturers;
please no stamps or 1st day covers.

Tom Osjecki
Phyllis' Philatelics
P.O. Box 792
Canyonville, OR 97417
ph: 541-839-4135 or 541-839-6151
Buys, sells and specializes in
postcards, paper Americana, stamps
and covers; over 25,000 covers and
postcards listed by state or topic.

Experts

James Kesterson
3881 Fulton Grove Rd.
Cincinnati, OH 45245-2504
ph: 513-752-0949
Wants 19th century US stamps on
envelopes (covers); also stampless and
illustrated covers; any amount.

Periodicals

Brookman Barrett & Worthen
Magazine: Brookman's Coverline
10 Chestnut Dr.
Bedford, NH 03110
ph: 800-332-3383 or 603-472-5575
fax: 603-472-8795
sales@coverspecialist.com
http://www.coverspecialist.com
Bi-monthly magazine about covers: US
first day covers, Akron and Macon
covers, Zeppelin covers, flight covers,
WWII patriotic covers, catapult
covers, Hawaii and Pacific Rim
covers, etc.

Covers (First Day)

Auction Services

Michael Mellone
FDC Publishing Co.
P.O. Box 206
Stewartsville, NJ 08886-0206
ph: 908-479-4617
fax: 908-479-6158
FDC@4-collectors.com
http://www.4-collectors.com
Conducts monthly mail auctions
exclusively for First Day Covers;
publishes price catalogs for first day
covers.

Clubs/Associations

American First Day Cover Society
Journal: First Days
P.O. Box 65960
Tucson, AZ 85728-5960
ph: 520-321-8080
fax: 520-321-0879
afdcs@aol.com
http://www.afdcs.org
First days, annual conventions,
chapters, cover exchange, auctions,
cachet information, awards, foreign
information, expertizing, question box,
archives, translation service, sales
department, slide programs, USPS
liaison.

Dealers

James T. McCusker
James T. McCusker, Inc.
804 Broadway
Raynham, MA 02767-1797
ph: 800-852-0076 or 508-822-7787
fax: 508-822-1230
mail@jamesmccusker.com
http://www.jamesmccusker.com
One of the world's largest online
retail offerings of US first day covers
complete with color illustrations; over
50,000 different items online.

Man./Prod./Dist.

Postal Commemorative Society
47 Richards Ave.
P.O. Box 57491
Norwalk, CT 06857-4910
ph: 203-853-2000 or 800-641-8026
fax: 203-855-8416
Sells a series of new first day covers.

Covers (Naval)

Clubs/Associations

Universal Ship Cancellation Society
Magazine: Log
747 Shard Ct.
Fremont, CA 94539
SeaBHall@aol.com
http://www.uscs.org
*Dedicated to the collection and study
of Naval and maritime Postal History;
interested in covers from ships and
related installations.*

Dogs

Clubs/Associations

Morris Raskin
Dogs On Stamps Study Unit of the
American Topical Association
Journal: DOSSU Journal
202A Newport Rd.
Monroe Township, NJ 08831-3920
ph: 609-655-7411
mraskin@nerc.com
http://www.dossu.org
*Purpose is to further the collection
and study of philatelic postal material
that pertains to dogs.*

Duck/Fish & Game

(see also PRINTS [MODERN];
STAMP COLLECTING, Revenue &
Tax Stamps)

Appraisers

David Boshart
National Wildlife Galleries
8504 Charter Club Blvd., Ste. 10
Fort Myers, FL 33919
ph: 239-275-0500 or 800-382-5278
fax: 239-936-2788
stamps@nationalwildlife.com
http://www.nationalwildlife.com
*Designs, produces and distributes
duck and other wildlife conservation
stamps, prints, and medallions; since
1976; also buys, sells, trades most
other prints and sculpture of all
subjects.*

Clubs/Associations

Tony Monico, Sec.
National Duck Stamp Collectors Society
Newsletter: Duck Tracks
P.O. Box 43
Harleysville, PA 19438-0043
ndscs@hwcn.org
http://www.NDSCS.org
*Promotes and encourages the
collecting and study of migratory
waterfowl hunting and conservation
stamps: Federal/state/foreign duck
stamps, first day covers, artist signed
stamps, duck stamp prints; visit Web
site for more info and to join.*

Dealers

David Boshart
National Wildlife Galleries
8504 Charter Club Blvd., Ste. 10
Fort Myers, FL 33919
ph: 239-275-0500 or 800-382-5278
fax: 239-936-2788
stamps@nationalwildlife.com
http://www.nationalwildlife.com
*Designs, produces and distributes
duck and other wildlife conservation
stamps, prints, and medallions; since
1976; also buys, sells, trades most
other prints and sculpture of all
subjects.*

Bob Dumaine
Sam Houston Duck Co.
Newsletter: Duck Report, The
P.O. Box 820087
Houston, TX 77282-0087
ph: 281-493-6386 or 800-231-5926
fax: 281-496-1445
bdhouduck@aol.com
http://www.shduck.com
*Handles all types of collector stamps
including United States and World
Wide; specialty is Duck Stamps (also
known as Hunting Permit stamps);
holds monthly auctions; attends nation
wide stamp shows; retail store; mail
order.*

Michael Jaffe
P.O. Box 61484
Vancouver, WA 98666-1484
ph: 360-695-6161 or 800-782-6770
fax: 360-695-1616
mjaffe@brookmanstamps.com
http://www.brookmanstamps.com
*Issues catalog of state and federal
duck stamps, and stamps issued by
Indian reservations.*

Michael Jaffe
Brookman Stamp Company
P.O. Box 61484
Vancouver, WA 98666-1484
ph: 360-695-6161 or 800-782-6770
fax: 360-695-1616
mjaffe@brookmanstamps.com
http://www.brookmanstamps.com

Experts

Lynn "Dr. Duck" Troute
Lynn Troute Decoys
3808 Kingsley Dr.
Springfield, IL 62707-7250
ph: 217-787-3595
fax: 217-726-1801
kstroute@yahoo.com
*Buys, sells, collects, appraises and
specializes in Federal and State duck
stamps; also buying duck stamps,
Illinois deer and turkey harvest pins,
and old wooden decoys and other
hunting and fishing artifacts.*

David R. Torre
P.O. Box 4298
Santa Rosa, CA 95402
ph: 707-525-8785
fax: 707-546-4859
drtorre@pacbell.net
Wants pictorial and non-pictorial

*waterfowl and fishing stamps; also
pre-1930 pictorial hunting & fishing
licenses from any state.*

Misc. Services

Federal Duck Stamp Office, US Fish &
Wildlife Service
1849 C. St., NW, Ste. 2058
Washington, DC 20240
ph: 202-208-4354
fax: 202-208-6269
terry_bell@fws.gov
http://duckstamps.fws.gov
*Proceeds from the sale of Federal duck
stamps go to the preservation of
national wetlands.*

Earth

Clubs/Associations

Fred Klein
Earth's Physical Features Study Unit of
the American Topical Association
Newsletter: Nature's Wonders
515 Magdalena Ave.
Los Altos, CA 94022
jyeaw@interests.com
http://www.philately.com/philately/
earths_physical.htm
*Earthquakes, environment, meteorol-
ogy, mountains, oceanography, rivers,
volcanoes.*

Errors

Clubs/Associations

Jim McDevitt
Errors, Freaks & Oddities Collectors
Club
Newsletter: EFO Collector
955 South Grove Boulevard,
Camden Point 65,
Kingsland, GA 31548-5263
ph: 912-729-1573
fax: 912-729-1585
cwouscg@aol.com
http://www.efoers.org
*Provides resources, publications,
regional & national meetings,
expertise service, heirs assistance, etc.,
to inform and guide those interested in
stamp errors, freaks and oddities.*

European

Clubs/Associations

Hank Klos
Europa Study Unit of the American
Topical Association
Newsletter: Europa News
P.O. Box 611
Bensenville, IL 60106
All aspects of a United Europe.

French

Clubs/Associations

Walter Parshall, Sec.
France & Colonies Philatelic Society
Journal: France & Colonies Philatelist
103 Spruce St.
Bloomfield, NJ 07003
d.r.stirrups@dundee.ac.uk
http://www.abel.co.uk/~stirrups/
FCPS.HTM

Gems & Jewelry

Clubs/Associations

George Young
Gems, Minerals, Jewelry Study Unit of
the American Topical Association
Newsletter: Philagems International
P.O. Box 632
Tewksbury, MA 01876-0632
ph: 978-851-8283
george-young@msn.com
http://www.philately.com/philately/
gems_minerals_su.htm
Gems, minerals, jewelry.

German

Clubs/Associations

Christopher Deterding, Sec. Treas.
Germany Philatelic Society
Journal: German Postal Specialist
P.O. Box 779
Arnold, MD 21012-4779
germanyphilatelic@juno.com
http://www.gps.nu
*Members have an interest in stamps
relating to Germany.*

Burt Miller, Sec.
Germany Philatelic Society, Golden Gate
Chapter
P.O. Box 911
Pacifica, CA 94044
danziger@aol.com

Golf

Clubs/Associations

Ron Spiers
International Philatelic Golf Society of
the American Topical Association
Newsletter: Tee Time
8025 Saddle Run
Powell, OH 43065
membership@ipgsonline.org
http://www.ipgsonline.org
*Provides golf philatelists from all over
the world the opportunity to
correspond with each other to build
their collections and increase their
knowledge about golf and philately.*

Graphics

Clubs/Associations

B.L. Johnson, Sec.
Graphics Philately Association
Newsletter: Philateli-Graphics
2138 Wilshire Rd.
Indianapolis, IN 46228-3252
bjohnson@indianahistory.org
*History of printing and graphic arts
as reflected in and on stamps and
postal stationary of the world.*

Guatemala

Clubs/Associations

Mae Vignola, Mem.
International Society of Guatemala
Collectors, Inc.
Journal: El Quetzal
105 22nd Ave.
San Francisco, CA 94121-1216
ph: 415-386-0819
*Quarterly journal; auction for
members only held once a year.*

Hawaii

Clubs/Associations

Hawaiian Philatelic Society
P.O. Box 10115
Honolulu, HI 96816-0115
ph: 808-521-5721
bannan@pixi.com
http://stampshows.com/hps.html

Hong Kong

Clubs/Associations

A. M. Chung, Sec.
Hong Kong Stamp Society
Journal: Hong Kong Philatelist
3300 Darby Rd., #503
Haverford, PA 19041-1064
hkstampsoc@yahoo.com
http://www.hkss.org

Hungary

Clubs/Associations

H. Alan Hoover
Society for Hungarian Philately
Newsletter: News of Hungarian Philately
2201 Roscomare Rd.
Los Angeles, CA 90077-2222
h.alan.hoover@1ycosmail.com
http://www.hungarianphilately.org

India

Clubs/Associations

Joyce Brand
India Study Circle for Philately
Journal: India Post
P.O. Box 145
High Wycombe, HP14 4PX U.K.
info@indiastudycircle.org
http://www.indiastudycircle.org
*Established in 1950 to promote the
study and research into the philatelic
and postal history of the Indian
subcontinent; over 500 members
worldwide; all those interested in
Indian philately are welcome to join.*

Irish

Dealers

David McCoy
Chrysalis Stamps
Ballymary
Milltown
Tuam, County Galway 999 Ireland
ph: +353 93 51625
fax: +353 93 51625
enquiry@chrysalis-stamps.com
http://www.chrysalis-stamps.com
*Dealers in classic mint postage stamps
of the British Empire to 1935; wants*

*list specialist for unmounted mint,
mounted mint and fine used postage
stamps of the British Commonwealth
to 1952.*

Israel

Clubs/Associations

Society of Israel Philatelists
Journal: Israel Philatelist
8358 Hitchcock Rd.
Youngstown, OH 44512
http://www.geocities.com/WallStreet/
2785
*For collectors of Forerunners, British
Mandate of Palestine, Israel Stamps.*

Experts

Israel I. Bick
P.O. Box 854
Van Nuys, CA 91408-0854
ph: 818-997-6496
fax: 818-988-4337
iibick@aol.com
http://www.bick.net
*A leading expert in the field of Holy
Land stamp collecting specializing in
Israel, Judaica and related materials.*

Japanese

Clubs/Associations

Kenneth Kamholz, Sec.
International Society for Japanese
Philately
Journal: Japanese Philately
P.O. Box 1283
Haddonfield, NJ 08033
isjp@comcast.net
http://www.isjp.org/isjp.html
*The society is nonpolitical and non-
commercial with one objective: to
promote intelligent interest in the
philately and postal history of Japan
and former Japanese colonies,
territories, and occupied areas.*

Dealers

Frank L. Allard, Jr.
Nippon Philatelics
P.O. Drawer 7300
Carmel, CA 93921-7300
ph: 831-625-2643
fax: 831-624-4617
*Buys and sells anything Japanese:
postcards, mail, stamps, posters,
postal stationary, First Day Covers,
photos, etc.; price lists available for
large SASE.*

Journalists/Authors

Clubs/Associations

Louis Forster
Journalists, Authors & Poets on Stamps
Unit of the American Topical
Association
Newsletter: JAPOS Bulletin
7561 East 24th Court
Wichita, KS 67226
Journalists, authors, poets.

Liechtenstein

Clubs/Associations

Ralph Schneider, Ed.
Liechtenstudy
Newsletter: Liechtenstudy
P.O. Box 23049
Belleville, IL 62223
ph: 618-277-6152 or 618-277-8543
fax: 618-277-1050
RSstamps@aol.com
http://www.rschneiderstamps.com/
lichtenstudy.htm
*Provides a broad range of services to
Liechtenstein collectors; postal
history, auctions, etc.*

Lighthouses

Clubs/Associations

Dalene Thomas
Lighthouse Stamp Society of the
American Topical Association
Newsletter: Philatelic Beacon, The
8612 West Warren Lane
Denver, CO 80227-2352
ph: 303-986-6620
dalene1@qwest.net
http://www.lighthousestampsociety.org
*Club promotes collecting stamps
depicting lighthouses; bi-monthly
journal discusses stamps, covers,
postmarks and all philatelic items that
picture lighthouses.*

Maps & Charts

Clubs/Associations

Miklos Pinther
Carto-Philatelists of the American
Topical Association
Newsletter: Carto-Philatelist
206 Grayson Place
Teaneck, NJ 07666
Maps, globes, charts.

Masks

Clubs/Associations

Carolyn Weber, Sec./Treas.
Mask Study Unit of the American
Topical Association
Newsletter: Mask Lore
kencar@vlnk.net
http://www.philately.com/philately/
masks.htm
*Discover the wide variety of masks on
postage stamps and correspond with
other collectors also interested in
masks on stamps.*

Masonic

Clubs/Associations

Masonic Study Unit of the American
Topical Association
Newsletter: Philatelic Freemason
1033 Hollytree Dr.
Cincinnati, OH 45231

Mathematics

Clubs/Associations

Monty J. Strauss
Mathematical Study Unit, an affiliate of
the American Topical Association
Newsletter: Philamath
Department of Math/Stat
Texas Tech University
Lubbock, TX 79409
m.strauss@ttu.edu
http://www.math.ttu.edu/msu
Computers, mathematics.

Medical

Clubs/Associations

Dr. Frederick Skvara
Medical Subjects Unit of the American
Topical Association
Journal: Scalpel & Tongs
P.O. Box 6228
Bridgewater, NJ 08807
fcskvara@bellatlantic.net
*Dentistry, nursing, physicians, Red
Cross, veterinary medicine.*

Meter Stamps

Collectors

Joel Hawkins
Meter Stamp Society
15261 W. Piccadilly Rd.
Goodyear, AZ 85338
joel5215@aol.com
http://members.aol.com/_ht_a/
msslibarch/M0000003.htm
*For those interested in the segment of
philately and postal history dealing
with stamps produced by meters and
similar equipment such as automat-
stamp vending machines.*

Mexico

Clubs/Associations

Mexico-Elmhurst Philatelic Society
International
Journal: Mexicana
P.O. Box 50997
Irvine, CA 92619-0997
*A philatelic society specializing in the
stamps of Mexico.*

Mobile Post Office

Clubs/Associations

Douglas N. Clark
Mobile Post Office Society
Newsletter: Transit Postmark Collector
P.O. Box427
Marstons Mills, MA 02648-0427
ph: 508-428-9132
dnc@alpha.math.uga.edu
http://www.eskimo.com/~rkunz/
mposhome.html
*Devoted to collecting of mail that has
been postmarked while in transit such
as while on a train, bus, boat,
streetcar, RFD carrier, etc.*

Music Related

Clubs/Associations

Philatelic Music Circle of the American
Topical Association
Newsletter: Baton, The
P.O. Box 1781
Sequim, WA 98382-1781
mwadem@hotmail.com
http://www.philatelicmusic.com
*For collectors of music related
philately.*

Napoleon

Clubs/Associations

Ken Berry
Napoleon Age Philatelist of the American
Topical Association
Newsletter: Campaign
7513 Clayton Dr.
Oklahoma City, OK 73132-5636
Life and time of Napoleon Bonaparte.

Pacific Islands

Clubs/Associations

John Ray
Pacific Islands Study Circle
Magazine: Pacifica
24 Woodvale Ave.
London, SE25 4AE U.K.
jray@dial.pipex.com
http://dspace.dial.pipex.com/jray/
pisc.html
*Caters to collectors of stamps and
postal history of the smaller Pacific
islands; Circle has group leaders who
can offer advice on the philately of
many islands; members dispose of
surplus material in their postal
auctions.*

Panama

Clubs/Associations

John C. Smith, Sec.
Canal Zone Study Group, The
Newsletter: Canal Zone Philatelist
408 Redwood Lane
Schaumburg, IL 60193-2748
balboa-hts@comcast.net
http://www.stampshows.com/czsg.html
*Organized in 1952 for the study of
stamps and postal history of the
Canal Zone and the Isthmus of
Panama.*

Perfins

Clubs/Associations

Floyd Walker, Ed.
Perfins Club
Newsletter: Perfins Bulletin
P.O. Box 3005
Alexandria, VA 22302
edit2001@aol.com
http://members.aol.com/perfins/
perfclub.htm
*Perfins are little holes in the
configuration of alphabet letters
which are punched into stamps as a
security, anti-theft measure.*

Petroleum

Clubs/Associations

Linda Corwin
Petroleum Philatelic Society Interna-
tional of the American Topical
Association
Newsletter: Petro-Philatelist, The
5427 Pinie Springs Court
Conroe, TX 77304
*Oil, natural gas, petrochemical
industry.*

Polar

Clubs/Associations

Janice Harvis, Treas.
American Society of Polar Philatelists
Newsletter: Ice Cap News
P.O. Box 2103
Riverton, NJ 08077-5103
jharvis@aol.com
http://www.south-pole.com/aspp.htm
*Focuses on worldwide polar stamps,
cancels, and covers.*

Possessions of the U.S.

Clubs/Associations

United States Possessions Philatelic
Society
Journal: Possessions
3604 Darice Lane
Jefferson City, MO 65109-6812

Postal Stationery

Clubs/Associations

Executive Secretary
United Postal Stationery Society
Journal: Postal Stationery
P.O. Box 1792
Norfolk, VA 23501
jsmajka@ameritech.net
http://www.upss.org
*For collectors of postal stationery,
namely embossed stamped envelopes
and government postal cards.*

Postmarks

Clubs/Associations

Jeffrey Hayward
Bullseye Cancel Collector's Club
163 Baden Place
Staten Island, NY 10306-6048
jeff@rockefeller.edu
http://www.jeffhayward.com/bccc

Bob Milligan, Mem.
Postmark Collectors Club
Newsletter: Bulletin
23381 Greenleaf Blvd.
Elkhart, IN 46514-4504
ph: 574-264-7660
bob.milligan@prodigy.net
http://www.postmarks.org
*National organization of collector of
postmarks, postal history, and covers;
supports the Margie Pfund Post Mark
Museum in Bellevue, OH, and the
Mittower Museum Building Fund;
annual convention and periodic
newsletter.*

Museums/Libraries

Dave Proulx, Curator
Margie Pfund Memorial Postmark
Museum & Research Library
7629 Homestead Dr.
Baldwinsville, NY 13027
stampdance@baldcom.net
http://www.postmarks.org/museum
*Has collection of over a million
different postal history items including
reference material on postmark
collecting around the world; museum
located near Bellevue, Ohio in the
Historic Lime Village.*

Periodicals

Paul Brenner
General Image, Inc.
Newsletter: Postmark Advisory
P.O. Box 335
Maplewood, NJ 07040
ph: 973-399-0708
postmark1@earthlink.net
http://home.earthlink.net/~postmark1

Railroad

Clubs/Associations

Oliver Atchison
Casey Jones Railroad Unit of the
American Topical Association
Newsletter: Dispatcher
P.O. Box 31631
San Francisco, CA 94131-0631
ph: 415-648-8057
CJRRU@att.net
http://www.uqp.de/cjr/index.htm
Trains, railroads, streetcars.

Dealers

Al Peterson
Rail Philatelist, The
P.O. Box 25505
Colorado Springs, CO 80936-5505
ph: 719-591-2341
railphil@aol.com
http://www.railphilatelist.com
*Carries everything philatelic relating
to trains or trolleys: stamps, covers,
postcards, Cinderellas (labels and
stickers), magazines, stock certificates,
specialty material.*

Religion Related

Clubs/Associations

Verna Shackleton
Collectors of Religion on Stamps
Magazine: COROS Chronicle
425 North Linwood Ave., #110
Appleton, WI 54914-3476
ph: 920-734-2417 or 920-734-6711
fax: 920-233-5604
corosec@powernetonline.com
http://www.powernetonline.com/
~corosec/coros1.htm
*COROS Chronicle is published bi-
monthly.*

Revenue & Tax Stamps

(see also BANK CHECKS; STAMP
COLLECTING, Duck/Fish & Game)

Clubs/Associations

Harold A. Effner, Jr., Treas.
State Revenue Society
Newsletter: State Revenue Newsletter
27 Pine St.
Lincroft, NJ 07738
haroldeffn@aol.com
http://www.hillcity-mall.com/SRS
*For collectors whose prime aim is the
collection, identification and
cataloging of state and local revenue
philately.*

Eric Jackson
American Revenue Association
Newsletter: American Revenuer
P.O. Box 728
Leesport, PA 19533-0728
ph: 610-926-6200
fax: 610-926-0120
eric@revenuer.com
http://www.revenuer.com
*Interested in US and foreign revenue
and tax stamps and stamped paper.*

Collectors

Hermann Ivester
5 Leslie Circle
Little Rock, AR 72205-2529
ph: 501-225-8565 or 501-688-8820
fax: 501-688-8807
ivesters@aol.com
*Collects all kinds of US Federal, state
and local revenue stamps including
special tax stamps and cigar,
cigarette, snuff and tobacco stamps;
especially wants stamps on documents
and packages.*

Dealers

Eric Jackson
Eric Jackson Revenue Stamps
P.O. Box 728
Leesport, PA 19533-0728
ph: 610-926-6200
fax: 610-926-0120
eric@revenuer.com
http://www.revenuer.com
*Buying US and foreign revenue and
tax stamps and stamped paper.*

Rotary Club

Clubs/Associations

Richard Dickson
Rotary on Stamps Unit of the American
Topical Association
Newsletter: Rotary-on-Stamps
P.O. Box 534
Irvington, VA 22480
ph: 804-438-6609
Rotary International.

Russian

Clubs/Associations

Gary A. Combs, Pres.
Rossica Society of Russian Philately
Journal: Rossica Journal of Russian
Philately
8241 Chalet Ct.
Millersville, MD 21108
gary.combs@rossica.org
http://www.rossica.org

Samoa

Clubs/Associations

Marty Miller
Fellowship of Samoa Specialists
Newsletter: Samoa Express, The
102-20 67 Dr.
Forest hills, NY 11375-2809
MMiller@LadasParry.com
http://members.aol.com/TongaJan/
foss.html

Scandinavia

Clubs/Associations

Don Brent, Ex. Sec.
Scandinavian Collectors Club
Newsletter: Posthorn
P.O. Box 13196
El Cajon, CA 92020
dbrent47@sprynet.com
http://www.scc-online.org
  *A non-profit philatelic society devoted
  to research and of stamps and postal
  history relating to Denmark, Danish
  West Indies, Finland, Faroes,
  Greenland, Iceland, Karelia, North
  Ingermanland, Norway, Slesvig, and
  Sweden.*

Scouting

Clubs/Associations

Lawrence E. Clay, Corr. Sec.
Scouts on Stamps Society International
Journal: SOSSI Journal
P.O. Box 6228
Kennewick, WA 99336
ph: 509-735-3731
fax: 509-735-2789
cclay@3-cities.com
http://www.sossi.org
  *A world-wide group of nearly 1,000
  collectors of Boy and Girl Scout
  related philatelic material; promotes
  friendship and fellowship through
  Scout philately; promotes stamp
  collecting for youth.*

Collectors

Lawrence E. Clay
P.O. Box 6228
Kennewick, WA 99336
ph: 509-735-3731
fax: 509-735-2789
cclay@3-cities.com
  *Specializes in Scout stamps and
  covers.*

Ships

Clubs/Associations

Robert Stuckert
Ships on Stamps Unit of the American
  Topical Association
Newsletter: Watercraft Philately
2750 Highway 21 East
Paint Lick, KY 40461
myron@turbonet.com
http://personal.palouse.net/hobbies/
  shipstamps
  All types of watercraft.

South Africa

Clubs/Associations

Bob Hisey
Philatelic Society for Greater Southern
  Africa, The
Magazine: Forerunners
7227 Sparta Rd.
Sebring, FL 33872
bobhisey@strato.net
http://www.homestead.com/psgsa
  *A world wide group of philatelists
  with interests in "British" Southern
  Africa, from Rhodesia to the Cape of
  Good Hope; magazine is published
  three times per year.*

Souvenir Cards

Clubs/Associations

Michael Padwee
Souvenir Card Collectors Society, Metro
  Chapter
Newsletter: SCCS Metro Chapter
  Newsletter
453 14th St.
Brooklyn, NY 11215
ph: 718-499-4307
souvenircard@mail.com
  *Members are collectors of souvenir
  cards in the New York, New Jersey
  and Connecticut area; Michael
  Padwee is author of "Catalog of
  Locally Issued USPS Souvenir
  Cards."*

Souvenir Card Collectors Society
Journal: Souvenir Card Journal
P.O. Box 4155
Tulsa, OK 74159-0155
ph: 918-664-6724
dmarr5569@aol.com
  *Souvenir cards are 8-1/2" x 11" cards
  with engraved reproductions of
  philatelic or numismatic designs from
  original plates.*

Space

Clubs/Associations

Carmine Torrisi, Sec.
Space Unit of the American Topical
  Association
Journal: Astrophile
P.O. Box 780241
Maspeth, NY 11378
ctorrisi1@juno.com
http://stargate.1usa.com/stamps
  *Hobbyists devoted to the collection
  and study of covers and stamps issued
  on space themes.*

Sports Related

Clubs/Associations

Margaret Jones
Sports Philatelists International of the
  American Topical Association
Journal: Journal of Sports Philately
5310 Lindenwood Ave.
Saint Louis, MO 6319-1758
membership@sportstamps.org
http://www.sportstamps.org
  *Promotes information on sports
  stamps, cancels; check lists & articles*
*related to sports and the Olympics;
Olympics, recreation, sports.*

Stamps on Stamps

Clubs/Associations

William E. Critzer
Stamps on Stamps Collectors Club
Newsletter: SOS Signal
1360 Trinity Dr.
Menlo Park, CA 94025
fax: 650-234-1136
wcritzer@avenidas.org
http://www.stampsonstamps.org
  *Collectors are interested in the
  postage stamp being used as a stamp
  motif.*

Supplies For

Suppliers

Lighthouse Publications
P.O. Box 705
Hackensack, NJ 07602-0705
ph: 201-342-1513 or 888-269-1513
fax: 201-342-7142
info@usa.leuchtturm.com
http://www.leuchtturm.com/us
  *Carries full line of products for the
  coin and stamp collector: albums,
  binders, blank pages, magnifiers,
  tongs, UV lamps.*

Brooklyn Gallery Coin & Stamp
8725 Fourth Ave.
P.O. Box 146
Brooklyn, NY 11209-0146
ph: 718-745-5701
fax: 718-745-2775
info@brooklyngallery.com
http://www.brooklyngallery.com
  Send $1.50 for 100+ page catalog.

Lou Montesano
Lincoln Coin & Stamp Company, Inc.
33 West Tupper
Buffalo, NY 14202
ph: 716-856-1884
fax: 716-856-4727
  Buys, appraises US coins.

Subway Stamp Shop, Inc.
2121 Beale Ave.
Altoona, PA 16601
ph: 800-221-9960 or 814-946-1000
fax: 814-946-9997
hugh@subwaystamp.com
http://www.subwaystamp.com
  *Supplies for the stamp and coin
  collector: albums, blank pages, cover
  protectors, clear sleeves, tongs, bags,
  illuminated magnifiers, SoftPRO
  stamp collectors software, coin boxes,
  currency holders, etc.*

Potomac Supplies
7720 Wisconsin Ave.
Bethesda, MD 20815
ph: 301-654-8828 or 800-426-5723
fax: 301-942-8778
jagrove@erols.com
http://www.potomacsupplies.com

Ron Kramer
RJI Philatelics
3105 Chamber Dr.
Raleigh, NC 28190-0439
ph: 704-291-9774 or 866-RJI-STAMP
fax: 704-296-9097
sales@rjiphilatelics.com
  Sells supplies for the stamp collector.

Michael Rogers
Michael Rogers, Inc.
199 E. Welbourne Ave., Ste. 3
Winter Park, FL 32789-4324
ph: 407-644-2290 or 800-843-3751
fax: 407-645-4434
mrogersinc@aol.com
http://www.michaelrogersinc.com

Scott Publishing Co.
P.O. Box 828
Sidney, OH 45365-0828
ph: 937-498-0802 or 800-5SC-OTT5
fax: 937-498-0807
cuserv@amospress.com
http://www.scottonline.com
  *Publisher of catalogs, albums and
  various stamp supplies, including
  Scott's US Stamp Collector's
  Database on CD-ROM.*

Warren Sankey
United States Stamp Company
368 Bush St.
San Francisco, CA 94104
ph: 415-421-7398
fax: 415-421-3167
usstamp@pacbell.net

Tonga

Clubs/Associations

Tom Jackson
Tonga & Tin Can Mail Study Circle
Newsletter: Tin Canner
121 Mullingar Ct., #1A
Schaumburg, IL 60193-3258
ph: 847-352-5842
tongajan@aol.com
http://members.aol.com/TongaJan/
  ttcmsc.html
  *Focuses on Tonga's postal history; an
  affiliate of the Society of Australasian
  Specialists/Oceania.*

Topical

Clubs/Associations

American Topical Association
Magazine: Topical Time
P.O. Box 57
Arlington, TX 76004-0057
ph: 817-274-1181
fax: 817-274-1184
americantopical@msn.com
http://home.prcn.org/~pauld/ata
  *Topicalists save stamps relating to a
  specific topic such as birds, space,
  buildings, transportation, etc.;
  affiliated with many specializing study
  units and clubs.*

STATE RELATED MEMORABILIA

Dealers

USID, Inc.
6175 NW 153rd St., Ste. 201
Hialeah, FL 33014
ph: 305-557-1832
usid@stampfinder.com
http://www.topicalstamps.com
Buys and sells topical stamps and covers, all with images.

Ukrainian

Clubs/Associations

Ukrainian Philatelic & Numismatic Society
Newsletter: Trident Visnyk
P.O. Box 303
Southfields, NY 10975-0303
Yurko@warwick.net
http://www.upns.org
Unites all collectors of Ukrainian materials; particularly dedicated to the promotion of the collecting of Ukrainian stamps, Ukrainian coins and medals, and Ukrainian banknotes; also publishes the journal "The Ukrainian Philatelist."

United Nations

Clubs/Associations

Blanton Clement
United Nations Philatelists of the American Topical Association
Newsletter: Journal of United Nations Philatelists
292 Springdale Terrace
Yardley, PA 19067
who@tiac.net
http://www.unpi.com
Worldwide U.N. related philately.

Windmills

Clubs/Associations

Orville Tysseling
Windmill Study Unit of the American Topical Association
Newsletter: Windmill Whispers
6125 Teagarden Circle
Dayton, OH 45449-3013
Molinology.

Wine

Clubs/Associations

James Crum
Wine on Stamps Study Unit of the American Topical Association
Journal: Enophilatelica
816 Kingsbury Ct.
Arroyo Grande, CA 93420-4517
ph: 805-489-3559
fax: 805-489-3559
jdakcrum@aol.com
http://home.prcn.com/~pauld/ata/units/wine.htm
Interested in stamps featuring vineyards, presses, barrels, wine bottles and glasses, chalices, wine in music, art, etc.

Women Related

Clubs/Associations

Hugh Gottfried
Women on Stamps Study Unit of the American Topical Association
Newsletter: Topical Woman
2232 26th St.
Santa Monica, CA 90405
dkristy@sprintmail.com

STAMPS

(see POSTER STAMPS; STAMP COLLECTING; SEALS & STAMPS)

STANHOPES

(see also OPTICAL ITEMS; PHOTOGRAPHS)

Collectors

Sheldon Katz
18 Cliffside Dr.
Port Jefferson, NY 11777-1118
ph: 631-928-1800

Brenda Macomber
RD 3 Box 201-K
Delta, PA 17314-9588
ph: 717-456-6116
cruzegal@aol.com
Wants to buy stanhope souvenirs, charms, unusual items; especially seeking 1939 World's Fair and domestic scenes, and color views.

John Andreae
P.O. Box 156
Granger, IN 46530-0156
ph: 219-675-9960
fax: 219-675-9961
jkandreae@aol.com

Mike & Gladys Kessler
25749 Anchor Circle
San Juan Capistrano, CA 92675-4002
ph: 949-661-3320
Wants to buy unusual items containing a microdot photograph in a tiny peephole: canes, walking sticks, parasols, sewing items, smoking paraphernalia, knives, jewelry, and souvenir items of all kinds.

Donald Gorlick
P.O. Box 24541
Seattle, WA 98124-0541
ph: 206-824-0508
Wants tiny viewers made of bone or metal sometimes found in crucifixes, pens, letter openers, needle holders, etc.

Dealers

Lucille Malitz
Lucid Antiques
P.O. Box KH
Scarsdale, NY 10583
ph: 914-636-7825 or 914-636-5171
fax: 914-636-7825
lithopha@optonline.net
These tiny photos, invented by Lord Stanhope in the 19th century, were found in many unusual souvenirs, such as pens, letter openers, sewing tapes, scissors, and charms.

STANLEY TOOLS

(see TOOLS, Stanley)

STAPLERS

Internet Resources

Curtis Scaglione
Stapler Exchange
curtscag@cs.com
http://www.geocities.com/typewriterexchange/staplers.htm
The first Web site dedicated to antique staplers.

STAR TREK

(see SCIENCE FICTION; TELEVISION SHOWS & MEMORABILIA, Star Trek)

STATE RELATED MEMORABILIA

(see also PLANNING; POSTCARDS, States; SOUVENIR & COMMEMORATIVE ITEMS)

Collectors

Dan DePalma
3 Burning Tree
Laguna Niguel, CA 92677
Wants CA, AZ, HI, NV, AK travel-related paper collectibles: brochures, menus, booklets, pamphlets, photographs, postcards; towns, cities, counties, roadside amusement spots, tourist attractions, Disneyland.

Alabama

Museums/Libraries

Alabama Department of Archives & History
624 Washington St.
P.O. Box 300100
Montgomery, AL 36130-0100
ph: 312-242-4363
fax: 312-240-3433
dpendlet@archives.state.al.us
http://www.archives.state.al.us

Alaska

Appraisers

Linda L. Halterman, ISA
Halterman's Appraisal Services
P.O. Box 672330
Chugiak, AK 99567
ph: 907-688-2175
fax: 907-688-2176
lllawson1@aol.com
Offers many services including awareness classes on a variety of items, complete home inventory sales, consultations, Appraiser locator for specialty items in required; second office located at P.O. Box 770581, Eagle River, AK 99577.

Collectors

Richard Reisinger
2610 Holgate St.
Tacoma, WA 98402-1204
ph: 253-272-7092
Buys, trades pre-1960 Alaska, Yukon, and N.W. Territories travel brochures, ephemera, postcards, city directories, telephone books, tourist souvenirs, china, bottles, pins, badges, posters, paintings, license plates, calendars, etc.

Dealers

Richard A. Wood
Alaskan Heritage Bookshop
P.O. Box 22165
Juneau, AK 99802-2165
ph: 907-789-8450
fax: 907-789-8450
dick@AlaskaWanted.com
http://www.ALaskaWanted.com
Buys/sells books, maps, stereo views, prints, photos, souvenirs, Klondike, letters, paintings, ephemera, etc.; anything Alaska/Yukon/Klondike; also wants Louis Potter bronze sculptures (1904-05) of Alaska subjects.

Experts

Richard Reisinger
2610 Holgate St.
Tacoma, WA 98402-1204
ph: 253-272-7092
Buys, trades pre-1960 Alaska, Yukon, and N.W. Territories travel brochures, ephemera, postcards, city directories, telephone books, tourist souvenirs, china, bottles, pins, badges, posters, paintings, license plates, calendars, etc.

Richard A. Wood
Alaskan Heritage Bookshop
P.O. Box 22165
Juneau, AK 99802-2165
ph: 907-789-8450
fax: 907-789-8450
dick@AlaskaWanted.com
http://www.ALaskaWanted.com
Buys/sells books, maps, stereo views, prints, photos, souvenirs, Klondike, letters, paintings, ephemera, etc.; anything Alaska/Yukon/Klondike; also wants Louis Potter bronze sculptures (1904-05) of Alaska subjects.

Museums/Libraries

Alaska State Museum
395 Whittier St.
Juneau, AK 99801-1718
ph: 907-465-2901
fax: 907-465-2976
bruce_kato@eed.state.ak.us
http://www.museums.state.ak.us
Alaskan history, ethnology, fine art and natural history; state-wide assistance to museums in Alaska; state-wide conservation services; grants-in-aid to Alaskan museums; purchase acquisitions; state-wide education services.

Arizona

Collectors

Sam Michael
P.O. Box 8025
Mesa, AZ 85214-8025
ph: 602-962-6523
Wants to buy pre-1920 Arizona related items: calendar plates, documents, advertising, badges, pins, posters, photographs, tins, signs, broadsides, real photo postcards, tokens, etc.

Bob Temarantz
2824 N. Bentley Ave.
Tucson, AZ 85716-5513
ph: 520-326-6704 or 520-741-9751
fax: 520-294-6052
azsnipe@hotmail.com
Wants to buy Arizona related memorabilia including photographs, advertising items, signs, hand mirrors, tokens, broadsides, and other ephemera.

Museums/Libraries

Arizona Historical Society
Journal: Journal of Arizona History
949 E. 2nd St.
Tucson, AZ 85719-4980
ph: 520-628-5774
ahsref@vms.arizona.edu
http://w3.arizona.edu/~azhist
Interprets Arizona history from the time of the Spanish arrival into the New World in 1540 through 50 years ago: collection includes US military uniforms, saddles, and accouterments 1846-1916; women's clothing, colonial silver, firearms.

Arkansas

Museums/Libraries

Old State House Museum
300 West Markham St.
Little Rock, AR 72201-1423
ph: 501-324-9685
fax: 501-324-9688
info@oldstatehouse.org
http://www.oldstatehouse.org

California

Collectors

Gil Schmidtmann
2346 Naples Ave.
Mentone, CA 92359-9569
ph: 909-794-1211
Wants San Bernardino County, CA pre-1930 stock certificates, postcards, postmarks, merchant tokens, badges, books, calendars, checks, currency, script, documents, newspapers, photos, promotional items, souvenir slates and spoons, etc.

Museums/Libraries

California Historical Society
678 Mission St.
San Francisco, CA 94105
ph: 415-357-1848
fax: 415-357-1850
info@calhist.org
http://www.calhist.org

Colorado

Dealers

Leo Stambaugh
Powder Cache Antiques
P.O. Box 984
612 6th St. Unit C - 2nd Floor
Georgetown, CO 80444-0779
ph: 303-569-2109
leomining@aol.com
http://www.powderchacheantiques.com
Buy, sell, trade Colorado historical photos, paper, medals, bottles, tokens, mining artifacts, paper and lamps, etc.; also wants mining items from any where.

Museums/Libraries

Colorado Historical Society
1300 Broadway
Denver, CO 80203-2137
ph: 303-866-3682
fax: 303-866-5739
membership@chs.state.co.us
http://www.coloradohistory.org

Connecticut

Museums/Libraries

Connecticut Historical Society
One Elizabeth St.
Hartford, CT 06105
ph: 860-236-5621
fax: 860-236-2664
ask_us@chs.org
http://www.chs.org

Delaware

Museums/Libraries

Historical Society of Delaware
505 Market St.
Wilmington, DE 19801
ph: 302-655-7161
fax: 302-655-7844
webmaster@hsd.org
http://www.hsd.org

Florida

Collectors

Douglas Hendriksen
P.O. Box 21153
Kennedy Space Center, FL 32815
ph: 407-452-0633
fl_collector@mpinet.net
Advanced collector wants to buy pre-1930 Florida items: photos, stereos, real photo and small town postcards, promotional pamphlets, paintings, souvenir china, license plates, RR and steamboat items; anything Florida.

Museums/Libraries

Holly Keris, Registrar
Museum of Arts & Sciences, The
1040 Museum Blvd.
Daytona Beach, FL 32114-4597
ph: 386-255-0285
fax: 386-255-5040
betty@moas.org
http://www.moas.org

Florida Historical Society
1320 Highland
Melbourne, FL 32935
ph: 407-690-1971
fax: 407-690-0099
Tebeaulib@aol.com
http://www.florida-historical-soc.org

Georgia

Museums/Libraries

Georgia Historical Society
501 Whitaker St.
Savannah, GA 31499
ph: 912-651-2128
fax: 912-651-2831
ghs@georgiahistory.com
http://www.georgiahistory.com

Hawaii

Collectors

Gene Snyder
991 McLean St.
Dunedin, FL 34699-3532
Wants Hawaiian memorabilia: ukuleles, Matson menus, nudes on black velvet, 1950s shirts.

Jim Stiso
31925 Sunset Ave.
S. Laguna, CA 92677
ph: 949-499-3667
Wants to buy Hawaiiana: vintage paintings, prints, shirts, lamps, dolls, etc.

Wayne Babcock
4846 Carpenteria Ave.
Carpinteria, CA 93013-1935
ph: 805-684-8148
oldsurfin@cs.com
Wants to buy pre-1960 Hawaiian items including cruise line menus, bamboo framed floral prints by Mundorff, Tip Freeman and others; Hula girls, Hawaiian-made ukuleles, surfing items, poi pounders, koa wood items, Duke Kahanamoku.

Rick Ralston
99-969 Iwaena St.
Aiea, HI 96701-3249
ph: 808-486-1243
fax: 808-486-1276
http://www.ralstonantiques.com
Wants Hawaiian prints, paintings, early wooden bowls, Hula girl lamps, dolls, etc.

John Honl
P.O. Box 1201
Kailua Kona, HI 96745-1201
ph: 808-325-9905
jhh@kona.net
Wants pre-1960 Hawaiian items

including lamps, Hula girls, postcard, menus, etc.

Bernie Berman
755 Isenberg St., 305
Honolulu, HI 96826-4504
ph: 808-941-8639
fax: 808-845-9638
Wants pre-1920 Hawaiiana, Oceania, Asian theater countries; postcards, photographs, advertising, memorabilia, broadsides, art books, historical, collectibles, postal covers, books, ephemera, screens, scrolls, prints, documents, etc.

Anne Moore
P.O. Box 604
Bingen, WA 98605-0604
ph: 509-493-4463
Wants all pre-1960 Hawaii memorabilia: Hula dolls, Hula lamps, ukuleles, books, menus, travel posters, paintings, prints, photos, postcards, clothing, artifacts, photos, sheet music, souvenirs, etc.

Dealers

Susan Mast
Susan Mast Enterprises
PMB 270
849 Almar Ave., Ste. C
Santa Cruz, CA 95060-5856
ph: 831-423-9786 or 800-366-9816
fax: 831-423-7001
sme@cruzio.com
http://www.cruzio.com/~alohasme
Buys and sells vintage 1860 to 1950s Hawaiiana: Ming's jewelry, Hakata figures, Hula lamps, menus, ephemera, books, Paradise of the Pacific magazine holiday issues, wood perfumes, Hula prints and posters, photos, ukuleles, etc.

Surf N Hula
P.. Box 812
Haiku, HI 96708-0812
ph: 800-410-7648 or 808-935-2341
info@surfNhula.com
http://www.surfNhula.com
Buys and sells everything that is vintage Hawaiian and surfing related; over 1,000 pieces in stock: paintings, posters, postcards, Hula figurines and nodders, artifacts, books, magazines, Duke Kahanamoku, surfboards, skateboards, etc.

Evan Olins
Hula Heaven
75-5744 Alii Dr.
Kailua Kona, HI 96740
ph: 808-329-7885
evan@hulaheaven.net
http://www.hulaheaven.net
Wants pre-1960s Hawaiian shirts; also wants souvenir and Hula girl items; visit the Aloha Museum for a look at some rare pieces from their private collection.

Mark Blackburn
Mauna Kea Galleries
65-1298 Kawaihae Rd.
Waimea, HI 96743
ph: 808-887-2244
fax: 808-887-2226
mkg@interpac.net
http://www.maunakeagalleries.com
*Wants Hawaiian artifacts, cala-
bashes, menus, souvenirs, Hula dolls,
lamps, ukuleles, quilts, vintage shirts,
ceramics, perfume bottles, souvenir
spoons, prints, engravings, jewelry,
books, ephemera, missionary, royalty,
diaries, etc.*

Museums/Libraries

Hawaiian Historical Society
560 Kawaiahao St.
Honolulu, HI 96813
ph: 808-537-6271
bedunn@lava.net
http://www.hawaiianhistory.org

Bishop Museum, The State Museum of
    Natural & Cultural History
1525 Bernice St.
Honolulu, HI 96817-0916
ph: 808-847-3511 or 888-777-7443
fax: 808-841-8968
museum@bishopmuseum.org
http://www.bishopmuseum.org

Hawaii (Hawaiian Shirts)

Dealers

Dan Kelley
Experienced Denim
P.O. Box 239
Fayetteville, AR 72702-0239
ph: 501-444-7541 or 800-336-4694
fax: 501-521-8331
exd@edenim.com
http://www.edenim.com
*Wants '30s-'50s Levis, denim wear of
all types, any brand or condition,
'40s-'50s gabardine shirts & jackets,
Hawaiian and bowling shirts; also
vintage fabrics, textiles, bedspreads,
tablecloths with Western or Mexican
theme.*

David Bailey
Bailey's Antiques & Aloha Shirts
517 Kapahulu Ave.
Honolulu, HI 96815-3854
ph: 808-734-7628
baileysantiques@webtv.net
*Buys and appraises pre-1960 Levis,
pre-1960 Aloha shirts, and
Hawaiiana; pre-1960 Aloha shirts can
be identified by double-stitched seams
around the armpit and along sides.*

Idaho

Museums/Libraries

Steve Guerber, Dir.
Idaho State Historical Society
1109 Main St., #250
Boise, ID 83702-5642
ph: 208-334-3987
fax: 208-334-2774
sguerber@ishs.state.id.us
http://www2.state.id.us/ishs

Illinois

Museums/Libraries

Illinois State Historical Society
210 1/2 S. Sixth
Springfield, IL 62701-1503
ph: 217-525-2781
fax: 217-525-2783
ishs@eosinc.com
http://www.prairienet.org/ishs

Illinois State Historical Library
Old State Capitol Plaza
Springfield, IL 62701-1507
ph: 217-524-7216
http://www.state.il.us/hpa/lib
*Created in 1889, the premier
repository for materials relating to the
history of Illinois.*

Illinois (Chicago)

Dealers

Bindy Bitterman
Eureka! Antiques, Nostalgia &
    Collectibles
705 W. Washington
Evanston, IL 60202-2214
ph: 847-869-9090
rbitt356@aol.com
*Specializes buying and selling early
paper advertising, catalogs,
calendars, etc. especially relating to
the Chicago area; a small but full
shop - they send no lists but will reply
by phone, email or letter; SASEs get
first attention.*

Indiana

Experts

Mark Roeder
305 Akron St.
Culver, IN 46511-1805
ph: 812-749-3490
*Wants to buy anything related to
Culver, IN and the Culver Military
Academy; especially postcards, books,
china, photos, and items of historical
interest; author of book "A History of
Culver and Lake Maxinkuckee."*

Museums/Libraries

Indiana Historical Society
450 West Ohio St.
Indianapolis, IN 46202-3269
ph: 317-232-1882 or 800-IHS-1830
fax: 317-233-3109
csmith@indianahistory.org
http://www.indianahistory.org

Iowa

Museums/Libraries

State Historical Society of Iowa
600 East Locust
Des Moines, IA 50319-0290
ph: 515-281-5111
Jerome.Thompson@dca.state.ia.us
http://www.iowahistory.org

Kansas

Dealers

Billy & Jeane Jones
Dearing Country Antiques
309 Independence Ave.
P.O. Box 82
Dearing, KS 67340-0082
ph: 620-948-6389
*Want ceramic or glass souvenirs,
plates, advertising items, calendars,
vases, view cards - anything related to
Dearing, Chanute, Coffeyville,
Independence, Cherryvale, Iola,
Fredonia, or Neodesha Kansas.*

Museums/Libraries

Kansas State Historical Society
6425 SW Sixth Ave.
Topeka, KS 66615-1099
ph: 785-272-8681
fax: 785-272-8682
webmaster@kshs.org
http://www.kshs.org
*Focuses on items associated with the
history of Kansas in particular or the
Great Plains in general; of particular
interest are objects made or invented
by Kansans.*

Kentucky

Collectors

Ed McDermott
1415 McKendree
Kevil, KY 42053
ph: 270-488-3420
emcdermott@brtc.net
*Wants pre-1920 advertising items
from Paducah, KY: signs, letterheads,
labeled bottles, corkscrews, shot
glasses, whiskey jugs, etc.*

Gary D. Gardner
200 College St.
Hodgenville, KY 42748-1404
ph: 270-358-3222
*Seeking to purchase Confederate relics
and documents pertaining to Kentucky
and Kentuckians, especially identified
personal effects, or anything related to
Breckenridge, Buckner, Jefferson
Davis.*

Museums/Libraries

J. Kevin Graffagnino, Ex. Dir.
Kentucky Historical Society
100 W. Broadway
Frankfort, KY 40602
ph: 502-564-1792
fax: 502-696-1999
kevin.graffagnino@mail.state.ky.us
http://www.kyhistory.org
*Consists of three museums: Kentucky
History Center, Old State Capitol,
Kentucky Military History Museum;
collections include rare prints, books,
manuscripts, artifacts, Kentucky based
or connected products.*

Louisiana

Museums/Libraries

Louisiana Historical Museum
P.O. Box 2448
New Orleans, LA 70176-2448
ph: 504-568-6968 or 800-568-6968
fax: 504-568-4995
lsm@crt.state.la.us
http://lsm.crt.state.la.us

Maine

Museums/Libraries

Maine Historical Society
c/o Center for Main History
485 Congress St.
Portland, ME 04101
ph: 207-774-1822
fax: 207-775-4301
mhistor1@maine.rr.com
http://www.mainehistory.com

Maryland

Museums/Libraries

Maryland Historical Society
201 West Monument St.
Baltimore, MD 21201-4674
ph: 410-685-3750
fax: 410-385-2105
webcomments@mdhs.org
http://www.mdhs.org

Massachusetts

Dealers

Gary Leveille
Antique Souvenir China
5 Brook Lane
Great Barrington, MA 01230
ph: 413-528-5490
garyleve@aol.com
http://www.berkshirecreative.com
*Wants to buy old souvenir china,
postcards and photos related to the
Massachusetts towns of Great
Barrington, Stockbridge, Sheffield,
Egremont, Ashley Falls, Hartsville,
New Marlboro, Glendale, Interlaken,
Alford, Monson.*

Museums/Libraries

Massachusetts Historical Society
1154 Boylston St.
Boston, MA 02215
ph: 617-536-1608
admin@masshist.org
http://www.masshist.org

Michigan

Museums/Libraries

Historical Society of Michigan
2117 Washtenaw Ave.
Ann Arbor, MI 48104-4599
ph: 734-769-1828 or 734-769-4267
fax: 734-769-1828
hsofmich@leslie.k12.mi.us

Michigan Historical Museum
717 West Allegan St.
Lansing, MI 48918-1800
ph: 517-373-3559
halexec@michigan.gov
http://www.michiganhistory.org
Persons wishing to donate artifacts should check the Web page or call the museum Collections Unit in advance.

Jesse Besser Museum
491 Johnson St.
Alpena, MI 49707
ph: 989-356-2202
fax: 989-356-3133
jbmuseum@northland.lib.mi.us
http://www.ogdennews.com/upnorth/
museum/home.html
Special Great Lakes collections: Native Americans, Great Lakes maps, Great Lakes (NE Michigan) photographs.

Minnesota

Museums/Libraries

Minnesota Historical Society
345 Kellog Blvd. West
Saint Paul, MN 55102-1906
ph: 651-296-6126
fax: 651-296-6126
webmaster@mnhs.org
http://www.mnhs.org

Mississippi

Museums/Libraries

Mississippi Historical Society
Journal: Journal of Mississippi History
P.O. Box 571
Jackson, MS 39205-0571
ph: 601-359-6850
fax: 601-359-6975
webmaster@mdah.state.ms.us
http://www.mdah.state.ms.us/admin/
mhistsoc.html

Missouri

Dealers

Trenton Boyd
P.O. Box 517
Columbia, MO 65205-0517
ph: 573-882-2461 or 573-442-5235
fax: 573-882-2950
vetlib@missouri.edu
Wants items from Missouri, except Kansas City and St. Louis.

Museums/Libraries

State Historical Society of Missouri
Magazine: Missouri Historical Review
1020 Lowry St.
Columbia, MO 65201-7298
ph: 573-882-7083
fax: 573-884-4950
shsofmo@umsystem.edu
http://www.system.missouri.edu/shs
The preeminent research facility for the study of Missouri and Missouri-ans; mission is to collect, preserve, make accessible, and publish material relating to the history of Missouri; does not hold memorabilia or artifacts.

Montana

Collectors

Tim Gordon, ISA
P.O. Box 5813
2717 Highland Dr.
Missoula, MT 59802
ph: 406-728-1812 or 888-720-1812
timbgordon@aol.com
http://www.xntrx.com
Wants any pre-1930 item marked "Montana:" calendars, advertising, photos, postcards, history books, tokens, trade cards, etc.

Museums/Libraries

Montana Historical Society
Journal: Montana the Magazine of Western History
225 North Roberts
P.O. Box 201201
Helena, MT 59620-1201
ph: 406-444-2694 or 800-243-9900
fax: 406-444-2692
mhslibrary@state.mt.us
http://www.montanahistoricalsociety.org
A state agency that collects, preserves, and interprets all aspects of Montana history through its museum, library, archives, photograph archives, oral history, and publications programs.

Nebraska

Museums/Libraries

Nebraska State Historical Society
15th & P Sts.
Lincoln, NE 68508
ph: 402-471-4754 or 800-833-6747
ednshs@inetnebr.com
http://www.nebraskahistory.org

Nevada

Collectors

Gil Schmidtmann
2346 Naples Ave.
Mentone, CA 92359-9569
ph: 909-794-1211
Wants pre-1930 stock certificates, postcards, postmarks, merchant tokens, badges, books, calendars, checks, currency, documents, newspapers, photos, promotional items, souvenir plates and spoons, etc.; also the same from Death Valley.

Museums/Libraries

Nevada Historical Society
1650 N. Virginia St.
Reno, NV 89503
ph: 775-688-1190
fax: 775-688-2917
arspence@clan.lib.nv.us
http://dmla.clan.lib.nv.us/docs/
museums/reno/his-soc.htm

New Hampshire

Museums/Libraries

New Hampshire Historical Society, Inc.
Journal: Historical New Hampshire
30 Park St.
Concord, NH 03301-6394
ph: 603-228-6688
fax: 603-224-0463
jdesmarais@nhhistory.org
http://www.nhhistory.org
Dedicated to preserving and sharing New Hampshire history.

New Jersey

Museums/Libraries

New Jersey Historical Society
52 Park Place
Newark, NJ 07102
ph: 973-596-8500
fax: 973-596-6957

New Jersey State Museum
205 West State St.
P.O. Box 530
Trenton, NJ 08625-0530
ph: 609-292-6464
fax: 609-599-4098
feedback@sos.state.nj.us
http://www.state.nj.us/state/museum

New Mexico

Museums/Libraries

Museum of New Mexico
107 West Palace Ave.
P.O. Box 2087
Santa Fe, NM 87501
ph: 505-827-6463
fax: 505-476-5076
jmarshall@mnm.state.nm.us
http://www.museumofnewmexico.org
Made up of four museums which house the country's most intriguing collection of New Mexico art, history and culture: Museum of Indian Arts & Culture, Museum of International Folk Art, Museum of Fine Arts, Palace of the Governors.

New York

Dealers

Scott Wagner
NY Memories Antiques & Collectibles
1410 Ave. S, Ste. 2-F
Brooklyn, NY 11229-3326
ph: 917-939-0148 or 718-375-3075
nymemories1@aol.com
Wants to buy antiques and collectibles relating to New York City, its five boroughs, the Statue of Liberty and the 1939 New York World's Fair; souvenirs, old relics of New York City's past, commemoratives.

Museums/Libraries

New-York Historical Society
Two West 77th St.
New York, NY 10024
ph: 212-873-3400
fax: 212-874-8706
nyhs@interport.net
http://www.nyhistory.org

Lori Sullivan
Adirondack Museum, The
Rte. 30
P.O. Box 99
Blue Mountain Lake, NY 12812-0099
ph: 518-352-7311
fax: 518-352-7653
lsullivan@adkmuseum.org
http://www.adirondackmuseum.org
The "Smithsonian" of the Adirondacks; 20 outdoor and indoor exhibit buildings; live programming tells the story of the Adirondacks from mid-1800s to present; new Visitors Center with Museum store, magnificent views, landscaped grounds.

New York State Historical Association
Magazine: Heritage
Lake Rd., Route 80
Cooperstown, NY 13326
ph: 607-547-1400 or 888-547-1450
carla@nysha.org
http://www.nysha.org
Private, non-profit educational institution chartered in 1899; purpose is to collect, preserve, interpret objects and documents significant to New York history and the American culture; collections of folk, fine, North Amer. Indian art.

New York (Brooklyn)

Collectors

Brian Merlis
P.O. Box 14
Lynbrook, NY 11563-0014
ph: 516-593-4505
Wants items relating to Brooklyn and Long Island: maps, LIRR, books, medals, prints, relics, badges, souvenirs, brochures, negatives, genealogy, histories, postcards, newspapers, artwork, atlases, letterheads, etc.

North Carolina

Collectors

J. Robert Boykin, III
P.O. Box 7440
Wilson, NC 27895
ph: 252-237-1700
fax: 252-237-2314
boykinappraisals@coastalnet.com
Wants to buy any pre-1930 items from North Carolina such as billheads, letterheads, postcards, history books, advertising, tokens, art, trade cards, bottles.

Museums/Libraries

North Carolina Museum of History
5 East Edenton St.
4650 Mail Service Center
Raleigh, NC 27699-4650
ph: 919-715-0200
fax: 919-733-8655
ncmoh@ncmail.net
http://www.ncmuseumofhistory.org
Promotes the understanding of the history and material culture of North Carolina for the educational benefit of North Carolinians.

North Dakota

Museums/Libraries

State Historical Society of North Dakota
612 East Blvd. Ave.
Bismarck, ND 58505-0830
ph: 701-328-2666
fax: 701-328-3710
histsoc@state.nd.us
http://www.state.nd.us/hist

Ohio

Museums/Libraries

Ohio Historical Society
1982 Velma Ave.
Columbus, OH 43211
ph: 614-297-2300
webmaster@ohiohistory.org
http://www.ohiohistory.org

Western Reserve Historical Society
10825 East Blvd.
Cleveland, OH 44106-1703
ph: 216-721-5722
fax: 216-721-0645
webmaster@wrhs.org
http://www.wrhs.org
*Oldest cultural institution in
Cleveland, with a research/
genealogical library, costume wing,
auto & aviation museum and restored
mansion under one roof; special
interest area in genealogical research.*

Oklahoma

Museums/Libraries

Oklahoma Historical Society
2100 N. Lincoln Blvd.
Oklahoma City, OK 73105-4997
ph: 405-521-2491
ohsmembers@ok-history.mus.ok.us
http://www.ok-history.mus.ok.us

Oregon

Museums/Libraries

Oregon Historical Society
1200 SW Park Ave.
Portland, OR 97205-2483
ph: 503-222-1741
fax: 503-221-2035
orhist@ohs.org
http://www.ohs.org

Pennsylvania

Museums/Libraries

Historical Society of Pennsylvania
1300 Locust St.
Philadelphia, PA 19107-5699
ph: 215-732-6200
fax: 215-732-2680
webmaster@hsp.org
http://www.hsp.org
*Holds many of the nation's most
important historical documents;
houses more than 500,000 books,
300,000 graphic works, and 15
million manuscript items; maintains
one of the largest family history
libraries in the nation.*

Suppliers

State Museum of Pennsylvania
3rd & North Sts.
P.O. Box 1026
Harrisburg, PA 17108-1026
ph: 717-772-4979 or 717-787-4980
museum@statemuseumpa.org
http://www.statemuseumpa.org

Pennsylvania German Heritage

Appraisers

C. Robert Harrison, ISA
Harrison Appraisals, LLC
3435 Uniontown Rd.
Westminster, MD 21158
ph: 410-775-1351
fax: 410-775-1351
bob@harrisonappraisals.com
http://www.harrisonappraisals.com
*Offers appraisals of antiques &
residential contents; specializes in
18th and 19th century American
furniture and Pennsylvania German
decorative arts, particularly American
"backcountry" furniture from the
Shenandoah Valley region.*

Museums/Libraries

James McMahon
Hershey Museum
170 W. Hersheypark Dr.
Hershey, PA 17033-2727
ph: 717-534-3439
fax: 717-534-8940
info@hersheymuseum.org
http://www.hersheymuseum.org
*Focused collection of objects detailing
the town of Hershey history, regional
PA German heritage, native American
material culture.*

Rhode Island

Museums/Libraries

Bernard Fishman, Ex. Dir.
Rhode Island Historical Society
110 Benevolent St.
Providence, RI 02906
ph: 401-331-8575
fax: 401-351-0127
bfishman@rihs.org
http://www.rihs.org

South Carolina

Dealers

Henry Barnet
Your Town, Inc.
516 Maverick Circle
Spartanburg, SC 29307-3707
ph: 864-579-2112
hbbarnet@cs.com
*Buys, sells and collects original
artwork done by southern artists and
those from South Carolina, especially
from the Piedmont area; wants prints,
ephemera, rare and collectible books,
etc.*

Museums/Libraries

South Carolina Historical Society
Magazine: South Carolina Historical
Magazine
100 Meeting St.
Charleston, SC 29401
ph: 843-723-3225
fax: 843-723-8584
info@schistory.org
http://www.schistory.org

South Dakota

Museums/Libraries

South Dakota State Historical Society/
Office of History
900 Governors Dr.
Pierre, SD 57501-2217
ph: 605-773-3458
fax: 605-773-6041
David.Hartley@state.sd.us
http://www.sdhistory.org

Deadwood Public Library
435 Wiliams St.
Deadwood, SD 57732-1113
ph: 605-578-2821
fax: 605-578-2170
dwd@sdln.net
http://dwdlib.sdln.net
*Wants Deadwood and Black Hills
history materials, both circulating and
archived; Deadwood newspapers from
1876 to present; historical photographs; oral histories.*

Tennessee

Collectors

Claude Bellar
1750 Keyes Rd.
Greenbrier, TN 37073
ph: 615-643-0290
fax: 615-643-0290
cbellar@aol.com
*Wants Tennessee bottles, stoneware,
advertising.*

Paul A. Jarrett
611 West Main
Waverly, TN 37185
ph: 615-296-3151
*Wants to buy pre-Prohibition
Tennessee jugs (miniature or full
size), embossed druggist bottles, pre-
1920 business letterhead, merchant
"good for" tokens.*

Peggy Dillard
P.O. Box 210904
Nashville, TN 37221-0904
ph: 615-646-1605
pdill43795@aol.com
*Wants Tennessee postcards and
historical items, especially Tennessee
Centennial Exposition (1897) items.*

Joe C. Copeland
P.O. Box 4221
Oak Ridge, TN 37831-4221
ph: 865-482-4215
joecopeland@comcast.net
*Wants to buy any Tennessee tokens
and other memorabilia, city and
county histories, pre-1950 phone
books and city directories, Dun &
Bradstreet directories, pins, medals,
badges, crocks, whiskey jugs,
gazetteers.*

Museums/Libraries

East Tennessee Historical Society
P.O. Box 1629
Knoxville, TN 37901-1629
ph: 423-544-5732
fax: 423-544-4319
eths@east-tennessee-history.org
http://www.east-tennessee-history.org

West Tennessee Historical Society
P.O. Box 111046
Memphis, TN 38111
lgundersen@jscc.cc.tn.us
http://www.wths.tn.org

Texas

Clubs/Associations

Ben Reynolds
Texas Centennial Collector
P.O. Box 8072
Longview, TX 75607
fax: 903-757-3043
bensbooks@worldnet.att.net
http://www.geocities.com/TheTropics/
6004
Free newsletter; no dues.

Collectors

James E. Kattner
P.O. Box 11132
Spring, TX 77391-1132
ph: 281-376-4826
victorio1sw@yahoo.com
*Wants to buy Texas tokens from
saloons, bars, military forts, post
traders, lumber companies, drug
stores, general stores, bakeries, etc.;
also wants Texas, pocket mirrors,
whiskey jugs and other Texas saloon
advertisement items.*

Museums/Libraries

Texas State Historical Association
2/306 Sid Richardson Hall
Austin, TX 78712
ph: 512-471-1525
fax: 512-471-1551
comments.tsha@lib.utexas.edu
http://www.tsha.utexas.edu

Utah

Museums/Libraries

Utah State Historical Society
300 Rio Grande
Salt Lake City, UT 84101-1143
ph: 801-533-3500
fax: 801-533-3503
cergushs@utah.gov
http://history.utah.gov

Vermont

Museums/Libraries

Vermont Historical Society
60 Washington St.
Barre, VT 05641-4209
ph: 802-479-8500
fax: 802-479-8510
vhs@vhs.state.vt.us
http://www.vermonthistory.org

Virginia

Museums/Libraries

Virginia Historical Society
428 North Boulevard
Richmond, VA 23220
ph: 804-358-4901
webadmin@vahistorical.org
http://www.vahistorical.org

Washington

Collectors

Richard Reisinger
2610 Holgate St.
Tacoma, WA 98402-1204
ph: 253-272-7092
*Wants 19th and early 20 century
Puget Sound region (Seattle, Tacoma,
Olympia, Mt. Rainier, etc.) travel
brochures, ephemera, postal history,
photos, view books, maps, tourist
souvenirs, china, bottles, pins,
badges, posters, etc.*

Museums/Libraries

Washington State Historical Society
1911 Pacific Ave.
Tacoma, WA 98402
ph: 253-272-3500 or 888-238-4373
http://www.wshs.org

Washington DC

Collectors

Jerry A. McCoy
800 Thayer Ave.
Silver Spring, MD 20910-4504
ph: 301-565-2519
sshistory@yahoo.com
*Wants to buy real photo (B & W)
postcards of 19th or early 20th
century Washington DC.*

Museums/Libraries

United States Capitol Historical Society
200 Maryland Ave., NE
Washington, DC 20002-5796
ph: 202-543-8919
fax: 202-544-8244
uschs@uschs.org
http://www.uschs.org
*Created in 1962 to promote the
history of the US Capitol and
Congress.*

Historical Society of Washington, D.C.
1307 New Hampshire Ave., N.W.
Washington, DC 20036-1507
ph: 202-785-2068
info@hswdc.org
http://www.hswdc.org
*Devoted to making the history of the
Washington metropolitan area and its*

*people accessible and understandable
to the public.*

West Virginia

Museums/Libraries

West Virginia State Museum
c/o WV Div. of Culture & History
1900 Kanawha Bouolevard East
Charleston, WV 25305-0300
ph: 304-558-0220
fax: 304-558-2779
mike.keller@wvculture.org
http://www.wvculture.org/museum/
index.html

Wisconsin

Museums/Libraries

George Vogt, Dir.
Wisconsin Historical Society
816 State St.
Madison, WI 53706
ph: 608-264-6400
libref@whs.wisc.edu
http://www.wisconsinhistory.org
*Museums contains collections
representing what is now Wisconsin
from pre-historic times to present.*

Wyoming

Museums/Libraries

Wyoming State Museum
Barrett Building
2301 Central Ave.
Cheyenne, WY 82002
ph: 307-777-7022
fax: 307-777-5375
wsm@state.wy.us
http://www.wyomuseum.state.wy.us

STATIONARY ENGINES

(see ENGINES, Gasoline)

STATUE OF LIBERTY COLLECTIBLES

(see also SOUVENIR &
COMMEMORATIVE ITEMS)

Clubs/Associations

Iris & Mort November
Statue of Liberty Collectors' Club
Newsletter: Statue of Liberty Collectors'
Club Newsletter
26601 Bernwood Rd.
Cleveland, OH 44122-7133
ph: 216-831-2646 or 216-831-0497
fax: 216-831-0497
lbrtyclub@aol.com
http://www.statueoflibertyclub.com
*For collectors or enthusiasts with an
interest in items relating to the Statue
of Liberty; dues help support the
Statue of Liberty Foundation; three
newsletters per year plus other Club
benefits including discounts, Club
meetings.*

Collectors

Jeffrey Eger
42 Blackberry Ln.
Morristown, NJ 07960-6404
ph: 973-455-1843
fax: 973-455-0186
*Writer/author/Statue of Liberty
historian looking for unusual early
items relating to the statue's history.*

Iris & Mort November
26601 Bernwood Rd.
Cleveland, OH 44122-7133
ph: 216-831-2646 or 216-831-0497
fax: 216-831-0497
lbrtyclub@aol.com
http://www.statueoflibertyclub.com
*Collects items relating to the Statue of
Liberty or its designer, Bartholdi.*

Mike Brooks
7335 Skyline
Oakland, CA 94611-1121
ph: 510-339-1751
deborahwb@aol.com
*Buying early souvenir models, books,
medals, advertising, donor certificates, unveiling invitations, Bartholdi
related items, etc.*

Dealers

Ronald Cutadean
1235 Kennedy Ave.
Louisville, CO 80027-1072
rcutadean@yahoo.com
*Buys, sells, trades Statue of Liberty
items.*

Experts

Harvey & Sandy Dolin
Harvey Dolin & Co.
111 Fulton St., Mezzanine Level
New York, NY 100386
ph: 212-267-0216
*Wants any item pertaining to the
Statue of Liberty.*

STEAM-OPERATED

Models & Equipment

(see also AUTOMOBILES, Steam;
BOATS, Steam; ENGINES; FARM
MACHINERY; GAUGES; HORNS &
WHISTLES; INDUSTRY RELATED
ITEMS; MACHINERY &
EQUIPMENT, Road Making;
RAILROADS; STEAMBOAT
COLLECTIBLES; TOYS, Farm;
TOYS, Steam/Hot Air)

Clubs/Associations

Hal H. Will
Northwest Steam Society
Newsletter: Steam Gage
3629 NW 64th St.
Seattle, WA 98107-2667
halathome@aol.com
http://www.northweststeamsociety.org
*Interested in steam-operated models,
equipment, and machinery; especially
railroads and steam steam boats.*

John Cook, Mem. Sec.
National Traction Engine Trust
Magazine: Steaming
c/o "Dolfarni," Church Lane
Kirkby la Thorpe
Sleaford, Lincolnshire NG34 9NU U.K.
ntet@ntet.co.uk
http://www.ntet.co.uk
*Based in the U.K.; dedicated to the
preservation of steam powered
traction and stationary engines and
ancillary equipment.*

Collectors

D.E. Haskins
1237 Alleghany Ln.
Northbrook, IL 60062
ph: 847-498-3516
*Wants old toy steam engines, parts
and literature (no railroad, please).*

Internet Resources

John Robertson
John's Steam & Stuff
johno@iglou.com
http://johno.myiglou.com
*Resources for the steam engine
builder.*

Museums/Libraries

Hamilton Museum of Steam &
Technology, The
900 Woodward Ave.
Hamilton, Ontario L8H 7N2 Canada
ph: 905-546-4797
fax: 905-546-4798
steammuseum@hamilton.ca
*Exhibits of industrial history;
children's activities.*

Periodicals

Village Press
Magazine: Live Steam Magazine
P.O. Box 1810
Traverse City, MI 49685-1810
ph: 231-946-3712 or 800-447-7367
fax: 231-946-9588
cmckinley@villagepress.com
http://www.livesteam.net
*A magazine for the amateur machinist,
or live steam hobbyist; steam
locomotives, marine vessels, tractors,
stationary steam engines, etc.; full
scale or models.*

George & Linda Broad
Magazine: Modeltec
P.O. Box 9
33247 154th Ave.
Avon, MN 56310
ph: 320-356-7255
fax: 320-356-7290
modeltec@cloudnet.com
*Monthly magazine for lovers of large-
scale trains, live steam, hot air and
antique gas engine models.*

Suppliers

James Humphrey
Mountain Car Company
P.O. Box 1073
1209 Colorado St.
Salem, VA 24153
ph: 540-387-0124 or 800-780-0124
fax: 540-387-4372
mcc@mountaincar.com
http://www.mountaincar.com
*Manufacturers 1-1/2" scale railroad
rolling stock and accessories,
passenger freight cars, trucks,
couplers, and more.*

Cannonball Ltd.
11501 E. Waterloo Rd.
Arcadia, OK. 73007
ph: 405-524-4400
fax: 405 396-8335
trains@cannonballltd.com
http://www.cannonballltd.com
*A 1-1/2" scale, 7-1/4 and 7-1/2 inch
gauge manufacturer and supplier of
model railroad locomotives, rolling
stock, power trucks, freight trucks,
rail, and miscellaneous accessories.*

MDM Locomotive Works
1931 NE 39th St.
Oklahoma City, OK 73111
ph: 405-478-0502
info@mdmlocomotiveworks.com
http://www.mdmlocomotiveworks.com
Precision 1-1/2" scale locomotives.

Allen Models
5994 Cuesta Verde
Goleta, CA 93117-1808
ph: 805-967-2095
*A supplier of live steam locomotives
and castings; 1-1/2" and 2-1/2" scale
models; catalog $5 ppd.*

Little Engines
131 La Grande Ave.
Moss Beach, CA 94038
ph: 650-728-1852
fax: 650-728-8050
locoworks@aol.com
*Supplier of 1/4" to 1" scale steam
locomotives, riding cars, trucks and
equipment; over 65 years in business.*

Steam Train Engines & Models
P.O. Box 123
Windsor, CA 95492-0123
ph: 707-838-8135
Steam4Me@aol.com
http://www.steam4me.com
*Specializes in live steam models of all
types, new and use, with an emphasis
on Gauge 1 and larger live steam
locomotives.*

STEAMBOAT COLLECTIBLES

(see also BOATS; OCEAN LINER
MEMORABILIA; SHIPPING; SHIP
RELATED)

Clubs/Associations

Sue Ewen
Steamship Historical Society of America,
Inc.
Magazine: Steamboat Bill
300 Ray Dr., Ste. #4
Providence, RI 02906
ph: 401-274-0805
http://www.sshsa.net
*For those interested in maritime
history; publishes high quality
quarterly magazine; has photo bank of
thousands of negatives of powered
vessels, national and regional
meetings.*

Tugboat Enthusiasts Society of the
Americas
Magazine: Tug Bitts
420 49th St. E, Lot 127
Palmetto, FL 34221
*Published quarterly; covers steamboat
& inland river history; packed with
news, photos, articles on all types of
tow boats, tugboats (harbor, ocean,
military) and work boat salvage,
restoration and history; a must for
tugboat enthusiasts.*

Steamboat Masters & Associations, Inc.
Journal: Egregious Steamboat Journal,
The
P.O. Box 3046
Louisville, KY 40201-3046
ph: 502-778-6784
fax: 502-776-9006
sbmaster@bellsouth.net
*Offers a wide variety of research and
consulting services; appraises
steamboat collections; sell them
through a bi-monthly journal of
steamboat history and technical
studies; a wealth of unpublished
information and photos.*

Sons & Daughters of Pioneer Rivermen
Magazine: S & D Reflector
126 Seneca Dr.
Marietta, OH 45750
http://sd.steamboats.org
*With about 1,100 members, this
organization is devoted to river
history; magazine published quarterly;
meets annually in Marietta, OH the
third weekend of September.*

Experts

Jack & Sandra Custer
P.O. Box 3046
Louisville, KY 40201-3046
ph: 502-778-6784
fax: 502-776-9006
sbmaster@bellsouth.net
*Experts, appraisers, dealers focusing
on steamboats and steamboat
collectibles; offers one-stop shopping
for collectibles, artifacts, art prints,
and resource books pertaining to
steamboats.*

Museums/Libraries

Steamship Historical Society Collection
at the University of Baltimore Library
1420 Maryland Ave.
Baltimore, MD 21201-5779
ph: 410-625-3134
thollowak@ubmail.ubalt.edu
http://archives.ubalt.edu/steamship/
collect.htm
*A 10,000-volume library of books,
periodicals, approx. 200,000
photographs, 25,000 printed
postcards, ship plans, and a brochure
collection devoted exclusively to the
history of engine-powered vessels.*

Amy Bannister, PR
Inland Rivers Library at the Public
Library of Cincinnati & Hamilton
County
800 Vine St.
Cincinnati, OH 45202-2071
ph: 513-369-6957
fax: 513-369-3123
amy.banister@cincinnatilibrary.org
http://www.cincinnatilibrary.org
*Specialty collections include rare book
collection (history of the Ohio and
Mississippi rivers and their tributaries
as commercial transportation routes),
clipping files, illustrations, maps,
photos, manuscripts, blueprints,
broadsides.*

John B. Briley, Mngr.
Ohio River Museum
601 Front St.
Marietta, OH 45750
ph: 740-373-3750 or 800-860-0145
fax: 740-860-3680
webmaster@ohiohistory.org
http://www.ohiohistory.org/places/
ohriver
*The Museum is the Ohio Historical
Society's interpretive center for river
history, especially steamboats; exhibits
include the 1918 steam towboat, W.P.
SNYDER JR., 19th century steamboat
artifacts, dioramas, photos, paintings,
videos.*

Yvonne Knight
Howard Steamboat Museum
1101 E. Market St.
P.O. Box 606
Jeffersonville, IN 47131-0606
ph: 812-283-3728
fax: 812-283-6049
david@reinhardt.com
http://www.steamboatmuseum.org
*Steamboat artifacts and models,
photographs, half-breadth models,
tools; 1894 mansion tour; original
Victorian furnishings; Moorish
parlor.*

Mississippi River Museum
350 E. 3rd St.
P.O. Box 266
Dubuque, IA 52004-0266
ph: 563-557-9545
fax: 563-583-1241
rivermuse@mwci.net
http://www.mississippirivermuseum.com
Focuses on the "William M. Black"

*(1934 side-wheeler river boat); also
collections relating to canoes,
flatboats, steamboats, steam engines,
and the Mississippi River.*

Murphy Library at the University of
Wisconsin, La Crosse
University of WI - La Crosse
1631 Pine St.
La Crosse, WI 54601
ph: 608-785-8505
fax: 608-785-8639
evans.anit@uwlax.edu
http://www.uwlax.edu/murphylibrary
*45,000 photographs of inland river
steamboats.*

John Neal Hoover, Lib.
St. Louis Mercantile Library Association
8001 Natural Bridge Rd.
Saint Louis, MO 63131-4401
ph: 314-621-0670
fax: 314-621-1782
*Specialty collections include the
National Inland Waterways Collection
consisting of books, manuscripts,
maps, photographs, reports and
pamphlets.*

Periodicals

Journal: Waterways Journal, The
319 N. 4th St.
Saint Louis, MO 63102-1906
ph: 314-241-7354
fax: 314-241-4207
hnspencer@waterwaysjournal.net
http://www.waterwaysjournal.net
*Weekly newspaper reporting on
current events.*

STEAMSHIP MEMORABILIA

(see OCEAN LINER MEMORABILIA;
SHIPPING; SHIP REPLATED;
STEAMBOAT COLLECTIBLES)

STEIFF

(see also DOLLS; TEDDY BEARS;
TOYS)

Appraisers

E. Adorjan
Imaginary Friends
P.O. Box 40601
Denver, CO 80204
ph: 303-761-7234
toyrep@aol.com
http://members.aol.com/toyrep
*Independent appraiser specializing in
Steiff and other stuffed toys and dolls.*

Clubs/Associations

Steiff Club USA
Magazine: Steiff Club USA Magazine
P.O. Box 460
Raynham Center, MA 02768-0460
ph: 800-830-0429
fax: 508-821-4477
clubinfo@steiffusa.com
http://www.steiffusa.com/club
Contemporary plush teddy bears with

trademark "button-in-ear;" a company-sponsored collectors club.

Beth B. Savino
Steiff Collectors Club
<u>Newsletter: Collector Life</u>
Westgate Village
3301 West Central Ave.
Toledo, OH 43606
ph: 419-531-2839 or 800-862-8697
fax: 419-531-2730
info@toystorenet.com
http://www.toystorenet.com
Focus is on collecting Steiff toys; sells exclusive Steiff Limited Edition; also buys old Steiff.

Collectors

Tadg Galleran
2911 4th St., #112
Santa Monica, CA 90405
ph: 310-314-0402
tadggalleran@hotmail.com
Wants to buy any and all Steiff animals, especially teddy bears and rabbits, from 1890s to 1950s; prefer excellent condition with button and/or chest tag; send photo.

Dealers

Barbara & Byron Baldwin
Old Friends Antiques
P.O. Box 754
Sparks, MD 21152
ph: 412-291-1024
fax: 412-291-1024
petsybar@aol.com
http://www.oldfriendsantiques.com
Specializing in Steiff bears and animals.

Rita Mueller
Grange Hall Antiques
1 South Eighth Alley
P.O. Box 263
New Market, MD 21774
ph: 301-865-5651
fax: 301-865-0518
Rita@newmarketmd.com
http://www.grangehallantiques.com
Quality Steiff animals from 1950s through 1980s; always buying one piece or entire collection: teddy bears, Schuco, Hermann, Steiff; also available - fine country graniteware from Germany available; mail orders and layaways.

Cheri Shivley
Cynthia's Country Store, Inc.
The Wellington Mall #15A
12794 W. Forest Hill Blvd.
West Palm Beach, FL 33414
ph: 561-793-0554
fax: 561-795-4222
cynbears@aol.com
http://www.cynthiascountrystore.com
Specializing in new, discontinued and antique Steiff, R. John Wright, and other manufacturers and artists bears.

E. Adorjan
Imaginary Friends
P.O. Box 40601
Denver, CO 80204
ph: 303-761-7234
toyrep@aol.com
http://members.aol.com/toyrep
Specializes repairs and restorations to Steiff and other stuffed toys and dolls; will advise if toy would be better off if left as-is; references and before-and-after photos available; official restoration specialist with Steiff.

Karen Strickland
Rare Bears
17831 Chase St.
Northridge, CA 91325-3808
ph: 818-993-9361
fax: 818-341-9316
Buys and sells Steiff, Schuco animals and vintage Teddy Bears; four quarterly listings for $20/yr.

Experts

Beth B. Savino
Toy Store, The
Westgate Village
3301 West Central Ave.
Toledo, OH 43606
ph: 419-531-2839 or 800-862-8697
fax: 419-531-2730
info@toystorenet.com
http://www.toystorenet.com
Buys, sells and specializes in Steiff toys; sells exclusive Steiff Limited Edition; also buys old Steiff.

E. Adjoran
Imaginary Friends
P.O. Box 40601
Denver, CO 80204
ph: 303-761-7234
toyrep@aol.com
http://members.aol.com/toyrep
"Dr." E is a Steiff authorized restorationist, independent appraiser and collector; specializes in Steiff and all other stuffed toys and teddy bears; buys, sells, trades, repairs, restores, appraises; consignment sales and custom-mades.

Internet Resources

Milton & Gayle Shaw
Steiff Collector Values & Reference Database
518 North Indian Rocks Rd.
Bellair Bluffs, FL 33770
ph: 727-584-7277
mshaw1@tampabay.rr.com
http://www.dollvalues.com
A searchable database with thousands of Steiff items pictured and valued.

Man./Prod./Dist.

Steiff USA, L.P.
P.O. Box 460
Raynham Center, MA 02768-0460
ph: 800-830-0429
fax: 508-821-4477
salesinfo@steiffusa.com
http://www.steiffusa.com
Manufacturer of collectible plush stuffed Steiff animals.

Margarete Steiff GmbH
P.O. Box 1560
Giengen/Brenz, D-89530 Germany
ph: +49 7322 131 452
fax: +49 7322 131 476
manuela.fustig@steiff.de
http://www.steiff.com
Started in 1880, manufactures high-quality mohair Teddy bears.

Repair Services

E. Adorjan
Imaginary Friends
P.O. Box 40601
Denver, CO 80204
ph: 303-761-7234
toyrep@aol.com
http://members.aol.com/toyrep
Specializes repairs and restorations to Steiff and other stuffed toys and dolls; will advise if toy would be better off if left as-is; references and before-and-after photos available; official restoration specialist with Steiff.

STEINS

(see also COLLECTIBLES [MODERN], Steins; GLASSES, Drinking)

Appraisers

George F. Adams
Steins Unlimited
Rt. 600 Box 7-B
Pamplin, VA 23958
ph: 434-248-6114
fax: 434-248-6114
Buys, sells, appraises and repairs (pewter) steins; Mettlach, Villeroy Boch, other German, Brewery, Bud, Millers, Coors, Strohs, Old Style, etc.

Auction Services

John McClain
York Town Auction Inc.
1625 Haviland Rd.
York, PA 17404
ph: 717-751-0211
fax: 717-767-7729
info@yorktownauction.com
http://www.yorktownauction.com
Antique & specialty auctions, lecture & appraisal services; antiques also purchased; American & English furniture, related specialties & accessories, Americana, folk art, jewelry, art, clocks & watches, militaria, steins, Oriental rugs.

Gary Kirsner
Gary Kirsner Auctions
P.O. Box 8807
Coral Springs, FL 33075-8807
ph: 954-344-9856
fax: 954-344-4421
gkirsner@garykirsnerauctions.com
http://www.garykirsnerauctions.com
Six to seven cataloged auctions per year; steins and related items; also specialty auctions of Limited Edition and retired collectibles.

Andre Ammelounx
Stein Auction Company
P.O. Box 136
Palatine, IL 60078
ph: 847-991-5927
fax: 847-991-5947
Conducts live and mail bid catalog stein auctions.

Clubs/Associations

Lawrence Beckendorff
Lone Star Chapter of the Stein Collectors International
labeck@txucom.net

Les Hopper, Ed.
Bayou Stein Verein
<u>Newsletter: Al E. Gator Sez</u>
ph: 504-394-3530
fax: 504-392-8937
leshopper@cox.net
http://www.bayousteinverein.org

Pennsylvania Keysteiners
keysteiner@att.net
http://keysteiners.8k.com
Dedicated to the study and collecting of beer steins.

Helmut Kister
Western Ohio Steinjager
president@steinjaeger.com
http://www.steinjaeger.com
Purpose is to teach the knowledge of beer stein and other drinking vessel collecting.

Jim DeMars
Sun Steiners
<u>Newsletter: Sun Steiner News</u>
P.O. Box 11782
Fort Lauderdale, FL 33339-1782
ph: 954-772-4490
fax: 954-772-4490
FLSteiners@aol.com
http://steincollectors.org/chapters/sunstein.html
Members collect beer steins; antique, brewery, character, Mettlach, etc.

Tom Seitz
Buckeye Stein Verein
2265 Bradley Rd.
Westlake, OH 44145-1737
ph: 419-841-3195
tseitz@buckeye-express.com

Stein Collectors International, Inc.
Magazine: Prosit
P.O. Box 342
Stevens Point, WI 54481-0342
ph: 360-598-6057
SASsteins@aol.com
http://www.steincollectors.org
Non-profit collectors' organization dedicated to the study and understanding of the art, culture, and manufacture of beer steins, drinking vessels, and related items from antiquity to modern times.

Pete McClintock
Rocky Mountain Steiners
ph: 303-978-9979
pete.mcclintock@ihsenergy.com
Rocky Mountaineer Steiners is a local chapter of Stein Collectors International which was founded in 1965 and is a non-profit organization dedicated to the study of the art, culture, and manufacture of beer steins, drinking vessels, etc.

Lyn Ayers
Pacific Stein Sammler
Newsletter: die Kunde
P.O. Box 6995
Bellevue, WA 98008-0995
ph: 425-747-9239
layers@wa-net.com
http://webhost.kendra.com/altekruge/pss

Collectors

Dr. Paul Rohe
P.O. Box 122
Martinville, NJ 08336-0122
Wants to buy old steins.

Michael G. Anderson
6761 N. Placita Bella
Tucson, AZ 85718-2530
ph: 520-299-3407
fax: 520-299-4917
mike3407@aol.com
Wants steins: blown glass, regimental, military, Mettlach, etc.

Steve Elliott
1600 Tennessee St.
Vallejo, CA 94590-4629
ph: 707-552-8400 or 707-642-1949
fax: 707-552-0881
Wants to buy antique beer steins.

Dealers

Heinz Roes
Heinz "N" Steins
7068 Aviation Blvd.
Glen Burnie, MD 21061-2442
ph: 410-760-0707 or 410-315-9831
fax: 410-760-0853
Buys, sells, appraises beer steins; military, Mettlach, character drinking vessels, cups, plaques, WWI, German, pipes, pictures, flasks, etc.; also occupational shaving mugs; also wants Black Forest wood carvings.

Thirsty Knight Antiques
7 & 9 East Main St.
P.O. Box 48
New Market, MD 21774
ph: 301-831-9889 or 301-865-5053
Specializing in beer steins since 1972: Mettlachs, regimentals, characters, glass, porcelain, silver, pewter, faience, stoneware from 1500s to late 1800s.

George F. Adams
Steins Unlimited
Rt. 600 Box 7-B
Pamplin, VA 23958
ph: 434-248-6114
fax: 434-248-6114
Buys, sells, appraises and repairs (pewter) steins; Mettlach, Villeroy Boch, other German, Brewery, Bud, Millers, Coors, Strohs, Old Style, etc.

Bill Cress
P.O. Box 989
Alton, IL 62002-0989
ph: 618-466-3513
williambud@webtv.net
Buys and sells all of the new and lots of the old steins; quarterly lists of modern steins and mugs for sale.

Experts

Ron Fox
416 Throop St.
North Babylon, NY 11704
ph: 631-376-0916
fax: 631-376-0916
oz@webspan.net
Specializes in Mettlach steins.

Thirsty Knight Antiques
7 & 9 East Main St.
P.O. Box 48
New Market, MD 21774
ph: 301-831-9889 or 301-865-5053
Specializing in beer steins since 1972: Mettlachs, regimentals, characters, glass, porcelain, silver, pewter, faience, stoneware from 1500s to late 1800s.

Gary & Beth Kirsner
Glentiques, Ltd.
P.O. Box 8807
Coral Springs, FL 33075-8807
ph: 954-344-9856
fax: 954-344-4421
gkirsner@garykirsnerauctions.com
http://www.garykirsnerauctions.com
Wants quality steins: Mettlach, regimentals, character, glass, etc.; author of "The Beer Stein Book," (1990.)

Jim DeMars
P.O. Box 11782
Fort Lauderdale, FL 33339-1782
ph: 954-772-4490
fax: 954-772-4490
FLSteiners@aol.com
http://steincollectors.org/chapters/sunstein.html

Les Paul
Les Paul, Steinologist
568 Country Isle M
Alameda, CA 94501-5614
ph: 510-523-7480
fax: 510-523-8755
oldsteins@aol.com
Contact for free antique beer stein appraisal or information without obligation; photos are helpful, but he can usually tell you retail and a fair dealer offer over the phone; call with the stein in your hands.

Internet Resources

Frank Loevi
BeerSteins America, Inc.
fjl@beerstein.net
http://www.beerstein.net
Great online library of beer stein related articles.

Stein Collectors International, Inc.
Magazine: Prosit
P.O. Box 342
Stevens Point, WI 54481-0342
ph: 360-598-6057
SASsteins@aol.com
http://www.steincollectors.org
Click on the library link for some great articles about collecting and identifying steins.

Mettlach

Experts

Joe & Pat Hartzler
J & P Collectibles
89 Brookhill Dr.
Howell, NJ 07731-1803
ph: 732-890-2887
Buys, sells and specializes in Mettlach steins; willing to share information.

Regimental

Experts

R. Ron Heiligenstein
3900 W. Brown Deer Rd., #A290
Milwaukee, WI 53209-1220
ph: 520-577-9607
ronheil@aol.com
http://www.regimentalbeerstein.com
Author of the definitive text on regimental steins, "Regimental Beer Steins of the Imperial German and Royal Bavarian Armies and the Imperial German Navy, 1890-1914."

STEREO VIEWERS & STEREOVIEWS

(see also 3-D PHOTOGRAPHICA; CAMERAS & CAMERA EQUIPMENT, Stereo Cameras; OPTICAL ITEMS; PAPER COLLECTIBLES; PHOTOGRAPHS)

Clubs/Associations

Susan Pinsky
Stereo Club of Southern California
Newsletter: 3D News
P.O. Box 2368
Culver City, CA 90231-2368
ph: 310-837-2368
fax: 310-558-1653
Reel3D@aol.com
http://www.la3dclub.com
A club for people interested in sharing 3-D (stereo) photography; some equipment listed in club newsletter classifieds.

Mary Ann Sell, Pres.
National Stereoscopic Association
Magazine: Stereo World
P.O. Box 86708
Portland, OR 97286
ph: 503-771-4440
vmmasell@cinti.net
http://www.stereoview.org
Members collect stereo views, stereoscopes, stereo cameras; View-Master reels, viewers, packets; all other 3-D collectibles; the glossy colorful magazine is published six timer per year.

Collectors

Norman Kulkin
Pixidiom
727 N. Fuller Ave.
Los Angeles, CA 90046-7504
ph: 323-653-6929
fax: 323-651-0640
pixidiom@aol.com
http://www.pixidiom.com
Buy, sell, trade vintage photographs: ambrotypes, tintypes, stereoviews, specialty is daguerreotypes; also early 19th century paper photos, early 20th century photos; also photographica including cameras.

Dealers

David L. Spahr
Maine Antique Photographica Gallery
51 High Holborn St.
Gardiner, ME 04345
ph: 207-582-0402
dspahr3d@stereoviews.com
http://www.stereoviews.com
19th and 20th century photograph specialist focusing on stereoviews.

Bryan W. Ginns
2109 Cty. Rte. 21
Valatie, NY 12184-6001
ph: 518-392-5805
fax: 518-392-7925
the3dman@aol.com

David Wood
Dave's Stereos
P.O. Box 838
Milford, PA 18337-0838
ph: 570-296-6176 or 845-856-5311 x397
fax: 845-856-5507
wood@pikeonline.net
http://www.daves-stereos.com
Collector and dealer wants stereoviews; wide range of interests, especially stereoviews by photographer

L. Hensel who took views of PA (especially Pike County, PA) and New York.

Christopher Perry
Photoplay Orchestra
7470 Church St., Ste. A
Yucca Valley, CA 92284-3248
ph: 760-365-0475
fax: 760-365-0495
evildoctor3d@yahoo.com
http://www.photoplayorchestra.com
Can transfer stereoviews to 3-D slides; also looking for views after 1900 and especially 1920 and after; no foreign travelogue of scenery; especially wants Hollywood, movie theaters, movie stars, World's Fair, magicians.

John Saddy
Jefferson Stereoptics
50 Foxborough Grove
London, Ontario N6K 4A8 Canada
ph: 519-641-4431
fax: 519-641-2899
john.saddy.3d@sympatico.ca
http://www3.sympatico.ca/
john.saddy.3d/home.htm
Specializes in stereoviews; buys, sells, and operates a specialized stereoview phone and mail auction; wants boxed sets, reels, quality accumulations, View-Master and Tru-Vue; specializes in consignments; also buys antique photography.

Tim McIntyre
Tim McIntyre's Antique Photographs
525 Nicola St., #908
Kamloops, British Columbia V2C 6J5
Canada
ph: 250-374-6610
timoni@orc.ca
http://www.timoni.net
Buys and sells 19th and early 20th century photographs, especially stereoviews, CDVs, cabinet cards, ambrotypes, tintypes, daguerreotypes and larger formats.

Experts

Russell Norton
Photographic Antiques
P.O. Box 1070
New Haven, CT 06504-1070
ph: 203-281-0066
http://www.stereoview.com
Buys, sells, trades, collects, specializes in stereo views; author of "Stereoviews Illustrated Vol. 1: 50 Early American;" $20 from author; full-size illustrations, great quality duotones.

John Waldsmith
Collector's Auctioneer, The
P.O. Box 83
Sharon Center, OH 44274
ph: 330-239-1944 or 330-239-2212
vansywalsy@aol.com
http://www.YourAuctionPage.com/
Waldsmith
Wants stereoscopic views, View-Master reels, photographica; conducts mail/phone auctions on regular basis;

also direct sales; author of "Stereo Views: An Illustrated History and Price Guide."

Chuck Reincke
Stereographica
2141 Sweet Briar Rd.
Tustin, CA 92780-6906
ph: 714-832-8563
fax: 714-832-8563
iam3dking@juno.com
Buy, sell stereo cards, View Master, Tru-Vue and viewers; prefer higher quality and more unusual items.

Mike Aversa, ISA
Aversa Estate & Appraisal Service
P.O. Box 863
Yorba Linda, CA 92885
ph: 717-777-3848 or 714-749-3887
AversaAntiques@mindspring.com
http://www.aversaantiques.com
Buys and sells stereo cards, stereo viewers, View Master viewers and reels, Tru-Vue, and all 3-D stereographica.

Misc. Services

Christopher Perry
Photoplay Orchestra
7470 Church St., Ste. A
Yucca Valley, CA 92284-3248
ph: 760-365-0475
fax: 760-365-0495
evildoctor3d@yahoo.com
http://www.photoplayorchestra.com
Can transfer a stereocard to an archival stereo slide.

Suppliers

David Starkman
Reel 3-D Enterprises, Inc.
P.O. Box 2368
Culver City, CA 90231-2368
ph: 310-837-2368
fax: 310-558-1653
reel3d@aol.com
http://stereoscopy.com/reel3d
Offers a catalog with complete line of items for the modern 3-D enthusiast: books, stereo viewers, mounting supplies, etc.

Craig Daniels
StereoType
2006 Highway 101, #167
Florence, OR 97439-9723
ph: 541-997-8879
fax: 541-997-8879
Supplier/publisher/designer of custom direct-mailable stereo viewer packages, the conversion of ordinary pictures into stereo pairs (!), and general information on stereoscopic resources (old viewers).

Alaska

Collectors

Richard A. Wood
P.O. Box 22165
Juneau, AK 99802-2165
ph: 907-789-8450
fax: 907-789-8450
dick@AlaskaWanted.com
http://www.ALaskaWanted.com
Wants stereoviews of Alaska and Klondike; especially by Muybridge, Maynard, Brodeck, Haynes, etc.; also photographer L. Hensel views of PA (especially Pike County, PA) and NY.

STERLING SILVER FLATWARE

(see FLATWARE)

STEVENGRAPHS

Appraisers

James S. Harriss
James S. Harris Antiques & Appraisals
P.O. Box 672
Richmond, KY 40475
ph: 859-623-9100
jimant@ipro.net
Specializes in the appraisal of coin and English hallmarked silver, American art pottery, stevengraphs, and English watercolors.

Clubs/Associations

Wayne R. Adams, Pres.
Stevengraph Collectors' Association
Newsletter: SCA Newsletter
29 War Bonnet Rd.
RFD #1, Box 29
Canaan, NH 03741
ph: 603-523-4276
fax: 603-523-4888
stevengraphs@yahoo.com
Approx. 140 members worldwide; focuses on the various jacquard woven silk works (Stevengraphs) by Thomas Stevens of Coventry, England but also has articles about other weavers.

Collectors

Frank J. Buono
P.O. Box 1535
Binghamton, NY 13902-1535
ph: 607-724-4444 or 800-527-8893
fax: 607-723-1656
fbuono@stny.rr.com
http://www.fjbstamps.com
Wants to buy Stevengraphs woven silk pictures and postcards.

Susan & Neil Laye
Sintra, 2 Hayloft Court
Limestone Hills, DE 19808
ph: 302-234-1660
smdkaye@aol.com

Dr. Mark Cottrill
Good Old Days, The
The Moat House
Lymm Hall
Lymm, Cheshire WA13 0AJ U.K.
ph: 01925-754097
mark.cottrill@which.net
Specializes in Stevengraphs, silk woven bookmarks and postcards; send for sales lists.

Dealers

Wayne R. Adams
American Decorative Arts/Crows Run
Gallery
29 War Bonnet Rd.
RFD #1, Box 29
Canaan, NH 03741-9746
ph: 603-523-4276
fax: 603-523-4888
stevengraphs@yahoo.com
Buys and sells individual and complete collections of stevengraphs; looking for good quality; a complete service to dealers and collectors.

Malcolm J. Roebuck
P.O. Box 11377
Chicago, IL 60611
ph: 312-467-1400
fax: 312-467-1900
info@stevengraphs.com
http://www.stevengraphs.com
Wants to buy Stevengraphs; one item or entire collections.

Edith & Jerry Horowitz
Pearl Antiques, Ltd., The
1551 Larimer St., #802
Denver, CO 80202
ph: 303-893-9778
fax: 303-893-9779
sjerryh@aol.com
http://www.pearlantiques.com
Specializes in Victorian and Georgian period jewelry, Stevensgraphs, inkwells, watch keeps and English brass; in business for over 30 years.

Internet Resources

Malcolm J. Roebuck
Stevengraphs Bookmarks & Postcards,
Etc.
P.O. Box 11377
Chicago, IL 60611
ph: 312-467-1400
fax: 312-467-1900
info@stevengraphs.com
http://www.stevengraphs.com
A Web site for Stevengraph collectors: Stevengraph dating, history, factory; also other silks.

Peter Daws
Victorian Silk
U.K.
peter@victoriansilk.com
http://www.victoriansilk.com
Web site with definitive lists and catalogs of Stevengraph silks portraits, silk pictures, silk bookmarks, and silk postcards.

Museums/Libraries

Herbert Art Gallery & Museum
U.K.
ph: 01203 832433
fax: 01203 832410
coventry.museums@dial.pipex.com
http://www.coventry.org/
coventrymuseums
*Has the largest collection of
Stevengraphs in public hands; also
has a very large silk ribbon collection.*

STICK PINS

(see CLOTHING & ACCESSORIES,
Vintage; CUFF LINKS; GEMS &
JEWELRY, Stick Pins)

STILL PHOTOGRAPHS

(see MOVIE MEMORABILIA;
PHOTOGRAPHS, Celebrity)

STOCK TICKERS

(see also TELEGRAPH ITEMS)

Collectors

Frank Guarino
P.O. Box 89
De Bary, FL 32713
ph: 407-668-5973

Jack Arnold
P.O. Box 2541
Reno, NV 89505-2541
ph: 775-786-0369 or 775-747-0311
fax: 775-787-8931
*Wants Wall St. stock tickers (Western
Union); also parts, stands, history,
and repair books.*

Dealers

Carl Ratner
94 Mechanic St.
Reinholds, PA 17569-9701
ph: 717-484-1021
artdeco@epix.net
*Buy, collects, sell, trade antique stock
tickers; interested in all types of
machines, parts and accessories, but
especially seeking Edison and Western
Union tickers with glass domes.*

Randy Donley
Donley's Wild West Town & Museum
8512 S. Union Rd.
Union, IL 60180-9661
ph: 815-923-9000
fax: 815-923-2253
mdonley@dls.net
http://www.wildwesttown.com
*Wants pre-1940 stock ticker tape
machines made by Edison or Brunnell.*

STOCKS & BONDS

(see also BANKING; CIVIL WAR
ARTIFACTS, Confederate Bonds;
COINS & CURRENCY, Paper
Money; PAPER COLLECTIBLES;
SCRIP; STOCK TICKERS)

Auction Services

R.M. Smythe & Company
26 Broadway, Ste. 271
New York, NY 10004-1701
ph: 212-943-1880 or 800-622-1880
fax: 212-908-4670
info@smytheonline.com
http://www.smytheonline.com
*Conducts auctions of Colonial
currency, Confederate currency,
federal essay notes, proof vignettes,
fractional and obsolete currency,
stocks, bonds, coins and autographs.*

Pierre Bonneau, CEO
Stock Search International, Inc.
4761 W. Waterbuck Dr.
Tucson, AZ 85742
ph: 800-537-4523 or 520-579-5635
fax: 520-579-5639
ssi@stocksearchintl.com
http://www.stocksearchintl.com
*Bi-annual Mail Bid auctions (Spring
and Fall) with fully-illustrated and
documented catalogs featuring more
than 600 collectible stocks and bonds
divided into ten categories:
Signatures, Finance, Food &
Beverage, Mining, Oil, Railroad, etc.*

Clubs/Associations

Richard Gregg
International Bond & Share Society
Magazine: Scripophily
15 Dyatt Place
Hackensack, NJ 07601-6004
ph: 201-489-2440
fax: 201-592-0282
president@scripophily.org
http://www.scripophily.org
*Focus is to provide information to
members through publications and
meetings, so as to encourage all
aspects of scripophily - the collection
and study of historic old stocks, bonds
and shares, antique financial
ephemera and autographs.*

George Teas, Ex. Dir.
Washington Historical Autograph &
    Certificate Organization (WHACO)
Newsletter: WHACO! News
P.O. Box 2428
Springfield, VA 22152-2428
ph: 703-866-0175
fax: 703-866-0175
gteas@earthlink.net
http://www.whaco.com
*Formed to bring collectors together to
promote the hobby of antique stock
and bond certificates and historical
autographs; database of prices,
featured articles, listings of dealers.*

Pierre Bonneau, Founder/Editor
Old Certificates Collector's Club
Newsletter: OCCC Newsletter
4761 W. Waterbuck Dr.
Tucson, AZ 85742
ph: 800-537-4523 or 520-579-5635
fax: 520-579-5639
ssi@stocksearchintl.com
http://www.stocksearchintl.com
Founded in 1994, this club offers a

*quarterly newsletter filled with
Scripophily news, trivia, tips,
biographies and auction reviews; also
exclusive right to consign material to
Mail Bid auctions of Stock Search
International.*

Collectors

Richard Urmston
Centennial Documents
P.O. Box 5262
Clinton, NJ 08809-0262
ph: 908-730-6009
fax: 908-730-9566
centdocs@postoffice.ptd.net
*Wants stocks & bonds; send
photocopy of items for sale; issues
periodic catalog of items for sale.*

Frederick Lingenfelser
814 Byram St.
Reading, PA 19606-1446
lingy@afo.net
*Grandson of an engraver, wants to
buy anything related to Western,
Republic, or Security bank note
companies: books, advertising,
histories, photographs, stock
certificates, etc.; will also share
information.*

Bob Schell
6804 Jeremiah Ct.
Fairfax, VA 22039
*Wants obsolete and antique stocks and
bonds, especially those with attractive
artwork; also wants fancy old bill
heads, invoices and stationary.*

Dealers

Paul Longo
Paul Longo Americana
P.O. Box 5510
Gloucester, MA 01930-0007
ph: 978-525-2290
*Wants pre-1910 stocks and bonds; any
amount.*

George H. LaBarre
George H. LaBarre Galleries, Inc.
P.O. Box 746
Hollis, NH 03049
ph: 800-717-9529 or 603-882-2411
fax: 603-882-4979
collect@glabarre.com
http://www.glabarre.com
*Specializes in collectible stocks and
bonds, autographs, paper money; also
deals with other areas of Americana;
retail and wholesale to other dealers
including large marketing companies;
inventory includes over 5.7 million
pieces in stock.*

Scott J. Winslow
Scott J. Winslow Associates, Inc.
P.O. Box 10240
Nashua, NH 03110-0240
ph: 603-641-8292 or 800-225-6233
fax: 603-641-5583
scott@scottwinslow.com
http://www.scottwinslow.com
*Buys and sells stocks certificates,
bonds and historical autographs; also
conducts mail bid auctions of same.*

Robert F. Kluge
American Vignettes
P.O. Box 155
Roselle Park, NJ 07204-0155
ph: 908-241-4209
*Specializes in buying and selling
stocks and bonds (scripophily);
established in 1980.*

R.M. Smythe & Company
26 Broadway, Ste. 271
New York, NY 10004-1701
ph: 212-943-1880 or 800-622-1880
fax: 212-908-4670
info@smytheonline.com
http://www.smytheonline.com
*Buys and sells and auctions
autographs, coins, paper money,
stocks, bonds, and related collectibles.*

D & D Scripophily International, Ltd.
P.O. Box 580063
Flushing, NY 11358
ph: 718-358-3447 or 800-941-0098
fax: 718-358-2849
*Wants holed, cancelled, obsolete stock
certificates.*

Frank Hammelbacher
Norrico Inc.
P.O. Box 660077
Flushing, NY 11366-0077
ph: 718-380-4009
fax: 718-380-9793
morrico@nyc.rr.com
http://www.morrico.com
*Buys, sells, collects in ephemera of all
kinds, especially old stocks and bonds
and Wild West posters.*

Frost & Robinson Collectables
P.O. Box 814
Richboro, PA 18954
ph: 215-377-6820
fax: 215-357-4847
fandr@voicenet.com
*Dealers in fine antique securities since
1980; specializing in old stocks,
bonds, and lottery tickets: specializing
in petroleum and mining companies;
also automobile, turnpikes, aviation,
railroads, banking.*

Bruce F. Heiner
P.O. Box 421
Hunt Valley, MD 21030
ph: 410-584-7090
fax: 420-771-1615
*Buys and sells antique share and bond
investments, stock certificates and
bonds: autos, airplanes, breweries,
buses, banks, canals, casinos,
computers, guns, hotels, insurance,
mining, movies, railroads, ships,
sports, theatre, etc.*

Jerry Neuman
P.O. Box 33
Ellicott City, MD 21041
ph: 410-465-6667
fax: 410-203-9033
loot@erols.com

Bob Kerstein
Scripophily.com
260 W. Broad St.
Falls Church, VA 22046
ph: 703-787-3552 or 888-STOCKS6
fax: 703-995-4422
information@scripophily.com
http://www.scripophily.com
A leading dealer in old stock and bond certificates.

Eric Drum
Collectible Stocks & Bonds
P.O. Box 559
Sandston, VA 23150
ph: 804-364-5076
fax: 804-364-5079
eric@oldstocks.com
http://www.oldstocks.com
Collector, dealer buys and sells old stock certificates; one of the leaders in the hobby of scripophily, collecting stock and bonds; Web site has online resource and catalog of offerings.

Hannelore Garrison
Antique Stocks & Bonds
P.O. Box 3632
Williamsburg, VA 23187-3632
ph: 800-451-4504 or 757-220-3838
fax: 757-220-4862
igarrison@antiquesecurities.com
http://www.antiquesecurities.com
Hannelore is a contributing author of "Insider's Guide to Antique Securities."

Barry Smith
Barry A. Smith, Inc.
P.O. Box 38306
Greensboro, NC 27438-8306
ph: 336-294-3262
fax: 336-299-3182
bsmith1707@aol.com
Buys and sells stock certificates: railroad, sports, oil, financial, mining, etc.

David M. Beach
Paper Americana
P.O. Box 471356
Lake Monroe, FL 32747
ph: 407-688-7403
fax: 407-688-7495
dbeach@cigarboxlabels.com
http://www.cigarboxlabels.com
Buys and sells antique US stocks and bonds; wants to buy stocks, letters, contracts, other documents signed by Jay Gould, James Fisk, Jr., Comm. Vanderbilt, Daniel Drew, Jay Cooke, Cyrus Field, Hetty Green and other Robber Barons.

Warren Anderson
America West Archives
P.O. Box 100
Cedar City, UT 84721-0100
ph: 435-586-9497 or 435-586-7323
awa@netutah.com
http://www.americawestarchives.com
Buys and sells issued American stocks & bonds 1840-1930; especially mining, energy, transportation; offers

mail order catalog; author of "Owning Western History."

Pierre Bonneau, CEO
Stock Search International, Inc.
4761 W. Waterbuck Dr.
Tucson, AZ 85742
ph: 800-537-4523 or 520-579-5635
fax: 520-579-5639
ssi@stocksearchintl.com
http://www.stocksearchintl.com
Deals essentially in stock and bond certificates issued between the American War of Independence and the latest tech boom; Collectors' Club, wish list and bi-annual mail bid auction catalogs also available.

Collectors Gallery, Inc.
2533 N. Cason St., Ste. 3531
Carson City, NV 89706
ph: 775-841-2735
admin@cgi-stocks.com
http://www.cgi-stocks.com
Has an inventory of over 60,000 antique stock and bonds from around the world.

Georgia Fox
Foxes' Den Antiques
P.O. Box 846
Sutter Creek, CA 95685-0846
ph: 209-267-0774
Wants old stocks & bonds, especially relating to gold mining in California or Nevada.

Tom Sluszkiewicz
ATS Numismatics
P.O. Box 54521
Burnaby, British Columbia V5E 4J6
Canada
ats@atsnotes.com
http://www.atsnotes.com
Buys and sells numismatic world banknotes, local and private paper money, collectibles bonds and stock certificates.

Experts

Pierre Bonneau, CEO
Stock Search International, Inc.
4761 W. Waterbuck Dr.
Tucson, AZ 85742
ph: 800-537-4523 or 520-579-5635
fax: 520-579-5639
ssi@stocksearchintl.com
http://www.stocksearchintl.com
A recognized authority in the field of financial investigation; a regular guest on national programs produced by CNN, CNBC and Bloomberg Financial; tracks down delisted securities to reactivate old investments; also appraises old stocks.

Ken Prag
Ken Prag Paper Americana
P.O. Box 14817
San Francisco, CA 94114-0817
ph: 415-586-9386
kprag@planeteria.net
Eager to buy old stocks and bonds, quality picture postcards, western

stereoviews, old timetables and brochures, etc.

Misc. Services

R.M. Smythe & Company
26 Broadway, Ste. 271
New York, NY 10004-1701
ph: 212-943-1880 or 800-622-1880
fax: 212-908-4670
info@smytheonline.com
http://www.smytheonline.com
A leading stock and bond research firm; will help to determine the value of old stocks and bonds and how to redeem them.

Stock Certificate Research Service
P.O. Box 490703
Atlanta, GA 30349
ph: 404-308-0096
stocks_researched@hotmail.com
http://www.welcome.to/stockresearch
Has been providing stock research service for over 10 years.

Cheryl Anderson
OldStockResearch.com
P.O. Box 100
Cedar City, UT 84721
ph: 435-586-9497
cheryl@oldstockresearch.com
http://www.oldstockresearch.com
Stock and bond certificate research service; tracing and researching old obsolete and obscure uncanceled stock certificates to determine if the companies are still in business and what the current value of the certificates might be.

Warren Anderson
America West Archives
P.O. Box 100
Cedar City, UT 84721-0100
ph: 435-586-9497 or 435-586-7323
awa@netutah.com
http://www.americawestarchives.com
A professional stock tracer who researches stock certificates and bonds to determine whether they have value on the current stock market or to a collector of worthless securities; author of "Owning Western History."

Pierre Bonneau, CEO
Stock Search International, Inc.
4761 W. Waterbuck Dr.
Tucson, AZ 85742
ph: 800-537-4523 or 520-579-5635
fax: 520-579-5639
ssi@stocksearchintl.com
http://www.stocksearchintl.com
Helping investors establish the value of old stocks & bonds for more than 30 years; has helped clients recover close to 6 million dollars from delisted securities they thought were worthless; free appraisals of stocks that cannot be sold.

Periodicals

Stacie Berger
Krause Publications
Newspaper: Bank Note Reporter
700 E. State St.
Iola, WI 54990-0001
ph: 715-445-2214
fax: 715-445-4087
stacie.berger@fwpubs.com
http://www.krause.com
Monthly news source and marketplace for collectors of US and world paper money, notes, checks and related fiscal paper.

Financial History

Museums/Libraries

Kristin Aguilera, Comm. Dir.
Museum of American Financial History, The
Magazine: Financial History
28 Broadway
New York, NY 10004
ph: 212-908-4519
fax: 212-908-4601
kaguilera@financialhistory.org
http://www.financialhistory.org
Dedicated to the development of the US capital markets and the people who made them famous; mission is to collect/preserve/display historical financial artifacts and to use them as an educational resource for schools & the public.

Mining Related

Dealers

Jeff J. Daly
Daly's Mining Shop
jdphoto33@aol.com
http://www.geocities.com/jdphoto33
Specializes in old mining company stock certificates.

Douglas McDonald
Gypsyfoot Enterprises, Inc.
P.O. Box 5833
Helena, MT 59604
ph: 406-449-8076
gypsyfoot@aol.com
Buying all pre-1933 mining stocks; please send photocopies for offer.

Experts

Chuck Voelker
844 Fairground St.
Plymouth, MI 48170
ph: 734-451-5911
Collector and researcher of 19th and early 20th century mining stock certificates, especially Michigan related.

STONE

(see MARBLE & STONE)

STONE CARVINGS

(see SCULPTURES)

STOVES

(see also CAST IRON ITEMS; KITCHEN COLLECTIBLES; RANGES)

Clubs/Associations

Antique Stove Association
Newsletter: Stove Parts Needed
 Newsletter
2617 Riverside
Houston, TX 77004-7610
ph: 713-528-2990
sales@antiquestoves.com
http://www.antiquestoves.com
 For those interested in antique stoves and related items; you must join to receive the benefits which are for members only.

Collectors

N.W. Neill, Jr.
Glascock Stove Co.
P.O. Box 38
Ennice, NC 28623-0038
fax: 336-657-8084
saddlemtn@skybest.com
 Historian wants cook stoves, heaters, etc. (complete or parts) made by the Glascock Stove Co. of Greensboro, NC; models include Carolina Beauty, Victor, Charter, Giant, Carolina Hot Blast, Blue Ridge, Plymouth, etc.

Dealers

Buck's Stove Palace
ph: 503-771-3374 or 888-237-8633
fax: 503-771-2311
sales@stoves.com
http://www.stoves.com
 Sells and restores vintage heaters and cook stoves; has a collection of over 400 including Heartland, Cawley/ LeMay, Monarch, Bridge Beach, Round Oak.

Richard Richardson
Good Time Stove Co.
P.O. Box 306
Goshen, MA 01032-0306
ph: 888-282-7506 or 413-268-3677
fax: 413-268-9284
rich@goodtimestove.com
http://www.antiquestoves.net
 Buys, sells and restores antique stoves and kitchen ranges.

Bob Brunelle
Brunelle Ent. Inc.
203 Union Rd.
Wales, MA 01081
ph: 413-245-7396
Bob@oldstoves.com
http://www.oldstoves.com
 Collector and dealer wants to buy pre-1920 fancy antique stoves with tiles or mica windows, or ornate castings.

Erickson's Antique Stoves, Inc.
P.O. Box 2275
At the Depot
Littleton, MA 01460
ph: 978-486-3589
fax: 978-486-3695
 Antique gas coal and wood stoves and ranges; bought, sold, restored.

Mike Trainor
Mike's Stove Works
98 Webster St.
Haverhill, MA 01830-4123
ph: 978-373-0767
 Buys, collects, sells and restores all types of coal, gas and wood stoves; old or new.

Barnstable Stove Shop
P.O. Box 472
West Barnstable, MA 02668
ph: 508-362-9913
 Buys, sells and restores antique wood, coal and gas stoves; large parts inventory; 20 years in business; expert restoration work.

Edward Semmelroth
Antique Stoves
415 Fleming Rd.
Tekonsha, MI 49092
ph: 517-278-2214
sales@antiquestoves.com
http://www.antiquestoves.com
 Appraises, buys, sells, restores antique stoves and ranges, 1700s to 1950; museum quality restorations; over 200 in stock; wood, coal, gas; also cookware, mica isinglass for sale.

Keokuk Stove Works
906 E. Co. Rd. 1120
Hamilton, IL 62341
ph: 212-847-2107
sales@keokukstoveworks.com
http://www.keokukstoveworks.com
 Buys and sells antique stoves and ranges.

Macy's Classic Stove Works
5515 Almeda Rd.
Houston, TX 77004-7443
ph: 713-521-0934 or 713-528-1297
fax: 713-521-0889
http://www.MacysClassicStoveWorks.com
 Buys, sells, brokers, repairs, and restores old ranges; also sells parts and publishes "Classic Ranges" newspaper.

Ron Schaffer
Classic Stoves Emporium
480 San Juan St.
P.O. Box 153
Pagosa Springs, CO 81147
ph: 970-264-2710
 Buys, sells and restores antique stoves; fabricates replacement parts as needed.

Experts

Clifford Boram
Antique Stove Information Clearinghouse
421 N. Main St.
Monticello, IN 47960-1932
ph: 574-583-6465
 Author of "How to Get Parts Cast for Your Antique Stove;" free consultation by phone; let phone ring 10 times; no mail inquiries, please; photocopies from 2,000-volume archive of stove manufacturers' literature 1860-1935.

Museums/Libraries

Beatrice & Joe Bryant
Bryant's Museum of Antique
 Woodburning Stoves
RR 2 Rich Rd.
P.O. Box 2048
Thorndike, ME 04986
ph: 207-568-3665
fax: 207-568-3666
 Hundreds of meticulously restored antique wood burning stoves from 1750s to 1850s.

Periodicals

Newsletter: Antique Stove Exchange,
 The
P.O. Box 2101
Waukesha, WI 53187
ph: 262-542-9190
fax: 262-542-9190
mail@theantiquestovexchng.com
http://www.theantiquestovexchng.com
 Since 1992, America's antique stove publication: source for those using, collecting, repairing and restoring antique stoves; informative articles, ads, locate a stove dealer, buy/sell/ trade cookstoves, heating stoves, parts.

Repair Services

Richard Richardson
Good Time Stove Co.
P.O. Box 306
Goshen, MA 01032-0306
ph: 888-282-7506 or 413-268-3677
fax: 413-268-9284
rich@goodtimestove.com
http://www.antiquestoves.net
 Buys, sells and restores antique stoves and kitchen ranges.

Beatrice & Joe Bryant
Bryant Stove Works & Music Inc.
RR 2 Rich Rd.
P.O. Box 2048
Thorndike, ME 04986
ph: 207-568-3665
fax: 207-568-3666
 Large collection on display; also sells parts and restores antique (1780s-1940s) cook stoves, parlor stoves, and gas stoves. In addition, restores player pianos.

Edward Semmelroth
Antique Stoves
415 Fleming Rd.
Tekonsha, MI 49092
ph: 517-278-2214
sales@antiquestoves.com
http://www.antiquestoves.com
 Appraises, buys, sells, restores antique stoves and ranges, 1700s to 1950; museum quality restorations; over 200 in stock; wood, coal, gas; also cookware, mica isinglass for sale.

Tomahawk Foundry, Inc.
2337 29th St.
Rice Lake, WI 54868
ph: 715-234-4498
ddirkes@tomahawkfoundry.com
http://www.tomahawkfoundry.com
 Makes replacement parts for cast iron stoves.

Antique Gas Stoves
P.O. Box 3175
Montclair, CA 91763
ph: 909-445-0300
cookin@antiquegasstoves.com
http://www.antiquegasstoves.com
 Sales, parts, repair and restoration of antique gas stoves, specializing in 1940s and 1950 O'Keefe & Merritt, Wedgewood, Roper and Western Holly; fully restored stoves are available.

Tom Lawson
Buckeye Appliance & Antiques
714 W. Fremont
Stockton, CA 95203-2702
ph: 209-464-9643
calbuck@aol.com
http://www.BuckeyeAppliance.com
 Specializes in the sales, parts and restoration of antique gas stoves; also sells kitchen collectibles, Hoosiers, 1950s chrome dinettes, and porcelain-top tables, architectural, garden.

Majolica

Experts

Laura Sussi
37 via Garzarolli
Gorizia, 34170 Italy
ph: +39-0481-531343
fax: +39-0481-531343
webmaster@stufantica.cjb.net
http://www.stufantica.com
 Skilled in majolica stoves (1750 to 1920) made during the former Austro-Hapsburg Empire; expert and collector wants to trade stoves and swap experiences in restoring.

Salesman Samples & Toys

Collectors

Andrew B. Golbert
RR 1 Box 1820
North Ferrisburg, VT 05473
ph: 802-453-2525
 Wants to buy children's cast iron toy stoves and salesmen's sample stoves and furnaces.

Sally Swanson
562 Shady Brook Circle W.
Girard, PA 16417
ph: 814-774-2166
Wants information on all cast iron toy stoves and salesman samples.

Judy Owen, ISA
Antique Appraisers - Grand Traverse
10332 Stoneybeach Pointe
Traverse City, MI 49686-8584
ph: 231-946-2534
fax: 231-946-2573
judy@antiqueappraisers.com
http://www.antiqueappraisers.com
Wants to buy miniature stoves.

Ralph C. Hylton
245 Hughes Ford Rd.
Sullivan, MO 63080-1924
ph: 573-468-8418
Wants to buy salesman samples and toy stoves; complete or in parts; also wants small cookware.

Dealers

Pamela Fullerton
Seven Sisters Antiques
14052 Lincoln Dr.
Athens, WI 54411
ph: 715-675-4115 or 715-675-3095
Buys and sells all kinds of salesman samples from architectural through stoves to machines and windmills.

Experts

Ed Hullet
5200 N. Lorraine
Hutchinson, KS 67502-2727
ph: 316-662-9381
Buys, sells, restores, and appraises exclusively salesmen's sample stoves.

STREETCAR LINE COLLECTIBLES

(see also RAILROAD
COLLECTIBLES)

Collectors

Seth Bramson
330 N.E. 96th St.
Miami, FL 33138-2718
ph: 305-757-1016
fax: 305-895-8178
sbramson@bellsouth.net
Buys railroad and trolleyana; postage paid on approvals.

Museums/Libraries

Seashore Trolley Museum
P.O. Box A
Kennebunkport, ME 04046-1690
ph: 207-967-2800
fax: 207-967-0867
carshop@gwi.net
http://www.trolleymuseum.org

Baltimore St.car Museum
1905 Falls Rd.
P.O. Box 4881
Baltimore, MD 21211
ph: 410-547-0264
samsmeatm@aol.com
http://baltimoremd.com/streetcar

STRING HOLDERS

Collectors

Bobbie & Alan Bryson
1 St. Eleanoras Ln.
Tuckahoe, NY 10707-1307
ph: 914-779-1405
napkindoll@aol.com
Wants string holders; Bobbie is co-author of the pictorial reference guide "Collectibles For The Kitchen, Bath & Beyond" (Krause Publications) which has an entire chapter on string holders with over 400 photos and vintage ads.

Emma Kretchek
5726 Terrace Park Dr.
Dayton, OH 45429-6048
ph: 937-434-9126

Al Little
151 Highway 173
Antioch, IL 60002
ph: 847-395-7752
fax: 847-395-7703
Buy, sells and trades string holders; single pieces or entire collections.

Dealers

John & Nancy Smith
American Sampler
P.O. Box 371
Barnesville, MD 20838-0371
ph: 301-972-6250
Wants ceramic, chalk, cast iron string holders.

Experts

Charles Reynolds
Reynolds Toys
2836 Monroe St.
Falls Church, VA 22042-2007
ph: 703-533-1322
reynoldstoys@erols.com
http://www.reynoldstoys.com
Wants string holders made of metal, glass or wood; not interested in chalk or china types.

STRIPTEASE

Collectors

Charles McCaghy
221 Williams St.
Bowling Green, OH 43402
ph: 419-352-7211
cmccagh@bgnet.bgsu.edu
Purchases paper items related to stripping in US and Canada: burlesque theaters, carnivals, clubs; belly dancing, carnival girl shows, shake dancing, striptease, table
dancing; photos, publications, postcards, programs.

Museums/Libraries

Exotic World Burlesque Hall of Fame Museum
29053 Wild Rd.
Helendale, CA 92342
ph: 760-243-5261
http://www.exoticworldusa.org

STUFFED TOYS

(see STEIFF; TEDDY BEARS; TOYS, Plush)

SUBWAY ITEMS

Museums/Libraries

New York Transit Museum
130 Livingston St., 9th Floor, Box E
Brooklyn, NY 11201
ph: 718-694-1068 or 718-243-8601
fax: 718-722-4316
orderhelp@imageexchange.com
http://www.mta.nyc.ny.us/museum
Features displays, exhibits, archive information regarding the New York Subway System.

SUGAR PACKETS

Clubs/Associations

Pam Miller, Mem. Sec.
UK Sucrologitsts Club
14 Marisfield Place
Selsey
West Sussex, PO20 0PD U.K.
info@uksucrologistclub.org.uk
http://www.uksucrologistclub.org.uk
Collectors of the little packets of sugar you get when you order tea or coffee in a cafe or restaurant.

Collectors

Phillip Miller
Sugar Packet Collector's Page, The
phillip@iquest.net
http://www.the.millerfamily.name/sugar
Collecting sugar packets since 1978.

SUGAR SHAKERS

Dealers

Glenda Ridgway
P.O. Box 231
Anna, IL 62906
ph: 618-833-7971

SUPER BOWL RINGS

(see SPORTS COLLECTIBLES, Jewelry)

SUPER HEROES

(see also COMIC BOOKS; POPULAR CULTURE; PREMIUMS; SCIENCE FICTION; TOYS, Super Hero)

Batman

Clubs/Associations

Fred Carini
Captain Action Society of Pittsburgh
Newsletter: Capt. Action News
516 Cubbage St.
Carnegie, PA 15106
ph: 412-276-6084
All Capt. Action club! Trading, buying, selling all Capt. Action items.

Collectors

David J. Anderson
5192 Dawes Ave.
Alexandria, VA 22311-1402
ph: 703-671-7422
fax: 703-578-1222
dja@erols.com
Aggressively seeks Batman and Superman items.

Dealers

Gotham Toys
P.O. Box 10098
Manassas, VA 20108
ph: 703-257-1220
fax: 323-417-4937
batmantoys@comcast.net
http://www.gothamtoys.com
Buys and sells Batman collectibles: action figures, toys and premiums, playsets, diecast, books and postgers, older toys, accessories and clothing, etc.

Captain Midnight

Clubs/Associations

John Samorajczyk
Air Heroes Fan Club
19205 Seneca Ridge Court
Gaithersburg, MD 20879-3135
ph: 301-869-1755
rasamora@aol.com
This club honors Captain Midnight.

Phantom

Collectors

Robert J. Griffin
P.O. Box 76
Mattawan, MI 49071
ph: 616-387-3024
griffinr@wmich.edu
Wants to buy memorabilia relating to The Phantom.

Superman

Collectors

David J. Anderson
5192 Dawes Ave.
Alexandria, VA 22311-1402
ph: 703-671-7422
fax: 703-578-1222
dja@erols.com
Aggressively seeks Batman and Superman items.

SWORDS

Dealers

Danny Fuchs
209-80 18th Ave., #4K
Bayside, NY 11360-1424
ph: 718-225-9030
fax: 718-225-3688
superdf62@aol.com
*Buys and sells all types of pre-1960
Superman collectibles: toys, games,
figurines, puzzles, novelties,
premiums, etc. rare or unusual; also
buying unusual/interesting collectibles
from other comic book characters.*

Experts

Danny Fuchs
209-80 18th Ave., #4K
Bayside, NY 11360-1424
ph: 718-225-9030
fax: 718-225-3688
superdf62@aol.com
*"America's foremost Superman
Collector;" co-author of "The
Adventures of Superman Collecting."*

Periodicals

Jim Nolt
Newsletter: Adventures Continue, The
220 N. Walnut St., #7
Lititz, PA 17543
ph: 717-625-4458
jimnolt@ptd.net
http://www.jimnolt.com
*Maintains a George Reeves (Super-
man) homepage on the World Wide
Web.*

SUPPLIERS

(see ANTIQUES DEALERS &
COLLECTORS; CLOCKS;
FIREARMS; KNIVES; MODELS;
REPAIR/RESTORATION/
CONSERVATION; STAMP
COLLECTING; TELEPHONES and
other individual categories)

SURVEYING INSTRUMENTS

(see also INSTRUMENTS &
DEVICES, Scientific)

Collectors

Stephen Buczko
27 Surrey Rd.
Salem, MA 01970-4362
ph: 978-744-4683
nsbuczko@aol.com
*Wants to buy surveying instruments
including compasses, solar instruments, mining instruments, early
transits, surveyors chains, early trade
catalogs related to surveying;
especially interested in early American
instruments.*

Ron Kiser
P.O. Box 621
Mars Hill, NC 28754
ph: 828-258-1380
fax: 828-689-4845
*Wants to buy antique brass surveying
instruments: transits, levels, alidades,*

plane tables, tripods, rods, chains,
surveyor's compasses, pocket
compasses, etc.

Michael S. Manier
100 E. Walnut
P.O. Box 110
Houston, MO 65483-0110
ph: 417-967-2777 or 417-962-5221
fax: 417-967-3026
msmanier@train.missouri.org
*Wants to buy compasses (both brass
and wooden), wire-link measuring
chains, theodolites, transits, levels,
octants, sextants, quadrants, solar
devices, calculating devices, and
drawing instruments.*

Paul H. Hayashi, PE
18 Tarabrook Dr.
Orinda, CA 94563-3121
ph: 925-254-5074 or 925-253-1038
fax: 925-253-0592
*Buys high precision theodolites, levels,
solar compasses, mining surveying
instruments, solar transits, US Coast
& Geodetic instruments.*

Donald Sanders
P.O. Box 1980
Granite Falls, WA 98252
ph: 360-691-5063
ddsanders@webtv.net
*Wants old surveying instruments:
transits, compasses, unusual plumb
bobs.*

Dealers

Al & Bobbie Roberts
Rational Past, The
221 Oceano Dr.
Los Angeles, CA 90049-4123
ph: 310-476-6277
fax: 310-476-6278
malinfo@therationalpast.com
http://www.therationalpast.com
*Organizer of West Coast Scientific &
Technical Antique and Collectible
Shows (Los Angeles and San
Francisco.)*

Experts

Dale R. Beeks
Perceptions Scientifica
P.O. Box 117
Mount Vernon, IA 52314-0117
ph: 800-880-5178 or 319-895-0506
dbeeksci@aol.com
*Expert, appraiser, wants pre-1900
compasses, transits, unusual
instruments, surveying ephemera;
offers museum services.*

SWANKYSWIGS

(see also GLASSES, Drinking)

Clubs/Associations

Martin Fountain
Swankyswigs Unlimited
201 Alvena St.
Wichita, KS 67203
ph: 316-943-1925

Collectors

Melvin Fountain
201 Alvena St.
Wichita, KS 67203
ph: 316-943-1925
*Avid collector with over 1,500;
Swankyswigs were decorated glasses
originally filled with Kraft Cheese
Spreads.*

Gary Kane
15006 Brookpoint
Houston, TX 77062
ph: 281-488-1537
gkane12345@prodigy.net
*Wants to buy or trade swankyswigs
with lids or labels, special issues,
with advertisements.*

Experts

Ian Warner
Mianco Partners
499 Main St. South
P.O. Box 93022
Brampton, Ontario L6Y 4V8 Canada
ph: 905-453-9074
*Specializing in Wade porcelain and
swankyswigs.*

SWAROVSKI

(see COLLECTIBLES [MODERN],
Crystal [Swarovski])

SWORDS

(see also ARMS & ARMOR; ARMS &
ARMOR, Japanese [Swords];
BAYONETS; CIVIL WAR
ARTIFACTS; EDGED WEAPONS;
MILITARIA)

Appraisers

Thomas Winter
817 N. Patton Ave.
Springfield, IL 62702-2430
ph: 217-523-8729
fax: 217-523-8729
tdw@warpnet.net
*Collector/appraiser of swords; wants
to buy quality Japanese swords &
high quality or rare German and US
swords, daggers, fighting knives &
any Samurai related items such as
armor, matchlocks, etc.; send SASE
for free evaluation.*

Clubs/Associations

Leonard J. Garigliano
Association of American Sword
Collectors, The
P.O. Box 288
Parsonsburg, MD 21849-0288
lgarswds@shore.intercom.net

Collectors

K. Wiley
719 Baldwin SE
Grand Rapids, MI 49503-4470
ph: 616-451-8410
*Wants Japanese swords, daggers,
sword parts; also German 3rd Reich*

daggers, swords, bayonets; references
available.

Thomas Winter
817 N. Patton Ave.
Springfield, IL 62702-2430
ph: 217-523-8729
fax: 217-523-8729
tdw@warpnet.net
*Collector/appraiser of swords; wants
to buy quality Japanese swords &
high quality or rare German and US
swords, daggers, fighting knives &
any Samurai related items such as
armor, matchlocks, etc.; send SASE
for free evaluation.*

Dealers

Fred Coluzzi
Frederick's Swords
6919 Westview Dr.
Oak Forest, IL 60452-1566
ph: 708-687-3647
fax: 708-687-3695
coluzzi113@aol.com
http://www.frederickantiqueswords.com
*Buys and sells antique swords and
daggers from all countries and all
periods; issues 2 to 3 major catalogs
per year: Japanese, US, German,
Turkish, Moro, Indonesian,
Philippine, Chinese.*

Robert B. Miller
LionGate Arms & Armour, Inc.
P.O. Box 14952
Scottsdale, AZ 85267
ph: 480-948-6348
hussar@antiqueswords.com
http://www.antiqueswords.com
*Buys and sells fine antique edged
weapons and armour; specializes in
European swords.*

Museums/Libraries

Fort Ticonderoga Museum
Newsletter: Bulletin of the Fort
Ticonderoga Museum
P.O. Box 390
Ticonderoga, NY 12883
ph: 518-585-2821
fax: 518-585-2210
fort@fort-ticonderoga.org
http://www.fort-ticonderoga.org
*10,000 volume research library
specializing in 18th century military
history and the history of the
Champlain Valley; museum depicts
history of the area and the campaigns
during the 7 Year War and the
Revolutionary War.*

Repair Services

Tom Nardi
Civil War Sword Rewrapping
711 Natalie Dr.
Windsor, CA 95492
ph: 707-838-1820
t.nardi@comcast.net
http://www.cds1.net/~nardi/swords
*Rewraps any Civil War of later sword
just like the originals; work in most
cases looks original; call only 10 am
to 6 pm PST only.*

Wilkinson

Clubs/Associations

Wilkinson Collectors Society
c/o Wilkinson Sword Limited, Sword
  Centre
19-21 Brunel Rd.
London, W3 7UH U.K.
ph: +44 181 749 2304
sales@wilkinson-swords.co.uk
http://www.wilkinson-swords.com
  Members receive free access to gun
  and sword records, historical advisory
  service, visits to the Sword Centre,
  advance information on new projects,
  preferential number allocation on
  limited editions; a company-sponsored
  club.

Here are some tips when contacting someone who is listed in this book:

When requesting information about a particular item, include a description (material, dimensions, maker's mark, model number, etc.) and a photo, sketch, digital image or photocopy of the item in question.

Always ask if there are charges for samples or for the services that you are requesting.

When corresponding by letter, please be sure to include a Large (#10 business size) Self-Addressed and Stamped Envelope (LSASE) if requesting a reply or the return of photographs.

Never call collect unless otherwise directed. When calling, be considerate of time zone differences and always ask if the party you are calling has time to talk. When leaving an answering machine message, always instruct the party to call you back collect.

TABLEWARE

(see also CERAMICS;
DINNERWARE; FLATWARE;
GLASS, Elegant; GLASS, Crystal)

Man./Prod./Dist.

New York Merchandise Mart
41 Madison Ave.
New York, NY 10010
ph: 212-686-1203
fax: 212-779-7105
http://www.41madison.com
*Showplace for purveyors of new
tableware including gifts, glassware,
ceramicware, silverware and
decorative accessories; sells exclusively
to the trade.*

Kristen Kuhnlein Blessman
225 Fifth Avenue - The International
   Showcase
225 Fifth Ave.
The New York Gift Building
New York, NY 10010-1102
ph: 212-685-6377 or 800-235-3512
fax: 212-684-3200
contactus@225-fifth.com
http://www.225-fifth.com
*Showplace for purveyors specializing
in the sale of new giftware &
decorative accessories; also tableware.*

Periodicals

Magazine: Gifts & Decorative Accessories
345 Hudson St., 4th Floor
New York, NY 10014
ph: 212-519-7200
fax: 212-519-7431
*Trade magazine for new gifts,
decorative accessories, collectibles,
stationery, gift baskets, and tabletop
wares; buyer's resource directory
guide available with subscription.*

Matching Services For

(see DINNERWARE; FLATWARE;
GLASS, Elegant; GLASS, Crystal)

TARGET SHOOTING
   MEMORABILIA

(see also SPORTING
COLLECTIBLES; TARGETS, Shooting
Gallery; TRAPSHOOTING)

Clubs/Associations

Rudi Prusok, Archivist
American Single Shot Rifle Association
Journal: Single Shot Rifle Journal
625 Pine St.
Marquette, MI 49855-3723
ph: 906-225-1828
fax: 906-227-1819
rprusok@nmu.edu
http://www.assra.com
*Organization dedicated to the
shooting and collecting of single shot
rifles from the turn of the century:
German Schuetzen, buffalo, benchrest,
and long range traditions; also
interested in related memorabilia; free
journal sample.*

Collectors

Dr. Anthony Sapienza
East 106 Ridgewood Ave.
Paramus, NJ 07652
ph: 201-262-6310
fax: 201-262-3990
siringo45@aol.com
*Serious collector wants anything
related to trick or exhibition shooting
(Annie Oakley, Doc Carver, Gus
Peret, etc.); wants posters, pinbacks,
glass target balls, souvenir targets;
plus shot items such as coins, playing
or business cards.*

David L. Hartline
P.O. Box 775
Columbus, OH 43085-0775
fax: 614-760-5427
*Wants to buy all types of pre-1920
shooting medals, badges and trophies
for marksmanship; will buy medals
whether complete or not; prefers items
that are engraved to winners; will
answer all letters.*

Target Balls

Collectors

Art Snyder
6086 W. Boggstown Rd.
Boggstown, IN 46110
ph: 317-835-7121
emshaw@in.net
*Buys/sells/trades antique glass target
balls, ball traps or throwers, glass
house or sporting ads pertaining to
same; anything related.*

Ralph Finch
34007 Hillside Ct.
Farmington, MI 48335-2513
ph: 248-476-4893 or 800-678-6400
   x6023
Wants glass target balls.

TARGETS

Shooting Gallery

(see also CAST IRON ITEMS;
TARGET SHOOTING MEMORABILIA)

Experts

Richard Tucker
Argyle Antiques
P.O. Box 262
Argyle, TX 76226-0262
ph: 940-464-3752
fax: 940-464-7293
lead1234@gte.net
*Buys and sells figural cast iron items
including shooting targets; no repros.
or repaired items wanted; also wants
catalogs, photographs and other
shooting gallery memorabilia*

TATTOO RELATED ITEMS

Experts

Lyle Tuttle
Tattoo Art Museum, The
841 Columbus Ave.
San Francisco, CA 94133
ph: 415-775-4991 or 707-462-4406
fax: 707-462-4433
http://www.lyletuttle.com
*Largest collection of tattoo art and
related antiques & collectibles; buys/
sells machines, designs, artifacts,
photos, paintings, etc.; mailing
address is 210 Clara Ave., Ukiah, CA
95482.*

Museums/Libraries

Lyle Tuttle
Tattoo Art Museum, The
841 Columbus Ave.
San Francisco, CA 94133
ph: 415-775-4991 or 707-462-4406
fax: 707-462-4433
http://www.lyletuttle.com
*Largest collection of tattoo art and
related antiques & collectibles; buys/
sells machines, designs, artifacts,
photos, paintings, etc.; mailing
address is 210 Clara Ave., Ukiah, CA
95482.*

TAXI RELATED COLLECTIBLES

Collectors

Nathan Willensky
Taxi Toys & Memorabilia
5 East 22nd St. #24C
New York, NY 10010-5329
ph: 212-982-2156
fax: 212-995-1065
taxitoys@aol.com
*Buy and trades anything Taxi - toys
and memorabilia; Taxis only.*

Henry Winningham
3205 S. Morgan St.
Chicago, IL 60608-6609
ph: 773-927-3796
*Wants anything pre-1950 that's
related to the Taxi industry.*

TAXIDERMY

(see ANIMAL TROPHIES)

TEA RELATED COLLECTIBLES

(see also CERAMICS; CHILDREN'S
THINGS, Dishes; KITCHEN
COLLECTIBLES; ORIENTALIA,
Japanese Items; SILVER; TOYS, Tin
Tea Sets)

Dealers

Alvin & Rose Mary Harper
Harpers Antiques & Interiors
236 Second St.
Lewes, DE 19958-1326
ph: 302-645-9750
*Buys and sells 19th and early 20th
century tea accessories such as
Staffordshire, Pearlware, Salopian,
and ironstone teapots, sterling and
plate silver, salesmen pottery samples,
European children's tea sets and
furniture.*

Dottie & Sy Shapiro
Great North Coast Tea Company
P.O. Box 2974
Miller Beach, IN 46403
ph: 219-938-1346
swsander@aol.com

Tea Balls

Collectors

Bobbie & Alan Bryson
1 St. Eleanoras Ln.
Tuckahoe, NY 10707-1307
ph: 914-779-1405
napkindoll@aol.com
*Wants to buy figural ceramic tea
balls.*

Tea Strainers

Dealers

Carol Payne
Carol's Antique Gallery
14455 Big Basin Way
Saratoga, CA 95070-6008
ph: 408-867-7055
*Wants to buy silver and silverplated
tea strainers, and other tea items such
as tea caddies (wood, silver, etc), tea
caddy scoops, tea infusers, and toast
racks; nothing dented, please.*

Teapots

Clubs/Associations

Vince McDonald
Totally Teapots
Newsletter: Let's Talk Teapots
Euxton
Chorley, Lancashire PR7 6EY U.K.
ph: 44-1257-450366
fax: 44-1257-450366
teapot.club@btinternet.com
http://www.totallyteapots.com

Experts

Tina M. Carter
882 South Mollison Ave.
El Cajon, CA 92020-6506
ph: 619-440-5043
premus2@aol.com
*Author of "Teapots, A Collectors
Guide" (available from the author for
$16 ppd.) and "Collectible Teapots, A*

Reference & Price Guide" (available from the author for $28.95 ppd.)

Internet Resources

Veilleuse-Theieres Collection
Gibson County Area Chamber of Commerce
P.O. Box 464
Trenton, TN 38382
ph: 901-855-0973
Collection of 525 European "Veilleuse-Theieres" (French for "night-light teapots") sickroom and nursery teapots used also as night lights and for the mixture of medications.

Museums/Libraries

Paul & Christine Gibbs
Cowry Teapot Museum
25 Castle St.
Conwy, North Wales LL32 8AY U.K.
ph: 01492 596533
fax: 01492 593429
info@teapotworld.com
http://www.teapotworld.co.uk
Over a thousand teapots from the classic 18th century pots, to the extraordinary novelties of the 20th century; in porcelain, bone china, pewter, glass, terra-cotta, earthenware, etc.

Teapots (Cardew)

Clubs/Associations

Cardew Collectors' Club - USA
200 S. 31st St.
Paducah, KY 42001
ph: 877-9TEAPOT or 800-808-5222
fax: 877-208-2565
collectorsclub@cardewdesign.com
http://www.cardewdesign.com/Pages/New2.40.html

Man./Prod./Dist.

Cardew Design North America, Inc.
190 Claremont Rd.
Bernardsville, NJ 07924 U.K.
ph: 877-983-2768
fax: 714-685-6914
cardewdesign@aol.com
http://www.cardewdesign.com
Maker of the highly detailed and collectible tea pots designed by Paul Cardew.

TEDDY BEARS

(see also BOOKS, Reference [Teddy Bears]; DOLLS; SMOKEY BEAR ITEMS; STEIFF; TEDDY BEARS [MODERN]; TOYS, Plush)

Appraisers

Ken Yenke
P.O. Box 36133
Strongsville, OH 44136
ph: 440-238-5363
kyleyk@flashmail.com
Author and collector; designated appraiser for Good Bears of the World; expert identification and

valuation of old teddy bears and plush animals;

Ann Miller, ISA
Bright-Miller Appraisals
19750 S.W. Peavine Mtn. Rd.
McMinnville, OR 97128
ph: 503-472-1092
Appraises, collects old Teddy Bears, Raggedy Ann & Andy dolls and books; belongs to "Good Bears of the World" and "Teddy Bear Boosters;" life member of United Federation of Doll Collectors; teaches antiques at State Comm. College.

Clubs/Associations

Donna Hearn, Sec./Treas.
Good Bears of the World
Magazine: Bear Tracks
P.O. Box 13097
Toledo, OH 43613-0097
ph: 419-531-5365 or 877-429-2327
tdbear2@comcast.net
http://www.goodbearsoftheworld.org
"Good Bears" spread love & understanding by giving away Teddy Bears to comfort every hurt, abused child or lonely, forgotten adult; quarterly newsletter.

Ann Miller
Teddy Bear Boosters Club
19750 S.W. Peavine Mtn. Rd.
McMinnville, OR 97128
ph: 503-472-1092

Hugglets Teddy Bear Association
P.O. Box 290
Brighton
East Sussex, BN2 1DR U.K.
ph: 01273 697974
fax: 01273 626255
info@hugglets.co.uk
http://www.hugglets.co.uk
For those interested in collecting and creating teddy bears.

Collectors

Barbara Wolters
Magazine: Teddy Tribune, The
254 W. Sidney
St. Paul, MN 55107-3494
ph: 651-291-7571
10 issues of Teddy Tribune per year; everything about teddy bears; send for free brochure.

Gwen Daniel
18 Belleau Lake Ct.
O Fallon, MO 63366-3144
ph: 636-978-3190
SimGirl200@aol.com
Wants to buy early, jointed teddy bears in good condition.

Bill Boyd
7408 Englewood Lane
Raytown, MO 64133-6913
ph: 816-356-7423
fax: 816-356-7423

Tadg Galleran
2911 4th St., #112
Santa Monica, CA 90405
ph: 310-314-0402
tadggalleran@hotmail.com
Wants to buy teddy bears made of mohair wool from 1980s to 1950s, in very good condition (send photo); also wants all Steiff animals before 1960 with button and/or chest tags.

Susan Murphy
29668 Orinda Rd.
San Juan Capistrano, CA 92675-1211
ph: 949-364-4333
Wants to buy old bears from early 1900s to 1950s; please enclose SASE.

Dealers

Rita Mueller
Grange Hall Antiques
1 South Eighth Alley
P.O. Box 263
New Market, MD 21774
ph: 301-865-5651
fax: 301-865-0518
Rita@newmarketmd.com
http://www.grangehallantiques.com
Quality Steiff animals from 1950s through 1980s; always buying one piece or entire collection: teddy bears, Schuco, Hermann, Steiff; also available - fine country graniteware from Germany available; mail orders and layaways.

Walter LaValley
Bachelor II Dolls & Bears
5130 Duke St., Ste. 6
Wheaton Plaza
Alexandria, VA 22304-2955
ph: 703-823-BEAR
fax: 703-823-1787
Specializes in dolls and bears.

Cheri Shivley
Cynthia's Country Store, Inc.
The Wellington Mall #15A
12794 W. Forest Hill Blvd.
West Palm Beach, FL 33414
ph: 561-793-0554
fax: 561-795-4222
cynbears@aol.com
http://www.cynthiascountrystore.com
Specializing in new, discontinued and antique Steiff, R. John Wright, and other manufacturers and artists bears.

Beth B. Savino
Toy Store, The
Westgate Village
3301 West Central Ave.
Toledo, OH 43606
ph: 419-531-2839 or 800-862-8697
fax: 419-531-2730
info@toystorenet.com
http://www.toystorenet.com
Focus is on collecting Steiff toys and teddy bears; sells exclusive Steiff Limited Edition; also buys old Steiff.

Myron Weis
Division St. Antiques
7 Division St. W
Buffalo, MN 55313
ph: 612-682-6453
Buys and sells a complete line of antiques with a specialty in Teddy Bears, Toys, and Folk Art.

World City, Inc.
6935 James Ave. South
Minneapolis, MN 55423-2147
Buys teddy bears; please send photo and asking price along with SASE for reply.

Experts

Patricia Snyder
My Dear Dolly
P.O. Box 303
Sparta, NJ 07871-0303
ph: 201-729-8087
dolly@sparta.csnet.net
http://www.mydeardolly.com
Wants older bears, parts, bear accessories, books, dolly-teddies; also wants Santas, bunnies, cloth Raggedy dolls; also appraises; on staff of two appraisal services; offers detailed lists of items for sale for $1 and LSASE.

Dee Hockenberry
Bears N Things
82 Timber Villa
Elizabethtown, PA 17022
ph: 717-367-4142
fax: 717-367-4143
Teddiesone@aol.com
http://www.deelor.com
Buys and sells; author of several books about Teddy Bears.

Marguerite Cantine
223 Southeast 37th Ave.
Ocala, FL 34471-3045
ph: 352-694-4514
fax: 352-694-4514
designbycantine@aol.com
An American Teddy Bear specialist; author of "American Teddy Bear Reference, Identification & Price Guide;" appraises American-made Teddy Bears from 1903-1946; SASE must accompany mailed requests; wants pre-1946 bears from original owners.

Terry & Doris Michaud
Carrousel by Michaud
505 West Broad St.
Chesaning, MI 48616-1210
ph: 517-845-7881
fax: 517-845-6650
dmmich217@aol.com
Teddy bear artists, authors and lecturers; write regular column about teddy bears for "Teddy Bear & Friends" magazine, and for the British magazine, "Teddy Bear Times."

E. Adjoran
Imaginary Friends
P.O. Box 40601
Denver, CO 80204
ph: 303-761-7234
toyrep@aol.com
http://members.aol.com/toyrep
"Dr." E is a Steiff authorized restorationist, independent appraiser and collector; specializes in Steiff and all other stuffed toys and teddy bears; buys, sells, trades, repairs, restores, appraises; consignment sales and custom-mades.

Man./Prod./Dist.

Bear-in-Mind, Inc.
Newsletter: Arctophile, The
3800 Williston Rd., Ste. 100
Hopkins, MN 55345
ph: 978-369-1167 or 800-222-6055
fax: 800-621-6055
info@bearinmind.com
http://www.bearinmind.com
A catalog company devoted to the consumer of new Teddy Bear related items; the first mail order company for Teddy Bears; started in 1977; send $1 for 40-page catalog; $5 for subscription to "The Arctophile."

Museums/Libraries

George B. Black, Jr.
Teddy Bear Museum, The
2511 Pine Ridge Rd.
Naples, FL 34109
ph: 239-598-2711
fax: 239-598-9239
info@teddymuseum.com
http://www.teddymuseum.com/about.htm
Collects and displays teddy bears and related items from teddy bear artists; developing teddy bear archives from the antique to present.

Bear Museum, The
38 Dragon St.
Petersfield, Hampshire GU31 4JY U.K.
ph: +44 (0) 1730 265108
bears@dial.pipex.com
http://www.bearmuseum.co.uk
History of Teddy Bears, identification tips, Teddy Bear links.

Teddy Bear Museum, The
19 Greenhill St.
Stratford-upon-Avon, Warwickshire CV37 6LF U.K.
ph: +44 (0) 1789 293160
info@theteddybearmuseum.com
http://www.theteddybearmuseum.com
A world famous teddy bear museum and shop.

Periodicals

Ashton International Media, Inc.
Magazine: Teddy Bear & Friends
P.O. Box 10545
Lancaster, PA 17605-0545
ph: 717-393-8371
fax: 717-393-8371
TBFedit@comcast.net
http://www.teddybearandfriends.com
Magazine dedicated to teddy bears and other plush friends; editorial coverage of bears - antique to modern artists; bear manufacturers, care and repair, display ideas, buying, selling, and insuring bears, new product arrivals, etc.

Jones Publishing, Inc.
Magazine: Teddy Bear Review
P.O. Box 5000
Iola, WI 54945
ph: 715-445-5000 or 800-331-0038
fax: 715-445-4053
jonespub@jonespublishing.com
http://www.teddybearreview.com
Embraces the joy of teddy bear and soft sculpture collecting: in-depth articles, collector tips, expert advice, show reports.

Repair Services

Clare Erickson
Auntie Clare's Doll Hospital Shop
2543 Seppela Blvd., N
North Saint Paul, MN 55109-3016
ph: 651-770-7522
clare@antieclares.com
http://www.antieclares.com
Offers professional restorations of dolls, bears, animals and plush, figurines and statues.

E. Adorjan
Imaginary Friends
P.O. Box 40601
Denver, CO 80204
ph: 303-761-7234
toyrep@aol.com
http://members.aol.com/toyrep
Specializes repairs and restorations to Steiff and other stuffed toys and dolls; will advise if toy would be better off if left as-is; references and before-and-after photos available; official restoration specialist with Steiff.

Jeri Cotherman
Doll & Bear's Paradise, A
855 1/2 N. Cedar
Laramie, WY 82072-2469
ph: 307-742-3429
dolls2fix@fiberpipe.net
http://www.adollsandbearsparadise.com
Restores dolls, stuffed animals; makes artist specialty bears; sells dolls and bears; buying dolls, patterns, old material, fur and fake fur.

Nisbet

Clubs/Associations

Howard & Sarah Wade
Peggy Nisbet International Collectors' Society
Newsletter: PNICS Newsletter
P.O. Box 325
Orrville, OH 44667-0325
ph: 330-682-8551
fax: 330-682-3655
RBCollectr@aol.com
Clearinghouse for information about Peggy Nisbet portrait and costume dolls and Nisbet bears from Britain, both primary and secondary markets.

Man./Prod./Dist.

Howard & Sarah Wade
Nisbet Dolls & Bears
P.O. Box 325
Orrville, OH 44667-0325
ph: 330-682-8551
fax: 330-682-3655
RBCollectr@aol.com
US distributor for Peggy Nisbet dolls and Nisbet bears from Britain.

TEDDY BEARS (MODERN)

(see also BOOKS, Reference [Teddy Bears]; DOLLS; SMOKEY BEAR ITEMS; STEIFF; TEDDY BEARS; TOYS, Plush)

Clubs/Associations

Teddy Bear Tymes
P.O. Box 21036
St. Catharines, Ontario L2M 7X2 Canada
tbt@vaxxine.com
http://www.teddybeartymes.com
A club for bear collectors, artists, and enthusiasts formed in 1987; hosts an annual Teddy Bear Show to raise funds for their Teddy Bear gifting program to area ambulances, fire departments, seniors' homes and family services.

Dealers

Mike Mellone
Essentially Bears
P.O. Box 25
Stewartsville, NJ 08886
ph: 908-479-4614
fdc@4-collectors.com
http://www.4-collectors.com
Specializing in Puffkins, current and retired; also Ganz Bears and Keepsake Resin Bears.

Nancy Pelham
Homestead Gift Shop
4 Hillwood Lane
Catskill, NY 12414
ph: 518-943-4371
fluffy@capital.net
http://www.homestead-gift-shop.com
Carries manufactured teddy bears from Boyds, Cottage Collectibles, Douglas, Mary Meyer, Orzek, and Ty;

also artist bears by Quite A. Bear and Nostalgic Bears.

John & Rosemary Gurney
Bearshop Exchange
2823 S.E. 35th Ave.
Okeechobee, FL 34974
ph: 863-7763-8728
fax: 863-763-2458
ringmaster@bearshop.net
http://www.bearshop.net
Buys and sells rare, vintage and collectible Teddy Bears, stuffed animals, and accessories: Dakin, Schuco, Steiff, Raikes, Gund, etc.

Bruce Kraemer
Da Bears Shop
7914 Gleason Dr., #1125
Knoxville, TN 37919
ph: 865-691-0140
dabearsshop@cs.com
http://dabearsshop.tripod.com
Sells contemporary miniature and artist teddy bears.

Judy Kuster
Bear Essentials Dolls, Bears & Collectible Toys
1502 Park St.
Paso Robles, CA 93446
ph: 805-237-8697
Offers vintage to present Barbie, GI Joe, action figures, Beanie Babies, Starting Lineup, Boyds Bears, Steiff, Muffy Vanderbear, Superman, Batman, Star Wars, Star Trek, and more.

Kitty Wilde
Bears by the Sea
680 Cypress St.
Pismo Beach, CA 93449
ph: 805-773-1952
fax: 805-773-5869
Bears@digitalwest.net
http://www.bearsbythesea.com
Specializing in Muffy and VanderBears, TY Plush and Beanie Babies, Boyds Plush Bears, Gund.

Richard Palmer
Teddy Bear Town
E-zine: Teddy Bear Town Newsletter
P.O. Box 58562
Seattle, WA 98138
ph: 206-764-0606
fax: 206-764-0808
richard@teddybeartown.com
http://www.teddybeartown.com
Offers a wide variety of collector's, gift and just plain old lovable bears.

Niki Ferraro
Bear St.
234-5149 Country Hills Blvd. NW, Ste. 154
Calgary, Alberta T3A 5K8 Canada
fax: 403-547-1018
mail@bearst.com
http://www.bearst.com
Specializes in Gund plush animals; Australian Animals, Christmas, Monkey Business, Signature Collection, baby GUND, Classic GUND, Jungle Cats, Pet Shop,

Snuffles, Whimsical Friends, Puppets, Mohair Collection, Bunnies, Classic Pooh.

Internet Resources

Debbie Kesling
debbie@PureGenius.com
http://www.cybearspace.com
Teddy bear designer maintains Web site with an incredible number of Teddy Bear links.

Kitty Wilde
Bears by the Sea
680 Cypress St.
Pismo Beach, CA 93449
ph: 805-773-1952
fax: 805-773-5869
Bears@digitalwest.net
http://www.bearsbythesea.com
Specializing in Muffy and VanderBears, TY Plush and Beanie Babies, Boyds Plush Bears, Gund; Web site provides valuable online resource information for collectors: price guides, online forums, historical data.

Teddybear NL
The Netherlands
wcoumans@cobweb.nl
http://www.cobweb.nl/wcoumans/teddie.htm
Great Web site for Teddy Bear information: history, general info, classic teddy bears, Paddington, Cherished Teddies, Fozzie Bear, Winnie the Pooh, Bear Baloo, Forever Friends, and lots more.

Periodicals

Atchison Literature Inc.
Magazine: Canadia Teddy Bear News Magazine
Box 457
Water Valley, Alberta T0M 2E0 Canada
ph: 877-280-2826
fax: 403-637-2616
patricia@teddybearnews.com
http://www.teddybearnews.com
A magazine for teddy bear artists and collectors.

Ashdown Publishing
Magazine: Teddy Bear Times
Avalon Court, Star Rd.
Partridge Green, West Sussex RH13 8RY U.K.
ph: +44 (0) 1403 711511 or 513-353-4052 (in US)
fax: +44 (0) 1403 711521
mark@ashdown.co.uk
http://www.teddybeartimes.com
Magazine with glossy color pages packed with news, information, ideas and inspiration for the growing bands of ardent teddy lovers.

Binkley

Man./Prod./Dist.

Binkley Toys
163 Beach Rd.
Hamilton, Ontario L8L 4A5 Canada
ph: 800-304-6642 or 905-547-4070
fax: 905-312-8962
info@binkley-toys.com
http://www.binkley-toys.com
Binkley bears are made in Canada.

Boyds

Clubs/Associations

Loyal Order of Friends of Boyds Collectors' Club, The
P.O. Box 4386
Gettysburg, PA 17325-4386
ph: 717-633-9898
t_houser@boydsstuff.com
http://www.boydsstuff.com
A company-sponsored collectors' club.

Dealers

Bailey King
Bloomin Boyds Bears
bloomin55@email.msn.com
http://www.bloominboydsbears.com
Carries a stock of over 700 Boyds resin bears & friends collectibles for sale.

Experts

Laurie Anne Greez
P.O. Box 1393
Easton, MA 02334-1393
fax: 508-230-9517
lag4boyds@aol.com
http://www.laurieannegreez.com
A professional writer whose Boyds expertise is widely respected.

Internet Resources

Kristin Sheaffer
Boyds Collector Forum
503 Lumpkin Rd.
Ft. Benning, GA 31905
KristinSheaffer@aol.com
http://www.boydsforum.com

Man./Prod./Dist.

Boyds Collections Ltd., The
P.O. Box 4385
Gettysburg, PA 17325
ph: 717-633-9898
t_houser@boydsstuff.com
http://www.boydsstuff.com

Periodicals

Laurie Anne Greez
Newsletter: Lions, Tigers, & Boyds, Oh, My!!!
P.O. Box 1393
Easton, MA 02334-1393
fax: 508-230-9517
lag4boyds@aol.com
http://www.laurieannegreez.com
Quarterly newsletter features articles relating to Boyds: Resin, Plus and Bear Necessity Lines; store exclusives, how to insure your Boyds, secondary

market information, photos, contests, retailer's spotlight, etc.

Muffy Vanderbear

Clubs/Associations

Michelle Sterling
Muffy VanderBear Club
Newsletter: Fanfare
401 North Wabash, Ste. 500
Chicago, IL 60611-5646
ph: 773-329-0020 or 800-682-3427
fax: 773-329-1417
bears@digitalwest.net
http://www.muffy.com/vbclub.htm
Muffy VanderBear, a seven-inch, golden pile plush stuffed dressed bear; the company-sponsored club provides information, services and limited edition bears exclusively to Club members.

TELECARDS

(see TELEPHONE CARDS)

TELEGRAMS

Collectors

Dr. Walter Brinker
Niedernfeld 2
Radevormwald, 42477 Germany
ph: 49-219540928
fax: 49-21956517
walter.brinker@t-online.de
A collector of international telegram forms; has about 400 from 202 countries.

TELEGRAPH ITEMS

(see also BROADCASTING; BUMPER STICKERS, Radio Station; ELECTRICITY RELATED ITEMS; FIRE FIGHTING MEMORABILIA, Fire Alarm Telegraphy; INSULATORS; RADIOS; STOCK TICKERS; TELEGRAMS)

Appraisers

Tom French
151 Barton Rd.
Stow, MA 01775
ph: 978-562-5573
tfrench@fiam.net
http://www.artifaxbooks.com
Can provide an informal opinion of value for old telegraph keys, sounders, etc.; send a letter including complete description, condition and photo if possible; please include a SASE; Vibroplex and McElroy instruments a specialty.

Clubs/Associations

Ed Gable
Antique Wireless Association
Newsletter: Old Timer's Bulletin
Box E
Breesport, NY 14816
ph: 607-739-5443
fax: 607-796-6230
k2mp@eznet.net
http://www.antiquewireless.org
One of the world's largest and oldest historical radio collector organizations; purpose is to document and preserve the history of radio, telegraph and television artifacts.

Harry Goldman
Tesla Coil Builders' Association
Newsletter: TCBA News
3 Amy Lane
Queensbury, NY 2804-9432
ph: 518-792-1003
stcole@deltanet.com
http://www.eskimo.com/~billb/tesla/tcba.html
TCBA is a clearinghouse on the history of electricity, wireless, electrotherapy, etc.; acts as consultants for high voltage historical equipment.

Ron Lawrence
Carolinas Chapter of the Wireless Association of America
P.O. Box 3015
Matthews, NC 28106-3015
ph: 704-289-1166
kc4yoy@trellis.net
http://www.cc-awa.org
Hosts five collector events each year.

International Morse Preservation Society, The
Newsletter: IMPS Newsletter
P.O. Box 47
Hadley, MI 48440-0047
kk4kf@cox.net
http://www.fists.org
FISTS exists to promote amateur CW activity; newcomers welcome; awards, nets (including beginners' net), dial-a-sked for beginners, straight key activities, QSL bureau, newsletter,

Keith LeBaron
Morse Telegraph Club, Inc.
Newsletter: Dots & Dashes
550 N. Greenfield Dr.
Freeport, IL 61032
ph: 815-232-2564
keithlebaron@att.net
http://members.tripod.com/morse_telegraph_club
For those with an interest in landline telegraphy; newspaper has articles having to do with stories and experiences of landline telegraphers, but also has some radiotelegraph articles as well.

Collectors

Roger W. Reinke
5301 Neville Ct.
Alexandria, VA 22310-1113
ph: 703-971-4095
rwreinke@cox.net
Wants telegraph instruments, stock tickers, and related items such as call boxes, signs, early paper; condition not important.

Howard Hazelcorn
6731 Ashley Ct.
Sarasota, FL 34241-9696
ph: 941-921-1815
mrpropane@aol.com
Wants rare early items.

Dale R. Beeks
Perceptions Scientifica
P.O. Box 117
Mount Vernon, IA 52314-0117
ph: 800-880-5178 or 319-895-0506
dbeeksci@aol.com
Wants pre-1900 telegraph keys, registers, and related items.

Jim
cd102@aol.com
http://members.aol.com/cd102
Collects and appraisers telegraphs and telephones as well as related documents.

Dealers

Jim & Felicia Kreuzer
New Wireless Pioneers
1541 Bronson Rd.
Grand Island, NY 14072
ph: 716-773-4999
fax: 716-773-5757
wireless@pce.net
http://www.marconi-wireless.com
Buys and sells 1850-1950 books, catalogs, magazines, autographs, and other literature dealing with early radio, telegraph, wireless, pre-1940 television, medical, telegraphy, early computers, television, X-ray and electricity.

Experts

Tom French
151 Barton Rd.
Stow, MA 01775
ph: 978-562-5573
tfrench@fiam.net
http://www.artifaxbooks.com
Will help you identify and date your telegraph instruments of all types; specialist in Martin, Vibroplex and McElroy items; wants to buy all kinds of telegraph instruments, including early railroad and Western Union keys and sounders.

Prof. Thomas Perera
P.O. Box 122
Hancock, VT 05748
ph: 802-767-3265
pererat@mail.montclair.edu
http://www.w1tp.com
Maintains Internet telegraph and scientific instrument museum and

collector's guide; author of "Perera's Telegraph Collector's Guide."

Russ Kleinman
Sparks Telegraph Key Review
P.O. Box 2474
Silver City, NM 88062
sparks@zianet.com
http://www.zianet.com/sparks/index.html
Collector with over 20 years experience in telegraphy and telegraph key collecting; strong Internet presence with fun, interactive, pictorial Web site; active research interest and specialty in spark keys.

Internet Resources

Neal McEwen, K5RW
Telegraph Office, The
nmcewen@metronet.com
http://fohnix.metronet.com/~nmcewen/ref.html
Lots of information about telegraphy, the history, links, instruments, etc.

Prof. Thomas Perera
Telegraph & Scientific Instrument On-Line Cyber-Museum
P.O. Box 122
Hancock, VT 05748
ph: 802-767-3265
pererat@mail.montclair.edu
http://www.w1tp.com
Online museum dedicated to the preservation of telegraph history, lore, and instrumentation; downloadable images; telegraph history, bibliography, and related links; email appraisals available.

Museums/Libraries

New England Wireless & Steam Museum, Inc.
1300 Frenchtown Rd.
East Greenwich, RI 02818
ph: 401-884-1710 or 401-885-0545
fax: 401-884-0683
newsm@ids.net
http://users.ids.net/~newsm
Composed of five buildings, the museum is a public, non-profit corporation run by volunteers; the wireless building shows the span of electrical communication from telegraph to TV: keys, sounders, crystal sets, tubes, ocean cable, etc.

American Radio Relay League Museum of Amateur Radio
225 Main St.
Newington, CT 06111-1494
ph: 860-666-1541
hq@arrl.org

Ed Gable
Antique Wireless Association's Electronic Communication Museum
Box E
Breesport, NY 14816
ph: 607-739-5443
fax: 607-796-6230
k2mp@eznet.net
http://www.antiquewireless.org
Open limited hours May through October; call or write before visiting;

please enclose SASE if requesting a reply.

Periodicals

John V. Terrey
Magazine: Antique Radio Classified
P.O. Box 2
Carlisle, MA 01741
ph: 978-371-0512
fax: 978-371-7129
arc@antiqueradio.com
http://www.antiqueradio.com
Antique radio's largest monthly about old radios, Art Deco, TVs, ham equip. - '40s, '50s, books, telegraph, etc.; lots of ads.

Carol McDougald
Magazine: Crown Jewels of the Wire
P.O. Box 1003
Saint Charles, IL 60174
ph: 630-513-1544
fax: 630-513-8278
editor@crownjewelsofthewire.com
http://www.crownjewelsofthewire.com
76-page monthly magazine of insulator and telephone and telegraph history; glass, porcelain; foreign columns; classified ads, show dates, etc.

Zyg Nilski
Nilski Partnership, The
Magazine: Morsum Magnificat
The Poplars
Wistanswick
Market Drayton, Shropshire TF9 2BA
U.K.
ph: +44 (0) 1630 638306
fax: +44 (0) 1630 638051
editor@morsemag.com
http://www.morsemag.com
A bi-monthly English publication; the international journal dedicated to Morse telegraphy, past, present, and future; for operators, historians, and collectors.

Telegraph Keys

Collectors

Prof. Thomas Perera
P.O. Box 122
Hancock, VT 05748
ph: 802-767-3265
pererat@mail.montclair.edu
http://www.w1tp.com
Wants to buy telegraph keys and apparatus; specializing in Civil War era, 19th century, land line, and wireless keys; has been collecting for over 40 years; has over 400 keys for trade.

Experts

Gil Schlehman
Gil Schleman Antiques
335 Indianapolis
Downers Grove, IL 60515-3119
ph: 630-968-2320
Noted collector and author of "Telegraph Key Review" column in the "Antique Radio Classified;" largest collection of "speed keys" in the world.

Suppliers

Tom French
Artifax Books
151 Barton Rd.
Stow, MA 01775
ph: 978-562-5573
artifaxbooks@yahoo.com
http://www.artifaxbooks.com
Carries vintage telegraph keys and sounders, also replacement knobs, paddles for old telegraph keys; knobs can be used on hand keys or "bugs;" paddles are good for Vibroplex, McElroy, Electric Specialty, Lionel, others; SASE for list.

TELEPHONE CARDS

(see also BANKING; CIVIL WAR ARTIFACTS, Currency; COINS & CURRENCY; CREDIT CARDS & CHARGE ITEMS; MONEYCARDS; WOODEN MONEY)

Clubs/Associations

Brian R. Lohmann, Dir. of Dev.
International Prepaid Communications Association
904 Massachusetts Ave. NE
Washington, DC 20002-6228
ph: 202-544-4448 or 800-958-7824
fax: 202-547-7417
inquiries@I-PCA.org
http://www.I-PCA.org
Trade association with collectors division; offers educational material.

Dealers

Steve Schwartz
MoneyCard.com Phone Cards
P.O. Box 677549
Orlando, FL 32867
ph: 407-898-7778
fax: 407-737-2996
manager@moneycard.com
http://www.moneycard.com/xcollect.htm
World's most comprehensive price list of USA phonecards, telephone cards and telecards for collectors; search by telephone company or theme.

James Moran
Telequest
1566 W. Algonquin, #165
Hoffman Estates, IL 60195-1575
ph: 847-991-1228
telequest@usa.net
http://www.telequest.biz
Sells US telephone cards and international cards with US themes; emphasis is on world, Disney, show cards, and scarce pre-1996 US cards.

Steve Eyer
P.O. Box 123 -MAC
Mount Zion, IL 62549-0123
ph: 217-864-4321
fax: 217-864-3021
steve@eyersworld.com
http://www.eyersworld.com
Specializes in Telephone Cards, and issues weekly price lists and

newsletters; write to subscribe at no charge.

Internet Resources

Steve Schwartz
MoneyCard.com Phone Cards
P.O. Box 677549
Orlando, FL 32867
ph: 407-898-7778
fax: 407-737-2996
manager@moneycard.com
http://www.moneycard.com/xcollect.htm
World's most comprehensive price list of USA phonecards, telephone cards and telecards for collectors; search by telephone company or theme.

Terry Stewart
Collector Link
71 John St. East
Waterloo, Ontario N2J 1G2 Canada
ph: 519-745-1745
stewart@collector-link.com
http://www.collector-link.com
Catalogs over 2,000 trading card related Web sites for: baseball, hockey, basketball, football, other sports, non-sports, phone cards, credit-debit cards, business cards, postcards.

TELEPHONE COMPANY ITEMS

Bell-Shaped Paperweights

Experts

Jacqueline C. Linscott
3557 Nicklaus Dr.
Titusville, FL 32780-5356
ph: 321-267-9170 or 321-480-1800
fax: 321-269-7767
bluebellwt@aol.com
Wants old, cobalt blue, bell-shaped paperweights used as giveaways by early telephone companies; author of "Blue Bell Paperweights, Telephone Pioneer Bells & Other Related Items," 2003 edition; $25 from the author.

TELEPHONES

(see also INSULATORS; TELEPHONE CARDS; TELEPHONE COMPANY ITEMS)

Clubs/Associations

Paul McFadden, Ed.
Telephone Collectors International, Inc.
Newsletter: Singing Wires
3207 E. Bend Dr.
Algonquin, IL 60102-9664
ph: 847-658-7855
fax: 847-658-9360
info@telephonecollectors.org
http://www.telephonecollectors.org
For antique telephone collectors; sponsors two shows annually where old phones and related items are displayed, bought and sold; newsletter published monthly; journal "Switchers Quarterly" published quarterly.

Cindy Krizek
Antique Telephone Collectors Association
Newsletter: Antique Telephone Collectors Newsletter
P.O. Box 94
Abilene, KS 67410-0094
ph: 785-263-1757
atca@atcaonline.com
http://www.atcaonline.com
Dedicated to the preservation of historical telephony; membership includes monthly 8-12 page newsletter with free advertising for members, numerous ATCA-sponsored antique telephone shows each year; nearly 1,500 members.

Telecommunications Heritage Group
Newsletter: TH News
P.O. Box 561
South Croydon, Surrey CR2 6YL U.K.
ph: 0870 321 2887
fax: 0870 321 2889
membership@thg.org.uk
http://www.thg.org.uk
Members are researchers, collectors, historians, operators of restored apparatus; interested in old telephones, telegraphs, phone kiosks and related hardware.

Collectors

William Boss
33 Hoffman Dr.
Kings Park, NY 11754-3601
ph: 631-269-7839
wbos@optonline.net
All types of telephones and related ephemera including blue glass paperweights, signs, pay phones, and parts.

Lydia M. Jackson-Fryer
608 Winans Way
Baltimore, MD 21229-1430
ph: 410-233-6231
fax: 410-233-6231
ljackson@umbc.edu
Wants to buy antique telephones from the 1920s through the 1950s.

Bob Hunter
15600 Andover Lane
Wake Forest, NC 27587-9778
ph: 919-528-3469
Collecting all types of phones: antique, novelty, toy, unusual; also wants related accessories and memorabilia.

Russ Pate
235 Sandpine Rd.
Indialantic, FL 32903-2117
ph: 407-777-1759 or 800-777-1759
rpate1@cfl.rr.com
Wants to buy telephones and related items from 1876 to present; condition not important.

Paul G. Engelke
23399 Rio Del Mar Dr.
Boca Raton, FL 33486-8504
ph: 561-338-3332
keytelco@bellsouth.net
Wants early wooden wall and candlestick phones, porcelain telephone signs, small coin phones, wooden coin phones, etc. but no paper.

Tom Vaughn
2016 Village Rd.
La Porte, IN 46350-7874
ph: 219-324-3494
fax: 219-325-4511
phoneman@adsnet.com
http://www.pcpages.com/phoneman/signpage.htm
Wants to buy pay-station and unusual old telephones; also wants porcelain telephone and telegraph company signs and badges.

John Huckeby
2440 W. CR 150 N
New Castle, IN 47362-9146
ph: 765-533-6369
fax: 765-533-6530
j.a.huckeby@worldnet.att.net
Wants old telephones, complete or parts.

Jerry Williams
104 N. Chicago
Salina, KS 67401
ph: 785-825-0578
Collector of old telephones, parts for old telephones, and related memorabilia.

Jon Kolger
6906 Meade Dr.
Colleyville, TX 76034-6416
ph: 817-329-5262
jkolger@gte.net
Always buying COLORED PLASTIC Art Deco style telephones from the 1920s through the 1950s; also seeking pre-1900 mechanical telephones that work on the "two tin cans on a string" principle; also wants telephone related paper, books, etc.

Dealers

Bruce & Charlotte Mager
Waves
251 W. 30th St.
New York, NY 10001
ph: 212-273-9616
c1wave@aol.com
http://www.wavesradio.com
Over 20 years experience specializing in vintage radios, phonographs, telegraphy, televisions, assorted electrical and mechanical apparatus, and related advertising memorabilia, books and pamphlets.

Jonathan Finder
Vintage Telephones
1203 East End Ave.
Pittsburgh, PA 15218
ph: 412-371-9608
jon@oldphones.com
http://www.oldphones.com
Buys, sells, repairs 1928-1960 vintage telephones; each is restored to work on modern lines; guaranteed and original; no reproductions; selection varies as does availability.

Bruce Patterson
Phone Wizard
23 South Berlin Pike
Lovettsville, VA 20180-8502
ph: 540-822-4730
fax: 540-822-4733
phonewizard@juno.com
Publishes a catalog ($3) providing genuine antique telephones, Art Deco telephones, and parts; offers restorations, conservation and repairs of all antique, old, and Western Electric telephones; visitors by appointment only.

Richard R. Marsh
Chicago Old Telephone Company
327 Carthage St.
Sanford, NC 27330-4206
ph: 800-843-1320 or 919-774-6625
fax: 919-774-7666
sales@chicagooldtelephone.com
http://www.chicagooldtelephone.com
Carries parts for old telephones; also repairs/restores and sells antique telephones; catalog available for free; also rents telephones to movies, TV and stage shows.

R. Wiltfong
Telephone Man
23709 West 95th
Lenexa, KS 66227
ph: 913-782-0607
IBuy@oldtelephone.com
http://www.oldtelephone.com
Wants to buy old telephones; sells working phones and parts; has one of the largest collections online; can repair most any telephone and can build any part.

Rainbow Hirsh
Hollywood Phones
2780 Northbrook Place
Boulder, CO 80304-1432
ph: 303-442-3304 or 888-212-3663 (orders)
One of the premier restorers of vintage (1910-1937) telephones; meticulous care and attention to authenticity is given to each instrument; also sells at major antique shows throughout the US.

Jim & Shirley's Antiques
2245 Faust Ave.
Long Beach, CA 90815-3354
ph: 562-598-1914
jimandshirley@webtv.net
Buys and sells antique telephones and Victrolas.

Ron Christianson
Antique Telephones & Parts
P.O. Box 43
Cave Junction, OR 97523
ph: 541-592-4123
bngholio@internetcds.com
http://www.cavejunction.com/phones
*Buys, sells, trades, repairs, restores,
wires to work, appraises, collects
antique telephones.*

Sheri Stritof
PhoneVault
P.O. Box 770
Ocean Park, WA 98640
ph: 360-665-4735
fax: 509-694-0491
info@phonevault.com
http://www.phonevault.com
*Collector, dealer, expert buys, sells
and repairs old telephones, including
novelty phones.*

Experts

Gregory R. Russell
Telephony Museum
russell@telephonymuseum.com
http://www.telephonymuseum.com
*Offers a variety of telephones for sale;
Web site provides fun and educational
look at the history of telephony and a
look at how the instrument was
developed and changed over the years;
consultant to telephony-related
museums.*

Internet Resources

Ron Christianson
Cyber Telephone Museum
P.O. Box 43
Cave Junction, OR 97523
ph: 541-592-4123
bngholio@internetcds.com
http://www.cavejunction.com/phones
*Virtual museum of old telephones
including images, history, interesting
facts, and more.*

Museums/Libraries

Tommy Smith, CEO
Georgia Rural Telephone Museum, The
P.O. Box 18878
Leslie, GA 31764
ph: 912-874-4786
http://www.sowega.net/%7Emuseum
*Has over 1,500 telephones from 1875
to present.*

Oliver P. Parks Telephone Museum
529 South 7th St.
Springfield, IL 62721
ph: 217-789-5303
*A private museum based on a personal
collection and including over 100
antique telephones.*

Robin Sherck, Dir.
Museum of Independent Telephony
412 S. Campbell
Abilene, KS 67410-2905
ph: 785-263-2681
fax: 785-263-0380
http://www.geocities.com/
museumofindependenttelephony
*Established to illustrate pioneer spirit
& ingenuity of the early independent
companies who pioneered rural phone
service; extensive collection of
telephones and associated memorabilia, artifacts, photographs,
documents.*

Periodicals

Carol McDougald
Magazine: Crown Jewels of the Wire
P.O. Box 1003
Saint Charles, IL 60174
ph: 630-513-1544
fax: 630-513-8278
editor@crownjewelsofthewire.com
http://www.crownjewelsofthewire.com
*76-page monthly magazine of
insulator and telephone and telegraph
history; glass, porcelain; foreign
columns; classified ads, show dates,
etc.*

Repair Services

Recollections
P.O. Box 768
Westford, MA 01886
ph: 978-692-6335
recollectn@aol.com
http://members.aol.com/recollectn
*Repairs and refurbishes pre-1980
collectible telephones: Ericofon,
Princess.*

Richard R. Marsh
Chicago Old Telephone Company
327 Carthage St.
Sanford, NC 27330-4206
ph: 800-843-1320 or 919-774-6625
fax: 919-774-7666
sales@chicagooldtelephone.com
http://www.chicagooldtelephone.com
*Sells old restored telephones to public
and collectors; restores old
telephones; provides old telephones to
movie companies, TV, stage shows,
etc.; displays at top antique shows in
major cities.*

Bill Wright
Antique Telephones
1307 Sixth Ave. North
Nashville, TN 37208
ph: 615-255-4672 or 615-256-1900
fax: 615-256-1902
Wrightghm@aol.com
*Collects, buys, repairs antique
telephones and old telephone PBX and
Central Office switching equipment.*

Ron & Mary Knappen
Phoneco, Inc.
19813 E. Mill Rd.
P.O. Box 70
Galesville, WI 54630-0070
ph: 608-582-4124 or 608-582-2263
fax: 608-582-4593
phonecoinc@aol.com
http://www.phonecoinc.com
*Buys, sells, refurbishes any old
telephone; also sells old and new
parts, character phones, novelty
phones; catalogs, history, price guide,
and diagrams.*

R. Wiltfong
Telephone Man
23709 West 95th
Lenexa, KS 66227
ph: 913-782-0607
IBuy@oldtelephone.com
http://www.oldtelephone.com
*Wants to buy old telephones; sells
working phones and parts; has one of
the largest collections online; can
repair most any telephone and can
build any part.*

Odis W. LeVrier
House of Telephones
2677 East Valley Dr.
San Angelo, TX 76905
ph: 325-482-0101
fax: 325-655-5681
olevrier@aol.com
*Repairs antique telephones and carries
parts including covered tinsel cords
and cordage.*

Sheri Stritof
PhoneVault
P.O. Box 770
Ocean Park, WA 98640
ph: 360-665-4735
fax: 509-694-0491
info@phonevault.com
http://www.phonevault.com
*Collector, dealer, expert buys, sells
and repairs old telephones, including
novelty phones.*

Suppliers

Ron & Mary Knappen
Phoneco, Inc.
19813 E. Mill Rd.
P.O. Box 70
Galesville, WI 54630-0070
ph: 608-582-4124 or 608-582-2263
fax: 608-582-4593
phonecoinc@aol.com
http://www.phonecoinc.com
*Buys, sells, refurbishes any old
telephone; also sells old and new
parts, character phones, novelty
phones; catalogs, history, price guide,
and diagrams.*

Art Deco

Dealers

Carl Ratner
94 Mechanic St.
Reinholds, PA 17569-9701
ph: 717-484-1021
artdeco@epix.net
*Buy, collects, sell, trade telephones
and parts; specializing in Art Deco
phones of the 1920s through 1940s.*

Candlestick

Experts

Howard Hazelcorn
6731 Ashley Ct.
Sarasota, FL 34241-9696
ph: 941-921-1815
mrpropane@aol.com
*Collects and specializes in candlestick
phones.*

Novelty

Dealers

Bob Roberts
P.O. Box 152
Guilderland, NY 12084-0152
*Wants to buy novelty transistor
radios, e.g. Atlas Battery, Brut
cologne, Budweiser, Pepsi, Coke,
McDonald's, etc.; also wants
telephones in unusual shapes, e.g. gas
pumps, food items, cartoon
characters, cars, movie related, TV,
etc.*

Western Electric

Dealers

Cliff Sullivan
4902 W. Monte Cristo
Glendale, AZ 85306-2638
ph: 602-978-3551
fax: 602-843-3391
suclif@worldnet.att.net
*Wants items marked "Western
Electric:" telephones, telegraph,
sound equipment, appliances, etc.;
also wants old or unusual telephones,
equipment, or telephone memorabilia.*

TELEVISION SHOWS & MEMORABILIA

(see also AUTOGRAPHS;
BROADCASTING; CHARACTER
COLLECTIBLES; COWBOY
HEROES; FAN CLUBS; GAMES,
Board [TV Related]; MOVIE
MEMORABILIA; PHOTOGRAPHS,
Celebrity; PREMIUMS; SCIENCE
FICTION; SPACE COLLECTIBLES;
SUPER HEROES; TELEVISIONS;
TOYS, Action Figures)

Auction Services

Bonhams & Butterfields
220 San Bruno Ave.
San Francisco, CA 94103
ph: 415-861-7500 or 800-223-2854
fax: 415-861-8951
info.US@butterfields.com
http://www.butterfields.com
Auctioneers and appraisers of antiques, fine art and collectibles in all categories; specialty sales include posters, toys, decorative arts, furniture, photography, etc.; the largest full service auction in the West.

Collectors

Daniel Wachtenheim
P.O. Box 480444
Los Angeles, CA 90048
ph: 323-848-3053
dwachte915@aol.com
Wants to buy '60s and '70s TV related toys.

Scott Weiss
1158 26th St., #489
Santa Monica, CA 90403
ph: 310-264-7202
fax: 310-264-7203
sweiss5905@aol.com
Wants to buy movie and TV imprinted promotional advertising objects; metal, wood, plastic, glass, ceramic: pin-back buttons, pins, paperweights, tokens, snowdomes, watches, radios, rings, matchbooks, flashlights, letter openers, etc.

Craig Dawson
115 Oakley Blvd.
Scarborough, Ontario M1P 3P8 Canada
baddog@thebulletin.net
http://www.thebulletin.net
Wants to buy anything related to 1960 through early 1980s television shows: Charlies Angels, Bewitched, Beverly Hillbillies, Laverne & Shirley, MASH, Gilligan's Island, The Rookies, Munsters, Adam-12, Bonanza, The Patty Duke Show, etc.

Dealers

Jon Allan
Elmer's Nostalgia, Inc.
3 Putnam St.
Sanford, ME 04073-2024
ph: 207-324-2166
elmers@gwi.net
http://www.elmers.net

Michael Torres
Howdy Do
72 E. 7th St.
New York, NY 10003
ph: 212-979-1618
howdy72@aol.com
http://members.aol.com/howdy72
A New York City shop that specializes in celebrity TV-related toys and other popular culture memorabilia.

Jerry Ohlinger
Jerry Ohlinger's Movie Material Store, Inc.
242 W. 14th St.
New York, NY 10011-7206
ph: 212-989-0869
fax: 212-989-1660
jomms@aol.com
http://www.moviematerials.com
Buys and sells motion picture photos and posters from 1920 to present; also TV photos; research services available; free lists available; complete lists of 100,000 black & white photos or of 100,000 color photos are $4 each.

Ken Farrell
Just Kids Nostalgia
310 New York Ave.
Huntington, NY 11743
ph: 631-423-8449
info@justkidsnostalgia.com
http://www.justkidsnostalgia.com
Wants to buy vintage TV toys: lunch boxes, board games, Batman, Green Hornet, Superman, Bonanza, Captain Video, Howdy Doody, Rootie Kazootie, Star Trek, etc.

Dennis & Mary Luby
Casey's Collectible Corner
HCR 31 Box 30
No. Blenheim, NY 12131
ph: 607-588-6464
caseyscc@aol.com
Buys and sells collectible toys: comic characters, TV shows and personalities; also space and monster toys, sports collectibles, etc.

Bill & Joanne Bruegman
Toy Scouts, Inc.
137 Casterton Ave.
Akron, OH 44303-1543
ph: 330-836-0668
orders@toyscouts.com
http://www.toyscouts.com
Specializes in Baby-Boomer era toys and television memorabilia.

Ron Davison
TV Toy Memories
618 South Northwest Hwy. #179
Barrington, IL 60010
ph: 847-542-7473
cerealboxman@yahoo.com
http://www.tvtoymemories.com
Buys and sells 1950s through 1990s TV related memorabilia: toys, coloring books, advertising memorabilia, paper dolls, cereal dolls; most items are unused and many are autographed by the TV celebrity.

Jon & Carolyn Thurmond
Collectorholics
15006 Fuller
Grandview, MO 64030-4522
ph: 816-322-0906

Ronald George
Classic TV Books
P.O. Box 524
Bountiful, UT 84011-0524
ph: 801-292-0351
fax: 801-292-1580
rgeorge@weber.edu
http://www.ClassicTVBooks.com
Offers out-of-print books and magazines relating to favorite TV shows of the 1950s through 1980s; including paperback novels, old issues of TV Guide and other entertainment magazines, hardcover Whitman TV tie-ins, Big Little Books.

Stephen Albert
TVC Enterprises
6704 Fruit Flower Ave.
Las Vegas, NV 89130
ph: 760-495-7956 or 702-369-4106
fax: 603-658-0184
tvcollector@excite.com
http://www.angelfire.com/ma/tvcollector
Specialize in TV, movie, rock 'n' roll, music, theater & other media-related collectibles & memorabilia.

Eddie Brandt's Saturday Matinee
5006 Vineland Ave.
North Hollywood, CA 91601
ph: 818-506-4242 or 818-506-7722
fax: 818-506-5649
A great source for stills, posters, and lobby cards.

Trudy Prescott
Star Struck International
2791 F. North Texas St., Ste. 112
Fairfield, CA 94533
ph: 707-426-0811
fax: 707-426-0811
sales@starcollectibles.com
http://www.starcollectibles.com
Buys and sells memorabilia from TV, film and music: costumes, autographs, memorabilia.

Harold Balde
Fungus Amungus
21 Wellington St.
Orangeville, Ontario L9W 2L2 Canada
ph: 519-938-8808
boardwalk12345@yahoo.com
http://www.fungus-amungus.com
Collector and dealer of Classic TV shows; mostly from 16mm film with original commercials; specialty is 1950s and 1960s; hard-to-find and obscure TV shows; over 20,000 shows.

Experts

Sue Fox
416 Throop St.
North Babylon, NY 11704
ph: 631-376-0916
fax: 631-376-0916
oz@webspan.net
Specializes in television show related memorabilia.

Ted Hake
Hake's Americana & Collectibles Auction
P.O. Box 1444
York, PA 17405-1444
ph: 717-848-1333
Ted@hakes.com
http://www.hakes.com
Author of "Hake's Guide to TV Collectibles" and several other books on collectibles; always purchasing items for mail-bid auctions of Disneyana, historical Americana, toys, premiums, political items, character and other collectibles.

David Welch
P.O. Box 714
Murphysboro, IL 62966-0714
ph: 618-687-2282
fax: 618-684-2243
PEZDude1@aol.com
http://www.pezheads.net/dwelch
Wants 1950s-1960s TV show related items such as lunch boxes, games, toys, etc.; paying $5,000+ for rare items, especially super heroes.

Stephen Albert
TVC Enterprises
6704 Fruit Flower Ave.
Las Vegas, NV 89130
ph: 760-495-7956 or 702-369-4106
fax: 603-658-0184
tvcollector@excite.com
http://www.angelfire.com/ma/tvcollector
Consultant, freelance writer or researcher for production companies, books publishers etc. on the subject of TV nostalgia.

Bill Morgan
World of TV Toys, The
P.O. Box 91-1491
Los Angeles, CA 90091
ph: 714-379-6791
ccmail@tvtoys.com
http://www.tvtoys.com
Co-author of "Collector's Guide to TV Toys & Memorabilia '60s & '70s;" Web site has items for sale, collector's guide, online articles, links to TV show fan pages and celebrity Web sites; has appeared on PAX TVs "Treasures in Your Home."

Internet Resources

Bill Morgan
World of TV Toys, The
P.O. Box 91-1491
Los Angeles, CA 90091
ph: 714-379-6791
ccmail@tvtoys.com
http://www.tvtoys.com
Co-author of "Collector's Guide to TV Toys & Memorabilia '60s & '70s;" Web site has items for sale, collector's guide, online articles, links to TV show fan pages and celebrity Web sites; has appeared on PAX TVs "Treasures in Your Home."

Museums/Libraries

American Museum of the Moving Image
35 Ave. at 36 St.
Astoria, NY 11106
ph: 718-784-4520 or 718-784-0077
fax: 718-784-4681
info@ammi.org
http://www.ammi.org
  The only museum in the US devoted to the art, history, technology of film, television, video, interactive media; collection includes costumes, dolls, movie posters, magazines, TV sets, movie cameras, and other items of film & TV history.

Periodicals

Stacie Berger
Antique Trader Publications, Inc.
Magazine: Big Reel
P.O. Box 1050
Dubuque, IA 52004-1050
ph: 800-334-7165 or 800-482-4155
fax: 800-531-0880
stacie.berger@fwpubs.com
http://www.bigreel.com
  A monthly tabloid for movie and television memorabilia collectors and fans: ads, news, current & nostalgic feature articles, obits, etc.

Charlie's Angels

Collectors

Jack Condon
P.O. Box 57468
Sherman Oaks, CA 91403
ph: 818-789-0862
fax: 818-501-1004
ChrlAngels@aol.com
http://www.charliesangelsfan.com
  Always looking to buy or trade "Charlie's Angels" memorabilia.

Dark Shadows

Clubs/Associations

Dark Shadows Festival
Newsletter: Shadow Gram
P.O. Box 92
Maplewood, NJ 07040-0092
ph: 973-762-7208
webmaster@mpimedia.com
  Interested in the "Dark Shadows" TV series; holds annual convention, Dark Shadows Festival.

Experts

Sue Ellen Wilson
6173 Iroquois Trail
Mentor, OH 44060-2903
ph: 440-946-6348
fax: 440-951-3056
sewilsonoh@aol.com
  Dark Shadow collector and former publisher of "Dark Shadows Collectables Classifieds."

Dennis The Menace

Collectors

Pete Nowicki
1531 39th Ave.
San Francisco, CA 94122-3015
ph: 415-566-7506
portfire86@aol.com
  Collector seeks all toys and collectibles relating to Dennis the Menace and his friends; no comics, please.

Doctor Who

Clubs/Associations

St. Louis Celestial Intervention Agency
Newsletter: Time Lord Times
P.O. Box 733
Saint Louis, MO 63188
fax: 314-872-9270
tltimes@aol.com
http://members.aol.com/tltimes/stlcia.html
  One of the largest strictly Doctor Who clubs with local meetings in North America; excellent source for news and articles.

Gilligan's Island

Clubs/Associations

Bob Denver
Gilligan Fan Club
P.O. Box 269
Princeton, WV 24740
Bob@BobDenver.com
http://bobdenver.com
  Created by Bob & Drema Denver themselves, this site is a jam-packed three-hour tour for Gilligan fans of all ages: GI info directly from Bob; visit Maynard's Coffee House, hear the Denver's' oldies radio show; a must for GI fans!

Official Gilligan's Island Fan Club
gilligan@san.rr.com
http://www.gilligansisle.com
  The Professor found a way to make a computer out of coconuts and bamboo shoots located near the lagoon; site contains a ton of information, chat, message board, classifieds, audio/video/games and episode guides.

Gunsmoke

Collectors

Hank Clark
P.O. Box 812
Waterford, CA 95386-0812
ph: 209-874-2640
fax: 209-874-5750
conchosmith@hotmail.com
  Wants television and radio "Gunsmoke" items; autographs, photos, advertising, etc.

I Dream Of Jeannie

Collectors

Richard D. Barnes
1520 West 800 North
Salt Lake City, UT 84116-2019
ph: 801-521-4400
fax: 801-292-1947
  Collector/historian wants "Jeannie" scripts, press photos, news articles, posters, books, toys, board games, etc.

Experts

Richard D. Barnes
1520 West 800 North
Salt Lake City, UT 84116-2019
ph: 801-521-4400
fax: 801-292-1947
  Author of I.D. of J. works including "Going Hollywood," a collectors guide to I.D. of J., Barbara Eden and other Hollywood collectibles; also "Jeannie Guide," and "Diary of a Genie."

Internet Resources

Richard David Barnes
1520 W. 800 North
Salt Lake City, UT 84116
ph: 801-521-4400
fax: 801-292-1947
  Jeannie trivia, photos, items for sale.

I Love Lucy

Clubs/Associations

Thomas J. Watson
We Love Lucy/The International Lucille Ball Fan Club
Magazine: Star Notes
P.O. Box 56234
Sherman Oaks, CA 91413-1234
ph: 818-981-0752
fax: 818-981-0757
info@lucyfan.com
http://www.lucyfan.com
  Quarterly magazine focusing on collectibles pertaining to the "I Love Lucy" TV show and to Lucille Ball and other characters.

Dealers

Cathy's Closet
101 Greenway
Mesquite, TX 75182-9597
ph: 972-226-1352 or 888-BUY-LUCY
iselllucy@aol.com
http://www.lucystore.com
  Sells new "I Love Lucy" collectibles: Lucy Barbies, books, stamps, ceramics, clothing and more.

Experts

Ric Wyman
P.O. Box 436
Falconer, NY 14733-0436
ph: 716-665-3311
  Expert within the world of Lucille Ball nostalgia; author of "For the Love of Lucy: The Complete Guide for Collectors & Fans," and "The 'I Love Lucy' Book of Trivia;" interested in purchasing any Lucille Ball or Desi Arnaz memorabilia.

Thomas J. Watson
P.O. Box 56234
Sherman Oaks, CA 91413-1234
ph: 818-981-0752
fax: 818-981-0757
info@lucyfan.com
http://www.lucyfan.com
  Collects and specializes in Lucille Ball memorabilia.

Internet Resources

Todd Fuller
I Love Lucy Online
todd@sitcomsonline.com
http://www.sitcomsonline.com/ilovelucy.html
  Dedicated to I Love Lucy: episode guides, sounds, pictures, Lucy trivia, Lucy's bio, message board and more.

Museums/Libraries

Lucy-Desi Museum
212 Pine St.
Jamestown, NY 14701
ph: 716-484-0800
fax: 716-484-1018
info@lucy-desi.com
http://www.lucydesi.com
  Located in Lucille Ball's hometown, the museum tells the personal story of Lucille Ball and Desi Arnaz.

Lassie

(see also ANIMAL COLLECTIBLES, Dogs [Collies])

Clubs/Associations

Joan L. Neidhardt
Lassie Fan Club
Newsletter: Lassie Star, The
P.O. Box 1000
Abingdon, MD 21009
JLNCollies@aol.com
http://www.lassie.net

Collectors

Joan L. Neidhardt
P.O. Box 1000
Abingdon, MD 21009
JLNCollies@aol.com
http://www.lassie.net
  Buys and sells anything relating to Collies or to Lassie; old, new, unique; toys, figurines, character collectibles.

Dealers

Joan L. Neidhardt
Colliewood Productions, LLC
P.O. Box 1000
Abingdon, MD 21009
JLNCollies@aol.com
http://www.lassie.net
  Buys and sells anything relating to Collies or to Lassie; old, new, unique; toys, figurines, character collectibles.

Lost In Space

Clubs/Associations

Flint Mitchell
Lost in Space Fannish Alliance
Newsletter: LISFAN
7331 Terri Robyn St.
Saint Louis, MO 63129-5233
ph: 314-846-2846
lisfanedtr@aol.com
http://www.lisfan.com
Membership is free.

Internet Resources

Museum of Lost in Space Collectibles
support@lostintoys.com
http://www.lostintoys.com/museum
A virtual museum dedicated to the classic television series" Lost in Space."

Partridge Family

Collectors

Daniel Wachtenheim
P.O. Box 480444
Los Angeles, CA 90048
ph: 323-848-3053
dwachte915@aol.com
Buys, sells, trades Partridge Family items: bus, record cabinet, guitar, dolls, etc.; also wants character drum sets (Monkees, Kaptain Kool, etc.) and '60s and '70s TV related toys.

Private Eye

Collectors

Gary Pimenta
64 Lakeside Dr.
Tiverton, RI 02878-3111
Wants to buy memorabilia related to television private eye shows such as 77 Sunset Strip, Surfside 6, Hawaiian Eye; wants related toys, magazines, comic books, etc.; send photos and asking prices.

Private Eye (Man From UNCLE)

Clubs/Associations

Sue Cole
U.N.C.L.E. Headquarters
Newsletter: U.N.C.L.E. Headquarters Newsletter
P.O. Box 8403
Rolling Meadows, IL 60008
cgs@prodigy.net
Official fan club for the man/girl from U.N.C.L.E.; focuses on the "Man from U.N.C.L.E." reruns, the program and its memorabilia.

Lynda Mendoza, Ed.
Official McCallum Observer Fan Club, The
Journal: McCallum Observer, The
P.O. Box 313
Lansing, IL 60438-0313
ph: 708-895-0736
fax: 708-895-1184
davidmccallum@fan.com
http://www.davidmccallum.org
An authorized journal that contains information about actor David McCallum's present and past career; published four times each year.

Sky King

Collectors

Rod W. Carnahan
537 El Paso St.
Jacksonville, TX 75766
ph: 903-586-1355
rodcarnahan_toys@tyler.net
http://www.antique-center.com/classic.htm

Star Trek

Clubs/Associations

Starfleet
Newsletter: Starfleet Communique
200 Hiawatha Blvd.
Oakland, NJ 07436-3643
Membership@sfi.org
http://www.sfi.org
International Star Trek and science fiction club with chapters in many major US cities and overseas.

Russ Haslage
International Federation of Trekkers
Magazine: Voyages
P.O. Box 242
Lorain, OH 44052-0242
ops@iftcommand.com
http://www.iftcommand.com
International club interested in Star Trek; numerous regional chapters; known for its public and charity work.

Dealers

David Roberts
D & S Sci-fi Toy World
4701 NE 72nd Ave. #J222
Vancouver, WA 98661
ph: 360-666-4774
fax: 360-666-4868
dave@dnstoys.com
http://www.dnstoys.com
Specializes in Star Wars, Star Trek, Aliens and other sci-fi movie related toys and collectibles.

Experts

Larry Brooks
Playmates Star Trek Action Figure Page
lbrooks2@email.unc.edu
http://www.unc.edu/~lbrooks2/playmate.html
Specializes in Star Trek Playmates action figures; Web site has a complete listing and price guide of all Star Trek Playmates figures; place and view buy/sell/trade ads.

Internet Resources

Star Trek: WWW
comments@stwww.com
http://www.stwww.com
Bills itself as "The Mother of All Star Trek sites."

The Fugitive

Clubs/Associations

Texas Bob Reinhardt
F.U.G.I.T.I.V.E.S., The
Newsletter: Stafford Chronicle, The
222 Soft Wind
New Braunfels, TX 78133-2414
ph: 830-935-4618
The Fugitives is a special interest group based upon the character of Dr. Richard Kimble as created by Roy Huggins, and brought to life by David Janssen; focus is on helping others as Dr. Kimble did; annual conventions.

Experts

Rusty Pollard
Newsletter: On The Run
P.O. Box 461402
Garland, TX 75046-1402
ph: 972-675-6964 or 214-397-3080
RustyPollard@ev1.net
No longer published but all 33 back issues of bi-monthly newsletter still available; devoted to the 1960s TV series "The Fugitive," its star, David Janssen, and his career.

The Waltons

Museums/Libraries

Walton's Mountain Museum
P.O. Box 124
Schuyler, VA 22969
ph: 804-831-2000
ralph@blueridgeweb.com
http://www.the-waltons.com/museum.html
School and hometown village of Earl Hammer, Jr., creator of "The Waltons" television series.

Westerns

(see also COWBOY HEROES)

Collectors

Gary Pimenta
64 Lakeside Dr.
Tiverton, RI 02878-3111
Wants to buy pre-1970 Western television program collectibles and comic books including board games and toys based on Western TV shows; send photos and asking prices.

TELEVISIONS

(see also AUDIO-VISUAL; ELECTRICITY RELATED ITEMS; RADIOS; RADIOS, Vacuum Tubes for; TELEVISION SHOWS & MEMORABILIA)

Clubs/Associations

Ed Gable
Antique Wireless Association
Newsletter: Old Timer's Bulletin
Box E
Breesport, NY 14816
ph: 607-739-5443
fax: 607-796-6230
k2mp@eznet.net
http://www.antiquewireless.org
One of the world's largest and oldest historical radio collector organizations; purpose is to document and preserve the history of radio, telegraph and television artifacts.

Paul R. Farmer, Mem.
Mid-Atlantic Antique Radio Club
Magazine: Radio Age
P.O. Box 352
Washington, VA 22747-0352
oldradiotime@hotmail.com
http://www.maarc.org
Published monthly since 1975 for collectors interested in the history of radio and television; restoration, articles by early experts; free buy and sell ads; free sample.

Dealers

Harry Poster
Vintage TVs
P.O. Box 1883
South Hackensack, NJ 07606-0483
ph: 201-794-9606
fax: 201-794-9553
hposter@att.net
http://www.harryposter.com
Collecting old TVs (has over 150) since 1985; buys and sells 1920s - 1970s b&w, color, and mirror-in-lid TVs, parts, kits, CRTs, books, empty boxes; color adapters, TV signs, displays, sales literature; buys complete shops & collections.

Bruce & Charlotte Mager
Waves
251 W. 30th St.
New York, NY 10001
ph: 212-273-9616
c1wave@aol.com
http://www.wavesradio.com
Over 20 years experience specializing in vintage radios, phonographs, telegraphy, televisions, assorted electrical and mechanical apparatus, and related advertising memorabilia, books and pamphlets.

P. Assenza
Retro Classic TVs
P.O. Box 2631
Lake Ronkonkoma, NY 11779
info@antiquetvs.com
http://www.antiquetvs.com

John Okolowicz
624 Cedar Hill Rd., Ste. 100
Ambler, PA 19002-1504
ph: 215-542-1597
john@grillecloth.com
http://www.grillecloth.com
Buys, sells, trades pre-1950 radios and TVs in unusual or ornate plastic

or wooden cabinets; especially those made by Emerson or Stromberg Carlson.

John E. Kendall
Vintage Electronics
P.O. Box 436
Fallston, MD 21047-0436
maloney@vintage-electronics.com
http://www.vintage-electronics.com
Wants radios from the 1920s through 1960s; buys, sells tube and transistor radios, unusual TVs, early miniature or handheld TVs, tube audio and other early odd electronics; also related items such as books, schematics, tubes, ads, etc.

Tommy Meers
GARMCo
fax: 404-297-8161
Buys and sells vintage electronics including antique tube, crystal and transistor radios, phonographs (record players), microphones, televisions and related collectibles; on Internet since 1996; worldwide insured shipping.

Ty Cutkomp
33 Oak Lane
Davenport, IA 52803
ph: 319-323-7263
Buys, sells, trades early televisions: Automatic, Atlas, Majestic, National Republic, Transvision, Silverton, Televue, Viewtone, and any 7" console TV.

Experts

Glenn F. Bubenheimer
Glenn's Vintage T.V. Service
27851 Terrence
Livonia, MI 48154-3498
ph: 734-421-5574
fax: 602-661-8304
Has collected pre-1953 and select 1950s TVs for over 15 years and has repaired them for twenty years; considers himself an expert in values, history and theory; has over 200 pieces in his collection.

Mike Brooks
7335 Skyline
Oakland, CA 94611-1121
ph: 510-339-1751
deborahwb@aol.com
Buying tiny screen early models, especially wants pre-WWII mechanical spinning disc sets and mirror-in-lid TVs.

Museums/Libraries

Museum of Television & Radio
25 West 52nd St.
New York, NY 10019
ph: 212-621-6800 or 212-621-6600
publicrelations@mtr.org
http://www.mtr.org
Museum had two locations, one in New York City and one in Los Angeles.

Ed Gable
Antique Wireless Association's Electronic Communication Museum
Box E
Breesport, NY 14816
ph: 607-739-5443
fax: 607-796-6230
k2mp@eznet.net
http://www.antiquewireless.org
Open limited hours May through October; call or write before visiting; please enclose SASE if requesting a reply.

Larry Auman
Auman Museum of Radio & Television (R)
215 N. Tuscarawas Ave.
Dover, OH 44622
ph: 330-343-2297 or 330-364-1058
latv@webtv.net
http://www.geocities.com/TelevisionCity/Set/1930
Museum shows early days of electronic entertainment: 1940s movie theater, 1920s-1930s radios, over 300 different 1930-1950 TVs, and related items.

Museum of Television & Radio
465 N. Beverly Dr.
Beverly Hills, CA 90210
ph: 310-786-1000
publicrelations@mtr.org
http://www.mtr.org
Museum had two locations, one in New York City and one in Los Angeles.

Periodicals

John V. Terrey
Magazine: Antique Radio Classified
P.O. Box 2
Carlisle, MA 01741
ph: 978-371-0512
fax: 978-371-7129
arc@antiqueradio.com
http://www.antiqueradio.com
Antique radio's largest monthly about old radios, Art Deco, TVs, ham equip. - '40s, '50s, books, telegraph, etc.; lots of ads.

Repair Services

David B. Johnson
2336 S. Kenilworth Ave.
Berwyn, IL 60402
ph: 708-484-2743
Vintage TV and radio repairs and restorations (electronics and cosmetics).

Suppliers

Antique Electronic Supply
6221 S. Maple Ave.
Tempe, AZ 85283-2856
ph: 480-820-5411
fax: 800-706-6789
info@tubesandmore.com
http://www.tubesandmore.com
Large catalog carrying tubes, supplies, capacitors, transformers, chemicals, test equipment, wire, parts, tools, books, old fabric lamp cords, etc.

TEXTILES

(see also CLOTHING & ACCESSORIES, Vintage; COVERLETS; FEED & GRAIN BAGS; LOOMS; MILITARIA, Uniforms; QUILTS; REPAIR/RESTORATION/CONSERVATION, Textiles; RUGS; SAMPLERS; SEWING ITEMS & GO-WITHS; SHAWLS; MILITARIA, Silk Embroideries; STEVENGRAPHS; TIE-BACKS)

Appraisers

Betsey Telford
Betsy Telford's Antique Quilts dba Rocky Mountain Quilts
130 York St.
York Village, ME 03909
ph: 800-762-5940
fax: 207-351-3381
betsey@btantiquequilts.com
http://www.rockymountainquilts.com
Dealer, appraiser, expert specializes in quilts, feedsacks and textile restoration; buys, sells and restores antique quilts; has over 400 quilts dating from 1740 to 1940 in stock; restores quilts and hooked using period fabrics.

Barbara Langston, ISA
11260 Beach Blvd.
Jacksonville, FL 32256
ph: 904-642-1003
linenlady@aol.com
Specializes in the appraisal of textiles including lace and linens.

Caroline Ashleigh
Caroline Ashleigh Associates, Inc.
800 E. Lincoln
Birmingham, MI 48009
ph: 248-613-4056
fax: 248-792-2545
carolineashleigh@appraiseyourart.com
http://www.appraiseyourart.com
Specializes in professional appraisals of fine art, antiques, textiles, residential contents; participating appraiser in the "Antiques Roadshow;" Certified Senior Member and Regional Representative of the Appraisers Association of America.

Juliene T. Neese, ISA
Juliene Neese Antiques
4343 Lindbergh
Addison, TX 75001
ph: 972-239-3392
fax: 972-934-8520
nescobro@wans.net
Appraises needlework: samplers, quilts, embroidery.

Terri Ellis, ISA
Mistletoe Estate Sales & Appraisals
1205 Mistletoe Dr.
Fort Worth, TX 76110-1018
ph: 817-926-9424
fax: 817-926-0386
tquilts@airmail.net
http://www.mistletoesales.net
Certified quilt appraiser by the American Quilter's Society; Accredited

Member of the ISA; also buys and sells vintage textiles.

Barbara Pickett, GCA, MCA, GGAC
Pickett Fence Productions
P.O. Box 771
Lakewood, CA 90714-0771
ph: 562-425-4149
fax: 562-425-4149
pickettB2@aol.com

Bette G. Bell, ISA CAPP
Guildmark Appraisal & Estate Sale Services, LLC
P.O. Box 952
Edmonds, WA 98020
ph: 425-775-5650
fax: 425-670-6957
stashn33@gte.net
http://www.guildmarkappraisal.com
Appraises quilts and other textiles such as samplers, ethnographic textiles, linens; handles estate sales throughout the NW; Certified Member of the International Society of Appraisers; appraising for over 16 years.

Auction Services

Jo Kris
Skinner, Inc.
63 Park Plaza
The Heritage on the Garden
Boston, MA 02116
ph: 617-350-5400
fax: 617-350-5429
info@skinnerinc.com
http://www.skinnerinc.com
Established in 1971, Skinner Inc. is the fourth largest auction house in the US; has offices in Boston and Bolton, MA.

Book Sellers

Dennis Marquand
Dennis B. Marquand Books
P.O. Box 1187
Culver City, CA 90232-1187
ph: 310-313-0177
fax: 310-915-9922
dennis@rugbooks.com
http://www.rugbooks.com
Specialize in books on ethnographic textiles from around the world with a focus on Oriental rugs, embroideries, textiles from Central Asian, Navajo, Tibet, Guatemala, Africa.

Clubs/Associations

Pat Funk, Ex. Dir.
Knitting Guild of America, The
Magazine: Cast On
ph: 859-268-2349
fax: 859-266-9396
patfunk@tkga.com
http://www.tkga.com
National association of hand and machine knitters; provides education for hand & machine knitters; "Cast On" contains articles, ads, seminars, correspondence courses, competition, etc.

Costume Society of America, The
Newsletter: CSA News
55 Edgewater Dr.
P.O. Box 73
Earleville, MD 21919-0073
ph: 410-275-1619x or 800-CSA-9447
fax: 410-275-8936
webmaster@costumesocietyamerica.com
http://www.costumesocietyamerica.com
*Dedicated to advancing the global
understanding of all aspects of dress
and appearance; also publishes the
journal "Dress."*

Stephanie Kline Morehouse
Textile Group of Los Angeles, Inc.
894 South Bronson Ave.
Los Angeles, CA 90005-3605
ph: 323-939-2240
fax: 323-939-2240
tglaincorp@aol.com
*Non-profit society formed in 1979 to
further interest in all and any type of
carpets, textiles or related arts;
regular meetings, lectures, viewing
private collections; textile design,
conservation, history.*

Margaret Geiss-Mooney
Bay Area Art Conservation Guild
1124 Clelia Court
Petaluma, CA 94954-5617
ph: 707-763-8694
mgmooney@moonware.net
http://palimpsest.stanford.edu/baacg
*Non-profit educational organization
with a membership reflecting the
various disciplines of the conservation
and preservation fields; promotes
general knowledge of cultural
preservation and conservation
activities.*

Dealers

Betsey Telford
Betsy Telford's Antique Quilts dba
  Rocky Mountain Quilts
130 York St.
York Village, ME 03909
ph: 800-762-5940
fax: 207-351-3381
betsey@btantiquequilts.com
http://www.rockymountainquilts.com
*Dealer, appraiser, expert specializes
in quilts, feedsacks and textile
restoration; buys, sells and restores
antique quilts; has over 400 quilts
dating from 1740 to 1940 in stock;
restores quilts and hooked using
period fabrics.*

M. Finkel & Daughter
936 Pine St.
Philadelphia, PA 19107
ph: 215-627-7797
fax: 215-627-8199
mailbox@finkelantiques.com
http://www.finkelantiques.com
*Specializes in schoolgirl samplers and
needlework from the 18th and 19th
centuries; publishes a catalog,
"Samplings," twice a year; available
by subscription.*

Marla Mallett
Marla Mallett Textiles
1690 Johnson Rd. NE
Atlanta, GA 30306
ph: 404-872-3356 or 877-542-0841
marlam@mindspring.com
http://www.marlamallett.com
*Specializes in antique flat woven
tribal Oriental rugs, bags, kilims
(kelims); also features handwoven
tapestries, embroideries and other
textile art from around the world;
2,800 photos illustrate a variety of
textile topics.*

Lydia Kulesov
Golden Thread Antiques
2634 West River Parkway
Minneapolis, MN 55406
ph: 888-645-0542 or 612-728-9696
marks@4insight.com
http://www.goldenthread.com

Diane McGee
Diane McGee Estate Clothing Company
5225 Jackson
Omaha, NE 68106-1331
ph: 402-551-0727
*Mail order only; specializing in
vintage linens and other textiles.*

Billie & John McBride
South Texas Trading Company
P.O. Box 857
Port Aransas, TX 78373
ph: 361-749-6149 or 800-484-9293
  x3474
STFNandTRADING@centurytel.net
http://www.southtexastrading.com
*Specializes in vintage textiles, lace and
accessories.*

Meg Andrews
Meg Andrews, Costumes & Textiles
U.K.
ph: +44 1582 460107
fax: +44 1582 461112
meg.andrews@cwcom.net
http://www.meg-andrews.com
*Specializes in 18th/19th c. English
costumes & accessories, 19th c.
paisley shawls, Arts & Crafts textiles
incl. William Morris, Chinese court
costumes and textiles, worldwide
hangings, 18th/19th c. samplers.*

Experts

Evelyn Kennedy
Sewtique, Inc.
391 Long Hill Rd.
P.O. Box 1293
Groton, CT 06340-1293
ph: 860-445-7320 or 800-332-9122
fax: 860-445-1448
sewtique@aol.com
http://www.sewtiqueonline.com
*Specialist in restoration, preservation
& conservation of apparel and
textiles; full service by mail/phone or
appt.; appraises textiles, laces,
tapestries, etc.; removes spots &
stains; teaches textile appraisal &
restoration workshops.*

Alda Horner
3700 Dean Dr., Unit #3301
Ventura, CA 93003
ph: 805-642-7953
*Author of "The Official Price Guide
to Linens, Lace, and Other Fabrics."*

Museums/Libraries

American Textile History Museum
491 Dutton St.
Lowell, MA 01854-4221
ph: 978-441-0400
fax: 978-441-1412
espear@athm.org
http://www.athm.org
*Outstanding collection of textiles and
textile making machinery and
equipment; tools, machines, prints,
photographs, business records,
industry periodicals, textiles,
swatches, sample books, trade
catalogs, etc.*

Rhode Island School of Design Museum
224 Benefit St.
Providence, RI 02903-2723
ph: 401-454-6500
fax: 401-454-6556
mshaw@risd.edu
http://www.risd.edu/museum.cfm
*Apparel, architecture, furniture,
graphic design, industrial design,
interior architecture, landscape
architecture.*

Shelburne Museum, Inc.
P.O. Box 10
Shelburne, VT 05482-0010
ph: 802-985-3346 or 802-985-3348
fax: 802-985-2331
info@shelburnemuseum.org
http://www.shelburnemuseum.org
*37 historic structures and exhibit
buildings; diverse collection of
American folk, fine, decorative and
utilitarian art.*

Hilary Jay, Dir.
Philadelphia University, The Goldey
  Paley Design Center
4200 Henry Ave.
Philadelphia, PA 19144
ph: 215-951-2860
fax: 215-951-2662
JayH@philau.edu
http://www.whatisdesigntoday.com
*A repository for over 200,000
historical textiles and textile-related
artifacts; serves as an educational
resource for students, faculty,
researchers, and the general public;
invites public to engage in learning
about contemporary design.*

Textile Museum, The
Newsletter: Textile Museum Bulletin,
The
2320 S St. NW
Washington, DC 20008
ph: 202-667-0441
fax: 202-483-0994
info@textilemuseum.org
http://www.textilemuseum.org
*Museum dedicated to furthering the
understanding of mankind's creative*

*achievements in the textile arts;
rotating exhibits drawn largely from
the museum's collections featuring
works from the eastern and western
hemispheres.*

Colleen Callahan
Valentine Richmond History Center
1015 East Clay St.
Richmond, VA 23219
ph: 804-649-0711
fax: 804-643-3510
info@richmondhistorycenter.com
http://www.richmondhistorycenter.com
*Largest costume and textile collection
in the South.*

Maryhill Museum of Art
35 Maryhill Museum Dr.
Goldendale, WA 98620-4601
ph: 509-773-3733
fax: 509-773-6138
MaryHill@gorge.net
http://www.maryhillmuseum.org
*Romanian folk textiles, ecclesiastical
embroideries, San Blas mola's and
1946 miniature haute couture
mannequins.*

Museum for Textiles, The
55 Centre Ave.
Toronto, Ontario M5G 2H5 Canada
ph: 416-599-5321 or 416-599-5515
fax: 416-599-2911
info@museumfortextiles.on.ca
http://www.museumfortextiles.on.ca
*The only museum in Canada
exclusively devoted to the collecting,
exhibition and documentation of
textiles from around the world.*

Mississippi Valley Textile Museum
3 Rosamond St. East
Almonte, Ontario K0A 1A0 Canada
ph: 613-256-3754
fax: 613-256-1307
mvtm@magma.ca
http://
  www.textilemuseum.mississippimills.com
*Museum provides information on the
early mills and their owners; features
displays of period offices, plus
artifacts and machinery related to the
beginnings of the textile industry.*

Periodicals

HALI Publications, Ltd.
Magazine: HALI
St. Giles House
50 Poland St.
London, W1F 4AX U.K.
ph: 020 7970 4600
fax: 020 7578 7222
hali@centaur.co.uk
http://www.hali.com
*"HALI" is the leading bi-monthly
international publication in the field
of carpet and textile art; an invaluable
encyclopedic source of information
with original research articles,
reviews of museum collections, etc.;
high color.*

Blankets

Experts

Barry Friedman
P.O. Box 55492
Valencia, CA 91385-0492
ph: 661-255-2365
BarryF@thevine.net
http://www.blanketboy.com
*Buys/sells pre-1945 Indian style wool
or cotton blankets by Pendleton,
Beacon, Capps, Esmond, Shuler &
Benninghofen, American Indian
Blanket Mills, Knight, Racine, Buell,
Jacobs Oregon City, Provo; plus
related catalogs and ads.*

Embroidery

Clubs/Associations

Embroiderers Guild of America
335 W. Braodway, Ste. 100
Louisville, KY 40202
ph: 502-589-6956
fax: 502-584-7900
egahq@aol.com
http://www.egausa.org
*Encourages the study of embroidery in
all its forms: regional chapters,
merchandise, news, needle arts,
children activities, gallery, seminars,
certification, etc.*

Experts

Ita Aber
4465 Douglas Ave, #8G
Bronx, NY 10471-3519
ph: 718-548-3355 or 212-877-7311
fax: 718-548-7888
*Specializes in old and new needle-
work; also repairs beadwork; author
of "The Art of Judaic Needlework."*

Museums/Libraries

Cooper-Hewitt Museum National
Museum of Design, Smithsonian
Institution
2 East 91st St.
New York, NY 10128
ph: 212-860-6868 or 212-849-8300
publicinfo@ch.si.edu
http://www.si.edu/ndm
*Can identify old lace, but are not
allowed to access value.*

Repro. Sources

Elizabeth Creeden
Sampler, The
84 Court St.
Plymouth, MA 02360
ph: 508-746-7077
fax: 508-747-7540
*Has knowledge of 17th, 18th and 19th
C. needlework in surface embroidery,
needlepoint (tent stitch) evenweave
stitching and crewel; reproduction and
adaptations can be drawn, charted or
designed and stitched; coat of arms,
samplers, etc.*

Fabric

Dealers

Dan Kelley
Experienced Denim
P.O. Box 239
Fayetteville, AR 72702-0239
ph: 501-444-7541 or 800-336-4694
fax: 501-521-8331
exd@edenim.com
http://www.edenim.com
*Wants '40s-'50s drapery (barkcloth)
with tropical, mod geometrics, large
flowered prints, many types of vintage
fabrics; send SASE for free list of
items wanted.*

Eugenie Gelman
Genie's Fab Fabrics
U.K.
genie@thebrighton.demon.co.uk
http://www.thebrighton.demon.co.uk
*Buys, sells, collects original fabric
from the 1950s to 1970s: curtains,
cushions, remnants, rolls.*

Lace & Linens

Appraisers

Barbara Langston, ISA
11260 Beach Blvd.
Jacksonville, FL 32256
ph: 904-642-1003
linenlady@aol.com
*Specializes in the appraisal of textiles
including lace and linens.*

Nance Searle, ISA
Searle Appraisal Practice
1355 Paige Ave.
Eugene, OR 97405
ph: 541-684-4038
fax: 541-683-6084
nms@jps.net
*Appraises all quilt and household
related textiles including linens, lace,
soft furnishings, antique/vintage
sewing notions and toy sewing
machines.*

Bette G. Bell, ISA CAPP
Guildmark Appraisal & Estate Sale
Services, LLC
P.O. Box 952
Edmonds, WA 98020
ph: 425-775-5650
fax: 425-670-6957
stashn33@gte.net
http://www.guildmarkappraisal.com
*Appraises quilts and other textiles
such as samplers, ethnographic
textiles, linens; handles estate sales
throughout the NW; Certified Member
of the International Society of
Appraisers; appraising for over 16
years.*

Clubs/Associations

International Old Lacers, Inc.
Magazine: International Old Lacers
  Bulletin
P.O. Box 554
Flanders, NJ 07836
iolinc@aol.com
http://members.aol.com/iolinc/ioli.html

Dealers

Marsha Manchester
Milady's Mercantile
17 South Main St.
Middleboro, MA 02346
ph: 508-946-2121
*Buys and sells linen and lace, and
ladies accessories, i.e., bridal
handkerchiefs, fans, shawls.*

Cynthia Cooper
Main St. Antiques Linen Room
P.O. Box 586
Farmington, CT 06034-0586
ph: 860-677-5423
fax: 860-677-5423
cynthia@antique-linens.com
http://www.antique-linens.com
*Extensive selection of antique and
vintage linens, most in pristine
condition: pillow cases, shams, linen
sheets, coverlets, tablecloths, napkins,
place mats, hand towels, handkerchiefs, curtains.*

Lydia Reed
Wyndham Needleworks
P.O. Box 248
Eastford, CT 06242
ph: 860-974-1214
fax: 860-974-1215
lydia@wyndhamneedleworks.com
http://www.wyndhamneedleworks.com
Buys and sells linen and lace.

Pahaka September
Pahaka
19 Fox Hill
Upper Saddle River, NJ 07458-1314
ph: 201-327-1464
pahakasept@aol.com
*Buys and sells quality lace, curtains,
bed and table linens, fabrics,
embroidery, etc.; by appointment or
mail order; sorry, no catalog.*

Pattyann Wilson
Patty's Prettys
P.O. Box 282
Roosevelt, NJ 08555-0282
ph: 609-443-6081
msnearmint@juno.com
*Specializes in antique and vintage
lace, quilts, linen and other findings;
buys, sells, trades.*

Susan & Michelle Horowitz
Quilted Corner, The
124 Fourth Ave.
New York, NY 10003-4903
ph: 212-505-6568
michelle@quiltedcorner.com
http://www.quiltedcorner.com
*Carries a wide assortment of vintage
linens, tablecloths, napkins, tea
towels, souvenir pillows, drapes and
textiles.*

Lois Lamb
Vintage Linens
4268 Persimmon Woods Dr.
Charleston, SC 29420
ph: 843-225-4268
vintagelinens@earthlink.net
http://www.vintagelinens.com
*Wants to buy antique linens that are
at least 50 years old; wants high
quality linens only including
pillowcases, sheets, bed covers,
doilies, runners, cloths, napkins, lace
curtains, etc.; linens with monograms
always a plus.*

Coria Fierbaugh
Sweethaven Lace
4681 Bloomfield Rd.
Taylorsville, KY 40071
ph: 502-477-8819
*Collector, dealer and expert in antique
lace and linen; also does repairs.*

Elizabeth M. Kurella
Lace Merchant, The
P.O. Box 244
Whiting, IN 46395
ph: 219-659-1124
ekurella@elizabethkurella.com
http://www.elizabethkurella.com
*Buys, sells, and appraises lace and
linens; offers many pieces of antique
lace for sale; author of "The Secrets
of Real Lace," and "Guide to Lace &
Linens."*

Sue Loomer
Grand Remnants
1136 Grand Ave.
Saint Paul, MN 55105
ph: 651-222-0221
grandremnants@aol.com
http://www.grandremnants.com
*Specializes in antique and vintage
fabric, linens and other textiles:
chenille, barkcloth, authentic quilt
cotton, lace, buttons and more.*

Sabine Casten
Lace Collection, The
558 Monroe
River Forest, IL 60305
ph: 708-366-0756
*Buys and sells linen and lace; also
interested in buttons.*

Karen Dawkins
Legacy Linens
1321 Dartmouth
Denton, TX 76201
ph: 940-382-5623 or 940-382-0181
fax: 940-591-0262
*Wants to buy lace and fancy white
linens in good condition; also baby
clothes, textiles and pre-1960 print
table cloths and kitchen towels gives
lectures and seminars on vintage
linens, lace, hats & jewelry.*

Rebecca Nohe
Quartermoon Market
315 East Pikes Peak Ave.
Colorado Springs, CO 80903
ph: 719-633-3999
Buys and sells linen and lace.

Jude Seyk
Vintage Collection
356 Main St.
Half Moon Bay, CA 94019-1724
ph: 650-712-0366
fax: 650-726-545
vintgecol@aol.com
http://www.vintagecollection.net
*Appraises, buys and sells linen and
lace; also old yardage, buttons, quilts,
sewing implements, sewing machines
and miniature sewing machines.*

Jules Kliot
Lacis
3163 Adeline St.
Berkeley, CA 94703-2401
ph: 510-843-7178
fax: 510-843-5018
staff@lacis.com
http://www.lacis.com
*Antique & historic textiles, lace from
the 16th century, vintage garments and
accessories; sells books and supplies
for costume, lace and embroidery; also
offers repairs and conservation
services.*

Jonathan Page
Honiton Lace Shop, The
44 High St.
Honiton
Devon, EX14 1PJ U.K.
ph: +44 (0)1404 42416
fax: +44 (0)1404 47797
shop@honitonlace.com
http://www.honitonlace.com
*Specializes in fine antique lace, lace
making equipment, bridal veils, and
related books and giftware.*

Experts

Marsha Manchester
Milady's Mercantile
17 South Main St.
Middleboro, MA 02346
ph: 508-946-2121
*Author of "Vintage White Linens, A
to Z" (Schiffer Pub.)*

Evelyn Kennedy
Sewtique, Inc.
391 Long Hill Rd.
P.O. Box 1293
Groton, CT 06340-1293
ph: 860-445-7320 or 800-332-9122
fax: 860-445-1448
sewtique@aol.com
http://www.sewtiqueonline.com
*Specialist in restoration, preservation
& conservation of apparel and
textiles; full service by mail/phone or
appt.; appraises textiles, laces,
tapestries, etc.; removes spots &
stains; teaches textile appraisal &
restoration workshops.*

Mary Beth Temple
Mary Beth Temple.com
P.O. Box 4
Tenafly, NJ 07670
ph: 201-569-5571
fax: 201-569-9170
VintageLin@aol.com
http://www.marybethtemple.com
*An expert in vintage linens and
textiles, especially in their care and
cleaning; also buys, sells vintage
linens, fabrics; offers lectures and
conservation supplies; author of
"Rescuing Vintage Textiles."*

Holly Van Sciver
130 Cascadilla Park
Ithaca, NY 14850
ph: 607-277-0498
vsblace@twcny.rr.com
*Specializes in bobbin lace and lace
making only; can help in identifying.*

Mary Lou Kueker
Heritage Lace Consulting
P.O. Box 15822
Arlington, VA 22215
ph: 301-490-5432
askus@laceconsultant.com
http://www.laceconsultant.com
*Specializing in antique lace and
linens; identification and appraisal
for all textiles; also cleaning and
repair of fine laces and linens.*

Elizabeth M. Kurella
Lace Merchant, The
P.O. Box 244
Whiting, IN 46395
ph: 219-659-1124
ekurella@elizabethkurella.com
http://www.elizabethkurella.com
*Author of "The Secrets of Real Lace,"
"Guide to Lace & Linens,"
"Complete Guide to Vintage
Textiles," and "Pocket Guide to
Valuable Old Lace & Lacy Linens."*

Internet Resources

Joeanna Smith
Heirloom Creations, Inc.
Joeanna@LegacyOfLace.com
http://www.legacyoflace.com
*This site is dedicated to the study of
antique lacy; designed to be a
reference for the study of mainly
Western European laces.*

Misc. Services

Unique Art Lace Cleaners
5926 Delmar Blvd.
Saint Louis, MO 63112
ph: 314-725-2900
fax: 314-725-3142
*Specializes in cleaning old textiles,
linens and lace.*

Museums/Libraries

Paula Harten
Lace Museum, The
552 South Murphy Ave.
Sunnyvale, CA 94086
ph: 408-730-4695
ronharten@earthlink.net
http://www.thelacemuseum.org
*Textiles, lace, linen; guild classes,
teaching, museum gift shop; purpose
is to keep the art of lace making alive
for future generations.*

Needlework

Appraisers

Cauleen Viscoff, ISA CAPP
Viscoff Appraisal Services, Inc.
266 Charlotte St., Ste. 277
Peterborough, Ontario K9J 2V4 Canada
ph: 866-221-3493 or 705-745-5514
fax: 705-745-5110
viscoffappraisals@on.aibn.com
http://www.viscoffappraisals.com
*Specializes in the appraisal of
needlework.*

Clubs/Associations

American Needlepoint Guild, Inc.
P.O. Box 1027
Cordova, TN 38088-1027
ph: 901-755-3728
fax: 901-755-3803
anginfo@needlepoint.org
http://www.needlepoint.org
*An educational, non-profit organiza-
tion whose purpose is educational and
cultural development through
participation in and encouragement of
interest in the art of needlepoint; for
all stitchers, whether amateur or
professional.*

Dealers

Carol Huber
40 Ferry Rd.
Old Saybrook, CT 06475
ph: 860-388-6809
fax: 860-434-9709
hubers@antiquesamplers.com
http://www.antiquesamplers.com
*Specializes in American and English
samplers, silk embroideries,
needlework pictures, and textile
accessories from the 17th, 18th and
19th centuries.*

Ruth J. Van Tassel
Van Tassel Baumann
690 Sugartown Rd.
Malvern, PA 19355
ph: 610-647-3330
http://www.antiquesandfineart.com/
tasselbaumann
*With Donald O. Baumann, specializes
in samplers and other schoolgirl
needlework; also offers needlework
conservation.*

Experts

Ita Aber
4465 Douglas Ave, #8G
Bronx, NY 10471-3519
ph: 718-548-3355 or 212-877-7311
fax: 718-548-7888
*Specializes in old and new needle-
work; also repairs beadwork; author
of "The Art of Judaic Needlework."*

Repro. Sources

Susan Bloomquist
Stitch Niche, The
208 Wild Tiger Rd.
Boulder, CO 80302
ph: 303-442-6556
fax: 303-546-6133
info@stitch1.com
http://www.stitch1.com
*Offers custom needlepoint textiles for
fine wood furniture; authentic
needlepoint reproduction of Berlin
wool work.*

Needlework (Judaic)

(see also JUDAICA)

Experts

Ita Aber
4465 Douglas Ave, #8G
Bronx, NY 10471-3519
ph: 718-548-3355 or 212-877-7311
fax: 718-548-7888
*Consultations, restorations and
commissions; works with architects
and decorators; lecturer, historian,
author of book and many articles on
same.*

Tablecloths

Clubs/Associations

Pam Glasell
Vintage Tablecloth Lover's Club
13541 Destino St.
Cerritos, CA 90703
ph: 562-440-7451
pam@gramasattic.net
http://www.vintagetableclothsclub.com
*For collectors of vintage printed
tablecloths of the 1930s through
1950s; online collecting club with chat
rooms, resource pages, photo albums,
stain guides and links to auction sites
and Web sites specializing in vintage
linens.*

Collectors

Chloe Ross
7553 Norton Ave. Apt. 4
Los Angeles, CA 90046-5500
ph: 213-874-3044
trstrap@aol.com
*Wants tablecloths with maps,
graphics or states, amusement parks,
locations; may be worn and some
stains OK; no AK or CA; especially
wants East Coast, Midwest, New
England or FL; buy or trade.*

Dealers

Helene Guarnaccia
52 Coach Lane
Fairfield, CT 06430
ph: 203-374-6034
greatstufftwo@aol.com
Specializes in handkerchiefs, scarves and tablecloths.

Susan & Michelle Horowitz
Quilted Corner, The
124 Fourth Ave.
New York, NY 10003-4903
ph: 212-505-6568
michelle@quiltedcorner.com
http://www.quiltedcorner.com
Carries a wide assortment of vintage linens, tablecloths, napkins, tea towels, souvenir pillows, drapes and textiles.

Paula Rubenstein
65 Prince St.
New York, NY 10012
ph: 212-966-8954
Specializes in vintage tablecloths.

Tapestries

Appraisers

James A. Ffrench
Beauvais Carpets
12 East 86th St., Apt. 736
New York, NY 10028
ph: 212-688-2265
Jaffrench@aol.com
http://www.beauvaiscarpets.com
Specializes in the appraisal of period carpets, tapestries and textiles of historical significance, both European and Eastern dating from 15th century to present.

Guido Muzzarelli
Appraisals & Valuations
4244 Laurelgrove Ave.
Studio City, CA 91604-1623
ph: 818-766-0605
fax: 818-766-3025
guidom@earthlink.net
Accredited Senior Member of the American Society of Appraisers and Appraisers Association of America; offers appraisals of Persian, Oriental and European carpets, rugs and tapestries for estates, insurance, donations.

Dealers

Marla Mallett
Marla Mallett Textiles
1690 Johnson Rd. NE
Atlanta, GA 30306
ph: 404-872-3356 or 877-542-0841
marlam@mindspring.com
http://www.marlamallett.com
Specializes in antique flat woven tribal Oriental rugs, bags, kilims (kelims); also features handwoven tapestries, embroideries and other textile art from around the world; 2,800 photos illustrate a variety of textile topics.

Allan Arthur
Cyber Rug Center
25 Bennett St.
Atlanta, GA 30309
ph: 800-686-7030 or 404-350-9560
aarthur@cyberrug.com
http://www.cyberrug.com
Buys and sells antique Oriental rugs, Persian rugs, Art Deco rugs, Chinese rugs, Kelim & flat woven rugs, Coptic and Asian textiles, European rugs and tapestries, Kashmir shawls, and American hooked and folk art rugs.

Ron Whaley
Her Castle Tapestry
134 Nelson St. #E
Arroyo Grande, CA 93420
ph: 800-350-3850
tapestry@fix.net
http://www.fix.net/~rwhaley
Sells large line of European tapestries: medieval, hunt scenes, nature scenes, florals, romantic scenes.

Experts

Evelyn Kennedy
Sewtique, Inc.
391 Long Hill Rd.
P.O. Box 1293
Groton, CT 06340-1293
ph: 860-445-7320 or 800-332-9122
fax: 860-445-1448
sewtique@aol.com
http://www.sewtiqueonline.com
Specialist in restoration, preservation & conservation of apparel and textiles; full service by mail/phone or appt.; appraises textiles, laces, tapestries, etc.; removes spots & stains; teaches textile appraisal & restoration workshops.

Repair Services

Hayko Restoration & Conservation
857 Lexington Ave., 2nd Floor
New York, NY 10021
ph: 212-717-5400
fax: 212-717-5400
info@hayko.com
http://www.hayko.com
Restoration and conservation of antique rugs; 20 years experience with carpets and tapestries; at your home or in the studio; references on request.

THANKSGIVING COLLECTIBLES

(see HOLIDAY COLLECTIBLES)

THEFT & FRAUD

(see ART THEFT & FRAUD)

THERMOMETERS

Clubs/Associations

Warren D. Harris
Thermometer Collectors Club of America
<u>Newsletter: Thermometer Reference</u>
6130 Rampart Dr.
Carmichael, CA 95608
ph: 916-966-3490 or 916-654-2097
fax: 916-966-3490
jockobwca@aol.com
http://www.angelfire.com/ma/thermo6

Experts

Richard Porter
49 Zarahelma Rd.
P.O. Box 944
Onset, MA 02558-0944
ph: 508-295-5504
thermometerman@aol.com
http://members.aol.com/
thermometerman/index.html
"The Thermometer Man;" his large collection featured in "Ripley's Believe It or Not" and the "Guiness Computer of World Records;" curator of the world's only thermometer museum; motto: "Always open, always free, with about 3,600 to see."

Warren D. Harris
6130 Rampart Dr.
Carmichael, CA 95608
ph: 916-966-3490 or 916-654-2097
fax: 916-966-3490
jockobwca@aol.com
http://www.angelfire.com/ma/thermo6
Wants decorative pre-1930 non advertising, non commercial, non clinical thermometers of every kind; mercury-in-the-tube type preferred; also wants thermometer related ephemera.

Museums/Libraries

Richard Porter, Curator
Porter Thermometer Museum
49 Zarahelma Rd.
P.O. Box 944
Onset, MA 02558-0944
ph: 508-295-5504
thermometerman@aol.com
http://members.aol.com/
thermometerman/index.html
World's largest private collection of thermometers from American and all over the world; representing over 100 manufacturers and featured in over 100 articles and 39 TV clips.

THERMOS BOTTLES

(see LUNCH BOXES)

THIRD REICH

(see MILITARIA, German)

TICKETS

(see also MOVIE MEMORABILIA; MUSIC; PAPER COLLECTIBLES; SPORTS COLLECTIBLES; TRANSPORTATION COLLECTIBLES; WORLD'S FAIRS & EXPOSITIONS)

Dealers

Jim Crump
Ticket Place Collectibles
P.O. Box 767
East Freetown, MA 02717
ph: 508-763-3502
fax: 508-763-9291
tickets@ticketplace.com
Specializes in unused tickets and stubs to sporting events, special events and concerts; wants to buy almost any kind of ticket or ticket stub out there; also has Elvis Presley ticket stubs for sale.

TIE BARS, CLIPS & TACKS

(see also CLOTHING & ACCESSORIES, Vintage; CUFF LINKS; GEMS & JEWELRY)

Collectors

Norman Landis
1315 Marbendale Ct.
Saint Louis, MO 63122
ph: 314-821-7933

Dean Hodgdon
2920 E. 77th St.
Tulsa, OK 74136-8723
ph: 918-494-0225 or 918-582-9918
d.hodgdon@worldnet.att.net
Wants company pins or tie tacks with years of services and company names; buys and trades; no tie bars, please.

TIE-BACKS

Collectors

Sandie Bush
516 N. Brian St.
Santa Maria, CA 93454
ph: 805-925-9756
Wants to buy glass and metal curtain tie-back holders.

TIFFANY ITEMS

(see also GEMS & JEWELRY; GLASS, Art; LAMPS & LIGHTING, Tiffany/Handel/Pairpoint; SILVER)

Appraisers

Arlie Sulka
Lillian Nassau Ltd.
220 E. 57th St.
New York, NY 10022
ph: 212-759-6062
fax: 212-832-9493
lilnassau@aol.com
http://www.lilliannassau.com
Specialist Tiffany appraiser: blown glass, lamps, windows and ceramics.

Paul G. Bailey, ISA
Antique Appraisal & Estate Services
12819 SE 38th St., PMB 320
Bellevue, WA 98006-1395
ph: 425-746-2777
fax: 425-746-3793
antiquabailey@aol.com
30 years experiencing appraising Tiffany.

Dealers

Bill Holland
William Holland Fine Arts
1554 Paoli Pike
PMB #300
West Chester, PA 19380
ph: 610-344-9848
fax: 610-344-0651
bill@hollandarts.com
http://www.hollandarts.com
Buys and sells Tiffany desk lamps and desk set pieces; no reproductions please.

Reyne Haines
Reyne Gallery
17 East 8th St.
Cincinnati, OH 45202
ph: 513-559-1405
fax: 513-651-0860
reyne@mindspring.com
http://www.reyne.com
Buys and sells Tiffany glass, lamps, bronze, jewelry and windows.

Paul G. Bailey, ISA
Antique Appraisal & Estate Services
12819 SE 38th St., PMB 320
Bellevue, WA 98006-1395
ph: 425-746-2777
fax: 425-746-3793
antiquabailey@aol.com
30 years buying, selling, appraising Tiffany.

Experts

Neustadt Museum of Tiffany Art, Inc., The
251 West 81st St., Ste. 7C
New York, NY 10024
ph: 212-874-0872
fax: 212-874-0872
nmtamuseum@aol.com
Permanent exhibition is at the Queens Museum of Art; also has traveling museum; offers research facilities.

Sylvia Kornblum
Team Antiques
P.O. Box 1052
Great Neck, NY 11023-0052
ph: 516-487-1826
Over 36 years experience in cataloging and selling Louis C. Tiffany, Tiffany Studios items by mail-order.

Carl Heck
Carl Heck Decorative Arts
P.O. Box 8416
Aspen, CO 81612-8416
ph: 970-925-8011
fax: 970-925-8011
carlheck5@aol.com
http://www.carlheck.com
Collector/dealer/expert specializing in

lamps by Tiffany, Pairpoint, Handel, Galle and Tiffany windows for over 32 years; currently Tiffany advisor for "Schroeder's," "Antique Trader" price guides.

Internet Resources

Paul Doros
Tiffany Studios Resource Center
tiffanystudios@comcast.net
http://www.geocities.com/Vienna/Choir/7564
A detailed Web site on the life and works of Louis Comfort Tiffany including a chronological history of Tiffany and Tiffany Studios; Paul was the first curator of glass for the Chrysler Museum in Norfolk, VA.

Man./Prod./Dist.

Tiffany Co.
5th Ave. at 57th St.
New York, NY 10022
ph: 212-755-8000 or 800-843-3269
http://www.tiffany.com
Main Tiffany store; Tiffany items also retailed through regional stores.

Museums/Libraries

Chrysler Museum of Art, The
245 West Olney Rd.
Norfolk, VA 23510-1587
ph: 757-664-6200
fax: 757-664-6201
museum@chrysler.org
http://www.chrysler.org

TILES

(see also BOOKS, Reference [Tiles]; CERAMICS)

Clubs/Associations

Alan Swade
Tiles & Architectural Ceramics Society
Magazine: Glazed Expressions
36 Friars Ave.
Stone, Staffordshire ST15 0AF U.K.
w.prescott@open.ac.uk
http://www.tilesoc.org.uk
Society serves the collector, historian, craftsman and conservator interested in decorated ceramics relating to buildings; also publishes biennial journal; magazine twice a year & a newsletter quarterly.

Collectors

Michael Padwee
453 14th St.
Brooklyn, NY 11215
ph: 718-499-4307
tileback101@mail.com
Tile historian who collects American antique ceramic tiles; author of "A Guide to the Patterns and Markings on the Backs of United States Ceramic Tiles, 1870s to 1930s," and "Field Guide to Key Patterns on US Ceramic Tiles" (1999).

Susan Frost
San Jose Tiles & Pottery
806 Rosedale Terrace
Austin, TX 78704-3159
ph: 512-447-2575 or 512-447-0407
fax: 512-447-2575
sfrost@austin.rr.com
http://www.io.com/~reuter
Wants to buy San Jose Pottery and San Jose Mission Crafts tiles.

Dealers

Sandie Fowler
Antique Articles
P.O. Box 72
North Billerica, MA 01862
ph: 978-663-8083
fax: 978-663-8083
artiles@earthlink.net
http://www.antiquearticles.com
With Wendy Harvey carries a full range of tiles dating primarily from 1880 to 1930s; has both American and European tiles; also has early Delft tiles c. 1700; has both single tiles and matching tiles including complete fireplace surrounds.

Pedro Leitao
Solar Antique Tiles
306 East 61st
New York, NY 10021
ph: 212-755-2403
fax: 212-980-2649
pleitao@aol.com
http://www.solarantiquetiles.com
Large selection of original antique tiles that have been removed from buildings and palaces dating back to 16th century; also has a line of reproduction tiles in antique designs.

Ken Forster
5501 Seminary Rd., Ste. 1311 South
Falls Church, VA 22041-3907
ph: 703-379-1142
kencforster@aol.com
Dealer in American art pottery and tiles, specializing in American tiles from 1860 to 1940; also Art Nouveau, Art Deco, Georg Jensen silver, and American Modernism.

Karen M. Guido
Karen Michelle Antique Tiles
1835 US 1 South #119, PMB 243
Saint Augustine, FL 32084
ph: 904-471-3226
karen@antiquetiles.com
http://www.antiquetiles.com
Over 3,000 antique & collectible tiles in stock; specializing in American and English tiles from 1870 to 1940; stock encompasses fireplace surrounds and mantle accents, border tiles, works of art in ceramics, tile-topped tables, etc.

Richard Mohr
Richard Mohr Antiques
402 S. Coler Ave.
Urbana, IL 61801
ph: 217-367-7856
kaospar@insightbb.com
Collects, buys, sells American art tiles, specializing in faience tiles,

particularly those of the Arts & Crafts movement.

Michael Swann
Tile Image Gallery
85 Curzon St.
Derby, Derbyshire DE1 1LN U.K.
ph: +44 1332 362770
captain@derbycity.com
Collector, dealer with Web site having full color images of tiles, each with a brief description and each dated; an essential reference source for anyone interested in ceramic art, history or design, method of surface decoration, etc.

Experts

Sandie Fowler
Antique Articles
P.O. Box 72
North Billerica, MA 01862
ph: 978-663-8083
fax: 978-663-8083
artiles@earthlink.net
http://www.antiquearticles.com
With partner Wendy Harvey are experts in the field of Tile and are one of the largest tile dealers in the country.

Karen M. Guido
Karen Michelle Antique Tiles
1835 US 1 South #119, PMB 243
Saint Augustine, FL 32084
ph: 904-471-3226
karen@antiquetiles.com
http://www.antiquetiles.com
Over 3,000 antique & collectible tiles in stock; specializing in American and English tiles from 1870 to 1940; stock encompasses fireplace surrounds and mantle accents, border tiles, works of art in ceramics, tile-topped tables, etc.

Norman Karlson
P.O. Box 769
Los Angeles, CA 90078
ph: 323-850-7632
fax: 323-883-0832
karlsonwp@aol.com
Specializes in American art tiles, c. 1920-1930; Spanish tiles, c. 1650-1800; Portuguese tiles c. 1780; Dutch tiles, c. 1750-1900; author of "American Art Tiles" (Rizzoli).

Chris Blanchett
Buckland Books
Holly Tree House
18 Woodlands Rd.
Littlehampton, West Sussex BN17 5PP U.K.
ph: (+44) 1903 717648
fax: (+44) 1903 717648
cblanchett@lineone.net
http://www.tiles.org/pages/bookshlf/BUCKLAND_BOOKS.html
Collector, historian and author on tiles and related subjects of all periods; research/identification undertaken; major library of tile-related materials; large reference collection of tiles, etc.

Internet Resources

Tom Colson
Tiles on the Web
U.K.
tom@tiles.org
http://www.tiles.org
This Web site provides a focus for Web resources to further the appreciation of ceramic tiles as an artistic media, historical artifacts, and architectural elements: tile organizations, resources for tile collectors, etc.

Man./Prod./Dist.

Dona Danziger
Clay Werks, Ltd.
4058 S. Main St.
P.O. Box 352
Exmore, VA 23350
ph: 757-414-0567
fax: 757-414-0571
info@clay werksltd.com
http://www.claywerksltd.com
Hand painted pottery and art tiles in current studio productions; brochures and shipping available.

Periodicals

Joseph Taylor
Tile Heritage Foundation
Newsletter: Flash Point
P.O. Box 1850
Healdsburg, CA 95448
ph: 707-431-8453
fax: 707-431-8455
foundation@tileheritage.org
http://www.tiles.org/pages/tileorgs/
thfinfo.htm
Dedicated to promoting the appreciation for tiled surfaces; promotes preservation of rare & unusual ceramics; has library on old tiles; also publishes a magazine entitled "Tile Heritage: A Review of American History."

Repro. Sources

Pedro Leitao
Solar Antique Tiles
306 East 61st
New York, NY 10021
ph: 212-755-2403
fax: 212-980-2649
pleitao@aol.com
http://www.solarantiquetiles.com
Large selection of original antique tiles that have been removed from buildings and palaces dating back to 16th century; also has a line of reproduction tiles in antique designs.

California

Experts

Steve Soukup
California Crazed
P.O. Box 7662
Van Nuys, CA 91409-7662
ph: 818-787-5990 or 818-781-9262
soukup@dfhaia.com
Collects, buys and sells California pottery and tiles: Catalina, Batchelder, Arequipa, Calco, Malibu,

Claycraft, California Faience, S&S, D&M, CCPCO, GMB, Tropico, Taylor, Tudor, etc.

California (Malibu Potteries)

Museums/Libraries

Malibu Lagoon Museum
23200 Pacific Coast Highway
P.O. Box 291
Malibu, CA 90265-0291
ph: 310-456-8432
http://www.adamsonhouse.org
Features the boldly hued tileworks of Southern California's Malibu Potteries (1926-1932); also tile books.

Drain

Museums/Libraries

Mike Weaver Drain Tile Museum
P.O. Box 464
Geneva, NY 14456
ph: 315-789-3848 or 315-789-5151
Large collection of over 350 drain tiles - ceramic pipes used to drain excess moisture from farm land - dating from 100 B.C.; this is the former home of John Johnston "Father of Tile Drainage in America."

Victorian

Experts

Pamela & Allan Luttig
Blue Boar Antiques
P.O. Box 423
Grand Ledge, MI 48837-0423
ph: 517-626-6432
blueboar@attglobal.net
http://www.blueboar.com

Zsolnay

Internet Resources

Federico Santi
Zsolnay Tile Museum, The Online
152 Spring St.
Newport, RI 02840-6806
ph: 401-841-5060
fax: 401-848-0953
zsolnay@drawrm.com
http://www.drawrm.com
An online museum of Zsolnay ceramic tiles from the 1870s through WWI; pictures, articles and tile links; browse to www.drawrm.com/ztilemus.htm.

TIME CAPSULES

Museums/Libraries

Chris Christofferson
Time Capsule Museum
904 South Roselle Rd.
Schaumburg, IL 60193
ph: 847-895-5901
fax: 847-895-3230
chris@timecapsulemuseum.com
http://www.timecapsulemuseum.com
Time capsules available; advice and research on 21st century collectibles; archival packaging, capsule selection,

preservation and storage; time capsule registry, archive, library and museum.

TIN COLLECTIBLES

(see ADVERTISING COLLECTIBLES; ADVERTISING COLLECTIBLES, Tins; COFFEE, Tins; FOLK ART, Tinware; KITCHEN COLLECTIBLES; MINING COLLECTIBLES, Cap Tins; PROPHYLACTICS, Tin; SMOKING COLLECTIBLES; TOYS, Tin; TYPEWRITERS, Ribbon Tins)

TITANIC MEMORABILIA

(see also NAUTICAL ANTIQUES; OCEAN LINER COLLECTIBLES)

Appraisers

James Corcoran, ISA
Corcoran Fine Arts Limited, Inc.
2915 Fairfax Rd.
Cleveland, OH 44118-4015
ph: 216-431-0025 or 216-397-0777
fax: 216-397-0222
corcoranfa@aol.com
http://www.corcoranfinearts.com
Appraises all types of Titanic and White Star Line memorabilia; appraised;Titanic Ship of Dreams" collection; other private collections; private dealers.

Clubs/Associations

Robert M. DiSogra, Pres.
Titanic International Society
Journal: Voyage
P.O. Box 7007
Freehold, NJ 07728-7007
ph: 732-462-1413 or 973-742-8747
fax: 732-462-1771
rdisogra@hotmail.com
http://www.titanicinternational.org
Members interested in the history of RMS TITANIC, her passengers and crew; a reference source for all Titanic artifacts; world wide society; annual meetings; speakers available on history, artifact recovery, educational displays.

Collectors

Gary Robinson
26 Richards Ave.
Oneonta, NY 13820
ph: 607-431-4437 or 607-432-6893
fax: 607-431-4105
robinson@digital-marketplace.net
http://www.titanicshipofdreams.com
Buys, sells and trades artifacts and ephemera relating to RMS Titanic and the White Star Line; also RMS Carpathia, Titanic's rescue ship.

Frederick Lingenfelser
814 Byram St.
Reading, PA 19606-1446
lingy@afo.net
Buying anything related to the Titanic: newspapers, postcards, menus, books, photographs, letters from survivors, paintings, artifacts, etc.

Experts

Edward Kamunda
208 Main St.
P.O. Box 51053
Indian Orchard, MA 01151-0053
ph: 413-543-4770
fax: 413-583-3633
titanicinfo@titanic1.org
http://www.titanic1.org
Wants newspapers, books, sheet music, artifacts; offers expert and knowledgeable appraisals of Titanic memorabilia for a fee.

Charles Ira Sachs
TransAtlantic Research
P.O. Box 8797
Universal City, CA 91618-8797
ph: 818-985-1345
fax: 818-985-1345
onrs@earthlink.net
Buys/sells/specializes/lectures on ocean liner and zeppelin history & memorabilia from the high seas (i.e., none from coastal or river steamers) dating from 1840 to 1960s; posters, postcards and related material for collectors/museums.

Internet Resources

Titanic Historical Society, Inc./Titanic Museum
208 Main St.
P.O. Box 51053
Indian Orchard, MA 01151-0053
ph: 413-543-4770
fax: 413-583-3633
titanicinfo@titanichistoricalsociety.org
http://www.titanichistoricalsociety.org
Online resources; focuses on all aspects of the "Titanic," "Britannic," "Olympic," and the White Star Line; premier source for information; finest collection anywhere; expert appraisals for a fee; open to the public.

Museums/Libraries

Edward Kamunda
Titanic Historical Society, Inc./Titanic Museum
Magazine: Titanic Commutator, The
208 Main St.
P.O. Box 51053
Indian Orchard, MA 01151-0053
ph: 413-543-4770
fax: 413-583-3633
titanicinfo@titanichistoricalsociety.org
http://www.titanichistoricalsociety.org
Founded in 1963, focuses on all aspects of the "Titanic," "Britannic," "Olympic," and the White Star Line; premier source for information; finest collection anywhere; expert appraisals for a fee; open to the public.

TOASTERS

(see also ELECTRICITY RELATED ITEMS; KITCHEN COLLECTIBLES)

Clubs/Associations

Toaster Collector Association
Newsletter: Saturday Evening Toast
P.O. Box 485
Redding Ridge, CT 06876
mac@toastercollector.com
http://www.toastercollector.com
*A club for toaster enthusiasts:
membership assists collectors with
research, preservation, documentation
of bread toasters.*

Collectors

William Blakeslee
116 S. Bethlehem Pike
P.O. Box 56
Ambler, PA 19002
ph: 215-646-6593
fax: 215-646-5459
readferry@snip.net
*Wants unusual electric toasters as
well as any pre-1910 electric
appliance: GE, Simplex, American
Electric Heat, Heinrichs.*

Howard & Jane Hazelcorn
6731 Ashley Ct.
Sarasota, FL 34241-9696
ph: 941-921-1815
mrpropane@aol.com
*Authors of "Price Guide to Old
Electric Toasters."*

Richard Mathes
P.O. Box 1408
Springfield, OH 45501-1408
*Wants unusual old fireplace, stove top
and pre-1940 electric toasters to add
to current collection.*

Oscar P. Barkhurst
3910 Brookside Dr.
Rapid City, SD 57702-2219
ph: 605-348-1354
*Wants old, electric pre-1950 toasters;
heart shaped, perch, roaster coffee pot
combination, very old toaster ovens,
unusual, odd. Send photo and
information printed on the item.*

Joe Lukach
7111 Deframe Ct.
Arvada, CO 80004-1168
ph: 303-422-8970
*Collector wants vintage toasters in
good condition; also wants items
related to toasters such as advertising,
catalogs, etc.*

Uwe H. Breker
Bonner Str. 528-530
Koln, D-50968 Germany
ph: 49 221 387049 or 941-925-0385 (US
Rep)
fax: 49 221 374878
auction@breker.com
http://www.breker.com
*Wants to buy toasters: porcelain,
ceramic, etc.*

Dealers

Michael Sheafe
Toaster Central
P.O. Box 20012
New York, NY 10021-0060
ph: 888-387-7730 or 212-744-3773
mac@toasterCentral.com
http://www.toasterCentral.com
*Toaster collector, dealer, expert,
restorer; buys and sells vintage
toasters: Sunbeam, Proctor,
Toastmaster, Dominion, Kenmore,
Toastwell, Westinghouse, GE,
Universal and others from the Golden
Age of chrome and Bakelite.*

Joseph & Elaine Paurel
P.O. Box 1466
Vallejo, CA 94590
ph: 707-554-2587
mtoaster@pacbell.net

Experts

Jim Barker
Toaster Master
P.O. Box 746
Allentown, PA 18102
ph: 610-439-0751
fax: 610-439-1925
jbar@enter.net
*Wants interesting electric toasters
1908-1940; Porcelier, GE, Toastrite,
Mecky, Pelouze; mechanical, push
button, crank type, drop down; highest
prices paid.*

Helen Greguire
Helen's Antiques
216 Mountain View Rd.
Landrum, SC 29356
ph: 864-457-7340

Museums/Libraries

Eric R. Norcross
Toaster Museum Foundation, The
Newsletter: Hotwire
1003 Carlton Ave., Ste. B
Charlottesville, VA 22902-5974
ph: 804-293-3569
eric@toaster.org
http://www.toaster.org
*A non-profit foundation dedicated to
preserving toasters and toast-related
paraphernalia.*

TOBACCO CARDS

(see ADVERTISING COLLECTIBLES,
Trade Cards [Tobacco]; CIGAR
BOXES, LABELS & BANDS;
CIGARETTE COLLECTIBLES;
CIGAR STORE COLLECTIBLES;
LIGHTERS; MATCHBOXES &
LABELS; MATCHCOVERS; MATCH
SAFES; PIPES; SMOKING
COLLECTIBLES)

TOBACCO COLLECTIBLES

(see also ADVERTISING
COLLECTIBLES, Trade Cards
[Tobacco]; MATCH SAFES; PAPER
COLLECTIBLES; SMOKING
COLLECTIBLES)

Clubs/Associations

Betty & Jim Ogburn
Piedmont Tobacco Memorabilia &
Collector's Club
185 Moser Rd.
King, NC 27021-8776
ph: 336-983-9729

Collectors

Dan Calandriello
10 Weston Place
Eatontown, NJ 07724
ph: 732-542-4770
danster-nj@comcast.net
*Wants 1880s-1910 American tobacco
posters showing card sets; tobacco
cards; leathers from 1880s-1905.*

David & Barbara Freiberg
Cerebro
P.O. Box 327
East Prospect, PA 17317-0327
ph: 717-252-2400 or 800-69L-ABEL
fax: 717-252-3685
cerebro@cerebro.com
http://www.cerebro.com
*Wants to buy tobacco paper items,
cigarette cards, tobacco trade cards.*

Betty & Jim Ogburn
185 Moser Rd.
King, NC 27021-8776
ph: 336-983-9729

Cindy Porman
22044 Roosevelt Rd.
South Bend, IN 46614
ph: 219-291-6414
imaporman@yahoo.com
*Wants Copenhagen Snuff, Weyman &
Sons, Weyman Bros., Skoal Snuff, and
Key Snuff tobacco items including
crocks, pocket tins, store displays,
metal and paper signs, and related
advertising items.*

Chris Cooper
F M Rd 1522
Pittsburg, TX 75686
ph: 903-856-7286
fax: 903-856-6879
*Wants tobacco tags, trade cards, tins,
cigar cutters, ashtrays, billheads,
caddies, labels, match safes, hammers,
box openers, pennants, felts, key
chains, bags, and most other tobacco
advertising and ephemera.*

Dealers

Lenore Monleon
33 Fifth Ave.
New York, NY 10003-4338
ph: 212-475-7871 or 212-675-7771
*Wants to buy tobacco collectibles:
pocket match safes, tobacco humidors,
enameled cigarette cases, etc.*

Stephen C. Jones
P.O. Box 267
Homer, NY 13077-0267
ph: 607-753-8822
*Wants cigar box labels, lithographers
sample books of cigar box labels,
cigarette cards, tobacco trade cards,*

*tobacco business cards, tobacco store
signs.*

J. Glen & Violet Moore
Main St. Antiques
47 W. Main St.
P.O. Box 627
New Market, MD 21774-0627
ph: 301-865-3710
*Buys and sells early American tobacco
collectibles; large selections of signs,
wood cigar boxes, pocket and other
tins, plug cutters, counter displays,
etc.; appointments preferred.*

Willisia Holbrook
Armbrook Antiques
531 Doub Rd.
Lewisville, NC 27023
ph: 888-393-8025 or 336-945-9477
fax: 336-945-9914
*Buys and sells early tobacco and
smoking antiques; specializes in pre-
1930s items; Web site has full online
catalog including descriptions and
photos.*

J. Jones
Hermit Tobacco Works Company
P.O. Box 669
Pioneer, OH 43554
ph: 517-567-2208
fax: 219-639-6035
pipestand@aol.com
http://www.pipestand.com
*Collector, dealer, expert buys and
sells trade pipes and all tobacciana;
anything Dunhill; cigar signs, fan
hangers, full tins of tobacco.*

Jeff Mogilner
Racine & Laramie, Ltd.
2737 San Diego Ave.
San Diego, CA 92110-2731
ph: 619-291-7833
fax: 619-297-6653
axracine@znet.com
*Buy, sell, collect antique tobacco
pipes: meerschaum, clay, briar,
porcelain, and related items.*

Experts

Mark Suozzi
P.O. Box 102
Ashfield, MA 01330
ph: 413-628-3241
fax: 413-628-3241
marklyn@valinet.com
http://www.marklynantiques.com
*Buys antique tin litho signs signs from
1860-1930, tobacco carvings, baseball
and political campaign subjects,
advertising iron cigar cutters, figural
lead counter top gas lighters, tobacco
wood trade signs and store cigar
figures.*

Jars

Clubs/Associations

Allen Gurst
Society of Tobacco Jar Collectors
Newsletter: Tobacco Jar Newsletter
1705 Chanticleer Dr.
Cherry Hill, NJ 08003
ph: 856-489-8363
fax: 856-489-8364
agurst@aol.com
http://www.tobaccojarsociety.com
Purpose is to promote the collection and dissemination of information related to the manufacture, design, artistic merit, and historic, educational and cultural aspects of antique tobacco jars; annual convention.

Collectors

Melinda Bagley
6370 Kirby Ridge Cove
Memphis, TN 38119

Sandie Goodman
3021 Courtland Blvd.
Cleveland, OH 44122-2805
ph: 216-921-0400
Focuses on collecting tobacco jars, especially figural jars.

Periodicals

Joe Horowitz
Newsletter: Tobacco Jar Quarterly
3011 Falstaff Rd., #307
Baltimore, MD 21209
jfigtobjar@aol.com

Mail Pouch

Collectors

Mike Boggs
2075 Beaver Valley Rd.
Dayton, OH 45434-6987
ph: 937-426-2171
fax: 937-426-3063
oatbox@erinet.com
Wants to buy anything related to Mail Pouch Tobacco - any size, any condition; also interested in any chewing tobacco items, any packs of tobacco, anything before 1965, all brands.

Tags

Clubs/Associations

Louis Storino
Tin Tag Collectors Club
Newsletter: Tin Tag Exchange, The
P.O. Box 189
Los Altos, CA 94023-0189
ph: 650-941-7663
fax: 650-941-8835
storino@ix.netcom.com
Dedicated to learning more about chewing tobacco tin tags.

Collectors

Chris Cooper
F M Rd 1522
Pittsburg, TX 75686
ph: 903-856-7286
fax: 903-856-6879
Wants tobacco tags, trade cards, tins, cigar cutters, ashtrays, billheads, caddies, labels, match safes, hammers, box openers, pennants, felts, key chains, bags, and most other tobacco advertising and ephemera.

Experts

Louis Storino
P.O. Box 189
Los Altos, CA 94023-0189
ph: 650-941-7663
fax: 650-941-8835
storino@ix.netcom.com
Collector and author of "Chewing Tobacco Tin Tags;" wants to buy tobacco tags - tin and paper used to identify brands of plug chewing tobacco; also wants related plug tobacco advertising, cards, posters, etc.

Tins

Dealers

Richard & Ann Lehmann
P.O. Box 123
Monrovia, MD 21770
ph: 301-253-3890
lehmann@tias.com
http://www.tias.com/stores/lehmann
Specializes in cigar and tobacco tins.

TOBY JUGS

(see CERAMICS [ENGLISH], Royal Doulton; COLLECTIBLES [MODERN], Toby Jugs)

TOKENS

(see also BANKING; CIVIL WAR ARTIFACTS, Tokens; COINS & CURRENCY; CREDIT CARDS & CHARGE ITEMS; GAMBLING COLLECTIBLES, Poker Chips & Gaming Tokens; MEDALS, ORDERS & DECORATIONS; SCRIP; WOODEN MONEY)

Auction Services

Lawrence Stack
Stack's Coin Galleries
123 West 57th St.
New York, NY 10019-2280
ph: 212-582-2580
fax: 212-245-5018
info@stacks.com
http://www.stacks.com
Specializes in the auctions of coins, medals, tokens, silver, paper currency.

David M. Gale
C & D Gale
2404 Berwyn Rd.
Wilmington, DE 19810-3525
ph: 302-478-0872
fax: 302-478-6866
cdgale@dol.net
http://www.cdgale.com/catalog/exonumia.htm
Conducts mail bid auctions of medals, tokens, religious items, trade checks, miscellaneous items, Civil War tokens and other exonumia; issues fixed-price exonumia catalogs.

H. Joseph Levine
Presidential Coin & Antique Co. Inc.
6550-I Little River Turnpike
Alexandria, VA 22312
ph: 703-354-5454
fax: 703-914-0547
JLevine968@aol.com
Conducts periodic auctions of Presidential and other medals, badges, decorations, tokens, World's Fair and other exonumia,

Kurt R. Krueger
Krueger Auctions
P.O. Box 275
Iola, WI 54945-0275
ph: 715-445-3845
fax: 715-445-4100
Specializing in the mail-bid auction of tokens, advertising, brewery items, Western Americana, postcards, World's Fair & Expo., autographs, sports, coins & currency, pinbacks, military memorabilia, automotive, Disneyana, toys, dolls, etc.

Dick Grinolds
P.O. Box 18002
Minneapolis, MN 55418
ph: 612-331-8246
Conducts periodic mail-in auctions of tokens, medals, GAR, ribbons.

Rich Hartzog
World Exonumia
P.O. Box 4143CNZ
Rockford, IL 61110-0643
ph: 815-226-0771
hartzog@exonumia.com
http://www.exonumia.com
Wants any tokens, medals, exonumia: badges, buttons, World's Fair items, political items, banners, etc.; sample auction catalog $4.

Exocoin
P.O. Box 720900
Oklahoma City, OK 73120-0900
ph: 800-860-7558
fax: 405-721-1194
rdmoc@cox.net
http://www.exocoin.com
Buys, sells merchant trade tokens, Civil War tokens; also political collectibles, World's Fair & Exposition items, rare coins, costume and estate jewelry, fine diamonds, and art glass.

Stephen P. Alpert
P.O. Box 66331
Los Angeles, CA 90066-0331
ph: 310-836-2482
fax: 310-836-5691
quadra@pacbell.net
https://home.pacbell.net/quadra
Conducts periodic auctions of tokens, medals, tags, credit cards, gambling chips, movie money, related coin-like items.

Clubs/Associations

Dennis P. Helmer
New Jersey Exonumia Society
Newsletter: Jerseyana
112 Carlton Ave.
Collingswood, NJ 08108-3501
D.P.Helmer@comcast.net
Collectors of New Jersey tokens, medals, paper, etc.; annual meeting at convention; regional meetings at different coin shows; quarterly newsletter.

Clark Rohmer, Sec.
National Token Collector's Association
Newsletter: Talkin' Tokens
P.O. Box 281
Ormond Beach, FL 32175
ph: 904-677-0420
fax: 904-677-0420
cjcoins@att.net
http://home.pacbell.net/tokenbob
For collectors of merchant and trade tokens.

Token & Medal Society
Journal: Token & Medal Society Journal
5224 West SR 46, #408
Sanford, FL 32771-9230
mlighter@bellsouth.net
http://www.angelfire.com/id/TAMS/index.html
Promotes and stimulates "exonumia," the study of non-government issue tokens and medals; an organization of collectors and researchers of tokens, medals and related items.

V. King
Indiana, Kentucky & Ohio Token & Medal Society
Newsletter: IKO-TAMS Newsletter
600 N. Colfax St., Apt. #233
Warsaw, IN 46580
ph: 219-372-3075
frjones@kconline.com
A non-profit society for collectors of tokens, medals and other exonumia; meets four times per year; members have bourse tables at each meeting.

Paul Manderscheil
Michigan Token & Medal Society
Newsletter: Junk Box, The
P.O. Box 256
Okemos, MI 48805
Dedicated to stimulating and maintaining interest in the exonumia of the state of Michigan.

Christopher Cipoletti, Ex. Dir.
American Numismatic Association
Magazine: Numismatist, The
818 N. Cascade Ave.
Colorado Springs, CO 80903-3279
ph: 719-632-2646 or 800-367-9723
fax: 719-634-4085
ana@money.org
http://www.money.org
Worldwide nonprofit assoc. chartered by US Congress to promote the study and collection of money including coins, tokens, paper currency, for research, interpretation, preservation of history and culture from ancient time to present.

Stephen P. Alpert
California Association of Token
  Collectors
Newsletter: Token Topics
P.O. Box 66331
Los Angeles, CA 90066-0331
ph: 310-836-2482
fax: 310-836-5691
quadra@pacbell.net
https://home.pacbell.net/quadra
An informal club for collectors of tokens, medals, and other exonumia; meets bi-monthly in southern California.

Scott E. Douglas, VP
Canadian Association of Token
  Collectors
Magazine: Numismatica Canada
273 Mill St. East
Acton, Ontario L7J 1J7 Canada
scott.douglas@sympatico.ca
http://www.nunetcan.net/catc.htm

Collectors

Jerome Schaeper, Jr.
365 Meadowlark Dr.
Edgewood, KY 41018-2608
ph: 859-341-3769
Collects and appraises merchant "good for" trade tokens; from saloons, dairies, military canteens, etc.

Donald G. Tritt
81 Donald Ross Dr.
Granville, OH 43023
ph: 740-587-0213
tritt@denison.edu
Wants to buy wooden exonumia (medals, plaques, political and advertising tokens, checkers, badges).

Rich Hartzog
World Exonumia
P.O. Box 4143CNZ
Rockford, IL 61110-0643
ph: 815-226-0771
hartzog@exonumia.com
http://www.exonumia.com
Wants any tokens, medals, exonumia: badges, buttons, World's Fair items, political items, banners, etc.; collections and quantities wanted.

James E. Kattner
P.O. Box 11132
Spring, TX 77391-1132
ph: 281-376-4826
victorio1sw@yahoo.com
Wants to buy tokens issued by Texas saloons, bars, military forts, post traders, lumber companies, drug stores, barbers, general stores, and other merchants; also tokens picturing steers, elephants, eagles, The Alamo; "Good for..."

Harold Fossum
P.O. Box 210127
Auke Bay, AK 99821
ph: 907-780-4472
hofossum@msn.com
Wants tokens that relate to the state of Alaska.

Dealers

Mark Gatcha
Token Trader, The
1225 Martha Custis Dr., Apt. 906
Alexandria, VA 22302
ph: 703-820-6025
Mgatcha@hotmail.com
http://www.arrowweb.com/gatcha/tokens.htm
Token dealer and collector.

Dan M. Jacobson
P.O. Box 277101
Sacramento, CA 95827-7101
Issues periodic lists of tokens for sale.

Experts

David E. Schenkman
P.O. Box 366
Bryantown, MD 20617-0366
ph: 301-274-3441
turtlehill@olg.com
Full time dealer recognized as one of the leading authorities in the field of tokens and medals; author of seven books, each of which is a standard reference; wants to buy tokens, medals, watch fobs, and advertising mirrors.

Joe C. Copeland
P.O. Box 4221
Oak Ridge, TN 37831-4221
ph: 865-482-4215
joecopeland@comcast.net
Wants to buy tokens from saloons, CCC camps, and all southeastern US; author of "Trade Tokens of Tennessee," listing over 2,500 tokens from over 350 towns; 260 pgs., $30 ppd.

Bob Temarantz
2824 N. Bentley Ave.
Tucson, AZ 85716-5513
ph: 520-326-6704 or 520-741-9751
fax: 520-294-6052
azsnipe@hotmail.com
Buys and specializes in western state "saloon," military, "post trader," Indian trader, territorial (i.e., Tucson, A.T., Yakima, W.T.) tokens,

"Good for" advertising pocket mirrors, etc.

Stephen P. Alpert
P.O. Box 66331
Los Angeles, CA 90066-0331
ph: 310-836-2482
fax: 310-836-5691
quadra@pacbell.net
https://home.pacbell.net/quadra
Co-author with Lawrence E. Elman of "Tokens and Medals, A Guide to the Identification and Values of United States Exonumia;" dealer in all types of tokens, medals, tags, credit cards, gambling chips, movie money, related coin-like items.

Internet Resources

Mark Gatcha
Token Trader, The
1225 Martha Custis Dr., Apt. 906
Alexandria, VA 22302
ph: 703-820-6025
Mgatcha@hotmail.com
http://www.arrowweb.com/gatcha/tokens.htm
This site is dedicated to providing token collectors with a centralized source for buying, selling, collecting and learning about every different category of the token collecting marketplace.

Museums/Libraries

Museum of the American Numismatic
  Association
Magazine: Numismatist, The
818 N. Cascade Ave.
Colorado Springs, CO 80903-3279
ph: 719-632-2646 or 800-367-9723
fax: 719-634-4085
ana@money.org
http://www.money.org
A museum collection including 400,000 items; largest numismatic circulating library with books and A/V material free to members.

Love

Clubs/Associations

Carbara Newhouse, Sec./Treas.
Love Token Society
Newsletter: Love Letter
5840 Tuttle Cove Rd.
Mandeville, LA 66503
ph: 913-539-1831
fax: 504-626-3867
For engraved coin (love token) collectors and enthusiasts; newsletter published bi-monthly.

Merchant

Collectors

Joe Hunt
2117 Bush Dr.
Huntsville, TX 77340
Wants all US "Good For" tokens; no casino tokens or wood tokens.

Dealers

Jim & Rita Hinton
Collector's Choice
P.O. Box 104284
Jefferson City, MO 65110-4284
ph: 573-636-7567
Wants merchant tokens that say "Good For;" prefers those listing town names.

Sales Tax

Clubs/Associations

Carl Cochrane
American Tax Token Society
Newsletter: ATTS Newsletter
12 Pheasant Dr.
Asheville, NC 28803
Interested in collecting tokens, scrip, punch cards, coupons, receipts, etc. relating to the history and collection of sales taxes.

Dealers

Tom Holifield
Whistle Stop
205 Railroad Ave.
P.O. Box 713
Alderson, WV 24910-0713
ph: 304-445-7120
fishnnut@hotmail.com
http://www.geocities.com/whistlestopstudio
Buys and sells sales tax tokens and related materials; also wants any tokens from the state of Mississippi.

Transportation (Fare)

Clubs/Associations

Bob Schneider
American Vecturist Association
Newsletter: Fare Box, The
2321 Londale Court
Virginia Beach, VA 23456
ph: 757-471-7433
fax: 757-200-3900
mykidsplay@aol.com
http://www.fantasticprices.com/token/AVAinfo.html
A source to buy, sell and trade all sorts of tokens; specializing in transportation tokens from the Atwood-Coffee catalog.

Dealers

Bob Schneider
2321 Londale Court
Virginia Beach, VA 23456
ph: 757-471-7433
fax: 757-200-3900
mykidsplay@aol.com
http://www.fantasticprices.com
Buys and sells transportation tokens.

Experts

John M. Coffee
P.O. Box 1204
Boston, MA 02104-1204
ph: 617-277-8111
Co-author of the Atwood-Coffee "Catalogue of Transportation Tokens."

John Hoffmann
8334 Heron Circle
Ooltewah, TN 37363-9794
Expert on railroad tie date nails and transportation tokens.

TOM'S PEANUTS
Dealers

Tina & Mark Richey
Spotted Horse Collectibles
12141 Couch Mill Rd.
Knoxville, TN 37932-1102
shcollect@aol.com
http://members.aol.com/shcollect/
homepage.html
Buys and sells memorabilia related to Tom Houston Peanut Co., maker's of Tom's Toasted Peanuts; interested in contacting other Tom's collectors.

TOOLS

(see also ARCHITECTURE & RELATED ITEMS; BLACKSMITHING ITEMS; DIAMOND EDGE; FARM COLLECTIBLES; FIREPLACE ITEMS; ICE INDUSTRY; HARDWARE; INDUSTRY RELATED ITEMS; KEEN KUTTER; LOGGING RELATED ITEMS; MACHINERY & EQUIPMENT)

Appraisers

Anthony Seo
Olde River Hard Goods
13A West Catawissa St.
Nesquehoning, PA 18240
ph: 570-669-9415
tonyseo@ptd.net
http://www.geocities.com/PicketFence/
1395
User, collector, and dealer in antique woodworking tools; specializes in wooden planes and good user tools; member of MWTCA, EAIA, and CRAFTS.

Lee Richmond
Best Things LLC, The
299 Herndon Parkway, Ste. 210
Herndon, VA 20170
ph: 703-796-5544
fax: 703-766-0966
lee@thebestthings.com
http://www.thebestthings.com
Specializes in the appraisal of vintage woodworking tools.

Steve Johnson
Union Hill Antique Tools
4521 243rd Ave. NE
Redmond, WA 98053
ph: 425-868-1532
fax: 425-868-1532
Tooltimer@msn.com
http://www.tooltimer.com
Appraiser, collector, dealer, expert specializing in the best hard-to-find antique woodworking, metalworking and turning tools and treadle equipment.

Auction Services

Barry Hurchalla
249 Creek Rd.
Boyertown, PA 19512
ph: 610-323-0333
threebid4@aol.com
Conducts monthly tool auctions in Eastern Pennsylvania; auctions include early wood through Stanley; also sells to beginner and the advanced collector; sales usually have over 1,000 tools; send $1 and SASE for list.

David Stanley
David Stanley Auctions
Stordon Grange, Osgathorpe
Loughborough, Leicestershire LE12 9SR
U.K.
ph: 01530 222320
fax: 01530-222523
david@davidstanley.com
http://www.davidstanley.com
Specializes in the buying, selling, collecting, appraising and auctioning antique and usable woodworking tools.

Book Sellers

Gary Roberts
Toolemera Press, The
1077 South St.
Roslindale, MA 02131
Buys and sells out-of-print books and ephemera on hand tools, machine tools, trades, industry and crafts; please send email request to be added to the private email list.

Jon Zimmers
Jon Zimmers Antique Tools
206 NE 24th
Portland, OR 97232
ph: 503-232-1565
jonz@teleport.com
http://www.teleport.com/~jonz
Collector and dealer specializing in antique tools for woodworkers and collectors; homepage has free classified ads, antique tools, tool-related books, and antique tool information.

Clubs/Associations

Marshall & Pat Stowell
New England Tool Collectors
Association
Newsletter: NETCA Newsletter
836 North King St.
Northampton, MA 01060-1127
ph: 413-586-2114
pstowell@resgs.umass.edu
Purpose is to promote and increase knowledge and understanding of early American trades and crafts, and of the tools with which they are associated; meeting held twice each year with swap and sale of tools.

Elton W. Hall, Ex. Dir.
Early American Industries Association,
The
Newsletter: Shavings, The
167 Bakersville Rd.
South Dartmouth, MA 02748-4198
ph: 508-993-4198
eaiainfo@worldnet.att.net
http://www.eaiainfo.org
Interested in old tools, implements, utensils, vehicles, "Whatsits;" and to discover, identify and preserve same; also publishes the magazine "Chronicle."

John Whelan
Collectors of Rare & Familiar Tools
Society (CRAFTS) of New Jersey
Newsletter: Tool Shed, The
38 Colony Ct.
New Providence, NJ 07974-2332
ph: 908-464-5424
jmwhelwdpl@aol.com
http://www.craftsofnj.org
Members share information on tools and implements used in early trades and industries; newsletter published five times per year.

Bill Hermanek
Long Island Antique Tool Collector's
Association
Newsletter: Workbench, The
31 Wildwood Dr.
Smithtown, NY 11787-3452
ph: 631-360-1216 or 516-333-2640
BHermanek@aol.com
Promotes knowledge, appreciation, collection and exchange of antique tools and machinery.

Ted Kinsey, Sec./Treas.
Western New York Antique Tool
Collector's Association
Newsletter: Talking Tools
3162 Avon Rd.
Geneseo, NY 14454
kinsey@uno.cc.geneseo.edu
http://physics.sci.geneseo.edu/
WNYATCA/info.htm

Bob Kendra, Pres.
Three Rivers Tool Collectors
Newsletter: TRTC Newsletter
310 Old Airport Rd.
Greensburg, PA 15601-5806
ph: 724-850-9444
Newsletter, four meetings per year, old tool sales.

John B. Cox
Potomac Antique Tools & Industries
Association (PATINA)
Newsletter: Patinagram
6802 Nesbitt Place
Mc Lean, VA 22101-2132
ph: 703-821-2931
Organization for men and women having an interest in the tools, crafts, techniques or manufacturing processes of the past.

Jim Hollins
Richmond Antique Tool Society
2208 Lochwood Ct.
Richmond, VA 23233
ph: 804-550-1010
jelliott@sycomtech.com
http://www.sycomtech.com/oldtool

Fred Bair, Jr.
Society of Workers in Early Arts &
Trades
Newsletter: Sweat Rag, The
606 Lake Lena Blvd.
Auburndale, FL 33823-2937
ph: 813-967-3262
fax: 813-967-3262
Members are largely those who do public demonstrations of early crafts, but membership is open to anyone; exchange knowledge of practices in crafts; promotes the finding, making and exchange of tools; annual directory.

George E. Woodard, Sec.
Ohio Tool Collectors Association
Newsletter: Ohio Tool Box
P.O. Box 261
London, OH 43140-0261
ph: 614-852-3180
Interested in tools used for any function including construction, writing, household, etc.

Carl Blair
Southwest Tool Collector's Association
712 South Lincoln Ln. Ct.
Mustang, OK 73064-4141
Purpose is to promote the collection and exchange of tools, implements and devices used by our forefathers.

Cliff Fales, Sec.
Rocky Mountain Tool Collectors
Newsletter: Shavings, Sawdust, &
Splinters
1435 S. Urban Way
Lakewood, CO 80228
cfales@idcomm.com
Approximately 200 members, generally, but not limited to, the Rocky Mountain area; promotes the collection, restoration, and study of tools of bygone crafts; about 6 meetings per year in Denver area, and 6 in Albuquerque area.

Laura Ptiney, Ed.
Preserving Arts & Skills of the Trades
(PAST)
Newsletter: Tooltalk
2535 Grambling Way
Riverside, CA 92507
ph: 909-686-5825
fax: 909-781-4731
editor@tooltalk.org
http://www.tooltalk.org
An organization for those interested in collecting old tools and learning about associated history.

John Wells
Mid-West Tool Collectors Association
Magazine: Gristmill
P.O. Box 8016
Berkeley, CA 94707-8016
admin@mwtca.org
http://www.mwtca.org
Club is dedicated to the study, preservation and understanding of the early tools, implements and devices used by our ancestors in their homes, shops, on the farms and on the seas.

Jean Racine, Treas.
Pacific Northwest Tool Collectors
12780 SW 231st Place
Hillsboro, OR 97123
ph: 503-628-1488
admin@tooltimer.com
http://www.tooltimer.com/PNTC.htm
For collectors and others interested in old tools; over 450 members.

Robert Bishop, Mem. Ch.
Tool Group of Canada
Newsletter: Yesterday's Tools
11 Beacourt Rd.
Torornto, Ontario M8Y 3G1 Canada
ph: 416-259-4768
rfbishopis@rogers.com
http://www.thetoolgroupofcanada.com
Members are interested in collecting antique tools: woodworking, metalworking, leatherworking, textiles, domestic tools, hunting/ trapping, nautical, fishing, scientific, medical, railway, farm, etc.; meets five times a year.

Tool & Trades History Society
Newsletter: Tools & Trades
22 Earlsbourne
Church Crookham
Fleet, Hampshire GU52 8XG U.K.
ph: 01252 617483
john@cottrell-family.org.uk
Founded in 1983 to further the knowledge and understanding of hand tools and the trades as well as the people who used them; investigates, records, interprets the history of these trades.

Collectors

Eric Brooker
611 First Crown Pt. Rd.
Rochester, NH 03867
ph: 603-335-2319
Wants to buy all-metal, flat handle screwdrivers with advertising; please send overall length and condition along with a description of both sides of the flat handle.

Jay Bolante
3058 North Honore St.
Chicago, IL 60657-2050
ph: 773-327-5091
jaybee47@msn.com
Collects and wants to buy foot or hand-operated tools and machines.

Larry Poffenberger
1604 E. 55th Place
Tulsa, OK 74105
ph: 918-745-9786
lkp@rosewoodandbrass.com
http://www.rosewoodandbrass.com
Part time dealer, full-time collector; specializes in Stanley (particularly Bed Rock planes) and other makes.

Dealers

Peter Habicht
Falcon-Wood Woodworking Tools
1985 S. Undermountain Rd.
Sheffield, MA 01257-9643
ph: 413-229-7745
peter@oldtools.com
http://www.oldtools.com
Buys and sells old woodworking tools.

Patrick Leach
Superior Works, The
P.O. Box 43
Ashby, MA 01431
ph: 978-386-2436
leach@supertool.com
http://www.supertool.com
Collector, dealer, expert, in antique tools from the mundane to the exotic; also manufacturer of high-quality reproduction tools; monthly email tool list of freshly picked goods sent upon request; shop where dealers, collectors, users shop.

Charles Bonanno
Vintage Tool House
http://www.vintagetoolhouse.com
Buys and sells a large variety of woodworking hand tools: hand planes, spoke shaves, hand saws, chisels, boring tools, measuring devices, etc.; also a authorized Stanley tools and parts dealer, even for old tools.

William A. Gustafson
William A. Gustafson Antiques
P.O. Box 104
11643 Rte. 22
Austerlitz, NY 12017-0104
ph: 518-392-2845
fax: 518-392-4436
oldtools@taconic.net
http://www.taconic.net/oldtools
Dealer, collector, specialist and appraiser of antique tools; also conducts tool auctions.

Martin J. Donnelly
Martin J. Donnelly Antique Tools
P.O. Box 281
Bath, NY 14810-0281
ph: 800-869-0695 or 607-566-2617
fax: 607-566-2575
mjd@mjdtools.com
http://www.mjdtools.com
Buys and sells antique tools of all sorts; publishes a catalog of antique tools for sale, a fully-indexed, photo-illustrated reference guide and sales catalog; used as a price guide for collectors and dealers worldwide

Anthony Seo
Olde River Hard Goods
13A West Catawissa St.
Nesquehoning, PA 18240
ph: 570-669-9415
tonyseo@ptd.net
http://www.geocities.com/PicketFence/1395
User, collector, and dealer in antique woodworking tools; specializes in wooden planes and good user tools; member of MWTCA, EAIA, and CRAFTS.

Frank J. Vasaturo
Hen House, The
2315 Marshall Rd.
Lansdowne, PA 19050
ph: 610-623-1075
fax: 610-623-1075
sales@hen-house.com
http://www.hen-house.com
Buying and selling tools for 45 years: wood, metal working, precision tools, instruments and kitchen tools.

James Leavenworth
118 Laurel Rd.
Boyertown, PA 19512
ph: 610-689-5024
Deals in antique tools from various time periods; handforged tools and artifacts as well as planes, shaves, knives, catalogs, and layout tools; from 200 years old to 20th century.

Lee Richmond
Best Things LLC, The
299 Herndon Parkway, Ste. 210
Herndon, VA 20170
ph: 703-796-5544
fax: 703-766-0966
lee@thebestthings.com
http://www.thebestthings.com
Carries a large selection of antique tools for sale: Stanley tools, molding planes, British metal planes, wooden planes, and more.

Don Boyer
141 Cottonwood Dr.
Franklin, TN 37069
ph: 615-794-7860
dnbyr@aol.com
http://www.cs.cmu.edu/~alf/en/tool-lists/boyer.txt
Collector, user of old tools with an emphasis on pre-WWII woodworking tools in excellent to new condition; always buying, selling, trading single tools or full shops; free online identification and appraisal from your descriptions.

Tom Witte
Witte's Antiques, Inc.
P.O. Box 399
Mattawan, MI 49071-0399
ph: 616-668-4161
fax: 616-668-5363
Full line tool dealer.

E.J. "Al" Renier
Renier's Antiques
P.O. Box 1323
Minnetonka, MN 55346-0323
ph: 952-937-0393
nordicAl@aol.com
Buys and sells old woodworking tools; expert in Nordic Tools (author and lecturer.)

John Walkowiak
3452 Humbolt Ave. S.
Minneapolis, MN 55408-3332
ph: 612-824-0785
Collecting woodworking tools, specializing in anything made by the Sandusky Tool Co., Ohio.

Paul Oltmanns
Tool Classics
Newsletter: Old Tool Nut Journal, The
475 S. 2100 Rd.
White City, KS 66872
ph: 785-349-2104
oldtoolnut@msn.com
http://www.fortunecity.com/meltingpot/zaire/91
Buys, sells, restores, repairs antique and collectible tools; also publishes "The Old Tool Nut Journal."

Bob Finch
Two Chiselers
1864 Glen Moore Dr.
Lakewood, CO 80215-3038
ph: 303-232-1932
fax: 303-232-4724
rffinch@aol.com
Buys, sells, collects tools; publishes periodic catalog, 36 to 40 pages, fully illustrated; authoring a book on the development of braces and boring tools.

David Zeidman
Tools 'n Rules
2828 Newlands Ave.
Belmont, CA 94002
ph: 650-591-4889
fax: 650-591-2587
dz@toolsrules.com
http://www.toolsrules.com
Buys and sells antique wood and metal working tools for the collector and craftsman; specializes in ivory and boxwood folding rules; the Web site has pictures of the actual tool available for sale.

E.D. "Dave" Paling
Tool Guy, The
227 Ney St.
San Francisco, CA 94112-1644
ph: 415-334-7295
Buys and sells quality used and antique woodworking and machinists tools

Carole & Larry Meeker
Antiques of a Mechanical Nature
5702 Vacation Blvd.
Somerset, CA 95684-9324
ph: 530-620-7019 or 888-607-6090
fax: 530-620-7020
clm@antiqbuyer.com
http://www.antiqbuyer.com
*Buy, sell, trade all manner of tools
and technology; not just woodworking
tools; especially wants mechanical
devices from home, shop, or office;
also wants related paper items and
occupational images.*

John Marshall
For Love or Money
16693 NW Meadowgrass Ct.
Beaverton, OR 97006
john@europa.com
http://home.europa.com/~john
*Buys and sells antique and collectible
woodworking and other trade tools;
member of PNTC and MWTCA.*

Jon Zimmers
Jon Zimmers Antique Tools
206 NE 24th
Portland, OR 97232
ph: 503-232-1565
jonz@teleport.com
http://www.teleport.com/~jonz
*Collector and dealer specializing in
antique tools for woodworkers and
collectors; homepage has free
classified ads, antique tools, tool-
related books, and antique tool
information.*

Steve Johnson
Union Hill Antique Tools
4521 243rd Ave. NE
Redmond, WA 98053
ph: 425-868-1532
fax: 425-868-1532
Tooltimer@msn.com
http://www.tooltimer.com
*Appraiser, collector, dealer, expert
specializing in the best hard-to-find
tools and treadle equipment.*

Bob Kaune
Antique & Used Tools
511 W. 11th
Port Angeles, WA 98362
ph: 360-452-2292
bktools@olympus.net
*Has a large selection of quality
vintage hand tools: planes, scrapers,
spokeshaves, chisels, slicks, draw
knives, saws, braces, drills, levels,
squares, bevels, parts and other hard-
to-find items; Stanley Bed Rock planes
a specialty.*

Charles Stirling
Bristol Design (Tools) Inc.
14 Perry Rd.
Bristol, BS1 5BG U.K.
ph: +44 177929 1740
tools@bristol-design.co.uk
http://www.bristol-design.co.uk
*Issues a woodworking catalog of tools
for sale with quality color illustrations of fine English and American
tools; subscription is $20 (partly*

*refundable) for 5 issues; stocks metal
planes, molding planes, plow planes,
chisels, etc.*

David Stanley
David Stanley Auctions
Stordon Grange, Osgathorpe
Loughborough, Leicestershire LE12 9SR
U.K.
ph: 01530-222320
fax: 01530-222523
david@davidstanley.com
http://www.davidstanley.com
*Specializes in the buying, selling,
collecting, appraising and auctioning
antique and usable woodworking
tools.*

Experts

William A. Gustafson
William A. Gustafson Antiques
P.O. Box 104
11643 Rte. 22
Austerlitz, NY 12017-0104
ph: 518-392-2845
fax: 518-392-4436
oldtools@taconic.net
http://www.taconic.net/oldtools
*Dealer, collector, specialist and
appraiser of antique tools; also
conducts tool auctions.*

Ed Hobbs
4417 Inwood Rd.
Raleigh, NC 27603-3315
ph: 919-828-2754
fax: 919-828-6697
*Appraises and specializes in tools;
writes column for Antique Week;
available for speaking and demonstrations on antique tools.*

Don Boyer
141 Cottonwood Dr.
Franklin, TN 37069
ph: 615-794-7860
dnbyr@aol.com
http://www.cs.cmu.edu/~alf/en/tool-lists/
boyer.txt
*Collector, user of old tools with an
emphasis on pre-WWII woodworking
tools in excellent to new condition;
always buying, selling, trading single
tools or full shops; free online
identification and appraisal from your
descriptions.*

John Walter
Tool Merchant, The
208 Front St.
P.O. Box 227
Marietta, OH 45750-0227
ph: 740-373-9973
fax: 740-373-9059
toolmerchant@sprynet.com
http://www.thetoolmerchant.com
*Buys, sells and appraises antique and
traditional woodworking tools; author
of "Antique & Collectible Stanley
Tools" (1990, The Tool Merchants).*

Internet Resources

Electronic Neanderthal, The
Allan.Fisher@cs.cmu.edu
http://www.cs.cmu.edu/~alf/en/en.html
*A repository of information on the use
and preservation of old and antique
woodworking tools: source of tools
and materials, events, schools,
organizations, books, and places to
visit, links to related Web sites.*

Museums/Libraries

Davistown Museum
58 Main St.
P.O. Box 346
Liberty, ME 04949
ph: 207-288-5126
fax: 207-288-2725
curator@davistownmuseum.org
http://www.davistownmuseum.org
*A regional history, tool and art
museum.*

American Precision Museum Association, Inc.
Newsletter: Tools & Technology
P.O. Box 679
196 Main St.
Windsor, VT 05089
ph: 802-674-5781
fax: 802-674-2524
curator@americanprecision.org
http://www.americanprecision.org
*The museum focuses on machine tools,
early American hand tools and their
products, such as sewing machines,
typewriters and guns.*

Bucks County Historical Society
Newsletter: Penny Lots
84 S. Pine St.
Doylestown, PA 18901-4930
ph: 215-345-0210
fax: 215-230-0823
info@mercermuseum.org
http://www.mercermuseum.org/bchs
*Operates three Nat. Historical
Landmarks; Mercer Museum has over
40,000 tools of Early American
trades/crafts; Spruance Library has
research material on trades & crafts;
Fonthill Museum is a concrete castle
laden with tiles & treasures.*

Hunter M. Pilkinton
World O' Tools Museum
2431 Hwy. 13 So.
Waverly, TN 37185-2930
ph: 931-296-3218
hunterp@usit.net
*Always interested in old or odd
mechanical tools; also related books
and catalogs.*

Periodicals

Clarence Blanchard
Magazine: Fine Tool Journal, The
27 Fickett Rd.
Pownal, ME 04069
ph: 207-688-4962
fax: 207-688-4831
ceb@finetoolj.com
http://www.FineToolJ.com
A quarterly magazine for tool

*collectors and craftsmen; features
biennial absentee tool auctions.*

Taunton Press
Magazine: Fine Woodworking
P.O. Box 5506
Newtown, CT 06470
ph: 800-283-7252 or 203-426-8171
fax: 203-426-3434
webeditor@taunton.com
http://www.taunton.com/fw/index.htm
*Publishes a bi-monthly "How-to"
magazine written and illustrated by
master craftsmen; also publishes a
related line of books and videos; free
catalog available.*

Barry Abel, Ed.
Newsletter: Tool Ads
P.O. Box 33
Hamilton, MT 59840-0033
ph: 406-363-3805
fax: 406-363-4117
airgunads@bitterroot.net
*A monthly newsletter for buyers and
sellers of all types of tools from hand
tools to machinery, parts, accessories
and related literature; contains only
ads and auction notices.*

Anvils

Experts

Dick Postman
10 Fisher Ct.
Berrien Springs, MI 49103-1163
ph: 616-471-5426
Author of "Anvils in America."

Blow Torches

Clubs/Associations

Ron Carr
Blow Torch Collectors Club
Newsletter: Torch, The
3328 258th Ave. SE
Sammamish, WA 98075-9173
ph: 425-557-0634 or 425-462-8603
fax: 425-462-8624
RMCarr@comocast.net
http://www.blowtorch.net
*A group of blow torch collectors
dedicated to preserving the history of
blow torches and related material;
new members always welcomed.*

Collectors

Samuel G. Scroggs
1073 Stonybridge Dr.
Chambersburg, PA 17201-9093
ph: 717-263-5422
Wants pre-1900 brass blow torches.

Ron Carr
3328 258th Ave. SE
Sammamish, WA 98075-9173
ph: 425-557-0634 or 425-462-8603
fax: 425-462-8624
RMCarr@comocast.net
http://www.blowtorch.net
*Wants to buy brass blow torches; turn
of the century brass torches, all
models including gasoline, alcohol,
and kerosene.*

Clamps

Experts

Milt Boyd
Rose Wood Dr.
Haverhill, MA 01832-1532
ph: 978-469-0973
fax: 978-469-0973
ClampGuy@clampguy.info
http://www.clampguy.info
*Collects and researches American
hand screw industry, from c. 1830 to
1930s; author of articles on clamp
makers; pamphlet on clamp collecting
available on request; wants to buy
catalogs of American clamp makers
and examples of their work.*

New Jersey

Experts

Alexander Farnham
Farnham Studio
78 Tumble Falls Rd.
Stockton, NJ 08559-1309
ph: 908-996-4179
*Author of "Search for Early New
Jersey Toolmakers," $27.50 ppd.,
hardbound, "Early Tools of New
Jersey and the Men Who Made Them,"
$22.50 ppd., hardbound, and "Tool
Collectors Handbook," $3.50 ppd.
softbound.*

Planes

Experts

Roger K. Smith
P.O. Box 177
Athol, MA 01331-0177
ph: 978-249-5990
tooltimer@msn.com
http://www.tooltimer.com/roger
*Buys, sells and specializes in planes;
send LSASE for free catalog; author
of "Patented Transitional & Metallic
Planes in America" - Vols. I and II;*

John Whelan
38 Colony Ct.
New Providence, NJ 07974-2332
ph: 908-464-5424
jmwhelwdpl@aol.com
*Author of "The Wooden Plane - Its
History, Form and Function"
(Astragal Press) and "Making
Traditional Wooden Planes"
(Astragal Press).*

Plumb Bobs

Collectors

R. Bruce Cynar
Old Technology Associates
10023 St. Clair's Retreat
Fort Wayne, IN 46825
ph: 260-489-5004
oldtchnlgy@msn.com
*Focuses on plumb bobs, plumb lines
and bobs with pulleys.*

Stanley

Collectors

Bill Hermanek
31 Wildwood Dr.
Smithtown, NY 11787-3452
ph: 631-360-1216 or 516-333-2640
BHermanek@aol.com
*Wants to buy planes, levels, rulers,
braces, marking gauges, etc.; also
wants tool literature, catalogs,
advertising; anything Stanley.*

Experts

John Walter
Tool Merchant, The
208 Front St.
P.O. Box 227
Marietta, OH 45750-0227
ph: 740-373-9973
fax: 740-373-9059
toolmerchant@sprynet.com
http://www.thetoolmerchant.com
*Author of the illustrated "Antique &
Collectible Stanley Tools: A Guide to
Identification and Value" - 1997
edition (8-1/2" x 5", 885 pages),
current values on 2,500 tools, over
1,500 illustrations.*

Periodicals

John Walter
Tool Merchant, The
Magazine: Stanley Tool Collector News
208 Front St.
P.O. Box 227
Marietta, OH 45750-0227
ph: 740-373-9973
fax: 740-373-9059
toolmerchant@sprynet.com
http://www.thetoolmerchant.com
*40-page user/collector magazine;
feature articles, research, 100s of
select quality tools for sale, all with
photos (lowest prices), user info.,
auction results, type studies, classified
ads.*

Tape Measures

Collectors

Janet Morphy
135 Wedgewood Dr.
Pittsburgh, PA 15229
ph: 412-366-6589
*Wants to buy figural tape measures of
metal, celluloid, porcelain.*

Sherry L. Werdon
400 N. Washington
Lowell, MI 49331-1465
ph: 616-897-9580
*Wants to buy figural tape measures;
also wants unusual sewing items such
as figural pin cushions, thimble
holders, etc.*

Wrenches

Collectors

Robert Rauhauser
P.O. Box 324
Thomasville, PA 17364-0324
ph: 717-792-0278
Wants wrenches with names;

*especially cutout (see throughs)
wrenches; any farm machinery
wrenches; specialty wrenches.*

Joe Greiwe
206 Albers St.
Batesville, IN 47006-1502
ph: 812-934-2747
*Has a collection of between 1,500 and
2,000 wrenches.*

Wrenches (Adjustable)

Collectors

Charles W. Wardell
P.O. Box 195
Trinity, NC 27370-0195
ph: 336-434-1145
*Wants early "monkey" wrenches of
unusual design. Many 1800-1900
inventors used clever schemes to make
the repair of machinery a more
pleasant task. Gripping a bolt or nut
securely and having a quick release
mechanism were important.*

TOOTH FAIRY

Experts

Dr. Rosemary Wells, Ph.D.
1129 Cherry St.
Deerfield, IL 60015
ph: 847-945-1129
fax: 847-945-1125
*Expert and researcher on the history
and lore surrounding the Tooth Fairy;
has a large collection of TF related
items.*

Museums/Libraries

Dr. Rosemary Wells, Ph.D.
Tooth Fairy Museum
Newsletter: Tooth Fairy Tabloid
1129 Cherry St.
Deerfield, IL 60015
ph: 847-945-1129
fax: 847-945-1125

TOOTHPICK HOLDERS

Clubs/Associations

National Toothpick Holder Collectors
Society
Newsletter: Toothpick Bulletin
P.O. Box 852
Archer City, TX 76351
ph: 408-252-8799
tpinfo@glass-works.com
http://www.collectoronline.com/club-
NTHCS.html
*Society members interested in
collecting toothpick holders of all
shapes and materials; monthly
newsletter, annual conventions.*

Collectors

Judy A. Knauer
1224 Spring Valley Lane
West Chester, PA 19380-5112
ph: 610-431-3477
winkjk@comcast.net
*Collector, lecturer, and author on old
glass toothpick holders; founder of*

*National Toothpick Holder Collectors
Society.*

Lorraine Holt
2892 Sand Creek Highway
Adrian, MI 49221
ph: 517-265-4777

Fred Phelps
P.O. Box 217
Colesburg, IA 52035-0217
ph: 319-856-2025

Richard & Nancy Ryan
8801 Thorndale Ct.
Fort Worth, TX 76180-1620
ph: 817-577-4341
fax: 817-788-4532
RARyan13@aol.com

Experts

Judy A. Knauer
1224 Spring Valley Lane
West Chester, PA 19380-5112
ph: 610-431-3477
winkjk@comcast.net
*Collector, lecturer, and author on old
glass toothpick holders; wants to add
to collection of old glass toothpick
holders; buying one piece or entire
collection; please describe, state
condition and price.*

TOURS/BUYING TRIPS

Internet Resources

Ron Heath
Antiques Web
U.K.
antiques-web@gifford.co.uk
http://www.antiques-web.co.uk
*This Web site lists antiques centers,
dealers and shows in the U.K.;
impartial advice for anyone planning
a U.K. antiques tour.*

Misc. Services

Peter Manston
Travel Keys Tours
P.O. Box 160691
Sacramento, CA 95816-0691
ph: 916-452-5200
*Buy antiques at the best fairs, flea
markets, warehouses and antique
centers in Europe; group tours or
individual escorted travel.*

TOWLETTES

Clubs/Associations

Michael Lewis
Modern Moist Towlette Collecting
3000 Highway 19A, Ste. 2
Mount Dora, FL 32757
MoistTwl@aol.com
http://members.aol.com/MoistTwl

TOY GUNS

BB Guns

(see also AIRGUNS)

Clubs/Associations

Jim Buskirk
Toy Gun Collectors of America
Newsletter: Toy Gun Collectors of
    America Newsletter
3009 Oleander Ave.
San Marcos, CA 92069-6128
ph: 760-599-1054
*Focuses on pre-WWII American cap
guns and spring/air BB guns (non-
pellet guns or other high powered air
guns); newsletter published quarterly:
photos, information, articles; also free
want ads for subscribers; quarterly
newsletter.*

Collectors

Bob Warner
P.O. Box 336
Lake George, MI 48633
ph: 517-588-4968
*Wants old BB and pellet guns, any
make: Daisy double barrel, Buffalo
Bill, Buck Jones, Buzz Barton, 25
Pump, Texas Ranger, NRA, and Daisy
toys.*

Terry Burger
2323 Lincoln
Beatrice, NE 68310-3306
ph: 402-228-2797
BarbieLJB@yahoo.com
*Wants pre-1915, preferably cast iron-
framed guns: Daisy, Atlas, Matchless,
New Rapid, etc.*

Mike Burleson
12048 CR 1168
Tyler, TX 75703
ph: 903-561-9343
bbguns@tyler.net
*Wants old or unusual American BB
guns by Markham, King, Heilprin,
Daisy or others.*

Clay Tontz
4043 Nora Ave.
Covina, CA 91722-3819
ph: 626-338-9976
Wants pre-1930 BB guns.

Experts

Jim Buskirk
3009 Oleander Ave.
San Marcos, CA 92069-6128
ph: 760-599-1054
*Buys, sells, collects and specializes in
BB guns and cap guns.*

Museums/Libraries

Customer Service
Daisy Manufacturing Co., Air Gun
    Museum
211 South 8th St.
P.O. Box 220
Rogers, AR 72757
ph: 501-636-1200 or 800-643-3458
fax: 501-636-1601
info@daisymuseum.com
http://www.daisymuseum.com
*World's oldest and largest manufac-
turer of BB and pellet air guns;
museum contains commemorative guns
and collectibles.*

Cap Guns

Clubs/Associations

Jim Buskirk
Toy Gun Collectors of America
Newsletter: Toy Gun Collectors of
    America Newsletter
3009 Oleander Ave.
San Marcos, CA 92069-6128
ph: 760-599-1054
*Focuses on pre-WWII American cap
guns and spring/air BB guns (non-
pellet guns or other high powered air
guns); newsletter published quarterly:
photos, information, articles; also free
want ads for subscribers; quarterly
newsletter.*

Collectors

George Fougere
67 East St.
North Grafton, MA 01536-1830
ph: 508-839-2701
*Interested in cast iron and die cast cap
pistols; no air rifles, please.*

Bob Williamson
190 Washington St.
East Stroudsburg, PA 18301-2819
ph: 570-421-6957 or 570-421-8550
fax: 570-421-8605
cboy@ptd.net
*Sells and buys rare and common cast
iron cap guns, bombs, canes, cannons,
BB guns (1860s to 1950s); also wants
caps, boxes, catalogs, literature, etc.*

Terry Burger
2323 Lincoln
Beatrice, NE 68310-3306
ph: 402-228-2797
BarbieLJB@yahoo.com

Bill Hamburg
P.O. Box 536
Woodland Hills, CA 91365
ph: 818-346-1269
fax: 818-346-0215
whamburg@aol.com
*Wants to buy excellent to mint-in-box
only; also buys cap gun boxes, pre-
1960 toy race cars, Smith-Miller and
MIC trucks, Tonka trucks, advertising
clocks, and old cowboy gear and
memorabilia.*

Experts

Rudy D'Angelo
P.O. Box 350
Farmington, CT 06034-0350
ph: 860-674-9422
fax: 860-677-7433
radpiimc44@aol.com
http://members.tripod.com/rudydangelo
*Author of "Television's Cowboys
Gunfighters & Cap Pistols."*

Jim Schleyer
P.O. Box 243
Burke, VA 22015-0243
*Wants to buy older toy and cap pistols
and holsters; will answer inquiries
that are accompanied by SASE; has
written extensively on the subject of
toy guns; author of "Backyard*

*Buckaroos - Collecting Western Toy
Guns."*

David Stanley
David's Cap Gun Collectables
P.O. Box 8
Hardy, KY 41531
ph: 606-353-8173
fordfanatic85@yahoo.com
http://www.geocities.com/fordfanatic85
*Collector, appraiser, repairer of
Western cowboy cap guns from the
1940s through the 1960s; designs and
manufacturers replica holsters.*

Brad Maxfield
maxfield@mcw.edu
http://members.nbci.com/bmaxfield/
    Marx/MarxMain.html
*Collector of miniature toy guns with
an expertise in miniature cap guns
made by the Louis Marx Company;
author/webmaster of Maxfield's Marx
Miniature Cap Guns, a Web based
collector's guide and reference.*

Charles W. Best
11523 Pine Valley Dr.
Franktown, CO 80116-8708
ph: 303-660-2318
Budbest@aol.com
*Collects 19th century cap guns; author
of "Cast Iron Toy Guns &
Capshooters;" advanced collector
interested in early toy guns.*

Jim Buskirk
3009 Oleander Ave.
San Marcos, CA 92069-6128
ph: 760-599-1054
*Buys, sells, collects and specializes in
BB guns and cap guns.*

Internet Resources

Brad Maxfield
Marx Miniature Cap Guns
maxfield@mcw.edu
http://members.nbci.com/bmaxfield/
    Marx/MarxMain.html
*A Web-based toy gun collector's guide
and reference.*

TOYS

(see also BANKS; CHARACTER
COLLECTIBLES; CHILDREN'S
THINGS; DISNEY COLLECTIBLES;
DOLLS; GAMES; KITS;
MINIATURES; MOVIE
MEMORABILIA; POPULAR
CULTURE; PREMIUMS; RIDING
TOYS; SOLDIERS, Toy; STEIFF;
SUPER HEROES; TEDDY BEARS;
TOY GUNS; TRAINS; TRUCKS)

Appraisers

AsktheAppraiser.com
4 Brussels St.
Worcester, MA 01610
ph: 781-821-0199
ata@collectingchannel.com
http://www.AsktheAppraiser.com
*The premiere online appraisal service
offered by CollectingChannel.com; all
appraisals comply with the "Uniform*

*Standards of Professional Appraisal
Practice" and with the standards of
the Association of Online Appraisers.*

Noel Barrett
Noel Barrett Antiques & Auctions, Ltd.
P.O. Box 300
Carversville, PA 18913-0201
ph: 215-297-5109
fax: 215-297-0457
toys@noelbarrett.com
http://www.noelbarret.com
*Specializes in the appraisal of toys,
games, vintage advertising and
country store items.*

Tim Luke, ISA
Treasure Quest Auction Galleries, Inc.
2581 Jupiter Park Dr., Ste. E5
Jupiter, FL 33458
ph: 561-741-0777 or 888-741-0777
fax: 561-741-0757
tim@tqag.com
http://www.tqag.com
*Specializes in the appraisal of toys,
dolls, and bears.*

Norbert Hernandez
Classic Animation
4524 Sterling Lane
Plano, TX 75093
ph: 214-641-4464 or 972-519-0066
nhernan770@aol.com
*Accredited member of the International
Society of Appraisers; specializes in
the appraisal of animation art, toys,
film mementoes.*

Nancy Burke Bosch, ISA
Bosch Appraisal Service
1610 Northstar Dr.
Petaluma, CA 94954-6607
ph: 707-773-3970
fax: 707-773-3974
nbbosch@pacbell.net
http://www.appraiseyourantiques.com
*Specializes in appraising European &
American furniture, fine art,
decorative art & accessories, china,
dolls, toys, crystal, silver, American
wicker, quilts, linen, other textiles,
other appreciable residential contents.*

Caren L. Carlson, ISA
Ask an Appraiser
31313 NW Paradise Park Rd.
Ridgefield, WA 98642-8754
ph: 360-887-8686
fax: 360-887-8909
carenscubbyhole@netscape.net
*Specializes in the appraisal of early
20th century dolls, toys and
accessories.*

Carol Sheehan, CPPA
SCA Appraisals
12 Burt Court
Stoney Creek, Ontario L8H 3H4 Canada
ph: 905-664-6712
fax: 905-664-6712
csheehan1@cogeco.ca
*Certified appraiser who appraises,
buys, sells toys and dolls.*

Auction Services

Martin Krim
New England Auction Gallery
P.O. Box 764
Middleton, MA 01949
ph: 978-304-3140
fax: 978-304-3140
mrkrim@attbi.com
http://www.old-toys.com
Conduct mail-bid auctions with full color illustrated catalogs; specializes in sales of Disney, TV and cartoon items from 1920-1970: toys, wind-ups, robots, space toys.

George Glastris
Skinner, Inc.
63 Park Plaza
The Heritage on the Garden
Boston, MA 02116
ph: 617-350-5400
fax: 617-350-5429
info@skinnerinc.com
http://www.skinnerinc.com
Established in 1971, Skinner Inc. is the fourth largest auction house in the US; has offices in Boston and Bolton, MA.

Richard W. Withington, Inc.
590 Center Rd.
Hillsboro, NH 03244
ph: 603-464-3232
fax: 603-464-4901
withington@conknet.com
http://www.withingtonauction.com

Herb & Barb Smith
Smith House Toy Sales
P.O. Box 336
Eliot, ME 03903
smithtoys@aol.com
http://www.smithhousetoys.com
Conducts four specialty mail-bid toys and collectibles auctions each year.

Randy Inman
Randy Inman Auctions, Inc.
P.O. Box 726
West Buxton, ME 04093
ph: 207-872-6900
fax: 207-872-6966
inman@inmanauctions.com
http://www.inmanauctions.com
Conducts specialty auctions for advertising, coin-op, gambling devices, automata, soda pop, Coca Cola, breweriana, robots and space toys, cast iron and tin toys, Disneyana, mechanical music, and mechanical and still banks.

James D. Julia Auctioneers Inc.
Rt. 201, Skowhegan Rd.
P.O. Box 830
Fairfield, ME 04937
ph: 207-453-7125
fax: 207-453-2502
jjulia@juliaauctions.com
http://www.juliaauctions.com
Conducts specialized auctions of toys and doll items and are one of the leaders in this field in North America.

Jeffrey Ralston
Lloyd Ralston Toy Auction
350 Long Beach Blvd.
Stratford, CT 06615
ph: 203-386-9399
fax: 203-386-9515
lrgallery@aol.com
http://www.lloydralstontoys.com
Specializes in auctioning toys, dolls, games and trains.

Bertoia Auctions
2141 DeMarco Dr.
Vineland, NJ 08360
ph: 856-692-1881
fax: 856-692-8697
bill@bertoiaauctions.com
http://www.bertoiaauctions.com
Specializing in the auctioning of antique toys, banks, trains, and doorstops; offers online auctions.

Sotheby's
1334 York Ave.
New York, NY 10021
ph: 212-606-7000
fax: 212-606-7107
http://www.sothebys.com
Over 70 collecting areas are featured at Sotheby's auctions including toys, dolls, porcelain, furniture, silver, art, books; exhibitions are free and everyone is welcome; for a free copy of "Sotheby's Newsletter," call 212-606-7245.

Henry Kurtz
Henry Kurtz Ltd.
163 Amsterdam Ave., Ste. 136
New York, NY 10023
ph: 212-642-5904
fax: 212-874-6018
Specializes in the sale of jewelry, paintings, prints, silver, coins, stamps, toys (especially lead soldiers), and movie memorabilia.

Amory Spizzirri, Client Svc.
William Doyle Galleries
175 E. 87th St.
New York, NY 10128-2205
ph: 212-427-2730
fax: 212-369-0892
info@doylegalleries.com
http://www.doylegalleries.com
Holds over 50 auctions annually of furniture and decorations, paintings and sculpture, jewelry, books and prints, couture and textiles, 20th century art & design, majolica, Lalique, Asian works of art and other specialty categories.

Ted Hake
Hake's Americana & Collectibles Auction
P.O. Box 1444
York, PA 17405-1444
ph: 717-848-1333
Ted@hakes.com
http://www.hakes.com
Always purchasing, consigning items for 5 mail-bid & online auctions per year; hundreds of categories including toys, character collectibles, Disney, cowboy heroes, premiums, television,

politicals, pin-back buttons, advertising and more.

Noel Barrett
Noel Barrett Antiques & Auctions, Ltd.
P.O. Box 300
Carversville, PA 18913-0201
ph: 215-297-5109
fax: 215-297-0457
toys@noelbarrett.com
http://www.noelbarret.com
Specializes in the auction of vintage toys, banks, trains and games; primarily this means items made prior to WWII with the exception of tin space and automotive toys made in the 1950s and early 1960s.

Ted Maurer
Successful Auction Management
1003 Brookwood Dr.
Pottstown, PA 19464-3022
ph: 610-323-1573 or 610-367-5024
ted@maurerail.com
http://www.maurerail.com
Specializes in the auctioning of toys, trains and railroad related items.

Richard W. Opfer, Jr.
Richard Opfer Auctioneering, Inc.
1919 Greenspring Dr.
Lutherville Timonium, MD 21093-4113
ph: 410-252-5035
fax: 410-252-5863
info@opferauction.com
http://www.opferauction.com
Specializes in auctioning paintings, furniture, antiques, toys, dolls, games, black memorabilia, and advertising items; monthly eclectic collector sales feature a wide variety of collectibles; weekly auctions include general estate merch.

Perry R. Eichor
Eichor Associates
703 N. Almond Dr.
Simpsonville, SC 29681-3453
ph: 864-967-8770
fax: 864-228-2541
kpmflyn@earthlink.net
Appraises and conducts auction sales of toys; member Antique Toy Collectors of America.

Ann Hays, ISA CAPP
Hays & Associates, Inc.
120 South Spring St.
Louisville, KY 40206-1953
ph: 502-584-4297
fax: 502-585-5896
annhays@haysauction.com
http://www.haysauction.com
Conducts specialty toy and doll auctions; Ann Hays is a Certified Appraiser of Personal Property with the International Society of Appraisers; director of auction house antique and collectible toy and doll department for over 25 years.

Lou & Sharon Daniels
American Eagle Auction Company
20030 US Highway 23N
Circleville, OH 43113
ph: 740-477-3900
fax: 740-927-5184
oakhouse@netpluscom.com
http://www.americaneagleauction.com

James L. Jackson, ISA
Jackson's Auctioneers & Appraisers
2229 Lincoln St.
P.O. Box 50613
Cedar Falls, IA 50613
ph: 319-277-2256
fax: 319-277-1252
jacksons@jacksonsauction.com
http://www.jacksonsauction.com
Conducts specialty auctions of antique toys (tin, cast iron, windup) and contemporary toys.

Kurt R. Krueger
Krueger Auctions
P.O. Box 275
Iola, WI 54945-0275
ph: 715-445-3845
fax: 715-445-4100
Specializing in the mail-bid auction of tokens, advertising, brewery items, Western Americana, postcards, World's Fair & Expo., autographs, sports, coins & currency, pinbacks, military memorabilia, automotive, Disneyana, toys, dolls, etc.

Joy Luke
Joy Luke Auction Gallery
300 E. Grove St.
Bloomington, IL 61701-5232
ph: 309-828-5533
fax: 309-829-2266
robert@joyluke.com
http://www.joyluke.com
Conducts periodic auctions specializing in the sale of toys, banks, trains and dolls.

Larry Martin
Larry Martin Toy Sales
6 Nancy Lane
Clinton, IL 61727
ph: 217-935-8211
fax: 217-935-3795
lmcs2000@yahoo.com
http://wwww.martinauctioncompany.com

Glenn Butler
Wallis & Wallis
West St. Auction Galleries
Lewes, East Sussex BN7 2NJ U.K.
ph: 01273-480208
fax: 01273-476562
wallisandwallis@mcmail.com
http://www.wallisandwallis.co.uk
Britain's specialist auctioneers of diecast & tin plate toys & models including model soldiers.

Sotheby's
34-35 New Bond St.
London, W1A 2AA U.K.
ph: 44 171 293 5000
fax: 44 171 293 5989
http://www.sothebys.com
Conducts specialty auctions of tinplate

toys, diecasts, trains, antique dolls,
teddy bears, automata.

Bryan Goodall
Vectis Auctions Ltd.
Fleck Way
Thornaby
Stockton on Tees, TS17 9JZ U.K.
enquiries@vectis.co.uk
http://www.vectis.co.uk
*A U.K. firm with offices in the US
specializing in the auction sale of
vintage toys and toy soldiers.*

Clubs/Associations

Association of Game & Puzzle Collectors
Journal: Game & Puzzle Collectors
  Quarterly
PMB 321
197M Boston Post Rd. West
Marlborough, MA 01752
juckett@attglobal.net
http://www.agpc.org
*Members are devoted to collecting,
researching, preserving games, jigsaw
puzzles, mechanical puzzles, and other
pastimes.*

Robert R. Grew
Antique Toy Collectors of America, Inc.,
  The
Newsletter: Toy Chest
c/o Carter, Ledyard & Milburn
Two Wall St. - 13th Floor
New York, NY 10005
ph: 212-238-8803
fax: 212-732-3232
grew@clm.com
*A non-profit organization focusing on
antique toys and games; since
membership is by invitation only for
established collectors, there is a
waiting list; bi-monthly newsletter
available only to members & to
libraries/museums on request.*

Canadian Toy Collectors' Society
Magazine: Toy Collector
91 Rylander Blvd., Unit 7, Ste. 245
Scarborough, Ontario M1B 5M5 Canada
ph: 905-389-8047
ctcsweb@hotmail.com
http://www.ctcs.org
*Association for toy collectors
worldwide; promoters of Canada's
greatest toy collector's show & sale,
promoter of C.T.C.S. "Limited
Edition" Brooklin models; CTCS
maintains large museum collection of
early Canadian toys.*

Collectors

Martin Krim
P.O. Box 764
Middleton, MA 01949
ph: 978-304-3140
fax: 978-304-3140
mrkrim@attbi.com
http://www.old-toys.com
*Wants wind-up and battery toys, toy
cars, robots and space toys.*

Mark Bergin
Mark Bergin Toys Ltd.
P.O. Box 3073
Peterborough, NH 03458-3073
ph: 603-924-2079
fax: 603-924-2022
mbergin@bergintoys.com
http://www.bergintoys.com
*Wants old toys: tin, metal, celluloid;
wind-up toys of all kinds, battery
operated toys, friction, robots, space
toys, space guns, cars, buses, racers,
motorcycles, boats, airplanes,
character toys, etc.*

William R. Strieder
335 South Green Haven Rd.
Stormville, NY 12570
ph: 845-221-9371
toybill@aol.com
*Wants to buy old toys: cast iron, tin
wind-ups, battery operated, banks, etc.*

Sanford Weltman
2 Roxbury Lane
Pittsford, NY 14534
ph: 585-249-9417 or 585-249-9499
*Buying old toys, one item or
collection.*

Larry Bruch
Larry Bruch Toys
P.O. Box 121
Mountain Top, PA 18707-0121
ph: 800-549-TOYS
bkinglar@aol.com
*All kinds of pre-1960 toys wanted:
German, American: metal cars,
airplanes, boats; comic characters,
cast iron toys and banks, etc.; also
buying Tootsietoys, Dinky, and Smith-
Miller; write for free 3-page
illustrated want list.*

Ronald Wiener
1650 Arch St., 22 Floor
Philadelphia, PA 19103-2097
ph: 215-977-2266
fax: 215-405-3866
rwiener@wolfblock.com
*Wants to buy toys, especially Marklin
German toy trains and other Marklin
toys, as well as other European toy
trains and transportation toys and
European and American tin toys (1890
to 1956).*

Lee Woolf
435 Sharpless St.
West Chester, PA 19382-3538
ph: 610-918-0620
*Wants to buy electric trains, toy trucks
and cars, lead figures and soldiers,
Daisy BB guns, model race cars.*

Jim Conley
2758 Coventry Lane
Canton, OH 44708-1320
ph: 330-477-7725
fax: 330-879-2950
*Buys and sells cars, trucks, tin wind-
ups, Buddy L, Metal Craft, Smith
Miller, Tonka, Lehmann, Bing, Ives,
Marx, etc.; also Fisher-Price, Gibbs
toys, Japanese tin cars from the '50s*

and '60s; OK for sellers to call
collect.

Jerry Peters
Chestnut Hollow, Ltd.
6060 Bordman Rd.
P.O. Box 6
Almont, MI 48003-0006
ph: 810-798-3158
jpeters@expression.org
*Wants to buy robots, sci-fi related,
aviation related, cars, trucks, wind-
ups, battery operated, etc.; Rocketeer,
Star Trek, Star Wars, Buck Rogers,
King Kong, Universal movie monsters,
actual movie props, autographs, movie
posters.*

Dr. Greg Zemenick
Dr. "Z"
1350 Kirts, Ste. 160
Troy, MI 48084-4852
ph: 248-642-8129 or 248-244-9430
fax: 248-244-9495
drzzeezz@aol.com
http://www.drzzeezzi.com
*Wants to buy early American (pre-
1910) toys, banks, cigar store
collectibles, tin toys, clocks;
appraises, collects, sells, repairs.*

Robert Manella
4441 Shari Ann Lane
Minneapolis, MN 55443
ph: 763-560-4290

Michael Sullivan
Route 1, Box 45
Jonesburg, MO 63351
ph: 636-488-5677
mandgee@socket.net
http://www.sully-has-it.com
*Buying and trading pressed steel
trucks, cars and airplanes.*

Kenneth R. Chane
9755 Independence Ave.
Chatsworth, CA 91311-4318
ph: 818-407-0855
fax: 818-407-0850
*Wants to buy ice cream vendors,
baggage carts with figures, graffiti
cars, tin lithograph toys.*

Dealers

Leila Dunbar
Dunbar's Gallery
76 Haven St.
Milford, MA 01757-3821
ph: 508-634-8697
fax: 508-634-8698
dunbars@dunbarsgallery.com
http://www.dunbarsgallery.com
*Mail order Americana - no reproduc-
tions; buys, sells and specializes in
vintage character and comic toys,
banks, advertising, automobilia, and
Halloween related items.*

George Newcomb
Plymouth Rock Toy Co.
P.O. Box 1202
Plymouth, MA 02362
ph: 508-746-2842 or 508-830-1880
fax: 508-830-0364
plyrocktoy@aol.com

Karen & Dan Dozier
ToyTent.com
23 Forest Ave.
Falmouth, MA 02540-4006
ph: 508-548-6342 or 508-548-0893
fax: 508-548-0893
tintoys@dozierdesigns.com
http://www.toytent.com
*Collector, dealer, appraiser of
Vintage and new collectible toys from
around the world; specializing in
robots, space toys, and high quality
handmade reproduction toy boxes;
also sells art posters made from toy
box graphics.*

Bob Gobeil
Bobby's Toys & Collectibles
P.O. Box 1416
Biddeford, ME 04005
bob@bobbystoys.com
http://www.bobbystoys.com
*Offers character toys from the 1970s
and 1980s from Alfs to Wuzzles; also
TV and movie memorabilia, cereal
premiums, fast food collectibles.*

Carl Lobel
P.O. Box 74A
Warren, VT 05674
ph: 802-496-4025
clobel@madriver.com
*Wants to buy comic character wind-
ups, Lehman, space toys, robots/
astronauts, TPS wind-ups, 1930-1960
Japanese, plush bear wind-ups,
unusual comic character items such as
figurines, radios, clocks, and dolls.*

Jeffrey Ralston
Lloyd Ralston Gallery
350 Long Beach Blvd.
Stratford, CT 06615
ph: 203-386-9399
fax: 203-386-9515
lrgallery@aol.com
http://www.lloydralstontoys.com

Ken Farrell
Just Kids Nostalgia
310 New York Ave.
Huntington, NY 11743
ph: 631-423-8449
info@justkidsnostalgia.com
http://www.justkidsnostalgia.com
*Buys and sells vintage toys; also
board games, lunch boxes, personality
dolls, character dolls, pinback
buttons, advertising figures, radio
premiums, bubble gum cards, baseball
cards.*

Raymond Schieber, Sr.
Toy Locators
5821 Diana Lane
Lake View, NY 14085
ph: 716-627-5840
RSchie7677@aol.com

Bob Smith
255 Tryon Pk.
Rochester, NY 14609-6814
ph: 585-288-7153
bob@oldtoysonline.com
http://www.oldtoysonline.com
Avid collector and dealer of 1870-1970 toys: wind-up, automotive, European tin, pressed steel, early diecast, cast iron; specializes in Oh Boy, Tootsietoys, Dinky Toys, Hillclimbers, Wyandotte, and German tin toys.

Jacqueline Henry
Antique Treasures, Toys & Dolls
2240 Academy St.
P.O. Box 17
Walworth, NY 14568-0017
ph: 315-986-1424
jhenry1@rochester.rr.com
http://www.cyberattic.com/~toysndolls
Buys and sells 1860-1960 toys; cast iron, lithographed tin, wind-ups, banks, candy containers, pressed steel toys, toy soldiers, dolls, games, etc.

Chris Savino
P.O. Box 419
Breesport, NY 14816-0419
ph: 607-739-3106
chrissavino@stny.rr.com
Wants to buy any childhood items: tin wind-ups, battery toys, cast iron toys, autos, trucks, marbles, robots; toys made in the US, Japan, Germany, France England; toys in original boxes bring more; call or write for an offer.

Phil McEntee
Where the Toys Are, Inc.
45 W. Pike St.
Canonsburg, PA 15317
ph: 724-745-4599
wheretoysr@aol.com
http://www.wherethetoysare.com
Expert and dealer in vintage and antique toys from Victorian era to baby boomer collectibles.

Bob Stevens
Keystone Toy Trader
529 N. Water St.
Masontown, PA 15461-1747
ph: 724-583-8234
fax: 724-583-0604
keystonetoytrader@charter.net
Wants quality antique toys in all categories: early comic character toys, cast iron and tin toys, diecast pre-WWII Tootsietoys, German penny toys, early German and European toys.

Jack L. Dempsey
Dempsey & Baster
1009 East 38th St.
Erie, PA 16504
ph: 814-825-7690 or 814-825-6381
info@dempseyandbaxter.com
http://www.dempseyandbaxter.com
Owns the only one-of-a-kind American coin in existence - the 11-cent coin; buys coins and currency; also tin toys, paper ephemera, fine estate jewelry.

Marianne Schneider
Schneider's Toys & Fancy Goods
2043 Bonnie Dr.
Lancaster, PA 17603
ph: 717-519-8888
fax: 717-519-8889
toy2biz@aol.com
Specializes in pre-WWII antique toys, primarily pre-1900: German handpainted tin, Lehmann, Martin, paper lithograph toys, Christmas, automata, early American tin and clockwork toys.

Jim Cox
Sussex Antique Toy Shop
107 Ave. L
Matamoras, PA 18336
ph: 570-491-2707
toyfolks@erols.com

Bill & Anne Shaner
Shaner's Antiques & Collectibles
403 N. Charlotte St.
Pottstown, PA 19464-5311
ph: 610-326-0165
Wants antique toys.

Sam Tressler
10301 Welty Rd.
Emmitsburg, MD 21727
ph: 301-447-2498
sdtressler@aol.com
Buys and sells antique toys.

Jim Abicht
Smithfield Antiques Center
131 Main St.
P.O. Box 157
Smithfield, VA 23431
ph: 757-365-0223
bobani@visi.net
Buys and sells old toys, specializing in Marx.

Ed Janey
1756 65th St.
Fernandina Beach, FL 32035-3112
ph: 904-491-8052
Always buying old toys, model kits, Western collectibles and toys, space toys, slot cars and car kits, lunch boxes, ad items, radios, Disney, soakies, etc.

Gordy Dutt
Gordy's
P.O. Box 201
Sharon Center, OH 44274-0201
ph: 330-239-1657
fax: 330-239-2991
Gordysmag@aol.com
http://www.gordyskitbuilders.com
Wants to buy toys from the '50s to

'80s: games, gum cards, model kits, gun sets, monsters, super heroes, cereal premiums, TV-related, cartoon toys, etc.

Bill & Joanne Bruegman
Toy Scouts, Inc.
137 Casterton Ave.
Akron, OH 44303-1543
ph: 330-836-0668
orders@toyscouts.com
http://www.toyscouts.com
Specializes baby-boom era toys from 1950s-60s: TV, cartoon, monsters, super heroes, games, cereal premiums, model kits, etc.; anything baby-boomer era.

Ed McDandal
Ed's Toy Shop
953 East Richmond
Kokomo, IN 46901
ph: 765-459-0325
fax: 765-459-0380
ed21131@aol.com
http://www.antiquetoy.net
Wants to buy old toys from the 1920s to 1930s; pressed steel cars and trucks, cast iron toys, wind-ups, live steam toys.

Tad Muscott
930 W. South St.
Mason, MI 48854
ph: 517-676-8697
fax: 517-676-8697
Wants childhood classic toys: windup, friction, battery operated, character, Disney, robots, space toys.

Richard Trautwein
Toys N Such
437 Dawson St.
Sault Sainte Marie, MI 49783-2119
ph: 906-635-0356
Collector, dealer, expert, appraiser wants tin and metal wind-up, battery operated, and electric toys: German, Japanese, or American; also gas operated toys and pedal cars and bikes.

Heinz Mueller
Continental Hobby House
P.O. Box 193
Sheboygan, WI 53082
ph: 920-693-3371
fax: 920-693-8211
continental@lsol.net
http://www.classictintoy.com
Dealers in classic toys, trains, high quality collectibles; buyers of toys, trains, Erector sets, steam engines, partial toys and parts.

Joe Morabito
Main St. Toys
P.O. Box 5211
Minneapolis, MN 55402
ph: 612-339-7321
fax: 612-375-0549
Joe@mainstreettoys.com
http://www.mainstreettoys.com
Sells vintage toys: space toys, pop culture, battery-powered, robots, windups, etc.

Jay Robinson
Chicago Kid
522 Rivershire Place
Lincolnshire, IL 60069
ph: 847-913-1106
fax: 847-913-1274
jay@thechicagokid.com
Wants to buy old electric and wind-up trains; also old toy trucks and cars; wind-up and battery-operated toys.

Sue Tarrant
Pretty Good Toys
67 May Valley Lane
Fenton, MO 63026
ph: 636-349-9057
fax: 636-349-9162
pgtoys@pgtoys.com
http://www.pgtoys.com
Buys and sells collectibles toys from 1960s to 1990s, specializing in Batman, Aliens, action figures, movie & TV collectibles, Star Trek, Star Wars, puzzles, records, advertising premiums.

Jon & Carolyn Thurmond
Collectorholics
15006 Fuller
Grandview, MO 64030-4522
ph: 816-322-0906
Buys, sells, trades TV Guides, Western items, Star Trek, military toys, banks, novelty radios, radio premiums, Disney, etc.

Jim Yeager
P.O. Box 413881
Kansas City, MO 64141
ph: 816-333-2839
Buys and sells antique toys from the 1870s to the 1950s.

Bill & Pam Shepardson
Shepardson's Vintage Toys
201 Schiller
Hermann, MO 65041
ph: 573-486-3903
Wants to buy toys: early tin, cast iron, paper litho, character toys.

Jim & Rita Hinton
Collector's Choice
P.O. Box 104284
Jefferson City, MO 65110-4284
ph: 573-636-7567

Timothy Ullmen
TTotalin Toys
P.O. Box 1188
Westlake, LA 70669-5414
ph: 337-430-0029
ttotalintoys@peoplepc.com
Buys and sells old pre-1970s toys, dolls, games, cars, etc.; tin, metal, friction, battery operated; collecting Flintstones, Hanna Barbera, Winnie the Pooh and any cartoon-related items.

Terri Mardis-Ivers
Terri's Toys & Nostalgia
114 Whitworth Ave.
Ponca City, OK 74601-3438
ph: 580-762-8697
toylady@cableone.net
Buying pre-1990 vintage toys and character collectibles: robots, space toys, any TV, movie, music personality items such as Gunsmoke, Jetsons, Munsters, Elvis, Beatles, Kiss, Barbie, tin toys, windups, battery operated, etc.

Marjorie Jeffreys
Going to Pieces
P.O. Box 390
Cibolo, TX 78108
ph: 210-659-2458
Buys and sells old games, toys, blocks and children's dishes and children's baking items.

John D. McKenna
McKenna Bros. Wholesale
801 W. Cucharras St., #803
Colorado Springs, CO 80905-1619
ph: 719-630-8732 or 719-488-0818
Buys, sells & collects pre-1960 toys in all categories especially early American tin, cast iron automotive and horse-drawn toys.

Brent Harelson
Santa Barbara Antique Toys
616 Bluelakes Blvd. N
PMB 133
Twin Falls, ID 83301
ph: 208-733-8229
fax: 208-732-8888
toys@antiquetoys.com
http://www.antiquetoys.com
Buys, sells and takes on consignment toys from 1890 to 1960: Hubley, Dent, Buddy L, Structo, Tonka, Bing, Marx, Schuco, Kingsbury, Dinky, Tootsietoy, Chein, Metalcraft, Smith-Miller.

Barrett Behnke
Barrett's Toys & Collectibles
7063 E. Blue Lake Dr.
Tucson, AZ 85715-3218
ph: 520-290-2864
barrettnan@aol.com
Wants to buy Wyandotte toys and other pressed steel and tin toys.

Richard Johnson
P.O. Box 27093
Prescott Valley, AZ 86312-7093
ph: 520-775-4714
fax: 520-771-9445
Tin toys, robots.

Wound & Wound Toy Company, The
7374 Melrose Ave.
Los Angeles, CA 90046
ph: 323-653-6703 or 800-937-0561
fax: 323-653-9089
info@thewoundandwound.com
http://www.thewoundandwound.com
Specializes in collectible tin and wind-up toys, and in novelties and music boxes from around the world.

Acme Vintage Toys & Animation Art
   Gallery
9976 Westwanda Dr.
Beverly Hills, CA 90210
ph: 310-276-5509
brad3845@aol.com
http://www.acmetoys.com
Specializes in mint and boxed tin toys, Japanese robots, cartoon cells, and classic animation art from Disney, Warner Brothers, 20th Century Fox, Dreamworks, Hanna Barbera and other legendary Hollywood studios.

Mike Stannard
Toys 'N' Stuff
P.O. Box 2037
San Bernardino, CA 92406
ph: 909-880-8558
fax: 909-880-8096
Wants to buy Star Wars, Gremlins, Planet of the Apes, GI Joe, Nightmare, Corgi & Dinky, character toys of all kinds, all other movie and TV related toys and memorabilia.

Kathleen Hehn
Gotta Have It! Collectible Toys
1215 S. Beach Blvd. #E
Anaheim, CA 92804
ph: 714-995-4151
toybunch@aol.com
http://www.got2haveit.com
Everything you could want in collectible toys: dolls, GI Joe, monsters, cartoon characters.

Keith Schneider
Gasoline Alley Antiques
6501 20th NE
Seattle, WA 98115
ph: 206-524-1606
fax: 206-524-6343
gasalley@nwlink.com
http://www.gasolinealleyantiques.com
Dealer in antique and collectible toys: toys, model kits, Disneyana, vintage sports, etc.

Carol Sheehan
I Remember That!!
12 Burt Court
Stoney Creek, Ontario L8H 3H4 Canada
ph: 905-664-6712
fax: 905-664-6712
csheehan1@cogeco.ca
Buys, sells, appraises toys, dolls, teddy bears, and collectibles.

Alicia & Jorge Valino
P.O. Box 1442
Montevideo, 11000 Uruguay
valino@valino.com
http://www.valino.com

Experts

Chick Darrow
Darrow's Fun Antiques
1101 1st Ave.
New York, NY 10021-8737
ph: 212-838-0730 or 888-DARROWS
fax: 212-838-3617
george@fun-antiques.com
http://www.fun-antiques.com
Buys & sells antique games, toys, ad

signs, animated art, jukeboxes, slot machines, comic watches, bicycles & memorabilia of all types; also prop rentals.

Judith Katz-Schwartz
Twin Brooks Antiques & Collectibles
E-zine: Antiques & Collectibles
   Newsletter
P.O. Box 6572
New York, NY 10128-0006
ph: 212-876-3512
fax: 212-876-3512
twinb@msjudith.net
http://www.msjudith.net
Buys, sells, appraises wind-ups, character toys, board games, battery operated, Chein, Marx, Disney, robots, Japanese celluloid, space toys, etc.; member Assoc. of Online Appraisers (AOA) & Inter. Soc. of Appraisers; free online newsletter.

Bob Smith
255 Tryon Pk.
Rochester, NY 14609-6814
ph: 585-288-7153
bob@oldtoysonline.com
http://www.oldtoysonline.com
Avid collector and dealer of 1870-1970 toys: wind-up, automotive, European tin, pressed steel, early diecast, cast iron; specializes in Oh Boy, Tootsietoys, Dinky Toys, Hillclimbers, Wyandotte, and German tin toys.

Ted Hake
Hake's Americana & Collectibles
   Auction
P.O. Box 1444
York, PA 17405-1444
ph: 717-848-1333
Ted@hakes.com
http://www.hakes.com
Author of "Hake's Guide to TV Collectibles" and several other books on collectibles; always purchasing items for mail-bid auctions of Disneyana, historical Americana, toys, premiums, political items, character and other collectibles.

Harry L. Rinker
Rinker Enterprises, Inc.
5093 Vera Cruz Rd.
Emmaus, PA 18049-9554
ph: 610-965-1122
fax: 610-965-1124
rinkeron@fast.net
http://www.harryrinker.com
Researches, writes about and appraises all forms of 19th and 20th century toys, games and puzzles.

Catherine Saunders-Watson
P.O. Box 454
Douglassville, PA 19518
golliqueen@aol.com
Writes on a variety of topics for antique publications in the US and the U.K.

Scott Smiles
Antique Toy Information Service
157 Yacht Club Way, Apt. #112
Hypoluxo, FL 33462-6048
ph: 561-582-6016
ssmiles664@aol.com
http://homepages.infoweek.com/
   ~antiquetoys/tintoys.htm
Toy collector, appraiser, expert; provides a toy evaluation service using 35mm photographs for $9.95 per toy; specializes in windups, friction and battery operated toys since 1983; consultant to antique toy price guides.

David Welch
P.O. Box 714
Murphysboro, IL 62966-0714
ph: 618-687-2282
fax: 618-684-2243
PEZDude1@aol.com
http://www.pezheads.net/dwelch
Wants 1950s-1960s tin robots; also 1930s-1960s Disney, Popeye, Betty Boop and monster toys; $10,000+ for rare items.

R. Bailey
P.O. Box 251
Coventry, CV5 9YT U.K.
ph: 0120 369 1212
Consultant to "Diecast Collector" magazine.

Internet Resources

About.com Hobbies
220 East 42nd St.
New York, NY 10017
pr@about-inc.com
http://home.about.com/hobbies
Online source for information about action figures, antiques, book collecting, coin collecting, collectibles, comic books, costume jewelry, dolls, mineral collecting, pin collecting, sports and trading cards, stamps, toy collecting.

Don Thompson
Vintage Toy Encyclopedia, The
P.O. Box 8701
Kansas City, MO 64114
http://www.toynfo.com
Great Web site with informative articles about scores and scores of action figures, dolls, toys and other collectibles.

Eric G. Myers
Raving Toy Maniac
1115 Autrey St.
Houston, TX 77006
ph: 713-529-1726
egm@toymania.com
http://www.toymania.com
Toy and action figure collector and expert with one of the Internet's most comprehensive toy collecting resources.

AntiqueTOY.com
204 Mize St.
Huntsville, TX 77340
travis@antiquetoy.com
http://www.antiquetoy.com
Internet magazine for toy collectors; toy classifieds.

Man./Prod./Dist.

International Toy Center
200 5th Ave.
New York, NY 10010
ph: 212-675-3535
fax: 212-727-2065
http://www.thetoycenter.com
Houses more than 1,500 manufacturers of toys, Christmas decorations, novelties, and products for every holiday.

Misc. Services

Scott Smiles
Antique Toy Information Service
157 Yacht Club Way, Apt. #112
Hypoluxo, FL 33462-6048
ph: 561-582-6016
ssmiles664@aol.com
http://homepages.infoweek.com/
~antiquetoys/tintoys.htm
Toy collector, appraiser, expert; you provide 2 35mm photos and he will provide a report on your toy including actual toy name, description, maker, history, age, and market value based on condition, rarity; cost is $9.95 per report.

Museums/Libraries

Robert Howarth, Jr.
Howie's Toy Museum
1930 Route 302
Lisbon, NH 03585-7100
ph: 603-838-6469
Toy museum open to the public and featuring trains, dolls, die cast vehicles, cap guns, western toys, sandbox toy, etc.

John Fawcett
Fawcett's Antique Toy Museum
P.O. Box 1156
Waldoboro, ME 04572-1156
ph: 207-832-7398
fawcetoy@gwi.net
http://home.gwi.net/~fawcetoy
Extensive collection of antique cartoon character toys; one of the finest Lone Ranger collections in the world on display.

Forbes Magazine Galleries
62 Fifth Ave.
New York, NY 10011-8882
ph: 212-620-5548
Permanent exhibits include over 500 toy boats, 12,000 miniature soldiers, twelve fabled Russian Imperial Easter Eggs made by the House of Faberge for the last two Russian czars, and over 300 jeweled items and objets d'art.

Sheila Clark
Museum of the City of New York
1220 5th Ave. at 103rd St.
New York, NY 10029-5221
ph: 212-534-1672
fax: 212-534-5974
http://www.mcny.org
Access by appointment; research fee charged.

Strong Museum, The
1 Manhattan Square
Rochester, NY 14607
ph: 585-263-2700
fax: 585-263-2493
http://www.strongmuseum.org
Collection contains more than 500,000 objects: toys, doll houses, miniatures, household furnishings, and the world's most comprehensive collection of dolls.

Toy & Miniature Museum of Delaware
P.O. Box 4053
Route 141
Wilmington, DE 19807
ph: 302-427-8697
fax: 302-427-8654
toys@thomes.net
http://www.thomes.net/toys

Delaware Toy & Miniature Museum
P.O. Box 4053
Wilmington, DE 19807
ph: 302-427-8697
fax: 302-427-8654
toys@thomes.net
http://www.thomes.net/toys
A historical reference of antique and contemporary doll houses, miniatures and sample furniture as well as dolls, toys, trains, boats and planes, both European and American from the 18th to 20th centuries.

Washington Dolls' House & Toy Museum
5236 44th St. NW
Washington, DC 20015-2101
ph: 202-244-0024
fax: 202-237-1659

Frances Kerber Walrond, Dir.
Eugene Field House & St. Louis Toy Museum
Newsletter: Field Notes
634 So. Broadway St.
Saint Louis, MO 63102
ph: 314-421-4689
ExecDir@EugeneFieldHouse.org
http://www.eugenefieldhouse.org
Birthplace and childhood home of Eugene Field, the children's poet; large collection of antique toys always on display; home of Roswell M. Field, lawyer for Dred Scott and his family when they sued for their freedom from slavery.

Roger Berg
Toy & Miniature Museum of Kansas City
5235 Oak St.
Kansas City, MO 64112-2877
ph: 816-333-2055 or 816-333-9328
fax: 816-333-2055
bergr@umkc.edu
http://www.umkc.edu/tmm
Museum housed in an elegant mansion features collections of miniatures, antique dolls' houses and antique toys.

Denver Museum of Miniatures, Dolls & Toys
1880 Gaylord St.
Denver, CO 80206-1211
ph: 303-322-1053
fax: 303-322-3704
dmmdt@juno.com
Displays miniatures, dolls and toys dating back to the 18th century.

Paul Gray
Bethnal Green Museum of Childhood
Cambridge Heath Rd.
London, E2 9PA U.K.
ph: 0181-980-2415
fax: 0181-983-5225
p.gray@vam.ac.uk
National collection of dolls, toys, games, puppets, and children's costumes.

Periodicals

Bob Yuhas
Magazine: Pressed Steel Toys
P.O. Box 1289
Mc Afee, NJ 07428-1289
ph: 973-697-4982 or 866-349-8697
pedalcar@netrom.com
http://www.pressedsteeltoysmonthly.com
A monthly magazine dedicated to all pressed steel toys from pedal cars to toy trucks.

Stacie Berger
Krause Publications
Magazine: Toy Shop
700 E. State St.
Iola, WI 54990-0001
ph: 715-445-2214
fax: 715-445-4087
stacie.berger@fwpubs.com
http://www.krause.com
A bi-weekly magazine offering complete coverage of baby-boomer toys, vintage toys, action figures, and TV toys; market trends, price guides, and auction updates included.

Stacie Berger
Krause Publications
Magazine: Toy Cars & Vehicles
700 E. State St.
Iola, WI 54990-0001
ph: 715-445-2214
fax: 715-445-4087
stacie.berger@fwpubs.com
http://www.krause.com
One-stop marketplace and information for collectors of scale vehicles: toy cars, trucks, military vehicles, and construction vehicles; model kits, diecasts, motor sports, promotional models.

Dale Kelley, Ed.
Magazine: Antique Toy World
P.O. Box 34509
Chicago, IL 60641-0509
ph: 773-725-0633
fax: 773-725-3449
http://www.antiquetoyworld.com
A monthly magazine serving toy collectors and dealers; 200 or more pages of all types of toys including antique toys, banks, cast iron toys, tin wind-ups, comic toys, pedal cars; ads, articles, etc.

Brian Savage
Fun Publications
Newspaper: Master Collector
225 Cattle Baron Parc Dr.
Fort Worth, TX 76108
ph: 800-772-6673 or 817-448-9863
fax: 817-448-9843
brian@mastercollector.com
http://www.mastercollector.com
Ads-only newspaper; dolls (antique and modern collectible), toys, banks, models, cars, Matchbox, monsters, puzzles, political, toy trains, etc.; subscribers receive free 30-word ad each month; published monthly; reaches 20,000.

Sandra Hood, Pub.
Krause Regional Antique Publications
Newsmagazine: Antique & Collectables
P.O. Box 12589
500 Fesler St., Ste. 201
El Cajon, CA 92022
ph: 619-593-2925 or 619-593-2927
fax: 619-447-7187
antiquequill@aol.com
The largest monthly newspaper in southern California covering the antiques & collectibles industry with focus sections on Nevada and Arizona; 64+ pages; events and show section, auctions, feature articles; columns, ads.

Repair Services

John Bogan
Bogan Restoration Services
ph: 972-445-4800
fax: 972-445-8207
jbogan@mindspring.com
http://www.mindspring.com/~dagmara/
deere.html
Buys, sells, restores vintage bicycles, pedal cars, toys and metalware.

Captain Bob's
9 Mohawk Dr.
Hampden, MA 01036
ph: 413-566-5109
Specializes in the repair of friction and windup toys.

Walter Allen
Specialty Castings
19 Mill Rd.
Boxford, MA 01921
ph: 978-887-9783
specialty@gis.net
http://www.gis.net/~specialty
Reproduces items for collectors by casting in cast iron, bronze, brass or aluminum; all items created through the lost wax process; also mold making, parts modification, and shrinkage compensation.

Marc Olimpio
Marc Olimpio's Antique Toy
Restoration Center
P.O. Box 1505
Wolfeboro, NH 03894
ph: 603-569-6739
Specializes in early handpainted German and French-American tin toys, iron and pressed steel, and cast iron.

Gary J. Moran
3 Finch Court
Commack, NY 11725-4901
ph: 516-864-9444
Antique toy repairs, including battery operated, friction and wind-up toys; call or write for free estimate; broken toys purchased.

Ron Hanley
Mini-Motors
130 Main
Hobart, NY 13788
ph: 607-538-9926
Repairs pedal cars and automotive toys: repair work, nickel plating, pressed-steel vehicles such as Tonka and Buddy L.

Joe Freeman
Tin Toy Works
1313 N. 15th St.
Allentown, PA 18102-1068
ph: 610-439-8268
fax: 610-439-1288
tintoyworks@enter.net
Specializes in the repair of tin toys; tin toy autos, boats, merry-go-rounds, etc.; repairs mechanisms, makes missing parts.

Jerry Shook
6528 Cedar Brook Dr.
New Albany, OH 43054-9715
ph: 614-855-7796
fax: 614-855-7796
surgeontoy@aol.com
Makes rubber & plastic replacement parts for toys: wind-ups, robots, space toys, battery operated, etc.; also for dolls; send SASE and $2 for parts list.

Randy Ibey
Randy's Toy Shop
165 North 9th St.
Noblesville, IN 46060
ph: 317-776-2220
fax: 317-776-9007
randy@randystoyshop.com
http://www.randystoyshop.com
Specializes in the repair of celluloid and composition toys, tin toys,

battery-operated, windup, friction, figural, Japanese, German, American, French toys; also restores the original boxes the toys came in.

2248 S. City Rd. 350 W.
Russiaville, IN 46979
ph: 765-453-1210
Restores pedal cars and pressed steel toys.

Heinz Mueller
Classic Tin Toy Company
P.O. Box 81
Cleveland, WI 53015
ph: 920-693-8417
fax: 920-693-8211
toys@classictintoy.com
http://www.classictintoy.com
Offers complete toy repair and restoration service: windup toys, battery operated toys, clockworks, cast iron toys and tin toys: painting, aging and matching colors, plating service, casting parts in cast iron, plastic, diecast, etc.

Classic Tin Toy Company Restoration Shop
P.O. Box 193
Sheboygan, WI 53082
ph: 920-693-3371
fax: 920-693-8211
toys@classictintoy.com
Repair and total restoration of all makes of old toys including tin, cast iron and tinplate trains; world's largest manufacturer of toy parts; catalog $10.

Mike Taylor
5545 Celestial Rd.
Dallas, TX 75240
ph: 972-788-1411
fax: 972-385-0779
Mike@rememwhen.com
http://www.rememwhen.com
Specializes in the restoration of metal collectibles, toys, pedal vehicles, etc.: cast iron, steel, aluminum, galvanized, brass, copper, tin, stainless steel and corrugated, stamped, rolled, pressed and pot metal.

Action Figures

(see also POPULAR CULTURE, Baby Boomer; TOYS, Playsets; TELEVISION SHOWS & MEMORABILIA, Star Trek)

Clubs/Associations

Texas Action Figure Ring
docgordo@mail.utexas.edu
http://www.angelfire.com/tx/afring

Society of Obsessive Female Toy Traders
jomina@pop.mindspring.com
http://www.geocities.com/Wellesley/5031

Michael Crawford
Action Toy Organization of Michigan
2884 Hawks
Ann Arbor, MI 48108
ph: 734-973-1904
For collectors of action figures; online images, toy reviews, and lots more for the action figure collector.

Collectors

Michael Crawford
2884 Hawks
Ann Arbor, MI 48108
ph: 734-973-1904
Action figure collector; also reviews new issues; check out the online museum of over 50 lines of action figures and more than 500 images.

Steve Almy
Galactic Highway
113 Colonial Parkway, Ste. B
Yorkville, IL 60560
ph: 630-553-2993
steve@galactic-hwy.com
http://www.galactic-hwy.com
Online Web store for the serious action figure/toy collector and gaming players.

Dealers

Action Comics & Toys
quirky@iname.com
Specializes in action figures including G.I. Joe and Star Wars; also comics and cards.

Doug Johnston
Northeast Comics/Action Figures
gtalon@hotmail.com
http://members.tripod.com/~gtalon/index.html
Over 10,000 Silver Age comics; also hundreds of action figures.

Dennis Barger
Men-In-Black Collectibles
ph: 734-483-8697
ypsitoys@aol.com
http://www.ypsitoys.com
Specializes in action figures.

Josh Vilensky
Plastic Dreams
34 S. Washington Ave.
Bergenfield, NJ 07621
ph: 201-387-2100 or 201-387-9186
fax: 201-387-0554
Pdstarwars@aol.com
http://www.plasticdreams.com
Specializing in 1960s to 1980s action figures and other plastic toys.

Edward Harsh
Hero Central
10070 San Clemente Dr.
Reno, NV 89511
ph: 775-852-1646
fax: 775-852-1647
Carries 1960s to 1970s G.I. Joe and Action Man, Mighty Dragon action figures, 21st century toys, Firebase Ryan accessories, 1990s HOF, Classic

Collection and POTF 12" Star Wars figures.

Rene Rivera
Rene's Action Figures, Toys & Collectibles
545 S. Atlantic Blvd., Ste. 6
Los Angeles, CA 90022
ph: 323-269-3933
mistertoys@aol.com
http://www.toyattack.com
An online source for 1,000s of action figures, toys and collectibles: Batman, cartoon, Simpsons, Spiderman, Marvel, superheroes, movie, comic, monsters and more.

411 Toys
16054 Sherman Way
Van Nuys, CA 91406
ph: 818-786-9760 or 888-411-TOYS
fax: 818-786-4655
http://www.411toys.com
Focuses on modern action figures, GI Joe, Star Wars; also Beanie Babies.

Brian Rachfal
Craddock's Non-Sports Cards & Collectibles
P.O. Box 7772
San Jose, CA 95150-3766
ph: 408-298-9070 or 408-629-3980
Buys, sells, trades Star Wars action figures, exclusive & regional playsets (Sears, J.C. Penney's, etc.), remote control items, diecast vehicles, gum cards and related memorabilia; also wants rare Star Trek & Indiana Jones toys & figures.

Experts

John Marshall
Toyzilla Enterprises
P.O. Box 340
Rancocas, NJ 08073-0340
jm@jmuniverse.com
http://www.jmuniverse.com
Author of "GI Joe And Other Backyard Heroes: Action Figures of the 1970s," "Action Figures of the 1980s," "Action Figures of the 1960s," "Comic Book Hero Toys," "Collecting Monster Toys;" writes articles for toy magazines.

Internet Resources

About.com Hobbies
220 East 42nd St.
New York, NY 10017
pr@about-inc.com
http://home.about.com/hobbies
Online source for information about action figures, antiques, book collecting, coin collecting, collectibles, comic books, costume jewelry, dolls, mineral collecting, pin collecting, sports and trading cards, stamps, toy collecting.

Don Thompson
Vintage Toy Encyclopedia, The
P.O. Box 8701
Kansas City, MO 64114
http://www.toynfo.com
*Great Web site with informative
articles about scores and scores of
action figures, dolls, toys and other
collectibles.*

Eric G. Myers
Raving Toy Maniac
1115 Autrey St.
Houston, TX 77006
ph: 713-529-1726
egm@toymania.com
http://www.toymania.com
*Toy and action figure collector and
expert with one of the Internet's most
comprehensive toy collecting
resources.*

Man./Prod./Dist.

Hasbro, Inc.
1011 Newport Ave.
Pawtucket, RI 02862
domains@hasbro.com
http://www.hasbro.com

Periodicals

James Tomlinson, Ed.
Lee Publications
Magazine: Action Figure News & Toy
Review
556 Monroe Turnpike
Monroe, CT 06468-2309
ph: 203-452-7286
fax: 203-452-0410
*AFN is a full size magazine dedicated
to the collecting of action figures
(plastic figures such as G.I. Joe,
Captain Action, Star Wars, etc.) and
toys from 1964 to present; articles,
ads, shows, etc.*

Tom Tumbusch
Tomart Publications
Magazine: Tomart's Action Figure
Digest
3300 Encrete Lane
Dayton, OH 45439-1944
ph: 937-294-2250
fax: 937-294-1024
office@tomart.com
http://www.tomart.com
*Devoted to action figure collectibles;
published bi-monthly.*

Mike Shuffield
Phase II Publishing
Magazine: G.I. Joe Patrol
P.O. Box 2362
Hot Springs National Park, AR 71914
ph: 501-525-7149
*A bi-monthly publication that brings
you up-to-date information on action
figure and related collectibles from
Hasbro, Marx, Mego, Kenner, Mattel
and many other action figure series;
identify loose accessories; ads.*

Repair Services

Michael Crawford
Western Action Figure Archive, The
2884 Hawks
Ann Arbor, MI 48108
ph: 734-973-1904
*Great archive of most all collectible
action figures.*

Suppliers

Mike Stefanik
Action Figure Supplies
P.O. Box 951
Chicopee, MA 01021
ph: 413-552-0413
fax: 413-534-6842
BanthaTrad@aol.com
http://www.digital-toys.com
*Action figure supplies, stands,
showcases, and more; carries over 100
different lines of collectible toys and
gifts.*

Action Figure Display Case Co.
512 North Spruce St.
Valley, NE 68064-9670
ph: 402-359-5539
fax: 773-395-3495
sales@usadisplay.net
http://www.usaidsplay.net
*Manufacturers display cases for
antiques and collectibles of all types.*

Action Figures (G.I. Joe)

Clubs/Associations

Brian Savage
Official G.I. Joe Collectors Club
Newsletter: G.I. Joe Collectors Club
Newsletter
225 Cattle Baron Parc Dr.
Fort Worth, TX 76108
ph: 800-772-6673 or 817-448-9863
fax: 817-448-9843
brian@mastercollector.com
http://www.gijoeclub.com
*Thousands of members worldwide; the
source for G.I. Joe information and
service; monthly newsletter; send SASE
for more information; membership
includes subscription to "Master
Collector" newspaper and 30-word ad
each month.*

James DeSimone
International G.I. Joe Collectors Club
150 S. Glenoaks Blvd.
Burbank, CA 91510-1314
ph: 818-563-1179
gijoe@gijoeinformation.com
http://www.gijoeinformation.com
*This unofficial club provides a
monthly newsletter with lots of info on
current Joe findings, happenings and
show info.*

Commander Lane
G.I. Joe: Steel Brigade Command
Newsletter: Ammo Box
8362 Lomay Ave.
Westminster, CA 92683-3327
ph: 714-297-5042
sbcommand@yahoo.com
http://www.steelbrigade.com
Longest running international fan

club for the 1982-1994 (3 3/4") G.I.
Joe: A Real American Hero collection;
newsletter published quarterly.

Collectors

Jeff Kowalski
P.O. Box 64
Pluckemin, NJ 07978
ph: 908-526-5033
*Wants G.I. Joe: dolls, clothing,
accessories, vehicles.*

Dealers

Dale Womer
Joe Depot, The
P.O. Box 228
Kulpsville, PA 19443-0228
ph: 215-721-9749
fax: 215-721-9749
gijoe@fast.net
http://www.ewtech.com/gijoe
*Carries a large selection of G.I. Joe
figures and accessories; new and
vintage accessories, loose Joes, boxed
figures, boxed foreigns, Hall of Fame,
prototypes, original art, patents,
vehicles, and more.*

Craig Polnoff
Old Joe Infirmary
PMB #474
14175 W. Indian School Rd., B4
Goodyear, AZ 85338
ph: 623-547-0181
fax: 623-547-0182
gijoedoctor@oldjoeinfirmary.com
http://www.oldjoeinfirmary.com
*Sells highly accurate 1/6th scale
uniforms and accessories under own
brand name, "Infirmary Exclusives."*

Bob Cummings
5669 Chelsea Ave.
La Jolla, CA 92037
ph: 858-456-2556
*Wants to buy old boys' toys, especially
GI Joe from the 1960s; pays most for
collections in excellent to mint-in-box
collection.*

Tina Windeler
Cotswold Collectibles, Inc.
1612 E. Main St.
P.O. Box 716
Freeland, WA 98249
ph: 360-331-5331 or 877-404-5637
fax: 360-331-5344
cotswold@whidbey.net
http://www.elitebrigade.com
*Buys and sells 12" G.I. Joe and
accessories, including replacement
parts such as boots, helmets, soldier
equipment, etc.; also a line of high
quality custom military 12" figures,
"The Elite Brigade;" free monthly
illustrated catalog.*

Experts

John Marshall
Toyzilla Enterprises
P.O. Box 340
Rancocas, NJ 08073-0340
jm@jmuniverse.com
http://www.jmuniverse.com
Author of "GI Joe And Other

*Backyard Heroes: Action Figures of
the 1970s," "Action Figures of the
1980s," "Action Figures of the
1960s," "Comic Book Hero Toys,"
"Collecting Monster Toys;" writes
articles for toy magazines.*

Joe Bodnarchuk
G.I. Joe Nostalgia Co.
62 McKinley Ave.
Kenmore, NY 14217-2414
ph: 716-873-0264 or 800-5GI-JOES
fax: 716-873-0264
webmaster@bodnarchuk.com
http://www.bodnarchuk.com/gijoe/
wwwfanclub.html
G.I. Joe enthusiast and collector since
1964; pays big for mint collections of
any size; quality a must.

James DeSimone
150 S. Glenoaks Blvd.
Burbank, CA 91510-1314
ph: 818-563-1179
gijoe@gijoeinformation.com
http://www.gijoeinformation.com
*Buys, collects, appraises, and
specializes in G.I. Joe; author of "The
New Official Identification Guide to
G.I. Joe" Vols. 1, 2, 3.*

Internet Resources

G.I. Joe
http://www.gijoe.com
*A Hasbro Co. Web site: G.I. Joe
images, supplies, FAQ, collector's
info, and a lot more.*

Joe Bodnarchuk
G.I. Joe Fun
62 McKinley Ave.
Kenmore, NY 14217-2414
ph: 716-873-0264 or 800-5GI-JOES
fax: 716-873-0264
webmaster@bodnarchuk.com
http://www.bodnarchuk.com/gijoe/
wwwfanclub.html
*A quarterly publication focusing of
G.I. Joe.*

Repair Services

Craig Polnoff
Old Joe Infirmary
PMB #474
14175 W. Indian School Rd., B4
Goodyear, AZ 85338
ph: 623-547-0181
fax: 623-547-0182
gijoedoctor@oldjoeinfirmary.com
http://www.oldjoeinfirmary.com
*Restoration service for 1960s to 1970s
Hasbro GI Joe; also retail sales of
figurines, uniforms, and accessories
for 12" action figures.*

Action Figures (Mego)

Dealers

Matthew
mattw2@bellsouth.net
http://mego.freeyellow.com/./index.html
*Great source to buy, sell, trade Mego
and other vintage action figures and
dolls.*

Internet Resources

Brian Heiler
Mego Museum
megomuseum@aol.com
http://www.toymania.com/megomuseum
Mego Corporation Toys (1971-1983) history, figures, accessories, Action Jackson, Dina-Mite, repair & customizing, buy, sell.

Agriculture Related

(see TOYS, Farm)

Airplane Related

(see also AIRLINE MEMORABILIA, Models [Desk])

Collectors

Perry R. Eichor
703 N. Almond Dr.
Simpsonville, SC 29681-3453
ph: 864-967-8770
fax: 864-228-2541
kpmflyn@earthlink.net
Wants aircraft toys and literature; member of Antique Toy Collectors of America.

Dealers

Dan Wells
Dan Wells Antique Toys
P.O. Box 7
Goshen, KY 40026
ph: 502-386-3453
jagdan@aol.com
Wants to buy all miniature/toy aircraft, especially travel agency and factory models.

Mike Bowen
704 St. James Place
Noblesville, IN 46060
ph: 317-773-9069
kbowen@iquest.net
Appraiser, dealer, collector, expert interested in any Aeromini/Aero Mini information or diecast planes.

Experts

G. R. Webster
P.O. Box 666
Frostproof, FL 33843
ph: 888-410-6353
fax: 888-410-6353
grwebster@aol.com
Interested in airplane toys and models: diecast toys, ID models, travel agency and desk models, etc.

Arcade

Experts

Al Aune
Mannolla Publishing
4441 Shari Ann Lane
Minneapolis, MN 55443-3461
ph: 612-560-4290 or 612-421-5151
fax: 612-421-3618
Author of "Arcade Toys;" contains hard-to-find information about dating Arcade toys.

Automotive

(see AUTOMOBILIA; TOYS, Cars)

Battery Operated

Collectors

Beau S. Cassity
Kid in Me, The
9502 Avenel Rd.
Silver Spring, MD 20903-2308
ph: 301-434-8293
nodkitty@msn.com
Specializes in pre and post WWII toys, especially battery operated; wants to buy all types of battery operated toys, including toys for parts; wants plastic toys and Japanese tin wind-ups.

Stuart Stein
P.O. Box 303
Frederick, MD 21705-0303
ph: 301-663-8369
fax: 301-663-8202
steincpa@ix.netcom.com
Wants to buy Japanese battery toys from the 1960s.

Mike Czerwinski
825 Vista Circle
Brea, CA 92621
ph: 714-990-4851
fax: 714-256-4525
nomadmikecz@yahoo.com
Expert repairs of battery operated toys; buys, sells, trades; has been collecting for over 20 years.

Experts

Don Hultzman
5026 Sleepy Hollow Rd.
Medina, OH 44256-8309
ph: 330-225-2668
Buys/sells pre-1970 battery operated and wind-up toys; wants toys in any condition; author of "Collector's Guide to Battery Toys;" also does expert repairs on battery operated toys; repairs are undetectable & guaranteed.

Repair Services

Dr. Jane Day
Toy Doctor(r), The
7658 Eades Rd.
Red Creek, NY 13143
ph: 315-754-8846
fax: 315-754-6238
janeday@zlink.net
http://www.thetoydoctor.com
Repairs battery operated toys; robots and space toys a specialty; dealer discounts; caring for all battery operated toys; "The Toy Doctor" is a registered trademark.

Don Hultzman
5026 Sleepy Hollow Rd.
Medina, OH 44256-8309
ph: 330-225-2668
Does expert repairs on battery operated toys; repairs are undetectable & guaranteed; also buys and sells pre-1970 battery operated and wind-up toys in any condition; wants comic

character toys: Disney, Hanna-Barbera, cartoon characters.

Randy King
Battery Operated Toy Repair
15232 So. 23rd St.
New Castle, IN 47362
ph: 765-521-0129
randyking4@hotmail.com
http://www.BatteryOperatedToyRepair.8m.com
Repairs old battery operated toys from the 1950s to the 1970s; tin and plastic toys, space robots, cars, trucks.

Mike Czerwinski
825 Vista Circle
Brea, CA 92621
ph: 714-990-4851
fax: 714-256-4525
nomadmikecz@yahoo.com
Expert repairs of battery operated toys; buys, sells, trades; has been collecting for over 20 years.

Bell

Collectors

Dr. Greg Zemenick
Dr. "Z"
1350 Kirts, Ste. 160
Troy, MI 48084-4852
ph: 248-642-8129 or 248-244-9430
fax: 248-244-9495
drzzeezz@aol.com
http://www.drzzeezzi.com
Wants bell toys.

Boats & Outboards

Collectors

Robert McDonald
K & O Toy Outboard Motors
166-12 29th Ave.
Flushing, NY 11358-1402
ph: 718-762-2541 or 718-520-3914
fax: 718-520-8577
jb6290@aol.com
http://members.fortunecity.com/jb6290
Wants to buy 1950s-1960s outboard motor toys: battery operated, metal motors only; Evinrude, Johnson, Mercury, Scottatwater, Gale, Buccaneer, Oliver.

Brent Simmons
3212 Severn Wharf Rd.
Hayes, VA 23072
ph: 804-642-2076
Wants to buy toy outboard boat motors; any condition.

Jack Browning
214 16th St. N.W.
Roanoke, VA 24017-5516
ph: 703-890-5083 or 703-982-8680
fax: 703-342-1283
jbrow9945@aol.com

Richard Gronowski
1100 Peninsula Dr.
Traverse City, MI 49686
ph: 231-941-2111
Wants to buy toy metal outboard boat motors: Gale, Oliver, Johnson,

Mercury, Scott, Evinrude, Wen-Mac, Sea-Fury.

Dealers

Keith Schneider
Gasoline Alley Antiques
6501 20th NE
Seattle, WA 98115
ph: 206-524-1606
fax: 206-524-6343
gasalley@nwlink.com
http://www.gasolinealleyantiques.com
Dealer in antique and collectible toys: toys, model kits, Disneyana, vintage sports, etc.

Bubble Blowers

Collectors

Judith Schulz
533 Milwaukee Ave.
Burlington, WI 53105-1232
ph: 262-763-3946
Wants old bubble blowers and related packages, literature, drawings and pictures of bubble blowing; conducts the International Bubble Blowing Extravaganza Event; gives bubble blower inventing workshops.

Canadian

Clubs/Associations

Betty Holland
CTM Farm Toy & Collectors Club
Magazine: Canadian Toy Mania
P.O. Box 489
Rocanville, Saskatchewan S0A 3L0
Canada
ph: 306-645-4566
fax: 306-645-4376
ctmtoys@sk.sympatico.ca
http://www.pin.ca/classics/default.htm
Focuses on farm toys and dolls.

Cannons

(see also CANNONS; FIREWORKS MEMORABILIA; TOY GUNS)

Experts

David Ross
Cannon-Mania
P.O. Box 552
Stratford, CT 06497
ph: 203-378-2582
cannon@cannon-mania.com
http://www.cannon-mania.com
Can identify and appraise older cast iron toy cannons.

Ray Brandes
1844 Mt. Cello Rd.
Norcross, GA 32448-5365
ph: 850-482-7562
rvb@ray-vin.com
http://www.ray-vin.com
Collector, dealer and expert on toy cannons; author of "Big-Bang Cannons - The Carbide Canon, A Unique American Toy" (Ray-Vin Publishing, 1993).

Internet Resources

David Ross
Cannon-Mania
P.O. Box 552
Stratford, CT 06497
ph: 203-378-2582
cannon@cannon-mania.com
http://www.cannon-mania.com
A Web site for those interested in small cannon, i.e., fine replicas that sit on a mantle, bookcase or desktop; also includes toys, salute cannon and cannon used on boats.

Museums/Libraries

Ray Brandes
Toy Cannon Museum
1844 Mt. Cello Rd.
Norcross, GA 32448-5365
ph: 850-482-7562
rvb@ray-vin.com
http://www.ray-vin.com
An online museum of toy carbide, firecracker, cap, blank and powder cannons; home of the world's most complete collection of Big Bang and Carbide Cannons; your source for information as well as repair parts and restoration items.

Suppliers

Conestoga Company
323 Sumner Ave.
P.O. Box 405
Bethlehem, PA 18016-0405
ph: 800-987-2264
fax: 610-433-0777
webmaster@bigbangcannons.com
http://www.bigbangcannons.com
Source for authentic Big-Bang cannons and parts.

Cars

(see also AUTOMOBILIA; MODELS, Cars; TOYS, Diecast)

Clubs/Associations

Tom Morgan
Post Car Registry
812 N. Third St.
Saint Peter, MN 56082
Dedicated to the preservation of plastic toy cars distributed through Post cereals from 1950-196; made by F&F Co. of Dayton, OH.

Richard Malinowski
Antique Miniature Race Car Collectors
Newsletter: Antique Miniature Race Car Collectors Newsletter
10711 S. Cicero Ave.
Oak Lawn, IL 60453
ph: 708-425-4463 or 708-425-2500
fax: 708-425-2633
spindizzy2@msn.com
An association for collectors of gas powered toy miniature race cars dating from the 1940s to 1950s; quarterly newsletter.

Mr. Dana Johnson
Toy Car Collectors Association
Newsletter: Toy Car Collector Magazine
P.O. Box 1824
Bend, OR 97701-1824
ph: 541-318-7176
toynutz@earthlink.net
http://www.toynutz.com/TCCA.html
Provides discounts on collector price guides, information on new products, model variations and values, resources for buying and selling, toy shows around the country; newsletter published monthly.

Collectors

David K. Bausch
252 N. 7th St.
Allentown, PA 18102-4024
ph: 610-432-3355
fax: 610-820-9368
oldtoy@aol.com
http://www.geocities.com/davidkbausch
Major collector of automobile related material, especially automobile art.

Rick Ralston
99-969 Iwaena St.
Aiea, HI 96701-3249
ph: 808-486-1243
fax: 808-486-1276
http://www.ralstonantiques.com
Buys and sells pre-WWII toy vehicles.

Dealers

Dan Wells
Dan Wells Antique Toys
P.O. Box 7
Goshen, KY 40026
ph: 502-386-3453
jagdan@aol.com
Wants to buy all tin, cast iron, and early pressed steel automotive toys; also excellent condition or better early diecast, especially Hot Wheels, Dinky, Corgi, Matchbox, etc.

Scott Gruenwald
Tin Car Garage Online
P.O. Box 436
Ingleside, IL 60041
ph: 847-356-1384
fax: 847-356-1870
http://www.tincargarage.com
Specializes in vintage tin toy cars and motorcycles; also automobilia, toy art, reproduction boxes for antique toys; research history about tin toys.

Experts

Steve Butler
2696 Brookmar Dr.
York, PA 17404-9489
ph: 717-792-4936
steve.b@earthlink.net
Buys, collects, appraises, specializes in automotive toys (cars and trucks) 1920-1960: iron, steel, cast metal, plastic; author & seller of "Promotionals 1934-1983;" promotional toy car and truck reference and price book; $22.65 ppd.

Clarence Young
Clarence Young Autohobby
302 Reems Creek
Weaverville, NC 28787-9792
ph: 828-645-5243
fax: 828-645-5243
clarenceyoung@carhobby.com
http://www.carhobby.com
Specializes in automotive promotional toys, mostly pot metal or plastic; sells "AUTOQUOTES;" also produces exclusive metal and/or resin toy cars.

Peter H. Foss
4301 Orchard Lake, 163
West Bloomfield, MI 48323
ph: 248-682-0272
fax: 248-682-5782
FossOhl@aol.com
Former President of the Toy Car Collectors Club.

Mr. Dana Johnson
Dana Johnson Enterprises
P.O. Box 1824
Bend, OR 97701-1824
ph: 541-318-7176
toynutz@earthlink.net
http://www.toynutz.com/TCCA.html
Diecast car expert; Matchbox collector since 1961; author of several books on the subject including "Matchbox Toys A to Z" (2004) and "Toy Car Collector's Guide" (2002), available from author.

Periodicals

Sue Elliott, Pub.
Challenge Publications, Inc.
Magazine: Car Toy Collectibles
8381 Canoga Ave.
Canoga Park, CA 91304-2605
ph: 818-700-6868 or 800-562-9182
fax: 818-700-6282
office@challengeweb.com
http://www.challengeweb.com/cartoys.html
Bi-monthly magazine covers model cars of all types, sizes, materials, and vintage; also covers automobilia from automotive art and racing collectibles to pedal cars, porcelain signs, neon clocks, apparel, literature, gas pumps, etc.

Cars (Racing)

Clubs/Associations

Jason Boye
National Slot Car Racing Club
1903 Middlefield Rd. #3
Redwood City, CA 94063-2252
ph: 650-365-9345
lemonzaco@aol.com
Regional chapters.

Collectors

Ira S. Kuperstein
22 Brush Hill Terrace
Butler, NJ 07405-2439
ph: 973-283-2420 or 800-526-5177
fax: 973-283-2426
kuperstein@nac.net
Wants to buy miniature gas powered racing car models.

Gabriel Bogdonoff
46 Porter Rd.
Howell, NJ 07731-8614
ph: 732-363-4064
Wants toy race cars, gas powered, any condition; also wants big tin friction race cars and Smith Miller trucks in any condition.

Jim Welytok
W241 N8938 Penny Lane
Sussex, WI 53089
ph: 262-246-7171
unievents@aol.com
Extensive collector of vintage slot cars; buys complete collections or single pieces.

Rick Burneson
435 1/2 South Orange St.
Mission Viejo, CA 92866-1611
ph: 714-997-1266
rb.housa@ix.netcom.com
http://pages.prodigy.com/housa
Collects and races H.O. scale electric slot cars.

Rod Thurgood
11 Perrins Lane
West Kempsey, New South Wales 2400
Australia
ph: (02) 6562 8209
fax: (02) 6562 6319
rodslot@midcoast.com.au
Wants 1:64 scale (HO size) model diecast, plastic, slot cars that depict the 1:1 scale Dodge Daytona, Plymouth Superbird range of vehicles.

Dealers

Ed Kipen
Slot Car Collectibles
ph: 773-539-0790
edscars@hotmail.com
http://www.homestead.com/slotcarcollectibles
Sells slot cars, parts, and track from 1960s through 1980s in HO and larger scales; Web site has pictures and descriptions; also buys.

William Sakas
P.O. Box 1725
Montclair, NJ 07042
ph: 973-783-7174
decobill@aol.com
http://members.aol.com/decobill
Buys and sells Aurora HO scale slot cars; buys one or entire collections.

Ron Bernstein
Toybaron, The
ph: 973-316-6845
toybaron@toybaron.com
http://www.toybaron2.com
*Buys and sells slot cars of all scales;
also toys, games and models from the
'60s to '80s.*

Robert Budano
Bud's HO Cars Inc.
2 Westbrook Dr.
Cortlandt Manor, NY 10567
ph: 914-526-4950
fax: 914-526-4950
budhocars@worldnet.att.net
http://www.homestead.com/budshocars/
budsho.html

Robert Molta
SlotCarCentral
113 Herz St.
Syracuse, NY 13208-3026
ph: 315-428-1724 or 315-490-2386
fax: 315-428-1282
rcmolta@msn.com
*In the slot car hobby for over 15
years; 400 cars on display; sells or
trades (preferred), appraises, collects,
repairs.*

John A. Clark
Slot Car Johnnie's
7634 Asden
Reynoldsburg, OH 43068
ph: 614-864-TJET
fax: 614-864-2800
afx1afx@aol.com
http://www.slotcarjohnnies.com
*Buys, sells, collects H.O. slot cars
from the 1960s, '70s, '80s; carries a
large supply & variety of slot cars in
all scales (HO, 1/32, 1/23) as well as
parts & accessories from used to
mint-in-box; author of "Aurora HO
Checklist" and others.*

Rad Trax Slot Car Headquarters
3650 S. Decatur Blvd., #6
Las Vegas, NV 89103
ph: 702-253-7568
fax: 702-253-7568
radtrax@radtrax.com
http://www.radtrax.com
*A slot car raceway and hobby store
since 1993; specializes in H.O., 1/32,
and 1/24 scales; huge selection of slot
cards and model car kits.*

Craig Reid
9116 E. Spraque #145
Spokane, WA 99206-3601
ph: 509-536-8489
crtoys@cet.com
http://www.cet.com/~crtoys
*Collector and dealer of HO slot cars;
also wants Star Trek, Transformers,
action figures, etc.*

Experts

Robert Molta
SlotCarCentral
113 Herz St.
Syracuse, NY 13208-3026
ph: 315-428-1724 or 315-490-2386
fax: 315-428-1282
rcmolta@msn.com
*In the slot car hobby for over 15
years; 400 cars on display; sells or
trades (preferred), appraises, collects,
repairs.*

John A. Clark
Slot Car Johnnie's
7634 Asden
Reynoldsburg, OH 43068
ph: 614-864-TJET
fax: 614-864-2800
afx1afx@aol.com
http://www.slotcarjohnnies.com
*Buys, sells, collects H.O. slot cars
from the 1960s, '70s, '80s; carries a
large supply & variety of slot cars in
all scales (HO, 1/32, 1/23) as well as
parts & accessories from used to
mint-in-box; author of "Aurora HO
Checklist" and others.*

Internet Resources

Chris Jennings
Slot Car Center, The
ph: 972-783-6792
joeslotz@excite.com
http://www2.clearlight.com/cgi-bin/
cgiwrap/chrisj/Ultimate.cgi
An H.O. Car Bulletin Board.

Ben Bell
Slotside
7 Elizabeth St.
Thornhill, Ontario L4J 1X7 Canada
ph: 905-731-2218
fax: 905-731-5374
slotside@slotside.com
http://www.slotside.com
*Provides technical information for the
dedicated slot racer together with a
world wide directory of commercial
tracks, interactive bulletin board, real
time chat, and links to every
meaningful slot car racing site on the
Web.*

Periodicals

Magazine: Slot Car Enthusiast
2482 Westhill Ct.
Norcross, GA 30071
ph: 770-263-8565
http://www.slotcar.org/sce
*Concentrates on all scales and sizes of
model race cars and racing, along
with the people who remain the
backbone of the commercial and club
scene, as well as the collectors across
the country.*

John Ford
Am/Slot Racing
Magazine: Scale Auto Racing News
2608 Robert Rd.
Aransas Pass, TX 78336
ph: 512-758-7223 or 800-797-7223
fax: 512-758-1640
fordpub@2fords.net
http://www.scaleautoracing.com
*Founded in 1979, world's oldest slot
car magazine: new products, how-tos,
race reports, etc.; for H.O., 1/32 and
1/24 scale.*

Rick Burneson
Newsletter: H.O. USA Newsletter
435 1/2 South Orange St.
Mission Viejo, CA 92866-1611
ph: 714-997-1266
rb.housa@ix.netcom.com
http://pages.prodigy.com/housa
*For H.O. scale slot cars; free ads with
membership.*

Scale Auto
Magazine: HO Journal
P.O. Box 2051
Redmond, WA 98073
fax: 425-868-9865
hoslots@scaleauto.com
http://www.scaleauto.com

Rod Thurgood, Ed.
Magazine: Australian Slot Car Review
11 Perrins Lane
West Kempsey, New South Wales 2400
Australia
ph: (02) 6562 8209
fax: (02) 6562 6319
rodslot@midcoast.com.au
*Published four times per year and
offering a comprehensive coverage of
slot car racing and collecting in
Australia; minimum of 52 pages;
informative articles and lots of
photos; free ads to subscribers; write
for info.*

Cast Iron

Dealers

Bob Smith
255 Tryon Pk.
Rochester, NY 14609-6814
ph: 585-288-7153
bob@oldtoysonline.com
http://www.oldtoysonline.com
*Avid collector and dealer of 1870-
1970 toys: wind-up, automotive,
European tin, pressed steel, early
diecast, cast iron; specializes in Oh
Boy, Tootsietoys, Dinky Toys,
Hillclimbers, Wyandotte, and German
tin toys.*

Bob Brady
Brady Toys & Banks
2341 Woodwick Rd.
Lancaster, PA 17601
ph: 717-569-7408
bobbra@comcast.net
http://www.mechanicalbanks.com
*Buys and sells mechanical and still
banks; also c. 1900 cast iron toys.*

Repair Services

Arnie Prince
Iron Man Toys
434 N. School St., #A
Lodi, CA 95240-1229
ph: 209-334-6101
fax: 209-334-6111
*Cast iron repair and restoration, cast
iron welding, fabrication, and
painting; buys cast iron toys and
parts.*

Character

(see also CHARACTER
COLLECTIBLES; DISNEY
COLLECTIBLES)

Auction Services

Martin Krim
New England Auction Gallery
P.O. Box 764
Middleton, MA 01949
ph: 978-304-3140
fax: 978-304-3140
mrkrim@attbi.com
http://www.old-toys.com
*Conduct mail-bid auctions with full
color illustrated catalogs; specializes
in sales of Disney, TV and cartoon
items from 1920-1970: toys, wind-ups,
robots, space toys.*

Clubs/Associations

Colleen Lewis
Figures Collectors Club
Newsletter: Figure Collector
10120 Main St.
Clarence, NY 14031-2049
ph: 716-741-8399
fax: 716-759-7462
bripvc@toyline.com
http://www.toyline.com/clubs/pcc
*International club for character/
cartoon figure collectors; quarterly
newsletter with information, reviews,
ads, etc. about figures including the
"Archives," a detailed listing of
figures by series with pictures; special
offers for members.*

Collectors

Martin Krim
P.O. Box 764
Middleton, MA 01949
ph: 978-304-3140
fax: 978-304-3140
mrkrim@attbi.com
http://www.old-toys.com
*Wants tin & celluloid toys from
Japan, Germany, etc.; character items
from TV shows, westerns, stars from
the 50-60s; robot & space toys;
plastic wind-up toys.*

Dealers

Leila Dunbar
Dunbar's Gallery
76 Haven St.
Milford, MA 01757-3821
ph: 508-634-8697
fax: 508-634-8698
dunbars@dunbarsgallery.com
http://www.dunbarsgallery.com
Mail order Americana - no reproductions; buys, sells and specializes in vintage character and comic toys, banks, advertising, automobilia, and Halloween related items.

Dennis & Mary Luby
Casey's Collectible Corner
HCR 31 Box 30
No. Blenheim, NY 12131
ph: 607-588-6464
caseyscc@aol.com
Buys and sells collectible toys: comic characters, TV shows and personalities; also space and monster toys, sports collectibles, etc.

Colleen Lewis
Buffalo Rd. Hobby
10120 Main St.
Clarence, NY 14031-2049
ph: 716-741-8399
fax: 716-759-7462
bripvc@toyline.com
http://www.toyline.com/clubs/pcc
Carries a huge selection of PVC cartoon figures from Animaniacs, Hanna Barbera, Looney Tunes, and Pink Panther to Little Lulu, Zorro and more; imported from all over the world; catalog $2.

Richard Trautwein
Toys N Such
437 Dawson St.
Sault Sainte Marie, MI 49783-2119
ph: 906-635-0356
Collector, dealer, wants wind-up, battery, tin, pull, cast iron toys: Barney Google, Charlie Chaplin, Mickey Mouse, Donald Duck, Popeye, etc.

Character (Mickey Mouse)

Collectors

Debra Krim
P.O. Box 764
Middleton, MA 01949
ph: 978-304-3140
fax: 978-304-3140
mrkrim@attbi.com
http://www.old-toys.com
Wants 1930s Mickey Mouse items: empty boxes, figurals, wind-ups, bisque figurines, games, jewelry, etc.

Comic

(see TOYS, Character)

Computer Programs For

Man./Prod./Dist.

Niche Software, Inc.
Software: Antique Toy & Die Cast Car Collector, The
7118 NW Terrace
Parkland, FL 33076
ph: 954-344-6561
marketing@collectiblesoftware.com
http://www.collectiblesoftware.com
Designed for collectors of antique and diecast toys.

Construction Sets

Collectors

Wally Krocsko
P.O. Box 307
Atlasburg, PA 15004-0307
ph: 724-947-5671
Sell construction sets (Erector, Meccano, American Model Builder); must enclose a LSASE to get a reply to buy/sell/trade inquiries; please call evenings.

Arlan Coffman
1223 Wilshire Blvd., Ste. 275
Santa Monica, CA 90403
ph: 310-453-2507
Wants architectural construction toys: Erector sets, building blocks, villages, Lincoln Logs & figures, etc.

Dealers

John Maleski
Space Toys
20289 Canal
Grosse Ile, MI 48138
ph: 734-675-8322

Joel Perlin
1111 Acapulco Ct.
Oxnard, CA 93035-2601
ph: 805-985-5498
fax: 805-382-7665
Specializes in antique Erector, Mecanno and other construction toys; complete, sets, ephemera, and spare parts; buys, sells, reproduces.

Experts

Joel Perlin
1111 Acapulco Ct.
Oxnard, CA 93035-2601
ph: 805-985-5498
fax: 805-382-7665
Specializes in antique Erector, Mecanno and other construction toys; complete, sets, ephemera, and spare parts; buys, sells, reproduces.

Construction Sets (Blocks)

Clubs/Associations

George Hardy
Anchor Block Foundation
Magazine: Anchor House News
1670 Hawkwood Ct.
Charlottesville, VA 22901
ph: 804-295-4863
fax: 804-295-4898
georgeh@ankerstein.org
http://www.ankerstein.org
Anchor House Foundation is a club whose members have interests in and build with Anchor Blocks; quarterly newsletter.

Collectors

Paul Neuman
173 Chrystie St.
New York, NY 10002
ph: 212-228-2444 or 212-734-4274
fax: 212-780-9338
sbogdonoff@aol.com
Wants to buy architectural toys, building block sets; wood, paper on wood, stone, metal, etc.

George Hardy
1670 Hawkwood Ct.
Charlottesville, VA 22901
ph: 804-295-4863
fax: 804-295-4898
georgeh@ankerstein.org
http://www.ankerstein.org
Collector of Richter's Anchor Stone Building Sets (Anker-Steinbaukasten).

Dealers

Arley Pett
Arley L. Pett Antiques
12 Beach Rd.
Gloucester, MA 09130-3214
ph: 978-283-2612
fax: 978-283-2612
apett92117@aol.com
Buys, sells and collects Anchor stone blocks and puzzles.

Construction Sets (Erector)

Clubs/Associations

A.C. Gilbert Heritage Society
Newsletter: A.C. Gilbert Heritage Society Newsletter
1440 Whalley, Ste. 252
New Haven, CT 06515
info@acghs.org
http://www.acghs.org
For A.C. Gilbert toy enthusiasts, all items except American Flyer trains; Erector sets, chemistry sets, magic sets, Gilbert appliances and tools; send SASE for membership info; newsletter published quarterly; over 400 members.

Frank Hare, Ed.
American Flyer Collectors Club
Magazine: Collector, The
P.O. Box 13269
Pittsburgh, PA 15243-0269
ph: 412-221-2250
fax: 412-221-8402
ironhorse@sgi.net
For collectors of A.C. Gilbert Co. American Flyer and other toy trains (all pre-1966 manufacturers); also contains information about Gilbert Erector sets.

Southern California Meccano & Erector Club
Newsletter: Southern CA Meccano & Erector Club Newsletter
P.O. Box 7653
Porter Ranch Station
Northridge, CA 91327-7653
pedwards@webnexus.com
http://www.erector.webnexus.com
Publishes a very good quarterly newsletter; holds regional meetings.

Collectors

Jay Smith
5 Whittier Rd.
Lexington, MA 02420
ph: 781-861-7547
LaserJay@aol.com
Former editor of the "A.C. Gilbert Heritage Society Newsletter."

Larry Yesner
285 Orchid Rd.
Levittown, NY 11756
ph: 516-579-7040
Wants Erector and Meccano sets; preferably the larger sets in mint or excellent condition.

James Mietlicki
146 Ridge Park Ave.
Cheektowaga, NY 14211
ph: 716-896-8047

Michael Wagner
Wagner & Sons Inc.
28 E. Willow St.
Carlisle, PA 17013
ph: 800-827-3948 or 800-821-7002
fax: 610-296-2258
mwagner@wagnerandsonstoys.com
http://www.wagnerandsonstoys.com
Purchasing A.C. Gilbert Erector set parts, manuals, catalogs, dealer items, etc.; also purchasing construction sets by Meccano, Marklin, Ives, Bing and Metalcraft.

Dealers

Jay Robinson
Chicago Kid
522 Rivershire Place
Lincolnshire, IL 60069
ph: 847-913-1106
fax: 847-913-1274
jay@thechicagokid.com
Buys construction sets; also wants electric trains of all types, toys, and robots.

Experts

Al Sternagle
400 RR 2
Hollidaysburg, PA 16648
ph: 814-695-7012
ams202@hotmail.com
*Sent $11.50 for "Erector Parts
Illustrated," $7.50 for "Erector
Advertising;" author of several
articles about Erector sets; send
LSASE for complete list of publications available.*

Bill Bean
439 Claxton Glen Ct.
Kettering, OH 45429
ph: 937-435-6196
ErectrBean@aol.com
http://www.erectorset.net
*Author of "Greenberg Guide to
Erector;" wants to buy Erector sets by
A.C. Gilbert, Ives, and Bing;
especially large sets in wood boxes
and chests; also store displays and
advertising pieces; collection featured
in Smithsonian Magazine.*

Museums/Libraries

William Brown, Dir.
Eli Whitney Museum
915 Whitney Ave.
Hamden, CT 06517-4036
ph: 203-777-1833
fax: 203-777-1229
wb@eliwhitney.org
http://www.eliwhitney.org
*Dedicated to helping children learn by
doing; uses Gilbert's construction and
chemistry ideas in their educational
program.*

Suppliers

Michael Wagner
Wagner & Sons Inc.
28 E. Willow St.
Carlisle, PA 17013
ph: 800-827-3948 or 800-821-7002
fax: 610-296-2258
mwagner@wagnerandsonstoys.com
http://www.wagnerandsonstoys.com
*The oldest and largest stock source of
original Erector parts, manuals,
catalogs and sets; send SASE for
catalog.*

Crayola Crayons

Museums/Libraries

Binney & Smith, Inc., Crayola Hall of
Fame
Two Rivers Landing
30 Centre Square
Easton, PA 18042-7744
ph: 423-515-8000 or 800-272-9652
webmaster@crayola.com
http://www.crayola.com/history/
history.html

Diecast

(see also AUTO RACING
MEMORABILIA; BANKS [MODERN];
MODELS; MODELS, Cars; MODELS,
Trucks & Equipment [Winross];
TOYS, Cars; TOYS, Ertl Replicas)

Clubs/Associations

Mr. Dana Johnson
Toy Car Collectors Association
Newsletter: Toy Car Collector Magazine
P.O. Box 1824
Bend, OR 97701-1824
ph: 541-318-7176
toynutz@earthlink.net
http://www.toynutz.com/TCCA.html
*Provides discounts on collector price
guides, information on new products,
model variations and values, resources
for buying and selling, toy shows
around the country; newsletter
published monthly.*

Collectors

Carl F. Pflanzer
205 US Hwy. 22
Green Brook, NJ 08812
ph: 732-424-7811
fax: 732-424-7814
ewa@ewacars.com
http://www.ewacars.com
Specializes in diecast cars.

Paul M. Provencher
Spring Garden House
20115 Woodfield Rd.
Gaithersburg, MD 20882-1229
ph: 301-948-2858
ppro@whitemetal.com
http://www.whitemetal.com
*Specializes in die cast vehicles of all
types; can provide information about
current and past die cast issues;
writes Die Cast Insider column for
Toy Trader magazine; contributor to
Antiques Weekly.*

Frank Kocinski III
912 Linwood
Delta, OH 43515
ph: 419-822-9028
*Collector and trader of Hot Wheels,
Matchbox, Johnny Lightning, and
Racing Champions diecast cars.*

David Lopez
P.O. Box 18023
San Jose, CA 95158
ph: 408-629-9928
fax: 408-972-1615
hwdave@yahoo.com
*Long time Hot Wheels collector also
wants Matchbox, Corgi, Dinky and
other brands of diecast toys; former
President of Northern California Hot
Wheels Collectors Club; always
interested in adding to his collection.*

Timothy G. Newman
P.O. Box 535
30911 Kodiak Lane
Bonanza, OR 97623
ph: 541-533-2300
fax: 208-723-4487
tnesplash@aol.com
*Specializes in Dinky toys and and
Meccano diecast toys made in
England; also deals in Corgi toys,
Matchbox, Hotwheels, Tootsie Toys,
Midetoys, NASCAR, Johnny
Lightning, Revell, Action and Road
Champs.*

British Diecast Model Collectors
Association
Magazine: CollectorLink
P.O. Box 11
Norwich, NR7 0SP U.K.
ph: +44 (0) 1603 505210
fax: +44 (0) 1603 507355
bmca@swapmeet.co.uk
http://www.swapmeet.co.uk/bmca
*For diecast collectors: Corgi, Dinky,
Matchbox, 00 and 0-gauge model
railway collectibles.*

Dealers

Toys for Collectors
P.O. Box 1406
North Attleboro, MA 02763
ph: 508-695-0588 or 888-445-3322
fax: 508-699-8649
tfcusa@northweb.com
http://www.tfcusa.com
*If you collect models of cars, trucks,
fire trucks, construction equipment,
cranes, buses, race cars, NASCARS,
etc. this is the source for better quality
1:43 scale models as well as 1:50,
1:18 and 1:14 scale models.*

Neil H. Waldmann
Neil's Wheels, Inc.
P.O. Box 374
Old Bethpage, NY 11804-0354
ph: 516-293-9659
fax: 516-420-0483
nw@neilswheels.com
http://www.neilswheels.com
*Authorized Matchbox collectibles
center; send SASE for list of 2000
models and brochure on Magic Box
Display System.*

Lisa Lynn Duffy
Duffys Diecast
1666 Scenery Dr.
Elizabeth, PA 15037
ph: 412-384-2081
fax: 412-384-1737
lissady@aol.com
http://www.duffysdiecast.com
*Sells Team Caliber, Action, Revell
discast.*

Ron Snyder
Diecast Toy Exchange
405 Carlisle Ave.
York, PA 17404
ph: 717-846-8097
fax: 717-845-2640
toys@diecasttoys.com
http://www.diecasttoys.com
*Sells and auctions diecast toys:
Matchbox, Hot Wheels, Dinky, Corgi,
and others.*

Steve Mullican
325 Elm Ave.
North Wales, PA 19454
ph: 215-699-2393
mulls64@aol.com
*Matchbox, Dinky, Corgi, early Lesney
products.*

Mike & Joyce Appnel
Kiddie Kar Kollectibles
1161 Perry St.
Reading, PA 19604
ph: 610-375-4780
info@kiddiekar.com
http://www.kiddiecar.com

Robert Lehmann
Reeded Edge, The
113-115 Baltimore St.
Cumberland, MD 21502
ph: 301-724-0400
fax: 301-724-0478
mail@reedededge.com
http://www.reedededge.com
*Appraises, collects, buys and sells all
pre-1970 diecast toys including Corgi,
Dinky, Matchbox, Schuco, Marklin,
Solido; prefer mint/boxed items;
especially interested in rare variants.*

Dan Wells
Dan Wells Antique Toys
P.O. Box 7
Goshen, KY 40026
ph: 502-386-3453
jagdan@aol.com
*Wants to buy Hot Wheels, Dinky,
Matchbox, Johnny Lightning, Corgi,
and Lesney cars; excellent or better
condition only.*

Toy Collector Club of America
1235 16th Ave. Court SW
Dyersville, IA 52040
ph: 800-452-3303 or 563-875-9263
fax: 563-875-8056
pkerker@speccast.com
http://www.toycollectorclub.com
*For collectors of contemporary diecast
banks and vehicles; gives collectors the
opportunity to purchase diecast metal
banks; newsletter lists what is
available for purchase and discounts
on products; a Spec-Cast company
sponsored club.*

Tom Lavely
Neat Olde Stuff
16935 N. Main St.
P.O. Box 9
Galesville, WI 54630-0009
ph: 608-582-2082
fax: 608-582-2180
tglavely@aol.com
*Collector of diecast Tootsietoy ships,
trains and airplanes (no cars or
trucks.)*

William Adorjan
P.O. Box 2494
Glenview, IL 60025
ph: 847-657-8502
iaretoys@aol.com
http://members.aol.com/iaretoys
*Buys, sells, collects and repairs
antique die-cast and tin vehicles.*

Thomas Mathews
T & D Toy & Hobby
116 S. Chicago Ave.
Freeport, IL 61032
ph: 815-232-1419 or 815-232-0096
fax: 815-232-0096
tdhobby@aol.com
Dealer of die cast toys, primarily racing memorabilia, but also trains, farm toys, model kits, and other types of toys.

3000toys.com - Stratton's Collector Toy
Network
4521 Reinmiller Rd.
Joplin, MO 64804
ph: 417-659-8697
fax: 417-659-9446
toys@3000toys.com
http://www.3000toys.com
Specializes in diecast banks, Caterpillar, Conrad, construction toys, Corgi, Ertl, First Gear trucks, John Deere, NASCAR, model trucks, Winross, etc.

Brent Powell
B & L Racing Collectibles
907 South Memorial Dr.
Tulsa, OK 74112
ph: 800-435-3570 or 918-664-3232
fax: 918-664-7018
brent@nascarshop.com
http://www.nascarshop.com
One of the largest racing collectibles companies in the US; specializes in diecast of all makes; also carries cards and many racing related souvenirs.

Bob Lowry
Foss Company, The
1224 Washington Ave.
Golden, CO 80401
ph: 303-279-3373
fax: 303-278-9556
BLowry@fossco.com
http://www.fossco.com
Carries a large selection of diecast toys.

Ernie Wilson
10262 Foothill Blvd.
Lake View Terrace, CA 91342
ph: 818-899-2634 or 888-845-9744
fax: 818-899-6764
NASCAR and NHRA diecast cars by Action and Revell.

Hu Arthur
Arthur's Collectible Toys
12422 107th Place NE
Kirkland, WA 98034
arthurhu@halcyon.com
http://www.arthurhu.com/collect.htm
Collector, dealer and expert in diecast and other model and toy cars: Hot Wheels, Matchbox, Sizzlers, Takara, Tomica, Siku, MicroMachines.

Ken Barrett
Ken's Diecast Car Gallery
7050 12th Ave. NW
Seattle, WA 98117
ph: 206-782-9877
Carries diecast collectibles: Hot

Wheels, Johnny Lightning, ERTL, Racing Champs, and more.

Kevin Pickell
Kevin's Hobbies
190 Hemlock
Anmore, British Columbia V3H 4W9
Canada
ph: 604-469-9718
fax: 604-469-9764
sales@scale18.com
http://www.scale18.com/diecast.html
Your source for information about 1/18th scale diecast cars; cars for sale, news, shows, collectors registry, chat room, manufacturers, limited edition companies, associations, collector homepages.

Experts

Richard L. Heuser
Heuser Publishing Div. of Heuser
Enterprises
508 Clapson Rd.
P.O. Box 300
West Winfield, NY 13491-0300
ph: 315-822-4804
fax: 315-822-4804
toybanks@heuser.com
http://www.heuser.com
Buys, collects, appraises and specializes in modern collectible toy banks and diecast toys.

Douglas R. Kelly
17920 Ashton Club Way
Ashton, MD 20861
ph: 301-570-2206
dandlk@erols.com
Author of "The Die Cast Price Guide;" Matchbox, Hot Wheels, Corgi, Tootsietoys, Winross, Schuco, Majorette, Burago, Danbury Mint, etc. from 1946 to present; regular contributor to magazines on diecast & tinplate toy cars.

Paul M. Provencher
Spring Garden House
20115 Woodfield Rd.
Gaithersburg, MD 20882-1229
ph: 301-948-2858
ppro@whitemetal.com
http://www.whitemetal.com
Specializes in die cast vehicles of all types; can provide information about current and past die cast issues; writes Hot Wheels Insider and other columns for collector periodicals.

Internet Resources

Custom Car Model Magazine
P.O. Box 2037
Garfield, NJ 07026
ph: 973-546-3305
fax: 973-546-7728
editor1@CARmodel.com
http://www.carmodel.com
Covers race cars in all forms: NASCAR, slotcars, diecast, static.

Jay Olins
Diecast Car Collectors Zone
1415 Dayton St.
Chicago, IL 60622
ph: 312-337-2010
mknab@priva.com
http://www.diecast.org
Dedicated to the collection of precision diecast cars, trucks, and motorcycles; Web site provides news, detailed illustrated reviews, comprehensive car lists, forums, auctions and pricing guide, collector ratings and more.

Toymart.com
1 Simmonds Rd.
Buckinghamshire, CT1 3RA U.K.
ph: 01227 472822
fax: 01227 768597
alan@toymart.com
http://www.toymart.com
Web site has on line price guide for mint and boxed Corgi, Crescent, Dinky, French Dinky, and Matchbox diecast toys.

Man./Prod./Dist.

Ted Burch
Burch Engineering PLLC Limited
Edition Die Cast
803 N. Dixie Ave., #119
Elizabethtown, KY 42701
info@4diecast.com
http://www.4diecast.com
Manufactures and sells high quality, low cost limited edition die cast vehicles.

Misc. Services

David L. Houston
Pro-Collectors System
webmaster@netdiecast.com
http://www.netdiecast.com/PCS
Great software program designed specifically for cataloging collections of diecast cars.

Periodicals

Richard L. Heuser
Heuser Publishing Div. of Heuser
Enterprises
Price Guide: Heuser's Price Guide to
  Official Collectible Banks
508 Clapson Rd.
P.O. Box 300
West Winfield, NY 13491-0300
ph: 315-822-4804
fax: 315-822-4804
toybanks@heuser.com
http://www.heuser.com
Quarterly price guide features Ertl, First Gear, Liberty Classics, Spec Cast, Action Racing Collectibles, Gearbox, Crown Premium/Vees Collectibles, DG Productions and others; listed by name, no., quantity, color, year made and value.

Richard L. Heuser
Heuser Publishing Div. of Heuser
Enterprises
Newsletter: Heuser's Quarterly
  Collectible Diecast Newsletter
508 Clapson Rd.
P.O. Box 300
West Winfield, NY 13491-0300
ph: 315-822-4804
fax: 315-822-4804
toybanks@heuser.com
http://www.heuser.com
Focuses on modern diecast collectible banks and custom imprinted replicas; new issues; articles of interest to collectors; listing of dealers and manufacturers; listing of upcoming toy shows.

Deb Sipe
Spec Cast
Newsletter: Spec Tacular News
P.O. Box 368
Dyersville, IA 52040-0368
ph: 319-875-8706
fax: 319-875-8056
info@speccast.com
http://www.speccast.com
A quarterly focusing on farm toys and collectibles.

Stacie Berger
Krause Publications
Magazine: Toy Cars & Vehicles
700 E. State St.
Iola, WI 54990-0001
ph: 715-445-2214
fax: 715-445-4087
stacie.berger@fwpubs.com
http://www.krause.com
One-stop marketplace and information for collectors of scale vehicles: toy cars, trucks, military vehicles, and construction vehicles; model kits, diecasts, motor sports, promotional models.

Jeff Atkinson
Newsletter: Traders Horn
1903 Schoettler Valley Rd.
Chesterfield, MO 63017-5203
ph: 636-532-3871
thorn@gloryroad.net
The oldest, largest bi-monthly periodical dedicated to the sales, trading of diecast toy vehicles, promotional models, model kits; obsolete, rare, current automotive & other transportation miniatures and related memorabilia; all scales.

Mike Forbes, Ed.
Magazine: Diecast Collector
The Maltings, West St.
Bourne, Lincs. PE10 9PH U.K.
ph: +44 (0) 1778 394748
mikef@warnersgroup.co.uk
http://www.diecast-collector.com
Monthly English magazine brings a colorful and nostalgic approach to the world of diecast transportation models.

Repro. Sources

Deb Sipe
Spec Cast
P.O. Box 368
Dyersville, IA 52040-0368
ph: 319-875-8706
fax: 319-875-8056
info@speccast.com
http://www.speccast.com
Manufacturer or discast replica belt buckles, banks, tractors, trucks, vehicle and airplane banks and non-banks, limited editions, and specialty items.

Suppliers

K & S Industries, Inc.
1801 Union Center Highway
Binghamton, NY 13905
ph: 877-742-5567 or 607-798-7156
fax: 607-798-7440
pleximan@888pickkns.com
http://www.888pickkns.com
Manufacturers of acrylic display cases for die-cast automotive collectors; made of clear acrylic with mirrored backs.

Diecast (Brooklin)

Clubs/Associations

Roger Mateo
San Francisco Bay Brooklin Club
Newsletter: SFBBC Newsletter
P.O. Box 61018
Palo Alto, CA 94306-6018
ph: 650-591-9580
fax: 650-591-9580
sfbbc@ix.netcom.com
http://www.netaccess.on.ca/~toys/sfbbc/baybrok.htm
Newsletter published every other month; current information on Brooklin models, upcoming specials; has international club membership.

Diecast (Corgi)

Clubs/Associations

Corgi Official Collector Club
Magazine: Corgi Collector
P.O. Box 323
Seansea, SA1 1BJ U.K.
ph: +44 (0) 116 282 6622
fax: +44 (0) 116 282 6633
webmaster@corgiclassics.co.uk
http://www.corgi.co.uk/front.ihtml
A company-sponsored collectors club; members receive monthly magazine, limited edition member-only Corgi models, membership card, invitations to Corgi previews in your area, and more.

Man./Prod./Dist.

Corgi Classics, Ltd.
P.O. Box 323
Seansea, SA1 1BJ U.K.
ph: +44 (0) 116 282 6622
fax: +44 (0) 116 282 6633
webmaster@corgiclassics.co.uk
http://www.corgi.co.uk/front.ihtml
Britain's leading diecast scale model manufacturer.

Diecast (Hot Wheels)

Clubs/Associations

David Conley
Blues City Hot Wheels Club
4807 Walden Glen
Memphis, TN 38128
ph: 901-386-6077
fax: 901-386-6077
A club for adults who are interested in a fair exchange of Hot Wheels product and knowledge.

John Boyd
Kentucky Hot Wheels Association
119 Etna St.
Russell, KY 41169
ph: 606-836-8815
khwa@zoomnet.net
http://www.zoomnet.net/~khwa
Die cast collectors Web site with real time classifieds, message board, news and information.

Heartland Hot Wheelers Club
P.O. Box 6372
Omaha, NE 68106-0372
ph: 402-345-1244
http://www.heartlandhotwheelers.com
A collectors club for Hot Wheels toy cars by Mattel; four quarterly shows per year in Omaha, NE.

Daryll Smith
Wheels of Fire - A Hot Wheels Club of Arizona
P.O. Box 86431
Phoenix, AZ 85080
onthepeg@cox.net
Club started in 1996 and caters to the Hot Wheels collector; monthly meetings; monthly newsletter; open to the public.

Wheels of Fire - A Hot Wheels Club of Arizona
P.O. Box 86431
Phoenix, AZ 86431
ph: 623-842-2680
JSutton666@aol.com

David Lopez, Pres.
Northern California Hot Wheels Collectors Club
P.O. Box 18023
San Jose, CA 95158
ph: 408-629-9928
fax: 408-972-1615
hwdave@yahoo.com
Meets monthly at different locations in the Silicon Valley; mostly new models are brought for sale and trade; members bring items for show and tell; all Hot Wheel enthusiasts are invited to attend.

Collectors

Jeff Hubbard
2900 91st St.
Sturtevant, WI 53177-2013
ph: 262-886-0477
jeffh27@yahoo.com
Buys older Hot Wheel cars and pre-1960 oil company highway maps.

Dealers

Russ Burke
Milezone's Toys
6824 N. 35th Ave., Ste. D
Phoenix, AZ 85017
ph: 602-864-3699
sales@milezone.com
http://www.milezone.com
Offers the finest in Hot Wheels, NASCAR, 1/18th scale diecast, dolls, action figures and more.

Experts

Tom Tumbusch
Tomart Publications
3300 Encrete Lane
Dayton, OH 45439-1944
ph: 937-294-2250
fax: 937-294-1024
office@tomart.com
http://www.tomart.com
Author of "Tomart's Price Guide to Hot Wheels."

Mike Strauss
26 Madera Ave.
San Carlos, CA 94070-2937
ph: 650-591-6482
fax: 650-591-7935
hwnewsltr@aol.com
http://members.aol.com/HWNEWSLTR
Hot Wheels collector and author; publisher of "Hot Wheels Newsletter," author of Tomart's Price Guide to Hot Wheels, produces annual Hot Wheels collector's convention.

Periodicals

Mike Strauss
Newsletter: Hot Wheels Newsletter
26 Madera Ave.
San Carlos, CA 94070-2937
ph: 650-591-6482
fax: 650-591-7935
hwnewsltr@aol.com
http://members.aol.com/HWNEWSLTR
Published bi-monthly; each issue contains articles covering history, new releases, club news, classified ads, promotions, Limited Editions, and anything else that has to do with Hot Wheels and the Hot Wheels collector community.

Diecast (Johnny Lightning)

Clubs/Associations

Johnny Lightning Club
Newsletter: NewsFlash
3618 Grape Rd.
Mishawaka, IN 46544
ph: 800-626-8478 or 219-256-0300
fax: 219-256-2657
lschlotfeldt@playingmantis.com
http://www.playingmantis.com
A company-sponsored club for collectors of Johnny Lightning cars.

Man./Prod./Dist.

Playing Mantis
3618 Grape Rd.
Mishawaka, IN 46544
ph: 800-626-8478 or 219-256-0300
fax: 219-256-2657
lschlotfeldt@playingmantis.com
http://www.playingmantis.com
Johnny Lighting, Sizzlers, Polar Lights model kits.

Diecast (Matchbox)

Clubs/Associations

Dorothy Colpitts
American-International Matchbox Collectors & Exchange Club
Newsletter: A.I.M. Newsletter
532 Chestnut St.
Lynn, MA 01904-2717
ph: 617-595-4135
fax: 617-595-4007
Monthly newsletter.

Charles Mack
Matchbox U.S.A.
Newsletter: Matchbox U.S.A. Newsletter
62 Saw Mill Rd.
Durham, CT 06422-2602
ph: 860-349-1655
fax: 860-349-3256
mtchboxusa@aol.com
Conducts annual conventions and shows; newsletter published monthly.

Everett Marshall
Matchbox Collectors Club
Newsletter: Matchbox Collectors Club Newsletter
17 Pearl St.
P.O. Box 977
Newfield, NJ 08344-0977
ph: 856-697-2800 or 800-976-7623
fax: 856-697-0762
mbroad@aol.com
http://www.mbxroad.com
Newsletter published quarterly.

Mike Appnel
Pennsylvania Matchbox Club
1161 Perry St.
Reading, PA 19604-2046

Bob Neumann, Sec.
Illinois Matchbox Collectors Club
P.O. Box 1582
Oak Lawn, IL 60455
ph: 630-257-0579
neuelectro@email.com
http://home.comcast.net/~rneumann25/imcc.html

Bay Area Matchbox Collectors Association
P.O. Box 1534
San Jose, CA 95109-1534
staff@bamca.org
http://www.bamca.org
Informal group of toy vehicle enthusiasts who hold meets to buy, sell, swap miniatures made by Matchbox, Hot Wheels, Dinky, Corgi, Ertl, Majorette, Tomica, and others as well as related items such as catalogs and boxes.

Tom Larson
Matchbox Northwest Collector's Club
1832 NE 25th Place
Renton, WA 98056
matchboxtom@cs.com
http://ourworld-top.cs.com/
 Matchboxtom/mbox.htm

Kevin McGimpsey
Matchbox International Collectors
 Association, The
Newsletter: MICA Newsletter
P.O. Box 120
Deeside, CH5 3HE U.K.
ph: 01244 539414
fax: 01244 539414
kevin@matchboxclub.com
http://www.matchboxclub.com
 *Formed to stimulate interest among
 collectors of Matchbox Diecast Models
 and Matchbox related items as
 manufactured originally by Lesney
 Products Ltd. and later by Matchbox
 Toys.*

Collectors

Charles Mack
62 Saw Mill Rd.
Durham, CT 06422-2602
ph: 860-349-1655
fax: 860-349-3256
mtchboxusa@aol.com

Tom Larson
1832 NE 25th Place
Renton, WA 98056
matchboxtom@cs.com
http://ourworld-top.cs.com/
 Matchboxtom/mbox.htm

Experts

Charles Mack
62 Saw Mill Rd.
Durham, CT 06422-2602
ph: 860-349-1655
fax: 860-349-3256
mtchboxusa@aol.com
 *Author of "Lesney's Matchbox Toys
 Regular Wheels Yrs. 1947-1969" and
 "Lesney's Matchbox Toys - The
 Superfast Years 1969-1982."*

Everett Marshall
17 Pearl St.
P.O. Box 977
Newfield, NJ 08344-0977
ph: 856-697-2800 or 800-976-7623
fax: 856-697-0762
mbroad@aol.com
http://www.mbxroad.com

Man./Prod./Dist.

Matchbox Inc.
8585 SW Hall Blvd.
Beaveton, WA 97008-6408
ph: 800-367-8926
http://www.matchboxtoys.com

Museums/Libraries

Charles Mack
Matchbox & Lesney Toy Museum
62 Saw Mill Rd.
Durham, CT 06422-2602
ph: 860-349-1655
fax: 860-349-3256
mtchboxusa@aol.com

Everett Marshall
Matchbox Rd. Museum
17 Pearl St.
P.O. Box 977
Newfield, NJ 08344-0977
ph: 856-697-2800 or 800-976-7623
fax: 856-697-0762
mbroad@aol.com
http://www.mbxroad.com

Diecast (Tomy)

Internet Resources

Jim Sutton
jbs3529@cs.com
http://tomypocketcars.freeservers.com
 *Web site devoted exclusively to
 blisterpacked, US-released Tomy/
 Tomica Pocket Cars; informative text
 and pictures, updated frequently.*

Ertl Replicas

(see also TOYS, Farm)

Clubs/Associations

Ertl Collectors Club
Newsletter: Replica, The
P.O. Box 500
Dyersville, IA 52040-0500
ph: 319-875-2000
fax: 319-875-5828
consumer_services@racn.com
http://www.rcertl.com
 *Provides new product and historical
 information to collectors of Ertl
 replica toys.*

Man./Prod./Dist.

Racing Champions Ertl, Inc.
P.O. Box 500
Dyersville, IA 52040-0500
ph: 319-875-2000
fax: 319-875-5828
consumer_services@racn.com
http://www.rcertl.com
 Manufacturer of Ertl diecast toys.

Periodicals

Richard L. Heuser
Heuser Publishing Div. of Heuser
 Enterprises
Newsletter: Heuser's Quarterly
 Collectible Diecast Newsletter
508 Clapson Rd.
P.O. Box 300
West Winfield, NY 13491-0300
ph: 315-822-4804
fax: 315-822-4804
toybanks@heuser.com
http://www.heuser.com
 *Focuses on modern diecast collectible
 banks and custom imprinted replicas;
 new issues; articles of interest to
 collectors; listing of dealers and
 manufacturers; listing of upcoming toy
 shows.*

Richard L. Heuser
Heuser Publishing Div. of Heuser
 Enterprises
Price Guide: Heuser's Price Guide to
 Official Collectible Banks
508 Clapson Rd.
P.O. Box 300
West Winfield, NY 13491-0300
ph: 315-822-4804
fax: 315-822-4804
toybanks@heuser.com
http://www.heuser.com
 *Quarterly price guide features Ertl,
 First Gear, Liberty Classics, Spec
 Cast, Action Racing Collectibles,
 Gearbox, Crown Premium/Vees
 Collectibles, DG Productions and
 others; listed by name, no., quantity,
 color, year made and value.*

Etch-A-Sketch

Man./Prod./Dist.

Ohio Art Company, The
1 Toy St.
P.O. Box 111
Bryan, OH 43506-0111
ph: 800-641-6226
info@world-of-toys.com
http://www.world-of-toys.com
 Maker of Etch-A-Sketch.

Farm

(see also BOOKS, Reference [Farm
Toys]; FARM COLLECTIBLES;
FARM MACHINERY; TOYS, Diecast;
TOYS, Ertl Replicas; TOYS,
Playsets; TRACTORS)

Clubs/Associations

David Semmel
Antique Engine, Tractor & Toy Club,
 Inc.
Newsletter: AETTC Newsletter
5731 Paradise Rd.
Slatington, PA 18080-4028
ph: 610-767-4768
 *Organized in 1986 with over 500
 members; dedicated primarily to
 collecting, preserving and enjoying old
 time farm engines and tractors; a
 lesser emphasis put on farm toys;
 newsletter three times per year.*

Collectors

Jim Proctor
1395 South Concord Rd.
West Chester, PA 193828343
ph: 610-399-0802

Dealers

George Mayer
Garden State Farm Toy Store
416 Route 40
Elmer, NJ 08318-2536
ph: 609-358-1144
fax: 609-358-1155
 *A complete hobby and collectors
 outlet: Ertl, Spec-Cast, Scale Models,
 1st Gear, banks, farm tractors, trucks,
 planes, D.C. cars, race cars, etc.*

Bossen Implement
300 Washburn Ave., Hwy 187 S
Lamont, IA 50650-9535
ph: 319-924-2880
fax: 319-924-2091
sales@bossenimp.com
http://www.bossenimp.com
 *Buys, sells, and appraises farm
 implements: John Deere, Case, New
 Holland, McCormick, Cat, AGCO,
 Ford, etc.*

Paul W. Jensen
Jensales Inc.
200 Main St.
Manchester, MN 56007-5000
ph: 507-826-3666 or 800-443-0625
fax: 507-826-3777
jensales@jensales.com
http://www.jensales.com
 *Sells new toy tractors; also repairs
 and modifies toy tractors to your
 specification.*

Museums/Libraries

National Farm Toy Museum
1110 16th Ave. SE
Dyersville, IA 52040
ph: 319-875-2727
http://www.dyersville.org/museum.htm
 *Large collection of cast iron toys,
 farm toys manufactured worldwide,
 first Ertl toy ever made, complete Tru-
 Scale collection, etc.*

Periodicals

Rick Larsen
Magazine: Toy Tractor Times, The
P.O. Box 156
Osage, IA 50461
ph: 641-732-3530
fax: 641-732-5135
 *Features farm toys with an emphasis
 on toy tractors; articles, ads, shows,
 new releases, etc.*

Deb Sipe
Spec Cast
Newsletter: Spec Tacular News
P.O. Box 368
Dyersville, IA 52040-0368
ph: 319-875-8706
fax: 319-875-8056
info@speccast.com
http://www.speccast.com
A quarterly focusing on farm toys and collectibles.

Claire Scheibe
Magazine: Toy Farmer
7496 106th Ave. SE
Lamoure, ND 58458-9404
ph: 701-883-5206 or 800-533-8293
fax: 701-883-5208
zekesez@aol.com
http://www.toyfarmer.com
Toy Farmer sponsors the annual National Farm Toy Shoy in Dyersville, IA.

Betty Holland
Magazine: Tractor Classics CTM
P.O. Box 489
Rocanville, Saskatchewan S0A 3L0
  Canada
ph: 306-645-4566
fax: 306-645-4376
ctmtoys@sk.sympatico.ca
http://www.pin.ca/classics/default.htm
Canada's bi-monthly farm toy magazine: toy show reviews, information on new and old farm toys, toy shows, collector of the month stories, price guides, cars, comics, dolls, display ads, classifieds.

Repair Services

Donald Walter
W2490 County Highway A
Curtiss, WI 54422
ph: 715-654-5440
Repairs tin trucks, pedal cars and tractors; removes old paint, repaints, adds needed parts, etc.

Suppliers

Dakotah Toys
RR 1 Box 157
Madison, SD 57042-9614
ph: 605-256-6676
fax: 605-256-9093
info@dakotahtoys.com
http://www.dakotahtoys.com
Catalog contains toy parts, decals, paints, kits, 1/64 items, books, scratch building materials, tools and diorama materials.

Fisher-Price

Clubs/Associations

Jeanne Kennedy
Fisher-Price Collectors Club
Newsletter: Gabby-Goose, The
1442 N. Ogden
Mesa, AZ 85205
ph: 480-396-2534
fpclub@aol.com
http://www.fpclub.org
Members study, research, discusses and write about Fisher-Price toys;

preserve and promote the collection of Fisher-Price toys and related items; annual convention in conjunction with ToyFest in August in East Aurora, NY.

Collectors

John J. Murray
P.O. Box 29
Eden, NY 14057-0029
The foremost collector of older Fisher-Price toys; co-author with Bruce R. Fox of "Fisher-Price 1931-63;" send SASE for information on book.

John Krupienski
5200 Hilltop Dr.
P.O. Box AA6
Brookhaven, PA 19015-1200
ph: 610-874-3003

Jeanne Kennedy
1442 N. Ogden
Mesa, AZ 85205
ph: 480-396-2534
fpclub@aol.com
http://www.fpclub.org

Internet Resources

Roy Summey
This Old Toy
P.O. Box 98393
Atlanta, GA 30359-8393
ph: 404-634-9086
fax: 404-633-7830
info@thisoldtoy.com
http://www.thisoldtoy.com
Great source for information on classic and antique Fisher-Price toys, products, history, and product identification and specs.

Man./Prod./Dist.

Fisher-Price, Inc.
636 Gerard Ave.
East Aurora, NY 14052
ph: 716-687-3000 or 800-432-5437
fax: 716-687-3667
http://www.fisherprice.com
Manufacturer of Fisher-Price toys; may still have parts for older toys, call 800-432-5437 to find out.

German & Japanese

Collectors

Martin Krim
P.O. Box 764
Middleton, MA 01949
ph: 978-304-3140
fax: 978-304-3140
mrkrim@attbi.com
http://www.old-toys.com
Wants German and Japanese toys c. 1900; also comic character toys, wind-ups, battery, etc.; celluloid, tin etc.

Guitars

Experts

Steve Evans
Jacksonville Guitar Center
1105 Burman Dr.
Jacksonville, AR 72076-4386
ph: 501-982-4933
jvilguitar@aol.com
http://members.aol.com/jvilguitar
Buys and collects toy guitars with pictures printed on the guitar; also wants crank models with built-in music boxes such as: Beany & Cecil, Popeye, Casper, and others.

Museums/Libraries

Steve Evans
Jacksonville Guitar Center
1105 Burman Dr.
Jacksonville, AR 72076-4386
ph: 501-982-4933
jvilguitar@aol.com
http://members.aol.com/jvilguitar
Large collection of vintage guitars on permanent display; includes over 100 cowboy guitars, c. 1930s-1950s, made with painted cowboy scenes showing Gene Autry, Roy Rogers, Buck Jones and others.

Horse-Drawn

Experts

Leon M. Weiss
Gemini Antiques Ltd.
P.O. Box 1752
2418 Montauk Highway
Water Mill, NY 11976
ph: 631-537-4565 or 212-316-6380
fax: 631-726-9366
julgert@geminiantiques.com
http://www.geminiantiques.com
Buys and sells mechanical still banks, cast iron toys, door stops, folk art and more.

Jack-in-the-Box

Collectors

Douglas Zimmerman
4413 Longford Dr.
Sarasota, FL 34232
ph: 941-378-3266
dnlzimm@webtv.net

Jacks

Collectors

Judith Schulz
533 Milwaukee Ave.
Burlington, WI 53105-1232
ph: 262-763-3946
Collects old and unusual jacks and pick-up sticks; coordinates the annual international jacks & pick-up sticks event and tournament each February.

Japanese

Internet Resources

Cool Japanese Toys
cjtadmin@cooljapanesetoys.com
News, editorial, articles, marketplace, buy and sell.

Kenner

Clubs/Associations

Ed Sterling
Girder & Panel Collectors Club
Newsletter: Girder & Panel Collectors
  Club Newsletter
P.O. Box 494
Bolton, MA 01740-0494
ph: 978-779-6058 or 978-779-6058
ed@ma.ultranet.com
http://www.ultranet.com/~ed
Club exists to document the history and production of Kenner Toys Girder and Panel toy sets; quarterly newsletter; buys and sell ads; ideal place to purchase and restore one of those 1960s toy construction sets.

Kinder Surprise

Collectors

Ann Brogley
P.O. Box 16033
Philadelphia, PA 19114-0033
ph: 215-824-4698 or 215-824-2350
fax: 215-824-4698
mostprod@erols.com
http://www.geocities.com/Heartland/
  Hills/2081
Collects Kinder Surprise figurines and toys, Kinder advertising and Kinder boxes; Kinder surprise toys are found in Ferrero chocolate eggs in many countries, but not in US.

Experts

Oliver Pink
Oliver's Kinder Paradise
Bauernfeldstr.28/5
Graz, A-8020 Austria
ph: +43 664 2201852
pink@magnet.at
http://kinder-surprise.hypermart.net
Kinder Surprise Toy collector, dealer, expert since 1992; has a huge collection of figurines; can help with Kinder questions.

Joachim Antona
Fuenfkirchener Str. 61
Tettnang, Baden-Wuerttemberg 88069
  Germany
joachim@antona.de
http://www.antona.de
Buys, sells, swaps Ferrero Kinder Surprise Egg toys; Web site has Kinder surprise toy online auction.

Kobe

Collectors

Bob Vargas
P.O. Box 1284
Los Altos, CA 94023
ph: 650-949-3959
Wants to buy Japanese Kobe toys; send good photo and price.

Mattel

Collectors

Joedi Johnson
P.O. Box 565
Billings, MT 59103
ph: 406-248-4875
fax: 407-248-4875
Joedi@dawndollsplus.com
http://www.dawndollsplus.com
*Buying Mattel Thingmakers, Maker
Paks, Play Paks, store displays,
Plastigoop, carded molds; Fright
Factory, Creep Crawlers, etc.;
newsletter available; also wants
Mattel Upsy Downsy dolls, accessories
and books.*

Monster

Collectors

Clayton Sayre
105 Francis St.
Portsmouth, VA 23702
ph: 757-487-8858
http://www.geocities.com/Hollywood/
Theater/1645
*Wants to buy classic movie monster
items: Frankenstein, Dracula,
Wolfman, Creature from the Black
Lagoon, etc.*

Neal Austinson
P.O. Box 1691
Windsor, CA 95492-1691
ph: 707-838-9015
*Wants movie monster toys: Franken-
stein, Wolfman, Creature From The
Black Lagoon, etc.*

Dealers

John Skerchock
P.O. Box 733
Bellefonte, PA 16823-0733
ph: 814-353-0565
*Specializes in monster and science
fiction collectibles from the 1960s to
present; writes articles for "Scary
Monsters" magazine and related
publications.*

Experts

John Marshall
Toyzilla Enterprises
P.O. Box 340
Rancocas, NJ 08073-0340
jm@jmuniverse.com
http://www.jmuniverse.com
*Author of "GI Joe And Other
Backyard Heroes: Action Figures of
the 1970s," "Action Figures of the
1980s," "Action Figures of the
1960s," "Comic Book Hero Toys,"
"Collecting Monster Toys;" writes
articles for toy magazines.*

Internet Resources

Gallery of Monster Toys, The
raycastile@aol.com
http://members.aol.com/raycastile/
page1.htm
*Dedicated to preserving a disappear-
ing facet of our popular culture; great
resources with pictures and history of*

monster toys from 1960s through
1980s.

Mr. Potato Head

Internet Resources

Dennis Martin
Mr. Potato Head Collector's Page
ph: 205-621-4167
fliptoppez@narrowgate.net
http://www.potatoheadcollector.com
*The Web's largest resource for Mr.
Potato Head information and history;
with over 100 pages, the Web site
covers history from 1952 to present;
includes images of almost all Mr.
Potato Head items ever made.*

Ohio Art Co.

Clubs/Associations

Sharon "Sherry" Lazane
Ohio Art Collectors Club
Newsletter: Ohio Art Beat
18203 Kristi Rd., West
Liberty, MO 64068
ph: 816-781-5452
slazane@aol.com
http://
www.ohioartcollectors.homestead.com/
AboutUs~nst.html
*Club is for those interested in
collecting toys made by the Ohio Art
Co.; especially sand toys including
pails, sieves or sifters, sprinkling
cans, water pumps, sand molds, sand
hoists or lifts, sand mills, tin litho tea
sets, drums, tops.*

Optical

(see also CAMERAS & CAMERA
EQUIPMENT; KALEIDOSCOPES;
MAGIC LANTERNS & SLIDES;
OPTICAL ITEMS; STANHOPES;
STEREO VIEWERS &
STEREOVIEWS)

Auction Services

Michael Pritchard
Christie's South Kensington, Ltd.
85 Old Brompton Rd.
London, SW7 3LD U.K.
ph: 020 7930 6074 or 020 7752 3279
fax: 020 7321 3321
info@christies.com
http://www.christies.com
*Specializes in the sale of optical toys
such as persistence of vision devices,
stereoscopes, magic lanterns/slides,
etc.*

Collectors

Uwe H. Breker
Bonner Str. 528-530
Koln, D-50968 Germany
ph: 49 221 387049 or 941-925-0385 (US
Rep)
fax: 49 221 374878
auction@breker.com
http://www.breker.com
*Wants to buy optical toys: magic
lanterns, mechanical slides,
stereoviewer, etc.*

Dealers

Bryan W. Ginns
2109 Cty. Rte. 21
Valatie, NY 12184-6001
ph: 518-392-5805
fax: 518-392-7925
the3dman@aol.com
*Wants large collections of stereo
views, old cameras, daguerreotypes,
magic lanterns, optical toys; anything
relating to photographics.*

Paper

(see also PAPER COLLECTIBLES)

Dealers

Barb & Jonathan Newman
Paper Soldier, The
8 McIntosh Lane
Clifton Park, NY 12065
ph: 518-371-9202 or 518-371-5130
*Paper toys bought and sold. Paper
dolls, paper soldiers, toy theaters,
planes, ships, paper and cardboard
houses, etc.*

Pedal Vehicles

(see BICYCLES & RELATED
MEMORABILIA; RIDING TOYS)

Penny

Dealers

Bob Stevens
Keystone Toy Trader
529 N. Water St.
Masontown, PA 15461-1747
ph: 724-583-8234
fax: 724-583-0604
keystonetoytrader@charter.net
*Wants quality antique toys in all
categories: early comic character toys,
cast iron and tin toys, diecast pre-
WWII Tootsietoys, German penny
toys, early German and European
toys.*

Pick-Up Sticks

Collectors

Judith Schulz
533 Milwaukee Ave.
Burlington, WI 53105-1232
ph: 262-763-3946
*Collects old and unusual jacks and
pick-up sticks; coordinates the annual
international jacks & pick-up sticks
event and tournament each February.*

Playsets

(see also SOLDIERS, Toy; TOYS,
Action Figures)

Collectors

Eric J. Reinkka
P.O. Box 190520
Jamaica, NY 11417-0520
ph: 718-219-4919
*Wants to buy old toy soldiers, sets,
playsets; Marx, Sears, Wards playsets,
1950s and 1960s model kits, battery/*

friction tinplate vehicles, G.I. Joe,
guns, etc.; any nice military theme toy.

Dave Gall
7180 Broadview
Parma, OH 44134
ph: 216-524-9514
*Wants Marx playsets: Gunsmoke,
Johnny Ringo, Ben-Hur, Blue and
Gray; also many others such as
westerns, military, space, etc.*

David W. Francis
148 King St.
Wadsworth, OH 44281
ph: 330-335-3717
fax: 330-335-3617
fphadv@bright.net
*Wants to buy zoo and farm animal
figures.*

Dealers

Paul Stadinger
STAD'S
815 North 12th St.
Allentown, PA 18102-1318
ph: 610-770-1140 or 610-433-7728
fax: 610-770-1740
toys@stadstoys.com
http://www.statstoys.com
*STAD'S is a leading source for plastic
figures from US makers (Marx, MPC,
Lido, Timmee, etc.) and foreign
(Britains, Timpo, etc.); twice monthly
catalog subscription is $4 for six
months.*

Stone Castle Imports
804 N. Third St.
P.O. Box 141
Bardstown, KY 40004
ph: 502-897-0207
fax: 502-897-6415
castle@toysoldiers.cc
http://www.toysoldiers.cc
*Carries a wide variety of toy soldiers
and playsets.*

Joseph Saine
Joseph Saine Toy Soldiers
P.O. Box 50506
Toledo, OH 43624
ph: 419-691-0008
josaine@att.net
http://home.att.net/~nostalgiarama
*Buys and sells antique and modern toy
soldiers, miniature figures, playsets:
lead, composition, and plastic toy
soldiers; any soldier or figure; issues
periodic listings.*

Tim Geppert
Colorado Quality Collectibles
2818 McKeag Dr.
Fort Collins, CO 80526
ph: 970-225-9782
cts@classictoysoldiers.com
http://www.classictoysoldiers.com
*Buys, sells, collects, appraises Marx
playsets, plastic toy soldiers and
figures; author of "Guide for Non-
Metallic Toy Soldiers of the US."*

Experts

Tim Geppert
Colorado Quality Collectibles
2818 McKeag Dr.
Fort Collins, CO 80526
ph: 970-225-9782
cts@classictoysoldiers.com
http://www.classictoysoldiers.com
*Buys, sells, collects, appraises Marx
playsets, plastic toy soldiers and
figures; author of "Guide for Non-
Metallic Toy Soldiers of the US."*

Periodicals

Thomas P. Terry, Ed.
Specialty Publishing Co.
Magazine: Plastic Figure & Playset
Collector
P.O. Box 1355
La Crosse, WI 54602-1355
ph: 608-781-1894
tompfpc@aol.com
http://www.hat.com/PFPC.html
*The only magazines devoted to Marx
Playsets (1950s-1970s) and related
plastic toys and figures of the era; bi-
monthly, 44+ pages, 8-1/2" x 11"
b&w format with articles, photos and
factory reprints, articles, Q&A, ads,
and more.*

Paul Stadinger
STAD'S
Magazine: Plastic Warrior
65 Walton Court
Woking, Surrey GU21 5EE U.K.
ph: (0) 1483 722778
fax: (0) 1483 772723
editor@plasticwarrior.freeserve.co.uk
http://www.plasticwarrior.com
*A British bi-monthly focusing on
leading European plastic figures,
firms (Britains, Timpo, etc.), reviews,
Q&A, letters, news, ads, etc.*

Plush

(see also)

Collectors

Johanna & Sean Billings
P.O. Box 244
Danielsville, PA 18038-0244
ph: 610-760-8134 or 610-760-1814
bankie@enter.net
*Wants to buy furry, plush stuffed
soccer balls; any size, any color, any
condition; will pay a couple dollars
for each plus shipping; also wants
unusual stuffed objects: stuffed
crayons, toothbrushes, guitars, etc.*

Periodicals

Scott Publications
Magazine: Soft Dolls & Animals
30595 Eight Mile
Livonia, MI 48152-1798
ph: 800-458-8237 or 248-477-6650
fax: 248-477-6795
concatus@scottpublications.com
http://www.scottpublications.com
*For people who love to make and
collect cloth dolls, animals, teddy
bears, and other plushes; each*

*bimonthly issue contains how-to
projects for every level of ability;
patterns included.*

Jones Publishing, Inc.
Magazine: Teddy Bear Review
P.O. Box 5000
Iola, WI 54945
ph: 715-445-5000 or 800-331-0038
fax: 715-445-4053
jonespub@jonespublishing.com
http://www.teddybearreview.com
*Embraces the joy of teddy bear and
soft sculpture collecting: in-depth
articles, collector tips, expert advice,
show reports.*

Pokemon

Man./Prod./Dist.

Nintendo's Pokemon World
http://www.pokemon.com
The official Pokemon Web site.

Periodicals

Hugh Murphy, PR
Beckett Publications, Inc.
Magazine: Beckett Pokemon & Anime
Collector
15850 Dallas Parkway
Dallas, TX 75248
ph: 972-448-9018 or 800-840-3137
hmurphy@beckett.com
http://www.beckett.com
*A monthly magazine with the most
comprehensive Pokemon coverage:
special price guides, checklists, video
game tips and tricks, coverage of all
150 monsters, Web site reviews,
tournament listings, merchandise, and
more.*

Pullstring

(see TOYS, Talking [Pullstring])

Racing

Internet Resources

Custom & Racing Model Magazine
Online
P.O. Box 2037
Garfield, NJ 07026
ph: 973-546-3305
fax: 973-546-7728
editor1@CARmodel.com
http://www.carmodel.com
*Covers race cars in all forms:
NASCAR, slotcars, diecast, static.*

Renwal

Collectors

Mary Soelberg
29126 Laro Dr.
Agoura Hills, CA 91301-1635
ph: 818-889-9909
*Advanced Renwal toy collector wants
hard-to-find pieces or boxed sets;
write with complete description and
price; no broken items.*

Dealers

Judy Mosholder
Dollhouse Furniture - Renwal
186 Pine Springs Camp Rd.
Boswell, PA 15531-2421
ph: 814-629-9277
jlytwins@floodcity.net
http://www.RenwalToys.com
*Buys and sells doll houses and plastic
doll house furniture, especially
Renwal, Ideal, and Marx; send LSASE
for list of items for sale.*

Russian

Dealers

George Francisco Paley
c/o Natural Way
Newsletter: Russian Toy Club
820-822 Massachusetts St.
P.O. Box 842
Lawrence, KS 66044-0842
ph: 785-865-5466
*Wholesale retailer and dealer;
periodically published a newsletter for
collectors of Russian toys - a rapidly
changing environment and usually a
situation of extremely limited
availability.*

Sand

Clubs/Associations

Sharon "Sherry" Lazane
Ohio Art Collectors Club
Newsletter: Ohio Art Beat
18203 Kristi Rd., West
Liberty, MO 64068
ph: 816-781-5452
slazane@aol.com
http://
www.ohioartcollectors.homestead.com/
AboutUs~nst.html
*Club is for those interested in
collecting toys made by the Ohio Art
Co.; especially sand toys including
pails, sieves or sifters, sprinkling
cans, water pumps, sand molds, sand
hoists or lifts, sand mills, tin litho tea
sets, drums, tops.*

Collectors

Doug & Pat Wengel
P.O. Box 305
Skillman, NJ 08558-0305
ph: 609-466-2461
fax: 609-466-8911
wengel@njcc.com
http://pluto.njcc.com/~wengel
Serious collectors of sand pails.

Patrick Batzler
8118 Virginia Circle North
St. Louis Park, MN 55426
ph: 952-525-9590
fax: 952-545-7662
patrickbatzler@aol.com
*Wants to buy children's tin sand box
play items: sand pails, watering cans,
shovels, etc. made by Ohio Art
Company, Chien and others.*

Donald Gorlick
P.O. Box 24541
Seattle, WA 98124-0541
ph: 206-824-0508
*Wants sand toys (not very old); small
box-like toy containing a clown or
trapeze artist which spins when the
box is inverted.*

Experts

Carole & Richard Smyth
Carole Smyth Antiques
P.O. Box 2068
Huntington, NY 11743-0861
ph: 631-673-8666
carolesmyth@yahoo.com
*Authors of "Pails by Comparison," a
study and price guide; available from
the author for $28.50 ppd.*

Schoenhut

Clubs/Associations

Pat Girbach, Sec./Mem.
Schoenhut Collectors Club
Newsletter: Schoenhut Newsletter
1003 W. Huron St.
Ann Arbor, MI 48103-4217
ph: 734-662-6676
fax: 734-662-6676
aawestie@provide.net
*Quarterly newsletter includes articles,
prices and announcements of shows
and events of interest to Schoenhut
collectors.*

Dealers

Harry R. McKeon, Jr.
18 Rose Lane
Flourtown, PA 19031-1910
ph: 215-233-4094
toyspost@aol.com
*Buys and sells Schoenhut items: dolls,
games, circus animals, toys,
accessories; anything Schoenhut except
pianos.*

Silly Putty

Man./Prod./Dist.

Binney & Smith, Inc.
1100 Church Lane
Easton, PA 18040
ph: 800-272-9652 or 610-253-6272
fax: 610-250-5768
webmaster@crayola.com
http://www.crayola.com
*This is the company that manufactures
Silly Putty today.*

Museums/Libraries

Crayola Hall of Fame, Binney & Smith,
Inc.
Two Rivers Landing
30 Centre Square
Easton, PA 18042-7744
ph: 423-515-8000 or 800-272-9652
webmaster@crayola.com
http://www.crayola.com/history/
history.html
*In addition to crayons, this museum
also honors Silly Putty.*

Space & Robot

(see also SPACE COLLECTIBLES)

Auction Services

Jeffrey Ralston
Lloyd Ralston Toy Auction
350 Long Beach Blvd.
Stratford, CT 06615
ph: 203-386-9399
fax: 203-386-9515
lrgallery@aol.com
http://www.lloydralstontoys.com

Collectors

Jim Welytok
W241 N8938 Penny Lane
Sussex, WI 53089
ph: 262-246-7171
unievents@aol.com
*Antique toy robot collector; looking
for tin toy robots and cars from the
1940s through 1960s.*

Christmas Catalog Collector, The
175 East Delaware, #7403
Chicago, IL 60611-1731
ph: 800-879-6948 or 312-337-3123
fax: 312-266-7982
*Wants to buy 1925-1970 space toys
and ray guns, Buck Rogers, Captain
Video, Space Patrol, etc.; also wants
toy/Christmas catalogs.*

Dealers

Karen & Dan Dozier
ToyTent.com
23 Forest Ave.
Falmouth, MA 02540-4006
ph: 508-548-6342 or 508-548-0893
fax: 508-548-0893
tintoys@dozierdesigns.com
http://www.toytent.com
*Collector, appraiser, dealer and
resource for antique collectible toys,
specializing in robots and space toys;
also expert toy box reproduction and
restorations.*

John Maleski
Space Toys
20289 Canal
Grosse Ile, MI 48138
ph: 734-675-8322
*Wants to buy space toy buildings, ray
guns, figures, premiums, 1950s TV
space series' toys, Archer slot handed
figures & accessories.*

Bill O'Neil
SkyScopes
1291B E. Woolford
Show Low, AZ 85901
ph: 520-537-2437
fax: 760-280-9965
skyscopes@aol.com
http://www.spacetoys.com
*Specializes in robots, ray guns, movie
posters, and other sci-fi related
collectibles.*

Space & Robot (Ray Guns)

Dealers

Gary Kraut
Alphaville
226 W. Houston St.
New York, NY 10014-4846
ph: 212-675-6850
fax: 212-741-2609
alphavil@mindspring.com
http://www.alphaville.com
*Along with partner Steve Karchin buys
and sells space toys.*

John Maleski
Space Toys
20289 Canal
Grosse Ile, MI 48138
ph: 734-675-8322
*Wants to buy space toy buildings, ray
guns, figures, premiums, 1950s TV
space series' toys, Archer slot handed
figures & accessories.*

Experts

Gene Metcalf
211 S. Elm #F
Oxford, OH 45056
metcalew@muohio.edu
http://www.toyraygun.com
Ray gun collector and expert.

Leslie Singer
7 Shackleford Plaza, Ste. C
Little Rock, AR 72211
ph: 501-221-2885
zenmotel@aol.com
*Collects and specializes in pre-1960
space toys; author of "ZAP! Ray Gun
Classics."*

Internet Resources

Gene Metcalf
Toy Ray Guns
211 S. Elm #F
Oxford, OH 45056
metcalew@muohio.edu
http://www.toyraygun.com
*Web site has images of hundreds of
toy ray guns from the US and abroad;
traces the development of this toy and
its social significance; lots of ray gun
pages plus bulletin boards, buy/sell/
trade pate, rotating gallery pages.*

Steam/Hot Air

Collectors

Robin Corsiglia
Toy Steam Engines
5200 NE 9th Lane
Ocala, FL 34470
ph: 352-236-2635 or 352-687-5950
marklinc1@earthlink.net
http://home.earthlink.net/~marklinc1/
index.html
*Buys, sells and collects toy steam
engines (stationary with real boilers
and flywheels) and tin pop-pop boats,
tin wind up boats, and tin battery
boats; mainly collects buy also buys,
sells, trades and gives out information.*

Dealers

Diamond Enterprises & Book Publishers
P.O. Box 537
Alexandria Bay, NY 13607-0537
ph: 613-475-1771 or 800-481-1353
fax: 613-475-3748
info@yesteryeartoys.com
http://www.yesteryeartoys.com
*American and Canadian distributors
of Mamod and Wilesco steam models;
sales, parts and service.*

Robin Corsiglia
Toy Steam Engines
5200 NE 9th Lane
Ocala, FL 34470
ph: 352-236-2635 or 352-687-5950
marklinc1@earthlink.net
http://home.earthlink.net/~marklinc1/
index.html
*Buys, sells and collects toy steam
engines (stationary with real boilers
and flywheels) and tin pop-pop boats,
tin wind up boats, and tin battery
boats; mainly collects buy also buys,
sells, trades and gives out information.*

Eureka, I Found It! Antiques &
Collectibles
P.O. Box 2192
Petaluma, CA 94953-2192
eureka@eureka-i-found-it.com
http://www.eureka-i-found-it.com
*An online dealer specializing in
vintage textiles and clothing, toy and
model steam engines, buttons, fans,
Art Deco, costume jewelry, toy sewing
machines.*

Experts

Richard Leach
26146 Redfield Rd.
Edwardsburg, MI 49112-9146
ph: 616-663-8844
*Expert and collector of toy steam
engines, hot air engines, toy electric
motors; author of "Weeden Steam Toy
Pictorial Guide" and steam toy
booklets and instruction sheets.*

Submarine Related

Dealers

Tom Lavely
Neat Olde Stuff
16935 N. Main St.
P.O. Box 9
Galesville, WI 54630-0009
ph: 608-582-2082
fax: 608-582-2180
tglavely@aol.com
*Collector, dealer of toy submarines,
sub memorabilia, photos, books,
related items,*

Super Hero

(see also CHARACTER
COLLECTIBLES; COMIC BOOKS;
PREMIUMS; SCIENCE FICTION;
TELEVISION SHOWS &
MEMORABILIA)

Collectors

Dale L. Ames
144 Russell St.
Worcester, MA 01610
ph: 508-755-3830

Experts

John Marshall
Toyzilla Enterprises
P.O. Box 340
Rancocas, NJ 08073-0340
jm@jmuniverse.com
http://www.jmuniverse.com
*Author, expert buys and sells action
figures and character collectibles from
1950s to present.*

Talking (Pullstring)

(see also DOLLS, Chatty Cathy)

Dealers

Bryin Dall
Pull This!
P.O. Box 2124
New York, NY 10009
ph: 212-777-1868
PullThis1@aol.com
*Buys and sells talking dolls and toys;
anything that has a pull-string and
talks (or used to); working or not;
will also buy empty boxes, advertising,
displays, and salesman samples.*

Repair Services

Rick Lehman
Speak-Up
25 Statler Dr.
Shirley, NY 11967
ph: 631-924-6256
*Source for repairing Chatty Cathy and
Mattel talkers.*

Kelly McIntyre
Chatty Cathy's Haven
19528 Ventura Blvd. #495
Tarzana, CA 91356-2917
ph: 818-881-3878
cchaven@aol.com
http://www.chattycathyshaven.com
*Repairs, buys and sells pullstring
talkers.*

Tin

Collectors

Tadg Galleran
2911 4th St., #112
Santa Monica, CA 90405
ph: 310-314-0402
tadggalleran@hotmail.com
*Wants to buy German tin "penny"
toys, German windups, trains, Steiff
and teddy bears, and cast iron toys.*

Dealers

Harry R. McKeon, Jr.
18 Rose Lane
Flourtown, PA 19031-1910
ph: 215-233-4094
toyspost@aol.com
*Buys and sells tin toys made by
Martin, Bing, Lehmann, Gutherman,
Ives, Strauss, etc.*

David A. Hull
Small Town Coins & Collectibles
7498 E. Davison Rd.
Davison, MI 48423-2014
ph: 810-658-1992
fax: 810-658-2977
towncoin@small-town.cnchost.com
http://small-town.cnchost.com
Dozens of original antique tin toys and Mint-In-Box for sale.

World City, Inc.
6935 James Ave. South
Minneapolis, MN 55423-2147
Wants pre-1960 old lithograph tin toys.

Scott Gruenwald
Tin Car Garage Online
P.O. Box 436
Ingleside, IL 60041
ph: 847-356-1384
fax: 847-356-1870
http://www.tincargarage.com
Specializes in vintage tin toy cars and motorcycles; also automobilia, toy art, reproduction boxes for antique toys; research history about tin toys.

John D. McKenna
McKenna Bros. Wholesale
801 W. Cucharras St., #803
Colorado Springs, CO 80905-1619
ph: 719-630-8732 or 719-488-0818
Buys, sells & collects pre-1960 toys in all categories especially early American tin, cast iron automotive and horse-drawn toys.

Richard Johnson
Richard Johnson Toys
121 N. Cortez
Prescott, AZ 86301
ph: 520-771-9438
fax: 520-771-9445
Specializes in tin toys.

Internet Resources

Mark Kerr
Tinplate Toys
75 Loates Lane
Watford, Hertfordshire WD17 2PA U.K.
mark@sable.co.uk
http://www.tinplatetoy.co.uk
The essential site for collectors and lovers of tinplate toys, clockwork devices, and automata; new and antique.

Repair Services

Joe Freeman
Tin Toy Works
1313 N. 15th St.
Allentown, PA 18102-1068
ph: 610-439-8268
fax: 610-439-1288
tintoyworks@enter.net
Specializes in the repair of tin toys; tin toy autos, boats, merry-go-rounds, etc.; repairs mechanisms, makes missing parts.

Tin Tea Sets

Experts

Cathy Cook
10 E. 13th St., #2D
New York, NY 10003-4467
ph: 212-691-2406
fax: 212-691-2406
ccook710@aol.com
Expert in history (late 19th century) of tin-lithographed toy tea sets; author on book on subject; seeks only rare sets.

Tinkertoys

Museums/Libraries

Evanston Historical Society
225 Greenwood St.
Evanston, IL 60201-4713
ph: 847-475-3410
fax: 847-475-3599
evanstonHS@northwestern.edu
http://www.evanstonhistorical.org
Tinkertoys originated in Evanston, IL; Evanston Historical Society has the largest collection of Tinkertoys and related information in the country.

Tonka

Collectors

George T. Kitchen
6708 El Parque
El Paso, TX 79912
ph: 915-584-7524
fax: 915-581-9519
webmaster@neatoldtoys.com
http://www.neatoldtoys.com
Tonka toy collector; has an online reference for collectors and enthusiasts of early Tonka trucks; restoration tips, identification guide, complete photo reference of Tonka Look Books produced from 1955 to 1971.

Dealers

Dave Montana
2265 Crestview Lane
Aston, PA 19014
tonkadave@aol.com
http://www.tonkadave.com
Buys and sells vintage Tonka toys, Matchbox, Corgi, Dinky, Ertl, Buddy L, Nylint and Structo.

Internet Resources

George T. Kitchen
Champion Toys
6708 El Parque
El Paso, TX 79912
ph: 915-584-7524
fax: 915-581-9519
webmaster@neatoldtoys.com
http://www.neatoldtoys.com
An online reference for collectors and enthusiasts of early Tonka trucks; restoration tips, identification guide, complete photo reference of Tonka Look Books produced from 1955 to 1971.

Suppliers

Thomas Toys
P.O. Box 405
Fenton, MI 48430
ph: 810-629-8707
Sells replacement parts for Tonka trucks.

Toonerville Trolley

Clubs/Associations

Bill Tait
Toonerville Trolley Collectors
Newsletter: Toonerville Times
4809 Listra Rd.
Rockville, MD 20853
ph: 301-933-0250
fax: 301-933-6582
wtait@comcast.net
Provides toy and trolley collectors with information on the Fontaine Fox cartoon series, Toonerville Folks; writings and drawings of F. Fox, history of Toonerville, cartoons, videos, values of collectible items, etc.

Experts

Asa Sparks
6045 Camelot Ct.
Montgomery, AL 36117-2555
ph: 334-270-0687
asasparks2@mindspring.com
http://toonerville1.homestead.com
Author of "The Compleat Toonerville," a definitive publication about Fontaine Fox and Tonnerville Folks.

Internet Resources

Scott McDonald
diesel@erols.com
http://users.erols.com/diesel/toonerville
A Web site for those who appreciate the humor and wit of the late Fontaine Fox.

Tops & Gyroscopes

(see also TOYS, Yo-Yos)

Collectors

Bruce R. Middleton
Top Secret
5 Lloyd Rd.
Newburgh, NY 12550-5028
ph: 914-564-2556
Buys, sells, trades tops, yo-yos, spinners, figurals, peg tops, supported tops, diablos, gyroscopes, etc.; seeks other collectors.

Don Olney
Toycrafter, The
1237 E. Main St.
Rochester, NY 14609-6941
ph: 716-288-9000 or 800-433-TOYS
fax: 716-654-7820
topman@toycrafter.com
http://www.toycrafter.com
Buys, sells, trades new and old tops; also wants top related ads, photos, books, photos and videos of people doing tricks with tops; author of "The

Little Book of Tops," and "The Tops Discovery Kit."

Experts

Judith Schulz
533 Milwaukee Ave.
Burlington, WI 53105-1232
ph: 262-763-3946
Wants to buy unusual tops, gyroscopes and yo-yos; also wants related ads, literature, and old packages; editor of "Spin-Offs," curator of a small museum about tops, gyros, and yo-yos; top expert of MGM's video "My Summer Story."

Museums/Libraries

Judith Schulz
Spinning Top Exploratory Museum
Journal: Spin-Offs
533 Milwaukee Ave.
Burlington, WI 53105-1232
ph: 262-763-3946
2,000 tops, gyroscopes & yo-yos on exhibit (antique and modern); top games & experiments to try; 35 types to spin; sales of unique tops; demos, live show at museum; "Spin-offs" is a playful research publication of history, facts, etc.

Transformers

Clubs/Associations

Tony Buchanan
TransMasters
Newsletter: Matrix
1215 S. Andrews Rd.
Yorktown, IN 47396-1002
autoforse@aol.com
http://www.geocities.com/Area51/
Dimension/8034
International club interested in Transformers, comics, cartoons and toys.

Collectors

Maret Webb
5101 E. Monterey Way
Phoenix, AZ 85018-6623
ph: 602-957-0653
fax: 602-957-1631
maret@vehrwebbstudio.com
Wants to buy Hasbro and Bandai Transformers (transformation robot toys), and related cards, books, cookie jars, games, posters, etc. - ANYTHING featuring Transformers.

Internet Resources

Transformers Collector, The
laser@erie.net
http://www.geocities.com/Area51/Zone/
6215
A Web site dedicated to transformers and the hobby of collecting them.

Renaud Lefebvre
Bigbot.com
Canada
rtlefebv@videotron.ca
http://www.bigbot.com
This site is dedicated to transformers (THE toys of the 1980s).

Transportation

Dealers

Tom Nefos
National Toy Connection
779 E. Merritt Island Cswy #1282
Merritt Island, FL 32952
NationalToy@aol.com
http://members.aol.com/NationalToy/
HessTrucks.html
*Publishes "Original Price Guide to
Hess Toys," and "Hess Photo Album
and Toys" on CD.*

Jim & Nancy Schaut
AutoHobbies
7147 W. Angela Dr.
Glendale, AZ 85308-8507
ph: 623-878-4293
fax: 801-697-9381
nancy@autohobbies.com
http://www.autohobbies.com
*Buys and sells transportation toys and
memorabilia; toys, trains; maintains a
Web site of one-of-a-kind items for
sale; authors of "American
Automobilia," an illustrated history
and price guide.*

Experts

Tom Nefos
National Toy Connection
779 E. Merritt Island Cswy #1282
Merritt Island, FL 32952
NationalToy@aol.com
http://members.aol.com/NationalToy/
HessTrucks.html
*Publishes "Original Price Guide to
Hess Toys," and "Hess Photo Album
and Toys" on CD.*

Trucks & Equipment

(see also GAS STATION
COLLECTIBLES; TOYS, Tonka;
TOYS, Transportation)

Collectors

Larry Bruch
Larry Bruch Toys
P.O. Box 121
Mountain Top, PA 18707-0121
ph: 800-549-TOYS
bkinglar@aol.com
*All kinds of pre-1960 toys wanted:
German, American: metal cars,
airplanes, boats; comic characters,
cast iron toys and banks, etc.; also
buying Tootsietoys, Dinky, and Smith-
Miller; write for free 3-page
illustrated want list.*

Bob Ford
4804 Bensalem Blvd.
Bensalem, PA 19020
ph: 215-638-0531
toytrucks@comcast.net
http://www.webvenues.net/modelts/
*Collects and sells Hess, Wilco,
Servco, Texaco and other gasoline
promotional toy trucks by Ertl and
others; also collects Hess memorabilia.*

N.W. Neill, Jr.
P.O. Box 38
Ennice, NC 28623-0038
fax: 336-657-8084
saddlemtn@skybest.com
*Wants to buy Tonka, Smith-Miller,
Doepke model toys, any make of toy
fire trucks.*

Bill Whelan
P.O. Box 617
Daly City, CA 94017-0617
ph: 650-756-1189
fax: 650-756-4772
slotdynasty@earthlink.net
*Wants to buy scale model
tractor/trailers & bobtails, 1/64th
down to 1/100th and smaller, with
company names, logos and advertising; especially Matchbox, Lledo,
promotionals, Herpa, Con-Cor,
Wiking, Winross, etc.*

Dealers

Brandon Lewis
Buffalo Rd. Imports
10120 Main St.
Clarence, NY 14031
ph: 716-759-7151
fax: 716-759-7462
bri@toyline.com
http://www.toyline.com/bri
*Specializing in construction scale
models since 1978 with the largest
selection available worldwide; stocks
both current and discontinued models:
NZG, Conrad, EMD, ATM, Old Cars,
Zon, Diapet, Arpra, Minimac, CCM
and more.*

Periodicals

Claire Scheibe
Magazine: Toy Trucker & Contractor
7496 106th Ave. SE
Lamoure, ND 58458-9404
ph: 701-883-5206 or 800-533-8293
fax: 701-883-5208
zekesez@aol.com
http://www.toytrucker.com
*Focuses on trucks and construction
toys; sponsors an annual National
Toy Truck and Construction Show in
August.*

Twist-Um

Collectors

Dale Abrams
960 Bryden Rd.
Columbus, OH 43205-1809
ph: 614-258-5258
fax: 614-258-6663
TLAntiques@aol.com
http://ourworld.cs.com/TeaLeafIronstone
*Wants to buy Twist-Um toys - jointed
figures, mostly animals, similar to
Schoenhuts; made in Oakland, CA in
the 1920s by the Twist-Um Toy Co.*

Water Pistols

Collectors

Jean B. Hall
10 Alden Dr.
Norwood, MA 02062
ph: 781-762-3779
fax: 781-278-9804
JeanBHall@aol.com
*Wants water pistols, especially
Captain Video, Ms. Pac-Man, St.
Louis Exposition 1904, etc.; also TV
Sci-Fi items.*

White Knob Wind-Ups

Dealers

Robert G. Johnson
Comet Toys
P.O. Box 26
Wayzata, MN 55391
ph: 763-544-596
fax: 763-544-596
comettoys@comettoys.com
http://www.comettoys.com
*New and reproduction and vintage tin
toy robots, space toys, wind-ups, life
size robot displays, advertising,
battery operated toys; Japanese and
European market toys.*

Richard Johnson
Richard Johnson Toys
121 N. Cortez
Prescott, AZ 86301
ph: 520-771-9438
fax: 520-771-9445

Alan Downhour
Great Wind-up, The
93 Pike #201
Seattle, WA 98101
ph: 206-621-9370
sales@greatwindup.com
http://www.greatwindup.com
*The Northwest's largest selection of
wind-up toys - plastic, tin toys and
other collectibles.*

Wooden

Collectors

Perry R. Eichor
703 N. Almond Dr.
Simpsonville, SC 29681-3453
ph: 864-967-8770
fax: 864-228-2541
kpmflyn@earthlink.net
*Wants to buy wooden toys made by
Hustler, Rich, Ted Toy, Toy Tinkers
and others.*

Yo-Yos

(see also TOYS, Tops & Gyroscopes)

Clubs/Associations

American Yo-Yo Association
Newsletter: Yo-Yo Times
P.O. Box 797
Spanaway, WA 33595
ph: 707-542-YOYO
fax: 707-542-9696
hobbymstr@utahyoyo.com
http://www.ayya.net
Association for yo-yo players and

*collectors; source for information and
two publications: "AYYA News"
(twice yearly) and "The Yo-Yo Times"
(quarterly); Mr. Stangle is also a
professional yo-yo entertainer!*

Collectors

Les Gordon, II
6475 E. 550 S
Whitestown, IN 46075-9696
ph: 317-769-3382
lgordon@egix.net
*Wants old yo-yos and related pins,
patches, advertisements, trophies,
strings, books, paper, memorabilia,
etc.*

Leigh Roger Rich
2209 W. 58th
Davenport, IA 52806
ph: 319-391-6503
*Has collection of 1,000 yo-yos, mostly
contemporary but also has 50 or so
antique yo-yos.*

Jason Colwell
3508 N. 2000 E. Country Rd.
Ludlow, IL 60949
ph: 217-396-5014 or 217-359-6081
*Want so buy old yo-yos (Duncan,
Flores, Goody, Jewel, Alox, Hiker,
Cheerio) and yo-yo-related items such
as string, patches, pins, trophies, etc.*

Bob Zeuschel
1638 Highland Valley Ctr.
Chesterfield, MO 63005-4919
ph: 636-537-3145
*Wants yo-yos by Duncan, Goody,
Royal, Ja-Do, Flores, etc.*

Bill Caswell
1512 Cherokee Place
Bartlesville, OK 74003
ph: 918-336-5130
rosicas@juno.com
*Wants old yo-yos by Flores, Festival,
Medalist, Cheerio, Hi-Ker, Duncan,
Goody, Royal; especially wants
jeweled and carved models.*

David Hall
Dave's Wonderful World of Yo-Yos
1304 Manzana NE
Albuquerque, NM 87110
ph: 505-268-5651
whistler@nmia.com
http://www.nmia.com/~whistler/yo-
yos.html
*Web site has chat board, museum, yo-
yo memorabilia, yo-yo mysteries,
image gallery, lings to more yo-yo
Web sites.*

Experts

Lucky Meisenheimer
7300 Sandlake Commons Blvd., Ste.
105
Orlando, FL 32819-8011
ph: 407-352-2444
fax: 407-363-2869
LuckyJ@msn.com
http://www.Yo-Yos.net
*Buys old yo-yos, singles, collections,
and yo-yo memorabilia; also contest*

kits, store displays, patches, pins, awards, advertising, etc.; author of "Lucky's Collectors Guide to 20th Century Yo-Yos."

John Stangle
YO-topia
634 Echo Lake Way
Santa Rosa, CA 95401
ph: 707-542-9696
fax: 707-528-9696
yotopia@yotopia.com
http://www.yotopia.com
YO-YO sales, service, collections, photos, events and much more: everything YO-YOs!

Internet Resources

Lucky Meisenheimer
Yo-Yo Net
7300 Sandlake Commons Blvd., Ste. 105
Orlando, FL 32819-8011
ph: 407-352-2444
fax: 407-363-2869
LuckyJ@msn.com
http://www.Yo-Yos.net
Web site has top prices paid for yo-yos, yo-yo grading, yo-yo articles, yo-yo links.

Museums/Libraries

Judith Schulz
Spinning Top Exploratory Museum
Journal: Spin-Offs
533 Milwaukee Ave.
Burlington, WI 53105-1232
ph: 262-763-3946
2,000 tops, gyroscopes & yo-yos on exhibit (antique and modern); top games & experiments to try; 35 types to spin; sales of unique tops; demos, live show at museum; "Spin-offs" is a playful research publication of history, facts, etc.

National Yo-Yo Museum
320 Broadway
Chico, CA 95928-5322
ph: 530-893-0545
info@nationalyoyo.org
http://www.nationalyoyo.org
Over 1,000 yo-yos on display; free admission.

Periodicals

Stuart F. Crump, Ed.
Creative Communications, Inc.
Newsletter: Yo-Yo Times
P.O. Box 1519 - MAC
Herndon, VA 22070-1519
ph: 703-715-6187
http://www.yoyotimes.com
A quarterly publication loaded with information about current yo-yo events, leading yo-yo'ers, the latest publications and videos, and anything else related to yo-yos.

TOYS (MODERN)

Clubs/Associations

Toy Industry Association
1115 Broadway, Ste. 400
New York, NY 10010
ph: 212-675-1141
fax: 212-633-1429
info@toy-tia.org
http://www.toy-tia.org
The toy, puzzle and game manufacturers' trade organization; sponsors the annual American International New York Toy Fair which is only open to the trade and to the press.

Periodicals

Maria Weiskott, Ed.
Chaners Business Information
Magazine: Playthings
345 Hudson St., 4th Floor
New York, NY 10014
ph: 212-519-7348
mweiskott@cahners.com
http://www.playthings.com
The unofficial trade journal for the toy industry; publishes a directory which lists manufacturers, their representatives, inventors and designers.

TRACTORS

(see also ENGINES; FARM MACHINERY; GAUGES; MACHINERY & EQUIPMENT, Road Making; TOYS, Farm)

Auction Services

Iron Horse Auction Co.
413 South Hancock St.
P.O. Box 1267
Rockingham, NC 28380
ph: 910-997-2248 or 800-997-2248
fax: 910-895-1530
horse@infoave.net
http://www.auctionweb.com/ironhorse
Conducts auctions specializing in the sale of antique steam engines, tractors and farm related items.

Clubs/Associations

Southern Antique Iron Association
P.O. Box 522
Wetumpka, AL 36092
info@southernantiqueiron.com
http://www.southernantiqueiron.com
A nonprofit organization founded in 2002 and dedicated to the collection, exhibiting and preservation of any antique tractor and engine as well as other various machinery of historical value.

Foothills Antique Tractor & Engine Club
P.O. Box 1127
Louisville, TN 37777-1127
tprather@utk.edu
http://web.utk.edu/~tprather/FoothillsTractorClub
Meets monthly to share information on all brands of antique tractors, engines and farmstead and homestead

equipment; several shows and community service projects as well; monthly newsletter; free classifieds on Web site.

Southern Illinois Antique Power Club
P.O. Box 144
Salem, IL 62881
jstorm@midwest.net
http://www.mountvernon.net/tractor/siapnav.htm
For tractor enthusiasts.

Ona Cook, Sec.
North Texas Antique Tractor & Engine Club
9112 Leaside Dr.
Dallas, TX 75238
ph: 214-341-4539
http://www.north-texas-antique-tractor-and-engine-club.org
Meet regularly to share knowledge and interest in the tractors, engines and farm equipment that mechanized our early 20th century farms; email address is info@http://www.north-texas-antique-tractor-and-engine-club.org

Jerry MacMartin, WebMaster
Early Day Gas Engine & Tractor Association, Inc.
Newsletter: National, The
1537 Weekend Villa Rd.
Ramona, CA 92065
ph: 760-789-3402
fax: 760-789-3769
rawarnock@sbcglobal.net
http://www.edgeta.org
A national organization with 90 regional "Branches" interested in early gas engines and tractors.

Collectors

Gary Dougherty
Gary's Antique Tractors
13502 92nd St.
Alto, MI 49302
ph: 616-765-3101
gdougher@rbc.org
http://www.angelfire.com/mi/GarysOldTractors
Collects and repairs tractors; Web site is a down home, personal, friendly, antique tractor page with pictures and great links to other tractor sites.

Dealers

Larry Sikes
Rock Ridge Farm - The Florida Tractor Connection
1813 NW 97th Terr.
Pompano Beach, FL 33071
ph: 954-527-7360
larry@rockridgefarm.com
http://www.rockridgefarm.com
Collects, restores, buys and sells antique tractors, stationary engines and farm equipment.

Classic Ag/Jones Salvage
RR 2, Box 171
Ainsworth, NE 69210
ph: 800-286-2171
fax: 402-387-0824
info@classicag.com
http://www.classicag.com
Buy classic tractor parts online; specializes in pre-1977 tractor parts, antique & vintage equipment, farm living and more.

Experts

Spencer Yost
Antique Tractor Internet Service
3160 MacBrandon Ln.
Pfafftown, NC 27040
ph: 910-924-6109
yostsw@atis.net
http://www.atis.net
Appraiser, collector, expert specializing in tractors; also does repairs.

Dave Mowitz
1716 Locust St.
Des Moines, IA 50336
ph: 515-243-3327
dmowitz@mdp.com
Author of "Ageless Iron, Restoring Your Legacy" and the "Ageless Iron Restoration Guide" which lists sources for parts, paint, etc.

Internet Resources

Kate Smalley
Antique Tractor Resource Page
P.O. Box 896
Branford, CT 06405
anttrac@antiquetractors.com
http://www.antiquetractors.com
A complete reference site for collectors and restorers of antique tractors, stationary engines and farm equipment; also provides Web sites and advertising services for businesses and individuals.

Spencer Yost
Antique Tractor Internet Service
3160 MacBrandon Ln.
Pfafftown, NC 27040
ph: 910-924-6109
yostsw@atis.net
http://www.atis.net
The oldest and most complete Web site on the Internet that specializes in antique tractors and farm equipment; thousands of people access the site monthly to buy and sell and research farm equipment.

Harry Matthews
Harry's Old Engine Page
P. O. Box 5612
Sarasota, FL 34277
oldengine@hotmail.com
http://www.old-engine.com
A pioneering Web site started in 1995 to present antique engines to the Web; collecting, restoring, showing antique stationary gas and steam engines; lots of resources for suppliers as well as a selection of books about engines.

Dave Haynes
Fastrac Antique Farm Tractor &
 Implement Support Group
P.O. Box 2297
Elkhart, IN 46515
dhaynes@adeptr.com
http://www.adeptr.com
*Source of people who are involved in
some way with the antique engine and
tractor hobby.*

Yesterday's Tractors
P.O. Box 160
Chimacum, WA 98325
fax: 360-385-6721
comments@yesterdaystractors.com
http://www.yesterdaystractors.com
*Tractor registry, resources, parts &
supplies, classifieds, hauling schedule,
discussion groups, tractor show
schedule, etc.*

Periodicals

Dennis Polk
Dennis Polk Equipment
Magazine: Polk's "The Antique Tractor
 Magazine"
72435 SR 15
New Paris, IN 46553
ph: 219-831-3555 or 800-795-3501
fax: 219-831-5717
sales@dennispolk.com
http://www.dennispolk.com
*Bi-monthly magazine covering the
world of antique tractors; restoration,
tractor pulls, auction results, collector
stories, etc.*

Chad & Katie Elmore
Magazine: Belt Pulley
P.O. Box 58
Jefferson, WI 53549
ph: 920-674-9732
elmore@jefnet.com
*Bi-monthly magazine featuring farm
machinery, all makes and models,
1900 to 1970: antique tractors, farm
machinery and related equipment.*

Magazine: Engineers & Engines
 Magazine
2240 Oak Leaf St.
P.O. Box 2757
Joliet, IL 60434-2757
ph: 815-741-2240
fax: 815-741-2243
barb@engineersandengines.com
http://www.engineersandengines.com
*Bi-monthly magazine: tractors, gas,
steam, farm machinery, railroad.*

Newsletter: Hook, The
P.O. Box 16
Marshfield, MO 65706
ph: 417-468-7000
thehook@pcis.net
http://www.pcis.net/thehook
*The magazine for antique and classic
tractor pullers.*

Ogden Publications, Inc.
Magazine: Gas Engine Magazine
1503 SW 42nd St.
Topeka, KS 66609-1265
ph: 785-274-4383 or 785-274-4300
fax: 785-274-4305
rbackus@ogdenpubs.com
http://www.gasenginemagazine.com
*G.E.M. is the leading magazine for
antique tractor and gas engine
collectors; articles, ads, auctions,
models, Maytag gas engines,
restoration tips, histories, auctions,
suppliers, parts, etc.; published
monthly.*

Magazine: Antique Power
P.O. Box 500
Missouri City, TX 77459
ph: 800-310-7047
fax: 281-261-5999
antique@antiquepower.com
http://www.antiquepower.com
*Has regular columns about farm toys,
tractor restoration, farm literature
collecting and tractor history; free ads
for subscribers.*

Newsletter: Western Antique Iron Trader
24696 SW Daniel Rd.
Beaverton, OR 97007
Irontrader@inetarena.com
http://www.irontrader.com
*A monthly newsletter for people
interested in antique tractors,
stationary engines, and related
equipment; contains many ads and
show announcements for the Western
states of WA, OR, and CA, as well as
for British Columbia.*

Suzanne Wright
Kelsey Publishing Ltd.
Magazine: Tractor & Machinery
 Magazine
Cudham Tithe Barn
Berry's Hill
Cudham, Kent TN16 3AG U.K.
ph: 01959 541444
fax: 01959 541400
info@kelsey.co.uk
http://www.kelsey.co.uk
*A 64-page monthly British magazine
dealing with all tractors and tractor-
driven machinery; restorations,
rallies, ploughing matches, auctions,
runs and club event.*

Repair Services

pratt@olympus.net
http://www.tractorlinks.com
*Almost 200 quality tractor links:
museums, Ford, Ferguson, Caterpillar, Case, Allis-Chalmers, John
Deere, Massey Harris, Minneapolis
Moline, Oliver, tractor pulling, and
more.*

Gary Dougherty
Gary's Antique Tractors
13502 92nd St.
Alto, MI 49302
ph: 616-765-3101
gdougher@rbc.org
http://www.angelfire.com/mi/
 GarysOldTractors
*Collects and repairs tractors; Web
site is a down home, personal,
friendly, antique tractor page with
pictures and great links to other
tractor sites.*

Suppliers

Restoration Supply
96 Mendon St.
Hopedale, MA 01747
ph: 508-634-6915
fax: 508-634-6613
resto@tractorpart.com
http://www.tractorpart.com
*World's largest supply of new
replacement, reproduction, and rebuilt
parts for North American farm
tractors built between 1935 and 1990;
no used parts.*

Steiner Tractor Parts, Inc.
G-10096 South Saginaw
Holly, MI 48442
ph: 810-695-1919
fax: 810-695-5032
sales@steinertractorparts.com
http://www.steinertractorparts.com
*Thousands of new replacement parts
in stock or manufactured for almost
any type of tractor, both new and old.*

Bert Ruprecht
Paynesville Tractor Parts
P.O. Box 231
30203 State Hwy. 55
Paynesville, MN 56362
ph: 320-243-7443 or 800-445-0061
fax: 320-243-7664
ptparts@lkdllink.net
http://www.lkdllink.net/~ptparts/
 ptparts.html
*Sells used tractors and parts for old
and collectible tractors.*

Walt Unger
Walt's Tractor Parts, LLC
5654 Highway 15
Mexico, MO 65265
ph: 888-414-4043 or 573-581-4345
fax: 573-581-1078
ungers@sockets.net
http://www.waltstractors.com
*Online replacement tractor parts
catalog.*

Allis-Chalmers

Periodicals

Nan Jones
Magazine: Old Allis News
10925 Love Rd.
Bellevue, MI 49021-9250
ph: 269-763-9770
fax: 269-763-9770
allisnews@aol.com
*A quarterly magazine for the Allis-
Chalmers collector and/or enthusiast;*

*Allis-Chalmers related articles,
photographs, histories, restoration
stories, suppliers ads, shows,
auctions, etc.*

Dennis Potter
Newsletter: Allis Connection, The
7011 E. Bethel Rd.
Elizabeth, IL 61028
ph: 815-598-3329
allisacres@blkhawk.net

Case

Clubs/Associations

J.I. Case Collectors Association
Magazine: Old Abe's News
400 Carriage Dr.
Plain City, OH 43064
http://www.mousetek.net/JICCA
*For those interested in antique farm
equipment (especially Case).*

J.I. Case Heritage Foundation, Inc.
Magazine: Heritage Eagle, The
P.O. Box 081156
Racine, WI 53408-1156
CaseHeritage@aol.com
http://www.marchofmachines.org

Caterpillar

Clubs/Associations

Antique Caterpillar Machinery Owners
 Club
P.O. Box 2220
East Peoria, IL 61611
cat@acmoc.org
http://www.acmoc.org

Collectors

James R. Owensby
190 Fernwood Rd.
Cochranville, PA 19330
ph: 610-869-3303
*Wants to buy Caterpillar tractor sales
literature, construction and farm
literature.*

Cockshutt

Clubs/Associations

International Cockshutt Club, Inc.
Magazine: Cockshutt Quarterly
1506 Indian Lakes Rd.
Kent City, MI 49330-9430
help@cockshutt.com
http://www.cockshutt.com
*Family-oriented club uniting people
interested in the education, preservation and exhibition of Cockshutt/CO-
OP tractors and farm equipment.*

Internet Resources

Dan Carpenter
Dandy's Dabblings
ph: 517-565-3060
hobsickle@aol.com
http://members.aol.com/Hobsickle/
 indexfix.html
*Rebuilds Cockshutt tractors and
engines; Web site has lots of good
Cockshutt information.*

Periodicals

John Kasmiski
Magazine: Golden Arrow Magazine
N7209 State Hwy. 67
Mayville, WI 53050
ph: 414-387-4578
Published quarterly; Cockshutt and Co-op.

Repair Services

Dan Carpenter
Dandy's Dabblings
ph: 517-565-3060
hobsickle@aol.com
http://members.aol.com/Hobsickle/indexfix.html
Rebuilds Cockshutt tractors and engines; Web site has lots of good Cockshutt information.

Ferguson

Clubs/Associations

Ferguson Club
Newsletter: Ferguson Club Journal
P.O. Box 20
Golspie, Sutherland KW10 6TE U.K.
ph: +44 1408 633108
ferguson.club@btinternet.com
http://www.fergusonclub.com

Ford (N-Models)

Internet Resources

Neil Reitmeyer
Nseries.com
207 Laurel Dr.
Shohola, PA 18458
neil@nseries.com
http://www.nseries.com

Daniel Dibben
Vintage Ford Tractor Resource, The
10905 East 241 Terrace
Peculiar, MO 64078
ph: 816-779-5804
naa60512@aol.com
http://members.aol.com/naa60512/naa.htm
Lots of technical information about Ford tractors 1953-1964: history, serial numbers, electrical, engine, specifications, paint, emblems, wheels, tires, brakes, photos, carburetor, hydraulics, model comparison, quick I.D., and more.

Periodicals

Rob Rinaldi
Magazine: N-News
P.O. Box 275
East Corinth, VT 05040-0275
infon@n-news.com
http://www.n-news.com
For those interested in old 9N-2N-8N-NAA through the 6000 Ford farm tractors and machinery; also for those with a general interest in antique farm tractors and machinery.

Fordson

Clubs/Associations

Ford/Fordson Registry & Collectors Association
645 Loveland Miamiville Rd.
Loveland, OH 45140
ph: 513-683-4935
info@ford-fordson.org
http://www.ford-fordson.org

Jack W. Heald
Fordson Tractor Club
Newsletter: FTC Newsletter
250 Robinson Rd.
Cave Junction, OR 97523-9719
ph: 541-592-3203
Dedicated to the restoration, preservation, exhibition of the Fordson tractor; bi-annual newsletter, manuals, service bulletins, etc.

Gibson

Clubs/Associations

Gibson Tractor Club
4200 Winwood Court
Floyds Knobs, IN 47119-9225
ph: 812-923-5822
dbaas@bluegrass.net
http://www.bluegrass.net/~dbaas
Over 400 members interested in preserving the heritage of the Gibson tractor.

Gravely

Clubs/Associations

Craig Seabrook
Gravely Tractor Club of America
Newsletter: Gravely Gazette, The
1444 Watt Rd.
Novelty, OH 44072
ph: 440-338-5950
seabrook@en.com
http://php.iupui.edu/~harrold/Gravely/tractor.html
The club represents a group of Gravely enthusiasts who are interested in the Model D Gravely, the Model L Gravely, and the 4-wheel tractors; members exchange information about history of the company, serial numbers, restoration tips.

John Deere

Clubs/Associations

Dave Trumbauer
Two-Cylinder Club Worldwide
Magazine: Two-Cylinder
P.O. Box 430
Grundy Center, IA 50638-0430
ph: 319-345-6060 or 888-7TC-CLUB
fax: 319-345-2662
memberservices@two-cylinder.com
http://www.two-cylinder.com
Over 20,000 members who collect John Deer literature and memorabilia, and who restore early John Deere tractors, engines, and implements; bi-monthly newsletter.

Upper Canada Two Cylinder Club
Newsletter: Upper Canada Two Cylinder Club Newsletter
Box 505
Drayton, Ontario N0G 1P0 Canada
uc2cc@hotmail.com
http://www.angelfire.com/ny/carrotpatch/page7.html
Dedicated to the preservation and enjoyment of antique John Deere tractors and related equipment.

Collectors

Jim Proctor
1395 South Concord Rd.
West Chester, PA 193828343
ph: 610-399-0802
Wants pre-1960 John Deere 2-cylinder tractors; also wants tractor sales literature.

Experts

Brenda Kruse
Bleeding Green
500 Cabezon Court
Gallup, NM 87301
ph: 505-722-2939 or 888-4JD-BOOK
fax: 505-722-4788
jdbook@bleedinggreen.com
http://www.BleedingGreen.com
Connected to major collectors across the country; author of "John Deere Collectibles" (Motorbooks/MBI Publishing 2001); Web site serves as an online community for collectors of John Deere memorabilia; also writes weekly JD column.

Museums/Libraries

John Deere Historic Site
8393 S Main St.
Dixon, IL 61021
ph: 815-652-4551
Tour the restored John Deere home, as well as the archaeological display of his original shop complete with functioning blacksmith.

Periodicals

Deere & Company
Magazine: JD Journal
One John Deere Place
Moline, IL 61265-8098
ph: 309-765-8000 or 800-765-9588
jdj@johndeere.com
http://www.deere.com/en_US/compinfo/publications
John Deere corporate magazine; contains columns on John Deere related collectibles.

Ogden Publications, Inc.
Magazine: John Deere Tradition
1503 SW 42nd St.
Topeka, KS 66609-1265
ph: 785-274-4380 or 800-678-4883
fax: 785-274-4305
editor@johndeeretradition.com
http://www.johndeeretradition.com
Monthly magazine with articles exploring the rich history of Deere & Company.

Magazine: Green Magazine
2652 Davey Rd.
Bee, NE 68314-9132
ph: 402-643-6269
fax: 402-643-3912
grnswap@aol.com
http://www.greenmagazineonline.com
For collectors of John Deere tractors, combines, implements, etc.; articles, ads, how-tos, restoration hints and tips, parts sources, farm toy auction notices, etc.

Massey-Harris

Clubs/Associations

Donald Snyder
Friends of Massey, Inc.
ph: 570-546-3996
snydonsherry@aol.com
For collectors interested in Massey Harris tractors and related memorabilia.

Rita Simmons, Treas.
Massey Collectors Association
2325 Massey Lane
Holts Summit, MO 65043
rsim101773@aol.com
http://www.masseycollectors.org
For collectors of Massey-Harris, Wallis, Massey Ferguson and Ferguson tractors and related equipment.

Periodicals

Keith Oltrogge
Newsletter: Wild Harvest
P.O. Box 529
Denver, IA 50622-0529
ph: 319-984-5292 or 319-352-5524
fax: 319-984-6408
keitho@sbt.net
Published bi-monthly.

Minneapolis-Moline

Clubs/Associations

Jean Fuder, Mem.
Minneapolis-Moline Collectors Club, The
Magazine: MM Corresponder
2805 - 290th Ave.
Foxhome, MN 56543-9315
moline@direcway.com
http://www.minneapolismolinecollectors.org
For Minneapolis-Moline collectors and enthusiasts organized to exchange knowledge, memorabilia, parts, and history of the MM legacy.

Collectors

Wayne Fuder
RR 2, Box 21
Foxhome, MN 56543
ph: 218-736-4769
Collects toys and memorabilia from Minneapolis Moline as well as items from Twin City, MTM, or Moline Plow Co.

Internet Resources

Tony Turner
Minneapolis-Moline Modern Machinery
111 CR 1752
Saltillo, MS 38866-9160
tony@minneapolis-moline.com
http://www.minneapolis-moline.com
Web site dedicated to Minneapolis-Moline tractors and equipment; lists part sources, serial number cross references, images, message board.

Periodicals

Ken Delap II
Magazine: Prairie Gold Rush
17390 S. SR 48
Seymour, IN 47274
kdelapmm@hsonline.net
http://www.minneapolis-moline
A quarterly magazine for Twin City, Minneapolis and Moline enthusiasts.

Oliver

Clubs/Associations

Hart-Parr/Oliver Collectors Association
Newsletter: Hart-Parr/Oliver Collector
P.O. Box 500
Missouri City, TX 77459-9903
ph: 618-664-2461 or 866-418-5548
fax: 618-664-2462
hartparroliverquest@mcmillencomm.com
http://www.hartparroliver.org
Publishes quarterly magazine as well as quarterly newsletter relating to all types of equipment built by Oliver Farm Equipment including brand names Hart-Parr, Nichols & Shepard, Cletrac, Farquar, Ann-Arbor, American Seeding & Be-Ge.

Collectors

Kevin Coers
Kevin's Oliver Haven
oliver77@hotmail.com
http://www.geocities.com/Heartland/
  Meadows/3420
Collector of Oliver tractors.

Rick & Andrew Garnhart
6372 E. Edwardsville Rd.
German Valley, IL 61039-9622
ph: 815-362-6531
Buy, sell, appraise Oliver tractors.

Dealers

Larry D. Harsin
Larry Harsin Olivers
3426 170th St.
Estherville, IA 51334-7451
ph: 712-362-2966
cobalt@rconnect.com
http://www.olivertractor.com
Oliver collector and restorer; parts & service; buy, sell, trade.

Rumely

Periodicals

Windstacker Productions
Magazine: Rumely Collector's News
12109 Mennonite Chruch Rd.
Tremont, IL 61568
ph: 309-925-3932
fax: 309-925-3312
agboy@dpc.net
http://www.rumely.com
Quarterly.

TRADING CARDS

Non-Sport

(see also ADVERTISING COLLECTIBLES, Trade Cards; BOTTLE CAPS, Milk; BUBBLE GUM CARDS; BUBBLE GUM & CANDY WRAPPERS; CARDS; COMIC BOOKS; PAPER COLLECTIBLES; SPORTS COLLECTIBLES)

Clubs/Associations

Christopher Benjamin
United States Cartophilic Society
Newsletter: Card Collectors Bulletin
P.O. Box 4020
Saint Augustine, FL 32085-4020
Focuses on non-sport cards.

Collectors

Dan Calandriello
10 Weston Place
Eatontown, NJ 07724
ph: 732-542-4770
danster-nj@comcast.net
Wants 1930s era non-sports cards: gum, candy, silks, Mickey Mouse, Indian gum, Superman, Lone Ranger, all war cards.

Walter Koenig
P.O. Box 4395
North Hollywood, CA 91617-0395
gineokw@aol.com
Wants to buy non-sports trading cards (gum, candy, character/comic) from the 1890s - 1950s.

Dealers

Mollie & John Witney
Non Sport Network
19 Lores Plaza #160
New Milford, CT 06776
ph: 860-355-0259 or 888-845-4846
fax: 860-355-0259
nonsport@aol.com
Carries full line of Non-Sport trading cards from 1950s to present; catalog of current sets available for $1.00 refundable with first order; thousands of older sets and singles available; interested in purchasing cards & sets; send list.

Gary S. Frisch
Non-Sports Cards
24 Peachtree Ct.
Monmouth Junction, NJ 08852
ph: 732-329-9203
Buys, sells, and trades non-sports

cards: sets, singles, wrappers, and boxes.

Jim Nicewander
Card Coach, The
P.O. Box 128
Plover, WI 54467-0128
ph: 715-341-5452
Wants Arm & Hammer/Church & Dwight trading cards, posters, and other related collectibles; publishes periodic catalog of cards and collectibles for sale; friendly, fast service since 1956.

Robert Conway
Card Attack, The
P.O. Box 260942
Lakewood, CO 80226-0942
ph: 303-988-7106
rgconway@earthlink.net
Buys, sells and trades bubble gum cards; non-sport specialist; also collects comics found in bubble gum, i.e., Bazooka Joe, Fleer Funnies, Archie, Tommy Swell, Henry, etc.

Doug Craddock
Craddock's Non-Sports Cards & Collectibles
P.O. Box 7772
San Jose, CA 95150-3766
ph: 408-298-9070 or 408-629-3980
Buys, sells and trades non-sports cards: 1930s - 1970s cards, singles, sets, wax packs, unopened boxes and wrappers. Main focus is 1950s-1960s. Finders fee paid for accumulations and collections purchased.

Ken Mitchell
710 Conacher Dr.
Willowdale, Ontario M2M 3N6 Canada
ph: 416-222-5808
Wants to buy gum, candy and non-sports trading cards.

Experts

Mollie & John Witney
Non Sport Network
19 Lores Plaza #160
New Milford, CT 06776
ph: 860-355-0259 or 888-845-4846
fax: 860-355-0259
nonsport@aol.com
Operates search service through many online systems helping collectors locate cards; specializes in pre-1970 cards; buys and sells throughout the world; posts informative "press releases" of new releases.

John Neuner
2189 Llewellyn Pkwy.
Forked River, NJ 08731-3704
gpnoons@bellatlantic.net
Author of "Non-Sport Wrapper Checklist and Price Guide."

Christopher Benjamin
P.O. Box 4020
Saint Augustine, FL 32085-4020
Appraiser identifies and evaluates all US and foreign trading cards (fee charged), private and insurance

inquiries welcome; author of "The Best Trading Card Guide Ever Issued," prices, descriptions, checklists, thousands of pictures.

Internet Resources

Robert Kohlbus
NonSport Card Collector
8706 Castlerock Ct.
Laurel, MD 20723
ph: 301-776-3769
An online source for information on the hobby of non-sport card collecting: release dates, new set descriptions, free classifieds, set reviews and contests.

Terry Stewart
Collector Link
71 John St. East
Waterloo, Ontario N2J 1G2 Canada
ph: 519-745-1745
stewart@collector-link.com
http://www.collector-link.com
Catalogs over 2,000 trading card related Web sites for: baseball, hockey, basketball, football, other sports, non-sports, phone cards, credit-debit cards, business cards, postcards.

Man./Prod./Dist.

Good Stuff Cards
P.O. Box 288
Katonah, NY 10536
ph: 914-666-7693
fax: 914-241-8270
info@goodstuffcards.com
http://www.goodstuffcards.com
Producer and distributor of Monster trading cards; also classic monsters, horror, and Sci-Fi of yesterday: Boris Karloff, Spaceships of the 1950s, alien invaders, mad science, Twilight Zone, Saturday serials, dinosaurs, etc.

Periodicals

Roxanne Toser
Roxanne Toser Non-Sport Enterprises, Inc.
Magazine: Non-Sport Update
4019 Green St.
P.O. Box 5858
Harrisburg, PA 17110-0858
ph: 717-238-1936
fax: 717-238-3220
feedback@nonsportupdate.com
http://www.nonsportupdate.com
The foremost bi-monthly publication for non-sport card collectors; original artwork covers, glossy paper, lots of articles by the experts, great variety of ads, includes a 32-page "pop-out" price guide and free cards.

Les Davis
Non-Sport Publication
Newsletter: Wrapper, The
1811 Moore Court
Saint Charles, IL 60174
ph: 630-443-9690
monsterwax@aol.com
http://www.thewrappermagazine.com
Focuses on non-sports cards,

wrappers and related items; 8 issues per year.

Wizards of the Coast, Inc.
Magazine: TopDeck
1801 Lind Ave., SW
Renton, WA 98055
ph: 800-395-7760
custserv@wizards.com
http://www.wizards.com
Focus on contemporary trading cards: Magic: The Gathering, Pokemon, Hercules: The Legendary Journeys, Xena: Warrior Princess, Star Trek, Star Wars, BattleTech, Dungeons & Dragons, etc.

TRAILERS & RVs

(see also GAS STATION
COLLECTIBLES; HIGHWAY
COLLECTIBLES; HOTEL
COLLECTIBLES; MOBILE HOMES)

Clubs/Associations

Todd & Kristin Kimmell
Lost Highways Classic Trailer &
  Motorhome Club
Magazine: Lost Highways Quarterly
P.O. Box 43737
Philadelphia, PA 19106-7737
ph: 215-925-2568
fax: 215-925-5646
info@losthighways.org
http://www.losthighways.org
A classic trailer and motor home club; archives collects material relating to trailers, motor homes and auto camping from 1920s to 1960s.

Vintage & Classic Travel Trailers
3802 E. Fernwood Ave.
Orange, CA 92869
creatived@vintage-vacations.com
http://www.vintage-vacations.com
A club for owners and admirers of 1920 through 1960s travel trailers; rallies, vintage trailers for sale, stories, archives.

Collectors

Todd & Kristin Kimmell
P.O. Box 43737
Philadelphia, PA 19106-7737
ph: 215-925-2568
fax: 215-925-5646
info@losthighways.org
http://www.losthighways.org
Wants 1920s to 1960s trailer, mobile home and RV related material: trailer parks, trailer travel, motor homes, autocamping, tincan tourists, etc.; magazines, books, pamphlets, promos, film (16mm-8mm), photos, even old trailers.

Periodicals

Don Nelson, Ed.
Deals on Wheels Publications
Magazine: Truck, Race, Cycle &
  Recreation
P.O. Box 205
Sioux Falls, SD 57101
ph: 605-338-7666 or 800-334-1886
fax: 605-338-5337
dkristja@dealsonwheels.com
http://www.dealsonwheels.com
Photo-ad magazine listing trucks, 4-wheel drives, cycles, race equipment, race cars, boats, recreation vehicles, trailers, jet-skis; classifieds.

Kelley Blue Book
Price Guide: Kelley Blue Book
5 Oldfield
Irvine, CA 92618
ph: 949-770-7704
fax: 949-837-1904
kelley@kbb.com
http://www.kbb.com/indexv.html
Web site offers current trade-in values for all makes and model cars for the past 21 years; also publishes printed value guides for cars, RVs, motorcycles, snowmobiles, motor homes, travel trailers, personal watercraft, etc.

Steve Ferguson, Ed.
National Automobile Dealers Association
Price Guide: N.A.D.A. Official Used Car
  Guide
P.O. Box 7800
Costa Mesa, CA 92628
ph: 800-544-6232 or 714-556-8511
fax: 714-556-8715
info@nadaguides.com
http://www.nada.org
A series of value guides for domestic and foreign cars, trucks, vans, RVs, mobile homes, motorcycles, snowmobiles, and boats, small and large; also Heavy Duty Trucks and Aircraft Book, car clubs & organizations, museums.

TRAINS

(see also MODELS; RAILROADS;
RAILROAD COLLECTIBLES)

Model

Appraisers

Brill Lee
Brill Lee Appraisal Services
P.O. Box 244
Bellevue, WA 98009-0244
ph: 425-885-4518
fax: 425-895-1022
brilllee@hotmail.com
Collects handheld kerosene railroad lanterns, padlocks, keys, telegraph equipment, stock certificates, signs, etc.; also model railroad items ("O" and "027" gauge Marx and Lionel trains and accessories.

Clubs/Associations

National Model Railroad Association,
  Inc.
Magazine: NMRA Bulletin, The
4121 Cromwell Rd.
Chattanooga, TN 37421
ph: 423-892-2846
fax: 423-899-4869
hq@hq.nmra.org
http://www.nmra.org
International association with regional and divisional organizations; monthly newsletter; the NMRA's Kalmbach Memorial Library offers an extensive collection of resource material on both model and prototype railroading.

Dealers

Chuck
Attic Fanatic Model Trains
19910 Viking Ave.
Poulsbo, WA 98370
ph: 360-779-3200
fax: 360-779-2210
Buys, sells, repairs, appraises and specializes in all kinds of model and toy trains.

Man./Prod./Dist.

Bob Gallegos
Walthers Trains
5601 W. Florist Ave.
Milwaukee, WI 53218
ph: 414-527-0770 or 800-877-7171
fax: 414-527-4423
custserv@walthers.com
http://www.walthers.com
Walthers has been a manufacturer and distributor of model railroad products since 1932; there are over 3,000 authorized Walthers dealers; distributes model railroad and related products from over 300 other manufacturers; reference book.

Periodicals

Andy Sperandeo, Ed.
Kalmbach Publishing Co.
Magazine: Model Railroader
P.O. Box 1612
21027 Crossroads Circle
Waukesha, WI 53187
ph: 262-796-8776 or 800-446-5489
fax: 262-796-1142
mrmag@mrmag.com
http://www2.modelrailroader.com
A monthly magazine for the toy train collector and model railroad enthusiast; articles, ads, hardware, models, track systems, structures, layout tips, techniques, plans and projects.

Marc Horovitz, Ed.
Kalmbach Publishing Co.
Magazine: Garden Railways
P.O. Box 1612
21027 Crossroads Circle
Waukesha, WI 53187
ph: 303-377-7785 or 800-446-5489
fax: 303-377-7785
mhorovitz@gardenrailways.com
http://www2.gardenrailways.com
Covers all aspects of outdoor model railroading, including building and operating model trains, designing and landscaping railways, and selecting and maintaining plant material; published bimonthly; for advanced to beginner.

Suppliers

Bob Gallegos
Walthers Trains
5601 W. Florist Ave.
Milwaukee, WI 53218
ph: 414-527-0770 or 800-877-7171
fax: 414-527-4423
custserv@walthers.com
http://www.walthers.com
Walthers has been a manufacturer and distributor of model railroad products since 1932; there are over 3,000 authorized Walthers dealers; distributes model railroad and related products from over 300 other manufacturers; reference book.

Con-Cor International, Ltd.
8101 E. Rersearch Court
Tucson, AZ 85710
ph: 520-721-8939
fax: 520-721-8940
concor@con-cor.com
http://www.con-cor.com
Unique source for thousands of model railroad products; also books and videos related to railroads and railroading.

Model (N Gauge)

Periodicals

Newsletter: N Scale Collector, The
31 Homesteader Lane
West Haven, CT 06516
ph: 203-932-3502
fax: 203-932-3502
FHoxsie@NScaleCollector.com
http://www.nscalecollector.com
Web site has lots of links to other N Scale resources.

Model (O Gauge)

Collectors

Joe Weber
604 Centre St.
Ashland, PA 17921-1332
ph: 570-875-4787 or 570-875-4401
Wants O-scale (Lionel size) toy trains, i.e., kits assembled by the enthusiast; made by Scalecraft, Lobaugh, Ferris, Hines, Max Gray.

Periodicals

<u>Magazine: O Gauge Railroading</u>
65 South Broad St.
P.O. Box 239
Nazareth, PA 18064-0239
ph: 610-759-0406
fax: 610-759-0223
info@ogaugerr.com
http://www.ogaugerr.com
A bi-monthly magazine exclusively for the O Gauge collector and market.

Model (S Gauge)

Clubs/Associations

Bill Moore, Treas
National Association of S Gaugers
<u>Newsletter: Dispatch, The</u>
220 Swedesboro Rd.
Gibbstown, NJ 08027-1504
ph: 609-423-0198
nasgdispatch@hotmail.com
http://trainweb.com/NASG

Internet Resources

Paul Yorke
7501 Springhaven Ave.
Indiantown, FL 34956
paul@s-trains.com
http://www.s-trains.com
Web site has message board, mailing list, Web links, Flyer related bookstore and chat sessions; information about American Flyer model trains collecting, restoring, selling and operating; also covered is "S" scale,

Periodicals

Donald Heimburger
Heimburger House Publishing Co.
<u>Magazine: S Gaugian</u>
7236 West Madison Ave.
Forest Park, IL 60130-1765
ph: 708-366-1973
fax: 708-366-1973
heimburgerhouse@heimburgerhouse.com
http://www.heimburgerhouse.com
The magazine focuses on S gauge (1:64 scale) model train operation, modeling, and collecting.

Toy

Appraisers

Brenda Wimperis
Greenberg Auctions
7566 Main St., Ste. 101
Sykesville, MD 21784-5826
ph: 410-795-7447
fax: 410-549-2553
info@greenbergshows.com
http://www.kalmbach.com/greenberg
Appraises and specializes in Lionel, American Flyer, Marx, LGB, Marklin, Williams, AMT, etc.

Bruce C. Greenberg
5233 Bessley Place
Alexandria, VA 22304
ph: 703-461-6991
brucegreenberg@comcast.net
Appraises and specializes in Lionel, American Flyer, Marx, LGB, Marklin, Williams, AMT, etc.; author of 22

books concerned with American toy trains; appraiser with litigation experience.

Auction Services

Bertoia Auctions
2141 DeMarco Dr.
Vineland, NJ 08360
ph: 856-692-1881
fax: 856-692-8697
bill@bertoiaauctions.com
http://www.bertoiaauctions.com
Specializing in the auctioning of antique toys, banks, trains, and doorstops; offers online auctions.

Brenda Wimperis
Greenberg Auctions
7566 Main St., Ste. 101
Sykesville, MD 21784-5826
ph: 410-795-7447
fax: 410-549-2553
info@greenbergshows.com
http://www.kalmbach.com/greenberg
Specialist in toy trains: Lionel, American Flyer, Marex, Ives, LGB, HO, Marklin, etc.; publishes an auction catalog and accepts mail bids.

Heinz Mueller
Continental Auctions
P.O. Box 193
Sheboygan, WI 53082
ph: 920-693-3371
fax: 920-693-8211
continental@lsol.net
http://www.classictintoy.com
Specializes in auctions of toy trains and all toy-related items.

Clubs/Associations

Louis A. Bohn, Mem. Ch.
Toy Train Collectors Society
<u>Newsletter: Century Limited</u>
109 Howedale Dr.
Rochester, NY 14616-1534
ph: 716-667-1548
New York State's largest and most active organization devoted to the collection, preservation and operation of the treasured electric trains of days gone by; runs toy train meets across NY state.

Train Collectors Association
<u>Magazine: Train Collectors Quarterly</u>
P.O. Box 248
Strasburg, PA 17579-0248
ph: 717-687-8976 or 717-687-8623
fax: 717-687-0742
toytrain@traincollectors.org
http://www.traincollectors.org
Purpose is to bring together persons interested in collecting and operating toy trains and related items; also publishes the "National Headquarters News" newsletter; contact toy reference library at ref-library@traincollectors.org.

Toy Train Operating Society, Inc.
<u>Magazine: TTOS Bulletin, The</u>
25 West Walnut St., Ste. 308
Pasadena, CA 91103
ph: 626-578-0673
fax: 626-578-0750
ttos@ttos.org
http://www.ttos.org
Formed to further the toy train hobby and to promote fellowship; members receive "The Bulletin" magazine and "Order Board" admagazine.

Collectors

Walter Makolandra
70 Cass Ave.
Woonsocket, RI 02895-4739
ph: 401-765-4756
Collector seeks Lionel, American Flyer, Marklin, Bing and other trains and related items.

Neil K. Yerger
Delaware Valley Hi-Railers
7 Farm Rd.
Wayne, PA 19087-3303
ph: 610-688-0689
Wants to buy Lionel, American Flyer, Williams, K-Line, Weaver, etc. toy trains and accessories.

Charles W. Casad
801 Tyler Ct.
Monticello, IL 61856-2246
ph: 217-762-2303
Wants Lionel toy trains in O-gauge, O-27 gauge, and standard gauge trains and any Lionel accessories; also wants any other toy train, either electric or key wind; all must be complete and operating, please.

Dealers

Evertt A. Chapman
Dad's Trains & Granddad's Too
7 Lee Rd.
Barrington, RI 02806
ph: 401-245-0523

Nathan Sonnheim
ph: 856-667-3796
fax: 856-667-9705
Buys Lionel & American Flyer trains; calls welcome.

Dave Boehm
Dave's Trains, Inc.
P.O. Box 367
Martinsville, NJ 08836-0367
ph: 732-271-5124
fax: 732-271-9285
dave@davestrains.com
http://www.davestrains.com
Specializes in postwar (1945 to 1969) Lionel trains; Web site offers trains, accessories, vintage tinplate, prewar Lionel, Marx; also repairs and service.

Bookbinder's Trains Unlimited
P.O. Box 660086
Flushing, NY 11366-0086
ph: 800-955-8729
fax: 718-657-2264
mhbookbinder@webtv.net
http://www.toy-electric-trains.com
Sells Lionel and American Flyer toy trains via his Internet Web site.

Charles Siegel
Train City
3133 Zuck Rd.
Erie, PA 16506
ph: 814-833-8313
fax: 814-838-3237
trainman@traincity.com
http://www.traincity.com
Buys, sells and repairs pre-owned Lionel, American Flyer, Marex, and other tin type toy trains.

Don Morris
HTrains, Inc.
6901 US Hwy. 19N
Pinellas Park, FL 33781
ph: 813-526-4682
fax: 813-526-3439
hrtrains@hrtrains.com
http://www.hrtrains.com
Full service model train shop; repair shop, research library, garden railroad, pre-owned antique trains, children's playroom, Brio, Thomas the Tank, classes, LGB, Lionel, Mikes Train House, Marklin.

Trains & Things
106 East Front St.
Traverse City, MI 49684
ph: 231-947-1353
fax: 231-947-1411
tctrains@traverse.net
http://www.tctrains.com
Buys and sells Lionel, American Flyer, Marx, Matchbox; also operates train rooms in toy train museum.

Jaehyun Kim
Train Shop
21027 Crossroads Circle
Waukesha, WI 53187
ph: 212-796-8776 x234
Jkim@kalmbach.com
http://www.trainshops.com/home.asp
Offers secure online shopping for model trains, model railroading products including HO, N scale, toy trains, Thomas the Tank, Lionel and more.

Jay Robinson
Chicago Kid
522 Rivershire Place
Lincolnshire, IL 60069
ph: 847-913-1106
fax: 847-913-1274
jay@thechicagokid.com
Wants to buy old electric and wind-up trains; also old toy trucks and cars; wind-up and battery-operated toys.

Pat Neil
Collectible Trains & Toys
10051 Whitehurst, Ste. 200
Dallas, TX 75243
ph: 214-373-9469 or 800-462-4902
fax: 214-373-1622
sales@trainsandtoys.com
http://www.trainsandtoys.com
Buys and sells pre-WWII Lionel, Marklin, K-line, American Flyer, and other trains including trains made in Germany; also does repairs on all toy trains made from 1900 to present.

Bill White
Vintage Lionel TrainXchange
1600 Smith, Ste. 4230
Houston, TX 77002
ph: 713-951-0230 or 888-624-5549
fax: 713-951-0022
comments@trainxchange.com
http://www.ghgcorp.com/lionel/
lionel.html
Buy, sell, appraise, repairs, trade old electric trains; helps individuals sell their train for top dollar; specializes in top quality collector items and original boxes; supplier of investment grade trains to discriminating collectors.

Train Shack, The
1030 N. Hollywood Way
Burbank, CA 91505
ph: 818-842-3330 or 800-572-9929
fax: 818-842-4562
info@trainshack.com
http://www.trainshack.com
Specializes in a wide variety of new, used, and collectible toy and model trains; trains and accessories in all scales, from G through Z: Lionel, LGB, Marklin, and others.

Experts

Ron Hollander
129 Lincoln St.
Montclair, NJ 07042-4405
Author of "All Aboard!" the story of the Lionel Train Company; will give free appraisal; send description, including manufacturer, type of car or engine, all numbers & lettering on any part of the car; include SASE for reply.

Bruce C. Greenberg
5233 Bessley Place
Alexandria, VA 22304
ph: 703-461-6991
brucegreenberg@comcast.net
Appraises and specializes in Lionel, American Flyer, Marx, LGB, Marklin, Williams, AMT, etc.; author of 22 books concerned with American toy trains; appraiser with litigation experience.

Allan W. Miller
1240-G Ivystone Way
Chesapeake, VA 23320
ph: 757-436-9710
fax: 757-436-9710
Former managing editor of Greenberg Books, Kalmbach Books, Landmark

Specialty Books; author of "Model Railroad Resources" directory, "Getting Started in Garden Railroading," and "Getting Started with Lionel Trains."

Internet Resources

Trains, Trams & Railroading
P.O. Box 5297
Ormond Beach, FL 32175-5297
ph: 904-672-4534
fax: 904-672-9214
trains@notry.com
http://www.notry.com/trains.htm
Lots of railroading and toy train links.

Jaehyun Kim
Trains.com
21027 Crossroads Circle
Waukesha, WI 53187
ph: 212-796-8776 x234
Jkim@kalmbach.com
http://www.trains.com/story/
story_list_homestyle.asp?idMenuCategory=1
Web site offers a wealth of information about toy train collecting, model trains, garden trains, train layouts, new product releases, scale railroading, collectible toy trains, news, and much more.

Man./Prod./Dist.

MTH Electric Trains
7020 Columbia Gateway Dr.
Columbia, MD 21046
ph: 410-381-2580
fax: 410-381-6122
sales@mth-railking.com
http://www.mth-railking.com
Manufacturer of the worlds finest O gauge trains; offers the best quality, variety, service, and value in the industry.

Museums/Libraries

National Toy Train Museum
P.O. Box 248
Strasburg, PA 17579-0248
ph: 717-687-8976 or 717-687-8623
fax: 717-687-0742
toytrain@traincollectors.org
http://www.traincollectors.org
Has trains on display dating from the late 1800s to present; five operating layouts (one with hands-on buttons); gift shop and reference library also available.

Periodicals

Neil Besougloff, Ed.
Kalmbach Publishing Co.
Magazine: Classic Toy Trains
P.O. Box 1612
21027 Crossroads Circle
Waukesha, WI 53187
ph: 262-796-8776 or 800-533-6644
fax: 262-796-1615
correspond@classtrain.com
http://www2.classtrain.com/ctt
A 9-times per year magazine with articles on collecting, repairing, & operating new & old Lionel, American Flyer, Marx, Ives, MTH, K-

Line & other toy trains; ads, layouts, museums, collectors.

Repair Services

JLM Toy Train Reproductions & Restorations
jlmtrains@aol.com
http://www.jlmtrains.com
Reproductions of early period Lionel trains and accessories; also repairs and restores all types of toy trains; offers machine shop services.

Joe Mania
Downtown Trains
17 Douglas Rd.
Freehold, NJ 07728
ph: 732-303-8299
fax: 732-303-8299
joe@jlmtrains.com
http://www.jlmtrains.com
Repairs and restores all makes of toy trains.

Jeffry DeSimone
307 Jefferson St.
Swedesburg, PA 19405
ph: 610-275-4664
desmone@bellatlantic.net
Restores Lionel, America Flyer, pre and post war engines serviced free with restoration.

Pat Neil
Collectible Trains & Toys
10051 Whitehurst, Ste. 200
Dallas, TX 75243
ph: 214-373-9469 or 800-462-4902
fax: 214-373-1622
sales@trainsandtoys.com
http://www.trainsandtoys.com
Buys and sells pre-WWII Lionel, Marklin, K-line, American Flyer, and other trains including trains made in Germany; also does repairs on all toy trains made from 1900 to present.

Repro. Sources

JLM Toy Train Reproductions & Restorations
jlmtrains@aol.com
http://www.jlmtrains.com
Reproductions of early period Lionel trains and accessories; also repairs and restores all types of toy trains; offers machine shop services.

Suppliers

Railroad Press Company, The
P.O. Box 2644
Novato, CA 94948
ph: 415-898-7030
fax: 415-897-2705
john@railpress.com
http://www.railpress.com
Toy train specialists carries books, stickers, signs, videos, whistles, stock certificates, coffee cups and much more for all Lionel, Flyer, Ives, Marx toy train fans.

Toy (American Flyer)

Clubs/Associations

Frank Hare, Ed.
American Flyer Collectors Club
Magazine: Collector, The
P.O. Box 13269
Pittsburgh, PA 15243-0269
ph: 412-221-2250
fax: 412-221-8402
ironhorse@sgi.net
For collectors of A.C. Gilbert Co. American Flyer and other toy trains (all pre-1966 manufacturers); also contains information about Gilbert Erector sets.

Internet Resources

Paul Yorke
7501 Springhaven Ave.
Indiantown, FL 34956
paul@s-trains.com
http://www.s-trains.com
Web site has message board, mailing list, Web links, Flyer related bookstore and chat sessions; information about American Flyer model trains collecting, restoring, selling and operating; also covered is "S" scale,

Toy (Floor)

Experts

Rick Ralston
99-969 Iwaena St.
Aiea, HI 96701-3249
ph: 808-486-1243
fax: 808-486-1276
http://www.ralstonantiques.com
Author of "Cast Iron Floor Trains;" available from the author by calling 800-486-9794.

Toy (Hornby)

Clubs/Associations

John Harwood, Mem.
Hornby Railway Collectors' Association
Journal: Hornby Railway Collector, The
PO Box 3443
Yeovil, Somerset BA21 4XR U.K.
ph: 01935 474830
colin@hrca.net
http://www.hrca.net
Members also receive "The Directory of Replacement and Repair Services."

Toy (Ives)

Clubs/Associations

Dave McEntarfer
Ives Train Society, The
21 Academy St.
Forestville, NY 14062
trainboy17@aol.com
http://hometown.aol.com/ivesboy/
index.html

Toy (LGB)

Clubs/Associations

David Snow
LGB Model Railroad Club
Newsletter: Big Train Operator
68 Hacienda Circle
Plantsville, CT 06479-1912
ph: 860-276-9324
david.e.snow@snet.net
http://www.lgbmrrc.com
A 2000+ member organization of LGB (Lehmann-Gross-Bahn) enthusiasts, mainly collectors.

Experts

Jack Barton
Buffington Publishing
P.O. Box 332
Hershey, PA 17033
ph: 717-312-0617 or 717-312-0717
fax: 717-312-0817
LGBTelegram@mindspring.com
http://www.lgbtelegram.com
Writes "LGB Kollector" column for the "LGB Telegram" magazine; internationally known LGB collector.

Periodicals

Frances Kehlbeck Civello
Buffington Publishing
Magazine: LGB Telegram
P.O. Box 332
Hershey, PA 17033
ph: 717-312-0617 or 717-312-0717
fax: 717-312-0817
LGBTelegram@mindspring.com
http://www.lgbtelegram.com
A quarterly magazine for LGB (Lehmann-Gross-Bahn) fans; features articles on collecting as well as a column called "LGB Kollector" in every issue.

Toy (Lionel)

Clubs/Associations

Lionel Operating Train Society
Magazine: Switcher
6376 West Fork Rd.
Cincinnati, OH 45247-5704
ph: 513-598-8240 or 847-398-3320
fax: 513-598-4778
lotsbusinessoffice@juno.com
http://www.lots-trains.org
The bi-monthly "Switcher" is loaded with layout designs, track plans, scenery construction, layout operating, maintenance, repair tips and techniques, building & rolling stock modification projects, club informa-tion & news.

Lionel Railroader Club
Newsletter: Inside Track, The
P.O. Box 748
New Baltimore, MI 48047-0748
ph: 810-949-4100 x1300
fax: 810-949-5429
lrrc@lionel.com
http://www.lionel.com/Clubs/LRRC
A Lionel company sponsored club; for model railroading enthusiasts; members receive newsletter published quarterly, club button, layout

accessories and other exclusive items; a company sponsored club.

Lionel Collectors Club of America
Newsletter: Lion Roars
P.O. Box 479
La Salle, IL 61301-0479
ph: 815-654-1705
mottlerm@conwaycorp.net
http://www.lionelcollectors.org
Purpose is to promote and foster interest in Lionel electric trains.

Collectors

Charles W. Casad
801 Tyler Ct.
Monticello, IL 61856-2246
ph: 217-762-2303
Wants American Lionel toy trains in O-gauge, O-27 gauge, and standard gauge trains; also wants any Lionel accessories; all must be complete and operating, please.

Dealers

Gary D. Mosholder
Gary's Trains
186 Pine Springs Camp Rd.
Boswell, PA 15531-2421
ph: 814-629-9277
gtrains@floodcity.net
http://www.GarysTrains.com
Buys and sells Lionel trains and accessories including Plasticville buildings; sends out periodical list of items for sale; also carries parts and does repairs.

Lionel Trainmaster
Newsletter: Trainmaster Newsletter
5001-B NW 34th St.
Gainesville, FL 32605
ph: 800-613-4222 or 352-373-4222
fax: 352-373-4468
Major dealer in Lionel trains; buys and sells; national market maker in secondary Lionel trains; published bi-monthly.

Bill White
Vintage Lionel TrainXchange
1600 Smith, Ste. 4230
Houston, TX 77002
ph: 713-951-0230 or 888-624-5549
fax: 713-951-0022
comments@trainxchange.com
http://www.ghgcorp.com/lionel/
lionel.html
Buy, sell, appraise, repairs, trade old electric trains; helps individuals sell their train for top dollar; specializes in top quality collector items and original boxes; supplier of investment grade trains to discriminating collectors.

Sam Mattes
Sam the Toy Train Man
7253 Pondera Circle
Canoga Park, CA 91307
ph: 818-347-4753 or 818-347-4753
sam@mattes.org
http://www.toytrains.com
Buys, sells, and appraises Lionel trains.

Experts

Ron Hollander
129 Lincoln St.
Montclair, NJ 07042-4405
Author of "All Aboard!" the story of the Lionel Train Company; will give free appraisal; send description, including manufacturer, type of car or engine, all numbers & lettering on any part of the car; include SASE for reply; by mail only.

Bill White
Vintage Lionel TrainXchange
1600 Smith, Ste. 4230
Houston, TX 77002
ph: 713-951-0230 or 888-624-5549
fax: 713-951-0022
comments@trainxchange.com
http://www.ghgcorp.com/lionel/
lionel.html
Buy, sell, appraise, repairs, trade old electric trains; helps individuals sell their train for top dollar; specializes in top quality collector items and original boxes; supplier of investment grade trains to discriminating collectors.

Man./Prod./Dist.

Lionel LLC
50625 Richard W. Blvd.
Chesterfield, MI 48051
ph: 810-949-4100
fax: 810-949-1013
http://www.lionel.com
The leading manufacturer of model trains; founded over 100 years ago, the success of this American icon is based on painstaking attention to quality and innovation.

Museums/Libraries

Charles W. Casad
Rayville Model Train Museum
801 Tyler Ct.
Monticello, IL 61856-2246
ph: 217-762-2303
Above is mailing address; physical location is 217 W. Washington St., Monticello, IL.

Toy (Marklin)

(see also TOYS, Marklin)

Clubs/Associations

Timothy Eckert
Marklin Enthusiasts of America
Newsletter: Handelspost
P.O. Box 217153
Charlotte, NC 28221
ph: 704-547-6058
eckertt@epri.com
Club limited to European prototype trains, toys or related items; not affiliated with Marklin, Inc. or Gebr Marklin & Cie GmbH.

Marklin Digital Special Interest Group
Newsletter: Digital SIG, The
16988 W. Victor Rd.
P.O. Box 510559
New Berlin, WI 53151-0559
ph: 414-784-8854
fax: 414-784-1095
webmaster@marklin.com
http://www.marklin.com/club
Provides its members with in-depth knowledge and insight into the advanced Marklin Digital control technology.

Marklin Club - North America
Magazine: Insider
16988 W. Victor Rd.
P.O. Box 510559
New Berlin, WI 53151-0559
ph: 414-784-8854
fax: 414-784-1095
webmaster@marklin.com
http://www.marklin.com/club
Dedicated to serving the interests of the Marklin enthusiast; helps enthusiasts get the most from Marklin trains and model railroading.

Collectors

Ronald Wiener
1650 Arch St., 22 Floor
Philadelphia, PA 19103-2097
ph: 215-977-2266
fax: 215-405-3866
rwiener@wolfblock.com
Wants Marklin (German) metal toys and toy trains, 1895-1960 in original and excellent condition, especially pre-1942 O gauge; also other old metal toys in excellent condition.

Grant A. Kreinberg
108 Brae Court
Suisun City, CA 94585-1304
ph: 707-864-1823 or 916-552-8736
fax: 707-864-9240
grantk@castles.com
Collector seeks "O" gauge Marklin and other European trains.

Man./Prod./Dist.

Fred Gates, Pres.
Marklin, Inc.
16988 W. Victor Rd.
P.O. Box 510559
New Berlin, WI 53151-0559
ph: 414-784-8854
fax: 414-784-1095
webmaster@marklin.com
http://www.marklin.com
Marklin, Inc. is the American subsidiary of Gebr. Marklin & Cie. GmbH and is the exclusive distributor in North America for Marklin products.

Toy (Marx)

Collectors

Bill Smith
56 Locust St.
East Douglas, MA 01516-2440
ph: 508-476-2015
Wants to buy all Marx trains and related items regardless of condition;

especially interested in Marx train catalogs.

Mark Whipple
102 Clarette Rd.
Pittsburgh, PA 15237-1058
ph: 412-366-9459
whip123@hotmail.com
Collects Marx trains and Marx accessories; also other Marx toys.

Toy (Plasticville)
Dealers

Gary D. Mosholder
Gary's Trains
186 Pine Springs Camp Rd.
Boswell, PA 15531-2421
ph: 814-629-9277
gtrains@floodcity.net
http://www.GarysTrains.com
Buys and sells Lionel trains and accessories including Plasticville buildings; sends out periodical list of items for sale; also carries parts and does repairs.

Bill Nole
319 Oak St.
Dunmore, PA 18512
ph: 570-343-2236

TRAMP ART

(see also FOLK ART)

Dealers

Michael Cornish
Cigar Box Antiques
92 Florence St.
Roslindale, MA 02131-2603
ph: 617-323-6029
cdissacorn@aol.com
Sells, brokers, consults on tramp art (objects made from cigar boxes and crate wood, usually edge-notched and stacked into pyramidal forms, c. 1880-1940); a recognized authority and author.

John Sholl
Sholl Antiques
P.O. Box 9
Norwood, NY 13668
ph: 315-353-2474
info@tramp-art.com
http://www.tramp-art.com
Specializes in folk crafts of the early 20th century: tramp art, penknife whimseys, marquetry, fretwork, pyrography.

Matt Lippa
Artisans
P.O. Box 256
Mentone, AL 35984-0256
ph: 256-634-4037
fax: 256-634-4037
artisans@folkartisans.com
http://www.folkartisans.com
Buy and sell folk art, outsider art, fine art; Internet WWW site offers links to additional dealers; also offers non-profit clubs and museums with an

outlet to post notices, press releases, calendar items, etc. at no charge.

Anne Foster
Hyde & Seek Antiques
1913 Hyde St.
San Francisco, CA 94109
ph: 415-776-8865
neilcalvin@aol.com
Wants all kinds of tramp art including frames, boxes, miniature pieces of furniture, etc.

Experts

Michael Cornish
Cigar Box Antiques
92 Florence St.
Roslindale, MA 02131-2603
ph: 617-323-6029
cdissacorn@aol.com
Sells, brokers, consults on tramp art (objects made from cigar boxes and crate wood, usually edge-notched and stacked into pyramidal forms, c. 1880-1940); a recognized authority and author.

Helaine Fendelman
Helaine Fendelman & Assoc.
60 Gramercy Park North
New York, NY 10010
ph: 212-228-6440
fax: 212-228-8577
HFendelman@aol.com
http://www.appraisersassoc.org/biography/HF0002/page.html
Co-author with Jonathan Taylor of "Tramp Art - An Art Phenomenon" (Stewart, Tabori & Chang, 1999); co-author with Joe Rosson of "Treasures in Your Attic" and of "Price it Yourself" (Harper Collins).

Clifford Wallach
81 Washington St., #7J
Brooklyn, NY 11201
ph: 718-596-5325
fax: 718-596-5581
info@trampart.com
http://www.trampart.com
Author of "Tramp Art, One Notch at a Time" published by Wallace-Irons; buys, sells exceptional forms of tramp art and other folk art and outsider art.

TRANSPORTATION COLLECTIBLES

(see also AIRLINE MEMORABILIA; AIRSHIPS; AUTOMOBILES; AUTOMOBILIA; AVIATION; BUS LINE COLLECTIBLES; BUSES; GAS STATION COLLECTIBLES; LUGGAGE LABELS; OCEAN LINER COLLECTIBLES; RAILROAD COLLECTIBLES; STEAMBOAT COLLECTIBLES; STREETCAR LINE COLLECTIBLES; TOYS; TRUCKS)

Clubs/Associations

Transport Ticket Society
Journal: Transport Ticket Society Journal
U.K.
davidrandell@btopenworld.com
http://www.btinternet.com/~transport.ticket
Interested in the collection and study of tickets, transfers, passes, tokens, and other items issued by companies in the fare collection process; also ticket issuing machines.

Collectors

Seth Bramson
330 N.E. 96th St.
Miami, FL 33138-2718
ph: 305-757-1016
fax: 305-895-8178
sbramson@bellsouth.net
Buys all US RR/trolley/steamship/airline and bus memorabilia; all Floridiana and US travel & destination material - things put out by boards of trade, chambers of commerce, cities, counties, towns, hotels, restaurants, businesses.

Dealers

Stephen Hansrote
Griffin Trading Company
159 Howell St.
Dallas, TX 75207
ph: 214-747-9234
fax: 214-747-0660
griffintc2@aol.com
http://www.griffintradingantiques.com
Buying and selling plane, train, automobile and ship collectibles; everything from advertising and signs to equipment and actual parts and supplies; also provides decor for national restaurant chains.

Ered Matthew
Cabin Class Collectibles
P.O. Box 740474
Dallas, TX 75374-0474
ph: 972-235-8639
fax: 972-235-8614
mailroom@cabinclass.com
http://www.cabinclass.com
Buys and sells fine ocean liner, airline, and other transportation memorabilia on the Internet.

Brad S. Lomazzi
Western Railroad Collectibles
1300 Liberty Ct.
Roseville, CA 95747-7440
ph: 916-782-6587
bslomazzi@att.net
Appraiser, dealer and expert in railroad and other transportation collectibles; author of "Railroad Timetables, Travel Brochures & Posters," and "Railroad Collectibles - A History and Price Guide."

Scott Arden
Antiques & Artifacts
20457 Highway 126
Noti, OR 97461-9706
ph: 541-935-1619
Leading RR mail order dealer for 31 years; catalog $1; buys and sells fine old transportation items, mostly non-paper; consignment.

Museums/Libraries

Lowell G. Kjenstad
Cole Land Transportation Museum
405 Perry Rd.
Bangor, ME 04401-6725
ph: 207-990-3600
fax: 207-990-2653
mail@colemuseum.com
http://www.colemuseum.org
200 antique Maine vehicles, 2,000 photos of life in early Maine communities, covered bridges, Maine state WWII memorial, Ertl-Coles express trucks, military collection.

Charles Chiarchiaro
Owls Head Transportation Museum
Rte. 73 Box 277
Owls Head, ME 04854
ph: 207-594-4418
fax: 207-594-4410
info@ohtm.org
http://www.ohtm.org
Founded in 1964 to collect, preserve and exhibit pioneer aircraft, ground vehicles, and engines significant to the evolution of transportation and/or the state of Maine.

Western Reserve Historical Society
10825 East Blvd.
Cleveland, OH 44106-1703
ph: 216-721-5722
fax: 216-721-0645
webmaster@wrhs.org
http://www.wrhs.org
Oldest cultural institution in Cleveland, with a research/genealogical library, costume wing, auto & aviation museum and restored mansion under one roof; special interest area in automobiles and aviation.

Henry Ford Museum & Greenfield Village
20900 Oakwood Blvd.
P.O. Box 1970
Dearborn, MI 48121-1970
ph: 313-982-6001 or 313-271-1620
fax: 313-271-9621
info@hfmgv.org
http://www.hfmgv.org
Museum houses a collection of over one million three-dimensional artifacts, defined by the following general categories: agricultural and industrial production, transportation, communication, and domestic life.

Pate Museum of Transportation
P.O. Box 711
840 N. Main St.
Pate, TX 76101
ph: 817-332-1161 or 817-396-4305

Forney Transportation Museum
4303 Brighton Blvd.
Denver, CO 80216
ph: 303-297-1113
fax: 303-297-3113
forney@frii.net
http://www.forneymuseum.com
*Over 100 antique automobiles plus
four steam locomotives (including
"Big Boy" #4005) and many other
transportation exhibits plus a gift
shop containing transportation
collectibles and souvenirs.*

China

Experts

Richard Luckin
621 Cascade Ct.
Golden, CO 80403-1581
ph: 303-278-0669
fax: 303-215-0099
rluckin@mindspring.com
*Collector of transportation china for
over 30 years; author of "Dining On
Rails," "Teapot Treasury," and
"Mimbres to Mimbreno;" also designs
and supplies china for private
railroad cars and for business cars
for various railroads.*

Barbara J. Conroy
P.O. Box 2343
Santa Clara, CA 95055
restaurant-china@comcast.net
http://restaurant-china.home.comcast.net
*Author of "Restaurant China, Vol. 1
and 2;" specializes in restaurant,
hotel, steam ship, railroad, airline,
and other commercial dinnerware.*

Timetables

(see also AIRLINE MEMORABILIA,
Timetables; RAILROAD
COLLECTIBLES, Timetables)

Clubs/Associations

Norbert Shacklette, Mem.
National Association of Timetable
Collectors
Newsletter: First Edition, The
125 American Inn Rd.
Villa Ridge, MO 63089-2153
crts@worldnet.att.net
http://www.rrhistorical.com/naotc
*Interested in timetables from airlines,
steamships, railroads, and bus lines.*

Collectors

Carl Loucks
P.O. Box 484
North Haven, CT 06473-0484
ph: 203-288-3765
fax: 203-234-2729
ct.direct.mail@snet.net
*Wants railroad timetables, brochures,
guides, maps, menus; also trolley, air
and bus.*

George Johnson
P.O. Box 1449
Lexington, VA 24450-1449
ph: 540-464-4326
fax: 540-464-4326
gnjo@rockbridge.net
*Wants to buy pre-1940 timetables;
railroad, trolley, airline or bus; any
quantity; also wants passes, catalogs,
and depot postcards.*

TRAPS

Clubs/Associations

Tom Parr
North American Trap Collectors
Association, Inc.
Newsletter: TRAPS
P.O. Box 94
Galloway, OH 43119-0094
ph: 614-878-6011
fax: 614-878-7621
*Members interested in the preservation
of all trapping devices (animal, fish,
bird, insect), trap operations,
trapping literature, fur trade industry
memorabilia, sporting collectibles,
trapping magazines and paper
ephemera, etc.*

National Trappers Association, Inc.
Magazine: American Trapper, The
P.O. Box 632018
Nachogdoches, TX 74963-2018
ph: 936-569-6444
trappers@aol.com
http://www.nationaltrappers.com
*Over 20,000 members promote
conservation to preserve the natural
resources of the US; magazine
published bi-monthly occasionally
contains articles about old trapping
equipment and techniques.*

Collectors

Ron Willoughby
2281 Lime Kiln Rd.
North Haverhill, NH 03774
ph: 603-787-2060
fax: 603-787-2060
swillo@together.net
*Wants to buy oddly-shaped traps and
bear traps; also buying all trapping
paper and memorabilia as well as lure
containers, smokers, advertising items,
etc.; a very serious buyer.*

Robert Kwalwasser
168 Camp Fatima Rd.
Renfrew, PA 16053-9104
ph: 724-789-7766
fax: 724-789-9771
robertk@tcis.net
*Wants old gopher, mole, mouse, fly,
minnow, and rat traps; also patent
models of same.*

Terry Swartz
RD 1 Box 197 A
Blain, PA 17006
ph: 717-536-3733

Chuck Clift
103 Duck Cove
Elmore, AL 36025-1007
ph: 334-285-6522
*Collects animal traps - everything
from mouse to bear traps; specializes
in mouse, rat, gopher, mole, killer,
glass minnows and glass fly traps,
bird and fish traps; odd shaped traps;
traps with teeth.*

Archie H. Stevens, Sr.
2196 AuSable Pt. Rd.
East Tawas, MI 48730
ph: 517-739-7006
*Wants antique traps: bear, wolf,
handforged, Newhouse, any size.*

Terry Burger
2323 Lincoln
Beatrice, NE 68310-3306
ph: 402-228-2797
BarbieLJB@yahoo.com

Clay Tontz
4043 Nora Ave.
Covina, CA 91722-3819
ph: 626-338-9976
*Wants traps - from mice to moose;
only the scarce and unusual.*

Dealers

William A. Russ
Russ Trading Post
23 William St.
Addison, NY 14801-1326
ph: 607-359-3896
*Buys and sells antique traps including
bear traps; also issues a catalog of
hunting and trapping supplies; send
$1 for catalog.*

Dennis Helman
6969 Wright Puthoff Rd.
Sidney, OH 45365
ph: 937-492-5769

Experts

Boyd Nedry
728 Buth Dr.
Comstock Park, MI 49321-8207
ph: 616-784-1513
*Specializes in unusual animal traps or
related items: fly, mouse, mole,
minnow, bear, rat, gopher, cockroach,
handcrafted; any material: wood,
glass, metal, etc.; any age; also books
and advertising on trapping; enclose
SASE.*

Museums/Libraries

Charles E. Hanson, Jr., Dir.
Museum of the Fur Trade
Magazine: MFT Quarterly
6321 Highway 20
Chadron, NE 69337-9501
ph: 308-432-3843
fax: 308-432-5963
museum@furtrade.org
http://www.furtrade.org
*Dedicated to the study of the American
fur trade from colonial times to the
present; furs, traps, trade guns, trade*

*goods, Indians; not involved with
present day trapping.*

Periodicals

Stacie Berger
Krause Publications
Magazine: Trapper & Predator Caller,
The
700 E. State St.
Iola, WI 54990-0001
ph: 715-445-2214
fax: 715-445-4087
stacie.berger@fwpubs.com
http://www.krause.com
*A monthly magazine about hunting,
trapping and predator calling, and
animal damage control.*

Fly

Collectors

Ralph Finch
34007 Hillside Ct.
Farmington, MI 48335-2513
ph: 248-476-4893 or 800-678-6400
x6023
*Wants to buy fly traps in odd colors,
shapes and sizes.*

Rat/Mouse/Fly

Collectors

Robert Kwalwasser
168 Camp Fatima Rd.
Renfrew, PA 16053-9104
ph: 724-789-7766
fax: 724-789-9771
robertk@tcis.net
*Wants old mouse, fly, minnow, and
rat traps.*

Tom Edmonds
6306 East Pea Ridge Rd.
Huntington, WV 25705-2526
ph: 304-736-8086
fax: 304-697-5282
cjedmondswv@aol.com
*Wants antique mousetraps; prefers
live catch or capture traps.*

TRAPSHOOTING

(see also SPORTING
COLLECTIBLES; TARGET
SHOOTING MEMORABILIA)

Museums/Libraries

Trapshooting Hall of Fame & Museum
601 W. National Rd.
Vandalia, OH 45377-1036
ph: 937-898-4638
fax: 937-898-5541
hof@shootata.com
http://www.traphof.org
*Located on the home grounds of the
Amateur Trapshooting Association's
home grounds (the governing body of
registered trapshooting; preserves the
artifacts and history of the sport of
trapshooting.*

TRAVEL COLLECTIBLES

(see GAS STATION COLLECTIBLES, Road Maps; HIGHWAY COLLECTIBLES; HOTEL COLLECTIBLES; PAPER COLLECTIBLES; PHOTOGRAPHS, Travel; SOUVENIR & COMMEMORATIVE ITEMS; STATE RELATED MEMORABILIA)

TREASURE HUNTING

(see also ARCHAEOLOGY; BOTTLES; CIVIL WAR ARTIFACTS; COINS & CURRENCY; NAUTICAL ANTIQUES; PREHISTORIC ARTIFACTS)

Clubs/Associations

Mary Lois VanSooy, Mem.
Federation of Metal Detector & Archeological Clubs, Inc.
Newsletter: Quest, The
5822 Barbanell St.
Long Beach, CA 90815-1303
chasrjones@earthlink.net
http://www.fmdac.com
The FMDAC is composed of over 190 clubs; goals include the promoting and protecting of the metal detecting hobby.

Federation of Independent Detectorists
44 Heol Dulais
Birchgrove
Swansea, South Wales SA7 9LT U.K.
fid.pro@dialin.net
U.K. based association of treasure hunters.

Internet Resources

Coin & Relic Gazette
sbuckner@enteract.com
http://www.enteract.com/~sbuckner/gazette.htm
An online e-zine for the metal detectorist.

Periodicals

George Streeter
Newsletter: Treasure Hunter's Gazette
14 Vernon St.
Keene, NH 03431
ph: 603-357-0607 or 800-447-6014
fax: 603-352-1147
gazette@monad.net
http://www.monad.net/~streeters/gazette/gazette.htm
An informative publication that discusses virtually any topic within the world of treasure hunting, including much metal detector information and prices.

Steve Anderson
People's Publishing Company
Magazine: Western & Eastern Treasures Magazine
P.O. Box 219
San Anselmo, CA 94979
ph: 800-999-9718 or 415-454-3936
treasurenet@prodigy.net
http://www.treasurenet.com/westeast
The world's treasure hunting

authority written by experts for metal detecting enthusiasts; improve your skills, upgrade equipment, research treasure sites, first hand accounts of coin, artifact, gold finds.

Greenlight Publishing
Magazine: Treasure Hunting Magazine
119 Newland St.
Witham, Essex CM8 1WF U.K.
ph: +44 (0) 1376 521900
fax: +44 (0) 1376 521901
info@treasurehunting.co.uk
http://www.acguk.com/treasure
Published since 1977, this is the biggest selling metal detecting magazine in the U.K.; how-tos, site research, machines and equipment, historical and finds identifications, etc.

Suppliers

George Streeter
Streeter's Treasure Hunting Supply
14 Vernon St.
Keene, NH 03431
ph: 603-357-0607 or 800-447-6014
fax: 603-352-1147
george.streeter@verizon.net
http://www.monad.net/~streeters
Vendor of treasure hunting equipment and supplies.

Computer Programs For

Man./Prod./Dist.

Niche Software, Inc.
Software: Treasure Hunter, The
7118 NW Terrace
Parkland, FL 33076
ph: 954-344-6561
marketing@collectiblessoftware.com
http://www.collectiblessoftware.com
Designed for anyone who hunts for treasures with a metal detector, or at auctions and garage sales.

TREES & SHRUBS

Clubs/Associations

American Society of Consulting Arborists
1524 Shady Grove Rd.
Rockville, MD 20850
ph: 301-947-0483
fax: 301-990-9771
asca@mgmtsol.com
http://www.asca-consultants.org
Call for referral to local appraisers of trees and shrubs.

International Society of Arboriculture
P.O. Box 3129
Champaign, IL 61826-1329
ph: 217-355-9411
fax: 217-355-9516
isa@isa-arbor.com
http://www2.champaign.isa-arbor.com
Publishes book "Guide for Establishing Values of Trees and Other Plants;" publishes catalog of arboriculture books, gifts, study guides, plant health manuals,

brochures and videos; some members are trained tree appraisers.

TRENCH ART

(see also AMMUNITION & EXPLOSIVE ORDNANCE, Shell Casings)

Collectors

Edward Mickel
5011 Briargrove Ln.
Dallas, TX 75287-7408
ph: 972-407-6960
eddolores@prodigy.net
Collector of WWI engraved shell casings and other items of art made from shell casings, parts of shell casings, projectiles, rotating bands or shrapnel.

Experts

Jane Kimball
Trench Art of the Great War
silverpenny@mindspring.com
http://www.trenchart.org
Focuses on trench art and other souvenirs made during WWI by soldiers, civilians, and prisoners of war during the war and afterwards.

TRIBAL

(see AFRICAN & TRIBAL ART; NATIVE AMERICAN; ART, Australia; ART, Oceanic; INDONESIA; PRECOLUMBIAN)

TRINKET BOXES

(see BOXES; FAIRINGS)

TROLLEY LINE COLLECTIBLES

(see RAILROAD COLLECTIBLES; STREETCAR LINE COLLECTIBLES)

TROLLS

(see also DOLLS; ELVES)

Collectors

Debbie Brown
541 South St. Clair St.
Painesville, OH 44077-3636
Wants old trolls & related items in any condition, any number: trolls, troll houses, handlebar covers, charms, outfits, animals, etc.; wants Greek God, PAN, statues, pictures, etc.

Sally Kimmel
1471 Lark Lane
Concord, CA 94521-2942
ph: 925-689-4138
sallyraek@yahoo.com
Troll lover wants 1960s to 1990s trolls, any size, tailed trolls, animal trolls (especially monkey), charms, pencil tops, clothes, houses, etc. -

anything with trolls; any condition; one piece or entire collections.

Marci Van Ausdall
4532 Fertile Valley Rd.
Newport, WA 99156
ph: 509-292-1311
betsymccallfanclub@hotmail.com
Wants to buy pre-1960 Trolls, clothing, accessories; jewelry; unusual items.

Experts

Jeanne Niswonger
305 West Beacon Rd.
Lakeland, FL 33803-7248
ph: 863-682-8484
Author of "Troll Dolls."

Man./Prod./Dist.

Minna & Johannes Kuuskoski
U.S. Trolls
2305 Market St.
Wilmington, NC 28403
ph: 910-251-2270
fax: 910-772-9038
trolls@trollforest.com
http://www.trollforest.com
The Kuuskoski family started making Trolls in Finland in 1952 - these were known as the FAUNI-Trolls; still making these Trolls and the collection has grown; each Troll is handmade and has a "personality;" each comes with story-card.

TROPHIES

(see ANIMAL TROPHIES; MORBID & ODD ITEMS; PINS, Award; SPORTING COLLECTIBLES)

TRUCK LINE COLLECTIBLES

(see TRANSPORTATION COLLECTIBLES; TRUCKS)

TRUCKS

(see also AUTOMOBILES; AUTOMOBILIA; FIRE FIGHTING MEMORABILIA, Apparatus; MILITARIA, Vehicles; TOYS, Hess; TOYS, Transportation; TRAILERS & RVs; TRANSPORTATION COLLECTIBLES)

Clubs/Associations

Antique Truck Club of America, Inc.
Magazine: Double Clutch
P.O. Box 291
Hershey, PA 17033-0291
ph: 717-533-9032
bpowell@atca-inc.net
http://www.atca-inc.net
Focuses on antique trucks and other commercial vehicles.

Larry L. Scheef, Gen. Mngr.
American Truck Historical Society
Magazine: Wheels of Time
P.O. Box 531168
Birmingham, AL 35253-1168
ph: 205-870-0566
fax: 205-870-3069
aths@mindspring.com
http://www.aths.org
Recognized by the American Trucking Association as the official archives for the trucking industry; collects & preserves the history of at least 25-year-old trucks and trucking; 83 chapters throughout the US, Canada and Australia.

Collectors

N.W. Neill, Jr.
P.O. Box 38
Ennice, NC 28623-0038
fax: 336-657-8084
saddlemtn@skybest.com
Wants to buy pre-1948 Dodge trucks, literature, ads, etc.; Dodge Power Wagons 1 ton 1946-1968; anything on Dodge cab-over trucks; also 1960-1970 big Dodge trucks.

Al Koenig
P.O. Box 6122
Rochester, MN 55903-6122
ph: 800-533-1702 or 507-367-4319
fax: 507-288-6859
hvyhlr@midspec.com
Wants 1930s to 1950s truck drivers' cap badges; also wants any other trucking company badges, trucking company lapel pins, cloth emblems, and other trucking company memorabilia.

Dealers

Leigh Knudson
719 Ohms Way
Costa Mesa, CA 92627
ph: 949-643-7601
fax: 949-646-6820
catruckman@aol.com
Buys and sells restored arrow style turn signals and glass era colored lights for commercial vehicles (no auto lights available); truck sales literature and photos; North American truck and bus emblems.

Museums/Libraries

Hays Antique Truck Museum & Old Truck Town
Newsletter: Old Truck Town News
1962 Hays Lane
Woodland, CA 95776
ph: 530-666-1044
fax: 530-666-5777
hatm@truckmuseum.com
http://www.truckmuseum.com
Dedicated to the preservation and display of antique trucks and the history of the trucking industry.

Periodicals

Magazine: Truck Buyers Guide
416 Green Lane, Ste. D
Bristol, PA 19007-9001
ph: 800-693-9928 or 215-826-9700
fax: 215-826-9901
info@tbg-truckbuyersguide.com
http://www.tbg-truckbuyersguide.com
Five separate East Coast regional editions mailed each month; photo-ad magazine listing wide assortment of trucks for sale.

Don Nelson, Ed.
Deals on Wheels Publications
Magazine: Truck, Race, Cycle & Recreation
P.O. Box 205
Sioux Falls, SD 57101
ph: 605-338-7666 or 800-334-1886
fax: 605-338-5337
dkristja@dealsonwheels.com
http://www.dealsonwheels.com
Photo-ad magazine listing trucks, 4-wheel drives, cycles, race equipment, race cars, boats, recreation vehicles, trailers, jet-skis; classifieds.

Magazine: This Old Truck
P.O. Box 500
Missouri City, TX 77459
ph: 800-310-7047
fax: 281-261-5999
antique@antiquepower.com
http://www.thisoldtruck.com
Full color magazine covering all makes of light trucks and commercial vehicles 1980 and earlier.

Steve Ferguson, Ed.
National Automobile Dealers Association
Price Guide: N.A.D.A. Official Used Car Guide
P.O. Box 7800
Costa Mesa, CA 92628
ph: 800-544-6232 or 714-556-8511
fax: 714-556-8715
info@nadaguides.com
http://www.nada.org
A series of value guides for domestic and foreign cars, trucks, vans, RVs, mobile homes, motorcycles, snowmobiles, and boats, small and large; also Heavy Duty Trucks and Aircraft Book, car clubs & organizations, museums.

Chevrolet

Clubs/Associations

National Chevy/GMC Truck Association
Newsletter: Pickups 'N Panels in Print
P.O. Box 607824
Orlando, FL 32860
ph: 407-880-1963 or 800-683-1961
fax: 407-886-7571
info@lategreatchevy.com
http://www.lategreatchevy.com
An organization by and for 1911 through 1972 Chevrolet/GMC enthusiasts; national and local shows, local clubs.

Ford

Clubs/Associations

Old Ford Truck Club
2675 Hamilton Mason Rd.
Hamilton, OH 45011
oftc@choice.net
http://users.choice.net/~oftc

White

Clubs/Associations

Leigh Knudson
Vintage White Trucks Association
719 Ohms Way
Costa Mesa, CA 92627
ph: 949-645-5938

TRUNKS

(see also LEATHER; LUGGAGE)

Dealers

Pat Morse
Trunk Shop, The
62 Canaan Back Rd.
Barrington, NH 03825
ph: 603-664-2205
fax: 603-664-9699
info@trunk.com
http://www.trunk.com
Refinishes and sells antique trunks.

Churchill Barton
Brettun's Village Trunk Shop
302 Lake St.
Auburn, ME 04210
ph: 207-782-0861 or 207-782-7863
Churchill@brettunsvillage.com
http://www.brettunsvillage.com/trunks
Sells and refinishes trunks, suitcases, toolboxes, toy boxes, and wardrobes; Web site has online help for do-it-yourselfer, info on trunk makers, and histories.

Stan Stevens, Jr.
Stevens Antique Trunks
61 Harrington Ave.
Closter, NJ 07624
ph: 201-768-1463
oldtrunx@aol.com
http://www.StevensAntiqueTrunks.com
Buys, sells and restores old trunk; author of "How to Refurbish Your Antique Trunk," $29.10 from author.

Harold & Sue Fox
Harold & Sue's Antique Trunks
10 "B" St.
Danville, PA 17821
ph: 570-275-2590
35 years experience restoring antique trunks; buys, sells, trades trunks.

Marvin Miller
This Old Trunk
P.O. Box 11352
Murfreesboro, TN 37129
info@thisoldtrunk.com
http://www.thisoldtrunk.com
Offers quality antique trunks and trunk restorations.

Antique Trunk Co.
3706 W. 169th St.
Cleveland, OH 44111
ph: 216-941-8618 or 440-835-9619
thebuda@msn.com
Buy, sell, trade, restore, and repairs old trunks; also carries repair supplies as well as instructional books of how to repair trunks.

Duane S. Bietz
Les Meilleurs
6461 S.E. Thorburn
Portland, OR 97215-1378
ph: 503-238-6888
fax: 503-233-1602
dbietz@aol.com
Collects and sells Louis Vuitton hard luggage and trunks; specialty pieces, cosmetic, cigar, liquor, shoe, hat, collar, car trunks; any Louis Vuitton memorabilia and promotional items; email or write with photos for appraisals or to sell.

Internet Resources

Churchill Barton
Brettun's Village Trunk Shop
302 Lake St.
Auburn, ME 04210
ph: 207-782-0861 or 207-782-7863
Churchill@brettunsvillage.com
http://www.brettunsvillage.com/trunks
Web site has online help for do-it-yourselfers, info on trunk makers, and histories.

Repair Services

Pat
Trunk Shop, The
62 Canaan Back Rd.
Barrington, NH 03825
ph: 603-664-2205
fax: 603-664-9699
info@trunk.com
http://www.trunk.com
Refinishes and sells antique trunks.

Marvin Miller
This Old Trunk
P.O. Box 11352
Murfreesboro, TN 37129
info@thisoldtrunk.com
http://www.thisoldtrunk.com
Offers quality antique trunks and trunk restorations.

Doris Harroff
AAA Antique Shop
953 W. Market
U.S. 6 West
Nappanee, IN 46550-1801
ph: 219-773-4912
Buys, sells and restores trunks.

Laurie A. Root
Original Woodworks
4631 Lake Ave.
Saint Paul, MN 55110
ph: 651-429-2222
orgwood@iaxs.net
http://www.originalwoodworks.com
Specializing in complete antique trunk repair and restoration; will transform

your trunk inside and out into a
treasured family heirloom.

Lawrence Lafary
Heirloom Restorations
ph: 309-694-0960
heirloom-restorations@insightbb.com
*Has over 20 years experience in trunk
restorations; goal is to make trunks
look like they have had excellent care
since first made; before and after
photographs available by email.*

Flora Keen
House of Antique Trunks
753 B Northport Dr.
P.O. Box 508
West Sacramento, CA 95691-0508
ph: 916-372-8228
*Antique trunk restoration parts &
accessories; doll trunk supplies;
chromolithographs for lids; linings,
adhesives, leather; repairs.*

Suppliers

Clifford Rufkahr
Rufkahr's
P.O. Box 56112
Virginia Beach, VA 23456
ph: 757-721-9154 or 800-545-7947
(orders)
fax: 757-426-8484
rufkahrs@rufkahrs.com
http://www.rufkahrs.com
*Reproduction hardware, lamp parts,
mirror supports and brackets, knobs,
pie safe tins, bed parts, Hoosier
cabinet parts, brass handles, brass
knobs, trunk hardware, caning
supplies, rocker runners, Simichrome,
Nev'r Dull, and more.*

Phyllis & Phil Kennedy
Phyllis Kennedy Hardware
10655 Andrade Dr.
Zionsville, IN 46077
ph: 317-873-1316
fax: 317-873-8662
philken@kennedyhardware.com
http://www.kennedyhardware.com
*Hardware for antique furniture, ice
boxes, Hoosier cabinets and trunks;
manufacturer of flour bins and sifters
for Hoosier cabinets; pulls, bails,
knobs, latches, chair seats and caning,
hinges, locks and keys, coat hooks, etc.*

Charlotte Ford Trunks
P.O. Box 536
Spearman, TX 79081
ph: 806-659-3027 or 800-553-2649
fax: 806-659-5614
trunks@charlottefordtrunks.com
http://www.charlottefordtrunks.com
*Trunk parts supplier, refinisher;
publishes a 60-page parts catalog.*

Gary Hahn
Muff's Antiques
135 S. Glassell St.
Orange, CA 92866-1421
ph: 714-997-0243
fax: 714-997-1601
muffs@earthlink.net
http://home.earthlink.net/~muffs
Buys, sells, trades, repairs old trunks;

also new and old repair parts, locks,
keys, supplies; catalog $5.

TUMBLERS

(see GLASSES, Drinking)

TURNPIKE COLLECTIBLES

(see HIGHWAY COLLECTIBLES)

TVs

(see TELEVISION SHOWS &
MEMORABILIA; TELEVISIONS)

TWINS

(see BIRTH RELATED ITEMS)

TYPEWRITERS

(see also ADDING MACHINES;
ADVERTISING COLLECTIBLES,
Typewriter Related; CALCULATORS;
OFFICE EQUIPMENT; PRINTING
EQUIPMENT)

Appraisers

Richard Polt
3800 Victory Pky.
Cincinnati, OH 45207-4443
polt@xavier.xu.edu
http://xavier.xu.edu/~polt/
typewriters.html
*Will help anyone estimate the value of
an antique typewriter; Web site
features classified ads for typewriters
and related items, repair shops
around the world, typewriter history,
and much more.*

Auction Services

Auction Team Breker
Bonner Str. 528-530
Koln, D-50968 Germany
ph: 49 221 387049 or 941-925-0385 (US
Rep)
fax: 49 221 374878
auction@breker.com
http://www.breker.com
*German auction company specializes
in the sale of old office equipment,
scientific instruments and devices,
photographica, and old technology
including toasters, typewriters, sewing
machines, tools, telecommunications,
etc.*

Clubs/Associations

Chuck Dilts, Ed.
Early Typewriter Collectors Association
Magazine: ETCetera
P.O. Box 286
Southborough, MA 01772
ph: 508-229-2064
etcetera@writeme.com
http://typewriter.rydia.net/etcetera.htm
*An international club for collectors of
old office equipment including*

typewriters, adding machines, pencil
sharpeners, staplers, ribbon tins, etc.;
provides contact with worldwide
network of members; free ads.

Collectors

Peter Frei
P.O. Box 500
Brimfield, MA 01010-0500
ph: 413-245-4660
peterfrei@prodigy.net
*Wants to buy handpowered vacuum
cleaners, pre-1875 sewing machines,
typewriters, calculators, and adding
machines.*

Anthony Casillo
Antique Typewriter Collecting
325 Nassau Blvd.
Garden City, NY 11530-5313
ph: 516-489-8300 or 516-742-4919
fax: 516-489-6501
typebar@aol.com
http://www.typewritercollector.com
*Wants early typewriters and related
items including adders, checkwriters,
pencil sharpeners and other early
office items including advertisements.*

Frank Briola
P.O. Box 44022
Pittsburgh, PA 15205-0222
ph: 412-937-8787 or 800-372-6509
fax: 412-937-1959
americana@mail.com
Wants early or unusual typewriters.

Howard Hazelcorn
6731 Ashley Ct.
Sarasota, FL 34241-9696
ph: 941-921-1815
mrpropane@aol.com
*Collects and specializes in early
typewriters; wants to buy typewriters
made between 1873 and 1910.*

Jerry Propst
P.O. Box 45
Janesville, WI 53547-0045
ph: 608-752-2816
fax: 608-752-7691
*When writing, please include a LSASE
if requesting a reply.*

Mike Brooks
7335 Skyline
Oakland, CA 94611-1121
ph: 510-339-1751
deborahwb@aol.com
*20 year collector buying early oddball
typewriters, braille writers, shorthand
machines and other 19th century office
machines; gladly provides free
appraisals by telephone; call evenings.*

Jim Rauen
6937 Glenview Dr.
San Jose, CA 95120-5437
ph: 408-268-2943
fax: 408-268-5667
*Collects typewriters and some related
office equipment, especially pre-1900;
will buy, sell, trade, and answer
inquiries on typewriter history and
values.*

Conrad & Terry Hamil
Typewriters
615 Grandridge
Grandview, WA 98930-1542
ph: 509-882-3617
ninwoham@quicktel.com
*Wants to buy typewriters, ribbon tins,
typing collectibles.*

Martin Howard
7 Queensgrove Rd.
Toronto, ON M1N 3AP Canada
ph: 416-690-7432
martinhoward@sympatico.ca
http://www.antiquetypewriters.com
*Wants to buy antique typewriters,
1880 to 1910; also ribbon tins,
company letterheads and typewriter
related ephemera.*

Experts

Rich Cincotta
P.O. Box 286
Southborough, MA 01772
ph: 508-229-2064
typewriter@writeme.com
http://typewriter.rydia.net
*Passionate typewriter collector,
dealer, expert, repairer building a
comprehensive collection; see portions
on the Web.*

Hobart D. Van Deusen
15 Belgo Rd.
Lakeville, CT 06039
ph: 860-435-0088
rtn.hoby@snet.net
*Collects and advises on antique
typewriters and typewriter-related
items: blotters, carbon paper boxes,
erasing shields, letter heads, rulers,
letter openers, etc.*

Richard Polt
Classic Typewriter Page, The
3800 Victory Pky.
Cincinnati, OH 45207-4443
polt@xavier.xu.edu
http://xavier.xu.edu/~polt/
typewriters.html
*Will help anyone estimate the value of
an antique typewriter; Web site
features classified ads for typewriters
and related items, repair shops
around the world, typewriter history,
and much more.*

Darryl Rehr
P.O. Box 641824
Los Angeles, CA 90064-6824
ph: 310-477-5229
fax: 310-268-8420
dcrehr@earthlink.net
http://home.earthlink.net/~dcrehr/
collecting.html
*Wants pre-1915 typewriters & related
advertising, especially typewriters w/o
keyboards; send SASE for free
information pamphlet.*

Internet Resources

Chuck Dilts
P.O. Box 286
Southborough, MA 01772
ph: 508-229-2064
typewriter@writeme.com
http://typewriter.rydia.net
Web site with links to keyboard machines, index machines, toys and other related collectibles; information about the TW list - an email group sharing information, tips, etc, on antique typewriters.

Museums/Libraries

John Lundstrom, Assoc. Cur.
Milwaukee Public Museum
800 W. Wells St.
Milwaukee, WI 53233
ph: 414-278-2702
jl@mpm.edu
http://www.mpm.edu
Museum has a large collection of antique typewriters.

Periodicals

Mike Brown
Newsletter: Typewriter Exchange, The
P.O. Box 52607
Philadelphia, PA 19115
ph: 215-934-7998 or 215-677-5879
typex1@aol.com
http://www.freenet.tlh.fl.us/~curtis7
For collectors of early office equipment; published quarterly.

Repair Services

Paul Robert
Typewriter Restoration Site
Oude Kerweg 9
Laren, 1251 NX The Netherlands
type@xs4all.nl
http://www.xs4all.nl/~catch55
Web site offers information about repairing antique typewriters; does not do repairs.

Ribbon Tins

Clubs/Associations

Hobart D. Van Deusen
Typewriter Ribbon Tin Group
Newsletter: Ribbon Tin News
15 Belgo Rd.
Lakeville, CT 06039
ph: 860-435-0088
rtn.hoby@snet.net
Serves as a resource for collectors looking for information, current news, exchange of views, social intercourse with fellow collectors; enhances the buying, selling, pricing typewriter ribbon tins and related items.

Collectors

Darryl Rehr
P.O. Box 641824
Los Angeles, CA 90064-6824
ph: 310-477-5229
fax: 310-268-8420
dcrehr@earthlink.net
http://home.earthlink.net/~dcrehr/
  tins.html
Wants tins of all sizes and makes,

especially those with unusual shapes & graphics; any amount; send description or photocopy.

Steve Hosier
44711 N. Cedar Ave.
Lancaster, CA 93534-3210
ph: 661-946-7118
antk-lvr@webtv.net
Wants typewriter ribbon tins.

Experts

Hobart D. Van Deusen
15 Belgo Rd.
Lakeville, CT 06039
ph: 860-435-0088
rtn.hoby@snet.net
Wants typewriter ribbon tins - small tin boxes used from 1880s to 1950 with graphic designs on them; has duplicates to sell; will help identify; also collects and advises on typewriter-related items: blotters, carbon paper boxes, etc.

Toy

Collectors

Steve Hosier
44711 N. Cedar Ave.
Lancaster, CA 93534-3210
ph: 661-946-7118
antk-lvr@webtv.net
Collects early toy typewriters from the 1890s through 1915: Simplex, Lord Baltimore, Practical, Eureka, Famos, and others.

U.S. POSTAL SERVICE ITEMS

(see POSTAL SERVICE ITEMS; POSTCARDS, Post Office Related; STAMP COLLECTING)

UFOs & UNEXPLAINED PHENOMENA

(see also BOOKS, Metaphysics; MAGICIANS PARAPHERNALIA; MORBID & ODD ITEMS; SCIENCE FICTION)

Book Sellers

Paul Hunt
Atlantis Books
3508 W. Magnolia Blvd.
Burbank, CA 91505
ph: 818-556-3441
BuyBook@pacbell.net
http://www.atlantisbookshop.com
Specializes in books about UFO, paranormal, occult, conspiracy.

Collectors

Lucius Farish
2 Caney Valley Dr.
Plumerville, AR 72127-8725
ph: 501-354-2558
ufobooks@webtv.net
Wants books, booklets, periodicals, and tapes on UFOs, extraterrestrial life, Atlantis, Bigfoot, occultism, unexplained phenomena.

Museums/Libraries

International U.F.O. Museum & Research Center
114 N. Main
P.O. Box 2221
Roswell, NM 88202-2221
ph: 505-625-9495
fax: 505-625-1907
iufomrc@iufomrc.org
http://iufomrc.org

Periodicals

Lucius Farish
Newsletter: UFO Newsclipping Service
2 Caney Valley Dr.
Plumerville, AR 72127-8725
ph: 501-354-2558
ufons@webtv.net
http://www.ozarkufo.iwarp.com
Current press reports of UFOs/ unexplained phenomena from around the world; news clippings compiled in 20-page monthly issues; since 1969.

UMBRELLA COVERS

Museums/Libraries

Nancy Hoffman, Dir.
Umbrella Cover Museum
62-B Island Ave.
Peaks Island, ME 04108
ph: 207-766-4496
nancy3@peaksisland.com
http://www.umbrellacovermuseum.org
Contains a collection of umbrella covers including sheaths, wrappers and pockets; donations welcome.

UNCLE SAM

(see also HISTORICAL AMERICANA; POLITICAL COLLECTIBLES)

Experts

Gerald E. Czulewicz
Antiques Americana
25699 Highway 65 NE
Isanti, MN 55040
ph: 763-444-9216
fax: 763-444-9218
charliezebra@msn.com
Author of "Foremost Guide to Uncle Sam Collectibles," featuring Uncle Sam images and objects: original paintings, watercolors, drawings, vintage posters, prints, folk art, banks, toys, games, etc.

UNICORNS

Collectors

Dianne Stephens
1104 Thistle Trail
Cedar Park, TX 78613-3470
dianne@unicorncollector.com
http://www.unicorncollector.com
Great Web site for the unicorn collector: legends, images of unicorn collectibles, bookstore, links, and more.

VACUUM CLEANERS

Collectors

Peter Frei
P.O. Box 500
Brimfield, MA 01010-0500
ph: 413-245-4660
peterfrei@prodigy.net
http://www.vacuumcleanermuseum.com
Wants to buy handpowered vacuum cleaners, pre-1875 sewing machines, typewriters, calculators, and adding machines.

Robert Kautzman
Kautzman Vacuum Cleaner Repair
3509 Fairchild St.
Alburtis, PA 18011-2631
ph: 610-682-4510 or 800-830-7996
vachunter@enter.net
http://www.vachunter.com
Collects hand crank and pump type vacuum cleaners: water, foot, steam and hand-powered; also 1900-1930 electric upright vacuum cleaners plus

tanks and hand vacuums; also wants primitive carpet stretchers and tackers; does repairs.

Billy Lipman
7428 Park Heights Ave.
Baltimore, MD 21208
ph: 410-486-1969
inkey@erols.com
Wants to buy antique vacuum cleaners: hand-pumped and hand-cranked vacuums; also VERY EARLY electric uprights and canister vacuums; also wants parts; call or send description; all calls returned.

Roger A. Proehl
205 East Joppa Rd. #1005
Baltimore, MD 21286-3221
ph: 410-296-4545
brendafan@aol.com
Buys, sells and trades pre-1940 vacuums; Hamilton Beach, Bee Vac, Kenmore, Apex, Hoover Duster; old parts needed such as bags, brushes, etc.; wants anything unusual.

Dealers

Grant Aslett
Don Aslett's Antiques
P.O. Box 39
Pocatello, ID 83204
ph: 208-232-6212
fax: 208-232-6286
Wants unique cleaning collectibles: vacuums, household items, cleaners, sweepers.

Internet Resources

Robert Kautzman
VacHunter Galleries
3509 Fairchild St.
Alburtis, PA 18011-2631
ph: 610-682-4510 or 800-830-7996
vachunter@enter.net
http://www.vachunter.com
Online museum of vacuums and related items: beaters, stretchers, carpet sweepers, vacuums of all types: upright, hand vacs, tank/canister, pumper, plunger, wheel, bellows, friction.

Museums/Libraries

Ann Haines, Operations
Hoover Historical Center
Newsletter: Center News
1875 Easton St. NW
North Canton, OH 44720-3331
ph: 330-499-0287 or 330-499-9200
fax: 330-494-4725
ahaines@hoover.com
http://www.hoovercompany.com/xq/asp/ qx/Company/hstcntr.htm
Restored Victorian farmhouse was boyhood home of W.H. Hoover, founder of The Hoover Co.; displays trace history of Hoover family and the evolution of cleaning devices with a focus on Hoover vacuum cleaner technology.

Veronica L. Krandl
Grand Rapids Public Museum
272 Pearl St. NW
Grand Rapids, MI 49504-5371
ph: 616-456-3977
fax: 616-456-3873
staff@grmuseum.org
http://www.grmuseum.org
World's largest collection of carpet sweepers representing over 150 manufacturers worldwide; archives and advertising collection of the Bissell Carpet Sweeper Company.

Don Aslett
Don Aslett's Cleaning Museum
311 South 5th Ave.
Pocatello, ID 83201
ph: 800-451-2402
fax: 208-232-6286
aslettdon@aol.com
http://www.cleanreport.com
Wants to buy vintage vacuums, commodes, cleaners in original packaging, ads, janitorial stuff, floor polishers, brooms, brushes, buckets, mops, posters suitable for museum.

Repair Services

Robert Kautzman
Kautzman Vacuum Cleaner Repair
3509 Fairchild St.
Alburtis, PA 18011-2631
ph: 610-682-4510 or 800-830-7996
vachunter@enter.net
http://www.vachunter.com
Collects hand crank and pump type vacuum cleaners: water, foot, steam and hand-powered; also 1900-1930 electric upright vacuum cleaners plus tanks and hand vacuums; also wants primitive carpet stretchers and tackers; does repairs.

VACUUM TUBES

(see RADIOS, Vacuum Tubes for)

VALENTINES

(see also CARDS; ELVES; HOLIDAY COLLECTIBLES; PAPER COLLECTIBLES)

Auction Services

Evalene Pulati
Pulati Auctions
P.O. Box 1404
Santa Ana, CA 92702-1404
ph: 714-547-1355

Clubs/Associations

Evalene Pulati
National Valentine Collectors Association
Newsletter: National Valentine Collectors Bulletin
P.O. Box 1404
Santa Ana, CA 92702-1404
ph: 714-547-1355
The quarterly newsletter focuses on

collecting valentines; identification, values, ads.

Experts

Evalene Pulati
P.O. Box 1404
Santa Ana, CA 92702-1404
ph: 714-547-1355
Author of "Illustrated Valentine Price Guides," updated in 1998, now available for $16.85 ppd.

VAMPIRES

(see HORROR, Dracula)

VAUDEVILLE MEMORABILIA

Collectors

Collector
American Vaudeville Museum
Newsletter: Vaudeville Times
P.O. Box 200772
Boston, MA 02120-0013
http://www.vaudeville.org
Wants original Vaudeville sheet music, posters, photos and movie memorabilia.

VENTRILOQUIST ITEMS

(see also PUPPETS; PERFORMING ARTS)

Collectors

J. Thomas
1208 Main St. North
Southbury, CT 06488
ph: 203-263-2233
fax: 203-263-2233
Wants to buy ventriloquist's dummies; child-size figures in handcarved wood, prefers with old clothing and full bodied; also wants sculptured heads; send photo and include phone contact.

T. Keppler
145 Lake Ave.
Nesconset, NY 11767-1049
ph: 631-361-4957
Wants ventriloquist dolls: Jerry Mahoney, Knucklehead Smiff, Moe Howard, and other uncommon vents.

Andy Gross
P.O. Box 6134
Beverly Hills, CA 90212-1134
ph: 310-362-4372 or 310-614-1944
fax: 310-680-6495
apedoll69@aol.com
http://www.lamagictoy.com
Wants ventriloquist dummies, any related items such as puppets, toys, games, photos, books, marionettes, and old pro & toy dummies, i.e., Jerry Mahoney, Knucklehead Smiff, Charlie McCarthy, Mortimer Snerd, Danny O'Day, Farfel, etc.

Museums/Libraries

Anne Roberts
Vent Haven Museum, The
33 West Maple Ave.
Ft. Mitchell, KY 41011-2616
ph: 606-341-0461
info@venthaven.com
http://www.venthaven.com
The museum is a collection of over 800 ventriloquist figures, pictures, playbills and memorabilia that is open to the public from May to September for guided tours by advanced appointment only.

VETERAN ITEMS

(see also BADGES; INDIAN WARS ITEMS; MEDALS, ORDERS & DECORATIONS; MILITARIA)

Clubs/Associations

Women's Army Corps Veterans' Association
Newsletter: Channel, The
P.O. Box 5577
Ft. McClellan, FL 32605-5577
ph: 256-820-6824
info@armywomen.org
http://www.armywomen.org
Object is to promote the general welfare of those personnel who have served honorably with the Women's Army Auxiliary Corps, or those who have served or are serving with the US Army, Army National Guard, Army Nurse Corps.

Civil War

Clubs/Associations

George G. Kane
Civil War Veterans Historical Association
Newsletter: Veteran, The
123 Springfield St.
Chicopee, MA 01013-2627
gkane1@prodigy.net
http://pages.prodigy.net/gkane1
For those interested in preserving the memory of Union and Confederate veterans of the American Civil War; also memorabilia.

Andrew Johnson, CIC
Sons of Union Veterans of the Civil War
405 So. Glebe Rd.
Arlington, VA 22204
amjohnson@juno.com
http://suvcw.org

Maitland Westbrook, Ex. Dir.
Sons of Confederate Veterans
Magazine: Confederate Veteran Magazine
P.O. Box 59
Columbia, TN 38402-0059
ph: 800-380-1896
fax: 931-381-6712
exedir@scv.org
http://www.scv.org

Collectors

George G. Kane
123 Springfield St.
Chicopee, MA 01013-2627
gkane1@prodigy.net
http://pages.prodigy.net/gkane1
Collector specializing in Grand Army of the Republic memorabilia.

Julie Brighenti
1036 Rostraver Rd.
Belle Vernon, PA 15012
ph: 724-929-7311
Wants Grand Army of the Republic items: badges, ribbons, canes, glass, gold testimonial badges, etc.; also W.R.C. and G.A.R. items.

David J. Maloney, ISA CAPP
P.O. Box 2049
Frederick, MD 21702-1049
ph: 301-228-2279
fax: 301-695-6491
dave@maloney.com
http://www.davidmaloney.com
Wants Union and Confederate veteran-related items: Grand Army of the Republic, United Confederate Veterans, WRC, SUV; any related item.

Peggy Dillard
P.O. Box 210904
Nashville, TN 37221-0904
ph: 615-646-1605
pdill43795@aol.com
Wants Confederate Veterans Reunion items.

Don Limpert
P.O. Box 524
Manchester, MI 48158
ph: 734-428-7400
delimpert@netzero.net

Dealers

Will Gorges
Battleground Antiques, Inc.
3910 US Highway 70 East
New Bern, NC 28560
ph: 252-636-3039 or 252-636-5445
fax: 252-637-1862
rebel@civilwarantiques.com
http://www.civilwarshop.com
Full time dealer buys, sells, collects and appraises authentic Civil War artifacts: firearms, accoutrements, edged weapons, dug items, documents, uniforms, coins, etc.; catalog available.

Charles Brecheisen
Trans-Mississippi Militaria
1004 Simon Dr.
Plano, TX 75025-2501
ph: 972-517-8111
fax: 972-517-8111
Buys, sells, trades anything to do with the Civil War, with a specialty in Civil War medical items: UCV, GAR, reunion items, paper, relics, photographs.

Museums/Libraries

Grand Army of the Republic Civil War Museum & Library
4278 Griscom St.
Philadelphia, PA 19124-3954
ph: 215-289-6484
garmuslib@aol.com
http://suvcw.org/garmus.htm
Civil War Museum & Library; artifacts, personal memorabilia, paintings, G.A.R. & S.U.V.C.W. records.

Wisconsin Veterans Museum, The
30 W. Mifflin St.
Madison, WI 53707-7843
ph: 608-267-1799
Veterans.Museum@dva.state.wi.us
http://badger.state.wi.us/agencies/dva/museum/wvmmain.html
Tells the story of men and women from the Badger State who served in America's conflicts from the Civil War to the Persian Gulf War; great collection of GAR memorabilia.

G.A.R. Hall & Museum/Meeker County Historical Society
Newsletter: G.A.R. Hall & Museum Newsletter
308 Marshall Ave. N
Litchfield, MN 55355
ph: 320-693-8911
Grand Army of the Republic (GAR) Hall built in 1885 by Union Veterans of the Civil War; maintained by Meeker Historical Society.

Grand Army of the Republic Memorial Museum
629 S. Seventh St.
Springfield, IL 62703
ph: 217-522-4373

VETERINARY MEDICINE ITEMS

Auction Services

Mike Smith, D.V.M.
7431 Covington Highway
Lithonia, GA 30058-7611
ph: 770-482-5100 or 770-482-5101
fax: 770-484-1304
petvet@mindspring.com
http://petvet.home.mindspring.com/VCR
Conducts periodic auctions of animal and veterinary medicine collectibles.

Clubs/Associations

Mike Smith, D.V.M.
Veterinary Collectibles Roundtable
Newsletter: Veterinary Collectibles Roundtable Newsletter
7431 Covington Highway
Lithonia, GA 30058-7611
ph: 770-482-5100 or 770-482-5101
fax: 770-484-1304
petvet@mindspring.com
http://petvet.home.mindspring.com/VCR
Seeking collectors and consignors for newsletter and twice-yearly auctions of antique veterinary patent medicines and advertising; for collectors of animal or veterinary medicine antiques.

Collectors

Dr. Fred Cesana
49 E. Main St.
Plainville, CT 06062
ph: 860-747-2759 or 860-379-0054
fax: 860-793-6019
Wants pre-1930 veterinary advertising items, cabinets, bottles with labels, etc.; also wants photographs of veterinarians, or their wagons or buildings and tintype or cabinet card photos of dogs and cats with their owners.

Paul Ferraglio
3332 W. Lake Rd.
Canandaigua, NY 14424-2441
ph: 585-394-7663
fax: 585-394-5424
p4alyo@aol.com
Wants to buy veterinary medicine items: old surgical instruments, animal medicine bottles and tins, pamphlets, display cabinets, signs.

Mike Smith, D.V.M.
7431 Covington Highway
Lithonia, GA 30058-7611
ph: 770-482-5100 or 770-482-5101
fax: 770-484-1304
petvet@mindspring.com
http://petvet.home.mindspring.com/VCR
Wants to buy animal and veterinary medicine collectibles.

Dealers

Willisia Holbrook
Armbrook Antiques
531 Doub Rd.
Lewisville, NC 27023
ph: 888-393-8025 or 336-945-9477
fax: 336-945-9914
Buys and sells early veterinarian antiques; specializes in pre-1930s items; Web site has full online catalog including descriptions and photos.

Jim Cole
October Farm Books
2609 Branch Rd.
Raleigh, NC 27610-9213
ph: 919-772-0482
fax: 919-779-6265
octoberfarm@bellsouth.net
http://www.octoberfarm.com
Buys and sells horse books and paper ephemera, especially relating to polo, carriages & driving, Morgan horses, American Saddlebred horses, and veterinary medicine; also old farm horse equipment and catalogs; mail order only.

Trenton Boyd
P.O. Box 517
Columbia, MO 65205-0517
ph: 573-882-2461 or 573-442-5235
fax: 573-882-2950
vetlib@missouri.edu
Interested in veterinary postcards including schools and military veterinary; also wants teratology cards that show animals with birth defects (e.g. five-legged calves); Red Cross dogs, Humane Association.

Military Related

Collectors

John N. Case, Jr., BS, DVM
Veterinary Corps Museum & Archives
5462 North University Dr.
Lauderhill, FL 33351-5006
ph: 954-749-0551 or 954-629-6688
fax: 954-749-5462
JCase74683@aol.com
http://hometown.aol.com/jcase74683/myhomepage/index.html
Wants military artifacts of the Veterinary Corps of each nation, any era; also military farriers, doghandlers, and Carrier pigeoneers: insignia, badges, medals, uniforms, hats/caps, documents, photos, IDs, books, etc., museum information.

VIETNAM ITEMS

(see also MILITARIA; SOCIAL CAUSES, Hippie Items)

Collectors

Sylvia Marcotte-Cloutier
Sylvia Charles of Blythe
218 W. Hobson Way
Blythe, CA 92225-1619
ph: 760-922-3456
fax: 760-922-5651
ru4flowerpower@aol.com
Wants 1960 to 1970 material relating to Vietnam, counterculture organizations, Civil Rights: diaries, letters, signed books, letters from military men sent home; documents, photos of sit-ins, marches, riots, demonstrations, etc.

Rick Synchef
208 Summit Dr.
Corte Madera, CA 94925-1342
ph: 415-927-8844
Wants 1960s "counterculture" memorabilia: beatnik, hippie, Black Panthers, Haight Ashbury, Tim Leary, Abbie Hoffman, Vietnam war, LBJ, Nixon, psychedelic, drugs, political, music, handbills, leaflets, books.

Periodicals

PRIMEDIA Enthusiast Group
Magazine: Vietnam
741 Miller Dr., SE, Ste. D-2
Leesburg, VA 20175
ph: 703-779-8318
fax: 703-779-8310
david.masini@primedia.com
http://www.thehistorynet.com/Vietnam
Covers the controversial Vietnam War from many perspectives for both veterans of the war and students of military and political history; published bi-monthly.

VIEW BOOKS

(see ALBUMS; PAPER COLLECTIBLES)

VIEW-MASTERS

(see 3-D PHOTOGRAPHICA, View-Masters)

VINTAGE CLOTHING

(see CLOTHING & ACCESSORIES, Vintage)

VIOLINS

(see MUSICAL INSTRUMENTS, String [Violins])

VISUAL AIDS

(see OPTICAL ITEMS)

VOLKSWAGEN RELATED ITEMS

Collectors

Dan Morris
1225 Ramblewood Dr.
Annapolis, MD 21401
ph: 410-757-6430
Collects European car club badges and vintage Volkswagon accessories.

Melissa Jess
3121 East Yucca St.
Phoenix, AZ 85028-2616
ph: 602-867-7672
fax: 602-867-7672
vwstuff@juno.com
http://www.vwstuff.us
Wants Volkswagen related items: models, literature, accessories, postcards, dealer items, Herbie Lovebug, VW memorabilia, etc.

Mike Wilson
P.O. Box 2176
Wilsonville, OR 97070
ph: 503-638-7074
fax: 503-550-5509
info@k-9agility.net
Wants Volkswagen toys, memorabilia, literature, etc.

Dealers

Frank Konisky
People Kars
290 Third Ave. Extension
Rensselaer, NY 12144
ph: 518-465-0477
fax: 518-465-0614
peoplekars@aol.com
http://www.peoplekars.com
Buy, sell, trade Volkswagen, Porsche and select European automobile models, toys and automobilia.

WAGONS

(see BICYCLES & RELATED MEMORABILIA; HORSE-DRAWN VEHICLES; RIDING TOYS)

WALKING STICKS

(see CANES & WALKING STICKS)

WALL POCKETS

Collectors

Bobbie & Alan Bryson
1 St. Eleanoras Ln.
Tuckahoe, NY 10707-1307
ph: 914-779-1405
napkindoll@aol.com
Wants to buy glass wall pockets.

Experts

Pam Brin
8 Park Lane
Minneapolis, MN 55416-4340
ph: 612-920-3030
fax: 612-920-3031

WALL STREET

(see STOCKS & BONDS, Financial History)

WALLACE NUTTING

(see also FURNITURE [ANTIQUE], Wallace Nutting; PRINTS, Wallace Nutting)

Auction Services

Michael Ivanovich
Ivankovich Antiques
P.O. Box 1536
Doylestown, PA 18901
ph: 215-345-6094
fax: 215-345-6692
ivankovich@wnutting.com
http://www.wnutting.com
Largest auction service for Wallace Nutting prints, books and furniture; conducts 3-4 auctions/yr., each with 300-500 Wallace Nutting pictures.

Clubs/Associations

Bob & Pam Franscella
Wallace Nutting Collectors Club
Newsletter: Wallace Nutting Collectors Newsletter
23 Newstar Ridge Rd.
Sparta, NJ 07871
ph: 973-726-9736
franscella@earthlink.net
Helps members learn more about Wallace Nutting, the man and his works; please include a SASE when requesting a reply.

Collectors

Bill Hamann
P.O. Box 22475
Cleveland, OH 44122
Past president of the Wallace Nutting Collectors Club.

Dealers

Sharon Lacasse
Sharon Lacasse Antiques
1424 Osterville - W. Barnstable Rd.
West Barnstable, MA 02668
ph: 508-428-0562
slacasse@capecod.net
http://www.capecod.net/wnutting
*Buying and selling pictures, books,
furniture and all memorabilia relating
to Wallace Nutting; also interested in
all other hand colored photographs by
any photographer.*

Bill & Anne Shaner
Shaner's Antiques & Collectibles
403 N. Charlotte St.
Pottstown, PA 19464-5311
ph: 610-326-0165
*Wants signed and titled Wallace
Nutting photographs.*

Experts

Michael Ivanovich
Ivankovich Antiques
P.O. Box 1536
Doylestown, PA 18901
ph: 215-345-6094
fax: 215-345-6692
ivankovich@wnutting.com
http://www.wnutting.com
*Wants pictures, books, furniture;
leading collector; conducts auctions of
Wallace Nutting items; author of
books on Nutting; also pictures that
resemble Wallace Nutting works, e.g.,
those by Fred Thompson, David
Davidson, Chas. Sawyer.*

Internet Resources

Jan K. Liberatore
Wallace Nutting Center, The
wncenter@aol.com
http://www.wallacenutting.com
*Great online Wallace Nutting
resource: classifieds, furniture, letters,
picture gallery, research material,
chat.*

WALLETS

(see BUSINESS CARD HOLDERS)

WARBIRDS

(see AVIATION, Military)

WASHING MACHINES

(see also ENGINES, Gasoline;
MAYTAG)

Experts

Robert Seger
4351 Harriet Ave., S.
Minneapolis, MN 55409
ph: 612-874-7960
*Collector of and expert in early
automatic clothes washing machines
from the mid-1940s to the early 1960s;*

*wants to buy vintage machines, parts
and literature.*

Lee Maxwell
Antique Washing Machines
35901 WCR 31
Eaton, CO 80615
ph: 970-454-1856
oldewash@aol.com
http://www.oldewash.com
*Collector of old and unusual washing
machines; has collection of over 960
pre-1940 washing machines having
wooden, copper or galvanized tubs;
send photos and description; machine
must be complete; does not do
appraisals.*

WATCH FOBS

Clubs/Associations

R.J. Rothlisberger
Midwest Watch Fob Collectors, Inc.
Newsletter: Watch Fob Collectors
  Newsletter
11895 Highway 99
Burlington, IA 52601-8521
ph: 319-752-6749
*A group organized to preserve, collect
and educate themselves about strap
advertising watch fobs.*

Jim Yowell
International Watch Fob Association,
  Inc.
Newsletter: International Watch Fob
Association Newsletter
601 Patriot Place
Holmen, WI 54636
ph: 608-526-2328
info@watchfob.com
http://www.watchfob.com
*Focus is on strap-type watch fobs;
members receive 2 fobs and 2
newsletter per year; membership roster
available; annual show in the
Cleveland, OH area.*

William "Bill" Mitchell
Canadian Association of Watch Fob
  Collectors
2 Elm Dr.
Stoney Creek, Ontario L8G 3B4 Canada
ph: 905-664-4576
wmitchell56@cogeco.ca
*Dedicated to the collection and
preservation of advertising-type watch
fobs.*

Collectors

John Cline
609 N. East St.
Carlisle, PA 17013-2012
ph: 717-249-4253
*Wants road or farm machinery-related
fobs, or fobs advertising fur, traps,
powder and gun companies.*

Gary Call
259 South 3rd St.
Pocatello, ID 83201-6442
ph: 208-232-0228
mrfob@webtv.net
*Wants to buy any strap-type
advertising watch fobs that are home*

*product related including food and
drink products; also wants livestock
commission and livestock related fobs,
and silo and grain elevator fobs.*

Advertising

Dealers

Dave Beck
P.O. Box 435
Mediapolis, IA 52637-0435
ph: 319-394-3943
fax: 319-394-3943
adman@mepotelco.net
*Buys and sells advertising watch fobs,
mirrors and pin-backs; send stamp for
illustrated mail auction catalog.*

Machinery & Equipment

Collectors

John Leite, Jr.
44 Glenwood Rd.
Brewster, MA 02631-2202
ph: 508-385-4905
*Wants to buy watch fobs dealing with
heavy equipment and trucking.*

WATCHES

(see also BOOKS, Reference
[Watches]; CLOCKS; GEMS &
JEWELRY; INSTRUMENTS &
DEVICES, Scientific; WATCH FOBS)

Appraisers

Gina D'Onofria, FGAA, ISA
GinaJewels
9615 Brighton Way
Beverly Hills, CA 90210
ph: 310-273-8471
ginala@earthlink.net
http://www.ginajewels.com
*Specializes in diamond grading,
gemstone and jewelry authentication,
and in the appraisal of watches and
jewelry; Accredited Member of the
Inter. Soc. of Appraisers.*

Rene Johnson
Accredited Gemological Appraisals
24681 La Plaza, Ste. 220
Dana Point, CA 92629
ph: 949-903-8841 or 949-933-0144
rene.johnson@cox.net
http://www.AGemAppraisals.com
*Graduate Gemologist through the
Gemological Institute of America
(GIA), Accredited Member of the
International Society of Appraisers;
jewelry and watch appraisals for
insurance and estate.*

Auction Services

George Horan
Jones & Horan Auction Team
453 Mast Rd.
Goffstown, NH 03045
ph: 603-623-5314
fax: 603-623-5314
pat@jones-horan.com
http://www.jones-horan.com
*Specializes in horological artifacts
and timepieces.*

Robert Schmitt
R. O. Schmitt Fine Arts
P.O. Box 1941
Salem, NH 03079
ph: 603-893-5915
fax: 603-893-9777
bob@roschmittfinearts.com
http://www.roschmittfinearts.com

Clubs/Associations

Jon Hanson, Pres.
Early American Watch Club, Chapter
  #149 NAWCC
P.O. Box 81555
Wellesley Hills, MA 02481-1333
jonontime@aol.com
*A specialty chapter within the
National Association of Watch &
Clock Collectors, Inc.; focuses on
early American watches.*

Paul Wadsworth, Pres.
American Watchmakers Institute,
  Chapter #102 NAWCC
64 South Ave.
P.O. Box 933
Hilton, NY 14468
*A specialty chapter within the
National Association of Watch &
Clock Collectors, Inc.*

Caroline M. Stuckert, PhD
National Association of Watch & Clock
  Collectors, Inc.
Magazine: Bulletin of the NAWCC
514 Poplar St.
Columbia, PA 17512-2130
ph: 717-684-8261
fax: 717-684-0878
jbland@nawcc.org
http://www.nawcc.org
*The NAWCC is a non-profit and
scientific-driven association founded
in 1943 and now serving the
horological interests of 38,000
members worldwide.*

American Watchmakers-Clockmakers
  Institute
Magazine: Horological Times
701 Enterprise Dr.
Harrison, OH 45030-1696
ph: 513-367-9800
fax: 513-367-1414
awi-info@awi-net.org
http://www.awi-net.org
*For those interested in horology as a
profession or avocation; monthly
technical magazine, technical
bulletins, training, public relations,
networking.*

Collectors

Bob Arnell
P.O. Box 313
Grandview, MO 64030-0313
ph: 816-966-0544 or 816-213-4999
bobstuff11@excite.com
*Wants to buy wrist and pocket
watches.*

Dealers

Robert Beaver
Classic Touch Antiques
P.O. Box 27
Newport, RI 02840-0001
ph: 401-849-1717 or 401-846-9663
fax: 401-849-1717
Buys and sells early and complicated watches, wrist and pocket.

Stewart Unger
Time Will Tell
twt@timewilltell.com
http://www.timewilltell.com
Specializes in high-end American wrist watches; appeared on PAX TVs "Treasures in Your Home."

Mark Stuart
P.O. Box 46
Skippack, PA 19474
ph: 610-631-6801
astrotrac@aol.com
http://welovewatches.com
Buys and sells vintage wrist watches; member of NAWCC for over 15 years.

Irv Temes
Temes & Co.
338 N. Charles St.
Baltimore, MD 21201
ph: 800-722-5274 or 410-347-7600
fax: 410-685-3299
itemes@aol.com
Buyers of high quality wrist watches and pocket watches, especially Rolex, Patek Philippe, Vacheron, Cartier, Tiffany, etc.; all conditions; please call or write for offer; member Jewelers Board of Trade, our 19th year.

N. Kenzie Smith
Clock Shop, The
119 East St.
Frederick, MD 21701
ph: 301-698-8252
http://www.frederickcounty.com/
  antiques/clock.htm
Sells, repairs and restores all mechanical clocks and watches; references upon request.

Greg A. Leveto
Antique Vintage Watches
1110 Winding Creek Trail
Atlanta, GA 30328
ph: 404-256-1121
fax: 404-252-3233
greg@antiquevintagewatches.com
http://www.antiquevintagewatches.com
Specializes in pre-1960 wrist watches.

Peter Thurber
Ritzi & Thurber, Inc.
160 S. Beach St.
Daytona Beach, FL 32114
ph: 904-252-2552 or 904-226-8489
fax: 904-226-8490
ritzi1881@earthlink.net
http://www.ritzi-thurber.com
Founded in 1881, restorations and repairs are done to all watches on premises; fine mechanical wrist and pocket watches are purchased as well as watches for parts; carries a

selection of pre-owned Rolex and other brands.

Don Baker
Finer Times Vintage Timepieces
P.O. Box 595
Tampa, FL 33548
ph: 813-909-7722
fax: 813-909-7722
donbaker@finertimes.com
http://www.finertimes.com
Buys and sells a large selection of vintage timepieces online: Rolex, Omega, LeCoultre, Hamilton, etc.; also sells a fine selection of horological related books and accessories.

Ashland
640 South Washington Blvd., Ste. 200
Sarasota, FL 34236-7108
ph: 800-424-5353 or 941-957-3760
fax: 941-365-4931
ashlandinvest@mindspring.com
Specializes in fine and important pocket and wrist watches.

Bill Marshall
Marshall Vintage Timepieces
255 Hiway Dr.
Clinton, TN 37716-4431
ph: 888-267-4886
fax: 423-457-0051
bill@timepast.com
http://www.timepast.com
Dealer, expert and repairer of vintage wrist and pocket watches.

Ed & Carolyn Sunday
Sunday & Sunday
P.O. Box 1240
Uniontown, OH 44685
ph: 330-966-6746
csunday@neo.rr.com
http://www.sundayandsunday.com
Specializes in pocket and wrist watches and in fine estate jewelry; has restored pocket watches for over 25 years.

David Lee
Clockworks, Inc., The
560 N. Western Ave.
Lake Forest, IL 60045-1920
ph: 847-234-7272
fax: 847-234-7286
davidlee@theclockworks.com
http://www.theclockworks.com
Buy, sell, repair, restore clocks, watches, barometers and music boxes.

Rick Chandler
Attic Antiques
P.O. Box 131
Algonquin, IL 60102
ph: 847-658-1433
ticktockchandler@earthlink.net
http://www.attic-antiques.net
Specializes in clocks, and wrist and pocket watches; over 35 years experience; 17th century to present; will answer questions about values and makers.

Ron Geweniger
Old World Jewelers Ltd.
1301 West 22nd St., Ste. 308
Oak Brook, IL 60523
ph: 630-990-0100 or 800-322-3871
fax: 630-928-0880
sales@oldworldjewelers.com
http://www.oldworldjewelers.com
Dealers specializing in luxury, vintage and pre-owned fine quality Swiss wrist watches and pocket watches.

Maundy International
P.O. Box 13028 - RAM
Shawnee Mission, KS 66212-3028
ph: 800-235-2866
mitime@hotmail.com
Watches - buying Patek Philippe pocket & wrist watches and fine watches from USA & Europe; since 1976; specializes in railroad pocket watches.

Mike Stute
World Wide Watch Brokers
626 Meadowbrooke
Duncanville, TX 75137
ph: 972-709-7960
lilthug@metronet.com
Selling all types of vintage and new wrist watches and pocket watches.

Robert M. Wingate
Wingate's Quality Watches
P.O. Box 59760
Dallas, TX 75229
ph: 800-842-8625 or 972-392-7676
fax: 972-392-2304
wingates@tic-tock.com
http://www.tic-tock.com
Specializes in the purchase, sale and restoration of antique watches; in business since 1976.

Tim Sweet
M.O.S.T. Watch & Clock Co.
3010 Forest Trail
San Angelo, TX 76904
ph: 915-947-8196
timsweet@cox.net
Dealer, collector, expert, auction and repair services, appraiser offering all aspects of antique clock and watch services; Web site has an Internet Horology Club.

Clark Davis
Colorado Gold & Silver
2644 W. Colorado Ave.
Colorado Springs, CO 80904
ph: 719-633-9109
xplore@earthlink.net
Watch dealer, appraiser, expert; has specialized in contemporary and vintage fine wrist and pocket watches for over 22 years.

Kenneth Jacobs
Wanna Buy a Watch?
7366 Melrose Ave.
Los Angeles, CA 90046
ph: 323-653-0467
fax: 323-653-9101
ken@wannabuyawatch.com
http://www.wannabuyawatch.com
Popular vintage and contemporary

watch site; sales and service; also carries an extensive selection of antique platinum diamond wedding and engagement rings.

Paul K. Lonnquist
Vintage Electronics & Other Collectibles
3076 Wauneta St.
Newbury Park, CA 91320-4446
ph: 805-498-5644 or 805-990-0557
paul@dock.net
Buys, sells, trades vintage watches, specializing in the more affordable brands; on the Internet for over 3 years.

Bill Porter
Vintage Time
P.O. Box 1155
Rancho Santa Fe, CA 92067
ph: 858-756-7769
fax: 858-756-5430
vintage@inetworld.net
http://www.vintagetime.com
Specializes in vintage pocket and wrist watches.

Howard Markham
Howard Markham Professional
  Numismatist
5225 Canyon Crest Dr., Ste. 20
Riverside, CA 92507-6319
ph: 909-686-2122 or 800-953-3027
Buys old pocket watches, either one piece or entire collections; wants railroad watches, wrist watches, older Rolex, Patek, Vacheron, etc.; will travel to buy larger collections.

Don Levison
Don Levison Antiques
P.O. Box 22262
San Francisco, CA 94122
ph: 415-753-0455
fax: 415-753-5206
dlevison@juno.com
http://www.antiquehorology.com
Buys and sells antique and better quality pocket and wrist watches, clocks, music boxes, singing birds, and other small automata; also mercury barometers from the 17th century to present.

Steve Bogoff
Bogoff Antique Timepieces
P.O. Box 408
Mill Valley, CA 94942
ph: 415-383-8100
fax: 415-383-8112
info@bogoff.com
http://www.bogoff.com
Buys, sells, appraises and has online catalog of complicated, rare, early, unusual, beautiful pocket watches, vintage wrist watches, small clocks, singing bird boxes and more.

Gloria Dekter
Ashton-Blakey Antiques & Collectibles
6021 Yonge St., Ste. 895
Toronto, Ontario M2M 3W2 Canada
ph: 905-886-5122
fax: 905-886-8566
ashtonb@netcom.ca
http://www.ashton-blakey-antiques.com
A complete Internet shop specializing in vintage wrist watches, antique pocket watches, watch fobs, chains; Web site contains images of all items; also specializes in scientific instruments.

Chris Hooper
Windy City Watch Collector
Singel 28 Boven
Amsterdam, 1015 The Netherlands
chris@chronometer.net
http://www.chronometer.net
Buys and sells vintage timepieces including pocket watches, wrist watches, marine chronometers, and ships' clocks.

Jonathan Wachsmann
Pieces of Time
1 - 7 Davies Mews
London, W1Y 2LP U.K.
ph: +44 020 7629 2422 or +44 020 7629 3272
fax: +44 020 7409 1625
info@antique-watch.com
http://www.antique-watch.com
One of London's leading dealers in antique, precision and pocket watches; has one of the largest specialist antique Internet sites in the world; has produced a quarterly catalog since 1984.

Experts

Philip M. Poniz
European Watch & Casemakers, Ltd.
P.O. Box 1314
Highland Park, NJ 08904-1314
ph: 732-777-0111
fax: 732-777-0118
horology@webspan.net
Does history and sales research on antique watches, clocks, musical boxes, and unusual mechanical objects of virtu.

Arthur Guy Kaplan
P.O. Box 1942
Baltimore, MD 21203
ph: 410-752-2090 or 410-664-8350
fax: 410-783-2723
Author of "The Official Price Guide to Antique Jewelry."

Joe Cohen
3090 North Couse Dr., Apt. #107
Pompano Beach, FL 33069
ph: 954-917-4676
jccohen3@attbi.com
Specializing in 17th, 18th, and 19th century clocks and watches; teaches course in identifying and researching antique clocks and watches.

Cooksey Shugart
P.O. Box 3147
Cleveland, TN 37320-3147
ph: 423-479-4813
fax: 423-479-4813
Author of "The Complete Price Guide to Watches," an annual price guide and mini encyclopedia for watch terminology; includes history of past watch manufacturers.

Internet Resources

WatchParadise.com
12900 Preston Rd., Ste. 1001
Dallas, TX 75230
ph: 899-392-0168
fax: 972-392-2304
admin@watchparadise.com
http://www.watchparadise.com
Web site provides a meeting place, market place and educational resource center for watch collectors, manufacturers, dealers, and jewelers; photo vault contains over 5,000 watch photos and descriptions; hundreds of useful links.

Museums/Libraries

American Clock & Watch Museum
Journal: Timepiece Journal
100 Maple St.
Bristol, CT 06010-5034
ph: 860-583-6070
fax: 860-583-1862
info@clockmuseum.org
http://www.clockmuseum.org
Preserves the history of American horology, especially Connecticut and Bristol's role; large displays of clocks & watches.

Caroline M. Stuckert, PhD
National Association of Watch & Clock Collectors Museum, Inc., The
514 Poplar St.
Columbia, PA 17512-2130
ph: 717-684-8261
fax: 717-684-0878
jbland@nawcc.org
http://www.nawcc.org
The National Watch & Clock Museum of the National Assoc. of Watch & Clock Collectors, documents the evolution of timekeeping around the world - from early sundials to atomic clocks with a collection of over 12,000 horological timepieces.

Periodicals

Magazine: Watch & Clock Review
2403 Champa St.
Denver, CO 80205-9903
ph: 303-296-1600
fax: 303-295-2159
print@goldenbellpress.com
http://www.goldenbellpress.com
Monthly magazine primarily for new and vintage watch and clock retailers; features articles on watches, clocks and shops; also ads for buyers, sellers, and restorers.

Magazine: Chronos
2403 Champa St.
Denver, CO 80205-9903
ph: 303-296-1600
fax: 303-295-2159
print@goldenbellpress.com
http://www.goldenbellpress.com
A quarterly publication primarily for the collector of fine timepieces, especially wrist watches.

Repair Services

Jan & Bill Kendzierski
Academy Timekeepers
226 S. Moore Ave.
Barrington, NJ 08007
ph: 856-547-7759
jmkwwk@aol.com

Philip M. Poniz
European Watch & Casemakers, Ltd.
P.O. Box 1314
Highland Park, NJ 08904-1314
ph: 732-777-0111
fax: 732-777-0118
horology@webspan.net
Restoration of watches, clocks, and music boxes; museum experience; can make any part and restore any watch; clients include Sotheby's, Cartier, collectors in USA, Asia and Europe; appraises, researches, lectures on watch making, fakes.

John Baer
John Baer - Watchmaker
215 East New St.
Lititz, PA 17543
ph: 717-627-1227
fax: 717-627-1227
jbaer@jbaer.com
http://www.jbaer.com
Specializes in the repair of Accutron watches and other fine watches.

N. Kenzie Smith
Clock Shop, The
119 East St.
Frederick, MD 21701
ph: 301-698-8252
http://www.frederickcounty.com/
antiques/clock.htm
Sells, repairs and restores all mechanical clocks and watches; references upon request.

Ferenc Bitt
European Watchworks, The
202 Loft Lane #185
Raleigh, NC 27609
ph: 919-845-4355
Specializes in the repair and restoration of fine and antique watches; Bitt is a Hungarian watchmaker educated in the old world model of European craftsmanship; over 25 years experience.

Peter Thurber
Ritzi & Thurber, Inc.
160 S. Beach St.
Daytona Beach, FL 32114
ph: 904-252-2552 or 904-226-8489
fax: 904-226-8490
ritzi1881@earthlink.net
http://www.ritzi-thurber.com
Founded in 1881, restorations and repairs are done to all watches on premises; fine mechanical wrist and pocket watches are purchased as well as watches for parts; carries a selection of pre-owned Rolex and other brands.

David Lee
Clockworks, Inc., The
560 N. Western Ave.
Lake Forest, IL 60045-1920
ph: 847-234-7272
fax: 847-234-7286
davidlee@theclockworks.com
http://www.theclockworks.com
Buy, sell, repair, restore clocks, watches, barometers and music boxes.

Felix Zaltsberg
Right Time International Watch Center
1485 S. Colorado Blvd.
Denver, CO 80222
ph: 888-TIME-388 or 303-691-2521
fax: 303-782-9316
felix@righttime.com
http://RightTime.com
A pre-owned and antique watch superstore; buys, trades, restores watches worldwide; four certified master watchmakers on premises to restore your favorite antique watch of clock; one year warranty on workmanship.

Alex Awakian
Monteau Gemological Services, Watch Repair Division
21250 Califa St., Ste. 203
Woodland Hills, CA 91367
ph: 818-712-9750
fax: 818-712-9755
Watch repair and refurbishing for wrist and pocket watches; American, Japanese, Swiss, French; dial refinishing, water resistant and water proof watches.

Suppliers

Harvey Schmidt
Watchmakers Tools
75-80 179 St.
Flushing, NY 11366
ph: 732-350-2084
wwlathlot@aol.com
http://www.toolpin.com
Specializes in selling antique and modern watchmaker's tools and machinery: lathes, lathe accessories, milling attachments, index plates, mandrels, rounding up tools, etc.

S. LaRose, Inc.
3223 Yanceyville St.
P.O. Box 21208
Greensboro, NC 27420-1208
ph: 336-621-1936
fax: 336-621-0706
info@slarose.com
http://www.slarose.com
Supplier of clock and watch parts.

Advertising

Dealers

Maggie Kenyon
M. Kenyon Co.
One Christopher St. 14-G
New York, NY 10014-3581
ph: 212-675-3213
mlkx@aol.com
*Buying, selling, collecting comic/
character watches for over 50 years;
included are sports, political and
product promotion watches in
addition to all comic watches;
interested in all regardless of age;
send SASE.*

Character/Comic

Collectors

Arthur Moore
1004 Cheyenne Blvd.
Madison, TN 37115-4212
ph: 615-865-4806
chance1@comcast.net
*Buys and sells comic character and
advertising watches in any condition.*

David Welch
P.O. Box 714
Murphysboro, IL 62966-0714
ph: 618-687-2282
fax: 618-684-2243
PEZDude1@aol.com
http://www.pezheads.net/dwelch
*Wants pre-1980 watches/clocks
relating to sports, TV, cartoon, comic,
movie characters with original boxes
ONLY; also wants empty boxes; no
political, please.*

Dealers

Maggie Kenyon
M. Kenyon Co.
One Christopher St. 14-G
New York, NY 10014-3581
ph: 212-675-3213
mlkx@aol.com
*Buying, selling, collecting comic/
character watches for over 50 years;
included are sports, political and
product promotion watches in
addition to all comic watches;
interested in all regardless of age;
send SASE.*

Man./Prod./Dist.

John J. Matteo, Jr.
Collectible Watch Co., Inc.
1100 Montrose Ave.
Charlottesville, VA 22902-6236
ph: 888-846-3101 or 804-984-5005
fax: 804-984-2777
jdematteo@collectiblewatch.com
http://www.collectiblewatch.com
*Producer of fine time pieces for the
serious collector; limited edition writs
and pocket watches; new collector tips
every month; sports, historical,
character.*

Mark Harbour
Fossil
2115 Campbell Creek
Richardson, TX 75082
ph: 800-449-3056
webguy@fossil.com
http://www.fossil.com
*Manufacturer of limited edition,
collectible, and antique-looking classic
watches and character watches
including Roy Rogers and Superman.*

Computer Programs For

Man./Prod./Dist.

John Christians
Software: WatchWare
4130 Terrace Dr.
Anchorage, AK 99502
ph: 907-243-8894
watch@watchware.net
http://www.watchware.org
*Horological software for collectors or
businesses; keep track of your
collections with easy-to-use software;
print reports for quick reference.*

Dials

Repair Services

Kirk Rich Dial Corporation
404 W. 7th St., Ste. 1215
Los Angeles, CA 90014
ph: 213-626-6840 or 213-626-6849
fax: 213-626-4302
info@krdial.com
http://www.krdial.com
*Specializes in restoring watch dials to
their original brilliance.*

Electric (Hamilton)

Dealers

Rene Rondeau
Rene Rondeau Hamilton Electric
  Watches
P.O. Box 391
Corte Madera, CA 94976-0391
ph: 415-924-6534
fax: 415-924-8423
rene@hamiltonwristwatch.com
http://www.hamiltonwristwatch.com
*Buys, sells, and repairs Hamilton
electric and mechanical wrist watches
from the 1920s and 1960s; author of
"The Watch of the Future," 3rd
edition and "Hamilton Wristwatches,
a Collector's Guide."*

Experts

Rene Rondeau
Rene Rondeau Hamilton Electric
  Watches
P.O. Box 391
Corte Madera, CA 94976-0391
ph: 415-924-6534
fax: 415-924-8423
rene@hamiltonwristwatch.com
http://www.hamiltonwristwatch.com
*Author of "The Watch of the Future,"
3rd edition and "Hamilton Wristwatches, a Collector's Guide."*

LED

Experts

Guy Ball
P.O. Box 345
Tustin, CA 92781-0345
ph: 714-730-6140
fax: 714-730-6140
mrcalc@usa.net
http://www.ledwatches.net
*Specializes in buying and selling LED
watches.*

Pocket

Appraisers

Jonathan Snellenburg
Jonathan Snellenburg Antiques, Inc.
594 Broadway, Ste. 507
New York, NY 10012
ph: 212-334-7270
fax: 212-334-7761
writeme@snellenburg.com
http://www.snellenburg.com
*Specializes in the appraisal of vintage
clocks, pocket watches, and scientific
instruments.*

Clubs/Associations

Jack Goldberg
Pocket Horology, Chapter #174
  NAWCC
5442 Valkeith Dr.
Houston, TX 77096
webmaster@pockethorology.org
http://www.pockethorology.org
*A national chapter of the NAWCC
dedicated to collaborative research on
the history and horology of pocket
watches.*

Collectors

Michael Sullivan
Route 1, Box 45
Jonesburg, MO 63351
ph: 636-488-5677
mandgee@socket.net
http://www.sully-has-it.com
*Buys, sells, trades quality pocket
watches; especially wants Illinois
Watch Company items.*

Dealers

Pocketwatch TIME!
admin@pocketwatchtime.com
http://www.pocketwatchtime.com
*Specializes in pocket watches, antique
and vintage: Hamilton, Illinois, Elgin,
American Waltham, AWW Co.,
Rockford, Howard, Ball, Gruen,*

*Hampden; also European and Swiss
manufacturers.*

Alan Altman
It's About Time
96 Harmati Lane
P.O. Box 537
Bearsville, NY 12409-0537
ph: 845-679-2832
fax: 845-679-2832
aaltman@hvc.rr.com
http://www.bearsystems.com/time
*Buys and sells American and
European pocket watches.*

Stephen Miles
Miles Pocketwatches
P.O. Box 366
Philmont, VA 20131
ph: 540-338-5482
fax: 540-338-5483
mileswatch@aol.com
http://www.miles-pocketwatches.com
*Internet site for the selling of
American and European pocket
watches; specializing in complications
such as repeaters and calendar
watches.*

Pat Gurley
Pat's Pocket Watches
744 N. Edward St.
Decatur, IL 62522
ph: 217-422-4427 or 217-875-9662
pgurley@tias.com
http://www.pocketwatch.com
*Carries a great selection of railroad
grade pocket watches; all original
antiques; Ball, Elgin, Waltham,
Illinois, Rockford, Hamilton, Howard,
Hampden, and many others.*

Robert Young
Pocket Watch.UK, The
U.K.
ph: 01795-843985
fax: 01795-843985
info@PocketWatch.co.uk
http://freespace.virgin.net/robert.young10
*Specialist mail order dealers buying
and selling the finest of antique and
vintage pocket watches from England
and Europe; also sells antique pocket
watch stands.*

Pocket Watch Stands

Dealers

Robert Young
Pocket Watch.UK, The
U.K.
ph: 01795-843985
fax: 01795-843985
info@PocketWatch.co.uk
http://www.pocketwatch.co.uk
*Specialist mail order dealer in fine
antique pocket watches stands.*

Swatch

Collectors

Carl F. Pflanzer
205 US Hwy. 22
Green Brook, NJ 08812
ph: 732-424-7811
fax: 732-424-7814
ewa@ewacars.com
http://www.ewacars.com
Wants Swatch watches and Swatch clothing; must be in excellent condition.

Internet Resources

Jerry S. Justianto
Jerry's Swatch Megalink
Indonesia
jsjxyz@msn.com
http://www.geocities.com/jsjxyz/swatch
Massive Swatch-related megalink Web site.

Timex

Appraisers

Carl Rosa
175 Union St.
Waterbury, CT 06706
ph: 203-757-8463 or 800-225-7742
fax: 203-755-8531
crosa@timexpo.com
http://www.timexpo.com
Collector and appraiser of Timex watches, Ingersoll watches, Waterbury clocks and related memorabilia; also director and curator of the Timexpo Museum.

Museums/Libraries

Carl Rosa
Timexpo Museum
175 Union St.
Waterbury, CT 06706
ph: 203-757-8463 or 800-225-7742
fax: 203-755-8531
crosa@timexpo.com
http://www.timexpo.com
A unique museum that combines the history of Timex and its predecessors with an archaeological exhibit; a Time Tunnel, a rich sensory experience taking you back in time to the ancient world, links the two themes; artifacts, memorabilia.

Wrist

Dealers

Jim Niederhofer
Sunburst - A Secret Treasure
jniederhofer4071@msn.com
http://www.newyorktime.com
Specializes in vintage wrist watches; member NAWCC.

Paul Duggan
Horological Artifacts
P.O. Box 63
Chelmsford, MA 01824-0063
ph: 978-256-5966
fax: 978-256-2497
paul@pduggan.com
http://www.pduggan.com
International watch buyers; wants fine

watches such as Rolex, Patek Philippe, Vacheron, Cartier, Tiffany, Gubelin, Jules Jurgenson, Breuget, E. Howard, American Watch Co., LeCoultre, etc.

Paul Duggan
Horological Artifacts
333 Washington St., Ste. 404
Boston, MA 02108
ph: 617-742-0221
fax: 617-742-0017
paul@pduggan.com
http://www.pduggan.com
International watch buyers; wants fine watches such as Rolex, Patek Philippe, Vacheron, Cartier, Tiffany, Gubelin, Jules Jurgenson, Breuget, E. Howard, American Watch Co., LeCoultre, etc.

Roger J. Foti
ModernWatches.net
1 Bery Lane
Wading River, NY 11792
ph: 516-929-3651
fax: 516-929-5499
rjfoti2@pipeline.com
http://www.modernwatches.net
Buys and sells vintage and contemporary watches with an emphasis on Hamilton, Omega, Baume & Mercier, Ebel, Audemars Piguet, Oris, Fortis, Krieger.

Delmas Minshew
We Love Watches
1 Industrial Dr.
Snow Hill, NC 28580
ph: 252-747-5252
Delmas@aol.com
http://www.welovewatches.com
Buys and sells quality vintage wrist watches.

Matthew Bain
Senzatempo
1655 Meridian Ave.
Miami Beach, FL 33139
ph: 305-534-5588
fax: 305-534-4545
matt@watchcommander.com
http://www.watchcommander.com
Specializes in vintage watches: Patek Philippe, Rolex, Cartier, Omega; all brands, new or old.

Timothy Haines
Got the Time?
405 Lafayette Ave.
Cincinnati, OH 45220
ph: 513-559-1405
fax: 513-651-0860
relostrat1@aol.com
http://members.aol.com/ReyneH
Buying men's wrist watches; vintage and new; Rolex, Patek, Universal Geneva, Breitling Chronographs, Doctors watches, etc.; please call or fax list of items for sale.

Girard Sensoli
Girards Vintage Watches
217 W. Main
Brighton, MI 48116
ph: 810-220-0011
fax: 810-220-0012
info@girards.com
http://girards.com
Watch collector, dealer repairer and watch show promoter for over 20 years; Rolex to Bulova; has an active Web site selling watches; also organizes watch and collectibles shows, also listed on his Web site.

Bruce Shawkey
Watch Store, The
P.O. Box 74
Evansville, WI 53536
ph: 608-882-4563
fax: 608-882-4563
brtime@inwave.com
http://www.thewatchstore.com
Buys, sells, consigns vintage watches; in business since 1989 offering medium- to high-grade watches.

Don Meyer
Vintage Timepieces Worldwide
12900 Preston Rd., Ste. 500
Dallas, TX 75230
ph: 972-392-4281 or 800-833-3159
donmeyeratvtw@aol.com
Buying vintage and modern Rolex, Patek, Vacheron, Breitling, Cartier, LeCoultre and any high grade Swiss watches.

Armand Gandara
Armand's Timeless Treasures, L.L.C.
P.O. Box 12752
Scottsdale, AZ 85267-2752
ph: 480-443-1310
fax: 480-948-2614
armand@armands-watches.com
http://www.armands-watches.com
Buys, sells, trades wrist watches, travel clocks, signs, wrist watch parts, movements and dials by Audemars Piguet, Boucheron, Breitling, Breuget, Cartier, Hamilton, Heuer, IWC, Jaeger LeCoultre, Longines, Patek Philippe, and others.

Internet Resources

TimeBeat.com
500 Fifth Ave., Ste. 215
New York, NY 10110
ph: 877-533-9778
fax: 212-730-5608
info@timebeat.com
http://www.watchzone.net
Worldwide community for wrist watch collectors and enthusiasts; sales, chat, watch reviews, watch auctions, etc.

Periodicals

Magazine: International Wristwatch
979 Summer St.
Stamford, CT 06905
ph: 203-352-1819 or 800-935-6171
fax: 203-352-1820
gary@internationalwristwatch.com
http://www.internationalwristwatch.com
A glossy magazine full of auction

reports, ads, articles about old and new wrist watches.

Bruce Shawkey
Newsletter: Vintage Wrist Watch Report
P.O. Box 74
Evansville, WI 53536
ph: 608-882-4563
fax: 608-882-4563
brtime@inwave.com
http://www.thewatchstore.com
Monthly newsletter.

WATER SPRINKLERS

(see CAST IRON ITEMS; CLOTHES SPRINKLERS; IRONS, Pressing)

WATKINS COMPANY

Clubs/Associations

Rose Weideman
Watkins Collectors Club
Newsletter: WCC Newsletter
Rt. 4 Box 161
Winona, MN 55987
rosew@hbci.com
For collectors of items, packaging and printed material made and distributed by the Watkins Company of Winona, MN.

WEANERS

Calf & Cow

(see also FARM COLLECTIBLES)

Collectors

Robert Rauhauser
P.O. Box 324
Thomasville, PA 17364-0324
ph: 717-792-0278
Wants calf and cow weaners; also hand milking machines.

WEAPONS

(see NATIVE AMERICAN, Tomahawks; ARMS & ARMOR; CIVIL WAR ARTIFACTS; EDGED WEAPONS; FIREARMS; KNIVES; MILITARIA; POWDER HORNS; SWORDS; TARGET SHOOTING MEMORABILIA)

WEATHERVANES

(see FOLK ART; LIGHTNING PROTECTION COLLECTIBLES)

WEAVING EQUIPMENT

(see COVERLETS; SPINNING WHEELS; TEXTILES)

WEDDING COLLECTIBLES

(see BRIDAL COLLECTIBLES)

WESTERN AMERICANA

(see also NATIVE AMERICAN; ART, Western; BARBED WIRE; BOTTLES, Western Whiskey; COWBOY HEROES; ANIMAL COLLECTIBLES, Horses; LAW ENFORCEMENT MEMORABILIA, Police & Sheriff; LEATHER; OUTLAWS & LAWMEN; PAPER COLLECTIBLES, Western; SADDLES)

Appraisers

Alvin O. Turner, ISA
Historical/Museum Services
115 N. Lazy Lane
Ada, OK 74820
ph: 580-436-5640
aoturner@adacomp.net
Regional specialist, collector and appraiser specializing in regional materials from Oklahoma and the American West.

Pierre G. Bovis
Bovis Primitive Arts
P.O. Box 5529
Santa Fe, NM 87502
ph: 505-989-1339 or 505-577-7992
fax: 505-989-1339
louberlugan@earthlink.net
http://www.bovisprimitivearts.com
Buy, sells, appraises cowboy memorabilia, primitive arts, American Indian arts, Napoleonic artifacts; also Polynesian, Hawaiian, New Guinea, Pacific Islands and African art including Shaman items, weapons, fine carvings.

Phil Moerschell
Western Collectables
P.O. Box 21
Bend, OR 97709
ph: 541-923-2140
fax: 541-923-9894
phm3@westerncollectables.com
http://www.westerncollectables.com
Collector, appraiser of Western Americana: cowboy spurs, bits and chaps, Indian baskets, beadwork, etc.

Brill Lee
Brill Lee Appraisal Services
P.O. Box 244
Bellevue, WA 98009-0244
ph: 425-885-4518
fax: 425-895-1022
brilllee@hotmail.com
Has collected, bought, sold vintage photography and art of Native Americans, Indian War soldiers, Western cowboy hats, boots, scarves, Western & military spurs, horse bits, horsehair items, and related cowboy gear for over 30 years.

Auction Services

High Noon
9929 Venice Blvd.
Los Angeles, CA 90034-5111
ph: 310-202-9010
Conducts periodic auctions of authentic cowboy and gunfighter memorabilia.

Clubs/Associations

Alvin G. Davis
American Cowboy Culture Association
4124 62nd Dr.
Lubbock, TX 79413-5116
ph: 806-795-2455
fax: 806-795-4749
adavis@cowboy.org
http://www.cowboy.org
Purpose is to promote all areas of cowboy culture; sponsors events relating to cowboys; sponsors National Cowboy Symposium & Celebration - held in September in Lubbock, TX.

National Bit, Spur & Saddle Collectors Association
Newsletter: NBSSCA Newsletter
P.O. Box 3035
Colorado Springs, CO 80934
ph: 719-520-9178
Members interested in western Americana memorabilia; supports shows and auctions; Western artifacts and collectibles show and auction schedules.

Collectors

Dr. Anthony Sapienza
East 106 Ridgewood Ave.
Paramus, NJ 07652
ph: 201-262-6310
fax: 201-262-3990
siringo45@aol.com
Wants Western Americana photos (CDVs, cabinet cards, real photo postcards) of famous Westerners such as outlaws, lawmen, Wild West performers; also wants photos of armed cowboys, Indians, lawmen, exhibition shooters posing with guns.

Jim Babchak
313 East 85 #4B
New York, NY 10028
ph: 212-861-1356
Wants to buy old cowboy stuff including cowboy boots, shirts, horsehair bridles, spurs, chaps, children's costumes from the 1940s and 1950s, anything Roy Rogers, Hopalong Cassidy or Gene Autry.

Lewis Leigh, Jr.
38785 Leighfield Ln.
Leesburg, VA 20175-6810
ph: 703-771-3081
fax: 703-771-1432
Wants papers, letters, journals, uniforms, weapons & flags of American soldiers, seamen, pioneers, adventurers: 1607-1919.

Howie Gross
407 Lincoln Rd.
Miami Beach, FL 33139
ph: 305-534-4757
fax: 305-538-5504
cowboyjudg@aol.com
Wants cowboy and Western memorabilia: buckles, collar tips, watch bands, cuff links, pendants, leather, etc.; Bohlin, R. Schaezlein, Soulages, McCabe, Hykes, Theis,

Garcia, Srour, Orms, Pecetti, Ellis, Silva.

Bob Maclin
1436 Lakewood
Lexington, KY 40502
ph: 859269-4450
Interested in corresponding with others who are interested in hitching posts; also horse bridles, bridle bits, boot jacks.

Ernest Hoodenpyle
P.O. Box 487
Walters, OK 73572
ph: 580-875-3080
Wants to buy old cowboy stuff: silver mounted spurs, horse hair bridles, rawhide items, gun belts, holsters, chaps, horn furniture, old catalogs, pre-1900 cowboy boots, etc.

Rusty Gilbert
P.O. Box 92
Adkins, TX 78101
ph: 210-649-3849
rusty@world-net.net
Wants highback saddles, chaps, fancy headstalls, old spurs and bits, rifle scabbards, iron stirrups, Western catalogs, cowboy items, Western style dinnerware.

George Foott
120 W. Park Ave.
Salida, CO 81201-1548
ph: 719-530-0344
sfgfco@chaffee.net
Wants to buy early Western mining memorabilia (especially Colorado): photographs, maps, promotional pamphlets, books, mining directories, miners' candleholders; also wants Old West cattle brand books, saddle catalogs, cowboy items.

Bill Mackin
1137 Washington St.
Craig, CO 81625-1613
ph: 970-824-6717 or 970-824-6360
fax: 970-824-7175
Wants pre-1940s cowboy and tack items: guns, cartridge belts, chaps, law badges, neckerchiefs, brands and brand books, spurs, knives, quirts, cowboy boots, hats, neckerchiefs, vests, cuffs, gauntlets, gun and saddle catalogs, etc.

Elizabeth Clair Flood
P.O. Box 1006
Wilson, WY 83014
Specializes in the history, fashion and gear of old time cowgirls and rodeo women.

William Manns
Cowboy Antiques
P.O. Box 6459
Santa Fe, NM 87502-6459
ph: 505-995-0102
fax: 505-995-0103
zon@nets.com
Wants to buy cowboy related antiques: pre-1930 spurs, holsters, hats, saddles, guns, catalogs, posters,

photos, chaps, wild west show items, etc.; send photos and prices; offers free identification service if LSASE is provided.

Maria E. Raymond
Plow & Pen, Inc.
P.O. Box 758
Knights Landing, CA 95645-0758
ph: 530-735-6596
mariaraymond@afes.com
Wants items relating to the history of women in the US West: 1st edition books, ephemera, photos, news articles, diaries, letters; especially interested in items relating to women of color.

Dealers

Leonard R. Kauffman
Treasure Hunt
P.O. Box 3862
Woodbridge, CT 06525-0862
ph: 203-387-8759
Wants pre-1900 western ephemera, view books, promotional booklets of towns and states; documents on mining, towns, Indians, Indian language material, emigrant guides, letters, etc.

Fred Neece, Jr.
1307 Hadtner St.
Williamsport, PA 17701-3707
ph: 570-323-4679
fax: 570-323-5293
Wants to buy old Western and cowboy items: boots, books, spurs, hats, leather cuffs, fancy shirts, chaps, holsters, art, Wells Fargo, Overland, Pony Express items, 1860s-1870s saddles, rodeo posters, etc.

Roger M. Crowley
Old West Shop
P.O. Box 5232
Vienna, WV 26105
ph: 304-295-3143
fax: 304-295-3143
oldwestshop@oldwestshop.com
http://www.oldwestshop.com
Buys and sells Western movie memorabilia, Western books, Remington prints, badges; old and new.

Gilbert Lewis
Frontier Americana
6348 Griffis Way
West Palm Beach, FL 33415
ph: 561-697-2459 or 561-655-3619
fax: 561-697-9608
shopro@bellsouth.net
http://www.frontieramericana.com
Buys and sells items from the Old West: gambling, saloon collectibles, weapons.

William Butts
Main Street Fine Books & Manuscripts
206 N. Main St.
Galena, IL 61036-2244
ph: 815-777-3749
fax: 815-777-8950
msfb@galenalink.com
http://www.wcinet.com/msfbooks
*Open shop dealing in autographs and
out-of-print books in most fields;
specializing in all aspects of American
history; book and autograph catalogs
issued regularly; member of A.B.A.A.;
author of "Sign Here" and other
autograph columns.*

Sharon Myers
J & S Oldwestern Store, Saddle Shop &
Museum
RR 1, Box 315-C-NT
Warsaw, MO 65355
ph: 660-438-2631
fax: 660-438-6517
oldwest@iland.net
http://www.jsoldwest.com
*Over 200 antique saddles, hibacks,
side-saddles, military, charro, etc.;
Admission to museum if free; also
1,300 Western collectibles for sale;
55-page catalog for $5.*

Dan Kelley
Experienced Denim
P.O. Box 239
Fayetteville, AR 72702-0239
ph: 501-444-7541 or 800-336-4694
fax: 501-521-8331
exd@edenim.com
http://www.edenim.com
*Wants Levis, denim jackets; also
fabrics, textiles, bedspreads, '40s-'50s
fancy cowboy boots and belts,
tablecloths with Western or Mexican
theme; will consider any condition;
send SASE for free list of items
wanted.*

Early West, The
P.O. Box 9292
College Station, TX 77842-9292
ph: 800-245-5841 or 409-775-6047
fax: 979-764-7758
*Buys, sells, trades Western American
including documents, photos, in-print
and out-of-print books, paper
ephemera; catalog includes items
relating to lawmen, cowboys, Indians,
Texans, soldiers, explorers, and
mountain men.*

Kurt House
Cowboy Collectibles
218 Country Wood
San Antonio, TX 78216-1607
ph: 210-490-2433
fax: 210-490-3433
cowboyhous@aol.com
*Life Member of National Bit, Spur,
Saddle Collectors Assoc.; author of
several articles on cowboy memorabilia; buys/sells all sorts of cowboy
items; author of "Hand Forged for
Texas Cowboys," a book on spur
maker Joe Bianci of TX.*

Paul E. Mix
P.O. Box 180182
Austin, TX 78718-0182
ph: 512-836-8005
fax: 512-835-1708
*Buys and sells Western Americana:
books on antique barbed wire,
Western Arcade cards, Tom Mix
memorabilia, pin-back buttons,
photos, branding irons, belt buckles;
catalog for $3, refundable with first
purchase.*

Bill Overly
P.P. Box 1394
Loveland, CO 80539
ph: 970-622-9612
*Web site provides links to Cowboy
art, poetry and rodeo; also has
available free advertising section for
sale or wanted to buy western art and
memorabilia.*

Lee Jacobs
P.O. Box 3098
Colorado Springs, CO 80934-3098
ph: 719-473-7101
*Buys, sells on commission high quality
cowboy collectibles; some appraisals
accepted; offers finders fee.*

John Hartman
Hartman's Mercantile
17897 Hwy. 160
Durango, CO 81301
ph: 970-247-5589
fax: 970-259-6020
*Buys and sells antique Frontier
memorabilia, Native American Indian
items, Cowboy items; also Ethnic
Rarities from around the world.*

Brian Lebel
Old West Antiques & Cowboy
Collectibles
1215 Sheridan Ave.
Cody, WY 82414-3629
ph: 307-587-9014
fax: 307-587-5393
oldwest@cody.wtp.net
http://www.codyoldwest.com
*Issues three catalogs per year of
western Americana collectibles:
saddles, chaps, spurs, bridles, etc.;
also auction news, ads.*

William L. King
Bozeman Trail Gallery
190 N. Main
Sheridan, WY 82801
ph: 307-672-3928
btg@bozemantrailgallery.com
http://www.bozemantrailgallery.com
*Buys, sells, appraises 19th-early 20th
c. Western art, especially by Joe
DeYong, E.W. Gollings, Hans
Kleiber; also wants No. Plains Indian
beadwork and related items, cowboy
equipment, Colt Bisley's, mod. 1885
Remington pistols.*

Mary Schmitt
Cayuse Western Americana
P.O. Box 1006
255 North Glenwood Ave.
Jackson, WY 83001
ph: 800-405-4096 or 307-739-1940
info@cayusewa.com
http://www.cayusewa.com
*Bits, spurs, bridles, saddles, gun
leather, ropes, books, skirts, chaps,
cuffs, gauntlets, hats, Indian
beadwork, Indian carvings, Indian
dolls.*

Sam Kennedy
Cisco's
212 N. 4th St.
Coeur d'Alene, ID 83814
ph: 208-769-7575
*Buys and sells Western Americana
including spurs, chaps, saddles, etc.*

Mike Turner
Cowboy Collectibles
912 W. Maple
Mapleton, UT 84664
ph: 801-489-9805
turnmkfox@cs.com
*Buys and sells Western Americana:
spurs, bits, leather, chaps, US
Cavalry, etc.*

Tyrone Campbell
Tyrone D. Campbell Gallery
8900 E. Pinnacle Peak Rd., B-2
Scottsdale, AZ 85255
ph: 480-502-8899 or 602-741-4505
fax: 480-502-4795
tyronecampbell@qwest.net
*Buys and sells antique American
Indian weavings: Navajo, Pueblo and
Hispanic weavings and folk art;
specializes in appraising collections,
consultations, and research of 19th &
20th C. Navajo weavings.*

Old West Cowboy Store
427 E. Allen St.
P.O. Box 129
Tombstone, AZ 85638
ph: 520-457-3166
cowboystore@theriver.com
http://www.oldwestcowboystore.com
*Specializing in Western and cowboy
memorabilia: cowboy gear, holsters,
spurs, Old West star badges, old
saddles, etc.*

Terry Schurmeier
Cowboys & Indians Antiques
4000 Central SE
Albuquerque, NM 87108
ph: 505-255-4054 or 505-255-5775
fax: 505-255-1730
cowgirls@rt66.com
http://www.cowboysandindiansnm.com
*Carries large inventory of pre-1940s
Native American pottery, baskets,
beadwork, jewelry, textiles; antique
devotional art, art of the Old West;
also Old West, Spanish Colonial, old
pawn & Mexican jewelry; buy, sell,
trade, appraise.*

Michael Kokin
Sherwoods Spirit of America
130 Lincoln Ave.
Santa Fe, NM 87501
ph: 505-988-1776
fax: 505-992-1812
americanwest1776@aol.com
http://www.sherwoodspirit.com
*Collector, dealer, expert, specializes
in exceptional and important American
history antiquities and collectibles:
antique guns, Native American, Civil
War, cowboy and Western memorabilia.*

Pierre G. Bovis
Bovis Primitive Arts
P.O. Box 5529
Santa Fe, NM 87502
ph: 505-989-1339 or 505-577-7992
fax: 505-989-1339
louberlugan@earthlink.net
http://www.bovisprimitivearts.com
*Buy, sells, appraises cowboy
memorabilia, primitive arts, American
Indian arts, Napoleonic artifacts; also
Polynesian, Hawaiian, New Guinea,
Pacific Islands and African art
including Shaman items, weapons,
fine carvings.*

High Noon
9929 Venice Blvd.
Los Angeles, CA 90034-5111
ph: 310-202-9010
*Wants to buy cowboy collectibles:
bits, spurs, chaps, braided horsehair,
silver saddles, saddle bags, cuffs, tack
catalogs, etc.*

Roger V. Baker
P.O. Box 620417
Redwood City, CA 94062-0417
ph: 650-851-7188
fax: 650-851-7188
*Buys, collects and sells Western
Americana: American Indian items,
cowboy paraphernalia, firearms,
knives, saloon antiques, gold rush,
mining and other related items.*

Chuck Wagon Antiques
P.O. Box 929
Morgan Hill, CA 95038
fax: 408-779-5701
cowboy@cowboygear.com
http://www.cowboygear.com
*Buys and sells cowboy memorabilia
and Western Americana: spurs, bits,
chaps, cuffs, prints, books, rawhide
and horsehair items, tack, branding
irons, saddle bags.*

Hank Clark
Argent Express
P.O. Box 812
Waterford, CA 95386-0812
ph: 209-874-2640
fax: 209-874-5750
conchosmith@hotmail.com
*Buys/sells Western American paper,
books, weapons, autographs, vintage
coins, photographs, gold &
silversmithing, conchos & buttons;
anything Western.*

Experts

Robert W.D. Ball
26 Byron Dr.
Avon, CT 06001-4507
Author of "Cowboy Collectibles and Western Memorabilia," and "Western Memorabilia and Collectibles."

Jay C. Lyndes
P.O. Box 31733
Billings, MT 59107-1733
ph: 406-652-7200 or 406-252-0237
fax: 406-652-8277
cowboymt@vcn.com
Wants to buy Western Americana including spurs, chaps, saddles, bridles, holsters, cartridge belts, vintage cowboy and Indian photos; also wants Montana books, documents and photos.

Bill Mackin
1137 Washington St.
Craig, CO 81625-1613
ph: 970-824-6717 or 970-824-6360
fax: 970-824-7175
Author of "Cowboy and Gunfighter Collectibles" price guide; sells books for Old West collectors by mail and at shows; over 45 years collecting; wants nice gun leather and cowboy gear; appraises, consults, lectures.

Warren Anderson
America West Archives
P.O. Box 100
Cedar City, UT 84721-0100
ph: 435-586-9497 or 435-586-7323
awa@netutah.com
http://www.americawestarchives.com
Buys and sells paper Americana associated with the Western US: old documents, letters, photos, stocks, maps, autographs, prints, etc.; author of "Owning Western History."

Museums/Libraries

Rockwell Museum, The
111 Cedar St.
Corning, NY 14830
ph: 607-937-5386
fax: 607-974-4536
info@rockwellmuseum.org
http://stny.lrun.com/rockwellmuseum
Collections include the finest in traditional and contemporary America Western and Native American art: paintings, sculpture, and more; considered by many to be "The Best of the West in the East."

Randy Donley
Donley's Wild West Town & Museum
8512 S. Union Rd.
Union, IL 60180-9661
ph: 815-923-9000
fax: 815-923-2253
mdonley@dls.net
http://www.wildwesttown.com
Large display of all kinds of Americana, especially from the Wild West.

Pony Express Museum
914 Penn St.
Saint Joseph, MO 64503
ph: 816-279-5059 or 800-530-5930
fax: 816-233-9370
Documents the history of the Pony Express.

National Cowgirl Hall of Fame & Western Heritage Center
1720 Gendy St.
Fort Worth, TX 76107
ph: 817-336-4475
fax: 817-336-2470
http://www.cowgirl.net
Only museum in the world dedicated to honoring women of the American West who have displayed extraordinary courage and pioneer spirit in their trail blazing efforts.

National Ranching Heritage Center, The
3121 Fourth St.
Lubbock, TX 79409-3200
ph: 806-742-0498
Jim.Pfluger@ttu.edu
http://www.ttu.edu/
RanchingHeritageCenter
Shows the evolution of ranching from the early trail driver's one room cabin (c. 1838) to a prosperous rancher's stylish Victorian house (c. 1909).

Museum of Northwest Colorado
590 Yampa St.
Craig, CO 81625-2612
ph: 970-824-6360
fax: 970-824-7175
musnwco@museumnwco.org
http://www.museumnwco.org
One of the world's most extensive collections of fine antique cowboy gear, frontier guns and gun leather, spurs, badges, saddles, chaps, etc.; a public county museum in historic state armory site; free admission.

Buffalo Bill Historical Center
Journal: Points West
720 Sheridan Ave.
Cody, WY 82414
ph: 307-587-4771
fax: 307-587-5714
janj@bbhc.org
http://www.bbhc.org
Dedicated to the study of the American West; four museums under one roof including the history of William F. Cody; large collection of personal belongings, photos and documents; offers no appraisal or evaluation services.

Autry Museum of Western Heritage
Magazine: Spur
4700 Western Heritage Way
Los Angeles, CA 90027-1462
ph: 323-667-2000
fax: 323-660-5721
tbailey@autry-museum.org
http://www.autry-museum.org
Explores, collects, and preserves objects and art relating to the mythology and history of the American West.

Wells Fargo Bank History Museum
333 S. Grand Ave.
Los Angeles, CA 90071-1504
ph: 213-253-7166
wfh@artmachine.com
http://www.wellsfargohistory.com/
museums
Documents the history of Wells Fargo: stories, Western fine art, documents, treasure boxes, stagecoaches, artifacts, early photos, gold coins, mining tools, balance scales, working telegraphs, and more.

Periodicals

PRIMEDIA Enthusiast Group
Magazine: Wild West
741 Miller Dr., SE, Ste. D-2
Leesburg, VA 20175
ph: 703-779-8318
fax: 703-779-8310
david.masini@primedia.com
http://www.thehistorynet.com/WildWest
A bi-monthly magazine covering America's westward expansion - major events, interesting characters, and little-known incidents, as well as Western art, artifacts, and collectibles.

Bobby Newton
Newspaper: Rope Burns
P.O. Box 35
Gene Autry, OK 73436-0035
ph: 405-389-5350
Largest listing of western events: bit-spur-collectible shows & auctions, rodeos, roundups, western trade & trappings, etc.

Reid Slaughter
Magazine: Cowboys & Indians
8214 Westchester Dr., Ste. 800
Dallas, TX 75225
ph: 972-750-8222 or 800-982-5370
fax: 972-750-4522
mail@cowboysindians.com
http://www.cowboysindians.com
The premier magazine of the West.

Sabot Publishing
Magazine: Southwest Art
5444 Westheimer, Ste. 1440
Houston, TX 77056
ph: 713-296-7900
fax: 713-850-1314
southwestart@southwestart.com
http://www.southwestart.com
The best in contemporary Western, traditional, Native American and impressionist artists; published monthly.

Magazine: American Cowboy
P.O. Box 54555
Boulder, CO 80322-4555
ph: 800-297-6933 or 850-682-7644
fax: 307-672-7766
editor@cowboy.com
http://www.americancowboy.com
The magazine of Western living: profiles of famous country-western singers, rodeo stars, artists, cowboys; coverage of today's western art & collectibles; auction results, history,

travel, cowboy poetry, etc.; bi-monthly.

Magazine: Western Horseman
P.O. Box 7980
Colorado Springs, CO 80933
ph: 719-633-5524
fax: 719-633-1392
edit@westernhorseman.com
http://www.westernhorseman.com
Monthly magazine focusing on western horsemanship and lifestyle.

Magazine: American Cowboy Poet Magazine
P.O. Box 326
Eagle, ID 83616
ph: 208-888-9838
fax: 208-887-2986
acpm@cowboyrudy.com
http://www.cowboyfudy.com/acpm.htm
Focusing on true cowboy music and poetry; articles, poetry, events, music offered by those who live the life and not by Hollywood or Nashville entertainers; great modern day cowboy artists featured in each issue.

Newspaper: Chronicle of the Old West
P.O. Box 2859
Show Low, AZ 85902
ph: 520-532-2875
fax: 520-532-5170
info@chronicleoftheoldwest.com
http://www.chronicleoftheoldwest.com
A monthly newspaper for Old West enthusiasts: historically accurate articles, reprints from 1800s newspapers and magazines, Old West events and activities.

William Manns
Newsletter: Cowboy Guide
P.O. Box 6459
Santa Fe, NM 87502-6459
ph: 505-995-0102
fax: 505-995-0103
zon@nets.com
Send SASE for Cowboy Guide which contains information about cowboy collectibles, upcoming cowboy auctions and shows, plus a list of dealers, museums and publications.

101 Ranch

Clubs/Associations

Ruth & Jerry Murphey
101 Ranch Collectors
10701 Timbergrove Lane
Corpus Christi, TX 78410
ph: 361-241-2213
fax: 361-241-6908
jmurphey1@aol.com
101 Ranch memorabilia collectors; for many years the 101 Ranch had a traveling wild west show; stars who worked on the ranch or appeared in the show included Buffalo Bill, Tom Mix, Will Rogers, Hoot Gibson, Buck Jones and many more.

Annie Oakley

(see also WESTERN AMERICANA, Buffalo Bill; WESTERN AMERICANA, Wild West Show)

Dealers

Vivian & James Karsnitz
1428 Jerry Lane
Manheim, PA 17545-9353
ph: 717-665-4202
Buys and sells anything Annie Oakley.

Bits

Collectors

Jean Gayle
Three Horses
7403 Blaine Rd.
Aberdeen, WA 98520-7409
ph: 360-533-3490
jgayle@techline.com
http://www.techline.com/~jgayle
*Buying fancy, ornamental, military,
iron horse bits; also wants to buy
bridle rosettes and old tack catalogs.*

Boots

Collectors

Ed Soost
1331 Weverton Rd.
Knoxville, MD 21758
ph: 301-694-7325
Wants to buy vintage Western boots.

Internet Resources

Jennifer June
Cowboy Boot Web Page, The
190 El Cerrito Plaza, Ste. 273
El Cerrito, CA 94530
ph: 510-435-5863
fax: 510-601-5852
newboots@dimlights.com
http://www.dimlights.com
*Boot collector and expert maintains a
Web site described as a "Tribute to
Cowboy Boots" and the folks who
make, wear, and admire them; updated
monthly; custom makers, events,
history, photos.*

Buffalo Bill

(see also WESTERN AMERICANA,
Annie Oakley; WESTERN
AMERICANA, Wild West Show)

Collectors

Michael Del Castello
23842 Cabot Blvd.
Hayward, CA 94545-1661
ph: 510-265-3506 or 510-851-3707
fax: 510-781-3468
mdc@mdcvacuum.com
http://www.wfcody.com
*Wants to buy Buffalo Bill Cody items:
posters, programs, photographs and
artifacts relating to Buffalo Bill, Wild
West Show memorabilia, Annie
Oakley, Wells Fargo.*

Museums/Libraries

Buffalo Bill Cody Museum Inc.
P.O. Box 284
LeClaire, IA 52753
ph: 319-289-5580
*LeClaire is the birthplace of Buffalo
Bill.*

Buffalo Bill Memorial Museum
987 1/2 Lookout Mountain Rd.
Golden, CO 80401
ph: 303-526-0747
pahaskateepee@aol.com
http://www.buffalobill.org

Buffalo Bill Historical Center
Journal: Points West
720 Sheridan Ave.
Cody, WY 82414
ph: 307-587-4771
fax: 307-587-5714
janj@bbhc.org
http://www.bbhc.org
*Dedicated to the study of the American
West; four museums under one roof
including the history of William F.
Cody; large collection of personal
belongings, photos and documents;
offers no appraisal or evaluation
services.*

Holsters

Repro. Sources

Old West Reproductions
446 Florence South Loop
Florence, MT 59833
ph: 406-273-2615
fax: 406-273-2615
rick@oldwestreproductions.com
http://www.oldwestreproductions.com
*Faithful reproductions of 1849-1900
holsters, cartridge belts, saddles and
more; send $3 for catalog; also
seeking to buy original Western
memorabilia, i.e., 1849-1900 holsters,
cartridge belts, wrist cuffs, etc.*

Photographs

Collectors

Tim Gordon, ISA
P.O. Box 5813
2717 Highland Dr.
Missoula, MT 59802
ph: 406-728-1812 or 888-720-1812
timbgordon@aol.com
http://www.xntrx.com
*Wants early photos of the West:
saloon interiors, cowboys, Indians,
lawmen, hangings, etc.; also offers
appraisal service.*

John McWilliams
P.O. Box 3655
Los Altos, CA 94024
ph: 650-949-2615
jmcwilliam@aol.com
*Long time collector of daguerreotypes
and early photographs of the
American West: wants images of
armed civilians, Texans, California
Gold Rush; especially wants images
showing large brimmed hats,
buckskins, pistols, and knives.*

Dealers

L.R. Kauffman
Treasure Hunt
P.O. Box 3862
Woodbridge, CT 06525-0862
ph: 203-387-8759
Wants pre-1900 western photos or

*stereo views of historical interest;
special wants include Watkins,
Jackson, Houseworth; stereos and
views of towns, streets, mining, shops,
etc. of 19th century Western America.*

Southwest

Appraisers

Joan Caballero, ISA
Joan Caballero Appraisals
P.O. Box 822
Santa Fe, NM 87504
ph: 505-982-8148
fax: 505-982-7048
joancaballero@msn.com
*Specializes in the appraisal of Native
American arts (antique & contemporary), New Mexican Hispanic arts,
and Southwest Regional fine arts
(Taos and Santa Fe schools and living
artists).*

Collectors

John W. Barry
Indian Rock Arts
P.O. Box 583
Davis, CA 95617-0583
ph: 530-758-2561
*Wants traditional Pueblo pottery
paintings, prints, photos; books on
Southwest Tribes & Pueblos,
Southwest archaeology, exploration
and surveys of the West, Yellowstone,
Grand Canyon, Yosemite tourism,
photographs, old tourist items.*

Dealers

Peter Eller, ISA
Peter Eller Gallery & Appraisers
206 Dartmouth
Albuquerque, NM 87106
ph: 505-268-7437
fax: 505-268-6442
pelgal@nmia.com
http://www.peterellergallery.com
*Specializes in works by Albuquerque
artists and minor New Mexico artists,
traditional and modernist, 1925-1965,
for beginning and intermediate
collectors; appraising art, antiques,
Spanish Colonial, religious and SW
Indian artifacts.*

Texas Rangers

Collectors

John McWilliams
P.O. Box 3655
Los Altos, CA 94024
ph: 650-949-2615
jmcwilliam@aol.com
*Long time collector of Texas Ranger
history and memorabilia; primarily
interested in original photographs and
documents from the period 1840 to
1910, but will consider all items
relating to Texas Ranger history.*

Museums/Libraries

Texas Ranger Hall of Fame & Museum
P.O. Box 2570
Waco, TX 76702-2570
ph: 254-750-8631
fax: 254-750-8629
bjohnson@eramp.net
http://www.texasranger.org
*Nonprofit and educational museum
and Hall of Fame dedicated to the
history of the Texas Rangers; artifact
collections, research library, and
audio-visual presentations.*

Wells Fargo

Collectors

Dennis Kurlander
P.O. Box 371
Santa Rosa, CA 95402
ph: 707-838-3800 or 707-584-1854
fax: 707-838-1086
dwkfargo@aol.com
*Wants "Wells Fargo Express" items,
or items from any other "Express"
Company such as Adams, American,
National, Pacific, or any other
obscure Express companies; collecting
for over 35 years.*

Wild West Show

(see also WESTERN AMERICANA,
Annie Oakley; WESTERN
AMERICANA, Buffalo Bill)

Auction Services

Kurt R. Krueger
Krueger Auctions
P.O. Box 275
Iola, WI 54945-0275
ph: 715-445-3845
fax: 715-445-4100
*Conducts periodic specialized auctions
of circus and Wild West Show
memorabilia.*

Collectors

Dr. Anthony Sapienza
East 106 Ridgewood Ave.
Paramus, NJ 07652
ph: 201-262-6310
fax: 201-262-3990
siringo45@aol.com
*Serious collector wants Wild West
Show memorabilia: posters,
programs, photographs, souvenir
targets, pin-backs, etc.; especially
dealing with trick shooters such as
Annie Oakley, Capt. Bogardus, Doc
Carver, Lillian Smith (Princess
Wenona).*

William Manns
Cowboy Antiques
P.O. Box 6459
Santa Fe, NM 87502-6459
ph: 505-995-0102
fax: 505-995-0103
zon@nets.com
*Wants to buy cowboy related antiques:
pre-1930 spurs, holsters, hats,
saddles, guns, catalogs, posters,
photos, chaps, wild west show items,
etc.; send photos and prices; offers*

free identification service if LSASE is provided.

Michael Del Castello
23842 Cabot Blvd.
Hayward, CA 94545-1661
ph: 510-265-3506 or 510-851-3707
fax: 510-781-3468
mdc@mdcvacuum.com
http://www.wfcody.com
Wants to buy Buffalo Bill Cody items: posters, programs, photographs and artifacts relating to Buffalo Bill, Wild West Show memorabilia, Annie Oakley, Wells Fargo.

Dealers

Art Sowin
Pahaska Books
8436 Samra Dr.
Canoga Park, CA 91304-3214
ph: 818-346-2171
pahaska@pacbell.net
Wants Wild West Show memorabilia: Buffalo Bill, Annie Oakley, Wild West Show books, advertising, photos, programs, tickets, passes, souvenir items, etc.

WHALING

(see also ENDANGERED SPECIES; NAUTICAL ANTIQUES; SCRIMSHAW)

Appraisers

Sara Conklin, ISA
Nautical Appraisals
P.O. Box 30203
Blairsden, CA 96103
ph: 415-467-6249 or 800-464-4208
fax: 415-467-6249
sconklin2@pngusa.net
http://home.earthlink.net/~sconklin2
Managed the collections of the National Maritime Museum in San Francisco for ten years and is an expert in appraising whaling objects and scrimshaw.

Experts

Sara Conklin, ISA
Nautical Appraisals
P.O. Box 30203
Blairsden, CA 96103
ph: 415-467-6249 or 800-464-4208
fax: 415-467-6249
sconklin2@pngusa.net
http://home.earthlink.net/~sconklin2
Managed the collections of the National Maritime Museum in San Francisco for ten years and is an expert in appraising whaling objects and scrimshaw.

Museums/Libraries

New Bedford Whaling Museum
18 Johnny Cake Hill
New Bedford, MA 02740-6317
ph: 508-997-0046
fax: 508-994-4350
abrengle@whalingmuseum.org
http://www.whalingmuseum.org
A whaling and local historical museum.

Cold Spring Harbor Whaling Museum
279 Main St.
P.O. Box 25
Cold Spring Harbor, NY 11724
ph: 631-367-3418
fax: 631-692-7037
info@cshwhalingmuseum.org
http://www.cshwhalingmuseum.org
A museum of local whaling history which is accredited by The American Association of Museums; extensive collections of scrimshaw and whalecraft, and archival materials relating to the maritime history of Cold Spring Harbor & LI North Shore.

Sag Harbor Whaling & Historical Museum
Main St.
P.O. Box 1327
Sag Harbor, NY 11963
ph: 516-725-0770
Large museum featuring 18th and 19th century whaling and other local artifacts: instruments, scrimshaw, ship models, tools, paintings.

San Francisco Maritime National Historical Park, Museum & Library
Bldg. E, Fort Mason Center
San Francisco, CA 94123
ph: 415-556-9870 or 415-556-9871
fax: 415-556-3540
safr_maritime_library@nps.gov
http://www.nps.gov/safr/local/lib/libtop.html

WHEEL TOYS

(see BICYCLES & RELATED MEMORABILIA; RIDING TOYS)

WHISKEY INDUSTRY ITEMS

(see also ADVERTISING COLLECTIBLES; DECANTERS, Figural Whiskey; CERAMICS [ENGLISH], Whisky Pitchers; GLASSES; PROHIBITION ITEMS; SALOON & BAR COLLECTIBLES)

Clubs/Associations

Deborah & Paul Inglis
Pub Jug/Whiskey Pitcher Collectors
P.O. Box 165
South Hadley, MA 01075-0165
ph: 413-533-0419
fax: 413-533-0419
bootleggers.nostalgia@worldnet.att.net
Members interested in buying, selling

and trading of whiskey pitchers/pub jugs and related items.

Collectors

Mike Strother
4677 Spring Creek Dr.
Lexington, KY 40515
ph: 859-272-6789
mstrother@att.net
Tax stamps, labels, letters & envelopes, documents, prohibition and anti-saloon papers, postcards (not drunks), licenses, etc.; wants almost anything paper dealing or related to the distilling industry.

Ronald Elfring
De Planck 7 E.
St. Martens-Voeren, 3790 Belgium
ph: 003 243 810603
fax: 003 1433 500485
elfringvanderheijden@belgacom.net
Wants whiskey industry related items: statues with whiskey brand, water pitchers, trays, any memorabilia related to whiskey distilleries; wants single items or entire collections.

Museums/Libraries

Seagram Museum Library, University of Waterloo
200 University Ave. West
Waterloo, Ontario N2L 3G1 Canada
ph: 519-888-4567
fax: 519-884-8009
lhasting@library.uwaterloo.ca
http://library.uwaterloo.ca/seagrams
Contains a large selection of documents donated by the Seagram Museum.

Jack Daniels

Collectors

Claude Bellar
1750 Keyes Rd.
Greenbrier, TN 37073
ph: 615-643-0290
fax: 615-643-0290
cbellar@aol.com

Old Crow

Collectors

Judith & Bob Walthall
P.O. Box 4465
Huntsville, AL 35815-4465
ph: 256-881-9198
Wants to buy Old Crow Whiskey items.

WHISTLERS

(see MUSIC BOXES, Birds & Bird Boxes [Singing])

WHISTLES

(see HORNS & WHISTLES)

WHITE HOUSE COLLECTIBLES

(see also PERSONALITIES [HISTORICAL]; POLITICAL COLLECTIBLES)

Clubs/Associations

White House Historical Association
c/o White House Visitor Center
1450 Pennsylvania Ave. NW
Washington, DC 20004-1005
ph: 800-717-1450 or 202-456-7041
webmaster@whha.org
http://www.whitehousehistory.org
The association was founded in 1961 as a charitable nonprofit institution for the purpose of enhancing the understanding, appreciation and enjoyment of the White House.

Dealers

H. Joseph Levine
Presidential Coin & Antique Co. Inc.
6550-I Little River Turnpike
Alexandria, VA 22312
ph: 703-354-5454
fax: 703-914-0547
JLevine968@aol.com
Wants include Presidential jewelry, Christmas cards, pens and White House glass, china, and paper items; also wants any item connected with Presidential inaugurations such as medals, ribbons, invitations, programs, buttons, etc.

China

Repro. Sources

United States Historical Society
25 E. Main St.
Richmond, VA 23219
ph: 804-648-4736 or 800-788-4478
fax: 804-648-0002
dolls@ushsdolls.com
http://www.ushsdolls.com

WICKER

Appraisers

Richard Saunders
894 Laurel Ave.
Pacific Grove, CA 93950
ph: 831-372-1273
fax: 831-372-7130
benfrank@redshift.com
Wicker expert and appraiser; author of five books and numerous articles on antique wicker.

Dealers

Antique Wicker
P.O. Box 69
Bernard, ME 04612
ph: 207-244-3983
fax: 207-244-7088
info@antiquewicker.com
http://www.antiquewicker.com
Over 28 years in the wicker business; 500 to 1,000 pieces in stock.

Gert Patterson
Wicker Repair by Gert Patterson
435 Comstock Lane N
Minneapolis, MN 55447-3656
ph: 763-476-2057 or 763-449-9505
fax: 763-449-9505
dgpebml@isd.net
Over 20 years experience in selling, buying and repairing all types of antique wicker furniture, lamps, buggies and other wicker items.

Cathryn Peters
Wicker Woman, The
E-zine: Wicker Woman's Weavings
1250 Hwy 25
Angora, MN 55703
ph: 218-666-6189
info@wickerwoman.com
http://www.wickerwoman.com
Wicker dealer and expert since 1975, specializing in the sale and restoration of wicker, cane and rush furniture; available to lecture, teach and write on antique wicker and seat weaving; online e-zine on wicker repair, weaving, basketry.

Experts

Richard Saunders
894 Laurel Ave.
Pacific Grove, CA 93950
ph: 831-372-1273
fax: 831-372-7130
benfrank@redshift.com
Wicker expert and appraiser; author of five books and numerous articles on antique wicker.

Repair Services

Veterans Chair Caning & Repair
442 10th Ave.
New York, NY 10001
ph: 212-564-4560
fax: 212-564-4560
info@veteranscaning.com
http://www.veteranscaning.com
Antique wicker restoration and repair; 13 years experience, by the piece or by the load; all expert work; no covering up.

Gert Patterson
Wicker Repair by Gert Patterson
435 Comstock Lane N
Minneapolis, MN 55447-3656
ph: 763-476-2057 or 763-449-9505
fax: 763-449-9505
dgpebml@isd.net
Over 20 years experience in selling, buying and repairing all types of antique wicker furniture, lamps, buggies and other wicker items.

Cathryn Peters
Wicker Woman, The
E-zine: Wicker Woman's Weavings
1250 Hwy 25
Angora, MN 55703
ph: 218-666-6189
info@wickerwoman.com
http://www.wickerwoman.com
Professional quality wicker furniture & seat weaving for over 26 years; specializing in all types of seat weaving: machine and hand cane, natural and paper rush, splint, seagrass, and cord; dealer, teacher, speaker, writer on wicker.

Gene & Deb Ruelle
Ruelle's
526 S. Broadway
Tyler, TX 75702
ph: 903-595-2176
fax: 903-595-1234
finishersformula@hotmail.com
http://www.ruelle.com
Offers antique furniture restorations, repairs, refinishing and appraising; also chair caning, seat weaving, rushing and wicker repair; member of Appraisers National Association.

Repro. Sources

Don Walker
Yesteryear Wicker
7616 Investment Ct.
Owings, MD 20736
ph: 410-257-1302
fax: 410-257-1306
gcp@chesapeake.net
http://www.chesapeake.net/wicker
World's only antique wicker reproduction specialist; over 13 years in business as distributors of high quality wicker reproductions.

Suppliers

Paige W. Beasley
Carolina Caning Supply
111 Fairfax Lane
Cary, NC 27513
ph: 800-346-0142 or 919-467-7773
Chair caning and repair supplies.

WIENER WERKSTATTE

(see MODERNISM)

WILDLIFE

(see ANIMAL TROPHIES; SPORTING COLLECTIBLES, Hunting & Fishing; TRAPS)

WINCHESTER COLLECTIBLES

(see also DIAMOND EDGE [SHAPLEIGH HARDWARE]; FIREARMS, Winchester; HARDWARE; KEEN KUTTER [SIMMONS HARDWARE])

Auction Services

Bob Simmons
Simmons & Company Auctioneers
40706 E. 144th St.
Richmond, MO 64085
ph: 816-776-2936 or 800-646-2936
fax: 816-470-5016
bob@simmonsauction.com
http://www.simmonsauction.com
Conducts annual specialty auctions of Winchester, Keen Kutter (E.C. Simmons Hardware) and Diamond Edge (Shapleigh Hardware)

collectibles; *has a well-established reputation for expertise and high quality merchandise.*

Clubs/Associations

Barbara Huhn, Mem.
Hardware Companies Kollectors' Klub, The
Newsletter: Winchester Keen Kutter Diamond Edge Chronicles
432 S. Gore St.
Saint Louis, MO 63119
ph: 314-968-0304
dhuhn@earthlink.net
http://www.thckk.org
A non-profit organization to serve as an interactive information distribution center for collectors of E.C. Simmons/ Keen Kutter, Winchester Store (non-gun), A.F. Shapleigh/Diamond Edge, Hibbard, and other hardware store brands.

Museums/Libraries

Shozo Kagoshima, Gen. Mngr.
Winchester Mystery House, Antique Products Museum
525 South Winchester Blvd.
San Jose, CA 95128
ph: 408-247-2000
fax: 408-247-2090
http://www.winchestermysteryhouse.com
Displays cutlery, flashlights, lawn mowers, fishing tackle, and farm tools manufactured by the Winchester Products company after WWI.

WINDMILL COLLECTIBLES

(see also FARM MACHINERY)

Collectors

Ohio Windmill & Pump, Inc.
Box 157 8389 S. Priceton Rd.
Berlin Center, OH 44401
ph: 330-547-6300
fax: 330-547-8213
Interested in anything windmill: literature, salesman samples, wooden wheel windmills, etc.

James Gress
13174 US 127
Paulding, OH 45879
ph: 419-399-5358
Wants to buy any kind of advertising or literature related to American windmills.

Dealers

Ohio Windmill & Pump Co.
Box 157 8389 S. Priceton Rd.
Berlin Center, OH 44401
ph: 330-547-6300
fax: 330-547-8213
Aermotor windmills & towers; hand pumps, cylinders & accessories; windmill books & historic literature; antique wood wheel windmills; custom fabrication & historic recreations and restorations; authentic original windmill weights.

T. Lindsay Baker
Windmill Books & Sales
P.O. Box 507
Rio Vista, TX 76093-0507
http://www.windmillersgazette.com
Always buying windmill trade catalogs, brochures, price lists, parts lists, and advertising ephemera.

Experts

T. Lindsay Baker
P.O. Box 507
Rio Vista, TX 76093-0507
http://www.windmillersgazette.com
Author of four books dealing with water-pumping windmills and the history of windmill use.

Museums/Libraries

Dalley Windmill Collection, The
E. Star Route, Box 7
Portales, NM 88130
ph: 505-356-6263 or 800-635-8036
Over 75 windmills from around the world.

Periodicals

T. Lindsay Baker
Newsletter: Windmillers' Gazette
P.O. Box 507
Rio Vista, TX 76093-0507
http://www.windmillersgazette.com
Only periodical in America devoted exclusively to windmills and wind power history; author of "A Field Guide to American Windmills."

Weights

(see also CAST IRON ITEMS)

Dealers

Doug Clemence
Treasure Chest
436 North Chicago
Salina, KS 67401-2020
ph: 785-827-9371 or 785-825-4111
Sells, sells and trades old and reproduction windmill weights.

Experts

Don Lawrence
P.O. Box 1141
Boise City, OK 73933-1141
ph: 580-544-3103
Co-author with Rick Nidey of "Windmill Weights," available from author for $17 ppd.

Richard Tucker
Argyle Antiques
P.O. Box 262
Argyle, TX 76226-0262
ph: 940-464-3752
fax: 940-464-7293
lead1234@gte.net
Buys and sells figural cast iron items: windmill weights, shooting targets, water sprinklers; no repros. or repaired items wanted.

WINES & WINE RELATED ITEMS

(see also CORKSCREWS)

Appraisers

William H. Edgerton
P.O. Box 88
Darien, CT 06820-0588
ph: 203-655-0566
fax: 203-655-8066
wedgerton@aol.com

Cris Drugan, ISA, PPS
809 White Pond Dr., Ste. D
Akron, OH 44310-2612
ph: 330-873-2513
fax: 330-867-8874
HopSing63@artserve.net
Wine collector and former chapter president of the AWS; accredited member of the International Society of Appraisers.

Auction Services

Amory Spizzirri, Client Svc.
William Doyle Galleries
175 E. 87th St.
New York, NY 10128-2205
ph: 212-427-2730
fax: 212-369-0892
info@doylegalleries.com
http://www.doylegalleries.com
Holds over 50 auctions annually of furniture and decorations, paintings and sculpture, jewelry, books and prints, couture and textiles, 20th century art & design, majolica, Lalique, Asian works of art and other specialty categories.

Michael Davis
Davis & Co. Wine Auctioneers, Ltd.
1440 N. Dayton St.
Chicago, IL 60622
ph: 312-587-9500
fax: 312-654-1800
Conducts six wine auctions per year.

Ben Ferdinand
Chicago Wine Company, The
5663 West Howard St.
Niles, IL 60714
ph: 847-647-8789
fax: 847-647-7265
tcwc@aol.com
http://www.tcwc.com
Specializes in the sale of rare and fine wines from around the world; wines offered in monthly live auctions and through various retail offerings; in business for over 25 years.

Bonhams & Butterfields
220 San Bruno Ave.
San Francisco, CA 94103
ph: 415-861-7500 or 800-223-2854
fax: 415-861-8951
info.US@butterfields.com
http://www.butterfields.com
Auctioneers and appraisers of antiques, fine art and collectibles in all categories; specialty sales include posters, toys, decorative arts, furniture, photography, etc.; the

largest full service auction in the West.

Auction Wine Sales, Riedel Sales
24801 SW Brentwood Dr.
West Linn, OR 97068
ph: 503-638-9463
fax: 503-638-6737
info@auctionvine.com
http://www.AuctionVine.com
Online auction service selling the very best in fine and rare wines.

David Richardson
Richardson's Wine Auctions
15 Kingston Ave.
Richmond, Adelaide 5033 Australia
ph: 8351-7373
fax: 8351-7374
david@erauctions.com.au
http://www.erauctions.com.au
Australia's largest auctioneers and valuers of fine wines; conducts some auctions live on the Internet.

Book Sellers

Warren R. Johnson
Second Harvest Books
P.O. Box 3306
Florence, OR 97439-3306
ph: 541-902-0215
fax: 541-902-0215
info@secondharvestbooks.net
http://www.secondharvestbooks.net
Specializes in wine books - used, old, hard-to-find and out-of-print.

Dealers

Derek White
10 Spring Dr.
Newtown, PA 18940
ph: 215-504-5552
dswhite@360youth.com
Active collector and dealer of antique corkscrews; specialty is rare, unusual mechanical and pocket figural corkscrews; will buy single items as well as entire collections; also wants wine-related items: funnels, bin labels, etc.

Stefan Blicker
NextWine.com
221 Devlin Rd., Ste. 225
Napa, CA 94558
ph: 860-680-9222 or 707-224-6453
fax: 707-224-6734
Offers hard-to-find, cult wines from the best vintners in the world; Web site offers full reviews and expert tasting notes; also buying cellared wines.

Experts

Mark Barlow
Winetiques
3107A Medlock Bridge Rd.
Norcross, GA 30071-1423
ph: 770-449-7610
fax: 770-449-1839
sales@wineaccessoriesmart.com
http://www.wineaccessoriesmart.com
Buys, sells, specializes in wine related antiques: corkscrews, tasters, bottle holders, old bottles, coasters,

advertising, books, art; anything related to wine or champagne.

Internet Resources

Michael J. Osborn
Wine.com
1200 NW Naito Parkway, Ste. 220
Portland, OR 97209
ph: 877-289-6886
michael@wine.com
http://www.wine.com
A complete wine Web site for the collector of fine and rare wines; online auctions, sales and information.

Museums/Libraries

Greyton H. Taylor Wine Museum
8843 Greyton H. Taylor Memorial Dr.
Hammondsport, NY 14840
ph: 607-868-3610
fax: 607-868-3205
bullyhil@ptd.net
http://www.bullyhill.com/heritage.asp
Museum contains a great collection of antiquated wine making equipment.

Computer Programs For

Man./Prod./Dist.

Niche Software, Inc.
Software: Wine Connoisseur, The
7118 NW Terrace
Parkland, FL 33076
ph: 954-344-6561
marketing@collectiblessoftware.com
http://www.collectiblessoftware.com
Specifically designed for anyone who collects or manages a wine cellar.

PrimaSoft PC, Inc.
Software: Wine Organizer
P.O. Box 456
Surrey, British Columbia V3T 5B7
Canada
ph: 800-371-7520 or 604-951-1085
fax: 604-951-7797
support@primasoft.com
http://www.primasoft.com
Designed for managing wine collections.

WINGS

(see AIRLINE MEMORABILIA, Junior Crew Member Wings; AIRLINE MEMORABILIA, Pilots Wings; AVIATION MEMORABILIA, Military Insignia)

WIRELESS TELEGRAPHY

(see TELEGRAPH ITEMS)

WITCHES

(see also GHOSTS & HAUNTINGS; HALLOWEEN COLLECTIBLES; HORROR)

Salem

Museums/Libraries

Salem Witch Museum
19 1/2 Washington Square North
Salem, MA 01970
ph: 978-744-1692
fax: 978-745-4414
facts@salemwitchmuseum.com
http://www.salemwitchmuseum.com
Depicts life in 1692 and the aftermath of the Salem Witch Trials.

WIZARD OF OZ

(see also MOVIE MEMORABILIA)

Clubs/Associations

International Wizard of Oz Club, The
Journal: Baum Bugle, The
P.O. Box 26249
San Francisco, CA 94126-6249
http://www.ozclub.org
Promotes the study and collecting of items relating to L. Frank Baum (1856-1919), The Oz Books, toys, movies, etc.; educates its members about the writings of L. Frank Baum and other authors and illustrators who contributed to Oz books.

Collectors

Bill Stillman
P.O. Box 167
Hummelstown, PA 17036
ph: 717-566-5538
fax: 717-566-7718
billstillman2@aol.com
Long time collector wants anything related to Wizard of Oz from 1900-1960s.

Michael Gessel
P.O. Box 748
Arlington, VA 22216-0748
ph: 703-524-0462
mgessel@cheerful.com
Wants books, posters, games, and advertising related to "The Wizard of Oz;" also wants items by W. W. Denslow.

Tod R. Machin
P.O. Box 3416
Kansas City, KS 66103
ph: 913-362-0528
Wants Oz items: old toys, books, dolls, paper and movie items dating from 1900 to 1970.

Margery Wilder
22 Dungeness Place
Port Townsend, WA 98368
wildem@olympus.net
Wants to buy Wizard of Oz books by any author; also wants related books, ephemera, and Baum non-Oz books.

Dealers

Elaine Willingham
Beyond the Rainbow Wizard of Oz
  Collectibles
P.O. Box 31672
Saint Louis, MO 63131-0672
ph: 314-799-1724
fax: 636-271-2727
oznews@i1.net
http://www.beyondtherainbow2oz.com
  *Specializing in current and older
  MGM Wizard of Oz and Judy Garland
  collectibles, videos, books, jewelry.*

Experts

Jay Scarfone
1815 Meadow Ridge Dr.
Hummelstown, PA 17036-7004
ph: 717-566-5538
fax: 717-566-7718
jscarfone@aol.com
  *Wants all kinds of memorabilia from
  the 1939 movie "The Wizard of Oz;"
  ads, souvenirs, posters, lobby cards,
  coat hangers, dolls, etc.*

WOOD

(see also PYROGRAPHY; REPAIR/
RESTORATION/CONSERVATION,
Furniture; REPAIR/RESTORATION/
CONSERVATION, Woodworking;
WOODEN MONEY)

Clubs/Associations

Bill & Myrtle Cockrell, Sec./Treas.
International Wood Collectors Society
Magazine: World of Wood
2300 West Rangeline Rd.
Greencastle, IN 46135-7875
ph: 765-653-6483
cockrell@indy.tds.net
http://www.woodcollectors.org
  *Dedicated to the advancement of
  information regarding wood; members
  enjoy wood sample collecting,
  identification (dendrology) and
  woodworking; trade, buy, sell and
  auction wood samples.*

Collectors

Donald G. Tritt
81 Donald Ross Dr.
Granville, OH 43023
ph: 740-587-0213
tritt@denison.edu
  *Wants to buy wooden exonumia
  (medals, plaques, political and
  advertising tokens, checkers, badges).*

Carvings

Collectors

Philly Rains
1401 Brentwood Dr.
Harrison, AR 72601
ph: 870-743-2040
fax: 419-735-0610
phillyr@anricarvings.com
http://www.anricarvings.com
  *Expert in antique ANRI Italian wood
  carvings, 1912 through 1960s; bottle
  stoppers, corkscrews, nutcrackers, bar*

sets, figurines, napkin rings, smoking
accessories, and more; appraisals
upon request.

Steve Elliott
1600 Tennessee St.
Vallejo, CA 94590-4629
ph: 707-552-8400 or 707-642-1949
fax: 707-552-0881
  *Wants to buy antique Black Forest
  wood carvings.*

Dealers

Joe Iozzia
Chameleon Collectibles
P.O. Box 1005
Pomona, NJ 08240-1005
ph: 609-652-8504
pinflyers@aol.com
http://members.aol.com/Pinflyers/
  WOODEN.html
  *Wants to buy figural wood
  handcarved people, animals, elves,
  pirates, monks, etc.; nutcrackers,
  cigarette boxes, bookends, ashtrays,
  pipe holders, figurines, bottle
  stoppers, humidors and unusual
  figural handcarved items.*

Heinz Roes
Heinz-N-Steins
7068 Aviation Blvd.
Glen Burnie, MD 21061-2442
ph: 410-760-0707 or 410-315-9831
fax: 410-760-0853
  *Buys, sells, appraises beer steins;
  military, Mettlach, character drinking
  vessels, cups, plaques, WWI, German,
  pipes, pictures, flasks, etc.; also
  occupational shaving mugs; also
  wants Black Forest wood carvings.*

Man./Prod./Dist.

Les Ramsay
Linden Tree Woodcarving Gallery
41 Bradley Rd.
Jackson Center, PA 16133
ph: 724-662-3523
comments@lindentree.com
http://www.lindentree.com
  *Hand carved wooden figures, doors,
  fireplace mantels and commissioned
  sculpture.*

Identification

Misc. Services

Wood Identification Workshop,
University of Massachusetts Div. of
Continuing Ed.
Goodell Bldg, Box 33260
Amherst, MA 01003-3260
ph: 413-545-2484
hoadley@forwild.umass.edu
  *Offers four-day workshops in wood
  identification; held in Jan. of each
  year.*

David P. Lindquist
Whitehall at the Villa
1213 E. Franklin St.
Chapel Hill, NC 27514-3307
ph: 919-942-3179 or 919-933-3305
fax: 919-942-6600
whchnc@aol.com
  Offers a wood identification course.

Regis Miller, Botanist
Center for Wood Anatomy Research,
  Dept. of Agriculture
One Gifford Pinchot Dr.
Madison, WI 53705-2398
ph: 608-231-9341 or 608-231-9200
fax: 608-321-9592
rmiller1@facstaff.wisc.edu
http://www.fpl.fs.fed.us/WoodID/
  idfact.html
  *Will identify a max of 5 wood samples
  per fiscal year (10/1-9/30) as a free
  public service to US citizens;
  noncitizen requests handled as time
  permits; if more than 5 identifications
  needed, inquire first to make
  arrangements.*

Turnings

Experts

Barry Friedman
P.O. Box 55492
Valencia, CA 91385-0492
ph: 661-255-2365
BarryF@thevine.net
http://www.blanketboy.com
  *Buys fine wooden bowls and vases by
  Bob Stocksdale, Ed Moulthrop, James
  Prestini, David Ellsworth and other
  famous turners.*

WOODBURNING CRAFT ITEMS

(see PYROGRAPHY ITEMS)

WOODEN MONEY

Clubs/Associations

Robbin Quinn
International Organization of Wooden
  Money Collectors
Newsletter: Bunyan's Chips
5295 Beechwood Rd.
Ravenna, OH 44266-9119
ph: 330-296-6783
rq83@aol.com
http://www.startext.net/homes/
  woodmoney/index.htm
  *Club of over 350 focuses on woods,
  wooden tokens, commemorative and
  official woods.*

Matt Welch
American Wooden Money Guild
Newsletter: Old Woody Views
P.O. Box 30444
Tucson, AZ 85751-0444
ph: 520-886-0505
matwelch@aol.com
  *"Lignadenarists" are interested in
  collecting wooden money.*

Collectors

Norman Boughton
P.O. Box 1
Macedon, NY 14502
ph: 315-986-3851
nbought1@rochester.rr.com
http://www.woodenmoney.com
  *Wants all forms of wooden money
  from the early flat wooden nickels
  shaped like real money to present day
  round wooden nickels; especially
  wants those for civic celebrations,
  centennials, anniversaries; Sambos,
  McDonald's, etc.*

Herb Hornung
Old Time Wooden Nickels
P.O. Box 18362
San Antonio, TX 78218-0362
ph: 877-464-2535 or 210-930-1677
fax: 210-832-8965
herb@wooden-nickel.com
http://www.wooden-nickel.com
  *Buy, sells and manufactures wooden
  nickels.*

Man./Prod./Dist.

Herb Hornung
Old Time Wooden Nickels
P.O. Box 18362
San Antonio, TX 78218-0362
ph: 877-464-2535 or 210-930-1677
fax: 210-832-8965
herb@wooden-nickel.com
http://www.wooden-nickel.com
  *Manufacturer of wooden nickels for
  business advertising, souvenirs,
  politics, tokens, clowns, banks, police,
  novelties, centennials, fairs and
  festivals, magicians, casinos, fraternal
  groups, Scouts, tourist attractions,
  etc.*

Museums/Libraries

Wooden Nickel Historical Museum
345 Old Austin Rd.
San Antonio, TX 78209
ph: 210-829-1291
fax: 210-832-8965
museum@wooden-nickel.net
http://www.wooden-nickel.net
  *Printing plates and dies, printing
  presses, engravings, and other
  memorabilia related to making
  wooden nickels; includes "round" and
  "flat" wooden nickels in various sizes
  from the beginning in 1930 to present;
  by appointment only.*

WOODSTOCK

(see also SOCIAL CAUSES, Hippie
Items)

Collectors

Cary Demont
P.O. Box 16013
Minneapolis, MN 55416
ph: 763-522-0957
  *Wants unusual Woodstock 69 concert
  related items: authentic T-shirt and
  windbreaker jackets worn by crew
  members, backstage passes, early*

fliers and mailers (especially for the Wallkill venue), 3-D items; no common tickets, posters.

WORKS ON PAPER

(see PAINTINGS & DRAWINGS; POSTERS; PRINTS; PRINTS [MODERN]; REPAIR/ RESTORATION/CONSERVATION, Paper Items)

WORLD WAR MEMORABILIA

(see MARINE CORPS ITEMS; MILITARIA, WWI Items; MILITARIA, WWII Items; RATIONING RELATED ITEMS)

WORLD'S FAIRS & EXPOSITIONS

Auction Services

H. Joseph Levine
Presidential Coin & Antique Co. Inc.
6550-I Little River Turnpike
Alexandria, VA 22312
ph: 703-354-5454
fax: 703-914-0547
JLevine968@aol.com
Conducts periodic auctions of Presidential and other medals, badges, decorations, tokens, World's Fair and other exonumia,

Clubs/Associations

Michael R. Pender, Pres.
World's Fair Collectors Society, Inc.
Newsletter: Fair News
P.O. Box 20806
Sarasota, FL 34276-3806
ph: 941-923-2590
wfcs@aol.com
http://members.aol.com/bbqprod/ wfcs.html
Focuses on collecting and preserving materials pertinent to the history of World's Fairs and International expositions; bi-monthly newsletter contains articles, ads, etc.

1904 World's Fair Society
Newsletter: World's Fair Bulletin
12934 Windy Hill Dr.
Saint Louis, MO 63128
admin@1904worldsfairsociety.org
http://www.1904worldsfairsociety.org
Purpose is to preserve the memories and memorabilia of the 1904 St. Louis World's Fair.

Collectors

Mark S. Waskow
95 St. Paul St., Ste. 440
Burlington, VT 05401
ph: 802-660-9522
fax: 802-862-8652
waskowgp@charter.net
Wants to to buy World's Fairs & Expositions: Crystal Palace, Corn Palace & Ice Palace Expos; 1901 West Indian & Pacific Expo in Charleston as well as the Florida

Subtropicals; 1933 and 1964 Sinclair Dinoland Exhibits and more.

Augyre T.
P.O. Box 1293
Bayonne, NJ 07002-6293
ph: 201-339-8375
augyret@yahoo.com
Buys 1939-40 and 1964-65 New York World's Fair, especially posters, signs and things unusual; also has some for trade/sale.

Ken Schultz
P.O. Box M753
Hoboken, NJ 07030
ph: 201-656-0966
fax: 201-418-8640
kschultz@midplains.net
http://userpages.chorus.net/kschultz
Wants all items relating to world's fairs and expositions.

Andy Rudoff
P.O. Box 111
Oceanport, NJ 07757-0111
ph: 732-542-3712
fax: 732-542-3712
shoreguy@comcast.net
Wants early (1851-1904) World's Fair items especially 1876 Centennial and 1893 Columbian Exposition; wants all items especially china, glass, and metal souvenirs; all other early US and foreign fairs also considered.

Steve Sheppard
2500 Johnson Ave., 20P
Bronx, NY 10463
ph: 718-549-6740
fax: 718-549-1571
xpo93@aol.com
Collects and sells World's Columbian Exposition items: advertising, documents, letters, diaries, photographs, and other ephemera; wants only World's Columbian Exposition items from the 1893 World's Fair.

Henry Heiman, III
P.O. Box 316
South Salem, NY 10590-0316
Wants 1939-1940 New York World's Fair items.

Rusty Olimpo
P.O. Box 363
Mechanicsville, PA 18934-0363
ph: 215-345-5768
oporx39@cs.com
Wants to buy anything relating to the 1939-40 New York World's Fair.

Frederick Lingenfelser
814 Byram St.
Reading, PA 19606-1446
lingy@afo.net
Wants to buy World's Fair items; specializes in 1893 Columbian Exposition: photographs, postcards, art work, maps, trinkets, tickets, etc.

Thomas J. Diddle
Worlds Columbian Exonumist, The
802 North Rd.
Boynton Beach, FL 33435-3238
ph: 561-738-1992
fax: 561-733-4127
Collects, buys, sells, trades 1893 Columbian Exposition collectibles and ephemera.

Paul A. Jarrett
611 West Main
Waverly, TN 37185
ph: 615-296-3151
Wants to buy any type of memorabilia from the 1897 Tennessee Centennial Exposition including china, paper, glassware, badges, pins, medals, ribbons, tickets, etc.

Ken Srail
ken@srail.com
http://www.srail.com
Wants to buy 1893 Columbian and 1901 Pan-American World's Fair memorabilia.

Rick Rann
P.O. Box 877
Oak Park, IL 60303-0877
ph: 708-442-7907
ukczech@aol.com
Wants to buy items from the 1933-1934 Chicago Century of Progress: uniforms, toys, ride tickets, pennants, etc.

Max Storm
529 Barcia Dr.
Saint Louis, MO 63119-1518
ph: 314-968-2810
storm@1904worldsfair.com
http://www.1904worldsfair.com
Wants any type of memorabilia from the 1904 St. Louis World's Fair: clocks, padlocks, postcards, watches, china, tickets, paper, stock certificates, etc.

Chuck Wasserman
11723 W. 101st
Shawnee Mission, KS 66214
ph: 913-492-5005
Well recognized expert, appraiser, collector of 1904 St. Louis World's Fair memorabilia; specializes in spoons, ceramics, and glass; especially foreign exhibit material such as jasperware, Haviland Limoges, Nippon, and moriage.

Dealers

Scott Wagner
NY Memories Antiques & Collectibles
1410 Ave. S, Ste. 2-F
Brooklyn, NY 11229-3326
ph: 917-939-0148 or 718-375-3075
nymemories1@aol.com
Buys and sells any and all items relating to the 1939-1940 New York World's fair; also wants to buy any old New York City memorabilia, souvenirs and collectibles.

Thomas J. Diddle
Worlds Columbian Exonumist, The
802 North Rd.
Boynton Beach, FL 33435-3238
ph: 561-738-1992
fax: 561-733-4127
Collects, buys, sells, trades 1893 Columbian Exposition collectibles and ephemera.

Bindy Bitterman
Eureka! Antiques, Nostalgia & Collectibles
705 W. Washington
Evanston, IL 60202-2214
ph: 847-869-9090
rbitt356@aol.com
Focuses on the Chicago World's Fairs and other Chicago memorabilia; a small shop - they send no lists but will reply by phone, email or letter; SASEs get first attention.

William "Bill" Pieber
Best of Times Antiques
1010 Mallow Dr.
Ballwin, MO 63011-2365
ph: 636-227-8930
Buys and sells St. Louis World's Fair (1904) and Louisiana Purchase Exposition items; also all World's Fair items from 1915 Pan-Pacific, 1939 New York, and 1939 San Francisco.

Vivian Briggs
Briggs Antiques
4443 Linwood Place
Riverside, CA 92506
ph: 909-781-3121
fax: 909-781-3121
Specializes in World's Fair items from 1856 to 1939 New York; has World's Fair items from 1856 to 1939 New York.

Alex Pancheco
Tipsico Coin LLC
P.O. Box 2067
Corvallis, OR 97339-2067
ph: 541-343-0091
tipsico@qwest.net
Appraises, buys World's Fair memorabilia, and all US and world tokens, medals, exonumia; especially interested in material from 1915 Panama-Pacific International Exposition.

Experts

Harvey & Sandy Dolin
Harvey Dolin & Co.
111 Fulton St., Mezzanine Level
New York, NY 100386
ph: 212-267-0216
Wants any item pertaining to the 1939 New York World's Fair and the Columbian Fair.

Judith Katz-Schwartz
Twin Brooks Antiques & Collectibles
E-zine: Antiques & Collectibles
  Newsletter
P.O. Box 6572
New York, NY 10128-0006
ph: 212-876-3512
fax: 212-876-3512
twinb@msjudith.net
http://www.msjudith.net
  *Buys, sells, appraises all categories of
  World's Fair memorabilia; looking
  for items from 1939 New York
  World's Fair; member Assoc. of
  Online Appraisers (AOA) & Inter.
  Soc. of Appraisers; free online
  newsletter.*

Steve Sheppard
2500 Johnson Ave., 20P
Bronx, NY 10463
ph: 718-549-6740
fax: 718-549-1571
xpo93@aol.com
  *Collects, specializes in World's
  Columbian Exposition items:
  advertising, documents, letters,
  diaries, photographs, and other
  ephemera; wants only World's
  Columbian Exposition items.*

Herbert Rolfes
2260 Chase Court
Mount Dora, FL 32757-6909
ph: 352-735-3947
fax: 352-735-3970
ny1939@aol.com
  *Co-author of "The World of
  Tomorrow: The 1939 New York
  World's Fair."*

Rich Hartzog
World Exonumia
P.O. Box 4143CNZ
Rockford, IL 61110-0643
ph: 815-226-0771
hartzog@exonumia.com
http://www.exonumia.com
  *Pre-1940 items preferred; collections
  and quantities wanted.*

Max Storm
529 Barcia Dr.
Saint Louis, MO 63119-1518
ph: 314-968-2810
storm@1904worldsfair.com
http://www.1904worldsfair.com
  *Collector, historian and appraiser;
  noted expert on the 1904 St. Louis
  World's Fair.*

Chuck Wasserman
11723 W. 101st
Shawnee Mission, KS 66214
ph: 913-492-5005
  *Well recognized expert, appraiser,
  collector of 1904 St. Louis World's
  Fair memorabilia; specializes in
  spoons, ceramics, and glass;
  especially foreign exhibit material
  such as jasperware, Haviland
  Limoges, Nippon, and moriage.*

Internet Resources

Terry Laupp
Terry's 1904 World's Fair Page
12934 Windy Hill Dr.
Saint Louis, MO 63128
terry.laupp@phoenixcreative.com
http://www.tlaupp.com
  *1905 St. Louis World's Fair
  information, fair buildings, fair maps,
  memorabilia, what's left, books in
  print, exhibits and statues, newspaper
  articles, link to World's Fair Society,
  and more.*

Museums/Libraries

Buffalo & Erie County Historical Society
25 Nottingham Ct.
Buffalo, NY 14216-3199
ph: 716-873-9644
fax: 716-873-1894
bechs@buffnet.net
http://intotem.buffnet.net/bechs

Atwater Kent Museum - the History
  Museum of Philadelphia
15 S. 7th St.
Philadelphia, PA 19106
ph: 215-685-4830
fax: 215-685-4937
http://www.philadelphiahistory.org
  *Founded in 1938 by radio pioneer A.
  Atwater Kent.*

Dan & Rose Amato
Christopher Columbus Museum
239 Whitney St.
P.O. Box 151
Columbus, WI 53925-0151
ph: 920-623-1992
fax: 920-623-1992
http://www.columbusantiquemall.com/
  #museum
  *Features a collection of souvenirs
  from the 1893 World's Columbian
  Exposition of Chicago; wants to buy
  all quality Christopher Columbus
  items, old and new.*

Dan & Rose Amato
1893 Chicago World's Columbian
  Exposition Museum
239 Whitney St.
P.O. Box 151
Columbus, WI 53925-0151
ph: 920-623-1992
fax: 920-623-1992
http://www.columbusantiquemall.com/
  #museum
  *Focuses on the World's Columbian
  Exposition of 1893; over 2,000 pieces.*

Keith R. Gill
Museum of Science & Industry
5700 S Lake Shore Dr.
Chicago, IL 60637
ph: 773-684-1414
fax: 773-684-0026
msi@msichicago.org
http://www.msichicago.org
  *Archives contains documents & photos
  of the 1893 Columbian Exposition and
  the 1933-1934 Century of Progress
  Exposition, including many pieces of
  the buildings and old exhibits from the
  Century of Progress.*

WRAPPERS

(see BUBBLE GUM & CANDY
WRAPPERS)

WRITING INSTRUMENTS

(see BLOTTERS; GLASS, Whimsies
[Pens]; INKWELLS & INKSTANDS;
OFFICE EQUIPMENT; PENCILS;
PENS; SEALS, Wax)

WWI

(see MILITARIA, WWI Items)

WWII

(see MILITARIA, WWII Items)

YACHTS

(see BOATS)

ZEPPELINS

(see AIRSHIPS)

**Here are some tips
when contacting
someone who is listed
in this book:**

When requesting
information about a
particular item, include
a description (material,
dimensions, maker's
mark, model number,
etc.) and a photo,
sketch, digital image or
photocopy of the item
in question.

Always ask if there are
charges for samples or
for the services that
you are requesting.

When corresponding
by letter, please be
sure to include a Large
(#10 business size)
Self-Addressed and
Stamped Envelope
(LSASE) if requesting a
reply or the return of
photographs.

Never call collect
unless otherwise
directed. When
calling, be considerate
of time zone differ-
ences and always ask
if the party you are
calling has time to talk.
When leaving an
answering machine
message, always
instruct the party to
call you back collect.

O

X - Y - Z

Maloney's Antiques & Collectibles Resource Directory
Listing Registraion and Change Form
This form is also available ONLINE at **www.davidmaloney.com/form.htm**
(Save and use this form for future additions or changes to your listings.)

1. List your SPECIALTY AREA (Please limit listings to five per Dealer or Collector). Make copies of this form if you have specialties in more than one area. _____

2. Check the ENTRY TYPE(S) that applies to this listing. More than one selection is OK:

_____ Appraiser	_____ Dealer	_____ Supplier of repair or replacement parts
_____ Auction Service	_____ Expert	_____ Repair/Restoration/Conservator Service
_____ Book Seller	_____ Matching Service	_____ Reproductions Source
_____ Club/Association	_____ Museum/Library	_____ Manufacturer, Producer or Distributor
_____ Collector	_____ Periodical	_____ On-line Service or Resource

Other (specify): _____

3. POINT-OF-CONTACT. Your name as you want it listed:_____

4. BUSINESS NAME of your company, club, association, publishing house, museum,

etc.:_____

5. ADDRESS (Note: for periodicals, include your **Editorial** or **Publisher's** address (not your subscription service) and your toll-free subscription telephone number, if any):

    Address: _____

    _____

    City: _____ State (or Province): _____ Zip (or Postal Code): _____

    Country : _____

6. TELEPHONE #1: (   )_____ TELEPHONE #2: (   )_____ FAX: (   )_____

7.   a. E-mail address: _____

    b. Internet website address: http:// _____

8. PERIODICALS (magazines, newsletters, newspapers, etc.) that you publish. **To ensure continued accuracy of your listing and to be eligible for preferred referral status, please make certain that complimentary subscriptions to your periodical are sent to Maloney's, Attn: File Editor, P.O. Box 2049, Frederick, MD 21702-1049 for review.**

    Periodical Name: _____

        Format (newsletter, magazine, journal, newspaper, etc.):_____

        Frequency of publication: _____

9. COMMENT LINE: (Describe your club, association, periodical, or service. For the collector or dealer, describe your wants. If you are an author, please list your most recent books dealing with this specialty area. Also, please attach catalogs, brochures, flyers, business cards, etc. that relate to this listing. 240 character limit.)

_____

_____

_____

The above information gives an accurate and realistic description of my business or areas of interest. I understand that this information is for distribution in electronic and written form including publication in *Maloney's Antiques & Collectibles Resource Directory* published by Krause Publications.

Date _____ Signature _____ Title_____

Please complete and mail or fax to: Maloney's, P.O. Box 2049, Frederick, MD 21702-1049
phone: (301) 228-2279, fax: (301) 695-6491, e-mail: dave@maloney.com